# McCORMICK ON EVIDENCE

## Seventh Edition

By
### Kenneth S. Broun
*General Editor*
*Henry Brandis Professor of Law Emeritus, University of North Carolina*

---

**Contributing Authors**
### George E. Dix
*George R. Killam, Jr. Chair of Criminal Law, The University of Texas*

### Edward J. Imwinkelried
*Edward L. Barrett, Jr. Professor of Law*
*University of California, Davis*

### David H. Kaye
*Regents' Professor of Law, Arizona State University College of Law*

### Robert P. Mosteller
*J. Dickson Phillips Distinguished Professor of Law,*
*University of North Carolina*

### E. F. Roberts
*Edwin H. Woodruff Professor of Law Emeritus, The Cornell Law School*

### Eleanor Swift
*Professor of Law, University of California at Berkeley School of Law*

## Volume 1

### Chapters 1–20

THOMSON REUTERS™

*For Customer Assistance Call 1-800-328-4880*

ISBN 978-0-314-81252-0

# Preface to the Seventh Edition

This edition of the book attempts to do what all of the prior editions accomplished: to set out the law of Evidence in as complete and understandable a manner as possible in a work of moderate length. The authors have tried to be faithful to the pragmatic approach to analyzing evidence issues taken by the original author of this book, Dean Charles McCormick.

Although the Federal Rules of Evidence and their state counterparts make up much of the basis for the law, many aspects depend heavily on case analysis. The book attempts to meld rules and case law in a way that is useful for practitioners, scholars, the courts and students. As in prior editions, important cases containing helpful discussions of precedent and policy are noted in the extensive footnotes found in the practitioner's edition.

As with the last three editions, there will be two versions of this edition, a two volume practitioner's edition, also intended to be useful for legal scholars and the judiciary, and a one-volume student edition. The only significant difference between the two editions is the absence of extensive footnoting in the student edition.

All of the authors of the Sixth Edition of the book have continued in this edition. Their responsibility for chapters has remained the same: Professor Edward Imwinkelried, Chapters 1-7, covering preparing and presenting evidence, examination of witnesses, procedure for admitting and excluding evidence, and competency; Professor Robert Mosteller, Chapter 12, privileges for governmental secrets and Chapters 24 to 34, dealing with the hearsay rule and its exceptions; Professor George Dix, Chapters 13-15, covering certain constitutional rights and privileges; Professor David Kaye, Chapters 16 to 20, dealing with relevancy considerations (including scientific evidence covered in Chapter 20); Professor Eleanor Swift, Chapters 21-23, dealing with real and demonstrative evidence and authentication and contents of writings; Professor Ernest Roberts, Chapter 35, judicial notice; and myself, Chapters 8-11, dealing with common law and statutory privileges and Chapter 36, the burdens of proof and presumptions.

This edition contains updates up to the present with regard to all of the matters covered in the treatise. The restyled Federal

Rules have been incorporated into the discussion. Special note should be taken of the discussion of developments in the forensic science community that affect how forensic science findings can and should be presented in court (Chapter 20); developments limiting federal constitutional exclusionary requirements (Chapter 15); the increased use of electronic evidence and its impact on evidentiary rules (Chapters 21 and 22); and the continuing evolution of the Confrontation Clause jurisprudence arising from the *Crawford* case (Chapter 24).

On behalf of all of the authors, I hope that we have both continued the traditional excellence of this treatise and taken steps to bring it fully up to date in terms of both the law and the age of technology in which we now live.

KENNETH S. BROUN

Chapel Hill, North Carolina
March, 2013

# Summary of Contents

## Volume 1

# Volume 2

# Table of Contents

## Volume 1

# CHAPTER 4. CROSS-EXAMINATION AND SUBSEQUENT EXAMINATIONS

# CHAPTER 5. IMPEACHMENT AND SUPPORT

# TITLE 3. ADMISSION AND EXCLUSION

# CHAPTER 6.  THE PROCEDURE OF ADMITTING AND EXCLUDING EVIDENCE

# TITLE 4. COMPETENCY

# CHAPTER 7.  THE COMPETENCY OF WITNESSES

# TITLE 5. PRIVILEGE: COMMON LAW AND STATUTORY

# CHAPTER 8. THE SCOPE AND EFFECT OF THE EVIDENTIARY PRIVILEGES

# CHAPTER 9. THE PRIVILEGE FOR MARITAL COMMUNICATIONS

# CHAPTER 10.  THE CLIENT'S PRIVILEGE: COMMUNICATIONS BETWEEN CLIENT & LAWYER

# CHAPTER 11.  THE PRIVILEGE FOR CONFIDENTIAL INFORMATION SECURED IN THE COURSE OF THE PHYSICIAN-PATIENT RELATIONSHIP

## CHAPTER 12. PRIVILEGES FOR GOVERNMENTAL SECRETS

## TITLE 6. PRIVILEGE: CONSTITUTIONAL

## CHAPTER 13. THE PRIVILEGE AGAINST SELF-INCRIMINATION

# CHAPTER 14. CONFESSIONS

# CHAPTER 15. THE PRIVILEGE CONCERNING IMPROPERLY OBTAINED EVIDENCE

# TITLE 7. RELEVANCY AND ITS COUNTERWEIGHTS

## CHAPTER 16. RELEVANCE

## CHAPTER 17. CHARACTER AND HABIT

## CHAPTER 18. SIMILAR HAPPENINGS AND TRANSACTIONS

# Volume 2

## TITLE 8. REAL EVIDENCE, OTHER NONTESTIMONIAL EVIDENCE, AND DEMONSTRATIVE AIDS

## CHAPTER 21. REAL EVIDENCE, OTHER NONTESTIMONIAL EVIDENCE, AND DEMONSTRATIVE AIDS

# TITLE 9. WRITINGS

# CHAPTER 22. AUTHENTICATION

# CHAPTER 23. THE REQUIREMENT OF THE PRODUCTION OF THE ORIGINAL WRITING, RECORDING, OR PHOTOGRAPH AS THE "BEST EVIDENCE"

# TITLE 10. THE HEARSAY RULE AND ITS EXCEPTIONS

# CHAPTER 24. THE HEARSAY RULE

# CHAPTER 25. ADMISSIONS OF A PARTY-OPPONENT

# CHAPTER 30. PUBLIC RECORDS, REPORTS, AND CERTIFICATES

# CHAPTER 31. TESTIMONY TAKEN AT A FORMER HEARING OR IN ANOTHER ACTION

# CHAPTER 32. DYING DECLARATIONS

# CHAPTER 33.   DECLARATIONS AGAINST INTEREST

# CHAPTER 34.   VARIOUS OTHER EXCEPTIONS AND THE FUTURE OF THE RULES ABOUT HEARSAY

# TITLE  11.  JUDICIAL NOTICE

# CHAPTER 35.   JUDICIAL NOTICE

# TITLE 12. BURDEN OF PROOF AND PRESUMPTIONS

# CHAPTER 36. THE BURDENS OF PROOF AND PRESUMPTIONS

# APPENDIX

# Title 1.  Introduction

## Chapter 1

# Preparing and Presenting the Evidence

### § 1  Planning and preparation of proof as important as the rules of evidence

The law of evidence is the system of rules and standards regulating the admission of testimony and exhibits at the trial of a lawsuit. The last section in this chapter, § 4, is an overview of the procedural regulations governing the sequence of evidentiary presentations at trial. However, the trial stage, when evidentiary rules govern, is a relatively late phase in a long litigation process. Thus, in every case dealing with a trial dispute over the application of a rule of evidence, the lawyers have already shouldered many other tasks in the planning and production of testimony and exhibits. The lawyers must perform these pretrial tasks in anticipation of problems of proof under the law of evidence—weeks, months, or years before any evidentiary question is submitted to a trial judge. Some of these earlier stages in the litigation process are mentioned in this chapter. In particular, the next to last section, § 3, discusses the use of formal discovery devices to prepare to gather evidence for trial while § 2 reviews the informal methods of readying for trial.

### § 2  Preparation for trial on the facts without resort to the court's aid[1]

In many cases, the lawyers collect evidence for trial without

---

**[Section 2]**

[1]For detailed practical suggestions, see Mauet, Pretrial (7th ed. 2008); Lane, Goldstein Trial Techniques (3d ed.); Belli, Modern Trials (2d ed. 1982); Keeton, Trial Tactics and Methods (2d ed. 1973).

resorting to formal discovery devices. The lawyer can either personally perform the collection task or delegate the task to an assistant such as a clerk or private investigator. Informal discovery techniques tend to be faster and less expensive than formal discovery. Moreover, the use of informal discovery methods can preserve the element of surprise. There is no element of surprise at trial when the lawyer deposes a witness to an accident; the opponent can attend the deposition and is entitled to a transcript of the deposition hearing. In contrast, the opponent may gain little or no advance notice if the lawyer is content to informally interview the witness. Although these investigative steps are informal, the attorney taking these steps must keep formal evidence law in mind.

As a starting point in informal discovery, the lawyer must interview the client to learn his version of the facts. At some point, these interviews should include a tactful but searching mock cross-examination to overcome the client's natural tendency to mention only the facts favorable to his side in the litigation. The lawyer conducting these interviews should endeavor to ensure that the attorney-client evidentiary privilege applies to these interviews.[2] The lawyer ought to contact not only the client but also other witnesses with personal knowledge of the relevant facts. The witnesses who have firsthand knowledge of the transaction in controversy must be interviewed; and where possible, their written statements ought to be taken.[3] The statement might become evidence at trial, or the lawyer could need to resort to the statement to refresh the witness's memory at trial if the witness has difficulty recalling the pertinent facts. In the case of statements by non-party witnesses, the lawyer should do his best to make certain that the evidentiary protection for work product attaches to the witnesses' statements.[4]

Apart from the ordinary lay eyewitnesses, it is increasingly necessary to arrange for experts such as epidemiologists in toxic tort actions, physicians in personal injury cases, chemists and physicists in patent litigation, engineers and architects in controversies over construction contracts, molecular biologists and psychiatrists in criminal cases, and handwriting experts in will contests. In one Rand Corporation study of California courts, 86% of the trials reviewed involved expert testimony.[5] Once again, the lawyer must keep evidence law in mind. In some jurisdictions, the attorney-client privilege extends to reports obtained

---

[2]See generally Ch. 9 infra.

[3]See § 3 infra concerning the right to interview witnesses.

[4]See § 96 infra.

[5]Gross, Expert Evidence, 1991 Wis. L. Rev. 1113, 1119.

from the lawyer's own experts.[6] Moreover, in many states the medical privilege forbids a civil defense lawyer from making ex parte contact with the plaintiff's treating physician.[7]

In addition to contacting potential expert and lay witnesses, it is often necessary to assemble exhibits. Exhibits can take the form of documentary evidence such as contracts, letters, receipts, certified copies of deeds, judgments, and decrees. In the computer age, it can also be crucial to print out electronic files and e-mail messages, which are often voluminous. Other physical evidence, such as the assailant's revolver or a sample of the goods in an action for breach of warranty, should be located and preserved for use at the trial. At trial the lawyer needs to be in a position to authenticate these items by, for example, proving a chain of custody to establish the identity of each item.[8] Chain of custody testimony can demonstrate that the exhibit tendered at trial is the same revolver found at the crime scene.

The lawyer is not restricted to objects which have an original, historical connection to the case such as the very weapon found at the homicide scene. The lawyer must be creative in planning aids to the senses such as still photographs, videotapes, motion picture films, X-rays, plats, diagrams, and models. Visual aids not only help the lawyer arrest the jurors' short-term attention; more importantly, they significantly increase the jurors' long-term memory of the data depicted by the aid. The use of visual aids is especially important when the lawyer contemplates offering scientific evidence. Jurors sometimes find scientific testimony confusingly complex and abstract. A visual aid such as a computer-generated animation (CGA) can powerfully simplify the testimony for the jury's benefit. If the lawyer hires a consultant to generate a CGA, the lawyer must ensure that consultant follows procedures that will enable the lawyer to lay an evidentiary foundation to justify the introduction of the item at trial.[9]

Where practicable, counsel should endeavor to lighten the task

---

[6]Beardslee, The Corporate Attorney-Client Privilege: Third-Rate Doctrine for Third-Party Consultants, 62 S.M.U. L. Rev. 727 (2009); Imwinkelried & Amoroso, The Application of the Attorney-Client Privilege to Interactions Among Clients, Attorneys, and Experts in the Age of Consultants: The Need for a More Premise, Fundamental Analysis, 48 Houst. L. Rev. 265 (2011).

[7]Imwinkelried & Blumoff, Pretrial Discovery: Strategy and Tactics § 4:4 (rev. 2008).

[8]See § 213 infra.

[9]The consultant will use software programs to generate the CGA. The software designer has included several scientific formula in the software. If the lawyer wants to use the CGA as substantive evidence of the events depicted in the CGA, the lawyer must lay a foundation establishing the judicial noticeability, general acceptance, or empirical validity of the formulae. Imwinkelried, Evidentiary Foundations § 4.09[4] (8th ed. 2012). See generally §§ 203 to 204 infra.

of proof at trial by securing the opponent's pretrial written stipulations to facts not in controversy such as the validity of the software used to generate a CGA, the authorship of documents, or the ownership of a vehicle involved in the suit. A stipulation can substitute for evidence and eliminate the need for counsel to present evidence at trial. In addition, if counsel will have to offer a copy to prove the terms of a document in the adversary's possession, counsel must give the opposing counsel written notice to produce the original at trial in order to satisfy the best evidence rule discussed in Chapter 23.

All these steps should be carefully planned with evidence law in mind. A tentative plan may emerge early in the litigation process. In any event, as the trial approaches, the lawyer must develop a theory of the case; and the lawyer ought to formulate a final plan to ensure that the attorney can prove up the theory at trial. Each essential factual element of the claim or defense ought to be listed, specifying the witnesses and documents by which it will be proved. The plan can be supplemented with (1) a list of the witnesses in the order in which they will be called, including the subject on which they will be testify, and (2) a master exhibit list, identifying the witnesses to authenticate each exhibit. Finally, on the eve of trial before the witnesses take the stand, the counsel calling a witness may need to reinterview the witness to confirm what he is prepared to swear to, to refresh his memory if necessary, and to ready him for the probable cross-examination. The counsel must keep evidence law in mind as he takes these preparatory pretrial steps. Every task must be performed with a view to the ultimate objective of ensuring that there will be ample, admissible evidence at trial.

Informal discovery has taken on added importance since 2007. In that year, the United States Supreme Court handed down its decision in *Bell Atlantic Corp. v. Twombly*,[10] an antitrust case. Prior to *Bell*, most American jurisdictions had endorsed the philosophy of notice pleading. Thus, in 1957, in *Conley v. Gibson*,[11] the Supreme Court had observed that "a complaint should not be dismissed for failure to state a claim unless it appears beyond doubt that the plaintiff can prove no set of facts in support of his claim which would entitle him to relief."[12] However, in *Bell Atlantic* the Court declared that "this famous observation has earned its retirement." In essence, the *Bell Atlantic* Court announced that in order to satisfy Federal Rule of Civil Procedure 8, the plaintiff must allege enough facts to demonstrate that he

---

[10]Bell Atlantic Corp. v. Twombly, 550 U.S. 544, 127 S. Ct. 1955, 167 L. Ed. 2d 929 (2007).

[11]Conley v. Gibson, 355 U.S. 41,

78 S. Ct. 99, 2 L. Ed. 2d 80 (1957).

[12]Conley, 355 U.S. at 45–46.

or she could plausibly win at trial.[13] In 2009 in *Ashcroft v. Iqbal*,[14] the Court indicated that the new standard applies across the board. After *Bell* and *Ashcroft,* the plaintiff may have to conduct additional discovery before filing in order to be in a position to draft a sufficient complaint. It is true that in rare cases, a litigant may conduct formal discovery before a complaint has been filed.[15] However, in the typical case the litigant will have to rely on the informal discovery methods discussed in this section to satisfy the enhanced pleading requirements.

## § 3    Invoking the court's aid in preparing for trial: Right to interview witnesses; discovery and depositions; requests for admission; pretrial conferences

### *The Right to an Opportunity to Interview Witnesses*

As the preceding section pointed out, one of the essential steps in informal trial preparation is interviewing the potential witnesses with firsthand knowledge of the relevant facts. From time to time the question arises whether counsel has a legal right to an opportunity to interview a witness. Counsel may have to resort to the court to settle the matter. The question usually arises when opposing counsel has instructed a witness not to "talk"[1] at all or only on certain conditions.[2] Several courts have ruled that a criminal defendant has such a right, enforceable against the prosecution in the limited sense that prosecutors may not pressure a potential witness to refuse to cooperate with the defense.[3]

---

[13]Davis, Just the Facts, But More of Them, 93 A.B.A.J. 16 (Oct. 2007); Joseph, Federal Practice: Pleading Requirements, Nat'l L.J., Sep. 3, 2007, at 13.

[14]Ashcroft v. Iqbal, 556 U.S. 662, 129 S. Ct. 1937, 173 L. Ed. 2d 868 (2009).

[15]Grenig, Taking and Using Depositions Before Action and Pending Appeal in Federal Court, 27 Am. J. Trial Advoc. 451, 458–59, 467–68 (2004); Solovy & Byman, Discovery: The Vestigial Rule, Nat'l L.J., Nov. 22, 2004, at 11. *See also* Cavanagh, Twombly's Seismic Disturbances, 38 Litigation, Wint. 2012, at 6, 7.

**[Section 3]**

[1]Vega v. Bloomsburgh, 427 F. Supp. 593 (D. Mass. 1977) (direction not to talk to opposing counsel without specific permission).

[2]Gregory v. U.S., 369 F.2d 185, 187 (D.C. Cir. 1966) ("it was my advice that they not speak to anyone about the case unless I was present").

[3]International Business Machines Corp. v. Edelstein, 526 F.2d 37 (2d Cir.1975) (court ordered that if opposing counsel was absent, stenographic report should be made for submission to the court). The courts often limit a lawyer's ability to conduct ex parte interviews. For example, in order to protect information covered by the medical privileges, numerous courts restrict interviews of treating physicians. Kelly, Glass & Erard, Ex Parte Interviews with Plaintiff's Treating Physicians: The Offensive Use of the Physician–Patient Privilege, 67 U.

Generally, under the Sixth Amendment[4] a criminal defendant has the right to an opportunity to interview witnesses privately.[5] There is respectable authority that the prosecution in a criminal case has a similar right.[6] There is also an emerging parallel right for both parties in civil cases.[7] Nevertheless, there are a situa-

---

Det. L. Rev. 502 (1990). In addition, to enforce the rules of legal ethics, many jurisdictions limit an attorney's ability to conduct ex parte interviews of employees of opposing corporations. Sonde & Gettman, Ex Parte Communication and Inadvertent Disclosures, Pract. Litig., May 1996, at 61, 65–69; Right of attorney to conduct ex parte interviews with corporate party's nonmanagement employees, 50 A.L.R. 4th 652.

[4]Imwinkelried & Garland, Exculpatory Evidence: The Accused's Constitutional Right to Introduce Favorable Evidence § 4-2a(2), at 103–04 n. 58 (3d ed. 2004) (collecting cases finding a Sixth Amendment violation when either the trial judge or prosecutor engaged in conduct which effectively denied the accused a potential defense witness). *See also* State v. Beecroft, 813 N.W.2d 814 (Minn. 2012) (the plurality held that a county attorney wrongfully interfered with defense forensic experts who were assistant medical examiners; the plurality characterized the assistant medical examiners as independent public officials).

[5]Fenenbock v. Director of Corrections for California, 692 F.3d 910, 916–19 (9th Cir. 2012); Gregory v. U.S., 369 F.2d 185 (D.C. Cir. 1966) (prosecutor stated, "it was my advice that they not speak to anyone about the case unless I was present"; trial court's failure to order prosecutor to permit the witnesses so advised to talk to defense counsel held error); Mota v. Buchanan, 26 Ariz. App. 246, 547 P.2d 517 (Div. 2 1976) (error to order that prosecutor be present at interview by defense counsel). *See* Accused's right to interview witness held in public custody, 14 A.L.R.3d 652; A.B.A. Standards Relating to the Administra-

tion of Justice, The Prosecution Function 3.1, and Discovery and Procedure Before Trial, 4.1. In *Gregory* the court mentioned due process and elemental fairness, the right that the prosecutor not frustrate the defense, the necessity for an opportunity to interview to find the truth in an adversary proceeding, the increasing trend to provide for discovery, and the duty to furnish witness lists.

The remedy is a court order countermanding any improper advice and instructing the witness that he may speak freely with opposing counsel if he wishes. Vega v. Bloomsburgh, 427 F. Supp. 593 (D. Mass. 1977); U.S. v. Mirenda, 443 F.2d 1351 (9th Cir. 1971).

U.S. v. Mendez–Rodriguez, 450 F.2d 1 (9th Cir. 1971), held that the government could not remove aliens to Mexico, placing them beyond subpoena power, without first giving defendant's counsel an opportunity to interview them. A similar issue arises when the government exercises its power to make a witness unavailable for subpoena. *See* U.S. v. Ballesteros–Acuna, 527 F.2d 928 (9th Cir. 1975).

[6]A.B.A. Standards Relating to The Administration of Criminal Justice, The Defense Function 4.3, and Discovery and Procedure Before Trial, 4.1; Hagan, Interviewing Witnesses in Criminal Cases, 28 Brooklyn L. Rev. 207 (1962). But it has been said that a witness has a right to have counsel present when interviewed by the prosecutor. U.S. v. Standard Oil Co., 316 F.2d 884 (7th Cir. 1963).

[7]International Business Machines Corp. v. Edelstein, 526 F.2d 37 (2d Cir.1975) (the appellate court reversed a trial judge's order that interviews with witnesses in the opposing counsel's absence must be had

tions in which a court will refuse to interfere even when counsel have suggested to witnesses that they limit or refuse interviews.[8] Absent a subpoena, on his own motion, the witness is generally free to refuse to submit to an informal interview.[9] As § 2 explained, despite the existence of formal discovery devices, the opportunity to informally interview witnesses is important in trial preparation. When the witness refuses to submit to an interview, the lawyer may need to resort to court to secure an opportunity to question the witness. At this juncture, the formal discovery devices come into play.

## Formal Discovery Devices

*Civil cases.* Adequate trial preparation often requires the use of the official fact-gathering procedures available after the lawsuit commences. The formal discovery procedures in the various

---

with stenographer present so that the interview could be made available to the court; interviews "may be conducted confidentially without the presence of opposing counsel or reporter, whenever the person interviewed is willing to proceed in this manner"). This case was cited in Vega v. Bloomsburgh, 427 F. Supp. 593 (D. Mass. 1977).

[8] Miscellaneous exceptional circumstances have been relied on in a few cases upholding denial of an interview. *See* Accused's right to interview witness held in public custody, 14 A.L.R.3d 652. For example, a security problem may be crucial if the witness sought to be interviewed is an informer. U.S. v. Murray, 492 F.2d 178 (9th Cir. 1973) (the court refused to order an interview six months before trial but without prejudice to renew a motion for interview twenty-four hours before trial). In U.S. v. Cook, 608 F.2d 1175 (9th Cir. 1979), the court sustained a refusal of access to government witnesses in the Federal Witness Protection Program on the ground that in the particular circumstances the defendant was not unfairly handicapped. But the court stated, "Our cases indicate that security concerns only justify a limitation upon the time and place of access."

[9] Fenenbock v. Director of Corrections for California, 692 F.3d 910, 916–919 (9th Cir. 2012); U.S. v.

Mirenda, 443 F.2d 1351 (9th Cir. 1971) (the court ordered that the witness be instructed that there was no restriction on talking to defense counsel but that the matter was for the witness to decide); Champlin v. Sargeant In and For County of Maricopa, 192 Ariz. 371, 965 P.2d 763 (1998).

There may be a factual question whether a refusal to interview or a limitation on an interview by the witness was the witness's own idea or the result of advice or instruction to the witness. Byrnes v. U.S., 327 F.2d 825 (9th Cir. 1964) (there was no limitation by party when party had first instructed persons to interview defendant's counsel only in the other counsel's presence, then opposing party had revoked that instruction, and the judge had also told the persons that no one had any objection to their speaking freely with defendant's counsel); U.S. v. Dryden, 423 F.2d 1175 (5th Cir. 1970) (the person to be interviewed was responsible for refusal to interview when he told a government agent to tell defense counsel he did not want to be interviewed and the agent merely related the message to defense counsel; a direction not to sign a statement was not an instruction to refuse an interview). *See also* U.S. v. Matlock, 491 F.2d 504 (6th Cir. 1974) (government attorney could tell witness he need not talk if he did not want to).

jurisdictions are treated at length in treatises and one-volume works concerning civil and criminal procedure.[10] Consequently, only a very short, summary review of these procedures is included here. Especially if the jurisdiction does not follow *Twombly* and *Iqbal*, the pleadings in civil cases may be fairly general and need not specify the facts in any great detail.[11] Notice pleadings give the defense little insight into the evidence that the plaintiff will adduce at trial. To furnish the necessary detail, the civil rules provide for fairly thorough post-pleading discovery processes by which each party can learn the possible evidence in the case, and ascertain which specific fact issues will be disputed at trial.[12]

In many states and federal judicial districts, the official procedures include a statute or court rule requiring mandatory pre-discovery disclosures. For example, under a 1993 amendment to Federal Rule of Civil Procedure 26(a), even absent a request by the opposing attorney, the litigant must reveal specified information about potential witnesses, relevant documents, and experts. The amendment forced plaintiffs to frontload their expenditures for expert services. If the mandatory disclosures do not satisfy the opposing attorney, the attorney can turn to formal discovery devices. The federal mandatory pre-discovery disclosure requirements were so controversial that when they were originally promulgated in 1993, the amendment provided that individual judicial districts could opt out of the requirements. However, in 2000, the rule was amended again to eliminate the opt-out provision. Especially after the amendment, the rule has had a major impact on the admissibility of expert testimony at trial. The rule requires experts to file a relatively completely report describing their anticipated testimony. If the expert does not file any report, the trial judge may altogether bar the expert's testimony as a discovery sanction. If the expert files a pretrial report but at trial the expert attempts to give testimony that was not revealed in the report, the judge may exclude that part of the expert's testimony.[13]

One of the most important discovery devices in civil cases is the deposition procedure enabling each party to orally examine

---

[10]*See* Wright and Miller's Federal Practice and Procedure, Civil §§ 2001 to 2293. For procedures in criminal cases, see Wright and Miller's Federal Practice and Procedure, Criminal, Rules 15, 16; 6–7, 25 Moore's Federal Practice (3d ed. 2010).

[11]*See* Wright & Kane, Federal Courts § 68 (7th ed. 2011); Hazard, Leubsdorf & Bassett, Civil Procedure §§ 4.11–.15 (6th ed. 2011) (5th ed.

2001). But see the discussion of *Bell Atlantic* and *Iqbal* in § 2, supra.

[12]The discovery processes summarized in this section also afford means to preserve evidence for the trial.

[13]Dairy Farmers of America, Inc. v. Travelers Ins. Co., 391 F.3d 936, 943 (8th Cir. 2004); Sih v. U.S., 90 Fed. Appx. 940, 944–47 (7th Cir. 2004). *But see* Thompson v. Doane Pet Care Co., 470 F.3d 1201, 1203 (6th Cir. 2006)

the other party under oath and likewise question other persons who have knowledge of the subject matter of the lawsuit. Over half the states have substantially copied the federal rules for this procedure.[14] Although a judicial order for a commission authorizing an officer to preside at an oral examination is still necessary in some states, the simplified procedure for taking oral depositions ordinarily requires only a notice to the person to be examined, a subpoena ordering him to appear at a certain time and place for the examination before a court reporter/notary public, and a notice of the examination for the opposing party if he is not the deponent.[15] In many jurisdictions, following the lead of the federal civil discovery process, at an oral deposition the examiner may seek any information "reasonably calculated to lead to the discovery of admissible evidence" even if the information will not be admissible at the trial.[16] Thus, at a deposition a lawyer can demand that the deponent disclose hearsay statements that would be inadmissible at trial. However, the lawyer cannot entirely ignore evidentiary doctrine during a deposition. To begin with, if the lawyer neglects to assert an evidentiary privilege during the deposition, the privilege may be waived for trial. Moreover, while most substantive evidentiary doctrines such as hearsay are inapplicable at a deposition, the opponent must make form objections such as the objection that the question is argumentative or misleading.[17] Effective use of depositions will enable a party to discover the evidence both for and against his position. Furthermore, the deposition of an opposing witness allows the attorney to evaluate the witness's demeanor: Will the deponent probably be an effective witness at trial? The witnesses' performance during their depositions can have a major impact on the settlement value of the case. That impact is especially likely if the deposition is videotaped. In 1993, Federal Rule of Civil Procedure 30(b)(2) was amended to give the moving party the presumptive right to specify "the method of recording." A videotaped deposition captures "that moment of shocked silence when the witness is confronted with an awful truth or incredible

---

("Section 26(a)(2) does not limit an expert's testimony simply to reading his report. No language in the rule would suggest such a limitation. The rule contemplates that the expert will supplement, elaborate upon, explain, and subject himself to cross-examination upon his report").

[14]Rules 26 to 37, Rules of Civil Procedure for the District Courts of the United States. At least 28 states have adopted the federal rules with variations. Oakley & Coon, The Federal Rules in State Courts: A Survey of State Court Systems of Civil Procedure, 61 Wash. L. Rev. 1367 (1986).

[15]Fed. R. Civ. P. 30.

[16]Fed. R. Civ. P. 26(b)(1). See detailed discussion in 6 Moore's Federal Practice ¶ 26.41 (3d ed. 2010).

[17]Imwinkelried & Blumoff, Pretrial Discovery: Strategy and Tactics § 7:21 (rev. 2004). See Ch. 2 infra.

surprise" or "the look of perplexed consternation or shocked embarrassment."[18] That demeanor may do irreparable damage to the witness's credibility.

Of course, depositions are not the only formal discovery devices. In many states in civil cases, written interrogatories may also be directed to the opponent, and he must answer them.[19] Interrogatories are usually employed hand in hand with oral depositions. For instance, if the opponent is a corporation, the lawyer might use interrogatories about the corporation's organizational structure to identify potential deponents. Further, a party often demands production, that is, that the adversary permit him to examine papers and things—even real property—relating to the subject matter of the suit.[20] The production context produces more published opinions dealing with the waiver of evidentiary privileges than any other setting. In many cases, the question presented is whether the opponent's inadvertent production of privileged documents waives the privilege.[21] Next, in over half the states in personal injury actions and sometimes other suits in which a party's physical or mental condition is in issue, the judge may issue an order for the physical or mental examination of a party.[22] Lastly, although not strictly speaking a discovery device, in many states a party can send requests for admissions to his opponent who must either admit or deny the specified fact.[23] For instance, a lawyer might ask that the opponent admit the facts necessary to lay the evidentiary foundation for introducing an exhibit at trial.

In many jurisdictions, after the close of discovery a pretrial hearing or conference is authorized for civil cases, although it is rarely used in some states.[24] When the time for trial approaches—usually two or three weeks before the date set for trial—the judge summons counsel for both sides and sometimes the parties. At the conference, the judge seeks to settle questions of pleading, define the scope of the dispute, and secure stipulations as to the facts not genuinely at issue. The original federal rule authorizing

---

[18]Neubauer, Videotaping Depositions, 19 Litig. 60, 60 (Sum. 1993).

[19]Fed. R. Civ. P. 33. See general discussion in Wright & Kane, Federal Courts § 86 (7th ed. 2011).

[20]Fed. R. Civ. P. 34.

[21]2 Imwinkelried, The New Wigmore: Evidentiary Privileges § 6.12.4b(4) (2d ed. 2010). Congress adopted new Federal Rule of Evidence 502 to address this problem.

[22]Fed. R. Civ. P. 35.

[23]This device is usually unavailable in states that have not adopted Federal Rule of Civil Procedure 36.

[24]For general discussion of pretrial conferences, see Manual for Complex Litigation § 21.2 (4th ed. 2004).

conferences[25] mentions, *inter alia,* the following objectives of the hearing:

(1) The simplification of the issues;

(3) The possibility of obtaining admissions of fact and of documents which will avoid unnecessary proof;

(4) The limitation of the number of expert witnesses; [and]

(5) The advisability of a preliminary reference of issues to a master for findings to be used as evidence when the trial is to be by jury.

The pretrial conference can serve as a vehicle for reaching agreement on various factual issues, although the conference does not always yield that result.[26] By process of elimination, the conference helps the parties identify the remaining disputed issues which the trial evidence will focus on.

One other procedure should be mentioned before concluding this summary: the procurement of the issuance and service of writs of subpoena for the witnesses who are to be called at trial. If a third party had custody of a relevant document or other physical evidence, the party who desires its production at trial may secure a subpoena duces tecum (SDT) addressed to the third party. The SDT commands him to attend the trial and to bring with him the document or other object. Once again evidence law comes into play. Like a party resisting a production request, a witness opposing a subpoena may occasionally assert an evidentiary privilege to quash the subpoena.

The use of some of these discovery devices can result in creating testimony and exhibits which can be introduced at trial. One of the risks of resorting to formal discovery is that the lawyer might inadvertently preserve unfavorable evidence for trial. (That risk explains why experienced litigators routinely conduct informal discovery before using formal discovery devices; a deposition is less risky if beforehand the lawyer gains at least a general sense of what the deponent is likely to testify to.) In certain circumstances, deposition testimony may be introduced at trial. Under the federal rules, an opposing party's deposition may be admitted virtually without any conditions.[27] The opposing party's statements at the deposition routinely fall within the hearsay exemption for statements by opposing parties (formerly called

---

[25]Fed. R. Civ. P. 16. The rule has been amended to state its purposes in more detail. The history of the pretrial conference is outlined in Sunderland, The Theory and Practice of Pre–Trial Procedure, 36 Mich. L. Rev. 215 (1937).

[26]See study of the pretrial conference in Rosenberg, The Pretrial Confer-ence and Effective Justice 23–71 (1964).

[27]Fed. R. Civ. P. 32(a)(3): "(3) An adverse party may use for any purpose the deposition of a party or anyone who, when deposed, was the party's officer, director, managing agent, or designee under Rule 30(b)(6) or

admissions of a party-opponent). The most common conditions for introducing the deposition testimony of non-party witnesses are the requirements set out in the Federal Rules of Civil Procedure.[28] The Federal Rules of Evidence also contain provisions regulating the admissibility of depositions under the former testimony hearsay exception.[29] By way of example, in most jurisdictions, a non-party deponent's deposition is admissible only if the deponent is unavailable to testify in person at trial.[30]

*Criminal cases.* Discovery procedures are also available to criminal defendants. However, extensive criminal discovery is a relatively recent development. Only in recent decades have rules or statutes been enacted to accord criminal defendants extensive discovery rights,[31] and even these procedures are limited. The 1970 Crime Control Act authorizes the defense to conduct witness depositions primarily for the preservation of the evidence (for future use as evidence), rather than merely for the purpose of discovery. To obtain judicial authorization for such a deposition or conditional examination, the defendant must make a preliminary showing that the prospective deponent will probably be unavailable at trial. Today some jurisdictions also authorize the prosecution to conduct such depositions.[32] Federal Rule of Criminal Procedure 16 is a broad discovery provision concerning defense discovery of reports, tests, grand jury testimony, books, papers, documents, tangible objects, and places.[33] There is a more limited provision for reciprocal discovery of similar matters by the government.[34] Rule 16 has been amended several times. The 1993 amendment is particularly noteworthy, since it expands the

---

31(a)(4)."

[28]Fed. R. Civ. P. 32(a)(2), (4) provides that depositions may be used at the trial in accordance with the following provisions:

(2) Any party may use a deposition to contradict or impeach the testimony given by the deponent as a witness, or for any other purpose allowed by the Federal Rules of Evidence.

* * * *

(4) A party may use for any purpose the deposition of a witness, whether or not a party, if the court finds: (A) that the witness is dead; (B) that the witness is more than 100 miles from the place of hearing or trial or is outside the United States, unless it appears that the witness's absence was procured by the party offering the deposition; (C) that the witness cannot attend or testify because of age, illness, infirmity, or imprisonment; (D) that the

party offering the deposition could not procure the witness's attendance by subpoena; or (E) on motion and notice, that exceptional circumstances make it desirable–in the interest of justice and with due regard to the importance of live testimony in open court–to permit the deposition to be used.

[29]See §§ 301 to 308 infra.

[30]Fed. R. Evid. 804(a).

[31]See discussion in Wright and Miller's Federal Practice and Procedure, Criminal § 251. See also § 97 infra.

[32]18 U.S.C.A. § 3503. *See* Wright and Miller's Federal Practice and Procedure, Criminal § 241.

[33]Fed. R. Crim. P. 16.

[34]Some provisions of Rule 16 limit government discovery rights to situations in which defendant has sought discovery under the rule. *See also* Fed.

discovery of expert testimony which either the government or the defense contemplates offering at trial. Unlike civil parties, however, criminal litigants do not have any duty to make mandatory pre-discovery disclosure; but one side can seek discovery from the other side.

The preceding paragraphs survey the most frequently used formal discovery devices. In various states, there are miscellaneous official discovery procedures, but no detailed review is attempted here.[35]

Whether the lawyer relies primarily on formal or informal discovery techniques to prepare for trial, the objective is the same: gathering a large quantity of believable, admissible evidence for trial. If the lawyer achieves that pretrial objective, the lawyer's client should gain either an advantageous settlement or a favorable trial verdict. In the vast majority of instances, the case settles without going to trial; in 2002 only 1.8% of the civil cases filed in federal court were disposed of by trial.[36] In most cases, pretrial is *the* trial of the attorney's case. The settlement is largely driven by the quantity and quality of the admissible evidence unearthed during formal and informal pretrial discovery.

## §4 The order of presenting evidence at the trial

If the case does not settle, the litigants proceed to trial. Evidence law figures even more prominently at this stage than it does during the pretrial phase.

If the hearing will be a jury trial, the jury must be selected before the lawyers present their evidence. Depending on the jurisdiction, during the voir dire examination of the panelists the judge might permit the attorney to question them about potential items of evidence in the case. A panelist could conceivably have such an adverse reaction to the item of evidence that he would be challengeable for cause, or the attorney might want to employ a peremptory strike to remove him from the jury.[1]

After the jury selection, the attorneys present opening statements. During the statements, the attorneys preview their evidence for the jury. According to American Bar Association

---

R. Crim. P. 26.

[35]See the various state provisions cited in Advisory Committee Note for Rule 16, Preliminary Draft of Proposed Amendments to the Federal Rules of Criminal Procedure, January 31, 1970.

[36]Refo, The Vanishing Trial, 30 Litigation, Wint. 2004, at 1, 2. *See also* A.B.A. Litigation Section, The Vanishing Trial (2004); Burns, The Death of the American Trial (2009); Galantner, The Vanishing Trial: An Examination of Trials and Related Matters in Federal and State Courts, 1 J. Emp. Legal Stud. 459, 460 (2004).

**[Section 4]**

[1]People v. Williams, 29 Cal. 3d 392, 174 Cal. Rptr. 317, 628 P.2d 869 (1981).

Model Rule of Professional Conduct 3.4(e), in opening a lawyer may not "allude to any matter that the lawyer does not reasonably believe . . . will . . . be supported by admissible evidence . . ." at trial. By far, the most common objection during opening statement is that a particular statement is argumentative. In this context, "argumentative" means that the statement is a conclusion which would be inadmissible under the evidence rules governing lay and expert opinion testimony.[2] As a rule of thumb, an attorney may not make a statement during opening unless, under the governing opinion rules, it would be permissible for one of the attorney's scheduled witnesses to make the statement on the stand. The attorney might be uncertain whether he or his opponent may refer to a particular item of potential evidence in opening. If so, even before opening statement the lawyer can file a pretrial in limine motion seeking an advance ruling on the admissibility of the evidence.[3] It is especially advisable to raise the issue before trial when the lawyer intends to rely on a novel type of expert testimony or an unconventional noncharacter or nonhearsay theory of admissibility.

After the opening statements, testimony begins. Under the usual order of proceeding at the trial, including a trial under the Federal Rules of Evidence, the plaintiff or prosecutor, with the burden of establishing his claim,[4] first introduces the evidence to prove the facts necessary to enable him to recover or obtain a conviction.[5] This initial phase is called the plaintiff's or prosecutor's case-in-chief. For instance, in a Contract lawsuit, the plaintiff would introduce evidence relating to the formation of the

---

[2]Jeans, Trial Advocacy § 8.13 (2d ed. 1993).

[3]See § 52 infra.

[4]Walker, Thibaut & Andresli, The Order of Presentation at Trial, 82 Yale L.J. 216, 216–26 (1992) (empirical research indicates that if jurors knows that an advocate's presentation will be followed by a contrary presentation, they adopt a more skeptical attitude toward the initial presentation; thus, by requiring the plaintiff to go first and alerting the jury that there will be a subsequent defense presentation, the judge places a real burden of proof on the plaintiff).

[5]This sequence is the usual order, since the plaintiff has the "burden of proof" in the sense of the duty of first proceeding with evidence to establish the facts pleaded in the com-

plaint. But this burden of opening the evidence usually carries with it the advantage called the "right to open and close," that is, the privilege of having the first and the last word in the closing argument to the jury. To obtain this advantage, the defendant occasionally admits the plaintiff's cause of action and rests solely on some affirmative defense in the answer; the defense thus assumes the burden of proceeding with the evidence first, but gains the right to open and close the argument. E.g., Liptak v. Security Ben. Ass'n, 350 Ill. 614, 183 N.E. 564 (1932); 6 Wigmore, Evidence § 1866 (Chadbourn rev. 1976) (a helpful chart showing the stages in presenting evidence and examining the individual witness), § 1867 (discussing the trial judge's power to permit deviations from the usual order).

contract, his fulfillment of the conditions to the defendant's duty, the defendant's breach of duty, and the amount of damages caused by the breach. At this stage the plaintiff calls all the witnesses on whom he relies to establish these facts, together with the pertinent documents. The documents are formally offered into evidence when they have been authenticated by a sponsoring witness's testimony. During this stage, each witness is initially questioned by the plaintiff's counsel on direct examination and then cross-examined by opposing counsel. These examinations can be followed by redirect and re-cross examinations. When all the plaintiff's or prosecutor's witnesses to his main case have been subjected to this process of questioning and cross-questioning, the plaintiff or prosecutor signals the completion of his case-in-chief by announcing that he rests.

In most jurisdictions, the judge presiding at trial has a discretionary power to permit testimony be presented out of normal order.[6] Thus, if it is impossible for a key defense witness to appear later in the hearing, the judge could allow the witness to testify early even before the plaintiff's or prosecutor's case-in-chief has concluded. Suppose, for example, that a civil defendant contemplates calling a doctor as a witness and that the physician is scheduled to conduct a life-or-death surgery on a day that will probably fall within the defense case-in-chief. In these circumstances, the trial judge might grant the defense leave to interrupt the plaintiff's case in order to present the surgeon's testimony.

Assume, though, that in the normal order, the plaintiff or prosecutor has rested. If the defense counsel believes that at this point the plaintiff or prosecutor has not presented a legally sufficient case, the counsel moves for a nonsuit, directed verdict, or judgment of acquittal as a matter of law. The counsel asserts the weakness of the plaintiff's or prosecutor's evidence and claims that the plaintiff or prosecutor has not met the initial burden of production or going forward.[7] For purposes of this motion, the judge assumes that all the evidence introduced by the plaintiff or prosecutor is admissible. The motion poses this question: If the trier of fact decides to believe all the plaintiff's or prosecutor's testimony, does the testimony have sufficient cumulative probative value to rationally sustain a plaintiff's verdict or conviction? If the testimony lacks adequate probative worth, the judge makes a peremptory ruling against the plaintiff or prosecutor. Otherwise, the trial continues.

If the trial continues, the next major phase is the defense case-

---

[6]Loinaz v. EG & G, Inc., 910 F.2d 1, 5 (1st Cir. 1990).

[7]See §§ 336, 338 infra.

in-chief or case in defense. The defendant now presents the witnesses and the tangible evidence supporting his case. At this stage the defendant produces evidence disputing the plaintiff's or prosecutor's claim. Thus, the defendant could present testimony that the alleged contract was never agreed on. Similarly, in a negligence case the defense might offer testimony that some bodily injury was not permanent as the plaintiff alleged. The defense can also support any properly pleaded affirmative defenses, such as fraud in the inducement of a contract sued on or the execution of a release of a personal injury claim. Here again each witness's story on direct examination is subject to being tested by cross-examination and supplemented on re-direct. When the defendant has completed the presentation of his proof of affirmative defenses, if any, and her evidence rebutting the plaintiff's or prosecutor's claims, the defendant announces that she rests.

At the conclusion of the defense case-in-chief, the defense could renew the motion for a directed verdict or nonsuit. At this point, the defense can argue alternatively that it has so weakened the plaintiff's or prosecutor's case that no rational juror could convict or find for the plaintiff or that the evidence of an affirmative defense is so strong that no rational juror could reject the defense.

The plaintiff or prosecutor now has another turn at bat; he may present a case in rebuttal. At this stage, the plaintiff or prosecutor is not entitled as of right to present witnesses who merely support the allegations of the complaint or accusatory pleading.[8] Rather, the plaintiff or prosecutor is confined to testimony refuting the defense evidence, unless the trial judge in her discretion permits him to depart from the regular scope of rebuttal.[9] The plaintiff's or prosecutor's rebuttal witnesses may be new ones, but he can also recall witnesses who testified for him during the case-in-chief to answer some point first raised by the defendant's witnesses. In this, as in the other stages, the witness may not only be examined on direct, but also cross-examined, redirected, and re-cross-examined. When the plaintiff's or prosecutor's case in rebuttal is finished, he closes his case. If new points are brought out in the plaintiff's or prosecutor's rebuttal, the defendant may meet them by evidence in rejoinder or

---

[8]Daly v. Far Eastern Shipping Co. PLC., 238 F. Supp. 2d 1231, 1238 (W.D. Wash. 2003), aff'd, 108 Fed. Appx. 476 (9th Cir. 2004) ("rebuttal evidence 'may not merely support the case-in-chief of the prosecution or plaintiff.' Rebuttal evidence is admissible only where the need for it could not have been foreseen at the time the plaintiff presented its case in chief.").

[9]U.S. v. Tejada, 956 F.2d 1256, 1267 (2d Cir. 1992) ("Trial judges have 'wide discretion' in permitting the introduction of evidence in rebuttal which might well have been brought out in the Government's case in chief.").

surrebuttal.[10] Otherwise, he closes his case. In a rare case, after a party has closed, the judge may permit the party to reopen the case to present additional evidence.[11]

When witnesses are called during the various phases of the case, the attorneys may not be the only ones to question the witnesses. To begin with, the judge may question the witnesses.[12]

---

[10]U.S. v. Barnette, 211 F.3d 803, 821 (4th Cir. 2000) (the defendant has the right to present surrebuttal to respond to "obviously . . . new matter" introduced during the rebuttal); U.S. v. Gaines, 170 F.3d 72, 83 (1st Cir. 1999) ("surrebuttal should be allowed 'only to explain away new facts brought forward by the proponent in rebuttal, or evidence to impeach witnesses who testified in rebuttal' ").

[11]U.S. v. Boone, 437 F.3d 829, 936–37 (8th Cir. 2006) ("Where the government has been allowed to reopen, the factors to be considered in reviewing that decision include whether the new evidence caused surprise to the defendant, whether the defendant was given adequate opportunity to rebut the new evidence, and whether the evidence was more detrimental to the defendant than it otherwise might have been because of the order in which it was presented"); U.S. v. Peterson, 233 F.3d 101 (1st Cir. 2000). By way of example, suppose that under Federal Rule of Evidence 404(b), a prosecutor proffered evidence of an accused's uncharged crimes in order to establish the *mens rea* of the charged offense. See § 190 infra. However, the defense counsel represented that the defense did not intend to dispute the existence of the mens rea. Based on that representation, the judge exercised her discretion under Federal Rule of Evidence 403 to exclude the evidence. Yet, for the first time during closing argument, the defense counsel challenged the sufficiency of the evidence of mens rea. In this scenario, it would be appropriate for the judge to allow the prosecution to reopen the evidence to present the testimony about the uncharged crimes

probative of the accused's mens rea. *See also* Peek v. State, 106 S.W.3d 72 (Tex. Crim. App. 2003) (under the governing statute, the judge must reopen the case if the proffered evidence would materially change the case). *But see* U.S. v. Nunez, 432 F.3d 573, 579–80 (4th Cir. 2005) (the trial judge abused discretion by permitting the government to reopen the case after the summations and the beginning of jury deliberations; "The party moving to reopen should provide a reasonable explanation for its failure to present the evidence in its case-in-chief . . . . The belated receipt of such testimony should not imbue the evidence with distorted importance . . . or preclude an adversary from having an adequate opportunity to meet the additional evidence . . . ."); Schafer v. Roe, 67 Fed. Appx. 388 (9th Cir. 2003) (if the judge reopens the case to permit the prosecution to present additional evidence, the judge must give the defense an opportunity to respond to the new evidence; but the defense may respond only to the subject covered by the new evidence) and People v. Whipple, 276 A.D.2d 829, 714 N.Y.S.2d 554 (3d Dep't 2000) (the trial judge erred in allowing the prosecution to reopen its case in order to present evidence essential to establishing a prima facie case of guilt).

If the trial judge denies the motion to reopen in order to preserve the alleged error for purposes of appeal, the litigant should make an offer of proof describing the additional evidence. Austin B. v. Escondido Union School Dist., 149 Cal. App. 4th 860, 57 Cal. Rptr. 3d 454 (4th Dist. 2007).

[12]Fed. R. Evid. 614.

The judge is not a mere umpire at trial.[13] The judge has discretion to exercise that power in order to clarify the witness's testimony and fill in important gaps in the record.[14] However, the judge must avoid giving the jury the impression that he or she has reached a conclusion as to the merits of the case or the witness's credibility.[15] In addition, in many jurisdictions, either the jurors have the right to pose questions or the trial judge has discretion to allow them to do so.[16] The judge typically screens juror questions and rules on their propriety before the question is put to the witness in open court.[17]

When both parties have announced that they have closed, the evidentiary hearing comes to a halt; and the trial proceeds with the closing arguments of counsel and the court's instructions to the jury. The instructions frequently include jury charges about the evidence in the case. For example, if the judge earlier ruled inadmissible certain proffered testimony the jury was exposed to, the judge might give the jury a *curative* instruction to disregard the testimony.[18] Even if the judge ruled certain evidence admissible, the judge might give the jury a *limiting* instruction that they may use the item of evidence only for a particular purpose or only against a particular party. Or the judge could read the jurors a *cautionary* instruction informing them that they should be especially wary in evaluating a certain type of evidence such as eyewitness or accomplice testimony.[19] Or, if an issue such as the authenticity of a document falls under Federal Rule of Evidence 104(b), the judge would tell the jury that they must decide the issue and disregard the evidence during the balance of their deliberations if they decide that the document is not genuine.[20]

To sum up, the major stages of the trial are:
  (1) the plaintiff's or prosecutor's main case or case-in-chief;
  (2) the defendant's case-in-chief or case in defense;

---

[13]U.S. v. Catalan-Roman, 585 F.3d 453 (1st Cir. 2009).

[14]U.S. v. Angulo-Hernandez, 565 F.3d 2, 9–10 (1st Cir. 2009); U.S. v. Thompson, 310 Fed. Appx. 485 (3d Cir. 2008); Lopez v. State, 297 Ga. App. 618, 677 S.E.2d 776 (2009).

[15]U.S. v. Melendez-Rivas, 566 F.3d 41, 45–51 (1st Cir. 2009).

[16]U.S. v. Smith, 569 F.3d 1209 (10th Cir. 2009); Ex parte Malone, 12 So. 3d 60 (Ala. 2008).

[17]U.S. v. Rawlings, 522 F.3d 403, 408–09 (D.C. Cir. 2008).

[18]Glenn v. State, 796 N.E.2d 322 (Ind. Ct. App. 2003) (the court recommended that the trial judge explain to the jurors the reason for the inadmissibility of the evidence; scholarly studies indicate that informing the jury of the reason for excluding the evidence can increase the effectiveness of the curative instruction).

[19]U.S. v. Telfaire, 469 F.2d 552 (D.C. Cir. 1972); U.S. v. Starzecpyzel, 880 F. Supp. 1027 (S.D. N.Y. 1995) (the appendix sets out a cautionary instruction on questioned document examination testimony); People v. Guzman, 47 Cal. App. 3d 380, 121 Cal. Rptr. 69 (2d Dist. 1975).

[20]See § 53 infra.

(3) the plaintiff's or prosecutor's rebuttal; and

(4) the defendant's rejoinder or surrebuttal.

In each stage, each witness's examination may pass through these steps:

(1) the direct examination conducted by the party who calls the witness;

(2) the cross-examination by the adversary;

(3) redirect;

(4) re-cross;[21] and

(5) questions by the judge or jurors.

The Federal Rules of Evidence do not prescribe an order for the presentation of evidence at trial. However, under Rule 611(a), the trial judge customarily follows the common law order.[22] According to Rule 611(a), the court "shall exercise reasonable control over the . . . order of examining witnesses and presenting evidence so as to (1) make those procedures effective for determining the truth, (2) avoid wasting time, and (3) protect witnesses from harassment or undue embarrassment." As a practical matter, judges rarely find a sufficient reason to depart from the normal sequence of the major stages of the hearing described above.[23] The primary focus of the explicit provisions of Rule 611 is the control of the steps in examining individual witnesses.[24] Hence, even trials conducted under the Federal Rules ordinarily follow

---

[21]In general, the order of presentation of evidence is similar in a criminal case, with the prosecution taking the role of "plaintiff."

[22]In Daubert v. Merrell Dow Pharmaceuticals, Inc., 509 U.S. 579, 113 S. Ct. 2786, 125 L. Ed. 2d 469 (1993), the Supreme Court noted that in at least some substantive doctrinal areas in evidence law, the provisions of the Federal Rules of Evidence supersede the common law and "occupy the field." 509 U.S. at 587–88. However, the Rules contain relatively few procedural provisions. For example, the Rules are silent on the scope of the cases-in-chief or the rebuttal stages of the case. In Beech Aircraft Corp. v. Rainey, 488 U.S. 153, 109 S. Ct. 439, 102 L. Ed. 2d 445 (1988), the Court held that the common law rule of completeness had survived the enactment of Federal Rule 106. Thus, the Court has recognized that the Rules are not a self-contained, comprehensive code on related procedures.

[23]Most often deviations from the normal sequence of a hearing concern the permission to call and question a witness out of order. See the cases cited in 3 Mueller & Kirkpatrick, Federal Evidence §§ 6.60 to 6.61 (3d ed. 2007). In Truman v. Wainwright, 514 F.2d 150 (5th Cir.1975), the court upheld the usual order by approving the constitutionality of a ruling that defendant had no right to call a witness during the presentation of the state's case.

[24]See cases cited in 4 Weinstein's Federal Evidence § 611.02 (rev. 2011). The Advisory Committee's Note, referring to Rule 611(a)(1), quoted in the text, takes the position that the clause "restates in broad terms the power and obligation of the judge as developed under common law principles." See 6 Wigmore, Evidence §§ 1866–67 (Chadbourn rev. 1976). See generally Geders v. U.S., 425 U.S. 80, 86–87, 96 S. Ct. 1330, 47 L. Ed. 2d 592 (1976) ("Our cases have consistently recog-

the traditional common law norms for the major stages of the case.

---

nized the important role the trial judge plays in the federal system of criminal justice. '[T]he judge is not a mere moderator, but is the governor of the trial for the purpose of assuring its proper conduct and of determining questions of law.' . . . A criminal trial does not unfold like a play with actors following a script; there is no scenario and can be none. The trial judge must meet situations as they arise and to do this must have broad power to cope with the complexities and contingencies inherent in the adversary process. To this end, he may determine generally the order in which parties will adduce proof; his determination will be reviewed only for abuse of discretion. Within limits, the judge may control the scope of rebuttal testimony . . .; may refuse to allow cumulative, repetitive, or irrelevant testimony . . .; and may control the scope of examination of witnesses . . . . If truth and fairness are not to be sacrificed, the judge must exert substantial control over the proceedings.").

# Title 2. Examination of Witnesses

## Chapter 2

## The Form of Questions on Direct; The Judge's Witnesses; Refreshing Memory

### § 5    The form of questions: (a) Questions calling for a free narrative versus specific questions

Any experienced litigator knows that at trial, the vast majority of objections relate to the issue of the form of the question rather than substantive evidence doctrines such as hearsay. Form objections can arise on either direct or cross-examination. Cross-examination can be more dramatic than direct examination, and skill in cross-examination may be more difficult to develop than the essential skill of direct examination, constructing a coherent, compelling narrative from the mouths of your own witnesses. However, the latter skill is far more important.[1]

One of the key tactical decisions on direct is whether a particular witness's testimony will better be elicited by several questions about particular facts rather than by a more open-ended question. In the latter case, the lawyer directs the witness's attention to the relevant incident by asking him whether he was on the scene at the time and then inviting him to generally recount what he saw and heard. This latter method, narrative testimony, is often more persuasive. From the jurors' perspective the account does not seem to come from the counsel, as it might when the counsel

---

[Section 5]

[1]*See* Mauet, Fundamentals of Trial Techniques Ch. 5 (8th ed. 2010); Wellman, Day in Court, Ch. 10 (1910), reprinted in Davenport, Voices in Court 86–98 (1958); Spellman, Direct Examination of Witnesses (1968).

poses very specific questions to the witness.[2] If the witness has a good memory, a pleasant personality, and an effective speaking style, his spontaneous narration of his own story may be more interesting and impressive. Narrative testimony allows the witness to put his honesty and intelligence on better display for the jury. Furthermore, empirical research indicates that spontaneous narrative is more accurate (because it is less influenced by suggestion).

However, the same studies show that fully interrogated testimony tends to be more complete.[3] Moreover, specific interrogation can be preferable to presenting complicated testimony in proper order, helping a nervous witness, and preventing boring testimony by a dull witness.[4] In addition, there are risks to relying on questions calling for narrative responses. When a witness is examined by the narrative method, counsel must be ready to interrupt with specific questions if the testimony becomes confusing, or to supplement the narrative with questions to bring out omitted facts. For example, if an expert uses a technical term of art, counsel should invite the expert to define the term for the jury.

Given these conflicting considerations, it is no surprise that

---

[2]Conley, Language in the Courtroom, 15 Trial, Sep. 1979, at 32 (the researchers in the Duke University Law and Language Project studied the impact of different questioning styles on the jurors; they found that the more acute jurors note the difference between questioning by one-ended queries and leading interrogation; in addition, the researchers discovered that some of those jurors infer that an attorney who leads his witness lacks faith in the witness; most importantly, the researchers concluded that once a juror infers that the attorney lacks faith in a witness, the juror tends to discount the witness's testimony); McElhaney, Straight Talk on Direct: When Done Well, Examining a Witness Is Like a Conversation, 84 A.B.A. J. 82 (Mar. 1998) ("even if the other side does not object, leading on direct sends the message that the witness is not a good source of information and needs to be told what to say").

[3]Gardner, The Perception and Memory of Witnesses, 18 Cornell L.Q. 391, 404 (1923), citing Marston, Studies in Testimony, 15 J. Crim. Law and Criminology, 1–31 (1924); Wigmore, The Science of Judicial Proof § 264 (3d ed. 1937). *But see* Marshall, Marquis & Oskamp, Effects of Kind of Question and Atmosphere of Interrogation on Accuracy and Completeness of Testimony, 84 Harv. L. Rev. 1620 (1971).

[4]Weinstein & Berger, Evidence ¶ 611[01] at 611–20 (1987) ("Often leading questions on direct will more quickly get the witness over preliminary matters. Combining this fact with McCormick's suggestion will lead to the following desirable sequences of forms of direct testimony: first leading questions to get to the central issue; then a request for the witness to tell what happened with appropriate instructions on avoiding hearsay and opinions; then searching non-leading questions; then refreshment by documents and the like; then leading questions to refresh; and, finally documents as past recollections recorded."). 4 Weinstein's Federal Evidence § 6.11.06[b] (rev. 2011) is generally to the same effect.

trial judges vary in their attitude toward questions calling for a narrative. Some trial judges enforce a general prohibition of questions calling for a narrative. These judges are concerned about the risk that the witness will narrate in a jumbled, confusing fashion. Under the prevailing view, though, there is no general rule of law requiring or even preferring either form of questioning. For example, there is no provision in the Federal Rules of Evidence forbidding narrative questions. Indeed, in rare situations in some states, the rules of legal ethics require the direct examiner to attempt to elicit the witness's testimony in narrative fashion.[5] Admittedly, a number of courts have correctly voiced concern about the possibility that when asked to narrate his story, the witness will mention hearsay or other inadmissible testimony.[6] However, together with counsel's careful phrasing of the question, a proper caution by counsel or court, on the adversary's request, can usually prevent this.

It is true that if the witness blurts out an improper statement, the only remedy is striking that part of the evidence and giving the jury a curative instruction to disregard the stricken testimony; and sometimes it is very difficult to unring the bell. There is a further danger that the opposing counsel may waive an objection if he does not interrupt promptly and move to strike. Opposing

---

[5]The situation is the case in which the direct examiner is convinced that the witness intends to commit perjury. In that event, some jurisdictions mandate that the direct examiner resort to the narrative method in order to minimize the attorney's involvement in the perjurious testimony. A.B.A. Defense Function Standard 7.7(c) formerly prescribed the procedures the direct examiner was to follow when she knew that the client contemplated perjury:

> The lawyer may identify the witness as the defendant and may ask appropriate questions of the defendant when it is believed that the defendant's answers will not be perjurious. As to matters for which it is believed the defendant will offer perjurious testimony, the lawyer should seek to avoid direct examination of the defendant in the conventional manner; instead, the lawyer should ask the defendant if he or she wishes to make any additional statement concerning the case to the trier or triers of fact.

See People v. Johnson, 62 Cal. App. 4th 608, 72 Cal. Rptr. 2d 805 (4th Dist.

1998); People v. Gadson, 19 Cal. App. 4th 1700, 24 Cal. Rptr. 2d 219 (2d Dist. 1993); Shockley v. State, 565 A.2d 1373, 1379–80 (Del. 1989) ("Recently the ABA has eschewed the use of the narrative approach. Nevertheless, the narrative continues to be a commonly accepted method of dealing with client perjury."); Com. v. Mitchell, 438 Mass. 535, 781 N.E.2d 1237 (2003); State v. McDowell, 2003 WI App 168, 266 Wis. 2d 599, 669 N.W.2d 204 (Ct. App. 2003); Aprile, Client Perjury: When Do You Know the Defendant Is Lying?, 19 Crim. Just. 14 (Fall 2004); Lefstein, Legal Ethics—Reflections on the Client Perjury Problem and Nix v. Whiteside, 2 Crim. Just. 27 (Sum. 1996).

[6]State v. Allemand, 153 La. 741, 96 So. 552, 553 (1923) (better practice is to ask definite questions, but here there was no prejudice); State v. Sullivan, 159 La. 589, 105 So. 631 (1925) (witness volunteered incompetent evidence in course of story which jury were instructed to disregard; no prejudice).

counsel must listen very intently to identify the objectionable parts of a narrative answer. However, the need to elicit the witness's knowledge in the most accurate way is a legitimate interest that trumps these dangers. The trial judge ought to have discretion, reviewable only for abuse,[7] to control the form of examination, to the end that the testimony is accurately presented. Hence, the judge may permit either method discussed.[8] On balance, whenever circumstances make narrative testimony feasible, its use is usually in the interest of both the examining party and the system; narrative testimony is not only more persuasive but it also can yield a more accurate account of the truth.

Enlightened judges rarely curb the use of questions calling for short narrative responses, except in criminal trials when it poses the risk of exposing the jury to constitutionally inadmissible testimony. As a practical matter, at the outset of a direct examination in a civil case many judges entertain a presumption that the lawyer may elicit the witness's testimony in narrative form. The presumption is rebutted—and the judge will insist on more specific questions—only if the witness's narrative becomes confused or the witness makes repeated references to inadmissible matter. So long as the witness avoids those two pitfalls during her testimony, the judge will permit the examiner to elicit the witness's testimony by questions calling for answers the length of a short paragraph. To ensure that the presumption remains unrebutted throughout the direct examination, the at-

---

[7]Denbeaux & Risinger, Questioning Questions: Objections to Form in the Interrogation of Witnesses, 33 Ark. L. Rev. 439, 465 (1979) ("We find no reported case in the last fifty years in which a reversal resulted solely from failure to control leading in the questioning process, and only one in which it was a major factor in the decision to reverse.").

[8]Northern Pac. R. Co. v. Charless, 51 F. 562 (C.C.A. 9th Cir. 1892), rev'd on other grounds, 162 U.S. 359 (1896) (leading case permitting free narrative in court's discretion); People v. Belcher, 189 Cal. App. 2d 404, 11 Cal. Rptr. 175 (2d Dist. 1961); Temple v. State, 245 Ind. 21, 195 N.E.2d 850 (1964); Pumphrey v. State, 84 Neb. 636, 122 N.W. 19, 21 (1909) (in court's discretion to require specific questions); Deams v. State, 159 Tex. Crim. 496, 265 S.W.2d 96 (1953) (judge in discretion could require specific questions). See also Ward v. City of Pittsburgh, 353 Pa. 156, 44 A.2d 553 (1945) (it was proper for judge to permit witness, whose power of speech had been affected by a stroke, to give his testimony by a written statement; the witness was present and could have been cross-examined). See generally U.S. v. Young, 745 F.2d 733, 761 (2d Cir. 1984) ("Generally speaking, a trial judge has broad discretion in deciding whether or not to allow narrative testimony. Fed. R. Evid. 611(a). We see no reason to apply a different rule here, where the narrative testimony accompanied and explained videotaped evidence."); Goings v. U.S., 377 F.2d 753, 762–63 (8th Cir. 1967) ("The trial judge should exercise his discretion with wide latitude to assure an atmosphere in which a witness will feel at ease in telling the truth. Ritualistic formality in presenting evidence should not deter untrained witnesses from telling their story in their own words.").

torney must properly prepare the witness before trial. The witness has to learn the chronology well, and the witness must know what not to mention—for example, inadmissible hearsay—unless the questioner asks point blank about that information.

These principles are consistent with former Federal Rule of Evidence 611(a),[9] which provides:

> The court shall exercise reasonable control over the mode and order of interrogating witnesses and presenting evidence so as to (1) make the interrogation and presentation effective for the ascertainment of the truth, (2) avoid needless consumption of time, and (3) protect witnesses from harassment or undue embarrassment.

Restyled Rule 611(a), effective December 1, 2011, is to the same effect:

> The court shall exercise reasonable control over the mode and order of examining witnesses and presenting evidence so as to:
>
> (1)  make those procedures effective for determining the truth;
>
> (2)  avoid wasting time; and
>
> (3)  protect witnesses from harassment or undue embarrassment.

Rule 611(a) does not purport to announce any categorical "rules" governing the form of the question. The accompanying Advisory Committee Note contains the sensible observation that "[s]pelling out detailed rules to govern the mode . . . of interrogating witnesses and presenting evidence is neither desirable nor feasible. The ultimate responsibility for the effective working of the adversary system rests with the judge."

## § 6 The form of questions: (b) Leading questions

The preceding section compared the technique of presenting the witness's free narrative on direct examination with that of eliciting testimony by specific questions. One danger of the latter method is that the witness may acquiesce in a false suggestion by the questioner. The same danger gives rise to another major form problem on direct examination, namely, leading or suggestive phrasing. The suggestion can plant the belief in its truth in the witness's mind. Some empirical studies confirm many judges' belief that this danger is greater than the average layperson

---

[9]The Advisory Committee's Note declares that the Federal Rule restates common law principles in broad terms. See § 4 supra.

supposes.[1] A friendly or pliant witness may follow suggestions on direct examination.[2] Yet, a case can be made that there is little reason to bar suggestive questions.[3] To be frank, before trial the witness is exposed to numerous, far more powerful suggestive influences. In that light, by the time of trial the "leading" objection seems comparatively trivial.

### *The Definition of "Leading"*

Nevertheless, subject to the limitations discussed in the remainder of this section, objections to leading questions are still permissible under the modern common law and Rule 611(c) of the Federal and Revised Uniform Rules of Evidence.[4] The first sentence of restyled Rule 611(c) announces a general norm that

---

**[Section 6]**

[1]Gardner, The Perception and Memory of Witnesses, 18 Corn. L.Q. 391, 405 (1933).

[2]State v. Hosey, 318 N.C. 330, 348 S.E.2d 805, 808 (1986) (leading questions are undesirable because of the "danger that they will suggest the desired reply to an eager and friendly witness. In effect, lawyers could testify, their testimony punctuated only by an occasional 'yes' or 'no' answer"). *See generally* Denroche, Leading Questions, 6 Crim. L.Q. 21, 22 (1963) ("[F]irst, that the witness is presumed to have a bias in favour of the party calling him; secondly, that the party calling a witness, knowing what that witness may prove, might by leading bring out only that portion of the witness' story favourable to his own case; and thirdly, that a witness, intending to be entirely fair and honest might assent to a leading question which did not express his real meaning.").

[3]Cleary, Evidence as a Problem in Communicating, 5 Vand. L. Rev. 277, 287 (1952) ("The witness is protected against suggestion only while on the stand, seemingly on the assumption either that intervening influences are unimportant or that he comes untouched from event to court. The former is directly contrary to the theory upon which leading questions are prohibited. The latter simply is not so. . . . Under the system of party responsibility for the production of

witnesses, no competent attorney dreams of calling witnesses who have not previously been interviewed. The preliminary interview affords full play to suggestion and context and evokes in advance of trial a complete verbalization, the importance of which cannot be overlooked. When the witness testifies, are his verbalizations at that time based upon his recall of the event or upon his recall of his former verbalizations.").

[4]Former Fed. R. Evid. 611(c) provides: "Leading questions should not be used on direct examination of a witness except as may be necessary to develop the witness' testimony. Ordinarily leading questions should be permitted on cross-examination. When a party calls a hostile witness, an adverse party, or a witness identified with an adverse party, interrogation may be by leading questions." Unif. R. Evid. 611(c) reads: "Leading questions should not be used on the direct examination of a witness except as is necessary to develop the witness's testimony. Ordinarily leading questions should be permitted on cross-examination. A party may interrogate a hostile witness, an adverse party, or a witness identified with an adverse party by leading questions." Effective December 1, 2011, Fed. R. Evid. 611(c) reads: "Leading questions should not be used on direct examination except as necessary to develop the witness's testimony. Ordinarily, the court should allow leading questions: (1) on cross-

"[l]eading questions should not be used on direct examination. . . ." The Advisory Committee Note underscores the choice of the verb "should" rather than "must" or "shall"; the Note emphasizes that the sentence is purposely "phrased in words of suggestion rather than command."

Although the norm against leading on direct is not an inflexible rule, it is still important to develop a working definition of "leading." A leading question is one that suggests to the witness the answer desired by the examiner.[5] A question may be leading because of its form, but sometimes the mere form of a question does not indicate whether it is leading. Some types of phrasing such as "Did he not?" are obviously leading,[6] but almost any other type of question can be leading, depending on its content and context. It is sometimes categorically asserted both that any question which can be answered yes or no is ipso facto leading[7] and that the neophyte attorney can always take refuge in neutral, alternative wording ("State whether or not . . .") to escape the charge of leading. However, sometimes the former kind of question is not leading, and often the latter type is.[8] The bottom line issue is whether an ordinary witness would get the impression

---

examination; and (2) when a party calls a hostile witness, an adverse party, or a witness identified with an adverse party."

[5]California Evidence Code § 764 states that "[a] 'leading question' is a question that suggests to the witness the answer that the examining party desires."

[6]There are degrees of leading:

- Some questions such as "Did he stop?" are mildly leading. The phrasing refers to an event and carries the suggestion that the event occurred. However, especially in bench trials, many judges routinely permit mildly leading questions on direct examination.

- However, the more negative phrasing, "Did he not?," carries a stronger suggestion. Fairly leading questions of this nature often prompts an objection, and especially in jury trials many judges sustain the objection.

- Worse still are brutally leading questions. A question can be made brutally leading in one of three ways. First, the examiner might use prefatory language such as "Isn't it true. . . .?" or "Won't you admit. . . .?" Second, the examiner might add a tag after a declarative sentence: "He came to a full stop. Right?" Finally, if the cross-examiner and a compliant witness get into a rhythm, the questioner utters the declarative sentence, drops the tag, and signifies that the statement is a question by raising his or her voice at the end of the sentence. Rutberg, Conversational Cross-Examination, 29 Am. J. Trial Adv. 353, 365–66 (2005).

[7]But see U.S. v. Hansen, 256 F. Supp. 2d 65, 70 n.10 (D. Mass. 2003), aff'd, 434 F.3d 92 (1st Cir. 2006) ("While not always the case, questions which can be answered either 'Yes' or 'No' are considered leading.").

[8]A question which can be answered yes or no is not leading unless it suggests which answer is desired. Harward v. Harward, 173 Md. 339, 196 A. 318 (1938); Implement Dealers Mut. Ins. Co. v. Castleberry, 368

that the questioner desired one answer rather than another. The form of a question, or previous questioning, may signal that desire, but the most important consideration can be the extent of the particularity of the question itself. When the question describes an incident in detail and asks if the incident happened, the natural inference is that the questioner expects an affirmative answer. Similarly, if one alternative branch of a question is concrete and detailed[9] but the other vague ("Was the sound like the loud scream of a woman in great fear or soft?"), the wording sends the message that the first alternative is preferred. In contrast, when the phrasing of a question is neutral ("At what time did this occur?") or balanced ("Was the water hot or cold?"), it is not leading.[10] To avoid leading question objections, experienced direct examiners consistently begin their questions with natural interrogatory words such as who, what, which, when, where, why, and how.

### The Propriety of Leading Questions

After we have defined the expression, "leading question," the next issue that arises is when it is permissible to employ leading phrasing. The courts have developed different norms for direct and cross-examination. As we have seen, before trial diligent lawyers normally informally interview all the witnesses whom

---

S.W.2d 249 (Tex. Civ. App. Beaumont 1963). It has been said that prefacing a question by "whether or not" seldom removes its leading character. State v. Murphy, 216 S.C. 44, 56 S.E.2d 736 (1949). For illustrative cases, see 3 Wigmore, Evidence §§ 769–72 (Chadbourn rev. 1970); West's Key Number Digest, Witnesses ⟶240(3) to (5). *Accord* Enfield, Direct Examination of Witnesses, 15 Ark. L. Rev. 32, 35 (1960) (" 'Did you subscribe the will in the testator's presence?' is not leading, nor is 'Do you know whether in handling paper from Callahan Tractor Company, and in particular, the contracts here, Ferguson relied on the financial statements and on the financial worth of Melvin Callahan?' The latter question may be objectionable on other grounds, but it is not leading even though the answer must be 'yes' or 'no'. The test is not that simple, and in fact an otherwise unobjectionable question may become leading merely by the tone or inflection of voice in which it is asked.").

[9]Melilli, Leading Questions on Direct Examination: A More Pragmatic Approach, 27 Am. J. Trial Advoc. 155, 167 (2003).

[10]*See generally* Morgan, Basic Problems of Evidence 58 (1961) ("There is no mechanical test for distinguishing a leading from a non-leading question. Usually a question that may be answered by yes or no is considered as leading, but it is not necessarily so. 'Did you or did you not' and 'state whether or not,' do not permit such an answer but they may be followed by matter that clearly indicates the desired answer. All that can be safely said is that a question so framed, or uttered with such an emphasis, or accompanied by such nonverbal conduct of the questioner as to suggest the desired answer, is leading. One form of leading is by assuming facts not conceded or not yet in evidence; such a question is often misleading as well.").

they expect to call for direct examination. This practice is perfectly ethical. However, the practice creates a probability that by the time of trial, the lawyer and the witness will have reached an *entente* making the witness susceptible to the lawyer's suggestions. In contrast, when a lawyer cross-examines a witness called by the adversary, the lawyer may have had no prior contact with the witness, and there is less likelihood of an understanding between them about the facts. Hence a common sense distinction evolved: On objection, the judge ordinarily forbids leading questions on direct examination but usually permits them on cross-examination.[11] The allowability of leading questions is discretionary,[12] and the judge's action will not be reversed unless it contributed to an unfair trial.[13]

---

[11]U.S. v. Smith, 378 F.3d 754, 755–56 (8th Cir. 2004).

[12]*E.g.,* People v. Harris, 43 Cal. 4th 1269, 78 Cal. Rptr. 3d 295, 185 P.3d 727, 740–41 (2008) (it was permissible for the prosecutor to use a leading question to direct a state witness's attention toward the defendant's location in the courtroom in order to make an in-court identification; due to a computer monitor blocking his line of sight, the witness was initially unable to see the defendant from the witness chair; the risk of improper suggestion was slight because the witness had already identified the defendant from a live lineup and at the preliminary hearing); Com. v. Sheppard, 313 Mass. 590, 48 N.E.2d 630 (1943); State v. Painter, 265 N.C. 277, 144 S.E.2d 6 (1965); West's Key Number Digest, Witnesses ☞240(2). Under Fed. R. Evid. 611(c), the matter is primarily entrusted to the trial judge's discretion. U.S. v. Brown, 603 F.2d 1022, 1025–26 (1st Cir. 1979) ("It has long been established that in the use of leading questions 'must be left to the sound discretion of the trial judge who sees the witness and can, therefore, determine in the interest of truth and justice whether the circumstances justify leading questions to be propounded to a witness by the party producing him.' St. Clair v. United States, 154 U.S. 134, 150 (1894)"). *See generally* Morgan, Basic Problems of Evidence 57 (1961) ("[T]he trial judge is free to exercise his discretion in almost all situations where he feels that leading will expedite the examination, and will do no harm to the adversary. Frequently, he realizes that to sustain the objection is only to require the proponent to reframe the question after he has by the leading question let the witness know what answer he wants. Consequently he rules that the question is leading but the answer may stand, and admonishes counsel to refrain from further leading."); Enfield, Direct Examination of Witnesses, 15 Ark. L. Rev. 32, 36 (1960) ("Obviously the damage is already done—the suggestion has been planted. Even so, the questioner will usually be allowed to rephrase and continue. The court, however, may refuse to allow continuation of the subject if in his discretion he feels that it would be improper or unfair to allow the examiner to continue on the same subject. True, such action by the court should be rare. The harm done is usually not very significant, and continued use of leading questions in such circumstances will soon draw sharp criticism from the court and embarrass the examiner before the jury. Constant leading of the witness makes a bad impression on judge and jury, even if opposing counsel does not object. The jury soon realizes that it is the lawyer and not the witness who is testifying.").

[13]The formula has been stated in

However, when the normal assumption about the relation between the witness and the examining counsel or his client does not hold true, the usual practice is reversed. Thus, if the witness on direct is legally identified with the opponent, appears hostile to the examiner, or is reluctant or uncooperative, the danger of suggestion disappears. In these circumstances, the judge will permit leading questions.[14] Conversely, when on cross-

various terms. In a leading case, U.S. v. Durham, 319 F.2d 590 (4th Cir. 1963) there was no abuse because there was no prejudice or clear injustice to a criminal defendant. However, leading questions which were prejudicial in substance caused a reversal in U.S. v. Meeker, 558 F.2d 387 (7th Cir. 1977) (leading questions implied prior misconduct, guilt as charged in the suit, and irrelevant conduct). Exaggerated use of leading questions can warp a case and amount to an abuse. Straub v. Reading Co., 220 F.2d 177 (3d Cir. 1955); U.S. v. Shoupe, 548 F.2d 636 (6th Cir. 1977) (the leading questions contained an extensive recitation of witness's unsworn and inadmissible statements inculpating the defendant). *See* West's Key Number Digest, Witnesses ☞240(2). *See generally* Miller v. Fairchild Industries, Inc., 876 F.2d 718, 734 (9th Cir. 1989) ("However, Rule 611(c) vests broad discretion in trial courts, and we will therefore reverse on the basis of improper leading questions only if the 'judge's action . . . amounted to, or contributed to, the denial of a fair trial;' " quoting earlier edition of treatise). The Advisory Committee Note to 611(c) states that "[a]n almost total unwillingness to reverse for infractions has been manifested by appellate courts."

The judge has authority to foreclose the witness from answering at all on a matter inquired into by a leading question (3 Wigmore, Evidence § 770, n. 4 (Chadbourn rev. 1970)) and a fortiori to prevent counsel from returning to the matter for a period of time long enough to dissipate the effect of the leading question. However, the authority is seldom exercised. After a judge sustains a leading question

objections, the judge usually permits the examiner to immediately rephrase the question.

[14]U.S. v. Nelson, 242 Fed. Appx. 164, 169 (5th Cir. 2007) (the prosecution may have its own witness declared hostile even if the unfavorable testimony does not "surprise" the prosecution); U.S. v. Meza-Urtado, 351 F.3d 301, 303 (7th Cir. 2003) ("Farias . . . became conveniently 'forgetful' . . . . In this situation, . . . he could have been treated as a hostile witness and asked leading questions until the cows came home"); U.S. v. Mora-Higuera, 269 F.3d 905, 912 (8th Cir. 2001) (the witness "became evasive and unclear"); People v. Gallery, 336 Ill. 580, 168 N.E. 650 (1929) (prosecutor's questions to unwilling state's witness; permissible to refresh memory, not to impeach); McNeill v. Fidelity & Cas. Co. of New York, 336 Mo. 1142, 82 S.W.2d 582 (1935) (plaintiff's examination of witness employed in agency of defendant insurance company); West's Key Number Digest, Witnesses ☞244; Comment Note.—Proper practice and relief on development of hostility by party's own witness, 117 A.L.R. 326. In many jurisdictions, a rule or statute permits a party to call the adverse party and interrogate him by leading questions. Fed. R. Evid. 611(c) states that leading questions may be used when "a party calls a hostile witness, an adverse party, or a witness identified with an adverse party." The judge decides whether the facts justify classifying the witness as hostile. U.S. v. Librach, 520 F.2d 550 (8th Cir. 1975) (the court approved leading questions to evasive government witness, whose testimony surprised the prosecutor). The term "adverse party" causes few

examination the witness appears biased in the cross-examining attorney's favor, the judge may prohibit counsel from leading.[15] In civil cases, the plaintiff can call the defendant as an adverse witness. After the plaintiff's direct examination of the defendant, the defendant's own counsel may conduct a cross-examination; the defendant's relationship with her own counsel is hardly hostile.

In many situations, judges routinely permit leading during direct examination.[16] For instance, leading questions may be used

---

problems. The expression, a person "identified with a hostile party," is a broad clause that automatically includes some witnesses such as a corporation's president within its ambit. The Advisory Committee Note to Rule 611(c) points out that under the prior law, Federal Rule of Civil Procedure 43(b), only the officers, directors, and managing agents of an entity were considered legally identified with the entity. The Note adds that the phrasing of Rule 611(c) "is designed to enlarge the category of persons thus callable." See dictum concerning an opponent's employee in Perkins v. Volkswagen of America, Inc., 596 F.2d 681 (5th Cir. 1979). *See generally* State v. Johnson, 784 P.2d 1135, 1142–43 (Utah 1989) (state counterpart of Fed. R. Evid. 611(c) was intended to enlarge categories of witnesses "automatically regarded as adverse"). *But see* Browne v. Signal Mountain Nursery, L.P., 286 F. Supp. 2d 904, 921 (E.D. Tenn. 2003) ("a district court is not required to allow counsel to ask leading questions of an adverse witness"); People v. Williams, 43 Cal. 4th 584, 75 Cal. Rptr. 3d 691, 181 P.3d 1035, 1069–70 (2008) (the trial judge did not err in refusing to allow the defense counsel to treat Polacek, the defendant's former prosecutor, as a hostile witness; the statute vests the judge with broad discretion; although Polacek interjected one inculpatory reference in response to an open-ended question, "Defendant does not explain why Polacek . . . would not have taken the opportunity to interject the same reference . . . under examination as a hostile witness or under cross-

examination by the prosecutor.").

Federal Rule 607 generally allows a direct examiner to impeach his own witness. There is authority that when the direct examiner properly invokes Rule 607, he may use leading questions about the impeaching facts. U.S. v. Ienco, 92 F.3d 564, 568 (7th Cir. 1996) (Rule 607 abolishes the voucher rule and "its corollaries").

[15]Moody v. Rowell, 34 Mass. 490, 17 Pick. 490, 498, 1835 WL 2374 (1835). "Ordinarily the court should allow leading questions . . . on cross-examination. . . ." Fed. R. Evid. 611(c) (1). The term "ordinarily" furnishes "a basis for denying the use of leading questions when the cross-examination is cross-examination in form only and not in fact, as for example the 'cross-examination' of a party by his own counsel after being called by his own opponent (savoring more of redirect) or of an insured defendant who proves to be friendly to the plaintiff." Advisory Committee's Note. However, the matter is in the trial court's discretion. Ardoin v. J. Ray McDermott & Co., Inc., 684 F.2d 335 (5th Cir. 1982) (on cross-examination of employee called by employer's opponent, trial court permitted leading questions by employer's counsel). See similar view in 3 Wigmore, Evidence § 773 (Chadbourn rev. 1970).

[16]U.S. v. Archdale, 229 F.3d 861, 866 (9th Cir. 2000) (the witness was experiencing difficulty due to the very personal nature of the topic). *See generally* Morgan, Basic Problems of Evidence 57–58 (1961) ("Among the situations in which the judge is most

to bring out preliminary matters such as the witness's name and occupation, or to elicit matters that are not seriously disputed.[17] Leading phrasing may also be employed to suggest a subject or topic, as distinguished from an answer.[18] Additional relaxations are justified on the ground of necessity. Thus, when the need appears, the judge ordinarily allows leading questioning of children[19] or adult witnesses who are so ignorant, timid, weak-minded, or deficient in the English language that they cannot otherwise convey the information they possess.[20] Admittedly, in

---

likely to permit leading because it will serve to elicit requisite information and expedite the proceeding are the following: (1) the witness has been asked non-leading questions until his recollection has been exhausted and counsel insists that that witness has further material information to which a leading question will direct his attention; (2) the witness is immature or timid or frightened; (3) the witness is in such physical or mental condition that he should be spared the effort of making long narrative answers; (4) the witness is illiterate or has difficulty in expressing himself in English, although he has sufficient understanding not to need an interpreter.").

[17]Southern Ry. Co. v. Hall, 209 Ala. 237, 96 So. 73 (1923) (introductory questions identifying time and place of incident in suit). The same holds true for preliminary matters triable to the court in the jury's absence. State v. Castelli, 92 Conn. 58, 101 A. 476, 479 (1917) (question whether threats were made or inducements given to secure confession); West's Key Number Digest, Witnesses ⟨=241. *See generally* 3 Wigmore, Evidence § 775 at 168 (Chadbourn rev. 1970) ("When a witness is asked about matters preliminary to the main topics of controversy—matters essential to be brought out, and yet not themselves in controversy—such as the witness' name, age, residence, relationship to the parties, and the like, it is obvious that there is usually no danger of improper suggestion, simply because there is no motive for it.").

The same view should obtain under Fed. R. Evid. 611(c). McClard v. U.S., 386 F.2d 495, 501 (8th Cir. 1967) ("Ofttimes leading questions are asked on preliminary and collateral matters to expedite the trial. In any event the control of leading questions is a matter left to the discretion of the trial judge."). *See* Advisory Committee Note, Fed. R. Evid. 611(c).

[18]Gerler v. Cooley, 41 Ill. App. 2d 233, 190 N.E.2d 488 (3d Dist. 1963); State v. Ward, 10 Utah 2d 34, 347 P.2d 865 (1959). The test should obviously apply under Fed. R. Evid. and Unif. R. Evid. 611(c).

[19]U.S. v. Carey, 589 F.3d 187, 191–92 (5th Cir. 2009) (the witness's youth and nervousness).

[20]U.S. v. Hernandez-Albino, 177 F.3d 33, 42 (1st Cir. 1999) ("at times, Ramirez was unresponsive and showed a lack of understanding . . . ."); U.S. v. Mulinelli-Navas, 111 F.3d 983, 990 (1st Cir. 1997) (the witness was unresponsive at times and showed a lack of understanding); U.S. v. Littlewind, 551 F.2d 244 (8th Cir. 1977) (leading questions to 13 and 14 year old prosecuting witnesses in rape cases were approved, citing Fed. R. Evid. 611(c)); Litherland v. Petrolane Offshore Const. Services, Inc., 546 F.2d 129 (5th Cir. 1977) (leading questions permitted to witness displaying difficulty in communicating by reason of obvious mental deficiency); Preston v. Denkins, 94 Ariz. 214, 382 P.2d 686 (1963) (78 year old witness in poor health and with defective independent recall); Legislative Note, Tex. R. Evid. 611 ("The

these cases, especially as to children,[21] there is a risk of false suggestion. However, it is better to run that risk than to abandon altogether the effort to elicit the witness's knowledge. Similarly, when a lawyer has directed a witness to the subject by non-leading questions without securing a complete account of the witness's knowledge, the witness's memory is said to be "exhausted." In that event, the judge may permit the examiner to ask more specific questions whose particularity can revive the witness's memory (but which simultaneously might suggest the desired answer).[22] Likewise, many courts liberally allow specific, leading questions during the direct examination of experts. These

---

purpose of the amendment is to permit, in the court's discretion, the use of leading questions . . . to ignorant or illiterate persons . . . ."); Saltzburg, Non-English Speaking Witnesses and Leading Questions, 13 Crim. Just. 37 (Sum. 1998); West's Key Number Digest, Witnesses ☞243.

[21]*See* U.S. v. Carey, 589 F.3d 187, 191–92 (5th Cir. 2009) (the witness's youth and nervousness); U.S. v. Wright, 540 F.3d 833, 844 (8th Cir. 2008) ("We generally allow leading questions during the examination of children who are reluctant to testify"); U.S. v. Rojas, 520 F.3d 876, 881–82 (8th Cir. 2008) (the child was 10 years old at the time of trial, and the record suggested that the child was distraught during her testimony); U.S. v. Johnson, 519 F.3d 816, 822 (8th Cir. 2008) (there is a child witness exception; the child was young, the subject matter was traumatic, and the child was reluctant to testify); U.S. v. Flute, 363 F.3d 676, 678 (8th Cir. 2004) (approvingly citing *Butler*, 56 F.3d 941 (8th Cir. 1955)); U.S. v. Grassrope, 342 F.3d 866, 869 (8th Cir. 2003) ("It is not uncommon that the precise physiological details of sexual assaults must be elicited by focused questioning. We have repeatedly upheld the use of leading questions to develop the testimony of sexual assault victims, particularly children"); U.S. v. Archdale, 229 F.3d 861 (9th Cir. 2000) (the minor was having difficulty testifying about a very sensitive personal matter); U.S. v. Butler, 56 F.3d 941 (8th Cir. 1995) (there is a "long-recognized" practice

permitting the proponent to pose leading questions to child witnesses); U.S. v. Longie, 984 F.2d 955, 958 (8th Cir. 1993) (although the child was "articulate," the record demonstrated the child "victim's hesitancy" to testify); Blasi v. Attorney General of Com. of Pennsylvania, 120 F. Supp. 2d 451, 472 (M.D. Pa. 2000) ("Pennsylvania permits 'direct, succinct, and even leading questions' when the witness is a child because children are easily intimidated by a courtroom"); Coon v. People, 99 Ill. 368, 370, 1881 WL 10553 (1881); Legislative Note, Tex. R. Evid. 611 ("The purpose of the amendment is to permit, in the court's discretion, the use of leading questions . . . to . . . children").

[22]U.S. v. Carboni, 204 F.3d 39, 45 (2d Cir. 2000) ("only after [the government] repeatedly attempted to elicit the same information through non-leading questions"); People v. Jones, 221 Cal. App. 2d 619, 34 Cal. Rptr. 618 (4th Dist. 1963); Gray v. Kelley, 190 Mass. 184, 76 N.E. 724 (1906); 3 Wigmore, Evidence § 777 (Chadbourn rev. 1970); West's Key Number Digest, Witnesses ☞242. This notion is included in Fed. R. Evid. 611(c) "to develop his testimony." Advisory Committee's Note. Where a hostile witness surprises the examiner by testimony contrary to his earlier pretrial statement, the examiner may ask leading questions about the former statement, not to discredit but to refresh his recollection. People v. Jehl, 150 Cal. App. 2d 665, 310 P.2d 495 (1st Dist. 1957). *But see* U.S. v. Berg, 178 F.3d 976, 981

courts reason that if the expert were allowed free rein, his testimony could easily become "complicated" and confuse the jury.[23]

In some jurisdictions, longstanding practice permits putting leading questions to a second witness who, for impeachment purposes, is called to testify about a previous witness's statement that is inconsistent with the previous witness's testimony.[24] Here too necessity is the stated justification. It might otherwise be difficult to quickly get to the point and direct the second witness's attention to the subject of the testimony.[25] It has been argued that the practice should be discontinued.[26] But most courts have rejected the argument and upheld the common practice.

---

(8th Cir. 1999) ("Although Berg may have had difficulty seeking some of the information he wanted from Clayton, the record does not indicate that Clayton is a hostile witness.").

   When refreshing recollection is by means of a leading question, counsel may not employ a leading question incorporating the content of the anticipated testimony in the jury's hearing if the matter under consideration is a pivotal issue in the litigation. The proper procedure is to show the witness a writing, if available, or to reduce the oral statement to writing, present it to the witness, and then inquire whether the witness now recalls. Alternatively counsel may attempt to refresh the witness's recollection by leading question after the jury is excused. On the other hand, when the witness cannot recall a preliminary or relatively unimportant matter, a leading question in open court incorporating the answer may be used. U.S. v. Socony-Vacuum Oil Co., 310 U.S. 150, 234, 60 S. Ct. 811, 84 L. Ed. 1129 (1940) ("[T]here would be error where under the pretext of refreshing witness' recollection the prior testimony was introduced as evidence."); Goings v. U.S., 377 F.2d 753, 760 (8th Cir. 1967) ("[I]f a party can offer a previously given statement to substitute for a witness's testimony under

the guise of 'refreshing recollection,' the whole adversary system of trial must be revised. *The evil of this practice hardly merits discussion. The evil is no less when an attorney can read the statement in the presence of the jury and thereby substitute his spoken work for the written document.*") (emphasis in original).

[23]Dunn v. Owens-Corning Fiberglass, 774 F. Supp. 929 (D.V.I. 1991), aff'd in part, vacated in part, 1 F.3d 1362, 1371 (3d Cir. 1993) ("complicated testimony").

[24]People v. Abair, 102 Cal. App. 2d 765, 228 P.2d 336 (4th Dist. 1951); Swanson v. McDonald, 58 S.D. 119, 235 N.W. 118 (1931) (citing authorities); West's Key Number Digest, Witnesses ⊜391.

[25]3 Wigmore, Evidence § 779 (Chadbourn rev. 1970). The practice is also justified as pinpointing the inquiry and thus avoiding bringing out incompetent matter which might result from general questions. Elgin, J. & E. Ry. Co. v. Lawlor, 229 Ill. 621, 82 N.E. 407 (1907). It is permissible under Fed. R. Evid. and Rev. Unif. R. Evid. 611(c) (1974). See note 18 supra.

[26]*See* Swoboda v. Union Pac. R. Co., 87 Neb. 200, 220, 221, 127 N.W. 215 (1910), which recognizes, but criticizes, the practice.

## § 7 The form of questions: (c) Argumentative, misleading, and indefinite questions

Sections 5 and 6 discussed form problems that arise mainly during direct examination. We turn now to form problems of primary importance on cross-examination. To begin with, the examiner may not ask a question that merely pressures the witness to assent to the questioner's inferences from or interpretations of the testimony already admitted. Rather than attempting to elicit new testimony, a cross-examiner might challenge a witness about an inference from the testimony already in the record. For instance, evincing disbelief in his demeanor, the cross-examiner might ask, "Do you really expect the jury to believe that?" or "How can you reconcile those statements?" This kind of question is objectionable as "argumentative"[1] or "badgering the witness." The trial judge has a wide range of discretion in enforcing the rule, particularly on cross-examination where such questions are more common. It is certainly fair for judges to enforce the rule during cross-examination. When the cross-examiner becomes argumentative, he is in effect previewing his summation, and he will later have an ample opportunity to argue the inferences during his summation to the jury.

Another common form problem occurs when the examiner words the question so that it assumes as true matters which no

---

**[Section 7]**

[1]Questions held argumentative: Smith v. Estelle, 602 F.2d 694, 700 n.7 (5th Cir. 1979) ("Dr. Grigson, you're kind of the hatchet man down here for the District Attorney's Office, aren't you?," and "Did you ever meet a person you didn't think was a sociopath?"); U.S. v. Micklus, 581 F.2d 612, 617 n.3 (7th Cir. 1978) ("I'm asking you. It wouldn't bother you any, to come in here and lie from the time you started to the time you stopped, would it?"); U.S. v. Cash, 499 F.2d 26 (9th Cir. 1974) ("As a matter of fact you drove the car that was parked outside the liquor store when he went in and stole some liquor, is not that a fact?", held argumentative but harmless error); Pettus v. Louisville & N. R. Co., 214 Ala. 187, 106 So. 807 (1925) ("If you had not been burning off the grass and weeds . . . on the right of way, it was still there?"); People v. Higgins, 119 Cal. Rptr. 3d 856, 873(Cal. App. 4th Dist. 2011); People v. Redd, 48 Cal. 4th 691, 108 Cal. Rptr. 3d 192, 229 P.3d 101 (2010); People v. Chatman, 38 Cal. 4th 344, 42 Cal. Rptr. 3d 621, 133 P.3d 534, 563 (2006) ("An argumentative question is a speech to the jury masquerading as a question. The questioner is not seeking to elicit relevant testimony. Often it is apparent that the questioner does not even expect an answer. The question may, indeed, be unanswerable."); White v. State, 22 Okla. Crim. 131, 210 P. 313 (1922) (in mayhem prosecution, question, "Isn't it a fact that [defendant's] mouth is so small that he could not reach up and get it wide enough open to get [complainant's] ear in there?", argumentative where both mouth and ear were visible to jury); Saltzburg, Rhetorical Questions, 17 Crim. Just. 38 (Spr. 2000) (argumentative questions pose special risks when the wording of the question uses legal terms and pressures the witness to draw a legal conclusion); Goff, Argumentative Questions, 49 Calif. St. Bar J. 140 (1974).

witness has yet testified to, and which are disputed between the parties.[2] The danger is two-fold. First, when the examiner puts the question to a friendly witness, the recitation of the assumed fact may be leading, suggesting the desired answer. Second, whether the witness is friendly or hostile, the answer can be misleading. The witness deserves a fair opportunity to affirm or deny the fact. If the witness is inattentive and answers the question without identifying the assumption, it may impossible for the trier of fact to later determine whether the witness affirmed or simply ignored the assumption. When the question suffers from this vice, the opposing counsel usually objects that the question "is misleading" or "assumes facts not in evidence."

Occasionally questions are considered objectionable because they are too broad or indefinite. Often this objection is in reality an objection of lack of relevancy.[3] Indefinite or ambiguous questions about a witness's personal background can be especially dangerous. Suppose, for instance, that the cross-examiner asks a witness whether he has had any "troubles," "brushes," "encounters," "problems," "difficulties," or "run-ins with the law." In response to that question, the witness might mention convictions admissible for impeachment as well as other misconduct that is both prejudicial and inadmissible. The witness's answer might violate the restrictions on credibility or character evidence.

The principles mentioned in this section are not expressly codified in the Federal or Revised Uniform Rules (1974), but they may be enforced in the trial judge's discretion under Rules 403 and 611(a).[4] As to Rule 403, see § 185 infra.

---

[2]Questions held objectionable: U.S. v. Medel, 592 F.2d 1305 (5th Cir. 1979) (question referring to specific facts not in evidence); Cherry v. Hill, 283 Ala. 74, 214 So. 2d 427 (1968) (question as to how long witness had seen pedestrians use a roadway assumed pedestrians had been using roadway); Reardon v. Boston Elevated Ry. Co., 311 Mass. 228, 40 N.E.2d 865 (1942) (question as to how many years water used to come through walls, bad as assuming that it had come through at all in the past); 3 Wigmore, Evidence §§ 771, 780 (Chadbourn rev. 1970); West's Key Number Digest, Witnesses ☞237.

The classic illustration is, "When did you stop beating your wife?"

But the questioner may properly assume the truth of a disputed fact previously testified to by the same witness. State v. Marshall, 105 Iowa 38, 74 N.W. 763 (1898); Graham v. McReynolds, 90 Tenn. 673, 18 S.W. 272 (1891) (question by court).

[3]E.g., People v. Williams, 200 Cal. App. 2d 838, 19 Cal. Rptr. 743 (3d Dist. 1962); West's Key Number Digest, Witnesses ☞236.

[4]See Fed. R. Evid. 403, 611(a).

## § 8 The judge may call witnesses; the judge and jurors may question witnesses

### *Judges*

Sections 5 to 7 deal with some of the form questions that arise when attorneys call and question witnesses. Problems can also materialize when judges call[1] or question[2] witnesses. Under the Anglo-American adversary trial system, the parties' counsel have the primary responsibility for finding, selecting, and presenting the evidence.[3] However, our system of party-investigation and party-presentation has limitations. The system is a means to the end of disclosing truth and administering justice.[4] In order to achieve that same end, the judge may exercise various powers to intervene to supplement the parties' evidence.

More specifically, the judge has the powers to call and question witnesses. Under the case law and Federal Rule of Evidence 614(b), the judge has discretion to examine any witness to clarify testimony or to bring out needed facts omitted by the parties.[5]

---

**[Section 8]**

[1]9 Wigmore, Evidence § 2484 (Chadbourn rev. 1981); Fed. R. Evid. and Rev. Unif. R. Evid. 614, 706 (1974); Calling and interrogation of witnesses by court under Rule 614 of the Federal Rules of Evidence, 53 A.L.R. Fed. 498; Court's witnesses (other than expert) in state criminal prosecution, 16 A.L.R.4th 352; Trial court's appointment, in civil case, of expert witness, 95 A.L.R.2d 390; West's Key Number Digest, Witnesses ⊜246(2).

[2]3 Wigmore, Evidence § 784 (Chadbourn rev. 1970); 9 Wigmore, Evidence § 2484 (1981); Propriety of conduct of trial judge in propounding questions to witnesses in criminal case, 84 A.L.R. 1172; West's Key Number Digest, Witnesses ⊜246.

[3]Landsman, Readings on Adversarial Justice: The American Approach to Adjudication 3–4 (1988). The adversary system should be compared with the inquisitorial system in some European countries where the judge has a wider responsibility for investigating the facts and presenting the proofs. *See* 9 Wigmore, Evidence § 2483 (Chadbourn rev. 1981). In the adversary system, the judge cannot bar a party from examining witnesses called by the party and conduct the entire direct examination himself. Dreyer v. Ershowsky, 156 A.D. 27, 140 N.Y.S. 819 (2d Dep't 1913).

[4]Professional Responsibility: Report of the Joint Conference, 44 A.B.A.J. 1159, 1159–61 (1958).

[5]U.S. v. Angulo-Hernandez, 565 F.3d 2, 9–10 (1st Cir. 2009); U.S. v. Thompson, 310 Fed. Appx. 485 (3d Cir. 2008) (the trial judge's seven questions were but a snippet in a two-week trial, the judge instructed the jury not to discern any opinion from the judge's questions, and the questions did not relate to the core of the defendant's insanity defense); U.S. v. Reyes, 227 F.3d 263 (5th Cir. 2000); U.S. v. Lankford, 196 F.3d 563, 573 (5th Cir. 1999) ("The judge's elicitation of 'damaging information' . . . is . . . by itself insufficient to demonstrate that the judge was engaged in misconduct"); U.S. v. Cisneros, 194 F.3d 626, 640 (5th Cir. 1999) ("a trial court has discretion to clarify testimony, even if that elicits facts harmful to the defendant"); U.S. v. Henry, 136 F.3d 12 (1st Cir. 1998) (the judge properly questioned an expert witness on the subject

of toxicity characteristic leaching procedure; there was a need to clarify the
witness's testimony because the witness had employed confusing, technical terms and jargon); U.S. v. Slone,
833 F.2d 595, 597 (6th Cir. 1987) ("In
[United States v. Hickman, 592 F.2d
931 (6th Cir.1979)], this circuit noted
that while potential prejudice lurks
behind every intrusion a presiding
judge makes into a trial, determining
when a trial judge oversteps his
bounds remains difficult. *Hickman*
identified three factors which determine whether a trial judge has good
reason to interject himself into the
trial. First, in a lengthy, complex trial,
judicial intervention is often necessary
for clarification. . . . Second, if the attorneys in a case are unprepared or
obstreperous or if the facts are becoming muddled and neither side is succeeding at attempts to clear them up,
judicial intervention may be necessary
for clarification. *Hickman,* 592 F.2d at
933. Third, if a witness is difficult, if a
witness' testimony is unbelievable and
counsel fails to adequately probe, or if
the witness becomes inadvertently
confused, judicial intervention may be
needed. . . ."); Lopez v. State, 297 Ga.
App. 618, 677 S.E.2d 776 (2009) (the
trial judge's questions were entirely
objective and did not suggest a particular answer to the witness); People v.
Galan, 151 Ill. App. 3d 481, 104 Ill.
Dec. 356, 502 N.E.2d 853, 855 (2d
Dist. 1986) ("It is an abuse of discretion for the trial judge to assume the
role of an advocate. However, he may
act to ensure that evidence essential
to the proper disposition of a case is
not inadvertently omitted. . . . Thus,
a trial judge may remind the prosecutor of the necessity to prove additional
elements . . . examine witnesses to
clarify material issues or eliminate
confusion . . . and advise counsel on
the proper phrasing of questions . . ."); 
State v. Cuevas, 288 N.W.2d 525, 531
(Iowa 1980) ("In fulfilling its role, occasions will arise when a trial court is
constrained to intervene on its own

volition to protect a witness from
abusive treatment or unnecessary humiliation, to stay the pursuit of a
patently irrelevant line of inquiry—
particularly when it may obfuscate the
issues and mislead the jury, to act to
avert unnecessary repetition, to require that the proceedings move forward without undue delay and to take
reasonable measure to insure that the
evidence is intelligibly presented to
the jury."); State v. Hibbs, 239 Mont.
308, 780 P.2d 182, 184 (1989) ("It is
true that under the rule, the court
may examine witnesses to fully elicit
or clarify facts."); Fed. R. Evid. 614(b)
& Unif. R. Evid. 614(b). *See generally*
Auger v. Auger, 149 Vt. 559, 546 A.2d
1373, 1375 (1988) ("It is the better
practice to allow counsel the opportunity to develop the facts in the first
instance. Counsel is in a better position to do so. As Judge Frankel has
noted: 'The judge views the case from
a peak of Olympian ignorance. His
intrusions will in too many cases result
from partial or skewed insights. He
may expose the secrets one side
chooses to keep while never becoming
aware of the other's. He runs a good
chance of pursuing inspirations that
better informed counsel have considered, explored, and abandoned after
fuller study. He risks at a minimum
the supplying of more confusion than
guidance by his sporadic intrusions.'
Frankel, The Search for Truth: An
Umpireal View, 123 U. Pa. L. Rev.
1031, 1042 (1975). While judges may
be tempted to succumb to the conceit
that their participation is essential to
the truth-seeking process, 'judicial
interrogation to search for the whole
truth or to complete the evidence presupposes that the judge knows the
truth better than the parties or their
counsel . . . . There is something
unseemly about a judge . . . who seeks
to elicit testimony in aid of those
answers.' Saltzburg, The Unnecessarily Expanding Role of the American
Trial Judge, 64 Va. L. Rev. at 57–58.").

   This part of the section dis-

The trial judge is not a mere umpire or passive moderator.[6] Some appellate courts have even gone to the length of stating that the trial judge may have a "duty" to question witnesses. If there were such a duty, an appellant could conceivably predicate error on the judge's failure to ask questions that would have yielded answers favorable to the appellant. However, the judicial references to "duty" seem to be rhetorical; the supposed duty does not appear to have been enforced by any appellate decision.[7]

---

cusses questioning only by the judge. A few jurisdictions flatly prohibit jurors from asking questions. State v. Zima, 237 Neb. 952, 468 N.W.2d 377 (1991). However, the prevailing view is that with the judge's leave, jurors may question the witnesses. U.S. v. Smith, 569 F.3d 1209 (10th Cir. 2009); U.S. v. Groene, 998 F.2d 604 (8th Cir. 1993); Ex parte Malone, 12 So. 3d 60 (Ala. 2008) (the overwhelming majority of courts permit the practice); State v. Hays, 256 Kan. 48, 883 P.2d 1093 (1994); Propriety of jurors asking questions in open court during course of trial, 31 A.L.R.3d 872. See O'Nellion v. Haynes, 122 Cal. App. 329, 9 P.2d 853 (1st Dist. 1932), where a juror asked the defendant "You carry liability insurance, don't you?" and was answered, "Yes," before objection could be made. However, in the view of many courts, the privilege of permitting jurors to question witnesses should be granted only when in the judge's sound discretion it appears that it will aid a juror in understanding a material issue involved, and ordinarily when some juror has indicated that he wishes the point clarified. State v. Anderson, 108 Utah 130, 158 P.2d 127 (1945). A judge's invitation to jurors to interrogate witnesses was condemned in State v. Martinez, 7 Utah 2d 387, 326 P.2d 102 (1958). But there are opposing views. U.S. v. Callahan, 588 F.2d 1078 (5th Cir. 1979) ("The proper handling of juror questions is a matter of procedure within the discretion of the trial judge;" judge invited questions to be written down by the judge). When questions are allowed, a requirement that they be submitted to the judge in writing facilitates consideration in the jury's absence and avoids prejudice to an objecting party. The latter part of this section contains an extended discussion the mechanics of questioning by jurors.

[6]U.S. v. Catalan-Roman, 585 F.3d 453 (1st Cir. 2009) (a trial judge is not a mere umpire; rather, he or she is the governor of the trial and has a perfect right to participate actively), cert.denied sub nom. Medina-Villegas v. U.S., 130 S. Ct. 3377, 176 L. Ed. 2d 1262 (2010); Stevenson v. District of Columbia Metropolitan Police Dept., 248 F.3d 1187, 1190 (D.C. Cir. 2001) ("Judges may do so repeatedly and aggressively to clear up confusion and manage trials . . . . moreover, '[t]he precepts of fair trial and judicial objectivity do not require a judge to be inert' "); U.S. v. Montas, 41 F.3d 775 (1st Cir. 1994); U.S. v. Rodriguez-Rodriguez, 685 F. Supp. 2d 293, 297 (D.P.R. 2010) (the judge is not a "bloodless automaton"). In one of the celebrated Watergate prosecutions, Judge John Sirica resorted to judicial questioning to elicit the true facts about the break-in. U.S. v. Liddy, 509 F.2d 428, 438 (D.C. Cir. 1974).

[7]U.S. v. Hinson, 585 F.3d 1328, 1339 (10th Cir. 2009); United States v. Brandt, 196 F.2d 653, 655 (2d Cir. 1952) ("He enjoys the prerogative, rising often to the standard of a duty, of eliciting those facts he deems necessary to the clear presentation of the issues. Pariser v. City of New York, 2 Cir., 146 F.2d 431."); U.S. v. Smith, 857 F. Supp. 1466, 1471 (D. Kan. 1994) (the Tenth Circuit has "encouraged" trial judges to exercise their power to question witnesses; when the record

In the great majority of states,[8] the judge has lost the traditional common law power to comment on the weight of the evidence. In those jurisdictions, the judge's questioning in jury cases must be cautiously guarded to avoid implied comment.[9] If the judge uses highly leading questions suggesting the desired answer, the questions may strongly imply that the desired answer is the truth and thus amount to comment.[10] Admittedly, courts have occasionally held that the policy against leading questions by counsel, namely, avoiding false testimony prompted by partisan suggestion,[11] does not apply to judges.[12] After all, the judge's office is supposed to be impartial. However, this reasoning is questionable.[13] Especially since the judge is an authority figure, there is a grave risk that the witness will adopt any suggestion implicit in the judge's question. Some witnesses are more likely to adopt the suggestion in a judge's question than in a question posed by counsel. Leading judicial questions clearly aimed at

---

in a criminal case needs clarification on facts determinative "of guilt or innocence," the "trial judge has an obligation, on his own initiative," to clarify the facts). See similar statements in federal opinions collected in 3 Mueller & Kirkpatrick, Federal Evidence § 6:105 (3d ed. 2007). All are dicta. Fed. R. Evid. 614(b) indicates the judge has discretion by stating the judge "may" interrogate witnesses. U.S. v. Trapnell, 512 F.2d 10 (9th Cir. 1975) (a trial judge did not have a duty to question although the defendant appeared pro se). *But see* State v. Beck, 2007 UT 60, 165 P.3d 1225, 1229 (Utah 2007) ("[t]he practice of questioning by a judge is not to be recommended or encouraged . . . . In questioning a witness, the judge should not engage in extensive examination . . . .").

[8]Kalven & Zeisel, The American Jury 419–21 (1966); N.M. R. Evid. 11-107 ("The court shall not comment to the jury upon the evidence or the credibility of the witnesses.").

[9]People v. De Lordo, 350 Ill. 148, 182 N.E. 726, 730–31 (1932); Risley v. Moberg, 69 Wash. 2d 560, 419 P.2d 151 (1966); Propriety of conduct of trial judge in propounding questions to witnesses in criminal case, 84 A.L.R. 1172, at 1181.

[10]Frangos v. Edmunds, 179 Or.

577, 173 P.2d 596 (1946); Anderson v. State, 83 Tex. Crim. 261, 202 S.W. 944 (1918). Research by Harvard psychologist Robert Rosenthal indicates that many jurors are sensitive to the judge's demeanor during trial and likely to be influenced if the demeanor suggests the judge's view of a witness's credibility or a litigant's position. Note, The Appearance of Justice: Judges' Verbal and Nonverbal Behavior in Criminal Jury Trials, 38 Stan. L. Rev. 89 (1985).

[11]See § 6 supra.

[12]Com. v. Galavan, 91 Mass. 271, 9 Allen 271, 1864 WL 3472 (1864); Connor v. Township of Brant, 31 Ont. L. Rep. 274 (1913). In the following cases, particular leading questions by the judge were held necessary and within his discretion: U.S. v. Seck, 48 Fed. Appx. 827 (2d Cir. 2002) (the trial judge's questions to the defendant did not deny her a fair trial even though most of the questions were framed in leading language); Stinson v. State, 125 Ark. 339, 189 S.W. 49 (1916) (carnal abuse, questions to victim); Driscoll v. People, 47 Mich. 413, 11 N.W. 221, 223 (1882); State v. Riley, 28 N.J. 188, 145 A.2d 601 (1958).

[13]See remark in Com. v. Berklowitz, 133 Pa. Super. 190, 2 A.2d 516 (1938).

discrediting or impeaching the witness, though allowable for counsel, can intimate the judge's belief that the witness has lied, and hence constitute a verboten implied comment.[14]

In the federal courts and the few states retaining the common law power to comment, these restrictions on judicial questions are relaxed. In all jurisdictions, the restrictions are enforced more laxly in judge-tried cases. Nevertheless, even then the judge must avoid extreme exercises of the power to question. In a judge-tried case, the judge's question might betray a premature judgment. In a jury trial, functionally the judge must not assume the role of an advocate or a prosecutor.[15] If his questions are too

---

[14]State v. Drew, 213 S.W. 106 (Mo. 1919) (questions indicating a purpose to discredit defendant and one of his witnesses). But not all questions bearing on credibility betray an adverse opinion, even though the answer might happen to be discrediting. Neutral questions about knowledge or interest might be needed and desirable. *See* Madison v. State, 200 Md. 1, 87 A.2d 593 (1952) (in a murder case, a judge's questioning of accused was proper: "A judge's right to ask questions is not confined to questions which have no possible bearing on credibility."). Accordingly, the court's view in State v. Perry, 231 N.C. 467, 57 S.E.2d 774 (1950), that "it is improper for a trial judge to ask questions for the purpose of impeaching," may need qualification.

[15]U.S. v. Tilghman, 134 F.3d 414, 416–21 (D.C. Cir. 1998) (the trial judge's questions could have suggested to the jury that the judge disbelieved the accused; "the central issue" in the case was whether the accused was "telling the truth"); Rivas v. Brattesani, 94 F.3d 802, 806–08 (2d Cir. 1996) (the trial judge asked one defense witness whether a particular exhibit was a "fraud made up at the end of the day;" although the judge instructed the jury to disregard any inferences from his comments, the instruction was insufficient to cure the prejudice to the accused); U.S. v. Filani, 74 F.3d 378 (2d Cir. 1996) (the trial judge stepped outside his proper role; he targeted the accused's credibility and

challenged the accused's story more like a prosecutor than an impartial judge); U.S. v. Edwardo-Franco, 885 F.2d 1002 (2d Cir. 1989) (there were enough questionable rulings and incidents in the instant case to support appellants' claim that the trial judge was biased and unfair); U.S. v. Mazzilli, 848 F.2d 384 (2d Cir. 1988) (court's questioning left the jury with the indelible impression that the court did not believe the witness's account of the facts); U.S. v. Hickman, 592 F.2d 931 (6th Cir. 1979); State v. Pharr, 44 Conn. App. 561, 691 A.2d 1081 (1997) (the trial judge made a prejudicial comment in the jury's hearing); Sparks v. State, 740 So. 2d 33 (Fla. 1st DCA 1999) (the trial judge crossed the line by calling the prosecutor's attention to evidence that the prosecutor then used to impeach the defendant); State v. Silva, 78 Haw. 115, 890 P.2d 702 (Ct. App. 1995) (the judge assumed the role of a prosecutor by conducting an unduly extensive examination of the complainant); State v. Beck, 2007 UT 60, 165 P.3d 1225, 1229 (Utah 2007) ("The judge must take particular care when the defendant takes the stand . . . . In this case, the trial judge overstepped these bounds. [A] judge commits error when, in a criminal case before a jury, he questions a defendant extensively about weak aspects of her defense. The trial court asked the defendant forty-eight questions"); Saltzburg, Judges Interrogate Witnesses: Crossing the Line, 13 Crim.Just. 40 (Wint. 1999) (discussing *Tilghman*, supra).

partisan and extensive, the judge runs the risk that the appellate court will find that he crossed the line between judging and advocacy.[16] However, the mere number of judicial questions is not dispositive. The nature of the questions and the identity of the witness are the most important considerations.[17]

Not only may the judge examine witnesses called by the parties.[18] In her discretion, again to bringing out needed facts, the judge may also call witnesses whom the parties have chosen not to call at all.[19] Judges most frequently exercise the power to call witnesses when a necessary witness will probably be hostile

---

[16]U.S. v. Melendez-Rivas, 566 F.3d 41, 45–51 (1st Cir. 2009) (the judge's question to a defense witness related to the defendant's involvement in a series of felony crimes; the question interjected prejudicial testimony that was not stricken; the jurors could easily have perceived the question as enhancing the prosecutor's effort to impeach the defense witness); Nationwide Mut. Fire Ins. Co. v. Ford Motor Co., 174 F.3d 801, 808 (6th Cir. 1999) (overruled on other grounds by, Adkins v. Wolever, 554 F.3d 650 (6th Cir. 2009)) (the court reversed the lower court judgment on the ground of judicial misconduct; the trial judge repeatedly interrupted the plaintiff's opening statement and often engaged in one-sided questioning of witnesses; the judge even invited objections by defense counsel; the judge's "interruptions were so numerous and his questions so one sided they must inevitably have left the jury with the impression that the judge believed Nationwide's actions were egregious and improper"); People v. Boone, 180 Ill. App. 3d 98, 128 Ill. Dec. 661, 534 N.E.2d 1266 (1st Dist. 1988) (reversal required where trial judge called witnesses, conducted the examinations, and asked questions directed at eliciting testimony against the defendant); Layne v. State, 542 So. 2d 237 (Miss. 1989) (reversal is required where the trial judge displays partiality, becomes an advocate, or, in any significant way, conveys to the jury the impression that he has sided with the prosecution).

[17]U.S. v. Santana-Perez, 619 F.3d 117, 124–26 (1st Cir. 2010) (the judge must be especially carefully in questioning the accused); U.S. v. Seeright, 978 F.2d 842, 847 (4th Cir. 1992); Moore v. U.S., 598 F.2d 439 (5th Cir. 1979) (the judge asked 105 questions compared to 41 by defense counsel and 66 by the prosecutor, but the questions of the judge were "unbiased, patient, temperate, never argumentative or accusatory"). See discussion of pertinent factors concerning the nature of questions in 4 Weinstein's Federal Evidence § 614.04[4][a] (rev. 2011), indicating that in the federal courts reversals for interrogation by the trial judge are rare.

[18]The previously stated conditions apply.

[19]Merchants' Bank v. Goodfellow, 44 Utah 349, 140 P. 759 (1914) (in a suit on bill of exchange, the trial judge called the last endorser). See Court's witnesses (other than expert) in state criminal prosecution, 16 A.L.R.4th 352; Trial court's appointment, in civil case, of expert witness, 95 A.L.R.2d 390; Fed. R. Evid. 614(a), 706(a) & Unif. R. Evid. 614(a), 706(a). Compare U.S. v. Ostrer, 422 F. Supp. 93 (S.D. N.Y. 1976) (the court observed that the power to call witness is rarely invoked).

There has been a suggestion that in some cases, in the interest of justice, the judge may have the duty as well as the power to call witnesses and hence may be reversed for a failure to do so. See Moore v. Sykes' Estate, 167 Miss. 212, 149 So. 789 (1933); Frankfurter, J., dissenting, in Johnson v. U.S., 333 U.S. 46, 55, 68 S. Ct. 391, 92 L. Ed. 468 (1948); 58 Yale L.J. 183

and the prosecutor desires to escape the necessity of calling him and being handicapped by the traditional rule against impeaching one's own witness.[20] Concededly, under the Federal Rules of Evidence,[21] the prosecutor has another option; the rules allow a party to impeach the party's own witness. Yet, as a practical

---

(1948). But efforts to obtain reversal on this ground have been unavailing. *E.g.*, U.S. v. Lester, 248 F.2d 329 (2d Cir. 1957); Steinberg v. U.S., 162 F.2d 120 (C.C.A. 5th Cir. 1947); State v. Hines, 270 Minn. 30, 133 N.W.2d 371 (1964); Halloran-Judge Trust Co. v. Carr, 62 Utah 10, 218 P. 138 (1923). Wigmore denies the existence of a duty. 9 Wigmore, Evidence § 2484 (Chadbourn rev. 1981). Fed. R. Evid. 614(a) states that the judge "*may*" call witnesses [emphasis added].

[20]People v. Rogers, 187 Ill. App. 3d 126, 135 Ill. Dec. 65, 543 N.E.2d 300 (2d Dist. 1989) (the primary purpose for the trial court to call a witness is to enable a party to obtain the testimony of an important witness whose veracity is doubtful without fear that the party will be unable to impeach the witness if he or she says something which damages the party's case); Beghtol v. Michael, 80 Md. App. 387, 564 A.2d 82 (1989) (the five factors used to determine when it is appropriate to call a court's witness are: (1) the prosecutor's inability to vouch for the witness's veracity or integrity; (2) the close relationship between the witness and the defendant; (3) the existence of contradictory or inconsistent statements by the witness; (4) the witness's hostility; and (5) the necessity for the testimony, i.e., where the witness possesses material evidence).

[21]Unif.R.Evid. 614 and the former version of Fed. R. Evid. 614 provide:
CALLING AND INTERROGATION OF WITNESSES BY COURT

(a) Calling by Court. The court may, on its own motion or at the suggestion of a party, call witnesses, and all parties are entitled to cross-examine witnesses thus called.

(b) Interrogation by Court. The court may interrogate witnesses, whether called by itself or by a party.

(c) Objections. Objections to the calling of witnesses by the court or to interrogation by it may be made at the time or at the next available opportunity when the jury is not present.

Effective December 1, 2011, the restyled Fed. R. Evid. 614 reads:

(a) Calling. The court may call a witness on its own or at a party's request. Each party is entitled to cross-examine the witness.

(b) Examining. The court may examine a witness regardless of who calls the witness.

(c) Objections. A party may object to the court's calling or examining a witness either at that time or at the next opportunity when the jury is not present.

A specific objection is required to preserve for appeal any alleged error in the court calling or interrogating a witness. However, the objection need not be made contemporaneously with the calling or interrogation if the jury is present. Thus counsel is relieved of the embarrassment attendant on objecting to the judge's action in the jury's presence. The objection can be made at the next available opportunity when the jury is absent, or preferably at the first reasonable opportunity for a sidebar conference. Objections so made will be considered timely. U.S. v. Evans, 994 F.2d 317, 324–25 (7th Cir. 1993) (the defense moved for a mistrial as the first order of business on the next day of trial); Hanson v. Waller, 888 F.2d 806 (11th Cir.1989); U.S. v. Kwiat, 817 F.2d 440, 447–48 (7th Cir. 1987).

If the court's questions are so extremely biased as to deprive a party of a fair trial and counsel fears that an objection might antagonize the court further, the absence of an objection will not preclude review on appeal. Stillman v. Norfolk & Western Ry. Co., 811 F.2d 834 (4th Cir.1987).

matter the prosecutor may not wish to call the witness and thereby be identified with the witness in the jurors' minds. If the witness has a long criminal record, his "affiliation" with the government might taint the prosecution case in the jurors' eyes. In these circumstances, the prosecutor could invoke the judge's discretion under Rule 614(a) to call the witness.[22] If the judge calls the witness, either party may cross-examine and impeach him.[23]

As we have seen, Rule 614(a) generally empowers the judge to call witnesses. Rule 706 deals specifically with court appointed expert witnesses. At common law another use of the judicial

---

*See* U.S. v. Alanis, 109 F.3d 1239, 1242–43 (7th Cir. 1997) (citing *Stillman* but finding it inapplicable); U.S. v. Gastiaburo, 16 F.3d 582 (4th Cir. 1994) (citing *Stillman* but finding it inapplicable).

[22]Under Fed. R. Evid. 614(a), the matter is largely in the court's discretion. *See* U.S. v. Cochran, 955 F.2d 1116, 1122 (7th Cir. 1992) ("We are unable to find, and counsel has not cited, a single example of a reversal because of a trial court's decision not to call a witness for the court"); U.S. v. Leslie, 542 F.2d 285 (5th Cir. 1976) (court approved the trial judge's calling three material witnesses on government requests made on the ground that the witnesses were adverse and hostile and that prosecutor did not wish to adopt their testimony, even though he could use leading questions and impeach them if he called them; citing Fed. R. Evid. 614, the appellate court observed that the trial court "could properly protect the prosecution from whatever tendency the jury might have had to associate the witness with the calling party"); State v. Medeiros, 80 Haw. 251, 909 P.2d 579 (Ct. App. 1995) (there is no bright-line rule governing the propriety of calling of witnesses by a trial judge). *But see* U.S. v. Karnes, 531 F.2d 214 (4th Cir. 1976) (it was error for the trial judge to call two witnesses when prosecutor would not call them and conceded he had no case without them) and People v. Arnold, 98 N.Y.2d 63, 745 N.Y.S.2d 782, 772 N.E.2d 1140 (2002) (a trial judge erred by calling a witness after

both sides rested; the judge's action deprived the defense of the ability to request that the trier of fact draw a negative inference from the prosecution's failure to call the witness). *See also* Graham, Examination of a Party's Own Witness Under the Federal Rules of Evidence: A Promise Unfulfilled, 54 Tex. L. Rev. 917, 991 n. 345 (1976) ("Having the court call the witness, moreover, does not directly serve the principles governing the propriety of leading questions, refreshing recollection, cross-examination, and impeachment in civil and criminal cases."). Calling witnesses at the defense's request has also been assumed to be in the court's discretion. U.S. v. Herring, 602 F.2d 1220 (5th Cir. 1979).

In civil cases, the calling of witnesses by the judge for this purpose is said to be in his discretion. McBride v. Dexter, 250 Iowa 7, 92 N.W.2d 443 (1958); Fed. R. Evid. 614(a). But the case authority in civil cases is relatively sparse.

[23]U.S. v. Browne, 313 F.2d 197, 199 (2d Cir. 1963) (with respect to witnesses called by the court, "either of the parties is entitled to impeach him by the usual methods including proof of prior inconsistent statements."); Chalmette Petroleum Corp. v. Chalmette Oil Distributing Co., 143 F.2d 826, 829 (C.C.A. 5th Cir. 1944) ("If neither party will risk calling a witness who knows important facts, it is in the power of the Court to call and examine such a witness—allowing both parties the right of cross-examination and impeachment.").

power to call witnesses, codified in some state statutes, is to mediate the battle of partisan expert witnesses employed by the parties. In effect, the practice resurrects the judge's ancient power to call an expert of his own choosing to give impartial testimony to aid him or the jury in resolving a scientific issue.[24] In its celebrated 1993 *Daubert* decision, the Supreme Court decided that in order to determine the admissibility of purportedly scientific testimony, federal trial judges must evaluate the extent and quality of the empirical validation of the underlying theory or technique.[25] In his concurring opinion in the 1997 *Joiner* case elaborating on *Daubert*, Justice Breyer encouraged trial judges to exercise their power under Rule 706.[26] Those decisions have prompted trial judges to appoint experts with greater frequency under Rule 706.[27] However, as we have seen, the scope of the judge's power of calling witnesses in aid of justice is broader and is not limited to expert testimony cases.[28]

### *Jurors*

The preceding section points out that judges may question witnesses called by the parties. Should jurors be allowed to do so?

There are conflicting policy considerations. On the one hand,

---

[24]*E.g.*, Scott v. Spanjer Bros., Inc., 298 F.2d 928 (2d Cir. 1962); Citizens' State Bank of Santa Monica v. Castro, 105 Cal. App. 284, 287 P. 559 (2d Dist. 1930) (handwriting expert, pursuant to statute); Polulich v. J. G. Schmidt Tool Die & Stamping Co., 46 N.J. Super. 135, 134 A.2d 29 (County Ct. 1957) (workmen's compensation: deputy having a judge's power may call impartial expert: extensive discussion); State v. Horne, 171 N.C. 787, 88 S.E. 433 (1916) (alienist in murder case: "expert witnesses . . . were originally regarded as amici curiae and were called generally by the court"); Trial court's appointment, in civil case, of expert witness, 95 A.L.R.2d 390; Fed. R. Evid. 706 & Rev. Unif. R. Evid. 706 (1974); Kaye, Bernstein & Mnookin, The New Wigmore: Expert Evidence § 1.3 (2d ed. 2011); Gross, Expert Evidence, 1991 Wis. L. Rev. 1113. If there is no statutory or court rule authority, there may be practical problems concerning costs and pretrial services of the expert. See discussion in § 17 infra.

[25]Daubert v. Merrell Dow Pharmaceuticals, Inc., 509 U.S. 579, 113 S. Ct. 2786, 125 L. Ed. 2d 469 (1993).

[26]General Elec. Co. v. Joiner, 522 U.S. 136, 147, 149–150, 118 S. Ct. 512, 139 L. Ed. 2d 508 (1997) (Breyer, J., concurring).

[27]Note, Fighting Fire with Firefighters: A Proposal for Expert Judges at the Trial Level, 93 Colum. L. Rev. 473, 483 (1993) ("increasing at a modest rate"). *See also* Jurs, Questions from the Bench and Independent Experts: A Study of State Court Judges (Mar. 22, 2012), available at http://ssrn.com/abstract=2027549 (last accessed Dec. 7, 2012) (22% of the responding judges had appointed an independent expert under their state equivalent of Rule 706).

[28]A judge is more likely to call a witness in a bench trial. *See* Cunningham v. Housing Authority of City of Opelousas, 764 F.2d 1097 (5th Cir.1985) (the judge's action in ordering a deposition in bench trial after party rested was equivalent to the judge calling witness on own).

there are obvious dangers to permitting jury questions. One fear is that if jurors actively participate in the trial, before they have heard all the evidence they may develop biases inconsistent with "their . . . role as neutral factfinders."[29] Moreover, there is the risk that the jurors will attach inordinate weight to the witnesses' answers to the jurors' questions and slight the testimony elicited by the parties. On the hand, there is a strong case for allowing the jurors to pose questions. The argument runs that if the jurors realize that they can pose questions, they will be motivated to be more engaged and attentive to the witnesses' testimony.[30] Furthermore, there are perils to the factfinding process if, even at the close of evidence, the jurors have nagging questions that are unanswered. One possibility is that the jurors will speculate as to the answer and base a verdict on conjecture. Another possibility is that the litigant might suffer a wrongful loss; even if the litigant could easily have supplied the missing evidence, the jurors may hold the gap in the evidence against the litigant and for that reason decide the case adversely to the litigant.

It is understandable that given these conflicting policies, there is a wide split of authority over the propriety of juror questions.

- At one extreme, a few jurisdictions such as Kentucky take the position that petit jurors have the right to ask questions.[31]
- The polar extreme view is that juror questions are absolutely forbidden,[32] at least in criminal cases.[33]
- However, both the majority view[34] and the growing trend[35] is to accord the trial judge discretion to allow juror

---

[29]U.S. v. Thompson, 76 F.3d 442 (2d Cir. 1996) (juror questioning creates the risk that jurors will jump to premature conclusions and develop an advocate mentality); U.S. v. Johnson, 892 F.2d 707, 713–14 (8th Cir. 1989) (Lay, J., dissenting).

[30]*See* Landsman, Of Mushrooms and Nullifers: Rules of Evidence and the American Jury, 21 St. Louis U. Pub. L. Rev. 65, 74–77 (2002).

[31]Stamp v. Com., 200 Ky. 133, 253 S.W. 242 (1923).

[32]State v. Zima, 237 Neb. 952, 468 N.W.2d 377 (1991); Morrison v. State, 845 S.W.2d 882 (Tex. Crim. App. 1992); Juries—Questioning by Jurors, 75 Cr.L. (BNA) 320 (Feb. 11, 2004) ("two states—Mississippi and Nebraska—have ruled that juror questioning is prohibited in all cases . . . .

See Wharton v. State, 734 So.2d 985 (Miss. 1998)").

[33]Juries—Questioning by Jurors, 75 Cr. L. (BNA) 320 (Feb. 11, 2004) ("Two other states—Minnesota and Texas—prohibit juror questioning in criminal cases. *See* State v. Costello, 646 N.W.2d 204 (Minn. 2002)").

[34]Juries—Questioning by Jurors, 75 Cr.L. (BNA) 320 (Feb. 11, 2004) ("The majority of courts"); U.S. v. Smith, 569 F.3d 1209 (10th Cir. 2009); U.S. v. Rawlings, 522 F.3d 403, 407 (D.C. Cir. 2008) (at least 10 federal appellate courts have ruled that such questions are within the trial judge's discretion); Ex parte Malone, 12 So. 3d 60 (Ala. 2008) (the overwhelming majority of courts); Tillotson v. Goodman, 154 Kan. 31, 114 P.2d 845, 853–54 (1941) (the empirical studies do not support the fears underlying

questioning.[36] Some courts restrict this discretion to complex cases,[37] While acknowledging that the complexity of a case makes it more appropriate for the judge to permit juror questioning, other courts do not strictly limit the discretion to complicated cases.[38] The latter position is the most sensible view. However, even in the jurisdictions following the majority view, the appellate courts often caution

---

the rationale for banning questions by jurors); MacLean, No Final Answer Over Juror Questions: U.S. Courts Allow It, But Don't Trust It, Nat'l L.J., May 12, 2008, at 1, 17 (the article lists the leading cases in each circuit; "Though eleven of the nation's 12 . . . federal circuits now allow jurors to pose questions to witnesses during trial, there's a big difference between allowing and encouraging. Only two circuits, the 7th and 9th U.S. circuit courts of appeal, have urged judges . . . to tell jurors at the outset of a civil trial that they may ask questions. Although nearly every circuit leaves the issue to a trial judge's discretion in case law, it comes with some strong cautions. The 4th Circuit said it is allowed 'but strongly discouraged.' The 1st Circuit said it is permitted, but it should be used 'sparingly,' and adds that it is 'fraught with peril.' Since Arizona pioneered the practice in 1995, courts in four states—Florida, Indiana, New Jersey, and Ohio—have started routinely telling jurors they are allowed to submit written questions during trials. Only two states, Mississippi, and Nebraska, bar the practice altogether and three more, Georgia, Minnesota, and Texas, limit it to civil trials only"); Marek, Study Tests Alternative Trial Methods (Sep. 29, 2008), available at http://www.law.com/jsp/article.jsp?id=1202424834469 (last accessed Dec. 7, 2012) (a Seventh Circuit Bar Association study found that "[m]ore than 80 percent of jurors reported that being able to submit written questions to the witnesses helped their understanding of the facts"); West, "The Blindfold of Justice Is Not a Gag": The Case for Allowing Controlled Questioning of Witnesses by Jurors, 38 Tulsa L. Rev. 529 (2003) (at least 31 jurisdictions permit juror questioning, and every federal circuit that has passed on the issue has concluded that the trial judge has discretion to allow juror questioning).

[35]Debarba, Maintaining the Adversary System: The Practice of Allowing Jurors to Question Witnesses During Trial, 55 Vand. L. Rev. 1521 (2002). *See also* U.S. v. Nivica, 887 F.2d 1110, 1123 (1st Cir. 1989) (stating that juror questioning is "perhaps coming into vogue").

[36]State v. Culkin, 97 Haw. 206, 35 P.3d 233 (2001); State v. Hays, 256 Kan. 48, 883 P.2d 1093 (1994); Com. v. Britto, 433 Mass. 596, 744 N.E.2d 1089 (2001); State v. Costello, 620 N.W.2d 924 (Minn. Ct. App. 2001) (acknowledging the majority view).

[37]U.S. v. Feinberg, 89 F.3d 333 (7th Cir. 1996); U.S. v. Thompson, 76 F.3d 442 (2d Cir. 1996) (the trial judge erred in allowing jury questioning in a relatively uncomplicated case); U.S. v. Ajmal, 67 F.3d 12 (2d Cir. 1995) (juror questioning is disfavored and to be used only in "extraordinary and compelling circumstances"; the trial judge erred by permitting extensive juror interrogation in a banal case which did not involve factual intricacies); U.S. v. Sutton, 970 F.2d 1001, 1005 (1st Cir. 1992) ("juror participation in the examination of witnesses should be the long-odds exception, not the rule").

[38]U.S. v. Collins, 226 F.3d 457 (6th Cir. 2000).

the trial bench that juror questioning is risky and should be carefully monitored by the trial judge.[39]

When the judge exercises discretion to permit juror questioning, the judge can monitor and minimize the risks by observing certain safeguards. The rules of evidence apply to juror questions, and there would be a substantial danger if, without prior screening, jurors could simply orally pose questions. Thus, the judge ought to instruct the jurors that when they want to ask a question, they should raise their hand. When a juror does so, the judge directs the juror to reduce the question to writing. The juror hands the slip of paper to the court reporter or bailiff, who in turn delivers the slip to the judge. At that point at sidebar the judge and attorneys can discuss the propriety of the question.[40] The judge ought to give the jury an additional instruction, cautioning them against reaching conclusions or taking positions before all the evidence had been presented to them. In addition, if a juror question is permitted, the attorneys should be allowed to follow-up[41] and examine the witness on the topic of the juror's question.[42]

## § 9   Refreshing recollection[1]

Whether the questioner is a counsel, the judge, or a juror, an

---

[39]U.S. v. Sykes, 614 F.3d 303, 313 (7th Cir. 2010); U.S. v. Rawlings, 522 F.3d 403, 409 (D.C. Cir. 2008) ("Permitting jury questions as a matter of course is ill-advised"); Ex parte Malone, 12 So. 3d 60 (Ala. 2008) (here the questions were "few in number" and "factual in nature"); MacLean, No Final Answer Over Jurors Questions: U.S. Courts Allow It, But Don't Trust It, Nat'l L.J., May 12, 2008, at 1, 17.

[40]U.S. v. Sykes, 614 F.3d 303, 313 (7th Cir. 2010); U.S. v. Rawlings, 522 F.3d 403, 407–08 (D.C. Cir. 2008) (the trial judge should inform counsel in advance that juror questions will be permitted, require that all juror questions be submitted in writing, review them with counsel outside the jury's presence, ask the question himself, permit counsel to requestion the witness, and, if appropriate, tell the jury to disregard the fact that a particular juror question was not asked); U.S. v. Groene, 998 F.2d 604 (8th Cir. 1993); U.S. v. Johnson, 914 F.2d 136 (8th Cir. 1990); State v. Graves, 274 Mont. 264, 907 P.2d 963 (1995); Knipes v. State,

124 Nev. 927, 192 P.3d 1178, 1181–82 (2008) (there should be a hearing on the record over the admissibility of the proposed juror question before the question is put to the witness); Williams v. Com., 24 Va. App. 577, 484 S.E.2d 153 (1997).

[41]State v. Costello, 620 N.W.2d 924 (Minn. Ct. App. 2001).

[42]U.S. v. Johnson, 914 F.2d 136 (8th Cir. 1990).

**[Section 9]**

[1]3 Wigmore, Evidence §§ 758–65 (Chadbourn rev. 1970); Maguire & Quick, Testimony, Memory and Memoranda, 3 How.L.J. 1 (1957); Fed. R. Evid. and Rev. Unif. R. Evid. (1974) 612; 4 Weinstein's Federal Evidence § 612.03 (2d ed. 1997); West's Key Number Digest, Witnesses ⚷253 to 260; Refreshment of recollection by use of memoranda or other writings, 125 A.L.R. 19 (supplemented by Refreshment of recollection by use of memoranda or other writings, 82 A.L.R.2d 473).

anxious witness may forget a relevant fact. Testifying is a novel, frightening experience for many witnesses. It is clear from every-day experience that the latent memory of an experience can sometimes be revived by a familiar image or statement. In the words of one court, the inspiration for the revival "may be a line from Kipling or the dolorous strain of 'The Tennessee Waltz'; a whiff of hickory smoke; the running of the fingers across a swatch of corduroy; the sweet carbonation of a chocolate soda; [or] the sight of a faded snapshot in a long-neglected album."[2] This is an illustration of the phenomenon that the classical psychologists called association. The retrieval of any part of a past experience helps to recall other parts in the same field of awareness, and a new experience can stimulate the recall of prior similar events.[3] The effect is a reminder. The reminder prompts our memory to retrieve associated experiences.[4]

As we have seen,[5] the interviewing of witnesses by counsel who will examine them in court is a necessary step in preparing for trial. Before trial, the counsel can best refresh the witness's memory about the facts of the case by giving her the opportunity to read her own previous written statements, letters, maps, or other documents. However, again testifying at trial can be an intimidating experience. On occasion, even if the attorney properly prepared the witness before trial, the witness becomes anxious and forgets on the stand. In that event, the attorney must attempt to refresh or revive the witness's memory in order to elicit the witness's testimony about the forgotten fact.

---

[2]Baker v. State, 35 Md. App. 593, 371 A.2d 699 (1977).

[3]These are the principles of contiguity and similarity. *See* Gardner, The Perception and Memory of Witnesses, 18 Corn.L.Q. 390, 392 (1933); Hutchins & Slesinger, Some Observations on the Law of Evidence—Memory, 41 Harv. L. Rev. 860 (1928).

[4]"In permitting a witness to refresh his recollection by consulting a memorandum, the courts are in accord with present psychological knowledge. A distinction is drawn, in the analysis of the memory process, between *recall,* which is the reproduction of what has been learned, and *recognition,* which is recall with a time-factor added, or an awareness that the recall relates to past experience. It is with recognition that the law is principally concerned in permitting a witness to revive his recollection. The psychological evidence is clear that in thus allowing to be brought to mind what has been forgotten, the law is following sound psychological procedure." Cairn, Law and the Social Sciences 200 (1935).

Refreshing recollection usually occurs on direct examination. However, refreshing recollection can arise on cross-examination of a witness who says he does not recall. In the judge's discretion, counsel may employ leading questions or a document to refresh recollection in the jury's presence provided that a prior inconsistent statement is not quoted in open court in the jury's hearing unless the requirements for impeachment by a prior inconsistent statement are complied with. To the extent refreshing recollection is in the nature of impeachment, the good faith basis and collateral non-collateral rules apply. See § 49 infra.

[5]See § 2 supra.

Suppose that at trial, when asked about a particular fact or event, the witness answers that she cannot remember. At least when the witness admits forgetfulness on the record,[6] it has long been the practice that counsel may hand her a memorandum to inspect for the purpose of "refreshing her recollection." When she speaks from a memory thus revived, her testimony is the evidence, not the writing.[7] This is the process of *refreshing recollection at trial* in the original, strict sense.

### Confusion with the Past Recollection Recorded Hearsay Exception

However, after the courts accepted this simple, uncontroversial practice, it was natural for counsel to seek to carry it a step further. Suppose that even after inspecting the writing, the witness states that her memory is not revived and that she cannot

---

[6]"Most jurisdictions require a foundation that the witness cannot recall all the facts or an event or that the witness's memory be exhausted." Tanford, The Trial Process: Law, Tactics and Ethics § 6.05[D][2], at 250–51 (4th ed. 2009); Rush v. Illinois Cent. R. Co., 399 F.3d 705, 716 (6th Cir. 2005); U.S. v. Balthazard, 360 F.3d 309, 318 (1st Cir. 2004) ("It is hornbook law that a party may not use a document to refresh a witness's recollection unless the witness exhibits a failure of memory.").

[7]Henry v. Lee, 2 Chitty 124 (1810), cited in 3 Wigmore, Evidence § 758 (Chadbourn rev. 1970). *See* People v. Seaton, 26 Cal. 4th 598, 110 Cal. Rptr. 2d 441, 28 P.3d 175, 211–12 (2001) ("There was no need to authenticate the tape recording and transcript because they were not introduced in evidence, but were used only to refresh Sergeant Mackey's recollection.").

The process of refreshing recollection must be conducted as provided in restyled Fed. R. Evid. 103(d) so as to prevent "inadmissible evidence" from being "suggested to the jury by any means" such as asking questions in the jury's hearing. Where refreshment of recollection is by means of a writing, this mandate is easily accomplished by handing the writing to the witness and requesting that the witness read the writing silently to himself. The witness may then be asked whether his recollection has been refreshed. If the answer is yes, the initial question is repeated. If the witness states that his recollection has not been refreshed, it is improper for counsel to read the writing aloud before the trier of fact. Rush v. Illinois Cent. R. Co., 399 F.3d 705, 716–18 (6th Cir. 2005) ("While we have authorized the use of leading questions to establish a witness's lack of memory as to a particular event, we have cautioned that the trial court may abuse its discretion when otherwise inadmissible evidence is introduced to the jury through the guise of refreshing a witness's recollection. *See* Shoupe, 548 F.2d at 641 ('[W]e find no precedent sanctioning the recitation in the presence of the jury of extended unsworn remarks . . . .')"); Gaines v. U.S., 349 F.2d 190 (D.C. Cir. 1965) (prior statements used to refresh may be read aloud only out of jury's presence); Westinghouse Elec. Corp. v. Wray Equipment Corp., 286 F.2d 491 (1st Cir. 1961) (jury improperly permitted to hear deposition read aloud); United States v. McKeever, 271 F.2d 669, 676 (2d Cir. 1959) (if a tape recording is to be used to refresh a witness's recollection, jury may not hear recording).

testify from a refreshed recollection. But she vouches that she recognizes the writing as a memorandum she made when the facts were fresh in her mind. She adds that although she has no present memory of the facts, she remembers correctly recording the facts in the memorandum. Here the writing itself becomes the evidence. This latter situation is quite different than the process of *refreshing recollection.* In refreshing recollection, after reviewing the memory aid the witness testifies orally on the basis of her present refreshed memory. In contrast, when her memory is not jogged, the counsel relies on the witness's voucher as a basis for introducing the writing.[8] The writing is the real evidence.

In both cases, the questioner tenders a memorandum to the witness, but the underlying justification in the second situation is fundamentally different. Here the justification rests on the reliability of a writing which the witness swears is a *record of her past recollection.* The writing itself is introduced into evidence. The courts formulated special foundational rules and restrictions for this kind of memorandum. Hence, the common law rules generally require that the memo must have been written by the witness or examined and found correct by her. There is a further restriction that the memo must have been prepared so promptly after the events recorded that the events were still fresh in the witness's mind when the record was made, or examined and verified by her. Memoranda satisfying these restrictions fall within the past recollection recorded exception to the hearsay rule.[9]

Apparently, the earlier English cases on genuine refreshment of recollection placed no comparable restrictions on the use of memoranda at the trial to revive a witness's memory.[10] Those memoranda were not required to have been written by the witness or under her direction, or to have been made near in time to the event. Theoretically, the questioner could use anything to fresh the witness's memory. However, in the case of the practice of introducing records of *past recollection,* the additional restrictions were prescribed with good reason. Unfortunately, since the old name of "refreshing recollection" was often applied indiscriminately to both practices, the two practices became confused. Predictably, the restrictions developed for one kind of memorandum (past recollection recorded) spilled over to the other (present recollection refreshed).

---

[8]*See* Jewett v. U.S., 15 F.2d 955, 956 (C.C.A. 9th Cir. 1926) and extended explanation in United States v. Riccardi, 174 F.2d 883 (3d Cir.1949).

[9]See Ch. 28 infra. But if the memorandum was prepared by the witness, it may be admissible as a non-hearsay statement. See § 251 infra.

[10]Henry v. Lee, 2 Chitty 124 (1810), cited in 3 Wigmore, Evidence § 758 (Chadbourn rev. 1970); Rex v. St. Martin's, (1834) 2 Ad. & El. 210, 111 Eng. Rep. 81 (K.B.).

*The Case for Distinguishing Between the Two Practices*

Which is the wiser practice: (1) the older rule, championed by Wigmore and most modern courts, that any memorandum, without restriction of authorship,[11] time, or correctness, is usable to revive memory, or (2) the doctrine requiring that a memorandum used to refresh meet the same restrictions as a record of past recollection? Even if the latter doctrine is an historical blunder, it could be a desirable practice enhancing the search for truth.

Any kind of stimulus, "a song, a face, or a newspaper item,"[12] can produce the "flash" of recognition, the subjective feeling that "it all comes back to me now." But the sincerity of the feeling is no guarantee of the objective correctness of the image recalled. There is a danger that the mind will "remember" something that never happened. That danger is at least as great here as in the case of leading questions.[13] "Imagination and suggestion are twin artists ever ready to retouch the fading daguerrotype of memory."[14] Thus, there is a plausible policy argument for extending to refreshing memory the safeguards developed for memoranda of past recollection recorded, namely, the requirements that the witness must have created the writing or recognized it as correct, and that the creation or recognition must have occurred while the event was still fresh in memory.[15]

Nevertheless, today most courts adhere to the "classical" view

---

[11]Many courts permit the witness to use documents prepared by third parties. U.S. v. Marrero, 651 F.3d 453, 472 (6th Cir. 2011), cert. denied, 132 S. Ct. 1042, 181 L. Ed. 2d 766 (2012); U.S. v. Carey, 589 F.3d 187, 190–91 (5th Cir. 2009) (the permissibility of using a writing to refresh recollection does not depend on its source, the identity of the author, or the truth of the writings' contents); In re Carolan, 204 B.R. 980 (B.A.P. 9th Cir. 1996) (an authenticated TRW report which the witness evidently had not seen previously); U.S. v. Darden, 70 F.3d 1507, 1540 (8th Cir. 1995) (a government report of the witness's account of a meeting with the accused); U.S. v. Conley, 503 F.2d 520 (8th Cir. 1974).

[12]*See* U.S. v. Summers, 422 Fed. Appx. 838 (11th Cir. 2011), cert. denied, 132 S. Ct. 195, 181 L. Ed. 2d 101 (2011) (a videotape); U.S. v. Ewald, 398 Fed. Appx. 657 (2d Cir. 2010) (a tape recording); Jewett v. U.S., 15 F.2d 955 (C.C.A. 9th Cir. 1926); Baker v. State, 35 Md. App. 593, 371 A.2d 699 (1977); Recent Decision, Evidence—Refreshed Recollection Testimony—Witness Must Refresh Memory by a Writing or Some Tangible Evidence, 62 Miss.L.J. 245 (1992) (criticizing a decision which precluded a witness from refreshing his memory by talking to another witness).

[13]Hutchins & Slesinger, Some Observations on the Law of Evidence—Memory, 41 Harv. L. Rev. 860, 868, 869 (1928). See also the telling passage quoted from Bentham, 3 Wigmore, Evidence § 758 (Chadbourn rev. 1970).

[14]Gardner, The Perception and Memory of Witnesses, 18 Corn.L.Q. 390, 401 (1933).

[15]*E.g.*, Putnam v. U.S., 162 U.S. 687, 695, 16 S. Ct. 923, 40 L. Ed. 1118 (1896) (transcript of witness's prior testimony not allowed to be used to refresh, because the transcript was not prepared contemporaneously with the

that any memorandum or object may be used as a stimulus to present memory without restriction as to authorship, guarantee of correctness, or time of making.[16] This liberal view is sounder. There are other, sufficient safeguards against abuse. The first safeguard is the trial judge's power under Federal Rule of Evidence 104(a). It is a preliminary question for her decision under Rule 104(a) whether the memorandum actually does refresh.

---

events the witness testified about); State v. Patton, 255 Mo. 245, 164 S.W. 223 (1914) (similar to last; "the ease with which, as Prof. Muensterberg tells us, the human mind is influenced by suggestion would seem to form an insuperable psychological objection to the use of data for this purpose, of the correctness of which the witness is ignorant"); N.L.R.B. v. Hudson Pulp & Paper Corporation, 273 F.2d 660 (5th Cir. 1960) (affidavit used was too remote in time; alternate ground of decision); State v. Winemiller, 411 N.W.2d 719, 721 (Iowa Ct. App. 1987) ("The necessary foundation for establishing the admissibility of a writing to refresh a witness's recollection is that the witness's recollection be exhausted, that the movant identify the time, place, and person to whom the statement is given, the court is satisfied the writing accurately reflects the witness's statements or the witness acknowledges the accuracy of the writing, and the court is satisfied the document will help in refreshing the person's memory.").

These requirements would create special difficulties in respect to the use of a transcript of the witness's own prior testimony. Hale, The Use by a Witness of His Own Prior Testimony for the Purpose of Refreshing His Recollection, 15 St. Louis L. Rev. 137, 146 (1930). However, most cases involving transcripts have not imposed the requirements. Refreshment of recollection by use of memoranda or other writings, 82 A.L.R.2d 473. See Ch. 31 infra, for introduction of the prior testimony itself into evidence.

[16]For the rule that witness need not have made the memorandum, see U.S. v. Conley, 503 F.2d 520 (8th Cir. 1974); People v. Griswold, 405 Ill. 533, 92 N.E.2d 91 (1950) (memorandum of conversation not made by witness); State v. Hale, 85 N.H. 403, 160 A. 95 (1932); 3 Wigmore, Evidence § 759 (Chadbourn rev. 1970); Refreshment of recollection by use of memoranda or other writings, 82 A.L.R.2d 473. *Compare* People v. Betts, 272 A.D. 737, 74 N.Y.S.2d 791 (1st Dep't 1947); 23 N.Y.U. L.Q. 529; 34 Va. L. Rev. 607. There the court held that a policeman who had destroyed his notes of a conversation with accused and his transcript from those notes, to avoid their use on cross-examination, was improperly allowed to refresh his memory from another version of his transcript embodied in the complaint. *Compare* Gardner v. Hobbs, 69 Idaho 288, 206 P.2d 539 (1949); State v. Peacock, 236 N.C. 137, 72 S.E.2d 612 (1952).

A memorandum need not be made at or near the time of the event recorded. Com. v. McDermott, 255 Mass. 575, 152 N.E. 704 (1926); Smith v. Bergmann, 377 S.W.2d 519 (Mo. Ct. App. 1964) (memorandum prepared by witness the night before testifying).

A witness need not vouch for the correctness of the memorandum. U.S. v. McKeever, 169 F. Supp. 426 (S.D. N.Y. 1958); Williams v. Stroh Plumbing & Elec., Inc., 250 Iowa 599, 94 N.W.2d 750 (1959). But some opinions contain a contrary implication. *E.g.*, Tebeau v. Baden Equipment & Const. Co., 295 S.W.2d 184 (Mo. Ct. App. 1956).

Fed. R. Evid. 612 and Unif. R. Evid. 612 adopt the view stated in the text. *E.g.*, U.S. v. Landof, 591 F.2d 36 (9th Cir. 1978) ("But, the law is clear that recollection can be refreshed from documents made by persons other than the witness.").

When there is no seeming connection between the contents of the memorandum and the witness's testimony, she may find that it does not;[17] she need not accept at face value the witness's claim that reviewing the memo revived the witness's memory. The judge has additional control under Rules 403 and 611(a). In the exercise of her discretion to control the manner of the witness's examination,[18] the judge may decline to permit the use of the memory aid when, under 403 and 611, she regards the danger of undue suggestion as substantially outweighing the probative value.

When the witness seeks to resort to the memorandum, another safeguard is the rule entitling the adverse party to inspect the memorandum so that she may (1) object to its use if a ground appears,[19] and (2) use the memorandum to cross-examine the

---

[17]U.S. v. Rinke, 778 F.2d 581 (10th Cir. 1985); Doty v. Elias, 733 F.2d 720 (10th Cir.1984). *See also* U.S. v. Scott, 701 F.2d 1340, 1346 (11th Cir. 1983) (witnesses instructed not to testify as to any statement contained in the refreshing material for which they did not have an independent recollection).

The witness's testimony is not conclusive when the circumstances show that his memory is in fact not revived. Hiskett v. Wal-Mart Stores, Inc., 180 F.R.D. 403 (D. Kan. 1998) (the trial judge does not have to accept the witness's statement). *Compare* United States v. Riccardi, 174 F.2d 883 (3d Cir.1949), holding that the memory of witnesses who testified while consulting a lengthy list of articles was actually refreshed.

[18]The element of discretion is recognized in U.S. v. Lonardo, 67 F.2d 883 (C.C.A. 2d Cir. 1933); U.S. v. Boyd, 606 F.2d 792 (8th Cir. 1979) (the propriety of permitting use of a writing prepared by another); State v. Bradley, 361 Mo. 267, 234 S.W.2d 556 (1950); West's Key Number Digest, Witnesses ⚷255. Under particular circumstances, though, there could be abuse of discretion. U.S. v. Shoupe, 548 F.2d 636 (6th Cir. 1977).

[19]Morris v. U.S., 149 F. 123 (C.C.A. 5th Cir. 1906); Shell Oil Co. v. Pou, 204 So. 2d 155 (Miss. 1967). *See also*

State v. Gadwood, 342 Mo. 466, 116 S.W.2d 42, 51 (1937) (it is in trial judge's discretion whether inspection should be postponed until the time of cross-examination); State v. Bean, 119 Vt. 184, 122 A.2d 744 (1956) (cites and applies State v. Gadwood, 342 Mo. 466, 116 S.W.2d 42 (1937)).

Former Fed. R. Evid. 612 provided:

Except as otherwise provided in criminal proceedings by section 3500 of title 18, United States Code, if a witness uses a writing to refresh memory for the purpose of testifying, either—

(1) while testifying, or

(2) before testifying, if the court in its discretion determines it is necessary in the interests of justice,

an adverse party is entitled to have the writing produced at the hearing, to inspect it, to cross-examine the witness thereon, and to introduce in evidence those portions which relate to the testimony of the witness. If it is claimed that the writing contains matters not related to the subject matter of the testimony the court shall examine the writing in camera, excise any portions not so related, and order delivery of the remainder to the party entitled thereto. Any portion withheld over objections shall be preserved and made available to the appellate court in the event of an appeal. If a writing is not produced or delivered pursuant to order under this rule, the court shall make any order justice requires, except that in criminal cases when the prose-

witness.[20] With the memorandum in hand, the cross-examiner has a good opportunity to test the credibility of the witness's claim that her memory has been revived, and to search out any discrepancies between the writing and the testimony. For instance, if there is no evident nexus between the contents of the writing and the fact purportedly remembered, the cross-examiner can attack the plausibility of the witness's testimony that viewing the writing helped the witness remember that fact. In the past, this inspection right was usually limited to writings used by the witness on the stand.[21] However, the policy reasons for inspection seem equally applicable to writings used by the witness to

cution elects not to comply, the order shall be one striking the testimony or, if the court in its discretion determines that the interests of justice so require, declaring a mistrial.

Effective December 1, 2011, restyled Rule 612 reads:

(a) Scope. This rule gives an adverse party certain options when a witness uses a writing to refresh memory:

(1) while testifying; or

(2) before testifying, if the court decides that justice requires the party to have those options.

(b) Adverse Party's Options; Deleting Unrelated Matter. Unless 18 U.S.C. § 3500 provides otherwise in a criminal case, an adverse party is entitled to have the writing produced at the hearing, to inspect it, to cross-examine the witness about it, and to introduce in evidence any portion that relates to the witness's testimony. If the producing party claims that the writing includes unrelated matter, the court must examine the writing in camera, deleted any unrelated portion, and order that the rest be delivered to the adverse party. Any portion deleted over objection must be preserved for the record.

(c) Failure to Produce or Deliver the Writing. If a writing is not produced or is not delivered as ordered, the court may issue any appropriate order. But if the prosecution does not comply in a criminal case, the court must strike the witness's testimony or—if justice so requires—declare a mistrial.

[20]Little v. U.S., 93 F.2d 401 (C.C.A. 8th Cir. 1937); People v. Gezzo, 307 N.Y. 385, 121 N.E.2d 380 (1954) (prejudicial error to refuse inspection); State v. Carter, 268 N.C. 648, 151 S.E.2d 602 (1966); West's Key Number Digest, Witnesses ☞256; Refreshment of recollection by use of memoranda or other writings, 125 A.L.R. 19 (supplemented Refreshment of recollection by use of memoranda or other writings, 82 A.L.R.2d 473); 3 Wigmore, Evidence § 762 (Chadbourn rev. 1970). See Fed. R. Evid. 612.

[21]State ex rel. Polytech, Inc. v. Voorhees, 895 S.W.2d 13 (Mo. 1995) (the court rejects the contrary federal view for the stated reason that the view "weakens the attorney-client and work product privileges"); Star Mfg. Co. v. Atlantic Coast Line R. Co., 222 N.C. 330, 23 S.E.2d 32 (1942) Refreshment of recollection by use of memoranda or other writings, 125 A.L.R. 19 (supplemented by Refreshment of recollection by use of memoranda or other writings, 82 A.L.R.2d 473).

The absolute right apparently extends to the situation where, after commencing his or her testimony, the witness refreshes recollection during a recess. See Cornwell v. State, 193 Ga. App. 561, 388 S.E.2d 353, 355 (1989) ("In an effort to eliminate confusion steming from its prior decisions concerning the circumstances under which defense counsel must be given access to such documents, the Supreme Court recently held, in Johnson

refresh her memory before she testifies. The subject of inspection and use of writings to which the witness referred before testifying at trial is discussed at the end of this section.

Not only may the adversary inspect the memoranda used to refresh memory during the witness's examination, but she may also submit them to the jury for their examination.[22] However, the party calling the witness may not do so unless the memorandum qualifies as independent evidence admissible under the hearsay rule.[23] The consensus is that unless they qualify as nonhearsay or fall within an exception to the hearsay rule, memoranda used to refresh are not substantive evidence that can be used to support a finding of fact. They are merely memory joggers or aids.[24] Consequently, the best evidence rule is inapplicable; and a copy may be used to refresh memory without accounting for the original.[25]

The line between using the writing merely as a memory jogger and treating it as a record of past memory can be shadowy. Must the proponent show that the witness has no present recollection whatsoever of the matters embodied in the memorandum before

---

v. State, 259 Ga. 403, 383 S.E.2d 118 (1989), that 'if a witness uses documents to refresh memory after the inception of a hearing or trial, then during that hearing or trial, the cross-examiner is entitled to examine such documents.' ").

[22]*See* Refreshment of recollection by use of memoranda or other writings, 125 A.L.R. 19 (supplemented by Refreshment of recollection by use of memoranda or other writings, 82 A.L.R.2d 473). The adversary may place it in evidence to let the jury compare it with the testimony. Riley v. Fletcher, 185 Ala. 570, 64 So. 85, 87 (1913); Refreshment of recollection by use of memoranda or other writings, 82 A.L.R.2d 473; Cal. Evid. Code § 771; Fed. R. Evid. 612. *Contra* Jurgiewicz v. Adams, 71 R.I. 239, 43 A.2d 310 (1945).

[23]Shear v. Rogoff, 288 Mass. 357, 193 N.E. 63 (1934); Miller v. Borough of Exeter, 366 Pa. 336, 77 A.2d 395 (1951); West Key Number Digest, Witnesses ⬤⮞257; Refreshment of recollection by use of memoranda or other writings, 125 A.L.R. 19 (supplemented Refreshment of recollection by use of memoranda or other writings, 82

A.L.R.2d 473). The text is a proper interpretation of Fed. R. Evid. 612. *See* 4 Weinstein's Federal Evidence § 612.03[5] (rev. 2011).

[24]Since the real evidence is the witness's testimony from refreshed memory, the exhibit is not formally admitted into evidence; rather, it remains an exhibit "for identification." U.S. v. Faulkner, 538 F.2d 724 (6th Cir. 1976). Although the exhibit should be neither quoted nor submitted to the jury, many trial judges insist that the exhibit be included in the record of trial in the event of an appeal.

[25]Atlanta & St. A.B. Ry. Co. v. Ewing, 112 Fla. 483, 150 So. 586 (1933); Com. v. Levine, 280 Mass. 83, 181 N.E. 851 (1932); West's Key Number Digest, Witnesses ⬤⮞255(5); Refreshment of recollection by use of memoranda or other writings, 125 A.L.R. 19 (supplemented by Refreshment of recollection by use of memoranda or other writings, 82 A.L.R.2d 473); Refreshment of recollection by use of memoranda or other writings, 82 A.L.R.2d 473. The statement applies to Fed. R. Evid. 612. 4 Weinstein's Federal Evidence § 612.03[5] (rev. 2011).

she can resort to it as a memory aid? Even in opinions issued under the Federal Rules of Evidence, it is sometimes asserted that that showing is required,[26] but that assertion is unsound. Restyled Rule 803(5) permits the proponent to rely on the past recollection recorded hearsay exception when, after viewing the writing, the witness "cannot recall well enough to testify fully and accurately." The courts should apply a similarly realistic standard under Rule 612. The witness may believe that she remembers completely; but, after reading the memorandum, she might well recall additional facts. As the ancient proverb has it, "The palest ink is clearer than the best memory." There is an undeniable danger that a suggestible witness may mistakenly think that she remembers a specific fact merely because she reads it. However, that danger is not so substantial that it justifies a categorical rule prohibiting the use of present recollection refreshed in these situations. The judge should enjoy discretion in the matter. Similarly, even if a witness recognizes from present memory the correctness of a set of facts recorded in a memorandum, the witness may be unable to detail the individual facts such as numbers from memory without consulting the writing. Accordingly, the generalization that, once refreshed, a witness must testify independently of the writing[27] is too inflexible. Again, the matter ought to be entrusted to the trial judge's discretion. The judge may permit the witness to consult the memorandum as she speaks, especially when it is so lengthy and detailed that even a witness with a fresh memory would realistically be unable to recite unaided all the items.[28]

As previously stated, many older cases refused to enforce a

---

[26]U.S. v. Morlang, 531 F.2d 183 (4th Cir. 1975) (case not decided under Fed. R. Evid.); Thompson v. U.S., 342 F.2d 137 (5th Cir. 1965); N.L.R.B. v. Hudson Pulp & Paper Corporation, 273 F.2d 660 (5th Cir. 1960); People v. Kraus, 377 Ill. 539, 37 N.E.2d 182 (1941); 3 Mueller & Kirkpatrick, Federal Evidence § 6.93 (3d ed. 2007); Tanford, An Introduction to Trial Law, 51 Mo. L. Rev. 623, 667 (1986) ("Most jurisdiction require a foundation that the witness cannot now recall all the facts about an event, or that the witness' memory is exhausted"); West's Key Number Digest, Witnesses ☞254; Refreshment of recollection by use of memoranda or other writings, 125 A.L.R. 19 (supplemented by Refreshment of recollection by use of memoranda or other writings, 82

A.L.R.2d 473). *Contra* U.S. v. Thompson, 708 F.2d 1294 (8th Cir. 1983).

Referring to Fed. R. Evid. 612, U.S. v. Jimenez, 613 F.2d 1373 (5th Cir. 1980) stated that there would not need to be a showing of need for use of material covered by the so-called Jencks Act, 18 U.S.C.A. § 3500. But see note 38, infra.

[27]Roll v. Dockery, 219 Ala. 374, 122 So. 630 (1929) (dictum).

[28]Taylor v. U.S., 19 F.2d 813, 817 (C.C.A. 8th Cir. 1927) ("It would be practically impossible for officers, making daily investigations of alleged violations of law, to remember the names, dates, and what took place, without referring to notes made by them at the time or immediately thereafter."); Kramer v. C. I. R., 389 F.2d

demand for production at trial of matter reviewed by a witness to refresh memory before testifying.[29] However, even prior to the enactment of the Federal Rules of Evidence, a growing number of cases reached the contrary conclusion.[30] The most important factor in accelerating this trend has been the adoption of Federal Rule of Evidence 612.[31] Rule 612 explicitly announces that when a witness uses a writing to refresh her memory even before testifying, an adverse party is entitled to have the writing produced at the hearing, to inspect it, to cross-examine the witness about the writing, and to introduce into evidence the portions relating to the witness's testimony, if the court in its discre-

---

236 (7th Cir. 1968) (accountant's computation); United States v. Riccardi, 174 F.2d 883 (3d Cir.1949) (list of articles). *See also* U.S. v. Boyd, 606 F.2d 792 (8th Cir. 1979) (statements in report concerning checks involved in three-year kickback scheme); Exxon Corp. and Affiliated Companies v. C.I.R., T.C. Memo. 1992–92, 1992 WL 28059 (1992) (the material was so detailed that the witness probably could not have committed it to memory); People v. Allen, 47 Cal. App. 2d 735, 118 P.2d 927 (1st Dist. 1941) (aged witness's prior testimony was read to her, and she assented to its correctness); Ward v. Morr Transfer & Storage Co., 119 Mo. App. 83, 95 S.W. 964 (1906) (itemized list of goods lost). *See generally* Goings v. U.S., 377 F.2d 753, 761 n.11 (8th Cir. 1967) ("Generally, doctors, engineers, accountants and other lay witnesses testifying should be allowed continuously to refer to data on their reports.").

But the witness must indicate that his memory is refreshed. Wolf v. Mallinckrodt Chemical Works, 336 Mo. 746, 81 S.W.2d 323 (1934); Freeland v. Peltier, 44 S.W.2d 404 (Tex. Civ. App. Galveston 1931); Weinstein & Berger, Evidence ¶ 612[01]. The witness may not read the writing aloud under the guise of refreshment, as a cloak for getting in evidence an inadmissible document. Freeland v. Peltier, 44 S.W.2d 404 (Tex. Civ. App. Galveston 1931); S.W. Bridges & Co. v. Candland, 88 Utah

373, 54 P.2d 842, 846, 847 (1936). Of course when the writing is otherwise admissible as evidence, it may be introduced and read by the witness. *See* Guiffre v. Carapezza, 298 Mass. 458, 11 N.E.2d 433 (1937).

[29]Tillman v. U.S., 268 F.2d 422 (5th Cir. 1959) (even given a request, it was not error not to produce narcotic agent's notes of conversation with defendant about six months before trial with which agent refreshed his recollection immediately before trial; matter was entrusted to the trial judge's discretion); Needelman v. U.S., 261 F.2d 802 (5th Cir. 1958) (no abuse of discretion in denying permission to see some of the notes and memoranda used for refreshing recollection). *Accord* Smith & Wesson, Div. of Bangor Punta Corp. v. U.S., 782 F.2d 1074 (1st Cir. 1986); Cosden Oil & Chemical Co. v. Karl O. Helm Aktiengesellschaft, 736 F.2d 1064 (5th Cir.1984).

[30]U.S. v. Smith, 521 F.2d 957 (D.C. Cir. 1975); In re Comair Air Disaster Litigation, 100 F.R.D. 350 (E.D. Ky. 1983) (prior to deposition); Prucha v. M & N Modern Hydraulic Press Co., 76 F.R.D. 207 (W.D. Wis. 1977); People v. Scott, 29 Ill. 2d 97, 193 N.E.2d 814 (1963); State v. Mucci, 25 N.J. 423, 136 A.2d 761 (1957) (noteworthy opinion by Heher, J.); State v. Bradshaw, 101 R.I. 233, 221 A.2d 815 (1966).

[31]Fed. R. Evid. 612.

tion determines production is necessary in the interests of justice.[32]

Consider the significance of the sweeping wording of Rule 612. A writing consulted to refresh memory could be a privileged one, such as a letter written by the client-witness to her attorney about the case. In this event, there is a possible conflict between Rule 612's disclosure requirement and the privilege for confidential communications between attorney and client. Should the pretrial act of consulting the writing effect a waiver of the privilege? Finding a waiver when the writing is consulted by the witness while testifying is obviously warranted; it would be patently unfair for a witness to consult the writing while testifying in open court but refuse to allow the opposing counsel to see the writing. The proper result is more debatable when a privileged writing is consulted before trial. Ordinarily the privilege involved will be either the absolute attorney-client privilege[33] or the qualified protection for "work product."[34] Section 93 of this treatise discusses the problem of waiver of those privileges.[35] At this point, it suffices to say that the clear trend in the federal cases has been to hold that Rule 612 overrides all privileges claims,[36] at least when the witness consulted the passage in the writing pretrial for the precise purpose of freshening his memory in order to testify.[37] Indeed, some of the more recent decisions override the privilege only when the record establishes that consulting the

---

[32]State v. Byrd, 35 Ohio App. 3d 100, 519 N.E.2d 852, 855 (8th Dist. Cuyahoga County 1987) ("In exercising its discretion whether to require the production of a writing which a witness reviewed before testifying, the court should consider (a) the apparent extent of the witness's reliance on that writing, (b) the significance of the data recalled by that reliance, (c) any resulting burden on another party, and (d) any potential disruption of orderly proceedings.").

[33]See generally Ch. 10 infra.

[34]See § 96 infra.

[35]See § 93 infra. *See also* U.S. v. Sai Keung Wong, 886 F.2d 252 (9th Cir. 1989) (a confidential informant's report privileged under Malaysian law need not be disclosed).

[36]Amerisure Ins. Co. v. Laserage Technology Corp., 1998 WL 310750 (W.D. N.Y. 1998) ("any privilege"); MaGee v. Paul Revere Life Ins. Co.,

954 F. Supp. 582 (E.D. N.Y. 1997) (psychiatrist-patient privilege); Audiotext Communications Network, Inc. v. US Telecom, Inc., 164 F.R.D. 250 (D. Kan. 1996) ("any privilege"); Redvanly v. NYNEX Corp., 152 F.R.D. 460, 471 (S.D. N.Y. 1993) (although the courts were previously reluctant to require disclosure, a line of case law spanning 16 years has reduced their reluctance); Belcour, Use it and Lose it—Privileged Documents, Preparing Witnesses, and Rule 612 of the Federal Rules of Evidence, 31 Fed.B.News & J. 171, 172 (1984).

[37]U.S. v. Sheffield, 55 F.3d 341 (8th Cir. 1995) (the more "cautious" cases hold that Rule 612 comes into play only when the record reflects both that the witness consulted the document and that the witness did so for the purpose of refreshing memory for trial; Rule 612 does not confer inspection rights unless the witness relied on the writing to refresh his or her

writing actually refreshed the witness's memory and affected the witness's trial testimony.[38]

A further matter connected to Federal Rule of Evidence 612 is the relationship between that rule and Federal Rule of Criminal Procedure 26.2. Rule 26.2 is the successor to the so-called Jencks Act, 18 U.S.C.A. § 3500. That relationship is explored in a later section.[39]

Lastly, hypnosis is sometimes employed as a technique to refresh a witness's recollection. That subject is analyzed in the chapter on scientific evidence.[40]

---

memory); Monticello Ins. Co. v. Kendall, 1998 WL 173194 (D. Kan. 1998) (there must be some showing, "however minimal, that the documents reviewed actually influenced the witness' testimony"); U.S. v. Bertoli, 854 F. Supp. 975 (D.N.J. 1994), aff'd in part, vacated in part, 40 F.3d 1384 (3d Cir. 1994) (Rule 612 did not apply simply because the prosecutor showed and explained some documents to the witness); Sauer v. Burlington Northern R. Co., 169 F.R.D. 120, 123 n.3 (D. Minn. 1996) ("our Court of Appeals has underscored the specificity with which a witness's reliance upon a privileged document must be established before a wholesale access to that document will be permitted"); Pack v. Beyer, 157 F.R.D. 226, 231 (D.N.J. 1994) (Rule 612 does not come into play merely because the witness mentions a document during his or her testimony); Butler Mfg. Co., Inc. v. Americold Corp., 148 F.R.D. 275, 278 (D. Kan. 1993) (although the witness initially answered affirmatively that he had used a writing to refresh his memory, he later claimed that he did not rely on the statement); Timm v. Mead Corp., 1992 WL 32280 (N.D. Ill. 1992) (standing alone, the witness's statement that he "glanced" at the document before testifying does not trigger Rule 612); Solovy & Byman, Preparing the Witness: Federal Rules of Evidence Pose an Unclear and Present Danger for Work Product, Legal Times, June 3, 2002, at 42–43 (Rule 612 "talks about production 'if a witness uses a writing to refresh memory.' What does that mean? Is it the actual refreshment of memory that is the test, or is it the act of attempting to refresh memory?"); Joseph, Experts and Privilege, Nat'l L.J., Feb. 8, 1999, at B6 ("In 1985, the 3d Circuit Court of Appeals limited this waiver analysis in Sporck v. Peil, 759 F.2d 312 (3d Cir. 1985), reasoning that Rule 612 authorizes disclosure not of the full document collation, but only of those specific facts, documents or excerpts that actually has been relied on by the witness"); Applegate, Preparing for Rule 612, 19 Litig., Spr. 1993, at 17, 20. As *Monticello Insurance* and the Joseph article indicate, some courts follow the narrow view that the witness must in fact have relied on the document to refresh the testimony he gives at trial.

[38]Rajanayagam v. Canada (Minister of Citizenship & Immigration), 159 F.T.R. 149, 1998 WL 1731194 (Fed. T.D. 1998); Joseph, Experts and Privilege, Nat'l L.J., Feb. 8, 1999, at B6.

[39]See § 97 infra.

[40]See § 206 infra.

# Chapter 3

# The Requirement of Firsthand Knowledge: The Opinion Rule & Expert Testimony

## § 10   The requirement of knowledge from observation[1]

The common law system of evidence is exacting in its insistence on the most reliable sources of information. This insistence is reflected in the hearsay rule, the documentary originals doctrine, and the opinion rule.[2] These doctrines are not absolute exclusionary rules; rather, each doctrine reflects a preference for a more reliable types of evidence. For example, by virtue of the opinion rule, the law prefers that a witness testify to facts, based on personal knowledge, rather than opinions inferred from such facts. One of the earliest and most pervasive manifestations of the common law insistence is the rule that a witness testifying about a fact which can be perceived by the senses must (1) have had an opportunity to observe, (2) have actually observed the fact, and (3) presently recall the observed fact.[3] The same general

---

**[Section 10]**

[1]2 Wigmore, Evidence §§ 650–70 (Chadbourn rev. 1979); 3 Weinstein's Federal Evidence Ch. 602 (rev. 2011); 4 Weinstein's Federal Evidence Chs. 701–06 (rev. 2011); West Key Number Digest, Witnesses ⚮37.

[2]Nance, The Best Evidence Principle, 73 Iowa L. Rev. 227 (1988).

[3]Daubert v. Merrell Dow Pharmaceuticals, Inc., 509 U.S. 579, 592, 113 S. Ct. 2786, 125 L. Ed. 2d 469 (1993) ("the usual requirement of firsthand knowledge—a rule which

requirement applies to declarations admitted under most exceptions to the hearsay rule; as a general proposition, the hearsay declarant must have had an opportunity to observe the fact declared.[4]

This requirement can easily be confused with the rule barring the repetition of out-of-court statements considered hearsay.[5] Technically, if the witness's testimony on its face purports to describe observed facts, but the testimony rests on statements of others, the objection is that the witness lacks firsthand knowledge. In contrast, when on its face the testimony indicates the witness is repeating out-of-court statements, a hearsay objection is appropriate.[6] Courts often blur this distinction.[7]

---

represents 'a most pervasive manifestation of the common law insistence upon the most reliable sources of information,' Advisory Committee's Notes on Fed. Rule. Evid. 602. . . ."); State v. Johnson, 92 Idaho 533, 447 P.2d 10 (1968); State v. Dixon, 420 S.W.2d 267 (Mo. 1967).

Unif. R. Evid. 602 and former Fed. R. Evid. 602 provide:

> A witness may not testify to a matter unless evidence is introduced sufficient to support a finding that the witness has personal knowledge of the matter. Evidence, to prove personal knowledge may, but need not, consist of the witness' own testimony. This rule is subject to the provisions of Rule 703, relating to opinion testimony by expert witnesses.

Effective December 1, 2011, restyled Fed. R. Evid. 602 reads:

> A witness may testify to a matter only if evidence is introduced sufficient to support a finding that the witness has personal knowledge of the matter. Evidence to prove personal knowledge may consist of the witness's own testimony. This rule does not apply to a witness's expert testimony under Rule 703.

[4]2 Wigmore, Evidence § 670 (Chadbourn rev. 1979); Adv. Com. Note, Fed. R. Evid. 803; and see the discussion here of the various exceptions. There are some instances, however, in which the requirement is not applied, e.g., an opposing party's statements (formerly called admissions of a

party-opponent), see § 254 infra. Where reputation is used as hearsay evidence of a fact (see § 322), while the witness who testifies to the reputation must know the reputation, the community-talk itself need not be shown to be based on knowledge. However, the reputation is limited to that in the locality where people would presumably know the reputed fact.

[5]See § 247 infra. See U.S. v. Reyes-Guerrero, 638 F. Supp. 2d 177, 185–90 (D.P.R. 2009) (the officer was not present at the time of the drug transaction he attempted to describe).

[6]Thus, the Advisory Committee's Note to Fed. R. Evid. 602 states:

> This rule does not govern the situation of a witness who testifies to a hearsay statement as such, if he has personal knowledge of the making of the statement. Rules 801 to 805 would be applicable. This rule would, however, prevent him from testifying to the subject matter of the hearsay statement, as he has no personal knowledge of it.

See Elizarraras v. Bank of El Paso, 631 F.2d 366 (5th Cir. 1980); Fox v. Allstate Ins. Co., 22 Utah 2d 383, 453 P.2d 701 (1969) (court states that counsel's hearsay objection should have been based on lack of knowledge). See also Morgan, Basic Problems of Evidence 60 (1961) ("[T]he trial judge was affirmed in refusing to allow a plaintiff to testify that to his own knowledge, during an operation for amoebic ulcer a portion of his intestine

The party offering the testimony has the burden of laying a foundational showing that the witness had an adequate opportunity to observe, actually observed, and presently recalls the observation.[8] Suppose that on direct examination, the witness initially appears to testify from personal knowledge. If it later appears for the first time that the witness lacked opportunity or did not actually observe the fact, his testimony will be stricken; and the jury will be given a curative instruction to disregard the stricken testimony.[9] Although the requirement for showing the witness's personal knowledge exists, the proponent's burden is a minimal one. The judge applies the Rule 104(b) procedure in deciding whether the proponent has made an adequate showing of personal knowledge.[10] As § 53 explains, the Rule 104(b) standard is relaxed. When under the circumstances reasonable persons could differ as to whether the witness had an adequate opportunity to observe, the witness's testimony is admissible; and

---

above the rectum was removed. Obviously he must have been giving the result of hearsay.").

It is especially important to distinguish the two objections under the Federal Rules of Evidence. Most foundational facts conditioning the application of hearsay exceptions fall under Fed. R. Evid. 104(a) and are assigned to the trial judge for decision. However, the foundational fact of personal knowledge under Rule 602 falls under Rule 104(b); and the trial judge plays only a limited, screening role, merely deciding whether the foundational testimony would permit a rational juror to find that the witness possesses the firsthand knowledge. Saltzburg, The Right Objection, 25 Crim. Just., Wint. 2011, at 54.

[7]Elizarraras v. Bank of El Paso, 631 F.2d 366, 374 (5th Cir. 1980) ("although appellant objected on hearsay grounds, not personal knowledge, we will not draw such a fine line"). *See* U.S. v. Stout, 599 F.2d 866 (8th Cir. 1979) (court upheld admission of testimony that was objected to as hearsay but a proper objection was arguably lack of personal knowledge).

[8]State v. Prescott, 70 R.I. 403, 40 A.2d 721 (1944) (it was not error to

exclude evidence where foundation not laid). This principle is adopted by Fed. R. Evid. and Rev. Unif. R. Evid. (1974) 602. See note 3 supra. But the judge has discretion to admit the evidence, deferring the proof of knowledge to a later stage. Sofas v. McKee, 100 Conn. 541, 124 A. 380 (1924).

[9]State v. Dixon, 420 S.W.2d 267 (Mo. 1967); Jamestown Plumbing & Heating Co. v. City of Jamestown, 164 N.W.2d 355 (N.D. 1968) (illustrates procedure). But it has been held that if there is no objection to the witness's testimony on direct examination and no effort to show lack of knowledge during cross-examination, the presumption is that the witness is testifying of his own knowledge. Canal Ins. Co. v. Winge Bros., Inc., 97 Ga. App. 782, 104 S.E.2d 525 (1958). These concepts are consistent with, and should be followed under, Fed. R. Evid. and Unif. R. Evid. 602.

Although Fed. R. Evid. 104(c) and Unif. R. Evid. 104(c) provide for a hearing on preliminary matters outside the jury's hearing when the interests of justice require, such hearings will often be unnecessary in applying Rule 602.

[10]Fed. R. Evid. 104(b).

the jury will then makes its own appraisal of his opportunity to know in evaluating the weight of the testimony.[11]

In laying the foundation, the examiner may elicit from the witness the particular circumstances which led him to notice, observe, or remember the fact.[12] What called the witness's attention to the fact or event? How clear a view did the witness have? Why was the fact so memorable for the witness? If the witness had a special reason to be attentive, the jury is likely to attach more weight to the witness's purported recollection.

While the law demands firsthand observation, the law does not unrealistically insist on either precise perception by the witness or certainty in recalling the facts.[13] Accordingly, even when a witness uses qualifying language such as "I think," "My impression

---

[11]*See* New England Environmental Technologies Corp. v. American Safety Risk Retention Group, Inc., 810 F. Supp. 2d 390, 396 (D. Mass. 2011) ("Evidence is inadmissible if the Court, in its discretion, determines that the witness 'could not have actually perceived or observed that which he testified to' "); Senecal v. Drollette, 304 N.Y. 446, 108 N.E.2d 602 (1952) (it was error to exclude testimony of 12-year-old boys as to speed and make of automobile, based on brief glance). Many decisions apparently assume the principle stated in the text without discussion.

The text applies under Fed. R. Evid. 104(b), 602. Fed. R. Evid. 602, Advisory Committee's Note ("It will be observed that the rule is in fact a specialized application of the provisions of Rule 104(b) on conditional relevancy."). See § 53 infra, for discussion related to Fed. R. Evid. 104(b).

*See generally* Uniform Rule of Evidence 19 (1953) ("The Judge may reject the testimony of a witness that he perceived a matter if he finds that no trier of fact could reasonably believe that the witness did perceive the matter."); Comment to Rule 104 of the Model Code of Evidence ("If the witness proposes to testify that he actually perceived a material matter, he must usually be permitted so to testify unless his story is inherently impossible or so fantastic that no rational person could reasonably believe it. The

mere fact that the opponent produces or offers to produce contradictory evidence of greater weight is immaterial, unless that evidence is of such overwhelming weight that no jury could reasonably believe that the witness did not perceive the matter.").

[12]People v. Neely, 163 Cal. App. 2d 289, 329 P.2d 357 (2d Dist. 1958) (witness may state reason he had occasion to recall a particular time, but erroneous exclusion was cured by cross-examination); Brown v. Chicago, B. & Q.R. Co., 88 Neb. 604, 130 N.W. 265 (1911) (witness may state that his attention was called to approaching vehicle by his little boy's remark).

The test is implied under Fed. R. Evid. 602. The Advisory Committee's Note for 602 states: "These foundation requirements [firsthand knowledge] may, of course, be furnished by the testimony of the witness himself; hence personal knowledge is not an absolute but may consist of what the witness thinks he knows from personal perception."

[13]Eitel v. Times, Inc., 221 Or. 585, 352 P.2d 485 (1960) (alleged insufficient inspection of wire did not render testimony about its source inadmissible); Ewing v. Russell, 81 S.D. 563, 137 N.W.2d 892 (1965) (testimony of condition of floor held admissible although witness testified she "didn't pay any particular attention to the floor").

A similar viewpoint should be

is," or "In my opinion," the testimony is admissible if he merely acknowledges an inattentive observation or an unsure memory.[14] However, an objection will be sustained if the judge concludes that the witness means that he speaks from conjecture or hearsay.[15] When the state of the record is unclear, the judge may exercise his power under Rule 614 to question the witness before making a final ruling on the objection.

Of course, a person who has no knowledge of a fact except what another has told him does not satisfy the requirement of knowledge from observation. However, when the witness bases his testimony partly on firsthand knowledge and partly on the accounts of others, the problem calls for a practical compromise. As a case in point, when a witness speaks about his own age[16] or his kinship with a relative,[17] the courts routinely allow the testimony. Strictly speaking, it is impossible for the witness to have personal knowledge of those facts; no matter how precocious a child might be, she will not recall her own birth. Hence, there is an element of necessity in this situation. Moreover, the witness's knowledge of this type of fact is likely to have a trustworthy basis, namely, reports from close relatives who possess firsthand knowledge. In

---

taken under Fed. R. Evid. 602. *See* M. B. A. F. B. Federal Credit Union v. Cumis Ins. Soc., Inc., 681 F.2d 930 (4th Cir. 1982) (witness's knowledge need not be positive; court must find witness could not have actually perceived or observed); U.S. v. Evans, 484 F.2d 1178 (2d Cir. 1973). There still should be support for a "finding" of personal knowledge under the test stated in the text at note 10 supra.

[14]Auerbach v. U.S., 136 F.2d 882 (C.C.A. 6th Cir. 1943) (witness testified to identity of man he saw, "to the best of my belief" but acknowledged he might be mistaken, allowed); Covey v. State, 232 Ark. 79, 334 S.W.2d 648 (1960) ("Seems like he said something like . . . ."); E.F. Enoch Co. v. Johnson, 183 Md. 326, 37 A.2d 901 (1944) ("It looked like that truck . . . swung in"); Tews v. Bamrick, 148 Neb. 59, 26 N.W.2d 499 (1947) ("I guess," as to speed of car); 2 Wigmore, Evidence § 658 (Chadbourn rev. 1979).

[15]U.S. v. Cox, 633 F.2d 871 (9th Cir. 1980) (witness had an impression of a matter); State v. Dixon, 420 S.W.2d 267 (Mo. 1967) ("I think"); State v. Thorp, 72 N.C. 186, 1875 WL 2639

(1875) ("my best impression"). *See generally* Morgan, Basic Problems of Evidence 60 (1961) ("In the usual situation the witness must speak as of his present memory. How clearly, how definitely must he purport to remember? What if he says, 'I am not sure, but my impression is,' or 'My recollection is hazy, but the best that I can remember is,'? Such cautious answers may mean that his perception was careless or inaccurate or that though he once had a reasonably clear picture of the matter, his memory has faded. Generally the courts have no hesitation in permitting the trier of fact to hear and consider such testimony, although, standing alone, it might not be sufficient to support a verdict or finding.").

[16]Antelope v. U.S., 185 F.2d 174 (10th Cir. 1950) (statutory rape: victim may testify to her age and date of birth); State v. Olson, 260 Iowa 311, 149 N.W.2d 132 (1967) (extra-judicial statement of age). See § 322 infra.

[17]State v. Schut, 71 Wash. 2d 400, 429 P.2d 126 (1967) (parentage of witness). See § 322 infra.

short, when the witness testifies to facts that he knows partly at firsthand and partly from hearsay reports, the judge should admit or exclude according to the overall reliability of the evidence.[18] By way of example, a witness's industry experience is a sufficient predicate for the witness's testimony about practices within the industry.[19] Similarly, lay employees of a business are often held to have enough "personalized knowledge" of the business' operation to testify about the amount of its profits.[20]

## § 11    The evolution of the rule against opinions: opinions of laymen

*The Original English View*

Although it is traceable to the British courts, the opinion rule was enforced more widely and far more inflexibly here than in

---

[18]The evidence was admitted in Hunt v. Stimson, 23 F.2d 447 (C.C.A. 6th Cir. 1928) (sales manager of lumber yard testified to amount of lumber on hand, based on his estimates from inspection and tallies made by other employees); Schooler v. State, 175 S.W.2d 664 (Tex. Civ. App. El Paso 1943) (geologist's testimony as to structure and oil prospects of land was based on inspection and reports by other geologists); Vogt v. Chicago, M., St. P. & P. R. Co., 35 Wis. 2d 716, 151 N.W.2d 713 (1967) (wife permitted to testify to her husband's earnings although books were incomplete).

An example under Fed. R. Evid. 602 is U.S. v. Mandel, 591 F.2d 1347 (4th Cir. 1979) (senator's feelings and beliefs on governor's position about certain legislation held inadmissible to the extent based upon hearsay; "The more difficult problem arises when the witness' belief is based in part on admissible testimony. We think this problem is one of degree. If the belief is primarily based upon hearsay, it is inadmissible. But if the belief is substantially based on admissible evidence, such as direct statements or acts by one of Governor Mandel's agents, then it should be admitted. The basis for the belief should be explored in each instance and a ruling on admissibility made when those

facts are before the trial court.").

Fed. R. Evid. 602 and Unif. R. Evid. 602 make clear that pursuant to Fed. R. Evid. and Unif. R. Evid. 703, an expert may testify without personal knowledge. See § 15 infra.

[19]U.S. v. Smith, 591 F.3d 974 (8th Cir. 2010).

[20]Mississippi Chemical Corp. v. Dresser-Rand Co., 287 F.3d 359, 373–74 (5th Cir. 2002) (collecting cases). More broadly, the courts tend to apply the personal knowledge requirement laxly in the business setting. Seltzer v. I.C. Optics, Ltd., 339 F. Supp. 2d 601 (D.N.J. 2004) (a former management employee could make assertions about the nature of the employer's advertising procedures; the employee had sufficient personal knowledge of company procedures to make the assertions); Mendoza v. Sysco Food Services of Arizona, Inc., 337 F. Supp. 2d 1172 (D. Ariz. 2004) (on the one hand, the head of the employer's human resources department was competent to testify that no one in that department knew of complaints by the plaintiff employee; on the other hand, the head had failed to establish that he had adequate personal knowledge to testify that no one in the employer's entire business knew of such complaints).

England.[1] The original rule against "opinions" had a different, limited meaning for the English judge. In English usage of the 1700's and earlier, the primary meaning of "opinion" was an unsupported "notion" or "persuasion of the mind without proof or certain knowledge."[2] Thus, the original expression implied a lack of grounds, which is quite different than the contemporary meaning of the term "opinion" in this country. Today we use the word to denote an inference, belief, or conclusion without necessarily suggesting that the inference is completely unfounded.

The requirement that witnesses have personal knowledge, discussed in the preceding section, has roots in medieval law.[3] The early courts demanded that witnesses testify about only "what they see and hear."[4] Coke's classic 1622 dictum, that "It is no satisfaction for a witness to say that he 'thinketh' or 'persuadeth himself' "[5] and Mansfield's 1766 statement, "It is mere opinion, which is not evidence"[6] ought to be understood as condemning only testimony not based on personal knowledge. Statements founded purely on hearsay or conjecture fall under this ban. But as Wigmore interprets the historical evidence, until the 1800's there was no judicial support for a more restrictive "opinion" rule excluding even inferences by witnesses possessing personal knowledge.[7]

### The Evolution of the American Law
*The early exclusionary rule.* However, by the middle of the

---

[Section 11]

[1]See for example the brief treatment of opinion evidence in Phipson, Evidence ch. 36 (10th ed. 1963). *See* Cowen & Carter, Essays on the Law of Evidence 163 (1956) ("In practice the English judges have paid little more than lip service to the rule."). *See also* King & Pillinger, Opinion Evidence in Illinois (1942) (a work valuable in any jurisdiction for its original analysis and creative ideas).

[2]Samuel Johnson's Dictionary (1st ed. 1755), cited in King & Pillinger, note 11, at p. 8.

[3]9 Holdsworth, Hist. Eng. L. 211 (1926).

[4]In 1349 it was held that witnesses were not challengeable "because the verdict will not be received from them, but from the jury; and the witnesses are to be sworn 'to say the truth,' without adding 'to the best of their knowledge,' for they should testify nothing but what they . . . know for certain, that is to say what they see and hear." Anon. Lib. Ass. 110, 11 (1349), quoted in Phipson Evidence ch. 36, at 475 (10th ed. 1963).

[5]Adams v. Canon, Dyer 53b, quoted in 7 Wigmore, Evidence § 1917, p. 2 (Chadbourn rev. 1979).

[6]Carter v. Boehm, 3 Burr. 1905, 1918 (1766), quoted in 7 Wigmore, Evidence § 1917, p. 7 (Chadbourn rev. 1978).

[7]7 Wigmore, Evidence § 1917 (Chadbourn rev.1979); King and Pillinger, supra note 11, at p. 7. The latter work cites Peake on Evidence, an English work published in 1801, as the source of the seminal statement that witnesses generally must state "facts" rather than "opinion."

1800's[8] the disparagement of "mere opinion" in the limited sense of conjecture not based on observation evolved into a broader. much more questionable canon of exclusion. This canon was the doctrine that witnesses generally must restrict their testimony to recitations of the "facts" and avoid "inferences, conclusions, or opinions,"[9] even ones drawn from their own personal knowledge of the facts.

That canon is based on the simplistic assumption that "fact" and "opinion" differ in kind and are readily distinguishable. The formula is a clumsy tools for regulating the examination of witnesses. It is clumsy because its basic assumption is an illusion. As the Supreme Court has remarked, "the distinction between statements of fact and opinion is, at best, one of degree."[10] The witness's words cannot "give" or "recreate" the facts, that is, the objective situations or events about which the witness is testifying. Drawings, maps, photographs, and even motion pictures are only remote, partial portrayals of those "facts." Word pictures—oral or written descriptions—of events are even more distant approximations of reality. No matter however seemingly specific, detailed, and "factual" it is, any conceivable statement is in some measure the product of inference as well as observation and memory. The distinction between the statement, "He was driving on the left-hand side of the road" (which would be categorized as "fact" under the rule), and "He was driving carelessly" (which would be called "opinion") is merely a difference

---

[8]*E.g.*, Donnell v. Jones, 13 Ala. 490, 511, 1848 WL 426 (1848) (the opinion of one acquainted with business whether levy of attachment had destroyed credit and forced business into assignment was excluded. "The general rule requires, that witnesses should depose only to facts, and such facts too as come within their knowledge. The expression of opinions, the belief of the witness, or deductions from the facts, however honestly made, are not proper evidence as coming from the witness; and when such deductions are made by the witness, the prerogative of the jury is invaded."). It is notable, however, that even in the 1850s, the Illinois court stated the matter hesitantly, "It is true, probably, that mere opinions, as opinions, when offered in evidence, should be confined to experts in the questions of skill or science as such, which are open to that kind of proof and for want of better." Butler v. Mehrling, 15 Ill. 488,

491, 1854 WL 4724 (1854). In the 1852, Sixth edition of his treatise, when he deals with opinions in § 440, Greenleaf cites no case support for his statement that "the opinions of witnesses are in general not evidence" but devotes numerous citations to cases receiving opinions.

[9]Among the leading cases which discussed the rule, in addition to the cases in the next preceding note, are Baltimore & O.R. Co. v. Schultz, 43 Ohio St. 270, 1 N.E. 324 (1885) (observer's opinion that fence unfit to keep stock off, excluded); Graham v. Pennsylvania Co., 139 Pa. 149, 21 A. 151 (1891) (the opinion of architect who had seen defendant's platform for alighting passengers, that because of construction and lighting it was unsafe was excluded).

[10]Beech Aircraft Corp. v. Rainey, 488 U.S. 153, 168, 109 S. Ct. 439, 102 L. Ed. 2d 445 (1988).

between a more concrete form of descriptive statement and a less specific form. The distinction between so-called "fact" and "opinion" is not a difference between opposites or contrasting absolutes, but instead a difference in degree with no bright line boundary.[11]

If trial judges must distinguish on the spur of the moment between "fact" and "opinion," no two judges, acting independently, will always reach the same results. Of course, many questions have recurred and have customarily been classified as calling for either "fact" or "opinion". But in a changing world there will be a myriad of new statements to which the judge must apply the distinction. Thus, good sense demands that the law accord the trial judge a wide range of discretion at least in classifying evidence as "fact" or "opinion," and probably also in admitting evidence classified as opinion. Several courts have expressed this viewpoint.[12] Federal Rule of Evidence and Uniform Rule of Evidence 701 reflect that the trial judge possesses such latitude.[13]

*The gradual relaxation of the admissibility standard.* The recognition of the impossibility of administering the opinion standard as a mandatory rule came slowly. The relaxation of the strictness of the standard was initially limited to cases of strict necessity.[14] A norm excluding opinion except in instances of strict necessity survives today as the "orthodox" view in a few state

---

[11]For a masterly exposition of this view, see 7 Wigmore, Evidence § 1919 (Chadbourn rev. 1978). Another discussion, with vivid illustrative material, is King & Pillinger, Opinion Evidence in Illinois 1–6, 21–23 (1942).

[12]Dersis v. Dersis, 210 Ala. 308, 98 So. 27 (1923) ("A certain discretion is rightly vested in the trial courts in directing the search for the truth by this class of evidence, and their action should not be disturbed unless it is apparent some right of a party has been invaded or suppressed. We think a man sitting up all night with a sick man, or one grievously wounded in the head may form an opinion whether he is conscious or unconscious, which may be given to the jury for what it is worth."); Grismore v. Consolidated Products Co., 232 Iowa 328, 5 N.W.2d 646 (1942) ("The courts and other authorities uniformly agree that the receipt of opinion evidence, whether lay or expert, and the extent to which it will be received in any particular

case, are matters resting largely in the administrative discretion of the court."); Osborn v. Lesser, 201 Kan. 45, 439 P.2d 395 (1968) (interpreting K.S.A. 60-456(a), i.e., original Uniform Rule 56(1)); Wilson v. Pennsylvania R. Co., 421 Pa. 419, 219 A.2d 666 (1966).

[13]U.S. v. Pierson, 503 F.2d 173 (D.C. Cir. 1974).

[14]*E.g.*, the following passage from a former leading case:

A few general propositions are submitted, which, it is believed, fairly reflect the current of authority on the subject of the admissibility of the opinions of witnesses as evidence. (1) That witnesses shall testify to facts and not opinions is the general rule. (2) Exceptions to this rule have been found to be, in some cases, necessary to the due administration of justice. (3) Witnesses shown to be learned, skilled, or experienced in a particular art, science, trade, or business may, in a proper case, give their opinions upon a given state of facts. This exception is limited to experts. (4) In matter more within

courts.[15] However, even in states which have not adopted the Federal Rules of Evidence or a similar statutory reform, the practice is becoming far more liberal than the older formulas. The practice is more accurately reflected in a formula used by some courts sanctioning the admission of opinions on grounds of "expediency" or "convenience" rather than "necessity." The so-called "collective fact" or "short-hand rendition" rule, permitting opinions on such subjects as a person's age,[16] a car's speed, or a person's intoxication,[17] rests on this more liberal notion.[18] The same notion underlies the acceptance of "skilled lay observer"

---

the common observation and experience of men, non-experts may, in cases where it is not practicable to place before the jury all the primary facts upon which they are founded, state their opinions from such facts, where such opinions involve conclusions material to the subject of inquiry. (5) In such cases the witnesses are required, so far as may be, to state the primary facts which support their opinions. Baltimore & O.R. Co. v. Schultz, 43 Ohio St. 270, 1 N.E. 324, 331 (1885). This is no longer the law of Ohio, which has since embraced Fed. R. Evid. 701. *See generally* Morgan, Basic Problems of Evidence 217 (1961) (under the orthodox rule, testimony in the form of opinion is allowed if the witness could not "accurately, adequately and with reasonable facility describe the fundamental facts upon which the opinion is erected.").

[15]*See* Whitney v. Central Paper Stock Co., 446 S.W.2d 415 (Mo. Ct. App. 1969) ("when it is impossible or extremely difficult for a witness to convey an actual and accurate meaning"; error to exclude opinion that wooden floor was "rotten"). The standard is stated in varying terms. *E.g.*, People v. Reed, 333 Ill. 397, 164 N.E. 847, 850 (1928) ("Most persons would probably find it difficult to describe the odor of a rose, whiskey, beer or limburger cheese, but this difficulty could scarcely be regarded as affecting the value of their testimony that they were familiar with and recognized the particular odor."); Beuttenmuller v. Vess Bottling Co. of St. Louis, 447 S.W.2d 519 (Mo. 1969) (opinion may be stated when "facts and circum-

stances are such that they may not be readily and accurately described").

[16]U.S. v. Yazzie, 976 F.2d 1252, 1253–55 (9th Cir. 1992) (the testimony would have supported the defendant's contention that he reasonably believed that the minor in question was at least 16 years of age).

[17]Although the courts assume that most American adults are competent to testify about alcohol intoxication, they distinguish drug intoxication. People v. Navarette, 30 Cal. 4th 458, 133 Cal. Rptr. 2d 89, 66 P.3d 1182, 1203 (2003) (a lay witness who has never seen someone under the influence of drugs may not express an opinion that a person looked like he was under the influence of cocaine); State v. Bealor, 187 N.J. 574, 902 A.2d 226, 234 (2006) (although lay opinion testimony regarding alcohol intoxication is admissible, the same is not true for marijuana intoxication). It can reasonably be assumed that the average law-abiding person has had substantial exposure to persons who were alcohol intoxicated; it is arguably improper to make a similar assumption about drug intoxication.

[18]A long-established "exception" to the opinion-rule in some states admits "opinions" where they can be justified as "short-hand renditions" of a total situation, or as "statements of collective facts": Dulaney v. Burns, 218 Ala. 493, 119 So. 21, 24 (1928) ("Did you ever say anything to influence him about not leaving anything to his kinfolks?"); Pollard v. Rogers, 234 Ala. 92, 173 So. 881 (1937) ("He looked like he was dying"; opinion has extensive

opinion on such topics as the identification of a person's handwriting style.[19] In the case of collective fact opinions, the proponent lays a foundation establishing an adequate opportunity for observation such as a sufficiently long period to observe the allegedly speeding car. In the case of skilled lay observer opinions, the proponent lays a foundation demonstrating a sufficiently large number of opportunities for prior observation such as previous occasions when the witness saw exemplars of the person's cursive writing. In effect Federal Rule of Evidence 701 codifies convenience as the standard.[20] Rather than restricting lay opinion to cases of strict necessity, by its terms Rule 701 authorizes the receipt of any lay opinion "helpful" to the trier of fact. As a general proposition,[21] Rule 701 liberalizes the common law standard.

The standard actually applied by many contemporary trial

---

discussion); State v. Morrow, 541 S.W.2d 738 (Mo. Ct. App. 1976) ("When a witness has personally observed events, he may testify to his 'matter of fact' comprehension of what he has seen in a descriptive manner which is actually a conclusion, opinion, or inference, if the inference is common and accords with the experience of everyday life."); City of Beaumont v. Kane, 33 S.W.2d 234, 241, 242 (Tex. Civ. App. Beaumont 1930) ("The situation at the end of Pearl Street presented such an appearance that a stranger on a rainy night would be liable to drive off into the river.").

[19]U.S. v. Tipton, 964 F.2d 650, 654–55 (7th Cir. 1992); Inbau, Lay Witness Identification of Handwriting, 34 Ill. L. Rev. 433 (1939).

[20]Fed. R. Evid. 701. But the text of Rule 701 does not limit lay opinion to statements which are permissible on the basis of "convenience." U.S. v. Leo, 941 F.2d 181, 193 (3d Cir. 1991) ("The modern trend favors the admission of opinion testimony. . . ."); U.S. v. Paiva, 892 F.2d 148, 157 (1st Cir. 1989); Young v. Illinois Cent. Gulf R. Co., 618 F.2d 332, 337–38 (5th Cir. 1980).

[21]In one respect, though, the Federal Rules may toughen the standard for the admission of lay opinions. At common law, the courts often allowed owners to testify about the value of their personal or real property. Some

courts extended the practice and permitted persons to testify about the value of their services. General Aggregate Corp. v. LaBrayere, 666 S.W.2d 901 (Mo. Ct. App. E.D. 1984). The courts admitted these opinions liberally, since the witness's status as owner was the only required foundation. Arkansas Oklahoma Gas Corp. v. Burton, 10 Ark. App. 419, 664 S.W.2d 894 (1984). The witness's proponent did not have to establish the witness's qualification as an expert. Citizens Elec. Corp. v. Amberger, 591 S.W.2d 736 (Mo. Ct. App. E.D. 1979). The witness could opine even though he was ignorant of market values in the general area. Arkansas Louisiana Gas Co. v. Cates, 10 Ark. App. 426, 664 S.W.2d 897 (1984). After the enactment of the Federal Rules, the federal courts have continued to admit these opinions. Gregg v. U.S. Industries, Inc., 887 F.2d 1462 (11th Cir. 1989); U.S. v. 215.7 Acres of Land, More or Less, Situate in Kent County, State of Del., 719 F. Supp. 273 (D. Del. 1989). However, to date the courts have overlooked a significant statutory construction problem. Although there is no mention of this type of testimony in the Advisory Committee Note to Rule 701 governing lay opinion, it is mentioned in Rule 702 governing expert opinion. Hence, there is an argument that the drafters intended to reclassify this type of opinion as expert testimony. If so, contrary to the prior com-

judges reflects Wigmore's position. His position was that lay opinions should be rejected only when they are superfluous in the sense that they will be of no value to the jury.[22] The value or helpfulness of opinions to the jury is the principal test of Federal Rule of Evidence and Uniform Rule of Evidence 701.[23] In light of Rule 701, the prevailing practice in respect to the admission of lay opinions should be described not as a rigid rule excluding opinions, but rather as a preference. The more concrete description is preferred to the more abstract. To be sure, to the extent reasonably feasible, the witness ought to attempt to convey the

---

mon law practice, the proponent of this type of valuation testimony will have to qualify the witness as an expert.

[22]7 Wigmore, Evidence § 1918 (Chadbourn rev. 1978). The test above is quoted in Allen v. Matson Nav. Co., 255 F.2d 273, 278 (9th Cir. 1958) (holding admissible testimony that floor was "slippery," a pre-Fed. R. Evid. decision).

[23]The text of Unif. R. Evid. 701 and former Fed. R. Evid. 701 incorporates the notion in the form of an affirmative limitation:

> If the witness is not testifying as an expert, the witness' testimony in the form of opinions or inferences is limited to those opinions of the witness which are (a) rationally based on the perception of the witness and (b) helpful to a clear understanding of the witness' testimony or the determination of a fact in issue.

Effective December 1, 2011, restyled Fed. R. Evid. 701 reads:

> If a witness is not testifying as an expert, testimony in the form of an opinion is limited to one that is:
> (a) rationally based on the witness's perception;
> (b) helpful to clearly understanding the witness's testimony or to determining a fact in issue; and
> (c) not based on scientific, technical, or other specialized knowledge within the scope of Rule 702.

Lay witnesses have been permitted to express opinions on extremely varied topics. The topics include "[t]he appearance of persons or things, identity, the manner of conduct, competency of a person, feelings, degrees of light or darkness, sound, size, weight, distance and an endless number of things that cannot be described factually in words apart from inferences." Ladd, Expert Testimony, 5 Vand. L. Rev. 414, 417 (1952). Also included are the speed of a vehicle, the value of personal property, the nature of substances or sounds, the witness's own physical, mental or emotional status, the identity and physical condition of another person including such things as age, condition of health, ability to work, sanity, knowledge, suffering, possession of mental facilities, hearing, eyesight, unconsciousness after an accident, and intoxication.

The Advisory Committee Notes (1972) observe:

> The rule assumes that the natural characteristics of the adversary system will generally lead to an acceptable result, since the detailed account carries more conviction than the broad assertion, and a lawyer can be expected to display his witness to the best advantage. If he fails to do so, cross-examination and argument will point up the weakness. See Ladd, Expert Testimony, 5 Vand. L. Rev. 414, 415–417 (1952). If, despite these considerations, attempts are made to introduce meaningless assertions which amount to little more than choosing up sides, exclusion for lack of helpfulness is called for by the rule.

See, e.g., U.S. v. Phillips, 600 F.2d 535 (5th Cir. 1979) (dictum that testimony of another's understanding amounted to little more than choosing up sides).

concrete primary facts to the trier of fact. However, when it is impractical for the witness to verbalize all the data supporting an inference,[24] the preference yields; and the witness's inferential testimony is admissible. Moreover, the principal impact of the rule is on the form of examination. The questions, while they cannot suggest the particular details desired,[25] should call for the most specific account that the witness can give. For example, the witness should not be asked, "Did they reach an agreement?" but rather "What did they say?" The opinion rule ought to be conceived as a matter of the form of the examination rather than the substance of the testimony—again, a difference of degree.[26] So conceived, like the form regulations of leading questions and questions calling for a free narrative, the opinion rule falls in the realm of discretion. The habit of Anglo-American lawyers to examine about specific details is a valuable tradition. The challenge is to preserve this habit while curbing time-wasting quibbles over trivial "opinion" objections. Unfortunately, those objections can still be voiced in jurisdictions wedded to a literal application of the older formulas.

A simple, clean solution would be to remove the matter of lay opinion from the category of matters governed by "rules."[27] Supporters of that solution find a sufficient substitute in lawyers' natural desire to present a detailed, convincing case[28] and the cross-examiner's ability to expose the non-existence or inconsistency of details not developed on direct. Federal Rule of Evidence 701 does not go quite that far, but it embraces a viable alternative short of altogether jettisoning the opinion doctrine. Under

---

[24]Government of Virgin Islands v. Knight, 989 F.2d 619 (3d Cir. 1993) ("It is difficult . . . to articulate all of the factors that lead one to conclude that a person did not intend to fire a gun"); U.S. v. Petrone, 185 F.2d 334 (2d Cir. 1950) ("Nothing is less within the powers of the ordinary witness than to analyze the agglomerate of sensations which combine in his mid to give him an 'impression' of the contents of another's mind. To require him to unravel that will, unless he is much practiced in self scrutiny, generally. . . paralyze his powers of expression"); Baltimore & O.R. Co. v. Schultz, 43 Ohio St. 270, 1 N.E. 324, 332 (1885) (lay opinions are admissible "where it is not practicable to place before the jury all the primary facts upon which they are founded. . . ."); Del. R. Evid. 701 (lay opinions are

admissible "when . . .[t]he witness cannot readily, and with equal accuracy and adequacy, communicate what he has perceived to the trier of fact without testifying in terms of inferences or opinions. . . .").

[25]That type of suggestive phrasing would render the question objectionably leading. See § 6 supra.

[26]Beech Aircraft Corp. v. Rainey, 488 U.S. 153, 168, 109 S. Ct. 439, 102 L. Ed. 2d 445 (1988).

[27]See 7 Wigmore, Evidence § 1929 (Chadbourn rev. 1978) (The Future of the Opinion Rule); Bozeman, Suggested Reforms of the Opinion Rule, 13 Temple U. L.Q. 296 (1939).

[28]Perlman, Preparation and Presentation of Medical Proof, 2 Trial Dip. J. 18 (Spr. 1979).

Rule 701 and Rule 602, the witness must have personal knowledge of matter forming the basis of testimony of opinion;[29] the testimony must be based rationally on the witness's perception;[30]

---

[29]Keyes v. Amundson, 391 N.W.2d 602, 606 (N.D. 1986) ("Rule 701, N.D. R. Ev., provides that opinion testimony by a lay witness is admissible if the opinion is rationally based on the perception of the witness and helpful to a clear understanding of his testimony or the determination of a fact in issue. *See* State v. Gill, 154 N.W.2d 791 (N.D. 1967); Knoepfle v. Suko, 108 N.W.2d 456 (N.D. 1961); State v. Mark G. Cohen, 538 A.2d 151, 153 (R.I. 1988) ("In State v. Bowden, 473 A.2d 275, 280 (R.I. 1984), we set out a two-part test for admitting lay opinion. First, the lay witness must have had an opportunity to view the person or event at issue. Second, the lay witness must be able 'to give concrete details on which the opinion was founded.' Id. The police officer's testimony in the case before us clearly satisfied both parts of this test. Accordingly, the trial justice correctly ruled his testimony admissible."). The degree of opportunity for observation and the extent of the observation do not affect the competency of the witness but go to the weight of the evidence. State v. Gill, supra; Knoepfle v. Suko, supra. In the instant case, we believe Beard's affidavits include a sufficient foundation to establish the admissibility of his testimony. Further, Beard's affidavit also indicates that he heard the motorcycle 'winding up or accelerating' for three seconds. The noise of a vehicle also may be a factor in a lay person's determination of speed. State v. Gill, supra.").

[30]Fed. R. Evid. 701 & Unif. R. Evid. 701. *E.g.*, Alexis v. McDonald's Restaurants of Massachusetts, Inc., 67 F.3d 341, 347 (1st Cir. 1995) ("there simply" was "no foundation" for the opinion that the defendant's employee acted with "race based animus"); U.S. v. Cox, 633 F.2d 871 (9th Cir. 1980) (impression voiced by witness did not rationally follow from facts she stated).

The requirement that the opinion be rationally based on the witness's perception mandates that the opinion be one which a lay person could normally form from observed facts.

In addition where relevancy requires, a foundation must be laid as to the witness's personal knowledge of facts to which the observed facts are being compared. Thus, a witness may not testify that something smelled like dynamite unless it is sufficiently established that the witness from prior experience knows what dynamite smells like. Another illustration of the concept that the witness must possess sufficient personal knowledge of facts to which to compare the testified to observation involves a car's speed. Before an occurrence witness can testify that the car was going about 70 m.p.h., a foundation must be laid establishing the witness's personal knowledge of how fast 70 m.p.h. really is. This is usually done by having the witness testify to having driven a car himself at such a speed while observing the speedometer or being in a car with someone else under similar circumstances. Although observing a car proceed at a certain speed while in the car is not the same perspective possessed by an occurrence witness standing on a street corner, the foundation is usually held sufficient. If further foundation is required, the witness could most likely testify to seeing cars go by on an interstate highway presumably proceeding at the speed of 65 m.p.h., if not faster. When the witness is older, he may recall the days before the 65 m.p.h. speed limit. Contrast the foregoing with a person who says that he has lived in the woods alone for the last thirty years and that the last time he was in a car was twenty years ago. On his first day back from isolation he just happens to see an accident involving the car in question. Under these circumstances, the occurrence witness's testimony as to the car going

and the opinion must be helpful to the jury (the principal test).[31] Under these statutory standards, many[32] courts have become more receptive to lay opinions about the state of mind of third parties.[33] Modernly, the courts tend to accept such opinions so long as the witness makes it clear to the jury that she is expressing an inference about the third party's apparent state of mind based on factors such as the third party's demeanor and behavior. Contrary to some early decisions,[34] if the proponent adequately establishes the witness's personal knowledge, the witness need not recite all the observed matters that are the bases of opinion,[35] although the judge has discretion to require preliminary

---

about 70 m.p.h. lacks a sufficient foundation. It is the same situation as the man saying something smelled like dynamite when he never had smelled dynamite before. *See* Eason v. Barber, 89 N.C. App. 294, 365 S.E.2d 672, 674–75 (1988) (witnesses 17 and 18 years old, with 9 and 14 months' driving experience respectively, properly permitted to testify as to vehicular speed).

[31]*See* U.S. v. Dellasera, 457 Fed. Appx. 876 (11th Cir. 2012) (the defendant's co-worker could express the opinion that in a conversation, the defendant had offered the co-worker the opportunity to make $10,000 by serving as a straw buyer in a real estate transaction); Mehus v. Emporia State University, 326 F. Supp. 2d 1213 (D. Kan. 2004) (the players on a college volleyball team were qualified to express an opinion as to the coach's ability).

[32]The trend is not universal. U.S. v. Guzzino, 810 F.2d 687, 699 n.15 (7th Cir. 1987).

[33]U.S. v. Ferguson, 676 F.3d 260, 293–94 (2d Cir. 2011) ("testimony by Houldsworth and Napier about what others . . . *meant* by certain statements" was "based on the perceptions that they formed from those communications. . . ."); Lightfoot v. Union Carbide Corp., 110 F.3d 898, 911 (2d Cir. 1997) (the witness cited "objective facts" supporting the opinion that age discrimination was a factor which influenced the decision to terminate the plaintiff); U.S. v. Meling, 47 F.3d

1546, 1550–56 (9th Cir. 1995) (given a 911 operator's experience dealing with other callers, the operator was properly permitted to opine that during the defendant's call, the defendant feigned grief); Government of Virgin Islands v. Knight, 989 F.2d 619, 629–30 (3d Cir. 1993) (the trend favors the admissibility of lay opinions, especially when it is difficult for the witness to articulate all the underlying facts; the witness was properly allowed to opine that the discharge of the gun was an accident); U.S. v. Hoffner, 777 F.2d 1423, 1425 (10th Cir. 1985) ("[C]ourts have been liberal in admitting witnesses' testimony as to another's state of mind. . . ."); John Hancock Mut. Life Ins. Co. v. Dutton, 585 F.2d 1289, 1294 (5th Cir. 1978); U.S. v. McClintic, 570 F.2d 685 (8th Cir. 1978) (the third party was aware of a particular fact); U.S. v. Smith, 550 F.2d 277, 281 (5th Cir. 1977) (the third party "knew and understood" certain requirements). *Compare* U.S. v. Kaplan, 490 F.3d 110, 119 (2d Cir. 2007) (the lay witness had an inadequate basis for an opinion about the defendant's state of mind; the basis was a single conversation) *with* U.S. v. Tsekhanovich, 507 F.3d 127, 129–30 (2d Cir. 2007) (the witness had known the defendant for several years before the conversation in question).

[34]See cases cited at C.J.S., Evidence § 718.

[35]Fed. R. Evid. 701 & Unif. R. Evid. 701.

testimony about those matters.[36] Of course, as parts of the same legislative scheme, Rules 701 and 403 must be harmonized. Thus, even if an inference passes muster under Rule 701, Rule 403 permits exclusion of an inference that is prejudicial, confusing, misleading, or time-wasting.[37]

The preceding paragraphs discuss the various requirements for admitting an inference as proper lay opinion. However, a proffered lay opinion can not only be excluded due to failure to satisfy those requirements; the opinion could also be barred for the stated reason that the topic of the testimony necessitates expert testimony. Effective December 1, 2000, Federal Rule of Evidence 701 was amended to provide that an admissible lay opinion may "not [be] based on scientific, technical, or other specialized knowledge within the scope of Rule 702." As the accompanying Advisory Committee Note explains, there were two reasons for the amendment. One was "to eliminate the risk that the reliability requirements of Rule 702 will be evaded through the simple expedient of proffering an expert in lay witness clothing." The other reason was to prevent litigants from evading the mandatory prediscovery disclosure requirements for expert testimony, set out in Federal Rule of Civil Procedure 26 and Criminal Rule 16.

Of course, the difficulty in administering the 2000 amendment is drawing the line between lay and expert testimony. Since 2000, the courts have frequently been called on to draw that line when prosecutors have offered "lay" opinions by experienced police officers.[38] Testimony by physicians in civil cases can pose the

---

[36]Fed. R. Evid. 701 does not require by its terms the preliminary disclosure of details by the lay witness in the process of establishing personal knowledge. However, the witness's opinion may not be sufficiently shown to be rationally based upon actual perception or considered by the court as helpful absent a preliminary disclosure of details. Thus in certain situations, the concrete details will be required prior to the rendering of the opinion. *See* Randolph v. Collectramatic, Inc., 590 F.2d 844 (10th Cir. 1979). *See also* Weinstein and Berger, Evidence ¶ 701[02] at 701–30 (1988) ("[T]he authority given a judge . . . to require a witness to state the basis for his opinion is available to a federal judge pursuant to Rules 104(a), 611(a)(1) and 614(b). Obviously the judge, at times, may be unable to determine whether an opinion is based on the witness' perception or is helpful without ascertaining the observed data. In other cases, where the judge feels the expression of an opinion could be neither misleading nor prejudicial, the judge may leave it to the adverse party to develop the basis on cross-examination."). 4 Weinstein's Federal Evidence §§ 701.02 and 701.05 (rev. 2011) are generally to the same effect.

[37]U.S. v. Calhoun, 544 F.2d 291 (6th Cir. 1976) (citing Fed. R. Evid. 403, the court excludes a prosecution witness's opinion as prejudicial because witness could not be fully subject to related cross-examination). See § 185 infra.

[38]*E.g.*, U.S. v. Jones, 218 Fed. Appx. 916, 917–18 (11th Cir. 2007) (under Rule 701, a police officer could testify that the quantity of drugs in

same line-drawing problems.[39] The line is critical because in many cases, lay and expert witnesses can testify on the same topic.[40] The judge can draw the line by focusing on the fundamental question of why the opinion is being admitted: Is it being accepted because it is impractical to verbalize the primary data such as the witness's personal experience (the rationale for lay opinion) or because the witness has a technique or method for drawing a more reliable inference from the primary data (the rationale for expert opinion)?[41] The note accompanying the 2000 amendment suggests that the trial judge ought to follow that approach. The note states that the amendment is not intended to

---

the instant case indicated that it was intended for distribution); U.S. v. Maher, 454 F.3d 13, 23–24 (1st Cir. 2006) (under Rule 701, a police officer was permitted to testify that the post-it note found in the defendant's van was a list of customer orders for drugs and was a "[d]rug distributors' way of being organized"); People v. Lewis, 43 Cal. 4th 415, 75 Cal. Rptr. 3d 588, 181 P.3d 947, 1010 (2008) (the detective's testimony about the significance of the marks on a shotgun shell was admissible lay opinion; "His opinion was rationally based on his perception and helpful to an understanding of his testimony . . . and the subject of his opinion—the significance of marks on the shell primer—was not so far 'beyond the common experience' that expert testimony was required"); People v. Maglaya, 112 Cal. App. 4th 1604, 6 Cal. Rptr. 3d 155, 158–59 (3d Dist. 2003) (a police officer, testifying as a non-expert, could properly testify that there were similarities between the defendant's shoe prints and the shoe prints found at the crime scene).

[39]U.S. v. Howell, 472 Fed. Appx. 245 (4th Cir. 2012) (a nurse's testimony about a victim's injuries required specialized knowledge not possessed by laypersons); Brown v. Ryan's Family Steak House, Inc., 113 Fed. Appx. 512, 515–16 (4th Cir. 2004) (under Rule 701, the court permitted a physician to testify that his patient lacked the mental capacity to enter into a binding contract due to brain atrophy and subclavian steal syndrome).

[40]Imwinkelried, Expert Witnesses: Lay and Expert Opinion, Nat'l L.J., Dec. 15, 2008, at 13 (in some circumstances, like a psychiatrist a lay witness can opine whether someone was behaving in an insane manner; likewise, like questioned document examiner a lay witness is sometimes permitted to opine whether a certain person wrote a particular document).

[41]"In the case of lay opinion testimony, the rationale is that there is necessity to resort to opinionated testimony because it is literally or virtually impossible for the witness to verbalize the primary data." Imwinkelried, The Taxonomy of Testimony Post-*Kumho*: Refocusing on the Bottomlines of Reliability and Necessity, 30 Cumber. L. Rev. 185, 194 (2000). In contrast, in the case of expert opinion, the percipient witnesses "may be able to verbalize 'the rudimental facts in elaborate detail.'" However, they cannot draw a reliable inference from those facts:

Suppose, for example, that the witness is a forensic pathologist in a medical examiner's office. Initially, the pathologist describes the condition of the cadaver at the time it was delivered to the morgue. At the time of the delivery of the cadaver, a technician took a large number of photographs of the cadaver. The photographs depict a pink discoloration in the lower regions of the body. Between the photographs and the witness's description of the condition of the cadaver, the trier of fact has all the primary data known to the pathologist. Should that bar the introduction of the pathologist's opinion about the significance of the discolor-

affect the "prototypical example[s]" of proper lay opinions such as inferences on the topics of "the appearance of persons or things, identity, the manner of conduct, competency of a person, degree of light or darkness, sound, size, weight, distance, or an endless number of things that cannot be described factually in words apart from inferences"—all examples of either "collective fact" or "skilled lay observer" opinion. However, more specifically, the note expressly endorses the reasoning of a 1992 Tennessee decision, *State v. Brown*.[42] The *Brown* court explained the distinction between the two types of opinions by stating that lay opinion "results from a process of reasoning familiar in everyday life" while expert opinion "results from a process of reasoning which can be mastered only by specialists in the field." *Brown* ruled that although a layperson could testify that a substance appeared to be blood, only an expert could opine that bruising around the eyes was indicative of skull trauma. The issue is not what topic the witness's opinion relates to; rather, the question is how the witness reaches the opinion on that topic.[43] It remains to be seen

---

ation? No. Over objection, the trial judge would undoubtedly permit the pathologist to explain that the discoloration was evidence of postmortem lividity and to make a time-of-death (TOD) estimate based on the extent of the lividity. The witness can convey the primary data about the condition of the cadaver to the trier of fact, but the trier lacks the expertise to draw a reliable inference from the data.

Imwinkelried, 30 Cumber. L. Rev. at 195–96.

[42]State v. Brown, 836 S.W.2d 530, 549 (Tenn. 1992). *See also* Compania Administradora de Recuperacion de Activos Administradora de Fondos de Inversion Sociedad Anonima v. Titan Intern., Inc., 533 F.3d 555, 559 (7th Cir. 2008) ("specialized or scientific techniques or processes of reasoning that can be mastered only by specialists in the field").

[43]Imwinkelried, Expert Witness: Lay and Expert Witness, Nat'l L.J., Dec. 15, 2008, at 13 ("Consider opinions about a document's authorship. The essence of a layperson's reasoning to that opinion is a comparison between the document in question and the person's handwriting style, which the witness is familiar with. The [lay] witness asks: How similar is this document to that writing style? In contrast, the expert uses a very different reasoning process to come to a conclusion on that topic. The expert may have no prior familiarity at all with either the alleged author or his or her handwriting style. Instead, the expert compares the questioned document with other exemplars of the alleged author's handwriting style. The expert then addresses this question: Do all these documents share a large number of rare writing characteristics? Since there are no reliable data as to the population frequency of various writing characteristics, the expert is implicitly comparing the documents to all the other documents he or she has studied to decide how common or rare the shared characteristics are"; there is a similar difference between lay and expert opinions on the topic of a person's sanity; the lay witness is comparing "the person's conduct at a particular time and the person's normal behavioral pattern"; although a psychiatrist may opine on the identical subject, he or she "resorts to a quite different reasoning process to derive his or her opinion"; the expert will compare the person's case history to

whether the lower courts will find the guidance in the note to be adequate.[44]

## § 12  The relativity of the opinion rule: Opinions on the ultimate issue

### *Questions of Fact*

As the preceding section pointed out, the terms "fact" and "opinion" denote merely a difference of degree[1] of concreteness of description or a distinction in nearness or remoteness of inference. The opinion rule prefers the more specific description to the less concrete, and the direct form of statement to the inferential. But there is still another variable in the equation: The purpose of the testimony has an impact on the required degree of concreteness. In the outer circle of collateral fact near the limit of relevancy, the courts receive evidence with relative freedom; but as the testimony moves closer to the central issue, the courts are more insistent on details instead of inferences.[2]

---

recognized diagnostic criteria).

Another example is the value of property. To establish the value of his or her property, an owner may call a valuation expert. However, at common law and under the Federal Rules, the courts permit owners to express an opinion about the value of their property. T-Mobile Northeast LLC v. City Council of City of Newport News, Va., 674 F.3d 380, 389 (4th Cir. 2012), cert. denied, 133 S. Ct. 264, 184 L. Ed. 2d 45 (2012); Echo, Inc. v. Timberland Machines & Irr., Inc., 661 F.3d 959 (7th Cir. 2011) ("a business owner or officer is allowed to testify 'to the value or projected profits of [their own] business, without [being qualified] as an accountant, appraiser, or similar expert' "); James River Ins. Co. v. Rapid Funding, LLC, 658 F.3d 1207, 1215–16 n.1 (10th Cir. 2011) (real property); Adams v. U.S., 823 F. Supp. 2d 1074, 1085–86 (D. Idaho 2011) (farmland).

[44]*See* Poulin, Experience-Based Opinion Testimony: Strengthening the Lay Opinion Rule, 39 Pepp. L. Rev. 552, 555–56, 566, 568–170, 617–118 (2011–12) (there is some overlap between lay and expert opinion; however, in defining the border between lay and expert opinion, the critical question is

not simply whether the witness has "an usual experience base" but rather whether the witness is using "a reliable and specialized mode of analysis"; if so, the witness's testimony should have to pass muster as expert testimony; "Most experience-based opinion [should] be evaluated as lay opinion . . . ."; the judge should classify the witness's opinion as expert only if "the expert has employed [a] . . . methodology—something beyond everyday reasoning—to draw inferences from the information base"; "Too often, witnesses with unusual or rich experience bases are permitted to testify as experts despite employing no reliable methodology or analysis. Absent such methodology, witnesses offering experience-based testimony merely apply ordinary lay reasoning to their experience base. Witnesses who derive their opinions by applying everyday reasoning to their personal experiences should be treated as lay witnesses").

**[Section 12]**

[1]Beech Aircraft Corp. v. Rainey, 488 U.S. 153, 168, 109 S. Ct. 439, 102 L. Ed. 2d 445 (1988).

[2]King & Pillinger, Opinion Evidence in Illinois 10 (1942).

Trial judges tend to be more liberal in exercising discretion to admit opinions and inferences about collateral matters and less indulgent when testimony relates to more crucial matters. But is it advisable to go further and to tie the judge's hands by a categorical rule forbidding opinion evidence as to "ultimate" matters?

Some highly opinionated statements by the witness amount to nothing more than an expression of his general belief as to how the case should be decided or the amount of damages which would be just. All courts exclude such extreme, conclusory expressions.[3] There is no necessity for this kind of evidence; its receipt would suggest that the judge and jury may shift responsibility for the decision to the witnesses. In any event, the opinion is worthless to the trier of fact.

But until about a half century ago, a large number of courts went far beyond this common sense reluctance to listen to the witness's views as to how the judge and jury should perform their functions; these courts announced a general doctrine that witnesses may never give their opinions or conclusions on an ultimate fact in issue.[4] The stated justification was sometimes that such testimony "usurps the function"[5] or "invades the province"[6] of the jury. These expressions were not meant to be taken literally. Rather, they were intended to convey the fear that the jury might forego independent analysis of the facts and bow too readily to the opinion of an expert or other influential witness.

Although many states followed the rule prior to 1942,[7] a trend later emerged to abandon it.[8] In most state courts, an expert may now express his opinion on an ultimate fact, provided that all the

---

[3]*E.g.*, Warren Petroleum Co. v. Thomasson, 268 F.2d 5 (5th Cir. 1959) (error to admit highway patrolman's statement after collision that owner of one of vehicles "should assume liability"); Duncan v. Mack, 59 Ariz. 36, 122 P.2d 215 (1942) (whether public convenience would be served by transfer of license); Grismore v. Consolidated Products Co., 232 Iowa 328, 5 N.W.2d 646 (1942) (opinions as to guilt, negligence, testamentary capacity, reasonable cause—dictum); Fed. R. Evid. 701, Advisory Committee's Note.

[4]U.S. v. Spaulding, 293 U.S. 498, 506, 55 S. Ct. 273, 79 L. Ed. 617 (1935); State v. Carr, 196 N.C. 129, 144 S.E. 698 (1928) and earlier cases collected in West's Key Number Digest, Evidence ⬥472, 506; West's Key Number Digest, Criminal Law ⬥450.

[5]Chicago & A.R. Co. v. Springfield & N.W.R. Co., 67 Ill. 142, 1873 WL 8152 (1873).

[6]De Groot v. Winter, 261 Mich. 660, 247 N.W. 69, 71 (1933). Michigan no longer follows the rule. See note 9 infra, and Federal Rule 704, text at note 10 infra, which Michigan has adopted.

[7]*See* Chicago & A.R. Co. v. Springfield & N.W.R. Co., 67 Ill. 142, 1873 WL 8152 (1873).

[8]The trend appears to have begun with the leading case of Grismore v. Consolidated Products Co., 232 Iowa 328, 5 N.W.2d 646 (1942).

other requirements for admission of expert opinion are met.[9] The trend culminated in the adoption of Federal Rule of Evidence 704, now subdivision 704(a). As restyled, Rule 704(a) reads: "In General—Not Automatically Objectionable. An opinion is not objectionable just because it embraces an ultimate issue."[10]

On its face, Rule 704(a) is not limited to expert opinions and thus seemingly authorizes the receipt of lay opinions on ultimate questions. Some courts had already adopted the view that laypersons' opinions on ultimate facts are permissible.[11] However, such opinions may run afoul of other restrictions in particular instances, e.g., opinions as to how the case should be decided and what amount of money damages would be appropriate.[12] Even under the most liberal rules, those opinions are excludable under

---

However, some states still adhere to the traditional rule. For example, the rule still survives to a degree in Connecticut. Connecticut Code of Evidence 7-3(a) provides:

> Testimony in the form of an opinion is inadmissible if it embraces an ultimate issue to be decided by the trier of fact, except that, other than as provided in subsection (b), an expert witness may give an opinion that embraces an ultimate issue where the trier of fact needs expert assistance in deciding the issue.

*See* State v. Finan, 275 Conn. 60, 881 A.2d 187, 193 (2005).

[9] Cases include Com., Dept. of Highways v. Widner, 388 S.W.2d 583 (Ky. 1965); Dudek v. Popp, 373 Mich. 300, 129 N.W.2d 393 (1964); Southern Pac. Co. v. Watkins, 83 Nev. 471, 435 P.2d 498 (1967); McKay Mach. Co. v. Rodman, 11 Ohio St. 2d 77, 40 Ohio Op. 2d 87, 228 N.E.2d 304 (1967); Groce v. Fidelity General Ins. Co., 252 Or. 296, 448 P.2d 554 (1968); Redman v. Ford Motor Co., 253 S.C. 266, 170 S.E.2d 207 (1969) (stating that the matter is in the trial judge's discretion); Rabata v. Dohner, 45 Wis. 2d 111, 172 N.W.2d 409 (1969) (abandoning rule that expert opinions on ultimate facts must be based upon hypothetical questions); In re Baxter's Estate, 16 Utah 2d 284, 399 P.2d 442 (1965). See review of the cases in Stoebuck, Opinions on Ultimate Facts: Status, Trends, and a Note of Caution, 41 Denver L. C. J. 226 (1964).

[10] Unif. R. Evid. 704 is identical in substance.

[11] Weber v. Chicago, R.I. & P. Ry. Co., 175 Iowa 358, 151 N.W. 852, 859 (1915) (lay opinion testimony as to whether spikes holding rails had been pulled with a crowbar, admissible), cited and discussed in Grismore v. Consolidated Products Co., 232 Iowa 328, 5 N.W.2d 646, 662 (1942); Model Code of Evidence Rule 401, adopted as case law in Church v. West, 75 Wash. 2d 502, 452 P.2d 265 (1969). *See also* Cal. Evid. Code § 805 reading, "Testimony in the form of an opinion that is otherwise admissible is not objectionable because it embraces the ultimate issue to be decided by the trier of fact."

[12] The fact that an opinion or inference is unobjectionable merely because it embraces an ultimate issue does not mean, however, that all opinions embracing the ultimate issue are admissible. Both Fed. R. Evid. 701 and 702 embody the criterion of helpfulness for lay and expert witnesses. Thus, an opinion that plaintiff should win is rejected as unhelpful. The Advisory Committee's Note to Fed. R. Evid. 704(a) states, "The abolition of the ultimate issue rule does not lower the bars so as to admit all opinions. Under Rules 701 and 702, opinions must be helpful to the trier of fact, and Rule 403 provides for exclusion of evidence which wastes time. These provisions afford ample assurances against the admission of opinions which would

Rule 403 on the ground that their value is outweighed by "the danger of unfair prejudice, confusion of issues, or misleading the jury, or by considerations of undue delay, waste of time, or needless presentation of cumulative evidence."[13] However, there is no categorical ban on opinions, either lay or expert, addressing ultimate facts.

This change in viewpoint concerning "ultimate fact" opinion resulted from the realization that the rule excluding opinion on ultimate facts is unduly restrictive, and can pose many close questions of application. The rule can unfairly obstruct the presentation of a party's case.[14] In jurisdictions where the traditional prohibition survives,[15] there can be time-consuming, wasteful arguments over whether an opinion concerns an ultimate fact.[16]

---

merely tell the jury what result to reach, somewhat in the manner of the oath-helpers of an earlier day." *See also* U.S. v. Perkins, 470 F.3d 150, 158 (4th Cir. 2006) ("conclusory testimony that a company engaged in 'discrimination,' or that an investment house engaged in a 'fraudulent and manipulative scheme' involves the use of terms with considerable legal baggage"; such testimony "nearly always invades the province of the jury"; however, "the legal meaning of some terms is not so distinctive from the colloquial meaning . . . ."); Kostelecky v. NL Acme Tool/NL Industries, Inc., 837 F.2d 828, 830 (8th Cir. 1988) (testimony "that the accident was caused by 'the injured's own conduct' and that the accident could have been avoided" held improperly admitted; "they are nothing more than legal conclusions of a lay witness and could not have assisted the trier of fact . . ."); Mitroff v. Xomox Corp., 797 F.2d 271, 276 (6th Cir. 1986) ("Although testimony which embraces an ultimate issue is not objectionable (Fed. R. Evid. 704), seldom will be the case when a lay opinion on an ultimate issue will meet the test of being helpful to the trier of fact since the jury's opinion is as good as the witness' and the witness turns into little more than an 'oath helper.' "). Moreover, to an extent Rule 704 (b) resurrects the ultimate fact prohibition, and there is authority that 704(b) applies to lay witnesses as well as experts. U.S.

v. Morales, 108 F.3d 1031 (9th Cir. 1997).

[13]Fed. R. Evid. 403 & Unif. R. Evid. 403; see § 185 infra. U.S. v. Milton, 555 F.2d 1198, 1203 (5th Cir. 1977) ("To be sure, Rule 704 does not paint with a broad brush, and expert opinion evidence may still be excluded if its prejudicial impact substantially outweighs its probative value, if it wastes time, see Rule 403, Fed. R. Evid., or if the trial court determines that the expert's specialized knowledge will not assist the trier of fact to understand the evidence."). *See also* U.S. v. Gutierrez, 576 F.2d 269 (10th Cir. 1978) (caution should be watchword in receiving opinions on the ultimate issue in criminal cases).

Even where the ban on opinions on the ultimate issue has been abolished, it is generally considered improper for either a lay or expert witness to testify as to whether another witness is telling the truth. State v. Myers, 382 N.W.2d 91 (Iowa 1986) (listing cases); State v. Logue, 372 N.W.2d 151 (S.D. 1985).

[14]See the discussion in Grismore v. Consolidated Products Co., 232 Iowa 328, 5 N.W.2d 646 (1942); 7 Wigmore Evidence §§ 1920–21 (Chadbourn rev. 1978).

[15]*E.g.*, Hubbard v. Quality Oil Co. of Statesville, Inc., 268 N.C. 489, 151 S.E.2d 71 (1966); Redman v. Community Hotel Corp., 138 W. Va.

## Questions of Law

Regardless of the rule concerning opinions on ultimate facts, at common law courts do not allow opinion on a question of law,[17] unless the issue concerns foreign law.[18] Nor do the Federal Rules of Evidence permit opinions on law except questions of foreign law.[19] One federal court voiced the typical judicial attitude when it wrote that "in a trial there is only one legal expert—the judge."[20]

---

456, 76 S.E.2d 759 (1953).

[16]Usually the process of breaking down general opinions concerning ultimate fact into more specific opinions is required to avoid opinions on ultimate facts. See, for example, disagreement between court and counsel in Spiezio v. Commonwealth Edison Co., 91 Ill. App. 2d 392, 235 N.E.2d 323 (1st Dist. 1968). This process tends to result in inconsistent or unexplainable decisions. *See, e.g.*, discussion of earlier Ohio cases, Note, 20 U. Cin. L. Rev. 484 (1951). The prohibitive rule, involving the concept of invading the province of the jury, is easily confused with the notion that experts should not be heard on commonplace matters. See § 13 infra. Few decisions intimate that the form of the testimony can be significant, in that a direct statement of fact in issue may be inadmissible, while a mere statement that it is the witness's opinion that the fact is so or a statement in the subjunctive mood, would be allowable. Turnbow v. Hayes Freight Lines, Inc., 15 Ill. App. 2d 57, 145 N.E.2d 377 (4th Dist. 1957); Hubbard v. Quality Oil Co. of Statesville, Inc., 268 N.C. 489, 151 S.E.2d 71 (1966) (expert can testify what "would produce the result"). This has rightly been called a mere quibble. Comment Note.—Testimony of expert witness as to ultimate fact, 78 A.L.R. 755. The two forms are mere expressions of belief and should be treated alike.

[17]H.M. ex rel. B.M. v. Haddon Heights Bd. of Educ., 822 F. Supp. 2d 439, 448 (D.N.J. 2011) ("An expert witness is prohibited from rendering a legal opinion."). The general rule is illustrated by Hawkins v. Chandler, 88

Idaho 20, 396 P.2d 123 (1964) (testimony that the law did not require the use of flares, but error was held not prejudicial) and Briney v. Tri-State Mut. Grain Dealers Fire Ins. Co., 254 Iowa 673, 117 N.W.2d 889 (1962) (testimony concerning legal effect of relationship between independent adjusters and fire insurance companies who hired them).

[18]See § 335 infra. *See also* State v. Grimes, 235 N.J. Super. 75, 561 A.2d 647, 649 (App. Div. 1989) ("Expert opinion testimony is not admissible concerning the domestic law of the forum. . . . Questions of law existing in the trial judge's mind may, of course, be resolved after considering briefs and arguments of counsel. Foreign law, on the other hand, is a proper subject for expert testimony.").

[19]Marx & Co., Inc. v. Diners' Club Inc., 550 F.2d 505 (2d Cir. 1977). For a discussion of the procedures for determining foreign law, see Fed. R. Civ. P. 44.1 and Fed. R. Crim. P. 26.1.

Some commentators have questioned whether the courts should continue to enforce a rigid ban on expert legal testimony. Baker, The Impropriety of Expert Witness Testimony on the Law, 40 U. Kan. L. Rev. 325 (1992); Ehrhardt, The Conflict Concerning Expert Witnesses and Legal Conclusions, 92 W. Va. L. Rev. 645 (1990); Friedland, Expert Testimony on the Law: Excludable or Justifiable?, 37 U. Miami L. Rev. 451 (1983). There is a plausible case for admitting such testimony when it is to be submitted to the judge. It can be argued that "with the increasing expansion and complexity of the law, it is no longer realistic to suppose that

Even a court which does not automatically ban opinion on the ultimate issue may condemn a question phrased in terms of a legal criterion that is not adequately defined by the questioner. Absent an adequate definition, the lay jurors may misunderstand the witness's answer.[21] Some jurisdictions still adhere to a general rule that a witness may never opine on a question of law or a mixed question of law and fact.[22] But it is often convenient or desirable to use questions partially phrased in terms of some legal standard familiar to lawyers. The problem is the jurors' in-

---

the trial court, left to its own devices," can easily determine the state of the law. Strong, Language and Logic in Expert Testimony: Limiting Expert Testimony by Restrictions of Function, Reliability, and Form, 71 Or. L. Rev. 349, 374 (1992). Moreover, expert legal testimony is routinely presented to juries in legal malpractice actions. However, outside that setting, as a matter of course courts generally adhere to the prohibition of submitting expert legal testimony to a jury. Specht v. Jensen, 853 F.2d 805, 810 (10th Cir. 1988) ("In no instance can a witness be permitted to define the law of the case"); Note: Expert Legal Testimony, 97 Harv. L. Rev. 797 ("it remains black-letter law that expert legal testimony is not permissible").

[20]Pivot Point Intern., Inc. v. Charlene Products, Inc., 932 F. Supp. 220, 225 (N.D. Ill. 1996).

[21]Andrews v. Metro North Commuter R. Co., 882 F.2d 705, 709 (2d Cir. 1989) ("Although testimony that embraces an ultimate issue to be decided by the jury is not inadmissible per se, Fed. R. Evid. 704, it should not be received if it is based on 'inadequately explored legal criteria.' "); U.S. v. Scop, 846 F.2d 135, 140 (2d Cir. 1988) (" 'The problem with testimony containing a legal conclusion is in conveying the witness' unexpressed, and perhaps erroneous, legal standards to the jury.' Torres v. County of Oakland, 758 F.2d 147, 150 (6th Cir. 1985)."); S.E.C. v. Badian, 822 F. Supp. 2d 352, 357 (S.D. N.Y. 2011); Rosen v. Protective Life Ins. Co., 817 F. Supp. 2d 1357, 1385–86 (N.D. Ga. 2011), aff'd, 2013 WL 104233 (11th Cir. 2013).

[22]Okland Oil Co. v. Conoco Inc., 144 F.3d 1308, 1328 (10th Cir. 1998); U.S. v. Espino, 32 F.3d 253, 257–58 (7th Cir. 1994) ("conspiracy" is a "legal conclusion"); Cryovac Inc. v. Pechiney Plastic Packaging, Inc., 430 F. Supp. 2d 346, 364 (D. Del. 2006) (an expert may not testify about patent and contract law); Casper v. SMG, 389 F. Supp. 2d 618, 621 (D.N.J. 2005) ("The district court must limit expert testimony so as not to allow experts to opine on 'what the law required' or to 'testify as to the governing law.' 'The rule prohibiting experts from providing their legal opinions or conclusions is so well established that it is often deemed a basic premise or assumption of evidence law—a kind of axiomatic principle.' In fact, every circuit has explicitly held that experts may not invade the court's province by testifying on issues of law"); Pinal Creek Group v. Newmont Mining Corp., 352 F. Supp. 2d 1037, 1044 (D. Ariz. 2005) (excluding a law professor's expert testimony about Maine law on "piercing the corporate veil"); Terrell v. Reinecker, 482 N.W.2d 428, 430 (Iowa 1992) (it was improper for an expert to testify that the plaintiff had "failed to yield the right-of-way;" the opinion "extend[ed] too far into the realm of legal conclusion"); Behlke v. Conwed Corp., 474 N.W.2d 351, 359 (Minn. Ct. App. 1991) ("legal analysis by an expert is 'ordinarily inadmissible' "); Davidson v. Prince, 813 P.2d 1225, 1231 (Utah Ct. App. 1991) ("an expert generally cannot give an opinion as to whether an individual was 'negligent' because such an opinion would require a legal conclusion"); Armstrong v. State, 826 P.2d 1106, 1111 (Wyo. 1992)

terpretation of the question.[23] How do we ensure that the jury properly interprets the part of the question alluding to the legal standard?

The problem frequently arises in relation to testimony on the issue of capacity to make a will. Thus, a court allowing opinions on an ultimate issue would approve a question, "Did X have mental capacity sufficient to understand the nature and effect of his will?"[24] That phrasing incorporates the substantive legal standard for testamentary capacity. However, even such a court would disapprove of the conclusory wording, "Did X have sufficient mental capacity to make a will?"[25] That question can easily be misunderstood by the witness and the jury if they do not know the law's definition of "capacity to make a will." But a court completely prohibiting opinions on the ultimate issue might condemn both forms of questions[26]—and perhaps even one where the questioner breaks down "testamentary capacity" into its legally defined elements.[27] This issue is by no means confined to estate litigation; similar problems might arise in respect to such

---

("The question that elicits the opinion testimony must be phrased to ask for a factual rather than a legal opinion"). The 1977 Committee Comment to Minnesota Rule 703 states: "[A] distinction should be made between opinions as to factual matters, and opinions involving a legal analysis or mixed questions of law and fact. Opinions of the latter nature are not deemed to be of any use to the trier of fact."

[23]Determining whether an opinion on the ultimate issue involves a pure question of law or unexplored legal criteria with respect to a mixed fact and law question (and is therefore inadmissible) is sometimes extremely difficult. *See, e.g.*, U.S. v. Unruh, 855 F.2d 1363 (9th Cir. 1987); U.S. v. Scop, 846 F.2d 135 (2d Cir. 1988). *See also* Comment, The Admissibility of Expert Witness Testimony: Time to Take the Final Leap?, 42 U. Miami L. Rev. 831, 872–74 (1988).

[24]*See* McDaniel v. Willis, 157 S.W.2d 672 (Tex. Civ. App. San Antonio 1941) (opinion that testator mentally incapable of transacting business); Scalf v. Collin County, 80 Tex. 514, 16 S.W. 314 (1891) (capacity to understand nature and effect of deed). *See*

*also* Slough, Testamentary Capacity: Evidentiary Aspects, 36 Texas L. Rev. 1, 5–16 (1957).

[25]Carr v. Radkey, 393 S.W.2d 806 (Tex. 1965); Brown v. Mitchell, 88 Tex. 350, 31 S.W. 621 (1895). Speaking of Fed. R. Evid. 701 and 702, the Advisory Committee's Note states:

They also stand ready to exclude opinions phrased in terms of inadequately explored legal criteria. Thus the question, "Did T have capacity to make a will?" would be excluded, while the question, "Did T have sufficient mental capacity to know the nature and extent of his property and the natural objects of his bounty and to formulate a rational scheme of distribution?" would be allowed. McCormick § 12.

[26]*See* Baker v. Baker, 202 Ill. 595, 67 N.E. 410 (1903) ("whether he was able understandingly to execute a will"); Schneider v. Manning, 121 Ill. 376, 12 N.E. 267 (1887) ("Had he mental capacity to dispose of his property by will or deed?"); King & Pillinger, Opinion Evidence in Illinois 225–28 (1942).

[27]Baddeley v. Watkins, 293 Ill. 394, 127 N.E. 725 (1920). *But see* Powell v. Weld, 410 Ill. 198, 101 N.E.2d 581 (1951).

issues as undue influence, total and permanent disability, and negligence.[28]

On the whole, the danger posed by these questions is slight, since attorneys seldom ask such questions except when the popular meaning is roughly the same as the legal meaning. In a jurisdiction where there is no general rule against opinions on the ultimate issue, a request by the adversary that the questioner define her terms should be the only recourse.[29] If the questioner makes the definition clear to the jury,[30] many jurisdictions accept opinions couched as conclusions on mixed questions of law and fact.[31]

Although the statutory provision which is now Rule 704(a) ap-

---

[28]*E.g.*, Shahid v. City of Detroit, 889 F.2d 1543 (6th Cir. 1989) (trial court properly excluded expert opinion that certain behavior by defendant officers amounts to negligence under law); U.S. v. McCauley, 601 F.2d 336 (8th Cir. 1979) (expert permitted to testify weapon was a machine gun required to be registered); U.S. v. Miller, 600 F.2d 498 (5th Cir. 1979) (in action for transporting securities knowing them to be taken by fraud, expert permitted to express opinion that securities were obtained by fraud); U.S. v. Davis, 564 F.2d 840 (9th Cir. 1977) (expert witness permitted to testify that the defendant doctor in prescribing drugs did not follow the usual course of professional procedure and that the prescriptions were not for a legitimate medical purpose); Alabama Power Co. v. Cantrell, 507 So. 2d 1295 (Ala. 1986) (the trial judge properly allowed the expert to state his opinion as to the proper maintenance and operation of an electrical system); McClellan v. French, 246 Ark. 728, 439 S.W.2d 813 (1969) (witness, in testifying a doctor was not guilty of malpractice, used the term in its connotation of "standard medical procedure in the community"); Sliman v. Aluminum Co. of America, 112 Idaho 277, 731 P.2d 1267 (1986) (testimony about extreme deviation from customary industry practices was properly introduced on the issue of punitive damages); Groce v. Fidelity General Ins. Co., 252 Or. 296, 448 P.2d 554 (1968) (no error in permitting witness

to testify to "good faith" of insurer-possibly dictum); Lindley v. Lindley, 384 S.W.2d 676 (Tex. 1964) (doctor not permitted to testify that a person's belief was an "insane delusion" because his medical concept might differ from the legal concept).

[29]This suggestion is cited in Groce v. Fidelity General Ins. Co., 252 Or. 296, 448 P.2d 554 (1968). It is in effect rejected in Carr v. Radkey, 393 S.W.2d 806 (Tex. 1965). The suggestion could be followed under Fed. R. Evid. and Rev. Unif. R. Evid. (1974) 701, 702, and 403, so long as the requirements of these rules are met.

[30]In some jurisdictions such as Texas, it is becoming customary to read the pertinent jury instruction aloud to the expert before eliciting the expert's opinion applying the legal standard set out in the instruction. Metot v. Danielson, 780 S.W.2d 283, 288 (Tex. App. Tyler 1989).

[31]Hines v. Denver and Rio Grande Western R. Co., 829 P.2d 419, 420 (Colo. App. 1991) (the expert could "express an opinion that [defendants'] conduct in the operation of the train constituted negligence."); Puente v. A.S.I. Signs, 821 S.W.2d 400, 402 (Tex. App. Corpus Christi 1991) ("This rule permits an expert to testify to ultimate issues which are mixed questions of law and fact, such as whether particular conduct constitutes negligence"); Harvey v. Culpepper, 801 S.W.2d 596, 601 (Tex. App. Corpus Christi 1990); Metot v. Danielson, 780 S.W.2d 283,

pears to abolish any ultimate fact prohibition, to a degree subdivision 704(b) resurrects the prohibition. 704(b) was enacted in part as a backlash against the acquittal of John Hinckley on insanity grounds after his attempted assassination of President Reagan. Federal Rule of Evidence 704(b)[32] provides that when an accused's mental state or condition is in issue (such as premeditation in homicide, lack of predisposition in entrapment, or the true affirmative defense of insanity),[33] an expert witness may not testify that the defendant did or did not have the mental state or condition constituting an element of the crime charged or of the defense.

Rule 704(b) seeks to eliminate the confusing spectacle of competing psychiatric and psychological experts testifying directly to contradictory conclusions on the ultimate legal issue to be resolved by the trier of fact. Even under Rule 704(b), presumably a mental health expert may answer the questions: "Was the accused suffering from a mental disease or defect?"; "Explain the characteristics of the mental disease and defect."; and "Was

---

288 (Tex. App. Tyler 1989) (in a medical malpractice action, a physician may be asked to assume the legal definitions of negligence and proximate cause and then opine as to whether the defendant physician's conduct "was negligent and a proximate case of" the plaintiff's injuries); Birchfield v. Texarkana Memorial Hosp., 747 S.W.2d 361, 365 (Tex. 1987) ("an expert may state an opinion on a mixed question of law and fact as long as the opinion . . . is based on proper legal concepts"); State v. Larsen, 828 P.2d 487 (Utah Ct. App. 1992) (in a securities fraud prosecution, the expert's testimony that a false statement was "material" may "be admitted as permissible fact-oriented testimony"); Jones v. Garnes, 183 W. Va. 304, 395 S.E.2d 548, 549–50 (1990) (a deputy may testify as to which party to an automobile accident failed to yield right-of-way).

[32]Former Fed. R. Evid. 704(b) provided:

(b) No expert witness testifying with respect to the mental state or condition may state an opinion or inference as to whether the defendant did or did not have the mental state or condition constituting an element of the crime

charged or of a defense. Such ultimate issues are matters for the trier of fact alone.

Effective December 1, 2011, restyled Fed. R. Evid. 704(b) reads:

In a criminal case, an expert witness may not state an opinion about whether the defendant did or did not have a mental state or condition that constitutes an element of the crime charged or of a defense. Those matters are for the trier of fact alone.

The courts have upheld the constitutionality of Rule 704(b). *E.g.*, U.S. v. Austin, 981 F.2d 1163 (10th Cir. 1992) (rejecting due process and equal protection challenges).

[33]18 U.S.C.A. § 17:

(a) Affirmative defense. It is an affirmative defense to a prosecution under any Federal statute that, at the time of the commission of the acts constituting the offense, the defendant, as a result of a severe mental disease or defect, was unable to appreciate the nature and quality or the wrongfulness of his acts. Mental disease or defect does not otherwise constitute a defense.

(b) Burden of proof. The defendant has the burden of proving the defense of insanity by clear and convincing evidence.

his act the product of that disease or defect?"[34] Those conclusions fall squarely within the domain of the witness's expertise. However, if Rule 704(b) is to have any teeth, it seems equally clear the expert may not directly answer the question: "Was the accused able to appreciate the nature and quality of his acts"; or "Did the accused appreciate the wrongfulness of his acts?"[35] To some extent, Rule 704(b) has had the intended effect of moderat-

---

[34]U.S. v. Brawner, 471 F.2d 969, 1011 (D.C. Cir. 1972) (en banc) (Bazelon, J., concurring and dissenting). *See also* U.S. v. Thigpen, 4 F.3d 1573 (11th Cir. 1993) (on direct examination, defense psychiatric experts opined that the defendant suffered from schizophrenia; on cross-examination, it was proper for the prosecutor to inquire whether schizophrenia necessarily implied that a person cannot appreciate the nature of his acts); U.S. v. Prickett, 604 F. Supp. 407, 409 (S.D. Ohio 1985) ("The legislative history of Rule 704 as amended explains the relationship of the new Rule 704(b) to the codification of the insanity defense in 18 U.S.C.A. § 20 as follows: The purpose of this amendment is to eliminate the confusing spectacle of competing expert witnesses testifying to directly contradictory conclusions as to the ultimate legal issue to be found by the trier of fact. Under this proposal, expert psychiatric testimony would be limited to presenting and explaining their diagnoses, such as whether the defendant has a severe mental disease or defect and what the characteristics of such a disease or defect, if any, may have been. H. Rep. No. 98-1030, 98th Cong., 2d Sess. 224, 232 U.S. Code Cong. & Admin. News 1984, p. 1. This and other relevant portions of the legislative history make it clear that while under Rule 704(b) an expert may testify as to the defendant's severe mental disease or defect and the characteristics of such a condition, he or she is not to offer the jury a conclusion as to whether said condition rendered the defendant 'unable to appreciate the nature and quality or the wrongful-

ness of his acts.' 18 U.S.C.A. § 20 (1984). Rather, under Rule 704(b), the latter is an 'ultimate issue' to be determined solely by the jury on the basis of the evidence presented. See, H.Rep. No. 98-1030, 98th Cong., 2d Sess. at 224 to 225, 227, and 233.").

[35]U.S. v. Frisbee, 623 F. Supp. 1217, 1223–24 (N.D. Cal. 1985) ("Pursuant to rule 704(b) of the Federal Rules of Evidence, the defendant's experts will not be allowed to state an opinion or inference as to whether the defendant did or did not form a specific intent to kill at the time the murder allegedly occurred. The legislative history of rule 704(b) states that the rule is intended to limit experts to 'presenting and explaining their diagnoses, such as whether the defendant had a severe mental disease or defect and what the characteristics of such a disease or defect, if any, may have been.' S. Rep. No. 225, 98th Cong., 2nd Sess. 230, reprinted in 1984 U.S. Code Cong. & Ad. News 3182, 3412. Thus, the Court will only allow the experts to testify concerning their diagnoses, the facts upon which those diagnoses are based, and the characteristics of any mental diseases or defects the experts believe the defendant possessed during the relevant time period. No testimony directly or indirectly opining on the issue of specific intent will be allowed."). The proponent may not escape from Rule 704(b) by the simple expedient of posing to the expert a hypothetical which "mirrors" the facts of the pending case. U.S. v. Smart, 98 F.3d 1379 (D.C. Cir. 1996); Saltzburg, Opinions on Intent: Mirroring Facts of the Case, 13 Crim. Just. 21 (Fall 1998).

ing courtroom battles of mental health experts,[36] but it has not made a dramatic difference. Rule 704(b) forbids dueling experts from expressing conflicting opinions on the ultimate topics, but many[37] courts still permit them to express diametrically opposed opinions on penultimate questions before the jury. Thus, most trial judges would allow the expert to testify about the defendant's mental illness, the classic symptoms of the illness, and the likely

---

[36]An expert is testifying with respect to an accused's mental state or condition constituting an element of the crime when that is the inference directly drawn from the expert's testimony. However if the expert leaves the inference to be drawn by the trier of fact, the testimony is not prohibited by Fed. R. Evid. 704(b). *See* U.S. v. Masat, 896 F.2d 88, 93 (5th Cir. 1990) (Rule 704(b) applies to "only a direct statement on the issue of intent"); U.S. v. Alvarez, 837 F.2d 1024 (11th Cir. 1988), U.S. v. Davis, 835 F.2d 274 (11th Cir. 1988); Note, Resurrection of the Ultimate Issue Rule: Federal Rule of Evidence 704(b) and the Insanity Defense, 72 Corn. L. Rev. 620, 639 (1987).

Query: Will a minor variation in breadth of admissible opinion significantly ameliorate problems arising when diametrically opposed expert witness opinions are rendered at trial? California Penal Code §§ 25(a), 28 and 29 are to the same effect as Rule 704(b). *But see* People v. McCowan, 161 Cal. App. 3d 822, 208 Cal. Rptr. 285, 291 (3d Dist. 1984) ("Examination of the record discloses defendant was permitted to present evidence suggesting that his mental condition prevented him from forming the required mental state at the time he committed the offenses. Dr. Galioni testified that his mental disorder, a 'major depressive episode,' had a significant impact on his mental process the night of the shootings. According to Galioni, defendant essentially was out of control, unable to think clearly or make judgments without great difficulty. The cause of his condition was the existence of numerous, intense pressures and stresses.").

While Rule 704(b) applies on its face solely to the criminal defendant, "the rationale of the amendment is equally applicable to one who is a 'witness.'" U.S. v. Cecil, 836 F.2d 1431, 1442 n.5 (4th Cir. 1988).

[37]While some courts find a violation of Rule 704(b) only when the witness attempts to opine directly whether the defendant did or did not have the required *mens rea*, other courts have gone farther. These courts use a "functional equivalence" test and apply Rule 704(b)'s prohibition to opinions such as the testimony that drivers of vehicles containing illegal drugs "usually" know of the drugs' presence. U.S. v. Gutierrez-Farias, 294 F.3d 657, 662–63 (5th Cir. 2002). *See also* U.S. v. Mendoza-Medina, 346 F.3d 121, 128–29 (5th Cir. 2003). Arguably, the best approach is the "probes the mind" standard developed by the Seventh Circuit:

> The third construction of Rule 704(b)'s scope begins from the premise that the provision is in response to confusing expert testimony from the behavioral sciences about states of mind. Seeking to limit the exclusionary rule to this legislative concern, the probes-the-mind test asks whether the inference or opinion flows from expertise in the psychological sciences. If the expert makes clear that any opinions or inferences—whether explicit or implicit, necessary or otherwise—result from expertise about matters that have nothing to do with human psychology or mental functioning, then the testimony lies outside the ban of Rule 704(b).

Kaye, Bernstein & Mnookin, The New Wigmore: Expert Evidence § 2.2.3, at 54 (2d ed. 2010).

impact of those symptoms on the defendant's cognitive and volitional capabilities.

## § 13   Expert witnesses:[1] Subjects of expert testimony, qualifications,[2] and cross-examination

In the past three decades, the use of expert witnesses has skyrocketed. In a Rand study of California Superior Court trials, experts appeared in 86% of the trials; and on average, there were 3.3 experts per trial.[3] Some commentators claim that the American judicial hearing is becoming trial by expert.[4] A lay observer is qualified to testify because he has firsthand knowledge of the situation or transaction at issue. The expert has something different to contribute. That something is the ability—the knowledge or skill—to draw inferences from the facts which a jury could not draw at all or as reliably.[5]

### Proper Subject for Expert Inference

Traditionally, to justify the admission of expert testimony, the proponent must first establish at least two general elements.[6] The threshold question relates to the subject matter of the expert's inference. In the past, it was sometimes asserted that the subject of the inference must be so distinctively related to a science, profession, business, or occupation as to be beyond the ken of lay persons.[7] Even at that time some cases held that the

---

**[Section 13]**

[1]*See* Kaye, Bernstein & Mnookin, The New Wigmore: A Treatise on Evidence: Expert Evidence (2d ed. 2010); Ladd, Expert Testimony, 5 Vand. L. Rev. 414 (1952); Voorhis, Expert Opinion Evidence, 13 N.Y.L.F. 651, 657 (1967); Smith v. Hobart Mfg. Co., 185 F. Supp. 751 (E.D. Pa. 1960), for possibilities of abuse in using witnesses supposedly learned in one subject.

[2]West's Key Number Digest, Criminal Law ☞477 to 481; West's Key Number Digest, Evidence ☞535 to 546; 7 Wigmore, Evidence §§ 1923, 1925 (Chadbourn rev. 1978); 4 Weinstein's Federal Evidence Ch. 702 (rev. 2011).

[3]Gross, Expert Evidence, 1991 Wis. L. Rev. 1113, 1118–19.

[4]Pizzi, Expert Testimony in the US, 145 New L.J. 82 (Jan. 27, 1995).

[5]However, as the Advisory Committee's Note for Fed. R. Evid. 702 states in part:

> Most of the literature assumes that experts testify only in the form of opinions. The assumption is logically unfounded. The rule [Rule 702] accordingly recognizes that an expert on the stand may give a dissertation or exposition of scientific or other principles relevant to the case, leaving the trier of fact to apply them to the facts.

[6]Coleman v. Parkline Corp., 844 F.2d 863, 865 (D.C. Cir. 1988) ("This court has recognized that Rule 702 prescribes a two part test. First, the witness must be qualified; i.e., he must have 'knowledge, skill, experience, training, or education' in the field. Second, the witness's testimony must be able to assist the trier of fact.").

[7]*Admissible:* Hagler v. Gilliland, 292 Ala. 262, 292 So. 2d 647 (1974) (manager of state employment service

judge has discretion in administering this rule.[8] In the middle of the 20th century, though, other cases began moving toward a more liberal standard, admitting expert opinion concerning matters about which the jurors may have general knowledge if the expert opinion would refine their understanding of the issue.[9] The latter standard is codified in Federal Rule of Evidence and Revised Uniform Rule of Evidence 702.[10] Rule 702 seems to permit expert opinion even when the matter is barely within the

---

testifying concerning plaintiff's employability); Harp v. Illinois Cent. R. Co., 370 S.W.2d 387 (Mo. 1963) (opinion on causation seems clearly admissible). *Inadmissible:* Wal-Mart Stores, Inc. v. White, 476 So. 2d 614 (Ala. 1985) (effect of rainwater on a store's floor); Housman v. Fiddyment, 421 S.W.2d 284 (Mo. 1967); Collins v. Zediker, 421 Pa. 52, 218 A.2d 776 (1966) (how fast does a person walk?); Hill v. Lee, 209 Va. 569, 166 S.E.2d 274 (1969) (whether automobile would make tracks in soil); West's Key Number Digest, Evidence ⊕508.

[8]Housman v. Fiddyment, 421 S.W.2d 284 (Mo. 1967); McCoid, Opinion Evidence and Expert Witnesses, 2 UCLA L. Rev. 356, 362–63 (1955).

[9]Har-Pen Truck Lines, Inc. v. Mills, 378 F.2d 705 (5th Cir. 1967) (economics professor's testimony as to value of housewife's life); Miller v. Pillsbury Co., 33 Ill. 2d 514, 211 N.E.2d 733 (1965) ("the trend is to permit expert testimony in matters which are complicated and outside the knowledge of the average person, and even as to matters of common knowledge and understanding where difficult of comprehension and explanation"); Currier v. Grossman's of N. H., Inc., 107 N.H. 159, 219 A.2d 273 (1966) (opinion of cause of accident admissible when it "might aid the jury"); Kaye, Bernstein & Mnookin, The New Wigmore: Expert Evidence § 2.1.2 (2d ed. 2010).

[10]Former Fed. R. Evid. 702 provided:

If scientific, technical, or other specialized knowledge will assist the trier of fact to understand the evidence or to determine a fact in issue, a witness qualified as an expert by knowledge, skill, experience, training, or education, may testify thereto in the form of an opinion or otherwise."

Effective December 1, 2011, restyled Fed. R. Evid. 702 reads:

A witness who is qualified as an expert by knowledge, skill, experience, training, or education may testify in the form of an opinion or otherwise if:

(a) the expert's scientific, technical, or other specialized knowledge will help the trier of fact to understand the evidence or to determine a fact in issue;

(b) the testimony is based on sufficient facts or data;

(c) the testimony is the product of reliable principles and methods; and

(d) the expert has reliably applied the principles and methods to the facts of the case.

As amended in 1999, Unif. R. Evid. 702 reads:

(a) General rule. If a witness's testimony is based on scientific, technical, or other specialized knowledge, the witness may testify in the form of opinion or otherwise if the court determines the following are satisfied:

(1) the testimony will assist the trier of fact to understand evidence or determine a fact in issue;

(2) the witness is qualified by knowledge, skill, experience, training, or education as an expert in the scientific, technical, or other specialized field;

(3) the testimony is based upon principles or methods that are reasonably reliable, as established under subdivision (b), (c), (d), or (e);

(4) the testimony is based upon sufficient and reliable facts or data; and

(5) the witness has applied the

jurors' competence if specialized knowledge will be "help[ful]."[11] Under this liberal reading of Rule 702, a psychologist may testify about the supposed unreliability of eyewitness testimony;[12] and human factors engineers may opine about the behavior of an average person in some settings.[13]

---

principles or methods reliably to the facts of the case.

(b) Reliability deemed to exist. A principle or method is reasonably reliable if its reliability has been established by controlling legislation or judicial decision.

(c) Presumption of reliability. A principle or method is presumed to be reasonably reliable if it has substantial acceptance within the relevant scientific, technical, or specialized community. A party may rebut the presumption by proving that it is more probable than not that the principle or method is not reasonably reliable.

(d) Presumption of unreliability. A principle or method is presumed not to be reasonably reliable if it does not have substantial acceptance within the relevant scientific, technical, or specialized community. A party may rebut the presumption by proving that it is more probable than not that the principle or method is reasonably reliable.

(e) Other reliability factors. In determining the reliability of a principle or method, the court shall consider all relevant additional factors, which may include:

(1) the extent to which the principle or method has been tested;

(2) the adequacy of research methods employed in testing the principle or method;

(3) the extent to which the principle or method has been published and subjected to peer review;

(4) the rate of error in the application of the principle or method;

(5) the experience of the witness in the application of the principle or method;

(6) the extent to which the principle or method has gained acceptance within the relevant scientific, technical, or specialized community; and

(7) the extent to which the witness's specialized field of knowl-

edge has gained acceptance within the general scientific, technical, or specialized community.

*But see* U.S. v. Amaral, 488 F.2d 1148 (9th Cir. 1973) (expert psychological testimony about the supposed unreliability of eyewitness identification would not be of "appreciable help" to the jury); U.S. v. Christophe, 833 F.2d 1296 (9th Cir. 1987) (although *Amaral* antedates the enactment of the Federal Rules of Evidence, *Amaral* is still good law); Johnson v. State, 236 Ga. App. 252, 511 S.E.2d 603 (1999), judgment aff'd, 272 Ga. 254, 526 S.E.2d 549 (2000) (excluding expert testimony about the supposed unreliability of eyewitness identification).

[11]4 Weinstein's Federal Evidence § 702.03[2] (rev. 2011); McCord, Syndromes, Profiles, and Other Mental Exotica: A New Approach to the Admissibility of Nontraditional Evidence in Criminal Cases, 66 Or. L. Rev. 19, 95 (1986) (testimony about expert testimony is admissible both when the expert can draw an inference completely beyond a layperson's capability—strict necessity—and when the expert can significantly augment an inference barely within a layperson's grasp—relative necessity).

[12]U.S. v. Downing, 753 F.2d 1224 (3d Cir. 1985). *See also* State v. Chapple, 135 Ariz. 281, 660 P.2d 1208, 1217–24 (1983); People v. McDonald, 37 Cal. 3d 351, 208 Cal. Rptr. 236, 690 P.2d 709 (1984); Gross, The Unfortunate Faith: A Solution to the Unwarranted Reliance Upon Eyewitness Testimony, 5 Tex. Wesleyan L. Rev. 307 (1999). See § 206 infra.

[13]Scott v. Sears, Roebuck & Co., 789 F.2d 1052, 1054–56 (4th Cir. 1986).

*The Witness's Qualification as an Expert*

Even if the inference relates to a proper subject, the witness must be competent to draw the inference. Hence, the second traditional requirement is that on objection[14] the witness's proponent show that the witness has sufficient skill or knowledge related to the pertinent field or calling that his inference will probably aid the trier in the search for truth.[15] The knowledge

---

[14]Some experienced litigators recommend that after listing the witness's qualifications, the proponent formally move that the judge accept the witness as an expert in a particular field. These attorneys believe that the judge's ruling increases the witness's credibility in the jurors' eyes. Precisely for that reason, though, some courts hold that it is improper for the judge to make a ruling absent an objection. *Compare* U.S. v. Bartley, 855 F.2d 547, 552 (8th Cir. 1988) ("Although it is for the court to determine whether a witness is qualified to testify as an expert, there is no requirement that the court specifically make that finding in open court upon proffer of the offering party. Such an offer and finding by the court might influence the jury in its evaluation of the expert and the better procedure is to avoid an acknowledgment of the witness's expertise by the court"), Standard 17, Sec. Litig., A.B.A., Civil Trial Practice Standards 46 (1998) ("Except in ruling on an objection, the court should not, in the presence of the jury, declare that a witness is qualified as an expert or to render an expert opinion, and counsel should not ask the court to do so"), and Commentary, Ky. R. Evid. 702 ("the official commentary states that "the practice of tendering a witness [as an expert] should be discontinued"; the commentary asserts that the judge's "anointing" or "approbation of the witness's expertise improperly conveys the impression 'that the witness's testimony is especially believable' "), *with* U.S. v. Vastola, 899 F.2d 211, 234 (3d Cir. 1990) ("the usual trial practice of moving for the admission of expert testimony"), vacated on other grounds, 497 U.S. 1001 (1990), and Ingram v.

State, 178 Ga. App. 292, 342 S.E.2d 765 (1986) (the preferred practice is to tender).

[15]Farner v. Paccar, Inc., 562 F.2d 518 (8th Cir. 1977) (person in trucking business for thirty years may testify on proper design of suspension system for trucks); U.S. v. Bermudez, 526 F.2d 89 (2d Cir. 1975) (special agent with four years' experience was permitted on basis of visual inspection to testify that substance contained "ricks," i.e., small lumps of compressed cocaine); Cunningham v. Gans, 507 F.2d 496 (2d Cir. 1974) (pipefitter with 33 years' experience was qualified to testify as expert on pipe hanger construction even though he was not a metallurgist); Panger v. Duluth, W. & P. Ry. Co., 490 F.2d 1112 (8th Cir. 1974) (employee injured in industrial accident may testify based upon his experience in the industry as to how accident could have been avoided); U.S. v. Atkins, 473 F.2d 308 (8th Cir. 1973) (addict was permitted to express opinion on whether substance was heroin).

Aid to the trier of fact is the basic test for admissibility of expert opinion under Fed. R. Evid. and Unif. R. Evid. 702. The Advisory Committee's Note indicates the intention of the federal rule:

Whether the situation is a proper one for the use of expert testimony is to be determined on the basis of assisting the trier. "There is no more certain test for determining when experts may be used than the common sense inquiry whether the untrained layman would be qualified to determine intelligently and to the best possible degree the particular issue without enlightenment from those having a specialized understanding of the subject involved in the dispute." Ladd, Expert Testimony, 5

may be derived from reading alone in some fields (education), from practice alone in other fields (experience),[16] or as is more commonly the case from both.[17] Of course, a statute may prescribe to the contrary and mandate both educational and experiential requirements as a condition to testifying as an expert on certain subjects.[18] However, such provisions are rare outside the medical malpractice context.[19] As a generalization, it is still

---

Vand. L. Rev. 414, 418 (1952). When opinions are excluded, it is because they are unhelpful and therefore a waste of time. 7 Wigmore § 1918.

Expert witnesses frequently express an opinion in response to a question such as "Do you have an opinion to a reasonable degree of [scientific, medical or other technical] certainty as to . . .?" While the expert today usually replies to follow up questions indicating his opinion in absolute terms such as "did" or "was caused," courts permit less than absolute certainty. Thus, opinions expressed in such terms as "could" or "most probable" are properly received. *See, e.g.,* U.S. v. Oaxaca, 569 F.2d 518 (9th Cir. 1978); U.S. v. Cyphers, 553 F.2d 1064 (7th Cir. 1977); U.S. v. Longfellow, 406 F.2d 415, 416 (4th Cir. 1969).

With respect to the requirement that the expert's opinion in certain matters such as causation satisfy the more probably true than not true standard, see Shumaker v. Oliver B. Cannon & Sons, Inc., 28 Ohio St. 3d 367, 504 N.E.2d 44 (1986).

[16]For example, the courts frequently allow experienced police officers to testify on such topics as the modus operandi for various crimes and the meaning of code words used by drug traffickers. Bamberger, The Dangerous Expert Witness, 52 Brooklyn L. Rev. 855 (1986); Schofield, Criteria for Admissibility of Expert Opinion Testimony on Criminal Modus Operandi, 3 Utah L. Rev. 547 (1978).

[17]Holmgren v. Massey-Ferguson, Inc., 516 F.2d 856 (8th Cir. 1975) (professor of mechanical engineering with little experience with corn pickers qualified as expert to testify about picker's design); Central Illinois Light

Co. v. Porter, 96 Ill. App. 2d 338, 239 N.E.2d 298 (3d Dist. 1968) (conservation officer and duck hunter qualified to give opinion as to effect of transmission lines on duck hunting); Grohusky v. Atlas Assur. Co., 195 Kan. 626, 408 P.2d 697 (1965) (one experienced in insurance business, but with little or no formal education, could testify as to practices and procedures in the insurance business); Norfolk & W. Ry. Co. v. Anderson, 207 Va. 567, 151 S.E.2d 628 (1966) (one expert qualified by experience and one by both experience and study as to cause of tomato crop damage).

"The rule [speaking of Fed. R. Evid. 702] is broadly phrased. The fields of knowledge which may be drawn upon are not limited merely to the 'scientific' and 'technical' but extend to all 'specialized' knowledge. Similarly, the expert is viewed, not in a narrow sense, but as a person qualified by 'knowledge, skill, experience, training or education.' Thus within the scope of the rule are not only experts in the strictest sense of the word, e.g. physicians, physicists, and architects, but also the large group sometimes called 'skilled' witnesses, such as bankers or landowners testifying to land values." Advisory Committee's Note, Fed. R. Evid. 702.

[18]Petrou v. South Coast Emergency Group, 119 Cal. App. 4th 1090, 15 Cal. Rptr. 3d 64 (4th Dist. 2004) (discussing the California Health and Safety Code provisions prescribing requirements for experts testifying in cases involving alleged emergency room malpractice).

[19]*See* Kaye, Bernstein & Mnookin, The New Wigmore: A Treatise on Evidence: Expert Evidence § 3.5.1.b,

true that while the court may rule that a certain subject of inquiry requires calling a member of a particular profession such as a doctor, engineer, or chemist, a specialist in a particular branch of a discipline or profession is usually not required.[20] The question is not whether this witness is more qualified than other experts in the field; that is not the standard of comparison. Rather, the issue is whether the witness is more competent to draw the inference than the lay jurors and judge. However, there is an incipient trend to toughen standards, especially in jurisdictions which have adopted the *Daubert*[21] standard for the admissibility of scientific testimony. In *Daubert* and its progeny, the Supreme Court emphasized that the witness must be competent to perform the specific "task at hand."[22] As a practical matter, that emphasis pressures the proponent to call a specialist to the

---

at 113 (2d ed. 2010), citing Ariz. Rev. Stat. Ann. § 12-2604; Ark. Code Ann. § 16-114-206(a); Colo. Rev. Stat. Ann. § 13-64-401; Del. Code Ann. tit. 18, § 6854; Idaho Code Ann § 6-1012, 6-1013; Iowa Code Ann. § 147.139; Mont. Code Ann. § 26-2-601; N.C. Gen. Stat. Ann. § 8c-7, Rule 702(B)-(E); Okla. Stat. Ann. tit. 63, § 1-1708.1I; 40 Pa. Cons. Stat. Ann. § 1303.512; S.C. Code Ann. § 15-36-100; Tenn. Code Ann. § 29-26-115(B).

[20]U.S. v. Viglia, 549 F.2d 335 (5th Cir. 1977) (physician with no experience in treating obesity could give opinion on use of controlled substance allegedly used for obesity); Wolfinger v. Frey, 223 Md. 184, 162 A.2d 745 (1960) (general practitioner may testify as to cause of kidney condition, citing many local cases). *See also* Hanson v. Baker, 534 A.2d 665 (Me. 1987); Letch v. Daniels, 401 Mass. 65, 514 N.E.2d 675 (1987); Mulholland v. DEC Intern. Corp., 432 Mich. 395, 443 N.W.2d 340, 345 n.4 (1989) ("Michigan has no statute prohibiting unlicensed professionals from testifying as experts. States which prohibit such testimony continue to constitute a small minority of the jurisdictions in this country"); Seawell v. Brame, 258 N.C. 666, 129 S.E.2d 283 (1963) (general practitioner may testify about whether injury caused or aggravated a neurosis, but testimony held inadmissible for other reasons); Parker v. Gunther, 122 Vt. 68, 164 A.2d 152 (1960) (gen-

eral practitioner could testify as to brain damage); Miller v. Peterson, 42 Wash. App. 822, 714 P.2d 695 (Div. 1 1986); West's Key Number Digest, Evidence ⊗537. The courts frequently assert that the test for qualification as an expert under Rule 702 is liberal. Waldorf v. Shuta, 916 F. Supp. 423, 429 (D.N.J. 1996); Kraft General Foods, Inc. v. BC-USA, Inc., 840 F. Supp. 344, 346–47 (E.D. Pa. 1993). *But see* Berger, Evidentiary Framework, in Reference Manual on Scientific Evidence 37, 58–59 (1994) (the author acknowledges that the courts frequently repeat the generalization that the expert witness need not be a specialist; however, the author contends that the generalization is misleading; she urges trial judges to more closely scrutinize the alleged qualifications of proffered expert witnesses).

[21]Daubert v. Merrell Dow Pharmaceuticals, Inc., 509 U.S. 579, 113 S. Ct. 2786, 125 L. Ed. 2d 469 (1993).

[22]Risinger, Defining the "Task at Hand": Non-Science Forensic Science After Kumho Tire Co. v. Carmichael, 57 Wash. & Lee L. Rev. 767 (2000). *See also* People v. Watson, 43 Cal. 4th 652, 76 Cal. Rptr. 3d 208, 182 P.3d 543, 571 (2008) ("The competency of an expert is relative to the topic and fields of knowledge about which the person is asked to opine").

stand.[23] Even post-*Daubert,* for the most part the substantive qualification standards have not crystallized into hard-and-fast rules. Instead, the appellate courts have entrusted the question to the trial judge's discretion reviewable only for abuse.[24] Reversals for abuse are rare.

At one time, at least if the witness's expertise was nonscientific character, most courts did not subject the expert's reasoning to scrutiny other than requiring that the opinion relate to a proper subject and that the witness qualify as an expert.[25] However, today most courts examine the expert's reasoning more carefully. To an extent, they scrutinize every essential element of the reasoning process. After the proponent qualifies the witness as an expert, the proponent elicits the expert's testimony on the merits. In the typical case,[26] the proponent invites the expert to describe a general technique or theory and then apply to the technique or

---

[23]Berry v. Crown Equipment Corp., 108 F. Supp. 2d 743 (E.D. Mich. 2000) (the trial judge should not " 'not the qualifications of the witness in the abstract, but whether those qualifications provide a foundation for the witness to answer a specific question' "); Alexander v. Smith & Nephew, P.L.C., 90 F. Supp. 2d 1225 (N.D. Okla. 2000) (the witness was not board certified in any relevant specialty); Broders v. Heise, 924 S.W.2d 148, 151–52 (Tex. 1996) ("Dr. Condos' medical expertise is undoubtedly greater than that of the general population, but the Heises do not establish that his expertise on the issue of cause-in-fact met the requisites of Rule 702 . . . . Just as a lawyer is not by general education and experience qualified to give an expert opinion on every subject of the law, so too a scientist or medical doctor is not presumed to have expert knowledge about every conceivable scientific principle or disease"); Giannelli, Forensic Science—Expert Qualifications: Traps for the Unwary, 36 Crim. L. Bull. 249 (2000).

In a number of cases, courts have ruled witnesses unqualified as experts on questioned document examination because the witness lacked membership in or certification by a professional organization. American General Life and Acc. Ins. Co. v. Ward, 530 F. Supp. 2d 1306, 1313 (N.D. Ga.

2008); Dracz v. American General Life Ins. Co., 426 F. Supp. 2d 1373, 1378 n.16 (M.D. Ga. 2006), aff'd, 201 Fed. Appx. 681 (11th Cir. 2006).

[24]Caisson Corp. v. Ingersoll-Rand Co., 622 F.2d 672, 682 (3d Cir. 1980) (trial court has broad discretion in admitting or excluding expert testimony); McKiernan v. Caldor, Inc., 183 Conn. 164, 438 A.2d 865 (1981) (meteorologist's opinion on whether ground was frozen on a certain date); Moore, Kelly & Reddish, Inc. v. Shannondale, Inc., 152 W. Va. 549, 165 S.E.2d 113 (1968); West's Key Number Digest, Evidence ⟲546.

[25]Strong, Language and Logic in Expert Testimony: Limiting Expert Testimony by Restrictions of Function, Reliability, and Form, 71 Or. L. Rev. 349 (1992).

[26]There are atypical cases. The proponent might call the expert simply because the expert happens to have firsthand knowledge of relevant facts. In that event, the foundation would be laid under Rule 602 rather than Rule 702. Alternatively, the proponent might elicit a lay opinion from someone who happens to be an expert. If a physician happened to observe the nonverbal demeanor of an alleged intoxicated person, the physician could express a lay opinion on that subject. Here, the foundation would be laid under Rule 701 rather than Rule 702.

theory to the specific facts of the case. In essence, the balance of the expert's testimony is a syllogism: The major premise is the validity of the expert's general theory or technique, the minor premise is the case specific data, and the application of major to minor yields a conclusion relevant to the merits of the case.[27] There are evidentiary restrictions on each step in the reasoning.

*The Validity of the Expert's Underlying Technique or Theory*

In addition to the traditional issues of the propriety of the topic for an expert opinion and the qualifications of the alleged expert, there is the question of whether the state of the art or scientific knowledge enables the expert to form a reliable opinion that will assist the trier of fact.[28] Is the expert's major premise reliable? As § 203 notes, prior to 1993 most jurisdictions held that purportedly scientific testimony has to be based on a generally accepted

---

Finally, the proponent might ask the expert simply to educate the jury about a theory or technique without inviting the expert to apply the theory to the facts of the case. The text of Rule 702 states that a qualified expert "may testify . . . in the form of an opinion or otherwise . . . ." The Advisory Committee Note states:

> Most of the literature assumes that experts testify only in the form of opinions. That assumption is logically unfounded. The rule accordingly recognizes that an expert on the stand may give a dissertation or exposition of scientific or other principles relevant to the case, leaving the trier of fact to apply them to the facts.

[27]Imwinkelried, The "Bases" of Expert Testimony: The Syllogistic Structure of Scientific Testimony, 67 N.C. L. Rev. 1 (1988). Consider, for example, a psychiatrist's testimony. The essential content of the testimony might consist of the following: (1) the major premise: If a person displays symptoms A and B, they have mental illness D; (2) the minor premise: This person's case history includes symptoms A and B; and (3) the conclusion: This person suffers from mental illness C. Although the typical direct examination follows this outline, there are at least three other ways that the proponent can use a witness who happens to be an expert:

- The proponent could call the witness under Rule 602 to testify to facts that she had observed. The witness's status as an expert does not disqualify the witness from giving factual testimony.
- The proponent might call the witness under Rule 701 to testify to a lay opinion.
- The proponent could call the witness under Rule 702 to lecture the jury about a theory or technique without asking the witness to apply the theory or technique to the facts of the instant case. The Advisory Committee Note accompanying Rule 702 explains that this possibility is the reason why the statute states that the expert "may testify in the form of an opinion or otherwise . . . ."

[28]U.S. v. Watson, 587 F.2d 365 (7th Cir. 1978); Tonkovich v. Department of Labor and Industries of State, 31 Wash. 2d 220, 195 P.2d 638 (1948). *See generally* State v. Woodburn, 559 A.2d 343, 346 (Me. 1989) (the trial court may consider whether the scientific propositions involved in the testimony have been generally accepted and whether the testimony has been demonstrated to have sufficient reliability as a predictor of untruthfulness). The principle in the text at least overlaps with the subject of the reli-

theory or technique. However, in its 1993 *Daubert* decision, the Supreme Court announced that when the proponent proffers the witness as a scientific expert, the proponent must establish that the witness's underlying theory or technique qualifies as reliable "scientific . . . knowledge" within the meaning of that expression in Federal Rule 702.[29] The Court explained that to qualify, the expert's hypothesis must be empirically validated. The Court stated that in evaluating the validation of the expert's hypothesis, trial judges should consider the following factors, *inter alia*: whether the proposition is testable and has been tested; whether the proposition has been subjected to peer review and publication; whether the methodology has a known error rate; whether there are accepted standards for using the methodology; and whether the methodology is generally accepted.

The question then arose as to whether *Daubert*'s reliability test for "scientific . . . knowledge" applies to other types of expert testimony. On its face, Rule 702 refers in the alternative to "scientific, technical, or other specialized knowledge." Thus, the wording of the statute suggests that there can be nonscientific "technical" and nonscientific, nontechnical "specialized" experts in addition to scientific experts.[30] Do *Daubert*'s test and list of relevant factors apply to nonscientific experts? In a copyright infringement case, the plaintiff might call an expert musician to testify about the degree of similarity between two songs. The musician is arguably testifying about "technical . . . knowledge." There are widespread conventions as to technique and methodology within the music field, but in most cases the musician's methodology cannot be validated in an empirical, scientific manner. Likewise, a prosecutor might call an experienced police

---

ability of an expert opinion which depends upon the validity of alleged scientific propositions, principles or techniques, and may conflict with results in this latter area. See § 203 infra.

Expert witnesses have been called upon to testify in child sexual abuse cases to educate the trier of fact about the symptoms of child sexual abuse, such as delay in reporting and the possibility of recantation, as well as to opine (1) that the child's testimony is consistent with abuse, or (2) that the child is telling the truth, or its equivalent—that the child has been abused. While most courts permit testimony to educate the trier of fact, courts differ as to the propriety of

opinion testimony as to consistency and that the child was abused. *See generally* State v. Moran, 151 Ariz. 378, 728 P.2d 248 (1986); State v. Spigarolo, 210 Conn. 359, 556 A.2d 112 (1989), State v. Newman, 109 N.M. 263, 784 P.2d 1006 (Ct. App. 1989).

[29]Daubert v. Merrell Dow Pharmaceuticals, Inc., 509 U.S. 579, 113 S. Ct. 2786, 125 L. Ed. 2d 469 (1993).

[30]*E.g.*, U.S. v. Shedlock, 62 F.3d 214, 219 (8th Cir. 1995) (police academy instructor); Grimm v. Lane, 895 F. Supp. 907, 913 (S.D. Ohio 1995) (a witness experienced in corrections).

officer to testify about the typical modus operandi for a crime.[31] Again, the officer's testimony may represent "specialized knowledge," but the officer will not be opining on the basis of systematic, controlled scientific research. Does the court nevertheless have to subject the reliability of the underlying assumptions of the musician and officer to scrutiny under *Daubert*?

Prior to 1999, the courts divided into three camps.[32] For their part, some courts ruled that "technical" and "specialized" expertise are exempt from the *Daubert* test.[33] In footnote 8 of its opinion, the *Daubert* Court disclaimed any intention to prescribe admissibility standards for nonscientific expert testimony. Under *Frye, Daubert's* predecessor, most courts took a laissez-faire attitude toward the reliability of the premises underlying nonscientific expert testimony; any doubts about the reliability of the expert's theory went "largely unregarded."[34]

At the polar extreme, other courts took the position that the entirety of the *Daubert* opinion extends to other types of expert testimony.[35] Some not only applied the general *Daubert* reliability test but also attempted to evaluate the reliability of nonscientific expertise in terms of the specific factors enumerated in *Daubert*.[36] The second camp, insisting that nonscientific testimony satisfy the *Daubert* factors, is wrong-minded. In effect, these cases endeavor to fit round pegs into square holes. It is meaningful to talk about error rates for scientific techniques, but that factor is hardly appropriate in the analysis of nonscientific expert testimony by musicians, police officers, lawyers, and farmers.

A third position is the most sensible: While the proponent of nonscientific testimony must demonstrate the reliability of the expert's underlying assumptions, the trial judge need not use the

---

[31]Schofield, Criteria for Admissibility of Expert Opinion Testimony on Criminal Modus Operandi, 3 Utah L. Rev. 547 (1978).

[32]Note, Inconsistent Gatekeeping in Federal Courts: Application of Daubert v. Merrell Dow Pharmaceuticals, Inc. to Nonscientific Expert Testimony, 30 Loy. L.A. L. Rev. 1379 (1997).

[33]McKendall v. Crown Control Corp., 122 F.3d 803 (9th Cir. 1997); Freeman v. Case Corp., 118 F.3d 1011 (4th Cir. 1997); U.S. v. Heath, 970 F.2d 1397, 1405 (5th Cir. 1992) (the "absence of scientific data" supporting the witness's opinion was not fatal to the admissibility of testimony by a real estate lawyer).

[34]Strong, Language and Logic in Expert Testimony: Limiting Expert Testimony by Restrictions on Function, Reliability, and Form, 71 Or. L. Rev. 349, 361 (1992).

[35]Watkins v. Telsmith, Inc., 121 F.3d 984 (5th Cir. 1997); Southland Sod Farms v. Stover Seed Co., 108 F.3d 1134, 1143 n.8 (9th Cir. 1997) ("*Daubert's* holding applies to all expert testimony, not just testimony based on novel scientific methods"); Claar v. Burlington Northern R. Co., 29 F.3d 499, 501 n.2 (9th Cir. 1994).

[36]Note, Inconsistent Gatekeeping in Federal Courts: Application of Daubert v. Merrell Dow Pharmaceuticals, Inc., 30 Loy. L.A. L. Rev. 1379 (1997).

*Daubert* factors to gauge reliability. Rather, the judge ought to engage in a more flexible analysis; the judge should pose such questions as whether in the real world members of the public routinely turn to this profession for services other than testimony and whether there is a feedback loop, alerting a member of the profession when she has erred.[37] An auto mechanic may lack the formal education to qualify as a scientific expert, but his customers are likely to provide him with feedback as to whether his repair work on their car was successful. Even before the Supreme Court's 1999 *Kumho* decision, the Judicial Conference had proposed an amendment to Rule 702 which in effect extended a foundational reliability requirement to major premises used by all types of experts, nonscientific as well as scientific.[38] The amendment was adopted in 2000.

Even before the amendment took effect, the issue reached the Supreme Court in 1999 in *Kumho Tire Co. v. Carmichael*.[39] In an majority opinion authored by Justice Breyer, the Court cited the proposed amendment to Rule 702 and essentially endorsed the

---

[37]Smith v. Haden, 872 F. Supp. 1040, 1045 (D.D.C. 1994); Imwinkelried, The Next Step After *Daubert*: Developing a Similarly Epistemological Approach to Ensuring the Reliability of Nonscientific Expert Testimony, 15 Cardozo L. Rev. 2271 (1994).

[38]The amendment read:

If scientific, technical, or other specialized knowledge will assist the trier of fact to understand the evidence or to determine a fact in issue, a witness qualified as an expert by knowledge, skill, experience or training, or education, may testify thereto in the form of an opinion or otherwise provided that (1) the testimony is sufficiently based upon reliable facts or data, (2) the testimony is the product of reliable principles and methods, and (3) the witness has applied the principles and methods reliably to the fact of the case.

The accompanying draft Advisory Committee Notes stated:

The amendment would not distinguish between scientific and other forms of expert testimony. The trial court's gatekeeping function applies to testimony by any expert. While the relevant factors for determining reliability will vary from expertise to expertise, the amendment rejects the premise that an expert's testimony should be treated

more permissively simply because it is outside the realm of science. An opinion from an expert who is not a scientist should receive the same degree of scrutiny for reliability as an opinion from an expert who purports to be a scientist.

As we shall see, the amendment took effect in 2000 after the Supreme Court's decision in *Kumho*.

[39]Kumho Tire Co., Ltd. v. Carmichael, 526 U.S. 137, 119 S. Ct. 1167, 143 L. Ed. 2d 238 (1999). The case was an appeal from the Eleventh Circuit's decision in Carmichael v. Samyang Tire, Inc., 131 F.3d 1433 (11th Cir. 1997). *Kumho* is a products liability case involving a car accident caused by a tire blowout. The plaintiff called a tire expert to testify that the tire in question was defective. Based on his experience and his visual inspection of the tire, the expert was prepared to testify that there was no sign that the tire had been overloaded or underinflated. The district court ruled the expert's testimony inadmissible because it did not satisfy the factors listed in *Daubert*. The Eleventh Circuit reversed, reasoning that it was improper to subject this type of expertise to the *Daubert* test.

third position. On the one hand, the Court stated that "a *Daubert*-style scrutiny" is appropriate for all types of expert testimony. As a matter of statutory construction, the Court argued that all kinds of expert testimony must amount to reliable "knowledge" to qualify for admission under Rule 702. In effect, the Court mandated that trial judges test the epistemological basis of proffered expert testimony. The expert is making a knowledge claim, and the judge must inquire whether there is a sufficient warrant for the expert's claim. The Court added that "the evidentiary rationale" underlying *Daubert* is a concern about reliability, and in the Court's judgment that rationale is equally applicable to non-scientific expertise. The Court asserted that "it would prove difficult, if not impossible, for judges to administer evidentiary rules under which a gatekeeping obligation depended upon a distinction between 'scientific' knowledge and 'technical' or 'other specialized' knowledge."

On the other hand, the *Kumho* majority made it clear that non-scientific testimony need not satisfy each of the *Daubert* factors in order to qualify for admission. The trial judge "may" consider the factors which he or she finds pertinent, but in a given case some or most of those factors might be inapposite. The Court commented that "we can neither rule out, nor rule in, for all cases . . . the applicability of the factors mentioned in *Daubert.* . . ." In 1997 in *General Electric Co. v. Joiner*,[40] the Court had ruled that abuse of discretion is the appropriate standard for appellate review of trial judge rulings under *Daubert*. *Joiner* made it clear that the trial judge enjoys discretion in applying the factors listed in *Daubert* to purportedly scientific testimony. In *Kumho*, the Court analogized to *Joiner*. The *Kumho* Court declared that "[t]he trial court must have the same kind of latitude in deciding how to test a [non-scientific] expert's reliability. . . ." The Court stressed that "whether *Daubert*'s specific factors are, or are not, reasonable measures of reliability in a particular case is a matter that the law grants the trial judge broad latitude to determine." Thus, *Kumho* goes beyond *Joiner*; in the case of non-scientific expertise, the judge has discretion to choose the factors to apply. In 2000, the proposed amendment to Rule 702 took effect, largely codifying *Kumho*'s prescriptions. However, *Kumho* and the amendment are such recent developments and the conceivable varieties of non-scientific expertise are so numerous that, understandably, the admissibility standards for such expertise are currently in flux. Nevertheless, some generalizations are possible. Three basic questions have been identified, and some consensus is developing on each question.

---

[40]General Elec. Co. v. Joiner, 522 U.S. 136, 118 S. Ct. 512, 139 L. Ed. 2d 508 (1997).

*What is the specific technique or theory that the expert will testify about?* It is certainly unacceptable for the expert to rely on a proposition or technique that is literally ineffable. An ineffable notion might be acceptable mysticism at a meeting of the Jedi Council, but it does not qualify as acceptable expertise in court. It is also clear that it is not enough for the witness to assert in conclusory fashion that she is relying on her general "expertise," "knowledge," or "education." Those considerations can qualify the witness as an expert, but they do not speak to the validity of the expert's theory or technique. To provide a useful expert insight, the witness must identify a more specific technique or theory. The witness must articulate that technique or theory. Otherwise, the witness is venturing nothing more than a guess.

Likewise, there is a growing consensus that in gauging the admissibility of the proffered opinion, the trial judge must focus on the specific theory or technique the expert relies on rather than the "global" reliability of the expert's discipline.[41] Admittedly, *Kumho* contains language carrying a contrary suggestion. In his lead opinion, citing the examples of astrology and necromancy, Justice Breyer commented that sometimes "the discipline itself lacks reliability."[42] However, most of the language in the *Daubert-Joiner-Kumho* trilogy indicates that the judge's focus should be narrow. In the formal summary at the end of his opinion in *Daubert*, Justice Blackmun stated that the proponent's foundation must convince the trial judge that the expert's theory or technique is sufficiently reliable "to perform the task at hand."[43] *Joiner* lends itself to the same interpretation. There Chief Justice Rehnquist analyzed the question of whether the animal studies cited by the plaintiff were an adequate basis for the expert's opinion as to the cause of Joiner's small-cell cancer. The Chief Justice initially listed the criticisms of the animal studies. He then wrote:

---

[41]*See generally* Risinger, Defining the "Task at Hand": Non-Science Forensic Science After Kumho Tire Co. v. Carmichael, 57 Wash. & Lee L. Rev. 767 (2000). *But see* Allen, Expertise and the Supreme Court: What Is the Problem?, 34 Seton Hall L. Rev. 1, 5–7 (2003) ("The testimony at trial must rest on something, obviously, and that 'something' must be true, whether it is the accumulated experience of an individual accurately summarized or knowledge of highly systematic disciplines. That global reliability is not sufficient to ensure local reliability is precisely why *Kumho* was decided as it was, but *Kumho* cannot stand for the proposition that global reliability is not a necessary element. Without global reliability, one has gibberish. Thus, the logical relationships underlying the Supreme Court's cases require that both the global and the local issues be resolved favorably before an expert should be allowed to testify.").

[42]Kumho Tire Co., Ltd. v. Carmichael, 526 U.S. 137, 151, 119 S. Ct. 1167, 143 L. Ed. 2d 238 (1999).

[43]Daubert v. Merrell Dow Pharmaceuticals, Inc., 509 U.S. 579, 597, 113 S. Ct. 2786, 125 L. Ed. 2d 469 (1993).

Respondent (plaintiff) failed to reply to this criticism. Rather than explaining how and why the experts could have extrapolated their opinions from these seemingly far-removed animal studies, respondent chose "to proceed as if the only issue [was] whether animal studies could ever be a proper foundation for an expert opinion." Of course, whether animal studies could ever be a proper foundation for an expert's opinion was not the issue. The issue was whether *these* experts' opinions were sufficiently supported by the animal studies on which they purported to rely.[44]

*Kumho* fits the same mold as *Daubert* and *Joiner*. In reviewing the foundation laid by the plaintiffs for the expert Carlson's opinion, Justice Breyer engaged in a highly particularized analysis:

> [C]ontrary to [plaintiffs'] suggestion, the specific issue before the [trial] court was not the reasonableness in general of a tire expert's use of a visual and tactile inspection to determine whether overdeflection had caused the tire's tread to separate from its steel-belted carcass. Rather, it was the reasonableness of using such an approach, along with Carlson's particular method of analyzing the data thereby obtained, to draw a conclusion regarding the particular matter to which the expert testimony was directly relevant.[45]

The Justice acknowledged that "as a general matter, tire abuse can be identified . . . through visual or tactile inspection of the tire." However, Carlson claimed to have developed a more "particular" method, namely, a theory that there are four characteristic signs of tire abuse and that the absence of at least two of the signs indicates that the accident was caused by a manufacturing defect in the tire.[46] Later in the opinion, the Justice stressed that Carlson had not rested his opinion: "simply [on] the general theory that, in the absence of evidence of abuse, a defect will normally have caused a tire's separation. Rather, the expert employed a more specific theory to establish the existence (or absence) of such abuse."[47] The Justice underscored that "the question before the trial court was specific, not general."[48]

As Professor Risinger has noted,[49] *United States v. Fujii*[50] is a perfect example of the narrow analytic focus demanded by the *Daubert* trilogy. There the issue was whether a questioned document examiner could identify the author of handprinting. The rub was that the defendant had learned to print in Japan where

---

[44]General Elec. Co. v. Joiner, 522 U.S. 136, 144, 118 S. Ct. 512, 139 L. Ed. 2d 508 (1997) (emphasis in the original).

[45]Kumho, 526 U.S. at 153–54.

[46]526 U.S. at 154.

[47]526 U.S. at 154.

[48]526 U.S. at 156.

[49]Risinger, Defining the "Task at Hand": Non-Science Forensic Science After Kumho Tire Co. v. Carmichael, 57 Wash. & Lee L. Rev. 767, 798–800 (2000).

[50]U.S. v. Fujii, 152 F. Supp. 2d 939 (N.D. Ill. 2000).

students are taught to eschew individuality in printing style and instead strictly follow a prescribed style. The court stated that it was not passing on the general trustworthiness of the discipline of forensic document examination. Rather, the issue before the court was whether the record established the examiner's ability to perform the specific task at hand. The court found the record lacking and excluded the testimony.

*Which type of use is the expert putting the theory or technique to?* There is a growing realization that after identifying the specific theory or technique the expert will testify about, the judge should categorize the use that the expert is making about the theory or technique. What type of use is the expert putting the theory or technique to? There are several possible categories, including a normative use.[51] However, most of the published opinions involve two other types of use.

One category is a descriptive or summational claim.[52] In this category, the expert merely describes or summarizes experience

---

[51]While most of the claims in the published opinions fall into the two categories discussed in text, these categories do not exhaust the possibilities. A third possibility is a normative claim. Risinger, Preliminary Thoughts on a Functional Taxonomy of Testimony of Expertise for the Post-*Kumho* World, in 1 Faigman, et al., Modern Scientific Evidence: The Law and Science of Expert Testimony § 2:12 (2011–12 ed.). For instance, a bioethicist might be proffered as a witness at a trial to determine whether to terminate a comatose patient's life support. Spielman & Agich, The Future of Bioethics Testimony: Guidelines for Determining Qualifications, Reliability, and Helpfulness, 36 San Diego L. Rev. 1043 (1999). Normative testimony is rarely admitted. Delgado & McAllen, The Moralist as Expert Witness, 62 B. U. L. Rev. 869 (1982).

Some have argued that in many instances when a litigator contemplates proffering for the normative purpose of persuading the judge to adopt a certain rule of law, the formal laws of evidence are inapplicable. The argument is that the litigator is submitting the information for a legislative purpose rather than an adjudicative one. Imwinkelried, Expert Testimony by Ethicists: What Should Be the Norm?, 76 Temple L. Rev. 91, 114–22 (2003), reprinted and revised, 33 Journal of Law, Medicine & Ethics 198 (Summer 2005). As the Advisory Committee Note to Federal Rule of Evidence 201(a) indicates, the formal evidentiary rules are inapplicable when information is tendered to a judge to enable the judge to perform an essentially legislative function such as formulating a common law rule. See § 331 infra. The formal rules of evidence should apply only in very circumscribed circumstances: The announced legal standard requires or invites the trier of fact to bring moral judgment to bear in order to make the decision; the standard in question ought to be interpreted as alluding to normative moral judgment; and the procedural law of the jurisdiction allocates the decision in question to the trier of fact. Imwinkelried, 76 Temple L. Rev. at 122–24. Although these situations are rare, in a given jurisdiction a decision whether to award punitive damages or whether to characterize certain police conduct as entrapment could satisfy these criteria. 76 Temple L. Rev. at 125–27.

[52]Risinger, Preliminary Thoughts on a Functional Taxonomy of Expertise for the Post-*Kumho* world, in Faigman, Kaye, Saks & Sanders, Science in the

in his or her field. Suppose, for instance, that in a contract lawsuit, there is a dispute as to the meaning of a term in the written agreement. To support her interpretation of the term, the plaintiff calls an experienced member of the industry as an expert witness. The witness proposes to testify that in the industry, there is a trade custom or usage as to the meaning of that term. The expert's specific theory is that the usage exists within the industry. So long as the witness testifies that she has been a member of the industry for a considerable period of time and has encountered the usage of the term by industry members on numerous occasions, the foundation is adequate.[53] (If she were testifying based solely on her personal experience, her testimony could be admitted as lay opinion under Rule 701. If she is also relying on conversations with other industry members and industry publications, her testimony will have to be admitted under Rule 702.)

The same rationale explains the approving mention of police testimony about drug argot in both Justice Breyer's *Kumho* opinion[54] and the 2000 Advisory Committee Note to Federal Rule 702.[55] Drug trafficking is a business. Just as a term can acquire a specialized meaning for members of a lawful commercial trade, a term can take on a peculiar significance for criminal drug traffickers. Hence, just as a veteran member of the meat scrap industry could explain the meaning of "50% protein" in a lawful contract between two industry members,[56] an experienced undercover narcotics officer may testify as to the meaning of "lid" in an unlawful agreement for the purchase of a contraband drug. As the 2000 Advisory Committee Note states, in this situation "experience alone . . . may . . . provide a sufficient foundation

---

Law: Standards, Statistics and Research Issues § 2-2.2.6 (2002).

[53]Frigaliment Importing Co. v. B.N.S. Intern. Sales Corp., 190 F. Supp. 116 (S.D. N.Y. 1960).

[54]Kumho Tire Co., Ltd. v. Carmichael, 526 U.S. 137, 150, 119 S. Ct. 1167, 143 L. Ed. 2d 238 (1999) ("experts in drug terms").

[55]2000 Adv. Comm. Note, Fed. R. Evid. 702, 28 U.S.C.A. ("when a law enforcement agent testifies regarding the use of code words in a drug transaction, the principle used by the agent is that participants in such transactions regularly use code words to conceal the nature of their activities. The method used by the agent is the application of extensive experience to

analyze the meaning of the conversations. So long as the principles and methods are reliable and applied reliably to the facts of the case, this type of testimony should be admitted").

[56]Hurst v. W.J. Lake & Co., 141 Or. 306, 16 P.2d 627 (1932) (the issue is whether 49.51% protein qualifies as "50% protein"). A complete foundation would include testimony that: The witness was involved or knew of a large number of transactions in which "50% protein" was used; in many instances during the performance phase of such agreements, suppliers tendered shipments of greater than 49.5% but less than 50.0% protein; and in the clear majority of such instances, the buyers willingly accepted the shipments.

for expert testimony." (If the officer were relying exclusively on personal experience, the proponent of the expert's testimony might be able to introduce the opinion under Rule 701. However, if the officer is relying on conversations with other officers and training manuals, Rule 702 will govern.)

However, in other cases the proponent of the expert testimony wants the expert to do more than merely recite or summarize experience as to fact *A*. It is not enough to establish the existence of fact *A*. Instead, the proponent contemplates inviting the expert to draw an inference from the witness's experience. The expert evaluates the experience and draws a further inference as to fact *B*. A drug dog handler may be prepared to go beyond describing the dog's behavior and add that the behavior was an "alert" indicating the presence of contraband drugs in the defendant's luggage. Likewise, a fingerprint examiner might be ready to go beyond describing the latent impressions found at a crime scene and add that a comparison with the defendant's inked impressions indicates that the defendant left the impression at the crime scene. In this category, the expert is making an inferential claim.

*How can the proponent validate that type of use of the expert's specific technique or theory?* Finally, having identified the expert's specific theory or technique and categorized the expert's claim about the theory or technique, in the words of *Daubert* the judge must determine whether the proponent has established "appropriate validation"[57] for that application of the theory. In effect, the answers to the first two questions specify the hypothesis or claim that must be validated: The expert asserts that by using a particular theory or technique, she can accurately draw a certain type of inference. The required validation varies with two factors: the type of claim the expert is making and the specificity of the claim.

As previously stated, one factor is the category or type of claim the expert is making. When the expert is making a simple descriptive claim, the trial judge should demand a foundation establishing that on a significant number of occasions, the witness or other members[58] of her specialty have had experiences similar to the incident in question. How many times has the

---

[57]Daubert v. Merrell Dow Pharmaceuticals, Inc., 509 U.S. 579, 590, 113 S. Ct. 2786, 125 L. Ed. 2d 469 (1993).

[58]Imwinkelried & Margolin, The Case for the Admissibility of Defense Testimony About Customary Political Practices in Official Corruption Prosecutions, 29 Am. Crim. L. Rev. 1,

20 (1991) (the authors discuss the admissibility of expert testimony about modus operandi; collecting cases, the authors state that the officer's opinion "rests on the officer's experience investigating crimes committed by third parties other than the accused, derived from an amalgam of firsthand experience, hearsay from other officers, and

industry member encountered a meat scraps transaction in which the expression, "50% protein," was used? How often has the undercover agent been involved in a contraband drug transaction in which the word, "lid," was employed? It is not enough for the witness to testify that she has been an industry member or an undercover agent for several years.[59] The experience must be sufficiently extensive and particularized enough to persuade the judge that the expert is competent to perform the specific "task at hand."

In contrast, if the expert is making an inferential claim, a foundation merely showing the expert's experience is inadequate. The judge should insist on a foundation demonstrating that the expert's technique or technique "works"; that is, it enables the expert to accurately make the determination as to which he or she proposes to testify. The foundation must include a showing of the results when the technique was used on prior occasions. Do the outcomes demonstrate a connection between facts $A$ and $B$? Neither the expert's personal voucher nor general acceptance in the field nor even long-term, repeated use of the theory suffices. Subdivision (b)(9) of Federal Evidence Rule 901 furnishes a helpful parallel. When the question is the authentication of "a process or system," the statute explicitly requires a "showing that the process or system produces an accurate result."[60] In *Kumho*, Justice Breyer asserted that in evaluating the reliability of an expert's methodology, the judge ought to consider "how often an

---

knowledge gained at special law enforcement schools").

[59]U.S. v. Hermanek, 289 F.3d 1076 (9th Cir. 2002) (although the witness was an experienced investigator, this evidently was the first occasion on which he had encountered certain allegedly coded references). In this respect the foundation is similar to the predicate for reputation character evidence. If the witness proposes testifying about a person's reputation for a character trait, it is not enough that the witness is a member of the same community as the person. In addition, the witness must vouch that he or she is familiar with the person's reputation in the community. See § 191 infra. Standing alone, residence in the person's community does not guarantee that the witness has heard any discussions or mention of the person's character. Similarly, membership in the industry does not guarantee that the witness has had any exposure to the usage of the expression, "50% protein" or "lid." *See* Imwinkelried, The Meaning of "Appropriate Validation" in *Daubert*—Interpreted in Light of the Broader Rationalist Tradition, Not the Narrow Scientific Tradition, 30 Fla. St. U. L. Rev. 735, 752 (2003).

[60]The Advisory Committee Note to the subdivision states that the subdivision applies to expert techniques such as X-rays and computers. Adv. Comm. Note, Fed. R. Evid. 901. In the macrocosm, society accepts science as a valid, useful enterprise because on an everyday basis, we witness the results of successful applications of scientific theories. John Ziman, Reliable Knowledge: An Exploration of the Grounds for Belief in Science 2, 6–7, 46, 75 (1978). The same reasoning is applicable in the microcosm when an expert proposes testifying about a scientific theory or technique at trial.

. . . expert's methodology has produced erroneous results . . . ."[61] The 2000 Advisory Committee Note to amended Rule 702 likewise states that a pertinent consideration is the "results" reached when the theory or technique is utilized. Under this standard, if the proffered expert is a drug or explosive dog handler, there should be a showing of the dog's track record.[62] In the past when the dog has alerted, what percentage of the alerts led to the seizure of contraband drugs? In the case of fingerprint examiners, on proficiency tests in what percentage of the cases have the examiners correctly identified the source of the impressions?[63]

The requisite validation varies not only with the type of claim but also with a second factor, the specificity of the expert's claim. The more specific the expert's theory, ordinarily the more extensive the foundation will have to be.[64] Consider the following, illustrative opinions:

- Opinion #1. Suppose that the expert proposes testifying only that a certain phenomenon exists. For instance, the expert might be prepared to opine that *mistaken eyewitness identifications are more common than most laypersons realize*. To validate that relatively general opinion, it would probably suffice if the foundation described empirical data from two types of studies. One type of study involved witnesses to simulated or staged crimes. This study estimated the incidence of mistaken eyewitness identifications. The second type of study would be a follow-up to the first; in this research, the witnesses testified at mock trials; and mock jurors were asked to decide whether to accept the witnesses' identifications. Assume that both studies were well designed, the first indicated that the incidence of mistaken identifications was 25%, but the second found that the jury concluded that only 10% of the identifications were erroneous. That foundation would arguably suffice to validate the expert's theory.

- Opinion #2. Now the expert proposes taking the next step and testifying to the more specific theory that certain factors can cause or prevent the phenomenon. By way of example, the expert might be prepared to testify that *a racial difference between the alleged perpetrator and the witness can*

---

[61]Kumho Tire Co., Ltd. v. Carmichael, 526 U.S. 137, 151, 119 S. Ct. 1167, 143 L. Ed. 2d 238 (1999). *See also* Colon ex rel. Molina v. BIC USA, Inc., 199 F. Supp. 2d 53, 70 (S.D. N.Y. 2001).

[62]U.S. v. Limares, 269 F.3d 794 (7th Cir. 2001); State v. White, 382 S.C. 265, 676 S.E.2d 684, 687 (2009) ("by experience the dog is found to be reliable . . . .").

[63]U.S. v. Llera Plaza, 188 F. Supp. 2d 549 (E.D. Pa. 2002).

[64]Imwinkelried, Expert Witness: The General and the Specific, Nat'l L.J., Oct. 6, 2008, at 13.

*cause a mistaken identification.* As a matter of logic, the foundation for opinion #1 does not validate this hypothesis. The expert would have to testify to a very different type of research project. Assume, though, that: The expert conducted a study involving two groups of subjects; with one exception, the two groups were similar—the same age and visual acuity and identical observation conditions; the exception was that while the first group was asked to identify a perpetrator of the same race, the second group was required to attempt to make a cross-racial identification; and the error rate for the second group was significantly higher than the rate for the first group. Now the foundation might be adequate. Similar experiments could demonstrate that conversely, improved lighting conditions reduce the probability that the phenomenon will occur.

- Opinion #3. The particular facts of the instant case are an illustration of the general phenomenon—*this witness is mistaken.* This opinion is even more specific and requires another, different foundation. The opinion demands a foundation establishing a more sophisticated understanding of the interplay and relationship among the various causal factors. The research supporting opinion #2 might indicate that the cross-racial factor can cause a mistaken identification but that excellent lighting conditions reduce the risk of error. In order to give opinion #3, the expert must explore the relationship between the factors. What is likely to occur if the identification is cross-racial but the lighting is excellent? The foundation must fit the specific theory advanced by the expert.

Although the courts have made progress in clarifying the meaning and reach of *Kumho,* there is still a remaining tension in the area. The pivotal question is this: If a controlled scientific experiment could feasibly have been devised to validate a non-scientific expert claim and the practitioners of the expertise have neglected to conduct the experimentation, how strongly, if at all, should that neglect cut against admissibility? By way of example, should the courts bar the introduction of fingerprint evidence even as non-scientific expertise if fingerprint experts have failed to conduct the rigorous scientific experiments that could verify their underlying premises?[65] In *Kumho,* Justice Breyer commented that the Court wanted to "make certain that an expert . . . employs in the courtroom the same level of intellectual rigor that

---

[65]U.S. v. Llera Plaza, 179 F. Supp. 2d 492 (E.D. Pa. 2002), withdrawn from bound volume and opinion vacated and superseded on reconsideration, 188 F. Supp. 2d 549 (E.D. Pa. 2002).

characterizes the practice of an expert in the relevant field."[66] If a certain type of testing is customary in the real world practice of the expert's discipline, the lack of testing could therefore be fatal to admissibility. Some of the foremost commentators on expert testimony have argued that Evidence law ought to be structured to create incentives for litigants to present "the best possible information"[67] and for experts to conduct desirable scientific research.[68] A number of courts have found this argument persuasive. It strikes these courts as "exactly backwards"[69] to approve the expert's validation reasoning when the expert has failed to resort to a superior, available validation methodology. Significantly, the 2000 Advisory Committee Note to amended Rule 702 evidences sympathy with the argument.[70] The note asserts that "[a]n opinion from an expert who is not a scientist should receive the same degree of scrutiny for reliability as an opinion from an expert who purports to be a scientist."

However, this line of argument arguably incorporates a best or better evidence principle into the analysis of the admissibility of expert testimony. At least prior to the 2000 amendment to Rule 702, it was difficult to discern such a principle in the text or legislative history of the Federal Rules of Evidence.[71] At trial, the opponent may certainly point to the factor of the expert's failure to use a superior, scientific methodology to validate his or her premises as a basis for attacking the weight of the expert's testimony. However, it is a very different question whether that

---

[66]Kumho Tire Co., Ltd. v. Carmichael, 526 U.S. 137, 152, 119 S. Ct. 1167, 143 L. Ed. 2d 238 (1999).

[67]1 Faigman, et al., Modern Scientific Evidence: The Law and Science of Expert Testimony § 30:2 (2012–2013 ed.); Faigman, Legal Alchemy: The Use and Misuse of Science in the Law 5, 82–83 (1999).

[68]1 Faigman, et al., Modern Scientific Evidence: The Law and Science of Expert Testimony § 30:2 (2012–2013 ed.); Faigman, Kaye, Saks & Sanders, How Good Is Good Enough?: Expert Evidence Under *Daubert* and *Kumho*, 50 Case W. Res. L. Rev. 645 (1999).

[69]*E.g.*, Watkins v. Telsmith, Inc., 121 F.3d 984, 991 (5th Cir. 1997). However, *Telsmith* could be read more narrowly to deal with an expert's attempt to avoid the necessity of showing a valid methodology by vague references to general engineering principles and practical experience.

[70]Adv. Comm. Note, Fed. R. Evid. 702. Approvingly citing *Watkins,* the note states:

> An opinion from an expert who is not a scientist should receive the same degree of scrutiny for reliability as an opinion from an expert who purports to be a scientist. See Watkins v. Telsmith, Inc., 121 F.3d 984, 991 (5th Cir. 1997) ("[I]t seems exactly backwards that experts who purport to rely on general engineering principles and practical experience might escape screening by the district court simply by stating that their conclusions were not reached by any particular method or technique").

[71]Imwinkelried, Should the Courts Incorporate a Best Evidence Rule Into the Standard Determining the Admissibility of Scientific Testimony?: Enough Is Enough Even When It Is Not the Best, 50 Case Wes. R. L. Rev. 19, 34–38 (1999).

failure should also factor into admissibility analysis. The question is not whether the proponent has presented the best possible validation, but rather enough validation to establish the reliability of the theory or technique. A scientific experiment can be devised to test virtually any proposition. The North Carolina Court of Appeals has declared that "there is . . . no requirement that a party offering [expert] testimony must produce evidence that the testimony . . . has been proven through scientific study."[72] In addition, several courts have expressly rejected the argument that the expert must base her opinion on the best available methodology.[73]

It remains to be seen how the courts will ultimately resolve this tension. In Justice Blackmun's original opinion in *Daubert,* he referred to the "liberal thrust"[74] of the Federal Rules and their "permissive"[75] approach. It is undeniable, though, that the federal courts are generally taking a harder line on expert testimony, including non-scientific evidence. In 2000, the Federal Judicial Center released a study of federal judges' receptivity to expert testimony.[76] In 1991, the Center had asked federal trial judges whether they had admitted all the expert testimony proffered to them in their last trial. In that year 75% of the respondents answered in the affirmative. In 1998 that figure had fallen to 58%. Again in 1991, the Center asked trial judges whether they had ever excluded expert testimony. In that year only 25% answered in the affirmative. In 1998 that number had risen to 41%. If the courts construe the 2000 amendment to Rule 702 as manifesting an intention to tighten the standards for the admissibility of non-scientific expertise, as a general proposition the proponents of expert testimony will find it more difficult to introduce such testimony over objection.

### The Trustworthiness of the Expert's Minor Premise

Expert opinion need not be admitted if the court believes that an opinion is premised on particular facts and it is unreasonable

---

[72]Taylor v. Abernethy, 149 N.C. App. 263, 560 S.E.2d 233 (2002).

[73]Colon ex rel. Molina v. BIC USA, Inc., 199 F. Supp. 2d 53, 81 n.21 (S.D. N.Y. 2001) ("the test for reliability is not whether the expert 'might have done a better job' "); ProtoComm Corp. v. Novell Advanced Services, Inc., 171 F. Supp. 2d 473, 478 (E.D. Pa. 2001); Lentz v. Mason, 32 F. Supp. 2d 733, 746 (D.N.J. 1999) ("For his testimony to be reliable, and, thus, admissible under *Daubert*, [the expert] need not have used the best method available,

only a reasonable one").

[74]Daubert v. Merrell Dow Pharmaceuticals, Inc., 509 U.S. 579, 588, 113 S. Ct. 2786, 125 L. Ed. 2d 469 (1993).

[75]Daubert, 509 U.S. at 589.

[76]Kaye, Bernstein & Mnookin, The New Wigmore: Expert Evidence § 7.4.1, at 331–32 (2d ed. 2010); Shaw, Study Reveals Judges Examine Expert Testimony Thoroughly, L.A. Daily J., Oct. 25, 2000, at 4.

to assume the truth of those facts.[77] If the expert proposes opining about an evaluation of the specific facts in the pending case, there must be a proper basis for the assumptions about those facts. Sections 14 to 16 discuss the potential sources for that information. As we shall see, there are three basic methods in which the expert can gain the minor premise information: She could acquire personal knowledge of the facts; other witnesses could provide admissible information of the facts, and the expert could be asked to hypothetically assume those facts; or the expert can rely on certain types of out-of-court reports about the facts.

*The Application of the Theory or Technique to the Minor Premise*

As previously stated, the expert's reasoning is often syllogistic in nature. Initially, the expert establishes her major premise, that is, the validity of the general theory or technique she contemplates using. Next, the expert describes her minor premise, the case-specific facts she is evaluating. To derive her final opinion, the expert applies the major premise to the minor. This application steps introduces another possibility of error in the expert's reasoning. A misapplication of the theory or technique can result in a flawed conclusion.

At common law, the prevailing view is that proof of proper test procedure or protocol is an essential element of the foundation for the expert's ultimate opinion.[78] There is a strong policy argument supporting that view. The proficiency studies in various

---

[77]Under Fed. R. Evid. 702, 703, and 705, the expert may testify only in terms of opinion subject to cross-examination and may base an opinion upon matters not of record—provisions seemingly indicating an intent that the questions about the basis for an opinion should usually go to the weight, not the admissibility of the opinion. *E.g.*, Singer Co. v. E. I. du Pont de Nemours & Co., 579 F.2d 433 (8th Cir. 1978). But if direct examination, cross-examination, and redirect examination reveal little or no factual basis for an opinion, it at least remains possible to have the opinion stricken as speculation and conjecture. In re Air Crash Disaster at New Orleans, La., 795 F.2d 1230 (5th Cir. 1986) (an award for damages cannot stand when the only evidence to support it is speculative or purely conjectural); Eastern Auto Distributors, Inc. v. Peugeot Motors of America, Inc., 795 F.2d 329 (4th Cir. 1986) (unsupported and speculative assumptions); Toubiana v. Priestly, 402 Mass. 84, 520 N.E.2d 1307 (1988) (a mere guess or conjecture by an expert witness is inadmissible). Or if the opponent is surprised by the calling of the expert to the stand due to opposing counsel's failure to comply with discovery requirements, it is possible the opinion may be excluded. Smith v. Ford Motor Co., 626 F.2d 784 (10th Cir. 1980). Considering Rule 403, expert opinion on marginally relevant subjects is less likely to be admissible when it might prejudice a criminal defendant. U.S. v. Green, 548 F.2d 1261 (6th Cir. 1977) (testimony as to effects of drug on users, in controlled substance prosecution).

[78]Imwinkelried, The Debate in the DNA Cases Over the Foundation for the Admission of Scientific Evidence: The Importance of Human

expert disciplines demonstrate that in many cases in which experts err, the root of the error is faulty test procedure.[79] The expert may be relying on a valid technique and applying the technique to trustworthy information about the case-specific facts, but sloppy test procedure can result in a misapplication of the theory and, hence, an erroneous final conclusion.

Nevertheless, after the Supreme Court's 1993 decision in *Daubert v. Merrell Dow Pharmaceuticals, Inc.*,[80] it was argued that the common law requirement had not survived the enactment of the Federal Rules. In *Daubert*, the Court ruled that the enactment of the Rules had impliedly overturned the *Frye* general acceptance test for the admissibility of scientific testimony. The Court reasoned that together with Rule 702, Rule 402 abolished the general acceptance test.[81] Rule 402 generally provided that relevant evidence is admissible unless it can be excluded under the Constitution, statute, a provision of the Federal Rules themselves, or other court rules adopted pursuant to statutory authority such as the Federal Rules of Civil and Criminal Procedure. The text of the Rules—in particular, the language of Rule 702—did not codify any general acceptance test, and consequently the Rules superseded that test. Citing *Daubert*, some commentators pointed out that the original statutory language also omitted any foundational requirement for proof that the expert correctly applied the theory or technique. These commentators contended that by parity of reasoning, just as Rule 402 overturned *Frye*, it impliedly repealed the common law view demanding a showing of proper test procedure.[82] In the words of one opinion, "[c]areless testing affects the weight of the evidence and not its admissibility . . . ."[83]

However, both at common law and under the Federal Rules, the trend has been to continue to enforce a foundational requirement for a showing that the expert properly applied the theory or technique. In several cases, the courts have recognized the

---

Error as a Cause of Forensic Misanalysis, 69 Wash. U. L.Q. 19, 23 (1991). There are caveats, though, about this generalization. To begin with, there was little case expressly addressing the issue. Moreover, neither courts nor attorneys strictly observed this requirement; attorneys made—and judges accepted—rather minimal showings.

[79]Imwinkelried, The Debate in the DNA Cases Over the Foundation for the Admission of Scientific Evidence at 25–27.

[80]Daubert v. Merrell Dow Pharmaceuticals, Inc., 509 U.S. 579, 113 S. Ct. 2786, 125 L. Ed. 2d 469 (1993).

[81]Daubert, 509 U.S. at 587–88.

[82]Harmon, How Has DNA Evidence Fared? Beauty Is in the Eye of the Beholder, 1 Expert Evidence Rep. (Shep./McG.-Hill) 149 (Feb. 1990).

[83]People v. Farmer, 47 Cal. 3d 888, 254 Cal. Rptr. 508, 765 P.2d 940, 956 (1989).

continuing existence of the foundational requirement.[84] Moreover, effective December 1, 2000, Rule 702 was amended to add a requirement that the proponent show that "the [expert] witness has applied the principles and methods reliably to the facts of the case." The accompanying Advisory Committee Note states that under the amendment, "the trial court must scrutinize not only the principles and methods used by the expert, but also whether those principles and methods have been properly applied to the facts of the case." The note approvingly cites a Third Circuit decision[85] declaring that the judge should exclude the expert testimony when the judge concludes that the expert has "misapplie[d] that methodology." The restyled rules now incorporate this foundational requirement in Rule 702(d).

### The Cross-Examination of Experts

There are not only special rules for an expert's direct examination; peculiar problems can also arise during cross. On cross-examination, opposing counsel may require the expert to reveal facts and data underlying the expert's opinion that were not disclosed on direct.[86] With respect to the facts and data forming the basis of the expert's opinion, the cross-examiner may explore whether, and if so how, the non-existence of any fact or the existence of a contrary fact, would or might affect the opinion. Counsel is permitted to test the expert's reasoning process by inquiring as to what changes of conditions would or might affect his opinion. In conducting that inquiry, the cross-examiner is not limited to facts supported by the record.[87]

However, there are limitations on the cross-examiner's ability

---

[84]People v. Venegas, 18 Cal. 4th 47, 74 Cal. Rptr. 2d 262, 954 P.2d 525 (1998); State v. Schwartz, 447 N.W.2d 422 (Minn. 1989); People v. Castro, 144 Misc. 2d 956, 545 N.Y.S.2d 985 (Sup 1989).

[85]In re Paoli R.R. Yard PCB Litigation, 35 F.3d 717, 745 (3d Cir. 1994).

[86]Former Fed. R. Evid. 705 provided: "The expert may testify in terms of opinion or inference and give reasons therefor without prior disclosure of the underlying facts or data, unless the court requires otherwise. The expert may in any event be required to disclose the underlying facts or data on cross-examination."

Effective December 1, 2011, restyled Fed. R. Evid. 705 reads: "Unless the court orders otherwise, an expert may state an opinion—and give the reasons for it—without first testifying to the underlying facts or data. But the expert may be required to disclose those facts or data on cross-examination."

[87]Bryan v. John Bean Division of FMC Corp., 566 F.2d 541, 545 (5th Cir. 1978) ("Since rule 705 shifts to the cross-examiner the burden of eliciting the bases of an expert witness' opinion, otherwise hearsay evidence that reveals the underlying sources of the expert's opinion should be as permissible on cross-examination as on direct. Moreover, otherwise hearsay evidence disclosing the basis of an expert witness' opinion should be admissible to impeach if strictly limited to that purpose by instructions and if, in the discretion of the judge, the impeach-

to use passages in published treatises and articles to attack the theory or technique underlying the expert's opinion. An expert witness may, of course, be confronted with a learned treatise, admissible as substantive evidence under the hearsay exception set out in Fed. R. Evid. 803(18).[88] As § 321 notes, at common law only a few jurisdictions recognized a learned treatise hearsay exception; but by virtue of the widespread adoption of state provisions patterned after Rule 803(18), the recognition of the exception is now the majority view. Many jurisdictions, though, go farther and allow the cross-examiner to use texts and articles for impeachment even when the publication does not fall within the scope of the hearsay exception. Some jurisdictions do so by statute.[89] Others allow the practice by case law.[90] Depending on the jurisdiction, the cross-examiner may confront the expert with a contrary passage in a publication: the expert relied on, the

---

ing evidence has sufficient guarantee of reliability that the prophylactic effect of the hearsay rule is not necessary to ensure trustworthiness."); State v. Goree, 762 S.W.2d 20, 23 (Mo. 1988) ("Normally, an expert witness may be cross-examined regarding facts not in evidence to test his qualifications, skills, credibility, or to test the validity and weight of his opinion."). Not all courts agree. Gordon v. St. Mary's Hosp., 769 S.W.2d 151, 156 (Mo. Ct. App. W.D. 1989) ("It is a matter of fundamental law that a hypothetical question must be based on facts supported by the evidence and assumptions in the question may not be outside the evidence, or reasonable inferences therefrom.").

[88]Former Fed. R. Evid. 803(18) provided:

> To the extent called to the attention of an expert witness upon cross-examination or relied upon by the expert witness in direct examination, statements contained in published treatises, periodicals, or pamphlets on a subject of history, medicine, or other science or art, established as a reliable authority by the testimony or admission of the witness or by other expert testimony or by judicial notice. If admitted, the statements may be read into evidence but may not be received as exhibits.

Effective December 1, 2011, restyled Fed. R. Evid. 803(18) reads:

> A statement contained in a treatise, periodical, or pamphlet if:
>
> (A) the statement is called to the attention of an expert witness on cross-examination or relied on by the expert on direct examination; and
>
> (B) the publication is established as a reliable authority by the expert's admission or testimony, by another expert's testimony, or by judicial notice.
>
> If admitted, the statement may be read into evidence but not received as an exhibit.

[89]Cal. Evid. Code § 721; Mich. Rules of Evidence 707. The Michigan Rule reads:

> To the extent called to the attention of an expert witness upon cross-examination, statements contained in published treatises, periodicals, or pamphlets on a subject of history, medicine, or other science or art, established as a reliable authority by the testimony or admission of the witness or by other expert testimony or by judicial notice, are admissible for impeachment purposes only. If admitted, the statements may be read into evidence but may not be received as exhibits.

McCarty v. Sisters of Mercy Health Corp., 176 Mich. App. 593, 440 N.W.2d 417, 418–20 (1989). These statutes deal with the use of the texts on a credibility theory of impeachment rather than as substantive evidence. Hence, on request, under a statute

expert consulted, the expert recognizes as authoritative, or is judicially noticeable as a standard authority in the field or which the cross-examiner has shown to be authoritative.[91] When the publication is used for the limited purpose of impeachment, it is admitted only to attack the quality of the expert's reasoning,[92] not as substantive evidence.[93] On request, the trial judge should give the jury a limiting instruction to that effect.

Cross-examination of an expert directed at establishing bias through financial interest is also quite common. The cross-examiner may seek to establish (1) financial interest in the instant case by reason of compensation for services, including services performed which enabled him to testify, (2) continued employment by a party, or (3) the fact of prior testimony for the same party or the same attorney. The common law authorities disagree over the propriety of cross-examination about such subjects as the amount of previous compensation from the same party, the percentage of the witness's total income generated by testifying on behalf of a party or a category of party, and the mere fact of prior testimony on behalf of other similarly situated persons or entities. However, financial interest can have a powerful biasing effect on an expert's testimony. Consequently, the better view is that such inquiries are permissible.[94]

The precise scope of cross-examination of expert witnesses rests

---

such as Federal Rule 105 the judge would be obliged to give the jury a limiting instruction as to the evidentiary status of the text.

[90]Habush, Cross—Examination of Non—Medical Experts 20–9–10 (1981); Hirsch, Morris & Moritz, Handbook of Legal Medicine 274 (5th ed. 1979).

[91]California Evidence Code § 721(b) allows the cross-examiner to employ the publication if:
  (1) The witness has referred to, considered, or relied upon such publication in arriving at or forming his or her opinion;
  (2) The publication has been admitted in evidence; [or]
  (3) The publication has been established as a reliable authority by the testimony or admission of the witness or by other expert testimony or by judicial notice.

[92]Cal. Law Revision Comm'n Comment, Cal. Evid. Code § 721. Since this practice permits resort to the text for the limited purpose of impeach-

ment rather than as substantive evidence, the text must be used for a purpose other than showing the truth of the assertions in the text. For example, the cross-examiner might utilize the test to show that: The expert carelessly misapplied the text he or she supposedly relied on; the expert prematurely rejected without good reason a contrary passage in a text he or she recognizes as authoritative; or the expert conducted incomplete research and neglected to find a contrary passage in an authoritative text. Imwinkelried, Rationalization and Limitation: The Use of Learned Treatises to Impeach Opposing Expert Witnesses, 36 Vt. L. Rev. 63, 70–77 (2011).

[93]Mich. R. Evid. 707 ("for impeachment purposes only").

[94]Sears v. Rutishauser, 102 Ill. 2d 402, 80 Ill. Dec. 758, 466 N.E.2d 210 (1984) (reversible error to preclude defense attorney from questioning plaintiff's medical expert as to number

in the trial judge's discretion. However, the judge should give the cross-examiner latitude, especially with respect to experts voicing opinions about matters clearly exceeding the common knowledge and experience of laymen.[95] In those situations, there is the greatest risk that the jurors will overvalue the direct testimony. Probing cross-examination can help reduce that risk.

## §14   Grounds for expert opinion: Hypothetical questions[1]

The traditional view has been that an expert may rest an opinion on two different types of bases: his firsthand knowledge of the facts, or facts shown by evidence already in the record at the time he states his opinion.[2] In the case of the second type of basis, the expert can learn the facts by sitting in court and listening to the trial testimony if the judge has exempted the expert from any sequestration order.[3] Alternatively, the facts may be furnished to the expert by including them in a hypothetical question. A hypothetical question asks the expert to assume their truth and then requests an opinion based on them:

Q Doctor, please assume facts *A, B,* and *C.* Assuming those facts, can you form an opinion about my client's diagnosis to a reasonable degree of medical probability?
Q What is that opinion?

---

of referrals received from plaintiff's lawyer and the financial benefits derived from them); Ford & Holmes, Exposure of Doctors' Venal Testimony, 1965 Trial Law. Guide 75, 79; Graham, Impeaching the Professional Expert Witness by a Showing of Financial Interest, 53 Ind. L.J. 35 (1977).

[95]*E.g.*, U.S. v. Preciado-Gomez, 529 F.2d 935, 942 (9th Cir. 1976) ("[E]xistence of bias or prejudice of one who has expressed an expert opinion can always be examined into on cross-examination of such expert; as well as the facts upon which his expert opinion was based."); Polk v. Ford Motor Co., 529 F.2d 259, 271 (8th Cir. 1976) ("[T]he weakness in the underpinnings of [expert's] opinions may be developed upon cross-examination and such weakness goes to the weight and credibility of the testimony."); Vermont Food Industries, Inc. v. Ralston Purina Co., 514 F.2d 456, 463 (2d Cir. 1975) ("The sufficiency of the [expert's] assumptions as well as the soundness of the opinion can be tested on cross-examination.").

**[Section 14]**

[1]2 Wigmore, Evidence §§ 672–86 (Chadbourn rev. 1979); 4 Weinstein's Federal Evidence Ch. 703 (rev. 2011); West's Key Number Digest, Criminal Law ☞482 to 489, West's Key Number Digest, Evidence ☞547 to 557; McElhaney, Expert Witnesses and the Federal Rules of Evidence, 28 Mercer L. Rev. 463 (1977).

[2]*See* 2 Wigmore, Evidence § 676 (Chadbourn rev. 1979). It is also possible to combine these two sources. If the witness had personal knowledge of some relevant facts, she can obviously supply admissible evidence of those facts; and it therefore be permissible to include those facts as well as facts testified to by other witnesses in a hypothetical question.

[3]*See* 2 Wigmore, Evidence § 681 (Chadbourn rev. 1979); Right of expert to give an opinion based on testimony of other witnesses not incorporated in a hypothetical question, 82 A.L.R. 1460; Fed. R. Evid. 615.

Although American litigators have posed hypothetical questions to experts for decades, the hypothetical question technique has been sharply criticized.[4] In response to the criticisms, these methods have been reformed in a growing number of jurisdictions, including those adopting the Federal and Revised Uniform Rules of Evidence. There have been two major changes. First, on direct examination an expert may state an opinion and the theoretical "reasons" for the opinion without prior disclosure of the underlying data or facts. This change eliminates the need for a lengthy statement of the underlying facts on direct examination. This change gives the cross-examiner the choice whether to expose the underlying data.[5] Second, the expert need not base her opinion on either firsthand knowledge or an hypothesis; in certain circumstances, otherwise inadmissible out-of-court reports are now considered proper grounds for the expert's opinion.[6] This change brings the legal practice more in line with the practice of experts outside the courtroom, since in their own practice they often rely on trustworthy out-of-court reports. At the same time,

---

[4]One of the major criticisms has been that attorneys use the hypothesis as a pretext for previewing their argument:

> To illustrate the lengths to which the hypothetical question has gone, I may mention a contested will case . . . tried in New York, in which a hypothetical question was propounded to three experts on each side. The . . . questions together consisted of about 36,000 words, that is, about 36 columns of newspaper print, and occupied more than four hours in reading.

Wellman, The Art of Cross—Examination 109 (4th ed. 1936).

[5]Former Fed. R. Evid. 705 provided: "The expert may testify in terms of opinions or inference and give reasons therefor without prior disclosure of the underlying facts or data, unless the court requires otherwise. The expert may in any event be required to disclose the underlying facts or data on cross-examination." Unif. R. Evid. 705 is identical in content. Effective December 1, 2011, restyled Fed. R. Evid. 705 reads: "Unless the court orders otherwise, an expert may state an opinion—and give the reasons for it—without first testifying to the underlying facts or data. But the expert may be required to disclose those facts or data on cross-examination." See also Cal. Evid. Code § 802; Kan. Stat. Ann. 60-456, 60-457; N.J.R.E. 705; N.Y. C.P.L.R. 4515.

[6]Former Fed. R. Evid. 703 provided:

> The facts or data in the particular case upon which an expert bases an opinion or inference may be those perceived by or made known to the expert at or before the hearing. If of a type reasonably relied upon by experts in the particular field in forming opinions or inferences upon the subject, the facts or data need not be admissible in evidence.

Unif. R. Evid. 703 is identical in content. Effective December 1, 2011, restyled Fed. R. Evid. 703 reads:

> An expert may base an opinion on facts or data in the case that the expert has been made aware of or personally observed. If experts in the particular field would rely on those kinds of facts or data in forming an opinion on the subject, they need not be admissible for the opinion to be admitted. But if the facts or data would otherwise be inadmissible, the proponent of the opinion may disclose them to the jury only if their probative value in helping the jury evaluate the opinion substantially outweighs their prejudicial effect.

See also Cal. Evid. Code §§ 801(b), 804.

in these more liberal jurisdictions a trial attorney may still employ the traditional methods of eliciting expert opinion, including the hypothetical question.[7] The use of the hypothetical question is not only permissible at contemporary common law; it is still popular and in widespread use. Since the proponent can specify the content of the hypothesis, the hypothetical question gives the proponent maximum control; and if the proponent keeps the hypothesis short and sweet, the jury will clearly understand the factual basis of the expert's opinion. The traditional views mentioned above are considered in this section while §§ 15 and 16 discuss the more modern liberal rule.

Of course, if an expert witness has firsthand knowledge of material facts, he may describe what he has observed and base his inferences on those facts under both traditional views and the Federal Rules of Evidence.[8] When the expert has no personal knowledge of the facts, the orthodox common law method of securing the benefit of the expert's skill is to ask the expert to assume certain facts and then, on the basis of this hypothesis, to state an opinion or inference.[9] These questions are known as hypothetical questions. In the judge's discretion, hypothetical questions are still permissible under the Federal Rules of Evidence and other liberal rules.[10]

In most jurisdictions committed to the more traditional views, the judge has discretion to allow an expert witness to remain in court during testimony by other witnesses. Later when the expert is called as a witness, the counsel can simplify a hypothetical question by merely instructing the witness to assume the truth of the previous testimony the witness has heard, or some specified part of it.[11] This practice is permissible under the Federal Rules

---

[7]See notes 5–6.

[8]*See* Fed. R. Evid. 703, Advisory Committee Note. The questions need not be couched in hypothetical form. Penn Fruit Co. v. Clark, 256 Md. 135, 259 A.2d 512 (1969); State v. Franks, 300 N.C. 1, 265 S.E.2d 177 (1980). Before the expert testifies to the inferences on this basis, a few courts require that the expert specify the basis of the opinion. See dictum in Cogdill v. North Carolina State Highway Commission, 279 N.C. 313, 182 S.E.2d 373 (1971). Substantial authority holds that data need not be specified before the statement of opinion. Fed. R. Evid. and Unif. R. Evid. 705; Com. v. Johnson, 188 Mass. 382, 74 N.E.

939, 940 (1905) (dictum). The judge should have a broad discretion. Fed. R. Evid. 705 and Unif. R. Evid. 705 (there need not be prior disclosure unless "the court requires otherwise").

[9]2 Wigmore, Evidence § 676 (Chadbourn rev. 1979).

[10]No authority requiring the use of a hypothetical question in any situation has been discovered. Depending upon the opportunity of a criminal defendant case to obtain adequate discovery, a hypothetical question of a prosecution expert might be required.

[11]*See* 2 Wigmore, Evidence § 681 (Chadbourn rev. 1979); Right of expert to give an opinion based on testimony of other witnesses not incorporated in

of Evidence and other contemporary state rules.[12] The practice has some advantages and some limitations. The assumed facts must be clear to the jury and not conflicting; otherwise, the witness's answer will not assist the jury. A question asking the witness to assume the truth of one previous witness's testimony usually meets these requirements.[13] However, as the range of assumption widens to cover the testimony of several witnesses[14] or all the testimony for one side,[15] the risk of confusing the jury increases. When a hypothetical question covers all the testimony in the case, the question can be approved only if the testimony on the issue relating to the question is consistent and simple enough for the jury to recall its basic outlines.[16]

---

a hypothetical question, 82 A.L.R. 1460.

[12]Fed. R. Evid. 703 & Unif. R. Evid. 703. See notes 5 to 6 supra.

[13]Bosse v. Ideco Division of Dresser Industries, Inc., 412 F.2d 567 (10th Cir. 1969).

Fed. R. Evid. 701 to 705 and Unif. R. Evid. 701 to 705 do not specify requirements for hypothetical questions, but the two requirements mentioned in the text follow from the statutory mandate that opinions should be helpful to the trier of fact. *See* 2 Wigmore, Evidence § 681 (Chadbourn rev. 1979); Right of expert to give an opinion based on testimony of other witnesses not incorporated in a hypothetical question, 82 A.L.R. 1460.

[14]Damm v. State, 128 Md. 665, 97 A. 645 (1916) (abortion: doctor's opinion based on evidence of attending and examining doctors, approved); Cornell v. State, 104 Wis. 527, 80 N.W. 745 (1899) (murder: defense, insanity: doctor's opinion based on 40 or 50 pages of testimony of other witnesses, approved on ground testimony not conflicting, and whether too voluminous and complicated was in trial judge's discretion).

[15]State v. Eggleston, 161 Wash. 486, 297 P. 162 (1931) (murder: defense, insanity: "assuming all of the testimony given by the defendant's witnesses is true . . . what is your opinion as to whether the defendant was sane . . .?" approved).

[16]Rhea v. M-K Grocer Co., 236 Ark. 615, 370 S.W.2d 33 (1963); Shouse, Doolittle & Morelock v. Consolidated Flour Mills Co., 132 Kan. 108, 294 P. 657 (1931) (opinion as to value of legal services, from all the testimony, disapproved, testimony conflicting; discussing the practice). *But compare* State v. Carroll, 52 Wyo. 29, 69 P.2d 542, 550–552 (1937) suggesting that more consideration should be given to the fact that the cross-examiner has an opportunity to clear up any ambiguity in the hypothesis flowing from the conflict in the testimony.

A question based on prior testimony might include the inference of a prior expert witness. If it is apparent that the question includes only prior expert's descriptions and statements of facts and not their inference or conclusions, the question is not objectionable. Cody v. Toller Drug Co., 232 Iowa 475, 5 N.W.2d 824 (1942) (question which asked expert witness to assume truth of testimony of previous witness, a chemist, as to result of tests conducted by that witness, was proper); Sepich v. Department of Labor and Industries, 75 Wash. 2d 312, 450 P.2d 940 (1969). In some cases, the phrasing of the questions leaves it unclear whether the testimony is actually based upon other opinion testimony. Dennis v. Prisock, 221 So. 2d 706 (Miss. 1969) ("she was being treated by doctors in Jackson and I had correspondence with doctors in Jackson" did not indicate the witness was relying on the opinions of others).

At common law, before posing a hypothetical question, the proponent must present admissible, independent evidence of every fact included in the hypothesis.[17] However, that requirement for hypothetical questions is no longer in effect in jurisdictions following the Federal Rules of Evidence.[18] The traditional requirement rests on the notion that if the opinion is premised on a fact which the jury, for lack of evidence, cannot find to be true, the jurors may not use the opinion as the basis for a finding. There must be admissible evidence supporting each assumed fact. Direct testimony is not required. It suffices if the fact is fairly inferable from the circumstances proved.[19] Moreover, at

---

In several cases it has been held that it is improper to ask the witness to assume the truth of testimony including prior opinions. Testimony of expert predicated in whole or in part upon opinions, inferences, or conclusions of others, 98 A.L.R. 1109. The second opinion may be but an academic echo. At least the judge should have discretion to draw the shadowy line between "fact" and "opinion" in this area. However, under Fed. R. Evid. 703 and Unif. R. Evid. 703, an expert may rely on facts or data reasonably relied upon by experts in the particular field, and under Rule 705 he need not even relate such matters before stating an opinion. By analogy, a case can be made that the traditional rule barring opinion based upon opinion in hypothetical questions is inapplicable if the expert indicates that the pertinent opinion is of a type relied on in the particular field, even when there is no such indication until cross-examination.

[17]Donaldson v. Buck, 333 So. 2d 786 (Ala. 1976); Nisbet v. Medaglia, 356 Mass. 580, 254 N.E.2d 782 (1970); Barnett v. State Workmen's Compensation Com'r, 153 W. Va. 796, 172 S.E.2d 698 (1970).

[18]It could be argued that material which may be relied upon by the expert under Fed. R. Evid. 703 should be includable in a hypothetical question if such material may be relied on in an opinion without the use of a hypothetical question under Rule 705. Neither Rule 703 nor Rule 705 expressly requires that an hypothesis be based

on admissible evidence. Furthermore, it has been urged that because an expert may state his opinion without specifying the elements of the hypothesis that the opinion rests on. Some judges think that these notions are impractical; they rule that so long as a hypothetical question is used, the proponent must indicate that such a question must be based on admissible evidence in the record. Logsdon v. Baker, 517 F.2d 174 (D.C. Cir. 1975); Iconco v. Jensen Const. Co., 622 F.2d 1291 (8th Cir. 1980). This position finds support in the California Law Revision Commission comment to California Evidence Code § 802:

[I]n some cases, a witness is required to [state the basis for his opinion on direct examination] in order to show that his opinion is applicable to the action before the court. Under existing law, where a witness testifies in the form of an opinion not based upon his personal observation, the assumed facts upon which his opinion is based must be stated . . . in order to permit the trier of fact to determine the applicability of the opinion in light of the existence or nonexistence of such facts. Evidence Code Section 802 will not affect the rule set forth in these cases, for it based essentially on the requirement that all evidence must be shown to be applicable—or relevant—to the action.

[19]State for Use and Benefit of Richardson v. Edgeworth, 214 So. 2d 579 (Miss. 1968); Farmers Co-op Exchange of Weatherford v. Krewall, 1969 OK 27, 450 P.2d 506 (Okla.

common law the supporting evidence need not have been already adduced if the interrogating counsel assures the judge that it will be forthcoming.[20]

Further, it is no objection that the supporting evidence is controverted.[21] The proponent is entitled to put his side of the case to the witness as the basis for the witness's opinion. However, there is a danger that by omitting some critical facts, the proponent may present an unfair, slanted version of the facts to the expert and that the jury may give undue weight to the opinion without considering its faulty basis. For instance, the proponent might elicit an unreliable estimate of a car's speed from an accident reconstruction expert if the proponent's hypothesis omitted any mention of undisputed evidence about the length of the skidmarks left by the car. Are there any safeguards against this danger? Some decisions require that all facts material to the question be mentioned in the hypothesis.[22] However, this rigid requirement is undesirable; it multiplies disputes over the sufficiency of the hypothesis and can cause counsel, out of excess of caution, to propound lengthy questions

---

1969); Friedman v. General Motors Corp., 411 F.2d 533 (3d Cir.1969); West's Key Number Digest, Evidence ☞553(3).

[20]Gibson v. Healy Bros. & Co., 109 Ill. App. 2d 342, 248 N.E.2d 771 (1st Dist. 1969) (practice is to be discouraged but is within the court's sound discretion). The rule was applied to cross-examination in Barretto v. Akau, 51 Haw. 383, 51 Haw. 461, 463 P.2d 917 (1969) (cross-examination hypothetical to demonstrate alternative theories or contest a substantive element in the case).

In most jurisdictions, the trial judge retains this common law discretion. For example, the judge has such discretion in any state with a statute tracking Federal Rule of Evidence 611. However, in some jurisdictions, the judge lacks this discretion. For example, the California Law Revision Commission Comment to Evidence Code § 802 indicates that the proponent must set out the hypothesis before eliciting the opinion based on the hypothesis.

[21]Fidelity & Cas. Co. of New York v. McKay, 73 F.2d 828 (C.C.A. 5th Cir.

1934) (jury should be instructed to disregard answer if they find facts are untrue); Louisville & N. R. Co. v. Self, 45 Ala. App. 530, 233 So. 2d 90 (Civ. App. 1970); Rasmussen v. Thilges, 174 N.W.2d 384 (Iowa 1970); Martin v. Frear, 184 Neb. 266, 167 N.W.2d 69 (1969) (facts conforming to examiner's theory may be included even if they are controverted); Kresha Const. Co. v. Kresha, 184 Neb. 188, 166 N.W.2d 589 (1969).

[22]Stumpf v. State Farm Mut. Auto. Ins. Co., 252 Md. 696, 251 A.2d 362 (1969) (question should contain a fair summary of the material facts in evidence essential to formulating a rational opinion); Ames & Webb, Inc. v. Commercial Laundry Co., 204 Va. 616, 133 S.E.2d 547 (1963) (question must embody all material facts which evidence tends to prove); West's Key Number Digest, Evidence ☞553(2).

Various courts have also held that undisputed material facts should not be ignored. Jackson v. Nelson, 382 F.2d 1016 (10th Cir. 1967); Christianson v. City of Chicago Heights, 103 Ill. App. 2d 315, 243 N.E.2d 677 (1st Dist. 1968).

that are tedious and confusing to the jury.[23] The sounder, prevailing view is that the hypothesis need not include all material facts.[24] However, even under the prevailing view, there are safeguards. One safeguard is the cross-examiner's rights; on cross-examination the adversary may supply omitted facts and ask the expert if those additional facts would modify his opinion or at least be relevant.[25] A further safeguard is the judge's authority; if she deems the question unfair, the trial judge may require that the questioner reword the hypothesis to supply an adequate basis.[26]

Section 12 of this chapter deals with the ultimate issue

---

[23]*E.g.,* Treadwell v. Nickel, 194 Cal. 243, 228 P. 25, 35 (1924) referring to a question "contained in some 83 pages of typewritten transcript, and an objection involved in 14 pages more of the record."

[24]U.S. v. Aspinwall, 96 F.2d 867 (C.C.A. 9th Cir. 1938); Virginia Beach Bus Line v. Campbell, 73 F.2d 97 (C.C.A. 4th Cir. 1934) (reviewing prior decisions); Napier v. Greenzweig, 256 F. 196 (C.C.A. 2d Cir. 1919); Dahlberg v. Ogle, 268 Ind. 30, 373 N.E.2d 159 (1978); Pickett v. Kyger, 151 Mont. 87, 439 P.2d 57 (1968); Gordon v. State Farm Life Ins. Co., 415 Pa. 256, 203 A.2d 320 (1964).

[25]See authorities cited in note 24 supra. *See also* Cunningham v. Gans, 507 F.2d 496, 501 (2d Cir. 1974) ("Then defense counsel should attack the expert's testimony by showing his conclusion would be different if certain facts were also assumed or if certain assumed facts were changed rather than by voicing picky objections to complicated hypothetical questions. Such a procedure has been advocated by many authorities. *See, e.g.,* Proposed Federal Rule of Evidence 705 and advisory committee's note; C. McCormick, Evidence § 78 (1972)."); People v. Fields, 170 Ill. App. 3d 1, 120 Ill. Dec. 285, 523 N.E.2d 1196, 1205 (1st Dist. 1988) ("In addition, an expert may be cross-examined for the purpose of explaining, modifying, or discrediting the expert's testimony . . . . An expert may be cross-examined to ascertain what factors were taken into account and what ones disregarded in

arriving at a conclusion, as well as to bring out any other relevant facts, and any pertinent fact, whether or not in evidence, may be assumed in a hypothetical question to test a witness's accuracy or skill. . . . The adversary may on cross-examination supply omitted facts and ask the expert if the expert's opinion would be modified by them.").

Many cross-examiners inquire only whether the new fact would be relevant to the analysis. They fear that a hostile, intelligent expert will refuse to concede that the new fact would "alter," "change," or "modify" the expert's opinion.

[26]See authorities cited in note 24 supra. For example, as the text suggests, the trial judge might require an accident reconstruction expert opining about a vehicle's speed to factor into his or her analysis evidence as to the length of the skidmarks left by the vehicle. *See also* Minneapolis, St. P. & S. S. M. R. Co. v. Metal-Matic, Inc., 323 F.2d 903, 910 (8th Cir. 1963) ("[T]rial court may . . . require counsel to supply additional facts if the question is framed inadequately. . . ."). Another view requires the phrasing of a question to incorporate some reasonable or supportable factual theory based upon the facts of record. *See* Vermont Food Industries, Inc. v. Ralston Purina Co., 514 F.2d 456 (2d Cir. 1975) ("any combination of the facts within the tendency of the evidence"; the case was not decided under the Fed. R. Evid.).

prohibition. That section notes that while the original version of Rule 704 purported to abolish the prohibition, to a degree the prohibition was resurrected when Congress amended the statute to add Rule 704(b). The question arises whether a direct examiner can in effect circumvent Rule 704(b) by using a hypothetical question. Suppose, for example, that the direct examiner crafts an hypothesis that mirrors the facts in the case.[27] After instructing the witness to assume the truth of the hypothesis, may the direct examiner elicit an ultimate opinion otherwise barred by Rule 704(b)? Admittedly, it is sometimes difficult to determine whether the opinion solicited by the question is one barred by Rule 704(b).[28] However, assuming that the judge decides that the opinion coincides with such a question, the trial judge should not permit the examiner to avoid Rule 704(b) by the simple expedient of resorting to a hypothetical question.[29]

## § 15   Expert's opinion based on reports of others and inadmissible or unadmitted data and facts[1]

As we have seen, at common law an expert could base an opinion either on personally known facts or facts stated in an hypothesis. However, those two bases do not exhaust the possibilities. The expert could also attempt to rest an opinion on third party out-of-court reports. However, the former majority view was that a question is improper if it calls for the witness's opinion on the basis of reports that are inadmissible in evidence under the hearsay rule.[2] The rationale for this view was that as a matter of logic, the jury could not accept the opinion based on the facts if the only evidence of the facts is inadmissible. This view applied even when the witness was asked to give an opinion, not merely on the basis of reports of this kind, but on those matters

---

[27]Saltzburg, Opinions on Intent: Mirroring Facts of the Case, 13 Crim. Just. 21 (Fall 1998).

[28]*E.g.*, U.S. v. Toms, 136 F.3d 176 (D.C. Cir. 1998); U.S. v. Boyd, 55 F.3d 667 (D.C. Cir. 1995); U.S. v. Mitchell, 996 F.2d 419 (D.C. Cir. 1993).

[29]Saltzburg, Opinion on Intent: Mirroring Facts of the Case, 13 Crim. Just. 21 (Fall 1998).

**[Section 15]**

[1]See § 324.3, infra.

[2]Davies v. Carter Carburetor, Division ACF Industries, Inc., 429

S.W.2d 738 (Mo. 1968) (opinion based on patient's history stated to physician-expert); Kraner v. Coastal Tank Lines, Inc., 26 Ohio St. 2d 59, 55 Ohio Op. 2d 68, 269 N.E.2d 43 (1971); Sykes v. Norfolk & W. Ry. Co., 200 Va. 559, 106 S.E.2d 746 (1959) (excluding opinion based on a study of figures furnished by others and not under expert's supervision or on subject matter observed by the expert, a railroad crossing); West's Key Number Digest, Criminal Law ⊨486; West's Key Number Digest, Evidence ⊨555; 4 Weinstein's Federal Evidence § 703.04 (rev. 2011).

supplemented by the witness's own observation.[3] However, today there has been a strong case law trend toward a contrary view.[4]

---

[3]Wild v. Bass, 252 Miss. 615, 173 So. 2d 647 (1965) (doctor may not base his opinion in part upon observation and in part upon patient's history related by patient's mother); Vick v. Cochran, 316 So. 2d 242 (Miss. 1975); West's Key Number Digest, Criminal Law ☜486; West's Key Number Digest, Evidence ☜555.

The status of basis statements, relied upon for expert opinions, as hearsay exceptions under the Federal Rules is discussed in § 324.3 infra.

[4]Trinity Universal Ins. Co. v. Town of Speedway, 137 Ind. App. 510, 210 N.E.2d 95 (1965) (estimate of cost of repair based in part upon reports of others; "an expert is competent to judge the reliability of statements made to him by other persons and taking these statements made to him by other persons together with his own first hand observations comprises a sufficient basis for a direct examination of his own professional opinion as to the cost of repairing the street."); Schooler v. State, 175 S.W.2d 664 (Tex. Civ. App. El Paso 1943) (geologist testified to opinion as to prospects for oil in a certain region, based on his own inspection and geological reports); Sutherland v. McGregor, 383 S.W.2d 248 (Tex. Civ. App. Fort Worth 1964) (opinion of petroleum engineer admissible though based partly on reports made by others). See Moore v. Cataldo, 356 Mass. 325, 249 N.E.2d 578 (1969) (dictum taking view that under Finnegan v. Fall River Gasworks Co., 159 Mass. 311, 34 N.E. 523 (1893), opinion testimony might rest in part on hearsay). Other decisions indicate a broader conclusion. Buckler v. Com., 541 S.W.2d 935 (Ky. 1976) (an expert may properly express an opinion "based upon information supplied by third parties which is not in evidence, but upon which the expert customarily relies in the practice of his profession"). Whether opinion can rest partially on hearsay may depend in part on the character of the subject matter of the opinion and the nature of the hearsay involved. The question of whether opinion may be based in part upon information from others (that is not in evidence) has arisen most often in connection with the testimony of medical experts and property valuation experts. Most courts permit the opinion of the medical expert who has treated the patient whose condition is the subject of his opinion, although the opinion is based in part upon history given by the patient. See Admissibility of opinion of medical expert as affected by his having heard the person in question give the history of his case, 51 A.L.R.2d 1051. As to the admissibility of the patient's history as substantive evidence, see §§ 277 to 278, infra. Some courts include within this rule information received from persons in the medical profession (or connected with it). See Gray v. Bird, 380 S.W.2d 908 (Tex. Civ. App. Tyler 1964) (psychiatrist's opinion). Some cases permit the treating medical expert to use in part a history furnished by a relative of the patient under particular circumstances. See Miller v. Watts, 436 S.W.2d 515 (Ky. 1969) (history furnished by mother of infant patient). In other jurisdictions the above extensions have not been accepted. E.g., Seawell v. Brame, 258 N.C. 666, 129 S.E.2d 283 (1963).

On the other hand, some courts refuse to permit opinion of so-called forensic medical experts, e.g., experts consulted only to prepare for trial, based in part on medical history related by the person examined or information received from third persons. See Brown v. Blauvelt, 152 Conn. 272, 205 A.2d 773 (1964); Briney v. Williams, 143 Ind. App. 691, 242 N.E.2d 132 (1968) (opinion based on "subjective symptoms" and statements of person who sought examination; otherwise patient's self-serving statements would be submitted to jury and bolstered by the expert opinion);

(There is also a related, incipient trend in the cases toward the view that opinions based on out-of-court reports are less objectionable when they concern subjects that have an indirect relation to the fact issues in the case, rather than directly concerning the central facts in issue.)[5]

The case law trend culminated in the broader modern view codified in Federal Rule of Evidence 703, adopted in many state jurisdictions. Under Rules 703 and 705, on direct examination an expert may give an opinion based on facts and data, including technically inadmissible reports, if the reports or other data are "of a type reasonably relied upon by experts in the particular field in forming opinions or inferences upon the subject."[6] These

---

Goodrich v. Tinker, 437 S.W.2d 882 (Tex. Civ. App. El Paso 1969) (patient's statements and subjective symptoms); Admissibility of opinion of medical expert as affected by his having heard the person in question give the history of his case, 51 A.L.R.2d 1051. Whether a medical expert is one in this latter category is sometimes a difficult problem and may not depend entirely upon whether treatment was prescribed. *See* Goodrich v. Tinker, 437 S.W.2d 882 (Tex. Civ. App. El Paso 1969). Some cases have attached weight to the time at which the expert was consulted. Admissibility of opinion of medical expert as affected by his having heard the person in question give the history of his case, 51 A.L.R.2d 1051, 1078.

For the wide variety of former views, see Comment, 35 So. Calif. L. Rev. 193 (1962); Rheingold, The Basis of Medical Testimony, 15 Vand. L. Rev. 473 (1962). There is a pronounced trend in case law to permit opinion of valuation experts based in part on personal knowledge and in part on information received from others. *See* Admissibility of testimony of expert, as to basis of his opinion, to matters otherwise excludible as hearsay—state cases, 89 A.L.R.4th 456. There is a similar trend in case law concerning expert opinion of mental states based on reports of others. *See* Admissibility on issue of sanity of expert opinion based partly on medical, psychological, or hospital reports, 55 A.L.R.3d 551.

The above trends are also evident in various states in which Fed. R. Evid. 703 has since been adopted. *See also* State v. Duell, 175 W. Va. 233, 332 S.E.2d 246 (1985) (expert witness on insanity should have been permitted to rely upon defendant's interview with another doctor).

[5]Town of Framingham v. Department of Public Utilities, 355 Mass. 138, 244 N.E.2d 281 (1969) (court approved expert's evaluation of studies on the effect of electromagnetic fields on human and animal systems).

[6]Former Fed. R. Evid. 703 provided:

The facts or data in the particular case upon which an expert bases an opinion or inference may be those perceived by or made known to the expert at or before the hearing. If of a type reasonably relied upon by experts in the particular field in forming opinions or inferences upon the subject, the facts or data need not be admissible in evidence.

Effective December 1, 2011, restyled Fed. R. Evid. 703 reads in pertinent part:

An expert may base an opinion on facts or data in the case that the expert has been made aware of or personally observed. If experts in the particular field would reasonably rely on those kinds of facts or data in forming an opinion on the subject, they need not be admissible for the opinion to be admitted.

*See generally* 5 Graham, Handbook of Federal Evidence § 703.1 (7th ed.

reports are arguably put to a nonhearsay use.[7] Rather than receiving the reports as substantive evidence, the judge admits the testimony about the reports for the limited purpose of show-ing the basis of the expert's opinion.[8] Irrespective of the truth of the reports, a consideration of the reports can assist the trier to assess the caliber of the expert's reasoning. The focus is on the effect of the report on the expert's state of mind; the fact that the expert has received the report indicates that his opinion is better grounded; the jury may consider the reports in the process of evaluating the quality of the expert's reasoning: Are the stated bases adequate to support the opinion? Did the expert commit any obvious logical fallacies in reasoning about the bases? Ac-cording to the Advisory Committee Note accompanying Rule 703, the primary rationale for permitting the expert to rely on such reports is that in the real world experts follow this practice: "The physician makes life-and-death decisions in reliance upon" such reports.[9] In the Note's words, Rule 703 "bring[s] the judicial practice into line with the practice of the experts themselves

---

2012) ("While only the terms 'facts or data' appear in Rule 703, opinions not in evidence, even those not admissible, may also form the bases of an expert's opinion if reasonably relied upon by experts in the particular field. Facts, data or opinions reasonably relied upon under Rule 703 may be disclosed to the jury on either direct or cross-examination to assist the jury in evalu-ating the expert's opinion by consider-ing its bases. This is true even if the facts, data or opinions have not them-selves been admitted and thus may not be considered for their truth. The court may instruct the jury that facts, data, or opinions reasonably relied upon by the expert under Rule 703 may be considered 'solely as a basis for the expert opinion and not as substantive evidence.' For most but not all practical purposes, Rule 703 operates as the equivalent of an ad-ditional exception to the rule against hearsay. For all purposes, Rule 703 creates an exception to the Original Writing Rule, Rule 1002, and serves as an alternative method of satisfying the requirement of authentication.").

[7]In Williams v. Illinois, 132 S. Ct. 2221, 183 L. Ed. 2d 89 (2012), a Sixth Amendment Confrontation Clause case, five justices—Justice

Thomas in concurrence and four dis-senters led by Justice Kagan—concluded that a report purportedly used under Rule 703 were in fact admitted for the hearsay purpose of proving the truth of the assertion. However, another five-justice majori-ty—Justice Thomas and the plurality led by Justice Alito—mooted that is-sue by ruling that the statement was not testimonial. The latter ruling mooted the issue of the use of the out-of-court statement. The latter ruling became the narrowest ground support-ing the Court's judgment affirming the defendant's conviction. Divided Supreme Court Says DNA Expert Can Testify About Profile Created by Others, 80 U.S.L.W. (BNA) 1747 (June 19, 2012).

[8]People v. Archuleta, 134 Cal. Rptr. 3d 727 (Cal. App. 4th Dist. 2011), review granted and opinion superseded, 139 Cal. Rptr. 3d 315, 273 P.3d 513 (Cal. 2012).

[9]The Advisory Committee's Note for Fed. R. Evid. 703 states in part:

The third source contemplated by the rule consists of presentation of data to the expert outside of court and other than by his own perception. In this re-spect the rule is designed to broaden the basis for expert opinions beyond

when not in court." If this type of data can be an acceptable basis for critical decisions in the operating room, it seems silly to preclude experts from relying on such reports in the courtroom.

### The Substantive Question Under Rule 703

The principal substantive problem presented by Rule 703 is the interpretation of the language quoted above. The key language consists of the words, "reasonably relied upon." The liberal approach is that the judge must accept the experts' view in deciding whether the rule is met at least in matters in which the judge is not equipped to "second guess" the expert.[10] The courts subscribing to this approach equate "reasonably" with "customarily." Under Rule 104(a) the judge makes a factual finding as to whether it is the customary practice of the expert's specialty to consider a certain type of report. If there is such a custom, the judge's hands are tied; the judge must allow the expert to rely on that type of report. There is a competing, restrictive approach to Rule 703 that even when it is the field's customary practice to consider a type of report, the trial judge has a residual discretion to decide that such reports are insufficiently reliable to serve as

---

that current in many jurisdictions and to bring the judicial practice into line with the practice of the experts themselves when not in court. Thus a physician in his own practice bases his diagnosis on information from numerous sources and of considerable variety, including statements by patients and relatives, reports and opinions from nurses, technicians and other doctors, hospital records, and X rays. Most of them are admissible in evidence, but only with the expenditure of substantial time in producing and examining various authenticating witnesses. The physician makes life-and-death decisions in reliance upon them. His validation, expertly performed and subject to cross-examination, ought to suffice for judicial purposes. Rheingold, supra, at 531 [Rheingold, The Basis of Medical Testimony, 15 Vand. L. Rev. 473 (1962), n. 9, supra]; McCormick § 15. A similar provision is California Evidence Code § 801(b). . . . If it be feared that enlargement of permissible data may tend to break down the rules of exclusion unduly, notice should be taken that the rule requires that the facts or data 'be of a type reasonably relied upon by experts in the particular field.' The language would not warrant admitting in evidence the opinion of an

'accidentologist' as to the point of impact in an automobile collision based on statements of bystanders, since this requirement is not satisfied. See Comment, Cal. Law Rev. Comm'n, Recommendation Proposing an Evidence Code 148–150 (1965).

[10]*E.g.*, In re Japanese Electronic Products Antitrust Litigation, 723 F.2d 238, 277 (3d Cir. 1983) ("In substituting its own opinion as to what constitutes reasonable reliance for that of the experts in the relevant fields the trial court misinterpreted Rule 703."); Peteet v. Dow Chemical Co., 868 F.2d 1428, 1432 (5th Cir. 1989) ("In making this determination, the trial court should defer to the expert's opinion of what data they find reasonably reliable."). In In re Paoli R.R. Yard PCB Litigation, 35 F.3d 717, 748 (3d Cir. 1994), the Third Circuit overruled its earlier decision in In re Japanese Electronic Products. Interestingly, Judge Edward Becker had been the trial judge reversed in the earlier case; and he later authored the opinion in *In re Paoli*.

the basis for an expert opinion.[11] Neither approach is flawless. The difficulty with the liberal approach is that a party can employ an expert witness to place untrustworthy facts, data, or opinions before the jury—a sort of "backdoor" hearsay exception. The criticism of the restrictive approach is that it seems presumptuous for an non-expert judge to tell a qualified expert the types of information that she may rely on to formulate an opinion.[12]

---

[11]*E.g.*, Shatkin v. McDonnell Douglas Corp., 727 F.2d 202 (2d Cir. 1984) (under Fed. R. Evid. 703 trial court is to determine whether the expert acted reasonably in making assumptions of fact upon which he would base his testimony); Viterbo v. Dow Chemical Co., 826 F.2d 420 (5th Cir. 1987) (Rule 703 requires courts to examine the reliability of expert witness sources). Of course, the data the expert proposes considering may be independently inadmissible for reasons other than a violation of the hearsay rule. D. Kaye, D. Bernstein & J. Mnookin, The New Wigmore: Expert Evidence §§ 4.6, 4.7.1 (2d ed. 2010) (when the data forming the expert's basis would have been excluded from evidence for some reason apart from its possible unreliability, the argument for deference underlying Rule 703 is less obvious).

[12]Consider this example. Assume the following facts: Plaintiff's warehouse burned to the ground. The insurance company asserts arson in defending an action on the insurance policy. The defendant insurance company lists as potential witnesses for trial an expert from the local fire department arson squad and an arson investigator employed by a company to conduct such investigations. The fire department arson expert arrived on the scene about twenty minutes after the first firefighter arrived. The expert is prepared to testify that the fire was deliberately set.

In support of this opinion, the fire department arson expert relies upon oral statements made by a firefighter on the scene describing observations during the first few minutes fighting the fire. The arson expert may reasonably rely on oral statements of another firefighter relating matters of personal knowledge. Arson experts customarily rely on such statements; and because the statements are made pursuant to a business duty to report, they are sufficiently trustworthy to make reliance reasonable. In addition, the fire department arson expert relies upon the results of laboratory tests on material the firefighters removed from the wreckage. Because these laboratory tests were conducted in the course of a regularly conducted business activity, the arson expert may reasonably rely on these results.

The arson expert also relies on two additional statements. The first statement, made by a firefighter on the scene, recounts that ten minutes after the firefighter arrived, a bystander calmly reported seeing a man run out of a building shortly before it caught fire. The second statement, made by another firefighter, relates that the firefighter saw Harold Jones standing at the corner watching the fire and that Harold Jones is rumored among the firefighters to be a professional arsonist. Although arson experts customarily may rely on these types of statements, neither statement is sufficiently trustworthy to render reliance reasonable. Applying the better restrictive approach to analyzing trustworthiness, the expert may not "reasonably" rely on the statement by a bystander without a business duty to report, possessing no indicia of trustworthiness beyond that of hearsay statements at large. Likewise, a statement by a member of the expert's organization reporting a rumor—a statement not based on personal knowledge of the underlying facts—is insufficiently trustworthy to be "reasonably"

On the whole, the restrictive approach is preferable both as a matter of policy and as a question of statutory construction.[13] To be sure, the judge should typically defer to the specialty's customary practice.[14] However, in an extreme case, the judge ought to have a residual power to second guess the customary practice and rule that a particular type of hearsay source is too untrustworthy. When the analogous Tort question arises as to whether an industrial practice is negligent, the courts consider evidence of the industry's customary practice; but the custom is not dispositive.[15] At most the existence of the custom should give rise to a presumption, but the presumption ought to be rebuttable.[16] The restrictive approach is also sounder as a matter of statutory interpretation. When the drafters wanted to make the application of an evidentiary rule dependent on the existence

---

relied upon even if experts in the field customarily consider such statements.

[13]Rule 703 deals with the facts or data on which an expert may base an opinion. Under the second sentence of the rule, if of a type "reasonably relied upon by experts in the particular field," the facts or data are exempt from compliance with the rules of evidence. The reliance by the experts in the field, if reasonable, is taken as a sufficient indication that the facts or data are worthy of being relied upon. Very clearly, then, two inquiries are required: (1) do experts in the field in fact rely upon this kind of facts or data? and (2) if so, is their reliance reasonable? Any other analysis would be at variance with the language and purpose of Rule 703's second sentence. *Accord* Head v. Lithonia Corp., Inc., 881 F.2d 941, 944 (10th Cir. 1989) ("Under Fed. R. Evid. 703 experts are given wide latitude to testify on facts otherwise not admissible in evidence and 'to broaden the acceptable bases of expert opinion.' Merit Motors, Inc. v. Chrysler Corp., 569 F.2d 666, 672–73 (D.C.Cir. 1977). Implicit in the rule, however, is the court's guidance to 'make a preliminary determination pursuant to Rule 104(a) whether the particular underlying data is of a kind that is reasonably relied upon by experts in the particular field in reaching conclusions.' 3 J. Weinstein & M. Burger, Weinstein's Evidence ¶ 703[03], at 703–16 (1982). This de-

termination must be made on 'a case-by-case basis and should focus on the reliability of the opinion and its foundation rather than merely on the fact that it was based, technically speaking, upon hearsay'. *Soden,* 714 F.2d at 503 (citation omitted). Thus, the district court 'may not abdicate its independent responsibilities to decide if the bases meet minimum standards of reliability as a condition of admissibility.' In re Agent Orange Prod. Liab. Litig., 611 F.Supp. 1223, 1245 (E.D. N.Y. 1985), aff'd, 818 F.2d 187 (2d Cir. 1987).").

The Advisory Committee's Note to Rule 703 lends support to the restrictive approach. In the Note, reasonable reliance is found with respect to the physician basing an opinion on "statements by patients and relatives, reports and opinions from nurses, technicians and other doctors, hospital records, and X rays", but denied with respect to an accidentologist attempting to rely on bystanders' statements as to the point of impact in an automobile collision.

[14]Ryan v. KDI Sylvan Pools, Inc., 121 N.J. 276, 579 A.2d 1241, 1247 (1990) (proof of the custom raises a rebuttable presumption that it is reasonable for the expert to rely).

[15]Prosser and Keeton on the Law of Torts § 33 (5th ed. 1984).

[16]Ryan, 579 A.2d at 1247.

of a custom or routine practice, as they did in Rules 406[17] and 803(17),[18] they found apt words to manifest their intention. In Rule 703, they opted to use the adverb "reasonably" rather than "customarily." "Reasonably" connotes an objective standard to be applied by the trial judge.

The judge and the attorneys may litigate this matter at a hearing under Rule 104.[19] A problem under Rule 703 in criminal cases is whether the defendant should or must have the opportunity to cross-examine the persons who originated the data on which an expert relies under Rule 703. On balance, the judge should probably apply Rule 703 unless a government expert is in effect being used to bring before the jury otherwise inadmissible matter (particularly hearsay implicating the confrontation clause).[20] The courts ought to employ a similar approach where the criminal defendant's mental health expert relies on the defendant's state-

---

[17]Fed. R. Evid. 406 ("the habit of a person or of the routine practice of an organization").

[18]Fed. R. Evid. 803(17) ("generally used an relied upon").

[19]The further question remains as to the division of responsibility with respect to the two inquiries mentioned in note 13 supra. First, as to determining what the experts' practice is, the primary sources of information must be testimony by the experts themselves, literature in the field, and perhaps judicial notice, presented to the judge, who will make the determination. The judge is ill-equipped to make the determination without assistance. For the experts alone to make the determination would be inconsistent with the judge's role under Rule 104(a) directing the judge generally to pass upon the qualifications of witnesses and the admissibility of evidence. Second, as to who determines the reasonableness of the experts' reliance, to allow the experts themselves to pass upon the reasonableness of their own practice would likewise be inconsistent with the judge's role under Rule 104(a). Plainly, the judge must make the finding of fact as to what the experts' practice is and then determine whether it is objectively reasonable. In the latter instance, a presumption of reasonableness would be consistent with the basis, purpose,

and language of Rule 703.

[20]An interesting question arises with respect to whether a witness qualified as an expert may reasonably rely upon facts, data or opinions under Rule 703 without herself providing additional expert input. With respect to such a summary expert, sometimes called a conduit expert, see U.S. v. Tomasian, 784 F.2d 782, 786 (7th Cir. 1986) ("Rule 703 does not sanction the simple transmission of hearsay; it only permits an expert opinion based on hearsay."); U.S. v. Williams, 431 F.2d 1168, 1172 (5th Cir. 1970) ("If the witness has gone to only one hearsay source and seeks merely to summarize the content of that source, then he is acting as a summary witness, not an expert. Since he is introducing the content of the extrajudicial statements or writings to prove truth, his testimony, like its source, is hearsay and is inadmissible unless the source qualifies under an exception to the hearsay rule. When, however, the witness has gone to many sources—although some or all be hearsay in nature—and rather than introducing mere summaries of each source he uses them all, along with his own professional experience, to arrive at his opinion, that evidence is regarded as evidence in its own right and not as an attempt to introduce hearsay in disguise.").

ments as support for an opinion about sanity.[21] It was hoped that the Supreme Court's decision in *Williams v. Illinois*[22] would shed some light on this issue; but, as we shall see at the end of this section, the Court decided *Williams* on another basis and, in the process, raised significant questions about the future of Rule 703.

### The Procedure for Administering Rule 703

In addition to the substantive question of the meaning of "reasonably" in Rule 703, the rule presents a procedural issue. Assuming that it is substantively permissible for an expert to rely on an out-of-court report as part of the basis of her opinion, how far may the expert go in describing the content of the report? The expert should certainly be allowed to generally indicate the type of report she is relying on. Thus, the expert could state that in forming her opinion, she considered reports from investigating police officers or findings from a toxicology laboratory. However, when the report is oral, may she quote the report in detail? If the report is in writing, may the proponent formally introduce the report, have the expert quote it, and even submit it to the jurors for their inspection? As § 324.3 points out, the courts have divided over this question. It has been argued that as a matter of logic, the jurors cannot thoroughly evaluate the expert's reasoning unless they have an in-depth understanding of all the bases of the opinion.[23] Further, a case can be made that the wording of Rule 705 indicates that the drafters contemplated that the expert should be permitted to give the jurors a detailed description of the content of the report.[24] That rule states that the expert "may" state the opinion and the reasons for the opinion "without first testifying to the underlying facts or data"—suggesting that the expert's proponent may choose to elicit the testimony about the underlying facts or data during the expert's direct examination.

However, the operative assumption here is that the report is not independently admissible; that is, it is not reliable enough to qualify for admission under any hearsay exception. With some support in the empirical studies,[25] several commentators caution that allowing the expert to detail the report's content creates a grave risk that the jurors will misuse the content as substantive

---

[21]*See generally* Noggle v. Marshall, 706 F.2d 1408, 1416 n.9 (6th Cir. 1983); People v. Coleman, 38 Cal. 3d 69, 211 Cal. Rptr. 102, 695 P.2d 189 (1985); People v. Finkey, 105 Ill. App. 3d 230, 61 Ill. Dec. 81, 434 N.E.2d 18 (4th Dist. 1982).

[22]Williams v. Illinois, 132 S. Ct. 2221, 183 L. Ed. 2d 89 (2012).

[23]Rice, Inadmissible Evidence as a Basis for Expert Opinion Testimony: A Response to Professor Carlson, 40 Vand. L. Rev. 583, 588–91 (1987).

[24]Epps, Clarifying the Meaning of Federal Rule of Evidence 703, 36 B. C. L. Rev. 53 (1994).

[25]Schuller, Expert Evidence and Hearsay: The Influence of

evidence.[26] Several jurisdictions have amended their version of Rule 703 to preclude the expert from elaborating on the content of the report,[27] and a December 1, 2000 amendment to Federal Rule 703 is to the same effect.[28]

---

"Secondhand" Information on Jurors' Decisions, 19 Law & Hum. Behav. 345 (1995).

[26]Carlson, Policing the Bases of Modern Expert Testimony, 39 Vand. L. Rev. 577 (1986); Carlson, Collision Course in Expert Testimony: Limitations on Affirmative Introduction of Underlying Data, 36 U. Fla. L. Rev. 234 (1984).

The risk of misuse of the third party's report is particularly great when expert #2 on the stand purports to base his or her opinion on an identical opinion voiced outside court by expert #1. Thus, a New York pathologist might purport to partially rest her opinion about time of death on an identical, out-of-court opinion expressed by a California colleague whom she consulted. The courts are split over the permissibility of this practice. Imwinkelried, Developing a Coherent Theory of the Structure of Federal Rule of Evidence 703, 47 Mercer L. Rev. 447. 457–61 (1996). Some courts refuse to permit expert #2 to serve as a "conduit" for the introduction of the identical opinion by expert #1. Carlson, Experts as Hearsay Conduits: Confrontation Abuses in Opinion Testimony, 76 Minn. L. Rev. 859 (1992). See Loeffel Steel Products, Inc. v. Delta Brands, Inc., 387 F. Supp. 2d 794 (N.D. Ill. 2005); Wantanabe Realty Corp. v. City of New York, 2004 WL 188088 (S.D. N.Y. 2004), aff'd, 159 Fed. Appx. 235 (2d Cir. 2005); People v. Bordelon, 162 Cal. App. 4th 1311, 77 Cal. Rptr. 3d 14, 25–26 (1st Dist. 2008) ("experts should generally be allowed to testify to all the facts upon which they base their testimony"; however, "[a]n expert witness may not, on direct examination, reveal the contents of reports prepared or opinions expressed by nontestifying experts"); Garibay v. Hemmat,

161 Cal. App. 4th 735, 74 Cal. Rptr. 3d 715 (2d Dist. 2008) ("Although experts may properly rely on hearsay in forming their opinions, they may not relate the out-of-court statements of another as independent proof of the fact. Physicians can testify as to the basis of their opinion, but that is not intended to be a channel by which testifying physicians can place the opinion of out-of-court physicians before the trier of fact"); Figlioli v. R.J. Moreau Companies, Inc., 151 N.H. 618, 866 A.2d 962, 968–69 (2005) (a testifying expert may not describe the substance of another expert's opinion).

[27]For example, Minnesota added the following subdivision (b) to its Rule 703:

> Underlying expert data must be independently admissible in order to be received upon direct examination; provided that when good cause is shown in civil cases and the underlying data is particularly trustworthy, the court may admit the data under this rule for the limited purpose of showing the basis for the expert's opinion.

Kentucky Rule 703 was amended along the same lines.

[28]The amendment to Federal Rule 703 added the following sentence at the end of the statute: "Facts or data that are otherwise inadmissible shall not be disclosed to the jury by the proponent of the opinion or inference unless the court determines that their probative value in assisting the jury to evaluate the expert's opinion substantially outweighs their prejudicial effect."

Effective December 1, 2011, the last sentence of restyled Fed. R. Evid. 703 reads:

> But if the facts or data would otherwise be inadmissible, the proponent of the opinion may disclose them to the jury only if their probative value in helping

Of course, in a broad sense almost all expert opinion about scientific propositions embodies hearsay indirectly.[29] Whenever an expert testifies, she implicitly draws on such material as lectures she heard and textbooks she read during her education. It would be ridiculous to apply the hearsay rule to that material:

> Would we require a modern accident reconstruction expert to replicate Newton's seventeenth century experiments to derive the laws of motion? Suppose that a physicist is testifying about the safety of a nuclear power plant. If the physicist contemplates relying on the words of Fermi or Oppenheimer, would we require that the physicist duplicate their research?[30]

However, that problem is distinguishable from the issue analyzed in this section. Newton's and Fermi's writings relate to the expert's major premise, that is, the research underpinning the expert's technique or theory. In this section, the question is quite different; the focus here is on the content of the expert's minor premise, namely, the case-specific information about how the traffic accident occurred or the accused's behavior just before he shot the decedent. There is less justification for lifting the bar of the hearsay rule when the expert rests her opinion on out-of-court reports about that kind of information. There is also greater probative danger because minor-premise data are more likely to overlap with the disputed facts on the historical merits in the case.

*The Impact of Williams v. Illinois on the Future of Rule 703*

In *Williams v. Illinois,*[31] a DNA expert opined that there was a match between the defendant's DNA profile and a profile extracted from a rape victim's vaginal swab. In her direct testimony, the expert referred to the profile that Cellmark had extracted from the vaginal swab. In particular, the expert referred to "the male DNA profile found in semen from vaginal swabs" of the victim. The question was whether that reference violated the defendant's Sixth Amendment rights.

Ultimately, the Court affirmed the defendant's conviction. The

---

the jury evaluate the opinion substantially outweighs their prejudicial effect.

[29]Thompson v. Underwood, 407 F.2d 994 (6th Cir.1969) (acceptable for medical expert to testify to partial permanent disability of about 37 percent, the expert used a manual published by the American Medical Association, but also reached his own independent opinion); Ryan v. Payne, 446 S.W.2d 273 (Ky. 1969) (acceptable that expert consulted skidmark distance tables prior to taking stand); 2 Wigmore, Evidence § 665(b) (Chadbourn rev. 1979).

[30]Imwinkelried, The "Bases" of Expert Testimony: The Syllogistic Structure of Scientific Testimony, 67 N.C. L. Rev. 1, 9 (1988).

[31]Williams v. Illinois, 132 S. Ct. 2221, 183 L. Ed. 2d 89 (2012).

Court did so because five justices—the plurality led by Justice Alito and Justice Thomas in concurrence—held that Cellmark's report was not testimonial. The plurality reasoned that the report was not testimonial because it did not target a specific defendant. In Justice Alito's words, the primary purpose of the report "was to catch a dangerous rapist who was still at large, not to obtain evidence for use against petitioner, who was neither in custody nor under suspicion at that time." Although Justice Thomas agreed that the report was not testimonial, he rejected the plurality's reasoning; instead, he contended that the report was not formal or solemn enough to trigger the Confrontation Clause. In any event, the characterization of the report as non-testimonial became the narrowest ground supporting the affirmance of the defendant's conviction.[32] Strictly speaking the affirmance moots all the other issues raised in the case.

Nevertheless, many lower courts will undoubtedly take note of the fact that five justices—the 703 majority—believed that any secondhand report relied on under Rule 703 must be used for the truth of the assertion. The disagreement between those justices and the plurality implicates significant questions about the future of Rule 703. Assuming that the proponent has otherwise satisfied Rule 703, does the proponent's failure to present independent, admissible evidence of 703 facts render the expert's opinion irrelevant and inadmissible or merely give the opponent an argument for attacking the weight of the opinion?

Initially, posit the 703 majority's view that the utilization of a report under Rule 703 necessarily entails the use of the report as substantive evidence. If the majority is right, there may be an admissibility problem; there is a strong argument that the jury ought to be permitted to consider the resulting opinion only when there is admissible, independent evidence of the 703 facts. If such evidence is lacking, the judge should bar the opinion. As in the case of a hypothetical question, when the proponent attempts to introduce the opinion, the opponent should have a parallel right to object on the ground that there is no extrinsic, admissible evidence of the 703 facts. Even when the judge exercises discretion to allow the proponent to submit the admissible evidence later— again as in the case of a hypothetical question—on the opponent's motion the judge should strike the opinion if the proponent rests without submitting the admissible evidence. At first blush, the view of the 703 majority seems to lead to the conclusion that the lack of independent evidence of the 703 facts creates an admissibility problem; and the judge ought to exclude the opinion.

---

[32]People v. Dungo, 55 Cal. 4th 608, 147 Cal. Rptr. 3d 527, 286 P.3d 442 (2012); People v. Lopez, 55 Cal. 4th 569, 147 Cal. Rptr. 3d 559, 286 P.3d 469 (2012); Divided Supreme Court Says DNA Expert Can Testify About Profile Created by Others, 80 U.S.L.W. (BNA) 1747 (June 19, 2012).

Alternatively, posit the conventional wisdom, endorsed by the plurality, that the utilization of a report under Rule 703 is a legitimate, nonhearsay use of the report. On that assumption, the proponent's failure to present independent, admissible evidence of the 703 facts creates a weight problem rather than an admissibility issue. The Advisory Committee Note to Rule 703 lends support to the plurality's view. The first paragraph of the Note discusses the hypothetical question. That discussion appears to contemplate that trial judges will continue to enforce the traditional, common law requirement that the proponent present independent, admissible evidence of the hypothesized facts. For instance, the Note mentions the situation in which an expert exempted from a sequestration order "hear[s] the testimony establishing the [hypothesized] facts."[33] Later the same paragraph turns to the expert's reliance on out-of-court reports. The Note expressly states that when an expert relies on this type of basis for the opinion, the proponent can dispense "with the expenditure of substantial time in producing and examining various authenticating witnesses." The Note adds that experts such as "physician[s] make[ ] life-and-death decisions in reliance" on such reports and that the expert's reliance on customary sources of information should "suffice" to warrant admitting the opinion.

However, even the plurality conceded that the proponent's failure to present independent, admissible evidence of a 703 secondhand report can sometimes render the opinion itself irrelevant. The plurality approvingly quoted a judicial instruction generally informing the jury that in assessing the weight of the expert's opinion, they may consider whether the 703 facts "are sustained by the [other] proof." More specifically, the plurality endorsed an instruction that if an essential assumption was "not supported by the proof," the expert's opinion deserves "no weight." Perhaps the best analogy is to the conditional relevance procedure codified in Federal Rule 104(b).[34] In the case of preliminary facts such as a lay witness's personal knowledge and an exhibit's authenticity, the jury ordinarily makes the ultimate relevance decision. The judge plays a limited, screening role and answers only this question: If the jury decides to accept the testimony at face value, does the foundational testimony possess sufficient probative value to support a rational jury finding that the fact exists? If the jury decides that the witness did not see the accident or that the writing is a forgery, common sense will lead the jury to disregard the evidence during the remainder of their deliberations. Similarly, even lay jurors without legal training can understand that the falsity of an essential premise renders

---

[33]Adv. Comm. Note, Fed. R. Evid. 703.

[34]See § 53 infra.

the opinion irrelevant and that they should ignore an irrelevant opinion. If so, the sort of jury instructions discussed in Justice Alito's plurality opinion will ordinarily be a satisfactory solution. The judge would have to intervene to exclude the opinion only when there is no or clearly insufficient independent, admissible evidence of an essential premise of the opinion.

The view of the 703 majority in *Williams* will probably muddy the 703 jurisprudence in the near future. On its face, *Williams* is a constitutional criminal procedure decision of interest only to criminal practitioners. However, civil practitioners must also pay attention to the language in *Williams* about the evidentiary status of reports relied on under Rule 703.

## § 16 Should the hypothetical question be retained?

In theory, the hypothetical question is an ingenious device for enabling the jury to apply the expert's scientific knowledge to the facts of the case. The device permits the judicial system to capitalize on the witness's expertise even when the expert has not had the time to acquire firsthand knowledge of the facts. Nevertheless in practice, it suffers from significant flaws and can be abused to obstruct the search for truth. If we require that it recite all the relevant facts, it becomes intolerably wordy. If we allow, as most courts do, the interrogating counsel to select whatever facts he sees fit,[1] we tempt him to shape a one-sided hypothesis. Many expert witnesses view this partisan slanting of the hypothesis as distasteful and a major weakness of the practice.[2] Many experts cite that partisanship as one of the reasons that they are reluctant to appear as witnesses. The legal writers who have studied the problem seem to concur in condemning the practice.[3]

What is the remedy? It hardly seems practical to require the

---

[Section 16]

[1]See § 14 supra.

[2]*E.g.*, White, Insanity and the Criminal Law 56 (1923) ("in a large experience, I have never known a hypothetical question, in a trial involving the mental condition of the defendant, which in my opinion offered a fair presentation of the case."); Hulbert, Psychiatric Testimony in Probate Proceedings, 2 Law & Contemp. Prob. 448, 455 (1935) ("But the present practice of misusing the hypothetical question as restatement of the case to re-impress the jury is bad strategy, though good tactics; bad strategy because it is so unfair, confusing and cause it is so unfair, confusing and degrading that it does not clarify the issue nor help achieve justice."); Roberts, Some Observations on the Problems of the Forensic Psychiatrist, 1965 Wis. L. Rev. 240, 258 (1965).

[3]*See, e.g.*, 2 Wigmore, Evidence § 686 (Chadbourn rev. 1979) ("Its abuses have become so obstructive and nauseous that no remedy short of extirpation will suffice. It is a logical necessity, but a practical incubus; and logic here must be sacrificed. . . . It is a strange irony that the hypothetical question, which is one of the few truly scientific features of the rules of evidence, should have become that feature which does most to disgust men of science with the law of Evidence.");

trial judge to undertake the thorough study of the case necessary to enable her to personally select the significant facts to be included in the hypothesis. It might be feasible for the questions to be framed by both counsel in conference with the judge, either at a pretrial hearing or during the trial in the jury's absence.[4] But that conferral process could be time-consuming. The only remaining expedient is the one generally advocated, namely, dispensing with the requirement that the question be accompanied by a recital of a hypothesis, unless the trial judge requires it. This is the procedure authorized by Federal and Uniform Rule of Evidence 705 and a few other statutes and rules.[5]

The cross-examiner has an election whether to bring out the

---

Judge Learned Hand, New York Bar Association Lectures on Legal Topics, 1921–1922 ("the most horrific and grotesque wen on the fair face of justice"). *See* Rabata v. Dohner, 45 Wis. 2d 111, 172 N.W.2d 409 (1969) stating in part:

> [M]oreover the members of this court, based upon their experience gleaned as practicing lawyers and trial judges, are satisfied that a mechanistic hypothetical question has the effect of boring and confusing the jury. Rather than inducing a clear expression of expert opinion and the basis for it, it inhibits the expert and forecloses him from explaining his reasoning in a manner that is intelligible to a jury.

[4]*See* Hulbert, Psychiatric Testimony in Probate Proceedings, 2 Law & Contemp. Prob. 448, 455 (1935).

[5]Former Fed. R. Evid. 705 provided: "The expert may testify in terms of opinion or inference and give reasons therefor without prior disclosure of the underlying facts or data, unless the court requires otherwise. The expert may in any event be required to disclose the underlying facts or data on cross-examination." Effective December 1, 2011, restyled Fed. R. Evid. 705 reads: "Unless the court orders otherwise, an expert may state an opinion—and give the reasons for it—without first testifying to the underlying facts or data. But the expert may be required to disclose those facts or data on cross-examination." *See also* Cal. Evid. Code § 802; Kan. Civ. Proc.

Code Ann. §§ 60-456 to 60-458; N.J.R.E. 705; N.Y. CPLR 4515.

The testimony may consist of anything from a full presentation (e.g., qualification, bases, opinion, reasoning) to a bare bones summary. *See* Hearings on Proposed Rules of Evidence Before the Special Subcomm. on Reform of Fed. Crim. Laws of the House Comm. on the Judiciary, 93d Cong., 1st Sess. 355–56 (Supp. 1973):

For example, one can envision the following dialogue immediately after the expert had been qualified as an orthopedic surgeon:

> Q. Doctor, do you have an opinion based upon a reasonable degree of medical certainty as to the extent [of] permanent disability suffered by the plaintiff as a result of this automobile accident?
>
> A. Yes.
>
> Q. What is your opinion?
>
> A. She is totally permanently disabled.
>
> Q. Thank, you doctor, that is all.

It is often necessary and desirable first to ask preliminary and explanatory foundation questions. *See* Weinstein & Berger, Evidence ¶ 705[01] at 705–10 (1988) ("In practice, the pressures of orderly presentation will often lead to divulgence of at least some of the supporting data. A witness with firsthand knowledge may be asked about the facts underlying his opinion because the facts themselves are needed to satisfy the burden of proof. A witness' acquaintance with certain data may have to be shown in

basis for the expert's opinion.[6] This approach does not lessen the partisanship of the question or the answer on direct examination. However, it simplifies the examination and removes the occasion for reversing the trial judgment by appellate disputes over deficiencies in the form of hypothetical questions. Rule 705 does, however, give the judge discretion to require prior disclosure of basis facts on direct. Judges tend to do so when there has not been adequate pretrial opportunity to discover them, especially in criminal cases.[7]

## § 17  Proposals for improvement of the practice relating to expert testimony[1]

### The Weaknesses

Common law countries employ the adversary or contentious system of trial, in which the opposing parties, not the judge as in other systems, have the responsibility and initiative in finding

---

qualifying him as an expert pursuant to Rule 702. And the necessity of making the evidence understandable to the jury will often result in the posing of some foundational questions before the opinion is requested."). 4 Weinstein's Federal Evidence § 705.03[1] (rev. 2011) is to the same effect. Of course Fed. R. Evid. 705 allows the more traditional methods of examining experts to the extent indicated in § 14. For more detailed treatment of these matters, see McElhaney, Expert Witnesses and the Federal Rules of Evidence, 28 Mercer L. Rev. 463 (1977).

[6]The various methods for cross-examination and the usual restrictions under the Fed. R. Evid. apply to the cross-examination of the expert. Rules 403 and 611 may be invoked to prevent irrelevant, confusing, or collateral matter. U.S. v. 10.48 Acres of Land, 621 F.2d 338 (9th Cir. 1980); U.S. v. Taylor, 510 F.2d 1283 (D.C. Cir. 1975). As to the cross-examination of expert witness, see generally § 13 at notes 86 to 95 supra.

[7]In civil cases, employment of Fed. R. Civ. P. 26(b)(4) and pretrial conferences will aid the conduct of the cross-examination. In criminal cases

discovery will also be necessary to the extent available in order to cross-examine the expert effectively. *See generally* Smith v. Ford Motor Co., 626 F.2d 784, 793 (10th Cir. 1980) ("The combined effect of [Rules 703 and 705] is to 'place the full burden of exploration of the facts and assumptions underlying the testimony of an expert witness squarely on the shoulders of opposing counsel's cross-examination. As stated in the Advisory Committee Note to Rule 705, and highlighted by the elimination of the foundation often provided by the hypothetical question," advance knowledge through pretrial discovery of an expert witness's basis for his opinion is essential for effective cross-examination." Graham, Discovery of Experts Under Rule 26(b)(4) of the Federal Rules of Civil Procedure: Part One, An Analytical Study, 1976 U. Ill. L. F. 895, 897.").

**[Section 17]**

[1]Comprehensive discussions are found in 2 Wigmore, Evidence § 563 (Chadbourn rev. 1979); Second Annual Report, New York Law Revision Commission, 795–910 (1936); Expert Testimony (a series of several articles), 2 Law & Contemp. Prob. 401–527 (1935).

and presenting proof.[2] Advantageous as this system is in many respects, its application to the procurement and presentation of expert testimony is widely considered a sore spot in judicial administration. The critics point to two chief weaknesses. The first is that the experts are chosen by the parties, who are naturally interested in finding not the best scientist, but the "best witness." As an English judge observed:

> [T]he mode in which expert evidence is obtained is such as not to give the fair result of scientific opinion to the Court. A man may go, and does sometimes, to half-a-dozen experts . . . . He takes their honest opinions, he finds three in his favor and three against him; he says to the three in his favor, "will you be kind enough to give evidence?" and he pays the three against him their fees and leaves them alone; the other side does the same . . . [T]he result is that the Court does not get that assistance from the experts which, if they were unbiased and fairly chosen, it would have a right to expect.[3]

The second weakness is that the adversary method of eliciting scientific testimony, frequently by hypothetical questions based on a partisan choice of facts, is ill-suited to the balanced presentation of technical data. In many cases, the net result is overemphasizing conflicts between experts' scientific opinions and making it more difficult for the jury to decide the case.[4]

### *Potential Remedies*

*The court appointment of experts to testify on the ultimate issues in the case.* A potential remedy for the first weakness lies in the use of trial judges' common law power to call experts. As early as the 14th century—before witnesses were heard by juries—there are recorded cases of judges summoning experts to aid them in determining scientific issues.[5] The existence of the judge's power to call witnesses generally and expert witnesses in

---

[2]*See* Millar, Legal Procedure, 12 Encyc. Soc. Sc. 439, 450 (1934), and Millar, The Formative Principles of Primitive Procedure, 18 Ill. L. Rev. 1, 4 (1923), where the two principles of party prosecution and judicial prosecution are contrasted, but it is pointed out that most systems of procedure use both principles in some degree.

[3]Jessel, M.R., in Thorn v. Worthington Skating Rink Co., L.R. 6 Ch.D. 415, 416 (1876), note to Plimpton v. Spiller, 6 Ch.D. 412 (1877). See also similar criticisms by Grier, J., in

Winans v. New York & E.R. Co., 62 U.S. 88, 101, 21 How. 88, 16 L. Ed. 68, 1858 WL 9350 (1858); Henshaw, J., in In re Dolbeer's Estate, 149 Cal. 227, 86 P. 695, 702 (1906) and Cartwright, C.J. in Opp v. Pryor, 294 Ill. 538, 128 N.E. 580 (1920).

[4]See criticism cited in notes 1 to 2, supra. *See also* Kaye, Bernstein & Mnookin, The New Wigmore: Expert Evidence § 4.4 (2d ed. 2010).

[5]Rosenthal, The Development of the Use of Expert Testimony, 2 Law & Contemp. Prob. 403, 406–11 (1935).

particular is well settled in this country.[6] The power is recognized by rules and statutes in a substantial number of states.[7] Some provisions apply to scientific issues in any case, civil or criminal,[8] others are limited to criminal cases,[9] and still others refer narrowly to sanity issues in criminal cases.[10] The principle is implemented in the Model Expert Testimony Act approved by the Commissioners on Uniform State Laws,[11] and embodied in Uniform Rule of Evidence and Federal Rule of Evidence 706.[12] Unfortunately, in the past judges have rarely exercised their power under Rule 706.[13] That reluctance is understandable. Before their appointment to the bench, most judges are schooled

---

[6]See § 8 supra; Kaye, Bernstein & Mnookin, The New Wigmore: Expert Evidence § 11.2 (2d ed. 2010); Notes, 51 Nw. U. L. Rev. 761 (1957), 12 Rutgers L. Rev. 375 (1957); Trial court's appointment, in civil case, of expert witness, 95 A.L.R.2d 390.

[7]See collection of statutes in 2 Wigmore, Evidence § 563 (Chadbourn rev. 1979).

[8]E.g., Cal. Evid. Code §§ 730 to 733; R.I. R. Evid. 708.

[9]E.g., Fla. R. Crim. P. Rule 3.210; Wis. Stat. Ann. 971.16.

[10]E.g., Ohio Rev. Code Ann. § 2945.40.

[11]The Act is set out in 1937 Handbook, Nat'l Conf. Com'rs on Unif. State Laws 339–48.

[12]Former Fed. R. Evid. 706 provided:

(a) Appointment. the court may on its own motion or on the motion of any party enter an order to show cause why expert witnesses should not be appointed, and may request the parties to submit nominations. The court may appoint any expert witnesses agreed upon by the parties, and may appoint expert witnesses of its own selection. An expert witness shall not be appointed by the court unless the witness consents to act. A witness so appointed shall be informed of the witness' duties by the court in writing, a copy of which shall be filed with the clerk, or at a conference in which the parties shall have opportunity to participate. A witness so appointed shall advise the parties of the witness' findings, if any; the witness' deposition may be taken by any party; and the witness may be called to testify by the court or any party. The witness shall be subject to cross-examination by each party, including a party calling the witness.

(b) Compensation. Expert witnesses so appointed are entitled to reasonable compensation in whatever sum the court may allow. The compensation thus fixed is payable from funds which may be provided by law in criminal cases and civil actions and proceedings involving just compensation under the fifth amendment. In other civil actions and proceedings the compensation shall be paid by the parties in such proportion and at such time as the court directs, and thereafter charged in like manner as other costs.

(c) Disclosure of appointment. In the exercise of its discretion, the court may authorize disclosure to the jury of the fact that the court appointed the expert witness.

(d) Parties' experts of own selection. Nothing in this rule limits the parties in calling expert witnesses of their own selection.

Effective December 1, 2011, restyled Fed. R. Evid. 706 superseded the above statute. However, the substantive provisions of the restyled rule are identical to those of the former rule. See also § 8, supra, and Fed. R. Evid. 614. Insofar as Fed. R. Crim. P. 28 concerned appointment of experts, it has been superseded by Fed. R. Evid. 706. Unif. R. Evid. 706 is the same as Fed. R. Evid. 706 except for minor stylistic difference.

[13]Cecil & Willing, Court-appointed Experts: Defining the Role of Experts Appointed under Federal Rule of

as litigators in the adversary tradition.[14] That tradition is so ingrained that some commentators believe that to overcome the judicial reluctance to appoint court experts, court appointment must be made mandatory in certain types of cases.[15]

*Limited court appointments of experts to provide the judge and jury with a primer on the relevant expertise.* It has been proposed that by adapting existing procedures, American courts could shift from a dialectic (adversary) to a more didactic (educational) model for presenting expert testimony.[16] One of the weaknesses in the current model is that at the typical trial, all the expert testimony is presented by witnesses hired by the litigants. When all the expert testimony comes from potentially biased sources, it is difficult for the trier of fact to separate the wheat from the chaff. Unlike many prior recommendations, this proposal does not contemplate that the judge will appoint an expert who would duplicate the work of the partisan experts and opine on the ultimate issue. Rather, the limited extent of the proposal is to modify existing procedures to give the trier of fact a primer on the basics in the relevant discipline. Armed with a primer, the trier would be in a better position to perform the task described by the *Joiner* Court, namely, deciding which partisan expert is making the more reasonable extrapolation and which is making "too great an analytical"[17] leap. Under this proposal, pursuant to Rule 201 the judge would judicially notice the well settled propositions in the discipline and instruct the jury about them. Then, pursuant to a very limited Rule 706 appointment, an independent expert would respond to the jury's questions about those propositions. In effect, the judge is the master teacher, the court-appointed expert is the teaching assistant, and the jurors are the students. After the judge's instructions and the jury's opportunity to question the court-appointed expert, the jury would hear the testimony by the partisan experts. These procedures would better enable the trier of fact to choose between the conflicting opinions advanced by the competing partisan experts. All of these procedures—judicial notice, court appointment, and juror

Evidence 706 47 (1992) (in a survey of over 400 federal district court judges, only 20% reported having ever invoked Rule 706).

[14] Cecil & Willing, Court-appointed Experts: Defining the Role of Experts Appointed under Federal Rule of Evidence 706, at 92 ("an unforgivable intrusion into the adversarial system"); Sheppard, Court Witnesses—A Desirable or Undesirable Encroachment on the Adversary System, 56

Aust. L.J. 234 (1982).

[15] Gross, Expert Evidence, 1991 Wis. L. Rev. 1113.

[16] Imwinkelried, The Next Step in Conceptualizing the Presentation of Expert Evidence as Education: The Case for Didactic Trial Procedures, 1 Int'l J. Evid. & Proof 128 (1997).

[17] General Elec. Co. v. Joiner, 522 U.S. 136, 146, 118 S. Ct. 512, 139 L. Ed. 2d 508 (1997).

questioning—are permissible under the current law in most jurisdictions.

*The establishment of panels of impartial experts.* Another possible antidote for the first weakness is establishing panels of impartial experts designated by groups in the appropriate specialty fields.[18] The judge could then select an expert from the panel. An American Bar Association committee approved in principle this procedure for impartial medical expert witnesses.[19] However, as we shall see, little headway has been made in implementing this procedure.

*The use of pretrial conferences to narrow the disagreements between the opposing experts.* The second weakness in the status quo may also be remediable. In the current system, lay jurors are often called on to arbitrate a "battle of experts." In some kinds of controversies, a well-devised plan of scientific investigation and report could greatly reduce the need for contested trials.[20] The Uniform Act provides that the court may require a conference of the experts, whether chosen by the court or the parties. The conference gives the experts an opportunity to resolve their disagreements in interpreting the data. The conference might lead to a complete agreement which practically settles the issue. If not, it may at least narrow the controversy. The Act provides that two or more experts may join in a single report. At the trial, the individual expert's report or a joint report can be read to the court and jury as a part of the expert's testimony, and he may be

---

[18]Review and discussion of various plans are found in Myers, "The Battle of the Experts": A New Approach to an Old Problem in Medical Testimony, 44 Neb. L. Rev. 539 (1965); Van Dusen, A United States District Judge's View of the Impartial Medical Expert System, 32 F.R.D. 498 (1963); Impartial Medical Testimony Plans, Alleghany County Medical Society Medico—Legal Committee (1961). *See also* Botein, The New York Medical Expert Testimony Project, 33 U. Det. L.J. 388 (1956). *See generally* Saltzburg, The Unnecessarily Expanding Role of the American Trial Judge, 64 Va. L. Rev. 1 (1978).

A further, and perhaps more questionable suggestion is the plan for medical-malpractice panels, staffed by physicians and attorneys. A claim could be voluntarily submitted to the panel. If the panel found it meritorious, the panel would aid in securing medical testimony.

[19]American Bar Association, Section of Judicial Administration, Committee on Impartial Medical Testimony, Report, 1956 (August); Handbook on the Improvement of the Administration of Justice, American Bar Association 79–80 (5th ed. 1971).

[20]In states where the statutes provide for the examination by psychiatrists of persons charged with serious crimes, the tendency has been for the prosecution, the defendant, and the court to acquiesce in the expert's conclusions many situations. *See* Weihofen, An Alternative to the Battle of Experts: Hospital Examination of Criminal Defendants Before Trial, 2 Law & Contemp. Prob. 419, 422 (1935); Overholser, The History and Operation of the Briggs Law of Massachusetts, 2 Law & Contemp. Prob. 436, 444 (1935).

cross-examined about the report. The Act dispenses with the requirement to use hypothetical questions.[21] There was a striking, if bizarre, example of the utility of joint reports in a New York DNA case, *People v. Castro*.[22] In that case,

> [i]n an unusual move, four of the expert witnesses—representing both the prosecution and the defense—met to review the scientific evidence after they had already testified. The result of this meeting was a two-page consensus statement that addressed the inadequacy of the scientific evidence and the legal procedures for assessing [the] evidence. Although the statement itself was not accepted as evidence in the pretrial hearing, the substance of the consensus document was introduced by the defense's recall of two prosecution expert witnesses to testify on its substance.[23]

Although these proposals addressing the two weaknesses have merit, the proposals themselves have been targets of criticism. For example, the expanded use of court appointed experts has its critics.[24] The critics argue that there is no such thing as a truly impartial expert and, even assuming such experts exist, courts lack the ability to identify and locate them.[25] To address this problem, the American Association for the Advancement of Science established the Court Appointed Scientific Experts (CASE) project.[26] At this stage, CASE is a pilot project to better enable federal judges to find suitably qualified, independent experts. In addition, critics contend that at trial identifying the witness as an appointed expert could result in excessive emphasis by the trier of fact on that expert's opinion.[27] Once the jury learns that one expert is the "court's" witness, the jurors might leap to the conclusion that they should accept her opinion.

---

[21]See note 1, supra.

[22]People v. Castro, 144 Misc. 2d 956, 545 N.Y.S.2d 985 (Sup 1989).

[23]Office of Technology Assessment, U.S. Cong., Genetic Witness: Forensic Uses of DNA Tests 103 (1990).

[24]*See* Levy, Impartial Medical Testimony—Revisited, 34 Temple L.Q. 416 (1961); Diamond, The Fallacy of the Impartial Expert, 3 Archives of Criminal Psychodynamics 221 (1959), excerpts reprinted in Allen, Furster and Rubin, Readings in Law and Psychiatry 145 (1968).

[25]Schuck, Techniques for Proof of Complicated Scientific and Economic Facts, 40 F.R.D. 33, 38 (1967) (The employment of court appointed experts "has value only where a fact of a scientific nature can be ascertained with some degree of definiteness by one well

versed in the field. If on the other hand there is any substantial room for interplay of theoretical attitude—as where the question concerns a so-called fact or theory in the field of economics such as in antitrust suits—then it is virtually impossible to find a 'neutral' expert and the very selection of the man usually will *predetermine* what his ultimate opinion will be and is 'tantamount' to a selection of the answer to the problem.") (emphasis in original).

[26]Kaye, Bernstein & Mnookin, The New Wigmore: Expert Evidence § 11.2.3, at 481 n. 36 (2d ed. 2010).

[27]Fed. R. Evid. 706(d) provides that the court, in its discretion, may authorize disclosure to the jury of the fact that the expert witness was appointed by the court. The Advisory Committee's Note states that "court appointed experts [may] acquire an

The two weaknesses mentioned above are not the only features of common law procedures which hamper the effectiveness of expert testimony. Other problem areas include: the unsuitability of the jury, a group of laypersons. as a tribunal for assessing scientific evidence;[28] the rules of privilege, especially the attorney-client privilege, the physician-patient privilege, and the privilege against self-incrimination which can block a full inquiry into the bases of the opinion;[29] and the use of legal standards of civil liability and criminal responsibility, which do not accord with the scientific standards which the experts are accustomed to, as in

---

aura of infallibility to which they are not entitled." The Advisory Committee's Note observes that disclosure "seems to be essential if the use of court appointed experts is to be fully effective." Nevertheless, Weinstein & Berger, Evidence ¶ 706[02] at 706–26 (1988), indicates that the question of disclosure was most strenuously debated in discussions among the Advisory Committee with some members of the bar expressing fear that "the court's imprimatur would overwhelm the jury and cause it to lose sight of the fact that the expert may have a professional bias towards one of the opposing views before it." Supporters of disclosure counter by pointing out that jurors should be encouraged to place special emphasis on the testimony of the court appointed experts for such reliance accords with the reasons for his appointment in the first place. Disclosure was apparently left discretionary to cover those situations where there exists two responsible schools of thought, or where disclosure of the fact of court appointment would tend to cause undue emphasis being placed on the expert's testimony. In any event, the arguments of those opposing the court appointment of experts as a solution to the problem of the battle of the venal experts are prevailing; as is also true generally at common law, the appointment of expert witnesses by the court under Fed. R. Evid. 706 is a relatively infrequent occurrence. Weinstein & Berger Evidence ¶ 701[01] at 706–14

(1988) ("Whether federal trial judges will react to Rule 706 by exercising their power to appoint more frequently remains doubtful. As a group they remain committed to adversarial responsibility for presenting evidence."). The latest edition of Weinstein takes a somewhat different view. 4 Weinstein's Federal Evidence § 706.02[1] (2d ed. 1997) ("It may be expected that, as the appearance of such neutral experts in the trial process becomes more common, the hostility toward them will begin to disappear"). *See* Kian v. Mirro Aluminum Co., 88 F.R.D. 351, 355 (E.D. Mich. 1980). In Wisconsin, the Judicial Council Committee added an explanatory note to that state's version of Rule 706. The note states that "[r]outine utilization of the power to appoint experts is an abuse of discretion."

[28]Many related problems exist. For example, psychiatric expert testimony may well differ, since it may depend upon whether the expert is "dynamically" or "organically" or otherwise oriented. *See* Allen, Furster, and Rubin, Readings in Law and Psychiatry 153 (1968).

[29]See §§ 99 and 134 infra. If the party who consulted an expert can assert a privilege to suppress any information about a non-testifying expert's analysis of the case, the party may "shop around" until he finds an expert willing to testify to precisely the opinion the party desires.

the case of the "understanding of right and wrong" test for legal sanity.[30]

More broadly, the courts' need for better employment of the technical resources goes beyond the use of expert witnesses. One judge has observed:

> The methods of courts might well be supplemented by the use of well tested examples of administrative tribunals, of expert investigators acting for the court—engineers, scientists, physicians, economic and social investigators, as needed—in addition to, not in substitute for, similar experts acting for the parties . . .
>
> Why should not judge and jury in cases involving multitudinous scientific exhibits, or scientific questions, have the benefit of the assistance of those competent to organize such data and analyze such questions? Why should not courts have adequate fact finding facilities for all kinds of cases? Boards of directors do. Administrative tribunals do. The parties, and in a large sense the public, have an interest in the decision of cases on whole truth, not on partial understanding. The machinery and expert staffs developed by the interstate commerce commission, state public service commissions, and workmen's compensation boards have values for fact finding which may profitably be studied in reference to judicial reorganization . . . .[31]

Even if in the long term we are unwilling to fundamentally reorganize the legal system to better integrate expertise, there are more modest steps that can be taken in the short term. The American legal tradition has devised a number of procedures which might conceivably be adapted to better utilize experts' services. For instance, special pretrial conferences could be tailored to deal exclusively with matters involving expert opinion. In addition, judges possess authority, often conferred by statute or rule but in any event an "inherent" judicial power,[32] to refer a question to a master, referee, auditor or similar officer, standing

---

[30]Weihofen, Insanity as a Defense in Criminal Law 64–68, 409–18 (1933). See also the body of literature which has grown up around Durham v. U.S., 214 F.2d 862 (D.C. Cir. 1954).

[31]Justice Harold M. Stephens, What Courts Can Learn from Commissions, 21 A.B.A. J. 141, 142 (1933). Also see generally Ch. 36 infra.

[32]See the opinion of Brandeis, J. in In re Peterson (State Report Title: Ex Parte Peterson), 253 U.S. 300, 312, 40 S. Ct. 543, 64 L. Ed. 919 (1920) (District Court may appoint auditor with provision that his report shall be used in evidence. "Courts have (at least in the absence of legislation to the contrary) inherent power to provide themselves with appropriate instruments required for the performance of their duties. *Compare* Stockbridge Iron Co. v. Cone Iron Works, 102 Mass. 80, 87–90 (1869). This power includes authority to appoint persons unconnected with the court to aid judges in the performance of specific judicial duties, as they may arise in the progress of a cause.")

A helpful discussion of the relative advantages and disadvantages of the use of adversary experts, masters, advisors, and court-appointed experts is found in Manual for Complex and Multidistrict Litigation § 21.5 (4th ed. 2004). *See* Fed. R. Civ. P. 53.

or special. The reference may contemplate merely an investigation and report, or a hearing followed by a report or a preliminary decision.[33] Even if the courts are reluctant to extend these procedures to expert testimony problems, the procedures could be prescribed by statute.[34] It has also been suggested that the courts make wider use of the executive branch's technical resources, specifically the administrative agencies and commissions.[35]

There are signs of progress. As previously stated, until recently most judges have been reluctant to resort to techniques such as court appointment under Rule 706.[36] However, in its 1993 *Daubert* decision,[37] the Supreme Court announced a new, reliability test for the admissibility of purportedly scientific testimony. That test requires trial judges to directly assess the validity of scientific hypotheses; the judges may no longer rely on "surrogates"[38] for validity such as the popularity or general acceptance of they hypothesis. The shift to the new validation test should encourage trial judges to appoint experts under 706. Indeed, in the course of its opinion, the *Daubert* Court mentioned the possibility that in applying the new test, judges would find it useful to appoint experts under the rule. In his concurrence in *Joiner*, Justice Breyer encouraged trial judges to exercise their appointment power.[39] There are signs that the incidence of court appointment is gradually increasing.[40] Moreover, there has been a dramatic increase in the number of continuing legal and judicial education programs devoted to scientific evidence. In addition, judges and attorneys now have far greater access to specialized scientific ev-

---

[33]Beuscher, The Use of Experts by the Courts, 54 Harv. L. Rev. 1105, 1111–20 (1941).

[34]Beuscher, 54 Harv. L. Rev. at 1126. There are, however, substantial general objections to the use of masters, and the like, even in a traditional way, in many types of cases.

[35]Beuscher, 54 Harv. L. Rev. at 1123.

[36]Cecil & Willging, Court-appointed Experts: Defining the Role of Experts Appointed under Federal Rule of Evidence 706, at 47 (1992).

[37]Daubert v. Merrell Dow Pharmaceuticals, Inc., 509 U.S. 579, 113 S. Ct. 2786, 125 L. Ed. 2d 469 (1993).

[38]Black, Ayala & Saffran—Brinks, Science and the Law in the Wake of *Daubert*: A New Search for Scientific Knowledge, 72 Tex. L. Rev. 715, 725–35 (1994).

[39]General Elec. Co. v. Joiner, 522 U.S. 136, 147, 149–50, 118 S. Ct. 512, 139 L. Ed. 2d 508 (1997) (Breyer, J., concurring).

[40]Note, Fighting Fire with Firefighters: A Proposal for Expert Judges at the Trial Level, 93 Colum. L. Rev. 473, 483 (1993) ("increasing at a modest rate"). *See* Jurs, Questions from the Bench and Independent Experts: A Study of State Court Judges (Mar. 22, 2012), available at http://ssr n.com/abstract=2027549 (last accessed Dec. 11, 2012) (22% of the state court judges responding indicated that they had appointed independent experts).

idence tools such as the *Reference Manual on Scientific Evidence* released by the Federal Judicial Center.[41]

## § 18   Application of the opinion rule to out-of-court statements

Does the opinion rule apply to out-of-court statements, offered in court under some exception to the hearsay rule? As we have seen, an early view[1] was that the opinion rule is a categorical rule of exclusion. Positing that view, it is natural to assume that if this kind of evidence is inadmissible when elicited from a witness on the stand, it certainly should be rejected when offered in hearsay form. Consequently, many older decisions analyze the admissibility of opinions contained in hearsay declarations as if they had been given by a witness on the stand, and reject or admit them accordingly.[2]

However, the emerging view is that the opinion doctrine should not be conceived as an absolute rule of exclusion. The doctrine is a relative norm for the examination of witnesses, preferring when it is feasible the more concrete testimony to the more general and inferential.[3] On that premise, the opinion rule has little or no sensible application to out-of-court statements. Sustaining an objection to counsel's question to a witness as calling for an "opinion" is usually not a serious matter; in most cases counsel can easily reframe the question on the spot to elicit the more concrete statement. But to automatically reject the same statement by an out-of-court declarant in a dying declaration mistakes the function of the opinion rule and may altogether shut out a valuable source of proof. When the source is an unavailable hearsay declarant, the stark choice facing the court may be between admitting the opinionated hearsay statement or denying the jury any information from that source. The legislatures and courts should opt for the first choice. Many of the cases and Wigmore take this enlightened view as to an opposing party's statements (formerly called admissions of a party-opponent),[4] and

---

[41]The third edition was released in 2011.

**[Section 18]**

[1]See § 11 supra.

[2]*E.g.*, Philpot v. Commonwealth, 195 Ky. 555, 242 S.W. 839 (1922); Pendleton v. Commonwealth, 131 Va. 676, 109 S.E. 201 (1921) (dying declaration).

[3]See §§ 11, 12 supra.

[4]Owens v. Atchison, T. & S. F. Ry. Co., 393 F.2d 77, 79 (5th Cir. 1968) ("It is well settled that the opinion rule does not apply to party's admissions."); Swain v. Oregon Motor Stages, 160 Or. 1, 82 P.2d 1084 (1938) (injured party's statement after collision that he considered driver of other car to blame); Taylor v. Owen, 290 S.W.2d 771 (Tex. Civ. App. San Antonio 1956) (statement that other driver was not at fault); 4 Wigmore, Evidence § 1053(3)

it is spreading to the other classes of declarations admitted under exceptions to the hearsay rule.[5]

Distinguish the superficially similar question of the declarant's lack of personal knowledge. If the out-of-court declarant had not observed at firsthand the fact declared, that deficiency goes not to form but to substance; and it is often fatal to admissibility when the declaration is offered as substantive evidence to prove the fact.[6]

---

(Chadbourn rev. 1972); and see § 256 infra. Compare the similar problem in respect to evidence of inconsistent statements to impeach, § 35 infra. See treatment of the various exclusions and exceptions to the hearsay rule in Chapters 25 to 33 infra.

[5]As to dying declarations, see § 313 infra. Federal Rule of Evidence 806(6), governing the admission of business entries, expressly authorizes the receipt of "opinions" and "diagno-

ses." The Supreme Court has construed Rule 803(8) (C) as permitting the introduction of opinions by expert investigators. Beech Aircraft Corp. v. Rainey, 488 U.S. 153, 109 S. Ct. 439, 102 L. Ed. 2d 445 (1988).

[6]See §§ 313 and 280 infra. But the state of law is to the contrary with respect to admissions, see § 255 infra and the entry of items in business records, see § 290 infra.

# Chapter 4

# Cross-Examination and Subsequent Examinations

## § 19   The right of cross-examination:[1] Effect of deprivation of opportunity to cross-examine

For two centuries, common law judges and lawyers have regarded the opportunity of cross-examination as an essential

---

**[Section 19]**

[1]As to cross-examination generally, see 5 Wigmore, Evidence §§ 1390–94 (Chadbourn rev. 1974), 6 Wigmore, Evidence §§ 1884–94 (1976); West's Key Number Digest, Witnesses ☞266 to 284.

However, the right to cross-examine a person comes into play only if the person becomes a witness and gives testimony. In the courtroom a person can engage in conduct, which has the practical effect of presenting information without testifying. For

safeguard of the accuracy and completeness of testimony.[2] They
have insisted that the opportunity is a right,[3] not a mere
privilege.[4] This right is available at the taking of depositions as
well as during the examination of witnesses at trial.[5] The premise
that the opportunity of cross-examination is an essential
safeguard has become the principal justification for the general
exclusion of hearsay statements.[6] It also underpins the recognition of a hearsay exception for former testimony taken at a prior
hearing where the present adversary was afforded the opportunity to cross-examine.[7] State constitutional provisions
guaranteeing the accused's right of confrontation have been
interpreted as codifying this right of cross-examination,[8] and the
Sixth Amendment confrontation clause of the federal constitution
has likewise been construed as guaranteeing the accused's right

---

example, a defendant may exhibit a
physical characteristic such as the
lack of tattoo (Display of physical
appearance or characteristic of defendant for purpose of challenging prosecution evidence as "testimony" resulting in waiver of defendant's privilege
against self-incrimination, 81 A.L.R.
Fed. 892) or engage in a non-verbal
demonstration without testifying and
thereby becoming subject to cross-
examination. U.S. v. Williams, 461
F.3d 441, 446–48 (4th Cir. 2006) (a
demonstration that a fanny pack was
too short to close around the defendant's waist); Lewis v. State, 725 So.
2d 183, 187–89 (Miss. 1998) (an in-
court demonstration).

[2]*See* 5 Wigmore, Evidence § 1367
(Chadbourn rev. 1974). *See also*
Hungate v. Hudson, 353 Mo. 944, 185
S.W.2d 646 (1945).

[3]Alford v. U.S., 282 U.S. 687, 51
S. Ct. 218, 75 L. Ed. 624 (1931); Cotto
v. Herbert, 331 F.3d 217 (2d Cir. 2003)
(at trial, the judge admitted a witness's pretrial identification because
the defendant had procured the witness's refusal to identify the defendant
in court; because of the defendant's
misconduct, the judge forbade the
defense from cross-examining the witness when the witness testified at
trial; despite the defendant's misconduct, the defendant had a right to
question the witness); U.S. v. Mills,
138 F.3d 928, 938 (11th Cir. 1998) ("A

trial judge may not totally deny a defendant the opportunity to cross-
examine a witness against him, whatever the time constraints, the number
of defendants, being tried, or relationship between defendants"). *But see* U.S.
v. Papajohn, 212 F.3d 1112 (8th Cir.
2000) (on direct examination, the witness refused to answer the prosecutor's
questions; the defendant was not entitled to cross-examine the witness,
since the witness did not give any
direct testimony to impeach); U.S. v.
Ellis, 156 F.3d 493, 498 (3d Cir. 1998)
(the defendant had no right to cross-
examine the witness; the witness "testified only as to the foundational basis
required to admit" a tape recording,
and the defendant had stipulated to
the authenticity of the tape).

[4]Resurrection Gold Min. Co. v.
Fortune Gold Min. Co., 129 F. 668
(C.C.A. 8th Cir. 1904).

[5]State ex rel. Bailes v. Guardian
Realty Co., 237 Ala. 201, 186 So. 168
(1939). Fed. R. Civ. P. 30(c) and Fed.
R. Crim. P. 15(b) recognize the right
at the taking of depositions.

[6]See § 245 infra.

[7]See § 302 infra.

[8]State v. Crooker, 123 Me. 310,
122 A. 865 (1923) (confrontation right
does not mean merely that accused
shall see the witness, but also guarantees the right to cross-examine), and
see § 252 infra.

to cross-examination in criminal proceedings.[9] Indeed, although other rights are subsumed under the confrontation clause,[10] in

---

[9]Crawford v. Washington, 541 U.S. 36, 124 S. Ct. 1354, 158 L. Ed. 2d 177 (2004); Smith v. State of Illinois, 390 U.S. 129, 88 S. Ct. 748, 19 L. Ed. 2d 956 (1968); Douglas v. State of Ala., 380 U.S. 415, 85 S. Ct. 1074, 13 L. Ed. 2d 934 (1965); Pointer v. Texas, 380 U.S. 400, 85 S. Ct. 1065, 13 L. Ed. 2d 923 (1965); Barber v. Page, 390 U.S. 719, 88 S. Ct. 1318, 20 L. Ed. 2d 255 (1968); California v. Green, 399 U.S. 149, 90 S. Ct. 1930, 26 L. Ed. 2d 489 (1970); Chambers v. Mississippi, 410 U.S. 284, 93 S. Ct. 1038, 35 L. Ed. 2d 297 (1973); Davis v. Alaska, 415 U.S. 308, 94 S. Ct. 1105, 39 L. Ed. 2d 347 (1974). *See generally* In re Oliver, 333 U.S. 257, 273, 68 S. Ct. 499, 92 L. Ed. 682 (1948) ("[T]hese rights [basic in our system of jurisprudence] include, as a minimum, a right to examine the witnesses against him.").

[10]The constitutional guarantee not only includes the right to cross-examine; in addition, the defendant generally has the right to personally confront the witness testifying against the defendant. Maryland v. Craig, 497 U.S. 836, 110 S. Ct. 3157, 111 L. Ed. 2d 666 (1990); Coy v. Iowa, 487 U.S. 1012, 108 S. Ct. 2798, 101 L. Ed. 2d 857 (1988). However, especially in the case of young child witnesses, the courts have relaxed this requirement in extreme cases when personal confrontation with the defendant would be so traumatic for the witness that the witness could not testify effectively. Thirty-seven states have enacted legislation authorizing alternative procedures for testimony by child witnesses (McAree, Voters OK Taped Child Testimony, Nat'l L.J., Nov. 10, 2003, at 6); and there is now a Uniform Child Witness Testimony by Alternative Methods Act. 71 U.S.L.W. (BNA) 2137 (Aug. 27, 2002). The showing of likely witness trauma must be "strong, specific, and persuasive." State v. Bray, 335 S.C. 514, 517 S.E.2d 714 (Ct. App. 1999). Expert testimony can

establish the requisite showing. Lomholt v. Iowa, 327 F.3d 748, 754 (8th Cir. 2003); People v. Powell, 194 Cal. App. 4th 1268, 124 Cal. Rptr. 3d 214 (6th Dist. 2011) (testimony by a social worker and the victim's mother established that the child victim would suffer such great emotional distress that she might be unable to provide a useful account of the events). When the requisite showing has been made, the courts have approved such procedures as two-way closed circuit television (Parkhurst v. Belt, 567 F.3d 995 (8th Cir. 2009); U.S. v. Etimani, 328 F.3d 493 (9th Cir. 2003); Ault v. Waid, 654 F. Supp. 2d 465, 486–90 (N.D. W. Va. 2009); Comment, Virtually Face-to-Face: The Confrontation Clause and the Use of Two-Way Video Testimony, 13 Roger Williams U. L. Rev. 565 (2008)), repositioning of courtroom chairs (Smith v. State, 340 Ark. 116, 8 S.W.3d 534 (2000)), and support persons for the witness. State v. T.E., 342 N.J. Super. 14, 775 A.2d 686 (App. Div. 2001).

In the case of child witnesses, given the requisite showing of likely trauma, the courts often permit the use of screens and shields. Lucas v. McBride, 505 F. Supp. 2d 329, 353 (N.D. W. Va. 2007) (during her testimony, the victim was positioned so that she did have to look directly at the defendant); State v. Vogelsberg, 2006 WI App 228, 297 Wis. 2d 519, 724 N.W.2d 649, 655 (Ct. App. 2006) (the defendant had threatened to harm the victim if the victim even told anyone about the abuse; the victim's trauma went beyond mere nervousness); Ebisike, The Evidence of Children, 44 Crim. L. Bull. 724, 737–39, 742–43 (2008) (summarizing the case law on shielding and screening procedures as well as the physical alteration of the courtroom). In many cases, the courts have also approved of support persons during the child's testimony. Lucas v. McBride, supra at 354 (the child's foster mother); People v.

the Supreme Court's 2004 decision in *Crawford v. Washington* a majority of the justices appeared to embrace the notion that the right to cross-examination is the primary interest secured by the confrontation clause.[11] Under the rubric of procedural due pro-

---

Stevens, 67 Cal. Rptr. 3d 567, 572–73 (Cal. App. 1st Dist. 2007) (a support person for a 16-year-old victim); People v. Ybarra, 57 Cal. Rptr. 3d 732, 739 (Cal. App. 5th Dist. 2007) (the support person was a victim advocate rather than a relative); Czech v. State, 945 A.2d 1088 (Del. 2008); Ebisike, 44 Crim. L. Bull. at 743 ("However, it is not permissible for a child to sit on the judge's or attorney's lap"). Some have even argued for the use of support dogs during testimony. Delinger, Using Dogs for Emotional Support of Testifying Victims of Crime, 15 Animal L. 171 (2009).

Even in the case of adult witnesses, the courts have sometimes authorized special steps to protect the witness from harm. In one case in which the defendant previously knew the foreign agent witnesses only by their pseudonyms, the court allowed the witnesses to testify under their pseudonyms and refused to permit the defense to cross-examine the witnesses about their actual names. U.S. v. Abu Marzook, 412 F. Supp. 2d 913, 923–24 (N.D. Ill. 2006). *See also* U.S. v. Ramos-Cruz, 667 F.3d 487, 500–01 (4th Cir. 2012) (Salvadoran citizens permitted to testify under psuedonyms); People v. Ramirez, 55 Cal. App. 4th 47, 64 Cal. Rptr. 2d 9 (1st Dist. 1997) (a rape victim was permitted to testify as "Jane Doe"). Some courts also permit witnesses to testify in disguise (People v. Brandon, 52 Cal. Rptr. 3d 427, 442 (Cal. App. 2d Dist. 2006)) at least so long as the use of such objects as sunglasses and cap does not interfere with the jury's ability to observe the witness's demeanor during cross-examination. Romero v. State, 173 S.W.3d 502 (Tex. Crim. App. 2005).

Some have argued that as a general proposition, the use of two-way videoconferencing or closed circuit television satisfies the right to personally confront adverse witnesses. Fuster-Escalona v. Florida Dept. of Corrections, 170 Fed. Appx. 627, 629–30 (11th Cir. 2006); U.S. v. Gigante, 166 F.3d 75, 79–83 (2d Cir. 1999) (two-way videoconferencing preserves rather than infringes face-to-face confrontation); Harmon, Child Testimony via Two-Way Closed Circuit Television: A New Perspective on Maryland v. Craig in United States v. Turning Bear and United States v. Bordeaux, 7 N.C. J. L. & Tech. 157 (2005) ("The Supreme Court's case-specific holding in Maryland v. Craig was directed at one-way closed circuit testimony"); Comment, Virtually Face-to-Face: The Confrontation Clause and the Use of Two-Way Video Testimony, 13 Roger Williams U. L. Rev. 565 (2008); Comment, Accusations from Abroad: Testimony of Unavailable Witnesses Via Live Two-Way Videoconferencing Does Not Violate the Confrontation Clause of the Sixth Amendment, 41 U.C. Davis L. Rev. 1671 (2008). *But see* Comment, Avoiding Virtual Justice: Video-Teleconference Testimony in Federal Criminal Trials, 56 Cath. U. L. Rev. 683, 684–86 (2007) (the courts have accepted this technology in civil trials; however, in "federal criminal trials . . . there is no clear evidentiary rule . . . . [T]here is dissonance among federal criminal decisions"); Comment, Virtual Confrontation: Is Videoconferencing Testimony by an Unavailable Witness Unconstitutional, 74 U. Chi. L. Rev. 1581, 1582–84 (2007).

[11]Crawford v. Washington, 541 U.S. 36, 124 S. Ct. 1354, 158 L. Ed. 2d 177 (2004); Ohio v. Roberts, 448 U.S. 56, 63, 100 S. Ct. 2531, 65 L. Ed. 2d 597 (1980); Dutton v. Evans, 400 U.S. 74, 94, 91 S. Ct. 210, 27 L. Ed. 2d 213 (1970) (Harlan, J., concurring).

cess, the courts have even granted a measure of constitutional protection to the right in civil cases.[12]

What are the consequences of a denial or failure of the right? There are several common, recurring situations.[13] First, a party testifying on his own behalf might unjustifiably refuse to answer questions necessary to a complete cross-examination. In this fact situation, the consensus is that the adversary is entitled to have the direct testimony stricken[14]—a result that seems fair. The party suffers the loss of the direct testimony, but the party himself is responsible for the denial of cross-examination.

Second, a non-party witness might similarly refuse to be cross-examined or to answer proper cross-examination questions. Here the proper result is less clear; the loss of the non-party witness's testimony can be a severe hardship to the party calling the witness, and the party may not be responsible in any way for the witness's refusal. Nevertheless, many courts and writers approve of the same drastic remedy of excluding the direct.[15] This remedy minimizes the party's temptation to procure the witness's

---

[12]Tribe, American Constitutional Law § 10–15 (2d ed. 1988); Friendly, Some Kind of Hearing, 123 U. Pa. L. Rev. 1267, 1285 (1975).

[13]See the analyses of these problems in 5 Wigmore, Evidence § 1390 (Chadbourn rev. 1974), and Degnan, Non—Rules Evidence Law: Cross-Examination, 6 Utah L. Rev. 323 (1959).

[14]U.S. v. $133,420.00 in U.S. Currency, 672 F.3d 629, 640–41 (9th Cir. 2012) ("a criminal defendant, like any other witness, must 'comply with the procedures used to give the jury a fair chance to evalute [the testimony's] truth' "); Williams v. Borg, 139 F.3d 737 (9th Cir. 1998); U.S. v. Bartelho, 129 F.3d 663, 673 (1st Cir. 1997) ("A trial judge may strike a witness's direct testimony if he flatly refuses to answer cross-examination questions related to the details of his direct testimony, thereby undermining the prosecution's ability to test the truth of his direct testimony. If the prosecutor's questions relate only to collateral matters, however, the trial judge should protect the defendant's right to present his defense, if possible"); U.S. v. Panza, 612 F.2d 432 (9th Cir. 1979) (defendant's refusal to answer prosecu-

tor's questioning went to the core of the defense); U.S. v. Colon-Miranda, 992 F. Supp. 86, 89 (D.P.R. 1998); People v. McGowan, 80 Cal. App. 293, 251 P. 643 (1st Dist. 1926) (accused's direct testimony to an alibi stricken when on cross-examination he refused to answer question about name of person who was with him at the time); Aluminum Industries v. Egan, 61 Ohio App. 111, 14 Ohio Op. 174, 22 N.E.2d 459 (1st Dist. Hamilton County 1938) (direct testimony of party-witness, refusing to answer pertinent cross-questions on unjustified ground of privilege). See also People v. Barthel, 231 Cal. App. 2d 827, 42 Cal. Rptr. 290 (4th Dist. 1965); In re Monaghan, 126 Vt. 53, 222 A.2d 665 (1966); West's Key Number Digest, Witnesses ☜284. Seemingly the cross-examiner could invoke the court's action to compel the witness to answer, if the privilege against self-incrimination has not been invoked or is inapplicable, but is not required to do so.

[15]U.S. v. Rosario Fuentez, 231 F.3d 700 (10th Cir. 2000); Klein v. Harris, 667 F.2d 274 (2d Cir. 1981) (witness recalled and refused to answer questions relevant to previous testimony); U.S. v. Frank, 520 F.2d 1287 (2d Cir. 1975) (cross-examination

refusal—a collusion which is often hard to prove; the remedy forcefully protects the right of cross-examination. However, there is a split of authority in the second situation. There is some precedent that the matter should be left to the judge's discretion.[16] In particular, there is support for the view that if the witness invokes the privilege against self-incrimination to refuse to answer cross-examination questions which are merely collateral,[17] that is, logically relevant only to the witness's credibility, the judge should not automatically strike the direct testimony. Here some cases give the judge a measure of discretion in ruling on the cross-examiner motion to strike.[18]

---

went directly to the heart of the direct examination); Whitley v. Ercole, 725 F. Supp. 2d 398, 422 (S.D. N.Y. 2010); Avincola v. Stinson, 60 F. Supp. 2d 133, 154–56 (S.D. N.Y. 1999); Mercado v. Stinson, 37 F. Supp. 2d 267 (S.D. N.Y. 1999) (although the witness generally testified about the robbery, the witness refused to give details about the defendant's involvement in the robbery); People v. Morgain, 177 Cal. App. 4th 454, 99 Cal. Rptr. 3d 301, 308 (1st Dist. 2009) ("[a] defendant's confrontation rights may be violated where a prosecutor examines a recalcitrant witness and poses questions that relate to prior statements made by that witness, in circumstances where the witness's recalcitrance effectively prevents cross-examination concerning those prior statements"); State v. Davis, 236 Iowa 740, 19 N.W.2d 655 (1945) (but here held that full opportunity was later accorded); Combs v. Com., 74 S.W.3d 738 (Ky. 2002) (the defense witness selectively invoked her Fifth Amendment privilege), amended (May 24, 2002); 5 Wigmore, Evidence § 1391 (Chadbourn rev. 1974).

[16]See Stephan v. U.S., 133 F.2d 87 (C.C.A. 6th Cir. 1943) (refusal to answer only a few of the cross-questions; judge in discretion properly refused to strike direct testimony); Moormeister v. Golding, 84 Utah 324, 27 P.2d 447 (1933) (the judge has discretion as to whether a deposition should be excluded for witness's failure to answer a question under nota-

ry's prompting). But in criminal cases, this rule raises constitutional questions. See text at note 9 supra.

[17]U.S. v. Wilmore, 381 F.3d 868, 873 (9th Cir. 2004), citing the leading case, U.S. v. Cardillo, 316 F.2d 606, 611 (2d Cir. 1963); U.S. v. Marzook, 435 F. Supp. 2d 708, 750 (N.D. Ill. 2006) ("the answer relate[d] only to collateral matters . . . ."). See notes 18–19 infra.

[18]The leading case is U.S. v. Cardillo, 316 F.2d 606 (2d Cir. 1963). See also U.S. v. Berrio-Londono, 946 F.2d 158, 160–61 (1st Cir. 1991); Bagby v. Kuhlman, 932 F.2d 131 (2d Cir. 1991); U.S. v. Stubbert, 655 F.2d 453 (1st Cir. 1981) (distinguishing between cross-examination questions closely related to crime at issue and questions involving collateral or repetitious matter); U.S. v. Seifert, 648 F.2d 557 (9th Cir. 1980) (judge had some discretion to decide when cross-examination went to direct or collateral matters); U.S. v. Williams, 626 F.2d 697 (9th Cir. 1980) (judge could refuse to strike direct when cross-examination in which witness refused to answer went only to collateral matters); Dunbar v. Harris, 612 F.2d 690 (2d Cir. 1979) (refusal to answer questions which went to credibility and were only collateral); U.S. v. Marcus, 401 F.2d 563 (2d Cir. 1968); Coil v. U.S., 343 F.2d 573 (8th Cir. 1965); U.S. v. Smith, 342 F.2d 525 (4th Cir. 1965) (repetitious cross-examination); Combs v. Com., 74 S.W.3d 738 (Ky. 2002) (although a defense witness invoked her Fifth

Third, the witness may become, or purport to become, sick or otherwise physically or mentally incapacitated, before cross-examination is begun or completed. The facts in many of these cases raise a suspicion of simulation, particularly when the witness is a party. Consequently, the party's direct examination is often stricken.[19] In the case of the non-party witness, the same result usually obtains.[20] However, at least in civil actions, a case can be constructed that the judge should not exclude the direct if he is clearly convinced that the incapacity is genuine. In that event he ought to let the direct testimony stand. He can then give the jury a cautionary instruction to explain the weakness of uncross-examined evidence.[21] (Temporary incapacity may change this result, as indicated below.)

In the fourth situation, the witness dies before the conclusion of the cross-examination. Here again it is usually held that the party denied cross-examination is entitled to have the direct testimony stricken,[22] unless, presumably, the death occurred during a postponement of the cross-examination consented to or procured by that party.[23] Indeed, its exclusion may be constitutionally compelled if the person was a state's witness in a crimi-

---

Amendment privilege with respect to some questions, those questions did not relate to essential details).

But the thwarted cross-examination may be pertinent to material issues as well as to credibility. Board of Trustees of Mount San Antonio Jr. College Dist. of Los Angeles County v. Hartman, 246 Cal. App. 2d 756, 55 Cal. Rptr. 144 (2d Dist. 1966) (but error held not prejudicial).

[19]U.S. v. Stalnaker, 571 F.3d 428, 434 (5th Cir. 2009) (the government witness was unable to complete her testimony because she suffered panic attacks on the stand); Louisville & N. R. Co. v. Gregory, 284 Ky. 297, 144 S.W.2d 519 (1940) (plaintiff suing for personal injuries testified from a cot and on cross-examination professed to be unable to proceed; judge refused to strike direct but offered to let defendant use cross-examination taken at former trial, which the defendant declined to do; it was error to refuse to strike).

[20]Wray v. State, 154 Ala. 36, 45 So. 697 (1908); People v. Cole, 43 N.Y. 508, 1871 WL 9590 (1871). But where the importance of the direct has been unusually emphasized by the proponent, the failure of cross-examination may require a mistrial. U.S. v. Malinsky, 153 F. Supp. 321 (S.D. N.Y. 1957).

[21]People v. Sanders, 189 Cal. App. 4th 543, 117 Cal. Rptr. 3d 140 (2d Dist. 2010), cert. denied, 132 S. Ct. 215, 181 L. Ed. 2d 117 (2011). This is suggested in Note, 27 Colum. L. Rev. 327 (1927). But it is doubtful that this procedure would be constitutional if the witness is one called by the prosecution in a criminal case. See note 9 supra.

[22]Kemble v. Lyons, 184 Iowa 804, 169 N.W. 117 (1918); Sperry v. Moore's Estate, 42 Mich. 353, 4 N.W. 13 (1880) (death during continuance procured by direct examiner); State v. Bigham, 133 S.C. 491, 131 S.E. 603 (1926); In re Sweeney's Estate, 248 Wis. 607, 22 N.W.2d 657 (1946) (right of cross-examination specially reserved by judge).

[23]See 5 Wigmore, Evidence § 1390, n. 6 (Chadbourn rev. 1974). The cases cited there, however, are instances of disabilities other than death.

nal case. Yet, at least in case of death, it has been suggested that striking the direct ought to be discretionary.[24] That suggestion has merit. No matter how valuable cross-examination may be, common sense tells us that the half-loaf of direct testimony is better than no bread at all.[25] It seems excessive to deny the jury all the testimony from a potential source of valuable information. It was the accepted practice in equity to let the direct testimony stand.[26] It is submitted that except for the testimony of prosecution witnesses, the judge should let the direct testimony stand but on request instruct the jury to consider the lack of opportunity to cross-examine in weighing the direct testimony.

The above results may be modified in certain situations. For instance, there is authority that where the incapacity is temporary, the cross-examiner may not insist on immediate exclusion of the direct testimony. Rather, he must be content with the offer of a later opportunity to cross-examine even when doing so makes it necessary for him to submit to a mistrial.[27] If the initial trial proceeded to decision without the benefit of the witness's testimony, the outcome might be a wrongful verdict. A second trial could avoid a miscarriage of substantive justice.

The preceding paragraphs assumed for simplicity's sake that although the witness answered some cross-questions, a failure to secure a complete cross-examination would be treated as if cross-examination had been wholly denied. That assumption is an oversimplification. Even when the cross-examination is cut off before it is finished, under the circumstances the questioning could be substantially complete enough to satisfy the requirement for an opportunity to cross-examine.[28] In a given case, cross-examination as to part of the direct testimony may be extensive enough to allow at least that part to stand though the rest must

---

[24]5 Wigmore, Evidence § 1390, p. 135 (Chadbourn rev. 1974) ("But the true solution would be to avoid any inflexible rule, and to leave it to the trial judge to admit the direct examination so far as the loss of cross-examination can be shown to him to be not in that instance a material loss") quoted approvingly in Kubin v. Chicago Title & Trust Co., 307 Ill. App. 12, 29 N.E.2d 859, 863 (1st Dist. 1940) (the judge's ruling striking the direct examination was affirmed absent showing of prejudice). *See also* Treharne v. Callahan, 426 F.2d 58 (3d Cir. 1970).

[25]*See* Note, 27 Colum. L. Rev. 327 (1927) pointing out that the testimony is more trustworthy than evidence admitted under many of the established hearsay exceptions.

[26]*See* Scott v. McCann, 76 Md. 47, 24 A. 536 (1892).

[27]Gale v. State, 135 Ga. 351, 69 S.E. 537 (1910) (where witness collapsed on defendant's cross-examination, it was not error to refuse to strike the evidence; defendant declined to consent to mistrial).

[28]Fuller v. Rice, 70 Mass. 343, 4 Gray 343, 1855 WL 5853 (1855).

be stricken.[29] If the cross-examination on a particular topic has been in depth, the trial judge should refuse to strike the direct testimony on that topic.

Although the preceding paragraphs deal with the conduct of parties and witnesses, the infringement of the right of cross-examination may result from the judge's action. The judge has wide discretionary control over the *extent* of cross-examination upon particular topics. However, the complete denial of cross-examination[30] or its arbitrary curtailment on a proper, important subject of cross-examination[31] is ground for reversal. In decisions

---

[29]U.S. v. Newman, 490 F.2d 139 (3d Cir. 1974) (a government witness's invocation of the Fifth Amendment to a question relevant to an important element should lead to the striking of the direct testimony going to that element—a partial striking of the direct). *See* Curtice v. West, 2 N.Y.S. 507 (Sup 1888); and *compare* People v. Visich, 57 A.D.3d 804, 870 N.Y.S.2d 376, 378–79 (2d Dep't 2008) (the trial judge refused to strike two witnesses' direct testimony after they invoked their privilege against self-incrimination during cross-examination; the refusal did not violate the defendant's confrontation right; the defendant was still able to cross-examine the witnesses concerning the instant crimes and explore each witness's bias and motivation to testify falsely through other evidence); and In re Mezger's Estate, 154 Misc. 633, 278 N.Y.S. 669 (Sur. Ct. 1935). *See also* Jaiser v. Milligan, 120 F. Supp. 599 (D. Neb. 1954) (a cross-examination begun but unfinished through no fault of the witness or her attorney suffices if its purposes have been substantially accomplished).

[30]Delaware v. Van Arsdall, 475 U.S. 673, 679, 106 S. Ct. 1431, 89 L. Ed. 2d 674 (1986) (trial court improperly "prohibited all inquiry into the possibility that [witness] would be biased as a result of the State's dismissal of his pending public drunkenness charge"); Alford v. U.S., 282 U.S. 687, 51 S. Ct. 218, 75 L. Ed. 624 (1931) (refusal to permit cross-examination of government witness about his present residence, in custody of U.S. mar-

shal, to show bias); Dixon v. U.S., 333 F.2d 348 (5th Cir. 1964) (judge should not have refused cross-examination when the judge questioned witness upon return of jury to open court to ask a question of the judge; the judge's questioning enhanced an informer's credibility); Fahey v. Clark, 125 Conn. 44, 3 A.2d 313 (1938) (refusal to permit cross-examination of plaintiff about prior injury); People v. Crump, 5 Ill. 2d 251, 125 N.E.2d 615 (1955) (refusal to permit cross-examination of accomplice witness to show that he was a drug addict or had used narcotics on day of crime).

The criminal defendant's right in such a case in both state and federal courts is a federal constitutional right. See § 29, infra.

[31]Alford v. U.S., 282 U.S. 687, 694, 51 S. Ct. 218, 75 L. Ed. 624 (1931) ("The extent of cross-examination with respect to an appropriate subject of inquiry is within the sound discretion of the trial court. It may exercise a reasonable judgment in determining when the subject is exhausted."); Delaware v. Van Arsdall, 475 U.S. 673, 679, 106 S. Ct. 1431, 89 L. Ed. 2d 674 (1986) ("[T]rial judges retain wide latitude insofar as the Confrontation Clause is concerned to impose reasonable limits on such cross-examination based on concerns about, among other things, harassment, prejudice, confusion of the issues, the witness' safety, or interrogation that is repetitive or only marginally relevant. And as we observed earlier this Term, 'the Confrontation Clause guarantees an *op-*

such as *Davis v. Alaska*,[32] the Supreme Court has emphasized that evidence of a witness's bias can have significant probative value on the question of a witness's credibility.[33] When a trial judge forecloses or severely limits cross-examination about a prosecution witness's bias, the trial judge is flirting with reversal on appeal.[34]

## § 20   Form of interrogation

Assuming that a litigant has the right to cross-examine, questions can arise as to the scope and form of the cross. In contrast to direct examination, cross-examination may usually be conducted by questions that are leading in form.[1] When the cross-examiner uses leading, narrowly-phrased questions, under the guise of asking questions the cross-examiner can make factual assertions on the record and force the witness to assent. The cross-examiner can virtually testify for the witness. The cross-examiner's purpose is often to weaken the effect of the direct

---

*portunity* for effective cross-examination, not cross-examination that is effective in whatever way, and to whatever extent, the defense might wish.' Delaware v. Fensterer, 474 U.S. 15, 20, 106 S.Ct. 292, 295, 88 L.Ed.2d 15 (1985) (per curiam) (emphasis in original)". *See also* U.S. v. Polk, 550 F.2d 1265 (10th Cir. 1977).

Notice the apparent change in tone between *Alford* and *Van Arsdall*. The latter case places a greater emphasis on the trial judge's discretion to impose reasonable limits.

[32]Davis v. Alaska, 415 U.S. 308, 94 S. Ct. 1105, 39 L. Ed. 2d 347 (1974).

[33]U.S. v. Sasson, 62 F.3d 874, 883 (7th Cir. 1995) ("where the defense is completely foreclosed from exposing the witness' bias or motive to testify, the limitation might directly implicate the defendant's constitutionally protected right to cross-examination"); Quinn v. Neal, 998 F.2d 526, 531 (7th Cir. 1993) ("[a] trial judge has no discretion to prevent cross-examination about . . . a prototypical form of bias . . . ."); Imwinkelried & Garland, Exculpatory Evidence: The Accused's Constitutional Right to Introduce Favorable Evidence § 8-7 (3d ed. 2004).

[34]U.S. v. Sasson, 62 F.3d 874, 883

(7th Cir. 1995) ("where the defense is completely foreclosed from exposing the witness' bias or motive to testify, the limitation may directly implicate the defendant's constitutionally protected right to cross-examination"); Quinn v. Neal, 998 F.2d 526, 531 (7th Cir. 1993) ("[a] trial judge has no discretion to prevent cross-examination about . . . a prototypical form of bias . . . ."); U.S. v. Williams, 892 F.2d 296, 301 (3d Cir. 1989) ("In this case, . . . the trial court prohibited all inquiry into the possibility that Boyd was biased. This we find to be . . . a violation of rights secured by the Confrontation Clause").

**[Section 20]**

[1]Ewing v. U.S., 135 F.2d 633 (App. D.C. 1942); In re Mitgang, 385 Ill. 311, 52 N.E.2d 807 (1944); 3 Wigmore, Evidence § 773 (Chadbourn rev. 1970); West's Key Number Digest, Witnesses ☞282.

Rev. Unif. R. Evid. (1974) 611(c) and Fed. R. Evid. 611(c) provide: "Ordinarily leading questions should be permitted on cross-examination." Effective December 1, 2011, restyled Fed. R. Evid. 611(c)(1) reads: "Ordinarily, the court should allow leading questions . . . on cross-examination . . . ."

testimony, and the witness is commonly assumed to be more or less uncooperative. Consequently there is little risk that the witness will acquiesce in the cross-examiner's suggestions.

The courts permit leading on cross-examination on the assumption that there is usually a hostile relationship between the witness and the cross-examiner. Given the nature of their relationship, the witness is unlikely to blindly accept the suggestions implicit in the questions' leading phrasing. However, in many jurisdictions when it appears that the witness is biased in the cross-examiner's favor and likely to yield to the suggestions of leading questions, the judge may forbid the cross-examiner from leading.[2] There are, however, a number of somewhat illogical decisions permitting leading questions on cross-examination even when the witness is biased in the cross-examiner's favor.[3]

In jurisdictions limiting the scope of cross-examination, if the examiner goes beyond the proper field of cross-examination he may be required to refrain from leading the witness as to the

---

[2]Moody v. Rowell, 34 Mass. 490, 498, 17 Pick. 490, 1835 WL 2374 (1835) ("So a judge may, in his discretion, prohibit certain leading questions from being put to an adversary's witness, where the witness shows a strong interest or bias in favor of the cross-examining party, and needs only an intimation, to say whatever is most favorable to that party."); 3 Wigmore, Evidence § 773 (Chadbourn rev. 1970); Cross-examination by leading questions of witness friendly to or biased in favor of cross-examiner, 38 A.L.R.2d 952. *See* Tolomeo v. Harmony Short Line Motor Transp. Co., 349 Pa. 420, 37 A.2d 511 (1944) (in a collision case where plaintiff called defendant's bus driver to show defendant's ownership, the trial judge improperly permitted defendant to cross-examine driver by leading questions about negligence). But it is largely a matter of discretion. Westland Housing Corp. v. Scott, 312 Mass. 375, 44 N.E.2d 959 (1942). In the case, a party was called by his adversary and cross-examined by his own counsel.

The text is applicable under Fed. R. Evid. 611 and Unif. R. Evid. 611(c). The Advisory Committee's Note states,

"The purpose of the qualification 'ordinarily' is to furnish a basis for denying the use of leading questions when the cross-examination is cross-examination in form only and not in fact, as for example the 'cross-examination' of a party by his own counsel after being called by the opposing counsel (savoring more of redirect) or of an insured defendant who proves to be friendly to the plaintiff." Accord Shultz v. Rice, 809 F.2d 643, 654 (10th Cir. 1986) ("The instant scenario involving the questioning of Dr. Rice by his own counsel is precisely that characterized in the note as 'cross-examination in form only and not in fact,' and therefore, should not have been allowed as a matter of right.").

[3]Martyn v. Donlin, 151 Conn. 402, 198 A.2d 700 (1964) (defense counsel permitted to use leading questions on cross-examination of defendant who had been called by plaintiff as an adverse witness); Wilcox v. Erwin, 49 S.W.2d 677 (Mo. Ct. App. 1932) (similar case); Cross-examination by leading questions of witness friendly to or biased in favor of cross-examiner, 38 A.L.R.2d 952.

new subject.[4] The cross-examiner "adopts" the witness with respect to the new topic. Although the questioning is formally cross-examination, it is functionally a direct examination; and the general prohibition against leading consequently comes into play.

## § 21   Scope of cross-examination: Restriction to matters opened up on direct: the various rules[1]

The practice varies widely in the different jurisdictions over the question of whether the cross-examiner is confined to the subjects testified about in the direct examination and, if so, to what extent. However, the differences of opinion should not be overstated. Although this section reviews those varying practices, there is a good deal of consensus over the proper scope of cross-examination. As § 22 notes, all the courts agree that the proper scope includes matters relevant to the witness's credibility. In addition, as we shall see again in § 24, most jurisdictions accord the trial judge a measure of discretion over the scope of cross-examination on the merits.[2] The point of sharpest disagreement is the normal scope of cross-examination on the historical merits of the case. There are three major schools of judicial thought on that topic.

### *The Traditional Rule of Wide-open Cross-examination*

In England and a few states, the simplest and freest practice prevails. In these jurisdictions, the cross-examiner is not limited

---

[4]Lis v. Robert Packer Hospital, 579 F.2d 819 (3d Cir. 1978); People v. Melone, 71 Cal. App. 2d 291, 162 P.2d 505 (1st Dist. 1945).

The rule in the text is adopted by former Fed. R. Evid. 611 and Unif. R. Evid. 611(b), which reads: "Cross-examination should be limited to the subject matter of the direct examination and matters affecting the credibility of the witness. The court may, in the exercise of discretion, permit inquiry into additional matters as if on direct examination."

Effective December 1, 2011, restyled Fed. R. Evid. 611(b) provides: "Cross-examination should not go beyond the subject matter of the direct examination and matters affecting the witness's credibility. The court may allow inquiry into additional matters as if on direct examination."

**[Section 21]**

[1]*See* 6 Wigmore, Evidence §§ 1886–91 (Chadbourn rev. 1976); Weinstein & Berger, Evidence ¶ 611[02]; West's Key Number Digest, Witnesses ☞269; Note, 37 Colum. L. Rev. 1373 (1937), Note, 24 Iowa L. Rev. 564 (1939).

[2]U.S. v. Vasquez, 858 F.2d 1387, 1392 (9th Cir. 1988) ("Federal Rule of Evidence 611(b) commits the scope of cross-examination to the trial judge's discretion. *See* United States v. Miranda—Uriarte, 649 F.2d 1345, 1353 (9th Cir. 1981); United States v. Green, 648 F.2d 587, 594 (9th Cir.1981). In exercising this discretion, the trial court may permit cross-examination 'as to all matters reasonably related to the issues (the defendant) put in dispute by his testimony on direct.' Miranda—Uriarte, 649 F.2d at 1353; Green, 648 F.2d at 594").

to the topics which the direct examiner has chosen to open.[3] The cross-examiner is free to question about any subject relevant to any issue on the merits of the entire case, including facts relating solely to the cross-examiner's own case or affirmative defense.

### The "Restrictive" Rule, in Various Forms, Limiting Cross-examination to the Scope of the Direct

The majority of the states agree that the cross-examination is limited to the matters testified to on the direct examination.[4] The Federal Rules of Evidence adopt this approach.[5] While all these jurisdictions purport to embrace the restrictive rule, they differ markedly in the rigor with which they enforce the rule:

- To begin with, one version of the doctrine strictly confines the cross-questions to those relating only to the same acts or facts mentioned on direct,[6] and, perhaps, those occurring at the same time and place. This version of the doctrine is

---

[3]Mayor and Corporation of Berwick-on-Tweed v. Murray, 19 L.J. Ch. 281, 286 (V.C., 1850); Morgan v. Brydges, (1818) 2 Stark, 314, 171 Eng. Rep. 657 (N.P.) (plaintiff's witness called for formal proof may be cross-examined by defendant, his employer, on the whole case); Ariz. R. Evid. 611(b) ("A witness may be cross-examined on any relevant matter"); Me. R. Evid. 611(b) (court may limit cross-examination "in the interests of justice").

[4]Among the leading cases which introduced this innovation in common law practice were Ellmaker v. Buckley, 16 S. & R. 72, 77 (Pa. 1827), People v. Horton, 4 Mich. 67, 82, 1856 WL 3893 (1856), and Philadelphia & Trenton R. Co. v. Stimpson, 39 U.S. 448, 461, 10 L. Ed. 535, 1840 WL 4631 (1840), by Story, J.

[5]Rev. Unif. R. Evid. (1974) 611(b) and former Fed. R. Evid. 611(b) provide: "Cross examination should be limited to the subject matter of the direct examination and matters affecting the credibility of the witness. The court may, in the exercise of discretion, permit inquiry into additional matters as if on direct examination."

Effective December 1, 2011, Fed. R. Evid. 611(b) reads: "Cross-examination should not go beyond the subject matter of the direct examination and matters affecting the witness's credibility. The court may allow inquiry into additional matters as if on direct examination."

*E.g.*, U.S. v. Caracappa, 614 F.3d 30, 42 (2d Cir. 2010); U.S. v. Brockenborrugh, 575 F.3d 726, 736 (D.C. Cir. 2009); U.S. v. Jackson, 576 F.2d 46, 49 (5th Cir. 1978) (within trial court discretion to limit cross-examination "to the subject matter of the direct examination and matters affecting the credibility of the witness"); Construction and application of provision of Rule 611(b) of Federal Rules of Evidence that cross-examination should be limited to subject matter of direct examination, 45 A.L.R. Fed. 639.

[6]State v. Guilfoyle, 109 Conn. 124, 145 A. 761 (1929) (doctor testified to general description of wound, cross-examination as to opinion whether wound caused by near or far shot properly precluded); Wheeler & Wilson Mfg. Co. v. Barrett, 172 Ill. 610, 50 N.E. 325 (1898) (plaintiff testified she bought and paid for sewing machine from defendant, cross-examination designed to show she took possession under written lease contract was properly excluded); McNeely v. Conlon, 216 Iowa 796, 248 N.W. 17 (1933) (eyewitness described accident; it was prejudicial error to permit defendant on

sometimes called the factual or historical test. Under this narrow view, the cross-examination is limited to "the same points" brought out on direct,[7] the "matters testified to,"[8] or the "subjects mentioned."[9]

- There is a slightly more expansive version of the restrictive rule. That version extends the scope to "facts and circumstances connected with" the matters stated on direct,[10] but even this phrasing still suggests a requirement of basic identity of transaction and proximity in time and space.

- Another variation gives cross-examination a still wider scope. Under this variation, the cross-examination may touch on the matters opened in direct and facts tending to explain, contradict, or discredit the direct testimony.[11]

- The broadest formula includes facts tending to "rebut" any inference or deduction from the matters testified on direct.[12]

---

cross to elicit that witness just after and at scene said to defendant, "It was not your fault"); Nagel v. McDermott, 138 Wash. 536, 244 P. 977 (1926) (witness testified to location of bicycle in collision incident, but could not testify to bicycle's speed on cross-examination).

[7]Carey v. City of Oakland, 44 Cal. App. 2d 503, 112 P.2d 714 (1st Dist. 1941).

[8]McAden v. State, 155 Fla. 523, 21 So. 2d 33 (1945); Nadeau v. Texas Co., 104 Mont. 558, 69 P.2d 586 (1937).

[9]State v. Bagley, 339 Mo. 215, 96 S.W.2d 331 (1936) (the English rule was not followed in criminal cases as to a defendant or his spouse; Mo. Ann. Stat. §§ 491.070, 546.260).

[10]Story, J., in Philadelphia & Trenton R. Co. v. Stimpson, 39 U.S. 448, 461, 10 L. Ed. 535, 1840 WL 4631 (1840); Austin v. State, 14 Ark. 555, 563, 1854 WL 606 (1854); Williams v. State, 32 Fla. 315, 13 So. 834 (1893).

[11]Krametbauer v. McDonald, 44 N.M. 473, 104 P.2d 900 (1940); Lewis v. State, 1969 OK CR 186, 458 P.2d 309 (Okla. Crim. App. 1969); State v. Ragonesi, 112 R.I. 340, 309 A.2d 851 (1973) ("facts and matters brought out in direct examination"). See also People v. Farley, 46 Cal. 4th 1053, 96 Cal. Rptr. 3d 191, 210 P.3d 361, 402 (2009)

("The cross-examination is not 'confined to a mere categorical review of the matters, dates, or times mentioned in the direct examination' "); People v. Hawthorne, 46 Cal. 4th 67, 92 Cal. Rptr. 3d 330, 205 P.3d 245, 268 (2009) ("A defendant cannot . . . limit cross-examination to the precise facts concerning which he testifies").

[12]A case expressing this view is Conley v. Mervis, 324 Pa. 577, 188 A. 350 (1936) (suit for damages for injury caused by a truck; defendant denies ownership; plaintiff calls defendant as witness and proves on direct that defendant owned license plates on truck; it was error to refuse to permit defendant to be cross-examined by his own counsel to show the plates were taken from his place of business without his knowledge or consent; this inquiry was allowable to rebut the inference of ownership of the truck and agency of the driver which would otherwise be drawn from ownership of the plates). See also Crosby v. De Land Special Drainage Dist., 367 Ill. 462, 11 N.E.2d 937 (1937); Eno v. Adair County Mut. Ins. Ass'n, 229 Iowa 249, 294 N.W. 323 (1940); and cases cited in Right to cross-examine witness in respect of facts not included in his direct examination, but which negative a prima facie case, presumption, or inference otherwise made by his testimony on direct examination, 108 A.L.R. 167.

There is little consistency in the phrasing and use of these formulas, even in the same jurisdiction.[13] All these express criteria are too vague to be employed with precision. Even assuming that cross-examination is limited to the subject matter of the direct examination, the subject matter of questions on direct examination can always be defined with greater or lesser generality regardless of the express formula.[14]

As previously stated, the Federal Rules codify a version of the restrictive approach. Federal Rule of Evidence 611(b) refers to "the subject matter of the direct examination." That statutory language should be interpreted as endorsing the broader, more liberal views described above.[15] That interpretation is consistent with the provision in Rule 611(b) that the court may permit inquiry into additional matters as if on direct.[16] As a practical matter, many federal trial judges apply the so-called legal test. This

---

[13]*See* Note, 37 Colum. L. Rev. 1373 (1937).

[14]Macaulay v. Anas, 321 F.3d 45, 53–54 (1st Cir. 2003) ("It is, of course, unrealistic to expect that direct examination and cross-examination will be perfectly congruent"). Two interesting theories, among others, are available for defining the scope of direct examination broadly. First, the scope of direct may be broadened to include the cross-examination by relating the direct and the cross to some legal issue in the case. *See* Graham v. Larimer, 83 Cal. 173, 23 P. 286 (1890) (in action on an illegal note, the issue was whether a former holder was a holder in due course; on direct former holder stated only that he had bought the note for value and on cross was questioned whether he knew that the consideration was illegal). Second, all possibly related events in real life could be treated as the scope or subject matter of direct, and the cross can be related to such events. *See* Security Ben. Ass'n v. Small, 34 Ariz. 458, 272 P. 647 (1928) (an issue in suit on life insurance policy was whether deceased was in good health when policy was taken out; deceased's mother stated on direct that she lived in California and that deceased's health was good when the policy was issued and, on cross, was asked why she returned with deceased to Arizona two months later).

[15]*E.g.*, U.S. v. Brockenborrugh, 575 F.3d 726, 736–37 (D.C. Cir. 2009) (the defendant's direct testimony suggested that he and a real estate agent had nothing more than a business relationship; on cross-examination, the prosecution was entitled to inquire about the defendant's sexual relationship with the agent); U.S. v. Lara, 181 F.3d 183, 199 (1st Cir. 1999) (the scope of cross-examination includes "other crimes he had committed"); U.S. v. Arnott, 704 F.2d 322 (6th Cir. 1983) (Rule 611(b) has been liberally construed to include all inferences and implications arising from the testimony); U.S. v. Giarratano, 622 F.2d 153, 156 (5th Cir. 1980); U.S. v. Whitson, 587 F.2d 948 (9th Cir. 1978). As § 190 of this treatise points out, under Federal Rule of Evidence 404(b), the prosecution may sometimes introduce an accused's uncharged crimes on a noncharacter theory of logical relevance to prove such facts of consequence as the accused's intent or identity as the perpetrator. Suppose that on direct examination, the accused denies the intent required for the charged offense. Under *Lara,* supra, on cross-examination the prosecutor could question the accused about uncharged acts relevant to establish the requisite mens rea. See also note 56 infra.

[16]The limits of cross-examination

test equates "the subject matter of the direct" with the essential elements of the cause of action, crime, or defense mentioned on direct. At the end of the trial, the judge gives the jury substantive law instructions on the pertinent causes of action, crimes, and defenses. These instructions list the essential legal elements which the burdened party must prove to prevail on that theory. One of the essential elements of a true crime is a *mens rea* element. Suppose that on direct examination, a defense witness testified about the accused's mens rea at the time of the *actus reus*. Under the legal test, on cross-examination the prosecutor could inquire about distinct acts by the accused so long as the other acts were logically relevant to the element of *mens rea*; the prosecution would not be limited to the historical events mentioned during the witness's direct examination.

All these limiting formulas share an escape valve, namely, the common law notion that where part of a transaction, contract, conversation, or event has been mentioned on direct, the remainder may be brought out on cross-examination.[17] This particular aspect of the rule of completeness is still in effect in modern federal practice.[18] In substance, this notion merely states the converse of the limiting rule itself. However, that does not detract from the notion's practical utility as an added argument to persuade a judge to expand the scope of cross-examination.

In civil cases, the trial judge sometimes exercises discretion to

---

by leading questions to the scope of direct are subject to the trial judge's discretion. U.S. v. Gaston, 608 F.2d 607 (5th Cir. 1979). See also § 20 at note 2, supra.

[17]Gilmer v. Higley, 110 U.S. 47, 3 S. Ct. 471, 28 L. Ed. 62 (1884) (transaction); Rosenberg v. Wittenborn, 178 Cal. App. 2d 846, 3 Cal. Rptr. 459 (2d Dist. 1960) (conversation); Johnson v. Cunningham, 104 Ill. App. 2d 406, 244 N.E.2d 205 (2d Dist. 1969) (conversations); Ah Doon v. Smith, 25 Or. 89, 34 P. 1093 (1893) (transaction); Glenn v. Philadelphia & W. C. Traction Co., 206 Pa. 135, 55 A. 860 (1903) (conversation); Vingi v. Trillo, 77 R.I. 55, 73 A.2d 43 (1950) (conversation); West's Key Number Digest, Witnesses ⚖268(3). *But see* In re Campbell's Will, 100 Vt. 395, 138 A. 725, 726 (1927) (will contest: proponents placed witness on stand who testified that Mrs. Campbell told her that instrument claimed to be a will was in trunk; contestants were allowed to bring out on

cross-examination that Mrs. Campbell told her on same occasion that she wanted her husband to destroy the instrument; it was error, but harmless. "The fact that the proponents had, in effect, put in evidence a part of a statement of Mrs. Campbell, did not, of itself, entitle the contestants to put in all of that statement. The latter could give in evidence whatever Mrs. Campbell then said that tended to qualify, explain, or contradict what Mrs. Stevens had testified to, but no more."). See also § 56 infra.

[18]See discussions in 1 Weinstein's Federal Evidence Ch. 106 (rev. 2011); Wright and Miller's Federal Practice and Procedure, Evidence § 5072. In Beech Aircraft Corp. v. Rainey, 488 U.S. 153, 109 S. Ct. 439, 102 L. Ed. 2d 445 (1988), the Court stated that Rule 106 merely partially codifies the rule of completeness. Thus, the common law aspect of the doctrine survived the enactment of Federal Rule 106.

adopt a "one-appearance" rule.[19] In the interest of judicial economy and the witness's convenience, the witness is called only once. After one side's direct examination of the witness, the other side is permitted to cross-examine the witness without being limited to the matter covered on direct examination. The judge is most likely to adopt this practice when the witness is of only marginal importance to the case and the practice will not substantially lengthen the cross-examination.

### The Half-open Door: Cross-examination Extends to Any Matters Except Cross-examiner's Affirmative Case

A third view as to the scope of cross-examination represents a middle course between the two extremes. Under this view, now mostly obsolete, the cross-examiner may question the witness about any matters relevant to any issue in the action *except* facts relating only to the cross-examiner's own affirmative case such as defendant's affirmative defenses or cross-claims or, in case of a plaintiff, his new matter in reply.[20] In some states, this compromise standard served as a temporary half-way house for courts which later embraced the "wide-open" practice.[21] Compared with the restrictive practice, the third view has the practical advantage

---

[19]Lyman v. St. Jude Medical S.C., Inc., 580 F. Supp. 2d 719, 727–28 (E.D. Wis. 2008).

[20]Legg v. Drake, 1 Ohio St. 286, 290, 1853 WL 29 (1853) (party may cross-examine "as to all matters pertinent to the issue on the trial; however, the scope of cross-examination was limited by the rule that a party cannot, before the time of opening his own case, introduce his distinct grounds of defense or avoidance" by cross-examination); Dietsch v. Mayberry, 70 Ohio App. 527, 25 Ohio Op. 315, 47 N.E.2d 404 (6th Dist. Williams County 1942). See also discussion of "Michigan rule" in Comment, 36 U. of Det. L.J. 162 (1958).

The objection that the cross-examination seeks matter proper only to the cross-examiner's own case has often, in the past, been given as a ground of decision in states following the more restrictive practice limiting the cross to the scope of the direct. See note 18 supra. But even under the more restrictive view, if the matter is opened in direct, it may be followed up in cross-examination, though this may

incidentally happen to sustain the cross-examiner's affirmative claim or defense. Garlich v. Northern Pac. Ry. Co., 131 F. 837 (C.C.A. 8th Cir. 1904).

[21]*E.g.*, Chandler v. Allison, 10 Mich. 460, 476, 1862 WL 1117 (1862) where this standard is perhaps first announced. There Campbell, J., in sustaining the propriety of cross-questions, said, "They were designed to determine the real character of the transaction in issue. They did not relate to matter in avoidance of it. . . . " See also Rush v. French, 1 Ariz. 99, 139, 140, 25 P. 816, 828 (1874) (witness may be cross-examined "upon all matters pertinent to the case of the party calling him, except exclusively new matter; and nothing shall be deemed new matter except it be such as could not be given under a general denial."). Arizona follows the "wide-open" practice, see note 2 supra. *But see* Silver v. London Assur. Corp., 61 Wash. 593, 112 P. 666 (1911) (apparently approving the "half-open door" rule). Washington now has adopted Fed. R. Evid. 611(b).

of reducing the incidence of disputes by widening the scope of examination. Its chief drawback is that, particularly under modern liberal pleading rules,[22] it is often difficult to determine whether the matter inquired about relates solely to the cross-examiner's "distinct grounds of defense or avoidance."[23]

## § 22   Cross-examination to impeach not limited to the scope of the direct

One of the main functions of cross-examination is to afford an opportunity to elicit answers impeaching the witness's veracity, capacity to observe, impartiality, and consistency. Even in jurisdictions adopting the most restrictive practice on the historical merits, impeaching cross-examination is not limited to matters brought out in the direct examination.[1] On direct examination, a witness's proponent ordinarily may not bolster the witness's credibility; during direct—before there has been any attack on the witness's credibility—the proponent generally may not elicit testimony which is logically relevant only to the witness's believability.[2] Until cross-examination, we often do not know whether the opponent will attack the witness's credibility; and if the opponent does not do so, it is a waste of time to receive testimony enhancing the witness's credibility. However, by the simple act of testifying, the witness places her credibility in issue. For that reason, the witness's credibility is fair game on cross-examination. Federal Rule of Evidence 611(b) adopts this view.[3]

---

[22]Until recently, Federal Rule of Civil Procedure 26 defined the scope of discovery as including information relevant to both issues already pleaded and issues which the pleadings could be amended to include. Oppenheimer Fund, Inc. v. Sanders, 437 U.S. 340, 98 S. Ct. 2380, 57 L. Ed. 2d 253 (1978); Imwinkelried & Blumoff, Pretrial Discovery: Strategy and Tactics § 2:3 (rev. 2010). However, in some instances the recent amendments to the Federal Rules of Civil Procedure limit the scope of discovery as of right to information relevant to issues actually pleaded. Pretrial Discovery: Strategy and Tactics § 3:2. As a practical matter, the discovery amendments pressure pleaders to include more specific allegations in their filings.

[23]See discussion in Note, 37 Colum. L. Rev. 1373, 1382 (1937).

**[Section 22]**

[1]Chicago City Ry. Co. v. Carroll, 206 Ill. 318, 68 N.E. 1087, 1089 (1903) (cross-question to doctor about who paid him); Beck v. Hood, 185 Pa. 32, 39 A. 842, 843 (1898) (that witness had talked at previous trial with foreman of jury); 6 Wigmore, Evidence § 1891 (Chadbourn rev. 1976).

[2]E.g., Fed. R. Evid. 608(a) ("But evidence of truthful character is admissible only after the witness's character for truthfulness has been attacked").

[3]Restyled Fed. R. Evid. and Unif. R. Evid. 611(b) permit cross-examination on "matters affecting the

## § 23 Formal and practical consequences of the restrictive rules: effect on order of proof: Side-effects

It is sometimes asserted that the only "essential" formal difference between the "wide-open" and the restrictive views of scope of cross-examination is the time or stage at which the witness may be called on to testify to the facts inquired about.[1] The primary difference among the views is supposedly their effect on the order of proof.[2] Under the "wide-open" rule the witness may be immediately questioned about the new matter during cross-examination. In contrast, under the restrictive rules the cross-examiner postpones the questions until his own next stage[3] of putting on proof and then calls the witness to prove the same facts.[4]

This assertion, though, overlooks the real world impact of the restrictive practice. At a given trial, timing can be critical; and even a "mere" postponement can be important. For dramatic effect, the questioner wants to strike while the iron is hot. Moreover, as a practical matter in many instances a postponement of the questions will not be the only result of a ruling excluding a cross-question as outside the scope of the direct; unless the question is vital and he is fairly confident of a favorable answer, the cross-examiner might be unwilling to run the risk of calling the adversary's witness at a later stage as his own witness. A cautious cross-examiner might well decide to abandon the inquiry. Getting concessions from the opponent's witness hot on the heels of the direct while his story is fresh is worth trying for. It is a much chancier and less attractive option to call an unfriendly witness later when her initial testimony is stale. Admittedly, to a

witness's credibility." *E.g.*, U.S. v. Palmer, 536 F.2d 1278, 1282 (9th Cir. 1976) ("The range of evidence that may be elicited for the purpose of discrediting a witness is very liberal. 3A Wigmore, Evidence § 944 at 778 (Chadbourn rev. 1970). Inquiry is permitted concerning his capacity to remember, to observe, and to recount, and for the purpose of testing his sincerity, truthfulness and motives.").

**[Section 23]**

[1]Valliant, J., in Ayers v. Wabash R. Co., 190 Mo. 228, 88 S.W. 608, 609 (1905); 6 Wigmore, Evidence § 1895 (Chadbourn rev. 1976).

[2]H.R. Rep. No. 93-650, 93d Cong., 2d Sess. remarks that the traditional rule embodied in Fed. R. Evid. 611(b)

at the instance of the House Committee on the Judiciary "facilitates orderly presentation by each party at trial."

[3]Grievance Committee of Bar of Fairfield County v. Dacey, 154 Conn. 129, 222 A.2d 339 (1966). As to the order of proof, by stages, of the respective parties, see § 4 supra.

[4]If a party avails himself of the opportunity to call the witness at a later stage, he cannot complain on appeal of a restriction on cross-examination. Clucas v. Bank of Montclair, 110 N.J.L. 394, 166 A. 311, 315 (N.J. Ct. Err. & App. 1933). *See also* State v. Savage, 36 Or. 191, 61 P. 1128 (1900) (same questions asked on re-call).

degree the restrictive rules promote the orderly presentation of proof. However, in some cases the application of those rules does not foster that policy. For example, suppose a direct examiner injects an issue by witness #1 but not by witness #2 who cannot be cross-examined on the issue although he has knowledge highly relevant to that issue.[5] In that situation, from the jury's perspective it might be more orderly and sensible to have both witnesses testify about the fact in the same phase of the case. However, the scope of rules will force the opponent to recall witness #2 later.

Moreover, postponing questions exceeding scope of direct is not the only formal consequence of the restrictive rule. There are many incidental effects. By way of example, the courts adopting the restrictive practice frequently say that if the cross-examiner, perhaps without objection, questions the witness about new matter, he makes the witness his own.[6] Although the questioning is formally cross-examination, the questioning about the new topic is functionally direct examination. The cross-examiner "adopts" the witness with respect to the new matter. Federal Rule of Evidence 611(b) embraces this adoption notion.[7] The cross-examiner normally may not ask leading questions about the new matter;[8] and under the traditional rule against impeaching one's own witness,[9] he may be precluded from impeaching the witness as to those facts.[10] However, since one may impeach one's own witness under Federal Rule of Evidence 607, the cross-examiner would

---

[5]This suggestion is made in Weinstein, Mansfield, Abrams & Berger, Cases and Materials on Evidence 370 (9th ed. 1997). The authors pose the question whether the scope of cross-examination should be determined by the posture of the whole case rather than by the scope of the direct examination of the second witness mentioned in the text.

[6]State v. Spurr, 100 W. Va. 121, 130 S.E. 81 (1925); 3A Wigmore, Evidence § 914 (Chadbourn rev. 1976) (critical of rule).

[7]See § 21 at note 16, supra.

[8]Lis v. Robert Packer Hospital, 579 F.2d 819 (3d Cir. 1978); People v. Melone, 71 Cal. App. 2d 291, 162 P.2d 505 (1st Dist. 1945); People ex rel. Phelps v. Court of Oyer & Terminer of New York County, 83 N.Y. 436, 459, 1881 WL 12757 (1881). But this result

rests on an assumption of a hard-and-fast rule that leading questions are always permissible in the proper field of cross-examination and never in the proper area of direct. 3A Wigmore, Evidence § 915 (Chadbourn rev. 1970.) The criterion should be whether the witness is probably willing to yield to suggestion. Under that criterion, there is usually no difference in the witness's attitudes, when the question is, or is not, within the scope of the direct. See § 6 supra.

[9]This rule, however, has been greatly liberalized in many jurisdictions. See § 38 infra.

[10]Pollard v. State, 201 Ind. 180, 166 N.E. 654 (1929); 3 Wigmore, Evidence § 914 (Chadbourn rev. 1970); West's Key Number Digest, Witnesses ⊶325.

not be precluded from impeaching the witness concerning the new matter brought out pursuant to Rule 611(b).[11]

Furthermore, the invocation of the restrictive rule to exclude unfavorable testimony from the plaintiff's witness which might otherwise be elicited on cross-examination, could have another critical formal effect: It might save the plaintiff from a directed verdict at the close of his case in chief.[12] Otherwise, during the plaintiff's case-in-chief, the defense could introduce new matter that arguably dictated a defense decision. In that light, the application of the restrictive rule can be a significant advantage for the plaintiff. The plaintiff both survives the directed motion and, during the later defense case, gains an opportunity to strengthen his case by eliciting favorable facts from his opponent's witnesses.

Finally, in one situation, the restrictive doctrine operates as a rule of complete exclusion, not a mere postponement. In this situation, the witness has a privilege not to be called as a witness by the cross-examiner. Thus, the privileges of the accused and the accused's spouse not to be called by the state may prevent the prosecutor from eliciting the new facts at a later stage, if the prosecutor cannot adduce them on cross-examination.[13]

## § 24   The scope of the judge's discretion under the wide-open and restrictive rules

In the early 19th century Gibson, C.J.[1] and Story, J.[2] modified the orthodox "wide-open" cross-examination by suggesting that questioning about new matter was improper at the stage of cross-examination. When they did so, they conceived of their modification as relating solely to the order of proof. Traditionally the order of proof[3] and the conduct and extent of cross-examination[4] were subject to the trial judge's discretionary control. In keeping with that tradition, restyled Federal Rule 611(a) empowers the judge to "exercise reasonable control over the . . . order of examining witnesses and presenting evidence. . . ." For its part,

---

[11]See § 21 at note 16 supra.

[12]Seemingly this was the result in the trial court of the judge's ruling limiting the cross-examination in Conley v. Mervis, 324 Pa. 577, 188 A. 350 (1936) described in § 21, note 12 supra. *See also* Ah Doon v. Smith, 25 Or. 89, 34 P. 1093 (1893), where the judge's ruling permitting the cross-examination about alleged new matter exposed the plaintiff to a dismissal of the action at the close of his testimony.

[13]See §§ 25, 26 infra.

[Section 24]

[1]In Ellmaker v. Buckley, 16 Serg. & Rawle 72, 1827 WL 2669 (Pa. 1827).

[2]In Philadelphia & Trenton R. Co. v. Stimpson, 39 U.S. 448, 10 L. Ed. 535, 1840 WL 4631 (1840).

[3]*See* 6 Wigmore, Evidence §§ 1867, 1885–86 (Chadbourn rev. 1976).

[4]*See* 3A Wigmore, Evidence §§ 944, 983(2) (Chadbourn rev. 1970).

Rule 611(b) allows the judge to a degree to "exercise . . . discretion" over the scope of cross.

The earlier decisions[5] and many contemporary cases[6] adopting the restrictive rule emphasize the trial judge's discretionary power to allow deviations.[7] Indeed, it has been said that both the courts following the wide-open view and those adopting the restrictive practice "recognize the discretionary power of the trial court to allow variations from the customary order and decline ordinarily to consider as an error any variation sanctioned by the trial court."[8] If this statement were completely accurate, the hazards of injustice at trial or appellate reversal would be relatively minor. But the statement paints too bright a picture.

In the states adopting "the scope of the direct" test, trial judges often find it easier to administer the test as a mechanistic rule rather than as a flexible standard of discretion. In the past, appellate courts reversed many cases for error in applying the test. Fortunately, the modern trend is to accord wider latitude to the trial judge.[9]

In jurisdictions following the traditional wide-open view, there

---

[5]*E.g.*, Chicago & R.I.R. Co. v. Northern Illinois Coal & Iron Co. of La Salle, 36 Ill. 60, 1864 WL 3099 (1864); Glenn v. Gleason, 61 Iowa 28, 15 N.W. 659 (1883); Blake v. People, 73 N.Y. 586, 1878 WL 12599 (1878); Kaeppler v. Red River Val. Nat. Bank, 8 N.D. 406, 79 N.W. 869 (1899); Schnable v. Doughty, 3 Pa. 392, 395, 1846 WL 4891 (1846); State v. Bunker, 7 S.D. 639, 65 N.W. 33 (1895); Lueck v. Heisler, 87 Wis. 644, 58 N.W. 1101 (1894).

[6]U.S. v. Diaz, 662 F.2d 713 (11th Cir. 1981) (extensive cross-examination permitted); U.S. v. Bright, 630 F.2d 804 (5th Cir. 1980); U.S. v. Gaston, 608 F.2d 607 (5th Cir. 1979) (many federal appellate opinions discuss specific reasons why it was proper to extend or limit cross-examination); State v. Brathwaite, 164 Conn. 617, 325 A.2d 284 (1973); Goodbody v. Margiotti, 323 Pa. 529, 187 A. 425 (1936).

While in Federal Rule 611(b) the Congress substituted the more restrictive language set forth in § 21 in lieu of the rule proposed by the Supreme Court, the present phrasing is the mildly hortatory "should," a guide-line rather than the mandatory style of the Ten Commandments. Additionally, the Rule expressly confers on the judge discretion to allow inquiry into additional matters. The effect is to confine the matter largely to the trial level and to remove it from the area of profitable appellate review. *See* Adv. Com. Note to Rule 611(b), Preliminary Draft, 46 F.R.D. 161, 304. Similarly as to Unif. R. Evid. 611(b).

[7]*See generally* Wills v. Russell, 100 U.S. 621, 626, 25 L. Ed. 607, 1879 WL 16569 (1879) ("Cases not infrequently arise where the convenience of the witness or of the court or the party producing the witness will be promoted by a relaxation of the rule, to enable the witness to be discharged from further attendance.").

[8]St. Louis, I.M. & S. Ry. Co. v. Raines, 90 Ark. 398, 119 S.W. 665, 668 (1909).

[9]*See* Note, 37 Colum. L. Rev. 1373, 1381 (1937) summarizing the results of a study of 810 decisions, including many reversals. Other examples include Papa v. Youngstrom, 146 Conn. 37, 147 A.2d 494 (1958); State ex rel. Rich v. Bair, 83 Idaho 475, 365 P.2d 216 (1961); Muscarello

has been little tendency to apply the notion that the order of proof is discretionary. Their tradition has not been shaped in terms of order of proof, but rather in the language of a right to cross-examine on the whole case.[10] The situation putting the greatest strain on the wide-open rule is the one in which a party, usually the plaintiff, finds himself compelled at the outset to call either the opposing party himself or an ally of the opponent to prove a formal fact not substantially in dispute.[11] Should the opponent then be allowed to disrupt the proponent's case at this stage by cross-examining the willing witness about defensive matters unrelated to the direct examination? This is an appealing situation for the exercise of discretion to deviate from the wide-open practice; to the prevent the disruption of the proponent's case, the trial judge could require the cross-examiner to recall the witness for these new matters when the cross-examiner later puts on his own case. Yet, as the decisions indicate, even in this extreme fact situation, trial judges rarely exercise their discretion in "wide-open" jurisdictions.[12]

---

v. Peterson, 20 Ill. 2d 548, 170 N.E.2d 564 (1960); Shupe v. State, 238 Md. 307, 208 A.2d 590 (1965); Golden Gate Corp. v. Providence Redevelopment Agency, 106 R.I. 371, 260 A.2d 152 (1969).

For cases emphasizing the court's discretion, see the cases in note 6, supra.

Where the adverse party is called as an adverse witness by his opponent, there seems to be a particularly strong tendency to emphasize the judge's discretion in limiting cross-examination. *See* City of Kotzebue v. Ipalook, 462 P.2d 75 (Alaska 1969) (restriction of cross-examination was harmless error when witness could be called as an adverse witness); Lindsay v. Teamsters Union, Local No. 74, 97 N.W.2d 686 (N.D. 1959); Kline v. Kachmar, 360 Pa. 396, 61 A.2d 825 (1948).

[10]*See* Morgan v. Brydges, (1818) 2 Stark. 314, 171 Eng. Rep. 657, 1818

WL 2843 (Assizes) (plaintiff's witness called for formal proof, may be cross-examined by defendant, his employer, on the whole case); Cowart v. Strickland, 149 Ga. 397, 100 S.E. 447 (1919) ("The rule in this state is that 'when a witness is called and examined, even to only a formal point, by one party, the other party has the right to cross-examine him as to all points.' "). However, the court's discretion is emphasized in Boller v. Cofrances, 42 Wis. 2d 170, 166 N.W.2d 129 (1969).

[11]There can be other reasons for calling the opposing party at the beginning of the proponent's case-in-chief. For example, some medical malpractice plaintiffs' attorneys believe that calling the defendant doctor first is a dramatic way to begin. The confrontation between the doctor and the plaintiff's attorney should immediately grab the jurors' attention.

[12]See § 25 infra.

## § 25    Application of wide-open and restrictive rules to the cross-examination of parties: (a) Civil parties[1]

In the cross-examination of party witnesses, two situations must be distinguished: (1) the hostile cross-examination by the adversary of a party who calls himself as a witness in his own behalf, and (2) the friendly cross-examination by the counsel of a party who has been called as an adverse witness by his opponent. In the first situation, in jurisdictions following the restrictive rules courts sometimes hold that while the range of discretion to permit the relaxation of the restrictive practice is wider,[2] the general limitation to the "scope of the direct" still applies.[3] However, relaxation of the restrictive practice *only* for parties as mentioned above does not appear to be authorized by Federal Rule of Evidence 611(b); on its face, 611(b) does not differentiate between the cross-examination of parties and non-parties.[4] Yet, without much discussion, a few cases have announced that the limitation to the scope of the direct is inapplicable during the hostile cross-examination of a party.[5] In the "wide-open" states, the courts routinely accord the cross-examiner the usual freedom from the restriction to the scope of direct.

Contrast the second situation: A statute or rule[6] provides that when a party calls the adverse party as a hostile witness, the party may question the witness "as upon cross-examination." Hence, the party may ask leading questions; and he is not "bound" by the adverse witness's answers—meaning chiefly that he may impeach the testimony by showing inconsistent

---

**[Section 25]**

[1]6 Wigmore, Evidence § 1890 (Chadbourn rev. 1976); 4 Weinstein's Federal Evidence § 611.03 (rev. 2011); West's Key Number Digest, Witnesses ☞275(5), (8).

[2]Roewe v. Lombardo, 76 Ill. App. 2d 164, 221 N.E.2d 521 (5th Dist. 1966); Ayres v. Keith, 355 S.W.2d 914 (Mo. 1962); Wagner v. Niven, 46 Tenn. App. 581, 332 S.W.2d 511 (1959).

[3]Banks v. Bowman Dairy Co., 65 Ill. App. 2d 113, 212 N.E.2d 4 (2d Dist. 1965); Maul v. Filimon, 315 S.W.2d 859 (Mo. Ct. App. 1958).

[4]The Advisory Committee's Note and the Congressional Committee Reports furnish no basis for reading this special relaxation into Rule 611(b). Nor does the text of the rule lead to such a result. Rather, the judge

has general discretion as to all witnesses, particularly to extend the scope of cross-examination. See § 24, note 6 supra. Some cases antedating the Federal Rules suggest the existence of a special discretion as to parties. *E.g.*, Rivers v. Union Carbide Corp., 426 F.2d 633 (3d Cir. 1970).

[5]Geelen v. Pennsylvania R. Co., 400 Pa. 240, 161 A.2d 595 (1960); Viens v. Lanctot, 120 Vt. 443, 144 A.2d 711 (1958).

[6]Fed. R. Evid. 611(c)(2) provides in part, "Ordinarily, the court should allow leading questions . . . when a party calls a hostile witness, an adverse party, or a witness identified with an adverse party." Under Fed. R. Evid. 607 a party may impeach a witness called by that party. Unif. R. Evid. 611(c) and 607 are virtually identical in substance.

statements. When this direct examination, savoring of cross, ends, some jurisdictions give the witness no right to be examined immediately by his own counsel; rather the judge has discretion to permit immediate questioning or to require that his examination be deferred until the witness-party's own case.[7] Most jurisdictions, though, allow the witness's immediate examination by his own counsel.[8] However, even if the witness's own counsel is permitted to conduct an immediate examination, on request the trial judge should forbid leading questions.[9] In restrictive jurisdictions, during this "cross-examination" of a friendly witness, there is no discernible judicial tendency to relax the usual limitation confining the questions to the scope of the direct.[10]

## § 26 Application of wide-open and restrictive rules to the cross-examination of parties: (b) The accused in a criminal case[1]

As a means of implementing the prescribed order of producing evidence, the restrictive rules limiting cross-examination to the scope of the witness's direct or to the proponent's case are burdensome, but understandable. The cross-examiner is temporarily blocked, but she has a theoretical remedy: She may later recall the witness for questioning when she puts on her own next stage of evidence. However, when the restrictive practice is applied to the criminal accused, as it is in most jurisdictions following that practice,[2] the accused can permanently preclude the prosecution from questioning the accused about facts outside the scope of the

---

[7]E.g., Davis v. Wright, 194 Ga. 1, 21 S.E.2d 88 (1942).

[8]E.g., Peters v. Shear, 351 Pa. 521, 41 A.2d 556 (1945). Fed. R. Evid. 611 and Unif. R. Evid. 611 seem to contemplate the immediate further examination. See note 9 infra.

[9]Fed. R. Evid. Rule 611(c)(1) ("Ordinarily, the court should allow leading questions . . . on cross-examination . . . .") The Advisory Committee's Note explains: "The purpose of the qualification 'ordinarily' is to furnish a basis for denying the use of leading questions when the cross-examination is cross-examination in form only and not in fact, as for example the 'cross-examination' of a party by his own counsel after being called by the opponent (savoring more of redirect) or of an insured defendant who proves to be friendly to the plain-

tiff." Rev. Unif. R. Evid. (1974) is the same as the Federal Rule. Accord Shultz v. Rice, 809 F.2d 643, 654 (10th Cir. 1986) ("cross-examination in form only and not in fact" not allowable as matter of right). See § 20 at note 2 supra.

[10]Grievance Committee of Bar of Fairfield County v. Dacey, 154 Conn. 129, 222 A.2d 339 (1966).

**[Section 26]**

[1]6 Wigmore, Evidence § 1890 (Chadbourn rev. 1976) 8 Wigmore, Evidence §§ 2276(d), 2278 (McNaughton rev. 1961); 4 Weinstein's Federal Evidence § 611.04 (rev. 2011); West's Key Number Digest, Witnesses ⊗277(4); Carlson, Cross-Examination of the Accused, 52 Cornell L.Q. 705 (1967).

[2]Tucker v. U.S., 5 F.2d 818 (C.C.A. 8th Cir. 1925); Enriquez v.

accused's direct. The accused may carefully limit his direct examination to a single aspect of the case such as age, sanity, or alibi[3] and then invoke the jurisdiction's rule normally restricting the cross-examination to that topic. At the very beginning of the direct examination, the defense counsel might expressly announce that she was going to question the accused "only" about a specified topic; counsel would do so to put herself in a better position to later urge scope objections. This application of the restrictive practice to the cross-examination of the accused has been criticized.[4] However, that criticism has not persuaded the courts to exempt prosecution cross-examination of the accused from the restriction. (Of course, the accused will not escape a searching inquiry on the whole case in a jurisdiction where the scope of cross-examination is "wide-open."[5])

Regardless of whether the result under the restrictive rule is desirable as a matter of policy, the scope of the accused's cross-examination might not be controlled solely by evidence case law,

---

U.S., 293 F.2d 788 (9th Cir. 1961); State v. Ragona, 232 Iowa 700, 5 N.W.2d 907, 909 (1942); Erving v. State, 174 Neb. 90, 116 N.W.2d 7 (1962). *See* 1 Imwinkelried, Giannelli, Gilligan & Lederer, Courtroom Criminal Evidence § 108, at 1–22 (5th ed. 2011) ("It is true that in electing to testify, the defendant waives the accused's privilege not to testify under the fifth amendment; and with the court's leave, the prosecutor may recall the defendant as a witness during the prosecution rebuttal. However, most judges take the position that the scope of the direct during the prosecution rebuttal must be confined to matters within the scope of cross during the defense case-in-chief. Thus, if the scope rules forbade the prosecutor from eliciting the testimony on cross-examination of the defendant during the defense case-in-chief, the prosecution similarly may be precluded from seeking the testimony later on any direct examination of the defendant during the prosecution rebuttal").

[3]Except, of course, that cross-examination to impeach is not confined to the scope of the direct (see § 22 supra). State v. Allnutt, 261 Iowa 897, 156 N.W.2d 266 (1968); State v. Shipman, 354 Mo. 265, 189 S.W.2d

273 (1945) (the accused may be cross-examined about prior convictions). Defendants are prone on direct to testify to their past "clean" records, which may open the door even wider to cross-examination on misconduct than the ordinary rule of impeachment would allow. *E.g.*, State v. Hargraves, 62 Idaho 8, 107 P.2d 854 (1940); State v. McDaniel, 272 N.C. 556, 158 S.E.2d 874 (1968).

[4]6 Wigmore, Evidence § 1890 n. 2 (Chadbourn rev. 1976).

[5]Clarke v. State, 78 Ala. 474, 480, 1885 WL 332 (1885) ("cross-examination relating to any matter connected with the transaction, or pertinent to the issue, and impeachment . . ."); State v. McGee, 55 S.C. 247, 33 S.E. 353 (1899); Brown v. State, 38 Tex. Crim. 597, 44 S.W. 176 (1898). In Missouri, however, where the wide-open practice prevails in civil cases (see § 21, note 2, supra), the legislature prescribed that the accused and his spouse shall be shielded from cross-examination except about matters referred to in the examination in chief. Mo. Stat. Ann. § 546.260, construed in State v. Davit, 343 Mo. 1151, 125 S.W.2d 47 (1938). *See also* State v. Harvey, 449 S.W.2d 649 (Mo. 1970).

statutes, or rules.[6] Federal Rule 611(b) does not purport to define the extent to which a testifying accused waives the constitutional privilege against self-incrimination.[7] Constitutional doctrine may well govern the outer limits of cross-examination concerning the degree to which the accused waives his privilege of self-incrimination by taking the stand and testifying.[8] Some judicial language suggests that under the Fifth Amendment of the United States Constitution, the waiver extends only to questions concerning matters mentioned upon direct examination.[9] If this position ultimately prevails, state practice will be partially controlled by the federal constitutional limits on waiver.[10] Those limits could render unconstitutional "wide-open" cross-examination of criminal defendants, and perhaps even liberal variations of the restrictive rules.

## § 27 Merits of the systems of wide-open and restricted cross-examination[1]

The principal virtue of the restrictive rules is that they pres-

---

[6]*See* Brown v. U.S., 356 U.S. 148, 78 S. Ct. 622, 2 L. Ed. 2d 589 (1958); Fitzpatrick v. U.S., 178 U.S. 304, 20 S. Ct. 944, 44 L. Ed. 1078, 1 Alaska Fed. 625 (1900); Tucker v. U.S., 5 F.2d 818 (C.C.A. 8th Cir. 1925); U. S. ex rel. Irwin v. Pate, 357 F.2d 911 (7th Cir. 1966). *But see* Johnson v. U.S., 318 U.S. 189, 63 S. Ct. 549, 87 L. Ed. 704 (1943). See generally § 132 infra.

[7]The Advisory Committee's Note states in part:

> The rule does not purport to determine the extent to which an accused who elects to testify thereby waives his privilege against self-incrimination . . . In all events, the extent of the waiver of the privilege against self-incrimination ought not to be determined as a by-product of a rule on the scope of cross-examination.

The scope of waiver by a testifying defendant is discussed in § 134 infra.

[8]See discussion in Carlson, Cross-Examination of the Accused, 52 Cornell L.Q. 705 (1967).

[9]See cases cited in § 26, note 6, supra.

[10]The privilege against self-incrimination under the Constitution of the United States was extended to the states in Malloy v. Hogan, 378 U.S. 1, 84 S. Ct. 1489, 12 L. Ed. 2d 653 (1964).

**[Section 27]**

[1]*See* 6 Wigmore, Evidence §§ 1887–88 (Chadbourn rev. 1976) (marshaling arguments pro and con, including judicial views, and favoring "wide-open" practice); Maguire, Evidence: Common Sense and Common Law 45–49 (1947) (something for both sides); 4 Weinstein's Federal Evidence § 611.03[1] (rev. 2011). The compilers of the Model Code of Evidence made no clear choice. Rule 105(h) would leave to the judge's discretion "to what extent and in what circumstances a party cross-examining a witness may be forbidden to examine him concerning material matters not inquired about on a previous examination by the judge or by an adverse party".

After initially favoring a restricted rule with discretion in the judge to depart from it (Fed. R. Evid. (P.D.1969) 611(b)), the Proposed Federal Rules of Evidence later opted for a wide-open rule, also with discretion to deviate. Fed. R. Evid. (R.D.1971) 611(b). The restricted rule was finally adopted by the Congress. § 21 supra, note 5.

sure the parties to present their facts in logical order: first the facts on which the plaintiff has the burden, then those which the defendant must prove, and so on.[2] The restrictive rules minimize the danger that one party's plan of presenting his facts will be interrupted by cross-examination interjecting new and damaging matters constituting his adversary's case. If permitted, such interjection can lessen the impact and persuasiveness of the proponent's case. The proponent planned to lay out an orderly case fact by fact. However, during its very presentation, the carefully crafted case is disrupted by contrary facts drawn out in cross-examination of the proponent's own witnesses. The proponent's "case," conceived as a single melody, is converted to counterpoint. The contemporary litigator views herself as a story-teller[3]—telling the jury a coherent, compelling narrative of the disputed events. The litigator understandably resents when the opposition attempts to disrupt the continuity and flow of the story. For that reason, most practitioners probably prefer the restrictive views of the scope of cross.[4]

Like all rules of order, the common law order of proof by "cases" or stages is to some extent arbitrary. Since two witnesses cannot speak at once, some rules must be worked out as to who shall call the witnesses and in what order. However, it seems artificial to impose a further restriction that a witness who knows many facts about the case may tell only certain facts at his first appearance, and as to others must be recalled later. There is a sort of natural order to the freer, wide-open practice; on direct examination the general order of proof of the respective parties' "cases" is maintained, but the adversary is free to draw out damaging facts on cross-examination. An alternative procedure would allow each witness successively to tell everything he knows about the case. That is the system which laypersons tend to follow in any informal investigation untrammeled by rules. Jeremy Bentham, the great critic of "artificial" procedural rules, favored a "natural" system of evidence. By that expression, he meant the practices which a lay family might use to investigate a factual question. That system better serves the witnesses' convenience and may strike the jury as a more natural way of developing the facts. Of course, it could be objected that a detour into new paths on cross-examination lessens the persuasiveness of the direct examiner's

---

[2]See § 4 supra.

[3]Old Chief v. U.S., 519 U.S. 172, 117 S. Ct. 644, 136 L. Ed. 2d 574 (1997); Lempert, Narrative Relevance, Imagined Juries, and a Supreme Court Inspired Agenda for Jury Research, 21 St. Louis U. Pub. L. Rev. 15, 16–17, 24 (2002); Reidinger, Spinning Yarns: Academics Ponder What Trial Lawyers Already Know—The Value of a Good Story, 82 A.B.A.J. 102 (June 1996).

[4]Carlson, Cross-Examination of the Accused, 52 Cornell L.J. 705, 706–07 (1967).

presentation of his story. However, it is hardly self-evident that the direct examiner has a right to the psychological advantage of presenting his facts in an oversimplified, one-sided way.[5] Is he entitled to make an favorable first impression on the jurors which, although answered later, can be hard to dislodge?

Another policy consideration is economy of time and energy. The wide-open rule leaves little or no opportunity for wrangling over its application at either the trial or appellate level.[6] In contrast, the restrictive practice can produce courtroom bickering over the choice among the numerous variations of the "scope of the direct" criterion, and the application of the chosen standard to particular cross-questions. These controversies often resurface on appeal, and there is the possibility of reversal for error.[7] Compliance with these ambiguous restrictions is a matter of constant concern to the cross-examiner. If these disputes and delays were necessary to guard substantive fundamental rights, they might be worth the cost. But as the price of enforcing a debatable regulation of the order of evidence, the sacrifice is misguided. The American Bar Association's Committee for the Improvement of the Law of Evidence remarked:

> The rule limiting cross-examination to the precise subject of the direct examination is probably the most frequent rule (except the Opinion rule) leading in trial practice today to refined and technical quibbles which obstruct the progress of the trial, confuse the jury, and give rise to appeal on technical grounds only. Some of the instances in which Supreme Courts have ordered new trials for the mere transgression of this rule about the order of evidence have been astounding. We recommend that the rule allowing questions upon any part of the issue known to the witness . . . be adopted . . . .[8]

In short, there is a strong case for the "wide-open" rule. Thus, while most practitioners favor the restrictive approach, the "wide-open" rule enjoys the support of many reformers, academics, and jurists.

---

[5]This query was first suggested by the late Professor Clarence Morris.

[6]A glance at the cases digested at West's Key Number Digest, Witnesses ☞269 demonstrates the almost entire absence of appellate dispute over the application of the wide-open practice and the large number of such questions from jurisdictions following the restrictive practice.

[7]See § 24 at note 9 supra.

[8]*See* 6 Wigmore, Evidence § 1888, at 711 (Chadbourn rev. 1976) where the relevant part of the Committee's report is set out in full.

## § 28   Cross-examination about witness's inconsistent past writings: Must examiner show the writing to the witness before questioning about its contents?

A fatal weakness of many liars is letter writing.[1] Betraying letters are often inspired by the liar's boastfulness or stupidity. Properly used, letters have exposed many a witness intent on perjury.[2] An eminent trial lawyer observed:

> . . . There is an art in introducing the letter contradicting the witness' testimony. The novice will rush in. He will obtain the false statement and then quickly hurl the letter in the face of the witness. The witness, faced with it, very likely will seek to retrace his steps, and sometimes do it skillfully, and the effect is lost.

> The mature trial counsel will utilize the letter for all it is worth. Having obtained the denial which he wishes, he will, perhaps, pretend that he is disappointed. He will ask that same question a few moments later, and again and again get a denial. And he will then phrase—and this requires preparation—he will then phrase a whole series of questions not directed at that particular point, but in which is incorporated the very fact which he is ready to contradict—each time getting closer and closer to the language in the written document which he possesses, until he has induced the witness to assert not once, but many times, the very fact from which ordinarily he might withdraw by saying it was a slip of the tongue. Each time he draws closer to the precise language which will contradict the witness, without making the witness aware of it, until finally, when the letter is sprung, the effect as compared with the other method is that, let us say, of atomic energy against a firecracker.[3]

### *The Rule in Queen Caroline's Case*

However, some courts have erected an obstacle to effectively

---

**[Section 28]**

[1] Of course, today the inconsistent statement could take the form of an email or a posting on social media.

[2] Probably the most famous instance is Sir Charles Russell's demolition of the witness Richard Pigott before the Parnell Commission in 1888, described in Wellman, The Art of Cross-Examination Ch. 20 (4th ed. 1936), and set out in Busch, Law and Tactics in Jury Trials § 350 (1949). This and many other striking instances are detailed in 4 Wigmore, Evidence § 1260 (Chadbourn rev. 1972).

[3] Nizer, The Art of Jury Trial, 32 Corn. L.Q. 59, 68 (1946). An instructive, similar suggestion as to the technique of "exposure by document" is found in Love, Documentary Evidence, 38 Ill. Bar J. 426, 429–30 (1950). See also 4 Belli, Modern Trials § 63.30 (2d ed. 1982). As described in text, the line of questioning is likely to draw an "asked and answered" objection; in the same line of questioning, the examiner covers the same topic several times. However, Federal Rule 611 does not codify a categorical prohibition of repetitive questioning; rather, the matter is entrusted to the judge's discretion. If the objection was forthcoming, the examiner might request permission to approach sidebar. At sidebar, the examiner would explain his objective. Based on that explanation, the trial judge would likely exercise discretion in favor of allowing the examiner to employ this technique.

using this impeachment technique. The obstacle is the rule in *Queen Caroline's Case,* pronounced by English judges in an 1820 advisory opinion.[4] The opinion announced that the cross-examiner cannot ask the witness about any written statements by the witness, or ask whether the witness has ever written a letter of a given tenor, without *first* both producing the writing *and* exhibiting it to the witness. The cross-examiner must permit the witness to read the writing or the part of it that the cross-examiner seeks to ask him about. In effect, the examiner must telegraph his punch. Thus, the potential trap is laid before the eyes of the intended prey. While reading the letter, the witness will be forewarned not to deny it. Worse still, a clever witness may be able to quickly weave a new web of deception to explain away the inconsistency.

As previously stated, *Queen Caroline's Case* announced that the writing must first be shown to the witness before he can be questioned about it. The judges conceived of the rule as an application of the best evidence doctrine requiring the production of the original document *when its contents are sought to be proved.*[5] This rule was a misconception in at least two respects. First, *at this stage* the cross-examiner is not seeking to prove the contents of the writing. On the contrary, his hope is that the witness will deny the existence of the letter. Second, the original documents rule requires the production of the document as proof of its contents to the judge and jury, not to the witness.[6] The Victorian barristers found the rule in the *Queen's Case* so obstructive that they lobbied and secured its abrogation by Parliament in 1854.[7]

However, this practice requiring exhibition to the witness was

---

[4]2 B. & B. 284, 286–90, 129 Eng. Rep. 976, 11 Eng. Rul. C. 183 (1820) (The House of Lords put the question to the judges: "First, whether, in the courts below, a party on cross-examination would be allowed to represent in the statement of a question the contents of a letter, and to ask the witness whether the witness wrote a letter to any person with such contents, or contents to the like effect, *without having first shown* to the witness the letter, and having asked that witness whether the witness wrote that letter and his admitting that he wrote such letter? . . ." Abbott, C.J., for the judges, answered the first question in the negative).

[5]This doctrine, called the best evidence rule, is analyzed in Ch. 23 infra.

[6]For these and other refutations of the theory of the *Queen's Case,* see the masterly discussion in 4 Wigmore Evidence § 1260 (Chadbourn rev. 1972). *See also* Stern & Grosh, A Visit with Queen Caroline: Her Trial and Its Rule, 6 Cap. U. L. Rev. 165 (1976).

[7]St. 17 & 18 Vict. c. 125, § 24 ("A witness may be cross-examined as to previous statements made by him in writing or reduced into writing, relative to the subject-matter of the cause, without such writing being shown to him; but if it is intended to contradict such witness by the writing, his attention must, before such contradictory proof can be given, be called to those parts of the writing which are to be used for the purpose of so contradicting him; providing always that it shall

unquestioningly accepted by many American courts[8] and occasionally by American legislatures.[9] The actual invocation of the rule at trial is relatively infrequent in most states in which the rule is still in effect. Even today some judges and practitioners in these jurisdictions are unaware of this pitfall in the cross-examiner's path.

The preceding paragraphs discussed the operation of the rule in situations in which the thrust of the attempted impeachment is the exposure of attempted perjury. In this situation, the rule seems to blunt one of counsel's most potent weapons. However, in the more typical case in the real world the weapon itself may be misdirected. Innocent witnesses write letters, forget their contents, and years later testify mistakenly to facts inconsistent with assertions in the letters. On the one hand, the cross-

---

be competent for the judge, at any time during the trial, to require the production of the writing for his inspection, and he may thereupon make such use of it for the purposes of the trial as he shall think fit.").

[8]*E.g.*, Washington v. State, 269 Ala. 146, 112 So. 2d 179 (1959) (cross-examination of accused as to statement signed by him; must be shown before questioning about contents); Glenn v. Gleason, 61 Iowa 28, 15 N.W. 659, 661 (1883) (whole letter must be read, relying on 1 Greenleaf on Evidence § 463, which popularized the rule in this country before judges here became aware that it had been abrogated in England); Bane v. State, 73 Md. App. 135, 533 A.2d 309, 319 (1987) ("Appellant's contention that the State was required to show him a prior statement before using it to impeach him would have been correct only if the prior statement had been a written one."); Price v. Grieger, 244 Minn. 466, 70 N.W.2d 421 (1955) (cited with approval in Hillesheim v. Stippel, 283 Minn. 59, 166 N.W.2d 325 (1969)); and cases collected 4 Wigmore, Evidence § 1263 (Chadbourn rev. 1972). West's Key Number Digest, Witnesses ⊙271(2), 271(4), 277(6).

The rule is often applied to cross-examination of parties about what they have written (see *Washington v. State*, supra). However, if the best evidence principle is the basis, it

has no application, since a party's oral admission of what he has written is a recognized exception to that rule. See § 242 infra.

The rule is arguably applicable to a signed deposition which may be classified as a writing, and it is sometimes applied to them, though this is an inconvenient practice. *See* 4 Wigmore, Evidence § 1262 (Chadbourn rev. 1972). But most courts distinguish depositions transcripts of oral testimony at a former trial, as to which the "show-me" rule is inapplicable. Toohey v. Plummer, 69 Mich. 345, 37 N.W. 297 (1888) (reporter's notes); Couch v. St. Louis Public Service Co., 173 S.W.2d 617, 622 (Mo. Ct. App. 1943); Charles v. McPhee, 92 N.H. 111, 26 A.2d 30 (1942). *Contra* Meadors v. Com., 281 Ky. 622, 136 S.W.2d 1066 (1940).

[9]*E.g.*, Ga. Code Ann. § 24-6-613(a) (the revised provision of the Georgia Code, which went into effect on January 13, 2013, reads: "In examining a witness concerning a prior statement made by the witness, whether written or not, the statement need not be shown nor its contents disclosed to the witness at that time; provided, however, upon request the same shall be shown or disclosed to opposing counsel."); Idaho R. Evid. 613. On the other hand, statutes and rules in various states have abrogated the rule. See note 12 infra.

examiner undeniably has a right to reveal their forgetfulness and discredit their present testimony to that extent. On the other hand, the cross-examiner arguably should not be allowed to encourage the witness by subtle questioning to widen the gap between their present testimony and their past writings. In this situation, the judge ought to have discretion whether to permit the questioning about the writing without requiring its exhibition to the witness.[10] When it seems clear to the judge that at most the witness is guilty of innocent misrecollection, the judge should have discretion to require the cross-examiner to show the writing to the witness.

In recognition of the disadvantages of the rule of *Queen Caroline's Case,* the Federal Rules of Evidence abolish the rule by permitting cross-examination without a prior showing of the writing to the witness.[11] Rule 613 substitutes a requirement that the writing be shown or disclosed to opposing counsel on request as an assurance of the cross-examiner's good faith.[12] However, there is federal authority that the trial judge retains discretion to require the exhibition of the writing to the witness.[13] As previously stated, it could be appropriate for the judge to exercise that

---

[10]Wash. R. Evid. 613(a) grants the judge discretion to require disclosure of the statement prior to cross-examination concerning the statement. For its part, Federal Rule 613(a) purports to eliminate any requirement to show the statement to the witness. However, some courts have construed Rule 403 as granting the trial judge discretion to require the cross-examiner to follow the common law practice. *E.g.,* U.S. v. Marks, 816 F.2d 1207, 1211 (7th Cir. 1987) (Posner, J.).

[11]The rule had for some time been "everywhere more honored in the breach than in the observance." U.S. v. Dilliard, 101 F.2d 829, 837 (C.C.A. 2d Cir. 1938).

[12]Former Fed. R. Evid. 613(a) provided: "In examining a witness concerning a prior statement made by the witness, whether written or not, the statement need not be shown nor its contents disclosed to the witness at that time, but on request the same shall be shown or disclosed to opposing counsel."

Unif. R. Evid. 613(a) is identical in content. Effective December 1, 2011, restyled Fed. R. Evid. 613(a) reads:

"When examining a witness about the witness's prior statement, a party need not show it or disclose its contents to the witness. But the party must, on request, show it or disclose its contents to an adverse party's attorney."

The federal Advisory Committee's Note observes:

> The rule does not defeat the application of Rule 1002 relating to production of the original when the contents of a writing are sought to be proved. Nor does it defeat the application of Rule 26(b)(3) of the Rules of Civil Procedure, as revised, entitling a person on request to a copy of his own statement, though the operation of the latter may be suspended temporarily.

*E.g.,* U.S. v. Lawson, 683 F.2d 688, 694 (2d Cir. 1982) ("At least in the absence of a claim of privilege or confidentiality, Rule 613(a) does not allow for the exercise of discretion. It flatly commands disclosure of a [prior statement used to cross-examine] to opposing counsel.").

[13]The trial judge retains discretion to require disclosure to the witness prior to questioning when in the court's discretion such disclosure will promote accuracy and fairness. U.S. v.

discretion in a case in which it is apparent that the essence of the impeachment is innocent misrecollection rather than outright perjury.

## § 29  The standard of relevancy as applied on cross-examination:[1] Trial judge's discretion[2]

There are three main functions of cross-examination: (1) to attack the credibility of the direct testimony of this witness and other opposing witnesses,[3] (2) to elicit additional facts on the historical merits related to those mentioned on direct,[4] and (3) in states following the "wide-open" rule,[5] to bring out additional facts elucidating any issue in the case.[6] The normal standard of

---

Marks, 816 F.2d 1207 (7th Cir. 1987).

**[Section 29]**

[1]West's Key Number Digest, Witnesses ☞270.

[2]West's Key Number Digest, Witnesses ☞267.

[3]The trustworthiness of a witness's testimony depends on the witness's willingness to tell the truth and his ability to do so. His ability to tell the truth as to an event of which he purports to possess personal knowledge is the product in turn of his physical and mental capacity, actual employment of the capacity to perceive, record, and recollect in the matter at hand, and his ability to narrate. On cross-examination the objectives pursued may be to draw into question the accuracy of the witness' perception, recordation and recollection, narration or sincerity. Tribe, Triangulating Hearsay, 87 Harv. L. Rev. 957 (1974); Morgan, Hearsay Dangers and the Application of the Hearsay Concept, 62 Harv. L. Rev. 177 (1948); Strahorn, A Reconsideration of the Hearsay Rule and Admissions, 85 U. Pa. L. Rev. 484 (1937). In assessing the witness's trustworthiness, the trier of fact looks not only to the content of the witness's testimony on direct and his answers to questions asked on cross-examination; the trier of fact also assesses the witness's demeanor.

[4]See § 21 supra.

[5]See § 21 supra.

[6]See generally 4 Graham, Handbook of Federal Evidence § 611.10 (7th ed. 2010) ("While cross-examination is commonly thought of as being destructive with the examining counsel attempting in one way or another to affect the trier of fact's assessment of the weight to be accorded the witness' testimony by discrediting the witness or his testimony, cross-examination entails much more. Counsel on cross-examination may (1) attempt to elicit disputed facts from the witness favorable to his case, (2) have the witness repeat those facts testified to on direct favorable to the cross-examiner, (3) have the witness testify to nondisputed facts essential to presentation of his theory of the case, (4) attempt to have the witness qualify, modify, or otherwise shed light upon his testimony with respect to unfavorable versions of disputed facts given on direct examination, (5) establish that the witness' testimony is not harmful to the advocate's case on the critical points under dispute, and/or (6) ask questions to the witness designed primarily to keep the cross-examiner's theory of the case before the trier of fact. Whether the cross-examiner chooses to attempt to elicit favorable facts from a witness called by an opponent, and/or ask questions designed to discredit the witness or his testimony, or have the witness testify to nondisputed fact, etc., naturally depends upon various factors, including the importance of the testimony of

relevancy governing testimony offered on direct examination applies to the subject-matter of cross-examination questions intended to serve the second and third functions.[7]

However, when she is performing the first function of attacking the credibility of the direct testimony, the cross-examiner's purpose is radically different than in pursuit of the other two functions. In the first function, the cross-examiner is not directly targeting the historical merits of the case. Here the common law test of relevancy is not whether the answer sought will shed light on any issue on the merits, but rather whether it aids the trier of fact in appraising the witness's credibility and assessing the probative value of the witness's direct testimony. In general the common law principles stated in this section also obtain under Federal Rule of Evidence and Revised Uniform Rule of Evidence 611(b). The restyled Federal Rule explicitly authorizes cross-examination about "matters affecting the witness's credibility." At common law and in modern federal practice there are many recognized lines of questioning for this purpose, none of which has any direct relevance to the historical merits.

For instance, one familiar type of credibility inquiry is the preliminary series of cross questions asking about residence and occupation, designed to place the witness in his setting. Either the witness's residence or occupation might give rise to an inference of bias.[8] Another common question is, "Have you talked to anyone

---

the witness in the context of the litigation considered in light of the realistic possibilities for a successful destructive cross-examination, given the ammunition available. Cross-examination is also sometimes much less; it is less because on cross-examination leading questions are sometimes prohibited, and certain kinds of impeachment will not always be allowed.").

[7]E.g., Moulton v. State, 88 Ala. 116, 6 So. 758, 759 (1889) (cross-examination must relate to facts in issue, except that otherwise irrelevant questions tending to test credibility may sometimes be asked); Marut v. Costello, 34 Ill. 2d 125, 214 N.E.2d 768 (1965).

[8]A leading case is Alford v. U.S., 282 U.S. 687, 51 S. Ct. 218, 75 L. Ed. 624 (1931) (abuse of discretion for the judge to refuse to allow cross-examination of government's witness

about his residence where the accused suspected that witness was detained in custody of federal authorities; "Cross-examination of a witness is a matter of right . . . Its permissible purposes, among others, are that the witness may be identified with his community so that independent testimony may be sought and offered of his reputation for veracity in his own neighborhood . . . that the jury may interpret his testimony in the light reflected upon it by knowledge of his environment . . . .").

Smith v. State of Illinois, 390 U.S. 129, 88 S. Ct. 748, 19 L. Ed. 2d 956 (1968) carried Alford farther by holding that a criminal defendant's Sixth Amendment and Fourteenth Amendment rights were violated when he was denied the right on cross-examination to ask the principal prosecution witness his correct name and address. The court quoted from Brookhart v. Janis, 384 U.S. 1, 3, 86

S. Ct. 1245, 16 L. Ed. 2d 314 (1966) to the effect that a denial of cross-examination "would be constitutional error of the first magnitude and no amount of showing of want of prejudice would cure it." However, the exact scope of the decision is uncertain. In a case in which the defendant was otherwise permitted full examination on the place of the witness in life, including the fact that he was staying in a motel at government expense, the court's sustaining an objection to a question about his "present" address was upheld. U.S. v. Teller, 412 F.2d 374 (7th Cir. 1969). *See also* U.S. v. Contreras, 602 F.2d 1237 (5th Cir. 1979); U.S. v. Lee, 413 F.2d 910 (7th Cir. 1969) (cross-examination as to present address barred); U.S. v. Lawler, 413 F.2d 622 (7th Cir. 1969) (inquiry barred as to where informer-witness was working at the time of trial); U.S. v. Palermo, 410 F.2d 468 (7th Cir. 1969) (name and address need not be given if threat to life of witness is shown by prosecution to the judge in camera); Iraola, The Sixth Amendment Right to Confront a Witness in a Federal Criminal Trial About His True Name, Address, and Place of Employment, 38 Crim. L. Bull. 396, 396–97 (May-June 2002) ("Generally, inquiries about a witness' name, address, and place of employment are deemed legitimate areas of cross-examination. Federal courts, however, uniformly have recognized that concern for the safety of a witness may lead to curtailment of the right to cross-examine the witness about that information in open court provided certain other conditions are met"; the balance of the article contains an excellent collection of the relevant case law).

With respect to the admissibility of background evidence, see Government of Virgin Islands v. Grant, 775 F.2d 508, 513 (3d Cir. 1985) ("The jurisprudence of 'background evidence' is essentially undeveloped. 'Background' or 'preliminary' evidence is not mentioned in the evidence codes, nor has it received attention in the treatises. One justification for its admission, at least in terms of the background of a witness *qua* witness, is that it may establish absence of bias or motive by showing the witness' relationship (or non-relationship) to the parties or to the case. It may also be said to bear on the credibility of the witness by showing the witness to be a stable person. The routine admission of evidence that an accused has never been arrested would thus seem to be a function of years of practice and of the common sense notion that it is helpful for the trier of fact to know something about a defendant's background when evaluating his culpability."); U.S. v. Blackwell, 853 F.2d 86, 88 (2d Cir. 1988) ("Certainly, the trial court is entitled to wide discretion concerning the admissibility of background evidence. Although it may be true that evidence of a lack of prior convictions or arrests may be of relatively low probative value, it is nevertheless something that the trier of the fact has a right to know in gauging the credibility of a witness. The opportunity to inform the trier of the fact of the accused's lack of a criminal record is clearly one of the factors which would motivate a defendant to testify. . . . Although it was error to strike the evidence of a prior clean record, the error was plainly harmless in this case."); Conway v. Chemical Leaman Tank Lines, Inc., 525 F.2d 927, 930 (5th Cir. 1976) ("The policy of the new Rules [of Evidence] is one of broad admissibility, and the generous definition of 'relevant evidence' in Rule 401 was specifically intended to provide that background evidence . . . is admissible.").

The admissibility of a witness's background information is subject to the court's discretion. Where the background information desired constitutes evidence of specific instances of conduct relating to character barred by Rules 404 and 405, discretion will normally be exercised in favor of exclu-

about this case?"[9] Like a witness's residence or occupation, a witness's pretrial contacts could have a biasing influence. Still another is the testing, exploratory question. In this kind of question, the cross-examiner (who may not have had the advantage of previously interviewing the witness) poses questions often remote from the main inquiry. The questions are designed to experimentally test the witness's ability to remember detailed facts of the same nature as those recited on direct, his capacity accurately to perceive facts, or his willingness to tell the truth without distortion or exaggeration.[10] This is part of the tradition and art of cross-examination, and some of the most famous instances of cross-examinations are of this variety.[11] The courts recognize that a rule strictly limiting cross questions to those relevant to the issues on the historical merits would cripple this kind of

---

sion. *See* U.S. v. Solomon, 686 F.2d 863 (11th Cir. 1982) (in its discretion, the trial court may prohibit inquiry into the extent of the witness's family and whether he had served in the military). *But see* Wilson v. Vermont Castings, 977 F. Supp. 691, 699 (M.D. Pa. 1997) ("Information about a party's or a witness' background, job and education is certainly appropriate and admissible in every action. Juries cannot make assessment of credibility in a vacuum. Such information gives background on the witness and a point of reference in assessing that individual's credibility. . . .").

[9] The question is usually approved. See cases cited in Crossexamination of witness in criminal case as to whether, and with whom, he has discussed facts of case, 35 A.L.R.2d 1045. In various instances, exclusion of similar questions has been deemed error. *See, e.g.,* U.S. v. Standard Oil Co., 316 F.2d 884 (7th Cir. 1963). *But see* State v. Yost, 241 Or. 362, 405 P.2d 851 (1965) (it was not error to exclude question asking witness with whom he had talked during recess when question did not shed any light on the witness's credibility under the circumstances).

[10] Kervin v. State, 254 Ala. 419, 48 So. 2d 204 (1950) (wide latitude to test witness's recollection is permitted subject to judge's discretion); People v. Sorge, 301 N.Y. 198, 93 N.E.2d 637 (1950) (proper for district attorney in cross-examining accused about other offenses to persist after denial "in the hope of inducing the witness to abandon his negative answers" and "on the chance that he may change his testimony"). *See also* Alford v. U.S., 282 U.S. 687, 692, 51 S. Ct. 218, 75 L. Ed. 624 (1931) ("Counsel often cannot know in advance what pertinent facts may be elicited on cross-examination. For that reason it is necessarily exploratory; and the rule that the examiner must indicate the purpose of his inquiry does not, in general, apply."). There are enlightening discussions and illustrations of the technique of "testing" cross-examination in Busch, Law and Tactics in Jury Trials § 303 (1949) and Lake, How to Cross-Examine Witnesses Successfully 137–151 (1957). But see § 41 infra.

[11] For instructive examples, see Wellman, The Art of Cross-Examination ch. 26 (4th ed. 1936) (by Littleton); Reed, Conduct of Law Suits §§ 423–39 (2d ed. 1912); Kiendl, Some Aspects of Cross-Examination, 51 Case and Comment, No. 6, pp. 27–30 (1946); Busch, Law and Tactics in Jury Trials § 303 (1949); Belli, The Voice of Modern Trials Vol. III (long play recording); Heller, Do You Solemnly Swear? Part VI (1968).

examination.[12] A final instance of credibility cross-examination is the attack by impeaching questions seeking to show such matters as inconsistent statements or conviction of crime.[13] Again, these facts have no necessary relevance to the historical merits.

As to all the lines of inquiry mentioned in the preceding paragraph, the criteria of relevancy are vague, since the cross-examiner's purpose is frequently exploratory.[14] Too tight a rein on the cross-examiner may rob the examination of its utility. However, dangers of undue prejudice[15] to the party or the witness and of potential waste of time are apparent. Consequently, the trial judge has a discretionary power to control the extent of examination.[16] Appellate courts overturn this exercise of discretion only for abuse resulting in substantial harm to the complain-

---

[12]Accordingly, some opinions point out that the rules of relevancy are not applied with the same strictness on cross-examination as on direct: State v. Smith, 140 Me. 255, 37 A.2d 246 (1944); O'Sullivan v. Simpson, 123 Mont. 314, 212 P.2d 435 (1949); Grocers Supply Co. v. Stuckey, 152 S.W.2d 911 (Tex. Civ. App. Galveston 1941 error refused) (during cross-examination, any fact bearing on witness's credit is relevant). Fed. R. Evid. 611(b) and Unif. R. Evid. 611(b) permit cross-examination upon "matters affecting the witness's credibility." Rule 611(a) clearly emphasizes the trial judge's discretion in these matters.

[13]See Ch. 5 infra, dealing with impeachment of witnesses.

[14]In recognition of the exploratory nature of cross-examination, a number of jurisdictions dispense with any need for an offer of proof on cross-examination. Cal. Evid. Code § 354(c). The underlying reasoning is that it is unrealistic to expect the cross-examiner to know the likely answer when she is pursuing a legitimate, but exploratory, line of questioning.

[15]Lee Won Sing v. U.S., 215 F.2d 680 (D.C. Cir. 1954) (question on cross whether accused had paid his co-defendant $20,000 to plead guilty was improper because it was asked without a reasonable foundation; the error was not adequately cured by instructions); State v. Lampshire, 74 Wash. 2d 888, 447 P.2d 727 (1968) (abuse of discre-

tion to permit question in regard to large telephone bill incurred by defendant-witness). See Fed. R. Evid. 403 & Unif. R. Evid. 403. See § 185 infra.

[16]Alford v. U.S., 282 U.S. 687, 694, 51 S. Ct. 218, 75 L. Ed. 624 (1931) ("The extent of cross-examination with respect to an appropriate subject of inquiry is within the sound discretion of the trial court. It may exercise a reasonable judgment in determining when the subject is exhausted."; but here, excluding inquiry as to place of residence of witness held an abuse of discretion); Casey v. U.S., 413 F.2d 1303 (5th Cir. 1969) (court barred questions implying United States gave covert support to defendant's enterprise); Hider v. Gelbach, 135 F.2d 693 (C.C.A. 4th Cir. 1943) (judge properly exercised discretion to curb repetitious cross-examination); State v. Cummings, 445 S.W.2d 639 (Mo. 1969) (court could exclude question to prosecuting witness concerning an insurance requirement that he file a criminal charge); Simpson v. State, 32 Wis. 2d 195, 145 N.W.2d 206 (1966) (objections to various questions to expert were sustained); West's Key Number Digest, Witnesses ⟐267. Fed. R. Evid. 611(a) grants the trial court discretion concerning cross-examination on the type of irrelevant subjects mentioned in the text, but questions may also be excluded on the ground that they are prejudicial or otherwise violate Rule 403. U.S. v. Lustig, 555 F.2d 737 (9th

ing party.[17] A survey of a large number of these cases reveals that in practice, the appellate courts more often find abuse when complaint is that the trial judge unduly limited the examination than when undue extension is alleged.[18] In a criminal case, the court is especially likely to find an abuse of discretion when the trial judge restricts cross-examination probing a prosecution witness's bias.[19]

## § 30 The cross-examiner's art

Section 5 of this treatise noted that although at the typical trial the direct examinations are more determinative of the outcome than the cross-examinations, many attorneys find it more difficult to master the art of cross-examination. An overview of the art of cross-examination, gleaned from the prolific writing on the subject,[1] may help the beginning advocate appreciate some of the wisdom lawyers have learned from hard experience. It may also aid in considering the topic of the next section, namely,

---

Cir. 1977).

[17]Bates v. Chilton County, 244 Ala. 297, 13 So. 2d 186 (1943); Com. v. Greenberg, 339 Mass. 557, 160 N.E.2d 181 (1959).

[18]For notable, instructive instances of holdings of abuse in curbing the accused's cross-examination of government witnesses, see Davis v. Alaska, 415 U.S. 308, 94 S. Ct. 1105, 39 L. Ed. 2d 347 (1974); District of Columbia v. Clawans, 300 U.S. 617, 57 S. Ct. 660, 81 L. Ed. 843 (1937); Alford v. U.S., 282 U.S. 687, 51 S. Ct. 218, 75 L. Ed. 624 (1931). Many kinds of rulings have been held an abuse of discretion. *E.g.*, U.S. v. Hogan, 232 F.2d 905 (3d Cir. 1956) (excluding cross-examination to the effect that witnesses had their sentences postponed, because they had agreed to testify for the government and hoped for preferential treatment); People v. Mason, 28 Ill. 2d 396, 192 N.E.2d 835 (1963) (limiting questions to show bias in a close case). On the other hand, restrictions have been upheld in particular circumstances on the ground that the cross-examination conducted was so substantial and thorough that further examination would have been cumulative or repetitious. *E.g.*, U.S. v. Headid, 565 F.2d 1029 (8th Cir. 1977).

[19]U.S. v. Sasson, 62 F.3d 874, 883 (7th Cir. 1995); Quinn v. Neal, 998 F.2d 526, 531 (7th Cir. 1993); U.S. v. Williams, 892 F.2d 296, 301 (3d Cir. 1989).

**[Section 30]**

[1]For a hundred years, lawyers have been fascinated with the topic, developed practical maxims, and collected dramatic instances. See the section on the "Theory and Art" in 5 Wigmore, Evidence § 1368 (Chadbourn rev. 1974). There are helpful, practical hints and examples in Busch, Law and Tactics in Jury Trials Ch. 15 (1959) and Lane, Goldstein Trial Technique §§ 19:1 to 19:96 (3d ed.). *See also* Reed, Conduct of Lawsuits (2d ed. 1912); Elliott, The Work of the Advocate (2d ed. 1912); Wellman, The Art of Cross-Examination (4th ed. 1936); Stryker, The Art of Advocacy Chs. 4, 5 (1954); Friedman, Essentials of Cross-Examination (1968); Mauet, Trial Techniques Ch. 7 (8th ed. 2010); Lubet, Modern Trial Advocacy (3d ed. 2010); Pozner & Dodd, Cross-Examination: Science and Techniques (2d ed. 2009); Bodin, ed., Trial Techniques Library (1967); Harolds, Kelner & Fuchsberg, Examination of Witnesses (1965); Lake, How to Cross-Examine Witnesses Successfully (1957);

evaluating the broader policy significance of cross-examination. The following are some of the most important generalizations.

*Pretrial preparation is the key.* Some lawyers seem to have a natural, intuitive talent for cross-examination. A great Victorian advocate, Montagu Williams, voiced this view when he said, "I am by trade a reader of faces and minds."[2] Today, however, the stress is on painstaking preparation, not divine inspiration.[3] Improvisation is often necessary, but its results are usually small compared to those achieved by planned questions based on facts methodically discovered before trial. The planning steps are explained in several classic works on cross-examination.[4] Not all steps have to be taken for all adverse witnesses; the testimony of some adverse witnesses is simply not damaging enough to warrant the expense of thorough preparation. Nevertheless, preparation before trial is the soil from which, in the average case, successful cross-examination grows.[5]

*At trial, listen intently to the direct testimony.* If you properly prepare before trial, during an opposing witness's direct examination you should have nothing to do other than concentrate on exactly what is being said. Some lawyers recommend that at trial, any notes in preparation for later questions be made by an associate or the client, rather than the cross-examiner. Oral sug-

---

Redfield, Cross-Examination and the Witness (1963); Wrottesley, The Examination of Witnesses in Court Ch. 3 (2d ed. 1926); Bailey & Rothblatt, Cross-Examination in Criminal Trials (1978); Carlson & Imwinkelried, Dynamics of Trial Practice Chs. 8, 10 (4th ed. 2010). Numerous readable articles include the following: Nizer, The Art of Jury Trial, 32 Corn. L.Q. 59 (1946); Comisky, Observations on the Preparation and Conduct of Cross-Examination, 2 Prac. Law. 24 (1956); Von Moschzisker, Some Maxims for Cross-Examination, 3 id. 78 (1957).

[2]Quoted Elliott, The Work of the Advocate 231 (2d ed. 1912).

[3]See especially the works of Busch and Lane, and the article of Nizer, The Art of Jury Trial, 32 Corn. L.Q. 59, 68 (1946). Nizer says:

Most lawyers who will tell you of brilliant cross-examination will not confess this: We are entranced by a brilliant flash of insight which broke the witness, but the plain truth of the matter is, as brother to brother, that ninety-

nine per cent of effective cross-examination is once more our old friend 'thorough preparation,' which places in your hands a written document with which to contradict the witness. That usually is the great gift of cross-examination.

[4]See particularly Busch, Law and Tactics in Jury Trials §§ 286–90 (1959); Friedman, Essentials of Cross-Examinations 15–36 (1968); Pozner & Dodd, Cross-Examination: Science and Techniques (2d ed. 2009).

[5]That most of the famous, devastating cross-examinations were grounded in pre-trial preparation is illustrated by such celebrated instances as Sir Charles Russell's cross-examination of Richard Pigott before the Parnell Commission. *See* 4 Wigmore, Evidence § 1260 (Chadbourn rev. 1972). It become even more evident in that storehouse of great cross-examinations, Aron Steuer, Max D. Steuer, Trial Lawyer (1950), especially in the account of People v. Gardner in the second chapter.

gestions at the counsel table to the cross-examiner should be avoided.[6] During the direct examination, the cross-examiner cannot afford to spend a good deal of time preparing notes or conversing; the task at hand for the cross-examiner is to listen intently to every word coming out of the mouth of the direct examiner and witness.

*Do not cross-examine unless you believe that you can probably achieve a specific strategic or tactical objective.* In the movies, desperate fishing expeditions on cross-examination routinely yield startling revelations. In the real world, they are usually ineffective and often counter-productive. The cross-examiner typically succeeds only in having the witness repeat the damaging testimony, and during cross hostile witnesses frequently add damning facts which were deliberately omitted on direct to set a trap for the cross-examiner.[7]

As a general proposition, the attorney should not cross at all unless, in his best professional judgment, he is convinced that he can probably achieve one of the useful purposes of cross. As we have seen, these purposes are: first, to elicit new facts on the historical merits, qualifying the direct or in some states bearing on any issue in the case; second, to test the witness's story by exploring its details and implications, in the hope of disclosing inconsistencies or implausibilities; and third, to elicit facts such as prior inconsistent statements, bias, and criminal convictions to impeach either this witness or another opposing witness. If you prepared thoroughly before trial, you are in position to predict whether you can probably achieve one or more of these objectives. The cross-examiner should rarely pose a question about a pivotal fact to an adverse witness unless the cross-examiner is reasonably confident the answer will be favorable. In deciding whether to pursue any of these objectives, but particularly the last two, the cross-examiner must be conscious that the odds are stacked against her. An unfavorable answer is more damaging when elicited on cross-examination. It is hard for an attorney to win his case on cross-examination, but it is easy for him to lose it. Hence, if the witness's direct testimony has done little or no harm, a cross-examination for the second or third purpose is often ill-advised. In many cases, when the direct examiner

---

[6]An often neglected phase of preparation is cautioning one's own witnesses about the probable line of cross-examinations, and especially warning them of such pitfall questions as "Whom have you talked to about this case?" and "When did you first know you would be called as a witness?" Lane, Goldstein Trial Technique §§ 19:25, 19:30 (3d ed.).

[7]Some court-wise expert witnesses hold back on direct examination in the hope that the cross-examiner will blunder and give the expert an opportunity to dramatically mention the damaging facts held in reserve.

tenders the witness to the cross-examiner, the cross-examiner should say only, "No questions, Your Honor. This witness may be excused."

But what if the witness's direct testimony has been damaging or even threatens to destroy the cross-examiner's case if the jury believes it? Suppose that although the testimony has been damaging, the cross-examiner has little ammunition against the witness.[8] Should the attorney launch an exploratory cross-examination? The cross-examiner must make a situational, on-the-spot judgment: Was the direct testimony so devastating that the jurors will probably regard a waiver of cross as an admission of the truth of the testimony, and, on that basis, find against the cross-examiner's client? In that situation cross-examination is usually necessary even if the chances of success are remote. To be blunt, if the direct testimony was devastating and the cross-examiner has no real ammunition against the witness, the cross-examiner must contemplate either launching a fishing expedition or seeking a recess to renew settlement discussions.

If out of desperation you decide to conduct a fishing expedition, it is inadvisable to follow the order of the witness's direct testimony. One commentator suggests: "If the witness is falsifying, jump quickly with rapid-fire questions from one point of the narrative to the other, without time or opportunity for a connected narrative: backward, forward, forward, backward from the middle to the beginning, etc."[9] Of course, there are common sense limits to this suggestion. If the cross-examiner jumps around too quickly and abruptly, the cross-examination will confuse the jurors rather than impressing them.

*Know when to conclude the cross-examination and try to end on a high note.* If the cross-examiner succeeds in eliciting a favorable fact, it is frequently better to wait and stress the inconsistency in closing argument than to continue to press the witness. If the cross-examiner presses immediately with a follow-up question, the additional question may give the witness an opportunity to recover and explain away the concession. When the cross-examiner has gained an important admission, she should not risk the witness's recantation by continuing the questioning to obtain

---

[8]See the enlightening discussion in Kiendl, Some Aspects of Cross-Examination, 51 Case and Comment, No. 6, p. 25 (1946), and see generally Lake, How to Cross-Examine Witnesses Successfully (1957).

[9]Ramage, A Few Rules for the Cross-Examination of Witnesses, 91 Cent. L.J. 354 (1920). For an illustra-

tion, see Reed, Conduct of Lawsuits 307–12 (2d ed. 1912). There is an important caveat, though. If the cross-examiners "jump[s]" from one topic to another too "quickly," the jurors might become confused. When they find the line of questioning confusing, they will probably forgive the witness for likewise seeming confused.

additional details or to demand a repetition of the admission.[10] Rather, she ought to move to another important point if she has one, and conclude the examination after her last big point. End on a high note: "When you have struck oil, stop boring."[11] The impact of a cross-examination depends on the overall impression left at the end of the cross rather the number of technical debating points which the cross-examiner scores against the witness.

*Cross-examine for the jury, not for your client.* As just stated, be conscious of the overall impression left by your cross-examination. It is often tempting for the cross-examiner to display his wit and skill for his client, or to satisfy the client's hostility toward an opposing witnesses by humiliating them.[12] Small victories on collateral matters are often easy to secure. However, the odds between the experienced advocate and the witness, nervous in new surroundings, are not even. The jury is keenly aware of this disparity, and most jurors are prone to imagine themselves in the witness's shoes. The jurors tend to sympathize—and side with—the witness. Impress the jury with your civility.[13]

The cross-examiner must be ultra polite in questioning sympathetic witnesses such as children, crime victims, and bereaved relatives. The cross-examiner usually obtains better results with the witness, and makes a better impression on the jury, with tact rather than bullying and sarcasm. However, in the rare case when the cross-examiner is convinced that a crucial witness has committed perjury and that he can expose it, the cross-examiner should press aggressively. Once it is clear to the jury that the cross-examiner has "the goods" on the witness, the cross-examiner can adopt a more overtly combative attitude toward the witness.

*Project sincerity.* While these generalities are worthwhile guidelines, the cross-examiner must adapt her techniques to the

---

[10] A question demanding the repetition of the answer may also be objectionable on the ground that the question has been "asked and answered."

[11] Credited to Josh Billings in Steeves, The Dangers of Cross-Examination, 86 Cent. L.J. 206, 207 (1918). "If you have made a homerun do not run around the bases twice." Ramage, A Few Rules, 91 Cent. L.J. 354, 356 (1920). *See also* Friedman, Essentials of Cross-Examination 119 (1968).

[12] "The object of cross-examination is not to produce startling effects, but to elicit facts which will support the theory intended to be put forward. Sir William Follett asked the fewest questions of any counsel I ever knew; and I have heard many cross-examinations from others listened to with rapture from an admiring client, each question of which has been destruction to his case." Sergeant Ballantine's Experiences, 1st Am. ed., 106, quoted in Reed, Conduct of Lawsuits 278 (2d ed. 1912).

[13] These points are especially well made by Kiendl, Some Aspects of Cross-Examination, 51 Case and Comment, No. 6, pp.24, 32 (1946). *See also* Lane, Goldstein Trial Technique §§ 19.39–.61 (3d ed. 1984).

specific situation she faces. Different seasoned litigators might use widely varying techniques in cross-examining the same witness.[14] As on direct, during cross-examination the litigator needs to adopt a questioning style suited to her personality. Whatever else the litigator does during trial, she must project sincerity to the jury. If the cross-examiner attempts to mimic another attorney's style and persona, her presentation may strike the jury as insincere.

## § 31    Cross-examination revalued

Early Victorian writers on advocacy waxed poetic about cross-examination and exaggerated its importance. One wrote, "There is never a cause contested, the result of which is not mainly dependent upon the skill with which the advocate conducts his cross-examination."[1] This romanticism contrasts with the realism of Scarlett, a great "leader" of a later day. Scarlett remarked, "I learned by much experience that the most useful duty of an advocate is the examination of witnesses, and that much more mischief than benefit generally results from cross-examination. I therefore rarely allowed that duty to be performed by my colleagues. I cross-examined in general very little, and more with a view to enforce the facts I meant to rely upon than to affect the witness's credit—for the most part a vain attempt."[2] Reed, one of the most sensible early 20th century writers on trial tactics, observed, "Sometimes a great speech bears down the adversary, and sometimes a searching cross-examination turns a witness inside out and shows him up to be a perjured villain. But ordinarily cases are not won by either speaking or cross-examining."[3] Yet, even today many lawyers who write concerning the art of cross-examination believe that failure to use this tool effectively

---

[14]*E.g.*, the cross-examination of the same witnesses by three different lawyers at a demonstration session in Examining the Medical Expert 143–48 (1969).

**[Section 31]**

[1]Quoted from Cox, The Advocate 434, in Reed, Conduct of Lawsuits 277 (2d ed. 1912).

[2]Memoir of Lord Abinger 75, quoted in Reed, Conduct of Lawsuits t 278 (2d ed. 1912).

[3]Reed, Conduct of Lawsuits 276 (2d ed. 1912). *See also* Kilner & McGovern, Successful Litigation Techniques § 14.01, at 14–1 (1981) ("The right to thoroughly cross examine all witnesses makes our adversary system work, because it is through that examination that the accuracy, truthfulness and trustworthiness of the testimony is tested. Some jurors, unfortunately, expect the cross examining attorney to pull a Perry Mason act on every witness and eventually to have him completely repudiate everything he said on direct examination. The trial practitioner, however, must recognize that things like that happen in television shows but seldom do they occur in a real courtroom.").

can lose a case.[4] That belief often holds true for criminal defense counsel.

Most contemporary commentators have a less romantic and more realistic view of the importance of cross-examination. To the modern advocate, cross-examination is more important as a means of gleaning additional facts on the merits to support the cross-examiner's theory of the case;[5] in the real world—as opposed to movies—the cross-examiner rarely destroys the credibility of an opposing witness. It is true that cross-examination of experts is critical in many cases. Federal Rule of Evidence 705 makes the opportunity to cross-examine particularly important when, as the rule permits, on direct examination an expert states only her opinion and the theoretical reasons for the opinion. In that situation, Rule 705 places the burden on the cross-examiner to explore the facts or data about the specific case on which the opinion is based. However, even in this context, the focus is ordinarily on the validity of the expert's reasoning process rather than the expert witness's personal credibility. In summary, while cross-examination can be an important tool at some trials, it does not loom as large a determinant of victory as direct examination in most cases.

We should not only consider this assessment in critiquing the norms and procedures for cross-examination. More broadly, a reappraisal of cross-examination as an engine for discovering truth should factor into any discussion of the reform of American evidence law, notably hearsay doctrine. The traditional assumption has been that if there is no opportunity for cross-examination, the statement of an out-of-court declarant is so lacking in reliability that it is not even worth hearing at trial. The traditional mindset is that the opportunity for cross-examination is essential. As we have seen, cross-examination is a useful device to ensure greater accuracy and completeness in the witness's testimony. In the hands of a skillful advocate, it will sometimes expose fraud or honest error. But it can also produce errors.[6] The litigator can use cross-examination to expose perjury; but it is sometimes the

---

[4]"Failure to examine a witness's background, recollection, bias and knowledge of the subject still can and often does lose a case that should have been won." Friedman, Essentials of Cross-Examination 6 (1968).

[5]"The type of cross-examination which is employed most frequently is that intended to discredit the direct testimony of the witness." Bodin, Principles of Cross-Examination, Trial Techniques Library 8 (1967).

[6]For accounts of staged experiments attempting to show comparative results as to accuracy and completeness of free narrative, direct examination and cross-examination, see Marston, Studies in Testimony, 15 J. Crim. Law & Criminology, 1 (1924); Cady, On the Psychology of Testimony, 35 Am. J. Psych. 10 (1924); Weld and Danzig, Study of Way in Which a Verdict is Reached by a Jury, 53 Am. J. Psych. 518 (1940) (effect of cross-

honest, timid witness[7] who goes down under the fire of cross-examination.[8] As a matter of fairness, every witness in judicial proceedings should be made available for cross-examination when it is feasible to do so. However, where cross-examination is impossible, as in the case of an out-of-court statement of a witness who dies before cross-examination, it is dubious to insist that the statement normally be excluded for that reason alone. Cross-examination ought to be considered useful, but not indispensable, as a means of discovering truth. The lack of an opportunity to cross-examine should be only one relevant factor in deciding whether to admit a statement. A modern, reformist approach to the hearsay doctrine might lead us to conclude that when the opportunity to cross-examine a witness is permanently cut off without either party's fault, the hearsay testimony should be admissible.[9] Hearsay statements arguably ought to be admitted if (1) the declarant based the statement on personal knowledge, and the declarant is now dead or unavailable for cross-examination or, (2) the declarant is alive and still available for cross-examination.[10] Perhaps written statements should be admit-

---

examinations upon jurors during progress of simulated trial); Snee and Lush, Interaction of the Narrative and Interrogatory Methods of Obtaining Testimony, 11 Am. J. Psych. 229 (1941); Gardner, The Perception and Memory of Witnesses, 18 Corn. L.Q. 391, 404 (1933); Burtt, Legal Psychology 147 (1931) ("It appears that when we really go after the observer in a rigorous fashion we tend to introduce some errors, perhaps through the mechanism of suggestion. . . .").

Some abuses of cross-examination are reflected in Erle Stanley Gardner, Confessions of a Cross-Examiner, 3 J. For. Sci. 374 (1958) (unfair questioning of a medical expert about compensation). Hazards of inadequate mastery of the art of cross-examination which can cause erroneous testimony error are pointed out in some of the references cited in § 30, supra note 1.

[7]In particular in the case of child abuse victims, there is a growing realization that forcing the victim to testify in the abuser's presence can impair the accuracy of the victim's testimony. A line of authority dispenses with the need for face-to-face confrontation during cross-examination when there has been a showing that such confrontation would traumatize the child and prevent the child from testifying effectively. Driggers v. State, 940 S.W.2d 699 (Tex. App. Texarkana 1996) (the trial judge made a finding that the complainant could not verbalize in her father's presence and that she would find direct confrontation traumatizing); State v. Foster, 81 Wash. App. 444, 915 P.2d 520 (Div. 1 1996) (the trial judge must make a specific finding as to whether "requiring the child to testify in the presence of the defendant will cause the child to suffer serious emotional or mental distress that will prevent the child from reasonably communicating at trial"). See § 19 note 10 supra.

[8]Elliott, The Work of the Advocate 235 (2d ed. 1911).

[9]Compare § 19, supra.

[10]Compare Ch. 34, infra.

ted wherever production for cross-examination can fairly be dispensed with.[11]

Although this reformist viewpoint is defensible, there are special constitutional concerns in criminal cases. The source of those concerns, of course, is the accused's right of cross-examination under the Fifth, Sixth, and Fourteenth Amendments.[12] Those constitutional guarantees constrain the liberalization of cross-examination practice and the hearsay rule.[13] To a degree, asymmetry between the hearsay rules in prosecutions and those in civil actions is inevitable.

## § 32   Redirect and subsequent examinations[1]

### Redirect Examination

The courts have developed what might be termed a "rule of first opportunity" to define the scope of redirect and recross-examination. As a general proposition, an attorney who calls a witness is normally required to elicit on the witness's first direct examination all the testimony that the attorney wishes to prove by the witness. This norm of proving everything feasible at the first opportunity is in the interest of fairness and efficiency. As previously stated, there is a split of authority over the question of whether the cross-examiner should be limited to answering the direct, with many more states favoring the restrictive approach.[2] However, when the question is the scope of redirect and the subsequent examinations, there is no such division; the uniform practice is that the party's examination is typically limited to answering any new matter drawn out in the adversary's immediately preceding examination.[3] It is true that under his general discretionary power to vary the normal order of proof, the judge may permit the redirect examiner to bring out relevant

---

[11]Compare Ch. 34, infra.

[12]See § 19 supra, and § 252, infra.

[13]Crawford v. Washington, 541 U.S. 36, 124 S. Ct. 1354, 158 L. Ed. 2d 177 (2004); Friedman, Adjusting to Crawford: High Court Decision Restores Confrontation Clause Protection, 19 Crim. Just., Sum. 2004, at 4, 7. See also Amar, Confrontation Clause First Principles: A Reply to Professor Friedman, 86 Geo. L.J. 1045 (1998); Imwinkelried, The Constitutionalization of Hearsay: The Extent to Which the Fifth and Sixth Amendments Permit or Require the Liberalization

of the Hearsay Rules, 76 Minn. L. Rev. 521 (1992).

**[Section 32]**

[1]See 6 Wigmore, Evidence §§ 1896–97 (Chadbourn rev. 1976), West's Key Number Digest, Witnesses ⬅285 to 291.

[2]See § 21 supra.

[3]The function of redirect examination is to meet new facts or rehabilitate a witness with respect to impeaching matter brought out on cross-examination through the introduction of redirect evidence tending to refute, deny, explain, qualify, disprove, repel,

matter which through oversight he failed to elicit on direct.[4] Under Federal Rule of Evidence 611(a), the judge has discretion over the scope of redirect.[5] However, even in Federal Rules jurisdictions, replying to new matter adduced on cross-examination is the customary, limited function of redirect. Exam-

---

or otherwise shed light on the evidence developed during cross-examination. U.S. v. Naiman, 211 F.3d 40, 51 (2d Cir. 2000) ("Redirect examination 'may be used to rebut false impressions arising from cross-examination . . . .'"); State v. Deshaw, 404 N.W.2d 156, 158 (Iowa 1987) ("Redirect examination questions that take the form of explanation, avoidance or qualification of matters brought out on cross-examination are permissible."). The scope of redirect includes questions: designed to explain apparent inconsistencies between statements made on direct and cross-examination; to deny or explain the making of an alleged prior inconsistent statement; to correct inadvertent mistakes made on cross-examination; to bring out circumstances repelling unfavorable inferences raised on cross-examination; to bring out admissible prior consistent statements; and to elicit other aspects of an event, transaction, conversation or document shedding light on the aspects previously developed during cross-examination.

[4]State v. Bennett, 158 Me. 109, 179 A.2d 812 (1962); Fisher Body Division, General Motors Corp. v. Alston, 252 Md. 51, 249 A.2d 130 (1969); State v. Conner, 97 N.J.L. 423, 118 A. 211 (N.J. Sup. Ct. 1922). See generally 6 Wigmore, Evidence § 1896 at 737 (Chadbourn rev. 1976) ("[T]he general principle of the *trial court's discretion* . . . is here fully recognized as sanctioning, when necessary, the exceptional allowance of new testimony which could have been put in before, or of a repetition of matters already testified to.") (emphasis in original).

[5]The judge's discretion is emphasized in Fed. R. Evid. 611(a), 403 and Unif. R. Evid. 611(a) and 403.

Former Rule 611(a) provided for the judge's discretion as follows:

The court shall exercise reasonable control over the mode and order of interrogating witnesses and presenting evidence so as to (1) make the interrogation and presentation effective for the ascertainment of the truth, (2) avoid needless consumption of time, and (3) protect witnesses from harassment or undue embarrassment.

Effective December 1, 2011, restyled Fed. R. Evid. 611(a) reads:

The court should exercise reasonable control over the mode and order of examining witnesses and presenting evidence so as to:

(1)    make those procedures effective for determining the truth;

(2)    avoid wasting time; and

(3)    protect witnesses from harassment or undue embarrassment.

*E.g.*, U.S. v. Taylor, 599 F.2d 832 (8th Cir. 1979) (the scope of redirect examination is within the trial judge's sound discretion and will be reversed only upon a showing of abuse of discretion); U.S. v. Lopez, 575 F.2d 681 (9th Cir. 1978) (". . . redirect is normally limited to the scope of cross-examination . . . The judge, in his discretion, may allow a new line of questioning on redirect.") (dictum).

ination for this purpose is often deemed a matter of right,[6] but even then its extent is subject to the judge's discretionary control.[7]

A skillful re-examiner can frequently remove the sting of an apparently devastating cross-examination.[8] The reply on redirect can take the form of explanation, avoidance, or qualification of the new substantive facts or impeachment matters elicited by the cross-examiner.[9] Suppose, for example, that on cross-examination, the witness conceded that he made an apparently inconsistent statement. On redirect, the examiner might invite the witness to explain away the apparent inconsistency by telling the jury that

---

[6]*See* U.S. v. Moran, 493 F.3d 1002, 1013 (9th Cir. 2007) (the trial judge allowed a defendant charged with tax violation to be cross-examined about a letter she had received from an expert who questioned the legality of her business practices; however, the judge forbade redirect examination about other expert opinions she had received which supported her practices; the judge took an unreasonably narrow view of the scope of redirect). Although no authority under Fed. R. Evid. 611(a) in point has been discovered, it is conceivable that redirect could be so important that it would be required. Villineuve v. Manchester St. Ry., 73 N.H. 250, 60 A. 748 (1905) (when inconsistent statement was mentioned on cross, the witness and party have right that witness be permitted to explain on redirect); Gray v. Metropolitan St. Ry. Co., 165 N.Y. 457, 59 N.E. 262 (1901); Martin's Adm'r v. Richmond, F. & P.R. Co., 101 Va. 406, 44 S.E. 695 (1903).

[7]People v. Kynette, 15 Cal. 2d 731, 104 P.2d 794 (1940); Com. v. Galvin, 310 Mass. 733, 39 N.E.2d 656 (1942). For federal authority, see note 5 supra.

[8]An interesting example is the examination by Sir Edward Carson quoted in 6 Wigmore, Evidence § 1896 (Chadbourn rev. 1976).

[9]U.S. v. Peters, 610 F.2d 338 (5th Cir. 1980) (defense cross-examination brought out that no photographs or recordings were made of defendant's conversations with government agent; on redirect it was pointed out that such recordings were not normal pro-

cedure on a "hand-to-hand buy"); Hawkins v. U.S., 417 F.2d 1271 (5th Cir. 1969) (redirect concerning defendant's brutal treatment of witness was permissible to rebut attempted impeachment of witness on cross-examination, citing Beck v. U.S., 317 F.2d 865 (5th Cir. 1963)); Abeyta v. People, 156 Colo. 440, 400 P.2d 431 (1965) (illustrating similar principle); Johnson v. Minihan, 355 Mo. 1208, 200 S.W.2d 334 (1947) (in a collision case plaintiff's witness, the driver of car in which plaintiff was guest, admitted signing, without reading, damaging statements mentioned on cross-examination; it was an abuse of discretion to deny redirect examination about fact that witness signed statement in order to secure settlement from defendant of witness's own claim); Long v. F. W. Woolworth Co., 232 Mo. App. 417, 109 S.W.2d 85 (1937) (proper to allow plaintiff, asked on cross if she had consulted doctor, to explain on redirect that she had not because she could not pay); Crowell v. State, 147 Tex. Crim. 299, 180 S.W.2d 343 (1944) (in prosecution for keeping bawdy house, the deputy sheriff on cross-examination admitted that he said he wanted to run defendant out of town; it was proper for him to explain on redirect that it was because of citizens' complaints against defendant).

Whether a witness who admits a conviction on cross-examination is allowed on redirect to explain the circumstances of the conviction is the subject of conflicting decisions. See § 43 infra.

he used a key term in the statement in a peculiar sense. The straightforward approach, such as "What did you mean by"[10] or "What was your reason for"[11] a witness's statement on cross-examination, is frequently effective. However, a mere reiteration of assertions made on the direct or cross-examination is usually prohibited,[12] although the judge has discretion in this matter.

The re-examiner often invokes the common law rule of completeness,[13] permitting proof of the remainder of a transaction, conversation, or writing when a part has been proven by the adversary[14] if the remainder relates to the same subject-matter.[15] In *Beech Aircraft Corp. v. Rainey,*[16] the Supreme Court announced that that aspect of the common law is still in effect in federal practice.[17] Moreover, the redirect examiner can frequently resort to the principle of curative admissibility,[18] permitting him to re-

---

[10]People v. Buchanan, 145 N.Y. 1, 39 N.E. 846, 853 (1895) (dictum).

[11]State v. Kaiser, 124 Mo. 651, 28 S.W. 182 (1894).

[12]Clayton v. Bellatti, 70 Ill. App. 2d 367, 216 N.E.2d 686 (4th Dist. 1966); Forslund v. Chicago Transit Authority, 9 Ill. App. 2d 290, 132 N.E.2d 801 (1st Dist. 1956). But where a witness on cross-examination was confronted with her written statement contradicting her story on direct, it was proper to ask her on redirect whether her direct testimony was true. Grayson v. U. S., 107 F.2d 367 (C.C.A. 8th Cir. 1939).

[13]See § 56 infra.

[14]State v. Kendrick, 173 N.W.2d 560 (Iowa 1970). See § 56 infra.

[15]U.S. v. Kopp, 562 F.3d 141, 144 (2d Cir. 2009) ("The rule 'does not . . . require the admission of portions of a statement that are neither explanatory of nor relevant to the admitted passages' "); White v. Commonwealth, 292 Ky. 416, 166 S.W.2d 873 (1942); State v. Williams, 448 S.W.2d 865 (Mo. 1970).

[16]Beech Aircraft Corp. v. Rainey, 488 U.S. 153, 109 S. Ct. 439, 102 L. Ed. 2d 445 (1988).

[17]Fed. R. Evid. 106 deals with the situation in which the direct examiner asks the judge to require the cross-examiner to read to the jury qualifying language in a writing in addition to the passage which the cross-examiner desires to read to impeach the witness. The judge may compel the cross-examiner to do so when the two parts of the writing are so closely connected that the qualifying language is an integral part of the context of the other passage. However, in Beech Aircraft Corp. v. Rainey, 488 U.S. 153, 109 S. Ct. 439, 102 L. Ed. 2d 445 (1988), the Court indicated that Rule 106 did not abolish the common law version of the rule of completeness, mentioned here. See § 56 infra.

[18]See § 57 infra. *See* Gilligan & Imwinkelried, Bringing the "Opening the Door" Theory to a Close: The Tendency to Overlook the Specific Contradiction Doctrine in Evidence Law, 41 Santa Clara L. Rev. 807, 824–36 (2001) (the authors differentiate in detail between specific contradiction impeachment and the curative admissibility doctrine; the authors note that: the trigger for curative admissibility is the opponent's presentation of inadmissible evidence; in curative admissibility cases the proponent's evidence need not expressly contradict the testimony previously introduced by the opponent; the proponent relying on curative admissibility should be required to demonstrate that a contemporaneous objection or

spond to irrelevant or inadmissible evidence elicited during cross-examination.[19]

## Re-cross Examination

Like redirect, recross-examination follows the rule of first opportunity. Consequently, the scope of recross as of right is normally confined to questions directed to explaining or avoiding new matter brought out on redirect.[20] Moreover, if the previous examinations of the witness have been lengthy, by this point the

---

motion to strike would have been an inadequate remedy; and as a general proposition the judge has discretion whether to invoke curative admissibility).

[19]U.S. v. Maultasch, 596 F.2d 19 (2d Cir. 1979); U.S. v. Maggio, 126 F.2d 155 (C.C.A. 3d Cir. 1942); Barrett v. U.S., 82 F.2d 528 (C.C.A. 7th Cir. 1936); Chamberlain v. State, 348 P.2d 280 (Wyo. 1960). But, according to some cases, the "open the gate" theory will not permit eliciting incompetent and prejudicial evidence on redirect. E.g., People v. Arends, 155 Cal. App. 2d 496, 318 P.2d 532 (2d Dist. 1957).

[20]U.S. v. Kenrick, 221 F.3d 19, 33 (1st Cir. 2000). Where no new matter was opened on redirect, the trial court's action in denying a recross was approved in Com. v. Gordon, 356 Mass. 598, 254 N.E.2d 901 (1970) and U.S. v. Fontenot, 628 F.2d 921 (5th Cir. 1980) (trial judge properly restricted recross-examination when not sought to meet new matter on direct and was unnecessary to a full and fair adjudication of the case). However, a recross, though not in reply to new matter on redirect, may be allowed in the court's discretion. Maryland Wrecking & Equipment Co. v. News Pub. Co., 148 Md. 560, 129 A. 836 (1925). See also Dege v. U.S., 308 F.2d 534 (9th Cir. 1962) (matter referred to on cross-examination but not in redirect examination).

Under Fed. R. Evid. 611(a) the judge has broad discretion. However, there is also a limited right to recross-examination. O'Brien v. Dubois, 145 F.3d 16, 26 (1st Cir. 1998) ("new matter elucidated for the first time on redirect examination"); U.S. v. Vasquez, 82 F.3d 574 (2d Cir. 1996) (on redirect examination, the police officer mentioned for the first time that he had never seen the accused's hands during the chase preceding the accused's apprehension; the testimony was relevant to the question of whether the accused was carrying a gun while running; it was error for the trial judge to deny the defense recross-examination to question the officer about that statement); U.S. v. Riggi, 951 F.2d 1368 (3d Cir. 1991) (when the prosecution elicited new information on redirect, the trial judge's absolute ban on recross violated the accused's right to confrontation); U. S. v. Caudle, 606 F.2d 451, 458 (4th Cir. 1979) ("Examining counsel is normally expected to elicit everything from a witness, so far as possible, at the first opportunity. Where, as here, new matter is brought out on redirect examination, the defendant's first opportunity to test the truthfulness, accuracy, and completeness of that testimony is on recross examination. 6 Wigmore, Evidence § 1896 (Chadbourn rev. 1976). To deny recross examination on matter first drawn out on redirect is to deny the defendant the right of any cross-examination as to that new matter. The prejudice of the denial cannot be doubted."). See also 6 Wigmore, Evidence § 1897 at 740–41 (Chadbourn rev. 1976) ("No doubt cases may arise in which redirect examination may make relevant certain new evidence for which there was no prior need or opportunity, and for this purpose a recross examination becomes proper; in such cases it is sometimes said to be a matter of right. But for

jury's patience may be exhausted. Even if the opposing counsel would be legally entitled to conduct recross, it may be foolish to exercise that right.

---

other matters there is ordinarily no such need, and the allowance of recross examination depends in such cases on the consent of the trial court.").

# Chapter 5

# Impeachment and Support

## § 33  Introduction: Bolstering, impeachment, and rehabilitation

Assume that a witness on the stand gives some testimony or
that a counsel introduces an out-of-court declarant's hearsay
statement as substantive evidence. As soon as the testimony or
hearsay statement[1] is admitted, the credibility of the witness or
declarant becomes a fact of consequence within the range of
dispute at trial under Federal Rule 401.

---

**[Section 33]**

[1]U.S. v. Moody, 903 F.2d 321,
328–29 (5th Cir. 1990); Brannon,
Successful Shadowboxing: The Art of
Impeachment of Hearsay Declarants,

13 Campbell L. Rev. 157 (1991);
Farham, Impeaching the Hearsay
Declarant, 12 Crim. Just., Wint. 1998,
at 4.

There are three groups of credibility rules.[2] The first relates to the attempts by a witness's proponent to bolster the witness's credibility even before it has been impeached. The second concerns the various techniques which the opponent may employ to attack or impeach the witness's credibility. Finally, a third set of rules addresses the methods which the witness's proponent may use to rehabilitate the witness's credibility after attempted impeachment, in effect to undo the damage done by impeachment.

Both at common law and under the Federal Rules, the general norm is that the witness's proponent may not bolster the witness's credibility before any attempted impeachment.[3] For example, on direct examination it would be improper for the witness's proponent to elicit the witness's own testimony that the witness "always tells the truth." Federal Rule of Evidence 608(a)(2) provides that the "evidence of [a witness's] truthful character is admissible only after the character . . . has been attacked . . . ." There are some exceptional situations discussed in § 47—fresh complaints and prior identifications—in which the witness's proponent is permitted to bring out bolstering evidence on direct examination.[4] However, as a general proposition, bolstering evidence is inadmissible. As of the time of the direct examination, it is uncertain whether the cross-examiner will attack the witness's credibility; the counsel might later waive cross-

---

[2]U.S. v. Toro, 37 M.J. 313, 315 (C.M.A. 1993)

[3]Fed. R. Evid. 608(a) ("But evidence of truthful character is admissible only after the witness's character for truthfulness has been attacked"); U.S. v. Martinez, 253 F.3d 251 (6th Cir. 2001) (it was improper bolstering for a prosecutor to elicit a narcotics deputy's testimony that the information provided by the informant in the past had always proved to be accurate); Woodard v. State, 269 Ga. 317, 496 S.E.2d 896, 899–900 (1998) (overruled by, Bunn v. State, 291 Ga. 183, 728 S.E.2d 569 (2012)) ("Unless a witness' veracity has affirmatively been placed in issue, the witness' prior consistent statement is pure hearsay evidence, which cannot be admitted merely to corroborate the witness, or to bolster the witness' credibility in the eyes of the jury"). *But see* Ochoa v. Breslin, 798 F. Supp. 2d 495, 505 (S.D.N.Y. 2011) ("While the practice of bolstering is prohibited in various states, including New York, it is not

[expressly] forbidden by the Federal Rules of Evidence").

[4]See the discussion of the fresh complaint and prior identification doctrines at the end of § 47. *See also* People v. Brown, 8 Cal. 4th 746, 35 Cal. Rptr. 2d 407, 883 P.2d 949 (1994) (fresh complaint); State v. Troupe, 237 Conn. 284, 677 A.2d 917 (1996) (discussing the "hue and cry" rationale for the constancy of accusation of doctrine); In re L.C., 41 A.3d 1261 (D.C. 2012) (the report-of-rape doctrine); Battle v. U.S., 630 A.2d 211 (D.C. 1993) (fresh complaint); Com. v. Aviles, 461 Mass. 60, 958 N.E.2d 37 (2011); Com. v. King, 445 Mass. 217, 834 N.E.2d 1175, 1181 (2005) (the court announced a "first complaint" doctrine; the testimony must be limited to the first person told of the assault); State v. Bethune, 117 N.J. 68, 563 A.2d 831 (1989) (fresh complaint); Marquez v. State, 165 S.W.3d 741, 745–47 (Tex. App. San Antonio 2005) (discussing the state "outcry" statute for statements by child sexual assault victims).

examination or cross-examine solely for the purpose of eliciting new facts on the historical merits which support that counsel's theory of the case. If the opposing counsel does so, all the time devoted to the bolstering evidence on direct examination will have been wasted. For that reason, the witness's proponent must ordinarily hold information favorable to the witness's credibility in reserve for rehabilitation on redirect.

Although the common law was hostile to bolstering evidence, the common law and the Federal Rules liberally admit impeaching evidence. There are five main modes of attack on a witness's credibility.[5] The first, and probably most frequently employed, is proof of a prior inconsistent statement or "self contradiction," as it is sometimes imprecisely described. That technique consists of proof that the witness previously made statements inconsistent with his present testimony. The second is an attack showing that the witness is biased on account of emotional influences such as kinship for one party or hostility to another, or motives of pecuniary interest, whether legitimate or corrupt. The third is an attack on the witness's character, but lack of religious belief is not available as a basis for this type of attack on credibility. The fourth is an attack showing a defect of the witness's capacity to observe, remember, or recount the matters testified about. The fifth is specific contradiction, that is, proof by other witnesses

---

[5]Credibility depends on the witness's willingness to tell the truth and his ability to do so. In turn, his ability to tell the truth as to an event of which he purports to possess personal knowledge is the product of his physical and mental capacity, actual employment of the capacity to perceive, record, and recollect, and his ability to narrate. Impeachment of a witness may be directed to one or more components of credibility. Thus the objective being pursued in any given situation may be to draw into question the accuracy of the witness's perception, recordation, recollection, narration, or sincerity. Tribe, Triangulating Hearsay, 87 Harv. L. Rev. 957 (1974); Morgan, Hearsay Dangers and the Application of the Hearsay Concept, 62 Harv. L. Rev. 177 (1948); Strahorn, A Reconsideration of the Hearsay Rule and Admissions, 85 U. Pa. L. Rev. 484 (1937). With respect to capacity and actuality of perception, recordation and recollection, and narration, discrediting may often be accomplished by the simple means of a leading question. For example, a witness may be asked if it was nighttime when the event occurred or whether he was over 400 feet away at the time. Where the attack is on sincerity, since a simple leading question will tend to be argumentative, resort to a specific mode of attack is generally required, such as a prior conviction or prior inconsistent statement. Of course with respect to certain modes of attack, particularly contradiction and prior inconsistent statements, the attack extends to personal knowledge. To illustrate, if the witness denies being 400 feet away and asserts instead that he was only 20 feet from the event, a prior inconsistent statement that he was 400 feet away constitutes an attack on not only sincerity but also perception and memory. In assessing the witness's credibility, the trier of fact looks not only to the content of the witness's testimony on direct and his answers to questions on cross-examination but also the witness's demeanor.

that material facts are not as testified to by the witness being impeached.[6] Some of these attacks such as bias are not specifically or completely treated by the Federal or Revised Uniform Rules of Evidence, but nevertheless they are implicitly authorized by those rules. Article VI of the Federal Rules contains several provisions expressly regulating impeachment techniques such as proof of prior inconsistent statements, and the admissibility of other facts logically relevant to witness credibility is governed by the general analytic framework set out in Federal Rules 401 to 403.

The process of impeachment can proceed in two different stages. First, the facts discrediting the witness or his testimony may be elicited from the witness himself on cross-examination. A good faith basis for the inquiry is required. Some modes of attack are limited to this stage; the shorthand expression is, "You must take his answer." When the mode of attack is limited in this manner, the cross-examiner is sometimes said to be restricted to "intrinsic" impeachment. Second, in other situations, the facts discrediting the witness may be proved by extrinsic evidence. For example, the plaintiff's witness to be impeached has already left the stand; and the impeaching defense attorney waits until her own case-in-chief and then proves the facts discrediting the testimony of the plaintiff's witness by a second witness or documentary evidence.[7]

There is a cardinal rule of impeachment. Never launch an attack implying that the witness has lied deliberately, unless the attack is provable and essential to your case. An unsuccessful attack often produces in the jury's mind an indignant sympathy for the witness. Unless you can show the jury that you have "the goods" on the witness, an aggressive attack on the witness can easily backfire. The attack will be worse than ineffective; it will be counterproductive.

In general, today there is less emphasis on impeachment of witnesses than formerly. The courts now apply the elaborate, common law system of rules regulating impeachment less strictly. The system has been simplified by relying less on rules and more on judicial discretion. Again, Article VI of the Federal Rules contains only a handful of provisions expressly regulating impeachment techniques. In the case of all other impeachment techniques, a federal judge applies the general relevancy principles codified in Federal Rules 401 to 403.[8]

---

[6]See § 49 infra.

[7]See §§ 45 and 49 infra.

[8]U.S. v. Abel, 469 U.S. 45, 105 S. Ct. 465, 83 L. Ed. 2d 450 (1984) (bias

## § 34 Prior inconsistent statement impeachment:[1] Degree of inconsistency required[2]

As § 33 noted, the most widely used impeachment technique is proof that the witness made a pretrial statement inconsistent with her trial testimony.[3] This generalization certainly holds true in civil actions where pretrial depositions are commonplace. Sections 34 and 35 address the threshold question of whether there is sufficient inconsistency between the witness's trial testimony and a pretrial statement to allow the opponent to resort to this impeachment technique. Section 36 discusses the question of when the proof of the inconsistent statement is restricted to intrinsic impeachment, that is, cross-examination. Finally, assuming that the opponent is not confined to cross-examination, § 37 addresses the other conditions that the opponent must satisfy before presenting extrinsic evidence of the inconsistent statement.

Before turning to this impeachment technique, though, we must distinguish the technique from the related issue of the substantive use of prior inconsistent statements. When a witness testifies to facts material in a case, the opponent may have available proof that the witness previously made statements inconsistent with his present testimony. Under a modern view of the hearsay rule, some or all such previous statements are exempt from the rule and consequently admissible as substantive evidence of the facts stated. This view is discussed in the chapter concerning hearsay.[4] However, under the more traditional views these previous statements are often inadmissible as evidence of what they assert because they constitute hearsay not within any exemption from or exception to the hearsay rule.[5] Even though the statements are inadmissible hearsay as evidence of the facts asserted, they are admissible for the limited purpose of impeaching the witness.[6] They may be admitted for that purpose with a limiting instruction under Federal Rule 105. The trial judge informs the jury that although they consider the statement for

---

impeachment).

**[Section 34]**

[1]3A Wigmore, Evidence §§ 1017–46 (Chadbourn rev. 1970); 4 Weinstein's Federal Evidence Chs. 607, 613 (rev. 2011); Hale, Prior Inconsistent Statements, 10 So. Cal. L. Rev. 135 (1937); West's Key Number Digest, Witnesses ⬅379 to 397.

[2]3A Wigmore, Evidence §§ 1040–43 (Chadbourn rev. 1970); 4 Weinstein's Federal Evidence

§ 613.04[1] (rev. 2011); West's Key Number Digest, Witnesses ⬅386.

[3]Uviller, Credence, Character, and the Rules of Evidence: Seeing Through the Liar's Tale, 42 Duke L.J. 776, 816–17, 927 (1993) (a survey of trial judges).

[4]See § 251 infra.

[5]See generally Chapter 24 infra.

[6]Any form of statement is acceptable. It may have been made orally as testimony at another trial or by depo-

whatever light it sheds on the witness's credibility, they may not treat the statement as substantive evidence of the facts asserted in the statement. Subject to the exception that some prior inconsistent statements are exempt from the hearsay rule if they were made under oath subject to the penalty of perjury at a trial, hearing, or deposition, the Federal and Revised Uniform Rules of Evidence preserve this traditional view.[7]

The treatment of inconsistent statements in this chapter is confined to the situation in which the statements are introduced for impeachment purposes but may not be used as substantive evidence (over the opponent's proper objection).[8] For this purpose, the previous statements may be drawn out in cross-examination of the witness himself; and at common law if on cross-examination the witness denied making the statement or failed to remember it,[9] the statement may later be proved by extrinsic evidence such as another witness's testimony. In contrast, under the Federal and Revised Uniform Rules of Evidence in some circumstances the making of the statement may also be brought out by the second witness without prior inquiry during the cross-examination of the witness who made it.[10]

This form of impeachment is sometimes imprecisely called "self-contradiction." It must be distinguished from "specific contradiction" impeachment, the mere production of other evidence as to material facts conflicting with the testimony of the assailed

---

sition, or in writing as a letter, report, witness-statement, or affidavit. Likewise, conduct evincing a belief inconsistent with the facts asserted on the stand is usable on the same principle. *E.g.*, State ex rel. State Highway Commission of Mo. v. Fenix, 311 S.W.2d 61 (Mo. Ct. App. 1958) (a purchase of property for particular purpose held consistent and inadmissible); West's Key Number Digest, Witnesses ⊜347. But settlements or offers to compromise are governed by other rules. See § 266 infra; Bratt v. Western Air Lines, 169 F.2d 214 (C.C.A. 10th Cir. 1948).

The use of unconstitutionally obtained evidence for purposes of impeachment is discussed in § 182 infra.

[7]The limited exemption admitting some inconsistent statements as substantive evidence, insofar as the hearsay rule is concerned, is contained in Rule 801(d)(1). Rule 613 outlines the procedure to use the witness's in-

consistent statements for impeachment purposes. For the text of Fed. R. Evid. 613 and Unif. R. Evid. 613, see § 37, note 13, infra.

[8]The use of prior inconsistent statements as substantive evidence is discussed in § 251 infra.

[9]See § 37 infra; People v. Perez, 82 Cal. App. 4th 760, 98 Cal. Rptr. 2d 522 (2d Dist. 2000) (the witness's testimony that she could not remember what happened on the night of the victim's murder was effectively inconsistent with her statement identifying the defendant as the shooter); Corbett v. State, 130 Md. App. 408, 746 A.2d 954 (2000) (a witness's profession of inability to recall is not inconsistent with a prior statement recounting events unless the trial judge concludes that the claimed memory loss is false).

[10]See § 37 infra. This discussion assumes the matter is noncollateral, §§ 36 and 49 infra.

witness. The production of other evidence conflicting with a witness's testimony is discussed in § 45.[11] The characterization of the prior inconsistent statement as "self" contradiction is accurate only in the sense that the inconsistent statement must be attributable to the witness to be impeached.[12] As we shall see, to be admissible, the prior statement need not flatly contradict the witness's trial testimony. The statement need be merely inconsistent with the testimony.

The attack by prior inconsistent statement is not based on the theory that the present testimony is false and the former statement true. Rather, the theory is that talking one way on the stand and another way previously is blowing hot and cold, raising a doubt as to the truthfulness of both statements.[13] Suppose that although at trial the witness testified that a car was going 70 miles an hour, pretrial she told the police that the car was going 50 miles an hour. The pretrial statement is relevant to the witness's credibility even if both that statement and the trial testimony are wrong. The fact *of* the inconsistent statement is relevant to the witness's credibility even when the fact asserted *in* the statement—the car's speed—is false. Even if in truth the car was going 60 miles an hour, the fact of the inconsistency gives the jury an insight into the witness's state of mind; the inconsistency shows that the witness is either uncertain or untruthful. In either event, the inconsistency calls into question the witness's believability. Assuming it is inadmissible as

---

[11]See § 45 infra.

[12]The attorney attempting the impeachment has the burden of establishing that the witness was the person who made the statement. Fed. R. Evid. 104(b) governs the sufficiency of the evidence. *See* U.S. v. Stadtmauer, 620 F.3d 238 n.35 (3d Cir. 2010) ("Several of our sister circuits have affirmed the exclusion, under Rule 613, of interview memoranda prepared by law enforcement that the witness had not adopted"); U.S. v. De La Cruz Suarez, 601 F.3d 1202 (11th Cir. 2010) (a witness may be impeached by a third party statement only if the witness has adopted it as his own); Williamson v. Moore, 221 F.3d 1177, 1183 (11th Cir. 2000) ("These non-verbatim, non-adopted witness statements were not admissible at trial as impeachment evidence"); Bank Brussels Lambert v. Credit Lyonnais (Suisse) S.A., 168 F.

Supp. 2d 57 (S.D. N.Y. 2001) (the party seeking to introduce notes to establish a witness's inconsistent statement has the burden of proving that the notes reflect the witness's own words rather than the note-taker's characterization). *But see* People v. Brown, 282 A.D.2d 312, 726 N.Y.S.2d 1 (1st Dep't 2001), order aff'd, 98 N.Y.2d 226, 746 N.Y.S.2d 422, 774 N.E.2d 186 (2002) (statements made by a defendant's prior counsel could be used to impeach the defendant).

[13]Compare to the discussion in 3A Wigmore, Evidence § 1017 (Chadbourn rev. 1970). *See* U.S. v. Winchenbach, 197 F.3d 548, 558 (1st Cir. 1999) ("the cross-examiner is permitted to show the discrepancy . . . not to demonstrate which of the two [statements] is true but, rather, to show that the two do not jibe (thus calling the declarant's credibility into question)").

substantive evidence under the hearsay rule,[14] the prior statement may be used in this context only as an aid in judging the credibility of the trial testimony inconsistent with the previous statement.[15] On request, the trial judge will give the jury a limiting instruction about the evidentiary status of the statement.

On an appropriate objection, the judge must make a preliminary determination whether the pretrial statement is inconsistent with the witness's trial testimony.[16] What degree of inconsistency between the witness's testimony and his previous statement is required to create a doubt about the witness's credibility? The language of some cases is too restrictive, suggesting that there must be a flat contradiction.[17] Under the more widely accepted view, any material variance between the testimony and the previous statement suffices.[18] The pretrial statement need "only bend in a different direction" than the trial testimony.[19] For instance, if the prior statement omits a material fact presently testified to and it would have been natural to mention that fact in the prior

---

[14]See notes 12–13 supra.

[15]See discussion in Chapter 24 infra.

[16]U.S. v. Avants, 367 F.3d 433 (5th Cir. 2004).

[17]E.g., Sanger v. Bacon, 180 Ind. 322, 101 N.E. 1001, 1003 (1913) (construing the statement most favorably to the witness, the statement must contradict the witness's testimony); State v. Bowen, 247 Mo. 584, 153 S.W. 1033, 1038 (1913) ("must be such as, either in their substance or their general drift, contradict").

[18]U.S. v. Gajo, 290 F.3d 922, 931 (7th Cir. 2002) ("the term 'inconsistent' . . . should not be confined to 'statements [that are] diametrically opposed or logically incompatible' "); Udemba v. Nicoli, 237 F.3d 8, 18 (1st Cir. 2001) ("Statements need not be directly contradictory in order to be deemed inconsistent within the purview of Rule 613(b)"); U.S. v. Rogers, 549 F.2d 490 (8th Cir. 1976) (when witness admitted making statement but testified he could not recollect it and other circumstances indicated witness was fully aware of contents of statement, the statement was sufficiently inconsistent; the trial court should have considerable discretion with respect to evasive answers); Com. v. West, 312

Mass. 438, 45 N.E.2d 260, 262 (1942) ("And it is not necessary that there should be a contradiction in plain terms. It is enough if the proffered testimony, taken as a whole, either by what it says or by what it omits to say, affords some indication that the fact was different from the testimony of the witness whom it is sought to contradict."); O'Neill v. Minneapolis St. Ry. Co., 213 Minn. 514, 7 N.W.2d 665, 669 (1942) ("Whether a prior statement does in fact impeach a witness does not depend upon the degree of inconsistency between his testimony and his prior statement. If there is any variance between them, the statement should be received and its effect upon the credibility of the witness should be left to the jury." Statement not inconsistent); Morgan v. Washington Trust Co., 105 R.I. 13, 249 A.2d 48 (1969); White, The Art of Impeachment and Rehabilitation, 13 The Pract. Litigator 29, 33 (Mar. 2002) ("Modern courts have interpreted the requirement to allow impeachment if at least one inference that may be drawn from the prior statements is that it is inconsistent with the statement testified to at trial").

[19]McNaught & Flannery, Massachusetts Evidence: A Courtroom Reference 13–5 (1988).

statement, the statement is sufficiently inconsistent.[20] In the same vein, the impeachment can take the form of a witness's earlier statement disavowing knowledge of facts that he now testifies to.[21] The test ought to be: Could the jury reasonably find that a witness who believed the truth of the facts testified to at trial would be unlikely to make a prior statement of this tenor?[22] The Federal and Uniform Rules of Evidence do not expressly pre-

---

[20]Jenkins v. Anderson, 447 U.S. 231, 239, 100 S. Ct. 2124, 65 L. Ed. 2d 86 (1980) ("Common law traditionally has allowed witnesses to be impeached by their previous failure to state a fact in circumstances in which that fact naturally would have been asserted. 3A Wigmore, Evidence § 1042, at 1056 (Chadbourn rev. 1970)"; defendant's prearrest silence not induced by governmental action is admissible to impeach); U.S. v. Bernier, 660 F.3d 543, 546 (1st Cir. 2011); U.S. v. Catalan-Roman, 585 F.3d 453 (1st Cir. 2009) (failure to mention), cert. denied sub nom. Medina-Villegas v. U.S., 130 S. Ct. 3377, 176 L. Ed. 2d 1262 (2010); U.S. v. Standard Oil Co., 316 F.2d 884 (7th Cir. 1963) (prior statement omitted matters about which witness testified at trial); Quinney v. Conway, 784 F. Supp. 2d 247, 256 (W.D. N.Y. 2011); Nomanbhoy Family Ltd. Partnership v. McDonald's Corp., 579 F. Supp. 2d 1071, 1088 (N.D. Ill. 2008) ("impeachment by omission"); Esderts v. Chicago, R. I. & P. R. Co., 76 Ill. App. 2d 210, 222 N.E.2d 117 (1st Dist. 1966) ("If a witness fails to mention facts under circumstances which make it reasonably probable he would mention them if true, the omission may be shown as an indirect inconsistency."); State v. Haga, 954 P.2d 1284 (Utah Ct. App. 1998) (an alibi witness's failure to come forward before trial); McElhaney, Impeachment by Omission, 14 Litigation 45 (Fall 1987). But see U.S. v. Zaccaria, 240 F.3d 75 (1st Cir. 2001) (the trial judge had discretion to preclude the cross-examination of a government witness about the fact that before trial, after being advised of his constitutional rights, he had been silent; the witness's silence was ambiguous, and there were no special

trappings imbuing his silence with probative value); U.S. v. Chandler, 197 F.3d 1198, 1202 (8th Cir. 1999) ("the omission . . . is an example of 'silence so ambiguous that it is of little probative'" value); Hall v. Phillips Petroleum Co., 358 Mo. 313, 214 S.W.2d 438 (1948).

[21]Hoagland v. Canfield, 160 F. 146, 171 (C.C.S.D. N.Y. 1908); In re Olson's Estate, 54 S.D. 184, 223 N.W. 41 (1929). Similarly, a previous statement denying recollection of facts testified to should be provable. But see Grunewald v. U.S., 353 U.S. 391, 77 S. Ct. 963, 1 L. Ed. 2d 931 (1957) (defendant's refusal to answer same questions before grand jury, on grounds the answers would tend to incriminate him, was inadmissible because refusal was not inconsistent under the circumstances); Lewis v. American Road Ins. Co., 119 Ga. App. 507, 167 S.E.2d 729 (1969) (witness refused to answer questions on prior deposition; inadmissible). The text should be applicable under the federal rules.

[22]Morgan v. Washington Trust Co., 105 R.I. 13, 249 A.2d 48 (1969). See generally State v. Dickenson, 48 Wash. App. 457, 740 P.2d 312, 317 (Div. 1 1987) ("Washington uses the following test for determining whether statements are inconsistent: 'Inconsistency is to be determined, not by individual words or phrases alone, but by the *whole impression or effect* of what has been said or done. On a comparison of the two utterances are they in effect inconsistent? Do the two expressions appear to have been produced by inconsistent beliefs?' 5 K. Tegland, Wash.Prac. § 256 (1982) (quoting Sterling v. Radford, 126 Wash. 372, 218 P. 205 (1923)).").

scribe a test for inconsistency. Under these statutory schemes, most courts apply the more liberal standards.[23] Thus, if the previous statement is ambiguous and according to one meaning inconsistent with the testimony, it ought to be admitted.[24] Reasonable judges can differ in applying the criterion of material inconsistency, and a fair range of discretion must be accorded the trial judge. Instead of restricting the use of prior statements by a mechanical test of inconsistency, in case of doubt the courts should lean toward receiving such statements to aid in evaluating the trial testimony. After all, the pretrial statements were made when memory was fresher and when there was less time

---

[23]U.S. v. Cody, 114 F.3d 772, 776–77 (8th Cir. 1997) (the pretrial statement need not be "diametrically opposed" to the trial testimony); U.S. v. Matlock, 109 F.3d 1313, 1319 (8th Cir. 1997) ("inconsistency is not limited to diametrically opposed answers"); U.S. v. Strother, 49 F.3d 869, 874 (2d Cir. 1995) ("statements need not be diametrically opposed to be inconsistent"); U.S. v. Gravely, 840 F.2d 1156, 1163 (4th Cir. 1988) ("The district court did not require flat contradiction. The court applied the standard:

> To be received as a prior inconsistent statement, the contradiction need not be in plain terms. It is enough if the "profferred testimony, taken as a whole, either by what it says or by what it omits to say" affords some indication that the fact was different from the testimony of the witness whom it sought to contradict.

Order, Joint Appendix at 2325 (quoting U.S. v. Barrett, 539 F.2d 244, 254 (1st Cir. 1976)). The standard was proper and its application not an abuse. U.S. v. McCrady, 774 F.2d 868, 873 (8th Cir. 1985) ("[T]he witness' out-of-court statement must be inconsistent with the witness' in-court testimony. '[I]nconsistency is not limited to diametrically opposed answers but may be found in evasive answers, . . ., silence, or changes of position.' United States v. Dennis, 625 F.2d 782, 795 (8th Cir. 1980); Laboy v. Demskie, 947 F.Supp. 733, 741 (S.D. N.Y. 1996) ("a prior statement need not directly and positively contradict a witness' testimony"); State v. Blake, 478 S.E.2d 550 (W.Va. 1996); see United States v. Rogers, 549 F.2d 490, 495–96 (8th Cir. 1976). The trial judge has considerable discretion in determining whether trial testimony is inconsistent with prior statements. United States v. Dennis, 625 F.2d at 795.").

The judge has discretion under Rule 403 to sustain objections if the risk that the jury will misuse an inconsistent statement in a particular instance as substantive evidence (and not restrict the use to judging credibility) is great. Shows v. M/V Red Eagle, 695 F.2d 114 (5th Cir. 1983).

[24]State v. Kingsbury, 58 Me. 238, 1870 WL 2976 (1870); Town of Concord v. Concord Bank, 16 N.H. 26, 1844 WL 2198 (1844); White, The Art of Impeachment and Rehabilitation, 13 The Prac. Litigator 29, 33 (Mar. 2002) ("Modern courts have interpreted the requirement to allow impeachment if at least one inference that may be drawn from the prior statements is that it is inconsistent with the statement testified to at trial"). But there are contrary decisions. State v. Bush, 50 Idaho 166, 295 P. 432 (1930) and cases cited. See also U.S. v. Reed, 167 F.3d 984, 988 (6th Cir. 1999) (a government witness made the allegedly inconsistent statements during a conversation in which he participated during an undercover operation; if the witness had been frank during the conversation, he "would have risked tipping" the defendant to the witness's "cooperation with the authorities"; in that setting, the witness's pretrial statements "cannot be taken at face value").

for the play of bias. Thus, they are often more trustworthy than the testimony.[25] A logical extension of this reasoning justifies the admission of prior testimony about an independent, unrelated event so strikingly similar to the present testimony as to raise a suspicion of fabrication.[26]

## § 35 Prior inconsistent statements: Opinion in form[1]

The question addressed in this section is a variation of the issue analyzed in § 34: What type of pretrial statement may be considered "inconsistent" with a witness's trial testimony? If a witness, such as an expert, testifies in terms of opinion, all courts permit impeachment by showing the witness's previous expression of an inconsistent opinion.[2] However, courts have struggled with the question which arises when the witness testifies to specific facts but then is sought to be impeached by prior inconsistent expressions of opinion. For example, in a collision case the plaintiff's witness testifies to particular facts indicating that the bus driver involved in the accident was at fault. The defense proposes to show that just after seeing the collision, the witness

---

[25]Com. v. Jackson, 281 S.W.2d 891 (Ky. 1955). See the comment by Davis, J. in Judson v. Fielding, 227 A.D. 430, 237 N.Y.S. 348, 352 (3d Dep't 1929), "In considering the evidence so sharply in dispute, the jury was entitled to know the contrary views the witness had expressed when the incident was fresh in his mind, uninfluenced by sympathy or other cause. Very often by calm reflection a witness may correct inaccurate observations or erroneous impressions hastily formed. But the jury should have all the facts in making an appraisement of the value and weight to be given the testimony."

See Ch. 24 infra.

[26]People v. Rainford, 58 Ill. App. 2d 312, 208 N.E.2d 314 (1st Dist. 1965) (prosecuting witness's testimony in prior rape case was exactly the same in unlikely details as witness's testimony in the instant prosecution against the same defendants for as-

sault with intent to rape the witness in a different, independent incident).

**[Section 35]**

[1]West's Key Number Digest, Witnesses ⟋384. As noted in § 34, this section assumes that inconsistent statements are sought to be introduced only for impeachment purposes. May a witness who testifies to facts be impeached by showing of prior inconsistent expressions of opinion by him, 66 A.L.R. 289 (supplemented by May a witness who testifies to facts be impeached by showing of prior inconsistent expressions of opinion by him, 158 A.L.R. 820).

[2]McGrath v. Fash, 244 Mass. 327, 139 N.E. 303 (1923) (doctor testified to moderate injuries; the doctor was impeached by his statement after examining plaintiff that "this was the worst accident case he handled in the last ten years"); Hutson v. State, 164 Tex. Crim. 24, 296 S.W.2d 245 (1956).

said, "The bus was not to blame."[3] The witness's pretrial, opinionated statement is inconsistent with the effect or impression created by the witness's trial testimony. Is that enough?

However, even before reaching the issue under Rule 613, we must confront another question: Should the opinion rule be invoked to exclude such an impeaching statement? The early, strict rule against opinions has been substantially relaxed in recent years.[4] Most courts appreciate that what was once supposed to be a fundamental difference in kind between fact and opinion is a mere difference in degree.[5] Wigmore considers that the rule goes no farther than excluding opinion as superfluous when the proponent can conveniently resort to more concrete statements.[6] Thus, at trial the principal value of the opinion rule is as a regulation requiring the examining counsel to bring out his facts by more specific questions if practicable, before introducing more general ones. It is often a mistake to apply the rule to out-of-court statements, since the out-of-court declarant might be unavailable and the proponent may not have the option to elicit the testimony in a more concrete form.[7] Moreover, when the out-of-court statement is not offered as evidence of the fact asserted but only to show the asserter's inconsistency, the essential purpose of the opinion rule, to improve the objectivity and hence reliability of testimonial assertions, is inapposite. Thus, the inconsistent opinion should be admitted for purposes of impeachment even if the proponent does not lay the normal opinion foundation discussed in Chapter 3. It is true that many earlier American decisions, influenced perhaps by a passage in Greenleaf[8] and a casual English *nisi prius* holding,[9] and some later opinions exclude impeaching statements in opinion form.[10] However, the trend and the majority view are in accord with the commonsense

---

[3]Judson v. Fielding, 227 A.D. 430, 237 N.Y.S. 348 (3d Dep't 1929) (impeachment allowed).

[4]See §§ 11, 12, 17 supra.

[5]Beech Aircraft Corp. v. Rainey, 488 U.S. 153, 168, 109 S. Ct. 439, 102 L. Ed. 2d 445 (1988). See §§ 11, 12 supra.

[6]7 Wigmore, Evidence § 1918 (Chadbourn rev. 1978).

[7]See § 18 supra.

[8]Greenleaf, Evidence § 449 (3d ed. 1846).

[9]Elton v. Larkins, 1832 WL 3722 (U.K. Assizes 1832) (suit on marine policy; the broker who effected policy for the plaintiff, called as defense witness, testified to facts showing material concealment; plaintiff sought to prove by extrinsic evidence after witness's denial that witness had said that "the underwriters had not a leg to stand on," excluded by Tindal, C.J. as "only a contradiction on a matter of judgment").

[10]*E.g.*, City Bank v. Young, 43 N.H. 457, 460, 1862 WL 1446 (1862); Morton v. State, 43 Tex. Crim. 533, 67 S.W. 115 (1902), and see cases cited May a witness who testifies to facts be impeached by showing of prior inconsistent expressions of opinion by him, 158 A.L.R. 820. *See also* Hirsh v. Manley, 81 Ariz. 94, 300 P.2d 588 (1956) (rule applied where court thought the out-of-court opinion re-

notion that if there is a substantial inconsistency, the form of the impeaching statement is immaterial.[11] Federal and Revised Uniform Evidence Rule 701 lends support to that view by codifying a broad version of the opinion rule.

## § 36 Prior inconsistent statements: Extrinsic evidence and previous statements as substantive evidence of the facts stated

Assume that there is sufficient inconsistency between the witness's pretrial statement and trial testimony to permit the opposing attorney to resort to this impeachment technique. The next question that arises is whether the attorney will be restricted to cross-examination or "intrinsic" impeachment. Strict rules of relevancy are relaxed on cross-examination.[1] Generally in his discretion the trial judge may permit the cross-examiner to inquire about any previous statements inconsistent with assertions that the witness has testified to on direct or cross. At the cross-examination stage, there is no categorical rule that the previous impeaching statements must not deal with "collateral" matters;[2] even if the matter has no relevance to the historical merits of the case, it bears on the witness's credibility, and cred-

---

quired expertise but witness had not been qualified as an expert); Dorsten v. Lawrence, 20 Ohio App. 2d 297, 49 Ohio Op. 2d 392, 253 N.E.2d 804 (6th Dist. Lucas County 1969); State v. Thompson, 71 S.D. 319, 24 N.W.2d 10 (1946).

[11]U.S. v. Barrett, 539 F.2d 244 (1st Cir. 1976); Tigh v. College Park Realty Co., 149 Mont. 358, 427 P.2d 57 (1967); and see the description of the trend and the collections of cases in May a witness who testifies to facts be impeached by showing of prior inconsistent expressions of opinion by him, 158 A.L.R. 820; Grady, The Admissibility of a Prior Statement of Opinion for Purposes of Impeachment, 41 Cornell L.Q. 224 (1956).

[Section 36]

[1]See § 29 supra. The present section deals with self-contradiction as a technique of impeachment. Contradiction by other witnesses is considered in § 45 infra.

[2]Dane v. MacGregor, 94 N.H. 294, 52 A.2d 290 (1947); Howard v. City Fire Ins. Co., 4 Denio 502, 506,

1847 WL 4118 (N.Y. Sup 1847); 3A Wigmore, Evidence § 1023 (Chadbourn rev. 1970).

Since the matter is within the trial judge's discretion, his ruling will usually be upheld on appeal. *E.g.*, Lenske v. Knutsen, 410 F.2d 583 (9th Cir. 1969); Wiesemann v. Pavlat, 413 S.W.2d 23 (Mo. Ct. App. 1967); State v. Brewster, 75 Wash. 2d 137, 449 P.2d 685 (1969) (trial judge permitted questions concerning collateral matter). Nevertheless, if the matter is clearly material, it has been held that the cross-examination must be permitted. Healy v. City of Chicago, 109 Ill. App. 2d 6, 248 N.E.2d 679 (1st Dist. 1969); State v. Thompson, 280 S.W.2d 838 (Mo. 1955). When the matter is immaterial and prejudicial, the trial judge may be reversed, at least if no appropriate requested instruction is given. Kantor v. Ash, 215 Md. 285, 137 A.2d 661 (1958).

An occasional opinion flatly states that cross-examination may not be had concerning an inconsistent statement on a matter that is collateral. Kantor v. Ash, 215 Md. 285, 137 A.2d 661 (1958); State v. Wilson, 158

ibility is in issue on cross. But as the next paragraph notes, at common law when the cross-examiner inquires about inconsistent statements on "collateral" matters, the cross-examiner must "take the answer"—he cannot later call other witnesses to prove the making of the alleged statement.[3] This restriction, the collateral fact rule, evolved as a creature of case law, but some courts continue to enforce it under the Federal and Revised Uniform Rules of Evidence.[4]

Extrinsic evidence of inconsistent statements, that is, the production of other witnesses' testimony about the statements, is restricted for obvious reasons of economy of time. The bromide, "You cannot contradict as to collateral matters," applies. Here the bromide means that to escape from the reach of the collateral fact rule, the subject of the statements must relate to the issues on the historical merits in the case.[5] Although the Federal and Revised Uniform Rules of Evidence do not codify a categorical prohibition on the use of extrinsic evidence to impeach about collateral matters, the judge may factor the same policy considerations (for example, balancing probative worth against time consumption) into her analysis under Rule 403.

Distinguish the collateral fact rule from a distinct but somewhat cognate notion. According to that notion, if a party questions a witness about a fact which would be favorable to the examiner if true, but receives a reply which has only a negative effect on examiner's case, the examiner may not introduce extrinsic evidence to prove that the witness earlier stated that the fact was true.[6] An affirmative answer would be material and subject to impeachment by an inconsistent statement. However,

---

Conn. 321, 260 A.2d 571 (1969).

[3]Denial on cross-examination of a statement relating to a "collateral" matter cannot be disputed by extrinsic evidence. State v. Mangrum, 98 Ariz. 279, 403 P.2d 925 (1965) (cross should have been permitted, but the extrinsic evidence was inadmissible); Montgomery v. Nance, 1967 OK 48, 425 P.2d 470 (Okla. 1967) cases cited in West's Key Number Digest, Witnesses ⬯383. It is important to understand the scope of the notion of "extrinsic evidence." Certainly, on cross-examination, the counsel may attempt to pressure the witness into a more truthful answer by reminding the witness of the penalties for perjury. Moreover, as we shall see in § 49, the trend in the case law is to permit the cross-

examiner to confront the witness with writings which document the impeaching fact so long as the witness is competent to authenticate the writing.

[4]The prohibition against contradiction on collateral matters is one of a number of assorted concepts subsumed under Fed. and Unif. R. Evid. 403. Dolan, Rule 403: The Prejudice Rule in Evidence, 49 S. Cal. L. Rev. 220 (1976). *See generally* §§ 49 and 185 infra. *E.g.*, U.S. v. Nace, 561 F.2d 763 (9th Cir. 1977).

[5]See § 49 infra.

[6]Miller v. Com., 241 Ky. 818, 45 S.W.2d 461 (1932) (defense witness denied she heard defendant say he was going to kill deceased; she was improperly impeached by proof that she had said she had heard such

a negative answer is not affirmatively damaging to the examiner; a negative answer is merely disappointing. According to this notion, a disappointing answer may not be impeached by extrinsic evidence; when the witness's only response is a negative answer, the opponent is limited to intrinsic impeachment on cross. In this situation the policy consideration is not saving time and preventing confusion, but rather the protection of the other party against the risk that the jury will misuse the statement as substantive proof in violation of the hearsay rule.[7] With respect to the Federal and Revised Uniform Rules of Evidence view, see § 38. As a general proposition, modern courts do not recognize this technical distinction between damaging and disappointing answers. Rather, under Rule 403 the judge makes a pragmatic judgment as to the importance of the impeachment.

As previously indicated,[8] a witness's inconsistent statements are analyzed in this chapter primarily on the assumption that they are inadmissible as substantive evidence under the traditional hearsay rule still administered in numerous states and under the limited exemption in the Federal and Revised Uniform Rules of Evidence (1974) 801(d)(1). Of course, under that exemption or special hearsay exceptions in various jurisdictions, some inconsistent prior statements of a witness are admissible as substantive evidence as well as for impeachment purposes. More broadly, under another view adopted in a few jurisdictions, despite the hearsay rule all prior inconsistent statements of trial witnesses may be considered substantive evidence and consequently are not restricted to their use as impeachment. Section 251 discusses the latter view.

---

threats); Woodroffe v. Jones, 83 Me. 21, 21 A. 177 (1890) (a wife sued for sprained ankle due to defective sidewalk; defense was that the plaintiff was negligent in wearing high-heeled shoes; husband, as witness, denied on cross-examination that he had warned his wife about her high heels; the court held that proof by another witness that he had said "that he told his wife about wearing such high heeled boots" was improperly admitted to impeach his denial which was merely negative and without probative significance).

[7]The pre-Rules decision of U.S. v. Cunningham, 446 F.2d 194 (2d Cir. 1971), reached this result with respect to a witness's prior statement, otherwise inadmissible as hearsay. Of course, if the witness's inconsistent statements are not hearsay under the more traditional rule or are defined as nonhearsay by modern rules such as Fed. R. Evid. 801(d)(1) and Unif. R. Evid. 801(d) (1), there would be no improper use. See generally § 251 infra.

[8]See § 34 supra.

## § 37  Prior inconsistent statements: Requirement of preliminary questions on cross-examination as "foundation" for proof by extrinsic evidence[1]

Assume both that there is sufficient inconsistency between the witness's pretrial statement and trial testimony and that the collateral fact rule does not confine the counsel to intrinsic impeachment on cross-examination. Even on those assumptions, there may be further conditions that the counsel must satisfy before the judge will permit the introduction of extrinsic evidence of the inconsistent statement. To be specific, before presenting the extrinsic evidence, the counsel might have to: (1) lay a foundation during the witness's cross-examination; and (2) elicit the witness's denial of making the inconsistent statement. At common law, the genesis for these conditions was *Queen Caroline's Case*.[2]

In 1820, in their answers in *Queen Caroline's Case,* the judges announced: "If it be intended to bring the credit of a witness into question by proof of anything he may have said or declared touching the cause, the witness is first asked, upon cross-examination, whether or not he has said or declared that which is intended to be proved."[3] The announcement crystallized a practice which had previously been occasional and discretionary. Later the practice was almost universally accepted in this country.[4] The rule came to be applied to both written and oral inconsistent statements.[5] The purposes of this traditional requirement are: to avoid unfair surprise to the adversary; to save time, since an admission by the witness may make extrinsic proof unnecessary; and to give the witness a fair chance to explain the discrepancy.

To satisfy the initial condition of a foundational question, the cross-examiner asks the witness whether the witness made the alleged statement, giving its substance and naming the time, the

---

[Section 37]

[1]3A Wigmore, Evidence §§ 1025–39 (Chadbourn rev. 1970); Hale, Inconsistent Statements, 10 So. Cal. L. R. 135–47 (1937); West's Key Number Digest, Witnesses ☞388 to 389.

[2]Ladd, Some Observations on Credibility: Impeachment of Witnesses, 52 Cornell L.Q. 239, 245 (1967).

[3](1820) 2 Brod. & Bing. 284, 313, 129 Eng. Rep. 976.

[4]3A Wigmore, Evidence § 1026 (Chadbourn rev. 1970). A foundation question has not been required in Massachusetts unless a party is attempting to impeach his own witness. Allin v. Whittemore, 171 Mass. 259, 50 N.E. 618 (1898) is a leading case. *See also* Mattox v. U.S., 156 U.S. 237, 245–50, 15 S. Ct. 337, 39 L. Ed. 409 (1895) (discussing the unanimity among the common law authorities with respect to the need to lay a foundation before impeaching the witness); Thompson v. J.P. Morin & Co., 80 N.H. 144, 114 A. 274 (1921) (citing earlier cases).

[5]See § 28 supra.

place, and the person to whom made.[6] The purpose of specifying these details is to refresh the witness's memory of the supposed statement by reminding the witness of the surrounding circumstances.[7] As a second condition, the witness's answer to the foundational question must necessitate the cross-examiner's resort to extrinsic evidence. If the witness denies making the statement or fails to admit it, for example by saying "I don't know" or "I don't remember,"[8] the element of necessity is satisfied. At the next stage of giving evidence, the cross-examiner may

---

[6]This is the usual formula. *See, e.g.*, Angus v. Smith, (1829) Mood. & M. 473, 173 Eng. Rep. 1228, 1829 WL 3479 (Assizes) ("you must ask him as to time, place, and person . . . it is not enough to ask him the general question whether he has ever said so and so"); Peyton v. State, 40 Ala. App. 556, 120 So. 2d 415 (1959). The use of leading questions in examining the impeaching witness is discussed in § 6 supra.

[7]Since the purpose of the foundation question is to focus the witness sufficiently on the out-of-court statement that he may remember it, the usual formula may be relaxed under circumstances in which the witness was adequately warned although the foundation question was not completely specific under the formula. State v. Caldwell, 251 La. 780, 206 So. 2d 492 (1968) (time not exactly specified).

[8]Some courts allow the introduction of extrinsic evidence in this situation on the theory that on the facts before it, the trial court properly found that the express claim of memory lapse was an implied denial of the prior statement. U.S. v. Insana, 423 F.2d 1165 (2d Cir. 1970); People v. Hovarter, 44 Cal. 4th 983, 81 Cal. Rptr. 3d 299, 189 P.3d 300, 319 (2008) (there is sufficient inconsistency if the proclaimed lack of memory is a deliberate evasion); People v. Gunder, 151 Cal. App. 4th 412, 59 Cal. Rptr. 3d 817 (3d Dist. 2007) ("In order to admit the prior extrajudicial statement of a forgetful witness as an inconsistent statement, the forgetfulness must be feigned . . . ."); People v. Ervin, 22

Cal. 4th 48, 91 Cal. Rptr. 2d 623, 990 P.2d 506 (2000) ("As long as there is a reasonable basis in the record for concluding that the witness's 'I don't remember' statements are evasive and untruthful, admission of his or her statements is proper"); People v. Perez, 82 Cal. App. 4th 760, 98 Cal. Rptr. 2d 522 (2d Dist. 2000) (the witness's testimony that she could not remember what happened on the night of the victim's murder was effectively inconsistent with her statement identifying the defendant as the shooter); People v. Green, 3 Cal. 3d 981, 92 Cal. Rptr. 494, 479 P.2d 998 (1971).

However, some courts take the position that if the witness's claimed lack of memory is truthful, the judge should exclude the evidence of the inconsistent statement. U.S. v. Shillingstad, 632 F.3d 1031, 1037 (8th Cir. 2011) ("Where a witness in good faith asserts that she cannot remember the relevant events, the trial court may, in its discretion, exclude the allegedly inconsistent statement"); Corbett v. State, 130 Md. App. 408, 746 A.2d 954 (2000) (a witness's profession of inability to remember is not inconsistent with a prior statement recounting events unless the trial judge concludes that the claimed memory loss is false).

More broadly, the view that forgetfulness suffices now has "a wide following among state and federal courts." U.S. v. Gajo, 290 F.3d 922 (7th Cir. 2002) ("many circuits . . . have held that in the context of a recalcitrant witness, a lack of memory is inconsistent with the description of specific details before the grand jury. In contrast, only one court has suggested that a prior statement should

then prove the making of the alleged statement.[9] When, however, the witness fully and unequivocally admits making the statement, may the cross-examiner still choose to prove it again by another witness? Surprisingly, with some support, Wigmore suggests that the cross-examiner may.[10] However, for the most part permitting cross-examination in these circumstances is a waste of time. Consequently, the prevailing view is to the contrary of Wigmore's suggestion,[11] and in the usual situation this is the wiser practice.[12]

Under Federal and Revised Uniform Rule 613, the only requirements for introducing a witness's prior inconsistent written or oral statements are that: (1) when the cross-examiner questions

---

not be admitted under Rule 801(d) (1) (A) if a witness genuinely cannot remember crucial facts related to the prior statement"); U.S. v. Milton, 8 F.3d 39, 47 (D.C. Cir. 1993); U.S. v. Billue, 994 F.2d 1562, 1565–66 (11th Cir. 1993) ("the answer of a witness that he does not remember having made a prior statement is as adequate a foundation as a flat denial"); Wassilie v. State, 57 P.3d 719 (Alaska Ct. App. 2002) (the court asserts that the majority of federal circuits refuse to distinguish between feigned and genuine memory loss); Note, 60 U. Chi. L. Rev. 167 (1993).

[9]People v. Perri, 381 Ill. 244, 44 N.E.2d 857 (1942) (denial); Reams' Adm'r v. Greer, 314 S.W.2d 511 (Ky. 1957) (witness stated he did not recall "Using those words"); West's Key Number Digest, Witnesses ⚷389.

[10]3A Wigmore, Evidence § 1037 n. 4 (Chadbourn rev. 1970). A case supporting this view is People v. Schainuck, 286 N.Y. 161, 36 N.E.2d 94 (1941) (arson: prosecution witness admitted on cross-examination that in Fire Marshal investigative hearing, he said he knew nothing about cause of fire; held, error to refuse defense counsel's request to inspect hearing-record with a view to proving witness's statements). Several Illinois cases support the view that the inconsistent statement is admissible; others seem contrary. See discussion in People v. Knowles, 91 Ill. App. 2d 109, 234 N.E.2d 149 (1st Dist. 1968).

[11]Rush v. Illinois Cent. R. Co., 399 F.3d 705, 723 (6th Cir. 2005); Alabama Elec. Co-op., Inc. v. Partridge, 284 Ala. 442, 225 So. 2d 848 (1969) (writing); State v. Jackson, 248 La. 919, 183 So. 2d 305 (1966) (writing; Art. 493 Code of Criminal Procedure applied).

[12]It saves time and minimizes the calling of witnesses on what is only a side issue. Yet circumstances may be such, especially when the statement is in writing, that the judge's discretion to allow the impeachment to proceed should be recognized.

However, see suggestion in Gordon v. U.S., 344 U.S. 414, 73 S. Ct. 369, 97 L. Ed. 447 (1953) (error to deny access to government witness's prior inconsistent written statements, despite his admission of inconsistency on cross-examination, since judge might nevertheless have admitted them "as a more reliable, complete and accurate source of information.").

Under Fed. R. Evid. 613, the judge may deny admission of extrinsic evidence of the inconsistent statement if the witness has already admitted making it. U.S. v. Jones, 578 F.2d 1332 (10th Cir. 1978). However, the liberality of the rule in permitting extrinsic evidence of the prior inconsistent statement before the witness's attention is called to the statement should be extended so that in the judge's discretion the extrinsic evidence can be introduced even if the witness has admitted the statement beforehand.

the witness concerning written statements or the substance of the statements, the statement must be shown or disclosed to the opposing counsel on request, and (2) at some point in time—even after the introduction of the extrinsic evidence—the witness is afforded a chance to deny or explain the statement, and the opposing counsel has the opportunity to question the witness about the statement.[13] Even the witness's opportunity to explain or deny later and the opposing counsel's opportunity to question later can be dispensed with in the judge's discretion in the interests of "justice."[14] For instance, suppose that despite the exercise of reasonable diligence the counsel did not discover the witness's inconsistent statement until after the witness was permanently excused from further testimony. Given those facts, on balance it serves the interest of substantive justice to permit counsel to introduce extrinsic evidence of the statement.

On their face, the Federal and Revised Uniform Rules of Evidence adopt a liberal view, abolishing the rigid notion that on cross-examination the witness must be shown an inconsistent statement or be advised of its contents before being questioned about its substance. Rule 613 goes even farther and abandons the traditional requirement that the foundational questions be put to the witness on cross-examination before extrinsic evidence of the statement is introduced, i.e., before other witnesses testify to it or before an inconsistent writing is introduced. As the Advi-

---

[13]Former Fed. R. Evid. 613 provided:

(a) Examining witness concerning prior statement. In examining a witness concerning a prior statement made by the witness, whether written or not, the statement need not be shown nor its contents disclosed to the witness at that time, but on request the same shall be shown or disclosed to opposing counsel.

(b) Extrinsic evidence of prior inconsistent statement of witness. Extrinsic evidence of a prior inconsistent statement by a witness is not admissible unless the witness is afforded an opportunity to explain or deny the same and the opposite party is afforded an opportunity to interrogate the witness thereon, or the interests of justice otherwise require. This provision does not apply to admissions of a party-opponent as defined in rule 801(d)(2).

Unif. R. Evid. 613 is identical in content. Effective December 1, 2011, restyled Fed. R. Evid. 613 reads:

(a) Showing or Disclosing the Statement During Examination. When ex-amining a witness about the witness's prior statement, a party need not show it or disclose its contents to the witness. But the party must, on request, show it or disclose its contents to an adverse party's attorney.

(b) Extrinsic Evidence of a Prior Inconsistent Statement. Extrinsic evidence of a witness's prior inconsistent statement is admissible only if the witness is given an opportunity to explain or deny the statement and an adverse party is given an opportunity to examine the witness about it, or if justice so requires. This subdivision (b) does not apply to an opposing party's statement under Rule 801(d) (2).

[14]The Advisory Committee's Note states: "In order to allow for such eventualities as the witness becoming unavailable by the time the statement is discovered, a measure of discretion is conferred upon the judge. See Comment to California Evidence Code § 770 and New Jersey Evidence Rule 22(b)."

sory Committee's Note to Federal Rule 613 indicates, "[t]he traditional insistence that the attention of the witness be directed to the statement on cross-examination is relaxed in favor of simply providing the witness an opportunity to explain and the opposite party an opportunity to examine on the statement, with no specification of any particular time or sequence." The Note approvingly cites California Evidence Code § 770. That statute expressly allows the counsel attacking the witness's credibility to offer extrinsic evidence of an inconsistent statement so long as the witness is excused subject to recall; excusing the witness in that manner obviates the need for any foundation during the witness's cross-examination.[15] The opposing party can later recall the witness to give the witness an opportunity to deny or explain away the statement. The Advisory Committee's Note suggests that Rule 613 facilitates the questioning of collusive witnesses by permitting several such witnesses to be examined before disclosure of a joint prior inconsistent statement. Such joint inconsistent statements are rare. That rather infrequent benefit hardly justifies Rule 613's general dispensation with the requirement that a foundation be laid on cross-examination. According to the Note, the rationale for Rule 613's general dispensation derives from two factors: (1) Rule 801(d)(1), as proposed by the Advisory Committee and the Supreme Court, gave substantive

---

[15]In a letter to the chair of the House subcommittee which studied the draft Federal Rules, Professor Edward Cleary, the Advisory Committee's Reporter, expressly stated that Rule 613 was intended to abolish the requirement that the counsel lay a foundation on cross before later introducing extrinsic evidence of the statement. Letter from Edward W. Cleary to Hon. William L. Hungate, May 8, 1973, in Supplement to Hearings Before Subcomm. Crim. Justice, House Comm. Jud., 93d Cong., 1st Sess., at 74–75 (1973). *See* U.S. v. Cruz-Rodriguez, 541 F.3d 19, 30 n.5 (1st Cir. 2008) ("the foundation requirements of 613(b) do not require that the witness be confronted with the statement while on the witness stand, but only that the witness be available to be recalled in order to explain the statement during the course of the trial"), cert.denied, 555 U.S. 1144 (2009); U.S. v. Libby, 475 F. Supp. 2d 73, 98 (D.D.C. 2007) ("at least four other [federal] circuits . . . have held that extrinsic evidence may be used in such a circumstance so long as the witness may be recalled to explain or deny the statement").

The rule gives the counsel attacking the witness's credibility a tactical choice that did not exist at common law. One option is to confront the witness immediately on cross-examination. Experienced attorneys tend to exercise this opinion when the basic thrust of the impeachment is the contention that the witness is lying. Lay jurors' basic sense of fairness leads them to expect the attorney to personally confront the witness when the attorney is leveling the serious accusation that the witness is committing perjury. The second option, though, is to excuse the witness subject to recall and later present the impeaching evidence. Veteran attorneys often select this option when the thrust of the impeachment is that the witness is merely mistaken.

effect to all prior inconsistent statements, and (2) widespread attorney incompetence.

To understand why the Advisory Committee originally proposed Rule 613, one must keep in mind that if prior inconsistent statements are admissible only for purposes of impeachment, the traditional foundation requirement serves the useful function of helping confine the use of such statements as to credibility and discouraging the trier of fact from misusing them as substantive evidence. The foundation requirement placed a prior pretrial statement in relatively immediate juxtaposition to the trial testimony of the witness sought to be impeached; in the same line of questioning, the cross-examiner mentions both the witness's statement on direct examination and the inconsistent pretrial statement. The juxtaposition makes it easier for the jurors to understand that they are to simply contrast the testimony and the statement for whatever insight that gives them into the witness's credibility. In addition, by giving the witness the opportunity to admit a prior statement, the foundation requirement reduces the likelihood that extrinsic evidence of the prior inconsistent statement will have to be introduced at all. It may be harder for the jury to avoid treating the extrinsic testimony as substantive; when the extrinsic evidence is introduced later during the trial, there may be no mention of the direct testimony that the extrinsic evidence is formally being admitted to impeach. However, if the witness fully admits the prior statement, at least in her discretion the judge could bar the extrinsic evidence.

It is critical to remember that, under the proposed evidence rules as originally drafted by the Advisory Committee, all prior inconsistent statements were admissible as substantive evidence pursuant to Rule 801(d)(1). The proposed substantive admissibility of all prior statements would have rendered the function served by the foundation requirement obsolete. A more practical consideration then became paramount. Again according to the Note, the practicality was that trial lawyers often forget to lay or never learned how to lay a proper foundation for the extrinsic evidence. The Advisory Committee politely referred to such forgetfulness or incompetence as "oversight." Positing wholesale substantive admissibility, though, these "oversight[s]" are less problematic. Even when the opponent does not lay a foundation on cross, the draft rule authorized the introduction of the inconsistent statement so long as the witness was eventually given an opportunity to deny or explain.

However, as finally enacted by Congress, Rule 801(d)(1) does not sanction the substantive admission of all prior inconsistent statements. Congress balked at embracing the Advisory Committee's sweeping position. Under the final versions of Rules 613 and

801, as at common law, some inconsistent statements are admissible only for the limited purpose of impeachment. Thus, the traditional foundation requirement still serves the useful function of encouraging the jury to consider a prior inconsistent statement solely as to credibility and not as substantive evidence. Since all prior inconsistent statements are not substantively admissible, counsel should not have the unfettered right to introduce extrinsic evidence of the statement before the witness has an opportunity to admit, deny, or explain the declaration. When the extrinsic evidence of the prior statement is admitted without relating it to the witness's trial testimony, the circumstances virtually invite the jury to treat the prior statement as substantive evidence. Accordingly, a strong case can be constructed that under Rules 403 and 611, federal courts and state courts with an identical scheme should require the traditional foundation be laid on cross-examination before the introduction of extrinsic evidence of prior statements admissible solely to impeach[16] unless the interests of justice require otherwise.[17] Admittedly, as a matter of statutory interpretation, it is difficult

---

[16]Laying the traditional foundation is clearly the "preferred method of proceeding." Wammock v. Celotex Corp., 793 F.2d 1518, 1522 (11th Cir. 1986) ("It is equally clear, however, that Rule 613(b) does not supplant the traditional method of confronting a witness with his inconsistent statement prior to its introduction into evidence as the preferred method of proceeding."). Accord U.S. v. McGuire, 744 F.2d 1197, 1204 (6th Cir. 1984) (the government did not cross-examine the defense witness as to the alleged prior inconsistent statement before introducing extrinsic proof: "We do not approve of the government not informing the defendants of this evidence, which we view as a questionable trial tactic."); Alexander v. Conveyors & Dumpers, Inc., 731 F.2d 1221, 1231 (5th Cir. 1984) ("While it may be the better practice to proffer the inconsistent statement while the witness is still on the witness stand, no such requirement is mandated by the Rule or its underlying rationale. Where, as in this case, opposing counsel has had full opportunity to cross-examine the witness regarding the prior inconsistent statements, no error exists in admitting the statements after the

witness has been discharged."); U.S. v. Praetorius, 622 F.2d 1054, 1065 (2d Cir. 1979) (after stating that Rule 613(b) does not specify any particular order for calling witnesses, the court notes that "the government asserts that even if the court did err with respect to Federal Rules of Evidence Rule 613, the court had the discretion to regulate the questioning as it did under Rule 403.").

In spite of the clear language of the Advisory Committee's Note, U.S. v. International Business Machines Corp., 432 F. Supp. 138 (S.D. N.Y. 1977), in requiring prior disclosure, stated that two circuits had taken the position that prior disclosure is required by Rule 613(b). The two cases cited at 432 F.Supp. at 140 n. 10—U.S. v. Truslow, 530 F.2d 257 (4th Cir. 1975), and U.S. v. Wright, 489 F.2d 1181 (D.C. Cir. 1973)—although involving trials occurring before the effective date of the federal rules, in fact support the proposition for which they are cited. Other circuits have made similar statements. *See* U.S. v. Franklin, 598 F.2d 954, 957 (5th Cir. 1979) ("As to some of the testimony, no proper predicate was laid. Fed. R. Evid. 613(b)."); U.S. v. Malatesta, 583

to find an invariable requirement that there be a foundation on cross-examination. However, several courts have held that under the statutes, they possess the discretion to mandate in light of the specific facts in a given case that the cross-examiner follow the traditional practice.[18] Indeed, some authorities assert that "most (though not all) of the circuits" which have passed on the question still adhere to "the traditional common law requirement" for a foundation on cross.[19]

If the witness attacked is not on the stand but the testimony introduced was given at a deposition or some other trial, at common law most prior decisions applying the traditional requirements exclude the inconsistent statement unless the foundation question was asked at the prior hearing.[20] In contrast, under the Federal and Revised Uniform Rule 613 the trial judge arguably has discretion to dispense with compliance with any general requirement that the opposing counsel have given the witness a

---

F.2d 748, 758 (5th Cir. 1978) ("Under Rule 613(b), Fed. R. Evid., once the witness had the opportunity 'to explain or deny' the prior statement, Lynch was free to introduce extrinsic evidence of it."); N.L.R.B. v. Adrian Belt Co., 578 F.2d 1304, 1310 n.7 (9th Cir. 1978) ("The employer's counsel never asked King what she had told the agencies about her employment status, although it was specifically suggested at the hearing that he do so. This failure would ordinarily have precluded any use of the agency records to impeach King because no proper foundation was laid. See Rule 613(b), Federal Rules of Evidence; 29 U.S.C.A. § 160(b) (N.L.R.B. hearings are to be conducted in accordance with the rules of evidence applicable in the district courts)."). Accord U.S. v. Bonnett, 877 F.2d 1450 (10th Cir. 1989); U.S. v. Elliott, 771 F.2d 1046 (7th Cir. 1985); U.S. v. Leslie, 759 F.2d 366 (5th Cir. 1985); Whitley v. Ercole, 725 F. Supp. 2d 398, 413 (S.D. N.Y. 2010) (citing Mattox v. U.S., 156 U.S. 237, 145–46, 15 S. Ct. 337, 39 L. Ed. 409 (1895)).

[17]As explained in the Advisory Committee's Note to Rule 613(b), the interests of "justice" would require ignoring the foundation requirements if the witness after testifying became unavailable by the time the prior statement was discovered or if counsel

wishes to examine several collusive witnesses before disclosing a joint prior inconsistent statement.

[18]Holmes v. Torguson, 41 F.3d 1251, 1260 (8th Cir. 1994) ("this procedure is not mandatory, but is optional at the trial judge's discretion"); U.S. v. Marks, 816 F.2d 1207, 1211 (7th Cir. 1987) (Posner, J.); U.S. v. Stewart, 325 F. Supp. 2d 474, 494 (D. Del. 2004), aff'd, 179 Fed. Appx. 814 (3d Cir. 2006) ("discretion to determine the sequence required to establish the proper foundation for Rule 613(b) evidence").

[19]U.S. v. Schnapp, 322 F.3d 564, 571 n.6 (8th Cir. 2003) ("impeachment of a witness by a prior inconsistent statement is normally allowed only when the witness is first provided an opportunity to explain or deny the statement"); U.S. v. Hudson, 970 F.2d 948, 959 (1st Cir. 1992) (Seyla, J., concurring). See also Schmertz, Article VI, in Emerging Problems Under the Federal Rules of Evidence 115, 191 (3d ed. 1998) (citing U.S. v. Bonnett, 877 F.2d 1450 (10th Cir. 1989) as "continuing the 'prior foundation' requirement of the common law").

[20]Doe ex dem. Hughes v. Wilkinson, 35 Ala. 453, 1860 WL 452 (1860); and cases cited 3A Wigmore, Evidence §§ 1031–32 (Chadbourn rev. 1970).

previous opportunity for denial or explanation.[21] Even when otherwise applicable, the traditional requirements ought to be abandoned in the case of depositions based on written interrogatories (which must be prepared in advance) and inconsistent statements made after the prior testimony was taken.[22]

If a party takes the stand as a witness and the adversary desires to use the party's prior inconsistent statement, the statement is receivable on two theories—first as an opposing party's statement (formerly termed the admission of a party-opponent)[23] and second as an inconsistent statement to impeach the witness. On the first theory, it is relevant to the factual issues on the historical merits of the case; on the second theory, it is not.[24] Yet even in jurisdictions requiring traditional foundational questions for impeachment, the prevailing view is that the requirement for

---

[21]The judge is already given discretion in the interests of "justice" to dispense with the witness's explanation or denial of the prior statement. See this section, note 66 supra.

[22]People v. Collup, 27 Cal. 2d 829, 167 P.2d 714, 718 (1946) (prosecution for rape: preliminary hearing testimony of state's witness read at trial; held, error to exclude evidence of witness's subsequent inconsistent statements, now absent from state; "the goal of all judicial proceedings is to bring before the trier of fact all pertinent evidence. Hence the rule allowing the use of former testimony is a salutary expedient . . . . But it is equally clear that by reason of the same principle the impeaching evidence should be admitted for what it is worth"). See approving Note, 20 So. Calif. L. Rev. 102. Cal. Evid. Code § 1202 provides that inconsistent statements of deponents in the same case may be introduced without a foundation question.

Similar questions arise with respect to impeachment by inconsistent statements of declarants whose hearsay declarations have been admitted under exceptions to the hearsay rule. Where foundation questions are otherwise required, they are ignored in connection with the use of inconsistent statements. State v. Debnam, 222 N.C. 266, 22 S.E.2d 562 (1942) (dying declaration); 3A Wigmore, Evidence § 1033 (Chadbourn rev. 1970) (declarations against interest). *Contra* Craig v. Wismar, 310 Ill. 262, 141 N.E. 766 (1923). *But see* People v. Hines, 284 N.Y. 93, 29 N.E.2d 483 (1940). Former Fed. R. Evid. 806 stated the flat rule:

> Evidence of a statement or conduct by the declarant at any time, inconsistent with the declarant's hearsay statement, is not subject to any requirement that the declarant may have been afforded an opportunity to deny or explain. If the party against whom a hearsay statement has been admitted calls the declarant as a witness, the party is entitled to examine the declarant on the statement as if under cross-examination.

Unif. R. Evid. 806 is identical in content. Effective December 1, 2011, restyled Fed. R. Evid. 806 reads: "The court may admit evidence of the declarant's inconsistent statement or conduct, regardless of when it occurred or whether the declarant had an opportunity to explain or deny it."

[23]See Chapter 26 infra.

[24]See discussion in § 34 supra. But Fed. R. Evid. 801(d) (1) and Uniform Rule 801(b) (1) (A) provide that an inconsistent statement is nonhearsay if given under oath and subject to the penalty of perjury at a trial, hearing, other proceeding, or a deposition. See § 251 infra.

a foundation is inapplicable here.[25] There is less danger of surprising a party than a witness. Furthermore, the party has an ample opportunity to deny or explain after the inconsistent statement is proved; as a litigant, the party can simply call himself as a witness later. In these jurisdictions, on occasion the courts inadvertently assume that the requirement applies to the party-witness.[26] Sometimes courts have imposed the requirement if the proponent offers the statement only for impeachment,[27] and one appellate court held the trial judge has discretion to impose the requirement for a foundational question as prerequisite to introducing an opposing party's admission.[28] These petty qualifications are hardly worthwhile. In jurisdictions which otherwise require the foundation question, the more sensible practice is entirely dispensing with the "foundation" for parties' admissions.

Federal Rule of Evidence 613 and the Revised Uniform Rule 613 have nothing to do with the introduction into evidence of parties' admissions, even if the admissions have some effect on the party's credibility as a witness.[29] Nor do the rules have any impact on the introduction of a statement pursuant to a hearsay exception in Federal and Revised Uniform Rules 803 when the out of court declarant testifies.[30] However, Federal and Revised Uniform Rule 613 applies when a prior inconsistent statement is admitted as substantive evidence solely by virtue of Federal and Revised Uniform Rule 801(d)(1)(A); the terms of Rule 801(d)(1)(A) render 613 applicable because they expressly refer to statements admitted as being "inconsistent with the declarant's [trial] testimony. . . ."

Again in jurisdictions in which a foundation question is required but the cross-examiner overlooks it, the judge should have discretion to consider such factors as the cross-examiner's ignorance of the inconsistent statement at the time when the wit-

---

[25]State v. Hephner, 161 N.W.2d 714 (Iowa 1968); and cases cited 4 Wigmore, Evidence § 1051 (Chadbourn rev. 1972); West's Key Number Digest, Witnesses ⟶388(3).

[26]*E.g.*, Wiggins v. State, 27 Ala. App. 451, 173 So. 890 (1937); Finn v. Finn, 195 S.W.2d 679 (Tex. Civ. App. Dallas 1946).

[27]Industrial Farm Home Gas Co. v. McDonald, 234 Ark. 744, 355 S.W.2d 174 (1962); Washington & O.D. Ry. Co. v. Smith, 289 F. 582 (App. D.C. 1923).

[28]Giles v. Valentic, 355 Pa. 108, 49 A.2d 384 (1946).

[29]The last sentence of Former Fed. R. Evid. 613(b) and Unif. R. Evid. 613(b) states: "This provision does not apply to admissions of a party-opponent as defined in rule 801(d) (2)."

Effective December 1, 2011, restyled Fed. R. Evid. 613(b) reads: "This subdivision (b) does not apply to an opposing party's statement under Rule 801(d) (2)."

*See* U.S. v. Cline, 570 F.2d 731 (8th Cir. 1978).

[30]The same is true at common law; a foundation is not required with respect to statements admitted pursuant to a common law hearsay exception regardless of whether the declarant testifies.

ness was cross-examined, the importance of the testimony under attack, and the practicability of recalling the witness. After weighing these factors, the judge ought to permit the impeachment without the foundation or allow a departure from the traditional time sequence if it seems fairer to do so.[31]

## § 38   Prior inconsistent statements: Rule against impeaching one's own witness[1]

### The Voucher Rule

The case law voucher rule forbidding a party to impeach her own witness is of obscure origin. It is probably a late manifestation of the evolution of the common law trial procedure from an inquisitorial to an adversary or contentious system.[2] The prohibition generally applied to all forms of impeachment. It applied not only to an attack by inconsistent statements but also to an attack on character or a showing of bias, interest, or corruption. However, the voucher rule never forbade the party from introducing other evidence specifically contradicting the facts testified to by her witness.[3]

Several reasons (or rationalizations) have been advanced for

---

[31]Model Code of Evidence Rule 106(2) leaves the enforcement of the requirement to the judge's discretion. Cal. Evid. Code § 770, and N.J.R.E. 613(b) likewise give the judge discretion. Although the California statute does not expressly use the term, "discretion," the reference to the "interests of justice" implicitly confers such discretion on the trial judge.

Although there is no particular time sequence for the witness's explanation or denial of an inconsistent statement under former Fed. R. Evid. 613(b) and Unif. R. Evid. 613(b), the judge may dispense entirely with the requirement for denial or explanation "in the interests of justice." See this section, note 13 supra.

In a jurisdiction requiring a foundation question, it has been indicated that it may be error for the cross-examiner to fail to follow up and produce extrinsic evidence of the inconsistent statement. People v. Williams, 105 Ill. App. 2d 25, 245 N.E.2d 17 (1st Dist. 1969) (error not reversible under circumstances). Fed. R. Evid. and Unif. R. Evid. 613(a)

requires disclosure of the statement to the opposing counsel on request, as an assurance of good faith.

**[Section 38]**

[1]3A Wigmore, Evidence §§ 896–918 (Chadbourn rev. 1970); 4 Weinstein's Federal Evidence Ch. 607 (rev. 2011); Ladd, Impeachment of One's Own Witness—New Developments, 4 U. Chi. L. Rev. 69 (1936); Hauser, Impeaching One's Own Witness, 11 Ohio St. L.J. 364 (1950); Comment, 49 Va. L. Rev. 996 (1963); West's Key Number Digest, Witnesses ⚷320 to 325.

[2]Ladd, Impeachment of One's Own Witness—New Developments, 4 U. Chi. L. Rev. 69, 70 (1936).

[3]Vondrashek v. Dignan, 200 Minn. 530, 274 N.W. 609 (1937) (principle recognized, but court refused to apply it to permit party to contradict by other witnesses his own testimony that he was not drunk—a picturesque case of behind the scenes conflict between the party and his insurer); Duffy v. National Janitorial Services, Inc., 429 Pa. 334, 240 A.2d 527 (1968); and

the voucher rule: first, by calling the witness the party vouches for the witness's trustworthiness; and second, the power to impeach is the power to coerce the witness to testify as desired, under the implied threat of assassinating the witness's character. Both rationales are flawed. The answer to the first is that, except in a few instances such as character witnesses or experts, the party has little or no choice of witnesses. The party may have to call the persons who happen to have observed the particular events in controversy. For the most part, you take your witnesses as you find them. The answers to the second reason are that: (a) it applies only to two kinds of impeachment, the attack on character and the showing of corruption, and (b) to forbid the attack by the calling party leaves that party at the mercy of the witness and the adversary. When the truth lies on the side of the calling party but the witness's character is bad, the adversary can attack the witness if the witness tells the truth; but when the witness lies, the adversary will not attack, and, under the rule, the calling party cannot impeach. The voucher rule should not be carried to an absurd extreme; if the witness has been bribed to change his story, the calling party ought to be allowed to expose the bribe.

As previously stated, the most frequently used kind of impeachment is by inconsistent statements. Most voucher cases involve this type of impeachment. It is difficult to see any justification for prohibiting proof of a prior inconsistent statement by a witness who has testified contrary to a previous statement. Perhaps there is a fear that the jurors will misuse the previous statement as substantive evidence of the facts asserted if, as in some jurisdictions, the use of the statement for that purpose would be inadmissible hearsay.[4] Except in those jurisdictions which have altogether abandoned it,[5] the common law rule against impeaching one's own witness persists largely with respect to proof of bias and attacks upon character.[6] By decision and statute, a number of jurisdictions have relaxed the rule insofar as it prohibits impeachment by inconsistent statements. A provision in the draft of the 1849 Field Code of Civil Procedure bore fruit in the 1854 English Common Law Procedure Act (St. 17 & 18 Vict. c. 125, § 22), reading: "[1] A party producing a witness shall not be allowed to impeach his credit by general evidence of bad character; [2] but he may, in case the witness shall in the opinion of the judge prove adverse, [3] contradict him by other evidence, [4] or by leave of the judge prove that he has made at other times a statement inconsistent with his present testimony." A few states cop-

---

cases cited in West's Key Number Digest, Witnesses ⟿320, 321, 400 to 402.

[4] See § 251 infra.

[5] See notes 15 to 16 infra.

[6] *See* Comment, 49 Va. L. Rev. 996, 1009 (1963).

ied this statute.[7] Other state legislatures, following the example of Massachusetts, adopted the English statute but omitted the statutory condition that the witness must have proved "adverse."[8] Still other courts reached a similar result by decision.[9]

These statutes and decisions open the door to the most important type of impeachment of one's own witness, namely, prior inconsistent statements. However, whether the reform is effected by statute or decision, some courts have imposed two troublesome limitations. One is that the party seeking to impeach must show that she is surprised at the witness's testimony.[10] The second is that she cannot impeach unless the witness's testimony is positively harmful or adverse to her cause. The witness's testimony must be worse than a mere failure ("I do not remember," "I do not know") to give expected favorable testimony.[11] A mere failure is simply disappointing, not positively damaging to her case.[12] These limitations are explicable only as attempts to safeguard the hearsay policy preventing the party from proving the witness's prior statement in situations where its only realistic value to the proponent is as substantive evidence of the facts asserted.[13] The rule against substantive use of the statements,

---

[7]Vt. Stat. Ann. tit. 12, § 1642; Va. Code Ann. § 8.01-403.

[8]*E.g.*, N.Y. CPL § 60.35; N.Y. CPLR 4514 (limited to writings).

[9]For example, note 10 infra.

[10]Surprise is required by several statutes, D.C. Code § 14-104; Ohio Evid. R. 607. The concept of "surprise," moreover, varies in the various jurisdictions. Sometimes "actual" or genuine surprise is required; in other decisions, it is not. *See* Comment, 49 Va. L. Rev. 996 (1963). There is a possible escape from the requirement if the judge will "call" the witness as a court's witness. See § 8 supra. *But see* Walker v. State, 144 Md. App. 505, 798 A.2d 1219 (2002), judgment rev'd on other grounds, 373 Md. 360, 818 A.2d 1078 (2003) (the state may impeach its own witness even though it cannot show surprise).

[11]Wurm v. Pulice, 82 Idaho 359, 353 P.2d 1071 (1960) (statute permits impeachment by inconsistent statement); Com. v. Strunk, 293 S.W.2d 629 (Ky. 1956) (rule permits inconsistent statement; court states "where the wit-ness testifies positively to the existence of a fact prejudicial to the party, or to a fact clearly favorable to the adverse party"); Roe v. State, 152 Tex. Crim. 119, 210 S.W.2d 817 (1948); Virginia Elec. & Power Co. v. Hall, 184 Va. 102, 34 S.E.2d 382 (1945); Ohio R. Evid. 607; *see* Comment, 49 Va. L. Rev. 996 (1963).

[12]See § 36, supra.

[13]For an argument in favor of retaining surprise and affirmative damage as prerequisites to impeachment by a party of its own witness by prior inconsistent statements, see 4 Graham, Handbook of Federal Evidence § 607:3 (7th ed. 2012).

Two matters concerning the common law rule where it persists even in modified form should be mentioned. First, a principal means of escape from the prohibition, insofar as it prevents introduction of inconsistent statements, is to question the witness about the previous statement not avowedly to discredit but to refresh the witness's memory, or as it is sometimes phrased, "to awaken his conscience." People v. Michaels, 335 Ill.

and the debatable soundness of its rationale, are the subject of a subsequent section.[14]

---

590, 167 N.E. 857 (1929). Or "for the purpose of probing his recollection, recalling to his mind the statements he has previously made and drawing out an explanation of his apparent inconsistency." Bullard v. Pearsall, 53 N.Y. 230, 231, 1873 WL 10363 (1873); Hicks v. Coleman, 240 S.C. 227, 125 S.E.2d 473 (1962).

Second, who is the party's own witness within the prohibition? It is not the mere calling of the witness but rather eliciting the witness's testimony that makes one the party's witness. Fall Brook Coal Co. v. Hewson, 158 N.Y. 150, 52 N.E. 1095 (1899). Moreover, in some jurisdictions restricting the cross-examination to the scope of the direct, if the cross-examiner elicits new matter the witness becomes the witness of the cross-examiner as to such testimony. 3A Wigmore, Evidence § 914 (Chadbourn rev. 1970); West's Key Number Digest, Witnesses ⟨325. In the case of deposition testimony it is the introduction of the deposition in evidence, not taking the deposition, that constitutes the adoption of the witness as the party's own. Adv. Comm. Note (1972), Fed. R. Civ. P. 32. In deleting former subdivision (c) to Rule 32, the Advisory Committee notes:

> The concept of "making a person one's own witness" appears to have had significance principally in two respects: impeachment and waiver of incompetency. Neither retains any vitality under the Rules of Evidence. The old prohibition against impeaching one's own witness is eliminated by Evidence Rule 607. The lack of recognition in the Rules of Evidence of state rules of incompetency in the Dead Man's area renders it unnecessary to consider aspects of waiver arising from calling the incompetent party-witness. Subdivision (c) is deleted because it appears to be no longer necessary in the light of the Rules of Evidence.

*See also* 3A Wigmore, Evidence §§ 912–13 (Chadbourn rev. 1970).

When a party calls an adverse party as a witness, the reasons for the prohibition seem inapplicable, and a few states expressly permit calling party to impeach. *See* N.H. R. Evid. 607. Absent such a provision, a few cases mechanically apply the prohibition. Price v. Cox, 242 Ala. 568, 7 So. 2d 288 (1942) (can contradict but not impeach). *See* 3A Wigmore, Evidence § 916 (Chadbourn rev. 1970); West's Key Number Digest, Witnesses ⟨324. *But see* Wells v. Goforth, 443 S.W.2d 155 (Mo. 1969) (rejecting former rule that adverse party witness cannot be impeached by inconsistent statement although statute permitted questioning as if on cross-examination). When the same witness is called twice, first by A and then by B, some courts have been troubled. *See* decisions collected 3A Wigmore, Evidence § 913 (Chadbourn rev. 1970). The most practical solution would be to hold that the prohibition does not apply at all, and both A and B may freely impeach. Next most sensible is to say, as some cases have indicated, that either A or B may impeach, at least by inconsistent statements, the testimony elicited during the other's call of the witness. *E.g.,* People v. Van Dyke, 414 Ill. 251, 111 N.E.2d 165 (1953); Arnold v. Manzella, 186 S.W.2d 882 (Mo. Ct. App. 1945); West's Key Number Digest, Witnesses ⟨380(9). Another view that the witness is the witness of A, and A in any event is precluded, has less to commend it. Hanrahan v. New York Edison Co., 238 N.Y. 194, 144 N.E. 499 (1924); West's Key Number Digest, Witnesses ⟨380(9). Surely the worst solution is to hold that both parties have adopted the witness, and neither may impeach. In re Campbell's Will, 100 Vt. 395, 138 A. 725 (1927).

[14] See § 251 infra.

More and more jurisdictions have abandoned the voucher rule prohibiting the impeachment of one's own witness.[15] Likewise, Federal Rule of Evidence 607 and Uniform Rule of Evidence 607 repeal the rule.[16] These rules permit resort to the standard methods of impeachment.[17] There is some dispute whether and under what circumstances impeachment of one's own witness is impermissible because of prejudice to the opposing party, particularly in criminal cases.[18] For instance, there is a sizeable body of precedent that a prosecutor may not employ a prior inconsistent statement to impeach a witness as a "mere subterfuge" or for the "*primary* purpose" of placing before the jury substantive evidence which is otherwise inadmissible.[19] The application of the "mere subterfuge" or "*primary* purpose" doctrine focuses on

---

[15]Cal. Evid. Code § 785; Kan. Stat. Ann. 60-420; Utah R. Evid. 607. *See* Rowe v. Farmers Ins. Co., Inc., 699 S.W.2d 423 (Mo. 1985) (overwhelming majority of jurisdictions have abandoned rule; listing provided). *But see* Slayton v. State, 481 N.E.2d 1300 (Ind. 1985) (hostility during examination required); N.J.R.E. 607 (the rule includes a provision allowing the use of prior consistent statements to rebut a charge of recent fabrication).

[16]Fed. R. Evid. 607 & Unif. R. Evid. 607. *See generally* U.S. v. Dennis, 625 F.2d 782, 795 n.6 (8th Cir. 1980) ("At common law, the party calling a witness at trial could not impeach his credibility unless the party could show both surprise and substantial harm. Bushaw v. United States, 353 F.2d 477 (9th Cir. 1965). But Rule 607 of the Federal Rules of Evidence allowed impeachment of one's own witness. So long as prior inconsistent statements are otherwise admissible, they may be used for impeachment; and surprise is no longer a prerequisite to their use. United States v. Long Soldier, 562 F.2d 601, 605 (8th Cir. 1977). The prosecution's ability to impeach its witness with prior inconsistent statements is crucial in cases where the 'turncoat' witness is afraid, United States v. Gerry, 515 F.2d 130, 139–40 (2d Cir. 1975) (loan sharking prosecution), or hostile, United States v. Rogers, 549 F.2d 490 (8th Cir. 1976) (charged with the same offense).").

[17]*See* U.S. v. Miller, 664 F.2d 94 (5th Cir. 1981) (inconsistent statement); Beard v. Mitchell, 604 F.2d 485 (7th Cir. 1979) (bias; dictum).

[18]*See* Weinstein & Berger, Evidence ¶ 607[01]. Citing authority, the authors suggest that the prejudicial effect of the impeachment should be considered under Rule 403, rather than the motive for impeachment pursuant to U.S. v. Morlang, 531 F.2d 183 (4th Cir. 1975). *See also* State v. Lavaris, 41 Wash. App. 856, 707 P.2d 134 (Div. 1 1985) (use by prosecution of prior inconsistent statement to impeach its own witness may be prohibited in light of the danger of unfair prejudice).

[19]U.S. v. Gilbert, 57 F.3d 709, 711–12 (9th Cir. 1995) ("the primary purpose of placing before the jury substantive evidence which is otherwise inadmissible"); U.S. v. Patterson, 23 F.3d 1239 (7th Cir. 1994) (the prosecution may not call a witness whom it knows will not give useful testimony just so that it can introduce otherwise inadmissible hearsay against the defendant in the hope that the jury will miss the subtle distinction between impeachment and substantive evidence); U.S. v. Ince, 21 F.3d 576, 581–82 (4th Cir. 1994) (at the first trial of the case, the witness claimed to suffer from memory loss; at the second trial, the prosecution again called the witness; once again the witness claimed memory loss; the judge

the content of the witness's testimony as a whole. If the witness's testimony is useful to establish any fact of consequence significant in the context of the litigation, the witness may be impeached by means of a prior inconsistent statement as to any other matter testified to.[20] In the words of one commentator, the pivotal

---

permitted the prosecution to impeach the witness with her pretrial statement that she heard the accused confess; the government used the impeachment as a guise for introducing inadmissible hearsay evidence of the accused's confession); U.S. v. Carter, 973 F.2d 1509, 1512–13 (10th Cir. 1992) (an attorney is entitled to assume that the witness will testify truthfully and consistently with a pretrial statement; the court should find an improper purpose only when the trial record "unequivocally" establishes the purpose); U.S. v. Kane, 944 F.2d 1406, 1412 (7th Cir. 1991) ("The test is whether the prosecution exhibited bad faith by calling a witness sure to be unhelpful to its case"); Hughes v. State, 4 S.W.3d 1 (Tex. Crim. App. 1999) (the trial judge should exclude statements which are offered under the guise of impeaching one's own witness but which are primarily useful to place otherwise inadmissible evidence before the jury); Saltzburg, Using Prior Statements, 24 Crim. Just. 45, 48 (Spr. 2009) ("it is presumptively improper for a direct examiner to call a witness to the stand for the sole purpose of offering an inconsistent statement for 'impeachment' ").

In U.S. v. Buffalo, 358 F.3d 519 (8th Cir. 2004), the court stated that it is more likely to find a violation of this rule when the proponent of the evidence is the prosecution. The court remarked that the risk of jury misuse of the evidence "is multiplied when the statement offered as impeachment testimony contains the defendant's alleged admission of guilt. Thus, a trial judge should rarely, if ever, permit the Government to 'impeach' its own witness by presenting what would otherwise be inadmissible hearsay if that hearsay contains an alleged confession to the crime for which the defendant

is being tried." The court contrasted the situation in which the defendant is the proponent: "Simply put, the prejudicial impact of the statement does not endanger the defendant's liberty by risking a conviction based on out-of-court statements that are not subject to confrontation by way of cross-examination."

[20]U.S. v. Hogan, 763 F.2d 697, 702 (5th Cir. 1985):

The rule in this Circuit, however, is that "the prosecutor may not use such a statement under the guise of impeachment for the primary purpose of placing before the jury substantive evidence which is not otherwise admissible." *Miller*, supra at 97 (emphasis in original); *Whitehurst v. Wright*, 592 F.2d 834, 839–40 (5th Cir. 1979); *United States v. Dobbs*, 448 F.2d 1262 (5th Cir. 1971). Every circuit to consider this question has ruled similarly. *See, e.g., United States v. Webster*, 734 F.2d 1191, 1192 (7th Cir. 1984); *United States v. Fay*, 668 F.2d 375, 379 (8th Cir. 1981); *United States v. DeLillo*, 620 F.2d 939, 946 (2d Cir.), *cert. denied*, 449 U.S. 835, 101 S.Ct. 108, 66 L.Ed.2d 41 (1980); *United States v. Morlang*, 531 F.2d 183, 190 (4th Cir. 1975); *United States v. Coppola*, 479 F.2d 1153, 1156–58 (10th Cir. 1973); *United States v. Michener*, 152 F.2d 880, 883 n. 3 (3d Cir. 1945); *Kuhn v. United States*, 24 F.2d 910, 913 (9th Cir.), *cert. denied*, 278 U.S. 605, 49 S.Ct. 11, 73 L.Ed. 533 (1928).

. . .

The danger in this procedure is obvious. The jury will hear the impeachment evidence, which is not otherwise admissible and is not substantive proof of guilt, but is likely to be received as such proof. The defendant thus risks being convicted on the basis of hearsay evidence that should bear only on a witness's credibility. Morlang, 531 F.2d at 190. *See also* FRE 403, 404.

United States v. Morlang, 531 F.2d 183, 190 (4th Cir. 1975) ("The over-

question is whether the "party [is] calling a witness with the reasonable expectation that the witness will testify something helpful to the party's case aside from the prior inconsistent statement."[21] Subject to that limitation, a rule excluding prior inconsistent statements of one's own witness can sometimes be a serious obstruction to the ascertainment of truth, even in criminal cases. In a given case, a criminal defendant might even urge that the application of the rule to prevent him from mounting a critical attack on a key defense witness is unconstitutional.[22]

## § 39   Bias and partiality[1]

Case law recognizes the powerful distorting effect on human testimony of the witness's emotions or feelings toward the parties or the witness's self-interest in the outcome of the case. Thus, the courts have long acknowledged that bias, or any acts, relationships, or motives reasonably likely to produce it, may be proved to impeach credibility.[2] Indeed, the right to cross-examine to ex-

---

whelming weight of authority is, however, that impeachment by prior inconsistent statement may not be permitted where employed as a mere subterfuge to get before the jury evidence not otherwise admissible."). *Accord* State v. Jasper, 200 Conn. 30, 508 A.2d 1387 (1986); State v. Rufener, 401 N.W.2d 740 (S.D. 1987); State v. Hancock, 109 Wash. 2d 760, 748 P.2d 611 (1988).

[21]Saltzburg, Using Prior Statements, 24 Crim. Just., Spr. 2009, at 45, 48 ("it is presumptively improper for a direct examiner to call a witness to the stand for the purpose of offering an inconsistent statement for 'impeachment' "); Saltzburg, Prior Inconsistent Statements: Fair and Unfair Use, 6 Crim. Just. 45, 46 (Sum. 1991). *See* U.S. v. Gilbert, 57 F.3d 709, 711–12 (9th Cir. 1995) (the witnesses in question observed the conduct for which the accused was convicted; their testimony for crucial, and the jury would have wondered if the prosecution had not called them to the stand); U.S. v. Eisen, 974 F.2d 246, 262–63 (2d Cir. 1992) (the witnesses provided "affirmative proof that was necessary to construct the Government's case").

[22]Chambers v. Mississippi, 410 U.S. 284, 93 S. Ct. 1038, 35 L. Ed. 2d 297 (1973); Imwinkelried & Garland, Exculpatory Evidence: The Accused's Constitutional Right to Introduce Favorable Evidence § 8-2 (3d ed. 2004).

**[Section 39]**

[1]3 A Wigmore, Evidence §§ 943–69 (Chadbourn rev. 1970); Weinstein & Berger, Evidence ¶ 607[03]; Hale, Bias as Affecting Credibility, 1 Hastings L.J. 1 (1949); West's Key Number Digest, Witnesses ☞363 to 78.

[2]*See generally* U.S. v. Abel, 469 U.S. 45, 52, 105 S. Ct. 465, 83 L. Ed. 2d 450 (1984) ("Bias is a term used in the 'common law of evidence' to describe the relationship between a party and a witness which might lead the witness to slant, unconsciously or otherwise, his testimony in favor of or against a party. Bias may be induced by a witness' like, dislike, or fear of a party, or by the witness' self-interest. Proof of bias is almost always relevant because the jury, as finder of fact and weigher of credibility, has historically been entitled to assess all evidence which might bear on the accuracy and

pose a prosecution witness's bias has a constitutional dimension.[3]

truth of a witness' testimony."); U.S. v. Greenwood, 796 F.2d 49 (4th Cir. 1986) (bias, defined as emotional partiality, is not a collateral issue; the point of a bias inquiry is to expose to the jury the witness's special motive to lie by revealing facts such as pecuniary interest in the trial, personal animosity, favoritism toward the defendant, or the witness's plea agreement with the government); U.S. v. Robinson, 530 F.2d 1076, 1079 (D.C. Cir. 1976) ("The dominant principle is that evidence showing the 'emotional partiality' of a witness 'is always significant in assessing credibility,' for 'the trier must be sufficiently informed of the underlying relationships, circumstances and influences operating on the witness so that, in light of his experience, he can determine whether a mutation in testimony could reasonably be expected as a probable human reaction.' ").

Partiality may be established by evidence of the witness's situation, making it "a priori" probable that he has some partiality of emotion for one party's cause. Bias can also be evidenced by the witness's conduct, indicating partiality; in situation, the inference is from the conduct apparently manifesting the feeling to the existence of the feeling itself. 3A Wigmore, Evidence § 945 at 782 (Chadbourn rev. 1970). See also Piscitelli v. Salesian Soc., 166 Cal. App. 4th 1, 82 Cal. Rptr. 3d 139 (2d Dist. 2008) (a witness may be impeached with evidence of a prior conviction showing bias without regard to the nature of the underlying crimes as it relates to the character traits of honesty and truthfulness; a showing of bias and proof of a conviction are alternative impeachment techniques, and the restrictions on the latter technique do not apply to a conviction logically relevant under the former technique).

The cross-examiner is not limited to questioning the witness concerning the circumstances of the witness's situation, his conduct, and his feelings about a party. The commission of prior acts of misconduct may give rise to an inference of partiality. Counsel may also inquire into the witness's statements concerning matters relating to possible partiality. U.S. v. Maynard, 476 F.2d 1170, 1174 (D.C. Cir. 1973) ("In certain situations . . . external facts from which may be inferred a specific bias, or motive to testify in a particular way, are admissible to impeach a witness—e.g., facts which show a familial, employment, or litigious relationship. Since the range of facts from which bias may be inferred is vast, hard and fast rules permitting or excluding specific types of impeachment evidence might be unwise."); Moody v. State, 495 So. 2d 104, 107 (Ala. Crim. App. 1986) ("Furthermore, in Alabama, '[t]he bias of a state's witness in favor of the State or against the accused may be shown by evidence of statements, acts, relationships or *charges of crime,* that would reasonably give rise to an inference that the witness is biased.' C. Gamble, McElroy's Alabama Evidence, 149.01(10) (3rd ed. 1977).").

[3]U.S. v. Abel, 469 U.S. 45, 50, 105 S. Ct. 465, 83 L. Ed. 2d 450 (1984); U.S. v. Recendiz, 557 F.3d 511, 530 (7th Cir. 2009) ("One such core value [of the Confrontation Clause] is the ability to expose a witness's motivation for testifying"), cert.denied sub nom. Navar v. U.S., 130 S. Ct. 340, 175 L. Ed. 2d 138 (2009); U.S. v. Carter, 313 F. Supp. 2d 921, 923 (E.D. Wis. 2004); Greene v. Wainwright, 634 F.2d 272 (5th Cir. 1981). When evidence of a complainant's prior sexual history is logically relevant on a bias theory, accused have occasionally successfully invoked this constitutional right to limit or override rape shield statutes. Com. v. Joyce, 382 Mass. 222, 415 N.E.2d 181, 186–87 (1981); State v. Jalo, 27 Or. App. 845, 557 P.2d 1359, 1362 (1976); Com. v. Black, 337 Pa. Super. 548, 487 A.2d 396, 401 (1985).

While Article VI of the Federal Rules of Evidence does not explicitly refer to attacking the witness by showing bias, interest, corruption, or coercion, the article impliedly authorizes the use of that ground of impeachment.[4] The inclusion of Article VI in the Federal Rules reflects the drafters' realization that a witness's credibility is a fact of consequence under Rule 401; and Rule 402 states that evidence logically relevant to a fact of consequence is admissible unless there is a statutory basis for exclusion. In short, Rule 402 is the only statutory authorization needed for the continued use of the bias impeachment technique in federal practice. In any event, though, the cross-examiner must have a good faith basis in fact for the inquiry about the fact or event.[5]

The kinds and sources of partiality are too varied to list exhaustively, but a few of the common instances will be mentioned. *Favor* or friendly feeling toward a party may be evidenced by family[6] or business relationship,[7] employment by a

---

[4]This fact was explicitly recognized in U.S. v. Abel, 469 U.S. 45, 51, 105 S. Ct. 465, 83 L. Ed. 2d 450 (1984) ("We think the lesson to be drawn from all of this is that it is permissible to impeach a witness by showing his bias under the Fed. Rules of Evid. just as it was permissible to do so before their adoption.").

The Uniform Rules of Evidence were amended to add Rule 616 entitled "Bias of Witness": "For the purpose of attacking the credibility of a witness, evidence of bias, prejudice, or interest of the witness for or against any party to the case is admissible." However, at the time of the *Abel* decision Federal Rule of Evidence 411 specifically referred to "proof of . . . bias or prejudice of a witness" as a legitimate theory for introducing evidence of liability insurance. In *Abel,* the Court and attorneys may have overlooked the reference to bias because the reference appears in Article IV rather than Article VI.

[5]See § 49 infra. *See also* People v. Rivera, 145 Ill. App. 3d 609, 99 Ill. Dec. 353, 495 N.E.2d 1088, 1095 (1st Dist. 1986) ("We address first the issue of whether error occurred when the State asked Rosario leading questions with impeaching overtones without presenting any evidence to sub-

stantiate those implications. It has long been recognized as error for the State to ask a defense witness questions presuming facts not in evidence as a precursor to impeachment of that witness, unless the State has evidence to substantiate the inquiry. (People v. Wallenberg (1962), 24 Ill.2d 350, 353, 181 N.E.2d 143). The asking of the leading question and the denial carry a harmful innuendo which is unsupported by any evidence. (People v. Burbank (1972), 53 Ill.2d 261, 270, 291 N.E.2d 161). The danger inherent in this situation is that the jury will ignore the denial and presume the accuracy of the impeaching insinuation contained in the question, substituting this presumption for proof. This result cannot be countenanced, as it would inevitably lead to a 'trial by insinuation and innuendo' rather than a trial by properly introduced evidence. (People v. Morris (1979), 79 Ill.App.3d 318, 330, 34 Ill.Dec. 363, 398 N.E.2d 38). We cannot elevate insinuation to the dignity of artful and proper cross-examination.").

[6]Williams v. State, 44 Ala. App. 503, 214 So. 2d 712 (1968) (court should have permitted defendant to show that state's witness was "kin" to defendant's alleged victim); Christie v. Eager, 129 Conn. 62, 26 A.2d 352 (1942) (in guest's suit against motorist, jury

party[8] or the party's insurer,[9] intimate[10] or sexual[11] relations, membership in the same organization,[12] or the witness's conduct or expressions evincing such feeling.[13] In auto collision cases, it is

could consider facts that the plaintiff is brother of motorist's wife, and that insurance company is the real defendant); 3A Wigmore, Evidence § 949 (Chadbourn rev. 1970).

[7]Aetna Ins. Co. v. Paddock, 301 F.2d 807 (5th Cir. 1962) (the witness had borrowed money from party); Curry v. Fleer, 157 N.C. 16, 72 S.E. 626 (1911) (that witness for party had sold his land to him at big price, admissible).

[8]Arnall Mills v. Smallwood, 68 F.2d 57 (C.C.A. 5th Cir. 1933) (witnesses' employment by defendant may be considered on credibility but is not, by itself, sufficient ground for disregarding their testimony); West's Key Number Digest, Witnesses ⊙369.

[9]It is usually held that the relevancy of the showing that the witness is an employee of defendant's liability insurer outweighs the danger of prejudice in disclosing the fact of insurance. Nunnellee v. Nunnellee, 415 S.W.2d 114 (Ky. 1967); and see numerous decisions, pro and con, collected in Admissibility of evidence, and propriety and effect of questions, statements, comments, etc., tending to show that defendant in personal injury or death action carries liability insurance, 4 A.L.R.2d 761.

[10]U.S. v. Baldridge, 559 F.3d 1126, 1135 (10th Cir. 2009).

[11]Olden v. Kentucky, 488 U.S. 227, 109 S. Ct. 480, 102 L. Ed. 2d 513 (1988) (charge that alleged victim of sex abuse concocted story of rape to protect her relationship with another); U.S. v. Jones, 766 F.2d 412 (9th Cir. 1985) (rebuffed homosexual advances); Parsley v. Com., 306 S.W.2d 284 (Ky. 1957) (rape; held evidence that defendant's fiancee who testified for him was pregnant by him was admissible to show her interest, since defendant's conviction would prevent his rendering aid and comfort to her); Propriety

of cross-examining witness as to illicit relations with defendant in criminal case, 25 A.L.R.3d 537; West's Key Number Digest, Witnesses ⊙370(4). One court has upheld this theory of admissibility when the evidence took the form of proof of a same-sex romantic relationship. McIntyre v. State, 934 P.2d 770 (Alaska Ct. App. 1997).

[12]U.S. v. Abel, 469 U.S. 45, 105 S. Ct. 465, 83 L. Ed. 2d 450 (1984) (membership of a party and a witness in the same secret prison organization which had a creed requiring members to lie for each other, even without proof that either one had adopted the organization's creed); U.S. v. Takahashi, 205 F.3d 1161 (9th Cir. 2000); Betts v. City of Chicago, Ill., 784 F. Supp. 2d 1020 (N.D. Ill. 2011) (common group membership). Likewise, the courts have held that a defense witness's membership in the same, uncharged conspiracy as the accused is relevant to show the witness's bias in the accused's favor. U.S. v. Robinson, 530 F.2d 1076 (D.C. Cir. 1976); Gilbert v. U.S., 366 F.2d 923 (9th Cir. 1966). See also People v. Anderson, 20 Cal. 3d 647, 143 Cal. Rptr. 883, 574 P.2d 1235, 1236–37 (1978) (joint arrests). But see People v. Bojorquez, 104 Cal. App. 4th 335, 128 Cal. Rptr. 2d 411, 415–16 (2d Dist. 2002) (although mutual gang membership is logically relevant to show bias, it is so prejudicial that "it has consistently been held that where other evidence shows the witness' association with the defendant, evidence of their gang membership should be excluded").

[13]U.S. v. Kerr, 464 F.2d 1367 (6th Cir. 1972) (witness paying certain bills of defendant's wife during defendant's imprisonment); People v. Layher, 238 Mich. App. 573, 607 N.W.2d 91 (1999) (the defendant in a child abuse prosecution hired a private investigator who testified at trial; the prosecution was properly allowed to question the inves-

commonly held that when a witness appears for defendant, the fact that he made a claim against the defendant and has already been paid a sum in settlement tends to show bias in defendant's favor.[14] Similarly, *hostility* toward a party may be shown by the fact that the witness has had a fight or quarrel with him,[15] has a lawsuit pending against him,[16] has contributed to the defense,[17] employed special counsel to aid in prosecuting the party,[18] or has a racial bias against (or in favor of) members of the party's ethnic group.[19] In criminal cases, the witness's attitude toward the

---

tigator about his arrest and prosecution for a similar charge involving his own daughter), aff'd, 631 N.W.2d 281 (Mich. 2001); Junior Hall, Inc. v. Charm Fashion Center, Inc., 264 N.C. 81, 140 S.E.2d 772 (1965) (witness, a friend of plaintiff, could be asked whether she had appeared as witness for plaintiff in similar suit of plaintiff against a third person); 3A Wigmore, Evidence § 950 (Chadbourn rev. 1970).

[14]See § 266 infra.

[15]U.S. v. Harvey, 547 F.2d 720 (2d Cir. 1976) (defendant was accused by government witness of being father of her child, refusing to support it, and beating the witness); 3A Wigmore, Evidence § 950 (Chadbourn rev. 1970).

In Jacek v. Bacote, 135 Conn. 702, 68 A.2d 144 (1949) a question asking whether witness was prejudiced against Afro-Americans, to which race defendant belonged, was held proper. *See also* U.S. v. Kartman, 417 F.2d 893 (9th Cir. 1969) (holding it was error to foreclose inquiry whether government witness had prejudice against persons who participated in anti-draft and anti-war demonstrations and hence against defendant); and cases cited therein.

[16]State v. Michelski, 66 N.D. 760, 268 N.W. 713 (1936) (manslaughter by automobile; held defendant entitled to show that state's witnesses had civil actions against defendant arising from same collision, on rather far-fetched ground that conviction would be admissible to impeach defendant in civil actions); Blake v. State, 365 S.W.2d 795 (Tex. Crim. App. 1963) (case involving embezzlement). But, on simi-

lar facts, the evidence was excluded in State v. Lawson, 128 W. Va. 136, 36 S.E.2d 26 (1945), and this was held a proper exercise of discretion. Cases are collected in 3A Wigmore, Evidence § 949 nn. 5, 6 (Chadbourn rev. 1970).

A past unsuccessful prosecution of a defense witness may be shown. U.S. v. Senak, 527 F.2d 129 (7th Cir. 1975).

[17]State v. Cerar, 60 Utah 208, 207 P. 597 (1922).

[18]Brogden v. State, 33 Ala. App. 132, 31 So. 2d 144 (1947); State v. Wray, 217 N.C. 167, 7 S.E.2d 468 (1940) (court assumes fact relevant on bias, but upholds exclusion as discretionary and not shown prejudicial).

[19]U.S. v. Figueroa, 548 F.3d 222 (2d Cir. 2008) (the trial judge erred in precluding a defendant, a member of a minority group, from questioning a government witness about his swastika tattoos); Brinson v. Walker, 547 F.3d 387, 393–95 (2d Cir. 2008) (evidence that the white complainant was a racist). *But see* U.S. v. Corbin, 73 Fed. Appx. 196 (9th Cir. 2003) (the exclusion of evidence of the arresting officer's alleged racial bias was not an abuse of discretion; the only proffered evidence was an unrelated, prior arrestee's subjective opinion); U.S. v. Willis, 43 F. Supp. 2d 873, 880–81 (N.D. Ill. 1999) (DEA agents testified at trial; there was "thin" evidence of "racial bias among other DEA personnel"; "Even assuming that racial prejudice existed, defendants have not pointed to one instance where such prejudice influenced the case"; "the lack of a link between alleged racism and concrete harm to defendants

victim sheds light on his feeling about the charge.[20] A defense witness's bias may arise from the fact that the same district attorney's office recently prosecuted one of the witness's relatives.[21] The witness's *self-interest* is evident when he is himself a party[22] or a surety on the debt sued on.[23] Similarly, it is relevant that he is being paid by a party to give evidence, even when, as in the case of an expert witness, a payment exceeding the regular witness fee is completely lawful.[24] *Self-interest* may also be shown in a criminal case when the witness testifies for the state and an indictment is pending against him,[25] the witness has not yet been

---

means the probative value of the alleged racism was substantially outweighed by the danger of sidetracking the jury and misusing time on a mini-trial on racism. . . ."); State v. Rankin, 191 N.C. App. 332, 663 S.E.2d 438, 443 (2008) (both the witness and the defendant were Muslim; the witness believed that "You're supposed to help them, assist them, if you can").

[20]Richardson v. State, 91 Tex. Crim. 318, 239 S.W. 218 (1922) (defense witness said deceased "was dead in hell, where he ought to be").

[21]U.S. v. Patterson, 68 Fed. Appx. 351 (3d Cir. 2003) (the United States Attorney's Office had recently prosecuted the son of the defense witness).

[22]Accordingly, it is held in some jurisdictions that the court, on request, must charge that the jury in weighing the party's testimony is to bear in mind his interest in the outcome. Denver City Tramway Co. v. Norton, 141 F. 599, 608 (C.C.A. 8th Cir. 1905).

[23]Southern Ry. Co. v. Bunnell, 138 Ala. 247, 36 So. 380, 383 (1903) (question whether employee witness had given indemnity bond to employer defendant, proper).

[24]Grutski v. Kline, 352 Pa. 401, 43 A.2d 142 (1945); 3A Wigmore, Evidence § 961, n. 2 (Chadbourn rev. 1970). A medical witness may be asked if the payment of his fee depends on the outcome of the case. Crowe v. Bolduc, 334 F.3d 124, 132 (1st Cir. 2003) ("Where witnesses under contingent fee arrangements are permitted to testify, examination on the contin-

gent fee is considered vital"). Most cases hold that the judge in his discretion may permit the opponent to bring out the amount of extra compensation the expert witness has received, will receive, or expects to receive. Current v. Columbia Gas of Ky., Inc., 383 S.W.2d 139 (Ky. 1964) (judge limited attack to showing that witness was paid unspecified extra compensation; affirmed); cases cited in Annot., Cross-examination of expert witness as to fees, compensation, and the like, 33 A.L.R.2d 1170. In Reed v. Philadelphia Transp. Co., 171 Pa. Super. 60, 90 A.2d 371 (1952) the judge sustained objection to the question, "How much do you expect to get paid for testifying here today?"; the ruling was held reversible error. A witness as to value may be asked how much he has received from the defendant city for similar testimony in the past year. U.S. v. Edwardo-Franco, 885 F.2d 1002, 1009–10 (2d Cir. 1989). *See also* Collins v. Wayne Corp., 621 F.2d 777 (5th Cir. 1980) (fees earned by expert in prior cases could be brought out); Graham, Impeaching the Professional Expert by a Showing of Financial Interest, 53 Ind. L.J. 35 (1977).

[25]U.S. v. Padgent, 432 F.2d 701 (2d Cir. 1970) (error to refuse to allow defense to bring out that government witness had jumped bail and was not being prosecuted for that offense); Mansfield v. Secretary, Dept. of Corrections, 601 F. Supp. 2d 1267, 1295–96 (M.D. Fla. 2009), rev'd on other grounds, 679 F.3d 1301 (11th Cir. 2012), cert. denied, 2013 WL 57319 (U.S. 2013); People v. Dillwood, 4 Cal.

charged with a crime,[26] has been promised leniency,[27] has been granted immunity,[28] is awaiting sentence,[29] is in protective custody,[30] or is an accomplice or co-indictee in the crime on trial.[31] Self-interest in an extreme form may be manifest in the witness's *corrupt* activity such as seeking to bribe another witness,[32] taking or offering to take a bribe to testify falsely,[33] or making similar

---

Unrep. 973, 39 P. 438 (Cal. 1895) (pendency of charges against witness as motive for testifying favorably to prosecution); State v. Ponthier, 136 Mont. 198, 346 P.2d 974 (1959) (same, citing many authorities); 3A Wigmore, Evidence § 967, n. 2 (Chadbourn rev. 1970). *But see* U.S. v. Thorn, 917 F.2d 170 (5th Cir. 1990) (in a federal case, the defense would have been permitted to cross-examine a prosecution witness about pending federal charges; however, the charges were pending in state court, and there was no evidence that the federal prosecutors could influence the disposition of the state charges).

The pressure to curry favor with the prosecutor is absent in a civil suit. In a collision suit where plaintiff called as witness the driver of one of the cars, it was held error to permit the defendant to impeach him by showing that he had been indicted for driving while intoxicated on the occasion in question and that the indictment was pending because of its liability to misuse as evidence of his guilt. Holden v. Berberich, 351 Mo. 995, 174 S.W.2d 791 (1943), annotated on this point. But if it had appeared that plaintiff had instigated and was controlling the prosecution of the criminal case, a different result might be warranted.

[26]U.S. v. Barrett, 766 F.2d 609 (1st Cir. 1985).

[27]Gordon v. U.S., 344 U.S. 414, 73 S. Ct. 369, 97 L. Ed. 447 (1953); U.S. v. Oliveros, 275 F.3d 1299, 1307 (11th Cir. 2001) ("When it comes to a witness' motive to lie, . . . what counts is not the actual extent of the benefit the witness has received or will receive, but the witness' belief about what he is getting. The bias of a witness is a subjective fact influenced by that wit-

ness' beliefs about the benefits he will receive if he testifies in a particular way and the value of it to him, which is measured by what he thinks will happen if he does not receive the benefit. A witness cannot be motivated to lie by something which the witness does not think will happen. The absolute truth about what Casanova received from the government and its value does not matter; what Casanova believed about it does"); Vogleson v. State, 250 Ga. App. 555, 552 S.E.2d 513 (2001) (the mandatory minimum sentence the witness was avoiding); State v. Mizzell, 349 S.C. 326, 563 S.E.2d 315 (2002) (the punishment the witness could receive if convicted).

[28]U.S. v. Walley, 567 F.3d 354, 361 (8th Cir. 2009) (a non-prosecution agreement); U.S. v. Wolfson, 437 F.2d 862 (2d Cir. 1970); Munchinski v. Wilson, 807 F. Supp. 2d 242, 287 (W.D. Pa. 2011) ("an archetypical form of impeachment evidence").

[29]Hughes v. U.S., 427 F.2d 66 (9th Cir. 1970).

[30]Alford v. U.S., 282 U.S. 687, 51 S. Ct. 218, 75 L. Ed. 624 (1931).

[31]People v. Simard, 314 Mich. 624, 23 N.W.2d 106 (1946) (defendant should have been allowed to ask state's witness if she had not been arrested for participation in same crime); 3A Wigmore, Evidence § 967 (Chadbourn rev. 1970).

[32]People v. Alcalde, 24 Cal. 2d 177, 148 P.2d 627 (1944); 3A Wigmore, Evidence § 960 (Chadbourn rev. 1970). Or writing a letter designed to intimidate another witness into giving perjured testimony. State v. Moore, 180 Or. 502, 176 P.2d 631 (1947).

[33]*See* Martin v. Barnes, 7 Wis. 239, 241–42, 1859 WL 6996 (1859)

baseless charges on other occasions.[34] The trial judge has a great deal of discretion in deciding whether particular evidence indicates bias. The large majority of published appellate decisions approve the trial judge's discretionary ruling on this score.[35]

### Foundational Question on Cross-examination[36]

At common law, most courts impose the requirement of a foundational question as in the case of impeachment by prior in-

---

(bargain between doctor-witness and plaintiff that she would pretend to be injured from fall, and they would share recovery); 3A Wigmore, Evidence § 961 (Chadbourn rev. 1970).

[34]But the cases are conflicting. *See* 3A Wigmore, Evidence § 963, note 2 (Chadbourn rev. 1970); Cross-examination of plaintiff in personal injury action as to his previous injuries, physical condition, claims, or actions, 69 A.L.R.2d 593. Among those supporting this kind of impeachment is People v. Evans, 72 Mich. 367, 40 N.W. 473 (1888) (rape upon daughter: other false charges by daughter against other men, allowed). Such charges may also evidence mental abnormality, see § 45 infra. Compare cases involving the question whether a plaintiff may be cross-examined about the previous institution of other suits and claims to show "claim-mindedness." Mintz v. Premier Cab Ass'n, 127 F.2d 744 (App. D.C. 1942) (yes); Cammarata v. Payton, 316 S.W.2d 474 (Mo. 1958) (no). See § 196 infra.

[35]*See generally* Delaware v. Van Arsdall, 475 U.S. 673, 106 S. Ct. 1431, 89 L. Ed. 2d 674 (1986) (the main and essential purpose of confrontation is to secure for the opponent the opportunity of cross-examination).

*Van Arsdall* emphasizes to a greater degree than prior decisions the trial judge's wide latitude to impose reasonable limits on cross-examination. 475 U.S. at 679 ("It does not follow, of course, that the Confrontation Clause of the Sixth Amendment prevents a trial judge from imposing any limits on defense counsel's inquiry

into the potential bias of a prosecution witness. On the contrary, trial judges retain wide latitude insofar as the Confrontation Clause is concerned to impose reasonable limits on such cross-examination based on concerns about, among other things, harassment, prejudice, confusion of the issues, the witness' safety, or interrogation that is repetitive or only marginally relevant. And as we observed earlier this Term, 'the Confrontation Clause guarantees an *opportunity* for effective cross-examination, not cross-examination that is effective in whatever way, and to whatever extent, the defense might wish.' Delaware v. Fensterer, 474 U.S. 15, 20 (1985) (per curiam) (emphasis in original).")*. See* U.S. v. Gomes, 177 F.3d 76, 81 (1st Cir. 1999) ("There was no indication that the government planned to revoke the agreement . . . ."); Swain v. Singletary, 42 F. Supp. 2d 1284 (M.D. Fla. 1999) (the charge had been dropped, the witness testified that there were no deals, and no charge was pending against the witness at the time of trial); People v. Bento, 65 Cal. App. 4th 179, 76 Cal. Rptr. 2d 412, 421 (2d Dist. 1998) (there was no evidence that the witness expected any help from the police in unrelated matters); Carpenter v. State, 979 S.W.2d 633, 639 (Tex. Crim. App. 1998) (the state trial judge properly barred questioning about federal charges; "[n]aked allegations which do no more than establish the fact that unrelated federal charges are pending do not, in and of themselves, show a potential for bias").

[36]3A Wigmore, Evidence § 964 (Chadbourn rev. 1970); Necessity and

consistent statements. Before the witness can be impeached by calling other witnesses to prove acts or declarations showing bias, the witness under attack must be asked about these facts during cross-examination.[37] There is pre-Rules federal case authority to this effect.[38] Fairness to the witness is most often cited as the reason for the requirement, but saving time by making extrinsic evidence unnecessary seems even more important. Analogizing to inconsistent statements, some courts distinguish between declarations and conduct evidencing partiality and require the preliminary question for the former but not as to the latter.[39] However, as suggested in a leading English case, words and conduct are usually intermingled in proof of partiality, and "nice and subtle distinctions" should be avoided in applying this rule.[40] It is better to require a "foundation" as to both or neither. However, even jurisdictions imposing the general requirement ought to accord the judge discretion to dispense with a foundation when matters of indisputable relationship, such as kinship, are concerned, where the foundation was overlooked and it is infeasible to recall the witness, or where other exceptional circumstances make it unfair to insist on the foundation.

At common law a minority of holdings do not require any foundational question on cross-examination of the principal witness as a preliminary to the introduction of extrinsic evidence of partiality.[41] The Federal and Uniform Rules are silent on the

---

sufficiency of foundation for discrediting evidence showing bias or prejudice of adverse witness, 87 A.L.R.2d 407; West's Key Number Digest, Witnesses ⊂⇒373; Schmertz & Czapanskiy, Bias Impeachment and the Proposed Federal Rules of Evidence, 61 Geo. L.J. 257, 262 (1972).

[37]State v. Shaw, 93 Ariz. 40, 378 P.2d 487 (1963); Washington v. U.S., 499 A.2d 95 (D.C. 1985); People v. Payton, 72 Ill. App. 2d 240, 218 N.E.2d 518 (5th Dist. 1966); Necessity and sufficiency of foundation for discrediting evidence showing bias or prejudice of adverse witness, 87 A.L.R.2d 407.

As in the case of inconsistent statements, the preliminary question about declarations showing partiality should call attention to time, place, and persons involved. See State v. Harmon, 21 Wash. 2d 581, 152 P.2d 314 (1944). See cases cited in Necessity and sufficiency of foundation for

discrediting evidence showing bias or prejudice of adverse witness, 87 A.L.R.2d 407.

[38]U.S. v. Harvey, 547 F.2d 720 (2d Cir. 1976) (foundation questions held sufficient); U.S. v. Marzano, 537 F.2d 257 (7th Cir. 1976) (reviewing prior federal cases)

[39]Necessity and sufficiency of foundation for discrediting evidence showing bias or prejudice of adverse witness, 87 A.L.R.2d 407; Schmertz & Czapanskiy, Bias Impeachment and the Proposed Federal Rules of Evidence, 61 Geo. L.J. 257, 265–69 (1972).

[40]See the excerpt from the opinion of Abbott, C.J. in Queen's Case, (1820) 2 Brod. & Bing. 284, 129 Eng. Rep. 976, 1820 WL 2043 (C.C.P.).

[41]Kidd v. People, 97 Colo. 480, 51 P.2d 1020 (1935) (witness's threat to "pin something on" another witness

subject. The discretion granted the judge in Rule 611(a)[42] is adequate authority to follow the same practice for partiality as that employed for prior inconsistent statements under Rule 613(b). However, given Rule 402, the judge could not announce the practice as a categorical, invariable requirement. Yet, she has discretion to require a foundation if the specific facts of the instant case warranted. Following the traditional method for impeachment by a prior inconsistent statement,[43] on cross-examination the witness under attack would first be asked about the acts or statements supposedly showing bias.

*Cross-examination and Extrinsic Evidence; Main Circumstances*

As we have seen, in many states the impeacher must inquire about the facts of partiality on cross-examination as the first step in impeachment. If the witness fully admits the facts, the impeacher should not be allowed to prolong the attack by calling other witnesses to the admitted facts.[44] At the very least, when the main circumstances from which the partiality proceeds have been proven, the trial judge has a discretion to determine how far the details may be probed, whether on cross-examination or by other witnesses.[45] After all, impeachment is not relevant to the historical merits of the case. Although he may not deny a reasonable opportunity at either stage to prove the witness's bias, the

---

unless he testified for the state); Necessity and sufficiency of foundation for discrediting evidence showing bias or prejudice of adverse witness, 87 A.L.R.2d 407.

[42]Former Fed. R. Evid. 611(a) and Unif. R. Evid. 611(a) provide:

The court shall exercise reasonable control over the mode and order of interrogating witnesses and presenting evidence so as to (1) make the interrogation and presentation effective for the ascertainment of the truth, (2) avoid needless consumption of time, and (3) protect witnesses from harassment or undue embarrassment.

Effective December 1, 2011, restyled Fed. R. Evid. 611(a) reads:

Control by the Court; Purposes. The court should exercise reasonable control over the mode and order of examining witnesses and presenting evidence so as to: (1) make those procedures effective for determining the truth; (2) avoid wasting time; and (3) protect wit-

nesses from harassment or undue embarrassment.

[43]See § 37 supra.

[44]This is the prevailing holding as to inconsistent statements, see § 37 supra, and similar reasons apply here, pro and con.

[45]People v. Dye, 356 Mich. 271, 96 N.W.2d 788 (1959) (trial court allowed examination into details; approved); Dods v. Harrison, 51 Wash. 2d 446, 319 P.2d 558 (1957) (trial court's refusal to permit examination as to details upheld); 3A Wigmore, Evidence § 951, note 2 (Chadbourn rev. 1970). A few courts have held that if the witness admits bias in general terms, the admission precludes further inquiry. *E.g.*, Walker v. State, 74 Ga. App. 48, 39 S.E.2d 75, 77 (1946); 3A Wigmore, Evidence § 951 n. 2 (Chadbourn rev. 1970).

trial judge has a discretion to control the extent of the proof.[46] He
has the responsibility to see that the sideshow does not take over
the circus. Several cases decided under the Federal Rules of Evidence confirm the existence of this discretion.[47] The discretion follows from the trial judge's power to "exercise reasonable control"
under the terms of Rule 611(a).[48]

Yet, if the witness on cross-examination denies or does not
fully admit the facts claimed to show bias, the attacker has a legitimate need to prove those facts by extrinsic evidence. In
courtroom parlance, facts showing bias are considered so highly
probative of credibility that they are never deemed "collateral";[49]
the cross-examiner is not required to "take the answer" of the
witness[50] but may call other witnesses to prove them.[51] There are
similar holdings under the Federal Rules of Evidence.[52]

---

[46]People v. Lustig, 206 N.Y. 162,
99 N.E. 183, 186 (1912) (extent of
testimony by other witnesses in court's
discretion). *See also* Marcus v. City of
Pittsburgh, 415 Pa. 252, 203 A.2d 317
(1964) (trial judge abused discretion
by permitting examination about prejudicial detail that was not impeaching); Glass v. Bosworth, 113 Vt. 303,
34 A.2d 113 (1943) (wide scope on
cross-examination in court's discretion).

[47]U. S. v. Hawkins, 661 F.2d 436
(5th Cir. 1981) (prosecution witnesses
who were examined about state of
mind while in foreign jails did not
have to be questioned about conditions
in the jails because the jury was adequately informed about states of
mind which were relevant to the issue
of bias for the government); U.S. v.
Singh, 628 F.2d 758 (2d Cir. 1980)
(similar test applied); U.S. v. Salsedo,
607 F.2d 318 (9th Cir. 1979) (defendant was denied inquiry into witness's
additional work for Drug Enforcement
Administration; test was whether jury
already had sufficient information to
appraise witness's bias and motives);
U.S. v. Diecidue, 603 F.2d 535 (5th
Cir. 1979) (probative value of additional evidence held very slight); U.S.
v. Fitzgerald, 579 F.2d 1014 (7th Cir.
1978) ("But a trial court has wide
discretion to limit cross-examination,
particularly when further cross-

examination into the witness' subjective thoughts would not be meaningful
because of previous testimony revealing the witness' bias.").

[48]See this section, note 42 supra.

[49]Smith v. Hockenberry, 146 Mich.
7, 109 N.W. 23, 24 (1906); State v.
Day, 339 Mo. 74, 95 S.W.2d 1183, 1184
(1936); Broadhead, Why Bias Is Never
Collateral: The Impeachment and
Rehabilitation of Witnesses in Criminal Cases, 27 Am. J. Trial Advoc. 235
(2003).

[50]Smith v. U.S., 283 F.2d 16 (6th
Cir. 1960) (dictum); 3A Wigmore,
Evidence § 1005(b), (c) (Chadbourn
rev. 1970). See references to "taking
the answer" in § 36 supra and §§ 45
and 49 infra.

[51]Smith v. Hornkohl, 166 Neb.
702, 90 N.W.2d 347 (1958) (dictum);
3A Wigmore, Evidence § 943 (Chadbourn rev. 1970).

[52]U.S. v. Abel, 469 U.S. 45, 52,
105 S. Ct. 465, 83 L. Ed. 2d 450 (1984)
("The 'common law of evidence' allowed the showing of bias by extrinsic
evidence, while requiring the cross-examiner to 'take the answer of the
witness' with respect to less favored
forms of impeachment."); U.S. v.
Delgado, 635 F.2d 889 (7th Cir. 1981);
U.S. v. Noti, 731 F.2d 610, 613 (9th
Cir. 1984) ("Evidence that happens to
include prior misconduct may be ad-

## § 40   Character: In general

The witness's character for truthfulness or mendacity is relevant circumstantial evidence on the question of the truthfulness of the witness's testimony. The fact that the witness previously engaged in deception tends to show the witness has a character trait for untruthfulness, and in turn the existence of that character trait at least slightly increases the probability that the witness lied during his testimony. The topic of character impeachment raises several questions, notably: In any particular situation, when does the danger of unfair prejudice against the witness and the party calling her from this type of impeachment outweigh the probative value of the light shed on credibility? Should character-impeachment be limited to an attack on the particular trait of truthfulness, or should it extend to "general" character for its undoubted, albeit more remote, bearing on truthfulness?[1]

The growing tendency is to use this form of attack more sparingly. The empirical studies of untruthfulness indicate that a person's general character trait for truthfulness is a poor predictor of whether she is untruthful on a specific occasion.[2] It was part of the melodrama of the pioneer trial to find "the villain of

---

missible, however, when it is offered to show the witness' possible bias or self-interest in testifying. Burr v. Sullivan, 618 F.2d 583, 586–87 (9th Cir. 1980). In such a case, the adverse party does not have to accept the witness' testimony, but may offer extrinsic evidence to rebut it."). *See also* Hale, Bias as Affecting Credibility, 1 Hastings L.J. 1 (1949) ("Evidence of bias is considered of such value that the existence of facts, implicit of it may be ascertained either by cross-examination or by extrinsic testimony. Considerations of auxiliary policy, such as surprise or collateral issue, have not been deemed relatively sufficient to limit the method of proof.").

Evidence showing lack of partiality is also non-collateral. See § 49 infra. *See also* U.S. v. Fusco, 748 F.2d 996, 998 (5th Cir. 1984) ("Because evidence of bias or lack of bias is substantive, rather than collateral, it may be developed on direct examination, as well as cross-examination, just like any other substantive evidence.").

Unlike impeachment prior conviction and prior inconsistent state-

ment upon a non-collateral matter, there is no obligation to later introduce extrinsic evidence if the witness fails to admit on cross-examination the matter asserted.

**[Section 40]**

[1]See the general discussion of relevancy and its counterweights in Ch. 16 infra, and of the relevancy of character evidence in various other situations in Ch. 17 infra.

[2]Lawson, Credibility and Character: A Different Look at an Interminable Problem, 50 Notre Dame L. Rev. 758, 779–85 (1975) (one leading study of the supposed consistency between the character trait and conduct on particular occasions found that "the most striking thing . . . is the amount of inconsistency exhibited"); Mendez, California's New Law on Character Evidence: Evidence Code Section 352 and the Impact of Recent Psychological Studies, 31 U.C.L.A. L. Rev. 1003 (1984) (challenging the psychological trait theory and surveying the empirical research supporting the competing situationist theory);

the piece." In all of Perry Mason's trials, he established his client's innocence by unmasking the real culprit. It fits less comfortably into the more realistic, businesslike atmosphere of the modern courtroom. Moreover, as a method of advocacy, the danger to the attacker is great if the attack misses its mark or is pressed too far. The jurors naturally sympathize with the witness, and the attacker should not level this accusation unless he has "the goods" on the witness. In this situation, the attack can easily backfire, and the jurors may resent the attacker. Finally, the legal ethics rules reinforce the trial advocacy lesson; lawyers must be conscious of their duty not to ask a question that the lawyer realizes is relevant only to degrade a witness.[3] For that matter, restyled Federal Rule 611(a)(3) directs the trial judge to protect the witness from "undue embarrassment."

## § 41   Character: Misconduct, for which there has been no criminal conviction[1]

The methods of proving a witness's character trait for untruthfulness include prior convictions (discussed in § 42) and proof of untruthful acts which have not resulted in a conviction, the subject of this section. As we shall see, evidence of prior convictions is more liberally admissible than the latter type of proof of bad character for truthfulness. The differential treatment of the two types of evidence is justifiable. To begin with, when the witness has already been convicted of the act, there is strong evidence[2] that the witness in fact committed the act calling his credibility into issue. Moreover, the availability of the written judgment of conviction reduces the risk that there will be a time-consuming, potentially distracting dispute over the question of whether the witness committed the act. In terms of the policy considerations recognized in Federal Rule of Evidence 403, there is a much stronger case for permitting conviction impeachment.

Yet, the English common law tradition of "cross-examination to credit" permits counsel to broadly inquire about the witness's as-

---

Spector, Rule 609: A Last Plea for Its Withdrawal, 32 Okla. L. Rev. 334, 351–53 (1979).

[3]*See* American Bar Association, Code of Professional Responsibility, Disciplinary Rule 7-106(C) (2), p. 88 (1969). Although the language of Model Rule 3.4 is not as explicit, its wording is broad enough to be construed as prohibiting this type of misconduct. *See also* Cal. Bus. & Prof. Code § 6068(f): "To advance no fact prejudicial to the honor or reputation of a party or witness, unless required by the justice of the cause with which he or she is charged."

**[Section 41]**

[1]3A   Wigmore,   Evidence §§ 981–87 (Chadbourn rev. 1970); 4 Weinstein's Federal Evidence § 608.12 (rev. 2011); West's Key Number Digest, Witnesses ☞344, 349.

[2]Note, Evidence of Other Crimes in Montana, 30 Mont. L. Rev. 235, 238 (1969) ("the strongest proof").

sociations and personal history including any misconduct tending to discredit his character, even though it has not been the subject of a conviction.[3] In the common law tradition the English courts trusted the bar's disciplined discretion to avoid abuse.[4] In this country, there is a confusing variety of decisions, occasionally even in the same jurisdiction. At present, however, the majority of courts limit the cross-examination attack on character to acts which have a significant relation to the witness's credibility.[5] By its terms, Federal Rule 608(b) permits the cross-examiner to inquire about acts which relevant only to "the witness's character [trait] for . . . untruthfulness. . . ."[6] However, a minority of courts permit a broader attack on character by wide-ranging

---

[3]3A Wigmore, Evidence §§ 983–86 (Chadbourn rev. 1970); Phipson, Evidence §§ 541, 1551–52 (10th ed. 1963).

The misconduct need not be criminal. U.S. v. Bagaric, 706 F.2d 42, 65 (2d Cir. 1983) ("[I]t is clear that the prior misconduct need not have created criminal liability or resulted in a conviction.").

[4]See quotations from Stephen and Birkenhead in 3A Wigmore, Evidence § 983 (Chadbourn rev. 1970); and 13 Halsbury's Laws of England, Evidence § 836 (2d ed. 1934) ("There are, also, certain limits, which must be determined by the discretion of the judge to the questions which may be asked affecting a witness's credit . . . .").

[5]Vogel v. Sylvester, 148 Conn. 666, 174 A.2d 122 (1961); Schreiberg v. Southern Coatings & Chemical Co., 231 S.C. 69, 97 S.E.2d 214 (1957).

[6]State v. Greer, 39 Ohio St. 3d 236, 530 N.E.2d 382 (1988) (evidence of a parole violation). Former Fed. R. Evid. 608(b) provided:

Specific instances of the conduct of a witness, for the purpose of attacking or supporting the witness' credibility, other than conviction of crime as provided in rule 609, may not be proved by extrinsic evidence. They may, however, in the discretion of the court, if probative of truthfulness or untruthfulness, be inquired into on cross-examination of the witness (1) concerning the witness' character for truthfulness or untruthfulness, or (2)

concerning the character for truthfulness or untruthfulness of another witness as to which character the witness being cross-examined has testified.

The giving of testimony, whether by an accused or by any other witness, does not operate as a waiver of his privilege against self-incrimination when examined with respect to matters which relate only to credibility.

Effective December 1, 2011, restyled Fed. R. Evid. 608(b) reads:

Specific Instances of Conduct. Except for a criminal conviction under Rule 609, extrinsic evidence is not admissible to prove specific instances of a witness's conduct in order to attack or support the witness's character for truthfulness. But the court may, on cross-examination, allow them to be inquired into if they are probative of the character for truthfulness or untruthfulness of:

  (1)  the witness; or

  (2)  another witness whose character the witness being cross-examined has testified about.

By testifying on another matter, a witness does not waive the privilege against self-incrimination for testimony that relates only to the witness's character for truthfulness.

Although Unif. R. Evid. 608(b) is lengthier than Federal Rule 608(b), the Uniform provision is essentially identical in content. See U.S. v. Cluck, 544 F.2d 195 (5th Cir. 1976) (extrinsic evidence of arrest and of crimes inadmissible).

Conduct satisfying this standard will normally involve dishonesty or false statement, i.e., active misrep-

cross-examination about acts of misconduct which show bad

---

resentation, as employed in Rule 609(a)(2). See § 42 infra. *E.g.*, U.S. v. Bayard, 642 F.3d 59, 63 (1st Cir. 2011), cert. denied, 131 S. Ct. 2944, 180 L. Ed. 2d 235 (2011) (use of the victim's credit cards); U.S. v. Weekes, 611 F.3d 68 (1st Cir. 2010), cert. denied, 131 S. Ct. 3021, 180 L. Ed. 2d 850 (2011) (use of false social security numbers); U.S. v. Whitmore, 359 F.3d 609, 619–20 (D.C. Cir. 2004) ("the witness has previously lied under oath"); Young v. James Green Management, Inc., 327 F.3d 616 (7th Cir. 2003) ("Stealing is probative Hynes v. Coughlin, 79 F.3d 285 (2d Cir. 1996) (the witness's incredible testimony at a deportation proceeding); U.S. v. Sherlin, 67 F.3d 1208, 1214–15 (6th Cir. 1995) (admitted lies); U.S. v. Veras, 51 F.3d 1365 (7th Cir. 1995) (a police officer's fraud in handling funds used to pay informants); U.S. v. Williams, 986 F.2d 86 (4th Cir. 1993) (possession of false identification); U.S. v. Farias-Farias, 925 F.2d 805 (5th Cir. 1991) (a lie to a customs agent); U.S. v. Beros, 833 F.2d 455 (3d Cir. 1987) (lie about marital status on a Nevada marriage license application); U.S. v. Amahia, 825 F.2d 177, 181 (8th Cir. 1987) ("Rule 608(b) will permit inquiry into the specific acts which may have led to an arrest if those acts related to *crimen falsi,* e.g., perjury, subornation of perjury, false statement, embezzlement, false pretense."); U.S. v. Fulk, 816 F.2d 1202 (7th Cir. 1987) (fact that defendant's chiropractor's license had been suspended for deceptive practices was probative of truthfulness); U.S. v. Page, 808 F.2d 723 (10th Cir. 1987) (acts admissible under Rule 608(b) include forgery, uttering forged instruments, bribery, suppression of evidence, false pretenses, cheating, and embezzlement); Andrade v. Walgreens-Optioncare, Inc., 784 F. Supp. 2d 533, 535–36 (E.D. Pa. 2011) (misrepresenting a Social Security number on an employment form); State v. Guenther, 181 N.J. 129, 854 A.2d 308 (2004) (the victim-witness has

made a prior false criminal accusation); State v. Clark, 2009 UT App 252, 219 P.3d 631 (Utah Ct. App. 2009) (a defendant may be entitled to an evidentiary hearing to determine the admissibility of a prior accusation of sexual abuse by the alleged victim if there is a legitimate reason to question the veracity of the prior accusation; however, there is no right to such a hearing absent a legitimate doubt). *See* Young v. James Green Management, Inc., 327 F.3d 616 (7th Cir. 2003) ("Stealing is probative of untruthfulness . . . ."); U.S. v. Simonelli, 237 F.3d 19 (1st Cir. 2001) (altering company time records and inflating bills to company clients); U.S. v. Munoz, 233 F.3d 1117 (9th Cir. 2000) (defendant's participation in a sale and lease-back scheme); U.S. v. Miles, 207 F.3d 988, 993 (7th Cir. 2000) (a witness's threats of violence which were intended to influence people's testimony against him); U.S. v. Manske, 186 F.3d 770 (7th Cir. 1999) (a witness's threats of violence against a person who might incriminate the witness called the witness's truthfulness into question); U.S. v. Davis, 183 F.3d 231 (3d Cir. 1999) (the defendant's misappropriation of police department gasoline for his personal car and the use of a false name); U.S. v. Willis, 43 F. Supp. 2d 873, 881 (N.D. Ill. 1999) (theft), aff'd sub nom. U.S. v. Martin, 248 F.3d 1161 (7th Cir. 2000); State v. West, 95 Haw. 452, 24 P.3d 648 (2001) (an accusation if the accusation is shown to be false). *See also* U.S. v. Fernandez, 353 Fed. Appx. 363, 373–74 (11th Cir. 2009) (a sexual relationship with an underage woman); U.S. v. Kenyon, 481 F.3d 1054, 1063–64 (8th Cir. 2007) (the trial judge did not err in refusing to allow the defendant to cross-examine the complainant about her prior allegedly false claims that a schoolmate and her uncle had sex with her; "A.L. 'May have been talking with other seventh graders about claimed sexual activities.' Since the alleged accusations were never made to an au-

moral character and have only an attenuated relation to credibility.[7] Finally, at the other extreme, a few jurisdictions

thority figure, the [trial] court reasoned, they amounted at most to childish gossip . . . ."); Tibbs v. Allen, 486 F. Supp. 2d 188, 195–96 (D. Mass. 2007) (under Massachusetts law, in rape cases, evidence of the complainant's false accusations "is admissible . . . only when there is a pattern of false accusations"); Winfred D. v. Michelin North America, Inc., 165 Cal. App. 4th 1011, 81 Cal. Rptr. 3d 756, 771–75 (2d Dist. 2008) (just as evidence of a woman's unchaste behavior is not admissible on the issue of credibility unless it shows bias, a man's sexual misconduct is generally inadmissible to impeach his credibility; evidence of illicit, intimate conduct is ordinarily not appropriate on the issue of a witness's credibility). *But see* U.S. v. Jeffers, 402 Fed. Appx. 601, 603 (2d Cir. 2010) (prior acts of violence); U.S. v. Johnson, 64 Fed. Appx. 596 (8th Cir. 2003) (it was proper to bar cross-examination of a police officer about domestic conflicts with his wife and police disciplinary actions); U.S. v. Meserve, 271 F.3d 314 (1st Cir. 2001) (assaultive conduct does not qualify); U.S. v. Miles, 207 F.3d 988 (7th Cir. 2000) (a witness's inadvertent failure to obey a gun-registration ordinance does not constitute deceptive conduct); Mason, The Use of Immigration Status in Cross-Examination of Witnesses: Scope, Limits, Objections, 33 Am. J. Trial Adv. 549 (2010) (although the courts should permit inquiry about specific instances of dishonest conduct such as the use of false documents, without more the witness's status as an illegal immigrant is not probative of untruthfulness); Zeigler, Harmonizing Rules 609 and 608(b) of the Federal Rules of Evidence, 2003 Utah L. Rev. 635, 666–67 ("Courts are . . . inconsistent in applying Rule 608(b). Commentators point out that courts take three different approaches. Courts taking the broad approach believe that 'virtually any conduct indicating bad

character also indicates untruthfulness.' Under the narrow approach, misconduct bears on truthfulness only if it directly involves lying or deception. Finally, under the middle approach, 'behavior seeking personal advantage by taking from others in violation of their rights' is seen as bearing on truthfulness. These positions have led courts to inconsistent rulings on the admissibility of such misconduct as theft, drug use, prostitution, bribery, fraud, and the use of excessive force).

Since the logical relevance of the evidence consists in the light which it sheds on the witness's willingness to testify truthfully at trial, in the case of a witness who is also a criminal defendant it is immaterial that the act occurred after the alleged crime. U.S. v. Chevalier, 1 F.3d 581, 584 (7th Cir. 1993). To make it even clearer that the focus is on the character trait for untruthfulness, the first and last sentences of Rule 608(b) were amended in 2003. In both sentences, the amendment deletes the term "credibility" and substitutes the expression, "character trait for truthfulness."

[7]Crenshaw v. Superintendent of Five Points Correctional Facility, 372 F. Supp. 2d 361 (W.D. N.Y. 2005) (under New York law, the trial judge has broad discretion in deciding whether to permit impeachment by inquiry about immoral, vicious, or criminal acts); People v. Sorge, 301 N.Y. 198, 93 N.E.2d 637 (1950); State v. Greer, 39 Ohio St. 3d 236, 530 N.E.2d 382 (1988) (evidence of a parole violation); State v. Jones, 215 Tenn. 206, 385 S.W.2d 80 (1964). *See* Right to impeach accused as a witness by proof of general bad moral character or reputation, 90 A.L.R. 870. The conduct need not be criminal. People v. Johnston, 228 N.Y. 332, 127 N.E. 186 (1920) (sending money to an accused prisoner for him to buy witnesses). The fact that the witness has been

altogether prohibit cross-examination as to acts of misconduct for impeachment purposes; the cross-examiner must have a conviction.[8] This latter view is arguably preferable given the dangers of prejudice (particularly if the witness is a party), of distraction and confusion, of abuse by asking unfounded questions, and the difficulties, as demonstrated in the appellate cases, of determining whether particular acts relate to character for truthfulness.[9]

This impeachment technique should be distinguished from showing conduct which indicates bias, conduct as an admission, and conduct for impeachment by contradiction. Those doctrines are analyzed in other sections of this treatise.[10]

In this country, the dangers of victimizing witnesses and of undue prejudice to the parties have led most courts permitting this character-impeachment technique to recognize that the trial judge has discretionary control over cross-examination concerning acts of misconduct.[11] To emphasize the existence of that control, the former version of Rule 608(b) expressly used the

---

dishonorably discharged from the Army was held so doubtful in its implications about "moral character" as to warrant the judge, in discretion, to exclude the inquiry. Kelley v. State, 226 Ind. 148, 78 N.E.2d 547 (1948).

[8]Com. v. Ornato, 191 Pa. Super. 581, 159 A.2d 223 (1960); Christie v. Brewer, 374 S.W.2d 908 (Tex. Civ. App. Austin 1964); Sparks v. State, 366 S.W.2d 591 (Tex. Crim. App. 1963). Statutes in some states prohibit the showing of acts of misconduct for impeachment. *E.g.*, Idaho Code Ann. § 9-1302; Cal. Evid. Code § 787; N.J.R.E. 608 (the New Jersey rule omits subdivision (b) of the federal rule); Or. Evid. Code 40.350, Rule 608(1)(b). Cal. Evid. Code § 787 is still in full force and effect in civil actions in that state. However, it has been overridden by an initiative measure applicable to criminal cases in that jurisdiction. People v. Harris, 47 Cal. 3d 1047, 255 Cal. Rptr. 352, 767 P.2d 619, 640–42 (1989).

[9]Former Uniform Rule 22(d) provides that "evidence of specific instances of his conduct relevant only as tending to prove a trait of his character, shall be inadmissible." For the text of the Rev. Unif. R. Evid. (1974) 608(b),

see this section note 6 supra. Another kindred theory, distinguishable from misconduct showing character, is the one that on cross-examination the examiner is entitled to place the witness in his setting by establishing his residence and occupation. See § 29, supra. As to whether this principle permits questions about a disreputable occupation, see cases pro and con collected in West's Key Number Digest, Witnesses ☞344(4); Right to inquire of witness as to his or her occupation for purposes of impeachment, 1 A.L.R. 1402.

[10]See § 39 supra re partiality, §§ 261 to 267 infra regarding admissions by conduct, and § 45 infra regarding impeachment by contradiction. Inconsistent conduct is yet another subject. See § 37 supra. *See* U.S. v. Hodnett, 537 F.2d 828 (5th Cir. 1976) (certain misconduct admitted to show bias).

[11]People v. Sorge, 301 N.Y. 198, 93 N.E.2d 637 (1950) (in abortion prosecution, accused properly cross-examined as to previous abortions; manner and extent in judge's discretion); State v. Neal, 222 N.C. 546, 23 S.E.2d 911 (1943) (accused in murder case properly asked about previous

phrase, "in the discretion of the court." Some of the factors that sway discretion are: (1) whether the witness's testimony is crucial or unimportant, (2) the relevancy of the act of misconduct to truthfulness,[12] (3) the nearness or remoteness of the misconduct to the time of trial,[13] (4) whether the matter inquired into is likely to lead to time-consuming, distracting explanations on cross-examination or re-examination,[14] and (5) whether there will be unfair humiliation of the witness and undue prejudice to the party who called the witness.[15] Of course, here too the cross-examiner must have a good faith basis in fact for the inquiry.[16]

In the formative period of evidence law, some courts recognized,

---

cutting affrays, larceny, vagrancy, nuisance and violation of the prohibition law, in judge's "sound discretion"). Fed. R. Evid. and Unif. R. Evid. 608(b), quoted in note 6 supra, specifically grant the judge discretion. *E.g.*, U.S. v. Nogueira, 585 F.2d 23 (1st Cir. 1978). Rules 403, 608(b), and 611(a) should be taken into account.

[12]See notes 5–7, supra. Illustrating Fed. R. Evid. 608(b), *see* Tigges v. Cataldo, 611 F.2d 936 (1st Cir. 1979); U.S. v. Estell, 539 F.2d 697 (10th Cir. 1976) (under the rule judge would have discretion to reject evidence that witness stole meat and passed worthless checks because such matters were not probative of truthfulness).

[13]U.S. v. McClintic, 570 F.2d 685, 691 n.6 (8th Cir. 1978) ("An incident's remoteness in time is no longer an explicit factor under Rule 608(b). . . . Nevertheless, remoteness in time remains a consideration relevant to the evidence's probative value."); U.S. v. Cox, 536 F.2d 65 (5th Cir. 1976).

[14]*See* Robinson v. Atterbury, 135 Conn. 517, 66 A.2d 593 (1949).

These considerations as well as the factor of undue prejudice may be taken into account under Fed. R. Evid. and Rev. Unif. R. Evid. (1974) 403.

[15]*See* U.S. v. Kizer, 569 F.2d 504 (9th Cir. 1978). Fed. R. Evid. and Rev. Unif. R. Evid. (1974) 403 and 611(a) are applicable. *See generally* State v. Morgan, 315 N.C. 626, 340 S.E.2d 84, 89–90 (1986) ("Rule 608(b) addresses the admissibility of specific instances of conduct (as opposed to opinion or

reputation evidence) only in the very narrow instance where (1) the *purpose* of producing the evidence is to impeach or enhance credibility by proving that the witness' conduct indicates his character for truthfulness or untruthfulness; and (2) the conduct in question *is in fact probative* of truthfulness or untruthfulness and is not too remote in time; and (3) the conduct in question *did not result in a conviction;* and (4) the inquiry into the conduct *takes place during cross-examination.* If the proffered evidence meets these four enumerated prerequisites, before admitting the evidence the trial judge must determine, in his discretion, pursuant to Rule 403, that the probative value of the evidence is not outweighed by the risk of unfair prejudice, confusion of issues or misleading the jury, and that the questioning will not harass or unduly embarrass the witness. Even if the trial judge allows the inquiry on cross-examination, extrinsic evidence of the conduct is not admissible. N.C.G.S. § 8C-1, Rule 608(b) and Commentary.").

[16]See § 49 infra. *See also* U.S. v. McBride, 862 F.2d 1316, 1320 (8th Cir. 1988) ("[T]he prosecutor may not, by innuendo, attack a witness' credibility by asking about a witness' criminal conduct when the prosecutor has no basis for the question.").

In the court's discretion counsel may be required to disclose his good faith basis outside the jury's presence prior to cross-examination. Michelson v. U.S., 335 U.S. 469, 472, 69 S. Ct. 213, 93 L. Ed. 168 (1948) ("The trial

as a sort of corollary of the privilege against self-incrimination, a witness's privilege not to answer questions calling for answers which would degrade or disgrace him when the questions were irrelevant to the historical merits in the case.[17] Though sporadically recognized during the 1800s,[18] today that privilege has been generally abandoned,[19] except as it is preserved by the codes of a few states.[20] Assume arguendo that the forum state still recognizes the privilege. Even in such a jurisdiction, although the privilege affords the witness some protection, the protection is not as effective as that afforded by a rule altogether prohibiting such cross-examination; the privilege must be claimed by the witness, and a claim in open court is almost as degrading as an affirmative answer. Taking an intermediate position, Federal and Uniform Rule of Evidence 611(a) gives the court discretion to prevent harassment or embarrassment of witnesses when they are cross-examined about acts of misconduct.[21]

In jurisdictions permitting character impeachment by proof of misconduct for which there has been no conviction, there is an important safeguard. The safeguard is the accepted rule limiting proof to intrinsic impeachment, that is, cross-examination. Thus,

---

court asked counsel for the prosecution, out of the presence of the jury, 'Is it a fact according to the best information in your possession, that Michelson was arrested for receiving stolen goods?' Counsel replied that it was, and to support his good faith exhibited a paper record which defendant's counsel did not challenge."); U.S. v. Crippen, 570 F.2d 535, 538 (5th Cir. 1978) ("In a recorded colloquy with counsel, the trial judge made certain that there was a factual basis for the attempted impeachment, as there was in the defendant's own statements to the grand jury in the four pages of the transcript then admitted."); Graham, Evidence and Trial Advocacy Workshop, 21 Crim. L. Bull. 495, 510–11 (1985). *But see* U.S. v. Davis, 609 F.3d 663, 680–81 (5th Cir. 2010), cert. denied, 131 S. Ct. 1676, 179 L. Ed. 2d 621 (2011) ("but "[t]hat does not mean that the basis in fact must be proved as a fact before a good faith inquiry can be made").

[17]*See* 3A Wigmore, Evidence §§ 984, 986(3) (Chadbourn rev. 1970).

[18]*See* 3A Wigmore, Evidence § 986(3) n. 13, § 987 (Chadbourn rev.

1970).

[19]Among decisions rejecting the privilege are State v. Carter, 1 Ariz. App. 57, 399 P.2d 191 (1965) (subject to court's discretion); Wallace v. State, 41 Fla. 547, 26 So. 713, 722 (1899); State v. Pfefferle, 36 Kan. 90, 12 P. 406, 408 (1886) (degrading character of question only a factor for judge's discretion); Carroll v. State, 32 Tex. Crim. 431, 24 S.W. 100 (1893).

[20]Ga. Code Ann. § 24-5-505(a); Utah Code Ann. § 78B-1-134(1).

[21]U.S. v. Marchesani, 457 F.2d 1291 (6th Cir. 1972). Fed. R. Evid. 611(a) and Unif. R. Evid. 611(a) provide, "The court shall exercise reasonable control over the mode and order of interrogating witnesses and presenting of evidence so as to . . . (3) protect witnesses from harassment or undue embarrassment." Effective December 1, 2011, restyled Fed. R. Evid. 611(a)(3) reads that "[t]he court shall exercise reasonable control over mode and order of examining witnesses and presenting evidence so as to . . . protect witnesses from harassment and undue embarrassment."

if the witness stands his ground and denies the alleged misconduct, the examiner must ordinarily[22] "take his answer." That expression does not mean that the cross-examiner may not press further to extract an admission,[23] for instance, by reminding the witness of the penalties for perjury. Rather, it means that the cross-examiner may not later call other witnesses to prove the discrediting acts.[24] This limitation is incorporated in Federal Rule of Evidence 608(b).[25] On the one hand, on cross-examination, the questioner should ask the witness directly and bluntly whether he committed the untruthful act. It is improper to inquire whether the witness was "fired," "disciplined," or "demoted" for the alleged act—those terms smuggle into the record implied hearsay statements by third parties who may lack personal knowledge.[26] On the other hand, if the witness himself authored

---

[22]Suppose that the "witness" being impeached is a hearsay declarant. The impeaching party has no opportunity to question the declarant about the impeaching act. In this situation, some courts hold that Federal Rule of Evidence 806 overrides the restriction on extrinsic evidence. U.S. v. Washington, 263 F. Supp. 2d 413, 423 (D. Conn. 2003) (noting the split of authority); Hornstein, On the Horns of an Evidentiary Dilemma: The Intersection of Federal Rules of Evidence 806 and 608(b), 56 Ark. L. Rev. 543 (2003).

[23]People v. Sorge, 301 N.Y. 198, 93 N.E.2d 637 (1950) (when witness denies, examiner in good faith may question further in hope of inducing witness to change answer). But the judge has discretion to limit further exploration of the matter. U.S. v. Bright, 630 F.2d 804 (5th Cir. 1980).

[24]U.S. v. Mahdi, 598 F.3d 883, 893 n.11 (D.C. Cir. 2010); State v. Bowman, 232 N.C. 374, 61 S.E.2d 107 (1950) (improper for state to attack credibility of defendant's witness by calling other witnesses to testify to her acts of misconduct); 3A Wigmore, Evidence § 979 (Chadbourn rev. 1970). See also § 49 infra.

[25]U.S. v. Abel, 469 U.S. 45, 55, 105 S. Ct. 465, 83 L. Ed. 2d 450 (1984) (Rule 608(b) "limits the inquiry to cross-examination of the witness, however, and prohibits the cross-examiner

from introducing extrinsic evidence of the witness' past conduct.").

As to preservation for appeal of alleged error with respect to a ruling on a motion in limine permitting use of a prior act of misconduct to impeach, see § 52 infra. at notes 23 to 27.

[26]Young v. James Green Management, Inc., 327 F.3d 616, 626 n.7 (7th Cir. 2003); U.S. v. Davis, 183 F.3d 231, 257 n.12 (3d Cir. 1999); State v. Mosley, 667 S.W.2d 767, 770–71 (Tenn. Crim. App. 1983); Saltzburg, Impeaching the Witness: Prior Bad Acts and Extrinsic Evidence, 7 Crim. Just. 28, 31 (Wint. 1993) ("counsel should not be permitted to circumvent the no-extrinsic-evidence provision by tucking a third person's opinion about prior acts into a question asked of the witness who has denied the act"). But see U.S. v. DeSantis, 134 F.3d 760 (6th Cir. 1998) (administrative agency finding); Schmertz, Article VI, in Emerging Problems Under the Federal Rules of Evidence 115, 162 (3d ed. 1998) (there is a "disturbing" trend in the cases permitting "counsel to ask witnesses who have already denied the bad conduct whether third parties have expressed their belief that the witness has engaged in the bad acts"; U.S. v. Whitehead, 618 F.2d 523 (4th Cir. 1980) ruled that the cross-examiner could question a defendant about his suspension from the practice of law).

The Advisory Committee Note

a writing mentioning the act, by the better view it is permissible for the cross-examiner to confront the witness with the writing.[27] The principal rationale for the collateral fact rule is that the presentation of extrinsic evidence on collateral matters entails an undue consumption of trial time. However, when the witness is competent to authenticate the writing in question during cross, there is little expenditure of additional time. Thus, it does not serve the purpose of the rule to apply it in this situation.

Another important safeguard against abuse is the privilege against self-incrimination. A witness who without objecting partially discloses incriminating matter cannot later invoke the privilege when she is asked to complete the disclosure.[28] However, the mere act of testifying does not waive the privilege as to criminal activities relevant solely to attacking the witness's

---

accompanying the 2003 amendment to Rule 608 states:

> It should be noted that the extrinsic evidence prohibition of Rule 608(b) bars any reference to the consequences that a witness might have suffered as a result of an alleged bad act. For example, Rule 608(b) prohibits counsel from mentioning that a witness was suspended or disciplined for the conduct that is the subject of impeachment, when that conduct is offered only to prove the character of the witness. See . . . Stephen A. Saltzburg, Impeaching the Witness: Prior Bad Acts and Extrinsic Evidence, 7 Crim. Just. 29, 31 (Winter 1993) ("counsel should not be permitted to circumvent the no-extrinsic-evidence prohibition by tucking a third person's opinion about prior acts into a question asked of the witness who has denied the act").

*But see* U.S. v. Cedeno, 644 F.3d 79, 81–82 (2d Cir. 2011), cert. denied, 132 S. Ct. 325, 181 L. Ed. 2d 201 (2011) and cert. denied, 132 S. Ct. 346, 181 L. Ed. 2d 217 (2011) and cert. denied, 132 S. Ct. 315, 181 L. Ed. 2d 194 (2011) (a prior adverse credibility finding by a state court), cert.denied sub nom. Diaz v. U.S., 132 S. Ct. 315, 181 L. Ed. 2d 194 (2011); U.S. v. Dawson, 434 F.3d 956, 957–58 (7th Cir. 2006) (a judicial determination); U.S. v. Nelson, 365 F. Supp. 2d 381, 387–91 (S.D. N.Y. 2005) (questions about adverse credibility findings against a witness in a previous hearing do not violate the ban on extrinsic evidence). In U.S. v. Holt, 486 F.3d 997, 1001–02 (7th Cir. 2007), the prosecution called a police officer as a witness. While the trial judge permitted the defense to cross-examine the officer about underlying conduct, the judge forbade the defense from questioning the officer "about complaints, investigations or discipline." The court distinguished *Dawson*, supra.

[27]Carter v. Hewitt, 617 F.2d 961, 970–71 (3d Cir. 1980); Schmertz, 21 Fed. Rules. Evid. News 96–106 ("if . . . the cross-examiner can lay a proper foundation as to otherwise relevant documents from the impeached witness's own mouth, there is no need for other extrinsic witnesses and little time is consumed"). *Contra* U.S. v. Martz, 964 F.2d 787, 789 (8th Cir. 1992). *See also* Schmertz, Article VI, in Emerging Problems Under the Federal Rules of Evidence 115, 159 n. 169 (3d ed. 1998) (even under this view, the cross-examiner could not question a witness about the contents of his or her medical records; "a patient rarely can qualify as a foundation witness, e.g., under Rule 803(6), even for his own medical file").

[28]For more detailed discussion, see § 140 infra.

credibility.[29] While an accused, unlike an ordinary witness, has an option whether to testify at all, exacting a waiver as the price of taking the stand is somewhat inconsistent with the right to testify in one's own behalf. Therefore Federal Rule of Evidence and Revised Uniform Rule of Evidence 608(b) provides that the giving of testimony by any witness, including an accused, does not waive the privilege as to matters relating only to credibility.[30]

## § 42    Character: Conviction of crime[1]

At common law a person's[2] conviction of treason, any felony, or a misdemeanor involving dishonesty or false statement (crimen falsi) or the obstruction of justice, rendered the convict completely incompetent as a witness. These were said to be "infamous" crimes.[3] Thanks to statutes or rules virtually universal in the common law world, this primitive absolutism has been abandoned. The disqualification for conviction of crime has been repealed, and by specific provision or decision it has been reduced to a mere ground for impeaching credibility. Unfortunately, just as the common law definition of disqualifying crimes was not very precise, many of the repealing statutes and rules suffer from indefiniteness.[4] In particular, the list of crimes for which a convic-

---

[29]Coil v. U.S., 343 F.2d 573 (8th Cir. 1965).

Statements in such cases as People v. Sorge, 301 N.Y. 198, 93 N.E.2d 637 (1950), that a witness, including an accused, may be asked on cross-examination "about any vicious or criminal act in his life that has a bearing on his credibility" arguably overlook the constitutional limitation. When the question was raised in People v. Johnston, 228 N.Y. 332, 127 N.E. 186 (1920), the court conceded that the waiver resulting from an accused taking the stand did not extend to facts affecting only credibility.

[30]Fed. R. Evid. 608(b) & Unif. R. Evid. 608(b). *See* Griffin v. California, 380 U.S. 609, 85 S. Ct. 1229, 14 L. Ed. 2d 106 (1965); Ferguson v. State of Ga., 365 U.S. 570, 81 S. Ct. 756, 5 L. Ed. 2d 783 (1961). The accused's right to testify in his own behalf is of constitutional dimension. *See* Rock v. Arkansas, 483 U.S. 44, 107 S. Ct. 2704, 97 L. Ed. 2d 37 (1987);

Washington v. Texas, 388 U.S. 14, 87 S. Ct. 1920, 18 L. Ed. 2d 1019 (1967).

**[Section 42]**

[1]3A Wigmore, Evidence §§ 980, 980a, 985–87 (Chadbourn rev. 1970); 4 Weinstein's Federal Evidence Ch. 609 (rev. 2011); Ladd, Credibility Tests, 89 U. Pa. L. Rev. 166, 174 (1940); West's Key Number Digest, Witnesses ⬥345.

[2]In most cases, the conviction was suffered personally by the witness. However, the cases suggest that a witness may be impeached by a corporation's conviction if the witness was a corporate agent who participated in the underlying criminal conduct. Walden v. Georgia-Pacific Corp., 126 F.3d 506, 523 (3d Cir. 1997).

[3]Greenleaf, Evidence § 373 (1842); 2 Wigmore, Evidence § 520 (Chadbourn rev. 1979).

[4]*E.g.* Conn. Gen. Stat. Ann. § 52-145:

(a) A person shall not be disqualified

tion[5] is a ground of impeachment varies widely among the states that have not adopted Federal Rule of Evidence 609.[6]

---

as a witness in any action because of, (1) his interest in the outcome of the action as a party or otherwise, (2) his disbelief in the existence of a supreme being, or (3) his conviction of crime.

(b) A person's interest in the outcome of the action or his conviction of crime may be shown for the purpose of affecting his credibility.

See other statutes and rules collected in 2 Wigmore, Evidence § 488 (Chadbourn rev. 1979).

[5]Conviction, of course, is the present requirement; and while it was once thought otherwise, today the opponent may not inquire about even an official accusation such as an arrest, indictment, or information falling short of a conviction. Hafner v. Brown, 983 F.2d 570, 576 (4th Cir. 1992); U.S. v. Dennis, 625 F.2d 782 (8th Cir. 1980); People v. Hardy, 70 Ill. App. 3d 351, 26 Ill. Dec. 212, 387 N.E.2d 1042 (1st Dist. 1979) (but questions as to pending charges which might show bias or interest are permissible); Johnson v. State, 82 Nev. 338, 418 P.2d 495 (1966) (arrest; cross-examination at preliminary hearing); Com. v. Ross, 434 Pa. 167, 252 A.2d 661 (1969) (arrest; opinion mentions exception as to indictment for same or closely related offense); 3A Wigmore, Evidence § 980a (Chadbourn rev. 1970). *Contra:* People v. Brocato, 17 Mich. App. 277, 169 N.W.2d 483 (1969) (holding defendant as witness may not be asked, but other witnesses may be in the judge's discretion); Comment Note.—Impeachment of witness by evidence or inquiry as to arrest, accusation, or prosecution, 20 A.L.R.2d 1421. In collision cases, proof is often sought to be made, under guise of impeachment, that one of the drivers was arrested for negligent driving at the time of the collision. It may have a remote bearing upon partiality, but its prejudicial use by the jury as hearsay evidence of guilt is a countervailing danger, and the courts usually exclude it.

*See* Holden v. Berberich, 351 Mo. 995, 174 S.W.2d 791 (1943) (cross-examination of driver as to indictment for driving while intoxicated at time of collision); Admissibility, on cross-examination or otherwise, of evidence that witness in a civil action had been under arrest, indictment, or other criminal accusation on a charge growing out of the accident, transaction, or occurrence involved in the civil action, 149 A.L.R. 935.

[6]A few jurisdictions adhere to the loose common law definition, described above, of "infamous crimes." *E.g.*, Md. Code Ann., Cts. & Jud. Proc. § 10-905. The California Code and some other codes specify only "felonies," a limitation which is at least simple to apply. Cal. Evid. Code § 788; Idaho R. Evid. 609; Nev. Rev. Stat. § 50.095 (the crime must be punishable by death or imprisonment for more than one year). This is the construction some courts have placed upon statutes worded in terms of "crime" or "any crime." *E.g.*, State v. Hurt, 49 N.J. 114, 228 A.2d 673 (1967). Some courts, unwilling to accept such simple tests, have read into general statutes a limitation that as to misdemeanors at least, the offense must involve "moral turpitude." Sims v. Callahan, 269 Ala. 216, 112 So. 2d 776 (1959); People v. Gabriel, 137 Cal. Rptr. 3d 382 (Cal. App. 2d Dist. 2012), opinion vacated, 206 Cal. App. 4th 450, 141 Cal. Rptr. 3d 784 (2d Dist. 2012) (possession of an assault weapon and cultivation of marijuana are crimes of moral turpitude); People v. Chavez, 84 Cal. App. 4th 25, 100 Cal. Rptr. 2d 680 (3d Dist. 2000) (sexual battery was a crime of moral turpitude); People v. Vera, 69 Cal. App. 4th 1100, 82 Cal. Rptr. 2d 128 (6th Dist. 1999) (opening or maintaining a place for the purpose of selling contraband drugs involves moral turpitude); Sapp v. State, 271 Ga. 446, 520 S.E.2d 462 (1999) (moral turpitude); Urtado v. State, 333 S.W.3d 418

This section initially discusses the types of convictions which

(Tex. App. Austin 2011) (interference with an emergency call is not a crime of moral turpitude); Smith v. State, 346 S.W.2d 611 (Tex. Crim. App. 1961) (conviction for selling and handling whiskey did not involve moral turpitude); Tasker v. Com., 202 Va. 1019, 121 S.E.2d 459 (1961) (misdemeanor did not involve moral turpitude); Vt. Stat. Ann. tit. 12, § 1608; Use of unrelated misdemeanor conviction (other than for traffic offense) to impeach general credibility of witness in state civil case, 97 A.L.R.3d 1150. Thus does the serpent of uncertainty crawl into the Eden of trial administration. The creation of a detailed catalog of crimes involving "moral turpitude" seems a waste of judicial energy. Moreover, shifting the burden to the judge's discretion raises problems as to the adequacy of his information or basis on which to exercise discretion. Still more uncertain is a rule giving the judge discretion on the question of whether the particular conviction substantially affects the witness's credibility. *See, e.g.,* Johnson v. State, 4 Md. App. 648, 244 A.2d 632 (1968). In California, the trial court has discretion to admit any conviction which necessarily involves moral turpitude, even if the immoral trait is one other than untruthfulness. People v. Castro, 38 Cal. 3d 301, 211 Cal. Rptr. 719, 696 P.2d 111 (1985). Moral turpitude is defined as a readiness to do evil. Id. The trial court must prohibit impeachment by prior conviction involving moral turpitude when in its discretion the court finds that the prior conviction's probative value is outweighed by its unduly prejudicial effect. Id. Although Cal. Evid. Code § 788 formerly limited the cross-examiner to felonies for impeachment purposes, by initiative criminal litigants may now inquire about misdemeanor-grade misconduct entailing moral turpitude. People v. Wheeler, 4 Cal. 4th 284, 14 Cal. Rptr. 2d 418, 841 P.2d 938 (1992); Blackburn, The Expansion of Allowable Impeachment:

Admission of Juvenile Priors, Misdemeanor Convictions, and Good Faith Cross-Examination by Prosecutors, 1 Chap. J. Crim. Just. 213 (2009) (California law after Proposition 8).

The making of various minor changes and a few major changes in Fed. R. Evid. 609(a) in states which have adopted the federal rules indicates the persistent tension between the considerations of simple administration and fairness to witnesses and parties.

In actions for injuries incurred in highway accidents, attempts are often made to cross-examine the participants about previous convictions for traffic offenses, but it is usually held that these convictions do not show moral turpitude or affect veracity. Nesbit v. Cumberland Contracting Co., 196 Md. 36, 75 A.2d 339 (1950) (allowing plaintiff to be cross-examined about traffic offenses was improper, notwithstanding he had answered on cross-examination that he considered himself a good driver). Some cases permit use of traffic offense convictions under various circumstances. Use of unrelated traffic offense conviction to impeach general credibility of witness in state civil case, 88 A.L.R.3d 74. Usually they would be inadmissible under Fed. R. Evid. 609(a).

Typically, convictions for violations of city ordinances cannot be used. Caldwell v. State, 282 Ala. 713, 213 So. 2d 919 (1968); Massen v. State, 41 Wis. 2d 245, 163 N.W.2d 616 (1969); Use of unrelated traffic offense conviction to impeach general credibility of witness in state civil case, 88 A.L.R.3d 74. *Contra* Scott v. State, 445 P.2d 39 (Alaska 1968) (violation of city ordinance is a "crime" as that term is used in governing rule; the present Alaska rule permits showing of a crime if it involves dishonesty or false statement).

Thus, the proposition that at least some crimes are relevant to credibility is generally accepted. The rea-

may be used for purposes of impeachment and the related question of the judge's discretion to bar the use of an otherwise admissible conviction. The section then takes up the topic of the mechanics of this impeachment technique, including the use of written copies of convictions and the extent to which the cross-examiner may elicit the details of the underlying criminal act.

### The Types of Convictions Usable for Impeachment

A rule strictly limiting impeachment to conviction of crimes involving deceit or false statement would have the virtue that those crimes have an obvious connection to truthfulness. It would have the further virtue that it is fairly definite and simple for administrative purposes.

However, the federal statutory scheme is more complex. The Federal Rule governing impeachment by proof of conviction of crime is the product of compromise.[7] Under Rule 609(a)(2), regardless of the imposable punishment, crimes of "dishonesty or false statement" may be used against any witness, including an

---

sons for limiting inquiry into specific instances of misconduct which have not resulted in a conviction, discussed in the preceding section, tend to disappear: danger of self-incrimination is usually absent; risks of confusion and surprise are lessened; and risk of prejudice to a party from proof of conviction of an ordinary witness is so slight as scarcely to deserve comment.

The preliminary part of this present section is devoted to witnesses generally; the more troublesome problems which arise when the witness is the accused in a criminal case are the subject of special discussion in the text beginning at note 68 infra.

[7]Former Fed. R. Evid. 609(a) provided:

(a) General Rule. For the purpose of attacking the credibility of a witness,

(1) evidence that a witness other than an accused has been convicted of a crime shall be admitted, subject to Rule 403, if the crime was punishable by death or imprisonment in excess of one year under the law under which the witness was convicted, and evidence that an accused has been convicted of such a crime shall be admitted if the court determines that the probative value of admitting this evidence outweighs its prejudicial effect to the accused; and

(2) evidence that any witness has been convicted of a crime shall be admitted if it involved dishonesty or false statement, regardless of the punishment.

Effective December 1, 2011, restyled Fed. R. Evid. 609(a) reads:

In General. The following rules apply to attacking a witness's character for truthfulness by evidence of a criminal conviction:

(1) for a crime that, in the convicting jurisdiction, was punishable by death or by imprisonment for more than one year, the evidence:

(A) must be admitted, subject to Rule 403, in a civil case or in a criminal case in which the witness is not a defendant; and

(B) must be admitted in a criminal case in which the witness is a defendant, if the probative value of the evidence outweighs its prejudicial effect to that defendant; and

(2) for any crime, regardless of the punishment, the evidence must be admitted if the court can readily determine that establishing the elements of the crime required proving—or the witness's admitting—a dishonest act or false statement.

accused.[8] Other misdemeanor-grade crimes (punishable by less than imprisonment in excess of one year) are never usable.[9] Under Rule 609(a)(1), against an accused who takes the stand, felony-grade crimes (punishable by death or imprisonment in excess of one year) may be used, if the court determines that the probative value of the conviction outweighs its prejudicial effect to the accused. In civil cases or against all criminal witnesses other than the accused, 609(a)(1) convictions are usable unless under the normal Rule 403 standard the court determines that the probative value of the conviction is substantially outweighed by its prejudicial effect.[10] In contrast, in the federal statutory

---

[8]See this section, note 7 supra.

[9]See this section, note 7 supra.

[10]The burden of establishing that probative value outweighs prejudice to the defendant is on the prosecution. Compare Rule 403 and other situations under Rule 609(a) (1), where the burden of showing that prejudice substantially outweighs probative value is on the objecting party. Trial judges are urged to make specific findings on prejudicial effect versus probative value. U.S. v. Mahone, 537 F.2d 922 (7th Cir. 1976).

The problems center on criminal defendants who elect to testify. Drawing on the *Luck* doctrine as refined in later cases (see this section, note 70, infra), factors appropriate for consideration in the balancing process are (1) the nature of the crime, (2) the recency of the prior conviction, (3) the similarity between the crime for which there was prior conviction and the crime charged, (4) the importance of defendant's testimony, and (5) the centrality of the credibility issue. U.S. v. Hayes, 553 F.2d 824 (2d Cir. 1977); U.S. v. Mahone, 537 F.2d 922 (7th Cir. 1976); 4 Weinstein's Federal Evidence § 609.04[2] (rev. 2011):

(1) The nature of the crime is pertinent because some crimes not within Rule 609(a)(2) are more "veracity-related" than others. U.S. v. Hayes, 553 F.2d 824 (2d Cir. 1977) (conviction for heroin smuggling more closely related to veracity than conviction for possession of narcotics or a violent crime); U.S. v. Ortiz, 553 F.2d 782 (2d Cir. 1977) (conviction for two separate heroin sales permits recognition "that a narcotics trafficker lives a life of secrecy and dissembling in the course of that activity, being prepared to say whatever is required by the demands of the moment, whether the truth or a lie").

(2) Recency of the conviction bears on the possibility of rehabilitation, which decreases with recency. Passage of time usually suggests some attenuation of the impact of the prior conviction.

(3) Similarity of the subject of the prior conviction to the crime charged bears strongly on the possibility of prejudice, as inviting an improper direct inference of guilt rather than directing attention to credibility. *See* U.S. v. Hayes, 553 F.2d 824 (2d Cir. 1977). *Compare* U.S. v. Hawley, 554 F.2d 50 (2d Cir. 1977).

(4) Fear of opening up his record may deter a defendant from taking the stand, and thus warrant exclusion so that the jury may have the benefit of his testimony. *See* Judge Mansfield dissenting in U.S. v. Ortiz, 553 F.2d 782 (2d Cir. 1977). This factor is closely related to the fifth.

(5) The factor of centrality of the credibility issue surfaces when the defendant's credibility is pitted against that of his accuser, with the verdict depending on the result. *See* U.S. v. Fountain, 642 F.2d 1083 (7th Cir. 1981) (excellent discussion affirming admission of conviction of premeditated murder conviction of defendant witness under particular circumstances); U.S. v. Ortiz, 553 F.2d 782 (2d Cir. 1977).

scheme regardless of the punishment or against whom used, crimes involving "dishonesty or false statement" are not subject to the balancing of probative value against prejudice; under 609(a)(2), they are automatically admissible.[11]

The meaning of the phrase "dishonesty and false statement" in Rule 609(a)(2) has been debated. The original Report of the Conference Committee stated:

> By the phrase "dishonesty and false statement" the Conference means crimes such as perjury or subornation of perjury, false statement, criminal fraud, embezzlement, or false pretense, or any other offense in the nature of *crimen falsi*, the commission of which involves some element of deceit, untruthfulness, or falsification bearing on the accused's propensity to testify truthfully.

Arguably, given the explicit language in the Conference Committee Report limiting the phrase "dishonesty or false statement" to offenses involving *crimen falsi*, even immediately after the enactment of the Federal Rules the courts should have ascribed little

---

Other lists of factors have been suggested. *See* State v. Fowler, 114 Wash. 2d 59, 785 P.2d 808, 814 (1990) ("In State v. Alexis, 95 Wash.2d 15, 621 P.2d 1269 (1980), we listed some of the factors a trial court should consider in weighing the value of the credibility against potential prejudice. They include: (1) the length of the defendant's criminal record; (2) remoteness of the prior conviction; (3) nature of the prior crime; (4) the age and circumstances of the defendant; (5) centrality of the credibility issue; and (6) the impeachment value of the prior crime. State v. Alexis, supra at 19, 621 P.2d 1269."). *See also* 2 Graham, Handbook of Federal Evidence § 609:3 (7th ed. 2012) ("In summary, the following factors should be considered in determining whether the probative value of admitting the evidence upon the credibility of the criminal defendant outweighs its prejudicial effect: (1) the nature of the prior crime; (2) the length of the defendant's criminal record; (3) defendant's age and circumstances; (4) the likelihood that the defendant would not testify; (5) the nearness or remoteness of the prior crime; (6) defendant's subsequent career; (7) whether the prior crime was similar to the one charged; (8) the centrality of the issue of credibility; and (9) the need for defendant's testimony. To this

one might add a tenth—facts surrounding the conviction including whether or not the defendant pled guilty or was convicted after trial, and whether the defendant testified at the trial.").

[11]U.S. v. Lester, 749 F.2d 1288, 1300 (9th Cir. 1984) ("Fed. R. Evid. 609(a) (2) provides that evidence of convictions of a crime involving dishonesty or false statement shall be admitted during cross-examination to attack the credibility of a witness. No discretion to exclude exists. United States v. Glenn, 667 F.2d 1269, 1272 (9th Cir. 1982).").

Rule 403 does not apply. U.S. v. Noble, 754 F.2d 1324, 1331 (7th Cir. 1985) ("Contrary to the defendant's assertion, the district court need not balance the prejudicial effect of the admission of the prior conviction against its probative value when admitting such evidence under Fed. R. Evid. Rule 609(a) (2) for the purpose of impeachment."); U.S. v. Kuecker, 740 F.2d 496, 501 (7th Cir. 1984) ("[A]ll circuits that have decided the issue have ruled that evidence of prior convictions for crimes involving dishonesty or false statement is admissible without a balancing of probative value versus prejudicial effect.").

meaning to the term "dishonesty" with the possible exception of embezzlement.[12] However, a controversy initially surfaced in reported decisions trying to determine whether the expression "dishonesty or false statement" applied to convictions involving petty larceny, robbery, shoplifting and narcotics.[13] Notwithstanding that controversy, it quickly became settled that negatively crimes involving solely the use of force such as assault[14] and battery,[15] and crimes such as drunkenness[16] and prostitution[17] do not involve "dishonesty or false statement," while affirmatively the crime of fraud does.[18] In 1990, when Rule 609 was amended, the Advisory Committee issued a new Note to the rule. The Note expressed disapproval of the minority of cases which read Rule 609(a)(2) broadly as including theft offenses.

Especially after the 1990 amendment, the published opinions display a willingness to follow the Conference Committee Report. Hence, the trend is to restrict "dishonesty or false statement" to a crime "which involves some element of deceit, untruthfulness, or falsification bearing on the accused's propensity to testify truthfully."[19] A few other crimes have now been held to categorically meet this definition.[20] However, federal courts and most state courts are unwilling to classify offenses such as petty

---

[12]In Preliminary Notes on Reading the Rules of Evidence, 57 Neb. L. Rev. 908, 917 (1978), the Reporter for the Advisory Committee, the late Professor Edward Cleary, wrote that the legislative history clearly established that the term "dishonesty" in Rule 609(a)(2) was "devoid of significant meaning."

[13]Hornstein, Harmonizing Rules 609 and 608(b) of the Federal Rules of Evidence, 2003 Utah L. Rev. 635, 664–66 ("Although courts generally admit convictions that directly involve lying or deceit, such as perjury, forgery, and various kinds of fraud, and exclude convictions for assault, traffic violations, weapons offenses, drunkenness, and sex offenses, they disagree about many other convictions that fall in the middle range, such as robbery, drug offenses, larceny, and burglary. Sometimes convictions that would not ordinarily fall under Rule 609(a)(2) are placed there if the crime involved elements of deceit or secrecy").

[14]U.S. v. Mahone, 328 F. Supp. 2d 77, 83-84 (D. Me. 2004), aff'd, 453 F.3d 68 (1st Cir. 2006).

[15]U.S. v. Harvey, 588 F.2d 1201 (8th Cir. 1978).

[16]U.S. v. Lossiah, 537 F.2d 1250 (4th Cir. 1976).

[17]U.S. v. Cox, 536 F.2d 65 (5th Cir. 1976).

[18]U.S. v. Brashier, 548 F.2d 1315 (9th Cir. 1976).

[19]S.E.C. v. Sargent, 229 F.3d 68 (1st Cir. 2000) ("lying to a government official"); U.S. v. Gomez, 772 F. Supp. 2d 1185, 1195–96 (C.D. Cal. 2011) (false personation); U.S. v. Mahone, 328 F. Supp. 2d 77, 82-83 (D. Me. 2004), aff'd, 453 F.3d 68 (1st Cir. 2006) (forgery). See also U.S. v. Colon-Ledee, 786 F. Supp. 2d 461 (D.P.R. 2010) (failure to pay child support).

[20]E.g., U.S. v. Agnew, 385 F.3d 288, 292 (3d Cir. 2004) (forgery); Altobello v. Borden Confectionary Products, Inc., 872 F.2d 215 (7th Cir. 1989) (meter tampering); U.S. v. Noble, 754 F.2d 1324 (7th Cir. 1985) (counterfeiting); U.S. v. Lester, 749 F.2d 1288 (9th Cir. 1984) (false police report); U.S. v. Harris, 738 F.2d 1068 (9th Cir. 1984) (passing counterfeit money); U.S. v.

larceny,[21] receipt of stolen property,[22] shoplifting,[23] robbery,[24] possession of a weapon,[25] and narcotic violations[26] as per se crimes of "dishonesty or false statement." Without more, a post-offense attempt to evade detection or arrest does not convert the prior offense into a crime involving dishonesty or false statement.[27]

---

Jackson, 696 F.2d 578 (8th Cir. 1982) (unlawfully transporting forged securities); U.S. v. Gellman, 677 F.2d 65 (11th Cir. 1982) (failure to file tax returns); U.S. v. Whitman, 665 F.2d 313 (10th Cir. 1981) (land fraud scheme); U.S. v. Kiendra, 663 F.2d 349 (1st Cir. 1981) (possession of a stolen vehicle and receiving stolen goods); Zukowski v. Dunton, 650 F.2d 30 (4th Cir. 1981) (willful failure to provide information for income tax purposes); U.S. v. Williams, 642 F.2d 136 (5th Cir. 1981) (bribery); U. S. v. O'Connor, 635 F.2d 814 (10th Cir. 1980) (forgery); U.S. v. Mucci, 630 F.2d 737 (10th Cir. 1980) (passing a bad check).

[21]Clarett v. Roberts, 657 F.3d 664, 669–70 (7th Cir. 2011) ("Retail theft lacks an element of an act of dishonesty . . . . As such, '[t]his circuit generally does not count retail theft as a crime of dishonesty' . . . ."); U.S. v. Estrada, 430 F.3d 606, 614 (2d Cir. 2005) ("While much successful crime [such as theft] involves some quantum of stealth, all such conduct does not, as a result, constitute crime of dishonesty or false statement for purposes of Rule 609(a) (2)"); U.S. v. Amaechi, 991 F.2d 374, 378–79 (7th Cir. 1993) (ten circuits have ruled that shoplifting is not a crime of dishonesty); U.S. v. Field, 625 F.2d 862 (9th Cir. 1980).

[22]U.S. v. Foster, 227 F.3d 1096 (9th Cir. 2000) (after all, the witness might have been completely truthful and straightforward in his or her dealings with the transferor of the stolen property). The decision brings to mind "honor among thieves."

[23]U.S. v. Owens, 145 F.3d 923, 927 (7th Cir. 1998) (the trial judge did not err in excluding a theft conviction although the court has 'declined to hold that all shoplifting is excludable under Rule 609"); U.S. v. Alexander,

48 F.3d 1477, 1488 (9th Cir. 1995); U.S. v. Dorsey, 591 F.2d 922 (D.C. Cir. 1978); Speers v. University of Akron, 196 F. Supp. 2d 551 (N.D. Ohio 2002). Contra U.S. v. Brackeen, 969 F.2d 827 (9th Cir. 1992) (bank robbery); People v. Jones, 971 P.2d 243 (Colo. App. 1998) (overruled by, People v. Segovia, 196 P.3d 1126 (Colo. 2008)); State v. Gallant, 307 Or. 152, 764 P.2d 920 (1988).

[24]U.S. v. Begay, 144 F.3d 1336 (10th Cir. 1998); U.S. v. Brackeen, 969 F.2d 827 (9th Cir. 1992) (bank robbery); U.S. v. Smith, 551 F.2d 348 (D.C. Cir. 1976); U.S. v. Mahone, 328 F. Supp. 2d 77, 83-84 (D. Me. 2004), aff'd, 453 F.3d 68 (1st Cir. 2006). Contra State v. Day, 91 N.M. 570, 577 P.2d 878 (Ct. App. 1978).

[25]U.S. v. Cameron, 814 F.2d 403 (7th Cir. 1987).

[26]U.S. v. Thompson, 559 F.2d 552 (9th Cir. 1977); U.S. v. Hastings, 577 F.2d 38 (8th Cir. 1978); State v. Calegar, 133 Wash. 2d 718, 947 P.2d 235, 237 (1997) (rejecting the State's argument that drug crimes "always involve some element of dishonesty"); State v. Hardy, 133 Wash. 2d 701, 946 P.2d 1175 (1997). Contra People v. Walker, 157 Ill. App. 3d 133, 109 Ill. Dec. 408, 510 N.E.2d 29 (1st Dist. 1987); State v. Giddens, 335 Md. 205, 642 A.2d 870 (1994) (drug distribution is relevant to a witness's credibility; the practical demands of that occupation require drug dealers to be ready to engage in whatever conduct is necessary to avoid detection, and in turn that indicates a willingness to lie).

[27]U.S. v. Mehrmanesh, 689 F.2d 822, 833 (9th Cir. 1982) ("We conclude that Mehrmanesh's prior conviction for smuggling or clandestinely introducing into the United States merchandise (hashish) in violation of 18

Suppose, though, that the party wishing to employ a conviction not considered per se a crime of "dishonesty or false statement" can show by going behind the face of the judgment that the particular offense was perpetrated by deceit, untruthfulness or falsification, i.e., involved some element of active misrepresentation. On that supposition, the prior conviction perhaps is logically relevant to impeach credibility.[28] However, until recently many, if not most, jurisdictions did not permit the party to go beyond the judgment.[29] As previously stated, the courts are receptive to this impeachment technique in part because the use of the written judgment reduces the risk of undue time consumption. If the parties were routinely allowed to go behind the judgment, the amount of time entailed by this technique could increase dramatically. To address this issue, the Evidence Rules Committee proposed amending Federal Rule 609(a)(2) to read: "evidence that any witness has been convicted of a crime shall be admitted, regardless of the punishment, if it readily can be determined that establishing the elements of the crime required proof or admission of an act of dishonesty or false

---

U.S.C. § 545 does not fall within the scope of Rule 609(a)(2). One is guilty of smuggling under 18 U.S.C. § 545 when he or she employs any method of introducing goods into this country surreptitiously with the intent to avoid and defeat United States customs laws. . . . Convictions for such surreptitious activity, not necessarily involving misrepresentations or falsification, do not bear *directly* on the likelihood that the defendant will testify truthfully."); State v. Reitz, 75 Or. App. 82, 705 P.2d 762, 763 (1985) ("The deceit involved is more than the mere effort of the criminal actor to hide the fact of crime or the identity of the actor from the authorities; by this reasoning all crimes would be crimes of deceit.").

[28]U.S. v. Mehrmanesh, 689 F.2d 822, 833 n.13 (9th Cir. 1982) ("Many Circuits, including the Ninth, have recognized that when a prior conviction by its definition is neither clearly covered nor clearly excluded by Rule 609(a) (2), the prosecution may invoke the automatic admissibility provision by demonstrating that a particular prior conviction rested on facts warranting the dishonesty or false statement description."); U.S. v. Barnes,

622 F.2d 107, 110 (5th Cir. 1980) ("[S]ome petty larceny offenses may involve dishonesty or false statement and some may not, and therefore it is necessary to look at the basis of the conviction to determine whether the crime embraced dishonesty."); U.S. v. Smith, 181 F. Supp. 2d 904, 909 (N.D. Ill. 2002) (the government did not show that the defendant's "convictions for robbery, burglary, theft, and drug possession . . . involved false statements or acts of deceit beyond the basic crime itself"); State v. Cheeseboro, 346 S.C. 526, 552 S.E.2d 300 (2001). *Accord* Altobello v. Borden Confectionary Products, Inc., 872 F.2d 215 (7th Cir.1989); U.S. v. Yeo, 739 F.2d 385 (8th Cir. 1984). *See* Green, Deceit and the Classification of Crimes: Federal Rule of Evidence 609(A)(2) and the Origins of Crimen Falsi, 90 J. Crim. L. & Criminology 1087 (2000).

[29]*See* U.S. v. Lipscomb, 702 F.2d 1049, 1062–68 (D.C. Cir. 1983). *But see* U.S. v. Payton, 159 F.3d 49, 57 (2d Cir. 1998) ("we will look beyond the elements of the offense to determine whether the conviction rested upon facts establishing dishonesty or false statement").

statement by the witness." The committee acknowledged that probing beyond the face of the judgment might consume some additional time, but the committee believed that the amendment was circumscribed enough to prevent "a 'mini-trial.'" The amendment took effect in 2006.[30] Restyled Rule 609(a)(1) incorporates the amendment.

Convictions[31] in any state or in federal court are usable to impeach. The trend is to hold that a conviction is sufficiently final as soon as the guilty verdict is entered even if sentence has not been imposed yet.[32] The fact of the conviction establishes the witness's commission of the underlying act; and for that purpose,

---

[30]The Advisory Committee Note accompanying the 2006 amendment states:

Ordinarily, the statutory elements of the crime will indicate whether it is one of dishonesty or false statement. Where the deceitful nature of the crime is not apparent from the statute and the face of the judgment—as, for example, where the conviction simply records a finding of guilt for a statutory offense that does not reference deceit expressly—a proponent may offer information such as an indictment, a statement of admitted facts, or jury instructions to show that the factfinder had to find, or the defendant had to admit, an act of dishonesty or false statement in order for the witness to have been convicted. But the amendment does not contemplate a "mini-trial" in which the court plumbs the record of the previous proceeding to determine whether the crime was in the nature of *crimen falsi*.

[31]At common law the term "conviction" has two accepted meanings—the jury verdict or the judgment entered following the verdict. Lewis v. Exxon Corp., 716 F.2d 1398 (D.C. Cir. 1983). For Rule 609 purposes, a jury verdict is sufficient. U.S. v. Vanderbosch, 610 F.2d 95, 97 (2d Cir. 1979) ("[W]e hold that a jury verdict of guilty prior to entry of judgment is admissible for impeachment purposes, if it meets the other requirements of Fed. R. Evid. 609. . . . As in the case of pending appeals, the defendant should be allowed to reveal to the jury the fact that judgment has not been entered as well as the pendency of motions for

acquittal and for a new trial before the sentencing court.").

Of course a judgment of conviction arising from a guilty plea is "fully equivalent for impeachment purposes to a determination of guilt following a trial." U.S. v. Pardo, 636 F.2d 535, 545–46 n.32 (D.C. Cir. 1980). A guilty plea prior to imposition of sentence may be employed to impeach. U.S. v. Chilcote, 724 F.2d 1498 (11th Cir. 1984); Com. v. Hill, 523 Pa. 270, 566 A.2d 252 (1989).

[32]U.S. v. Klein, 560 F.2d 1236, 1239 (5th Cir. 1977); People v. Castello, 65 Cal. App. 4th 1242, 77 Cal. Rptr. 2d 314, 321 (4th Dist. 1998) ("The ordinary legal meaning of conviction is a verdict of guilty or the confession of the defendant in open court, and not the sentence or judgment"); People v. Martinez, 62 Cal. App. 4th 1454, 73 Cal. Rptr. 2d 358, 361–64 (5th Dist. 1998) (there is a conviction on the return of a guilty verdict); Specht v. State, 734 N.E.2d 239 (Ind. 2000) (the defendant may be impeached with a prior guilty plea which has not yet been reduced to judgment); Jewel v. Com., 260 Va. 430, 536 S.E.2d 905 (2000) (an accepted guilty plea is a "conviction" even before the trial judge issues a finding of guilty and imposes sentence). *See also* U.S. v. Faison, 61 F.3d 22 (11th Cir. 1995) (a guilty verdict is a conviction for purposes of the offense of being a convicted felon in possession of a firearm). *But see* State v. McFadden, 772 So. 2d 1209 (Fla. 2000) (unless there is a final judgment of conviction or an adjudication of

the verdict suffices.[33] Though a civil judgment against a lawyer of suspension or disbarment for criminal misconduct is not technically a conviction, there is authority that either is provable to impeach.[34] Statutes relating to juvenile court proceedings frequently provide that a finding of delinquency shall not be used in evidence against the child in any other court and is not deemed a "conviction." These statutes are usually construed as precluding the finding from being employed to impeach credibility.[35] In various jurisdictions, as under the Federal Rules of Evidence, this matter is expressly dealt with by evidence rules or statutes.[36] Under such provisions, juvenile adjudications are admissible only in limited, defined circumstances.[37]

---

guilt, a defendant or witness may not be impeached with evidence of a guilty plea or jury verdict).

[33]*But see* Pettijohn v. Wusinich, 705 F. Supp. 259, 261 (E.D. Pa. 1989) ("The cases require, however, that the fact that judgment has not yet been entered . . . be revealed to the jury").

[34]Lansing v. Michigan Cent. R. Co., 143 Mich. 48, 106 N.W. 692 (1906); State v. Pearson, 39 N.J. Super. 50, 120 A.2d 468 (App. Div. 1956) (and cases cited therein).

[35]State v. Coffman, 360 Mo. 782, 230 S.W.2d 761 (1950); People v. Peele, 12 N.Y.2d 890, 237 N.Y.S.2d 999, 188 N.E.2d 265 (1963); Shephard, Collateral Consequences of Juvenile Proceedings: Part II, 15 Crim. Just. 41, 41–42 (Fall. 2000) (citing numerous cases, the author asserts that "[a] juvenile adjudication is not normally deemed to be a conviction of a crime . . . and, thus, does not impugn the truthfulness of the person"); Use of judgment in prior juvenile court proceeding to impeach credibility of witness, 63 A.L.R.3d 1112. But compare the views expressed in 3A Wigmore, Evidence §§ 924a, 980 (Chadbourn rev. 1970). He collects the statutes in § 196 n. 5. Application of Gault, 387 U.S. 1, 87 S. Ct. 1428, 18 L. Ed. 2d 527 (1967), mandating certain procedural requirements in juvenile cases, does not bear directly upon this subject.

[36]Former Fed. R. Evid. 609(d) provided:

Evidence of juvenile adjudications is generally not admissible under this rule. The court may, however, in a criminal case allow evidence of a juvenile adjudication of a witness other than the accused if conviction of the offense would be admissible to attack the credibility of an adult and the court is satisfied that admission in evidence is necessary for a fair determination of the issue of guilt or innocence.

In the revised Uniform Rule, the phrase "Except as otherwise provided by statute" is inserted at the beginning of the second sentence; otherwise the rules are the same. Effective December 1, 2011, restyled Fed. R. Evid. 609(d) reads:

Juvenile Adjudication. Evidence of a juvenile adjudication is admissible under this rule only if:

(1) it is offered in a criminal case;

(2) the adjudication was of a witness other than the defendant;

(3) an adult's conviction for that offense would be admissible to attack the adult's credibility; and

(4) admitting the evidence is necessary to fairly determine guilt or innocence.

[37]See notes 35 to 36 supra. A juvenile adjudication has been said to be admissible to impeach by contradiction when the subject of lack of convictions was "opened up" by the witness (U.S. v. Canniff, 521 F.2d 565 (2d Cir. 1975)) and to impeach by showing bias. Davis v. Alaska, 415 U.S. 308, 94 S. Ct. 1105, 39 L. Ed. 2d 347 (1974)

There are several miscellaneous issues related to conviction impeachment. By case law, a pardon does not prevent the use of the conviction to impeach.[38] The Federal Rules of Evidence adopt the same rule under stated conditions.[39] The primary condition is that under Rule 609(c)(2), a pardon bars the use of the conviction only if the pardon "or other equivalent procedure" was "based on a finding that the person has been rehabilitated" or "a finding of innocence." By the predominant view, including the Federal Rules of Evidence, the pendency of an appeal does not preclude the use of the conviction.[40] Most courts hold that lapse of time may

---

(as a matter of constitutional right).

[38]Richards v. U.S., 192 F.2d 602 (D.C. Cir. 1951) (one judge dissenting); Vedin v. McConnell, 22 F.2d 753, 5 Alaska Fed. 394 (C.C.A. 9th Cir. 1927); Pardon as affecting impeachment by proof of conviction of crime, 30 A.L.R.2d 893. *Contra* Cal. Evid. Code, § 788.

[39]Former Fed. R. Evid. 609(c) and Unif. R. Evid. 609(c) distinguish between pardons based upon findings of rehabilitation and subsequent good behavior or pardons based on findings of innocence, and other pardons. They provide:

> Evidence of a conviction is not admissible under this rule if (1) the conviction has been the subject of a pardon, annulment, certificate of rehabilitation, or other equivalent procedure based on a finding of the rehabilitation of the person convicted, and that person has not been convicted of a subsequent crime which was punishable by death or imprisonment in excess of one year, or (2) the conviction has been the subject of a pardon, annulment, or other equivalent procedure based on a finding of innocence.

Effective December 1, 2011, restyled Fed. R. Evid. 609(c) reads:

> Effect of a Pardon, Annulment, or Certificate of Rehabilitation. Evidence of a conviction is not admissible if:
>
> (1) the conviction has been the subject of a pardon, annulment, certificate of rehabilitation, or other equivalent procedure based on a finding that the person has been rehabilitated, and the person has not been convicted of a later crime punishable by death or by imprisonment for more than one year; or

> (2) the conviction has been the subject of a pardon, annulment, or other equivalent procedure based on a finding of innocence.

*See* Wal-Mart Stores, Inc. v. Regions Bank Trust Dept., 347 Ark. 826, 69 S.W.3d 20 (2002) ("the Fifth Circuit has noted that Rule 609 'draw[s] a distinction between pardons based on actual innocence or a finding of rehabilitation (which makes the underlying conviction inadmissible for impeachment) and pardons granted solely to restore civil rights (which have no relevance to character and do not impair the admissibility of the underlying conviction)' "). *Compare* Zinman v. Black & Decker (U.S.), Inc., 983 F.2d 431, 435–36 (2d Cir. 1993) (evidence of the witness's community-mindedness and lawful conduct were insufficient; a formal finding of rehabilitation is required) *with* U.S. v. Thorne, 547 F.2d 56 (8th Cir. 1976) (trial court could determine the witness had been rehabilitated on the basis of his activities and treatment and refuse to permit a showing of his prior conviction although the witness had no certificate of rehabilitation of any kind). *See* Construction and application of Rule 609(c) of the Federal Rules of Evidence, providing that evidence of conviction is not admissible to attack credibility of witness if conviction has been subject of pardon, annulment, or other procedure based on finding of rehabilitation or innocence, 42 A.L.R. Fed. 942.

[40]People v. Bey, 42 Ill. 2d 139, 246 N.E.2d 287 (1969); Suggs v. State, 6 Md. App. 231, 250 A.2d 670 (1969),

prevent use of a conviction too remote in time from trial when the judge in his discretion finds that under the circumstances it lacks sufficient probative value.[41] The Federal Rule of Evidence is more specific; under Rule 609(b), convictions are presumptively remote and inadmissible when more than 10 years have elapsed.[42]

---

and the many cases cited therein. Contra cases cited in *Suggs v. State*, supra; Permissibility of impeaching credibility of witness by showing former conviction, as affected by pendency of appeal from conviction or motion for new trial, 16 A.L.R.3d 726.

Former Fed. R. Evid. 609(e) and Unif. R. Evid. 609(e) provide: "The pendency of an appeal therefrom does not render evidence of a conviction inadmissible. Evidence of the pendency of an appeal is admissible." Effective December 1, 2011, restyled Fed. R. Evid. 609(e) reads: "Pendency of an Appeal. A conviction that satisfies this rule is admissible even if an appeal is pending. Evidence of the pendency is also admissible."

[41]Lanier v. State, 43 Ala. App. 38, 179 So. 2d 167 (1965) (it was not an abuse of discretion to admit a conviction 30 years entered before trial). Right to impeach credibility of accused by showing prior conviction, as affected by remoteness in time of prior offense, 67 A.L.R.3d 824.

[42]Former Fed. R. Evid. 609(b) provided:

Evidence of a conviction under this rule is not admissible if a period of more than ten years has elapsed since the date of the conviction or of the release of the witness from the confinement imposed for that conviction, whichever is the later date, unless the court determines, in the interests of justice, that the probative value of the conviction supported by specific facts and circumstances substantially outweighs its prejudicial effect. However, evidence of a conviction more than 10 years old as calculated herein, is not admissible unless the proponent gives to the adverse party sufficient advance written notice of intent to use such evidence to provide the adverse party with a fair opportunity to contest the use of such evidence.

The Uniform Rule contains similar language. Effective December 1, 2011, restyled Fed. R. Evid. 609(b) reads:

Limit on Using the Evidence After 10 Years. This subdivision applies if more than 10 years have passed since the witness's conviction or release from confinement for it, whichever is later. Evidence of the conviction is admissible only if:

(1) its probative value, supported by specific facts and circumstances, substantially outweighs its prejudicial effect; and

(2) the proponent gives an adverse party reasonable written notice of the intent to use it so that the party has a fair opportunity to contest its use.

*See* Boomsma v. Star Transp., Inc., 202 F. Supp. 2d 869 (E.D. Wis. 2002) (more than 14 years); Bizmark, Inc. v. Kroger Co., 994 F. Supp. 726 (W.D. Va. 1998) (in Rule 609, "release from confinement" means release from actual imprisonment; neither parole nor probation constitutes "confinement"); State v. Ihnot, 575 N.W.2d 581 (Minn. 1998) (the question presented was when the ten-year period ends; the court noted that there is a three-way split of authority—the date the trial begins, the date the witness testifies, or the date of the offense being litigated; the courts opts for the third view, since the other two possibilities are subject to manipulation; in addition, the third date is more relevant to the question of the length of the period of good behavior). See remarks indicating that the degree by which probative value must outweigh prejudicial effects is greater under the above rule than in the case of the weighing process under the somewhat similar terms of Rule 609(a). U.S. v. Beahm, 664 F.2d 414 (4th Cir. 1981). *See* Construction and application of

Case authority is divided over the use of a judgment based on a plea of *nolo contendere*.[43] The Federal Rule of Evidence should be interpreted as permitting the use of such a judgment.[44] Other

---

Rule 609(b) of Federal Rules of Evidence, setting time limit on admissibility of conviction of crime to attack credibility of witness, 160 A.L.R. Fed. 201. *See also* Simpson v. Thomas, 528 F.3d 685 (9th Cir. 2008) (the question is "whether prior convictions more than ten years old may be used for impeachment . . . if those prior convictions are used to enhance a sentence for a separate conviction that falls within the ten-year limit of Rule 609(b). We hold that such convictions do not endure for the purposes of Rule 609(b) . . . ."). Holland, It's About Time: The Need for a Uniform Approach to Using a Prior Conviction to Impeach a Witness, 40 St. Mary's L.J. 455 (2008), discusses four issues relating to the use of stale convictions under the Texas version of Rule 609(b):

- What is the end point for measuring the ten year period? "Texas courts have measured the end point from the age of a conviction from several different points in time. Those various points on the timeline, which may be called 'as of' dates, include: (1) the date(s) of the offense(s) currently being tried; (2) the date the defendant-witness was arrested for the offense(s) currently being tried; (3) the start date of the trial in which the prior conviction is used as impeachment evidence; and (4) the date when the witness testifies and the prior conviction is offered as impeachment evidence." The author favors the last option.

- Is "tacking" appropriate? "Under this doctrine, if a witness had a remote conviction A, that conviction could be 'tacked' onto a later conviction B that was within the ten-year window. As a result of this tacking, the older conviction

was effectively 'revitalized' or, in other words, was constructively transformed from a remote to a fresh conviction." The author opposes this doctrine.

- In one of the leading Texas cases, Theus v. State, 845 S.W.2d 874 (Tex. Crim. App. 1992), the court stated that in assessing the probative value of the conviction, the trial judge should consider both temporal proximity and the witness's subsequent history, that is, other crimes suggesting "a propensity for running afoul of the law." Some subsequent cases have concluded that the conviction possesses high probative value only when both elements are satisfied—a two-pronged, conjunctive test. The author believes that those cases misread *Theus*.

- Do the *Theus* factors apply both when the conviction is less than 10 years old and when the conviction is more than 10 years old? The author contends that the factors apply in both situations.

[43]Pfotzer v. Aqua Systems, 162 F.2d 779 (C.C.A. 2d Cir. 1947) (admissible); Lacey v. People, 166 Colo. 152, 442 P.2d 402 (1968); Strickland v. State, 498 So. 2d 1350, 1352 (Fla. 1st DCA 1986) (admissible); Com. v. Snyder, 408 Pa. 253, 182 A.2d 495 (1962) (admissible); Cal. Evid. Code, § 788. *Contra* Clinkscales v. State, 104 Ga. App. 723, 123 S.E.2d 165 (1961). *See* Conviction upon plea of *nolo contendere* as admissible for purpose of impeaching witness, 146 A.L.R. 867. Many jurisdictions do not recognize the plea. Attitudes toward it are mixed.

[44]Fed. R. Evid. 609(a) is silent as to whether convictions based on pleas of *nolo contendere* may be used to

Federal Rules such as Rules 410 and 803(22) expressly refer to *nolo* pleas. Those references suggest that the drafters purposely omitted any reference to such pleas in Rule 609 and decided against excluding convictions resting on such pleas from the scope of Rule 609.

### The Mechanics of Using a Conviction for Impeachment

Assume that the conviction in question is usable for impeachment purposes. What mechanical steps should the attorney follow to employ the conviction for that purpose? Of course, the attorney must establish that the witness is the person who suffered the proffered conviction. However, the identity between the

---

impeach. However, Rule 410 renders a *nolo* plea inadmissible against the person making it, and Rule 803(22) recognizes a hearsay exception for felony convictions except on *nolo* pleas. While these two provisions might be thought to preclude the use of *nolo* convictions to impeach, convincing factors strongly indicate a contrary answer. If Rule 410 applies to convictions used to impeach, then a *nolo* conviction could be used to impeach any witness except a party. No reason for such an anomalous result is apparent. Rule 803(22) recognizes a hearsay exception for felony convictions, yet certain misdemeanors are usable for impeachment under Rule 609 which, if applicable, Rule 803(22) would exclude as hearsay. The conclusion must be that Rule 609 is a complete scheme; since it does not exclude *nolo* convictions, they are usable. This conclusion is reinforced by the history of the Federal Rule. In the Preliminary Draft of 1969, no mention of *nolo* convictions appeared. In the 1971 Draft they were expressly excluded. However, the reference to *nolo* convictions did not appear in the Rules adopted by the Supreme Court in 1972 or in the Rules as enacted by the Congress. Since to a large extent the Congress drew on the 1971 Draft in making changes in the Rules, it must be assumed that it was aware that at one stage convictions based on *nolo* pleas were expressly excluded from the Rule. *Accord* Brewer v. City of Napa, 210 F.3d 1093, 1096 (9th Cir. 2000) ("Rule 410 by its terms prohibits only evidence of plea (includ-

ing no contest pleas), insofar as pleas constitute statements or admissions. Rule 609, by contrast, permits admission for impeachment purposes of evidence of convictions"); U.S. v. Sonny Mitchell Center, 934 F.2d 77, 79 (5th Cir. 1991); U.S. v. Williams, 642 F.2d 136, 140 n.3 (5th Cir. 1981) ("The commentators uniformly support the position that a nolo conviction is admissible under Rule 609."); State v. Outlaw, 326 N.C. 467, 390 S.E.2d 336 (1990). *Contra* U.S. v. Morrow, 537 F.2d 120 (5th Cir. 1976) (conviction based upon plea of *nolo contendere* may not be used to impeach credibility of witness). *See also* U.S. v. Graham, 325 F.2d 922 (6th Cir. 1963) (in narcotics prosecution use of plea of *nolo contendere* in prior narcotics case to show that defendant was an addict not permitted).

It is unconstitutional to impeach a defendant by a prior conviction which was not constitutional because the accused had been denied counsel. Loper v. Beto, 405 U.S. 473, 92 S. Ct. 1014, 31 L. Ed. 2d 374 (1972). *See also* U.S. v. Reece, 797 F. Supp. 843, 848 (D. Colo. 1992) (the defendant introduced evidence that at the prior trial, the judge failed to inform him of his Fifth Amendment privilege before he testified; once the defendant presented that evidence, the burden shifted to the government to produce evidence that the conviction was constitutionally valid; the government neglected to do so).

witness's name and the name stated on the judgment can support a permissive inference that the witness is the convict.[45]

The general rule in other situations is that if feasible, proof of an official record must be made by a certified or examined copy rather than oral testimony about its contents.[46] That rule was applied in England to proof of records of conviction and precluded the cross-examiner from asking about convictions.[47] This practice still persists in a few states.[48] However, the inconvenience of the requirement, and the obvious reliability of the witness's answer acknowledging his own conviction, have led most jurisdictions to abandon that practice; by statute, rule, or decision, the vast majority of jurisdictions permit the proof by either production of the record or a copy, or the oral acknowledgment by the convicted witness himself.[49] Hence, the cross-examiner need not "lay a foundation" by copy or record.[50] Nor is she bound to "take the answer" if the witness denies the conviction, but may prove it by introducing the record.[51]

---

[45]State v. Ivy, 710 S.W.2d 431, 434 (Mo. Ct. App. E.D. 1986).

[46]*E.g.*, Jones v. Melindy, 62 Ark. 203, 36 S.W. 22, 23–24 (1896), and discussion § 240 infra, and 4 Wigmore, Evidence § 1269 (Chadbourn rev. 1972).

[47]R. v. The Inhabitants of Castell Careinion, 1806 WL 1401 (K.B.).

[48]Carroll v. Crawford, 218 Ga. 635, 129 S.E.2d 865 (1963); People v. McCrimmon, 37 Ill. 2d 40, 224 N.E.2d 822 (1967) (to impeach defendant as a witness in a criminal case; dictum). Arguably the practice lessens the adverse impact of the evidence when the witness is the accused and affords some amelioration of his unfortunate predicament.

[49]Gaskill v. Gahman, 255 Iowa 891, 124 N.W.2d 533 (1963); State v. Wolfe, 343 S.W.2d 10 (Mo. 1961). Authorities are collected in 4 Wigmore, Evidence § 1270, n. 5 (Chadbourn rev. 1972). A few courts have permitted impeachment by showing of a verdict of guilty without judgment, and a few have rejected such proof. Permissibility of impeaching credibility of witness by showing verdict of guilty without judgment of sentence thereon, 28 A.L.R.4th 647.

[50]Moe v. Blue Springs Truck Lines, Inc., 426 S.W.2d 1 (Mo. 1968).

Fed. R. Evid. 609(a) does not require any "foundation" question before the record is introduced. S. Rep. No. 93-1277 93d Cong., 2d Sess. 14 (1974) states: "It is to be understood however, that a court record of a prior conviction is admissible to prove that conviction if the witness has forgotten or denies its existence." This statement does not necessarily seem to require a "foundation" question as a matter of routine.

[51]See notes 49 to 50 supra. A few cases have addressed the question whether there is error if the prosecutor fails to introduce the record after the witness upon cross-examination denies the existence of a conviction. State decisions seem inconclusive. See Effect of prosecuting attorney asking defense witness other than accused as to prior convictions where he is not prepared to offer documentary proof in event of denial, 3 A.L.R.3d 965. Federal decisions indicate that if the witness fails on cross-examination to admit the conviction in any respect, for example by specifically denying or claiming a lack of recollection, the government must introduce evidence of the conviction, preferably the public

Sometimes the direct examiner elicits the testimony about the witness's conviction. It is a common tactic for the party who calls a witness with a provable criminal record to bring out the prior conviction on direct examination.[52] This practice is not true impeachment of a party's own witness but rather as anticipatory, preemptive disclosure designed to reduce the prejudicial effect of a revelation of the evidence for the first time on cross-examination.[53] It is "a time-honored trial tactic"[54] to attempt to

---

record of conviction, as well as evidence proving that the witness was the individual convicted. Shaw v. Johnson, 786 F.2d 993, 999 (10th Cir. 1986) ("Insofar as federal crimes are concerned, we have held that the United States does not discharge its burden of proving a prior conviction by merely introducing court records pertaining to a person of the same or similar name, and that such record must be supported by some independent evidence tending to support its trustworthiness in order to become 'sufficient in law.' "); U.S. v. Wolf, 561 F.2d 1376 (10th Cir. 1977) (improper to inquire of witness on cross-examination as to whether he was ever convicted of any other felony where prosecution unprepared to prove an undisclosed conviction); Ciravolo v. U.S., 384 F.2d 54, 55 (1st Cir. 1967) ("[T]o ask a defendant whether he has had criminal convictions, without possessing a certified copy of the record, is fraught with possibilities of error."); U.S. v. Haskell, 327 F.2d 281, 284 (2d Cir. 1964) ("As a general rule, of course, it is grossly improper for a cross-examiner to suggest that a witness has been convicted of crimes, especially felonies, when he has no support for the question."); Carlton v. U.S., 198 F.2d 795 (9th Cir. 1952) (better practice to produce the public record where available). *Compare* U.S. v. Scott, 592 F.2d 1139 (10th Cir. 1979) (reliance on FBI "rap sheet" as basis upon which to cross-examine as to prior convictions is proper). *See also* Barcomb v. State, 68 So. 3d 412 (Fla. 4th DCA 2011) (the Florida cases are divided; "Some recent appellate decisions have relaxed the requirement

that counsel possess a certified copy of the judgment of conviction if a 'good faith effort' has been made to obtain the judgment of conviction. Under the rationale of these cases, counsel can attack credibility based on a 'rap sheet.' Others have rejected the relaxation and continue to require the certified copy").

[52]U.S. v. Countryman, 758 F.2d 574, 577 (11th Cir. 1985) ("[I]t is permissible for the government to disclose guilty pleas of co-conspirator government witnesses in order to blunt the impact of expected attacks on the witnesses' credibility."); U.S. v. Dixon, 547 F.2d 1079, 1082 n.2 (9th Cir. 1976) ("It seems clear from the legislative history that on direct examination, a party may elicit the evidence of a prior conviction from his own witness; if the witness has forgotten or denies the existence of the conviction, the party may then introduce evidence of the conviction by public record, even though this does not take place on cross-examination. Moreover, Rule 607, by its terms, places no limitation on the manner in which a party may impeach his own witness, and there is no reason to believe that such a witness cannot be impeached by evidence of a prior conviction.").

[53]U.S. v. Medical Therapy Sciences, Inc., 583 F.2d 36, 39 (2d Cir. 1978) ("[E]ven in jurisdictions where a party may not discredit his own witness, it has been held that the fact of prior convictions may be brought out on direct examination for non-impeachment purposes."); People v. Lankford, 210 Cal. App. 3d 227, 258 Cal. Rptr. 322, 323 (1st Dist. 1989) ("Appellant chose to disclose that prior

beat the opposing attorney to the punch; when the witness's proponent discloses the impeaching fact on direct, the jury may have a higher regard to the proponent's candor, and the disclosure might take some of the sting out of the later cross-examination. Anticipatory disclosure is particularly common when the criminal defendant testifies on his own behalf.[55] Section 55 of this treatise discusses the question of whether the direct examiner's mention of the evidence waives any objection that the direct examiner's client would otherwise have to the opponent's introduction of the conviction.

However, more often than not the initial mention of the conviction occurs on cross-examination. How far may the cross-examiner go in inquiring about convictions? There is consensus that he may ask about the name of the crime committed,[56] i.e. murder or embezzlement. The name is stated on the face of the

---

felony conviction on his direct examination rather than have such disclosure made on the prosecution's cross-examination. Such trial strategy is believed by some to minimize the expected adverse effect of the conviction, inevitably to be exposed, by demonstrating to the jury defendant's honesty and candor as to adverse matters."); Quinones v. State, 528 So. 2d 46, 47 (Fla. 3d DCA 1988) ("[T]he Florida supreme court has approved the use of anticipatory rehabilitation by the defense to mitigate the harmful consequences of damaging facts 'by explaining something about the nature or character of the damaging information,' Lawhorne v. State, 500 So.2d 519, 521 (Fla.1986) . . . .").

As to impeaching one's own witness, see § 38 supra.

[54] U.S. v. Ewings, 936 F.2d 903, 909–10 (7th Cir. 1991); St. John v. State of N.C. Parole Com'n, 764 F. Supp. 403, 414 (W.D. N.C. 1991), aff'd, 953 F.2d 639 (4th Cir. 1992).

[55] U.S. v. Holly, 167 F.3d 393, 395 (7th Cir. 1999) ("the government is allowed to 'front' the expected cross-examination of witnesses"); U.S. v. Freeman, 164 F.3d 243 (5th Cir. 1999) (the prosecution may "steal the defense's thunder by presenting a prior inconsistent statements as part of its direct examination of a witness"); U.S. v. Bad Cob, 560 F.2d 877, 883 (8th Cir.

1977) ("The introduction by a witness himself, on his direct, of a prior conviction is a common trial tactic, recommended by textwriters on trial practice. There is a paucity of authority justifying in theory this well accepted practice, but it has been justified on the ground that it serves a twofold purpose; (a) to bring out the witness' 'real character,' the whole person, particularly his credibility, and (b) to draw the teeth out of the adversary's probable use of the same evidence on cross-examination.").

As to preservation for appeal of alleged error with respect to a ruling on a motion in limine permitting the use of a prior conviction to impeach, see infra § 52, at notes 23 to 27. There is authority that if the defendant testifies and preempts the cross by mentioning a conviction on direct, the defendant has not waived the right to challenge the judge's pretrial ruling that the conviction is admissible. Wilson v. Groaning, 25 F.3d 581, 586 n.10 (7th Cir. 1994) (finding a waiver under the circumstances would be a "harsh response to a party's reasonable tactical decision to soften the impact of prior convictions which the trial court has already ruled are admissible").

[56] U.S. v. Headbird, 461 F.3d 1074, 1078 (8th Cir. 2006) ("little beyond the fact and nature of . . . [the] prior offenses"); U.S. v. Tumblin, 551 F.2d

copy of the judgment of conviction. Where the crime was aggravated. it would certainly add force of the impeachment if he could also ask about any lurid circumstances, for example, whether the murder victim was both a baby and the witness's own niece.[57] A few courts have suggested that since proof by record is allowable, cross-examination should be permitted to disclose all the facts mentioned in the record of trial.[58] On balance, however, the more reasonable position restricts the cross-examiner to the basic facts reflected on the face of the judgment: the name of the crime,[59] the time and place of conviction,[60] and sometimes the punishment.[61] That position minimizes the risks

---

1001 (5th Cir. 1977); State v. Phillips, 102 Ariz. 377, 430 P.2d 139 (1967); People v. Terry, 57 Cal. 2d 538, 21 Cal. Rptr. 185, 370 P.2d 985 (1962) (dictum); Barnett v. State, 240 Ind. 129, 161 N.E.2d 444 (1959).

[57]Choice v. State, 54 Tex. Crim. 517, 114 S.W. 132, 133 (1908) (properly excluded).

[58]*See* State v. Garvin, 44 N.J. 268, 208 A.2d 402 (1965) ("the statute has been consistently construed to authorize proof by cross-examination of what the record for conviction disclosed," citing cases); State v. Rodia, 132 N.J.L. 199, 39 A.2d 484 (N.J. Ct. Err. & App. 1944) ("Were you ever convicted of the crime of atrocious assault and battery by cutting," approved over objection that "by cutting" was improper, on ground that the charge of cutting would have been shown by the record of conviction); State v. Lindsey, 27 Wash. 2d 186, 177 P.2d 387 (1947) (court upheld cross-examination to show nature of offense and punishment "for the reason that these matters were set forth in the judgment of conviction"). Very often, however, the "record" includes only the so-called Judgment of Conviction and Sentence showing no more than the nature of a crime in terms of the governing criminal statute and no details of the punishment except the length of imprisonment, amount of fine, and probation, if any. *But see* Com. v. Kalhauser, 52 Mass. App. Ct. 339, 754 N.E.2d 76, 80 (2001) (the trend in the case law has "moved away from

the position that the impeaching party can mention anything in the record of conviction, toward recommending that the better practice is to avoid mentioning potentially prejudicial material in the criminal record").

[59]See this section, note 53 supra. Unfortunately, the name of a crime does not always indicate its nature. When it is sought to classify a conviction as one involving dishonesty or false statement under Federal Rule 609(a), supra note 7, either because it is a misdemeanor or in order to avoid balancing probative value against prejudice, further inquiry may be required. U.S. v. Papia, 560 F.2d 827 (7th Cir. 1977) (original charge of forgery shown to have been bargained down to "some sort of false statement forgery in application for loan" from savings and loan association, with guilty plea to "some sort of theft under $100").

[60]Hadley v. State, 25 Ariz. 23, 212 P. 458, 462 (1923) ("Were you ever convicted of a felony in Oklahoma," approved).

[61]*Compare* U.S. v. Albers, 93 F.3d 1469, 1480 (10th Cir. 1996); U.S. v. Robinson, 8 F.3d 398, 409 (7th Cir. 1993) ("whether the defendant had previously been convicted of a felony, . . . what the felony was and . . . when the conviction was obtained"); U.S. v. Wesley, 990 F.2d 360 (8th Cir. 1993) (whether a conviction was obtained, when the conviction was obtained, and what the conviction was for); Campbell v. Greer, 831 F.2d 700,

of prejudice and distraction from the central issues in the case. Further details such as the victim's name[62] and the aggravating circumstances may not be inquired into[63] unless the specific circumstance in question is independently admissible under another theory of logical relevance such as Rule 404(b) or 608(b).

It could be argued that if the impeacher is foreclosed from showing aggravating details, even-handedness dictates that the witness be precluded from explaining or extenuating the conviction or denying his guilt. It is unquestionably impractical and forbidden to retry the case on which the conviction was based. Many decisions completely prohibit any explanation, extenuation,

---

707 (7th Cir. 1987) ("Essentially all the information that the cross-examiner is permitted to elicit is the crime charged, the date, and the disposition."); U.S. v. Wolf, 561 F.2d 1376, 1381 (10th Cir. 1977) ("The cross-examination should be confined to a showing of the essential facts of convictions, the nature of the crimes, and the punishment."); U.S. v. Chaco, 801 F. Supp. 2d 1217, 1222 (D.N.M. 2011) ("[F]urther damaging details . . . [a]re not fair game") *with* Tucker v. U.S., 409 F.2d 1291, 1294 n.1 (5th Cir. 1969) ("He was required to give answers only as to whether he had been previously convicted of a felony, as to what the felony was and as to when the conviction was had."); Beaudine v. U.S., 368 F.2d 417, 421 (5th Cir. 1966) ("Number of convictions, the nature of each of the crimes charged, the date and time of conviction"); State v. Bloomer, 156 Ariz. 276, 751 P.2d 592 (Ct. App. Div. 2 1987) (impeaching party may not inquire as to the length of sentence); People v. Szadziewicz, 161 Cal. App. 4th 823, 74 Cal. Rptr. 3d 416 (2d Dist. 2008).

[62]Stevens v. State, 138 Tex. Crim. 59, 134 S.W.2d 246 (1939).

[63]U.S. v. Osazuwa, 564 F.3d 1169 (9th Cir. 2009) (the Ninth Circuit rejected the prosecution argument that since only Rule 608(b) incorporates an extrinsic evidence limitation, the prosecution may freely inquire about collateral details under Rule 609); U.S. v. White, 222 F.3d 363, 370 (7th Cir. 2000) ("Ordinarily, 'the details of the prior conviction should not

[be] exposed to the jury"); U.S. v. Hursh, 217 F.3d 761 (9th Cir. 2000) (the evidence of the prior conviction was "sanitized"); U.S. v. Cox, 536 F.2d 65 (5th Cir. 1976) (reviews cases); Cooper v. McNeil, 622 F. Supp. 2d 1242, 1257 (M.D. Fla. 2008) (under Florida law, "[t]he general rule . . . is that the State is restricted to asking a witness if he or she has been previously convicted of a crime, and if so, the number of times"); U.S. v. Brown, 606 F. Supp. 2d 306, 312 (E.D. N.Y. 2009) ("the government 'is generally limited to establishing the bare [or essential] facts of the conviction: usually the name of the offense, the date of the conviction, and the sentence"); U.S. v. Ramos-Cartagena, 9 F. Supp. 2d 88, 91 (D.P.R. 1998) ("the gruesome details of" the underlying offense are inadmissible); State v. Norgaard, 272 Minn. 48, 136 N.W.2d 628 (1965) (age of girl involved in conviction for assault with intent to rape; but error not prejudicial in this instance); White v. State, 202 Miss. 246, 30 So. 2d 894 (1947) (inquiry whether conviction for wilful trespass followed a withdrawn guilty plea of burglary, improper). But according to some courts, if the witness testifies to matters pertaining to a conviction on direct examination, he "opens the door" to some cross-examination about the circumstances. *E.g.*, U.S. v. Wolf, 561 F.2d 1376 (10th Cir. 1977); State v. Rush, 248 Or. 568, 436 P.2d 266 (1968) (dictum); State v. Wilson, 26 Wash. 2d 468, 174 P.2d 553 (1946).

or denial of guilt even by the witness himself on redirect.[64] This prohibition is a logical consequence of the premise of finality or conclusiveness of the judgment. However, that prohibition does not satisfy our feeling that the witness ought to have some opportunity for self-defense, if it can be done without too much distraction from the business at hand. Accordingly, while not opening the door to retry the conviction, numerous courts accord the witness the right to make a brief, general statement in explanation, mitigation, or denial of guilt,[65] or grant the trial judge a discretion to permit it.[66] Wigmore aptly terms it a "harmless charity to allow the witness to make such protestations on his own behalf as he may feel able to make with a due regard to the penalties of perjury."[67]

The most prejudicial impact of conviction impeachment (as is true also of cross-examination as to misconduct, see § 42, above) is on one particular type of witness, namely, the criminal accused who elects to take the stand. Suppose that the accused is forced to admit that he has a "record" of past convictions, particularly convictions for crimes similar to the one on trial. In this situation, despite any limiting instructions, there is an obvious danger of misuse of the evidence. The jurors might give more weight to the past convictions as evidence that the accused is the kind of man who would commit the crime charged or even that he ought to be imprisoned without much concern for present guilt, than to

---

[64]Mayo v. State, 32 Ala. App. 264, 24 So. 2d 769 (1946) (accused-witness not allowed to show he was given probation for offense for which convicted); State v. Gregg, 230 S.C. 222, 95 S.E.2d 255 (1956) (defendant-witness not permitted to state mitigating details on redirect examination).

[65]4 Wigmore, Evidence § 1117 n. 3 (Chadbourn rev. 1972).

[66]See generally U.S. v. Plante, 472 F.2d 829, 832 (1st Cir. 1973) ("Within the limits of not disputing the offense, occasionally the opponent of the witness, and occasionally the proponent, wish to go into the details in order to enhance, or diminish the effect of the conviction. There is a split of authority as to whether the proponent may do so. . . . We believe that neither party should be able to develop the details. To permit the opponent to do so tends unduly to prejudice the witness, cf. United States v. Tomaiolo, 2

Cir., 1957, 249 F.2d 683, 687, and in all cases it leads to a collateral issue, with frequently one party or the other being at a disadvantage."). However, if the defendant exercises this right and goes too far, the defendant's testimony may open the door to a further prosecution inquiry about the details of the underlying offense. See U.S. v. Jackson, 876 F. Supp. 1188, 1198 (D. Kan. 1994) (the defendant went to some length in minimizing his role in the drug transaction which led to the prior conviction).

[67]4 Wigmore, Evidence § 1117, at 251 (Chadbourn rev. 1972).

It is not uncommon for the criminal defendant to testify to having pleaded guilty to the prior offense, thereby suggesting his willingness to "own up" to what he does and the further inference that he is innocent of the current charges.

the convictions' legitimate bearing on credibility.[68] The accused with a "record," who has a meritorious defense to the present charge, thus faces a harsh dilemma. One horn of the dilemma is that if he stays off the stand, his silence alone might prompt the jury to believe him guilty. The other horn is that if he elects to testify, his "record" becomes provable to impeach him, and this again could doom his defense.

Where does the proper balance lie? Most prosecutors argue forcefully that it is misleading to permit the accused to implicitly portray himself as having led a blameless life, and this argument has prevailed widely. One intermediate position, between routinely admitting all the convictions and excluding them all, is that the convictions should be restricted to those bearing directly on character for truthfulness.[69] Another intermediate view—but with the disadvantage of uncertainty—permits the introduction of the defendant's prior convictions in the judge's discretion. In each instance, the judge would have to balance the possible prejudice against the probative value of the conviction as to credibility.[70] As already noted, the Federal Rule of Evidence is a compromise.[71] Federal Rule 609 essentially embraces the latter intermediate view. However, even these intermediate views do

---

[68]Griswold, The Long View, 51 A.B.A.J. 1017, 1021 (1965); Schaefer, Police Interrogation and the Privilege Against Self—Incrimination, 61 NW. U. L. Rev. 506, 512 (1966); McGowan, Impeachment of Criminal Defendants by Prior Convictions, 1970 Ariz. St. L.J. 1. Statistical support is found in Kalven & Zeisel, The American Jury 124, 126–30, 144–46, 160–62 (1966); Beaver & Marques, A Proposal to Modify the Rule on Criminal Conviction Impeachment, 58 Temp. L.Q. 585, 602 (1985) (discussing part of the Chicago Jury Project described in The American Jury, supra); Wissler & Saks, On the Inefficacy of Limiting Instructions—When Jurors Use Prior Conviction Evidence to Decide Guilt, 9 Law & Hum. Behav. 37 (1985).

[69]Original Uniform Rule 21 limited provable convictions with respect to witnesses generally to crimes involving dishonesty or false statement.

[70]In Luck v. U.S., 348 F.2d 763 (D.C. Cir. 1965), the court found authority for such an approach in the provision then in D.C. Code Ann. 1981, § 14-305 that conviction "may" be given in evidence to impeach. Brown v. U.S., 370 F.2d 242 (D.C. Cir. 1966) and Gordon v. U.S., 383 F.2d 936 (D.C. Cir. 1967), developed standards for the exercise of discretion, including the nature of the crime, nearness or remoteness in time, the person's subsequent career, and the similarity of the crime to the one charged. The present D.C. Code, § 14-305 contains provisions similar to those in Fed. R. Evid. 609 but with differences.

As amended, Rule 609 distinguishes between the balancing test when the witness is the criminal defendant and the governing balancing test for all other types of witnesses. U.S. v. Tse, 375 F.3d 148, 159–64 (1st Cir. 2004).

[71]See text at notes 7 to 27 supra.

Where a witness is impeached by means of prior conviction, the immediate giving of a limiting instruction is appropriate as is the repetition of the instruction concerning the proper use of the prior conviction when the jury is instructed on the law at the conclusion of the case. U.S. v. Diaz, 585 F.2d 116, 118 (5th Cir. 1978)

not exhaust the possibilities. In Pennsylvania,[72] under certain circumstances, the accused who takes the stand is shielded from cross-examination as to misconduct or conviction of crime when it is offered to impeach but not from proof by the record of conviction. Finally, the former Uniform Rule[73] provided that if the accused does not offer evidence supporting his own credibility, the prosecution may not, on cross-examination or otherwise, use his conviction for impeachment purposes. The very variety of proposed solutions indicates the thorny nature of the problem.

In view of that difficulty, the suggestion has been made that the "mere fact" method be employed for convictions punishable by death or imprisonment in excess of one year.[74] The method is described as follows:

---

("This court has repeatedly indicated that when evidence of prior similar crimes is properly introduced, the jury must be able to distinguish between credibility evidence and affirmative evidence.").

[72]42 Pa. Cons. Stat. Ann. § 5919.

In England, the Criminal Evidence Act, 1898 (61 & 62 Vict. c. 36), subs. 1(f) provided:

> A person charged and called as a witness in pursuance of this Act shall not be asked, and if asked shall not be required to answer, any question tending to show that he has committed or been convicted of or been charged with any offence other than that wherewith he is then charged, or is of bad character, unless—(i) the proof that he has committed or been convicted of such other offence is admissible evidence to show that he is guilty of the offence wherewith he is then charged; or (ii) he has personally or by his advocate asked questions of the witnesses for the prosecution with a view to establish his own good character, or has given evidence of his good character, or the nature or conduct of the defence is such as to involve imputations on the character of the prosecutor or the witnesses for the prosecution; or (iii) he has given evidence against any other person charged with the same offence.

See analysis and discussion, 1 Wigmore, Evidence § 194a; Cross, Evidence ch. 15 (5th ed. 1979).

[73]Former Uniform Rule 21: ". . . If the witness be the accused in a criminal proceeding, no evidence of his

conviction of a crime shall be admissible for the sole purpose of impairing his credibility unless he has first introduced evidence admissible solely for the purpose of supporting his credibility."

[74]*See generally* Watts v. State, 160 Fla. 268, 34 So. 2d 429 (1948); State v. Shepherd, 94 Idaho 227, 486 P.2d 82 (1971); Sebastian v. Com., 436 S.W.2d 66 (Ky. 1968); State v. Quinlan, 126 Mont. 52, 244 P.2d 1058 (1952); State v. Craig, 192 Neb. 347, 220 N.W.2d 241 (1974); State v. Hungerford, 54 Wis. 2d 744, 196 N.W.2d 647 (1972). *See also* 2 Graham, Handbook of Federal Evidence § 609:6 (6th ed. 2006); Ehrhardt, A Look at Florida's Proposed Code of Evidence, 2 Fla. St. U. L. Rev. 681, 698–99 (1974); Note, Admissibility of Prior Crimes Evidence to Impeach a Witness in Florida, 15 U. Fla. L. Rev. 220, 225–26 (1962); Comment, Impeachment of Witness Credibility by Use of Past Conviction Evidence—Kentucky Court of Appeals Adopts a New Rule, 59 Ky. L.J. 514, 525–26 (1970); Naylor, Section 609 of the Nebraska Evidence Rules: A Need for Clarification, 57 Neb. L. Rev. 26, 28–29 (1978); Comment, Impeachment of a Witness' Credibility by Proof of a Prior Criminal Conviction, 1959 Wis. L. Rev. 312 (1959). The Illinois courts have expressly rejected this approach. People v. Cox, 195 Ill. 2d 378, 254 Ill. Dec. 720, 748 N.E.2d 166 (2001); People v. Atkinson, 186 Ill. 2d 450, 239 Ill. Dec. 1, 713 N.E.2d 532 (1999).

[T]he proper procedural approach is simply to ask the witness the straight-forward question as to whether he had ever been convicted of a crime. The inquiry must end at this point unless the witness denies that he has been convicted. In the event of such denial the adverse party may then in the presentation of his side of the case produce and file in evidence the record of any such conviction. If the witness admits prior conviction of a crime, the inquiry by his adversary may not be pursued to the point of naming the crime for which he was convicted. If the witness so desires he may of his own volition state the nature of the crime and offer any relevant testimony that would eliminate any adverse implications; for example, the fact that he had in the meantime been fully pardoned or that the crime was a minor one and occurred many years before.[75]

The suggestion has also been made that impeachment of the accused by showing prior convictions is unconstitutional. Under the Sixth Amendment the accused has a constitutional right to testify,[76] and the admissibility of convictions for impeachment purposes pressures the accused to forego exercising that right. However, to date, no federal or state court has embraced the suggestion.[77]

---

[75]McArthur v. Cook, 99 So. 2d 565, 567 (Fla. 1957).

Applying the "mere fact" method, on direct examination of the criminal defendant, counsel would inquire:

Q: Have you ever been convicted of an offense punishable by death or imprisonment in excess of one year?

A: Yes.

Q: How many times?

A: Twice.

No further questions on either direct or cross-examination would normally be asked about the prior convictions. The standard limiting instruction would be given. Resort to the "mere fact" method is particularly appropriate where the defendant's prior conviction is similar to the offense for which he is then on trial and thus the risk of prejudice extremely high.

The "mere fact" method may also be applied with respect to crimes of dishonesty or false statement. Accordingly, the following questions would be posed to the witness on direct examination:

Q: Have you ever been convicted of an offense punishable by death or imprisonment in excess of one year?

A: Yes.

Q: How many times?

A: Once.

Q: Have you ever been convicted of an offense involving dishonesty or false statement?

A: Yes.

Q: How many times?

A: Once.

If the nature of the particular offense was felt by the court to be particularly helpful to the jury in assessing credibility, the following could be asked:

Q: What was the nature of that offense?

A: Perjury.

Few courts have adopted this method.

[76]Rock v. Arkansas, 483 U.S. 44, 107 S. Ct. 2704, 97 L. Ed. 2d 37 (1987).

[77]See discussion in Note, 37 U. Cin. L. Rev. 168 (1968). See Spencer v. State of Tex., 385 U.S. 554, 87 S. Ct. 648, 17 L. Ed. 2d 606 (1967), sustaining the constitutionality of presenting evidence of prior convictions on an habitual criminal issue at the trial of the principal charge, may be pertinent.

## § 43  Character: Impeachment by Proof of Opinion or Bad Reputation[1]

In most jurisdictions the impeacher may attack a prior witness's character by posing the following formulaic questions to a second witness:

> Q. "Do you know William Witness's current general reputation for truth and veracity in the community in which he lives?"
> A. "Yes."
> Q. "What is that reputation?"
> A. "It is bad."
> Q. "Given that reputation, would you believe William Witness under oath?"
> A. "No."

This formula is the product of traditions which became established in a majority of American courts.[3] The common law tradition is the result of choices between alternative solutions. As we shall see, some of the traditional choices were wise, but others were misguided.

One misguided choice was the threshold decision that this attack on character for truth must be limited to the abstract, debilitated form of proof of reputation. By what is apparently a misreading of legal history,[4] at common law the American courts generally prohibited proof of character by having a witness describe his opinion of the prior witness's character even when the opinion is based on extensive personal experience with the witness under attack and observation of his conduct.[5] The courts

---

However, in People v. Castro, 38 Cal. 3d 301, 211 Cal. Rptr. 719, 696 P.2d 111 (1985), the lead opinion stated that it would violate due process to impeach an accused with convictions which did not entail moral turpitude—to say the least, a highly debatable conclusion. Based on that reasoning, the court adopted a narrowing interpretation of an initiative measure which seemingly allowed prosecutors to use any felony conviction for purposes of impeachment.

**[Section 43]**

[1]See 3A Wigmore, Evidence §§ 920–30 (Chadbourn rev. 1970); 4 Weinstein's Federal Evidence §§ 608. 10–.11 (rev. 2011); Ladd, Techniques of Character Testimony, 24 Iowa L. Rev. 498 (1939); West's Key Number

Digest, Witnesses ☞333 to 343, 356 to 358.

[3]Creech, Adducing Proof of Character or Reputation: A Precise Methodology, Case & Com. 32 (July to Aug. 1975).

[4]See 7 Wigmore, Evidence §§ 1981–82 (Chadbourn rev. 1978), and further discussion infra § 186.

[5]Gifford v. People, 148 Ill. 173, 35 N.E. 754 (1893) (dictum); State v. Polhamus, 65 N.J.L. 387, 47 A. 470 (N.J. Sup. Ct. 1900); State v. Steen, 185 N.C. 768, 117 S.E. 793 (1923). See also cases in which direct opinion was sought in connection with attempts to obtain reputation testimony. Parasco v. State, 168 Tex. Crim. 89, 323 S.W.2d 257 (1959) ("In your opinion is the testimony of . . . under oath worthy of

defended the limitation to reputation on the ground that admitting an opinion would provoke distracting side disputes about the witness's specific conduct, since the impeaching witness may be cross-examined about the basis of his opinion.[6] That danger undoubtedly exists, and the judge would need to confine the disputes to reasonable limits. However, the choice of reputation (instead of opinion based on observation) eliminated much of the objectivity from the attempt to appraise character, and it encouraged the parties to select character witnesses who, under the guise of reputation, voiced prejudice and ill-will. The hand is that of Esau, but the voice is Jacob's. In addition, reputation in modern, impersonal urban centers is often evanescent or non-existent.

The Federal Rules of Evidence and the Revised Uniform Rules of Evidence break with tradition and permit attack by opinion, while at the same time continuing to authorize the traditional reputation attack.[7] Indeed, the Federal Rules seem to authorize the admission of expert opinion on the topic. Although Article VII

---

belief?"; held error); People v. Wendt, 104 Ill. App. 2d 192, 244 N.E.2d 384 (1st Dist. 1968).

Many courts, however, perhaps conscious of the weakness of reputation evidence, have compromised by permitting the injection of personal opinion by such questions as these (after proving bad reputation): "From that reputation, would you believe him on oath?" Burke v. Zwick, 299 Ill. App. 558, 20 N.E.2d 912 (4th Dist. 1939). Or an even more curious straddle: "From your association with W. and from what you know about his reputation . . . do you believe him entitled to credit under oath?" *See* Bowles v. Katzman, 308 Ky. 490, 214 S.W.2d 1021 (1948). This type of testimony has been approved under Fed. R. Evid. 608(a). U.S. v. Davis, 639 F.2d 239 (5th Cir. 1981); U.S. v. Lollar, 606 F.2d 587 (5th Cir. 1979); Attacking or supporting credibility of witness by evidence in form of opinion or reputation, under Rule 608(a) of Federal Rules of Evidence, 52 A.L.R. Fed. 440. However, the first type of question mentioned above which is asked upon the basis of the witness's previous reputation testimony may be doubtful as not being based upon the impeaching witness's rational perception of the witness attacked, a requirement under

Fed. R. Evid. 701. *See* Fed. R. Evid. 608(a).

[6]*See* People v. Van Gaasbeck, 189 N.Y. 408, 82 N.E. 718, 721 (1907) (discussing the analogous problem as to character-evidence offered by the accused on the issue of guilt). The contrary policy argument is powerfully presented in 7 Wigmore, Evidence § 1986. The current trend favoring proof in the form of opinion is reflected in Fed. R. Evid. 608(a) and Unif. R. Evid. 608(a), infra note 7.

[7]Former Fed. R. Evid. 608(a) and Unif. R. Evid. 608(a) provide:

The credibility of a witness may be attacked or supported by evidence in the form of opinion or reputation, but subject to these limitations: (1) the evidence may refer only to character for truthfulness or untruthfulness, and (2) evidence of truthful character is admissible only after the character of the witness for truthfulness has been attacked by opinion or reputation evidence or otherwise.

Effective December 1, 2011, restyled Fed. R. Evid. 608(a) reads:

Reputation or Opinion. A witness's credibility may be attacked or supported by testimony about the witness's reputation for having a character for truthfulness or untruthfulness, or by testimony about that character. But evidence of truthful character is admis-

of the Federal Rules expressly distinguishes between lay and expert opinion, Rule 608(a) refers generally to "opinion."[8] The argument runs that if the drafters had wanted to limit Rule 609(a) opinions to lay testimony, the drafters would have said so.

At common law, the courts faced a further choice. The choice related to the question of whether the inquiry should extend to "general character" and other specific bad traits such as sexual immorality, or whether it ought to be directed solely to the trait of veracity. In the realm of "character," it is best to insist on a high degree of relevancy. Fortunately the great majority of courts limit the inquiry to "reputation for truth and veracity."[9] Under Federal and Revised Uniform Rule of Evidence 608(a), both opinion and reputation are similarly restricted; the rule mentions solely "character for truthfulness or untruthfulness."[10] Only a few

---

sible only after the witness's character for truthfulness has been attacked.

At least four states which have generally adopted the federal rules do not permit the use of opinion testimony to attack character.

[8]U.S. v. Jewell, 614 F.3d 911, 926 (8th Cir. 2010), cert. denied, 131 S. Ct. 1677, 179 L. Ed. 2d 621 (2011); U.S. v. Gonzalez-Maldonado, 115 F.3d 9, 16–17 (1st Cir. 1997).

[9]McHargue v. Perkins, 295 S.W.2d 301 (Ky. 1956); 3A Wigmore, Evidence § 923 (Chadbourn rev. 1970); West's Key Number Digest, Witnesses ⮑342.

[10]Fed. R. Evid. and Unif. R. Evid. 608(a), supra note 7 (character for "truthfulness or untruthfulness"). *See also* U.S. v. Schmitz, 634 F.3d 1247, 1268–70 (11th Cir. 2011); U.S. v. Harris, 471 F.3d 507 (3d Cir. 2006) (nearly all the federal circuits that have passed on this issue have found such questions improper); U.S. v. Freitag, 230 F.3d 1019, 1024 (7th Cir. 2000) ("it is improper to ask one witness to comment on the veracity of the testimony of another witness); U.S. v. Henke, 222 F.3d 633 (9th Cir. 2000); Athridge v. Iglesias, 167 F. Supp. 2d 389, 398 (D.D.C. 2001) ("Under . . . 608(a) one witness may testify as to the credibility of another witness only in the form of an opinion as to the latter's character for truth telling. Hence,

one witness may not express the opinion that another witness is not telling the truth"); Saltzburg, Opening the Door to Bolstering, 16 Crim.Just. 50, 55 (Sum. 2001) ("The opinion by one witness that another witness's information is truthful is off limits"). *But see* People v. Johnigan, 196 Cal. App. 4th 1084, 128 Cal. Rptr. 3d 190, 202 (2d Dist. 2011) ("It is settled that a criminal defendant can be asked whether prosecution witnesses are lying"); State v. Pilot, 595 N.W.2d 511 (Minn. 1999) (where the defendant claimed that the state's case against him was fabricated, it was permissible to ask him whether the prosecution witnesses were lying); State v. Hart, 2000 MT 332, 303 Mont. 71, 15 P.3d 917 (2000) (in a case in which someone had to be lying, it was permissible for the prosecutor to ask the defendant whether the state's witnesses were lying); Saltzburg, Cross-Examining the Defendant About Other Witnesses, 22 Crim. Just., Wint. 2012, at 46, 48 ("Like most general rules, the prohibition . . . is always subject to an exception when a defendant opens the door by voluntary testimony on direct examination. A defendant who volunteers testimony that other witnesses are lying is subject to cross-examination that may address the defendant's opinion about these other witnesses").

jurisdictions open the door to reputation for "general character"[11] or "general moral character."[12] Fewer still permit proof of reputation for specific traits other than veracity.[13]

As we shall see in Chapter 17, the common law and the Federal Rules allow an accused to introduce character evidence on the historical merits of the case; when the accused does so, the evidence must relate to the accused's character at the time of the alleged *actus reus*. However, here the temporal focus is different. The crucial time when the witness's character influences his truth-telling is the time he testifies.[14] But obviously reputation takes time to form and is the result of the witness's earlier conduct. Hence, the reputation does not reflect character precisely at the trial date. The practical solution is to do what most courts do, that is, (1) to permit the reputation-witness to testify about the impeachee's "present" reputation as of the time of the trial,[15]

---

[11]Grammer v. State, 239 Ala. 633, 196 So. 268, 272 (1940) (but reputation for specific traits of character is not permitted).

[12]Ind. Code Ann. § 34-45-2-12, 35-37-4-2.

[13]Among decisions excluding the evidence are Pugh v. State, 42 Ala. App. 499, 169 So. 2d 27, 28 (1964) (bad reputation for being a thief); State v. Alberts, 241 Iowa 1000, 43 N.W.2d 703 (1950) (bad reputation for an honest, upright citizen and industrious man; dictum); State v. Mondrosch, 108 N.J. Super. 1, 259 A.2d 725 (App. Div. 1969) (reputation with regard to a propensity or inclination to be accusatory against others, applying former Evidence Rules 22 and 47); N.J.R.E. 608 (the New Jersey rule omits subdivision (b) of the federal rule).

In prosecutions for sexual offenses, the victim's reputation for lack of chastity is often excluded for the purpose of attacking credibility. Fed. R. Evid. 608(a) by its very terms should dictate that result. Moreover, Fed. R. Evid. 412, the "rape shield" rule, limits the use of reputation or opinion evidence of the victim's lack of chastity. A complete summary of state "rape shield statutes" is contained in Tanford & Bocchino, Rape Victim Shield Laws and the Sixth Amendment, 128 U. Pa. L. Rev. 544, 591–602 (1980). Most of the opinions admitting evidence of reputation for specific traits to attack credibility are prosecutions for sexual offenses in which reputation for lack of chastity is the reputation introduced. Wheeler v. State, 148 Ga. 508, 97 S.E. 408 (1918); Modern status of admissibility, in forcible rape prosecution, of complainant's general reputation for unchastity, 95 A.L.R.3d 1181; Modern status of admissibility, in statutory rape prosecution, of complainant's prior sexual acts or general reputation for unchastity, 90 A.L.R.3d 1300.

[14]See U.S. v. Null, 415 F.2d 1178 (4th Cir. 1969) (when accused proves good character on issue of guilt, it is reputation at the time of act that counts; but if his credibility as a witness is in question, it is reputation at the time of trial).

Decisions as to time are collected in 3A Wigmore, Evidence § 928 (Chadbourn rev. 1970); West's Key Number Digest, Witnesses ⟨⟩343.

[15]Carter v. State, 226 Ala. 96, 145 So. 814 (1933) (time to which the character relates is "the time of trial and prior thereto"); Goehring v. Com., 370 S.W.2d 822 (Ky. 1963) (time must be time of trial "and a reasonable period thereafter;" 9 months before trial was a reasonable period). See also Frith v. Commonwealth, 288 Ky. 188, 155

and (2) to accept testimony about reputation as of any pretrial time period which the judge in his discretion finds is not too remote.[16] Most courts follow this practice under Federal Rule of Evidence 608(a).[17] A witness's opinion permitted by the rule must have a similar temporal relation to the trial.[18]

As to the place of reputation,[19] the traditional inquiry is about general reputation for veracity "in the community where he (the witness to be impeached) lives." The purpose of this geographic limitation is to restrict evidence to reputation among the people who know the witness best.[20] The residential limitation was appropriate for the living conditions in England (and less so in America) before the Industrial Revolution, when most people resided in small towns or rural villages. But as an exclusive limitation, it is inappropriate today. A person may be virtually anonymous in the suburb or city neighborhood where he lives, but well known in another locality where he works or several localities where he regularly does business. Thus, the courts now generally agree that proof may be made of the witness's reputation not only where he lives, but also in any substantial group of people among whom he is well known,[21] such as the persons with

---

S.W.2d 851 (1941) (manslaughter: held impeachment by showing reputation for bad moral character as of time of trial ordinarily proper but error to admit where witness impeaching witness testifies bad reputation was due to the homicide).

[16]U.S. v. Whitmore, 359 F.3d 609, 616–18 (D.C. Cir. 2004) (the witness was a newspaper reporter; the witness was prepared to testify about an arresting officer's reputation for untruthfulness; however, the witness had not had direct contact with the officer's community for some time); Snow v. Grace, 29 Ark. 131, 136, 1874 WL 1151 (1874) (character seven years before properly received); Shuster v. State, 62 N.J.L. 521, 41 A. 701 (N.J. Sup. Ct. 1898) (reputation 18 years before, properly excluded); State v. Thomas, 8 Wash. 2d 573, 113 P.2d 73 (1941) (sodomy, evidence that prosecuting witness 13 years old had bad reputation for truth two years before trial, held, exclusion, in view of child's age, not abuse of discretion; careful opinion by Driver, J.).

[17]U.S. v. Lewis, 482 F.2d 632, 641 (D.C. Cir. 1973) (dictum; "at the time of trial and during a prior period not remote thereto").

[18]The same results are dictated by relevancy principles.

[19]See 3A Wigmore, Evidence § 930 (Chadbourn rev. 1970); West's Key Number Digest, Witnesses ⚷343; Admissibility of testimony as to general reputation at place of employment, 82 A.L.R.3d 525.

[20]See Brill v. Muller Bros., Inc., 40 Misc. 2d 683, 243 N.Y.S.2d 905 (Sup 1962), rev'd because evidence rules inapplicable in arbitration proceeding, 17 A.D.2d 804, 232 N.Y.S.2d 806 (1st Dep't 1962), judgment aff'd, 13 N.Y.2d 776, 242 N.Y.S.2d 69, 192 N.E.2d 34 (1963) (trial court stated that reputation testimony cannot come from a stranger sent out by the adverse party to investigate the reputation).

[21]Craven v. State, 22 Ala. App. 39, 111 So. 767 (1927).

The question of place is often es-

whom he works,[22] does business,[23] or goes to school.[24] Even a large jail population can qualify as a community.[25] To give reputation testimony, the witness must be a member of such a "community," not a mere acquaintance of the witness being impeached.[26] These standards apply under Federal Rule of Evidence 608(a).[27] The rule gives the trial judge a measure of discretion to determine whether the group in question meets these standards[28] and whether the witness has a sufficient nexus to the group.

Other problems arise when the attack on character is by opinion, as authorized by Federal Rule of Evidence 608(a). To

---

sentially a matter of the time when the reputation was acquired, discussed in the preceding paragraph. *See, e.g.,* Lee v. State, 179 Miss. 122, 174 So. 85 (1937) (reputation in place where witness lived six months before trial, provable).

[22]Hamilton v. State, 129 Fla. 219, 176 So. 89 (1937) (reputation could be proved by fellow-employees at hotel where accused worked); State v. Axilrod, 248 Minn. 204, 79 N.W.2d 677 (1956) (not error to admit testimony confined primarily to community in which impeached witness worked).

[23]Hubert v. Joslin, 285 Mich. 337, 280 N.W. 780 (1938) (reputation in locality 15 miles away from home, where he owned a farm, visited frequently, and had many business dealings).

[24]People v. Colantone, 243 N.Y. 134, 152 N.E. 700, 702 (1926) (error to exclude evidence of reputation of ex-soldier, by instructors at vocational school, members of his company in army, and member of disabled veterans' post of 250 men. "The determining factor is whether the community in which the defendant has lived his life is sufficiently large for the persons to become acquainted with his character and to form a general opinion of it. This we call general reputation. The cases are quite right which exclude evidence of reputation among such a small class of persons or business associates, as to make it, not a general reputation, but rather the evidence of individual and independent dealings."). *Compare* Williams v. U.S., 168 U.S. 382, 18 S. Ct. 92, 42 L. Ed. 509

(1897) (error to permit evidence of reputation of immigration inspector "in the custom house;" evidence as to his reputation "among the limited number of people in a particular public building" was inadmissible); State v. Swenson, 62 Wash. 2d 259, 382 P.2d 614 (1963) (error to allow showing of reputation in the church of which impeached witness was a member or among people of that church).

[25]People v. Bieri, 153 Mich. App. 696, 396 N.W.2d 506 (1986).

[26]U.S. v. George, 201 F.3d 370 (5th Cir. 2000).

[27]*E.g.,* U.S. v. Oliver, 492 F.2d 943 (8th Cir. 1974) (error to exclude reputation testimony by former roommates who had known witness for seven weeks). See also remarks in U.S. v. Mandel, 591 F.2d 1347 (4th Cir. 1979) (reputation in law office where witness worked).

[28]Ulrich v. Chicago, B. & Q.R. Co., 281 Mo. 697, 220 S.W. 682, 684 (1920) (judge did not abuse discretion in admitting evidence of plaintiff's reputation at time of trial in locality where he formerly lived and continued to do business); State v. McEachern, 283 N.C. 57, 194 S.E.2d 787 (1973) (extensive discussion, concluding that reputation from "any community or society in which the person has a well known or established reputation" qualifies).

Hearsay aspects of reputation evidence are analyzed in § 248 infra. Cross-examination of the character witness is discussed in § 48 infra.

begin with, the opinion must relate to the prior witness's character trait for untruthfulness, not the question of whether the witness's specific trial testimony was truthful.[29] Moreover, a lay person's opinion should rest on some firsthand knowledge pursuant to Rule 602; the opinion ought to be based on rational perception and aid the jury, as required by Rule 701. The lay witness must be sufficiently familiar with the person to make it worthwhile to present the witness's opinion to the jury.[30] However, specific untruthful acts cannot be elicited during the witness's direct examination even for the limited purpose of showing the basis of the opinion.[31] An adequate preliminary showing to meet the requirements of Rule 701 consists of evidence of suf-

---

[29]The prevailing view is that one witness may not be asked whether another witness lied or was untruthful. U.S. v. Harris, 471 F.3d 507 (3d Cir. 2006) (nearly all the federal circuits that have passed on this issue have found such questions improper); U.S. v. Worley, 94 Fed. Appx. 44, 48–49 (3d Cir. 2004); Athridge v. Iglesias, 167 F. Supp. 2d 389 (D.D.C. 2001), judgment rev'd on other grounds, 312 F.3d 474 (D.C. Cir. 2002)Athridge v. Iglesias, 167 F. Supp. 2d 389, 398 (D.D.C. 2001) ("one witness may not express the opinion that another witness is not telling the truth"); State v. Graves, 668 N.W.2d 860 (Iowa 2003) (the prosecutor may not ask a defendant whether the state's witnesses are lying); Daniel v. State, 119 Nev. 498, 78 P.3d 890 (2003) (the court prohibited prosecutors from asking a defendant on cross-examination whether the prosecution witnesses were lying). But see U.S. v. Martin, 454 F. Supp. 2d 278, 286 (E.D. Pa. 2006) ("Courts are split on whether or not such questions are proper . . . ."); People v. Johnigan, 196 Cal. App. 4th 1084, 128 Cal. Rptr. 3d 190, 202 (2d Dist. 2011) ("It is settled that a criminal defendant can be asked whether prosecution witnesses are lying"); Saltzburg, Cross-Examining the Defendant about Other Witnesses, 26 Crim. Just., Wint. 2012, at 46, 48 ("Like most general rules, the prohibition on [such] questions . . . is always subject to an exception when a defendant opens the door by voluntary testimony on direct examination. A de-

fendant who volunteers testimony that other witnesses are lying is subject to cross-examination that may address the defendant's opinion about these other witnesses.").

[30]Ricketson v. Seaboard Airline R. Co., 403 F.2d 836, 839 (5th Cir. 1968) (although the defendant's brother had not communicated with the defendant for over a decade, the brother was competent to testify to his own opinion of the defendant's honesty; the long break in family relations was a proper subject for cross-examination and argument). But see U.S. v. Garza, 448 F.3d 294, 296–98 (5th Cir. 2006) (the court upheld the exclusion of an investigator's opinion about the credibility of a police officer; while the investigator had investigated the officer over a two-month period, the trial judge did not abuse discretion in concluding that the investigator lacked an adequate basis for an opinion as to the officer's truthfulness).

[31]U.S. v. Hoskins, 628 F.2d 295 (5th Cir. 1980); State v. Freeland, 316 N.C. 13, 340 S.E.2d 35 (1986) (the trial court erred in allowing a mother to refer to specific acts and occurrences tending to show that her child has a good character for truthfulness and can distinguish fantasy from reality). Federal Rule 405 refers to the use of opinion to prove character. The Advisory Committee Note to Rule 405 states that the statutory scheme "contemplate[s] that testimony of specific instances is not generally permissible on the direct examination of an ordi-

ficient acquaintance with the witness to be attacked.[32] Impeachment by expert opinion rather than lay opinion testimony is considered in the next section.

## § 44   Defects of capacity: Sensory or mental[1]

Assume that the witness has a sensory deficiency but not one which is so extreme that it renders the person incompetent as a witness under the standards discussed in Chapter 7. Any deficiency of the senses, such as deafness or color blindness, which would substantially lessen the ability to perceive the facts which the witness purports to have observed, ought to be provable to attack the witness's credibility. The opposing attorney may launch the attack either on cross-examination or by producing other witnesses to prove the defect. (More broadly, the limits of human powers of perception should be studied more intensively in the interest of a more accurate, objective administration of justice.[2])

As to the mental qualities of intelligence and memory, a distinction must be made between attacks on competency[3] and attacks on credibility, the subject of this section. Sanity in a general sense is no longer a test of competency, and a so-called "insane" person is generally permitted to testify if he can report correctly the matters to which he testifies and understand the duty to

---

nary opinion witness to character." *But see* Comment, A Comparison of the Use of Character Witness Testimony in Maryland Versus the Federal Practice: Distinguishing Reasonable Basis from Specific Instances of Conduct After Jensen v. State, 355 Md. 692, 736 A.2d 307 (1999), 30 U. Balt. L. Rev. 127, 129, 151 (2000) ("It is undisputed that a character witness [in federal court] is strictly prohibited from testifying about specific acts of the principal witness's conduct on direct examination"; however, Maryland rule 5-608 states that "on direct examination, a character witness may give a reasonable basis as to reputation or an opinion . . . .").

[32]U.S. v. Turning Bear, 357 F.3d 730 (8th Cir. 2004) (the witness was prepared to opine about the victim's truthfulness; the foundation was sufficient, since the witness had daily contact with the victim during the four to six months in which the witness had served as the victim's foster mother); U.S. v. Watson, 669 F.2d 1374 (11th

Cir. 1982); Honey v. People, 713 P.2d 1300 (Colo. 1986). *But see* U.S. v. Goldwire, 55 M.J. 139 (C.A.A.F. 2001) (on cross, Green admitted that his opinion rested on a single instance in which the defendant lied).

**[Section 44]**

[1]*See* 3A Wigmore, Evidence §§ 931–35, 989–95 (Chadbourn rev. 1970); 4 Weinstein's Federal Evidence § 607.05[1]-[3] (rev. 2011); Necessity and admissibility of expert testimony as to credibility of witness, 20 A.L.R.3d 684.

[2]*See* C.C. Moore, A Treatise on Facts (1908); Wigmore, Principles of Judicial Proof ch. 22 (3d ed. 1937); Sobel, Eye—Witness Identification: Legal and Practical Problems (1972); Gardner, The Perception and Memory of Witnesses, 18 Corn. L.Q. 391 (1933); Moore, Elements of Error in Testimony, 28 Or. L. Rev. 293 (1943); Trankell, Reliability of Evidence (1972).

[3]See § 62 infra.

speak the truth.[4] Federal Rule of Evidence 601, applicable at least in federal question cases in federal court, precludes the trial judge from treating insane persons as automatically incompetent to testify. However, a prospective witness could conceivably be treated as incompetent if in an extreme case he did not have the capacity to recall, understand the duty to tell the truth, or acquire personal knowledge.[5] More commonly, in the judge's discretion both at common law and under the Federal Rules,[6] the fact of mental "abnormality"[7] at either the time of observing the facts or testifying can serve as a basis for impeachment on cross or by extrinsic evidence.[8] The use of expert opinion as extrinsic evidence in this situation is discussed in the last part of this section.

---

[4]People v. Dixon, 81 Ill. App. 2d 330, 225 N.E.2d 445 (1st Dist. 1967); People v. Nash, 36 Ill. 2d 275, 222 N.E.2d 473 (1966); West's Key Number Digest, Witnesses ⊂➝41; and § 62, infra.

[5]Excluding civil actions in which state law supplies the rule of decision as to an element of a claim or defense, former Rule 601 provided, "Every person is competent to be a witness except as otherwise provided in these rules." Effective December 1, 2011, restyled Rule 601 reads: "Every person is competent to be a witness unless these rules provide otherwise." The remaining rules do not mention defects of capacity.

However, in at least extreme cases, one could be so incompetent as to make one's testimony irrelevant under Rules 401 and 402, or so incompetent that Rule 403 would bar testimony. Likewise a defect of capacity could be so severe that one could not understand the concept of truth-telling duties under Rule 603 or would be incapable of having firsthand knowledge under Rule 602. For an example illustrating that mental incompetency is more likely to go to credibility, *see* U.S. v. Lightly, 677 F.2d 1027 (4th Cir. 1982) (person not held incompetent to be a witness because of a prior finding that he was criminally insane and incompetent to stand trial and also suffered from hallucinations).

[6]"Interest in the outcome of litigation and mental capacity are, of course, highly relevant to credibility and require no special treatment to render them admissible along with other matters bearing upon the perception, memory, and narration of the witnesses." Fed. R. Evid. 601, Advisory Committee's Note. Extrinsic evidence of mental capacity would be permissible in the judge's discretion under Rule 403. The court has similar discretion in controlling cross-examination. *E.g.*, U.S. v. Lopez, 611 F.2d 44 (4th Cir. 1979) (judge upheld in refusing cross-examination concerning a psychiatric examination).

[7]Revels v. Vincenz, 382 F.3d 870, 877 (8th Cir. 2004) (cross-examination as to whether in the past the witness had "heard voices").

[8]U.S. v. Lindstrom, 698 F.2d 1154 (11th Cir. 1983) (trial court improperly limited cross-examination as to mental condition of key prosecution witness with a history of psychiatric disorders manifesting themselves in violent threats and destructive conduct); U.S. v. Partin, 493 F.2d 750 (5th Cir. 1974) (evidence of insanity or mental derangement is admissible to impeach); U.S. v. Wilson, 493 F. Supp. 2d 464, 467 (E.D. N.Y. 2006) (the defense could question a government witness about mental health problems that might affect the witness at the time of trial); State v. Miskell, 161

What about defects of mind within the range of normality, such as a slower than average mind or a poorer than usual memory? A skilled questioner can sometimes expose these qualities in a testing cross-examination.[9] May they be proved by other witnesses? The decisions are divided.[10] It is eminently a question for the judge's discretion.[11] The trial judge determines whether the relative importance of the testimony attacked and the insight gained into the witness's credibility outweigh the time and potential distraction involved in opening this side-dispute. The development of standardized tests for intelligence and their widespread

---

N.W.2d 732 (Iowa 1968) (permitting cross-examination showing witness had been adjudged senile); State v. Vigliano, 50 N.J. 51, 232 A.2d 129 (1967) (error to sustain objection to cross-examination to show witness was committed to psychiatric ward during trial); Com. v. Towber, 190 Pa. Super. 93, 152 A.2d 917 (1959) (admission of hospital record showing commitment for mental treatment improperly refused); State v. Barnes, 703 S.W.2d 611 (Tenn. 1985) (error to prohibit cross-examination as to hospitalizations in mental institutions occurring in close proximity to underlying event and testimony at trial). Cases are collected in 3A Wigmore, Evidence § 932, n. 1 (Chadbourn rev. 1970); West's Key Number Digest, Witnesses ☞377; Cross-examination of witness as to his mental state or condition, to impeach competency or credibility, 44 A.L.R.3d 1203. See also cases cited in n. 28, infra. *But see* U.S. v. Wilson, 493 F. Supp. 2d 477 (E.D. N.Y. 2006) (the defense could not introduce evidence of a witness's childhood history of mental health problems); Comment, Admitting Mental Health Evidence to Impeach the Credibility of a Sexual Assault Complainant, 153 U. Pa. L. Rev. 1373 (2005) (it is true that in the past, the courts have sometimes admitted evidence that the complainant was "a pathological liar," had made a suicide attempt, or suffered from post-traumatic stress disorder for impeachment purposes; however, the author argues that these facts have so little to do with credibility that the courts ought to bar such evidence); Adams v.

Ford Motor Co., 103 Ill. App. 2d 356, 243 N.E.2d 843 (5th Dist. 1968) (sustaining rejection of offer of records of witness's prior commitments to mental institution).

[9]That a cross-examination to test intelligence is usually allowable, *see* dicta in Blanchard v. People, 70 Colo. 555, 203 P. 662 (1922) and Henry v. State, 1911 OK CR 321, 6 Okla. Crim. 430, 119 P. 278 (1911); Cross-examination of witness as to his mental state or condition, to impeach competency or credibility, 44 A.L.R.3d 1203.

[10]Admissible: State v. Armstrong, 232 N.C. 727, 62 S.E.2d 50 (1950) (expert testimony that witness was a moron should have been admitted). Excluded: Fries v. Berberich, 177 S.W.2d 640 (Mo. Ct. App. 1944) (expert testimony as to weak memory). Decisions are collected in 3A Wigmore, Evidence § 935, note 1 (Chadbourn rev. 1970); Necessity and admissibility of expert testimony as to credibility of witness, 20 A.L.R.3d 684.

[11]*E.g.*, Mangrum v. State, 227 Ark. 381, 299 S.W.2d 80 (1957) (trial court rejection of counselor's testimony where witness had been a pupil, showing intelligence test score and counselor's conclusion, was properly within range of the trial court's discretion). *See also* Polson v. State, 246 Ind. 674, 207 N.E.2d 638 (1965) (rejection of cross-examination question whether witness was "a little behind in school" was proper exercise of discretion). Fed. R. Evid 403 and 611, and Unif. R. Evid 403 and 611 grant similar discretion.

use in business, government and the armed forces, suggest that they may eventually serve as useful aids in evaluating courtroom testimony.[12] However, that day has not yet arrived.

Abnormality is a horse of a different color. It is a standard ground of impeachment.[13] One form of abnormality comes into play when a person is under the influence of drugs or alcohol. If the witness was under the influence at the time of the events which he testifies to or at the time he testifies, this condition is provable to impeach on cross or by extrinsic evidence.[14] The courts, though, treat habitual addiction differently. Standing alone, the mere fact of chronic alcoholism is ordinarily not provable on credibility.[15] Apart from the minimal probative value of evidence of alcoholism, its admission arguably violates the gen-

---

[12]See Hutchins & Slesinger, The Competency of Witnesses, 37 Yale L.J. 1017, 1019 (1928); Gardner, The Perception and Memory of Witnesses, 18 Corn. L.Q. 391, 409 (1933); Redmount, The Psychological Bases of Evidence Practices: Intelligence, 42 Minn. L. Rev. 559 (1958).

[13]See this section note 8 supra.

[14]*Drink*. Rheaume v. Patterson, 289 F.2d 611 (2d Cir. 1961) (dictum); Walker's Trial, 23 How. St. Tr. 1157 (1794) ("Do you know whether he had drunk any [liquor]?" "He had had a little; he knew what he was saying and doing." "Just as much as he knows now?" "He was not half so much in liquor then as he is now."); Olstad v. Fahse, 204 Minn. 118, 282 N.W. 694 (1938) (that the witness had been drinking beer at the time of the accident, and was under influence; extrinsic evidence allowable); Blumhagen v. State, 11 P.3d 889 (Wyo. 2000); 3A Wigmore, Evidence § 933 (Chadbourn rev. 1970). However, there is a variety of decisions whether particular evidence is admissible to prove intoxication at the time of the incident about which the witness testifies. *See* Impeachment of witness with respect to intoxication, 8 A.L.R.3d 749.

*Drugs*. Wilson v. U.S., 232 U.S. 563, 34 S. Ct. 347, 58 L. Ed. 728 (1914) (witness, having admitted addiction and that she had taken a dose in the morning before testifying, was asked how often she used it and whether she

had with her the "implements;" held, proper, to show whether at the moment of testifying she was under its influence); Roberts v. Hollocher, 664 F.2d 200, 203 (8th Cir. 1981) ("The cross-examination concerning Roberts' use of drugs was permissible in light of his previous testimony. The questions were relevant to Roberts' physical state at the time of the alleged incidents and to his ability to accurately recall those incidents."); U.S. v. Hodges, 556 F.2d 366 (5th Cir. 1977) (witness admitted smoking marijuana cigarettes before a meeting; evidence of second witness excluded when no showing a second witness had expertise concerning effect of use of marijuana cigarettes); State v. Carrera, 528 A.2d 331, 333 (R.I. 1987) ("We hold that evidence of use of drugs is admissible *to show that the witness was under the influence of those drugs at the time of the events to which he or she is testifying*."); Use of drugs as affecting competency or credibility of witness, 65 A.L.R.3d 705.

[15]U.S. v. Gallardo, 497 F.3d 727, 733 (7th Cir. 2007) ("The defendants presented no evidence that the government's witnesses were using drugs during the events to which they testified, or that they were ever addicted to drugs"); Dobson v. Walker, 150 Fed. Appx. 49, 52 (2d Cir. 2005) (there was no evidence that the witness "had already used drugs at the time she witnessed the murder"); U.S. v. DiPaolo, 804 F.2d 225, 230 (2d Cir.

eral prohibition against using character as circumstantial proof of conduct; in the final analysis, the attorney is simply arguing that since the witness was intoxicated on previous occasions, it is more likely that the witness was intoxicated when he observed the relevant events.[16] Yet, when the abnormality is a drug addiction carrying even more social odium, some decisions routinely allow it to be shown, even without expert testimony that addiction to the particular drug affects some aspect of credibility such as perception or memory.[17] However, more courts exclude it, absent a showing of a specific effect on the witness's veracity.[18]

---

1986) ("As Wigmore points out, however, 'a general *habit of intemperance* tells us nothing of the witness's testimonial incapacity [unless it involves] actual intoxication at the time of the event observed or at the time of testifying.' Hence, because its bearing on moral character 'does not involve the veracity trait . . ., it will usually not be admissible.' Id. § 933 at 762 (citation & footnote omitted)."); Poppell v. U.S., 418 F.2d 214 (5th Cir. 1969) (general reputation for intemperance could be excluded); Springer v. Reimers, 4 Cal. App. 3d 325, 84 Cal. Rptr. 486 (1st Dist. 1970) (must be shown that intoxication occurred contemporaneously with events about which witness testifies); State v. Burke, 522 A.2d 725, 732 (R.I. 1987) ("Generally, chronic alcoholism is not admissible for the purpose of impeaching a witness's credibility."); Indemnity Ins. Co. of North America v. Marshall, 308 S.W.2d 174 (Tex. Civ. App. Beaumont 1957) (similar case); Impeachment of witness with respect to intoxication, 8 A.L.R.3d 749. But it seems that where general moral character may be shown to impeach (see § 44 supra), habitual drunkenness is also let in. Willis v. Wabash R. Co., 284 S.W.2d 503 (Mo. 1955) (permitted showing of incidents of drunkenness as immoral acts); Impeachment of witness with respect to intoxication, 8 A.L.R.3d 749.

[16]1 Jefferson's California Evidence Benchbook § 28.21 (3d ed. 1997).

[17]*E.g.,* People v. Crump, 5 Ill. 2d 251, 125 N.E.2d 615 (1955) (but in Illinois, cross-examiners must be pre-pared to make a showing concerning intended questions to bring out addiction; People v. Brown, 76 Ill. App. 2d 362, 222 N.E.2d 227 (1st Dist. 1966)). See the valuable descriptions and analyses of the cases in Hale, Comment, 16 So. Calif. L. Rev. 333 (1943); 3A Wigmore, Evidence § 934 (Chadbourn rev. 1970); Use of drugs as affecting competency or credibility of witness, 65 A.L.R.3d 705; Note, 1966 Utah L. Rev. 742.

[18]*E.g.* U.S. v. Hodge, 594 F.3d 614, 618 (8th Cir. 2010) ("Prior drug abuse or drug addiction . . . has no automatic effect on the credibility of a witness"); Kelly v. Maryland Casualty Co., 45 F.2d 782 (W.D. Va. 1929) (scholarly and comprehensive opinion by McDowell, J.) without passing on this question, on the ground that the evidence offered did not show excessive use); Use of drugs as affecting competency or credibility of witness, 65 A.L.R.3d 705. *See also* Doe v. State, 487 P.2d 47 (Alaska 1971); State v. Ballesteros, 100 Ariz. 262, 413 P.2d 739 (1966); People v. Wilson, 44 Cal. 4th 758, 80 Cal. Rptr. 3d 211, 187 P.3d 1041, 1063 (2008) (evidence of habitual narcotics use is inadmissible for impeachment absent expert testimony on the probable effect of such use on perception and memory); People v. Balderas, 41 Cal. 3d 144, 222 Cal. Rptr. 184, 711 P.2d 480 (1985) (evidence of habitual narcotics or alcohol use is inadmissible to impeach perception or memory unless there is expert testimony on the probable effect of such use on those faculties); Edwards v. State, 548 So. 2d 656, 658 (Fla. 1989)

Most federal cases concur with the majority view.[19] The majority courts have the better of the argument. There is insufficient scientific consensus to warrant judicial notice that addiction in and of itself usually affects credibility.[20] Worse still, the evidence is pregnant with prejudice.[21]

### Psychiatric Testimony

In recent decades with the growth of psychiatry, expert testimony about issues of sanity in cases of wills and crimes has become commonplace. The use of expert psychiatric testimony about mental disorders and defects is a potential aid in determining a witness's credibility in any kind of litigation.[22] In one type of litigation, namely sex offense prosecutions, Wigmore and several other commentators characterized this kind of testimony as indispensable, and in the distant past it was routinely approved

---

("This view excludes the introduction of evidence of drug use for the purpose of impeachment unless: (a) it can be shown that the witness had been using drugs at or about the time of the incident which is the subject of the witness's testimony; (b) it can be shown that the witness is using drugs at or about the time of the testimony itself; or (c) it is expressly shown by other relevant evidence that the prior drug use affects the witness's ability to observe, remember, and recount.").

[19]See discussion in 4 Weinstein's Federal Evidence § 607.05[4][b] (rev. 2011), suggesting counsel desiring to introduce drug use should first notify the court of all the details of usage and be ready to show its effect upon the credibility by expert testimony or recognized literature. The majority of federal cases have excluded evidence of general drug usage. *Compare* U.S. v. Sampol, 636 F.2d 621 (D.C. Cir. 1980) (inquiry into general drug usage barred); U.S. v. Kizer, 569 F.2d 504 (9th Cir. 1978), U.S. v. Boyd, 833 F. Supp. 1277, 1359 (N.D. Ill. 1993) ("As a general rule, a witness 'past drug use is not probative of veracity. . . .' ") with U.S. v. Jackson, 576 F.2d 46 (5th Cir. 1978) (only general dictum that drug usage goes to credibility).

[20]In Kelly v. Maryland Casualty Co., 45 F.2d 782 (W.D. Va. 1929), Judge McDowell marshals the medical

opinions pro and con (45 F.2d at 784, 785). See also the lengthy discussion in People v. Williams, 6 N.Y.2d 18, 187 N.Y.S.2d 750, 159 N.E.2d 549 (1959).

There is disagreement whether expert opinion is admissible to show the effect of narcotic addiction upon credibility. People v. Williams, 6 N.Y.2d 18, 187 N.Y.S.2d 750, 159 N.E.2d 549 (1959) reviewing authorities at length. *See also* Necessity and admissibility of expert testimony as to credibility of witness, 20 A.L.R.3d 684.

[21]U.S. v. Simpson, 910 F.2d 154, 158 (4th Cir. 1990) ("the insinuation of drug crimes" can be "highly prejudicial"); U.S. v. Kearney, 420 F.2d 170, 174 (D.C. Cir. 1969) ("hostility based on the general odium of narcotics use. [T]he matter of drug addiction, which involves social transgression and the possibility of illegal conduct, is properly approached with awareness of the potential for prejudice of the jury"); People v. Moten, 229 Cal. App. 3d 1318, 280 Cal. Rptr. 602, 606 (5th Dist. 1991) (evidence of drug usage can be "highly inflammatory and prejudicial"); People v. Mullins, 79 Mich. App. 515, 261 N.W.2d 67, 68 (1977); People v. Dowdell, 88 A.D.2d 239, 453 N.Y.S.2d 174, 177 (1st Dep't 1982).

[22]Sutherland & Henderson, Expert Psychiatrists and Comments on Witness Credibility, Trial, July 1998, at 82.

by the courts.[23] Wigmore asserted that women who testify they
have been sexually attacked *often* report such matters falsely and
that a judge should *always* be sure that the female victim's
mental history is closely scrutinized by a mental health expert.
Today we know that those assertions are both chauvinist and
inaccurate.[24] Most courts now hold that the admission of psychiatric testimony is in the judge's discretion. More often than not
judges exercise the discretion to exclude evidence of the witness's
past psychiatric problems.[25] Further, many appellate courts hold
that a trial judge should exercise the power to order an examination to generate such testimony only for compelling reasons in
exceptional circumstances.[26] The criteria for identifying such cir-

---

[23]*See* 3A Wigmore, Evidence
§§ 934a, 924a, and 924b (Chadbourn
rev. 1970), which substantially preserve the original Wigmore text. The
discussion is divided into separate
headings for impeachment by attack
on moral character and by showing
mental derangement or defects. However, insofar as use of expert opinion
on the complainant's "social history
and mental makeup" in cases charging sexual crimes is concerned, the
sections are related.

Comments include the
following: Machtinger, Psychiatric
Impeachment in Sex Cases, 39 J. Crim.
L. 750 (1949); Notes, 26 Ind. L.J. 98
(1950), 43 Iowa L. Rev. 650 (1958).

The following are pertinent
cases: People v. Bastian, 330 Mich.
457, 47 N.W.2d 692 (1951); State v.
Wesler, 137 N.J.L. 311, 59 A.2d 834
(N.J. Sup. Ct. 1948) (doctors' testimony
that girls are psychopaths and immoral and that psychopaths are prone
to be untruthful did not require rejection of girls' stories); Miller v. State,
49 Okla. Crim. 133, 295 P. 403 (1930)
(testimony of superintendent of insane
hospital that girl, said to be nympho-
maniac, was normal, admissible on
credibility). The expert was not court-
appointed in the above cases.

[24]Bienen, A Question of
Credibility: John Henry Wigmore's
Use of Scientific Authority in Section
924a of the Treatise on Evidence, 19
Calif. Western L. Rev. 235 (1983).
Various other important articles are

cited. The author emphasizes sex
crimes in which young females are the
victims.

[25]U.S. v. Smith, 77 F.3d 511, 516
(D.C. Cir. 1996); U.S. v. Beasley, 72
F.3d 1518, 1528 (11th Cir. 1996) ("Expert medical testimony concerning the
truthfulness or credibility of a witness
is generally inadmissible. . . ."); U.S.
v. Annigoni, 68 F.3d 279, 282 (9th Cir.
1995); U.S. v. Sasso, 59 F.3d 341, 348
(2d Cir. 1995); U.S. v. Hinkle, 37 F.3d
576, 579 (10th Cir. 1994); U.S. v. Butt,
955 F.2d 77 (1st Cir. 1992) ("federal
courts appear to have found mental instability relevant to credibility only
where, during the time-frame of the
events testified to, the witness exhibited a pronounced disposition to lie or
hallucinate, or suffered from a severe
illness, such as schizophrenia, that
dramatically impaired her ability to
perceive and tell the truth").

[26]Among the cases indicating
there should be compelling reasons for
the judge to order an examination are:
U.S. v. Skorniak, 59 F.3d 750, 759 (8th
Cir. 1995) (an examination "is a drastic
measure," and the defendant offered
"insufficient evidence" of the witness's
mental illness to justify an examination); U.S. v. Roebuck, 46 V.I. 292, 334
F. Supp. 2d 833, 833–34 (D.V.I. 2004)
("the type of examination requested by
Defendant is an 'extraordinary measure' and generally is not permitted.
While the Court has authority to order a witness to undergo psychiatric
or psychological examination to aid in

cumstances are unclear; if compelled examinations are to be permitted at all, the courts ought to specify strict limiting condition. Indeed, there is respectable state authority that judges have no inherent power to order a psychiatric examination with a view to possibly admitting testimony about the findings in rape trials.[27]

Although the use of psychiatric testimony in sex offense cases

---

its competency determination, the 'exercise of this power is neither frequent nor common, and never lightly undertaken'"); U.S. v. Roman, 884 F. Supp. 126, 127 (S.D. N.Y. 1995) (ordering an examination is a "drastic measure" that is "particularly within the discretion of the trial court," since it can "seriously impinge" on the witness's privacy; here the defendant did not provide the court with any information to support the inference that the witness's mental capacity was impaired); Com. v. Gibbons, 378 Mass. 766, 393 N.E.2d 400 (1979) (rape case; interpreting statute giving judge power to order an examination and considering various factors affecting that power); State v. Eighth Judicial Dist. Court of State of Nev., in and for County of Clark (Romano), 120 Nev. 613, 97 P.3d 594 (2004) (overruled by, Abbott v. State, 122 Nev. 715, 138 P.3d 462 (2006)) (compelling need); Washington v. State, 96 Nev. 305, 608 P.2d 1101 (1980) (implies lack of corroboration is a compelling reason); State v. Clasey, 252 Or. 22, 446 P.2d 116 (1968) (cites Ballard v. Superior Court of San Diego County, 64 Cal. 2d 159, 49 Cal. Rptr. 302, 410 P.2d 838 (1966), as stating lack of corroboration or showing of some mental or emotional instability as compelling reason); In re Michael H., 360 S.C. 540, 602 S.E.2d 729 (2004) (rejecting an absolute bar on psychological testing); State v. Carlson, 392 N.W.2d 89 (S.D. 1986) (discretion granted only upon a substantial showing of need and justification); Forbes v. State, 559 S.W.2d 318 (Tenn. 1977); Necessity or permissibility of mental examination to determine competency or credibility of complainant in sexual offense prosecution, 45 A.L.R.4th 310. See also Government of Virgin Islands v. Scuito, 623 F.2d 869 (3d Cir. 1980) (alleged use of drugs causing some unusual behavior considered insufficient basis for examination in rape case; citing Benn below, countervailing considerations include infringement of right of privacy, trauma caused by order, possible harassment; embarrassment; deterrence of complaints by victims; see this section note 27 infra); U.S. v. Benn, 476 F.2d 1127 (D.C. Cir. 1972) (corroborating circumstances justified failure to order examination; matter must be decided in the light of particular facts).

[27]See this section note 26, supra. Strict limiting conditions for an order of examination are advocated in O'Neale, Court Ordered Psychiatric Examination of a Rape Victim in a Criminal Rape Prosecution—Or How Many Times Must a Woman Be Raped?, 18 Santa Clara L. Rev. 119 (1978). In State v. Clontz, 305 N.C. 116, 286 S.E.2d 793 (1982), a second degree rape case, the court held that absent statute the trial judge does not have power to order a psychiatric examination of an unwilling witness, stating in part that an order would be contrary to the public policy of a rape shield statute to prevent unnecessary intrusion into sex crime victims' privacy. See Cal. Penal Code § 1112: "[T]he trial court shall not order any prosecuting witness, complaining witness, or any other witness, or victim in any sexual assault prosecution to submit to a psychiatric or psychological examination for the purpose of assessing his or her credibility."

In rather sweeping fashion, Fed. R. Evid. 412 purports to bar evidence of the past sexual behavior of the victim of certain sexual offenses including rape or an assault with intent

has garnered the most attention, psychiatric testimony has been offered in other types of cases. A number of courts have taken the position that the use of expert psychiatric testimony to impeach a principal witnesses is not confined to sexual assault cases.[28] However, as a general proposition the federal courts are disinclined to exercise their discretion to broadly permit attacks by experts on mental capacity.[29] When there is a solid ground for

---

to commit rape (as well as other evidence of past sexual behavior, under certain conditions). It may be urged that Rule 412's provisions implicitly bar psychiatric opinion based in any part upon "past sexual behavior," although the legislative history does not specifically indicate such a conclusion. For further material concerning Fed. R. Evid. 412, and rape shield statutes, see § 193 infra.

In *Scuito,* the appellate court mentioned that the trial judge's opinion "was not based on the letter but on the spirit of Rule 412," although the defense evidently sought expert testimony of complainant's ability generally to perceive reality and to separate fact from fancy, rather than fantasizing about sex in particular. 623 F.2d at 875. *See generally* State v. Coe, 521 So. 2d 373, 375–76 (Fla. 2d DCA 1988) ("The parties correctly point out that there is a split in the decisions on these issues in other jurisdictions. *See* Necessity or permissibility of mental examination to determine competency or credibility of complainant in sexual offense prosecution, 45 A.L.R.4th 310. The rationale in jurisdictions holding that a court does not have authority to require such examinations is (1) that appointing a psychiatrist to examine a witness for credibility usurps the factfinder's role; (2) that to require a psychiatrist to 'vouch' for the witness' credibility would be another form of required corroboration of sex offenses which has been repealed by the legislatures in these jurisdictions; and (3) that such a requirement would invade the victim's privacy and would likely result in few victims reporting a sexual battery for fear of having to subject themselves to a psychiatric examina-

tion. *E.g.,* People v. Souvenir, 373 N.Y.S.2d 824 (N.Y.Crim.Ct. 1975). Even in jurisdictions holding that the trial court does have the authority to require such examinations, the courts emphasize that such authority should only be exercised for 'strong and compelling' reasons. *E.g.,* State v. Gregg, 602 P.2d 85 (Kan. 1979); Forbes v. State, 559 S.W.2d 318 (Tenn. 1977); State v. Lederer, 299 N.W.2d 457 (Wis. 1980).").

[28]U.S. v. Hiss, 88 F. Supp. 559 (S.D. N.Y. 1950) (expert permitted to testify to diagnosis formed from courtroom observation that the government's star witness was a psychopathic personality with "a tendency towards making false accusations"). *See also* Ingalls v. Ingalls, 257 Ala. 521, 59 So. 2d 898 (1952) (doctor's opinion based upon a previous examination should have been admitted); Taborsky v. State, 142 Conn. 619, 116 A.2d 433 (1955) (opinion of psychiatrist in prosecution for murder, regarding prosecuting witness's hallucinations and delusions, would be admissible in a new trial); Necessity and admissibility of expert testimony as to credibility of witness, 20 A.L.R.3d 684. However, a number of cases (primarily older cases) hold these opinions inadmissible. *See, e.g.,* note 33, supra; Thompson v. Standard Wholesale Phosphate & Acid Works, 178 Md. 305, 13 A.2d 328 (1940). See criticism of the earlier cases in Weihofen, Testimonial Competence and Credibility, 34 Geo. Wash. L. Rev. 53, 68 (1965).

[29]U.S. v. Ciocca, 106 F.3d 1079 (1st Cir. 1997); U.S. v. Smith, 77 F.3d 511, 516 (D.C. Cir. 1996); U.S. v. Beasley, 72 F.3d 1518, 1528 (11th Cir.

believing that a principal witness suffers from a severe mental abnormality affecting credibility, there may be a legitimate need to employ the resources of psychiatry.[30] Many contemporary courts accept the principle that psychiatric evidence should be received, at least in the judge's discretion, whenever its probative value outweighs the cost in time, distraction, and expense.[31]

The value[32] of such evidence depends, *inter alia*, on the importance of the witness's testimony and the adequacy of the expert's opportunity to form a reliable opinion. This first factor, the importance of the testimony, is relevant to the justifiability of subjecting witnesses (even party-witnesses) to the ordeal of psychiatric attack.[33] The second factor is the adequacy of the opportunity to form a trustworthy opinion. An opinion based solely on a hypothetical question is virtually worthless. Only slightly more reliable is an opinion resting on the expert's observation of the subject's courtroom demeanor and testimony. The courtroom is not only a foreign environment for most witnesses; worse still, the prospect of testifying can create anxiety which distorts the witness's normal demeanor. Most psychiatrists agree that a sat-

---

1996) ("Expert medical testimony concerning the truthfulness of credibility of a witness is generally inadmissible. . . ."); U.S. v. Annigoni, 68 F.3d 279, 282 (9th Cir. 1995); U.S. v. Sasso, 59 F.3d 341, 348 (2d Cir. 1995); U.S. v. Hinkle, 37 F.3d 576, 579 (10th Cir. 1994); U.S. v. Demma, 523 F.2d 981 (9th Cir. 1975). See discussion in 4 Weinstein's Federal Evidence § 607.05[6] (rev. 2011).

[30]These are classified and described in Comment, Psychiatric Evaluation of the Mentally Abnormal Witness, 59 Yale L.J. 1324, 1326 (1950); Weihofen, Testimonial Competence and Credibility, 34 Geo. Wash. L. Rev. 53 (1965). See suggestions for future studies in Juviler, Psychiatric Opinions as to Credibility of Witnesses: A Suggested Approach, 48 Calif. L. Rev. 648 (1960). The American Psychiatric Association promulgates a Diagnostic and Statistical Manual. The A.P.A. is now at work on the fifth edition of the DSM.

[31]U.S. v. Butler, 481 F.2d 531 (D.C. Cir. 1973). See discussion in People v. Williams, 6 N.Y.2d 18, 187 N.Y.S.2d 750, 159 N.E.2d 549 (1959) and Weihofen, Testimonial Competence and Credibility, 34 Geo. Wash.

L. Rev. 53, 75–76 (1965). *See also* Juviler, Psychiatric Opinions as to Credibility of Witnesses: A Suggested Approach, 48 Calif. L. Rev. 648 (1960).

[32]Although this section discusses two factors affecting the value of the evidence, there are other considerations. In Daubert v. Merrell Dow Pharmaceuticals, Inc., 509 U.S. 579, 113 S. Ct. 2786, 125 L. Ed. 2d 469 (1993), the Supreme Court announced a new empirical test to determine the admissibility of purported scientific testimony. Some courts have applied that test to "soft" science such as testimony by mental health experts. Comment, Admissibility of Expert Psychological Evidence in the Federal Courts, 17 Ariz. St. L.J. 1315 (1995).

[33]Other factors should be pertinent. These include the invasion of the witness's privacy, the showing that there is a relation between the asserted mental condition and the witness's credibility, and the possibility of entering into collateral matter that is confusing to the jury. U.S. v. Lopez, 611 F.2d 44 (4th Cir. 1979) (but the court was dealing with cross-examination of the witness sought to be impeached).

isfactory opinion can be formed only after the witness has been subjected to a thorough clinical examination.[34] A few decisions have held that the trial judge has a discretionary power to order an examination of a prosecuting witness, but the conditions for exercising that discretion are unclear.[35] Many of those decisions involve sexual assault prosecutions, but the decisions at least

---

[34]Comment, 59 Yale L.J. 1324, 1339 (1950); Note, 30 Neb. L. Rev. 513, 519 (1951); Weihofen, cited supra, note 30. A slashing cross-examination of the psychiatrist witness in United States v. Hiss, note 28, supra, illustrates the difficulties of reliance upon observance of courtroom demeanor and a reading of the record. *See* McCord, Syndromes, Profiles, and Other Mental Exotica: A New Approach to the Admissibility of Nontraditional Psychological Evidence in Criminal Cases, 66 Or. L. Rev. 19, 47 (1987) ("[w]hile several cases suggest support . . . . for Hiss, only one court seems to follow it").

[35]*See generally* Evans v. State, 304 Md. 487, 499 A.2d 1261, 1272 (1985) ("[A] trial judge has the authority to order a mental examination of a witness to assist in the determination of competency when the issue cannot be satisfactorily resolved by reference to existing information and voir dire of the witness. In determining whether a request for a mental examination should be granted, however, a trial judge should carefully balance the demonstrated necessity for a compelled examination against the existence of important countervailing considerations. In affirming the denial of a motion for a psychiatric examination of a government witness, the United States Court of Appeals for the District of Columbia Circuit, in United States v. Benn, 476 F.2d 1127, 1131 (D.C.Cir. 1972), listed some of the factors to be considered: '[A] psychiatric examination may seriously impinge on a witness' right to privacy; the trauma that attends the role of complainant . . . is sharply increased by the indignity of a psychiatric examination; the examination itself could serve as a tool

of harassment; and the impact of all these considerations may well deter the victim of . . . a crime from lodging any complaint at all. Since there is no exact measure for weighing these kinds of dangers against the need for an examination, the decision must be entrusted to the sound discretion of the trial judge in light of the particular facts.' "). Most of the cases seem to recognize the discretion although they usually reject any contention that the trial judge's failure to order an examination was an abuse of discretion. U.S. v. Bari, 750 F.2d 1169, 1178–79 (2d Cir. 1984); U.S. v. Riley, 657 F.2d 1377 (8th Cir. 1981); U.S. v. Stout, 599 F.2d 866 (8th Cir. 1979); U.S. v. Jackson, 576 F.2d 46 (5th Cir. 1978); People v. Stice, 165 Cal. App. 2d 287, 331 P.2d 468 (2d Dist. 1958); State v. Cox, 352 S.W.2d 665 (Mo. 1961); State v. Klueber, 81 S.D. 223, 132 N.W.2d 847 (1965); State v. Miller, 35 Wis. 2d 454, 151 N.W.2d 157 (1967) (but court may not compel if witness refuses). In State v. Butler, 27 N.J. 560, 143 A.2d 530 (1958), the court stated that the state's witness should have been examined for competency and that evidence at the competency hearing would be admissible on the issue of credibility. On the other hand, for the view that the court has no power to order examination of witnesses, *see* U.S. v. Ramirez, 871 F.2d 582, 584 (6th Cir. 1989) (a witness may not be ordered to be examined; "The most the court could do is condition such witness's testimony on a prior examination."); State v. Walgraeve, 243 Or. 328, 412 P.2d 23 (1966). See additional authority in Necessity or permissibility of mental examination to determine competency or credibility of complainant in sexual offense prosecution, 45 A.L.R.4th 310.

implicitly recognize a broader principle. If it exists at all, the discretionary power ought to extend to any type of case. The exercise of the discretion should be informed by such factors as whether undue expenditure of time or expense will result, whether the witness is a key witness, and whether there are solid indications that the witness is suffering from mental abnormality at the time of trial or the time of the relevant event. An expert opinion based on courtroom observation and reading the trial record ought to be admitted only as a last resort if the judge lacks the power to order an examination.[36] Even then, permitting opinion based on such flimsy bases is dubious.

Expert opinion on character for truthfulness or untruthfulness authorized by Federal and Revised Uniform Rule 608(a) must be distinguished from the topic discussed above, opinion about the witness's mental capacity to tell the truth. Rule 608(a) is not direct authority for the admission of the type of opinion testimony discussed in this section.[37]

## § 45   Impeachment by "specific contradiction"[1]

"Specific contradiction" may be explained as follows. In the

---

[36]*See* similar suggestion, Weihofen, Testimonial Competence and Credibility, 34 Geo. Wash. L. Rev. 53, 77–78 (1965).

[37]It could be urged that the suggested distinction would often be merely illusory because an expert testifying in terms of opinion of "character" for truthfulness or untruthfulness would only be speaking of mental or emotional conditions associated with mental capacity for truth-telling but in a more direct way. Whether there could be expertise on "character" for veracity is questionable. Whether the jury would be aided by such claimed expertise might also be questionable in many instances. For a discussion of other difficulties in using expert opinion of character for truthfulness or untruthfulness, *see* 3 Mueller & Kirkpatrick, Federal Evidence § 6:32 (3d ed. 2007). In any event, expert opinion as to the witness's character for truthfulness is inadmissible. U.S. v. Scop, 846 F.2d 135, 142 (2d Cir. 1988) ("We believe that expert witnesses may not offer opinions on relevant events based on their personal assessment of the credibility of another

witness's testimony. The credibility of witnesses is exclusively for the determination by the jury, United States v. Richter, 826 F.2d 206, 208 (2d Cir. 1987), and witnesses may not opine as to the credibility of other witnesses at the trial."); U.S. v. Cecil, 836 F.2d 1431, 1441 (4th Cir. 1988) ("Beyond this, while [Rule 704] permits an expert to testify on ultimate issues if the district judge finds such evidence helpful, that principle has never been extended to the right of a psychiatrist to give an opinion on the credibility of a witness. That determination of credibility is one strictly for the jury. Many cases, decided after the adoption of the Federal Rules of Evidence, have so held. In fact, the authorities seem uniform that a psychiatrist may not testify to the credibility of a witness; that issue is one for the jury.").

**[Section 45]**

[1]3A Wigmore, Evidence §§ 1000–07 (Chadbourn rev. 1970); 4 Weinstein's Federal Evidence § 607.06 (rev. 2011); West's Key Number Digest, Witnesses ⊘398 to 409.

The extent to which evidence obtained in violation of a constitu-

course of testifying about an accident or crime, Witness One mentions that at the time he witnessed the event, the day was snowy and he was wearing a green sweater. Suppose that the statements about the snow and the sweater can be "disproved." Disproof can happen in several ways. Witness One on direct or cross-examination may later acknowledge that he was in error. Or the judge might take judicial notice that at the time and place—Tucson in July—it was not snowing. But often disproof or "contradiction" involves calling Witness Two to testify to the contrary that the day was sunny and warm. This is the sense in which the term "contradiction" is meant in this section.[2]

What impeaching value does the contradiction have in the above situation? If Witness One is wrong and Witness Two right, it tends to show that Witness One has erred about or falsified certain facts, and therefore is capable of error or lying. That showing should be considered negatively in weighing other testimony by Witness One. But that insight has negligible probative value. After all, all human beings are fallible; and all testimony ought to be discounted to some extent for this weakness. It is true that the trial judge in his discretion may permit the cross-examiner to test the power of Witness One to observe, remember and recount facts unrelated to the case to "explore" these capacities.[3] However, to permit a prolonged dispute about such extraneous, "collateral" facts as the weather and the witness's clothing by allowing the attacker to call other witnesses to disprove them, is impractical. There are evident dangers of surprise, jury confusion,[4] and waste of time.[5]

To combat these dangers, at common law many courts enforced

---

tional right may be used to impeach is treated in § 182 infra. The use of treatises to impeach experts is dealt with in § 321 infra.

    [2] In the courtroom and the cases, "contradiction" is loosely extended to include impeachment by proof of a prior inconsistent statement of the first witness ("self-contradiction"). *E.g.*, Calley v. Boston & Maine R.R., 92 N.H. 455, 33 A.2d 227 (1943). The proof by a second witness of the prior inconsistent statement usually entails a contradiction too, but it is the witness's inconsistency that is the heart of the attack. See § 37 supra.

    [3] See § 29 supra.

    [4] ". . . Witnesses are not expected to come prepared to sustain all the statements they have made upon sub-

jects not involved in the controversy, and because its admission would involve the trial of too many issues as to the truth of the statements the determination of which would at last have little effect upon the decision of the cause." Williams, J., in Gulf, C. & S.F. Ry. Co. v. Matthews, 100 Tex. 63, 93 S.W. 1068, 1070 (1906).

    This is one of the very things that Fed. and Unif. R. Evid. 403 are designed to guard against.

    [5] "If we lived for a thousand years, instead of about sixty or seventy, and every case were of sufficient importance, it might be possible and perhaps proper to throw a light on matters in which every possible question might be suggested, for the purpose of seeing by such means whether the whole was unfounded, or what por-

the restriction that a witness may not be impeached by producing extrinsic evidence of "collateral" facts "contradicting" the first witness's assertions about those facts.[6] § 49 discusses the collateral fact rule in detail. A matter is deemed "collateral" if the matter itself is irrelevant to establish any fact of consequence in the litigation,[7] i.e., irrelevant for a purpose other than mere contradiction of the prior witness's in-court testimony. When the collateral fact sought to be contradicted is elicited on cross-examination, this restriction is often expressed by saying that the answer is conclusive or that the cross-examiner must "take the answer."[8] By the better view, if the "collateral" fact happens to have been drawn out on direct, the rule against extrinsic contradiction still applies.[9] The danger of surprise is lessened, but the policy considerations of waste of time and confusion of issues are still present.

Article VI of the Federal Rules does not expressly mention specific contradiction as a permissible method of impeachment. However, the federal courts continue to permit resort to this

---

tion of it was not, and to raise every possible inquiry as to the truth of the statements made. But I do not see how that could be; in fact, mankind find it to be impossible. Therefore, some line must be drawn." Rolfe, B., in Attorney General v. Hitchcock, 1847 WL 5862 (U.K. Ex Ct 1847). Justice Holmes expressed the same sentiment when he described a rule as "a concession to the shortness of life." Reeve v. Dennett, 145 Mass. 23, 11 N.E. 938, 944 (1887). See this section note 4, supra.

[6]Klein v. Keresey, 307 Mass. 51, 29 N.E.2d 703 (1940). *See also* U.S. v. Jackson, 540 F.3d 578, 587–88 (7th Cir. 2008) (one may not impeach by contradiction on collateral matters; merely attempting to prove that the witness is lying is not a proper purpose of impeachment by contradiction); U.S. v. Miller, 159 F.3d 1106, 1112 (7th Cir. 1998) ("Though contradiction is a valid method of impeachment, 'one may not contradict for the sake of contradiction' "); U.S. v. McCafferty, 801 F. Supp. 2d 605, 616 (N.D. Ohio 2011), aff'd, 482 Fed. Appx. 117 (6th Cir. 2012); U.S. v. Forest, 729 F. Supp. 2d 403, 411 (D. Me. 2010).

The prohibition against contra-

diction as to collateral matters is one of the concepts subsumed under Rule 403. Dolan, Rule 403: The Prejudice Rule in Evidence, 49 So. Cal. L. Rev. 220 (1976).

The rule against impeaching on collateral matters occasionally yields to the theory that inadmissible evidence may be rebutted by evidence which otherwise would be inadmissible. See § 57 infra.

[7]See generally § 49 infra.

[8]Howard v. State, 234 Md. 410, 199 A.2d 611 (1964).

[9]Lambert v. Hamlin, 73 N.H. 138, 59 A. 941 (1905); State v. Price, 92 W. Va. 542, 115 S.E. 393, 405 (1922); 3A Wigmore, Evidence § 1007 (Chadbourn rev. 1970). But many courts hold to the contrary. *E.g.*, Howell v. State, 141 Ark. 487, 217 S.W. 457 (1920) (carnal knowledge; complainant's direct testimony that she had never had intercourse with anyone but defendant should have been allowed to be contradicted, distinguishing situation where brought out on cross-examination) and cases cited by Wigmore, Evidence § 1007. See § 57 infra.

technique.[10] They are correct in doing so. The Supreme Court's reasoning in *United States v. Abel*[11] is apposite. As in the case of specific contradiction, Article VI is silent on the bias impeachment technique. However, the *Abel* Court noted that bias is logically relevant to a witness's credibility; and consequently, Rule 402 is sufficient statutory authorization for the continuation of the practice of bias impeachment. Like bias, specific contradiction is relevant to impeach a prior witness's credibility. The judge may exercise her discretion under Rule 403 to limit specific contradiction impeachment;[12] but when it is logically relevant, specific contradiction evidence is presumptively admissible under Rule 402.[13]

## § 46    Beliefs concerning religion[1]

As § 63 indicates,[2] the common law competency rules required a belief in a God who would punish untruth as a qualification for taking the witness's oath. This requirement arose in a religious climate which has weakened with the passage of time. Most common law jurisdictions have abandoned the requirement. Many jurisdictions have general provisions such as that in the Illinois constitution to the effect that "no person shall be denied any civil or political rights, privilege or capacity on account of his religious opinions."[3] The courts have construed these provisions as abrogat-

---

[10]Common v. City of Chicago, 661 F.3d 940 (7th Cir. 2011); U.S. v. Gilmore, 553 F.3d 266, 271–72 (3d Cir. 2009) (impeachment by contradiction is a means of policing a witness's obligation to speak the truth; the limitations set out in Rule 609 are inapplicable when a conviction is used for the purpose of contradicting a witness's testimony); U.S. v. Perez-Perez, 72 F.3d 224, 227 (1st Cir. 1995) ("Impeachment by contradiction is a recognized mode of impeachment. . . ."); U.S. v. Tarantino, 846 F.2d 1384, 1409 (D.C. Cir. 1988); U.S. v. Welker, 44 M.J. 85 (C.A.A.F. 1996).

[11]U.S. v. Abel, 469 U.S. 45, 105 S. Ct. 465, 83 L. Ed. 2d 450 (1984).

[12]U.S. v. Tarantino, 846 F.2d 1384, 1409 (D.C. Cir. 1988).

[13]Gilligan & Imwinkelried, Bringing the "Opening the Door" Theory to a Close: The Tendency to Overlook the Specific Contradiction Doctrine in Evidence Law, 41 Santa Clara L. Rev. 807, 810–16 (2001).

**[Section 46]**

[1]*See* 2 Wigmore, Evidence § 518 (Chadbourn rev. 1979) (competency), 3A Wigmore, Evidence § 936 (Chadbourn rev. 1970) (impeachment), 8 Wigmore, Evidence § 2213 (McNaughton rev. 1961) (privilege); 3 Weinstein's Federal Evidence Ch. 603 (2d ed. 1997); 4 Weinstein's Federal Evidence Ch. 610 (rev. 2011); Comment by Chadbourn on State v. Beal, 154 S.E. 604 (N.C.1930), 9 N.C. L. Rev. 77 (1930); Swancara, Impeachment of Non—Religious Witnesses, 13 Rocky Mt. L. Rev. 336 (1941); Propriety and prejudicial effect of impeaching witness by reference to religious belief or lack of it, 76 A.L.R.3d 539; West's Key Number Digest, Witnesses ⬤340(2).

[2]See § 63 infra.

[3]Starks v. Schlensky, 128 Ill. App. 1, 4, 1906 WL 2026 (2d Dist.

ing the rule of incompetency to take the oath.[4] Nor is belief in God required by the Federal Rules of Evidence.[5]

As indicated in §§ 43 and 65, the overall trend has been to convert the old grounds of testimonial incompetency, such as interest and infamy, into bases for impeaching credibility. This principle of conversion has sometimes been expressly enacted in constitutional provisions and statutes.[6] Should the same principle be applied to permit a witness's credibility to be attacked by showing that she is an atheist or agnostic and does not believe in divine punishment for perjury? Most courts that have addressed the question have said no; they reached that conclusion by interpreting either general provisions such as that in the Illinois constitution, or more specific constitutional, statutory, or rule language.[7] Thus, many states recognize a witness's privilege not to be examined about her own religious faith or beliefs, except so far as the judge[8] finds that the relevance of the inquiry to some fact of consequence in the case outweighs the interest of privacy

---

1906). Illinois constitutions have contained this provision since 1818.

[4]*See* the constitutional and statutory provisions, and decisions interpreting them, from twenty-four states, compiled in 70 C.J. 98, 99, and § 63 infra. A compilation of specific references to the articles and sections of the constitutions dealing with Witnesses appears in 3 Constitutions, 1813 (1938) published by N.Y. State Const. Committee. Forty jurisdictions are listed as having abolished by statute or constitutional provision the requirement for witnesses of religious belief. Torpey, Judicial Doctrines of Religious Rights 278 (1948).

[5]Former Fed. R. Evid. 601 provided:

Every person is competent to be a witness except as otherwise provided in these rules. However, in civil actions and proceedings, with respect to an element of a claim or defense as to which State law supplies the rule of decision, the competency of a witness shall be determined in accordance with State law.

The corresponding revised Uniform Rule consists of only the first sentence. Effective December 1, 2011, restyled Fed. R. Evid. 601 reads: "Every person is competent to be a witness unless these rules provide otherwise. But in a civil case, state law governs the witness's competency regarding a claim or defense for which state law supplies the rule of decision." Former Fed. R. Evid. 603 provided: "Before testifying, every witness shall be required to declare that the witness will testify truthfully, by oath or affirmation administered in a form calculated to awaken the witness' conscience and impress the witness' mind with the duty to do so." *See* Advisory Committee's Note. Revised Uniform Rule of Evidence (1974) 603 is identical in content. Effective December 1, 2011, restyled Fed. R. Evid. 603 reads: "Before testifying, a witness must give oath or affirmation to testify truthfully. It must be in a form designed to impress that duty on the witness's conscience."

Neither set of rules contains any competency requirement of religious belief.

[6]Chadbourn, Comment, 9 N.C. L. Rev. 77, 78 n. 5 (1930).

[7]Government of Virgin Islands v. Petersen, 553 F.2d 324 (3d Cir. 1977); Propriety and prejudicial effect of impeaching witness by reference to religious belief or lack of it, 76 A.L.R.3d 539.

[8]Searcy v. Miller, 57 Iowa 613,

and the danger of prejudice.[9] A few old cases, either reasoning from the conversion of grounds of incompetency into bases for impeachment or following the peculiar language of specific statutory provisions, seemingly allowed this ground of impeachment.[10] But those cases are badly dated and have little modern precedential value. Even under the old cases, courts would not permit inquiry about particular creeds, faiths, or affiliations except as they shed light on the witness's belief in a God who will punish untruthfulness.[11]

There is a strong argument that, in addition to recognizing a witness's privilege not to answer questions about her own religious beliefs, the legislatures and courts should forbid the party to impeach by bringing other witnesses to attack the first witness's faith. Today, there is no basis for believing that the lack of faith in God's avenging wrath is an indication of greater than average untruthfulness. Without that basis, the evidence of atheism is irrelevant to the question of credibility.[12]

---

10 N.W. 912, 916 (1881) ("He is not to be questioned as to his religious belief . . ."); Com. v. Burke, 82 Mass. 33, 16 Gray 33, 1860 WL 6925 (1860) (improper to question witness about his beliefs on voir dire or cross-examination, despite statute permitting impeachment on this ground); Free v. Buckingham, 59 N.H. 219, 225, 1879 WL 4197 (1879) ("This is not because the inquiry might tend to disgrace him, but because it would be a personal scrutiny into the state of his faith and conscience, contrary to the spirit of our institutions"); 8 Wigmore, Evidence § 2213 (McNaughton rev. 1961).

[9]Examples of situations where relevancy did outweigh: McKim v. Philadelphia Transp. Co., 364 Pa. 237, 72 A.2d 122 (1950) (under statute recognizing privilege, judge properly permitted cross-examination of personal injury plaintiffs to show they were ministers in Jehovah's Witnesses sect and what their duties were, on issue of damages); Ft. Worth & D.C. Ry. Co. v. Travis, 45 Tex. Civ. App. 117, 99 S.W. 1141 (1907) (personal injury plaintiff could be cross-examined as to her Christian Scientist beliefs about suffering, and as to whether her faith caused her not to take medicine pre-

scribed). But compare cases where inquiry into the plaintiff's faith as Christian Scientist was found to be insufficiently relevant to the substantive issues. City of Montgomery v. Wyche, 169 Ala. 181, 53 So. 786 (1910); Adams v. Carlo, 101 S.W.2d 753 (Mo. Ct. App. 1937).

[10]Allen v. Guarante (State Report Title: Allen v. Guarente), 253 Mass. 152, 148 N.E. 461 (1925) and decisions cited from Georgia, Indiana, Iowa, and Massachusetts in Religious belief or lack of it as affecting credibility of witness, 95 A.L.R. 726, superseded by Propriety and prejudicial effect of impeaching witness by reference to religious belief or lack of it, 76 A.L.R.3d 539. Most of the cases in the earlier annotation, however, are obsolete.

[11]"The credibility of witnesses can be affected only by evidence of their disbelief in the existence of God. . . . Adherence to any particular sect is no basis for argument in this respect." Allen v. Guarante (State Report Title: Allen v. Guarente), 253 Mass. 152, 148 N.E. 461, 462 (1925).

[12]"Unorthodox religious convictions, including agnosticism and atheism, quite often exist because of honest intellectual doubts. It is untenable to argue that there is a correlation be-

Restyled Federal Rule of Evidence 610 provides: "Evidence of a witness's religious beliefs or opinions is not admissible to attack or support the witness's credibility."[13] A juror might wrongfully discount the credibility of the member of an unconventional or unusual religion. Rule 610 guards against that type of prejudice.[14] However, the prohibition is not complete. In some cases, evidence of the witness's religion will be admissible on an alternative theory of logical relevance. For example, the Advisory Committee Note to Rule 610 adds that "disclosure of affiliation with a church which is a party to the litigation would be allowable under the rule," since it could bear on the witness's bias.[15]

## § 47 Supporting the witness

As § 33 noted, there are three stages in credibility analysis: bolstering before attempted impeachment, impeachment, and rehabilitation after attempted impeachment. Impeachment is not a dispassionate study of the witness's capacities and character, but rather an *attack* on his credibility. Under our adversary system of trials, the witness's proponent must be given an opportunity to meet this attack by presenting evidence rehabilitating the witness. As we have seen, one general principle, recognized under

---

tween this kind of unorthodoxy and inveracity. That correlation which may exist between what Pope calls 'blind unbelief' and untruthfulness is so slight that the value of the evidence is outweighed by the possibilities for prejudice with which it is pregnant." Chadbourn, Comment, 9 N.C. L. Rev. 77, 81 (1930).

[13]The prior version of Fed. R. Evid. 610 and Unif. R. Evid. 610 were to the same effect. *See* Malek v. Federal Ins. Co., 994 F.2d 49 (2d Cir. 1993) (it was error for the defense counsel to suggest during the cross-examination of one of plaintiffs' witnesses that his Hassidic affiliation affected his truthfulness; the error was prejudicial because "the impeached witness' religious affiliation is the same as that of the plaintiffs"); U.S. v. Sampol, 636 F.2d 621, 666 (D.C. Cir. 1980); Government of Virgin Islands v. Petersen, 553 F.2d 324 (3d Cir. 1977).

[14]The Advisory Committee's Note to the Federal Rule points out that the rule does not bar disclosure of affiliation with a church which is a party to the litigation for the purpose of show-

ing interest or bias. *E.g.*, U.S. v. Hoffman, 806 F.2d 703, 708 (7th Cir. 1986) (evidence of defendant's religious affiliation with the Reverend Sun Yung Moon established a possible motive to send threatening letter to the President); Mauldin v. Upjohn Co., 697 F.2d 644 (5th Cir. 1983) (witness permitted to testify as to hardship imposed on him in attempting to attend church by the injury he sustained). *But see* U.S. v. Teicher, 987 F.2d 112 (2d Cir. 1993) (the trial judge properly found that the witness's views about Jewish people were not probative of a relevant bias).

Uniform Rule of Evidence 610 is identical in substantive content.

[15]*See also* People v. Bautista, 163 Cal. App. 4th 762, 77 Cal. Rptr. 3d 824 (6th Dist. 2008) (the statute did not prohibit the admission of evidence of religious beliefs and practices of the defendant lay pastor and his churchgoers; the evidence provided a context for the defendant's actions and the complaining witnesses' delay in reporting the alleged incidents).

both case law and the Federal Rules of Evidence, is that absent an attack upon credibility, no bolstering evidence is allowed.[1]

---

**[Section 47]**

[1]U.S. v. Spriggs, 996 F.2d 320 (D.C. Cir. 1993) (collecting cases to the effect that when a cooperating conspirator testifies on direct, the prosecutor may not elicit the details of the cooperation agreement that are more likely to bolster than impeach); U.S. v. Awkard, 597 F.2d 667 (9th Cir. 1979) (bolstering of witness by calling expert on hypnosis); U.S. v. Jackson, 588 F.2d 1046 (5th Cir. 1979) (reputation for truthfulness; see Fed. R. Evid. and Unif. R. Evid. 608(a), providing in part, ". . . (2) evidence of truthful character is admissible only after the character of the witness for truthfulness has been attacked by opinion or reputation evidence or otherwise."); McPhearson v. State, 271 Ala. 533, 125 So. 2d 709 (1960) (defendant properly denied permission to show defense witness's good reputation for truth and veracity); State v. Harmon, 278 S.W. 733 (Mo. 1925) (testimony offered to support unimpeached character for truth of accused as witness, properly excluded); State v. Parsons, 83 N.J. Super. 430, 200 A.2d 340 (App. Div. 1964) (state properly refused permission to support state's witness by showing he changed his story after being shown results of a polygraph test, thus anticipating an attack on the witness's credibility); Martin v. Crow, 372 S.W.2d 724 (Tex. Civ. App. Texarkana 1963) (not error to refuse to permit plaintiff's witness to testify that he had no interest in the suit); Registration in Federal District Court of Judgment of Another Federal Court Under 28 U.S.C.A. sec. 1963, 194 A.L.R. Fed. 531; Admissibility of evidence of good reputation for truth and veracity of witness who has not been impeached, 15 A.L.R. 1065 (supplemented by Admissibility of evidence of good reputation for truth and veracity of witness who has not been impeached, 33 A.L.R. 1220). However, when a prosecution witness is testifying pursuant to an agreement, during direct examination some courts permit the witness to testify about the agreement and, in particular, allow the witness to mention that the agreement requires him or her to testify truthfully. U.S. v. McClellon, 578 F.3d 846 (8th Cir. 2009); U.S. v. Alviar, 573 F.3d 526 (7th Cir. 2009). The courts sometimes advance the justification that otherwise, the jury might speculate as to why a witness connected with the crime has not been charged. Woods v. U.S., 987 A.2d 451 (D.C. 2010).

The exclusion of character-support, absent attack, is frequently explained as the corollary of a presumption that the witness's character is good. E.g., Johnson v. State, 129 Wis. 146, 108 N.W. 55, 58 (1906). 4 Wigmore, Evidence § 1104 n. 1 (Chadbourn rev. 1972), says that the character is simply unknown.

It has been held that a witness's act consistent with his testimony about the main fact is admissible, even absent attack, as corroborating the testimony. State v. Slocinski, 89 N.H. 262, 197 A. 560 (1938) (witness to arson threat, allowed to testify that he reported the threat to the police and to his own lawyer, at the time it was made). Such evidence is often justified as furnishing relevant corroboration. Mahoney v. Minsky, 39 N.J. 208, 188 A.2d 161 (1963) (witness's testimony that he made a cash payment of $2,500 and cashed a check to obtain the cash amount; error to refuse admission of the check).

Nor can the party bolster his witness by proof, in the case in chief, that the witness has previously told the same story that he tells on the stand. State v. Herrera, 236 Or. 1, 386 P.2d 448 (1963) (prosecution witness's prior consistent statement was admitted; error, however, was not reversible because defendant later impeached the witness); Newton v. State, 147

Conversely, after the witness's opponent has introduced evidence of impeaching facts, the witness's proponent may present contradictory evidence disproving the alleged impeaching facts. Such disproof is relevant and generally allowable.[2]

---

Tex. Crim. 400, 180 S.W.2d 946 (1944) (prosecuting witness in attempted murder, where issue is assailant's identity, allowed to recite his report to guests of identity of telephone caller on night of attack, held error); 4 Wigmore, Evidence § 1124 (Chadbourn rev. 1972). This can be justified on grounds of saving of time by avoiding a defense of the witness before a need for one appears. In addition, the prior statement may be inadmissible as substantive proof on the issues because it is hearsay for that purpose. However, if the statement is offered to meet an express or implied charge of recent fabrication or improper influence or motive, Fed. R. Evid. 801(d) (1) (B) provides that the statement is not hearsay. Unif. R. Evid. 801(b) (1) (B) is to the same effect. See § 251 infra. But when the principal fact to which this "bolstering" evidence is addressed is later denied by the adversary's witness (as in the *Newton* case, 180 S.W.2d 946 (Tex. Crim. 1944), does this furnish the "attack" and convert the present point into one of mere order of proof? Usually mere contradiction in relevant testimony is not an attack. *See* text at note 384 infra. *But see* Ochoa v. Breslin, 798 F. Supp. 2d 495, 505 (S.D. N.Y. 2011) ("While the practice of bolstering is prohibited in various states, including New York, it is not [expressly] forbidden by the Federal Rules of Evidence").

[2]Thus, evidence of bad character to impeach may be rebutted by evidence of good character. *See* Fed. R. Evid. 608(a) and Unif. R. Evid. 608(a) quoted in part in note 366 supra; Prentiss v. Roberts, 49 Me. 127, 137, 1860 WL 2764 (1860); 4 Wigmore, Evidence § 1105 (Chadbourn rev. 1972). Some courts permit at least the witness's summary denial or explanation of guilt where he has been impeached by conviction. See § 42 notes

64–67 supra. Of course, the witness might deny (4 Wigmore, Evidence § 1119 (Chadbourn rev. 1972)) or attempt to explain (U.S. v. Mitchell, 556 F.2d 371 (6th Cir. 1977); People v. Burke, 52 Ill. App. 2d 159, 201 N.E.2d 636 (2d Dist. 1964)) the facts allegedly showing bias. *See also* U.S. v. Lopez, 100 Fed. Appx. 32, 34–35 (2d Cir. 2004); U.S. v. Henderson, 337 F.3d 914 (7th Cir. 2003) ("Henderson argues that evidence of McPhaul's cooperation in other cases was not relevant because McPhaul did not yet have other 'bargaining chips' with which to negotiate a lesser sentence, thereby giving McPhaul a greater motive to frame him. We do not agree. McPhaul's cooperation in other cases made it less probable that he framed Henderson because Henderson was the first of several 'bargaining chips' which McPhaul could work. The fact that Henderson was McPhaul's first deal does not remove this case from [that] rationale. By the time he arranged the deal with Henderson, McPhaul had given other names to the government and eventually assisted with the investigations of those people. McPhaul knew that he would have multiple bargaining chips, beginning with Henderson, and the evidence of his further cooperation casts doubt on Henderson's argument that McPhaul had a greater to falsely implicate Henderson"); U.S. v. Sumlin, 271 F.3d 274, 281–82 (D.C. Cir. 2001) ("In United States v. Smith, 232 F.3d 236 (D.C-.Cir. 2000), we dismissed a relevance challenge . . . on grounds that the fact that a paid informant 'has informed and testified truthfully in the past under his plea agreement certainly bears on his response to similar pressures and temptations in the present" case; the evidence was a proper method of rebutting the bias impeachment); U.S. v. Scott, 267 F.3d 729, 735 (7th Cir. 2001) (the defense attacked

## The General Ban on Bolstering

As just stated, absent the introduction of impeaching facts, the witness's proponent ordinarily may not bolster the witness's credibility. The rationale is that we do not want to devote court time to the witness's credibility and run the risk of distracting the jury from the historical merits unless and until the opposing attorney attacks the witness's credibility. Admittedly, there are exceptions to this general norm. For instance, the fact of a complaint of rape and in some instances certain details of the complaint have been held admissible. If a person has been raped, they will normally make a complaint about the incident. Both the fact of complaint and, where allowed, the details of the complaint may be admissible on the theory of bolstering the complaining witness.[3] However, since this evidence may sometimes come in as substantive evidence under some theories, the matter is dealt

---

an informant's credibility for bias; to rebut the attack, the prosecution was entitled to show the witness's cooperation in unrelated cases; "Burns' successful participation in numerous other cases meant that at the time he was negotiating over his plea deal, he had lots of information to use as bargaining chips. That fact was relevant . . . because it made less probable the assertion that Burns was lying in Lindermann's case out of self interest"); U.S. v. Brown, 547 F.2d 438 (8th Cir. 1977) (proper to admit extrinsic evidence to rebut incident relied upon to show bias (*cf.* U.S. v. Scholle, 553 F.2d 1109 (8th Cir. 1977)); Ryan v. Dwyer, 33 A.D.2d 878, 307 N.Y.S.2d 565 (4th Dep't 1969) (party calling witness may prove any fact tending to show witness's absence of interest or bias; here after a showing that witness settled a claim with plaintiff arising out of the accident, a similar settlement with defendant may be proved); Fishman, Informant Credibility and Evidence of Cooperation in Other Cases, 26 Am. J. Trial Advoc. 363 (2002). The making of an inconsistent statement may also be denied or explained. Tri-State Transfer Co. v. Nowotny, 198 Minn. 537, 270 N.W. 684 (1936) (rebutting witness may testify that complaint introduced as prior witness's inconsistent statement was not drawn by him but by attor-

ney); Ryan v. Dwyer, 33 A.D.2d 878, 307 N.Y.S.2d 565 (4th Dep't 1969) (witness may explain inconsistent statement; dictum that he may deny making it). *See also* U.S. v. Holland, 526 F.2d 284 (5th Cir. 1976) (later correction of misstatement before grand jury).

The generalization in the text finds support under the Federal and Revised Uniform Rules, since such evidence undoubtedly falls within the definition of "relevant evidence" in Rule 401.

It seems clear from the context of Rule 608(b) and the tenor of the federal Advisory Committee's Note that the statutory limitations on the use of specific instances of conduct are intended to apply only with respect to character for truthfulness, not with respect to other kinds of credibility attacks such as bias or motive to falsify. For text of Rule 608(b), see § 41, note 6 supra. *Compare* U.S. v. Scholle, 553 F.2d 1109 (8th Cir. 1977).

[3]*See* 4 Wigmore, Evidence §§ 1134–40 (Chadbourn rev. 1972), 6 id. §§ 1760–61 (Chadbourn rev. 1976); West's Key Number Digest, Rape ☞48. *See* In re L.C., 41 A.3d 1261 (D.C. 2012) (the report-of-rape doctrine); Com. v. McCutcheon, 51 Mass. App. Ct. 715, 748 N.E.2d 489 (2001) (a complaint was admissible in a statutory rape case although the 14-year-

with at length later.[4] Likewise, prior consistent statements of identification can be admissible substantively or to bolster; but precisely because prior identifications may be introduced as substantive evidence and trigger constitutional requirements, that subject is also discussed elsewhere.[5] With the exception of fresh complaints and prior identifications, the witness's proponent may proffer evidence of the witness's truthfulness as rehabilitation only after attempted impeachment.

### Corroboration

Suppose that the witness completes his or her testimony about fact *A* and that the opposing attorney does not attempt any impeachment. As we shall soon see, absent attempted impeachment, the witness's proponent cannot offer later testimony for the purpose of rehabilitating the witness's credibility. Thus, the proponent could not call witness #2 to testify that witness #1 has a reputation as a truthful person. However, the proponent may call witness #2 to give additional testimony about fact *A*. On its face, that testimony is relevant to the historical merits rather than witness #1's credibility. This type of testimony is classified as corroborating rather than rehabilitating. Under Federal Rule of Evidence 403, the trial judge has discretion to limit the amount of corroborating testimony about fact *A*, but such testimony is not subject to the limitations on either bolstering or rehabilitation.

### Rehabilitation

A discussion of rehabilitation is best organized around the techniques employed. The two most common rehabilitative methods are: (1) introduction of supportive evidence of good character of the witness attacked, and (2) proof of the witness's consistent statements. The basic question is whether these two types of rehabilitation evidence represent a proper response in kind to the specific methods of impeachment that have been used. The general test of admissibility is whether evidence of the witness's good character or consistent statements is logically relevant to explain the impeaching fact. The rehabilitating facts must meet the impeachment with relative directness. The wall, attacked at one point, may not be fortified at another, distinct

---

old complainant was a "consenting" partner to the sexual encounters).

[4]See § 272.

[5]See § 251 infra. *See also* Robinson v. Graham, 671 F. Supp. 2d 338, 348–49 (N.D. N.Y. 2009) (New York law on prior identification); People v. Tisdel, 201 Ill. 2d 210, 266 Ill. Dec. 849, 775 N.E.2d 921 (2002) (the prosecutor may not only elicit testimony that the witness identified the defendant; the prosecutor may also present testimony that the witness did not pick out anyone else).

point.[6] Credibility is a side issue, and the circle of relevancy should be drawn narrowly in this context. When we reach the stage of rehabilitation after impeachment, we are rather far afield from the historical merits of the case; and the courts justifiably insist on a stronger showing of relevance to minimize the risk that the jury will lose sight of the merits. As a rule of thumb, the courts demand that the rehabilitation be a response in kind to the impeachment. Precisely how responsive is a question of degree as to which reasonable courts differ.

*Proof of the witness's character trait for truthfulness.*[7] When may the party supporting the impeached witness offer evidence of the witness's good character for truth? Certainly attacks by evidence of bad reputation,[8] bad opinion of character for truthfulness,[9] conviction of crime,[10] or misconduct which has not resulted

---

[6]*See* Holmes, J., in Gertz v. Fitchburg R. Co., 137 Mass. 77, 78, 1884 WL 10541 (1884). In holding that the plaintiff, impeached as a witness by conviction of crime, could give evidence of his good reputation for truth, Holmes stated:

> We think that the evidence of his reputation for truth should have been admitted, and that the exception must be sustained. There is a clear distinction between this case and those in which such evidence has been held inadmissible, for instance, to rebut evidence of contradictory statements; Russell v. Coffin, 8 Pick. 143; Brown v. Mooers, 6 Gray 451; or where the witness is directly contradicted as to the principal fact by other witnesses. Atwood v. Dearborn, 1 Allen, 483.
>
> In such cases, it is true that the result sought to be reached is the same as in the present,—to induce the jury to disbelieve the witness. But the mode of reaching the result is different. For, while contradiction or proof of contradictory statements may very well have the incidental effect of impeaching the character for truth of the contradicted witness in the minds of the jury, the proof is not directed to that point. The purpose and only direct effect of the evidence are to show that the witness is not to be believed in this instance. But the reason why he is not to be believed is left untouched. That may be found in forgetfulness on the part of the witness, or in his having been deceived, or in any other possible cause. The disbe-

lief sought to be produced is perfectly consistent with an admission of his general good character for truth, as well as for the other virtues; and until the character of a witness is assailed, it cannot be fortified by evidence.

[7]Of course, the character evidence must take the form of reputation or opinion testimony. Evidence of the witness's specific, prior truthful acts is inadmissible even if the opponent has attacked the witness's character for truthfulness. U.S. v. Murray, 103 F.3d 310, 321 (3d Cir. 1997) (the defense attacked an informant's character trait for truthfulness; even then it was improper for the prosecution to elicit testimony of 65 or 66 prior occasions when the informant had furnished reliable leads to make a case for the police).

[8]See this section, note 2 supra. *See* Fed. R. Evid. 608(a), Advisory Committee's Note.

[9]Fed. R. Evid. 608(a) and Advisory Committee's Note.

[10]See this section, note 6, supra; Fed. R. Evid. 608(a), Advisory Committee's Note. *See* Derrick v. Wallace, 217 N.Y. 520, 112 N.E. 440 (1916); 4 Wigmore, Evidence § 1106 (Chadbourn rev. 1972). *But see* Com. v. Ford, 199 Pa. Super. 102, 184 A.2d 401 (1962) (affirming rejection of reputation evidence and stating matter was within the trial judge's discretion).

in conviction,[11] all open the door to character support.[12] The evidence of good character for truth is a logically relevant response in kind to all these modes of impeachment. Moreover, a slashing cross-examination[13] can carry strong accusations of misconduct and bad character, which even the witness's forceful denial will not remove from the jury's mind. If the judge considers that fairness requires it, he may admit evidence of good character as a palliative for the insinuation of an accusatory cross-examination.[14]

---

[11]Fed. R. Evid. 608(a), Advisory Committee's Note; First Nat. Bank v. Blakeman, 1907 OK 76, 19 Okla. 106, 91 P. 868 (1907) ("when the witness has been impeached by evidence of particular acts of criminal or moral misconduct, either on cross-examination or by record of conviction," citing cases); Com. v. Fulton, 574 Pa. 282, 830 A.2d 567 (2003) (the prosecution's questioning about a specific instance of a witness's untruthfulness impugned the witness's character for truthfulness); 4 Wigmore, Evidence § 1106 (Chadbourn rev. 1972).

[12]*See generally* Renda v. King, 347 F.3d 550, 554–55 (3d Cir. 2003) ("Direct attacks on a witness' veracity in the particular case do not open the door for evidence of the witness' good character. For example, evidence of bias or prior inconsistent statements do not open the door . . . . Evidence of bias only relates to a motive to lie in the particular case, not a general predisposition to lie. Similarly, prior inconsistent statements do not open the door . . . because there can be a number of reasons for the error, such as defects in knowledge or memory, a bias or interest in this particular case, or a general character trait for untruthfulness. Indirect attacks . . . open the door for evidence of a witness' good character for truthfulness. As the Advisory Committee Notes for Rule 608(b) state: '[o]pinion or reputation that the witness is untruthful specifically qualifies as an attack under the rule, and evidence of misconduct, including conviction of crime, and of corruption also fall within this category. Evidence of bias or interest does not. The reason that an indirect attack

. . . opens the door . . . is because such attacks directly call into question the witness' moral character for truthfulness. Likewise, '[a]n act of corruption directly affects moral character; and the corroboration should therefore depend upon the rule for acts involving character' ").

[13]U.S. v. Valletto, 58 Fed. Appx. 931, 934 (3d Cir. 2003) ("Lopa's reputation for truthfulness was attacked during a vigorous cross-examination . . . ."). *See also* U.S. v. Lechoco, 542 F.2d 84 (D.C. Cir. 1976) (a defense psychiatrist based his testimony in part on information provided by the defendant; the prosecution called into question the reliability of the information; the trial judge erred in refusing to allow the defense "to elicit testimony relating to the defendant's reputation for truthfulness and honesty" in response to the prosecution cross-examination).

[14]U.S. v. Scholle, 553 F.2d 1109 (8th Cir. 1977) (dictum); Harris v. State, 49 Tex. Crim. 338, 94 S.W. 227 (1906) (a stern cross-examination, tending to bring witness into disrepute before jury and indirectly attacking his testimony). *Contra* U.S. v. Thomas, 768 F.2d 611, 618 (5th Cir. 1985) ("Under Rule 608, evidence of a truthful character is admissible only after the character of the witness for truthfulness has been attacked by opinion or reputation evidence or otherwise. Vigorous cross-examination and/or the fact that a witness is contradicted by other evidence in the case does not constitute such an attack."). *See also* Com. v. Ingraham, 73 Mass. 46, 49, 7 Gray 46, 1856 WL 5779 (1856), sanctioning proof of good character after a

A witness's corrupt conduct showing bias should also be regarded as an attack on veracity-character and thus warrant character support.[15] However, impeachment for bias or interest by facts not involving corruption, such as proof of family relationship,[16] does not open the door to proof of good character for truthfulness.[17]

The courts divide over the propriety of supporting the witness by showing his good character for truthfulness when the witness has been impeached only by evidence of an inconsistent statement or the opponent's evidence specifically contradicting the facts to which the witness testified. If the witness has been impeached by an inconsistent statement, in the past perhaps the numerical majority of courts routinely permitted a showing of his good character for truthfulness.[18] However, if the adversary has merely introduced evidence contradicting the facts to which the witness testified, most cases forbade a showing of the witness's good character for truthfulness.[19] Convenient as hard-and-fast answers to these questions may be, it is unsound to resolve those

---

mere abortive attempt to prove the witness's bad character. Mere inconsistencies in the witness's testimony, exposed by cross-examination, were held insufficient to justify good character reputation evidence in Royal v. Cameron, 382 S.W.2d 335 (Tex. Civ. App. Tyler 1964).

[15]Fed. R. Evid. 608(a), Advisory Committee's Note; People v. Ah Fat, 48 Cal. 61, 64, 1874 WL 1218 (1874) (evidence that state's witness had offered to identify killer "if there was any coin in it"). *See also* Rodriguez v. State, 165 Tex. Crim. 179, 305 S.W.2d 350 (1957) (where attempt has been made to show witness's corrupt motives).

[16]Fed. R. Evid. 608(a), Advisory Committee's Note; Lassiter v. State, 35 Ala. App. 323, 47 So. 2d 230 (1950), Note, 3 Ala. L. Rev. 206 (1950).

[17]Renda v. King, 347 F.3d 550, 554–55 (3d Cir. 2003).

[18]Dickson v. Dinsmore, 219 Ala. 353, 122 So. 437 (1929); Turner v. State, 112 Tex. Crim. 245, 16 S.W.2d 127 (1929). *Contra* State v. Hoffman, 134 Iowa 587, 112 N.W. 103 (1907). *See* 4 Wigmore, Evidence § 1108 (Chadbourn rev. 1972); Testimony tending to show that party or witness

has made contradictory statements as ground for evidence as to his truth and veracity, 6 A.L.R. 862. But the preferable approach, at least under the Fed. R. Evid., is to place this matter in the discretion of the judge who can consider the circumstances under which each inconsistent statement was made. *See* Beard v. Mitchell, 604 F.2d 485 (7th Cir.1979); Outlaw v. U.S., 81 F.2d 805 (C.C.A. 5th Cir. 1936).

[19]U.S. v. Dring, 930 F.2d 687, 691 (9th Cir. 1991) ("the presentation of contradiction evidence, in the form of contravening testimony by other witnesses, does not trigger rehabilitation"); Louisville & N. R. Co. v. McClish, 115 F. 268 (C.C.A. 6th Cir. 1902), opinion by Day, J. (witness who testified he saw decedent pass along railway track shortly before train passed, contradicted by witness who testified first witness was not at the scene but was in opera house at the time; held error to admit character-support, though contradiction "admits of no reconciliation . . . upon any theory of honest mistake or failure of memory"); People v. Wheatley, 805 P.2d 1148 (Colo. App. 1990); Whaley v. State, 157 Fla. 593, 26 So. 2d 656 (1946) (murder: material conflict between testimony of accused and of officers as to terms of

questions in a mechanical fashion. A more sensible view is that in each case the judge should consider whether a particular impeachment for inconsistency or a conflict in testimony[20] amounts in effect to an attack on the witness's character trait for truthfulness.[21] It may be more realistic to treat the impeachment as a limited attack on the veracity of the specific testimony the witness has given in the instant case, rather than a broader assault on the witness's truthfulness.[22] One relevant consideration is whether the inconsistency or contradiction relates to a matter on which the witness could be innocently mistaken. Is the inconsistency or contradiction so flat that the irresistible common sense inference is a lie rather than an innocent mistake? Another pertinent consideration is the number of inconsistencies mentioned by the cross-examiner. The larger the number, the stronger is the inference that by character the witness is a liar, not simply a witness who has told an isolated lie.[23] Under the Federal Rules of Evidence, the trial judge may arguably consider the factor of

---

alleged oral confession, does not warrant admission of defendant's good reputation for truth). *Contra* Redd v. Ingram, 207 Va. 939, 154 S.E.2d 149 (1967). *See* 4 Wigmore, Evidence § 1109 (Chadbourn rev. 1972).

Again, the Federal Rules of Evidence entrust the matter to the judge's discretion. *See* Rule 608(a), Advisory Committee's Note, which states in part: "Whether evidence in the form of contradiction is an attack upon the character of the witness must depend in part upon the circumstances." *See also* discussion in U.S. v. Medical Therapy Sciences, Inc., 583 F.2d 36 (2d Cir. 1978). *But compare* U.S. v. Jackson, 588 F.2d 1046 (5th Cir. 1979).

Wigmore, supra, suggests that the argument for supporting character here is weaker than in the case of impeachment for inconsistency. This may be so if one insists on an attack on character as a condition precedent. However, from the view of the administration of justice, can one imagine a greater need for the jury to know "what type of man" the witness is than in these cases of irreconcilable conflicts?

[20]In many cases of inconsistent statements, there will be both an inconsistency and a conflict of evidence in the sense that the witness denies the making of the inconsistent statement and also in the sense that the witness's substantive story is contradicted.

[21]See the stress placed on discretion in Outlaw v. U.S., 81 F.2d 805, 808 (C.C.A. 5th Cir. 1936) and First Nat. Bank v. Blakeman, 1907 OK 76, 19 Okla. 106, 91 P. 868, 871 (1907). *See also* U.S. v. Drury, 344 F.3d 1089 (11th Cir. 2003) (the prosecutor's pointing out inconsistencies in the defendant's testimony did not amount to an attack on the defendant's character trait for truthfulness).

[22]Renda v. King, 347 F.3d 550, 554–55 (3d Cir. 2003).

[23]State v. Eugenio, 219 Wis. 2d 391, 579 N.W.2d 642 (1998) (evidence of the witness's truthful character is admissible only when the judge concludes "that a reasonable person would consider the attack on the witness to be an assertion that the witness is not only lying in this instance, but is a liar generally").

the number of inconsistencies in deciding whether to permit the rehabilitation.[24]

*Proof of the witness's prior consistent statements.* Turning to attempts to rehabilitate an attacked witness by introducing a prior statement consistent present testimony, a similar threshold question arises: What kinds of attack on the witness open the door to evidence of the witness's prior statements consistent with his present testimony?[25] When the attack takes the form of character impeachment by showing misconduct, convictions, or bad reputa-

---

[24]See mention of Fed. R. Evid. in note 19, supra.

Only reputation or opinion testimony is permitted; specific instances of conduct in support of the principal witness's character for truthfulness are inadmissible. See § 43 supra.

The number of reputation or opinion witnesses who will be permitted to testify as to untruthfulness or truthfulness is within the court's discretion. Since the testimony of such witnesses is to a great degree cumulative, a court may limit to one the number allowed to testify. U.S. v. Haynes, 554 F.2d 231 (5th Cir. 1977) (untruthfulness). Nevertheless, the usual practice is to permit several character witnesses to testify especially where the criminal defendant offers such witness in support of his character for truthfulness. U.S. v. Jackson, 696 F.2d 578 (8th Cir. 1982) (defendant permitted seven character witnesses at first trial and four "live" and two "read" at second trial).

Sometimes opinion or reputation evidence in support of truthful character consists of testimony of prominent figures or pillars of society. U.S. v. Crippen, 570 F.2d 535, 538 (5th Cir. 1978) ("The defendant called a number of eminent people as character witnesses. While the testimony of each was slightly different, the first, a Roman Catholic Sister who was president of a college on whose board Crippen sat, was typical. She said Crippen's reputation for truth and veracity was good. He was regarded with great trust. He was regarded by 'all of us' as 'honest and sincere' in his efforts."); U.S. v. Wright, 542 F.2d 975,

979 (7th Cir. 1976) (the defendant called "as character witnesses his minister, a history professor, and the executive director of a Boys Club."); Wolfson v. Baker, 444 F. Supp. 1124, 1129 n.3 (M.D. Fla. 1978) ("These 'character' witnesses were called for the purpose of establishing Wolfson's reputation in the community for truthfulness. The witnesses were tendered under the rule of evidence now codified in Rule 608(a), Fed. R. Evid. A substantial number of witnesses was called for the sole purpose of establishing Wolfson's reputation for truth and veracity, and the list was impressive. It included many figures of national or local prominence, including sports figures Joe DiMaggio and Sid Luckman, television personality Ed Sullivan, and former Florida governor Fuller Warren.").

[25]Tombroek v. State, 2009 WY 126, 217 P.3d 806 (Wyo. 2009) (the requirement "does not mandate a specific allegation during cross-examination; rather it may be made by implication or innuendo, and it may be found in the thrust of" the impeachment).

In various states there still is a rule that a witness's consistent statements cannot be introduced as "substantive evidence" but must be confined to the purpose of "rehabilitating" a witness. In other words such evidence is regarded as inadmissible hearsay if within the definition of hearsay but not within any exception to the hearsay rule. See § 251 infra. On the other hand, Fed. R. Evid. 801(d)(1)(B) provides that a prior statement of a witness, who testifies at a trial or

tion, there is no justification for rehabilitating by consistent statements.[26] The rehabilitation does not meet the attack and fails the response-in-kind rule of thumb.

---

hearing and is subject to cross-examination concerning the statement, is not hearsay if the statement is "(B) consistent with the declarant's testimony and is offered to rebut an express or implied charge against the declarant of recent fabrication or improper influence or motive." Unif. R. Evid. 801(b)(1)(B) is identical.

There is an important question under the Federal and Uniform Rules whether the above conditions for using consistent statements as nonhearsay substantive evidence govern the use of consistent statements merely to support the credibility of a witness whose credibility has been attacked. There is federal authority that Rule 801(d)(1)(B) also governs the conditions under which consistent statements can be used merely to bolster the credibility of the attacked witness. *See* U.S. v. Quinto, 582 F.2d 224 (2d Cir. 1978) and discussions in opinions in United U.S. v. Rubin, 609 F.2d 51 (2d Cir. 1979). *See also* Effect of Rule 801(d)(1)(B) of the Federal Rules of Evidence upon the admissibility of a witness' prior consistent statement, 47 A.L.R. Fed. 639 for cases seeming to assume this conclusion. The opposing viewpoint is that the question of admission of consistent statements merely for rehabilitation purposes is a matter of discretion of the trial judge, who, as a matter of relevancy under Rule 401, should decide whether a consistent statement will sufficiently tend to meet the particular credibility attack(s). Rule 403. A similar theory regarding the admission of consistent statements when an attack has been made by inconsistent statements is discussed in 4 Weinstein's Federal Evidence § 607.09 (rev. 2011).

No matter which of the above theories in applying the Federal Rules of Evidence is followed, the conclusions stated in the instant text paragraph should be correct under the federal rules. *See, e.g.*, U.S. v. Williams,

573 F.2d 284 (5th Cir. 1978) (bias attack suggesting that testimony had been influenced by government actions permitted showing of witness's consistent statement). This latter case can be interpreted to mean, contrary to other cases indicated above, that Rule 801(d) (1) (B) itself does not necessarily require that the consistent statement or motives mentioned in the rule exist *before* the inconsistent statement. *See also* Effect of Rule 801(d)(1) (B) of the Federal Rules of Evidence upon the admissibility of a witness' prior consistent statement, 47 A.L.R. Fed. 639.

[26]Stanford v. State, 34 Tex. Crim. 89, 29 S.W. 271 (1895) (bad reputation); 4 Wigmore, Evidence § 1125 (Chadbourn rev. 1972); Admissibility of impeached witness' prior consistent statement—modern state civil cases, 59 A.L.R.4th 1000; Admissibility of impeached witness' prior consistent statement—modern state criminal cases, 58 A.L.R.4th 1014; Effect of Rule 801(d)(1)(B) of the Federal Rules of Evidence upon the admissibility of a witness' prior consistent statement, 47 A.L.R. Fed. 639. *See* U.S. v. Bishop, 264 F.3d 535, 548 (5th Cir. 2001) (the defense lawyers implied that the witness, Locus, made mistakes or lied during testimony; however, they did not indicate that "his supposed fabrications were recent or made with an improper motive. Rule 801(d)(1)(B) cannot be construed to allow the admission of what would otherwise be hearsay every time a law enforcement officer's credibility or memory is challenged"); U.S. v. Lozada-Rivera, 177 F.3d 98, 104 (1st Cir. 1999) ("Generally speaking, a charge of improper motive or recent fabrication need not be expressly made . . . . But the proponent . . . must point to specific questions during his adversary's presentation which suggest recent fabrication or bias").

Further, at common law under the prevailing temporal priority doctrine, if the attacker has charged bias, interest, corrupt influence, contrivance to falsify, or want of capacity to observe or remember, the prior consistent statement is deemed irrelevant to refute the charge unless the consistent statement was made *before* the source of the bias, interest, influence or incapacity originated.[27] If the statement was made later, proof of the statement does not assist the jury to evaluate the witness's testimony because the reliability of the consistent statement is subject to the same doubt as the trial testimony. Many courts continue to

---

[27]Government of Virgin Islands v. Muiruri, 340 Fed. Appx. 794 (3d Cir. 2009) (the alleged victim's purported motive to fabricate arose before she gave the statement to the police); U.S. v. Prieto, 232 F.3d 816 (11th Cir. 2000) (there is no per se rule that a witness's statement following arrest is necessarily made with a motive to fabricate; the court noted that the other circuits have split over the question). Excluded on the ground of timing: Sesterhenn v. Saxe, 88 Ill. App. 2d 2, 232 N.E.2d 277 (1st Dist. 1967) (consistent statement held inadmissible when impeachment attempt went to showing bias and not a recent fabrication); People v. Gardineer, 2 Mich. App. 337, 139 N.W.2d 890 (1966) (statement after alleged bias held inadmissible). Admitted where statement was made before the alleged influence arose: People v. Hillhouse, 27 Cal. 4th 469, 117 Cal. Rptr. 2d 45, 40 P.3d 754, 769 (2002) (a prior consistent statement is admissible if it predates any of the improper motives that the opposing party expressly or impliedly suggests may have influenced the witness's testimony); People v. Kynette, 15 Cal. 2d 731, 104 P.2d 794 (1940); Burns v. Clayton, 237 S.C. 316, 117 S.E.2d 300 (1960) (witness's consistent statement "prior to the existence of his relation to cause"; impeachment suggesting witness had been paid to testify falsely). *See* Admissibility of impeached witness' prior consistent statement—modern state civil cases, 59 A.L.R.4th 1000; Graham, Prior Consistent Statements: Rule 801(d)(1)(B) of the Federal Rules of Evidence, Critique and Proposal, 30 Hast. L.J. 575 (1979).

The charge, triggering the doctrine, need not be made by the opposing attorney. *See* Klein v. State, 273 S.W.3d 297, 315–16 (Tex. Crim. App. 2008) (on direct examination, the victim testified that her father had sexually assaulted her; later in the direct she stated that the earlier testimony was false and that the prosecutor's earlier questions had been confusing and tricky; that statement amounted to a charge of improper influence or motive; given that charge, the prosecution could introduce her earlier statements to a police officer and a Child Protective Services investigator that her father had sexually abused her).

If the witness's accuracy of memory is challenged, a consistent statement made shortly after the event and before he had time to forget, could arguably be received in support. ". . . The accuracy of memory is supported by proof that at or near the time when the facts deposed to have transpired, and were fresh in the mind of the witness, he gave the same version of them that he testified to on the trial." Smith, C.J. in Jones v. Jones, 250 (N.C. 1879). Relying upon particular circumstances, the judge could use this theory to permit introduction in spite of the fact that accuracy of memory is not referred to in either Fed. R. Evid. 801(d)(1)(B) or Unif. R. Evid. 801(b)(1)(B). *See also* Cross v. State, 118 Md. 660, 86 A. 223, 227 (1912). Admissibility of impeached witness' prior consistent statement—modern state civil cases, 59 A.L.R.4th 1000.

enforce the temporal priority doctrine under the Federal Rules;[28] but there is a large body of contra authority.[29] In 1995 in *Tome v. United States*,[30] the Supreme Court held that Rule 801(d)(1)(B), governing the admission of consistent statements as substantive evidence, incorporates the temporal priority doctrine. Although the Court disclaimed ruling on the question of whether the doctrine applies when the consistent statement under "any other evidentiary principle" such as rehabilitation, some commentators read the opinion as a signal that the Court will eventually extend the same limitation to consistent statements proffered for the limited purpose of rehabilitation.[31]

There is a further division of opinion over the question whether impeachment by inconsistent statements opens the door to support by proving consistent statements.[32] A few courts usually rule that this type of support is permissible.[33] This holding has the merit of easy application. At the opposite extreme, since the in-

---

[28]See this section, note 25, supra; U.S. v. Williams, 264 F.3d 561, 575 (5th Cir. 2001) ("[B]ecause the motive for Love to lie arose prior to his testimony in the first trial, the testimony was inadmissible . . . ."); U.S. v. Bao, 189 F.3d 860 (9th Cir. 1999) (although the defendant had not yet been arrested at the time of the statement, he was already motivated to lie because the police had searched the premises and found counterfeit manuals); U.S. v. Miller, 874 F.2d 1255, 1271 (9th Cir. 1989) ("rehabilitative prior statements are admissible . . . only if they were made before the witness had a motive to fabricate"); U.S. v. McCaskey, 30 M.J. 188, 192 (C.M.A. 1990) ("[T]o be logically relevant to rebut such a charge, the prior statement typically must have been made before the point at which the story was fabricated or the improper influence or motive arose. Otherwise, the prior statement normally is mere repetition which, if made while still under the improper influence or after the urge to lie has reared its ugly head, does nothing to 'rebut' the charge.").

[29]U.S. v. Montague, 958 F.2d 1094, 1098 (D.C. Cir. 1992) ("We join the Fifth and Eleventh Circuits in holding that the prior consistent statement need not have preceded the appearance of the motive. . . ."); U.S. v.

Casoni, 950 F.2d 893, 904–06 (3d Cir. 1991) ("the evidence was offered only for rehabilitative purposes"); U.S. v. Farmer, 923 F.2d 1557 (11th Cir. 1991) ("appellant's argument that the prior consistent statements were inadmissible because they were not made before the motive to fabricate arose has repeatedly been rejected by this circuit"); Bullock & Gardner, Prior Consistent Statements and the Premotive Rule, 24 Fla. St. U. L. Rev. 509 (1997).

[30]Tome v. U.S., 513 U.S. 150, 115 S. Ct. 696, 130 L. Ed. 2d 574 (1995).

[31]Garland & Schneider, Prior Consistent Statements as Evidence in the United States and Canada—a Small Part of the Story of How Sex Crimes Cases Continue to Generate Law Reform: Herein of a Comparison of Tome v. United States and R. v. Khan, 2 Sw. J. Law & Trade in Americas 451, 467 (1995).

[32]See decisions collected in 4 Wigmore, Evidence § 1126 (Chadbourn rev. 1972); Weinstein & Berger, Evidence ¶ 607[08]; Admissibility of impeached witness' prior consistent statement—modern state civil cases, 59 A.L.R.4th 1000; West's Key Number Digest, Witnesses ⊕395, 414(2).

[33]*E.g.*, Stafford v. Lyon, 413 S.W.2d 495 (Mo. 1967); State v. Bethea,

315

consistency remains despite all consistent statements, some courts hold generally that impeachment by prior inconsistent statement does not permit rehabilitation by prior consistent statement.[34] That general holding seems preferable, but certain qualifications should be recognized. In particular, when the attacked witness denies making the inconsistent statement, evidence of consistent statements very near the time of the alleged inconsistent one is relevant to corroborate his denial.[35] Again, if in the specific situation, the attack by inconsistent statement is accompanied by or interpretable as a charge of a recent plan or contrivance to give false testimony, proof of a consistent statement antedating the plan or contrivance tends to disprove that the testimony was the result of contrivance; the testimony could not be the product of the alleged contrivance because the witness said the same thing before the supposed contrivance. Here all courts agree.[36] It is up to the judge to decide whether the impeachment at least implies a charge of contrivance. Most courts agree

---

186 N.C. 22, 118 S.E. 800 (1923) (allowable after any form of impeachment); Admissibility of impeached witness' prior consistent statement—modern state civil cases, 59 A.L.R.4th 1000.

[34]*E.g.*, Com. v. Jenkins, 76 Mass. 485, 488, 10 Gray 485, 1858 WL 6356 (1858).

[35]U.S. v. Khan, 821 F.2d 90 (2d Cir. 1987); Twardosky v. New England Tel. & Tel. Co., 95 N.H. 279, 62 A.2d 723 (1948); Donovan v. Moore-McCormack Lines, 266 A.D. 406, 42 N.Y.S.2d 441 (1st Dep't 1943); Admissibility of impeached witness' prior consistent statement—modern state civil cases, 59 A.L.R.4th 1000. *Contra* Burks v. State, 78 Ark. 271, 93 S.W. 983 (1906). *See also* Com. v. White, 340 Pa. 139, 16 A.2d 407 (1940), suggesting that where the witness denies the inconsistent statement, the admission of the supporting statement is in the judge's discretion.

There seems to be no direct authority under the Fed. R. Evid. although Rule 613(b) provides that the witness must be afforded an opportunity to explain or deny comes very close. The matter should be treated as one of relevancy under Rule 401, subject to the limitations of Rule 403.

[36]State v. Galloway, 247 A.2d 104 (Me. 1968); People v. Mirenda, 23 N.Y.2d 439, 297 N.Y.S.2d 532, 245 N.E.2d 194 (1969) (witness himself testified to consistent statement on redirect); People v. Singer, 300 N.Y. 120, 89 N.E.2d 710 (1949), noted 35 Cornell L.Q. 867. In the last case the court points out that though the common phrase is "recent" fabrication or contrivance, the term "recent" is misleading. It is not required to be near in point of time to the trial, but only that the alleged contrivance be closer to the trial in point of time than the consistent statement. See cases collected 4 Wigmore, Evidence § 1129 (Chadbourn rev. 1972); Admissibility of impeached witness' prior consistent statement—modern state civil cases, 59 A.L.R.4th 1000. Some decisions mention that the consistent statement should have been made before the witness would foresee its effect upon the fact issue, *see* Admissibility of impeached witness' prior consistent statement—modern state civil cases, 59 A.L.R.4th 1000, or before motive to falsify even if made before an inconsistent statement, Giordano v. Eastern Utilities, Inc., 9 A.D.2d 947, 195 N.Y.S.2d 753 (2d Dep't 1959).

When made before the occurrence of the matters mentioned in the

that there has been such a charge if the cross-examiner asks the witness to admit that he "didn't come up with this story" until the witness spoke with an attorney or party. However, if there is no such charge, the attack often amounts to a mere imputation of inaccurate memory. If so, only consistent statements made when the event was recent and memory fresh should be admitted.[37] Recognition of these qualifications still allows the courts to exclude statements procured after the inconsistent statement, and thus to discourage pressure on witnesses to furnish counter-statements.[38]

---

text, consistent statements are admissible under Fed. R. Evid. 801(d)(1)(B) and Unif. R. Evid. 801(b) (1) (B), quoted in note 25 supra. If admissible as substantive evidence under that rule, such statements must be admissible simply for rehabilitation purposes as well. However, the judge has a certain amount of practical discretion because the authority for admissibility is Rule 801 subject to Rule 403. See this section note 39 infra.

There is authority that if the inconsistent statement used to impeach is part of a larger statement, the remainder may be introduced to explain or negate the inconsistent part. Affronti v. U.S., 145 F.2d 3 (C.C.A. 8th Cir. 1944). Fed. R. Evid. 106 is a related principle. See also U.S. v. Denton, 246 F.3d 784, 789 (6th Cir. 2001) ("[T]he use of prior consistent statements for rehabilitation is particularly appropriate where, as here, those statements are part of a report or interview containing inconsistent statements which have been used to impeach the credibility of the witness . . . . The rehabilitative use of prior consistent statements is . . . in accord with the principle of completeness promoted by Rule 106").

See § 56 infra for a further related principle.

[37] See this section, note 27 supra.

[38] These after-statements have often been excluded. See, e.g., U.S. v. Sherman, 171 F.2d 619 (2d Cir. 1948)

(opinion by L. Hand, J.); Crawford v. Nilan, 289 N.Y. 444, 46 N.E.2d 512 (1943) (consistent statement procured from witness on morning of trial, held improperly admitted); Weiler v. Weiler, 336 S.W.2d 454 (Tex. Civ. App. Eastland 1960); Sweazey v. Valley Transport, 6 Wash. 2d 324, 107 P.2d 567 (1940). The *Crawford* and *Sweazey* cases exemplify the stresses of the race for statements in accident controversies. See Maguire, Evidence: Common Sense and Common Law 63 (1947). Investigators hired by defendants and insurance companies often secure from witnesses one-sided statements in defendants' favor; and if the witness's testimony diverges in plaintiff's favor, these come in as inconsistent statements. The obviously needed opportunity to counter these statements comes in the form of the witness's opportunity to deny or explain on cross-examination and redirect. In a New York case where the plaintiff raised doubts as to the accuracy of his signed inconsistent statement prepared defendant's investigator and testified that the investigator "talked him into giving it," the court admitted the plaintiff's consistent statement made five days later to plaintiff's employer and not for the purpose of the action, as bearing on the issue as to the accuracy of the inconsistent statement. One judge dissented in a vigorous opinion. Donovan v. Moore-McCormack Lines, 266 A.D. 406, 42 N.Y.S.2d 441 (1st Dep't 1943).

These qualifications can be recognized consistently with the text of the Federal Rules of Evidence.[39] Under a broader viewpoint, the common law temporal priority doctrine does not apply to all consistent statements offered for the limited purpose of rehabilitation in federal practice;[40] and the judge has discretion under Rules 401 and 403 to determine whether the particular circumstances justify admission of consistent statements to rehabilitate the witness. Suppose, for instance, that the cross-examiner forced the witness to concede that the witness had made a seemingly inconsistent statement. To rehabilitate the witness, it would be logically relevant to elicit the witness's description of other out-of-statements in which he used a key term in a peculiar sense which eliminated the seeming inconsistency. The other statements would be relevant on that theory even if they were made after the apparently inconsistent statement. Of course, this result would obtain only when the proponent offers the evidence for the limited purpose of rehabilitation and not as substantive evidence under Rule 801.[41]

Even when part of a witness's prior statement is logically relevant to the witness's rehabilitation, only that part of the witness's earlier overall narrative is admissible for that purpose.[42] The witness's proponent does not have carte blanche to introduce the entire narrative simply because one passage has legitimate evidentiary value as rehabilitation.

---

[39]*E.g.*, U.S. v. Quinto, 582 F.2d 224 (2d Cir. 1978) (opinion states consistent statement must meet the requirements listed in Rule 801(d)(1)(B) and that consistent statement must be made before motive to fabricate). The text statement assumes that Rule 801(d)(1)(B) prescribes the conditions for use of inconsistent statements to rehabilitate a witness as well as the conditions under which such statements may be considered substantive evidence, i.e., non-hearsay. Even under this notion, the judge should have discretion. *See* discussion in note 25 supra.

[40]U.S. v. Castillo, 14 F.3d 802, 806 (2d Cir. 1994) ("the standard for admitting" the statement as rehabilitation "is less onerous than the standard used to determine whether the statement qualifies . . . under Fed. R. Evid. 801(d) (1) (B)).

[41]This view assumes that Rule 801(d)(1)(B) does not prescribe the conditions under which consistent statements may be used to rehabilitate a witness. See this section, note 390. Rules 401 and 403 would be applied to the circumstances in each individual situation. For example, an inconsistent statement alone might constitute sufficient reason to introduce a consistent statement. *See* U.S. v. Payne, 944 F.2d 1458 (9th Cir. 1991) ("The consistent statements had probative force . . . because they placed the inconsistencies brought out by Payne in a broader context, demonstrating that the inconsistencies were a minor part of an otherwise consistent account"). *But see* United States v. Quinto, note 404 supra. The consistent statement could be made after the contrivance or occurrence of improper influence or motive to testify. *See* Hanger v. U.S., 398 F.2d 91 (8th Cir. 1968).

[42]People v. DelGuidice, 199 Colo. 41, 606 P.2d 840, 844–45 (1979), disapproved on other grounds by People v. Harlan, 8 P.3d 448 (Colo. 2000).

## § 48 Attacking the supporting character witness

As § 41 explained, Rule 608(b)(1) permits the cross-examiner to impeach a witness by forcing the witness to admit that she had committed an untruthful act, even if the act has not resulted in a conviction. Rule 608(b)(2) also deals with impeachment, but now the target of the impeachment is different.

Under Fed. R. Evid. 608(b)(2) and Uniform Rule 608(b)(ii)[1] and at common law, a character witness who has testified to his favorable opinion or the good reputation of another witness ("principal witness") for truth and veracity[2] can be cross-examined about the principal witness's specific prior acts if the acts are probative of untruthfulness.[3] The courts usually deem specific instances of conduct involving dishonesty or false statement sufficiently proba-

---

[1]Former Fed. R. Evid. 608(b) provided:

Specific instances of the conduct of a witness, for the purpose of attacking or supporting the witness' credibility, other than conviction of crime as provided in rule 609, may not be proved by extrinsic evidence. They may, however, in the discretion of the court, if probative of truthfulness or untruthfulness, be inquired into on cross-examination of the witness (1) concerning the witness' character for truthfulness or untruthfulness, or (2) concerning the character for truthfulness or untruthfulness of another witness as to which character the witness being cross-examined has testified.

Uniform Rule of Evidence 608(b) is identical in content. Effective December 1, 2011, restyled Fed. R. Evid. 608(b) reads:

Specific Instances of Conduct. Except for a criminal conviction under Rule 609, extrinsic evidence is not admissible to prove specific instances of a witness's conduct in order to attack or support the witness's character for truthfulness. But the court may, on cross-examination, allow them to be inquired into if they are probative of the character for truthfulness or untruthfulness of:

(1) the witness; or

(2) another witness whose character the witness being cross-examined has testified about.

By testifying on another matter, a witness does not waive any privilege against self-incrimination for testimony that relates only to the witness's character for truthfulness.

[2]For a discussion of when good character testimony is admissible to support a witness's character for truth and veracity, see § 47 at notes 8 to 24 supra.

[3]U.S. v. Bah, 574 F.3d 106, 118 (2d Cir. 2009) (a defense character witness gave his personal opinion; it was permissible for the prosecutor to question the witness about a former customer's complaint accusing the defendant of fraud); The prior acts of misconduct may but need not be criminal. U.S. v. Bright, 588 F.2d 504 (5th Cir. 1979) (reprimand for unprofessional conduct); U.S. v. Crippen, 570 F.2d 535 (5th Cir. 1978) (altering automobile odometers which was not at time criminal offense).

While it seems to happen rarely, with respect to a witness who testifies as to his unfavorable opinion or the bad reputation of the principal witness for truth and veracity, cross-examination is permitted as to specific instances of the principal's witness's conduct probative of truthfulness. *See* Rule 608(b)(2), note 1 supra.

tive of untruthfulness;[4] such specific acts are fair game on cross-examination even if they have not resulted in a conviction.[5] However, extrinsic evidence with respect to specific instances of the principal witness's conduct not resulting in a conviction is inadmissible; the cross-examiner must take the character witness's answer.[6] The Advisory Committee Note accompanying the 2003 amendment to Rule 608 states that "the absolute prohibition on extrinsic evidence applies . . . when the sole reason for proffering that evidence is to attack the witness' character for truthfulness." In this line of inquiry, the only legitimate relevance of the answers is to impeach the character witness's credibility.

To be sure, a character witness testifying about the principal witness's reputation for truthfulness may be cross-examined concerning with whom, where, and when the witness has discussed the principal witness's reputation. Opinion testimony must be based on the character witness's personal knowledge of the principal witness; and consequently, the extent of his relationship with the principal witness is a proper subject of inquiry on cross-examination. Moreover, as the next paragraph explains, the cross-examiner may go farther and ask about specific acts by the principal witness.

When a character witness testifies on direct as to the principal witness's reputation for truthfulness, at the common law the traditional phasing of the cross-examination question about specific instances of the principal witness's untruthful conduct is "Have you heard?" In contrast, where the direct testimony of the character witness takes the form of an opinion, according to the common law the proper form of the question is either "Do you know?" or "Are you aware?" The distinction, while correct in theory, is of such slight practical importance that it could easily be eliminated at common law. For their part, the Federal Rules abandoned the distinction.[7] The character witness may be asked directly not only about the principal witness's specific acts probative of untruthfulness, but also about his familiarity with the

---

[4]See § 41 supra. *Cf.* Fed. R. Evid. 609(a) (2).

[5]See § 42 supra with respect to the admissibility of prior convictions to impeach.

[6]U.S. v. Herzberg, 558 F.2d 1219, 1223 (5th Cir. 1977) (the language of Fed. R. Evid. 608(b) "prohibits proof by extrinsic evidence even where the prosecutor 'inquiries into' prior acts on cross-examination. The cross-examining attorney must take the witness' answer."). See also § 49 infra.

[7]See § 191 infra. The Advisory Committee Note to Rule 405(b) comments on the distinction in the context of character evidence on the historical merits:

The theory is that, since the reputation witness relates what he has heard, the inquiry tends to shed light on the accuracy of his hearing and reporting. Accordingly, the opinion witness would be asked whether he knew, as well as whether he had heard. The fact is, of course, that these distinctions are of slight if any practi-

principal witness's convictions, arrests, and indictments. All these matters have a natural bearing on the principal witness's reputation and character witness's opinion of the principal witness. They are disreputable acts, inconsistent with the good reputation for truthfulness which the character witness has vouched for. Lack of familiarity with such matters is relevant to an assessment of the basis for the character witness's testimony.[8] If the witness answers that he is unfamiliar with these matters, the witness's answer impeaches the extent of the witness's knowledge of the principal witness's character. Alternatively, familiarity with the matters impeaches the character witness' standard of "truthfulness" or "untruthfulness"; if the witness answers that he is familiar with the unfavorable fact and yet vouches for the principal witness's good character, the character witness is either lying or using a rather strange standard for evaluating good character. Whatever the form of the question, the cross-examiner must have a good faith basis supporting the inquiry.[9]

The judge may preclude inquiry on cross-examination of the character witness about principal witness's acts probative of untruthfulness not resulting in a conviction if the judge determines that the probative value of such cross-examination is substantially outweighed by the danger of unfair prejudice.[10] The tenuous relevance of character testimony to veracity, coupled with the risk of unfair prejudice when the principal witness is also a party, militate in favor of the court exercising discretion to prohibit inquiry into specific acts. In principle, a strong case can be made for a blanket prohibition of cross-examination about specific acts allegedly committed by the principal witness. However, to date there is neither judicial holding nor even dictum approving such a sweeping prohibition.

---

cal significance, and the second sentence of subdivision (a) eliminates them as a factor in formulating questions.

[8] It is, however, improper to ask the character witness whether his testimony would change if he knew that the defendant had committed the acts for which on trial. Such questions lack probative value, assume facts which are the subject of the litigation, and destroy the presumption of innocence. U.S. v. Morgan, 554 F.2d 31 (2d Cir. 1977); U.S. v. Candelaria-Gonzalez, 547 F.2d 291 (5th Cir. 1977).

[9] U.S. v. Bright, 588 F.2d 504 (5th Cir. 1979); U.S. v. Wells, 525 F.2d 974 (5th Cir. 1976); U.S. v. Beno, 324 F.2d 582 (2d Cir. 1963). See also § 49

infra.

Examining counsel may be required to disclose his good faith basis out of the jury's hearing prior to inquiry. U.S. v. Reese, 568 F.2d 1246, 1249 (6th Cir. 1977) ("In passing, we hold that the better practice would have been for the trial judge to have had a voir dire examination to determine whether there were actually such rumors before permitting the cross-examination. This would avoid any random shots to the prejudice of the appellant.").

[10] U.S. v. Bright, 588 F.2d 504 (5th Cir. 1979) (cross-examination permitted after reference to applicability of Fed. R. Evid. 403).

## § 49 Contradiction: Collateral and non-collateral matters; good faith basis

On cross-examination, one of the purposes of every permissible type of impeachment is to test the witness's credibility.[1] The use of extrinsic evidence[2] to contradict is more restricted due to considerations of confusion of the issues, misleading the jury, and undue consumption of time. If a matter is considered collateral, the counsel may be limited to intrinsic impeachment. In other words, the witness's testimony on direct or cross-examination stands—the cross-examiner must take the witness's answer; and contradictory extrinsic testimony, evidence offered other than through the witness himself, is barred.[3] When the matter is not collateral, extrinsic evidence may be introduced to dispute the witness's testimony on direct examination or cross.

The topic of the collateral fact rule can be confusing. It is helpful to approach the topic in the following sequence. First, we shall explore the limited procedural significance of a determination that the rule bars extrinsic evidence to impeach a witness. Second, we will identify the impeachment techniques exempt from the rule and, by process of elimination, the techniques subject to the rule. Finally, we shall explore how the courts determine whether a particular matter is "collateral" for purposes of the rule.

### The Procedural Significance of a Determination that the Rule Bars Extrinsic Evidence

The rule does not limit cross-examination. During cross-

---

[Section 49]

[1]Davis v. Alaska, 415 U.S. 308, 316, 94 S. Ct. 1105, 39 L. Ed. 2d 347 (1974) ("Cross-examination is the principal means by which the believability of a witness and the truth of his testimony are tested. Subject always to the broad discretion of a trial judge to preclude repetitive and unduly harassing interrogation, the cross-examiner is not only permitted to delve into the witness' story to test the witness' perceptions and memory, but the cross-examiner has traditionally been allowed to impeach, i.e., discredit, the witness.").

[2]U.S. v. McNeill, 887 F.2d 448, 453 (3d Cir. 1989) ("Extrinsic evidence is evidence offered through other witnesses, rather than through cross-

examination of the witness himself or herself.").

[3]U.S. v. Adams, 799 F.2d 665 (11th Cir. 1986). *Accord* State v. Gore, 299 S.C. 368, 384 S.E.2d 750 (1989) ("When a witness denies an act involving a matter collateral to the case in chief, the inquiring party is not permitted to introduce contradictory evidence to impeach the witness."). *See generally* 1 Starkie, Evidence 160 (1824) ("If a question as to collateral fact be put to a witness for the purpose of discrediting his testimony, his answer must be taken as conclusive, and no evidence can be afterward admitted to contradict it. This rule does not exclude the contradiction of the witness as to any facts immediately connected with the subject of inquiry.").

examination, the questioner may attempt to challenge virtually any aspect of the witness's direct testimony. An error in any facet of the direct examination can reflect adversely on the witness's perceptual ability, memory, narrative ability, or sincerity; and all those factors are relevant to the jury's assessment of the witness's credibility. Subject to the trial judge's discretionary control under Rule 403, the cross-examiner can question about these factors to her heart's content. Moreover, even if the witness initially gives the cross-examiner an unfavorable answer, the questioner may apply pressure during cross by, for example, reminding the witness of the penalties for perjury. The courts sometimes say that when the collateral fact rule applies, the cross-examiner must "take the witness's answer," but that expression does not mean that the cross-examiner is obliged to accept the initial answer out of the witness's mouth. Lastly, although there is a split of judicial sentiment on the issue,[4] there is modern authority that to apply further pressure for a truthful answer, the cross-examiner may confront the witness with any contrary writing which the witness would be competent to authenticate.[5] The witness might have made the relevant statement in a letter that she personally authored. Again, one of the principal justifications for the rule is the courts' desire to minimize the amount of court time devoted to matters relevant only to a witness's credibility. There might be a considerable time expenditure if, after the witness leaves the stand, the attorney calls a second witness to impeach the prior witness. However, little additional time will be consumed if the cross-examiner presents the witness with a writing he can authenticate.[6]

What then is the procedural significance of the rule? The core prohibition applies when the witness to be impeached has already left the stand and the former cross-examiner later calls a second witness or proffers an exhibit[7] to impeach the earlier witness's credibility. At common law if the collateral fact rule applies at this juncture, the second witness's testimony or the exhibit is automatically inadmissible.

---

[4]U.S. v. Jackson, 882 F.2d 1444, 1448–49 (9th Cir. 1989).

[5]Carter v. Hewitt, 617 F.2d 961, 970–71 (3d Cir. 1980).

[6]Schmertz, 21 Fed. Rules Evid. News 96–168, citing U.S. v. Ureta, 44 M.J. 290 (C.A.A.F. 1996). The author asserts that prior writings should not be considered " 'extrinsic' in this impeachment context if the witness . . . admits making the statement. This authenticates the document, making it unnecessary to waste trial time by calling a third party witness to do this job".

[7]The counsel would not necessarily need to call a second witness to lay the foundation for the exhibit. The responses to pretrial requests for admission or a trial stipulation might suffice to establish the foundation. The remaining objection would be that the collateral fact rule barred the introduction of the exhibit.

### Which Impeachment Techniques Are Exempt from, and Which Subject to, the Collateral Fact Rule?

Most impeachment techniques are exempt from the collateral fact rule. In some cases, the exemption arises from the very nature of the impeachment technique. Suppose, for instance, that the question arises in one of the few jurisdictions which admits polygraph evidence. As a matter of policy, a jurisdiction has decided to permit impeachment by polygraphists or the testimony of other persons about a prior witness's character trait for untruthfulness. Those impeachment techniques necessarily involve extrinsic evidence: After the witness to be impeached leaves the stand, the former cross-examiner calls the polygraphist or the bad character witness. If the policy decision has been made to countenance these impeachment techniques, the techniques must necessarily be exempted from the collateral fact rule.

Moreover, other techniques are exempted because the impeaching facts are deemed highly probative of credibility. For example, proof of (1) bias,[8] interest, corruption, or coercion, (2) alcohol or drug use, (3) deficient mental capacity, (4) want of physical capacity or lack of exercise of the capacity to acquire personal knowledge[9] and (5) a prior conviction[10] are exempt. These matters can possess such great probative worth on the issue of the witness's credibility that the courts tolerate the expenditure of the additional time entailed in the subsequent presentation of extrinsic evidence.

Which techniques are then subject to the collateral fact rule? By process of elimination, we conclude that there are only three: proof the witness has committed untruthful act which has not resulted in a conviction, proof that the witness made an inconsistent pretrial statement, and specific contradiction.

### When Is a Particular Topic Deemed Collateral?

Assume both that the former cross-examiner is proffering extrinsic evidence to impeach the prior witness and that the counsel is using one of the impeachment techniques subject to the collateral fact rule. When is the specific impeaching evidence deemed collateral and inadmissible?

In the case of proof of the witness's untruthful acts which have not resulted in a conviction, the answer is relatively simple. With

---

[8]Broadhead, Why Bias Is Never Collateral: The Impeachment and Rehabilitation of Witnesses in Criminal Cases, 27 Am. J. Trial Advoc. 235 (2003).

[9]Prior inconsistent statements

relevant to establish such matters bearing directly upon credibility are non-collateral; extrinsic proof is admissible.

[10]See § 42 supra.

one exception, extrinsic evidence of such acts is always deemed collateral.[11] On the one hand, if the witness initially denies perpetrating the act, the cross-examiner may pressure the witness for an honest answer by reminding the witness of the penalties of perjury and perhaps by confronting the witness with his own writing mentioning the act. On the other hand, when the witness sticks to his guns and adamantly refuses to concede the act, the cross-examiner must "take the answer" even though it would be relatively easy for the cross-examiner to expose the perjury. Even if a person with personal knowledge of the witness's act were sitting in the courtroom, the cross-examiner could not later call that person to the stand to prove the prior witness's commission of the deceitful act.

The solitary exception to this general rule applies when the witness's testimony triggers the curative admissibility or "door opening" doctrine. Extrinsic evidence concerning a collateral matter may be admitted under the doctrine of "door opening." The courts tend to admit evidence under this doctrine where the government seeks to introduce evidence on rebuttal to contradict specific factual assertions raised during an accused's direct examination.[12] Suppose, for example, that on direct examination, an accused witness made a sweeping, superlative assertion that he had "never" committed a deceitful act. That assertion is such a serious violation of the rules limiting bolstering evidence that on a curative admissibility theory, many courts allow the opposing counsel to both cross-examine about the assertion and later

---

[11]People v. Rosenthal, 289 N.Y. 482, 46 N.E.2d 895 (1943) (accused was asked on cross-examination about other like crimes, and denied them, held state cannot produce other witnesses to contradict); State v. Broom, 222 N.C. 324, 22 S.E.2d 926 (1942) (similar); Com. v. Boggio, 204 Pa. Super. 434, 205 A.2d 694 (1964) (party cannot contradict answer to question whether witness ever had intercourse with another man). See § 4 supra.

Fed. R. Evid. 608(b) contains the following provision:

Specific instances of the conduct of a witness, for the purpose of attacking or supporting the witness' credibility, other than conviction of crime as provided in rule 609, may not be proved by extrinsic evidence. They may, however, in the discretion of the court, if probative of truthfulness or untruthfulness, be inquired into on cross-examination of the witness (1) concerning the witness' character for

truthfulness or untruthfulness, or (2) concerning the character for truthfulness or untruthfulness of another witness as to which character the witness being cross-examined has testified.

Unif. R. Evid. 608(b) is identical in content. Effective December 1, 2011, restyled Fed. R. Evid. 608(b) reads:

Specific Instances of Conduct. Except for a criminal conviction under Rule 609, extrinsic evidence is not admissible to prove specific instances of a witness's conduct in order to attack or support the witness's character for truthfulness. But the court may, on cross-examination, allow them to inquired into if they are probative of the character for truthfulness or untruthfulness of:

(1)   the witness; or

(2)   another witness whose character the witness being examined has testified about.

[12]See § 57 infra.

introduce extrinsic evidence rebutting the assertion. However, with this single exception, impeaching evidence of a witness's other untruthful acts which have not resulted in a conviction is always subject to the collateral fact rule.

The determination of whether the extrinsic impeachment evidence relates to a collateral matter is more complex when the former cross-examiner resorts to extrinsic evidence to prove a prior inconsistent statement or specifically contradict the earlier witness's testimony. Although extrinsic evidence of untruthful acts is almost always considered collateral, extrinsic evidence offered for these purposes is sometimes collateral but sometimes non-collateral.

In these situations, there are two ways in which the extrinsic impeaching evidence can qualify as non-collateral. To begin with, the matter is non-collateral and extrinsic evidence consequently admissible if the matter is itself relevant to a fact of consequence on the historical merits of the case.[13] When the fact is logically relevant to the merits of the case as well as the witness's credibility, it is worth the additional court time entailed in hearing extrinsic evidence. Moreover, the extrinsic evidence is non-collateral and again admissible when it relates to a so-called "linchpin" fact. Under this prong of the test, for purposes of impeachment a part of the witness's story may be attacked where as a matter of human experience, he could not be mistaken about that fact if the thrust of his testimony on the historical merits was true.

Consider the following illustration. Bob is called to testify that the color of the traffic light facing Apple Street was red at the time of an automobile accident he witnessed at the corner of Apple and Main. On direct examination, Bob testifies that he distinctly recalls that when he witnessed the accident, he was driving on the street Piagano's Pizza Restaurant is situated on and indeed was heading toward the restaurant. He adds that Piagano's is located on the corner of Apple and Peach. On cross-examination counsel asks, "Isn't it true that Piagano's Pizza Restaurant is located on Apple three blocks east of Peach at

---

[13]People v. Wadley, 169 Ill. App. 3d 1036, 120 Ill. Dec. 338, 523 N.E.2d 1249, 1257 (1st Dist. 1988) ("The test to determine whether a matter is collateral is whether it could be introduced for any purpose other than to contradict. . . . The trial court is vested with broad discretion when applying this 'collateral' test."); Henson v. State, 530 N.E.2d 768, 770 (Ind. Ct. App. 1988) ("A matter is collateral if the party seeking to introduce it for purposes of contradiction would not be entitled to prove it as part of his case-in-chief."); State v. Watkins, 227 Neb. 677, 419 N.W.2d 660, 665 (1988) (evidence is noncollateral if it tends to establish a matter the party could prove independent of self-contradiction). With respect to prior inconsistent statements, see also § 36 supra.

Maple?" This cross-examination question is permissible as potentially affecting the jury's assessment of Bob's powers of perception and recollection. However, if Bob continues to maintain that the restaurant is on Peach Street, extrinsic evidence may not be offered during the cross-examiner's case in chief as to the location of the restaurant. The matter is collateral because the location of the restaurant is not relevant in the litigation other than to contradict Bob's testimony. Even if Bob denied on cross-examination making a prior statement in which he allegedly said that the restaurant was on Apple and Maple, extrinsic evidence of the prior statement would be inadmissible because the matter is collateral.

On the other hand, the color of the traffic light facing Apple is non-collateral; the color of the traffic light is itself relevant in the case. Thus, specific contradiction evidence that the light facing Apple Street was green is admissible. Likewise, if Bob denies on cross-examination having previously stated that the traffic light was green, extrinsic evidence of Bob's prior inconsistent statement is admissible. Assuming Bob is then asked on cross-examination if he was wearing his glasses while driving, a yes answer may be contradicted by extrinsic evidence that his only pair of glasses was being repaired at the time of the accident. Evidence disputing the witness's ability to gain personal knowledge of facts relevant in the case is non-collateral. Similarly, if Bob denied on cross-examination that his wife was related to the plaintiff, extrinsic evidence of that fact would be admissible. Evidence of the witness's partiality is non-collateral. Extrinsic evidence offered to establish the witness's bias, interest, corruption, or coercion may be admitted following a witness's denial of a fact giving rise to an inference of bias.

Finally, vary the initial illustration. Again, on direct Bob testified that when he witnessed the accident, he was driving on the very street on which Piagano's is located. Now the specific contradiction evidence is that Piagano's Pizza Restaurant is situated on Main Street. If Bob was on Main, not Apple, as he approached the intersection, extrinsic evidence of the location of the restaurant would be admissible. In this variation of the illustration, an error as to the location of the restaurant brings into question the trustworthiness of Bob's testimony on the historical merits of the case. Bob may have seen the light facing Main, not the light facing Apple.[14] The location of the restaurant would be considered a "linchpin" fact, and extrinsic evidence would

---

[14]To illustrate, assume no left turn is allowed from Apple onto Main. To go left, you have to turn right before the intersection and then left onto Main, thus winding up on Main and not Apple when approaching the intersection. This type of left turn structure is found in New Jersey.

therefore be admissible to impeach Bob. A fact negating the assumption that the witness was in the right place at the right time to observe what he testified to is a classic example of a "linchpin" fact.

What is the status of the common law collateral fact rule under the Federal Rules? The continued application of the standard theory of collateral contradiction in federal practice has been criticized on the ground that it is a mechanistic doctrine which ignores pertinent policy considerations. It has been urged that the courts should substitute the discretionary approach of Rule 403.[15] That approach is the better construction of the federal statutes. Although Rule 608(b) expressly prohibits extrinsic evidence of a witness's untruthful acts, the Federal Rules do not expressly codify a categorical collateral fact restriction. For example, there is no mention of that restriction in Rule 613 governing prior inconsistent statement impeachment. Given Rule 402, there is a powerful argument that the enactment of the Federal Rules impliedly overturned the collateral fact rule.[16] Under this reading of the Federal Rules, there is no rigid prohibition of introducing extrinsic evidence to impeach a witness on a collateral matter; rather, under Rule 403, the judge would make a practical judgment as to whether the importance of the witness's testimony and the impeachment warrants the expenditure of the additional trial time. However, the collateral fact rule was so ingrained at common law that many federal opinions continue to mention "collateral" evidence.[17]

The abolition of the collateral fact doctrine by the Federal Rules

---

[15]Speaking of "Recasting the 'collateral matter' rule into a rule of discretion . . .," Weinstein & Berger, Evidence ¶ 607[05] concludes, "The Federal Rules, while silent on the subject of impeachment by contradiction, should be used to reach results analogous to those reached under the [former] Uniform Rules by substituting the discretion approach of Rule 403 for the collateral test advocated by case law."

[16]In Daubert v. Merrell Dow Pharmaceuticals, Inc., 509 U.S. 579, 113 S. Ct. 2786, 125 L. Ed. 2d 469 (1993) and U.S. v. Abel, 469 U.S. 45, 105 S. Ct. 465, 83 L. Ed. 2d 450 (1984), the Supreme Court approvingly quoted the statement by the late Professor Edward Cleary, the Reporter for the Advisory Committee, that "in principle, no common law of evidence re-

mains." The Federal Rules were patterned after the parallel provisions in the California Evidence Code. The California Law Revision Commission Comment states:

The effect of Section 780 (together with 351) is to eliminate this inflexible rule of exclusion. This is not to say that all evidence of a collateral nature offered to attack the credibility of a witness would be admissible. Under Section 352, the court has substantial discretion to exclude collateral evidence. The effect of Section 780, therefore, is to change the present inflexible rule of exclusion to a rule of discretion to be exercised by the trial judge.

Cal. Evid. Code § 351 corresponds to Federal Rule 402, and § 352 is the counterpart to Rule 403.

[17]E.g., U.S. v. Pisari, 636 F.2d 855

is a two-edged sword. The preceding paragraph noted that under Rule 403, the witness's testimony and the impeaching evidence could have such importance that the judge might permit extrinsic evidence which would have been barred at common law. The judge must make a pragmatic judgment call.[18] However, it is equally true that the judge could conceivably bar evidence which would technically have been considered non-collateral and admissible at common law.[19] Thus, standing alone, compliance with the common law rule does not guarantee the admissibility of extrinsic evidence under the federal statutes.[20] Even if the evidence is

---

(1st Cir. 1981).

[18]Saltzburg, Prior Inconsistent Statements and Collateral Matters, 19 Crim.Just. 45, 46 (Fall 2004).

[19]U.S. v. Pisari, 636 F.2d 855 (1st Cir. 1981).

[20]The classic statement of the test of "collateralness" appears in the opinions in Attorney General v. Hitchcock, 1847 WL 5862 (U.K. Ex Ct 1847). That case was an information under the revenue laws. A witness for the plaintiff was asked on cross-examination if he had not said he had been offered 20 pounds to testify by officers of the Crown, which he denied. Held, the defendant could not call a witness to testify that the first witness had made the alleged statement. Pollock, C.B. said: "A distinction should be observed between those matters which may be given in evidence by way of contradiction as directly affecting the story of the witness touching the issue before the jury, and those matters which affect the motives, temper, and character of the witness, not with respect to his credit, but with reference to his feelings towards one party or the other. It is certainly allowable to ask a witness in what manner he stands affected toward the opposite party in the cause . . . and whether he has not used expressions importing that he would be revenged on some one or that he would give such evidence as might dispose of the cause in one way or the other. If he denies that, you may give evidence as to what he said, not with the view of having a direct effect on the issue, but to show what is the state

of mind of that witness in order that the jury may exercise their opinion as to how far he is to be believed." The alleged statement was that the witness had been *offered* a bribe, not that he had accepted one. But query as to evidence of attempted bribery of a witness as an admission by conduct? See § 265 infra.

Another illuminating discussion is the opinion of Rutledge, J. in Ewing v. U.S., 135 F.2d 633, 640–42 (App. D.C. 1942). Here a witness for defendant accused of rape swore to facts which, if believed, made it impossible to believe complainant's story. Over the witness's denial, the government was (it was held) properly allowed to prove that the witness had said (1) I believe the defendant guilty but (2) he is facing the electric chair, and I must be on his side. The court rejected the test of collateralness used in some cases (*see, e.g.,* Butler v. State, 179 Miss. 865, 176 So. 589 (1937)), whether the party would have been entitled to prove the matter "as part of his case," and approved Wigmore's statement of the test as follows: "Could the fact as to which the prior self-contradiction is predicated have been shown in evidence for any purpose independently of the self-contradiction?" 3A Wigmore, Evidence § 1020 (Chadbourn rev. 1970). This seems to be equivalent to saying that the fact which is the subject of the previous statement must be (1) relevant to an issue, or (2) provable under impeachment practice by extrinsic evidence. Of course, the second previous statement in the *Ewing* case is not a prior inconsistent state-

otherwise admissible, it could be vulnerable to a Rule 403 objection.[21]

## § 50   Exclusion and separation of witnesses

The immediately preceding paragraphs discuss the evidentiary techniques which counsel may use to either attack or support a witness's credibility. However, there are also procedural steps which the judge can take to help ensure credible testimony. Judicial exclusion and separation orders are illustrative. There is no constitutional right to the exclusion of witnesses from the courtroom.[1] However, exclusion orders are available in virtually very jurisdiction. If a witness hears the testimony of others before she takes the stand, it is much easier for the witness to deliberately tailor her own story to that of other witnesses. Witnesses may also be influenced subconsciously. In either event, the cross-examiner will find it more difficult to expose fabrication, collusion, inconsistencies, or inaccuracies in the testimony of a witness who has already heard other witnesses testify.[2] Separation prevents improper influence during the trial by prohibiting

---

ment but a direct expression of bias, provable as such for impeachment regardless of self-contradiction. Somewhat similar is State v. Sandros, 186 Wash. 438, 58 P.2d 362 (1936). There, despite a defense witness's denials, the state was allowed to prove that the witness, claimed to be the accused's accomplice in forging a will, had (1) said that he had carried the will in his pocket for three weeks (which was material as tending to show it could not have been made at the time it was dated) and (2) made efforts to persuade a person to testify falsely to the genuineness of the signature. The court approved the Wigmore test, above.

[21]The only type of evidence invulnerable to Rule 403 is seemingly a conviction qualifying under Rule 609(a) (2). *See* Green v. Bock Laundry Mach. Co., 490 U.S. 504, 109 S. Ct. 1981, 104 L. Ed. 2d 557 (1989); Rothstein, Some Themes in the Proposed Federal Rules of Evidence, 33 Fed. B.J. 21, 29 (1974).

**[Section 50]**

[1]U.S. v. Edwards, 526 F.3d 747, 758 (11th Cir. 2008).

[2]Perry v. Leeke, 488 U.S. 272, 281, 109 S. Ct. 594, 102 L. Ed. 2d 624 (1989) ("The reason for the rule is one that applies to all witnesses—not just defendants. It is a common practice for a judge to instruct a witness not to discuss his or her testimony with third parties until the trial is completed. Such nondiscussion orders are a corollary of the broader rule that witnesses may be sequestered to lessen the danger that their testimony will be influenced by hearing what other witnesses have to say, and to increase the likelihood that they will confine themselves to truthful statements based on their own recollections. The defendant's constitutional right to confront the witnesses against him immunizes him from such physical sequestration. Nevertheless, when he assumes the role of a witness, the rules that generally apply to other witnesses—rules that serve the truth-seeking function of the trial—are generally applicable to him as well. Accordingly, it is entirely appropriate for a trial judge to decide, after listening to the direct examination of any witness, whether the defendant or a nondefendant, that cross-

witness-to-witness communication both inside and outside the courtroom.[3]

At common law the court in its discretion may exclude witnesses.[4] The court is empowered to order exclusion on its own motion; but in many, if not most, cases the judge enters the order at the request of a party. Rather than adopting a discretionary approach, Federal and Uniform Rule of Evidence 615 treats the exclusion of witnesses as a matter of right. Restyled Fed. R. Evid. 615 states: "At a party's request, the court must order witnesses excluded . . . ."[5] A request to exclude witnesses is often referred

---

examination is more likely to elicit truthful responses if it goes forward without allowing the witness an opportunity to consult with third parties, including his or her lawyer."); Geders v. U.S., 425 U.S. 80, 87, 96 S. Ct. 1330, 47 L. Ed. 2d 592 (1976) ("The aim of imposing 'the rule on witnesses,' as the practice of sequestering witnesses is sometimes called, is twofold. It exercises a restraint on witnesses 'tailoring' their testimony to that of earlier witnesses; and it aids in detecting testimony that is less than candid."); Clark v. State, 480 N.E.2d 555, 558 (Ind. 1985) ("The primary reason for a separation of witnesses order is to prevent witnesses from gaining knowledge of questions actually posed to, and answers actually given, by prior witnesses, and adjusting their own testimony as a result thereof.").

[3]U.S. v. Romano, 736 F.2d 1432 (11th Cir. 1984), vacated on other grounds 755 F.2d 1401 (11th Cir. 1985). *But see* U.S. v. Guthrie, 557 F.3d 243, 247–49 (6th Cir. 2009) (the trial judge did not err in permitting the prosecutor to speak with the victim during a recess in her cross-examination; "Sequestration orders, even when granted, do not prohibit witnesses from speaking with counsel"; however, the trial judge had announced limits on the prosecutor's conversation with the witness; the judge forbade the prosecutor from "coach[ing] the witness").

[4]Kaufman v. U.S., 163 F.2d 404 (C.C.A. 6th Cir. 1947); Wisehart v. State, 484 N.E.2d 949 (Ind. 1985).

[5]Former Fed. and Rev. Unif. R. Evid. 615 provide:

At the request of a party the court shall order witnesses excluded so that they cannot hear the testimony of other witnesses and it may make the order of its own motion. This rule does not authorize exclusion of (1) a party who is a natural person, or (2) an officer or employee of a party which is not a natural person designated as its representative by its attorney, or (3) a person whose presence is shown by a party to be essential to the presentation of the party's cause.

Effective December 1, 2011, restyled Fed. R. Evid. 615 reads:

At a party's request, the court must order witnesses excluded so that they cannot hear other witnesses' testimony. Or the court may do so on its own. But this rule does not authorize excluding:

(a) a party who is a natural person;

(b) an officer or employee of a party that is not a natural person, after being designated as the party's representative by its attorney;

(c) a person whose presence a party shows to be essential to presenting the party's claim or defense; or

(d) a person authorized by statute to be present."

At least since the days of Susanna and the Elders, forbidding communication between witnesses has been recognized as a means of preventing the tailoring of testimony and exposing inconsistency. The Story of Susanna and the Elders is one of the apocryphal books of the Old Testament. For an abbreviated version, *see* 6 Wigmore, Evidence § 1837 (Chadbourn rev. 1976). *See also* Graham, "The Rule":

to as "invoking the rule on witnesses." Rule 615 does not specify a deadline for making the request.[6] The appellate courts have ap-

---

Exclusion and Separation of Witnesses for Dummies, 46 Crim. L. Bull. 1357 (2010); Levenson, Sequestration, Nat'l L.J., A13, Apr. 3, 2006 (many trial judges issue "supplemental orders" forbidding the witnesses from discussing their testimony outside the courtroom, "others will not construe a Rule 615 order . . . broadly. *See* United States v. Scharstein, 531 F.Supp. 460 (E.D.Ky. 1982). For example, some courts have held that a standard Rule 615 order does not in itself bar witnesses from being in the same holding cell where they can easily discuss their testimony. For these courts, a supplemental order from the judge is required. *See, e.g.*, United States v. Collins, 340 F.3d 672, 681 (8th Cir. 2003). It is widely accepted that courts have the power to issue such supplemental orders but they must be requested."). *But see* Comment, Exclusion of Justice: The Need for a Consistent Application of Witness Sequestration Under Federal Rule of Evidence 615, 30 U. Dayton L. Rev. 63, 65 (2004) ("Some courts have applied Rule 615 narrowly, holding that witnesses are to be excluded from the courtroom but may not be separated outside the courtroom"); Note, Rule 615–Beyond the Walls of the Courtroom Proper: Efficacious Truth-Seeking Devices or Toothless Tiger?, 10 Suffolk J. Trial & App. Advoc. 115, 116, 123–28 (2005) (according to one strand of authority, "Rule 615 requires only that witnesses be physically excluded from the courtroom and does not proscribe communication between witnesses outside the courtroom proper"; other courts read the statute more broadly as empowering trial judges to proscribe reading transcripts and discussing testimony outside the courtroom).

[6]*See* U.S. v. Brown, 547 F.2d 36 (3d Cir. 1976) (request to exclude prior to opening is discretionary; no error in failing to exclude after opening as the request was not renewed). *Compare* 6

Wigmore, Evidence § 1840 at 470 (Chadbourn rev. 1976) ("[T]he *time* for sequestration begins with the delivery of testimony upon the stand and ends with the close of testimony. It is therefore not appropriate during the reading of the pleadings or the opening address of counsel; . . . . It continues for each witness after he had left the stand, because it is frequently necessary to recall a witness in consequence of a later witness' testimony. It need not be demanded at the very opening of the testimony, at any time later, when the supposed exigency arises, the order may be requested."), *with* 4 Weinstein's Federal Evidence § 615.02[2][a], at 617–7–8 (2d ed. 1997) ("The customary practice is to exercise discretion to exclude prospective witnesses during openings and any arguments or offers of proof when a witness's testimony may be summarized. Thus, Rule 615 is commonly applied at suppression hearings. However, at least one court has found that Rule 615 does not apply to a sentencing hearing").

There is authority that Rule 615 applies to pretrial suppression hearings (U.S. v. Warren, 578 F.2d 1058 (5th Cir. 1978)) and depositions, Williams v. Electronic Control Systems, Inc., 68 F.R.D. 703 (E.D. Tenn. 1975). *Compare* U.S. v. West, 607 F.2d 300 (9th Cir. 1979) (exclusion of witnesses at a preliminary evidentiary hearing rests in the court's discretion; the mandatory exclusion of Rule 615 commences with the presentation of evidence at trial). However, effective December 1, 1993, Federal Rule of Civil Procedure 30(c) was amended to read: "Examination and cross-examination of witnesses at depositions may proceed as permitted at the trial under the provisions of the Federal Rules of Evidence except Rule . . . 615." The Advisory Committee Note explains that since Rule 615 is inapplicable, "other witnesses are not automatically excluded from a deposi-

plied several standards in determining whether a trial judge's failure to order a witness's exclusion constitutes reversible error.[7]

Even if a litigant makes a Rule 615 motion, not all witnesses may be excluded and separated. Neither case law nor Rule 615 authorizes exclusion of: (1) a party who is a natural person,[8] (2) an officer or employee of a party which is not a natural person[9] designated as its representative by its attorney which includes a government's investigative agent,[10] (3) a person whose presence is shown by the party to be essential to the presentation of the

---

tion simply by the request of a party." The judge has discretion to enter such an order under Civil Rule 26(c) (5).

Exclusion extends through closing arguments at trial. U.S. v. Juarez, 573 F.2d 267 (5th Cir. 1978). *Compare* 6 Wigmore, Evidence § 1840 at 470 (Chadbourn rev. 1976) (ends with close of testimony).

[7]U.S. v. Ell, 718 F.2d 291, 293–94 (9th Cir. 1983) ("A number of circuits have held that the district court's erroneous denial of an exclusion request does not mandate reversal absent a showing of prejudice. *E.g.*, Wood v. Southwestern Bell Telephone Co., 637 F.2d 1188, 1194 (8th Cir. [1981]); Virgin Islands v. Edinborough, 625 F.2d 472, 474 (3d Cir. 1980); United States v. Warren, 578 F.2d 1058, 1076 (5th Cir. 1978). Other courts have suggested, without reaching the question, that noncompliance with the rule may mandate automatic reversal. United States v. Burgess, 691 F.2d 1146, 1157 (4th Cir. 1982); State v. DiModica, 192 A.2d 825, 830 (N.J. 1963). Finally, several states have adopted an approach which presumes that a violation of the rule prejudiced the defendant and thus requires reversal unless the contrary is manifestly clear from the records or unless the prosecution proves that there was no prejudice. *See* State v. Roberts, 612 P.2d 1055, 1057 (Ariz. 1980); Reynolds v. State, 497 S.W.2d 275, 277 (Ark. 1973); Montos v. State, 95 S.E.2d 792, 794 (Ga. 1956); Givens v. State, 657 P.2d 97, 100 (Nev. 1983).").

[8]Varlack v. SWC Caribbean, Inc., 550 F.2d 171 (3d Cir. 1977) (exclusion of party held reversible error).

The possibility that numerous parties, each similarly situated as to an event or controversy, may present an appropriate case for exclusion was raised in N.L.R.B. v. Stark, 525 F.2d 422 (2d Cir. 1975), but not decided. However, if a natural person is disruptive in court, he or she may forfeit the right to be present during the trial. Illinois v. Allen, 397 U.S. 337, 343, 90 S. Ct. 1057, 25 L. Ed. 2d 353 (1970).

[9]Doll v. U.S. West Communications, Inc., 60 Fed. Appx. 253, 254–55 (10th Cir. 2003) (a corporate defendant's designated representative was not subject to exclusion from trial as a witness). *See* U.S. v. Green, 324 F.3d 375, 380–81 (5th Cir. 2003) ("this Court has never decided whether the Government can designate more than one individual as its case agent . . . .").

[10]Hampton v. Kroger Co., 618 F.2d 498 (8th Cir. 1980) (one representative of each Kroger store implicated in suit was properly permitted to remain in courtroom even though each was called to testify); U.S. v. Jones, 687 F.2d 1265, 1268 (8th Cir. 1982) ("Defendant contends that subdivision (2) includes only federal officers and does not encompass local police officers. Although the issue has not been squarely decided, there is nothing in the cases or legislative history of the rule that suggests state or local officers should be treated differently than federal officers."); U.S. v. Boyer, 574 F.2d 951 (8th Cir. 1978) (FBI agents fit under second exception); U.S. v. Auten, 570 F.2d 1284 (5th Cir. 1978) (government investigator). *See generally* U.S. v. Machor, 879 F.2d 945, 953

cause,[11] or (4) as of 1997, the victim of the offense an accused is charged with when the prosecution contemplates calling the victim as a witness during a subsequent sentencing hearing.[12] In criminal cases, judges routinely invoke (2) to permit the attendance of the investigating case agent at trial.[13] Sometimes the courts classify an expert as a witness whose presence is essential

(1st Cir. 1989) ("Defendants maintain, however, that even after the promulgation of the new Federal Rules of Evidence, the court retained discretion to exclude a person who falls within the 615(2) exception. The courts are divided on this issue. Some cases support defendants' view that the trial court has discretion to exclude the government case agent. United States v. Thomas, 835 F.2d 219, 223 (9th Cir. 1987); United States v. Woody, 588 F.2d 1212, 1213 (8th Cir. 1978). The majority view, however, is that Fed. R. Evid. 615(2) has severely curtailed the discretion of the trial court to sequester the government's case agent. The practical and policy concerns inherent in the promulgation of the rule support this view. Thus, we reject defendants' argument.").

[11]The courts sometimes apply this provision to case agents or experts whom the attorney needs "at the elbow" during trial. See U.S. v. Ratfield, 342 Fed. Appx. 510 (11th Cir. 2009) (the trial judge properly excused two I.R.S. agents from the rule and allowed them to remain in the courtroom; they testified as summary witnesses, based on other witnesses' testimony and documents introduced into evidence). Since such witnesses do not purport to testify from personal knowledge, there is less danger that their testimony will be distorted by their presence in court.

[12]In 1997, Congress enacted the Victim Rights Clarification Act. In pertinent part, the Act reads:

(a) Non—Capital Cases. Notwithstanding any statute, rule, or other provision of law, a Untied States District Court shall not order any victim of an offense excluded from the trial of a defendant accused of that offense because the victim may, during the

sentencing hearing, make a statement or present any information in relation to the sentence.

(b) Capital Cases. Notwithstanding any statute, rule, or to the provision of law, a United States District Court shall not order any victim of an offense excluded from the trial of a defendant accused to that offense because such victim may, during the sentencing hearing, testify as to the effect of the offense on the victim or the victim's family or as to any other factor for which notice is required under section 3593(A).

See U.S. v. McVeigh, 958 F. Supp. 512 (D. Colo. 1997).

[13]U.S. v. Green, 293 F.3d 886 (5th Cir. 2002) (the complexity of the case justified exempting investigators from the F.B.I., the state police, and the county sheriff's office); U.S. v. Berry, 133 F.3d 1020, 1024 (7th Cir. 1998); U.S. v. Jackson, 60 F.3d 128 (2d Cir. 1995) (noting the split of authority over the question of whether the trial judge may exempt more than one case agent); U.S. v. Pulley, 922 F.2d 1283 (6th Cir. 1991); Long v. State, 743 N.E.2d 253 (Ind. 2001) (the court indicates that it is questionable to permit a party to retain more than one witness in the courtroom); Schmertz, Article VI, in Emerging Problems Under the Federal Rules of Evidence 115, 202 (3d ed. 1998) ("The Circuits are divided on whether more than one person may serve as designated representative under Rule 615(2)").

In some cases in which the judge exempts the case agent from the sequestration order, the judge requires the agent to testify first in order to eliminate the risk that the agent will modify his or her testimony to conform to that of the other witnesses. However, requiring the agent to testify first can interfere with the prosecution's

under (3). It can be vital to give counsel the benefit of an expert's assistance while an opposing expert is testifying. In particular, assistance may be necessary in connection with technical matters as to which counsel lacks sufficient familiarity to try the case effectively on his own. When the counsel lacks that familiarity, she may need an expert "at her elbow" during the opposing expert witnesses' testimony;[14] without the expert's assistance, the counsel would be handicapped in preparing to conduct an immediate cross-examination. A strong argument can also be made for permitting the presence of an expert witness who intends to give an opinion based in part on evidence presented at trial.[15] Congress added exception (4) to Rule 615 in the 1997 Victim Rights Clarification Act. In addition to these four exceptions, there is a further limitation on the scope of Rule 615; several courts have held that the rule does not apply to rebuttal witnesses[16] or witnesses called to impeach credibility.[17]

On its face, Rule 615 authorizes only the exclusion of the prospective witness from the courtroom. While Rule 615 does not explicitly provide for the separation of witnesses, the prevailing view is that courts have inherent procedural authority to take further steps designed to prevent communication between witnesses such as ordering them to remain physically apart,[18] not to discuss the case with one another,[19] and not to read a transcript of another witness's trial testimony.[20]

---

trial strategy. The courts are divided over the question of whether the judge should ordinarily mandate that the agent testify first. U.S. v. Drummond, 69 Fed. Appx. 580 (3d Cir. 2003).

    Although it is typically the prosecution which invokes 615(2) in criminal cases, the defense may also do so. U.S. v. Ortiz, 10 F. Supp. 2d 1058 (N.D. Iowa 1998) (the defense was entitled to the exemption of a court-appointed investigator who had intimate knowledge of the facts of the case; without the investigator's presence, the defense could not function effectively at trial).

[14]People v. Valdez, 177 Cal. App. 3d 680, 223 Cal. Rptr. 149, 152–54 (5th Dist. 1986).

[15]U.S. v. Conners, 894 F.2d 987 (8th Cir. 1990); U.S. v. Burgess, 691 F.2d 1146 (4th Cir. 1982); Miller v. Universal City Studios, Inc., 650 F.2d 1365 (5th Cir.1981); T. J. Stevenson &

Co., Inc. v. 81,193 Bags of Flour, 629 F.2d 338 (5th Cir. 1980). *See also* § 15 supra.

[16]U.S. v. Bramlet, 820 F.2d 851 (7th Cir. 1987).

[17]U.S. v. Shurn, 849 F.2d 1090 (8th Cir. 1988).

[18]*But see* U.S. v. Collins, 340 F.3d 672 (8th Cir. 2003) (the placement of two prosecution witnesses in the same holding cell while they awaited their turns to testify did not violate the sequestration order; neither could tell the other about the nature of his testimony, since neither had testified before they were placed in the cell).

[19]U.S. v. Shaver, 607 F. Supp. 2d 1168, 1175 (S.D. Cal. 2009) ("A circumvention of Rule 615 occurs when witnesses indirectly defeat its purpose by either discussing testimony they have given or events in the courtroom with other witnesses who are to testify. Rule 615 applies equally to rebuttal

If a witness violates an order of exclusion or sequestration, the trial judge has discretion to select the appropriate remedy.[21] The

---

witnesses and to witnesses who have already testified. [T]rial information is not to be revealed by witnesses to other witnesses . . . .").

[20]U.S. v. Magana, 127 F.3d 1, 5-6 (1st Cir. 1997) (although the "heartland" of sequestration is the order that the witness remain outside the courtroom, the judge may also regulate the witness's conduct outside the courtroom; by way of example, the judge may "order that witnesses not converse with each other about the case" or "prohibit counsel from conferring with a witness during the witness's testimony, including any recesses"); U.S. v. Sepulveda, 15 F.3d 1161, 1176 (1st Cir. 1993) ("such nondisclosure orders are generally thought to be a standard concomitant of basic sequestration fare. . . ."); U.S. v. Johnston, 578 F.2d 1352, 1355 (10th Cir. 1978) ("[A] circumvention of the rule does occur where witnesses indirectly defeat its purpose by discussing testimony they have given and events in the courtroom with other witnesses who are to testify. . . . This should be avoided by instructions to counsel and the witnesses when the rule's invocation is announced, making it clear that witnesses are not only excluded from the courtroom but also that they are not to relate to other witnesses what their testimony has been and what occurred in the courtroom."); Zeigler v. Fisher-Price, Inc., 302 F. Supp. 2d 999, 1011–18 (N.D. Iowa 2004) (the defendant manufacturer's attorneys alerted its expert witness prior to his testimony that they had learned from the consumer's offer of proof that the expert had misinterpreted the X-rays on which the expert contemplated basing his testimony; the alert permitted the expert to reshape his testimony); O'Kelley v. State, 175 Ga. App. 503, 333 S.E.2d 838, 841 (1985) ("[O]bviously, if the purpose of the rule is to be adequately served, witnesses may not be *told* what prior witnesses have

said either. Otherwise the same undesired influence can result to impurify their testimony and thereby render its credibility questionable. The clear import of the statute is to preserve the integrity of testimony, with the ultimate goal of arriving at the truth. Thus, 'the rule extends to communications, direct and indirect, between witnesses outside the courtroom, . . . .' Lackey, supra 246 Ga. at 335, 271 S.E.2d 478.").

The court in U.S. v. Buchanan, 787 F.2d 477, 485 (10th Cir. 1986) concluded that Rule 615 implicitly incorporates a prohibition against witness to witness communication out of court—witnesses should be clearly instructed that they "are not to discuss the case or what their testimony has been or would be or what occurs in the courtroom with anyone other than counsel for either side."

With respect to the criminal defendant's right to discuss his testimony with counsel, Geders v. U.S., 425 U.S. 80, 96 S. Ct. 1330, 47 L. Ed. 2d 592 (1976), held that prohibiting the defendant from consulting his attorney during an overnight recess denied the accused the effective assistance of counsel. Whether counsel may be prohibited from discussing case with defendant "during a brief routine recess during the trial day" was expressly reserved. Id. at 89 n. 2. This question was addressed in Perry v. Leeke, 488 U.S. 272, 109 S. Ct. 594, 102 L. Ed. 2d 624 (1989), where the Supreme Court ruled that barring the criminal defendant from consulting with his counsel during a fifteen minute break between direct and cross-examination did not violate the Sixth Amendment.

[21]Holder v. U.S., 150 U.S. 91, 14 S. Ct. 10, 37 L. Ed. 1010 (1893); U.S. v. Rossetti, 768 F.2d 12 (1st Cir. 1985); U.S. v. Eastwood, 489 F.2d 818 (5th Cir. 1973); Leidel v. Ameripride Services, Inc., 291 F. Supp. 2d 1241, 1248 (D. Kan. 2003) ("There are a

court may refuse to permit a witness to testify,[22] declare a mistrial, or give the jury a cautionary instruction to weigh the witness's credibility in light of the witness's presence in court or discussions with another witness.[23] The court can also hold the witness in contempt. The courts are markedly reluctant to resort to the drastic remedy of disqualifying the witness.[24] The strongest

---

number of remedies a court may employ during the trial, when such a violation arises. Although Rule 615 does not specify remedies, courts have inter alia, cited the witness in contempt, permitted opposing counsel to comment on the witness's violation of the rule, allowed opposing counsel to impeach the witness with cross examination on the issue, or given a curative jury instruction. In the Tenth Circuit, a witness's intentional disregard of the order, or a showing of resulting prejudice, may warrant the court excluding or striking the witness's testimony"); Swope v. State, 490 N.E.2d 736 (Ind. 1986).

[22]U.S. v. Smith, 318 Fed. Appx. 780 (11th Cir. 2009).

[23]U.S. v. Eastwood, 489 F.2d 818 (5th Cir. 1973).

[24]Holder v. U.S., 150 U.S. 91, 92, 14 S. Ct. 10, 37 L. Ed. 1010 (1893) ("If a witness disobeys the order of withdrawal, while he may be proceeded against for contempt, and his testimony is open to comment to the jury by reason of his conduct, he is not thereby disqualified, and the weight of authority is that he cannot be excluded on that ground, merely, although the right to exclude under particular circumstances may be supported as within the discretion of the trial court."); U.S. v. Rhynes, 218 F.3d 310 (4th Cir. 2000) (it was an abuse of discretion to exclude a defense witness when the violation was caused by the defense counsel, not the defendant); Rowan v. Owens, 752 F.2d 1186, 1191 (7th Cir. 1984) ("It is true that enforcing such a rule might, by making it impossible for the defendant to put on a meritorious defense, be a disproportionate sanction for its violation, and if so it would be impermissible . . .");

U.S. v. Gibson, 675 F.2d 825, 836 (6th Cir. 1982) ("Most authorities agree that 'particular circumstances' sufficient to justify exclusion of a witness are indications that the witness has remained in court with the 'consent, connivance, procurement or knowledge' of the party seeking his testimony."); U.S. v. Warren, 578 F.2d 1058 (5th Cir. 1978); Ex parte Faircloth, 471 So. 2d 493, 497 (Ala. 1985) ("In this case, petitioner himself invoked the rule, he was then informed that he was responsible for his own witnesses, he failed to meet this responsibility, and he failed to make any showing of the materiality of the witness's expected testimony. Under these circumstances, we find no abuse of discretion in the trial court's refusal to permit this witness to testify."); Blaylock v. Strecker, 291 Ark. 340, 724 S.W.2d 470, 472–73 (1987) ("The third phase, and third different standard, arises when a witness has been ordered sequestered, but does not comply. The rule does not mention the consequences of noncompliance with an order of exclusion, and therefore the sanctions are a matter of case law. The three possible methods of enforcement available to the trial judge are: (1) citing the witness for contempt, (2) permitting comment on the witness's noncompliance in order to reflect on her credibility, and (3) refusing to let her testify. See 4 Weinstein's Federal Evidence § 615.07[2] (2d ed. 1997). The first option, citing the witness for contempt, was not a viable alternative under the facts of this case. The second option, and the one favored in this State since 1855, Pleasant v. State, 15 Ark. 624, 650 (1855), and favored by federal courts since 1893, Holder v. United States, 150 U.S. 91 (1893) was available, and its use would have been

case for altogether barring the witness's testimony is a fact situation in which the witness heard testimony which could influence his own testimony and the party or counsel calling the witness colluded in the witness's violation of the sequestration order.[25] Unfortunately once it is decided to permit the witness to testify, the alternatives of comment or contempt have their drawbacks.[26] The best approach is to avoid the problem beforehand. Before trial, the judge should emphatically impress on both the witnesses and counsel the importance of obeying the court's ruling excluding and separating the witness. If the witness is absent at the hearing at which the judge issues the order, the judge should direct the attorney to inform the witness of the order.

---

proper. It was error to use the third option, exclusion."). *Compare* Jefferson v. State, 256 Ga. 821, 353 S.E.2d 468, 472 (1987) ("A violation of the rule goes to the credibility of the witness, and renders him amenable to the court for contempt in disobeying the court's order, but does not render him incompetent or permit the exclusion of his testimony. May v. State, 90 Ga. 793, 800(2), 17 S.E. 108 (1892); Shelton v. State, 111 Ga.App. 351(1), 141 S.E.2d 776 (1965); Thomas v. State, 7 Ga.App. 615(1), 67 S.E. 707 (1910).").

[25]U.S. v. Smith, 318 Fed. Appx. 780 (11th Cir. 2009); U.S. v. Gibson, 675 F.2d 825 (6th Cir. 1982); Childs v. State, 761 N.E.2d 892 (Ind. Ct. App. 2002) (the witness waited until after the victim took the stand to tell anyone what the victim had allegedly said to her, the witness spoke to the defendant, and the witness's proposed testimony represented a shift in defense strategy that could have left the prosecution at a disadvantage). *See also* U.S. v. Washington, 653 F.3d 1251,

1267–70 (10th Cir. 2011), cert. denied, 132 S. Ct. 1039, 181 L. Ed. 2d 765 (2012) ("There are no indicia of 'consent, connivance, procurement, or knowledge' of Ms. Warrior's violation by defense counsel . . . , and the district court never paused to conduct even a semblance of a 'probable prejudice' inquiry").

[26]4 Weinstein's Federal Evidence § 615.07[2][b], at 615-31-32 (rev. 2011) ("although a contempt citation punishes the witness and may perhaps deter future misconduct, it 'does nothing to extinguish any false testimony which the witness may have fabricated by listening to other witnesses.' An instruction or comment, while useful, may have unwarranted repercussions if the witness remained in the courtroom and had a discussion with another witness but his or her testimony was unaffected. A derogatory comment on the witness's credibility under these circumstances may actually distort the truth").

# Title 3.   Admission and Exclusion

## Chapter 6

# The Procedure of Admitting and Excluding Evidence

## § 51   Presentation of evidence: Offer of proof

To gain a working knowledge of evidence law, you must appreciate the procedural framework within which evidence doctrine operates. Our adversary system requires the parties to present trial evidence pursuant to rules that make it clear when proof has been formally proffered before it is introduced and then may be considered by the trier of fact.[1] The procedural rules impact every participant in the trial process, and a matter of procedural fairness the rules must be sufficiently clear for all the participants: The proponent needs to know how to introduce evidence, the opponent must know when to object, and the judge has to know when to rule. The rules of practice concerning presentation of evidence, offers of proof, and objections all are designed to secure this result.

---

**[Section 51]**

[1]The fact issues at the trial should be decided based on the evidence "in the record", i.e., facts officially introduced in accordance with the rules of practice and those which the court may judicially notice. See Ch. 35 infra.

The presentation of exhibits such as writings, photographs, knives, guns, and other tangible objects often proves troublesome to neophytes.[2] There are variations in local procedures, but the general process may be briefly described here.[3] The party wishing to introduce evidence of this type should first have the object marked "for identification" as an exhibit.[4] After the proponent has the thing marked by the clerk for identification as an exhibit, the proponent submits the proposed exhibit to the opposing attorney for his inspection, at least on his request.[5] After showing the exhibit to the opponent, the proponent approaches the witness.[6] At this point, the proponent "lays the foundation" for its introduction as an exhibit by having it appropriately authenticated or identified by the witness's testimony.[7] Although the courts often speak of laying "the foundation" in the singular, in truth the proponent may have to lay multiple foundations. Thus, a single exhibit such as a letter might require authentication, best evidence, and hearsay foundations.

The procedures for handling exhibits vary to a degree not only from jurisdiction to jurisdiction but also even between judges sitting in the same jurisdiction. However, the following generalizations hold true in most jurisdictions. After laying all the required foundations or predicates, the proponent tenders the exhibit to the judge by stating, "Plaintiff offers this (document or object, describing it), marked 'Plaintiff's Exhibit No. 2' for identification, into evidence as Plaintiff's Exhibit No. 2." At this juncture, the

---

[2]In ordinary practice, introduction of depositions does not require the procedures described in the subsequent text.

[3]The techniques for introducing exhibits are described and illustrated in detail in Imwinkelried, Evidentiary Foundations Ch. 4 (8th ed. 2012); Mauet, Trial Techniques Ch. 6 (8th ed. 2010); Lane, Goldstein Trial Technique §§ 12:1 to 12:58 (3d ed.); Keeton Trial Tactics and Methods 63–70 (1973); Virgie v. Stetson, 73 Me. 452, 461, 1882 WL 3723 (1882).

[4]The purpose of having the clerk mark proposed exhibits "for identification" is to make them part of the record in case they are refused as exhibits. *See* Duncan v. McTiernan, 151 Conn. 469, 199 A.2d 332 (1964) (it is error for the trial court to refuse to permit a proposed exhibit to be marked for identification). Tags may be used for marking, if needed. The inclusion of the exhibit in the record enables the appellate court to make a more informed decision whether a ruling excluding the exhibit was error.

[5]In many jurisdictions, at this point it is customary for the proponent to ask the judge to have the record reflect that the proponent has shown the exhibit to the opposing counsel. When the record reflects that fact, on appeal it will be easier for the proponent to argue that the opponent waived any objections evident on the face of the exhibit.

[6]In some courts, especially federal courts, courtroom etiquette dictates that the attorney request the judge's permission to approach the witness.

[7]Certain items are "self-authenticating." See generally Authentication, Ch. 22 infra and Fed. R. Evid. 902.

opponent can object to its receipt in evidence, and the judge will rule on the objection. Assuming the judge rules the exhibit admissible, if the item of evidence is a writing, with the judge's permission it may be read to the jury by the counsel offering it or by the witness. Again, with the judge's permission, the writing could also be passed to the jury or displayed on a screen. In the judge's discretion or in accordance with local custom or rule, when the exhibit is a gun or knife, it may be shown or passed to the jurors for their physical inspection.[8] (Some judges do not permit the proponent to submit his exhibits to the jury until the conclusion of the proponent's case-in-chief.)

When the courtroom is fully equipped with computer technology, the mechanics are even simpler.[9] The court staff may include a technologist to operate the computer, and there will be monitor screens in front of the judge, at the counsel tables, on the witness stand, and in the jury box. Even before the trial session begins, the attorney can present an electronic version of the exhibit to the technologist. Initially, the attorney asks that the technologist "display," "release," or "show" the exhibit to the judge. Next, the attorney requests that it be shown to opposing counsel. Then the attorney asks the technologist to show the exhibit to the witness. At this point the attorney elicits the witness's foundational testimony for the exhibit. If the judge rules that the foundation is complete, the attorney lastly requests that the exhibit be displayed on the monitor screens in the jury box.

Of course, the usual way of presenting oral testimony is to call the witness to the stand and ask him questions. Normally (but not always), the opponent must challenge the admissibility of the testimony by voicing objections to the questions before the wit-

---

[8]In some jurisdictions, although the proponent marks the exhibits for identification during the sponsoring witnesses' testimony, it is customary to formally move them into evidence all together at the end of the case-in-chief.

When the proponent requests permission to read an exhibit to the jury, the opponent sometimes objects that "the document itself is the best evidence." Brockett & Keker, Effective Direct & Cross–Examination § 11.11, at 248–49 (1986). That objection is spurious. Cole, A Judge's Answers on Evidence, 38 Litigation, Wint. 2012, at 7, 8. The best evidence rule generally requires that the proponent produce the original in the courtroom. However, once the proponent does so, the best evidence rule has spent its force. At this point, the trial judge's discretion under Federal Rule 611(a) comes into play. The judge has discretion to regulate the manner in which the evidence is presented to the jury. Moss, Beyond the Fringe: Apocryphal Rules of Evidence in Texas, 43 Baylor L. Rev. 701, 726 (1991). An alternative view is that the rule generally requires the document to be shown to the jury but that the trial judge has discretion to permit the writing to be read to the jurors.

[9]Imwinkelried, Evidentiary Foundations § 4.01[3] (8th ed. 2012).

ness answers the question.[10] Ordinarily, the admissibility of testimony is decided by the judge's sustaining or overruling objections to questions. If the court sustains an objection to a question, the witness is prevented from answering the question and from testifying to that extent.

When the judge sustains an objection, the proponent of the question should usually make "an offer of proof." The usual practice is for the proponent to explain to the judge what the witness would say if the witness were permitted to answer the question and what the expected answer is logically relevant to prove.[11] There are two reasons for this practice. One is that it permits the

---

[10]See § 52 infra.

[11]Former Fed. R. Evid. 103 provided:

(a) Effect of Erroneous Ruling. Error may not be predicated upon a ruling which admits or excludes evidence unless a substantial right of the party is affected, and

* * *

(2) Offer of Proof. In case the ruling is one excluding evidence, the substance of the evidence was made known to the court by offer or was apparent from the context within such questions were asked.

(b) Record of Offer and Ruling. The court may add any other or further statement which shows the character of the evidence, the form in which it was offered, the objection made, and the ruling thereon. It may direct the making of an offer in question and answer form.

(c) Hearing of Jury. In jury cases, proceedings shall be conducted, to the extent practicable, so as to prevent inadmissible evidence from being suggested to the jury by any means, such as making statements or offers of proof or asking questions in the hearing of the jury.

Unif. R. Evid. 103 is identical in content. Effective December 1, 2011, restyled Fed. R. Evid. 103 reads:

(a) Preserving a Claim of Error. A party may claim error in a ruling to admit or exclude evidence only if the error affects a substantial right of the party and:

* * *

(2) if the ruling excludes evidence, a party informs the court of its sub-

stance by an offer of proof, unless the substance was apparent from the context.

(b) Record of offer and ruling. The court may add any other or further statement which shows the character of the evidence, the form in which it was offered, the objection made, and the ruling thereon. It may direct the making of an offer in question and answer form.

(c) Hearing of jury. In jury cases, proceedings shall be conducted, to the extent practicable, so as to prevent inadmissible evidence from being suggested to the jury by any means, such as making statements or offers of proof or asking questions in the hearing of the jury.

* * *

The term "proffer" is sometimes used to describe an offer of proof.

For cases stating the requirement for an offer of proof, *see* Philadelphia Record Co. v. Sweet, 124 Pa. Super. 414, 188 A. 631 (1936) (it was reversible error to deny counsel opportunity of making offer); D'Acchioli v. Cairo, 87 R.I. 345, 141 A.2d 269 (1958) (rule was applied in a bench trial). *See generally* 1 Weinstein's Federal Evidence §§ 103.20.21 (rev. 2011); U.S. v. Yarrington, 634 F.3d 440 (8th Cir. 2011) (the defense counsel made a sufficient offer of proof; the counsel both described the proposed testimony and explained how the testimony would impeach a government witness); West's Key Number Digest, Trial ⚷44 to 49; Comment Note.— Ruling on offer of proof as error, 89 A.L.R.2d 279. See also note 23, infra.

trial judge to reconsider the claim for admissibility.[12] Before the offer of proof, the judge might not have realized the logical relevance of the line of inquiry. However, the second, formal reason is to preserve the issue for appeal by including the expected answer in the official record of trial. In the event of an appeal from the judge's ruling, the appellate court can better understand the scope and effect of the question and proposed answer. That understanding enables the appellate court in a better position to decide: whether the judge's ruling sustaining an objection was error,[13] whether the error was prejudicial, and what final disposi-

---

When an offer of proof is proper, the trial court must permit it to be made. *See* Comment Note.—Ruling on offer of proof as error, 89 A.L.R.2d 279, § 5.

On occasion under Fed. R. Evid. 103(b), circumstances may call for the judge to direct that the offer be made by questions and the witness's answers out of the jury's hearing. Doubts as to what the witness might say are settled. The trial judge might insist that the proponent use this method when the judge is skeptical about the proponent's description of the evidence. For his part, the questioner should seek to make offers by questions and answers if the accuracy of the offer could become an important issue on appeal. . It has been suggested that the better practice is to make the offer of proof by questioning the witness. State v. Goad, 707 S.W.2d 846 (Tenn. 1986). *See also* U.S. v. Adams, 271 F.3d 1236, 1242 (10th Cir. 2001) (discussing the various methods of making an offer, including examination of the witness, "the least favored method" of a statement by counsel, and a documentary offer of proof, signed by the witness, marked as an exhibit, and introduced into the record). There are at least four different methods of making an offer of proof of a witness's anticipated testimony:

(1) Dictation of statement into the record of the testimony anticipated from the excluded question. . . . This statement is properly made at the reporter's desk so that it may be heard by the court and opposing counsel, if he de-

sires, but not heard by the jury or witness. . . .

(2) Introduction of statement written by examining counsel containing the answer the witness would give, in the opinion of questioner, if permitted to testify.

(3) A written statement of the witness's testimony signed by the witness and offered as part of the record. This would occur principally when witness was friendly and available before trial and the testimonial issue is known as a pivotal problem during preparation for trial. It is desirable when matter of competency or privilege of witness is in issue, for then the excluded testimony may be easily presented in the record. It is suggested in using this and the preceding method that the writing be marked as an exhibit and introduced into the record for proper identification on appeal.

(4) Request the court to excuse the jury temporarily, examine the witness before the court, and have the answers reported in the record. If it were not for the inconvenience, this would be by far the most desirable method.

Ladd, The Need in Iowa of an Offer of Excluded Testimony for Appeal, 18 Iowa L. Rev. 304, 318 n. 28 (1933); Graham, Preserving Error for Appeal: Objections and Offers of Proof, 44 Crim. L. Bull. 609, 621 (July-Aug. 2008).

[12]Once the judge realizes the logical relevance of the line of inquiry, on his own motion the judge may reconsider the ruling, overrule the objection, and permit the questioning.

[13]Parliament Ins. Co. v. Hanson, 676 F.2d 1069, 1074 (5th Cir. 1982)

tion to make on appeal.[14] The trial judge usually requires the offer of proof to be made outside the jury's hearing. The judge has already ruled the evidence inadmissible; and if the offer were made in the jury's hearing, the jurors would be exposed to inadmissible testimony which could improperly influence their deliberation. Federal Rule of Evidence 103(c) imposes the requirement for an offer of proof.[15] Significantly, on cross-examination, the requirement is often relaxed; some jurisdictions entirely eliminate the need for an offer of proof on cross-examination[16] while most courts accept less specific offers on cross than they demand on direct.[17] The courts realize that it is often more difficult to predict the answers on cross-examination than on direct, since cross-

---

("The purpose of this rule is to alert the court and opposing counsel to the thrust of the excluded evidence, enabling them to take appropriate action; and to provide an appellate court with a record allowing it to determine whether the exclusion was erroneous or not."); Fortunato v. Ford Motor Co., 464 F.2d 962, 967 (2d Cir. 1972) ("The main purposes for this rule are to permit the trial judge to reevaluate his decision in light of the actual evidence to be offered, . . . and to permit the reviewing court to determine if the exclusion affected the substantial rights of the party offering it . . . .").

[14]The offer of proof might help the appellate court decide whether to remand for further proceedings in the lower court or to enter a final judgment for one of the parties.

[15]Fed. R. Evid. and Unif. R. Evid. 103(c). Delaying an offer of proof until the day after exclusion of testimony has been held justified on the ground that counsel did not wish to make the offer of proof in the jury's hearing. U.S. v. Robinson, 544 F.2d 110 (2d Cir. 1976). Usually the offer of proof can be made immediately after the ruling by requiring counsel to approach the bench so the jury cannot hear or by recessing the trial.

While motions in limine and related procedures are most commonly employed to obtain an advance ruling excluding evidence, see § 52 infra, text at notes 13–30, nothing in their nature precludes resort to them as a means of obtaining an advance ruling in favor of the proponent of evidence.

[16]Cal. Evid. Code § 354(c).

[17]On cross-examination, the examining counsel is ordinarily assumed not to have had an advance opportunity to learn how the witness will answer, and the requirement of a detailed offer will not usually be applied. Cohen v. Cohen, 196 Ga. 562, 27 S.E.2d 28, 30 (1943); Higgins v. Pratt, 316 Mass. 700, 56 N.E.2d 595 (1944); Calci v. Brown, 95 R.I. 216, 186 A.2d 234 (1962) (dictum). Cal. Evid. Code § 354(c) completely eliminates the need for an offer of proof on cross-examination. *But see* People v. Foss, 155 Cal. App. 4th 113, 65 Cal. Rptr. 3d 790 (3d Dist. 2007) (the exception for objections sustained on cross-examination does not apply if the cross-examiner's question exceeds the scope of the direct examination; in that event, the cross-examiner must make an offer of proof, as specific and non-speculative as possible).

Unlike § 354(c), Federal Rule 103 does not carve out any exception for questions posed on cross. *See* Saltzman v. Fullerton Metals Co., 661 F.2d 647 (7th Cir. 1981) (not recognizing an exception). Even on cross-examination the court in its discretion may require counsel to hint her purpose far enough to show the materiality of the answer hoped for. Lavieri v. Ulysses, 149 Conn. 396, 180 A.2d 632 (1962) (insufficient hint); Perry v. Carter, 332 Mass. 508, 125 N.E.2d 780 (1955)

examination is sometimes exploratory. It would therefore be unfair to demand the same degree of specificity in offers of proof during cross-examination.

Occasionally, in the context of the record, the question itself can so clearly indicate the tenor of the expected answer that the appellate court will consider the propriety of the ruling on the question without an offer of proof.[18] However, when an offer of proof is typically required before the appellate court will consider a ruling sustaining an objection to a question, the statement constituting the offer of proof must be reasonably specific;[19] the offer should factually describe the witness's probable answer and

---

(there was no apparent error in excluding questions). This discretion probably exists under Fed. R. Evid. 103(a) (2), note 11 supra. A possible example is U.S. v. Medel, 592 F.2d 1305 (5th Cir. 1979). *Compare* State v. Affeld, 307 Or. 125, 764 P.2d 220, 222 (1988) ("The only justification for the exception offered by any of these cases is that a cross-examiner has no idea what the answer to the question will be. While this might be so, there is no reason that the cross-examiner should not determine the answer by asking the question as part of the offer of proof."). If an objection is sustained, and the cross-examiner believes the matter is of sufficient importance in making a record or persuading the judge to change the ruling, the cross-examiner should not take the risk of continuing the cross-examination without making an offer of proof or indicating the general purpose of the questioning.

There is a practical difficulty in making an offer of proof. If it is important not to warn the witness concerning answers desired, an attempt should be made to make the offer of proof out of the witness's hearing. It has been held that the cross-examiner may make an offer of proof if she desires to do so. Abbadessa v. Tegu, 122 Vt. 338, 173 A.2d 153 (1961). This should be the federal rule as well.

[18]Fed. R. Evid. 103(a)(2). *See* Beech Aircraft Corp. v. Rainey, 488 U.S. 153, 174, 109 S. Ct. 439, 102 L. Ed. 2d 445 (1988) ("Rule 103(a)(2) requires, in the first place, that to

preserve an argument that evidence was wrongly excluded the proponent must make known the substance of the evidence sought to be admitted by an offer of proof unless it 'was apparent from the context within which questions were asked'. Here the nature of the proposed testimony was abundantly apparent from the very question put . . . ."); Hartwig v. Olson, 261 Iowa 1265, 158 N.W.2d 81 (1968) (dictum); Manning v. Redevelopment Agency of Newport, 103 R.I. 371, 238 A.2d 378 (1968) (court held that the answer to particular question was not apparent in part).

Obviously, the skillful trial lawyer will make an offer rather than gambling on a successful invocation of this approach, which is often the resort of those who forgot.

[19]U.S. v. Winkle, 587 F.2d 705 (5th Cir. 1979); Kane v. Carper–Dover Mercantile Co., 206 Ark. 674, 177 S.W.2d 41 (1944) ("we offer to prove . . . that C.D. is not the proper plaintiff for recovery or damage;" too indefinite; must be so specific as to give the judge an opportunity to rule on particular testimony); Ostmo v. Tennyson, 70 N.D. 558, 296 N.W. 541 (1941) (must show what facts are sought to be introduced, so that court may see whether they have any bearing); Shoemaker v. Selnes, 220 Or. 573, 349 P.2d 473 (1960) (one offer so vague it could not be understood; second offer stated counsel "believed" witness would testify as specified). *Compare* Moran v. Levin, 318 Mass. 770, 64 N.E.2d 360 (1945) (the case was an ac-

identify the purpose of the proffered testimony.[20] Thus, the proponent must tell the judge what the tenor of the evidence would be and why the evidence is logically relevant. Where the sustained objection challenges the relevancy of the testimony, the offer of proof should indicate the facts on which relevancy depends.[21] When the objection is on a ground other than relevancy, the offer must also explain why the objection is unsound.[22] These general guidelines apply under Federal Rule of Evidence 103 as well as at common law.[23] Effective December 1, 2000, Rule 103 was amended. By virtue of the amendment to Rule 103(a), if

---

tion for deceit in a sale of dairy cows, one of which was alleged not to produce milk due to disease; plaintiff's offer to show by plaintiff and wife "certain representations made by defendant with reference to the condition, the health of these cows, as to whether they were milk producers" was held sufficient even though it was a "summary" or "abstract" of the proposed evidence).

[20]Davey Bros., Inc. v. Stop & Shop, Inc., 351 Mass. 59, 217 N.E.2d 751 (1966) (offer of proof failed to indicate purpose for which the testimony would be relevant); Holman v. Kemp, 70 Minn. 422, 73 N.W. 186, 188 (1897) (counsel asked plaintiff if he did not drink a good deal before the accident; the question was excluded; appellant claimed this was relevant to explain plaintiff's physical condition at time of trial; the claim was an insufficient offer. "If such was the real purpose of the evidence, it was not apparent upon the record, and the trial court's attention should have been specifically called to the object of the evidence.").

Fed. R. Evid. 103(a)(2) speaks of a showing of the substance of the "evidence." Nevertheless, to make sure error is shown, where appropriate, the purpose and theory of the evidence should be stated. Fed. R. Civ. P. 46 requires that the party make known to the court "the action which the party desires the court to take or the party's objection to the action of the court *and the grounds therefor . . . .*" (italics supplied.) Fed. R. Crim. P. 51 contains the same language. Both rules apply to evidentiary matters.

[21]Braman v. Wiley, 119 F.2d 991 (C.C.A. 7th Cir. 1941) (in a collision case, there was evidence that defendant was drunk; defendant offered a witness to testify to a conversation with defendant soon after; on appeal defendant contended this was material to negate drunkenness; the court held that the evidence was irrelevant for the purpose stated); Ex parte Taylor, 322 S.W.2d 309 (Tex. Civ. App. El Paso 1959) (statement that "the whole matter is relevant to this matter" held insufficient when judge inquired as to purpose of question); Fuchs v. Kupper, 22 Wis. 2d 107, 125 N.W.2d 360 (1963) (question was immaterial absent offer of proof of additional facts). Unless relevancy must have been apparent: Creighton v. Elgin, 387 Ill. 592, 56 N.E.2d 825 (1944) (question itself showed purposes and materiality).

[22]Deaton & Son v. Miller Well Servicing Co., 231 S.W.2d 944 (Tex. Civ. App. Amarillo 1950) (party offering evidence which would ordinarily be hearsay—here an agent's declarations—must show facts bringing it under some exception); Clements v. Jungert, 90 Idaho 143, 408 P.2d 810 (1965) (party offering evidence excluded as hearsay was required to show declarant's authority).

[23]See notes 11–17 supra.

Unless excused because the answer is apparent from the context, the proponent's failure to make an offer of proof precludes raising the question on appeal. Yost v. A. O. Smith Corp., 562 F.2d 592, 595 (8th Cir. 1977) (claim of error was rejected; the court

before trial the proponent makes a proper offer of proof and the trial makes a purportedly final ruling excluding the evidence, the proponent need not renew the offer at trial to preserve the issue for appeal.

Under these guidelines, the proponent has significant burdens. If the proponent counsel specifies a purpose for which the proposed evidence is inadmissible and the judge excludes, counsel cannot complain of the ruling on appeal although it could have been admitted for another purpose.[24] Likewise, if part of the evidence offered such as a deposition, letter, or conversation is admissible but a part is not, it is incumbent on the proponent, not the judge, to separate out the admissible part. When counsel offers both the admissible and inadmissible matter together and the judge rejects the entire offer, the proponent may not complain on appeal.[25]

The offer of proof methodology described above assumes that a

---

stated that absent offer of proof it had "no way of knowing whether the excluded evidence would be helpful or harmful to appellants."); Mills v. Levy, 537 F.2d 1331 (5th Cir. 1976) (error may not be predicated on exclusion of testimony allegedly falling within the "dying declaration" hearsay exception, since no offer of proof was made); U.S. v. Muncy, 526 F.2d 1261 (5th Cir. 1976) (court does not have to pass on question of refusal to allow extrinsic evidence impeaching government witness absent an offer of proof showing what excluded evidence would be).

A proper offer of proof by one party preserves the question for review on appeal when raised by a co-party aligned in interest. Howard v. Gonzales, 658 F.2d 352 (5th Cir. 1981). The co-party's offer fills the appellate court's information need.

[24]U.S. v. Grapp, 653 F.2d 189 (5th Cir. 1981); Huff v. White Motor Corp., 609 F.2d 286 (7th Cir. 1979). Fed. R. Evid. 103(a)(2) does not mention the principle in the text, but the notion of waiver is easily distilled from Fed. R. Civ. P. 46 and Fed. R. Crim. P. 51. Other authority includes Deitrich v. Kettering, 212 Pa. 356, 61 A. 927 (1905). Likewise, if a specific ground for admission is claimed in the offer of proof but is inapplicable and the judge

excludes the evidence, the proponent cannot complain that there was another ground for admission. U.S. v. Anderson, 618 F.2d 487 (8th Cir. 1980); U.S. v. Sims, 617 F.2d 1371 (9th Cir. 1980); Johnson v. Rockaway Bus Corp., 145 Conn. 204, 140 A.2d 708 (1958) (claim of admissibility as a declaration against interest precluded consideration on appeal of admissibility as an admission of a party); Watkins v. Watkins, 397 S.W.2d 603 (Mo. 1965) (on cross-examination questioner made an offer of proof apparently on basis matter was relevant to issues; on appeal, the court refused to consider an alternative theory of logical relevance bearing on credibility); Comment Note.—Ruling on offer of proof as error, 89 A.L.R.2d 279.

[25]For federal rule purposes, see note 23 supra. Other cases include Sooner Pipe & Supply Corp. v. Rehm, 1968 OK 164, 447 P.2d 758 (Okla. 1968) (offer of incompetent evidence included); Morris v. E. I. Du Pont De Nemours & Co., 346 Mo. 126, 139 S.W.2d 984 (1940) (motion picture, in part irrelevant); Williams v. Rhode Island Hospital Trust Co., 88 R.I. 23, 143 A.2d 324 (1958); Comment Note.— Ruling on offer of proof as error, 89 A.L.R.2d 279.

single witness is being questioned on the stand.[26] Suppose that there are several other available witnesses, but not yet in court, to prove a fact. Assume further that the judge's rulings already indicate that he will probably exclude this entire line of testimony, or the judge rules in advance that the line of testimony is inadmissible. Must the party produce each witness, question him, and on exclusion, describe each expected answer? A few decisions mandate this procedure.[27] Obviously that procedure wastes time. The better view is that it is not invariably required to call the other witnesses. Under this view, an adequate offer of proof can be made without producing all the witnesses if the offer is sufficiently specific[28] and there is nothing in the record to indicate the proponent's bad faith or inability to produce the proof.[29]

---

[26]In the case of a single witness, an offer of proof is usually held premature and ineffective it is made before putting a question to the witness (to which objection may be taken). Some cases hold that a witness must ordinarily be placed on the stand and questioned in connection with the offer of proof. See other cases cited in Comment Note.—Ruling on offer of proof as error, 89 A.L.R.2d 279. However, Fed. and Unif. R. Evid. 103(c) contemplate that later questions in a line of inquiry need not be asked before the jury if the judge barred earlier questions in the same line. Rather, the federal Advisory Committee's Note states: "The judge can foreclose a particular line of testimony and counsel can protect the record without a series of questions before the jury, designed at best to waste time and at worst 'to waft into the jury box' the very matter sought to be excluded." For other supporting cases involving one witness, see Missouri Pac. Ry. Co. v. Castle, 172 F. 841 (C.C.A. 8th Cir. 1909); Garvey v. Chicago Rys. Co., 339 Ill. 276, 171 N.E. 271, 274–75 (1930) (offer of evidence on new trial motion without producing witness held sufficient, distinguishing Chicago City Ry. Co. v. Carroll, 206 Ill. 318, 68 N.E. 1087 (1903)).

[27]Chicago City Ry. Co. v. Carroll, 206 Ill. 318, 68 N.E. 1087 (1903);

Eschbach v. Hurtt, 47 Md. 61, 66, 1877 WL 6980 (1877) ("If the defendant had at the trial witnesses who could have proved . . . it was his duty to have called them or one of them to the stand and propounded appropriate questions. . . . ."). Fed. and Unif. R. Evid. 103(b) and 611(a) may permit a judge to require this procedure, but in his discretion he should rarely do so.

[28]It would seem wise to name the witness or witnesses and to indicate the particulars that each would prove.

[29]See comment concerning the federal rules in note 26 supra. Scotland County v. Hill, 112 U.S. 183, 186, 5 S. Ct. 93, 28 L. Ed. 692 (1884) ("If the trial court has doubts about the good faith of an offer of testimony, it can insist on the production of the witness, and upon some attempt to make the proof, before it rejects the offer; but if it does reject it, and allows a bill of exceptions which shows that the offer was actually made and refused, and there is nothing else in the record to indicate bad faith, an appellate court must assume that the proof could have been made. . . . " [of course bills of exception are mostly obsolete; see § 52, infra]); Witt v. Voigt, 162 Wis. 568, 156 N.W. 954 (1916) (when counsel said he had witnesses in court who would testify to certain facts, court said such evidence would not be received; the counsel had made a suf-

## § 52 Objections[1]

If the administration of the exclusionary rules of evidence is to be fair and workable, the judge must be informed promptly of any contention that evidence should be rejected, and the reasons supporting the contention. This burden is placed on the party opponent, not the judge. Accordingly, the general approach is that a failure to make a specific objection at the time the evidence is proffered, is a waiver on appeal of any ground of complaint against its admission. However, this general approach is modified by the doctrine of plain error, discussed at the end of this section.

### Time of Making: Motions to Strike

The opponent may not gamble on the possibility of a favorable answer.[2] Rather, the opponent must object to the admission of evidence as soon as the ground for objection becomes apparent.[3] Usually, during a witness's testimony, an objection is apparent as soon as the question is asked, since the wording of the ques-

---

ficient offer).

**[Section 52]**

[1] 1 Wigmore, Evidence § 18 (3d ed. 1940); 1 Weinstein's Federal Evidence §§ 103.10–.14 (rev. 2011); West's Key Number Digest, Trial ⬥73 to 97; Aprile, How to Be a Conscientious Objector, 27 Crim. Just., Fall 2011, at 40 (the article discusses in detail the various facets of a good objection: the hail to the judge, the objection itself, the statement of grounds, a description of prejudice, constitutionalization, and the request for relief).

[2] Unif. R. Evid. 103(a)(1) and former Fed. R. Evid. 103(a)(1) embody the principles set forth in this paragraph of the text:

(a) Effect of Erroneous Ruling. Error may not be predicated upon a ruling which admits or excludes evidence unless a substantial right of the party is affected, and

(1) Objection. In case the ruling is one admitting evidence, a timely objection or motion to strike appears of record, stating the specific ground of objection, if the specific ground was not apparent from the context;
. . . .

Effective December 1, 2011, restyled Fed. R. Evid. 103(1)(1) reads:

Preserving a Claim of Error. A party may claim error in a ruling to admit or exclude evidence only if the error affects a substantial right of the party and:

(1) if the ruling admits evidence, a party, on the record:

(A) timely objects or moves to strike; and

(B) states the specific ground, unless it was apparent from the context . . . .

See Reagan v. Brock, 628 F.2d 721 (1st Cir. 1980); U.S. v. Armedo–Sarmiento, 545 F.2d 785 (2d Cir. 1976). See also Hastings v. Serleto, 61 Cal. App. 2d 672, 143 P.2d 956 (2d Dist. 1943); Kuiken v. Garrett, 243 Iowa 785, 51 N.W.2d 149 (1952).

[3] See Fed. R. Evid. 103(a)(1) and Unif. R. Evid. 103(a)(1). See also People v. Dykes, 46 Cal. 4th 731, 95 Cal. Rptr. 3d 78, 209 P.3d 1, 29 (2009) (the requirement for a timely objection applies in capital as well as non-capital cases); Cheffer v. Eagle Discount Stamp Co., 348 Mo. 1023, 156 S.W.2d 591 (1941). But see U.S. v. Meserve, 271 F.3d 314, 324 (1st Cir. 2001) (it became obvious later that the conviction in question was a 20-year-old misdemeanor; "[t]he general principle that an objection should be made after a question has been asked but before an

tion is likely to indicate that it calls for inadmissible evidence. If there is an opportunity, counsel must then state her objection before the witness answers.[4] But sometimes an objection before an answer is infeasible. An eager witness may answer so quickly that counsel does not have enough time and a fair chance to object.[5] In that event, the counsel may move to strike the answer for the purpose of interposing an objection to the question; if the judge thinks that the witness "jumped the gun" and grants the motion, the counsel then states her objection to the question. Or a question which is unobjectionable may be followed by a partially or completely nonresponsive answer.[6] In this situation, the questioner[7] has the right to have the nonresponsive material stricken. Or after the evidence is received, a ground of objection to the evidence may later surface for the first time.[8] For example, although on direct examination the witness purported to testify from personal knowledge, it might become evident for the first time on cross that in reality, the witness is relying on inadmissible hearsay. In all these cases, an "after-objection" may be stated as soon as the ground appears. The proper technique is to move to strike the objectionable evidence and request a curative instruc-

---

answer has been given . . . is flexible in deference to the 'heat of a hotly contested criminal trial' . . . . Meserve's objection, although delayed, was sufficiently contemporaneous . . . .").

[4]See federal cases cited in note 31 supra. *See also* Stark's Adm'x v. Herndon's Adm'r, 292 Ky. 469, 166 S.W.2d 828 (1942) (question asked by juror); Lineberry v. Robinett, 446 S.W.2d 481 (Mo. Ct. App. 1969).

[5]A motion to strike should then be made. Wightman v. Campbell, 217 N.Y. 479, 112 N.E. 184 (1916) (but in the particular situation an objection sufficed); Sorenson v. Smith, 65 Or. 78, 129 P. 757 (1913). These rules are undoubtedly effective under Fed. R. Evid. 103(a)(1).

[6]Brown v. Parker, 375 S.W.2d 594 (Mo. Ct. App. 1964) (dictum); Wallace v. American Toll Bridge Co., 124 Or. 179, 264 P. 351 (1928) (when the is question is proper but the answer is improper. the approved practice is to move to strike the answer).

The mere fact that the answer is unresponsive is not an objection available to the opponent. Hester v.

Goldsbury, 64 Ill. App. 2d 66, 212 N.E.2d 316 (1st Dist. 1965) and cases cited therein; Isham v. Birkel, 184 Neb. 800, 172 N.W.2d 92 (1969) (exclusion by trial judge on opponent's objection held reversible error under particular circumstances). The objection is available to only the questioner, who may move to strike. Davidson v. State, 211 Ala. 471, 100 So. 641 (1924).

Again, these principles are applicable under Fed. R. Evid. 103(a)(1).

[7]If the only vice in the answer is that it is nonresponsive to the question, it would seem that the only aggrieved party is the questioner. If the answer is otherwise admissible, the other party arguably lacks standing to move to strike the nonresponsive material. However, many trial judges permit both parties to move to strike on the ground of nonresponsiveness; and in pertinent part, Cal. Evid. Code § 766 provides that "answers that are not responsive shall be stricken on motion of any party." According to the Cal. Evid. Code § 11, " 'Shall' is mandatory. . . ."

[8]*See* Young v. Dueringer, 401 S.W.2d 165 (Mo. Ct. App. 1966).

tion to the jury to disregard the evidence. Ideally, counsel should use the term of art "motion to strike," but any phraseology directing the judge's attention to the grounds as soon as they appear suffices.[9]

Suppose that the evidence is a transcript of an earlier deposition. The time when objections must be made to deposition questions varies, depending on the type of objection.[10] Usually objections going to the "manner and form" of the questions or answers, such as challenges to leading questions or nonresponsive answers—sometimes opinions and secondary evidence are put in this class—must be made during the deposition hearing.[11] The rationale is that in these cases, if the opponent had objected on the spot, the proponent could have cured the problem. For instance, the proponent might have rephrased the question or established an excuse for the non-production of the original writing. In contrast, objections going to the "substance," such as relevancy and hearsay, may ordinarily be urged for the first time when the deposition is offered at trial.[12]

Assume that there was a prior trial rather than a prior deposition hearing. Suppose further that evidence was introduced at the earlier trial of the case, and an available objection was not made then. In those circumstances, may the opponent object for the first time when the same evidence is tendered at a second

---

[9]Mere labels should not make a difference under Fed. R. Evid. 103(a)(1). *See also* Hackenson v. City of Waterbury, 124 Conn. 679, 2 A.2d 215 (1938) (plaintiff-witness "jumped the gun" and answered a question before defendant objected, and court sustained the objection; the court held that the objection was sufficient to preserve the issue even though there was no formal motion to strike); Wightman v. Campbell, 217 N.Y. 479, 112 N.E. 184 (1916) (when the first question in series proving the making of a land survey was answered before objection and objection was then made "to all that proof," the trial judge overruled the objection; the appellate court held that the objector had sufficiently raised the issue even without a motion to strike).

As to the adequacy of instructions to disregard, see § 58 at note 17 and § 59 infra.

[10]*See* Fed. R. Civ. P. 32(b) and (d), adopted in many states and Fed. R.

Crim. P. 15 and 16.

[11]Fed. R. Civ. P. 32(b) and (d); 1 Wigmore, Evidence § 18, nn. 7–14 (3d ed. 1940).

If the opponent raises an objection to a question during the deposition and further instructs the deponent not to answer, before trial the proponent may file a motion to compel the deponent to answer the question. The proponent may need to know the answer in order to properly prepare for trial.

A fair rule of thumb is to include in this category objections which probably could have been obviated by the examiner if raised at the time. The rationale is that in all these cases, if the opponent had made an objection on the spot, the proponent could have cured the problem by, for instance, rephrasing the question or establishing an excuse for the non-production of the original writing. *But see* Fed. R. Crim. P. 16.

[12]See references, note 10 supra.

trial? The trial and deposition settings differ markedly. As previously stated, the opponent can forego most types of objections at a deposition hearing while, at a trial, the opponent must generally urge the objections. § 259 addresses this issue.

### Pretrial Motions in Limine

A motion for an advance ruling on the admissibility of evidence is a relatively modern device for obtaining rulings on evidence even before the evidence is proffered at trial.[13] The proponent of evidence can file an in limine motion to obtain an advance ruling that an item of evidence is admissible. However, in the vast majority of cases, the opponent files the motion to obtain an advance ruling that a particular item of evidence is inadmissible. The purpose of such motions may be to shield the jury from exposure to prejudicial inadmissible evidence or to afford a basis for strategic decisions.[14] For instance, an advance ruling might help the counsel decide whether to mention an item of evidence during opening statement[15] or advise her client whether to take the stand.[16] Advance rulings on objections can be sought before or during trial prior to the presentation of the evidence.[17] Although there is some old authority forbidding advance rulings,[18] today

---

[13]Carlson, Successful Techniques for Civil Trials Ch. 1 (2d ed. 1992); Hazel, The Motion in Limine: A Texas Proposal, 21 Hous. L. Rev. 919 (1984); Gamble, The Motion *In Limine:* A Pretrial Procedure That Has Come of Age, 33 Ala. L. Rev. 1 (1981); Miller, To Argue Is Human, to Exclude Divine: The Role of Motions in Limine and the Importance of Preserving the Record on Appeal, 32 Am. J. Trial Adv. 541 (2009); Rothblatt & Leroy, The Motion in Limine in Criminal Trials, 60 Ky. L.J. 611 (1972); Comments, 29 Ark. L. Rev. 247 (1975), 27 U. Fla. L. Rev. 531 (1975), 9 Gonzaga L. Rev. 780 (1974), 35 Mont. L. Rev. 362 (1974); Modern status of rules as to use of motion in limine or similar preliminary motion to secure exclusion of prejudicial evidence or reference to prejudicial matters, 63 A.L.R.3d 311.

[14]Luce v. U.S., 469 U.S. 38, 40 n.2, 105 S. Ct. 460, 83 L. Ed. 2d 443 (1984) (" '*In limine*' has been defined as: '[o]n or at the threshold; at the very beginning; preliminarily.' Black's Law Dictionary 708 (5th ed. 1979). We use the term in a broad sense to refer to any motion, whether made before or during trial, to exclude anticipated prejudicial evidence before the evidence is actually offered.").

[15]If during opening the counsel mentions prejudicial evidence which is later ruled inadmissible, the opponent might be entitled to a mistrial.

[16]Suppose, for example, that the accused has a prior conviction but the judge rules the conviction inadmissible for impeachment purposes. It is then safer for the counsel to advise the client to testify.

[17]Motions at the trial may be untimely if an intolerable, extensive interruption at the trial is required. U.S. v. Murray, 492 F.2d 178 (9th Cir. 1973).

[18]*E.g.*, State v. Flett, 234 Or. 124, 380 P.2d 634 (1963); Modern status of rules as to use of motion in limine or similar preliminary motion to secure exclusion of prejudicial evidence or reference to prejudicial matters, 63 A.L.R.3d 311.

the prevailing rule is that the judge has considerable discretion[19] to make or refuse to make advance rulings,[20] Unless the resolution of the motion requires a prediction of the state of the evidence at the later trial, and as long as the matter is left primarily within the trial judge's discretion, a pretrial ruling on a motion in limine should be encouraged.[21] In the pretrial setting, the judge has more time to carefully think through the evidentiary issue; there are no jurors impatiently waiting for the sidebar conference to end. In addition, an in limine motion may prevent the jurors' exposure to prejudicial information and thereby avoid a mistrial.

When a party files an in limine motion, the judge can make three different types of rulings. First, the judge can refuse to entertain the motion and defer the issue until trial. In most but

---

[19]*But see* Ponder v. Conway, 748 F. Supp. 2d 183, 193 (W.D. N.Y. 2010) (under New York law, "a defendant is entitled to an in limine ruling setting forth the extent to which the prosecution may cross-examine him regarding prior crimes and acts bearing on his credibility . . . should he choose to testify"); People v. Mullins, 242 Ill. 2d 1, 350 Ill. Dec. 819, 949 N.E.2d 611 (2011); People v. Patrick, 233 Ill. 2d 62, 330 Ill. Dec. 149, 908 N.E.2d 1 (2009) (citing Settles v. State, 584 So. 2d 1260 (Miss. 1991), State v. McClure, 298 Or. 336, 692 P.2d 579 (1984), and State v. Ritchie, 144 Vt. 121, 473 A.2d 1164 (1984), the court noted that several jurisdictions recognize a general rule that a trial judge should not defer ruling on a defense motion challenging the admissibility of a defendant's conviction offered for purposes of impeachment; in order to make an intelligent decision whether to testify, the defendant needs to know whether the conviction will be admissible; in the instant case, the trial judge erred in deferring the ruling).

[20]U.S. v. Oakes, 565 F.2d 170 (1st Cir. 1977); U.S. v. Kahn, 472 F.2d 272 (2d Cir. 1973); U.S. v. Evanchik, 413 F.2d 950 (2d Cir. 1969); People v. Owen, 299 Ill. App. 3d 818, 233 Ill. Dec. 900, 701 N.E.2d 1174 (4th Dist. 1998). These cases involve an advance

motion to exclude alleged prejudicial, inadmissible evidence on cross-examination of a defendant if he takes the stand. *See also* U.S. v. Palumbo, 401 F.2d 270 (2d Cir. 1968). Compare People v. Lytal, 415 Mich. 603, 329 N.W.2d 738 (1982) (defendant is entitled to know before he takes the stand whether a prior conviction can be used to impeach).

Authority under the Federal and Revised Uniform Rules Evid. may be found in Rules 103(c), 104(c), and 611(a), the rules on pretrial conference and other pretrial proceedings, and the court's general power to control proceedings before them.

Like other interlocutory orders, rulings on these matters ordinarily remain subject to reconsideration by the judge at any time during the trial. However, when strategy has been developed in reliance on the ruling, as when an accused takes the stand in reliance on a ruling excluding impeachment by prior convictions, a trial judge's subsequent reversal of his ruling may well be an abuse of discretion.

[21]U.S. v. Oakes, 565 F.2d 170 (1st Cir. 1977) (it is within the trial judge's discretion whether to make advance ruling on admissibility of prior convictions to impeach accused if he takes the stand, but practice is strongly encouraged).

not all cases,[22] the judge has discretion whether to rule on the issue before trial. Secondly, the judge can make a preliminary or tentative ruling on the motion. By way of example, suppose that the opponent moves to exclude an item of evidence as unduly prejudicial under Rule 403. Although the judge agrees that the evidence might prejudice the jury, the judge can conceive of a state of the record in which the proponent's need for the evidence would be so great that the need would trump the risk of prejudice. If so, the judge might tentatively exclude the evidence. However, the judge would also inform the proponent that the ruling is not final; if at any point during trial, the proponent thought that the state of the record had sharpened the need for the evidence, the proponent could approach sidebar and request permission to introduce the evidence. Thirdly, the judge could make a definitive or final ruling on the merits of the motion.

Suppose that a party moves in limine to exclude certain evidence but the judge denies the motion. To preserve the issue for appeal, must the party repeat the objection at trial when the opposing party offers the evidence? There is a split of authority over this question.[23] At common law the traditional, prevailing view was that if she loses a pretrial in limine motion, the opponent

---

[22]See note 19 infra.

[23]1 Weinstein's Federal Evidence § 103.11[2][b][iii] (rev. 2011); 1 Graham, Handbook of Federal Evidence § 103:8 (7th ed. 2012); Brosnahan, Using Motions in Limine in the Federal Courts, The Practical Litigator, Sep. 1997, at 13 (collecting cases on both sides of the split of authority). In state court, where a motion in limine is made and ruled upon, the point raised is sometimes treated as preserved for appeal despite the lack of an offer of proof or trial objection. *See* Palmerin v. City of Riverside, 794 F.2d 1409, 1412 n.3 (9th Cir. 1986) ("State courts are split on whether a contemporaneous objection during trial is required to preserve a right to appeal on an evidentiary matter admitted over a denied motion *in limine*. *Compare* Reeve v. McBrearety, 660 P.2d 75, 77 (Kan. App. 1983); State v. Harper, 340 N.W.2d 391, 393 (Neb. 1983); Kaiser v. State, 673 P.2d 160, 161–62 (Okla. Crim. 1983); State v. Lesley, 672 P.2d 79, 82 (Utah 1983); Gamble, The Motion *in Limine*: A Pretrial Procedure That Has Come of

Age, 33 Ala. L. Rev. 1, 16 (1981) (objection during trial required); with State v. Sisneros, 670 P.2d 721, 723 (Ariz. 1983); Harley–Davidson Motor Co. v. Daniel, 260 S.E.2d 20, 22 (Ga. 1979) (*in limine* motion preserves objection for appeal).").

With respect to the interlocutory or final nature of a ruling on a motion in limine, see Euroholdings Capital & Inv. Corp. v. Harris Trust & Sav. Bank, 602 F. Supp. 2d 928, 935 (N.D. Ill. 2009) ("'[T]he [in limine] ruling is subject to change when the case unfolds . . . . 'Indeed, even if nothing unexpected happens at trial, the district judge is free, in the exercise of sound judicial discretion, to alter a previous in limine ruling'"); Saltzburg, Impeachment of Witnesses and the Federal Rules of Evidence, 22 Crim. L. Bull. 101, 115 (1986) ("Trial judges in many cases have rendered final rulings for litigants prior to a trial event so that the litigants may prepare. Despite the language of *Luce*, it would be unfortunate if trial judges could not assist the parties in their preparation with some definitive rulings. This is not to say that the trial judge must or

must renew the objection at trial in order to preserve the issue for appeal.[24] Of course, that view robs the in limine motion of much of its utility. One of the foremost advantages of an in limine motion is that the opponent makes the motion outside the jury's hearing, and there is no risk that the jury will form the impression that the opponent is objecting to hide the truth. If the opponent must renew the motion in the jury's presence, that risk rears its ugly head again.

However, even at common law some appellate courts dispensed with a requirement for renewal when the trial judge's ruling is explicit[25] and purportedly definitive.[26] In 2000, Federal Rule of Evidence 103 was amended to codify that approach, and restyled Federal Rule of Evidence 103(a)(2) provides that "(o)nce the court rules definitively on the record—either before or at trial—a party need not renew an objection or offer of proof to preserve a claim of error for appeal." The Advisory Committee Note accompanying the 2000 amendment adds that the opponent has an "obligation

---

should rule finally prior to trial or prior to a part of a trial. It is only to acknowledge that some rulings can be made once and for all early in a case, and that trial judges should have the authority to make them.") (reprinted with permission from Criminal Law Bulletin, March/April 1986, vol. 22, No. 2. Copyright © 1986, Warren, Gorham & Lamont, Inc., 210 South Street, Boston, MA. 02111). All Rights Reserved. There is considerable support for the notion that if the motion in limine is fully briefed and a definitive ruling made, it is *not* necessary for the opposing party to object at trial to preserve error for appeal with respect to evidence held admissible on the motion in limine. *E.g.*, Freeman v. Package Machinery Co., 865 F.2d 1331 (1st Cir. 1988); Palmerin v. City of Riverside, 794 F.2d 1409 (9th Cir. 1986).

Evidence offered in violation of an order in limine must be objected to at trial. U.S. Aviation Underwriters, Inc. v. Olympia Wings, Inc., 896 F.2d 949 (5th Cir. 1990).

[24]Gill v. Thomas, 83 F.3d 537 (1st Cir. 1996); U.S. v. Wiman, 77 F.3d 981 (7th Cir. 1996); U.S. v. Blum, 65 F.3d 1436 (8th Cir. 1995); U.S. v. Birbal, 62 F.3d 456 (2d Cir. 1995).

[25]Rosenfeld v. Basquiat, 78 F.3d 84 (2d Cir. 1996).

[26]U.S. v. Collier, 527 F.3d 695, 699 (8th Cir. 2008) (the trial judge made a definitive ruling); U.S. v. McVeigh, 153 F.3d 1166, 1200 (10th Cir. 1998) ("A motion in limine will not preserve an objection if it is not renewed at the time the evidence is introduced unless 'the issue (1) is fairly presented to the district court, (2) is the type of issue that can be fairly decided in pretrial hearing, and (3) is ruled upon without equivocation by the trial judge' "); Pandit v. American Honda Motor Co., Inc., 82 F.3d 376 (10th Cir. 1996). See also Bradford & Wyrsch, Making the Record in the Trial Court, 64 J. Mo. Bar 284, 286 (Nov.-Dec. 2008) ("Trial counsel has the obligation to clarify whether an in limine ruling . . . is 'definitive' "). *But see* U.S. v. Lillie, 669 F. Supp. 2d 903, 906 (N.D. Ill. 2009); Euroholdings Capital & Inv. Corp. v. Harris Trust & Sav. Bank, 602 F. Supp. 2d 928, 935 (N.D. Ill. 2009) ("[T]he [in limine] ruling is subject to change when the case unfolds . . . . 'Indeed, even if nothing unexpected happens at trial, the district judge is free, in the exercise of sound judicial discretion, to alter a previous in limine ruling.").

. . . to clarify whether an in limine or other evidentiary ruling is definitive when there is doubt on that point."[27]

An in limine motion is distinguishable from a motion to suppress.[28] Suppression motions typically rest on constitutional grounds such as the Fourth Amendment exclusionary rule rather than statutory and common law evidence rules. Moreover, in most jurisdictions, the party must make suppression motions before trial under pain of waiver.[29] Further, if the suppression motion is timely, the judge ordinarily must dispose of it before trial. As previously stated, in the case of in limine motions, the judge usually[30] has discretion whether to rule on the merits of the motion before trial.

### General and Specific Objections[31]

To help the judge make an intelligent ruling on the merits, the opponent should make a specific objection. Specificity has three aspects: specificity as to grounds, part, and party.

*Specificity as to grounds.* Objections have to be accompanied by a definite statement of the grounds;[32] in other words, objections must reasonably indicate the appropriate rules of evidence relied on as reasons for the objections.[33] These objections are labeled "specific" objections in contrast to so-called general objections.

---

[27]U.S. v. Hargrove, 625 F.3d 170, 177 (4th Cir. 2010), cert. denied, 132 S. Ct. 292, 181 L. Ed. 2d 177 (2011); U.S. v. Parish, 606 F.3d 480, 485 (8th Cir. 2010); Micro Chemical, Inc. v. Lextron, Inc., 317 F.3d 1387 (Fed. Cir. 2003) ("Here, the district court made definitive rulings either before or at trial on all of the defendant's objections to Fiorito's testimony").

[28]See § 180 infra.

[29]See § 55 infra.

[30]*But see* U.S. v. Lubell, 301 F. Supp. 2d 88 (D. Mass. 2004) (in a limited class of cases, the judge is required to rule on the pretrial motion; a pretrial ruling is necessary only when the evidence needed to decide the motion is entirely segregable from questions of guilt or innocence; when the evidence is not completely segregable such as in cases where the evidence overlaps, the judge may postpone the ruling until trial unless the overlap is de minimis); People v. Patrick, 233 Ill. 2d 62, 330 Ill. Dec. 149, 908 N.E.2d 1 (2009) (citing Settles

v. State, 584 So. 2d 1260 (Miss. 1991), State v. McClure, 298 Or. 336, 692 P.2d 579 (1984), and State v. Ritchie, 144 Vt. 121, 473 A.2d 1164 (1984), the court notes that several jurisdictions recognize a general rule that a trial judge should not defer ruling on a defense motion challenging the admissibility of a defendant's conviction offered for purposes of impeachment; in order to make an intelligent decision whether to testify, the defendant needs to know whether the conviction will be admissible; in the instant case, the trial judge erred in deferring the ruling).

[31]1 Wigmore, Evidence § 18(c)(1)(2) (3d ed. 1940); 1 Weinstein's Federal Evidence § 103.12 (rev. 2011); West's Key Number Digest, Trial ⊕81 to 84.

[32]*See* Fed. and Unif. R. Evid. 103(a)(1). *See also, e.g.,* Craig v. Citizens Trust Co., 217 Ind. 434, 26 N.E.2d 1006 (1940).

[33]Ferguson v. Secretary for Dept. of Corrections, 580 F.3d 1183, 1212

The specificity requirement serves two important purposes at the trial level. First, the requirement helps to ensure that the trial judge understands the objection raised and that the adversary has a fair opportunity to remedy the defect, if possible.[34] However, the requirement for a specific objection does not *per se* ban the use of general trial objections (objections which state no distinct grounds).[35] When the evidence is objectionable on some ground, the judge has discretion to entertain and sustain a general objection. However, as we shall soon see, the requirement is enforced to a certain extent on appeal. The second purpose of the requirement is to make a proper record for the reviewing court in the event of an appeal.

If the judge *overrules* a general objection, on appeal the objecting party ordinarily may not attack the ruling by urging a ground not mentioned when the objection was made at trial.[36] Yet, there are three exceptional situations in which the appellate court will disregard this requirement and consider a meritorious objection that was not voiced to the trial judge. First, if the ground for exclusion should have been obvious to judge and the proponent, the lack of specification of the ground is immaterial for purpose of appealing the judge's action overruling the general objection.[37] This exception is simple good sense. Second, some courts hold that if the evidence is inadmissible for any purpose, a general

---

(11th Cir. 2009) ("Though 'magic words are not needed to make a proper objection,' counsel must articulate his concern with sufficient specificity 'to inform the trial judge of the alleged error' ").

[34]City of Yuma v. Evans, 85 Ariz. 229, 336 P.2d 135 (1959).

[35]Fed. R. Evid. 103(a)(1) does not ban the use of general objections at trial because the rule governs treatment of rulings on appeal and motions for new trial. *See also* Graham, Preserving Error for Appeal: Objections and Offers of Proof, 44 Crim. L. Bull. 609, 614–15 (July-Aug. 2008).

[36]Fed. R. Evid. 103(a)(1) embodies this general rule. For case law, see, *e.g.*, Reed v. Trainor, 142 Ind. App. 192, 233 N.E.2d 685 (1968).

[37]Restyled Fed. R. Evid. 103(a)(1) (error may not be predicated on a ruling admitting evidence absent a specific, timely objection "unless the [objection] was apparent from the context"); former Fed. and Unif. R.

Evid. 103(a)(1) (error may not be predicated upon a ruling admitting evidence unless a timely specific objection was made "if the specific ground was not apparent from the context"). Case law is to the same effect. Styblo v. McNeil, 317 Ill. App. 316, 45 N.E.2d 1011 (1st Dist. 1943) ("An objection, except where it is obvious, should be stated in such a manner as to inform the court of the point being urged."); Johnson v. Jackson, 43 Ill. App. 2d 251, 193 N.E.2d 485 (1st Dist. 1963) ("it is difficult to show that a particular defect cannot be cured or that the ground for objection is obvious;" held not obvious in this case); Floy v. Hibbard, 227 Iowa 149, 287 N.W. 829 (1939) (general objection sufficient "where the grounds of the objection are discernible").

On appeal, however, reliance on this doctrine may indicate oversight in failing to "protect the record" or ignorance of a supposedly apparent specific objection.

objection suffices to secure appellate review of the judge's overruling the objection.[38] This exception makes little sense if the
ground is not apparent; when the ground is not evident, there is
still a need for specification.[39] If the opponent had put the
proponent on notice of the dispute over the admissibility of the
evidence, the proponent might have substituted alternative proof
to establish the fact. Third, it has been suggested that if the
omitted ground could not have been obviated, a general objection
permits appellate consideration of an unstated, specific objection.[40]
The case for this exception overlooks an important consideration.
Assume arguendo that the objection to the particular evidence
could not have been obviated. Nevertheless, if the objection had
been stated and the proponent realized the validity of the objection, again the proponent might have withdrawn the inadmissible evidence and substituted other evidence to fill the gap.[41]
Fortunately, Federal Rule of Evidence 103(a)(1) does not codify
the third exception.[42]

The cumulative impact of the above rules is that the appellate
court typically upholds a trial judge's action in overruling a general objection. If the trial judge *sustains* a general objection, the
appellate court is again charitable to the trial judge's ruling.
"When evidence is *excluded* upon a mere general objection, the
ruling will be upheld, if any ground in fact existed for the
exclusion. It will be assumed, in the absence of any request by
the opposing party or the court to make the objection definite,
that it was understood, and that the ruling was placed upon the
right ground."[43]

---

[38]Granberry v. Gilbert, 276 Ala.
486, 163 So. 2d 641 (1964) (if illegal
for any purpose and incurable by other
evidence or by reframing question);
Scally v. Flannery, 292 Ill. App. 349,
11 N.E.2d 123 (4th Dist. 1937); State
ex rel. State Highway Commission v.
Rauscher Chevrolet Co., 291 S.W.2d
89 (Mo. 1956).

[39]The qualification arises from
the fact that some courts treat the
objection "I object" as raising a relevancy objection. See note 51 infra.

[40]Floy v. Hibbard, 227 Iowa 149,
287 N.W. 829 (1939); Smith v. Fine,
351 Mo. 1179, 175 S.W.2d 761 (1943).

[41]*See* Campbell v. Paschall, 132
Tex. 226, 121 S.W.2d 593 (Comm'n
App. 1938).

[42]Fed. and Unif. R. Evid. 103(a)
(1). *See* U.S. v. Ashton, 555 F.3d 1015,
1019 (D.C. Cir. 2009) ("when the party
offering evidence does not request that
the court clarify its decision to exclude
that evidence, a reviewing court will
sustain the exclusion on any ground
that the district court could have invoked").

[43]Tooley v. Bacon, 70 N.Y. 34, 37,
1877 WL 12006 (1877). *See* 1 Wigmore,
Evidence § 18. If the offering counsel
requests a statement of the specific
grounds for excluding the evidence,
the trial judge is obligated either to
furnish it himself or to require objecting counsel to furnish it. Colburn v.
Chicago, St. P., M. & O.R. Co., 109
Wis. 377, 85 N.W. 354 (1901). *See also*
U.S. v. Dwyer, 539 F.2d 924 (2d Cir.

Examples of general objections are "I object;"[44] objections on the ground that the evidence is "inadmissible,"[45] "illegal,"[46] "incompetent,"[47] "foundation,"[48] is not "proper" testimony,[49] or an objection "on all the grounds ever known or heard of."[50] One of the most overworked objections is the formula that the evidence is "incompetent, irrelevant and immaterial." Its rhythm and alliteration seduce some lawyers to employ it as a routine ritual. Courts frequently treat this formula as merely equivalent to the general objection,[51] "I object." As applied to evidence, the word "incompetent" means no more than inadmissible and thus does not state a ground of objection. However, although somewhat general in wording, the expression "irrelevant and immaterial" states a distinct, substantive ground for exclusion.[52] A requirement that the objector state specifically the reason why the evidence is irrelevant or immaterial, as some courts demand, can be unduly burdensome; it requires the opponent to prove a negative. It is more practical to consider the irrelevancy objection in this form as a specific objection with one qualification. The qualification is that if the judge has any doubt as to relevancy, before ruling she may ask the proponent to explain the purpose of the proof.[53]

To make a sufficiently specific objection, the opponent should name the generic evidentiary rule being violated: "calls for infor-

---

1976); U.S. v. Hibler, 463 F.2d 455 (9th Cir. 1972). If in doubt, offering counsel should follow this procedure. While in terms, Federal Rule 103(a) strictly applies only to saving error for review, its principal purpose is to promote precision and clarity of evidence rulings at trial. 1 Saltzburg, Martin & Capra, Federal Rules of Evidence Manual 103-5 (10th ed. 2011). The suggested procedure is available under the Federal Rules.

Once the general objection has been converted into a specific one, the later treatment of the objection should follow the rules prescribed for specific objections.

[44]See language in Bandera v. City of Quincy, 344 F.3d 47 (1st Cir. 2003) ("objection") and U.S. v. Hutcher, 622 F.2d 1083 (2d Cir. 1980). The wordings at notes 45-50 are clearly not specific objections for the purposes of Fed. R. Evid. 103(a)(1). See also notes 31 to 41 supra. Gerald v. Caterers, Inc., 382 S.W.2d 740 (Mo. Ct. App. 1964).

[45]Fowler v. Wallace, 131 Ind. 347, 31 N.E. 53 (1892).

[46]Johnston v. Johnston, 174 Ala. 220, 57 So. 450 (1912).

[47]Minchen v. Hart, 72 F. 294 (C.C.A. 8th Cir. 1896).

[48]U.S. v. Barker, 27 F.3d 1287, 1292 (7th Cir. 1994).

[49]Itasca Lumber Co. v. Martin, 230 F. 584 (C.C.A. 8th Cir. 1916).

[50]Johnston v. Clements, 25 Kan. 376, 1881 WL 834 (1881) (possibly a world's record).

[51]Vogel v. Sylvester, 148 Conn. 666, 174 A.2d 122 (1961) (objection on basis of irrelevancy); Goldfoot v. Lofgren, 135 Or. 533, 296 P. 843 (1931); West's Key Number Digest, Trial ⚏83(2).

[52]See 1 Graham, Handbook of Federal Evidence § 103:2 (7th ed. 2012). As to relevancy and materiality generally, see Ch. 16 infra.

[53]Ample authority for this approach is found in Fed. R. Civ. P. 46

mation protected by the attorney-client privilege," "lack of authentication," "not the best evidence," or "hearsay"—the level of specificity found in the phrasing of the titles of the various articles in the Federal Rules of Evidence. Under the prevailing view, it is unnecessary to be any more specific. From a tactical perspective, it is usually[54] undesirable to be more specific. If the opponent names the specific deficiency in the foundation, the opponent has in effect educated the proponent, and the proponent now knows exactly how to cure the defect in the foundation. However, a minority view requires the opponent to specify the missing foundational element.[55] This view has the advantage of forcing the opponent to get right to the point and thereby saving trial time. In the pretrial setting when the judge is ruling on an in limine motion, the judge is more likely to follow the minority view.[56] At trial, an objection can surface unexpectedly; and it is often impractical to insist that the opponent specify the precise deficiency in the proffered testimony. In contrast, when the context is pretrial, the opponent typically has more time to formulate a specific objection. Understandably, the judge demands more precise objections in the latter context.

While an "irrelevancy" objection has occasionally been held sufficient to preserve a claim of prejudice in the sense of arousing personal animus against the party,[57] that holding is questionable; that phrasing does not explicitly raise the policy concerns listed in Federal Rule 403.[58] Those concerns can easily be raised specifically, and a reference to one of those concerns does not require

---

and Fed. R. Crim. P. 51, supra § 51, note 23. At this stage, each party desires the court to act in her favor and is obliged to state her grounds.

[54]There are exceptions to that proposition. In most cases, after the judge sustains the objection, the proponent may rephrase. If the proponent does so, a prejudicial line of questioning can potentially continue. If the opponent wants to cut off the line of questioning, the opponent might: (1) make a very specific objection, identifying the deficiency in the proponent's foundation; and (2) assert that the deficiency is incurable. In this situation, the opponent sometimes asks for permission to approach sidebar and presents her argument outside the jury's hearing.

[55]U.S. v. Fendley, 522 F.2d 181 (5th Cir. 1975) (it is insufficient to object that evidence is inadmissible

hearsay; the opponent must specify that the evidence is inadmissible as a business entry because there is no evidence that it was the regular practice of the business to prepare this type of record); People v. Wright, 48 Cal. 3d 168, 255 Cal. Rptr. 853, 768 P.2d 72 (1989) ("although defendant made a general best-evidence-rule objection, he failed to object on foundational grounds to the prosecution's failure to establish the original writing was lost or destroyed"); People v. Dorsey, 43 Cal. App. 3d 953, 118 Cal. Rptr. 362 (5th Dist. 1974).

[56]Imwinkelried, The Pretrial Importance and Adaptation of the "Trial" Evidence Rules, 25 Loy. L.A. L. Rev. 965, 983–84 (1992).

[57]E.g., Hungate v. Hudson, 353 Mo. 944, 185 S.W.2d 646 (1945).

[58]Grounds for objection available under Rule 403 include "unfair preju-

the opponent to establish a negative.[59] The judge should demand that the opponent cite Rule 403 or identify a probative danger mentioned in Rule 403. By the same token, many courts hold that a "hearsay" objection is insufficient to raise a Sixth Amendment Confrontation Clause objection.[60]

In the above cases, the judge pressures the objecting party to be more specific. In other cases, though, the objector faces exactly the opposite problem: the judge might make it difficult for the attorney to verbalize a sufficiently specific objection to make the record for appeal. As we shall see, the trial judge has a right to preclude "speaking" objections, in which under the guise of objecting the objector endeavors to make a speech to the jury. In an effort to prevent a speaking objection, the trial judge sometimes unduly interferes with the attorney's ability to articulate a complete objection satisfactory to the appellate court. When the record shows that the trial judge is responsible for the generality of the objection stated in the court below, the appellate courts are more liberal in deciding whether the objection was sufficiently specific with respect to ground.

A variation of the problem of specificity as to ground arises when an evidentiary rule limits the purposes for which an item of evidence may be admitted. Assume that evidence offered is properly admissible on a particular issue but not upon some other issue, or is admissible against one party but not against another.[61] Here, although she assigns grounds, an objector who simply asks that this evidence be excluded cannot complain on appeal if her objection is overruled. Instead, she should request that the admission of the evidence be limited to the particular purpose or party.[62]

*Specificity as to part.* Objections ought to be specific not only

---

dice, confusing the issues, misleading the jury, undue delay, wasting time, or needlessly presenting cumulative evidence." *See* U.S. v. Eagle, 515 F.3d 794, 803 (8th Cir. 2008); U.S. v. Adkins, 196 F.3d 1112, 1116 n.3 (10th Cir. 1999) (a "relevance" objection did not raise a Rule 403 issue); § 185 infra.

[59]Of the objections listed in Rule 403, note 58 supra, only the first three are likely candidates for success on review.

[60]U.S. v. Cabrera-Beltran, 660 F.3d 742, 751 (4th Cir. 2011), cert. denied, 132 S. Ct. 1935, 182 L. Ed. 2d 775 (2012); U.S. v. Meises, 645 F.3d 5 (1st Cir. 2011). *See also* Saltzburg, The Right Objection, 25 Crim.Just., Wint.

2011, at 54 (discussing the relationship between the hearsay and lack of personal knowledge objections).

[61]*Issues.* Finley v. Smith, 240 Ark. 323, 399 S.W.2d 271 (1966); Curtin v. Benjamin, 305 Mass. 489, 26 N.E.2d 354 (1940); West's Key Number Digest, Trial ⌐86.

*Parties.* Solomon v. Dabrowski, 295 Mass. 358, 3 N.E.2d 744 (1936); West's Key Number Digest, Trial ⌐87.

If such a limitation is not requested, the objection lacks the specificity mandated by Rule 103(a)(1).

[62]Finley v. Smith, note 61 supra; Walls v. Clark, 252 Or. 414, 449 P.2d 141 (1969) (parties).

with regard to the ground, but also with respect to the particular part of an offer. Suppose that evidence sought to be introduced consists of several statements or items tendered as a unit in a deposition, letter, conversation, or trial transcript. Assume that the opponent objects to the whole of the evidence when some parts are subject to the objection made but other parts are not. In this situation, the judge does not err by overruling the objection.[63] It is not the judge's responsibility to sever the bad parts if some are good.[64] That is the opponent's burden. Obviously this rule should not be administered rigidly by the appellate courts; rather, the courts ought to apply the rule realistically with a sensitivity to the realities of the particular trial situation.

*Specificity as to party.* When the counsel represents only one party at trial, she is obviously claiming that the evidence is inadmissible against her client. However, when counsel appears on behalf of multiple clients at the same trial, the evidence might be admissible as against one but inadmissible as against the other. In this situation, counsel runs the risk of waiving the objection if she does not identify the client whom the evidence is inadmissible against.

Assume that the opponent makes an objection that lacks specificity with respect to ground, part, or party. On appeal, the court will uphold the *overruling* of an untenable specific objection even if there was a tenable ground for exclusion which was not urged in the trial court.[65] In an adversary system of litigation, it is the opponent's responsibility to specifically articulate a justifiable basis for excluding the proponent's evidence.

---

[63]U.S. v. McGrath, 622 F.2d 36 (2d Cir. 1980); Clayton v. Prudential Ins. Co. of America, 4 N.C. App. 43, 165 S.E.2d 763 (1969) (an objection to letter as a whole was insufficient although part was inadmissible on hearsay and opinion grounds); Jacobson v. Bryan, 244 Wis. 359, 12 N.W.2d 789 (1944) (part of a traffic officer's report of accident was based on personal knowledge, but another part was not; an objection to whole report was insufficient); West's Key Number Digest, Trial ⟨⟩85.

[64]An objection which fails to separate out the objectionable part as the target of the objection lacks the specificity mandated by Rule 103(a)(1). *See* United States v. McGrath, note 60 supra; Wright and Miller's Federal Practice and Procedure, Evidence § 5036. *See also* Mucci v. LeMonte, 157

Conn. 566, 254 A.2d 879 (1969). The judge may sustain the objection without error, since he has no duty to separate the good from the bad. See § 51 supra.

[65]This is the result both at common law and under Fed. and Unif. R. Evid. 103(a)(1). An untenable specific objection is the same as no objection at all. Gray v. Lucas, 677 F.2d 1086, 1099 n.13 (5th Cir. 1982) (hearsay claim not considered on appeal because not raised below); U.S. v. Brady, 595 F.2d 359 (6th Cir. 1979); U.S. v. Ruffin, 575 F.2d 346, 355 (2d Cir. 1978) (objection below of irrelevancy did not support an appellate claim of hearsay); People ex rel. Blackmon v. Brent, 97 Ill. App. 2d 438, 240 N.E.2d 255 (1st Dist. 1968); State v. Dietz, 115 N.W.2d 1 (N.D. 1962).

When an untenable specific objection is *sustained,* there is authority that the appellate court will uphold the ruling if there is any other ground for doing so, even though the ground was not cited below.[66] There is no point in ordering a retrial if the evidence would have to be excluded on the proper ground. However, some qualifications are necessary. When the correct objection, had it been made, could have been obviated,[67] or admissible evidence could have been substituted, a retrial is appropriate. If a ruling on the proper objection at the second trial would involve the judge's discretion, again a new trial is appropriate unless the judge determines that on remand her discretion would be exercised in favor of exclusion.[68] A similar result should follow where findings of fact are required as a preliminary to determining admissibility.[69]

### *Repetition of Objections*

A offers one witness's testimony which his adversary, B, thinks is inadmissible. B objects, and the objection is *sustained.* In that event, when A offers similar testimony by the same or another witness, B must repeat her objection if she is to complain about the later evidence.[70] Suppose, however, the first objection is *overruled.* Must B repeat her objection when other similarly objectionable evidence is offered? A few decisions intimate that she must[71]—a requirement which wastes time and casts B in the unenviable role of an obstructionist in the jurors' eyes. However, most courts sensibly hold that B is entitled to assume that the judge will continue to make the same ruling and she need not repeat the objection.[72] The logical consequences of this view are that the first objection is not waived by the objector's subsequent

---

[66]*See* 1 Wigmore, Evidence § 18 at 345 (3d ed. 1940).

[67]*See* Morgan, Basic Problems in Evidence 54 (1962).

[68]*See* Saltzburg, Another Ground for Decision—Harmless Trial Court Errors, 47 Temple L.Q. 193 (1974). This reasoning would apply if, at the hearing on a new trial motion after the first hearing, the judge realized that there is a tenable specific objection to the evidence.

[69]Saltzburg, Another Ground for Decision–Harmless Trial Court Errors, 47 Temple L.Q. 193 (1974).

[70]Frost v. Goddard, 25 Me. 414, 1845 WL 1274 (1845); Wagner v. Jones, 77 N.Y. 590, 1879 WL 12215 (1879).

The instant rule is embodied in Fed. R. Evid. 103(a)(1) and Unif. R. Evid. 103(a)(1).

[71]Shelton v. Southern Ry. Co., 193 N.C. 670, 139 S.E. 232 (1927).

[72]Tucker v. Reil, 51 Ariz. 357, 77 P.2d 203 (1938); West–Nesbitt, Inc. v. Randall, 126 Vt. 481, 236 A.2d 676 (1967); West's Key Number Digest, Trial ⟨key⟩79; Ladd, Common Mistakes in the Technique of Trial, 22 Iowa L. Rev. 609, 612–17 (1937).

The "continuing objection" is not specifically mentioned by Fed. and Unif. R. Evid. 103(a)(1). The federal Advisory Committee's Note indicates it is authorized by its reference to California Code § 353. *See* Wright and Miller's Federal Practice and Proce-

conduct and that in addition, the reach of this objection extends to all subsequent, similar evidence vulnerable to the same objection. In any jurisdiction where the law on this point is at all unsettled, it is a wise precaution for objecting counsel to ask the judge to have the record reflect a "running" or "continuing" objection, going to all other like evidence.[73]

## The Exception[74]

Closely associated with the objection but distinct from it was the classic common law exception;[75] if the objector disagreed with the judge's overruling of the objection, the objector had to "except"

---

dure, Evidence § 5037. *Accord* U.S. v. Lynn, 608 F.2d 132 (5th Cir. 1979); Squyres v. Hilliary, 599 F.2d 918 (10th Cir. 1979).

[73]U.S. v. Roach, 164 F.3d 403, 410 (8th Cir. 1998) ("A standing objection may be appropriate to cover the same recurring issue, but it cannot protect a party where there are distinct foundation questions involved"); U.S. v. Fortenberry, 919 F.2d 923 (5th Cir. 1990); State v. Guloy, 104 Wash. 2d 412, 705 P.2d 1182 (1985) (counsel requested continuing objection). Reliance on a continuing objection can be risky. *See* U.S. v. McVeigh, 153 F.3d 1166 (10th Cir. 1998) (continuing objections are generally considered inappropriate for Rule 403 challenges, since the probativity/prejudice balance can vary from question to question); Hall v. State, 119 Md. App. 377, 705 A.2d 50 (1998) (a continuing objection "is effective only as to questions clearly within its scope").

[74]1 Wigmore, Evidence § 20 (3d ed. 1940); West's Key Number Digest, Trial ☞99 to 104, 105.

[75]The function and procedure of bills of exception are described in Green, Basic Civil Procedure 254–55 (2d ed. 1979):

. . . [T]he only function of the appellate court was to review alleged errors of law, and in so doing it was confined to the common law record which consisted of the writ (summons), the return, pleadings, verdict and judgment. The court could not review the facts since they were the sole province of the jury, and furthermore no record of the

testimony was kept. Consequently the scope of review was very narrow, at least until the year 1285 when Parliament passed the famous Statute of Westminster II which, among other things, provided for Bills of Exceptions. The purpose of a Bill of Exceptions was to bring before the appellate court for review matters which otherwise would not appear on the common law record due to the fact that there were no court reporters to record the testimony and the proceedings at the trial. This was before the days of shorthand and recording devices. After the Statute of Westminster II if a litigant believed the court had erred in a ruling, he could make it a matter of record by "saving his exception." For example, if counsel had objected to a question asked of a witness and the court had overruled the objection and counsel thought the ruling was erroneous, he could say, "If the court please, I desire to save an exception to your honor's ruling." The judge was then obliged to stop the trial and call the scrivener who, with his quill pen, would make a record on parchment which would read something like the following: (after giving the caption of the case) "Elmer Zilch, a witness sworn in the above entitled case, was asked the following question, 'Have you stopped beating your wife?' to which counsel for the defendant objected on the ground the question was improper because an answer either way would incriminate him; whereupon, after argument the court overruled the objection, to which ruling the defendant duly saved his exception." When this document was completed, it would be signed by the judge. During the course of the trial numerous exceptions might be "saved." At the conclusion of the trial they

to the ruling on the record to preserve the issue for purpose of appeal. The federal rules and the practice in most states dispense with exceptions, and provide that for all purposes, "it is sufficient to 'inform[ ] the court—when the court ruling or order is made or sought—of the action the party wishes the court to take, or the party's objection to the court's action and the grounds for that objection."[76] Nevertheless, for motivations such as a desire to impress a jury, some attorneys persist in announcing that they "except" to rulings at jury trials even in jurisdictions where exceptions are unnecessary. These attorneys do so at the risk of irritating the trial judge—and having the trial judge admonish them in the jury's hearing.

### The Tactics of Objecting

Jurors want to know the facts. They may resent objections as attempts to hide the facts, and view sustained objections as the successful suppression of the truth.[77] If this description of the jury's attitude is accurate, certain conclusions as to desirable tactics follow.

Even when a question is technically objectionable, the opponent should not object unless making the objection will do more good than harm. Conduct a cost/benefit analysis. In some situations, an objection can be counterproductive. Objections to leading questions or opinion evidence frequently result in strengthening the examiner's case by requiring her to elicit the testimony in more concrete, convincing form.[78] In a given case, an authentication, best evidence, or hearsay objection can have the same result and backfire. Further, if an objection has little chance of being sustained at trial or on appeal, it usually should not be made. An

---

would be bound together and certified by the trial judge as the Bill of Exceptions in the case, and they would be attached to and become a part of the record on appeal. Today, with modern methods of court reporting, this antiquated method of preserving a record has become obsolete and court rules make "exceptions" unnecessary. (Footnotes omitted.)

[76]Fed. R. Crim. P. 51(b). The analogous provision in the Federal Rules of Civil Procedure, Rule 46, refers to "the action that it wants the court to take or objects to, along with the ground for the request or objection."

[77]See general discussion in Keeton, Trial Tactics and Methods 166–90 (2d ed. 1973); Mauet, Trial Techniques § 10.3, at 449-50 (8th ed. 2010); Carlson & Imwinkelried, Dynamics of Trial Practice § 6.3, at 170–71 (4th ed. 2010). The National Law Journal and LEXIS funded a large survey of juror attitudes. The researchers reported:

> When a lawyer made an objection, 46 percent of the jurors thought the lawyer was trying to hide something the jurors felt would have been helpful to know. . . . Young jurors were particularly suspicious of objections—59% of those in the 18–34 age group thought that lawyers had something to hide.

Panelists Give Tip to Lawyers, Nat'l L.J., Feb. 22, 1993.

[78]Ladd, Common Mistakes in the Technique of Trial, 22 Iowa L. Rev. 609, 617 (1937).

unsuccessful objection may succeed only in magnifying the importance of unfavorable evidence; the jurors might think that the opponent must have thought that the evidence was damning because he went to the length of trying to exclude it. Objections ought to be few in number, and they should target only evidence which will do substantial harm to the objector's theory of the case.[79]

Finally, when objections are made in the jury's presence, the objector's demeanor and the phrasing of the objection are important. An objection ought to be phrased to prevent the objection from sounding as if it rests exclusively on some technical rule.[80] Thus, an objection to a copy under the best evidence rule should not be stated solely in terms of "secondary evidence" but should also mention the unreliability of an incomplete copy. Likewise, the objection "hearsay" ought to be expanded to mention the need to produce the declarant so that the jury can see him and evaluate his credibility. The art of making effective objections at a jury trial consists in adding a short adjective, adverb, or phrase which signals the jury that the ground of the objection relates to substantive justice. However, most judges do not tolerate lengthy "speaking" objections. If a counsel is foolish enough to attempt such an objection, the judge might admonish counsel in the jury's hearing.

### Withdrawal of Evidence

The Federal and Uniform Rules of Evidence do not deal explicitly with the subject of withdrawal of evidence. However, reasonably construed, Rule 611(a) permits withdrawal as an aspect of the court's discretionary control over the presentation of evidence. The discretion could be exercised in accordance with the principles historically recognized in the case law. The cases sometimes imply that if a party has introduced evidence which is not objected to and which turns out to be favorable to the adversary, the offering party may withdraw the evidence as of right.[81] The accepted rule, however, is that withdrawal is not of right. Rather, the adversary is entitled to have the benefit of the

---

[79]Lane, Goldstein Trial Technique § 13:8 (3d ed.).

[80]See examples of objections in Busch, Law and Tactics in Jury Trials §§ 488, 492 (1949); Keeton, Trial Tactics and Methods 210–15 (2d ed. 1973); Mauet, Trial Techniques Ch. 10 (8th ed. 2010); Bright, Carlson &

Imwinkelried, Objections at Trial (5th ed. 2008); Imwinkelried, Evidentiary Foundations § 2.03[3], at 17-18 (8th ed. 2012).

[81]See Young v. U.S., 97 F.2d 200, 205 (C.C.A. 5th Cir. 1938), and Note, 17 Tex. L. Rev. 373, 374 (1939).

testimony,[82] unless exceptional facts make it fair for the judge in her discretion to allow withdrawal.[83] However, if the evidence is admitted over the adversary's objection, and the proponent later decides to yield to the objection and asks to withdraw the evidence, the court may revoke its ruling and permit the withdrawal.[84]

### Plain Error Rule

Many of the criteria for so-called "plain error" and "harmful error" (as opposed to harmless error) are similar. Yet, the two concepts should be distinguished. Like Uniform Rule of Evidence 103(a), restyled Federal Rule Evidence 103(a) codifies the "harmless error" concept with the statement, "A party may claim error only if the error affects a substantial right of the party . . . ." Thus, only harmful errors warrant relief. Plain error is defined in restyled Rule 103(e): "A court may take notice of a plain error even if the claim of error was not properly preserved." In contrast to harmful error, harmless error denotes a ruling which is incorrect but which is not cause for reversal. Plain error denotes a harmful error that is sufficiently serious to justify considering it on appeal despite the opponent's failure to observe the usual procedures for preserving error for review.[85]

There are several key distinctions between plain and harmful error. To begin with, there is a difference in degree between harmful and plain error. For error to be harmful, the error must be prejudicial to the appellant; but for plain error, the error must have *very* prejudicial effects.[86] To qualify as plain error, the error

---

[82]Page v. Payne, 293 Mo. 600, 240 S.W. 156 (1922) (defendant had no right to withdraw parts of documents introduced by him); Looman Realty Corp. v. Broad St. Nat. Bank of Trenton, 74 N.J. Super. 71, 180 A.2d 524 (App. Div. 1962) (no withdrawal unless evidence irrelevant or immaterial); 1 Wigmore, Evidence § 17c (3d ed. 1940); West's Key Number Digest, Trial ⊕58.

[83]Maas v. Laursen, 219 Minn. 461, 18 N.W.2d 233, 235 (1945) (withdrawal is discretionary; it may be allowed if evidence irrelevant or if favorable only to withdrawing party; court here did not err in denying withdrawal).

[84]Alabama Great Southern R. Co. v. Hardy, 131 Ga. 238, 62 S.E. 71, 72

(1908); McCarty v. Bishop, 231 Mo. App. 604, 102 S.W.2d 126 (1937) (evidence may be withdrawn in the court's discretion despite a protest by the opposing party).

[85]*See* 1 Weinstein's Federal Evidence § 103.42 (rev. 2011) (exclusion without a proper offer of proof may be plain error); Adv.Com. Note, Fed. R. Evid. 103(d).

[86]*E.g.*, U. S. v. Frady, 456 U.S. 152, 163, 102 S. Ct. 1584, 71 L. Ed. 2d 816 (1982) ("particularly egregious errors"); U.S. v. Atkinson, 297 U.S. 157, 160, 56 S. Ct. 391, 80 L. Ed. 555 (1936) ("seriously affect the fairness, integrity or public reputation of judicial proceedings"); U.S. v. Douglas, 818 F.2d 1317, 1320 (7th Cir. 1987) ("such a great magnitude that it probably

must be a "blockbuster."[87] Harmful error is the genus, and plain error is the species. Moreover, to trigger the plain error doctrine, the error must create a risk of a miscarriage of substantive justice.[88] Some exclusionary rules of evidence bar the admission of relevant, reliable evidence in order to promote an extrinsic social policy. While those rules are certainly legitimate, it may be difficult to persuade an appellate court that a ruling admitting relevant, trustworthy evidence was likely to cause justice to miscarry. Despite the fundamental theoretical distinctions between the two concepts, surprisingly little difference can be found in the way the harmful and plain error concepts are applied in the published opinions.[89]

The published opinions clearly demonstrate the appellate courts' hesitancy to overturn the trial judge's evidentiary decisions.[90] There are many reasons for that hesitancy. The appellate courts are loathe to second guess the trial judge who usually has a better feel for the case.[91] Moreover, appellants frequently fail to marshal facts demonstrating that the alleged error was prejudicial.[92] This judicial reluctance is evident even in criminal cases.[93] However, a holding of plain error is far more likely in cases involving the constitutional rights of criminal defendants.[94] Reversals on the basis of plain error are much less

---

changed the outcome of the trial").

[87]U.S. v. Olivo-Infante, 938 F.2d 1406 (1st Cir. 1991).

[88]U.S. v. Shorty, 159 F.3d 312, 313 (7th Cir. 1998); U.S. v. Yamin, 868 F.2d 130 (5th Cir. 1989); U.S. v. Solomon, 856 F.2d 1572 (11th Cir. 1988).

[89]Wright and Miller's Federal Practice and Procedure, Criminal § 856 ("Indeed the cases have given the distinct impression that 'plain error' is a concept appellate courts find impossible to define, save that they know it when they see it.").

[90]Berger, When, If Ever, Does Evidentiary Error Constitute Reversible Error?, 25 Loy. L.A. L. Rev. 893 (1992); Swift, The Hearsay Rule at Work: Has It Been Abolished De Facto by Judicial Decision?, 76 Minn. L. Rev. 473 (1992).

[91]Of course, the trial judge may object or suggest objections to the at-

torney. See § 55 infra.

[92]1 Weinstein's Federal Evidence § 103.42 (rev. 2011), quoting Sykes v. U.S., 373 F.2d 607 (5th Cir. 1966); Graham, Preliminary Questions of Admissibility, Fed. R. Evid. 103 and 104; Motions in Limine, 44 Crim. L. Bull. 108 (Jan.-Feb. 2008).

[93]See cases cited in Wright and Miller's Federal Practice and Procedure, Evidence § 5036; Berger, When, If Ever, Does Evidentiary Error Constitute Reversible Error?, 25 Loy. L.A. L. Rev. 893 (1990). But there are many cases in which plain error was cause for reversal. See sources cited in note 114 supra.

[94]Chapman v. California, 386 U.S. 18, 87 S. Ct. 824, 17 L. Ed. 2d 705 (1967) indicates that "before a federal constitutional error can be harmless, the court must be able to declare a belief that it was harmless beyond a reasonable doubt . . . "

common in civil suits than in criminal cases, in part because liberty and life are not at stake in a civil action.[95]

The application of the plain error doctrine depends upon a fact intensive, case specific analysis.[96] Findings of plain error are not only rarities; they also have very limited precedential value.

## § 53 Preliminary questions of fact arising on objections[1]

Most evidentiary rules operate to exclude relevant evidence.[2] Examples are the hearsay doctrine, the rule preferring original writings, and the privileges for confidential communications. All these exclusionary rules are "technical" in the sense that they were developed by a special professional group, judges and lawyers, and in the further sense that for long-term ends they sometimes obstruct the ascertainment of truth in the particular case. Most of these technical exclusionary rules and their exceptions are conditioned on the existence of certain facts. These are not the facts on the historical merits of the case under Federal Rule of Evidence 401. Rather, these are foundational, preliminary, or predicate facts falling under Rule 104. For example, a copy of a writing will not be received unless the original is lost, destroyed, or otherwise unavailable.[3] Suppose a copy is offered and there is conflicting evidence as to whether the original is destroyed or intact. It is, of course, the judge who decides that there is a rule of evidence law establishing the criterion of admission or exclusion. However, who decides whether the original is lost, destroyed or unavailable—the preliminary question of fact on which the *application* of the rule of evidence law hinges?

Procedural law usually assigns "issues of fact" to the jury, but there are strong reasons for not doing so here. If the special question of fact were submitted to the jury when objection was made, cumbersome problems about unanimity would arise. More

---

[95]In civil cases, reversal for plain error is rare. 1 Mueller & Kirkpatrick, Federal Evidence § 1:22 (3d ed. 2007). The Federal Rules of Criminal Procedure contain a plain error rule, Fed. R. Crim. P. 52(b), but the Federal Rules of Civil Procedure do not.

[96]*E.g.*, 1 Weinstein's Federal Evidence § 103.42 (rev. 2011).

**[Section 53]**

[1]9 Wigmore, Evidence § 2550 (Chadbourn rev. 1981); 1 Weinstein's Federal Evidence Ch. 104 (rev. 2011); Maguire, Evidence: Common Sense and Common Law 211–30 (1947); Maguire and Epstein, Preliminary Questions of Fact, 40 Harv. L. Rev. 392 (1927); Morgan, Functions of Judge and Jury in Preliminary Questions, 43 Harv. L. Rev. 165 (1929); West's Key Number Digest, Trial ⬤138; West's Key Number Digest, Criminal Law ⬤736.

[2]"And chiefly it [the law of evidence] determines as among probative matters . . . what classes of things shall not be received. This excluding function is the characteristic one in our law of evidence." Thayer, Preliminary Treatise on Evidence 264 (1898).

[3]See § 230 infra.

importantly, if the judge submitted the evidence (such as the copy in the hypothetical) to the jury and directed them to disregard it unless they found that the disputed fact existed, the aim of the exclusionary rule might be frustrated for two reasons. First, the jury would often be unable to erase the evidence from their minds even after, at a conscious level, they found that the conditioning fact did not exist. For instance, even if the jury found that an accused's statement to his attorney was technically privileged and inadmissible, common sense suggests that they would have a difficult time forgetting that they had learned that the accused admitted committing the charged offense. Second, some jurors might be unwilling to perform the mental gymnastic of "disregarding" the evidence. They are primarily intent on reaching a verdict in accord with what they believe to be true, rather than in promoting the long-term policies of evidence law. The law-trained judge appreciates that the policy of protecting privacy interests justifies enforcing privileges, but the lay jurors might view a privilege unfavorably as an impediment to their tasks to find the truth and do justice in the case before them.

### *Foundational Facts Conditioning the Application of Technical Exclusionary Rules*

Accordingly, under the traditional and still generally accepted view, the trial judge finally decides the preliminary questions of fact conditioning the admissibility of evidence objected to under exclusionary rules such as the hearsay doctrine.[4] This principle is

---

[4]The following situations are illustrative. Bartlett v. Smith, 1843 WL 5781 (U.K. Ex Ct 1843) (the question whether bill drawn in London or Dublin, which conditioned its admissibility under the Stamp Act should have been decided by judge instead of submitting it to jury); Sylvania Elec. Products, Inc. v. Flanagan, 352 F.2d 1005 (1st Cir. 1965) (under the best evidence rule, the judge must decide that the original has become unavailable); W.A. Manda v. City of Orange, 82 N.J.L. 686, 82 A. 869 (N.J. Ct. Err. & App. 1912) (in an eminent domain proceeding, evidence of prices paid for other properties admissible if the other properties are substantially the property being condemned; the question of whether there is sufficient similarity should be decided by the judge); State v. Maynard, 184 N.C. 653, 113 S.E. 682 (1922) (the issue was the admissibility in criminal case of witness's former testimony; the judge properly decided and refused to submit to jury the preliminary question whether the defendant had procured the witness's absence); Potter v. Baker, 162 Ohio St. 488, 55 Ohio Op. 389, 124 N.E.2d 140 (1955) (accuracy of words testified to and nature of occurrence are preliminary questions for judge in deciding admissibility of spontaneous exclamations under hearsay exception).

If reasonably supported by the evidence, his decision will not be reversed. Smith v. U.S., 106 F.2d 726 (C.C.A. 4th Cir. 1939) (sufficiency of showing of unavailability, where witness temporarily ill); People v. Centers, 56 Cal. App. 2d 631, 133 P.2d 29 (2d Dist. 1943) (sufficiency of showing of diligence in search for absent witness).

incorporated in Federal and Uniform Rule of Evidence 104(a).[5] The same practice extends to the determination of preliminary facts conditioning the application of the rules as to witnesses' competency[6] and privileges.[7] On all these preliminary questions, on request the judge will hold a hearing at which each side may

---

Determinations are reviewed on appeal under the clearly erroneous standard. U.S. v. Wilson, 798 F.2d 509 (1st Cir. 1986); U.S. v. Pecora, 798 F.2d 614 (3d Cir. 1986).

    See § 162 infra, for rules concerning the admission of a criminal defendant's confession.

[5]Former Fed. and Unif. R. Evid. 104(a) provide:

> Preliminary questions concerning the qualification of a person to be a witness, the existence of a privilege, or the admissibility of evidence shall be determined by the court, subject to the provisions of subdivision (b). In making its determination it is not bound by the rules of evidence except those with respect to privileges.

    Effective December 1, 2011, Fed. R. Evid. 104(a) reads:

> In General. The court must decide any preliminary question about whether a witness is qualified, a privilege exists, or evidence is admissible. In so deciding, the court is not bound by evidence rules, except those on privilege.

Subdivision (b) of Federal Rule 104, to which reference is made, states a special rule for so-called "conditionally relevant" evidence. See text accompanying note 13, infra.

    The Uniform Rules now include a special provision for the determination of privileges. Subdivision 104(b) reads:

> A person claiming a privilege must prove that the conditions prerequisite to the existence of the privilege are more probably true than not. A person claiming an exception to a privilege must prove that the conditions prerequisite to the applicability of the exception are more probably true than not. If there is a factual basis to support a good faith belief that a review of the allegedly privileged material is necessary, the court, in making its determi-

nation, may review the material outside the presence of any other person.

[6]Bell v. State, 164 Ga. 292, 138 S.E. 238 (1927) (the issue of the competency of nine-year-old boy as witness was for judge, and it was error to submit the issue to jury); Moosbrugger v. Swick, 86 N.J.L. 419, 92 A. 269 (N.J. Sup. Ct. 1914) (the question of whether assignor of claim sued on had assigned in good faith and hence escaped incompetency under Dead Man's Act was for judge).

    Unless the witness's competency is determined under state law in connection with testimony relating to an element of a claim or defense as to which state law supplies the rule of decision, Fed. R. Evid. 601 will rarely raise a matter of competency. However, an expert's qualification to testify pursuant to Fed. R. Evid. 702 is a matter to be decided by the judge. *E.g.*, U.S. v. Haro-Espinosa, 619 F.2d 789 (9th Cir. 1979).

[7]Robinson v. U.S., 144 F.2d 392 (C.C.A. 6th Cir. 1944) (attorney-client communications); Phelps Dodge Corporation v. Guerrero, 273 F. 415 (C.C.A. 9th Cir. 1921) (physician-patient privilege). The last case holds that the burden of proof for the facts of privilege is on the party asserting the privilege.

    Whether common law principles or state law govern privileges under Fed. R. Evid. 501, Rule 104(a) assures the result in the text. In 1999, Uniform Rule of Evidence 104(b) was amended to read:

> Determination of privilege. A person claiming a privilege must prove that the conditions prerequisite to the existence of the privilege are more probable true than not. A person claiming an exception to a privilege must prove

produce evidence.[8] When the opponent objects, she can request

that the conditions prerequisite to the applicability of the exception are more probably true than not. If there is a factual basis to support a good faith belief that a review of the allegedly privileged material is necessary, the court, in making its determination, may review the material outside the presence of any other person.

Simpson & Huang, Procedural Rules Governing the Admissibility of Evidence, 54 Okla. L. Rev. 513, 523 (2001).

[8]What should be the burden of proof, the required measure of persuasion, at the hearing? The Federal and Revised Uniform Rules (1974) are silent. The most commonly accepted standard is the preponderance of the evidence, i.e., more probably true than not true. U.S. v. Enright, 579 F.2d 980 (6th Cir. 1978) (introduction of statement of co-conspirator); Admissibility of statement by coconspirator under Rule 801(d)(2)(E) of Federal Rules of Evidence, 44 A.L.R. Fed. 627. The Supreme Court held in Lego v. Twomey, 404 U.S. 477, 92 S. Ct. 619, 30 L. Ed. 2d 618 (1972), that even a confession's voluntariness as a constitutional matter need be established by only a preponderance of the evidence. In view of the strict precautions surrounding the admission of confessions, it is highly unlikely that a higher standard would be required in other situations. However, while the national constitution prescribes a floor, it does not set the ceiling. Hence, it is open to the states to choose to impose more rigorous standards. A persuasive argument has been made that the standard should depend in all situations, as well as in those involving constitutional issues, on the type of case, the purpose of the rule giving rise to the preliminary fact question, and whether the rule relates to the reliability of the evidence. Saltzburg, Standards of Proof and Preliminary Questions of Fact, 27 Stan. L. Rev. 271 (1975). However, the United States Supreme Court disagrees. According to the Court, Fed.

R. Evid. 104(a) issues are determined by the judge in all cases applying the preponderance of the evidence standard, i.e., more probably true than not true. Bourjaily v. U.S., 483 U.S. 171, 173–77, 107 S. Ct. 2775, 97 L. Ed. 2d 144 (1987) ("We are therefore guided by our prior decisions regarding admissibility determinations that hinge on preliminary factual questions. We have traditionally required that these matters by established by a preponderance of proof. Evidence is placed before the jury when it satisfies the technical requirements of the evidentiary Rules, which embody certain legal and policy determinations. The inquiry made by a court concerned with these matters is not whether the proponent of the evidence wins or loses his case on the merits, but whether the evidentiary Rules have been satisfied. Thus, the evidentiary standard is unrelated to the burden of proof on the substantive issues, be it a criminal case, see In re Winship, 397 U.S. 358 (1970), or a civil case. . . . Therefore, we hold that when the preliminary facts relevant to Rule 801(d)(2)(E) are disputed, the offering party must prove them by a preponderance of the evidence.").

As a general proposition, the proponent of the evidence has the burden of establishing the preliminary facts, but the opposing party has the burden of producing evidence to show the existence of grounds for objection otherwise. Wright and Miller's Federal Practice and Procedure, Evidence § 5053. The allocation of burdens on constitutional issues is discussed in § 180 infra.

As to keeping preliminary fact matter from coming to the jury's attention, Fed. R. Evid. 104(c) provides:

Hearings on the admissibility of confessions shall in all cases be conducted out of the hearing of the jury. Hearings on other preliminary matters shall be so conducted when the interests of justice so require or, when an accused is a witness and so requests.

Unif. R. Evid. 104(d) is identical in

the opportunity to conduct voir dire in support of the objection.[9] In effect, the voir dire is a mini cross-examination. During the voir dire, the opponent questions the witness solely about the foundational fact which the proponent attempted to establish. Between the proponent's foundation and the opponent's voir dire, the judge hears all the testimony both pro and con on the foundational issue. The judge acts as a factfinder in determining the existence of the foundational fact.[10] The judge may consider the credibility of the foundational testimony. Hence, the judge can decide to disbelieve the proponent's testimony even if it is facially sufficient.

### Foundational Facts Conditioning the Logical Relevance of the Evidence

The preceding discussion involves situations where the evidence is sought to be excluded under a "technical" exclusionary rule. Those situations must be distinguished from another type of situation, namely one in which the logical relevancy—the fundamental probative value—of the evidence depends on the existence of a preliminary fact. As the Advisory Committee's Note to Federal Rule of Evidence 104(b) observes:

> Thus when a spoken statement is relied upon to prove notice to X, it is without probative value unless X heard it. Or if a letter purporting to be from Y is relied upon to establish an admission by him, it has no probative value unless Y wrote . . . it. Relevance in this

---

content. Effective December 1, 2011, Fed. R. Evid. 104 (c) reads:

Conducting a Hearing So That the Jury Cannot Hear It. The court must conduct hearing on a preliminary question so that the jury cannot hear it if:
(1) the hearing involves the admissibility of a confession;
(2) a defendant in a criminal case is a witness and so requests; or
(3) justice so requires.

As the Federal Advisory Committee's Note to Rule 104(c) observes with respect to preliminary matters other than the accused's confessions and testimony:

Otherwise, detailed treatment of when preliminary matters should be heard outside the hearing of the jury is not feasible. The procedure is time consuming. Not infrequently the same evidence which is relevant to the issue of establishment of a condition precedent to admissibility is also relevant to

weight or credibility, and time is saved by taking foundation proof in the presence of the jury. Much evidence on preliminary questions, though not relevant to jury issues, may be heard by the jury with no adverse effect. A great deal must be left to the discretion of the judge who will act as the interests of justice require.

[9]This is the second sense of "voir dire" at trial. "Voir dire" is also the term used to describe the questioning of the panelists to determine whom will be selected to serve as a petit juror.

[10]Imwinkelried, Trial Judges–Gatekeepers or Usurpers? Can the Trial Judge Critically Assess the Admissibility of Expert Testimony Without Invading the Jury's Province to Evaluate the Credibility and Weight of the Testimony?, 84 Marq. L. Rev. 1 (2000).

sense has been labelled "conditional relevancy." Morgan, Basic Problems of Evidence 45–56 (1962).[11]

These factual questions of conditional relevancy under Rule 104(b) not only differ from questions falling under Rule 104(a). They also differ from questions whether particular evidence is relevant as a matter of law under Rule 401, such as the issue of whether evidence that on the day before a murder the accused purchased a weapon of the type used in the killing is relevant. Questions of the latter nature are, of course, for the judge. Distinguish that Rule 401 question of law from the Rule 104(b) question of fact whether the gun marked as prosecution exhibit #3 for identification is the very gun the accused purchased.

Conditional relevancy questions under 104(b) are well within the jurors' competency; they involve the kind of questions which jurors are accustomed to decide. Did A say such-and-such? Did B sign the letter offered in evidence? The jury's role and power on the merits would be greatly curtailed if judges made the final decisions on these questions. The judge is not, however, entirely eliminated from the picture; rather, the judge divides responsibility with the jury in the following manner. The judge requires the proponent to bring forward evidence from which a rational jury could find the existence of the preliminary fact. At this point, the judge plays a limited, screening role. The judge cannot pass on the credibility of the foundational testimony. Rather, the test is a hypothetical jury finding. The judge must accept the testimony at face value and ask only this question: If the jury decides to believe the testimony, is there a rational, permissive inference of the existence of the preliminary fact? When the judge determines that the jury could not find the existence of the preliminary fact, he excludes the evidence. Otherwise, the question is for the jury. Although in fact some trial judges permit the opponent to conduct voir dire on conditional relevance issues, strictly speaking the opponent has no right to voir dire on this type of issue. When the opponent has contrary evidence, the opponent submits it to the jury rather than the judge. On request, in the final instructions the judge directs the jury to determine the existence of the foundational fact and to disregard the evidence if they find that the foundational fact has not been proven.

This procedure is followed at modern common law[12] and prescribed by Federal Rule of Evidence 104(b) and Uniform Rule

---

[11]Adv. Com. Note, Fed. R. Evid. 104(b). *See also* Morgan, Functions of Judge and Jury in Preliminary Questions of Fact, 43 Harv. L. Rev. 164, 164–75 (1929). See the general treatment of authentication as an aspect of conditional relevancy, Ch. 22 infra.

[12]Patton v. Bank of La Fayette, 124 Ga. 965, 53 S.E. 664 (1906) (in a suit on a note, the defendant denied executing the note; the note was ad-

of Evidence 104(c) and Federal Rule 104(b). Restyled Federal Rule 104(b), reads:

When the relevance of evidence depends on whether a fact exists, proof must be introduced sufficient to support a finding that the fact does exist. The court may admit the proposed evidence on the condition that the proof be introduced later.[13]

---

missible if the proponent presented foundational testimony from which the note could be found to be genuine); Coleman v. McIntosh, 184 Ky. 370, 211 S.W. 872 (1919) (in a breach of promise, the defendant offered in evidence plaintiff's purported letter to another man; plaintiff denied she wrote it, and trial judge excluded it; the trial judge erred, since there was some evidence of genuineness; the letter should have been admitted and authenticity left to jury); Winslow v. Bailey, 16 Me. 319, 1839 WL 761 (1839) (in an action on a note, the defense was fraudulent misrepresentation; the defendant offered as evidence of the false statement, a third person's certificate as to the amount of timber on a tract; the court held that the trial judge properly ruled that he should not determine whether the certificate was used as an inducement to plaintiff, but should require only prima facie evidence of this, before admitting the certificate); Coghlan v. White, 236 Mass. 165, 128 N.E. 33 (1920) (whether required statutory written notice was delivered to defendant was not for judge as fact preliminary to admitting notice in evidence, but rather for jury on the conflicting testimony).

But the distinction is one over which the courts occasionally stumble. Gila Valley, G. & N. Ry. Co. v. Hall, 232 U.S. 94, 34 S. Ct. 229, 58 L. Ed. 521 (1914) (there was an issue whether plaintiff knew of defect in appliance; defendant offered evidence of remark about defect made when plaintiff was less than 20 yards away: on objection judge excluded on the ground that it had not been proved that the plaintiff heard the statement: there was no error, since the issue was a preliminary question for judge); Dexter v. Thayer,

189 Mass. 114, 75 N.E. 223 (1905) (the question was whether agreement between parties alleged to have been made for one by purported agent was authorized; the question was a preliminary fact for judge). See also Cal. Evid. Code § 403; N.J.R.E. 104(b).

[13]Federal Rule of Evidence 104(b) and Uniform Rule of Evidence 104(c) provide merely that evidence will be admitted if a party has introduced evidence "sufficient to support a finding that the fact does exist." No explanation or definition is provided as to the term "finding." "Finding" should not vary according to the nature of the matter or the particular evidence involved. In all matters, the condition is fulfilled when in light of all the evidence admitted as to the condition (including evidence admitted on any voir dire of the witness), viewed most favorably to the party seeking to fulfill the condition, a reasonable juror could find the condition in question to be more probably true than not true. See Huddleston v. U.S., 485 U.S. 681, 689, 108 S. Ct. 1496, 99 L. Ed. 2d 771 (1988) ("In determining whether the Government has introduced sufficient evidence to meet Rule 104(b), the trial court neither weighs credibility nor makes a finding that the Government has proved the conditional fact by a preponderance of the evidence. The court simply examines all the evidence in the case and decides whether the jury could reasonably find the conditional fact . . . by a preponderance of the evidence. See 21 C. Wright & K. Graham, Federal Practice and Procedure § 5054, p. 269 (1977).").

Where the admissibility of evidence depends upon connecting facts, the order of proof is largely within the trial judge's discretion. Evidence ad-

Federal Rule 602 expressly applies this procedure to the preliminary issue of a lay witness's personal knowledge, and Rule 901(a) extends the procedure to the foundational issue of the authenticity of exhibits. The drafters reasoned that the jurors could be trusted to decide these preliminary issues. If the jurors find that a lay witness did not see the accident he testified about or that a letter allegedly written by the accused is a forgery, common sense should lead them to disregard the witness's testimony or the letter during their deliberations. These preliminary facts condition the logical relevance of the evidence in a fundamental sense that is obvious even to lay jurors who lack legal training. In short, it is safe to allow the jurors to make these determinations.

Some situations have not readily lent themselves to classification as falling in either of the two categories of facts and accordingly require further discussion.[14]

First, confessions are subject to their own special rules, which are treated elsewhere.[15]

Second, in cases involving dying declarations some jurisdictions assign the jury a role in deciding the preliminary question whether declarant had the settled, hopeless expectation of death

---

mitted upon a promise to connect it up will later be excluded on a motion to strike if the appropriate connection is not established. Huddleston v. U.S., 485 U.S. 681, 689, 108 S. Ct. 1496, 99 L. Ed. 2d 771 (1988) ("The trial court has traditionally exercised the broadest sort of discretion in controlling the order of proof at trial, and we see nothing in the Rules of Evidence that would change this practice. Often the trial court may decide to allow the proponent to introduce evidence concerning a similar act, and at a later point in the trial assess whether sufficient evidence has been offered to permit the jury to make the requisite finding. If the proponent has failed to meet this minimal standard of proof, the trial court must instruct the jury to disregard the evidence.").

[14]In Huddleston v. U.S., 485 U.S. 681, 108 S. Ct. 1496, 99 L. Ed. 2d 771 (1988), the Court held that Rule 104(b) governs the foundational question of whether the accused committed an act of uncharged misconduct proffered under Rule 404(b), for example, another murder allegedly committed

with the same distinctive modus operandi. At the prior common law, the prevailing view had been that the judge resolved that foundational question. U.S. v. Kenney, 598 F. Supp. 883, 887 (D. Me. 1984) ("[t]he clear majority view"). A number of courts have refused to follow Huddleston. *E.g.*, People v. Garner, 806 P.2d 366 (Colo. 1991); Phillips v. State, 591 So. 2d 987 (Fla. 1st DCA 1991). At least when the prosecution offers only one uncharged incident, *Huddleston* probably reaches the right result. The contra state decisions argue that the judge must resolve the question because the evidence is so highly prejudicial. However, that argument misses the point. The issue is whether the jury is likely to disregard the evidence if they find that the foundational fact does not exist. If the jury concludes that the accused did not commit the act—either the act did not occur or a third party perpetrated the act—common sense ought to lead them to the conclusion that they should not utilize the evidence against the accused.

[15]See § 162 infra.

required for that hearsay exception.[16] This practice is not followed under Federal and Uniform Rule of Evidence 104.[17]

In a third, troublesome group of cases, the preliminary fact question coincides with one of the ultimate disputed fact-issues that the jury normally decides. There are several examples. (1) In a bigamy prosecution, the first marriage is disputed, the second wife is called as a state's witness, and defendant objects under a statute disqualifying the wife to testify against her husband. (2) Plaintiff sues on a lost writing, and defendant raises a best evidence objection and contends that it was not lost because it never existed. (3) In a prosecution, the state offers an alleged co-conspirator's declaration made during the course of and in furtherance of the conspiracy. Defendants deny that the conspiracy ever existed. The published common law opinions on these three issues are split.

In Example (1) the preliminary question involves the witness's competency. Competency would be a question for the judge at common law or under Rule 104(a) if it were not for the overlap with the jury issue on the merits of whether she was validly mar-

---

[16]The nature of the requirement is discussed in § 310 infra. Some decisions have admitted dying declarations if reasonable persons could differ as to whether declarant was conscious of impending death. Emmett v. State, 195 Ga. 517, 25 S.E.2d 9, 19 (1943); People v. Denton, 312 Mich. 32, 19 N.W.2d 476 (1945). Sometimes the practice has been for the judge to determine the preliminary question, but require him, if he admits the evidence, to instruct the jury to disregard if they find no consciousness. State v. Garver, 190 Or. 291, 225 P.2d 771 (1950).

A majority, however, follow the practice that issues with respect to this requirement are preliminary issues for the judge. Comer v. State, 212 Ark. 66, 204 S.W.2d 875 (1947); Tillman v. State, 44 So. 2d 644 (Fla. 1950); People v. Hubbs, 401 Ill. 613, 83 N.E.2d 289 (1948) (admissibility for court, weight for jury); State v. Rich, 231 N.C. 696, 58 S.E.2d 717 (1950); Cal. Evid. Code § 405. But if the judge admits the declaration, in appraising its weight the jury may consider whether they believe that the declaration was made under a sense of impending death. Com. v. Knable, 369 Pa. 171, 85 A.2d 114 (1952). Hence they are entitled to hear the evidence as to the circumstances surrounding the making of the declaration. Conway v. State, 177 Miss. 461, 171 So. 16 (1936); State v. Dotson, 96 W. Va. 596, 123 S.E. 463 (1924).

Cases pro and con are collected in 5 Wigmore, Evidence § 1451 (Chadbourn rev. 1974), and in West's Key Number Digest, Homicide ☞1092.

[17]No provision excludes the dying declaration hearsay exception from the scope of Fed. and Unif. R. Evid. 104(a), for determination by the judge. It should, however, be noted that Former Federal Rule 104(e) and Uniform Rule 104(f) provide: "This rule does not limit the right of a party to introduce before the jury evidence relevant to weight or credibility."

Effective December 1, 2011, restyled Fed. R. Evid. 104(e) reads: "Evidence Relevant to Weight and Credibility. This rule does not limit a party's right to introduce before the jury evidence that is relevant to the weight or credibility of other evidence."

The rule thus follows the majority view described in note 16 supra.

ried to the accused. Allowing the judge to decide her competency does not interfere with the jury's function in any way; his decision need not be disclosed to the jury, and additional relevant evidence may be made available to the jury. Accordingly the cases tend to leave the competency decision to the judge.[18] Even if the judge decides to overrule the competency objection and permit the spouse's testimony, the accused can litigate the question of the validity of the second marriage to the jury during the trial on the merits.

In Example (2) the preliminary question whether a writing was lost is ordinarily for the judge at common law or under Rule 104(a), but the writing obviously cannot have been lost if it never existed. Aside from the question of loss, the execution of the document would be a jury question; the preliminary question of authentication under Rule 901 is allocated to the jury at common law and under Rule 104(b). The basic issue in the case is whether the original writing ever existed; the question whether it has been lost is subsidiary. Sound judgment dictates assigning the decision of the basic question to the jury, rather than subsuming it under the judge's authority to determine the application of the best evidence rule. This is the result both by case law[19] and under Rule 1008.[20] If the judge decided that the writing never existed

---

[18]Matz v. U.S., 158 F.2d 190 (App. D.C. 1946). *See also* State v. Lee, 127 La. 1077, 54 So. 356 (1911) (murder by Mack Lee conceded, but defendant claimed he is not Mack Lee; defense offers as a witness the wife of Mack Lee, who presumably would have testified defendant was not her husband; after a preliminary hearing, the trial judge excluded a witness under statute forbidding wife to testify for husband on the ground that he was satisfied that the accused was Mack Lee; the court held that there was no error, since the general rule applied).

[19]Stowe v. Querner, L.R. 5 Exch. 155 (1870); St. Croix Co. v. Sea Coast Canning Co., 114 Me. 521, 96 A. 1059 (1916); Fauci v. Mulready, 337 Mass. 532, 150 N.E.2d 286 (1958). *See* Maguire & Epstein, Preliminary Questions, 40 Harv. L. Rev. 392, 415–20 (1927).

[20]Former Fed. and Unif. R. Evid. 1008 provide:

When the admissibility of other evidence of contents of writings, recordings, or photographs under these rules depends upon the fulfillment of a condition of fact, the question whether the condition has been fulfilled is ordinarily for the court to determine in accordance with the provisions of rule 104. However, when an issue is raised (a) whether the asserted writing ever existed, or (b) whether another writing, recording, or photograph produced at the trial is the original, or (c) whether other evidence of contents correctly reflects the contents, the issue is for the trier of fact to determine as in the case of other issues of fact.

Effective December 1, 2011, restyled Fed. R. Evid. 1008 reads:

Ordinarily, the court determines whether the proponent has fulfilled the factual conditions for admitting other evidence of the content of a writing, recording, or photograph under Rule 1004 or 1005. But, in a jury trial, the jury determines—in accordance with Rule 104(b)—any issue about whether:
 (a) an asserted writing, recording, or photograph ever existed;

and excluded the secondary evidence, the case would end without ever going to the jury on the central issue.[21]

In Example (3), the common law cases divide over whether the judge should make the preliminary determination whether a conspiracy existed and defendant and declarant were members of it, or whether the judge ought to admit the evidence upon a prima facie showing, instructing the jury to disregard it if they find these matters not proved.[22] Supporting the first position is the argument that the judge is dealing with the applicability of a hearsay doctrine, the exemption for co-conspirator declarations. This reasoning points to the application of Rule 104(a) under the Federal and Revised Uniform Rules. In contrast, under one view of the hearsay definition, virtually all co-conspirator declarations qualify as "verbal acts"[23] and hence nonhearsay in the first place. This reasoning cuts in favor of empowering the jury to make the determination, after screening by the judge, as a question of conditional relevancy.[24] Whatever the relative merits of these conflicting positions, in *Bourjaily v. United States*[25] the Supreme Court declared authoritatively that determining the admissibility of a co-conspirator's statement is solely a matter for the judge under Rule 104(a)[26] and that the judge must apply the more probably true than not (preponderance) standard of proof. This result reflects two considerations: the awkward procedural consequences of submitting the preliminary question to the jury, and the courts' understandable wish to limit the use of conspiracy charges by prosecutors.

A closely related question is whether Rule 104(a) or 104(b)

---

   (b)   another one produced at the trial or hearing is the original; or

   (c)   other evidence of content accurately reflects the content.

In U.S. v. Gerhart, 538 F.2d 807 (8th Cir. 1976), the court extended the rule to include the question whether an original is lost.

[21]Levin, Authentication and Content of Writings, 10 Rutgers L. Rev. 632, 644 (1956). The questions of personal knowledge under Rule 602 and of authenticity under Rule 901 both are decided under Rule 104(b), rather than solely by the judge under Rule 104(a). Adv. Com. Notes, Fed. R. Evid. 602, 901.

[22]1 Weinstein's Federal Evidence § 104.16 (rev. 2011).

[23]See § 259 infra.

[24]Cal. Evid. Code § 1223 treats these foundational questions as conditional relevance issues. After subdivisions (a) and (b) enumerate the foundational facts, § 1223(c) announces that the question is whether the proponent has introduced foundational testimony "sufficient to sustain a finding of the facts specified in subdivisions (a) and (b). . . ."

[25]Bourjaily v. U.S., 483 U.S. 171, 107 S. Ct. 2775, 97 L. Ed. 2d 144 (1987).

[26]Under Fed. R. Evid. 801(d)(2)(E) and Rev. Unif. R. Evid. 801(d)(2)(E), a statement is not hearsay if it is offered against a party and is a statement by a co-conspirator of a party during the course and in furtherance of the conspiracy.

governs the foundational facts conditioning the hearsay exemption for authorized admissions in civil cases. One would think that the same procedure should govern the foundations for both hearsay exemptions; after all, a conspiracy is a criminal agency. However, even after the Supreme Court rendered its decision in *Bourjaily*, there was a strong statutory construction argument that Rule 104(b) controlled the foundational facts for the civil exemption. The original Advisory Committee Note to Rule 104 approvingly quotes Professor Morgan as indicating that it is a conditional relevance question whether a principal "authorized" an admission made by an alleged agent. Some jurisdictions remain firmly committed to the view that these are conditional relevance questions.[27] However, a 1997 amendment to Federal Rule 801 makes it clear that the federal courts are to apply the same procedure to both sets of foundational facts. Since *Bourjaily* squarely holds that Rule 104(a) governs the facts conditioning the coconspirator exemption, a fortiori 104(a) now controls the preliminary facts for authorized admissions.

## § 54  Availability as proof of evidence admitted without objection

As § 52 indicated, a failure to make a sufficient objection to incompetent evidence waives any ground of complaint as to the admission of the evidence.[1] But it has another equally important effect. If the testimony is received without objection, the testimony becomes part of the evidence in the case and is usable as proof to the extent of its rational persuasive power.[2] The fact that it was inadmissible does not prevent its use as proof so far as it has probative value. The inadmissible evidence, unobjected to, may be relied on in argument,[3] and alone or in part it can support a verdict or finding.[4] At the trial court level, a party may rely on the evidence to defeat a directed verdict motion; and on

---

[27]After subdivision (a) lists the requisite foundational facts, Cal. Evid. Code § 1222(b) applies the conditional relevance procedure to the facts. *See* Kaus, All Power to the Jury—California's Democratic Evidence Code, 4 Loy. L.A. L. Rev. 233, 237 (1971) (criticizing the California statute).

**[Section 54]**

[1]This generalization is subject to the "plain error" rule. See § 52 supra.

[2]McWilliams v. R & T Transport, Inc., 245 Ark. 882, 435 S.W.2d 98 (1968) (hearsay); Old v. Cooney Detective Agency, 215 Md. 517, 138 A.2d 889

(1958). Again the text is subject to the "plain error" rule. See § 52 supra.

[3]Birmingham Railway & Electric Co. v. Wildman, 119 Ala. 547, 24 So. 548 (1898); Chicago & E.I.R. Co. v. Mochell, 193 Ill. 208, 61 N.E. 1028 (1901).

[4]Indianapolis Blue Print & Mfg. Co. v. Kennedy, 215 Ind. 409, 19 N.E.2d 554 (1939); Department of Employment Sec. v. Minnesota Drug Products, Inc., 258 Minn. 133, 104 N.W.2d 640 (1960) (dictum); Dafoe v. Grantski, 143 Neb. 344, 9 N.W.2d 488 (1943) (hearsay standing alone may sustain a finding); Gregoire v. Insurance Co. of

appeal, the party may use the evidence to uphold the legal sufficiency of the evidence to support a judgment. This principle is almost universally accepted.[5] The Federal and Revised Uniform Rules of Evidence are silent on this subject but raise no doubt as to the continued viability of the common law rule. The principle applies to any ground of incompetency under the exclusionary rules. It is most often invoked with respect to hearsay,[6] but it has also been applied to secondary evidence of writings,[7] opinions,[8] evidence elicited from incompetent witnesses,[9] privileged infor-

---

North America, 128 Vt. 255, 261 A.2d 25 (1969). *See* decisions collected in West's Key Number Digest, Trial ☞105. *But see* Pearson v. Stevens, 446 S.W.2d 381 (Tex. Civ. App. Houston 1st Dist. 1969) (contra as to hearsay forming basis of finding of fact or judgment). However, the Texas courts seem to be moving toward the majority view. Comment, Hearsay Admitted Without Objection: A Reassessment of Its Probative Value, 33 Baylor L. Rev. 983 (1981). See note 5 infra.

[5]See references in note 4, supra. However, in Texas and Georgia, hearsay admitted without objection is said to have no probative force. *See* extensive discussion in Consideration, in determining facts, of inadmissible hearsay evidence introduced without objection, 79 A.L.R.2d 890. This notion is also expressed in Wheelock Bros. v. Lindner Packing & Provision Co., 130 Colo. 122, 273 P.2d 730 (1954) (hearsay was an insufficient basis for holding that the plaintiff had made out a prima facie case).

[6]U.S. v. Alvarez, 584 F.2d 694, 697 (5th Cir. 1978) ("Absent plain error, hearsay that is not subjected to proper objection is ordinarily admissible at trial for any relevant purpose."); Ventromile v. Malden Electric Co., 317 Mass. 132, 57 N.E.2d 209 (1944) (plaintiff's statement after accident made in presence of defendant's employee); De Moulin v. Roetheli, 354 Mo. 425, 189 S.W.2d 562 (1945) (statement by manager of defendant's grocery store after plaintiff's fall); People v. McCoy, 101 Ill. App. 2d 69, 242 N.E.2d 4 (4th Dist. 1968) (unusual

case in which prosecuting attorney took stand and presented state's case). *See* note 157 supra, for contrary view. Consideration, in determining facts, of inadmissible hearsay evidence introduced without objection, 79 A.L.R.2d 890, collects numerous cases.

[7]Elster's Sales v. Longo, 4 Cal. App. 3d 216, 84 Cal. Rptr. 83 (2d Dist. 1970); Carter v. Com., 450 S.W.2d 257 (Ky. 1970); Glover v. Mitchell, 319 Mass. 1, 64 N.E.2d 648 (1946) (federal price regulations); West's Key Number Digest, Trial ☞105(5).

[8]Curtin v. Franchetti, 156 Conn. 387, 242 A.2d 725 (1968) (opinion as to ownership of property); Word v. City of St. Louis, 617 S.W.2d 479 (Mo. Ct. App. E.D. 1981) (plaintiff knew a hole had been there for a long time because of presence of cracks in the asphalt); Dieter v. Scott, 110 Vt. 376, 9 A.2d 95 (1939) (defendant's testimony that he acted as lessee's agent is a conclusion; however, since the testimony was not objected to, the testimony is entitled to consideration if it is not in conflict with underlying facts regarding the relationship); West's Key Number Digest, Trial ☞105(3). But the Georgia court did weaken when the opinion was on the ultimate issue. Morgan v. Bell, 189 Ga. 432, 5 S.E.2d 897 (1939) (mental capacity to make will).

[9]Estate of Berg, 34 Ill. App. 3d 379, 340 N.E.2d 51 (1st Dist. 1975); Walker v. Fields, 247 S.W. 272 (Tex. Comm'n App. 1923) (interested survivor's testimony, which had not been objected to, was "not without probative force"). *Contra* Brittian v. McKim, 204 Ark. 647, 164 S.W.2d 435 (1942)

mation,[10] and evidence objectionable due to the lack of authentication of a writing,[11] firsthand knowledge,[12] or expert qualification.[13]

However, relevancy and probative worth stand on a different footing. If the evidence has no probative force or insufficient probative value to sustain the proposition for which it is offered, the lack of objection adds nothing to its worth;[14] and the evidence will not support a finding. It is still irrelevant or insufficient. However, the failure to object to evidence related to the controversy but not covered by the pleadings, can informally frame new issues and impliedly amend the pleadings.[15] When this occurs, the failure to object on the ground that the evidence is irrelevant

---

(result based on fact that incompetency rule was contained in the constitution), but disapproved in Starbird v. Cheatham, 243 Ark. 181, 419 S.W.2d 114 (1967).

[10]Gruner v. Gruner, 183 Mo. App. 157, 165 S.W. 865 (1914) (marital communications).

[11]Collins v. Streitz, 95 F.2d 430 (C.C.A. 9th Cir. 1938); Elswick v. Charleston Transit Co., 128 W. Va. 241, 36 S.E.2d 419 (1945) (city ordinance: failure to object waives proof of existence and authenticity); West's Key Number Digest, Trial ⊂⇒105(4).

[12]See Winsor v. Hawkins, 130 Conn. 669, 37 A.2d 222 (1944) (plaintiff's testimony that she had neuritis and water on the knee, was received without objection; even though she probably had received the information secondhand from doctor, the testimony could be given such weight as it deserved).

[13]McGuire v. Baird, 9 Cal. 2d 353, 70 P.2d 915 (1937) (in a malpractice action, by not objecting defendant admitted qualifications of plaintiff's doctor to testify to skill ordinarily exercised in that community); Woods v. Siegrist, 112 Colo. 257, 149 P.2d 241 (1944) (testimony by chiropractor-witness, whose qualifications were not objected to, sustains findings though contradicted by qualified neurologists); Jones v. Treegoob, 433 Pa. 225, 249 A.2d 352 (1969); West's Key Number Digest, Trial ⊂⇒105(3).

[14]Marshall v. Kleinman, 186 Conn. 67, 438 A.2d 1199 (1982); Danahy v. Cuneo, 130 Conn. 213, 33 A.2d 132 (1943); Craig v. Citizens Trust Co., 217 Ind. 434, 26 N.E.2d 1006 (1940); De Long v. Iowa State Highway Com'n, 229 Iowa 700, 295 N.W. 91 (1940) (but here the court goes on to adopt the untenable view that inadmissible hearsay, standing alone, can never have sufficient probative worth to support a finding).

[15]Many jurisdictions have adopted Rule 15(b) of the Federal Rules of Civil Procedure. Pursuant to this rule, pleadings are deemed amended when issues not raised by the pleadings are "tried by the express or implied consent of the parties" at the trial. By virtue of this rule, evidence not objected to can raise new issues not within the pleadings. E.g., Niedland v. U.S., 338 F.2d 254 (3d Cir. 1964). See Wright and Miller's Federal Practice and Procedure, Civil § 1493. Cases not governed by the rule have also reached a similar result. Phillips v. New Amsterdam Cas. Co., 193 La. 314, 190 So. 565 (1939). Under the federal rule, however, even if the evidence outside the issues is not objected to, there is not necessarily implied consent to the new issue. For example, there is no implication of consent when the opposing party was not and should not have been aware that a new issue was being raised by the evidence. This situation is most likely to occur when the evidence in question relates to both an issue already raised

to any issue raised by the original pleadings is waived,[16] and the evidence can support the proponent's position on the new informal issue.[17]

## § 55 Waiver of objection

As a general proposition, the party's failure to assert an objection promptly and specifically effects a waiver.[1] What other conduct constitutes a waiver?

### A Failure to Testify After the Loss of a Motion in Limine

When a party has unsuccessfully[2] moved in limine motion to exclude credibility evidence, some authorities require the party to

---

by the pleadings and a new issue. *See* Otness v. U.S., 23 F.R.D. 279 (Terr. Alaska 1959).

[16]See note 15 supra. This result was reached absent Fed. R. Civ. P. 15(b) in Atlanta Enterprises v. James, 68 Ga. App. 773, 24 S.E.2d 130 (1943).

[17]See note 15 supra. Again this result is reached absent Fed. R. Civ. P. Rule 15(b) in Wood v. Claxton, 199 Ga. 809, 35 S.E.2d 455 (1945).

**[Section 55]**

[1]See § 52 supra. The use of a term, "waiver," in the situations discussed generally in this section has been strongly criticized. Wright and Miller's Federal Practice and Procedure, Evidence § 5039. Many courts have apparently not used the term in its strictly technical sense, but as a convenient label for various doctrines of preclusion. Many of the original case citations in the instant section indicate no confusion with the strictly orthodox terms, "waiver" and "estoppel," as used in other areas of the law.

Some courts recognize vicarious objections; "[w]hen one co-party objects [to an evidentiary issue] and thereby brings the matter to the attention of the court, further objections by other co-parties are unnecessary." U.S. v. Irving, 665 F.3d 1184, 1206–1207 (10th Cir. 2011), cert. denied, 132 S. Ct. 1873, 182 L. Ed. 2d 656 (2012). Moreover, a failure to object can be excused when the trial judge's prior rulings make it futile to object. State

v. Barajas, 247 Or. App. 247, 268 P.3d 732 (2011). See further § 137 infra.

[2]*See generally* Luce v. U.S., 469 U.S. 38, 41–42, 105 S. Ct. 460, 83 L. Ed. 2d 443 (1984) ("Any possible harm flowing from a district court's *in limine* ruling permitting impeachment by a prior conviction is wholly speculative. The ruling is subject to change when the case unfolds, particularly if the actual testimony differs from what was contained in the defendant's proffer. Indeed even if nothing unexpected happens at trial, the district judge is free, in the exercise of sound judicial discretion, to alter a previous *in limine* ruling."). Thus, in federal courts, the defendant must testify to preserve error for review with respect to a claim of improper impeachment with a prior conviction. Luce v. United States, id.; U.S. v. Gunter, 551 F.3d 472, 483–84 (6th Cir. 2009); U.S. v. Fallon, 348 F.3d 248, 253–54 (7th Cir. 2003) (by failing to testify, the defendant waived the right to challenge the impeachment use of convictions outside the normal ten-year period); Government of Virgin Islands v. Fonseca, 44 V.I. 336, 274 F.3d 760, 765 (3d Cir. 2001) (collecting cases applying *Luce*); U.S. v. Kozeny, 643 F. Supp. 2d 415, 417 (S.D. N.Y. 2009) ("a court's ruling regarding a motion in limine 'is subject to case when the case unfolds' . . . . [E]ven if nothing unexpected happens at trial the district court is free, in the exercise of sound judicial discretion, to alter a previous in limine ruling"); Brumfield v. Stinson, 297 F. Supp. 2d

testify to preserve the issue for appeal. When the testimony is logically relevant only to credibility, the party can preclude the admission of the testimony by foregoing the witness's testimony. Thus, the cost of a ruling admitting the evidence can be the loss of the witness's testimony. The argument runs that the appellate court cannot intelligently gauge that cost unless the court has the benefit of the testimony; the appellate courts reason that without the benefit of the witness's actual testimony, they cannot properly evaluate the trial judge's ruling denying the in limine motion.

However, the holdings in those authorities are limited in scope; many[3] of these authorities relate to evidence logically relevant only on a credibility theory. Moreover, in some jurisdictions, a voir dire of the witness outside the jury's presence obviates the need for the witness to testify at trial to preserve the issue for purposes of appeal.[4] Finally, some jurisdictions flatly reject the

---

607, 619–20 (W.D. N.Y. 2003).

Although *Luce* involved Rule 609 impeachment with a conviction, some jurisdictions have extended the scope of the case's holding beyond that context. U.S. v. Ferrer, 441 Fed. Appx. 867 (3d Cir. 2011) ("our sister circuits have extended *Luce* beyond the Rule 609(a) context"); State v. Romar, 221 Ariz. 342, 212 P.3d 34 (Ct. App. Div. 1 2009) (the defense waived its objection to the cross-examination of defense character witnesses; after the judge's ruling, the defense elected not to call the witnesses; the appellate court refused to rule "based on purely hypothetical testimony"); State v. Smyers, 207 Ariz. 314, 86 P.3d 370 (2004). The same is true with respect to impeachment by prior acts of misconduct not leading to a conviction. U.S. v. Weichert, 783 F.2d 23 (2d Cir. 1986). The rule has also been applied to post-arrest silence offered for impeachment purposes. People v. Boyd, 470 Mich. 363, 682 N.W.2d 459 (2004).

[3]There is an argument that the *Luce* reasoning applies only when the challenged evidence is logically relevant only on a credibility theory. Under *Luce,* the trial judge must consider the probative value of the testimony the party contemplates giving. The ruling can deter the party from testify-

ing precisely because the party can preclude the introduction of credibility evidence by not testifying. If the party does not testify, his or her credibility does not become an issue; and evidence bearing only on the party's credibility is irrelevant and consequently inadmissible under Federal Rule 401. The *Luce* reasoning does not apply when the evidence can be admitted even if the party does not testify. For example, in many instances, evidence of a defendant's uncharged misconduct can be admitted under Federal Rule 404(b) even if the defendant decides against testifying. Rule 404(b) evidence is ordinarily relevant to the historical merits rather than credibility. Nevertheless, some courts assume that a defendant must testify in order to preserve a Rule 404(b) ruling for appeal. 2 Imwinkelried, Uncharged Misconduct Evidence § 9:15, at 9-96-99 (rev. 2009) (collecting authorities).

[4]"[T]he First Circuit has indicated that a voir dire of the defendant out of the presence of the jury may be sufficient to preserve the issue for appellate review . . . ." May & Cohen, Staying Luce, 27 The Champion 30, 32 (Nov. 2003) (citing U.S. v. Griffin, 818 F.2d 97, 105 (1st Cir. 1987) and U.S. v. Nivica, 887 F.2d 1110, 1116 (1st Cir. 1989)).

view that the party must call the witness in order to preserve the issue.[5]

### Demand for Inspection of a Writing

Federal Rule of Civil Procedure 34 authorizes a litigant to demand that the opponent produce writings and objects for pretrial inspection. Suppose that one party, D, gives notice to his opponent, O, to produce a document, and O produces it. Then D asks to inspect it and is allowed to do so. Assume that under some evidentiary doctrine the document, if offered by O, would be inadmissible except for the facts of notice, production, and inspection. Do these facts preclude D from objecting when O offers the document into evidence? Old precedents in England, Massachusetts, and a few other states said yes: D is precluded from objecting.[6] This result was originally rationalized on the notion that it would be unconscionable to permit the demanding party to examine the producing party's private papers without incurring some corresponding risk.[7] A later case, however, attempted to justify the result on another theory; according to that case, at least when the demand is made in open court, the jury may suspect the party who is called on to produce the writing of evasion or concealment unless he can introduce the writing.[8] That argument has limited validity, though; that risk is present

---

[5]Warren v. State, 121 Nev. 886, 124 P.3d 522 (2005); Graham, Motions in Limine: Anticipatory Disclosure of Prior Conviction, 41 Crim. L. Bull. 539, 549 (Sep.-Oct. 2005) ("Tennessee law provides that a defendant need not testify to preserve error for appeal . . . State v. Galmore, 994 S.W.2d 120, 122-25 (Tenn. 1999)").

[6]Wharam v. Routledge, 1805 WL 1043 (U.K. Assizes 1805); Calvert v. Flower, 1836 WL 3607 (K.B.); Clark v. Fletcher, 83 Mass. 53, 1 Allen 53, 1861 WL 4380 (1861) (leading case); Leonard v. Taylor, 315 Mass. 580, 53 N.E.2d 705 (1944); and cases cited in Production, in response to call therefor by adverse party, of document otherwise inadmissible in evidence, as making it admissible, 151 A.L.R. 1006. However, as remarked in Zimmerman v. Zimmerman, 12 N.J. Super. 61, 79 A.2d 59 (App. Div. 1950), the spirit of the federal discovery rules adopted in New Jersey "seems to run counter" to the older practice. This Zimmerman view-

point should apply in states which have adopted in substance the federal discovery rules. See also West's Key Number Digest, Evidence ⟪368(14).

But the rule does not apply in any event when the writing is used by one party to refresh his witness's memory: the other party is entitled to inspect the writing without being penalized by being required to permit its introduction in evidence. Clearly the supposed reason of the rule does not apply. Nussenbaum v. Chambers & Chambers, 322 Mass. 419, 77 N.E.2d 780 (1948). See § 9 supra.

[7]Clark v. Fletcher, 83 Mass. 53, 1 Allen 53, 57, 1861 WL 4380 (1861), quoted in Production, in response to call therefor by adverse party, of document otherwise inadmissible in evidence, as making it admissible, 151 A.L.R. 1006, 1013.

[8]Leonard v. Taylor, 315 Mass. 580, 53 N.E.2d 705 (1944) This shifting of ground, however tenuous the new justification may seem, at least

only when, under local procedure, the demand must be made in the jury's hearing. Modernly, the demand is ordinarily made out of court before trial.

The modern cases recognize that the old policy against compelled disclosure of relevant writings in a party's possession is outmoded.[9] The contemporary policy is just the opposite, namely, that of pressuring full disclosure except for privileged matter.[10] Accordingly, today the overwhelming majority of states reject the old rule[11] and permit D to assert any pertinent objection if O later offers the writing. This rule is consistent with Federal and Uniform Rule of Evidence 103(a)(1). The older view is at odds with the liberal pretrial discovery policy of the federal civil rules, which have been adopted widely in the states.[12] In this fact situation, it is silly to infer that the party requesting production has waived all evidentiary objections to the introduction of the writing; the party cannot forecast the potential objections until she has had an opportunity to review the contents of the writing.

### Failure to Object to Earlier Similar Evidence

A party has introduced evidence of particular facts without objection. Later he offers additional evidence, perhaps by other witnesses or writings, of the same facts. May the adversary now object, or has he waived his right by his earlier quiescence? Some opinions summarily state that he may not object.[13] However, in the more carefully reasoned opinions, courts usually conclude

---

implies that the rule should be restricted to the limits of the new reason, namely, to jury trials where request for inspection is made in the jury's presence.

[9]See the vigorous criticism of the rule in 7 Wigmore, Evidence § 2125 (Chadbourn rev. 1978).

[10]Fed. R. Civ. P. 26.

[11]Scully v. Morrison Hotel Corp., 118 Ill. App. 2d 254, 254 N.E.2d 852 (1st Dist. 1969) (rejecting "English" rule in Illinois); Morgan v. Paine, 312 A.2d 178 (Me. 1973) (overruling prior cases); Smith v. Rentz, 131 N.Y. 169, 30 N.E. 54, 56 (1892) ("The party who has in his possession books or papers which may be material to the case of his opponent has no moral right to conceal them from his adversary. . . . The party calling for books and papers would be subjected to great hazard if an inspection merely, without more,

would make them evidence in the case. That rule tends rather to the suppression than the ascertainment of truth, and the opposite rule is, as it seems to us, better calculated to promote the ends of justice."); Merlino v. Mutual Service Cas. Ins. Co., 23 Wis. 2d 571, 127 N.W.2d 741 (1964).

[12]See Zimmerman v. Zimmerman, 12 N.J. Super. 61, 79 A.2d 59 (App. Div. 1950); Oakley & Coon, The Federal Rules in State Courts: A Survey of State Court Systems of Civil Procedure, 61 Wash. L. Rev. 1367 (1986).

[13]Star Realty v. Strahl, 261 Iowa 362, 154 N.W.2d 143 (1967); State v. Tranchell, 243 Or. 215, 412 P.2d 520 (1966) (matter is in court's discretion); Rash v. Waterhouse, 124 Vt. 476, 207 A.2d 130 (1965).

But no court would hold that because earlier evidence was subject to an objection under a particular exclusionary rule, e.g., hearsay, and

that standing alone, the earlier failure to object to other like evidence is not a waiver of objection to the new inadmissible evidence.[14] This conclusion should be reached under the Federal and Revised Uniform Rules of Evidence.[15] (Of course, overruling the new objection will sometimes be harmless error, since the earlier evidence could render the error harmless; but that is a different question.)[16] As § 52 points out, even when evidence is technically objectionable, experienced trial attorneys do not object unless the evidence is clearly damaging. Their practice is in the interest of judicial economy and encouraged by the nonwaiver rule. The conventional wisdom is that an attorney should not assert every technically available objection; to avoid alienating the jury, the attorney ought to object only when the objection is both legally meritorious and tactically sound—such as when the evidence in question would do major damage to the attorney's theory of the case. It might have been tactically inadvisable to object to the earlier evidence; although the testimony was technically objectionable under evidence law, its contents might have been innocuous or positively helpful. It would be wrong-minded to infer a waiver from the earlier failure to object.

However, when the evidence of the fact, admitted without objection, is extensive,[17] and the evidence though inadmissible has some probative value, the trial judge should have discretion to find that the objector's conduct amounted to a waiver. Again, this approach can be followed under the Federal and Revised Uniform Rules of Evidence.

---

was received without objection, the prior lack of objection precludes the adversary from asserting this ground of objection against new evidence. *E.g.*, New York Life Ins. Co. v. Neasham, 250 F. 787 (C.C.A. 9th Cir. 1918) (consent to use transcript of one witness's testimony at coroner's hearing, did not waive the right to object to transcript of another witness's testimony at same hearing).

[14]Lowery v. Jones, 219 Ala. 201, 121 So. 704 (1929) ("If these [later] objections had been sustained, the force of the former testimony would probably have been weakened in the mind of the jury"); Slocinski v. Radwan, 83 N.H. 501, 144 A. 787 (1929); Bobereski v. Insurance Co. of Pennsylvania, 105 Pa. Super. 585, 161 A. 412, 415 (1932) (". . . the fact that incompetent, irrelevant, and immaterial evidence may be introduced on a trial by one party, without objection

from the other party, because he may deem it of no importance and harmless, does not prevent the latter from objecting to the further introduction and elaboration of such evidence when he is of opinion that it is both important and harmful. The principle of estoppel does not apply in such case."); McLane v. Paschal, 74 Tex. 20, 11 S.W. 837, 839 (1889).

[15]This position is also taken in Wright and Miller's Federal Practice and Procedure, Evidence § 5039.

[16]As pointed out by Phillips, C.J. in Slayden v. Palmo, 108 Tex. 413, 194 S.W. 1103, 1104 (1917).

[17]Of course, evidence and counterevidence may make the fact material, though not pleaded. *E.g.*, Sweazey v. Valley Transport, 6 Wash. 2d 324, 107 P.2d 567 (1940), and see § 54 note 3 supra.

### *The Offering of Like Evidence by the Objector*

If a party who has objected to evidence of a certain fact himself later produces affirmative evidence of the same fact from his own witness, he has waived his earlier objection.[18] This result should obtain under the Federal and Revised Uniform Rules of Evidence.[19] However, when his objection is made and overruled, he is entitled to treat this ruling as the "law of the trial" and to negatively rebut or explain, if he can, the evidence admitted over his protest. Consequently, as a general rule there is no waiver if he cross-examines the adversary's witness about the matter.[20] There is no waiver even though the cross-examiner repeats the fact,[21] or even meets the testimony with other evidence which, under the theory of his objection, would be inadmissible.[22] Here

---

[18]U.S. v. Silvers, 374 F.2d 828, 832 (7th Cir. 1967) (defense counsel objected to testimony of prior convictions but relied on defendant's long prison experiences in presenting insanity defense; "a defendant's reference to or use of an erroneously admitted line of evidence cures or waives the error."); Trouser Corp. of America v. Goodman & Theise, Inc., 153 F.2d 284 (C.C.A. 3d Cir. 1946) (the court recognized the general principle, but in this case it was unclear whether the testimony was elicited in effort to rebut); In re Forsythe's Estate, 221 Minn. 303, 22 N.W.2d 19 (1946) (other letter from same person giving similar but more prejudicial facts, a waiver); Inter–City Trucking Co. v. Mason & Dixon Lines, 38 Tenn. App. 450, 276 S.W.2d 488 (1954); City of Houston v. McFadden, 420 S.W.2d 811 (Tex. Civ. App. Houston 14th Dist. 1967, error refused n.r.e.); and cases in 1 Wigmore, Evidence § 18 n. 35 (3d ed. 1940). *See also* Russian v. Lipet, 103 R.I. 461, 238 A.2d 369 (1968) (the party elicited the same testimony from the same witness).

[19]The party should not be permitted "to blow hot and cold" in this way. Perhaps the result can be viewed as a simple lack of objection under Fed. R. Evid. 103(a).

[20]Chester v. Shockley, 304 S.W.2d 831 (Mo. 1957); Sayner v. Sholer, 77 N.M. 579, 425 P.2d 743 (1967); Haase v. Ryan, 100 Ohio App. 285, 60 Ohio Op. 251, 136 N.E.2d 406, 410 (6th Dist. Lucas County 1955). There are some holdings to the contrary. *See, e.g.*, Grain Dealers Mut. Ins. Co. v. Julian, 247 S.C. 89, 145 S.E.2d 685 (1965) (previous objection must be reserved).

Similarly, when the evidence objected to is elicited on cross-examination, the objector may seek to explain or refute on redirect without a waiver. Tucker v. Reil, 51 Ariz. 357, 77 P.2d 203 (1938).

[21]While calling for a repetition is a permissible part of a testing, as a matter of tactics exploratory cross-examination and repetition should be held to a minimum.

[22]Salt Lake City v. Smith, 104 F. 457, 470 (C.C.A. 8th Cir. 1900); State v. Tiedemann, 139 Mont. 237, 362 P.2d 529 (1961); Glennon v. Great Atlantic & Pacific Tea Co., 87 R.I. 454, 143 A.2d 282 (1958). *See generally* U.S. v. DeCarlo, 458 F.2d 358, 372 n.1 (3d Cir. 1972) ("It has long been the rule that when a party's objection is made and overruled, he is entitled to treat that ruling as the 'law of the case' and to explain or rebut, if he can, the evidence which has come in over his protest. Consequently, a party does not waive his objection if he meets the evidence to which he objected with other evidence which under the theory of the objection would be incompe-

too the courts can reach the same result under the Federal and Revised Uniform Rules of Evidence.[23]

However, some courts have carved out an exception to the above general rule. Suppose that the defense counsel believes that the prosecutor will attempt to use an inadmissible conviction to impeach the defendant but unsuccessfully moves in limine to bar the use of the conviction. Assume further that to blunt the impact of the expected impeachment, during the defendant's direct examination the defense counsel has the defendant acknowledge the conviction. In 2000 in *Ohler v. United States,*[24] the Court held that by mentioning her conviction on direct, the defendant waived any error in the in limine ruling. The Court's syllabus states:

> A defendant who preemptively introduces evidence of a prior conviction on direct examination may not challenge the admission of such evidence on appeal. Ohler attempts to avoid the well-established commonsense principle that a party introducing evidence cannot complain on appeal that the evidence was erroneously admitted by invoking the Federal Rules of Evidence 103 and 609. However, neither Rule addresses the question at issue here. She also argues that applying such a waiver rule in this situation would compel a defendant to forgo the tactical advantage of preemptively introducing the conviction in order to appeal the in limine ruling. But both the Government and the defendant in a criminal trial must make choices as the trial progresses.

The Court's holding has been sharply criticized.[25] The essence of the criticism is that it is an accepted trial tactic to blunt anticipated damaging evidence and that the cost of resorting to such a legitimate tactic should not include forfeiting the right to challenge an erroneous trial court ruling. Since the decision is non-constitutional in character, the states are free to adopt a contrary view. Several have done so.[26]

---

tent.").

[23]See general agreement in Wright and Miller's Federal Practice and Procedure, Evidence § 5039; 1 Mueller & Kirkpatrick, Federal Evidence § 1:12, at 79–82 (3d ed. 2007); U.S. v. DeCarlo, 458 F.2d 358, 372 n.1 (3d Cir. 1972).

[24]Ohler v. U.S., 529 U.S. 753, 120 S. Ct. 1851, 146 L. Ed. 2d 826 (2000). *See also* Clarett v. Roberts, 657 F.3d 664 (7th Cir. 2011); U.S. v. McConnel, 464 F.3d 1152, 1160–1162 (10th Cir. 2006) (as a matter of trial strategy, the defendant admitted the conviction on direct examination); U.S. v. Watler, 461 F.3d 1005 (8th Cir. 2006) (the defendant waived the issue, even though the defendant had already lost a motion in limine to exclude the evidence and the defendant mentioned the evidence on direct only to limit the damage that might be inflicted on cross-examination); U.S. v. Decoud, 456 F.3d 996, 1011 (9th Cir. 2006).

[25]Perrin, Pricking Boils, Preserving Error: On the Horns of a Dilemma After Ohler v. United States, 34 U.C. Davis L. Rev. 615 (2000).

[26]State v. Daly, 623 N.W.2d 799

*Exclusion by Judge on Her Own Motion Absent an Objection*

A party's failure to object usually waives the objection and forecloses that party from complaining if the evidence is admitted.[27] But the party's failure does not preclude the trial judge from excluding the evidence on her own motion if the prospective witness is incompetent or the evidence is inadmissible, and the judge believes the interests of justice require the exclusion of the testimony.[28] The judge is especially likely to intervene in criminal cases to bar inadmissible evidence that might severely prejudice the defendant. The judge can step in both to protect the accused's rights and to decrease the risk that any conviction will be vulnerable to collateral attack on the ground of ineffective representation of counsel. The Federal and Revised Uniform Rules of Evidence grant the judge sufficiently broad power to intervene *sua sponte* in such circumstances.[29]

However, many types of evidence such as reliable affidavits or

---

(Iowa 2001); State v. Thang, 145 Wash. 2d 630, 41 P.3d 1159 (2002).

[27]See § 52 supra.

[28]Bodholdt v. Garrett, 122 Cal. App. 566, 10 P.2d 533 (1st Dist. 1932) (the trial judge excluded a truck driver's unexcited statement that broken spring was cause of collision; the judge did not err; "The court on its own motion in the interest of justice may exclude. . . . " Query, whether the ruling was in the interest of justice.); South Atlantic S. S. Co. of Del. v. Munkacsy, 37 Del. 580, 187 A. 600 (1936) (in a suit by seaman for injury, the trial judge excluded a boatswain's opinion as to safe character of work; there was no error; "the trial judge is something more than a mere umpire;" careful exposition of judge's authority); King v. Baker, 109 Ga. App. 235, 136 S.E.2d 8 (1964) (judge excluded answer which was nonresponsive but otherwise admissible); City of Detroit v. Porath, 271 Mich. 42, 260 N.W. 114 (1935) (irrelevant picture); Wisniewski v. Weinstock, 130 N.J.L. 58, 31 A.2d 401 (N.J. Sup. Ct. 1943) (a truck driver's testimony as to speed from tire-tracks was excluded for lack of qualification); Best v. Tavenner, 189 Or. 46, 218 P.2d 471 (1950) (where witness died from stroke after direct testimony was partly completed, judge had dis-cretion to withdraw testimony from jury on own motion or declare mistrial); Barber v. State Highway Commission, 80 Wyo. 340, 342 P.2d 723 (1959). Cases are collected at West's Key Number Digest, Trial ☞105(6).

It is even sometimes said that the judge at the close of the case may of his own motion withdraw incompetent evidence from the jury though not objected to when received. *E.g.*, American Workmen v. Ledden, 196 Ark. 902, 120 S.W.2d 346 (1938). But an opposite result is advocated "to prevent unfairness, in that, if the counsel offering the testimony were made aware of the objection to the testimony at the time, he would have had an opportunity to cure it." Electric Park Amusement Co. v. Psichos, 83 N.J.L. 262, 83 A. 766, 768 (N.J. Sup. Ct. 1912).

[29]The judge has broad power to control the presentation of evidence to make the interrogation and presentation "effective for determining the truth," under Fed. and Unif. R. Evid. 611(a). Coupled with the plain error provisions of Rule 103(d), those powers afford a base for the principle in the text. *See* U.S. v. Wright, 542 F.2d 975 (7th Cir. 1976) (trial judge could on own initiative bar line of questioning as irrelevant).

copies of writings, albeit technically inadmissible, are probative and trustworthy. In that case, absent an objection, the trial judge would be unjustified in excluding the evidence. The judge should exercise her discretionary power to intervene only when the evidence is irrelevant, unreliable, misleading, or prejudicial as well as technically inadmissible.

However, privileged evidence, such as confidential communications between husband and wife, ought to be treated differently. The privileges protect the holder's outside interests, not the parties' interest in securing justice in the present litigation. Accordingly, when a question calls for privileged matter and the holder is present, if necessary the judge may explain the privilege to the holder; but the judge should not assert it on her own motion if the holder decides against claiming the privilege. In contrast, when the holder is absent, the judge in some jurisdictions has a discretionary power to assert it on the holder's behalf.[30]

## § 56 The effect of the introduction of part of a writing or conversation[1]

The preceding sections discuss the procedures applicable when the opposing attorney negatively attempts to exclude the evidence proffered by the proponent. In some cases, though, the opponent endeavors to turn the proponent's proffer to affirmative advantage; the opponent argues that the proponent's proffer allows the opponent to introduce evidence that might otherwise be inadmissible. Sections 56 and 57 discuss these cases. Like § 32, this section addresses the rule of completeness while § 57 describes the curative admissibility doctrine.

Two competing considerations come into play when a party offers in evidence only a portion of a writing, oral statement, or conversation. One consideration is the danger of admitting only a portion of the expression, wresting that part out of its context.

---

[30]People v. Atkinson, 40 Cal. 284, 1870 WL 908 (1870) (where witness, an attorney, on examination was unable to say whether communications from client were public or private, over the defendant-client's objection the trial judge admitted the evidence, the appellate court held that the trial judge had erred; and by way of dictum the appellate court added that the trial court should have excluded on its own motion); Hodges v. Mullikin, 1 Bland Ch. 503, 509 (Md. Ch. 1831) ("if the client be no party . . . the lips of his attorney must remain closed and the Court cannot allow him to speak . . . "). Cal. Evid. Code § 916 requires the judge to exclude privileged information if no person authorized to claim the privilege is present.

**[Section 56]**

[1]7 Wigmore, Evidence §§ 2094–2125 (Chadbourn rev. 1978); West's Key Number Digest, Evidence ⊙155(8), (10).

"The fool hath said in his heart, there is no God,"[2] where only the last phrase is quoted, is Wigmore's classic example of the possibilities of distortion.[3] You can indeed quote the Bible as saying "there is no God;" but to do so would be a misleading half-truth because it rips the quotation from its context. Moreover, this danger may not be completely averted by a later, separate reading of the omitted parts. The distorted impression can sometimes linger and work its influence at the subconscious level. The second consideration is the countervailing danger of requiring that the whole be offered, possibly wasting time and cluttering the trial record with passages which have no bearing on the present controversy.

What is the proper balance between these two considerations? In the light of the dangers, is a party who seeks to introduce part of a writing or statement required to offer it in its entirety, or at least all that is relevant to the facts sought to be proved? The common law version of the rule of completeness permits the proponent to prove such part as he desires.[4] At common law, the opponent cannot force the proponent to broaden the scope of his questioning of the witness. However, when the proponent turns the witness over to the opponent for questioning, the opponent can then elicit the other parts relevant to the same topic. Although the Federal Rules of Evidence do not expressly codify this facet of the rule of completeness, under the Supreme Court's 1988 decision in *Beech Aircraft v. Rainey* the opponent can still invoke this doctrine in modern federal practice.[5]

However, there is a strong policy argument that to guard

---

[2]For the oft-repeated classic illustration, see 7 Wigmore, Evidence § 2094 (Chadbourn rev. 1978).

[3]Interpretation is a contextual process. "The setting of a word or words gives character to them, and may wholly change their apparent meaning. A notable instance of such practice is that of the minister, displeased with the manner of hairdressing used by the women of his congregation, who preached from the text, 'Topknot come down!' which was found to be the latter part of the scriptural injunction, 'Let them that are upon the *housetop not come down.*' " Lattimore, J., in Weatherred v. State, 129 Tex. Crim. 514, 89 S.W.2d 212, 214 (1935).

[4]*E.g.*, State Highway Dept. v. Thomas, 115 Ga. App. 372, 154 S.E.2d 812 (1967) (attorney could introduce part of a lease contract); Melnick v. Melnick, 154 Pa. Super. 481, 36 A.2d 235 (1944) (plaintiff could offer a part of the petition and admission in corresponding paragraph of answer without including other matters in that paragraph by way of avoidance or defense). *But see* Flood v. Mitchell, 68 N.Y. 507, 511, 1877 WL 11890 (1877) (the whole instrument creating or transferring rights should be introduced). *See also* 7 Wigmore, Evidence § 2099 (Chadbourn rev. 1978). With respect to testimony given at a former trial, it is fairly common to require that the substance of all of a witness's testimony on the particular subject be given, though there are contrary holdings. 7 Wigmore, Evidence § 2098, n. 4, § 2099(4) (Chadbourn rev. 1978).

[5]In Beech Aircraft Corp. v. Rainey, 488 U.S. 153, 109 S. Ct. 439,

against the danger of an ineradicable, false first impression, the adversary should have an additional right—the adversary ought to be permitted to require the proponent to introduce both the part which the proponent desires to introduce and other passages which are an essential part of its context.[6] Federal and Uniform Rule of Evidence 106 go beyond the common law completeness rule and grant the opponent the further right to demand that the proponent expand the scope of his questioning of the witness to avoid creating a misleading initial impression. The statutes prescribe this rule for writings or recorded statements.[7] The party invoking Rule 106 must specify the omitted portion of the writing

---

102 L. Ed. 2d 445 (1988), the Court indicated that Rule 106 "partially codified" the completeness doctrine. The implication is that the uncodified aspect of the doctrine is still in effect in federal court.

[6]See note 7 infra. *See also* U.S. v. Bollin, 264 F.3d 391, 414 (4th Cir. 2001) ("The fact that some of the omitted testimony arguably was exculpatory does not, without more, make it admissible under the rule of completeness"); U.S. v. Burns, 162 F.3d 840, 853 (5th Cir. 1998) (Rule 106 "guards against 'the danger that an out-of-context statement may create such prejudice that it is impossible to repair by a subsequent presentation of additional material'"); Bowers v. State, 298 Md. 115, 468 A.2d 101 (1983) (to explain or shed light on the meaning of the part already received). Fed. R. Civ. P. 32(a)(6) contains the following, flexible rule for depositions: "If a party offers in evidence only part of a deposition, an adverse party may require the offeror to introduce other parts that in fairness should be considered with the part introduced, and any part may itself introduce any other parts." The fairness concept originated in Ill. Sup. Ct. R. 212(c).

[7]Former Fed. R. Evid. 106 provided:

When a writing or recorded statement or part thereof is introduced by a party, an adverse party may require the introduction at that time of any other part or any other writing or recorded statement which ought in fairness to be considered contemporaneously with it.

Uniform Rule of Evidence 106 is identical in content. Effective December 1, 2011, restyled Fed. R. Evid. 106 reads:

If a party introduces all or part of a writing or record statement, an adverse party may require the introduction, at that time, of any other part—or any other writing or recorded statement—that in fairness ought to be considered at the same time.

*E.g.*, Beech Aircraft Corp. v. Rainey, 488 U.S. 153, 171, 109 S. Ct. 439, 102 L. Ed. 2d 445 (1988) ("The common-law 'rule of completeness', which underlies Federal Rule of Evidence 106, was designed to prevent exactly the type of prejudice of which Rainey complains. In its aspect relevant to this case, the rule of completeness was stated succinctly by Wigmore: 'the opponent, against whom a part of an utterance has been put in, may in his turn complement it by putting in the remainder, in order to secure for the tribunal a complete understanding of the total tenor and effect of the utterance'. 7 J. Wigmore, Evidence in Trials at Common Law § 2113, p. 653 (J. Chadbourn rev. 1978)."); U.S. v. Soures, 736 F.2d 87, 91 (3d Cir. 1984) ("Under this doctrine of completeness, a second writing may be required to be read if it is necessary to (1) explain the admitted portion, (2) place the admitted portion in context, (3) avoid misleading the trier of fact, or (4) insure a fair and impartial understanding. United States v. Marin, 669 F.2d 73, 84 (2d Cir. 1982).").

It has been properly assumed that a "recorded" statement includes a tape recording. U.S. v. Salsedo, 607 F.2d 318 (9th Cir. 1979); In re Air Crash Disaster at John F. Kennedy Intern. Airport on June 24, 1975, 635 F.2d 67 (2d Cir. 1980). The term "writing" encompasses correspondence. Flint v. Youngstown Sheet & Tube Co., 143 F.2d 923 (C.C.A. 2d Cir. 1944). *See* DesJardins v. State, 759 N.E.2d 1036, 1037 (Ind. 2001) (under Rule 106, "all modes of conveying information, including videotapes, constitute writings or recordings . . . , even if they are defined by Rule 1001 as 'photographs' ").

Fed. R. Evid. 106 has been applied when the contents of a writing have effectively been presented to the jury during a witness's cross-examination even though the writing itself was not formally received in evidence. U.S. v. Pendas–Martinez, 845 F.2d 938 (11th Cir. 1988).

With respect to determining which "other" written or recorded statements are included, see U.S. v. Boylan, 898 F.2d 230, 257 (1st Cir. 1990) ("[I]n determining the admissibility of various units contained in document collections, a preliminary decision must be made as to what grouping constitutes a fair and reasonably complete unit of material. In some cases, that unit may be a single document; in others, all the documents; or in a third class, some subpart of a document or collection. [Citations omitted] We believe that the only sound approach is to accord the district court, within its usual evidentiary discretion, the task of determining what reasonable unit of wholeness must be preserved in order to comply with Rule 106's mandate of completeness.").

The party seeking admission of any other part or any other writing or recorded statement must specify the portion sought to be introduced and explain why in fairness that portion ought to be considered contemporaneously. U.S. v. Sweiss, 814 F.2d 1208, 1212 (7th Cir. 1987).

The Advisory Committee's Note for Rule 106 states, "For practical reasons, the rule is limited to writings and recorded statements and does not apply to conversations." Some courts insist that the rule is limited to writings and recordings. U.S. v. Branch, 91 F.3d 699 (5th Cir. 1996) (most circuits have held that Rule 106 does not apply to testimony about oral conversations); U.S. v. Blakeney, 942 F.2d 1001, 1029 (6th Cir. 1991); 1 Weinstein's Federal Evidence para. 106.03[1] (rev. 2011). Nevertheless, the trial judge appears to have the same power to require the introduction of remainder of oral conversations under Federal and Revised Uniform Rule of Evidence (1974) 611(a). U.S. v. Li, 55 F.3d 325, 329 (7th Cir. 1995) ("Fed. R. Evid. 611(a) grants district courts the same authority regarding oral statements. . . ."); U.S. v. Alvarado, 882 F.2d 645, 650 n.5 (2d Cir. 1989) ("This rule is stated as to writings in Fed. R. Evid. 106, but Fed. R. Evid. 611(a) renders it substantially applicable to oral testimony as well"); U.S. v. Castro, 813 F.2d 571 (2d Cir. 1987) ("in practice verbal precision cannot be expected when the source of evidence as to an utterance is the memory of a witness"); U.S. v. Goldwire, 55 M.J. 139 (C.A.A.F. 2001) (under Rule 611(a), the judge has discretion to extend Rule 106 to oral statements); Sipary v. State, 91 P.3d 296 (Alaska Ct. App. 2004); State v. Cabrera-Pena, 361 S.C. 372, 605 S.E.2d 522, 525–26 (2004) ("We find the state's assertion of a distinction between written and oral conversations in this case to be one without a difference. This is not a case in which the defendant gave numerous written and oral statements to police over several hours, days or weeks. [T]his was a one-hour conversation with police wherein Cabrera-Pena 'gave a statement–a written statement and vocal statements.' The Court of Appeals held that Rule 106, by its terms, applies only to written or recorded statements. We find the common law of this state

or tape which supposedly serves as essential, integral context for the part the opposing party wants to introduce.[8]

It is sometimes stated that the additional material may be introduced only if it is otherwise admissible.[9] However, as a categorical rule, that statement is unsound.[10] In particular, the statement is sometimes inaccurate as applied to hearsay law. At

---

extends the rule of completeness to oral communications. Accordingly, where, as here, the state elects to use a witness to elicit portions of a conversation (and incriminating statements therein) made by a defendant, the rule of completeness requires the defendant be permitted to inquire into the full substance of that conversation").

[8]U.S. v. Flentge, 151 Fed. Appx. 490, 492 (8th Cir. 2005) (the defendant never identified the portions of the record and explained how those portions would place the government's evidence in context); U.S. v. Ramos-Caraballo, 375 F.3d 797, 802 (8th Cir. 2004); U.S. v. King, 351 F.3d 859 (8th Cir. 2003); U.S. v. Webber, 255 F.3d 523, 526 (8th Cir. 2001) ("the party urging admission of an excluded conversation must 'specify the portion of the testimony that is relevant to the issue at trial and that qualifies or explains portions already admitted").

[9]*See generally* U.S. v. Pendas–Martinez, 845 F.2d 938, 944 n.10 (11th Cir. 1988):

Following 21 C. Wright & K. Graham, Federal Practice and Procedure, §§ 5072, 5078 (1977 & Supp. 1987), several courts have held that Rule 106 can fulfill its function adequately only if otherwise inadmissible evidence can be admitted under the rule. See, e.g., United States v. Sutton, 801 F.2d 1346, 1368–69 (D.C. Cir. 1986); see also United States v. LeFevour, 798 F.2d 977, 981 (7th Cir. 1986) (either otherwise inadmissible evidence becomes admissible or if inadmissible (perhaps because of privilege), then the misleading portion must be excluded as well) (dictum). This analysis emphasizes the rule's provision that "any other portion" may be admitted, with the only stated limitation being that the other portion "in fairness ought to be admitted." Fed. R. Evid. 106.

Other Circuits have followed 1 J. Weinstein & M. Berger, Weinstein's Evidence, ¶ 106[02] at p. 106–12 (1985), to hold that Rule 106 addresses only an order of proof problem and does not make admissible what is otherwise inadmissible. See, e.g., United States v. Costner, 684 F.2d 370, 373 (6th Cir. 1982); United States v. Burreson, 643 F.2d 1344, 1349 (9th Cir. 1981), cert. denied, 454 U.S. 830, 102 S.Ct. 125, 70 L.Ed.2d 106, 454 U.S. 847, 102 S.Ct. 165, 70 L.Ed.2d 135 (1981).

This Court has not addressed this issue, and we find it unnecessary to do so here . . . .

*See also* U.S. v. Shaver, 89 Fed. Appx. 529, 532–33 (6th Cir. 2004) (the court emphasized that Beech Aircraft Corp. v. Rainey, 488 U.S. 153, 109 S. Ct. 439, 102 L. Ed. 2d 445 (1988) "did not allow hearsay in"; "Completeness . . . does not outweigh the hearsay rules . . . . Exculpatory hearsay may not come in solely on the basis of completeness"); Echo Acceptance Corp. v. Household Retail Services, Inc., 267 F.3d 1068 (10th Cir. 2001) (the rule of completeness does not allow a party to introduce otherwise inadmissible hearsay); U.S. v. Giles, 67 F. Supp. 2d 947, 951 (N.D. Ill. 1999) ("the Rule of Completeness does not 'render admissible the evidence which otherwise is inadmissible under hearsay rules' ").

[10]U.S. v. Collicott, 92 F.3d 973, 983 (9th Cir. 1996); Barrett v. U.S., 965 F.2d 1184, 1194 (1st Cir. 1992) ("there is considerable disagreement whether Fed. R. Evid. 106 can ever serve as a basis for admitting evidence which is inadmissible on other grounds"); U.S. v. Boylan, 898 F.2d 230, 257 n.16 (1st Cir. 1990); Hickson Corp. v. Norfolk Southern Ry. Co., 227 F. Supp. 2d 903, 909 n.6 (E.D. Tenn. 2002), aff'd, 124 Fed. Appx. 336 (6th Cir. 2005) ("a split of opinion"); Sipary

least when the other passage of the writing or statement is so closely connected to the part the proponent contemplates introducing that it furnishes essential context[11] for that part, the passage becomes admissible on a nonhearsay theory.[12] For that matter, the contextual nonhearsay theory does not exhaust the proponent's arguments. As we shall see, the complex of admissibility doctrines includes the concept of waiver of objection through "door opening."[13] In some cases, under that doctrine the proponent can successfully argue that the adversary's prior conduct has "opened the door" and rendered an otherwise inadmissible part admissible.[14] Ultimately, whether an otherwise

---

v. State, 91 P.3d 296 (Alaska Ct. App. 2004); Nance, Verbal Completeness and Exclusionary Rules Under the Federal Rules of Evidence, 75 Tex. L. Rev. 51, 127, 129 (1996) (the author concedes that under the case law, it is unsettled whether Rule 106 has a "trumping function" to override "an otherwise valid objection"; however, the author argues in favor of recognizing that function).

[11]U.S. v. Hoffecker, 530 F.3d 137, 192–93 (3d Cir. 2008) (while one tape was intended to recruit prospective telemarketers, the other tape consisted of instructions to telemarketers who had already been recruited); U.S. v. Ramos-Caraballo, 375 F.3d 797, 803 (8th Cir. 2004) ("the rule does not complete into play when 'a few inconsistencies between out-of-court and in-court statements are revealed through cross-examination; rather, it operates to ensure fairness where a misunderstanding or distortion created by the other party can only be averted by the introduction of the full text of the out-of-court statement' ").

[12]In a closely analogous situation, when prosecutors offer tape recordings including both accused's admissions and third party's statements to the accused, the courts routinely rule that the statements are admissible for the nonhearsay purpose of establishing the interpretive context of the accused's admissions. Wright v. Quarterman, 470 F.3d 581, 585–86 (5th Cir. 2006) ("Under the rule of optional completeness, hearsay is admissible

when it serves to clarify other hearsay evidence elicited by the opposing party"); U.S. v. Sorrentino, 72 F.3d 294 (2d Cir. 1995) (overruled by, U.S. v. Abad, 514 F.3d 271 (2d Cir. 2008)) (the third party's statements to the accused make the accused's statements more intelligible); U.S. v. Catano, 65 F.3d 219 (1st Cir. 1995) ("into context"); U.S. v. Beal, 940 F.2d 1159 (8th Cir. 1991) ("explanatory in interpreting" the admissions); U.S. v. Ailsworth, 948 F. Supp. 1485 (D. Kan. 1996). Of course, under this theory of admissibility, on request the judge would give the jury a limiting instruction as to the evidentiary status of the other passage.

[13]U.S. v. Corrigan, 168 F.2d 641, 645 (C.C.A. 2d Cir. 1948) ("[T]he doctrine of 'opening the door' is an application of the 'principle of completeness;' that is, if one party to litigation puts in evidence part of a document, or a correspondence or a conversation, which is detrimental to the opposing party, the latter may introduce the balance of the document, correspondence or conversation in order to explain or rebut the adverse inferences which might arise from the fragmentary or incomplete character of the evidence introduced by his adversary."). For further discussion of "opening the door," see § 57 infra.

[14]U.S. v. Sutton, 801 F.2d 1346, 1368 (D.C. Cir. 1986) ("Rule 106 can adequately fulfill its function only by permitting the admission of some otherwise inadmissible evidence when the court finds in fairness that the

inadmissible part offered to explain, modify, or qualify the part already received is admitted should turn on whether its probative value for that purpose is substantially outweighed by dangers of unfair prejudice, confusion of the issues, misleading the jury, or waste of time.[15]

The adversary has another alternative, namely, later invoking the more limited, common law completeness rule. The state of the law governing this alternative is clearer and more consistent. The adversary may wait until her own next opportunity to present evidence. Then merely by virtue of the fact that the first party has earlier introduced a part, she has the right to introduce the remainder of the writing, recording, statement, correspondence, former testimony, or conversation relating to the same subject matter.[16] The more drastic doctrine, Rule 106, does not come into play unless the other passage is so closely related to the part the proponent offers that presenting only that part to the jury would be a half-truth which might mislead the jury. In contrast, the common law right applies so long as the other pas-

---

proffered evidence should be considered contemporaneously. A contrary construction raises the specter of distorted and misleading trials, and creates difficulties for both litigants and the trial court."). *E.g.*, Polk v. Yellow Freight System, Inc., 876 F.2d 527 (6th Cir. 1989) (conclusion in report that incident was "fabrication and exaggeration" properly admitted under Rule 106); Grobelny v. W.T. Cowan, Inc., 151 F.2d 810 (C.C.A. 2d Cir. 1945) (hearsay statements in medical report admitted as explanatory aid to a proper understanding of segments of the medical report offered by the opponent).

[15]Fed. R. Evid. 403. Either the additional evidence offered to dispel the misleading effect or the evidence originally offered that created the misleading impression may be excluded. U.S. v. LeFevour, 798 F.2d 977, 981 (7th Cir. 1986) ("If otherwise inadmissible evidence is necessary to correct a misleading impression, then either it is admissible for this limited purpose by force of Rule 106, the view taken in 21 Wright & Graham, Federal Practice and Procedure § 5072, at p. 344 (1977), or, if it is inadmissible (maybe because of privilege), the misleading evidence

must be excluded too."); U.S. v. Gold, 743 F.2d 800 (11th Cir. 1984) (questions and answers can be deleted from a transcript in order to avoid prejudice to codefendant over defendant's objection that inclusion was required by Rule 106).

[16]Fed. R. Evid. 106, Advisory Committee's Note states, "The rule does not in any way circumscribe the right of the adversary to develop the matter on cross-examination or as part of his own case." *See generally* Beech Aircraft Corp. v. Rainey, 488 U.S. 153, 172, 109 S. Ct. 439, 102 L. Ed. 2d 445 (1988) ("In proposing Rule 106, the Advisory Committee stressed that it 'does not in any way circumscribe the right of the adversary to develop the matter on cross-examination or as part of his own case'. Advisory Committee's Notes on Fed. Rule Evid. 106, 28 U.S.C. App., p. 682. We take this to be a reaffirmation of the obvious: that when one party has made use of a portion of a document, such that misunderstanding or distortion can be averted only through presentation of another portion, the material required for completeness is *ipso facto* relevant and therefore admissible under Rules 401 and 402.").

sage is logically relevant to the same topic as the part the proponent offers. This right is subject to the previously mentioned qualification which comes into play when there is an independent evidentiary objection to the remainder.[17]

## § 57  Fighting fire with fire: Inadmissible evidence as opening the door[1]

One party successfully offers inadmissible evidence. There are various potential explanations for the introduction of the inadmissible evidence: The evidence might come in because the adversary neglects to object, he has no opportunity to object, or the judge erroneously overrules an objection.[2] Is the adversary entitled to answer this evidence, with testimony by way of denial or explanation? The question has prompted a sharp split of authority. In some jurisdictions the adversary is not entitled to meet the evidence, in others he may do so, and in still others he may do so if he would be prejudiced by denying him an opportunity to meet the evidence. However, it may be significant that in reaching these results, many, if not most, decisions seem merely to affirm the trial judge's action.[3] The majority of courts appear to subscribe to the general proposition that "one who

---

[17]*E.g.*, Socony Vacuum Oil Co. v. Marvin, 313 Mich. 528, 21 N.W.2d 841 (1946) (when part of transcribed interview between plaintiff's investigator and defendant was introduced by plaintiff, defendant not entitled to offer another part describing his poor financial condition and stating that he was not insured); Jeddeloh v. Hockenhull, 219 Minn. 541, 18 N.W.2d 582 (1945) (although part of a conversation after accident was proved, the door not opened to proof of part showing that the defendant was insured); State v. Skaug, 63 Nev. 59, 161 P.2d 708 (1945) (separable part of confession showing commission of other unconnected crimes should have been excluded). See also notes 8–15 supra.

**[Section 57]**

[1]*See* 1 Wigmore, Evidence § 15 ("Curative Admissibility") (3d ed. 1940); 1 Weinstein's Federal Evidence § 103.14 (rev. 2011); Note, 35 Mich. L. Rev. 636 (1937); West's Key Number Digest, Evidence ☞155(5).

The kinship between the subject matter of the present section and

waiver of objections, § 55 supra, is apparent, but cognizance must be taken of differences noted in the text.

[2]The party introducing the inadmissible evidence may not complain. All American Life and Cas. Co. v. Oceanic Trade Alliance Council Intern., Inc., 756 F.2d 474, 479 (6th Cir. 1985) ("Under the 'invited error' doctrine, it is an accepted matter of law that where the injection of allegedly inadmissible evidence is attributable to the action of the party seeking to exclude that evidence, its introduction does not constitute reversible error. See United States v. Lerma, 657 F.2d 786, 788 (5th Cir. 1981); United States v. Martinez, 604 F.2d 361, 366 (5th Cir. 1979).").

[3]1 Wigmore, Evidence § 15 (3d ed. 1940). Comment, Evidence—Curative Admissibility in Missouri, 32 Mo. L. Rev. 505, 505–08 (1967) (reviewing the split of authority).

The principle is often referred to as "door opening", "curative admissibility", or "invited error."

induces a trial court to let down the bars to a field of inquiry that is not competent or relevant to the issues cannot complain if his adversary is also allowed to avail himself of the opening."[4] Federal cases occasionally apply the same general notion.[5]

---

[4]Warren Live Stock Co. v. Farr, 142 F. 116, 117 (C.C.A. 8th Cir. 1905). To like effect, *see, e.g.*, St. Clair County v. Bukacek, 272 Ala. 323, 131 So. 2d 683 (1961) (irrelevant evidence; "rule is that irrelevant, incompetent or illegal evidence may be admitted to rebut evidence of like character"); Corley v. Andrews, 349 S.W.2d 395 (Mo. Ct. App. 1961) (the counter evidence was hearsay; the counter evidence "should have been allowed"); Hartman v. Maryland Cas. Co., 417 S.W.2d 640 (Tex. Civ. App. Waco 1967).

Some courts, however, have, at least occasionally, expressed the view that the introduction of inadmissible evidence does "not open the door" to answering inadmissible evidence. People v. McDaniel, 59 Cal. App. 2d 672, 140 P.2d 88 (2d Dist. 1943); Savannah News–Press, Inc. v. Hartridge, 110 Ga. App. 203, 138 S.E.2d 173 (1964) (the introduction of immaterial evidence did not entitle opponent to rebuttal evidence; "there can be no equation of errors in the trial of a case").

Other courts have stated that the introduction of inadmissible evidence "opens the door" only if the opponent is prejudiced unless he can meet the evidence. U.S. v. Nardi, 633 F.2d 972 (1st Cir. 1980) ("no prejudice to be rebutted"); Thurman v. Pepsi–Cola Bottling Co., 289 N.W.2d 141 (Minn. 1980) (if evidence is inadmissible and non-prejudicial, rebutting evidence is inadmissible); 1 Wigmore, Evidence § 15 (3d ed. 1940).

[5]In re Aircrash In Bali, Indonesia on April 22, 1974, 684 F.2d 1301 (9th Cir. 1982) (alternate reason for admission of evidence of pilot's incompetency was opponent's evidence that pilot was competent); CCMS Pub. Co., Inc. v. Dooley–Maloof, Inc., 645 F.2d 33 (10th Cir. 1981) (appellant introduced evidence of compromise on cross-examination of opponent; opponent "was entitled to rebut"); Croce v. Bromley Corp., 623 F.2d 1084 (5th Cir.1980) (approval of trial court's decision admitting pilot's past conduct to rebut previous evidence to the contrary; all such evidence went to inadmissible purpose of showing pilot's reputation); U.S. v. Giese, 597 F.2d 1170 (9th Cir. 1979) (defendant introduced the acts of selling, owning, and reading various books to show peaceable character, opening door to cross-examination as to contents of a particular book); U.S. v. Doran, 564 F.2d 1176 (5th Cir. 1977) (defendant testified he refused plea bargain deal; on cross-examination, government could ask him about otherwise inadmissible counter-offer); U.S. v. James, 555 F.2d 992 (D.C. Cir. 1977) ("ordinarily evidence inadmissible to prove the case-in-chief is rendered admissible only if the defendant himself introduces the evidence or is in some manner estopped from objecting to its use;" but principle held inapplicable on the facts at hand). The rule was applied to justify government evidence contradicting defendant's statement although the government evidence was introduced first in time. U.S. v. Benedetto, 571 F.2d 1246 (2d Cir. 1978).

Inadmissible matters brought out on cross-examination cannot be used by the cross-examiner to open the door to otherwise inadmissible rebuttal evidence. U.S. v. Pantone, 609 F.2d 675, 681 (3d Cir. 1979) ("[W]e disapprove of the practice of using cross-examination beyond the scope of the direct testimony for the purpose of laying a foundation for the introduction, as rebuttal, of otherwise inadmissible evidence."); U.S. v. Lambert, 463 F.2d 552, 557 (7th Cir. 1972) ("The general rule is that a witness may not be impeached by contradiction as to col-

Unfortunately, the published appellate opinions afford little guidance on the question as to how the trial judge should deal with the problem.[6] Because of the many variable factors affecting the solution in a particular case, the diverse situations do not lend themselves easily to neat generalizations. However, the published decisions identify two key factors, the prejudicial nature of the evidence and whether the opponent made a timely objection to block the admission of the evidence. Given those two factors, the following generalizations, having some support in the decisions, are reasonable:

(1) If the inadmissible evidence sought to be answered is irrelevant and not prejudice-arousing, to save time and to avoid distraction from the issues the judge should refuse to hear answering evidence. However, under the prevailing view, if he does admit it, the party opening the door has no standing to complain.[7] Consider, for example, a case in which one party improperly injects evidence of the good character of one of his

---

lateral or irrelevant matters elicited on cross-examination."). *See also* note 228 infra.

[6]The following cases illustrate the various approaches:

- *Discretionary:* U.S. v. Whitworth, 856 F.2d 1268, 1285 (9th Cir. 1988) ("Under the rule of curative admissibility, or the 'opening the door' doctrine, the introduction of inadmissible evidence by one party allows an opponent, in the court's discretion, to introduce evidence on the same issue to rebut any false impression that might have resulted from the earlier admission."). Accord State v. Small, 301 N.C. 407, 272 S.E.2d 128 (1980).
- *Exclude:* U.S. v. Duran, 886 F.2d 167, 169 (8th Cir. 1989) (" '[T]he remedy of the defense is to object when the victim [makes a statement about her past sexual behavior]; [he] may not use the prosecution's violation of Rule 412 as an excuse for further inquiry into the victim's past sexual behavior.' ").
- *Admit:* U.S. v. Garcia, 900 F.2d 571 (2d Cir. 1990) (where a defendant in his direct testimony falsely states a specific fact,

the prosecution may prove, either through cross-examination or by calling its own witnesses, that he lied *as to that fact*). *Accord*, State v. Crosman, 125 N.H. 527, 484 A.2d 1095 (1984).*See generally* Gilligan & Imwinkelried, Bringing the "Opening the Door" Theory to a Close: The Tendency to Overlook the Specific Contradiction Doctrine in Evidence Law, 41 Santa Clara L. Rev. 807, 824–36 (2001) (distinguishing in detail between specific contradiction impeachment and the curative admissibility doctrine).

[7]If the evidence sought to be answered is irrelevant, the rule against contradicting on a collateral issue generally dictates the exclusion of the answering evidence. See § 49 supra. The opening the door theory operates in a very real sense as an exception. U.S. v. Ochoa, 609 F.2d 198, 205 (5th Cir. 1980) ("In United States v. Caron, 474 F.2d 506 (5th Cir. 1973), the defendant, charged with giving false testimony before a grand jury by denying that he was a bookmaker, testified in his own defense and categorically denied that he was a bookmaker or engaged in bookmaking operations. On cross-examination, the

distant relatives who played a minor role in the litigated event.[8] That type of evidence is unlikely to change the outcome of the trial. It would hardly be an abuse of discretion for the judge to exclude the opponent's evidence attacking the relative's character.

(2) Suppose alternatively that, although inadmissible, the evidence is relevant to the issues and hence presumably damaging to the adversary's case, or though irrelevant is materially prejudicial and the adversary seasonably objected or moved to strike. Here the adversary should be entitled to present answering evidence as of right.[9] By objecting, he did his best to save the court from mistake. His remedy of assigning appellate error to the ruling is inadequate.[10] He needs a fair opportunity to win his case at the trial level by refuting the damaging evidence. In many cases, the adversary simply cannot afford the expense of a second trial after an appeal. Assume that the opponent succeeds in introducing inadmissible evidence of his own good character.[11] That type of evidence is much more likely to affect the verdict than testimony about a distant relative's character. (This situation should be distinguished from the question, considered in § 55, whether the prior objection is waived if the answering evidence is permitted.)

(3) Suppose that the first inadmissible evidence is relevant or that albeit irrelevant, the evidence is prejudicial and the adversary failed to object or to move to strike out where an objection might have avoided the harm. Here in principle the admission of answering evidence should rest in the judge's discretion.[12] The judge ought to weigh the probable impact of the first evidence, the time and distraction incident to answer-

---

court allowed the introduction of evidence showing defendant's dealings with another bookmaker though it was collateral to the issues raised by the indictment and for which defendant was on trial.").

[8]*E.g.*, Fortner v. Bruhn, 217 Cal. App. 2d 184, 31 Cal. Rptr. 503 (1st Dist. 1963).

[9]Bremhorst v. Phillips Coal Co., 202 Iowa 1251, 211 N.W. 898, 904 (1927) ("It was the duty of the court to give both parties the benefit of the same rules of evidence."); Mattechek v. Pugh, 153 Or. 1, 55 P.2d 730 (1936). Contra: Buck v. St. Louis Union Trust Co., 267 Mo. 644, 185 S.W. 208, 213 (1916) (" . . . his objection will save him on appeal and he needs no other

protection."). *See* Note, 35 Mich. L. Rev. 636, 637 (1937).

[10]Note, 35 Mich. L. Rev. 636, 637 (1937). Wigmore takes the opposite view. 1 Wigmore, Evidence § 15 (3d ed. 1940).

[11]People v. Matlock, 11 Cal. App. 3d 453, 89 Cal. Rptr. 862 (1st Dist. 1970).

[12]Grist v. Upjohn Co., 16 Mich. App. 452, 168 N.W.2d 389 (1969) (permitting introduction of hearsay concerning same conversation was within the court's discretion); Crosby v. Keen, 200 Miss. 590, 28 So. 2d 322 (1946); Biener v. St. Louis Public Service Co., 160 S.W.2d 780 (Mo. Ct. App. 1942) (semble); Franklin Fire Ins. Co. v. Coleman, 87 S.W.2d 537 (Tex. Civ.

ing it, and the likely effectiveness of a curative instruction to the jury to disregard it.[13] However, here several courts have indicated that introduction of the answering evidence is a matter of right and not allowed merely in the judge's discretion.[14]

(4) In any event, if the inadmissible evidence or even the inquiry eliciting it is so prejudice-arousing that an objection or motion to strike would not have erased the harm, the adversary should be entitled to answer it as of right.[15]

This section is devoted to the question of rebutting inadmissible evidence. That question differs from the issue of whether a

---

App. Waco 1935) (in a suit on a fire policy, the defense was arson; defendant's witness volunteered statement that he arrested plaintiff after the fire; the court held that the trial judge had discretion to permit the defendant to show the dismissal of complaint on which he was arrested).

[13]One factor in a court's decision to permit rebuttal evidence under the doctrine of "opening the door" is the recognition that inadmissible evidence once heard by the jury sometimes cannot be removed from consideration merely because it is formally stricken from the record and the jury instructed to disregard it. Accordingly, refutation of inadmissible evidence is occasionally for this reason alone permitted. Counsel, aware that refutation may be allowed if no objection is made but will not be permitted if the evidence is stricken, may consciously refrain from objecting.

[14]London v. Standard Oil Co. of California, Inc., 417 F.2d 820 (9th Cir. 1969); Moschetti v. City of Tucson, 9 Ariz. App. 108, 449 P.2d 945 (1969); Com. v. Wakelin, 230 Mass. 567, 120 N.E. 209, 212–13 (1918); Sprenger v. Sprenger, 146 N.W.2d 36 (N.D. 1966); Shoup v. Mannino, 188 Pa. Super. 457, 149 A.2d 678 (1959).

Illustrative are the cases in which an accused takes the stand and makes an overly-broad denial of guilt ("I never"). Such evidence is not irrelevant in the sense used in Fed. R. Evid. 401 but is rather inadmissible as going to establish character by specific instance prohibited by Fed. R. Evid.

404 and 405. Numerous decisions allow the prosecutor to rebut by evidence of otherwise inadmissible other offenses. People v. Westek, 31 Cal. 2d 469, 190 P.2d 9 (1948); State v. Barnett, 156 Kan. 746, 137 P.2d 133 (1943). In Walder v. U.S., 347 U.S. 62, 74 S. Ct. 354, 98 L. Ed. 503 (1954) this principle was carried to the extreme of allowing the results of an unconstitutional search and seizure to be introduced. See § 178 infra. If the statement is elicited on cross-examination, much authority refuses to allow it to be used as a door opener. State v. Goldsmith, 104 Ariz. 226, 450 P.2d 684 (1969), Dalton v. People, 224 Ill. 333, 79 N.E. 669 (1906), and Agnello v. U.S., 269 U.S. 20, 46 S. Ct. 4, 70 L. Ed. 145 (1925) disallowed use of the results of an unconstitutional search and seizure under these circumstances. See also note 5 supra.

[15]Thus, in State v. Witham, 72 Me. 531, 536, 1881 WL 4001 (1881) a child's birth to an unmarried woman was improperly admitted as evidence of defendant's adultery, and counterevidence of other men's intercourse was received to rebut it. The court said: "The introduction of immaterial testimony to meet immaterial testimony on the other side is generally within the discretion of the presiding judge. But if one side introduces evidence irrelevant to the issue, which is prejudicial and harmful to the other party, then, although it comes in without objection, the other party is entitled to introduce evidence which will directly and strictly contradict it."

party's introduction of evidence inadmissible under some exclusionary rule (such as hearsay) gives the adversary license to introduce other evidence which (1) is inadmissible under the same exclusionary rule but (2) bears on a different issue or is irrelevant to the original inadmissible evidence.[16] The "opening the door" doctrine has not been extended that far; the door does not swing open that widely.

## § 58   Admissibility of evidence dependent on proof of other facts: "Connecting up"[1]

The relevancy or admissibility of evidence of a particular fact frequently hinges on the proof of other facts. Thus, proof that a speeding automobile passed a particular spot at a certain time,[2] or that there was a conversation between the witness and an unidentified stranger at a given time and place,[3] will become relevant only when the automobile is identified as the defendant's or the stranger is shown to be the plaintiff. In the same manner, evidence of certain acts and declarations might not become material until they are shown to be those of the defendant's agent.[4] Likewise, a copy of a writing does not become admissible until the original is proven to be lost or destroyed.[5] In terms of logic, some of these missing facts may be thought of as preliminary to the fact offered, and others as coordinate with it. In either event, often only one fact can be proven at a time or by a witness. In a given case, the most convenient sequence of calling witnesses might not coincide with the order of strict logic.[6] Logic might dictate that a doctor testify first, but logic might have to yield to an emergency surgery.

Who decides the order of facts? In the first instance, the offering counsel does so by making the offer. However, in his general

---

[16]The distinction is applied in Daniels v. Dillinger, 445 S.W.2d 410 (Mo. Ct. App. 1969).

[Section 58]

[1]1 Wigmore, Evidence § 14 (3d ed. 1940), 6 id. § 1871 (Chadbourn rev. 1976); Note, 32 Ill. L. Rev. 882 (1938); Necessity and sufficiency of renewal of objection to, or offer of, evidence admitted or excluded conditionally, 88 A.L.R.2d 12; West's Key Number Digest, Trial ☞51, 79, 90.

[2]State v. Freeman, 93 Utah 125, 71 P.2d 196 (1937).

[3]Atlanta & W. P. R. Co. v. Truitt, 65 Ga. App. 320, 16 S.E.2d 273 (1941).

[4]Smith v. Ohio Millers' Mut. Fire Ins. Co., 320 Mo. 146, 6 S.W.2d 920 (1928).

[5]See Ch. 23 infra.

[6]See the remarks of Miller, J. in a conspiracy case: "The logical sequence of events—from agreement in a common purpose to perpetration of an act designed to carry it out—does not require that introduction of the evidence must follow that same rigorous sequence." McDonald v. U.S., 133 F.2d 23 (App. D.C. 1942).

discretionary supervision over the order of proof avoid confusion,[7] the judge may require that the missing fact be proved first.[8] But the trial judge seldom does so. At common law, when the adversary objects to the relevancy or the competency of the offered fact, the everyday method of handling the situation is to admit it conditionally; that is, the judge accepts the evidence on the proponent's express or implied assurance as an officer of the court that she will "connect up" the tendered evidence by proving the missing facts later.[9] Federal Rule of Evidence 104(b), Uniform Rule 104(c), and Rule 611(a) in both codes grant the trial judge this same authority.[10]

However, in a long trial with many witnesses and complex facts, it is easy for the offering counsel to later forget the need to present the required "connecting" proof, and for the judge and the adversary to overlook this gap in the evidence. Who has the burden of invoking the failure of the condition subsequent? The burden is on the objecting party to renew the objection and invoke the condition.[11] According to the majority view, the opponent

----

[7]Fed. R. Evid. 103 and Unif. R. Evid. 103; Matz v. U.S., 158 F.2d 190 (App. D.C. 1946) (order of prosecution's evidence in a bigamy case); 6 Wigmore, Evidence §§ 1867, 1871 (Chadbourn rev. 1976).

[8]Gerber v. Columbia Palace Corp., 183 A.2d 398 (Mun. Ct. App. D.C. 1962) (judge ruled evidence inadmissible without proof of other facts).

[9]For decisions approving the practice, see, for example, Innes v. Beauchene, 370 P.2d 174 (Alaska 1962); Brown v. Neal, 283 N.C. 604, 197 S.E.2d 505 (1973).

[10]Former Federal Rule 104(b) and Uniform Rule 104(c) provide that when relevancy depends upon a condition of fact, the court may admit the evidence "subject to" the introduction of evidence to support a finding of fulfillment of the condition. Effective December 1, 2011, restyled Fed. R. Evid. 104(b) states that "[w]hen the relevance of evidence depends on whether a fact exists, proof must be introduced sufficient to support a finding that the fact does exist." See the rule at § 53, note 12. Rule 611(a) recognizes the judge's authority to control the mode and order of interrogating witnesses

and presenting evidence. See Huddleston v. U.S., 485 U.S. 681, 690, 108 S. Ct. 1496, 99 L. Ed. 2d 771 (1988) ("The trial court has traditionally exercised the broadest sort of discretion in controlling the order of proof at trial, and we see nothing in the Rules of Evidence that would change this practice. Often the trial court may decide to allow the proponent to introduce evidence concerning a similar act, and at a later point in the trial assess whether sufficient evidence has been offered to permit the jury to make the requisite finding. If the proponent has failed to meet this minimal standard of proof, the trial court must instruct the jury to disregard the evidence").

[11]U.S. v. Dougherty, 895 F.2d 399, 403 (7th Cir. 1990) ("If a condition attached to the admission of evidence is not satisfied by the offering party, the burden properly rests with the objecting party to renew the objection. Such a practice affords the trial judge an opportunity to ensure that the evidentiary record is complete and to give proper consideration to any defects or omissions in proof."); Necessity and sufficiency of renewal of objection to, or offer of, evidence admitted or excluded conditionally, 88 A.L.R.2d

must move to strike the evidence conditionally received,[12] when the failure of condition becomes apparent. The failure becomes apparent when the offering party completes the particular stage of the case in which the evidence was offered.[13] When the proponent "rests" without introducing the missing proof, the adversary should then "move to strike"; if the opponent fails to do at that juncture, she cannot later as of right invoke the condition. Although some courts have considered the difference in form dispositive, a motion to strike, a motion to withdraw the fact from the jury, and a request for a curative instruction to disregard the evidence all should be regarded as a sufficient invocation of the condition. This analysis is compatible with Federal and Revised Uniform Rules of Evidence 104(b) and 611(a).

However, the proponent assumed some responsibility by promising to furnish the connecting proof. That responsibility can best be recognized by according the trial judge a discretion to allow the adversary to invoke the condition at any time before the case is submitted to the jury or before final judgment in a bench case, so long as the continued availability of the missing proof

---

12; West's Key Number Digest, Trial ⊕79.

[12]Arnold v. Ellis, 5 Mich. App. 101, 145 N.W.2d 822 (1966) (in judge-tried case, judge could consider evidence when no motion to strike was made); State v. Freeman, 93 Utah 125, 71 P.2d 196 (1937) (a motion to strike was necessary; a mere request for instruction to disregard, at close of case, was insufficient: the decision contains a full discussion with one judge dissenting). But it has been said that in a jury case a motion for an instruction to disregard the evidence is the proper recourse. Kolka v. Jones, 6 N.D. 461, 71 N.W. 558, 564 (1897). *See also* Caley v. Manicke, 29 Ill. App. 2d 323, 173 N.E.2d 209 (2d Dist. 1961) (dictum that failure to connect "at the very least would occasion an instruction to disregard"). As a practical matter, both a motion to strike and a request for a curative instruction to disregard should be made. Decisions are collected in 6 Wigmore, Evidence § 1871 n. 6 (Chadbourn rev. 1976); Necessity and sufficiency of renewal of objection to, or offer of, evidence admitted or excluded conditionally, 88 A.L.R.2d 12.

Normally, it is assumed when evidence is improperly received or not "connected up," an instruction to disregard is a sufficient corrective. But the evidence may be so prejudicial that realistically, an instruction will not cure the harm. National Cash Register Co. v. Kay, 119 S.W.2d 437 (Mo. Ct. App. 1938). "Human nature does not change merely because it is found in the jury box. The human mind is not a slate, from which can be wiped out, at the will and instruction of another, ideas and thoughts written thereon." People v. Deal, 357 Ill. 634, 192 N.E. 649, 652 (1934). Fed. and Unif. R. Evid. 403 authorizes the court to weigh the prejudice and the efficacy of an instruction. See the discussion of the adequacy of curative and limiting instructions in § 59 infra.

[13]In Keber v. American Stores Co., 116 N.J.L. 437, 184 A. 795 (N.J. Ct. Err. & App. 1936) this was said to be the proper time and that an earlier motion was premature. *See also* Note, 32 Ill. L. Rev. 882, 883 (1938); Necessity and sufficiency of renewal of objection to, or offer of, evidence admitted or excluded conditionally, 88 A.L.R.2d 12.

makes it fair to litigate the issue later.[14] It is especially appropriate for the judge to exercise discretion in the adversary's favor when the offering party's case-in-chief was a lengthy one. The longer the case-in-chief is, the greater the probability that the adversary will innocently forget about the issue; and hence, the adversary's failure is relatively excusable.

Distinguish between the practice of conditional receipt pending further proof and the provisional admission of evidence where objection is made, taking the objection under advisement subject to a later ruling when the record has been more amply developed. Here, to preserve the objection, the objecting counsel must renew the objection before the case concludes.[15] The practice seems appropriate enough in a judge-tried case.[16] However, in a jury trial there is a danger that letting the evidence in, even provisionally, might make an impression on the jury that a later instruction cannot erase[17]—a risk that seems unnecessary to incur. Understandably, this practice has been criticized.[18] Although the published opinions sometimes indicate that the trial judge has discretion to employ this procedure, in many, if not most, instances resort to this practice is unnecessary and should be avoided.

### § 59   Evidence admissible for one purpose, inadmissible for another: "Limited admissibility"[1]

#### A Limitation as to Purpose

An item of evidence may be logically relevant in several aspects, leading to distinct inferences or bearing upon different issues.

---

[14]Note, 32 Ill. L. Rev. 882, 884 (1938).

[15]McGee v. Maryland Cas. Co., 240 Miss. 447, 127 So. 2d 656 (1961) (jury case). See cases collected in Necessity and sufficiency of renewal of objection to, or offer of, evidence admitted or excluded conditionally, 88 A.L.R.2d 12.

[16]Its advantages are pointed out by Sanborn, Cir. J., in Builders Steel Co. v. C.I.R., 179 F.2d 377, 379 (8th Cir. 1950).

[17]McKee v. Bassick Min. Co., 8 Colo. 392, 8 P. 561 (1885). Though sometimes criticized, this practice has been used in jury cases. See cases in, Necessity and sufficiency of renewal of objection to, or offer of, evidence admitted or excluded conditionally, 88

A.L.R.2d 12; West's Key Number Digest, Trial ☞51. It is forbidden by statute in Connecticut even in judge-tried cases. Conn. Gen. Stat. Ann. § 52-208 is construed in Kovacs v. Szentes, 130 Conn. 229, 33 A.2d 124 (1943). See note 12 supra, as to the effectiveness of instructions to disregard.

[18]E.g., Missouri Pac. Transp. Co. v. Beard, 179 Miss. 764, 176 So. 156 (1937); West's Key Number Digest, Trial ☞51; Necessity and sufficiency of renewal of objection to, or offer of, evidence admitted or excluded conditionally, 88 A.L.R.2d 12.

**[Section 59]**

[1]1 Wigmore, Evidence § 13 (3d ed. 1940); Weinstein & Berger, Evidence ¶ 105 [01]–[07]; West's Key Number Digest, Trial ☞48.

For one of these purposes it may be admissible but for another inadmissible.[2] In this common situation, subject to the limitations outlined below, the normal practice in case law and under the Federal and Uniform Rules of Evidence is to admit the evidence.[3] The opponent's legitimate interest is protected, not by an objection to its admission,[4] but by a request at the time of the offer for a limiting instruction that the jury consider the evidence

---

[2]*See* Leonard, The New Wigmore: Selected Rules of Limited Admissibility (rev. ed. 2002).

[3]U.S. v. Abel, 469 U.S. 45, 56, 105 S. Ct. 465, 83 L. Ed. 2d 450 (1984) ("But there is no rule of evidence which provides that testimony admissible for one purpose and inadmissible for another purpose is thereby rendered inadmissible; quite the contrary is the case. It would be a strange rule of law which held that relevant, competent evidence which tended to show bias on the part of a witness was nonetheless inadmissible because it also tended to show that the witness was a liar."). *E.g.*, Lubbock Feed Lots, Inc. v. Iowa Beef Processors, Inc., 630 F.2d 250 (5th Cir. 1980) (evidence constituting inadmissible hearsay to show agency was admissible for impeachment by contradiction); Sprinkle v. Davis, 111 F.2d 925 (C.C.A. 4th Cir. 1940) (the action was a suit for injury to plaintiff highway workman by defendant's automobile: the trial judge erred in excluding defendant's evidence that plaintiff had been compensated by Highway Department; the evidence was inadmissible on issue of liability or damages but admissible to show bias of witnesses who were highway employees); Williams v. Milner Hotels Co., 130 Conn. 507, 36 A.2d 20 (1944) (a guest sued a hotel for having been bitten by rat while guest lying in bed; the guest could prove that rat-holes in room were later closed by tin patches; although the evidence was inadmissible as admission of fault, it was admissible to show control, existence of rat-holes, and to corroborate guest's evidence); Low v. Honolulu Rapid Transit Co., 50 Haw. 582, 445 P.2d 372 (1968); Stoeppelman v.

Hays–Fendler Const. Co., 437 S.W.2d 143 (Mo. Ct. App. 1968) (evidence showing insurance existed properly admissible to show control of the property).

See the qualifications in the text in this section. Fed. and Unif. R. Evid. 105 assume the practice.

It seems, however, that to complain of the judge's exclusion of evidence inadmissible in one aspect, the proponent must have stated the purpose for which it is competent (Archer v. Sibley, 201 Ala. 495, 78 So. 849 (1918)), unless the admissible purpose is apparent. Kansas City Southern Ry. Co. v. Jones, 241 U.S. 181, 36 S. Ct. 513, 60 L. Ed. 943 (1916). The rule was applied where both an admissible and an inadmissible purpose were stated. Richter's Bakery, Inc. v. Verden, 394 S.W.2d 230 (Tex. Civ. App. Waco 1965 error refused). These rules merely apply the normal requirements for making an offer of proof in other situations in which an objection is sustained. *See* analogous rules at § 51 at notes 24 and 25 supra.

[4]Scott v. Missouri Ins. Co., 361 Mo. 51, 233 S.W.2d 660 (1950) (in an action on life policy, defendant offered its investigators' report on the death; plaintiff objected as hearsay, and judge excluded; held error to exclude, should have admitted to show good faith in denying liability with limiting instruction, if requested); Bialek v. Pittsburgh Brewing Co., 430 Pa. 176, 242 A.2d 231 (1968) (it was proper to admit evidence to show article was not defective with instruction indicating evidence should not be used for improper purpose of establishing due care, which was not in issue).

only for the allowable purpose.[5] Realistically, the instruction may not always be effective,[6] but admission of the evidence with the limiting instruction is normally the best reconciliation of the competing interests.[7] However, consider situations where the danger of the jury's misuse of the evidence for the inadmissible purpose is acute, and the value of the evidence for the legitimate purpose is slight or the point for which it is admissible can readily be proved by other evidence. In such situations, both the cases and the Federal and Revised Uniform Rules of Evidence 403 recognize the judge's power to exclude the evidence altogether.[8] Some hearsay problems cry out for the invocation of Rule 403.

---

[5]Former Fed. R. Evid. 105 and Unif. R. Evid. 105 provide: "When evidence which is admissible as to one party or for one purpose but not admissible as to another party or for another purpose is admitted, the court, upon request, shall restrict the evidence to its proper scope and instruct the jury accordingly."

Effective December 1, 2011, restyled Fed. R. Evid. 105 reads: "If the court admits evidence that is admissible against a party or for a purpose—but not against another party or for another purpose—the court, on timely request, must restrict the evidence to its proper scope and instruct the jury accordingly."

The rule does not purport to determine when such evidence should be admitted but assumes that a ruling has been made in favor of admissibility. See note 8 infra, as to admissibility. Under the federal rule, the judge may give an instruction on his own initiative without any request. See discussion in 1 Weinstein's Federal Evidence § 105.07[3] (2d ed. 1997). This source also discusses whether omission of an instruction might be plain error.

Pertinent cases include U.S. v. Vitale, 596 F.2d 688 (5th Cir. 1979); Sims v. Struthers, 267 Ala. 80, 100 So. 2d 23 (1957) (admission not error when instruction was not requested on ground that the remedy was a request for an instruction); Hatfield v. Levy Bros., 18 Cal. 2d 798, 117 P.2d 841 (1941) (opponent, not having requested instruction, waived right to instruction); Bouchard v. Bouchard, 313 Mass. 531, 48 N.E.2d 161 (1943); State ex rel. State Highway Commission v. Yackel, 445 S.W.2d 389 (Mo. Ct. App. 1969) (if party feared improper use of the evidence, he should have requested an instruction); Rynar v. Lincoln Transit Co., 129 N.J.L. 525, 30 A.2d 406, 409 (N.J. Ct. Err. & App. 1943) (" . . . The party . . . may summon the court's assistance by request for charge or other appropriate means.").

[6]Beaver & Marques, A Proposal to Modify the Rule on Criminal Conviction Impeachment, 58 Temp. L.Q. 585, 602 (1985) (discussing the Chicago Jury Project); Wissler & Saks, On the Inefficacy of Limiting Instructions— When Jurors Use Prior Conviction Evidence to Decide Guilt, 9 Law & Hum. Behav. 37 (1985).

[7]Richardson v. Marsh, 481 U.S. 200, 107 S. Ct. 1702, 95 L. Ed. 2d 176 (1987) (there is an almost invariable assumption that jurors follow their instructions); Lakeside v. Oregon, 435 U.S. 333, 340 n.11, 98 S. Ct. 1091, 55 L. Ed. 2d 319 (1978) ("As this Court has remarked before: '[W]e have not yet attained that certitude about the human mind which would justify us in . . . a dogmatic assumption that jurors, if properly admonished, neither could nor would heed the instructions of the trial court . . . Bruno v. United States, 308 U.S., at 294").

[8]Fed. and Unif. R. Evid. 403 clearly authorize the court to consider the overall prejudicial effect of the evidence and whether an instruction

Assume that the proponent offers an out-of-court statement for a nonhearsay purpose but on its face the declaration asserts facts directly relevant to a critical issue in the case and the declarant would presumably have personal knowledge of the facts. Here common sense suggests that there is a grave risk that the jurors will misuse the testimony as substantive evidence.[9]

### A Limitation as to Party

Similarly, subject to the restrictions stated in the above and following paragraphs, evidence is frequently admissible as against one party, but not as against another. In that event, the accepted practice is to admit the evidence with an instruction, if requested, that the jurors are to consider it only as to the party against whom it is properly admissible.[10]

However, even limiting instructions are insufficient to insure against jury misuse of the confessions or admissions of a codefendant who does not take the stand when the confession implicates

---

would be sufficient to avoid prejudice. The potentially prejudicial effect is particularly important in criminal cases, especially when the prosecution attempts to show the accused's other crimes under Fed. and Unif. R. Evid. 404(b) as evidence of motive or intent. See § 190 infra. In distinguishing Fed. R. Evid. 105 from other rules, the Advisory Committee's Note states, "The wording of the present rule . . . [repels] any implication that limiting or curative instructions are sufficient for all situations."

Case law is to the same effect. Adkins v. Brett, 184 Cal. 252, 193 P. 251, 254 (1920) (in husband's action for alienation, evidence of wife's statement about parties with and gifts from defendant, though ordinarily competent to show wife's feelings, might be excluded if danger great that jury would use it as evidence of defendant's conduct). See also Shepard v. U.S., 290 U.S. 96, 103, 54 S. Ct. 22, 78 L. Ed. 196 (1933); State v. Goebel, 40 Wash. 2d 18, 240 P.2d 251 (1952) (evidence of other crimes admissible for specific purpose should be excluded in court's discretion if unduly prejudicial).

[9]E.g., Bruton v. U.S., 391 U.S. 123, 88 S. Ct. 1620, 20 L. Ed. 2d 476 (1968). See also Shepard v. U.S., 290 U.S. 96, 54 S. Ct. 22, 78 L. Ed. 196

(1933); Carlson & Imwinkelried, Dynamics of Trial Practice: Problems and Materials § 15.3, at 439–41 (4th ed. 2010).

[10]Chesapeake & O. Ry. Co. v. Boyd's Adm'r, 290 Ky. 9, 160 S.W.2d 342 (1942) (statement of engineer, codefendant, admissible against him, if not against railway; a general objection without request to limit the evidence was insufficient); Grimm v. Gargis, 303 S.W.2d 43 (Mo. 1957) (evidence properly admissible against one party with proper instruction); Fort Worth Hotel Co. v. Waggoman, 126 S.W.2d 578 (Tex. Civ. App. Fort Worth 1939) (evidence admissible against one defendant, joint tortfeasors, was not subject to objection by other defendant; the other defendant's proper relief is a request to have the evidence limited).

But if the evidence is offered generally and excluded there is no error (Hudson v. Smith, 391 S.W.2d 441 (Tex. Civ. App. Houston 1965, error refused)), unless of course, undue prejudice results or a constitutional rule is involved. With the same limitations, when there is only an objection and no request for instruction, there is no error. American Medical Ass'n v. U.S., 130 F.2d 233 (App. D.C. 1942).

the defendant. In this situation, the confession is admissible against the non-testifying codefendant as an opposing party's statement (formerly termed a personal admission). But it may be inadmissible against the defendant, as when a codefendant made the statement after he had been arrested and ceased being an active member of the conspiracy with the defendant.[11] In similar situations, at a joint trial the traditional solution was to admit the evidence with a limiting instruction barring its use against the defendant. However, when the other evidence in the record indicates that there is a close relationship between the two and that the codefendant had personal knowledge of the facts asserted in his confession, there is an intolerable risk that the jury will disregard any limiting instruction and misuse the confession as proof of the defendant's guilt. A violation of the Sixth Amendment right to confront witnesses results.[12] Since the due process clause of the Fourteenth Amendment incorporates the Sixth Amendment confrontation guarantee, this rule is directly enforceable in state courts.[13] However if, apart from the codefendant's confession, the case against the defendant was so overwhelming that its admission was harmless beyond a reasonable doubt, the appellate court will not reverse.[14]

It would be a mistake, though, to generalize that if one purpose of two or more uses of evidence against a criminal defendant violates the defendant's constitutional rights, the evidence is

---

[11]The statement would be vicariously admissible against the defendant if the codefendant made the statement during and in furtherance of the conspiracy. Fed. R. Evid. 801(d)(2)(E). However, given the timing, this statement falls outside the scope of that exemption from the hearsay rule.

[12]If the jury misuses the codefendant's confession against the defendant, functionally the codefendant becomes an accuser of the defendant; but since the codefendant elects not to testify, the defendant cannot confront (cross-examine) the accuser. Bruton v. U.S., 391 U.S. 123, 88 S. Ct. 1620, 20 L. Ed. 2d 476 (1968). See The Supreme Court, 1967 Term, 82 Harv. L. Rev. 95, 231–38 (1968). The decision was held retroactive in Roberts v. Russell, 392 U.S. 293, 88 S. Ct. 1921, 20 L. Ed. 2d 1100 (1968).

So-called "interlocking confessions" (when defendant's own confession is also before the jury) are not by virtue of being "interlocking" ipso facto admissible. Cruz v. New York, 481 U.S. 186, 107 S. Ct. 1714, 95 L. Ed. 2d 162 (1987). As to redacted confessions, see Gray v. Maryland, 523 U.S. 185, 118 S. Ct. 1151, 140 L. Ed. 2d 294 (1998); Richardson v. Marsh, 481 U.S. 200, 107 S. Ct. 1702, 95 L. Ed. 2d 176 (1987). When the co-defendant takes the stand subject to cross-examination and his testimony exculpates the defendant, his confession may be used. Nelson v. O'Neil, 402 U.S. 622, 91 S. Ct. 1723, 29 L. Ed. 2d 222 (1971). See § 279 infra.

[13]Harrington v. California, 395 U.S. 250, 89 S. Ct. 1726, 23 L. Ed. 2d 284 (1969).

[14]Harrington v. California, 395 U.S. 250, 89 S. Ct. 1726, 23 L. Ed. 2d 284 (1969); Chapman v. California, 386 U.S. 18, 87 S. Ct. 824, 17 L. Ed. 2d 705 (1967), Comment, 83 Harv. L. Rev. 814 (1970). See § 182 infra.

completely inadmissible.[15] For example, in several cases, the Supreme Court has ruled that although a constitutional exclusionary rule precluded the use of an item of evidence as substantive proof, the evidence was admissible for impeachment purposes subject to a limiting instruction.[16]

## § 60 Admission and exclusion of evidence in bench trials without a jury

The evidentiary rules at common law and under the Federal and Uniform Rules of Evidence apply in bench trials without a jury.[1] Nevertheless as Thayer states the conventional wisdom, the law of evidence is to a great extent a "product of the jury system . . . where ordinary untrained citizens are acting as judges of fact."[2] The Advisory Committee Note to Federal Rule of Evidence 104 reiterates the received orthodoxy that the common law courts developed the exclusionary rules in large part due to their doubts about the capacity of lay jurors.[3] For their part, judges possess professional experience in valuing evidence, greatly lessening the need for exclusionary rules. At common law, there was a sense that it was inexpedient to apply these restrictions to judges; that sense caused appellate courts to say that the same strictness need not be observed in applying the rules of evidence in bench trials as in jury trials. An appellate court should arguably reach the same result under the Federal and Uniform Rule of Evidence.[4]

The most important influence encouraging trial judges to take

---

[15]*E.g.*, U.S. v. Havens, 446 U.S. 620, 100 S. Ct. 1912, 64 L. Ed. 2d 559 (1980) (evidence illegally obtained and inadmissible as proof of government case was admissible to impeach defendant by contradiction under certain circumstances); Harris v. New York, 401 U.S. 222, 91 S. Ct. 643, 28 L. Ed. 2d 1 (1971) (voluntary statements inadmissible under Miranda v. Arizona, 384 U.S. 436, 86 S. Ct. 1602, 16 L. Ed. 2d 694 (1966), could be used to impeach by inconsistent statement technique).

[16]See cases cited in note 15 supra.

**[Section 60]**

[1]*E.g.*, Stewart v. Prudential Ins. Co. of America, 147 Pa. Super. 296, 24 A.2d 83 (1942).

[2]Preliminary Treatise on Evidence 509 (1898).

[3]*But see* Langbein, The Criminal Trial Before the Lawyers, 45 U. Chi. L. Rev. 263 (1978); Nance, The Best Evidence Principle, 73 Iowa L. Rev. 277 (1998) (challenging that assumption).

[4]*E.g.*, Clark v. U.S., 61 F.2d 695 (C.C.A. 8th Cir. 1932); Weisenborn v. Rutledge, 233 Mo. App. 464, 121 S.W.2d 309, 313 (1938); and numerous cases collected in West's Key Number Digest, Trial ⊕377(1).

The rules contain no special provision for judge-tried cases. However, Rules 102 (statement of purpose), 103 (error in admitting or excluding must affect substantial right), and 611 (broad powers to control trial), all point to the conclusion that failure to follow the earlier case law would violate the spirit and to a degree the letter of the Rules.

a relaxed attitude toward evidence rules in nonjury cases is a doctrine recognized by most appellate courts. According to this doctrine, on an appeal from a bench trial, the receipt of inadmissible evidence over objection is ordinarily not ground for reversal if there was other, admissible evidence sufficient to support the findings. The judge is presumed to have disregarded the inadmissible evidence and relied on the admissible evidence.[5] However, when the judge errs in the opposite direction by excluding evidence which ought to have been received, the judge's ruling is subject to reversal[6] if it is substantially harmful to the losing party. But some appellate decisions decline to apply the presumption when the evidence was objected to and the objection overruled.[7] The judge's action in overruling the objection suggests that the trial wanted to consider the evidence in question. Moreover, the presumption may be rebutted by a contrary showing. The rebuttal showing could take the form of statements from the bench during trial, or references to improperly admitted evidence in specific findings of fact prepared either separately or as part of an opinion or memorandum of decision.[8]

In practice, considerations of waste of time, predictability and consistency lead most trial judges to apply the rules of evidence in a nonjury trial to exclude evidence that "is *clearly* inadmissible, privileged, or too time consuming in order to guard against reversal."[9] However, where the admissibility of evidence proffered at a bench trial is debatable, many experienced, cautious judges

---

[5]Plummer v. Western Intern. Hotels Co., Inc., 656 F.2d 502 (9th Cir. 1981); Clark v. U.S., 61 F.2d 695 (C.C.A. 8th Cir. 1932); General Metals, Inc. v. Truitt Mfg. Co., 259 N.C. 709, 131 S.E.2d 360 (1963); Lenahan v. Leach, 245 Or. 496, 422 P.2d 683 (1967); Tolbert v. State, 743 S.W.2d 631 (Tex. Crim. App. 1988); West's Key Number Digest, Appeal & Error ☞931(6); Maguire & Epstein, Preliminary Questions of Fact, 36 Yale L.J. 1100, 1115 (1927). See explanation of harmless error in § 52, at notes 115-16, supra.

[6]Examples of reversals where the exclusion was found prejudicial: Kelly v. Wasserman, 5 N.Y.2d 425, 185 N.Y.S.2d 538, 158 N.E.2d 241 (1959) (tried before referee); McCloskey v. Charleroi Mountain Club, 390 Pa. 212, 134 A.2d 873 (1957). *See* West's Key Number Digest, Appeal & Error ☞1056.5.

[7]Farish v. Hawk, 241 Ala. 352, 2 So. 2d 407 (1941) (equity case) (*but compare* Bessemer Theatres v. City of Bessemer, 261 Ala. 632, 75 So. 2d 651 (1954) nonjury law case); People v. De Groot, 108 Ill. App. 2d 1, 247 N.E.2d 177, 181–82 (1st Dist. 1969) ("Where an objection has been made to the evidence and overruled, it cannot be presumed that the evidence did not enter into the court's consideration. The ruling itself indicates that the court thought the evidence proper."); Bellew v. Iowa State Highway Commission, 171 N.W.2d 284 (Iowa 1969) (prejudice presumed unless record affirmatively shows evidence was later discarded; record so indicated).

[8]People v. Gilbert, 68 Ill. 2d 252, 12 Ill. Dec. 142, 369 N.E.2d 849 (1977); Gray v. Grayson, 76 N.M. 255, 414 P.2d 228 (1966).

[9]Eagle–Picher Industries, Inc. v. Liberty Mut. Ins. Co., 682 F.2d 12, 18

follow a practice calculated to minimize the risk of reversal. That practice is to provisionally admit all arguably admissible evidence, even if objected to,[10] with the announcement that all admissibility questions are reserved until all the evidence is in. In considering any objections renewed by motion to strike at the end of the case, the judge leans toward admission rather than exclusion[11] but seeks to find clearly admissible testimony on which to base his findings of fact.[12] To minimize the risk of appellate reversal, a prudent trial judge will explicitly identify on the record the admissible evidence that she is basing her factual findings on. The practice lessens the time spent in arguing objections and helps ensure that appellate courts have in the record the evidence that was rejected as well as that which was admitted. A more complete trial record sometimes enables the appellate court to dispose of the case by entering a final judgment rather than merely remanding to the trial court for further proceedings.

---

(1st Cir. 1982).

[10]Multi–Medical Convalescent and Nursing Center of Towson v. N. L. R. B., 550 F.2d 974 (4th Cir. 1977) (if in doubt, let it in); Builders Steel Co. v. C.I.R., 179 F.2d 377, 379 (8th Cir. 1950) (valuable discussion); Simpson v. Vineyard, 324 S.W.2d 276 (Tex. Civ. App. El Paso 1959); Holendyke v. Newton, 50 Wis. 635, 7 N.W. 558, 559 (1880) (referee or judge should be very careful in rejecting evidence, and where there is reasonable doubt, though he thinks it inadmissible, ought to receive it subject to objections).

But occasionally appellate courts disapprove. *See* Kovacs v. Szentes, 130 Conn. 229, 33 A.2d 124 (1943) (based on Conn. Gen. Stat. Ann. § 52-208 forbidding court to admit evidence subject to objection unless parties agree; "A judge has not such control over his mental faculties that he can definitely determine whether or not inadmissible evidence he has heard will affect his mind . . . "); Holcombe v. Hopkins, 314 Mass. 113, 49 N.E.2d 722 (1943); Havas v. 105 Casino Corp., 82 Nev. 282, 417 P.2d 239 (1966) ("We disapprove the practice of trial courts holding in abeyance rulings on evidence. It precipitates all manners of difficulty.") West's Key Number Digest, Trial ⬦51, 379.

[11]*See* Holendyke v. Newton, 50 Wis. 635, 7 N.W. 558 (1880).

[12]As in Hatch v. Calkins, 21 Cal. 2d 364, 132 P.2d 210 (1942) where the judge's memorandum decision recited that his decision was based on the competent portion of certain affidavits.

# Title 4.   Competency

## Chapter 7

# The Competency of Witnesses

### § 61   Competency of witnesses, in general[1]

Most evidentiary rules regulate the content of proposed testimony. However, competency rules address the threshold question of whether a prospective witness is qualified to give any testimony at all in the case. For the most part, the competency standards relate to the prospective witness's status and personal capacities[2] rather than the content of the testimony the witness is prepared to give. The early common law rules of incompetency were harsh, but they have been undergoing a process of piecemeal statutory liberalization for well over a century. During that period, most of the former grounds for altogether barring a wit-

---

**[Section 61]**

[1]2 and 3 Wigmore, Evidence §§ 483–721 (Chadbourn rev. 1979); 1 Weinstein's Federal Evidence Ch. 601 (rev. 2011); Allen, The Law of Evidence in Victorian England (1997). The history of the subject is fully treated in 9 Holdsworth Hist. Eng. Law 177–97 (1926) and briefly in Rowley, The Competency of Witnesses, 24 Iowa L. Rev. 482 (1939).

[2]U.S. v. Phibbs, 999 F.2d 1053, 1069 (6th Cir. 1993).

ness[3] have been converted into mere bases for impeaching his credibility.[4]

Since the disqualification of witnesses for incompetency is thus dwindling in importance, and since the statutory reforms of the

---

[3]As a general proposition, the competency standards apply to hearsay declarants as well as in-court witnesses. If a person would be incompetent to testify under the standard, his hearsay statement is usually inadmissible. However, in the past many jurisdictions have held excited utterances admissible even when the declarant was a small child who would have been in competent to testify at trial. State v. Breyer, 40 Idaho 324, 232 P. 560 (1925); Admissibility of testimony regarding spontaneous declarations made by one incompetent to testify at trial, 15 A.L.R.4th 1043. Moreover, many jurisdictions now admit hearsay statements by alleged victims of child abuse without requiring a showing that the victim would be competent at trial. People v. District Court of El Paso County, 776 P.2d 1083 (Colo. 1989). *See also* Schmertz, Article VI, in Emerging Problems Under the Federal Rules of Evidence 115, 121 (3d ed. 1998) ("there is the question of whether a hearsay declarant must be competent under Rules 601–606 in some way other than having personal knowledge. The Rules do not specifically address this question").

[4]In 1998, a panel of the United States Court of Appeals for the Tenth Circuit held that prosecutors violated the federal bribery statute, 18 U.S.C. § 201(c)(2), by offering lighter sentences to cooperating witnesses and that, as a remedy, the cooperating witness's testimony had to be altogether excluded. U.S. v. Singleton, 144 F.3d 1343 (10th Cir. 1998). However, the en banc court took the extraordinary step of vacating the decision on its own motion. 165 F.3d 1297 (10th Cir. 1999); U.S. v. Lara, 181 F.3d 183, 197 (1st Cir. 1999) (the initial *Singleton* decision was "nothing more than an aberration . . . . [T]he opinion has been overruled in the circuit of its birth . . ., and several other courts of appeal have disavowed its . . . reading of section 201(c)(2) . . . ."); Johnson, Judicial Nullification-Denial of Equal Access to Witnesses Is Denial of Due Process, 28 The Champion 20 (Feb. 2004) ("every United States Circuit Court has now held that a federal prosecutor may promise a criminal defendant leniency in exchange for testimony, and three circuits have held that such a prosecutor may pay a witness money for testifying. One approves payments by local law enforcement agencies"). Of course, the defense counsel may still inquire about these concessions and payments as a basis for establishing the witness's bias. See § 39 supra.

common law competency rules[5] vary from state to state, this treatise does not assay a detailed review of the law in the different jurisdictions. Instead, the following sections summarize the common law grounds of incompetency and describe the general directions of reform.

## § 62    Mental incapacity[1] and immaturity:[2] Oath or affirmation

### *The Common Law*

At modern common law, there is no rule automatically precluding an insane person as such[3] from testifying. Moreover, although some states base a youth's competency or presumed competency on the child's chronological age, most jurisdictions do not preclude a child of any specified age from testifying.[4] In each case, the test is whether the witness has enough intelligence to make it

---

[5]*See generally* Fryer, Note on Disqualification of Witnesses, Selected Writings on Evidence and Trial 345 (Fryer ed. 1957); Orfield, Competency of Witnesses in Federal Criminal Cases, 46 Marq. L. Rev. 324 (1963); 2 Wigmore, Evidence §§ 475–531, 575–620 (Chadbourn rev. 1979); 6 id. §§ 1815–29 (Chadbourn rev. 1976).

**[Section 62]**

[1]2 Wigmore, Evidence §§ 492–501 (Chadbourn rev. 1979); 3 Weinstein's Federal Evidence § 601.40[1] (rev. 2011); Mental condition as affecting competency of witness, 148 A.L.R. 1140; Mental condition as affecting competency of witness, 26 A.L.R. 1491; West's Key Number Digest, Witnesses ⬤39 to 41; Weihofen, Testimonial Competence and Credibility, 34 Geo. Wash. L. Rev. 53 (1965).

[2]2 Wigmore, Evidence §§ 505–09 (Chadbourn rev. 1979); 3 Weinstein's Federal Evidence § 601.04[2] (rev. 2011); Competency of young child as witness in civil case, 81 A.L.R.2d 386 (sec. 9 superseded in part Witnesses: child competency statutes, 60 A.L.R. 4th 369); West's Key Number Digest, Witnesses ⬤40, 45.

[3]People v. McCaughan, 49 Cal. 2d 409, 317 P.2d 974 (1957); Truttmann v. Truttmann, 328 Ill. 338, 159

N.E. 775 (1927) (mental defective competent); People v. Lambersky, 410 Ill. 451, 102 N.E.2d 326 (1951); State v. Wildman, 145 Ohio St. 379, 31 Ohio Op. 5, 61 N.E.2d 790 (1945) (imbecile child competent). *See also* Schmertz, Article VI, in Emerging Problems Under the Federal Rules of Evidence 115, 117 (3d ed. 1998) ("This study . . . has revealed no reported federal case under the Rules upholding a challenge to a witness' competency based upon such once-accepted grounds as mental incapacity . . . .").

[4]Radiant Oil Co. v. Herring, 146 Fla. 154, 200 So. 376, 377 (1941) ("not an arbitrary age but the degree of intelligence . . . is the test . . . ."); State v. Poole, 124 Idaho 346, 859 P.2d 944, 947 (1993) (the "trend of the law favors general competency"); Rueger v. Hawks, 150 Neb. 834, 36 N.W.2d 236, 244 (1949) ("There is no precise age which determines the question of a child's competency"); Litzkuhn v. Clark, 85 Ariz. 355, 339 P.2d 389 (1959); Artesani v. Gritton, 252 N.C. 463, 113 S.E.2d 895 (1960) (error to exclude seven-year old child as witness solely "by reason of age"). The statutes referring to "children under ten years of age who appear incapable of receiving just impressions of the facts respecting which they are examined, or of relating them truly," do not change the rule stated in the text. *See, e.g.,*

worthwhile to hear him at all and whether he recognizes a duty to tell the truth.[5] Does he possess enough capacity to perceive,

---

Litzkuhn v. Clark, supra. In some jurisdictions, children above a certain age are presumed competent. *E.g.*, State v. Fears, 659 S.W.2d 370, 375 (Tenn. Crim. App. 1983) (overruled by, State v. Harrison, 270 S.W.3d 21 (Tenn. 2008)) ("The rule is that at the age of 14 years a witness is presumed to be competent . . . .").

[5]With respect to a child of tender years, the traditional test of competency involves four fundamental elements, all of which must be present for the child to be competent to testify: (1) present understanding or intelligence to understand, on instruction, the duty to speak the truth; (2) mental capacity at the time of the occurrence in question truly to perceive and to register the perception; (3) memory sufficient to retain an independent recollection of the observations made; and (4) capacity to translate into words the memory of such observations. Burnam v. Chicago Great Western R. Co., 340 Mo. 25, 100 S.W.2d 858 (1936). *See also* State v. Segerberg, 131 Conn. 546, 41 A.2d 101, 102 (1945) ("The principle . . . is that the child shall be sufficiently mature to receive correct impressions by her senses, to recollect, and narrate intelligently and to appreciate the moral duty to tell the truth."). A preliminary finding that the child knows the difference between the truth and a lie or fantasy is essential. Common questions asked to children to determine the child's ability to distinguish truth from a lie or fantasy are inquiries such as "If I told you my robe was white, would that be a lie or the truth?" and "Is Santa Claus real or just make believe?"

The published opinions indicate that the courts tend to resolve doubts in favor of finding children competent as witnesses. *See generally* Kentucky v. Stincer, 482 U.S. 730, 739–42, 107 S. Ct. 2658, 96 L. Ed. 2d 631 (1987) ("Under Kentucky law, when a child's competency to testify is raised, the

judge is required to resolve three basic issues: whether the child is capable of observing and recollecting facts, whether the child is capable of narrating those facts to a court or jury, and whether the child has a moral sense of the obligation to tell the truth. *See* Moore v. Commonwealth, 384 S.W.2d 498, 500 (Ky.1964) ('When the competency of an infant to testify is properly raised it is then the duty of the trial court to carefully examine the witness to ascertain whether she (or he) is sufficiently intelligent to observe, recollect and narrate the facts and has a moral sense of obligation to speak the truth.'); Capps v. Commonwealth, 560 S.W.2d 559, 560 (Ky.1977); Hendricks v. Commonwealth, 550 S.W.2d 551, 554 (Ky.1977); *see also* Thomas v. Commonwealth, 189 S.W.2d 686, 687 (Ky.1945); Comment, An Overview of the Competency of Child Testimony, 13 No. Ky. L. Rev. 181, 184 (1986). Thus, questions at a competency hearing usually are limited to matters that are unrelated to the basic issues of the trial. Children often are asked their names, where they go to school, how old they are, whether they know who the judge is, whether they know what a lie is, and whether they know what happens when one tells a lie. *See* Comment, The Competency Requirement for the Child Victim of Sexual Abuse: Must We Abandon It?, 40 U. Miami L. Rev. 245, 263, and n. 78 (1985); Comment, Defendants' Rights in Child Witness Competency Hearings: Establishing Constitutional Procedures for Sexual Abuse Cases, 69 Minn. L. Rev. 1377, 1381–1383, and nn. 9–11 (1985)."). Although *Stincer* cites primarily Kentucky precedents, other jurisdictions are in accord. Haliym v. Mitchell, 492 F.3d 680, 703 (6th Cir. 2007) (the seven-year-old was prompted to say "I do" and did not know what it meant to swear to God; however, he stated that he would tell the truth, that it was good to tell the truth, and that he would be punished

record, recollect, and narrate to probably add valuable knowledge of the facts to the record?[6] At common law, following the procedure for foundational facts conditioning the competency of evidence,[7] the trial judge determines as a matter of fact whether the prospective witness possesses the requisite testimonial qualities,

---

if he lied); People v. L.G., 18 Misc. 3d 243, 844 N.Y.S.2d 846, 848 (City Crim. Ct. 2007) (the prosecution interviewed the child to demonstrate the child's understanding of the nature of an oath).

A preliminary hearing, especially with respect to children, is sometimes held in chambers with only the judge, the witness, and a court reporter present. On other occasions the attorneys for both sides are present while the parties are excluded. Shanks, Evaluating Children's Competency to Testify: Developing a Rational Method to Assess a Young Child's Capacity to Offer Reliable Testimony in Cases Alleging Child Sex Abuse, 58 Cleve. St. L. Rev. 575 (2010). The question whether the criminal defendant has a constitutional right to be present in addition to his counsel was answered in the negative in Kentucky v. Stincer, 482 U.S. 730, 107 S. Ct. 2658, 96 L. Ed. 2d 631 (1987). *But see* Medina v. Diguglielmo, 461 F.3d 417 (3d Cir. 2006), rev'd on other grounds, 461 F.3d 417 (3d Cir. 2006) (under Pennsylvania law, "[w]hile adult witnesses are assumed to be competent, when the witness is under 14 years of age, there must be a searching judicial inquiry as to mental capacity"); Ebisike, The Evidence of Children, 44 Crim. L. Bull. 723, 724–25 (2008) (" 'the 1770 decision in Rex v. Brasier [, 168 Eng. Rep. 202 (1770)'; solidified the principle that there is no age below which children are automatically . . . disqualified from testifying.' In this case, it was held that 'an infant, though under the age of seven years, may be sworn in a criminal prosecution, provided such infant appears, on strict examination by the court, to possess a sufficient knowledge of the nature and

consequences of an oath . . . .' In 1895, following on from Rex v. Brasier, the U.S. Supreme Court in Wheeler v. United States [, 159 U.S. 523 (1895)] upheld the competency of children as witnesses and stated that there is no minimum age for child competency. Addressing the competency of a five-year-old to testify in a murder trial, the Supreme Court stated 'that the boy was not by reason of his youth, as a matter of law, absolutely disqualified as a witness, is clear. While no one would think of calling an infant of only two or three years old, there is no precise age which determines the question of competency . . . . In 1918, the Court in Rosen v. United States [, 245 U.S. 467 (1918)] reaffirmed the competency of children as witnesses").

[6]The test has sometimes been phrased as a requirement that the witness must have enough intelligence to "understand the nature and obligation of an oath." This requirement is inappropriate. It confounds a religious standard with a mental standard. If this test were literally applied, even the most intelligent lay witness could hardly meet the standard, much less a child or an insane person. Examples of decisions in which the court purports to recognize this test are Bielecki v. State, 140 Tex. Crim. 355, 145 S.W.2d 189 (1940), and Mullins v. Com., 174 Va. 472, 5 S.E.2d 499 (1939). *See also* People v. Augustin, 112 Cal. App. 4th 444, 5 Cal. Rptr. 3d 171 (4th Dist. 2003) (the victim witness had both cerebral palsy and a speech impediment).

[7]See § 53 supra. *See* People v. Wittrein, 221 P.3d 1076 (Colo. 2009) (there is no per se rule against conducting the hearing to determine a child's competency in front of the jury).

that is, the capacities to perceive,[8] remember, narrate, and understand the duty to tell the truth under oath. Children as young as three years old have been ruled competent as witnesses.[9]

---

[8]To a degree, the application of the competency standard turns on the content of the proposed testimony. The question is whether the prospective witness had the capacity to perceive the facts which she contemplates testifying about. Thus, a deaf person can testify about what she saw (U.S. v. Barnes, 30 F.3d 575, 577 (5th Cir. 1994)); and a blind person is competent to testify about what he heard. *See* U.S. v. Bell, 367 F.3d 452, 464 (5th Cir. 2004) ("the Rules do not provide that deaf and mute individuals are somehow lacking in competency to be witnesses in federal court").

[9]Houff v. Blacketter, 402 Fed. Appx. 167 (9th Cir. 2010), cert. denied, 132 S. Ct. 138, 181 L. Ed. 2d 57 (2011) (a hearsay statement by a four-year-old victim), cert.denied sub nom. Houff v. Coursey, 132 S. Ct. 138, 181 L. Ed. 2d 57 (2011); Bradburn v. Peacock, 135 Cal. App. 2d 161, 286 P.2d 972, 974 (1st Dist. 1955) (error for judge to rule a three-year-old child incompetent without conducting voir dire examination); Evans v. State, 117 Nev. 609, 28 P.3d 498 (2001) (a child witness was competent even though the child was only four at the time of the crimes); State v. Meadows, 158 N.C. App. 390, 581 S.E.2d 472 (2003) (while the witness was only five at the time of the trial, he still permitted to testify about his mother's shooting two years earlier); State v. Dwyer, 149 Wis. 2d 850, 440 N.W.2d 344, 346 (1989) ("many three-and four-year-old children can recognize a lie . . . ."); Baldas, When Children Take the Stand, Nat'l L.J., Sep. 1, 2003, at 1 (Professor Lucy McGough is the author of Child Witnesses: Fragile Voices in the American Legal System (1994); her perception is that the legislatures and courts have liberalized the competency standards to the point that "prosecutors now might use a 3-year-old to testify where they wouldn't dream of it 20 years ago"). *Compare* Walters v. McCormick, 108 F.3d 1165 (9th Cir. 1997) (four year old child competent), State v. Anderson, 154 Ohio App. 3d 789, 2003-Ohio-5439, 798 N.E.2d 1155 (7th Dist. Mahoning County 2003) (the four-year-old was competent even though she incorrectly stated her birthday, did not know how hold her brother was, believed in Santa Claus, and said that she saw monsters; she answered many questions correctly, and a child that young can be expected to have an imagination and play make-believe), and In Interest of J.R., 436 Pa. Super. 416, 648 A.2d 28 (1994) (four year old child competent) *with* Delacruz v. State, 734 So. 2d 1116 (Fla. 1st DCA 1999) (the four-year-old girl verbally answered only 17 of 78 qualifying questions and responded to the remaining questions by shrugging her shoulders or nodding her head) and Townsend v. State, 613 So. 2d 534 (Fla. 5th DCA 1993) (two year old child incompetent). The empirical research has strengthened the argument for treating even very young children as competent witnesses. People v. Jones, 51 Cal. 3d 294, 270 Cal. Rptr. 611, 792 P.2d 643, 655 (1990) (contemporary studies "have produced results indicating that most of the . . . traditional assumptions are . . . unfounded"); Bessner, The Competency of the Child Witness: A Critical Analysis of Bill C-15, 31 Crim. L.Q. 481, 500–06 (1989); Lyon & Saywitz, Young Maltreated Children's Competence to Take the Oath, 3 Applied Develop. Sci. 16 (1999) (although young children have difficulty defining truth and falsehood, in responding to questions they can demonstrate that they appreciate the difference); 1 Myers, Evidence in Child Abuse and Neglect Cases §§ 2.10–.11 (2d ed. 1992). *See* Com. v. Delbridge, 578 Pa. 641, 855 A.2d 27 (2003) (at a competency hearing in a child abuse case, the opposing counsel may attempt to establish that the pro-

Similarly, persons suffering from disabilities[10] such as deafness and muteness may be competent witnesses.[11] Likewise, persons suffering from mental disorders often satisfy the competency standards.[12] Without more, neither past drug use nor even drug addiction is automatically disqualifying; and a crack cocaine user with the intelligence of a seven-year-old has been held to be a competent witness.[13] The upshot is that a person is deemed

---

spective witness's testimony had been irrevocably tainted by suggestive questioning); Lyon, Applying Suggestibility Research to the Real World: The Case of Repeated Questions, 65 Law & Contemp. Probs. 97 (2002); Warren & Marsil, Why Children's Suggestibility Remains a Serious Concern, 65 Law & Contemp. Probs. 127 (2002); Walker, Forensic Interviews of Children: The Components of Scientific Validity and Legal Admissibility, 65 Law & Contemp. Probs. 149 (2002); Ceci & Friedman, The Suggestibility of Children: Scientific Research and Legal Implications, 86 Cornell L. Rev. 33 (2000) (the authors argue that except in extreme cases, the fact that a child has been subjected to suggestive questioning should not render the child incompetent as a witness; however, they also contend that the problem of suggestibility is so substantial that the courts ought to be more receptive to expert evidence on the suggestibility of children); Lyon, The New Wave in Children's Suggestibility Research: A Critique, 84 Cornell L. Rev. 1004 (1999).

[10]Vasquez v. Kirkland, 572 F.3d 1029 (9th Cir. 2009) (the victim was deaf, could not speak, and had never learned standard sign language; however, the trial judge utilized the services of both a court-certified American Sign Language interpreter and a certified intermediary interpreter, who used signs, gestures, and facial expressions to communicate with the witness).

[11]U.S. v. Bell, 367 F.3d 452, 464 (5th Cir. 2004). See also People v. Augustin, 112 Cal. App. 4th 444, 5 Cal. Rptr. 3d 171 (4th Dist. 2003) (an assault victim with cerebral palsy and

speech disability was a competent witness; the burden of proving the prospective witness's incompetency lies with the objecting party; a witness who is merely difficult to understand is not automatically incompetent). But see Anderson v. Franklin County, Mo., 192 F.3d 1125 (8th Cir. 1999) (the person did not know any standardized system of sign language).

[12]Dorsey v. Chapman, 262 F.3d 1181 (11th Cir. 2001) (the witness suffered from multiple personality disorder); Andrews v. Neer, 253 F.3d 1052, 1062–63 (8th Cir. 2001) (schizophrenic witness); Loeblein v. Dormire, 229 F.3d 724 (8th Cir. 2000) (multiple personality disorder); Tromello v. DiBuono, 132 F. Supp. 2d 82 (E.D. N.Y. 2000) (under New York law, the fact that a prospective witness is insane or mentally ill does not per se disqualify the witness); People v. Gipson, 117 Cal. App. 4th 1065, 12 Cal. Rptr. 3d 478 (6th Dist. 2004) (the fact that a prospective witness may have suffered from mental disorders does not by itself establish that the person is incompetent to be a witness).

[13]People v. Lewis, 26 Cal. 4th 334, 110 Cal. Rptr. 2d 272, 28 P.3d 34, 53–54 (2001). See also U.S. v. Cross, 430 F.3d 406, 411 (7th Cir. 2005) ("A witness' history of drug abuse does not necessarily render his testimony . . . unworthy of consideration. [T]here is no evidence that the witness' memory was 'impaired by a history of cocaine addiction' "); U.S. v. Cook, 949 F.2d 289, 293 (10th Cir. 1991) ("drug abuse alone does not render a witness incompetent"). One court even permitted an intoxicated person to testify so long as the witness's blood alcohol level had dropped below the legal limit for driv-

incompetent only in extreme cases such as when he experiences insane delusions directly relevant to the subject-matter of his testimony[14] or suffers from a psychosis likely to grossly distort his testimony.[15]

The major reason for the severe, early common law disqualification standards was the judges' distrust of a jury's ability to assess the words of a small child or a deranged person. Conceding *arguendo* the jury's deficiencies, the remedy of excluding such a witness—who may be the only person possessing the facts—is primitive and Draconian. Even if the trier of fact lacks legal training and the testimony is difficult to evaluate, on balance it is still better to let the evidence come in for what it is worth with cautionary instructions.

### The Federal Rules of Evidence

Although the more contemporary common law rules are relatively lax, the statutory reforms go even farther. Many states have enacted statutes specifically providing that the alleged victim is per se a competent witness in a child abuse prosecution.[16] Furthermore, most modern evidence codes contain general provisions radically liberalizing the competency standards. Federal Rules 601-03 and 403 are pertinent.

*Rules 601–03.* Revised Uniform Rule of Evidence 601 and the first sentence of Federal Rule of Evidence 601 typify such codes. Restyled Rule 601 announces that "every person is competent to be a witness unless these rules provide otherwise."[17] The only general competency requirements expressly "otherwise provided" by the Federal and Revised Uniform Rules of Evidence are

---

ing. People v. Alley, 232 P.3d 272 (Colo. App. 2010).

[14]People v. Jackson, 273 Cal. App. 2d 248, 78 Cal. Rptr. 20, 24–25 (2d Dist. 1969). *But see* People v. Anderson, 25 Cal. 4th 543, 106 Cal. Rptr. 2d 575, 22 P.3d 347 (2001) (although the witness suffered from delusions, the witness's account was plausible and included many details corroborated by independent evidence).

[15]Greyhound Lines, Inc. v. Wade, 485 F.3d 1032, 1085 (8th Cir. 2007) (the witness had a serious brain impairment "that makes normal thinking and processing almost impossible"); State v. Slimskey, 257 Conn. 842, 779 A.2d 723 (2001) (the victim was prone to distort his perception of reality with paranoid and persecuto-

rial ideas); Helge v. Carr, 212 Va. 485, 184 S.E.2d 794, 796–98 (1971).

[16]State v. James, 211 Conn. 555, 560 A.2d 426 (1989); State v. Williams, 729 S.W.2d 197 (Mo. 1987). *See also* Ziegler, The Child as Victim/Witness in Missouri, 49 J. Mo. B. 303, 304 (July–Aug. 1993) ("automatic competency"); Comment, The Competency Requirement for the Child Victim of Sexual Abuse: Must We Abandon It?, 40 U. Miami L. Rev. 245, 273 (1985) (collecting the statutes); Witnesses: child competency statutes, 60 A.L.R. 4th 369.

[17]Unif. R. Evid. 601 adopts the first sentence of former Fed. R. Evid. 601: "Every person is competent to be a witness except as otherwise provided in these rules." The first sentence of

restyled Fed. R. Evid. 601, effective December 1, 2011, reads: "Every person is competent to be a witness unless these rules provide otherwise." As in Fed. R. Evid., only judges (Rule 605) and jurors (Rule 606) are made incompetent to be witnesses in the trials in which they act as such. See § 68 infra.

The Advisory Committee's Note to Fed. R. Evid. 601 states:

> No mental or moral qualifications for testifying as a witness are specified. Standards of mental capacity have proved elusive in actual application. A leading commentator observes that few witnesses are disqualified on that ground. Weihofen, Testimonial Competence and Credibility, 34 Geo. Wash. L. Rev. 53 (1965). Discretion is regularly exercised in favor of allowing the testimony. A witness wholly without capacity is difficult to imagine. The question is one particularly suited to the jury as one of weight and credibility, subject to judicial authority to review the sufficiency of the evidence. 2 Wigmore §§ 501, 509. Standards of moral qualification in practice consist essentially of evaluating a person's truthfulness in terms of his own answers about it. Their principal utility is in affording an opportunity on voir dire examination to impress upon the witness his moral duty. This result may, however, be accomplished more directly, and without haggling in terms of legal standards, by the manner of administering the oath or affirmation under Rule 603.

In the federal courts in civil cases, Fed. R. Evid. 601 poses an interpretive problem because of its second sentence, reading, "But in a civil case, state law governs the witness's competency regarding a claim or defense for which state law supplies the rule of decision." *Compare* Foucher v. First Vermont Bank & Trust Co., 821 F. Supp. 916 (D. Vt. 1993) (since state law governed, the court applied a state dead man's statute) *with* Donovan v. Sears Roebuck & Co., 849 F. Supp. 86 (D. Mass. 1994) (although state law governed, the federal court refused to apply a special state hear-say exception for decedent's statements).

The provision for applying state law to the competency of witnesses is not absolutely clear. The congressional Conference Report on the Federal Rules states:

> If an item of proof tends to support or defeat a claim or defense, or an element of a claim or defense, and if state law supplies the rule of decision for that claim or defense, then state competency law applies to that item of proof. For reasons similar to those underlying its action on Rule 501, the Conference adopts the House provision.

The Conference Report for Fed. R. Evid. 501 takes the position, under a similar provision in that rule, that in "nondiversity jurisdiction civil cases, federal privilege law will generally apply . . . . When a federal court chooses to absorb state law, it is applying the state law as a matter of federal common law." H.R., Fed.Rules of Evidence, Conf. Rep. No. 1597, 93d Cong., 2d Sess. *But see* Barton v. American Red Cross, 829 F. Supp. 1290 (M.D. Ala. 1993) (although the basis of jurisdiction was federal question under special legislation concerning the Red Cross, state tort law supplied the rule of decision, and the court therefore applied state evidence law to determine the competency of a proffered expert). On the other hand, the same Conference Report pointed out that if in diversity cases a claim or defense is based upon federal substantive law, federal privilege law privilege law would govern such claims or defenses cases. Assuming the above statements represent Congress' intention and the true meaning of Rule 601, Congress probably has the power to enact such a statute, limiting reference to state competency law to diversity cases. See cases cited in the Conference Report. *But see* Wright & Kane, The Law of Federal Courts § 60 (6th ed. 2002).

Thus the apparent intent is that application of state competency rules in diversity cases depends upon

contained in Rule 603[18] (prescribing that every witness declare that he will testify truthfully by oath or affirmation) and Rule 602[19] (mandating that the witness possess personal knowledge). A plain meaning interpretation of Rule 601 is that there are no remaining competency standards[20] and that all the prospective witness need do is to take the oath.[21] The very first sentence of the Advisory Committee Note to Rule 601 confirms that plain

---

whether such issues are governed by state substantive law. Under this view, state competency law governs when the witness testifies on any issues controlled by state law. This view has the virtue that it is relatively straightforward and should pose few problems in most diversity cases (which do not involve issues dependent upon federal law). In diversity cases, the testimony of witnesses who are incompetent under state law could be limited to testimony on federal issues. If the same witness's testimony were relevant to both the state and federal issues, the matter could be handled by proper limiting instructions to the jury in a jury-tried case. *But see* Estate of Chlopek by Fahrforth v. Jarmusz, 877 F. Supp. 1189, 1193 (N.D. Ill. 1995) (the court quotes a passage in a Judiciary Committee report to the effect that when the two bodies of law apply but conflict, the one favoring admission should govern).

[18]Former Fed. R. Evid. 603 provided: "Before testifying, every witness shall be required to declare that the witness will testify truthfully, by oath or affirmation administered in a form calculated to awaken the witness' conscience and impress the witness' mind with the duty to do so." Uniform Rules of Evidence 603 is identical in content. Effective December, 1, 2011, restyled Fed. R. Evid. 603 reads: "Before testifying, a witness must give an oath or affirmation to testify truthfully. It must be in a form designed to impress that duty on the witness's conscience."

[19]Former Fed. R. Evid. 602 provided:

A witness may not testify to a matter unless evidence is introduced sufficient to support a finding that the witness has personal knowledge of the matter. Evidence to prove personal knowledge may, but need not, consist of the witness' own testimony. This rule is subject to the provisions of Rule 703, relating to opinion testimony by expert witnesses.

Uniform Rules of Evidence 602 is identical in content. Effective December 1, 2011, restyled Fed. R. Evid. 602 reads:

A witness may testify to a matter only if evidence is introduced sufficient to support a finding that the witness has personal knowledge of the matter. Evidence to prove personal knowledge may consist of the witness's own testimony. This rule does not apply to a witness's expert testimony under Rule 703.

[20]Schmertz, Article VI, in Emerging Problems Under the Federal Rules of Evidence 115, 116 (3d ed. 1998) ("a very strong—if not conclusive—presumption of general witness competency").

[21]State v. Ward, 242 S.W.3d 698, 703–04 (Mo. 2008) (the defendant refused to affirm that he would promise to tell the truth under the pains and penalties of perjury; he added that there was no form of oath or affirmation that he would take that would have a binding effect on his conscience).

meaning interpretation. The Note states that "[n]o mental or moral qualifications for testifying as a witness are specified."[22]

That sweeping interpretation of Rule 601 has evidently struck some courts as too revolutionary. Rather than construing Rule 601 literally, they take the more conservative position that the rule has a more limited impact, merely creating a presumption of competency.[23] Some have suggested that the judge has implicit authority to bar a potential witness's testimony under Rule 603. That rule requires that the witness take an oath or make an affirmation that he will testify truthfully. The argument runs that to ensure that the oath is meaningful rather than a empty ritual, the trial judge should be empowered to determine in common law fashion whether the prospective witness is qualified to take the oath or make the affirmation.

However, the conservative argument does violence to the statutory language of Rules 601 and 602. At the very most, the Federal Rules can be construed as adopting an intermediate position, imposing only four substantive requirements: (1) the witness have the capacity to accurately perceive, record, and recollect impressions of fact (physical and mental capacity), (2) the witness perceived, recorded, and recollects impressions tending to establish a fact of consequence in the litigation (personal knowledge), (3) the witness declare that he will tell the truth, understands the duty to tell the truth (oath or affirmation), and appreciates the difference between the truth and a lie or fantasy, and (4) the witness possesses the capacity to comprehend questions and express himself intelligibly, if necessary with an interpreter's aid[24] (narration).[25] Rule 602 requires personal knowledge, and Rule 603 mandates an oath. In light of the text of Rules 601 to 603, an argument can be made that on an appropri-

---

[22]U.S. v. Hyson, 721 F.2d 856, 864 (1st Cir. 1983) ("There is no provision in the rules for the exclusion of testimony because a witness is mentally incompetent. The question of competency goes to the issue of credibility, which is for the trier of fact."); U.S. v. Roach, 590 F.2d 181, 185 (5th Cir. 1979) ("[U]nder the new Federal Rules of Evidence it is doubtful that mental incompetence would ever be grounds for disqualification of a prospective witness."). See also note 21 supra.

[23]U.S. v. Blankenship, 923 F.2d 1110 (5th Cir. 1991); Government of the Virgin Islands v. Leonard A., 922 F.2d 1141 (3d Cir. 1991); U.S. v. Bloome, 773 F. Supp. 545, 546 (E.D.

N.Y. 1991) ("an initial presumption of competency").

[24]Former Fed. R. Evid. 604 provided: "An interpreter is subject to the provisions of these rules relating to qualification as an expert and the administration of an oath or affirmation to make a true translation." Uniform Rules of Evidence (1974) 604 is identical in content. Effective December 1, 2011, restyled Fed. R. Evid. 604 reads: "An interpreter must be qualified and must give an oath or affirmation to make a true translation." *E.g.*, State v. Randolph, 698 S.W.2d 535 (Mo. Ct. App. E.D. 1985) (deaf mute may testify with aid of interpreter).

ate objection, the witness's proponent must make this four-fold showing to satisfy both the letter and spirit of those rules. The statutes expressly require the proponent to show that the witness acquired firsthand knowledge. The argument runs that as a matter of logic, the witness could not have gained that knowledge unless she possessed the substantive capacities listed in this foundation. After all, how can you perceive anything unless you have the capacity to perceive? However, given the wording of Rules 601 and 602, it is untenable to require anything more than this minimal foundation. It is certainly indefensible to announce any hard-and-fast rules concerning the incompetency of children of a specified age or adults suffering from a particular mental disorder. Moreover, especially since Rule 602 indicates that the judge must use the Rule 104(b) conditional relevance procedure for determining whether the proponent's showing of personal knowledge is satisfactory, the judge should apply the same lax procedure to all four substantive requirements.[26]

Even the intermediate interpretation of the Federal Rules, though, leads to a substantial relaxation of the common law competency standards. As previously stated, at common law the trial judge decided as a question of fact whether the prospective witness possessed all the requisite capacities—the preliminary factfinding procedure now employed under Federal Rule 104(a).[27] However, if the common law requirements have survived to an extent, as a matter of statutory interpretation they must largely be implied from the statutory scheme including Rule 602. As

---

[25]*See generally* State v. McNeely, 314 N.C. 451, 333 S.E.2d 738, 740 (1985) ("The test of competency is whether the witness understands the obligation of an oath or affirmation and has sufficient capacity to understand and relate facts which will assist the jury in reaching its decision."); Jenkins v. Snohomish County Public Utility Dist. No. 1, 105 Wash. 2d 99, 713 P.2d 79, 81 (1986) ("The test to determine child competency is set out in State v. Allen, 70 Wash.2d 690, 692, 424 P.2d 1021 (1967). The five-part test states the child must exhibit (1) an understanding of the obligation to speak the truth on the witness stand; (2) the mental capacity at the time of the occurrence concerning which he is to testify to receive an accurate impression of it; (3) a memory sufficient to retain an independent recollection of the occurrence; (4) the capacity to express in words his memory of the oc-

currence; and (5) the capacity to understand simple questions about it. This test, read in conjunction with the statute, must be applied by the trial court to determine whether the child witness is competent to testify. State v. Ryan, 691 P.2d 197 (Wash.1984)."); Larsen v. State, 686 P.2d 583, 585 (Wyo. 1984) (competency requires "(1) an understanding of the obligation to speak the truth on the witness stand; (2) the mental capacity at the time of the occurrence concerning which he is to testify, to receive an accurate impression of it; (3) a memory sufficient to retain an independent recollection of the occurrence; (4) the capacity to express in words his memory of the occurrence; and (5) the capacity to understand simple questions about it.").

[26]See § 53.

[27]See § 53.

previously stated, Rule 602 expressly indicates that the judge is to apply the conditional relevance procedure set out in Rule 104(b). To qualify a person as a witness, the witness's proponent need introduce only evidence sufficient to support a permissive inference of personal knowledge, i.e., that the witness had the capacity to and actually did observe, receive, record, and can now recollect and narrate impressions obtained through any sense. That minimalist intermediate approach is consistent with the Advisory Committee's Note to Rule 601. The Note asserts that the common law standards of mental capacity proved elusive, few witnesses were actually disqualified, and a witness wholly without mental capacity is difficult to imagine.[28]

*Rule 403.* Despite this analysis of Rules 601 and 602, the testimony of a witness whose mental capacity has been seriously impaired could still conceivably be excluded under Rule 403 on the ground that no reasonable juror could possibly believe that the witness possesses personal knowledge, or understands the difference between the truth and a lie or fantasy.[29] With the exception of convictions qualifying under Federal Rule 609(a)(2), all evidence is subject to discretionary exclusion under Rule 403.[30] The opponent's evidence of the prospective witness's deficiencies could be so strong that the trial judge could justifiably bar the witness under Rule 403.[31] For instance, if the prospective witness

---

[28]See note 22 supra.

[29]Uniform Rule of Evidence 19 (1953) ("The judge may reject the testimony of a witness that he perceived a matter if he finds that no trier of fact could reasonably believe that the witness did perceive the matter."); Comment to Rule 104 of the Model Code of Evidence ("If the witness proposes to testify that he actually perceived a material matter, he must usually be permitted so to testify unless his story is inherently impossible or so fantastic that no rational person could reasonable believe it. The mere fact that the opponent produces or offers to produce contradictory evidence of greater weight is immaterial, unless that evidence is of such overwhelming weight that no jury could reasonably believe that the witness did not perceive the matter."); Morgan, Basic Problems of Evidence 59–60 (1961) ("A witness other than an expert, must confine his testimony to

matters of which he purports to have first hand knowledge, that is, to matters which he has perceived. The court may not refuse to permit a witness to testify that he perceived a material matter merely because the court believes the witness to be obviously mistaken or obviously falsifying. It is only where no reasonable trier of fact could believe that the witness perceived what he claims to have perceived that the court may reject the testimony. Not improbability but impossibility is the test."). *See* Anderson v. Franklin County, Mo., 192 F.3d 1125 (8th Cir. 1999) (the trial judge did not err in excluding the testimony of a potential witness, a deaf mute who could not read, write, or communicate through standard sign language).

[30]Rothstein, Some Themes in the Proposed Federal Rules of Evidence, 33 Fed. B.J. 21, 29 (1974).

[31]U.S. v. Phibbs, 999 F.2d 1053, 1069 (6th Cir. 1993) (in response to a

is virtually incoherent, his testimony would have minimal probative value and pose a significant danger of jury confusion.

In sum, a witness's competency to testify at most requires only a minimal ability to observe, recollect, and recount as well as an understanding of the duty to tell the truth.[32] Where a witness's capacity is brought into question, the ultimate issue is whether a reasonable juror must believe that the person's powers of perception, recollection, or narration are so deficient that it is not worth the time listening to his testimony. This test of competency requires only minimum credibility.[33] The marked trend is to resolve doubts about the witness's credibility in favor of permitting the jury to hear the testimony and evaluate the witness's credibility for itself.[34] Thus, proof of mental deficiency ordinarily has the effect of reducing the weight to be given to testimony

---

challenge to a prospective witness's competency, the court commented that "the authority of this court to control the admissibility . . . [evidence] is to be found outside of Rule 601").

[32]U.S. v. Gutman, 725 F.2d 417, 420 (7th Cir. 1984) ("Although insanity as such is no longer a ground for disqualifying a witness, see Fed. R. Evid. 601, a district judge has the power, and in an appropriate case the duty, to hold a hearing to determine whether a witness should not be allowed to testify because insanity has made him incapable of testifying in a competent fashion."); U.S. v. Banks, 520 F.2d 627, 630 (7th Cir. 1975) (the test is "whether a proffered witness is capable of testifying in any meaningful fashion whatsoever."); U.S. v. Benn, 476 F.2d 1127, 1130 (D.C. Cir. 1972) ("Competency depends upon the witness' capacity to observe, remember, and narrate as well as an understanding of the duty to tell truth.").

[33]Weinstein and Berger, Evidence ¶ 601[01] at 601-9 to 601-11 (1988) ("In such cases, since there are no longer artificial grounds for disqualifying a witness as incompetent, the traditional preliminary examination into competency is no longer required. But a trial judge still has broad discretion to control the course of a trial (Rule 611) and rule on relevancy (Rules 401 and 403). If competency is defined as the minimum standard of credibility necessary to permit any reasonable man to put any credence in a witness's testimony, then witnesses must be competent as to the matters they are expected to testify about; it is the court's obligation to insure that the minimum standard is met. In making this determination the court will still be deciding competency. It would, however, in view of the way the rule is cast, probably be more accurate to say that the court will decide not competency but minimum credibility. This requirement of minimum credibility is just one aspect of the requirement of minimum probative force—i.e., relevancy. Regardless of terminology, the trial judge may exclude all or a part of the witness' testimony on the ground that no one could reasonably believe the witness could have observed, remembered, communicated or told the truth with respect to the event in question. The judge may use the *voir dire* to make this determination. . . . Thus the practice remains much as it has been in determining that the witness meets minimum credibility standards."). 3 Weinstein's Federal Evidence § 601.03[1][a] (rev. 2011) is to the same effect.

[34]U.S. v. Villalta, 662 F.2d 1205 (5th Cir. 1981) (a person's lack of total fluency in translating Spanish to English went to weight and not competency to testify as a lay witness); U.S. v. Jones, 482 F.2d 747, 751 (D.C. Cir. 1973) ("[I]t has become the modern

rather than keeping the witness off the stand. Nevertheless, as previously stated, in an extreme case under Rule 403 the judge might exclude the testimony of a witness passing the test of minimum credibility on the basis of perceived probative dangers such as misleading or confusing the jury.[35]

## § 63    Religious belief[1]

At early common law, as a prerequisite to taking the oath the witness had to believe in a divine being who, in this life or hereafter, will punish false swearing.[2] Members of many major religions met the test, but followers of other religions, as well as atheists and agnostics, could not. That early approach is obviously inconsistent with the democratic principle of freedom of conscience. The state courts[3] have invoked various theories for overturning this ground of incapacity. For example, the courts have: relied on explicit state constitutional or statutory provisions,[4] expansively interpreted state provisions forbidding deprivation of rights for religious beliefs,[5] adopted Federal Rules of

---

trend to limit the trial court's power to exclude testimony because of incompetency and to make the pivotal question one of credibility.").

[35]U.S. v. Gutman, 725 F.2d 417, 424–25 (7th Cir. 1984); Huff v. White Motor Corp., 609 F.2d 286, 294 n.12 (7th Cir. 1979) ("In the extreme case in which the witness' incompetence is clear, the judge could exercise his balancing authority under Rule 403 to exclude the evidence."); U.S. v. Benn, 476 F.2d 1127, 1130 (D.C. Cir. 1972) (competency "also requires an assessment of the potential prejudicial effects of allowing the jury to hear the testimony. Mental retardation may be so severe, capabilities so impaired, and the testimony so potentially prejudicial that it should be barred completely by the judge. Or there may be sufficient indications of a witness' capacity and of the reliability of her testimony that it should be heard and assessed by the jury, albeit with a cautionary instruction.").

**[Section 63]**

[1]2 Wigmore, Evidence § 518 (Chadbourn rev. 1979), 6 id. §§ 1816–29 (Chadbourn rev. 1976); 3

Weinstein's Federal Evidence § 601.02[1] (rev. 2011); West's Key Number Digest, Witnesses ⊙44, 227.

[2]Attorney-General v. Bradlaugh, [1885], L.R. 2 Q.B.D. 697; 6 Wigmore, Evidence § 1817 (Chadbourn rev. 1976).

[3]See the constitutional and statutory provisions listed in 6 Wigmore, Evidence § 1828 note 1 (Chadbourn rev. 1976).

[4]E.g., Cal. Const.1879, art. I, § 4 ("No person shall be rendered incompetent to be a witness or juror on account of his opinions on matters of religious belief"); New York Const. 1895, Art. I, § 3 (similar to last, as to witnesses); Texas Const.1876, Art. I, § 5 ("No person shall be disqualified to give evidence in any of the Courts of this State on account of his religious opinions, or for the want of any religious belief . . . ."); 42 Pa. Cons. Stat. Ann. § 5902 ("The capacity of any person to testify in any judicial proceeding shall not be affected by his opinions on matters of religion.").

[5]E.g., Hroneck v. People, 134 Ill. 139, 24 N.E. 861, 865 (1890) (under a state constitution provision that "no

Evidence or Revised Uniform Rules of Evidence 601 and 603,[6] or modified the common law "in the light of reason and experience"[7] because such a requirement is inconsistent with the tolerant spirit of our institutions.[8] In any event, the enforcement of this early common law rule of incapacity appears prohibited in any state or federal court by the first and fourteenth amendments of the national constitution.[9]

The witness himself can object to an oath that directly or inferentially requires him to avow a belief in God. If the witness has a scruple against oaths, the witness may "affirm" under penalty of perjury rather than "swear."[10] No particular form of

---

person shall be denied any civil or political right, privilege or capacity, on account of his religious opinions" a witness is qualified though he lacked the religious belief required at common law; see Ill. Const., Art. I, § 3); State v. Levine, 109 N.J.L. 503, 162 A. 909 (N.J. Sup. Ct. 1932), 33 Col. L. Rev. 539 (under former Art. 1, § 4 [now N.J. Const., Art. 1, § 5], providing that no person shall be denied enjoyment of civil rights because of religious principles, it was error to deny the accused the privilege of affirming as a witness on account of his want of religious belief, even though he was allowed to tell his story to the jury.).

[6]See Fed. R. Evid. (1st sentence) and Unif. R. Evid. 601, § 62 at note 21 supra. Fed. R. Evid. 603 confirms the text. Former Fed. R. Evid. 603 provides: "Before testifying, every witness shall be required to declare that the witness will testify truthfully, by oath or affirmation in a form calculated to awaken his conscience and impress the witness' mind with his duty to do so." Unif. R. Evid. 603 is identical in content. Effective December 1, 2011, restyled Fed. R. Evid. 603 reads: "Before testifying, a witness must give an oath or affirmation to testify truthfully. It must be in a form designed to impress that duty on the witness's conscience."

[7]See Gillars v. U.S., 182 F.2d 962, 969, 970 (D.C. Cir. 1950) (proper to allow a witness to "affirm" and testify though he did not believe in

divine punishment for perjury and though D.C.Code, Title 14, § 101 provided that "all evidence shall be given under oath according to the forms of the common law," except that a witness with conscientious scruples against an oath may affirm). See also Flores v. State, 443 P.2d 73 (Alaska 1968) (witness who was sworn under the usual oath competent although on cross-examination he stated he did not believe in God); People v. Wood, 66 N.Y.2d 374, 497 N.Y.S.2d 340, 488 N.E.2d 86 (1985).

[8]See note 7 supra.

[9]The textual statement may be inferred from Torcaso v. Watkins, 367 U.S. 488, 81 S. Ct. 1680, 6 L. Ed. 2d 982 (1961) (belief in God, as a Maryland test of eligibility for public office, was unconstitutional under the First and Fourteenth Amendments of the federal constitution).

[10]U.S. v. Moore, 217 F.2d 428 (7th Cir. 1954), rev'd on other grounds, 348 U.S. 966 (1955). If a lawyer anticipates that her witness will refuse to swear, before calling the witness the lawyer should alert the court official who administers the oath. If without incident the witness affirms, the jury will probably not even notice that the witness did not swear. However, if the court official attempts to administer a typical oath and then the witness refuses to take the oath, not only may the witness be embarrassed; in addition, some jurors might discount the witness's credibility.

oath or affirmation is necessary.[11] However, it has been held that
routinely swearing witnesses to tell the truth by using the phrase,
"so help me God," does not warrant reversal when the witnesses
themselves did not object;[12] requiring the use of that phrase might
violate the witness's freedom of conscience, but in the typical
case the losing litigant probably lacks standing to object on
appeal. However, in some circumstances, as when it is evident to
the jury that the losing party shared the beliefs which prevented
the witness from swearing, the party could make a plausible
argument that he was prejudiced. Inquiry into the witness's
religious opinions for impeachment purposes is discussed in another section.[13]

## § 64   Conviction of crime[1]

The common law disqualified altogether a prospective witness
who had been convicted of certain offenses, namely, treason,
felony, or a crime involving fraud or deceit.[2] In England and most
states during the last hundred years, legislation has swept away
this disqualification.[3] In 1917, the United States Supreme Court
determined that "the dead hand of the common law rule" of
disqualification no longer applies in federal criminal cases.[4] The
disqualification is not recognized in Federal Rule of Evidence and
Uniform Rule of Evidence 601.[5] However, a few states retain the
disqualification for conviction of perjury and subornation.[6] Even
these statutes are now of questionable validity under the

---

[11]U.S. v. Thai, 29 F.3d 785 (2d
Cir. 1994); U.S. v. Armijo, 5 F.3d 1229,
1235 (9th Cir. 1993) ("there is no
constitutional or statutorily required
form of oath"); Ferguson v. C.I.R., 921
F.2d 588, 589–90 (5th Cir. 1991) ("alternative statement"). See U.S. v.
Ward, 989 F.2d 1015 (9th Cir. 1992)
("fully integrated Honesty").

[12]State v. Albe, 10 Ariz. App. 545,
460 P.2d 651 (Div. 1 1969).

[13]See § 46 supra.

**[Section 64]**

[1]2 Wigmore, Evidence §§ 488,
519–24 (Chadbourn rev. 1979); 3
Weinstein's Federal Evidence
§ 601.05[1] (rev. 2011); West's Key
Number Digest, Witnesses ⊂⊃48, 49.

[2]Wigmore, Evidence §§ 519, 520
(Chadbourn rev. 1979).

[3]See the statutes collected in 2
Wigmore, Evidence § 488 (Chadbourn
rev. 1979). Some of the cited statutes
retaining vestiges of the common law
rule have been amended since the collection was compiled. See generally
Allen, The Law of Evidence in Victorian
England (1997).

[4]Rosen v. U.S., 245 U.S. 467, 38
S. Ct. 148, 62 L. Ed. 406 (1918).

[5]See § 62 note 21 supra.

[6]The majority of courts have denied disqualification by reason of a
conviction in another state, although
conviction in the forum would result
in disqualification. See Conviction in
another jurisdiction as disqualifying
witness, 2 A.L.R.2d 579. Any of the
remaining statutes would be abrogated
by Unif. R. Evid. 601, supra § 62 at
note 22.

Supreme Court's decision in *Washington v. Texas.*[7] There the Court invalidated Texas legislation that barred persons charged or convicted as co-participants in the same crime from testifying for each other. The Court found that it was irrational to permit such persons to testify for the prosecution while categorically barring their testimony for the defense.

## § 65 Parties and persons interested: The dead man statutes[1]

By far the most drastic common law incompetency rule was the doctrine excluding testimony by parties to the lawsuit and all persons with a direct pecuniary or proprietary interest in the outcome. In effect, this rule both imposed a disability on the party to testify in his own behalf and granted him a privilege not to be called as a witness against himself by the adversary. The disability had the specious justification of preventing self-interested perjury. The privilege lacked even that dubious rationale. It is almost unbelievable that the rule continued in force in England until the middle of the 19th century—and in this country for a few decades longer. In England, the reform was sweeping, and no shred of disqualification remains in civil cases.

In this country, however, the reformers were forced to accept a compromise. An objection was raised with respect to controversies over consensual transactions, such as contracts, or other events such as traffic accidents where one party died but the other survived. The thrust of the objection was that fraud might result if the surviving parties or interested persons could testify about the transaction or the event.[2] The survivor could still testify although death had sealed the adverse party's lips. This is a seductive argument. It was accepted in nearly all the states, at a time

---

[7]Washington v. Texas, 388 U.S. 14, 87 S. Ct. 1920, 18 L. Ed. 2d 1019 (1967). The counterargument is that the Court invalidated the Texas statutes primarily because they irrationally differentiated between the witness's appearance of the prosecution and defense. That policy concern is inapplicable if the statute bars the convict from appearing as a witness for either side.

**[Section 65]**

[1]2 Wigmore, Evidence §§ 575–80 (Chadbourn rev. 1979); 3 Weinstein's Federal Evidence § 601.05[1] (rev. 2011); West's Key Number Digest, Witnesses ⊶125 to 183.5; Ray, Dead Man's Statutes, 24 Ohio St. L.J. 89 (1963).

[2]Greene v. U.S., 447 F. Supp. 885, 890 (N.D. Ill. 1978) ("The purpose of the statute is 'to protect the estates of deceased persons and the interests of parties suing or defending as executor, administrator, heir, legatee, or devisee, against the possibility of false testimony and fraudulent claims by survivors.' 6 Callaghan's Illinois Evidence § 1202 at 3–4 (1964). The Illinois cases are clear that the statute is not intended to exclude testimony which would augment the estate."); In re Estate of Hall, 517 Pa. 115, 535 A.2d 47, 53 (1987) ("The purpose of the Act is to prevent the injustice that

when the real policy dispute was whether the general disqualification should be abolished or retained. At that time, the recognition of the exception for survivors' cases undoubtedly struck the reformers as a minor concession. Minor or not, the concession survives in many states.

Accordingly, statutes in numerous states still provide that the common law disqualification of parties and interested persons is abolished with a single exception. The exception was that they remain disqualified to testify concerning a transaction or communication with a person since deceased in a suit prosecuted or defended by the decedent's executor or administrator.[3] However, there is often a proviso by statute or case law that the surviving party or interested person may testify if called by the adversary, that is, the decedent's executor or administrator; the proviso abrogates the privilege feature of the common law rule. The practical consequence of these statutes comes into play when a survivor has rendered services, furnished goods, or lent money to a person whom he trusted without an independent, corroborating witness or admissible written evidence. The survivor is helpless if the other dies and the representative of his estate declines to pay. The statute may close the survivor's mouth in an action arising from a fatal automobile collision,[4] or a suit on a note or account which the survivor paid in cash without obtaining a receipt.[5]

Today, these restrictions are purely creatures of statute.

---

would result from permitting a surviving party to a transaction to testify favorably to himself and adversely to the interest of a decedent, when the decedent's representative would be hampered in attempting to refute the testimony or be in no position to refute it, by reason of the decedent's death.").

[3]This is the most common general form, but the variants are so numerous that no statute can be said to be "typical." Recent Development, Evidence–The Dead Man's Statute: State Legislatures and Courts Conflict, 25 Am.J.Trial Advoc. 213, 221 (2001) (collecting statutes). The cases interpreting one statute must be cited with great caution in construing another statute, and there is a good deal of conflicting interpretive case law. Some statutes apply to suits by or against other persons deriving interests from a deceased person, as well as suits by or against guardians of incompetents.

The variations in the statutes were summarized and graphically charted in Vanderbilt, Minimum Standards of Judicial Administration 334–41 (1949). *See also* Yaeger, The Pennsylvania Dead Man's Statute, 18 Widener L. Rev. 53 (2012). For an opinion describing the operation of a relatively "typical" statute, see Melvin v. Parker, 472 So. 2d 1024 (Ala. 1985).

[4]Testimony to facts of automobile accident as testimony to a "transaction" or "communication" with a deceased person, within dead man statute, 80 A.L.R.2d 1296; West's Key Number Digest, Witnesses ⚖159(3); Stout, Should the Dead Man's Statute Apply to Automobile Collisions, 38 Texas L. Rev. 14 (1959).

[5]*See* Building Services Unlimited Inc. v. Riley, 238 F. Supp. 2d 255 (D.D.C. 2002) (the District of Columbia statute barred a condominium owner's testimony that her deceased

Consequently, when a case raises a dead man's issue, the primary task is statutory construction. As Felix Frankfurter said, "Read the statute."[6] To dissect the statute, keep the following questions in mind:

- What types of proceedings does the statute apply to? Must the decedent's personal representative be formally joined as a party? Does the statute apply only to causes of action derived from the decedent such as suits for the decedent's pain and suffering prior to death, or does it also extend to causes of action for wrongful death which are conferred by statute directly on the heirs?

- Who is disqualified? All statutes disqualify the surviving party. Some statutes also bar the surviving party's spouse. Many similarly exclude testimony by "interested persons."[7] The courts tend to limit the scope of the latter expression to persons such as a surviving party's business partner who would benefit by the direct legal operation of the judgment in the case.[8]

- What is the nature of the competence? Is the statute's bar limited to "communications" with the decedent? Or does the statute use broader language, typically "transactions"? How expansively should the term "transaction" be interpreted? Since the decedent's death has deprived the estate of the decedent's testimony based on personal knowledge, there is a strong argument that the "transaction" should purposively be construed broadly to include any fact or event which the decedent had firsthand knowledge of.[9]

- Are there any special exceptions to the scope of the prohibition? Many statutes lift the bar of the statute when the survivor and the decedent stood in the relationship of employer and employee or partners. If the statute applied to such relationships, it would be difficult to enforce routine agreements between such parties. Those are important

---

co-owner did not in fact make a 50% contribution to the mortgage payments on the condominium).

[6]Quoted in Friendly, Benchmarks.

[7]Comment, The Deadman's Statute—Who Is an Interested Party in Wisconsin?, 87 Marq. L. Rev. 1025 (2004).

[8]Maltas v. Maltas, 197 F. Supp. 2d 409, 426 (D. Md. 2002), rev'd on other grounds, 65 Fed. Appx. 917 (4th Cir. 2003) ("Although those of Ben's children not presently named as par-

ties may have some interest in the outcome of this case (as they are not named in Ben's will), this interest does not render them incompetent to testify" under the Maryland statute).

[9]Although the survivor may not testify directly as to the forbidden topics, some courts permit the survivor to authenticate documentary evidence which contain information relevant to those topics. Clark v. Meyer, 188 F. Supp. 2d 416, 422 n.34 (S.D. N.Y. 2002) ("The [New York] dead man's statute does not apply to documentary and other tangible evidence").

relationships in the business world, and the law should not impede them.

● What acts constitute a waiver of the statute? The estate certainly loses the protection of the statute when it calls an otherwise disqualified person as a witness at trial.[10] Is there also a waiver if the estate merely deposes the person before trial? In some states, there is deep-seated judicial hostility to the continued existence of the statutes; and that hostility translates into the courts' willingness to strain to find a waiver.

More fundamentally, most commentators agree that the expedient of refusing to listen to the survivor is, in Bentham's words, "blind and brainless."[11] In seeking to avoid injustice to one side, the statutory drafters ignored the equal possibility of creating injustice to the other. The survivor's temptation to fabricate a claim or defense is evident enough—so obvious that any juror should realize that his story must be evaluated cautiously. In case of fraud, a searching cross-examination will often reveal discrepancies in the "tangled web" of deception. In any event, the survivor's disqualification is more likely to disadvantage the honest than the dishonest survivor. A litigant who would resort to perjury will hardly hesitate at suborning a third person, who is not disqualified, to swear to the false story.

Legislators and courts are gradually coming to realize the stupidity of the traditional survivors' evidence acts, and adopting liberalizing changes. A few states provide that the survivor may testify, but that his testimony is legally insufficient to support a judgment unless the testimony is corroborated by other evidence.[12] Others authorize the trial judge to permit the survivor to testify

---

[10]Paul v. Gomez, 118 F. Supp. 2d 694 (W.D. Va. 2000) (applying the Virginia statute). *See also* Yeager, The Pennsylvania Dead Man's Statute, 18 Widener L. Rev. 53, 62–69 (2012) (discussing both the waiver of and exceptions to the Pennsylvania state statute).

[11]Ladd, Witnesses, 10 Rutgers L. Rev. 523, 526 (1956); Ray, Dead Man's Statutes, 24 Ohio St. L.J. 89, 105–08 (1963).

[12]Statutes and cases are collected in Corroboration required under statute prohibiting judgment against representative of deceased person on uncorroborated testimony of his adversary, 21 A.L.R.2d 1013 and Recent Development, Evidence–The Dead

Man's Statute: State Legislatures and Courts Conflict, 25 Am.J.Trial Advoc. 213, 220 (2001).

These statutes do not concern the witness's competency to testify but only the effect of his testimony. Therefore, Fed. R. Evid. 601 should not apply insofar as it refers to state law issues in diversity cases. Whether such statutes would be per se applicable on state issues in federal court under the *Erie* doctrine is a different question. Arguably they would not be. *See* Byrd v. Blue Ridge Rural Elec. Co-op., Inc., 356 U.S. 525, 78 S. Ct. 893, 2 L. Ed. 2d 953 (1958). An analogy might be made to diversity cases concerning sufficiency of evidence, in which more often than not a federal test (not a state test) governs. Wright & Miller,

when it appears that his testimony is necessary to prevent injustice.[13] Both of these solutions have evident drawbacks[14] which are avoided by a third type of statute. The third kind of statutory scheme sweeps away the disqualification entirely and allows the survivor to testify without restriction. However, the scheme even-handedly minimizes the danger of injustice to the decedent's estate by admitting any relevant writings or oral statements by the decedent, both of which would ordinarily be excluded as hearsay.[15]

Except in diversity cases, Federal Rule of Evidence and Uniform Rule of Evidence 601 completely abandon the instant disqualification.[16] However, not all states that have generally copied the Federal Rules have followed suit.[17] The disqualification not only survives in some states; the disqualification can also come into play in federal court. The second sentence of restyled Federal Rule 601 reads: "But in a civil case, state law governs the witness's competency regarding a claim or defense for which state law supplies the rule of decision."

In short, interest as a disqualification in civil cases has been discarded, except for the relic of the survivors' evidence statutes. The common law disqualification which prevented the criminal

---

Federal Practice and Procedure: Civil § 2525. A contrary view is implied in 3 Weinstein's Federal Evidence § 601.05[2] (rev. 2011).

[13]*See* Ariz. Rev. Stat. Ann. § 12-2251.

Since this statute affects the witnesses' competency to testify, Fed. R. Evid. 601, insofar as it speaks of state issues, should govern. See § 62 at note 22 supra.

[14]Ray, Dead Man's Statutes, 24 Ohio St. L.J. 89 (1963).

[15]This solution was recommended by the American Bar Association in 1938:

> That the rule excluding testimony of an interested party as to transactions with deceased persons, should be abrogated by the adoption of a statute like that of Connecticut, which removes the disqualification of the party as a witness and permits the introduction of declarations of the decedent, on a finding by the trial judge that they were made in good faith and on decedent's personal knowledge.

For discussions of the problem and the alternative solutions, see 2 Wigmore, Evidence § 578 (Chadbourn rev. 1979); Morgan et al. The Law of Evidence, Some Proposals for Its Reform, Ch. III (1927); Ladd, The Dead Man Statute, 26 Iowa L. Rev. 201 (1941); Ray, Dead Man's Statutes, 24 Ohio St. L.J. 89 (1963).

The comment in note 12 supra, applies except that "sufficiency of evidence cases" are inapplicable.

[16]See § 62 note 17 supra. Recent Development, Evidence–Dead Man's Statute: State Legislatures and Courts Conflict, 25 Am. J. Trial Advoc. 213, 220 (2001) (collecting the statutes and court rules). However, even in jurisdictions where Rule 601 arguably has superseded the dead man's statute, courts occasionally refer to the dead man's restriction. 25 Am. J. Trial Advoc. at 221 (collecting cases).

[17]At least seven states retained a dead man's statute in some form. The majority did not do so. *See* 1 Joseph & Saltzburg, Evidence in America: The Federal Rules in the States § 35.3, at 4 (1987) (Florida, Idaho, North Carolina, Texas, Utah, Vermont, and Wisconsin).

accused from being called as a witness by either side has been abrogated in England and this country to the extent it disabled the defendant from testifying in his own behalf. However, it survives in that the prosecution cannot call the defendant. In this form, it is a privilege and constitutes one aspect of the broader Fifth Amendment privilege against self-incrimination, discussed in §§ 116 and 131.[18]

While the disqualification of parties and persons interested in the result of the lawsuit has been almost entirely swept away, evidence law still acknowledges the relevance of the fact of a witness's interest. Interest or bias may still be proved to impeach credibility.[19] Indeed, under the Sixth Amendment Confrontation Clause a criminal defendant has a constitutional right to cross-examine a prosecution witness to expose the witness's bias.[20] In most jurisdictions the trial judge instructs the jury that a party's testimony may be weighed in the light of his self-interest and stake in the outcome of the trial.[21]

## § 66  Husbands and wives of parties[1]

Closely related to the parties' disqualification and even more arbitrary and misguided, was the early common law disqualification of the party's husband or wife. This disqualification prevented the party's husband or wife from testifying either for or against the party in any case, civil or criminal.[2] The disability of the husband or wife as a witness to testify *for* the party-spouse was a disqualification, based on the supposed infirmity of interest. In contrast, the rule enabling the party-spouse to prevent the

---

[18]See §§ 116, 131, infra.

[19]See § 39 supra.

[20]Davis v. Alaska, 415 U.S. 308, 94 S. Ct. 1105, 39 L. Ed. 2d 347 (1974). *See* U.S. v. Sasson, 62 F.3d 874, 883 (7th Cir. 1995) ("where the defense is completely foreclosed from exposing the witness' bias or motive to testify, the limitation may directly implicate the defendant's constitutionally protected right to cross-examination"); Quinn v. Neal, 998 F.2d 526, 531 (7th Cir. 1993) ("[a] trial judge has no discretion to prevent cross-examination about . . . a prototypical form of bias . . . .").

[21]Hancheft v. Haas, 219 Ill. 546, 76 N.E. 845 (1906); Lovely v. Grand Rapids & I.R. Co., 137 Mich. 653, 100 N.W. 894 (1904); State v. Turner, 320 S.W.2d 579 (Mo. 1959).

**[Section 66]**

[1]2 Wigmore, Evidence §§ 488 (statutes), 600–20 (Chadbourn rev.1979) (marital disqualification to testify for the spouse), 8 Wigmore, Evidence §§ 2227–45 (privilege of party-spouse to prevent other spouse from testifying against the party) (McNaughton rev.1961); 3 Weinstein's Federal Evidence § 601 App. 102[6] (rev. 2011); West's Key Number Digest, Witnesses ⌐51 to 65; Hutchins & Slesinger, Some Observations on the Law of Evidence: Family Relations, 13 Minn. L. Rev. 675 (1929); Note, 56 NW. L. Rev. 208 (1961).

[2]See authorities in note 1 supra.

husband or wife from testifying *against* the party functioned as a privilege.[3]

Of course, the common law rule has been modified. In the majority of jurisdictions, statutes make the husband or wife fully competent to testify for or against the party-spouse in civil cases.[4] In criminal cases, the disqualification of the husband or wife to testify for the accused spouse has been removed everywhere; but in many states the prosecution may not call the spouse, without the accused spouse's consent, thus preserving the accused's privilege to keep the spouse off the stand altogether.[5] In some jurisdictions either spouse may assert the privilege.[6] In its 1980 *Trammel* decision, the Supreme Court announced that in federal criminal cases, only the witness spouse (the spouse who is to be called by the prosecution as a witness) may claim the privilege.[7]

---

[3] 8 Wigmore, Evidence § 2227 (McNaughton rev. 1961).

[4] See statutes collected in 2 Wigmore, Evidence § 488 (Chadbourn rev.1979), 8 Wigmore, Evidence § 2245 (McNaughton rev. 1961), and summary of statutes in Note, 38 Va. L. Rev. 359 (1952).

[5] See tabulation in Trammel v. U.S., 445 U.S. 40 n.9, 100 S. Ct. 906, 63 L. Ed. 2d 186 (1980). See also sources cited in note 4 supra. State v. Dunbar, 360 Mo. 788, 230 S.W.2d 845, 849 (1950) (this was a prosecution of husband for shooting wife in arm, so that it had to be amputated; under the statute, wife, though competent, was not compellable to testify; the case overlooks the principle that a party cannot complain of the infringement of a witness's privilege; the husband arguably lacked standing to appeal on the ground of a violation of the wife's privilege; see § 73 infra). Many jurisdictions do not recognize this privilege at a grand jury hearing. In re A Grand Jury Subpoena, 849 A.2d 797, 800–05 (Mass. 2006).

[6] See sources cited in note 5 supra.

[7] Trammel v. U.S., 445 U.S. 40, 100 S. Ct. 906, 63 L. Ed. 2d 186 (1980). The result reached in this opinion is contrary to Rule 505 as promulgated by the Supreme Court but deleted by Congress.

In 1986, Uniform Rule of Evidence 504 (1974) was amended. Rev. Paragraph (a) of the amended rule provides a privilege for confidential communications between husband and wife; for text see infra § 78. The remainder of the revised rule is as follows:

(b) Spousal testimony in criminal proceedings. The spouse of an accused in a criminal proceeding has a privilege to refuse to testify against the accused spouse.

(c) Exceptions. There is no privilege under this rule in any civil proceeding in which the spouses are adverse parties, in any criminal proceeding in which a prima facie showing is made that the spouses acted jointly in the commission of the crime charged; or in any proceeding in which one spouse is charged with a crime or tort against the person or property of (i) the other, (ii) a minor child of either, (iii) an individual residing in the household of either, or (iv) a third person if the crime or tort is committed in the course of committing a crime or tort against any of the individuals previously named in this sentence. The court may refuse to allow invocation of the privilege in any other proceeding if the interests of a minor child of either spouse may be adversely affected."

Those provisions were redesignated

The identification of the holder of the privilege is critical because it also determines who is competent to waive the privilege.[8]

The privilege has occasionally been defended on the ground that it protects family harmony. However, family harmony is almost always past saving when the witness spouse is willing to aid the prosecution. There are not only serious questions about the soundness of the policy rationale for the doctrine; at least at first blush, it is also difficult to defend the recognition of the doctrine as a matter of statutory construction. In recognizing the existence of the witness spouse's privilege, the Supreme Court looked to Rule 501 rather than Rule 601. Initially, one might think that Rule 601 on competency would govern. If Rule 601 governed and the Court gave 601 a literal interpretation, 601 would preclude the recognition of any privilege. After all, as the Advisory Committee Note accompanying Rule 601 states, "[n]o . . . qualifications" are "specified" in the text of the rule. However, in *Trammel* the Court correctly noted that its original draft of Article V of the Federal Rules touched on this privilege and that Congress had not objected to the treatment of the issue as an Article V problem.[9] If Rule 501 controls, the Court had the power to recognize the privilege. Some states, though, have gone beyond *Trammel* and taken the step of abolishing the privilege in crimi-

---

subdivisions (c) and (d), and their wording was slightly changed in the 1999 amendment of the Uniform Rules.

There is authority that the trial judge must inform the spouse of the spouse's right to refuse to testify. Henness v. Bagley, 644 F.3d 308, 326–27 (6th Cir. 2011), cert. denied, 132 S. Ct. 1970, 182 L. Ed. 2d 822 (2012) (Ohio law), cert. denied sub nom. Henness v. Robinson, 132 S. Ct. 1970, 182 L. Ed. 2d 822 (2012).

[8]U.S. v. Bad Wound, 203 F.3d 1072 (8th Cir. 2000) (the defendant's putative wife entered into a plea agreement; the provisions of the agreement were specific enough to waive her privilege).

[9]Fed. R. Evid. 601 should govern the question of whether one spouse may testify *for* the other. See text accompanying note 3 supra.

Fed. R. Evid. 501 governs the possible disqualification of one spouse to testify *against* the other. Former Fed. R. Evid. 501 stated:

Except as otherwise required by the Constitution of the United States or provided by Act of Congress or in rules prescribed by the Supreme Court pursuant to statutory authority, the privilege of a witness, person, government, State or political subdivision thereof shall be governed by the principles of the common law as they may be interpreted by the courts of the United States in the light of reason and experience. However, in civil actions and proceedings, with respect to an element of a claim or defense as to which State law supplies the rule of decision, the privilege of a witness, person, government, State, or political subdivision thereof shall be determined in accordance with State law.

Effective December 1, 2011, restyled Fed. R. Evid. 501 reads:

The common law–as interpreted by United States courts in the light of reason and experience–governs a claim of privilege unless any of the following provides otherwise:
- the United States Constitution;
- a federal statute; or
- rules prescribed by the Supreme Court.

nal cases; in those jurisdictions, spouses may be called to the stand to testify in criminal cases just as any other witness.[10]

Even when this privilege would otherwise apply, the prosecution may be able to defeat the privilege claim by invoking the so-called injured spouse exception. Even at common law the instant privilege was denied an accused husband in prosecutions for wrongs directed against the wife's person.[11] In these cases, the spouse is the victim named in the indictment or information. The application of the privilege in these prosecutions would frustrate the enforcement of the criminal statutes in question, since the victim spouse is typically an important or even essential[12] source of prosecution evidence. Most statutes retaining the instant privilege broaden the scope of the exception to encompass prosecution of any "crime committed by one against the other" and various other offenses,[13] including crimes against children or the marital relation such as adultery.[14]

Most jurisdictions limit the privilege in another respect, that

---

But in a civil case, state law governs privilege regarding a claim or defense for which state law supplies the rule of decision.

Trammel v. U.S., 445 U.S. 40, 100 S. Ct. 906, 63 L. Ed. 2d 186 (1980), confirms the legislative history indicating that Fed. R. Evid. 501 governed the instant privilege relating to the calling of a spouse to the stand. It also held as described in note 7 supra. There is no suggestion that the privilege will be applied in federal question civil cases.

Of course, in diversity cases the standard for applying the instant privilege is state law as described in the rule. As to the conflict of laws rule applicable in such cases, see § 76.1 infra.

Pre-*Trammel* federal cases on various aspects of the federal privilege are collected in What constitutes such discriminatory prosecution or enforcement of laws as to provide valid defense in federal criminal proceedings, 45 A.L.R. Fed. 732, 735.

[10]See sources cited in note 5 supra.

[11]1 Blackstone, Commentaries 443 (1765); 8 Wigmore, Evidence § 2239 (McNaughton rev.1961).

[12]In some cases, without the benefit of the other spouse's testimony, the prosecution will be unable to satisfy the initial burden of production and make out a submissible case.

[13]Lynch v. Com., 74 S.W.3d 711 (Ky. 2002) (the Kentucky statute extends the exception to offenses against "an individual residing in the household"; that expression includes a person who kept his belongings at the spouse's house and lived there whenever he was in town).

[14]2 Wigmore, Evidence § 488 (Chadbourn rev.1979) 8 Wigmore, Evidence §§ 2239, 2240 (McNaughton rev.1961). The statutes frequently go farther and expressly except particular crimes (aside from crimes against the spouse's person or property) such as bigamy, adultery, rape, crimes against the children of either or both, and abandonment and support proceedings. People v. Bogle, 41 Cal. App. 4th 770, 48 Cal. Rptr. 2d 739, 745 (3d Dist. 1995) ("cohabitant"); State v. Michels, 141 Wis. 2d 81, 414 N.W.2d 311 (Ct. App. 1987) (foster child); 38 Va. L. Rev. 359, 364, 365 (1952); 8 Wigmore, Evidence § 2240 (McNaughton rev.1961); Competency of One Spouse to Testify Against Other in Prosecution for Offense Against Child of Both or Either or Neither, 119 A.L.R.5th 275; Competency of one spouse to testify against other in prose-

is, its duration. There is some disagreement over the duration of the privilege. However, most courts regard the initial time at which it comes into existence as the date of the creation of the marriage and the terminus as the date of termination of marriage, as by divorce.[15]

Several procedural questions arise. Of course, the holder of the privilege must be identified.[16] As previously stated, there is a division of authority over the identity of the holder. There is a further disagreement whether it is error for the prosecution to call the spouse to the stand, thereby forcing the accused spouse or the witness's spouse to object in the jury's presence.[17] Most courts reinforce the privilege by precluding comment on its exercise.[18]

The privilege is sometimes applied to the spouse's extra-judicial

---

cution for offense against third party as affected by fact that offense against spouse was involved in same transaction, 74 A.L.R.4th 277. Occasionally similar results are reached even absent express exceptions in the statute. State v. Kollenborn, 304 S.W.2d 855 (Mo. 1957) (in prosecution of husband for assault on their minor child, wife could testify for state). *See also* Wyatt v. U.S., 362 U.S. 525, 80 S. Ct. 901, 4 L. Ed. 2d 931 (1960) (transportation of wife for purpose of prostitution in violation of Mann Act is crime against her, and she can be compelled to testify).

A number of jurisdictions lift the bar of the disqualification when both spouses are alleged to have been members of the same criminal conspiracy and the prosecution seeks testimony about the conspiracy. U.S. v. Freeman, 694 F. Supp. 190, 191 (E.D. Va. 1988) ("[t]he Seventh Circuit [was] the first to extend the joint participants exception to the privilege not to testify against a spouse. United States v. Clark, 712 F.2d 299 (7th Cir. 1983)"). However, the support for this exception is far from unanimous. U.S. v. Ramos-Oseguera, 120 F.3d 1028 (9th Cir. 1997); U.S. v. Keck, 773 F.2d 759, 766 (7th Cir. 1985); U.S. v. Archer, 733 F.2d 354, 359 n.3 (5th Cir. 1984). The prosecution had urged this exception on the Supreme Court in Trammel v. U.S., 445 U.S. 40, 100 S. Ct. 906, 63

L. Ed. 2d 186 (1980). The Court bypassed relying on the proposed exception. The Court's refusal to rely on the exception may be a signal that the majority did not favor the exception.

[15]8 Wigmore, Evidence § 2237 (McNaughton rev.1961). See dictum in Pereira v. U.S., 347 U.S. 1, 74 S. Ct. 358, 98 L. Ed. 435 (1954). Pre-*Trammel* decisions held that a defendant who has left his wife may not claim privilege under the particular circumstances. U.S. v. Cameron, 556 F.2d 752 (5th Cir. 1977); U.S. v. Brown, 605 F.2d 389 (8th Cir. 1979).

[16]See sources cited in note 5 supra; also § 73 infra.

[17]State v. Tanner, 54 Wash. 2d 535, 341 P.2d 869 (1959) (it was improper to force objection before jury, but case may be limited to its facts); Hignett v. State, 168 Tex. Crim. 380, 328 S.W.2d 300 (1959) (requiring defendant to object in jury's presence is error); State v. Hixson, 237 Or. 402, 391 P.2d 388 (1964) (contra; it was not error to call spouse to stand and request defendant's permission to examine her); Calling or offering accused's spouse as witness for prosecution as prejudicial misconduct, 76 A.L.R.2d 920.

[18]See cases cited at 8 Wigmore, Evidence § 2243 (McNaughton rev. 1961).

statements.[19] However, in *Trammel* the Supreme Court indicated that the federal version of the privilege is limited to in-court testimony.[20]

Limiting the scope of the privilege in these various respects is a step in the right direction. The privilege is an archaic survival of a mystical dogma.[21] The privilege reflects an outmoded social attitude toward marriage.[22] The Supreme Court's draft of Federal Rule of Evidence 504 would have abolished the privilege; and on the balance, the abolition of the privilege would probably be desirable.

Both the instant privilege and the ancient disqualification must be distinguished from another, narrower privilege—the privilege against disclosure of confidential communications between husband and wife. The spousal communications privilege is discussed in Chapter 9.[23] The disqualification and the instant privilege can have the effect of keeping the spouse altogether off the witness stand. In contrast, the communications privilege has a more limited procedural effect; while the spouse is on the stand, the communications privilege merely bars the spouse from disclosing certain communications passing between the spouses.

### § 67    Incompetency of husband and wife to give testimony on non-access[1]

In 1777, in an ejectment case involving the issue of the claimant's legitimacy, Lord Mansfield delivered a pronouncement

---

[19]See cases cited in 8 Wigmore, Evidence § 2232 (McNaughton rev. 1961), but vicarious admissions and a few other exceptions are noted. A contrary decision is Eubanks v. State, 242 Miss. 372, 135 So. 2d 183 (1961) (wife's extra-judicial statement admitted as part of the res gestae).

[20]Trammel v. U.S., 445 U.S. 40, 52 n.12, 100 S. Ct. 906, 63 L. Ed. 2d 186 (1980). *See also* U.S. v. James, 164 F. Supp. 2d 718 (D. Md. 2001) (the spouse's statements were admissible under the excited utterance hearsay exception); State v. Rush, 340 N.C. 174, 456 S.E.2d 819 (1995).

[21]Coke, Commentary on Littleton 6b (1628) (". . . a wife cannot be produced either for or against her husband," *"quia sunt duae animae in carne una"* ("for they are two souls in one flesh")).

[22]*See* Hutchins & Slesinger, Some Observations on the Law of Evidence: Family Relations, 13 Minn. L. Rev. 675, 678 (1929), but compare Note, 17 U. Chi. L. Rev. 525, 530 (1950) and § 86 infra. See also the criticisms of the privilege in 8 Wigmore, Evidence § 2228 (McNaughton rev. 1961), ranging from Jeremy Bentham's 1827 philippic to the recommendation for its abolition by the A.B.A. Committee on the Improvement of the Law of Evidence of the American Bar Association in 1937.

[23]See Ch. 9 infra.

**[Section 67]**

[1]7 Wigmore, Evidence §§ 2063–64 (Chadbourn rev. 1978); West's Key Number Digest, Witnesses ⬿57; Comment Note.—Rule as regards competency of husband or wife to testify as to nonaccess, 49 A.L.R.3d 212.

which apparently was new-minted doctrine. He declared "that the declarations of a father or mother cannot be admitted to bastardize the issue born after marriage . . . [I]t is a rule founded in decency, morality and policy, that they shall not be permitted to say after marriage that they have had no connection and therefore that the offspring is spurious . . . ."[2] Wigmore criticized Mansfield's invention as obstructive.[3] Yet, the doctrine was followed by later English decisions[4] until overruled by statute,[5] and has been accepted by some American courts.[6] A few courts have wisely rejected it by construing the general statutes abolishing the incompetency of parties and of spouses as overturning this eccentric incompetency,[7] but other courts have rejected the argument.[8]

Even the jurisdictions which recognize the exclusionary rule differ over the scope of the rule. The points of controversy about the rule's scope are: (a) whether it is limited strictly to evidence of non-access,[9] or whether it reaches other types of evidence show-

---

[2]Goodright v. Moss, 1777 WL 9 (K.B.).

[3]7 Wigmore, Evidence § 2064 (Chadbourn rev. 1978). See also § 205 as to conclusive effect of negative results of scientific tests for paternity.

[4]E.g., Russell v. Russell, [1924] App.C. 687 (H.L.)

[5]St.1949, 12, 13, and 14 Geo. 6, ch. 100, Law Reform (Miscellaneous Provisions) Act, 1949, § 7 ("evidence of a husband or wife shall be admissible in any proceedings to prove that marital intercourse did or did not take place between them during any period . . . husband or wife shall not be compellable in any proceeding to give evidence of the matters aforesaid"). Similar provisions are contained in St.1950, 14 Geo. 6, ch. 25, Matrimonial Causes Act, 1950, § 32.

[6]See 7 Wigmore, Evidence § 2065 (Chadbourn rev. 1978). The realistic opinion of Smith, C.J., in Moore v. Smith, 178 Miss. 383, 172 So. 317 (1937), rejects outright the reasoning in Goodright v. Moss, 1777 WL 9 (K. B.). Likewise, the reasoning is not accepted by the Fed. R. Evid. or the Rev. Unif. R. Evid.

[7]In re McNamara's Estate, 181 Cal. 82, 183 P. 552 (1919); Ventresco v. Bushey, 159 Me. 241, 191 A.2d 104 (1963) (overruling Hubert v. Cloutier, 135 Me. 230, 194 A. 303 (1937) and citing additional cases); State v. Soyka, 181 Minn. 533, 233 N.W. 300 (1930); Loudon v. Loudon, 114 N.J. Eq. 242, 168 A. 840 (Ct. Err. & App. 1933) (extensive discussion by Perskie, J.); State v. Schimschal, 73 Wash. 2d 141, 437 P.2d 169 (1968).

[8]E.g., State v. Wade, 264 N.C. 144, 141 S.E.2d 34 (1965); State ex rel. Worley v. Lavender, 147 W. Va. 803, 131 S.E.2d 752 (1963). Specific statutes, however, often limit or abrogate the rule in particular proceedings. E.g., the statutes described in Sayles v. Sayles, 323 Mass. 66, 80 N.E.2d 21, 22 (1948) (statutes permitting spouse's testimony to non-access in prosecutions for non-support and in illegitimacy proceedings).

[9]Hall v. State, 176 Md. 488, 5 A.2d 916 (1939). See also Shelley v. Smith, 249 Md. 619, 241 A.2d 682 (1968); Com. v. Gantz, 128 Pa. Super. 97, 193 A. 72 (1937); Com. v. Ludlow, 206 Pa. Super. 464, 214 A.2d 282 (1965).

ing that someone other than the husband is the father;[10] (b) whether the rule applies only in proceedings where legitimacy is in issue[11] or extends to divorce suits where the question is adultery rather than the child's legitimacy;[12] and (c) whether it prohibits only the testimony of husband and wife on the stand,[13] or also excludes evidence of the spouse's previous out-of-court declarations.[14] In view of the unsoundness of the rule, in each instance the courts should adopt the narrower view of the scope of the doctrine.

## § 68   Judges,[1] jurors[2] and lawyers

### Judges

A judicial officer called to the stand in a case in which she is not sitting as a judge is not disqualified by his office from testifying.[3] For example, if an assault occurred during trial, the judge at that trial could appear as a witness in a subsequent assault prosecution presided over by another judge. But when a judge is called as a witness in a trial before her, her appearance

---

[10]As in Grates v. Garcia, 20 N.M. 158, 148 P. 493 (1915); Esparza v. Esparza, 382 S.W.2d 162 (Tex. Civ. App. Corpus Christi 1964).

[11]The reasoning, if not the holding, in Sayles v. Sayles, 323 Mass. 66, 80 N.E.2d 21 (1948), supports the view that a suit for divorce for adultery is outside the scope of the rule. Biggs v. Biggs, 253 N.C. 10, 116 S.E.2d 178 (1960), seems a holding to that effect.

[12]As in Gonzalez v. Gonzalez, 177 S.W.2d 328 (Tex. Civ. App. El Paso 1943).

[13]As held in Sayles v. Sayles, 323 Mass. 66, 80 N.E.2d 21 (1948).

[14]Zakrzewski v. Zakrzewski, 237 Mich. 459, 212 N.W. 80 (1927) (pursuant to the rule, the court excluded a wife's admission that a child was not her husband's); Schmidt v. State, 110 Neb. 504, 194 N.W. 679, 681 (1923) (wife's declarations); West v. Redmond, 171 N.C. 742, 88 S.E. 341 (1916). See Admissibility, on issue of child's legitimacy or parentage, of declarations of parents, relatives, or the child, deceased or unavailable, 31 A.L.R.2d 989; Comment Note.—Rule as regards competency of husband or wife to testify as to nonaccess, 49 A.L.R.3d 212.

[Section 68]

[1]6 Wigmore, Evidence § 1909 (Chadbourn rev. 1976); 3 Weinstein's Federal Evidence § 601 App.102[2] (rev. 2011); West's Key Number Digest, Witnesses ☞68 to 70; Judge as a witness in a cause on trial before him, 157 A.L.R. 315.

[2]6 Wigmore, Evidence § 1910 (Chadbourn rev. 1976), 8 Wigmore, Evidence §§ 2345–56 (McNaughton rev. 1961); 3 Weinstein's Federal Evidence § 601 App.102[2] (rev. 2011); West's Key Number Digest, Witnesses ☞73; West's Key Number Digest, New Trial ☞141 to 143.

[3]Thus, judges commonly testify about matters occurring in former trials at which they presided. Hamilton v. Vasquez, 17 F.3d 1149 (9th Cir. 1994) (in a federal habeas corpus proceeding, a state trial judge testified about the judge's decision to shackle the accused during the state trial); Steele v. Duckworth, 900 F. Supp. 1048 (N.D. Ind. 1994); Woodward v. City of Waterbury, 113 Conn. 457, 155 A. 825 (1931). Judges should be competent

as witness is obviously inconsistent with her impartial role in the adversary system of trial.[4] Nevertheless, under the older common law view she was generally regarded as a competent witness,[5] although she had a discretion to decline to testify.[6] Shockingly, this view seems to be still in effect under a few state statutes.[7] The

---

witnesses in subsequent habeas corpus proceedings. *See* Leighton v. Henderson, 220 Tenn. 91, 414 S.W.2d 419 (1967); Judge as witness in cause not on trial before him, 86 A.L.R.3d 633; Report of the Special Committee on the Propriety of Judges Appearing as Witnesses, 36 A.B.A. J. 630 (1950).

The problem can arise when, at a bench trial, the judge relies on his or her personal knowledge of facts which are not judicially noticeable. U.S. v. Berber-Tinoco, 510 F.3d 1083, 1089–93 (9th Cir. 2007) (at a suppression hearing, the judge improperly injected his own observation regarding the location of stop signs along a certain road near the border and the narrowness of the road; those facts were not in the record, and they were not reasonable inferences from the record; "[a] trial judge is prohibited from relying on his personal experience to support the taking of judicial notice"); U.S. v. Nickl, 427 F.3d 1286, 1292–94 (10th Cir. 2005) (an accomplice testified at the defendant's trial; in a previous proceeding, the judge had taken the accomplice's guilty plea; during cross-examination, the defense counsel asked the accomplice whether she had pleaded guilty just to get the matter behind her; at that point, the judge improperly interjected the comment that he would never have accepted her guilty plea unless she had convinced him that she had the requisite *mens rea*); U.S. v. Lewis, 833 F.2d 1380, 1385 (9th Cir. 1987) (the trial judge's personal experience with "a general anesthetic"). Similarly, the problem can arise if one of the counsel attempts to read into the record the judge's statements at a prior hearing. U.S. v. Blanchard, 542 F.3d 1133, 1147–49 (7th Cir. 2008) (the prosecutor read into the record the judge's comments

at a prior suppression hearing; "While it is true that the prosecutor, rather than the trial judge, read the . . . comments into the record at trial, this in no way alters our conclusion. In the presence of the jury, the judge acknowledged that the . . . comments were his . . . . Under such circumstances, Rule 605 is violated; the rule would serve little purpose if it were violated only where a judge observes all the formalities—taking of an oath, sitting in the witness chair, etc.—of an ordinary witness).

Moreover, a judge's testimony might be excludable under Federal Rule of Evidence 403. U.S. v. Munoz-Franco, 203 F. Supp. 2d 102 (D.P.R. 2002) (Rule 403 applied; the probative value of character testimony by an active federal district court judge from the same district was substantially outweighed by the attendant probative dangers; the jurors passed by the judge's courtroom every day, and some of the proceedings in the trial had been held in the proposed witness's courtroom).

[4]"The two characters are inconsistent with each other and their being united in one person is incompatible with the fair and safe administration of justice." Parker, J., in Morss v. Morss, 11 Barb. 510, 511, 1851 WL 5343 (N.Y. Gen. Term 1851)

[5]See examples in the English practice in the 1600s and 1700s, described in 6 Wigmore, Evidence § 1909 n. 1 (Chadbourn rev. 1976).

[6]*See* O'Neil & Hearne v. Bray's Adm'x, 262 Ky. 377, 90 S.W.2d 353 (1936); O'Neal v. State, 106 Tex. Crim. 158, 291 S.W. 892 (1927).

[7]See similar statutes described in 6 Wigmore, Evidence § 1909 (Chadbourn rev. 1976). The Tennessee stat-

view is obviously subject to criticism.[8] The criticism led to a decided shift toward a second view that the judge is disqualified from testifying about material, disputed facts but may testify as to matters merely formal and undisputed.[9] Although the second view is a step in the right direction, it can be hard to distinguish between material and formal matters. Moreover, there seems little need for the judge's testimony on these topics, since formal matters nearly always can be proved by other witnesses. Accordingly, there is growing support for a third view that a judge is incompetent to testify in a case which she is trying.[10] The view is as sensible as it is simple. This view is codified in Federal Rule of Evidence 605 and Revised Uniform Rule of Evidence 605.[11] The rule provides for an "automatic" objection.[12]

---

ute is applied in State ex rel. Phillips v. Henderson, 220 Tenn. 701, 423 S.W.2d 489 (1968).

Under the view that a judge is competent as a witness, he should give his evidence under the same procedures applicable to other witnesses. Great Liberty Life Ins. Co. v. Flint, 336 S.W.2d 434 (Tex. Civ. App. Fort Worth 1960).

[8]The Advisory Committee's Note for Fed. R. Evid. 605 posed a series of rhetorical questions to illustrate the practical problems that arise when the presiding judge appears as a witness:

> Who rules on objections? Who compels him to answer? Can he rule impartially on the weight and admissibility of his own testimony? Can he be impeached or cross-examined effectively? Can he, in a jury trial, avoid conferring his seal of approval on one side in the eyes of the jury? Can he, in a bench trial, avoid an involvement destructive of impartiality?

[9]Wingate v. Mach, 117 Fla. 104, 157 So. 421 (1934) (testimony as to formal matter did not make the judge a "material" witness under disqualifying statute); State ex rel. Smith v. Wilcoxen, 1957 OK CR 51, 312 P.2d 187 (Okla. Crim. App. 1957) (judge incompetent to testify to material facts and, if he is called, he should disqualify himself). This view seems to be advocated by Wigmore. See 6

Wigmore, Evidence § 1909 (Chadbourn rev. 1976).

[10]See the general statements of the rule of disqualification or the impropriety of judicial testimony in State v. Sandquist, 146 Minn. 322, 178 N.W. 883, 885 (1920); State v. Eubanks, 232 La. 289, 94 So. 2d 262 (1957), rev'd on other grounds, 356 U.S. 584 (1958); Brashier v. State, 197 Miss. 237, 20 So. 2d 65 (1944); Maitland v. Zanga, 14 Wash. 92, 44 P. 117 (1896). See Report of the Special Committee on the Propriety of Judges Appearing as Witnesses, 36 A.B.A. J. 630, 633 (1950) ("The modern rule is that a judge is not a competent witness in a case in which he is presiding, unless there is a statute permitting it.").

Nevertheless, even though the judge may be incompetent, his testimony, if harmless, is not ground for reversal. E.g., McCaffrey v. State, 105 Ohio St. 508, 138 N.E. 61, 63 (1922), and cases cited in Judge as a witness in a cause on trial before him, 157 A.L.R. 315.

[11]Fed. R. Evid. 605 and Unif. R. Evid. 605 provides: "The judge presiding at the trial may not testify in that trial as a witness. No objection need be made in order to preserve the point."

State v. Baird, 259 Neb. 245, 609 N.W.2d 349 (2000) (at a hearing to determine whether there was good

*Jurors*

Three distinct doctrines relate to the question of when a juror can be a source of evidence.

*The incompetency.* On occasion, persons who formerly served as jurors testify to events that occurred at the previous hearing.[13] Like a judge at a prior trial, a person who had served as a juror at that trial could appear as a witness in a subsequent prosecution to testify about an assault that occurred during the earlier trial. However, a threat to the tribunal's impartiality arises when a juror sitting in a case is called as a witness. Nevertheless, some early common authorities allowed such testimony. To eliminate that danger, Federal and Revised Uniform Rule of Evidence (1974) 606(a) overturned the common law by providing that the juror is incompetent as a witness.[14] Many jurisdictions have adopted statutes and court rules patterned after Rule 606(a). Consequently, substantial inroads have been made on the traditional common law and the early statutes that had been construed as allowing juror testimony.[15] Modernly these problems rarely arise, since in the vast majority of cases panelists with

---

cause to delay the defendant's trial, the judge recited facts within his personal knowledge for the record; the government had not presented any evidence of the court's scheduling difficulties). *See also* Kennedy v. Great Atlantic & Pacific Tea Co., Inc., 551 F.2d 593 (5th Cir. 1977) (citing Rule 605, the court holds that it was error to allow judge's law clerk to testify as to private view of premises where accident occurred).

[12]The Advisory Committee's Note explains:

> To require an actual objection would confront the opponent with a choice between not objecting, with the result of allowing the testimony, and objecting, with the probable result of excluding the testimony but at the price of continuing the trial before a judge likely to feel that his integrity had been attacked by the objector.

For a general discussion of the judge as a witness, see State v. Simpson, 314 N.C. 359, 334 S.E.2d 53 (1985).

[13]U.S. v. Awadallah, 436 F.3d 125, 131–35 (2d Cir. 2006) (the defendant was charged with committing perjury before a grand jury; a former grand juror was a competent witness at the perjury trial).

[14]Former Fed. R. Evid. 606(a) provided:

> A member of the jury may not testify as a witness before that jury in the trial of the case in which the juror is sitting. If the juror is called so to testify, the opposing party shall be afforded an opportunity to object out of the presence of the jury.

Rev.Unif. R. Evid. (1974) is identical in content. Effective December 1, 2011, restyled Fed. R. Evid. 606(a) reads: "A juror may not testify as a witness before the other jurors at the trial. If a juror is called to testify, the court must give a party an opportunity to object outside the jury's presence." *See also* Cal. Evid. Code § 704.

[15]Statutes frequently provide to the contrary. *E.g.*, State v. Cavanaugh, 98 Iowa 688, 68 N.W. 452 (1896) (juror was allowed to testify, under former Iowa Code Ann. § 780.17, but Iowa. R. Evid. 2.19(5)(b) now provides to the contrary). Of course, instances in which jurors will be called as ordinary witnesses are rare because of the procedures for selection of the jurors.

pre-knowledge of the facts of the case are identified and stricken during jury selection.

*The exclusionary rule.* While Rule 606(a) deals with the question of whether a sitting juror can give any testimony in the case, there is a separate traditional doctrine that a juror may not furnish an affidavit or testify to impeach the juror's verdict.[16] By virtue of this doctrine, the juror is barred from testifying about matters that "inhere"[17] in the deliberation process. Although occasionally criticized, this doctrine is now firmly entrenched.[18] The

---

[16]Like the rule forbidding parents to bastardize their issue (see § 67, supra), this dogma was an innovation introduced by Lord Mansfield. The seminal case was Vaise v. Delaval, 1785 WL 83 (K.B.). There jurors' affidavits that their verdict was based on chance were rejected. Lord Mansfield remarked: "The Court cannot receive such an affidavit from any of the jurymen themselves, in all of whom such conduct is a very high misdemeanor; but in every such case the Court must derive their knowledge from some other source, such as some person having seen the transaction through a window or by some such other means". The weaknesses of this position are pointed out in 8 Wigmore, Evidence §§ 2352–53 (McNaughton rev. 1961).

[17]Miles v. City of Minneapolis, 185 F. Supp. 2d 1026, 1029–30 (D. Minn. 2002).

[18]*E.g.*, Hoffman v. City of St. Paul, 187 Minn. 320, 245 N.W. 373 (1932) (affidavits as to quotient verdict excluded) and cases collected in 8 Wigmore, Evidence § 2354 (McNaughton rev. 1961) and in West's Key Number Digest, New Trial ⊙142 to 143.

The various problems are analyzed and the lines of authority identified in Impeachment of Jury Verdicts, 25 U. Chi. L. Rev. 360 (1958).

Some courts following the dogma of the juror's incompetency to impeach his verdict limit the disqualification to testimony about matters occurring within the jury room, and allow the juror to testify to irregularities

occurring outside. Pierce v. Brennan, 83 Minn. 422, 86 N.W. 417 (1901) (jurors' affidavits as to their privately viewing the scene); *and see* Welshire v. Bruaw, 331 Pa. 392, 200 A. 67 (1938) (while jurors cannot testify to misconduct among themselves in jury room, they may testify as to outsiders' misconduct there—here a drunken tipstaff puts pressure on them for a verdict by remarks in jury room). At common law, the disqualification to "impeach" the verdict does not preclude the juror from testifying in support of the verdict, when it is attacked by testimony of outsiders. Morakes v. State, 201 Ga. 425, 40 S.E.2d 120, 127 (1946); Iverson v. Prudential Ins. Co. of America, 126 N.J.L. 280, 19 A.2d 214 (N.J. Ct. Err. & App. 1941). The proper distinction is intrinsic versus extrinsic, not inside versus outside the jury room. *See also* U.S. v. Hernandez-Escarsega, 886 F.2d 1560, 1579 (9th Cir. 1989) ("Rule 606(b) of the Federal Rules of Evidence, however, prohibits the use of juror testimony to impeach a verdict when that testimony relates to intrinsic matters—that is, the internal, mental processes by which the verdict was reached. *See* Tanner v. United States, 483 U.S. 107, 116–127, 107 S.Ct. 2739, 2745–51, 97 L.Ed.2d 90 (1987). Whether the juror was literally inside or outside the jury room when the irregularity occurred has no bearing on the determination that a particular influence was external or internal. Id. at 117, 107 S.Ct. at 2746.").

The traditional doctrine barring juror impeachment disqualifies jurors but not officers and eavesdroppers with knowledge of misconduct. Reich

traditional version of the doctrine, often termed the Mansfield rule,[19] broadly prohibits jurors from testifying about both their subjective mental processes and objective events that transpire during deliberations. Barring juror impeachment of the verdict promotes the finality of verdicts and encourages frank jury deliberation, while discouraging later harassment of jurors by losing parties.[20]

At common law a few courts have abandoned the Mansfield rule, and permit jurors to testify to misconduct and irregularities which are ground for new trial.[21] Under this so-called Iowa view,[22]

---

v. Thompson, 346 Mo. 577, 142 S.W.2d 486 (1940), annotated on this point. In *Reich*, the testimony of the clerk, who overheard from adjoining room statements made in the jury room, was held admissible.

[19]Carlson, Impeaching Jury Verdicts, Litigation, Fall 1975, at 31–33.

[20]Tanner v. U.S., 483 U.S. 107, 119, 107 S. Ct. 2739, 97 L. Ed. 2d 90 (1987) ("There is little doubt that post-verdict investigation into juror misconduct would in some instances lead to the invalidation of verdicts reached after irresponsible or improper juror behavior. It is not at all clear, however, that the jury system could survive such efforts to perfect it. Allegations of juror misconduct, incompetency, or inattentiveness, raised for the first time days, weeks, or months after the verdict seriously disrupt the finality of the process. *See, e.g.*, Government of Virgin Islands v. Nicholas, 759 F.2d at 1081 (one year and eight months after verdict rendered, juror alleged that hearing difficulties affected his understanding of the evidence). Moreover, full and frank discussion in the jury room, jurors' willingness to return an unpopular verdict, and the community's trust in a system that relies on the decisions of laypeople would all be undermined by a barrage of post verdict scrutiny of juror conduct. *See* Note, Public Disclosures of Jury Deliberations, 96 Harv. L. Rev. 886, 888–892 (1983)."); Government of Virgin Islands v. Gereau, 523 F.2d 140, 148 (3d Cir. 1975) ("The rule was formulated to fos-

ter several public policies: (1) discouraging harassment of jurors by losing parties eager to have the verdict set aside; (2) encouraging free and open discussion among jurors; (3) reducing incentives for jury tampering; (4) promoting verdict finality; (5) maintaining the viability of the jury as a judicial decision-making body."); People v. Force, 89 Cal. Rptr. 3d 50, 68–70 (Cal. App. 4th Dist. 2009) (the statute bars evidence of "deliberative error" in the jury's collective mental process—confusion, misunderstanding, and misinterpretation of the law"; "the only 'overt' evidence' presented concerned the comments of some jurors about their own personal sexual activities and the purported 'pressure' imposed on hold-out jurors to change their votes"; "the jurors' comments about their own personal sexual experiences were based on their life experiences, not any specialized knowledge they had acquired about human sexuality"; likewise, the statute does not permit proof that some jurors applied even "intense" pressure on other jurors or lost their tempers during deliberation). See also note 25 infra.

[21]The following are some of the leading opinions favoring this view: Whyte, J., in Crawford v. State, 10 Tenn. 60, 2 Yer. 60, 67, 1821 WL 402 (Ct. Err. & App. 1821); Cole, J., in Wright v. Illinois & Mississippi Tel. Co., 20 Iowa 195, 210, 1866 WL 140 (1866). For other decisions and statutes in the various jurisdictions see 8 Wigmore, Evidence § 2354 notes 1, 2; (McNaughton rev. 1961); Admissibility, in civil case, of juror's affidavit or

jurors may testify about "objective" facts and events occurring during deliberation—occurrences which are objective in the sense that other jurors could observe them and independently corroborate the juror's testimony about the fact or event. To protect finality, these courts rely on a narrower doctrine excluding evidence of the jurors' arguments during deliberations and evidence as to their own subjective motives, beliefs, mistakes, and mental operations.[23] The juror cannot testify as to the subjective impact of the objective event on the juror's state of mind; rather, the judge inquires whether the event was likely to affect a hypotheti-

---

testimony to show bias, prejudice, or disqualification of a juror not disclosed on voir dire examination, 48 A.L.R.2d 971.

[22]Carlson, Impeaching Jury Verdicts, Litigation, Fall 1975, at 31–33.

[23]Davis v. U.S., 47 F.2d 1071 (C.C.A. 5th Cir. 1931) (excluding jurors' testimony that defendant's failure to take stand was discussed as indicating guilt and that this was given weight); U.S. v. Davis, 612 F. Supp. 2d 48, 53 (D.D.C. 2009), aff'd, 377 Fed. Appx. 19 (D.C. Cir. 2010) ("pressure among jurors, misunderstanding of instructions, a compromise verdict, or a self-imposed time limit"); Caldwell v. E.F. Spears & Sons, 186 Ky. 64, 216 S.W. 83 (1919) (jury misunderstood instructions); Collings v. Northwestern Hosp., 202 Minn. 139, 277 N.W. 910 (1938) (same as last); State v. Best, 111 N.C. 638, 15 S.E. 930 (1892) (five jurors' affidavit that they assented to verdict of guilty on belief that recommendation to mercy would save accused from death penalty). Such matters are said to "inhere in the verdict." Decisions are collected in 8 Wigmore, Evidence § 2349 (McNaughton rev. 1961); West's Key Number Digest, New Trial ⊙143(4), (5).

While these expressions and mental operations are no ground for attacking the verdict, when an allowable attack is made for misconduct such as an unauthorized view, jurors' evidence as to whether the misconduct actually influenced their finding (and this evidence would usually support

the verdict) has sometimes been received. Caldwell v. Yeatman, 91 N.H. 150, 15 A.2d 252 (1940). However, most decisions are to the contrary. People v. Stokes, 103 Cal. 193, 37 P. 207, 209 (1894) (dictum); City of Houston v. Quinones, 142 Tex. 282, 177 S.W.2d 259 (1944). See Admissibility and effect, in criminal case, of evidence as to juror's statements, during deliberations, as to facts not introduced into evidence, 58 A.L.R.2d 556. Accord Rushen v. Spain, 464 U.S. 114, 121 n.5, 104 S. Ct. 453, 78 L. Ed. 2d 267 (1983) ("A juror may testify concerning any mental bias in matters unrelated to the specific issues that the juror was called upon to decide and whether extraneous prejudicial information was improperly brought to the juror's attention. . . . But a juror generally cannot testify about the mental process by which the verdict was arrived . . ."). Absent evidence of the actual jurors' reaction, the judge inquires whether the error was likely to influence a hypothetical reasonable juror. As to the influence on the jurors of erroneous instructions and improper arguments of counsel, as distinguished from juror misconduct, the considerations may differ. The test may be, not were the jurors influenced, but rather was the instruction or the argument calculated to mislead. See, e.g., People v. Duzan, 272 Ill. 478, 112 N.E. 315 (1916) (error in refusing instruction, jurors' evidence that they did not notice that instruction was marked refused, rejected); 8 Wigmore, Evidence § 2349 (McNaughton rev. 1961).

cal reasonable juror.[24] Federal and Uniform Rule of Evidence 606(b) generally accord with prior federal case law following the traditional, Mansfield doctrine.[25]

It is important to appreciate the limits to the scope of statutory provisions such as Rule 606(b). First, these rules do not specify the substantive grounds for a new trial. These rules merely govern the jurors' competency to testify to establish such grounds.[26] Second, in addition to jurors' subjective thought processes, discus-

---

[24]U.S. v. Blackwell, 459 F.3d 739, 769 (6th Cir. 2006).

[25]Former Fed. R. Evid. 606(b) provided:

Upon an inquiry into the validity of a verdict or indictment, a juror may not testify as to any matter or statement occurring during the course of the jury's deliberations or to the effect of anything upon that or any other juror's mind or emotions as influencing the juror to assent to or dissent from the verdict or indictment or concerning the juror's mental processes in connection therewith, except that a juror may testify on the question whether extraneous prejudicial information was improperly brought to the jury's attention or whether any outside influence was improperly brought to bear upon any juror. Nor may a juror's affidavit or evidence of any statement by the juror concerning a matter about which the juror would be precluded from testifying be received for these purposes.

Unif. R. Evid. 606(b) is substantially the same. Effective December 1, 2011, restyled Fed. R. Evid. 606(b) reads:

During an Inquiry into the Validity of a Verdict or Indictment.

(1) Prohibited Testimony or Other Evidence. During an inquiry into the validity of a verdict or indictment, a juror may not testify about any statement made or incident that occurred during the jury's deliberations; the effect of anything on that juror's or another juror's vote; or any juror's mental processes concerning the verdict or indictment. The court may not receive a juror's affidavit or evidence of a juror's statement on these matters.

(2) Exceptions. A juror may testify whether:

(A) extraneous prejudicial information was improperly brought to the jury's attention;

(B) an outside influence was improperly brought to bear on any juror; or

(C) a mistake was made in entering the verdict on the verdict form.

By insulating jury decisionmaking and juror mental processes, Rule 606(b) adopts the philosophy expressed in McDonald v. Pless, 238 U.S. 264, 267–68, 35 S. Ct. 783, 59 L. Ed. 1300 (1915) that "[j]urors would be harassed and beset by the defeated party in an effort to secure from them evidence of facts which might establish misconduct sufficient to set aside a verdict. If evidence thus secured could be thus used the result would be to make what was intended to be a private deliberation, the constant subject of public investigation—to the destruction of all frankness and freedom of discussion and conference."

An interesting question arises when a federal habeas corpus proceeding is a challenge to a state court conviction. In this situation, does Rule 606(b) control, or should the federal judge apply the state law governing jurors' competency? The courts have tended to apply federal law. McDowell v. Calderon, 107 F.3d 1351 (9th Cir. 1997); Schmertz, Article VI, in Emerging Problems Under the Federal Rules of Evidence 115, 139–40 (3d ed. 1998) ("the Second, Fourth and Seventh Circuits had also taken this stance").

[26]The Advisory Committee's Note states: "This rule does not purport to specify the substantive grounds for setting aside verdicts for irregularity; it deals only with the competency of

sions, motives, beliefs, and mistakes, the rules exclude testimony about most irregular juror conduct in the jury room.[27] Again, Rule 606(b) is a version of the Mansfield approach. Thus, the federal courts have held that the rule bars testimony about racist

---

jurors to testify concerning those grounds."

[27]The federal Advisory Committee's Note cites concrete instances illustrating the operation of Rule 606(b):

Under the federal decisions the central focus has been upon insulation of the manner in which the jury reached its verdict, and this protection extends to each of the components of deliberation, including arguments, statements, discussions, mental and emotional reactions, votes, and any other feature of the process. Thus testimony or affidavits of jurors have been held incompetent to show a compromise verdict, Hyde v. U.S., 225 U.S. 347, 382, 32 S. Ct. 793, 56 L. Ed. 1114 (1912); a quotient verdict, McDonald v. Pless, 238 U.S. 264, 35 S. Ct. 783, 59 L. Ed. 1300 (1915); speculation as to insurance coverage, Holden v. Porter, 405 F.2d 878 (10th Cir. 1969), Farmers Co-op. Elevator Ass'n Non-Stock of Big Springs, Neb. v. Strand, 382 F.2d 224, 230 (8th Cir. 1967), misinterpretation of instructions, Farmers Coop. Elev. Ass'n v. Strand, supra; mistake in returning verdict, U.S. v. Chereton, 309 F.2d 197 (6th Cir. 1962); interpretation of guilty plea by one defendant as implicating others, U.S. v. Crosby, 294 F.2d 928, 949 (2d Cir. 1961). The policy does not, however, foreclose testimony by jurors as to prejudicial extraneous information or influences injected into or brought to bear upon the deliberative process. Thus a juror is recognized as competent to testify to statements by the bailiff or the introduction of a prejudicial newspaper account into the jury room, Mattox v. U. S., 146 U.S. 140, 13 S. Ct. 50, 36 L. Ed. 917 (1892). See also Parker v. Gladden, 385 U.S. 363, 87 S. Ct. 468, 17 L. Ed. 2d 420 (1966). See also Gotti v. U.S., 622 F. Supp. 2d 87, 98 (S.D. N.Y. 2009) (jury tampering).

Other illustrations of matters to which the jurors may testify are collected in 3 Weinstein's Federal Evidence § 606.04[4] (rev. 2011). See 3 Graham, Handbook of Federal Evidence § 606:2 (7th ed. 2012) ("A juror thus may not attack his verdict for example on the grounds of a quotient verdict, that a fellow juror was intoxicated, that jury instructions were misinterpreted, or on the basis of speculation as to insurance. Similarly excluded as grounds of attack are internal discussions, arguments, mental and emotional reactions, votes, or statements, even a statement purporting to relate specific factual information which was incorrect. Jurors may however attack their verdict on the grounds that prejudicial extraneous influence or information was injected into or brought to bear upon the deliberation process, Rule 606(b). Thus a juror may testify on the question whether extraneous prejudicial information was brought to the jury's attention (e.g., a radio newscast or a newspaper account), whether any outside influence which improperly had been brought to bear upon a juror (e.g., a threat to the safety of a member of his family), as well as whether an unauthorized view or improper jury investigation transpired. In addition a verdict may be attacked on the grounds of juror bias."). See also Schmertz, Article VI, in Emerging Problems Under the Federal Rules of Evidence 115, 142 (3d ed. 1998) ("Where a question is raised as to threats and coercion within the jury room, the prevailing view under Rule 606(b) has been that juror testimony about these aspects of deliberation is not admissible . . . .").

remarks during deliberations[28] and jurors' consumption of alcohol at lunch.[29] Third, in one respect, Federal Rule 606 appears to broaden the scope of the common law rule. While that rule barred juror testimony and affidavit only when it was offered to impeach a verdict, the wording of 606(b) is so expansive that it seemingly applies whether the evidence is offered to impeach or support the verdict. Fourth, the rules do not exclude juror testimony about outside influences or extraneous prejudicial information.[30] Thus, a criminal juror could testify that he had received a threatening phone call;[31] and in a civil case involving accident reconstruction testimony, one juror could supply an affidavit indicating that another juror had brought a text on accident reconstruction into the deliberation room and read aloud passages to the other jurors. Fifth, the rules appear to apply only post-indictment or post-verdict. On their face, the rules do not apply directly to a hearing to determine whether to discharge a juror during deliberations for misconduct.[32] Sixth, some jurisdictions interpret even the original, unamended version of Rule 606(b) as permitting the

---

[28]Shillcutt v. Gagnon, 827 F.2d 1155 (7th Cir. 1987); Dobbs v. Zant, 720 F. Supp. 1566, 1571–79 (N.D. Ga. 1989), aff'd, 963 F.2d 1403 (11th Cir. 1991), rev'd on other grounds, 506 U.S. 357 (1993). However, the defendant might argue that the Constitution trumps the common law or statutory restriction. West, 12 Racist Men: Post-Verdict Evidence of Juror Bias, 27 Harv. J. Racial & Ethnic Just. 165, 184 (2011) (citing authorities from the First, Seventh, and Ninth circuits); Goldman, Post-Verdict Challenges to Racial Comments Made During Juror Deliberations, 61 Syracuse L. Rev. 1 (2010); Comment, Fleshner v. Pepose Vision Institute: Eviscerating the Mansfield Rule, 46 New Engl. L. Rev. 649 (2011–12) (racial, ethnic, or religious comments).

[29]Tanner v. U.S., 483 U.S. 107, 107 S. Ct. 2739, 97 L. Ed. 2d 90 (1987).

[30]See note 27 supra.

Although the rule allows evidence of the extraneous influence itself, it does not permit jurors' testimony about the impact of the influence on their subjective state of mind. Rather, the court inquires how the extraneous information would have influenced a hypothetical juror. U.S. v.

Greer, 285 F.3d 158, 173 (2d Cir. 2002); U.S. v. Lloyd, 269 F.3d 228, 237–38 (3d Cir. 2001); U.S. v. Elias, 269 F.3d 1003, 1020 (9th Cir. 2001) (as a general proposition, "juror testimony about the effect of extraneous information or improper contacts on a juror's state of mind is prohibited"); TIG Ins. Co. v. Liberty Mut. Ins. Co., 250 F. Supp. 2d 1197, 1199 (D. Ariz. 2003) (the "existence" of the extraneous influence, not how the jurors were "affected" by it).

[31]See People v. Wadle, 97 P.3d 932 (Colo. 2004) (a juror downloaded from the Internet information about a medication taken by the defendant and shared the information with other jurors); Scott, Internet-Surfing Jurors Vex Judges, Nat'l L.J., Dec. 2, 2002, at A8.

[32]People v. Allen, 53 Cal. 4th 60, 133 Cal. Rptr. 3d 548, 264 P.3d 336 n.10 (2011); People v. Cleveland, 25 Cal. 4th 466, 106 Cal. Rptr. 2d 313, 21 P.3d 1225 (2001) (the court noted that "the provisions of Evidence Code section 1150 apply only to the postverdict situation and not to an inquiry conducted during jury deliberations"; however, by analogy to the statute the court to adopt a narrow scope of inquiry).

jurors to correct an improperly transmitted or announced verdict.[33] Finally, the rules do not preclude testimony of other persons who know of jury misconduct.[34] The bar applies only to jurors. Hence, if the door to the jury deliberation room was ajar and a passing bailiff heard one juror threaten another, the bailiff would be competent to testify about the threat.

*The privilege.* Distinguish these rules of incompetency and exclusion, codified in Rules 606(a)–(b), from a third doctrine supported by Wigmore[35] and a few judicial opinions[36] According to this doctrine, each juror has a personal privilege against disclosing in court her communications to the other jurors during their deliberations. There is little judicial support for this doctrine.

### Lawyers

Although in some instances an attorney's testimony can violate the rules of legal ethics, those rules do not govern the admissibil-

---

[33]Munafo v. Metropolitan Transp. Authority, 277 F. Supp. 2d 163, 170–71 (E.D. N.Y. 2003) ("banning inquiry into the deliberative process makes sense only if the verdict reflects the true intent of the jury. As recognized by the Second Circuit, Rule 606(b) 'is silent regarding inquiries designed to confirm the accuracy of a verdict.' Accordingly, 'juror testimony is admissible to show that the verdict delivered was not that actually agreed upon.' A court may interview jurors and consider their testimony 'to correct the mistaken transmission of the verdict from the jury,' so long as the inquiry is limited 'to ascertain what the jury decided [rather than] why they did so'"). *See also* 75 Cr. L. Rep. (BNA) 607 (Sep. 15, 2004) (the Administrative Office of the U.S. Courts has released for comment a proposed amendment to Federal Rule 606(b); "Rule 606(b) would be amended to provide, in conformity with case law, that juror testimony may be used to prove that the verdict reported was the result of a clerical mistake. But the amended rule rejects a broader exception, adopted by some courts, permitting use of juror testimony to prove that jurors were operating under a misunderstanding about the consequences of the result that they agreed upon"). The amendment, adding subsection (3) to

Rule 606(b), took effect in 2006.

[34]*See* Advisory Committee Note to Rule 606(b). The rule does not relate to secrecy or disclosure but only to the jurors' competency as witnesses and certain evidence such as affidavits provided by jurors.

[35]8 Evidence § 2346 (McNaughton rev. 1961).

[36]In Clark v. U.S., 289 U.S. 1, 53 S. Ct. 465, 77 L. Ed. 993 (1933), on appeal from a juror's conviction for contempt in giving false answers, Justice Cardozo wrote: "The books suggest a doctrine that the arguments and votes of jurors, the *media concludendi*, are secrets, protected from disclosure unless the privilege is waived. . . . Freedom of debate might be stifled and independence of thought checked if jurors were made to feel that their arguments and ballots were to be freely published to the world. The force of these considerations is not to be gainsaid. . . . Assuming that there is a privilege which protects from impertinent exposure the arguments and ballots of a juror while considering his verdict, we think the privilege does not apply where the relation giving birth to it has been fraudulently begun or fraudulently continued." The privilege was held inapplicable because of the fraudulent conduct.

ity of the testimony under evidence law. At common law and under Federal and Revised Uniform Rule of Evidence 601, a lawyer for a party is not per se incompetent to testify.[37] Nevertheless, the court has wide discretion to bar testimony by a lawyer presently in the case,[38] especially when the lawyer endeavors to testify in his client's favor.[39] Judges routinely exercise this discretion to prevent such testimony where other sources of evidence about the fact of consequence are available or where the necessity for the lawyer's testimony could easily have been avoided.[40]

---

[37]U.S. v. Fiorillo, 376 F.2d 180, 185 (2d Cir. 1967) ("Testimony of the attorney for a party is not incompetent in federal court."). *See* Fryer, Note on Disqualification of Witnesses, Selected Writings on Evidence and Trial 345 (Fryer ed. 1957).

[38]Ramey v. District 141, Intern. Ass'n of Machinists and Aerospace Workers, 378 F.3d 269, 282 (2d Cir. 2004) ("there is no hard-and-fast rule against testimony by attorneys who have represented clients in the past. The advocate-witness rule applies, first and foremost, where the attorney representing the client before a jury seeks to serve as a fact witness in that very proceeding").

[39]U.S. v. Brown, 417 F.2d 1068 (5th Cir. 1969); Travelers Ins. Co. v. Dykes, 395 F.2d 747 (5th Cir. 1968). *See generally* U.S. v. Prantil, 764 F.2d 548 (9th Cir. 1985).

In the court's discretion, a party may call to the stand the attorney for an opposing party upon a showing of "compelling need." U.S. v. Roberson, 897 F.2d 1092 (11th Cir. 1990). *See also* State v. Simpson, 314 N.C. 359, 334 S.E.2d 53 (1985); People v. Gendron, 41 Ill. 2d 351, 243 N.E.2d 208 (1968).

A government attorney may testify in a case that he has neither prepared nor tried. U.S. v. McCrady, 774 F.2d 868 (8th Cir. 1985).

With respect to the use of a stipulation to avoid the opposing lawyer being called as a witness and disqualified as counsel, see U.S. v. Diozzi, 807 F.2d 10 (1st Cir. 1986). *But see* U.S. v. Kliti, 156 F.3d 150, 156 (2d Cir. 1998)

(the defense attorney could have furnished testimony to support the defendant's claim that the defendant had made a certain exculpatory statement; the trial judge erred in failing to conduct a hearing to determine whether the defendant was willing to change counsel in order to make the defense attorney's testimony available; "[w]hen faced with an attorney as a sworn . . . witness, the proper recourse is to disqualify the attorney, not to exclude the testimony").

[40]U.S. v. Ziesman, 409 F.3d 941, 950 (8th Cir. 2005) (requests for testimony by the U.S. Attorney trying the case are disfavored; " 'the party seeking such testimony must demonstrate that the evidence is vital to his case and that his inability to present the same or similar facts from another source creates a compelling need for the testimony"); U.S. v. Martinez, 151 F.3d 384, 393 (5th Cir. 1998) ("it is a general rule in this circuit that a party's attorney may not be called as a witness unless his testimony is both necessary and unobtainable from other sources"); U.S. v. Regan, 103 F.3d 1072, 1083 (2d Cir. 1997) ("A defendant who wishes to call a prosecutor must demonstrate a compelling . . . reason to do so"); U.S. v. Oreto, 37 F.3d 739, 746 (1st Cir. 1994) ("A defendant must establish a 'compelling need' before being allowed to call a prosecutor as a trial witness, a step that will usually require the prosecutor to step aside"); U.S. v. Brown, 417 F.2d 1068 (5th Cir. 1969); U.S. v. Fiorillo, 376 F.2d 180 (2d Cir. 1967); U.S. v. Alu, 246 F.2d 29 (2d Cir. 1957); Supreme Beef Processors, Inc. v.

Even where no other witness is available and the lawyer is willing to withdraw, judges usually exercise their discretion to preclude the lawyer from testifying.[41] Permitting the lawyer to withdraw and substituting new counsel will delay, if not disrupt, the proceeding. The judicial discretion is ordinarily exercised in that manner whether the lawyer is being called by her client's side[42] or the opposition.[43] If the lawyer both testified and continued to try the case, there is a risk that the jury might

American Consumer Industries, Inc., 441 F. Supp. 1064 (N.D. Tex. 1977); People v. Garcia, 84 Cal. App. 4th 316, 100 Cal. Rptr. 2d 789, 799–800 (1st Dist. 2000) ("Only in extraordinary circumstances should an attorney in the action be called as a witness, and before the [prosecuting] attorney is called the defendant has an obligation to demonstrate that there is no other source for the evidence he seeks"). *See also* People v. Donaldson, 93 Cal. App. 4th 916, 113 Cal. Rptr. 2d 548 (5th Dist. 2001) (the defense counsel was guilty of ineffective representation in failing to object when the prosecutor took the stand to testify about a pretrial conversation with a key prosecution witness).

One situation that can usually be avoided is the offering of lawyer testimony as to the existence of a witness's alleged inconsistent statement. U.S. v. Dennis, 843 F.2d 652 (2d Cir. 1988). As a precaution during the pretrial investigation, the attorney should have a third party present when she interviews a prospective witness. The third party is then available to testify about the allegedly inconsistent statement.

[41]See generally notes 38 to 40 supra. *Compare* Bickford v. John E. Mitchell Co., 595 F.2d 540, 544 (10th Cir. 1979) ("Attorneys appearing as witnesses on behalf of their clients have been required to withdraw as counsel to avoid ethical improprieties, as was done in this case. . . . We find no error in permitting Mr. Rogers to testify in light of the facts that (1) he had not previously participated in the trial; (2) he withdrew from the case before he was allowed to take the wit-

ness stand; and (3) the trial was to the court and not to a jury.").

[42]Riddle v. Cockrell, 288 F.3d 713, 721 (5th Cir. 2002) ("It is an almost universally frowned upon practice for a prosecutor to testify at the trial of the case he is prosecuting . . . . Such a practice should only be permitted in extraordinary circumstances or for compelling reasons").

[43]Bogosian v. Woloohojian Realty Corp., 323 F.3d 55, 66 (1st Cir. 2003) ("Although not strictly forbidden, procurement of trial testimony from opposing counsel is generally disfavored"; the court lists the factors the trial judge should consider in exercising discretion); U.S. v. Martinez, 151 F.3d 384, 393 (5th Cir. 1998) ("it is a general rule in this circuit that a party's attorney may not be called as a witness unless his testimony is both necessary and unobtainable from other sources . . . ."); U.S. v. Sattar, 314 F. Supp. 2d 279, 315 (S.D. N.Y. 2004), aff'd, 590 F.3d 93 (2d Cir. 2009) (" 'A defendant who wishes to call a prosecutor as a witness must demonstrate a compelling and legitimate reason to do so' "); People v. Garcia, 84 Cal. App. 4th 316, 100 Cal. Rptr. 2d 789, 799–800 (1st Dist. 2000) ("Only in extraordinary circumstances should an attorney in an action be calling as a witness, and before the [prosecuting] attorney is called, defendant has an obligation to demonstrate that there is no other source for the evidence he seeks"; the defendant attempted to call the prosecutor as a percipient witness to an interview with another witness; however, another person was present at the interview, and the interview was taped); State v. Peeler, 265 Conn. 460,

confuse the lawyer's testimony as a witness with the lawyer's arguments as an advocate—a risk that brings Federal Rule of Evidence 403 into play.

ABA Model Rule of Professional Conduct, 3.7, Lawyer as Witness, originally promulgated in 1983, reads:

(a) A lawyer shall not act as advocate at a trial in which the lawyer is likely to be a necessary witness unless:

(1) the testimony relates to an uncontested issue

(2) the testimony relates to the nature and value of legal services rendered in the case; or

(3) disqualification of the lawyer would work substantial hardship on the client.

(b) A lawyer may act as advocate in a trial in which another lawyer in the lawyer's firm is likely to be called as a witness unless precluded from doing so by [conflict of interest] Rule 1.7 or Rule 1.9.[44]

---

828 A.2d 1216 (2003) (the prosecutor lacked a compelling need to call the defendant's attorney as a witness).

[44]Rules 1.7 and 1.9 of the A.B.A. Model Rules of Professional Conduct provide:

**Rule 1.7.**

**Conflict of Interest: Current Clients**

(a) Except as provided in paragraph (b), a lawyer shall not represent a client if the representation involves a concurrent conflict of interest. A concurrent conflict of interest exists if:

(1) the representation of one client will be directly adverse to another client; or

(2) there is a significant risk that the representation will be materially limited by the lawyer's responsibility to another client, a former client or a third person or by a personal interest of the lawyer.

(b) Notwithstanding the existence of a concurrent conflict of interest under paragraph (a), a lawyer may represent a client if:

(1) the lawyer reasonably believes that the lawyer will be able to provide competent and diligent representation to each affected client;

(2) the representation is not prohibited by law;

(3) the representation does not involve the assertion of a claim by one client against another client represented by the lawyer in the same litigation or other proceeding before a tribunal; and

(4) each affected client gives informed consent, confirmed in writing.

**Rule 1.9.**

**Duties to Former Clients**

(a) A lawyer who has formerly represented a client in a matter shall not thereafter represent another person in the same or a substantially related matter in which that person's interests are materially adverse to the interests of the former client unless the former client gives informed consent, confirmed in writing.

(b) A lawyer shall not knowingly represent a person in the same or a substantially related matter in which a firm with which the lawyer formerly was associated had previously represented a client

(1) whose interests are materially adverse to that person; and

(2) about whom the lawyer had acquired information protected by Rules 1.6 and 1.9(c) that is material to the matter; unless the for-

Subdivision (a) generally bars the attorney's testimony when the attorney is personally involved in the trial of the case. However, subdivision (b) rejects vicarious disqualification—the attorney may testify at a trial being conducted by another member of the attorney's firm.

California has gone even farther in liberalizing the advocate-witness prohibition.[45] California Rule of Professional Conduct 5-210 lifts even the personal disqualification by providing that a lawyer-advocate may testify before a jury if the lawyer "has the informed, written consent of the client." As previously stated, the courts which routinely bar such testimony reason that there is a danger that the jury will confuse the lawyer's testimony and lawyer's arguments. However, the proponents of the California rule counter that the courts often permit the same witness to testify about facts as well as opinions. By way of example, the cases are legion allowing an experienced police officer to both describe an accused's conduct and voice an opinion that the conduct fits the modus operandi for a particular type of crime.[46] If anything, such testimony presents the risk to a greater degree than a lawyer-advocate's testimony. When a police officer testifies in that manner, during the same direct examination the officer states both opinions and facts. In contrast, if the lawyer's testimony is restricted to facts, at least there is a gap between the factual testimony and the opinionated summation. That gap should reduce the risk of confusion.

---

mer client gives informed consent, confirmed in writing.

(c)  A lawyer who has formerly represented a client in a matter or whose present or former firm had represented a client in a matter shall not thereafter:

  (1)  use information relating to the representation to the disadvantage of the former client except as these Rules would permit or require with respect to a client, or when the information has become generally known; or

  (2)  reveal information relating to the representation except as these Rules would permit or require with respect to a client.

*See* U.S. v. Presgraves, 658 F. Supp. 2d 770, 785 (W.D. Va. 2009) (the "advocate-witness rule").

[45]People v. Earp, 20 Cal. 4th 826, 85 Cal. Rptr. 2d 857, 978 P.2d 15, 49 (1999) (there is no categorical rule against testimony by trial counsel,

notwithstanding the Rules of Professional Conduct).

[46]U.S. v. Thomas, 896 F.2d 589 (D.C. Cir. 1990); Bamberger, The Dangerous Expert Witness, 52 Brook. L. Rev. 855 (1986). However, a number of courts have prescribed procedural steps to minimize the risk that the jurors will confuse the witness's dual roles. For example, various courts have required that: The proponent first elicit the witness's lay testimony; the proponent phrase the questions in a way to flag the difference between the two types of testimony ("Based on what you observed" as opposed to "Drawing on your training and experience"); and the trial judge give the jury an instruction emphasizing the difference. *See* U.S. v. Baptiste, 596 F.3d 214, 223 (4th Cir. 2010); U.S. v. York, 572 F.3d 415, 425 (7th Cir. 2009); U.S. v. Anchrum, 590 F.3d 795, 803 (9th Cir. 2009).

## §69 Firsthand knowledge and expertness

Two other rules, previously mentioned, relate to the general subject of witnesses' competency. These rules are the requirement that a witness testifying to objective facts must have had the means of learning them from observation,[1] and the doctrine that one testifying to an inference or opinion in matters requiring special knowledge or skill must qualify as an expert in the field.[2] Unlike most other competency doctrines going to the capacity to testify at all, these two rules are directed at the person's capacity as a witness to testify to a particular matter, not the person's fundamental competency to be a witness.

## §70 The procedure of disqualification[1]

Under the common law practice, the witness is not sworn until she is placed on the stand to begin her testimony. At early common law, before the oath was administered, the adversary had an opportunity to object to the prospective witness's competency. The judge or counsel would then examine the witness about her qualifications, before she was sworn as a witness. This was known as a voir dire examination. Traditionally when the witness was first called to the stand to testify, the opponent had to immediately challenge her competency if the opponent was then aware of grounds of challenge.[2] If the opponent did not voice a competency objection before the witness took the oath, the objection was waived.

---

**[Section 69]**

[1]See § 10 supra. The requirement of firsthand knowledge on the part of lay witnesses is not a question of competency in the traditional sense. Thus Fed. R. Evid. 104(a), stating that a person's qualification to be a witness is a question for the court, is inapplicable to issues of first-hand knowledge. Rather, as the Advisory Committee Note to Rule 602 notes, these are questions of conditional relevancy, with the judge playing a limited, screening role and the jury making the final determination. *See* Joy Mfg. Co. v. Sola Basic Industries, Inc., 697 F.2d 104 (3d Cir. 1982); § 53 supra as to conditional relevancy generally.

[2]See § 13 supra.

**[Section 70]**

[1]2 Wigmore, Evidence §§ 483–87 (Chadbourn rev. 1979); 3 Weinstein's Federal Evidence § 601.03 (rev. 2011); West's Key Number Digest, Witnesses ⊸76 to 79, 121 to 124, 180 to 183.

[2]2 Wigmore, Evidence § 586 (Chadbourn rev. 1979). If it is error for the prosecution to call a spouse to the stand and require the accused spouse to object before the jury, as it is in some courts, see § 66, supra, and § 76, infra, prior voir dire examination outside the jury's presence is necessary. In some courts, voir dire examination may also be required of proposed infant witnesses and prospective witnesses who are allegedly mentally incompetent. Saucier v. State, 156 Tex. Crim. 301, 235 S.W.2d 903 (1950) (challenge to witness's mental competency). It often seems assumed that the examination should be held in the jury's presence presumably because it can affect credibility. If the grounds of incompetency are unknown when the witness takes the stand but are disclosed in the testimony, the challenge may be made later. Nunn v. Slemmons'

As we have seen, Federal and Uniform Rules of Evidence 601 significantly liberalize the substantive standards for witness competency. That substantive liberalization has a procedural impact. Except possibly for federal diversity cases, the procedure followed under either Federal Rule of Evidence 601[3] or Revised Uniform Rule of Evidence 601[4] differs sharply from the common law procedure described in the preceding paragraph. Under those rules, the common law incompetency standards have largely been supplanted by specific provisions such as Rules 602 and 603. Rule 602 requires that a witness possess firsthand knowledge. An objection premised on 602 must be urged after the witness takes the oath but before he answers a question relating to a fact which he lacks personal knowledge of. Rule 603 mandates that the prospective witness take an oath, but again the opponent could not object before the person took the oath; quite to the contrary, an objection would usually be appropriate only after the person refused to take the oath. The procedure for challenging judges and jurors as witnesses is prescribed by Rules 605 and 606.[5] Hence, under the new statutes, there appears to be only one case in which the opponent must routinely follow the common law procedure; in federal criminal cases, objections based on the spouse witness's privilege not to be called by the prosecution must still arguably be asserted before the spouse witness takes the oath. In jurisdictions giving Rule 601 a literal, plain meaning interpretation, there are no competency objections to be raised independently of Rules 602 and 603; and there would be no challenge to interpose before the witness begins to testify.[6] Even in federal diversity cases, the judge need not comply with the

---

Adm'r, 298 Ky. 315, 182 S.W.2d 888 (1944). When the challenge is based on general mental incompetency, the burden rests on the objector to show by examination of the challenged witness or other evidence that the disqualification exists. State v. Barker, 294 Mo. 303, 242 S.W. 405 (1922); 2 Wigmore, Evidence §§ 484, 497 (Chadbourn rev. 1979).

[3]See the prior sections in this chapter.

[4]See the rule at § 62, note 21 supra.

[5]See § 68 supra.

[6]See § 62 at note 21 supra.

As to ordering a witness's psychiatric examination to aid the court's determination of the witness's competency in the sense of minimum cred-

ibility, see § 62 at note 33 supra. *See generally* Evans v. State, 304 Md. 487, 499 A.2d 1261, 1272 (1985) ("[A] trial judge has the authority to order a mental examination of a witness to assist in the determination of competency when the issue cannot be satisfactorily resolved by reference to existing information and voir dire of the witness. In determining whether a request for a mental examination should be granted, however, a trial judge should carefully balance the demonstrated necessity for a compelled examination against the existence of important countervailing considerations. In affirming the denial of a motion for a psychiatric examination of a government witness, the United States Court of Appeals for the District of Columbia Circuit, in United States v. Benn, 476 F.2d 1127, 1131

procedures followed in any particular state for disposing of competency objections. It is one thing to require the federal judge to apply the state's substantive competency standard, as Rule 601 sometimes mandates. It is quite another matter to import state procedure into a federal courtroom.

Under both case law and the Federal and Uniform Rules of Evidence, before eliciting an expert opinion from a witness, the offering party must first show the witness's knowledge or skill. The proponent usually establishes the witness's expert status by eliciting the witness's own testimony about her qualifications.[7] However, those requirements come into play after the witness has begun to testify. Although the opponent could raise the issue in advance of the witness's testimony by filing an in limine motion, the opponent is not required to do so. Thus, here again the opponent would not waive the objection by neglecting to raise the issue before the witness takes her oath.

In the competency context, when a foundational question of fact is disputed or doubtful on the evidence, the trial judge sitting with a jury ordinarily does not submit this question of fact to the jury. The solitary exception is the question of whether the witness possesses firsthand knowledge.[8] Hence, if a spousal disqualification objection raises the preliminary question of whether the party and witness spouse are validly married, the judge follows the procedure prescribed by Rule 104(a).[9] In contrast, the judge would apply Rule 104(b)'s conditional relevance procedure to the preliminary question of whether the witness had personal knowledge. In federal court the procedure for determining the competency of a child witness is governed by statute, 18 U.S.C. § 3509(c).[10]

---

(D.C.Cir. 1972), listed some of the factors to be considered: '[A] psychiatric examination may seriously impinge on a witness' right to privacy; the trauma that attends the role of complainant . . . is sharply increased by the indignity of a psychiatric examination; the examination itself could serve as a tool of harassment; and the impact of all these considerations may well deter the victim of . . . a crime from lodging any complaint at all. Since there is no exact measure for weighing these kinds of dangers against the need for an examination, the decision must be entrusted to the sound discretion of the trial judge in light of the particular facts.' *Accord* United States v.

Butler, 481 F.2d 531 (D.C.Cir. 1973). *See* Rasnick v. State, 256 A.2d 543 (Md.App.1969), cert. denied, 400 U.S. 835, 91 S.Ct. 70, 27 L.Ed.2d 67 (1970).").

[7]See §§ 10, 13 supra.

[8]See § 69, note 1 supra.

[9]See § 53.

[10]18 U.S.C.A. § 3509(c) provides as follows with respect to determining the competency of a child witness:

  (1)  Effect of Federal Rules of Evidence. Nothing in this subdivision shall be construed to abrogate rule 601 of the Federal Rules of Evidence.

(2) Presumption. A child is presumed to be competent.

(3) Requirement of a Written Motion. A competency examination regarding a child witness may be conducted by the court only upon written motion and offer of proof of incompetency by a party.

(4) Requirement of Compelling Reasons. A competency examination regarding a child may be conducted only if the court determines, on the record, that compelling reasons exist. A child's age alone is not a compelling reason.

(5) Persons Permitted to be Present. The only persons who may be permitted to be present at a competency examination are—

(A) the judge;

(B) the attorney for the government;

(C) the attorney for the defendant;

(D) a court reporter; and

(E) persons whose presence, in the opinion of the court, is necessary to the welfare and well-being of the child, including the child's attorney, guardian an ad litem or adult attendant.

(6) Not Before Jury. A competency examination regarding a child witness shall be conducted out of the sight and hearing of a jury.

(7) Direct Examination of Child. Examination of a child related to competency shall normally be conducted by the court on the basis of questions submitted by the attorney for the Government and the attorney for the defendant including a party acting as an attorney pro se. The court may permit an attorney but not a party acting as an attorney pro se to examine a child directly on competency if the court is satisfied that the child will not suffer emotional trauma as a result of the examination.

(8) Appropriate Questions. The questions asked at the competency examination of a child shall be appropriate to the age and developmental level of the child, shall not be related to issues at trial, and shall focus on determining the child's ability to understand and answer simple questions.

(9) Psychological and Psychiatric Examinations. Psychological and psychiatric examinations to assess the competency of a child witness shall not be ordered without a showing of a compelling need.

As previously stated in § 62, there is a strong statutory construction argument that Rule 601 abolishes the common law competency standards, even for children. In that light, § 3509(c)(2) is puzzling. There is no need for a presumption of competency if child witnesses do not have to satisfy competency standards. The general thrust of the legislation in question was to liberalize the admissibility of evidence in prosecutions involving child victims; and given that, it is difficult to believe that Congress intended to reinstate the competency requirements which had earlier been abolished. Subdivision (1) of the statute expressly disclaims any intention to abrogate Rule 601. Nevertheless, one commentator has asserted:

> Regardless of its disclaimer, Section 3509 has seemingly revived an elaborate version of the common law tests of child competency that Rule 601 had tried to abolish. It is far from clear whether this backtracking specifically tailored for child abuse proceedings is a sound development.

Schmertz, Article VI, in Emerging

## § 71  Probable future of the rules of competency

The rules disqualifying witnesses with knowledge of relevant facts and mental capacity to convey that knowledge are serious obstructions to the ascertainment of truth. In the first edition of this treatise, Dean McCormick famously remarked, "The manifest destiny of evidence law is a progressive lowering of the barriers to truth."[1] For a century, the steady course of legal reform has been in the direction of sweeping away these obstructions. To that end all states should adopt Federal Rules of Evidence 601 to 606 or the similar provisions of the Revised Uniform Rules of Evidence. For its part, Congress ought to exercise the power to mandate these rules without qualification for diversity cases.[2]

---

Problems Under the Federal Rules of Evidence 115, 120 (3d ed. 1998). Congress might have enacted § 3509 without carefully considering the significance of Rule 601 or perhaps even out of an excess of caution.

**[Section 71]**

[1]McCormick, Handbook of the Law of Evidence § 81 (1954).

[2]The second sentence of Fed. R. Evid. 601 was added by Congress. During the congressional deliberations, it was pointed out that the original Rule's making so-called Dead Man's Statutes of the states inapplicable in federal courts was a center of controversy. House Comm. on Judiciary, Fed.Rules of Evidence, H.R. Rep. No. 650, 93d Cong., 1st Sess., p. 9 (1973).

# Title 5.  Privilege: Common Law and Statutory

## Chapter 8

# The Scope and Effect of the Evidentiary Privileges

## § 72   The purposes of rules of privilege:[1] (a) Other rules of evidence distinguished

The overwhelming majority of all rules of evidence have as

---

[Section 72]

[1]As to the basis of privileges generally, *see* 8 Wigmore, Evidence §§ 2192, 2197, 2285 (McNaughton rev. 1961), Imwinkelried, The New Wigmore: Evidentiary Privileges §§ 1.3, 5.1–5.4 (2d ed. 2010) and the opinion of Learned Hand, Circuit Judge, in McMann v. Securities and
Exchange Commission, 87 F.2d 377, 378 (C.C.A. 2d Cir. 1937) (denying the claim of a customer to a privilege against the disclosure of his broker's records relating to his trading account: "The suppression of truth is a grievous necessity at best, more especially when as here its inquiry concerns the public interest; it can be justified at

465

their ultimate justification some tendency to promote the objectives set forward by the conventional witness' oath, the presentation of "the truth, the whole truth, and nothing but the truth." Thus such prominent exclusionary rules as the hearsay rule, the opinion rule, the rule excluding bad character as evidence of crime, and the original documents (or "Best Evidence") rule, have as their common purpose the elucidation of the truth, a purpose that these rules seek to effect by operating to exclude evidence which is unreliable or which is calculated to prejudice or mislead.

By contrast the rules of privilege, of which the most familiar are the rule protecting against self-incrimination and those shielding the confidentiality of communications between husband and wife, attorney and client, and physician and patient, are not designed or intended to facilitate the fact-finding process or to safeguard its integrity. Their effect instead is clearly inhibitive; rather than facilitating the illumination of truth, they shut out the light.[2]

Rules that serve to render accurate ascertainment of the truth more difficult, or in some instances impossible, may seem anomalous in a rational system of fact-finding.[3] Nevertheless, rules of privilege are not without a rationale. Their warrant is the protec-

---

all only when the opposed private interest is supreme."). *See also* Barnhart, Theory of Testimonial Competency and Privilege, 4 Ark. L. Rev. 377 (1950); Donnelly, The Law of Evidence: Privacy and Disclosure, 14 La. L. Rev. 361 (1954); Falknor, Extrinsic Policies Affecting Admissibility, 10 Rutgers L. Rev. 574 (1956); Katz, Privileged Communications: A Proposal for Reform, 1 Dalhousie L.J. 597 (1974); Ladd, Privileges, 1969 L. & Soc. Order 555; Louisell, Confidentiality, Conformity, and Confusion: Privileges in Federal Court Today, 31 Tul. L. Rev. 101 (1956); Scallen, Relational and Informational Privileges and the Case of the Mysterious Mediation Privilege, 38 Loy. L. A. Law. Rev. 537 (2004); Tacon, A Question of Privilege: Valid Protection or Obstruction of Justice, 17 Osgoode Hall L.J. 335 (1979). For discussions of privilege under modern codifications, including the Federal Rules of Evidence, see § 76 infra. *And see* Developments in the Law—Privileged Communications, 98 Harv. L. Rev. 1450 (1985).

[2]State ex rel. State Highway Dept. v. 62.96247 Acres of Land, More or Less, in New Castle Hundred, New Castle County, 57 Del. 40, 193 A.2d 799, 806 (Super. Ct. 1963) (Lynch, J.): "There are many exclusionary rules of evidence that are intended to withhold evidence which is regarded as unreliable or regarded as prejudicial or misleading, but rules of privileged communications have no such purpose. Such rules of privilege preclude the consideration of competent evidence which could aid in determining the outcome of a case, and privilege in no way can be justified as a means of promoting a fair settlement of disputes.").

[3]*See* Elkins v. U.S., 364 U.S. 206, 80 S. Ct. 1437, 4 L. Ed. 2d 1669 (1960) (Frankfurter, J., dissenting: privileges justified "only to the very limited extent that permitting a refusal to testify or excluding relevant evidence has a public good transcending the normally predominant principle of utilizing all rational means for ascertaining truth.").

tion of interests and relationships which, rightly or wrongly, are regarded as of sufficient social importance to justify some sacrifice of availability of evidence relevant to the administration of justice.[4]

The interests allegedly served by privileges, as might be expected, are varied. The great constitutional protections that have evolved around self-incrimination, confessions, and unlawfully obtained evidence are considered elsewhere.[5] They are commonly classed as privileges.

Of the rules treated here, a substantial number operate to protect communications made within the context of various professional relationships, e.g., attorney and client, physician and patient, clergyman and penitent. The rationale traditionally advanced for these privileges is that public policy requires the encouragement of the communications without which these relationships cannot be effective. This rationale, today sometimes referred to as the utilitarian justification for privilege, found perhaps its strongest supporter in Dean Wigmore who seems to have viewed it as the chief, if not the exclusive, basis for privilege.[6] Wigmore's views have been widely accepted by the courts, and have largely conditioned the development of thinking about privilege.[7]

More recently other, and analytically distinct, rationales for privilege have been advanced. According to one theory, certain

---

[4]*See* State v. 62.96247 Acres of Land in New Castle Hundred, 193 A.2d at 807 (Lynch, J.: "Thus, the duty of the confidant of nondisclosure of confidential communications is imposed to protect the reliance interest of the communicant, with an assent of the community. This reliance interest is protected because such protection will encourage certain communications. Encouraging these communications is desirable because the communications are necessary for the maintenance of certain relationships. It is socially desirable to foster the protected relationships because other beneficial results are achieved, such as the promotion of justice, public health and social stability. These goals are promoted in furtherance of a well-organized, peaceful society, which in turn is considered necessary for human survival.").

[5]See Chs. 13, 14, and 15 infra.

[6]*See* Louisell, Confidentiality, Conformity, and Confusion: Privileges in Federal Court Today, 31 Tul. L. Rev. 101, 111 (1956).

[7]Particularly influential have been Wigmore's stated four essential conditions for the establishment of a privilege. *See* 8 Wigmore, Evidence § 2285 (McNaughton rev. 1961):

(1) The communications must originate in a confidence that they will not be disclosed;

(2) This element of confidentiality must be essential to the full and satisfactory maintenance of the relation between the parties;

(3) The relation must be one which in the opinion of the community ought to be sedulously fostered; and

(4) The injury that would inure to the relation by the disclosure of the communications must be greater than the benefit thereby gained for the correct disposal of litigation.

privacy interests in society are deserving of protection by privilege irrespective of whether the existence of such privileges actually operates substantially to affect conduct within the protected relationships.[8] Thus, while it has been suggested that communications between husband and wife and physician and patient are not primarily induced by the privileges accorded them, some form of these privileges is nevertheless seen as justified on the alternative basis that they serve to protect the essential privacy of certain significant human relationships.[9] Similarly, but not identically, other writers have formulated humanistic theories of privilege that emphasize autonomy, creating privacy enclaves with particular types of consultants to enable the citizen to make more intelligent, independent life preference choices.[10] Given their comparatively recent origin, these latter rationales probably have not operated as a conscious basis for either the judicial or legislative creation of existing privileges. Today's judicial tendency to pour new wine into old bottles, however, may serve to make nonutilitarian theories factors in the subsequent development of thinking about privilege.[11]

It is open to doubt whether all of the interests and relationships that have sometimes been urged as sufficiently important to justify the creation of privileges really merit this sort of protection bought at such a price. Moreover, even if the importance of given interests and relationships be conceded, there remain questions as to whether evidentiary privileges are appropriate, much less sufficient, mechanisms for accomplishing the desired objectives. In any event, it is clear that in drawing their justifications from considerations unrelated to the integrity of the adjudication process, rules of privilege are of a different order than the great bulk of evidentiary rules.

---

[8]*See* Black, The Marital and Physician Privileges—Reprint of a Letter to a Congressman, 1975 Duke L.J. 45; Note, 56 Ind. L.J. 121 (1980).

[9]Austin, The Use of Privileged Communications for Impeachment Purposes, 49 N.Y.S. B. J. 564 (1977); Saltzburg, Privileges and Professionals: Lawyers and Psychiatrists, 66 Va. L. Rev. 597 (1980); Comment, 9 U.C.D. L. Rev. 477 (1976).

[10]*See, e.g.*, Imwinkelried, The New Wigmore: Evidentiary Privileges § 5.3.3 (2d ed. 2010); Wydick, The Attorney-Client Privilege: Does It Really Have Life Everlasting, 87 Ky. L.J. 1165, 1174 (1999).

[11]*See* Roberts v. Superior Court, 9 Cal. 3d 330, 107 Cal. Rptr. 309, 508 P.2d 309 (1973) ("Potential encroachment upon constitutionally protected rights of privacy" required liberal construction of California psychotherapist-patient privilege.). *See also* Scallen, Relational and Informational Privileges and the Case of the Mysterious Mediation Privilege, 38 Loy. L. A. Law. Rev. 537, 568–76 (2004) (arguing that privileged categorized as relational (such as the attorney-client privilege) and informational (such as work product protection) have different rationales and should be interpreted in light of those rationales).

## § 72.1  The purposes of rules of privilege: (b) Certain rules distinguished

As developed in a subsequent section,[1] true rules of privilege may be enforced to prevent the introduction of evidence even though the privilege is that of a person who is not a party to the proceeding in which the privilege is involved. This characteristic serves to distinguish certain other rules which, like privileges, are intended to encourage or discourage certain kinds of conduct. Among these latter rules may be included those excluding offers of compromise[2] and subsequent remedial measures following an injury.[3]

Functionally, the policies toward which these latter rules are directed may be fully realized by implementing the rules only in litigation to which the person sought to be actuated by the rule is a party. For example, the rule excluding evidence of offers of compromise is designed to encourage compromise; admitting the evidence in a case to which the offeror is not a party will in no wise operate to discourage compromises. Accordingly, such rules may be asserted only by a party. This consideration, in addition to the fact that these rules are also justified in part by considerations relating to relevancy, makes classification as rules of privilege analytically imprecise.

Again, true rules of privilege operate generally to prevent revelation of confidential matter within the context of a judicial proceeding.[4] Thus, rules of privilege do not speak directly to the question of unauthorized revelations of confidential matter outside the judicial setting,[5] and redress for such breaches of confidence must be sought in the law of torts or professional responsibility.[6]

## § 73  Procedural recognition of rules of privilege

In one important procedural respect, rules of privilege are similar to other evidentiary rules. The fact that most exclusionary rules are intended to protect the integrity of the fact-finding pro-

---

[Section 72.1]

[1] § 73 infra.

[2] See § 266 infra.

[3] See § 267 infra.

[4] Some modern statutes, however, do take the form of general prohibitions of disclosure. See, e.g., Cal. Evid. Code § 954.

[5] Rules of privilege have on occasion been held to imply a cause of ac-

tion for unauthorized extra-judicial disclosure. See Berry v. Moench, 8 Utah 2d 191, 331 P.2d 814 (1958).

[6] Note, Breach of Confidence: An Emerging Tort, 82 Colum. L. Rev. 1426 (1982). The admissibility of evidence derived from an unauthorized extra-judicial disclosure is considered in Comment, Evidentiary Privileges and the Exclusion of Derivative Evidence: Commentary and Analysis, 26 San Diego L. Rev. 625 (1989).

cess while rules of privilege look toward the preservation of confidences might lead the casual reflector to conclude that the former will operate inexorably to exclude untrustworthy evidence while the latter will only be enforced at the option of the holder of the privilege. Such, we know, is not the case. Neither set of rules is self-executing:[1] rules of exclusion, no less than rules of privilege, must be asserted to be effective, and if not asserted promptly will ordinarily be waived.[2] Instead, the distinction in purpose between the two types of rules is reflected by a difference in the persons who may claim their benefit and, perhaps today, in what forum.

### § 73.1    Procedural recognition of rules of privilege: (a) Who may assert?[1]

This difference in foundation between the two groups of rules manifests itself in another line of cleavage. The rule of exclusion or preference, being designed to make the trial more efficient as a vehicle of fact disclosure, may be invoked as of right only by the person whose interest in having the verdict follow the facts is at stake in the trial. Thus, when evidence condemned by one of these rules is offered, only the adverse party may object, unless the judge elects to interpose. But by contrast, if the evidence is privileged, the right to object does not attach to the opposing party as such, but to the person vested with the outside interest or relationship fostered by the particular privilege.[2] True, other

---

[Section 73]

[1]*See, e.g.,* Rosado v. Bridgeport Roman Catholic Diocesan Corp., 292 Conn. 1, 970 A.2d 656, 689 (2009) (failure to assert privilege at the time of disclosure operates as a waiver); Morgan, Some Problems of Proof 100–101 (1956).

[2]Diaz v. U.S., 223 U.S. 442, 32 S. Ct. 250, 56 L. Ed. 500 (1912) (hearsay); Halley v. Brown, 92 N.H. 1, 24 A.2d 267 (1942) (same); Southland Equipment Co. v. Hooks, 8 N.C. App. 98, 173 S.E.2d 641 (1970); 1 Wigmore, Evidence, § 18 n. 1 (3d ed. 1940); Fed. R. Evid. 103(a)(1). And see §§ 52, 55 supra.

[Section 73.1]

[1]*See* Imwinkelried, The Alienability of Evidentiary Privileges: Of Property and Evidence, Burden and Benefit, Hearsay and Privilege, 80 St. John's L. Rev. 497 (2006); Note, 34 Ky. L.J. 213 (1946); Note, 20 U. Cin. L. Rev. 76 (1951); Right of one against whom testimony is offered to invoke privilege of communication between others, 2 A.L.R.2d 645; 81 Am. Jur. 2d, Witnesses § 279; West's Key Number Digest, Privileged Communications and Confidentiality, ⊙19, 84, 167, 262, 322.

[2]U.S. v. Ortega, 150 F.3d 937 (8th Cir. 1998) (prosecutor had no standing to raise attorney-client privilege on behalf of witness who was being cross-examined by defense); Henard v. Superior Court, 26 Cal. App. 3d 129, 102 Cal. Rptr. 721 (5th Dist. 1972) (party opponent not entitled to claim physician-patient privilege of others); Womack v. State, 260 Ga. 305, 393 S.E.2d 232 (1990) (defendant could not assert his witness'

persons present at the trial, including the adverse party,[3] may call to the court's attention the existence of the privilege, or the judge may choose to intervene of his own accord to protect it, but this is regarded as having been done on behalf of the owner of the privilege.[4]

The right to complain on appeal is a more crucial test. If the court erroneously recognizes an asserted privilege and excludes proffered testimony on this ground, clearly the tendering party has been injured in his capacity as litigant and may complain on appeal. But if a claim of privilege is wrongly denied, and the privileged testimony erroneously let in, the distinction that we have suggested between privilege and a rule of exclusion would seem to be material. If the adverse party to the suit is likewise the owner of the privilege, then, while it may be argued that the party's interest as a litigant has not been infringed,[5] most courts decline to draw so sharp a line, and permit him to complain of the error.[6]

Where, however, the owner of the privilege is not a party to the

---

attorney-client privilege); Stetson v. Silverman, 278 Neb. 389, 770 N.W.2d 632 (2009) (privilege covering reports and investigatory records of Department of health belonged to the department, not a physician); State v. Echols, 152 Wis. 2d 725, 449 N.W.2d 320 (Ct. App. 1989) (psychologist-patient privilege claimable only by statutorily enumerated persons); 8 Wigmore, Evidence § 2196 (McNaughton rev. 1961); Imwinkelried, The New Wigmore: Evidentiary Privileges § 6.5.1, at 608-11(2d ed. 2010).

[3]People v. Vargas, 53 Cal. App. 3d 516, 126 Cal. Rptr. 88 (1st Dist. 1975) (in absence of defendant privilege holder his attorney, or court, had duty to raise privilege); Mayer v. Albany Medical Center Hospital, 56 Misc. 2d 239, 288 N.Y.S.2d 771 (Sup 1968) (privilege of non-party may be raised by any party); Comment, 30 Colum. L. Rev. 686, 690 (1930).

[4]Colorado State Bd. of Accountancy v. Raisch, 960 P.2d 102 (Colo. 1998) (accounting firm may raise privilege on client's behalf pending decision by client to waive privilege). Touma v. Touma, 140 N.J. Super. 544, 357 A.2d 25 (Ch. Div. 1976) (marriage counselor not entitled to assert

privilege waived by both spouses); State v. Chenette, 151 Vt. 237, 560 A.2d 365 (1989) (physician's power to invoke physician-patient privilege ceases once it is clear physician does not speak for patient). See also Bond v. Bond, 887 S.W.2d 558 (Ky. Ct. App. 1994) (custodial father not permitted to claim psychotherapist-patient privilege on behalf of child where mental state of child was at issue in child custody case); State v. Jarvis, 199 W. Va. 38, 483 S.E.2d 38 (1996) (defendant's son had no standing to claim attorney-client privilege on behalf of deceased victim/wife).

[5]Wigmore, Evidence § 2196 (McNaughton rev. 1961).

[6]People v. Werner, 225 Mich. 18, 195 N.W. 697 (1923) (privilege not to have husband testify); Garrett v. State, 118 Neb. 373, 224 N.W. 860 (1929) (same); People v. Brown, 72 N.Y. 571, 1878 WL 12522 (1878) (self-disgracing testimony). Submission to a contempt citation of the witness whose testimony is claimed to be privileged will, under the prevailing view, establish immediate appealability. Cobbledick v. U.S., 309 U.S. 323, 60 S. Ct. 540, 84 L. Ed. 783 (1940). Even where the witness is unwilling to submit to a con-

suit, it is somewhat difficult to see why this invasion of a third person's interest should be ground of complaint for the objecting party, whose only grievance can be that the overriding of the outsider's rights has resulted in a fuller fact-disclosure than the party desires. It has not been thought necessary to afford this extreme sanction in order to prevent a break-down in the protection of privilege.[7] In at least two classes of privileges, the privileges against self-incrimination[8] and against the use of evidence secured by unlawful search or seizure,[9] this distinction has been clearly perceived and the party is quite consistently denied any ground for reversal, despite the constitutional bases of the two privileges. The results in cases of erroneous denials of other privileges are more checkered; a considerable number of the older cases seem to allow the party to take advantage of the error on appeal.[10]

The California Code of Evidence, one of the few modern codifications to address the question, is clear-cut. It provides: "A party may predicate error on a ruling disallowing a claim of privilege only if he is the holder of the privilege, except that a party

---

tempt citation, immediate appeal will frequently be allowed since the opposite holding would subject the privilege holder to partial loss of the value of the privilege, i.e., confidentiality. *See* In re Sealed Case, 737 F.2d 94 (D.C. Cir. 1984), relying on Perlman v. U.S., 247 U.S. 7, 38 S. Ct. 417, 62 L. Ed. 950 (1918). *But see* In re Grand Jury Subpoena, 190 F.3d 375, 385–88 (5th Cir. 1999) (no immediate appeal under *Perlman* doctrine where party in possession of document had an interest in preserving confidentiality and therefore a reason to risk a contempt citation).

[7]But see the vigorous expression of an opposing view by the dissenting judges in State v. Snook, 94 N.J.L. 271, 109 A. 289, 290 (N.J. Ct. Err. & App. 1920).

[8]See § 119 infra.

[9]See § 175 infra.

[10]Many of the cases are explainable by the fact that the question of the party's standing to raise the point was not noticed, e.g., Bell v. State, 88 Tex. Crim. 64, 224 S.W. 1108 (1920) (marital communications; witness'

privilege denied; defendant allowed to assign as ground of error on appeal). In other cases the court assumes that the evidence usually classified as privileged is "unlawful" or incompetent, e.g., Kaye v. Newhall, 356 Mass. 300, 249 N.E.2d 583 (1969).

A few opinions in cases permitting the party to complain place it expressly on ground of public policy. State v. Barrows, 52 Conn. 323, 1885 WL 8744 (1885) (client's privilege); Bacon v. Frisbie, 80 N.Y. 394, 1 Ky. L. Rptr. 128, 1880 WL 12404 (1880) (client's privilege). The more recent cases where the point is considered seem to be gravitating, under the influence of the Wigmore treatise, to the contrary holding. Matthews v. McNeill, 98 Kan. 5, 157 P. 387 (1916); Martin v. State, 203 Miss. 187, 33 So. 2d 825 (1948). But a few contrary decisions continue to appear. Stauffer v. Karabin, 30 Colo. App. 357, 492 P.2d 862 (App. 1971). *See also* Comment, 30 Colum. L. Rev. 686, 694 (1930); Right of one against whom testimony is offered to invoke privilege of communication between others, 2 A.L.R.2d 645.

may predicate error on a ruling disallowing a claim of privilege by his spouse . . . ."[11]

## § 73.2    Procedural recognition of rules of privilege: (b) Where may privilege be asserted? Rules of privilege in conflict of laws[1]

Under traditional choice of law doctrine all rules of evidence, including those of privilege, were viewed as procedural and thus appropriately supplied by the law of the forum.[2] This approach naturally tended to suppress any consideration of the differences in purpose clearly existing between rules of exclusion and preference on the one hand, and rules of privilege on the other.

Modern conflict of laws analysis, by contrast, inclines toward resolution of choice of law questions through evaluation of the policy interests of the respective jurisdictions that have some connection with the transaction in litigation. Under this approach, the forum will almost invariably possess a strong interest in a correct determination of the facts in dispute before its courts, and therefore a strong interest in the application of its rules of exclusion and preference. By contrast, the forum may have virtually no interest in applying its rules of privilege in a case where the relationship or interest sought to be promoted or protected by the privilege had its contacts exclusively with another jurisdiction.[3]

Thus, for example, if a given professional relationship is car-

---

[11]Cal. Evid. Code § 918.

**[Section 73.2]**

[1]*See generally* Dunham, Testimonial Privileges in State and Federal Courts: A Suggested Approach, 9 Willamette L.J. 26 (1973); Reece & Leiwant, Testimonial Privileges and Conflict of Laws, 41 Law & C.P. 85 (1977); Sterk, Testimonial Privileges: An Analysis of Horizontal Choice of Law Problems, 61 Minn. L. Rev. 461 (1977); Weinstein, Recognition in the United States of Privileges of Another Jurisdiction, 56 Colum. L. Rev. 537 (1956).

Choice of law questions arising in federal courts are further treated infra at § 76.1.

[2]Restatement (First) of Conflict of Laws § 597 (1934). Metropolitan Life Ins. Co. v. McSwain, 149 Miss. 455, 115 So. 555 (1928). The traditional rule continues to be applied in criminal cases, though the same result would here presumably be reached by modern analysis. *See* Bussard v. State, 295 Ark. 72, 747 S.W.2d 71 (1988) (applying Arkansas rather than Missouri physician-patient privilege to permit testimony of Missouri physician concerning Missouri surgery); People v. Thompson, 950 P.2d 608 (Colo. App. 1997) (Oregon marital privilege inapplicable in Colorado murder prosecution even though marriage centered in Oregon and communication took place there; no special reason why forum policy should not be given effect under Restatement (2d) § 139(2)).

[3]Dunham, Testimonial Privileges in State and Federal Courts: A Suggested Approach, 9 Willamette L.J. 26 (1973); Reece & Leiwant, Testimonial Privileges and Conflict of Laws, 41 Law & C.P. 85 (1977); Sterk, Testimonial Privileges: An Analysis of Horizontal Choice of Law Problems,

ried out exclusively in State X which itself does not extend a privilege to protect that relationship, there would seem to be no compelling reason for the forum, State Y, to apply its own rules of privilege, thus denying its court the benefit of helpful evidence. No interest either of the forum or of State X argues for recognition of the forum's privilege in such a case.[4]

On the other hand, if the relationship is carried out exclusively in State X, which does extend a privilege to the communication in question, circumstances may exist in which in which the forum, State Y, may want to recognize that privilege even though there would be no comparable privilege under its law.[5]

## § 74  Limitations on the effectiveness of privileges: (a) Risk of eavesdropping and interception of letters

Since privileges operate to deny litigants access to every person's evidence, the courts have generally construed them no more broadly than necessary to accomplish their basic purposes. One manifestation of this tendency is to be seen in the general rule that a privilege operates only to preclude testimony by parties to the confidential relationship. Accordingly, a number of older decisions held that an eavesdropper may testify to confiden-

---

61 Minn. L. Rev. 461 (1977); Weinstein, Recognition in the United States of Privileges of Another Jurisdiction, 56 Colum. L. Rev. 537 (1956).

[4]*See* Restatement (Second) of Conflict of Laws § 139(1) (1971):

Evidence that is not privileged under the local law of the state which has the most significant relationship with the communication will be admitted, even though it would be privileged under the local law of the forum, unless the admission of such evidence would be contrary to the strong public policy of the forum.

*But see* Hare v. Family Publications Service, Inc., 334 F. Supp. 953 (D. Md. 1971) (holding Maryland accountant-client privilege applicable to protect communications made in New York which recognized no privilege.).

[5]Restatement (Second) of Conflict of Laws § 139(2) (1971):

Evidence that is privileged under the local law of the state which has the most significant relationship with the communication but which is not privileged under the local law of the forum will be admitted unless there is some

special reason why the forum policy favoring admission should not be given effect.

*See* Compuware Corp. v. Moody's Investors Services, Inc., 222 F.R.D. 124, 131–33 (E.D. Mich. 2004) (New York journalist's privilege applied where New York had a strong public interest in the outcome); State v. Lipham, 2006 ME 137, 910 A.2d 388, 392 (Me. 2006) (Maine law applied where Maine had most significant relationship to the marital communication); Ford Motor Co. v. Leggat, 904 S.W.2d 643 (Tex. 1995) (Michigan's broader interpretation of attorney-client privilege would govern in Texas case). *See also* Golden Trade, S.r.L. v. Lee Apparel Co., 143 F.R.D. 514 (S.D. N.Y. 1992) (foreign law with regard to confidentiality governed questions of communications to foreign patent agents concerning applications in those countries); Comment, A Choice of Law Analysis of Evidentiary Privileges, 50 La. L. Rev. 157 (1989) arguing that the differential policies underlying various privileges should be considered for choice of law purposes.

tial communications,[1] and that a letter, otherwise confidential and privileged, is not protected if it is stolen or otherwise intercepted by a third person.[2] This principle, however, has only infrequently been carried to the extent of allowing a privilege to be breached if the interception is made possible by the connivance of a party to the confidential relationship.[3]

Though the same general rule is still sometimes applied,[4] most modern decisions do no more than hold that a privilege will not protect communications made under circumstances in which interception was reasonably to be anticipated.[5] Certainly, a qual-

---

**[Section 74]**

[1]This seems to have been the holding even when the overhearing was not due to carelessness on the part of the confidants. Com. v. Griffin, 110 Mass. 181, 1872 WL 8901 (1872) (conversation in jail of husband and wife, overheard by officers in concealment); Com. v. Wakelin, 230 Mass. 567, 120 N.E. 209 (1918) (dictograph hidden in cell of husband and wife); Clark v. State, 159 Tex. Crim. 187, 261 S.W.2d 339 (1953) (conversation of accused with attorney over long distance telephone reported by operator who eavesdropped in violation of company rule); Effect of knowledge of third person acquired by overhearing or seeing communication between husband and wife upon rule as to privileged communication, 63 A.L.R. 107; 81 Am. Jur. 2d, Witnesses §§ 321306, 365; West's Key Number Digest, Privileged Communications and Confidentiality ⬅158 to 159.

[2]Intercepted letters, admitted: Hammons v. State, 73 Ark. 495, 84 S.W. 718 (1905); People v. Dunnigan, 163 Mich. 349, 128 N.W. 180 (1910); Com. v. Smith, 270 Pa. 583, 113 A. 844 (1921). Testimony of person who saw letters without recipient's connivance, admitted: Harris v. State, 72 Tex. Crim. 117, 161 S.W. 125 (1913). But a conflicting view excludes the letters, whether secured with or without the addressee's consent. McKie v. State, 165 Ga. 210, 140 S.E. 625 (1927) (letters of wife to husband, produced at trial of wife for husband's murder, by temporary administrator appointed

during trial to secure the letter from husband's deposit box offered by state, held inadmissible.) See also 8 Wigmore, Evidence §§ 2325, 2326, 2329 (McNaughton rev. 1961); Imwinkelried, The New Wigmore: Evidentiary Privileges § 6.5.1, at 608–11 (2d ed. 2010); 81 Am. Jur. 2d, Witnesses § 321.

[3]See, e.g., State v. Sysinger, 25 S.D. 110, 125 N.W. 879 (1910). The majority rule declines to allow privilege to be vitiated through connivance: U.S. v. Neal, 532 F. Supp. 942 (D. Colo. 1982) (collecting cases and citing majority rule); People v. Dubanowski, 75 Ill. App. 3d 809, 31 Ill. Dec. 403, 394 N.E.2d 605 (1st Dist. 1979); Hunter v. Hunter, 169 Pa. Super. 498, 83 A.2d 401 (1951).

[4]State v. Szemple, 135 N.J. 406, 640 A.2d 817 (1994) (marital privilege does not apply to written communication coming into possession of third party without consent of recipient spouse); Erlich v. Erlich, 278 A.D. 244, 104 N.Y.S.2d 531 (1st Dep't 1951) (wiretaps of attorney-client communications held admissible); State v. Slater, 36 Wash. 2d 357, 218 P.2d 329 (1950) (testimony of officer overhearing husband-wife communication from adjacent hotel room).

[5]A number of cases upholding admissibility on the facts before them state or imply that a reasonable expectation of privacy will bar the eavesdropper's testimony. U.S. v. Madoch, 149 F.3d 596 (7th Cir. 1998) (no expectation of privacy in conversation at jail); Proffitt v. State, 315 So. 2d 461,

ification of the traditional rule in terms of the reasonable expectations of the privileged communicator may provide a desirable common law readjustment to cope with the alarming potential of the modern eavesdropper. While in earlier times the confidentiality of privileged communications could generally be preserved by a modest attention to security,[6] homespun measures will hardly suffice against the modern panoply of electronic paraphernalia.[7]

The vastly enhanced technology of eavesdropping has drawn a variety of legislative reactions more directly responsive to the problem. These have included state statutes prohibiting wiretapping and electronic surveillance and denying admissibility to evidence obtained in violation.[8] Such provisions are of course in addition to the protection that may rest on constitutional grounds. Moreover, statutes and rules defining the privileges have begun to include provisions entitling the holder to prevent anyone from disclosing a privileged communication.[9]

---

464 (Fla. 1975) (court characterizes issue as whether "appellant and his wife knew or should have known that their privileged communication was being overheard."), 4 Fla. St. L. Rev. 553 (1976). *See also* 3 Weinstein & Berger, Evidence ¶ 503.15[3] (2012) (noting trend away from traditional rule and toward honoring of privilege where reasonable precautions taken); Comment, Applicability of the Attorney-Client Privilege to Communications Intercepted by Third Parties, 69 Iowa L. Rev. 263 (1983).

[6]*See* Wolfle v. U.S., 291 U.S. 7, 54 S. Ct. 279, 78 L. Ed. 617 (1934) (noting that husband-wife communications may generally easily be kept confidential; testimony of public stenographer to whom husband dictated letter, not barred by privilege).

[7]Lanza v. New York State Joint Legislative Committee on Government Operations, 5 Misc. 2d 324, 164 N.Y.S.2d 531, 534, (Sup 1957), rev'd on other grounds, 3 N.Y.2d 92, 164 N.Y.S.2d 9, 143 N.E.2d 772 (1957) ("who could foresee the development of electronic devices making useless the most elaborate precautions to safeguard the confidences of attorney and client"); 42 Minn. L. Rev. 664, 37 Neb. L. Rev. 472, 106 Pa. L. Rev. 307, 36 Texas L. Rev. 505, 32 N.Y.U. L.

Rev. 1309. *See also* Morrow v. Superior Court, 30 Cal. App. 4th 1252, 36 Cal. Rptr. 2d 210 (2d Dist. 1994) (prosecutor's deliberate eavesdropping on conversation between attorney and client cause for dismissal of indictment); State v. Cory, 62 Wash. 2d 371, 382 P.2d 1019 (1963) ("odious practice of eavesdropping on privileged communications between attorney and client" violated privilege as well as constitutional right to counsel; prosecution dismissed). A different issue arises where what is sought to be excluded is evidence derived from an overheard conversation as opposed to the conversation itself. *See, e.g.*, U.S. v. Squillacote, 221 F.3d 542, 558–60 (4th Cir. 2000) (government intercepted telephone calls between defendants and psychotherapists as to which privilege applied; no suppression of evidence derived from conversations).

[8]Cal. Penal Code §§ 631(c), 632(d); 720 Ill. Comp. Stat. 5/14-1(a). So strictly drawn is the Illinois statute that a specific exemption was included in order to allow the hard-of-hearing to wear hearing aids. *See also* Federal Wiretap Act, 18 U.S.C.A. §§ 2510 to 2522.

[9]With respect to the attorney-client privilege, Cal. Evid. Code § 954. *See also* Menendez v. Superior Court,

## § 74.1 Limitations on the effectiveness of privileges: (b) Adverse arguments and inferences from claims of privilege

The underlying conflict comes most clearly in view in the decisions relating to the allowability of an adverse inference from the assertion of privilege. Plainly, the inference may not ordinarily be made against a party when a witness for that party claims a privilege personal to the witness, for this is not a matter under the party's control.[1] But where the party himself suppresses evidence by invoking a privilege given to him by the law, should an adverse inference be sanctioned? The question may arise in various forms, for example, whether an inquiry of the witness, or of the party, calling for information obviously privileged, may be pressed for the pointed purpose of forcing the party to make an explicit claim of the privilege in the jury's hearing, or again, whether the inference may be drawn in argument, and finally, whether the judge in the instructions may mention the inference as a permissible one.

Under familiar principles an unfavorable inference may be drawn against a party not only for destroying evidence, but for the mere failure to produce witnesses or documents within his control.[2] No showing of wrong or fraud seems to be required as a foundation for the inference that the evidence if produced would have been unfavorable. Why should not this same conclusion be drawn from the party's active interposing of a privilege to keep out the evidence? A leading case for the affirmative is *Phillips v. Chase*,[3] where the court said:

> It is a rule of law that the objection of a party to evidence as incompetent and immaterial, and insistence upon his right to have his case tried according to the rules of law, cannot be made a subject of comment in argument.[4] . . . On the other hand, if evidence is material and competent except for a personal privilege of one of the parties to have it excluded under the law, his claim of the privilege may be referred to in argument and considered by the jury, as indicating his opinion that the evidence, if received, would be prejudicial to him.

An oft-quoted statement by Lord Chelmsford gives the contrary view:

---

3 Cal. 4th 435, 11 Cal. Rptr. 2d 92, 834 P.2d 786 (1992) (statute prevents eavesdropper from disclosing communications between patient and psychotherapist).

**[Section 74.1]**

[1] See § 73.1 supra, and more particularly as to self-incrimination § 119 infra.

[2] See § 264 infra.

[3] Phillips v. Chase, 201 Mass. 444, 87 N.E. 755, 758 (1909).

[4] *See also* 5 Busch, Law and Tactics in Jury Trials § 658 (1963).

The exclusion of such evidence is for the general interest of the community, and therefore to say that when a party refuses to permit professional confidence to be broken, everything must be taken most strongly against him, what is it but to deny him the protection which, for public purposes, the law affords him, and utterly to take away a privilege which can thus only be asserted to his prejudice?[5]

The first of these arguments is based upon an unfounded distinction between incompetent and privileged evidence, namely, a supposition that the privilege can be waived and the incompetency cannot.[6] As we have seen, both may be waived with equal facility. As to the second, it may be an overstatement to say that permitting the inference "utterly takes away" the privilege. A privilege has its most substantial practical benefit when it enables a party to exclude from the record a witness, document, or line of proof that is essential to the adversary's case, lacking which he cannot get to the jury at all on a vital issue. The inference does not supply the lack of proof.[7] In other situations, the benefit accruing from a successful claim of privilege will depend upon circumstances.[8] It is evident, however, that in a case that survives a motion for a directed verdict or its equivalent, allowing comment upon the exercise of a privilege or requiring it to be claimed in the presence of the jury tends greatly to diminish its value. In *Griffin v. California*[9] the Supreme Court held that allowing comment[10] upon the failure of an accused to take the stand violated his privilege against self-incrimination "by making its assertion costly." Whether one is prepared to extend this protection to all privileges probably depends upon her attitude towards privileges in general and towards the particular privilege involved. The cases, rather naturally, are in dispute.[11] It is submitted that the best solution is to recognize only privileges that are soundly based in policy and to accord those privileges

---

[5]Wentworth v. Lloyd, 10 H.L.Cas. 589, 591 (1864).

[6]See § 73 supra. In fact both can be waived.

[7]See § 264 infra.

[8]O'Brien, Judicial Responses When a Civil Litigant Exercises a Privilege: Seeking the Least Costly Remedy, 31 St. L. U. L.J. 323 (1987), surveys other remedies which the courts have occasionally used to eliminate unfairness occasioned by claims of privilege.

[9]Griffin v. California, 380 U.S. 609, 85 S. Ct. 1229, 14 L. Ed. 2d 106 (1965).

[10]The comment assumed the form both of a jury instruction and argument by the prosecutor, but the Court indicated that either alone would be a violation.

[11]For cases *see* Right to insist that opponent's claim of privilege shall be made in presence of jury, or to ask him if he is willing to waive privilege, 144 A.L.R. 1007 (requiring claim to be made or asking party if he will waive, in presence of jury); Calling or offering accused's spouse as witness for prosecution as prejudicial misconduct, 76 A.L.R.2d 920 (calling of spouse of accused by prosecution); Propriety and prejudicial effect of comment by counsel

the fullest protection. Thus comment, whether by judge or by counsel, or its equivalent of requiring the claim to be made in the presence of the jury, and the drawing of inferences from the claim, all would be foreclosed.[12]

## § 74.2 Limitations on the effectiveness of privileges: (c) Constitutional limitations on privilege

A previously unrecognized source of limitations on privilege in criminal cases has in recent years emerged as a result of decisions of the Supreme Court dealing with the Compulsory Process and Confrontation Clauses of the Constitution of the United States.

The three cases that have figured in this development are *Washington v. Texas*,[1] *Davis v. Alaska*,[2] and *United States v. Nixon*.[3] In *Washington v. Texas*, the Court held the provisions of the Compulsory Process Clause binding upon states as a component of due process, and struck down a Texas statute that rendered persons charged or convicted as co-participants in the same crime incompetent to testify for one another. The Court's decision stressed the "absurdity" of the statute and specifically held only that the constitutional provision is violated by "arbitrary rules that prevent whole categories of defense witnesses from testifying . . . ."[4] The Court expressly disclaimed any implied disapproval of testimonial privileges that it noted are based upon quite different considerations.

In *Davis v. Alaska*, the Court held that the Confrontation Clause was violated by application of a state statute privileging juvenile records where the result was to deny the defendant the opportunity to elicit on cross-examination the probationary status of a critical witness against him. Recognizing the strength of the state policy in favor of preserving the confidentiality of juveniles' records, the Court nevertheless held that this policy must yield to the superior interest of the defendant in effective confrontation. Significantly, the Court's decision did not compel disclosure of the

---

as to refusal to permit introduction of privileged testimony, 32 A.L.R.3d 906 (comment in argument on exercise of privilege); Propriety and prejudicial effect of comment or instruction by court with respect to party's refusal to permit introduction of privileged testimony, 34 A.L.R.3d 775 (comment by judge in summing up or instructing).

[12]*See* Cal. Evid. Code § 913; N.J.Rules of Evid. 532; Proposed Fed. R. Evid. 513, 56 F.R.D. 260, not en-

acted by the Congress.

**[Section 74.2]**

[1]Washington v. Texas, 388 U.S. 14, 87 S. Ct. 1920, 18 L. Ed. 2d 1019 (1967).

[2]Davis v. Alaska, 415 U.S. 308, 94 S. Ct. 1105, 39 L. Ed. 2d 347 (1974).

[3]U.S. v. Nixon, 418 U.S. 683, 94 S. Ct. 3090, 41 L. Ed. 2d 1039 (1974).

[4]Washington v. Texas, 388 U.S. 14, 22, 87 S. Ct. 1920, 18 L. Ed. 2d 1019 (1967).

juvenile record, but only remanded the case for further proceedings not inconsistent with the Court's opinion.

Finally, in *United States v. Nixon*, the Court held that a claim of absolute privilege of confidentiality for general presidential communications in the performance of the office would not prevail "over the fundamental demands of due process of law in the fair administration of criminal justice. The generalized assertion of privilege must yield to the demonstrated, specific need for evidence in a pending criminal trial."[5]

Taken together, and despite the somewhat distinctive fact situations involved, these cases fairly raise the question as to the viability of a claim of privilege when a criminal defendant asserts: (1) a need to introduce the privileged matter as exculpatory, or (2) a need to use the privileged matter to impeach testimony introduced by the state.[6] The question is of course not altogether a novel one. Privileges running in favor of the government, such as the informer's privilege, have long been qualified to accommodate the defendant's rights of confrontation.[7] Similarly, the state has frequently been precluded from relying upon the testimony of a witness whose claim of privilege on self-incrimination grounds prevents effective cross-examination.[8]

A number of state decisions, purporting to give effect to the constitutional holdings of *Davis* and *Nixon*, have resolved conflicts between the rights of a defendant on the one hand and claims of private privilege on the other by overriding the latter and forcing (or attempting to force) the testimony of the privilege holder.[9]

Despite such decisions, the extent to which protection of the interests of a criminal defendant constitutionally requires invasion of private privilege was never clear, and has been placed even further in doubt in the decision of the Supreme Court in

---

[5]U.S. v. Nixon, 418 U.S. 683, 713, 94 S. Ct. 3090, 41 L. Ed. 2d 1039 (1974).

[6]*See generally* Clinton, The Right to Present a Defense: An Emergent Constitutional Guarantee in Criminal Trials, 9 Ind. L. Rev. 713 (1976); Westen, The Compulsory Process Clause, 73 Mich. L. Rev. 71 (1974); Notes, 73 Mich. L. Rev. 1465 (1975), 30 Stan. L. Rev. 935 (1978).

[7]Roviaro v. U.S., 353 U.S. 53, 77 S. Ct. 623, 1 L. Ed. 2d 639 (1957).

[8]See § 19 supra.

[9]Salazar v. State, 559 P.2d 66 (Alaska 1976); Hammarley v. Superior Court, 89 Cal. App. 3d 388, 153 Cal. Rptr. 608 (3d Dist. 1979); People v. Pate, 625 P.2d 369 (Colo. 1981); State v. Hembd, 305 Minn. 120, 232 N.W.2d 872 (1975); Matter of Farber, 78 N.J. 259, 394 A.2d 330 (1978). *See also* M. v. K., 186 N.J. Super. 363, 452 A.2d 704 (Ch. Div. 1982) (statutory privilege for communications between marriage counselor and persons counseled denies child's due process rights to all material evidence in custody proceeding; Davis not cited).

*Pennsylvania v. Ritchie.*[10] In *Ritchie*, the defendant, charged with rape and other related crimes, sought pretrial access to files of a state child protective agency. The defendant's chief interest in the files, which were protected by a qualified privilege under state statute, was to discover material of possible use in the cross-examination of his daughter, the complaining witness. The state supreme court, relying on *Davis*, held that the defendant had the right to inspect the files in question by virtue of the Confrontation and Compulsory Process clauses. The Supreme Court reversed this portion of the state judgment, a majority of the court concurring that the defendant was entitled only to have the file inspected in camera by the trial court. Only four justices, however, joined in the plurality opinion which based this result on due process grounds and stated that the Pennsylvania court's reliance on *Davis* was "misplaced" and that the Confrontation Clause creates only a "trial" right.

Not surprisingly, the *Ritchie* decision has been accorded a variety of interpretations. One approach adopted by several courts is to require that the defendant make a showing that there is reasonable ground to believe that failure to produce material which has been found privileged will be likely to impair defendant's right of confrontation.[11] Once such a showing is made, the state must then obtain the privilege holder's waiver for purposes of an in camera inspection and, if the matter is found relevant, for trial presentation; otherwise the privilege-holder's testimony will be

---

[10]Pennsylvania v. Ritchie, 480 U.S. 39, 107 S. Ct. 989, 94 L. Ed. 2d 40 (1987).

[11]*See, e.g.,* Burns v. State, 968 A.2d 1012, 1025–26 (Del. 2009) (defendant established his entitlement to an in camera review of private therapy records by making a "plausible showing" that the records sought were material and relevant); State v. Juarez, 570 A.2d 1118 (R.I. 1990) (defendant failed to show that privileged matter contained anything beneficial to him); State v. Cardall, 1999 UT 51, 982 P.2d 79, 86 (Utah 1999) (defendant made a sufficient showing of materiality in victim's school psychological records to require in camera review of records); State v. Rehkop, 180 Vt. 228, 2006 VT 72, 908 A.2d 488, 497 (2006) (defendant made a sufficient particularized preliminary showing entitling him to an in camera review of victim's school

counselor records). Even beneficial matter may not possess substantial importance within the context of the case. *See* Mills v. State, 476 So. 2d 172 (Fla. 1985) (application of attorney-client privilege to prevent impeachment of witness against defendant by prior inconsistent statement made to attorney's investigator held not to violate defendant's right to confrontation where witness was impeached with other inconsistent statements).

As generally supporting the view that the defendant's constitutional right should be proportioned to the importance of the matter sought, *see* Hill, Testimonial Privilege and Fair Trial, 80 Colum. L. Rev. 1173 (1980); Note, 30 Stan. L. Rev. 935, 964 (1978). *But see* Westen, Compulsory Process II, 74 Mich. L. Rev. 191, 211 (1975).

inadmissible.[12] However, many decisions have failed to find that the defendant's constitutional rights require even so limited an intrusion on private privilege.[13]

Even more dubious today is any right of the criminal defendant to obtain and present matter protected by private privilege that is relevant to the issues of the case but has no direct bearing upon the credibility of a witness for the prosecution.[14]

## § 75  The sources of privilege

The earliest recognized privileges were judicially created, the origin of both the husband-wife and attorney-client privileges being traceable to the received common law.[1] The development of judge-made privileges, however, virtually halted over a century ago.[2] Though it is impossible definitely to ascribe a reason for

---

[12]State v. Whitaker, 202 Conn. 259, 520 A.2d 1018 (1987) (sexual assault counselor privilege); State v. Trammell, 231 Neb. 137, 435 N.W.2d 197 (1989) (physician-patient privilege); People v. Stanaway, 446 Mich. 643, 521 N.W.2d 557 (1994) (one defendant's case remanded for determination of whether there was a reasonable probability of various privileged records containing material necessary to the defense; another defendant failed to make such a showing; court emphasizes that waiver required because privileges were absolute).

[13]People v. Hammon, 15 Cal. 4th 1117, 65 Cal. Rptr. 2d 1, 938 P.2d 986 (1997) (court not required to review privileged information in hands of third party psychotherapy providers); Dill v. People, 927 P.2d 1315 (Colo. 1996) (no in camera inspection required of private psychologist's report); People v. Foggy, 121 Ill. 2d 337, 118 Ill. Dec. 18, 521 N.E.2d 86 (1988) (defendant's constitutional right must yield to absolute legislative privilege even where privileged matter shown significant to defense; dictum); In re Crisis Connection, Inc., 949 N.E.2d 789 (Ind. 2011) (defendant had no right to document protected by statutory victim-advocate privilege); In re Maraziti, 233 N.J. Super. 488, 559 A.2d 447 (App. Div. 1989) (attorney-client privilege); Com. v. Wilson, 529

Pa. 268, 602 A.2d 1290 (1992) (no inspection required of report of sexual assault counselor). In the federal courts, compare, e.g., U.S. v. Shrader, 716 F. Supp. 2d 464 (S.D. W. Va. 2010) (psychotherapist-patient privilege not subordinate to defendant's Sixth Amendment Rights) with U.S. v. W.R. Grace, 439 F. Supp. 2d 1125, 1137–43 (D. Mont. 2006) (attorney-client privilege may yield to defendant's Sixth Amendment right to present evidence based upon a weighing of the value of the evidence against the purposes served by the privilege).

[14]For an attempt to state principles controlling after Ritchie, see White, Evidentiary Privilege and the Defendant's Constitutional Right to Introduce Evidence, 80 J. Crim. L. & Criminology 377 (1989).

[Section 75]

[1]See §§ 78 and 87 infra.

[2]A significant exception to this statement is, of course, the development of privileges in the federal courts. Fed. R. Evid. 501 tells the federal courts to develop privileges under "the principles of the common law as they may be interpreted . . . in the light of reason and experience." The most notable decision under that rule has been the recognition of a psychotherapist-patient privilege in Jaffee v. Redmond, 518 U.S. 1, 116 S.

this cessation, a contributing factor was undoubtedly a judicial tendency to view privileges from the standpoint of their hindrance to litigation. Certainly the vantage point of the legal profession in general, and of the judiciary in particular, is such as to force into prominence the more deleterious aspects of privilege as impediments to the fact-finding process. By contrast, many of the beneficial consequences claimed for privilege can be expected to be observable only outside the courtroom, and even then are often difficult to demonstrate empirically.[3]

Perhaps as a consequence, during the 19th century the source of newly created privileges shifted decisively from the courts to the legislatures. New York enacted the first physician-patient privilege in 1828,[4] and the vast majority of new privileges created since that time have been of legislative origin. The trend extended to codification even of the preexisting common law privileges, and today the husband-wife and attorney-client privileges are statutorily controlled in most states.[5]

It may be argued that legitimate claims to confidentiality are more equitably received by a branch of government not preeminently concerned with the factual results obtained in litigation, and that the legislatures provide an appropriate forum for the balancing of the competing social values necessary to sound decisions concerning privilege.[6] At the same time, while there is no doubt that some of the statutorily created privileges are soundly

---

Ct. 1923, 135 L. Ed. 2d 337 (1996). *See also, e.g.*, Deitchman v. E.R. Squibb & Sons, Inc., 740 F.2d 556 (7th Cir. 1984) (scientific researcher-subject privilege); Reichhold Chemicals, Inc. v. Textron, Inc., 157 F.R.D. 522 (N.D. Fla. 1994) (self-critical analysis). *See also* State v. Sandstrom, 224 Kan. 573, 581 P.2d 812 (1978) (recognizing limited newsperson's privilege "although such does not exist by statute or common law"); Opinion of the Justices, 117 N.H. 390, 373 A.2d 642 (1977) (semble). Most proposals for new privileges, not surprisingly, look toward legislative action. *See, e.g.*, Coburn, Child-Parent Communications: Spare the Privilege and Spoil the Child, 74 Dick. L. Rev. 599 (1970).

[3]*See* Saltzburg, Privileges and Professionals: Lawyers and Psychiatrists, 66 Va. L. Rev. 597, 599–600 (1980). *See also* Rosenburg, The New Tools in Law, 52 Marq. L. Rev. 539 (1969) (urging greater use of

social science research techniques to validate assumptions underlying privilege.) For an effort to secure this type of data, *see* Blasi, The Newsman's Privilege: An Empirical Study, 70 Mich. L. Rev. 229 (1971).

[4]N.Y. Rev. Stats. 1829, Vol. II, Part III, c-7, Tit. 3, art. eight, § 73.

[5]Many of the statutes are collected in Imwinkelried, The New Wigmore: Evidentiary Privileges App. D (2d ed. 2010).

[6]People v. Sanders, 99 Ill. 2d 262, 75 Ill. Dec. 682, 457 N.E.2d 1241 (1983) (expansion and creation of privileges should be left to the legislature for the reasons advanced by the text); Com., Cabinet for Health and Family Services v. Chauvin, 316 S.W.3d 279, 286–89 (Ky. 2010) (rules that predominately foster accuracy in fact-finding by affecting what happens inside a courtroom are procedural and within the exclusive authority of the Court; however those that predominately fos-

based, legislatures have on occasion been unduly influenced by powerful groups seeking the prestige and convenience of a professionally based privilege.[7] One result of the process has been that the various states differ substantially in the numbers and varieties of privilege that they recognize.

Until very recently, the heavy consensus among commentators has favored narrowing the field of privilege,[8] and attempts have been made, largely without success, to incorporate this view into the several 20th century efforts to codify the law of evidence. The draftsmen of both the Model Code of Evidence[9] and the 1953 Uniform Rules of Evidence[10] favored limitations on the number and scope of privileges. The final versions of both of these codifications, however, contained the generally recognized common law and statutory privileges substantially unimpaired.[11]

The Federal Rules of Evidence as proposed by the Advisory Committee and approved by the Supreme Court contained provisions recognizing and defining nine non-constitutional privileges: required reports,[12] attorney-client,[13] psychotherapist-patient,[14] husband-wife,[15] clergyman-communicant,[16] political vote,[17] trade secrets,[18] secrets of state and other official information,[19] and identity of informer.[20] In addition, proposed Rule 501 specifically limited the privileges to be recognized in the federal courts to those provided for by the Rules or enacted by the Congress.[21] When the Rules were submitted to the Congress the privilege

---

ter other objectives, like privileges, have an out-of-court effect are substantive and within the power of the legislature).

[7] *See* 8 Wigmore, Evidence § 2286 at 532 (McNaughton rev. 1961); Wright and Miller's Federal Practice and Procedure, Evidence § 5522 (discussing the enactment of statutes establishing a psychotherapist-patient privilege).

[8] Maguire, Common Sense and Common Law 99–101 (1947); 8 Wigmore, Evidence §§ 2285–86 (McNaughton rev. 1961); Chafee, Privileged Communications: Is Justice Served By Closing the Doctor's Mouth on the Witness Stand?, 52 Yale L.J. 607 (1943); McCormick, The Scope of Privilege in the Law of Evidence, 16 Tex. L. Rev. 447 (1938); Radin, "The Privilege of Confidential Communication Between Lawyer and Client, 16 Calif. L. Rev. 487 (1928). *And see* 5

Bentham, Rationale of Judicial Evidence 302 (J.S. Mill ed. 1827).

[9] American Law Institute Proceedings 187 (1941–1942).

[10] *See* Uniform Rules of Evidence, Prefatory Note (1953).

[11] Model Code of Evidence, Foreword, 17 (1942); Uniform Rules of Evidence, Rules 23 to 39 and Comments (1953).

[12] Deleted Rule 502, 56 F.R.D. 234.

[13] Deleted Rule 503, 56 F.R.D. 235.

[14] Deleted Rule 504, 56 F.R.D. 240.

[15] Deleted Rule 505, 56 F.R.D. 244.

[16] Deleted Rule 506, 56 F.R.D. 247.

[17] Deleted Rule 507, 56 F.R.D. 249.

[18] Deleted Rule 508, 56 F.R.D. 249.

[19] Deleted Rule 509, 56 F.R.D. 251.

[20] Deleted Rule 510, 56 F.R.D. 255.

[21] Deleted Federal Rule 501, 56

provisions excited particular controversy,[22] with the result that all of the specific rules of privilege were excised from the finally enacted version of the Rules.[23] Indeed, Congress went a step further than simply rejecting the proposed rules. It enacted a statute that requires that any "rule creating, abolishing, or modifying an evidentiary privilege" must be approved by an Act of Congress' rather than through the usual Court initiated rulemaking process.[24]

The Congressional action reflects the policy considerations discussed earlier in this section. Although some evidentiary privileges arose out of the common law, most have been the result of legislative action involving the balancing of competing social values. The federal courts are free to deal with privileges on a case by case basis in the context of the facts before them, but the development of broader rules has been left to the legislative process.

The failure of Congress to enact specific rules of privilege left the Federal Rules of Evidence with a large gap when viewed as a potential model code for possible adoption by the states. Therefore, in promulgating the Revised Uniform Rules of Evidence (1974), based almost entirely on the Federal Rules, the National Conference of Commissioners on Uniform State Laws included specific rules of privilege.[25] These rules were substantially rules submitted to Congress, but contained some notable changes.[26] Some states adopting rules or codes based upon the Federal Rules have adopted the proposed Federal Rules concerning privilege, others have adopted the 1974 Uniform Rules on this subject, and some have retained their antecedent rules of privilege.[27]

---

F.R.D. 230, reads:

> Except as otherwise required by the Constitution of the United States or provided by Act of Congress, and except as provided in these rules or in other rules adopted by the Supreme Court, no person has a privilege to:
>
> > (1) Refuse to be a witness; or
> >
> > (2) Refuse to disclose any matter; or
> >
> > (3) Refuse to produce any object or writing; or
> >
> > (4) Prevent another from being a witness or disclosing any matter or producing any object or writing.

With some slight modification to adapt it to State use and to substitute the term "record" for writing, the proposed federal rule is now Unif. R. Evid. 501.

[22]A summary of the controversy may be found in Broun, Giving Codification a Second Chance—Testimonial Privileges and the Federal Rules of Evidence, 53 Hastings L.J. 769, 772–78 (2002).

[23]For the text of Fed. R. Evid. 501 as adopted by the Congress, see § 76.1 infra.

[24]28 U.S.C.A. § 2074(b).

[25]See Revised Uniform Rules of Evidence (1999) 502 to 508.

[26]The changes are presented in detail in 2 Weinstein and Berger, Evidence §§ 502–510 (2012).

[27]The Uniform Rules of Evidence were amended in 1999. Unif. R. Evid.

## § 76    The current pattern of privilege

The failure of Congress to enact specific rules of privilege for the federal courts effectively precluded any immediate prospect of substantial national uniformity in this area. It is arguable that, in light of the strength and contrariety of views which the subject generates, hope for such a consensus was never realistic.[1] In any event, the present form of Federal Rule of Evidence 501 perpetuates a fluid situation in the federal law of privilege and affords the states little inducement to adopt identical or similar schemes of privilege. The variegated pattern of privilege in both federal and state courts, described below, thus seems likely to remain the case for the foreseeable future.

## § 76.1    The current pattern of privilege: (a) Privilege in federal courts; what law applies?

The Proposed Federal Rules of Evidence recognized only privileges emanating from federal sources and their enactment would have created a unitary scheme of privilege applicable to all cases regardless of jurisdictional ground.[1] The congressionally enacted rules, however, establish a bifurcated system of privilege rules. Federal Rule of Evidence 501 provides:

> The common law—as interpreted by United States courts in the light of reason and experience—governs a claim of privilege unless any of the following provides otherwise:
> • the United States Constitution;
> • a federal statute; or
> • rules prescribed by the Supreme Court.

---

501 to 511. As amended, the Rules deviate even more significantly from the Proposed Federal Rules of Evidence with regard to privilege than the rules promulgated in 1974 and 1986.

[Section 76]

[1]It is noteworthy that even Nevada, a state so enthusiastic over the prospects afforded by the project that it adopted the rules embodied in the Preliminary Draft of Federal Rules of Evidence for United States District Courts and Magistrates (1969), substituted its own preexisting rules of privilege. Advocacy for federal codification of the privilege rules has not entirely gone away. *See* Broun, Giving Codification a Second Chance—Testimonial Privileges and the Federal Rules of Evidence, 53 Hastings L.J. 769 (2002);

Glynn, Federalizing Privilege, 52 Am. U. L. Rev. 59 (2002); Glynn, One Privilege to Rule Them All? Some Post-Sarbanes-Oxley and Other Reflections on a Federally Codified Attorney-Client Privilege, 38 Loy. L.A. L. Rev. 597 (2004); Kirgis, A Legisprudential Analysis of Evidence Codification: Why Most Rules of Evidence Should Not be Codified—But Privilege Law Should Be, 38 Loy. L.A. L. Rev. 809 (2004). For an argument against codification, *see* Rice, Back to the Future with Privileges: Abandon Codification, Not the Common Law, 38 Loy. L.A. L. Rev. 739 (2004).

[Section 76.1]

[1]The text of deleted Fed. R. Evid. 501 appears in § 75 supra.

But in a civil case, state law governs privilege regarding a claim or defense for which state law supplies the rule of decision.[2]

Under Rule 501, then, common law, "as interpreted . . . in the light of reason and experience," will determine the privileges applicable in federal question and criminal cases, while privileges in diversity actions will derive from state law. In the former types of cases, it seems likely that the rules promulgated by the Supreme Court will prove influential as indicators of "reason and experience."[3] But it is also apparent that the intent of Rule 501 is not to limit the number and type of privileges recognized to those

---

[2]This is the restyled rule, effective Dec. 1, 2011. The rule before restyling read:

Except as otherwise required by the Constitution of the United States or provided by Act of Congress or in rules prescribed by the Supreme Court pursuant to statutory authority, the privilege of a witness, person, government, State, or political subdivision thereof shall be governed by the principles of the common law as they may be interpreted by the courts of the United States in the light of reason and experience. However, in civil actions and proceedings, with respect to an element of a claim or defense as to which State law supplies the rule of decision, the privilege of a witness, person, government, State, or political subdivision thereof shall be determined in accordance with State law.

[3]See the statement of Weinstein, J., in U.S. v. Mackey, 405 F. Supp. 854, 857 (E.D. N.Y. 1975):

Despite their deletion by Congress, the privilege rules promulgated by the Supreme Court remain of considerable utility as standards. Congress expressed no disagreement with their substance; it eliminated them primarily because they were considered substantive in nature and not a fit subject for rule making.

The specific rules on privilege promulgated by the Supreme Court are reflective of "reason and experience." They are the culmination of three drafts prepared by an Advisory Committee consisting of judges, practicing lawyers and academicians. In its many years of work, the Committee considered hundreds of suggestions received in response to the circulation of the

drafts throughout the legal community. Finally, they were adopted by the Supreme Court by an eight to one vote. The rule against advisory opinions is only slightly more violated by giving weight to this vote than it would have been had Congress not vetoed these provisions, and had they become "Rules," rather than "standards."

As its commentary indicates, the Advisory Committee in drafting the privilege rules was for the most part restating the law applied in the federal courts. These rules or standards, therefore, are a convenient comprehensive guide to the federal law of privileges as it now stands, subject of course to a considerable flexibility of construction.

This view is reinforced by the rationale of the Supreme Court in deciding Jaffee v. Redmond, 518 U.S. 1, 116 S. Ct. 1923, 135 L. Ed. 2d 337 (1996). The Court, in finding the existence of a federal psychotherapist-patient privilege, noted with approval the inclusion of such a privilege in the proposed rules as well as the statement of the Senate Judiciary committee that its action in rejecting the proposed rules "should not be understood as disapproving any recognition of a psychiatrist-patient . . . privilege contained in the [proposed] rules." Id. at 14–15 (citing S. Rep. No. 93-1277 at 13). *See also* Imwinkelried, Draft Article V of the Federal Rules of Evidence on Privileges, One of the Most Influential Pieces of Legislation Never Enacted: The Strength of the Ingroup Loyalty of the Federal Judiciary, 58 Ala. L. Rev. 41 (2006); Imwinkelried, An Hegelian Approach to Privileges Under Federal Rule of Evidence 501: The Restrictive Thesis,

included in the proposed rules.[4] A significant question exists whether this freedom should be used to recognize and apply state privileges in cases where Rule 501 does not require such to be done.[5]

The situation with respect to cases in which state law provides the rule of decision, primarily diversity cases, is somewhat clearer. Presumably a federal court today would not, as was sometimes done prior to the enactment of Rule 501, enforce a privilege in a diversity case that is not recognized by applicable state law. A major question remains, however, as to the process by which the existence or absence of an "applicable" state privilege will be determined in conflict of law situations.

It has been argued that, given the status of Rule 501 as an Act of Congress, the federal courts, in determining the applicable

---

the Expansive Antithesis, and the Contextual Synthesis, 73 Neb. L. R. 511 (1994); Schwartz, Privileges Under The Federal Rules of Evidence—A Step Forward?, 38 U. Pitt. L. Rev. 79 (1976); Krattenmaker, Interpersonal Testimonial Privilege—A Suggested Approach to the Federal Rules, 64 Geo. L.J. 613 (1976); Federal Rules of Evidence Symposium, 49 Temp. L. Q. 860 (1976).

[4]Trammel v. U.S., 445 U.S. 40, 100 S. Ct. 906, 63 L. Ed. 2d 186 (1980) ("In rejecting the proposed rules and enacting Rule 501, Congress manifested an affirmative intention not to freeze the law of privilege. Its purpose rather was to 'provide the courts with the flexibility to develop rules of privilege on a case-by-case basis' . . ."). *See also* Imrinkelried, An Hegelian Approach to Privileges Under Federal Rule of Evidence 501: The Restrictive Thesis, the Expansive Antithesis, and the Contextual Synthesis, 73 Neb. L. R. 511 (1994), where the author describes Congressional intent on the expansion or restriction of privileges as neutral, but argues that the law of privileges should develop in light of the context of the Federal Rules of Evidence, which are biased in favor of the admissibility of evidence. For examples of federal cases recognizing new privileges, see § 75.

[5]It has been argued that Rule 501 envisions that even in federal

question cases federal courts should defer to state privilege law absent overriding federal policy to the contrary. Kaminsky, State Evidentiary Privileges for Federal Civil Litigation, 43 Ford. L. Rev. 923 (1975). The concept that state privileges should be considered in this context has received some judicial support. Lora v. Board of Ed. of City of New York, 74 F.R.D. 565 (E.D. N.Y. 1977) (Weinstein, J. "If the state holds out the expectation of protection to its citizens they should not be disappointed by a mechanical or unnecessary application of the federal rule;" but privilege denied). See also Dudley, Federalism and Federal Rule of Evidence 501: Privilege and Vertical Rule of Law, 82 Geo. L.J. 1781 (1994) where the author argues that, with a few exceptions based on overriding federal policy considerations, the law of the jurisdiction with the power to regulate the relationship or activity giving rise to the privilege should govern. *See, however*, American Civil Liberties Union of Mississippi, Inc. v. Finch, 638 F.2d 1336, 1343 (5th Cir. 1981) ("That the courts of a particular state would recognize a given privilege will not often of itself justify a federal court in applying that privilege."); Jenkins v. DeKalb County, Georgia, 242 F.R.D. 652 (N.D. Ga. 2007) (court declined to enforce state peer review privilege in federal civil rights case).

state law of privilege, are not constrained to accept state conflict of laws principles. Though this position has been supported by a number of commentators,[6] a majority of the cases decided since enactment of the Federal Rules have continued to follow the doctrine of *Klaxon Co. v. Stentor Electric Manufacturing Co.*[7] and thus to look to state choice of law rules in determining what state's privilege should be applied.[8]

Issues of the application of state or federal privilege law also arise in cases in which there are both federal and state claims. In such instances, the better practice would seem to be to consider the predominant nature of the claims and the issues to which the arguably privileged information would be relevant. Most federal courts facing that question have applied the federal law of privileges, although the problem has most commonly arisen in situations where the predominant claims are federal.[9] A few courts have considered the predominant nature of the claims and the issues to which the arguably privileged information would be relevant.[10]

---

[6]Berger, Privileges, Presumptions, and Competency of Witnesses in the Federal Court: A Federal Choice of Law Rule, 42 Brooklyn L. Rev. 417 (1976). Also supporting a federal choice of law rule, *see* Dunham, Testimonial Privileges in State and Federal Courts: A Suggested Approach, 9 Willamette L.J. 26 (1973). A contrary view is Wellborn, The Federal Rules of Evidence and the Application of State Law in the Federal Courts, 55 Tex. L. Rev. 371 (1977).

[7]Klaxon Co. v. Stentor Electric Mfg. Co., 313 U.S. 487, 61 S. Ct. 1020, 85 L. Ed. 1477 (1941).

[8]*See, e.g.,* Samuelson v. Susen, 576 F.2d 546 (3d Cir. 1978); Tartaglia v. Paul Revere Life Ins. Co., 948 F. Supp. 325 (S.D. N.Y. 1996); Anas v. Blecker, 141 F.R.D. 530 (M.D. Fla. 1992). *But see* Mitsui & Co. (U.S.A.) Inc. v. Puerto Rico Water Resources Authority, 79 F.R.D. 72 (D.P.R. 1978). *See also* Yasmin & Yaz (Drospirenone) Mktg, Sales Practice and Products Liability Litigation, 2011 WL 1375011 (S.D.Ill. 2011) (applying choice of law rules in multi-district litigation; analyzes choice of law rules in all states).

[9]*See, e.g.,* Memorial Hosp. for McHenry County v. Shadur, 664 F.2d 1058 (7th Cir. 1981); Hancock v. Dodson, 958 F.2d 1367 (6th Cir. 1992); Perrignon v. Bergen Brunswig Corp., 77 F.R.D. 455 (N.D. Cal. 1978).

[10]Garza v. Scott and White Memorial Hosp., 234 F.R.D. 617, 625 (W.D. Tex. 2005) (state peer review privilege applied to state law claims where evidence applied exclusively to those claims); Platypus Wear, Inc. v. K.D. Co., Inc., 905 F. Supp. 808 (S.D. Cal. 1995) (state privilege law applied where diversity claims predominated); Scott v. McDonald, 70 F.R.D. 568 (N.D. Ga. 1976). For a discussion of the policy considerations involved in the decision to apply either state or federal privilege law in mixed claim cases, *see* Broun, Giving Codification a Second Chance-Testimonial Privileges and the Federal Rules of Evidence, 53 Hastings L.J. 769, 810–812 (2002). *See also* Dudley, Federalism and Federal Rule of Evidence 501: Privilege and Vertical Rule of Law, 82 Geo. L.J. 1781, 1839–1840 (1994), where the author would have the decision turn primarily on the question of what jurisdiction regulated the relationship

## § 76.2   The current pattern of privilege: (b) State patterns of privilege; recognizing new privileges

State patterns in the recognition of privileges vary greatly. As developed in succeeding chapters, all states possess some form of husband-wife,[1] and attorney-client privilege.[2] All afford some protection to certain government information.[3] Most, though not all, allow at least a limited privilege to communications between physician and patient.[4] In addition several other privileges are worthy of specific mention.

Though probably not recognized at common law, a privilege protecting confidential communications between clergymen and penitents has now been adopted in all 50 states.[5] Wigmore's seemingly grudging acceptance of the privilege perhaps reflects the difficulty of justifying its existence on exclusively utilitarian grounds,[6] since at least where penitential communications are required or encouraged by religious tenets, they are likely to continue to be made irrespective of the presence or absence of evidentiary privilege. A firmer ground appears available in the inherent offensiveness of the secular power attempting to coerce an act violative of religious conscience.[7] Implementing a decent regard for religious convictions while at the same time avoiding making individual conscience the ultimate measure of testimonial obligation has proved to be attended by some difficulties. Early statutory forms of the privilege undertook to privilege only penitential communications "in the course of discipline enjoined

---

or activity giving rise to the privilege.

[Section 76.2]

[1]See Ch. 9 infra.

[2]See Ch. 10 infra.

[3]See Ch. 12 infra.

[4]See Ch. 11 infra.

[5]Walsh, The Priest–Penitent Privilege: An Hibernocentric Essay in Postcolonial Jurisprudence, 80 Ind. L.J. 1037 (2005); Comment, Striking Down the Clergyman-Communicant Statutes: Let Free Exercise of Religion Govern, 62 Ind. L.J. 397 (1987).

Concerning the privilege generally, *see* Callahan, Historical Inquiry into the Priest-Penitent Privilege, 36 Jurist 328 (1976); Hogan, A Modern Problem on the Privilege of the Confessional, 6 Loy. L. Rev. 1 (1951); Kuhlman, Communications to Clergymen—When are They Privileged?, 2

Val. U. L. Rev. 265 (1968); Reece, Confidential Communications to the Clergy, 24 Ohio St. L.J. 55 (1963); Shetreet, Exemptions and Privileges on the Grounds of Religion and Conscience, 62 Ky. L.J. 377 (1974); Developments in the Law—Privileged Communications, 98 Harv. L. Rev. 1450, 1555–1563 (1985); Who Are "Clergy" or Like Within Privilege Attaching to Communications to Clergy Members or Spiritual Advisers, 101 A.L.R.5th 619; Subject Matter and Waiver of Privilege Covering Communications to Clergy Member or Spiritual Adviser, 93 A.L.R.5th 327.

[6]8 Wigmore, Evidence § 2396 (McNaughton rev. 1961).

[7]*See* 4 Bentham, Rationale of Judicial Evidence 588 (J.S. Mill ed. 1827) ("But with any toleration, a coercion of this nature is altogether inconsistent and incompatible.").

by the church" to which the communicant belongs.[8] This limitation, however, has been urged to be unduly, perhaps unconstitutionally, preferential to the Roman Catholic and a few other churches.[9] The statutes have, accordingly, generally been broadened. Uniform Rule of Evidence 505, as promulgated in 1974, is typical in extending the privilege generally to "confidential communication[s] by a person to a clergyman in his professional character as spiritual advisor."[10]

The states are split on the question of who can waive the clergyman-penitent privilege.[11] Some provide that the privilege belongs only to the communicant,[12] others provide that it belongs to the clergy member[13] and still others hold that it belongs to both.[14]

---

[8]The privilege still appears in this form in some statute books. *See, e.g.,* Ariz.Rev.Stat. § 12-2233. *See also* State v. Martin, 137 Wash. 2d 774, 975 P.2d 1020 (1999) where the court interpreted language in this form to require only that clergy member be enjoined to receive confidential communications and to provide counseling.

[9]*See* Kuhlman, Communications to Clergymen—When are They Privileged?, 2 Val. U. L. Rev. 265 (1968)

[10]The language of the Uniform Rule was modified in 1999 to read: An individual has a privilege to refuse to disclose and to prevent another from disclosing a confidential communication by the individual to a cleric in the cleric's professional capacity as spiritual adviser. Unif. R. Evid. 505. *See also* Scott v. Hammock, 870 P.2d 947 (Utah 1994), where the court held that nonpenitential communications were within the Utah privilege if intended to be confidential and made for the purpose of seeking spiritual counseling from a cleric acting pursuant to the discipline of his or her church.

Constitutional questions have not been not fully resolved concerning the application of the privilege under various clauses of the United States Constitution, including the free exercise and establishment clauses. See the discussion in Mockaitis v. Harcleroad, 104 F.3d 1522 (9th Cir.

1997), where the court enjoined state officials from monitoring prison confessions made to Roman Catholic priests, relying both on the Fourth Amendment and on the Religious Freedom Restoration Act (RFRA). *See also* Varner v. Stovall, 500 F.3d 491, 494–99 (6th Cir. 2007) (state did not violate establishment clause in refusing to apply clergy-penitent privilege to private journal entries); In re Lifschutz, 2 Cal. 3d 415, 85 Cal. Rptr. 829, 467 P.2d 557 (1970). In *Lifschutz* the court avoided what it characterized as a "potentially difficult constitutional question" under the establishment clause by holding that only one seeking material protected by the privilege has standing to raise the constitutional issue.

[11]See the compilation of statutes in Comment, Should Clergy Hold the Priest-Penitent Privilege?, 82 Marq. L. Rev. 171, 187–190 (1998).

[12]*See, e.g.,* Nicholson v. Wittig, 832 S.W.2d 681 (Tex. App. Houston 1st Dist. 1992). *See also* De'udy v. De'udy, 130 Misc. 2d 168, 495 N.Y.S.2d 616 (Sup 1985) (extended discussion of history and rationale of privilege, finding no independent privilege in clergyman).

[13]*See, e.g.,* Nestle v. Com., 22 Va. App. 336, 470 S.E.2d 133 (1996). In State v. Szemple, 135 N.J. 406, 640 A.2d 817 (1994), the court reached the same result. The New Jersey rule was amended the same year to provide

One of the most persistently advocated privileges for many years, but particularly during the past decade, has been one shielding journalists from being testimonially required in court to divulge the identities of news sources.[15] The rationale asserted for this privilege is analogous to that underlying the long-standing governmental informers privilege and is exclusively utilitarian in character.[16] Thus, it is contended that the news sources essential to supply the public's need for information will be "dried up" if their identities are subject to compelled disclosure.[17] Numerous attempts to have the privilege enacted by federal statute have failed, and it is not one of those privileges that was incorporated into the Revised Uniform Rules of Evidence (1974).[18] Moreover, the argument that a journalist's privilege is constitutionally to be implied from the First Amendment

---

specifically that both the clergyman and the penitent hold the privilege. N.J. Stat. Ann. § 2A:84A-23. *See also* Note, 25 Seton Hall L. Rev. 1591 (1995).

[14]*See, e.g.,* People v. Burnidge, 279 Ill. App. 3d 127, 216 Ill. Dec. 19, 664 N.E.2d 656 (2d Dist. 1996).

[15]Cases and statutes are collected in 8 Wigmore, Evidence § 2286, nn. 9, 21 (McNaughton rev. 1961); Imwinkelried, The New Wigmore: Evidentiary Privileges § 7.5, App. D (2d ed. 2010). The innumerable law review treatments include: Blasi, The Newsman's Privilege: An Empirical Study, 70 Mich. L. Rev. 229 (1971); Eckhardt & McKey, Reporter's Privilege: An Update, 12 Conn. L. Rev. 434 (1980); Fargo and McAdoo, Common Law or Shield Law? How Rule 501 Could Solve the Journalist's Privilege Problem, 33 Wm. Mitchell L. Rev. 1347 (2007); Monk, Evidentiary Privilege for Journalists' Sources: Theory and Statutory Protection, 51 Mo. L. Rev. 1 (1986); Comment, Piercing the Shield: Reporter Privilege in Minnesota Following State v. Turner, 82 Minn. L. Rev. 1563 (1998); Note, 80 Yale L.J. 336 (1970). Some recent state court decisions with regard to the privilege include Miller v. Superior Court, 21 Cal. 4th 883, 89 Cal. Rptr. 2d 834, 986 P.2d 170, 178–79 (1999) (newsperson's shield law protected unpublished information, whether confidential or not, from subpoena by State); Gordon

v. Boyles, 9 P.3d 1106, 1117–20 (Colo. 2000) (qualified journalist's privilege applied in defamation case); People v. Pawlaczyk, 189 Ill. 2d 177, 244 Ill. Dec. 13, 724 N.E.2d 901, 912 (2000) (reporters properly divested of statutory privilege based upon compelling interest of grand jury proceeding).

[16]The nature of the objective professed would appear to necessitate an absolute, or almost absolute privilege. *See* Note, 80 Yale L.J. 336 (1970).

[17]For an extended articulation of the asserted justification for the privilege, *see* U.S. v. Criden, 633 F.2d 346, 355–56 (3d Cir. 1980). *See also* In re Madden, 151 F.3d 125 (3d Cir. 1998) (wrestling commentator was an entertainer, not a journalist entitled to qualified privilege); Alexander, Looking Out for the Watchdogs: A Legislative Proposal Limiting the Newsgathering Privilege to Journalists in the Greatest Need of Protection for Sources and Information, 20 Yale L. & Pol'y Rev. 97 (2002).

[18]No journalist privilege is included in the revised Uniform Rules, just as none was included in the Supreme Court's version of the Federal Rules. Federal statutes do not deal with the subject, though numerous bills have been introduced. For a compilation of state statutes, *see* Caldero v. Tribune Pub. Co., 98 Idaho 288, 562 P.2d 791, 794 n.1 (1977). *See also* Shield Laws, Council of State Governments

guarantee of a free press was seemingly rejected by the Supreme Court in *Branzburg v. Hayes*.[19] However, taking note that this rejection did not command an absolute majority of the Court,[20] a substantial number of lower federal courts have undertaken to recognize a qualified journalist's privilege[21] that may be penetrated by appropriate showings on the part of the party desiring the privileged information.[22] Though occasionally referred to as a common law creation, despite *Branzburg*, the privilege has generally been said to derive from the First Amendment.[23] Some form of privilege for journalists has been created by statute,[24] nor in a few cases by judicial decision,[25] in a substantial number of states. A few state courts have also found the privilege to be

------

(1973).

[19]Branzburg v. Hayes, 408 U.S. 665, 92 S. Ct. 2646, 33 L. Ed. 2d 626 (1972). *See also* Herbert v. Lando, 441 U.S. 153, 99 S. Ct. 1635, 60 L. Ed. 2d 115 (1979) (rejecting First Amendment "editorial process" privilege.)

[20]Mr. Justice Powell, who cast the deciding vote in Branzburg, authored a concurring opinion favoring a "balancing test," i.e., a qualified privilege. This fact has not been lost upon the lower federal courts. *See* Riley v. City of Chester, 612 F.2d 708 (3d Cir. 1979) (adopting Powell formulation).

[21]U.S. v. Burke, 700 F.2d 70 (2d Cir. 1983); Ashcraft v. Conoco, Inc., 218 F.3d 282, 287 (4th Cir. 2000) (qualified privilege for confidential sources based on First Amendment); Cervantes v. Time, Inc., 464 F.2d 986 (8th Cir. 1972); Silkwood v. Kerr-McGee Corp., 563 F.2d 433 (10th Cir. 1977); U.S. v. Ahn, 231 F.3d 26, 37 (D.C. Cir. 2000) (qualified journalist's privilege not overcome where reporter's testimony was not "essential and crucial" to defendant's case); Lee v. Department of Justice, 401 F. Supp. 2d 123, 135–42 (D.D.C. 2005) (no common law reporter's privilege). There is a split in the circuits to whether even a qualified privilege should apply to nonconfidential information. *Compare, e.g.*, U.S. v. Smith, 135 F.3d 963 (5th Cir. 1998) (no privilege) *with* Gonzales v. National Broadcasting Co., Inc., 194

F.3d 29, 33–35 (2d Cir. 1999) (privilege).

[22]In the Third Circuit the requirements for overcoming the privilege are said to be three:

"First, the movant must demonstrate that he has made an effort to obtain the information from other sources. Second, he must demonstrate that the only access to the information sought is through the journalist and her sources. Finally, the movant must persuade the Court that the information sought is crucial to the claim." United States v. Cuthbertson, 651 F.2d 189, 195–6 (3d Cir. 1981).

[23]*See, e.g.*, Ashcraft v. Conoco, Inc., 218 F.3d 282 (4th Cir. 2000). The source of the privilege has obvious implications for its potential applicability to diversity and state litigation. *See* The New York Times Co. v. Gonzales, 459 F.3d 160, 168–74 (2d Cir. 2006) (any common law or First Amendment privilege would be qualified and overcome under these facts); Miller v. Transamerican Press, Inc., 621 F.2d 721 (5th Cir. 1980) (stating First Amendment privilege available in diversity case but holding discovery permissible on facts).

[24]Cases and statutes are collected in 8 Wigmore, Evidence § 2286, nn. 9, 21 (McNaughton rev. 1961); Imwinkelried, The New Wigmore: Evidentiary Privileges § 7.5, App. D (2d ed. 2010).

[25]*See, e.g.*, Opinion of the Justices, 117 N.H. 390, 373 A.2d 642 (1977).

implied by state constitutional provision.[26] Unlike other professional privileges, it is generally conceived as belonging to the journalist, to be claimed or waived irrespective of the wishes of the news source.

Communications to accountants are privileged in perhaps a third of the states.[27] This privilege is most closely analogous to that for attorney-client,[28] though the social objective to be furthered is arguably a distinguishable and lesser one.

In recent years much attention has been bestowed upon the plight of the rape victim, and some sort of sexual assault victim-counselor privilege has been created by statute or court decision in a substantial number of states.[29] Such a privilege can claim a

---

[26]Matter of Contempt of Wright, 108 Idaho 418, 700 P.2d 40 (1985) (three of five separate opinions finding state constitutional privilege); State ex rel. Green Bay Newspaper Co. v. Circuit Court, Branch 1, Brown County, 113 Wis. 2d 411, 335 N.W.2d 367 (1983) (recognizing and applying qualified journalist's privilege based on state constitution); State v. Rinaldo, 36 Wash. App. 86, 673 P.2d 614 (Div. 1 1983) (recognizing "absolute" journalist's privilege based upon state constitution).

[27]See statutes listed in Imwinkelried, The New Wigmore: Evidentiary Privileges App. D (2d ed. 2010). See also Inspector General of U.S. Dept. of Agriculture v. Glenn, 122 F.3d 1007 (11th Cir. 1997) (no accountant-client privilege under federal law); Sears, Roebuck & Co. v. Gussin, 350 Md. 552, 714 A.2d 188 (1998) (thorough discussion of privilege in Maryland); Notes, 28 Okla. L. Rev. 637 (1975), 46 N.C. L. Rev. 419 (1968). And see U.S. v. Kovel, 296 F.2d 918 (2d Cir. 1961) (accountant as attorney's agent; disclosures privileged).

I.R.C. 7525, enacted in 1998, provides for a privilege with regard to communications between taxpayers and federal authorized tax practitioners, including certified public accountants. See U.S. v. Frederick, 182 F.3d 496, 500 (7th Cir. 1999) (tax

practitioner's privilege inapplicable where practitioner engaged in other than lawyer's work); Gillet, The Federal Tax Practitioner-Client Privilege (I.R.C. Section 7525): A Shield to Cloak Confidential Communications or a Dagger for Both the Practitioner and the Client?, 70 UMKC L. Rev. 129 (2001). See also Cavallaro v. U.S., 284 F.3d 236, 249 (1st Cir. 2002) (documents generated by accountant not within attorney-client privilege where accountant's services not necessary, or at least not highly useful, for the effective consultation between client and lawyer).

[28]But see U.S. v. Arthur Young & Co., 465 U.S. 805, 104 S. Ct. 1495, 79 L. Ed. 2d 826 (1984) (reversing court of appeals decision and finding no "work product" privilege for public accountants).

[29]In re Crisis Connection, Inc., 949 N.E.2d 789 (Ind. 2011) (applying state victim-counselor privilege); Albuquerque Rape Crisis Center v. Blackmer, 2005-NMSC-032, 138 N.M. 398, 120 P.3d 820 (2005) (upholding victim-counselor privilege); Note, The Constitutionality of an Absolute Privilege for Rape Crisis Counseling, 30 B.C. L. Rev. 411 (1989). See also discussion of related privileges in Jaffee v. Redmond, 518 U.S. 1, 116 S. Ct. 1923, 135 L. Ed. 2d 337 (1996).

substantial basis in public policy, but inevitably comes into conflict with the constitutional rights of the criminal defendant.[30]

Even broader acceptance has been achieved by the principle that protection by evidentiary privilege is necessary for the deliberations of medical review committees.[31]

There is occasional recognition of privilege for communications to confidential clerks, stenographers and other "employees" generally, school teachers, school counselors, participants in group psychotherapy, nurses, marriage counselors, private detectives, and social workers.[32] A privilege for parent-minor child communications has been recommended[33] but has received little judicial approval.[34] Privileges for scientific researcher-subject[35] and self-critical analysis[36] have fared only somewhat better.

---

[30]See § 74.2 supra.

[31]Cruger v. Love, 599 So. 2d 111 (Fla. 1992); Stalker v. Abraham, 69 A.D.3d 1172, 897 N.Y.S.2d 250 (3d Dep't 2010) (testimony from medical review committee member protected in medical malpractice case); Trinity Medical Center, Inc. v. Holum, 544 N.W.2d 148 (N.D. 1996); HCA Health Services of Virginia, Inc. v. Levin, 260 Va. 215, 530 S.E.2d 417, 420 (2000) (discussion of scope of privilege); Cate, Physician Peer Review, 20 J. Legal Med. 479 (1999); Comment, The Medical Review Committee Privilege: A Jurisdictional Study, 67 N.C. L. Rev. 179 (1988) (noting the existence of some form of such a privilege in 46 states). See also Virmani v. Novant Health Inc., 259 F.3d 284 (4th Cir. 2001) (no peer review privilege where information sought by physician against hospital for discrimination claim).

[32]See 8 Wigmore, Evidence § 2286 (McNaughton rev. 1961); Imwinkelried, The New Wigmore: Evidentiary Privileges § 6.2.8 (2d ed. 2010). See also Bearden v. Boone, 693 S.W.2d 25 (Tex. App. Amarillo 1985) (communications by private investigator to attorney or to client privileged under attorney-client privilege, though not under local statute affording limited protection to information acquired by private investigators).

[33]See H.R. 3577, 105th Cong., 2nd Sess. (1998); S. 1721, 105th Cong., 2nd Sess. (1998). Bauer, Recognition of a Parent-Child Testimonial Privilege, 23 St. L. U. L.J. 676 (1979); Coburn, Child-Parent Communications; Spare the Privilege and Spoil the Child, 74 Dick. L. Rev. 599 (1970); Kandoian, The Parent-Child Privilege and the Parent-Child Crime, 36 Me. L. Rev. 59 (1984); Kraft, The Parent-Child Testimonial Privilege: Who's Minding the Kids?, 18 Fam. L. Q. 505 (1985); Stanton, Child-Parent Privilege for Confidential Communications: An Examination and Proposal, 16 Family L. Q. 1 (1982); Stern, Don't Tell Mom The Babysitter's Dead: Arguments for Federal Parent-Child Privilege and a Proposal to Amend Article V, 99 Geo. L.J. 605 (2011); Note, Parent-Child Loyalty and Testimonial Privilege, 100 Harv. L. Rev. 910 (1986).

[34]See, e.g., In re Grand Jury, 35 V.I. 516, 103 F.3d 1140 (3d Cir. 1997) (rejecting privilege); U.S. v. Davies, 768 F.2d 893 (7th Cir. 1985) (collecting numerous federal and state authorities rejecting the privilege); In re Grand Jury Subpoena, 430 Mass. 590, 722 N.E.2d 450, 451 (2000) (court refused to create a child-parent privilege, deferring to legislature). A few cases have recognized the privilege. See In re Agosto, 553 F. Supp. 1298 (D. Nev. 1983); Application of A and M, 61 A.D.2d 426, 403 N.Y.S.2d 375

495

An attempt to obtain recognition of a federal privilege protecting against disclosure of confidential peer review materials of academic institutions has been rejected by the Supreme Court.[37]

## § 77   The future of privilege

Despite the rejection by the Congress of the Proposed Federal Rules of Evidence relating to privilege and the resultant failure to effect substantive changes in this area, several concurrent developments may portend certain new directions in the development of the law of privilege.

The vehemence of the attacks leveled at certain of the proposed Federal Rules on privilege suggests that the basic concept of evidentiary privilege, despite its deleterious consequences for the administration of justice, will not be abandoned in the foreseeable future. Many of these attacks, predictably, came from groups specifically interested in the preservation or creation of particular privileges.[1] Much more significantly, the cause of privilege was also espoused by an unprecedentedly large segment of the academic community.[2] The latter response was in large part precipitated by a generalized concern over the increasing intrusive-

---

(4th Dep't 1978).

[35]Deitchman v. E.R. Squibb & Sons, Inc., 740 F.2d 556 (7th Cir. 1984). *See* Weinstein & Wimberly, Secrecy in Law and Science, 23 Cardozo L. Rev. 1 (2001); Delgado & Millen, God, Galileo, and Government: Toward Constitutional Protection for Scientific Inquiry, 53 Wash. L. Rev. 349 (1978); Nejelski & Lerman, A Researcher-Subject Testimonial Privilege, 1971 Wis. L. Rev. 1085; O'Neil, Court-Ordered Disclosure of Academic Research: A Clash of Values of Science and Law, 59-SUM Law & Contemp. Probs. 35 (1996); 81 A.L.R.Fed. 897. *See also* Wilkinson v. F.B.I., 111 F.R.D. 432 (C.D. Cal. 1986) (doubting the existence of the privilege).

[36]*Compare* Reichhold Chemicals, Inc. v. Textron, Inc., 157 F.R.D. 522 (N.D. Fla. 1994) (recognizing qualified privilege) *with* Spencer Sav. Bank, SLA v. Excell Mortg. Corp., 960 F. Supp. 835 (D.N.J. 1997) (refusing to recognize privilege). *See also* Lara v. Tri-State Drilling, Inc., 504 F. Supp. 2d 1323 (N.D. Ga. 2007) (court finds no self-critical analysis privilege under

state law outside of statutory medical peer-review privilege); Zoom Imaging, L.P. v. St. Luke's Hosp. and Health Network, 513 F. Supp. 2d 411, 417 (E.D. Pa. 2007) (court rejects application of self-critical analysis privilege to protect outside consultant's organizational study of radiology practice); Vandergrift, The Privilege of Self-Critical Analysis: A Survey of the Law, 60 Alb. L. Rev. 171 (1996); Comment, Critical Analysis Privilege for Products Liability: What Is It and How Can It Be Achieved in Wisconsin, 1999 Wis. L. Rev. 119.

[37]University of Pennsylvania v. E.E.O.C., 493 U.S. 182, 110 S. Ct. 577, 107 L. Ed. 2d 571 (1990).

**[Section 77]**

[1]*See generally* Hearings Before the Special Subcommittee on Reform of Federal Criminal Laws of the House Committee on the Judiciary on Proposed Rules of Evidence, 93d Cong., 1st Sess., ser. 2 (1973).

[2]This reaction was expressed not only in communications to Congress, id. at 195, 240, but in a variety of

ness of modern society into human privacy, a concern reflected in several Supreme Court decisions conferring constitutional status upon certain aspects of privacy.[3]

While the ultimate strategic significance of evidentiary privilege as a bastion for defending privacy values may be doubted, the focus on privacy or on similar humanistic justifications as an operative basis for the recognition of many privileges is believed to be a healthy and overdue development. At the optimum, such a focus may offer a theoretical basis for a more satisfactory accommodation than has heretofore been achieved between the legitimate demands for freedom against unwarranted intrusion on the one hand and the basic requirements of the judicial system on the other.

The traditionally felt need, stemming largely from Wigmore's dictum, to justify all privileges in terms of their utilitarian value leads not only to the assertion of highly questionable sociological premises but also affords little prospect for meaningful reconciliation of values in this area. Traditional evidentiary privilege necessarily paints with a broad brush since the achievement of utilitarian objectives requires privileges that are essentially absolute in character.[4] But if it is recognized that not all privileges are based on identical considerations or will have identical effects if allowed in litigation, it will be seen that not all privileges need make such large demands.[5] If the object aimed at is not the inducement of conduct in certain relationships but the protection of individual privacy from unnecessary or trivial intrusions, the implementation of the privilege is amenable to the finer touch of the specific solution. Thus, a decision in the particular case that

---

publications. *See, e.g.*, Black, The Marital and Physician Privileges—Reprint of a Letter to a Congressman, 1975 Duke L.J. 45; Krattenmaker, Testimonial Privilege in Federal Courts: An Alternative to the Federal Rules of Evidence, 62 Geo. L.J. 61 (1973).

[3]*E.g.*, Griswold v. Connecticut, 381 U.S. 479, 85 S. Ct. 1678, 14 L. Ed. 2d 510 (1965); Roe v. Wade, 410 U.S. 113, 93 S. Ct. 705, 35 L. Ed. 2d 147 (1973).

[4]*See* Note, 91 Harv. L. Rev. 464, 468 (1977) (excellent though critical statement of the rationale of absolute privilege). The United States Supreme Court, emphasizing the utilitarian justifications for the attorney-client and psychotherapist-patient privi-

leges, has maintained that an "uncertain privilege . . . is little better than no privilege at all." Upjohn Co. v. U.S., 449 U.S. 383, 393, 101 S. Ct. 677, 66 L. Ed. 2d 584 (1981) (attorney-client); Jaffee v. Redmond, 518 U.S. 1, 18, 116 S. Ct. 1923, 135 L. Ed. 2d 337 (1996) (psychotherapist-patient).

[5]*See* Saltzberg, Privileges and Professionals: Lawyers and Psychiatrists, 66 Va. L. Rev. 597, 622 (1980) ("Privileges are not all equally important; they vary with the interests they protect and the policies they promote."); Scallen, Relational and Informational Privileges and the Case of the Mysterious Mediation Privilege, 38 Loy. L.A. L. Rev. 537 (2004) (informational and relational privileges should receive different treatment).

sufficiently grave considerations demand disclosure will, to be sure, impact adversely on the privilege holder, but no more extended societal interest will be impaired.

Another factor may also contribute to a greater use of qualified or conditional privileges that are subject to suspension on ad hoc determination of particular need for evidence in a given case. It is already clear that the law of privilege must to some extent accommodate to the developing rights of criminal defendants under the Confrontation and Compulsory Process Clauses.[6] At the same time it is desirable, whenever possible, to avoid a choice between the automatic and total override of privilege whenever a criminal defendant asserts a need for privileged matter, and the dismissal of the charges if the privilege is to be sustained. At least in those instances where accomplishment of the privilege objective does not necessitate absolute protection, an in camera weighing of the potential significance of the matter sought as against the considerations of privacy underlying the privilege may represent a desirable compromise.

Though necessarily entailing a certain amount of procedural inconvenience and a considerable amount of judicial discretion, this solution has recommended itself to a number of commentators and courts. It is perhaps reasonable to predict that an increased involvement of judges in the general area of privacy and confidentiality may be in the making.

---

[6]See § 74.2 supra.

# Chapter 9

# The Privilege for Marital Communications

### § 78    History and background, and kindred rules[1]

We are dealing here with a late offshoot of an ancient tree. The older branches are discussed in another chapter.[2] Those earlier rules, to be sharply distinguished from the present doctrine, are first, the rule that the spouse of a party or person interested is disqualified from testifying in favor of the other spouse, and second, the privilege of a party against having the party's husband or wife called as an adverse witness. These two earlier rules forbid the calling of the spouse as a witness at all, for or against the party, regardless of the actual testimony to be elicited, whereas the privilege presently discussed is limited to a certain class of testimony, namely communications between the spouses or more broadly in some states, information gained on account of the marital relation.

The movement for procedural reform in England in the first half of the 1800s found expression in the evidence field in agitation for the break up of the system of disqualification of parties and spouses. One of the auxiliary reasons that had been given to

---

**[Section 78]**

[1]8 Wigmore, Evidence §§ 2332–2341 (McNaughton rev. 1961); Imwinkelried, The New Wigmore: Evidentiary Privileges § 6.2.1 (2d ed. 2010); Developments in the Law—Privileged Communications, 98 Harv. L. Rev. 1450, 1563–1571 (1985); 81 Am. Jur. 2d, Witnesses §§ 284 to 324; 98 C.J.S., Witnesses §§ 299 to 315.

[2]See § 66 supra.

justify the disqualification of spouses was that of preserving marital confidences.[3] As to the disqualification of spouses the reform was largely accomplished by the Evidence Amendment Act, 1853. On the eve of this legislation, Greenleaf, writing in this country in 1842, clearly announced the existence of a distinct privilege for marital communications, and this pronouncement was echoed in England by Best in 1849,[4] though seemingly there was little or no support for such a view in the English decisions.[5] Moreover, the Second Report of 1853 of the Commissioners on Common Law Procedure, after rejecting the arguments for the outmoded rules of disqualification, calls attention to the special danger of "alarm and unhappiness occasioned to society by . . . compelling the public disclosure of confidential communications between husband and wife . . ." and declares that "[a]ll communications between them should be held to be privileged."[6]

However, though the policy supporting a privilege for marital communications had thus been distinctly pointed out, there had been little occasion for its judicial recognition, since the wider disqualifications of the spouses of parties left small possibility for the question of the existence of such a privilege to arise.[7]

Nevertheless, the English Act of 1853, mentioned above, after it abolished the disqualification of husbands and wives of the parties, enacted that "no husband shall be compellable to disclose any communication made to him by his wife during the marriage, and no wife shall be compellable to disclose any communication made to her by her husband during the marriage."[8] Moreover, nearly all the states in this country, while making spouses competent to testify, have included provisions disabling them from testifying to communications between them.[9]

In the light of this history the Court of Appeal in England has

---

[3]See 8 Wigmore, Evidence § 2333 (McNaughton rev. 1961); Taylor, Evidence, 899 (1848) (recounting this as a reason given but rejecting it as "too large"), quoted Shenton v. Tyler, L.R. 1939 Ch.D. 620, 634.

[4]See the citations to these early editions of Greenleaf and Best in Shenton v. Tyler, L.R. 1939 Ch.D. 620, 633, 634.

[5]The English decisions before 1853 are carefully dissected in the opinion of Greene, M.R. in Shenton v. Tyler, L.R. 1939 Ch.D. 620.

[6]See quotation from this report, 8 Wigmore, Evidence § 2332 (McNaughton rev. 1961).

[7]See 8 Wigmore, Evidence § 2333 (McNaughton rev. 1961).

[8]St. 16 & 17 Vict. c. 83, § 3.

[9]See, e.g., Cal. Evid. Code §§ 980 to 987:

§ 980. Privilege for confidential marital communications.

Subject to Section 912 [waiver] and except as otherwise provided in this article, a spouse (or his guardian or conservator when he has a guardian or conservator), whether or not a party, has a privilege during the marital relationship and afterwards to refuse to disclose, and to prevent another from disclosing, a communication if he claims the privilege and the communication was made in confidence between

denied that there was any common law privilege for marital communications.[10] In this country, however, the courts have frequently said that the statutes protecting marital communications from disclosure are declaratory of the common law.[11] Moreover, some courts have even held the "common law" rule to be in

---

him and the other spouse while they were husband and wife.

§ 981. Exception: Crime or fraud.

There is no privilege under this article if the communication was made, in whole or in part, to enable or aid anyone to commit or plan to commit a crime or a fraud.

§ 982. Exception: Commitment or similar proceeding.

There is no privilege under this article in a proceeding to commit either spouse or otherwise place him or his property, or both, under the control of another because of his alleged mental or physical condition.

§ 983. Exception: Proceeding to establish competence.

There is no privilege under this article in a proceeding brought by or on behalf of either spouse to establish his competence.

§ 984. Exception: Proceeding between spouses.

There is no privilege under this article in:

(a) A proceeding brought by or on behalf of one spouse against the other spouse.

(b) A proceeding between a surviving spouse and a person who claims through the deceased spouse, regardless of whether such claim is by testate or intestate succession or by inter vivos transaction.

§ 985. Exception: Certain criminal proceedings.

There is no privilege under this article in a criminal proceeding in which one spouse is charged with:

(a) A crime committed at any time against the person or property of the other spouse or of a child of either.

(b) A crime committed at any time against the person or property of a third person committed in the course of committing a crime against the person or property of the other spouse.

(c) Bigamy.

(d) A crime defined by Section 270 or 270a of the Penal Code. [Nonsupport of child or wife.]

§ 986. Exception: Juvenile court proceeding.

There is no privilege under this article in a proceeding under the Juvenile Court Law, . . . .

§ 987. Exception: Communication offered by spouse who is criminal defendant.

There is no privilege under this article in a criminal proceeding in which the communication is offered in evidence by a defendant who is one of the spouses between whom the communication was made.

N.Y. CPLR 4502 provides, in part:

\* \* \*

(b) Confidential communication privileged. A husband or wife shall not be required, or, without consent of the other if living, allowed, to disclose a confidential communication made by one to the other during marriage.

*See also* Imwinkelried, The New Wigmore: Evidentiary Privileges App. D (2d ed. 2010); Note, The Marital Privilege in the Twenty-First Century, 32 U. Mem. L. Rev. 137, 169–77 (2001) for compilations of state statutes with regard to both marital privileges.

[10]Shenton v. Tyler, L.R. 1939 Ch. D. 620; *see* Notes, 55 Law Q. Rev. 329, Holdsworth, 56 Law Q. Rev. 137. In this case the court held that the English statute, quoted at note 8, supra, providing that "husbands" and "wives" shall not be compellable to testify to communication, did not apply to exempt a surviving widow from interrogation as to conversations with her husband claimed to have created a secret trust in favor of the plaintiff, a third person.

[11]Hopkins v. Grimshaw, 165 U.S. 342, 17 S. Ct. 401, 41 L. Ed. 739 (1897); Hagerman v. Wigent, 108 Mich.

effect without benefit of statute,[12] at least until legislatively abrogated.[13]

In addition to the vitality that it has displayed in the courts, the rule discussed here has been viewed by some legal commentators as the most defensible of the various forms of marital privilege. However, Federal Rule of Evid. 505 as approved by the Supreme Court but deleted by the Congress, recognized no privilege for confidential communications between spouses, limiting the privilege to that of an accused in a criminal proceeding to prevent his spouse from testifying against him.[14] The marital privilege under the Revised Uniform Rules, limited under the 1974 version of those rules to a privilege of the accused to prevent disclosure of confidential communications, was subsequently broadened by amendment of Uniform Rule of Evidence 504.[15] The revised rule recognizes a privilege on the part of a spouse to re-

---

192, 65 N.W. 756, 757 (1896); Gjesdahl v. Harmon, 175 Minn. 414, 221 N.W. 639, 641 (1928); 98 C.J.S., Witnesses § 299.

[12]Arnold v. State, 353 So. 2d 524 (Ala. 1977) (common law marital communications privilege recognized in presence of statute codifying marital privilege but containing no communications privilege).

[13]See State v. Angell, 122 R.I. 160, 405 A.2d 10 (1979) (holding common law privilege impliedly repealed in criminal cases; statute relating to competency of spouses in civil cases contained communications provision, while similar statute for criminal cases did not). But compare Burton v. State, 501 S.W.2d 814 (Tenn. Crim. App. 1973) (retaining communications privilege under similar statutory configuration).

[14]Deleted Rule 505, 56 F.R.D. 244, read:

(a) General Rule of Privilege. An accused in a criminal proceeding has a privilege to prevent his spouse from testifying against him.

(b) Who May Claim the Privilege. The privilege may be claimed by the accused or by the spouse on his behalf. The authority of the spouse to do so is presumed in the absence of evidence to the contrary.

(c) Exceptions. There is no privilege under this rule (1) in proceedings in which one spouse is charged with a crime against the person or property of the other or of a child of either, or with a crime against the person or property of a third person committed in the course of committing a crime against the other, or (2) as to matters occurring prior to the marriage, or (3) in proceedings in which a spouse is charged with importing an alien for prostitution or other immoral purpose in violation of 8 U.S.C. § 1328, with transporting a female in interstate commerce for immoral purpose or other offense in violation of 18 U.S.C. §§ 2421 to 2424, or with violation of other similar statutes.

[15]Unif. R. Evid. 504 (1986). The Rule, as amended in 1999 without significant substantive change from the 1986 version, reads:

Rule 504. Spousal Privilege.

(a) Confidential communication. A communication is confidential if it is made privately by an individual to the individual's spouse and is not intended for disclosure to any other person.

(b) Marital communications. An individual has a privilege to refuse to testify and to prevent the individual's spouse or former spouse from testifying as to any confidential communication made by the individual to the spouse during their marriage. The privilege may be waived only by the individual holding the privilege or by the holder's guardian or conservator, or the individual's personal rep-

fuse to testify against an accused spouse in a criminal proceeding[16] as well as one for confidential communications in criminal and civil cases. Under Federal Rule of Evidence 501, as adopted by Congress, the federal courts have continued to recognize a marital communications privilege as effective by common law.[17]

## § 79   What is privileged: Communications only, or acts and facts?[1]

Greenleaf, arguing in 1842 for a privilege distinct from marital incompetency, and furnishing the inspiration for the later statutes by which the privilege was formally enacted, spoke only of "communications" and "conversations."[2] Those later statutes themselves (except one or two)[3] sanctioned the privilege for "com-

---

resentative if the individual is deceased.

(c) Spousal testimony in criminal proceeding. The spouse of an accused in a criminal proceeding has a privilege to refuse to testify against the accused spouse.

(d) Exceptions. There is no privilege under this rule:

(1) in any civil proceeding in which the spouses are adverse parties;

(2) in any criminal proceeding in which an unrefuted showing is made that the spouses acted jointly in the commission of the crime charged;

(3) in any proceeding in which one spouse is charged with a crime or tort against the person or property of the other, a minor child of either, an individual residing in the household of either, or a third person if the crime or tort is committed in the course of committing a crime or tort against the other spouse, a minor child of either spouse, or an individual residing in the household of either spouse; or

(4) in any other proceeding, in the discretion of the court, if the interests of a minor child of either spouse may be adversely affected by invocation of the privilege.

[16]The cognate privilege for adverse spousal testimony is treated in § 66 supra.

[17]Cases are collected in Marital privilege under Rule 501 of Federal Rules of Evidence, 46 A.L.R. Fed. 735.

**[Section 79]**

[1]8 Wigmore, Evidence § 2337 (McNaughton rev. 1961); Imwinkelried, The New Wigmore: Evidentiary Privileges §§ 6.7.1, 6.7.3 (2d ed. 2010); 35 Corn. L. Q. 187 (1949), 57 J. Crim. L. & Cr. 205 (1956), 34 Minn. L. Rev. 257 (1950), 3 Vand. L. Rev. 656 (1950), 35 Va. L. Rev. 1111; "Communications" Within Testimonial Privilege of Confidential Communications Between Husband and Wife as Including Knowledge Derived from Observation by One Spouse of Acts of Other Spouse, 23 A.L.R.6th 1.

[2]See § 78 supra.

[3]Ohio Rev.Code § 2317.02 ("communication made by one to the other, or an act done by either in the presence of the other, during coverture unless . . . in the known presence or hearing of a third person competent to be a witness; . . . ."); Tenn.Code Ann. § 24-1-201 (". . . neither husband nor wife shall testify to any matter that occurred between them by virtue of or in consequence of the marital relation"; note that the current version of this statute refers only to "confidential communications").

munications" and for nothing beyond.[4] Accordingly it would seem that the privilege should be limited to expressions intended by one spouse to convey a meaning or message to the other. These expressions may be by words, oral, written or in sign-language, or by expressive acts, as where the husband opens a trunk before his wife and points out objects in the trunk to her.[5] Moreover, the protection of the privilege will shield against indirect disclosure of the communication,[6] as where a husband is asked for his wife's whereabouts which he learned only from her secret communication.[7] It seems, nevertheless, that logic and policy should cause the courts to halt with communications as the furthest boundary of the privilege, and a substantial number have held steadfast at this line.[8]

---

[4]See the statutes compiled in 2 Wigmore, Evidence § 488 (Chadbourn rev. 1979).

[5]*See* State v. Smith, 384 A.2d 687 (Me. 1978) (husband's display of items to wife was, under circumstances, said by court to be equivalent to assertion, "I have stolen a gun and a camera"). *See also* U.S. v. Bahe, 128 F.3d 1440 (10th Cir. 1997) (sexual touching of wife by husband viewed as a communication).

[6]See by analogy Quarfot v. Security Nat. Bank & Trust Co., 189 Minn. 451, 249 N.W. 668 (1933) (in action against executor to recover note alleged to constitute gift, plaintiff's testimony stating reason why he left note in decedent's possession held inadmissible as conclusion and as concerning conversation with deceased). *But see* Alexander v. State, 759 So. 2d 411, 421 (Miss. 2000) (no error to permit expert to use letters written by defendant to his wife as samples of defendant's handwriting).

[7]Blau v. U.S., 340 U.S. 332, 71 S. Ct. 301, 95 L. Ed. 306 (1951) (witness's wife was hiding out to avoid service of subpoena in connection with Communist investigation; held, since witness got his knowledge of his wife's whereabouts from what she "secretly told" him, he could refuse to disclose); In re Grand Jury Investigation, 603 F.2d 786 (9th Cir. 1979) (witness asked nature of husband's duties; government made no showing that knowledge came other than from husband).

[8]Pereira v. U.S., 347 U.S. 1, 74 S. Ct. 358, 98 L. Ed. 435 (1954); U.S. v. Estes, 793 F.2d 465 (2d Cir. 1986); U.S. v. Lofton, 957 F.2d 476 (7th Cir. 1992); U.S. v. Smith, 533 F.2d 1077 (8th Cir. 1976) (testimony of wife that husband placed package of heroin in her underclothing did not violate communications privilege; while acts may constitute communications, for privilege to apply some message must be conveyed); State v. Drury, 110 Ariz. 447, 520 P.2d 495 (1974) (defendant urged expansion of privilege to cover acts as well as communications; extension denied, as "the privilege serves no real function in the reality of married life"); People v. Krankel, 131 Ill. App. 3d 887, 87 Ill. Dec. 75, 476 N.E.2d 777 (4th Dist. 1985) (acts of defendant in entering and leaving burglary victim's home, and returning to car where wife waited and pulling out stolen wallet not within privilege); Gordon v. State, 609 N.E.2d 1085 (Ind. 1993) (privilege does not cover acts not intended to carry a message); State v. Palubicki, 700 N.W.2d 476 (Minn. 2005) (husband's acts not within privilege where they did not constitute assertive conduct intended to convey a message); State v. Edwards, 2011 MT 210, 361 Mont. 478, 260 P.3d 396, 401 (2011) (privilege protects only communications, not mere conduct); Com. v. Chiappini, 566 Pa. 507, 782 A.2d

An equal or greater number of courts, however, have construed their statutes that say "communications" to extend the privilege to acts, facts, conditions, and transactions not amounting to communications at all. One group seems to announce the principle that acts done privately in the wife's presence amount to "communications."[9] Another would go even further and say that any information secured by the wife as a result of the marital relation and which would not have been known in the absence of such relation is protected.[10] Some at least of this latter group would hold that information secured by one spouse through observation during the marriage as to the health,[11] or intoxica-

---

490, 496 (2001) (privilege did not apply to acts except where the spouse intended to convey a message by the actions).

[9]Smith v. State, 344 So. 2d 915 (Fla. 1st DCA 1977) (wide variety of acts and comments incident to an elaborate attempt to dispose of body of husband's murder victim held to be communications); Shepherd v. State, 257 Ind. 229, 277 N.E.2d 165 (1971) (husband's testimony against former wife to the effect that she had driven car for him during burglary held improperly admitted; participation in crime was a matter of confidence); Com. v. Byrd, 689 S.W.2d 618 (Ky. Ct. App. 1985) (drawing clear distinction between acts done in private and acts which "may have been known or seen by any person"; privilege limited to former); Menefee v. Com., 189 Va. 900, 55 S.E.2d 9 (1949), 34 Minn. L. Rev. 257 (1950) (wife's testimony as to husband's leaving home before robbery, as to time of returning, as to his placing pistol on mantel-piece, and as to her driving with him near where stolen safe was hid, held privileged as "communication privately made"). Perhaps the reductio ad absurdum of the "acts" cases is State v. Robbins, 35 Wash. 2d 389, 213 P.2d 310 (1950). There the husband was charged with automobile theft, and evidence of his former wife that when she was presenting application for license for the stolen car at the office her husband was waiting outside in an automobile was a "communication" and privileged.

The court said, "It is obvious that he would not have waited in the automobile had he not relied on the confidence between them by reason of the marital relation."

In People v. Melski, 10 N.Y.2d 78, 217 N.Y.S.2d 65, 176 N.E.2d 81 (1961) the New York Court of Appeals held by a four to three decision that there was no privilege for the wife's observation of her husband, the defendant, and several of his friends in defendant's kitchen with stolen guns. The dissent asserted that the presence of the third persons did not destroy confidentiality but was "part of the very fact confidentially communicated."

[10]Prudential Ins. Co. of America v. Pierce's Adm'x, 270 Ky. 216, 109 S.W.2d 616 (1937) (formula held to apply to knowledge gleaned by the wife from the entry of husband's birth in his family Bible).

[11]Griffith v. Griffith, 162 Ill. 368, 44 N.E. 820 (1896) (impotence); Willey v. Howell, 168 Ky. 466, 182 S.W. 619 (1916) (venereal disease). But it has been held that testimony as to the general condition of health, accessible to other persons, would not be privileged. Supreme Lodge of Mystic Workers of the World v. Jones, 113 Ill. App. 241, 1903 WL 3483 (3d Dist. 1903), and see "Communications" Within Testimonial Privilege of Confidential Communications Between Husband and Wife as Including Knowledge Derived from Observation by One Spouse of Acts of Other Spouse, 23 A.L.R.6th 1.

tion, habitual or at a particular time,[12] or the mental condition[13] of the other spouse, would be protected by the privilege.

All extensions beyond communications seem unjustified under either the instrumental or humanistic justifications for this privilege. The attitude of the courts in these cases seems to reflect a confusion with the quite distinguishable purpose of preserving family harmony by disqualifying one spouse from giving any testimony whatsoever against the other.[14] It is unrealistic to think that it would occur to anyone other than an attorney would consider the existence of the privilege before taking action in the presence of a spouse or, even more certainly, that a spouse would not even have entered into a marital relation but for the existence of the broader privilege—a premise one would have to believe in order to justify the exclusion of all information received as a result of the marital relation. Furthermore, it seems equally difficult to justify a private enclave between spouses that extends beyond confidential communications and information obtained through marital confidence.[15]

A specific instance of development in a direction consistent with the underlying policies behind the privilege has recently been evident in statutes and cases that exclude from the protection of the privilege communications in furtherance of crime or fraud.[16] This exception, long recognized to restrict the cognate

---

[12]Monaghan v. Green, 265 Ill. 233, 106 N.E. 792 (1914). *Contra* State v. Johnston, 133 Wis. 2d 261, 394 N.W.2d 915 (Ct. App. 1986) (drinking of alcohol in wife's presence was not a communication and not privileged).

[13]McFadden v. Welch, 177 Miss. 451, 170 So. 903 (1936). *Contra* Lanham v. Lanham, 62 Tex. Civ. App. 431, 146 S.W. 635 (Texarkana 1910) (husband's demeanor in wife's presence on train); "Communications" Within Testimonial Privilege of Confidential Communications Between Husband and Wife as Including Knowledge Derived from Observation by One Spouse of Acts of Other Spouse, 23 A.L.R.6th 1

[14]See § 66, supra.

[15]Imwinkelried, The New Wigmore: Evidentiary Privileges § 6.7.3 at 665 (2d ed. 2010).

[16]A few states have recognized this exception by statute. *See e.g.,* West's Ann.Cal.Evid.Code § 981, quoted supra § 78, note 10; Kan.Stat. Ann. 60-437(b)(5). Several federal circuits and some states have adopted the exception by judicial decision. *See also* U.S. v. Miller, 588 F.3d 897, 905 (5th Cir. 2009) (conversations between defendant and his wife not privileged where they involved joint criminal activity); U.S. v. Darif, 446 F.3d 701, 706–07 (7th Cir. 2006) (communications between husband and wife not privileged where both implicated in marriage fraud scheme); U.S. v. Bey, 188 F.3d 1, 4–5 (1st Cir. 1999) (privilege did not apply where spouses were joint participants in a criminal conspiracy); U.S. v. Mendoza, 574 F.2d 1373 (5th Cir. 1978) (adopting rule that interspousal communications about crimes in which spouses are jointly participating do not come within the privilege); State v. Smith, 384 A.2d 687, 693 (Me. 1978) ("We do not believe that the purpose behind the marital privilege is served by

privilege for attorney-client communications, seems amply justified in the present context as well.

## § 80  The communication must be confidential[1]

Most statutes expressly limit the privilege to "confidential communications."[2] However, even where the words used are "any communication" or simply "communications," the notion that the privilege is born of the "common law" and the fact that the prestatutory descriptions of the privilege had clearly based it upon the policy of protecting confidences,[3] have caused most courts to read into such statutes the requirement of confidentiality.[4] Communications in private between husband and wife are assumed to be confidential,[5] though of course this assumption will be strengthened if confidentiality is expressly affirmed, or if the

---

permitting spouses engaged in criminal activity to raise a cloud of secrecy around their communications regarding that activity. Such communications do not foster the type of honesty and mutual trust upon which fulfilling marital relations ought to be predicated"); State v. Witchey, 388 N.W.2d 893 (S.D. 1986) (collecting authorities and adopting exception by decision); Hermansen v. Tasulis, 2002 UT 52, 48 P.3d 235, 243 (Utah 2002) (sufficient evidence to determine that communications fell within exception for statements made for purposes of committing a tort). *But compare* Smith v. State, 344 So. 2d 915 (Fla. 1st DCA 1977) (rejecting furtherance of crime exception on ground of harm it would inflict on policy of privilege). Communications between spouses as to joint participation in crime as within privilege of interspousal communications, 62 A.L.R.4th 1134. *See also* U.S. v. Rakes, 136 F.3d 1 (1st Cir. 1998) (privilege still exists where husband and wife were both victims of a crime); U.S. v. Montgomery, 384 F.3d 1050 (9th Cir. 2004) (exception did not apply where joint criminal activity not undertaken at the time of the communication).

Of course even where recognized the exception does not render admissible confessions of crime by one spouse to a nonparticipating spouse. U.S. v. Estes, 793 F.2d 465 (2d Cir.

1986) (husband's initial statement that he had stolen money remained privileged, though subsequent statements made after wife became accessory were not); State v. Holt, 223 Kan. 34, 574 P.2d 152 (1977) (Kansas statute cited above did not remove privilege with respect to note confessing completed crime left by defendant for wife; but admission harmless error).

**[Section 80]**

[1]8 Wigmore, Evidence § 2336 (McNaughton rev. 1961); West's Key Number Digest, Privileged Communications and Confidentiality ⬳80, 81; 98 C.J.S., Witnesses § 303.

[2]See statutes compiled in 2 Wigmore, Evidence § 488 (Chadbourn rev. 1979). See also California and New York provisions, § 78 supra.

[3]See § 78 supra.

[4]New York Life Ins. Co. v. Mason, 272 F. 28 (C.C.A. 9th Cir. 1921) ("any communications" in [former] R.C.M. 1947, § 93-701-3 should be interpreted as limited to confidential statements); Shepherd v. Pacific Mut. Life Ins. Co., 230 Iowa 1304, 300 N.W. 556 (1941); Thayer v. Thayer, 188 Mich. 261, 154 N.W. 32, 35 (1915). Contra: Pugsley v. Smyth, 98 Or. 448, 194 P. 686 (1921) (reviewing statutes and decisions in various states). *See generally* 98 C.J.S., Witnesses § 303.

[5]Blau v. U.S., 340 U.S. 332, 71

subject is such that the communicating spouse would probably desire that the matter be kept secret, either because its disclosure would be embarrassing or for some other reason. However, a variety of factors, including the nature of the message or the circumstances under which it was delivered, may serve to rebut a claim that confidentiality was intended.[6] In particular, if a third

---

S. Ct. 301, 95 L. Ed. 306 (1951); In re Grand Jury Investigation, 603 F.2d 786 (9th Cir. 1979); Cal. Evid. Code § 917. *But compare* People v. Burton, 6 Ill. App. 3d 879, 286 N.E.2d 792 (1st Dist. 1972) ("presumption" of confidentiality for statements does not attach to acts even where communicative).

[6]For general discussions, *see* Reserve Fund Derivative and Securities Litigation, 275 F.R.D. 154 (S.D.N.Y.2011) (court examines various aspects of system to determine that there was no reasonable expectation of confidentiality with regard to emails); Russell v. State, 743 N.E.2d 269, 272 (Ind. 2001) (attempts to persuade wife to communicate with third person not within privilege); Parkhurst v. Berdell, 110 N.Y. 386, 18 N.E. 123, 127 (1888) ("such communications as are expressly made confidential, or such as are of a confidential nature, or induced by the marital relation"); Mitchell v. Mitchell, 80 Tex. 101, 15 S.W. 705 (1891) ("determined by the subject-matter of the communication or the circumstances under which it was made or both"). *See also* Story, Twenty–First Century Pillow–Talk: Applicability of the Marital Communications Privilege to Electronic Mail, 58 S.C. L. Rev. 275 (2006).

*See* Yoder v. U.S., 80 F.2d 665 (C.C.A. 10th Cir. 1935) (husband left note for wife at their home written on large cardboard; held not privileged); Lynch v. State, 2 So. 3d 47, 65 (Fla. 2008) (letter to wife telling her to disclose information to victim's family not confidential); Resnover v. State, 267 Ind. 597, 372 N.E.2d 457 (1978) (husband's communication to wife of jail-break plan held not confidential where plan was to be communicated to additional participants); Guyette v. State,

84 Nev. 160, 438 P.2d 244 (1968) (letters written by husband in jail awaiting trial handed to sheriff for delivery to wife and not folded, sealed, or otherwise arranged to suggest confidentiality held not privileged); Com. v. May, 540 Pa. 237, 656 A.2d 1335, 1342 (1995) (no expectation of confidentiality where husband had signed form permitting prison officials to read mail); State v. Fiddler, 57 Wash. 2d 815, 360 P.2d 155 (1961) (husband sent letters to illiterate wife knowing someone would have to read them to her). *But see* U.S. v. Montgomery, 384 F.3d 1050 (9th Cir. 2004) (note left by wife for husband in kitchen of home confidential where no showing that the note was likely to have been seen by the couple's children); Winstead v. Com., 327 S.W.3d 386, 394–395 (Ky. 2010), as modified, (Dec. 16, 2010) and as corrected, (Dec. 17, 2010) (request to give false information to authorities within privilege; harmless error); St. Clair v. Com., 174 S.W.3d 474, 480 (Ky. 2005) (statement made in public place may be confidential if circumstances indicate others could not hear).

In People v. Dudley, 24 N.Y.2d 410, 301 N.Y.S.2d 9, 248 N.E.2d 860 (1969) the court held that husband's acts and statements concerning murder committed by him were not privileged where husband's threats to kill wife if she disclosed information indicated that husband did not rely upon the confidentiality of the relationship.

Threats of bodily harm, though in secret, being a violation of marital duty, should not, it seems, be privileged. *See* Rubalcada v. State, 731 N.E.2d 1015, 1022 (Ind. 2000) (threats to wife not within privilege). *Contra* O'Neil v. O'Neil, 264 S.W. 61 (Mo. Ct. App. 1924) (private threats privileged, unless accompanied by violence). In a

person is present to the knowledge of the communicating spouse, this stretches the web of confidence beyond the marital pair, and the communication is unprivileged.[7] Even the presence of children of the family will deprive the conversation of protection unless the children are too young to understand what is said.[8] The

---

New York suit for separation, the husband defended on grounds of cruelty and testified that the wife said she had committed adultery with another man and they were going away. Two judges thought the communication not privileged because not prompted by confidentiality of marriage relation; three judges concurred in result but on grounds of an exception for wrongs by one spouse against the other; two dissented. Poppe v. Poppe, 3 N.Y.2d 312, 165 N.Y.S.2d 99, 144 N.E.2d 72 (1957); Note, Confession of Adultery to Spouse Held Not a Privileged Confidential Communication, 58 Colum. L. Rev. 126 (1958).

[7]Pereira v. U.S., 347 U.S. 1, 74 S. Ct. 358, 98 L. Ed. 435 (1954) ("The presence of a third party negatives the presumption of privacy."); U.S. v. Strobehn, 421 F.3d 1017, 1021 (9th Cir. 2005) (note to wife and others not confidential); U.S. v. Mitchell, 137 F.2d 1006 (C.C.A. 2d Cir. 1943) (threats against wife in presence of others); Shepherd v. Pacific Mut. Life Ins. Co., 230 Iowa 1304, 300 N.W. 556 (1941) (negotiations between husband, wife, and her father); Meece v. Com., 348 S.W.3d 627, 676 (Ky. 2011), cert. denied, 133 S. Ct. 105, 184 L. Ed. 2d 49 (2012) (no privilege where another occupant of the house was within earshot); Gutridge v. State, 236 Md. 514, 204 A.2d 557 (1964) (defendant in jail sent oral message to wife by a trusty); People v. Ressler, 17 N.Y.2d 174, 269 N.Y.S.2d 414, 216 N.E.2d 582 (1966) (conversation between husband and wife in presence of victim of homicide before he was slain by husband); West's Key Number Digest, Witnesses ⚷193; 98 C.J.S., Witnesses § 312.

A letter from a husband to his wife, dictated by him to a stenographer, has been held not privileged.

"Normally husband and wife may conveniently communicate without stenographic aid, and the privilege of holding their confidences immune from proof in court may be reasonably enjoyed and preserved without embracing within it the testimony of third persons to whom such communications have been voluntarily revealed. . . . The privilege suppresses relevant testimony, and should be allowed only when it is plain that marital confidence cannot otherwise reasonably be preserved. Nothing in this case suggests any such necessity." Wolfle v. U.S., 291 U.S. 7, 16, 17, 54 S. Ct. 279, 78 L. Ed. 617 (1934) (Stone, J.).

In Breimon v. General Motors Corp., 8 Wash. App. 747, 509 P.2d 398 (Div. 1 1973), it was held that the presence of a third person cannot be established, and the privilege thus destroyed, by the unsupported testimony of the spouse receiving the communication. *Compare* Stafford v. State, 1983 OK CR 131, 669 P.2d 285 (Okla. Crim. App. 1983) (wife's testimony allowed to establish presence of third person where wife's testimony was corroborated in "other areas").

[8]People v. Sanders, 99 Ill. 2d 262, 75 Ill. Dec. 682, 457 N.E.2d 1241 (1983) (in presence of three children, the oldest 13; not privileged); Hicks v. Hicks, 271 N.C. 204, 155 S.E.2d 799 (1967) (presence of 8 year old daughter did not destroy privilege); State v. Muenick, 26 Ohio App. 3d 3, 498 N.E.2d 171 (9th Dist. Summit County 1985) (statements in presence of wife's sons, 10 and 11, not privileged); Fuller v. Fuller, 100 W. Va. 309, 130 S.E. 270 (1925) (in presence of 13 year old daughter, not privileged); 98 C.J.S., Witnesses § 312. Presence of child at communication between husband and wife as destroying confidentiality of

fact that the communication relates to business transactions may show that it was not intended as confidential.[9] Examples are statements about business agreements between the spouses,[10] or about business matters transacted by one spouse as agent for the other,[11] or about property[12] or conveyances.[13] Usually such state-

---

otherwise privileged communication between them, 39 A.L.R.4th 480.

[9]"So, too, it cannot be that the rule of privilege must be held to extend so far as to exclude all communications between husband and wife having reference to business relations existing either as between them directly, or as between them—one or both—and others. Certainly as to business relations existing between husband and wife directly, there can be no adverse consideration of public policy. Quite to the contrary, public policy, as reflected by statute and by our decisions, permits of such relations to the fullest extent. And it would be shocking to say that a contract thus made, or rights or liabilities thus accruing, could not be enforced because, forsooth, a communication between the parties having relation thereto, and essential to proof, was privileged. The cases are almost unanimously against such a conclusion." Bishop, J. in Sexton v. Sexton, 129 Iowa 487, 105 N.W. 314, 316 (1905). *See* 98 C.J.S., Witnesses § 306; Conversations between husband and wife relating to property or business as within rule excluding private communications between them, 4 A.L.R.2d 835.

[10]Hanger Orthopedic Group, Inc. v. McMurray, 181 F.R.D. 525 (M.D. Fla. 1998) (no reason to believe that statements relating to business were confidential); Appeal of Spitz, 56 Conn. 184, 14 A. 776 (1887) (claim of wife against insolvent estate of husband: held, wife's testimony as to husband's promises and representations which induced her to advance money, not privileged; "they were no more privileged than a promissory note would have been if he had made his contract in that form"); Brooks v. Brooks, 357 Mo. 343, 208 S.W.2d 279 (1948) (wife

sues husband for proceeds of joint adventure. "In actions between a husband and wife involving property rights the rule excluding relevant conversations . . . yields to the necessity of the situation for the prevention of injustice. . . ."); Bietman v. Hopkins, 109 Ind. 177, 9 N.E. 720 (1887) (in suit by husband's creditor to set aside husband's deed to wife, plaintiff objects to wife's testimony that deed given to repay advances—seemingly could be based on ground that the plaintiff is not the holder of the privilege); Ward v. Oliver, 129 Mich. 300, 88 N.W. 631 (1902) (similar to last). *But see* U.S. v. Montgomery, 384 F.3d 1050 (9th Cir. 2004) (note left by wife indicating that sister was acting improperly with regard to a business in which both husband and wife were involved held to be within privilege—even where the note implored husband to communicate the substance of her concerns to husband's sister).

[11]Schmied v. Frank, 86 Ind. 250, 257, 1882 WL 6459 (1882) (wife's testimony that she authorized husband to buy note as her agent, not privileged: such authority "is intended to be known and would be worthless unless known"); People v. Byrd, 207 Mich. App. 599, 525 N.W.2d 507 (1994) (husband's statements to wife asking her to sell marijuana to undercover policeman not within privilege); Lurty's Curator v. Lurty, 107 Va. 466, 59 S.E. 405 (1907) (husband's account of money due wife on sale of their joint property not privileged).

[12]Hagerman v. Wigent, 108 Mich. 192, 65 N.W. 756 (1896) (wife's delivery of mortgage to husband with instructions to give to plaintiff after wife's death, not privileged, as it was expected to be disclosed); Parkhurst v. Berdell, 110 N.Y. 386, 18 N.E. 123

ments relate to facts that are intended later to become publicly known. To cloak them with privilege when the transactions come into litigation would be productive of special inconvenience and injustice.

## §81   The time of making the communication:[1] Marital status

The privilege is created to encourage marital confidences and is limited to them. Consequently, communications between the husband and wife before they were married,[2] or after their divorce,[3] are not privileged. And attempts to assert the privilege by participants in living arrangements argued to be the functional equivalents of marriage have to date uniformly been rejected by the courts.[4] The requirement of a valid marriage may be satisfied by a valid common law marriage,[5] if it can be proved, but a

---

(1888) (husband's conversation with wife as to securities in his hands belonging to third person, not privileged; "they were ordinary conversations, relating to matters of business, which there is no reason to suppose he would have been unwilling to hold in the presence of any person").

[13]Eddy v. Bosley, 34 Tex. Civ. App. 116, 78 S.W. 565 (1903) (communication by husband to second wife preceding his deed to her advising her of the interest of his children in the property will be received to show notice to her; claim of privilege overruled on ground that the conveyance "if accomplished would operate as a fraud" upon the children).

**[Section 81]**

[1]Imwinkelried, The New Wigmore: Evidentiary Privileges § 6.9 (2d ed. 2010); 98 C.J.S., Witnesses §§ 302, 314 to 315.

[2]U.S. v. Pensinger, 549 F.2d 1150 (8th Cir. 1977); Thurman v. Com., 975 S.W.2d 888 (Ky. 1998) (no privilege for communications preceding marriage); Hood v. State, 17 So. 3d 548, 553 (Miss. 2009) (conversation before marriage not protected by privilege); State v. Keithley, 227 Neb. 402, 418 N.W.2d 212 (1988) (semble).

[3]Yoder v. U.S., 80 F.2d 665 (C.C.A. 10th Cir. 1935).

[4]See State v. Watkins, 126 Ariz. 293, 614 P.2d 835 (1980) (equal protection does not require recognition of privilege for other than married couples); People v. Delph, 94 Cal. App. 3d 411, 156 Cal. Rptr. 422 (2d Dist. 1979); State v. Lard, 86 N.M. 71, 519 P.2d 307 (Ct. App. 1974); Greenwald v. H & P 29th Street Associates, 241 A.D.2d 307, 659 N.Y.S.2d 473 (1st Dep't 1997) (privilege did not apply to single sex couple in a spousal relationship); Communication between unmarried couple living together as privileged, 4 A.L.R.4th 422. Compare Comment, 1977 Ariz. St. L.J. 411 (advocating continued denial of the privilege) with Glover, Evidentiary Privileges for Cohabiting Parents: Protecting Children Inside and Outside of Marriage, 70 La. L. Rev. 751 (2010) (argues for expanding the privilege to include unmarried cohabiting parents).

[5]People v. Schmidt, 228 Mich. App. 463, 579 N.W.2d 431 (1998) (privilege applied where common law marriage recognized in home state, even though not in forum). See also U.S. v. Boatwright, 446 F.2d 913 (5th Cir. 1971) (claimant failed to establish

bigamous marriage will not suffice.[6] Although this latter holding should probably, by analogy to other privileges, be relaxed where the party seeking the benefit of the privilege was ignorant of the status of the other purported spouse,[7] the courts have not consistently done so.[8]

What of a husband and wife living apart? It has been urged that communication in this context is far more likely to be related to preservation of the marriage[9] than are the vast bulk of admittedly privileged communications. This fact, coupled with the pragmatic difficulty involved in determining when hostility between the spouses has become implacable, argues for the more easily administered approach of terminating the privilege only upon a decree of divorce. Some courts have adopted such a view.[10] However, other courts, especially the federal circuits, have

---

valid common law marriage); Com. v. Wilson, 543 Pa. 429, 672 A.2d 293 (1996) (semble). *Compare* U.S. v. Acker, 52 F.3d 509 (4th Cir. 1995) (no privilege where the states involved did no recognize common law marriages).

[6]U.S. v. Neeley, 475 F.2d 1136 (4th Cir. 1973) (marriage claimed to support communications privilege not only bigamous but probably known to be so by both "spouses"); People v. Mabry, 71 Cal. 2d 430, 78 Cal. Rptr. 655, 455 P.2d 759 (1969) (distinguishing People v. Godines, infra n. 8, on ground that bigamous marriage is void rather than voidable); People v. Catlin, 26 Cal. 4th 81, 26 Cal. 4th 1060c, 109 Cal. Rptr. 2d 31, 26 P.3d 357, 388–89 (2001) (no marital communications privilege where husband's divorce from previous wife was not final); Conley v. Reisinger, 713 So. 2d 1113 (Fla. 5th DCA 1998) (no privilege where marriage bigamous).

[7]For a criticism of the holding of People v. Mabry, supra note 6, on this ground, *see* Comment, 9 U.C.D. L. Rev. 569, 600 (1976).

[8]*See, e.g.,* U.S. v. Hamilton, 19 F.3d 350 (7th Cir. 1994) (privilege did not exist even though husband made statement in reliance on the existence of a valid marriage). It is suggested that there is no meaningful distinction to be drawn between this situation and that in which a communication

made during a purported marriage, later annulled for fraud by the victim of the fraud, has been held privileged. *See* People v. Godines, 17 Cal. App. 2d 721, 62 P.2d 787 (2d Dist. 1936); 25 Calif. L. Rev. 619 (1937). *But see* People v. Van Dorsten, 202 Mich. App. 293, 507 N.W.2d 831 (1993) (privilege did not exist, regardless of whether marriage was void or voidable).

[9]This seems to be assumed without discussion in McCoy v. Justice, 199 N.C. 602, 155 S.E. 452 (1930).

[10]*See* Coleman v. State, 281 Md. 538, 380 A.2d 49 (1977) (holding privilege applicable to communication made after husband had been served in divorce proceeding); People v. Fields, 38 A.D.2d 231, 328 N.Y.S.2d 542 (1st Dep't 1972) (citing practical difficulty of ascertaining "genuine" existence of marriage); Muetze v. State, 73 Wis. 2d 117, 243 N.W.2d 393 (1976) (impending dissolution of marriage has no effect on communications privilege). *See also* Glover v. State, 836 N.E.2d 414, 419 (Ind. 2005) (communications between husband and wife privileged despite claim that marriage was entered into to defraud immigration authorities); Effect, on competency to testify against spouse or on marital communication privilege, of separation or other marital instability short of absolute divorce, 98 A.L.R.3d 1285.

refused to apply the privilege where the parties are separated at the time of the communication.[11]

## § 82 Hazards of disclosure to third persons against the will of the communicating spouse[1]

The weight of decision seems to support the view that the privilege does not protect against the testimony of third persons who have overheard (either accidentally or by eavesdropping) an oral communication between husband and wife,[2] or who have secured possession or learned the contents of a letter from one spouse to another by interception,[3] or through loss or misdelivery by the custodian.[4]

In addition, several courts, especially more recently, have held that particular statutes provide only that a spouse may not be

---

[11]In U.S. v. Murphy, 65 F.3d 758 (9th Cir. 1995), the court refused to apply the privilege where the couple was separated and the marriage irreconcilable. Other courts have required only separation to destroy the privilege. U.S. v. Porter, 986 F.2d 1014 (6th Cir. 1993). *See also* U.S. v. Byrd, 750 F.2d 585 (7th Cir. 1984) (rejecting contention that marital deterioration destroys privilege, but holding that proof of "permanent separation" at the time of the communication automatically renders privilege inapplicable); U.S. v. Singleton, 260 F.3d 1295, 1300 (11th Cir. 2001) (privilege not available where parties are living separately with no reasonable expectation of reconciliation); In re Grand Jury Investigation, 431 F. Supp. 2d 584, 592–93 (E.D. Va. 2006) (privilege ends with permanent separation); Note, "Honey, The Judge Says We're History": Abrogating the Marital Privilege Via Modern Doctrines of Marital Worthiness, 77 Cornell L. Rev. 843 (1992).

[Section 82]

[1]8 Wigmore, Evidence § 2339 (McNaughton rev. 1961); Imwinkelried, The New Wigmore: Evidentiary Privileges §§ 6.6.2, 6.6.3 (2d ed. 2010); Effect of knowledge of third person acquired by overhearing or seeing communication between husband and wife upon rule as to privileged

communication, 63 A.L.R. 107; 98 C.J.S., Witnesses §§ 312

[2]Helton v. State, 217 Ga. App. 691, 458 S.E.2d 872 (1995) (eavesdropper); State v. Slater, 36 Wash. 2d 357, 218 P.2d 329 (1950) (same); Nash v. Fidelity-Phenix Fire Ins. Co., 106 W. Va. 672, 146 S.E. 726 (1929) (same). *See* discussion below in this section with regard to sophisticated electronic interceptions.

[3]Howton v. State, 391 So. 2d 147 (Ala. Crim. App. 1980) (jailhouse letter read by officer); Batchelor v. State, 217 Ark. 340, 230 S.W.2d 23 (1950) (letter to wife intercepted by jailer); People v. Dunnigan, 163 Mich. 349, 128 N.W. 180 (1910) (abrogated by, People v. Fisher, 442 Mich. 560, 503 N.W.2d 50 (1993)) (spy entering prisoner's cell ostensibly to cut his hair promises to take letter to wife but gives it to sheriff).

[4]State v. Myers, 230 Kan. 697, 640 P.2d 1245 (1982) (letters found under mattress on premises vacated by wife three months earlier not within privilege); Zimmerman v. State, 750 S.W.2d 194 (Tex. Crim. App. 1988) (letter taken from bureau by wife's mother without wife's knowledge or consent not privileged; letter's admission found erroneous on other grounds); Waiver of evidentiary privilege by inadvertent disclosure—state law, 51 A.L.R.5th 603.

examined about confidential statements. Under such statutes, the privilege does not prevent another person from testifying to the statements or the introduction of documents containing references to such communications.[5]

Such rulings are perhaps best sustained on the view that, since the privilege has as its only effect the suppression of relevant evidence, its scope should be confined as narrowly as is consistent with reasonable protection of marital communications. In this view, it seems, since the communicating spouse can ordinarily take effective precautions against overhearing, he should bear the risk of a failure to use such precautions.[6] Moreover, if he sends a messenger with a letter, he should ordinarily assume the risk that the chosen emissary may lose or misdeliver the message.[7] The rationale that the spouses may ordinarily take effective measures to communicate confidentially tends to break down where one or both are incarcerated.[8] However, communications in the jailhouse are frequently held not privileged, often on

---

[5]*See, e.g.*, Kidd v. State, 330 Ark. 479, 955 S.W.2d 505 (1997) (statement by defendant's wife to detective); People v. Fisher, 442 Mich. 560, 503 N.W.2d 50 (1993) (wife's statement contained in pre-sentencing report); State v. Clark, 1997 ND 199, 570 N.W.2d 195 (N.D. 1997) (wife's statements to police officer). *See also* earlier cases such as Com. v. Wakelin, 230 Mass. 567, 120 N.E. 209, 212 (1918); Connella v. Territory, 1906 OK 2, 16 Okla. 365, 86 P. 72, 75 (1906). In Rumping v. Director of Public Prosecutions, H.L. (1962) 3 All E.R. 256 (1962), the accused, a mate on a Dutch ship, wrote a letter to his wife amounting to a confession of murder, handed the letter in a sealed envelope to a member of the ship's crew to post when the ship reached a port outside England. When the accused was arrested the man gave the letter to the captain who turned it over to the police. The House of Lords held the letter admissible on the ground that the Criminal Evidence Act, 1898, does not recognize a privilege for confidential communications under these circumstances in providing that: "No husband shall be compellable to disclose any communication made to him by his wife during the marriage, and no wife shall be compellable to disclose any communication made to her by her husband during the marriage."

[6]Commonwealth v. Everson, 123 Ky. 330, 29 Ky. L. Rptr. 760, 96 S.W. 460, 461 (1906) (likened to attorney-client privilege as to which "it has been said that if persons wish the communications they have with their attorneys to be kept secret, they should be careful not to talk in the hearing of others"); 8 Wigmore, Evidence §§ 2339(1), 2326 (McNaughton rev. 1961). *See also* State v. Countryman, 572 N.W.2d 553 (Iowa 1997) (no privilege where notes written between spouses left in stolen car).

[7]Hammons v. State, 73 Ark. 495, 84 S.W. 718 (1905) (letter to wife from defendant in jail delivered by messenger to wife's father: two judges dissenting); O'Toole v. Ohio German Fire Ins. Co., 159 Mich. 187, 123 N.W. 795 (1909) (overruled by, People v. Fisher, 442 Mich. 560, 503 N.W.2d 50 (1993)) (letter from wife to husband, dropped and lost by husband).

[8]Com. v. Wakelin, 230 Mass. 567, 120 N.E. 209 (1918) (dictograph planted in cell where husband and wife were held).

the theory that no confidentiality was or could have been expected.[9]

As has been observed elsewhere, the development of sophisticated eavesdropping techniques has led to curbs upon their use and upon the admissibility of evidence obtained thereby.[10] It has also led to inclusion in rules governing privileged communications provisions against disclosure by third persons.[11]

Except in those jurisdictions where the privilege is held only to prevent the spouse from testifying and not the introduction of other testimony or documents,[12] most of the cases have held that the privilege will not be lost if the eavesdropping,[13] or the delivery or disclosure of the letter[14] is due to the betrayal or connivance of

---

[9]U.S. v. Griffin, 440 F.3d 1138, 1144–45 (9th Cir. 2006) (letter written by inmate to his attorney/wife not confidential); People v. Von Villas, 11 Cal. App. 4th 175, 15 Cal. Rptr. 2d 112 (2d Dist. 1992); Fields v. State, 125 Nev. 785, 220 P.3d 709, 717 (2009) (privilege did not apply to recorded telephone conversations between defendant and incarcerated wife when both were warned that call was being recorded); State v. Smyth, 7 Wash. App. 50, 499 P.2d 63 (Div. 2 1972). *But compare* Ward v. State, 70 Ark. 204, 66 S.W. 926 (1902) (letter to wife and enclosure to third person given by husband in jail to wife and seized from her by officers, held, the former privileged, the latter not); North v. Superior Court, 8 Cal. 3d 301, 104 Cal. Rptr. 833, 502 P.2d 1305 (1972) (privilege upheld where detective induced belief that conversation would be private), 61 Cal. L. Rev. 457 (1973). *See also* State v. Rollins, 363 N.C. 232, 675 S.E.2d 334 (2009) (conversation between husband and wife on prison grounds not within privilege because "no expectation of privacy"). The *Rollins* case has been criticized for its confusion of the test for privilege with the test for Fourth Amendment violations, *see* Broun and Mosteller, The Danger to Confidential Communications in the Mismatch between the Fourth Amendment's "Reasonable Expectation of Privacy" and the Confidentiality of Evidentiary Privileges, 32 Campbell L. Rev. 147(2009).

[10]See § 74 supra, and §§ 169, 176 infra.

[11]Cal. Evid. Code § 980, quoted in § 78.

[12]See discussion in People v. Fisher, 442 Mich. 560, 503 N.W.2d 50, 65 (1993) (especially the dissent by Levin, J).

[13]Hunter v. Hunter, 169 Pa. Super. 498, 83 A.2d 401 (1951) (husband suing wife for divorce offers wire-recordings of their conversation in bed: the wire-recorder having been set up by plaintiff's son, with plaintiff's connivance without wife's knowledge, held privileged); Spouse's betrayal or connivance as extending marital communications privilege to testimony of third person, 3 A.L.R.4th 1104.

[14]U.S. v. Neal, 532 F. Supp. 942 (D. Colo. 1982) (collecting cases and following majority rule); People v. Dubanowski, 75 Ill. App. 3d 809, 31 Ill. Dec. 403, 394 N.E.2d 605 (1st Dist. 1979). *See also* Spouse's betrayal or connivance as extending marital communications privilege to testimony of third person, 3 A.L.R.4th 1104; McCoy v. Justice, 199 N.C. 602, 155 S.E. 452 (1930) (husband's letters disclosed by wife to third persons). Nevertheless, there are a number of cases which disregard this element of betrayal and hold the privilege not applicable. State v. Sysinger, 25 S.D. 110, 125 N.W. 879 (1910) (prisoner's letter to wife, delivered by her to State's attorney); Effect of knowledge

the spouse to whom the message is directed. Just as that spouse would not be permitted, against the will of the communicating spouse, to betray the confidence by testifying in court to the message, so he or she may not effectively destroy the privilege by out-of-court betrayal.

If the spouse to whom a letter is addressed dies and it is found among the effects of the deceased, may the personal representative be required or permitted to produce it in court? Here there is no connivance or betrayal by the deceased spouse, and on the other hand this is not a disclosure against which the sender could effectively guard. If the privilege is to be held, as most courts do,[15] to survive the death of one of the spouses, it seems that only a court that strictly limits the effect of the statute to restraining the spouses themselves from testifying, could justify a denial of the privilege in this situation.[16]

### § 83 Who is the holder of the privilege? Enforcement and waiver

Greenleaf in 1842, in foreshadowing the protection of marital communications, wrote of the projected rule as a "privilege" based on "public policy." Many legislatures, however, when they came to write the privilege into law phrased the rule simply as a survival in this special case of the ancient incompetency of the spouses, which the same statutes undertook to abolish or restrict. So it is often provided that the spouses are "incompetent" to testify to marital communications. Consequently, the courts frequently overlook this "common law" background[1] of privilege, and permit any party to the action to claim the benefit of the rule by objection. Doubtless counsel often fail to point out that privilege, not incompetency, is the proper classification, and that the distinctive feature of privilege is that it can only be claimed by the holder or beneficiary of the privilege, not by a party as such.[2] The latter principle is clearly correct.[3]

Who is the holder? Wigmore's argued that the policy of

---

of third person acquired by overhearing or seeing communication between husband and wife upon rule as to privileged communication, 63 A.L.R. 107.

[15]See § 85 infra.

[16]Privilege applied: Bowman v. Patrick, 32 F. 368 (C.C.E.D. Mo. 1887); McKie v. State, 165 Ga. 210, 140 S.E. 625 (1927) (trial of wife for murder of husband; wife's letter to husband, produced by his temporary administrator, held improperly admitted, two

judges dissenting), noted critically, 37 Yale L.J. 669. Privilege denied: Dickerson v. U.S., 65 F.2d 824 (App. D.C. 1933) (trial of husband for murder of wife; letter to wife found by third person among her effects, held admissible).

**[Section 83]**

[1]See § 78 supra.

[2]See § 73.1 supra.

[3]Luick v. Arends, 21 N.D. 614, 132 N.W. 353, 362, 363 (1911) (statutory phrase, "nor can either be . . .

encouraging freedom of communication points to the communicating spouse as the holder.[4] Under this view, in the case of statement of a husband to his wife, only the husband could assert the privilege, where the sole purpose is to show the expressions and attitude of the husband. However, even under this limited view, if the object were to show the wife's adoption of the husband's statement by her silence, the husband's statement and her conduct both become her communication and she can claim the privilege. Similarly, if a conversation or an exchange of correspondence between them is offered to show the collective expressions of them both, either could claim privilege as to the entire exchange.

Despite Wigmore's argument, most jurisdictions now provide that both spouses hold the privilege. More than half of the states reach this result by statute or rule.[5] Most federal circuit decisions have reached the same conclusion.[6] The rationale articulated by one court in its decision to disregard earlier precedent placing the privilege only in the communicating spouse was that a failure to permit the non-communicating spouse to assert the privilege would eviscerate the privilege by inviting attempts to prove the statements of the other spouse circumstantially.[7] Despite the view expressed in earlier editions of this text,[8] the rationale expressed is convincing.[9]

A failure by the holder to assert the privilege by objection, or a

---

without consent of the other examined as to any communication" creates a privilege, not a disqualification, which only a spouse can assert, and the defendant, in the alienation suit here, cannot assert the privilege or complain on appeal of its denial); Coles v. Harsch, 129 Or. 11, 276 P. 248, 253–255 (1929) (alienation action, plaintiff's wife having later married defendant; defendant, not being the holder of the privilege, could not object at the trial or on appeal to plaintiff's disclosure of marital communications); Patterson v. Skoglund, 181 Or. 167, 180 P.2d 108 (1947) (only husband or wife, not the defendant, can assert the privilege).

[4] 8 Wigmore, Evidence § 2340(1) (McNaughton rev. 1961).

[5] E.g., Ala. R. Evid. 504; Cal. Evid. Code § 980. The statutes and rules are collected in U.S. v. Montgomery, 384 F.3d 1050, 1058 n.1 (9th Cir. 2004). See also Unif. R. Evid. 504(b) (1999 amendment), which pro-

vides for a privilege for "any confidential communication made by the individual to the spouse during their marriage."

[6] E.g., U.S. v. Porter, 986 F.2d 1014, 1018 (6th Cir. 1993); U.S. v. Lea, 249 F.3d 632, 641 (7th Cir. 2001); United States v. Montgomery, supra note 5 at 1057–59; U.S. v. Bahe, 128 F.3d 1440, 1442 (10th Cir. 1997).

[7] U.S. v. Montgomery, 384 F.3d 1050, 1059 (9th Cir. 2004), citing 2 Mueller & Kirkpatrick, Federal Evidence § 207 (2d ed. 1994).

[8] See, most recently, Strong et al, McCormick on Evidence § 83 at 336 (5th ed. 1999).

[9] See also Imwinkelried, The New Wigmore: Evidentiary Privileges § 6.5.1.b, at 633–35 (2d ed. 2010) (arguing that, under an autonomy-based humanistic rationale for the privilege, it would make sense to treat both spouses as holders of the privilege).

voluntary revelation by the holder of the communication,[10] or of a material part, is a waiver. The judge, however, may in some jurisdictions in his discretion protect the privilege[11] if the holder is not present to assert it, and objection by a party not the holder may serve the purpose of invoking this discretion, though the party may not complain[12] if the judge fails to protect this privilege belonging to the absent spouse.

## § 84  Controversies in which the privilege is inapplicable[1]

The common law privilege against adverse testimony of a spouse was subject to an exception in cases of prosecution of the husband for offenses against the wife, at least those of violence.[2] When nineteenth century statutes in this country limited and regulated this privilege and the incompetency of spouses as witnesses and defined the new statutory privilege for confidential communications, the common law exception above mentioned

---

[10]U.S. v. Figueroa-Paz, 468 F.2d 1055 (9th Cir. 1972) (communications privilege must be continuously asserted or it will be waived); State v. Beavers, 290 Conn. 386, 963 A.2d 956, 973 (2009) (failure to object at time of offer of evidence waived privilege); Pendleton v. Pendleton, 103 Ohio App. 345, 3 Ohio Op. 2d 370, 145 N.E.2d 485 (2d Dist. Montgomery County 1957) (privilege may be waived, and once waived may not later be asserted in the same cause); West's Ann.Cal. Evid.Code § 912(a). It is suggested in Fraser v. U.S., 145 F.2d 139, 144 (C.C.A. 6th Cir. 1944) that when the husband claims the privilege on the stand, but answers when ordered by the court to do so, this is a waiver, but this conclusion seems questionable. See, e.g., U.S. v. Lilley, 581 F.2d 182 (8th Cir. 1978) (disclosure by holder spouse waives privilege); People v. Worthington, 38 Cal. App. 3d 359, 113 Cal. Rptr. 322 (3d Dist. 1974); Cummings v. People, 785 P.2d 920 (Colo. 1990) (accusation on opening statement of husband's attorney that wife had committed the murder charged waived privilege); Glover v. State, 836 N.E.2d 414, 420 (Ind. 2005) (wife could waive privilege as to husband's confidential communication). But see Brown v. State, 359 Md. 180, 753 A.2d 84, 98 (2000) (defendant did

not waive privilege by claiming that wife had committed the crime); See also Arizona statute, A.R.S. § 13-4062(1)(a) (2010) (no privilege if testifying spouse makes a voluntary statement to a law enforcement officer during the investigation of the offense in question) and State v. Carver, 227 Ariz. 438, 258 P.3d 256 (Ct. App. Div. 1 2011) (interpreting statute).

If both spouses are holders of the privileges, as discussed earlier in this section, the disclosure of the communication by one of the spouses without the involvement of the other should not constitute a waiver. See § 82 supra.

[11]Coles v. Harsch, 129 Or. 11, 276 P. 248, 255 (1929); Model Code of Evidence Rule 105(e).

[12]See decisions cited note 3 supra.

**[Section 84]**

[1]8 Wigmore, Evidence § 2338 (McNaughton rev. 1961); Imwinkelried, The New Wigmore: Evidentiary Privileges §§ 6.13.2, 6.13.5 (2d ed. 2010); 98 C.J.S., Witnesses § 301; 81 Am. Jur. 2d, Witnesses §§ 285 to 287; Model Code of Evidence Rule 216.

[2]See § 66, supra, and 8 Wigmore, Evidence § 2239 (McNaughton rev. 1961).

was usually incorporated and extended, and frequently other exceptions were added. Under these statutes[3] it is not always clear whether the exceptions are intended to apply only to the provisions limiting the competency of the spouses as witnesses, or whether they apply also to the privilege for confidential communications. Frequently, however, in the absence of a contrary decision, it is at least arguable that the exception does have this latter application, and in some instances this intent is clearly expressed. Any other result would, in principle, indeed be difficult to justify.

The types of controversies in which the marital communication privilege is made inapplicable vary, of course, from state to state. They may be derived from express provision, from statutory implication, or from decisions based upon common law doctrine.[4] They may be grouped as follows:[5]

- Prosecutions for crimes committed by one spouse against the other or against the children of either.[6] Besides statutes in general terms, particular crimes, most frequently family desertion and pandering, are often specified, and as to these

---

[3]See the compilation of statutes in 2 Wigmore, Evidence § 488 (Chadbourn rev. 1979).

[4]See e.g., U.S. v. Walker, 176 F.2d 564, 568 (2d Cir. 1949) (L. Hand, C.J.: "We do not forget that a wife from the earliest times was competent to testify against her husband, when the crime was an offense against her person. . . . The same exception probably extends to the privilege against the admission of confidential communications"); People v. McCormack, 278 A.D. 191, 104 N.Y.S.2d 139, 143 (1st Dep't 1951) (common law exception for testimony as to assaults on wife is to be read into statute creating privilege, though exception not mentioned).

[5]Compare the exceptions in the California statute quoted in § 78. See also Crimes against spouse within exception permitting testimony by one spouse against other in criminal prosecution—modern state cases, 74 A.L.R. 4th 223; Competency of One Spouse to Testify Against Other in Prosecution for Offense Against Child of Both or Either or Neither, 119 A.L.R.5th 275.

[6]It has been held that the phrase

"children of either" is not limited to the natural children of the spouses, but includes a foster child. Daniels v. State, 681 P.2d 341 (Alaska Ct. App. 1984). See also Reaves v. State, 284 Ga. 236, 664 S.E.2d 207, 210 (2008) (privilege inapplicable in prosecution for crimes against 11-year-old stepdaughter); State v. Anderson, 636 N.W.2d 26, 34 (Iowa 2001) (statutory exception to marital privilege did not apply where allegedly abused child not in care of husband); Stevens v. State, 806 So. 2d 1031, 1050 (Miss. 2001) (statutory exception to privilege applies with regard to crime against child regardless of whether child part of household). But see U.S. v. Banks, 556 F.3d 967, 976 (9th Cir. 2009) (exception did not apply to crimes against grandchild). See also Cassidy, Reconsidering Spousal Privileges After Crawford, 33 Am. J. Crim. L. 339 (2006) (arguing for broad application of the exception in domestic violence cases); Goodno, Protecting "Any Child": The Use of Confidential Marital Communications Privilege in Child-Molestation Cases, 59 Kan. L. Rev. 1 (2010).

latter the withdrawal of the privilege for communications is usually explicit.

- Actions by one of the spouses against an outsider for an intentional injury to the marital relation. Thus far this exception has been applied, sometimes under statutes, sometimes as a continuation of common law tradition, chiefly in actions for alienation of affection or for criminal conversation.[7] It is usually applied to admit declarations expressive of the state of affection of the alienated spouse.[8]

- Actions by one spouse against the other. Some of the statutes are in this broader form. Some apply only to particular kinds of actions between them, of which divorce suits are most often specified. This exception for controversies between the spouses,[9] which should extend to controversies between the representatives of the spouses, seems worthy of universal acceptance. In the analogous case of clients who jointly consult an attorney, the clients are held to have no privilege for such consultation in controversies between themselves.[10] So here it seems that husband and wife, while they would desire that their confidences be shielded from the outside world, would ordinarily anticipate that if a controversy between themselves should arise in which their mutual conversations would shed light on the merits, the interests of both would be served by full disclosure.

---

[7]Stocker v. Stocker, 112 Neb. 565, 199 N.W. 849, 36 A.L.R. 1063 (1924); Hafer v. Lemon, 1938 OK 240, 182 Okla. 578, 79 P.2d 216 (1938). *Contra* Gjesdahl v. Harmon, 175 Minn. 414, 221 N.W. 639 (1928); McKinnon v. Chenoweth, 176 Or. 74, 155 P.2d 944 (1945). Cases are collected in Applicability and effect in suit for alienation of affections of rule excluding confidential communications between husband and wife, 36 A.L.R. 1068 (supplemented by Admissibility of statements or declarations of plaintiff's spouse in an action for alienation of affections for the purpose of showing his or her mental state, 82 A.L.R. 825).

[8]Applicability and effect in suit for alienation of affections of rule excluding confidential communications between husband and wife, 36 A.L.R. 1068 (supplemented by Admissibility of statements or declarations of plaintiff's spouse in an action for alienation of affections for the purpose of

showing his or her mental state, 82 A.L.R. 825)

[9]See statutes in 2 Wigmore, Evidence § 488 (Chadbourn rev. 1979). *See* Poppe v. Poppe, 3 N.Y.2d 312, 165 N.Y.S.2d 99, 144 N.E.2d 72, 76 (1957); 58 Colum. L. Rev. 126 (1958), where, absent an explicit statutory exception, an exception was recognized in a separation suit for the wife's declaration that she had committed adultery and "they thought they would go away together," which was relied on as an act of cruelty by the defending husband. See also the reference to this case in § 80 n. 6 supra. *Compare* Oliver v. Oliver, 325 S.W.2d 33 (Mo. Ct. App. 1959) (divorce action; communications held privileged); T.C.H. v. K.M.H., 693 S.W.2d 802 (Mo. 1985) (privilege not to be applied in cases where custody of children in issue; judicially created exception to statutory privilege).

[10]See § 91.1 infra.

● A criminal prosecution against one of the spouses in which a declaration of the other spouse made confidentially to the accused would tend to justify or reduce the grade of the offense.[11]

## § 85 If the communication was made during the marriage, does death or divorce end the privilege?[1]

The incompetency of husband or wife to testify for the other, and the privilege of each spouse against adverse testimony are terminated when the marriage ends by death or divorce.[2] The privilege for confidential communications of the spouses, however, was based, in the mind of its chief sponsor, Greenleaf, upon the policy of encouraging confidences, who thought that encouragement required not merely temporary but permanent secrecy.[3] The courts in this country have accepted this need for permanent protection[4] and about one-half of the statutes codifying the privi-

---

[11]Wigmore argues for such an exception. 8 Wigmore, Evidence § 2338(4) (McNaughton rev. 1961). And he calls attention to the "cruel absurdity" of excluding the communication in these circumstances in Steeley v. State, 17 Okla. Crim. 252, 187 P. 821 (1920) (defendant charged with murder of wife's paramour could not testify to wife's communications to him disclosing deceased's conduct in debauching her) and other cases cited. This view is adopted in Model Code of Evidence Rule 216(d) and Comment. *See also* Alaska R.Evid. 505(b)(2)(D).

**[Section 85]**

[1]8 Wigmore, Evidence § 2341 (McNaughton rev. 1961); Imwinkelried, The New Wigmore: Evidentiary Privileges § 6.9.1.a (2d ed. 2010); 98 C.J.S., Witnesses § 314; 81 Am. Jur. 2d, Witnesses § 289; West's Key Number Digest, Privileged Communications and Confidentiality ☞83.

[2]See § 66 supra.

[3]"The happiness of the married state requires that there should be the most unlimited confidence between husband and wife; and this confidence the law secures by providing that it shall be kept forever inviolable; that nothing shall be extracted from the bo-

som of the wife which was confided there by the husband. Therefore, after the parties are separated, whether it be by divorce or by the death of the husband, the wife is still precluded from disclosing any conversations with him . . . ." 1 Greenleaf, Evidence 296 (13th ed. 1876).

[4]*See, e.g.*, U.S. v. Pensinger, 549 F.2d 1150 (8th Cir. 1977) (divorce does not terminate privilege, but communications not protected because in presence of third persons); Shepherd v. State, 257 Ind. 229, 277 N.E.2d 165 (1971) (divorced wife barred by privilege from testifying about acts which were matter of confidence); In re Petition for Disciplinary Action Against Westby, 639 N.W.2d 358, 366–367 (Minn. 2002) (privilege survives divorce but did not apply to former husband's observations concerning ex-wife's representation of clients); Com. v. May, 540 Pa. 237, 656 A.2d 1335 (1995) (conversation held with now divorced wife in front of two-year-old child within privilege; harmless error); Breimon v. General Motors Corp., 8 Wash. App. 747, 509 P.2d 398 (Div. 1 1973) (divorced wife precluded from testifying concerning admission made by former husband; "A spouse should not be placed in fear that a future change in marital status would find

lege explicitly provide that it continues after death or divorce.[5] In fact, this characteristic accounts for a large proportion of the attempted invocations of the communications privilege, since if the marriage has not been terminated one of the other, more embrasive marital privileges will frequently apply.

In earlier editions of this text, the opinion was given that, "where the marital tie has been severed that the supposed policy of the privilege has the most remote and tenuous relevance, and the possibilities of injustice in its application are most apparent."[6] The text quoted Wigmore, who stated, "there must arise occasional instances of hardship where ample flexibility should be allowed in the relaxation of the rule."[7] The English case of *Shenton v. Tyler*,[8] was cited as an example of an instance of hardship. There, the plaintiff sued a widow and alleged that her deceased husband had made an oral secret trust, known to the widow, for the benefit of plaintiff, and sought to interrogate the widow. The widow relied on section 3 of the Evidence Amendment Act, 1853, as follows: ". . . no wife shall be compellable to disclose any communication made to her during the marriage." The court rejected the Greenleaf theory of a common law privilege for communications surviving the end of the marriage, and was "unable to find any warrant for extending the words of the section by construction so as to include widowers and widows and divorced persons."[9] The earlier versions of this text then stated: "However debatable may be the court's position that there was no common law privilege for marital communications,[10] it seems clear that the actual holding that the privilege for communications ends when the marriage ends is preferable in policy to the contrary result reached under American statutes and decisions."[11]

The present authors take a somewhat different position with regard to the survival of the privilege after death or divorce. Rather than concluding that a holding that the privilege ends when the marriage ends is preferable in policy, we would argue that a humanitarian, rather than utilitarian, justification for the privilege may call for a qualified privilege generally. Such a privilege would survive death or dissolution of the marriage but might

---

his innermost secrets broadcast.").

[5]See the compilation of statutes in 2 Wigmore, Evidence § 488 (Chadbourn rev. 1961).

[6]See, most recently, Strong, et al. McCormick on Evidence, § 85 at 339 (5th ed. 1999).

[7]Strong, et al. McCormick on Evidence, § 85 at 339 citing 8 Wigmore, Evidence § 2341 (McNaughton rev.

1961).

[8]Shenton v. Tyler, L.R. [1939] Ch.Div. 620 (C.A.).

[9]Shenton v. Tyler, L.R. [1939] Ch.Div. 620, 652 (by Luxmoore, L.J.).

[10]See § 78 supra.

[11]See, most recently, Strong, et al. McCormick on Evidence, § 85 at 339 (5th ed. 1999).

give way in circumstances such as *Shenton v. Tyler*. The possibility of a qualified privilege is discussed in the next section.

## § 86    Policy and future of the marital communications privilege[1]

The argument traditionally advanced in support of the marital communications privilege is that the privilege is needed to encourage marital confidences, which confidences in turn promote harmony between husband and wife. This argument, now reiterated for almost a century and a half, obviously rests upon certain assumptions concerning the knowledge and psychology of married persons. Thus it must be assumed that spouses will know of the privilege and take its protection into account in determining to make marital confidences, or at least, which is not the same thing, that they would come to know of the absence of the privilege if it were withdrawn and be, as a result, less confiding than at present.

In the absence of any empirical validation, these propositions have appeared highly suspect to many,[2] though not all,[3] commentators. The most convincing answer to the argument of policy appears to be that the contingency of courtroom disclosure would almost never (even if the privilege did not exist) be in the minds of the parties in considering how far they should go in their secret conversations. What encourages them to fullest frankness is not the assurance of courtroom privilege, but the trust they place in the loyalty and discretion of each other. If the secrets are not told outside the courtroom there will be little danger of their being elicited in court. In the lives of most people appearance in court as a party or a witness is an exceedingly rare and unusual event, and the anticipation of it is not one of those factors which materially influence in daily life the degree of

---

**[Section 86]**

[1]8 Wigmore, Evidence § 2332 (McNaughton rev. 1961); 97 C.J.S., Witnesses § 266; 81 Am. Jur. 2d, Witnesses § 296; The foregoing give the supporting arguments of policy.

[2]Hutchins & Slesinger, Some Observations on the Law of Evidence: Family Relations, 13 Minn. L. Rev. 675, 682 (1929); Hines, Privileged Testimony of Husband and Wife in California, 19 Calif. L. Rev. 390, 410–414 (1931); Comment, 7 Cumb. L. Rev. 307, 319 (1976) (". . . it could not

be said that the parties normally would have anticipated such an event as being forced to testify when they made the communication."); Note, 86 Dick. L. Rev. 491 (1982).

[3]Krattenmaker, Interspousal Testimonial Privileges Under the Federal Rules of Evidence: A Suggested Approach, 64 Geo. L.J. 613 (1976); Reutlinger, Policy, Privacy, and Prerogatives: A Critical Examination of the Proposed Federal Rules of Evidence as They Affect Marital Privilege, 61 Calif. L. Rev. 1353 (1973).

fullness of marital disclosures.[4] Thus, while the danger of injustice from suppression of relevant proof is clear and certain,[5] the probable benefits of the rule of privilege in encouraging marital confidences and wedded harmony are marginal.

But probably the policy of encouraging confidences is not the prime influence in creating and maintaining the privilege. It is really a much more natural and less devious matter. It is a matter of emotion and sentiment. All of us have a feeling of indelicacy and want of decorum in prying into the secrets of husband and wife.[6]

---

[4]". . . Very few people ever get into court, and practically no one outside the legal profession knows anything about the rules regarding privileged communications between spouses. As far as the writers are aware (though research might lead to another conclusion) marital harmony among lawyers who know about privileged communications is not vastly superior to that of other professional groups." Hutchins & Slesinger, Some Observations on the Law of Evidence: Family Relations, 13 Minn. L. Rev. 675, 682 (1929).

Proposed Fed. R. Evid. 505 (1971), did not include a privilege for confidential communications. The Advisory Committee's Note to this proposed rule states with respect to the privilege:

> The rule recognizes no privilege for confidential communications. The traditional justifications for privileges not to testify against a spouse and not to be testified against by one's spouse have been the prevention of marital dissension and the repugnancy of requiring a person to condemn or be condemned by his spouse. 8 Wigmore §§ 2228, 2241 (McNaughton rev. 1961). These considerations bear no relevancy to marital communications. Nor can it be assumed that marital conduct will be affected by a privilege for confidential communications of whose existence the parties in all likelihood are unaware. The other communication privileges, by way of contrast, have as one party a professional person who can be expected to inform the other of the existence of the privilege. Moreover, the relationships from which those privi-

leges arise are essentially and almost exclusively verbal in nature, quite unlike marriage. See Hutchins & Slesinger, Some Observations on the Law of Evidence: Family Relations, 13 Minn. L. Rev. 675 (1929). Cf. McCormick § 90; 8 Wigmore § 2337 (McNaughton rev. 1961).

[5]Examples of cases where the possibilities of injustice seem conspicuous are In re De Neef, 42 Cal. App. 2d 691, 109 P.2d 741 (1st Dist. 1941) (wife sues on life insurance policy taken out in her favor by deceased husband. Defense: fraudulent representations by husband as to his health. Held, wife cannot be interrogated as husband's statements to her as to his physical condition. "We are not concerned with the reason for the rule or its effect on the administration of justice"); McKie v. State, 165 Ga. 210, 140 S.E. 625 (1927) (wife's conviction for murder of husband reversed because of admission of wife's letters to husband, found in his effects after he was killed); Todd v. Barbee, 271 Ky. 381, 111 S.W.2d 1041 (1937) (excluding husband's testimony that he gave wife money to pay rent) and People v. Daghita, 299 N.Y. 194, 86 N.E.2d 172 (1949) (error to allow wife to testify in prosecution of husband for grand larceny, that she saw him bringing stolen property into their home and hiding it under his bed).

[6]See, e.g., Black, The Marital and Physician Privileges—A Reprint of a Letter to a Congressman, 1975 Duke L.J. 45, 48–49.

As pointed out in an earlier section,[7] such humanistic considerations in support of the marital communications and other privileges have been widely advanced in recent years. Increasing recognition of the true operative basis for affording privilege to the marital partners may argue for the treatment of the privilege as qualified rather than absolute. The humanistic need for the creation of a private enclave within a marital relationship may not stand in the balance where there is a need for otherwise unobtainable evidence critical to the ascertainment of significant legal rights.[8]

However, neither the courts nor the legislatures have made moves to convert the marital communications privilege from absolute to qualified. Indeed, the most recent pronouncements of the United States Supreme Court with regard to other privileges suggest a rejection of any notion that the more commonly accepted privileged be anything other than absolute.[9] And the trend with regard to the marital communications privilege seems to be going in the direction of continuing recognition of the privilege in a fairly broad and certainly absolute form.[10]

---

[7]See § 72 supra. See also, Borden, In Defense of the Privilege for Confidential Marital Communications, 39 Ala. Law. 575, 581 (1978) (". . . the benefit of the privilege derives not from its encouragement of confidence, but from the recognition that the confidence once having existed, deserves protection").

[8]See, e.g., Imwinkelried, The New Wigmore: Evidentiary Privileges § 6.2.1 (2d ed. 2010) (emphasizing the strength of the humanistic case for the privilege).

[9]"[A]n uncertain privilege . . . is little better than no privilege at all." Upjohn Co. v. U.S., 449 U.S. 383, 393, 101 S. Ct. 677, 66 L. Ed. 2d 584 (1981)

(attorney client privilege). See also Jaffee v. Redmond, 518 U.S. 1, 17, 116 S. Ct. 1923, 135 L. Ed. 2d 337 (1996), where the Court made the same point with regard to the psychotherapist-patient privilege.

[10]Uniform Rule of Evidence 504, amended in 1999, provides absolute protection for marital communications except that the privilege may be abrogated "in the discretion of the court, if the interests of a minor child or either spouse may be adversely affected by invocation of the privilege." Unif.R. Evid. 504(d)(4). See also U.S. v. Montgomery, 384 F.3d 1050 (9th Cir. 2004) (broad and absolute application of the privilege).

# Chapter 10

# The Client's Privilege: Communications Between Client & Lawyer

## § 87  Background and policy of the privilege: (a) Theoretical considerations

The notion that the loyalty owed by the lawyer to his client disables him from being a witness in his client's case is deep-rooted in Roman law.[1] This Roman tradition may or may not

---

**[Section 87]**

[1]*See* Radin, The Privilege of Confidential Communication between Lawyer and Client, 16 Calif. L. Rev. 487, 488 (1928). As to the history and foundations of the privilege generally, see also Cain, The Attorney's Obligation of Confidentiality—Its Effect on the Ascertainment of Truth in an Adversary System of Justice, 3 Glendale L. Rev. 81 (1978); Fried, The Lawyer as Friend: The Moral Foundations of the Attorney-Client Relation, 85 Yale L.J. 1060 (1976); Hazard, An Historical Perspective on the Attorney-Client Privilege, 66 Calif. L. Rev. 1061

have been influential in shaping the early English doctrine of which we find the first traces in Elizabeth's time, that the oath and honor of the barrister and the attorney protect them from being required to disclose, upon examination in court, the secrets of the client.[2] But by the eighteenth century in England the emphasis upon the code of honor had lessened and the need of the ascertainment of truth for the ends of justice loomed larger than the pledge of secrecy. So a new justification for the lawyer's exemption from disclosing his client's secrets was found. This theory, which continues as the principal rationale of the privilege today, rests upon three propositions. First the law is complex and in order for members of the society to comply with it in the management of their affairs and the settlement of their disputes they require the assistance of expert lawyers. Second, lawyers are unable to discharge this function without the fullest possible knowledge of the facts of the client's situation. And last, the client cannot be expected to place the lawyer in full possession of the facts without the assurance that the lawyer cannot be compelled, over the client's objection, to reveal the confidences in court.[3] The consequent loss to justice of the power to bring all pertinent facts before the court is, according to the theory, outweighed by the benefits to justice (not to the individual client) of a franker disclosure in the lawyer's office.

This clearly utilitarian justification, premised on the power of the privilege to elicit certain behavior on the part of clients, has a compelling common-sense appeal. The tendency of the client in giving his story to his counsel to omit all that he suspects will work against him is a matter of every day professional observation. It makes it necessary for the prudent lawyer to cross-examine his client searchingly about possible unfavorable facts. In criminal cases the difficulty of obtaining full disclosure from the accused is well known, and would certainly become an absolute impossibility if the defendant knew that the lawyer could be compelled to repeat what he had been told.

---

(1978); Note, The Attorney-Client Privilege: Fixed Rules, Balancing, and Constitutional Entitlement, 91 Harv. L. Rev. 464 (1977).

[2] 8 Wigmore, Evidence § 2290 (McNaughton rev. 1961) (history of the privilege); Imwinkelried, The New Wigmore: Evidentiary Privileges § 2.2 (2d ed. 2010).

[3] ". . . An increase of legal business, and the inabilities of parties to transact that business themselves, made it necessary for them to employ . . . other persons who might transact that business for them; that this necessity introduced with it the necessity of what the law hath very justly established, an inviolable secrecy to be observed by attorneys, in order to render it safe for clients to communicate to their attorneys all proper instructions. . . ." Mounteney, B. in Annesley v. Earl of Anglesea, 17 How. St. Tr. 1225 (1743) quoted in 8 Wigmore, Evidence § 2291 (McNaughton rev. 1961) (policy of the privilege).

These justifications, however, have never been convincing to all. Jeremy Bentham, perhaps the most famous of the privilege's critics to date, argued that the privilege is not needed by the innocent party with a righteous cause or defense, and that the guilty should not be given its aid in concerting a false one.[4] Bentham's apocalyptic division of the client world into righteous and guilty seems somewhat naive in a time when even the best-intended may doubt their compliance with an ever more overwhelming body of law. Nevertheless, none can deny the privilege's unfortunate tendency to suppress the truth, and it has commonly been urged that it is only the greater benefit of increased candor that justifies the continuation of the privilege. Wigmore, the great champion and architect of the privilege, subscribed to this view, though he acknowledged that "Its benefits are all indirect and speculative; its obstruction is plain and concrete."[5]

The trend of recent years toward attempted empirical verification of the intuitive judgments of the past has lent a special cogency to Wigmore's assessment. For the degree of efficacy of the privilege in achieving its avowed aims, speculated to be quite low by critics, is ironically likely to prove indemonstrable by reason of the privilege itself.[6] Despite these difficulties, it is of course possible to proceed from the Cartesian postulate that the privilege effects some unknown and unknowable marginal alteration in client behavior.[7] But such minimal claims, even when combined with efforts to structure the privilege so as to confine its opera-

---

[4]See Bentham, Rationale of Judicial Evidence (1827), 7 The Works of Jeremy Bentham 473, 474, 475, 477, 479 (Bowring ed. 1842), passages quoted 8 Wigmore, Evidence § 2291. See also Fischel, Lawyers and Confidentiality, 65 U. Chi. L. Rev. 1 (1998), where the author suggests that the privilege may in fact harm the innocent by making it more difficult for them to communicate that they have nothing to hide.

[5]8 Wigmore, Evidence § 2291, p. 554 (McNaughton rev. 1961). For an opposing view see Barnhart, Privilege in the Uniform Rules of Evidence, 24 Ohio St. L.J. 131 (1963). The "loss" occasioned by the privilege may be challenged on the ground that absent the privilege no useful evidence would have been created. See Saltzburg, Privileges and Professionals: Lawyers and Psychiatrists, 66 Va. L. Rev. 597 (1980).

[6]Either the presence of an investigator during an attorney-client conference, or the disclosure of the substance of such a conference, would presumably destroy the privilege. See Alexander, The Corporate Attorney-Client Privilege: A Study of the Participants, 63 St. John's L. Rev. 191 (1989); Danet, Hoffman & Kermish, Obstacles to the Study of Lawyer-Client Interaction: The Biography of a Failure, 14 Law & Soc. Rev. 905 (1980). See also Imwinkelried, A Psychological Critique of the Assumptions Underlying the Law of Evidentiary Privileges: Insights from the Literature on Self-Disclosure, 38 Loy. L.A. L. Rev. 707 (2004).

[7]See, e.g., Saltzburg, Corporate and Related Attorney-Client Privilege Claims: A Suggested Approach, 12 Hof. L. Rev. 279 (1984) ("Although it is conceivable that if there were no privilege clients would reveal almost

tion to contexts in which it will most probably have an effect,[8] seem to fall short of an adequate justification.

As a possible ancillary justification, it is today suggested with increasing frequency that considerations of privacy should play a role in supporting and ultimately defining the privilege.[9] To date, this rationale has achieved only very little recognition in the courts[10] as a supporting, much less a sufficient, justification for the attorney-client privilege. It is probable that the ultimate fate of this theory will depend upon the success of its advocates in suggesting what implications for the parameters for the privilege are implied by such a rationale.[11]

At the present time it seems most realistic to portray the attorney-client privilege as supported in part by its traditional utilitarian justification, and in part by the integral role it is perceived to play in the adversary system itself.[12] Our system of litigation casts the lawyer in the role of fighter for the party

---

as much information to their attorneys as they would do when a privilege protects them, it is not unreasonable to assume that some communication would be repressed").

[8]Saltzburg, Corporate and Related Attorney-Client Privilege Claims: A Suggested Approach, 12 Hof. L. Rev. 279 (1984) represents a creative effort of this sort with respect to the privilege in the corporate context.

[9]See Louisell, Confidentiality, Conformity and Confusion: Privileges in Federal Court Today, 31 Tul. L. Rev. 101, 110 (1956) ("[I]t is . . . submitted that there are things even more important to human liberty than accurate adjudication. One of them is the right to be left by the state unmolested in certain human relationships"; implying that the attorney client relationship is such a relationship). See also Krattenmaker, Testimonial Privileges in Federal Courts: An Alternative to the Proposed Federal Rules of Evidence, 62 Geo. L.J. 61 (1973); Developments in the Law—Privileged Communications, 98 Harv. L. Rev. 1450, 1486, 1504 (1985).

[10]But see State v. Sugar, 84 N.J. 1, 417 A.2d 474 (1980) ("interference with the intimate relationship between attorney and client may do profound violence to the individual privacy of the client"). And see State ex rel. Great American Ins. Co. v. Smith, 574 S.W.2d 379 (Mo. 1978) (en banc) (suggesting possibility of such a rationale in case of corporations).

[11]There seems no reason why a privilege, like any other rule of law, cannot be supported by multiple justifications. Alexander, The Corporate Attorney-Client Privilege: A Study of the Participants, 63 St. John's L. Rev. 191, 219 (1989) ("There is no reason why instrumental and noninstrumental rationales must be viewed as mutually exclusive; it is perhaps a question of emphasis"); Developments in the Law—Privileged Communications, 98 Harv. L. Rev. 1450, 1504 (1985) ("The utilitarian and non-utilitarian justifications of the privilege are not as irreconcilable as their proponents imply"). Use of multiple rationales will, of course, tend to raise doubt as to the scope of the rule.

[12]Many commentators have suggested such a connection. Among the most helpful, see Alschuler, The Search for Truth Continued, The Privilege Retained: A Response to Judge Frankel, 54 U. Colo. L. Rev. 67 (1982) (noting various alterations in the adversary system which would be necessitated by abolition of the privilege); Uviller, The Advocate, the Truth, and

whom he represents. A strong tradition of loyalty attaches to the relationship of attorney and client, and this tradition would be outraged by routine examination of the lawyer as to the client's confidential disclosures regarding professional business. To the extent that the evidentiary privilege, then, is integrally related to an entire code of professional conduct,[13] it is futile to envision drastic curtailment of the privilege without substantial modification of the underlying ethical system to which the privilege is merely ancillary.[14]

The foregoing state of affairs is clearly less than optimum from the standpoint that predictability in the application of the privi-

---

Judicial Hackles: A Reaction to Judge Frankel's Idea, 123 U. Pa. L. Rev. 1067, 1074 (1975) ("[F]or better or worse, our view of the lawyer's duty is bound to our history and cultural traditions").

[13]The privilege discussed in this chapter must be distinguished from the duty imposed by the rules governing a lawyer's professional conduct requiring that information received in the course of a lawyer's representation of a client be kept confidential. *See* discussion in Zacharias, Harmonizing Privilege and Confidentiality, 41 S. Tex. L. Rev. 69 (1999). The distinction was clearly made under the American Bar Association Model Code of Professional Responsibility, Disciplinary Rule 4-101. The distinction between privileged and confidential information is implicit in the more recent American Bar Association Model Rules of Professional Conduct, Rule 1.6 (as amended in August, 2002), which deals with confidential information, not privilege:

Confidentiality of Information

(a) A lawyer shall not reveal information relating to the representation of a client unless the client gives informed consent, the disclosure is impliedly authorized in order to carry out the representation or the disclosure is permitted by paragraph (b)

(b) A lawyer may reveal information relating to the representation of a client to the extent lawyer reasonably believes necessary:

(1) to prevent reasonably certain death or substantial bodily harm;

(2) to prevent the client from committing a crime or fraud that is reasonably certain to result in substantial injury to the financial interests or property of another and in furtherance of which the client has used or is using the lawyer's services;

(3) to prevent, mitigate or rectify substantial injury to the financial interests or property of another that is reasonably certain to result or has resulted from the client's commission of a crime or fraud in furtherance of which the client has used the lawyer's services;

(4) to secure legal advice about the lawyer's compliance with these Rules;

(5) to establish a claim or defense on behalf of the lawyer in a controversy between the lawyer and the client, to establish a defense to a criminal charge or civil claim against the lawyer based upon conduct in which the client was involved, or to respond to allegations in any proceeding concerning the lawyer's representation of the client; or

(6) to comply with other law or a court order.

\* \* \*

[14]*See generally* Zacharias, Rethinking Confidentiality, 74 Iowa L. Rev. 351 (1989). *But see* Fischel, Lawyers and Confidentiality, 65 U. Chi. L. Rev. 1 (1998) (the attorney-client privilege, as well as the work-product privilege and the rules governing confidentiality should be abolished as serving only lawyers rather than their clients or society as a whole).

lege, logically indispensable for any utilitarian effect, is largely lacking in many areas.[15] Advocates of the supposedly inviolate privilege of yesteryear perceive even greater uncertainties interjected by the increasing uses of in camera inspection to determine the legitimacy of claims of privilege,[16] and even in some jurisdictions the use of a balancing test to determine whether the privilege will be honored.[17] While a balancing approach to the privilege is not consistent with the privilege's current rationales,[18] one could argue that increased use of these expedients may ultimately result in a more rational administration of the privilege than could be achieved through the tradi-

---

[15]It is generally recognized that it is unreasonable to expect reliance on an uncertain privilege. See, e.g., Upjohn Co. v. U.S., 449 U.S. 383, 393, 101 S. Ct. 677, 66 L. Ed. 2d 584 (1981) ("But if the purpose of the attorney-client privilege is to be served, the attorney and client must be able to predict with some degree of certainty whether particular discussions will be protected"). But lack of definition has been the principal criticism directed at the Upjohn extension of the privilege. See Upjohn at 403–404 (Burger, C.J., concurring). And see Dobbins, Great (and Reasonable) Expectations: Fourth Amendment Protection for Attorney–Client Communications, 32 Seattle U. L. Rev. 35 (2008) (arguing that recognizing Fourth Amendment protection for attorney-client communications would provide more consistent protection); Saltzburg, Corporate and Related Attorney-Client Privilege Claims: A Suggested Approach, 12 Hof. L. Rev. 279 (1984).

[16]See Freedman, Corporate Attorney-Client Privilege Since Upjohn, at Home and Abroad, 9 U. Dayton L. Rev. 425 (1984) ("One recalls with nostalgia that the privilege once operated as a virtually impregnable bar to disclosure"; citing personally observed instance of federal judge's refusal to examine allegedly privileged document in camera). See also American College of Trial Lawyers, The Erosion of the Attorney Client Privilege and Work Product Doctrine in Federal Criminal Investigations at

27 (2002). In camera inspection has now become almost routine with respect to some questioned applications of the privilege. See, for example, § 95, infra.

[17]Matter of Jacqueline F., 47 N.Y.2d 215, 417 N.Y.S.2d 884, 391 N.E.2d 967 (1979) (privilege not absolute under New York precedents; Fuchsberg, J., dissenting, argues forcefully for "inviolable" privilege as integral to adversary role of lawyer). See also Note, The Attorney-Client Privilege: Fixed Rules, Balancing and Constitutional Entitlement, 91 Harv. L. Rev. 464 (1977) (advocating balancing, particularly of corporate claims of privilege).

[18]See, e.g., Swidler & Berlin v. U.S., 524 U.S. 399, 409, 118 S. Ct. 2081, 141 L. Ed. 2d 379 (1998) (balancing "ex post the importance of the information against client interest, even limited to criminal cases, introduces substantial uncertainty into the privilege's application"); Upjohn Co. v. U.S., 449 U.S. 383, 393, 101 S. Ct. 677, 66 L. Ed. 2d 584 (1981) ("an uncertain privilege . . . is little better than no privilege at all"). See also In re Dow Corning Corp., 261 F.3d 280, 284 (2d Cir. 2001) (protective order will not substitute for invocation of privilege); Berger, Comment: The Privileges Article in the New York Proposed Code of Evidence, 47 Brooklyn L. Rev. 1405 (1981) (noting that balancing approach is more consistent with privacy rationale than with traditional utilitarian theory).

tional methodology of controlling its scope through the liberal extension of exceptions and application of waiver doctrine.

A clear statement of the scope of the privilege as now generally accepted is embodied in the Uniform Evid. Rules as amended in 1999.[19]

---

[19]Unif. R. Evid. 502:

(a) Definitions. In this rule:

(1) "Client" means a person for whom a lawyer renders professional legal services or who consults a lawyer with a view to obtaining professional legal services from the lawyer.

(2) A communication is "confidential" if it is not intended to be disclosed to third persons other than those to whom disclosure is made in furtherance of the rendition of professional legal services to the client or those reasonably necessary for the transmission of the communication.

(3) "Lawyer" means a person authorized, or reasonably believed by the client to be authorized, to engage in the practice of law in any State or country.

(4) "Representative of the client" means a person having authority to obtain professional legal services, or to act on legal advice rendered, on behalf of the client or a person who, for the purpose of effectuating legal representation for the client, makes or receives a confidential communication while acting in the scope of employment for the client.

(5) "Representative of the lawyer" means a person employed, or reasonably believed by the client to be employed, by the lawyer to assist the lawyer in rendering professional legal services.

(b) General rule of privilege. A client has a privilege to refuse to disclose and to prevent any other person from disclosing a confidential communication made for the purpose of facilitating the rendition of professional legal services to the client:

(1) between the client or a representative of the client and the client's lawyer or a representative of the lawyer;

(2) between the lawyer and a representative of the lawyer;

(3) by the client or a representative of the client or the client's lawyer or a representative of the lawyer to a lawyer or a representative of a lawyer representing another party in a pending action and concerning a matter of common interest therein;

(4) between representatives of the client or between the client and a representative of the client; or

(5) among lawyers and their representatives representing the same client.

(c) Who may claim privilege. The privilege under this rule may be claimed by the client, the client's guardian or conservator, the personal representative of a deceased client, or the successor, trustee, or similar representative of a corporation, association, or other organization, whether or not in existence. A person who was the lawyer or the lawyer's representative at the time of the communication is presumed to have authority to claim the privilege, but only on behalf of the client.

(d) Exceptions. There is no privilege under this rule:

(1) if the services of the lawyer were sought or obtained to enable or aid anyone to commit or plan to commit what the client knew or reasonably should have known was a crime or fraud;

(2) as to a communication relevant to an issue between parties who claim through the same deceased client, regardless of whether the claims are by testate or intestate succession or by transaction inter vivos;

(3) as to a communication relevant to an issue of breach of duty by a lawyer to the client or by a client to the lawyer;

(4) as to a communication necessary for a lawyer to defend in a legal proceeding an accusation that the lawyer assisted the client in criminal or fraudulent conduct;

## § 87.1　Background and policy of the privilege: (b) Applications in corporate, governmental and other entity settings

The application of the privilege for the benefit of a corporate client, as distinguished from a natural person, was never questioned until a federal district court in 1962 held that a corporation is not entitled to claim the privilege.[1] The decision attracted wide attention and much comment, most of which was adverse, until reversed on appeal.[2] There seems to be little reason to believe that the issue will arise soon again.

The scope of the privilege in the corporate context, however, has presented an exceptionally troublesome question that is even yet not fully resolved. The difficulty is basically one of extrapolating the essential operating conditions of the privilege from the paradigm case of the traditional individual client who both supplies information to, and receives counsel from, the attorney.[3] Are both of these aspects of the relationship to be protected in the corporate setting, in which the corporate agents in a position to furnish the pertinent facts are not necessarily those empowered to take action responsive to legal advice based upon those facts? Early decisions focused upon the first half of this dichotomy, and extended the privilege expansively to communications from any

---

(5) as to a communication relevant to an issue concerning an attested document to which the lawyer is an attesting witness;

(6) as to a communication relevant to a matter of common interest between or among two or more clients if the communication was made by any of them to a lawyer retained or consulted in common, when offered in an action between or among any of the clients; or

(7) as to a communication between a public officer or agency and its lawyers unless the communication concerns a pending investigation, claim, or action and the court determines that disclosure will seriously impair the ability of the public officer or agency to act upon the claim or conduct a pending investigation, litigation, or proceeding in the public interest.

**[Section 87.1]**

[1]Radiant Burners, Inc. v. American Gas Ass'n, 207 F. Supp. 771 (N.D. Ill. 1962).

[2]Radiant Burners, Inc. v. American Gas Ass'n, 320 F.2d 314 (7th Cir. 1963). The case is remarkable for the number of *amici curiae* briefs urging reversal including briefs from the Chicago Bar Ass'n., the Illinois State Bar Ass'n., and the American Bar Ass'n.

For comment on the District Court decision, see 76 Harvard L. Rev. 655 (1963), 52 Ill.B.J. 666 (1963), 61 Mich. L. Rev. 603 (1963), 57 NW. U. L. Rev. 596 (1962).

On the privilege as applied to corporations generally, see Simon, The Attorney-Client Privilege as Applied to Corporations, 65 Yale L.J. 953 (1956).

[3]*See* Higley, Jones & Buck, Confidentiality of Communications by In-House Counsel for Financial Institutions, 6 N.C. Banking Inst. 265 (2002); Sexton, A Post-Upjohn Consideration of the Corporate Attorney-Client Privilege, 57 N.Y.U. L. Rev. 443, 478 (1982).

"officer or employee" of the client corporation.[4] This emphasis was dramatically reversed by the case of *City of Philadelphia v. Westinghouse Electric Corp.,*[5] which propounded a "control group" test under which the privilege was restricted to communications made by those corporate functionaries "in a position to control or even to take a substantial part in a decision about any action which the corporation may take upon the advice of the attorney."[6]

The "control group" theory was widely,[7] though not universally,[8] followed by the courts until the 1981 decision of the Supreme Court in *Upjohn Co. v. United States.*[9] While the Court specifically declined in Upjohn to attempt the formulation of a definitive rule,[10] it did specifically reject the control group principle as one which "cannot . . . govern the development of the law in this area."[11] The principal deficiency that the Court noted as inherent in the control group test is its failure to recognize the function of the privilege as protecting the flow of information to the advising attorney.[12] The opinion does suggest limitations however, in that such information will be privileged only if: (1) it is communicated for the express purpose of securing legal advice for the corporation; (2) it relates to the specific corporate duties of the communicating employee; and (3) it is treated as confidential within the corporation itself.[13]

The *Upjohn* decision evoked a large amount of commentary,[14] much of which has been critical. In addition to the decision's fail-

---

[4]U.S. v. Aluminum Co. of America, 193 F. Supp. 251 (N.D. N.Y. 1960); Zenith Radio Corp. v. Radio Corp. of America, 121 F. Supp. 792 (D. Del. 1954); U.S. v. United Shoe Machinery Corp., 89 F. Supp. 357 (D. Mass. 1950).

[5]City of Philadelphia v. Westinghouse Elec. Corp., 210 F. Supp. 483 (E.D. Pa. 1962).

[6]City of Philadelphia v, Westinghouse Electric Corp. 210 F.Supp. at 485.

[7]In re Grand Jury Investigation, 599 F.2d 1224 (3d Cir. 1979); Virginia Elec. & Power Co. v. Sun Shipbuilding & Dry Dock Co., 68 F.R.D. 397 (E.D. Va. 1975); Garrison v. General Motors Corp., 213 F. Supp. 515 (S.D. Cal. 1963).

[8]*See* Harper & Row Publishers, Inc. v. Decker, 423 F.2d 487 (7th Cir. 1970), affirmed by an equally divided Court 400 U.S. 348).

[9]Upjohn Co. v. U.S., 449 U.S. 383, 101 S. Ct. 677, 66 L. Ed. 2d 584 (1981).

[10]Upjohn, 449 U.S. at 386, 396. This failure was strenuously criticized by Chief Justice Burger in a concurring opinion. 449 U.S. at 402 (". . . I believe that we should articulate a standard that will govern similar cases and afford guidance to corporations, counsel advising them, and federal courts." Burger, C.J., concurring in part and concurring in the judgment).

[11]449 U.S. at 402.

[12]449 U.S. at 390.

[13]449 U.S.at 394.

[14]An extensive collection of law review notes on *Upjohn* may be found in Freedman, Corporate Attorney-Client Privilege Since Upjohn, at Home and Abroad, 9 U. Dayton L. Rev. 425, 427 (1984). *See also* Glynn, One Privilege to Rule Them all? Some

ure to articulate the scope of the privilege of corporations more clearly, another frequent criticism has been *Upjohn's* reliance upon a utilitarian rationale without at the same time limiting the privilege to instances where it is likely to be effective for its stated purpose. Thus a lower level corporate employee sufficiently sophisticated to factor an evidentiary privilege into his decision to communicate with a corporate attorney is unlikely to be reassured by a privilege which is waivable in the exclusive discretion of the corporation.[15] At a minimum, the privilege should apply only to corporate employees who either have, or are expressly conferred, the power to assert the privilege.[16]

Though the *Upjohn* decision is not rested upon constitutional grounds, and is thus not binding upon the states, it has had considerable influence outside the federal system.[17] At the same

---

Post-Sarbanes-Oxley and Other Reflections on a Federally Codified Attorney-Client Privilege, 38 Loy. L.A. L. Rev. 597 (2004) (argues for a codified privilege that would, among other things, clarify the application of the privilege in a corporate setting).

[15]Many commentators have noted this point. *See, e.g.,* Alexander, The Corporate Attorney-Client Privilege: A Study of the Participants, 63 St. John's L. Rev. 191, 227 (1989); Sexton, A Post-Upjohn Consideration of the Corporate Attorney-Client Privilege, 57 N.Y.U. L. Rev. 443, 467 (1982).

[16]*See* Saltzburg, Corporate and Related Attorney-Client Privilege Claims: A Suggested Approach, 12 Hofstra L. Rev. 279 (1984) (presenting a detailed proposal as to how the scope of the privilege should be tailored in the corporate context). *See also* Brown, Reconsidering the Corporate Attorney–Client Privilege: A Response to the Compelled–Voluntary Waiver Paradox, 34 Hofstra L. Rev. 897 (2006) (similarly arguing for a narrowing of the privilege in the corporate context); Geisel, Upjohn Warnings, the Attorney-Client Privilege, and Principles of Lawyer Ethics: Achieving Harmony, 65 U. Miami L. Rev. 109 (2010) (calling for reassessment of the analysis of whether an attorney represents the individual interviewed on behalf of the corporation).

[17]*See, e.g.,* Southern Bell Tel. & Tel. Co. v. Deason, 632 So. 2d 1377 (Fla. 1994) (analyzing Florida's subject matter test for application of privilege); Note, Oregon Expands the Protections of the Attorney-Client Privilege for Corporations and Other Business Entities, 24 Willamette L. Rev. 1 (1988) (discussing enactment of Upjohn-type statute proposed by major local corporation).

Uniform Rule of Evidence 502 was amended in 1986 by the Conference of Commissioners on Uniform State Laws in an attempt to track the *Upjohn* decision. *See* Unif. R. Evid. 502 (comment to 1986 amendment). The 1986 rule arguably exceeds the *Upjohn* privilege in breadth in that it imposes no requirement that the subject matter of a corporate employee's communication concern the employee's duties. The Rule was amended again in 1999, but with no change in the language dealing with the Upjohn issue. *See* the current rule supra § 87, n. 19. The more conventional response is that the employee fortuitously witnessing an event unconnected with his duties is not within the privilege. *See* Leer v. Chicago, M., St. P. & P. Ry. Co., 308 N.W.2d 305 (Minn. 1981). For discussion of the problem of the bystander witness, *see* Comment, Beyond Upjohn: Achieving Certainty by Expanding the Scope of the Corporate Attorney-Client Privilege, 50 Ford. L.

time, some states continue to subscribe to the control group test,[18] thus adding the identity of the forum in which the privilege will ultimately be asserted to other sources of uncertainty as to its scope.

An *Upjohn* extension of the corporate attorney-client privilege almost necessitates extension of the privilege in other organizational structures.[19] While under the control group test the scope of the corporate privilege might be roughly likened to that available to a proprietorship,[20] extension to lower level employees without a corresponding extension to employees of various other entities is probably politically as well as theoretically indefensible.

Where the entity in question is governmental, however, significantly different considerations appear,[21] which have led a number of states substantially to limit the privilege for such

---

Rev. 1182 (1982).

In Samaritan Foundation v. Goodfarb, 176 Ariz. 497, 862 P.2d 870 (1993), the court adopted a subject matter test more limited than *Upjohn*, at least in instances where the inquiry was initiated by the corporation rather than the employee. Under such circumstances, the communication must have concerned the employee's own conduct in order to come within the privilege. However, the next year, the Arizona legislature amended the state's privilege statute to provide a more expansive version of the privilege in the corporate setting, requiring only that the communication be made for the purpose of obtaining legal advice. Ariz. Rev. Stat. Ann. § 12-2234. *See also* Comment, An Analysis of the Troubling Issues Surrounding In-House Counsel and the Attorney-Client Privilege, 23 Hamline L. Rev. 289 (1999); Note, Arizona's Attorney-Client Communication Privilege for Corporations, 27 Ariz. St. L.J. 335 (1995).

[18]*See, e.g.,* Consolidation Coal Co. v. Bucyrus-Erie Co., 89 Ill. 2d 103, 59 Ill. Dec. 666, 432 N.E.2d 250 (1982); National Tank Co. v. Brotherton, 851 S.W.2d 193 (Tex. 1993).

[19]*See* Sexton, A Post-Upjohn Consideration of the Corporate Attorney-Client Privilege, 57 N.Y.U. L. Rev. 443, 463 n. 86 (1982) (. . . arguments justifying a corporate

attorney-client privilege also justify a privilege for government agencies, labor unions, non-profit corporations, associations, and partnerships. Hence, Upjohn may foreshadow the development of an "enterprise" privilege). Unif. R. Evid. 502 would appear to provide for such an "enterprise" privilege by virtue of its definitions of "client" and "representative of the client." The question, of course, is not whether entities other than corporations may claim the privilege, but whether the privilege extends to cover communications by non-management employees. *Compare* Benge v. Superior Court, 131 Cal. App. 3d 336, 182 Cal. Rptr. 275 (5th Dist. 1982) (holding labor union to be within Cal. Evid. Code's definition of person and thus entitled to privilege, and extending privilege to all communications made at closed local meeting with attorneys. *See also* Chambliss, The Scope of In-Firm Privilege, 80 Notre Dame L. Rev. 1721 (2005) (discusses the application of the attorney-client privilege with regard to in-house counsel employed by a law firm).

[20]*See, e.g.,* Alaska R. Evid. 503(a) (2) commentary ("The restrictive [control group] view adopted brings the corporate privilege more in line with the privilege available to unincorporated business concerns.").

[21]*See* Note, Attorney-Client Privilege for the Government Entity, 97

entities.[22] On the federal level, cases arising from the investigation of President Clinton have held that any privilege applicable to communications between government attorneys and government officials will not apply to prevent disclosure in the face of a grand jury subpoena.[23]

As noted above, there are situations which draw into question the application of the conventional rule that a corporation's privilege may be asserted or waived by the management of the corporation. One such situation is the derivative stockholder's action, in which both parties claim to be acting in the corporate interest. In the leading case of *Garner v. Wolfinbarger*,[24] the court addressed the problem thus raised by recognizing a qualified privilege on the part of the corporate management, but one which may be pierced by a showing of good cause by the shareholders. Several federal Courts of Appeal[25] and some states[26] have explicitly adopted the *Garner* approach and some cases have

---

Yale L.J. 1725 (1988) (arguing against the extension of the privilege to government entities).

[22]Unif. R. Evid. 502(d)(7), supra § 87, adopted in a number of states, effectively limits the government entity's privilege in this area. However, the privilege will be held to exist in various contexts, especially in cases involving municipal governments. *See, e.g.,* Roberts v. City of Palmdale, 5 Cal. 4th 363, 20 Cal. Rptr. 2d 330, 853 P.2d 496 (1993) (letter from city attorney to members of city council); Shew v. Freedom of Information Com'n, 245 Conn. 149, 714 A.2d 664 (1998) (communication to town manager from attorney retained by town); Tausz v. Clarion-Goldfield Community School Dist., 569 N.W.2d 125 (Iowa 1997) (meeting of school board with attorney). *See also* In re County of Erie, 473 F.3d 413 (2d Cir. 2007) (emails from county officials to county attorney with regard to prison policies were privileged).

[23]In re Lindsey, 158 F.3d 1263 (D.C. Cir. 1998); In re Grand Jury Subpoena Duces Tecum, 112 F.3d 910 (8th Cir. 1997). *See also* In re Witness Before Special Grand Jury 2000–2, 288 F.3d 289, 294 (7th Cir. 2002) (no attorney-client privilege existed between state officeholder and state government lawyer as to federal grand

jury subpoena); Ellinwood, "In the Light of Reason and Experience": The Case for a Strong Government Attorney-Client Privilege, 2001 Wis. L. Rev. 1291; Note, In Defense of the Government Attorney-Client Privilege, 84 Cornell L. Rev. 1682 (1999); Note, Should the Federal Government Have an Attorney-Client Privilege?, 51 Fla. L. Rev. 695 (1999).

[24]Garner v. Wolfinbarger, 430 F.2d 1093 (5th Cir. 1970).

[25]*See, e.g.,* Fausek v. White, 965 F.2d 126, 130 (6th Cir. 1992) (quoting at length from *Garner* because "it is the seminal case, and we agree with its rationale and adopt its holding"); Weil v. Investment/Indicators, Research and Management, Inc., 647 F.2d 18, 23 (9th Cir. 1981) (recognizing *Garner*, but limiting the exception to shareholder derivative suits). District Court cases from other circuits have also applied the doctrine. *See, e.g.,* Henry v. Champlain Enterprises, Inc., 212 F.R.D. 73, 85 (N.D. N.Y. 2003) (applying the *Garner* exception to derivative action). *But see* Shirvani v. Capital Investing Corp., Inc., 112 F.R.D. 389, 390 (D. Conn. 1986) (declining to adopt the *Garner* exception, finding that attorney-client privilege has never protected the type of misconduct which would underlay any genuinely appealing *Garner* claim and that

expanded it beyond derivative shareholder actions.[27] Yet, although probably the prevailing doctrine in dealing with disputes between shareholders and corporations,[28] the *Garner* approach has been criticized as injecting too much uncertainty into the application of the privilege.[29]

---

the proper test of disclosure in that instance would not be a vague "good cause" checklist).

[26]*See, e.g.,* Zirn v. VLI Corp., 621 A.2d 773, 781 (Del. 1993) (*Garner* applied); Omega Consulting Group, Inc. v. Templeton, 805 So. 2d 1058, 1060 (Fla. 4th DCA 2002) (citing *Garner* in refusing to reverse lower court holding that attorney-client privilege did not apply to communications in question).

[27]*See* Solis v. Food Employers Labor Relations Ass'n, 644 F.3d 221 (4th Cir. 2011) (adopts the fiduciary exception for documents subpoenaed in response to ERISA investigations); In re Occidental Petroleum Corp., 217 F.3d 293, 297–98 (5th Cir. 2000) (Garner doctrine applied to action by employees who were participants in stock ownership plan suing for breach of fiduciary duty); Ward v. Succession of Freeman, 854 F.2d 780, 786 (5th Cir. 1988) (holding *Garner* applicable to nonderivative shareholder actions, but finding no good cause for disclosure shown on facts). I Ferguson v. Lurie, 139 F.R.D. 362, 365–66 (N.D. Ill. 1991) (considering *Garner* factors after finding that general partners have a fiduciary obligation to limited partners in a limited partnership); Aguinaga v. John Morrell & Co., 112 F.R.D. 671, 676–81 (D. Kan. 1986) (applying *Garner* to a labor union and the employees it represented). *But see* U.S. v. Jicarilla Apache Nation, 131 S. Ct. 2313, 180 L. Ed. 2d 187 (2011) recognizes exception but refuses to apply it to U.S. government holding property in trust for Apache tribe).

[28]*See* Restatement (Third) of the Law Governing Lawyers § 85 (2000).

[29]*See* Friedman, Is the Garner Qualification of the Corporate Attorney-Client Privilege Viable After Jaffee v. Redmond?, 55 Bus. Law. 243, 272–73 (1999). *See also* Saltzburg, Corporate Attorney-Client Privilege in Shareholder Litigation and Similar Cases: *Garner* Revisited, 12 Hofstra L. Rev. 817 (1984) (*Garner* inhibits flow of information from corporate officers to corporation's attorney); Saltzberg, Martin & Capra, Federal Rules of Evidence Manual, § 501.02[5][l][ii] (8th ed. 2002) (*Garner* should be limited to shareholders derivative litigation); Santoni, Application of the Attorney-Client Privilege to Disputes Between Owners and Managers of Closely-Held Entities, 31 Creighton L. Rev. 849 (1998) (argues that attorney-client privilege in closely-held corporations be treated as an asset of the corporation).

The *Garner* exception should be distinguished from the exception applied by many courts with regard to communications made by a fiduciary on behalf of the beneficiaries of a trust or similar arrangements. *See* Restatement (Third) of the Law Governing Lawyers § 84 (2000). The seminal case is Riggs Nat. Bank of Washington, D.C. v. Zimmer, 355 A.2d 709, 712–14 (Del. Ch. 1976). The exception is often invoked in ERISA cases. *See e.g.,* U.S. v. Mett, 178 F.3d 1058, 1063 (9th Cir. 1999). The fiduciary exception does not require the showing of good cause required under *Garner*, see, e.g., Hudson v. General Dynamics Corp., 186 F.R.D. 271, 274 (D. Conn. 1999). *See also* Henry v. Champlain Enterprises, Inc., 212 F.R.D. 73, 85 (N.D. N.Y. 2003), where the court applied the Garner exception to a derivative action and the fiduciary exception to ERISA claims.

## § 88    The professional relationship

The privilege for communications of a client with her lawyer hinges upon the client's belief that she is consulting a lawyer in that capacity and her manifested intention to seek professional legal advice.[1] It is sufficient if she reasonably believes that the person consulted is a lawyer, though in fact she is not.[2] Communications in the course of preliminary discussion with a view to employing the lawyer are privileged though the employment is in the upshot not accepted.[3] The burden of proof rests on the person asserting the privilege to show that the consultation was a professional one.[4] Payment or agreement to pay a fee, however,

---

**[Section 88]**

[1]*See* Note, 24 Iowa L. Rev. 538 (1939).

[2]People v. Barker, 60 Mich. 277, 27 N.W. 539 (1886) (confession to detective pretending to be an attorney); Unif. R. Evid. 502(a) (3), supra § 87.

A surprising number of cases have involved attempted assertions of the privilege for communications to "jailhouse" lawyers, i.e., inmates with no formal legal training. Such claims have uniformly been rejected, frequently on the ground that a reasonable person could not have believed that the confidant was an attorney. *See* People v. Velasquez, 192 Cal. App. 3d 319, 237 Cal. Rptr. 366 (5th Dist. 1987); People v. Barber, 116 Ill. App. 3d 767, 72 Ill. Dec. 472, 452 N.E.2d 725 (3d Dist. 1983); State v. Fleury, 545 So. 2d 1208 (La. Ct. App. 4th Cir. 1989); Richardson v. State, 744 S.W.2d 65 (Tex. Crim. App. 1987), cert. granted and judgment vacated on other grounds, Richardson v. Texas, 492 U.S. 914.

[3]Constand v. Cosby, 232 F.R.D. 494 (E.D. Pa.2006) (communications privileged where plaintiff was consulting counsel for advice on a problem that has legal implications); In re Dupont's Estate, 60 Cal. App. 2d 276, 140 P.2d 866 (1st Dist. 1943) (preliminary negotiations fell within language of [former] Cal. Code Civ. Proc. § 1881,

subd. 2 conferring privilege to communications, "in the course of professional employment," "no person could ever safely consult an attorney for the first time * * * if the privilege depended on the chance of whether the attorney after hearing the statement of the facts decided to accept the employment or decline it"); Denver Tramway Co. v. Owens, 20 Colo. 107, 36 P. 848 (1894); Keir v. State, 152 Fla. 389, 11 So. 2d 886 (1943) (letters); State v. Iwakiri, 106 Idaho 618, 682 P.2d 571 (1984); Mixon v. State, 224 S.W.3d 206 (Tex. Crim. App. 2007) (privilege applied even though lawyer declined to represent defendant). Of course, statements made after the employment is declined are not privileged. McGrede v. Rembert Nat. Bank, 147 S.W.2d 580 (Tex. Civ. App. Texarkana 1941). Unif. R. Evid.502(b) covers the matter by extending the privilege to communications "for the purpose of facilitating the rendition" of legal services.

[4]U.S. v. Landof, 591 F.2d 36 (9th Cir. 1978); McKnew v. Superior Court of City and County of San Francisco, 23 Cal. 2d 58, 142 P.2d 1 (1943); McGrede v. Rembert Nat. Bank, 147 S.W.2d 580 (Tex. Civ. App. Texarkana 1941). *See also* U.S. v. Martin, 278 F.3d 988, 1000 (9th Cir. 2002) (defendant failed to show that attorney represented him at the time of communication); U.S. v. Munoz, 233 F.3d 1117, 1128 (9th Cir. 2000) (same).

is not essential.[5] But where one consults an attorney not as a lawyer but as a friend[6] or as a business adviser[7] or banker,[8] or negotiator,[9] or as an accountant,[10] or where the communication is

---

[5]U.S. v. Costanzo, 625 F.2d 465 (3d Cir. 1980); Matters v. State, 120 Neb. 404, 232 N.W. 781 (1930); Hodge v. Garten, 116 W. Va. 564, 182 S.E. 582 (1935); 98 C.J.S., Witnesses § 322.

[6]Modern Woodmen of America v. Watkins, 132 F.2d 352 (C.C.A. 5th Cir. 1942) (disclosure of suicidal intent); G & S Investments v. Belman, 145 Ariz. 258, 700 P.2d 1358 (Ct. App. Div. 2 1984); Lifsey v. Mims, 193 Ga. 780, 20 S.E.2d 32 (1942) (lawyer drawing deed as a "friendly act"); State v. Parker, 747 N.W.2d 196 (Iowa 2008) (no privilege where meeting between defendant and lawyer was social); In re Estate of Conner, 33 N.W.2d 866 (Iowa 1948), modified on other grounds 36 N.W.2d 833 (Iowa 1949) (divulging grandson's illegitimacy, to secure friend's help in telling boy); State v. Gordon, 141 N.H. 703, 692 A.2d 505 (1997) (statements made in seeking advice from an attorney-instructor not within privilege).

[7]U.S. v. United Shoe Machinery Corp., 89 F. Supp. 357 (D. Mass. 1950) (a communication soliciting business advice, not privileged, and attorney-client privilege does not extend to attorneys employed in a department of corporation which functions as a business branch, but does exist between corporation and attorneys in its legal department who perform substantially the same service as outside counsel); U.S. v. Vehicular Parking, 52 F. Supp. 751 (D. Del. 1943) (business advice and directions by attorney who was promoter, director and manager of corporation concerned); E.I. du Pont de Nemours & Co. v. Forma-Pack, Inc., 351 Md. 396, 718 A.2d 1129 (1998) (collection of debts other than through litigation not legal activity); Clayton v. Canida, 223 S.W.2d 264 (Tex. Civ. App. Texarkana 1949) (attorney acting as accountant, income tax return). And whether the attorney was acting

as such on different occasions may require individual assessment. Payton v. New Jersey Turnpike Authority, 148 N.J. 524, 691 A.2d 321 (1997) (in camera review required to determine whether investigation was for purposes of litigation). However, where business and legal advice are intertwined and the legal component predominates, the privilege has been held to apply. Sedco Intern., S. A. v. Cory, 683 F.2d 1201 (8th Cir. 1982). *See also* Rehling v. City of Chicago, 207 F.3d 1009, 1019 (7th Cir. 2000) (general counsel of police department acted as a lawyer, not business advisor, when advising high ranking police officers with regard to personnel matters); Montgomery County v. MicroVote Corp., 175 F.3d 296, 303–04 (3d Cir. 1999) (lawyer employed as an "election consultant" was in fact performing legal services; communications between county and lawyer were privileged); Giesel, The Legal Advice Requirement of the Attorney-Client Privilege: A Special Problem for In-House Counsel and Outside Attorneys Representing Corporations, 48 Mercer L. Rev. 1169 (1997).

[8]U.S. v. Horvath, 731 F.2d 557 (8th Cir. 1984); Belcher v. Somerville, 413 S.W.2d 620 (Ky. 1967).

[9]Myles E. Rieser Co. v. Loew's Inc., 194 Misc. 119, 81 N.Y.S.2d 861 (Sup 1948) (attorneys acting both as lawyers and as negotiators; communications in latter capacity not privileged); Henson v. State, 97 Okla. Crim. 240, 261 P.2d 916 (1953) (communication between defendant and attorney sharing office and secretary with defendant's attorney, not privileged and no attorney-client relationship existed where defendant knew attorney represented another and attorney tried to settle differences between his client and defendant).

to the attorney acting as a "mere scrivener"[11] or as an attesting witness to a will or deed,[12] or as an executor[13] or as agent,[14] the consultation is not professional nor the statement privileged.

---

[10]Olender v. U.S., 210 F.2d 795 (9th Cir. 1954) (attorney engaged as an accountant to prepare financial statement and income tax returns).

[11]The phrase is often used as a justification for denying the privilege, see e.g., In re Grand Jury Subpoena (Mr. S.), 662 F.3d 65 (1st Cir. 2011), cert. denied, 133 S. Ct. 43, 183 L. Ed. 2d 680 (2012) (no privilege where attorney in real estate transactions acted as a "mere scrivener"); Benson v. Custer, 236 Iowa 345, 17 N.W.2d 889 (1945); Sparks v. Sparks, 51 Kan. 195, 32 P. 892 (1893); Aetna Cas. and Sur. Co. v. Certain Underwriters at Lloyd's London, 176 Misc. 2d 605, 676 N.Y.S.2d 727 (Sup 1998) (no privilege attached to meeting of industry-wide group to discuss economic problems). The distinction is usually drawn between instances where the lawyer is employed merely to draft the document and cases where his advice is sought as to terms and effect. Mueller v. Batcheler, 131 Iowa 650, 109 N.W. 186, 187 (1906) (conveyances); Dickerson v. Dickerson, 322 Ill. 492, 153 N.E. 740 (1926) (deed); Cranston v. Stewart, 184 Kan. 99, 334 P.2d 337 (1959); Wilcox v. Coons, 359 Mo. 52, 220 S.W.2d 15 (1949); Shelley v. Landry, 97 N.H. 27, 79 A.2d 626 (1951). Bolyea v. First Presbyterian Church of Wilton, 196 N.W.2d 149 (N.D. 1972) (privilege held inapplicable where attorney employed as scrivener offered legal advice which was rejected by client). Usually it will be found that an attorney asked to draw a will, is not a mere scrivener, but is acting professionally. Booher v. Brown, 173 Or. 464, 146 P.2d 71 (1944). And the strict view of privilege in respect to the employment of lawyers as conveyancers seems somewhat inconsistent with the bar's present-day emphasis upon the importance of this as a lawyer's function. See Houck, Real Estate Instruments and the Bar, 5 Law & Contemp. Prob. 66 (1938).

[12]Smith v. Smith, 222 Ga. 694, 152 S.E.2d 560 (1966) (lawyer may testify as to client's mental condition, his knowledge of the contents and other pertinent facts attending execution of contract, prepared and attested to by him); In re Heiler's Estate, 288 Mich. 49, 284 N.W. 641 (1939) (lawyer attesting will could testify to what he learned in his capacity as witness); Larson v. Dahlstrom, 214 Minn. 304, 8 N.W.2d 48 (1943) (lawyer attesting deed could testify to statements made by client at time of execution as bearing on mental condition); Anderson v. Thomas, 108 Utah 252, 159 P.2d 142 (1945) (deed; attesting lawyer may testify to conversations at time of execution).

[13]Peyton v. Werhane, 126 Conn. 382, 11 A.2d 800 (1940).

[14]U.S. v. Bartone, 400 F.2d 459 (6th Cir. 1968) (services consisted of tracing funds); Pollock v. U.S., 202 F.2d 281 (5th Cir. 1953) (money deposited with attorney to be applied on purchase of real estate); Hansen v. Janitschek, 31 N.J. 545, 158 A.2d 329 (1960) (attorney-client relationship held not to exist where attorney employed solely to assist in obtaining loan). See also Zenith Radio Corp. v. Radio Corp. of America, 121 F. Supp. 792 (D. Del. 1954) critically noted 23 Geo. Wash. L. Rev. 786 (1955) (attorney-employee of corporate patent department would be regarded as "acting as a lawyer" within discovery rule when preponderantly engaged in giving legal advice but not when largely concerned with technical aspects of a business or engineering character). In Sperti Products, Inc. v. Coca-Cola Co., 262 F. Supp. 148 (D. Del. 1966) the same court held that the rule of Zenith did not extend to take communications between clients and outside attorneys who represent them before the Patent Office outside the privilege. The Court cited Chore-Time Equipment,

There is some conflict in the decisions as to whether the privilege is available for communications to an administrative practitioner who is not a lawyer.[15] However, the privilege will generally be applicable even where the services performed by a lawyer are not necessarily available only from members of the legal profession.[16]

Ordinarily an attorney can lawfully hold herself out as qualified to practice only in the state in which she is licensed, and consultation elsewhere on a continuing basis would traditionally not be privileged,[17] but exceptionally by custom she might lawfully be consulted elsewhere in respect to isolated transactions, and Uniform Evidence Rule 502(a)(3) requires only that she be authorized or reasonably be believed to be authorized "in any State or country."[18]

Traditionally, the relationship sought to be fostered by the

---

Inc. v. Big Dutchman, Inc., 255 F. Supp. 1020 (W.D. Mich. 1966) (communications between outside patent attorney and client privileged).

For cases on the above as well as related categories, *see* 98 C.J.S., Witnesses § 324.

[15]Decisions denying the privilege to administrative practitioners include: U.S. v. Zakutansky, 401 F.2d 68 (7th Cir. 1968) (work papers used by accountant in preparing tax return); Falsone v. U.S., 205 F.2d 734 (5th Cir. 1953) (certified public accountant having the same rights as an enrolled attorney under Treasury Department regulations); U.S. v. United Shoe Machinery Corp., 89 F. Supp. 357 (D. Mass. 1950) (patent solicitors not members of bar employed in corporation's patent department); Kent Jewelry Corp. v. Kiefer, 202 Misc. 778, 113 N.Y.S.2d 12 (Sup 1952) (patent agent authorized to practice before the United States Patent Office). *But compare* In re Ampicillin Antitrust Litigation, 81 F.R.D. 377 (D.D.C. 1978) (privilege applicable to communications to patent agents registered with the U.S. Patent Office; collecting authorities to the same effect); Golden Trade, S.r.L. v. Lee Apparel Co., 143 F.R.D. 514 (S.D. N.Y. 1992) (communication by attorneys to foreign patent agents privileged). *See also* Naffier. Attorney-Client Privilege for Nonlawyers? A Study of Board of Immigration

Appeals-Accredited Representatives, Privileges and Confidentiality, 59 Drake L. Rev. 583 (2011).

[16]U.S. v. Frederick, 182 F.3d 496, 500 (7th Cir. 1999) (documents prepared for use in connection with tax returns not privileged); U.S. v. Summe, 208 F. Supp. 925 (E.D. Ky. 1962) (lawyer employed to fill out tax return). *Compare* U.S. v. Merrell, 303 F. Supp. 490 (N.D. N.Y. 1969) (schedule of income and expenses furnished by client, and attorney's working papers, intended to be disclosed in returns and not confidential). *See generally* Petersen, Attorney-Client Privilege in Internal Revenue Service Investigations, 54 Minn. L. Rev. 67 (1969); What matters are protected by attorney-client privilege or are proper subject of inquiry by Internal Revenue Service where attorney is summoned in connection with taxpayer-client under federal tax examination, 15 A.L.R. Fed. 771.

[17]U.S. v. United Shoe Machinery Corp., 89 F. Supp. 357 (D. Mass. 1950).

[18]Paper Converting Mach. Co. v. FMC Corp., 215 F. Supp. 249 (E.D. Wis. 1963) (patent counsel member of Ohio bar but not of California bar where employed, communications held privileged); Georgia-Pacific Plywood Co. v. U.S. Plywood Corp., 18 F.R.D. 463 (S.D. N.Y. 1956) (where house counsel of corporation not licensed in state where suit pending was actively engaged in legal service to corporation

privilege has been that between the lawyer and a private client, but more recently the privilege has been held to extend to communications to an attorney representing the state.[19] However, disclosures to the public prosecuting attorney by an informer are not within the attorney-client privilege,[20] but an analogous policy of protecting the giving of such information has led to the recognition of a privilege against the disclosure of the identity of the informer, unless the trial judge finds that such disclosure is necessary in the interests of justice.[21] Communications to an attorney appointed by the court to serve the interest of a party are of course within the privilege.[22] A communication by a lawyer to a member of the Board of Governors of the state bar association, revealing a fraudulent conspiracy in which he had been engaged and expressing his desire to resign from the practice of law was held not privileged.[23]

Wigmore argued for a privilege analogous to the lawyer-client privilege for "confessions or similar confidences" made privately by persons implicated in a wrong or crime to the judge of a court.[24] As to judges generally there seems little justification for such a

---

in multi-state litigation communications with him relating to legal service were privileged); Zenith Radio Corp. v. Radio Corp. of America, 121 F. Supp. 792, 794 (D. Del. 1954) ("Bar membership should properly be of the court for the area wherein the services are rendered, but this is not a sine qua non, e.g., visiting counsel, long distance services by correspondence, pro hac vice services, 'house counsel' who practice law only for the corporate client and its affiliates and not for the public generally, for which local authorities do not insist on admission to the local bar."). In theory, making existence of the privilege dependent upon the technicalities of the attorney's admission status appears dubious. Absent such a limitation, the client is afforded more protection when consulting an imposter than when consulting an attorney unlicensed in the jurisdiction.

[19]People By and Through Dept. of Public Works v. Glen Arms Estate, Inc., 230 Cal. App. 2d 841, 41 Cal. Rptr. 303 (1st Dist. 1964); Hartford Acc. & Indem. Co. v. Cutter, 108 N.H. 112, 229 A.2d 173 (1967); Riddle Spring Realty Co. v. State, 107 N.H. 271, 220

A.2d 751 (1966) (appraisals and reports confidentially made at request of attorney for state held privileged. See Unif. R. Evid. 502(a)(1), supra § 87, note 19. See also Prior Lake American v. Mader, 642 N.W.2d 729, 737–39 (Minn. 2002) (discusses relationship between attorney-client privilege and Open Meetings Law; exception to Open Meetings Law held inapplicable).

[20]Fite v. Bennett, 142 Ga. 660, 83 S.E. 515 (1914); Cole v. Andrews, 74 Minn. 93, 76 N.W. 962 (1898); Application of Heller, 184 Misc. 75, 53 N.Y.S.2d 86 (Sup 1945).

[21]Wilson v. U.S., 59 F.2d 390 (C.C.A. 3d Cir. 1932); 8 Wigmore, Evidence §§ 2374, 2375 (McNaughton rev. 1961); Imwinkelried, The New Wigmore: Evidentiary Privileges § 7.3 (2d. ed. 2010). See § 111 infra.

[22]Jayne v. Bateman, 1942 OK 298, 191 Okla. 272, 129 P.2d 188 (1942) (lawyer appointed as guardian ad litem of incompetent party apparently expected to act as attorney also).

[23]Steiner v. U.S., 134 F.2d 931 (C.C.A. 5th Cir. 1943).

[24]8 Wigmore, Evidence § 2376 (McNaughton rev. 1961).

privilege if the policy-motive is the furtherance of the administration of justice by encouraging a full disclosure.[25] Unlike the lawyer the judge needs no private disclosures in advance of trial to enable her to perform her functions. In fact such revelations would ordinarily embarrass rather than aid her in carrying out her duties as a trial judge.[26] The famous case of *Lindsey v. People*,[27] however, raised the question whether the judge of a juvenile court does not stand in a special position with regard to confidential disclosures by children who come before her. The majority of the court held that when a boy under promise of secrecy confessed to the judge that he had fired the shot that killed his father the judge was compellable, on the trial of the boy's mother for murder, to divulge the confession. The court pointed out that a parent who had received such a confidence would be compellable to disclose.[28] In the case of this particular court the need for encouraging confidences is clear, but in most cases the most effective encouragement will come from the confidence-inspiring personality of the judge, even without the aid of assurances of secrecy.[29] The court's conclusion that the need for secrecy for this type of disclosure does not outweigh the sacrifice to the administration of justice from the suppression of the evidence seems justifiable.

### § 89    Subject-matter of the privilege: (a) Communications

The modern justification of the privilege, namely, that of encouraging full disclosure by the client for the furtherance of

---

[25]There is limited authority on the issue. People v. Pratt, 133 Mich. 125, 94 N.W. 752 (1903) tends to support the privilege. Opposed are People v. Sharac, 209 Mich. 249, 176 N.W. 431 (1920) and Agnew v. Agnew, 52 S.D. 472, 218 N.W. 633 (1928).

[26]Prichard v. U.S., 181 F.2d 326 (6th Cir. 1950) (communications between judge and attorney seeking legal advice concerning his conduct which was to be investigated by a grand jury called by the judge to investigate election frauds, not privileged and attorney-client relationship did not arise).

[27]Lindsey v. People, 66 Colo. 343, 181 P. 531 (1919) (three judges dissenting), 33 Harv. L. Rev. 88, 35 id. 693, 29 Yale L.J. 356, 4 Minn. L. Rev.

227; State v. Bixby, 27 Wash. 2d 144, 177 P.2d 689 (1947).

[28]The continuing strength of the court's argument by analogy will, of course depend on the future of the parent-child privilege. See § 76 supra.

[29]The special nature of juvenile court proceedings with respect to the need for confidentiality of reports and records is recognized by modern juvenile court statutes. See statutes set out in 8 Wigmore, Evidence § 2376 n. 3 (McNaughton rev. 1961).

Cases recognizing the application of the informer's privilege for information given to judges (see cases pro and con collected in Evidence: privilege of communications made to public officer, 59 A.L.R. 1555) are to be distinguished.

the administration of justice,[1] might suggest that the privilege is only a one-way one, operating to protect communications of the client or his agents[2] to the lawyer or his clerk[3] but not vice versa. However, it is generally held that the privilege will protect at least those attorney to client communications which would have a tendency to reveal the confidences of the client.[4] In fact, only rarely will the attorney's words be relevant for any purpose other than to show the client's communications circumstantially, or to establish an admission by the client by his failure to object.[5] Accordingly, the simpler and preferable rule, adopted by a number

---

**[Section 89]**

[1]See § 87 supra.

[2]Anderson v. Bank of British Columbia [1876] L.R. 2, Ch.D. 644 (Ct. App.); Wheeler v. Le Marchant [1881] L.R. 17 Ch.D. 675 (Ct.App.); State ex rel. State Highway Dept. v. 62.96247 Acres of Land, More or Less, in New Castle Hundred, New Castle County, 57 Del. 40, 193 A.2d 799 (Super. Ct. 1963) (expert appraiser employed by client who aided attorney in preparation of case barred by privilege from testifying for opponents); Privilege as to communications between lay representative in judicial or administrative proceedings and client, 31 A.L.R.4th 1226; Persons other than client or attorney affected by, or included within, attorney-client privilege, 96 A.L.R.2d 125 (sec. 16 superseded in part Privilege as to communications between lay representative in judicial or administrative proceedings and client, 31 A.L.R.4th 1226); Note, 1943 Wis. L. Rev. 424.

[3]U.S. v. Kovel, 296 F.2d 918 (2d Cir. 1961) (statements to accountant in employ of attorney); State v. Krich, 123 N.J.L. 519, 9 A.2d 803 (N.J. Sup. Ct. 1939) (communication to attorney's secretary); 8 Wigmore, Evidence § 2301 (McNaughton rev. 1961); Imwinkelried, The New Wigmore: Evidentiary Privileges § 6.6.4 (2d ed. 2010); Persons other than client or attorney affected by, or included within, attorney-client privilege, 96 A.L.R.2d 125 (sec. 16 superseded in part Privilege as to communications between lay representative in judicial or

administrative proceedings and client, 31 A.L.R.4th 1226).

[4]Matter of Fischel, 557 F.2d 209 (9th Cir. 1977). *See also* Rice, Attorney-Client Privilege: Continuing Confusion About Attorney Communications, Drafts, Pre-Existing Documents, and the Source of the Facts Communicated, 48 Amer. U. L. Rev. 967 (1999).

[5]A defamatory statement made by the lawyer in declining employment and sought to be proved solely as a basis for an action against the lawyer for slander was held privileged in Minter v. Priest, [1929] 1 K.B. 655. It is criticized as unwarranted by the policy of the privilege in a Note, 43 Harv. L. Rev. 134.

Communications upon their respective clients' business between counsel defending them against a common charge have been said to be within the privilege. Continental Oil Co. v. U.S., 330 F.2d 347 (9th Cir. 1964) (exchange of confidential memoranda between counsel for several clients summoned before grand jury investigating antitrust violations); In re Felton, 60 Idaho 540, 94 P.2d 166 (1939); 98 C.J.S., Witnesses § 321; Attorney-client privilege as affected by communications between several attorneys, 9 A.L.R.3d 1420. *See also* U.S. v. United Shoe Machinery Corp., 89 F. Supp. 357 (D. Mass. 1950) (privilege extends to communications to and from corporation's outside counsel or general counsel and staff and employees in its patent department); General Acc. Fire & Life Assur. Corp. v. Mitchell, 128 Colo. 11, 259 P.2d 862 (1953) (order for production of all cor-

of statutes and the Uniform Evidence Rules[6] and by the better reasoned cases,[7] extends the protection of the privilege also to communications by the lawyer to the client.

An even more embracive view, adopted by statute in a few states,[8] would protect against disclosure by the attorney of any knowledge he has gained while acting as such, even information obtained from sources other than the client. Such an extension finds no justification in the modern utilitarian theory of the privilege. In any event, the more widely prevailing rule does not bar divulgence by the attorney of information communicated to him or his agents by third persons.[9] Nor does information so obtained become privileged by being in turn related by the attorney to the client in the form of advice.[10]

The commonly imposed limitation of protection to communications passing between client and attorney, while logically derived from the policy rationale of the privilege, does raise certain problems of construction where the information acquired by the attorney does not come in the conventional form of oral or writ-

---

respondence between home office and local counsel and local agents and all telegrams and written memoranda between home office, its attorneys and agents and insured, should have been denied on ground of privilege); Missouri, K. & T. Ry. Co. of Texas v. Williams, 43 Tex. Civ. App. 549, 96 S.W. 1087 (1906) (general counsel of railway writes to local attorney). Unif. R. Evid. 502(b)(3), dealing with "pooled information" cases, supra § 87, n. 19. See infra § 91.1.

[6]See statutes set out in 8 Wigmore, Evidence § 2292 n. 2 (McNaughton rev. 1961) and Unif. R. Evid. 502(b), supra § 87.

[7]Sprague v. Thorn Americas, Inc., 129 F.3d 1355, 1369–70 (10th Cir. 1997); U.S. v. Amerada Hess Corp., 619 F.2d 980 (3d Cir. 1980); In re LTV Securities Litigation, 89 F.R.D. 595 (N.D. Tex. 1981) (strongly criticizing rule that attorney-client communications are protected only where revelatory of client confidence on grounds that all attorney advice tends to reveal client communications, that rule does not recognize fact-gathering role of attorney, and that narrower rule makes scope of privilege uncertain); In re Navarro, 93 Cal. App. 3d 325, 155 Cal.

Rptr. 522 (4th Dist. 1979) (applying California statute); Gillard v. AIG Ins. Co., 609 Pa. 65, 15 A.3d 44 (2011) (interpreting state statute; privilege applies to communications from attorney to client); *contra* Potts v. Allis-Chalmers Corp., 118 F.R.D. 597, 602 (N.D. Ind. 1987) (extending the privilege to all communications from the attorney is "contrary to the expressed intention of the Seventh Circuit to confine the privilege to the narrowest limits consistent with the privilege's purpose").

[8]See statutes quoted in 8 Wigmore, Evidence § 2292, n. 2 (McNaughton rev. 1961).

[9]Matter of Walsh, 623 F.2d 489 (7th Cir. 1980); Morrell v. State, 575 P.2d 1200 (Alaska 1978).

[10]Giordani v. Hoffmann, 278 F. Supp. 886 (E.D. Pa. 1968). The general rule is seemingly applied to the situation in which the attorney is called upon to testify as to whether he told client of required court appearance, time and date of trial, etc. State v. Breazeale, 11 Kan. App. 2d 103, 713 P.2d 973 (1986) (adopting theory that in making such communications attorney serves merely as conduit).

ten assertions by the client. Initially it is fairly easy to conclude, as most authority holds, that observations by the lawyer that might be made by anyone, and which involve no communicative intent by the client, are not protected.[11] Conversely, testimony relating intentionally communicative acts of the client, as where he rolls up his sleeve to reveal a hidden scar or opens the drawer of his desk to display a revolver, would as clearly be precluded as would the recounting of statements conveying the same information. Much more problematic are cases in which the client delivers tangible evidence such as stolen property to the attorney, or confides facts enabling the attorney to come into the possession of such evidence. Here the decisions are somewhat conflicting,[12] reflecting the virtual impossibility of separating the

---

[11]U.S. v. Pipkins, 528 F.2d 559 (5th Cir. 1976) (identification of physical characteristics readily observable by anyone not within privilege); Clark v. Skinner, 334 Mo. 1190, 70 S.W.2d 1094 (1934) (attorney's knowledge of client's mental capacity and of want of any undue influence and that deeds were delivered, not privileged); State v. Fitzgerald, 68 Vt. 125, 34 A. 429 (1896) (attorney's testimony to client's intoxication, observable by all, not privileged); 8 Wigmore, Evidence § 2306 (McNaughton rev. 1961); Imwinkelried, The New Wigmore: Evidentiary Privileges § 6.7.1, at 737–39 (2d ed. 2010).

The same principle has almost invariably been applied to allow testimony by the attorney as to the client's competency to stand trial. People v. Kinder, 126 A.D.2d 60, 512 N.Y.S.2d 597 (4th Dep't 1987); Manning v. State, 766 S.W.2d 551 (Tex. App. Dallas 1989). However, communications from clients to lawyers are within the privilege even in such hearings. See Cohen, The Attorney-Client Privilege, Ethical Rules and the Impaired Criminal Defendant, 52 U. Miami L. Rev. 529 (1998) (author argues for relaxation of privilege where issue is competency to stand trial).

[12]The privilege is not generally viewed as affording the attorney license to withhold evidence from the judicial system. See In re January 1976 Grand Jury, 534 F.2d 719 (7th Cir. 1976) (privilege not applicable to resist subpoena for money, turned over to attorney by clients suspected of bank robbery); In re Ryder, 263 F. Supp. 360 (E.D. Va. 1967) (attorney suspending from practice for taking possession of gun and money and secreting them in safe deposit box pending termination of trial); State ex rel. Sowers v. Olwell, 64 Wash. 2d 828, 394 P.2d 681 (1964). However, the apparent weight of authority holds that the privilege prevents the attorney from being required to reveal his source. Anderson v. State, 297 So. 2d 871 (Fla. 2d DCA 1974) (delivery of stolen merchandise to attorney's receptionist by defendant was privileged communication); State v. Green, 493 So. 2d 1178 (La. 1986) (attorney's knowledge that gun had been in defendant's possession within privilege); Rubin v. State, 325 Md. 552, 602 A.2d 677 (1992) (privilege attached where attorney's investigator took bullets from defendant/client's purse and gave them to attorney; admission harmless error); People v. Nash, 418 Mich. 196, 341 N.W.2d 439 (1983) (holding by sharply divided court that testimony revealing that items of physical evidence were obtained from attorney's office violated privilege). But see Hughes v. Meade, 453 S.W.2d 538 (Ky. 1970) (lawyer required to divulge identity of person delivering stolen property to him). And see People v. Meredith, 29 Cal. 3d 682, 175 Cal. Rptr. 612, 631 P.2d 46 (1981) in which

act of confidence which may legitimately be within the privilege from the preexisting evidentiary fact which may not. To resolve the dilemma, one carefully reasoned argument is that the privilege should not operate to bar the attorney's disclosure of the circumstances of acquisition,[13] since to preclude the attorney's testimony would offer the client a uniquely safe opportunity to divest himself of incriminating evidence without leaving an evidentiary trail.[14]

Difficulties also arise in applying the communications-only theory when one assisting the lawyer, e.g., an examining physician, learns and communicates to the lawyer matters not known to the client. The privilege seems to apply with respect to the communication itself. If the physician is considered as aligned with the client, his knowledge would be that of the client and not privileged; but if aligned with the lawyer, the privilege seems to apply, as held in the leading case.[15]

The application of the privilege to writings presents practical problems requiring discriminating analysis. A professional communication in writing, as a letter from client to lawyer for example, will of course be privileged.[16] These written privileged communications are readily to be distinguished from preexisting

---

defendant told attorney that he had burned murder victim's wallet and placed it in a trash can, and attorney sent investigator to retrieve wallet. The court held that while the initial communication was within the privilege, once the attorney sent the investigator to retrieve the property the testimony of the latter concerning the location and condition of the property was unprotected.

Since withholding of evidence is itself a crime, collusion between attorney and client to retain the evidence in order to hide it has been held to forfeit the privilege as to source by operation of the crime or fraud exception. State v. Taylor, 502 So. 2d 537 (La. 1987). The exception is treated § 95 infra. Cases are collected in State ex rel. Sowers v. Olwell, 64 Wash. 2d 828, 394 P.2d 681 (1964).

[13]Saltzburg, Communications Falling Within the Attorney-Client Privilege, 66 Iowa L. Rev. 811 (1981).

[14]Saltzburg, Communications Falling Within the Attorney-Client Privilege, 66 Iowa L. Rev. at 838.

"Only by having the lawyer transfer the evidence to the government for her is the client able to 'launder' the evidence—that is, remove it from her possession and place it in the hands of the government without having the government connect it up with its source." *Compare* Lefstein, Incriminating Physical Evidence, The Defense Attorney's Dilemma, and the Need for Rules, 64 N.C. L. Rev. 897 (1986) (arguing for an expanded application of the privilege).

[15]City & County of San Francisco v. Superior Court In and For City and County of San Francisco, 37 Cal. 2d 227, 231 P.2d 26 (1951). Unless this is regarded as privileged, Fed. R. Civ. P. 26(b)(4)(B) seems to permit discovery in such case if hardship is shown. Distinguish the situation of the expert who examines for the purpose of testifying, thus contemplating disclosure and eliminating the privilege. See § 91, note 6 infra.

[16]Peyton v. Werhane, 126 Conn. 382, 11 A.2d 800 (1940).

An interesting case presented

documents or writings, such as deeds, wills, and warehouse receipts, not in themselves constituting communications between client and lawyer. As to these preexisting documents two notions come into play. First, the client may make communications about the document by words or by acts, such as sending the document to the lawyer for perusal or handing it to him and calling attention to its terms. These communications, and the knowledge of the terms and appearance of the documents that the lawyer gains thereby are privileged from disclosure by testimony in court.[17] Second, on a different footing entirely, stands the question, shall a lawyer who has been entrusted with the possession of a document by his client be subject to an order of court requiring him to produce the document at the trial or in pretrial discovery proceedings whether for inspection or for use in evidence? The policy of encouraging full disclosure does of course apply to encouraging the client to apprise his lawyer of the terms of all relevant documents, and the disclosure itself and the lawyer's knowledge gained thereby as we have seen are privileged. It is true also that placing the documents in the lawyer's hands is the most convenient means of disclosure. But the next step, that of adding to the privilege for communications a privilege against production of the preexisting documents themselves, when they would be subject to production if still in the possession of the client, would be an intolerable obstruction to justice. To prevent the court's gaining access to a relevant document a party would only have to send it to his lawyer. So here this principle is controlling: if a document would be subject to an order for production if it were in the hands of the client it will be equally subject to such an order

---

the question whether confidential letters of the client were usable, not as evidence of their contents but as specimens for comparison by expert witnesses with an anonymous letter charged to have been written by the client. People v. Smith, 318 Ill. 114, 149 N.E. 3 (1925) (not privileged against use for this purpose).

[17]Wheatley (Survivors of William Stewart) v. Williams, 1836 WL 4584 (U.K. Ex Ct 1836) (attorney not required to testify whether paper shown him by client bore a stamp); U.S. v. Hankins, 631 F.2d 360 (5th Cir. 1980) (tax counsel not required to reveal which books of client's he had examined); Kobluk v. University of Minnesota, 574 N.W.2d 436 (Minn. 1998) (draft of letter sent to counsel for review may be a privileged communi-

cation); Virginia Elec. and Power Co. v. Westmoreland-LG & E Partners, 259 Va. 319, 526 S.E.2d 750, 755 (2000) (draft letter sent to counsel for legal opinion before it was to be sent to others was privileged). But see the varied treatment given to preliminary drafts of documents intended for dissemination to others discussed in § 91 infra.

But the act of the execution of a document by the client in the lawyer's presence is not ordinarily intended as a confidential communication and thus is usually not privileged. Chapman v. Peebles, 84 Ala. 283, 4 So. 273 (1888). A fortiori, when the attorney signs as a witness and takes the acknowledgment of the client as a notary. McCaw v. Hartman, 1942 OK 50, 190 Okla. 264, 122 P.2d 999 (1942).

if it is in the hands of his attorney.[18] An opposite conclusion would serve the policy of encouraging the client to make full disclosure to his lawyer right enough, but reasonable encouragement is given by the privilege for communications about documents, and the price of an additional privilege would be intolerably high. There are other doctrines which may impel a court to recognize a privilege against production of a preexisting document,[19] but not the doctrine of privilege for lawyer-client communications.

## § 90    Subject-matter of the privilege: (b) Fact of employment and identity of the client

When a client consults an attorney for a legitimate purpose, he will seldom, but may occasionally, desire to keep secret the very fact of consultation or employment of the lawyer. Nevertheless, consultation and employment are something more than a mere private or personal engagement. They are the calling into play of the services of an officer licensed by the state to act in certain ways in furtherance of the administration of justice, and vested with powers of giving advice on the law, of drafting documents, and of filing pleadings and motions and appearing in court for his client, which are limited to this class of officers.

Does the privilege for confidential communications extend to the fact of consulting or employing such an officer, when intended to be confidential? The traditional and still generally applicable rule denies the privilege for the fact of consultation or employment,[1] including the component facts of the identity of the client,[2]

---

[18]Fisher v. U.S., 425 U.S. 391, 96 S. Ct. 1569, 48 L. Ed. 2d 39 (1976); U.S. v. Robinson, 121 F.3d 971 (5th Cir. 1997). Sovereign Camp, W.O.W. v. Reed, 208 Ala. 457, 94 So. 910 (1922); Andrews v. Ohio & M.R. Co., 14 Ind. 169, 174, 1860 WL 4065 (1860); Palatini v. Sarian, 15 N.J. Super. 34, 83 A.2d 24 (App. Div. 1951); Pearson v. Yoder, 1913 OK 515, 39 Okla. 105, 134 P. 421 (1913); State v. Guthrie, 2001 SD 89, 631 N.W.2d 190, 194 (S.D. 2001) (suicide note in lawyer's possession was not privileged); Rice, Attorney-Client Privilege: Continuing Confusion About Attorney Communications, Drafts, Pre-Existing Documents, and the Source of the Facts Communicated, 48 Amer. U. L. Rev. 967 (1999); Imwinkelried, The New Wigmore: Evidentiary Privileges § 6.7.1, at 733 (2d ed. 2010). 8 Wigmore, Evidence § 2307 (McNaughton rev. 1961).

And as a necessary incident the attorney may be required to testify whether he has possession of such a document of the client. Guiterman, Rosenfield & Co. v. Culbreth, 219 Ala. 382, 122 So. 619 (1929).

[19]See § 96 infra.

**[Section 90]**

[1]Behrens v. Hironimus, 170 F.2d 627 (4th Cir. 1948). See authorities collected in 8 Wigmore, Evidence § 2313 (McNaughton rev. 1961); 98 C.J.S., Witnesses § 332.

[2]U.S. v. Ricks, 776 F.2d 455 (4th Cir. 1985), on rehearing U.S. v. Ricks, 802 F.2d 731 (4th Cir. 1986) (privilege did not preclude proof that defendants paid attorney fees for members of drug

such identifying facts about him as his address and occupation,[3] the identity of the lawyer,[4] and the payment and amount of fees.[5] Similarly, factual communications by the lawyer to the client concerning logistical matters such as trial dates are not privileged.[6]

---

ring arrested on narcotics charges); U.S. v. Pape, 144 F.2d 778 (C.C.A. 2d Cir. 1944) (prosecution for violation of Mann Act; lawyer-witness properly allowed to be asked by prosecution whether accused employed him to represent the woman whom he was charged with transporting and himself; Learned Hand, Cir. J., dissenting); Tenet Healthcare Corporation v. Louisiana Forum Corporation, 273 Ga. 206, 538 S.E.2d 441, 444 (2000) (identity of client informing lawyer of cause of action against defendant not privileged); In re Richardson, 31 N.J. 391, 157 A.2d 695 (1960) (attorney-client relation does not privilege lawyer from disclosing the identity of the person who retained him, or of the person who paid his fee); Priest v. Hennessy, 51 N.Y.2d 62, 431 N.Y.S.2d 511, 409 N.E.2d 983 (1980) (privilege inapplicable to prevent disclosure of identity of person paying attorney to represent prostitutes; strong dissent); People ex rel. Vogelstein v. Warden of County Jail of New York County, 150 Misc. 714, 270 N.Y.S. 362 (Sup 1934), affirmed without opinion 271 N.Y.S. 1059 (App. Div. 1934) (attorney who entered appearance for fifteen defendants charged with violation of gambling laws, required in grand jury investigation to testify as to whether one person, the man behind the scene, had not employed him to act for all these defendants; opinion by Shientag, J., is the best on the question); Lemley v. Kaiser, 6 Ohio St. 3d 258, 452 N.E.2d 1304 (1983) (identity of clients retaining attorney to effect "unlawful" adoption not privileged in habeas action by natural mother).

[3]U.S. v. Lee, 107 F. 702 (C.C.E.D. N.Y. 1901); Falkenhainer v. Falkenhainer, 198 Misc. 29, 97 N.Y.S.2d 467 (Sup 1950); Dike v. Dike, 75 Wash. 2d

1, 448 P.2d 490 (1968) (whereabouts of client who had possession of child in violation of custody order); Disclosure of name, identity, address, occupation, or business of client as violation of attorney-client privilege, 16 A.L.R.3d 1047. *But compare* Matter of Nackson, 114 N.J. 527, 555 A.2d 1101 (1989).

[4]Dyson v. Hempe, 140 Wis. 2d 792, 413 N.W.2d 379 (Ct. App. 1987).

[5]O'Neal v. U.S., 258 F.3d 1265, 1276 (11th Cir. 2001) (information with regard to receipt of attorney's fee not privileged); Hampton Police Ass'n, Inc. v. Town of Hampton, 162 N.H. 7, 20 A.3d 994 (2011) (no privilege where only a general description of services); Seventh Elect Church in Israel v. Rogers, 102 Wash. 2d 527, 688 P.2d 506 (1984). *But see* State ex rel. Dawson v. Bloom-Carroll Local School Dist., 131 Ohio St. 3d 10, 2011-Ohio-6009, 959 N.E.2d 524 (2011) (itemized billing statements were privileged); Lane v. Sharp Packaging Systems, Inc., 2002 WI 28, 251 Wis. 2d 68, 640 N.W.2d 788, 804–05 (2002) (billing records, containing detailed description of the nature of the legal services provided, were privileged).

[6]Watkins v. State, 516 So. 2d 1043 (Fla. 1st DCA 1987); State v. Breazeale, 11 Kan. App. 2d 103, 713 P.2d 973 (1986). *Compare* In re Grand Jury Subpoena Bierman, 765 F.2d 1014 (11th Cir. 1985) (upholding privilege under circumstances, but suggesting that basic fact of notice to client of surrender date not within privilege).

An attorney may testify as to the terms of employment on an issue as to whether some act done by the attorney was authorized, In re Michaelson, 511 F.2d 882 (9th Cir. 1975) (attorney's authority to file public document; no privilege); Pacific Tel. &

Several reasons have been advanced as a basis for denying protection to the client's identity, most notably that "the mere fact of the engagement of counsel is out of the rule [of privilege] because the privilege and duty of silence do not arise until the fact is ascertained."[7] Additionally, it is said that a party to legal proceedings is entitled to know the identity of the adversary who is putting in motion or staying the machinery of the court.[8] Such propositions, however, shed little light on the real issue, i.e., whether client anonymity is in some cases essential to obtaining the proper objectives of the privilege.

The inadequacy of a purely simplistic rule excluding client identity from the coverage of the privilege was revealed by the facts of the leading case of *Baird v. Koerner*,[9] in which the court upheld a claim of privilege by an attorney who had mailed a check for back taxes to the IRS on behalf of an anonymous client. Any other result on the facts of *Baird* would seem inconceivable, and the decision has served a wholesome purpose by introducing an element of flexibility into the general rule. However, a number of decisions following *Baird* arguably vastly extended the exceptions to the rule. Thus it was variously stated that exception is made "when the disclosure of the client's identity by his attorney would have supplied the last link in a existing chain of incriminating evidence . . . ,"[10] or "where . . . a strong probability exists that disclosure of such information would implicate the client in the very criminal activity for which legal advice was sought."[11] Such decisions may have blazed a false trail in making the exceptions to the rule turn too largely upon the question of the severity

---

Tel. Co. v. Fink, 141 Cal. App. 2d 332, 296 P.2d 843 (2d Dist. 1956) (authority to enter into stipulation under which default judgment was taken); Sachs v. Title Ins. & Trust Co., 305 Ky. 154, 202 S.W.2d 384 (1947) (on question whether defendant in prior judgment was before court, attorney who appeared for her can testify to employment to defend suit).

[7]Shientag, J. in People ex rel. Vogelstein v. Warden of County Jail of New York County, 150 Misc. 714, 270 N.Y.S. 362 (Sup 1934). But the party propounding the question as to the identity of the client may state and assume that the relationship exists, so that there is no need to establish it. In

re Shawmut Min. Co., 94 A.D. 156, 87 N.Y.S. 1059, 1062 (4th Dep't 1904).

[8]"Every litigant is in justice entitled to know the identity of his opponents." 8 Wigmore, Evidence § 2313 (McNaughton rev. 1961).

[9]Baird v. Koerner, 279 F.2d 623 (9th Cir. 1960). The case is noted in 49 Calif. L. Rev. 382 (1961); 39 Tex. L. Rev. 512 (1961); 47 Va. L. Rev. 126 (1961).

[10]In re Grand Jury Proceedings, 680 F.2d 1026, 1027 (5th Cir. 1982) (en banc).

[11]U.S. v. Hodge and Zweig, 548 F.2d 1347, 1353 (9th Cir. 1977).

of potential harm to the client rather than upon considerations germane to the privilege.[12]

Today there is a marked trend toward refocusing upon the essential purpose of the privilege by extending its protection to client identity and fee arrangements only if the net effect of the disclosure would be to reveal the nature of a client communication.[13] Protection should certainly be denied where agencies performed by attorneys are no necessary part of the attorney's unique role nor appropriate for immunization from public disclosure and scrutiny.[14] Arguably, general application of a rule of disclosure seems the approach most consonant with the

---

[12]See, e.g., Tornay v. U.S., 840 F.2d 1424 (9th Cir. 1988) (noting criticism of U.S. v. Hodge and Zweig, 548 F.2d 1347, 1353 (9th Cir. 1977) and restating rule: "A careful reading of Baird, and close examination of subsequent cases, indicates that Baird applies only when it is shown that, because of exceptional circumstances, disclosure of the client's identity or the existence of a fee arrangement would reveal information that is tantamount to a confidential professional communication").

[13]See, e.g., In re Subpoenaed Grand Jury Witness, 171 F.3d 511, 514 (7th Cir. 1999) (identity privilege where its revelation would reveal client's motive); Lefcourt v. U.S., 125 F.3d 79 (2d Cir. 1997) (privilege applicable to report of payment of fees to attorney only if confidentiality would be compromised); U.S. v. Blackman, 72 F.3d 1418 (9th Cir. 1995); In re Grand Jury Proceedings 88-9 (MIA), 899 F.2d 1039 (11th Cir. 1990) (privilege denied where disclosure of client identity would not reveal other privileged information); Matter of Grand Jury Proceeding, Cherney, 898 F.2d 565 (7th Cir. 1990) (fact that disclosure would incriminate client insufficient to invoke privilege, but privilege applicable where disclosure would reveal substance of confidential communication). See also In re Grand Jury Subpoena, 204 F.3d 516, 519 (4th Cir. 2000) (identity of client not privileged where lawyer had already disclosed

purpose of representation); U.S. v. Sindel, 53 F.3d 874 (8th Cir. 1995) (cash payments made by one client within privilege where disclosure would reveal confidential information; payments made to second client not within exception). See also the interesting case of Matter of Grand Jury Subpoena of Stewart, 144 Misc. 2d 1012, 545 N.Y.S.2d 974 (Sup 1989), in which a claim of privilege for the identity of a third party benefactor was supported by an affidavit from the client that if the name were revealed he would no longer trust his attorney. This attempt to utilize the "adversary system" theory of the privilege to extend its scope was rejected by the court, on the ground that counsel could readily have avoided the problem.

[14]Saltzburg, Communications Falling Within the Attorney-Client Privilege, 66 Iowa L. Rev. 811, 823 (1981) ("It is a different matter . . . when the client seeks to have the lawyer perform an act as the client's agent that would be subject to scrutiny by courts if performed by other agents—for example, transmitting money from the client to someone else—without the lawyer having to reveal the identity of the principal. In this type of case, the concealment of identity would tend to allow persons to engage in activities that ordinarily would be subject to inquiry and to insulate themselves from otherwise proper scrutiny.").

preservation of the repute of the lawyer's high calling.[15] At the same time, much should depend upon the client's objective in seeking preservation of anonymity, and cases will arise in which protection of the client's identity is both proper and in the public interest.[16]

## § 91 The confidential character of the communications: Communications intended to be made public; presence of third persons and agents

It is of the essence of the privilege that it is limited to those communications that the client either expressly made confidential or which he could reasonably assume under the circumstances would be understood by the attorney as so intended. This common law requirement seems to be read into those statutes that codify the privilege without mentioning the confidentiality requirement.[1] A mere showing that the communication was from client to attorney does not suffice, but the circumstances indicating the intention of secrecy must appear.[2] Wherever the matters communicated to the attorney are intended by the client to be

---

[15]"The conclusion reached would seem to be inevitable, if we are to maintain the honor of the profession, and make an officer of the court an agency to advance the ends of justice, rather than to be used as an instrument to subvert them. The identity of an employer or client who retains a lawyer to act for him or for others in a civil or criminal proceeding should not be veiled in mystery. The dangers of disclosure are shadowy and remote; the evils of concealment are patent and overwhelming. As between the two social policies competing for supremacy, the choice is clear. Disclosure should be made if we are to maintain confidence in the bar and in the administration of justice." Shientag, J. in People ex rel. Vogelstein v. Warden of County Jail of New York County, 150 Misc. 714, 270 N.Y.S. 362, 371 (Sup 1934).

[16]State v. Gonzalez, 290 Kan. 747, 234 P.3d 1 (2010) (identity protected where attorney had already disclosed communication itself and identity of client would complete disclosure of confidence); In re Kaplan, 8 N.Y.2d 214, 203 N.Y.S.2d 836, 168 N.E.2d 660 (1960) (client's communication to at-torney for purpose of disclosing wrong-doing by others communicated by at-torney to public officials held to justify protection of identity of client); 10 Buffalo L. Rev. 364 (1961), 46 Iowa L. Rev. 904 (1961), 59 Mich. L. Rev. 791 (1961), 12 Syracuse L. Rev. 408 (1961).

[Section 91]

[1]See statutes, privileging "communications" generally, quoted in 8 Wigmore, Evidence § 2292, n. 2 (McNaughton rev. 1961). See also Imwinkelried, The New Wigmore: Evidentiary Privileges § 6.8 (2d ed. 2010).

[2]Gardner v. Irvin, L.R.4 Ex.D. 49, 53 (1878); U.S. v. (Under Seal), 748 F.2d 871 (4th Cir. 1984). For discussions of confidentiality problems in the age of the Internet, see Rand, What Would Learned Hand Do?: Adapting to Technological Change and Protecting the Attorney-Client Privilege on the Internet, 66 Brook. L. Rev. 361 (2000); Comment, 69 U. Colo. L. Rev. 851 (1998). See also Leslie, The Costs of Confidentiality and the Purpose of Privilege, 2000 Wis. L. Rev. 31; Rice, Attorney-Client Privilege: The Eroding Concept of Confidentiality Should be Abolished, 47 Duke L.J. 853 (1998).

made public or revealed to third persons, obviously the element of confidentiality is wanting.[3] Similarly, if the same statements have been made by the client to third persons on other occasions this is persuasive that like communications to the lawyer were not intended as confidential.[4]

A split of authority has arisen, especially in federal court cases, about the status of preliminary conversations concerning documents that are to be published to third parties as well as drafts of those documents. Some courts have held that such conversations and drafts are not confidential based upon the intent of the client ultimately to publish the information.[5] Other courts have found them to be within the privilege at least to the extent that the information was not ultimately disclosed.[6] At least one court has held that privilege may attach to preliminary drafts, but only "if they were prepared or circulated for the purpose of giving or obtaining legal advice and contain information or provisions not included in the final version."[7] If the goal of the attorney-client privilege is to encourage a free flow of communications between attorney and client, preliminary conversations and drafts reflect-

---

[3]Colton v. U.S., 306 F.2d 633 (2d Cir. 1962) (information for inclusion in tax return not privileged; dictum); U.S. v. Tellier, 255 F.2d 441 (2d Cir. 1958), (attorney's advice to client where client expected attorney to prepare letter to third person setting forth his objections); Hill v. Hill, 106 Colo. 492, 107 P.2d 597 (1940) (letters by wife to attorney giving data on alimony in arrears, with intention that he should present the information to delinquent husband); Spencer v. Burns, 413 Ill. 240, 108 N.E.2d 413 (1952) (statement of true marital status made by client for purpose of transmission to seller and examiner of title to property client wished to purchase); Walsh v. Barcelona Associates, Inc., 16 Ohio App. 3d 470, 476 N.E.2d 1090 (10th Dist. Franklin County 1984) (attorney's authority to enter into agreement on behalf of client not privileged); Anderson v. Thomas, 108 Utah 252, 159 P.2d 142 (1945) (suit to cancel deed of deceased for mental incapacity, testimony of attorney that deceased asked him to arrange for bank not to cash his checks without attorney's approval, not privileged).

[4]Solon v. Lichtenstein, 39 Cal. 2d 75, 244 P.2d 907 (1952); Bryan v. Barnett, 205 Ga. 94, 52 S.E.2d 613 (1949); Travelers Indem. Co. v. Cochrane, 155 Ohio St. 305, 44 Ohio Op. 302, 98 N.E.2d 840 (1951).

[5]E.g., U.S. v. (Under Seal), 748 F.2d 871, 875 n.7 (4th Cir. 1984); U.S. v. Naegele, 468 F. Supp. 2d 165, 170–71 (D.D.C. 2007) (communications with regard to bankruptcy filing and draft filings not privileged); North Carolina Elec. Membership Corp. v. Carolina Power & Light Co., 110 F.R.D. 511, 517 (M.D. N.C. 1986).

[6]E.g., In re Grand Jury Subpoena Duces Tecum Dated Sept. 15, 1983, 731 F.2d 1032, 1037 (2d Cir. 1984) (no basis for inferring that client did not intend the drafts to be confidential); Schenet v. Anderson, 678 F. Supp. 1280, 1283 (E.D. Mich. 1988) ("Preliminary drafts may reflect not only client confidences, but also the legal advice and opinions of attorneys, all of which is protected by the attorney-client privilege."); U.S. v. Schlegel, 313 F. Supp. 177, 179 (D. Neb. 1970).

[7]Andritz Sprout-Bauer, Inc. v. Beazer East, Inc., 174 F.R.D. 609, 633 (M.D. Pa. 1997).

ing those conversations ought to be protected. The client and her attorney ought to be able to discuss the precise terms of the disclosure, including drafting wording reflecting the best way to communicate the information, without the risk that matters ultimately determined not to be disclosed would be unprivileged.[8]

Questions as to the effect of the presence of persons other than the client and the lawyer often arise. At the extremes answers would be clear. Presumably the presence of a casual disinterested third person within hearing to the client's knowledge would demonstrate that the communication was not intended to be confidential.[9] On the other hand if the help of an interpreter is necessary to enable the client to consult the lawyer his presence would not deprive the communication of its confidential and privileged character.[10] Moreover, in cases where the client has

---

[8]*See also* discussions in Northrop, The Attorney-Client Privilege and Information Disclosed to an Attorney with the Intention that the Attorney Draft a Document to be Released to Third Parties: Public Policy Calls for at Least the Strictest Application of the Attorney-Client Privilege, 78 Fordham L. Rev. 1481(2009); Rice, Attorney-Client Privilege in the United States § 5:13 (2012 ed.); Imwinkelried, The New Wigmore, Evidentiary Privileges § 6.8.2.b, at 815 (2d ed. 2010).

[9]Mason v. Mason, 231 S.W. 971 (Mo. 1921); In re Quick's Estate, 161 Wash. 537, 297 P. 198 (1931), and cases collected in 8 Wigmore, Evidence § 2311, n. 6 (McNaughton rev. 1961); Imwinkelried, The New Wigmore: Evidentiary Privileges § 6.8.1 (2d ed. 2010); 97 C.J.S., Witnesses § 290; Note, 36 Mich. L. Rev. 641 (1938); Privilege as to communications between lay representative in judicial or administrative proceedings and client, 31 A.L.R.4th 1226. *See also* U.S. v. Lentz, 419 F. Supp. 2d 820, 828 (E.D. Va. 2005) (jail inmate had no reasonable expectation of confidentiality in telephone conversations with his attorney where he was notified that calls were recorded and subject to monitoring). *But see* U.S. v. DeFonte, 441 F.3d 92, 95 (2d Cir. 2006) (inmate's memorialization of conversations with attorney were privileged).

In the case of persons overhearing without the knowledge of the client, it seems that the more reasonable view if there is to be any privilege at all, would protect the client against disclosure, unless he has failed to use ordinary precautions against overhearing, and this result has been reached in some modern cases. Blackmon v. State, 653 P.2d 669 (Alaska Ct. App. 1982) (conference between attorney and client in courthouse corridor overheard by state trooper; privilege upheld where circumstances indicated reasonable precautions). Unif. R. Evid. 502(b) adopts this position. The older cases allowed the eavesdropper to speak. Vanhorn v. Com., 239 Ky. 833, 40 S.W.2d 372 (1931); Schwartz v. Wenger, 267 Minn. 40, 124 N.W.2d 489 (1963) (conversation between client and attorney in public corridor of courthouse overheard by third person, held not privileged).

[10]Du BarrAa v. Livette, 1791 WL 602 (U.K. Assizes 1791); State v. Loponio, 85 N.J.L. 357, 88 A. 1045 (N.J. Ct. Err. & App. 1913). *See also* State v. Aquino-Cervantes, 88 Wash. App. 699, 945 P.2d 767 (Div. 2 1997) (interpreter may not testify about observations made during confidential attorney-client communications).

In U.S. v. Kovel, 296 F.2d 918 (2d Cir. 1961), the court relied upon the analogy of an interpreter, in ap-

one of his agents attend the conference,[11] or the lawyer calls in his clerk[12] or confidential secretary,[13] the presence of these intermediaries will be assumed not to militate against the confidential nature of the consultation, and presumably this would not be made to depend upon whether the presence of the agent, clerk or secretary was in the particular instance reasonably necessary to the matter in hand.[14] It is the way business is generally done and that is enough. As to relatives and friends of

---

plying the privilege to an accountant employed by the lawyer to assist in the litigation.

[11]In re Busse's Estate, 332 Ill. App. 258, 75 N.E.2d 36, 38 (2d Dist. 1947) (client's agent who was nurse and business caretaker present at conference with attorney); Foley v. Poschke, 137 Ohio St. 593, 19 Ohio Op. 350, 31 N.E.2d 845 (1941) (detective employed by divorce plaintiff to investigate husband's conduct present at conference with lawyer).

Of course, the presence of additional counsel to participate in the consultation does not detract from confidentiality. Dickerson v. Dickerson, 322 Ill. 492, 153 N.E. 740 (1926).

[12]Sibley v. Waffle, 16 N.Y. 180, 1857 WL 7096 (1857); Hunt v. Taylor, 22 Vt. 556, 1850 WL 3501 (1850); Privilege as to communications between lay representative in judicial or administrative proceedings and client, 31 A.L.R.4th 1226.

A substantial number of state statutes provide that communications to the employees of the attorney are privileged. See statutes collected and quoted, 8 Wigmore, Evidence § 2292, n. 2 (McNaughton rev. 1961). And disclosures to a physician employed by the client's attorney to examine the client have been held subject to the attorney-client privilege. City & County of San Francisco v. Superior Court In and For City and County of San Francisco, 37 Cal. 2d 227, 231 P.2d 26 (1951); Applicability of Attorney-Client Privilege to Communications Made in Presence of or Solely to or by Other Attorneys, Coparties, and Their Staff, 64 A.L.R. 6th 655.

A law student in the office is not within the rule, unless she acts as clerk. Wartell v. Novograd, 48 R.I. 296, 137 A. 776 (1927). See also Allen Cty. Bar Assn. v. Williams, 95 Ohio St. 3d 160, 2002-Ohio-2006, 766 N.E.2d 973, 974 (2002) (attorney monitoring actions of attorney under probationary status may not view privileged materials without client's waiver of the

[13]Taylor v. Taylor, 179 Ga. 691, 177 S.E. 582 (1934) ("Under modern practice of law the business of an attorney in most offices cannot be conducted without such an assistant."). A Texas case would seemingly give the privilege only when the secretary or stenographer is the medium of communication. Otherwise, the court suggests "it could as well be claimed that the rule would extend to the employee, who swept the attorney's floor." Morton v. Smith, 44 S.W. 683, 684 (Tex. Civ. App. 1898) (stenographer allowed to testify to statements made by client to attorney).

[14]Today the necessities of litigation may extend considerably beyond agents such as stenographers and clerks. Jenkins v. Bartlett, 487 F.3d 482, 491 (7th Cir. 2007) (presence of representative of police liaison officer did not destroy privilege in consultation between an officer and attorney); State v. Pratt, 284 Md. 516, 398 A.2d 421, 423 (1979) ("[G]iven the complexities of modern existence, few if any lawyers could, as a practical matter, represent the interest of their clients without a variety of nonlegal assistance; upholding privilege for psychiatrist employed by counsel)." Where the expert is a psychiatrist, the privilege is generally extended, but a distinct question exists as to whether the priv-

the client, the results of the cases are not consistent,[15] but it seems that here not only might it be asked whether the client reasonably understood the conference to be confidential but also

---

ilege is waived by the raising of a defense of mental defect. See § 93, infra. Unif. R. Evid. 502(a)(4) adopts a broad version of the privilege by defining a "representative of the lawyer" as "one employed by the lawyer to assist the lawyer in the rendition of professional legal services"). The 1999 amendment to the Uniform Rules of Evidence makes clear that a "representative of a lawyer" is anyone "reasonably believed by the client to be" so employed. Unif. R. Evid. 402(a)(4). *See also* Olson v. Accessory Controls and Equipment Corp., 254 Conn. 145, 757 A.2d 14, 27–28 (2000) (communications with environmental company hired by attorney to assist in providing client with legal advice with regard to government order, were privileged). *But see* U.S. v. Richey, 632 F.3d 559 (9th Cir. 2011) (some communications with appraiser hired by attorney may not have been for the purpose of obtaining legal advice and therefore were not privileged); Cavallaro v. U.S., 284 F.3d 236, 248 (1st Cir. 2002) (attorney-client privilege did not apply with regard to communications with accountants where accountants hired to give accounting advice rather than assisting attorneys in providing legal advice); U.S. v. Ackert, 169 F.3d 136, 139 (2d Cir. 1999) (conversations between attorney and investment banker not privileged even though attorney was assisted by banker in giving legal advice); In re Lindsey, 158 F.3d 1263 (D.C. Cir. 1998) (government lawyer was not acting as an intermediary where his actions constituted an independent contribution to the President Clinton's representation); Rubin v. State, 325 Md. 552, 602 A.2d 677 (1992) (privilege did not apply where investigator consulted independently of his relationship with attorney). *See also,* Imwinkelried & Amoroso, The Application of the Attorney-Client Privilege to Interactions Among Clients, Attorneys,

and Experts in the Age of Consultants: The Need For a More Precise Fundamental Analysis, 48 Hous. L. Rev. 265 (2011); Murphy, Spin Control and the High–Profile Client–Should the Attorney–Client Privilege Extend to Communications With Public Relations Consultants?, 55 Syracuse L. Rev. 545 (2005).

[15]U.S. v. Bigos, 459 F.2d 639 (1st Cir. 1972) (privilege upheld for communication in presence of client's father; presence of 3rd persons only indicative of non-confidentiality, not determinative); Cafritz v. Koslow, 167 F.2d 749 (App. D.C. 1948) (sister accompanies brother, client, to attorney's office; "There was no identity of interest between [brother and sister] nor can it be said that [sister] stood in relation of agent to [brother]"); Lynch v. Hamrick, 968 So. 2d 11, 16 (Ala. 2007) (daughter's presence at meeting between mother and attorney with regard to conveyance of property to daughter destroyed privilege); State v. Gordon, 197 Conn. 413, 504 A.2d 1020 (1985) (wife's testimony not barred by attorney-client privilege since wife's status bore no relationship to legal associate of defense counsel; query whether this test is the appropriate one); Gerheiser v. Stephens, 712 So. 2d 1252 (Fla. 4th DCA 1998) (defendant mother's conversation with attorney protected by privilege where she acted as agent for her son in securing legal representation); Smith v. State, 204 Ga. 184, 48 S.E.2d 860 (1948) (murder prosecution, evidence of what was said in conference with attorney by wife of defendant, when deceased was present, held privileged, without discussion); People v. Doss, 161 Ill. App. 3d 258, 112 Ill. Dec. 839, 514 N.E.2d 502 (4th Dist. 1987) (friend present at conference with attorney to lend "moral support"; privilege held inapplicable).

whether the presence of the relative or friend was reasonably necessary for the protection of the client's interests in the particular circumstances.[16]

## § 91.1  The confidential character of the communications: Joint consultations and employments; controversies between client and attorney

When two or more persons, each having an interest in some problem, or situation, jointly consult an attorney, their confidential communications with the attorney, though known to each other, will of course be privileged in a controversy of either or both of the clients with the outside world, that is, with parties claiming adversely to both or either of those within the original charmed circle.[1] But it will often happen that the two original clients will fall out between themselves and become engaged in a controversy in which the communications at their joint consultation with the lawyer may be vitally material. In such a controversy it is clear that the privilege is inapplicable. In the first place the policy of encouraging disclosure by holding out the promise of protection seems inapposite, since as between themselves neither would know whether he would be more helped or handicapped, if in any dispute between them, both could invoke

---

[16]Compare the remarks of the court in Bowers v. State, 29 Ohio St. 542, 546, 1876 WL 123 (1876): "We think it is only a dictate of decency and propriety to regard the mother in such a case as being present and acting in the character of confidential agent of her daughter. The daughter's youth and supposed modesty would render the participation of her mother appropriate and necessary."

**[Section 91.1]**

[1]U.S. v. BDO Seidman, LLP, 492 F.3d 806, 816–17 (7th Cir. 2007) (communications protected even though not in anticipation of litigation); International Broth. of Teamsters, Chauffeurs, Warehousemen and Helpers of America v. Hatas, 287 Ala. 344, 252 So. 2d 7 (1971); State v. Maxwell, 10 Kan. App. 2d 62, 691 P.2d 1316, 1320 (1984) (communications between joint clients and attorney "will be privileged in controversies of either or both with the outside world"); Applicability of attorney-client privilege to evidence or testimony in

subsequent action between parties originally represented contemporaneously by same attorney, with reference to communication to or from one party, 4 A.L.R.4th 765.

It is generally held that the client making the communication is the only joint client who can waive the privilege. See, e.g., In re Grand Jury Subpoenas, 89-3 and 89-4, John Doe 89-129, 902 F.2d 244, 248–49 (4th Cir. 1990) (no unilateral waiver of privilege); Matter of Grand Jury Subpoena Duces Tecum Dated November 16, 1974, 406 F. Supp. 381, 394 (S.D. N.Y. 1975) (waiver of privilege by one co-client did not destroy privilege as to communications by other co-clients). But a somewhat different issue is presented where one joint client is prosecuted and the other is willing to testify as to the joint consultations. The issue in such an instance is whether the co-client is now the equivalent of an "opposing party." The courts are divided. See State v. Cascone, 195 Conn. 183, 487 A.2d 186 (1985) (collecting cases but declining to choose either "rule").

the shield of secrecy. And secondly, it is said that they had obviously no intention of keeping these secrets from each other, and hence as between them it was not intended to be confidential. In any event, it is a qualification of frequent application[2] and of even wider potentiality, not always recognized. Thus, in the situation mentioned in the previous section where a client calls into the conference with the attorney one of the client's agents, and matters are discussed which bear on the agent's rights against the client, it would seem that in a subsequent controversy between client and agent, the limitation on the privilege accepted

---

[2]Estate of Swantee, 90 Misc. 2d 519, 394 N.Y.S.2d 547 (Sur. Ct. 1977); Netzley v. Nationwide Mut. Ins. Co., 34 Ohio App. 2d 65, 63 Ohio Op. 2d 127, 296 N.E.2d 550 (2d Dist. Montgomery County 1971); Unif. R. Evid. 502(d)(5). Cases are collected in Applicability of attorney-client privilege to evidence or testimony in subsequent action between parties originally represented contemporaneously by same attorney, with reference to communication to or from one party, 4 A.L.R.4th 765. *See also* Pagano v. Ippoliti, 245 Conn. 640, 716 A.2d 848 (1998) (employee consulted lawyer on behalf of employer; privilege did not apply in later dispute between the two).

It has been held that the beneficiary of a contract made by the jointly consulting clients stands in the shoes of the parties and is entitled to disclosure. Allen v. Ross, 199 Wis. 162, 225 N.W. 831 (1929). So also as to personal representatives and others in privity. Hurlburt v. Hurlburt, 128 N.Y. 420, 28 N.E. 651 (1891) (action by administrator of one client against administratrix of the other).It would seem that judgment creditors should be treated the same. *See* Applicability of attorney-client privilege to evidence or testimony in subsequent action between parties originally represented contemporaneously by same attorney, with reference to communication to or from one party, 4 A.L.R.4th 765.

The analogy to two persons consulting the same lawyer on a common matter has been invoked to deny a claim of privilege by management in stockholder's derivative suits with respect to communications between management and corporate counsel prior to the litigation. Garner v. Wolfinbarger, 430 F.2d 1093 (5th Cir. 1970); Pattie Lea, Inc. v. District Court of City and County of Denver, 161 Colo. 493, 423 P.2d 27 (1967) (accountant privilege). Saltzburg, Corporate Attorney-Client Privilege in Shareholder Litigation and Similar Cases: Garner Revisited, 12 Hof. L. Rev. 817 (1984). *See* supra § 87.1. *See also* In re Teleglobe Communications Corp., 493 F.3d 345, 387 (3d Cir. 2007) (resolution of privilege dispute between corporation and former subsidiary would depend upon a factual determination of whether the parties were represented by the same attorneys on a matter of common interest that is the subject-matter of the disputed documents); In re Grand Jury Subpoena, 274 F.3d 563, 574 (1st Cir. 2001) (even though both corporation and employees were represented by attorney and within joint defense rule, where communications affected both corporation and employees, corporation's waiver of privilege waived privilege for all); Miller, Morton, Caillat & Nevis v. Superior Court (Curry), 215 Cal. Rptr. 365 (App. 6th Dist. 1985) (privilege subject to joint client exception upon formation of general partnership on theory that consulting general partners were acting for benefit of every general partner).

in the joint consultation cases should furnish a controlling analogy.[3]

A step beyond the joint consultation where communications by two clients are made directly in each other's hearing is the situation where two parties separately interested in some contract or undertaking, as in the case of borrower and lender or insurer and insured, engage the same attorney to represent their respective interests, and each communicates separately with the attorney about some phase of the common transaction. Here again it seems that the communicating client, knowing that the attorney represents the other party also, would not ordinarily intend that the facts communicated should be kept secret from him.[4] Whether the doctrine of limited confidentiality should be applied to communications by an insured to a nonlawyer agent of the insurer bound by contract to provide the defense for both has provoked differing judicial reactions.[5] Where the statement is made directly to the attorney hired by the insurer, there is no question that the privilege applies in an action brought by a third person, nor does it seem disputed that there is no privilege where the controversy

---

[3]But in the only cases encountered in which this situation was presented the analogy was not discussed and the privilege was sustained against the agent. In re Busse's Estate, 332 Ill. App. 258, 75 N.E.2d 36, 38 (2d Dist. 1947) (client's agent who was nurse and business caretaker present at conference with attorney); Foley v. Poschke, 137 Ohio St. 593, 19 Ohio Op. 350, 31 N.E.2d 845 (1941) (detective employed by divorce plaintiff to investigate husband's conduct present at conference with lawyer).

The *Busse* case is criticized on this point in Note, 61 Harv. L. Rev. 717, and on another point in Note, 15 U. Chi. L. Rev. 989.

Finding that the agent was in fact a joint client will of course reverse the result. *See* Manella v. First Nat. Bank & Trust Co. of Barrington, 173 Ill. App. 3d 436, 122 Ill. Dec. 109, 526 N.E.2d 368 (2d Dist. 1988).

[4]*See, e.g.,* Gottwald v. Medinger, 257 A.D. 107, 12 N.Y.S.2d 241 (4th Dep't 1939) (in suit on bond where attorney originally represented borrower and lender in arranging loan, statement of borrower to attorney of amount owed, not privileged.)

[5]An apparent majority holds that such statements are privileged, usually on the ground that the insurer is bound under the policy to defend the insured. *See, e.g.,* Gene Compton's Corp. v. Superior Court In and For City and County of San Francisco, 205 Cal. App. 2d 365, 23 Cal. Rptr. 250 (1st Dist. 1962); People v. Ryan, 30 Ill. 2d 456, 197 N.E.2d 15 (1964); Brakhage v. Graff, 190 Neb. 53, 206 N.W.2d 45 (1973); Thomas v. Harrison, 634 P.2d 328 (Wyo. 1981). Cases holding that such statements are not within the privilege include: DiCenzo v. Izawa, 68 Haw. 528, 723 P.2d 171 (1986); Jacobi v. Podevels, 23 Wis. 2d 152, 127 N.W.2d 73 (1964). Additional cases are collected in Insured-insurer communications as privileged, 55 A.L.R.4th 336.

Where the insurer's agent is acting under the direction of an attorney hired to represent the insured, the minority jurisdictions would accord the privilege. *See* Langdon v. Champion, 752 P.2d 999, 1004 (Alaska 1988) (privilege does not extend "except in those cases where it can be shown that the adjustor received the communication at the express direction of counsel for the insured.

is between the insured, or someone claiming under him, and the company itself over the company's liability under the policy.[6]

Another step beyond the joint client situation is the instance where two or more clients, each represented by their own lawyers, meet to discuss matters of common interest—commonly called a joint defense agreement or pooled information situation. Such communications among the clients and their lawyers are within the privilege.[7] Although it originated in the context of criminal cases,[8] the doctrine has been applied in civil cases[9] and to plaintiffs in litigation as well as defendants.[10] It is commonly said

---

[6]Vicor Corp. v. Vigilant Ins. Co., 674 F.3d 1 (1st Cir. 2012) (no privilege in controversy between insured and insurer); Simpson v. Motorists Mut. Ins. Co., 494 F.2d 850, 854 (7th Cir. 1974) (statement made by insurer defending an insured not privileged in a coverage action against insurer); Henke v. Iowa Home Mut. Cas. Co., 249 Iowa 614, 87 N.W.2d 920 (1958) (action by insured against insurer for negligent failure to settle claims against insured); Klefbeck v. Dous, 302 Mass. 383, 19 N.E.2d 308 (1939) (suit by injured party after judgment to subject policy to payment of judgment, defended by insurer on ground automobile not legally registered in state of issuance; held, plaintiff, claiming under insured, entitled to use letter of attorney, acting for both, to insurer); Travelers Indem. Co. v. Cochrane, 155 Ohio St. 305, 44 Ohio Op. 302, 98 N.E.2d 840 (1951); Shafer v. Utica Mut. Ins. Co., 248 A.D. 279, 289 N.Y.S. 577 (4th Dep't 1936) (action by injured party after judgment to subject policy to payment of judgment contested by company on ground of failure of insured to cooperate; held, company entitled to prove statements of insured to joint attorney); Liberty Mut. Ins. Co. v. Engels, 41 Misc. 2d 49, 244 N.Y.S.2d 983 (Sup 1963); Hoffman v. Labutzke, 233 Wis. 365, 289 N.W. 652 (1940) (on motion to set aside verdict against automobile liability insurer for damages to injured party, on ground of non-cooperation by insured, statement of insured to joint attorney not privileged); Insured-insurer communications as privileged, 55 A.L.R.4th 336.

[7]The classic case is Chahoon v. Commonwealth, 62 Va. 822, 21 Gratt. 822, 1871 WL 4931 (1871). See also U.S. v. Henke, 222 F.3d 633, 637 (9th Cir. 2000); U.S. v. Hsia, 81 F. Supp. 2d 7, 16 (D.D.C. 2000); Unif. R. Evid. 502(b)(3).

There is some question as to whether the privilege is applicable in subsequent litigation between formerly allied parties. Compare Welles, A Survey of Attorney-Client Privilege in Joint Defense, 35 U. Miami L. Rev. 321, 337 (1981) (privilege inapplicable) with Mueller & Kirkpatrick, Evidence § 5:20 (3d ed.) (matter not yet settled; some justification for application of the privilege).

[8]For a discussion of the joint defense doctrine in criminal cases, see Bartel, Reconceptualizing the Joint Defense Doctrine, 65 Fordham L. Rev. 871 (1996).

[9]E.g., In re LTV Securities Litigation, 89 F.R.D. 595 (N.D. Tex. 1981) (administrative proceedings). Hanover Ins. Co. v. Rapo & Jepsen Ins. Services, Inc., 449 Mass. 609, 870 N.E.2d 1105 (2007) (joint defense exception applied despite lack of clients' express consent to such an agreement).

[10]E.g., Schachar v. American Academy of Ophthalmology, Inc., 106 F.R.D. 187, 191 (N.D. Ill. 1985) (plaintiffs involved in different lawsuits).

that the doctrine applies only where the parties are involved in litigation,[11] but some courts have applied it in other instances.[12]

The burden of showing the common interest is on the party claiming the privilege.[13] Such an agreement may not be found to exist even where two clients jointly consult lawyers with regard to related matters. For example, in a matter involving the Whitewater investigation, the court held that matters discussed between Hilary Rodham Clinton and her lawyers and lawyers representing the Office of the President were not within the common interest doctrine. Mrs. Clinton's interests were in avoiding personal liability, criminal or civil; the White House as a governmental institution did not have a similar interest.[14]

The weight of authority seems to support the view that when client and attorney become embroiled in a controversy between themselves, as in an action by the attorney for compensation or by the client for damages for the attorney's negligence, the seal is removed from the attorney's lips.[15] Though sometimes rested

---

[11]*See, e.g.,* In re Santa Fe Intern. Corp., 272 F.3d 705, 713 (5th Cir. 2001) (joint defense rule did not apply where no litigation or threat of litigation). Unif. R. Evid. 502(b)(3) requires a "pending action."

[12]*See, e.g.,* In re Regents of University of California, 101 F.3d 1386, 1389–90 (Fed. Cir. 1996) (patent application).

[13]*See* U.S. v. Weissman, 195 F.3d 96, 99 (2d Cir. 1999) (defendant failed to establish existence of a joint defense agreement); U.S. v. Bay State Ambulance and Hosp. Rental Service, Inc., 874 F.2d 20, 29 (1st Cir. 1989) (client failed to show that communication was for purposes involving the joint defense).

[14]In re Grand Jury Subpoena Duces Tecum, 112 F.3d 910, 922 (8th Cir. 1997).

[15]Willy v. Administrative Review Bd., 423 F.3d 483, 494–501 (5th Cir. 2005) (privilege did not protect communications in retaliatory discharge claim brought by in-house counsel); Sokol v. Mortimer, 81 Ill. App. 2d 55, 225 N.E.2d 496 (1st Dist. 1967) (attorney's suit for fee); Nave v. Baird, 12 Ind. 318, 1859 WL 4663 (1859) (suit by client for negligence); Weinshenk v.

Sullivan, 100 S.W.2d 66 (Mo. Ct. App. 1937) (attorney's suit for compensation); Stern v. Daniel, 47 Wash. 96, 91 P. 552 (1907) (lawyer's suit for fee; client's letters to lawyer not privileged though it discloses client's improper conduct. "They would have been privileged, no doubt as between either of the parties to this suit and third parties; but as between the attorney and client the rule of privilege will not be enforced where the client charges mismanagement of his cause by the attorney, as was the case here, and where it would be a manifest injustice to allow the client to take advantage of the rule of privilege to the prejudice of the attorney, or when it would be carried to the extent of depriving the attorney of the means of obtaining or defending his own rights."); State v. Markey, 259 Wis. 527, 49 N.W.2d 437 (1951).

Under Unif. R. Evid. 502(d)(3) (1986), there was no privilege as to "a communication relevant to a breach of duty by the lawyer to his client or by the client to his lawyer." 502(d)(3) was left intact when the rule was amended in 1999 and a provision was added, 503(d)(4), providing that there is no privilege under the rule "as to a communication necessary for a lawyer to defend in a legal proceeding a charge

upon other grounds[16] it seems that here again the notion that as between the participants in the conference the intention was to disclose and not to withhold the matters communicated offers a plausible reason.[17] As to what is a controversy between lawyer and client the decisions do not limit their holdings to litigation between them, but have said that whenever the client, even in litigation between third persons, makes an imputation against the good faith of his attorney in respect to his professional services, the curtain of privilege drops so far as necessary to enable the lawyer to defend his conduct.[18] Perhaps the whole doctrine, that in controversies between attorney and client the privilege is relaxed, may best be based upon the ground of practical necessity that if effective legal service is to be encouraged the privilege must not stand in the way of the lawyer's just enforcement of his rights to be paid a fee and to protect his reputation. The only question about such a principle is whether in all cases the privilege ought not to be subject to the same qualification, that it should yield when the evidence sought is necessary to the attainment of justice.

## §92 The client as the holder of the privilege: Who may assert, and who complain on appeal of its denial?[1]

A rule regulating the competency of evidence or of witnesses—a so-called "exclusionary" rule—is normally founded on the policy of safeguarding the fact-finding process against error, and it is assertable by the party against whom the evidence is offered. The

---

that the lawyer assisted the client in criminal or fraudulent conduct." *See also,* Pappas v. Holloway, 114 Wash. 2d 198, 787 P.2d 30 (1990) (suit by attorney for fee with counterclaim by client for malpractice and third-party complaint against other attorneys involved in underlying case; held that client's privilege was waived as to all attorneys involved in earlier action).

[16]E.g., that a contract for compensation is not a communication from the client, and is "collateral" to the professional relation. Baskerville v. Baskerville, 246 Minn. 496, 75 N.W.2d 762 (1956); Strickland v. Capital City Mills, 74 S.C. 16, 54 S.E. 220 (1906).

When the client claims that the attorney has given incompetent advice the lawyer may testify as to the advice given. Leverich v. Leverich, 340 Mich. 133, 64 N.W.2d 567 (1954); Chase v. Chase, 78 R.I. 278, 81 A.2d 686 (1951).

[17]Minard v. Stillman, 31 Or. 164, 49 P. 976 (1897); *see* 8 Wigmore, Evidence § 2312(2) (McNaughton rev. 1961; Imwinkelried, The New Wigmore: Evidentiary Privileges § 6.13.2.a (2d ed. 2010).

[18]Meyerhofer v. Empire Fire & Marine Ins. Co., 497 F.2d 1190 (2d Cir. 1974); Pierce v. Norton, 82 Conn. 441, 74 A. 686 (1909); Hyde v. State, 70 Ga. App. 823, 29 S.E.2d 820 (1944); Moore v. State, 231 Ind. 690, 111 N.E.2d 47 (1953); State v. Journey, 207 Neb. 717, 301 N.W.2d 82 (1981); Doll v. Loesel, 288 Pa. 527, 136 A. 796 (1927); Chase v. Chase, 78 R.I. 278, 81 A.2d 686 (1951).

**[Section 92]**

[1]*See* 8 Wigmore, Evidence § 232 (McNaughton rev. 1961); Note, 30 Colum. L. Rev. 686 (1930); 81 Am. Jur. 2d, Witnesses §§ 332 to 333.

earmarks of a privilege, as we have seen, are first, that it is not designed to protect the fact-finding process but is intended to protect some "outside" interest, other than the ascertainment of truth at the trial, and second, that it cannot be asserted by the adverse party as such, but only by the person whose interest the particular rule of privilege is intended to safeguard.[2] While once it was conceived that the privilege was set up to protect the lawyer's honor, we know that today it is agreed that the basic policy of the rule is that of encouraging clients to lay the facts fully before their counsel. They will be encouraged by a privilege that they themselves have the power to invoke. To extend any benefit or advantage to someone as attorney, or as party to a suit, or to people generally, will be to suppress relevant evidence without promoting the purpose of the privilege.

Accordingly it is now generally agreed that the privilege is the client's and his alone, and Uniform Rule 502(b) vests the privilege in the client.[3] It is thought that this would be recognized even in those states that, before modern notions of privilege and policy were adequately worked out, codified the rule in terms of inadmissibility of evidence of communications, or of incompetency of the attorney to testify thereto.[4] These statutes are generally held not to be intended to modify the common law doctrines.[5]

It is not surprising that the courts, often faced with statutes drafted in terms of obsolete theories, and reaching these points

---

[2]See the discussion in § 72, supra of the distinction between competency and privilege. Of course, a party may be the holder of a privilege.

[3]Among the many cases where this is recognized are Minter v. Priest, [1930] A.C. 558, 579 (By Lord Atkin: "But the right to have such communications so protected is the right of the client only. In this sense it is a 'privilege,' the privilege of the client"); Abbott v. Superior Court in and for Alameda County, 78 Cal. App. 2d 19, 177 P.2d 317 (1st Dist. 1947) (where client has no privilege because of his illegal purpose, attorney has none); Foster v. Hall, 29 Mass. 89, 12 Pick. 89, 1831 WL 2760 (1831); Russell v. Second Nat. Bank of Paterson, 136 N.J.L. 270, 55 A.2d 211 (N.J. Ct. Err. & App. 1947); Ex parte Lipscomb, 111 Tex. 409, 239 S.W. 1101 (1922).

[4]See the statutes collected and quoted in 8 Wigmore, Evidence § 2292, n. 2 (McNaughton rev. 1961).

[5]See, e.g., In re Young's Estate, 33 Utah 382, 94 P. 731, 732 (1908) where the court said:

Subdivision 2 of section 3414, Rev. St. 1898, so far as material to the present inquiry, provides as follows: 'An attorney cannot, without the consent of his client, be examined as to any communication made by the client to him, or his advice given therein in the course of professional employment.' It will be observed that, under the foregoing provision, the privilege therein given, as at common law, is purely personal, and belongs to the client. If the client waives the privilege, neither the attorney nor any one else may invoke it. It is likewise apparent that the privilege given by the statute is simply declaratory of that existing at common law. Without this statute, therefore, in view of section 2488, Rev. St. 1898, in which the common law of England is adopted, the privilege would exist and be in force in this state. The mere fact that the common-law privilege is declared in statutory form does not extend the scope of its operation.

rarely and usually incidentally, have not worked out a consistent pattern of consequences of this accepted view that the rule is one of privilege and that the privilege is the client's. It is believed that the applications suggested below are well grounded in reason and are supported by some authority, whether of text or decision.

First, it is clear that the client may assert the privilege even though he is not a party to the cause wherein the privileged testimony is sought to be elicited.[6] Second, if he is present at the hearing whether as party, witness, or bystander he must assert the privilege personally or by attorney, or it will be waived.[7] Third, it is generally held that, if he is not present at the taking of testimony, nor a party to the proceedings, the privilege may be called to the court's attention by anyone present, such as the attorney[8] for the absent client, or a party in the case,[9] or the court of its own motion may protect the privilege.[10] Fourth: While if an asserted privilege is erroneously sustained, the aggrieved party may of course complain on appeal of the exclusion of the testimony, the erroneous denial of the privilege can only be complained of by the client whose privilege has been infringed. This opens the door to appellate review by the client if he is also

---

[6]*See* Ex parte Martin, 141 Ohio St. 87, 25 Ohio Op. 225, 47 N.E.2d 388 (1943) (client who was a witness whose testimony by deposition was sought, allowed to test question of privilege).

[7]Steen v. First Nat. Bank, 298 F. 36 (C.C.A. 8th Cir. 1924) (client's testimony on preliminary hearing to conversation with lawyer, a waiver); Hill v. Hill, 106 Colo. 492, 107 P.2d 597 (1940) (client as witness asked for production of documents to refresh her memory, waiver of privilege, if any, for documents). See § 93 infra.

[8]Republic Gear Co. v. Borg-Warner Corp., 381 F.2d 551 (2d Cir. 1967), "Not only may an attorney invoke the privilege in his client's behalf when the client is not a party to the proceeding in which disclosure is sought, (citations omitted) but he should do so, for he is 'duty-bound to raise the claim in any proceeding in order to protect communications made in confidence.' . . ."); Chicago Great Western Ry. Co. v. McCaffrey, 178

Iowa 1147, 160 N.W. 818 (1917) (attorney for railway, party to present suit, asked to produce correspondence with client properly claimed privilege). Unif. R. Evid. 502(c) provides: "The person who was the lawyer at the time of the communication may claim the privilege but only on behalf of the client. His authority to do so is presumed in the absence of evidence to the contrary." Cal. Evid. Code §§ 954, 956 require the lawyer to claim the privilege unless instructed otherwise by the holder.

[9]O'Brien v. New England Mut. Life Ins. Co., 109 Kan. 138, 197 P. 1100 (1921) (absent client's privilege asserted, apparently by lawyer-witness or by party).

[10]Tingley v. State, 16 Okla. Crim. 639, 184 P. 599 (1919). And the judge may advise the witness of the privilege. *See* State v. Madden, 161 Minn. 132, 201 N.W. 297, 298 (1924). See § 73 supra.

a party and suffers adverse judgment.[11] If he is not a party, the losing party in the cause, by the better view is without recourse.[12] Relevant, competent testimony has come in, and the privilege was not created for his benefit. But the witness, whether he is the client or his attorney, may refuse to answer and suffer an adjudication of contempt and may, in some jurisdictions at least, secure review on habeas corpus if the privilege was erroneously denied.[13] This remedy, however, is calculated to interrupt and often disrupt progress of the cause on trial. Does a lawyer on the witness stand who is asked to make disclosures that she thinks may constitute an infringement of her client's privilege, owe a duty to refuse to answer and if necessary to test the judge's ruling on habeas corpus or appeal from a judgment of contempt? It seems clear that, unless in a case of flagrant disregard of the law by the judge, the lawyer's duty is merely to present her view that the testimony is privileged, and if the judge rules otherwise, to submit to her decision or pursue the possibility of an appeal.[14]

---

[11]Ex parte Lipscomb, 111 Tex. 409, 239 S.W. 1101, 1105 (1922) (attorney for one of the parties when required by judge to testify to transaction with client, refused and sought to raise question of privilege on habeas corpus; held, writ denied because of client's adequate remedy by appeal).

[12]Schaibly v. Vinton, 338 Mich. 191, 61 N.W.2d 122 (1953); Appeal of McNulty, 135 Pa. 210, 19 A. 936 (1890).

[13]Ex parte Martin, 141 Ohio St. 87, 25 Ohio Op. 225, 47 N.E.2d 388 (1943); Elliott v. U.S., 23 App. D.C. 456, 1904 WL 19086 (App. D.C. 1904); 39 C.J.S., Habeas Corpus § 203. But not if the client is a party and so has an adequate remedy by appeal. Ex parte Lipscomb, 111 Tex. 409, 239 S.W. 1101, 1105 (1922).

Appeal from the judgment of contempt is ordinarily available as a means of reviewing the ruling, and enforcement of the judgment will be stayed pending review. *But see* Dike v. Dike, 75 Wash. 2d 1, 448 P.2d 490 (1968), 45 Wash. L. Rev. 181 (1970) in which the trial judge had the lawyer handcuffed, removed to the county jail, fingerprinted, "mugged," and held until released on $5,000 bail. The

court on appeal vacated the contempt order, while ruling at the same time that the order to disclose was not erroneous.

[14]*Compare* the remarks of Shaw, C.J., in Foster v. Hall, 29 Mass. 89, 12 Pick. 89, 1831 WL 2760 (1831): "Mr. Robinson [an attorney-witness] very properly submitted it to the court to determine, on the facts disclosed, whether he should answer, or not, having no wish either to volunteer or withhold his testimony. The rule in such case is, that the privilege of confidence is the privilege of the client, and not of the attorney, and, therefore, whether the facts shall be disclosed or not, must depend on the just application of the rule of law, and not upon the will of the witness."

The former A.B.A. Code of Professional Responsibility, Disciplinary Rule 4-101(C) provided: "A lawyer may reveal . . . (2) Confidences or secrets when . . . required by law or court order." Although there was no comparable language in the Model Rules of Professional Conduct as originally drafted, the Rules were amended in 2002. Rule 1.6(b)(4) provides that a lawyer may reveal confidential information "to comply with other law or a court order." See § 87, note 13. Com-

## § 93   Waiver[1]

Since as we have seen, it is the client who is the holder of the privilege, the power to waive it is his, and he alone, or his attorney or agent acting with his authority, or his representative, may[2] exercise this power. In the case of the corporation, the power to claim or waive the privilege generally rests with corporate management, i.e., ultimately with the board of directors.[3]

Waiver may be found, as Wigmore points out, not merely from

---

ment 20 to rule 1.6, providing that a lawyer "must comply with the final orders of a court or other tribunal of competent jurisdiction requiring the lawyer to give information about the client," was eliminated. In its place, Comment [11] directs the lawyer to consult with the client about the possibility of appeal and states that unless review is sought, the lawyer is permitted to comply with the court's order.

**[Section 93]**

[1]*See* 8 Wigmore, Evidence §§ 2327–2329 (McNaughton rev. 1961); Imwinkelried, The New Wigmore: Evidentiary Privileges § 6.12 (2d ed. 2010); Note, 16 Minn. L. Rev. 818 (1932); West's Key Number Digest, Privileged Communications and Confidentiality ☞168; 81 Am. Jur. 2d, Witnesses §§ 282, 334 to 342.

[2]Lietz v. Primock, 84 Ariz. 273, 327 P.2d 288 (1958) (guardian ad litem, in controversy with attorney); Wilcox v. Coons, 359 Mo. 52, 220 S.W.2d 15 (1949) (either personal representative or devisee of deceased may waive); Yancy v. Erman, 45 Ohio Op. 208, 99 N.E.2d 524 (C.P. 1951) (guardian of an incompetent client may waive his privilege), 36 Minn. L. Rev. 408 (1952); Waiver of attorney-client privilege by personal representative or heir of deceased client or by guardian of incompetent, 67 A.L.R.2d 1268. *See* Unif. R. Evid. 502(c), supra § 87.

[3]*See* Commodity Futures Trading Com'n v. Weintraub, 471 U.S. 343, 105 S. Ct. 1986, 85 L. Ed. 2d 372 (1985), holding that management power to waive the privilege passes to a trustee in bankruptcy of the corporation, even

with respect to prebankruptcy communications. *See also* In re Grand Jury Subpoena, 274 F.3d 563, 574 (1st Cir. 2001) (corporations waiver of privilege effective as to employees who consulted attorney under joint defense agreement where communications concerned both affairs of the corporation and the individuals); Goodrich v. Goodrich, 158 N.H. 130, 960 A.2d 1275, 1283 (2008) (corporation's new ownership gained control of preexisting attorney-client privilege); Lane v. Sharp Packaging Systems, Inc., 2002 WI 28, 251 Wis. 2d 68, 640 N.W.2d 788, 802 (2002) (former director could not waive privilege on behalf of corporation); Cummings, The Ethical Mine Field: Corporate Internal Investigations and Individual Assertions of the Attorney–Client Privilege, 109 W.Va. L. Rev. 669 (2007) (arguing that an employee who reasonably believed he was communicating to his own attorney should be able to prevent the corporation from waiving the privilege); Taggart, Parent-Subsidiary Communications and the Attorney-Client Privilege, 65 U. Chi. L. Rev. 315 (1998). *See also* Ross v. City of Memphis, 423 F.3d 596 (6th Cir. 2005) (municipality, not employee, held privilege which could be claimed despite employee's reliance on advice of counsel defense); Inter–Fluve v. Montana Eighteenth Judicial Dist. Court, 2005 MT 103, 327 Mont. 14, 112 P.3d 258 (2005) (although former director had no power to waive corporate privilege, he was joint-client with corporation so that privilege would not prevent him from gaining access to communications with corporate counsel).

words or conduct expressing an intention to relinquish a known right, but also from conduct such as partial disclosure which would make it unfair for the client to invoke the privilege thereafter.[4] Finding waiver in situations in which forfeiture of the privilege was not subjectively intended by the holder is consistent with the view, expressed by some cases and authorities, that the essential function of the privilege is to protect a confidence that, once revealed by any means, leaves the privilege with no legitimate function to perform.[5] Logic notwithstanding, it would appear poor policy to allow the privilege to be overthrown by theft[6] or fraud,[7] and in fact most authority requires that to effect a waiver a disclosure must at least be voluntary.[8]

Given the scope of modern discovery and the realities of contemporary litigation, a question of great practical importance today is whether a voluntary but inadvertent disclosure should result in waiver.[9] In earlier times, the burden of avoiding such a disclosure of privileged matter was relatively slight compared to

---

[4]*See, e.g.,* Greenberg v. State, 421 Md. 396, 26 A.3d 955 (2011) (case remanded for a determination of the extent to which client had waived privilege in discussing dealings with attorney). *See also* 8 Wigmore, Evidence § 2327 (McNaughton rev. 1961); Imwinkelried, The New Wigmore: Evidentiary Privileges § 6.12.4 (2d ed. 2010).

Traditionally, waiver is described as intentional relinquishment of a known right. Johnson v. Zerbst, 304 U.S. 458, 464, 58 S. Ct. 1019, 82 L. Ed. 1461 (1938). However, voluntary disclosure, regardless of knowledge of the existence of the privilege, deprives a subsequent claim of privilege based on confidentiality of any significance. *But see* Frease v. Glazer, 330 Or. 364, 4 P.3d 56, 60 (2000) (client did not waive privilege by fleeing jurisdiction).

[5]U.S. v. Kelsey-Hayes Wheel Co., 15 F.R.D. 461, 464 (E.D. Mich. 1954); People v. Bloom, 193 N.Y. 1, 85 N.E. 824, 826 (1908) ("[W]hen a secret is out, it is out for all time, and cannot be caught again like a bird, and put back in its cage").

[6]Wigmore took the position that disclosures resulting from theft are not within the privilege, basing this conclusion on the argument that the risk of inadequate precautions is upon the client. 8 Wigmore, Evidence § 2325 at 633 (3d ed. 1940). For a modern application of this view, *see* Suburban Sew 'N Sweep, Inc. v. Swiss-Bernina, Inc., 91 F.R.D. 254 (N.D. Ill. 1981). *Compare* In re Grand Jury Proceedings Involving Berkley and Co., Inc., 466 F. Supp. 863 (D. Minn. 1979) (citing modern trend toward protection of privilege in stolen documents).

[7]*See, e.g.,* State v. Schmidt, 474 So. 2d 899 (Fla. 5th DCA 1985) (disclosure obtained through deceit did not waive privilege).

[8]Unif. R. Evid. 510 provides:

Waiver of Privilege

(a) Voluntary disclosure. A person upon whom these rules confer a privilege against disclosure waives the privilege if the person or the person's predecessor, while holder of the privilege, voluntarily discloses or consents to disclosure of any significant part of the privileged matter. This rule does not apply if the disclosure itself is privileged.

(b) Involuntary disclosure. A claim of privilege is not waived by a disclosure that was compelled erroneously or made without an opportunity to claim the privilege.

[9]Scholarly treatments of the problem include: Ayres, Attorney-

that encountered today where enormous quantities of documents may be sought by an opponent through discovery.[10] Under current conditions, some privileged material is likely to pass through even the most tightly woven screen. Since the consequences of such an oversight are potentially staggering, the question is raised as to whether traditional waiver doctrine ought to be modified. Not surprisingly, the decisions in the area have been somewhat divergent. However, while some courts apparently still adhere to a rather strict approach to waiver,[11] others have considered factors such as the excusability of the error, whether prompt attempt to remedy the error was made, and whether preservation of the privilege will occasion unfairness to the opponent.[12] The costs of attempting to avoid waiver under a strict rule would argue strongly for modification along these lines, and it is believed that the decisions are tending in this direction.

Closely related to the inadvertent waiver issue is the question

---

Client Privilege: The Necessity of Intent to Waive the Privilege in Inadvertent Disclosure Cases, 18 Pac. L.J. 59 (1986); Davidson and Voth, Waiver of Attorney-Client Privilege, 64 Or. L. Rev. 637 (1986); Grippando, Attorney-Client Privilege: Implied Waiver Through Inadvertent Disclosure of Documents, 38 U. Miami L. Rev. 511 (1985); Marcus, The Perils of Privilege: Waiver and the Litigator, 84 Mich. L. Rev. 1605 (1986); Rand, What Would Learned Hand Do?: Adapting to Technological Change and Protecting the Attorney-Client Privilege on the Internet, 66 Brook. L. Rev. 361 (2000). See also Note, Jennifer A. Hardgrove, Scope of Waiver of Attorney-Client Privilege: Articulating a Standard That Will Afford Guidance to Courts, 1998 U. Ill. L. Rev. 643, 659; Note, Waiver of evidentiary privilege by inadvertent disclosure—federal law, 159 A.L.R. Fed. 153.

[10]See Marcus, The Perils of Privilege: Waiver and the Litigator, 84 Mich. L. Rev. 1605, 1608–1615 (1986) for a discussion of the problems generated by large cases.

[11]See, e.g., Texaco Puerto Rico, Inc. v. Department of Consumer Affairs, 60 F.3d 867 (1st Cir. 1995); Underwater Storage, Inc. v. U. S. Rubber Co., 314 F. Supp. 546 (D. D.C. 1970); Duplan Corp. v. Deering

Milliken, Inc., 397 F. Supp. 1146 (D.S.C. 1974).

[12]Alldread v. City of Grenada, 988 F.2d 1425 (5th Cir. 1993) (party properly ordered to return privileged documents inadvertently turned over); Gomez v. Vernon, 255 F.3d 1118, 1133 (9th Cir. 2001) (privilege maintained even though inmates' legal papers contained in file in prison library; confidentiality existed to reasonable extent under circumstances). See also Continental Cas. Co. v. Under Armour, Inc., 537 F. Supp. 2d 761, 767 (D. Md. 2008) (applying state law in diversity case to consider circumstances of disclosure); Hydraflow, Inc. v. Enidine Inc., 145 F.R.D. 626, 637 (W.D. N.Y. 1993); Edwards v. Whitaker, 868 F. Supp. 226, 229 (M.D. Tenn. 1994); Kanter v. Superior Court (Safeco Ins. Co. of America), 253 Cal. Rptr. 810 (App. 2d Dist. 1988); Farm Credit Bank of St. Paul v. Huether, 454 N.W.2d 710 (N.D. 1990); Walton v. Mid-Atlantic Spine Specialists, P.C., 280 Va. 113, 694 S.E.2d 545 (2010) (court used multi-factor test to determine that disclosure resulted in waiver); Note, Inadvertent Disclosure and the Attorney-Client Privilege: Looking to the Work-Product Doctrine for Guidance, 22 Cardozo L. Rev. 1315 (2001).

of the scope of waiver. The traditional rule has been that waiver as to one document waives the privilege for other documents relating to the same subject matter.[13] However, under modern practice, where the volume of documents may be enormous, a broad subject matter waiver may be inappropriate. Thus, in instances of inadvertent waiver, even some courts applying a strict waiver policy have limited the scope of the waiver to the document itself rather than extending it to all documents dealing with the same subject matter.[14] Others have narrowed the scope of the subject matter significantly.[15] A persuasive argument has been made that the treatment of the inadvertent and scope of waiver issues be analyzed in terms of fairness and that the "principal concern is selective use of privileged material to garble the truth, which mandates giving the opponent access to related privileged material to set the record straight."[16]

In 2008, Congress sought to alleviate some of the more troublesome aspects arising from both inadvertent waiver and the broad scope of waiver in some courts. Federal Rule of Evidence 502[17] now provides that inadvertent disclosures do not operate as waivers, provided the privilege holder took reasonable steps to prevent

---

[13]*E.g.,* Matter of Estate of Baker, 139 Misc. 2d 573, 528 N.Y.S.2d 470 (Sur. Ct. 1988).

[14]*See* Golden Valley Microwave Foods, Inc. v. Weaver Popcorn Co., Inc., 132 F.R.D. 204 (N.D. Ind. 1990); International Digital Systems Corp. v. Digital Equipment Corp., 120 F.R.D. 445, 449–50 (D. Mass. 1988). *Contra* In re Grand Jury Proceedings, 727 F.2d 1352 (4th Cir. 1984); In re Sealed Case, 877 F.2d 976 (D.C. Cir. 1989).

[15]*See, e.g.,* Hercules, Inc. v. Exxon Corp., 434 F. Supp. 136, 156 (D. Del. 1977) ("The privilege or immunity has been found to be waived only if facts relevant to a particular, narrow subject matter have been disclosed in circumstances in which it would be unfair to deny to the other party an opportunity to discover other relevant facts with respect to that subject matter."); In re Grand Jury Proceedings Oct. 12, 1995, 78 F.3d 251 (6th Cir. 1996) (intentional, non-litigation disclosure; waiver of subject matter, but subject matter limited under the circumstances); Weil v. Investment/

Indicators, Research and Management, Inc., 647 F.2d 18 (9th Cir. 1981) (subject matter waiver; however, because disclosure made early in proceedings and to opposing counsel rather than the court the subject matter of the waiver is limited to the matter actually disclosed and not related matters).

[16]Marcus, The Perils of Privilege: Waiver and the Litigator, 84 Mich. L. Rev. 1605, 1607–08 (1986).

[17]*See generally* Broun and Capra, Getting Control of Waiver of Privilege in the Federal Courts: A Proposal for a Federal Rule of Evidence 502, 58 S.C. L. Rev. 211 (2006). More recent articles trace the reaction of the lower federal courts to the rule, *see, e.g.* Grimm, Bergstrom & Kraeuter, Federal Rule of Evidence 502: Has It Lived Up To Its Potential?, 17 Richmond Journal of Law and Technology 8 (2011); Murphy, Federal Rule of Evidence 502: The "Get Out of Jail Free" Provision – Or Is It?, 41 N. Mex. L. Rev. 193(2011).

disclosure and to rectify the error.[18] The Rule also provides that the scope of waiver is limited to other disclosures of the same subject matter that "ought in fairness to be considered together."[19] The rule applies in federal courts to disclosures made in either federal or state proceedings.[20] Rule 502 also provides that a federal court order finding that there is no waiver is binding in other federal or state proceedings, even with regard to third parties.[21]

Turning then to the specific contexts in which waiver may be argued to occur, it will be recalled that as noted in an earlier section the commencement of a malpractice action against the attorney by the client will constitute a waiver of the privilege by the latter.[22] There are, in addition, a variety of other types of actions in which the advice of an attorney will sometimes be relied upon in support of a claim or defense. It has accordingly become established that if a party interjects the "advice of counsel" as an essential element of a claim or defense, then that party waives the privilege as to all advice received concerning the same subject matter.[23] While there can be no doubt of the desirability of a rule preventing a party from relying upon the advice of counsel as the basis of a claim or defense while at the same time frustrating a full exploration of the character of that advice, the problem of defining when such an issue has been interjected is an extremely difficult one. The cases are generally agreed that filing or defending a lawsuit does not waive the privilege.[24] By contrast, specific reliance upon the advice either in pleading or testimony will gen-

---

[18]Fed. R. Evid. 502(b). *Compare* Coburn Group, LLC v. Whitecap Advisors LLC, 640 F. Supp. 2d 1032 (N.D. Ill. 2009) and Rhoads Industries, Inc. v. Building Materials Corp. of America, 254 F.R.D. 216 (E.D. Pa.2008) (both construing Rule 502 to find no waiver from inadvertent production of documents)

[19]Fed. R. Evid. 502(a).

[20]Fed. R. Evid. 502(c).

[21]Fed. R. Evid. 502(d). *See* Rajala v. McGuire Woods, LLP, 2010 WL 2949582 (D. Kan. 2010) (court entered protective order over objection of party). *See also* Buffmire, The (Unappreciated) Multidimensional Benefits of Rule 502(d): Why and How Litigants Should Better Utilize the New Federal Rule of Evidence, 79 Tenn. L. Rev. 141 (2011).

[22]Section 91.1, supra.

[23]Hunt v. Blackburn, 128 U.S. 464, 9 S. Ct. 125, 32 L. Ed. 488 (1888); U.S. v. Bauer, 551 F.3d 786 (8th Cir. 2008) (privilege waived where attorney's performance was the central element of defense); U.S. v. Workman, 138 F.3d 1261 (8th Cir. 1998); Skelton v. Spencer, 98 Idaho 417, 565 P.2d 1374 (1977) (extensively collecting state authorities).

[24]Chase Manhattan Bank N.A. v. Drysdale Securities Corp., 587 F. Supp. 57 (S.D. N.Y. 1984); Barr Marine Products, Co., Inc. v. Borg-Warner Corp., 84 F.R.D. 631 (E.D. Pa. 1979). *See also* Frontier Refining, Inc. v. Gorman-Rupp Co., Inc., 136 F.3d 695 (10th Cir. 1998) (bringing of a suit against indemnitor did not waive attorney-client privilege where communications with regard to settlement were not vital to defense); Home Indem. Co. v. Lane Powell Moss and Miller,

erally be seen as waiving the privilege.[25] Some decisions have gone much further, and have extended the doctrine broadly to cases in which a mental state asserted by the client is sought to be shown inconsistent with the advice of counsel.[26] Such extensions seem dubious lacking full acceptance of the Benthamite principle that the privilege ought to be overthrown to facilitate the search for truth.[27]

Of course, if the holder of the privilege fails to claim his privilege by objecting to disclosure by himself or another witness when he has an opportunity to do so, he waives his privilege as to the communications so disclosed.[28]

---

43 F.3d 1322 (9th Cir. 1995) (privileged information not vital to defense of bad faith failure to settle claim); Ex parte State Farm Fire and Cas. Co., 794 So. 2d 368, 373–74 (Ala. 2001) (plaintiff did not waive privilege by filing action claiming attorney's fees based upon insurance company's failure to defend); Metropolitan Life Ins. Co. v. Aetna Cas. and Sur. Co., 249 Conn. 36, 730 A.2d 51, 54–55 (1999) (insurance company did not waive privilege by asserting that it acted reasonably with regard to settlement). *But see* Pamida, Inc. v. E.S. Originals, Inc., 281 F.3d 726, 729–31 (8th Cir. 2002) (under Nebraska law, client waived privilege by seeking indemnification for legal expenses).

[25]U.S. v. Miller, 600 F.2d 498 (5th Cir. 1979); Wender v. United Services Auto. Ass'n, 434 A.2d 1372 (D.C. 1981); Kaarup v. St. Paul Fire and Marine Ins. Co., 436 N.W.2d 17 (S.D. 1989). *See also* Livingstone v. North Belle Vernon Borough, 91 F.3d 515 (3d Cir. 1996) (claim that plaintiff did not appreciate legal implications of release raised advice of counsel defense and constituted waiver of privilege); Cazanas v. State, 270 Ga. 130, 508 S.E.2d 412 (1998) (defendant attacking validity of guilty plea as not entered knowingly and intelligently may not use privilege to block testimony of lawyer who represented him at plea hearing); Waldrip v. Head, 272 Ga. 572, 532 S.E.2d 380, 387 (2000) (ineffective assistance of counsel claim resulted in limited waiver of privilege

with regard to matters relevant to the specific allegations of ineffectiveness); Petition of Dean, 142 N.H. 889, 711 A.2d 257 (1998) (filing ineffective assistance of counsel claim constitutes limited waiver of privilege). *But see* In re Lott, 424 F.3d 446 (6th Cir. 2005) (petitioner's assertion of actual innocence in habeas petition did not waive privilege).

[26]Connell v. Bernstein-Macaulay, Inc., 407 F. Supp. 420 (S.D. N.Y. 1976); Pitney-Bowes, Inc. v. Mestre, 86 F.R.D. 444 (S.D. Fla. 1980); League v. Vanice, 221 Neb. 34, 374 N.W.2d 849 (1985).

[27]For alternative suggestions for limiting the scope of waiver through issue interjection, *see* Restatement (Third) of the Law Governing Lawyers § 80 comments b (2000); Davidson & Voth, Waiver of the Attorney-Client Privilege, 64 Or. L. Rev. 637 (1986). *See also* Rhone-Poulenc Rorer Inc. v. Home Indem. Co., 32 F.3d 851 (3d Cir. 1994) (advice of counsel must be affirmatively asserted as claim or defense).

[28]Nguyen v. Excel Corp., 197 F.3d 200, 207 (5th Cir. 1999) (client waived privilege by failing to object to all questions designed to elicit information about privileged communications and by selectively disclosing confidential communications); Steen v. First Nat. Bank, 298 F. 36 (C.C.A. 8th Cir. 1924); Hurley v. McMillan, 268 S.W.2d 229 (Tex. Civ. App. Galveston 1954); 98 C.J.S., Witnesses, § 383. *But see* People v. Kor, 129 Cal. App. 2d 436, 277 P.2d 94 (2d Dist. 1954) (failure of

By the prevailing view, which seems correct, the mere voluntary taking the stand by the client as a witness in a suit to which he is party and testifying to facts which were the subject of consultation with his counsel is no waiver of the privilege for secrecy of the communications to his lawyer.[29] It is the communication that is privileged, not the facts. If on direct examination, however, he testifies to the privileged communications, in part, this is a waiver as to the remainder of the privileged consultation or consultations about the same subject.[30]

What if the client is asked on cross-examination about the communications with his lawyer, and he responds without asserting his claim of privilege? Is this a waiver? Unless there are some circumstances which show that the client was surprised or misled, it seems that the usual rule that the client's failure to claim the privilege when to his knowledge testimony infringing it is offered,[31] would apply here,[32] and that the decisions treating such testimony on cross-examination as being involuntary and not constituting a waiver[33] are hardly supportable.

How far does the client waive by calling the attorney as a wit-

---

one of defendants, who jointly consulted a lawyer, to claim his privilege when examined about disclosures to attorney, does not waive his right to claim privilege against examination of attorney about the same disclosures). The decision is criticized, it seems soundly, in Note, 2 UCLA L. Rev. 573.

[29]People v. Tamborrino, 215 Cal. App. 3d 575, 263 Cal. Rptr. 731 (2d Dist. 1989); Brookings v. State, 495 So. 2d 135 (Fla. 1986); Com. v. Goldman, 395 Mass. 495, 480 N.E.2d 1023 (1985). But a contrary result is sometimes held to be dictated by statute. Inzano v. Johnston, 33 Ohio App. 3d 62, 514 N.E.2d 741 (11th Dist. Lake County 1986).

[30]U.S. v. Bollin, 264 F.3d 391, 412 (4th Cir. 2001) (defendant waived privilege by testifying to the same transactions and communications as attorney testified to); Hollins v. Powell, 773 F.2d 191 (8th Cir. 1985); U.S. v. McCambridge, 551 F.2d 865 (1st Cir. 1977); U.S. v. Pauldino, 487 F.2d 127 (10th Cir. 1973); Howell v. U.S., 442 F.2d 265 (7th Cir. 1971); Chase v. Chase, 78 R.I. 278, 81 A.2d 686 (1951); Similarly, if the party-client introduces part of his correspondence with

his attorney, the production of all the correspondence could be demanded. Kunglig Jarnvagsstyrelsen v. Dexter & Carpenter, 32 F.2d 195 (C.C.A. 2d Cir. 1929).

[31]See, e.g., Rock v. Keller, 312 Mo. 458, 278 S.W. 759 (1925); Weisser v. Preszler, 62 N.D. 75, 241 N.W. 505 (1932).

[32]General Accident, Fire & Life Assur. Corporation v. Savage, 35 F.2d 587, 592 (C.C.A. 8th Cir. 1929); Steen v. First Nat. Bank, 298 F. 36, 43 (C.C.A. 8th Cir. 1924); Kelly v. State, 493 So. 2d 356 (Miss. 1986); Raleigh & C.R. Co. v. Jones, 104 S.C. 332, 88 S.E. 896, 898 (1916) (failure to object on cross-examination entitles other party to call attorney). It is clear, of course, that the party-witness may claim the privilege during the cross-examination. Ex parte Bryant, 106 Or. 359, 210 P. 454 (1922). With regard to deposition testimony, see Hawkins v. Stables, 148 F.3d 379 (4th Cir. 1998) (client's answering question at deposition concerning what attorney had told her waived privilege).

[33]Seaboard Air Line Ry. v. Parker, 65 Fla. 543, 62 So. 589 (1913); Lauer v. Banning, 140 Iowa 319, 118 N.W.

ness? If the client elicits testimony from the lawyer-witness as to privileged communications this obviously would waive as to all consultations relating to the same subject,[34] just as the client's own testimony would.[35] It would seem also that by calling the lawyer as a witness he opens the door for the adversary to impeach him by showing his interest.[36] And it seems reasonable to contend as Wigmore does[37] that if the client uses the lawyer to prove matter that he would only have learned in the course of his employment this again should be considered a waiver as to related privileged communications.[38] But merely to call the lawyer to testify to facts known by him apart from his employment should not be deemed a waiver of the privilege. That would attach too harsh a condition on the exercise of the privilege.[39] Unless the lawyer-witness is acting as counsel in the case on trial,

---

446, 450 (1908); Foley v. Poschke, 66 Ohio App. 227, 19 Ohio Op. 563, 32 N.E.2d 858, 861 (8th Dist. Cuyahoga County 1940); State v. James, 34 S.C. 49, 12 S.E. 657 (1891). In none of these opinions is there any discussion of why the usual rule of waiver from failure to object does not apply. In most of them, however, the testimony on cross-examination consisted of a denial of having made to the attorney the statement inquired about, and it is arguable that a layman might not realize when he anticipated making such an answer, that there was any occasion to claim privilege.

[34]GFI, Inc. v. Franklin Corp., 265 F.3d 1268, 1273 (Fed. Cir. 2001) (patentee waived privilege for purposes of patent infringement suit where patent attorney testified in earlier trial concerning state of mind, knowledge of prior art and communications with client); Brooks v. Holden, 175 Mass. 137, 55 N.E. 802 (1900); 8 Wigmore, Evidence § 2327 (McNaughton rev. 1961); Imwinkelried, The New Wigmore: Evidentiary Privileges § 6.12.4.c (4) (2d ed. 2010).

[35]See e.g., U.S. v. Bollin, 264 F.3d 391, 412 (4th Cir. 2001) (defendant waived privilege by testifying to the same transactions and communications as attorney testified to); Hollins v. Powell, 773 F.2d 191 (8th Cir. 1985); U.S. v. McCambridge, 551 F.2d 865 (1st Cir. 1977); U.S. v. Pauldino, 487

F.2d 127 (10th Cir. 1973); Howell v. U.S., 442 F.2d 265 (7th Cir. 1971); Chase v. Chase, 78 R.I. 278, 81 A.2d 686 (1951).

[36]Conyer v. Burckhalter, 275 S.W. 606 (Tex. Civ. App. Dallas 1925) (error to exclude cross-examination as to attorney's fee-interest in outcome of suit); Moats v. Rymer, 18 W. Va. 642, 1881 WL 3854 (1881).

[37]8 Wigmore, Evidence § 2327 (McNaughton rev. 1961).

[38]This view seems supported by the result in Jones v. Nantahala Marble & Talc Co., 137 N.C. 237, 49 S.E. 94 (1904) (action for attorney's fees; defendant called attorney formerly associated with plaintiff in employment for which fee is claimed, to testify that fee claimed is excessive; held, this waived defendant's right to object to plaintiff's introducing letter from witness during pendency of employment which would otherwise have been privileged).

But there is authority for the view that if the lawyer's testimony does not relate to the privileged communications themselves, there is no waiver. Drayton v. Industrial Life & Health Ins. Co., 205 S.C. 98, 31 S.E.2d 148 (1944).

[39]See 8 Wigmore, Evidence § 2327 (McNaughton rev. 1961); Imwinkelried, The New Wigmore: Evidentiary Privileges § 6.12.4.c (4) (2d ed. 2010);

there is no violation of the Model Rules of Professional Conduct,[40] and if he is, it recognizes that his testifying may be essential to the ends of justice. Moreover, these are matters usually governed not by the client but by the lawyer, to whom the ethical mandate is addressed.

In an earlier section[41] discussing a witness' use of a writing to refresh his recollection for purposes of testifying, it was pointed out that, under both common law and Federal Evidence Rule 612, if a witness consulted a writing to refresh his recollection while testifying, opposing counsel is entitled to inspect it, to cross-examine the witness upon it, and to introduce in evidence portions that relate to the testimony of the witness. It was further pointed out that if the document were privileged, e.g. an attorney-client communication, such act of consultation would effect a waiver of the privilege.[42] And finally, the problem area was said to be when the privileged writing was consulted by the witness prior to testifying. At common law, authority generally was against requiring disclosure of writings consulted prior to testifying, and under that view the problem of waiver of privilege does not arise. However, an increasing number of cases have allowed disclosure, and Federal Evidence Rule 612 gives the trial judge discretion to order disclosure.[43] Should this discretionary power of the judge extend also to deciding whether a waiver of privilege has occurred? Or should it be said that on the one hand waiver never occurs, or on the other that it always occurs? The Report of the House Committee on the Judiciary took a strict no-waiver position,[44] but no language to that effect was incorporated in Rule 612. Nor was there included any specific provision that privilege should always be waived. The discretionary provision was inserted almost as a matter of necessity to limit disclosure of the potentially vast volume and variety of documents that might be consulted before testifying to those truly bearing on the testimony

---

Note, 16 Minn. L. Rev. 818, 827 (1932). *But see* Martin v. Shaen, 22 Wash. 2d 505, 156 P.2d 681, 685 (1945) (where attorney-executor testified that he received a certain deed from the deceased client, and the court said that when he "voluntarily took the stand and testified upon a vital issue in the case, he waived the privilege of withholding his testimony as to all matters relevant to that issue" including communications between lawyer and client at the time the deed was placed in the lawyer's hands.).

[40]A.B.A. Model Rules of Professional Conduct 3.7. *See also* former A.B.A. Code of Professional Responsibility, Disciplinary Rules 5-101(B), 5-102.

[41]See § 9 supra.

[42]See § 9 supra.

[43]Fed. R. Evid. 612, Adv. Comm. Note.

[44]"The Committee intends that nothing in the Rule be construed as barring the assertion of a privilege with respect to writings used by a witness to refresh his memory." House Comm. on Judiciary, Fed.Rules of Evidence, H.R. Rep. No. 650, 93d Cong., 1st Sess., p. 13 (1973).

of the witness, and similar considerations are pertinent to the waiver question. While the cases are mixed, the preferred view seems to be that the judge's discretion extends not only to the threshold question whether connection with the testimony is sufficient to warrant disclosure but also to the question whether its importance is sufficient to override the privilege, given all the circumstances.[45]

When at an earlier trial or stage of the case the privilege has been waived and testimony as to the privileged communications elicited without objection, the prevailing view is that this is a waiver also for any subsequent hearing of the same case.[46]

This result has traditionally been justified on the ground that once the confidence protected by the privilege is breached the privilege has no valid continuing office to perform.[47] It should be noted, however, that the same result may here be supported by the distinguishable consideration that to allow a subsequent claim of the privilege would unfairly disadvantage the opponent who has reasonably assumed that the evidence would be available. The same reasons seem to apply where the waiver was publicly made upon the trial of one case, and the privilege later sought to be asserted on the hearing of another case.[48]

Should the same rule of once published, permanently waived,

---

[45]Marshall v. U.S. Postal Service, 88 F.R.D. 348 (D.D.C. 1980) (waiver of attorney-client privilege extends only to documents consulted, not to genesis of those documents); Joseph Schlitz Brewing Co. v. Muller & Phipps (Hawaii), Ltd., 85 F.R.D. 118 (W.D. Mo. 1980) (entire file not opened up by merely "looking at it;" must show documents were actually examined; privileged documents should have "special discretionary safeguards against disclosure"); Wheeling-Pittsburgh Steel Corp. v. Underwriters Laboratories, Inc., 81 F.R.D. 8 (N.D. Ill. 1978) (employee-witness reviewed file "Communications with Counsel" prior to testifying; held, attorney-client privilege waived). *See* U.S. v. American Tel. and Tel. Co., 642 F.2d 1285 (D.C. Cir. 1980), suggesting a stricter standard of waiver for work product than for attorney-client in inter-party disclosure situations. *See also* Weinstein & Berger, Evidence ¶ 612[04].

[46]Green v. Crapo, 181 Mass. 55, 62 N.E. 956, 959 (1902) (waiver at

probate court hearing, effective at subsequent hearing on appeal); In re Whiting, 110 Me. 232, 85 A. 791 (1913) (similar); 8 Wigmore, Evidence § 2328 (McNaughton rev. 1961); Imwinkelried, The New Wigmore: Evidentiary Privileges § 12.4.b (4) (2d ed. 2010); Note, 16 Minn. L. Rev. 818, 829 (1932). See also discussions of the question as applied to waiver of objections generally by waiver at an earlier trial: 81 Am. Jur. 2d, Witnesses § 155; Waiver of objection to testimony or evidence at one trial as affecting right to make objection on subsequent trial of same case, 79 A.L.R. 173.

[47]Green v. Crapo, 181 Mass. 55, 62 N.E. 956, 959 (1902) (Holmes, C.J.: "[T]he privacy for the sake of which the privilege was created was gone by appellant's own consent, and the privilege does not remain in such circumstances for the mere sake of giving the client an additional weapon to use or not at his choice.").

[48]Thus in Steen v. First Nat. Bank, 298 F. 36 (C.C.A. 8th Cir. 1924) it was held that a failure to object to ques-

apply to out-of-court disclosures made by the client or with his consent? Authority is scanty, but it seems that if the client makes or authorizes public disclosure, this should clearly be a waiver.[49] Even where the privileged matter is privately revealed,[50] or authorized to be revealed,[51] to a third person, waiver has generally resulted and this conclusion may be supported by analogy to the cases which deny privilege when a third person is present at the

tions to the client's representative about privileged matter at the preliminary hearing in a criminal prosecution, prevented assertion of the privilege at the trial of an action for malicious prosecution. *Compare* Alden v. Stromsem, 347 Ill. App. 439, 106 N.E.2d 837 (1st Dist. 1952) (in suit for engineering fees, communications disclosed by both parties at previous trial for attorney fees, not privileged). *But see* Matison v. Matison, 95 N.Y.S.2d 837 (Sup 1950) (in action by third party, communications between attorney and client were privileged, though attorney had testified thereto in previous action by him for attorney fees).

[49]U.S. v. Dakota, 197 F.3d 821, 826 (6th Cir. 1999) (consent to inspection of documents containing communications with attorney waived privilege); In re von Bulow, 828 F.2d 94 (2d Cir. 1987) (publication of book by attorney waived privilege as to communications revealed; no waiver as to other undisclosed communications); In re Burnette, 73 Kan. 609, 85 P. 575, 583 (1906) (procured stranger to read, published contents in newspaper interview, and spread substance on record of a court in a pleading). *See also* U.S. v. Jacobs, 117 F.3d 82 (2d Cir. 1997) (inaccurate public disclosure of communications still waives privilege); Rice, Attorney-Client Privilege: Continuing Confusion About Attorney Communications, Drafts, Pre-Existing Documents, and the Source of the Facts Communicated, 48 Amer. U. L. Rev. 967 (1999).

[50]Holland v. State, 17 Ala. App. 503, 86 So. 118 (1920) (oral disclosure by defendant to witness of advice given him by lawyers); and *see* Seeger v. Odell, 64 Cal. App. 2d 397, 148 P.2d 901, 906 (2d Dist. 1944).

With regard to disclosures by client to government investigators, see U.S. v. Billmyer, 57 F.3d 31 (1st Cir. 1995) (privilege waived by discussions with government investigator); In re Grand Jury Proceedings Oct. 12, 1995, 78 F.3d 251 (6th Cir. 1996) (telling government agent that client had given detailed description of marketing plan to attorney waived privilege as to specific elements of plan); Smith, Be Careful How You Use It or You May Lose It: A Modern Look at Corporate Attorney-Client Privilege and the Ease of Waiver in Various Circuits, 75 U. Det. Mercy L. Rev. 389 (1998). *See also* Byrnes v. IDS Realty Trust, 85 F.R.D. 679 (S.D. N.Y. 1980) (semble). However, in Permian Corp. v. U.S., 665 F.2d 1214 (D.C. Cir. 1981), the court found this "limited waiver" theory "wholly unpersuasive." *See also* U.S. v. Rockwell Intern., 897 F.2d 1255 (3d Cir. 1990) (record inadequate to determine waiver by disclosure to SEC and independent auditors). *See also* Marks, Corporate Investigations, Attorney–Client Privilege, and Selective Waiver: Is a Half–Privilege Worth Having at All?, 30 Seattle U. L. Rev. 155 (2006).

[51]Phillips v. Chase, 201 Mass. 444, 87 N.E. 755 (1909) (deceased client had requested attorney to communicate facts disclosed to him, to her brothers after her death). *But see* Wesp v. Everson, 33 P.3d 191, 199 (Colo. 2001) (client's suicide note did not waive privilege where disclosures in note were not of privileged material).

consultation.[52] The federal courts are split on the issue of whether
a disclosure to a government agency necessarily constitutes a
complete waiver of the privilege. One Court of Appeals has held
that it does not, announcing in effect a rule of selective waiver.[53]
A few courts have at least suggested that the waiver may not apply as to others if the client has clearly communicated its intent
to retain the privilege, such as by entering into a confidentiality
agreement with the federal agency.[54] The majority of courts dealing with the issue have found a complete, rather than selective
waiver.[55]

It has been pointed out that considerations of fairness to the
opponent rarely enter in where the disclosure is neither public
nor made in the context of the litigation.[56]

---

[52]See § 91 supra.

[53]Diversified Industries, Inc. v.
Meredith, 572 F.2d 596 (8th Cir. 1977)
(en banc), the court declined to apply
the rule cited where disclosure of
privileged information had been made
voluntarily to the SEC in a separate
investigation.

[54]In re Steinhardt Partners, L.P.,
9 F.3d 230 (2d Cir. 1993); Dellwood
Farms, Inc. v. Cargill, Inc., 128 F.3d
1122 (7th Cir. 1997).

[55]*E.g.,* Westinghouse Elec. Corp.
v. Republic of Philippines, 951 F.2d
1414, 1419 (3d Cir. 1991), the court
rejected the possibility of selective
waiver even though disclosures made
to the Securities and Exchange Commission were made subject to a confidentiality agreement. *See also* In re
Pacific Pictures Corp., 679 F.3d 1121
(9th Cir. 2012) A(disclosure of documents to government resulted in complete waiver); In re Qwest Communications Intern. Inc., 450 F.3d 1179 (10th
Cir. 2006) (disclosure to SEC resulted
in complete waiver of privilege); In re
Columbia/HCA Healthcare Corp.
Billing Practices Litigation, 293 F.3d
289 (6th Cir. 2002); Permian Corp. v.
U.S., 665 F.2d 1214 (D.C. Cir. 1981);
U.S. v. Massachusetts Institute of

Technology, 129 F.3d 681 (1st Cir.
1997).

[56]Note, Fairness and the Doctrine
of Subject Matter Waiver of the
Attorney-Client Privilege in
Extrajudicial Disclosure Situations,
1988 U. Ill. L. Rev. 999 (arguing
against subject matter waiver except
where prejudice to opponent is shown).

## § 94   The effect of the death of the client[1]

The accepted theory is that the protection afforded by the privilege will in general survive the death of the client.[2] This settled view was fixed more firmly by the United States Supreme Court in *Swidler & Berlin v. United States*.[3] In *Swidler*, the Court held that the government, which sought information about an interview between the late Deputy White House Counsel Vincent W. Foster and his attorney shortly before Foster's suicide, had failed to make a showing sufficient to justify an overturning of the common law rule. The government had urged that the survival of the privilege be balanced against the government's need for the information in a criminal investigation. The Court rejected the concept of a privilege so qualified, emphasizing that the knowledge that communications will remain confidential even after death "encourages the client to communicate fully and frankly with counsel."[4]

In reaching its decision in *Swidler*, the Court acknowledged the existence of exceptions to the privilege both in instances where the communications are in furtherance of crime or fraud[5] and in cases involving the validity or interpretation of a will or other dispute between parties claiming by succession from the testator at his death.[6] This testamentary exception has been reached by different routes. Sometimes the testator will be found to have waived the privilege in his lifetime, as by directing the

---

[Section 94]

[1]*See* 8 Wigmore, Evidence §§ 2314, 2329 (McNaughton rev. 1961); Imwinkelried, The New Wigmore: Evidentiary Privileges § 6.5.2.b (2d ed. 2010); Imwinkelried, The Alienability of Evidentiary Privileges: Of Property and Evidence, Burden and Benefit, Hearsay and Privilege. 80 St. John's L. Rev. 497 (2006); Involuntary disclosure or surrender of will prior to testator's death, 75 A.L.R.4th 1144; Privileges as to communications to attorney in connection with drawing of will, 64 A.L.R. 184 (supplemented by Privilege as to communications to attorney in connection with drawing of will, 66 A.L.R.2d 1302 (sec. 2 superseded in part Involuntary disclosure or surrender of will prior to testator's death, 75 A.L.R.4th 1144)); 81 Am. Jur. 2d, Witnesses § 347.

[2]State v. Macumber, 112 Ariz. 569, 544 P.2d 1084 (1976); Hitt v. Stephens, 285 Ill. App. 3d 713, 221 Ill. Dec. 368, 675 N.E.2d 275 (4th Dist. 1997); Martin v. Shaen, 22 Wash. 2d 505, 156 P.2d 681 (1945); 8 Wigmore, Evidence § 2323 (McNaughton rev. 1961). Unif. R. Evid. 502(c) allows the personal representative of a deceased client to claim the privilege, but is subject to 503(d)(2) as between persons who claim through the same deceased client.

[3]Swidler & Berlin v. U.S., 524 U.S. 399, 118 S. Ct. 2081, 141 L. Ed. 2d 379 (1998).

[4]Swidler & Berlin v. U.S., 524 U.S. at 407.

[5]See § 95, infra.

[6]Swidler & Berlin v. United States, at 402–405. Indeed, the Court noted that the existence of the privilege in testamentary situation was further evidence that the privilege ordinarily survives the death of the client.

attorney to act as an attesting witness.[7] Wigmore argues, as to the will contests, that communications of the client with his lawyer as to the making of a will are intended to be confidential in his lifetime but that this is a "temporary confidentiality" not intended to require secrecy after his death[8] and this view finds approval in some decisions.[9] Other courts say simply that where all the parties claim under the client the privilege does not apply.[10] The distinction is taken that when the contest is between a "stranger" and the heirs or personal representatives of the deceased client, the heirs or representatives can claim privilege,[11]

---

[7]In re Landauer's Estate, 261 Wis. 314, 52 N.W.2d 890 (1952); Privileges as to communications to attorney in connection with drawing of will, 64 A.L.R. 184 (supplemented by Privilege as to communications to attorney in connection with drawing of will, 66 A.L.R.2d 1302 (sec. 2 superseded in part Involuntary disclosure or surrender of will prior to testator's death, 75 A.L.R.4th 1144)).

[8]8 Wigmore, Evidence § 2314 (McNaughton rev. 1961). *See also* Imwinkelried, The New Wigmore: Evidentiary Privileges § 6.13.2.b (2d ed. 2010) (discussing exception for decedent's statements relevant in estate litigation)

[9]*See, e.g.,* Dickerson v. Dickerson, 322 Ill. 492, 153 N.E. 740 (1926) (communications between client and attorneys concerning deed, intended to be confidential during client's lifetime only); Hecht's Adm'r v. Hecht, 272 Ky. 400, 114 S.W.2d 499 (1938) (death removes the pledge of secrecy); Snow v. Gould, 74 Me. 540, 543, 1883 WL 3387 (1883); In re Graf's Estate, 119 N.W.2d 478 (N.D. 1963).

[10]Russell v. Jackson, (1851) 9 Hare 387, 392, 68 Eng. Rep. 558, 560 (V.C.) ("The disclosure in [testamentary] cases can affect no right or interest of the client. The apprehension of it can present no impediment to the full statement of his case to his solicitor. . . . In the cases of testamentary dispositions the very foundation on which the rule proceeds seems to be wanting . . . ."); Trustees of Baker University v. Trustees of Endowment Ass'n of Kansas State College of Pittsburg, 222 Kan. 245, 564 P.2d 472 (1977) (privilege not applicable in suit to determine whether bequest to one beneficiary had been adeemed); Succession of Norton, 351 So. 2d 107 (La. 1977) (no privilege in suit between executor and forced heirs); Herrig v. Herrig, 199 Mont. 174, 648 P.2d 758 (1982) (rule in text adopted in suit by decedent's children by former marriage seeking to enforce rights to life insurance proceeds required under divorce decree); Stevens v. Thurston, 112 N.H. 118, 289 A.2d 398 (1972) (no privilege in will contest); In re Crook's Estate, 87 N.J. Super. 210, 208 A.2d 655 (County Ct., P. Div. 1965) (semble); Tanner v. Farmer, 243 Or. 431, 414 P.2d 340 (1966) (action by administrator to recover *inter vivos* gift to grandnephew); Unif. R. Evid. 502(d)(2); Privileges as to communications to attorney in connection with drawing of will, 64 A.L.R. 184 (supplemented by Privilege as to communications to attorney in connection with drawing of will, 66 A.L.R.2d 1302 (sec. 2 superseded in part Involuntary disclosure or surrender of will prior to testator's death, 75 A.L.R.4th 1144)). *Contra* In re Coons' Estate, 154 Neb. 690, 48 N.W.2d 778 (1951).

[11]Briggs v. Clinton County Bank & Trust Co. of Frankfort, Ind., 452 N.E.2d 989 (Ind. Ct. App. 1983) (privilege available to administrator in action against decedent's former conservator); Stegman v. Miller, 515 S.W.2d 244 (Ky. 1974) (implied contract to make will); McCaffrey v. Brennan's Estate, 533 S.W.2d 264 (Mo. Ct. App.

and they can waive it.[12] Even if the privilege were assumed to be applicable in will contests, it could perhaps be argued that since those claiming under the will and those claiming by intestate succession both equally claim under the client, each should have the power to waive.[13]

The doctrine that the privilege is ineffective, on whatever ground, when both litigants claim under the deceased client has been applied to suits by the heirs or representatives to set aside a conveyance by the deceased for mental incapacity[14] and to suits for the enforcement of a contract made by the deceased to make a will in favor of plaintiff.[15] The cases encountered where the party is held to be a "stranger" and hence not entitled to invoke this doctrine are cases where the party asserts against the estate a claim of a promise by the deceased to pay, or make provision in his will for payment, for services rendered.[16]

None of this authority would seem to be eroded by the *Swidler* case. But certainly the survival of the privilege in the ordinary situation is now entrenched. The *Swidler* case is, of course, bind-

---

1976); Clark v. Second Judicial Dist. Court, 101 Nev. 58, 692 P.2d 512 (1985) (breach of contract to make will); In re Smith's Estate, 263 Wis. 441, 57 N.W.2d 727 (1953); Privileges as to communications to attorney in connection with drawing of will, 64 A.L.R. 184 (supplemented by Privilege as to communications to attorney in connection with drawing of will, 66 A.L.R.2d 1302 (sec. 2 superseded in part Involuntary disclosure or surrender of will prior to testator's death, 75 A.L.R.4th 1144)).

[12]Phillips v. Chase, 201 Mass. 444, 87 N.E. 755 (1909) (in controversy with stranger, either personal representative or heir may waive—dictum).

[13]*See* Wilcox v. Coons, 359 Mo. 52, 220 S.W.2d 15 (1949) (privilege of deceased client accrues to his personal representatives and may be waived either by his grantees under deed or his devisees under will.) *See also* Walton v. Van Camp, 283 S.W.2d 493 (Mo. 1955).

[14]Olsson v. Pierson, 237 Iowa 1342, 25 N.W.2d 357 (1946).

[15]Eicholtz v. Grunewald, 313 Mich. 666, 21 N.W.2d 914 (1946) (suit by children to enforce contract of

parents to make mutual wills and to set aside conveyance by father); Cummings v. Sherman, 16 Wash. 2d 88, 132 P.2d 998 (1943) (similar); Allen v. Ross, 199 Wis. 162, 225 N.W. 831 (1929) (similar). *But see* In re Smith's Estate, 263 Wis. 441, 57 N.W.2d 727 (1953) (in suit against estate based upon breach of contract by testatrix in making her last will, attorney's testimony privileged on ground that claimants were not claiming through testatrix but asserting adverse claim against the estate) and Spence v. Hamm, 226 Ga. App. 357, 487 S.E.2d 9 (1997) (communication by decedent concerning contract to make will privileged).

[16]*See* Briggs v. Clinton County Bank & Trust Co. of Frankfort, Ind., 452 N.E.2d 989 (Ind. Ct. App. 1983) (privilege available to administrator in action against decedent's former conservator); Stegman v. Miller, 515 S.W.2d 244 (Ky. 1974) (implied contract to make will); McCaffrey v. Brennan's Estate, 533 S.W.2d 264 (Mo. Ct. App. 1976); Clark v. Second Judicial Dist. Court, 101 Nev. 58, 692 P.2d 512 (1985) (breach of contract to make will); In re Smith's Estate, 263 Wis. 441, 57 N.W.2d 727 (1953).

ing in the federal courts, and likely to be persuasive to the states, especially those that have held that way in the past.[17] The principal question remaining is whether there will be other inroads on the privilege in special situations. For example, in *Swidler*, the dissent raised the specter of a deceased client's confession to a crime with which another is now charged.[18] In apparent response, the majority suggested that constitutional considerations might compel disclosure in such a situation.[19] It is difficult to imagine that the privilege would survive such a set of facts.

The issue of survival of the privilege may also be affected by state statutes. Almost half of the states have statutes giving the personal representative the right to claim the privilege, thus acknowledging its survival.[20] Presumably, the right to claim the privilege would also give the representative the right to waive it.[21] California's statute provides that the privilege survives only so long as the estate is still in administration.[22]

## § 95 Consultation in furtherance of crime or fraud[1]

Since the policy of the privilege is that of promoting the

---

[17]*E.g.,* Wesp v. Everson, 33 P.3d 191, 200–01 (Colo. 2001) (privilege survives death of client; court refuses to read into privilege an exception for "manifest injustice"); People v. Vespucci, 192 Misc. 2d 685, 745 N.Y.S.2d 391 (County Ct. 2002) (privilege applied in criminal case after death of client). *See also* In re Miller, 357 N.C. 316, 584 S.E.2d 772 (2003) (privilege survives, but would be applied only there is a need to protect the client's concerns for his criminal or civil liability or harm to reputation or loved ones).

[18]Swidler & Berlin v. U.S., 524 U.S. 399, 413, 118 S. Ct. 2081, 141 L. Ed. 2d 379 (1998) (dissent by O'Connor, J).

[19]Swidler & Berlin v. United States, 524 U.S. at 409, n. 3.

[20]*E.g.,* Ala. R. Evid. 502(c); Fla. Stat. Ann. § 90.502(3)(c); N.J. Stat. Ann. § 2A:84A-20(1).

[21]Some courts have specifically so held. In re Curtis' Estate, 193 Kan. 431, 394 P.2d 59 (1964); Scott v. Grinnell, 102 N.H. 490, 161 A.2d 179 (1960). *But see* U.S. v. Yielding, 657

F.3d 688 (8th Cir. 2011), cert. denied, 132 S. Ct. 1777, 182 L. Ed. 2d 534 (2012) (personal representative could not waive privilege where the information could damage the deceased client's reputation).

[22]Cal. Evid. Code § 954.

**[Section 95]**

[1]8 Wigmore, Evidence §§ 2298, 2299 (McNaughton rev. 1961); Imwinkelried, The New Wigmore: Evidentiary Privileges § 6.13.2.d (2d ed. 2010); Brown, The Crime-Fraud Exception to the Attorney-Client Privilege in the Context of Corporate Counseling, 88 Ky. L.J. 1191 (1999); Fried, Too High a Price for Truth: The Exception to the Attorney-Client Privilege for Contemplated Crimes and Frauds, 64 N.C. L. Rev. 443 (1986); Gardner, The Crime or Fraud Exception to the Attorney-Client Privilege, 47 A.B.A.J. 708 (1961); West's Key Number Digest, Privileged Communications and Confidentiality ⊸154; 98 C.J.S., Witnesses § 336; 81 Am. Jur. 2d, Witnesses §§ 377 to 385; Attorney-client privilege as affected by wrongful or criminal character of contemplated acts or course of conduct, 125 A.L.R.

administration of justice, it would be a perversion of the privilege to extend it to the client who seeks advice to aid him in carrying out an illegal or fraudulent scheme. Advice given for those purposes would not be a professional service but participation in a conspiracy. Accordingly, it is settled under modern authority that the privilege does not extend to communications between attorney and client where the client's purpose is the furtherance of a future intended crime or fraud.[2] Advice secured in aid of a legit-

---

508.

[2]Queen v. Cox, (1884) 14 Q.B.D. 153, 1884 WL 19016 (C.C.R.) (prosecution for conspiracy to defraud judgment creditor by transfer of debtor's property; communications between debtor and solicitor in respect to preventing collection of judgment by transfer of assets, not privileged); Matter of Doe, 551 F.2d 899 (2d Cir. 1977) (conversation disclosing client's plan to bribe juror); Fidelity-Phenix Fire Ins. Co. of N. Y. v. Hamilton, 340 S.W.2d 218 (Ky. 1960) (conversation tending to show fraudulent claim under fire insurance policy); Standard Fire Ins. Co. v. Smithhart, 183 Ky. 679, 211 S.W. 441 (1919) (communications by insured in fire policy tending to show arson and fraudulent claim); Gebhardt v. United Rys. Co. of St. Louis, 220 S.W. 677, 679 (Mo. 1920) (client asserting personal injury on street car, discloses to attorney that she was not on car; "The law does not make a law office a nest of vipers in which to hatch out frauds and perjuries"); Ott v. State, 87 Tex. Crim. 382, 222 S.W. 261 (1920) (husband consults attorney as to what punishment would probably be incurred if he killed his wife); Applicability of attorney-client privilege to communications with respect to contemplated tortious acts, 2 A.L.R.3d 861. See also Callan & David, Professional Responsibility and the Duty of Confidentiality: Disclosure of Client Misconduct in an Adversary System, 29 Rutgers L. Rev. 332 (1976).

A leading case recognizes the rule, but places a seemingly unjustifiable restriction upon it in holding that the client may assert the privilege when he is sued or prosecuted for a different crime from the one involved in the consultation. Alexander v. U.S., 138 U.S. 353, 11 S. Ct. 350, 34 L. Ed. 954 (1891) (client on trial for murder of his partner; error to admit communications to lawyer asserted to show plan to convert murder-victim's property). This restriction was called a "dictum" and rejected in Petition of Sawyer, 229 F.2d 805 (7th Cir. 1956). See also U.S. v. Alexander, 287 F.3d 811, 816 (9th Cir. 2002) (attorney may testify to threats made to him and others by client during his representation of him on fraud charges); U.S. v. Reeder, 170 F.3d 93, 106 (1st Cir. 1999) (consultations with attorney not privileged under the crime/fraud exception even though consultations involved conduct that covered up rather than directly involved the crimes charged).

In order to protect the client who acts upon professional advice in committing what later is ruled to be a crime or fraud, Unif. R. Evid. 502(d)(1) applies the furtherance of crime or fraud exception only when the client knew or reasonably should have known the act to be a crime or fraud.

To the same effect is State ex rel. North Pac. Lumber Co. v. Unis, 282 Or. 457, 579 P.2d 1291 (1978). Conversely, the attorney's misuse of confidential information to defraud will not defeat the privilege. Glade v. Superior Court, 76 Cal. App. 3d 738, 143 Cal. Rptr. 119 (3d Dist. 1978).

The exception discussed in this section must be distinguished from the corresponding duty of an attorney to keep information relating to the representation of a client confidential. Under A.B.A. Model Rule of Professional Conduct 1.6, a lawyer may reveal in-

imate defense by the client against a charge of past crimes or past misconduct, even though he is guilty, stands on a different footing and such consultations are privileged.[3] If the privilege is to be denied on the ground of unlawful purpose, the client's guilty intention is controlling, though the attorney may have acted innocently and in good faith.[4] As to when the client must be shown to have had the guilty purpose, the traditional and apparent majority rule is that the purpose must exist at the time the legal advice is sought.[5] However, some cases have held that the exception applies where the client has used the lawyer's advice to

---

formation to the extent reasonably believed to be necessary to prevent reasonably certain death or substantial bodily harm. The former A.B.A. Model Code of Professional Responsibility, Disciplinary Rule 4-101(C) (3) provided that a lawyer may reveal the intention of a client to commit a crime and the information necessary to prevent the crime.

[3]"The privileged communications may be a shield of defense as to crimes already committed, but it cannot be used as a sword or weapon of offense to enable persons to carry out contemplated crimes against society." Gebhardt v. United Rys. Co. of St. Louis, 220 S.W. 677, 679 (Mo. 1920). Clark v. State, 159 Tex. Crim. 187, 261 S.W.2d 339 (1953); State ex rel. Sowers v. Olwell, 64 Wash. 2d 828, 394 P.2d 681 (1964) (knife obtained by attorney as result of confidential communication from client held not privileged from production but prosecution barred from disclosing source); Attorney-client privilege as affected by its assertion as to communications, or transmission of evidence, relating to crime already committed, 16 A.L.R.3d 1029.

[4]Queen v. Cox, (1884) 14 Q.B.D. 153, 1884 WL 19016 (C.C.R.); In re Grand Jury Investigation, 445 F.3d 266 (3d Cir. 2006) (communications from attorney to client with regard to destruction of documents were not privileged despite absence of showing that attorney had knowledge of potential wrongdoing; In re Grand Jury Proceedings, 102 F.3d 748 (4th Cir.

1996); U.S. v. Chen, 99 F.3d 1495 (9th Cir. 1996); U.S. v. Hodge and Zweig, 548 F.2d 1347 (9th Cir. 1977); In re Selser, 15 N.J. 393, 105 A.2d 395 (1954); 24 Fordham L. Rev. 290 (1955), 30 N.Y.U. L. Rev. 1251 (1955); Orman v. State, 22 Tex. App. 604, 3 S.W. 468 (Ct. App. 1886); Attorney-client privilege as affected by wrongful or criminal character of contemplated acts or course of conduct, 125 A.L.R. 508. A converse question is raised in Clark v. State, 159 Tex. Crim. 187, 261 S.W.2d 339 (1953). The accused called his lawyer and told him that he had just killed his former wife. Though seemingly the call was for counsel in his defense, the lawyer volunteered advice that he should get rid of the fatal weapon. Apparently this advice was taken, as the weapon was not found. The court held that "the conversation was admissible as not within the realm of legitimate professional counsel and employment".

Where the matter claimed to be privileged reveals criminality only by the lawyer, it has been held that limited invasion of the client's privilege is justified. In re Impounded Case (Law Firm), 879 F.2d 1211 (3d Cir. 1989).

[5]E.g., In re BankAmerica Corp. Securities Litigation, 270 F.3d 639, 643–44 (8th Cir. 2001) (crime-fraud exception did not apply where client sought legal advice concerning disclosure obligation and thereafter commits an unintentional disclosure violation); In re Sealed Case, 754 F.2d 395 (D.C. Cir. 1985). See also Note, 60 Tulane L. Rev. 1061 (1986).

engage in or assist a crime or fraud, irrespective of the client's intention at the time of consultation.[6]

Both the procedure and standard for determining the application of the crime-fraud exception have been troublesome for the courts. The question of whether and when the court can examine documents in camera in aid of its application of the exception was decided for the federal courts in *United States v. Zolin*.[7] The judge may inspect documents in camera when there is a "factual basis adequate to support a good faith belief by a reasonable person" that such an inspection "may reveal evidence to establish the claim that the crime-fraud exception applies."[8] Although the Supreme Court has not addressed the quantum of proof necessary for the second stage of the inquiry—the determination of whether the exception in fact applies—the federal[9] and state[10] courts considering the issue have used a similar standard. Al-

---

[6]*See* U.S. v. Ballard, 779 F.2d 287, 292–93 (5th Cir. 1986) (conversations with attorney concerning the disclosure of transfer of assets prior to bankruptcy filing not within privilege where client hired another lawyer who filed bankruptcy without disclosing assets); Fidelity-Phenix Fire Ins. Co. of N. Y. v. Hamilton, 340 S.W.2d 218 (Ky. 1960) (no privilege where client consulted lawyer who told him that insurance policy did not cover a fire because of coverage limitations; client then had another lawyer file suit on policy relating a different set of facts). These cases must be distinguished from situations where there is simply proof that the client committed a crime or fraud after consulting the lawyer. *See, e.g.,* In re Sealed Case, 107 F.3d 46, 50 (D.C. Cir. 1997) (mere fact that a person commits a crime after consulting with counsel does not establish a prime facie case that the consultation was in furtherance of the fraud; showing "temporal proximity between the communication and a crime is not enough"); Pritchard-Keang Nam Corp. v. Jaworski, 751 F.2d 277, 281–82 (8th Cir. 1984) (that communications with attorneys may help prove that a fraud occurred does not mean that the communications were used in perpetrating the fraud).

[7]U.S. v. Zolin, 491 U.S. 554, 109 S. Ct. 2619, 105 L. Ed. 2d 469 (1989).

[8]U.S. v. Zolin, 491 U.S. at 572.

[9]*E.g.,* In re Grand Jury Proceedings (Gregory P. Violette), 183 F.3d 71, 75 (1st Cir. 1999) ("[T]he party invoking [the crime-fraud exception] must make a prima facie showing: (1) that the client was engaged in (or was planning) criminal or fraudulent activity when the attorney-client communications took place; and (2) that the communications were intended by the client to facilitate or conceal the criminal or fraudulent activity."); In re Sealed Case, 107 F.3d 46 (D.C. Cir. 1997) (burden of proof satisfied if the government offers evidence that if believed by the trier of fact would establish the elements of an ongoing or imminent crime or fraud); U.S. v. Chen, 99 F.3d 1495 (9th Cir. 1996) (reasonable cause to believe that clients where using their lawyers as part of an ongoing scheme to evade taxes); U.S. v. Neal, 27 F.3d 1035 (5th Cir. 1994) (prima facie showing). See also a frequently cited case on this point that actually involved a petit juror: Clark v. U.S., 289 U.S. 1, 53 S. Ct. 465, 77 L. Ed. 993 (1933) ("There must be a showing of a prima facie case sufficient to satisfy the judge that the light should be let in.").

[10]*E.g.,* United Services Auto. Ass'n v. Werley, 526 P.2d 28 (Alaska 1974); Olson v. Accessory Controls and Equipment Corp., 254 Conn. 145, 757 A.2d

though variously expressed, what is required is a prima facie case that the communication was in furtherance of crime or fraud, or in other words, that the one who seeks to avoid the privilege bring forward evidence from which the existence of an unlawful purpose could reasonably be found.[11] Although the trial judge may consider information offered by the party opposing review, there is no requirement that such consideration be given.[12] On the other hand, the court must determine that the communication was itself in furtherance of the crime or fraud, not merely that it has the potential of being relevant evidence of criminal or fraudulent activity.[13]

---

14, 34–35 (2000) (trial court properly held that plaintiff failed to meet burden of showing probable cause to believe that the proponent of the privilege intended to commit a fraud); First Union Nat. Bank of Fla. v. Whitener, 715 So. 2d 979 (Fla. 5th DCA 1998) (no prima facie proof of fraud); State ex rel. Nix v. Cleveland, 83 Ohio St. 3d 379, 1998-Ohio-290, 700 N.E.2d 12 (1998) (insufficient showing of probable cause); Frease v. Glazer, 330 Or. 364, 4 P.3d 56, 61–62 (2000) (insufficient showing of probable cause); Lane v. Sharp Packaging Systems, Inc., 2002 WI 28, 251 Wis. 2d 68, 640 N.W.2d 788, 809 (2002) (trial court abused discretion in not conducting in camera review of documents once it had determined that a prima facie case of fraud had been established). *See also* O'Rourke v. Darbishire, [1920] App.C. 581, 604, 614, 622 (H.L.) (evidence and not mere pleading of fraud required).

[11]The various standards articulated by the federal circuits for the requirement of a prima facie case are set forth in In re Grand Jury Subpoenas, 144 F.3d 653 (10th Cir. 1998). *See also* Bricker, Revisiting the Crime Fraud Exception to the Attorney Client Privilege: A Proposal to Remedy the Disparity in Protections for Civil and Criminal Privilege Holders, 82 Temple L. Rev. 149 (2009) (discussion of procedure in civil and criminal cases for determining the existence of the crime-fraud exception and proposing legislature to provide more safeguards in summary judgment cases); Mottley

and Player, Issues in "Crime-Fraud" Practice and Procedure: The Tobacco Litigation Experience, 49 S.C. L. Rev. 187 (1998).

[12]*See, e.g.,* In re Napster, Inc. Copyright Litigation, 479 F.3d 1078 (9th Cir. 2007) (in a civil case, court must allow both parties to present evidence relevant to the exception before ordering outright disclosure; burden of proof to vitiate privilege is by a preponderance of the evidence; In re Grand Jury Subpoena 92-1(SJ), 31 F.3d 826 (9th Cir. 1994). Special problems arise in the grand jury setting. *See* In re Impounded, 241 F.3d 308, 318 n.9 (3d Cir. 2001) ("Because the need for secrecy in grand jury proceedings prohibits an adversarial proceeding regarding ex parte, in camera evidence, courts may rely exclusively on ex parte materials in finding sufficient prima facie evidence to invoke the crime-fraud exception . . .").

[13]In re Grand Jury Subpoena, 419 F.3d 329 (5th Cir. 2005) (exception applies only to those communications made in further of crime or fraud); In re Richard Roe, Inc., 68 F.3d 38 (2d Cir. 1995).

Of course, the inference of the client's wrongful intent will often be a circumstantial one. *See, e.g.,* U.S. v. Wonderly, 70 F.3d 1020, 1023 (8th Cir. 1995) (stating that "[i]ntent to defraud need not be shown by direct evidence; rather, it may be inferred from all the facts and circumstances surrounding the defendant's actions."); Sawyer v. Stanley, 241 Ala. 39, 1 So. 2d 21 (1941)

Concern has been expressed by the criminal defense bar about the uncertainty and seeming ease with which the crime-fraud exception has been applied.[14] But especially given the courts' concern for secrecy in grand jury proceedings—the most common setting in which the exception is raised—it seems unlikely that it will become more difficult for the prosecution to establish the existence of the exception.

Questions arise fairly frequently under this limitation upon the privilege in the situation where a client has first consulted one attorney about a claim, and then employs other counsel and brings suit. At the trial the defense seeks to have the first attorney testify to disclosures by the client which reveal that the claim was fabricated or fraudulent. This of course may be done,[15] but if the statements to the first attorney would merely reveal variances from the client's later statements or testimony, not sufficient to evidence fraud or perjury, the privilege would stand.[16]

It has been questioned whether the traditional statement of the area of the limitation, that is in cases of communications in aid of crime or fraud, is not itself too limited. Wigmore argued that the privilege should not be accorded to communications in furtherance of any deliberate scheme to deprive another of his rights by tortious or unlawful conduct.[17] A few courts have

where a will was contested for forgery and evidence of an attorney was admitted that the purported beneficiary asked him whether decedent had left a will, without disclosing existence of purported will.

[14]American College of Trial Lawyers, The Erosion of the Attorney-Client Privilege and Work Product Doctrine in Federal Criminal Investigations 27 (2002) ("The current rules allow prosecutors to obtain an in camera review based on unsubstantiated information that they may have collected through an unlawful intrusion into the privilege, without giving defendants an opportunity to challenge the reliability or validity of that evidence.") See also Brown, The Crime-Fraud Exception to the Attorney-Client Privilege in the Context of Corporate Counseling, 87 Ky. L.J. 1191, 1259–60 (1999).

[15]In re Koellen's Estate, 167 Kan. 676, 208 P.2d 595 (1949) (client admitted to first lawyer that he had forged

will which he later sought to probate, not privileged); Standard Fire Ins. Co. v. Smithhart, 183 Ky. 679, 211 S.W. 441 (1919) (client sought first lawyer to sue on fire policy, disclosing that she had connived in burning her house; not privileged); Gebhardt v. United Rys. Co. of St. Louis, 220 S.W. 677 (Mo. 1920) (fabricated personal injury claim: no privilege).

[16]Nadler v. Warner Co., 321 Pa. 139, 184 A. 3 (1936) (offer to show statement of personal injury claimant, merely inconsistent with present position but not claimed to show fraud, rejected); Thomas v. Jones, 105 W. Va. 46, 141 S.E. 434 (1928) (inconsistency not such as to show fraud).

[17]8 Wigmore, Evidence § 2298, p. 577 (McNaughton rev. 1961). See also Fellerman v. Bradley, 99 N.J. 493, 493 A.2d 1239 (1985) (containing lengthy discussion of "fraud" as contemplated by the exception, and holding that the term should be given an "expansive" reading); Coleman v. American

expanded the exception to include intentional torts;[18] most courts considering the issue have not.[19]

Stricter requirements such as that the intended crime be malum in se or that it involve "moral turpitude," suggested in some of the older decisions,[20] seem out of place here where the only sanction proposed is that of opening the door to evidence concededly relevant upon the issue on trial. There further seems no apparent reason why the exception should not be applied equally to the work product privilege.[21]

## § 96 Protective rules relating to materials collected for use of counsel in preparation for trial: Reports of employees, witness-statements, experts' reports, and the like

A heavy emphasis on the responsibility of counsel for the management of the client's litigation is a characteristic feature of the adversary or contentious system of procedure of the Anglo-American tradition. The privilege against disclosure in court of confidential communications between lawyer and client, as we have seen, is largely supported in modern times by the policy of encouraging free disclosure by the client in the attorney's office to

---

Broadcasting Companies, Inc., 106 F.R.D. 201 (D.D.C. 1985) (expressing agreement with Wigmore position, but finding insufficient evidence of tort to invoke exception).

Cal. Evid. Code § 956 and Unif. R. Evid 502(d)(1), however, say "fraud" in lieu of "tort," in view of the technical nature of many torts.

[18]The federal cases are primarily from the District of Columbia Circuit in instances where the courts have articulated a broader definition but in which the activities involved were probably criminal or fraudulent, rather than simply tortious. See In re Sealed Case, 754 F.2d 395, 399 (D.C. Cir. 1985); In re Sealed Case, 676 F.2d 793, 812 (D.C. Cir. 1982); Recycling Solutions, Inc. v. District of Columbia, 175 F.R.D. 407, 409 (D.D.C. 1997).

[19]See Motley v. Marathon Oil Co., 71 F.3d 1547, 1551 (10th Cir. 1995) (crime/fraud exception did not apply to statements even if in furtherance of illegal racial discrimination if not criminal or fraudulent); Bulk Lift Intern.

Inc. v. Flexcon & Systems, Inc., 122 F.R.D. 493, 496 (W.D. La. 1988) (fraud, not mere inequitable conduct must be involved); Oil, Chemical and Atomic Workers Intern. Union v. Sinclair Oil Corp., 748 P.2d 283 (Wyo. 1987) (declining to extend exception to torts generally). See generally the cases collected in Applicability of attorney-client privilege to communications with respect to contemplated tortious acts, 2 A.L.R.3d 861.

[20]Bank of Utica v. Mersereau, 3 Barb. Ch. 528, 598, 5 N.Y. Ch. Ann. 998, 1848 WL 4466 (N.Y. Ch. 1848) (limited to felony or malum in se); Hughes v. Boone, 102 N.C. 137, 9 S.E. 286, 292 (1889) (similar dictum).

[21]See, e.g., In re Sealed Case, 107 F.3d 46 (D.C. Cir. 1997); In re Grand Jury Proceedings, 102 F.3d 748 (4th Cir. 1996). But compare Menton v. Lattimore, 667 S.W.2d 335 (Tex. App. Fort Worth 1984) (no exception applicable to work product material; holding based upon state work product statute).

enable the lawyer to discharge that responsibility.[1] The need for this encouragement is understood by lawyers because the problem of the guarded half-truths of the reticent client is familiar to them in their day-to-day work.

Closely allied to this felt need of promoting a policy of free disclosure by the client to permit the managing of the lawyer's affairs most effectively in the interests of justice, is a feeling by lawyers of a need for privacy in their work and for freedom from interference in the task of preparing the client's case for trial. Certainly if the adversary were free at any time to inspect all of the correspondence, memoranda, reports, exhibits, trial briefs, drafts of proposed pleadings, and plans for presentation of proofs, which constitute the lawyer's file in the case, the attorney's present freedom to collect for study all the data, favorable and unfavorable, and to record his tentative impressions before maturing his conclusions, would be cramped and hindered.

The natural jealousy of the lawyer for the privacy of her file, and the court's desire to protect the effectiveness of the lawyer's work as the manager of litigation, have found expression, not only as we have seen in the evidential privilege for confidential lawyer-client communications, but in rules and practices about the various forms of pretrial discovery.[2] Thus, under the old chancery practice of discovery, the adversary was not required to disclose, apart from her own testimony, the evidence that she would use, or the names of the witnesses she would call in support of her own case.[3] The same restriction has often been embodied in, or read into, the statutory discovery systems.[4]

Counterbalancing this need for privacy in preparation, of course, is the very need from which the discovery devices spring, namely, the need to make available to each party the widest possible sources of proof as early as may be so as to avoid surprise and facilitate preparation.[5] The trend has been in the direction of wider recognition of this latter need, and the taboo against the

---

**[Section 96]**

[1]See § 87 supra.

[2]General discussions of discovery will be found in Hazard, Leubsdorf & Bassett, Civil Procedure, Ch. 8 (6th ed. 2011); Developments in the Law—Discovery, 74 Harv. L. Rev. 940 (1961).

[3]Ragland, Discovery Before Trial Ch. 15 (1932); 6 Wigmore, Evidence § 1856 (Chadbourn rev. 1976); Sunder-

land, Scope and Method of Discovery Before Trial, 42 Yale L.J. 862, 866 (1933).

[4]Ragland, Discovery Before Trial Ch. 15 (1932); 6 Wigmore, Evidence §§ 1856a, 1856b (Chadbourn rev. 1976).

[5]6 Moore, Federal Practice ¶ 26.02 (2012); Wright, Law of Federal Courts § 81 (5th ed. 1994); Goodrich, J., in Hickman v. Taylor, 153 F.2d 212, 217 (C.C.A. 3d Cir. 1945).

"fishing expedition"[6] has yielded increasingly to the proposition that the ends of justice require a wider availability of discovery than in the past. Accordingly there has developed an impressive arsenal of instruments of discovery, including interrogatories to the adverse party, demands for admissions, oral and written depositions of parties and witnesses, production of documents or things, entry upon land, and physical and mental examinations.[7] In recent years some disenchantment with discovery has surfaced with claims that it was used as an instrument of harassment, was unduly time-consuming, and was excessively costly.[8] In an effort to reduce the abuse of discovery and to attempt to insure the flow of information from party to party, the Federal Rules of Civil Procedure were amended in 1993 and again in 2000, principally to provide for mandatory disclosure of information without the need for invocation of particular discovery devices.[9] These amendments have some impact on the application of the privileges discussed later in this chapter.

*Attorney-Client privilege.* In the first place, of course, it is recognized that if the traditional privilege for attorney-client communications applies to a particular writing which may be found in a lawyer's file, the privilege exempts it from pretrial discovery proceedings,[10] such as orders for production or questioning about its contents in the taking of depositions. On the other hand, if the writing has been in the possession of the client or his agents and was there subject to discovery, it seems axiomatic that the client cannot secure any exemption for the document by sending it to an attorney to be placed in his files.[11]

How do these distinctions apply to a report made by an agent to the client of the results of investigation by himself or another agent of facts pertinent to some matter that later becomes the

---

[6]Hickman v. Taylor, 329 U.S. 495, 507, 67 S. Ct. 385, 91 L. Ed. 451 (1947).

[7]*See* Fed. R. Civ. P. 26 to 37. Many states have followed the lead of these highly influential rules.

[8]Wright, Law of Federal Courts § 81 (5th ed. 1994).

[9]Fed. R. Civ. P. 26(a). The 1993 amendments to Rule 26(a) provided that individual districts could opt out of its provisions. Many districts did so. The 2000 amendments eliminated the opt-out provisions in order to establish a nationally uniform practice. Fed. R. Civ. P. 26 advisory committee note to

2000 amendments. The scope of the mandatory disclosure provisions was narrowed by the 2000 amendments from information "relevant to disputed facts alleged with particularity in the pleadings" to information "that the disclosing party may use to support its claims or defenses, unless solely for impeachment."

[10]Upjohn Co. v. U.S., 449 U.S. 383, 101 S. Ct. 677, 66 L. Ed. 2d 584 (1981) (IRS summons). Fed. R. Civ. P. 26(b)(1) specifically excludes privileged matter from the reach of discovery.

[11]See § 89 supra.

subject of litigation,[12] such as a business dispute or a personal injury. It has usually been held that an agent's report to his principal though made in confidence is not privileged as such,[13] and looked on as a mere preexisting document it would not become privileged when sent by the client-principal to his lawyer for his information when suit is brought or threatened.[14] The problem frequently arises in connection with proceedings for discovery of accident reports by employees, with lists of eyewitnesses, and in connection with signed statements of witnesses attached to such reports or secured separately by investigators employed in the client's claim department or by an insurance company with whom the client carries insurance against liability.[15] Uniform Evidence Rule 502(b) extends the privilege to confidential communications for the purpose of facilitating the rendition of legal services to the client to communications "(4) between representatives of the client or between the client and representatives of the client . . . ." The import of this provision remains largely unexplored.

Whether a communication by the client's agent, on behalf of the client, to the latter's attorney would be privileged, has been discussed elsewhere.[16] Under the Supreme Court decision in *Upjohn Co. v. United States*[17] the attorney-client privilege will protect intra-corporate communications made for the purpose of securing legal advice if, additionally, the communication relates to the communicating employee's[18] assigned duties and is treated as confidential by the corporation. In *Upjohn*, the communications in question were made by the employees directly to General Counsel and other lawyers representing the corporation in the investigation. An analogous rule would seem appropriate for application to agency situations not involving corporations.

By contrast, routine reports of agents made in the regular course of business, before suit is brought or threatened, have usually, though not always, been treated as pre-existing docu-

---

[12]*See* Simon, Attorney-Client Privilege as Applied to Corporations, 65 Yale L.J. 953 (1956).

[13]Southwark and Vauxhall Water Co v. Quick, 1877 WL 17063 (CA 1878); Evidence: statement or report by servant or agent to master or principal, in respect of matters then or afterward involved in litigation, as a privileged communication, 146 A.L.R. 977.

It should be borne in mind that the problem here is one of privilege, not of admissibility in evidence. As to

the latter, see § 267 infra.

[14]See § 89 supra.

[15]Cases involving the claim of privilege for such reports and statements are collected in Note, 26 Minn. L. Rev. 744 (1942); Insured-insurer communications as privileged, 55 A.L.R.4th 336.

[16]See §§ 87.1, 91 supra.

[17]Upjohn Co. v. U.S., 449 U.S. 383, 101 S. Ct. 677, 66 L. Ed. 2d 584 (1981).

[18]See § 87.1 supra.

ments which not being privileged in the client's hands do not become so when delivered into the possession of his attorney.[19] It is clear, however, that these classifications are not quite mutually exclusive and that some cases will fall in a doubtful borderland.[20] And the law is in the making on the question whether a report of accident or other casualty, by a policy-holder or his agents to a company insuring the policy-holder against liability, is to be treated as privileged when the insurance company passes it on to the attorney who will represent both the company

---

[19]Woolley v. North London R. Co., L.R. 4 C.P. 602 (1869) (court allowed inspection of reports of accident by guard of train, an inspector, and the locomotive superintendent to the general manager; significant question was not time of reports nor whether confidential, but whether made in ordinary course of duty); Anderson v. Bank of British Columbia, L.R. 2 Ch.D. 644 (C.A. 1876) (letter from manager of branch bank to head office in response to telegram, reporting on transfer of funds from one account to another, written before suit filed though litigation then probable, not privileged against production, since there was no suggestion in the telegram that the report was for submission to counsel); Hurley v. Connecticut Co., 118 Conn. 276, 172 A. 86 (1934) (motorman's report of accident subject to inspection; mere fact that it was made for preparation against possibility of litigation not sufficient for privilege); Wise v. Western Union Telegraph Co., 36 Del. 456, 178 A. 640 (Super. Ct. 1935) (report from one branch office to another, at latter's request, upon complaint of patron that forged telegram transmitted in his name; held not privileged from discovery in absence of clear showing that document was prepared with bona fide intention of laying before attorney); Wylie v. Consolidated Rail Corp., 198 A.D.2d 884, 605 N.Y.S.2d 700 (4th Dep't 1993) (reports resulting from regular internal operation of business were subject to disclosure); Robertson v. Com., 181 Va. 520, 25 S.E.2d 352 (1943) (motorman's report of accident made in course of ordinary duty before suit brought or threatened required to be produced at trial by counsel from his files); 8 Wigmore, Evidence § 2318 (McNaughton rev. 1961); Imwinkelried, The New Wigmore: Evidentiary Privileges § 6.7.1, at 733 (2010); Evidence: statement or report by servant or agent to master or principal, in respect of matters then or afterward involved in litigation, as a privileged communication, 146 A.L.R. 977.

[20]See, e.g., The Hopper No. 13, [1925] Prob. 52 (shipmaster's report required by general rule, of a collision, on a printed form headed "confidential report . . . in view of anticipated litigation," sent to solicitors; held, privileged); Jessup v. Superior Court In and For Santa Clara County, 151 Cal. App. 2d 102, 311 P.2d 177 (1st Dist. 1957) (father of boy drowned in municipal pool not entitled to inspect report of investigation made for use of city attorney for defense purposes, where that was dominant purpose though it might also be used for study in accident prevention); Lifshutz v. Citizens and Southern Nat. Bank of Florida, 626 So. 2d 252 (Fla. 4th DCA 1993) (information gathered in anticipation of claims was within privilege). Note, 88 U. Pa. L. Rev. 467, 469 (1940).

Resolving the question according to the dominant purpose of the report, as in Holm v. Superior Court, 42 Cal. 2d 500, 267 P.2d 1025 (1954), will often pose difficulties of practical application. A suggested solution is to apply the privilege only to reports having no purpose except use in litigation. Note, 21 U. Chi. L. Rev. 752 (1954).

and the insured.[21] Reasonably, the insurance company may be treated as an intermediary to secure legal representation for the insured, by whom the confidential communications can be transmitted as through a trusted agent. A report to a liability insurer can have no purpose other than use in potential litigation.[22]

*Work product.* The discussion thus far has centered upon the extent to which the attorney-client privilege, just as any other privilege, can be invoked as a bar to discovery. Another, and much more frequently encountered limitation upon discovery of materials contained in the files of counsel, is furnished by the so-called "work product" doctrine, exempting trial preparations, in varying degrees, from discovery.

The seminal case on the work product privilege is *Hickman v. Taylor*,[23] decided by the Supreme Court in 1947. The case involved a suit under the Jones Act arising out of the deaths of crew members in a tugboat sinking. After a public hearing on the incident at which the surviving crew members testified, an attorney for the tug owners obtained signed statements from the survivors. The lawyer also interviewed other persons, in some instances making memoranda. Plaintiffs sought the statements, both written and oral. The defendants and their attorney refused and were held in contempt.

The United States Supreme Court affirmed the judgment of the Court of Appeals, which had reversed the contempt citation. The problem, said the Court, was to balance the interest in privacy of a lawyer's work against the interest supporting reasonable and necessary inquiries. Proper preparation of a client's case demands that information be assembled and sifted, legal theories be prepared, and strategy be planned "without undue and needless

---

[21]Privilege denied: Lamar Advertising of S.D., Inc. v. Kay, 267 F.R.D. 568 (D.S.D. 2010); Aiena v. Olsen, 194 F.R.D. 134 (S.D. N.Y. 2000); Virginia-Carolina Chemical Co. v. Knight, 106 Va. 674, 56 S.E. 725, 727 (1907); Brown v. Meyer, 137 Kan. 553, 21 P.2d 368 (1933). Privilege accorded: People v. Ryan, 30 Ill. 2d 456, 197 N.E.2d 15 (1964); Brakhage v. Graff, 190 Neb. 53, 206 N.W.2d 45 (1973); In re Klemann, 132 Ohio St. 187, 7 Ohio Op. 273, 5 N.E.2d 492 (1936); New York Casualty Co. v. Superior Court of City and County of San Francisco, 30 Cal. App. 2d 130, 85 P.2d 965 (1st Dist. 1938). Notes, 48 Mich. L. Rev. 364 (1950); Insured-insurer communications as privileged, 55 A.L.R.4th 336.

[22]The case for applying the privilege is particularly appealing when the report contains incriminating statements, as in People v. Ryan, 30 Ill. 2d 456, 197 N.E.2d 15 (1964). If the attorney-client privilege is denied, the insured is confronted with an unhappy choice between breaching the clause of his policy requiring him to co-operate in the defense of claims and waiving his privilege against self-incrimination.

[23]Hickman v. Taylor, 329 U.S. 495, 67 S. Ct. 385, 91 L. Ed. 451 (1947).

interference."[24] If the product of this work (interviews, statements, memoranda, etc.) were available merely on demand, the effect on the legal profession would be demoralizing. Discovery may be had where relevant and non-privileged facts, necessary for preparation of the opposing party's case, remain hidden, or the witness unavailable. The burden is on the party seeking to invade the privacy of the lawyer to show justification; this is "implicit in the rules as now [in 1947] constituted."[25] There had been no attempt in *Hickman* to show need for the written statements. And as for the oral statements, to require the attorney to reproduce them would have a highly adverse effect upon the legal profession, making the lawyer more an ordinary witness than an officer of the court. Under the circumstances of this case, no showing could be made that would justify requiring disclosure of the mental impressions of counsel as to what the witnesses told him.

Considerable disagreement in the lower courts as to the meaning of *Hickman v. Taylor* followed that decision, no doubt resulting at least in part from the labored path followed by the Court to the conclusion that the matter of a qualified work product privilege was in fact covered by its own rules as then written. Finally after more than 20 years, the Court in 1970 adopted an amended Rule 26(b), with subdivision (3) directed in specific terms to the scope of the qualified work product protection.[26] Nonetheless, *Hickman v. Taylor* remains a "brooding omnipresence," much cited and quoted by the courts, and in fact still

---

[24]Hickman, 329 U.S. at 511.

[25]Hickman, 329 U.S. at 512.

[26]Fed. R. Civ. P. 26(b)(3) now provides:

**(3)** *Trial Preparation: Materials.*

**(A)** *Documents and Tangible Things.* Ordinarily, a party may not discover documents and tangible things that are prepared in anticipation of litigation or for trial by or for another party or its representative (including the other party's attorney, consultant, surety, indemnitor, insurer, or agent). But, subject to Rule 26(b)(4), those materials may be discovered if:

    **(i)** they are otherwise discoverable under Rule 26(b)(1); and

    **(ii)** the party shows that it has substantial need for the materials to prepare its case and cannot, without undue hardship, obtain their substantial equivalent by other means.

**(B)** *Protection Against Disclosure.* If the court orders discovery of those materials, it must protect against disclosure of the mental impressions, conclusions, opinions, or legal theories of a party's attorney or other representative concerning the litigation.

**(C)** *Previous Statement.* Any party or other person may, on request and without the required showing, obtain the person's own previous statement about the action or its subject matter. If the request is refused, the person may move for a court order, and Rule 37(a)(5) applies to the award of expenses. A previous statement is either:

    **(i)** a written statement that the person has signed or otherwise adopted or approved; or

    **(ii)** a contemporaneous stenographic, mechanical, electrical, or other recording—or a transcription of it—that recites substantially verbatim the person's oral statement.

governs an important area of the qualified work product protection.[27]

These salient provisions of Rule 26(b)(3) should be noted:[28]

(1) The document or thing must have been "prepared in anticipation of litigation or for trial." If this scope seems unduly limited, it must be remembered that litigation is the frame of reference for work product. When the lawyer is engaged in rendering other services, e.g., the drafting of a contract, information that she needs will most likely be communicated by the client, falling within the attorney-client privilege. Information from outside sources is viewed as a peculiar characteristic of the litigation situation.[29]

(2) *Hickman v. Taylor* on its facts dealt only with work produced by an attorney, leaving open a troublesome question as to the status of the product of claim adjusters, investigators, and the like. The rule, however, is specific, speaking of documents prepared "by or for another party or by or for that other party's representative (including the other party's attorney, consultant, surety, indemnitor, insurer, or agent)."

(3) The opposing party can obtain work product only if "the party shows that it has substantial need for the materials to prepare its case and cannot, without undue hardship, obtain their substantial equivalent by other means."[30]

(4) The judge in ordering discovery of covered materials is directed to "protect against disclosure of the mental impressions, conclusions, opinions, or legal theories of a party's attorney or other representative concerning the litigation."[31] Literally read, the rule appears to protect mental impressions

---

[27]*See* Upjohn Co. v. U.S., 449 U.S. 383, 397–402, 101 S. Ct. 677, 66 L. Ed. 2d 584 (1981).

[28]For more extended coverage, see Wright & Kaye, Law of Federal Courts § 82 (6th ed. 2002)).

[29]*See, e.g.,* Upjohn Co. v. United States, 449 U.S.at 397. *See also* In re Professionals Direct Ins. Co., 578 F.3d 432, 439–40 (6th Cir. 2009) (documents prepared for insurance coverage decision rather than litigation, not protected).

[30]Among the many cases construing the "substantial need" requirement are: Director, Office of Thrift Supervision v. Vinson & Elkins, LLP, 124 F.3d 1304 (D.C. Cir. 1997) (showing inadequate); Marchello v. Chase Manhattan Auto Finance Corp., 219 F.R.D. 217

(D. Conn. 2004) (same); K.W. Muth Co. v. Bing-Lear Mfg. Group, L.L.C., 219 F.R.D. 554 (E.D. Mich. 2003) (showing adequate); Coogan v. Cornet Transp. Co., Inc., 199 F.R.D. 166 (D. Md. 2001) (same). *See also* Cohn, The Work-Product Doctrine: Protection, Not Privilege, 71 Geo. L.J. 917 (1983). Cases on the sufficiency of showings of necessity are compendiously collected in Wright and Miller's Federal Practice and Procedure, Civil § 2025.

The language of Rule 26(b)(3) was restyled in 2007 with no intent to change the meaning of the rule. No court has since found any different result based on the new language.

[31]The work product defined by this phrase is today often referred to as "opinion" (as opposed to "fact") work product. *See* Comment, The Potential

and the like of the lawyer only against disclosure that would be incidental to disclosure of documents and tangible things, in this regard being absolute in terms. If, however, counsel had not reduced a witness' statement to writing and counsel's deposition were taken in an effort to discover what the witness had said, Rule 26(b)(3) literally would not apply. Under these circumstances, however, it seems inconceivable that courts would not fall back upon *Hickman v. Taylor* and require an extraordinarily strong showing of need, as has indeed been the case.[32]

(5) A person, whether a party or a witness, is entitled to a copy of his or her own statement merely by requesting it; no showing of need is required.

The rule, it should be observed, does not immunize facts, or the identities of persons having knowledge of facts, or the existence of documents as contrasted with the documents themselves.[33] Nor does the rule spell out the breadth of application or the duration of the qualified privilege that it recognizes. Case law is meager on such significant questions as whether the privilege applies at trial[34] or whether it can be invoked in other proceedings.[35]

Amendments to Rule 26 since1993 affect claims of privilege

---

for Discovery of Opinion Work Product Under Rule 26(b)(3), 64 Iowa L. Rev. 103 (1978).

[32]*See, e.g.,* U.S. v. One Tract of Real Property Together With all Bldgs., Improvements, Appurtenances and Fixtures, 95 F.3d 422, 428 n.10 (6th Cir. 1996). The Court in Upjohn Co. v. U.S., 449 U.S. 383, 400–401, 101 S. Ct. 677, 66 L. Ed. 2d 584 (1981) avoided a ruling on the question of whether the privilege to against disclosure of opinion was absolute, holding simply that the magistrate in that case had used the clearly inappropriate "substantial need" and "undue hardship" standards in determining the application of the privilege. Prior to the *Upjohn* decision, some federal courts had held the protection of opinion work product to be absolute, or nearly so. Since *Upjohn*, a few courts have held that discovery may be ordered where the attorney's opinion is "directly in issue," as in an advice of counsel case. *See, e.g.,* Ferrara & DiMercurio, Inc. v. St. Paul Mercury Ins. Co., 173 F.R.D. 7 (D. Mass. 1997). Others have maintained that the privilege is nearly absolute. *See, e.g.,* In re Allen, 106 F.3d 582 (4th Cir. 1997).

*See* authorities collected in Wright and Miller's Federal Practice and Procedure, Civil §§ 2024, 2026.

[33]Hickman v. Taylor, 329 U.S. 495, 507–08, 67 S. Ct. 385, 91 L. Ed. 451 (1947). Fed. R. Civ. P 26(a)(1)(A) calls for the mandatory disclosure of the identity of persons having knowledge of facts relevant to party's claim or defense.

[34]U.S. v. Nobles, 422 U.S. 225, 239, 95 S. Ct. 2160, 45 L. Ed. 2d 141 (1975) suggests that the qualified privilege may be invoked at trial.

[35]Duplan Corp. v. Moulinage et Retorderie de Chavanoz, 487 F.2d 480 (4th Cir. 1973) recognized the qualified privilege in another unrelated case. *See also* In re Grand Jury Proceedings, 43 F.3d 966 (5th Cir. 1994) (work-product privilege continued protection in subsequent, expanded grand jury investigation); Federal Election Com'n v. Christian Coalition, 179 F.R.D. 22 (D.D.C. 1998) (work-product protection applies to material prepared for any litigation); Wright and Miller's Federal Practice and Procedure, Civil § 2024 at 350–354.

and work product protection, especially with regard to documents and the preparation of experts to testify. Rule 26(a)(1)(ii) now requires at least a description of all documents, electronically stored information and tangible things in the possession or control of a party that the disclosing party may use to support its claims or defenses, unless solely for impeachment. Although the Advisory Committee Note to the 1993 amendment stresses that the disclosing party does not, by describing documents, waive its right to object to production on the basis of privilege or work product protection,[36] Rule 26(b)(5)(A) now requires that any claim of privilege or protection must be made expressly and describe the nature of the documents, communications, or things not produced or disclosed in a manner that, without revealing information itself privileged or protected, will enable other parties to assess the applicability of the privilege claim.[37]

Rule 26(a)(2) now requires experts whose testimony may be used at trial to submit a report disclosing the expert's opinions and other related information, including all data or other information considered by the witness in forming opinions. The Advisory Committee Note emphasizes that the amendment means that litigants should not be able to argue that "materials" furnished to their experts used in forming their opinions are protected from disclosure.[38] Courts considering the issue under the amended rule have differed as to whether "materials" includes mental-impressions communications between the attorney and the expert.[39]

---

[36]Advisory Committee Note to Fed. R. Civ. P. 26, as amended (1993).

[37]*See* In re Grand Jury Subpoena, 274 F.3d 563, 576 (1st Cir. 2001) (failure to file privilege log, even one that was less than precise, fatal to claim of attorney-client and work product privileges). *See also* cases collected with regard to the creation of a "privilege log" in Wright and Miller's Federal Practice and Procedure, Civil § 2016.1.

Fed. R. Civ. P. 26 was amended in 2006, in large measure to add specific procedures for dealing with electronically stored information. The amendment also added Rule 26(b)(5)(B) setting forth a procedure for dealing with information produced in discovery as to which there is a claim of privilege–a problem that is most acute in dealing with electronically stored information. In addition,

Rule 26(f)(3)(D) now directs the parties to discuss privilege issues in their discovery conference and to discuss whether to ask the court to incorporate in a court order any agreement on dealing with claims made after production. The inadvertent production of documents, as well as the agreements of parties and court orders regarding production, are now dealt with in Fed. R. Evid. 502. See § 93.

[38]Advisory Committee Note, to Fed. R. Civ. P. 26, as amended (1993).

[39]*Compare* Haworth, Inc. v. Herman Miller, Inc., 162 F.R.D. 289 (W.D. Mich. 1995) (mental impressions protected); Chopper, Estate of, ex rel. Chopper v. R.J. Reynolds Tobacco Co., 195 F.R.D. 648, 651–52 (N.D. Iowa 2000) (same), *with* Karn v. Ingersoll-Rand Co., 168 F.R.D. 633 (N.D. Ind. 1996) (Rule 26(a)(2) disclosure provi-

## § 97    Discovery in criminal cases: Statements by witnesses

The development of discovery in criminal cases has, for a variety of reasons, lagged far behind that available in the civil area.[1] The pros and cons of the continuing debate on the subject are outside the scope of the present treatment, though it is pertinent to observe that the trend seems clearly in the direction of more liberal discovery in the criminal area.[2] This expansion of criminal discovery, like its earlier civil analog, has raised the question whether "work product" should be afforded protection, and even the more advanced rules and proposals on the subject do undertake to provide such protection.[3]

A distinguishable question which has drawn considerable attention is whether disclosure should be granted of material at, as

---

sions "trump" work product protections); Weil v. Long Island Sav. Bank FSB, 206 F.R.D. 38, 40 (E.D. N.Y. 2001). *See also* Joseph, Emerging Expert Issues Under the 1993 Disclosure Amendments to the Federal Rules of Civil Procedure, 164 F.R.D. 97 (1996).

**[Section 97]**

[1]*See generally* Brennan, The Criminal Prosecution: Sporting Event or Quest for Truth?, 1963 Wash. U. L. Q. 279; Brennan, The Criminal Prosecution: Sporting Event or Quest for Truth? A Progress Report, 68 Wash. U. L.Q. 1 (1990); Everett, Discovery in Criminal Cases—In Search of a Standard, 1964 Duke L.J. 477; Fletcher, Pretrial Discovery in State Criminal Cases, 12 Stan. L. Rev. 293 (1960); Goldstein, The State and the Accused: Balance of Advantage in Criminal Procedure, 69 Yale L.J. 1149 (1960); Krantz, Pretrial Discovery in Criminal Cases: A Necessity for Fair and Impartial Justice, 42 Neb. L. Rev. 127 (1963); Louisell, Criminal Discovery: Dilemma Real or Apparent?, 49 Calif. L. Rev. 56 (1961); Montoya, A Theory of Compulsory Process Clause Discovery Rights, 70 Ind. L.J. 845 (1995); Nakell, Criminal Discovery for the Defense and the Prosecution—The Developing Constitutional Considerations, 50 N.C. L. Rev. 437 (1972); Traynor, Ground Lost and Found in Criminal Discovery,

39 N.Y.U. L. Rev. 228 (1964); 6 Wigmore, Evidence §§ 1850–1855b, 1859g, 1863 (Chadbourn rev. 1976); Wright and Miller's Federal Practice and Procedure, Criminal §§ 251 to 261, 436 to 439; West's Key Number Digest, Criminal Law ⊚⇒6.

[2]*See* Wright and Miller's Federal Practice and Procedure, Criminal § 251(2009): "Discovery in criminal cases is a matter of course."

[3]Fed. R. Crim. P. 16 provides for disclosure by the government of statements made by the defendant and the defendant's prior record. Both the defense and the government are required to disclose certain documents and tangible objects and reports of examinations and tests. The Rule requires the disclosure by both parties of written summaries of expert testimony intended for use at trial. Subdivisions (a)(2) and (b)(2) protect from discovery reports, memoranda or other internal documents prepared by government or defense attorneys or the agents of either. Subdivision (a)(2) also excludes from discovery witness statements except as provided by 18 U.S.C.A. § 3500. See discussion below in this section with regard to the relationship between 18 U.S.C.A. § 3500 and Fed. R. Crim. P. 26.2.

*See also* ABA Standards for Criminal Justice, Discovery and Procedure Before Trial, Parts II and III.

opposed to before, trial. At a fairly early date, both federal and state decisions[4] had espoused the view that when the statements of prosecution witnesses contradicting their trial testimony are shown to be in the hands of the government the defendant is entitled to demand their production at the trial. But despite this background, the famous *Jencks*[5] case was widely viewed as a startling incursion into new territory. The Supreme Court held in that case that the trial court had erroneously denied defense requests to inspect reports of two undercover agents who were government witnesses. It was not required, said the Court, that defendant show that the reports were inconsistent with the witnesses' testimony; if they related to the same subject, defendant was entitled to make the decision whether they were useful to the defense. The dissent condemned the holding as affording the criminal "a Roman holiday for rummaging through confidential information [in government files] as well as vital national secrets."[6] This view was echoed in widespread protests by the press, by the Department of Justice, and in the halls of Congress where the so-called Jencks Act of 1959[7] was hastily enacted.[8] Despite this background, the Act was for the most part a codification of the decision which had been so vehemently attacked.

Federal Rule of Criminal Procedure 26.2 was adopted in 1980 and covers much of the same ground as the Jencks Act,[9] but with some significant differences.[10] A highly significant change effected by Rule 26.2 was the expansion of coverage to include statements by defense witnesses and prospective witnesses as well as those

---

[4]Gordon v. U.S., 344 U.S. 414, 73 S. Ct. 369, 97 L. Ed. 447 (1953); People v. Riser, 47 Cal. 2d 566, 305 P.2d 1, 13 (1956).

[5]Jencks v. U.S., 353 U.S. 657, 77 S. Ct. 1007, 1 L. Ed. 2d 1103 (1957) (prosecution of labor union official for filing false non-Communist affidavit with NLRB).

[6]Jencks, 353 U.S. at 681–682.

[7]18 U.S.C.A. § 3500.

[8]The history of the legislation is graphically recounted in Keeffe, Jinks and Jencks, 7 Cath. U. L. Rev. 91 (1958).

[9]Arguments have been made that the adoption of Fed. R. Crim. P. 26.2 effectively supersedes the Jencks Act. *See* 4 Weinstein & Berger, Evidence § 612[02] (2d ed. 2012). However, the Act has not been repealed.

[10]Fed. R. Crim. P. 26.2 provides:

Rule 26.2. Producing a Witness's Statement

(a) Motion to Produce. After a witness other than the defendant has testified on direct examination, the court, on motion of a party who did not call the witness, must order an attorney for the government or the defendant and the defendant's attorney to produce, for the examination and use of the moving party, any statement of the witness that is in their possession and that relates to the subject matter of the witness's testimony.

(b) Producing the Entire Statement. If the entire statement relates to the subject matter of the witness's testimony, the court must order that the statement be delivered to the moving party.

(c) Producing a Redacted Statement. If the party who called the witness claims that the statement contains information that is privileged or does not relate to the subject matter of the witness's testimony, the court must

for the government.[11] This change was stimulated by the Supreme Court's decision in *United States v. Nobles*.[12] As under the Act, the penalty for refusal is striking of the testimony, with the further provision that if the refusing party is the government a mistrial may be declared if justice requires.[13] A defendant cannot, of course, be allowed to abort a trial by refusing to deliver a statement.

The difference between the Act and Rule 26.2 with regard to a definition of a "statement" may also be significant. Subsection (a) of the Act as amended provides that no statement by a government witness or prospective witness should be the subject of subpoena, discovery, or inspection until the witness has testified

---

inspect the statement in camera. After excising any privileged or unrelated portions, the court must order delivery of the redacted statement to the moving party. If the defendant objects to an excision, the court must preserve the entire statement with the excised portion indicated, under seal, as part of the record.

(d) Recess to Examine a Statement. The court may recess the proceedings to allow time for a party to examine the statement and prepare for its use.

(e) Sanction for Failure to Produce or Deliver a Statement. If the party who called the witness disobeys an order to produce or deliver a statement, the court must strike the witness's testimony from the record. If an attorney for the government disobeys the order, the court must declare a mistrial if justice so requires.

(f) "Statement" Defined. As used in this rule, a witness's "statement" means:

(1) a written statement that the witness makes and signs, or otherwise adopts or approves;

(2) a substantially verbatim, contemporaneously recorded recital of the witness's oral statement that is contained in any recording or any transcription of a recording; or

(3) the witness's statement to a grand jury, however taken or recorded, or a transcription of such a statement.

(g) Scope. This rule applies at trial, at a suppression hearing under Rule 12, and to the extent specified in the following rules:

(1) Rule 5.1(h) (preliminary hearing);

(2) Rule 32(i)(2) (sentencing);

(3) Rule 32.1(e) (hearing to revoke or modify probation or supervised release);

(4) Rule 46(j) (detention hearing); and

(5) Rule 8 of the Rules Governing Proceedings under 28 U.S.C. § 2255.

[11] Fed. R. Crim. P. 26.2(a).

[12] U.S. v. Nobles, 422 U.S. 225, 95 S. Ct. 2160, 45 L. Ed. 2d 141 (1975). A defense investigator had interviewed government identification witnesses before trial, and the defense proposed to call him to impeach them. The judge ruled that this would be allowed only if his interview report was given to the government. The defense refused, and the testimony was excluded. The Supreme Court ruled that the work product protection was waived as to the subject matter of the testimony by the "testimonial" use of the report in cross-examination of the identification witnesses and attempting to refresh the recollection of one of them.

As to the inclusion of statements by defense witness in Rule 26.2, see Pulaski, Extending the Disclosure Requirements of the Jencks Act to Defendants: Constitutional and Nonconstitutional Considerations, 64 Iowa L. Rev. 1 (1978), Federal Rule 26.2 and the New Mutuality of Discovery: Constitutional Objections and Tactical Suggestions, 17 Crim. L. Bull. 285 (1981). See § 133. infra.

[13] Fed. R. Crim. P. 26.2(e).

on direct examination in the trial. Subsection (b) provides that after a witness called by the government has testified on direct the court should, on motion of defendant, order the government to produce any statement (as later defined) relating to the subject matter of his testimony. Under subsection (c) the court will in case of question examine the statement and excise portions not related to the testimony. If, under subsection (d), the government elects not to comply with the order to produce, the testimony is to be stricken or, if justice requires, a mistrial is to be declared. In subsection (e), "statement" as used in subsections (b), (c), and (d) is defined; the definition is very precise and narrow, designed to include only statements that beyond any reasonable question represent with a very high precision the words used by the witness. It will be observed that subsection (a) was designed to bar disclosure of any statement of a witness, regardless of how precise or imprecise a rendition it might be, unless and until the witness had testified for the government. After that testimony had been given, then disclosure was allowed and required but only as to highly precise statements, as defined in (e). If a writing were not a statement at all, in the broad sense of (a), the Act does not affect it.[14] As determined by the Supreme Court in *Palermo v. United States,*[15] writings that were statements in the broad sense of (a), but not within the strict definition of (e), or within (e) but whose maker did not testify, remain locked away, except as they might be obtainable under *Brady v. Maryland,*[16] or possibly under Evidence Rule 612 as discussed below.

Rule 26.2 does not contain the prohibition of subsection (a) of the Act against compelling disclosure of a statement, in the broad sense, unless and until the witness has testified on direct. Thus Rule 26.2 deals only with compelling production of statements within the strict definition of subsection (e) of the Act, which is essentially repeated as subdivision (f) of the Rule. As a companion to Rule 26.2, there was at the same time added to Rule 17 of the Criminal Rules, which deals with subpoenas, a new subdivision

---

[14]Simmons v. U.S., 390 U.S. 377, 88 S. Ct. 967, 19 L. Ed. 2d 1247 (1968) (photograph not attached to a statement); Communist Party of U.S. v. Subversive Activities Control Bd., 254 F.2d 314 (D.C. Cir. 1958) (Department of Justice records of payments made to informant-witness).

[15]Palermo v. U.S., 360 U.S. 343, 351, 79 S. Ct. 1217, 3 L. Ed. 2d 1287 (1959) (government agent's summary of interview with witness not a "statement" within subsection (e) of Act and production not required). Although

agreeing with the result, four members of the Court disagreed with the ruling of exclusivity.

Note also the work product protections of Fed. R. Crim. P. 16(a)(2) and (b)(2).

[16]Brady v. Maryland, 373 U.S. 83, 83 S. Ct. 1194, 10 L. Ed. 2d 215 (1963). See § 252 infra.

For a discussion of the relationship between the *Brady* rule and the Jencks Act, see U.S. v. Starusko, 729 F.2d 256 (3d Cir. 1984).

(h) Rule 17(h) now reads: "No party may subpoena a statement of a witness or of a prospective witness under this rule. Rule 26.2 governs the production of the statement."[17]

It is unclear whether Rule 17(h) means a statement only as defined in Rule 26.2(f) or a statement within the broader definition of subsection (a) of the Jencks Act.

In an earlier section[18] attention was directed to the need to examine the relationship between Criminal Rule 26.2 and Evidence Rule 612. That section pointed out that when a witness while testifying refers to a writing to refresh his or her memory, an opposing party is entitled to inspect it, to cross-examine upon it, and to introduce in evidence portions related to the testimony of the witness; if the reference for refreshing was prior to testifying, access to and use of the writing is subject to the court's discretion.[19] If the writing consulted for refreshment is the statement of a witness or prospective witness, the potential for conflict between Criminal Rule 26.2 and Evidence Rule 612 exists. If the writing is a statement within the strict definition of Rule 26.2(f), the conflict is in reality no more than an overlap, as under either rule disclosure is required once the witness has testified on direct. But when the statement is a statement in the broad sense, as under subsection (a) of the Act, but not within the strict definition of subsection (e) of the Act, the construction in *Palermo*[20] as previously observed, was that no disclosure was available. The confusion is compounded by the fact that Rule 612 opens with the phrase, "Except as otherwise provided in criminal proceedings by section 3500 of title 18, United States Code . . ." and has not been amended. What is the effect of the exception? Does subsection (a) of the Act continue with its former effect? Did *Palermo* survive, pro tanto, the subsequent enactment of Rule 612? A fully satisfactory resolution probably lies only in the legislative sphere. But if one accepts the argument that Rule 26.2 fully supersedes the Jencks Act,[21] the problem goes away. If a statement comes within Rule 26.2 it must be produced after the witness testifies. If it is not within Rule 26.2, it may be produced in the discretion of the court under Rule 612. However, if subsection (a) of the Jencks Act is still alive and the *Palermo* case is still good law, there is no power in the court to order production

---

[17]Fed. R. Crim. P. 17(h). Rule 12(h) extends the provisions of Rule 26.2 to pretrial hearings on motions to suppress evidence. The production provisions of Rule 26.2 apply to hearings on motions to suppress as well as other adversary hearings. *See* Fed. R. Crim. P. 26.2(g).

[18]See § 9 supra.

[19]Fed. R. Evid. 612.

[20]Palermo v. U.S., 360 U.S. 343, 351, 79 S. Ct. 1217, 3 L. Ed. 2d 1287 (1959).

[21]See discussion above.

of a statement that comes within the Jencks Act and does not come within Rule 26.2.[22]

---

[22]For further discussion of this issue *see* Foster, The Jencks Act—Rule 26.2—Rule 612 Interface—"Confusion Worse Compounded," 34 Okla. L. Rev. 679 (1981); Mueller and Kirkpatrick, Federal Evidence § 6:97 (3d ed.).

The federal court opinions have not dealt with the issue frequently. In instances in which it has potentially arisen, the court has simply held that the material consulted was not a statement even within the broader Jencks Act definition and ruled that production was in the discretion of the court under Rule 612. *See* U.S. v. Blas, 947 F.2d 1320, 1327 (7th Cir. 1991); U.S. v. Soto, 711 F.2d 1558, 1562 n.7 (11th Cir. 1983).

Although the Supreme Court disclaimed a constitutional base for *Jencks*, U.S. v. Augenblick, 393 U.S. 348, 89 S. Ct. 528, 21 L. Ed. 2d 537 (1969), one cannot be unmindful of the constitutional support that has been given to the defense right to attack the credibility of prosecution witnesses, whether by cross-examination, Alford v. U.S., 282 U.S. 687, 51 S. Ct. 218, 75 L. Ed. 624 (1931), or testimony of impeaching witnesses, Davis v. Alaska, 415 U.S. 308, 94 S. Ct. 1105, 39 L. Ed. 2d 347 (1974).

# Chapter 11

# The Privilege for Confidential Information Secured in the Course of the Physician-Patient Relationship

## § 98   The statement of the rule and its purpose

The common law knew no privilege for confidential information imparted to a physician. When a physician raised the question before Lord Mansfield whether he was required to disclose professional confidences, the great Chief Justice drew the line clear. "If a surgeon was voluntarily to reveal these secrets, to be sure, he would be guilty of a breach of honor and of great indiscretion; but to give that information in a court of justice, which by the law of the land he is bound to do, will never be imputed to him as any indiscretion whatever."[1]

---

[Section 98]

[1]The Duchess of Kingston's Trial, 20 How. St. Trials 573 (1776). See, in general, the able treatise, DeWitt, Privileged Communications Between Physician and Patient (1958); 8 Wigmore, Evidence §§ 2380–2391 (McNaughton rev. 1961); Model Code of Evidence Rules 220 to 223 and commentary; 98 C.J.S., Witnesses §§ 341 to 355; West's Key Number Digest, Privileged Communications and Confidentiality ⬅200 to 276. See also Developments in the Law—Privileged Communications, 98 Harv. L. Rev. 1450, 1530–1555 (1985); Comments, 33 U. Fla. L. Rev. 394 (1981).

Helpful local treatments include, Quinn, The Physician-Patient Privilege in Colorado, 37 U. Colo. L. Rev. 349 (1965); Olson, A Look at Indiana Code 34-1-14-5: Indiana's Physician-

The pioneer departure from the common law rule was the New York statute of 1828 which in its original form was as follows: "No person authorized to practice physic or surgery shall be allowed to disclose any information which he may have acquired in attending any patient, in a professional character, and which information was necessary to enable him to prescribe for such patient as a physician, or to do any act for him as a surgeon."[2]

Another early act which has been widely copied is the provision of the California Code of Civil Procedure of 1872, § 1881, ¶ 4, "A licensed physician or surgeon cannot, without the consent of his patient, be examined in a civil action as to any information acquired in attending the patient which was necessary to enable him to prescribe or act for the patient."

The rationale traditionally asserted to justify suppression in litigation of material facts learned by a physician is the encouragement thereby given to the patient freely to disclose all matter which may aid in the diagnosis and treatment of disease and injury. To obtain this end, so the argument runs, it is necessary to secure the patient from disclosure in court of potentially embarrassing private details concerning health and bodily condition.[3] The validity of this utilitarian justification of the privilege has been questioned by many on the ground that the average patient, in consulting a physician, will have his or her thoughts centered upon his illness or injury and the prospects for betterment or cure, and will spare little thought for the remote possibility of some eventual disclosure of his condition in court.[4] Other, more recent analyses, recognize the weakness of the utili-

---

Patient Privilege, 8 Val. U. L. Rev. 38 (1973); Note, 55 Or. L. Rev. 459 (1976); Note, 7 Tulsa L. Rev. 157 (1971).

[2] N.Y. Rev. Stats. 1829, vol. II, Part III, c. 7, Tit. 3, art. eight, § 73.

[3] Piller by Piller v. Kovarsky, 194 N.J. Super. 392, 476 A.2d 1279 (Law Div. 1984) (purpose of the privilege is "to enable patient to secure medical services without fear of betrayal and unwarranted disclosure in court of information which might deter him from revealing his symptoms to a doctor to the detriment of his health"); State ex rel. Grimm v. Ashmanskas, 298 Or. 206, 690 P.2d 1063 (1984) (opinion by Jones, J., discussing history, purpose, and criticisms of privilege).

[4] Morgan, Foreward to Model Code of Evidence 28 (1942) ("The ordinary citizen who contemplates consult-ing a physician not only has no thought of a lawsuit, but he is entirely ignorant of the rules of evidence. He has no idea whether a communication to a physician is or is not privileged. If he thinks at all about the matter, he will have no hesitation about permitting the disclosure of his ailments except in case of a disease which he considers disgraceful."). See also Lora v. Board of Ed. of City of New York, 74 F.R.D. 565, 574 (E.D. N.Y. 1977) (privilege has "been object of nearly unanimous scholarly criticism"). Nor, in the view of at least some physicians, will absence of privilege work any effect on the doctor. Comment, Privileged Communications, 197 J.A.M.A. 257, 258 (1966) ("[T]he physician being called upon with comparative infrequency to make disclosures, would not be consciously affected in his relation

tarian justification for the privilege but find the privilege supportable on the basis of humanitarian concerns that support creation of a private enclave that enables the patient to make informed, independent choices among medical options.[5]

Whatever the rationale for the privilege, the number of states adhering to the common law and refusing any general physician-patient privilege has slowly but steadily dwindled. Only six states[6] and the federal courts[7] now fail to recognize a general physician patient privilege.

Over the same period, there has been a strong trend toward the recognition of a related privilege protecting communications between psychotherapists of various descriptions and their patients. Although psychiatrists, being medically trained, have always come within the ambit of the older physician-patient privilege where that privilege is recognized, it has been argued that accepted practice in the treatment of mental illness involves considerations not encountered in other medical contexts. The following statement is frequently quoted in this regard.

> Among physicians, the psychiatrist has a special need to maintain confidentiality. His capacity to help his patients is completely dependent upon their willingness and ability to talk freely. This makes it difficult if not impossible for him to function without being able to assure his patients of confidentiality and, indeed, privileged communication . . . . A threat to secrecy blocks successful treatment.[8]

The uniqueness of this relationship led to the inclusion in the proposed Federal Rules of Evidence of a psychotherapist-patient privilege even though no general physician-patient privilege was proposed.[9] The Uniform Rules of Evidence have retained this privilege, but make the rule optionally one extending to confidential communication to a physician as well as to a psychotherapist

---

with the patient.")

[5]Imwinkelried, The New Wigmore: Evidentiary Privileges § 6.2.6(a) (2d ed. 2010). *See also* Charles L. Black, The Marital and Physician Privileges—A Reprint of a Letter to a Congressman, 1975 Duke L.J. 454.

[6]Imwinkelried, The New Wigmore: Evidentiary Privileges App. D (2d ed. 2010).

[7]*See, e.g.,* U.S. v. Moore, 970 F.2d 48 (5th Cir. 1992); Hancock v. Dodson, 958 F.2d 1367 (6th Cir. 1992); U.S. v. Bercier, 848 F.2d 917 (8th Cir. 1988).

[8]Report No. 45, Group for the Advancement of Psychiatry 92 (1960). *See also* Taylor v. U.S., 222 F.2d 398, 401 (D.C. Cir. 1955); Slovenko, Psychiatry and a Second Look at the Medical Privilege, 6 Wayne L. Rev. 175 (1960); Slovenko, Psychotherapy and Confidentiality, 24 Clev. St. L. Rev. 375 (1975); Note, 47 NW. L. Rev. 384 (1952). The recognition of a psychotherapist-patient privilege, while failing to recognize a general physician-patient privilege, has not been without its critics. *See, e.g.,* Wright and Miller's Federal Practice and Procedure, Evidence § 5522.

[9]Deleted Fed. R. Evid. 504.

or mental health provider.[10] In the same vein, all of the states

---

[10]Unif. R. Evid. 503 reads:

Rule 503. [Psychotherapist] [Physician and Psychotherapist] [Physician and Mental-Health Provider] [Mental-Health Provider]-Patient Privilege.

(a) Definitions. In this rule:

(1) A communication is "confidential" if it is not intended to be disclosed to third persons, except those present to further the interest of the patient in the consultation, examination, or interview, those reasonably necessary for the transmission of the communication, and persons who are participating in the diagnosis and treatment of the patient under the direction of a [psychotherapist] [physician or psychotherapist] [physician or mental-health provider] [mental-health provider], including members of the patient's family.

[(2) "Mental-health provider" means a person authorized, in any State or country, or reasonably believed by the patient to be authorized, to engage in the diagnosis or treatment of a mental or emotional condition, including addiction to alcohol or drugs.]

[(3) "Patient" means an individual who consults or is examined or interviewed by a[psychotherapist] [physician or psychotherapist] [physician or mental-health provider] [mental-health provider].]

[(4) "Physician" means a person authorized in any State or country, or reasonably believed by the patient to be authorized to practice medicine.]

[(5) "Psychotherapist" means a person authorized in any State or country, or reasonably believed by the patient to be authorized, to practice medicine, while engaged in the diagnosis or treatment of a mental or emotional condition, including addiction to alcohol or drugs, or a person licensed or certified under the laws of any State or country, or reasonably believed by the patient to be licensed or certified, as a psychologist, while similarly engaged.]

(b) General rule of privilege. A patient has a privilege to refuse to disclose and to prevent any other person from disclosing confidential communications made for the purpose of diagnosis or treatment of the patient's [physical,] mental[,] or emotional condition, including addiction to alcohol or drugs, among the patient, the patient's [psychotherapist] [physician or psychotherapist] [physician or mental-health provider] [mental-health provider] and persons, including members of the patient's family, who are participating in the diagnosis or treatment under the direction of the [psychotherapist] [physician or psychotherapist] [physician or mental-health provider] [mental-health provider].

(c) Who may claim the privilege. The privilege under this rule may be claimed by the patient, the patient's guardian or conservator, or the personal representative of a deceased patient. The person who was the [psychotherapist] [physician or psychotherapist] [physician or mental-health provider] [mental-health provider] at the time of the communication is presumed to have authority to claim the privilege, but only on behalf of the patient.

(d) Exceptions. There is no privilege under this rule for a communication:

(1) relevant to an issue in proceedings to hospitalize the patient for mental illness, if the [psychotherapist] [physician or psychotherapist] [physician or mental-health provider] [mental-health provider], in the course of diagnosis or treatment, has determined that the patient is in need of hospitalization;

(2) made in the course of a court-ordered investigation or examination of the [physical,] mental[,] or emotional condition of the patient, whether a party or a witness, with respect to the particular purpose for which the examination is ordered, unless the court orders otherwise;

(3) relevant to an issue of the [physical,] mental[,] or emotional

that continue to reject a general physician-patient privilege have enacted privileges applicable to the more limited psychotherapeutic context.[11] Most expand the privilege to cover communications to social workers.[12]

The action of the states was bolstered by the recognition of a psychotherapist-patient privilege by the United States Supreme Court in *Jaffee v. Redmond*.[13] Relying on a utilitarian rationale, the Court emphasized that "the mere possibility of disclosure may impede development of the confidential relationship necessary for successful treatment."[14] The Court also noted the appropriateness of the recognition of the privilege in the federal courts in light of the universal recognition of such a privilege in the states. The holding extended the privilege not only to psychiatrists and psychologists but, over the dissent of two justices,[15] to licensed social workers as well. The Court also held that the privilege it recognized was absolute, rejecting the balanc-

---

condition of the patient in any proceeding in which the patient relies upon the condition as an element of the patient's claim or defense or, after the patient's death, in any proceeding in which any party relies upon the condition as an element of the party's claim or defense;

(4) if the services of the [psychotherapist] [physician or psychotherapist] [physician or mental-health provider] [mental-health provider] were sought or obtained to enable or aid anyone to commit or plan to commit what the patient knew, or reasonably should have known, was a crime or fraud or mental or physical injury to the patient or another individual;

(5) in which the patient has expressed an intent to engage in conduct likely to result in imminent death or serious bodily injury to the patient or another individual;

(6) relevant to an issue in a proceeding challenging the competency of the [psychotherapist] [physician or psychotherapist] [physician or mental-health provider] [mental-health provider];

(7) relevant to a breach of duty by the [psychotherapist] [physician or psychotherapist] [physician or mental-health provider] [mental-health provider]; or

(8) that is subject to a duty to disclose under [statutory law].

[11]Alabama, Maryland, Massachusetts, South Carolina, Tennessee and West Virginia protect such communications while having no general physician-patient privilege. Imwinkelried, The New Wigmore: Evidentiary Privilege, App. D (2d ed. 2010).

[12]*See* Jaffee v. Redmond, 518 U.S. 1, 16–17, 116 S. Ct. 1923, 135 L. Ed. 2d 337 (1996).

[13]Jaffee v. Redmond, 518 U.S. 1, 116 S. Ct. 1923, 135 L. Ed. 2d 337 (1996). Several federal courts had recognized the existence of such a privilege even before *Jaffee*. *See* In re Zuniga, 714 F.2d 632 (6th Cir. 1983) (collecting federal cases and recognizing privilege, but holding it generally inapplicable to protect the identity of the patient or the fact or time of his treatment). *But compare* U.S. v. Corona, 849 F.2d 562 (11th Cir. 1988).

[14]Jaffee v. Redmond, 518 U.S. at 10.

[15]Jaffee at 18 (dissenting opinion by Justice Scalia, joined on this point by Chief Justice Rehnquist).

ing test applied by the Court of Appeals in the *Jaffee* case[16] and by some states.[17]

The Court, confined to the facts before it, could not detail all of the contours of the privilege it announced. It explicitly left open the application of the privilege if a serious threat of harm to the patient or to others can be averted only by means of a disclosure by the therapist.[18] The lower federal courts have just begun to flesh out the dimensions of the privilege.[19] The remaining sections of this chapter will discuss the general physician-patient privilege, but note specifically cases dealing specially with the psychotherapist-patient privilege.

One theory absent from the Court's analysis in *Jaffee* was any suggestion that the recognition of the privilege was constitutionally required.[20] However, there have been arguments made that certain aspects of the physician-patient relationship involve some sort of a federal constitutional guarantee of a right of privacy. In

---

[16]Jaffee v. Redmond, 51 F.3d 1346 (7th Cir. 1995).

[17]*E.g.,* N.C. Gen. Stat. § 8-53.7. See also discussion § 105, infra.

[18]Jaffee v. Redmond, 518 U.S.at 18, n. 19. The issue is still not fully resolved in the federal courts. *Compare* U.S. v. Auster, 517 F.3d 312 (5th Cir. 2008) (communications not privileged where patient knew that psychotherapist would communicate his threats to the victims) and U.S. v. Glass, 133 F.3d 1356 (10th Cir. 1998) (recognized exception that would apply to a threat that was serious when uttered and where disclosure was the only means of averting harm) *with* U.S. v. Hayes, 227 F.3d 578 (6th Cir. 2000) (privilege still exists when raised at a court hearing after the threat had passed); U.S. v. Chase, 340 F.3d 978 (9th Cir. 2003) (en banc) (same). *See also* Sellers, United States v. Landor: The Federal Circuit Split Over the Dangerous Patient Exception to the Psychotherapist-Patient Privilege, 34 Am. J. Trial Advoc. 417 (2010).

[19]*See, e.g.,* Oleszko v. State Compensation Ins. Fund, 243 F.3d 1154, 1157 (9th Cir. 2001) (psychotherapist-patient privilege extended to Employee Assistance Program counselors); In re Grand Jury

Proceedings (Gregory P. Violette), 183 F.3d 71 (1st Cir. 1999) (crime-fraud exception applied to psychotherapist-patient privilege); U.S. v. Schwensow, 151 F.3d 650 (7th Cir. 1998) (privilege did not apply where communications made to persons who were no physicians, psychotherapists, counselors or social workers); Barrett v. Vojtas, 182 F.R.D. 177 (W.D. Pa. 1998) (privilege did not apply where examination ordered by public officials). *See* Broun, The Medical Privilege in the Federal Courts-Should It Matter Whether Your Ego or Your Elbow Hurts?, 38 Loy. L.A. L. Rev. 657 (2004). *See also* Amann & Imwinkelried, The Supreme Court's Decision to Recognize a Psychotherapist Privilege in Jaffee v. Redmond, 116 S.Ct. 1923 (1996): Nelken, The Limits of Privilege: The Developing Scope of Federal Psychotherapist-Patient Privilege Law, 20 Rev. Litig. 1 (2000); The Meaning of "Experience" and the Role of "Reason" Under Federal Rule of Evidence 501, 65 U. Cin. L. Rev. 1019 (1997); Note, 46 Cath. U. L. Rev. 963 (1997); Note, 47 DePaul L. Rev. 701 (1998); Note, 110 Harv. L. Rev. 287 (1996).

[20]See discussion of *Jaffee* in U.S. v. Glass, 133 F.3d 1356, 1358 (10th Cir. 1998).

*Whalen v. Roe*,[21] the constitutionality of a New York statute creating a state data bank of the names and addresses of persons obtaining certain drugs by medical prescription was challenged, inter alia, on the ground that patients would be deterred from obtaining appropriate medication by the apprehension that disclosure of their names would stigmatize them as drug addicts. Though garbed in constitutional vestments as an impairment of the right to make personal decisions, this argument bears a striking resemblance to the traditional rationale of privilege. While upholding the statute in *Whalen*, the Supreme Court did so on the basis of reasoning which seemed to suggest the existence of some constitutional right on the part of patients to preserve confidentiality with respect to medical treatment.

Subsequent decisions of lower federal and state courts evidence considerable disagreement concerning the nature and scope, and even the existence, of the constitutionally based right intimated to exist in *Whalen*.[22] A majority of the cases considering the point have involved information conveyed during psychotherapeutic treatment, a context in which the traditional utilitarian justification has been urged to possess particular validity.[23] Nevertheless, even cases of the latter sort have generally been resolved on the particular facts against the claimant of privilege,[24] and it would appear clear that any constitutional right to privacy in medical

---

[21]Whalen v. Roe, 429 U.S. 589, 97 S. Ct. 869, 51 L. Ed. 2d 64 (1977).

[22]*See* Borucki v. Ryan, 827 F.2d 836 (1st Cir. 1987) (§ 1983 action based on disclosure of plaintiff's psychiatric examination to determine competence to stand trial; held: defendant's actions did not violate a clearly established constitutional right of privacy). *See also* Hansen v. Lamontagne, 808 F. Supp. 89 (D.N.H. 1992) (§ 1983 action; police officer had no clearly established constitutional privacy right to nondisclosure of confidential information from his personnel file); King v. State, 272 Ga. 788, 535 S.E.2d 492, 494–95 (2000) (even in absence of physician-patient privilege, federal and state constitutional right of privacy protected defendant's medical records).

[23]*See* Smith, Constitutional Privacy in Psychotherapy, 49 Geo. Wash. L. Rev. 1 (1980). But compare Developments in the Law—Privileged Communications, 98 Harv. L. Rev.

1450, 1548 (1985) (criticizing the special status urged for psychotherapy on ground that it tends to promote a fragmented model of health care).

[24]Seaton v. Mayberg, 610 F.3d 530 (9th Cir. 2010), cert. denied, 131 S. Ct. 1534, 179 L. Ed. 2d 309 (2011) (medical evaluation of prisoner facing civil commitment not protected); Borucki v. Ryan, 827 F.2d 836 (1st Cir. 1987); Caesar v. Mountanos, 542 F.2d 1064 (9th Cir. 1976) (recognizing constitutional protection for qualified psychotherapist-patient confidentiality, but upholding contempt citation of psychiatrist); U. S. ex rel. Edney v. Smith, 425 F. Supp. 1038 (E.D. N.Y. 1976) (discussing and implicitly accepting constitutional status of psychotherapist-patient privilege but finding no violation on facts); In re Lifschutz, 2 Cal. 3d 415, 85 Cal. Rptr. 829, 467 P.2d 557 (1970) (confidentiality of psychotherapeutic session falls within constitutionally protected "zone of privacy," but protection not absolute; contempt citation of psychiatrist

information is a highly qualified one. In any event, the courts have consistently failed to refer to any protection afforded as a "privilege."[25]

The matter of the protection of patient privacy and its relationship to a physician-patient privilege has been further muddled by the adoption of the Health Insurance Portability and Accountability Act of 1996 (HIPAA) and its implementing regulations.[26] The HIPAA regulatory scheme recognizes a patient's privacy interests but contemplates the disclosure of protected health information in the course of a judicial or administrative proceeding[27] or for law enforcement purposes.[28] Although the issue has been raised, courts asked to consider the question have not been hesitant to find that HIPAA does not codify a general federal physician-patient privilege; nor have they found a limitation on the disclosure of the information in court or grand jury proceedings as provided in the act and regulations.[29]

## § 99   Relation of physician and patient

The first requisite for the privilege is that the patient must have consulted the physician[1] for treatment or for diagnosis look-

---

affirmed). *Contra* J. P. v. DeSanti, 653 F.2d 1080 (6th Cir. 1981) (declining to read "isolated" comments in Whalen as creating constitutionally based right); State ex rel. D.M. v. Hoester, 681 S.W.2d 449 (Mo. 1984) (child abuse exception to statutory privilege within legislative power to enact as privilege has no constitutional basis). *But see* In re T.R., 557 Pa. 99, 731 A.2d 1276, 1281–82 (1999) (parent had a privacy right under Pennsylvania constitution to prevent her psychological evaluation and disclosure of results in juvenile dependency matter).

[25]*See, e.g.,* U.S. v. Burzynski Cancer Research Institute, 819 F.2d 1301, 1304, 1310 (5th Cir. 1987) (applying privacy considerations but not privilege to the information sought in an action against a doctor for shipment of non-FDA approved anti-cancer drug).

[26]Pub. L. No. 104-191, 110 Stat. 1936 (1996). For an example of pertinent regulations under HIPAA, see 45 C.F.R. § 164.512.

[27]45 C.F.R. § 164.512(e).

[28]45 C.F.R. § 164.512(f).

[29]*See* U.S. ex rel. Stewart v. Louisiana Clinic, 2002 WL 31819130, *2–*6 (E.D. La. 2002) (noting the absence of a federal physician-patient privilege while interpreting HIPAA regulations); In re Grand Jury Subpoena John Doe No. A01-209, 197 F. Supp. 2d 512, 514–15 (E.D. Va. 2002) (finding no federal physician-patient privilege and that HIPAA regulations do not protect patient's privacy interests in the face of a legitimate law enforcement inquiry). *See also* Broun, The Medical Privilege in the Federal Courts-Should It Matter Whether Your Ego or Your Elbow Hurts?, 38 Loy. L.A. L. Rev. 657, 694–99 (2004).

**[Section 99]**

[1]The statutes usually specify "physician" or "physician and surgeon," and sometimes require that they be "licensed" or "authorized." Accordingly, the decisions usually deny the privilege for communications to other practitioners, such as dentists, Buchanan v. Mayfield, 925 S.W.2d 135 (Tex. App. Waco 1996); optometrists,

ing toward treatment.[2] If consulted for treatment it is immaterial by whom the doctor is employed.[3] Usually, however, when the

---

People v. Baker, 94 Mich. App. 365, 288 N.W.2d 430 (1979); druggists, Green v. Superior Court, In and For San Joaquin County, 220 Cal. App. 2d 121, 33 Cal. Rptr. 604 (3d Dist. 1963); paramedics, Rogers v. State, 255 P.3d 1264, 127 Nev. Adv. Op. No. 25 (Nev. 2011); physician assistant, U.S. v. Ghane, 673 F.3d 771 (8th Cir. 2012), cert. denied, 133 S. Ct. 477, 184 L. Ed. 2d 299 (2012); social workers, Fitzgerald v. A. L. Burbank & Co., 451 F.2d 670 (2d Cir. 1971); chiropractors, In re Polen, 108 Ohio App. 3d 305, 670 N.E.2d 572 (10th Dist. Franklin County 1996). *Contra,* Collins v. Bair, 256 Ind. 230, 268 N.E.2d 95 (1971) (chiropractor). *See also* Classes of persons within term "physician" in rule as to privileged communications, 68 A.L.R. 176. An intern may be a "physician" though not yet licensed to practice. Franklin Life Ins. Co. v. William J. Champion & Co., 353 F.2d 919 (6th Cir. 1965).

Where a distinct privilege is granted to a related profession, the same principle is usually applied. State v. Gotfrey, 598 P.2d 1325 (Utah 1979) (psychologist-patient privilege unavailable because psychologist not licensed as required by statute).

As to nurses, assistants, and technicians, see § 101 infra. For privileged aspects of hospital records, see § 293 infra.

A patient's reasonable belief that he was consulting a licensed medical practitioner is sufficient to create privilege under some statutes. Cal. Evid. Code § 1010. *See* Comment, Underprivileged Communications: Extension of the Psychotherapist–Patient Privilege to Patients of Psychiatric Social Workers, 61 Calif. L. Rev. 1050 (1973).

[2]Doe v. Sex Offender Registry Bd., 459 Mass. 603, 947 N.E.2d 9 (2011) (statement to psychologist not privileged where patient refused to participate in treatment); U.S. v. Romo, 413 F.3d 1044 (9th Cir. 2005) (counselor

not consulted for diagnosis or treatment); City & County of San Francisco v. Superior Court In and For City and County of San Francisco, 37 Cal. 2d 227, 231 P.2d 26 (1951); Osborn v. Fabatz, 105 Mich. App. 450, 306 N.W.2d 319 (1981); West's Key Number Digest, Privileged Communications and Confidentiality ⟐227. The consultation contemplated remedial measures if possible in Bassil v. Ford Motor Co., 278 Mich. 173, 270 N.W. 258 (1936) (husband and wife consult doctor to ascertain why child not born of their union). *Compare* Vaughan v. Martin, 145 Ind. App. 455, 251 N.E.2d 444 (1969) (Christian Scientist examined by physician to obtain certificate to enter nursing home; privilege held created under local statute). If treatment was the object of the communication, the fact that treatment did not occur will not destroy privilege. However, information gained by the physician before subject became a patient is not privileged. Ranger, Inc. v. Equitable Life Assur. Soc. of U.S., 196 F.2d 968 (6th Cir. 1952).

The Court in Jaffee v. Redmond, 518 U.S. 1, 15, 116 S. Ct. 1923, 135 L. Ed. 2d 337 (1996) confined the psychotherapist-patient privilege to statements made "in the course of diagnosis or treatment." Deleted Federal Rule of Evidence 504 limited the privilege to communications made "for the purposes of diagnosis or treatment." *See also* Unif. R. Evid. 503. In In re Grand Jury Proceedings (Gregory P. Violette), 183 F.3d 71, 77 n.4 (1st Cir. 1999), the court noted the significance of the "more expansive formulation" of the rule in *Jaffee* as a justification for the imposition of a crime-fraud exception. *See* Note, Role of Jaffee v. Redmond's "Course of Diagnosis or Treatment" Condition in Preventing Abuse of the Psychotherapist-Patient Privilege, 35 Ga. L. Rev. 345 (2000).

[3]Russell v. Penn Mut. Life Ins. Co., 70 Ohio App. 113, 24 Ohio Op. 440, 41 N.E.2d 251 (1st Dist. Hamilton

doctor is employed by one other than the patient, treatment will not be the purpose and the privilege will not attach. Thus, when a driver at the request of a public officer is subjected to a blood test for intoxication,[4] or when a doctor is appointed by the court[5] or the prosecutor[6] to make a physical or mental[7] examination, or

County 1941) (doctors who attended insured, apparently employed by life insurance company). *See also* State v. More, 382 N.W.2d 718 (Iowa Ct. App. 1985) (suspect taken to emergency by police following complaint of chest pain; privilege applied). And when a patient goes, or is taken unconscious, to a hospital for care or treatment, the hospital doctors who are charged with the duties of examination, diagnosis, care or treatment are within the purview of the privilege statute. State v. Staat, 291 Minn. 394, 192 N.W.2d 192 (1971); Branch v. Wilkinson, 198 Neb. 649, 256 N.W.2d 307 (1977). Competency of hospital physician or attendant to testify as to condition of patient, 22 A.L.R. 1217. Where the defendant, after being involved in a fatal automobile accident was taken to the county hospital by police after his arrest for examination, statements given by him to hospital physician as to his medical history of epilepsy were, under the circumstances, communications for the purpose of treatment and were privileged. People v. Decina, 2 N.Y.2d 133, 157 N.Y.S.2d 558, 138 N.E.2d 799 (1956); Note, 43 Cornell L. Q. 295 (1958). So also if the doctor, though employed by the defendant, examines the plaintiff in the hospital under circumstances causing the patient to believe that the examination is part of the hospital's care. Ballard v. Yellow Cab Co., 20 Wash. 2d 67, 145 P.2d 1019 (1944).

[4]The decisions are somewhat conflicting, but may generally be reconciled on the ground that tests run for medical reasons are privileged while those without medical purpose at request of police are not. *See* State v. Santeyan, 136 Ariz. 108, 664 P.2d 652 (1983) (urinalysis performed for diagnosis and not at request of law enforcement officer privileged); State v. McElroy, 553 So. 2d 456 (La. 1989) (blood test ordered by physician for diagnosis within privilege). State in Interest of M.P.C., 165 N.J. Super. 131, 397 A.2d 1092 (App. Div. 1979) (results of tests requested by police not within privilege). If the test is made pursuant to an implied consent statute the privilege generally will not attach. State v. Erickson, 241 N.W.2d 854 (N.D. 1976). *See also,* De Witt, Privileged Communications Between Physician and Patient 114 (1958).

[5]State v. Cole, 295 N.W.2d 29 (Iowa 1980) (where court order for examination clearly specified limited purpose, physician precluded from establishing confidential relationship); State v. Prince, 688 So. 2d 643 (La. Ct. App. 2d Cir. 1997), modified on other grounds, 701 So.2d 965 (La. 1997).

[6]State v. Steelman, 120 Ariz. 301, 585 P.2d 1213 (1978) (defendant's claim that he expected examining physicians to help him with drug withdrawal symptoms held question of fact within discretion of trial court; denial of privilege upheld); People v. Henderson, 19 Cal. 3d 86, 137 Cal. Rptr. 1, 560 P.2d 1180 (1977) (psychiatrist interviewing on instruction of prosecutor clearly indicated status; no privilege). *But see* State v. Toste, 178 Conn. 626, 424 A.2d 293 (1979) (privilege available where psychiatrist examined at request of state but not pursuant to court order as required by local statute).

[7]When the purpose of the examination is solely to ascertain the person's mental condition, the physician-patient relationship is not created, and there is no privilege on that score for the person's disclosures. Williamson v. State, 330 So. 2d 272 (Miss. 1976); State

is employed for this purpose by the opposing party,[8] or is selected by a life insurance company to make an examination of an applicant for a policy[9] or even when the doctor is employed by plaintiff's own lawyers in a personal injury case to examine plaintiff solely to aid in preparation for trial,[10] the information secured is not within the present privilege. But when the patient's doctor calls in a consultant physician to aid in diagnosis or treatment, the disclosures are privileged.[11] Moreover, cases decided under the federal psychotherapist privilege have held that

---

v. Fouquette, 67 Nev. 505, 221 P.2d 404 (1950); State v. Fears, 86 Ohio St. 3d 329, 1999-Ohio-111, 715 N.E.2d 136, 150 (1999) (privilege did not attach where licensed psychologist consulted in preparation for testimony at criminal trial); State v. Riggle, 76 Wyo. 1, 298 P.2d 349 (1956); Simecek v. State, 243 Wis. 439, 10 N.W.2d 161 (1943); West's Key Number Digest, Privileged Communications and Confidentiality ⟷227. *See also* Com. v. Lamb, 365 Mass. 265, 311 N.E.2d 47 (1974) (statute creating exception for examinations of this type required patient to be informed; privilege applied where patient not informed). But where the purpose of the committal to the hospital includes treatment as well as diagnosis, the disclosures will be protected. Taylor v. U.S., 222 F.2d 398, 401, 402 (D.C. Cir. 1955); State v. O'Neill, 274 Or. 59, 545 P.2d 97 (1976) (privilege available to patient involuntarily committed under dangerous person statute). Notes, 54 Mich. L. Rev. 423, 40 Minn. L. Rev. 621, 1955 Wash. U. L. Q. 405, Selected Writings on Evidence and Trial 258 (Fryer ed. 1957). And where the appointed panel includes the defendant's own psychiatrist who shared with the others his information gained in previous treatment, their testimony as to their findings is privileged. People v. Wasker, 353 Mich. 447, 91 N.W.2d 866 (1958).

[8]VanSickle v. McHugh, 171 Mich. App. 622, 430 N.W.2d 799 (1988) (examination at request of plaintiff's no-fault insurance carrier; context known to be potentially adversary and examination not for betterment of health); Briglia v. Exxon Co., USA, 310 N.J. Super. 498, 708 A.2d 1246 (Law Div. 1997) (no privilege where independent medical examination ordered). But when the patient supposes that the doctor is a hospital specialist acting on his behalf, the privilege has been held to apply. Arizona & N. M. Ry. Co. v. Clark, 207 F. 817 (C.C.A. 9th Cir. 1913).

[9]McGinty v. Brotherhood of Railway Trainmen, 166 Wis. 83, 164 N.W. 249 (1917); 70 C.J. 441, n. 94. And so of an examination by employer's physician of an applicant for employment. Moutzoukos v. Mutual Ben. Health & Accident Ass'n, 69 Utah 309, 254 P. 1005 (1927). Similarly examination of a juvenile directed by subject's probation officer was held not privileged in Rusecki v. State, 56 Wis. 2d 299, 201 N.W.2d 832 (1972).

[10]City & County of San Francisco v. Superior Court In and For City and County of San Francisco, 37 Cal. 2d 227, 231 P.2d 26 (1951) (but held that the communications were privileged under the attorney-client privilege), 25 So. Cal. L. Rev. 237, 13 U. Pitt. L. Rev. 428; State v. Pratt, 284 Md. 516, 398 A.2d 421 (1979) (semble); Lindsay v. Lipson, 367 Mich. 1, 116 N.W.2d 60 (1962). *See also* State v. Rhomberg, 516 N.W.2d 803 (Iowa 1994) (overruled by, State v. Heemstra, 721 N.W.2d 549 (Iowa 2006)) (no privilege where psychiatrist retained by party for use at juvenile court hearing).

[11]Leonczak v. Minneapolis, St. P. & S.S.M. Ry. Co., 161 Minn. 304, 201 N.W. 551 (1924); 98 C.J.S., Witnesses § 350.

therapy session mandated by a patient's employer will be privileged.[12]

If the patient's purpose in the consultation is an unlawful one, as to obtain narcotics in violation of law,[13] or as, by some authority, a fugitive from justice to have his appearance disguised by plastic surgery,[14] the law withholds the shield of privilege.

It has been held that where a doctor has attended a childbirth, the child is a patient and can claim privilege against the doctor's disclosure of facts as to the apparent maturity of the child at birth.[15]

After the death of the patient the relation is ended and the object of the privilege can no longer be furthered. Accordingly, it seems the better view that facts discovered in an autopsy examination are not privileged.[16]

---

[12]*See* Speaker ex rel. Speaker v. County of San Bernardino, 82 F. Supp. 2d 1105, 1116–17 (C.D. Cal. 2000) holding that the fact that the session is mandatory does not destroy the privilege where the patient is told by his employer that the session would be confidential); Caver v. City of Trenton, 192 F.R.D. 154, 162 (D.N.J. 2000) (holding that the privilege applied where no confidential information was disclosed by psychologist to employer).

[13]The rule is codified in Uniform Narcotic Drug Act (1932, as amended 1958), § 17, par. 2, which provides that information given to a doctor "in an effort unlawfully to procure a narcotic drug, or unlawfully to procure the administration of any such drug" shall not be privileged. The Act has largely been replaced by the Uniform Controlled Substances Act (1970), which is silent on the subject. Such a provision scarcely seems necessary as no treatment is involved. *See* State v. Garrett, 8 Ohio App. 3d 244, 456 N.E.2d 1319 (10th Dist. Franklin County 1983) (false statement to physician made for purpose of obtaining drugs "not within the relation" of physician-patient and therefore not privileged).

[14]*See* Model Code of Evidence Rule 222: "No person has a privilege under Rule 221 if the judge finds that

sufficient evidence, aside from the communication, has been introduced to warrant a finding that the services of the physician were sought or obtained to enable or aid anyone to commit or to plan to commit a crime or a tort, or to escape detection or apprehension after the commission of a crime or a tort." *But see* Mutual of Omaha Ins. Co. v. American Nat. Bank and Trust Co., 610 F. Supp. 546 (D. Minn. 1985) (general rule stated in text does not necessarily extend to disclosure to a psychotherapist of an intent to commit a future crime).

[15]Jones v. Jones, 208 Misc. 721, 144 N.Y.S.2d 820 (Sup 1955); Note, 28 Rocky Mt. L. Rev. 425 (1956); Note, 7 Syracuse L. Rev. 347 (1956).

[16]Estate of Green v. St. Clair County Road Com'n, 175 Mich. App. 478, 438 N.W.2d 630 (1989) (privilege inapplicable to results of blood test during autopsy; no physician-patient relationship arise when patient is not alive); Zueger v. Public Hosp. Dist. No. 2 of Snohomish County, 57 Wash. App. 584, 789 P.2d 326 (Div. 1 1990) (semble). Decisions pro and con are cited in 8 Wigmore, Evidence § 2382 n. 11 (McNaughton rev. 1961). The point should not be confused with the distinct question of the preservation of inter vivos confidences after the patient's death. See § 102, infra.

## § 100 Subject matter of the privilege: Information acquired in attending the patient and necessary for prescribing

Statutes conferring a physician-patient privilege vary extensively, though probably a majority follow the pioneer New York and California statutes in extending the privilege to "any information acquired in attending the patient."[1] Understandably, these provisions have been held to protect not only information explicitly conveyed to the physician by the patient, but also data acquired by examination and testing.[2] Other statutes appear facially to be more restrictive and to limit the privilege to communications by the patient.[3] This appearance, however, may frequently be misleading, for statutes of this sort have been construed to provide a privilege fully as broad as that available elsewhere.[4] The confusion is further compounded by a line of

---

**[Section 100]**

[1]See § 98 supra. Statutes are collected in 8 Wigmore, Evidence 2380 (McNaughton rev. 1961).

[2]State v. Pitchford, 10 Kan. App. 2d 293, 697 P.2d 896 (1985) (statute protecting "information" held to apply to blood test administered to handcuffed patient violently resisting treatment); Sarphie v. Rowe, 618 So. 2d 905 (La. Ct. App. 1st Cir. 1993) ("when an individual walks into a doctor's office and opens his mouth . . . everything spilling out of it, whether it be his identity or his false teeth . . . is presumptively privileged").

[3]See, e.g., Ohio Rev.Code § 2317.02. In Jaffee v. Redmond, 518 U.S. 1, 10, 116 S. Ct. 1923, 135 L. Ed. 2d 337 (1996), discussed supra § 98, the Count referred to the need to protect "confidential communications," relying on the need for an "atmosphere of confidence and trust in which the patient is willing to make a frank and complete disclosure of facts, emotions, memories and fears." Arguably, the Court was signaling a limited scope to the application of the subject matter of the privilege. See also Boudreau ex rel. Boudreau v. Ryan, 2001 WL 1001156 (N.D. Ill.2001) (psychotherapist-patient privilege did not apply where there was no showing that the records contained confidential communications).

[4]See, e.g., In re D.H. ex rel. Powell, 319 Ill. App. 3d 771, 253 Ill. Dec. 826, 746 N.E.2d 274, 281 (1st Dist. 2001) (privilege protects facts as well as communications); Burns v. City of Waterloo, 187 Iowa 922, 173 N.W. 16 (1919), on rehearing Burns v. City of Waterloo, 174 N.W. 644 (Iowa 1919) (observations of intoxication included within privilege); State v. Schroeder, 524 N.W.2d 837 (N.D. 1994) ("communications" includes information and observations made for purposes of diagnosis and treatment); McKee v. New Idea, 44 N.E.2d 697 (Ohio Ct. App. 3d Dist. Mercer County 1942) (submission to examination is "communication"). But some courts have drawn a distinction. Com. ex rel. Platt v. Platt, 266 Pa. Super. 276, 404 A.2d 410 (1979) (privilege not applicable to observations as opposed to communications). And see Oxford v. Hamilton, 297 Ark. 512, 763 S.W.2d 83 (1989) (holding adoption of Unif. R. Evid. 503, privileging only communications in place of former "information" statute, rendered results of blood test admissible).

Cases involving discovery by medical personnel of physical objects on patient's person have failed to develop a satisfactory rationale. State v. Staat, 291 Minn. 394, 192 N.W.2d

authority that holds that facts observable by anyone without professional knowledge or training are not within the privilege.[5]

While the information secured by the physician may be privileged, the fact that the physician has been consulted by the patient and has treated him or her,[6] and the number and dates of visits,[7] are not within the shelter of the privilege.

---

192 (1971) (bottles of narcotics discovered by hospital orderly; privilege held not available on ground orderly not shown conclusively to be acting as physician's agent); State v. McCoy, 70 Wash. 2d 964, 425 P.2d 874 (1967) (bag of marijuana found in patient's sock by nurses in emergency room; privilege not available because discovery occurred before arrival of physician); People v. Fonseca, 134 Misc. 2d 1078, 514 N.Y.S.2d 189 (Sup 1987) (70 packets of cocaine removed from patient's body during surgery held a "communication," but outside the privilege on grounds of public policy). See § 101 infra.

[5]See, e.g., People v. Hedges, 98 A.D.2d 950, 470 N.Y.S.2d 61 (4th Dep't 1983). But see People v. Covington, 19 P.3d 15, 21 (Colo. 2001) (matter privileged where information in photographs taken by physician's assistant at request of sheriff's officer was not "readily discernible" to officer).

[6]Carondelet Health Network v. Miller, 221 Ariz. 614, 212 P.3d 952 (Ct. App. Div. 2 2009) (name of decedent's hospital roommate not privileged); Cranford v. Cranford, 120 Ga. App. 470, 170 S.E.2d 844 (1969) (records incidentally revealing patient's names sought to determine husband's income in divorce action). See also De Witt, Privileged Communications Between Physician and Patient § 47 (1958); Privileged Communications-Physician and Patient-Patients' Names and Addresses Are Not Privileged in Income Tax Investigation, 67 Harv. L. Rev. 1272 (1954). But see Falco v. Institute of Living, 254 Conn. 321, 757 A.2d 571, 576 (2000) (identity of patient attacking plaintiff privileged under psychiatrist-patient privilege statute); Dorris v. Detroit Osteopathic Hosp.

Corp., 460 Mich. 26, 594 N.W.2d 455, 459 (1999) (identity of patient within physician-patient privilege statute).

Some state courts have distinguished between the general physician-patient relationship and that of psychotherapist-patient. Revelation of the patient's identity in the latter context necessarily exposes something concerning the nature of the condition and treatment, and some statutes have therefore undertaken to privilege the patient's identity in this context. See Ex parte Abell, 613 S.W.2d 255 (Tex. 1981) (statute precluded discovery of names of other patients of psychiatrist in suit by two patients alleging psychiatrist induced them to engage in sexual relations with him). And see Rudnick v. Superior Court, 11 Cal. 3d 924, 114 Cal. Rptr. 603, 523 P.2d 643 (1974) (patient's identity privileged only if context will reveal nature of illness); Hetter v. Eighth Judicial Dist. Court of State In and For County of Clark, 110 Nev. 513, 874 P.2d 762 (1994) (privacy action against plastic surgeon; names of patients may be protected where nature of the problem or treatment is disclosed by disclosure of name).

Federal cases decided with regard to the psychotherapist-patient privilege have held that the identity of the patient or the date of his or her treatment is not within the privilege. See Santelli v. Electro-Motive, 188 F.R.D. 306 (N.D. Ill. 1999); Vanderbilt v. Town of Chilmark, 174 F.R.D. 225 (D. Mass. 1997); Hucko v. City of Oak Forest, 185 F.R.D. 526 (N.D. Ill. 1999); Booker v. City of Boston, 1999 WL 734644 (D. Mass. 1999). See also In re Zuniga, 714 F.2d 632 (6th Cir. 1983) (privilege "as a general rule" does not cover patient's identity, or the fact or time of treatment; pre-Jaffee).

The extent to which the privilege attaches to the information embodied in hospital records is discussed in the chapter on Regularly Kept Records.[8]

### § 101    The confidential character of the disclosure: Presence of third persons and members of family; information revealed to nurses and attendants; public records

We have seen that the statutes existing in many states codifying the privileges for marital communications and those between attorney and client usually omitted the requirement that to be privileged such communications must have been made in confidence. Nevertheless, the courts have read this limitation into these statutes, assuming that the legislatures must have intended this common law requirement to continue.[1] The statutes giving the patient's privilege for information gained in professional consultations again omit the adjective "confidential."[2] Should it nonetheless be read in, not as a continuation of a common law requirement, but as an interpretative gloss, spelled out from policy and analogy? Certainly the policy arguments are strong. First is the policy of holding all privileges within reasonable bounds since they cut off access to sources of truth. Second, the argument that the purpose of encouraging those who would otherwise be reluctant, to disclose necessary facts to their doctors, will be adequately served by extending a privilege for only such disclosures as the patient wishes to keep secret.

This principle of confidentiality[3] is supported by those decisions that hold that if a casual third person is present with the acquiescence of the patient at the consultation, the disclosures made in his presence are not privileged,[4] and thus the stranger, the patient and the doctor may be required to divulge them in court.

---

[7]Padovani v. Liggett & Myers Tobacco Co., 23 F.R.D. 255 (E.D. N.Y. 1959) ("The mere facts that on certain occasions the plaintiff submitted himself for diagnosis and treatment, as well as the dates of same, the names and addresses of the physicians, whether or not diagnoses were reduced to writing, and related matters, are subject to disclosure so long as the subject communicated is not stated."); Polish Roman Catholic Union of America v. Palen, 302 Mich. 557, 5 N.W.2d 463 (1942); Jenkins v. Metropolitan Life Ins. Co., 171 Ohio St. 557, 15 Ohio Op. 2d 14, 173 N.E.2d 122 (1961); Matter of Judicial Inquiry

(Anonymous N), 8 A.D.2d 842, 190 N.Y.S.2d 633 (2d Dep't 1959).

[8]See § 293 infra.

[Section 101]

[1]See §§ 80, 91 supra.

[2]See § 98 supra.

[3]See 8 Wigmore, Evidence § 2381 (McNaughton rev. 1961); Imwinkelried, The New Wigmore: Evidentiary Privileges § 6.8 (2d ed. 2010). 98 C.J.S., Witnesses § 348; West's Key Number Digest, Privileged Communications and Confidentiality ⬥260.

[4]Horowitz v. Sacks, 89 Cal. App. 336, 265 P. 281 (1st Dist. 1928) (sev-

Whether this principle is to be applied when the stranger is a police officer who has escorted the patient to the hospital or doctor's office should, it would seem, turn on whether meaningful acquiescence on the patient's part is to be found on the facts.[5]

If, however, the third person is present as a needed and customary participant in the consultation, the circle of confidence may be reasonably extended to include him and the privilege will be maintained. Thus the presence of one sustaining a close family relationship to the patient should not curtail the privilege.[6] And the nurse present as the doctor's assistant during the consultation or examination, or the technician who makes tests or X-ray photographs under the doctor's direction, will be looked on as the doctor's agent in whose keeping the information will

---

eral family members present); State v. LaRoche, 122 N.H. 231, 442 A.2d 602 (1982) (statement made in presence of paramedic lingering in emergency room out of curiosity); State v. Harris, 51 Wash. App. 807, 755 P.2d 825 (Div. 1 1988) (statement to psychologist in lobby of building); Presence of third person as affecting privileged character of communications between patient and physician, 96 A.L.R. 1419; 98 C.J.S., Witnesses § 350. *See also* Crawford ex rel. Goodyear v. Care Concepts, Inc., 2001 WI 45, 243 Wis. 2d 119, 625 N.W.2d 876, 882–83 (2001) (information concerning assaults by nursing home resident against other residents was not confidential under physician-patient privilege statute).

[5]The decisions, however, are varied. Among those supporting the view expressed in the text are People v. Covington, 19 P.3d 15, 21 (Colo. 2001) (presence in emergency room of sheriff's officer who asked physician's assistant to take photographs of victim's wounds did not abrogate privilege); Secrest v. State, 679 A.2d 58 (Del. 1996) (privilege attached where defendant disoriented and did not know officer was present); People v. Decina, 2 N.Y.2d 133, 157 N.Y.S.2d 558, 138 N.E.2d 799 (1956) (leading case upholding privilege and stating question is whether under circumstances confidentiality was intended). *See also* State v. Deases, 518 N.W.2d 784 (Iowa 1994) (presence of prison guards did not destroy privilege). Others have appar-

ently found consent under dubious circumstances, People v. Marquez, 692 P.2d 1089 (Colo. 1984) (noting that defendant was conscious while police observed physician remove bullet, but basis for denying privilege unclear). And some courts seemingly consider officers like casual strangers. State v. Thomas, 78 Ariz. 52, 275 P.2d 408 (1954); State v. Lewis, 735 S.W.2d 183 (Mo. Ct. App. S.D. 1987) (statement made in presence of officer not privileged; alternate holding).

[6]Grosslight v. Superior Court, 72 Cal. App. 3d 502, 140 Cal. Rptr. 278 (2d Dist. 1977) (privilege covers confidential communications to psychiatric personnel by intimate family members); Bassil v. Ford Motor Co., 278 Mich. 173, 270 N.W. 258 (1936) (husband and wife consult doctor about their childlessness: but the principle of joint consultation could have been relied on); Denaro v. Prudential Ins. Co. of America, 154 A.D. 840, 139 N.Y.S. 758, 761 (2d Dep't 1913) ("when a physician enters a house for the purpose of attending a patient, he is called upon to make inquiries, not alone of the sick person, but of those who are about him and who are familiar with the facts, and communications necessary for the proper performance of the duties of a physician are not public, because made in the presence of his immediate family or those who are present because of the illness of the person").

remain privileged.[7] But the application of strict agency principles in this context would seem inconsistent with the realities of modern medical practice,[8] and the preferable view is that of the courts that have based their decisions upon whether the communication was functionally related to diagnosis and treatment.[9]

---

[7]Shultz v. State, 417 N.E.2d 1127 (Ind. Ct. App. 1981) (technician who drew blood for testing under direction of physician covered by privilege, though privilege waived); Ostrowski v. Mockridge, 242 Minn. 265, 65 N.W.2d 185 (1954) (nurse assisting doctor at examination; decisions cited and analyzed); Branch v. Wilkinson, 198 Neb. 649, 256 N.W.2d 307 (1977) (privilege extends to agents of physicians); In re Kathleen M., 126 N.H. 379, 493 A.2d 472 (1985) (presence of additional members of "treatment team" does not prevent privilege); Evidence: privilege of communications by or to nurse or attendant, 47 A.L.R.2d 742.

A few courts will deny the privilege even when the nurse is acting as the doctor's assistant. *See, e.g.,* State v. McKinnon, 38 Ohio App. 3d 28, 525 N.E.2d 821 (9th Dist. Summit County 1987) (testimony as to results of blood test ordered by physician but performed by technician did not violate privilege). On the topic generally see Evidence: privilege of communications by or to nurse or attendant, 47 A.L.R.2d 742.

The patient-privilege statute occasionally specifically includes information given to nurses and other specified health care workers. State v. Raymond, 139 Vt. 464, 431 A.2d 453 (1981). *See also* 8 Wigmore, Evidence 2380 n. 5 (McNaughton rev. 1961).

If the statement is not one looking toward diagnosis or treatment, or is made to one not concerned with the patient's medical care, the privilege generally will not attach. State v. Tornquist, 254 Iowa 1135, 120 N.W.2d 483 (1963) (statement overheard by nursing director not concerned with treatment) (alternative holding); State v. Anderson, 247 Minn. 469, 78 N.W.2d 320 (1956) (statement to nurse as to identity of driver of car); State v. Sweet, 142 Vt. 238, 453 A.2d 1131 (1982) (nurse acting in administrative capacity; distinguishing *State v. Raym*).

[8]Thus cases suggesting that the privilege does not attach until such time as a physician arrives, e.g., Ramon v. State, 387 So. 2d 745 (Miss. 1980) (nurse in emergency room not agent of physician); State v. Shirley, 731 S.W.2d 49 (Mo. Ct. App. S.D. 1987) (statements to nurse employed by hospital and not working under direction of physician not privileged; but dissenting opinion states preference for rule suggested in text); State v. McCoy, 70 Wash. 2d 964, 425 P.2d 874 (1967) (nurses undressing patient in emergency room not subject to physician's direction), or that the actions of medical personnel must be specifically directed by a physician, *e.g.,* Block v. People, 125 Colo. 36, 240 P.2d 512 (1951) (blood test taken by technician); Myers v. State, 251 Ga. 883, 310 S.E.2d 504 (1984) (nurse acting as agent for hospital and not physician in administering questionnaire); State v. Staat, 291 Minn. 394, 192 N.W.2d 192 (1971), would seem at odds with modern emergency room procedure. In virtually all of the cases applying this rationale, better alternative grounds of admissibility were available, generally that the statement or communication did not relate to diagnosis or treatment.

[9]Franklin Life Ins. Co. v. William J. Champion & Co., 350 F.2d 115 (6th Cir. 1965) (revelation of statement of medical history to intern on hospital admission held just as contrary to policy of statute as statement to physician); Blue Cross v. Superior Court, 61 Cal. App. 3d 798, 132 Cal. Rptr. 635 (3d Dist. 1976) (claims filed with health insurer to obtain payment for

Many courts on the other hand do not analyze the problems in terms of whether the communications or disclosures were confidential and professional, but rather in terms of what persons are intended to be silenced as witnesses. This seems to be sticking in the bark of the statute, rather than looking at its purpose. Thus these courts, if casual third persons were present at the consultation, will still close the mouth of the doctor but allow the visitor to speak.[10] And if nurses or other attendants or technicians gain information necessary to treatment they will be allowed by these courts to speak (unless the privilege statute specifically names them) but the physician may not.[11]

When the attending physician is required by law to make a certificate of death to the public authority, giving his opinion as to the cause, the certificate should be provable as a public record, despite the privilege. The duty to make a public report overrides the general duty of secrecy, and in view of the availability of the record to the public, the protection of the information from general knowledge, as contemplated by the privilege, cannot be attained. Accordingly, under the prevailing view, the privilege does not attach.[12]

Today, state and local laws increasingly impose upon physi-

---

medical services held "reasonably necessary" to obtain diagnosis and treatment); Darnell v. State, 674 N.E.2d 19 (Ind. Ct. App. 1996) (test is whether third party worked under close supervision of physician).

[10]Iwerks v. People, 108 Colo. 556, 120 P.2d 961 (1941) (deputy sheriff present at doctor's examination of injured prisoner may testify as to what examination disclosed and prisoner's statements to doctor); Springer v. Byram, 137 Ind. 15, 36 N.E. 361, 363 (1894) (ambulance drivers could testify to accident victim's statements to doctor); Indiana Union Traction Co. v. Thomas, 44 Ind. App. 468, 88 N.E. 356, 359 (1909) (patient privileged not to disclose communications with doctor, though in presence of daughter and friend); Leeds v. Prudential Ins. Co. of America, 128 Neb. 395, 258 N.W. 672 (1935) (bringing friend to consultation does not waive privilege); Presence of third person as affecting privileged character of communications between patient and physician, 96 A.L.R. 1419; 98 C.J.S., Witnesses § 350.

And, as in the case of the other privileges for confidential communications, the eavesdropper is permitted to testify to what he overhears. Ryan v. Industrial Com'n of Ohio, 72 N.E.2d 907 (Ohio Ct. App. 8th Dist. Cuyahoga County 1946) (dictum).

[11]First Trust Co. of St. Paul v. Kansas City Life Ins. Co., 79 F.2d 48, 52 (C.C.A. 8th Cir. 1935) (nurse and dietician could testify as to information gained in carrying out doctors' instructions for care of patient); Collins v. Howard, 156 F. Supp. 322 (S.D. Ga. 1957); Weis v. Weis, 147 Ohio St. 416, 34 Ohio Op. 350, 72 N.E.2d 245 (1947) (similar to last); Prudential Ins. Co. of America v. Kozlowski, 226 Wis. 641, 276 N.W. 300 (1937) (testimony of nurse and X-ray operator received); Note, 22 Marq. L. Rev. 211 (1938); Evidence: privilege of communications by or to nurse or attendant, 47 A.L.R.2d 742.

[12]Polish Roman Catholic Union of America v. Palen, 302 Mich. 557, 5 N.W.2d 463 (1942); Engel v. Starry, 268 Minn. 252, 128 N.W.2d 874 (1964); Randolph v. Supreme Liberty Life Ins.

cians requirements to report various types of patient information related to the public health and safety, e.g., the treatment of gunshot wounds, venereal disease, HIV and AIDS, mental illness, and the occurrence of fetal death.[13] Generally, state schemes for the collection and preservation of such data and its use by appropriate authorities have been upheld as against challenges based either upon a constitutional right of privacy or the professional privilege.[14] In some instances, e.g., the reporting of gunshot wounds, the privilege has been held to be qualified to the extent of the reporting requirement, with the result that the physician may testify to any fact included within the report.[15] Conversely, where the physician's report is not required the physician would remain precluded from testifying to the facts in the report, though there is some authority that the privilege, being testimonial, does not bar use of the report to generate other admissible evidence.[16] Many of the reporting systems, however, obviously do not envi-

---

Co., 359 Mo. 251, 221 S.W.2d 155 (1949); Perry v. Industrial Commission, 160 Ohio St. 520, 52 Ohio Op. 387, 117 N.E.2d 34 (1954); and cases cited 8 Wigmore, Evidence § 2385a (McNaughton rev. 1961). *Contra* Davis v. Supreme Lodge Knights of Honor, 165 N.Y. 159, 58 N.E. 891 (1900) (two judges dissenting). *Compare* the similar question about the records of public hospitals, discussed in 8 Wigmore, Evidence § 2382(3) (McNaughton rev. 1961).

[13]Compare the list of types of required reports noted by the United States Supreme Court in Whalen v. Roe, 429 U.S. 589, 602, 97 S. Ct. 869, 51 L. Ed. 2d 64 (1977). Physician-patient privilege as applied to physician's testimony concerning wound required to be reported to public authority, 85 A.L.R.3d 1196.

[14]Whalen v. Roe, 429 U.S. 589, 97 S. Ct. 869, 51 L. Ed. 2d 64 (1977) (upholding constitutionality of New York statute requiring recordation of names and addresses of all persons obtaining certain drugs by prescription); Planned Parenthood of Central Missouri v. Danforth, 428 U.S. 52, 96 S. Ct. 2831, 49 L. Ed. 2d 788 (1976) (semble; abortions); State v. Russo, 259 Conn. 436, 790 A.2d 1132, 1145–46 (2002) (state statute requiring that prescriptions be open for inspection by

drug enforcement personnel constitutional); Gabor v. Hyland, 166 N.J. Super. 275, 399 A.2d 993 (App. Div. 1979) (injunctive relief denied where sought to eliminate clause in Medicaid benefit form authorizing release of all medical information by providers of reimbursable services); Volkman v. Miller, 52 A.D.2d 146, 383 N.Y.S.2d 95 (3d Dep't 1976). *But see* Hawaii Psychiatric Soc., Dist. Branch of American Psychiatric Ass'n v. Ariyoshi, 481 F. Supp. 1028 (D. Haw. 1979).

[15]People v. Lay, 254 A.D. 372, 5 N.Y.S.2d 325 (2d Dep't 1938); State v. Antill, 176 Ohio St. 61, 26 Ohio Op. 2d 366, 197 N.E.2d 548 (1964); People v. Covington, 19 P.3d 15 (Colo. 2001) (duty to report gunshot wounds abrogated physician patient privilege). *See also* N.J. Stat. Ann. § 2A:84A-22.2 (privilege does not extend to reports required to be filed by physician or patient). Physician-patient privilege as applied to physician's testimony concerning wound required to be reported to public authority, 85 A.L.R.3d 1196.

[16]Bryson v. State, 1985 OK CR 107, 711 P.2d 932 (Okla. Crim. App. 1985), (claim that evidence deriving from physician's voluntary report was barred by statutory privilege rejected; court in dictum states that physician would have been barred from testify-

sion general disclosure of the data collected, and maintenance of some degree of confidentiality may in fact be indispensable to constitutionality.[17]

## § 102    Rule of privilege, not incompetency: Privilege belongs to the patient, not to an objecting party as such; effect of the patient's death

As has been pointed out in the discussion of privileges generally,[1] the rule which excludes disclosures to physicians is not a rule of incompetency of evidence serving the end of protecting the adverse party against unreliable or prejudicial testimony. It is a rule of privilege protecting the extrinsic interest of the patient and designed to promote health, not truth. It encourages free disclosure in the sickroom by preventing disclosure in the courtroom. The patient is the person to be encouraged and he is the holder of the privilege.[2]

Consequently, the patient alone during his or her lifetime has the right to claim or to waive the privilege. If the patient is in a position to claim it and does not, it is waived[3] and no one else may assert it.[4] If the patient is not present, is unaware of the situation, or for some other reason is unable to claim the privilege,

---

ing to facts).

[17]In Whalen v. Roe, 429 U.S. 589, 97 S. Ct. 869, 51 L. Ed. 2d 64 (1977), the Supreme Court, in upholding the New York statute, placed considerable emphasis on the restricted number of persons who would have access to the reported information. *See also* U.S. v. Oberle, 136 F.3d 1414 (10th Cir. 1998) (drug treatment records may be disclosed only after a showing of good cause); State ex rel. C.J.V. v. Jamison, 973 S.W.2d 183 (Mo. Ct. App. E.D. 1998) (drug abuse records may be disclosed for good cause, but there is a strong presumption against disclosure). *Compare* Carr v. Schmid, 105 Misc. 2d 645, 432 N.Y.S.2d 807 (Sup 1980) (allowing discovery of record of plaintiff's venereal disease from public agency on basis of litigant-patient exception).

**[Section 102]**

[1]See § 72 supra.

[2]Metropolitan Life Ins. Co. v. Kaufman, 104 Colo. 13, 87 P.2d 758 (1939) (physician compelled to give

testimony where privilege had been waived by patient; "Privileged communications are personal to the patient only."); Cal. Evid. Code § 1014(c); 8 Wigmore, Evidence § 2386 (McNaughton rev. 1961); Imwinkelried, The New Wigmore: Evidentiary Privileges § 6.5 (2d ed. 2010); West's Key Number Digest, Privileged Communications and Confidentiality ⊙262, 322.

[3]People v. Bloom, 193 N.Y. 1, 85 N.E. 824 (1908) (patient who fails to claim privilege against testimony of his physicians, at first trial, a civil case, waives permanently and cannot object to similar testimony at his later trial for perjury).

[4]Mosteller v. Stiltner, 727 S.E.2d 601 (N.C. Ct. App. 2012) (privilege belongs to the patient, not the therapist). *See also* State v. Thomas, 1 Wash. 2d 298, 95 P.2d 1036 (1939) (defendant charged with carnal knowledge of child, could not object to physician's testimony where child and mother did not; but here physician made examination at instance of

it is generally held that the privilege may be asserted on his or her behalf by a guardian, personal representative, or the health care provider,[5] the latter being frequently held to have an enforceable duty to invoke the privilege in the absence of waiver by the patient.[6] This necessary rule has unfortunately demonstrated considerable potential for allowing health care providers to advance personal interests under the guise of vindicating the privilege.[7] It is to be hoped that it will not ultimately prove beyond judicial ingenuity in cases of this sort to allow the patient the ultimate decision as to whether the privilege will be invoked.[8]

---

county and doctor-patient relation probably did not exist). A similar holding on similar facts is State v. Fackrell, 44 Wash. 2d 874, 271 P.2d 679, 681 (1954). *And see* People v. Palomo, 31 P.3d 879, 884–85 (Colo. 2001) (defendant had no standing to raise any privilege with regard to victim's medical records); State v. Echols, 152 Wis. 2d 725, 449 N.W.2d 320 (Ct. App. 1989) (defendant not entitled to assert witness' psychotherapist-patient privilege).

[5]*See* Unif. R. Evid. 503(c): "The privilege under this rule may be claimed by the patient, the patient's guardian or conservator, or the personal representative of a deceased patient. The person who was the [psychotherapist] [physician or psychotherapist] [physician or mental-health provider] [mental-health provider] at the time of the communication is presumed to have authority to claim the privilege, but only on behalf of the patient." *And see*, Matter of K.S., 137 Wis. 2d 570, 405 N.W.2d 78 (1987) (counsel representing incompetent has authority to claim privilege of patient). *But see* In re Berg, 152 N.H. 658, 886 A.2d 980, 987 (2005) (court must determine whether assertion or waiver of privilege is in minor child's best interests); Ellison v. Ellison, 1996 OK 64, 919 P.2d 1 (Okla. 1996) (custodial parent may not invoke child's psychotherapist-patient privilege in a custody proceeding).

[6]*See, e.g.,* St. Louis Little Rock Hosp., Inc. v. Gaertner, 682 S.W.2d 146 (Mo. Ct. App. E.D. 1984) (failure of provider to assert privilege on behalf of patient in absence of waiver may give rise to action for damages). *See also* Cal. Evid. Code §§ 994, 995, which requires the physician to claim the privilege unless otherwise instructed by the patient. The obligation may extend beyond the term of the professional relationship. *See* Clark v. Clark, 220 Neb. 771, 371 N.W.2d 749 (1985) (sale of physician's practice and records does not affect existence of privilege).

[7]*See* Parkson v. Central DuPage Hosp., 105 Ill. App. 3d 850, 61 Ill. Dec. 651, 435 N.E.2d 140 (1st Dist. 1982) (hospital had standing to assert privilege of non-party patients who had received same drug as plaintiff); State v. Jaggers, 506 N.E.2d 832 (Ind. Ct. App. 1987) (chiropractor could assert privilege of patients in suit to enjoin him from practicing acupuncture). *But compare* Burns v. Boyden, 2006 UT 14, 133 P.3d 370, 379 (Utah 2006) (court denied privilege where chiropractor found to have asserted it in his own self-interest); Matter of Application to Quash a Subpoena Duces Tecum in Grand Jury Proceedings, 56 N.Y.2d 348, 452 N.Y.S.2d 361, 437 N.E.2d 1118 (1982) (hospital being investigated for possible crimes against patients not entitled to privilege for deceased patients' records); State v. McGriff, 109 Ohio App. 3d 668, 672 N.E.2d 1074 (3d Dist. Logan County 1996) (defendant doctor not permitted to invoke patients' privilege to shield himself from criminal investigation).

[8]*See., e.g.,* Goldstein v. St. Paul

The adverse party as such has no interest to protect if he or she is not the patient, and thus cannot object as of right.[9]

In order to facilitate full disclosure as well as to protect the privacy of the decedent, most courts hold that the privilege continues after death.[10] However, in contests of the survivors in interest with third parties, e.g., actions to recover property claimed to belong to the deceased, actions for the death of the deceased, or actions upon life insurance policies, the personal representative, heir or next of kin, or the beneficiary in the policy may waive the privilege,[11] and, by the same token, the adverse

---

Fire & Marine Ins. Co., 665 So. 2d 1267 (La. Ct. App. 4th Cir. 1995) (nursing home sued based upon injury caused by patient could not claim privilege on behalf of patient); Med. Mut. of Ohio v. Schlotterer, 122 Ohio St. 3d 181, 2009-Ohio-2496, 909 N.E.2d 1237 (2009) (patients' broad consent to release of medical records to insurer waived privilege asserted by physician on their behalf).

[9]Thus, after the death of the patient, in a suit on an insurance policy, the insurer cannot assert the privilege. Olson v. Court of Honor, 100 Minn. 117, 110 N.W. 374, 377 (1907); Hier v. Farmers Mut. Fire Ins. Co., 104 Mont. 471, 67 P.2d 831 (1937). *Contra* Westover v. Aetna Life Ins. Co., 99 N.Y. 56, 1 N.E. 104 (1885). *See* Right of one against whom testimony is offered to invoke privilege of communication between others, 2 A.L.R.2d 645. At least one court has held that an accused may claim error in the denial of the privilege to another person where the patient had properly raised the privilege at the trial, Cotton v. State, 675 So. 2d 308 (Miss. 1996), effectively overruling state precedent to the contrary, Davenport v. State, 143 Miss. 121, 108 So. 433 (1926).

[10]Bassil v. Ford Motor Co., 278 Mich. 173, 270 N.W. 258 (1936). *Accord* Cal. Evid. Code § 993. The utilitarian reasons given in most cases are not dissimilar to those articulated by the United States Supreme Court in Swidler & Berlin v. U.S., 524 U.S. 399, 118 S. Ct. 2081, 141 L. Ed. 2d 379 (1998)

(see discussion § 94, supra) with regard to the general survival of the attorney-client privilege after the death of the client. *But see* U.S. v. Hansen, 955 F. Supp. 1225 (D. Mont. 1997), reversed on other grounds, 145 F.3d 1342 (9th Cir. 1998) (unpublished opinion) (psychotherapist-patient privilege announced in *Jaffee v. Redmond* does not survive as against claim for information by defendant in criminal case).

[11]Emmett v. Eastern Dispensary and Cas. Hospital, 396 F.2d 931 (D.C. Cir. 1967) (next of kin had right to waive privilege and obtain medical records of deceased in support of possible malpractice action); Harvey v. Silber, 300 Mich. 510, 2 N.W.2d 483 (1942) (administrator suing for death due to defendants' alleged malpractice); Colwell v. Dwyer, 20 Ohio Op. 320, 35 N.E.2d 789 (Ct. App. 2d Dist. Madison County 1940) (administrator plaintiff in death action); State ex rel. Calley v. Olsen, 271 Or. 369, 532 P.2d 230 (1975) (beneficiary under life policy allowed to waive over opposition of personal representative). In Fleet Messenger Service, Inc. v. Life Ins. Co. of North America, 205 F. Supp. 585 (S.D. N.Y. 1962), an action to recover the proceeds of a life policy, the claim of privilege by the widow and the personal representative, neither of whom was a beneficiary, was rejected on ground that only parties may claim the privilege. But the result here would better have been justified as a waiver by the beneficiary.

party may not effectively assert the privilege.[12] In contests over the validity of a will, where both sides—the executor on the one hand and the heirs or next of kin on the other—claim under and not adversely to the decedent, the assumption should prevail that the decedent would desire that the validity of his or her will should be determined in the fullest light of the facts.[13] Accordingly in this situation either the executor or the contestants may effectively waive the privilege without the concurrence of the other.[14]

---

[12]Wimberley v. State, 217 Ark. 130, 228 S.W.2d 991 (1950); Jasper v. State, 1954 OK CR 45, 269 P.2d 375 (Okla. Crim. App. 1954); West's Key Number Digest, Privileged Communications and Confidentiality ☞19, 84, 167. *See also* Hale v. Superior Court, 28 Cal. App. 4th 1421, 34 Cal. Rptr. 2d 279 (4th Dist. 1994) (attorneys for patient's estate should have been permitted to contact treating physicians). An early New York case, however, holds that any party may raise the objection, and it remains for the patient to waive. Westover v. Aetna Life Ins. Co., 99 N.Y. 56, 1 N.E. 104, 105, 106 (1885). This position seems insupportable.

[13]"If he did not have testamentary capacity, then the paper was not his will, and it is not the policy of the law to maintain such an instrument. It is undoubtedly the policy of the law to uphold the testamentary disposition of property, but not until it is ascertained whether such a disposition has been made. . . . And no one can be said to represent the deceased in that contest, for he could only be interested in having the truth ascertained, and his estate can only be protected by establishing or defeating the instrument as the truth so ascertained may require. The testimony of the attending physician is usually reliable, and often controlling, and to place it at the disposal

of one party to such a proceeding and withhold it from the other would be manifestly partial and unjust." Ladd, J., in Winters v. Winters, 102 Iowa 53, 71 N.W. 184, 185 (1897).

[14]Hyatt v. Wroten, 184 Ark. 847, 43 S.W.2d 726 (1931) (heirs); Gorman v. Hickey, 145 Kan. 54, 64 P.2d 587 (1937) (heir contesting will could waive though executor opposed waiver); Lembke v. Unke, 171 N.W.2d 837 (N.D. 1969) (heirs entitled to waive in will contest; overruling prior decision denying waiver after patient's death); Haverstick v. Banet, 267 Ind. 351, 370 N.E.2d 341 (1977) (semble); Extrajudicial admissions of fact by attorney as binding client, 97 A.L.R. 374. *And see* Note, 39 Minn. L. Rev. 800 (1955).

Suits attacking conveyances by the deceased are generally held to be governed by the same principle. Calhoun v. Jacobs, 141 F.2d 729 (App. D.C. 1944); McDonald v. McDonald, 53 Wis. 2d 371, 192 N.W.2d 903 (1972).

An alternative approach in will contest cases is suggested in Winters v. Winters, 102 Iowa 53, 71 N.W. 184 (1897), namely that neither side may assert the privilege since the determination of who steps into the shoes of the decedent must await the outcome of the suit. See also § 95 supra, where the attorney-client privilege is involved.

## § 103  What constitutes a waiver of the privilege?

The physician-patient statutes, though commonly phrased in terms of incompetency, are nevertheless held to create merely a privilege for the benefit of the patient, which he or she may waive.[1]

Generally[2] it is agreed that a contractual stipulation waiving the privilege, such as is frequently included in applications for life or health insurance, or in the policies themselves, is valid and effectual.[3]

Another context in which the privilege is waived anticipatorily is that in which a testator procures an attending doctor to subscribe his or her will as an attesting witness. This action constitutes a waiver as to all facts affecting the validity of the will.[4]

The physician-patient privilege, like most other privileges, may also be waived in advance of trial by a disclosure of the privileged information either made or acquiesced in by the privilege holder.[5] Obviously, the law has no reason to conceal in court what has

---

**[Section 103]**

[1] 8 Wigmore, Evidence § 2388 (McNaughton rev. 1961); Imwinkelried, The New Wigmore: Evidentiary Privileges § 6.12 (2d ed. 2010).

[2] In Michigan such an agreement was early held to be invalid as against public policy. Gilchrist v. Mystic Workers of the World, 196 Mich. 247, 163 N.W. 10 (1917). Such provisions continue to be ineffective. Drouillard v. Metropolitan Life Ins. Co., 107 Mich. App. 608, 310 N.W.2d 15 (1981).

[3] Jones v. Prudential Ins. Co. of America, 388 A.2d 476 (D.C. 1978); Murphy v. Mutual Life Ins. Co. of New York, 62 Idaho 362, 112 P.2d 993, 994 (1941); Templeton v. Mutual Life Ins. Co. of New York, 1936 OK 394, 177 Okla. 94, 57 P.2d 841 (1936); 1 Wigmore, Evidence § 7a (3d ed. 1940); Imwinkelried, The New Wigmore: Evidentiary Privileges § 6.12.4.a (1) (2d ed. 2010); Note, 16 N.C. L. Rev. 53 (1938); Validity, construction, and effect of stipulation in application or policy of insurance waiving privilege as to communication to or testimony by physician, 54 A.L.R. 412; West's Key Number Digest, Privileged Communications and Confidentiality ☞266. See also State v. Ross, 89 Wash. App. 302, 947 P.2d 1290 (Div. 1 1997)

(release of treatment related records effective to waive privilege). But occasionally a court by an eccentric interpretation may emasculate the waiver. Noble v. United Ben. Life Ins. Co., 230 Iowa 471, 297 N.W. 881 (1941) (consent to doctor's furnishing to insurer information gained in attending patient is not waiver of privilege as to doctor's testimony in court.).

[4] In re Mullin's Estate, 110 Cal. 252, 42 P. 645 (1895); Stormon v. Weiss, 65 N.W.2d 475, 512 (N.D. 1954); 8 Wigmore, Evidence § 2390(1) (McNaughton rev. 1961).

[5] See, e.g., Tex. R. Evid. 511:

A person upon whom these rules confer a privilege against disclosure waives the privilege if:

(1) the person or a predecessor of the person while holder of the privilege voluntarily discloses or consents to disclosure of any significant part of the privileged matter unless such disclosure itself is privileged; or

(2) the person or a representative of the person calls a person to whom privileged communications have been made to testify as to the person's character or character trait insofar as such communications are relevant to such character or character trait.

Judicial statements are generally

been freely divulged on the public street, and the only question in such cases becomes the voluntariness of the revelation and the scope of the waiver.[6]

Waiver in connection with litigation is an area in which substantial changes have occurred in recent years. A shrinking from the embarrassment which comes from exposure of bodily disease or abnormality is human and natural. It is arguable that legal protection from exposure is justified to encourage frankness in consulting physicians. But it is not human, natural, or understandable to claim protection from exposure by asserting a privilege for communications to doctors at the very same time when the patient is parading before the public the mental or physical condition as to which the patient consulted the doctor by bringing an action for damages arising from that same condition.[7] This, in the oft-repeated phrase, is to make the privilege not a shield only, but a sword.

The conclusion mandated by these considerations clearly is that a patient voluntarily placing his or her physical or mental condition in issue in a judicial proceeding waives the privilege with respect to information relative to that condition. Failure to find a waiver from assertion of a claim or defense predicated upon a physical or mental condition has the awkward consequence of effectively frustrating discovery on a central issue of the case unless one of a variety of temporizing expedients is pressed into service to accommodate the outmoded rule.[8]

Today the once prevalent rule that no waiver results from rais-

---

similar. Cates v. Wilson, 321 N.C. 1, 361 S.E.2d 734 (1987).

[6]U.S. v. Crews, 781 F.2d 826 (10th Cir. 1986) (threat to kill president made to nurse in psychiatric ward; privilege, if any, waived by subsequent voluntary discussion of statement with F.B.I. agent); Thomas v. State, 656 N.E.2d 819 (Ind. Ct. App. 1995) (disclosure to police officer waived privilege as to same subject matter).

But clearly not all disclosures to third persons will effect waiver. See State ex rel. Gonzenbach v. Eberwein, 655 S.W.2d 794 (Mo. Ct. App. E.D. 1983) (authorization of release of medical records to medical and liability insurers did not clearly and unequivocally demonstrate purpose to abandon privilege).

[7]"The patient-litigant exception precludes one who has placed in issue his physical condition from invoking the privilege on the ground that disclosure of his condition would cause him humiliation. He cannot have his cake and eat it too." City & County of San Francisco v. Superior Court In and For City and County of San Francisco, 37 Cal. 2d 227, 231 P.2d 26, 28 (1951) (by Traynor, J.). *But see* State ex rel. Crowden v. Dandurand, 970 S.W.2d 340 (Mo. 1998) (patient-litigant waiver extends only to medical records bearing on the condition put into issue); Hageman v. Southwest Gen. Health Ctr., 119 Ohio St. 3d 185, 2008-Ohio-3343, 893 N.E.2d 153 (2008) (waiver of privilege for purposes of litigation is limited to that case).

[8]These expedients have included

ing a claim or defense has been widely reversed by statute.[9] Thus, at present, the crucial questions concern the types of issues which sufficiently implicate a party's physical or mental condition, and what actions by a party serve to raise these issues within the meaning of the modern statutes. A claim for damages for personal injuries is of course the paradigm example,[10] and will clearly waive the privilege in all jurisdictions where such waiver by filing is possible at all.[11] Claims for damages for mental suffering have been treated similarly,[12] but here some discernment is called for unless the privilege be seen to evaporate upon the filing of any claim whatsoever.[13] In addition, cases applying the

---

staying the proceeding until such time as the party will permit pretrial examination of the doctor, Mariner v. Great Lakes Dredge & Dock Co., 202 F. Supp. 430, 20 Ohio Op. 2d 341 (N.D. Ohio 1962) and holding that commencement of the action effects a qualified waiver of the privilege for discovery purposes, leaving the ultimate scope of the waiver to be determined by the nature of the privileged party's evidence at trial, Eberle v. Savon Food Stores, Inc., 30 Mich. App. 496, 186 N.W.2d 837 (1971).

[9]See Cal. Evid. Code § 996. Unif. R. Evid. 503(d)(3) provides:

There is no privilege under this rule for a communication relevant to an issue of the [physical,] mental[,] or emotional condition of the patient in any proceeding in which the patient relies upon the condition as an element of the patient's claim or defense or, after the patient's death, in any proceeding in which any party relies upon the condition as an element of the party's claim or defense;

The rule embodied in these statutes is often referred to as the "patient-litigant" exception to the physician-patient privilege. Some form of the Uniform Rule is now in effect in a substantial number of states. See 13A U.L.A. 278 et seq. See also Ortega v. Colorado Permanente Group, P.C., 265 P.3d 444 (Colo. 2011) (under statute, privilege did not apply in action brought by patient against HMO); State v. Rieflin, 558 N.W.2d 149 (Iowa 1996) (overruled by, State v. Lyman, 776 N.W.2d 865 (Iowa 2010)) (giving

notice of insanity and diminished responsibility defenses waived privilege under "patient-litigant" exception).

[10]Arctic Motor Freight, Inc. v. Stover, 571 P.2d 1006 (Alaska 1977); Hartmann v. Nordin, 147 P.3d 43 (Colo. 2006) (plaintiff waived privilege for her medical condition including to medical history of her relatives by filing medical malpractice action); State ex rel. McNutt v. Keet, 432 S.W.2d 597 (Mo. 1968); Christensen v. Munsen, 123 Wash. 2d 234, 867 P.2d 626 (1994) (privilege waived in medical malpractice claim; defendant could call plaintiff's treating physician as a witness). See also Wigmore's caustic denunciation of the older rule, 8 Wigmore § 2389 (McNaughton rev. 1961).

[11]Pennsylvania, for example, appears to limit its waiver rule exclusively to civil actions for personal injuries. 42 Pa. Cons. Stat. Ann. § 5929.

[12]Haney v. Mizell Memorial Hosp., 744 F.2d 1467 (11th Cir. 1984) (explicit prayer for damages for mental anguish waived privilege); Wimberly Resorts Property, Inc. v. Pfeuffer, 691 S.W.2d 27 (Tex. App. Austin 1985) (semble).

[13]Johnson v. Trujillo, 977 P.2d 152, 157 (Colo. 1999) (generic claim for damages for mental anguish, etc., incident to physical injuries did not waive physician-patient or psychotherapist-patient privilege); Reda v. Advocate Health Care, 199 Ill. 2d 47, 262 Ill. Dec. 394, 765 N.E.2d

psychotherapist-patient privilege established in *Jaffee v. Redmond*[14] have not agreed as to whether and when a plaintiff who asserts a claim involving distress waives that privilege.[15] With respect to defenses, a distinction is clearly to be seen between the allegation of a physical or mental condition, which will effect the waiver, and the mere denial of such a condition asserted by the adversary, which will not.[16]

---

1002, 1009 (2002) (patient does not waive privilege against disclosure of mental health records merely by claiming damages for neurological injury of a stroke or other brain damage); Thiele v. Ortiz, 165 Ill. App. 3d 983, 117 Ill. Dec. 530, 520 N.E.2d 881 (1st Dist. 1988) (claim for loss of society in wrongful death case did not place decedent's mental condition in issue; court notes that construction of exception to apply to all issues involving mental condition would lead to virtual extinction of privilege); Laznovsky v. Laznovsky, 357 Md. 586, 745 A.2d 1054, 1073 (2000) (person seeking child custody claiming to be a fit parent does not, without more, waive psychiatrist/psychologist privilege with respect to past mental health). *See also* D.C. v. S.A., 178 Ill. 2d 551, 227 Ill. Dec. 550, 687 N.E.2d 1032 (1997) (plaintiff did not waive privilege by asserting in complaint that he was in exercise of ordinary care and free from contributory negligence).

[14]Jaffee v. Redmond, 518 U.S. 1, 116 S. Ct. 1923, 135 L. Ed. 2d 337 (1996). *See* discussion in § 98, supra.

[15]*Compare* Vanderbilt v. Town of Chilmark, 174 F.R.D. 225 (D. Mass. 1997) (no waiver unless plaintiff introduces evidence of the substance of her communication) *with* Sarko v. Penn-Del Directory Co., 170 F.R.D. 127, 21 A.D.D. 270 (E.D. Pa. 1997) (plaintiff in action under Americans with Disabilities Act alleging that employer failed to reasonably accommodate her clinical depression waived any applicable privilege). *See also* Santelli v. Electro-Motive, 188 F.R.D. 306, 308–09 (N.D. Ill. 1999) (mere claim of emotional distress not sufficient to waive privilege; party must

elect to inject into a case either the fact of her treatment or any symptoms or conditions that she may have experienced); Vasconcellos v. Cybex Intern., Inc., 962 F. Supp. 701 (D. Md. 1997) (plaintiff entitled to some protection under privilege even in a case in which she alleges emotional injuries); State ex rel. Dean v. Cunningham, 182 S.W.3d 561 (Mo. 2006) (mere claim of emotional distress does not waive privilege). *See generally* Broun, The Medical Privilege in the Federal Courts—Should It Matter Whether Your Ego or Your Elbow Hurts?, 38 Loy. L.A. L. Rev. 657, 670–75 (2004); Smith, An Uncertain Privilege: Implied Waiver and the Evisceration of the Psychotherapist-Patient Privilege in the Federal Courts, 58 DePaul L. Rev. 79 (2008); Note, Certainty Thwarted: Broad Waiver Versus Narrow Waiver of the Psychotherapist-Patient Privilege After Jaffee v. Redmond, 52 Hastings L.J. 1369 (2001); Note, Implying Plaintiffs' Waivers of the Psychotherapist-Patient Privilege after Jaffee v. Redmond, 59 U. Pitt. L. Rev. 901 (1998).

[16]Clark v. District Court, Second Judicial Dist., City and County of Denver, 668 P.2d 3 (Colo. 1983) (mere denial of allegation in wrongful death action that individual defendant had long history of mental illness known to corporate defendant did not waive psychiatrist patient privilege); Branch v. Wilkinson, 198 Neb. 649, 256 N.W.2d 307, 315 (1977) ("We do not believe that this [patient-litigant] exception should be invoked where the patient merely denies the allegations of the opposing party concerning his condition.").

A much litigated point since the conversion to more liberal rules of waiver has been whether a waiver effected by filing a claim or defense will permit the waiving party's adversary in litigation to contact physicians on an ex parte basis. Those decisions approving such contacts stress the economies of informal discovery and the anomaly of treating any witness as "belonging" to a party,[17] considerations which suffice to make permissibility of ex parte contact the better rule. A contrary position, however, has been taken by a greater number of courts,[18] and possesses a substantial rationale in the consideration that the waiver following upon the filing of a claim or defense extends only to information relevant to the condition relied upon.

In the criminal area, waiver under the modern statutes has been seen to flow from assertion of the defenses of insanity and diminished responsibility.[19]

Because of the principles discussed above, there will today be

---

[17]Leading authorities for this position include Doe v. Eli Lilly & Co., Inc., 99 F.R.D. 126 (D.D.C. 1983); Brandt v. Pelican, 856 S.W.2d 658 (Mo. 1993); Moses v. McWilliams, 379 Pa. Super. 150, 549 A.2d 950 (1988). See also Lee Memorial Health System v. Smith, 40 So. 3d 106 (Fla. 2d DCA 2010) (communications between the hospital and the physicians were not "disclosures" and did not trigger privilege).

[18]Horner v. Rowan Companies, Inc., 153 F.R.D. 597 (S.D. Tex. 1994) (private ex parte interviews between defendant's counsel and plaintiff's treating physicians prohibited unless specifically authorized by plaintiff); Cua v. Morrison, 626 N.E.2d 581 (Ind. Ct. App. 1993) (ex parte interviews with party-patient's health care providers prohibited); Scott By and Through Scott v. Flynt, 704 So. 998 (Miss. 1996) (ex parte interviews prohibited unless authorized by plaintiff); State ex rel. Kitzmiller v. Henning, 190 W. Va. 142, 437 S.E.2d 452 (1993) (ex parte interviews prohibited; opposing counsel restricted to formal discovery methods). Some courts have permitted interviews by opposing counsel of treating physicians, but with limitations. See Samms v. District Court, Fourth Judicial Dist. of State of Colo., 908 P.2d 520 (Colo. 1995) (ex parte

interviews between defendant's counsel and plaintiff's treating physicians could be authorized by the court provided discussions limited to relevant, non-privileged information and plaintiff was given notice permitting her or her attorney to attend); Baker v. Wellstar Health System, Inc., 288 Ga. 336, 703 S.E.2d 601 (2010) (defendant's interviews with plaintiff's health care providers limited in light of privilege); Steinberg v. Jensen, 194 Wis. 2d 439, 534 N.W.2d 361 (1995) (defense counsel may communicate ex parte with plaintiff's treating physician so long as the communication does not involve disclosure of confidential information). Discovery: right to ex parte interview with injured party's treating physician, 50 A.L.R.4th 714.

[19]Post v. State, 580 P.2d 304, 307 (Alaska 1978) ("When one claims to be insane in a public trial . . . the humiliation which may be associated with the exposure of one's inner self is disregarded in order to achieve another end and the basis for the psychotherapist-patient privilege is largely eliminated"); State v. Koon, 704 So. 2d 756 (La. 1997) (plea of not guilty by reason of insanity waives physician-patient privilege as to information relevant to that issue); State v. Johnson, 968 S.W.2d 123 (Mo. 1998) (defendant waive physician-patient privilege by raising posttraumatic

fewer occasions in which a cause will come on for trial with the patient's privilege still intact. Since the possibility still exists, however, it should be briefly considered how the privilege may be waived in trial.

How far does the patient's testifying waive the privilege? Doubtless, if the patient on direct examination testifies to,[20] or adduces other evidence of,[21] the communications exchanged or the information furnished to the doctor consulted this would waive in respect to such consultations. When, however, the patient in his or her direct testimony does not reveal any privileged matter respecting the consultation, but testifies only to physical or mental condition, existing at the time of such consultation, then one view is that, "where the patient tenders to the jury the issue as to his physical condition, it must in fairness and justice be held that he has himself waived the obligation of secrecy."[22] This view has the merit of curtailing the scope of a privilege that some view as obstructive, but there are a number

---

stress disorder defense to murder charge); State v. Valley, 153 Vt. 380, 571 A.2d 579 (1989) (defendant waived privilege by filing notice of defense of insanity; citing treatise) Contra: Ex parte Day, 378 So. 2d 1159 (Ala. 1979) (no waiver by plea of insanity alone).

[20]Mauro v. Tracy, 152 Colo. 106, 380 P.2d 570 (1963) (plaintiff's testimony concerning treatment waived privilege in personal injury case); Dennis v. Prisock, 254 Miss. 574, 181 So. 2d 125 (1965), appeal after remand 221 So.2d 706 (privilege waived where patient testifies in detail about nature of injuries and consultations with physician). Epstein v. Pennsylvania R. Co., 250 Mo. 1, 156 S.W. 699 (1913) (". . . since plaintiff had himself voluntarily gone upon the stand, and in his case in chief, as a witness for himself, laid bare for lucre's sake all of the secrets of his sickroom, since he had told and retold what Dr. Elston, his physician, said to him, and what he said to Elston, since he had told the precise nature of his alleged hurts as he said Elston found them, and since he had also voluntarily related the treatment professionally given to him by Elston, he waived the competency of other physicians, also there present, having knowledge of the identical facts."); State v. Smith, 84 Wash. App.

813, 929 P.2d 1191 (Div. 1 1997) (defendant's testimony at first trial waived privilege for second trial); When testimony by patient deemed to waive physician-patient privilege, 114 A.L.R. 798. The principle is applicable irrespective of whether the witness is a party. *See* People v. Lowe, 96 Misc. 2d 33, 408 N.Y.S.2d 873 (City Crim. Ct. 1978) (defendant in criminal prosecution allowed to obtain victim's records of mental treatment; victim's testimony that he suffered brain injury during WWII held to constitute waiver). But the court's readiness to find waiver in this case may have been increased by a desire to avoid conflict between the privilege and defendant's constitutional rights.

[21]Buckminster's Estate v. C.I.R., 147 F.2d 331 (C.C.A. 2d Cir. 1944) (executrix introducing statements and diagnosis of physician who attended decedent waived privilege). *And see* Fishboats, Inc. v. Welzbacher, 413 So. 2d 710 (Miss. 1982) (plaintiff's display of injured portions of his body to jury waived privilege).

[22]Andrews, J. in Hethier v. Johns, 233 N.Y. 370, 135 N.E. 603 (1922); 8 Wigmore, Evidence § 2389(2) (McNaughton rev. 1961).

of courts that hold that the patient's testimony as to his or her condition without disclosure of privileged matter is not a waiver.[23] If the patient reveals privileged matter on cross-examination, without claiming the privilege, this is usually held not to be a waiver of the privilege enabling the adversary to make further inquiry of the doctors, on the ground that such revelations were not "voluntary."[24]

If the patient examines a physician as to matters disclosed in a consultation, or course of treatment, of course this is a waiver and opens the door to the opponent to examine the patient about any other matters then disclosed.[25] And if several doctors participated jointly in the same consultation or course of treatment the calling of one to disclose part of the shared information waives objection to the adversary's calling any other of the joint consultants to testify about the consultation, treatment or the results thereof.[26] Some courts go further and hold that calling by the patient of one doctor and eliciting privileged matter from that doctor opens the door to the opponent's calling other doctors consulted by the patient at other times to bring out any facts relevant to the issue on which the privileged proof was adduced.[27] Arguably, it is not consonant with justice and fairness to permit

---

[23]Bryan Bros. Packing Co. v. Grubbs, 251 Miss. 52, 168 So. 2d 289 (1964) (no waiver arising from plaintiff's testimony in personal injury case that she had been treated by a particular doctor); Harpman v. Devine, 133 Ohio St. 1, 9 Ohio Op. 347, 10 N.E.2d 776 (1937) (two judges dissenting), critically noted 51 Harv. L. Rev. 931; Clawson v. Walgreen Drug Co., 108 Utah 577, 162 P.2d 759 (1945) (no waiver when patient testified concerning nature and extent of injury, but did not give evidence of what doctors told him nor of details of treatment); West's Key Number Digest, Privileged Communications and Confidentiality ⬤⟞265.

[24]Buffa v. Scott, 147 Ariz. 140, 708 P.2d 1331 (Ct. App. Div. 1 1985) (approving general rule that privilege not waived by testimony of patient on cross-examination, but holding waiver properly found where in context testimony was "contrary to true medical facts"). Iseman v. Delmar Medical-Dental Bldg., Inc., 113 A.D.2d 276, 495 N.Y.S.2d 747 (3d Dep't 1985) (no waiver by testimony on cross-

examination on deposition where plaintiff did not rely on condition as basis for recovery; two judges dissenting).

[25]Care and Protection of Bruce, 44 Mass. App. Ct. 758, 694 N.E.2d 27 (1998) (privileged status of psychiatric records waived by extensive cross-examination of psychiatrist about records); Maas v. Laursen, 219 Minn. 461, 18 N.W.2d 233 (1945); Demonbrun v. McHaffie, 348 Mo. 1120, 156 S.W.2d 923 (1941); Unick v. Kessler Memorial Hospital, 107 N.J. Super. 121, 257 A.2d 134 (Law Div. 1969).

[26]Jimerson v. Prendergast, 697 P.2d 804 (Colo. App. 1985). Doll v. Scandrett, 201 Minn. 316, 276 N.W. 281 (1937) (three judges dissenting), 22 Minn. L. Rev. 580; Morris v. New York, O. & W. Ry. Co., 148 N.Y. 88, 42 N.E. 410 (1895). *Contra:* Jones v. City of Caldwell, 20 Idaho 5, 116 P. 110 (1911). *See* Waiver of privilege as regards one physician as a waiver as to other physicians, 5 A.L.R.3d 1244.

[27]De Groff v. Clark, 358 Mich. 274, 100 N.W.2d 214 (1960) (waiver in such circumstances provided for by lo-

the patient to reveal his or her secrets to several doctors and then when the condition comes in issue to limit the witnesses to the consultants favorable to the claims.[28] But a substantial number of courts balk at this step.[29]

Though the privilege continues after death of the patient, it may then be waived by the personal representative of the decedent.[30] And where the personal representative is involved in litigation over the decedents estate with other persons claiming through the decedent, or where heirs-at-law are in opposition to one another, any one of the parties may waive the privilege.[31]

---

cal statute); Weissman v. Wells, 306 Mo. 82, 267 S.W. 400 (1924) (personal injury plaintiff who claimed nervous state due to injury, by calling doctor to testify to her condition after injury waived objection to defendant's proving by other doctor her same condition before injury); Steinberg v. New York Life Ins. Co., 263 N.Y. 45, 188 N.E. 152 (1933), (plaintiff suing on disability policy puts doctor on stand to prove that he has had disability from tuberculosis since time of claim; held this warrants defendant in proving by another doctor that plaintiff had same disease several years before, in support of its plea of misrepresentation); Robinson v. Lane, 1971 OK 9, 480 P.2d 620 (Okla. 1971) (plaintiff's testimony concerning injuries waived privilege with respect to physicians other than those called by him; earlier precedent to the contrary overruled); McUne v. Fuqua, 42 Wash. 2d 65, 253 P.2d 632 (1953) (lucid discussion by Hamley, J.); Comment, Evidence: The Physician-Patient Privilege: Alternatives to the Rule as it Now Exists in Oklahoma, 24 Okla. L. Rev. 380 (1971); and cases cited in Waiver of privilege as regards one physician as a waiver as to other physicians, 5 A.L.R.3d 1244. *See also* Hogan, Waiver of the Physician-Patient Privilege in Personal Injury Litigation, 52 Marq. L. Rev. 75 (1968).

[28]"A litigant should not be allowed to pick and choose in binding and loosing; he may bind or he may loose. . . . He may choose a serviceable and mellow one out of a number of physicians to fasten liability upon the defendant, and then, presto! change! exclude the testimony of those not so mellow and serviceable, to whom he has voluntarily given the same information and the same means of getting at a conclusion on the matter already uncovered by professional testimony to the jury. There is no reason in such condition of things, and where reason ends the law ends." Lamm, J. in Smart v. Kansas City, 208 Mo. 162, 105 S.W. 709, 722 (1907).

[29]No waiver as to doctors consulted separately. Mays v. New Amsterdam Cas. Co., 40 App. D.C. 249, 46 L.R.A.N.S. 1108, 1913 WL 20000 (App. D.C. 1913); Acme-Evans Co. v. Schnepf, 214 Ind. 394, 14 N.E.2d 561 (1938); Brown v. Guiter, 256 Iowa 671, 128 N.W.2d 896 (1964) and cases cited in Waiver of privilege as regards one physician as a waiver as to other physicians, 5 A.L.R.3d 1244; 81 Am. Jur. 2d, Witnesses § 474; West's Key Number Digest, Privileged Communications and Confidentiality ⟳265.

[30]*See* Revised Uniform R. Evid. (1986 amendment) 503. *See also* District Attorney for Norfolk Dist. v. Magraw, 417 Mass. 169, 628 N.E.2d 24 (1994) (executor or administrator of estate may waive psychotherapist-patient privilege).

[31]In re Wilson's Estate, 416 A.2d 228 (D.C. 1980); Haverstick v. Banet, 267 Ind. 351, 370 N.E.2d 341 (1977). Who may waive privilege of confidential communication to physician by person since deceased, 97 A.L.R.2d 393.

## § 104 Kinds of proceedings exempted from the application of the privilege[1]

The wide variation among state statutes creating and defining the physician-patient privilege renders it difficult to generalize usefully concerning the types of proceedings exempted from the operation of the privilege.[2] Even where the Uniform Rule has been adopted, one or more qualifications have commonly been engrafted upon it.[3] And though the now widely-adopted patient-litigant exception has undoubtedly reduced somewhat the differential application of the privilege, there remain many instances in which the holder of the privilege will not come within that exception. In short, it is indispensable to consult local statutes on the present point.

Probably the most common pattern to be observed in the statutes is that of a broadly defined privilege, applicable to both civil and criminal proceedings,[4] to which a variety of specific exceptions are then attached. But there are states which deny the privilege in criminal cases generally,[5] or in felony cases,[6] or in cases of homicide.[7]

With respect to other exceptions, the privilege has long been viewed as unworkable in worker compensation cases,[8] and in medical malpractice[9] cases and will generally be unavailable in these contexts. In more recent years, proceedings involving child abuse have claimed the attention of the legislatures, and these proceedings are now the most commonly singled out as involving policy considerations more weighty than those underlying the

---

[Section 104]

[1]98 C.J.S., Witnesses § 344 to 345; 81 Am. Jur. 2d, Witnesses § 431 to 435; West's Key Number Digest, Privileged Communications and Confidentiality ☞213 to 214.

[2]The statutes are collected in 8 Wigmore § 2380 (McNaughton rev. 1961).

[3]See 13A U.L.A. 278 to 284.

[4]In the absence of specific limiting language, the privilege will generally be held to apply to criminal as well as civil cases. See People v. Reynolds, 195 Colo. 386, 578 P.2d 647 (1978); 8 Wigmore, Evidence § 2385 (McNaughton rev. 1961); Imwinkelried, The New Wigmore: Evidentiary Privileges § 6.4.2.a (2d ed. 2010).

[5]See, e.g., Cal. Evid. Code § 998; Idaho Code § 9-203(4). And on occa-

sion the physician-patient privilege is denied in criminal cases, but the psychotherapist-patient privilege allowed.

[6]Kan. Stat. Ann. § 60-427(b).

[7]Wis. Stat. Ann. § 905.04(4)(d).

[8]More than half the states which have the privilege provide that it shall not apply in Workmen's Compensation proceedings. See the statutes compiled in 8 Wigmore, Evidence § 2380, n. 6 (McNaughton rev. 1961).

[9]8 Wigmore, Evidence § 2385 n. 3 (McNaughton rev. 1961). But as Wigmore points out in the cited section, there is probably no need for such a specific statutory exclusion provided the jurisdiction recognizes the patient-litigant exception. See also Imwinkelried, The New Wigmore: Evidentiary Privileges § 6.13.3 (2d ed. 2010).

privilege.[10] Other types of proceedings found withdrawn from the operation of the privilege are commitment proceedings,[11] prosecutions for some types of drug offenses,[12] and will contests.[13] The privilege is also sometimes withdrawn in child custody proceedings.[14]

## § 105    The policy and future of the privilege[1]

Some statements of Buller, J., in 1792 in a case involving the application of the attorney-client privilege seem to have furnished the inspiration for the pioneer New York statute of 1828 on the doctor-patient privilege. He said:

> The privilege is confined to the cases of counsel, solicitor, and attorney. . . . It is indeed hard in many cases to compel a friend to disclose a confidential conversation; and I should be glad if by law such evidence could be excluded. It is a subject of just indignation where persons are anxious to reveal what has been communicated to them in a confidential manner. . . . There are cases to which it is much to be lamented that the law of privilege is not extended; those in which medical persons are obliged to disclose the information which they acquire by attending in their professional characters.[2]

These comments reveal attitudes which have been influential

---

[10]8 Wigmore, Evidence § 2380 (McNaughton rev. 1961); Imwinkelried, The New Wigmore: Evidentiary Privileges §§ 6.13.2, at 963-66; 6.13.5.a. (2d ed. 2010).

[11]E.g., Rev. Unif. R. Evid. 503(d)(1).

[12]Neb. Rev. Stat. § 27-504(4)(e).

[13]Idaho Code § 9-203(4)(C).

[14]Mass. Gen. Laws Ann. ch. 210, § 3(b). See Matter of Von Goyt, 461 So. 2d 821 (Ala. Civ. App. 1984) (holding a psychologist-patient privilege "outweighed" in child custody case though no such exception existed in the statute). But see Petition of Catholic Charitable Bureau of Archdiocese of Boston, Inc., to Dispense with Consent to Adoption, 392 Mass. 738, 467 N.E.2d 866 (1984) (distinguishing between child custody and termination of parental rights cases and holding privilege available in latter).

**[Section 105]**

[1]There is a wealth of cogent discussion of the policy of the privilege. Most of the older treatments are ad-

verse. Wigmore's scalpel cuts deepest. 8 Evidence § 2380a (McNaughton rev. 1961). Other excellent discussions: De Witt, Privileged Communications Between Physician and Patient, Ch. IV (1958); Chafee, Is Justice Served by Closing the Doctor's Mouth?, 52 Yale L.J. 607 (1943); Purrington, An Abused Privilege, 6 Colum. L. Rev. 388 (1906) (historical, comparative, critical); Notes, 33 Ill. L. Rev. 483 (1939), 12 Minn. L. Rev. 390 (1928). See also for worthwhile treatments: Welch, Another Anomaly—the Patient's Privilege, 13 Miss. L.J. 137 (1941) (emphasis on local decisions); Curd, Privileged Communications between Doctor and Patient—an Anomaly, 44 W.Va. L. Q. 165 (1938); Long, Physician-Patient Privilege Obstructs Justice, 25 Ins. Counsel J. 224 (1958). But compare the commentaries cited infra at note 4.

[2]Wilson v. Rastall, (1792) 4 Term. Rep. 753, 759, 100 Eng. Rep. 1287 (K. B.).

The Revisers who drafted the New York statute, supported it in their report as follows:

ever since in the spread of statutes enacting the doctor-patient privilege. One attitude is the shrinking from forcing anyone to tell in court what he or she has learned in confidence. It is well understood today, however, that no such sweeping curtain for disclosure of confidences in the courtroom could be justified. Another is the complete failure to consider the other side of the shield, namely, the loss which comes from depriving the courts of any reliable source of facts necessary for the right decision of cases.

Perhaps the main burden of Justice Buller's remarks, however, is the suggestion that since the client's disclosures to the lawyer are privileged, the patient's disclosures to the doctor should have the same protection. This analogy has probably been more potent than any other argument, particularly with the lawyers in the legislatures. They would be reluctant to deny to the medical profession a recognition which the courts have themselves provided for the legal profession. Manifestly, however, the soundness of the privilege may not be judged as a matter of rivalry of professions, but by the criterion of the public interest.

Some of the analytical weaknesses of the utilitarian rationale of the privilege, except perhaps in the psychotherapeutic context, have been noted earlier.[3] To these must be added the perplexities and confusions arising from judicial and legislative attempts to render tolerable a rule which essentially runs against the grain of truth. The uncertainties of application of a privilege so extensively and variously qualified and restricted certainly undermine any effort to justify it on utilitarian grounds. One familiar with the vagaries of its operation may not be disposed to repose confidence in its protection. Those not so knowledgeable will often find it a snare and a delusion.

---

In 4 Term, Rep. 580, Buller, J. (to whom no one will attribute a disposition to relax the rules of evidence), said it was 'much to be lamented' that the information specified in this section was not privileged. Mr. Phillips expresses the same sentiment in his treatise on evidence, p. 104. The ground on which communications to counsel are privileged, is the supposed necessity of a full knowledge of the facts, to advise correctly, and to prepare for the proper defense for prosecution of a suit. But surely the necessity of consulting a medical adviser, when life itself may be in jeopardy, is still stronger. And unless such consultations are privileged, men will be incidentally punished by being obliged to suffer the consequences of injuries without relief from the medical art and without con-viction of any offense. Besides, in such cases, during the struggle between legal duty on the one hand, and professional honor on the other, the latter, aided by a strong sense of the injustice and inhumanity of the rule, will in most cases furnish a temptation to the perversion or concealment of truth, too strong for human resistance. In every view that can be taken of the policy, justice or humanity of the rule, as it exists, its relaxation seems highly expedient. It is believed that the proposition in the section is so guarded, that it cannot be abused by applying it to cases not intended to be privileged.

Original Reports of Revisers, vol. 5, p. 34, quoted Purrington, op. cit., 6 Colum. L. Rev. 392, 393 (1906).

[3] See § 98 supra.

A more tenable argument, however, has been increasingly advanced in recent years. This view holds that the privilege should not be viewed as operating to inspire the making of medical confidences but rather as protecting such confidences once made.[4] The legitimate interest in the privacy of the physician-patient relationship should not be subject to casual breach by every litigant in single-minded pursuit of the last scrap of evidence which may marginally contribute to victory in litigation. Arguably the privilege does, at least on occasion, operate to prevent such unwarranted intrusions.[5] The issue is whether the value of such protection is sufficiently great to justify both the suppression of critical evidence in other cases and the costs of administering a highly complex rule.

Regardless of how such a debate might be resolved in one's own mind, complete abolition of the privilege is unlikely given current political realities. One alternative resolution is legislation such as that which exists in North Carolina, which qualifies its statutory privilege with the provision that "the court, either at trial or prior thereto . . . may, subject to G.S. 8-53.6, compel such disclosure when, in his opinion disclosure is necessary to a proper administration of justice."[6] Such a balancing was expressly

---

[4]Black, Marital and Physician Privileges—A Reprint of a Letter to a Congressman, 1975 Duke L.J. 45, 50 ("But evaluation of a rule like this [privilege] entails not only a guess as to what conduct it will motivate, but also an estimate of its intrinsic decency . . . Why does this judgment of decency altogether vanish, sink to absolute zero, as soon as somebody files any kind of non-demurrable complaint . . ."); Krattenmaker, Testimonial Privileges in Federal Courts: An Alternative to the Proposed Federal Rules of Evidence, 62 Geo. L.J. 61, 92 (1973) ("Proponents of testimonial privileges need not carry the burden of proving what factors influence behavior. Privileges are important for other reasons as well . . . . Most important . . . is the simple fact that when a particular confidant's claim of privilege is upheld, so is his very right of privacy."). See discussion supra § 98.

[5]See Grey v. Superior Court, 62 Cal. App. 3d 698, 133 Cal. Rptr. 318 (2d Dist. 1976) (insurer presented with claim under accidental death policy sought to depose psychiatrist on "surmise" that result might be evidence of suicide). See also Broun, The Medical Privilege in the Federal Courts—Should It Matter Whether Your Ego or Your Elbow Hurts?, 38 Loy. L.A. L. Rev. 657, 701–05 (2004).

[6]N.C. Gen. Stat. Ann. § 8-53. Such a proviso was recommended for enactment by other states by Committee on the Improvement of the Law of Evidence of the American Bar Association for 1937–38. 8 Wigmore, Evidence § 2380a, n. 4 (McNaughton rev. 1961). See Sims v. Charlotte Liberty Mut. Ins. Co., 257 N.C. 32, 125 S.E.2d 326 (1962) where Moore, J., in a perceptive opinion observed with respect to the application of G.S. § 8-53, "It seems to us that the privilege statute, when strictly applied without the exercise of discretion on the part of the judge, is more often unjust than just . . . Our Legislature intended the statute to be a shield and not a sword. It was careful to make provision to avoid injustice and suppression of truth by putting it in the power of the trial judge to

rejected by the Court in *Jaffee v. Redmond*,[7] in connection with the psychotherapist-patient privilege. However, the adoption of such a limitation by statute is certainly possible and may be effective in protecting privacy against trivial intrusion while permitting the use of critical evidence.[8]

---

compel disclosure. Judges should not hesitate to require the disclosure where it appears to them to be necessary in order that the truth be known and justice be done. The Supreme Court cannot exercise such authority and discretion, nor can it repeal or amend the statute by judicial decree. If the spirit and purpose of the law is to be carried out, it must be at the superior court level."

The Sims case is noted in Note, Hearsay-Admissibility of Hospital Records, 41 N.C. L. Rev. 621 (1963).

[7]Jaffee v. Redmond, 518 U.S. 1, 116 S. Ct. 1923, 135 L. Ed. 2d 337 (1996), see discussion supra § 98.

[8]Some courts appear to take this approach even in the absence of stat-ute. *See* Bond v. District Court, In and For Denver County, 682 P.2d 33 (Colo. 1984) (though psychotherapist-patient privilege waived by bringing of suit, trial court erred in not considering patient's interests in ruling on protective order); Moss v. State, 925 So. 2d 1185 (La. 2006) (Louisiana health care provider-patient privilege interpreted as permitting balancing of interests before application of privilege); State v. Elwell, 132 N.H. 599, 567 A.2d 1002 (1989) (physician-patient privilege will yield where disclosure is "essential;" "This qualification serves the dual objectives of providing essential information while protecting the confidentiality of the relationship.").

# Chapter 12

# Privileges for Governmental Secrets

## § 106  Other principles distinguished

In discussing the evidentiary privileges and rules of exclusion regarding the production and admission of writings and information in the possession of government officers, other principles should be noted, which may hinder the litigant seeking facts from the government but which are beyond our present inquiry. Among these are: (a) questions of substantive privilege of government officers from liability for their acts and words,[1] (b) questions as to executive immunity from liability,[2] (c) issues regarding the

---

**[Section 106]**

[1]*See, e.g.,* Spalding v. Vilas, 161 U.S. 483, 16 S. Ct. 631, 40 L. Ed. 780 (1896) (exemption of Postmaster General from civil liability for official statement); Dobbs, Hayden & Bublick, The Law of Torts ch. 28 (2d ed. 2011) (discussing traditional immunities and liabilities of government entities, officers, and employees); Imwinkelried, The New Wigmore: Evidentiary Privileges § 1.3.3, at 36–43 (2d ed. 2010) (discussing legislators' immunity for

statements and acts, immunity for government employees for official conduct related to civil rights actions, and certain immunities for witnesses and prosecutors); 8 Wigmore, Evidence § 2368 (McNaughton rev. 1961).

[2]*See* Clinton v. Jones, 520 U.S. 681, 117 S. Ct. 1636, 137 L. Ed. 2d 945 (1997); Mitchell v. Forsyth, 472 U.S. 511, 105 S. Ct. 2806, 86 L. Ed. 2d 411 (1985); Nixon v. Fitzgerald, 457 U.S. 731, 102 S. Ct. 2690, 73 L. Ed. 2d 349 (1982); Harlow v. Fitzgerald, 457 U.S.

irremovability of official records,[3] (d) prohibition against suits based on certain types of information,[4] and (e) denial of information on basis of separation of powers.[5]

## § 107    The common law privileges for military or diplomatic secrets and other facts the disclosure of which would be contrary to the public interest[1]

As the activities of modern government have expanded, the need of litigants for the disclosure and proof of documents and other information in the possession of government officials has

---

800, 102 S. Ct. 2727, 73 L. Ed. 2d 396 (1982); Butz v. Economou, 438 U.S. 478, 98 S. Ct. 2894, 57 L. Ed. 2d 895 (1978); State of Mississippi v. Johnson, 71 U.S. 475, 18 L. Ed. 437, 1866 WL 9457 (1866); Halperin v. Kissinger, 807 F.2d 180 (D.C. Cir. 1986); Smith v. Nixon, 807 F.2d 197 (D.C. Cir. 1986); Ellsberg v. Mitchell, 807 F.2d 204 (D.C. Cir. 1986); Zweibon v. Mitchell, 720 F.2d 162 (D.C. Cir. 1983); Chemerinsky, Constitutional Law: Principles and Policies § 4.4 (4th ed. 2011); Imwinkelried, The New Wigmore: Evidentiary Privileges § 1.3.4, at 51–52 (2d ed. 2010) (discussing partial immunity from process for a sitting president).

[3]See, e.g., Dunham v. City of Chicago, 55 Ill. 357, 1870 WL 6429 (1870) (court will not order removal where certified copies will serve as well); 8 Wigmore, Evidence § 2373 (McNaughton rev. 1961).

[4]See Tenet v. Doe, 544 U.S. 1, 125 S. Ct. 1230, 161 L. Ed. 2d 82 (2005) (dismissing spy's law suit based on espionage agreements); Kash & Indrisano, In the Service of Secrets: The U.S. Supreme Court Revisits Totten, 39 J. Marshall L. Rev. 475 (2006).

[5]See Cheney v. U.S. Dist. Court for Dist. of Columbia, 542 U.S. 367, 383–85, 124 S. Ct. 2576, 159 L. Ed. 2d 459 (2004) (ruling that separation of powers arguments could be raised without first invoking executive privilege); Kitrosser, Secrecy and Separated Powers: Executive Privilege Revisited, 92 Iowa L. Rev. 489 (2007); Radsan, Second-Guessing the Spymasters with

a Judicial Role in Espionage Deals, 91 Iowa L. Rev. 1259 (2006).

**[Section 107]**

[1]Imwinkelried, The New Wigmore: Evidentiary Privileges ch. 8 (2d ed. 2010); 6 Moore's Federal Practice ¶ 26.52(2) (3d ed. 2012); 26 Wright & Graham, Federal Practice & Procedure: Evidence §§ 5663 to 5670, 5672, 5683, 5691 (1992); 2 Greenwald, et al., Testimonial Privileges §§ 9:14 to 9:17 (2012 ed.); 8 Wigmore, Evidence §§ 2378, 2379 (McNaughton rev. 1961); Askin, Secret Justice and the Adversary System, 18 Hastings Const. L. Q. 745 (1991); Cheh, Judicial Supervision of Executive Secrecy: Rethinking Freedom of Expression for Government Employees and the Public Right of Access to Government Information, 69 Cornell L. Rev. 690 (1984); Chesney, Legislative Reform of the State Secrets Privilege, 13 Roger Williams U. L. Rev. 443 (2008); Chesney, State Secrets and the Limits of National Security Litigation, 75 Geo. Wash. L. Rev. 1249 (2007); Cox, Executive Privilege, 122 U. Pa. L. Rev. 1383 (1974); Crook, From the Civil War to the War on Terror: The Evolution and Application of the State Secrets Privilege, 72 Alb. L. Rev. 57 (2008); Donohue, The Shadow of State Secrets, 159 U. Pa. L. Rev. 77 (2010); Fein, Access to Classified Information: Constitutional and Statutory Dimensions, 26 Wm. & Mary L. Rev. 805 (1985); Frost, The State Secrets Privilege and Separation of Powers, 75 Fordham L. Rev. 1931 (2007); Hansen, Extraordinary Renditions and the State Secrets Privilege: Keeping Focus on the Task at Hand,

correspondingly increased. When this need is asserted and opposed, the public interest in the secrecy of "classified" information comes into direct conflict with the public interest in the protection of the claim of the individual to due process of law in the redress of grievances.[2] The proper resolution of this conflict requires careful judicial scrutiny.

A privilege and a rule of exclusion has been recognized for writings and information constituting military or diplomatic secrets of state.[3] The justification for secrecy is obviously extremely strong when the material is vital to national security. In addition to military matters, the privilege has been extended to intelligence-gathering methods or capabilities and sensitive information concerning diplomatic relations with foreign governments.[4] The courts have declined, however, to extend the

---

33 N.C. J. Int'l L. & Com. Reg. 629 (2008); Iraola, Congressional Oversight, Executive Privilege, and Requests for Information Relating to Federal Criminal Investigations and Prosecutions, 87 Iowa L. Rev. 1559 (2002); Kinkopf, The State Secrets Problem: Can Congress Fix It?, 80 Temp. L. Rev. 489 (2007); Rozell, Executive Privilege Revived?: Secrecy and Conflict During the Bush Presidency, 52 Duke L.J. 403 (2002); Schwinn, The State Secrets Privilege in the Post-9/11 Era, 30 Pace L. Rev. 778 (2010); Telman, Intolerable Abuses: Rendition for Torture and the State Secrets Privilege, 63 Ala. L. Rev. 429 (2012); Telman, Our Very Privileged Executive: Why the Judiciary Can (and Should) Fix the State Secrets Privilege, 80 Temp. L. Rev. 499 (2007).

[2]"Besides, the public good is in nothing more essentially interested, than in the protection of every individual's private rights, as modeled by the municipal law." 1 Blackstone, Commentaries 139 (1765). *See also* Pound, Administrative Discretion and Civil Liberties in England, 56 Harv. L. Rev. 806, 814 (1943).

[3]Imwinkelried, The New Wigmore: Evidentiary Privileges § 8.2 (2d ed. 2010); 8 Wigmore, Evidence § 2378(2) (McNaughton rev. 1961). *See* Aaron Burr's Trial, Robertson's Rep. I,

121, 127, 186, 255, II, 536 (1807); 8 Wigmore, Evidence (3d ed. 1940) § 2379, p. 799. The subpoena duces tecum was issued by Chief Justice Marshall to President Jefferson to produce correspondence with General Wilkinson, over objection of government that it involved relations with France and Spain. Marshall wrote: "There is certainly nothing before the Court which shows that the letter in question contains any matter the disclosure of which would endanger the public safety; . . . if it does contain any matter which it would be imprudent to disclose, which it is not the wish of the Executive to disclose, such matter, if it be not immediately and essentially applicable to the point, will of course be suppressed."

[4]In re U.S., 872 F.2d 472, 476 (D.C. Cir. 1989). Examples of matters over which the privilege was affirmed or assumed: C.I.A. v. Sims, 471 U.S. 159, 105 S. Ct. 1881, 85 L. Ed. 2d 173 (1985) (seemingly innocuous information which, when combined with other information, poses a reasonable danger of "divulging too much to a sophisticated intelligence analyst"); U.S. v. Reynolds, 345 U.S. 1, 73 S. Ct. 528, 97 L. Ed. 727 (1953) (details of aircraft radar and recently developed electronics); Totten v. U.S., 92 U.S. 105, 23 L. Ed. 605, 1875 WL 17758 (1875) (spy services during Civil War under contract with President Lincoln); Kasza v.

privilege to matters that are not related to the national defense or international relations.[5]

The Supreme Court has ruled that the government as holder of the privilege[6] must assert it.[7] The government may assert the privilege in actions to which it is not a party.[8] Generally, private parties cannot claim the privilege.[9] When a claim of state secrets privilege would be appropriate but is not made due to oversight

---

Browner, 133 F.3d 1159 (9th Cir. 1998) (information related to the operating location of a military facility); Black v. U.S., 62 F.3d 1115 (8th Cir. 1995) (plaintiff's alleged contacts with government officers); Zuckerbraun v. General Dynamics Corp., 935 F.2d 544 (2d Cir. 1991) (radar system technology); Bowles v. U.S., 950 F.2d 154 (4th Cir. 1991) (documents on the purchase, insurance, and inspection of a government vehicle involved in a personal injury suit); In re Under Seal, 945 F.2d 1285 (4th Cir. 1991) (documents related to alleged collusion between defense contractors); Patterson by Patterson v. F.B.I., 893 F.2d 595 (3d Cir. 1990) (FBI file of a sixth-grader); Fitzgerald v. Penthouse Intern., Ltd., 776 F.2d 1236 (4th Cir. 1985) (information regarding the use of dolphins for military and intelligence purposes); Northrop Corp. v. McDonnell Douglas Corp., 751 F.2d 395 (D.C. Cir. 1984) (military contracts and military employee's job responsibilities); Salisbury v. U.S., 690 F.2d 966 (D.C. Cir. 1982) (material reflecting communications intercepted through electronic surveillance and relating to the national defense and international relations); Halkin v. Helms, 690 F.2d 977 (D.C. Cir. 1982) (information concerning interception of communications under CIA project); Farnsworth Cannon, Inc. v. Grimes, 635 F.2d 268 (4th Cir. 1980) (military related contracts); Clift v. U.S., 597 F.2d 826 (2d Cir. 1979) (contracts for cryptographic devices); Halkin v. Helms, 598 F.2d 1 (D.C. Cir. 1978) (information concerning whether international communications were intercepted and disseminated to other federal agencies); Machin v. Zuckert, 316 F.2d 336 (D.C. Cir. 1963) (conclusions based upon privileged informa-tion and reports reflecting military deliberations or recommendations as to policies to be pursued); Bentzlin v. Hughes Aircraft Co., 833 F. Supp. 1486 (C.D. Cal. 1993) (missile capabilities and aircraft tactics); Maxwell v. First Nat. Bank of Maryland, 143 F.R.D. 590 (D. Md. 1992) (information relating to an alleged covert relationship between a bank and the CIA); Nejad v. U.S., 724 F. Supp. 753 (C.D. Cal. 1989) (rules of engagement and military operational orders).

[5]King v. U. S., 112 F. 988 (C.C.A. 5th Cir. 1902) (conversations of government detectives with witnesses for the purpose of inducing and influencing the evidence of such witnesses not protected); In re Grand Jury Subpoena dated August 9, 2000, 218 F. Supp. 2d 544, 560–61 (S.D. N.Y. 2002) (ruling that privilege if otherwise applicable does not cover sovereign acts not implicating military or intelligence issues); Kinoy v. Mitchell, 67 F.R.D. 1 (S.D. N.Y. 1975) (domestic intelligence investigations which do not relate to the national defense or international relations not protected).

[6]U.S. v. Reynolds, 345 U.S. 1, 7, 73 S. Ct. 528, 97 L. Ed. 727 (1953); Deleted Fed. R. Evid. 509(a). However, this privilege may also be held by foreign governments in United States courts. See Kessler v. Best, 121 F. 439, 440 (C.C.S.D. N.Y. 1903).

[7]Reynolds, 345 U.S. at 7.

[8]In re U.S., 872 F.2d 472, 475 (D.C. Cir. 1989); Fitzgerald v. Penthouse Intern., Ltd., 776 F.2d 1236, 1241–43 (4th Cir. 1985).

[9]Reynolds, 345 U.S. at 7. But see 26 Wright & Graham, Federal Practice and Procedure: Evidence § 5670 (1992) (arguing that it does not follow from

or lack of knowledge, the court should assure that notice is given to the appropriate government officer.[10]

The Court has also held that the privilege cannot be waived by a private party.[11] However, when the government is prosecuting a criminal case, it may be forced to forego the privilege for documents essential to the litigation.[12] The fact that similar information has been disclosed earlier does not constitute waiver[13] or prevent the government from claiming the privilege in a later case.[14] However, if the prior disclosure of confidential information revealed the same specific information, then the privilege is waived.[15]

Congress has enacted two statutes that interact with and mirror the state secrets privilege: the national security exemption in

---

*Reynolds* or from the fact that only the holder can waive the privilege that only the holder of the privilege can claim it).

Some authority suggests that a private party may be able to claim the privilege when the information is protected by a statute or military regulation. *See* Clift v. U.S., 597 F.2d 826, 828–29 (2d Cir. 1979).

[10]*See* U.S. ex rel. Schwartz v. TRW, Inc., 211 F.R.D. 388, 392–94 (C.D. Cal. 2002) (giving government 60 days to claim apparently available state secret privilege); In re Westinghouse Elec. Corp. Uranium Contracts Litigation, 76 F.R.D. 47, 59 (W.D. Pa. 1977); Deleted Fed. R. Evid. 509(c). In the criminal context this has been codified in the Classified Information Procedures Act. 18 U.S.C.A. App. 3 § 5.

[11]Reynolds, 345 U.S. at 7.

[12]Reynolds, 345 U.S. at 12; U.S. v. Andolschek, 142 F.2d 503, 506 (C.C.A. 2d Cir. 1944).

[13]Students Against Genocide v. Department of State, 257 F.3d 828, 836–37 (D.C. Cir. 2001) (ruling in FOIA case that displaying a number of reconnaissance photographs did not waive privilege with respect to others in the series where CIA Director asserted national security claim); Salisbury v. U.S., 690 F.2d 966, 971 (D.C. Cir. 1982); Halkin v. Helms, 598

F.2d 1, 9 (D.C. Cir. 1978); National Lawyers Guild v. Attorney General, 96 F.R.D. 390, 402 (S.D. N.Y. 1982).

[14]Halkin, 598 F.2d at 9.

[15]Spock v. U.S., 464 F. Supp. 510, 520 (S.D. N.Y. 1978). However, the privilege is not waived by a disclosure which was compelled erroneously or made without opportunity to claim the privilege, Deleted Fed. R. Evid. 512; Unif. R. Evid. 511. Additionally, the privilege remains intact even if a criminal defendant had access to the information. The government interest protected includes disclosure to the general public. *See* U.S. v. Smith, 780 F.2d 1102, 1109 (4th Cir. 1985). The privilege also survives granting access to disputed documents to attorneys for defense contractors, see N.S.N. Intern. Industry v. E.I. Dupont de Nemours & Co., Inc., 140 F.R.D. 275, 279–81 (S.D. N.Y. 1991), and accidental disclosures, see Maxwell v. First Nat. Bank of Maryland, 143 F.R.D. 590, 597 (D. Md. 1992). *See also* Students Against Genocide, 257 F.3d at 837–38 (holding in FOIA case that displaying of some reconnaissance photographs by the Secretary of State to the UN Security Council did not waive privilege in that the photos were displayed rather than distributed and were shown only to a limited number of foreign governments).

the Freedom of Information Act (FOIA)[16] and the Classified Information Procedures Act (CIPA).[17]

Although the national security exemption of FOIA is similar to the state secrets privilege, it neither expands nor contracts existing privileges, nor does it create any new privileges.[18] Additionally, important differences exist between the privilege and the FOIA exemptions.[19]

Similarly, CIPA does not create a new evidentiary rule.[20] It recognizes a power in the executive branch to determine that public disclosure of classified information shall not be made in a crimi-

---

[16] 5 U.S.C.A. § 552(b)(1). This provision provides that FOIA does not apply to information that "(A) is specifically authorized under criteria established by an Executive order to be kept secret in the interest of national defense or foreign policy and (B) are in fact classified pursuant to such Executive order." See generally Greenwald, et al., Testimonial Privileges § 9:17 (2012 ed.); United States Dep't of Justice, Justice Dep't Guide to the Freedom of Information Act, available at http://www.justice.gov/oip/exemption1.htm (discussing exemption 1).

[17] 18 U.S.C.A. App. 3. See also Yaroshefsky, Secret Evidence is Slowly Eroding the Adversary System: CIPA and FISA in the Courts, 34 Hofstra L. Rev. 1063 (2006); Yaroshefsky, The Slow Erosion of the Adversary System: Article III Courts, FISA, CIPA and Ethical Dilemmas, 5 Cardozo Pub. L. Pol'y & Ethics J. 203 (2006).

[18] See John Doe Agency v. John Doe Corp., 493 U.S. 146, 153, 110 S. Ct. 471, 107 L. Ed. 2d 462 (1989); Chamber of Commerce of U.S. v. Legal Aid Soc. of Alameda County, 423 U.S. 1309, 1310–11, 96 S. Ct. 5, 46 L. Ed. 2d 14 (1975) (Douglas, Circuit Justice); Association for Women in Science v. Califano, 566 F.2d 339, 342 (D.C. Cir. 1977). However, the FOIA exemptions may be considered in construing other privileges. Rice v. Black, 112 F.R.D. 620, 630 (D. Neb. 1986).

[19] Halkin v. Helms, 690 F.2d 977, 996 (D.C. Cir. 1982). The D.C. Circuit noted that the claim of privilege is made by the highest officer of the executive department after careful consideration of the particular situation. As a result, "the risk of permitting relatively unaccountable 'invisible' bureaucratic decisions as to the national security value of information (specifically, the decisions to classify information which trigger the FOIA exemption) to bar disclosure on a wholesale basis is not presented in a state secrets case." Halkin, 690 F.2d at 996. Further, the privilege operates on a different premise than the FOIA exemption, being "rooted in the careful consideration by an executive officer in a policy making role, entirely different from those governing the routine classification of information by lesser officials." 690 F.2d at 996. Additionally, the state secrets privilege, unlike the FOIA exemption, applies regardless of whether the material has been formerly classified. 690 F.2d at 996.

[20] U.S. v. Smith, 780 F.2d 1102, 1106 (4th Cir. 1985); U.S. v. Collins, 720 F.2d 1195, 1199 (11th Cir. 1983). See also Salgado, Government Secrets, Fair Trials, and the Classified Information Procedures Act, 98 Yale L.J. 427, 433 (1988); H.R. Rep. No. 831, 96th Cong. 2d Sess., pt. 2 at 3 (1980). But cf. U.S. v. Aref, 533 F.3d 72, 78–79 (2d Cir. 2008) (while recognizing that CIPA creates no privilege, it presupposes a governmental privilege against disclosing classified information, which the court concluded was most likely the state secrets privilege).

nal trial[21] and outlines procedures to protect against the threat of disclosure or the unnecessary disclosure of classified information.[22] CIPA procedures are intended to address situations where a criminal defendant is already in possession of classified information; it does not provide for discovery of classified information.[23] CIPA applies to classified testimony as well as classified documents.[24] It requires a criminal defendant to give particularized notice of an intention to reveal classified information as part of the defense.[25] Upon receiving such notice, the government can seek a ruling that some or all of the information is immaterial, move for substitution of a non-sensitive summary for the information, or admit the facts sought to be proven and thereby eliminate the need for disclosure.[26] Where a determination of privilege prevents the defendant from disclosing classified information, the court may dismiss charges or provide the defendant appropriate lesser relief.[27]

Wigmore seems to regard it as doubtful whether the denial of disclosure should go further than this,[28] but some state statutes

---

[21]18 U.S.C.A. App. 3 § 6(e)(1). The circuit courts disagree on whether the head of the department must assert the privilege. *Compare* Aref, 533 F.3d at 80 (requiring privilege to be asserted by the head of the department as mandated by *Reynolds*), *with* U.S. v. El-Mezain, 664 F.3d 467, 521–22 (5th Cir. 2011), cert. denied, 133 S. Ct. 525, 184 L. Ed. 2d 338 (2012) and cert. denied, 133 S. Ct. 525 (2012) (concluding that the absence of a requirement in CIPA that the Attorney General act indicates asserting privilege need not be made by the head of the department); U.S. v. Rosen, 557 F.3d 192, 198 (4th Cir. 2009) (concluding that agency head did not need to invoke privilege in criminal matters under CIPA).

[22]*See* El-Mezain, 664 F.3d at 521–22 (fashioning test for disclosure influenced by *Reynolds* and Roviaro v. U.S., 353 U.S. 53, 77 S. Ct. 623, 1 L. Ed. 2d 639 (1957), which concerned the informer privilege); Aref, 533 F.3d at 79–80 (utilizing the *Roviaro* standard to determine when the government's claim of privilege must give way); U.S. v. Yunis, 867 F.2d 617, 623–24 (D.C. Cir. 1989) (utilizing

*Roviaro* to establish test for disclosure); U.S. v. Hanjuan Jin, 791 F. Supp. 2d 612, 618–20 (N.D. Ill. 2011) (developing standards for granting protective order). *See also* 2 Greenwald, et al., Testimonial Privileges § 9:16 (2012 ed.).

[23]U.S. v. Pringle, 751 F.2d 419, 427 (1st Cir. 1984); U.S. v. LaRouche Campaign, 695 F. Supp. 1290, 1316 (D. Mass. 1988).

[24]U.S. v. North, 708 F. Supp. 399, 400 (D.D.C. 1988).

[25]U.S. v. Collins, 720 F.2d 1195, 1199 (11th Cir. 1983).

[26]Collins, 720 F.2d at 1197. *See also* Aref, 533 F.3d at 80 (affirming district court's determination to deny discovery and issue a protective order because the information was not helpful to the defense).

[27]18 U.S.C.A. App. 3 § 6(e)(2). *See* U.S. v. Moussaoui, 382 F.3d 453, 471–82 (4th Cir. 2004) (finding dismissal not appropriate sanction for government refusal to produce enemy combatant witness where substitutes for testimony were adequate).

[28]*See* 8 Wigmore, Evidence § 2378, at 796 n.7 (McNaughton rev.

occasionally describe the privilege in broader terms,[29] and the English decisions seem to have accepted the wide generalization that official documents and facts will be privileged whenever their disclosure would be injurious to the public interest.[30] Whether this wider principle is justified in point of policy is open to serious question.

## § 108   Qualified privileges for government information: The constitutional presidential privilege; common law privileges for agency deliberations and law enforcement files

The case of *United States v. Nixon*[1] brought into sharp focus both the limits of the long-standing executive privilege protecting diplomatic and military secrets and the distinguishable question as to whether some broader privilege protects confidential communications between the President and his immediate advisors. In *Nixon*, the Supreme Court recognized a constitutionally based privilege of this nature but held it to be qualified and subject to invasion upon a showing of demonstrable need for evidence relevant to a criminal proceeding.[2] The presidential privilege has occasioned considerable discussion by constitutional scholars,[3] and

---

1961).

[29]*See* Cal. Evid. Code § 1040 (providing a privilege against disclosure of official information that "is against the public interest because there is a necessity for preserving the confidentiality of the information that outweighs the necessity for disclosure in the interest of justice"); 8 Wigmore, Evidence § 2378, at 799 n.9 (McNaughton rev. 1961) (giving other statutes). The Uniform Rules of Evidence (2005) contain no provision of this nature.

[30]The opinion of Viscount Simon, L.Ch., for the House of Lords in Duncan v. Cammell, Laird & Co., (1942) A.C. 624, accepts this principle and reviews the supporting precedents.

**[Section 108]**

[1]U.S. v. Nixon, 418 U.S. 683, 94 S. Ct. 3090, 41 L. Ed. 2d 1039 (1974).

[2]In the aftermath of *Nixon*, some refinement and clarification of the privilege has taken place. *See generally* Nixon v. Administrator of General

Services, 433 U.S. 425, 97 S. Ct. 2777, 53 L. Ed. 2d 867 (1977); In re Sealed Case, 121 F.3d 729 (D.C. Cir. 1997); U.S. v. North, 910 F.2d 843 (D.C. Cir. 1990); Dellums v. Powell, 561 F.2d 242 (D.C. Cir. 1977); Senate Select Committee on Presidential Campaign Activities v. Nixon, 498 F.2d 725 (D.C. Cir. 1974) (en banc); U.S. v. Poindexter, 727 F. Supp. 1501 (D.D.C. 1989).

[3]Berger, Executive Privilege: A Constitutional Myth (1974); Chemerinsky, Constitutional Law: Principles and Policies § 4.3 (4th ed. 2011); Cox, Executive Privilege, 122 U. Pa. L. Rev. 1383 (1974); Dorsen & Shattuck, Executive Privilege, the Congress and the Courts, 35 Ohio St. L.J. 1 (1974); Freund, On Presidential Privilege, 88 Harv. L. Rev. 13 (1974); Kitrosser, Secrecy and Separated Powers: Executive Privilege Revisited, 92 Iowa L. Rev. 489 (2007); Lee, The President's Secrets, 76 Geo. Wash. L. Rev. 197 (2008); Miller, Congressional Inquests: Suffocating the Constitutional Prerogative of Executive Privilege, 81 Minn. L. Rev. 631 (1997); Nathanson, From

although of great importance when invoked, it is only occasionally encountered.

Of much greater everyday significance is the enormous quantity of information produced, collected, and compiled by the governmental agencies. Only an extremely small percentage of this governmental information will fall within the previously discussed privilege protecting military and diplomatic secrets.[4] What then of the vast remainder?

Although not within any well-defined evidentiary privilege, securing information from this great store of information was often extremely difficult or impossible. Before amended in 1958, the Federal Housekeeping Act[5] was assumed by administrators to authorize the issuance of regulations requiring governmental personnel in the actual possession of governmental documents and records to decline to produce them even when served with a subpoena issued by a court. These regulations were consistently upheld by the Supreme Court,[6] and although the cases never

---

Watergate to Marbury v. Madison: Some Reflections on Presidential Privilege in Current Historical Perspective, 16 Ariz. L. Rev. 59 (1974); Rozell, Executive Privilege: The Dilemma of Secrecy and Democratic Accountability (1994); Shane, Legal Disagreement and Negotiation in a Government of Laws: The Case of Executive Privilege Claims Against Congress, 71 Minn. L. Rev. 461 (1987); Symposium, United States v. Nixon: Presidential Power and Executive Privilege Twenty-Five Years Later, 83 Minn. L. Rev. 1061 (1999). Regarding issues during the Clinton administration, see Symposium: Executive Privilege and the Clinton Presidency, 8 Wm. & Mary Bill Rts. J. 535 (2000); Miller, Presidential Sanctuaries after the Clinton Sex Scandals, 22 Harv. J. L. & Pub. Pol'y 647 (1999); Turley, Paradise Lost: The Clinton Administration and the Erosion of Executive Privilege, 60 Md. L. Rev. 205 (2001).

[4]*See* Comment, Executive Privilege at the State Level, 1974 U. Ill. L.F. 631 (pointing out that exclusive federal responsibility for war and foreign relations makes military and diplomatic secrets privilege inapplicable to state context). Other qualified governmental privileges, however,

may apply. *See* discussion infra sections (a) and (b).

[5]5 U.S.C.A. § 822, R.S. § 161 (1875) provided as follows: "The head of each department is authorized to prescribe regulations, not inconsistent with law, for the government of his department, the conduct of its officers and clerks, the distribution and performance of its business, and the custody, use, and preservation of the records, papers, and property appertaining to it."

[6]U.S. ex rel. Touhy v. Ragen, 340 U.S. 462, 71 S. Ct. 416, 95 L. Ed. 417 (1951) (similar regulations of Attorney General approved, following above decision, in its application to subordinate officers; "When one considers the variety of information contained in the files of any government department and the possibilities of harm from unrestricted disclosure in court, the usefulness, indeed the necessity, of centralizing determination as to whether subpoenas duces tecum will be willingly obeyed or challenged is obvious."); Boske v. Comingore, 177 U.S. 459, 20 S. Ct. 701, 44 L. Ed. 846 (1900) (statute conferring rulemaking power on heads of departments valid under the "necessary and proper" clause and Treasury regulation prohib-

went so far as to hold that the Act created a statutory privilege, the practical effect was that private litigants were unable to obtain the information. The 1958 amendment to the Act included a provision removing any possible implication that it was intended to create a statutory privilege,[7] and this intent has been followed in subsequent court decisions.[8]

Access to governmental information was even more substantially increased with the enactment by Congress[9] and many state legislatures of freedom of information legislation. While these statutes are directed toward availability of information for the public in general and the news media in particular, they have importance in clearing the way for discovery in litigation. To proceed under the federal Freedom of Information Act, no standing or particularized need for the desired information is required, and any person is eligible to proceed under the provisions of the statute. For present purposes, however, the important question is the extent to which FOIA affects the question of evidentiary privilege for governmental information.

At the time of the enactment of the original federal FOIA in 1966, there was clearly some protection extended by the courts to sensitive government information which did not constitute a military or diplomatic secret. Thus, a qualified common law privilege protected some aspects of government agency policy delibera-

---

iting production of records by collector of internal revenue valid; collector punished for contempt by state court for nonproduction discharged on habeas corpus).

[7] Pub. L. No. 85-619, 72 Stat. 547 (1958). The Act in its present form reads:

The head of an Executive department or military department may prescribe regulations for the government of his department, the conduct of its employees, the distribution and performance of its business, and the custody, use, and preservation of its records, papers, and property. This section does not authorize withholding information from the public or limiting the availability of records to the public.

5 U.S.C.A. § 301.

[8] Sperandeo for and on Behalf of N. L. R. B. v. Milk Drivers and Dairy Emp. Local Union No. 537, 334 F.2d 381 (10th Cir. 1964); Olson Rug Company v. N.L.R.B., 291 F.2d 655

(7th Cir. 1961); Rosee v. Board of Trade of City of Chicago, 35 F.R.D. 512 (N.D. Ill. 1964) (reports of commodity transactions held not privileged from disclosure under Commodity Exchange Act authorizing the Secretary of Agriculture to make investigations and to "publish from time to time, in his discretion, the result of such investigation and such statistical information gathered therefrom as he may deem of interest to the public, except data and information which would separately disclose the business transactions of any person and trade secrets or names of customers . . . ." The Court pointed out that where Congress has intended to prohibit the use of government-held data in judicial proceedings it has not talked in terms of "publish" or "publication" but has expressed the prohibition explicitly, citing examples of such statutes).

[9] 5 U.S.C.A. § 552.

tions,[10] and another, less clearly defined privilege shielded agency investigative files.[11] In enacting FOIA, Congress recognized the desirability of maintaining some degree of confidentiality in these areas and included them within the exemption provisions of the act.[12]

FOIA itself does not address the question of evidentiary admissibility,[13] and thus cannot be said to be a statutory enactment of the privileges in question.[14] At the same time, it is obvious that the two are critically interrelated and that the exemption provisions mark the outermost limits of the privileges.[15] It would be anomalous in the extreme to deny evidentiary admission on

---

[10]Environmental Protection Agency v. Mink, 410 U.S. 73, 86, 93 S. Ct. 827, 35 L. Ed. 2d 119 (1973) ("[T]he legislative history of Exemption 5 demonstrates that Congress intended to incorporate generally the recognized rule that 'confidential intra-agency advisory opinions . . . are privileged from inspection,' " quoting Kaiser Aluminum & Chemical Corp. v. U.S., 141 Ct. Cl. 38, 157 F. Supp. 939 (1958)). A distinct deliberative process privilege probably originated in Morgan v. U.S., 304 U.S. 1, 58 S. Ct. 773, 82 L. Ed. 1129 (1938). *See* Weaver & Jones, The Deliberative Process Privilege, 54 Mo. L. Rev. 279 (1989).

[11]*See* 8 Wigmore, Evidence 2378 (McNaughton rev. 1961) (citing cases privileging investigative files, but treating privilege as merged with that protecting deliberative processes); Imwinkelried, The New Wigmore: Evidentiary Privileges § 7.4.2, at 1294 (2d ed. 2010) (noting that both Congress and lower federal courts have been reluctant to recognize a formal investigatory privilege). The congeries of rationale today asserted to underlie a privilege for investigative files seem never to have coalesced in a single authority prior to the enactment of FOIA. Not surprisingly, protection of the flow of information to government was the dominant theme. *See* Machin v. Zuckert, 316 F.2d 336, 339 (D.C. Cir. 1963) ("We agree with the Government that when disclosure of investigative reports obtained in large part through promises of confidentiality would hamper the efficient operation

of an important Government program" the reports should be privileged.). The preexistence of the privilege is discussed, and apparently assumed, in Cooney v. Sun Shipbuilding & Drydock Co., 288 F. Supp. 708 (E.D. Pa. 1968).

[12]5 U.S.C.A. § 552(b)(5) & (7).

[13]N. L. R. B. v. Sears, Roebuck & Co., 421 U.S. 132, 143, 95 S. Ct. 1504, 44 L. Ed. 2d 29 (1975) (stating that FOIA "is fundamentally designed to inform the public about agency action and not to benefit private litigants").

[14]John Doe Agency v. John Doe Corp., 493 U.S. 146, 153, 110 S. Ct. 471, 107 L. Ed. 2d 462 (1989) ("The FOIA was not intended to supplement or displace the rules of discovery."); Association for Women in Science v. Califano, 566 F.2d 339, 342 (D.C. Cir. 1977) ("FOIA neither expands nor contracts existing privileges, nor does it create any new privileges"); Forest Products Northwest, Inc. v. U.S., 62 Fed. Cl. 109, 113–14 (2004), aff'd, 453 F.3d 1355 (Fed. Cir. 2006) (refusing to treat failure to meet FOIA exemption as basis for private party's assertion of privilege). The privileges may, of course, be recognized without FOIA. *See* McClain v. College Hosp., 99 N.J. 346, 492 A.2d 991 (1985) (recognizing the two privileges here discussed in absence of comprehensive state FOIA).

[15]*See generally* United States Dep't of Justice, Freedom of Information Act Guide, May 2004, available at http://www.justice.gov/oip/exemption 5.htm (discussing exemption 5).

grounds of confidentiality to material available on request to even the casually interested.[16] However, the converse is not necessarily true, and the evidentiary privileges may reasonably protect *less* than the total sum of information denied the general public under the FOIA exceptions. Such a differentiation is justifiable on the ground that the litigant's interest in access to evidence will sometimes be stronger than the ordinary citizen's interest in obtaining information.[17] Accordingly, not all information exempt from disclosure under the FOIA exceptions will necessarily be protected by privilege if sought by discovery processes for purposes of litigation.[18] As the foregoing synopsis suggests, the numerous decisions construing FOIA's exception provisions will be of varying precedential value concerning the scope of the privileges discussed below.

*(A) The Deliberative Process Privilege.*[19]

This privilege protects communications made between governmental personnel, or between governmental personnel and outside consultants, which consist of advisory opinions and recommendations preliminary to the formulation of agency

---

[16]N. L. R. B. v. Sears, Roebuck & Co., 421 U.S. 132, 95 S. Ct. 1504, 44 L. Ed. 2d 29 (1975) ("Exemption 5 withholds from a member of the public documents which a private party could not discover in litigation with the agency."); U.S. v. Weber Aircraft Corp., 465 U.S. 792, 801, 104 S. Ct. 1488, 79 L. Ed. 2d 814 (1984) ("[R]espondents' contention that they can obtain through the FOIA material that is normally privileged would create an anomaly in the FOIA . . . ."). *See also* Rothstein & Crump, Federal Testimonial Privilege § 5:1, at 390 (2d ed. 2011) (noting that FOIA sets a floor for the claim of executive privilege).

[17]"The problems of what a citizen should be able to get from a Government agency when he has simply the general interest of the citizen in finding out what is going on and the problems of the litigant who has a particular need are obviously very different and almost by hypothesis what is the right solution for the first cannot be the right solution for the second." Hearings on Proposed Federal Rules of Evidence, Subcommittee on Reform of Federal Criminal Laws of the H. Comm. on the Judiciary, 93rd Congress

274 (1973) (statement of Friendly, J.).

Proposed Fed. R. Evid. 509(a)(2) would have created at least qualified evidentiary privilege for matter covered by any of the FOIA exceptions.

[18]N. L. R. B. v. Sears, Roebuck & Co., 421 U.S. 132, 95 S. Ct. 1504, 44 L. Ed. 2d 29 (1975); Maclay v. Jones, 208 W. Va. 569, 542 S.E.2d 83, 88–89 (2000) (concluding that state FOIA provisions regarding law enforcement investigatory material do not control the scope of civil discovery but rather address confidentiality as to the public generally).

[19]*See generally* Greenwald, et al., Testimonial Privileges §§ 9:8 to 9:13 (2012 ed.); Berger, The Incarnation of Executive Privilege, 22 UCLA L. Rev. 4 (1974); Cox, Executive Privilege, 122 U. Pa. L. Rev. 1383 (1974); Weaver & Jones, The Deliberative Process Privilege, 54 Mo. L. Rev. 279 (1989); Wetlaufer, Justifying Secrecy: An Objection to the General Deliberative Privilege, 65 Ind. L.J. 845 (1990). Sometimes this privilege is called the "agency policy deliberations privilege," the "official information privilege," or simply "executive privilege."

policy.[20] Like other communications privileges, that protecting governmental agency deliberations seeks to encourage a free flow of communication in the interest of some larger end—here, establishing agency policy only after consideration of the full array of contrasting views on the subject.[21] As with other privileges, the assumption is that total candor will be enhanced, and the quality of governmental decision-making correspondingly improved, by an assurance of at least qualified confidentiality. Also, this privilege is justified by its avoidance of premature and potentially misleading public disclosure of possible agency action and by helping to assure that governmental decision-makers will be judged solely upon the quality of their decisions without regard to the quality of other options considered and discarded.[22]

To come within the rationale of the privilege, the matter sought to be kept confidential must have been communicated prior to finalization of the policy,[23] and must have constituted opinion or

---

[20]Formaldehyde Institute v. Department of Health and Human Services, 889 F.2d 1118 (D.C. Cir. 1989); CNA Financial Corp. v. Donovan, 830 F.2d 1132 (D.C. Cir. 1987); Daily Gazette Co., Inc. v. West Virginia Development Office, 198 W. Va. 563, 482 S.E.2d 180, 189 (1996). Department of Interior v. Klamath Water Users Protective Ass'n, 532 U.S. 1, 121 S. Ct. 1060, 149 L. Ed. 2d 87 (2001), the Supreme Court noted, but declined to rule on, the view of some courts of appeal that the FOIA exemption applies to communications by consultants as intra-agency memoranda when the consultant functions much as an employee of the agency might. Klamath, 532 U.S. at 9–12. Because the communications at issue were made by an Indian tribe with its own interest in mind, rather than by uninterested consultants, the exemption clearly did not apply. 532 U.S. at 12–13.

[21]N. L. R. B. v. Sears, Roebuck & Co., 421 U.S. 132, 150–51, 95 S. Ct. 1504, 44 L. Ed. 2d 29 (1975); McKinley v. Board of Governors of Federal Reserve System, 647 F.3d 331, 340 (D.C. Cir. 2011), cert. denied, 132 S. Ct. 1026, 181 L. Ed. 2d 738 (2012) (ruling that Board had sufficiently demonstrated that disclosure of the withheld

material would discourage candid internal discussion and undermine policy development and also made a specific showing disclosure would harm the decision-making process); State of Mo. ex rel. Shorr v. U.S. Army Corps of Engineers, 147 F.3d 708, 710 (8th Cir. 1998); Assembly of State of Cal. v. U.S. Dept. of Commerce, 968 F.2d 916, 920 (9th Cir. 1992); In re Franklin Nat. Bank Securities Litigation, 478 F. Supp. 577 (E.D. N.Y. 1979).

[22]City of Virginia Beach, Va. v. U.S. Dept. of Commerce, 995 F.2d 1247, 1252–53 (4th Cir. 1993); Jordan v. U.S. Dept. of Justice, 591 F.2d 753 (D.C. Cir. 1978) (en banc); Cook v. Watt, 597 F. Supp. 545 (D. Alaska 1983).

[23]Hongsermeier v. C.I.R., 621 F.3d 890, 904 (9th Cir. 2010), cert. denied, 131 S. Ct. 1604, 179 L. Ed. 2d 500 (2011) and cert. denied, 131 S. Ct. 2887, 179 L. Ed. 2d 1190 (2011) (ruling that the material must be both pre-decisional and deliberative); U.S. v. Fernandez, 231 F.3d 1240, 1246–47 (9th Cir. 2000) (shielding pre-decisional death penalty evaluation form containing recommendations); State of Mo. ex rel. Shorr v. U.S. Army Corps of Engineers, 147 F.3d 708, 710 (8th Cir. 1998); Tax Analysts v. I.R.S.,

evaluation as opposed to the mere reporting of objective facts.[24] However, factual information that reflects or reveals the deliberative processes of the agency is protected by the privilege.[25]

---

117 F.3d 607, 616 (D.C. Cir. 1997); Maricopa Audubon Soc. v. U.S. Forest Service, 108 F.3d 1089, 1093 (9th Cir. 1997); Redland Soccer Club, Inc. v. Department of Army of U.S., 55 F.3d 827, 854 (3d Cir. 1995); Ethyl Corp. v. U.S. E.P.A., 25 F.3d 1241, 1248 (4th Cir. 1994); U.S. v. Farley, 11 F.3d 1385, 1389 (7th Cir. 1993); Town of Norfolk v. U.S. Army Corps of Engineers, 968 F.2d 1438, 1458 (1st Cir. 1992); Hopkins v. U.S. Dept. of Housing and Urban Development, 929 F.2d 81, 84 (2d Cir. 1991); Florida House of Representatives v. U.S. Dept. of Commerce, 961 F.2d 941, 945 (11th Cir. 1992). Some courts have ruled that documents created after the decision date can still qualify as predecisional when they recount predecisional deliberations, see Ford Motor Co. v. U.S., 94 Fed. Cl. 211, 223 (2010); reflect continuing examination of an existing policy, see S.E.C. v. Nacchio, 704 F. Supp. 2d 1099, 1110–11 (D. Colo. 2010); or relate a decision to future decisions regarding application of the policy, see Citizens Against Casino Gambling In Erie County v. Stevens, 814 F. Supp. 2d 261, 269–70 (W.D. N.Y. 2011).

Courts have also extended protection of the privilege to situations not generally deliberative, but that are in particular instances a part of the decision-making process. *See* Dow Jones & Co., Inc. v. Department of Justice, 917 F.2d 571, 575 (D.C. Cir. 1990) (documents created by non-agency personnel); North Dartmouth Properties, Inc. v. U.S. Dept. of Housing and Urban Development, 984 F. Supp. 65, 70 (D. Mass. 1997) (communications from superior to subordinate); Lurie v. Department of Army, 970 F. Supp. 19, 34 (D.D.C. 1997) (witness statements); Capital Information Group v. State, Office of Governor, 923 P.2d 29, 37–38 (Alaska 1996) (one-way communications).

[24]*See* Environmental Protection Agency v. Mink, 410 U.S. 73, 87–88, 93 S. Ct. 827, 35 L. Ed. 2d 119 (1973); Grand Cent. Partnership, Inc. v. Cuomo, 166 F.3d 473, 481 (2d Cir. 1999); Redland Soccer Club, Inc. v. Department of Army of U.S., 55 F.3d 827, 854 (3d Cir. 1995); City of Virginia Beach, Va. v. U.S. Dept. of Commerce, 995 F.2d 1247, 1253 (4th Cir. 1993); Town of Norfolk v. U.S. Army Corps of Engineers, 968 F.2d 1438, 1458 (1st Cir. 1992); Skelton v. U.S. Postal Service, 678 F.2d 35, 38 (5th Cir. 1982); Playboy Enterprises, Inc. v. Department of Justice, 677 F.2d 931, 935 (D.C. Cir. 1982); E.B. v. New York City Bd. of Educ., 233 F.R.D. 289, 292–93 (E.D. N.Y. 2005) (excluding information from the privilege that involved routine operating decisions and did not relate to policy formulation); Allocco Recycling, Ltd. v. Doherty, 220 F.R.D. 407, 412–13 (S.D. N.Y. 2004).

[25]U.S. v. Fernandez, 231 F.3d 1240, 1247 (9th Cir. 2000) (protecting factual material so interwoven with deliberative material as not to be severable); Mapother v. Department of Justice, 3 F.3d 1533, 1537–39 (D.C. Cir. 1993); Petroleum Information Corp. v. U.S. Dept. of Interior, 976 F.2d 1429, 1434–35 (D.C. Cir. 1992); U.S. Dep't of Commerce, 995 F.2d at 1254; Assembly of State of Cal. v. U.S. Dept. of Commerce, 968 F.2d 916, 921 (9th Cir. 1992); National Wildlife Federation v. U.S. Forest Service, 861 F.2d 1114, 1117–19 (9th Cir. 1988); Florida House of Representatives, 961 F.2d at 950; Chisler v. Johnston, 796 F. Supp. 2d 632, 640–42 (W.D. Pa. 2011) (ruling that factual information within investigative document is not protected by privilege and must be produced); Loving v. U.S. Dept. of Defense, 496 F. Supp. 2d 101, 109–10 (D.D.C. 2007), aff'd, 550 F.3d 32 (D.C. Cir. 2008) (noting that unlike the presidential communication privilege, the

Whether the communication reflected the view that ultimately became embodied in agency policy, or even whether the communication was considered or totally ignored by the decisionmaker is immaterial.[26] Also, the government is not required to identify a particular decision to which the communication contributed as long as the deliberative process involved and the role played by the communication are identified.[27] The privilege, which must be claimed by the agency head, or in most circuits some carefully delegated subordinate,[28] is that of the govern-

---

deliberative process privilege does not apply to purely factual portions of a document that can be segregated from the opinions it contains, but denying disclosure because all reasonably segregable factual information had been provided).

[26]Lead Industries Ass'n, Inc. v. Occupational Safety and Health Administration, 610 F.2d 70 (2d Cir. 1979); Citizens for Responsibility and Ethics in Washington v. Office of Admin., 249 F.R.D. 1, 7–8 (D.D.C. 2008) (ruling that mere reliance on a document's conclusions does not constitute adoption of the document's analysis as agency policy and therefore did not destroy its privileged status); California Native Plant Society v. U.S. E.P.A., 251 F.R.D. 408, 411–12 (N.D. Cal. 2008) (observing that privilege does not require final action to adopt a policy, only that the communications were part of a decision-making process). However, if the communication is expressly adopted or incorporated by reference in the decision, the communication may lose protected status. *See* Florida House of Representatives, 961 F.2d at 945 n.4; North Dartmouth Properties, Inc. v. U.S. Dept. of Housing and Urban Development, 984 F. Supp. 65, 69 (D. Mass. 1997); Weaver & Jones, The Deliberative Process Privilege, 54 Mo. L. Rev. 279, 294 (1989).

[27]Access Reports v. Department of Justice, 926 F.2d 1192, 1196 (D.C. Cir. 1991); U.S. Dep't of Commerce, 995 F.2d at 1255; Hunt v. U.S. Marine Corps, 935 F. Supp. 46, 51 (D.D.C. 1996); Manna v. U.S. Dept. of Justice, 815 F. Supp. 798, 815 (D.N.J. 1993).

*Cf.* Moye, O'Brien, O'Rourke, Hogan, & Pickert v. National R.R. Passenger Corp., 376 F.3d 1270, 1280 (11th Cir. 2004) (ruling that as to deliberative process exemption to FOIA, agency need not show the specific policy decision to which material related); California Native Plant Society v. U.S. E.P.A., 251 F.R.D. 408, 412–14 (N.D. Cal. 2008) (requiring that the agency provide sufficiently detailed information to demonstrate generally how the document fit into the deliberative process, finding conclusory statements in initial submission inadequate, and requiring further specification).

[28]Marriott Intern. Resorts, L.P. v. U.S., 437 F.3d 1302, 1306–08 (Fed. Cir. 2006) (describing the reasons why with the absolute state secrets privilege the agency head must claim the privilege, but adopting the "majority" position that authority can be delegated as to the deliberative process privilege described in Landry v. F.D.I.C., 204 F.3d 1125, 1134–36 (D.C. Cir. 2000); Pacific Gas & Elec. Co. v. U.S., 70 Fed. Cl. 128, 137–38 (2006) (refusing to recognize the privilege, inter alia, because delegation of authority inadequate in that it was extremely broad in scope and provided little, if any, criteria for invoking the privilege); In re Methyl Tertiary Butyl Ether (MTBE) Products Liability Litigation, 643 F. Supp. 2d 439, 443 (S.D. N.Y. 2009) (ruling that attorney for agency could not invoke privilege and neither could high-level official without delegation from head of agency under official guidelines).

ment,[29] and apparently may be claimed indefinitely. It is not terminated by the adoption of the policy concerned and likely not by the death of the author of the privileged matter.[30] As further discussed below, the privilege is not absolute and is therefore subject to invasion upon a sufficient showing of necessity.[31] The privilege also does not protect communications which demonstrate government misconduct,[32] which are themselves the subject of the litigation,[33] or which become the formally adopted policy.[34]

---

[29]First Eastern Corp. v. Mainwaring, 21 F.3d 465, 474 (D.C. Cir. 1994). The privilege may also be claimed by foreign governments in United States courts. *See* LNC Investments, Inc. v. Republic of Nicaragua, 1997 WL 729106 (S.D. N.Y. 1997).

[30]Fisher v. Renegotiation Bd., 473 F.2d 109, 115 (D.C. Cir. 1972); Manna, 815 F. Supp. at 815; Kaiser Aluminum & Chemical Corp. v. U.S., 141 Ct. Cl. 38, 157 F. Supp. 939 (1958); Capital Information Group v. State, Office of Governor, 923 P.2d 29, 36 (Alaska 1996).

[31]Redland Soccer Club, Inc. v. Department of Army of U.S., 55 F.3d 827, 854 (3d Cir. 1995); Texaco Puerto Rico, Inc. v. Department of Consumer Affairs, 60 F.3d 867, 885 (1st Cir. 1995); May v. Department of Air Force, 777 F.2d 1012 (5th Cir. 1985); In re Pharmaceutical Industry Average Wholesale Price Litigation, 254 F.R.D. 35, 40–43 (D. Mass. 2008) (concluding that as to some documents sufficient necessity had been shown to overcome deliberative process privilege where those documents were relevant to proving knowledge which was an element of false claims act litigation). Timeliness of the claim may also be relevant to upholding the privilege. *See* Sikorsky Aircraft Corp. v. U.S., 106 Fed. Cl. 571, 584–86 (2012) (applying the rationale of Federal Rule 502 to find privilege waived).

[32]Texaco Puerto Rico, 60 F.3d at 885; Tri-State Hosp. Supply Corp. v. U.S., 226 F.R.D. 118, 134–36 (D.D.C. 2005); In re Grand Jury Subpoena dated August 9, 2000, 218 F. Supp. 2d 544, 561 (S.D. N.Y. 2002).

[33]In re Subpoena Duces Tecum Served on Office of Comptroller of Currency, 145 F.3d 1422, 1424 (D.C. Cir. 1998); New York v. Salazar, 701 F. Supp. 2d 224, 237–38 (N.D. N.Y. 2010), aff'd, 2011 WL 1938232 (N.D. N.Y. 2011) (ruling privilege cannot bar discovery where central theme of claims is that the deliberative process itself was infected by arbitrary conduct); Qamhiyah v. Iowa State University of Science and Technology, 245 F.R.D. 393, 397 (S.D. Iowa 2007) (denying privilege because the suit for unlawful discrimination put into issue the government's intent in making the decision resulting from the deliberative process); Jones v. City of College Park, Ga., 237 F.R.D. 517, 520–21 (N.D. Ga. 2006) (ruling that deliberative process privilege is inapplicable when government misconduct is the focus of the lawsuit as it is in a suit alleging racial discrimination in decision not to renew plaintiff's employment); Anderson v. Marion County Sheriff's Dept., 220 F.R.D. 555, 561 (S.D. Ind. 2004) (deliberative process involved in alleged employment discrimination that was subject of the suit not protected); Scott v. Board of Educ. of City of East Orange, 219 F.R.D. 333, 337 (D.N.J. 2004) (ruling privilege did not protect deliberations in civil rights suit where deliberative process itself is genuinely in dispute). In In re Delphi Corp., 276 F.R.D. 81, 85 (S.D. N.Y. 2011), the court took a slightly different view, concluding that, rather than creating an exception when the agency motivation is challenged, a balancing test is still involved under which the need for the deliberative documents will generally

The question of privilege for government agency deliberations has arisen relatively infrequently in the context of state government.[35] Many of the states enacting FOIA statutes have included exemption provisions protecting policy development materials from mandatory disclosure.[36] Where the question of a true evidentiary privilege has arisen, i.e., where the material is sought for introduction into evidence rather than simply as information, a majority of the cases have upheld the existence of a qualified privilege on the federal model.[37] The root of the privilege on the state level has almost invariably been said to be the doctrine of separation of powers.[38]

(B) *The Privilege for Information and Files Relating to Law Enforcement.*

Prior to the enactment of the federal FOIA and its state counterparts, a privilege protecting the investigative results of government agencies appears to have been sporadically recognized but ill-defined,[39] frequently being treated as an aspect of a more comprehensive but amorphous privilege for "government information."[40] Clearly, however, disclosure of the files of law

---

outweigh the governmental interest.

[34]*See, e.g.*, National Council of La Raza v. Department of Justice, 339 F. Supp. 2d 572, 585 (S.D. N.Y. 2004).

[35]The privilege has, however, been asserted successfully by state and municipal executives in federal court. *See* Wainwright v. Washington Metropolitan Area Transit Authority, 163 F.R.D. 391 (D.D.C. 1995); Gomez v. City of Nashua, N.H., 126 F.R.D. 432 (D.N.H. 1989); Moorhead v. Lane, 125 F.R.D. 680 (C.D. Ill. 1989). *But see* U. S. v. Gillock, 445 U.S. 360, 371, 100 S. Ct. 1185, 63 L. Ed. 2d 454 (1980).

[36]*See, e.g.*, 5 Ill. Comp. Stat. 140/7(1)(f); Ky. Rev. Stat. 61.878(h); N.Y. Pub. Off. Law § 87(2)(g).

[37]Capital Information Group v. State, Office of Governor, 923 P.2d 29 (Alaska 1996); Killington, Ltd. v. Lash, 153 Vt. 628, 572 A.2d 1368 (1990); Daily Gazette Co., Inc. v. West Virginia Development Office, 198 W. Va. 563, 482 S.E.2d 180 (1996). *But see* District Attorney for Norfolk Dist. v. Flatley, 419 Mass. 507, 646 N.E.2d 127 (1995); Sands v. Whitnall School Dist., 2008 WI 89, 312 Wis. 2d 1, 754 N.W.2d 439,

456–58 (2008) (concluding there is no deliberative process privilege in Wisconsin and finding it inconsistent with the state's strong policy of transparency and openness).

[38]*See* Capital Information Group, 923 P.2d at 39–40.

[39]*See, e.g.*, U. S. v. Mackey, 36 F.R.D. 431, 433 (D. D.C. 1965) ("[T]he records of law enforcement agencies, such as the Metropolitan Police Department, are regarded as confidential and are not subject to public inspection. This is in the interest of law enforcement both for the protection of the public as well as for the protection of individual members of the public who might be under investigation."); Capitol Vending Co. v. Baker, 35 F.R.D. 510 (D. D.C. 1964).

[40]*See* Imwinkelried, The New Wigmore: Evidentiary Privileges § 7.4.2, at 1074 nn. 31 & 32 (2d ed. 2010) (citing limited case law that recognizes a qualified investigatory privilege for law enforcement purposes); 8 Wigmore, Evidence § 2378 (McNaughton rev. 1961) (treating investigatory records together with policy deliberations and stating limits of

enforcement agencies may seriously hamper enforcement efforts by discouraging or compromising confidential informants; disclosing the existence, targets, or methods of investigation; endangering witnesses or law enforcement personnel; or undermining a criminal prosecution or civil enforcement proceeding by revealing the nature of the case in preparation.[41] Congress recognized the legitimacy of these concerns in the enactment of a highly specific exemption to FOIA, which in the most recent iteration of the statute expands its protection to "records or information compiled for law enforcement purposes."[42] Today the exemption and the privilege, at least in federal law, seem inextricably intertwined, leaving no practical reason for distinguishing between them.[43]

To come within the ambit of the privilege, the materials must have been compiled for law enforcement purposes and the agency must demonstrate that disclosure would have one of the six specified results in FOIA Exemption 7.[44] The privilege is qualified and,

---

privilege are unclear).

[41]*See* In re Department of Investigation of City of New York, 856 F.2d 481, 484 (2d Cir. 1988). *See generally* Dorsen & Shattuck, Executive Privilege, the Congress, and the Courts, 35 Ohio St. L.J. 1 (1974).

[42]5 U.S.C.A. § 552(b)(7) exempts:

\* \* \* \*

(7) records or information compiled for law enforcement purposes, but only to the extent that the production of such law enforcement records or information (A) could reasonably be expected to interfere with enforcement proceedings, (B) would deprive a person of a right to a fair trial or an impartial adjudication, (C) could reasonably be expected to constitute an unwarranted invasion of personal privacy, (D) could reasonably be expected to disclose the identity of a confidential source, including a State, local, or foreign agency or authority or any private institution which furnished information on a confidential basis, and, in the case of a record or information compiled by criminal law enforcement authority in the course of a criminal investigation or by an agency conducting a lawful national security intelligence investigation, information furnished by a confidential source, (E) would disclose techniques and procedures for law enforcement investigations or prosecutions, or would disclose guidelines for law en-

forcement investigations or prosecutions if such disclosure could reasonably be expected to risk circumvention of the law, or (F) could reasonably be expected to endanger the life or physical safety of any individual.

\* \* \* \*

A detailed discussion of the development of and case law interpreting exemption 7 and each of its subsections may be found in United States Dep't of Justice, Justice Dep't Guide to the Freedom of Information Act, available at http://www.usdoj.gov/oip/foi-act.htm.

[43]*See generally* Greenwald, et al., Testimonial Privileges §§ 9:18, 9:25 (2012 ed.). However, procedures for claiming the privilege are different from those prescribed under FOIA. *See* Hartford Fire Ins. Co. v. U.S., 857 F. Supp. 2d 1356, 1365–66 (Ct. Int'l Trade 2012) (ruling that FOIA preempts common law right of disclosure of law enforcement investigations under material misrepresentation claim); McQueen v. U.S., 179 F.R.D. 522, 526 (S.D. Tex. 1998).

[44]F.B.I. v. Abramson, 456 U.S. 615, 622, 102 S. Ct. 2054, 72 L. Ed. 2d 376 (1982). The privilege also protects materials originally collected for non-law enforcement purposes as long as they have been used for law enforce-

as with other privileges, may be overcome through a showing of sufficient need.[45] Though it has been said that the privilege, unlike that for agency policy deliberations, expires with the governmental undertaking to which the privileged matter relates,[46] this seems an overly broad generalization.[47] However, the protection will not attach absent an initial government demonstration that production "could reasonably be expected to" bring about one or more of the harms specified by the statute.[48]

With regard to state law in this area, some states expressly confer privilege upon law enforcement records.[49] Others have "classical" official information statutes, which cover at least some of such records under the rubric of communications made by or to a public officer in official confidence when the public interest would suffer from disclosure.[50] Where, however, a state FOIA is in effect, courts appear to accord it primacy in determining the maximum sweep of this privilege.[51]

---

ment purposes prior to the claim of privilege. John Doe Agency v. John Doe Corp., 493 U.S. 146, 153, 110 S. Ct. 471, 107 L. Ed. 2d 462 (1989) (treating exemption 7).

[45]Torres v. Kuzniasz, 936 F. Supp. 1201, 1209 (D.N.J. 1996); In re United Telecommunications, Inc. Securities Litigation, 799 F. Supp. 1206, 1208 (D.D.C. 1992); U.S. v. Davis, 131 F.R.D. 391 (S.D. N.Y. 1990); Kay v. Pick, 711 A.2d 1251, 1256 (D.C. 1998). Ten widely cited illustrative factors considered in this balancing of interests are presented in Frankenhauser v. Rizzo, 59 F.R.D. 339, 344 (E.D. Pa. 1973). See Jones v. City of Indianapolis, 216 F.R.D. 440, 444–49 (S.D. Ind. 2003) (applying factors).

[46]See, e.g., Frankenhauser, 59 F.R.D. 339.

[47]See Black v. Sheraton Corp. of America, 564 F.2d 531 (D.C. Cir. 1977) (noting adverse effect on candor of witnesses if remarks would become public after proceeding); Morrissey v. City of New York, 171 F.R.D. 85, 90 (S.D. N.Y. 1997) (investigation need not be ongoing for privilege to be applicable); Borchers v. Commercial Union Assur. Co., 874 F. Supp. 78, 80 (S.D. N.Y. 1995) (privilege may apply even if investigation is closed). To the extent that the

privilege here is redundant with the informer's privilege, it may persist following the proceeding. See Swanner v. U.S., 406 F.2d 716 (5th Cir. 1969) (in an action by informer against government for failing to protect him, material relating to other informers remained protected).

[48]The showing, however, need not be specific to the case at hand, but may be based on the likelihood of the apprehended interference as indicated by experience. Manna v. U.S. Dept. of Justice, 51 F.3d 1158, 1164 (3d Cir. 1995) (construing exemption 7); Kanter v. Internal Revenue Service, 478 F. Supp. 552 (N.D. Ill. 1979).

[49]See, e.g., Wis. Stat. Ann. § 905.09. But see Maclay v. Jones, 208 W. Va. 569, 542 S.E.2d 83, 86 (2000) (observing that the state has no general law enforcement privilege, only one covering confidentiality of informants).

[50]See Cal. Evid. Code § 1040; Neb. Rev. Stat. § 27-509.

[51]See, e.g., State ex rel. Shanahan v. Iowa Dist. Court for Iowa County, 356 N.W.2d 523 (Iowa 1984) (court relies on FOIA exemption to determine scope of statutory privilege for law enforcement records); State ex rel. Multimedia, Inc. v. Whalen, 48 Ohio

## § 109   Effect of the presence of the government as a litigant[1]

To the extent that the Freedom of Information Act is available as a means for obtaining government records and information for use in evidence, as discussed in the preceding section, no distinction is made between situations where the litigation is between parties other than the government and those where the government is a party. However, when procedures other than under the Act are used, the difference may be substantial.

When the government is not a party and successfully resists disclosure sought by a party, the result is generally that the evidence is unavailable, as, for example, if a witness died, and the case will proceed accordingly, with no consequences save those resulting from the loss of the evidence.[2] This approach to dealing with the impact of governmental privilege upon litigation between third parties causes no insuperable difficulties where the privilege is a conditional one and a balancing of interests has been made, or where an absolute privilege is involved and the privileged matter does not bear critically on the central issues of the case. The approach may be inappropriate, however, where the invocation of the absolute privilege, such as for military secrets, makes impossible any approximation of a full presentation of the issues.[3] Whether dismissal of the case is warranted where the sovereign has rendered its courts incapable of fairly trying the issues, dismissal has been granted at the behest of the government where continued litigation by adversary means threatens partial or indirect exposure of the protected secret.[4]

The presence of the government in court as a litigant, whether

---

St. 3d 41, 549 N.E.2d 167 (1990) (where FOIA extends access, judicial weighing as required in discovery is inappropriate).

**[Section 109]**

[1]*See generally* Askin, Secret Justice and the Adversary System, 18 Hastings Const. L. Q. 745 (1991); Brancart, Rethinking the State Secrets Privilege, 9 Whittier L. Rev. 1 (1987); Gardner, The State Secrets Privilege Invoked for Civil Litigation: A Proposal for Statutory Relief, 29 Wake Forest L. Rev. 567 (1994).

[2]Farnsworth Cannon, Inc. v. Grimes, 635 F.2d 268, 270–71 (4th Cir. 1980) (original panel opinion).

[3]*See* Zuckerbraun v. General Dynamics Corp., 935 F.2d 544, 547 (2d

Cir. 1991); Farnsworth Cannon, 635 F.2d at 280 (Phillips, J., specially concurring and dissenting) (dismissal appropriate when privilege deprives the "litigation process of its essential utility for fair resolution of those issues").

[4]*See* Weinberger v. Catholic Action of Hawaii/Peace Educ. Project, 454 U.S. 139, 146–47, 102 S. Ct. 197, 70 L. Ed. 2d 298 (1981); Mohamed v. Jeppesen Dataplan, Inc., 614 F.3d 1070, 1087–89 (9th Cir. 2010), cert. denied, 131 S. Ct. 2442, 179 L. Ed. 2d 1235 (2011) (en banc) (dismissing action by foreign national against company allegedly aiding an extraordinary rendition program because no feasible way to litigate the case without unjustified risk of divulging state secrets); El-Masri v. U.S., 479 F.3d 296, 306–11

as the moving party in a civil or criminal proceeding or by virtue of consenting to be sued as a defendant,[5] raises the possibility that an exercise of privilege may be handled by ordinary judicial enforcement measures.[6] Accordingly, in a criminal prosecution, the court may give the government the choice of disclosing matters of significance to the defense or having the case dismissed.[7] However, where too many relevant facts remain obscured by the state-secrets privilege to reach a reliable judgment, a government contract as a matter of last resort may be declared unenforceable leaving the parties where they were when the suit was filed.[8]

As the plaintiff in a civil action, the government is subject to the ordinary rules of discovery, and may face dismissal of its action if through the invocation of privilege it deprives the defendant of evidence useful to the defense.[9] There would, however, seem to be no reason why the government, as distinguished from other litigants, should necessarily face dismissal for failure to provide discovery under all circumstances.[10] Only where the governmental claim of privilege shields evidence of such impor-

---

(4th Cir. 2007) (ruling that dismissal was required because litigation could not be fairly conducted without disclosure of material covered by the state secrets privilege); Kasza v. Browner, 133 F.3d 1159, 1166 (9th Cir. 1998); In re Under Seal, 945 F.2d 1285, 1289–90 (4th Cir. 1991); Fitzgerald v. Penthouse Intern., Ltd., 776 F.2d 1236 (4th Cir. 1985); Ellsberg v. Mitchell, 709 F.2d 51, 58 (D.C. Cir. 1983); Fazaga v. F.B.I., 884 F. Supp. 2d 1022, 1039-49 (C.D. Cal. 2012) (dismissing case because privileged information essential to government's defense and because privileged and nonprivileged information so inextricably intertwined that deciding the merits would present an unacceptable risk of disclosing state secrets); Black v. U.S., 900 F. Supp. 1129, 1133 (D. Minn. 1994).

[5]For example, under the Tort Claims Act, 28 U.S.C.A. § 2674.

[6]Thus it may fairly be said, "[t]he Government as a litigant is, of course, subject to the rules of discovery." U. S. v. Procter & Gamble Co., 356 U.S. 677, 681, 78 S. Ct. 983, 2 L. Ed. 2d 1077 (1958). *See also* Bank Line v. U.S., 163 F.2d 133 (C.C.A. 2d Cir. 1947).

[7]*See* U.S. v. Reynolds, 345 U.S. 1, 12, 73 S. Ct. 528, 97 L. Ed. 727 (1953); U.S. v. Pringle, 751 F.2d 419, 425–28 (1st Cir. 1984); U.S. v. Andolschek, 142 F.2d 503, 506 (C.C.A. 2d Cir. 1944).

[8]General Dynamics Corp. v. U.S., 131 S. Ct. 1900, 1908–10, 179 L. Ed. 2d 957 (2011).

[9]In U.S. v. Cotton Valley Operators Committee, 9 F.R.D. 719 (W.D. La. 1949), a civil antitrust action, the Government failed to comply with the order to produce certain reports and correspondence and the action was dismissed. *See also* U. S. v. Procter & Gamble Co., 356 U.S. 677, 78 S. Ct. 983, 2 L. Ed. 2d 1077 (1958).

[10]Fed. R. Civ. P. 37 provides for a number of sanctions short of dismissal, and the latter has been held a drastic remedy, appropriate only in extreme circumstances. Further, it is significant that Fed. R. Civ. P. 26(b)(1) exempts from discovery matters which are privileged. Some courts have held that the government may use privileged information to establish a fact upon which it has the burden of producing evidence and maintain secrecy through in camera review. *See* Patterson by Patterson v. F.B.I., 893 F.2d 595, 599–600 (3d Cir. 1990); In re U.S., 872 F.2d 472, 476 (D.C. Cir.

tance as to deny the defendant due process should dismissal automatically result.[11]

Where the government is the defendant, as under the Tort Claims Act, an adverse finding cannot be rendered against it as the price of asserting an evidentiary privilege. This is not one of the terms upon which Congress has consented that the United States be subjected to liability.[12] Accordingly, where the plaintiff's action cannot be proved without disclosure of the privileged matter, the plaintiff will remain remediless,[13] although in light of the extreme nature of this result, some courts seek ways to avoid it.[14]

## § 110    The scope of the judge's function in determining the validity of the claim of privilege

When the head of department has made a claim of privilege for documents or information under his control as being military or diplomatic secrets is this claim conclusive upon the judge? *United States v. Reynolds*,[1] which remains the Supreme Court's most comprehensive ruling on this privilege, has been extensively mined for the answer to this question. The generally accepted conclusions are that, while the judiciary is not to defer totally to the "caprice" of the executive,[2] the judicial role is a limited one, focused largely upon the process of claiming the privilege rather

---

1989).

[11]Attorney General of U.S. v. Irish People, Inc., 684 F.2d 928 (D.C. Cir. 1982). *See also* Kasza v. Browner, 133 F.3d 1159, 1166 (9th Cir. 1998) (setting out general analysis).

[12]U.S. v. Reynolds, 345 U.S. 1, 73 S. Ct. 528, 97 L. Ed. 727 (1953); Tenenbaum v. Simonini, 372 F.3d 776, 777–78 (6th Cir. 2004); McDonnell Douglas Corp. v. U.S., 323 F.3d 1006, 1022–24 (Fed. Cir. 2003); In re U.S., 872 F.2d 472, 476 (D.C. Cir. 1989); Salisbury v. U.S., 690 F.2d 966 (D.C. Cir. 1982).

[13]Zuckerbraun v. General Dynamics Corp., 935 F.2d 544, 547 (2d Cir. 1991); Molerio v. F.B.I., 749 F.2d 815 (D.C. Cir. 1984); Guong v. U.S., 860 F.2d 1063 (Fed. Cir. 1988); Hayden v. National Sec. Agency/Central Sec. Service, 608 F.2d 1381 (D.C. Cir. 1979); Edmonds v. U.S. Dept. of Justice, 323 F. Supp. 2d 65, 77–81 (D.D.C. 2004); Zoltek Corp. v. U.S., 86 Fed. Cl. 738, 747–50 (2009) (permitting the government to move for summary

judgment on a claim that patent was invalid on grounds of obviousness despite having asserted the state secrets privilege because it was the defendant in the civil action). *Cf.* In re Sealed Case, 494 F.3d 139, 143–54 (D.C. Cir. 2007) (ruling in a *Bivens* action brought against the government the state secrets privilege may be invoked but even though the privilege was properly invoked the proceedings could continue because the case could be fairly litigated without disclosing the privileged material).

[14]In re U.S., 872 F.2d 472, 477 (D.C. Cir. 1989) (denying mandamus requiring dismissal of suit in which district court had ordered further discovery; dismissal "draconian" and to be avoided if suit can proceed without disclosure of secrets).

**[Section 110]**

[1]U.S. v. Reynolds, 345 U.S. 1, 73 S. Ct. 528, 97 L. Ed. 727 (1953).

[2]"Judicial control over the evidence in a case cannot be abdicated to the caprice of executive officers." Rey-

than upon the merits of its invocation.[3] Thus, the privilege must be asserted through a formal claim by the head of the executive department having charge of the material, and the statement of this official must indicate personal consideration of the claim, the identity (so far as possible) of the privileged material, and the reasons supporting the claim.[4] In some instances, no more will be necessary in order to enable the court to rule in favor of the claim,[5] but it is not unusual for the government to further support its claim with an affidavit, and perhaps other matter, to be reviewed by the court in the absence of opposing counsel.[6]

---

nolds, 345 U.S. at 9–10.

[3]The "mechanical" application of the standards derived from *Reynolds* is criticized in Note, 91 Yale L.J. 570 (1982).

[4]For a comprehensive discussion of the *Reynolds* requirements, see Ellsberg v. Mitchell, 709 F.2d 51 (D.C. Cir. 1983); National Lawyers Guild v. Attorney General, 96 F.R.D. 390 (S.D. N.Y. 1982). It is not necessary that the department head personally review each document or each page of a disputed document. *See* Maxwell v. First Nat. Bank of Maryland, 143 F.R.D. 590, 598 (D. Md. 1992); N.S.N. Intern. Industry v. E.I. Dupont de Nemours & Co., Inc., 140 F.R.D. 275, 280–81 (S.D. N.Y. 1991). Additionally, where federal law prohibits disclosure of certain information, the personal objection of an executive officer may be unnecessary. Clift v. U.S., 597 F.2d 826, 828–29 (2d Cir. 1979).

Whether the assertion of the privilege must come from the highest level of the executive department appears to vary between governmental privileges. When the "more sensitive and absolute privilege" for state and military secrets is invoked, the cases impose a more stringent requirement as to invocation by the "head of the department" than as to the deliberative process and law enforcement privileges, where lesser officials have been permitted to assert the privilege. *See* U.S. v. Abu-Jihaad, 630 F.3d 102, 140–41 (2d Cir. 2010), cert. denied, 131 S. Ct. 3062, 180 L. Ed. 2d 892 (2011) (concluding that refusing to provide

information under CIPA, which has its origins in the state secrets privilege, requires invocation by department head); Marriott Intern. Resorts, L.P. v. U.S., 437 F.3d 1302, 1306–08 (Fed. Cir. 2006) (describing the reasons why with the absolute state secrets privilege the agency head must claim the privilege but adopting the "majority" position that authority can be delegated as to the deliberative process privilege); Landry v. F.D.I.C., 204 F.3d 1125, 1136 (D.C. Cir. 2000) (finding assertion of deliberative process privilege by regional director sufficient and describing the difference in treatment for state secrets privilege). *But see* Chao v. Westside Drywall, Inc., 254 F.R.D. 651, 656–58 (D. Or. 2009) (requiring that Secretary of Labor claim informant privilege for claimant-employees when bringing action against employers under Fair Labor Standards Act).

[5]*See* Halkin v. Helms, 690 F.2d 977 (D.C. Cir. 1982) (holding public affidavit sufficient to support claim of privilege, thus rendering unnecessary any consideration of contentions concerning in camera affidavit which had also been submitted).

[6]Despite its anomalousness in adversary proceedings, the propriety of ex parte in camera submissions in the present context is well established. *See, e.g.*, Doe v. C.I.A., 576 F.3d 95, 105–07 (2d Cir. 2009) (ruling that party could not avoid this limitation by arguing that its reason for seeking access was to enable it to argue that the alleged state secrets are not really state secrets); U.S. v. Klimavicius-

Whatever material is considered by the court, the standard applied is whether there exists a reasonable danger that disclosure will damage national security.[7] If this danger is found, the privilege is absolute and is not affected by the extent of the litigant's need for the confidential information.[8] That need is considered only when determining how deeply the court will probe to satisfy itself that a privilege claim is justified.[9] Any relevant non-confidential information should be disentangled from other classified information when possible.[10] However, if the information forms a mosaic and disclosure of an apparently innocuous part could lead to the disclosure of classified information, disentangling is not required.[11]

Once outside the restricted area of military and diplomatic secrets, however, a greater role for the judiciary in the determination of governmental claims of privilege becomes not only desirable, but necessary. The head of an executive department or in most circuits a carefully delegated subordinate, who claims the privilege,[12] can appraise the public interest of secrecy as well (or perhaps better) than the judge, but predictably the official's posi-

---

Viloria, 144 F.3d 1249, 1261 (9th Cir. 1998); Black v. U.S., 62 F.3d 1115, 1119 (8th Cir. 1995); Jabara v. Webster, 691 F.2d 272 (6th Cir. 1982) (holding that trial court could properly consider in camera submissions without granting access to plaintiff or counsel); Halkin v. Helms, 598 F.2d 1 (D.C. Cir. 1978) (noting that permissibility of in camera inspections is well established and protective orders are inadequate to prevent disclosure). But it has been held that a public record as complete as feasible under the circumstances should precede any in camera submissions. Ellsberg v. Mitchell, 709 F.2d 51 (D.C. Cir. 1983).

[7]U.S. v. Reynolds, 345 U.S. 1, 10, 73 S. Ct. 528, 97 L. Ed. 727 (1953). For further discussion of the rationale of the standard, see Zagel, The State Secrets Privilege, 50 Minn. L. Rev. 875, 910 (1966) ("There is no greater reason for secrecy than protecting the military and diplomatic welfare of the nation.").

[8]See Berger, The Incarnation of Executive Privilege, 22 UCLA L. Rev. 4 (1974) (criticizing inflexible character of privilege). But see New York Times Co. v. U.S., 403 U.S. 713, 719,

91 S. Ct. 2140, 29 L. Ed. 2d 822 (1971) (once the press obtains classified information, the First Amendment establishes a qualified right to publish). See generally Fein, Access to Classified Information: Constitutional and Statutory Dimensions, 26 Wm. & Mary L. Rev. 805, 822 (1985).

[9]Ellsberg v. Mitchell, 709 F.2d at 51, 58–59 (D.C.Cir. 1983); Halkin v. Helms, 690 F.2d 977, 990 (D.C. Cir. 1982). The more compelling a litigant's need, the more deeply the court should probe. Conversely, the more plausible the government's claim, the more deferential the court should be.

[10]In re U.S., 872 F.2d 472, 476 (D.C. Cir. 1989); Ellsberg, 709 F.2d at 63.

[11]C.I.A. v. Sims, 471 U.S. 159, 178–79, 105 S. Ct. 1881, 85 L. Ed. 2d 173 (1985); Kasza v. Browner, 133 F.3d 1159, 1166 (9th Cir. 1998).

[12]In Marriott Int'l Resorts, 437 F.3d at 1308, the Federal Circuit altered its position and concluded that "the head of an Agency can, when carefully undertaken, delegate authority to invoke the deliberative process privilege on the Agency's behalf." See also Cobell v. Norton, 213 F.R.D. 1, 8

tion will tend to minimize the individual's interest. Under the normal routine, the question will come to chief administrators with recommendations from cautious subordinates against disclosure, and in the press of business, they are likely to approve the recommendations about apparently minor matters without much independent consideration.[13] The determination of questions of fact and the applications of legal standards in passing upon the admissibility of evidence and the validity of claims of privilege are traditionally the trial judge's responsibility. As a public official, the judge should have respect for the executive's concern about disclosure, but, at the same time, judicial duties require an appraisal of private interests that must be reconciled with conflicting public policies. A judge may thus be better qualified than the executive to weigh both interests and to strike a proper balance.

The foregoing considerations largely explain why privileges running in favor of government, other than that for military and diplomatic secrets, are uniformly held to be qualified.[14] Thus, where these privileges are claimed, the judge must determine whether the interest in governmental secrecy is outweighed in the particular case by the litigant's interest in obtaining the evidence. Striking a satisfactory balance will, on the one hand, require consideration of the interests giving rise to the privilege and an assessment of the extent to which disclosure will realistically impair those interests. On the other hand, factors which will affect the litigant's need include the significance of the evidence sought for the case, the availability of the desired information from other sources, and the nature of the right being as-

---

(D.D.C. 2003) (observing that D.C. Circuit's law is not to interpret "head of the department" too narrowly).

[13]See the graphic comments of Wigmore to like effect. 8 Evidence § 2378, at 796 n.7 (McNaughton rev. 1961). *See also* Imwinkelried, The New Wigmore: Evidentiary Privileges § 8.4.1, at 1417–18 (2d ed. 2010) (noting a distinction between procedures followed for major and minor government secrets under which as to the former the chief department head must claim the privilege and the judge has less participation, and as to the latter, an attorney representing the government may claim the privilege and the judge's participation is greater); Duncan v. Cammell, Laird & Co., (1942) A.C. 624, 642 (identifying the grounds that should influence the ex-

ecutive).

[14]Rothstein and Crump, Federal Testimonial Privileges §§ 5:8 & 5:9 (2d ed. 2011) (noting that other that executive privileges other than state secrets are not absolute); Greenwald, et al., Testimonial Privileges §§ 9:1 to 9:2, 9:8 to 9:11, 9:16 (2012 ed.). *See also* Dorsen & Shattuck, Executive Privilege, the Congress, and the Courts, 35 Ohio St. L.J. 1 (1974). *Cf.* Imwinkelried, The New Wigmore: Evidentiary Privileges § 8.4.2, at 11424–25 (2d ed. 2010) (noting that government officials tend to overclassify information, citing the comical example of the classification of a study of the bow and arrow, and that judges are generally more impartial in making such decisions).

serted in the litigation. Here, as with other qualified privileges, in camera inspection by the court offers a practical way for testing the claim of privilege without destroying irretrievably the secrecy which the privilege is designed to preserve.[15]

## § 111    The privilege against the disclosure of the identity of an informer[1]

For entirely understandable reasons, informers fear disclosure, and if their names were subject to being readily revealed, this important aid to law enforcement would be seriously compromised. On this ground of policy, a privilege is recognized for disclosure of the identity of an informer[2] who has given information about suspected crimes to a prosecuting or investigating officer or to another person to be relayed to such an officer.[3] The privilege runs to the government and may be invoked by its of-

---

[15]Environmental Protection Agency v. Mink, 410 U.S. 73, 93, 93 S. Ct. 827, 35 L. Ed. 2d 119 (1973).

**[Section 111]**

[1]Imwinkelried, The New Wigmore: Evidentiary Privileges § 7.3 (2d ed. 2010); 1 LaFave Search and Seizure § 3.3(g) (5th ed.); 8 Wigmore, Evidence § 2374 (McNaughton rev. 1961); Grano, A Dilemma for Defense Counsel: Spinelli-Harris Search Warrants and the Possibility of Police Perjury, 1971 U. Ill. L.F. 405; Katz, The Paradoxical Role of Informers within the Criminal Justice System: A Unique Perspective, 7 U. Dayton L. Rev. 51 (1981); Quinn, McCray v. Illinois: Probable Cause and the Informer's Privilege, 45 Denver L.J. 399 (1968); Wohl, Confidential Informants in Private Litigation: Balancing Interests in Anonymity and Disclosure, 12 Fordham J. Corp. & Fin. L. 551 (2007).

[2]The privilege has long been recognized. See, e.g., Worthington v. Scribner, 109 Mass. 487, 1872 WL 8824 (1872) (in action for false charges made to U.S. Treasury that plaintiff was an imposter, defendant held privileged not to answer interrogatories as to his giving this information); Dellastatious v. Boyce, 152 Va. 368, 147 S.E. 267, 274–75 (1929) (in action for trespass and false arrest, held er-

ror to require disclosure of identify of person from whom officer secured information supporting warrant); Marks v. Beyfus, 1890 WL 9837 (CA 1890) (judge should exclude identity of informer under policy except where the evidence is needed to establish the innocence of an accused).

Uniform Rule of Evidence 509 (2005) sets out a privilege for the identity of informers. Deleted Federal Rule 510, which varies somewhat in other details, contained an additional provision that permitted the court to require the informer's identity to be disclosed when information provided by the informer was used to establish the legality of obtaining evidence and the judge was not satisfied with the information provided. Upon request of the government, it established a method for disclosing this information in camera. See State v. Veburst, 156 Vt. 133, 589 A.2d 863, 868 (1991) (discussing different scope of exceptions in Deleted Federal Rule and Uniform Rule).

[3]See Hardy's Trial, 24 How. St. Tr. 99 (1794), quoted in 8 Wigmore, Evidence (3d ed. 1940) § 2374, p. 751 (Erie, L.C.J.: "I cannot satisfy myself that there is any substantial difference between the case of this man's going to a justice of the peace . . . or to some other person who communicated with a justice.").

ficers who, as witnesses or otherwise, are asked for the information.[4] According to some authority, the privilege also may be asserted by the alleged informer.[5] In some jurisdictions when neither the government nor the informer is represented at the

---

While typically the privilege is applied in criminal prosecutions, it is applicable in civil litigation as well when the disclosure involves an informant involved in criminal investigation. *See* Michelson v. Daly, 590 F. Supp. 261, 264 (N.D. N.Y. 1984). Similar considerations may be present in cases involving informants providing information regarding law violation beyond the criminal law. Thus, the privilege has frequently been upheld in contexts in which enforcement depends upon reporting. *See* Brennan v. Engineered Products, Inc., 506 F.2d 299 (8th Cir. 1974) (applicable to Fair Labor Standards Act cases); Westinghouse Elec. Corp. v. City of Burlington, Vt., 351 F.2d 762 (D.C. Cir. 1965) (civil antitrust action, but filing of action held to have eliminated any privilege where complaints were material to a defense of statute of limitations); Fruchtman v. Town of Dewey Beach, 886 F. Supp. 2d 427 (D. Del. 2012) (ruling privilege inapplicable to information provided to mayor who has no law enforcement responsibilities). Although recognized as stronger in civil suits, Elnashar v. Speedway SuperAmerica, LLC, 484 F.3d 1046, 1053 (8th Cir. 2007) (observing that privilege is stronger in civil cases because the countervailing constitutional guarantees assured to criminal defendants are not present); In re U. S., 565 F.2d 19, 22 (2d Cir. 1977), the privilege must nevertheless give way if disclosure is essential to a fair determination of the issues. *See* Westinghouse Elec. Corp., 351 F.2d at 762; Michelson, 590 F. Supp. at 261.

[4]This is probably the most frequent source of objection. *See, e.g.*, Wilson v. U.S., 59 F.2d 390 (C.C.A. 3d Cir. 1932) (prohibition officer properly refused to answer question as to source of information on raid); Bocchicchio v.

Curtis Pub. Co., 203 F. Supp. 403 (E.D. Pa. 1962) (local police officer not represented by counsel successful in claiming the privilege when called as witness in civil libel action); Marks v. Beyfus, 1890 WL 9837 (CA 1890). *Cf.* Gill v. Gulfstream Park Racing Ass'n., Inc., 399 F.3d 391, 401–02 (1st Cir. 2005) (finding that under state law informer's privilege could not be invoked by private entity in discovery dispute); Uniform Rule of Evidence 509 (2005) allows the privilege to be claimed only by public entities. *But cf.* Chao v. Westside Drywall, Inc., 254 F.R.D. 651, 656–58 (D. Or. 2009) (requiring that Secretary of Labor claim informant privilege for claimant-employees when bringing action against employers under Fair Labor Standards Act).

[5]Worthington v. Scribner, 109 Mass. 487, 1872 WL 8824 (1872); Wells v. Toogood, 165 Mich. 677, 131 N.W. 124 (1911) (action for slander against alleged informer; when officer was asked about complaint of theft made to him by defendant, defendant's counsel objected). *But see* Roviaro v. U.S., 353 U.S. 53, 59, 77 S. Ct. 623, 1 L. Ed. 2d 639 (1957) ("What is usually referred to as the informer's privilege is in reality the Government's privilege to withhold from disclosure the identity of persons who furnish information of violations of law to officers charged with enforcement of that law. . . . The purpose of the privilege is the furtherance and protection of the public interest in effective law enforcement. The privilege recognizes the obligation of citizens to communicate their knowledge of the commission of crimes to law-enforcement officials and, by preserving their anonymity, encourages them to perform that obligation.").

trial, the judge may invoke it for the absent holder,[6] as in other cases of privilege.[7] Whether the privilege is confined to disclosure of identity[8] or extends also to the contents of the communication[9] is in dispute. The policy of the privilege does not appear to require shielding the communication from disclosure, but shielding the contents is required if revealing those contents would likely identify the informer, which is often the case.[10]

The privilege has two important qualifications. The first is that when the identity has already become known to "those who would

---

[6]*See* Marks v. Beyfus, (1890) 25 Q.B.D. 494, 500, 1890 WL 9837 (C.A.) (statement of Bowen, L.J.) ("[T]he privilege does not depend upon the witness claiming it when asked the question; but the judge should refuse to allow the question as soon as it is asked.").

[7]See supra § 73.1.

[8]This is the view of 8 Wigmore, Evidence § 2374, p. 765 (McNaughton rev. 1961) and the form in which the doctrine is stated in many of the leading opinions. *See, e.g.*, Scher v. U.S., 305 U.S. 251, 254, 59 S. Ct. 174, 83 L. Ed. 151 (1938) ("public policy forbids disclosure of an informer's identity"). *See also* Bowman Dairy Co. v. U.S., 341 U.S. 214, 221, 71 S. Ct. 675, 95 L. Ed. 879 (1951) (ruling in an antitrust case that the government could be required to produce complaints and statements received from third persons but that the court must be "solicitous to protect against disclosures of the identity of informants." While Professor Imwinkelried agrees with Wigmore that the privilege extends only to the protection of an informant's identity, and not to the content of communications, he notes two exceptions. One covers communicated content that would reveal an informant's identity, and the other protects the location of surveillance equipment and posts. Imwinkelried, The New Wigmore: Evidentiary Privileges § 7.3.1, at 1268–69 (2d ed. 2010).

[9]Numerous opinions state the doctrine as including the contents of

the statement but usually in situations where the wider coverage is not material. *See, e.g.*, Michael v. Matson, 81 Kan. 360, 105 P. 537 (1909); Wells v. Toogood, 165 Mich. 677, 131 N.W. 124 (1911). *Cf.* U.S. v. Jackson, 345 F.3d 59, 70 (2d Cir. 2003) (ruling that where disclosure required, *Roviaro* principle covers only identity of the informant and not communications).

[10]*See* U.S. v. Cartagena, 593 F.3d 104, 113 (1st Cir. 2010) (protecting content were defendant failed to explain why it would not reveal identity of informant); U.S. v. Wilburn, 581 F.3d 618, 625 (7th Cir. 2009) (ruling on whether specific types of questions would be prohibited because likely to reveal identity of informant); U.S. v. Gil, 58 F.3d 1414, 1421 (9th Cir. 1995) (cross-examination limitations regarding location information given in tip because information might have revealed identity of informant); In re Apollo Group, Inc. Securities Litigation, 251 F.R.D. 12, 34–35 (D.D.C. 2008) (approving withholding the content of informer's communications under informant privilege that might reveal the informer's identity); People v. Hobbs, 7 Cal. 4th 948, 30 Cal. Rptr. 2d 651, 873 P.2d 1246, 1252 (1994) (finding this extension a well-established corollary to privilege); State v. Hosey, 134 Idaho 883, 11 P.3d 1101, 1107 (2000) (ruling that request for transcript of in camera hearing of informant was properly denied on ground that the identity of informant could be ascertained from its contents).

have cause to resent the communication,"[11] the privilege ceases. The second is that, when the privilege is asserted by the state in a criminal prosecution and the evidence of the identity of the informer becomes important to the establishment of the defense, the court will require the disclosure,[12] and if it is still withheld, will dismiss of the prosecution.[13]

---

[11]Roviaro, 353 U.S. at 60 (followed by Uniform Rule of Evidence 509 (2005)). Obviously, not all disclosures, such as those to other law enforcing agencies, are inconsistent with its policies. See U.S. v. Smith, 780 F.2d 1102 (4th Cir. 1985) (in cases involving the Classified Information Procedures Act, see supra § 107, it was held that defendant's knowledge of the information did not destroy the privilege in an espionage case because foreign informants, unlike most domestic ones, may not even know who is likely to resent their disclosures); U.S. v. Long, 533 F.2d 505 (9th Cir. 1976) (holding privilege still effective after disclosure of informer's name to defense by government because others in community likely to resent informer's conduct).

The privilege likely should cease to exist with the death of the informant. Smith v. City of Detroit, 212 F.R.D. 507, 510 (E.D. Mich. 2003).

[12]In Roviaro v. U.S., 353 U.S. 53, 77 S. Ct. 623, 1 L. Ed. 2d 639 (1957), a narcotics conviction was reversed for refusal to require disclosure of an informer's identity. The informer was in fact far more than an informer; he was present at the transportation and participated in the sale, on both of which counts accused was charged. The Court pointed out that the "informer" might have testified to an entrapment, thrown doubt on the identity of the accused or the package, testified as to accused's lack of knowledge of the contents, or contradicted the government's version of an important conversation. Merely being an informer does not insulate against disclosure when the informer's activities go beyond informing. See Elliott v. State, 417 Md. 413, 10 A.3d 761, 780–81 (2010) (disclosure required where

informant was participant and testimony was potentially relevant to intent and proving entrapment in drug offense); Com. v. Mello, 453 Mass. 760, 905 N.E.2d 562, 564–66 (2009) (approving denial of disclosure of informer to support the defendant's entrapment defense where the defendant only showed that the informer encouraged her to meet with an undercover officer to whom she sold drugs, but failed to show that the informer either induced her to commit the crime or participated in the undercover officer's inducement); Com. v. Dias, 451 Mass. 463, 886 N.E.2d 713, 718–22 (2008) (approving trial court's determination to order disclosure where informant was participant in crime and his version as recited in warrant deviated from that of anticipated government witness and concluding trial court was not required to grant prosecution's motion for in camera hearing to determine whether informant had valid Fifth Amendment privilege since informant's identity might provide important information to defense even if privilege were ultimately asserted); State v. Vanmanivong, 2003 WI 41, 261 Wis. 2d 202, 661 N.W.2d 76, 86–87 (2003) (ruling that Roviaro's balancing approach requires disclosure only if the evidence is necessary to the defense to the degree it would create a reasonable doubt).

The polarity often employed by the courts contrasts the "mere tipster" on the one hand with the "participant" on the other. See U.S. v. Robinson, 144 F.3d 104, 106 (1st Cir. 1998); U.S. v. Moore, 129 F.3d 989, 992 (8th Cir. 1997). See also U.S. v. Gaston, 357 F.3d 77, 84–85 (D.C. Cir. 2004) (ruling that Roviaro does not apply to informant who saw fruits of search prior to execution of warrant but did not par-

While the inherent fairness of this second exception is apparent, its implementation is challenging if the privilege is not to be rendered meaningless by automatic defense allegations of the informer's potential value as a witness. To avoid this result, an in camera hearing is widely used, and sometimes required, to determine the nature of the informer's probable testimony.[14] With or without an in camera hearing, the trial court's task is to assess the balance between the value of that testimony to the

---

ticipate in the crime). Labels, while useful, should not, however, obscure the real issue, which is the potential value of the informant's testimony to the defendant. *See* U.S. v. Mabry, 953 F.2d 127, 131–32 (4th Cir. 1991) (noting that informants often play intermediate role between participant and tipster); State v. Hernandez, 254 Conn. 659, 759 A.2d 79, 86 (2000) (concluding that status as "tipster" does not preclude disclosure, which was properly ordered because informant witnessed events that could have been important to defendant's claim).

[13]"It is a sound rule to keep secret information furnished to the state of violations of its laws, but this commendable public policy must yield to a higher, or at least an equal, right accorded to an accused to have a court investigate the facts material to his offense in a criminal prosecution, and sometimes the departments of government will be put to a choice of either foregoing a criminal prosecution or disclosing the source of material information necessary to the conduct of orderly judicial procedure." U.S. v. Keown, 19 F. Supp. 639, 646 (W.D. Ky. 1937). Relief less than dismissal may also be appropriate. *See* U.S. v. Jenkins, 4 F.3d 1338, 1341–42 (6th Cir. 1993) (identity kept confidential, but failure of informant to corroborate part of detectives' testimony in testimony given during in camera hearing disclosed to the jury).

Where the prosecution is required under *Roviaro*, whether the prosecution has any further duty to produce the informant will depend

upon several factors, including the degree of the prosecution's control over the informant and the importance of the informant's testimony. *See* U.S. v. Williams, 496 F.2d 378 (1st Cir. 1974). *See also* U.S. v. Martinez-Figueroa, 363 F.3d 679, 681 (8th Cir. 2004) (ruling that prosecution satisfied its duty in notifying the defendant pretrial of the informant's identity and that he was a fugitive).

[14]*See* U.S. v. Ramirez-Rangel, 103 F.3d 1501, 1508 (9th Cir. 1997) (trial judge erred in not holding in camera hearing before denying motion to reveal informant's identity who observed critical transaction). In camera proceedings for this purpose are commonly referred to in the cases as *Roviaro* hearings. For a helpful discrimination between those cases in which such a hearing is and is not required, see Suarez v. U.S., 582 F.2d 1007 (5th Cir. 1978). As to the factors to be considered by the trial court in such a hearing, see U.S. v. Rutherford, 175 F.3d 899, 902 (11th Cir. 1999) (remanding to the district court to conduct an in camera hearing to determine if informants would support a plausible misidentification defense for a defendant who was arrested three months after the drug transaction, where the informants participated in the transaction and were in a better position than the government agents to identify the guilty party); U.S. v. Gonzales, 606 F.2d 70 (5th Cir. 1979); Heard v. Com., 172 S.W.3d 372, 374–75 (Ky. 2005) (relying on broad availability of in camera hearing).

defense and the significance of the considerations underlying the privilege in the particular case.[15]

A variant of the second situation occurs when a search or seizure is challenged under the Fourth Amendment and the statement of an informant is essential to probable cause. Although resting less clearly on constitutional grounds,[16] courts frequently employ in camera hearings when they determine that in order to decide probable cause they must resolve questions concerning the informer's existence or nature of the information actually provided by the informer.[17] In recent years, courts have recognized a privilege analogous to the informer's privilege that protects the confidentiality of police surveillance locations so that private citizens permitting the police to use their property will not be

---

[15]See, e.g., U.S. v. Fairchild, 122 F.3d 605, 609 (8th Cir. 1997) (disclosure denied by weighing factors after in camera hearing); U.S. v. Sanchez, 988 F.2d 1384, 1391 (5th Cir. 1993) (describing basic three-factor test of informant's involvement in crime, helpfulness of disclosure to defense, and government's interest in nondisclosure).

[16]See McCray v. State of Ill., 386 U.S. 300, 87 S. Ct. 1056, 18 L. Ed. 2d 62 (1967) (neither due process nor right of confrontation was violated by Illinois rule that shielded informer's identity from disclosure when issue involved probable cause; trial judge not required to assume officers who testified regarding the informer were committing perjury). Compare U.S. v. Cummins, 912 F.2d 98, 103 (6th Cir. 1990) (due process does not require disclosure of informant's identity at suppression hearing, but rather left to discretion of trial court), with State v. Casal, 103 Wash. 2d 812, 699 P.2d 1234, 1237 (1985) (accepting argument of Professor LaFave that McCray only held that Constitution did not always require disclosure and that it may under a proper showing be required to determine Fourth Amendment issue).

[17]Supporting the propriety of trial courts conducting in camera proceedings on probable cause issues, see for example, U.S. v. Moore, 522 F.2d 1068, 1072 (9th Cir. 1975); People v. Vauzanges, 158 Ill. 2d 509, 199 Ill.

Dec. 731, 634 N.E.2d 1085 (1994); People v. Edwards, 95 N.Y.2d 486, 719 N.Y.S.2d 202, 741 N.E.2d 876, 880 (2000) (holding that, in the absence of several specific exceptions, in camera hearing is not discretionary but is required where the informant is essential to establish probable cause); People v. Darden, 34 N.Y.2d 177, 356 N.Y.S.2d 582, 313 N.E.2d 49, 52 (1974); State v. Casal, 103 Wash. 2d 812, 699 P.2d 1234, 1238 (1985). Some courts caution that even an in camera hearing entails risks of disclosure. See State v. Richardson, 204 Conn. 654, 529 A.2d 1236, 1242 (1987) (risks great where informant required to personally appear). In most jurisdictions, in camera hearings are not automatically granted upon defense allegations but require some specific justification. See, e.g., U.S. v. Kime, 99 F.3d 870, 878–79 (8th Cir. 1996) (defendant's burden entails more than mere speculation that informant's identity would be helpful and disclosure properly denied without in camera hearing); State v. Robertson, 494 N.W.2d 718, 726 (Iowa 1993) (in camera examination not required because defendant failed to make substantial preliminary showing that police perjury occurred). But see People v. Adrion, 82 N.Y.2d 628, 606 N.Y.S.2d 893, 627 N.E.2d 973, 975 (1993) (in camera hearing required if informant essential to probable cause and defense challenge made); Casal, 699 P.2d at 1238 (same).

subject to retaliation,[18] and to aspects of sensitive surveillance equipment used.[19]

## § 112    Statutory privileges for certain reports of individuals to government agencies: Accident reports, tax returns, etc[1]

A somewhat similar policy to that supporting the privilege for the identity of informers applies to reports that individuals are required by law to make to government agencies for the administration of their public functions. If such statements are admissible against those reporting the information, full and true reporting may be discouraged.[2] On the other hand, these reports often deal with facts highly material in litigation, and an early report

---

[18]*See, e.g.*, U.S. v. Green, 670 F.2d 1148 (D.C. Cir. 1981); Valentin v. U.S., 15 A.3d 270, 273–75 (D.C. 2011) (applying privilege to protect observation post information, balancing the interests of the government and defendant); People v. Price, 404 Ill. App. 3d 324, 343 Ill. Dec. 544, 935 N.E.2d 552, 558–60 (1st Dist. 2010) (applying privilege recognized in the state but finding trial court misapplied balancing inquiry in particular case); Church v. State, 408 Md. 650, 971 A.2d 280, 290–93 (2009) (recognizing surveillance location privilege but imposing an initial burden on the prosecution to demonstrate a legitimate interest in preventing disclosure in that the location is still in use or that revealing the location would put someone in danger); Com. v. Lugo, 406 Mass. 565, 548 N.E.2d 1263 (1990); State v. Garcia, 131 N.J. 67, 618 A.2d 326 (1993). For limitations on scope of this privilege, see U.S. v. Foster, 986 F.2d 541, 542–44 (D.C. Cir. 1993). *But see* State v. Darden, 145 Wash. 2d 612, 41 P.3d 1189, 1196–97 (2002) (ruling that no surveillance location privilege exists under state statutory or common law and that the court has no authority to create such a privilege).

[19]*See* U.S. v. Van Horn, 789 F.2d 1492, 1507–08 (11th Cir. 1986) (protecting nature and location of surveillance equipment under *Roviaro* principle); U.S. v. Rigmaiden, 844 F. Supp. 2d 982, 996–1003 (D. Ariz. 2012) (protecting under *Roviaro* doctrine information about various elements of search for computer aircard that located laptop used in fraudulent scheme).

**[Section 112]**

[1]Imwinkelried, The New Wigmore: Evidentiary Privileges §§ 7.2 & 7.4 (2d ed. 2010); 8 Wigmore, Evidence § 2377 (McNaughton rev. 1961); Greenwald, et al., Testimonial Privileges § 9:28 (2012 ed.); 3 Weinstein's Federal Evidence §§ 502A.01–502A.07 (2d ed. 2012).

[2]Association for Women in Science v. Califano, 566 F.2d 339, 343–44 (D.C. Cir. 1977); New York State Dept. of Taxation and Finance v. New York State Dept. of Law, Statewide Organized Crime Task Force, 44 N.Y.2d 575, 406 N.Y.S.2d 747, 378 N.E.2d 110, 112–14 (1978). Additionally, required reports may be privileged to avoid the undue weight a jury may give to such a report. Torchia v. Burlington Northern, Inc., 174 Mont. 83, 568 P.2d 558 (1977). *See* Imwinkelried, The New Wigmore: Evidentiary Privileges § 7.4.1 (2d ed. 2010) (citing several state statutes that extend such protection to confidential information submitted by private citizens). *Cf.* Chao v. Westside Drywall, Inc., 254 F.R.D. 651, 655–56 (D. Or. 2009) (applying informant privilege to claimant-employees who filed complaints under Fair Labor Standards Act brought by the Secretary of Labor).

to government may be reliable and important to ascertain the facts. The latter interest has generally prevailed with the courts, and in the absence of statutory authority, such reports are not privileged.[3]

Policy arguments that a privilege is needed to encourage frank and full reporting have frequently prevailed with legislatures, and statutory privileges for reports of highway and industrial accidents; tax returns; selective service reports; social security, health, unemployment compensation, and census data; and bank records are common.[4] Whether such privileges are absolute or qualified depends largely on the individual statute, but courts have construed many statutes as granting only a qualified privilege that may be overcome in appropriate circumstances.[5] The privilege is held either by the reporter, the government, or both.[6]

---

[3]Baldrige v. Shapiro, 455 U.S. 345, 360, 102 S. Ct. 1103, 71 L. Ed. 2d 199 (1982) ("A statute granting a privilege is to be strictly construed so as 'to avoid a construction that would suppress otherwise competent evidence.' "); Villa v. Burlington Northern and Santa Fe Railway Co., 397 F.3d 1041, 1047 (8th Cir. 2005) (refusing to extend privilege to parallel information on different report form and stating that only Congress may expand the current narrow privilege); Association for Women in Science v. Califano, 566 F.2d 339, 344 (D.C. Cir. 1977) (privilege must be statutorily based even to be considered; simply holding out report as "confidential" is insufficient). *See also* Branch v. Phillips Petroleum Co., 638 F.2d 873 (5th Cir. 1981); Wiener v. NEC Electronics, Inc., 848 F. Supp. 124, 128–29 (N.D. Cal. 1994); In re Domestic Air Transp. Antitrust Litigation, 141 F.R.D. 556, 560 (N.D. Ga. 1992). A legislature, by specifically designating instances in which materials are privileged, has by implication expressed its intention not to protect undesignated materials from disclosure. In re Story, 159 Ohio St. 144, 50 Ohio Op. 116, 111 N.E.2d 385, 388 (1953). Executive orders and regulations promulgated pursuant to specific statutory authority achieve the same result as statutory privileges. *See* Califano, 566 F.2d at 344 (executive orders); Tobias v. Kwiatek, 98 F.R.D. 513 (D. Vt. 1983) (regulations).

[4]For cases collected on these specific subjects, see 8 Wigmore, Evidence § 2377 (McNaughton rev. 1961).

[5]*See, e.g.*, American Civil Liberties Union of Mississippi, Inc. v. Finch, 638 F.2d 1336, 1344 (5th Cir. 1981); Califano, 566 F.2d at 346 (discussing different classes of statutes and holding that statutes that bar disclosure but do not specify from whom the materials are to be withheld are accorded only a qualified privilege); Tobias v. Kwiatek, 98 F.R.D. 513, 516 (D. Vt. 1983); Ideal Toy Corp. v. Tyco Industries, Inc., 478 F. Supp. 1191, 1193 (D. Del. 1979).

[6]*See* 3 Weinstein's Federal Evidence § 502A.03[2] (2d ed. 2012); Washington Post Co. v. U.S. Dept. of Health and Human Services, 603 F. Supp. 235 (D.D.C. 1985). For a discussion of "Reverse FOIA" actions by private parties to enjoin the government from releasing allegedly protected materials, see United States Dep't of Justice, Freedom of Information Act Guide, May 2004, available at http://www.usdoj.gov/oip/foi-act.htm.

The soundness of a policy extending greater protection to these reports than is required by constitutional guarantees[7] is dubious, and in some instances seems to imply a greater need for accuracy in governmental statistic gathering than in judicial fact-finding. But where the policy has been adopted by statute, any lack of wisdom does not justify judicial incursions against the protection afforded.[8] While federal courts are not obliged to honor privileges created by state statute or court rule,[9] they have occasionally done so, applying a variety of balancing tests to determine whether to honor the privilege.[10]

## § 113    The secrecy of grand jury proceedings: Votes and expressions of grand jurors; testimony of witnesses

The taking of evidence by grand jurors and their deliberations have traditionally been shrouded in secrecy.[1] The ancient oath

---

[7]Required reports may, of course, raise problems of self-incrimination. *See* infra § 142. The privileges discussed in the present section may to some degree represent an effort to meet that problem. *See generally* Saltzburg, The Required Records Doctrine: Its Lessons for the Privilege Against Self-Incrimination, 53 U. Chi. L. Rev. 6 (1986).

[8]Hickok v. Margolis, 221 Minn. 480, 22 N.W.2d 850 (1946).

[9]*See* Matter of Grand Jury Impaneled January 21, 1975, 541 F.2d 373 (3d Cir. 1976).

Proposed Federal Rule 502 would have provided a privilege in federal court for information privileged by state statutes of the type covered in this section. 56 F.R.D. at 234 to 235. However, it was not adopted. The Uniform Rules of Evidence (2005) do not contain such a provision.

[10]*See, e.g.,* In re Grand Jury Subpoena Dated Nov. 14, 1989, 728 F. Supp. 368 (W.D. Pa. 1990); Unger v. Cohen, 125 F.R.D. 67, 69 (S.D. N.Y. 1989); King v. Conde, 121 F.R.D. 180, 187–91 (E.D. N.Y. 1988); Kelly v. City of San Jose, 114 F.R.D. 653, 655–56 (N.D. Cal. 1987). While a federal statute creates a similar privilege, some courts have applied a state statutory privilege modified to correspond to the

federal model. *See, e.g.,* In re Grand Jury Subpoena Dated Nov. 14, 1989, 728 F. Supp. at 371–74 (applying qualified privilege applicable under federal law rather than absolute privilege appropriate under state law); In re Grand Jury Empanelled January 21, 1981, 535 F. Supp. 537 (D.N.J. 1982) (same). Additionally, states recognize the statutory privileges of other states. *See* Davidson v. Great Nat. Life Ins. Co., 737 S.W.2d 312 (Tex. 1987).

[Section 113]

[1]1 Beale et al., Grand Jury Law and Practice, Ch.5 (2d ed. 2012); 8 Wigmore, Evidence § 2360 (McNaughton rev. 1961); Kadish, Behind the Locked Door of an American Grand Jury: Its History, Its Secrecy, and Its Process, 24 Fla. St. U. L. Rev. 1 (1996); Levy, The Patriot Act Grand Jury Disclosure Exception: A Proposal for Reconciling Civil Liberty and Law Enforcement Concerns, 5 J.I.C.L. 2 (2005); Shaw, The USA Patriot Act of 2001, the Intelligence Reform and Terrorism Prevention Act of 2004, and the False Dichotomy Between Protecting National Security and Preserving Grand Jury Secrecy, 35 Seton Hall L. Rev. 495 (2005). *See also* In re Special Grand Jury 89-2, 450 F.3d 1159, 1163–66 (10th Cir. 2006) (recounting extensive efforts of members of grand jury investigating environmental

administered to the grand jurors bound them to keep secret "the King's counsel, your fellows' and your own."[2]

crimes by government contractors at Rocky Flats Nuclear Weapons Plant in Colorado to disclose aspects of the investigation). However, statements by the prosecution about its investigation that do not reveal matters occurring before the grand jury do not violate the secrecy principle. *See* In re Sealed Case No. 99-3091, 192 F.3d 995, 1001–03 (D.C. Cir. 1999) (finding no violation of secrecy requirement in revelation by attorney for independent counsel that not long after the Senate concludes its impeachment trial of President Clinton, Ken Starr should indict Clinton for lying under oath in his January 1998 deposition in the Paula Jones case).

[2]Fed. R. Crim.P. 6(e)(2) states that "[n]o obligation of secrecy may be imposed on any person except in accordance with Rule (6)(e)(2)(B)." Unless specifically provided otherwise in the rules, it imposes a secrecy requirement on grand jurors, those who receive and record the proceedings, and attorneys for the government.

Fed. R. Crim. P. 6(e)(3) provides exceptions from the secrecy requirement as follows:

(A) Disclosure of a grand-jury matter—other than the grand jury's deliberations or any grand juror's vote—may be made to:

(i) an attorney for the government for use in performing that attorney's duty;

(ii) any government personnel—including those of a state, state subdivision, Indian tribe, or foreign government—that an attorney for the government considers necessary to assist in performing that attorney's duty to enforce federal criminal law . . . .

(B) A person to whom information is disclosed under Rule 6(e)(3)(A)(ii) may use that information only to assist an attorney for the government in performing that attorney's duty to enforce federal criminal law. An attorney for the government must promptly provide the court that impaneled the grand jury with the names of all persons to whom a disclosure has been made, and must certify that the attorney has advised those persons of their obligation of secrecy under this rule.

(C) An attorney for the government may disclose any grand-jury matter to another federal grand jury.

(D) An attorney for the government may disclose any grand-jury matter involving foreign intelligence, counterintelligence . . . , or foreign intelligence information . . . to any federal law enforcement, intelligence, protective, immigration, national defense, or national security official to assist the official receiving the information in the performance of that official's duties. An attorney for the government may also disclose any grand-jury matter involving, within the United States or elsewhere, a threat of attack or other grave hostile acts of a foreign power or its agent, a threat of domestic or international sabotage or terrorism, or clandestine intelligence gathering activities by an intelligence service or network of a foreign power or by its agent, to any appropriate Federal, State, State subdivision, Indian tribal, or foreign government official, for the purpose of preventing or responding to such threat or activities.

(i) Any official who receives information under Rule 6(e)(3)(D) may use the information only as necessary in the conduct of that person's official duties subject to any limitations on the unauthorized disclosure of such information. Any State, State subdivision, Indian tribal, or foreign government official who receives information under Rule 6(e)(3)(D) may use the information only consistent with such guidelines as the Attorney General and the Director of National Intelligence shall jointly issue.

Several objectives are commonly suggested as being promoted by the policy of secrecy: to guard the independence of action and freedom of deliberation of the accusatory body, to protect the reputations of those investigated but not indicted, to prevent the forewarning and flight of those accused before publication of the indictment, and to encourage free disclosure by witnesses.[3] The procedure for attaining them assumes two forms, somewhat loosely described as "privilege." The first is a privilege against disclosure of the grand jurors' communications to each other during their deliberations and of their individual votes.[4] The propriety of such a measure as an assurance of free and independent deliberation can scarcely be doubted, though it may be of slight practical importance in view of the infrequency with which these communications and votes will be relevant to any material inquiry.[5] The second of these privileges involves disclosure of the testimony given by witnesses before the grand jury, and as an area of substantial controversy, deserves thoughtful scrutiny.

---

(ii) Within a reasonable time after disclosure is made under Rule 6(e)(3)(D), an attorney for the government must file, under seal, a notice with the court in the district where the grand jury convened stating that such information was disclosed and the departments, agencies, or entities to which the disclosure was made.

. . . .

[3]The classical justifications for grand jury secrecy are set forth in U.S. v. Rose, 215 F.2d 617, 628–629 (3d Cir. 1954). Cf. Rehberg v. Paulk, 132 S. Ct. 1497, 1509–10, 182 L. Ed. 2d 593 (2012) (ruling that grand jury witnesses enjoy absolute immunity from suit in § 1983 civil actions to encourage voluntary, full, and frank testimony of witnesses).

[4]Fed. R. Crim. P. 6(e)(3)(A) (exceptions not permitted for deliberations and votes of grand jurors); U.S. v. Sigma Intern., Inc., 244 F.3d 841, 871 (11th Cir. 2001) (en banc) (holding that rule was violated where prosecutor revealed to second grand jury that first had wanted to indict, which was considered tantamount to disclosing grand jury deliberations); Wm. J. Burns International Detective Agency v. Holt, 138 Minn. 165, 164 N.W. 590 (1917) (in action to recover for detective services allegedly rendered at request of grand jurors, conversations among members during deliberations about employing detectives excluded); Opinion of the Justices, 96 N.H. 530, 73 A.2d 433 (1950) (power of legislative investigating committee does not extend to inquiring into grand jurors' votes and opinions); 8 Wigmore, Evidence § 2361 (McNaughton rev. 1961). The privilege does not extend to deliberations in the course of preparing a report which was outside the lawful functions of the grand jury. Bennett v. Stockwell, 197 Mich. 50, 163 N.W. 482 (1917). Neither of the privileges discussed in this section applies to prevent public access to purely "ministerial" records of a grand jury. In re Special Grand Jury (for Anchorage, Alaska), 674 F.2d 778 (9th Cir. 1982). Also, privilege does not prevent grand juror from being called as a witness at trial to testify to the purpose of the grand jury inquiry in order to show materiality of testimony of the witness in a perjury prosecution. See U.S. v. Conley, 186 F.3d 7, 17 (1st Cir. 1999).

[5]8 Wigmore, Evidence §§ 2361, 2364 (McNaughton rev. 1961). But see Wm. J. Burns International Detective Agency v. Holt, 138 Minn. 165, 164 N.W. 590 (1917).

While the grand jury in its origins may have been an instrument of, and subservient to, the crown, its position as an important bulwark of the rights of English citizens was established by the end of the 17th century.[6] This latter aspect is evident in the provision of the Fifth Amendment of the Constitution of the United States requiring presentment or indictment as a precondition of prosecution for a capital or infamous crime.[7] During this period, the grand jury's independence from incursion by both prosecution and defense appears to have been well recognized, and prosecutors were admitted only by sufferance.[8] However, the decline in the perceived need for the grand jury as a protector of individual liberties, which caused its abolition in England,[9] seems in this country to have led to predominant emphasis on aiding the prosecution in investigating crime and serving as a powerful instrument of discovery. Thus, we find statutes and rules providing for the presence of prosecuting attorneys and stenographers except when the grand jury is deliberating or voting.[10]

The veil of secrecy surrounding grand jury proceedings does not preclude all subsequent disclosure and use of the testimony and other material presented there.[11] In the federal system, prosecutors have long had the use of grand jury material in crim-

---

[6]1 Holdsworth, A History of English Law 321–23 (7th ed. 1956); Younger, The People's Panel (1963); Goldstein, The State and the Accused: Balance of Advantage in Criminal Procedure, 69 Yale L.J. 1149, 1170 (1960). The key case is Earl of Shaftesbury's Trial, (1681) 8 How. St. Tr. 759 (quoted in 8 Wigmore, Evidence § 2360, at 729 (McNaughton rev. 1961)).

[7]See Leipold, Why Grand Juries Do Not (and Cannot) Protect the Accused, 80 Cornell L. Rev. 260, 283–85 (1995).

[8]People v. Klaw, 53 Misc. 158, 104 N.Y.S. 482 (Gen. Sess. 1907); Younger, The People's Panel 77 (1963).

[9]Administration of Justice Act of 1933, 23 & 24 Geo. 5, c. 36.

[10]See, e.g., Fed. R. Crim. P. 6(d): "Attorneys for the government, the witness under examination, interpreters when needed and, for the purpose of taking the evidence, a stenographer or operator of a recording device may be present while the grand jury is in session, but no person other than the jurors may be present while the grand jury is deliberating or voting."

[11]See Dassault Systemes, SA v. Childress, 663 F.3d 832, 845–46 (6th Cir. 2011), cert. denied, 133 S. Ct. 286, 184 L. Ed. 2d 168 (2012) (ruling that mere contact of materials with grand jury did not cause document to be a matter "occurring before a grand jury" because the production of a discrete portion of preexisting records would likely not reveal the scope or nature of the grand jury inquiry); In re Petition of Kutler, 800 F. Supp. 2d 42, 45–50 (D.D.C. 2011) (granting release of President Nixon's decades-old Watergate grand jury testimony to historian under special circumstances exception); Oracle Corp. v. SAP AG, 566 F. Supp. 2d 1010, 1011–13 (N.D. Cal. 2008) (ruling that grand jury witness may not resist disclosure of evidence in private litigation because the evidence was disclosed to a grand jury investigation where doing so would not reveal the inner workings of the grand jury); Dexia Credit Local v. Rogan, 395

inal prosecutions stemming from the grand jury's investigations.[12] Such use is perfectly consistent both with the practical operation of the grand jury[13] and with the central purpose of that body which justifies its broad investigatory powers. However, government use of grand jury material for purposes other than criminal prosecution, such as in a regulatory proceeding dealing with the same facts, would generally be an abuse of the grand jury system[14] and the federal statutory provisions.[15]

Several decisions of the Supreme Court have examined the statutory provisions and imposed limitations on access to grand jury materials by government agencies. In the first of these decisions, *United States v. Sells Engineering, Inc.*,[16] the Court held that government attorneys, other than those working on the crim-

---

F. Supp. 2d 709, 714–17 (N.D. Ill. 2005) (grand jury secrecy does not protect documents presented to the grand jury that do not reveal grand jury proceedings); Lockheed Martin Corp. v. Boeing Co., 393 F. Supp. 2d 1276, 1280 (M.D. Fla. 2005) (ruling that privilege not available to private party as a grand jury seeking to resist production of documents in civil litigation where documents do not reveal undisclosed information about the investigation, the subjects or targets of the investigation, or the identities of the grand jurors and where the prosecutors have not asserted that disclosure would undermine the investigation).

[12]*See, e.g.*, U.S. v. Socony-Vacuum Oil Co., 310 U.S. 150, 233, 60 S. Ct. 811, 84 L. Ed. 1129 (1940) (refreshing recollection of government witness); People v. Goldberg, 302 Ill. 559, 135 N.E. 84 (1922) (impeachment of defense witness); Izer v. State, 77 Md. 110, 26 A. 282 (1893) (proving perjury before grand jury). *See generally* 1 Beale et al., Grand Jury Law and Practice § 5:8 (2d ed. 2012). This general authorization includes disclosure to an Assistant United States Attorney in another district for use in enforcing federal criminal law, Impounded, 277 F.3d 407, 412–14 (3d Cir. 2002), and upon court order to state governmental personnel, including quasi-governmental investigative agencies, when assisting in enforcing federal criminal law, U.S. v. Pimental, 380

F.3d 575, 592–96 (1st Cir. 2004).

[13]"Government attorneys are allowed into grand jury rooms . . . because both the grand jury's functions and their own *prosecutorial* duties require it . . . [T]he same reasoning applies to disclosure of grand jury materials outside the grand jury room." U.S. v. Sells Engineering, Inc., 463 U.S. 418, 429, 103 S. Ct. 3133, 77 L. Ed. 2d 743 (1983).

[14]U. S. v. Procter & Gamble Co., 356 U.S. 677, 78 S. Ct. 983, 2 L. Ed. 2d 1077 (1958) (use of "criminal procedures to elicit evidence in a civil case . . . would be flouting the policy of the law").

[15]*See* Fed. R. Crim. P. 6(e)(3)(C) (I). *See generally* 1 Beale et al., Grand Jury Law and Practice § 5:8 (2d ed. 2012).

[16]U.S. v. Sells Engineering, Inc., 463 U.S. 418, 103 S. Ct. 3133, 77 L. Ed. 2d 743 (1983). The same requirement was imposed with respect to state officials who request federal grand jury material in Illinois v. Abbott & Associates, Inc., 460 U.S. 557, 103 S. Ct. 1356, 75 L. Ed. 2d 281 (1983). Grand jury secrecy requirements under *Sells Engineering* apply within the federal government to the filing of a summary of the proceedings before one grand jury with a judge in a different, but related, case (the qui tam court). *See* In re Sealed Case, 250 F.3d 764, 768–70 (D.C. Cir. 2001).

inal matters before the grand jury, are not automatically entitled to access to grand jury materials without a court order, and further that to obtain such an order, not only must the requirements of the statute be met, but also a "particularized need" for the material must be shown. In *United States v. Baggot*,[17] the Court held that the Internal Revenue Service was not entitled to court ordered access to grand jury materials in connection with a civil tax investigation because such an investigation is not "preliminary to or in connection with a judicial proceeding" as required by the rule.

Finally, in *United States v. John Doe, Inc. I*,[18] the Court qualified somewhat the impact of *Sells Engineering*. First, it allowed the attorney who conducted the grand jury investigation to continue using grand jury materials in civil proceedings related to the investigation. Second, although continuing to recognize that "particularized need" must be shown before disclosure to other government attorneys, the Court noted that the policy concerns supporting grand jury secrecy were "implicated to a much lesser extent" when disclosure involved other government attorneys.[19]

In the federal system, both government agencies and private parties must show a "particularized need" for grand jury material before it is to be released.[20] This requirement, though sometimes criticized by commentators,[21] has consistently been reasserted by

---

[17]U.S. v. Baggot, 463 U.S. 476, 103 S. Ct. 3164, 77 L. Ed. 2d 785 (1983).

[18]U.S. v. John Doe, Inc. I, 481 U.S. 102, 107 S. Ct. 1656, 95 L. Ed. 2d 94 (1987).

[19]Doe, 481 U.S. at 112; In re Grand Jury Subpoenas Dated Feb. 28, 2002, March 26, 2003, Oct. 4, 2004, 472 F.3d 990, 996–99 (8th Cir. 2007) (finding no prohibition against FBI investigator who was working simultaneously on criminal and civil investigation having access to grand jury materials as necessary to assist in criminal investigation and no showing of breach of grand jury secrecy unless the materials were disclosed to other parties or put to use in some way other than to further the criminal investigation).

[20]U. S. v. Procter & Gamble Co., 356 U.S. 677, 78 S. Ct. 983, 2 L. Ed.

2d 1077 (1958). *See* U.S. v. Aisenberg, 358 F.3d 1327, 1349–50 (11th Cir. 2004) (ruling that district court failed to require showing of particularized need when it granted blanket disclosure even though it determined the prosecution was conducted in bad faith); In re Grand Jury Proceedings, 503 F. Supp. 2d 800, 804–06 (E.D. Va. 2007) (ruling that SEC's claims to need grand jury potentially to impeach and refresh recollection of grand jury witnesses and because of limitations imposed on depositions by another court were insufficient to satisfy the "particularized need" requirement of completed grand jury).

[21]*See, e.g.*, Knudsen, Pretrial Disclosure of Grand Jury Testimony, 48 Wash. L. Rev. 423 (1973) (advocating doing away with secrecy except where government shows good cause).

the Supreme Court.[22] Clearly, federal grand jury secrecy will enjoy substantial protection for the foreseeable future.

Among others having a potential need for access to transcripts of testimony before a grand jury, perhaps the strongest case may be made for the criminal defendant. The right of an accused to a copy of his or her own recorded grand jury testimony is today recognized by statute or rule in a number of states[23] and in the federal courts.[24] Considerations of basic fairness (and the inapplicability of the justifications for grand jury secrecy in this context) argue strongly for this access. The defense is guaranteed access to the testimony of other grand jury witnesses who testify at trial by the Jencks Act,[25] which requires production of such testimony once they have testified on direct. No infringement of the objectives of secrecy mentioned at the beginning of this section can result from such disclosure, which constitutes the least acceptable minimum.[26]

Despite the stringent language of the federal rule imposing se-

---

[22]Douglas Oil Co. of California v. Petrol Stops Northwest, 441 U.S. 211, 99 S. Ct. 1667, 60 L. Ed. 2d 156 (1979) ("It is clear from *Procter & Gamble* and *Dennis* [*v. United States*, 384 U.S. 855 (1966)] that disclosure is appropriate only in those cases where the need for it outweighs the public interest in secrecy, and that the burden of demonstrating this balance rests upon the private party seeking disclosure. It is equally clear that as the considerations justifying secrecy become less relevant, a party asserting a need for grand jury transcripts will have a lesser burden in showing justification. For an examination of the meaning of "particularized need," see 1 Beale et al., Grand Jury Law and Practice § 5:10 (2d ed. 2012).

[23]*See, e.g.*, Kan. Stat. Ann. § 22-3212(a)(3); W. Va. R. Crim. P. 16(a)(1)(A).

[24]Fed. R. Crim. P. 16(a)(1)(B)(iii). Rule 6(e)(1) requires the recording of all grand jury proceedings except when deliberating or voting.

[25]18 U.S.C.A. § 3500; Fed. R. Crim. P. 26.2.

[26]A.B.A. Standards for Criminal Justice, Discovery Standards, Standard 11-2.1(ii) & Commentary 20–21 (3d ed. 1996) propose that writ-

ten statements be provided before trial so as not to delay the trial or to deny effective assistance of counsel. *See also* Harris v. U.S., 433 F.2d 1127, 1129 (D.C. Cir. 1970) ("We note with particular approval the Government's current practice of making the grand jury testimony of its prospective witnesses available to defense counsel at the commencement of the trial . . . .").

However, delay in providing or failure to provide grand jury material as required by the Jencks Act results in reversal only upon a finding of prejudice. *See* U.S. v. Elem, 269 F.3d 877, 882 (7th Cir. 2001) (ruling that, although Jencks Act does not by its terms require a showing of prejudice from failure to produce grand jury transcript, such a requirement has been judicially imposed); U.S. v. Montgomery, 210 F.3d 446, 451–52 (5th Cir. 2000) (noting that although production is not excused under a good faith argument, delayed production after verdict did not require reversal where there were no material deviations between trial testimony of witness and grand jury transcript). Also, where the grand jury witness does not testify at trial, a criminal defendant, like other litigants, is required to demonstrate a particularized need for access to the grand jury testimony. *See, e.g.*, U.S. v. Wilkinson, 124 F.3d 971,

crecy on grand jury proceedings,[27] witnesses are pointedly omitted from the list of those bound by its provisions.[28] Whether a federal judge has authority to order grand jury witnesses not to disclose their own testimony in order to protect the integrity of an investigation is unclear.[29] Absent such atypical orders, witnesses are free to divulge their testimony as they see fit after testifying. Indeed, the Supreme Court held that a state statute prohibiting a grand jury witness from ever disclosing testimony before the grand jury violated the First Amendment as applied to a witness who wished to disclose information independently acquired by him to which he had testified.[30] On the other hand, some authorities suggest that witnesses may not be compelled to disclose what their testimony was before the grand jury.[31]

---

977 (8th Cir. 1997) (holding that showing of particularized need not made).

[27]Fed. R. Crim. P. 6(e).

[28]Fed. R. Crim. P. 6(e) para. 2 (Original Committee Note); In re Grand Jury, 490 F.3d 978, 985–90 (D.C. Cir. 2007) (ruling over government objection that witnesses have a right to review the transcript of their own testimony, but leaving unanswered whether they have a right to a copy of that transcript).

[29]*Compare* In re Subpoena to Testify Before Grand Jury Directed to Custodian of Records, 864 F.2d 1559, 1563–64 (11th Cir. 1989) (upholding practice), *with* Beale et al., Grand Jury Law and Practice § 5:5 (2d ed. 2012)

(questioning validity of general practice).

[30]Butterworth v. Smith, 494 U.S. 624, 110 S. Ct. 1376, 108 L. Ed. 2d 572 (1990). *See* Hoffmann-Pugh v. Keenan, 338 F.3d 1136, 1138–40 (10th Cir. 2003) (ruling that statute that prohibited witness from disclosing information gained though participation in grand jury process but permitted her to disclose information she previously possessed was constitutional).

[31]*See* Application of Eisenberg, 654 F.2d 1107, 1113 (5th Cir. 1981); In re Swearingen Aviation Corp., 605 F.2d 125, 127 (4th Cir. 1979); Beale et al., Grand Jury Law and Practice § 5:5 (2d ed. 2012).

# Title 6.   Privilege: Constitutional

## Chapter 13

# The Privilege Against Self-Incrimination

## § 114   The history and development of the privilege

The legal right of a person to be free of compelled self-incrimination has traditionally been described as a privilege, although it is embodied in federal and state constitutional provisions that do not explicitly use that terminology. The Supreme Court has noted that "[t]he term 'privilege against self-incrimination' is not an entirely accurate description of a person's [Fifth Amendment] constitutional protection against being 'compelled in any criminal case to be a witness against himself.' "[1] Nevertheless, since the most fundamental part of that protection is the right of an accused in a criminal trial not to be compelled to be a witness for the prosecution, it is appropriate to continue to regard the right as a privilege albeit with implications beyond those of other evidentiary privileges.

Because of considerable dispute as to the wisdom of the privilege against self-incrimination, the origin and development of the rule have been of special interest to legal scholars. Unfortunately

---

**[Section 114]**

[1]U.S. v. Hubbell, 530 U.S. 27, 34, 120 S. Ct. 2037, 147 L. Ed. 2d 24 (2000). See generally the opinions in Chavez v. Martinez, 538 U.S. 760, 123 S. Ct. 1994, 155 L. Ed. 2d 984 (2003), discussed in § 117 infra.

important aspects of the matter are still clouded with doubt. What is known suggests that the privilege had its roots in opposition to the use of the ex officio oath by the English ecclesiastical courts and that its development was intimately intertwined with the political and religious disputes of early England. The most significant ambiguity is whether the privilege as finally applied in the common law courts after 1700 represented a logical extension of principle underlying earlier opposition to the procedures of ecclesiastical courts, or rather, whether it reflected condemnation by association of a procedure not inherently inconsistent with prevailing values.

Prior to the early 1200s, trials in the ecclesiastical courts had been by ordeal or compurgation oath, the formal swearing by the party and his oath helpers. Under the "inquisitorial oath," there was active interrogation of the accused by the judge in addition to the accused's uncomfortable consciousness of his oath to reveal the entire truth of the matter under inquiry. There was some formal limitation upon the power of the ecclesiastical courts to use this device.

The oath procedure was subsequently adopted by two controversial courts and used for essentially political purposes. In 1487 the Court of the Star Chamber was authorized to pursue its broad political mandate by means of the oath. The Star Chamber was not even subjected to the requirement of presentation that theoretically provided protection from use of the oath to engage in broad "fishing inquisitions" by the ecclesiastical courts. About one hundred years later the same procedure was authorized for the Court of the High Commission in Causes Ecclesiastical, established to maintain conformity to the recently established church.[2] The freewheeling methods of these politically-minded courts, including the use of torture,[3] undoubtedly stimulated a great deal of additional opposition to the oath procedures.

Required self-incrimination and the use of the oath were not confined to the ecclesiastical courts and the courts of High Commission and Star Chamber. In criminal trials the accused was expected to take an active part in the proceedings, often to his own detriment.[4] He was examined before trial by justices of the peace, and the results of this examination were preserved for use by the judge at trial. Only in limited classes of cases was the ex-

---

[2]1 Eliz. I, ch. 1; M. Maguire, Attack of the Common Lawyers on the Oath Ex Offico, in Essays in History and Political Theory in Honor of Charles H. McIlwain, 213–16 (1936).

[3]Pittman, The Colonial and Constitutional History of the Privilege Against Self-Incrimination in America, 21 Va. L. Rev. 763, 773 (1935).

[4]Morgan, The Privilege Against Self-Incrimination, 34 Minn. L. Rev. 1, 12–23 (1949); 8 Wigmore, Evidence § 2250 (McNaughton rev. 1961), p. 285–86.

amination under oath. This was not out of tenderness for the accused, but rather because it was believed that administering an oath would unwisely permit the accused to eventually place before the jury an influential denial of guilt made under oath.[5]

After 1641, the common law courts began to apply to their own procedure some of the restrictions on use of the oath that had been urged for their ecclesiastical counterparts. By 1700, extraction of an answer in any procedure in matters of criminality or forfeiture was improper.[6] This was the privilege against compelled self-incrimination.

It is difficult to draw many helpful conclusions from the historical origin of the privilege. Wigmore accepts Bentham's suggestion that the privilege as ultimately applied in the common law courts was essentially an overreaction to abusive use of the oath procedure without proper presentment of charges.[7] But perhaps this is too narrow a reading of the historical material. Even if the initial objection was only to the impropriety of putting individuals to their oath without presentation, this policy suggests at least limited objection to the use of information extracted from the mouth of the accused as the basis for a criminal prosecution. This early suspicion of compulsory self-incrimination, even if it extended only to situations where compulsion was exerted before an accusation had been made by some other method, seems to be based upon a perception that compelling an individual to provide the basis for his own penal liability should be limited because the position in which it places the individual, making a choice between violating a solemn oath and incurring penal liability, weighs against important policies of individual freedom and dignity.

There is significant disagreement regarding the early development of the privilege in America. Some evidence of the privilege in early colonial America exists.[8] In any case, it was inserted in the constitutions or bills of rights of seven American states before

---

[5] 8 Wigmore, Evidence § 2250 at p. 285.

[6] 8 Wigmore, Evidence § 2250 at 290–91.

[7] 8 Wigmore, Evidence § 2250 at 292, citing J. Bentham, Rationale of Judicial Evidence, in 7 The Works of Jeremy Bentham 456, 462 (Bowring ed. 1843). This view was also accepted in the first edition of this text. McCormick, Evidence 255 (1954).

Later scholarship has suggested that no privilege was recognized in common law criminal procedure until the late eighteenth century, and that its development then was related to the increased involvement of defense counsel in criminal proceedings and their success in making trial a meaningful stage of the proceedings. See Langbein, The Historical Origin of the Privilege Against Self-Incrimination at Common Law, 92 Mich. L. Rev. 1047 (1994).

[8] Pittman, The Colonial and Constitutional History of the Privilege, 21 Va. L. Rev. at 776–79.

1789,[9] and has since spread to all state constitutions except those of Iowa and New Jersey. In both of the latter states, however, it was accepted as a matter of nonconstitutional law.[10]

## § 115   Current nature and status of the privilege

The privilege is, of course, embodied in that portion of the Fifth Amendment to the United States Constitution providing, "No person . . . shall be compelled in any criminal case to be a witness against himself. . . ." The precise nature of the federal constitutional right created by this language divided the justices of the United States Supreme Court in *Chavez v. Martinez*.[1]

Justice Thomas, writing for four members of the Court, took the view that the literal terms of the Fifth Amendment mean that no violation of the provision itself occurs until or unless an accused's in-court testimony as a witness is compelled in the course of a criminal trial or a statement made out-of-court or in another proceeding is used in that trial.[2] The Court has authority under the Fifth Amendment to create "prophylactic rules" to safeguard the core constitutional rights, he added. One of these rules is an evidentiary privilege that protects a person who is not on trial for a criminal offense from being compelled to give testimony, because that testimony may later be used in a manner that violates the core of Fifth Amendment protection.[3]

Justice Kennedy, writing for three justices, read the Fifth Amendment provision more broadly:

> [T]he Self-Incrimination Clause is a substantive constraint on the conduct of the government, not merely an evidentiary rule governing the work of the courts . . . . The Clause protects an individual from being forced to give answers demanded by an official in any

---

[9]Virginia (1776), Pennsylvania (1776), Maryland (1776), North Carolina (1776), Vermont (1777), Massachusetts (1780), and New Hampshire (1784). *See* Pittman, The Colonial and Constitutional History of the Privilege Against Self-Incrimination in America, 21 Va. L. Rev. 763, 765 (1935).

[10]*See* State v. Height, 117 Iowa 650, 91 N.W. 935 (1902) (state constitutional guarantee of due process includes protection from compelled self-incrimination); State v. White, 27 N.J. 158, 142 A.2d 65 (1958) (no state constitutional prohibition against compelled self-incrimination but statutory provisions are "no less urgent and protective").

**[Section 115]**

[1]Chavez v. Martinez, 538 U.S. 760, 123 S. Ct. 1994, 155 L. Ed. 2d 984 (2003).

[2]Chavez, 538 U.S. at 766–67 (Thomas, J., announcing the judgment of the Court) (joined by the Chief Justice, and Justices O'Connor and Scalia).

[3]538 U.S. at 770–71.

context where the answers might give rise to criminal liability in the future.[4]

The provision, in other words, "provides both assurance that a person will not be compelled to testify against himself in a criminal proceeding and a continuing right against government conduct intended to bring about self-incrimination."[5]

Justice Souter, joined by Justice Breyer, indicated that evidentiary use of testimony or statements by the accused is "the core of Fifth Amendment protection."[6] He appeared to also believe that this Fifth Amendment core protection could be extended to include protection against other governmental activity if that is shown to be desirable to protect the basic or core guarantee.[7]

Whether this doctrinal division among the justices makes much practical difference is open to question. *Chavez* itself involved an effort to establish civil liability for damages on the basis of coercive out-of-court interrogation. A majority declined to impose such liability on the basis of Fifth Amendment law; four justices reasoned that under Justice Thomas's analysis such expansion was doctrinally prohibited and two reasoned that Chavez had not shown that the conceptually-permissible expansion was appropriate. Justice Thomas commented that even under his approach, the prophylactic nature of the privilege of one not on trial on criminal charges to withhold an answer would not alter the case law addressing penalties for violating that privilege.[8]

For many and perhaps most purposes, it is probably of no significance whether the constitutional right of a witness to refuse to engage in testimonial and incriminating conduct is based on a "prophylactic rule" developed to safeguard the core Fifth Amendment right, as Justice Thomas argued, or is itself an aspect of that core Fifth Amendment right.[9] Courts might, however, be persuaded to less vigorously develop the protections afforded one not at the time an accused in a criminal case if convinced that the right at issue is a judicially-promulgated prophylactic rule rather than a core Fifth Amendment provision.

The Fifth Amendment privilege is, of course, applicable to the states by virtue of the Fourteenth Amendment. So holding in

---

[4]538 U.S. at 791 (Kennedy, J., concurring in part and dissenting in part) (joined by Justices Stevens and Ginsburg).

[5]538 U.S. at 791.

[6]538 U.S. at 777 (Souter, J., concurring in the judgment).

[7]538 U.S. at 777.

[8]538 U.S. at 772 n. 3 (Thomas, J., announcing the judgment of the Court).

[9]Justice Thomas's distinction does at least coincide with a distinction sometimes drawn in privilege discussion between the privilege of an accused and that of a witness; see generally § 117 infra.

*Malloy v. Hogan*,[10] decided in 1964, the Supreme Court relied heavily upon the basic proposition that "the American system of criminal prosecution is accusatorial, not inquisitorial." "[T]he Fifth Amendment privilege," the Court continued, "is its essential mainstay . . . . Governments, state and federal, are thus constitutionally compelled to establish guilt by evidence independently and freely secured, and may not by coercion prove a charge against an accused out of his own mouth."[11]

*Malloy* also rejected as "incongruous" the contention that the availability of the federal privilege to a witness in a state proceeding should be determined according to a less stringent standard than is applicable in a federal proceeding. "[T]he same standards," it concluded, "must determine whether an accused's silence in either a federal or state proceeding is justified."[12]

Much recent self-incrimination discussion has focused upon the Supreme Court's construction of the Fifth Amendment's privilege. In some senses, this is unfortunate. Similar privileges are recognized in all states as a matter of either or both state constitutional provision or case law, and versions of the privilege are sometimes embodied in statutory provisions[13] or court rule.[14] Commentators and courts have increasingly recognized state courts' right and perhaps duty to construe state constitutional and statutory provisions "independently" of the Supreme Court's construction of even identically-phrased federal constitutional provisions.[15] This jurisprudence of "new federalism" emphasizes that there is no single privilege against compelled self-incrimination. Specifically, discussion of legal protection against compelled self-incrimination must recognize the possibility that state law provides citizens with greater protection than does the Fifth Amendment privilege.

State privileges sometimes differ in phraseology from the Fifth Amendment. Seldom, however, do these differences in terminology strongly suggest how current questions of construction should be resolved. The Fifth Amendment provides that no person is to be "compelled in any criminal case to be a witness against

---

[10]Malloy v. Hogan, 378 U.S. 1, 84 S. Ct. 1489, 12 L. Ed. 2d 653 (1964).

[11]Malloy, 378 U.S.at 7–8.

[12]378 U.S. at 9–14.

[13]Md. Code Ann., Cts. & Jud. Proc. § 9-107 ("A person may not be compelled to testify in violation of his privilege against self-incrimination"); Tex. Code Crim. Proc. Ann. art. 1.05 ("In all criminal prosecutions the accused . . . shall not be compelled to give evidence against himself.").

[14]N.J.R.E. 503 ("every natural person has a right to refuse to disclose in an action or to a police officer or other official any matter that will incriminate him").

[15]*See generally* Abrahamson, Criminal Law and State Constitutions: The Emergence of State Constitutional Law, 63 Texas L. Rev. 1141 (1985).

himself." State constitutional provisions, in contrast, sometimes specify that no person may be "compelled to give evidence against himself."[16] While this suggests the possibility that the protection afforded by the state provisions is broader, it is difficult to regard the difference in language as necessarily controlling.

## § 116  Policy foundation of the privilege under federal constitutional and state law[1]

Inquiry into the policies that do or might support the privilege often seems a frustrating and perhaps fruitless task. Despite the privilege's rich history, vigorous arguments have been made that the dangers of the Court of Star Chamber no longer exist and that the privilege has outlived its rationale.[2] Even proponents of the privilege acknowledge that its popularity and acceptance was not based upon a careful scrutiny of its rationale and that its incorporation into our legal tradition occurred without thorough examination.[3] Modern discussion has tended to undertake largely de novo development of justifications.

Whether a conceptually adequate justification exists may have little significance to the basic questions under modern law. Stuntz noted that judicial and academic writings tend to be dominated by standard explanations for the privilege that fail to explain adequately even the basic aspects of Fifth Amendment privilege law. This, he added, "lead[s] to a widespread sense that many of [the Fifth Amendment privilege's] rules and limitations are simply inexplicable."[4]

Critics of the privilege, of course, stress that the privilege may

---

[16]*E.g.* Texas Const. Art. I, § 10; Utah Const. Art. I, § 12.

**[Section 116]**

[1]*See generally* 8 Wigmore, Evidence § 2251 (McNaughton rev. 1961); Dolinko, Is There A Rationale for the Privilege Against Self-Incrimination?, 33 UCLA L. Rev. 1063 (1986); Greenawalt, Silence as a Moral and Constitutional Right, 23 William & Mary L. Rev. 15 (1981); Clapp, Privilege Against Self-Incrimination, 10 Rutgers L. Rev. 541 (1956). *See also* Allen and Mace, The Self-Incrimination Clause Explained and Its Future Predicted, 94 J. Crim. L. & Crim. 243 (2004); Dripps, Foreword, Against Police Interrogation, And the Privilege Against Self-Incrimination, 78 J. Crim. L. & C. 699, 711–18 (1988); Stuntz,

Self-Incrimination and Excuse, 88 Colum. L. Rev. 1227, 1233–40 (1988); Taslitz, Confessing in the Human Voice: A Defense of the Privilege Against Self–Incrimination, 7 Cardozo Pub. L., Policy & Ethics J. 121 (2008).

[2]Carman, A Plea for Withdrawal of Constitutional Privilege from the Criminal, 22 Minn. L. Rev. 200 (1937); Pound, Legal Interrogation of Persons Accused or Suspected of Crime, 24 J. Crim. L., C. & P.S. 1014 (1934); Terry, Constitutional Provisions Against Forcing Self-Incrimination, 15 Yale L.J. 127 (1905); Wigmore, Nemo Tenetur Seipsum Prodere, 5 Harv. L. Rev. 71, 85–87 (1891).

[3]Gerstein, Privacy and Self-Incrimination, 80 Ethics 87, 87 (1970).

[4]Stuntz, Self-Incrimination and

lack a satisfactory and principled basis. In addition, they urge that the privilege involves disruptive difficulties of application and excessive costs. First, the privilege deprives the state of access to a valuable source of reliable information, the subject of the investigation himself, and therefore purchases whatever values it attains at too great a cost to the inquiry for truth. The subject may be an especially valuable source of information when the alleged crime is one of the sophisticated "white collar" offenses, and in such situations the privilege may deny the prosecution access to the only available information.[5]

Moreover, the privilege may as a practical matter be impossible to implement effectively. Although the law may extend the theoretical right to remain silent at no or minimal cost, in fact it is inevitable that inferences will be drawn from silence and that the inferences will be acted upon. Since these inferences are drawn from inherently ambiguous silence, they are less reliable than inferences from other sources, including compelled self-incriminatory testimony. The result is that one who chooses to invoke the privilege is not protected, but rather is subjected to potential prejudice in a manner ill designed to promote even the person's own best interest.

Rationales for the privilege can usefully be divided into systemic ones, based on the role of the privilege in maintaining an appropriate criminal justice system, and individual ones, resting on the value of the privilege in implementing the interests or values of those suspected or accused of crime.[6] These rationales may overlap, as is demonstrated by the argument that the privilege serves as a valuable means of preventing the conviction of innocent criminal defendants.[7]

One who is under the strain of actual or potential accusation, although innocent, may be unduly prejudiced by his own testimony for reasons unrelated to its accuracy. For example, he may have physical traits or mannerisms that would cause an adverse reaction from the trier of fact. He might, under the strain of interrogation, become confused and thereby give an erroneous impression of guilt. Or, his act of testifying may permit the prosecution to introduce his prior criminal convictions, ostensibly for impeachment purposes, and the trier of fact may uncritically

---

Excuse, 88 Colum. L. Rev. at 1228.

[5]*See* Terry, Constitutional Provisions Against Forcing Self-Incrimination, 15 Yale L.J. 127 (1905).

[6]Dolinko, 33 UCLA L. Rev. at 1065–66.

[7]*E.g.* Griswold, The Fifth Amend-ment Today 20–21 (1955). Dean Griswold later, however, suggested that it had been a mistake to defend the privilege on the ground that it is "basically designed to protect those innocent of crime, at least in any numerical sense." Griswold, The Right to be Let Alone, 55 NW. U. L. Rev. 216, 223 (1960).

infer his guilt from these. The privilege affords such an individual the opportunity to avoid these dangers possibly flowing from
discussing an incriminating situation and thereby creating an
unreliable but prejudicial impression of guilt.[8]

Whether these considerations support the privilege is at best
problematic. Few defendants may give misleading impressions of
guilt, and juries may be more skilled at evaluating evidence than
is sometimes believed. Even when there is a significant risk that
testifying will create an erroneous impression of guilt, practical
considerations are likely to lead many defendants to testify
nevertheless.[9] To the extent that these risks are real ones, other
reforms in criminal procedure might better protect against them;
the admissibility of prior convictions to impeach, for example,
might be limited.[10]

The privilege may also protect the innocent in less direct ways.
It constitutes one part, but an important part, of our accusatorial
system which requires that no criminal punishment be imposed
unless guilt is established by a large quantum of especially reliable evidence. By denying the prosecution access to what is
regarded as an inherently suspect type of proof, the self-
incriminating admissions of the accused, the privilege forces the
prosecution to establish its case on the basis of more reliable
evidence.[11] This arguably creates an additional assurance that
every person convicted is in fact guilty as charged. Some,
however, argue that the privilege is an ineffective means of
encouraging the making of the guilt-innocence decision on reliable evidence.[12] In many situations, for example, it denies
defendants the right to call witnesses whose testimony might
well be reliable and exculpatory.[13]

Other systemic arguments run that the privilege serves to deny
governments powers that might otherwise be abused,[14] particu-

---

[8]Wilson v. U.S., 149 U.S. 60, 66,
13 S. Ct. 765, 37 L. Ed. 650 (1893).

[9]Dolinko, 33 UCLA L. Rev. at
1075.

[10]Dolinko, 33 UCLA L. Rev. at
1075–76.

[11]The classic statement of this position was reported by Sir James Fitz-
James Stephen and attributed by him
to an experienced Indian civil officer.
Explaining why prisoners were sometimes tortured, the officer stated:

There is a great deal of laziness in

it. It is far pleasanter to sit comfortably in the shade rubbing red pepper
into a poor devil's eyes than to go about
in the hot sun hunting up evidence.

Stephen, A History of the Criminal
Law of England 442 n. 1 (1883).

[12]Dolinko, 33 UCLA L. Rev. at
1076–77.

[13]Dripps, 78 J. Crim. L. & C. at
716.

[14]Dolinko, 33 UCLA L. Rev. at
1077–87.

larly in especially sensitive areas.[15] It may also serve to maintain public confidence in the legal system by preventing the degeneration of trials into spectacles that many would find offensive.[16] Of course, the privilege may in fact do neither. Public confidence in the legal system, to the contrary, may even be reduced when courts are compelled to eschew what appears to be the most reliable sources of information. To the extent that the privilege does accomplish these purposes, it may do so inefficiently, as by failing to identify and restrain those governmental powers most offensive and likely to be abused or those aspects of criminal procedure most offensive to the population in general.

Recent defenses of the privilege have tended to rely less upon systemic rationales than upon individual ones.[17] These arguments, which again somewhat overlap, suggest that the privilege prevents the treatment of suspects and defendants in ways that would be offensive to notions of "privacy" or "individual autonomy." As the privilege applies to out-of-court law enforcement interrogation, for example, it may serve to prohibit interrogation techniques that, given the public's increased sensitivities, may now be as offensive as physical torture was at an earlier time in the privilege's development.

As applied in either the in-court or out-of-court situations, the privilege may prevent the treatment of suspects and accuseds in ways that are unacceptably "cruel." Intolerable cruelty may arise simply from compelling the accused to participate in the process itself.[18] Or, the privilege may prevent the treatment of such persons in ways unacceptable because such treatment is inconsistent with developed notions of human dignity. Even a guilty person, for example, may be regarded as retaining aspects of dignity that are violated when that person is compelled to actively

---

[15]Griswold, 55 NW. U. L. Rev. at 223. Compelled self-incrimination, as history demonstrates, can serve as a valuable tool for suppressing dissent, opposition to the existing political authorities, and freedom of thought and opinion. In view of the difficulty, and perhaps impossibility, of making the right to compel incriminating answers available only in those situations in which no danger is posed to these areas of broad social concern, denying this right to the state in all situations is justified.

[16]*See* Stephen, 1 A History of the Criminal Law of England 441 (1883).

[17]Dolinko, 33 UCLA L. Rev. at 1066–67.

[18]Dolinko, although ultimately finding the argument unconvincing, acknowledges:

[I]f it is cruel to inflict a certain harm on a person at all, it does seem even more cruel to compel him to inflict that harm on himself. That is, compelling the victim to inflict the harm on himself *aggravates* the cruelty of simply inflicting it on him without his participation.

*See* Dolinko, 33 UCLA L. Rev. at 1102 (emphasis in original).

participate in the process of bringing punitive sanctions down upon the person.[19]

Gerstein[20] has developed a somewhat similar argument based on privacy concerns: Most persons apprehended for a crime which they have committed regard themselves as a part of the same moral community as those who are the victims of criminal offenses. They regard the commission of an offense as a moral as well as a legal matter. For such persons, a confession involves not simply submission to legal liability but the acknowledgement of moral wrongdoing and often the revelation of remorse.[21] A person's judgments of his own moral blameworthiness is special and perhaps unique and thus peculiarly private.[22] This sort of "information," self-acknowledgment of moral blameworthiness, is so "private" that the individual ought to have full control over it.[23] Even if the courts are empowered to convict an accused of a crime, they should not be empowered to force the accused to publicly make the judgment by which the accused condemns himself in his own conscience. An accused ought to be able to decide whether to share this only with his God or those to whom he feels bound by trust and affection.[24]

A related argument runs that compelling even a guilty person to choose among incriminating himself, committing perjury, or suffering penalties such as contempt citation requires such a difficult or offensive choice that the privilege is justified by the need to prevent that choice. Exactly why the choice presented by this

---

[19]"[W]e do not make even the most hardened criminal sign his own death warrant, or dig his grave, or pull the lever that springs the trap on which he stands. We have through the course of history developed a considerable feeling of the dignity and intrinsic importance of the individual man. Even the evil man is a human being." Griswold, The Fifth Amendment Today, at 7.

[20]Gerstein, Privacy and Self-Incrimination, 80 Ethics 87, 87 (1970). *See also* Gerstein, The Demise of Boyd: Self-Incrimination and Private Papers in the Burger Court, 27 UCLA L. Rev. 343, 345–56 (1979); Gerstein, Punishment and Self-Incrimination, 16 Am. J. Juris. 84 (1971).

[21]Gerstein, 16 Am. J. Juris. at 90–92.

[22]Gerstein, 16 Am. J. Juris. at 91.

[23]Gerstein, 16 Am. J. Juris. at 92. Dolinko, 33 UCLA L. Rev. at 1125–27; suggests that Gerstein has not adequately supported his contention that revelation of self-condemnation is peculiarly private and Dolinko contends that it is not. He regards Gerstein's position as ultimately resting on the proposition that each person should have the exclusive right to control his own moral development. Dolinko questions whether this is so.

[24]Gerstein, 16 Am. J. Juris. at 92. Efforts to compel self-incrimination may be viewed as intruding upon privacy with particular vigor because they seek access to "mental" aspects of the subject, i.e., private thoughts, feelings and beliefs. *See* Arenella, Schmerber and The Privilege Against Self-Incrimination: A Reappraisal, 20 Am. Crim. L. Rev. 31, 40–42 (1982).

"cruel trilemma"[25] is so offensive is not entirely clear. Perhaps it is because a person's natural instincts and personal interests so strongly suggest that the person should lie in an effort to avoid criminal liability that it is somehow unfair to punish the person for following those instincts. If no reasonable person could be expected to do other than what the witness did, fairness seems offended by punishing the individual. Perhaps the choice is offensive simply because the state is forcing the person to act. In many cases, Judge Frank argued, "the state would be forcing him to commit a crime and then punishing him for it."[26] Yet the law often puts witnesses and others to choices that seem no less difficult or "unfair." To single out a group of persons for solicitude, most of whom find themselves in their position because of their own criminal acts, may be inappropriate.[27]

Stuntz[28] argues that other efforts to explain the privilege unsatisfactorily assume that the activity protected is in some sense "justified." He suggests that a more satisfactory explanation rests on quite different excuse grounds. Were the privilege not recognized, our legal system would be compelled to make available an excuse defense to those defendants who, when called as prosecution witnesses, perjured themselves rather than admit guilt. But such a defense would invoke quite heavy systemic costs. By removing the deterrents to perjury, for example, the defense would lead to a flood of perjurious testimony impairing juries' ability to accurately resolve cases. Recognizing the privilege avoids the need to pay those costs.

Allen and Mace[29] attempt to explain[30] the Supreme Court's Fifth Amendment privilege law. Keying on the requirement that the compelled activity be testimonial, they conclude that the federal constitutional privilege means "the government may not compel revelation of the incriminating substantive results of com-

---

[25]See Murphy v. Waterfront Com'n of New York Harbor, 378 U.S. 52, 55, 84 S. Ct. 1594, 12 L. Ed. 2d 678 (1964) (Fifth Amendment privilege reflects, among other things, "our unwillingness to subject those suspected of crime to the cruel trilemma of self-accusation, perjury or contempt"). The role of the "trilemma" in both supporting the privilege and determining its applicability was stressed in Pennsylvania v. Muniz, 496 U.S. 582, 597, 110 S. Ct. 2638, 110 L. Ed. 2d 528 (1990).

[26]U.S. v. Grunewald, 233 F.2d 556, 591 (2d Cir. 1956), judgment rev'd, 353 U.S. 391, 77 S. Ct. 963, 1 L. Ed. 2d 931 (1957) (Frank J. dissenting).

[27]See Dolinko, 33 UCLA L. Rev. at 1093–95.

[28]Stuntz, Self-Incrimination and Excuse, 88 Colum. L. Rev. 1227 (1988).

[29]Allen and Mace, The Self-Incrimination Clause Explained and Its Future Predicted, 94 J. Crim. L. & Crim. 243 (2004).

[30]Allen and Mace, 94 J. Crim. L. & Crim. at 248 (theory is a "positive" one and thus "not normative or justificatory, and to be clear, we largely leave such inquiry to others").

pelled cognition."[31] They thus construe the case law as stressing official responsibility for generating an incriminating thought process at least as much as the manner in which the government obtains the results of that thought process. Perhaps this indicates an implicit focus upon a notion of autonomy in thought—the privilege should appropriately limit the government's ability to generate and then exploit thoughts because this impinges upon the most central of peoples' autonomous functioning.

Modern versions of the privilege must be regarded as supported by varying combinations of the considerations discussed above. Particular requirements imposed by them often must rest upon combinations of some but less than all of the considerations. The core situation covered by all versions of the privilege, direct trial examination of the sworn defendant under threat of contempt citations as to whether the defendant committed the crime charged, implicates all of these considerations to a singularly significant degree. Whether or not other situations come within the privilege, however, must depend upon what considerations are implicated, the comparative weight given those considerations, and the degree to which they are implicated. The variety of purposes and rationales that can be called into play and the absence of historical or other guidelines for applying those purposes and rationales, however, mean that courts have extraordinary flexibility in constructing policy analyses with which to address particular issues presented by the privilege in its various forms.

With regard to the Supreme Court's development of the Fifth Amendment privilege, the Court's expansive discussion in *Murphy v. Waterfront Comm'n of N.Y. Harbor*,[32] suggested that the Court regarded a broad and flexible array of policy considerations as both supporting the federal constitutional privilege and as relevant to its content:

> [The privilege] reflects many of our fundamental values and most noble aspirations: our unwillingness to subject those suspected of crime to the cruel trilemma of self-accusation, perjury or contempt; our preference for an accusatorial rather than an inquisitorial system of criminal justice; our fear that self-incriminating state-

---

[31]Allen and Mace, 94 J. Crim. L. & Crim. at 268.

They pose a hypothetical in which officers stimulate a suspect into addressing in his own mind whether a murder victim's body is concealed at various locations. By monitoring his physical reactions to being asked about those locations, the officers determine in which location he believes the body

is hidden. This would violate the privilege under their approach, Allen and Mace, 94 J. Crim. L. & Crim. at 268–69, although the suspect was not compelled to engage in communicatively "testimonial" conduct.

[32]Murphy v. Waterfront Com'n of New York Harbor, 378 U.S. 52, 84 S. Ct. 1594, 12 L. Ed. 2d 678 (1964).

ments will be elicited by inhumane treatment and abuses; our sense of fair play which dictates a fair state-individual balance by requiring the government to leave the individual alone until good cause is shown for disturbing him and by requiring the government in its contest with the individual to shoulder the entire load; our respect for the inviolability of the human personality and of the right of each individual to a private enclave where he may lead a private life, our distrust of self-deprecatory statements; and our realization that the privilege, while sometimes a shelter to the guilty, is often a protection to the innocent.[33]

In *United States v. Balsys*,[34] however, a majority deprecatingly characterized the *Murphy* discussion as at most a "catalog [of] aspirations furthered by the [Fifth Amendment Self-Incrimination] Clause." The values reflected in the decision, it continued, are not "reliable"—or, almost certainly in the Court's view, appropriate—"guides to the actual scope of protection under the Clause."[35]

Most specifically, *Balsys* construed *Murphy's* discussion as asserting that the federal constitutional privilege is designed to protect, and should be construed as protecting, "personal inviolability and the privacy of a testimonial enclave."[36] This "comparatively ambitious conceptualization of personal privacy underlying the Clause,"[37] it concluded, rested upon *Murphy's* incorrect conclusion that earlier and narrower views of the Clause as reflecting the Framers' intent to embody the English common-law privilege in the Constitution were mistaken. With regard to the specific issue raised by *Balsys* and addressed by the *Murphy* discussion, *Balsys* concluded—contrary to the *Murphy* discussion—that the common-law rule, embodied in the English common-law privilege, was clear. Considerations of personal testimonial integrity or privacy, as stressed in the *Murphy* discussion, would not support "a significant change in the scope of traditional . . . [Fifth Amendment] protection" as is suggested by the common-law rule.[38]

What, then, is the significance for Fifth Amendment purposes of the policies that support the privilege or, in *Balsys'* terms, the aspirations furthered by the federal constitutional privilege? The Supreme Court has acknowledged that "the privilege has never been given the full scope which the values it helps to protect suggest."[39] Moreover, "[t]he policies behind the privilege are varied, and not all are implicated in any given application of the

---

[33]Murphy, 378 U.S. at 55.

[34]U.S. v. Balsys, 524 U.S. 666, 118 S. Ct. 2218, 141 L. Ed. 2d 575 (1998).

[35]Balsys, 524 U.S. at 691–92.

[36]524 U.S. at 691.

[37]524 U.S. at 684.

[38]524 U.S. at 693.

[39]Schmerber v. California, 384 U.S. 757, 762, 86 S. Ct. 1826, 16 L. Ed.

privilege."[40] *Balsys* suggests that the Court regards the major consideration in defining the content of the Fifth Amendment as the Framers' apparent intent to embody in the Fifth Amendment the English common-law privilege as then understood. More "ambitious conceptualization[s]" of the policies that might be furthered by the privilege are unlikely to move the Court to particular interpretations of that privilege as broader than its English common-law predecessor. As *Balsys* itself acknowledged, the *Balsys'* discussion rejects a reading of *Murphy* that if accepted would "invest[ ] the Clause with a more expansive promise."[41]

### § 117   Where the privilege applies: Distinction between the privilege of an accused in a criminal case and the privilege of a "witness"

When the English common law courts began to apply the privilege in their own proceedings, it soon became clear that the privilege could be invoked not only by a defendant in a criminal prosecution but also by a witness whose conviction could not procedurally be a consequence of the proceeding.[1] There is no historical indication that this was recognized as an important step in the growth of the privilege, and the written decisions offered no rationale.

The Fifth Amendment prohibits compelling a person "in any criminal case to be a witness against himself." This and the terms of early state constitutional provisions as well can be read as prohibiting only compulsion to cause an individual to give oral testimony in a criminal proceeding in which that person is the defendant. Several authorities have argued that this was their original meaning.[2] Nevertheless, in 1924 the Supreme Court rejected the contention that the Fifth Amendment applied only where the prosecution in a criminal trial sought to compel the testimony of the accused:

> The privilege is not ordinarily dependent upon the nature of the proceeding in which the testimony is sought or is to be used. It ap-

---

2d 908 (1966).

[40]McGautha v. California, 402 U.S. 183, 214, 91 S. Ct. 1454, 28 L. Ed. 2d 711 (1971).

[41]U.S. v. Balsys, 524 U.S. 666, 683, 118 S. Ct. 2218, 141 L. Ed. 2d 575 (1998).

[Section 117]

[1]8 Wigmore, Evidence § 2250 (McNaughton rev. 1961), p. 290. Levy, Origins of the Fifth Amendment 313

(1968) reported that the privilege had been extended to witnesses in the trial of King Charles in 1649.

[2]Corwin, The Supreme Court's Interpretation of the Self-Incrimination Clause, 29 Mich. L. Rev. 1, 2 (1930); Mayers, The Federal Witness' Privilege Against Self-Incrimination: Constitutional or Common-Law, 4 Am. J. Legal History 107 (1960).

plies alike to civil and criminal proceedings, wherever the answer might tend to subject to criminal responsibility him who gives it. The privilege protects a mere witness as fully as it does one who is also a party defendant.[3]

Courts now universally accept that state constitutional provisions as well as the Fifth Amendment applies to and may be invoked by one who is not the defendant in an actual trial of a criminal case.[4] Some discussion refers to what might be two different privileges: that of the accused in a criminal case itself and that of a witness.[5]

Justice Thomas, joined by three other members of the United States Supreme Court suggested in *Chavez v. Martinez*[6] that this distinction might at least coincide with Fifth Amendment doctrine. No violation of the provision itself occurs, he reasoned until or unless an accused's in-court testimony as a witness is compelled in the course of a criminal trial or a statement made out-of-court or in another proceeding is used in that criminal trial.[7] This is arguably the privilege of an accused in a criminal case. Under its authority to create "prophylactic rules" to safeguard the core constitutional rights, he added, the Court has created an evidentiary privilege that protects a person who is not on trial for a criminal offense from being compelled to give testimony, because that testimony may later be used in a manner that violates the core of Fifth Amendment protection.[8] This is arguably the privilege of one not an accused but rather a witness.

Justice Thomas's view was not accepted by the Supreme Court as a whole, and whether it is may have little practical significance. There is a real possibility, however, that the courts may less rigorously develop and apply what the judges perceive is only a "prophylactic" privilege protecting those who are not the accused in an actual criminal case.

Precisely what the right to refuse to engage in compelled self-incriminating conduct means undoubtedly differs in various situations. Perhaps some general distinctions can usefully be

---

[3]McCarthy v. Arndstein, 266 U.S. 34, 40, 45 S. Ct. 16, 69 L. Ed. 158 (1924).

[4]8 Wigmore, Evidence § 2252 (McNaughton rev. 1961), pp. 326–27.

[5]*E.g.* U.S. v. Echeles, 352 F.2d 892, 897 (7th Cir. 1965) (referring to the "plain difference between the privilege of witness and accused"). *Cf.* State v. Maestas, 2012 UT App. 53, 272 P.3d 769, 786 (Utah Ct. App. 2012) ("the protections provided a witness claim-

ing the privilege of the Fifth Amendment and a defendant in his own criminal trial are very different") (emphasis removed).

[6]Chavez v. Martinez, 538 U.S. 760, 123 S. Ct. 1994, 155 L. Ed. 2d 984 (2003).

[7]Chavez, 538 U.S.at 766–67 (Thomas, J., joined by the Chief Justice, and Justices O'Connor and Scalia).

[8]538 U.S. at 770–71.

drawn depending upon whether the person relying on the right is an accused in a criminal action or in some sense merely a witness. It is unlikely, however, that in any meaningful sense there are two different rights or privileges. Nevertheless, this chapter does address separately for some purposes the privilege as it applies to the accused in a criminal case and as it applies to others.

Insofar as it is important to determine whether a situation implicate the privilege of an accused in a criminal case or that of others, it is necessary to identify when a criminal case commences. The *Chavez* plurality declined to offer a definitive answer as to the precise moment a "criminal case" commences. It did, however, indicate that "a 'criminal case' at the very least requires the initiation of legal proceedings"[9] and therefore police interrogation during an investigation does not occur in a criminal case.[10]

The privilege of the accused, then, is best considered as implicated when a person's compelled testimonial conduct may immediately contribute to a judicial finding that the person is guilty of a criminal offense. In other situations, the person can invoke the privilege but not the status of an accused and thus has the privilege of a witness.

The term "privilege of a witness" suggests that the privilege is limited to proceedings of some formality in which a person can be a witness. This is clearly not the case. In *Miranda v. Arizona*,[11] the Supreme Court made clear that the privilege has application to out-of-court custodial interrogation by law enforcement officers.[12] Concern is sometimes expressed over whether the privilege applies to situations in which, out-of-court, a suspect is not in custody within the meaning of *Miranda*, not interrogated within *Miranda's* meaning of that term, or both.

In fact, the Fifth Amendment privilege probably applies to any situation in which a person might engage in testimonial self-incriminating conduct. As Justice Marshall argued, there is simply no logic in suggesting that the right to remain silent created by the privilege applies only if some governmental official attempts to compel a person to speak.[13] What protection the so-called privilege of a witness provides to someone in the out of court presence (but not the custody) of a law enforcement officer may, however, be much different than the protection the privilege provides to one who is a witness before a legislative committee.

---

[9]538 U.S. at 766.

[10]538 U.S. at 767.

[11]Miranda v. Arizona, 384 U.S. 436, 86 S. Ct. 1602, 16 L. Ed. 2d 694 (1966).

[12]See § 149 infra.

[13]Jenkins v. Anderson, 447 U.S. 231, 250 n.4, 100 S. Ct. 2124, 65 L. Ed. 2d 86 (1980) (Marshall, J., dissenting).

## § 118 Asserting the privilege

The privilege against compelled self-incrimination "is not self-executing," and "may not be relied upon unless it is invoked in a timely manner."[1] A taxpayer who makes incriminating admissions on a tax form rather than refusing to provide the information on the basis of the privilege, for example, cannot later successfully claim that those admissions are inadmissible because they constituted compelled self-incrimination.[2] This is not a matter of waiver, but rather a substantive requirement of the right to be free from compelled self-incrimination.[3]

In some situations, the need to so assert the Fifth Amendment privilege is relaxed. Where any response by the person is likely to be testimonially self-incriminating, the person need not affirmatively invoke the privilege. Thus a gambler was not required to invoke the privilege rather than simply fail to file a return required by federal gambling tax statutes, because any response to the statutory demand—including the submission of a claim of privilege—was likely to be incriminating.[4] Nor must a person invoke the privilege if an official penalty is placed on the very action of invoking it.[5]

An actual accused person involved in a criminal action is less likely to be required to affirmatively invoke the privilege than one who is only a witness. The accused's privilege is violated if in a jury trial the jury attention is called to the accused's failure to testify even if the accused has taken no affirmative action to invoke the right to not testify under the privilege.[6] The privilege of one undergoing custodial interrogation by law enforcement officers is violated if the officers do not warn the person of the Fifth Amendment's application and before any interrogation elicit an effective waiver of the right to the presence of counsel.[7] In these contexts, the privilege is truly one to remain silent or completely passive, not simply a right to invoke the privilege and thus avoid compelled self-incrimination.

When the privilege must be invoked, how explicitly must be

---

[Section 118]

[1]Roberts v. U. S., 445 U.S. 552, 559, 100 S. Ct. 1358, 63 L. Ed. 2d 622 (1980).

[2]Garner v. U. S., 424 U.S. 648, 665, 96 S. Ct. 1178, 47 L. Ed. 2d 370 (1976).

[3]Garner, 424 U.S.at 654 n. 9.

[4]Marchetti v. U.S., 390 U.S. 39, 88 S. Ct. 697, 19 L. Ed. 2d 889 (1968); Grosso v. U.S., 390 U.S. 62, 88 S. Ct. 709, 19 L. Ed. 2d 906 (1968).

[5]Garrity v. State of N.J., 385 U.S. 493, 87 S. Ct. 616, 17 L. Ed. 2d 562 (1967) (police officer called before grand jury and threatened with discharge for claiming the privilege could first raise the privilege when testimony given without invoking the privilege was later offered against the officer in a criminal trial).

[6]See § 126 infra.

[7]See § 149 infra.

person invoke it? On the infrequent occasions when this has arisen, the courts have been inconsistent. Where a witness stated he was acting on his "preference" to not testify rather than asserting any privilege, he was held nevertheless to have invoked the privilege, since "[a] witness can invoke his Fifth Amendment rights by the act of refusing to testify."[8] On the other hand, a defendant who had previously declined to reveal the identity of his associate in crime was held not to have invoked the privilege during a sentencing hearing when he again refused to do so. Defense counsel stated, "I have to object to that for a number of reasons . . . I think it's totally inappropriate . . . . There could be many reasons for not disclosing [the information]. . . . [I]t could be that it could incriminate him, it could be other reasons as well."[9] The controlling question should be whether the witness or defendant made sufficiently clear to the trial judge the reliance on the privilege to alert the judge to the need to make whatever inquiries necessary to determine whether reliance on the privilege was appropriate on the facts.

The matter was apparently raised by *Hiibel v. Sixth Judicial Dist. Court of Nev., Humboldt Cty.*,[10] in which the Supreme Court held that the Fifth Amendment did not bar Hiibel's prosecution for refusing to provide his name to a police officer. Although the Court relied primarily upon its conclusion that Hiibel had failed to show that providing his name posed a sufficient risk of incrimination to trigger the privilege, it also noted that Hiibel had apparently refused to provide his name "only because he thought his name was none of the officer's business."[11] Perhaps, particularly in situations involving a minimal risk of incrimination, a person seeking to bar penalization for out-of-court conduct must at the time of that conduct have articulated reliance on the privilege or at least upon a legal right to act or not act on the basis of a risk of incrimination.[12]

---

[8]State v. Lingle, 140 S.W.3d 178 (Mo. Ct. App. S.D. 2004). *Accord* Doe ex rel. Rudy-Glanzer v. Glanzer, 232 F.3d 1258 (9th Cir. 2000) (witness being deposed invoked the privilege where counsel for witness stated that witness should not answer because doing so would violate his "fundamental due process" rights and witness was entitled to raise "a Fifth Amendment objection" to the line of questioning).

[9]U.S. v. Lyons, 54 Fed. Appx. 113 (3d Cir. 2002). In the police interrogation context, one court has held that the suspect's motive for expressing a

desire to remain silent is irrelevant to the effectiveness of this invocation of the privilege. Munson v. State, 123 P.3d 1042, 1046–55 (Alaska 2005).

[10]Hiibel v. Sixth Judicial Dist. Court of Nevada, Humboldt County, 542 U.S. 177, 124 S. Ct. 2451, 159 L. Ed. 2d 292 (2004).

[11]Hiibel, 542 U.S. at 190.

[12]In *Hiibel*, the parties did not put at issue whether if the Fifth Amendment provides a right to refuse to identify oneself, Hiibel adequately asserted that right when his identification was demanded and when he was

## § 119    Personal nature of the privilege[1]

Courts frequently describe the privilege against compelled self-incrimination as being personal in nature.[2] These often offhand comments are, however, somewhat misleading.

The privilege is clearly personal in the sense that only the person who is at risk of incrimination can rely upon it. A witness, therefore, cannot refuse to provide information on the ground that it would incriminate someone else and thus intrude upon their interests. If a lawyer is called as a witness before a grand jury, for example, he cannot rely on the privilege as a basis for refusing to respond to questions on the ground that the answers would incriminate his client.[3] A criminal defendant cannot invoke the privilege of witnesses,[4] codefendants,[5] or even co-conspirators[6]

---

tried for failing to provide it. *See* Brief for the United States as Amicus Curiae Supporting Respondent at 27–28, Hiibel v. Sixth Judicial Dist. Court of Nevada, Humboldt County, 542 U.S. 177, 124 S. Ct. 2451, 159 L. Ed. 2d 292 (2004).

**[Section 119]**

[1]*See generally* West's Key Number Digest, Witnesses ⟿306.

[2]*E.g.* U.S. v. Agajanian, 852 F.2d 56, 58 (2d Cir. 1988) ("The privilege against self-incrimination is personal"); State v. Bryan, 551 A.2d 807, 813 (Del. Super. Ct. 1988), reversed on other grounds 571 A.2d 170 (Del. 1990) (it is an "established proposition" that the privilege against compulsory self-incrimination is a personal one").

[3]*E.g.* In re Grand Jury Proceedings, 760 F.2d 26, 27 (1st Cir. 1985) (rejecting argument that under Fifth Amendment, an attorney can refuse to answer any questions which client, if asked those questions, could decline to answer on self-incrimination grounds); In re Grand Jury Proceedings-Gordon, 722 F.2d 303, 308–09 (6th Cir. 1983) (legal precedent in Sixth Circuit holds that attorney may not plead that his client might be incriminated by attorney's testimony). The Supreme Court has noted the issue under the Fifth Amendment privilege but has not resolved it. Fisher v. U.S., 425 U.S.

391, 402 n.8, 96 S. Ct. 1569, 48 L. Ed. 2d 39 (1976).

[4]*E.g.* U.S. v. Agajanian, 852 F.2d 56, 58 (2d Cir. 1988) (because privilege is personal, a criminal defendant cannot assert the right of a prosecution witness to be informed of her self-incrimination rights before being compelled to testify); State v. Bailey, 292 Kan. 449, 255 P.3d 19, 27–28 (2011) (criminal defendant lacked standing to complain of possible violation of prosecution witnesses' privilege); Com. v. Morganti, 455 Mass. 388, 917 N.E.2d 191, 205 (2009). "[T]he ancient common law understanding that a husband and wife are a single person" does not give one spouse the ability to raise the other spouse's privilege. Carpenter v. Com., 51 Va. App. 84, 654 S.E.2d 345, 352 (2007).

[5]Scherrer v. State, 294 Ark. 227, 742 S.W.2d 877, 881 (1988) (defendant does not have standing to complain of admission of codefendant's allegedly coerced statements, because the right not to incriminate oneself "is personal"); Dowtin v. U.S., 999 A.2d 903, 909–10 (D.C. 2010) ("a co-defendant lacks standing to challenge an asserted violation of his co-defendant's Fifth Amendment right against compulsory self-incrimination").

[6]Poole v. U.S., 329 F.2d 720, 721 (9th Cir. 1964).

or accomplices.[7] Nor, generally speaking, can a criminal defendant successfully complain that the self-incrimination rights of such persons were violated in the litigation process.[8]

There has been some suggestion that the personal nature of the privilege means that it can only be invoked by the personal act or statement of the holder and thus that a lawyer cannot invoke it on behalf of the holder.[9] This is unnecessary and undesirable. When a lawyer, acting under authorization of the client and on behalf of the client, invokes the client's privilege, there is nothing to be gained by requiring the client to invoke the privilege himself.[10] On the other hand, it is reasonable (and perhaps necessary) to require that the decision as to whether or not to invoke the privilege be made by the client and not the lawyer.[11] If the lawyer's authorization is in reasonable doubt, the

---

[7]Lawton v. State, 259 Ga. 855, 388 S.E.2d 691, 693 (1990) (defendant may not on appeal complain of trial court's action in requiring accomplice Lee to testify because "the defendant lacks standing to assert Lee's privilege against self-incrimination"); State v. Tiessen, 354 N.W.2d 473, 477 (Minn. Ct. App. 1984) (defendant could not seek suppression of confession of accomplice because he "cannot vicariously assert a violation of [another's] Fifth Amendment rights").

[8]*E.g.* People v. Adams, 283 Ill. App. 3d 520, 218 Ill. Dec. 805, 669 N.E.2d 1331, 1333 (1st Dist. 1996) ("the constitutional privilege against self-incrimination is a personal privilege belonging only to the person testifying, even where that person's testimony also incriminates defendant," so defendant cannot complain on appeal of trial court's refusal to permit witness to invoke privilege).

[9]*See, e.g.*, U.S. v. Schmidt, 816 F.2d 1477, 1481 n.3 (10th Cir. 1987) ("Only the appellants, not their counsel, are the proper parties to interpose a claim of privilege personal to themselves to prevent compelled disclosures that appellants 'reasonably believe[ ] could be used [against them]' "); Cleary v. Shahan, 2001 WL 1823428 (Del. C.P. 2001), rev'd on other grounds 2002 WL 499879 (Del.Super.2002) (claim of privilege was inadequate

where record showed that privilege was asserted by counsel rather than by party). In at least some of these cases, the real issue is whether the person can invoke the privilege without being sworn and submitting to specific questions. See § 130 infra.

[10]U.S. v. Smart, 501 F.3d 862, 866 (8th Cir. 2007) ("Representation by the witness's counsel that the witness will invoke his Fifth Amendment rights 'is sufficient for the district court to refuse to compel that witness to appear.' "); (U.S. v. Johnson, 752 F.2d 206, 210–11 (6th Cir. 1985) (lawyer's assertion of reliance by client on privilege was authorized by client and therefore effective where lawyer had represented client for some time, client was present, and client indicated no disapproval of lawyer's actions); State v. Nieves, 89 Conn. App. 410, 873 A.2d 1066, 1069 (2005) (trial court did not err in allowing witness to invoke privilege "through the representation of counsel"); State v. Wilson, 323 Or. 498, 918 P.2d 826, 834 n.8 (1996) ("A criminal defendant may invoke the right to be free from compelled self-incrimination through counsel . . . . ").

[11]*See generally* People v. Fernandez, 219 Cal. App. 3d 1379, 269 Cal. Rptr. 116, 121 (2d Dist. 1990) (witness's privilege "is a personal privilege held by [him], not by his counsel," and

trial judges should have authority to require that the client's authorization be established.

## §120 Incrimination: A "real and appreciable" risk of contributing to prosecution and convictions

The privilege applies only if compelled action is incriminating. As is developed later in this chapter,[1] this means that it protects only against criminal liability. Two other aspects of the requirement of incrimination are also important.

First, and despite the terminology of the Fifth Amendment and many other formulations of the privilege, the privilege is not limited to compelled testimony that is actually introduced into evidence at a criminal trial. Rather, it protects against any conduct meeting the other requirements that would furnish a link in the chain of evidence usable to prosecute the person. This means that it protects against compulsion to engage in conduct that may lead to evidence that could be used in the trial of a criminal offense.[2]

Second, the danger of incrimination in the above sense must be "real and appreciable." Early in the development of the Fifth Amendment privilege, the courts established that a danger only "imaginary and unsubstantial" will not support invocation of the privilege.[3]

In several early decisions, the United States Supreme Court invoked this formulation of the required risk as a basis for holding the privilege inapplicable,[4] and "real and appreciable" risk language is sometimes repeated. As now applied, however, the requirement is probably of little if any significance. Courts, for example, sustain claims of the privilege where criminal liability

---

consequently trial court erred in barring defendant from calling as a witness a codefendant who was willing to testify although codefendant's counsel "objected").

**[Section 120]**

[1]See §§ 121 to 123 infra.

[2]U.S. v. Hubbell, 530 U.S. 27, 37–38, 120 S. Ct. 2037, 147 L. Ed. 2d 24 (2000), discussing Hoffman v. U. S., 341 U.S. 479, 486, 71 S. Ct. 814, 95 L. Ed. 1118 (1951).

[3]Brown v. Walker, 161 U.S. 591, 608, 16 S. Ct. 644, 40 L. Ed. 819

(1896), drawing upon Queen v. Boyles, (1861) 1 B. & S. 311, 121 Eng. Rep. 730 (K.B.).

[4]Rogers v. U.S., 340 U.S. 367, 374–75, 71 S. Ct. 438, 95 L. Ed. 344 (1951) (after witness had admitted holding office of treasurer of Communist Party, disclosure of acquaintance with her successor presents no more than a mere imaginary possibility of increasing the danger of prosecution); Brown, 161 U.S. at 626 (possibility of conviction under laws of another sovereign a danger of an imaginary and unsubstantial character).

would rest on prohibitions against sexual activity seldom and perhaps never enforced.[5]

Some courts have expressly embraced what is clearly the functional rule: Whether a sought disclosure is incriminating turns on the possibility rather than the likelihood of its use to prosecute. If a court finds the possibility of future prosecution and that the disclosure would contribute to any such prosecution, that ends the inquiry. The court should not attempt to assess how likely it is there will be a prosecution.[6]

The Supreme Court restated and applied the requirement in *Hiibel v. Sixth Judicial Dist. Court of Nev., Humboldt Cty.*[7] The privilege applies, *Hiibel* stated, only if the person reasonably believed the disclosures sought could be used in a criminal prosecution or could lead to other evidence that might be so used. A reasonable person cannot have a reasonable apprehension that the person's name will be incriminating, at least without any support. Disclosure of one's name, the Court explained, "is so likely to be so insignificant in the scheme of things as to be incriminating only in unusual circumstances."[8] Hiibel himself had not offered even an after-the-fact explanation as to how the disclosure of his name could have been used against him in a criminal case. Had he offered such an explanation, apparently, the trial court would have been required to determine whether a reasonable person could believe that the name could itself be

---

[5]Gunn v. Hess, 90 N.C. App. 131, 367 S.E.2d 399 (1988) (witness may invoke privilege in response to questions concerning sexual activity constituting misdemeanors of adultery and fornication); Hollowell v. Hollowell, 6 Va. App. 417, 369 S.E.2d 451, 453 (1988); Matter of Grant, 83 Wis. 2d 77, 264 N.W.2d 587, 591 (1978).

[6]Johnson v. Fabian, 735 N.W.2d 295, 311 (Minn. 2007) ("many federal circuits have held that the inquiry into whether a statement is incriminating should not consider the actual likelihood of prosecution," and " 'once incriminating potential is found to exist, courts should not engage in raw speculation as to whether the government will actually prosecute' ") (quoting U.S. v. Sharp, 920 F.2d 1167, 1171 (4th Cir. 1990)); Empire Wholesale Lumber Co. v. Meyers, 192 Or. App. 221, 85 P.3d 339, 343 (2004) ("A person's assertion of the Fifth Amendment privilege does not depend on the court's assessment of the likelihood of prosecution."); Ac-

cord, U.S. v. Jones, 703 F.2d 473, 478 (10th Cir. 1983) ("Once the court determines that the answers requested would tend to incriminate the witness, it should not attempt to speculate whether the witness will in fact be prosecuted."). *See also* U.S. v. Edgerton, 734 F.2d 913, 921 (2d Cir. 1984); Carter v. U.S., 684 A.2d 331, 336–37 (D.C. 1996) (en banc) ("the overwhelming majority of cases . . . have determined that the trial judge should not speculate about or predict the likelihood of prosecution in relation to an assertion of the constitutional privilege against self-incrimination," so "a court may only assess the possibility of future prosecution not the probability").

[7]Hiibel v. Sixth Judicial Dist. Court of Nevada, Humboldt County, 542 U.S. 177, 124 S. Ct. 2451, 159 L. Ed. 2d 292 (2004).

[8]Hiibel, 542 U.S. at 189–90.

used or could lead to other evidence that might be used in a criminal case.[9]

Application of the general requirement of a real and appreciable risk to some more specific problems in the administration of the privilege does present difficulties. These are considered elsewhere in this chapter in connection with the compulsory production of documents and tangible items[10] and the task of determining whether a witness's response to a question is sufficiently related to criminal liability to support invocation of the privilege.[11]

## §121 Limitation of the privilege to protection against criminal liability: (a) In general

The privilege protects its holders only against the risk of legal criminal liability. It provides no protection against the disgrace and practical excommunication from society which might result from disclosure of matter which, under the circumstances, could not give rise to criminal liability.[1]

If the risk of criminal liability is removed there is no privilege. It is clear, then, that the privilege does not apply when prosecution and conviction is precluded by passage of the period of limitations,[2] pardon,[3] prior acquittal,[4] or a grant of immunity.[5] When prior conviction removes the risk of criminal liability, then the privilege is similarly rendered inapplicable. Whether that risk is

---

[9]*Hiibel's* analysis may have been affected by doubt as to whether his refusal to make disclosure was in fact motivated by self-incrimination concerns. See § 118 supra.

[10]See § 138 infra.

[11]See § 132 infra.

[Section 121]

[1]Whether the privilege protects against particular possibilities, the subject of this section, must be distinguished from the acceptability of burdens placed on a person's exercise of the privilege, discussed in §§ 126, 127, and 136 infra.

The subject of this section must also be distinguished from whether the privilege can be invoked in a particular kind of proceedings, and whether in particular kinds of proceedings the person has the privilege of an accused in a criminal case or that of a witness,

distinguished in § 117 supra. *See* In re Scott, 29 Cal. 4th 783, 129 Cal. Rptr. 2d 605, 61 P.3d 402, 419 (2003) (in post-conviction habeas corpus, convicted defendant does not have the right not to be called as a witness but if called to testify may invoke the privilege in response to particular questions).

[2]MacFarland v. State, 929 So. 2d 549, 551 (Fla. 5th DCA 2006); Home Ins. Co. v. Manufacturers Hanover Trust Co., 208 A.D.2d 458, 617 N.Y.S.2d 311 (1st Dep't 1994).

[3]Moore v. Backus, 78 F.2d 571, 577 (C.C.A. 7th Cir. 1935).

[4]Ex parte Critchlow, 11 Cal. 2d 751, 81 P.2d 966, 971 (1938); People ex rel. Gross v. Sheriff of City of N.Y., 277 A.D. 546, 101 N.Y.S.2d 271 (2d Dep't 1950), aff'd on other grounds 96 N.E.2d 763 (N.Y. 1951).

[5]See § 142 infra.

actually removed by prior conviction, however, presents some special problems.

If direct appeal from a conviction is pending or remains available, a convicted defendant might, despite his conviction, harbor hope that his conviction will be reversed on appeal and that any disclosures he makes would be used to incriminate him upon any retrial that follows. Because of this possibility, the courts have generally held that a convicted defendant retains the protection of the privilege until appeal is exhausted or until the time for appeal expires.[6] The risk of a reversal and retrial is not so remote as to constitute a negligible risk under the prevailing standard.[7]

Whether the possibility that a conviction might be invalidated in collateral attack should render the privilege available is another matter. Collateral attack is generally available at any time, so regarding the risk of retrial after a successful attack of this sort as preserving protection would dramatically expand the protection of the privilege. The best solution is to treat the possibility of successful collateral attack and retrial as raising the question of whether the facts present a "real and appreciable" danger of incrimination.[8] In the absence of some specific showing that collateral attack is likely to be successful, a conviction should be regarded as removing the risk of incrimination and conse-

---

[6]*E.g.* Johnson v. Fabian, 735 N.W.2d 295, 310 (Minn. 2007) (convicted defendant can invoke the privilege as long as a direct appeal of conviction is pending, or as long as the time for direct appeal has not expired). *Accord* People v. Fonseca, 36 Cal. App. 4th 631, 42 Cal. Rptr. 2d 525, 528 (2d Dist. 1995) (convicted witness could invoke privilege where appeal could still be filed); Martin v. Flanagan, 259 Conn. 487, 789 A.2d 979, 984–85 (2002) ("The weight of authority permits a witness whose conviction has not been finalized on direct appeal to invoke the privilege against self-incrimination and refuse to testify about the subject matter which formed the basis of his conviction.").

The Supreme Court, without discussing collateral attack, has stated that no further incrimination can occur, and the privilege cannot be invoked, if "the sentence has been fixed and the judgment of conviction has become final." Mitchell v. U.S., 526 U.S. 314, 326, 119 S. Ct. 1307, 143 L. Ed. 2d 424 (1999).

[7]Ellison v. State, 310 Md. 244, 528 A.2d 1271, 1277–78 (1987).

If a defendant has pleaded guilty, of course, this quite likely reduces the likelihood that the conviction will be reversed on appeal and admissions will be incriminating on retrial. Mitchell, 526 U.S. at 326, implicitly held that this reduction was not enough to remove the risk of incrimination. Compare, State v. Bailey, 292 Kan. 449, 255 P.3d 19, 29 (2011) (no privilege where witness had entered a guilty plea, been sentenced, and filed a notice of appeal).

[8]See § 120 supra.

This approach was characterized as involving "practical difficulties," at least where it would require a trial judge asked to compel a witness to testify to review the judge's own prior decision. James v. State, 75 P.3d 1065, 1069 (Alaska Ct. App. 2003) (applying this approach where defendant was called in probation revocation would require trial judge to review his earlier dismissal of application for post-conviction relief pending on ap-

quently the protection of the privilege.[9] Most courts, however, treat the finality of a conviction as unqualifiedly removing the risk of incrimination.[10]

The privilege does not protect against all adverse determinations in criminal litigation other than a finding of guilt. The Supreme Court reasonably assumed in *Estelle v. Smith*[11] that a finding of competency to stand trial would not be incrimination. Clearly removal of a procedural barrier to continuation of a prosecution should not be incrimination.

Whether the privilege protects against more severe punishment is less clear. *Minnesota v. Murphy*[12] indicated—albeit in dictum—that revocation of probation is not be incrimination for

---

peal). Compare, Johnson v. Fabian, 735 N.W.2d 295, 311 (Minn. 2007) (noting but not reaching "the issue of whether the possibility of Henderson's conviction being overturned in a yet-to-be commenced collateral attack presents the requisite real and appreciable risk of incrimination").

[9]Several courts have taken this approach. *See* People v. Edgeston, 157 Ill. 2d 201, 191 Ill. Dec. 84, 623 N.E.2d 329, 339 (1993) (where witness expressed intent to challenge his guilty plea and renege on the plea agreement, and prosecutor expressed intent, in the absence of the plea agreement, to prosecute witness for murder and use any statements he made at defendant's trial against him in that proceeding, it was not an abuse of the trial court's discretion to find that a real danger of incrimination existed which allowed witness to assert privilege); State v. Marks, 194 Wis. 2d 79, 533 N.W.2d 730, 735 (1995) (privilege sometimes extends beyond sentencing and appeal, as "as where the defendant intends to or is in the process of moving to modify his or her sentence and can show an appreciable chance of success"). *Accord* State v. Verdugo, 124 Ariz. 91, 602 P.2d 472, 473–74 (1979); Com. v. Rodgers, 472 Pa. 435, 372 A.2d 771, 781 (1977).

[10]Roth v. Commissioner of Corrections, 759 N.W.2d 224, 229 (Minn. Ct. App. 2008) ("extending the Fifth Amendment privilege to the period of collateral review would extend the privilege almost indefinitely," and therefore protection ends after appeal or expiration of period for appeal). *Accord* Archer v. State, 383 Md. 329, 859 A.2d 210, 219 (2004) (witness was compellable "because no appeal or sentence review was pending and the time for appeal and sentence review had expired); Lewis v. Department of Corrections, 365 N.J. Super. 503, 839 A.2d 933, 935 (App. Div. 2004) (where witness was convicted and sentenced and direct appeals were exhausted, witness was not at risk for incrimination despite his intention in the future to attack the conviction by post-conviction proceedings).

In Mitchell v. U.S., 526 U.S. 314, 326, 119 S. Ct. 1307, 143 L. Ed. 2d 424 (1999), the Supreme Court simply ignored the possibility of a conviction being invalidated on collateral attack.

The result is that in post-conviction proceedings, the State may be able to call the defendant and compel his testimony. *See* Keough v. State, 356 S.W.3d 366, 372 n.7 (Tenn. 2011) (noting that courts differ on "whether, and in what manner, the right against self-incrimination applies in the post-conviction context").

[11]Estelle v. Smith, 451 U.S. 454, 101 S. Ct. 1866, 68 L. Ed. 2d 359 (1981).

[12]Minnesota v. Murphy, 465 U.S. 420, 104 S. Ct. 1136, 79 L. Ed. 2d 409 (1984).

Fifth Amendment privilege purposes despite the fact that it increases the severity of the punishment inflicted for a crime.[13]

On the other hand, *Estelle v. Smith* appeared to regard a defendant as protected by the privilege from having to reveal information usable only to establish a fact—his "dangerousness"—that could lead to imposition of death rather than life for the crime of which he was convicted.[14]

A defendant's Fifth Amendment privilege applies at sentencing, the Supreme Court held in *Mitchell v. United States*.[15] Further, it applies as the privilege of an accused insofar as the sentencing entity cannot draw an adverse inference from the defendant's failure to testify "in determining the facts of the offense."[16] This reaffirmed that a trial court cannot at sentencing compel the defendant to admit guilt or penalize the defendant's refusal to do so. Despite the conviction, acknowledgement of facts relating to the crime might later prove incriminating regarding that offense.

But *Mitchell's* language left unclear whether the Fifth Amendment privilege provides protection against being compelled to make admissions that would only increase the severity of punishment.[17] Could the sentencing judge in *Mitchell* draw an adverse inference regarding facts that would not indicate liability for additional convictions but would support the assessment of a more severe sentence? Does the incrimination from which the defendant is protected include an increase in the severity of punishment?

In actual fact, at issue in *Mitchell* was whether Mitchell was protected by the privilege from having to disclose facts related to the amount of drugs attributable to Mitchell for federal sentencing purposes. The Government did not contend that these facts were not incriminating, but rather argued that by pleading guilty she had waived her Fifth Amendment protection. A fair reading of *Mitchell* makes clear that the Court assumed that facts that would tend to increase the severity of the punishment imposed

---

[13]Murphy, 465 U.S. at 435 n. 7. *Accord* People v. Bell, 296 Ill. App. 3d 146, 230 Ill. Dec. 704, 694 N.E.2d 673, 676–77 (4th Dist. 1998); State v. Sites, 231 Neb. 624, 437 N.W.2d 166, 168 (1989).

[14]Murphy, 451 U.S. at 461–63 (rejecting argument that privilege did not apply because information "was used only to determine punishment after conviction, not to establish guilt").

[15]Mitchell v. U.S., 526 U.S. 314, 119 S. Ct. 1307, 143 L. Ed. 2d 424 (1999).

[16]Mitchell, 526 U.S. at 330.

[17]The major uncertainty arises from the Court's emphasis on the trial court's use of the defendant's silence "in determining the facts of the offense."

by the trial court were incriminating for purposes of Fifth Amendment law.[18]

*Mitchell* explicitly disclaimed addressing whether a sentencing judge or jury might properly give weight to a defendant's silence at sentencing insofar as it tended to show lack of remorse or failure to accept responsibility for the crime.[19] Lower courts have sometimes attempted to read *Mitchell* as permitting sentencing authorities to consider silence in these ways, but doing so is difficult if not impossible.[20] Some courts bar sentencing authorities from giving any such effect to silence.[21]

---

[18]The Court's reference to the improper inference as one made "in determining the facts of the offense" most likely reflected the Court's effort to narrow its discussion so as not to address whether a defendant's silence at sentencing might be considered as bearing on remorse or acceptance of responsibility.

[19]Mitchell, 526 U.S. at 330.

[20]Ketchings v. Jackson, 365 F.3d 509, 514 (6th Cir. 2004) (state courts unreasonably found that trial judge acted only on the basis of lack of remorse and was not improperly influenced by defendant's failure to admit guilt). *See generally* Miller v. Lafler, 2012 WL 5519677 (6th Cir. 2012) (discussing *Ketchings* and other courts' application of *Mitchell*).

Another court noted that "a significant number of jurisdictions has recognized the subtle, yet meaningful, distinction between imposing a harsher sentence upon a defendant based on his or her lack of remorse, on the one hand, and punishing a defendant for his or her refusal to admit guilt, on the other." It held that the trial court in the case before it "inferred a poor prognosis for rehabilitation on the sole basis of [the defendant's] refusal to admit guilt" and "[i]n so doing, . . . penalized [the defendant] for his refusal to admit guilt." State v. Kamanao, 103 Haw. 315, 82 P.3d 401, 407–10 (2003). *Compare,* Green v. State, 84 So. 3d 1169, 1171 (Fla. 3d DCA 2012) ("Although a defendant's expression of remorse and acceptance of responsibility are appropri-

ate factors for the court to consider in mitigation of a sentence, a lack of remorse, the failure to accept responsibility, or the exercise of one's right to remain silent at sentencing may not be considered by the trial court in fashioning the appropriate sentence."); State v. Kellis, 148 Idaho 812, 229 P.3d 1174, 1177 (Ct. App. 2010) review denied ("[I]t is impermissible for a trial court to attempt to coerce a defendant into acknowledging guilt through threats of harsher punishment, [but] a court is not entirely prohibited from considering continued assertions of innocence as a factor in the sentencing decision. Rather, a court may properly consider a defendant's refusal to acknowledge guilt when evaluating the defendant's rehabilitation potential because acknowledgment of guilt is a critical first step toward rehabilitation."). *Contra* State v. Souder, 105 S.W.3d 602 (Tenn. Crim. App. 2002) (trial court did not err in relying on the defendant's assertion of the privilege in denying probation).

[21]State v. Trujillo, 227 Ariz. 314, 257 P.3d 1194, 1198 (Ct. App. Div. 1 2011) review denied (in considering Trujillo's lack of remorse and his failure to admit guilt, the trial court deprived him of a right essential to his defense) (citing *Mitchell*); State v. Willey, 163 N.H. 532, 44 A.3d 431, 441 (2012) ("just as it is unconstitutional to increase a defendant's punishment because he refuses to admit guilt, so too is it unconstitutional for a court to draw an adverse inference of lack of remorse from a defendant's silence at

## § 122 Limitation of the privilege to protection against criminal liability: (b) Distinguishing criminal and noncriminal legal liability[1]

It is clear that the privilege does protect against the risk of conviction for what are technically criminal offenses and equally clear that it does not protect against the imposition of liability for damages on the basis of traditionally civil causes of action. Whether it protects against types of liability that are between these two poles is less certain.[2]

In 1886, the Supreme Court held that "proceedings instituted for the purpose of declaring the forfeiture of a man's property by reason of offenses committed by him, though they may be civil in form, are in their nature criminal."[3] Thus the Fifth Amendment privilege protects against forfeiture, at least where such action is based on conduct that could also serve as the basis for a criminal prosecution. In *Application of Gault*,[4] the Court held that the federal constitutional privilege protected against compelled disclosures that could lead to a finding that a child was delinquent. This determination apparently rested largely upon the fact that such a finding could result in a loss of liberty which the Court concluded was indistinguishable from the imprisonment that might follow criminal conviction.[5]

But in *Baxter v. Palmigiano*,[6] the Court almost offhandedly held that disciplinary penalties imposed upon convicted prison inmates were not "incrimination" and did not themselves invoke the protection of the Fifth Amendment privilege. Two years later, the Court held that a civil penalty imposed under the Federal Water Pollution Control Act for discharge of harmful substances

---

sentencing").

**[Section 122]**

[1]*See generally* West's Key Number Digest, Witnesses ⊕294, 295.

[2]Whether a type of liability is "criminal" for purposes of the Fifth Amendment privilege against compelled self-incrimination is not necessarily determined by whether it invokes other federal constitutional protections afforded to those subjected to criminal action. *See* U.S. v. Regan, 232 U.S. 37, 50, 34 S. Ct. 213, 58 L. Ed. 494 (1914).

[3]Boyd v. U.S., 116 U.S. 616, 634, 6 S. Ct. 524, 29 L. Ed. 746 (1886). *See also* U.S. v. U.S. Coin and Currency, 401 U.S. 715, 718, 91 S. Ct. 1041, 28 L. Ed. 2d 434 (1971); Lees v. U.S., 150 U.S. 476, 480–81, 14 S. Ct. 163, 37 L. Ed. 1150 (1893).

[4]Application of Gault, 387 U.S. 1, 87 S. Ct. 1428, 18 L. Ed. 2d 527 (1967).

[5]Gault, 387 U.S. at 50.

[6]Baxter v. Palmigiano, 425 U.S. 308, 96 S. Ct. 1551, 47 L. Ed. 2d 810 (1976).

into navigable waters was not "incrimination" within the Fifth Amendment meaning.[7]

This line of decisions came to a head in *Allen v. Illinois*,[8] in which the Court considered whether the Fifth Amendment protected against being found a sexually dangerous person under the nominally civil Illinois Sexually Dangerous Persons Act. Under the Act, a person may be found a sexually dangerous person only upon proof that he has engaged in criminal sexual misconduct. If such a finding is made, the person can be committed for an indeterminate period to a maximum-security institution run by correctional authorities. Generally, the Court held, the legislature's designation of liability as civil in nature will be sufficient to take it out of Fifth Amendment coverage.[9] A "civil" label must be disregarded and the Fifth Amendment applied, however, upon " 'the clearest proof' that 'the statutory scheme [is] so punitive either in purpose or effect as to negate [the State's] intention' that the proceeding be civil . . . ."[10] The Illinois courts had determined that the proceedings were essentially civil in nature. Allen failed to make the required showing that the scheme was punitive in purpose or effect. Contrary to indications in *Gault*, the fact that liability may result in involuntary incarceration is insufficient to require application of the privilege.[11]

Under *Allen*, a litigant seeking to establish that the Fifth Amendment protects against a nominally civil form of liability has a difficult task and is unlikely to succeed. In that case, the Court assumed that the Fifth Amendment privilege does not protect against compulsory hospitalization for mental illness.[12] Lower courts have held that the privilege does not protect

---

[7]U.S. v. Ward, 448 U.S. 242, 100 S. Ct. 2636, 65 L. Ed. 2d 742 (1980).

[8]Allen v. Illinois, 478 U.S. 364, 106 S. Ct. 2988, 92 L. Ed. 2d 296 (1986).

[9]Allen, 478 U.S.at 368–69 (quoting from U.S. v. Ward, 448 U.S. 242, 249, 100 S. Ct. 2636, 65 L. Ed. 2d 742 (1980)).

[10]478 U.S. at 369.

[11]478 U.S. at 372. Allen might have made such a case, the Court offered, had he shown that incarceration under the Act was under conditions no different from those of persons convicted of crimes for sexual misconduct. 478 U.S. at 373–74. *Gault*, the Court concluded, rested upon a determina-

tion that delinquency proceedings were intended to punish those found delinquent, unlike *Allen* in which the State's intent to treat rather than punish had not been disproved. 478 U.S. at 373.

[12]People v. Wilkinson, 185 Cal. App. 4th 543, 110 Cal. Rptr. 3d 776, 779 (5th Dist. 2010) ("the potential committee [in a section 6500 mentally retarded person commitment] may not refuse to testify, although the Fifth Amendment privilege against self-incrimination applies, as it does in all civil proceedings"); People ex rel. Strodtman, 2011 WL 5084951 (Colo. App. 2011), cert. denied, 2012 WL 3964660 (Colo. 2012) ("the Fifth Amendment privilege against self-

members of the bar against disciplinary proceedings[13] or judges against judicial discipline.[14] Nor is protection afforded against civil penalties for practicing dentistry without a license,[15] termination of parental rights,[16] or liability for civil contempt of court.[17] Criminal contempt, however, is probably incrimination within the meaning of the privilege.[18]

Although the privilege does not protect against a certain type of legal liability, one who is the subject of a proceeding to impose that liability can still invoke the privilege. Most likely, the person does not have the privilege of an accused in a criminal case. A

---

incrimination does not extend to patients in Colorado's civil commitment proceedings"); In re Kister, 194 Ohio App. 3d 270, 2011-Ohio-2678, 955 N.E.2d 1029, 1052 (4th Dist. Athens County 2011) ("an involuntary-commitment proceeding is not penal in nature"). *Contra* In re United Health Services Hospitals, Inc., 6 Misc. 3d 447, 785 N.Y.S.2d 313, 317 (Sup 2004) (privilege protects against loss of liberty due to allegations of mental illness or incapacity).

[13]Matter of Shannon, 179 Ariz. 52, 876 P.2d 548, 566 (1994) (where the only possible penalty is disciplinary sanctions, the salient constitutional inquiry is whether disciplinary sanctions are "penalties affixed to criminal acts," and "[c]ourts that have considered this question have unanimously responded negatively"). *Accord* DeBock v. State, 512 So. 2d 164, 166 (Fla. 1987) (bar discipline is "remedial" and for the protection of the courts and the public and consequently a witness can be compelled to testify under a grant of immunity that does not protect him from such discipline).

[14]In re Hill, 149 Vt. 431, 545 A.2d 1019, 1022 (1988).

[15]Richardson v. Tennessee Bd. of Dentistry, 913 S.W.2d 446, 461 (Tenn. 1995). *See also* Roach v. National Transp. Safety Bd., 804 F.2d 1147, 1152–55 (10th Cir. 1986) (administrative proceeding to suspend a commercial pilot's license was criminal or "quasi-criminal" so as to invoke the Fifth Amendment privilege).

[16]In re Pittman, 149 N.C. App.

756, 561 S.E.2d 560, 564–65 (2002); In re B.P., 2000 MT 39, 298 Mont. 287, 995 P.2d 982, 989 (2000). *Accord* Matter of C.C., 1995 OK CIV APP 127, 907 P.2d 241, 243 (Ct. App. Div. 4 1995); In re Interest of Clifford M., 6 Neb. App. 754, 577 N.W.2d 547, 552 (1998); Murray v. Texas Dept. of Family & Protective Services, 294 S.W.3d 360, 367 (Tex. App. Austin 2009). *Cf.* In re Care and Protection of Sharlene, 445 Mass. 756, 840 N.E.2d 918, 926–27 (2006) ("The privilege against self-incrimination applicable in criminal proceedings is not applicable to child custody proceedings.").

[17]Ex parte Hulsey, 536 So. 2d 75, 76 (Ala. Civ. App. 1988) (respondent in contempt proceeding for failure to comply with court order directing child support could be called as adverse witness by movant and jailed until he complied with order). *Accord* In re Contemnor Caron, 110 Ohio Misc. 2d 58, 744 N.E.2d 787, 834 (C.P. 2000).

[18]Carter v. Brodrick, 750 P.2d 843, 845 (Alaska Ct. App. 1988) (contempt proceeding resulting in penalty for definite term was "criminal" and hence trial court erred in requiring respondent to testify as the prosecution's "chief witness"). *Accord* People v. Hixson, 2012 IL App (4th) 100777, 358 Ill. Dec. 376, 965 N.E.2d 447, 452 (App. Ct. 4th Dist. 2012) (defendant in proceedings on allegation of direct criminal contempt was entitled to the right to testify or to remain silent); In re J.T.R., 47 Kan. App. 2d 91, 271 P.3d 1262, 1269 (2012) (a person charged with indirect criminal contempt has the right against self-incrimination").

refusal to respond to particular questions must be addressed on the basis of the answers tending to create criminal liability, not simply their tendency to increase the risk of the proceeding itself being successful.[19]

## § 123 Limitation of the privilege to protection against criminal liability: (c) Incrimination under the laws of another jurisdiction[1]

A witness may assert the privilege on the basis of concern regarding criminal liability in the courts of a jurisdiction other than the one in which the witness's testimony is being sought. These situations can be divided as follows: (a) a witness in either state or federal court claims danger of incrimination under the laws of a foreign country; (b) a witness in a state court claims danger of incrimination under the laws of another state; (c) a witness in a state court claims danger of incrimination under federal law; and (d) a witness in a federal court claims a danger of incrimination under state law.

Traditionally, most courts took the position that the privilege protected only against incrimination under the laws of the sovereign which was attempting to compel the incriminating information.[2] In part, the basis for such holdings was the view that the risk of prosecution by another sovereign was so low as not to invoke protection under the privilege.[3] It has also been argued, however, that this result follows from the rationale for the privilege. To the extent that the privilege is based upon concern regarding brutality and other such excesses that a sovereign might commit when attempting to compel a person's assistance in achieving his own conviction, that risk is seldom presented when the only potential criminal liability lies under the laws of another jurisdiction. In such cases, the compelling sovereign is unlikely to have sufficient interest in incriminating

---

[19]*Cf.* People v. Hall, 378 Ill. App. 3d 666, 317 Ill. Dec. 511, 882 N.E.2d 85, 88–89 (3d Dist. 2007) ("a motorist can be required to testify as an adverse witness at a hearing on his petition to rescind statutory summary suspension of his driving privileges, but any incriminating statements made during such testimony cannot be used against him in a criminal prosecution").

**[Section 123]**

[1]*See generally* West's Key Number Digest, Witnesses ⊕297(14).

[2]*See, e.g.,* Knapp v. Schweitzer, 357 U.S. 371, 380, 78 S. Ct. 1302, 2 L. Ed. 2d 1393 (1958); U.S. v. Murdock, 284 U.S. 141, 149, 52 S. Ct. 63, 76 L. Ed. 210 (1931). *See also* Feldman v. U.S., 322 U.S. 487, 492, 64 S. Ct. 1082, 88 L. Ed. 1408 (1944) (testimony compelled by a state could be introduced into evidence in federal prosecution).

[3]Brown v. Walker, 161 U.S. 591, 608, 16 S. Ct. 644, 40 L. Ed. 819 (1896); In re Werner, 167 A.D. 384, 152 N.Y.S. 862 (1st Dep't 1915).

the person to perform acts that invoke the rationale for the privilege.[4]

With regard to the Fifth Amendment privilege, this traditional position was rejected by the Supreme Court in *Murphy v. Waterfront Commission*.[5] Murphy and several others had been subpoenaed to testify before the Waterfront Commission of New York Harbor regarding a work stoppage at certain New Jersey piers. They were granted immunity from prosecution under New York and New Jersey law but invoked their Fifth Amendment privilege on the ground that their responses would tend to incriminate them under federal law. The Supreme Court agreed that the Fifth Amendment privilege protects state witnesses from liability under federal as well as state law. Noting the high degree of cooperation among jurisdictions, it reasoned without extended discussion that most and perhaps all of the policies and purposes of the Fifth Amendment privilege are defeated when a witness possessing protection against incrimination under both state and federal law can be "whipsawed" into incriminating himself under both bodies of law by simply being called as a witness in the courts of first one and then the other jurisdiction.[6] The defense of the traditional view noted earlier was dismissed as based upon too narrow a view of those policies supporting the Fifth Amendment privilege.[7]

The court recognized, however, that to expand Murphy's Fifth Amendment protection in state courts to include protection against incrimination under federal law without providing the states with a means of obtaining his testimony would ignore the interests that both levels of Government have in investigating and prosecuting crime.[8] Consequently, it held that when a state compels testimony incriminating under federal law, as for example under a grant of immunity, the Federal Government is prohibited from making any incriminating use of that compelled testimony and its fruits. Since Murphy and his companions were thus adequately protected against the use of their compelled testimony in securing their federal convictions, they could be compelled to testify.

*Murphy* expressly resolved only situation (c) above. But it removed any conceptual basis for the traditional view that the

---

[4]8 Wigmore, Evidence § 2258, at 345 (McNaughton rev. 1961).

[5]Murphy v. Waterfront Com'n of New York Harbor, 378 U.S. 52, 84 S. Ct. 1594, 12 L. Ed. 2d 678 (1964).

[6]Murphy, 378 U.S.at 55–56.

[7]378 U.S. at 56 n. 5.

[8]378 U.S. at 79. *Accord* In re Contempt of Ecklund, 636 N.W.2d 585 (Minn. Ct. App. 2001) (witness in state proceeding with final conviction could invoke privilege on the basis of potential incrimination under federal law, because *Murphy* had not been overruled although the Court has questioned some of its reasoning).

privilege was inapplicable in situations (b) and (d). In both situations, witnesses have protection. But the jurisdiction seeking their testimony may nevertheless compel it if the witness can be assured that the compelled testimony and evidence derived from it cannot be used to incriminate him under the laws of the other jurisdiction. This assurance is provided by the federal constitutional prohibition against the use of involuntary statements in either federal or state protections.[9]

There is, then, general agreement that a federal witness is protected against incrimination under state law[10] and that a state witness is protected against incrimination under the law of other states. Similarly, it is clear that in either situation the witness can be granted immunity by the forum jurisdiction and compelled to answer. Neither the testimony nor evidence derived from it, however, will be usable in the other jurisdiction.[11]

Situation (a) above was addressed by the Supreme Court in *United States v. Balsys.*[12] *Murphy*, as construed in *Balsys*, did not reject either the reading of the common-law privilege as limited to incrimination under the law of the sovereign seeking to compel the testimony or the significance of the common-law rule in defining the content of the Fifth Amendment privilege. Rather, *Murphy* rested on the limited rationale that since the Fifth Amendment privilege is binding on the States as well as the federal government, for purposes of applying this aspect of the Fifth Amendment "the state and federal jurisdictions were as one."[13] There is, however, no reason to similarly regard the federal government and a foreign sovereign "as one," and therefore the common-law derived "same sovereign principle" applies. Since the foreign sovereign is not the same as that seeking the testimony, incrimination under the law of that sovereign does not trigger the privilege.

---

[9]*Cf.* Shotwell Mfg. Co. v. U.S., 371 U.S. 341, 347, 83 S. Ct. 448, 9 L. Ed. 2d 357 (1963) (admission of guilt obtained from a person under a governmental promise of immunity must be excluded from evidence under the self-incrimination clause of the Fifth Amendment).

[10]U.S. v. Mahar, 801 F.2d 1477, 1496 (6th Cir. 1986) (federal witness who had been acquitted in prior federal prosecution could have invoked his privilege on the basis of potential liability under state law).

[11]Whether statements made pursuant to less formal arrangements, such as plea bargains in which the prosecution agrees not to prosecute or use testimony given by the defendant, are involuntary and hence inadmissible may pose a difficult problem. *See* McKay v. Great American Ins. Co., 876 So. 2d 666, 674 (Fla. 4th DCA 2004) (testimony given pursuant to state plea agreement purporting to give defendant immunity "may or may not" be inadmissible as involuntary if federal prosecution were to arise).

[12]U.S. v. Balsys, 524 U.S. 666, 118 S. Ct. 2218, 141 L. Ed. 2d 575 (1998).

[13]Balsys, 524 U.S. at 683.

If the matter turned instead on a comparison of the likely costs and benefits of expanding the Fifth Amendment privilege to cover incrimination under the laws of foreign sovereigns, *Balsys* reasoned alternatively, the result would be the same. Despite the relatively few cases in which claims of incrimination under the laws of a foreign sovereign might be raised, expansion of the privilege would result in loss of some evidence that might cause serious adverse consequences for domestic law enforcement. Since the Court has no role in conducting foreign relations, it could not properly assume expansion of the privilege would stimulate legislation and international agreements that would minimize this cost. Expansion of the privilege might not benefit those who might invoke an expanded privilege. Their silence in reliance on an expanded privilege might be used to deport them to countries where they would face criminal prosecution.[14]

*Balsys* left open the possibility that the Fifth Amendment privilege could be invoked on the basis of a showing that a potential foreign prosecution that would be in essence brought by the foreign sovereign on behalf of the American jurisdiction seeking the testimony. Merely showing that the American jurisdiction supports foreign prosecution by treaty agreement to provide that foreign jurisdiction with evidence of criminal guilt is not sufficient. Rather, *Balsys* suggests, the issue would be raised only by a showing that the two jurisdictions had enacted substantively similar criminal codes targeting "offenses of international character," and that the American jurisdiction was seeking the testimony "for the purpose of obtaining evidence to be delivered to other nations as prosecutors of a crime common to both nations."[15]

## § 124    Limitation of the privilege to compelled "testimonial" activity[1]

The Fifth Amendment privilege and those of almost all states

---

[14]524 U.S.at 696–98.

An Illinois court reasoned that the state's constitutional privilege "guarantees a right of fundamental decency and dignity which precludes a court from extracting testimony from a witness who reasonably fears a subsequent criminal prosecution by another sovereign, be it in a different domestic jurisdiction or in a foreign country." Relsolelo v. Fisk, 317 Ill. App. 3d 798, 251 Ill. Dec. 21, 739 N.E.2d 954, 959 (1st Dist. 2000). This was rejected on further appeal. Relsolelo v. Fisk, 198 Ill. 2d 142, 260 Ill. Dec. 190, 760 N.E.2d 963 (2001) (no basis exists for construing state provision as providing more protection than is provided by Fifth Amendment).

[15]Balsys, 524 U.S. at 698–700.

[Section 124]

[1]*See generally* West's Key Number Digest, Criminal Law ⚖393(1). Allen and Mace, The Self-Incrimination Clause Explained and Its Future Predicted, 94 J. Crim. L. & Crim. 243, 259 (2004), note that the requirement of testimonial conduct is the source of most modern theoretical problems

protect only against compulsion to engage in testimonial self-incriminating activity. Exploration of what the courts mean by testimonial activity is necessary to consideration of the basis and wisdom of this limitation.

As early as 1910, the United States Supreme Court held that the Fifth Amendment prohibits only the compelled extraction of "communications."[2] This was reaffirmed in *Schmerber v. California*,[3] which explained that the privilege "protects an accused only from being compelled to testify against himself, or otherwise provide the state with evidence of a testimonial or communicative nature."[4] The word "witness" in the Fifth Amendment text, the Court noted in *United States v. Hubbell*,[5] explains the application of protection to communications "that are 'testimonial' in character."[6]

In *Doe v. United States*,[7] the Court approved the approach urged by the Government: an act is "testimonial" within the meaning of the Fifth Amendment privilege if it "explicitly or implicitly, relate[s] a factual assertion or disclose[s] information."[8] It then elaborated that this means that compelled action is "testimonial" only if the action is sought as an indication of the subject's intentional expression of his knowledge or belief concerning factual matters.[9] This approach was reaffirmed in *Pennsylvania v. Muniz*.[10]

Therefore, the privilege is implicated when, but only when, the Government imposes compulsion to cause the subject to act in a manner that the subject intends as a disclosure of his perception of, or belief as to, factual matters. Consequently, the government is not prohibited from compelling actions because it does so to

---

with the privilege.

[2]Holt v. U.S., 218 U.S. 245, 252–53, 31 S. Ct. 2, 54 L. Ed. 1021 (1910).

[3]Schmerber v. California, 384 U.S. 757, 86 S. Ct. 1826, 16 L. Ed. 2d 908 (1966).

[4]Schmerber, 384 U.S.at 761.

[5]U.S. v. Hubbell, 530 U.S. 27, 120 S. Ct. 2037, 147 L. Ed. 2d 24 (2000).

[6]Hubbell, 530 U.S. at 34. The use of the term "testimonial" in self-incrimination law must be distinguished from the use of that term in the Supreme Court's relatively new construction of the confrontation clause of the Sixth Amendment. Crawford v. Washington, 541 U.S. 36, 124 S. Ct. 1354, 158 L. Ed. 2d 177 (2004) (confrontation clause is violated by admission into evidence of testimonial out-of-court statements unless the declarant is unavailable and the defendant had a prior opportunity for cross-examination).

[7]Doe v. U.S., 487 U.S. 201, 108 S. Ct. 2341, 101 L. Ed. 2d 184 (1988).

[8]Doe, 487 U.S. at 210.

[9]487 U.S. at 211, citing only 8 J. Wigmore, Evidence § 2265 p. 386 (McNaughton rev. 1961).

[10]Pennsylvania v. Muniz, 496 U.S. 582, 594–95, 110 S. Ct. 2638, 110 L. Ed. 2d 528 (1990).

learn the subject's thoughts. The privilege prohibits only compulsion to require the subject to intentionally reveal his thoughts.[11]

Physical as well as verbal activity may be testimonial under this definition.[12] The "vast majority" of verbal statements will be testimonial, however, because "[t]here are very few instances in which a verbal statement, either oral or written, will not convey information or assert facts."[13]

Thus the privilege does not bar compulsion upon a suspect to put on a blouse for purposes of determining whether it fits him,[14] to cause a suspect to cooperate in the extraction of a blood sample which would suggest his guilt,[15] to require a suspect to participate in a lineup,[16] or to obtain a voice sample[17] from a suspect. When compelled production of documents or other items involves compelled testimonial activity is a specialized problem considered elsewhere.[18]

Some of these generalizations may be too broad. *United States v. Mara*,[19] for example, seemed to treat compelled production of a

---

[11]Moore v. State, 323 Ark. 529, 915 S.W.2d 284, 289 (1996) ("In determining whether evidence is testimonial in nature the courts look to see if the activity performed is *for the purpose of communication*, such as a gesture; if it is, the activity is privileged.") (emphasis supplied). *Accord* Smith v. State, 829 N.E.2d 64, 75–76 (Ind. Ct. App. 2005) (suspect's conduct in removing money from her body cavity and placing them in her shoe revealed she was in possession of that money but was not testimonial, because she did not intend those actions to be an admission that she was in possession of the money).

The Massachusetts court held that a suspect's refusal to comply with police requests for cooperation is testimonial, and generalized: "Conduct evidence admitted to show consciousness of guilt is always testimonial because it tends to demonstrate that the defendant knew he was guilty." Com. v. Conkey, 430 Mass. 139, 714 N.E.2d 343, 348 (1999).

[12]Muniz, 496 U.S. at 595 n. 9 (definition applies to both verbal and nonverbal conduct, and "nonverbal conduct contains a testimonial component whenever the conduct reflects the

actor's communication of his thoughts to another").

Whether compelled decryption of a computer hard drive would involve testimonial activity was discussed at length in In re Grand Jury Subpoena Duces Tecum Dated March 25, 2011, 670 F.3d 1335, 1346 (11th Cir. 2012) ("the decryption and production of the hard drives would require the use of the contents of Doe's mind and could not be fairly characterized as a physical act that would be nontestimonial in nature").

[13]Doe v. U.S., 487 U.S. 201, 213, 108 S. Ct. 2341, 101 L. Ed. 2d 184 (1988).

[14]Holt v. U.S., 218 U.S. 245, 252–53, 31 S. Ct. 2, 54 L. Ed. 1021 (1910).

[15]Schmerber v. California, 384 U.S. 757, 765, 86 S. Ct. 1826, 16 L. Ed. 2d 908 (1966).

[16]U.S. v. Wade, 388 U.S. 218, 221–22, 87 S. Ct. 1926, 18 L. Ed. 2d 1149 (1967).

[17]U.S. v. Dionisio, 410 U.S. 1, 6–7, 93 S. Ct. 764, 35 L. Ed. 2d 67 (1973).

[18]See § 138 infra.

[19]U.S. v. Mara, 410 U.S. 19, 93 S.

handwriting sample as nontestimonial.[20] Some subsequent lower court decisions, however, have reasonably concluded such compelled activity becomes testimonial under certain circumstances. "Obtaining a handwriting sample by dictation," one court explained, "allows the examiner to pose spelling questions to the subject, which are answered in the written exemplar. It also allows the examiner to assess the degree of the subject's sophistication, the level of his education, the scope of his vocabulary, and his educational level." This most likely makes the production of the exemplar a testimonial act.[21]

Even during trial, a criminal defendant can be compelled to engage in incriminating conduct before the jury if that conduct is not testimonial. The defendant can, of course, be compelled to be in the courtroom.[22] Courts have upheld trial judges' requirements that defendants display a tattoo to a witness on the stand,[23] show the jury the defendant's teeth,[24] and put on the jacket, mask and cap worn by the perpetrator of the charged crime and say the words spoken by the perpetrator—"Give me the money" and "Hurry up."[25]

In *Muniz*, the Supreme Court addressed the testimonial nature of several aspects of a stationhouse sobriety test. The officer conducting the test first asked Muniz his name, address, height, weight, eye color, date of birth, and current age. Next, in an apparent effort to test Muniz' ability to calculate, he asked, "Do you know what the date was of your sixth birthday?" Finally, the officer instructed him, as he performed several physical dexterity tests, to count.

The *Muniz* majority assumed that the first questions, as to Muniz' name, address, height, weight, eye color, date of birth,

---

Ct. 774, 35 L. Ed. 2d 99 (1973).

[20]Mara, 410 U.S. at 21–22.

[21]U.S. v. Kallstrom, 446 F. Supp. 2d 772, 776 (E.D. Mich. 2006) (following U.S. v. Campbell, 732 F.2d 1017 (1st Cir. 1984)). *Accord* State v. Cooke, 914 A.2d 1078, 1109–1110 (Del. Super. Ct. 2007) (excluding exemplars produced in response to dictation of the words to be written).

[22]People v. Frye, 18 Cal. 4th 894, 77 Cal. Rptr. 2d 25, 959 P.2d 183, 249 (1998) (trial court's ruling requiring defendant's presence at the penalty phase did not compel defendant to be a witness against himself in violation of his state and federal constitutional guarantee against self-incrimination

even if it resulted in his demeanor in court being considered by the jury when it made its penalty determination, since "the constitutional guarantee against self-incrimination is a prohibition against compelling an accused to give statements that are testimonial in nature" and thus the privilege is not implicated by order); State v. Moore, 308 S.C. 349, 417 S.E.2d 869, 870 (1992).

[23]Walker v. State, 706 So. 2d 1303 (Ala. Crim. App. 1997).

[24]State v. Gilmer, 604 So. 2d 117, 120 (La. Ct. App. 2d Cir. 1992).

[25]Holder v. State, 837 S.W.2d 802, 805 (Tex. App. Austin 1992).

and current age, did call for testimonial responses.[26] It made clear, however, that the Fifth Amendment did not bar the officers from compelling Muniz to speak in order to determine whether he would slur his words. Slurred speech and other evidence of lack of muscular coordination do not involve testimonial components and thus their compelled demonstration does not invoke the Fifth Amendment privilege.[27]

Controversy focused upon the second question—concerning whether Muniz knew the date of his sixth birthday—to which Muniz had responded, "No, I don't." Justice Brennan, speaking for a bare majority of five justices, explained that this question did not require exploration of the "outer boundaries of what is 'testimonial,'" because the "core meaning" of that concept made clear that Muniz' response to the question was testimonial. That the police were seeking to ascertain the physical nature of Muniz' brain processes was not controlling, he continued, if that inquiry was pursued by means that called for testimonial responses from the suspect. The question posed to Muniz called for a testimonial response, because it demanded that he communicate his perception or belief concerning the result of his mental processes. Functionally, he was communicating that he believed or knew that he was unaware of the date of his sixth birthday.[28]

Applying *Muniz*, a California court held impermissible the "Romberg [field sobriety] test." An officer administering the test has the suspect stand, tilt his head back, close his eyes, and tell the officer when he thinks 30 second has passed. "The probative value of the Romberg test, the court explained, "lies firmly in the accuracy of the subject's estimation as communicated to police. Because the test requires the suspect to communicate an implied assertion of fact or belief (i.e., that 30 seconds has elapsed), the test is similar to the sixth birthday question in *Muniz*, which called for a testimonial response."[29]

A response to a police demand that a person state that person's name, it was argued in *Hiibel v. Sixth Judicial District Court of*

---

[26]Pennsylvania v. Muniz, 496 U.S. 582, 601, 110 S. Ct. 2638, 110 L. Ed. 2d 528 (1990) (further holding that the questions asked were within a "routine booking question" exception to *Miranda*; see generally § 149 infra).

[27]Muniz, 496 U.S. at 590–92.

[28]496 U.S. at 596–600.

Allen and Mace, The Self-Incrimination Clause Explained and Its Future Predicted. 94 J. Crim.

L. & Crim. 243, 274–76 (2004), argue that Justice Marshall's concurrence should not be construed as supporting the plurality's approach, and that consequently *Muniz* did not resolve whether this question called for a testimonial response.

[29]People v. Bejasa, 205 Cal. App. 4th 26, 140 Cal. Rptr. 3d 80, 93 (4th Dist. 2012).

*Nevada, Humboldt County,*[30] is no more testimonial than a response to a demand that a person stand to reveal their height. The Supreme Court did not reach the question, but offered that this "may qualify as an assertion of fact related to identity" and thus might be testimonial. Production of demanded identity documents, it added, might also be testimonial.[31]

Whether a suspect's refusal to participate in a breath test for blood alcohol level is testimonial remains uncertain. The Supreme Court commented in *South Dakota v. Neville*[32] that there is "considerable force" in the argument that a suspect's refusal to participate in a breath test for blood alcohol is like flight and thus noncommunicative conduct rather than a testimonial communication. It did not reach the issue because the Court held that in any case the refusal was not compelled.[33] Lower courts have tended to characterize refusals as nontestimonial.[34] The Massachusetts court, perhaps the leading authority to the contrary, has reasoned that a refusal is akin to the refusing person's stating, "I have had so much to drink that I know or at least suspect that I am unable to pass the test."[35]

Best analyzed, such conduct is not testimonial. Although it does reveal the suspect's perception that he is too intoxicated to pass the test, it does not do so by compelling the suspect's intentional communication of his perception that he is so intoxicated. The suspect does not intend the response as an assertion of the fact inferred from it—that the suspect is conscious of his state of intoxication.

*Muniz* left unresolved whether recitation of letters or numbers in a specified sequence—reciting the alphabet, for example—is

---

[30]Hiibel v. Sixth Judicial Dist. Court of Nevada, Humboldt County, 542 U.S. 177, 124 S. Ct. 2451, 159 L. Ed. 2d 292 (2004).

[31]Hiibel, 542 U.S. at 189. *Compare* Com. v. Haskell, 438 Mass. 790, 784 N.E.2d 625, 630–31 (2003) (demanding that one found in possession of a firearm produce a license for the firearm does not trigger the privilege, but asking the person whether he has a license does).

[32]South Dakota v. Neville, 459 U.S. 553, 103 S. Ct. 916, 74 L. Ed. 2d 748 (1983).

[33]Neville, 459 U.S. at 561. See § 125 infra (requirement of compulsion).

[34]*E.g.* State v. Busciglio, 976 So. 2d 15, 21-22 (Fla. 2d DCA 2008) (following decisions from other jurisdictions, holding refusal nontestimonial "whether analyzed under article I, section 9, of the Florida Constitution or the Fifth Amendment of the United States Constitution").

[35]Com. v. Lopes, 459 Mass. 165, 944 N.E.2d 999, 1003 (2011) (quoting Opinion of the Justices to the Senate, 412 Mass. 1201, 591 N.E.2d 1073, 1077 (1992)).

testimonial.[36] Arguably these recitations involve implied assertions of the suspects' beliefs. Such a recitation of the alphabet can be viewed as an implied—but testimonial—assertion, "I believe E follows C." Nevertheless, most lower courts have held that such action is not testimonial. This is best based on the proposition that such a recitation does not involve an intentional disclosure of the person's beliefs but are rather a rote recitation of "a set of generic symbols"[37] or—in the words of the Massachusetts court—"the reflexive functioning of the [person's] mental processes."[38]

*Muniz* suggested that the testimonial requirement should be applied—at least in part—by using a functional analysis based on the rationale for the privilege. At its core, the privilege is designed to protect those suspected of crime from modern-day analogues of the historic trilemma of self-accusation, perjury or contempt. "Whatever else it may include . . . ," Justice Brennan explained in *Muniz*, "the definition of 'testimonial' evidence . . . must encompass all responses to questions that, if asked of a sworn suspect during a criminal trial, could place the suspect in the 'cruel trilemma.' "[39] Arguably neither suspects asked to consent to tests nor those commanded to recite numbers or letters are placed in this posture. Offering what the persons perceive as more favorable but false answers to the officers' demands are simply not options.

Precisely why the privilege should be limited to compulsion to engage in "testimonial" activity has seldom been addressed. Certainly the language of most if not all constitutional provisions does not require this result. To the contrary, a broader construction of the privilege is somewhat suggested by the terms of some

---

[36]Pennsylvania v. Muniz, 496 U.S. 582, 603 n.17, 110 S. Ct. 2638, 110 L. Ed. 2d 528 (1990). During one test, Muniz counted accurately and therefore his response was not incriminating. During the other, he did not count at all and failed to argue that his silence had "any independent incriminating significance."

[37]*See, e.g.*, State v. Randy J., 150 N.M. 683, 2011-NMCA-105, 265 P.3d 734, 741 (Ct. App. 2011), cert. denied, 269 P.3d 903 (N.M. 2011) (observing that "[t]he majority of states that have considered the issue have concluded that counting or reciting the alphabet during a field sobriety test is not testimonial under the Fifth Amendment," and following these decisions). *Contra* Allred v. State, 622 So. 2d 984,

987 (Fla. 1993) (under Florida constitutional self-incrimination provision, reciting of alphabet is testimonial because the incriminating inference is drawn not from the physical characteristics of the speech but rather from the incorrect contents—the inaccurate ordering if the letters); State v. Fish, 321 Or. 48, 893 P.2d 1023, 1030 (1995) (counting and reciting alphabet are testimonial under state constitution).

[38]Vanhouton v. Com., 424 Mass. 327, 676 N.E.2d 460, 466 (1997). *Accord* People v. Berg, 92 N.Y.2d 701, 685 N.Y.S.2d 906, 708 N.E.2d 979, 982 (1999).

[39]Pennsylvania v. Muniz, 496 U.S. 582, 596–97, 110 S. Ct. 2638, 110 L. Ed. 2d 528 (1990).

formulations of it, as for example those providing that no person "shall be compelled to give evidence against himself."[40] Such nuances in terminology have not, however, been regarded as of much significance.[41]

In *Doe*, the Supreme Court noted that so limiting the privilege is consistent with the history of the Fifth Amendment privilege and its predecessors, which were historically intended to prevent the use of legal compulsion to extract sworn communications from accuseds of facts, which would incriminate them.[42] The Court acknowledged that the policies supporting the privilege would be served to some extent by applying the privilege more broadly. It did not, however, develop precisely why that does not argue persuasively for a broader formulation of the privilege's protection. "[T]he scope of the privilege," the *Doe* majority simply observed, "does not coincide with the complex of values it helps to protect."[43] But this observation is of little help in explaining why the testimonial requirement is imposed to determine the extent to which the scope will coincide with those values.

*Doe* conceded that the privilege is based in part upon the need to limit the Government's ability to compel the accused to "assist in his prosecution" in a broader sense, and that this purpose would be served by expanding the privilege to nontestimonial situations. It then simply assumed that the protected interests in "privacy, fairness, and restraint of governmental power" are not impermissibly offended by compelling the accused to cooperate in the prosecution's use of his body to develop "highly incriminating testimony."[44] Apparently this assumption was based in part at least on the conclusions that other federal Constitutional provisions also serve that same purpose,[45] apparently so effectively that the Fifth Amendment need not be developed so as to provide additional limits.

States remain free, of course, to define the protection afforded by their constitutional, statutory, or case law privileges more broadly and as not limited to compelled testimonial conduct. Traditionally, there was considerable authority that some state privileges prohibited any compelled activity, whether testimonial

---

[40]*E.g.* Conn. Const. Art. 1, § 8.

[41]*E.g.* State v. Asherman, 193 Conn. 695, 478 A.2d 227, 240–41 (1984) (rejecting the argument that "to give evidence" covers all actions resulting in evidence, whether those actions were testimonial or not).

[42]Doe v. U.S., 487 U.S. 201, 211, 108 S. Ct. 2341, 101 L. Ed. 2d 184 (1988).

[43]Doe, 487 U.S. at 213.

[44]487 U.S. at 213 n. 11.

[45]487 U.S. at 214 (emphasizing the Fourth Amendment prohibition against compulsion to consent to a "search" and the Due Process clause's "limitation on the Government's ability to coerce individuals into participating in criminal prosecutions").

or not, giving rise to incriminating evidence or information implicating the person so compelled. After the Utah Supreme Court's rejection of this position in 1985,[46] however, apparently only Georgia still adheres to this approach.[47]

Under the approach of the Georgia courts, the privilege prohibits only compulsion to engage in certain affirmative actions that are self-incriminating but not necessarily testimonial. It does, therefore, prohibit compelling a suspect to produce a handwriting exemplar.[48] But it does not bar compelled but passive submission to a surgical procedure required for removal of a bullet from the suspect's body,[49] the taking of blood samples for chemical analysis,[50] or the removal of a suspect's shoes.[51] A person cannot be compelled to engage in an act which will create evidence incriminating the person, although the person can be compelled to act so as to assist authorities in obtaining already existing evidence of this sort.[52]

Perhaps the rationales of the privilege simply cannot support a broad construction of the privilege that would expand its application to nontestimonial compelled activity. To the extent that the privilege is designed to minimize cruelty, arguably that purpose might be best effectuated by prohibiting compulsion to engage in any volitional affirmative act, since such situations provide an incentive to engage in potentially abusive persuasion until the subject complies. As the Utah court noted in the leading rejection of this position, however, other constitutional provisions are available to condemn excessive coercion.[53] Moreover, the incentive for extreme, and thus cruel, persuasive measures is greatest in situations where communicative cooperation is sought, because there the subjects retain the power to control the contents of the sought responses.

---

[46]See American Fork City v. Crosgrove, 701 P.2d 1069 (Utah 1985).

[47]See generally Com. v. Hayes, 544 Pa. 46, 674 A.2d 677, 682–83 (1996) (rejecting argument that force used to extract evidence that new scientific advances make conclusive on guilt is unacceptable and should be prohibited by the privilege).

[48]State v. Armstead, 152 Ga. App. 56, 262 S.E.2d 233, 234 (1979).

[49]Creamer v. State, 229 Ga. 511, 192 S.E.2d 350, 354 (1972).

[50]Robinson v. State, 180 Ga. App. 43, 348 S.E.2d 662, 669 (1986), reversed on other grounds 350 S.E.2d 464 (Ga. 1986). Compelling a urine sample, similarly, does not violate the privi-

lege. Green v. State, 260 Ga. 625, 398 S.E.2d 360, 362 (1990). See also Price v. State, 194 Ga. App. 453, 390 S.E.2d 663, 664 (1990) (removal of leg hair pursuant to search warrant involved compelled submission to an act and thus did not violate privilege).

[51]Batton v. State, 260 Ga. 127, 391 S.E.2d 914, 917 (1990).

[52]Georgia Peace Officers Standards and Training Council v. Anderson, 290 Ga. App. 91, 658 S.E.2d 840, 843 (2008), relying upon Dempsey v. Kaminski Jewelry, Inc., 278 Ga. App. 814, 630 S.E.2d 77 (2006).

[53]American Fork City v. Crosgrove, 701 P.2d 1069, 1074 (Utah 1985).

Any use of a suspect himself to develop evidence with which to bring about the suspect's own downfall might be regarded as offending privacy concerns underlying the privilege; the more the compelled participation by the suspect intrudes upon the privacy of the person's thoughts, the greater this privacy intrusion might be. It is doubtful, however, whether today privacy considerations are of sufficient significance in supporting the privilege to serve as a foundation for defining its scope.

Difficulties in determining what forms of cooperation are sufficiently affirmative to come within a prohibition against compelled affirmative cooperation argue against defining the scope of a privilege in those terms.[54] Yet, as *Muniz* illustrated, defining the privilege as limited to testimonial activity itself presents serious difficulties.

## §125 Requirement of compulsion

The privilege protects against "compelled" self-incriminatory and testimonial activity.[1] What compulsion means varies with the context of the testimonial activity, although the recent history of the privilege has involved significant expansion of the concept of compulsion.

Traditionally, the privilege was limited to situations in which "legal" compulsion, compulsion imposed under authority of law, was exerted upon the witness.[2] Consequently, the privilege was inapplicable to police questioning, since law enforcement officers have no authority to compel answers to their inquiries. In *Miranda v. Arizona*,[3] however, the Supreme Court rejected this approach as a matter of Fifth Amendment law and held the privilege implicated in out-of-court custodial interrogation by police. Reasoning that coverage of such activity was necessary to avoid rendering the privilege at trial a mere empty formality, the Court rejected the requirement that the compulsion be legal. The Fifth Amendment privilege applies to and protects citizens in situa-

---

[54]The Utah court concluded that "the affirmative act standard requires the state to make overly fine distinctions that may not further significantly the policies of the privilege." Cosgrove, 701 P.2d at 1075.

**[Section 125]**

[1]The conceptual differences among the Supreme Court justices as to the nature of the Fifth Amendment

privilege, developed in Chavez v. Martinez, 538 U.S. 760, 123 S. Ct. 1994, 155 L. Ed. 2d 984 (2003), include differences as to the precise role of compulsion. See generally §115 supra.

[2]*See generally* Note, 5 Stan. L. Rev. 459 (1953).

[3]Miranda v. Arizona, 384 U.S. 436, 86 S. Ct. 1602, 16 L. Ed. 2d 694 (1966).

tions in which their freedom to abstain from self-incrimination "is curtailed in any significant way."[4]

On the other hand, the requirement of compulsion is the conceptual basis for many of the procedural requirements that must be met for successful reliance upon the privilege and consequently serves to limit its effect. Most important, as a general rule, compulsion is present only if a witness has asserted a right to refuse to disclose self-incriminating information and this refusal has been overridden.[5] The need for compulsion also explains the recent holdings that the Fifth Amendment privilege does not protect the contents of self-incriminatory documents from compelled production.[6]

Application of the requirement of compulsion has presented special difficulties when the offered evidence tends to show a suspect's refusal to submit to a procedure such as a blood alcohol or breath test. Much of the difficulty arises from failure to recognize that the leading Supreme Court decision, *South Dakota v. Neville,*[7] holds that—at least in this context—compulsion triggers the privilege only if it is "impermissible,"

At issue in *Neville* was the admissibility of a driver's refusal to submit to a blood alcohol test, offered by the prosecution as evidence of the driver's intoxication. To the extent that the refusal may have been testimonial,[8] the Court held, any compulsion exerted upon the driver to take the test did not render the refusal compelled within the meaning of the Fifth Amendment privilege. The criminal process often requires suspects and defendants to make choices, the Court explained, and the Fifth Amendment does not necessarily preclude this:

> [T]he values behind the Fifth Amendment are not hindered when the state offers a suspect the choice of submitting to the blood-alcohol test or having his refusal used against him. . . . [T]he state could legitimately compel the suspect, against his will, to accede to the test. Given, then, that the offer of taking a blood-alcohol test is clearly legitimate, the action becomes no *less* legitimate when the State offers a second option of refusing to take the test, with the attendant penalties for making that choice.[9]

The refusal, therefore, is not an act compelled by the officer and trial use of evidence of that refusal is not barred by the privilege.

---

[4]Miranda, 384 U.S. at 467. To put the matter another way, see § 117 supra, the privilege "applies"—but is not necessarily violated—in any situation in which a person might engage in self-incriminating testimonial conduct and could conceivably be compelled to do so.

[5]See § 118 supra.

[6]See generally §§ 137 to 138 infra.

[7]South Dakota v. Neville, 459 U.S. 553, 103 S. Ct. 916, 74 L. Ed. 2d 748 (1983).

[8]See § 124 supra.

[9]Neville, 459 U.S. at 565 (emphasis in original).

The leading state court analyses concluding that refusals are compelled do not take issue with *Neville's* function requirement of impermissible compulsion. Rather, they find that at least as a matter of state law the compulsion involved is impermissible.

The Oregon Supreme Court in *State v. Fish*,[10] for example, addressed evidence of a refusal to submit to field sobriety test. The court regarded the tests as calling for testimonial self-incriminating responses and thus beyond the power of the state to require. Although South Dakota could compel Neville to submit to the blood draw, Oregon could not permissibly compel Fish to submit to the field sobriety tests. The compulsion upon Fish, unlike that on Neville, was not *permissible* compulsion and thus *Fish* held it triggered the privilege.[11]

## § 126 Privilege as applied to an accused in a criminal proceeding: (a) Inferences from and comment upon the accused's reliance upon the privilege in the trial[1]

A defendant's refusal to testify in a criminal case itself, the most basic invocation of the privilege imaginable, cannot be penalized by use of that action as tending to prove the defendant's guilt in that trial.[2] Implementing this, however, has proven somewhat troublesome.

---

[10]State v. Fish, 321 Or. 48, 893 P.2d 1023 (1995).

[11]Fish, 893 P.2d at 1029–30.

The Massachusetts court's analysis in Opinion of the Justices to the Senate, 412 Mass. 1201, 591 N.E.2d 1073, 1078 (1992), has been described as "conclud[ing] that evidence of a refusal to submit to a breathalyzer test is testimonial in nature, and that there is compulsion because both alternatives, refusal or submission, require the suspect to furnish evidence against himself." Wyatt v. State, 149 Md. App. 554, 573, 817 A.2d 901, 913 (2003). In other words, as in *Fish*, the compulsion was impermissible.

**[Section 126]**

[1]*See generally* West's Key Number Digest, Criminal Law ☞656(7).

[2]The Supreme Court refused to recognize an exception that would have permitted a sentencing court to draw adverse inferences from the defendant's silence regarding the factual matters respecting the circumstances and details of the crime. "The concerns which mandate the rule against negative inferences at a criminal trial," it explained, "apply with equal force at sentencing." Mitchell v. U.S., 526 U.S. 314, 329, 119 S. Ct. 1307, 143 L. Ed. 2d 424 (1999). It carefully reserved comment on whether trial courts could rely on silence as tending to show lack of remorse or failure to accept responsibility in applying federal sentencing law. Mitchell, 526 U.S. at 330.

In *Griffin v. California*,[3] the Supreme Court held that the Fifth Amendment privilege was violated[4] by a prosecutor's argument which urged the jury to draw an inference of guilt from a defendant's failure to testify when his testimony could reasonably have been expected to deny or explain matters proved by the prosecution and a jury instruction that authorized the jury to draw that suggested inference. So encouraging the jury to infer guilt from the defendant's reliance upon the privilege, the Court concluded, constituted an impermissible penalty for exercising the privilege, despite the risk that even without argument or instruction the jury might do it anyway.[5] "What the jury may infer given no help from the court is one thing," noted the Court. "What they may infer when the court solemnizes the silence of the accused into evidence against him is quite another."[6]

In 1999, the Court reaffirmed *Griffin*. Rejecting the argument that the rule is useless because jurors will inevitably draw adverse inferences from defendants' silence, it explained:

> The rule against adverse inferences from a defendant's silence in criminal proceedings . . . is of proven utility . . . . It is far from clear that citizens, and jurors, remain today so skeptical of the principle or are often willing to ignore the prohibition against adverse inferences from silence . . . . [T]he rule prohibiting an inference of guilt from a defendant's rightful silence has become an essential feature of our legal system . . . [and] is a vital instrument for teaching that the question in a criminal case is not whether the defendant committed the act of which he is accused. The question is

---

[3]Griffin v. California, 380 U.S. 609, 85 S. Ct. 1229, 14 L. Ed. 2d 106 (1965).

[4]Statues may also bar reliance upon invoking the privilege to prove guilt. For example, the federal statute making defendants competent witnesses, 18 U.S.C.A. § 3481, and its predecessors have, since 1878, provided that the accused's failure to request to testify "shall not create any presumption against him." This was held in Wilson v. U.S., 149 U.S. 60, 13 S. Ct. 765, 37 L. Ed. 650 (1893) to prohibit prosecutorial comment on the defendant's failure to testify.

[5]Griffin, 380 U.S. at 614. *Griffin* errors, however, are subject to federal constitutional "harmless error" analysis and thus may not require that a conviction be held invalid. *See* Chapman v. California, 386 U.S. 18, 21–24, 87 S. Ct. 824, 17 L. Ed. 2d 705 (1967); U.S. v. Hasting, 461 U.S. 499, 507–09, 103 S. Ct. 1974, 76 L. Ed. 2d 96 (1983).

[6]Griffin, 380 U.S. at 614.

Despite the implications of *Griffin*, defendants are seldom able to attack a conviction on the direct basis that their failures to testify in their own defense were taken into account in finding them guilty. Courts will generally not permit efforts to establish that jurors actually relied upon such impermissible considerations, and even apparently unambiguous admissions by trial judges sitting without juries have failed to persuade appellate courts to overturn convictions. *E.g.* State v. DeGrat, 128 Idaho 352, 913 P.2d 568, 570 (1996) (right not to testify does not give a defendant a right to attack a verdict by showing via juror testimony that the jurors did in fact consider his failure to testify).

whether the Government has carried its burden to prove the allegations while respecting the defendant's individual rights.[7]

Under *Griffin*, any explicit—or "direct"—invitation to a jury—by the trial judge, the prosecutor, or even counsel for a co-defendant[8]—to consider the defendant's failure to testify as tending to prove guilt is prohibited. Arguments and instructions that have other primary functions are often held permissible, even though they may also serve to call juries' attention to defendants' failure to testify. For example, the Supreme Court upheld an instruction permitting the jury to infer knowledge that property was stolen from evidence of possession of recently-stolen property, if the possession was not satisfactorily explained. Without elaboration, it simply observed that the instruction could not fairly be understood as a comment on the defendant's failure to testify.[9]

A prosecutor improperly commented on the accused's reliance on the privilege by observing to the jury, "Mr. Marshall [the defendant] did not take the stand" and "[w]e don't have Mr. Marshall's thoughts."[10] Another also did so by arguing "[I]n order to have self-defense, what has to happen is someone says, 'Yeah, I committed this crime [but] I intended to do this because I was in fear of my life.' "[11]

Courts have, however, had some difficulty identifying those arguments by prosecutors that are at most prohibited "indirect" references to the defendant's failure to testify. Lower courts have generally held that arguments possibly referring to the defendant's failure to testify must be considered in context and are impermissible under *Griffin* only if the prosecutor "manifestly intended" to comment on the defendant's silence or if the character of the argument was such that a jury would "naturally and necessarily" construe it as a comment on the defendant's failure to testify.[12]

Generally, prosecutors may safely argue that the State's evi-

---

[7]Mitchell v. U.S., 526 U.S. 314, 329–30, 119 S. Ct. 1307, 143 L. Ed. 2d 424 (1999).

[8]*See* People v. Estrada, 63 Cal. App. 4th 1090, 75 Cal. Rptr. 2d 17, 24 (4th Dist. 1998) (comment on defendant's silence by counsel for codefendant violated *Griffin*).

[9]Barnes v. U.S., 412 U.S. 837, 846 n.12, 93 S. Ct. 2357, 37 L. Ed. 2d 380 (1973).

[10]Marshall v. State, 415 Md. 248, 999 A.2d 1029, 1030 (2010).

[11]Hunter v. State, 956 S.W.2d 143 (Tex. App. Amarillo 1997). Inexplicably, a split court on rehearing found no constitutional defect in the argument, "The only person who knows where [the fatal] shot was fired from exactly is the person sitting in that chair over there [indicating the defendant] and he hasn't seen fit to tell us." Ragland v. Com., 191 S.W.3d 569, 588–91 (Ky. 2006).

[12]*E.g.* Lampley v. State, 284 Ga. 37, 663 S.E.2d 184, 186 (2008); State v. Madkins, 42 Kan. App. 2d 955, 219

dence, or particular parts of it, are "uncontradicted."[13] If the state of the evidence is that the only possible contradictory testimony would be from the defendant, however, such argument constitutes an impermissible indirect comment on the defendant's failure to testify.[14] Similarly, an argument stressing the lack of any evidence becomes impermissible if the only evidence that might be presented would be the testimony of the accused.[15]

Otherwise proper comment on the defendant's silence at trial is permissible if it is a fair response to evidence or argument made by the defendant. Thus in United States v. Robinson[16] when defense counsel argued to the jury that the prosecution had unfairly denied the defendant the opportunity to explain his actions, the prosecutor was permitted to respond in argument that the defendant had "every opportunity," if he chose to use it, "to explain this to the ladies and gentlemen of the jury."[17]

---

P.3d 831, 835 (2009).

[13]Timberlake v. State, 690 N.E.2d 243, 254 (Ind. 1997) ("A comment based upon uncontradicted evidence is not equivalent to an impermissible comment upon a defendant's decision not to testify."). *Accord, e.g.*, State v. Hawkins, 328 S.W.3d 799, 813–14 (Mo. Ct. App. S.D. 2010).

The Supreme Court did not pass on the question in U.S. v. Robinson, 485 U.S. 25, 30, 108 S. Ct. 864, 99 L. Ed. 2d 23 (1988), discussed later in this section.

[14]*E.g.* Landreth v. State, 331 Ark. 12, 960 S.W.2d 434, 435 (1998) (*Griffin* was violated when prosecutor, referring to testimony by Laura Baker about a telephone conversation with the defendant, argued, "Have you heard anything about that conversation other than what Laura said was said? No."); State v. Scutchings, 2009 ND 8, 759 N.W.2d 729, 732 (N.D. 2009) (where the evidence was that only C.M. and the defendant were present, prosecutor agued improperly by posing to jury the question "What do you have to refute C.M.'s testimony? Nothing.").

[15]U.S. v. Williams, 112 Fed. Appx. 581, 583 (9th Cir. 2004) (improper for prosecutor, referring to evidence that

the defendant had fled when approached by an officer, to ask, "[W]as there any evidence why this defendant did not stop there?" because only defendant could testify to this).

[16]U.S. v. Robinson, 485 U.S. 25, 108 S. Ct. 864, 99 L. Ed. 2d 23 (1988).

[17]Robinson, 485 U.S. at 30. *Accord* Lockett v. Ohio, 438 U.S. 586, 595, 98 S. Ct. 2954, 57 L. Ed. 2d 973 (1978) (where defense counsel had focused the jury's attention on the defendant's failure to testify by outlining in opening argument what appeared to be the defendant's version of the events and stating to the jury that the defendant would be the "next witness," any tendency of the prosecutor's argument that the prosecution's evidence was unrefuted to comment on the defendant's failure to testify "added nothing to the impression" already created by defense counsel); U.S. v. Ivory, 532 F.3d 1095, 1102 (10th Cir. 2008) (where defense counsel argued that no witness testified in support of prosecution's theory as to meaning of word used by defendant in recorded conversation, prosecutor could respond by mentioning defendant's failure to testify in explaining need to rely on circumstantial evidence in ascertaining meaning).

## § 127 Privilege as applied to an accused in a criminal proceeding: (b) Impeachment and substantive use of prior invocation of the privilege or silence

A criminal defendant may have invoked the privilege prior to the trial on the criminal accusation. This may have occurred out of court during the pretrial events that led to the present trial, it may have occurred in a prior trial of the same case, or it may have happened in a different proceeding. May the prosecution use any of those prior invocations of the privilege against the defendant, perhaps only to impeach the defendant if he testifies or perhaps as affirmative proof of guilt?

*Griffin v. California*[1]—discussed in the last section—prohibits use of a defendant's invocation of the privilege in the present trial to prove guilt. It does not, however, address the prosecution's ability to use evidence that the accused invoked the privilege in other contexts. A defendant who testifies and thus waives the privilege is generally held to have waived it for—but only for—the trial in which this occurs.[2] Does this approach work against the accused as well as for him, so that an invocation of the privilege in an earlier context can be used by the prosecution in the present—and arguably different—proceeding?

In *Raffel v. United States*,[3] the Supreme Court held that a defendant who testified at trial had no federal constitutional protection against cross-examination concerning his failure to testify at a prior trial on the same charge. This seemed to rest largely on a waiver notion—the Court stressed that a defendant who takes the witness stand subjects himself to such cross-examination as is generally permitted.[4] But other language in the opinion suggested that the basis of decision was rather that such a defendant has no right that warrants protection. Any Fifth Amendment right to be free from penalties for invoking the privilege, the Court suggested, extends only to penalties imposed in the same trial or proceeding in which the defendant invoked the privilege.[5]

Precisely when and how the privilege protects out-of-court silence remains somewhat unclear.[6] Under *Jenkins v. Anderson*,[7] *Raffel* permits a testifying defendant to be cross-examined about

---

[Section 127]

[1]Griffin v. California, 380 U.S. 609, 85 S. Ct. 1229, 14 L. Ed. 2d 106 (1965).

[2]See § 129 infra.

[3]Raffel v. U.S., 271 U.S. 494, 46 S. Ct. 566, 70 L. Ed. 1054 (1926).

[4]Raffel, 271 U.S.at 496–97.

[5]"We can discern nothing in the policy of the law against self-incrimination which would require the extension of immunity to any trial or to any tribunal other than that in which the defendant preserves it by refusing to testify." 271 U.S. at 499.

[6]Silence after the *Miranda* warning that the person has a right to

prior out-of-court silence even if that silence is, as a general matter, protected. *Jenkins* left open whether it is in fact protected.[8] Impeachment of a testifying defendant with prior in-court reliance on the privilege or out-of-court invocations of it is clearly permissible as a matter of privilege law.

Whether the prosecution can make substantive use of the defendant's prior invocations is less clear. Insofar as *Raffel* suggested that neither the letter nor the reason for the privilege suggests that invoking the privilege has any effect in any trial or tribunal other than that in which it occurs, it was simply wrong. This is clear from the quite complicated case law on the validity of various burdens on the exercise of the privilege.[9]

If the prior invocation was in a formal proceeding, the question should probably be whether permitting its substantive use in a later criminal prosecution is an unacceptable burden on an exercise of the privilege. Given the significant chilling effect this would undoubtedly have, such use of a prior formal invocation of the privilege should be barred.

Whether the prosecution may use out-of-court silence or invocation of the privilege is less certain. Discussion tends to become mired in whether the privilege protects silence in such situations and, if so, whether the situations involved any necessary compulsion to trigger its protection.[10]

In fact, the privilege almost certainly applies in out-of-court situations, whether the person is in custody or not.[11] As applied, however, it does not require affording the person a right to counsel or even a right to warnings. But it does protect the person's right to refuse to make self-incriminating admissions. Invocations of that right should be treated the same as more explicit in-court invocations of the right to refuse to give self-incriminating testimony under oath. Thus the prosecution should be barred from using as substantive evidence of guilt proof that the defendant expressly invoked that right ("I refuse to say anything because I believe there is too great a risk that anything

---

remain silent, however, cannot be used even to impeach because of the "fundamental unfairness" inherent in informing a suspect that he has a right to remain silent and then using that silence against him. Doyle v. Ohio, 426 U.S. 610, 96 S. Ct. 2240, 49 L. Ed. 2d 91 (1976). See generally § 161 infra.

[7]Jenkins v. Anderson, 447 U.S. 231, 100 S. Ct. 2124, 65 L. Ed. 2d 86 (1980).

[8]Jenkins, 447 U.S. at 235 n. 2.

[9]See generally § 136 infra.

[10]*E.g.*, State v. Leach, 102 Ohio St. 3d 135, 2004-Ohio-2147, 807 N.E.2d 335, 339–42 (2004).

[11]See § 117 supra, discussing the application of the privilege of a "witness," and § 161 infra.

I say will be incriminating.") or that the defendant indicated a desire to consult with counsel.[12]

If the prosecution offers evidence that the accused, before trial and out of court, was silent in the face of circumstances that would cause a reasonable person to protest, the question under the self-incrimination privilege[13] should be whether it is likely enough that the silence reflects reliance on the privilege's right to refuse to respond. This is considered in Section 161. In view of the widespread public perception that such persons do have a right to refuse to respond and the difficulty of determining on a case-by-case basis what motivated silence, such silence should be treated as an invocation of the privilege. The prosecution should be barred by the privilege from using it to prove the guilt of the defendant on trial.

## § 128    Privilege as applied to an accused in a criminal proceeding: (c) Instructing the jury regarding the privilege

Whether instructions directing jurors to give no weight to a defendant's failure to testify can in fact be effective, of course, is open to dispute. In *Carter v. Kentucky*,[1] the Supreme Court nevertheless held that the Fifth Amendment requires trial judges upon request to instruct juries that no inferences are to be drawn from defendants' failures to testify. "No judge can prevent jurors from speculating about why a defendant stands mute in the face of a criminal accusation," the Court reasoned, "but a judge can, and must if requested to do so, use the unique power of the jury instruction to reduce that speculation to a minimum."[2]

It is widely recognized, however, that reasonable persons differ with regard to when, if ever, such an instruction is likely to do

---

[12]Invocations of a perceived right to counsel should be treated as assertions of the right to remain silent. *Cf.* Wainwright v. Greenfield, 474 U.S. 284, 295 n.13, 106 S. Ct. 634, 88 L. Ed. 2d 623 (1986) ("With respect to post-*Miranda* warnings 'silence,' we point out that silence does not mean only muteness; it includes the statement of a desire to remain silent as well as of a desire to remain silent until an attorney has been consulted."); Combs v. Coyle, 205 F.3d 269, 279 (6th Cir. 2000) (suspect's rely to officer that officer should "talk to [my] lawyer" "is best understood as communicating a desire to remain silent outside the presence of an attorney").

[13]Of course, even if the privilege does not bar admission of such silence it may be inadmissible as a matter of federal Due Process or evidence law. See § 161 infra.

[Section 128]

[1]Carter v. Kentucky, 450 U.S. 288, 101 S. Ct. 1112, 67 L. Ed. 2d 241 (1981).

[2]Carter, 450 U.S. at 303. In James v. Kentucky, 466 U.S. 341, 344, 104 S. Ct. 1830, 80 L. Ed. 2d 346 (1984), the Court held that a defense request for an "admonition" was sufficient to invoke the *Carter* right, despite the state's technical characterization of what was at issue as an "instruction."

more good than harm. The instruction, of course, reminds jurors of the defendant's failure to testify and emphasizes it albeit by stressing the law's demand that the failure be given no significance. Some lawyers, in at least some situations, believe that the giving of such an instruction increases rather than decreases the likelihood that the jury will actually consider the defendant's failure to testify. In light of this, may or should such an instruction be given if the defendant does not request it or if the defendant actively opposes it?

In *Lakeside v. Oregon*,[3] the Supreme Court found no Fifth Amendment defect in a trial judge's giving of such an instruction over the defendant's objection. *Griffin* was concerned only with adverse comment, the Court reasoned. It then rejected as "speculative" Lakeside's argument that the jury might, in the absence of instructions, take no notice of his failure to testify but if given cautionary instructions might totally disregard those directives and draw an inference from his failure to testify. Sound nonconstitutional policy may direct that a trial judge respect a defendant's desire that cautionary instructions not be given, the Court commented, and states remain free to prohibit cautionary instructions over defendants' objection as a matter of state law.[4]

---

At least one court has held that a trial judge is not required to avoid in the instruction reference to the defendant's "failure to testify," at least where the defendant did not explicitly suggest equally effective but more neutral language. State v. Casanova, 255 Conn. 581, 767 A.2d 1189, 1201–02 (2001).

The instruction need not address possible reasons for defendants' failure to testify. *See* People v. Roberts, 2 Cal. 4th 271, 6 Cal. Rptr. 2d 276, 826 P.2d 274, 296 (1992) ("We see no reason to require a court to outline every hypothetical reason for a defendant's failure to testify: such comments may be left for a defendant's closing argument if counsel desires to explain the matter further," and therefore trial judge did not err in failing to tell jury defendant might have declined to testify because of fear or nervousness).

Courts have differed regarding whether a trial judge may suggest that the decision not to testify may have been a "tactical" one. *Compare* People v. Rose, 223 A.D.2d 607, 637 N.Y.S.2d 172, 174 (2d Dep't 1996) (trial court's "expansive no-adverse-inference charge implied that the defendant's exercise of his right not to testify was a tactical decision," and therefore was reversible error) *with* State v. James, 342 N.C. 589, 466 S.E.2d 710, 716 (1996) (trial court did not commit constitutional error by telling jury, "[A defendant's choice not to take the stand] may . . . be a trial tactic that the defendant not present evidence, for if the defendant makes that decision not to present evidence, not to take the stand, the defendant would get the final argument or closing to the jury.").

[3]Lakeside v. Oregon, 435 U.S. 333, 98 S. Ct. 1091, 55 L. Ed. 2d 319 (1978).

[4]Lakeside, 435 U.S. at 340.

It is difficult to find any significant interests furthered by the giving of such an instruction over the defendant's objection.[5] Moreover, in light of the uncertainty as to whether and when such an instruction is more favorable to an accused than the absence of any instruction, there is little reason to permit the instruction if the defendant affirmatively objects. As the Pennsylvania Supreme Court noted, permitting the trial judge to decide whether to give the instruction removes the judge from the role of impartial presider and inserts that judge into the role of advocate for the defendant. This is clearly undesirable.[6]

An increasing number of jurisdictions require trial judges to omit the instruction if the defendant objects.[7] This is sometimes by statute,[8] and sometimes by constitutional[9] or nonconstitutional case law.[10]

---

[5]A prohibition against the instruction over defense objection arguably creates the risk that proper convictions will have to be reversed for insufficient reason. But this can be avoided by application of the harmless error rule. *See* Roberts, 826 P.2d at 297 ("We must assume that the jury followed the admonition not to take into account defendant's failure to testify," so "it is inconceivable that the giving of the instruction led to a less favorable outcome for defendant" and giving of the instruction over the defendant's objection is not reversible error).

[6]Com. v. Edwards, 535 Pa. 575, 637 A.2d 259, 261 (1993).

[7]In these jurisdictions, it is generally not error to give the instruction where the defendant has neither requested it nor objected to it. Kissinger v. State, 117 Md. App. 372, 700 A.2d 795, 797 (1997). Contra, State v. Gomez, 721 N.W.2d 871, 881 (Minn. 2006) (applying Minnesota rule that giving of the no-adverse-inference instruction is error if the record does not contain the defendant's consent).

[8]*E.g.* Conn. Gen. Stat. Ann. § 54-84(b) (instruction to be given "[u]nless the accused requests otherwise"); N.Y. Crim. Proc. Law § 300.10(2) (instruction to be given at request of the defendant "but not otherwise").

[9]Bush v. State, 775 N.E.2d 309, 310–11 (Ind. 2002) (giving of instruction over defendant's objection was violation of state constitutional right against self-incrimination); People v. Anderson, 153 Ill. App. 3d 542, 106 Ill. Dec. 512, 505 N.E.2d 1303, 1306 (1st Dist. 1987); Conn v. State, 535 N.E.2d 1176, 1182–83 (Ind. 1989). The Vermont court, however, refused to construe the state constitution as going beyond *Lakeside* and barring the instruction if the defendant objects. State v. Martin, 182 Vt. 377, 2007 VT 96, 944 A.2d 867, 885 (2007). Some other courts follow the same approach. Lewis v. State, 518 So. 2d 214, 219 (Ala. Crim. App. 1987); State v. Wheeler, 108 Wash. 2d 230, 737 P.2d 1005, 1010 (1987). *Compare* Com. v. Rivera, 441 Mass. 358, 805 N.E.2d 942, 951–53 (2004) (reaffirming that trial judges should not give the instruction when asked by defendants not to do so, but overruling case law that doing so is per se reversible error).

[10]Roberts, 826 P.2d at 297; Hardaway v. State, 317 Md. 160, 562 A.2d 1234 (1989); Com. v. Buiel, 391 Mass. 744, 463 N.E.2d 1172, 1174 (1984); *Edwards*, 637 A.2d at 261. The Minnesota Supreme Court has held that ordinarily a trial judge should obtain a defendant's personal permission, not simply that of defense counsel, before instructing the jury on the

## § 129  Privilege as applied to an accused in a criminal proceeding: (d) "Waiver" of the privilege by voluntary testimony[1]

The extensive protection afforded by the privilege to one who is the accused in a criminal case is diminished by the act of the accused in testifying during the trial. Unlike the situation of a witness, who loses the privilege only by testifying to incriminating facts, the accused suffers this reduction in his rights merely by testifying, regardless of the incriminatory content of his testimony. In *Brown v. United States*[2] the Supreme Court explained:

> [The accused] has the choice, after weighing the advantage of the privilege against self-incrimination against the advantage of putting forward his version of the facts and his reliability as a witness, not to testify at all. He cannot reasonably claim that the Fifth Amendment gives him not only this choice but, if he elects to testify, an immunity from cross-examination on the matters he has himself put in dispute. It would make of the Fifth Amendment not only a humane safeguard against judicially coerced self-disclosure but a positive invitation to mutilate the truth a party offers to tell.[3]

The diminution of the accused's rights under the privilege occurs only if the accused testifies in the criminal case itself. Pretrial and out-of-court disclosure of incriminating facts, as to law enforcement officers, does not impair the defendant's protection at the trial itself.[4] Moreover, testimony at a hearing before trial or even during trial on an issue other than guilt will not affect the accused's protection under the privilege with regard to the trial itself.[5] Participating during trial in a demonstration not involving testimony does not impair the accused's ability to remain off the witness stand and avoid cross-examination or com-

---

defendant's failure to testify. State v. Thompson, 430 N.W.2d 151, 153 (Minn. 1988).

**[Section 129]**

[1]*See generally* West's Key Number Digest, Witnesses ☞301, 305(2).

[2]Brown v. U.S., 356 U.S. 148, 78 S. Ct. 622, 2 L. Ed. 2d 589 (1958).

[3]Brown, 356 U.S. at 155–56. *Accord* Mitchell v. U.S., 526 U.S. 314, 322, 119 S. Ct. 1307, 143 L. Ed. 2d 424 (1999) ("The justifications for the rule of waiver . . . are evident: A witness may not pick and choose what aspects of a particular subject to discuss without casting doubt on the trustworthiness of the statements and diminish-

ing the integrity of the factual inquiry.").

[4]Ginyard v. U.S., 816 A.2d 21, 33 (D.C. 2003) ("a suspect who voluntarily makes admissions to the police at the time of arrest does not thereby waive his Fifth Amendment privilege for future proceedings").

[5]Simmons v. U.S., 390 U.S. 377, 393–94, 88 S. Ct. 967, 19 L. Ed. 2d 1247 (1968) (trial judge erred by admitting at trial testimony given by defendant at hearing on motion to suppress evidence); Wells v. Com., 32 Va. App. 775, 531 S.E.2d 16, 21 (2000) ("An accused does not waive his privilege against self-incrimination by testifying before trial or, in a jury trial,

ment on the failure to testify.[6] Of course, having testified in another trial of even the same exact criminal charge does not prevent the accused from relying on the privilege.[7]

The effect of a defendant's participating in entry of a plea of guilty was explored by the Supreme Court in *Mitchell v. United States*.[8] Despite the offer of such a plea, the Court made clear, a criminal defendant has the right to refuse to take the witness stand at a hearing on whether the plea should be accepted. Apparently the defendant may even refuse to participate in an in-court plea colloquy at which the accused is not sworn.[9] If the defendant participates in such a colloquy, even under oath, admissions so made will not be given the same effect as testimony at a contested trial. This is because the defendant's participation in the colloquy does not selectively put matters related to the offense into issue and thus involves no risk of misleading the court as to matters put into issue by the defendant.[10]

The major problem in applying this rule has been defining the extent to which an accused loses the protection of the privilege by testifying. Traditionally, many courts have taken the position that a defendant who testifies becomes subject to cross-examination under the jurisdiction's applicable rules and loses the right to invoke the privilege in response to any question proper under that jurisdiction's rules concerning the permissible

---

outside the presence of the jury as to 'collateral matters,' such as venue or admissibility of a confession.").

[6]*Cf.* Williams v. State, 991 So. 2d 593 (Miss. 2008) ("The formal exhibition of defendant's gold teeth before the jury was not 'testimonial' and, therefore, did not, in and of itself, open the door to cross-examination or self-incrimination."); State v. Fivecoats, 251 Or. App. 761, 284 P.3d 1225, 1228 (2012) (allowing defendant to walk in front of jury would not have been "testimonial" and would not have required defendant to submit to cross-examination).

[7]City of Liberal, Kansas v. Witherspoon, 28 Kan. App. 2d 649, 20 P.3d 727, 730 (2001) (defendant's testimony in municipal court trial was admissible at trial de novo held on appeal, but court assumed defendant testimony in first trial did not impair defendant's ability to decline to testify in second trial).

[8]Mitchell v. U.S., 526 U.S. 314, 119 S. Ct. 1307, 143 L. Ed. 2d 424 (1999). But see § 127 supra (impeachment of a testifying defendant by questions concerning failure to testify at prior trial on same charge).

[9]Mitchell, 526 U.S. at 324 (noting that by refusing to participate in such a colloquy, a defendant runs the risk of having the plea rejected as without adequate basis).

[10]526 U.S. at 322–23. In *Mitchell*, at the defendant's guilty plea proceeding, the factual basis for the charges was put on the record and the judge, after putting Mitchell under oath, asked, "Did you do that?" Mitchell replied, "Some of it." Neither Mitchell's plea of guilty nor her statement during the "narrow inquiry" of the specific plea colloquy, the Court held, amounted to a waiver of her privilege preventing her from refusing to provide information about the details of her offense.

scope of cross-examination.[11] Under this approach, a testifying defendant may be questioned concerning all matters permitted by that rule and credibility.[12] Such a defendant may not invoke the privilege on the ground that answers to such questions would incriminate the defendant further regarding the offenses on which the trial is being held. Nor can the defendant invoke it on the ground that the answers would create liability for other offenses.

This last statement is subject to one exception. Courts generally enforce the position adopted by Federal Rule 608(b)[13] that a criminal defendant, like other witnesses, does not by testifying lose the right to invoke the privilege regarding criminal misconduct relevant to the case only because that conduct tends to show the accused's lack of credibility.[14] If such misconduct is relevant to some other issue, however, the privilege cannot be invoked by the defendant to avoid incriminating answers to questions about it.[15]

Under the traditional approach, the extent to which a testifying accused's protection is diminished is determined by the

---

[11]*E.g.* U.S. v. Spinelli, 551 F.3d 159, 167 (2d Cir. 2008) ("By choosing to testify, however, the defendant gives up his right to refuse to answer questions that fall within the proper scope of cross examination."): Blackman v. Com., 45 Va. App. 633, 613 S.E.2d 460, 465 (2005) (when an accused testifies the privilege is waived for the matters covered by the testimony "and the scope of the waiver is determined by the scope of relevant cross-examination").

Thus a federal district court erred in ruling that a defendant who testified as to one of several counts could be cross-examined only regarding the count as to which he testified. U.S. v. Fernandez, 559 F.3d 303, 330–31 (5th Cir. 2009) ("The proper line is between what on cross-examination is relevant and irrelevant to the scope of the direct examination.").

Some judicial discussions approve of extremely broad cross-examination without linking that to the general rule concerning scope of cross-examination. *E.g.* Com. v. Gaynor, 443 Mass. 245, 820 N.E.2d 233, 256 (2005) (trial judge had discre-

tion to refuse to permit defendant, charged with four rape-murders, to testify about and be cross-examined regarding only one of those charges).

[12]*E.g.* People v. Coffman, 34 Cal. 4th 1, 17 Cal. Rptr. 3d 710, 96 P.3d 30, 84–88 (2004) (defendant's testimony on direct that he did not want to kill the victim "or anyone else" "open[ed] the door" to cross-examination about other killings).

[13]Fed. R. Evid. 608(b).

[14]*E.g.* Whitman v. State, 316 Ga. App. 655, 729 S.E.2d 409, 413 (2012) ("The right against self-incrimination is retained as to collateral matters, therefore, so long as the defendant does not somehow waive that right in his direct examination."). See § 41 supra as to claiming the privilege on cross-examination directed to impeachment.

[15]*See* U.S. v. Cuozzo, 962 F.2d 945, 948 (9th Cir. 1992) (testifying defendant could not invoke the privilege regarding questions as to prior fraudulent activities because those activities tended to rebut her claim that she lacked the fraudulent intent required by the charged offense).

jurisdiction's choice of a rule for cross-examination in general. If the jurisdiction limits cross-examination to the scope of direct examination, a defendant on trial for several offenses could, at least in theory, testify regarding less than all of the charged offenses and avoid cross-examination concerning those not addressed on direct. In practice, the courts in these jurisdictions tend to require only a reasonable relationship to matters covered by direct and thus and to find no right to refuse to respond to questions with relatively attenuated relation to the matters inquired into on direct examination.[16] At least occasionally, however, courts hold cross-examination exceeds the permissible limits and the defendant can thus invoke the privilege.[17]

A defendant's loss of protection by virtue of testifying in his own defense should not be tied to the jurisdiction's rules concerning permissible cross-examination. There is no reason why the scope of an important constitutional right should vary depending upon the jurisdiction's choice of a cross-examination rule. Determining the scope of cross-examination is essentially a matter of control over the order of production of evidence. The pri-

---

[16]Rhoden v. Rowland, 10 F.3d 1457, 1461 (9th Cir. 1993) (state court properly held rape defendant testifying as to good faith belief that victim consented could not invoke privilege in response to questions about prior rapes, as those questions would be reasonably related to his direct testimony); U.S. v. Rackstraw, 7 F.3d 1476, 1480 (10th Cir. 1993) (defendant charged with traveling in interstate commerce to distribute drugs who testified that he did not know drugs were in the car could not invoke privilege regarding questions concerning prior sales of drugs, as these were reasonably related to his direct testimony); State v. Grazian, 144 Idaho 510, 164 P.3d 790, 798 (2007) (trial court did not abuse discretion in ruling that if defendant testified regarding incidents on which three counts of attempted procurement for prostitution were based, prosecution could cross-examine on events giving rise to other counts of procurement for prostitution because that questioning would be on matters relevant to the testimony); Wells v. Com., 32 Va. App. 775, 531 S.E.2d 16, 21 (2000) (where defendant charged with possession of marijuana testified about how he was em-

ployed at the time of the alleged offense, waiver extended to possession of marijuana and prosecution could properly comment on his failure to deny possession). *See also* Com. v. Judge, 420 Mass. 433, 650 N.E.2d 1242, 1251 n.10 (1995) (after defendant testified that his confession was involuntary, questions concerning the truth of the admissions made in the confession were reasonably related to his direct testimony and proper under the approach cited in the text, so that constitutionality of broader state law approach permitting questions about any aspect of the case would not be reached).

[17]Holman v. State, 372 Ark. 2, 269 S.W.3d 815, 825–26 (2007) (trial court erred in permitting testifying defendant to be questioned about items belonging to others found in his home where on direct testimony he did not testify as to the identity thefts to which those items related); State v. Epefanio, 156 Wash. App. 378, 234 P.3d 253, 259 (Div. 3 2010) (rape defendant's testimony about sexual activity involving other did not preclude relying on privilege concerning confrontation at different time).

743

mary policy served by limiting cross-examination is the orderly conduct of the trial; ordinary witnesses usually have no legitimate interest that is affected by the scope of permitted cross-examination. Defining the protection of the privilege, on the other hand, involves the fairness of requiring defendants to forfeit the protection of the privilege in order to place their own versions of the facts before triers of fact. This affects defendants' interests which are, generally speaking, protected by the privilege. The scope of protection retained by a testifying defendant should not be tied to the scope of cross-examination of the ordinary witness.[18]

Testifying defendants are required to submit to cross-examination to provide reasonable assurance that their testimony, like that of other witnesses, is subjected to procedures providing assurance of accuracy. The extent to which a defendant forfeits the privilege by testifying should be related to this rationale for decreased protection because of his testifying. Thus a defendant who testifies should have no right to invoke the privilege regarding questions on cross-examination that the trial court, in the exercise of discretion, determines are necessary to provide the prosecution with a reasonable opportunity to test the defendant's assertions on direct.[19]

If a defendant has testified in his own defense and impermissibly refused to respond to cross-examination in mistaken reliance upon his privilege, what action should or may the trial court take? As in the case where an ordinary witness invokes the privilege on cross-examination,[20] the trial court has substantial

---

[18]This was recognized in Neely v. State, 97 Wis. 2d 38, 292 N.W.2d 859 (1980). The drafters of the Federal Rules of Evidence expressly disclaimed any intent to affect the scope of waiver of the privilege by defining the scope of cross-examination of a witness. Fed. R. Evid. 611(b), Advisory Committee Note. *See* U.S. v. Beechum, 582 F.2d 898, 907 (5th Cir. 1978) (en banc).

[19]A few cases acknowledge the possibility of "limited waivers" by testimony restricted to relatively narrow collateral purposes. Com. v. Camm, 443 Pa. 253, 277 A.2d 325, 331 (1971) (where defendant took witness stand for limited purpose of testifying to involuntariness of confession, trial court properly sustained his claim to the privilege in response to questions concerning guilt or innocence). Several decisions have held that in a capital

trial, a defendant may testify as to matters that might mitigate punishment without waiving the privilege regarding other matters. State v. Riels, 216 S.W.3d 737, 745–46 (Tenn. 2007) (when defendant testified in punishment phase of trial as to his remorse and relationship with his family, trial court erred in permitting prosecution to cross-examine him regarding the details of the offense of which he had been convicted). *Accord* Lesko v. Lehman, 925 F.2d 1527, 1542–43 (3d Cir. 1991). The cases are, at best, "divided," People v. Monterroso, 34 Cal. 4th 743, 22 Cal. Rptr. 3d 1, 101 P.3d 956, 974–76 (2004), and most courts have rejected this. *E.g.* State v. Lee, 189 Ariz. 590, 944 P.2d 1204, 1216 (1997).

[20]See § 134 infra.

discretion as to how to respond.[21] But in view of a defendant's particularly important interest in having his version of the events go to the trier of fact, a trial judge should be especially reluctant to strike the defendant's testimony on direct examination. A judge should strike the testimony only after considering and rejecting alternative measures such as striking only part of the testimony on direct examination or directing that the jury consider in assessing the defendant's credibility his improper reliance upon his privilege.[22]

The loss of protection has traditionally been regarded as effective throughout the trial in which the accused testifies. During that proceeding the privilege does not reattach if the accused physically leaves the witness stand, and the accused can be recalled and required to testify again if this is otherwise procedurally proper.[23] On the other hand, the trial on guilt is regarded by some courts as a different proceeding than the sentencing hearing, so a defendant's waiver of the privilege by testifying at trial does not affect that defendant's ability to decline to testify at the sentencing.[24]

---

[21]The judge may hold the defendant in contempt or instruct the jury to consider the defendant's failure to testify in assessing credibility. If the defendant has asserted in advance an improper refusal to respond to cross-examination questions, the judge may require the defendant to invoke the privilege before the jury. Rackstraw, 7 F.3d at 1480.

[22]Schnelle v. State, 103 S.W.3d 165, 175 (Mo. Ct. App. W.D. 2003) (defense counsel's representation was defective because counsel failed to oppose striking of defendant's testimony, it was far from clear that refusal to answer a question on cross-examination warranted striking defendant's entire testimony). *Accord* Williams v. Borg, 139 F.3d 737, 740–42 (9th Cir. 1998) (striking testimony of defendant who testified to innocent version of events but refused to respond to questions concerning prior convictions was "a measured response to serve an important purpose," per-

mitting assessment of the defendant's credibility, and thus within the trial judge's discretion). *Compare* People v. Hunter, 250 Cal. Rptr. 443, 445–47 (App. 4th Dist. 1988) (opinion ordered not officially published) (trial court abused its discretion in striking defendant's testimony on direct examination, where the defendant refused to respond to some but not all questions asked on cross-examination and trial court did not consider alternatives).

[23]Cuba v. State, 905 S.W.2d 729, 733 (Tex. App. Texarkana 1995) (trial court properly permitted State to reopen its case, recall the defendant, and impeach that defendant). *Accord* State v. Coty, 229 A.2d 205, 215 (Me. 1967).

[24]Carroll v. State, 68 S.W.3d 250, 253 (Tex. App. Fort Worth 2002) (defendant's waiver of privilege at the guilt/innocence phrase of trial does not extend to punishment phase); People v. Ramirez, 98 Ill. 2d 439, 75 Ill. Dec. 241, 457 N.E.2d 31, 35–36 (1983) (same).

## § 130   The privilege as applied to a witness: (a) Invoking the privilege[1]

The privilege, as applied to persons who are not defendants in a criminal prosecution, provides only a right to decline to respond to certain inquiries. It provides no right to be free from all inquiries designed to elicit self-incriminatory responses. Further, although the Supreme Court has unfortunately referred offhandedly to a witness's "privilege of silence,"[2] in fact the privilege provides a witness no absolute right to remain silent but only a right to refuse to respond to incriminating questions.

Generally, a witness must submit to questioning and invoke the privilege in response to each specific question.[3] A witness has no right to refuse either to appear or to be sworn as a witness.[4] Ordinarily, then, a witness must submit to a series of questions and assert the privilege in response to each one.

Courts justify the requirement that witnesses so raise their privilege on the basis of the limited protection afforded witnesses by the privilege in this context and the need to accommodate considerations other than the witnesses' interest in avoiding compelled self-incrimination. Parties to litigation have obvious interests in being able to produce relevant testimony, and society as a whole has an important interest in the accurate and efficient resolution of litigation.[5] The trial judge and not the witness himself must determine whether a witness's claim of the privilege is justified.[6] Requiring specific assertion of the privilege when the testimony or information is sought permits efficient resolu-

---

[Section 130]

[1]*See generally* West's Key Number Digest, Witnesses ⊸307. Invoking the privilege is considered in general terms in § 118 supra.

[2]Rogers v. U.S., 340 U.S. 367, 375, 71 S. Ct. 438, 95 L. Ed. 344 (1951).

[3]Vazquez-Rijos v. Anhang, 654 F.3d 122, 129 (1st Cir. 2011) (although witness might have been entitled to invoke privilege in response to specific questions during deposition, privilege did not entitle witness to refuse to appear for deposition). *See also* Simmons v. State, 392 Md. 279, 896 A.2d 1023, 1035 (2006) (witness did not make "a bona fide assertion of her Fifth Amendment privilege against self-incrimination" by sending letters to parties saying "I . . . effective im-

mediately choose to assert my 5th Amendment rights and not testify for or against my husband in the afore mentioned case," because "letters are, at best, a statement of her intention to assert her privilege against self-incrimination if called to testify . . . , not a genuine assertion of the privilege").

[4]*See* Campbell v. Schroering, 763 S.W.2d 145, 147 (Ky. Ct. App. 1988) (witness's privilege was only to refuse to respond to particular questions and did not entitle witness to relief from measures to assure her appearance at trial such as contempt citation or pretrial incarceration).

[5]*See generally* North River Ins. Co., Inc. v. Stefanou, 831 F.2d 484, 486–87 (4th Cir. 1987).

[6]See § 132 infra.

tion of witnesses' claims in a manner that accommodates these other interests. A claim of the privilege by a witness alerts the court and the parties to the need to immediately inquire into the basis for that claim when the facts are fresh and can most accurately be developed. It also guides that inquiry by identifying the nature of the possible incriminatory risks that must be investigated.[7]

In criminal trials, the rights of the accused necessarily affect the matter of witnesses' invocations of the privilege. If such action by a witness interferes with a defendant's ability to present the testimony of that witness, this may infringe upon the defendant's right to produce testimony and thus make a defense to the charges. If the action interferes with a defendant's ability to cross-examine a prosecution witness, this may infringe upon the defendant's right to confront witnesses produced against that defendant.

In some situations, a trial judge may properly permit a witness to make what is often called a "blanket" invocation of the privilege. Such action excuses the witness from invoking the privilege on a question-by-question basis and may even excuse the witness from being required to take the stand and oath. Although a defendant's right to compel the testimony of witnesses argues against permitting a witness called by the defendant to such a blanket invocation generally,[8] a trial judge may in exceptional circumstances permit even a witness called by the defense in a criminal trial to make a blanket invocation of the privilege. Such blanket invocations are clearly disfavored.[9]

---

[7]*See generally* U.S. v. Hatchett, 862 F.2d 1249, 1251 (6th Cir. 1988) (party must respond to particular interrogatories in order to permit a judicial determination whether he has an adequate fear of incrimination); People v. Ford, 45 Cal. 3d 431, 247 Cal. Rptr. 121, 754 P.2d 168, 173 (1988) (requirement that witness be called and sworn to invoke privilege assures that court and not witness determine whether reliance upon privilege is justified and permits determination whether witness's fear of incrimination is justified).

[8]Johnson v. U.S., 746 A.2d 349, 355 (D.C. 2000) ("as a general rule, when a witness' invocation of his Fifth Amendment privilege conflicts with a defendant's right to compulsory process under the Sixth Amendment, the trial court must 'rule on the claim of privilege one question at a time' "). *Accord* Davis v. Straub, 421 F.3d 365, 372–73 (6th Cir. 2005) (state trial court's acceptance of witness's blanket invocation of privilege violated defendant's Sixth Amendment right); Littlejohn v. U.S., 705 A.2d 1077, 1083 (D.C. 1997) (trial judge erred in permitting defense witness to make blanket invocation of the privilege, because only a question-by-question inquiry could adequate resolve the conflict between the defendant's rights and those of the witness).

[9]U.S. v. McAllister, 693 F.3d 572, 583 (6th Cir. 2012) ("There is a presumption against blanket assertions of Fifth Amendment privilege . . . ."); Butler v. U.S., 890 A.2d 181, 187 (D.C.

In *Carter v. Commonwealth*,[10] for example, the defendant offered a witness to testify that he was not present at the charged
shooting. The witness had admitted herself shooting the victim,
the witness's attorney advised the judge that she intended to
exercise her privilege, and the witness (not under oath) confirmed
that intention to the judge. By accepting this as a proper blanket
invocation of the privilege, the trial judge erred. The judge was
required to consider how the witness would have responded to
particular questions, whether some or all of the answers would
be incriminating, and whether the defense might have been
entitled to answers to some relevant questions despite the
witness's right to refuse to answer others.[11]

A trial judge properly permits a witness to make a blanket
invocation of the privilege only if the judge, after adequate inquiry, determines the witness could legitimately refuse to answer
essentially all relevant questions.[12] In making this determination, and in deciding how rigorously to press for support for the
claim that the privilege would be available to all questions, the
judge may properly consider whether requiring the witness to attempt to explain or justify the claim of a right to avoid all questions would itself "result in injurious disclosure."[13] The judge may
also consider whether the witness would be entitled to so invoke
the privilege on cross-examination as to require that any relevant direct testimony elicited be struck.[14] It is also relevant—if it
is the case—that denial of a blanket invocation would result in
putting before a jury only the witness's invocation of the
privilege.[15]

Whether to permit blanket invocations of the privilege necessarily involves considerable discretion, and trial judges' decisions

---

2006).

[10]Carter v. Com., 39 Va. App. 735,
576 S.E.2d 773 (2003).

[11]Carter, 576 S.E.2d at 779–81.
*Accord* State v. Lougin, 50 Wash. App.
376, 749 P.2d 173, 176 (Div. 1 1988)
(trial judge erred in permitting witness to invoke the privilege by an announcement that she would not testify
regarding any aspect of the "transactions" relating to the theft for which
the defendant was on trial, because
the right of a witness cannot be raised
"as a blanket foreclosure of testimony").

[12]U.S. v. Highgate, 521 F.3d 590,

594 (6th Cir. 2008) (trial judge abused
his discretion when witness took the
stand and made a blanket assertion of
his privilege, and the judge credited
the assertion "without further probing"); U.S. v. Mares, 402 F.3d 511, 514
(5th Cir. 2005).

[13]State v. Jordan, 719 So. 2d 556,
564 (La. Ct. App. 4th Cir. 1998).

[14]Johnson, 746 A.2d at 356 (trial
judge properly ruled that witness
would be entitled to avoid cross-
examination).

[15]*Cf.* Com. v. Doolin, 2011 PA
Super 133, 24 A.3d 998, 1002 (2011).

to permit this action will be reversed only for abuse of discretion.[16] Nevertheless, a trial judge by failing to inquire into the merits of a witness's blanket assertion of the privilege may abuse that discretion.[17]

Ordinarily, it is desirable that the jury not know that a witness has invoked the privilege, since neither party to litigation is entitled to draw any inference from a witness's invocation.[18] Therefore, if a party anticipates that his witness will invoke the privilege, he should alert the trial court of this. The witness's invocation and the court's inquiry into the justification for the witness's reliance on the privilege should take place out of the presence of the jury.[19] But where it is not clear in advance whether a witness will invoke the privilege, a trial judge has discretion whether to interrupt the presentation of the case to conduct an anticipatory inquiry or, instead, to proceed despite the risk that the jury will therefore observe the witness's reliance on the privilege.[20]

## § 131    The privilege as applied to a witness: (b) Rights to be warned and to counsel[1]

A witness at risk of losing the privilege against self-incrimination by testifying to self-incriminating facts generally has no "right" to be warned of the privilege and its potential loss by the testimony the witness is about to give.

A trial judge who becomes aware that the questioning of a witness raises the risk that the witness by responding will incrimi-

---

[16]Mares, 402 F.3d at 514–15 (prosecution had already introduced substantial evidence of witness's involvement in robbery, burglary and other crimes and defenses strategy made clear defense sought to elicit admissions by witness of involvement in offenses).

[17]U.S. v. Highgate, 521 F.3d 590, 594 (6th Cir. 2008) (trial judge abused his discretion when witness took the stand and made a blanket assertion of his privilege, and the judge credited the assertion "without further probing").

[18]Ellis v. State, 683 S.W.2d 379, 382–83 (Tex. Crim. App. 1984) (trial court did not err in refusing to permit defendant to call codefendant to invoke his privilege before jury); Tovar v. State, 777 S.W.2d 481, 488–89 (Tex. App. Corpus Christi 1989) (prosecutor

erred in commenting upon witness's action in invoking the privilege). If the witness invokes the privilege on cross-examination and thus limits his inquiry into the credibility of his testimony, some courts have suggested that the witness is properly required to invoke the privilege in front of the jury. See State v. Sidebottom, 753 S.W.2d 915, 922–23 (Mo. 1988).

[19]See People v. Ford, 45 Cal. 3d 431, 247 Cal. Rptr. 121, 754 P.2d 168, 174 n.6 (1988) (recommending use of "pretestimonial hearing" out of presence of jury for this purpose).

[20]Hutson v. State, 747 S.W.2d 770, 772 (Mo. Ct. App. E.D. 1988).

**[Section 131]**

[1]See generally West's Key Number Digest, Witnesses ⊕302.

nate himself, however, has substantial discretion[2] as to whether and how to respond. The judge may, for example, stop the questioning briefly to warn the witness that she may decline to give self-incriminating answers and perhaps assure that the witness has a clear opportunity to assert a desire to withhold answers.[3] In addition, the judge may suggest that the witness may wish to consult with an attorney. The judge may also take more drastic steps as, for example, by temporarily stopping the trial so that the witness may consult with an attorney[4] and even by appointing an attorney to consult with the witness.[5]

Appellate courts sometimes advise trial judges to exercise their discretion sparingly and in light of the loss of relevant and reliable evidence that may result from such action.[6] In any case,

---

[2]At least one court has indicated that a trial judge sometimes has a duty to so intervene. People v. Berry, 230 Cal. App. 3d 1449, 281 Cal. Rptr. 543, 544 (4th Dist. 1991) (trial judge who becomes aware of the potential for self-incrimination on the part of a witness "has a duty to protect the witness by either informing that person of his or her constitutional rights or by appointment of counsel for that purpose"). *Compare* All Modes Transport, Inc. v. Hecksteden, 389 N.J. Super. 462, 913 A.2d 814, 819 (App. Div. 2006) ("[T]he trial court's apparent view that it had an obligation to warn [a testifying witness] that continuation of his cross-examination could result in him incriminating himself was mistaken. A trial court has no obligation to warn even a potential witness who is not represented by counsel that his or her testimony may be self-incriminating.").

[3]*E.g.* People v. Siegel, 87 N.Y.2d 536, 640 N.Y.S.2d 831, 663 N.E.2d 872, 875 (1995) ("Our precedents approve the conduct of a trial court in advising a witness, who it can be reasonably anticipated will give self-incriminating testimony, of the possible legal consequences of giving such testimony and of the witness' Fifth Amendment privilege to refuse to testify.").

[4]People v. Green, 74 A.D.3d 1899, 903 N.Y.S.2d 844, 847 (4th Dep't 2010)

("the [trial] court did not err in sua sponte advising a prosecution witness that his trial testimony on direct examination appeared to contradict his grand jury testimony and that he may wish to consult with an attorney under those circumstances")

[5]People v. Dyer, 425 Mich. 572, 390 N.W.2d 645, 649 (1986) (trial judge acted properly in appointing an attorney for a witness, taking a brief recess, and then entertaining a statement from that attorney as to the witness's position); People v. McDaniel, 233 A.D.2d 466, 650 N.Y.S.2d 755 (2d Dep't 1996) (trial court "did not act improperly by assigning counsel to two of the defendant's witnesses to advise them of the legal consequences of perjury [after they had testified at the pretrial hearing on the motion to suppress evidence]").

[6]Attor v. Attor, 384 N.J. Super. 154, 894 A.2d 83, 89 (App. Div. 2006) ("The judge is not barred from alerting the witness of her self-incrimination right, but the judge's authority to caution the witness should be exercised sparingly and with caution. To the extent that evidence is suppressed through assertion of the privilege, 'justice is denied because the truth has been suppressed. To justify so serious an insult to the judicial process, some compensating gain should be incontestable.' ") (quoting from State v. Bogus, 223 N.J. Super. 409, 538

warning or other action to protect the privilege of witnesses is best done out of the presence of the trial jury.[7]

Ordinarily, this process protects only the interests of the witness. Noncompliance with any requirements as might apply does not prejudice the legitimate interests of the parties, so they may not complain of the trial judge's failure to take adequate steps to protect the interests of the witnesses.[8] This rule applies in criminal litigation as well as civil, and generally speaking the accused has no standing to object to or seek relief simply from the trial court's disregard of a witness's rights under the privilege.[9] If a defendant can show that the violation of a witness's rights under the privilege affected the reliability of the testimony, however, the defendant may have a due process basis for complaint.[10]

A trial judge's admonitions of a witness in a criminal trial may also infringe the defendant's Sixth Amendment right to present all potentially exculpatory evidence. As the Supreme Court recognized in *Webb v. Texas*,[11] trial judges' efforts to protect defense witnesses' interests may impermissibly intrude upon defendants' right to produce evidence.[12]

Perhaps the most that can be generally said with confidence in such situations is that trial judges have a special duty to seek an accommodation between witnesses' self-incrimination interests and defendants' interests in full production of relevant evidence.[13] The judge is not barred from alerting the witness to her self-incrimination right, but the judge's authority to caution the wit-

---

A.2d 1278 (App. Div. 1988)).

[7]*See* People v. Tanner, 255 Mich. App. 369, 660 N.W.2d 746, 752 (2003), decision rev'd on other grounds, 469 Mich. 437, 671 N.W.2d 728 (2003) (if judge finds warning of Fifth Amendment rights necessary, "the court should inform the witness of his right not to incriminate himself . . . out of the presence of the jury").

[8]Bailey v. State, 398 So. 2d 406, 412 (Ala. Crim. App. 1981) (defendant cannot complain on appeal of failure of trial judge to warn state witness as to danger of self-incrimination).

[9]U.S. v. Howard, 124 Fed. Appx. 415, 419–20 (6th Cir. 2005) (convicted defendant lacked standing to complain on appeal that witness was improperly compelled to testify without immunity); State v. Austin, 87 S.W.3d 447, 479 (Tenn. 2002).

[10]People v. Jenkins, 22 Cal. 4th 900, 95 Cal. Rptr. 2d 377, 997 P.2d 1044, 1090 (2000) (defendant failed to show coercion and thus unreliability).

[11]Webb v. Texas, 409 U.S. 95, 93 S. Ct. 351, 34 L. Ed. 2d 330 (1972).

[12]In *Webb*, the Supreme Court held that the trial judge violated the defendant's Sixth and Fourteenth Amendment rights by gratuitously singling out one defense witness, administering a lengthy lecture on perjury to that witness, implying that he expected the witness to lie, and assuring the witness that if he lied he would be prosecuted, probably convicted, and given a sentence consecutive to the one he was already serving, and that his parole opportunities would be impaired.

[13]State v. Reedy, 177 W. Va. 406, 352 S.E.2d 158, 165–66 (1986).

ness "should be exercised sparingly and with great caution." In deciding whether and how to proceed, the judge should consider, among other factors, the actual risk of the witness being prosecuted,[14] and must take special care[15] to assure that any decision not to testify is that of the witness herself.[16] Of course, the prosecution's interest in being able to challenge the credibility of defense testimony must also be given adequate consideration. The witness must therefore be alerted to the duty after testifying on direct examination to submit to appropriate cross-examination.

A neutral and objective warning, however, is within the court's discretionary authority. For example, no violation of *Webb* or abuse of discretion occurred when, prior to trial, the trial judge contacted a proposed defense witness by telephone, explained to the witness that she was implicated in the offense of which the defendant was accused, that she had a right not to incriminate herself or to waive that right and testify on the defendant's behalf.[17]

## § 132    The privilege as applied to a witness: (c) Resolving a witness's claim of the privilege[1]

When a witness claims a right under the privilege to refuse to answer questions, determining whether the witness must be excused from providing the demanded response is sometimes a difficult task. Usually the question is whether the demanded response, if given, would be incriminatory. Sometimes this is clearly the case because the question on its face calls for an incriminat-

---

[14]State v. Johnson, 223 N.J. Super. 122, 538 A.2d 388, 392 (App. Div. 1988).

[15]The judge might, for example, make clear that the witness understands that even if she begins testifying, she can invoke the privilege, and thus that the decision to begin testifying does not result in compete loss of protection. *See* Reedy, 352 S.E.2d at 165–66.

[16]*See* Knotts v. State, 61 S.W.3d 112, 116–17 (Tex. App. Houston 14th Dist. 2001) (trial judge improperly repeatedly warned witness that if witness's testimony deviated from that of police officers, witness would be prosecuted for perjury, although perjury is not simply testifying to a version of the facts that contradicts the prosecution's theory of the case); People

v. Radovick, 275 Ill. App. 3d 809, 212 Ill. Dec. 82, 656 N.E.2d 235, 240 (1st Dist. 1995) (trial judge violated defendant's right to due process and fair trial by six times warning witness who reported he had consulted counsel, repeatedly offering to provide another attorney for witness, and generally conveying the impression that the judge believed the witness had received bad advice from his attorney, where these admonishments caused the witness to refuse to testify on self-incrimination grounds).

[17]U.S. v. Talib, 347 Fed. Appx. 934, 939 (4th Cir. 2009).

**[Section 132]**

[1]*See generally* West's Key Number Digest, Witnesses ⟜297(1), (2).

ing response.[2] The difficulties arise from facially innocent questions, as, for example, "Do you know John Bergoti?"[3]

The witness himself, of course, is not the final arbiter of whether his invocation is proper. Rather, the court itself must determine whether the refusal to answer is in fact justifiable under the privilege. Any other position would subordinate the effective operation of the judicial system to the desires of witnesses.[4]

Traditionally, a witness invoking the privilege was required to produce information from which the court could find a sufficient risk of incrimination and perhaps even to convince the court that such a risk existed.[5] In order to sustain the witness's reliance on the privilege the court was required to "see, from the circumstances of the case, and the nature of the evidence which the witness is called to give, that there is reasonable ground to apprehend danger to the witness from his being compelled to answer."[6]

Traditional analysis, however, was cast into doubt by *Hoffman v. United States*,[7] which must be the point of reference for modern application of witnesses' Fifth Amendment privilege. "To sustain the privilege," the Supreme Court explained in *Hoffman*, "it need only be evident from the implications of the question, in the setting in which it was asked, that a responsive answer to the question or an explanation of why it cannot be answered might be dangerous because injurious disclosure could result."[8] The trial court erred in rejecting Hoffman's claim of a right to refuse to answer the question there at issue, the Court concluded, because "it was not *'perfectly clear*, from a careful consideration of all the circumstances in the case, that the witness is mistaken,

---

[2]In re Boiardo, 34 N.J. 599, 170 A.2d 816, 819 (1961) ("Did you bribe Officer Smith?"); Com. v. Koehler, 36 A.3d 121, 153 (Pa. 2012) (witness asked whether on specific occasion, she used illegal drugs).

[3]Malloy v. Hogan, 378 U.S. 1, 11–14, 84 S. Ct. 1489, 12 L. Ed. 2d 653 (1964).

[4]Hoffman v. U. S., 341 U.S. 479, 486, 71 S. Ct. 814, 95 L. Ed. 1118 (1951).

One court, rejecting an earlier decision, confirmed that the fact that the witness's invocation of the privilege was "provoked" by advice of counsel did not alone justify a trial court's sustaining the invocation. Walters v.

State, 359 S.W.3d 212, 216 (Tex. Crim. App. 2011).

[5]*E.g.*, Presta v. Owsley, 345 S.W.2d 649, 653 (Mo. Ct. App. 1961) (witness has burden of proof on issue of incriminatory nature of answer).

[6]Mason v. U.S., 244 U.S. 362, 365, 37 S. Ct. 621, 61 L. Ed. 1198, 4 Alaska Fed. 571 (1917). The phrase was initially used by Cockburn, J., in The Queen v. Boyes, (1861) 1 B. & S. 311, 330, 121 Eng. Rep. 730, 738 (Q. B.).

[7]Hoffman v. U. S., 341 U.S. 479, 71 S. Ct. 814, 95 L. Ed. 1118 (1951).

[8]Hoffman, 341 U.S. at 486–87.

and that the answer[s] *cannot possibly* have such tendency' to incriminate."[9]

Despite *Hoffman's* prominence, its precise significance is not entirely clear. The Court's first statement is consistent with traditional doctrine: Unless the court can conclude that further inquiry would create a danger of injurious disclosure it cannot sustain a claim of privilege. If this conclusion cannot be drawn from circumstances already available for scrutiny, the witness has the obligation to bring the necessary circumstances to the attention of the court. But the Court's second statement indicates that a trial judge must permit the witness to refuse to answer in reliance on the privilege unless the judge can conclude that the witness's invocation is improper. This, of course, would reallocate at least the burden of producing information and indicates that in the absence of a sufficient factual basis for the conclusion, the claim of privilege must be allowed.

Lower courts disagree on how *Hoffman* is to be read. Some construe it as requiring that a witness's claim to the privilege be sustained unless it is perfectly clear from all the circumstances that the answer to the question cannot possibly have any tendency to incriminate the witness.[10] This suggests that the party seeking the witness's testimony over the witness's claim of the privilege has both the burden of producing information or evidence on which the witness's claim can be evaluated and—once that information or evidence is produced—of persuading the trial judge that the required risk of incrimination is absent.[11] Other courts read *Hoffman* as sometimes at least imposing upon a witness invoking the privilege some obligation to support that claim.[12]

The difficulty with placing any burden on the witness relying

---

[9]341 U.S at 488 (emphasis in original).

[10]*See, e.g.*, People v. Williams, 43 Cal. 4th 584, 75 Cal. Rptr. 3d 691, 181 P.3d 1035, 1058 (2008) (judge must be perfectly clear that the answer cannot possibly have a tendency to incriminate witness); State v. Cecarelli, 32 Conn. App. 811, 631 A.2d 862, 866 (1993) ("before refusing to allow the privilege, the trial court must find that the answers to any questions proposed cannot possibly have a tendency to incriminate"); In re Speer, 965 S.W.2d 41, 45 (Tex. App. Fort Worth 1998).

[11]*See* State v. Manley, 664 N.W.2d 275, 285–86 (Minn. 2003) (trial court should not require witness to prove

the hazard of incrimination, as this would require the witness to surrender the protection the privilege guarantees); State ex rel. Nothum v. Kintz, 333 S.W.3d 512, 515 (Mo. Ct. App. E.D. 2011) ("The privilege against self-incrimination extends not only to refusing to answer the question asked, but also to refusing to explain how the answer might incriminate the witness.").

[12]Pixley v. Com., 453 Mass. 827, 906 N.E.2d 320, 325 (2009) ("The burden is on the witness to show 'a real risk that his answers to questions will tend to indicate his involvement in illegal activity, "and not a mere imaginary, remote or speculative possibility of prosecution." ' ") (quoting

on the privilege, of course, is that sometimes meeting this burden will itself require disclosure of self-incriminating facts. In light of this, *Hoffman* is best read as follows: A witness invoking the privilege need not carry a burden of persuasion requiring the witness to persuade the judge that the answer sought would be incriminating. But where the question, considered in light of the evidence in the case and other information properly taken into account, is one which the trial judge could reasonably regard as presenting no more than an imaginary and unsubstantial risk of incrimination, the witness has the burden of putting into the record—by evidence, logical argument, or persuasion—a basis for regarding that conclusion as insufficiently supported. In the words of the Idaho courts, such a witness "must sketch a plausible scenario" under which the answer would be incriminating.[13] Although a witness might produce evidence in support of a claim of the privilege under this approach, such evidence is not necessary. Argument of counsel presenting logical possibilities may well be sufficient.[14] But a conclusory assertion by or on behalf of the witness that responses "may well include" or "could easily include" incriminating information is not enough.[15]

Although there are some suggestions that a trial court is required to hold a hearing on whether a witness's claim of privilege protection is proper,[16] courts generally find that trial judges have discretion as to how to resolve such claims and whether to hold a specific type of factual hearing is a matter within that

---

Com. v. Martin, 423 Mass. 496, 668 N.E.2d 825, 830 (1996), quoting In re Morganroth, 718 F.2d 161, 167 (6th Cir. 1983)). *Accord* Tyson v. Equity Title & Escrow Co. of Memphis, LLC., 282 F. Supp. 2d 820, 824 (W.D. Tenn. 2003) (witness presents sufficient evidence to establish Fifth Amendment protection if the evidence permits the court, by reasonable inference or judicial imagination, to conceive of a sound basis for a reasonable fear of incrimination); State v. Rosas-Hernandez, 202 Ariz. 212, 42 P.3d 1177, 1182 (Ct. App. Div. 1 2002) ("The witness must provide the court with a factual predicate from which the court can evaluate the claim of privilege.").

[13]Whiteley v. State, 131 Idaho 323, 955 P.2d 1102, 1106 (1998) (quoting McPherson v. McPherson, 112 Idaho 402, 732 P.2d 371, 374 (Ct. App.

1987)). *Accord* State ex rel. Harry Shapiro, Jr., Realty & Inv. Co. v. Cloyd, 615 S.W.2d 41, 45 (Mo. 1981) (where risk of incrimination is not otherwise obvious, witness or attorney must describe in general terms a "rational basis" for concluding that the answer would be incriminating).

[14]*See* In re J.M.V., Inc., 90 B.R. 737, 740 n.5 (Bankr. E.D. Pa. 1988); Brock v. Gerace, 110 F.R.D. 58, 65 (D.N.J. 1986).

[15]In re Commitment of Sutton, 884 So. 2d 198, 203 (Fla. 2d DCA 2004).

[16]People v. Craig, 334 Ill. App. 3d 426, 268 Ill. Dec. 206, 778 N.E.2d 192, 209 (1st Dist. 2002) ("the court is required to conduct a hearing" on whether a witness has reasonable cause to apprehend incrimination).

discretion.[17] Claims to privilege protection are often resolved on the basis of proffers of counsel and this is apparently appropriate.[18] A trial judge would probably act impermissibly in rejecting a witness's claim to the privilege without granting the witness's request for a factual hearing at which the witness would have an opportunity to establish the basis for his claim. In a criminal trial, a defendant's right to compel testimony undoubtedly entitles the defendant to at least a minimally fair procedure for determining whether a defense witness can avoid testifying by invoking the privilege.[19]

*Hoffman* itself made clear a judge is not limited to the formal record in the case but may consider news media reports, general information, and perhaps even specific factual information which he has from other sources. In an effort to minimize the risk that a witness will have to make incriminatory disclosures to establish that he is not required to do so, some courts have entertained ex parte submissions and conducted in camera proceedings.[20]

As in other situations, state courts are of course free to construe state formulations of the privilege as more protective of the

---

[17]People v. Katsigiannis, 171 Ill. App. 3d 1090, 122 Ill. Dec. 249, 526 N.E.2d 508, 516 (2d Dist. 1988). *Cf.* State v. Rosas-Hernandez, 202 Ariz. 212, 42 P.3d 1177, 1182 (Ct. App. Div. 1 2002) (a trial judge need not personally question a witness asserting the privilege if the judge can gain the necessary information by other means).

[18]Brown v. U.S., 864 A.2d 996, 1004–05 (D.C. 2005) (trial court did not err in sustaining witness's claim of privilege protection on the basis of proffer by counsel). The *Brown* court added: "[T]rial judges often rely on proffers by counsel instead of formal questioning procedure to make privilege determinations. We have never forbidden the practice of relying on proffers in such situations, and we see no reason to disapprove it here." Brown, 864 A.2d at 1005. *Accord* State v. Manley, 664 N.W.2d 275, 285–86 (Minn. 2003) (trial court did not abuse discretion in failing to make inquiry of witness invoking privilege, where witness's counsel indicated witness was invoking Fifth Amendment privilege and counsel could not reveal the witness's reasons for doing so without violating attorney-client privilege).

[19]State v. Nieves, 89 Conn. App. 410, 873 A.2d 1066, 1072 (2005) (defendant failed to establish that right to present a defense was violated when trial court sustained witness's claim of the privilege without requiring the witness to personally invoke the privilege at a hearing but after "a thorough colloquy with the attorneys").

[20]Com. v. Pixley, 77 Mass. App. Ct. 624, 933 N.E.2d 645, 649 (2010) ("In exceptional circumstances, the information made available to the judge in open court will not be adequate to permit the judge to assess the validity of the asserted privilege. When this is the case, the judge may conduct an in camera hearing with the witness and the witness's counsel at which the witness will be required to disclose enough additional information to permit the judge to make the determination."). *Accord* U.S. v. Duncan, 704 F. Supp. 820, 822–23 (N.D. Ill. 1989) (at claimant's suggestion, court will entertain in camera submission on which to resolve claimant's assertion of self-incrimination privilege in response to I.R.S. subpoena for business records); King v. Olympic Pipeline Co., 104 Wash. App. 338, 16 P.3d 45, 54 n.34

underlying interests than the Fifth Amendment as applied in *Hoffman*.[21]

## § 133   Privilege as applied to a witness: (d) "Waiver" by disclosure of incriminating facts[1]

A witness may lose the protection of the privilege by certain disclosures of the incriminating facts about which the privilege entitles the witness to refuse to testify. In *Mitchell v. United States*,[2] the Supreme Court stated:

> It is well established that a witness, in a single proceeding, may not testify voluntarily about a subject and then invoke the privilege against self-incrimination when questioned about the details. The privilege is waived for the matters to which the witness testifies, and the scope of the waiver is determined by the scope of relevant cross-examination.[3]

*Mitchell* and other discussions refer to this as a rule of "waiver." That may not be strictly accurate. It does not require that the witness at the time of the testimony actually have understood and intended to give up a known right to invoke the privilege when questioned about details. The rule is perhaps based in part on a somewhat waiver-like rationale that a witness *should know* that by voluntarily testifying the witness loses the protection of the privilege as provided by the rule.[4]

The rule rests primarily on the need to avoid leaving a trier of fact with the limited version of relevant information that would be before it if a witness was permitted to at will pick a point at which to invoke the privilege. In the leading case, *Rogers v.*

---

(Div. 1 2000) ("The procedure for ruling on the propriety of an invocation of a Fifth Amendment privilege is ordinarily an in camera proceeding on a closed record.").

[21]*See* State ex rel. Harry Shapiro, Jr., Realty & Inv. Co. v. Cloyd, 615 S.W.2d 41, 45 (Mo. 1981) (federal approach creates an unacceptable risk that the privilege will be lost in the process of establishing its applicability, so under state privilege a party seeking an answer from a witness who had invoked the privilege must establish that the answer cannot possibly have a tendency to incriminate the witness).

**[Section 133]**

[1]*See generally* West's Key Number Digest, Witnesses ☞305(1).

[2]Mitchell v. U.S., 526 U.S. 314, 119 S. Ct. 1307, 143 L. Ed. 2d 424 (1999).

[3]Mitchell, 526 U.S. at 321.

[4]In *Mitchell* itself, the language quoted above was followed by the apparently explanatory comment, "The witness himself, certainly if he is a party, determines the area of disclosure and therefore of inquiry." 526 U.S. at 321.

*United States*,[5] the Supreme Court explained that to permit a claim of the privilege on questions asked on proper cross-examination "would open the way to distortion of facts by permitting a witness to select any stopping place in the testimony."[6]

Most discussions agree that loss of the privilege is not based primarily on waiver considerations, and thus the witness's actual knowledge that further disclosure will be required is neither a requirement for finding the witness has lost protection or for determining the scope of a witness's loss of protection. In *Garner v. United States*,[7] the Supreme Court stated explicitly that a person may lose the protection of the Fifth Amendment privilege without making a knowing and intelligent waiver as that term in ordinarily used in constitutional analysis.[8] Nevertheless, courts sometimes refuse to find that disclosure by a witness costs the witness the privilege if the facts show that the witness made the disclosure without awareness of the legal significance of doing so or regard the witness's actual understanding of the result of the original testimony in determining the effect of that testimony.[9]

At least one influential discussion of the rule suggests that a witness loses the protection of the privilege only by testifying to actually incriminating matters.[10] But clearly the question is not whether the voluntary testimony was itself incriminating but rather whether the further questions are necessary to test the accuracy of what was disclosed in the testimony, whether incriminating or not.

The privilege's protection is not lost simply by any disclosure by a witness of incriminating knowledge. It is clear, for example, that a witness cannot be denied the right to refuse to answer a question asked in court because the witness previously answered

---

[5]Rogers v. U.S., 340 U.S. 367, 71 S. Ct. 438, 95 L. Ed. 344 (1951).

[6]Rogers, 340 U.S. at 371.

[7]Garner v. U. S., 424 U.S. 648, 96 S. Ct. 1178, 47 L. Ed. 2d 370 (1976).

[8]Garner, 424 U.S. at 654 n. 9.

[9]State v. Iverson, 48 Conn. App. 168, 708 A.2d 615 (1998) (witness's blurted statement did not result in loss of the privilege, because it was made without knowledge of privilege); Safari v. State, 961 S.W.2d 437, 443–44 (Tex. App. Houston 1st Dist. 1997) (witness did not lose privilege by his testimony because he did not understand the significance of his decision to give that testimony).

The Massachusetts court has applied a complex standard for determining whether the original testimony was "voluntary" as is required for loss of the privilege. Whether a witness was informed that the testimony given would require responding to the question at issue or whether the witness actually understood this are factors to be considered but are not necessarily dispositive. Com. v. King, 436 Mass. 252, 763 N.E.2d 1071, 1078–79 (2002).

[10]Rogers, 340 U.S. at 373 ("where criminating facts have been voluntarily revealed, the privilege cannot be invoked to avoid disclosure of the details").

that question in out-of-court discussion with an investigator.[11] On the other hand, actual in-court testimony is not the only way in which the privilege's protection might be lost. An admission made in an affidavit submitted in a proceeding may result in the affiant's inability to invoke the privilege when asked about the substance of that admission later in the proceeding.[12] Apparently loss of protection can be incurred only by testimony or sworn submissions.

How is the scope of a witness's loss of protection properly determined? Some courts read the Supreme Court's case law as directing a relatively mechanical inquiry whether, in view of the witness's prior disclosures, the answer to the question at issue would increase the risk of incrimination. Only if the answer would not increase the risk of incrimination has the witness lost the right to invoke the privilege in response to the question.[13]

Some courts have applied a more functional approach based upon the Second Circuit's decision in *Klein v. Harris*.[14] *Klein* reasoned that the Supreme Court's rationale for holding that testimony may lead to loss of the privilege's protection should inform the criterion to be applied both to determine when protec-

---

[11]Nationwide Life Ins. Co. v. Richards, 541 F.3d 903, 911 (9th Cir. 2008) (witness's statements to investigating officers in the days following victim's death did not waive her privilege against self-incrimination with respect to the later criminal proceeding against victim's killer or with respect to the civil proceeding based on victim's death); U.S. v. Rivas-Macias, 537 F.3d 1271, 1280 (10th Cir. 2008) (pretrial unsworn statement by witness to authorities did not waive right of witness to invoke privilege at trial); Com. v. Dias, 451 Mass. 463, 886 N.E.2d 713, 722 (2008) (contrary to the apparent view of trial judge, a person does not waive his or her Fifth Amendment privilege by disclosing facts to the police).

[12]*E.g.*, OSRecovery, Inc. v. One Groupe Intern., Inc., 262 F. Supp. 2d 302, 309 (S.D. N.Y. 2003) (admission made in affidavit deprived witness of protection of the privilege in responding to deposition questions during discovery). *See* Com. v. Slonka, 42 Mass. App. Ct. 760, 680 N.E.2d 103, 109–10 (1997) (if sworn statement made to defense counsel was given vol-

untarily, disclosure in it waived privilege). Generally, "[a]n affidavit operates like other testimonial statements to raise the possibility that the witness has waived the Fifth Amendment privilege." In re Edmond, 934 F.2d 1304, 1309 (4th Cir. 1991).

[13]Johnson v. U.S., 746 A.2d 349, 356 (D.C. 2000) (witness who testified he had exclusive possession over an automobile for several hours before the arrest of the occupants did not lose the right to invoke the privilege when asked about his presence in the car when contraband was found in it and his knowledge of that contraband or its origin, because answering the questions posed a "substantial incremental risk of incrimination"); Com. v. Farley, 443 Mass. 740, 824 N.E.2d 797, 805 (2005) (witness who testified to having sold drugs at a past time did not lose the right to refuse to answer questions about his current employment status, because the answers would tend to incriminate him concerning current drug activities).

[14]Klein v. Harris, 667 F.2d 274 (2d Cir. 1981).

tion is lost and to determine the scope of any loss that occur. Thus:

> A court should only infer a waiver of the fifth amendment's privilege against self-incrimination from a witness' prior statements if (1) the witness' prior statements have created a significant likelihood that the finder of fact will be left with and prone to rely on a distorted view of the truth, and (2) the witness had reason to know that his prior statements would be interpreted as a waiver of the fifth amendment privilege against self-incrimination.[15]

This approach has been criticized as inconsistent with the Supreme Court's analyses of self-incrimination law.[16] Nevertheless, some courts have used it.[17]

A witness's loss of the privilege by testifying applies throughout but not beyond the "proceeding" in which the witness has given the incriminating testimony.[18] This is apparently because the shift from one proceeding to another sufficiently increases the risk of further incrimination that the witness should be entitled to decide anew whether to disclose incriminating information.[19]

---

[15]Klein, 667 F.2d at 287.

[16]See In re A & L Oil Co., Inc., 200 B.R. 21, 25 (Bankr. D. N.J. 1996) (Supreme Court jurisprudence requires neither that trier of fact be left with distorted view of truth or the witness have had reason to know the initial testimony would result in loss of protection).

[17]Boler v. State, 177 S.W.3d 366, 371 (Tex. App. Houston 1st Dist. 2005) (witness was properly permitted to refuse to answer some questions after answering others, because questioning party did not show that testimony given left jury with distorted view of the truth or that witness had reason to know testimony would be construed as waiver of privilege protection); DeMauro v. DeMauro, 142 N.H. 879, 712 A.2d 623, 628 (1998) (where witness's testimony left jury with no information on witness's assets, his invocation of the privilege regarding his assets did not leave the jury with an inaccurate assessment of those assets).

[18]Dickson v. State, 188 Md. App. 489, 982 A.2d 850, 863 (2009) ("The law is well established that a person's waiver of his or her Fifth Amendment

privilege in one trial or proceeding does not preclude him or her from asserting the claim of privilege as to the same subject matter in a subsequent trial or proceeding."). Accord Martin v. Flanagan, 259 Conn. 487, 789 A.2d 979, 985 (2002) ("It is well settled that a waiver of the self-incrimination privilege is one proceeding does not affect the rights of a witness in another, separate proceeding."); DeMauro v. DeMauro, 142 N.H. 879, 712 A.2d 623, 628 (1998) (testimony in a collateral proceeding did not preclude witness from invoking the privilege, because "waiver of the privilege is limited to the particular proceeding in which the witness appears"); Myers v. State, 2007 OK CR 8, 154 P.3d 714 (Okla. Crim. App. 2007) (co-defendant by testifying at his own trial did not waive the right to assert privilege against self-incrimination in trial of defendant).

The witness's earlier testimony, of course, may be admissible in the second proceeding; see §§ 254 to 261 infra.

[19]Cf. State v. Whiting, 136 Wis. 2d 400, 402 N.W.2d 723, 728–730 (Ct. App. 1987) (relying on increased risk of legal detriment in retestifying and

Applying this approach, the courts agree that testimony in one trial does not bar a witness from refusing to testify as to those same matters in another trial.[20] More dispute exists concerning the effect of testifying at an early stage of what might be regarded as a single unit of litigation. Most courts hold that testimony at a grand jury proceeding,[21] or other pretrial event or hearing[22] does not preclude a witness from invoking the privilege at trial.

---

the need for a rule that encourages witnesses to provided needed testimony).

[20]State v. Linscott, 521 A.2d 701, 703 (Me. 1987) (witness who had previously at his own criminal trial testified about events was entitled to invoke privilege in subsequent trial of accomplice); In re Knapp, 536 So. 2d 1330, 1336 (Miss. 1988).

[21]The leading case is In re Neff, 206 F.2d 149, 152 (3d Cir. 1953). *See also* Cordeck Sales, Inc. v. Construction Systems, Inc., 382 Ill. App. 3d 334, 320 Ill. Dec. 330, 887 N.E.2d 474, 492 (1st Dist. 2008) ("a witness does not waive his right to invoke his fifth amendment privilege against self-incrimination at trial simply because he provided prior testimony before a grand jury in the same case"); Com. v. Martin, 423 Mass. 496, 668 N.E.2d 825, 830 (1996) ("testimony before a grand jury should not be considered a waiver of a witness's privilege against self-incrimination for the purpose of offering testimony at a subsequent trial on an indictment returned by that grand jury"). *Contra* Marshall v. U.S., 15 A.3d 699, 708 (D.C. 2011) ("it has long been the law in the District of Columbia that 'a witness who voluntarily testifies before a grand jury without invoking the privilege against self-incrimination, of which [she] has been advised, waives the privilege and may not thereafter claim it when [she] is called to testify as a witness at the trial on the indictment returned by the grand jury, where the witness is not

the defendant, or under indictment' herself") (quoting Ellis v. U.S., 416 F.2d 791, 800 (D.C. Cir. 1969)).

[22]Slutzker v. Johnson, 393 F.3d 373, 388–89 (3d Cir. 2004) (witness who testified at coroner's inquest could invoke Fifth Amendment when called as a witness in a prosecution arising from the death at issue in the inquest); People v. Williams, 43 Cal. 4th 584, 75 Cal. Rptr. 3d 691, 181 P.3d 1035, 1058 (2008) ("a witness's failure to invoke the privilege against self-incrimination during one hearing within a proceeding does not necessarily constitute a waiver for the purpose of subsequent hearings"); State v. Roberts, 136 N.H. 731, 622 A.2d 1225, 1235 (1993) (answering questions during deposition does not cost a witness the right to invoke the privilege at trial because "[t]he majority rule preserves a witness's right to assert the privilege in subsequent, distinct stages of a single proceeding.").

One court, however, has held that testimony at a pretrial hearing could deprive a witness of the ability to invoke the Fifth Amendment privilege when later the same day the witness was called to testify in the trial itself. Com. v. King, 436 Mass. 252, 763 N.E.2d 1071, 1078 n.6 (2002) ("A voir dire hearing, held on the day of trial, is the same proceeding as the trial for purposes of the doctrine of waiver by testimony, and the Commonwealth does not contend otherwise.").

## § 134 The privilege as applied to a witness: (e) Effect in a criminal trial of prosecution witness's reliance on the privilege

Special problems of potentially constitutional dimensions are presented in a criminal case if a prosecution witness invokes the privilege. These situations implicate criminal defendants' right to cross-examine witnesses who testify against them, as protected by the Sixth Amendment and many state constitutional provisions.[1]

In *Namet v. United States*,[2] the Supreme Court suggested that prosecution misconduct sufficient to render a conviction invalid might occur if the prosecution, knowing that a witness will invoke the privilege, calls that witness before the jury and then makes a "conscious and flagrant attempt to build its case out of inferences arising from use of the [self-incrimination] privilege."[3] Alternatively, such action creates significant risk that the jury will rely upon an inference of the defendant's guilt from the questions themselves or from the witness's invocation of the privilege in response to them. This might constitute an impermissible use of "testimony" not subject to cross-examination by the defendant.[4]

In *Douglas v. Alabama*,[5] the Court gave constitutional status to the second possibility identified in *Namet*. *Douglas* held that a defendant's Sixth Amendment right to effective cross-examination was violated when the prosecution was permitted to extensively question a witness regarding a pretrial statement implicating the

---

**[Section 134]**

[1]*Cf.* Pointer v. Texas, 380 U.S. 400, 85 S. Ct. 1065, 13 L. Ed. 2d 923 (1965) (right to confrontation was violated by admission into evidence at trial of transcript of testimony taken at a preliminary hearing at which the accused lacked counsel and therefore was unable effectively to cross-examine).

Whether the witness had a right to rely on the privilege is probably of little or no significance, since the impact on the defendant is not affected by this. *See* State v. Morales, 788 N.W.2d 737, 752–53 (Minn. 2010) ("Courts . . . agree that a defendant is unfairly prejudiced when a witness refuses to answer, regardless of whether

the witness was protected by a valid privilege.").

[2]Namet v. U.S., 373 U.S. 179, 83 S. Ct. 1151, 10 L. Ed. 2d 278 (1963).

[3]Namet, 373 U.S. at 186. *Compare* Frazier v. Cupp, 394 U.S. 731, 736–37, 89 S. Ct. 1420, 22 L. Ed. 2d 684 (1969) (where prosecutor believed in "good faith" that witness would testify rather than invoke the privilege, no need to address whether calling and examining witness was misconduct constituting constitutional error).

[4]Namet, 373 U.S. at 187.

[5]Douglas v. State of Ala., 380 U.S. 415, 85 S. Ct. 1074, 13 L. Ed. 2d 934 (1965).

defendant and the witness refused on self-incrimination grounds to respond to all questions.[6]

If the prosecution calls a witness who simply invokes the privilege but gives no actual testimony harmful to the defendant, the lower courts have been reluctant to grant defendants relief, at least where little more than the witness's reliance on the privilege is put before the jury. In *People v. Gearns*,[7] for example, the prosecution was permitted to call a witness other testimony made clear was an associate of the defendant. As he had previously indicated he would, the witness refused to answer questions despite being ordered to so. The Michigan Supreme Court found harmless evidentiary error[8] but no confrontation violation because the prosecution had not elicited any testimony from the witness.[9] On federal habeas corpus review,[10] the Sixth Circuit held that the state court had mistakenly assumed that a confrontation violation could occur only if substantive testimony was elicited. In some situations, the Court of Appeals made clear, simply putting a witness's invocation of the privilege before the jury violates confrontation by permitting an inference that the witness and the defendant engaged in criminal conduct together or that the witness has knowledge of the defendant's guilt. This was not shown to have occurred in *Gearns*.[11]

If the prosecution is permitted to ask numerous and perhaps

---

[6]Douglas, 380 U.S. at 419–20. The basic risk, the Court noted, was that although the prosecutor's unanswered question of the witness inquiring whether he had made the statement read to the jury was "not technically testimony," the jury may have regarded the reading of the statement as the equivalent of testimony. 380 U.S. at 419. *Compare* Frazier, 394 U.S. at 735–36 (limiting instructions prevented confrontation violation where witness was on the stand only a short period, only a paraphrase of witness's statement was put before jury, that paraphrase of the statement was presented to jury during opening argument and not when witness was called and invoked the privilege, statement was not a vitally important part of prosecution's case, and jury was told that the opening statement should not be considered as evidence). If the witness is merely asked about preliminary matters and thus the questions put no testimony or its equivalent before the jury, a violation is unlikely

to be found. People v. Gearns, 457 Mich. 170, 577 N.W.2d 422, 432 (1998).

[7]People v. Gearns, 457 Mich. 170, 577 N.W.2d 422 (1998).

[8]Gearns, 577 N.W.2d at 436 (ethical prohibition against calling witness who is known to be unwilling to testify makes doing so evidentiary error).

[9]577 N.W.2d. at 437.

[10]Thomas v. Garraghty, 18 Fed. Appx. 301 (6th Cir. 2001).

[11]Thomas, 18 Fed.Appx. at 309–10. Violations were also found in State v. Register, 375 S.W.3d 99, 103–104 (Mo. Ct. App. W.D. 2012) transfer denied (emphasizing prosecutor's reliance in argument that jury show infer from witness's invocation of privilege that she knew defendant was guilty and was protecting him); State v. Morales, 788 N.W.2d 737, 756 (Minn. 2010) (questions asked of witness who invoked privilege "provided the only detailed narrative of the crime that was consistent with the State's theory

leading questions, the question is whether this shows a sufficient effort by the prosecution to build or shore up its case by inferences from the witness's reliance on the privilege. Among the relevant considerations are the prosecutor's certainty that the witness will invoke the privilege, the number and nature of the questions as to which the privilege is invoked, the importance to the prosecution's case of those matters as to which the jury might have drawn an inference from the witness's invocation of the privilege, whether other evidence has been introduced on those matters, and the giving, and likely effectiveness, of an instruction to the jury to draw no inference from the witness's action.[12]

If a prosecution witness invokes the privilege only after having given considerable testimony, a somewhat different problem—also involving confrontation considerations—is presented. In such situations, the trial court must appraise the impact of the witness's action upon the defendant's ability to test the credibility of the testimony already given. The assessment must include the nature of the precluded inquiry and the directness of its relationship to critical aspects of the witness's direct testimony, whether the area of inquiry was adequately covered by the other questions that were answered, and the overall quality of the cross-examination viewed in relation to the issues actually litigated at trial.[13]

If the witness's invocation of the privilege does preclude effective cross-examination, the witness's testimony on direct exami-

---

of the case"); State v. Sanlin, 2005 WL 1105227 (Tenn. Crim. App. 2005) (witness was identified in other testimony as a "codefendant," the exchange during the witness's appearance on the stand suggested he was afraid, and during argument the prosecutor referred to the witness's invocation of the privilege).

[12]See generally U.S. v. Victor, 973 F.2d 975, 979 (1st Cir. 1992). Accord People v. Newton, 966 P.2d 563, 571 (Colo. 1998) ("given the leading questions which allowed the prosecution to advance its theory of the case, the sheer number of times Cummins invoked her privilege, the lack of any explanation or instruction to the jury from the trial court, the significance of Cummins's testimony, and the possible adverse inferences that a jury could draw from her refusal to answer the questions, we conclude that Newton was unfairly prejudiced in viola-

tion of Namet and Douglas"); Silva v. State, 113 Nev. 1365, 951 P.2d 591, 595 (1997) (trial court committed Douglas error by permitting prosecution to continue to question witness despite witness's intent to invoke privilege).

[13]Bagby v. Kuhlman, 932 F.2d 131, 135 (2d Cir. 1991); State v. Roma, 199 Conn. 110, 505 A.2d 717, 720 (1986).

Some courts emphasize that a defendant has a particularly difficult task in establishing error if a witness's reliance on the privilege precludes cross-examination only matters "collateral" to the witness's direct testimony. E.g., State v. Hill, 382 S.C. 360, 675 S.E.2d 764, 768 (Ct. App. 2009) (admission of witness's direct testimony was proper where witness invoked privilege only in response to questions concerning "collateral matters" bearing on credibility).

nation—or at least that part not subject to challenge by cross-examination—must be struck. On the other hand, if the witness's action does not have this effect, the trial judge can properly take measures short of striking the witness's direct testimony. These might include having the witness invoke the privilege before the jury or instructing the jury to consider the testimony in light of the defendant's reduced ability to cross-examine.[14] Trial courts have considerable discretion both in evaluating the effect of witness's invocation of the privilege and in fashioning an appropriate remedy.[15]

### § 135 The privilege as applied to a witness: (f) Effect in a criminal trial of defense witness's invocation of the privilege

If in a criminal trial a potential or actual defense witness invokes the privilege, problems with significant constitutional ramifications are raised. Several situations must be distinguished. All implicate a criminal defendant's right to produce evidence and compel testimony in defense against criminal charges. This right, of course is guaranteed by the Sixth Amendment and many state constitutional provisions.

The first is where the circumstances make clear a potential defense witness will not testify for the defense unless granted immunity. As a general rule, whether to seek immunity for a witness is the prerogative of the prosecution. Trial courts thus gen-

---

[14]People v. Ray, 109 P.3d 996, 1001–02 (Colo. App. 2004) (trial court did not abuse its discretion in refusing to strike testimony where witness invoked privilege on matters concerning credibility "that were only marginally related, at best, to commission of the crime charged in the case"). A defendant who fails to cross-examine as much as possible but instead contends only that the witness should not have been permitted to testify at all fails to present the issue. Adkins v. Com., 96 S.W.3d 779, 788–90 (Ky. 2003).

[15]People v. Vargas, 88 N.Y.2d 363, 645 N.Y.S.2d 759, 668 N.E.2d 879, 887 (1996) (although trial court should strike testimony only where no less drastic alternatives exist, trial court erred when it did not consider full range of options after prosecution witness was recalled, asked about possible recantation, and invoked the privilege). See Cody v. State, 278 Ga. 779, 609 S.E.2d 320, 322–23 (2004) (if witness's invocation of the privilege relates only to a collateral matter or general credibility, testimony on direct generally need not be stricken); Schnelle v. State, 103 S.W.3d 165, 174–75 (Mo. Ct. App. W.D. 2003) (extreme sanction of striking witness's entire testimony may be used only if witness invokes privilege in response to questions pertaining to matters "directly affecting the witness's testimony," and may not be imposed if question concerns collateral matter).

erally lack authority to grant immunity at the request of criminal defendants.[1]

In some situations, a defendant's inability to secure testimony from a defense witness may make the prosecution a violation of the defendant's constitutional rights. Trial courts thus may have inherent power to grant immunity to defense witnesses or to dismiss criminal charges or otherwise penalize the prosecution unless the prosecution seeks immunity for a defense witness. An accused faces a difficult task in establishing that the constitutional right to compel testimony means that the trial court has authority to grant immunity or must put pressure on the prosecution to initiate immunity.[2] Most likely this is permissible only upon a finding that the prosecution's refusal to grant immunity is a bad faith effort to use its discretion to distort the judicial fact-finding process.[3] At least one court, however, has recognized a broader power in the courts to grant use immunity to defense witnesses at the defense request.[4]

A second type of situation occurs where a defense witness

---

**[Section 135]**

[1]*E.g.,* Dennard v. State, 313 Ga. App. 419, 721 S.E.2d 610, 612 (2011) (no error in refusing to grant immunity to defense witness because under Georgia law the district attorney and not the court have discretion to grant immunity and statutes make no provision for grant of immunity to defense witnesses). See generally § 142 infra.

[2]The leading decision is Government of Virgin Islands v. Smith, 615 F.2d 964 (3d Cir. 1980). *Accord* Carter v. U.S., 684 A.2d 331 (D.C. 1996). *See also* People v. Samuels, 36 Cal. 4th 96, 30 Cal. Rptr. 3d 105, 113 P.3d 1125, 1146 (2005) (although it is doubtful that California trial courts have inherent authority to grant immunity, it is possible that they may be able to grant use immunity where necessary to vindicate a criminal defendant's right to compulsory process and a fair trial).

Alaska courts have recognized limited authority of this sort. Blair v. State, 42 P.3d 1152, 1155 (Alaska Ct. App. 2002) (trial court may dismiss charges for prosecution's refusal to grant immunity to defense witness only where that refusal undermines the fundamental fairness of the trial).

*Compare* Myomick v. State, 2011 WL 3369272 (Alaska Ct. App. 2011) (unreported) (detailing limited exercise of power recognized in *Blair*).

Courts are perhaps increasingly willing to acknowledge defendants' right to relief, usually in situations not presented by the cases before the courts. State v. Ayuso, 105 Conn. App. 305, 937 A.2d 1211, 1223 (2008) (because defendant failed to show prosecutorial misconduct, court need not decide whether due process includes right to immunity when such misconduct is shown); State ex rel. Nothum v. Walsh, 380 S.W.3d 557, 564 n.7 (Mo. 2012) ("Although some other jurisdictions hold that judges have inherent authority to grant immunity in certain circumstances, Missouri courts never have so held, nor has this Court been asked to address that issue here.").

[3]State v. Haner, Sr., 182 Vt. 7, 2007 VT 49, 928 A.2d 518, 522 (2007) ("The *Smith* approach, insofar as it does not rely on prosecutorial misconduct, has been uniformly rejected by other federal circuit courts, as well as numerous state courts, that have addressed judicial use immunity.")

[4]State v. Belanger, 2009-NMSC-025, 146 N.M. 357, 210 P.3d 783

improperly and in violation of the trial judge's directions insists on invoking the privilege. As a general rule, a defendant is not entitled to have a witness invoke the privilege before the jury.[5] But the lack of any other appropriate relief for a defendant wronged in this way may mean in this limited situation putting the witness on the stand to improperly refuse to testify may be appropriate. This is especially likely to be the case if the defense presents sufficient evidence to permit the jury to find that the witness rather than the defendant committed the charged offense.[6]

The third type of situation is presented if a defense witness invokes the privilege only in response to the prosecution's efforts to cross-examine. The prosecution, of course, is entitled to a fair opportunity to test the credibility of defense testimony. Consequently, in an appropriate case the trial court can properly strike a defense witness's testimony on direct examination. But such ac-

---

(2009). The court explained:

> Before granting use immunity to a defense witness over the opposition of the prosecution, district courts should perform a balancing test which places the initial burden on the accused. The defendant must show that the proffered testimony is admissible, relevant and material to the defense and that without it, his or her ability to fairly present a defense will suffer to a significant degree. If the defendant meets this initial burden, the district court must then balance the defendant's need for the testimony against the government's interest in opposing immunity . . . . In opposing immunity, the State must demonstrate a persuasive reason that immunity would harm a significant governmental interest. If the State fails to meet this burden, and the defendant has already met his burden, the court may then exercise its informed discretion to grant use immunity which our appellate courts would review for abuse of discretion.

Belanger, 210 P.3d at 793.

[5]State v. Sale, 110 Haw. 386, 133 P.3d 815, 822 (Ct. App. 2006) ("courts in other jurisdictions have routinely held that the trial court properly prohibited a criminal defendant from calling a witness to have the witness invoke his or her Fifth Amendment privilege in front of the jury"); Stephenson v. State, 864 N.E.2d 1022, 1047 (Ind. 2007) ("defendants do not have a right to force a witness to invoke the Fifth Amendment privilege before the jury"). *Contra* Edmonds v. State, 955 So. 2d 787, 793 (Miss. 2007) ("Under the Sixth Amendment's guarantee of the right to call witnesses, it is generally accepted that a defendant may call a witness who intends to invoke the Fifth to the stand in order that the jury can observe the witness's responses.").

[6]Gray v. State, 368 Md. 529, 796 A.2d 697, 714–18 (2002) (noting that court may alternatively instruct jury that witness has invoked privilege). *Accord* People v. Lopez, 71 Cal. App. 4th 1550, 84 Cal. Rptr. 2d 655 (4th Dist. 1999). *See also* State v. Whitt, 220 W. Va. 685, 649 S.E.2d 258, 269–70 (2007) (trial court has discretion to compel defense witness to invoke privilege before the jury if "the defendant has presented sufficient evidence to demonstrate the possible guilt of the witness for the crime the defendant is charged with committing" and in exercising this discretion "the trial court should consider whether the defendant will be unfairly prejudiced by not allowing the potentially exculpatory witness to invoke this privilege in the jury's presence").

tion endangers the defendant's Sixth Amendment right to present testimony.

Trial judges have considerable discretion in dealing with these situations. If the witness's actions frustrate the entire cross-examination process, the trial court may and should strike the testimony or, if this is addressed before the witness testifies, bar the witness from testifying.[7] But they should be reluctant to impose this drastic remedy.[8] Less severe alternatives, such as striking only those portions of the testimony on direct which cannot be adequately tested on cross-examination or barring in advance questioning on those matters which cannot be so tested, should first be considered. Excluding or striking the testimony without careful consideration of these alternatives can be error.[9]

## § 136   Burdens on exercise of the privilege[1]

The Fifth Amendment privilege, according to *Malloy v. Hogan*,[2] gives one enjoying it not only the right to remain silent in the face of incriminatory questions but also a right "to suffer no penalty . . . for such silence."[3] This undoubtedly overstates the Fifth Amendment's protection. Nevertheless, it is clear that on some occasions the privilege bars the imposition of penalties for, or burden on, exercising the privilege.[4]

The Supreme Court has exercised particular care in protecting

---

[7]*See* U.S. v. Rosario Fuentez, 231 F.3d 700, 705–08 (10th Cir. 2000) (where witness who testified in support of entrapment defense refused to answer questions about the defendant's involvement in the events, the trial court properly struck the testimony); People v. Brown, 119 P.3d 486 (Colo. App. 2004), vacated and remanded for reconsideration on other grounds 2005 WL 697079 (Colo.2005) (trial court properly excluded testimony of defense witness who indicated he would refuse to answer questions necessary for prosecution to inquire into the details of the matter and examine the reliability of the witness's observations); People v. Siegel, 87 N.Y.2d 536, 640 N.Y.S.2d 831, 663 N.E.2d 872, 874–76 (1995) (where defense witness made clear he would invoke privilege in response to all questions regarding the subject matter of his direct testimony, prosecution was "entitled" to have all his direct testimony stricken, but trial judge

acted acceptably in adopting the less drastic remedy of instructing the jury that it could consider witness's invocation of the privilege on witness's credibility).

[8]*See generally* Combs v. Com., 74 S.W.3d 738, 743 (Ky. 2002) (striking all of defense witness's testimony is a "drastic remedy not lightly invoked"); Lawson v. Murray, 837 F.2d 653, 656 (4th Cir. 1988).

[9]Combs, 74 S.W.3d at 745 (trial court erred in barring all testimony by witness without considering whether it could admit testimony on direct and limit cross-examination).

**[Section 136]**

[1]*See generally* West's Key Number Digest, Witnesses ⬤309.

[2]Malloy v. Hogan, 378 U.S. 1, 84 S. Ct. 1489, 12 L. Ed. 2d 653 (1964).

[3]Malloy, 378 U.S. at 8.

[4]Identifying improper penalties or burdens must be distinguished from

an accused in a criminal case against one burden—the drawing of adverse inferences from the accused's reliance on the privilege.[5] Even the privilege of an accused in a criminal case itself,[6] however, does not mean that an accused is constitutionally entitled to be completely free of any penalty or burden in that criminal case itself from the accused's reliance on the privilege in that case.[7]

The case law does not attempt to distinguish which privilege is at issue. In *McKune v. Lile*,[8] for example, the imprisoned defendant complained regarding pressure to speak regarding the offense of which he was convicted, possible perjury for testifying at his trial on that offense, and other offenses for which no charges had been brought. Depending on how a "criminal case" is defined,[9] the first might have involved complaints regarding the privilege of an accused, since his punishment for the convicted offense would be increased in harshness. No member of the Court argued that the permissibility of the burdens at issue depended on whether he relied on his privilege as the accused in the criminal case or his privilege as a witness. On the other hand, the Court has clearly treated the drawing of an adverse inference in a criminal proceeding as more dangerous to the privilege than the drawing of such an inference in a civil proceeding.[10]

A line of older cases invalidated a number of penalties for invoking the Fifth Amendment privilege. A teacher cannot be discharged for invoking the privilege before a congressional committee.[11] Similarly, an attorney cannot be disbarred for relying upon the privilege and refusing to produce documents during

---

defining what constitutes "incrimination," as discussed in §§ 121 to 123 supra. The privilege's basic requirements are violated if a person is compelled to testify in a criminal trial in which that person is a defendant or the person's out-of-court testimonial communications are compelled and then used as evidence of guilt in such a trial. Where this does not occur but the person is placed at a disadvantage because the person demand the protection of these basic requirements, the issue is a burden or penalty one.

[5]See § 126 supra.

[6]See § 117 supra (distinction between privilege of accused in a criminal case and privilege of a witness).

[7]*E.g.*, Bordenkircher v. Hayes, 434 U.S. 357, 98 S. Ct. 663, 54 L. Ed. 2d 604 (1978) (plea bargaining system withholding leniency from defendants who exercise their Fifth Amendment right and put the prosecution to its proof does not violate Fifth Amendment).

[8]McKune v. Lile, 536 U.S. 24, 122 S. Ct. 2017, 153 L. Ed. 2d 47 (2002).

[9]See § 117 supra.

[10]Mitchell v. U.S., 526 U.S. 314, 329, 119 S. Ct. 1307, 143 L. Ed. 2d 424 (1999).

[11]Slochower v. Board of Higher Ed. of City of New York, 350 U.S. 551, 558, 76 S. Ct. 637, 100 L. Ed. 692 (1956).

a judicial investigation into his alleged professional misconduct,[12] a police officer was improperly dismissed for refusing to sign a general waiver of immunity during an investigation of the "fixing" of traffic tickets,[13] architects called before grand juries investigating public contracts could not on the basis of their refusal to waive their privilege be barred from state public contracting for five years,[14] and an officer of a political party cannot be barred from party or public office for five years for refusing to testify or waive immunity when called before a grand jury to testify concerning the conduct of his office.[15]

On the other hand, the Fifth Amendment does not forbid the drawing of adverse inferences against parties to civil actions when they invoke the privilege during that litigation. This appropriately "accommodates the right not to be a witness against oneself while permitting civil litigation to proceed." The accommodation reflects in part that the party against whom the privilege is invoked in civil litigation cannot avoid the impact of this by granting immunity, while that option is available to at least one party in a criminal case. It also reflects that the holder of the privilege has a somewhat less important interest in being able to avoid "be[ing] a witness" in civil litigation, because less is at stake than in criminal cases and the litigant is not pervasively influenced by the Government's sole interest in convicting the person.[16]

In *Baxter v. Palmigiano*,[17] a 7 to 2 majority held that in a prison disciplinary proceeding, prison authorities could consider an inmate's invocation of the privilege as tending to show the alleged disciplinary infraction. No majority could be reached in McKune v. Lile,[18] however, on how to evaluate a convicted and imprisoned defendant's claim that a reduction of the quality of the conditions of his confinement as a result of his reliance on the privilege was an impermissible burden on his exercise of his rights.

The *McKune* plurality found guidance in the case law determin-

---

[12]Spevack v. Klein, 385 U.S. 511, 514, 87 S. Ct. 625, 17 L. Ed. 2d 574 (1967).

[13]Gardner v. Broderick, 392 U.S. 273, 278–79, 88 S. Ct. 1913, 20 L. Ed. 2d 1082 (1968). *See also* Uniformed Sanitation Men Ass'n v. Commissioner of Sanitation of City of New York, 392 U.S. 280, 283, 88 S. Ct. 1917, 20 L. Ed. 2d 1089 (1968) (sanitation department employees could not be discharged for refusal to sign similar "waiver").

[14]Lefkowitz v. Turley, 414 U.S. 70, 83, 94 S. Ct. 316, 38 L. Ed. 2d 274 (1973).

[15]Lefkowitz v. Cunningham, 431 U.S. 801, 807, 97 S. Ct. 2132, 53 L. Ed. 2d 1 (1977).

[16]*See* Mitchell, 526 U.S. at 328.

[17]Baxter v. Palmigiano, 425 U.S. 308, 96 S. Ct. 1551, 47 L. Ed. 2d 810 (1976).

[18]McKune v. Lile, 536 U.S. 24, 122 S. Ct. 2017, 153 L. Ed. 2d 47 (2002).

ing when prison conditions can support a due process challenge. It suggested that reducing the quality of an inmate's prison life in reaction to the inmate's reliance on the privilege does not violate the Fifth Amendment if the reductions are related to legitimate penological objectives and "do not constitute atypical and significant hardships in relations to the ordinary incidents of prison life."[19] Justice O'Connor disagreed with the plurality's reliance on due process case law and was troubled at the plurality's failure to base its approach on a comprehensive theory of the Fifth Amendment privilege. She agreed with the plurality that no violation of the privilege occurred because in her view the alterations in the defendant's prison conditions were not so "great" as to constitute compulsion.[20]

Although *McKune* failed to provide a framework for determining whether a penalty upon an exercise of the Fifth Amendment privilege is constitutionally invalid, it made clear that a majority of the Court was willing to be more flexible than the earlier case law suggested. Specifically, the majority is clearly willing to give considerable weight to the social values served by burdening exercise of the privilege and to balance these against the impact of the burden on the privilege.

*Baxter* and the earlier case law suggested that when an adverse inference was permissible, it nevertheless could not be the sole basis on which to penalize the party invoking the privilege.[21] *McKune* cast considerable doubt on whether this is the case. The plurality explicitly rejected the argument that a burden on the exercise of the privilege is necessarily improper if that burden is imposed "automatically" as a result of invocation of the privilege.

---

[19]McKune, 536 U.S. at 37–38.

[20]536 U.S. at 49 (O'Connor, J., concurring in the judgment).

[21]536 U.S. at 318 (prison disciplinary authorities could consider inmate's invocation of privilege as tending to show disciplinary infraction, as long as a finding that the disciplinary infraction was established was not based entirely upon the inference from the inmate's invocation of the privilege). *Accord* Minnesota v. Murphy, 465 U.S. 420, 438, 104 S. Ct. 1136, 79 L. Ed. 2d 409 (1984) (probation's invocation of the privilege could be among factors to be considered in deciding whether probationer's was to be revoked but could not be the automatic consequence of invoking it); Langley v. Langley, 617 So. 2d 678, 680 (Ala. Civ. App. 1992) (although husband's invocation of self-incrimination privilege raises an inference, this alone is not enough in divorce proceeding to support a finding that husband committed adultery); Gabriel v. Columbia Nat. Bank of Chicago as T/U/T 2292, 228 Ill. App. 3d 240, 170 Ill. Dec. 120, 592 N.E.2d 556, 561 (1st Dist. 1992) (in action for fraud seeking reformation of land trust, "it is a violation of [the defendant's] State constitutional privilege against self-incrimination to grant judgment on the pleadings for defendant's invocation of the privilege in her answer to allegations of forgery contained in [the plaintiff's] complaint); Frizado v. Frizado, 420 Mass. 592, 651 N.E.2d 1206, 1210 (1995).

The severity of the burden as well as its automatic nature must be considered.[22] Justice O'Connor appeared to agree.[23]

Penalty issues may arise in civil litigation during trial. Unlike the case in criminal litigation, comment on reliance on the privilege by a party or witness is often permissible.[24] One court explained: "In a civil proceeding [an adverse inferences that may logically be drawn from exercise of the privilege] is permissible, where appropriate, not as a sanction or remedy for any unfairness created by exercise of the privilege but simply because the inference is relevant and outside the scope of the privilege."[25] Some courts reason that the spirit if not the letter of self-incrimination law dictates that some limit be placed—even in the civil context—of adverse inferences drawn from reliance on the privilege. The Tennessee court, for example, concluded:

> [T]he trier of fact may draw a negative inference from a party's invocation of the Fifth Amendment privilege in a civil case only when there is independent evidence of the fact to which a party refuses to answer by invoking his or her Fifth Amendment privilege. In instances when there is no corroborating evidence to support the fact under inquiry, no negative inference is permitted.[26]

Special issues may also arise in the civil context when a party is called upon to plead or participate before trial.[27] They most commonly occur as a result of a party's invocation of the privilege during discovery. When this occurs, courts have the power to respond appropriately even if the response results in a disadvantage being placed upon the party who invoked the privilege. The purpose of such action, and the objective of the court in fashioning an appropriate response for a particular case, should not be to sanction the party who invoked the privilege but rather to

---

[22]McKune, 536 U.S. at 44.

[23]536 U.S. at 52 (O'Connor, J., concurring in the judgment).

[24]E.g. In re H.T., 2012 OK CIV APP 49, 276 P.3d 1054, 1058 (Div. 3 2011), cert. denied, 133 S. Ct. 329, 184 L. Ed. 2d 195 (2012) ("allowing comment on the exercise of the privilege [by a party] in a civil proceeding is not prohibited").

[25]Diaz v. Washington State Migrant Council, 165 Wash. App. 59, 265 P.3d 956, 970 (Div. 3 2011).

[26]Akers v. Prime Succession of Tennessee, Inc., 387 S.W.3d 495, 506

(Tenn. 2012), cert. denied, 2013 WL 656075 (U.S. 2013). Cf. Blake v. Dorado, 211 S.W.3d 429, 433–34 (Tex. App. El Paso 2006) (negative inference from defendants invocation of privilege in response to two interrogatory questions was not sufficient to create contested question of fact and to avoid summary judgment).

[27]See S.E.C. v. Leach, 156 F. Supp. 2d 491 (E.D. Pa. 2001) (granting motion of individual defendant in action for injunctive relief and civil penalties for protective order excusing defendant from answering complaint).

provide a remedy for the party disadvantaged by his opponent's reliance upon the privilege.[28]

Trial courts have considerable discretion in fashioning relief in these situations. Dismissal, judgment against the party invoking the privilege or the striking of pleadings is clearly permissible, at least in some situations.[29] But the constitutionally-based need to minimize penalization of the exercise of a fundamental right requires that alternatives be considered. These include delaying the civil litigation pending resolution of criminal matters,[30] excluding evidence on matters about which one party invoked the privilege,[31] and permitting impeachment of a party by pre-trial invocation of the privilege be considered first.[32] The remedy imposed should be no more burdensome on the party invoking the privilege than is necessary to prevent unfair and unnecessary prejudice to the other party.[33]

Arguably courts should be particularly willing to impose vigor-

---

[28]*See generally* Sparks v. Sparks, 768 S.W.2d 563, 566–567 (Mo. Ct. App. E.D. 1989).

[29]*See* Serafino v. Hasbro, Inc., 82 F.3d 515, 517 (1st Cir. 1996) (rejecting contention that legitimate exercise of Fifth Amendment privilege can never justify dismissal of civil claim).

[30]*See* Louis Vuitton Malletier S.A. v. LY USA, Inc., 676 F.3d 83, 98–99 (2d Cir. 2012) (discussing multi-factor tests for use by district courts in deciding whether to exercise their discretion to delay civil proceedings to protect civil defendants from being penalized in those proceedings by reliance on the privilege); Armstrong v. Tanaka, 228 P.3d 79, 85 (Alaska 2010) ("where an individual threatened by criminal charges brings a civil action, and either party to the civil action requests a stay of civil proceedings pending resolution of the related criminal proceedings, a trial court must balance the parties' interests to determine whether a stay is appropriate").

[31]Trial testimony, for example, may be excluded if during discovery a party invoked the privilege regarding the matter. Nationwide Life Ins. Co. v. Richards, 541 F.3d 903, 910 (9th Cir. 2008) ("Trial courts generally will not permit a party to invoke the privilege against self-incrimination with respect

to deposition questions and then later testify about the same subject matter at trial.").

[32]Harris v. City of Chicago, 266 F.3d 750, 754–55 (7th Cir. 2001) (where civil defendant refused on self-incrimination grounds to respond to discovery requests, trial court erred in refusing to permit plaintiff to introduce evidence of this action).

Civil protective orders may be issued, but these have been rejected as ineffective. *See* Steiner v. Minnesota Life Ins. Co., 85 P.3d 135, 142 (Colo. 2004) (parties may leak information despite order, order may be modified, and information protected by order may be disclosed at trial).

[33]Montoya v. Superior Court In and For County of Maricopa, 173 Ariz. 129, 840 P.2d 305, 307 (Ct. App. Div. 1 1992) (striking pleadings and entry of default judgment against party in juvenile dependency proceedings for invoking privilege regarding drug use was excessively harsh). *Compare* Serafino v. Hasbro, Inc., 82 F.3d 515, 518–19 (1st Cir. 1996) (trial court did not err in dismissing civil action because of plaintiff's refusal on self-incrimination grounds to answer questions during discovery, where the withheld information was central to the defendants' defense, there was no alternative means of obtaining the in-

ous penalties such as dismissal where a civil plaintiff invokes the privilege, and thus uses the privilege's shield as a sword to force an unfair advantage. Fundamental notions of fairness are violated if a party comes into court seeking relief from another and then relies upon his privilege to conceal information that might defeat his claim.[34] A civil litigant's involuntary involvement in a lawsuit, in contrast, suggests that in fashioning a remedy for the litigant's invocation of the privilege more weight be given to that litigant's self-incrimination interests.[35]

Nevertheless, the appellate courts have recently required that trial judges carefully consider whether means short of dismissal can provide sufficient relief even where a civil plaintiff invokes the privilege. A Colorado court, agreeing with this "modern trend," held that a trial judge faced with a civil plaintiff's invocation of the privilege must consider (1) whether the defendant has a substantial need for the withheld information; (2) whether the defendant has alternative means of obtaining the withheld information; and (3) whether the court can fashion a remedy short of dismissal that will prevent unfair and unnecessary prejudice to the defendant.[36]

---

formation, and in light of the hardship on the defendants a stay of the proceedings was not an adequate alternative).

[34]Johnson v. Missouri Bd. of Nursing Adm'rs, 130 S.W.3d 619, 630 (Mo. Ct. App. W.D. 2004) (courts have long approved dismissal of a claim by litigant who seeks relief but refuses on Fifth Amendment grounds to reveal relevant information in discovery). *Accord* Behrens v. Blunk, 280 Neb. 984, 792 N.W.2d 159, 167 (2010) ("federal courts have recognized that due process precludes plaintiffs [in civil cases] from proceeding to trial while denying the very materials needed by their adversaries to mount a defense [by invoking the privilege]."). As *Behrens* recognized, however, even in these situation the trial court must balance the parties' competing interests and con-

sider less drastic remedies. Behrens, 792 N.W.2d at 167 (dismissal on only a finding that delay would prejudice the defendants was application of "a rule of automatic dismissal when a plaintiff invokes his or her privilege against self-incrimination during discovery" and error).

[35]*See* Stubblefield v. Gruenberg, 426 N.W.2d 912, 915 (Minn. Ct. App. 1988).

[36]Steiner v. Minnesota Life Ins. Co., 85 P.3d 135, 141 (Colo. 2004) (trial court erred in dismissing case without applying balancing test). *Accord* McMullen v. Bay Ship Management, 335 F.3d 215, 218–19 (3d Cir. 2003) (trial court erred in dismissing action when plaintiff invoked privilege and defendant suggested stay as alternative to dismissal).

## § 137    The privilege as related to documents and tangible items: (a) Protection of contents and limits on use of "private" papers

*Boyd v. United States*[1] indicated that the Fifth Amendment privilege against compelled self-incrimination prohibited the seizure and use in evidence of a person's private papers to prove the person's criminal guilt. This suggested the privilege protected the substantive contents of documents and perhaps other physical items. The conceptual basis for this position was never entirely clear, but it seemed to rest upon combined Fourth and Fifth Amendment protection.

In *Fisher v. United States*[2] and decisions following it the Supreme Court has rejected the conceptual basis of *Boyd* by making clear that no violation of the Fifth Amendment privilege occurs in the absence of compulsion to put incriminating thought into the contents of documents.[3] "[A] person may be required to produce specific documents even though they contain incriminating assertions of fact or belief because the creation of those documents was not "compelled" within the meaning of the privilege."[4] Thus *Boyd's* notion that the Fifth Amendment privilege protects a privacy interest in the contents of certain private or personal document is no longer viable. The privilege, as generally construed, does not protect any interest in the contents of private papers or documents voluntarily created.[5]

Therefore, where officers learned that a suspect had kept a journal in which he had made entries indicating his guilt of a

---

[1]Boyd v. U.S., 116 U.S. 616, 6 S. Ct. 524, 29 L. Ed. 746 (1886).

[2]Fisher v. U.S., 425 U.S. 391, 96 S. Ct. 1569, 48 L. Ed. 2d 39 (1976).

[3]U.S. v. Doe, 465 U.S. 605, 104 S. Ct. 1237, 79 L. Ed. 2d 552 (1984) (only Fifth Amendment issue raised by compelled production of business records is whether the act or production is a compelled testimonial act). *See Doe*, 465 U.S. at 618 (O'Connor, J., concurring) ("the Fifth Amendment provides absolutely no protection for the contents of private papers of any kind"); Andresen v. Maryland, 427 U.S. 463, 470–77, 96 S. Ct. 2737, 49 L. Ed. 2d 627 (1976) (where business papers were obtained in a permissible search, the Fifth Amendment prohibited neither their seizure nor their use).

[4]U.S. v. Hubbell, 530 U.S. 27, 35, 120 S. Ct. 2037, 147 L. Ed. 2d 24 (2000).

[5]*See* Barrett v. Acevedo, 143 F.3d 449, 458–60 (8th Cir. 1998) (majority view is that the Fifth Amendment does not protect the contents of voluntarily prepared documents, whether business or personal); Moyer v. Com., 33 Va. App. 8, 531 S.E.2d 580, 587 (2000) (opinion on rehearing en banc) ("neither the seizure nor admission into evidence of appellant's diaries violated his Fifth Amendment privilege against compelled self-incrimination"). *Contra* U.S. v. (Under Seal), 745 F.2d 834, 840 (4th Cir. 1984) (Fifth Amendment protects "the individual's right to keep at least that aspect of himself which is reflected in his private papers free from the intrusive hands of the government"); Moyer, 531 S.E.2d at 594–98 (Benton, J., dissenting).

double murder, the suspect had no protected privacy interest in the content of that private document. He consequently was not entitled to resist a subpoena for its production, or to oppose its offer into evidence at his trial, on the ground that the Fifth Amendment prohibits the seizure or use against him of the contents of his private papers.[6]

States remain free, of course, to construe state privileges more broadly and as protecting the privacy of personal papers. The New Jersey Supreme Court has construed the state's common law privilege as retaining a *Boyd*-like protection for the content of at least some private papers.[7] Other jurisdictions, however, have shown no inclination to follow this approach.

## § 138   The privilege as related to documents and tangible items: (b) Compulsory production and incrimination by the "act of production"[1]

One in possession of documents or tangible items may have a right under the privilege to refuse a demand—usually made by subpoena—to produce those items. Under *Fisher v. United States*,[2] *United States v. Doe*,[3] and *United States v. Hubbell*[4] this is the case, however, only if the act of production involves a self-incriminating testimonial communication.

By producing an item in response to a subpoena a person may make one or more of several explicit or implicit representations: (a) the person believes that items described by the subpoena exist; (b) the person believes that such items are within the person's possession or control; and (c) the person believes that the items

---

[6]Barrett, 143 F.3d at 460.

[7]Matter of Grand Jury Proceedings of Guarino, 104 N.J. 218, 516 A.2d 1063, 1070 (1986) ("We affirm our belief in the *Boyd* doctrine and hold that the New Jersey common law privilege against self-incrimination protects the individual's right "to a private enclave where he may lead a private life." . . . To determine whether [documentary] evidence sought by the government lies within that sphere of personal privacy . . . a court must look to their contents, not to the testimonial compulsion involved

in the act of producing them . . . .").

**[Section 138]**

[1]*See generally* West's Key Number Digest, Criminal Law ⚷393(1); West's Key Number Digest, Witnesses ⚷306.

[2]Fisher v. U.S., 425 U.S. 391, 96 S. Ct. 1569, 48 L. Ed. 2d 39 (1976).

[3]U.S. v. Doe, 465 U.S. 605, 104 S. Ct. 1237, 79 L. Ed. 2d 552 (1984).

[4]U.S. v. Hubbell, 530 U.S. 27, 120 S. Ct. 2037, 147 L. Ed. 2d 24 (2000).

produced are within the description of the subpoena.[5] Any such representations are unquestionably testimonial communications. Under *Fisher*, *Doe*, and *Hubbell*, whether the Fifth Amendment applies to a demand for production of items depends upon whether any communications of these sorts as might be involved in a particular case involve a real and appreciable risk of incrimination.

Under *Fisher* and *Doe*, if the information available to the prosecution is such that the item's existence, the person's possession of it, and its authenticity as what the demand calls for are "foregone conclusion[s]," the act of production does not add significantly to the incriminating information available to the government. In this event, testimonial communications involved in production do not create the "real and appreciable risk" of self-incrimination necessary to invoke the privilege. Thus, the privilege provides no basis for refusing the demand for production.[6]

*Hubbell* made clear that the question is whether the prosecution's derivative use of the testimonial aspects of the act of production would be incriminating.[7] Further, *Hubbell's* willingness to find incriminating derivative use[8] and depreciating reference to the foregone conclusion analysis[9] suggest that at least as applied pre-*Hubbell* that analysis may have been insufficiently sensitive to the risks that demanded productions would be derivatively incriminating.

To overcome an assertion of the privilege made in response to a subpoena calling for production of documents, then, the prosecution must establish two things. First it must show that it already has sufficient information that the documents exist and are in the person's possession.[10] The broader the language of the subpoena, the more difficult this task becomes. The prosecution must establish the existence and possession of the documents

---

[5]Fisher, 425 U.S. at 410.

[6]425 U.S. at 411; Doe, 465 U.S. at 614 n. 13.

[7]Hubbell, 530 U.S. at 41.

[8]In *Hubbell*, the defendant produced 13,120 pages of records in response to a subpoena issued to determine whether he had violated a prior plea agreement. The contents of those documents led to his prosecution for tax crimes. Although the Government argued that the testimonial aspects of his production of the documents—as distinguished from the substantive contents of the documents—were not incriminating with regard to the tax offenses, the Court rejected this. The Government made no showing it knew of the existence or location of the 13,120 pages of documents, and it obtained the records leading to the prosecution only through the defendant's response to the subpoena. 530 U.S. at 42–45.

[9]530 U.S. at 44 ("Whatever the scope of his 'foregone conclusion' rationale . . .").

[10]In re Grand Jury Subpoena, Dated April 18, 2003, 383 F.3d 905, 910–12 (9th Cir. 2004).

with reasonable particularity, although this does not require actual knowledge of each and every responsive document.[11]

Second, it must show that it can establish independent of the act of production that the documents are in fact what they purport to be.[12] This showing may, for example, be that prosecution handwriting experts will be able to establish (if it is the case) that produced documents were written by the witness asserting the privilege.[13] Under *Hubbell*, the prosecution must negate the possibility that by selecting and assembling documents for production, the witness will not be tacitly providing information that will contribute to the prosecution's ability later to authenticate those documents.[14]

An in camera examination of the documents by the court may be an appropriate manner of resolving whether the act of production is sufficiently likely in the specific case to be testimonially incriminating.[15]

Although many of the cases involve demands for documents, the protection of the privilege extends to other demands. The privilege was violated, therefore, by compelled production of re-

---

[11]In re Grand Jury Subpoena Dated July 6, 2005, 256 Fed. Appx. 379, 381–82 (2d Cir. 2007) (compelled production of recording was permissible although "the government does not know the exact number of recordings or conversations, or the precise location of the recordings"). On the other hand, an "overbroad argument" that people like the witness always possess documents that would come within the terms of the subpoena is not sufficient. Hubbell, 530 U.S. at 45.

[12]In re Grand Jury Subpoena Dated April 18, 2003, 383 F.3d at 912–13.

[13]In re Grand Jury Subpoena Dated July 6, 2005, 256 Fed.Appx. at 382 (subpoenaed tapes "could be authenticated using one of the several alternatives proposed by the government—for instance, that individuals familiar with [the] voices could identify them, that the government could ask [another participant in the recorded conversation] to identify his voice, or that the government could rely upon experts to authenticate the voices on the tapes").

[14]In re Grand Jury Subpoena Dated April 18, 2003, 383 F.3d. at 912. An in camera examination of the documents by the court may be an appropriate manner of resolving whether the act of production is sufficiently likely to be testimonially incriminating. 383 F.3d at 910 (district court erred in refusing to examine documents in camera to determine whether witness's act of production would be incriminating); U.S. v. Cianciulli, 2002-2 U.S. Tax Cas. (CCH) P 50,555, 90 A.F.T.R.2d 2002-5203, 2002 WL 1484396 (S.D. N.Y. 2002) (concluding after in camera review of documents that production of them could furnish a link in the chain of evidence needed to convict the witness).

[15]383 F.3d at 910 (district court erred in refusing to examine documents in camera to determine whether witness's act of production would be incriminating); U.S. v. Cianciulli, 2002-2 U.S. Tax Cas. (CCH) P 50,555, 90 A.F.T.R.2d 2002-5203, 2002 WL 1484396 (S.D. N.Y. 2002) (concluding after in camera review of documents that production of them could furnish a link in the chain of evidence needed to convict the witness).

cordings[16] and a court's order of protection requiring a subject possibly in illegal possession of a pistol to "[s]urrender any and all firearms owned or possessed."[17] Perhaps more questionable, at least one court held a suspect was protected against a subpoena duces tecum directing the suspect to decrypt a computer and produce the contents of the computer's hard drive.[18]

If one on whom a demand for production is made can decline to comply in reliance on the privilege, this basis for refusal to comply can be eliminated by giving the person immunity from the results of the acknowledgments made by the act of production of the item sought.[19] This is the case even it the item is a document with incriminating contents, since one in possession of a document with self-incriminating contents has no Fifth Amendment protection for the contents of those documents. Immunity must be as broad as the protection of the privilege. Thus under *Hubbell* it must provide protection against even derivative use of the testimonial aspects of the act of production.[20]

### § 139    The privilege as related to documents and tangible items: (c) "Required records" and items possessed pursuant to regulatory schemes[1]

Compelled production of documents that would otherwise be prohibited by the Fifth Amendment privilege is permitted if those documents are "required records."[2] Further, compelled production of items or even persons may be permitted if the items or persons are in the witness's custody pursuant to a regulatory scheme similar to those making documents required records.

---

[16]In re Grand Jury Subpoena Dated July 6, 2005, 256 Fed. Appx. 379, 381–82 (2d Cir. 2007).

[17]People v. Havrish, 8 N.Y.3d 389, 834 N.Y.S.2d 681, 866 N.E.2d 1009, 1014–16 (2007).

[18]In re Grand Jury Subpoena Duces Tecum Dated March 25, 2011, 670 F.3d 1335, 1345–46 (11th Cir. 2012) ("We hold that the act of Doe's decryption and production of the contents of the hard drives would sufficiently implicate the Fifth Amendment privilege. We reach this holding by concluding that (1) Doe's decryption and production of the contents of the drives would be testimonial, not merely a physical act; and (2) the explicit and implicit factual communications associated with the decryption and production are not foregone conclusions.").

[19]U.S. v. Doe, 465 U.S. 605, 614–15, 104 S. Ct. 1237, 79 L. Ed. 2d 552 (1984).

[20]U.S. v. Hubbell, 530 U.S. 27, 45–46, 120 S. Ct. 2037, 147 L. Ed. 2d 24 (2000). (grant of immunity required dismissal of indictment where act of production of documents contributed to investigation and indictment of witness).

**[Section 139]**

[1]*See generally* West's Key Number Digest, Criminal Law ☞393(1).

[2]The required records doctrine also may render unavailable self-incrimination "defenses" to criminal liability for failing to comply with regulatory schemes. This use of the doctrine is beyond the scope of concern here.

In *Shapiro v. United States*,[3] the Supreme Court held that the Fifth Amendment privilege against compelled self-incrimination was no barrier to the compelled production of documents that were required records, that is, records that the law requires the witness to keep.[4] As later developed, the *Shapiro* doctrine permits compelled production only if all of three additional requirements be met. First, the purposes of the government's activity that imposes the requirement that the records be kept must be "essentially regulatory." Second, the records required and demanded must be of the sort that the regulated persons or businesses would customarily keep. Third, the records must have some "public aspects."[5]

The first requirement focuses upon the nature of the government's purpose in imposing the regulatory scheme. Usually, the judicial inquiry is simply whether the regulatory scheme is a generally permissible one. If so, a demand for records kept pursuant to it meets the first *Shapiro* requirement.[6] Simply because the government relies in part upon criminal sanctions does not mean that the scheme is not essentially regulatory. However, if the scheme focuses upon those selected for attention because

---

[3]Shapiro v. U.S., 335 U.S. 1, 68 S. Ct. 1375, 92 L. Ed. 1787 (1948).

[4]In some situations, such records will also be held by the witness as an agent of an organization and thus the "collective entity" rule, discussed in § 141 infra, will also render Fifth Amendment protection unavailable. Since the required records doctrine does not require that the witness have the records as agent of a sufficiently meaningful organizational entity, however, it will apply in situations not covered by the collective entity rule.

[5]Marchetti v. U.S., 390 U.S. 39, 56–57, 88 S. Ct. 697, 19 L. Ed. 2d 889 (1968); Grosso v. U.S., 390 U.S. 62, 67–68, 88 S. Ct. 709, 19 L. Ed. 2d 906 (1968). *Accord, e.g.*, In re Special February 2011-1 Grand Jury Subpoena Dated September 12, 2011, 691 F.3d 903, 906 (7th Cir. 2012); Metro Equipment Corp. v. Com., 74 Mass. App. Ct. 63, 904 N.E.2d 432, 438–39 (2009).

[6]Rajah v. Mukasey, 544 F.3d 427, 442–43 (2d Cir. 2008) (federal immigration statutes and regulations are regulatory rather than criminal); U.S. v. Lehman, 887 F.2d 1328, 1333 (7th Cir. 1989) (Packers and Stockyards

Act of 1921, 7 U.S.C. §§ 181 et seq., "is a valid regulatory scheme"); In re Grand Jury Proceedings, 801 F.2d 1164, 1168 (9th Cir. 1986) (state regulation of purchase, sale and prescription of various drugs meets first *Shapiro* requirement); Craib v. Bulmash, 49 Cal. 3d 475, 261 Cal. Rptr. 686, 777 P.2d 1120, 1130 (1989) (Labor Code was intended not to punish violators but to assure that employees are not required or permitted to work under substandard conditions and to protect employers who comply with the Code from unfair competition from those who do not, and therefore is essentially regulatory under *Shapiro*); People ex rel. Public Utilities Com'n v. Entrup, 143 P.3d 1120, 1123 (Colo. App. 2006) (statutory requirements that motor vehicle carriers maintain and file insurance policies to demonstrate that they have liability insurance in required amounts are regulatory in nature); Metro Equipment Corp. v. Commonwealth, 904 N.E.2d at 439 (state Minimum Fair Wage Law is regulatory); State v. Gomes, 162 Vt. 319, 648 A.2d 396, 401 (1994) (day-care licensing scheme is essentially "regulatory in nature" under *Shapiro* analysis).

they are suspected of criminal activities[7] or upon conduct which is criminal,[8] the scheme is not regulatory and the exception does not apply.[9]

The second requirement is met if the documents sought are the type of records usually kept in connection with the regulated activity.[10] A subpoena for records and contracts relating to an attorney's representation of a named client called for records within the rule, for example, because these are required and customarily kept by persons engaged in the practice of law.[11]

The third requirement may be the most troublesome to apply, because of uncertainty as to what public aspects must exist and what is required to establish them.[12] Unquestionably, the records need not be "public" in the sense that the general public has access to them or a right of access.[13] Rather, the question is generally posed as whether the records are closely enough related to a sufficiently important "public" interest.[14] In an unusual refusal to apply the required records rule, for example, the Seventh Circuit

---

[7]Marchetti v. U.S., 390 U.S. 39, 57, 88 S. Ct. 697, 19 L. Ed. 2d 889 (1968).

[8]Baltimore City Dept. of Social Services v. Bouknight, 493 U.S. 549, 560, 110 S. Ct. 900, 107 L. Ed. 2d 992 (1990).

[9]Curran v. Price, 334 Md. 149, 638 A.2d 93, 106–07 (1994) (statutory scheme regulating contracts with persons accused of crimes focuses upon persons suspected of criminal behavior and is intended to ameliorate effects of criminal conduct and thus is not a noncriminal regulatory scheme sufficient to invoke required records doctrine; attorney general could therefore not compel defendant to produce any contract into which he had entered).

Records required by the federal Bank Secrecy Act of 1970, 31 U.S.C.A. § 5311, are exempt from Fifth Amendment protection although providing assistance to law enforcement was "prominent" in the minds of members of Congress. Congress was equally concerned with identifying undetected civil liability. In re M.H., 648 F.3d 1067, 1074–75 (9th Cir. 2011), cert. denied, 133 S. Ct. 26, 183 L. Ed. 2d 676 (2012). Accord In re Grand Jury Subpoena, 696 F.3d 428, 434–35 (5th Cir. 2012).

[10]See In re January, 1986 Grand Jury, No. 217, 155 Ill. App. 3d 445, 108 Ill. Dec. 116, 508 N.E.2d 277 (1st Dist. 1987) (rejecting the argument that the rule requires a showing that the witness himself ordinarily kept the records and is met by proof that persons in the business would generally keep them).

[11]Unnamed Attorney v. Attorney Grievance Com'n of Maryland, 349 Md. 391, 708 A.2d 667, 679 (1998).

[12]U.S. v. Lehman, 887 F.2d 1328, 1333 (7th Cir. 1989) (third requirement "does not lend itself to analytical precision").

[13]See State v. Gomes, 162 Vt. 319, 648 A.2d 396, 401 (1994) ("public aspects" criterion does not require records to be open to public inspection or subject to a filing requirement and is met in most instances if law makes the records subject to inspection by authorities, so attendance records kept by day care center have the necessary public aspects).

[14]Unnamed Attorney, 708 A.2d at 679 (records kept by attorneys have public aspects, because the purpose of regulation and discipline of attorneys is to protect the public); Gomes, 648 A.2d at 402 (public's interest in regulatory oversight of day-care facilities

held that even if the Internal Revenue Code required taxpayers to keep records supporting claims made in tax returns, the limited nature of the taxpayer-Internal Revenue Service relationship was insufficient to give the records the "public aspects" that the *Shapiro* rule requires.[15]

The required records rule is of questionable wisdom. One court summarized the case for the rule:

> [W]hen the criteria for the required-records exception are met, the exception applies regardless of whether the act of producing the requested records would involve self-incriminating testimony by the record holder.
>
> The courts have cited several reasons for [compelling the production of documents under the required-records regardless of whether the act of producing the requested records would involve self-incriminating testimony by the record holder]: (1) a person engaged in a regulated activity in which record keeping is required by statute or law is deemed to have waived the privilege against self-incrimination with respect to the act of producing the required records; (2) the record holder admits little of significance in the way of existence or authentication by producing records that the law requires to be kept in furtherance of public policy; and (3) the public interest in obtaining records required by a regulatory scheme normally outweighs the private interest in nondisclosure because invocation of the privilege frustrates the regulatory purpose of the scheme.[16]

This is essentially a conclusion that the need for disclosure outweighs the relatively minimal intrusion upon protected interests caused by compelled production.

A balancing analysis of this sort may have been appropriate when *Shapiro* was decided, given the then-current assumption that the Fifth Amendment protected against the self-incriminating contents of documents.[17] Such broad protection is perhaps properly limited by balancing analyses of this sort. Now that the federal constitutional privilege applies only to the act of production, however, the quite limited protection afforded self-incrimination interests may not justify limitation by such a balancing of interests. Nevertheless, the courts have refused to read post-*Shapiro* developments in Fifth Amendment doctrine as superseding the required records rule or so undermining its justification as to demand that it be abandoned.[18]

State courts remain free, of course, to construe their state priv-

---

gives records of those facilities public aspects).

[15]U.S. v. Porter, 711 F.2d 1397, 1405 (7th Cir. 1983).

[16]Gomes, 648 A.2d at 401.

[17]See generally § 137 supra.

[18]U.S. v. Lehman, 887 F.2d 1328, 1332 (7th Cir. 1989); Unnamed Attorney, 708 A.2d at 675.

ileges as embodying no similar exception. They have not, however, done so.[19]

*Baltimore City Department of Social Services v. Bouknight*[20] suggests that the principle underlying the *Shapiro* required records rule will apply beyond the limited area of production of documents.

*Bouknight* upheld the compelled production by Bouknight of a child placed by a juvenile court with her, over her Fifth Amendment objections that by producing the child she would be acknowledging control over the child and that this might aid her prosecution. The Court relied heavily upon *Shapiro*. It explained *Shapiro* as resting on the principle that "[w]hen a person assumes control over items that are the legitimate object of the government's non-criminal regulatory powers, the ability to invoke the privilege is reduced."[21] This same principle, the Court continued, applied in *Bouknight*. By finding the child within the jurisdiction of the juvenile court, the state subjected him to a noncriminal regulatory scheme. When Bouknight accepted custody, she assumed certain obligations attending that custody, including that of producing the child for "inspection."[22]

The required records exception, or at least the principle on which it is based, is obviously not limited to documentary records. It may render the privilege unavailable as a bar to compelled production of other items or even persons where custody of the items or persons is pursuant to a noncriminal regulatory scheme of the same sort as renders documentary records subject to compelled production.

As applied, the required records rule or principle operates to deprive a witness of the power to successfully resist a demand that an item or person be produced. *Bouknight* noted the possibility that in these situations, as where an organizational agent is compelled to produce organizational property despite the self-incriminating effects of doing so,[23] the incriminating testimonial admissions made by the production cannot be used against the

---

[19]*See* Craib v. Bulmash, 49 Cal. 3d 475, 261 Cal. Rptr. 686, 777 P.2d 1120, 1130 n.15 (1989), in which the California Supreme Court, by a 4-3 vote, found no persuasive reason for departing from what it read as its own precedents recognizing a *Shapiro*-like exception to the state constitutional privilege.

[20]Baltimore City Dept. of Social Services v. Bouknight, 493 U.S. 549, 110 S. Ct. 900, 107 L. Ed. 2d 992 (1990).

[21]Bouknight, 493 U.S. at 558.

[22]493 U.S. at 559.

[23]*See* § 141 infra, discussing Braswell v. U.S., 487 U.S. 99, 108 S. Ct. 2284, 101 L. Ed. 2d 98 (1988).

witness.[24] Whether compelled production under the required records approach in fact generates what is in effect use immunity has not been resolved.

## § 140   Privilege as related to corporations, associations, and their agents: (a) The privilege of the organization[1]

Only natural persons have the Fifth Amendment privilege against compelled self-incrimination. Neither corporations[2] nor unincorporated associations such as labor unions[3] have a privilege.[4]

Many of the rationales for the privilege support its limitation to "natural individuals." Organizations, for example, do not possess the "dignity" which is offended by compelled self-incrimination. An organization cannot be subjected to torture or "equally reprehensible methods that are necessary to compelling self-incrimination or that are invited by the right to do so."[5]

Further, a corporation, unlike a natural person, is "a creature of the State" holding privileges subject to the laws of the State and the terms of its charter. Legislatures reasonably reserve a right to investigate such organizations to assure that they have not exceeded their powers and to conduct such investigations by demanding even self-incriminating information from the

---

[24]Bouknight, 493 U.S. at 562–63 (citing *Braswell*). *See* Hastings v. State, 560 N.E.2d 664, 669 n.4 (Ind. Ct. App. 1990) (*Bouknight* "expressly acknowledged" that the Fifth Amendment could be invoked to limit the admission into evidence of information properly compelled under its holding).

Several other courts have noted but not resolved the issue. In re M.H., 648 F.3d 1067, 1079 (9th Cir. 2011), cert. denied, 133 S. Ct. 26, 183 L. Ed. 2d 676 (2012) ("[b]ecause M.H.'s Fifth Amendment privilege is not implicated, we need not address his request for immunity"); U.S. v. Oxfort, 44 M.J. 337, 342 (C.A.A.F. 1996) (court is not called upon to define the limits of the Government's ability to use testimonial aspects of producing a document in a prosecution); People v. Kroncke, 70 Cal. App. 4th 1535, 83 Cal. Rptr. 2d 493, 506 (1st Dist. 1999) ("in this case, we are not called upon to define the precise limitations on the State's ability to *use* the 'testimonial' aspect of the required disclosures") (emphasis

in original); Kil v. Com., 12 Va. App. 802, 407 S.E.2d 674, 677 (1991).

**[Section 140]**

[1]*See generally* West's Key Number Digest, Witnesses ⊸306.

[2]Hale v. Henkel, 201 U.S. 43, 74–75, 26 S. Ct. 370, 50 L. Ed. 652 (1906); Ex parte Ebbers, 871 So. 2d 776, 801–02 (Ala. 2003).

[3]U.S. v. White, 322 U.S. 694, 704, 64 S. Ct. 1248, 88 L. Ed. 1542 (1944).

[4]People v. Appellate Div. of Superior Court (World Wide Rush, LLC), 197 Cal. App. 4th 985, 130 Cal. Rptr. 3d 116, 123 (2d Dist. 2011) ("organizations of any sort, corporate or otherwise . . . lack the privilege against self-incrimination"); PCS4LESS, LLC v. Stockton, 291 Mich. App. 672, 806 N.W.2d 353, 357 (2011) ("organizations generally are not protected by the privilege").

[5]White, 322 U.S. at 698–99.

organizations.[6] If this is not permitted, many necessary investigations into possible abuses by corporations of their immense power would necessarily fail, because such abuses could can sometimes—and perhaps often—only be ascertained by information obtained from the organizations themselves.[7]

Thus if a demand for production of documents or items is made upon an organization, the officers or agents of the organization who respond have no right to refuse to respond because doing so will incriminate the organization.

State courts remain free, of course, to construe state privileges as affording protection to such entities. They have not, however, tended to do so.[8]

## § 141 The privilege as related to corporations, associations, and their agents: (b) Agents' ability to invoke their personal privilege and the "collective entity" rule[1]

An officer or agent of an association is, of course, protected by that person's own Fifth Amendment privilege against compelled self-incrimination, even though the association itself has no privilege. Such a person's ability to invoke that protection in response to a demand for production of documents or other items, however, is limited by the so-called "collective entity" rule.

Under the collective entity rule, an organization agent who holds items or documents of the organization may not invoke the person's personal privilege in response to demands for production of the items or documents of the organization.[2] When a corporation custodian produces corporation documents, "the custodian's

---

[6]Hale, 201 U.S. at 75.

[7]201 U.S. at 74. *Accord* In re Grand Jury Subpoena Issued June 18, 2009, 593 F.3d 155, 158–59 (2d Cir. 2010) (rule that a one-person corporation cannot avail itself of the Fifth Amendment privilege is sensible in part because "it avoids creating a category of organizations effectively immune from regulation by virtue of being beyond the reach of the Government's subpoena power").

[8]*See* Metro Equipment Corp. v. Com., 74 Mass. App. Ct. 63, 904 N.E.2d 432, 438 (2009) ("Much like the Fifth Amendment privilege, the [Massachusetts state constitutional] privilege against self-incrimination extends only to natural persons, and not to a corporation . . ."); In re Nassau County Grand Jury Subpoena Duces Tecum Dated June 24, 2003, 4 N.Y.3d 665, 797 N.Y.S.2d 790, 830 N.E.2d 1118, 1123–24 (2005) (finding no reason to depart from federal approach and holding that partnership has no privilege under state constitution).

**[Section 141]**

[1]*See generally* West's Key Number Digest, Witnesses ⟐306.

[2]Wilson v. U.S., 221 U.S. 361, 382, 31 S. Ct. 538, 55 L. Ed. 771 (1911).

act of production is not regarded as a personal act, but rather an act of the corporation."[3]

The Supreme Court first justified the collective entity rule on the grounds that significant public interests justified limiting the protection afforded organizational agents by the privilege, and that those agents in effect assumed the risk of this reduced protection by becoming agents of the organization. Permitting a claim of privilege by a corporation agent, the Court explained, would be "tantamount to a claim of privilege by the corporation," and thus would circumvent the privilege's inapplicability to such organizations.[4] This, moreover, "would have a detrimental impact on the Government's efforts to prosecute 'white collar crime,' one of the most serious problems confronting law enforcement authorities."[5] Further, by accepting the position as agent of the organization, a person incurs certain obligations, including that of producing organizational documents regardless of the self-incriminating repercussions.[6]

In *Braswell v. United States*,[7] the Supreme Court held that the personal protection afforded the organizational agent who is compelled to produce organizational items requires that the agent's act of production not be used against him individually.[8] Suppose, for example, the Government subpoenas the records of Corporation A from X, president of that corporation. X produces the records. Later, X is prosecuted and the prosecution wishes to show that X possessed the records and was aware of their contents. To prove this, the prosecution may show: (a) X was president of Corporation A; (b) documents of this sort are generally in possession of and familiar to the president of an organization like Corporation A; and (c) these documents were produced by an agent of Corporation A in response to a subpoena for docu-

---

[3]Braswell v. U.S., 487 U.S. 99, 110, 108 S. Ct. 2284, 101 L. Ed. 2d 98 (1988). Whether a former employee or officer of a collective entity is subject to the rule has somewhat divided the courts. *See* Gloves, Inc. v. Berger, 198 F.R.D. 6, 10 (D. Mass. 2000) (noting split but concluding former employee who leaves corporation's employment continues to hold corporate records in representative capacity and may be required to produce them); Jung Chul Park v. Cangen Corp., 416 Md. 505, 7 A.3d 520, 533 (2010) (a former employee of a corporation cannot assert the privilege against compelled incrimination to the act of producing corporate documents in his possession). If

the entity is dissolved, whoever retains the records most likely retains them in a representative capacity and can be compelled to produce them. Amato v. U.S., 450 F.3d 46, 53–54 (1st Cir. 2006) ("the district court committed no error in concluding that [corporation's] records remained corporate records after the corporation's dissolution").

[4]Braswell, 487 U.S. at 110.

[5]487 U.S. at 115.

[6]487 U.S. at 110.

[7]Braswell v. U.S., 487 U.S. 99, 108 S. Ct. 2284, 101 L. Ed. 2d 98 (1988).

[8]487 U.S. at 118.

ments of this sort. But the prosecution may not show in support that X himself personally produced the documents on behalf of Corporation A.[9]

*Braswell* in effect mandates that an organizational agent who in response to compulsion produces organizational documents or items be given automatic use immunity protecting the agent from the use against him of testimonial communications made by the act of production. Under this approach, the collective entity rule can be regarded as based on the lack of any significant risk of incrimination by whatever testimonial communications are made by production.

The Supreme Court has indicated that the collective entity rule requires the custodian of organizational property to do no more than produce the document or item or explain under oath the nonproduction of the items. A custodian, the Court said, "may decline to utter upon the witness stand a single self-incriminating word."[10] Subsequently, however, the Court suggested an organizational agent obligated to produce items might also have no right to resist giving testimony merely "auxiliary to the production" of the items because such testimony would not involve an increased risk of incrimination beyond what resulted from the act of production.[11] A witness who has explained nonproduction by testifying the witness does not have the items sought most likely cannot, however, be compelled to testify as to where the items

---

[9]The Court left open what might be required if, under particular circumstances, a jury would inevitably conclude from proof that the documents were produced that the defendant himself produced them. This might be the case, for example, if the evidence had otherwise shown that the defendant was the sole employee and officer of a corporation. 487 U.S. at 118 n. 11.

[10]Wilson v. U.S., 221 U.S. 361, 385, 31 S. Ct. 538, 55 L. Ed. 771 (1911).

[11]Curcio v. United States, 354 U.S. 118, 125, 77 S. Ct. 1145, 1 L. Ed. 2d 1225 (1957). The leading case for the proposition that oral testimony can sometimes be compelled is U.S. v. Austin-Bagley Corporation, 31 F.2d 229, 234 (C.C.A. 2d Cir. 1929). *See* In re Prosser, 50 Bankr. Ct. Dec. (CRR) 29, 59 Collier Bankr. Cas. 2d (MB) 1393, 2008 WL 2388378, *6 n.7 (Bankr.

D. V.I. 2008) (discussing *Austin-Bagley Corp.*).

In Braswell v. U.S., 487 U.S. 99, 108 S. Ct. 2284, 101 L. Ed. 2d 98 (1988), Justice Kennedy believed the majority read *Curcio* as drawing a strict line between the act of production, which can be compelled, and "oral testimony," which cannot be. *See* 487 U.S. at 126 (Kennedy, J., dissenting). Most courts, however, read *Curcio* and *Braswell* as permitting the compulsion of an organizational agent to give oral testimony simply providing in that form the information conveyed implicitly by the act of production. In re Custodian of Records of Variety Distributing, Inc., 927 F.2d 244, 247–52 (6th Cir. 1991) (authentication testimony could, under *Curcio*, be compelled, and therefore custodian could be required to give oral testimony necessary to establish admissibility of produced documents under business records exception to the hearsay rule).

are now located if that information would be personally incriminating.[12]

A witness is deprived of the right to rely on his personal privilege to resist a demand for documents or items only if there is a collective entity sufficient to invoke the collective entity rule. Under *Bellis v. United States*,[13] whether a unit is sufficient to trigger the rule depends upon whether the unit is recognizable as an entity apart from its individual members, probably on the basis of its performance of organized and institutional activity. *Bellis* added:

> The group must be relatively well organized and structured, and not merely a loose, informal association of individuals. It must maintain a distinct set of organizational records, and recognize rights in its members of control and access to them.[14]

A corporation will generally if not always be a sufficient collective entity.[15] Unincorporated associations present greater difficulties.[16] A labor union, of course, is a sufficient unit to invoke the rule.[17] *Bellis* itself makes clear that a partnership will often be sufficient.

The partnership in *Bellis* was a law firm that had been in exis-

---

[12]*See* Grand Jury Subpoena Dated April 9, 1996 v. Smith, 87 F.3d 1198, 1201 (11th Cir. 1996) (under Curcio v. United States, 354 U.S. 118, 77 S. Ct. 1145, 1 L. Ed. 2d 1225 (1957), a witness cannot be compelled to testify as to location of the items, once witness claims not to have possession).

[13]Bellis v. U. S., 417 U.S. 85, 94 S. Ct. 2179, 40 L. Ed. 2d 678 (1974).

[14]Bellis, 417 U.S. at 92–93.

[15]*See generally* U.S. v. Stone, 976 F.2d 909, 912 (4th Cir. 1992) (corporation that is a one-person operation is sufficient entity to trigger collective entity doctrine).

Braswell, 487 U.S. at 117 n. 11, left open the possibility that the privilege may apply if the custodian is the sole person associated with the corporation so that a jury would inevitably conclude that since the records had been produced, the person must have produced them. Apparently this exception, if it exists, has never been applied. *See* U.S. v. Milligan, 371 F. Supp. 2d 1127 (D. Ariz. 2005) (if *Braswell* dicta recognizes an exception, collective entity rule would nevertheless

be applied where record indicated shareholder's wife was associated with the corporation). *Compare* In re Grand Jury Subpoena Issued June 18, 2009, 593 F.3d 155, 157–159 (2d Cir. 2010) (reaffirming pre-*Braswell* holding that collective entity rule is necessarily invoked if entity is an actual corporation, even if corporation is essentially a one-person operation).

[16]*See* In re Grand Jury Subpoena, 973 F.2d 45, 47–50 (1st Cir. 1992) (Massachusetts nominee trust was collective entity, although beneficiaries retained control over trustees, where trustees had some authority to act independently on behalf of the trust and fiduciary obligations to the trust, and such a trust is held out to the outside world as separate and apart from the beneficiaries).

[17]U.S. v. White, 322 U.S. 694, 64 S. Ct. 1248, 88 L. Ed. 1542 (1944). A governmental organization may be sufficient. *See* U.S. v. Blackman, 72 F.3d 1418, 1427 (9th Cir. 1995) ("no reason" not to extend *Braswell* to governmental records held by witness as a custodian).

tence for nearly fifteen years and had three partners and six employees. It maintained a bank account and held itself out as an entity with an independent institutional identity. Size is relevant but not necessarily determinative, the Court commented.[18] "[A]n insubstantial difference in the form of [a] business enterprise," it continued, should not control.[19] Despite their noncorporate nature, partnerships such as law and stock brokerage firms are often large, impersonal, and perpetual in duration. The personal interest of any particular partner in the financial records of the organization is "highly attenuated."[20] A different case might be presented, the Court noted, if the partnership had been a "small family" one or if "there were some other pre-existing relationship of confidentiality among the partners."[21]

Single-member limited liability companies—or LLCs—have been described in this context as "hybrids of both corporations and sole proprietorships."[22] As might be expected, they are sufficient to trigger the collective entity rule.[23]

A person loses the right to invoke the person's own privilege only if the demand is for items belonging to the organization held by the person in his capacity as an agent of the entity.[24] With regard to records, the agency rationale for the collective entity rule indicates that agency law provides an appropriate source for standards. Records are organizational ones possessed as an agent of the organization if the person in developing and possessing them acted within the scope of his agency relationship with the entity.[25]

States, of course, remain free to construe state privileges as af-

---

[18]Bellis v. U. S., 417 U.S. 85, 100, 94 S. Ct. 2179, 40 L. Ed. 2d 678 (1974).

[19]Bellis, 417 U.S. at 101.

[20]417 U.S. at 93–94.

[21]417 U.S. at 101. *Accord* In re Nassau County Grand Jury Subpoena Duces Tecum Dated June 24, 2003, 4 N.Y.3d 665, 797 N.Y.S.2d 790, 830 N.E.2d 1118, 1124–25 (2005) (small law firm was collective entity under *Bellis*). One court noted that "in the thirty-six years since *Bellis* was decided, the Supreme Court has done nothing to transform this hypothetical musing into a substantive limitation on the applicability of the collective-entity principle." U.S. v. Roe, 421 Fed. Appx. 881, 884–85 (10th Cir. 2011) (joining other circuits in declining to develop such a limitation without further direction from Supreme Court).

[22]U.S. v. Feng Juan Lu, 248 Fed. Appx. 806, 808 (9th Cir. 2007).

[23]Feng Juan Lu, 248 Fed.Appx. at 808 (noting that state law required an LLC to have a statutory agent and witness "clearly intended the businesses to be separate from her in the event of a lawsuit" and thus "intentionally took advantage of the corporate characteristics of the LLC structure to obtain asset-protection advantages"). *Accord* S.E.C. v. Ryan, 747 F. Supp. 2d 355, 364–365 (N.D. N.Y. 2010).

[24]Bellis, 417 U.S at 93.

[25]*See* U.S. v. Wujkowski, 929 F.2d 981, 983–84 (4th Cir. 1991) (remanding for inquiry into whether diaries were personal documents or rather corporate documents held in a representative capacity, which depends on "who prepared the document, the na-

fording broader protection to organizational agents than is provided by the Fifth Amendment.[26]

## § 142 Removing the danger of incrimination by granting immunity: (a) In general[1]

The privilege protects only against formal legal liability. Consequently, if the risk of criminal liability is removed by a grant of effective immunity, the privilege no longer applies.

Generally, the availability of formal immunity to witnesses is closely tied to statutory authority for such immunity and statutorily-provided procedures for conferring and enforcing it.[2] Early statutes sometimes provided for immunity for a witness who simply testified about a matter, permitting witnesses to insulate themselves from prosecution by volunteering information. Modern statutes, in contrast, tend to provide for immunity only if a witness invokes the privilege,[3] the prosecution seeks a grant of immunity,[4] and the trial judge grants it.[5] This is the case, for example, under the federal statute.[6]

---

ture of its contents, its purpose or use, who maintained possession and who had access to it, whether the corporation required its preparation, and whether its existence was necessary to or in furtherance of the conduct of the corporation's business," as well as any other relevant considerations). *Compare* U.S. v. Stone, 976 F.2d 909, 911 (4th Cir. 1992) (appeal after remand) (diaries contained "some unspecified personal entries" which were "not enough to alter the character of the documents as business ones"). *See also* In re Sealed Case, 877 F.2d 83, 88–91 (D.C. Cir. 1989) (records of bank account opened by witness in corporation's name were corporate ones held as agent of corporation, although they were used to hold funds stolen from corporation).

[26]*See* Com. v. Doe, 405 Mass. 676, 544 N.E.2d 860, 862 (1989) (organizational agent loses personal protection of state constitutional privilege only if agent's assumption of responsibility for organizational items was a knowing and intelligent waiver of agent's protection under the privilege). *Compare* In re Nassau County Grand Jury Subpoena Duces Tecum Dated June

24, 2003, 4 N.Y.3d 665, 797 N.Y.S.2d 790, 830 N.E.2d 1118, 1124–25 (2005) (holding, after discussion, that *Bellis* would be adopted for purposes of state constitutional privilege and law firm partner could be compelled to produce firm records).

**[Section 142]**

[1]*See generally* West's Key Number Digest, Witnesses ⚿303, 304.

[2]*See* Com. v. Dalrymple, 428 Mass. 1014, 699 N.E.2d 344, 345–46 (1998) (prosecutor has no inherent authority, based on common law, to grant immunity to a witness in proceedings covered by statutory provision for granting immunity).

[3]State v. Korkowski, 312 N.J. Super. 429, 712 A.2d 210 (App. Div. 1998) (revised immunity statute no longer provides immunity for testimony given without first invoking privilege against self-incrimination).

[4]Whether a defendant can ever successfully demand the granting of immunity to a witness the defendant wishes to call is considered in § 135 supra.

[5]The trial judge's role is often

Most jurisdictions appear to assume that formal immunity sufficient to permit compelling a witness to testify can be conferred only where and as authorized by statute.[7] Under this approach, courts have no authority to themselves develop systems for granting immunity. The New Mexico Supreme Court in *State v. Belanger*,[8] however, characterized "use" immunity—distinguished in the next section from "transactional" immunity—as essentially a matter of evidence. "New Mexico courts," it noted, "control issues of evidence and testimony . . . ." Further, "[i]n granting use immunity, courts are acting upon their inherent power to control their courtroom and to establish procedural rules." Thus, it concluded, the court itself "controls use immunity rules."[9] Pursuant to this authority, it promulgated an evidence rule authorizing trial courts to grant use immunity on request of criminal defendants.

Many courts recognize prosecutors' power independent of statutory authorization to confer "informal"—or "pocket"—immunity by entering into an agreement with a witness.[10] The immunity provided by these arrangements most likely does not supplant the privilege. A witness can invoke the privilege despite the agreement not to do so.[11]

Immunity does not protect the witness from prosecution for

---

very limited. *See* People v. Ousley, 235 Ill. 2d 299, 335 Ill. Dec. 850, 919 N.E.2d 875, 886 (2009) (as in the federal system, "the court's role in considering a motion for use immunity essentially is ministerial, so that a court cannot decide whether a procedurally proper motion is necessary or advisable").

[6]18 U.S.C.A. §§ 6001 to 6005 (witness in judicial proceeding receives immunity only if witness invokes privilege against self-incrimination, prosecutor seeks order compelling the witness to testify or provide information, court issues such an order, and court communicates to the witness that the witness may not refuse to comply with the order on the basis of self-incrimination). The court has no discretion to deny a proper request for an order. *See* Ullmann v. U.S., 350 U.S. 422, 432–34, 76 S. Ct. 497, 100 L. Ed. 511 (1956).

[7]*Cf.* State v. Belanger, 2009-NMSC-025, 146 N.M. 357, 210 P.3d 783, 789 (2009) ("the federal rule on witness immunity is purely

statutory-a grant of authority from Congress to prosecutors").

[8]State v. Belanger, 2009-NMSC-025, 146 N.M. 357, 210 P.3d 783 (2009).

[9]Berlanger, 210 P.3d at 791.

[10]*See generally* State v. Edmondson, 714 So. 2d 1233, 1237–39 (La. 1998) (discussing informal or "pocket" immunity and characterizing it as enforceable "not because of the self-incrimination clause but because the due process clause requires prosecutors to scrupulously adhere to commitments made to suspects in which they induce the suspects to surrender their constitutional rights"). A witness who testifies under pocket immunity is most likely entitled at most to whatever protection the witness has under the immunity agreement. *See* U.S. v. Mendizabal, 214 Fed. Appx. 496, 501–02 (6th Cir. 2006).

[11]Kincy v. Dretke, 92 Fed. Appx. 87, 91 (5th Cir. 2004) (prosecutor could not compel testimony from codefendant who had entered into plea agreement committing codefendant to tes-

perjury committed in the giving of the immunized testimony. In such a prosecution, the testimony relied upon as being false may, of course, be used against the witness.[12] It is less clear whether immunized testimony may be used to prove that the witness committed perjury other than during the immunized testimony.[13] Almost certainly it must protect the witness against prosecution for perjury committed prior to the immunized testimony.[14]

Immunity creates special difficulties when a person's suspected behavior may constitute crimes subject to prosecution by different prosecutors.[15] Massachusetts requires a prosecutor seeking

---

tify and had pleaded guilty pursuant to that agreement, but had not yet been sentenced). *Accord* U.S. v. McFarlane, 309 F.3d 510, 514 (8th Cir. 2002) (criminal defendant may, by plea agreement, give up the right to assert the privilege and if defendant later invokes it the defendant must "face the consequences of breaching the immunity agreement").

[12]Glickstein v. U.S., 222 U.S. 139, 143, 32 S. Ct. 71, 56 L. Ed. 128 (1911) (witness may be prosecuted for perjury committed while testifying pursuant to statute directing that "no testimony given [under immunity] . . . shall be offered in evidence against him in any criminal proceeding," and the witness's alleged perjurious testimony may be admitted in evidence in the perjury prosecution); Altieri v. Holden, 231 A.D.2d 369, 663 N.Y.S.2d 602 (2d Dep't 1997) (witness who received transactional immunity for testimony before grand jury could nevertheless be prosecuted for perjury committed by that testimony and testimony given before grand jury could be used in perjury prosecution).

One court has held that the jurisdiction gives trial courts no authority to immunize a witness for prospective perjury and that that a prosecutor's effort to confer informal immunity for such perjury was "unacceptable behavior and an abuse of discretion." State v. Radcliffe, 9 Haw. App. 628, 859 P.2d 925, 933 (1993).

[13]The majority's language in U. S. v. Apfelbaum, 445 U.S. 115, 131, 100 S. Ct. 948, 63 L. Ed. 2d 250 (1980),

suggests that the Fifth Amendment poses no barrier to the use of immunized testimony in either situation: "[N]either the [federal] immunity statute nor the Fifth Amendment precludes the use of [a witness'] immunized testimony at a subsequent prosecution for making false statements, so long as that testimony conforms to otherwise applicable rules of evidence." Three members of the Court, however, expressed reservations concerning the implications of this broad dictum. Apfelbaum, 445 U.S. at 132–133 (immunized testimony might not be admissible in prosecution for perjury committed after the immunized testimony rather than in the course of it) (Brennan, J., concurring in the judgment); 445 U.S. at 133 (Blackmun, J., joined by Marshall, J., concurring in the judgment).

[14]State v. Adams, 153 Ohio App. 3d 134, 2003-Ohio-3086, 791 N.E.2d 1045, 1051 (7th Dist. Harrison County 2003) (state immunity statute must be read as conferring protection against prosecution for perjury based on earlier testimony inconsistent with immunized immunized testimony). *See also* In re Grand Jury Proceedings, 644 F.2d 348, 350–51 (5th Cir. 1981) ("well established" that federal immunity statute and its perjury exception "forecloses the government from prosecuting an immunized witness for perjury based upon prior false statements").

[15]Situations involving potential incrimination under the laws of other jurisdictions are addressed in § 123 su-

formal immunity for a witness to notify other prosecutors and the attorney general. This provides them with an opportunity to be heard on whether the court should grant the request.[16] Whether formal procedures of this sort can be circumvented by informal immunity agreements is not settled.[17]

## § 143   Removing the danger of incrimination by granting immunity: (b) "Testimonial" versus "use" immunity

Immunity is of two kinds. "Transactional" immunity confers full immunity from prosecution for all offenses related to matters about which the witness testifies, that is, often all offenses arising out of the "transaction" that was the subject of the compelled testimony.[1] "Use" immunity, on the other hand, provides no bar to prosecution but protects the witness from use against that witness of the compelled testimony and evidence directly or indirectly derived from that testimony.[2]

Some immunity statutes permit only the granting of transactional immunity or only both transactional and use immunity.[3] Others, such as the federal statute, authorize only the granting of use immunity.[4] The Vermont court has construed its statute as authorizing use immunity but also as giving the trial judge discretion to find—on the facts of the particular case—that use immunity would not adequately protect the witness and thus to refuse to compel testimony unless the prosecution seeks transactional immunity.[5]

---

pra.

[16]Mass. Gen. L. ch. 233, § 20E(d).

[17]See Frawley v. Watson, 14 Mass. L. Rptr. 141, 2001 WL 1631719 (Mass. Super. Ct. 2001) (given statutory procedure, letter commitments from one prosecutor and attorney general were not sufficient to confer effective immunity). See also, State v. Bryant, 146 Wash. 2d 90, 42 P.3d 1278, 1284 (2002) (informal agreement between one prosecuting attorney and defendant for use immunity was not binding on neighboring prosecuting attorney).

[Section 143]

[1]Allen v. Iowa Dist. Court for Polk County, 582 N.W.2d 506, 508 (Iowa 1998).

[2]Allen, 582 N.W.2d at 508.

[3]582 N.W.2d. at 509–10 (Iowa

Rule of Criminal Procedure 19(3) [now Iowa. R. Crim. P. 2.20(3)] authorizes only the granting of both transaction and use immunity, because without a grant of use immunity a witness receiving transactional immunity would not be protected from use of the testimony in future civil, administrative or forfeiture actions).

[4]18 U.S.C.A. § 6002 (effect of order compelling testimony is that "no testimony or other information compelled under the order (or any information directly or indirectly derived from such testimony or other information) may be used against the witness in any criminal case, except a prosecution for perjury, giving a false statement, or otherwise failing to comply with the order").

[5]State v. Ely, 167 Vt. 323, 708 A.2d 1332, 1340 (1997).

*Counselman v. Hitchcock*,[6] decided in 1892, was widely regarded as indicating that the Fifth Amendment privilege permitted compelled testimony over a claim of the privilege only upon a granting of transactional immunity. In *Kastigar v. United States*,[7] however, the Supreme Court held that a grant of transactional immunity is not necessary in order to compel a witness to testify over an assertion of his privilege. The sole concern of the privilege, reasoned the majority, is the prevention of compulsion to give testimony that leads to the infliction of penalties affixed to criminal acts. "Immunity from the use of compelled testimony, as well as evidence derived directly and indirectly therefrom," it concluded, "affords this protection."[8]

Use immunity that does not provide protection against derivative use is not sufficient to supplant the privilege and compel testimony by one with a right to claim it.[9]

The *Kastigar* dissenters and other critics of use immunity argue that even use immunity extending to derivative use is inadequate because, given practical realities, use immunity cannot eliminate or sufficiently minimize the possibility that in actuality compelled testimony will contribute to conviction of the immu-

---

[6]Counselman v. Hitchcock, 142 U.S. 547, 12 S. Ct. 195, 35 L. Ed. 1110 (1892).

[7]Kastigar v. U.S., 406 U.S. 441, 92 S. Ct. 1653, 32 L. Ed. 2d 212 (1972). *See also* Zicarelli v. New Jersey State Commission of Investigation, 406 U.S. 472, 92 S. Ct. 1670, 32 L. Ed. 2d 234 (1972) (companion case to *Kastigar* upholding a state immunity statute providing for use immunity).

[8]Kastigar, 406 U.S. at 453. The distinction between direct and indirect use was explained by one court as follows:

> Evidentiary use of immunized testimony includes the direct presentation of immunized testimony to the grand or petit jury, as well as any derivative (or indirect) use of the immunized testimony. Derivative evidentiary use includes the exposure of witnesses to immunized testimony "to refresh their memories, or otherwise to focus their thoughts, organize their testimony, or alter their prior or contemporaneous statements." Evidentiary use also includes the use of immunized testimony to obtain investigatory leads and to influence a witness to testify.

U.S. v. Slough, 677 F. Supp. 2d 112,

130–31 (D.D.C. 2009), vacated on other grounds, 641 F.3d 544 (D.C. Cir. 2011), cert. denied, 132 S. Ct. 2710, 183 L. Ed. 2d 84 (2012) (citations omitted).

[9]State v. Adams, 153 Ohio App. 3d 134, 2003-Ohio-3086, 791 N.E.2d 1045, 1049 (7th Dist. Harrison County 2003). Statutory immunity not including protection from evidence indirectly derived from immunized statements is insufficient to require testimony. Com. v. Brown, 2011 PA Super 47, 26 A.3d 485, 500 (2011).

But if a defendant does not assert the privilege and instead enters into an informal agreement that gives the defendant immunity, the scope of that immunity is governed by the terms of the agreement. It may not be as broad as would be required to override the defendant's assertion of the privilege. *See* U.S. v. McFarlane, 309 F.3d 510, 514 (8th Cir. 2002) (where agreement did not provide for full derivative use immunity, immunized statements could be used to deny downward departure from sentencing guidelines).

nized witness.[10] In response, the *Kastigar* majority held that once a defendant establishes that he has previously testified under a grant of immunity concerning matters related to his prosecution, the prosecution, upon defense objection, must affirmatively prove that the evidence it offers against the defendant is derived from a legitimate source wholly independent of the previously compelled testimony. This burden of proof is adequate, the Court concluded, to assure that compelled testimony will not be used to incriminate the witness forced to give it.[11] At such a so-called *Kastigar* hearing, the prosecution must prove its nonuse of the immunized testimony by a preponderance of the evidence.[12]

Lower courts agree that under *Kastigar*, the prosecution must prove that it will make no "evidentiary" use of immunized testimony if it proceeds against a witness who has given immunized testimony. All evidence offered at trial and before any indicting grand jury, then, must be shown to have had a source other than—or independent of—the immunized testimony. A general assertion by the prosecution that its evidence has an independent source is not sufficient. Rather, the prosecution must proceed item-by-item and witness-by-witness and demonstrate its source for the proffered testimony. The same is true regarding evidence elicited by cross-examination; *Kastigar* is violated if a prosecutor's consideration of a defendant's immunized testimony enables the prosecutor to elicit significant testimony on cross-examination of defense witnesses.[13]

When the evidence at issue as potentially derived from immunized testimony is testimony of a witness, the prosecution's task is often quite difficult, especially if the evidence shows that the witness has been exposed to the immunized testimony. At least in those situations, the prosecution may be required to proceed line-by-line through the witness's testimony and demonstrate that the substance of the testimony was not affected by the immunized testimony. As a practical matter, the prosecution may be able to meet its burden only if it has "canned" the testi-

---

[10]Kastigar, 406 U.S. at 468 (Marshall, J., dissenting). Justice Douglas expressed a similar view. 406 U.S. at 462–67 (Douglas, J., dissenting).

[11]406 U.S. at 460–61.

[12]*See* State v. Beard, 203 W. Va. 325, 507 S.E.2d 688, 691 (1998). *Accord,* State ex rel. Heidelberg v. Holden, 98 S.W.3d 116, 120 (Mo. Ct. App. S.D. 2003) (rejecting contention that defendant was entitled to *Kastigar* hearing "only upon pointing to some particular piece of allegedly tainted evidence").

*Kastigar* itself referred only to a "heavy burden" on the prosecution. 406 U.S. at 462.

[13]*See* U.S. v. Byrd, 765 F.2d 1524, 1531 (11th Cir. 1985).

mony—by producing and filing a sworn version of it—before the witness was exposed to the immunized testimony.[14]

Lower courts disagree on whether use immunity does—and constitutionally must—prohibit the prosecution from all "nonevidentiary" use of immunized testimony. One court explained the term:

> Nonevidentiary use . . . is that which does not culminate directly or indirectly in the presentation of evidence against the immunized person. Such use includes "assistance in focusing the investigation, deciding to initiate prosecution, refusing to plea bargain, interpreting evidence, planning cross-examination and otherwise generally planning trial strategy."[15]

Some courts regard use immunity as sufficient to negate the Fifth Amendment right not to testify to self-incriminating matters only if it prohibits nonevidentiary use.[16] Most, however, reject this approach.[17] The prosecution's burden at a *Kastigar* hearing is, of course, greatly increased if it must prove that it is making no nonevidentiary use of immunized testimony.

Probably the leading decision regarding nonevidentiary use as

---

[14]*See* State v. Vallejos, 118 N.M. 572, 883 P.2d 1269, 1276–78 (1994) (commenting that prosecution must be aware when it grants immunity that such action creates a "grave risk" that future prosecution of the witness "may, as a practical matter, be impossible").

[15]U.S. v. Slough, 677 F. Supp. 2d 112, 131 (D.D.C. 2009), vacated on other grounds, 641 F.3d 544 (D.C. Cir. 2011), cert. denied, 132 S. Ct. 2710, 183 L. Ed. 2d 84 (2012) (quoting U.S. v. North, 910 F.2d 843, 857 (D.C. Cir. 1990)). *See* State v. Brocious, 2003-Ohio-4708, 2003 WL 22060162 (Ohio Ct. App. 2d Dist. Clark County 2003) (evidence showed "[a]t the least," that prosecutor used immunized statements in solidifying prosecutor's decision to charge defendant).

[16]U.S. v. Morrissette, 70 M.J. 431, 438 (C.A.A.F. 2012) ("Both the Supreme Court and this Court in the military context have interpreted 'use' to include evidentiary and nonevidentiary uses, including the indirect use of testimony to alter the investigative strategy or to inform the decision to prosecute."); People v. Stevenson, 228 P.3d 161, 166 (Colo. App. 2009) (Colo-

rado case law appears to adopt the "broad view that *Kastigar* proscribes even non-evidentiary uses of immunized testimony"); State v. Jackson, 125 Ohio St. 3d 218, 2010-Ohio-621, 927 N.E.2d 574, 578–79 (2010) ("the 'use' against which [the Fifth Amendment] protects is broad, encompassing evidentiary and nonevidentiary use of any compelled statement"); State v. Gault, 551 N.W.2d 719, 724–25 (Minn. Ct. App. 1996) (nonevidentiary use of immunized testimony is prohibited because only that construction of use immunity makes it coextensive with the privilege).

[17]State v. Koehn, 2001 SD 144, 637 N.W.2d 723, 728 (S.D. 2001) (majority of courts reject *McDaniel* rule prohibiting all nonevidentiary use of immunized testimony). The District of Columbia Circuit joined those courts not prohibiting all nonevidentiary use, at least for purposes of a case in which the witness argued his indictment reflected prohibited nonevidentiary use of his testimony. U.S. v. Slough, 641 F.3d 544, 553–54 (D.C. Cir. 2011), cert. denied, 132 S. Ct. 2710, 183 L. Ed. 2d 84 (2012).

impermissible,[18] *United States v. McDaniel*,[19] has been read as holding that proof that prosecutors were exposed to and aware of immunized testimony of the defendant is sufficient to establish that nonevidentiary use was made of that testimony.[20] This is apparently on the rationale that the prosecution cannot, as a practical matter, produce satisfactory evidence that prosecutors so exposed to immunized testimony did not make use of that testimony.[21] Opponents of the nonevidentiary use approach argue, of course, that at least if that approach is applied as required by this reading of *McDaniel*, use immunity effectively precludes prosecution and thus becomes transactional immunity.[22]

A significant number of state courts have construed state constitutions as requiring transactional immunity.[23] Most often, this is based on conclusions that practical difficulties in applying use immunity mean that in actual fact use immunity does not provide adequate assurance that immunized testimony will not be used against the witness in a subsequent prosecution. The Alaska Supreme Court, for example, stressed that faded memories and other difficulties of proof will often make impossible ac-

---

[18]*Compare* Brocious, 2003 WL 22061162 (*McDaniel* approach is "better approach") with Koehn, 637 N.W.2d at 728 (apparently rejecting *McDaniel* approach).

[19]U.S. v. McDaniel, 482 F.2d 305 (8th Cir. 1973).

[20]*See* People v. Reali, 895 P.2d 161, 166 (Colo. App. 1994). This may require a showing by prosecutors that prosecutors and law enforcement officers exposed to the immunized statements did not after that exposure further participate in the case. State v. Carapezza, 293 Kan. 1071, 272 P.3d 10, 17 (2012) (approving trial court's application of such an approach); State v. Vallejos, 118 N.M. 572, 883 P.2d 1269, 1274 (1994). *Compare* U.S. v. Daniels, 281 F.3d 168, 181–82 (5th Cir. 2002) (rejecting per se rule but adding "[t]here may be some cases in which the exposure of a prosecution team to a defendant's immunized testimony is so prejudicial that it requires disqualification of the entire prosecution team").

The leading federal decision rejecting this approach is probably U.S. v. Byrd, 765 F.2d 1524, 1531 (11th Cir. 1985).

[21]*See* U.S. v. Mapelli, 971 F.2d 284, 288 (9th Cir. 1992) (Government's showing was inadequate under *McDaniel*, because it failed to show that prosecutors' decisions to present or not present witnesses or exhibits and not to cross-examine the defendant were not affected by knowledge of immunized testimony).

[22]*See* U.S. v. Byrd, 765 F.2d 1524, 1531 (11th Cir. 1985) (if prosecution must negate all nonevidentiary use of immunized testimony, "the realistic difference between transactional and use immunity [becomes] hopelessly blurred if not totally extinguished").

[23]State v. Ely, 167 Vt. 323, 708 A.2d 1332, 1337–38 (1997) (collecting decisions). *Accord* State v. Vondehn, 348 Or. 462, 236 P.3d 691, 696–97 (2010) (under Oregon case law, "the state could not compel the statements of a witness without granting transactional immunity because, without protecting the witness from all evidentiary and nonevidentiary use of compelled statements, the state would not afford the witness the same protection that the constitution confers—the right to remain silent").

curate determinations as to whether immunized testimony in fact affected the prosecution's evidence[24] and that no procedural way is available to adequately protect witnesses from nonevidentiary use against them of compelled testimony.[25]

Some courts have found use immunity adequate under state constitutional standards only if it involves safeguards more stringent than those required by *Kastigar* as a matter of Fifth Amendment law. The Pennsylvania Supreme Court, for example, upheld use immunity but only on the condition that the prosecution is required to prove that its evidence "arose *wholly* [from] independent sources" and to prove this by clear and convincing evidence.[26] States may in other ways exceed what is required by Fifth Amendment law. Kansas, for example, requires that at a *Kastigar* hearing the prosecution prove by clear and convincing evidence it made no use of immunized testimony.[27]

---

[24]State v. Gonzalez, 853 P.2d 526, 530 (Alaska 1993).

[25]Gonzalez, 853 P.2d at 531–32. *Accord* State v. Thrift, 312 S.C. 282, 440 S.E.2d 341, 350–51 (1994) (use immunity creates unacceptable difficulty and confusion in determining when sufficient use has been made of immunized testimony, such as for example when the grand jury that heard immunized testimony then indicts the testifying witness). *Contra* Ely, 708 A.2d at 1339 (state constitution does not require transactional immunity, in part because twenty-five years of experience with *Kastigar* standards shows that use immunity can provide adequate protection for immunized witnesses).

[26]Com. v. Swinehart, 541 Pa. 500, 664 A.2d 957, 969 (1995) (emphasis in original).

[27]Kan. Stat. Ann § 22-3102(b)(2). *See* State v. Carapezza, 293 Kan. 1071, 272 P.3d 10, 15 (2012) (noting that statute requires more than the constitutional minimum).

# Chapter 14

# Confessions

## § 144  "Confessions" and admissibility

Among the most frequently raised evidentiary issues in criminal litigation are those relating to the admissibility of self-incriminating admissions by the defendant. These issues are the subject of the present chapter.

Traditional analysis sometimes required inquiry into whether a self-incriminating statement by a defendant was a "confession"—a statement admitting all facts necessary for conviction of the crime at issue[1]—or an "admission"—an acknowledgment of one or more facts tending to prove guilt but not of all the facts necessary to do so.[2] Most major limitations upon the admissibility of confessions now also apply to admissions and even exculpatory statements. This chapter, therefore, will assume unless a particular discussion requires otherwise that no distinction need be drawn among self-incriminating acknowledgements.

Confessions are out-of-court statements quite frequently offered to prove the truth of matters asserted therein and thus are potentially subject to exclusion pursuant to the prohibition against hearsay. Nevertheless, there is general agreement that the prosecution is entitled to introduce confessions, although the conceptual basis for this position is somewhat unclear.[3]

Given the general principle that defendants' confessions are admissible to prove guilt, confession law becomes primarily a collection of rules that prevent the use of particular categories of confessions. To some extent, some confession law rules are examples of the sort of exclusionary sanctions discussed in Chapter 15. Under these, exclusion of confessions is mandated by a perceived need to implement policies other than the accurate ascertainment of the "truth." For example, the requirement that confessions be excluded if they are shown to be sufficiently related to an unlawful arrest is designed to maximize compliance with the rules governing arrest and prompt presentation.

The traditional voluntariness mandate,[4] on the other hand, is more closely related to the objective of accurate ascertainment of guilt or innocence at trial. Whether the modern voluntariness demand and other confession law requirements—such as the well-known *Miranda v. Arizona*[5] rules[6]—still do and should serve that function, perhaps among others, is a major issue in modern confession law.

---

**[Section 144]**

[1]Gladden v. Unsworth, 396 F.2d 373, 375 n.2 (9th Cir. 1968); People v. Fitzgerald, 56 Cal. 2d 855, 17 Cal. Rptr. 129, 366 P.2d 481, 484 (1961).

[2]People v. Wytcherly, 172 Mich. App. 213, 431 N.W.2d 463, 466 (1988) ("an admission does not by itself show guilt in the absence of proof of other facts not admitted by the defendant").

[3]*See* Wigmore, Evidence § 816 (Chadbourn rev. 1970) ("[T]he ground for receiving admissions in general . . . suffices also for confessions."); Morgan, Admissions as an Exception to the Hearsay Rule, 30 Yale L.J. 355 (1921). *See also* Maguire, Evidence of Guilt § 1.02 (1959) (confessions "a specialized sort of admission").

[4]See § 149 infra.

[5]Miranda v. Arizona, 384 U.S. 436, 86 S. Ct. 1602, 16 L. Ed. 2d 694 (1966).

[6]See §§ 150 to 153 infra.

## § 145   *Corpus delicti* or corroboration requirement: (a) In general[1]

All American jurisdictions have some form of a rule requiring corroboration of at least some out-of-court statements by the accused otherwise admissible against that accused in a criminal prosecution.[2] The rule has sometimes been incorporated into statute or court rule.[3] Constitutional considerations, however, most likely do not demand it.[4]

There are several quite different formulations of the requirement, some of which are variations of what is often called the requirement of independent proof of the *corpus delicti*. Another, applied by the federal courts and some state tribunals, is a more flexible approach. The two basic approaches are described in two sections that follow.[5]

This section addresses some general aspects of the rule, focusing upon the rationale for it, whether it does (and should) address evidence sufficiency, admissibility, or both, and whether it is a matter for the judge, the jury, or perhaps both.

*Rationale for Requirement.*[6] The requirement has traditionally been based upon concern that convictions might result from false

---

**[Section 145]**

[1]*See generally* West's Key Number Digest, Criminal Law ⊜413.70 to 417.81.

[2]People v. Alvarez, 27 Cal. 4th 1161, 119 Cal. Rptr. 2d 903, 46 P.3d 372, 376 (2002); *See* Greenleaf, Law of Evidence § 217 (3rd ed. 1846); DeJesus v. State, 655 A.2d 1180, 1199 (Del. 1995) (all American jurisdictions apply some version of the requirement).

[3]*E.g.*, Ark. Code Ann. § 16-89-111(d) (confession must be accompanied by "other proof that the offense was committed"); Iowa R. Crim. Proc. 2.21(4) (confession not sufficient for conviction "unless accompanied by other proof that the defendant committed the offense"); N.Y. Crim. Proc. Law § 60.50 (conviction requires in addition to a confession or admission "additional proof that the offense charged has been committed").

[4]*See* Lucas v. Johnson, 132 F.3d 1069, 1077 (5th Cir. 1998) (state defendant's complaint that state corrobora-

tion requirement was not met raised no issue of federal constitutional dimensions); State v. Mauchley, 2003 UT 10, 67 P.3d 477, 488 (Utah 2003) (*corpus delicti* corroboration rule is not constitutionally mandated); State v. Dow, 168 Wash. 2d 243, 227 P.3d 1278, 1280 (2010) ("Washington's *corpus delicti* rule, particularly the requirement that the State present independent, corroborative evidence that the offense occurred, is judicially created and not constitutionally mandated."). *Contra* State v. Housler, 193 S.W.3d 476, 490 (Tenn. 2006) ("Due Process is violated when the jury convicts on the basis of the defendant's confession absent corroborating evidence of the *corpus delicti*.").

[5]See § 146 (*corpus delicti* approach), § 147 (truthfulness approach) infra.

[6]Different formulations of the requirement, see §§ 146 and 147 infra, might, of course, be supported by somewhat different rationales.

confessions.[7] Widespread agreement remains that the need to assure accuracy of convictions remains at least a major basis for the requirement. There has, however, been no consensus on the nature and sources of inaccuracy that support the rule.

Traditionally and generally, the requirement appears to have a relatively modest objective—protecting against the risk of conviction for a crime that never occurred.[8] Thus the target inaccuracies are very limited. A Maryland court, for example, commented that the requirement serves the limited purpose of preventing a mentally unstable person from confessing to and being convicted of a crime that never occurred.[9]

Sometimes, however, the objectives are stated more broadly although frequently quite generally. The Delaware court, for example, asserted that its rule "serves to protect those defendants who may be pressured to confess to crimes that they either did not commit or crimes that did not occur."[10] The Washington court indicated that the rule is designed to combat, first, risks of inaccuracy arising from misinterpretation or misreporting by witnesses who testify to what defendants admitted and, second, risks of inaccuracy with regard to what defendants said. These latter sources of inaccuracy, the court continued, include not only force or coercion but also the possibilities that a confession was "based upon a mistaken perception of the facts or law."[11] The Michigan Supreme Court indicated that the requirement serves "to minimize the weight of a confession and require collateral evidence to support a conviction,"[12] which it regarded as desirable on the apparent assumption that confessions are of dubious reli-

---

[7]See 7 Wigmore, Evidence § 2070, p. 510 (Chadbourn rev. 1978). The corroboration requirement rests upon the dual assumptions that such risks of inaccuracy are serious ones and that juries are likely to accept confessions uncritically and thus are unable or disinclined to recognize and accommodate these risks. See State v. Parker, 315 N.C. 222, 337 S.E.2d 487, 494 (1985).

[8]See, e.g., People v. Jones, 17 Cal. 4th 279, 70 Cal. Rptr. 2d 793, 949 P.2d 890, 902–03 (1998) ("The purpose of the corpus delicti rule is to assure that 'the accused is not admitting to a crime that never occurred.' "); State v. Daugherty, 173 Ariz. 548, 845 P.2d 474, 477 (Ct. App. Div. 1 1992) (potential "that a suspect might falsely confess to a nonexistent crime" led to

development of requirement).

[9]Crouch v. State, 77 Md. App. 767, 551 A.2d 943, 944 (1989). See also People v. Booden, 69 N.Y.2d 185, 513 N.Y.S.2d 87, 505 N.E.2d 598, 600 (1987) (Bellacosa, J., dissenting) (statutory requirement is "designed essentially to protect unfortunate individuals from their own criminal fantasies").

[10]DeJesus v. State, 655 A.2d 1180, 1202 (Del. 1995).

[11]City of Bremerton v. Corbett, 106 Wash. 2d 569, 723 P.2d 1135, 1139 (1986).

[12]People v. McMahan, 451 Mich. 543, 548 N.W.2d 199, 201 (1996), (quoting from Hall, General Principles of Criminal Law (2d ed.), ch. VII, p. 226).

ability and prosecutors should be encouraged to develop and use other evidence of guilt.[13]

Whether considerations beyond accuracy can also support the requirement is doubtful. It has been argued that the corroboration requirement serves to combat improper police practices in securing confessions generally,[14] and thus serves to discourage law enforcement actions offensive for reasons other than inaccuracy. At best, however, the requirement achieves this objective indirectly, and the function is almost certainly more effectively accomplished by other legal requirements relating to confessions.[15]

*Admissibility, Evidence Sufficiency, or Both?* Many formulations of the corroboration rule put it as a matter of admissibility of a confession, often in addition to its role as a measure of evidence sufficiency.[16] Reported decisions often contain appellate courts' expressions of expectation that trial judges will demand sufficient other evidence before permitting the prosecution to put evidence of an out-of-court confession before the jury.[17] Despite their general statements, appellate courts have been unwilling to enforce any requirement of admissibility by reversing convictions supported by sufficient evidence because the trial court failed to require that evidence before admitting the confession.[18] Trial judges' discretion regarding the order of proof permits them to in effect admit confessions subject to later presentation by the pros-

---

[13]*See also* State v. Parker, 315 N.C. 222, 337 S.E.2d 487, 494 (1985) (requirement might be supported on the basis that it tends to encourage other and more desirable police investigatory practices than interrogation of suspects, although this rationale has rarely been offered).

[14]*See* Comment, 1984 Wis. L. Rev. 1121, 1128–30.

[15]*See* Parker, 337 S.E.2d at 494 (this rationale largely undercut by *Miranda* and other federal constitutional limits on confessions).

[16]*E.g.,* Corona v. State, 64 So. 3d 1232, 1244 (Fla. 2011) ("the State is required to present evidence that a crime occurred and evidence establishing each element of the crime before the defendant's confession can be admitted"); People v. McMahan, 451 Mich. 543, 548 N.W.2d 199, 201 (1996) ("In Michigan, it has long been the rule that proof of the *corpus delicti* is required before the prosecution is al-

lowed to introduce the inculpatory statements of an accused.").

Clearly some trial courts assume that they can and perhaps must address application of the rule pretrial, State v. Mauchley, 2003 UT 10, 67 P.3d 477, 490 (Utah 2003), when evidence sufficiency is seldom open to challenge but admissibility in a later trial is often resolved.

[17]*E.g.,* State v. Fundalewicz, 2012 ME 107, 49 A.3d 1277, 1278 n.1 (Me. 2012) ("Although we have noted a 'strong preference for proof of *corpus delicti* prior to admitting evidence of a defendant's confession or admission,' we have also noted that a trial court has 'discretion to control the order of proof pursuant to the *corpus delicti* rule.' ") (quoting State v. Knight, 2002 ME 35, 791 A.2d 110, 114 (Me. 2002)).

[18]*E.g.,* King v. State, 908 N.E.2d 673, 688 (Ind. Ct. App. 2009) (prosecution need not prove the *corpus delicti* by the required independent evidence prior to the admission of a confession

ecution of the required corroborating evidence. It may be that any formal requirement of admissibility is relatively meaningless as a practical matter because trial judges will know that noncompliance will seldom or never lead to appellate reversal.

Appellate reversals of convictions on the basis of the rule are sometimes put as reversals for the procedural error of admitting a confession in violation of the rule.[19] This, of course, indicates the rule is only a procedural one and appellate reversals for its violation are not findings of evidence sufficiency automatically requiring acquittals.

The Alaska Court of Appeals in *Langevin v. State*[20] addressed the matter at length. It acknowledged that "the majority position in this country is that a defendant is entitled to an acquittal if the government introduces evidence of the defendant's out-of-court confession but fails to satisfy the *corpus delicti* rule."[21] This, it concluded, is based on a perception of the rule that makes adequate corroborating evidence an "implicit element" of the charged offense. Alaska, however, has an "evidentiary foundation" conception of the corroboration rule under which the rule simply addresses whether a trial judge should permit the prosecution to introduce an out-of-court admission or confession as part of its case. When raised on appellate review of a conviction, the rule permits at most a finding that the trial judge procedurally erred and the convicted appellant is entitled to a new trial.[22]

As *Langevin* recognized, most appellate courts treat the corroboration requirement as applied on appellate review as relating to evidence sufficiency, perhaps as well as admissibility. Consequently, a convicted defendant who prevails on appeal is entitled to acquittal.[23]

Nevertheless, the theoretical admissibility requirement of the

---

as long as the evidence presented at trial meets the requirement).

Mullen, Rule Without Reason: Requiring Independent Proof of the Corpus Delicti as a Condition of Admitting an Extrajudicial Confession, 27 U.S.F. L. Rev. 385, 395 (1993), asserted that "no court has ordered a new trial for failure to comply" with the frequently-made admonition that trial judges should demand proof of the *corpus delicti* before admitting a confession.

[19]A Pennsylvania court held that a defendants could be retried after appellate reversal of a conviction on *corpus delicti* grounds, reasoning that the reversal was for procedural error in admitting the confession and the evidence—although including the improperly admitted confession—had not been found insufficient so as to trigger a federal constitutional right to acquittal. Com. v. McMullen, 2000 PA Super 38, 745 A.2d 683, 685, 689 (2000). The Pennsylvania court's analysis was held in federal habeas corpus to have been a reasonable application of federal law. McMullen v. Tennis, 562 F.3d 231, 240–45 (3d Cir. 2009).

[20]Langevin v. State, 258 P.3d 866 (Alaska Ct. App. 2011).

[21]Langevin, 258 P.3d at 873.

[22]258 P.3d at 783–84.

[23]*E.g.*, Reinlein v. State, 75 So. 3d

corroboration rule remains firmly entrenched. When the Utah court jettisoned the *corpus delicti* approach and adopted the trustworthiness standard, for example, it turned explicitly to whether the rule as retained should continue to serve a "gatekeeping" function by imposing an admissibility requirement. Citing only its recognition that no other type of evidence is as potentially prejudicial to defendants as confessions, it held:

> [B]efore a confession may be admitted, the trial court must determine as a matter of law that the confession is trustworthy. When making its determination, the trial court must review the totality of the circumstances. Only after a confession is deemed trustworthy by a preponderance of the evidence may it be admitted into evidence.[24]

The rationale generally given for the corroboration requirement, as discussed above, does not argue for the rule as a limit on admissibility. A rule of admissibility has been defended as encouraging objective jury determinations of whether the prosecution has proved crimes were committed,[25] but unless jury verdicts on that matter are required mid-trial, a rule of admissibility does not well serve this objective.

The only possible basis for an admissibility requirement must rest on a need to encourage the trial judge to scrutinize carefully the non-confession evidence before deciding to let the prosecution prove a confession and, in all probability, go to the jury. A judge may do this more objectively if forced to do it towards the end of the prosecution's case by marshaling the evidence to decide if the prosecution should be permitted to introduce the confession as the finale of its presentation.

Whether this is a needed practice by trial judges, and if so whether it can actually be compelled by a rule of confession admissibility, is at best doubtful. On balance, there is no reason for the corroboration requirement to be framed or discussed as one of admissibility. The courts should stop pretending that it is a rule of this sort.

*Judge, Jury, or Both?* Is the requirement only for the court or should the jury be instructed to apply it as well? Wigmore assumes that the trial judge applies the rule first, and if the case goes to the jury the "same question" is then posed for the jury. The jury must then address, "without reference to the judge's rul-

---

853, 856 (Fla. 2d DCA 2011) (remanding for discharge of defendant); State v. Smith, 362 N.C. 583, 669 S.E.2d 299 (2008) (conviction reversed and remanded with instructions to dismiss charge).

[24]State v. Mauchley, 2003 UT 10,

67 P.3d 477, 490 (Utah 2003) (noting that similar requirements are imposed by other jurisdictions adopting the trustworthiness approach).

[25]*See* Mullen, 27 U.S.F. L. Rev. at 395–96.

ing, whether the corroboration exists to satisfy them."[26] Some courts certainly regard the jury as playing a role in applying the requirement.[27] At least a few appear to conceptualize the jury's evaluation as the major one, with the judge's ruling merely a preliminary screening decision.[28] Insofar as the rule is one of evidence sufficiency, its nature suggests that the jury should at least play a role in its application.[29]

Other courts have taken far different approaches. The Court of Appeals for the District of Columbia Circuit reasoned that as applied in the federal system, the corroboration requirement is "something of a hybrid rule having elements both of admissibility and sufficiency." Juries, of course, are to evaluate the credibility of confession evidence and the sufficiency of the evidence as a whole, but the corroboration rule does not add anything specific to the jury's consideration of these matters. Thus, it concluded, a jury charge is not required[30] or, apparently, even appropriate. Several other federal courts of appeals have agreed.[31]

The District of Columbia Court of Appeals in 2011 joined "[t]he majority of jurisdictions that have considered this issue" and held that the sufficiency of corroboration evidence is not a matter for jury consideration. It relied in large part on the unacceptability of an approach that would empower juries to "overrule" trial

---

[26]7 Wigmore, Evidence § 2073, p. 531 (Chadbourn rev. 1978).

[27]*E.g.,* State v. Sweat, 727 S.E.2d 691, 697 (N.C. 2012) ("Whether a confession is sufficiently corroborated under the *corpus delicti* doctrine is a legal question of admissibility to be determined by the trial judge.") (citing Wigmore).

The California Supreme Court held that an amendment to the state constitution removing the bar to admission of an insufficiently corroborated confession did not affect the need to instruct the jury on the requirement of corroboration to convict. People v. Fuiava, 53 Cal. 4th 622, 137 Cal. Rptr. 3d 147, 269 P.3d 568, 642 (2012), cert. denied, 133 S. Ct. 788 (2012).

[28]State v. Ervin, 731 S.W.2d 70, 72 (Tenn. Crim. App. 1986) ("The question of whether the State has sufficiently established the *corpus delicti* of a crime is primarily a jury question."). *See also* State v. Origer, 418 N.W.2d 368, 371 (Iowa Ct. App. 1987) (Under Iowa rule, "[t]he existence of

corroborative evidence is an issue for the court, and its sufficiency is ordinarily for the jury."), reaffirmed in *Polly*, 657 N.W.2d at 467.

[29]Perhaps Pennsylvania stresses the jury's role more than does any other jurisdiction, since it requires that the *corpus delicti* be proved to the trier of fact beyond a reasonable doubt. *See* Com. v. Reyes, 545 Pa. 374, 681 A.2d 724, 729 (1996).

[30]U.S. v. Dickerson, 163 F.3d 639, 641–43 (D.C. Cir. 1999). *Accord* Watkins v. Com., 238 Va. 341, 385 S.E.2d 50, 55 (1989). *See also* State v. Kelley, 308 A.2d 877, 885 (Me. 1973) (trial judge should not have instructed jury not to consider defendant's confession until and if it had determined that the *corpus delicti* existed).

[31]*See* U.S. v. McDowell, 687 F.3d 904, 912 (7th Cir. 2012) (following the First and District of Columbia circuits in holding that no jury instruction is required). The Sixth Circuit holds otherwise. *E.g.,* U.S. v. Adams, 583 F.3d 457, 469–70 (6th Cir. 2009).

judges' decisions that confessions are adequately corroborated.[32] Characterization of the rule as one of substantive law defining evidence sufficiency does not require that the issue be submitted to the jury, a Maryland court concluded. It is best viewed as establishing a requirement of sufficient evidence to go the jury rather than one of sufficiency of evidence to convict for jury application.[33]

An instruction demanding the jury consider whether the prosecution has presented sufficient corroborating evidence may be too ambitious to be of practical value. The Alaska Court of Appeals explained:

> Under this approach, if the trial judge rules that *corpus delicti* is satisfied, the jury would hear the defendant's confession, only to later be asked to set the confession to one side and determine whether the government's remaining evidence is sufficient to establish the *corpus delicti*. One might doubt whether jurors, having heard the defendant's confession to a heinous crime, could dispassionately discharge this duty.[34]

*Statements to Which the Requirement Applies.* There is widespread agreement that the requirement, whatever the local formulation of it, applies not only to "confessions", defined as complete and conscious admissions of guilt of a crime, but also to "admissions"—acknowledgments of facts relevant to guilt—because these involve the risks which the requirement is designed to reduce.[35] Most courts at least assume it applies to statements intended when made to be exonerating—so-called "exculpatory statements"[36]—but this position has been challenged.[37] The requirement is not limited to statements made to law enforce-

---

[32]Fowler v. U.S., 31 A.3d 88, 91–93 (D.C. 2011).

[33]Riggins v. State, 155 Md. App. 181, 843 A.2d 115, 141 (2004).

[34]Langevin v. State, 258 P.3d 866, 870 (Alaska Ct. App. 2011) (quoting Dodds v. State, 997 P.2d 536, 540–41 (Alaska Ct. App. 2000)).

[35]*See* Opper v. U.S., 348 U.S. 84, 90–92, 75 S. Ct. 158, 99 L. Ed. 101 (1954). *See also* State v. Polly, 657 N.W.2d 462, 466 n.1 (Iowa 2003) ("admissions made after the crime must also be supported with sufficient corroborating evidence"); In re J.H., 928 A.2d 643, 652 n.12 (D.C. 2007) ("The corroboration rule applies not only to strict confessions that contain a complete and conscious admission of guilt, but also to admissions of essential facts or elements of the offense."); State v. Aten, 79 Wash. App. 79, 900 P.2d 579, 582 (Div. 2 1995) (Washington corroboration requirement applies to admissions as well as confessions). *Contra* Lowe v. State, 267 Ga. 180, 476 S.E.2d 583, 585 (1996) (since an admission, by its nature, cannot prove the crime without additional evidence, corroboration requirement does not apply).

[36]The seminal Supreme Court decision, Opper v. U.S., 348 U.S. 84, 75 S. Ct. 158, 99 L. Ed. 101 (1954), discussed in § 147 infra, applied the federal requirement to exculpatory statements. *See* Wong Sun v. U.S., 371 U.S. 471, 487, 83 S. Ct. 407, 9 L. Ed. 2d 441 (1963) ("we held in [*Opper*] that even where exculpatory statements are voluntary and thus clearly admis-

ment officers and consequently applies to statements made to private persons.[38] It does not, however, apply to incriminating statements made prior to or during the offense.[39]

---

sible, they require at least the same degree of corroboration required of incriminating statements"). State courts have often simply assumed that state versions of the rule applies to exculpatory statements. *E.g.,* State v. Johnson, 291 S.C. 127, 352 S.E.2d 480, 482 (1987) (per curiam).

One leading analysis stated the general rule in the course of concluding that exculpatory statements could not constitute the corroboration necessary for an inculpatory statement to which the requirement unquestionably applied. Aten, 900 P.2d at 584.

The rationale of the rule most clearly applies if the prosecution offered a statement exculpatory in part because that statement contains some overtly incriminating admissions. Johnson, 352 S.E.2d at 482 (statement acknowledged that defendant's companion robbed and killed victim but denied participation). *Cf.* Com. v. McMullen, 545 Pa. 361, 681 A.2d 717, 720–21 (1996) (*corpus delicti* rule applies only to incriminatory statements, but statement in which defendant admitted being present but not participating when another killed the victim was "inculpatory for purposes of the *corpus delicti* rule"). The rationale is less obviously applicable if a statement is wholly exculpatory but offered with proof of its falsity to show the defendant's consciousness of guilt.

[37]A Florida court reasoned that the policies furthered by the *corpus delicti* rule would not be furthered by applying it to evidence of the defendant's exculpatory and inconsistent out-of-court statements. Price v. State, 776 So. 2d 1100, 1101 (Fla. 5th DCA 2001) (if accused was convicted on the basis of these statements, he could not be said to have been convicted "out of derangement, mistake, or official fabrication"). *See also* People v. Hooker, 64 Cal. Rptr. 2d 723, 729 (App. 2d Dist. 1997) review denied and ordered

not officially published ("some authority" supports claim that *corpus delicti* rule applies even to denial of guilt and explanations of innocence, "but it is unanalytical and we believe misguided"); Shipley v. State, 570 A.2d 1159, 1169 (Del. 1990) ("questionable" whether exculpatory statements fall within the reach of *corpus delicti* rule).

[38]Bishop v. State, 294 Ark. 303, 742 S.W.2d 911 (1988) (overruled on other grounds by, Matthews v. State, 2009 Ark. 321, 319 S.W.3d 266 (2009)) (corroboration requirement applied to defendant's out-of-court admission to his mother that he had robbed a store because he needed Christmas money). But a sufficient risk of unreliable admissions to justify applying the rule may not be present when a person makes admissions before arrest or even before police begin an investigation. State v. Hauk, 2002 WI App 226, 257 Wis. 2d 579, 652 N.W.2d 393, 399–400 (Ct. App. 2002) (rule did not apply to admissions made to friend before police investigation).

[39]Warszower v. U.S., 312 U.S. 342, 346, 61 S. Ct. 603, 85 L. Ed. 876 (1941) (admissions as to facts that later became incriminatory did not raise the danger of inaccurate conviction, and therefore such admissions need not be corroborated); State v. Johnson, 821 P.2d 1150, 1162 (Utah 1991) (majority position, supported by "sound policy," is that the requirement does not apply to statements made prior to or during the commission of a crime). The California Supreme Court has applied its requirement to pre-crime statements showing criminal intent, reasoning that the risk of an unjust conviction is less but sufficient to justify application of the requirement. It has not, however, applied the requirement to a statement—even showing intent—made during the offense. People v. Carpenter, 15 Cal. 4th 312, 63 Cal. Rptr. 2d 1, 935 P.2d 708,

## §146 *Corpus delicti* or corroboration requirement: (b) Requirement of independent proof of the *corpus delicti*

The traditional formulation of the corroboration requirement, still applied by most jurisdictions, demands that there be some evidence other than the confession that tends to establish the *corpus delicti*.[1] Generally, the evidence need not do so beyond a reasonable doubt. If sufficient independent evidence exists, that independent evidence and the confession may both be considered in determining whether guilt has been proved beyond a reasonable doubt. Only "slight" corroborating evidence is often required,[2] and this can be circumstantial as well as direct.[3]

There is some dispute regarding the definition of *corpus delicti*, which literally means the "body of the crime." To establish guilt in a criminal case, the prosecution must ordinarily show that (a) the injury or harm constituting the crime occurred; (b) this injury or harm was done in a criminal manner; and (c) the defendant was the person who inflicted the injury or harm. Wigmore maintains that *corpus delicti* means only the first of these, that is, "the fact of the specific loss or injury sustained," and does not require proof that this was occasioned by anyone's criminal agency.[4] Some courts have agreed.[5]

Most courts, however, define *corpus delicti* as involving both (a) and (b). This means that the corroborating evidence must tend to

---

755 (1997) (corroboration requirement did not apply to evidence that during attack defendant told victim that he wanted to rape her).

[Section 146]

[1]*E.g.,* People v. Sargent, 239 Ill. 2d 166, 346 Ill. Dec. 441, 940 N.E.2d 1045, 1055–56 (2010) (despite more flexible language in some opinions, corroborating evidence must "tend to show that a crime occurred").

[2]*E.g.,* State v. Hill, 333 S.W.3d 106, 134 (Tenn. Crim. App. 2010) ("the State needs 'only slight evidence of the *corpus delicti* . . . to corroborate a confession and sustain a conviction' ") (quoting State v. Smith, 24 S.W.3d 274, 281 (Tenn. 2000)). *Accord* People v. Jones, 17 Cal. 4th 279, 70 Cal. Rptr. 2d 793, 949 P.2d 890, 902–03 (1998) ("The amount of independent proof of a crime required . . . is quite small; we have described this quantum of evidence as 'slight' or 'minimal' ");

Watkins v. Com., 238 Va. 341, 385 S.E.2d 50, 54 (1989).

[3]State v. Meyers, 799 N.W.2d 132, 139 (Iowa 2011) ("Corroborating evidence may be either direct or circumstantial." *Accord, e.g.,* Jones v. State, 2010 WY 44, 228 P.3d 867, 870 (Wyo. 2010).

One extrajudicial uncorroborated statement, however, cannot be used to corroborate another extrajudicial statement. *E.g.,* Ross v. State, 268 Ind. 471, 376 N.E.2d 1117 (1978); State v. Charity, 587 S.W.2d 350 (Mo. Ct. App. S.D. 1979).

[4]Wigmore, Evidence § 2072, pp. 524–25 (Chadbourn rev. 1978).

[5]State v. Tillman, 152 Conn. 15, 202 A.2d 494, 496–97 (1964) (traditional definition of *corpus delicti* "creates complications and difficulties in the trial of cases" which "tend to produce unjust results," so Wigmore definition adopted); Com. v. Forde, 392

show the harm or injury and that it was occasioned by criminal activity. It need not, however, in any manner tend to show that the defendant was the guilty party. Thus in a homicide case, the *corpus delicti* consists of proof that the victim died and that the death was caused by a criminal act, but it need not tend to connect the defendant on trial with that act.[6]

The traditional approach has been to require that the elements of the offense be carefully distinguished and that the corroborating evidence tends to show each of those elements.[7] A growing number of courts, however, are abandoning the strict requirement that the corroborating evidence always tend to prove all elements of the *corpus delicti*. Thus the corroborating evidence need only tend to show the "major" or "essential" harm involved in the offense charged and not all of the elements technically distinguished.[8] This tendency is most pronounced in homicide cases, where defendants are often tried for offenses that involve requirements beyond simply the causing of death in a criminal manner.[9]

This approach is somewhat troublesome as applied to certain modern crimes that—unlike homicide offenses—do not involve a

---

Mass. 453, 466 N.E.2d 510, 513 (1984) (objective of the corroboration requirement is the limited one of guarding against convictions for "imaginary crimes," and the restrictive definition of *corpus delicti* best tailors the requirement to serve this limited purpose).

[6]*E.g.,* Shipley v. State, 570 A.2d 1159, 1169 (Del. 1990); Watkins v. Com., 238 Va. 341, 385 S.E.2d 50, 55 (1989). In contrast, a jurisdiction adopting the Wigmore definition of *corpus delicti* requires only that the corroborating evidence tend to show that the victim in fact is dead. Forde, 466 N.E.2d at 513–514.

[7]Florida applies this approach. *See* State v. Carwise, 846 So. 2d 1145, 1146 (Fla. 2003) (Cantero, J., dissenting from dismissal of review).

[8]*See* Riggins v. State, 155 Md. App. 181, 843 A.2d 115, 134 (2004) (corroborating evidence must only tend to prove "the major or essential harm involved in the charged offense"). *Accord* Hart v. State, 301 Ark. 200, 783 S.W.2d 40, 42–43 (1990) ("The state need not independently prove each specific element of the offense of

theft by receiving to establish the *corpus delicti*."); People v. Jones, 17 Cal. 4th 279, 70 Cal. Rptr. 2d 793, 949 P.2d 890, 904 (1998) ("independent evidence of every physical act constituting an element of an offence" is not necessary); DeJesus v. State, 655 A.2d 1180, 1199 n.11 (Del. 1995).

Where the penalty for transporting narcotics was enhanced upon proof that the transportation was from one county to a noncontiguous county, the *corpus delicti* did not include the noncontiguous county matter. People v. Miranda, 161 Cal. App. 4th 98, 73 Cal. Rptr. 3d 759, 765–66 (3d Dist. 2008).

[9]*See* People v. Weaver, 26 Cal. 4th 876, 111 Cal. Rptr. 2d 2, 29 P.3d 103, 132–34 (2001) (*corpus delicti* rule inapplicable to felonies used to determine the degree of a homicide); State v. Bishop, 753 P.2d 439, 477–78 (Utah 1988) (*corpus delicti* in first degree murder case includes only death of victim and causing of death by criminal means and does not include aggravating circumstances such as the purpose of silencing a witness or commission of the killing in an especially heinous manner).

single and tangible injury or loss that readily be characterized as constituting the "major" or "essential" harm involved in the offense.[10] This is arguably the case, for example, where the crime is an inchoate one, such as conspiracy or attempt. Nevertheless, creative analysis in defining the essential features of even such crimes permits application of the modern *corpus delicti* approach to such offenses.[11]

*State v. Angulo*,[12] illustrates the trend and its possible implication. Defendant Angulo's confession to penetration and thus rape of a child was used although the corroborating evidence did not tend to establish penetration but only acts constituting molestation or attempted rape. Finding no error, the appellate court relied in part on the fact that the gravamen of the child rape—a sexual act with a minor—was corroborated.[13] Perhaps the *corpus delicti* should be so defined as including only the gravamen of the offense. *Angulo* went on, however, to more questionably add that the corroboration requirement is designed to assure only whether *a* crime was committed, not *which* crime was committed. Thus the corroborating evidence need only indicate that the events or incident on which the prosecution is based involved some crime.[14] This is quite likely an erroneous conclusion regarding the function served by the requirement and an overstatement of implications of general trend toward flexible definitions of the *corpus delicti* needing corroboration.

Felony murder cases have presented special difficulty. Under the traditional application of the *corpus delicti* formulation, the elements of felony murder include the predicate felony as well as the fact of death and the causing of it in a criminal way; thus, corroborating evidence would have to tend to prove that predicate felony.[15] Most courts, however, have balked at this and have held that the corroborating evidence need not tend to prove the predicate felony.[16]

The general rule in felony murder cases is sometimes regarded

---

[10]*See* State v. Parker, 315 N.C. 222, 337 S.E.2d 487, 493 (1985).

[11]*See* DeJesus, 655 A.2d at 1199 n. 11 ("in an attempted robbery case, the State must establish some evidence, aliunde the defendant's confession, which tends to show that the defendant (1) attempted to take, exercise control over or obtain the property of another (2) by the use or threat of immediate force").

[12]*E.g.*, State v. Angulo, 148 Wash. App. 642, 200 P.3d 752 (Div. 3 2009).

[13]Angulo, 200 P.3d at 759.

[14]200 P.3d at 759. *Compare* State v. Bircher, 156 Wash. App. 1005, 2010 WL 1953583 (Div. 1 2010) (*Angulo* not followed because it relieves prosecution of need to corroborate all elements of charged offense).

[15]People v. Allen, 390 Mich. 383, 212 N.W.2d 21 (1973).

[16]Hall v. State, 361 Ark. 379, 206 S.W.3d 830, 834–35 (2005) ("so long as the *corpus delicti* of the homicide (i.e., death caused by a criminal agency) is established by independent evidence, the predicate felony may be shown by confession alone"); Dawson v. State,

as reflecting the general principle that elements affecting only the degree or seriousness of the crime are not part of the *corpus delicti* that needs to be corroborated.[17] Thus in a prosecution for burglary that would be first degree burglary because it was committed in the nighttime, the time of the entry could be proved by the confession alone because the time of entry determined only the degree of burglary committed.[18]

Situations involving multiple related crimes have also posed difficulty under the *corpus delicti* rule. Where an accused is being tried for several offenses, must the prosecution support the application of the *corpus delicti* requirement to each offense, one by one? Under such an approach, the statement may be used only to convict of those offenses also shown by the corroborating evidence. Some courts have clearly relaxed the rule's requirements for these situations. The Pennsylvania court, for example, held that if a statement incriminates the defendant regarding multiple offenses and the prosecution complies with the *corpus delicti* rule regarding one offense, the statement can be used to establish guilt of other offenses if two requirements are met. First, the connection between the crimes must be close. Second, permitting such use of the statement must, on the facts, pose no significant risk of convicting the accused for crimes that did not occur.[19]

Some courts assume that *mens rea* is part of the *corpus delicti*

---

23 So. 3d 841, 843 (Fla. 4th DCA 2009) ("in a felony murder case, the *corpus delicti* is the fact of death through criminal agency, and proof of the underlying felony is not required") (quoting Foster v. State, 886 So. 2d 1037, 1038 (Fla. 4th DCA 2004); State v. Bishop, 753 P.2d 439, 477–78 (Utah 1988). *Contra DeJesus*, 655 A.2d at 1202 (since "a person is just as likely to confess to a non-existing felony as he is to confess to a non-existing murder," requiring proof of the underlying felony is most consistent with the objectives of the *corpus delicti* rule).

[17]*E.g.*, People v. Miller, 37 Cal. 2d 801, 236 P.2d 137, 140 (1951) (uncorroborated admission can be used "to establish the degree of the crime committed"); State v. Cutwright, 626 So. 2d 780, 783 (La. Ct. App. 2d Cir. 1993) (commenting in the felony murder context that "the confession can prove the elements essential to determining the degree of the crime").

[18]State v. Cook, 26 Ariz. App. 198, 547 P.2d 50, 53 (Div. 1 1976), vacated on other grounds 564 P.2d 877 (Ariz. 1977).

[19]State v. Chatelain, 347 Or. 278, 220 P.3d 41, 45 (2009) (burglary proof "requires corroboration of defendant's intent to commit a crime, in addition to corroboration of the unlawful entry," since defendant intent to commit a crime is central to the crime of burglary); Com. v. Taylor, 574 Pa. 390, 831 A.2d 587, 596 (2003) (statement was admissible to prove criminal homicide and related robbery, kidnapping and conspiracy.

An Arizona court concluded that many courts adhering to the *corpus delicti* formulation generally have been willing to accept "what is, in essence, a trustworthiness approach for closely related offenses." State v. Morgan, 204 Ariz. 166, 61 P.3d 460, 465 (Ct. App. Div. 2 2002). In *Morgan*, the confession admitted oral sexual activity with

and must be shown by at least some independent evidence.[20] This has not been critically considered, however, and at least several courts have disagreed.[21] On principle, corroboration should be required since *mens rea* is generally necessary to show that the injury or harm constituting the crime was done in a criminal manner. Given the ease of meeting the requirement, requiring some independent proof—which may be circumstantial, of course—from which the necessary mental state can be inferred should not be a difficult burden.

## § 147 *Corpus delicti* or corroboration requirement: (c) Requirement of evidence tending to establish truthfulness of statement

Some jurisdiction have, to some extent at least, rejected the traditional requirement of independent evidence tending to prove the *corpus delicti* of the charged offense in favor of an alternative standard for determining whether a confession is adequately corroborated. This alternative approach is based on the United States Supreme Court's analysis developed in *Opper v. United States*.[1]

In *Opper,* the Court held as a matter of federal evidence law that a conviction in federal court could not rest upon an uncor-

---

a minor and that was one of the charged offenses. The corroborating evidence tended to show anal and vaginal sexual activity, but not oral conduct. The confession was properly considered on the oral conduct charges, the court held, because it was "sufficiently corroborated to eliminate any concern that it could be untrue and, thus, supported a 'reasonable inference' that the offense had occurred." Morgan, 61 P.3d at 467.

[20]People v. Dessauer, 38 Cal. 2d 547, 241 P.2d 238, 241 (1952) (assuming that proof of premeditated murder requires independent evidence of premeditation); People v. Parich, 256 Ill. App. 3d 247, 194 Ill. Dec. 647, 627 N.E.2d 1289, 1291 (2d Dist. 1994) (possession of cocaine with intent to deliver corroborated by proof that cocaine was packaged into multiple baggies showing intent to deliver); State v. Bircher, 156 Wash. App. 1005, 2010 WL 1953583 (Div. 1 2010) (conviction of attempted trafficking in stolen prop-

erty reversed because of lack of corroboration of intent to traffic).

[21]State v. C.M.C., 110 Wash. App. 285, 40 P.3d 690, 692 (Div. 1 2002) ("While the *mens rea* is an essential element of the offense, it is separate and distinct from the initial question of whether the body of the crime has been established); DeJesus v. State, 655 A.2d 1180, 1200, 1204 (Del. 1995) (since the independent evidence need not tend to prove all elements of an offense, in attempted robbery as in homicide cases *mens rea* can be proved by the confession alone); Finchum v. State, 463 N.E.2d 304, 306 (Ind. Ct. App. 1984) ("the State is not required to independently prove the mental elements of a particular crime if the defendant has given a confession which admits them").

**[Section 147]**

[1]Opper v. U.S., 348 U.S. 84, 75 S. Ct. 158, 99 L. Ed. 101 (1954).

roborated confession.[2] The "better rule," *Opper* continued without extensive explanation, would not require that the corroborating evidence establish the *corpus delicti* but rather that it be "substantial independent evidence which would tend to establish the truthfulness of the statement."[3] Some state courts[4] and a few legislatures[5] have adopted this position. In 2003, for example, the Utah Supreme Court carefully examined the matter in *State v. Mauchley*[6] and adopted *Opper's* analysis.

The major advantage of the trustworthiness approach is that its flexibility permits it to provide some—and arguably ade-

---

[2]In Smith v. U.S., 348 U.S. 147, 156, 75 S. Ct. 194, 99 L. Ed. 192 (1954), the Court added that *Opper* requires corroboration for those elements of an offense "established by admissions alone."

[3]Opper, 348 U.S. at 93.

[4]Perhaps the leading earlier case is State v. Parker, 315 N.C. 222, 337 S.E.2d 487, 495 (1985). Other adoptions of the trustworthiness approach include Armstrong v. State, 502 P.2d 440, 447 (Alaska 1972); People v. LaRosa, 2013 CO 2, 293 P.3d 567, 573-77 (Colo. 2013); State v. Hafford, 252 Conn. 274, 746 A.2d 150, 174 (2000); State v. Yoshida, 44 Haw. 352, 354 P.2d 986, 990 (1960); State v. Meyers, 799 N.W.2d 132, 139 (Iowa 2011); State v. Heiges, 806 N.W.2d 1, 13 (Minn. 2011); State v. Zysk, 123 N.H. 481, 465 A.2d 480, 483 (1983); State v. Wilson, 2011-NMSC-001, 149 N.M. 273, 248 P.3d 315, 321 (2010) (overruled by, State v. Tollardo, 2012-NMSC-008, 275 P.3d 110 (N.M. 2012)); Fontenot v. State, 1994 OK CR 42, 881 P.2d 69, 77 (Okla. Crim. App. 1994) (reaffirming adoption of *Opper* standard in 1976); (Tenn. Crim. App. 1986); State v. Osborne, 335 S.C. 172, 516 S.E.2d 201, 204–05 (1999); State v. Mauchley, 2003 UT 10, 67 P.3d 477 (Utah 2003).

Wisconsin has not expressly adopted the "federal approach," but it has rejected the *corpus delicti* formulation in favor of an *Opper*-like approach which requires only "corroboration of any significant fact." Holt v. State, 17 Wis. 2d 468, 117 N.W.2d 626, 633

(1962).

Several courts have declined to abandon the *corpus delicti* analysis for the *Opper* approach. State v. Carwise, 846 So. 2d 1145 (Fla. 2003) (dismissing as improvidently granted review on certified question asking whether Florida should adopt *Opper* approach); People v. McMahan, 451 Mich. 543, 548 N.W.2d 199, 201 (1996) ("This Court remains unconvinced that the protection afforded an accused by the common-law *corpus delicti* standard is no longer needed."); State v. Aten, 130 Wash. 2d 640, 927 P.2d 210, 222 (1996) (although an increasing number of state courts have followed the trend towards adopting the *Opper* approach, "[w]e are not among them").

[5]In 2003, Washington provided by statute for a trustworthiness approach "where independent proof of the corpus delicti is absent, and the alleged victim of the crime is dead or incompetent to testify . . . ." Wash. Rev. Code Ann. § 10.58.035(1).

Florida provides by statute that in prosecutions for certain offenses, a confession may be introduced if the prosecution establishes it is unable to establish the *corpus delicti* and there is sufficient corroborating evidence tending to establish the trustworthiness of the confession. *E.g.* Fla. Stat. Ann. § 92.565. This adopts the trustworthiness approach. *See* Geiger v. State, 907 So. 2d 668, 672 (Fla. 2d DCA 2005).

[6]State v. Mauchley, 2003 UT 10, 67 P.3d 477 (Utah 2003).

quate[7]—protection against conviction on the basis of inaccurate confessions while avoiding serious problems sometimes involved in the *corpus delicti* formulation. Application of the *corpus delicti* formulation may have been a relatively simple task that accomplished the purpose of the corroboration requirement when crimes were few and were defined in simple and concise terms. But modern statutory criminal law has increased the number and complexity of crimes. Simply identifying the elements of the *corpus delicti* thus provides fertile ground for dispute. Requiring that the corroborating evidence tends to establish each element once the *corpus delicti* is defined may pose an unrealistic burden upon the prosecution without significantly furthering the requirement's objective of providing assurance against conviction on the basis of inaccurate confessions. This is especially the case with regard to crimes that may not have a tangible *corpus delicti*, such as attempt offenses, conspiracy, tax evasion and similar offenses.[8] The modern approach of requiring corroboration of only the "major" or "essential" harm involved in an offense, although conceptually reasonable, may often founder on difficulty in identifying the major or essential harm.

As the Utah court stressed in *Mauchley*, the prosecution may under the trustworthiness approach use independent evidence of the crime to show a statement's trustworthiness. Where such evidence is lacking, it added, the prosecution may rely on the same types of evidence used in other areas to bolster the credibility and reliability of an out-of-court statement:

> [These f]actors * * * include the following: evidence as to the spontaneity of the statement; the absence of deception, trick, threats, or promises to obtain the statement; the defendant's positive physical and mental condition, including age, education, and experience; and the presence of an attorney when the statement is given.[9]

As applied to modern crimes, in summary, the trustworthiness approach is supported as most likely easier than the *corpus delicti* rule to apply, as effective in accomplishing the modest realistic objectives of the requirement, and less likely to lead to occasionally unreasonable results.

---

[7]*See* Mauchley, 67 P.3d at 488. *Contra* McMahan, 548 N.W.2d at 201 (constitutional protections against conviction on the basis of confessions "are not foolproof," and insufficient to justify dispensing with the protection provided by the traditional *corpus delicti* rule).

[8]*See* Parker, 337 S.E.2d at 493. Connecticut first applied the *Opper* approach to crimes prohibiting conduct that do not require harm, loss or in-

jury, because the traditional rule was difficult or impossible to apply in this context. State v. Harris, 215 Conn. 189, 575 A.2d 223 (1990). Ten years later it adopted the *Opper* approach for all situations. Hafford, 746 A.2d at 174 (cautioning that if a crime requires injury or loss, proof of that will often be necessary to showing trustworthiness).

[9]Mauchley, 67 P.3d at 489.

## § 148 *Corpus delicti* or corroboration requirement: (c) Future of the requirement

Wigmore maintains that no corroboration rule is needed and that existing corroboration requirements are, in the hands of unscrupulous defense counsel, "a positive obstruction to the course of justice."[1] Commentators have often agreed.[2]

Given the development of other confession law doctrines, especially Fifth Amendment protections as promulgated in *Miranda v. Arizona*[3] and the voluntariness requirement, concerns regarding law enforcement interrogation practices do not provide significant support for the corroboration requirement. Whether courts can justify retaining the doctrine for the purpose of encouraging investigatory techniques other than interrogation with reasonable expectation of success is at best questionable; the corroboration requirement as applied most likely provides little significant pressure for pursuing such alternatives.

Similarly, the requirement as administered is quite unlikely to provide much protection against inaccuracies resulting from mistakes in reporting, suspects' misunderstandings of the law or facts, or pressures too subtle to invoke *Miranda* or voluntariness

---

**[Section 148]**

[1]7 Wigmore, Evidence § 2070 p. 510 (Chadbourn rev. 1978).

[2]Comment, 20 U.C.L.A. L. Rev. 1055 (1973) (rule is ineffective in preventing convictions on false testimony and "pragmatic scrutiny" indicates it should be abolished); Developments in the Law, Confessions, 79 Harv. L. Rev. 938, 1084 (1966) ("serious consideration should be given to elimination of the corpus delicti requirement"); Note, 46 Fordham L. Rev. 1205, 1235 (1978) (rule is duplicative of other confession doctrines). See People v. Robson, 80 P.3d 912, 914 (Colo. App. 2003) (prosecution's authorities "present sound arguments" why the rule should be abandoned or modified on public policy grounds, but intermediate court is bound by precedent). *Contra* Moran, In Defense of the *Corpus Delicti* Rule, 64 Ohio St. L.J. 817 (2003).

Sangero and Halpert, Why a Conviction Should Not Be Based on a Single Piece of Evidence: A Proposal for Reform, 48 Jurimetrics J. 43 (2007), in contrast, argue that the risk of error when the prosecution relies heavily upon a single piece of evidence—such as a confession—demands more protection than is provided by American courts' application of the *corpus delicti* rule. They urge a requirement of "strong corroboration" mandating corroborating evidence relating to "all three elements that must be proven in a criminal trial: (1) the occurrence of the injury or harm constituting the crime; (2) that the injury or harm was done in a criminal manner; and (3) that the defendant was the person who inflicted the injury or harm." 48 Jurimetrics J. at 86. *See also* Sangero and Halpert, Proposal to Reverse the View of a Confession: From Key Evidence Requiring Corroboration to Corroboration for Key Evidence, 44 U. Mich. J. L. Reform 511 (2011); Sangero, *Miranda* Is Not Enough: A New Justification for Demanding "Strong Corroboration" to a Confession, 28 Cardozo L. Rev. 2791 (2007).

[3]Miranda v. Arizona, 384 U.S. 436, 86 S. Ct. 1602, 16 L. Ed. 2d 694 (1966). See generally § 150 infra.

protection. Any protection the requirement provides against false confessions by mentally disturbed persons could as well be provided by careful scrutiny of the evidence by conscientious judges. The requirement may, however, serve to trigger such scrutiny in appropriate cases by trial judges otherwise too rushed by the press of business to recognize such evidentiary deficiencies. Generally speaking, there is still some reason to be concerned about convictions for offenses never committed,[4] and a reasonable corroboration requirement serves to provide some protection at minimal cost.

If a requirement of corroboration is to be retained, the complexity of the *corpus delicti* approach—as discussed in Section 146— tends only to detract from the requirement's real function. The "truthfulness" approach—discussed in Section 147—is best designed to pursue the realistic objectives of a corroboration requirement.

There is insufficient justification for treating the rule as one related to admissibility of defendant's admissions. The requirement should be only one of evidence sufficiency. If juries are adequately instructed on the prosecution's burden of proof, there is no need to submit the corroboration requirement to those juries. Finally, the rule should be one to be applied by trial judges and appellate courts, not juries.

Thus a trial judge should have a duty to assure, if the prosecution's case rests for all practical purposes upon the defendant's out-of-court confession or admission, that the prosecution has produced reasonable evidence other than that confession or admission to establish the trustworthiness of the confession or admission. On appeal from a conviction, the issue should be whether the record contains sufficient evidence to justify a reasonable judge or jury in concluding the confession or admission is trustworthy.

## § 149   Voluntariness, in general[1]

The common law rule requiring voluntariness of an out-of-court confession as a condition for admission into evidence was

---

[4]In one case, a medical examiner first concluded that the probable cause of a child's death was Sudden Infant Death Syndrome, but when told the mother had confessed to smothering the child the physician amended the finding to add that asphyxia due to smothering could not be ruled out and was a possible cause of death. State v. Nieves, 207 Ariz. 438, 87 P.3d 851, 854 (Ct. App. Div. 1 2004) (reversing conviction for lack of independence evidence of the *corpus delicti* of death by criminal means).

**[Section 149]**

[1]*See generally* West's Key Number Digest, Criminal Law ⟷410.75 to 410.93.

developed only in the mid-1700s.[2] Early discussions made clear that the rationale for the requirement was the perceived lack of reliability of statements motivated not by guilt but by a desire to avoid discomfort or to secure some favor.[3]

In its first confession case, *Hopt v. Utah*,[4] the Supreme Court of the United States adopted as a matter of federal evidence law what it characterized as the well-developed common law requirement of voluntariness. That requirement, the Court explained, commands that a confession be held inadmissible

> when the confession appears to have been made either in consequence of inducements of a temporal nature, held out by one in authority, touching the charge preferred, or because of a threat or promise by or in the presence of such a person, which, operating upon the fears or hopes of the accused, in reference to the charge, deprives him of that freedom of will or self-control essential to make his confession voluntary within the meaning of the law.[5]

Thirteen years later, in *Bram v. United States*,[6] the Court commented that whenever an issue arises in federal criminal trials as to the voluntariness of a confession, "the issue is controlled by that portion of the Fifth Amendment to the Constitution of the United States, commanding that no person 'shall be compelled in any criminal case to be a witness against himself.' "[7] This, the Court continued, embodies the common law rule of voluntariness.[8]

Because the Fifth Amendment was not held binding on the states until 1964,[9] the *Bram* analysis did not impose the voluntariness requirement upon the states as a matter of federal constitutional law. The Court's 1936 holding in *Brown v. Mississippi*,[10] however, made clear that a state court conviction resting upon a confession extorted by brutality and violence violated the accused's general right to due process guaranteed by the

---

[2]Rudd's Case, (1775) 1 Leach Cr.C. 115, 118, 168 Eng. Rep. 160, 161 ("The instance has frequently happened, of persons having made confessions under threats or promises: the consequence as frequently has been, that such examinations and confessions have not been made use of against them on their trial.").

[3]Warickshall's Case, (1783) 168 Leach Cr.C. 263, 263–64, 168 Eng. Rep. 234, 234–35 (K.B.):

> Confessions are received in evidence, or rejected as inadmissible, under a consideration whether they are or are not entitled to credit. . . . [A] confession forced from the mind by the flattery of hope, or by the torture of fear,

comes in so questionable a shape when it is to be considered as the evidence of guilt, that no credit ought to be given to it.

[4]Hopt v. People, 110 U.S. 574, 4 S. Ct. 202, 28 L. Ed. 262 (1884).

[5]Hopt, 110 U.S. at 585.

[6]Bram v. U.S., 168 U.S. 532, 18 S. Ct. 183, 42 L. Ed. 568 (1897).

[7]Bram, 168 U.S. at 542.

[8]168 U.S. at 548.

[9]See § 115 supra.

[10]Brown v. State of Mississippi, 297 U.S. 278, 56 S. Ct. 461, 80 L. Ed. 682 (1936).

Fourteenth Amendment. Subsequent cases established that any use in a state criminal proceeding of a coerced confession violated the federal standard.[11] After the Fifth Amendment was applied to the states, the Court characterized the due process standard developed in *Brown* and its progeny as "the same general standard which [is] applied in federal prosecutions, a standard grounded in the policies of the privilege against self-incrimination."[12]

Despite the traditional emphasis upon the federal constitutional requirement of voluntariness, state constitutional and evidence law in most if not all jurisdictions also imposes similar requirements.

In *Blackburn v. Alabama*,[13] the Supreme Court explained that "a complex of values underlies the stricture against use by the state of confessions which, by way of convenient shorthand, this Court terms involuntary."[14] The traditional criterion for determining the admissibility of a confession challenged under the federal constitutional voluntariness requirement was articulated by Justice Frankfurter in 1961:

> The ultimate test . . . [is] voluntariness. Is the confession the product of an essentially free and unconstrained choice by its maker? If it is, if he has willed to confess, it may be used against him. If it is not, if his will has been overborne and his capacity for self-determination critically impaired, the use of his confession offends due process.[15]

Physical coercion or the threat of it, of course, necessarily shows that the defendant's will was overborne and his confession involuntary.[16] But the Court was increasingly presented with claims of "psychological" rather than physical coercion.[17] Application of the voluntariness standard became more difficult as cases increasingly relied upon these claims of more subtle influences than were presented by the earlier decisions.

---

[11]*See* Lynumn v. Illinois, 372 U.S. 528, 83 S. Ct. 917, 9 L. Ed. 2d 922 (1963); Payne v. State of Ark., 356 U.S. 560, 78 S. Ct. 844, 2 L. Ed. 2d 975 (1958).

[12]Davis v. State of N.C., 384 U.S. 737, 740, 86 S. Ct. 1761, 16 L. Ed. 2d 895 (1966).

[13]Blackburn v. State of Ala., 361 U.S. 199, 80 S. Ct. 274, 4 L. Ed. 2d 242 (1960).

[14]Blackburn, 361 U.S. at 207.

[15]Culombe v. Connecticut, 367 U.S. 568, 602, 81 S. Ct. 1860, 6 L. Ed. 2d 1037 (1961).

[16]*E.g.*, Brown v. State of Mississippi, 297 U.S. 278, 56 S. Ct. 461, 80 L. Ed. 682 (1936). *See also* U.S. v. Jenkins, 938 F.2d 934, 938–939 (9th Cir. 1991) (confessions made "substantially concurrent" with physical violence are per se involuntary without inquiry as to whether on the totality of the circumstances the defendant's will was overborne).

[17]*Cf.* Ashcraft v. State of Tenn., 322 U.S. 143, 64 S. Ct. 921, 88 L. Ed. 1192 (1944).

Since 1961 the constitutional question of voluntariness has been carefully distinguished from the question of the accuracy or reliability of particular confessions. In *Rogers v. Richmond*,[18] the Court held that due process did not permit a trial court to resolve the admissibility of a confession challenged on voluntariness grounds by using "a legal standard which took into account the circumstances of probable truth or falsity."[19] Evidence that a challenged confession (or some subpart of it) is accurate, then, is totally irrelevant to the voluntariness inquiry.

In *Colorado v. Connelly*,[20] the Court held that the Fourteenth Amendment's due process requirement of voluntariness imposed no absolute requirement that a confession reflect "an essentially free and unconstrained choice" by the defendant.[21] Official and coercive activity "is a necessary predicate to the finding that a confession is not 'voluntary' within the meaning of the Due Process Clause of the Fourteenth Amendment."[22] In the absence of this predicate, a showing that a confession reflected little or no meaningful choice by the defendant—because of private coercion or undisclosed mental impairment, for example—does not does not even raise an issue as to federal due process voluntariness.

*Connelly* provided little guidance for determining what constitutes the official coercion necessary to require the Fourteenth Amendment analysis to proceed to the mind of the suspect. *Connelly's* facts illustrate the difficulty. Connelly's statement was made in response to hallucinatory voices, but the officer who took it was unaware of Connelly's impairment. The Court summarily concluded that the taking and later the trial use of Connelly's statement to the officer did not violate the Fourteenth Amendment.[23] It appeared to distinguish *Blackburn v. Alabama*[24] on the basis that in *Blackburn* police learned during interrogation that Blackburn had a history of mental problems. Nevertheless they continued the interrogation and "exploited this weakness with coercive tactics" such as prolonged questioning in a tiny room. Exploitation of a known impairment in a manner that impairs the suspect's ability to decide whether to confess can constitute the coercion necessary for involuntariness.

Pre-*Connelly* Supreme Court case law reflected consideration of

---

[18]Rogers v. Richmond, 365 U.S. 534, 81 S. Ct. 735, 5 L. Ed. 2d 760 (1961).

[19]Rogers, 365 U.S. at 543. *See also* Haynes v. State of Wash., 373 U.S. 503, 83 S. Ct. 1336, 10 L. Ed. 2d 513 (1963) (error to suggest to jury that if confession was involuntary it might nevertheless be considered if corroborated by other evidence).

[20]Colorado v. Connelly, 479 U.S. 157, 107 S. Ct. 515, 93 L. Ed. 2d 473 (1986).

[21]Connelly, 479 U.S. at 166–167.

[22]479 U.S. at 167.

[23]479 U.S. at 167.

[24]Blackburn v. State of Ala., 361 U.S. 199, 80 S. Ct. 274, 4 L. Ed. 2d 242 (1960).

numerous factors in evaluating a voluntariness challenge. The Court gave significant weight to the time of the day or night of the interrogation,[25] the length of interrogation,[26] the quality of the conditions in which the defendant was held before confessing,[27] and similar matters. These have been evaluated in light of various characteristics of the accused that presumably affect the impact of these factors upon the accused. Thus the Court has found suggestion of involuntariness in the accused's youth,[28] physical illness, injury, or infirmity,[29] low educational level,[30] and little or no prior experience with law enforcement practices and techniques.[31] Whether or not officers warned the suspect of his right to silence and explained that right, where there is no specific obligation to do so, is relevant to voluntariness; in any case, the extent of the suspect's actual appreciation of his rights is clearly significant.[32] These factors remain relevant under *Connelly*, but only after official coercive activity has been found.

More recently, on the other hand, the Court in *Bobby v. Dixon*[33] disapproved of the lower court's position that involuntariness was at least strongly suggested by proof that officers urged the defendant to "cut a deal" before his accomplice did so. Nothing in

---

[25]*Cf.* Greenwald v. Wisconsin, 390 U.S. 519, 520, 88 S. Ct. 1152, 20 L. Ed. 2d 77 (1968) (per curiam) (arrest at 10:45 p.m. and interrogation from then until midnight).

[26]Watts v. State of Ind., 338 U.S. 49, 52–53, 69 S. Ct. 1347, 93 L. Ed. 1801 (1949) (5 days of interrogation); Turner v. Com. of Pa., 338 U.S. 62, 63–64, 69 S. Ct. 1352, 93 L. Ed. 1810 (1949) (4 days of interrogation).

[27]Greenwald, 390 U.S. at 520 (defendant spent night in jail cell with plank as bed); Brooks v. Florida, 389 U.S. 413, 88 S. Ct. 541, 19 L. Ed. 2d 643 (1967) (per curiam) (subject confined for 14 days in "punishment cell," with no external windows and no bed or furnishing except a hole flush with the floor that served as a commode).

[28]Gallegos v. Colorado, 370 U.S. 49, 54, 82 S. Ct. 1209, 8 L. Ed. 2d 325 (1962) (14 year old youth "cannot be compared with an adult in full possession of his senses and knowledgeable of the consequences of his admissions").

[29]Mincey v. Arizona, 437 U.S. 385, 398–99, 98 S. Ct. 2408, 57 L. Ed. 2d 290 (1978) (suspect wounded by gunshot and undergoing medical treatment at time of interrogation); Greenwald, 390 U.S. at 520 (suspect had high blood pressure and was without medication).

[30]Greenwald, 390 U.S. at 520 (defendant had only ninth grade education). *Compare* Crooker v. State of Cal., 357 U.S. 433, 438, 78 S. Ct. 1287, 2 L. Ed. 2d 1448 (1958) (evidence that suspect was a college graduate who had attended one year of law school considered in holding confession voluntary).

[31]Lynumn v. Illinois, 372 U.S. 528, 534, 83 S. Ct. 917, 9 L. Ed. 2d 922 (1963) (suspect had no prior experience with criminal law).

[32]Greenwald, 390 U.S. at 521 (failure to advise suspect of constitutional rights tended to show involuntariness). *Compare* Frazier v. Cupp, 394 U.S. 731, 739, 89 S. Ct. 1420, 22 L. Ed. 2d 684 (1969), (emphasizing, in holding confession admissible, that such advice was given.)

[33]Bobby v. Dixon, 132 S. Ct. 26, 181 L. Ed. 2d 328 (2011).

the Court's holdings suggests, it explained, that officers may not do this.[34]

The Supreme Court's due process voluntariness law contains no hint that voluntariness necessarily and always requires awareness of the legal right to refuse to make a self-incriminating statement. To the contrary, in a general review of voluntariness law, the Court commented that in none of its decisions had the Court required that the prosecution prove "as part of its initial burden" on voluntariness that the defendant was aware of his right to refuse to answer police queries.[35] Although the defendant's awareness of his right is relevant, like nearly all other considerations it is to be considered in evaluating the totality of the circumstances.

One court effectively summarized the analysis:

> Many factors can bear on the voluntariness of a confession. . . . [W]e look to all elements of the interrogation, including the manner in which it was conducted, the number of officers present, and the age, education, and experience of the defendant. Not all of the multitude of factors that may bear on voluntariness are necessarily of equal weight, however. Some are transcendent and decisive. We have made clear, for example, that a confession that is preceded or accompanied by threats or a promise of advantage will be held involuntary, notwithstanding any other factors that may suggest voluntariness, unless the State can establish that such threats or promises in no way induced the confession. A confession that is preceded or accompanied by any physical mistreatment would obviously be regarded in the same way. Those kinds of factors are coercive as a matter of law. When shown to be present, the State has a very heavy burden, indeed, of proving that they did not induce the confession.
>
> Other factors, such as the length of interrogation, team or sequential questioning, the age, education, experience, or physical or mental attributes of the defendant, do not have that broad, decisive kind of quality but assume significance, and may become decisive, only in the context of a particular case—based on the actual extent of their coercive effect. Lying between these two kinds of factors is a third—factors that may not be coercive as a matter of law but that need to be given special weight whenever they exist.[36]

As this makes clear, the analysis has considerable flexibility.

State constitutional, statutory or case law requirements of voluntariness need not, of course, be construed as having the same contents as the due process requirement.[37] As lower courts confront the implications of *Connelly's* limitations on federal due

---

[34]Dixon, 132 S.Ct. at 30.

[35]Schneckloth v. Bustamonte, 412 U.S. 218, 226–27, 93 S. Ct. 2041, 36 L. Ed. 2d 854 (1973).

[36]Williams v. State, 375 Md. 404, 825 A.2d 1078, 1092–93 (2003).

[37]*See* State v. Smith, 933 S.W.2d 450, 455 (Tenn. 1996) ("The test of

process voluntariness, they may be receptive to arguments that statutory or state constitutional voluntariness requirements are not subject to an absolute requirement of official coercion.[38] Such arguments may find support in pre-*Connelly* state cases imposing absolute requirements that confessing defendants have made meaningful decisions to confess.[39]

## § 150 Self-incrimination (*Miranda*) requirements: (a) In general[1]

In 1966, the Supreme Court, clearly dissatisfied with the due process voluntariness requirement, decided *Miranda v. Arizona*.[2] This decision revolutionized federal constitutional confession law

---

voluntariness for confessions under Article I, § 9 of the Tennessee Constitution is broader and more protective of individual rights than the test of voluntariness under the Fifth Amendment.").

[38]*See* State v. Bowe, 77 Haw. 51, 881 P.2d 538 (1994) (state constitution, unlike federal provision under Connelly, is concerned with unreliability of involuntary confessions regardless of the source of the involuntariness, so confession coerced by private person is involuntary under state constitutional law); People v. Westmorland, 372 Ill. App. 3d 868, 310 Ill. Dec. 447, 866 N.E.2d 608, 615 (2d Dist. 2007) ("under Illinois law, a confession may be deemed involuntary in the absence of police misconduct, based entirely on the defendant's personal characteristics"). *Accord* Mirabal v. State, 698 So. 2d 360, 361 (Fla. 4th DCA 1997). *Contra* Mills v. Com., 996 S.W.2d 473, 481 (Ky. 1999) (overruled on other grounds by, Padgett v. Com., 312 S.W.3d 336 (Ky. 2010)) (state action required before confession can be found involuntary under state constitution).

State statutory provisions have been similarly construed as rendering privately coerced confessions involuntary and hence inadmissible. State v. Conde, 174 Ariz. 30, 846 P.2d 843, 848 (Ct. App. Div. 1 1992); Griffin v. State, 230 Ga. App. 318, 496 S.E.2d 480, 484 (1998); People v. Barham, 5 Misc. 3d 227, 781 N.Y.S.2d 870 (Dist. Ct. 2004).

As to common law requirements see, Pappaconstantinou v. State, 352 Md. 167, 721 A.2d 241 (1998) (primary purpose of Maryland common law voluntariness requirement is to protect against government overreaching, so state action is required).

[39]*See* People v. Sorbo, 170 Misc. 2d 390, 649 N.Y.S.2d 318, 319 (Sup 1996) ("it has long been the law in New York that a Defendant's involuntary statement, whether obtained by the police or a private individual, may not be used").

[Section 150]

[1]*See generally* West's Key Number Digest, Criminal Law ⟨key⟩517.2, 518.

[2]Miranda v. Arizona, 384 U.S. 436, 86 S. Ct. 1602, 16 L. Ed. 2d 694 (1966). Two years earlier, in Escobedo v. State of Ill., 378 U.S. 478, 84 S. Ct. 1758, 12 L. Ed. 2d 977 (1964), the Court had applied the Sixth Amendment right to counsel to a stationhouse interrogation situation, but did so in terms that left quite unclear the nature and scope of the protection afforded. *Miranda* clearly reflected the Court's decision to abandon the Sixth Amendment as the major federal constitutional limitation in this area and to instead develop the Fifth Amendment. The present role of the Sixth Amendment is, perhaps as a result, somewhat unclear; see generally § 154 infra.

The Court explicitly declined to

and has become the focus of subsequent confession law development and analysis.

On the doctrinal level, *Miranda's* significance lies, first, in its holding that custodial law enforcement interrogation implicates the Fifth Amendment's privilege against compelled self-incrimination even though police have no legal authority to compel answers to their questions. "As a practical matter," the Court reasoned, "the compulsion to speak in the isolated setting of the police station may well be greater than in courts or other official investigations [where the legal power to compel answers may be exercised]."[3]

The focus of the Court's concern in *Miranda* was what the Court perceived as the "inherently compelling pressures" of custodial interrogation. Without proper safeguards, the Court reasoned, these will inevitably work "to undermine the individual's will to resist and to compel him to speak where he would not otherwise do so freely."[4] Modern in-custody interrogation, it stressed, is "psychologically rather than physically oriented"[5] and inherently involves "compulsion."[6] In the absence of protective devices, therefore, "no statement obtained from the defendant [in this context] can truly be the product of free choice."[7]

To provide the protective devices necessary to protect the privilege in the custodial interrogation context, the Court developed what have come to be characterized as per se or "prophylactic" rules. These are requirements designed to assure that specific decisions are legally acceptable but which, for protective purposes, apply even to situations where on the facts the suspects' decisions may not have fallen below standards imposed by the law. A confession obtained in violation of these requirements must, as a matter of Fifth Amendment law, be excluded from evidence even if application of voluntariness standards to the particular facts of the case would not lead to a finding that the confession was involuntary.[8]

Although this has been somewhat overshadowed by later developments, it is clear that the *Miranda* Court regarded the major source of protection for those undergoing custodial inter-

---

overrule *Miranda* in 2000. Dickerson v. U.S., 530 U.S. 428, 443–44, 120 S. Ct. 2326, 147 L. Ed. 2d 405 (2000) (declining to overrule *Miranda* "[w]hether or not we would agree with *Miranda's* reasoning and its resulting rule, were we addressing the issue in the first instance").

[3]Miranda, 384 U.S. at 461.

[4]384 U.S. at 467.

[5]384 U.S. at 448.

[6]384 U.S. at 458.

[7]384 U.S. at 458.

[8]Dickerson, 530 U.S. at 442 (Congressional statutory directive that compliance with *Miranda* requirements is to be treated only as a factor in determining whether a confession is voluntary and hence admissible is constitutionally ineffective).

rogation to be the right to an attorney. The suspect's Fifth Amendment interests, reasoned the majority, can only be protected by affording the suspect an attendant right to counsel.[9] This means not simply the right to consult with counsel before questioning, "but also to have counsel present during any interrogation . . . ."[10] Counsel must be available regardless of the financial ability of the suspect. Consequently, an attorney must be provided at public expense for those indigent defendants who wish the assistance of counsel.[11]

The most well-known *Miranda* requirement is that of warnings. While "no talismanic incantation" of the language used in the opinion is necessary,[12] officers must give the suspect essentially the following admonitions:

1. You have the right to remain silent;
2. Anything you say can [and will] be used against you in court;
3. You have the right to consult with a lawyer and to have the lawyer with you during interrogation; and
4. If you cannot afford an attorney, one will be appointed for you prior to any questioning if you so desire.

The first three elements are "absolute prerequisite[s]" to acceptable custodial interrogation. Failure to give even one of them cannot be "cured" by evidence that the suspect was already aware of the substance of the omitted warning[s].[13] Omission of the fourth element, on the other hand, is not fatal if the suspect was known to already have an attorney or to have ample funds to secure one. If, however, there is any doubt as to the applicability of the fourth element, this will be resolved against the prosecution.[14] The warnings must be given prior to any interrogation.[15]

Neither the right to remain silent nor its attendant right to counsel during interrogation is mandatory. Both are subject to waiver. In all cases where the prosecution offers at trial a self-incriminating statement made during custodial interrogation, it must show a voluntary and intelligent waiver of the privilege against self-incrimination itself, that is, the right to silence. If the statement was made during interrogation at which no lawyer

---

[9]Miranda, 384 U.S. at 469 (right to counsel "is indispensable to the protection of the Fifth Amendment privilege under the system we delineate today").

[10]384 U.S. at 470.

[11]384 U.S. at 472–73.

[12]California v. Prysock, 453 U.S.

355, 359, 101 S. Ct. 2806, 69 L. Ed. 2d 696 (1981).

[13]Miranda, 384 U.S. at 471–72.

[14]384 U.S. at 473 n. 43.

[15]384 U.S. at 467–68 (if person in custody is to be interrogated, the person must "first" be provided warnings).

was present on the suspect's behalf, the prosecution must also show an effective waiver of the right to counsel.

*Miranda* waivers need not be "express," the Court reaffirmed in *North Carolina v. Butler*.[16] Obviously, evidence that the suspect specifically articulated that she was aware of the right and was choosing not to exercise it constitutes strong, but not necessary, evidence of waiver. At the other extreme, *Miranda* itself expressly stated that waivers would not be presumed from a suspect's silence after the warnings or from the fact that the suspect eventually provided a confession.[17] The showing required of the fact of waiver, and the possible need under some circumstances to assert the *Miranda* rights, are addressed more fully in Section 152; the voluntariness and intelligence required is considered in Section 153.

Special problems are presented if officers interrogate a suspect in violation of *Miranda*, they then comply with *Miranda* and again interrogate the suspect, and the prosecution offers only incriminating admissions made after compliance. A split majority of the Court in *Missouri v. Seibert*[18] addressed these situations. Seven years later a unanimous Court applied *Seibert* in *Bobby v. Dixon*.[19]

In *Seibert* itself, the first interrogation was quite productive and Seibert gave a quite complete confession which she repeated after the interrogating officer complied with *Miranda*.[20] Further, the testimony indicated that the officer had been trained to do this for the explicit purpose of obtaining incriminating admissions in disregard of *Miranda*, then complying with *Miranda*, and finally soliciting admissions after this compliance on the assumption that the later admissions could be used in evidence. *Seibert* clearly disapproved of this activity, but the majority split on the rationale.

---

[16]North Carolina v. Butler, 441 U.S. 369, 99 S. Ct. 1755, 60 L. Ed. 2d 286 (1979) (state court erred in applying a per se rule requiring an express waiver).

[17]Miranda, 384 U.S. at 475.

Once an effective waiver is found, further problems may be presented by the need to define its scope. A waiver apparently extends to whatever a reasonable person in the situation would anticipate. *See* Wyrick v. Fields, 459 U.S. 42, 47, 103 S. Ct. 394, 74 L. Ed. 2d 214 (1982) (per curiam) (waiver of counsel for purposes of polygraph examination included waiver for purposes of post-examination inter-

rogation, because "it would have been unreasonable for Fields and his attorneys to assume that Fields would not be informed of the polygraph readings and asked to explain any unfavorable result").

[18]Missouri v. Seibert, 542 U.S. 600, 124 S. Ct. 2601, 159 L. Ed. 2d 643 (2004).

[19]Bobby v. Dixon, 132 S. Ct. 26, 181 L. Ed. 2d 328 (2011) (per curiam).

[20]The issue developed because of the general rule that an admission is not rendered inadmissible simply because it was the "fruit" of an earlier admission obtained in violation of *Miranda*. See generally § 159 infra.

The *Seibert* plurality reasoned that the key consideration was whether the *Miranda* warnings could be effective in this context involving a single coordinated and continuing interrogation. The warnings could not be effective, the plurality concluded, because a warned suspect led through questions the suspect answered shortly before is unlikely to understand the warning as giving the suspect a meaningful right to remain silent during the latter part of the interrogation.[21] The officer's subjective intention is apparently relevant but it is not the focus of the analysis.[22] Justice Kennedy, the fifth member of the *Seibert* majority, found controlling the officer's deliberate use of a two-step strategy to undermine the *Miranda* requirements. Where an officer acts with such an intention, the postwarning admissions should be inadmissible unless the officer has taken effective curative measures before those admissions were elicited.[23]

*Dixon*, an unsigned opinion, found *Seibert* inapplicable to the facts before the Court with no discussion of the effect of the split Court in *Seibert*. *Dixon* stressed that the prewarning statement did not admit involvement in the murder at issue and police did not use that statement to elicit the postwarning confession to the murder. Moreover, four hours passed and circumstances dramatically changed between the two interrogation sessions. Thus "Dixon received *Miranda* warnings before confessing to [the] murder [and] the effectiveness of those warnings was not impaired by the sort of 'two-step interrogation technique' condemned in *Seibert* . . . ."[24]

Despite the rigor with which the *Miranda* Court fashioned per se Fifth Amendment requirements out of the very general language of the constitutional provision, post-*Miranda* decisions have shown no inclination to continue this approach by developing more such requirements.[25] This was made obvious in *Moran v. Burbine*,[26] rejecting a per se rule requiring police to inform a suspect of an attorney's efforts to reach him. The Court acknowledged that such a rule "might add marginally to *Miranda's* goal of dispelling the compulsion inherent in custodial interrogation." "[O]verriding practical considerations," however, argued against such a rule. The complexity that would accompany any such rule

---

[21]Siebert, 542 U.S. at 612–14.

[22]542 U.S. at 616.

[23]542 U.S. at 620–21 (Kennedy J., concurring in the judgment).

[24]Dixon, 132 S.Ct. at 32.

[25]The one exception is the strict prohibition against approaching a suspect who invokes the right to counsel. See § 152 infra.

[26]Moran v. Burbine, 475 U.S. 412, 106 S. Ct. 1135, 89 L. Ed. 2d 410 (1986).

would decrease *Miranda's* clarity and ease of application.[27] Further, such a requirement would cause some suspects to decline to make voluntary but self-incriminating statements and thus "work a substantial and . . . inappropriate shift in the subtle balance struck in [*Miranda*]."[28]

State courts are, of course, free to read state constitutional self-incrimination provisions as imposing the same requirements which *Miranda* found in the Fifth Amendment privilege. Such action would seem to be a prerequisite to state law holdings that state law imposes more stringent versions of specific *Miranda* requirements than are demanded by Supreme Court case law. A few state courts have explicitly embraced a version of the *Miranda* requirements as independently required by their state constitutions.[29]

## § 151 Self-incrimination (*Miranda*) requirements: (b) Applicability of *Miranda*; "custody," "interrogation," and exceptions

*Miranda v. Arizona*[1] applies only if a suspect is in "custody" and is "interrogated." Only if both of these prerequisites exist does a situation present the extreme risks to the suspect's privilege against compelled self-incrimination that justifies the extraordinary protection afforded by the *Miranda* requirements.[2] Each of these terms has become something of a term of art, and their definitions are considered in this section. In addition, the Supreme Court has recognized several exceptional situations in which, despite the existence of both custody and interrogation, either the extreme risks with which *Miranda* is concerned are lacking or those risks are outweighed by countervailing considerations. These exceptions are also addressed here.

*Custody.* Custody is not limited to "stationhouse custody," but

---

[27]Burbine, 475 U.S. at 425.

[28]475 U.S. at 426.

[29]*See* Traylor v. State, 596 So. 2d 957, 965–66 (Fla. 1992) ("[b]ased on [the history of voluntariness under Florida law] and the experience under *Miranda* and its progeny, we hold that to ensure the voluntariness of confessions, the Self-Incrimination Clause of Article I, Section 9, Florida Constitution, [imposes the same requirements as *Miranda*]"). *Accord* State v. Barrett, 205 Conn. 437, 534 A.2d 219, 225 (1987); State v. Santiago, 53 Haw. 254, 492 P.2d 657, 665 (1971); State v.

Vondehn, 348 Or. 462, 236 P.3d 691, 699 (2010); State v. Brunelle, 148 Vt. 347, 534 A.2d 198, 204 n.11 (1987).

**[Section 151]**

[1]Miranda v. Arizona, 384 U.S. 436, 86 S. Ct. 1602, 16 L. Ed. 2d 694 (1966).

[2]Oregon v. Mathiason, 429 U.S. 492, 495, 97 S. Ct. 711, 50 L. Ed. 2d 714 (1977) (per curiam) (lower court erred in applying *Miranda* because interrogation took place in a "coercive environment" where suspect was not in custody).

can occur in a suspect's own home.[3] It does not require that the officers' purpose in detaining the suspect relate to the offense which is the subject of the interrogation.[4] On the other hand, not every deprivation of a suspect's liberty constitutes custody.

Custody exists only if the circumstances are such as would cause a reasonable person to perceive that his freedom has been curtailed to a degree associated with a formal arrest. This depends on the objective circumstances of the situation, not on the subjective views of the officer or the suspect.[5]

If an officer makes a formal arrest by explicitly informing the suspect that an arrest has been made, of course, this constitutes custody.[6] In addition, however, a suspect is in custody despite the lack of a formal arrest if the officer detaining the suspect treats the suspect in a manner that a reasonable person would regard as involving an arrest "for practical purposes." Relevant considerations include the length of the detention, any express or implied communication by the officer of the officer's intent to arrest the suspect, and the length, vigor, and subject of questioning and other investigatory efforts by the officer.[7]

Under this approach, a person detained for brief field investigation under what is often called a *Terry* stop is usually not in custody. A motorist subjected to a "traffic stop"—a detention that a reasonable person would perceive as involving issuance of a citation and release—is similarly not in custody.[8]

*Interrogation.* The meaning of interrogation was addressed in *Rhode Island v. Innis,*[9] refusing to limit *Miranda* to situations involving "express interrogation:"

> [T]he term "interrogation" under *Miranda* refers not only to express questioning, but also to any words or actions on the part of the police (other than those normally attendant to arrest and custody) that the police should know are reasonably likely to elicit an incriminating response from the suspect.[10]

Whether law enforcement conduct is the "functional equivalent" of express questioning focuses primarily upon the perspec-

---

[3]Orozco v. Texas, 394 U.S. 324, 89 S. Ct. 1095, 22 L. Ed. 2d 311 (1969) (*Miranda* applied to questioning of a suspect in his own bedroom, where officers had entered and surrounded the bed in which he was lying).

[4]Mathis v. U.S., 391 U.S. 1, 88 S. Ct. 1503, 20 L. Ed. 2d 381 (1968).

[5]Stansbury v. California, 511 U.S. 318, 323, 114 S. Ct. 1526, 128 L. Ed. 2d 293 (1994) (per curiam).

[6]Berkemer v. McCarty, 468 U.S. 420, 435, 104 S. Ct. 3138, 82 L. Ed. 2d 317 (1984) (formal arrest for even minor offense constitutes custody).

[7]Berkemer, 468 U.S. at 435.

[8]Howes v. Fields, 132 S. Ct. 1181, 182 L. Ed. 2d 17 (2012)

[9]Rhode Island v. Innis, 446 U.S. 291, 100 S. Ct. 1682, 64 L. Ed. 2d 297 (1980).

[10]Innis, 446 U.S. at 301.

tive of the suspect. Evidence that the words or conduct at issue were intended by the officer to elicit self-incriminating admissions from the suspect does not itself establish that interrogation took place. It may, however, tend to show that the officer knew or should have known that the words or conduct were sufficiently likely to elicit the desired response.[11]

Applying the *Innis* standard, the Court has been quite reluctant to characterize situations as involving the functional equivalent of express questioning. *Innis* itself illustrates this approach. A comment by one officer to another—"God forbid one of [the neighborhood's impaired children] might find a weapon . . . and . . . hurt themselves."—in a suspect's presence was held in *Innis* not to constitute interrogation; the facts did not establish that the officers should have been aware that their comments would move the suspect to make a self-incriminating admission as to the location of a gun he had hidden in the area.[12] Permitting a suspect's wife to talk to a suspect arrested for the murder of the couple's young son was similarly held not to constitute interrogation.[13]

Even express questions put to a suspect may not constitute interrogation, if—given the other purposes of the questioning—the risk of those questions eliciting a self-incriminating response is minimal. Police inquiry of a suspect whether he would submit to a blood alcohol test, for example, does not constitute "interrogation."[14] No interrogation took place when an officer explained to a suspect how a breathalyzer examination worked, the legal aspects of the applicable Implied Consent Law and then inquired whether he understood and will be willing to submit to the test.[15] Nor was there interrogation when, during a videotaping, an officer instructed the suspect how he was to perform physical sobriety tests and inquired whether the suspect understood the instructions.[16]

*Exceptions to Miranda Requirements. Miranda* does not apply to some situations involving both custody and interrogation as those are defined under the Court's case law.

---

[11]446 U.S. at 301 n. 7.

[12]446 U.S. at 302–03.

[13]Arizona v. Mauro, 481 U.S. 520, 107 S. Ct. 1931, 95 L. Ed. 2d 458 (1987).

[14]South Dakota v. Neville, 459 U.S. 553, 564 n.15, 103 S. Ct. 916, 74 L. Ed. 2d 748 (1983).

[15]Pennsylvania v. Muniz, 496 U.S. 582, 603, 110 S. Ct. 2638, 110 L. Ed. 2d 528 (1990).

[16]Muniz, 496 U.S. at 604.

If the questioning is done by an officer functioning in an undercover capacity, the Court held in *Illinois v. Perkins*,[17] *Miranda* has no application. Where a suspect is unaware that he is conversing with his captors, the majority reasoned, the situation does not present the interaction between custody and interrogation creating the risk of coercion that justifies the extraordinary *Miranda* protections.[18] *Miranda* also does not apply, the Court held in *New York v. Quarles*,[19] in certain situations in which police inquiries are supported by particularly pressing concerns for public safety. Where compliance with *Miranda's* mandates would create an immediate and high risk to public safety, the costs are excessive.[20]

A plurality of the Court in *Pennsylvania v. Muniz*[21] recognized another exception for "routine booking questions" asked during the processing of an arrested suspect.[22] This exception, which is almost certain to be accepted by a majority of the Court, covers questions designed to elicit biographical data necessary to complete the booking process and to provide pretrial services. Thus in *Muniz*, *Miranda* was regarded by the plurality as inapplicable to questions concerning Muniz's name, address, height, weight, eye color, date of birth, and current age.

### § 152 Self-incrimination (*Miranda*) requirements: (c) Prohibition against interrogation

Under certain—and limited—circumstances, *Miranda v. Arizona*[1] gives a person undergoing custodial interrogation a right not to be interrogated at all. Essentially, the right is one to be free of efforts by officers to persuade the defendant to make a self-incriminating admission or otherwise give up the right to remain silent. In these situations, the risk of any admission being involuntary is sufficient to justify barring all efforts to elicit such an admission.

As an initial matter, interrogation of a suspect in custody is barred until the person has been adequately warned and has waived one or more rights. The case law, however, initially focused on situations in which defendants affirmatively asserted their rights.

---

[17]Illinois v. Perkins, 496 U.S. 292, 110 S. Ct. 2394, 110 L. Ed. 2d 243 (1990).

[18]Perkins, 496 U.S. at 297.

[19]New York v. Quarles, 467 U.S. 649, 104 S. Ct. 2626, 81 L. Ed. 2d 550 (1984).

[20]Quarles, 467 U.S. at 657–58.

[21]Pennsylvania v. Muniz, 496 U.S. 582, 110 S. Ct. 2638, 110 L. Ed. 2d 528 (1990).

[22]Muniz, 496 U.S. at 601–02 (plurality portion of opinion by Brennan, J.).

**[Section 152]**

[1]Miranda v. Arizona, 384 U.S. 436, 86 S. Ct. 1602, 16 L. Ed. 2d 694 (1966).

*Edwards Rule and Reassertion of Waived Right to Counsel.* A suspect who has initially waived counsel may, of course, change his mind. If the suspect during permissible interrogation indicates "in any manner" that the suspect now wishes to have the assistance of counsel, interrogation must cease until counsel is present.[2]

In *Edwards v. Arizona*[3] the Supreme Court held that a suspect who had affirmatively invoked his right to counsel could not be further approached by officers until a lawyer was present,[4] even if that approach did not consist of efforts to persuade him to waive his right but only an inquiry regarding his continued unwillingness to do so. Under *Edwards*, police-initiated inquiries regarding possible admissions or questioning are barred until a lawyer is present. *Arizona v. Roberson*[5] made clear that a reapproach is impermissible even if it concerns a different offense than that under actual or possible discussion when the suspect invoked his right to counsel. The unacceptable risk that an officer's eagerness to secure the suspect's waiver will result in an involuntary waiver is not eliminated because the reapproach is for a different offense.[6]

After a suspect has initially waived the right to counsel, *Davis v. United States*[7] held, *Edwards* is triggered only by a clear and unambiguous request for counsel. A suspect's words are sufficiently clear under *Davis* only if a reasonable officer hearing them would, given the circumstances, understand them to be a request for the assistance of counsel. An ambiguous or equivocal reference to counsel that a reasonable officer would at most construe as indicating that the suspect might be invoking the right to counsel—such as Davis' statement, "Maybe I should talk to a lawyer."—is of no legal significance. Stressing the need for bright lines to guide officers, *Davis* rejected the argument that an ambiguous or equivocal reference to counsel, although not triggering *Edwards'* total bar to reapproaching the suspect, should require officers to limit further inquiries of the suspect to

---

[2]Miranda, 384 U.S. at 473–74.

[3]Edwards v. Arizona, 451 U.S. 477, 101 S. Ct. 1880, 68 L. Ed. 2d 378 (1981).

[4]That the suspect consulted with counsel does not permit officers to reapproach the suspect after counsel has left; counsel must be present. Minnick v. Mississippi, 498 U.S. 146, 153–55, 111 S. Ct. 486, 112 L. Ed. 2d 489 (1990).

[5]Arizona v. Roberson, 486 U.S. 675, 108 S. Ct. 2093, 100 L. Ed. 2d 704 (1988).

[6]Invoking the right to counsel by a suspect not in custody, however, does not raise a bar to approaching that suspect later when the suspect is taken into custody. Bobby v. Dixon, 132 S. Ct. 26, 29, 181 L. Ed. 2d 328 (2011).

[7]Davis v. U.S., 512 U.S. 452, 114 S. Ct. 2350, 129 L. Ed. 2d 362 (1994).

ascertaining whether in fact the suspect does desire to invoke his right to assistance of counsel.[8]

A suspect's request for counsel may be sufficiently limited that continued questioning of some sort does not violate *Edwards*. In *Connecticut v. Barrett*,[9] for example, Barrett made clear to officers that he would not give a written statement until his lawyer was present, but that he had "no problem" in talking orally with the officers about the incident. This, the Supreme Court held, invoked Barrett's right to counsel only with regard to interrogation designed to produce a written statement. Thus *Edwards* did not bar further interrogation reasonably designed only to elicit an oral statement.[10]

*Edwards* prohibits only a reapproach by police. If the suspect—without being so reapproached—takes action that demonstrates a desire on the suspect's part for further generalized discussion about the investigation, the *Edwards* bar to further interrogation disappears.[11] In *Oregon v. Bradshaw*,[12] a plurality indicated that the suspect's question—"Well, what is going to happen to me now?"—made while he was being transferred from the station-house to jail could have been reasonably interpreted by the officer as evidencing the suspect's desire to open up further discussion concerning the investigation.[13] Although the suspect had previously invoked his right to counsel, police acceptably again warned him of his rights and, when he waived the right to counsel, interrogated him.

A significant change in circumstances may end an *Edwards* prohibition against reapproaching the suspect. This occurs, under *Maryland v. Shatzer*[14] if the suspect is released from custody, remains at liberty for at least fourteen days and is then rearrested. This period of liberty eliminates the coercive impact

---

[8]Davis, 512 U.S. at 462 ("If the suspect's statement is not an ambiguous or unequivocal request for counsel, the officers have no obligation to stop questioning him.").

[9]Connecticut v. Barrett, 479 U.S. 523, 107 S. Ct. 828, 93 L. Ed. 2d 920 (1987).

[10]Barrett, 479 U.S. at 529–30.

[11]Oregon v. Bradshaw, 462 U.S. 1039, 1045, 103 S. Ct. 2830, 77 L. Ed. 2d 405 (1983) (plurality opinion) (inquiry is insufficient if it "cannot fairly be said to represent a desire on the

part of the accused to open up a more generalized discussion relating directly or indirectly to the investigation), 1055 (Marshall, J., dissenting) ("an accused's inquiry must demonstrate a desire to discuss the subject matter of the criminal investigation").

[12]Oregon v. Bradshaw, 462 U.S. 1039, 103 S. Ct. 2830, 77 L. Ed. 2d 405 (1983).

[13]Bradshaw, 462 U.S. at 1045–46.

[14]Maryland v. Shatzer, 559 U.S. 98, 130 S. Ct. 1213, 175 L. Ed. 2d 1045 (2010).

of the initial custody and thus the need for the extraordinary
protection afforded by the *Edwards'* bar to reapproach.[15]

*Invoking the Right to Silence. Edwards'* bar to reapproaching a
suspect does not apply to a suspect who invokes the right to
remain silent but not the *Miranda* right to counsel. A suspect
who—for example, asserts, "I have nothing to say."—is not, under
*Michigan v. Mosley,*[16] protected by a per se or total prohibition
against reapproach. Interrogation must cease for the moment,[17]
but officer may later reapproach the suspect. If after reapproach
the suspect waives his rights, however, the situation may require
an unusually effective demonstration that the waiver was
voluntary.[18]

The *Davis* requirement that an invocation of a *Miranda* right
be unambiguous and unequivocal, under *Berghuis v. Thompkins,*[19]
applies to invocations of the right to remain silent as well as to
the right to counsel.[20]

If counsel is in fact present, *Miranda* itself suggested there
"may be some circumstances in which further questioning would
be permissible" although the suspect indicated he wished to
remain silent. The fact that the interrogation was over objection,
of course, would be a circumstance tending to show that any
admissions ultimately made were involuntary and hence
inadmissible.[21]

*Waiver Compared to Invocation of Miranda Rights. Miranda*
itself suggested that no custodial interrogation could occur unless
and until the suspect was warned and both (a) had counsel present or effectively waived the right to counsel; and (b) had effectively waived the right to remain silent. Waiver could be

---

[15]Shatzer, 130 S.Ct. at 1223.

[16]Michigan v. Mosley, 423 U.S.
96, 96 S. Ct. 321, 46 L. Ed. 2d 313
(1975). *See* Edwards v. Arizona, 451
U.S. 477, 485, 101 S. Ct. 1880, 68 L.
Ed. 2d 378 (1981) (*Mosley* noted *Miranda's* distinction between the effect
of requesting counsel and that of "a
request to remain silent").

[17]Mosley, 423 U.S. at 103 (police
must " 'scrupulously hono[r]' this 'critical safeguard' when the accused invokes his or her 'right to cut off questioning' ") (quoting *Miranda,* 384 U.S.
at 474, 479).

[18]§ 153 infra.

[19]Berghuis v. Thompkins, 130 S.
Ct. 2250, 176 L. Ed. 2d 1098 (2010).

[20]Thompkins, 130 S.Ct. at 2260
("there is no principled reason to adopt
different standards for determining
when an accused has invoked the *Miranda* right to remain silent and the
*Miranda* right to counsel"). *Compare*
Com. v. Clarke, 461 Mass. 336, 960
N.E.2d 306, 320 (2012) (rejecting this
approach as a matter of state law
because it unacceptably "permits police to continue questioning a person
in custody who has never waived his
right to remain silent until such time
as that person articulates with utmost
clarity his desire to remain silent").

[21]Miranda, 384 U.S. at 474 n. 44.

implied rather than express.[22] Do the requirements of unambiguous and unequivocal assertions of rights apply only after the rights have been initially waived and during interrogation the suspect seeks to undo those waivers?

This was considered in *Thompkins*, addressing whether the prosecution showed the required initial waiver of the right to silence. The Court acknowledged that *Miranda* itself suggested even an implied waiver must be in some sense "specifically made," but it added the Court had retreated from that position.[23] Further, "the law can presume that an individual who, with a full understanding of his or her rights, acts in a manner inconsistent with their exercise has made a deliberate choice to relinquish the protection those rights afford . . . ." As a result:

> Where the prosecution shows that a *Miranda* warning was given and that it was understood by the accused, an accused's uncoerced statement establishes an implied waiver of the right to remain silent.[24]

*Thompkins* involved only the right to silence and not the right to counsel. Much of the Court's language was broad and general and the Court's rationale would seem to apply to the right to counsel as well.

Under *Thompkins*, officers who have warned a suspect and laid the basis for a finding the suspect understood the right to counsel and—to some extent—to avoid interrogation need not also elicit an affirmative answer to questions such as, "And are you willing to talk with us?" Instead, they may simply begin interrogation.

This comes close to requiring as an initial matter that a suspect wishing after being warned to rely on the *Miranda* rights to invoke them and to do so with the clarity demanded by *Davis*.

State courts need not, of course, follow *Thompkins* in developing state law. The Supreme Judicial Court of Massachusetts rejected the *Thompkins* approach as inappropriately placing on a defendant who has made an uncoerced admission the burden of proving he did not effectively waive his interrogation rights.[25]

*Anticipatory Assertions of the Rights.* Can a suspect bar officers from approaching the suspect by anticipatorily asserting that the suspect wishes the presence of counsel at any interrogation? In *Montejo v. Louisiana*,[26] the Court strongly suggested this could not be done.

---

[22]See § 150 supra.

[23]Thompkins, 130 S.Ct. at 2261.

[24]130 S.Ct. at 2261.

[25]Com. v. Clarke, 461 Mass. 336, 960 N.E.2d 306, 320 n.12 (2012).

[26]Montejo v. Louisiana, 556 U.S. 778, 129 S. Ct. 2079, 173 L. Ed. 2d 955 (2009).

Courts need not struggle with whether defendants' statements at preliminary court appearances constitute invocations of the *Miranda* right to counsel at interrogations, *Montejo* reasoned, because the *Miranda* rights cannot be invoked in this manner. "What matters," the Court explained, "is what happens when the defendant is approached for interrogation, and (if he consents) what happens during the interrogation—not what happened at any preliminary hearing."[27]

If the *Miranda* rights cannot be anticipatorily invoked during a court appearance, they certainly cannot be anticipatorily invoked during law enforcement custody that proceeds an approach for interrogation.[28]

## § 153 Self-incrimination (*Miranda*) requirements: (d) Effectiveness of waivers; voluntariness and intelligence

The Fifth Amendment as construed in *Miranda v. Arizona*[1] requires for admission of a self-incriminating statement that the prosecution show that the making of the statement itself was an effective waiver of the right to remain silent and, unless a lawyer were present, that before and during the interrogation the person waived the right to assistance of counsel. To be effective, waivers must be both "voluntary" and "intelligent.

The requirement that waivers of self-incrimination rights during custodial interrogation be "intelligent" is separate and distinct from the demand that such waivers be "voluntary."[2] As best defined, the demand that the waivers be intelligent addresses the information of which a suspect must have actually been aware for the suspect's decision to be effective. The requirement that the waivers be "voluntary," on the other hand, requires that the suspect's decision have been free of unacceptable influences.

The basic question is whether the standards for determining the effectiveness of such waivers are stricter than those imposed

---

[27]Montejo, 556 U.S. at 797.

[28]*Cf.* Bobby v. Dixon, 132 S. Ct. 26, 29, 181 L. Ed. 2d 328 (2011) ("this Court has 'never held that a person can invoke his *Miranda* rights anticipatorily, in a context other than "custodial interrogation" ' ") (quoting McNeil v. Wisconsin, 501 U.S. 171, 182 n.3, 111 S. Ct. 2204, 115 L. Ed. 2d

158 (1991)).

**[Section 153]**

[1]Miranda v. Arizona, 384 U.S. 436, 86 S. Ct. 1602, 16 L. Ed. 2d 694 (1966).

[2]Edwards v. Arizona, 451 U.S. 477, 482–483, 101 S. Ct. 1880, 68 L. Ed. 2d 378 (1981).

by the due process requirements of voluntariness.[3] The fact of custodial interrogation argues for stricter standards than are embodied in due process voluntariness, since suspects' interests are placed at greater risk by custodial interrogation than they are under in those situations to which only the more general due process standard applies. Correspondingly appropriate protection might best be afforded by imposing stricter requirements for determining the acceptability of suspects' decisions to provide the prosecution with evidence or with access to them for questioning without the protection of counsel.

On the other hand, suspects protected by the privilege against self-incrimination as construed in *Miranda* will have been provided warnings, and they are protected against interrogation until they waive their right to counsel. Perhaps these aspects of self-incrimination law provide adequate protection against the increased threat generated by custodial interrogation. Stricter standards for voluntariness, then, may be unnecessary. Moreover, given the difficulty of articulating useful standards in this area, courts may be unable to distinguish meaningfully between two standards, one applicable to custodial interrogation situations and another applicable to other situations.

In fact, the Supreme Court has made clear, voluntariness in *Miranda* waiver law is generally the same as in the due process standard. "There is obviously no reason," the Court commented in *Colorado v. Connelly*,[4] "to require more in the way of a 'voluntariness' inquiry in the *Miranda* waiver context than in the Fourteenth Amendment confession context."[5] No notice was taken of arguments that such reasons exist, no authority was cited, and no discussion was provided.

*Voluntariness. Connelly* held specifically that a waiver of *Miranda* rights, like a decision to confess under due process voluntariness, need not constitute an exercise of "free will" or "free choice" by the suspect. "Voluntariness" as is required for a *Miranda* waiver is only put into question if the facts show official coercion or overreaching and, as a result, the decision was not voluntary in the more ordinary sense of that term.

The prosecution's burden of showing *Miranda* voluntariness is especially heavy if the suspect was reapproached after earlier invoking his right to remain silent. Under *Michigan v. Mosley*,[6] the admissibility of any statements so obtained depends upon the effectiveness of that waiver, which in turn depends upon "whether

---

[3]See § 149 supra.

[4]Colorado v. Connelly, 479 U.S. 157, 107 S. Ct. 515, 93 L. Ed. 2d 473 (1986).

[5]Connelly, 479 U.S. at 169–70.

[6]Michigan v. Mosley, 423 U.S. 96, 96 S. Ct. 321, 46 L. Ed. 2d 313 (1975).

[the suspect's] 'right to cut off questioning' was 'scrupulously honored.' "[7] What constitutes sufficient respect for this right is not entirely clear.

Generally, the prosecution can meet its burden of proving at least a prima facie showing of voluntariness by eliciting from the interrogating officer that the suspect had not been threatened or promised anything, and appeared to freely decide for himself to forego the assistance of counsel and to provide an incriminating statement. If the defense introduces evidence suggesting official overreaching and a significant impact of that overreaching upon the suspect, of course, the prosecution may well have to respond with more detailed and persuasive evidence in order to meet its burden of persuasion.

*Intelligence.* "Intelligence," as used in *Miranda's* waiver criteria, involves only an understanding of the basic abstract Fifth Amendment rights of which a suspect must be informed: that there is a legal right to remain silent during custodial interrogation; that anything said can be used in evidence to convict her of a crime; that she is entitled to consult with a lawyer and to have a lawyer present during custodial interrogation; and that if she decides to speak to law enforcement officers she is entitled to discontinue such discussion at any time she wishes.[8] It is not necessary that she be aware of factual or legal matters bearing upon the wisdom of exercising any of those options. In fact, ignorance of any or all of those matters is totally irrelevant to the effectiveness of the waiver.[9]

Consequently, a defendant who has previously made an incriminating statement which is in fact inadmissible against her need not understand the inadmissibility of that statement in order to effectively waive her rights and again admit those same facts.[10] The Court has strongly hinted that a defendant who acknowledges participation in a robbery under circumstances that, unknown to her, create felony murder liability for a killing committed by a companion has made intelligent waivers of her rights despite ignorance as to the legal effect of the admissions.[11] A suspect's waiver of the right to counsel is not rendered ineffec-

---

[7]Mosley, 423 U.S. at 104.

[8]*See* Colorado v. Spring, 479 U.S. 564, 574, 107 S. Ct. 851, 93 L. Ed. 2d 954 (1987). *See also* Moran v. Burbine, 475 U.S. 412, 427, 106 S. Ct. 1135, 89 L. Ed. 2d 410 (1986) (*Miranda* holds that "full comprehension of the rights to remain silent and request an attorney" is sufficient to accomplish its purpose of dispelling coercion inherent in custodial interrogation).

[9]*See* Spring, 479 U.S. at 569–77 (defendant's awareness of subjects to be covered in interrogation "is not relevant" to determining the effectiveness of his waiver of Fifth Amendment rights).

[10]Oregon v. Elstad, 470 U.S. 298, 316–18, 105 S. Ct. 1285, 84 L. Ed. 2d 222 (1985).

[11]California v. Beheler, 463 U.S. 1121, 103 S. Ct. 3517, 77 L. Ed. 2d

tive by ignorance concerning the subjects about which the officers intended to question her if she waived counsel's help.[12] In *Moran v. Burbine*,[13] the Court held that a suspect's waiver of counsel was not rendered unintelligent by his unawareness that there was a specific attorney ready and willing to represent him during questioning if he wished representation.

In light of *Connelly*, which held that a *Miranda* waiver can be rendered involuntary only by official coercion, is official coercion also a prerequisite to consideration of the possibility that a *Miranda* waiver is insufficiently intelligent or knowing? The issue was not addressed in *Connelly* itself.[14] *Connelly's* general discussion, however, suggests that official misconduct is necessary. If the "voluntariness" of a waiver is put into issue only by a preliminary showing of official coercion, a similar showing would seem necessary to challenge the "intelligence" of that waiver. Thus *Connelly* apparently means that a trial court need not consider a defendant's claim that because of mental illness or retardation, intoxication or emotional distress she failed to actually understanding the warnings, unless the court first finds that official coercion occurred and played a causal role in this failure to develop the required understanding.

The Court's position that an intelligent waiver of *Miranda* rights requires at most only an abstract understanding of those legal matters covered in the *Miranda* warnings serves several purposes. First, it avoids the difficult task of determining and articulating what broader information would be required. Second, it eliminates what would sometimes be an impossible task for the prosecution. Officers in some situations would simply be unable to provide a suspect with sufficient information concerning a crime, their investigation of it, or the suspect's legal position to render any waivers effective. They would, then, be barred from productive interrogation of the suspect. A construction of *Miranda* that so limits officers can reasonably be viewed as exces-

---

1275 (1983) (per curiam), discussed with approval in the *Miranda* context in Elstad, 470 U.S. at 317.

[12]Colorado v. Spring, 479 U.S. 564, 574, 107 S. Ct. 851, 93 L. Ed. 2d 954 (1987).

[13]Moran v. Burbine, 475 U.S. 412, 106 S. Ct. 1135, 89 L. Ed. 2d 410 (1986).

[14]The evidence in *Connelly* was that Connelly's mental illness did not significantly impair his cognitive abilities. Connelly, 479 U.S. at 161. The Supreme Court addressed only "volun-

tariness" and not "intelligence." It acknowledged that the lower court decision could be read as finding Connelly's waiver invalid "on other grounds," but concluded that if this was the case the state court's analysis was influenced by its mistaken perception of constitutional "voluntariness" and required reconsideration. 479 U.S. at 171 n. 4. The dissenters expressed the view that the unidentified "other grounds" included lack of intelligence. 479 U.S. at 188 (Brennan, J., dissenting).

sively solicitous of those interests of suspects that the self-incrimination privilege properly protects.

On the other hand, this position arguably renders *Miranda* ineffective in assuring that suspects' confession decisions reflect what in ordinary terms are "meaningful" decisions. In many situations, awareness of the abstract law would for most persons be only a relatively minor consideration in deciding whether to invoke either or both the rights to representation or counsel.

Assuring that suspects' choices are meaningful in such a broad, tactical sense, however, is most likely beyond the purposes of the *Miranda* requirements. The exceptional risks to suspects' privilege caused by custodial interrogation that justify the *Miranda* requirements probably arise exclusively from potential improper influences on suspects' volition. Custodial interrogation may not pose similarly severe risks to suspects' access to factual information or their abilities to intellectually assimilate or use it. Since the *Miranda* requirements are imposed for reasons at most indirectly related to suspects' ability to make intellectually informed and reasoned decisions, waiver criteria are appropriately formulated so as to require relatively minimal intellectual understanding of facts useful in making "wise" decisions.

States, of course, remain free to construe state constitutional requirements differently and some have done so. Several, for example, have held that police failure to permit an attorney to consult with a client undergoing interrogation renders the client's waivers ineffective.[15]

## § 154   General right to counsel requirements

*Miranda v. Arizona*[1] and analogous state self-incrimination decisions recognize a right to counsel based upon the privilege against self-incrimination as it applies during custodial law enforcement interrogation. General constitutional rights to counsel, such as that in the Sixth Amendment, focus upon representation at trial, but they also apply to certain pretrial situations in which suspects may make self-incriminating admissions. Since an exclusionary sanction attaches to violations of these rights to counsel, failures to comply with them permit challenges to the admissibility of confessions. Two primary issues are presented: first, under what circumstances is a confessing suspect

---

[15]*See* Ajabu v. State, 693 N.E.2d 921, 934–35 (Ind. 1998) (summarizing the split among state courts and holding that refusing a lawyer's request to be present during interrogation did not invalidate the client's waivers).

**[Section 154]**

[1]Miranda v. Arizona, 384 U.S. 436, 86 S. Ct. 1602, 16 L. Ed. 2d 694 (1966).

protected by these general rights to counsel; and second, what protections are afforded a suspect by these provisions?

*Sixth Amendment Right to Counsel.* The Sixth Amendment applies if adversary judicial proceedings against the suspect have begun[2] and police attempt to deliberately elicit self-incriminating admissions from the suspect.[3] "Deliberate elicitation" of admissions probably differs minimally if at all from "interrogation" as defined in case law under *Miranda*.[4]

When adversary judicial proceedings begin is not entirely clear. Detention by the police or even formal arrest is not sufficient. On the other hand, a formal charge, as by the filing of an indictment, is clearly enough. It is not, however, required. In *Michigan v. Jackson*,[5] the Court held that an "arraignment", by which it apparently meant an arrested person's post-arrest appearance before a judicial officer, does trigger the Sixth Amendment right.[6] In most situations, this post-arrest appearance will be the definitive point.[7]

The Sixth Amendment right does not, generally speaking, protect a suspect from being approached in the absence of counsel by officers seeking to persuade him to provide a self-incriminating statement.[8] A suspect entitled to Sixth Amendment protection is apparently entitled to at least the same admonishments required by *Miranda*, although generally not more. The Court has left

---

[2]*See* Brewer v. Williams, 430 U.S. 387, 398, 97 S. Ct. 1232, 51 L. Ed. 2d 424 (1977). *See also* Moore v. Illinois, 434 U.S. 220, 98 S. Ct. 458, 54 L. Ed. 2d 424 (1977).

[3]*See* Kuhlmann v. Wilson, 477 U.S. 436, 457, 106 S. Ct. 2616, 91 L. Ed. 2d 364 (1986).

[4]*Cf.* Wilson, 477 U.S. at 459 ("the primary concern of the [Sixth Amendment] line of decisions is secret interrogation by investigatory techniques that are the equivalent of direct police interrogation"). *Compare* Fellers v. U.S., 540 U.S. 519, 524–25, 124 S. Ct. 1019, 157 L. Ed. 2d 1016 (2004) (despite finding that officers did not interrogate defendant, those officers clearly deliberately elicited information from defendant where they came to defendant's home, informed him that their purpose was to discuss defendant's involvement in drug activities, and engaged him in discussion).

[5]Michigan v. Jackson, 475 U.S.

625, 106 S. Ct. 1404, 89 L. Ed. 2d 631 (1986) (overruled on other grounds by, Montejo v. Louisiana, 556 U.S. 778, 129 S. Ct. 2079, 173 L. Ed. 2d 955 (2009)).

[6]Jackson, 475 U.S. at 629 n. 3. *Cf.* Williams, 430 U.S. at 399 (Sixth Amendment was triggered where arrest warrant had been issued, defendant had been arrested and "arraigned" on the warrant, and judge "committed" defendant to jail).

[7]The Sixth Amendment is triggered by the filing of a preliminary complaint and the defendant's appearance before a magistrate on that preliminary complaint. Rothgery v. Gillespie County, Tex., 554 U.S. 191, 128 S. Ct. 2578, 171 L. Ed. 2d 366 (2008) (prosecutorial involvement in deciding to file complaint not necessary).

[8]Patterson v. Illinois, 487 U.S. 285, 290–91, 108 S. Ct. 2389, 101 L. Ed. 2d 261 (1988).

open the possibility that a waiver of the Sixth Amendment right to counsel may require that the defendant be informed, or perhaps that the suspect know from some source, that the matter has progressed beyond general police investigation to adversary judicial proceedings.[9]

The Sixth Amendment embodies a version of the *Edwards* rule.[10] A suspect who invokes his Sixth Amendment right to counsel as it applies in the law enforcement interrogation context cannot be re-approached by officers.[11] But the Sixth Amendment right to counsel, unlike *Miranda's* right to representation, is "offense-specific." Therefore, a suspect who has by requesting counsel invoked his Sixth Amendment version of the *Edwards* rule may be approached by officers concerning other offenses as to which matters have not progressed sufficiently so as to give him a Sixth Amendment right to counsel as to those other offenses.[12]

The Sixth Amendment right to counsel during questioning, like the Fifth Amendment right, can be waived.[13] A waiver of the Sixth Amendment right must, of course, be both voluntary and

---

[9]*Cf.* Patterson, 487 U.S. at 293–94 (any possible Sixth requirement that suspect be made aware of the gravity of his situation was met when officer informed suspect that he had been indicted for the offense). *See* State v. Anson, 2002 WI App 270, 258 Wis. 2d 433, 654 N.W.2d 48, 54–55 (Ct. App. 2002), aff'd after review on other grounds 698 N.W.2d 776 (Wis.2005) (after Sixth Amendment attaches, suspect "must be made aware that the adversarial process has begun . . . by informing the accused that he or she has been formally charged with a crime, by reading to the accused the *Miranda* warnings, or by anything else that would inform the accused that the adversarial process has begun").

[10]See § 152 supra.

[11]Michigan v. Jackson, 475 U.S. 625, 632-33, 106 S. Ct. 1404, 89 L. Ed. 2d 631 (1986) (overruled by, Montejo v. Louisiana, 556 U.S. 778, 129 S. Ct. 2079, 173 L. Ed. 2d 955 (2009)), held the Sixth Amendment version of the *Edwards* rule was triggered by a general request for counsel made at "arraignment" or even acceptance at that point of representation by counsel. *Montejo* read *Jackson* as barring

police-initiated interrogation after the Sixth Amendment attaches of any suspect represented by counsel and overruled it as so construed. Montejo, 556 U.S. at 797. *Montejo* seems to establish that the Sixth Amendment right to counsel like the Fifth Amendment right cannot be invoked anticipatorily. See § 152 supra. It also suggests that—contrary to *Jackson*—invocation of the Sixth Amendment requires the suspect to unambiguously indicate he desires representation during interrogation.

[12]McNeil v. Wisconsin, 501 U.S. 171, 175–76, 111 S. Ct. 2204, 115 L. Ed. 2d 158 (1991) (suspect who invoked Sixth Amendment right to counsel during court appearance on robbery charge could be approached by officers seeking to question him about an unrelated robbery-murder as to which his Sixth Amendment rights had not yet attached).

[13]*Cf.* Brewer v. Williams, 430 U.S. 387, 405–06, 97 S. Ct. 1232, 51 L. Ed. 2d 424 (1977) (declining to hold that suspect could not waive his right to counsel but holding on facts that he did not do so).

intelligent.[14] The Supreme Court has rejected the arguments that "because a Sixth Amendment right may be involved, it is more difficult to waive than the Fifth Amendment counterpart."[15] Generally, then, a waiver of the Sixth Amendment right to counsel requires no more than an effective waiver of *Miranda* rights.[16]

Sixth Amendment protection differs—and exceeds—Fifth Amendment-*Miranda* protection in three primary ways. First, a suspect whose Sixth Amendment right has attached has a Sixth Amendment right to counsel if efforts are made to elicit a self-incriminating admission from the suspect by a police officer functioning in an undercover capacity or a private citizen acting under the direction of law enforcement officers without disclosing that purpose;[17] *Miranda* does not apply where the interrogator's official status is concealed from the suspect.[18]

Second, the Sixth Amendment right to counsel, unlike *Miranda*, does not require that the suspect be in "custody." Thus a suspect from whom an officer seeks to elicit a self-incriminating admission after the suspect had been released on post-indictment bail is protected by the Sixth Amendment right to counsel.[19]

Finally, if a suspect is in fact represented by counsel and the Sixth Amendment has attached, the Sixth Amendment protects the defendant-counsel relationship more rigorously than it is protected by the Fifth Amendment and *Miranda*. In *Moran v. Burbine*[20] the Supreme Court indicated that officers' interference with defense counsel's efforts to contact a client undergoing custodial interrogation, although not discovered by the client until later, would render the client's waiver of his right to counsel ineffective.[21] Officers' simple failure to inform such a client that defense counsel is attempting to contact the client would apparently have the same effect.[22]

Despite *Burbine's* emphasis on existing attorney-client relation-

---

[14]*See* Patterson v. Illinois, 487 U.S. 285, 292, 108 S. Ct. 2389, 101 L. Ed. 2d 261 (1988).

[15]Patterson, 487 U.S. at 297–98.

[16]As a general matter an:

accused who is admonished with the warnings prescribed by this Court in *Miranda* . . . has been sufficiently apprised of the nature of his Sixth Amendment rights, and of the consequences of abandoning those rights, so that his waiver on this basis will be considered an intelligent one.

487 U.S. at 296. *Accord* U.S. v. Hernandez, 281 F.3d 746, 748 (8th Cir. 2002).

[17]*Cf.* Illinois v. Perkins, 496 U.S. 292, 299–300, 110 S. Ct. 2394, 110 L. Ed. 2d 243 (1990).

[18]See § 151 supra.

[19]*E.g.,* State v. Anson, 2002 WI App 270, 258 Wis. 2d 433, 654 N.W.2d 48, 55 (Ct. App. 2002), aff'd after review on other grounds 698 N.W.2d 776 (Wis.2005).

[20]Moran v. Burbine, 475 U.S. 412, 106 S. Ct. 1135, 89 L. Ed. 2d 410 (1986).

[21]Burbine, 475 U.S. at 428.

[22]Patterson v. Illinois, 487 U.S. 285, 296 n.9, 108 S. Ct. 2389, 101 L.

ships, the Sixth Amendment does not mean that law enforcement officers are barred from approaching suspects simply because those suspects are represented.[23]

*State Constitutional Rights to Counsel.* State courts seeking to impose greater limits upon law enforcement questioning though their state constitutions have tended to rely upon explicit constitutional rights to counsel rather than rights derived from constitutional self-incrimination privileges. This has been the case even if so applying the state rights requires construing them as applicable earlier in the criminal process than the analogous Sixth Amendment right.

State courts' willingness to so apply state constitutional rights has been most common where officers have either or both interfered with counsel's access to a suspect undergoing interrogation or have failed to inform such a suspect of counsel's ready availability. The New York court has vigorously developed that state's right to counsel and held that under certain circumstances a suspect's right to counsel during questioning is "indelible," meaning that it can only be effectively waived in the presence of counsel.[24] The New Jersey court has applied the state's right to counsel to the period between the filing of a complaint (or issuance of an arrest warrant) and indictment. During that period, prosecutors or police can initiate conversations with defendants, but they must inform the defendants that a complaint has been filed or a warrant issued.[25]

## § 155   Special problems: Promises made to suspects[1] and deception of suspects[2]

Promises and deception, two types of circumstances at least relevant to the effectiveness of defendants' decisions to confess, have presented special difficulty. Courts have tended to draw no

---

Ed. 2d 261 (1988) (in the Sixth Amendment context, a waiver would not be valid "where a suspect was not told that his lawyer was trying to reach him").

[23]Montejo v. Louisiana, 556 U.S. 778, 797, 129 S. Ct. 2079, 173 L. Ed. 2d 955 (2009) (overruling Michigan v. Jackson, 475 U.S. 625, 106 S. Ct. 1404, 89 L. Ed. 2d 631 (1986), (insofar as *Jackson* held to the contrary).

[24]The seminal case is People v. Donovan, 13 N.Y.2d 148, 243 N.Y.S.2d 841, 193 N.E.2d 628 (1963). *See generally* People v. Grice, 100 N.Y.2d 318, 763 N.Y.S.2d 227, 794 N.E.2d 9 (2003) (police are barred from approaching a

suspect only if the suspect informs them the suspect is represented or there is direct communication of representation by the attorney or a professional associate of the attorney).

[25]State v. A.G.D., 178 N.J. 56, 835 A.2d 291, 297–98 (2003) (such information is indispensable to a knowing and intelligent waiver of rights).

**[Section 155]**

[1]*See generally* West's Key Number Digest, Criminal Law ☞411.53 to 411.55.

[2]*See generally* West's Key Number Digest, Criminal Law ☞411.59.

distinction between whether the matter at issue is the effectiveness of the defendant's waiver of a constitutional right to remain
silent or the right to counsel to protect the right to silence, on the
one hand,[3] or the more general voluntariness of the defendant's
statement[4] on the other.

*Promises.* Early voluntariness law placed particular emphasis
on "promises" of some benefit in the criminal prosecution as
among the influences rendering confessions inadmissible.[5] Modern voluntariness standards, self-incrimination demands, and
right to counsel requirements have incorporated at least some of
this early "promise law."

During the vigorous application of the voluntariness requirement in the early 1800s, what today would be regarded by most
courts as quite innocuous references to possible benefits were
regarded as per se tainting subsequent confessions.[6] *Bram v.
United States*[7] arguably incorporated such an approach into
federal due process voluntariness,[8] on the apparent ground that
suspects are particularly sensitive to such inducements and the
impact on particular defendants of particular promises is "too difficult to assess."[9]

But in *Arizona v. Fulminante*[10] the Supreme Court indicated
that this early language suggesting a rigid rule that promises
render a confession involuntary does not state the current standard for determining the federal constitutional voluntariness of a

---

[3]See § 153 supra (effectiveness of
Miranda v. Arizona, 384 U.S. 436, 86
S. Ct. 1602, 16 L. Ed. 2d 694 (1966)
waivers).

[4]See § 149 supra (voluntariness).

[5]Hopt v. People, 110 U.S. 574,
585, 4 S. Ct. 202, 28 L. Ed. 262 (1884)
(emphasizing "inducements of a temporal nature, held out by one in authority, touching on the charge preferred").

Benefits on matters collateral to
the charge and prosecution, in contrast, were and sometimes still are
treated as less significant. Pasuer v.
State, 271 Ga. App. 259, 609 S.E.2d
193, 196 (2005) (overruled on other
grounds by, Vergara v. State, 283 Ga.
175, 657 S.E.2d 863 (2008)) (any promise of a reduction in bond would be one
of a collateral benefit and would not
make otherwise admissible confession
involuntary).

[6]*See* Greenleaf, A Treatise on the
Law of Evidence § 219 (3rd ed. 1846).

[7]Bram v. U.S., 168 U.S. 532, 18
S. Ct. 183, 42 L. Ed. 568 (1897).

[8]Bram, 168 U.S. at 564–65
(statement to the accused that, "If you
had an accomplice, you should say so,
and not have the blame of this horrible
crime on your own shoulders," might
have been understood by the accused
as holding out the encouragement that
by disclosing his accomplice and
thereby acknowledging his own guilt
he might obtain mitigation of his
punishment, and therefore rendered
his confession involuntary).

[9]Brady v. U.S., 397 U.S. 742,
754, 90 S. Ct. 1463, 25 L. Ed. 2d 747
(1970).

[10]Arizona v. Fulminante, 499 U.S.
279, 111 S. Ct. 1246, 113 L. Ed. 2d 302
(1991).

confession.[11] Instead, the Court approved an approach under which the federal constitution requires no more than that courts consider promises as part of the totality of the circumstances when they determine the voluntariness of defendants' confessions.[12]

Some state courts have been reluctant to abandon traditional law's special concern for promises. They are, however, often unclear on whether they are defining requirements of state constitutional or evidence law as demanding more than federal constitutional law, or rather applying federal constitutional law with minimal significance given to *Fulminante*.[13]

Any theoretical remaining emphasis on promises is mitigated by an increasing willingness to define "promise" narrowly and perhaps artificially as limited to what purport on their faces to be guarantees of some benefit to be delivered if the suspect confesses.[14] What is often characterized as an exhortation to tell the truth,[15] a prediction that confessing will result in more lenient treatment,[16] or even an indication that in return for a confession an officer will "do what he can" or that "things will go easier" are

---

[11]Fulminante, 499 U.S. at 285.

[12]499 U.S. at 286–87 (approving analysis used by court below).

[13]*E.g.*, People v. Kellerman, 337 Ill. App. 3d 781, 272 Ill. Dec. 60, 786 N.E.2d 599, 605 (3d Dist. 2003), vacated on other grounds 789 N.E.2d 303 (Ill.2003) (proof that officer offered defendant three or four years imprisonment if he confessed to arsons made confession involuntary and inadmissible); State v. Thomas, 711 So. 2d 808, 811 (La. Ct. App. 2d Cir. 1998) ("promises or inducements will void a defendant's confession").

In contrast, the Maryland courts have made clear that they are applying that state's common law requirement of voluntariness. Knight v. State, 381 Md. 517, 850 A.2d 1179, 1183 (2004) ("A confession made in reliance on an improper promise of assistance by an interrogating officer or an agent of the police always will be deemed involuntary under Maryland nonconstitutional common law.").

[14]Pugliese v. Com., 16 Va. App. 82, 428 S.E.2d 16, 21 (1993) ("A 'promise' has been defined as 'an offer to perform or withhold some future ac-

tion within the control of the promisor.'").

[15]Rogers v. State, 289 Ga. 675, 715 S.E.2d 68, 71 (2011) (telling defendant "you are not trying to help yourself" did not make confession involuntary because exhortation to tell the truth and telling suspect that truthful cooperation may be considered by others is permissible); Thomas, 711 So.2d at 811 ("a mild exhortation to tell the truth, or an indication that if the defendant cooperates the officer will 'do what he can' or 'things will go easier,' will not negate the voluntary nature of a confession"). *Compare* State v. McCoy, 692 N.W.2d 6, 27–28 (Iowa 2005) (officer can tell a suspect that it is better to tell the truth, but if officer tells the suspect what advantage is to be gained or is likely from making a confession the officer's statement become a promise of leniency rendering a statement involuntary).

[16]State v. Evans, 2009-NMSC-027, 146 N.M. 319, 210 P.3d 216, 225 (2009) ("threats that merely highlight potential real consequences, or are 'adjurations to tell the truth,' are not characterized as impermissibly coercive' . . . It is not per se coercive for

held not to constitute promises within the meaning of a rule giving specific effect to promies.[17] One court was probably accurate when it commented that an "express promise" can itself render a confession inadmissible but evidence of an "implied promise" is simply one factor in a totality of the circumstances voluntariness analysis.[18]

Even if a prohibited promise is found, the evidence may not satisfactorily prove that the suspect relied upon it in deciding to confess.[19] If the defendant first raised the possibility of the benefit he authorities later promised, the promise is less likely to render the defendant's decision legally ineffective.[20] This is apparently on the ground that the defendant's initiative shows that the effect of the promise was not such as to impair the defendant's decisionmaking in the manner or degree necessary to render the confession involuntary.[21]

There is general agreement that a promise of complete im-

---

police to truthfully inform an accused about the potential consequences of his alleged actions."); Pugliese v. Com., 16 Va. App. 82, 428 S.E.2d 16, 21 (1993) ("A 'promise' does not . . . include 'a prediction about future events beyond the parties' control or regarded as inevitable.' ").

Thus an officer's statement to a suspect that that "he was interested in the truth, as were the courts, and that the courts were interested in whether suspects showed remorse or were cooperative" was held to contain "no explicit or implicit promise of possible leniency." State v. Nicklasson, 967 S.W.2d 596, 606 (Mo. 1998).

[17]State v. Thomas, 711 So. 2d 808, 811 (La. Ct. App. 2d Cir. 1998).

[18]State v. Gutierrez, 2011-NMSC-024, 150 N.M. 232, 258 P.3d 1024, 1036 (2011).

[19]Carney v. State, 249 P.3d 308, 312–13 (Alaska Ct. App. 2011) (promise not to arrest suspect did not render confession inadmissible, where suspect nevertheless expected to be arrested and did not rely on the promise); State v. Trostle, 191 Ariz. 4, 951 P.2d 869, 880 (1997) (detective's statement, "Help us out the best you can. That's all we ask. Be honest with us and help us out and it'll work out in the long run." did not induce his confession

where suspect did not confess until after other persistent questioning and did not otherwise react to the statement as if he believed it a promise); Knight v. State, 381 Md. 517, 850 A.2d 1179, 1189 (2004) (if an improper promise was made, statement is inadmissible only if there was a causal nexus between that promise and the statement).

[20]E.g., Baker v. State, 71 So. 3d 802, 815–16 (Fla. 2011), cert. denied, 132 S. Ct. 1639, 182 L. Ed. 2d 238 (2012) ("whether a deal that resulted in a confession was proposed by the defendant; is relevant to the voluntariness of the statement); Drew v. State, 503 N.E.2d 613, 617 (Ind. 1987) (reviewing cases). Accord Eakes v. State, 387 So. 2d 855, 860 (Ala. Crim. App. 1978) ("a confession is not rendered involuntary by a promise of a benefit that was solicited freely and voluntarily by the accused"); Jacobs v. State, 787 S.W.2d 397, 399 (Tex. Crim. App. 1990) (claim of promise would be evaluated in light of defendant's "role of dealmaker").

[21]Bivins v. State, 642 N.E.2d 928, 940 (Ind. 1994) (defendant's "specific request" for leniency subsequently promised showed the defendant had a pre-promise propensity and willingness to make a voluntary statement and thus that the statement made was freely given).

munity from prosecution or its equivalent in return for a confession will render a resulting confession involuntary.[22] A promise not to pursue charges for the most serious offenses committed by admitted actions may have the same effect.[23] Furthermore, a promise that a confession would be kept confidential has been held to similarly render a confession inadmissible.[24]

Some approaches emphasize the risk of inaccuracy. Several statutes[25] and some case law[26] provide that confessions are inadmissible if made in response to promises likely to stimulate a

---

[22]State v. Sturgill, 121 N.C. App. 629, 469 S.E.2d 557, 559–69 (1996) (because "defendant reasonably relied on police promises not to prosecute, and those promises were disregarded by the State, we hold that traditional notions of substantial justice and fair play, as well as defendant's substantive due process rights, mandate a new trial, and suppression of defendant's confession"); State v. Aguilar, 133 Or. App. 304, 891 P.2d 668, 670 (1995) ("If a person in the defendant's circumstances reasonably would have believed that the officer was promising immunity and reasonably would have relied on that promise in making the confession, then the confession is considered to have been induced by the promise of immunity and as a matter of law is involuntary and must be suppressed.").

[23]See Foster v. State, 283 Ga. 484, 660 S.E.2d 521, 524 (2008) (statements connecting defendant to weapon were inadmissible because detectives promised to not press any charges related to weapon if defendant confessed); State v. Strain, 779 P.2d 221, 226 (Utah 1989) (defendant guaranteed that if he admitted homicide, he would not be prosecuted for first degree murder). Accord State v. Rezk, 150 N.H. 483, 840 A.2d 758 (2004) (confession was involuntary because made in response to officer's promise not to prosecute defendant for several offenses, including the one for which he was arrested, because this was so attractive an offer it was likely to strip the defendant of his capacity for self-determination). Compare State v. Unga, 165 Wash. 2d 95, 196 P.3d 645,

652 (2008) ("An unqualified promise not to prosecute that in fact induces a confession may be 'of such a nature that it can easily be found to have overcome a person's resistance to giving a statement to authorities.' . . . However . . . a promise does not per se render a confession involuntary; it is one factor among the totality of the circumstances.").

[24]Jones v. State, 65 P.3d 903, 909 (Alaska Ct. App. 2003) (officer's agreement that conversation would be "off the record" made statement inadmissible); Lee v. State, 418 Md. 136, 12 A.3d 1238, 1250 (2011) (officer's statement, "This is between you and me, bud. Only me and you are here, all right? All right?," "directly contradict the [earlier] advisement that "anything you say can and will be used against you in a court of law" and rendered confession inadmissible); State v. McDermott, 131 N.H. 495, 554 A.2d 1302, 1305 (1989) (officer's assurance that suspect's admissions concerning a homicide would "not leave the office" required exclusion). One court has noted that case law suggests an improper assurance of confidentiality may be remedied but it contains no "bright line rule" on what is required. State v. Dodge, 2011 ME 47, 17 A.3d 128, 134–35 (Me. 2011).

[25]N.Y. Crim. Proc. Law § 60.45(1) (statement involuntary if obtained "by means of any promise or statement of fact, which promise or statement creates a substantial risk that the defendant might falsely incriminate himself"). See also Kan. Stat. Ann. § 60-460(f) (confession admissible if not induced by threats or promises "likely

false confession by an innocent suspect. Whether this is consistent with federal due process voluntariness law's position that the accuracy of a particular confession is irrelevant to its voluntariness[27] is open to question.[28]

Several courts have suggested that although officers may inform a suspect that cooperation may benefit the suspect, they may not tell that suspect that lack of cooperation—and a failure to confess—may result harsher treatment.[29] "The first may contribute to the informed nature of the decision. But the second has no legitimate purpose 'and can only be intended to coerce.' "[30] Thus a confession was inadmissible because interrogators told the defendant that if he did not cooperate they would ask for a "lot of jail time" and would make it "real uncomfortable" for him and that they would file a "recommendation that he was uncooperative."[31]

Despite the apparent relaxation of promise law, some appellate courts sustain convicted defendants' claims that promises of leniency—perhaps in combination with other factors—rendered

---

to cause the accused to make such a statement falsely").

[26]State v. Brown, 285 Kan. 261, 173 P.3d 612, 626 (2007) ("in order to render a confession involuntary as a product of a promise of some benefit to the accused, including leniency, the promise . . . must be such that it would be likely to cause the accused to make a false statement to obtain the benefit of the promise"); Garcia v. State, 919 S.W.2d 370, 387 (Tex. Crim. App. 1994) ("A promise made by a law enforcement officer may render a confession involuntary if it was positive, made or sanctioned by someone with apparent authority, was of some benefit to the defendant and was of such a character as would likely cause a person to speak untruthfully. To determine if the promise of a benefit was likely to influence appellant to speak untruthfully, an appellate court must look to whether the circumstances of the promise made the defendant 'inclined to admit a crime he didn't commit.' ").

[27]See § 149 supra.

[28]Perhaps the tendency of promise of a particular sort to generate false admissions in general can be used to

determine the weight to be given to a promise in determining—without regard to the accuracy of the admission at issue—whether the decision to make the admission was voluntary. This is a terribly fine line to draw.

[29]State v. Swanigan, 279 Kan. 18, 106 P.3d 39, 51 (2005) (growing number of courts have disapproved of law enforcement threatening to convey suspects lack of cooperation to the prosecutor, some finding it coercive per se and others considering it as part of the totality of the circumstances). Accord U.S. v. Leon Guerrero, 847 F.2d 1363, 1366 (9th Cir. 1988); U.S. v. Tingle, 658 F.2d 1332, 1336 n.5 (9th Cir. 1981); State v. Strayhand, 184 Ariz. 571, 911 P.2d 577, 585 (Ct. App. Div. 1 1995), relying on U.S. v. Harrison, 34 F.3d 886, 891 (9th Cir. 1994);

[30]Strayhand, 911 P.2d at 585.

[31]911 P.2d at 585. Accord State v. Tuttle, 2002 SD 94, 650 N.W.2d 20, 32–36 (S.D. 2002) (statement was inadmissible because officer told defendant his failure to cooperate would be noted in police report, suggesting that refusal to admit guilt might result in harsher treatment).

confessions inadmissible.[32] One court—characterizing the situation as involving "false" promises because the promised leniency did not materialize—explained:

> The reason we treat a false promise differently than other somewhat deceptive police tactics (such as cajoling and duplicity) is that a false promise has the unique potential to make a decision to speak irrational and the resulting confession unreliable. Police conduct that influences a rational person who is innocent to view a false confession as more beneficial than being honest is necessarily coercive, because of the way it realigns a suspect's incentives during interrogation. "An empty prosecutorial promise could prevent a suspect from making a rational choice by distorting the alternatives among which the person under interrogation is being asked to choose." The ultimate result of a coercive interrogation is unreliable.[33]

The task of a court considering a defendant's claim of involuntariness "is to examine whether [the defendant] was not able to make a rational decision due to promises made by the interrogating [officer]."[34]

*Deception.* If evidence that officers deceived the defendant convincingly demonstrates that the defendant lacked some information necessary to make his confession admissible under the applicable legal standard, of course, the evidence necessarily demonstrates that this legal standard was not met.[35] The legal standards apparently require quite little in terms of a defendant's

---

[32]State v. Polk, 812 N.W.2d 670, 676 (Iowa 2012) (interrogating officer "crossed the line by combining statements that county attorneys 'are much more likely to work with an individual that is cooperating' with suggestions Polk would not see his kids 'for a long time' unless he confessed."); State v. Bordeaux, 207 N.C. App. 645, 701 S.E.2d 272, 278 (2010) ("[D]etectives promised that they would speak on the Defendant's behalf and a benefit would result. When viewed in their totality, the Detectives' statements during the course of the interview aroused in Defendant 'an "emotion of hope"' of lighter, more lenient sentence" and rendered confession inadmissible); State v. Jenkins, 192 Ohio App. 3d 276, 2011-Ohio-754, 948 N.E.2d 1011, 1018–19 (2d Dist. Montgomery County 2011) (officer's promise to defendant that if defendant admitted to residen-

tial burglaries officer would recommend that defendant receive drug treatment rather than incarceration made defendant's confession involuntary; treatment in lieu of conviction was statutorily unavailable to a person convicted of residential burglaries).

[33]U.S. v. Villalpando, 588 F.3d 1124, 1128–29 (7th Cir. 2009) (quoting U.S. v. Montgomery, 555 F.3d 623, 629 (7th Cir. 2009), quoting Sprosty v. Buchler, 79 F.3d 635, 646 (7th Cir. 1996)).

[34]Villalpando, 588 F.3d at 1129

[35]*Cf.* U.S. v. Degaule, 797 F. Supp. 2d 1332, 1380 (N.D. Ga. 2011) (trickery or deceit in interrogation is prohibited by voluntariness law only if it deprives the suspect of knowledge essential to understanding his rights and the consequences of abandoning them).

awareness.[36] however, and this approach therefore gives little significance to proof of deception.

Officers' misrepresentations that the criminal law does not cover what the defendants are being asked to admit are likely to render the confession inadmissible.[37] If confessing defendants need not know the law criminalizes what they are confessing, apparently officers are barred from misrepresenting the criminal law does not cover the conduct. Perhaps such misrepresentations are, or are akin to, promises of nonprosecution.

Courts sometimes seem open to arguments that deception should have some significance beyond disproving that the defendant had the awareness required to make an admissible confession. Some courts put the possible rule as one prohibiting notions of fairness or due process.[38] No consensus has developed, however, on how to implement this.

The uncertain state of the law is almost certainly the result of uncertainty as to why law enforcement deception of suspects might be inappropriate and—if it is inappropriate at all—how inappropriate it is. Is it undesirable because—and thus only when—it might or does lead to an inaccurate confession? Or is it simply "wrong"—perhaps immoral in some sense—for public officials to lie and to exploit those lies? Even if such action is wrong, it is inappropriate enough to demand condemnation by excluding confessions to serious criminal conduct?

Common law voluntariness appears, from the minimal case law available, to have regarded proof of deception as largely if not entirely irrelevant to admissibility.[39] The Supreme Court addressed the issue under Fourteenth Amendment due process voluntariness in *Frazier v. Cupp*.[40] Officers falsely told Frazier that a companion (Rawls) had been taken into custody and had confessed. Rejecting the attack on the later confession almost offhandedly, the Supreme Court—offering no authority, discus-

---

[36]See §§ 149 (voluntariness), 153 (waiver of *Miranda* rights) supra.

[37]McGhee v. State, 899 N.E.2d 35, 38 (Ind. Ct. App. 2008) (confession to incestual sex with adult niece was rendered inadmissible by officer's misrepresentation that it was not against the law for an uncle to have consensual sex with a niece); Light v. State, 20 So. 3d 939, 941 (Fla. 1st DCA 2009) (confession to sex with 16 year old girl inadmissible because officer misrepresented age of consent in the applicable law).

[38]See State v. Faruqi, 344 S.W.3d 193, 204 (Mo. 2011) ("Statements obtained by subterfuge on the part of police 'are admissible unless the deception offends societal notions of fairness or is likely to produce an untrustworthy confession.' ") (quoting State v. Davis, 980 S.W.2d 92, 96 (Mo. Ct. App. E.D. 1998)).

[39]See generally Dix, Mistake, Ignorance, Expectation of Benefit, and the Modern Law of Confessions, 1975 Wash. U. L.Q. 275, 282.

[40]Frazier v. Cupp, 394 U.S. 731, 89 S. Ct. 1420, 22 L. Ed. 2d 684 (1969).

sion, or rationale—simply stated, "[T]he fact that the police misrepresented the statements that Rawls had made is, while relevant, insufficient in our view to make this otherwise voluntary confession inadmissible."[41]

In *Miranda v. Arizona*,[42] the Court, again with no substantive discussion or citation of authority, commented, "[A]ny evidence that the accused was . . . tricked . . . into a waiver [of the *Miranda* rights] will, of course, show that the defendant did not voluntarily waive his privilege."[43] Although *Frazier* was decided after *Miranda*, the Court in *Frazier* amazingly made no mention of the obvious tension between the implications of the *Miranda* dictum and the *Frazier* analysis. In several subsequent cases presenting *Miranda* issues, the Court has failed to respond to or reach defendants' claims that their *Miranda* waivers were rendered ineffective by police deception.[44] In *Colorado v. Spring*,[45] the Court recognized and left open the possibility that affirmative misrepresentations by officers might have significance for the effectiveness of a *Miranda* waiver beyond its logical relevance to the intelligence of that waiver.[46]

Lower courts generally say that deception is not necessarily sufficient by itself to make an otherwise admissible confession inadmissible,[47] but deception is a factor to consider in determining whether necessary voluntariness has been demonstrated.[48] Under what circumstances deception is sufficient to tip the scales

---

[41]Frazier, 394 U.S. at 739.

[42]Miranda v. Arizona, 384 U.S. 436, 86 S. Ct. 1602, 16 L. Ed. 2d 694 (1966).

[43]Miranda, 384 U.S. at 476.

[44]Michigan v. Mosley, 423 U.S. 96, 99 n.5, 96 S. Ct. 321, 46 L. Ed. 2d 313 (1975) (holding confession admissible despite claim that it was induced by "trickery," but without addressing why that claim was rejected); Oregon v. Mathiason, 429 U.S. 492, 493, 97 S. Ct. 711, 50 L. Ed. 2d 714 (1977) (per curiam) (officer's misrepresentation to defendant that his fingerprints had been found at scene was not relevant to whether he was in "custody" and was not otherwise discussed by Court).

[45]Colorado v. Spring, 479 U.S. 564, 107 S. Ct. 851, 93 L. Ed. 2d 954 (1987).

[46]Spring, 479 U.S. at 576 n. 8 ("we are not confronted with an affirmative misrepresentation by law enforcement officers . . . and do not reach the question whether a waiver of *Miranda* rights would be valid in such a circumstance").

[47]People v. Klausner, 74 P.3d 421, 425 (Colo. App. 2003) (where only factor suggesting confession was involuntary was single misrepresentation, this did not make confession involuntary); State v. Barner, 486 N.W.2d 1, 3 (Minn. Ct. App. 1992) (trial court erred in suppressing a confession simply because police lied to the suspect).

[48]*E.g.*, U.S. v. Lopez, 437 F.3d 1059, 1066 (10th Cir. 2006) (confession was, on totality of the circumstances, involuntary in light of misrepresentations of strength of evidence and promise that if killing was mistake defendant would spend 6 rather than 60 years in prison); State v. Swanigan, 279 Kan. 18, 106 P.3d 39, 54 (2005) (falsely telling suspect his fingerprints were found at crime scene might not

in favor of involuntariness is not clear. What is clear is that it will not be easily or frequently found.[49]

One court commented that deception will not have this effect simply because it influenced the suspect's decision to confess, "as long as the decision [to confess] results from the suspect's balancing of competing interests."[50] Perhaps the inquiry must be—in part at least—whether the deception and other circumstances so affected the defendant's emotion or reasoning as to prevent the suspect from making a minimally sufficient balance between those considerations militating against the wisdom of confessing and those favoring such action.[51] The inquiry may, however, need to go beyond this.

Some courts have turned to the risk of deception leading to unreliability as the controlling factor—or at least one of the controlling considerations. Thus "a confession induced by deception or trickery . . . is not inadmissible, unless the method used was calculated to produce an untruthful confession or was offensive to due process."[52] The Nebraska court has focused not on the general tendency of the deception used to produce inaccurate confessions, but rather on whether on the facts of the specific case the particular deception used "produced a false or untrustworthy

---

be enough to show coercion, but this together with threats, promises, low intellect and anxiety did show statement was involuntary).

[49]*E.g.,* U.S. v. Degaule, 797 F. Supp. 2d 1332, 1380 (N.D. Ga. 2011) ("trickery can sink to the level of coercion, but this is a relatively rare phenomenon") (quoting U.S. v. Flemmi, 225 F.3d 78, 91 n.5 (1st Cir. 2000)); State v. Lawrence, 282 Conn. 141, 920 A.2d 236, 259 (2007) ("statements by the police designed to lead a suspect to believe that the case against him is strong are common investigative techniques and would rarely, if ever, be sufficient to overbear the defendant's will and to bring about a confession to a serious crime that is not freely self-determined . . . .") (quoting State v. Lapointe, 237 Conn. 694, 678 A.2d 942, 961 (1996)).

[50]State v. Register, 323 S.C. 471, 476 S.E.2d 153, 158 (1996).

[51]*Cf* State v. Mayes, 251 Mont. 358, 825 P.2d 1196, 1208 (1992) (where suspect had been awake for more than 30 hours when he confessed, questioned continually, separated from his children, and lied to about the strength of the evidence against him, "[t]he combination of the circumstances surrounding [the] confession mandates suppression").

[52]Rodriquez v. State, 934 S.W.2d 881, 890–91 (Tex. App. Waco 1996) (officer's misrepresentation that victim had identified defendant as the assailant was neither calculated to produce an untrue statement nor in violation of due process). *Accord* Thorpe v. State, 285 Ga. 604, 678 S.E.2d 913, 921 (2009) ("We have long held that the mere fact that an incriminating statement was procured through artifice or deception does not render the statement involuntary as long as the means employed were not calculated to elicit an untrue statement."); State v. Baylor, 423 N.J. Super. 578, 34 A.3d 801, 807 (App. Div. 2011) ("law enforcement officers may employ deception or trickery in an interrogation of a suspect unless such deception or trickery was calculated to produce an untruthful confession or was offensive to due process").

confession."[53] This reference to accuracy poses the same problems here as when it is used to address the significance of promises.

The Seventh Circuit has indicated deception will render a statement involuntary if it "destroy[s] the information that [the suspect] require[s] for a rational choice" in at least part because it renders the confession unreliable.[54] Applying this approach, it held a confession to killing an infant by violent shaking involuntary because officers misrepresented to the defendant (who had acknowledged gently shaking the baby) that medical reports excluded all other possible causes of the child's death. The court explained:

> In this case a false statement did destroy the information required for a rational choice. Not being a medical expert, Aleman could not contradict what was represented to him as settled medical opinion. He had shaken Joshua, albeit gently; but if medical opinion excluded any other possible cause of the child's death, then, gentle as the shaking was, and innocently intended, it must have been the cause of death. Aleman had no rational basis, given his ignorance of medical science, to deny that he had to have been the cause.
>
> * * **
>
> A trick that is as likely to induce a false as a true confession renders a confession inadmissible because of its unreliability even if its voluntariness is conceded. If a question has only two answers—A and B—and you tell the respondent that the answer is not A, and he has no basis for doubting you, then he is compelled by logic to "confess" that the answer is B. That was the vise the police placed Aleman in. They told him the only possible cause of Joshua's injuries was that he'd been shaken right before he collapsed; not being an expert in shaken-baby syndrome, Aleman could not deny the officers' false representation of medical opinion. And since he was the only person to have shaken Joshua immediately before Joshua's collapse, it was a logical necessity that he had been

---

[53]State v. Nissen, 252 Neb. 51, 560 N.W.2d 157, 170 (1997) (per curiam) (trial court did not err in admitting confession despite evidence that officers falsely told suspect that they knew he had told his wife to lie about the time he returned home the night of the crime, because in light of what the suspect was aware the officers knew the trial judge was not clearly wrong "in finding that the falsehood in question did not render Nissen's [confession] false or unreliable").

An additional consideration is involved if the deception becomes a trial matter. In State v. Patton, 362 N.J. Super. 16, 826 A.2d 783 (App. Div. 2003), police fabricated an audiotape implicating the defendant, used this to procure a confession, and then at trial introduced the tape in support of the voluntariness of the confession. This was held to violate state constitutional due process. Patton, 826 A.2d at 805.

[54]Aleman v. Village of Hanover Park, 662 F.3d 897, 906–07 (7th Cir. 2011), cert. denied, 133 S. Ct. 26, 183 L. Ed. 2d 676 (2012) (quoting U.S. v. Rutledge, 900 F.2d 1127, 1129–30 (7th Cir. 1990)).

responsible for the child's death. Q.E.D. A confession so induced is worthless as evidence . . . .[55]

Some courts distinguish between deception regarding "intrinsic" facts—facts relating to the crime to which the suspect confessed and the suspect's guilt of it—and misrepresentation as to "extrinsic" facts—facts concerning other matters. Deceiving a suspect regarding extrinsic facts creates a particularly high risk, first, of overbearing the suspect's will by distorting what would otherwise be a rational choice whether to confess or remain silent, and, second, that the confession will be unreliable.[56] Misrepresentations as to extrinsic facts are generally treated as entitled to more weight as tending to show involuntariness than misrepresentations as to intrinsic facts.[57]

## § 156  Delay in presenting arrested person before magistrate[1]

Statutes and court rules in virtually every state as well as Rule

---

[55]Aleman, 662 F.3d at 906–07.

[56]Holland v. McGinnis, 963 F.2d 1044, 1051–52 (7th Cir. 1992). The Hawaii Supreme Court adopted a similar approach:

[E]mployment by the police of deliberate falsehoods intrinsic to the facts of the alleged offense in question will be treated as one of the totality of circumstances surrounding the confession or statement to be considered in assessing its voluntariness; on the other hand, deliberate falsehoods extrinsic to the facts of the alleged offense, which are of a type reasonably likely to procure an untrue statement or to influence an accused to make a confession regardless of guilt, will be regarded as coercive per se, thus obviating the need for a "totality of circumstances" analysis of voluntariness.

State v. Kelekolio, 74 Haw. 479, 849 P.2d 58, 73 (1993).

[57]Holland, 693 F.2d at 1052 (misrepresentations as to the strength of the evidence against the suspect did not, on the facts, render confession involuntary); Sheriff, Washoe County v. Bessey, 112 Nev. 322, 914 P.2d 618, 619–20 (1996) (misrepresentation to sexual assault suspect that laboratory report indicated his semen stains on sofa at scene of assault was only factor suggesting involuntariness and

thus confession was voluntary); Green v. State, 934 S.W.2d 92, 100–01 (Tex. Crim. App. 1996) (misrepresentations as to existence of eyewitness did not render confession involuntary).

**[Section 156]**

[1]*See generally* West's Key Number Digest, Criminal Law ☞413.14.

Whether a confession is to be excluded because of unreasonable delay in presentation must be distinguished from a closely related question. As a matter of Fourth Amendment law, a suspect arrested without a warrant must be afforded a judicial determination of probable cause, usually within 48 hours of the initial detention. This determination need not be made at the defendant's presentation before a magistrate, although as a matter of local practice it often is made then. County of Riverside v. McLaughlin, 500 U.S. 44, 111 S. Ct. 1661, 114 L. Ed. 2d 49 (1991); Gerstein v. Pugh, 420 U.S. 103, 95 S. Ct. 854, 43 L. Ed. 2d 54 (1975). Must a confession obtained during custody after the 48 hour period expires be excluded? This is a question of Fourth Amendment exclusionary remedy law, and the Supreme Court has left it open. Powell v. Nevada, 511 U.S. 79, 84 n.*, 114 S. Ct. 1280, 128 L. Ed. 2d 1 (1994).

5(a) of the Federal Rules of Criminal Procedure require that arrested persons be brought with some dispatch before judicial officers for what, under the Federal Rules, is called the "initial appearance." Controversy continues as to the appropriate effect of violation of the applicable requirement on the admissibility of a confession obtained during the delay.[2] The Supreme Court's development of the so-called *McNabb-Mallory* Rule and Congress's modification of it have served as a basis for analysis.

These cases present two distinguishable issues that are sometimes not separated by the courts. First is whether particular delay is improper, especially if that delay is for purposes of questioning the suspect prior to the appearance before the magistrate and the resulting judicial warnings, appointment of counsel and perhaps release from custody on bail. Second is the effect of delay determined to be improper on the admissibility of a confession given during that improper delay.

*McNabb-Mallory Rule.* In *McNabb v. United States,*[3] the Supreme Court held that statements elicited from a defendant during a period in which federal officers had failed to comply with what is now Federal Rule of Criminal Procedure 5(a)'s requirement of presentation before a magistrate without "unnecessary delay" were inadmissible at the defendant's subsequent federal criminal trial.[4] This holding, the Court made clear, was not of constitutional dimensions but rather was an exercise of the Court's supervisory power.[5] The impact of this exclusionary requirement was increased by the Court's construction of the

---

*Compare* Powell, 511 U.S. at 89–90 (Thomas, J., dissenting) (failure to afford a judicial probable cause hearing does not trigger an exclusionary sanction if probable cause in fact existed and, alternatively, exclusion is not required unless the defendant shows "but for" causation between the denial of a probable cause determination and the making of the challenged confession). *See* People v. Willis, 215 Ill. 2d 517, 294 Ill. Dec. 581, 831 N.E.2d 531, 541–42 (2005) (although some courts have looked to whether the taint of an unreasonable delay was attenuated, court adopted approach of most courts and holds that confession given during delay that has become unreasonable under *Gerstein* is admissible if voluntary).

[2]There is little likelihood that a confession given *before* any delay in presenting a defendant had become

improper will be affected by later improper delay. Under the *McNabb-Mallory* rule, the Supreme Court held that a confession obtained before delay became improper was admissible despite further and improper delay. U.S. v. Mitchell, 322 U.S. 65, 70, 64 S. Ct. 896, 88 L. Ed. 1140 (1944).

[3]McNabb v. U.S., 318 U.S. 332, 63 S. Ct. 608, 87 L. Ed. 819 (1943).

[4]McNabb, 318 U.S. at 344. *See also* Upshaw v. U.S., 335 U.S. 410, 69 S. Ct. 170, 93 L. Ed. 100 (1948) (applying *McNabb* to prompt presentation requirement moved from federal statute to Federal Rule of Criminal Procedure 5(a)).

[5]The requirement of prompt presentation is applicable only to persons under arrest or detention on federal charges. Thus no prompt presentation issue is presented by delay of a suspect held by state authorities on a state

substance of the Rule 5(a) requirement. In *Mallory v. United States*,[6] the Court held that if officers delayed presenting a defendant before a magistrate in order to interrogate him, the delay was "unnecessary" within the meaning of Rule 5(a).

Thus the so-called *McNabb-Mallory* Rule was in part a substantive rule—any delay in presentation for purposes of interrogation was unnecessary under Rule 5(a)—and in part a remedial rule—a confession obtained during delay that had become unnecessary for Rule 5(a) purposes was for that reason automatically inadmissible. Whether the Court in fact possessed a supervisory power sufficient to support its development of an exclusionary sanction of this sort has been questioned.[7] The Supreme Court has never suggested that the *McNabb-Mallory* Rule or any similar prophylactic rule is required by the federal Constitution. Rather, the Court has assumed that delay is merely a factor in constitutional analysis of the voluntariness of a confession[8] and presumably the effectiveness of waivers of Fifth and Sixth Amendment rights. In any case, a violation of a state prompt presentation requirement does not constitute an automatic violation of any federal constitutional requirement and, generally speaking, goes only to the voluntariness of the confession.[9]

*Congressional Modification or Rejection of McNabb-Mallory.* In 1968, Congress responded to the *McNabb-Mallory* Rule by enacting what was codified as Section 3501 of Title 18 of the United States Code.[10] Section 3501(c) provides that in a federal criminal prosecution, a voluntary confession made by an arrested person within six hours of arrest or detention "shall not be inadmissible solely because of delay in bringing such person before a magistrate . . . ." Under Section 3501(a), a confession "shall be admissible [in a federal prosecution] if it is voluntarily given." Section 3501(b) specifies that among the factors to be considered in determining voluntariness is "the time elapsing between arrest and arraignment[11] of the defendant . . . ."

Under Section 3501, a confession made within six hours of ar-

---

charge, unless state authorities act in collusion with federal officers to frustrate the suspect's right to a prompt federal presentment. U.S. v. Alvarez-Sanchez, 511 U.S. 350, 358–59, 114 S. Ct. 1599, 128 L. Ed. 2d 319 (1994).

[6]Mallory v. U.S., 354 U.S. 449, 77 S. Ct. 1356, 1 L. Ed. 2d 1479 (1957).

[7]*See generally* Beale, Reconsidering Supervisory Power in Criminal Cases: Constitutional and Statutory Limits on the Authority of the Federal Courts, 84 Colum. L. Rev. 1433 (1984).

[8]*See* Culombe v. Connecticut, 367 U.S. 568, 601–02, 81 S. Ct. 1860, 6 L. Ed. 2d 1037 (1961).

[9]*E.g.,* West v. Johnson, 92 F.3d 1385, 1403 (5th Cir. 1996).

[10]Pub. L. 90-351, Title II, § 701(a), 82 Stat. 210 (1968), codified as 18 U.S.C.A. § 3501.

[11]Here, as in much discussion, the term "arraignment" is not being used in its technically correct sense, which means the appearance before the trial court at which the defendant is called

rest cannot be excluded from a federal prosecution simply because of delay in presenting the defendant and will be inadmissible only upon a determination that it is involuntary. When a confession given during a period of improper delay lasting longer than the six hour "safe haven" in the statute was addressed by the Supreme Court in *Corley v. United States*.[12] Sections 3501(a) and (b), *Corley* held, simply do not address the *McNabb-Mallory* situation. Section 3501(c) means that delay in presentment is not itself a basis for excluding a confession given during the six-hour period after arrest. But if a confession is given after the expiration of that six-hour period and the delay in presentment was unreasonable or unnecessary "under the *McNabb-Mallory* cases," the delay alone still requires exclusion.[13]

In reaching this result, the *Corley* majority stressed that reading the statute otherwise would leave the federal prompt presentation requirement "without any teeth." This, in turn, was particularly significant since that requirement is not "just some administrative nicety." Rather, it is an important safeguard against the risk of governmental overreaching by extended secret questioning. The prompt presentation demand "has always mattered in very practical ways and still does."[14]

*State Positions.* State courts and legislatures have taken a wide variety of approaches. Agreement that *McNabb-Mallory* is not constitutionally-based and thus binding on the states assures that states are free to reject the Supreme Court's approach.

A few state courts, acting under supervisory authority, have adopted state versions of *McNabb-Mallory*, requiring suppression of confessions obtained during delay that has become improper because of failure to present the accused before a judicial officer.[15] Maximum flexibility is provided by the approach of the Kansas court, which has held that trial courts have broad discretion to fashion and apply remedies for violation of the right of prompt presentation, including exclusion of statements made during impermissible delay.[16]

The requirement of exclusion is sometimes qualified by a requirement that the defendant show that the delay caused or at

---

upon to plead. *See, e.g.,* Fed. R. Crim. P. 10. Rather, it refers to the appearance made to comply with the requirement that an arrested person be presented before a magistrate, as is still required by Fed. R. Crim. P. 5(a).

[12]Corley v. U.S., 556 U.S. 303, 129 S. Ct. 1558, 173 L. Ed. 2d 443 (2009).

[13]Corley, 556 U.S. at 322.

[14]556 U.S. at 320.

[15]The leading decision is probably Johnson v. State, 282 Md. 314, 384 A.2d 709 (1978), which was later legislatively negated. *See also* Vorhauer v. State, 59 Del. 35, 212 A.2d 886, 891 (1965) (adopting "the prevailing federal rule, known as the *McNabb-Mallory* rule").

[16]*See* State v. Crouch, 230 Kan. 783, 641 P.2d 394, 398 (1982). Even dismissal of the prosecution is avail-

contributed to the defendant's decision to confess.[17] Under the Montana court's approach, the prosecution can escape exclusion by making a showing that the evidence at issue was not reasonably related to the delay.[18] Given that for other reasons compliance with *Miranda v. Arizona*[19] and other requirements must be shown, defendants under this approach have a difficult and perhaps impossible task in making cases for exclusion.[20]

Several state legislatures have, in varying degrees, followed Congress' lead. In several jurisdictions, state statures follow the federal model.[21] Other states provide unqualifiedly by statute that delay in presenting a defendant does not by itself render inadmissible those confessions obtained during improper delay.[22] The Maryland court, to reconcile such a statutory provision with

---

able, the court indicated, but this is to be used only if no other remedy would "protect against abuse." *Accord* State v. Strong, 2010 MT 163, 357 Mont. 114, 236 P.3d 580, 584 (2010) (dismissal may sometimes be ordered as a remedy for a violation of prompt presentation requirements).

[17]McAdory v. State, 98 Ark. App. 181, 253 S.W.3d 16, 21 (2007) ("When a suspect's first appearance is delayed, incriminating statements taken during the delay will be suppressed only if the delay is unnecessary, the statement is prejudicial, and the statement is reasonably related to the delay.") (citing Duncan v. State, 291 Ark. 521, 726 S.W.2d 653, 657 (1987)); White v. State, 76 So. 3d 335, 338–39 (Fla. 3d DCA 2011) (delay must be shown to have induced the confession); State v. Wallace, 351 N.C. 481, 528 S.E.2d 326, 348 (2000) (confession need not be excluded where defendant failed to show the delay caused defendant to confess); State v. Barros, 24 A.3d 1158, 1182 (R.I. 2011) ("our well-settled case law . . . unambiguously indicates that a defendant who seeks to have an inculpatory statement suppressed because of an unnecessary delay in presentment 'must demonstrate both: (1) that the delay in presentment was unnecessary and (2) that such delay was 'causative' with respect to' the making of the inculpatory statement"); Jones v. State, 944 S.W.2d 642, 650 n.10 (Tex. Crim. App. 1996).

[18]State v. Benbo, 174 Mont. 252, 570 P.2d 894, 900 (1977).

[19]Miranda v. Arizona, 384 U.S. 436, 86 S. Ct. 1602, 16 L. Ed. 2d 694 (1966), discussed in § 150 supra. The criteria for determining the effectiveness of defendants' decisions in these situations is addressed in § 153.

[20]If *Miranda* warnings were given, "it is generally difficult for defendants to show that their post-arrest statements were tainted by the lack of a prompt initial appearance." State v. Owen, 2007 SD 21, 729 N.W.2d 356, 366 (S.D. 2007) (quoting Riney v. State, 935 P.2d 828, 834 (Alaska Ct. App. 1997)).

[21]State legislation similar to 18 U.S.C.A. § 3501 was passed in 1969 by Arizona, 1969 Sess. Laws ch. 23, § 1, codified at Ariz. Rev.Stat. § 13-3988, and Indiana, Ind. 1969 Ind. Sess. Laws ch. 312. Indiana repealed its provision in 1981. 1981 Ind. Acts 298, Sec. 9(a).

[22]Earlier Maryland case law was negated by 1981 legislation. Md. Code Ann., Cts. & Jud. Proc. § 10-912. *See* Woods v. State, 315 Md. 591, 556 A.2d 236, 247 (1989). Louisiana legislation provides that the failure of law enforcement officers to present a defendant "shall have no effect whatsoever upon the validity of the proceedings thereafter against the defendant." La. Code Crim. Proc. art. 230.1(D). Apparently this bars exclusion of confessions

the right of presentation, concluded that any deliberate and unnecessary delay in presenting a defendant before a magistrate as required by state law "must be given very heavy weight in deciding whether a confession is voluntary."[23]

The majority of state courts treat delay in presentation as merely a factor to consider in determining the voluntariness of decisions made during the delay and thus in deciding the admissibility of challenged confessions.[24] Given the flexibility of the voluntariness analysis, weight may be given to showings that delay was for purposes of using the delay to interrogate.[25] Nevertheless, successful challenges to admissibility under the approach are unusual.[26]

The Massachusetts Supreme Judicial Court effectively articulated in *Commonwealth v. Rosario*[27] that the basic question for state courts having authority to embrace or reject *McNabb-Mallory* as a matter of state law: Is prompt presentation important enough to protecting suspects' self-incrimination rights to justify enforcing the requirement by excluding all statements made after delay becomes improper.[28] Relying heavily upon the federal statute, the Massachusetts court concluded that *Miranda*

---

because of such delay.

[23]Williams v. State, 375 Md. 404, 825 A.2d 1078, 1095 (2003) (explaining that the violation of the prompt presentation requirement "creates its own aura of suspicion").

[24]*E.g.,* People v. Willis, 215 Ill. 2d 517, 294 Ill. Dec. 581, 831 N.E.2d 531, 538 (2005) (in "vast majority of jurisdictions," "an inculpatory statement obtained during an unreasonably long delay between a warrantless arrest and a probable cause hearing must be suppressed only if it was involuntary"); Williams v. State, 375 Md. 404, 825 A.2d 1078, 1092 (2003) (most state hold that unnecessary delay "is simply a factor to be considered in determining voluntariness"); People v. DeCampoamor, 91 A.D.3d 669, 936 N.Y.S.2d 256, 258 (2d Dep't 2012) ("an undue delay in arraignment is but one factor in assessing the voluntariness of a confession").

[25]*E.g.,* State v. McCartney, 228 W. Va. 315, 719 S.E.2d 785, 795–96 (2011), cert. denied, 133 S. Ct. 122, 184 L. Ed. 2d 58 (2012) (proper to consider evidence that the purpose for

the delay was to obtain incriminating admission from arrestee concerning the crime for which the arrest was made).

[26]An Illinois appellate court, however, upheld suppression of a confession where the defendant was detained without presentation for 72 hours—an "enormously long time"—and was interrogated sporadically despite his denials of involvement. "This process eventually wore defendant down and created a lack of free will." People v. Sams, 367 Ill. App. 3d 254, 305 Ill. Dec. 267, 855 N.E.2d 158, 161–62 (1st Dist. 2006).

[27]Com. v. Rosario, 422 Mass. 48, 661 N.E.2d 71 (1996). *Rosario* was reaffirmed in Com. v. Morganti, 455 Mass. 388, 917 N.E.2d 191, 201 (2009).

[28]A relevant consideration is whether the courts will be pressed to develop exceptions and qualifications to a basic rule of exclusion. *See* Perez, 845 A.2d at 785 (while "professing to follow a rule of automatic exclusion based on the passage of time," Pennsylvania courts in fact recognized so many exceptions that the rule func-

and voluntariness requirements were sufficient to protect suspects' self-incrimination rights during brief post-arrest questioning, and therefore otherwise admissible statements made within six hours of arrest are not to be excluded on presentation delay grounds. To minimize the need to define what delays are reasonable, the court held that statements obtained after delay has exceeded six hours are to be excluded, unless the delay is caused by "reasons not attributable to the police, such as a natural disaster."[29]

*Waivers of Right to Prompt Presentation.* The courts agree that whatever rights defendants have in the jurisdiction to exclusion of a confession based at least in part on delay in presentation is lost if the prosecution shows the defendants effectively waived the right to prompt presentation.[30] Thus they ignore the warnings of Massachusetts Chief Justice Liacos in *Rosario.* He argued that giving effect to waivers, particularly those made after nonpresentation has become improper, will "undoubtedly eviscerate the [general] rule."[31] In any case, he also argued that the need for a meaningful and bright-line requirement of presentation suggests the right to prompt presentation be nonwaivable.[32]

Whether giving effect to waivers is defensible on sound policy grounds depends in part on whether the courts will require proof that offered waivers reflected meaningful choices.[33] There seems, however, no possible defense of the position taken by the District of Columbia Court of Appeals in *Brown v. United States*[34] that a waiver of *Miranda* rights is also necessarily a waiver of prompt presentation rights.[35] Such an approach gives virtually no independent significance to the right of prompt presentation.

---

tioned "as no rule at all").

[29]Rosario, 661 N.E.2d at 76–77.

[30]*E.g.,* U.S. v. McDowell, 687 F.3d 904, 910–11 (7th Cir. 2012) (setting out signed waiver).

[31]Rosario, 661 N.E.2d at 78 (Liacos, Chief Justice, dissenting).

[32]661 N.E.2d at 78–79.

[33]The Maryland Court of Special Appeals held that execution of a summary waiver form was inadequate:

There was no evidence that any of the investigating officers gave the appellant an oral explanation of his prompt presentment right. What is stated in the [form] was not sufficient to advise the appellant of all of his rights with regard to prompt presentment. The written waiver form stated only, "You have been in the custody of the Prince George's County Police for over 23 [or 24] hours. You have a right to be presented before a District Court Commissioner within 24 hours of your apprehension." The form did not advise the appellant of any of the information he needed to know in order to intelligently waive his prompt presentment right.

Perez v. State, 168 Md. App. 248, 896 A.2d 380, 399 (2006).

[34]Brown v. U.S., 979 A.2d 630 (D.C. 2009).

[35]Brown, 979 A.2d at 635–36 (relying on Crawford v. U.S., 932 A.2d 1147, 1157 (D.C. 2007)).

## § 157 Reliability or trustworthiness as admission requirement

A major theme of American confession law is the ambiguity of the role that a trial judge's assessment of a confession's accuracy, reliability or trustworthiness plays in determining the admissibility of that confession.

The federal due process requirement is clearly unconcerned with inaccuracy that cannot be attributed to official action. Even when official action is involved, the Supreme Court has mandated a focus on voluntariness that is divorced from the accuracy of the confession.[1] If a defendant's Fifth Amendment rights under *Miranda v. Arizona*[2] or Sixth Amendment right to counsel[3] is implicated, there is no more emphasis on reliability. State courts applying what appear to be state law voluntariness requirements sometimes look to the tendencies of the type of official action to stimulate a false confession.[4] Generally, the legal literature assumes that the trustworthiness of a confession is a matter for the jury.

The real problem in a jury trial system of course is whether juries are unlikely to recognize the untrustworthiness of at least some confessions, so that exclusion is appropriate to avoid jury misuse of them. In 1986, the Supreme Court offhandedly commented that the reliability of a criminal defendant's out-of-court admissions "is a matter to be governed by the evidentiary laws of the forum,"[5] thereby suggesting the existence of a body of law addressing this. In fact, little law of this sort exists.

As Richard Leo has pointed out,[6] the most obvious source of such a body of law would be trial courts' authority to exclude evidence on the ground that its probative value is outweighed by its danger of undue prejudice.[7] State courts have occasionally com-

---

**[Section 157]**

[1] See § 149 supra.

[2] Miranda v. Arizona, 384 U.S. 436, 86 S. Ct. 1602, 16 L. Ed. 2d 694 (1966), discussed in § 150 supra. The criteria for determining the effectiveness of defendants' decisions in these situations is addressed in § 153.

[3] See § 154 supra.

[4] See § 149 supra.

[5] Colorado v. Connelly, 479 U.S. 157, 167, 107 S. Ct. 515, 93 L. Ed. 2d 473 (1986).

[6] Leo, *Miranda* and the Problem of False Confessions, in The *Miranda* Debate (Leo and Thomas eds. 1998) at 279.

[7] See generally § 185 supra.

Milhizer, Confessions After Connelly: An Evidentiary Solution for Excluding Unreliable Confessions, 81 Temple L. Rev. 1, 34–36 (2008), argues that this body of law is insufficient in large part because it does not provide trial courts with sufficient guidance for resolving challenges to confessions. Further, it does not compel trial courts to give confessions the "vigorous" scrutiny they should be given when their reliability is placed at issue. He suggests adoption of the following:

Evidence of a defendant's confession or

mented that defendants can challenge confessions on this basis[8] and on rare occasions have reviewed admissibility under this approach.[9]

Defendants seldom argue specifically why particular confessions might create a risk of jury misuse or undue prejudice. The mere fact that a jury is likely to consider an out-of-court statement as devastating to a defendant's case, of course, is not enough to trigger this analysis. Defendants must point out why juries are not likely to recognize indicia of unreliability and thus properly determine probative value.[10]

As a practical matter, and regardless of the doctrine, it seems

---

admission is not admissible in any criminal proceeding if, in the judge's determination, considering all of the relevant evidence pertaining to the confession, no reasonable juror by a preponderance of the evidence could conclude that the confession is reliable. 81 Temple L. Rev. at 47.

[8]State v. Moss, 2003 WI App 239, 267 Wis. 2d 772, 672 N.W.2d 125, 130 (Ct. App. 2003) (defendant "could have availed himself of Wisconsin's rules of evidence to challenge the reliability of his statement," but he did not do so); People v. Cox, 221 Cal. App. 3d 980, 270 Cal. Rptr. 730, 733 n.3 (4th Dist. 1990) (evidence that defendant was psychotic at time of admission may have rendered it excludable on the ground that it was so unreliable or untrustworthy that its probative value was outweighed by its prejudicial impact"); In re Sanborn, 130 N.H. 430, 545 A.2d 726, 732–33 (1988) ("there may well be grounds for probative unreliability for excluding a statement under State law," but nothing in case before court raises any questions regarding reliability of statement); State v. Honaker, 193 W. Va. 51, 454 S.E.2d 96, 103 (1994) (defendant failed to raise available attack on confession obtained by private person based on its unreliability under Rules 401 through 403 of state rules of evidence).

[9]See State v. Tucker, 157 Ariz. 433, 759 P.2d 579, 591–92 (1988) (statements made by defendant while intoxicated were not so unreliable that they had to be excluded); Pappaconstantinou v. State, 352 Md. 167, 721

A.2d 241, 248 (1998) (trial court did not err in finding privately obtained statement "sufficiently reliable to be admissible"); State v. Schulz, 691 N.W.2d 474, 479 (Minn. 2005) (trial court did not err in admitting recorded message left by defendant identifying himself as "Kill" and saying he had lived up to his name, because no indication it gave prosecution an unfair advantage and thus involved undue prejudice); State v. Griffith, 660 A.2d 704, 707 (R.I. 1995) (trial court did not err in admitting statement, because "[t]he probative value of the confession is not outweighed by any danger of unfair prejudice to defendant"); *Accord* Phillips v. State, 344 Ark. 453, 40 S.W.3d 778, 782 (2001) (where letter written by defendant was capable of being construed as an admission or as involving a grammatical error, interpretation was for the jury and trial court did not err in admitting it over rule 403 objection); Davis v. State, 330 Ark. 610, 955 S.W.2d 705, 708 (1997) (trial court did not err in admitting entirety of recorded conversation involving defendant over Rule 403 objection). *Cf.* State v. Allen, 126 Wash. App. 1017, 2005 WL 536082 (Div. 2 2005), aff'd, 159 Wash. 2d 1, 147 P.3d 581 (2006) (not published) (jury's playing of tape recorded confession during deliberations was not unduly prejudicial because tapes were likely to promote jury's resolution of issues "rather than incite an emotional response").

[10]Schulz, 691 N.W.2d at 478 ("while it is clear the [recorded] voice mail message [from the defendant

like that lower courts often apply a requirement of voluntariness as at least implicating trustworthiness. It is also likely that this application occurs with the attitude that generally trustworthiness is a matter for the factfinder, and the implicit trustworthiness aspect of voluntariness is invoked only by a showing of extraordinary factors that strongly suggest unreliability.[11]

Insofar as the requirement of corroboration is an admissibility demand,[12] it may require what amounts to an admissibility inquiry into trustworthiness. This is clearly the result of the Utah court's adoption of the trustworthiness approach to corroboration in *State v. Mauchley*.[13] *Mauchley* also developed[14] how a preliminary inquiry into trustworthiness might proceed:

> In cases . . . where there is no evidence of a crime independent of the confession, the State may nevertheless "establish the trustwor-

---

introduced into evidence by the prosecution] had a devastating impact on the defendant's case, principally because a confession recorded in the defendant's own voice is highly incriminating, there is no support in the record for the assertion . . . that introduction of such a confession is evidence giving one party an unfair advantage").

[11]In a Connecticut prosecution, for example, defense counsel moved to suppress the defendant's confession, relying on the defendant's fatigue, the duration of custody, the length of the interrogation, and certain aspects of the statement that counsel asserted were inaccurate. The trial judge overruled the motion, explaining he found no hint of coercion and believed the confession was "the product of an essentially free and unconstrained choice by its maker." Defense counsel asked if the court intended to address "the reliability issue that I raised." The judge responded that he thought he had and counsel commented that the ruling was only on "voluntariness." The judge then continued in further explanation of his ruling: "[T]here is nothing . . . that would diminish the reliability of the confession." Clearly this trial judge regarded voluntariness as including consideration of trustworthiness. State v. Rivet, 2005 WL 1756341 (Conn. Super. Ct. 2005) (not reported).

A few appellate decisions have addressed the matter. An Illinois appellate court concluded that the state's voluntariness case law required consideration of both whether a statement was voluntary and whether it was reliable. People v. Braggs, 335 Ill. App. 3d 52, 268 Ill. Dec. 861, 779 N.E.2d 475 (1st Dist. 2002). On further review, the Illinois Supreme Court resolved the case on other grounds. 810 N.E.2d 472 (Ill.2004). *See also* State v. Farley, 192 W. Va. 247, 452 S.E.2d 50, 57 (1994) (reliability is relevant to voluntariness but it is not the "primary consideration"). *Compare* Com. v. DiGiambattista, 442 Mass. 423, 813 N.E.2d 516, 528 n.15 (2004) (voluntariness is not assessed based on the reliability of the confession itself, but "it is nevertheless troublesome that this particular confession has been shown to be inaccurate in so many important respects").

[12]See § 145 supra.

[13]State v. Mauchley, 2003 UT 10, 67 P.3d 477 (Utah 2003). See generally § 148 supra.

[14]The court relied heavily upon Leo and Ofshe, Criminal Law: The Consequences of False Confessions: Deprivation of Liberty and Miscarriages of Justice in the Age of Psychological Interrogation, 88 J. Crim. L. & Criminology 429 (1998).

thiness of the confession with other evidence typically used to bolster the credibility and reliability of an out-of-court statement."

Factors used in other areas of the law to bolster the credibility and reliability of an out-of-court statement include the following: evidence as to the spontaneity of the statement; the absence of deception, trick, threats, or promises to obtain the statement; the defendant's positive physical and mental condition, including age, education, and experience; and the presence of an attorney when the statement is given. We conclude that these factors also have applicability in determining the trustworthiness of confessions.

We emphasize, however, that since a demonstrably wrong statement may indicate that a confession is false, the overall facts and circumstances related in the confession must be consistent with " 'facts otherwise known or established.' " For example, if a man spontaneously confesses that he fondled a child, but the evidence demonstrates he was never in physical proximity with the child, his confession is likely untrustworthy because the facts related in the confession are inconsistent with otherwise known or established facts.[15]

If the facts contain independent evidence of the offense, that of course may also be used to evaluate trustworthiness:

One of the ways a confession may be bolstered by independent evidence is by showing a person's confession demonstrates the individual has specific personal knowledge about the crime.

While not exclusive, three factors tending to demonstrate personal knowledge include the following: (1) providing information that "lead[s] to the discovery of evidence unknown to the police," (2) providing information about "highly unusual elements of the crime that have not been made public," and (3) providing "an accurate description of the mundane details of the crime scene which are not easily guessed and have not been reported publicly," because "mundane details [are] less likely to be the result of [suggestion] by the police." Examples of mundane details may include the following: "how the victim was clothed, disarray of certain furniture pieces, presence or absence of particular objects at the crime scene," "or which window was jimmied open."

Here, too, the degree of "fit between the specifics of a confession and the crime facts" is critical because the "fit" determines whether a confession should be deemed trustworthy. If a person merely provides information already known by the police or the public, or if the information provided is inaccurate, a confession may be untrustworthy.[16]

It would be preferable for courts to explicitly recognize that a defendant may reasonably object to the admissibility of an out-of-court statement on the ground that there are significant indications that the statement is untrustworthy, the jury is not likely to properly consider these indications, and thus that the jury will

---

[15]Mauchley, 67 P.3d at 488–89 (citations omitted).

[16]67 P.3d at 489 (citations omitted).

give the evidence regarding the statement more weight than it is entitled to be given. Such an objection calls for an inquiry and this inquiry is distinct from that into voluntariness.

The approach set out in *Mauchley* is an excellent framework for an inquiry of this sort. Reality dictates, however, that application of this approach accommodate the traditional notion that the credibility of evidence that the defendant confessed is ordinarily for the trier of fact. A defendant seeking to exclude a confession as untrustworthy must establish to the satisfaction of the judge that unusual considerations mean that the jury is unlikely to objectively evaluate the trustworthiness and hence the weight properly given to the prosecution's evidence in the case before the court.

## § 158   Mandatory recording of confessions

Traditionally, the means by which law enforcement and prosecution authorities preserve and present at trial a criminal defendant's out-of-court incriminating statements goes to the weight of the evidence rather than to its admissibility.[1] Some have long urged, however, that law enforcement be required to record such statements and perhaps also the interrogations that lead to them, and that such requirements be enforced by limits on admissibility of evidence of such statements.

Proponents of a recording requirement argue that criminal defendants' rights to have involuntary admissions excluded and to have law enforcement misconduct during questioning identified and penalized can be enforced only if courts can be provided a specific and accurate record of what occurred during law enforcement interviews of defendants. Only recordings can provide such records.[2] Others contend that such a requirement is often impractical, and generally expensive.[3] Moreover, recording may discourage suspects from making admissions for reasons

---

[Section 158]

[1]*E.g.,* State v. Knight, 369 N.J. Super. 424, 849 A.2d 209, 219 (App. Div. 2004), judgment rev'd on other grounds, 183 N.J. 449, 874 A.2d 546 (2005).

[2]Stephan v. State, 711 P.2d 1156, 1161 (Alaska 1985) ("In the absence of an accurate record [of the interrogation], the accused may suffer an infringement upon his right to remain silent and to have counsel present during the interrogation."). *See generally,* *e.g.,* Drizin & Reich, Heeding the

Lessons of History: The Need for Mandatory Recording of Police Interrogations to Accurately Assess the reliability and Voluntariness of Confessions, 52 Drake L. Rev. 619 (2004); Leo & Ofshe, The Consequences of False Confessions: Deprivation of Liberty and Miscarriages of Justice in the Age of Psychological Interrogation, 88 J. Crim. L. & Criminology 429, 494-95 (1998).

[3]*See* State v. Cook, 179 N.J. 533, 847 A.2d 530, 545 (2004).

entirely unrelated to those interests the legal limits on interrogations and the use of admissions are designed to further.[4]

What authority courts have to impose requirements that admissions be recorded or to exclude evidence where such requirements have been violated is questionable. There is universal agreement that federal constitutional considerations demand neither recording nor exclusion of evidence of admissions because questioning or statements were not recorded.[5]

In 1980, the Alaska Supreme Court announced that law enforcement officers were required to record interrogation of suspects, when recording was feasible.[6] Five years later in *Stephan v. State*,[7] the court made clear this was an aspect of state constitutional due process, which required that it be enforced by an exclusionary rule barring the use of evidence of admissions related to a violation of that rule.[8]

Several courts have imposed somewhat similar requirements in the exercise of their supervisory authority. In what is probably the leading decision, *State v. Scales*,[9] the Minnesota Supreme Court held that all custodial interrogations including any information about rights, any waiver of those rights, and all questioning were to be electronically recorded where feasible and must be recorded when questioning occurs at a place of detention. Suppression is required of any statements obtained in violation of the recording requirement if—but only if—the violation is found "substantial."[10]

The Massachusetts Supreme Judicial Court, emphasizing the complexities of the undertaking in *Scales*, nevertheless found

---

[4]Suspects may simply have an emotional aversion to being recorded that generates anxiety when recording occurs. Of course, this must be distinguished from any tendency of a recording to simply focus a defendant's attention on the legal significance of the actions at issue. *See* Cook, 847 A.2d at 544 ("A technique, like recording, that reinforces a suspect's understanding and appreciation of that portion of the *Miranda* warnings [that anything he says can be used against him in a court of law] is not to be eschewed because it would have that desirable reinforcing effect.").

[5]*E.g.*, Martin v. Lord, 378 F. Supp. 2d 184, 185 n.1 (W.D. N.Y. 2005); U.S. v. Owlboy, 370 F. Supp. 2d 946, 949 (D.N.D. 2005); Clark v. State, 374 Ark. 292, 287 S.W.3d 567, 574–76

(2008) (summarizing case law). *Accord, e.g.*, People v. Childres, 60 A.D.3d 1278, 875 N.Y.S.2d 662, 664 (4th Dep't 2009) (no federal—or state—due process requirement that interrogations and confessions be electronically recorded).

[6]Mallott v. State, 608 P.2d 737, 743 n.5 (Alaska 1980).

[7]Stephan v. State, 711 P.2d 1156 (Alaska 1985).

[8]Stephan, 711 P.2d at 1161–62.

[9]State v. Scales, 518 N.W.2d 587 (Minn. 1994).

[10]Scales, 518 N.W.2d at 592. The court refused to expand the requirement to include noncustodial interrogations. State v. Conger, 652 N.W.2d 704, 709 (Minn. 2002).

that lack of responsiveness to its expressed preference for recording justified some supervisory action. It found sufficient action
short of that taken in *Scales*:

> [W]hen the prosecution introduces evidence of a defendant's confes-
> sion or statement that is the product of a custodial interrogation or
> an interrogation conducted at a place of detention (e.g., a police sta-
> tion), and there is not at least an audiotape recording of the
> complete interrogation, the defendant is entitled (on request) to a
> jury instruction advising that the State's highest court has
> expressed a preference that such interrogations be recorded when-
> ever practicable, and cautioning the jury that, because of the
> absence of any recording of the interrogation in the case before
> them, they should weigh evidence of the defendant's alleged state-
> ment with great caution and care. Where voluntariness is a live is-
> sue . . ., the jury should also be advised that the absence of a re-
> cording permits (but does not compel) them to conclude that the
> Commonwealth has failed to prove voluntariness beyond a reason-
> able doubt.[11]

The New Jersey Supreme Court in *State v. Cook*,[12] decided in
2004, indicated a willingness to exercise its supervisory authority.
It established an advisory committee to study and make recommendations on the use of electronic recordings of custodial
interrogations. In 2005, after receiving the report of that committee,[13] it adopted New Jersey Court Rule 3:17 directing recording.[14]
Law enforcement's failure to record a statement as required by
the rule "shall be a factor for consideration by the trial court in
determining the admissibility of a statement, and by the jury in
determining whether the statement was made, and if so, what
weight, if any, to give to the statement."[15] Where a required recording was not made, "the court shall, upon request of the defendant, provide the jury with a cautionary instruction."[16]

Since *Stephan*, *Scales* and *Cook*, courts have generally been
unwilling to adopt recording requirements, either as mandates of
state constitutional law or pursuant to judicial supervisory
authority. The Connecticut Supreme Court, for example, after an
extensive discussion, stressed that its unwillingness to impose recording requirements under either authority was due in large
part to the complexity of the matter and its perception that the
nature of the relevant considerations made the matter better

---

[11]Com. v. DiGiambattista, 442
Mass. 423, 813 N.E.2d 516, 533–34
(2004). The court five years later refused to hold unrecorded statements
per se inadmissible. Com. v. Pimental,
454 Mass. 475, 910 N.E.2d 366, 372
(2009).

[12]State v. Cook, 179 N.J. 533, 847

A.2d 530 (2004).

[13]*See* State v. Delgado, 188 N.J.
48, 902 A.2d 888, 896 (2006).

[14]N.J. Ct. Rule 3:17.

[15]N.J. Ct. Rule 3:17(d).

[16]N.J. Ct. Rule 3:17(e).

suited to legislative resolution.[17] It also expressed reservations concerning the use of its supervisory authority to promulgate requirements impacting so dramatically matters outside the judicial process.[18]

A number of legislatures have, however, acted. Illinois now provides by statute that in a homicide prosecution a statement made during custodial interrogation at a place of detention that is not recorded is presumed inadmissible.[19] This presumption "may be overcome by a preponderance of the evidence that the statement was voluntarily given and is reliable, based on the totality of the circumstances."[20]

The District of Columbia legislation requires police to tape custodial interrogations of persons suspected of crimes of violence.[21] Maine requires that all law enforcement agencies adopt written policies "regarding procedure to deal with. . . . recording of law enforcement interviews of suspects in serious crimes . . . ."[22] Neither provision addresses the evidentiary consequences of failures to record.

---

[17]State v. Lockhart, 298 Conn. 537, 4 A.3d 1176, 1181–91 (2010). *Accord* State v. Barros, 24 A.3d 1158, 1166 (R.I. 2011) (Rhode Island criminal due process clause does not afford defendants right to have custodial interrogations recorded).

[18]Lockhart, 4 A.3d at 1191–92 (court normally exercises supervisory authority "with regard to judicial actors" and proposal "would directly effect all law enforcement agencies"). *Accord* Barros, 24 A.3d at 1166 (declining to exercise supervisory power to promulgate a mandatory recording requirement). Other courts have declined to reverse earlier holdings that no constitutional right to recording exists, People v. Pearson, 53 Cal. 4th 306, 135 Cal. Rptr. 3d 262, 266 P.3d 966, 976 (2012); State v. Eli, 126 Haw. 510, 273 P.3d 1196, 1203 (2012), or have held for as a matter of first impression that no right to recording exists, State v. Madsen, 813 N.W.2d 714, 722 (Iowa 2012); State v. Goebel, 2007 ND 4, 725 N.W.2d 578, 584 (N.D. 2007).

The Wisconsin Supreme Court held that all custodial interrogations of juveniles at a place of detention be electronically recorded and "where feasible" when conducted elsewhere. In re Jerrell C.J., 2005 WI 105, 283 Wis. 2d 145, 699 N.W.2d 110, 123 (2005). Explaining its exercise of its supervisory power, the Wisconsin Supreme Court explained that the requirement imposed was not one regulating police practice. Law enforcement questioning in violation of the requirement would not be in any sense "illegal." Rather, the court's power to regulate the flow of evidence permitted it to adopt requirements for the use of evidence resulting from police interrogations. Jerrell C.J., 699 N.W.2d at 119–20.

[19]725 Ill. Comp. Stat. Ann. 5/103-2.1(b). *See generally* People v. Harris, 2012 IL App (1st) 100678, 364 Ill. Dec. 902, 977 N.E.2d 811, 820–26 (App. Ct. 1st Dist. 2012) (discussing statute at length).

[20]725 Ill. Comp. Stat. Ann. 5/103-2.1(f). The Connecticut statute is similar. Conn. Pub. Act. 11-174, § 1, codified at Conn. Gen. Stat. Ann. § 54.1o (effective Jan. 1, 2014); Conn. Gen Stat. Ann. § 54.1o.

[21]D.C. Code Ann. § 5-116.01.

[22]Me. Rev. Stat. tit. 25 § 2803-B(1)(k).

Missouri, as a result of 2009 legislation, provides that all custodial interrogation of persons suspected of specified serious offenses "shall be recorded when feasible."[23] The governor is authorized (by subsection 5 of the statute) to withhold funds from a law enforcement agency that in bad faith fails to attempt to comply with this directive.[24] Then the statute minimizes the evidentiary and procedural effects of nonrecording:

> Nothing in this section shall be construed as a ground to exclude evidence, and a violation of this section shall not have impact other than that provided for in subsection 5 of this section. Compliance or noncompliance with this section shall not be admitted as evidence, argued, referenced, considered or questioned during a criminal trial.[25]

If a recording requirement is to be imposed, perhaps the major question is how complete a recording should be required. Should it be sufficient that the prosecution has a recording of the statement it wishes to introduce? Or should the record also include all custodial interrogation, the warnings and waivers before custodial interrogation begins, or perhaps even all interaction between the defendant and officers in which improper influences on the defendant might be brought to bear?[26] The New Hampshire Supreme Court focused on this and held—pursuant to its supervisory power—that although it would impose no requirement of a recording, the prosecution could use a recording to prove a statement made during custodial interrogation only if the entire interrogation was recorded.[27]

A further question is whether any recording requirement imposed should be made enforceable by exclusion of some or all

---

[23]Mo. Rev. Stat. § 590.700(2).

[24]Mo. Rev. Stat. § 590.700(5).

[25]Mo. Rev. Stat. § 590.700(6).

Texas requires the recording of statements made during custodial interrogation for the statement to be admissible, but provides some exceptions. Tex. Code Crim. Proc. art. 38.22, § 3.

[26]Sullivan, Recording Custodial Interrogations: The Police Experience, 52 Fed. Law. 20, 23 (2005) ("A number of [police] departments record suspects' final statements or confessions but not the preceding questioning.").

[27]State v. Barnett, 147 N.H. 334, 789 A.2d 629, 632–33 (2001). Accord State v. Dupont, 149 N.H. 70, 816 A.2d

954, 958 (2003) (where police warned defendant, obtained waivers, interrogated him, obtained a statement, and only then audiotaped his confession, trial judge erred in admitting the recording). Barnett does not require that the recording include the warnings and the defendant's waivers.

Of course, other recording-related issues may arise as well, including some about the mechanics of the recording process. One court noted that if a statement is videorecorded, jurors' response may be affected by whether the camera was focused on the defendant or rather showed both the defendant and the interrogator. Cook, 847 A.2d at 545 n. 6.

statement unrecorded in violation of the requirement.[28] An exclusionary penalty, of course, might reasonably be regarded as the only way of providing an effective incentive for law enforcement compliance with any recording mandate imposed. On the other hand, some courts or legislatures may find a recording requirement acceptable only if it is not burdened by the complexities and costs of an exclusionary sanction. A recording requirement without an exclusionary penalty may have some value and is perhaps preferable to no such requirement.

Insofar as a recording requirement is enforced by a rule excluding evidence, perhaps the major question is what should be required to trigger the right to have evidence excluded? The evidence rule would provide the maximum motivation, of course, if the fact of noncompliance alone is sufficient to require exclusion.[29] But the courts have been reluctant to so mandate the exclusion of evidence of potentially reliable confessions.[30] Under the Minnesota approach as adopted in *Scales*, for example, a defendant's failure to claim that an unrecorded statement was tainted by a violation of the requirements of *Miranda v. Arizona*[31] or was involuntary or otherwise inadmissible means the violation of the recording requirement is not substantial and need not (and perhaps must not) result in exclusion.[32] In *Stephan*, the Alaska Supreme Court indicated that the due process recording requirement did not require exclusion "if no testimony is presented that

---

[28]Two leading advocates of recording have abandoned their earlier contention that failure to record should require exclusion of a confession. Sullivan and Vail, The Consequences of Law Enforcement Officials' Failure to Record Custodial Interviews as Required by Law, 99 J. Crim. L. & Criminology 215, 221 (2009) ("The better approach is to allow testimony by both prosecution and defense as to what occurred during the unrecorded interviews, but require that trial judges give jury instructions about the legal requirement of electronically recording custodial interviews, and the superior reliability of recordings as compared to testimony about what was said and done.").

[29]This is the approach suggested by the model of Miranda v. Arizona, 384 U.S. 436, 86 S. Ct. 1602, 16 L. Ed. 2d 694 (1966), under which the failure

to comply with the warning and waiver requirements requires exclusion regardless of whether the defendant claims that the offered admission was involuntary; see § 150 supra.

[30]*Cf.* State v. Tilt, 2004 UT App 395, 101 P.3d 838, 841–42 (Utah Ct. App. 2004) (noting Utah Supreme Court's earlier recognition that rule requiring recording of confessions "would deprive the courts of much evidence that is generally reliable").

[31]Miranda v. Arizona, 384 U.S. 436, 86 S. Ct. 1602, 16 L. Ed. 2d 694 (1966).

[32]State v. Inman, 692 N.W.2d 76, 81 (Minn. 2005) (exclusion was not required where at hearing on admissibility of confession defendant created no evidentiary dispute regarding issues relating to confession).

the [unrecorded] statement is inaccurate or was obtained improperly."[33]

In the absence of any formal requirement that a statement or interrogation be recorded, the absence of a recording is evidence bearing on whatever issues may be presented. Officers' unexplained failure to record an interrogation where recording was possible might sufficiently impair their credibility that their testimony will not suffice to meet the prosecution's burden of proving compliance with *Miranda v. Arizona*[34] or voluntariness.[35]

## § 159   Evidence obtained as a result of inadmissible confessions[1]

At early common law, the involuntariness of a confession did not affect the admissibility of other evidence obtained by use of that statement.[2] If, for example, a suspect was coerced into confessing to a murder and also into revealing the location of the murder weapon, the weapon, if located, could be used in evidence. The rationale for this position was that the confession was excluded because of its untrustworthiness. If the "fruits" of that confession were themselves sufficiently probative of the defendant's guilt, the reason for excluding the confession did not extend to that derivative evidence and hence it was admissible. American courts applying the voluntariness requirement adopted this position.[3]

As criminal evidence became permeated with exclusionary flavor after *Mapp v. Ohio*[4] and *Miranda v Arizona*,[5] American courts quite uncritically adopted for confession cases the "fruit of the poisonous tree" doctrine as developed in Fourth Amendment

---

[33]Stephan v. State, 711 P.2d 1156, 1165 (Alaska 1985).

[34]Miranda v. Arizona, 384 U.S. 436, 86 S. Ct. 1602, 16 L. Ed. 2d 694 (1966).

[35]*E.g.*, U.S. v. Lewis, 355 F. Supp. 2d 870, 873–74 (E.D. Mich. 2005) (experienced officers' failure to memorialize interviews by video or audio record, where equipment was available, contributed to finding that prosecution had not complied with *Miranda* despite their testimony that they had done so).

**[Section 159]**

[1]*See generally* West's Key Number Digest, Criminal Law ☞394.1(3),

413.38, 413.49, 413.96.

[2]3 Wigmore, Evidence § 859 (Chadbourn rev. 1970).

[3]Osborn v. People, 83 Colo. 4, 262 P. 892, 900–01 (1927); State v. Brauner, 239 La. 651, 119 So. 2d 497, 500 (1960); State v. Herring, 200 N.C. 306, 156 S.E. 537, 537 (1931).

[4]Mapp v. Ohio, 367 U.S. 643, 81 S. Ct. 1684, 6 L. Ed. 2d 1081 (1961), discussed in § 166 infra.

[5]Miranda v. Arizona, 384 U.S. 436, 86 S. Ct. 1602, 16 L. Ed. 2d 694 (1966).

case law.[6] This was apparently on the rationale that voluntariness law had come to serve purposes other than assuring the reliability of evidence, and encouraging law enforcement compliance with rules designed to accomplish these broader objectives required exclusion of "fruits" as well as involuntary confessions themselves.[7]

The Supreme Court made clear that at least the Fifth Amendment issue is not that easily resolved. In *United States v. Patane*,[8] the Court held that federal constitutional law did not require the exclusion of physical evidence obtained by using information in a statement itself inadmissible because it was tainted by a violation of the requirements of *Miranda*. No majority of the justices agreed on a rationale for this, however.

Justice Thomas, writing for three members of the Court, reasoned that the nature of the Fifth Amendment privilege precluded a rule requiring exclusion. The Self-Incrimination Clause is violated only by the use at trial of a defendant's compelled testimony, and thus the clause itself cannot be violated by the evidentiary use of nontestimonial evidence obtained as a result of a voluntary out-of-court statement. Prophylactic rules such as those imposed by *Miranda* are justified only if they are necessary to assure that compelled statements themselves will not be used at trial. Permitting the use of the fruits of a statement creates no danger that the statement itself will be used at trial.[9]

The *Miranda* requirements do not constitute "a direct constraint on the police," Justice Thomas continued. Thus there is no reason to apply a fruit of the poisonous tree as a means of encouraging police compliance with those requirements themselves.[10]

---

[6]*E.g.,* Gladden v. Holland, 366 F.2d 580, 584 (9th Cir. 1966) (despite involuntary confession, state defendant could be retried but at such a trial that confession and "any of the fruits thereof" cannot be used); People v. O'Leary, 45 Ill. 2d 122, 257 N.E.2d 112, 114 (1970) (after struggling with voluntariness of confession to burglary and holding it involuntary, court simply assumes that this also requires suppression of pry bar which defendant revealed to officers during and after confession).

[7]*See generally* People v. Ditson, 57 Cal. 2d 415, 20 Cal. Rptr. 165, 369 P.2d 714, 725–27 (1962).

[8]U.S. v. Patane, 542 U.S. 630, 124 S. Ct. 2620, 159 L. Ed. 2d 667 (2004).

[9]542 U.S. at 643.

[10]542 U.S. at 642.

At least one court has found a bar to use of a later statement triggered not by *Miranda's* "procedural" requirement of warnings but rather a failure to honor the right to counsel when that right was asserted by the suspect. Osburn v. State, 2009 Ark. 390, 326 S.W.3d 771, 783 (2009) (this showed a violation of a Fifth Amendment right the triggered a fruit of the poisonous tree doctrine). *Accord* State v. Venegas, 79 So. 3d 912, 915 (Fla. 2d

Justice Souter, writing for three and perhaps four justices,[11] reasoned that the *Miranda* requirements are closely enough related to the core protections afforded by the Fifth Amendment that the need to encourage law enforcement compliance with them justifies the exclusion of the fruit of a statement obtained in violation of them.[12] Justice Kennedy, writing for himself and Justice O'Connor, did not reach whether the need to deter *Miranda* violations themselves could justify a constitutional rule excluding the fruit of a statement. Assuming that deterrence of *Miranda* violations was a proper consideration, he concluded that "the important probative value of reliable physical evidence" meant that proponents of a fruit of the poisonous tree rule had failed to make their case.[13]

*Patane* involved physical evidence obtained as a result of a statement tainted by a *Miranda* violation. But the result confirmed the Court's earlier holdings that no fruit of the poisonous tree analysis applied to the testimony of witnesses found as a result of such a statement[14] or an incriminating out-of-court statement by the accused made after compliance with *Miranda* but made subsequent to the tainted and inadmissible statement.[15]

*Patane* reaffirmed the indications given nearly twenty years earlier in *Oregon v. Elstad*[16] that the same approach would not be taken to evidence obtained as a factual consequence of an involuntary out-of-court statement.

*Elstad* and *Patane* make clear that if a confession is involuntary, neither the rule permitting evidentiary use of the fruits of a *Miranda* violation nor its rationale apply. Consequently, at least a subsequent confession given by the defendant is not free from challenge as tainted by the events stimulating the first confession. On the other hand, *Elstad* reaffirmed that a suspect from whom a confession has been coerced is not, as a result, perpetually disabled from thereafter giving an admissible confession,[17] and *Patane* gave no reason to question this.

Precisely what standard determines whether a subsequently

---

DCA 2012) (physical evidence must be suppressed where case did not involve a "mere failure[ ] to warn" but rather continuing uncounseled interrogation after defendant invoked the right to counsel).

[11]Justice Breyer relied on reasons he described as similar to those set forth in Justice Souter's opinion. Patane, 542 U.S. at 647–48 (Breyer, dissenting).

[12]542 U.S. at 646–47 (Souter, J., dissenting).

[13]542 U.S. at 645 (Kennedy, J., concurring in the judgment).

[14]Michigan v. Tucker, 417 U.S. 433, 94 S. Ct. 2357, 41 L. Ed. 2d 182 (1974).

[15]Oregon v. Elstad, 470 U.S. 298, 105 S. Ct. 1285, 84 L. Ed. 2d 222 (1985).

[16]Oregon v. Elstad, 470 U.S. 298, 105 S. Ct. 1285, 84 L. Ed. 2d 222 (1985).

[17]Elstad, 470 U.S. at 311–12.

given confession is suppressible because of successful voluntariness challenge to the admissibility of the initial confession, however, is not entirely clear. The major question is whether the prosecution establishes admissibility by proving that the second and challenged confession is itself voluntary or whether it must prove more. There are two major possibilities.

First, a defendant may simply need to persuade a court that the prosecution has failed to establish the voluntariness of the challenged subsequent confession. While the Court has left open whether there is a formal presumption that a confession is involuntary if it was given after an initial involuntary statement,[18] the prosecution's burden of proving voluntariness at least imposes a practical need to overcome an inference of involuntariness.[19] As a practical matter, then, the prosecution may need to establish that the influences rendering the first statement involuntary were no longer operative or controlling at the time of the second.

Second, a more conventional fruit of the poisonous tree analysis, as used in Fourth Amendment exclusionary sanction analysis, may apply. If the defendant—perhaps aided by a presumption—establishes that "but for" having made the first and involuntary statement the defendant would not have made the second and challenged confession as and when he did, the second confession becomes inadmissible fruit unless the prosecution establishes that the taint of the coercion was attenuated. Whether this approach really differs in substance from the first is by no means clear.[20]

If a defendant challenges nonconfession evidence as the inadmissible result of an involuntary confession, presumably the second approach distinguished above will apply. Such evidence is inadmissible fruit of the involuntary confession if "but for" the

---

[18]*See* Lyons v. State of Okl., 322 U.S. 596, 604, 64 S. Ct. 1208, 88 L. Ed. 1481 (1944) (not reaching suggestion that Court adopt "a presumption that earlier abuses render subsequent confessions involuntary unless there is clear and definite evidence to overcome the presumption").

[19]At least some lower courts apply such a presumption. *E.g.,* Mirabal v. State, 698 So. 2d 360, 361 (Fla. 4th DCA 1997) ("Generally, where it is established that the initial confession was involuntary, the coercion is presumed to continue 'unless clearly shown to have been removed prior to a subsequent confession.'").

[20]People v. Ornelas, 937 P.2d 867,

871 (Colo. App. 1996):

To demonstrate the admissibility of a subsequent confession that may be tainted by a prior involuntary confession, the prosecution must establish that the connection between the initial illegality and the evidence has become so attenuated as to dissipate the initial taint. The illegal taint may be purged if the voluntariness of the second statement is shown.

Thus a showing of voluntariness accomplished attenuation of the taint. *Accord* U.S. v. Jenkins, 938 F.2d 934, 941 (9th Cir. 1991) ("Determining whether the taint had dissipated sufficiently is merely another way of asking whether the subsequent confession was, itself, voluntary.").

confession the evidence would not have been obtained as it was. The prosecution can escape exclusion by showing an exception, such as attenuation of taint or inevitable discovery, applies.

State law, of course, need not track the Supreme Court's federal constitutional law. After *Elstad*, some state courts incorporated the Supreme Court's approach into any *Miranda*-like requirement of state law.[21] Other state tribunals, however, rejected *Elstad*.[22] Massachusetts has also rejected *Patane*, reasoning that "[t]o apply the *Patane* analysis to the broader rights embodied in [our state constitution] would have a corrosive effect on them, undermine the respect we have accorded them, and demean their importance to a system of justice chosen by the citizens of Massachusetts in 1780."[23] The court adopted "a common-law rule" making physical evidence obtained as a result of a statement inadmissible.[24] Several other state courts have also rejected *Patane* as a matter of state law.[25]

The Wisconsin Supreme Court held that state constitutional considerations bar the use of physical evidence obtained as a result of a deliberate *Miranda* violation. It stressed the need for a strong deterrent of the "particularly repugnant" law enforcement conduct involved.[26] In addition, however, it emphasized that the scope of the exclusionary penalty imposed by state constitutional law would be determined in part by what is appropriate to assure the integrity of the state judiciary. That judiciary would be "systemically corrupted" by an exclusionary sanction encourag-

---

[21]State v. Aubuchont, 141 N.H. 206, 679 A.2d 1147, 1149 (1996); State v. Hicks, 333 N.C. 467, 428 S.E.2d 167, 177 (1993).

[22]People v. Bethea, 67 N.Y.2d 364, 502 N.Y.S.2d 713, 493 N.E.2d 937, 938 (1986) (State constitutional protection against compelled self-incrimination "would have little deterrent effect if the police know that they can as part of a continuous chain of events question a suspect in custody without warning, provided only they thereafter question him or her again after warnings have been given"). *Accord* State v. Pebria, 85 Haw. 171, 938 P.2d 1190, 1193 (Ct. App. 1997); Com. v. Prater, 420 Mass. 569, 651 N.E.2d 833, 841 (1995); State v. Smith, 834 S.W.2d 915, 919 (Tenn. 1992).

[23]Com. v. Martin, 444 Mass. 213,

827 N.E.2d 198, 203 (2005).

[24]Martin, 827 N.E.2d at 200.

[25]State v. Farris, 109 Ohio St. 3d 519, 2006-Ohio-3255, 849 N.E.2d 985 (2006) ("physical evidence obtained as a result of the unwarned statements . . . is inadmissible pursuant to Section 10, Article I of the Ohio Constitution"); State v. Vondehn, 348 Or. 462, 236 P.3d 691, 700 (2010) ("when the police violate Article I, section 12, by failing to give required *Miranda* warnings, the state is precluded from using physical evidence that is derived from that constitutional violation to prosecute a defendant"); State v. Peterson, 181 Vt. 436, 2007 VT 24, 923 A.2d 585, 590–93 (2007).

[26]State v. Knapp, 2005 WI 127, 285 Wis. 2d 86, 700 N.W.2d 899, 918 (2005).

ing law enforcement "to intentionally take unwarranted investigatory shortcuts to obtain convictions."[27]

## § 160    Judicial confessions,[1] guilty pleas, and admissions made in plea bargaining[2]

Most confession law involves self-incriminating admissions made by suspects to law enforcement officers during the prejudicial stages of a criminal investigation. But the prosecution sometimes seeks trial use of self-incriminating admissions made by the defendant during what is essentially the judicial processing of a case. These admissions can usefully be broken down into three categories: "judicial" confessions, guilty pleas, and admissions made in connection with plea bargaining.

*Judicial Confessions.* A so-called "judicial confession" is an incriminating admission made in court or judicial proceedings.[3] It may consist of a defendant's testimony in a different (and perhaps civil) proceeding[4] or in a prior hearing during the criminal prosecution in which it is offered.[5] It may also be a "stipulation" or even the pleadings in this or other litigation.[6] Under the general rules governing admissions,[7] these judicial confessions are admissible, subject of course to compliance with such requirements as any right to counsel the defendant may have had at the time.

*Guilty Pleas.* A defendant's guilty plea and statements made in connection with its offer to and acceptance by the trial court are

---

[27]Knapp, 700 N.W.2d at 921.

**[Section 160]**

[1]*See generally* West's Key Number Digest, Criminal Law ⟊410.20 to 410.29.

[2]*See generally* West's Key Number Digest, Criminal Law ⟊410.46.

[3]*Cf.* People v. Watson, 2012 IL App (2d) 91328, 358 Ill. Dec. 403, 965 N.E.2d 474, 487 (App. Ct. 2d Dist. 2012).

[4]*E.g.,* U.S. v. McClellan, 868 F.2d 210, 215 (7th Cir. 1989) (prosecution permitted to introduce defendant's own testimony and admissions by defendant and his attorney, all made in earlier civil proceeding by creditors to have certain debts declared nondischargeable in bankruptcy).

[5]People v. Thomas, 191 Ill. App. 3d 187, 138 Ill. Dec. 568, 547 N.E.2d 735, 740 (4th Dist. 1989) (prosecution

permitted to prove that at a pretrial hearing on defense counsel's motion to withdraw, the defendant testified to his irritation at having to attend several pretrial hearings and explained, "[A]ll this stuff ain't necessary, you know, especially when I know that I am not guilty of nothing but aggravated battery, you know?"); People v. Rose, 224 A.D.2d 643, 639 N.Y.S.2d 413, 414 (2d Dep't 1996) (prosecution properly permitted to use admissions made by defendant during testimony before grand jury).

[6]*E.g.,* State v. Irving, 114 N.J. 427, 555 A.2d 575, 580 (1989) (testifying defendant could be cross-examined concerning contents of his notice-of-alibi "bill of particulars," because factual assertions in pleadings may be used against the person making the assertions).

[7]See § 266 infra.

admissible as admissions.[8] Pleas of guilty to minor offenses may sometimes constitute questionable evidence of actual guilt, but this is best handled by considering on a case-by-case basis the probative value of particular pleas weighed against the risk of undue prejudice likely to arise from their admission into evidence.[9]

Federal Rule 410[10] prohibits the use of a withdrawn guilty plea and also bars the use of statements made in the course of proceedings in which such pleas are submitted to and accepted by the trial court. This is apparently on the rationale that permitting use of the plea would frustrate the policy objectives supporting the right to withdraw that plea.[11] State statutes or court rules generally are similar.[12]

*Admissions Made in Connection With Plea Bargaining.* There is general agreement that admissions made in connection with plea negotiations that do not result in final pleas of guilty must be excluded in order to encourage the desirable or at least necessary process of plea bargaining. This is provided for in federal litigation by Federal Rule 410.[13] State statutes and court rules often address the matter as well, although there is considerable variation among the provisions.[14]

These provisions typically make inadmissible statements made

---

[8]*E.g.,* U.S. v. Jose, 359 Fed. Appx. 813, 814 (9th Cir. 2009) ("The guilty plea was an admission by a party-opponent of his having assaulted the victim. *See* Fed. R. Evid. 801(d)(2)(A) ."); U.S. v. Gotti, 641 F. Supp. 283, 289 (E.D. N.Y. 1986) (guilty pleas and accompanying "allocutions" would be accepted as admission by a party); People v. Latham, 90 N.Y.2d 795, 666 N.Y.S.2d 557, 689 N.E.2d 527, 528 (1997) (defendant's admissions made during entry of plea of guilty to attempted murder were admissible in prosecution for murder, brought after victim died).

[9]Gotti, 641 F.Supp. at 290 (pleas of guilty to misdemeanors would not be excluded per se but would be evaluated under Fed. R. Evid. 403).

[10]Fed. R. Evid. 410. See § 266 infra.

[11]Kercheval v. U.S., 274 U.S. 220, 223–24, 47 S. Ct. 582, 71 L. Ed. 1009 (1927) (prohibiting pre-Rules use of withdrawn plea on this ground). *Accord* People v. Alt, 50 A.D.3d 1164, 854 N.Y.S.2d 591, 592 (3d Dep't 2008) ("It

is well settled that where a defendant's plea is withdrawn, it is out of the case for all purposes and the People may not use the plea or the contents of the plea allocution on either their direct case or for purposes of impeachment.").

[12]*E.g.,* Mich. R. Evid. 410; Neb. Rev. Stat. Ann. § 27-410; S.D. Codified Laws § 19-12-12. *See* Hill v. State, 1995 OK CR 28, 898 P.2d 155, 164 (Okla. Crim. App. 1995) (trial court erred in permitting prosecutor to prove and question defendant regarding withdrawn guilty plea).

[13]Fed. R. Evid 410(a)(4). Prior to 2002, similar language appeared in Fed. R. Crim. P. 11(e)(6)(D). Fed. R. Crim. P. 11(f) now provides: "The admissibility or inadmissibility of a plea, a plea discussion, and any related statement is governed by Federal Rule of Evidence 410."

[14]*E.g.,* Cal. Evid. Code § 1153 ("offer to plead guilty" inadmissible); Ind. Code Ann. § 35-35-3-4 (verbal or written communication "concerning [a] plea agreement" not admissible if the

"in the course of plea discussions."[15] Considerable difficulty arises in determining what are "plea discussions," and when particular statements are made "in the course" of such discussions.

Some provisions, such as the federal ones, limit protection to statements made in connection with discussions with a prosecutor,[16] on the rationale that discussions between law enforcement officers and defendants do not involve the sort of negotiations that should be encouraged by exclusion of admissions made during those negotiations.[17] Thus generally no protection is afforded admissions made to law enforcement officers,[18] even under versions of the rule that are not explicitly limited to statements made to prosecutors.[19] Nevertheless, admissions made to a law enforcement officer will be protected if the evidence shows that the officer was apparently acting as the authorized agent of a prosecutor.[20]

---

plea agreement does not culminate in approval by court).

[15]These provisions protect only statement made in the process of reaching a plea bargain. If a bargain is reached and obligates the defendant to make certain statements, those statements are not protected. The provisions' purpose of encouraging free and open discussion and settlement would not be served by construing them as covering matters developing after settlement was reached. U.S. v. Watkins, 85 F.3d 498, 500 (10th Cir. 1996) (both language of and policy underlying federal provision "verify that once a plea agreement is reached, statements made thereafter are not entitled to the exclusionary protection of the Rule"). *Accord* U.S. v. Gonzalez, 608 F.3d 1001, 1005–06 (7th Cir. 2010), cert. denied, 131 S. Ct. 952, 178 L. Ed. 2d 786 (2011); State v. Campoy, 220 Ariz. 539, 207 P.3d 792, 800–01 (Ct. App. Div. 2 2009); Wainwright v. State, 704 So. 2d 511, 514 (Fla. 1997); People v. Connery, 296 Ill. App. 3d 384, 230 Ill. Dec. 689, 694 N.E.2d 658, 662 (3d Dist. 1998).

[16]Fed. R. Evid 410(a)(4) (protecting statements "made during plea discussions with an attorney for the prosecuting authority"). Similar state provisions, although probably modeled upon the earlier federal rules, have

not always been similarly limited. *E.g.,* Minn. R. Evid. 410 ("Evidence of . . . an officer to plead guilty or nolo contendere . . . or of statements made in connection with any of the foregoing . . . offers, is not admissible . . . ."). *Compare* R.I. R. Evid. 410(4) (limiting exclusion to statements related to discussions "with an attorney for the prosecuting authority").

[17]Advisory Committee Note to proposed amendment of Fed. R. Crim. P. 11(e)(6), 77 F.R.D. 533–37 (1978).

[18]U.S. v. Lewis, 117 F.3d 980, 983 (7th Cir. 1997) (statements made by defendant to IRS agent at meeting between defendant, his attorney, and agent were not covered by federal provisions); Weil v. State, 936 So. 2d 400, 404 (Miss. Ct. App. 2006) (rule did not cover statements made to arresting officer who had no authority to negotiate the charges).

[19]Banther v. State, 823 A.2d 467, 485 (Del. 2003) (police made clear they could not tell defendant what was going to happen to him); Owen v. Crosby, 854 So. 2d 182, 189–90 (Fla. 2003) (officer repeatedly told defendant officer could not make any promises). *Accord* People v. Martinez, 36 P.3d 154, 160–61 (Colo. App. 2001).

[20]*See* U.S. v. Millard, 139 F.3d 1200, 1205 n.4 (8th Cir. 1998) (statements were protected although made

Whether statements were sufficiently related to actual or perceived plea discussions—and thus are protected—is frequently disputed. Admissions made by defendants in the hopes of obtaining information from authorities rather than negotiating a plea bargain are, of course, not covered.[21] More significantly, there is no protection for statements made by defendants who are simply seeking to obtain leniency.[22]

These situations are frequently addressed by using a two part analysis often attributed to *United States v. Richardson.*[23] Under this approach, an admission is protected only if both of two requirements are met. First, the defendant must have made the admission with an actual expectation that he was in the process of negotiating a plea bargain. Second, was that expectation must have been objectively reasonable given the totality of the circumstances.[24]

Perhaps most troublesome are situations in which defendants made admissions in what might be characterized as efforts to begin or simply interest the prosecution in beginning plea negotiations. Some courts seem to require that before the admissions are made, the prosecutors have somewhat explicitly entered into discussions of specific possible quid pro quo exchanges.[25] The

---

to federal law enforcement agent, where agent told defendant that he was working directly with a specific Assistant United States Attorney and during the course of the discussions the agent telephoned the prosecutor); Richardson v. State, 706 So. 2d 1349, 1354 (Fla. 1998) (per curiam) (protection extended to statements made to police officer who approached defendant with proposed agreement signed by prosecutor, even though officer did not have authority to modify the proposal during discussions with the defendant); Clutter v. Com., 364 S.W.3d 135, 138 (Ky. 2012) ("plea discussions 'with an attorney for the prosecuting authority' include discussions . . . with law enforcement officials who are either acting with the express authority of the prosecutor or who state they are acting with such authority"); Kreps v. Com., 286 S.W.3d 213, 219–20 (Ky. 2009) (protection held applicable where during discussion officer telephoned prosecutor and informed defendant what prosecutor was willing to do); Com. v. Stutler, 2009 PA Super

30, 966 A.2d 594, 598 (2009) (statements to officer protected where prosecutor authorized officer to communicate offer to defendant).

[21]People v. Taylor, 289 Ill. App. 3d 399, 224 Ill. Dec. 749, 682 N.E.2d 310, 314 (4th Dist. 1997).

[22]*E.g.,* People v. Beler, 327 Ill. App. 3d 829, 261 Ill. Dec. 676, 763 N.E.2d 925, 928–29 (4th Dist. 2002) (defendant's discussion with officer may have shown a hope of gaining leniency but not of negotiating a plea agreement).

[23]U.S. v. Robertson, 582 F.2d 1356 (5th Cir. 1978) (en banc).

[24]*E.g.,* Clutter v. Com., 364 S.W.3d 135, 138 (Ky. 2012); Calabro v. State, 995 So. 2d 307, 314 (Fla. 2008); State v. Hatch, 165 Wash. App. 212, 267 P.3d 473, 476 (Div. 1 2011).

[25]U.S. v. Morgan, 91 F.3d 1193 (8th Cir. 1996) (federal provisions did not extend to statements made during meeting among the defendant, defense counsel, FBI agents, and an Assistant United States Attorney, although the

Florida Supreme Court, however, has reasonably rejected an absolute requirement that a plea offer have been made.[26]

Under the most reasonable approach, plea negotiations do not require any express or actual formal agreement by the parties that they are negotiating a possible plea bargain.[27] Admissions should be protected if the defendant believes prosecution authorities to whom the admissions are made are receptive to bargaining and prosecution authorities have by words or conduct justified this belief. Thus protection was properly extended to statements made at a meeting "orchestrated" by the defendant because he "wanted to orchestrate a deal" and law enforcement officers and a prosecutor agreed to and did attend without informing the defendant they would be present only to collect incriminating statements to be used against defendant at trial.[28]

*Waiver of Protection for Admissions Made in Connection With Plea Bargaining.* The Supreme Court held in *United States v.*

---

prosecutor explained the charges the defendant could face, the process of sentencing in federal cases, and the effect of cooperation on sentence). *Accord* State v. Crockett, 886 So. 2d 1139, 1146–48 (La. Ct. App. 5th Cir. 2004) (no plea negotiations where defendant offered information and prosecutor agreed to "consider" that information but stated that no deals were on the table and she did not want the discussion to be construed as a "deal in progress"); State v. Curry, 153 N.C. App. 260, 569 S.E.2d 691, 693–94 (2002) (no plea negotiations where assistant district attorney told defendant and counsel that she did not have authority to negotiate a deal, the prosecution might consider an offer if the defendant cooperated, and there were "possibilities" of the defendant pleading to a string of minor charges).

[26]Calabro v. State, 995 So. 2d 307, 317 (Fla. 2008) ("neither the statute nor the rule contains any requirement that a defendant's offer to plead must be in response to a State offer before it will receive the protection of exclusion from evidence"). In *Calabro*, after arraignment and in open court with the prosecutor present, the defendant stated, "I will like to avoid the trial and have some kind of plea agreement set earlier . . .," and shortly thereafter added, "I know this is unusual but

unfortunately, I'm guilty of this." This admission was held protected.

At least one court has indicated the lack of formal charges at the time of the admissions precludes a finding that plea negotiations were under way. Green v. State, 870 N.E.2d 560, 565–66 (Ind. Ct. App. 2007) (no plea negotiations were involved during discussions leading to agreement with prosecutor not to seek death penalty because no charges had yet been filed).

[27]State v. Hatch, 165 Wash. App. 212, 267 P.3d 473, 476 (Div. 1 2011) (rejecting contention that "plea negotiations do not occur until the parties formally agree that they are negotiating").

[28]State v. Brabham, 413 N.J. Super. 196, 994 A.2d 526, 533–34 (App. Div. 2010). *Accord, e.g,* People v. Garcia, 169 P.3d 223, 228 (Colo. App. 2007) (admissions was protected when made to polygraph operator during test requested by prosecution to see "what type of plea may or may not be made at that point"); Nunes v. State, 988 So. 2d 636, 638 (Fla. 2d DCA 2008) (statement protected "[a]lthough no plea offer was made at the time of the statement, the State repeatedly expressed to Mr. Nunes the process that would be followed to decide whether a plea offer would be made. And, the State, in fact, did offer a plea deal later

---

*Mezzanatto*[29] that the protection of the federal provisions is subject to waiver.[30] This has encouraged development of "proffer" agreements in which defendants before entering into negotiations waive some or all statutory or rule protection for admissions made in connection with those negotiations.[31]

*Mezzanatto* held a waiver effective when the prosecution offered an otherwise-protected admission to impeach a testifying defendant. Lower courts have generally held, however, that its rationale also applies when the prosecution offers otherwise-protected admission in its case-in-chief to prove guilt. So enforcing waivers will not frustrate the general purpose of Rule 410 to encourage plea negotiations.[32]

The admissibility of admissions made pursuant to these proffer agreements is determined by the terms of the agreement.[33] If a plea is entered pursuant to the agreement and the defendant exercises his right to withdraw the plea, the agreement is probably breached and otherwise-protected admissions may be used.[34] Agreements often provide that the defendant must be completely

---

in the course of the case.").

[29]U.S. v. Mezzanatto, 513 U.S. 196, 115 S. Ct. 797, 130 L. Ed. 2d 697 (1995).

[30]Mezzanatto, 513 U.S. at 206–09 (protection waived by defendant's pre-discussion agreement that any statements made during the negotiations could be used to impeach any contradictory testimony he might give at trial).

[31]U.S. v. Parra, 302 F. Supp. 2d 226, 230–32 (S.D. N.Y. 2004), aff'd, 249 Fed. Appx. 226 (2d Cir. 2007) (setting out terms of standard proffer agreement form used by United States Attorney's office). *See generally* Del Giono, Pitfalls of Proffers in the Second Circuit, United States v. Velez, Champion, July, 2004.

[32]*See generally* U.S. v. Mitchell, 633 F.3d 997, 1004–06 (10th Cir. 2011) (after thorough discussion, "join[ing] other] . . . courts, agreeing that case-in-chief waivers will not undermine voluntary plea negotiations or compromise the fact-finding process at trial"); U.S. v. Hardwick, 544 F.3d 565, 570 (3d Cir. 2008); State v. Campoy, 220 Ariz. 539, 207 P.3d 792, 802–03 (Ct. App. Div. 2 2009). *Accord* U.S. v. Annette, 2012 WL 1890237 (D. Vt.

2012) (holding enforceable a "Total Waiver Clause" giving the government the right to introduce any statements made by the defendant "against him without limitation and for any purpose in any proceeding" triggered by— among other things—"knowingly provid[ing] false or misleading statements" to the government).

[33]*See, e.g.,* U.S. v. Sanders, 341 F.3d 809, 817 (8th Cir. 2003) (statements made after proffer agreement were admissible at sentencing because agreement so provided). *Accord* U.S. v. Rebbe, 314 F.3d 402, 406–08 (9th Cir. 2002) (statement admissible in rebuttal under agreement); Hood v. Com., 269 Va. 176, 608 S.E.2d 913, 915–16 (2005) (pursuant to proffer agreement, prosecution could use statement of defendant because it was inconsistent with information elicited at trial by defendant on cross-examination of prosecution witness).

[34]*E.g.,* U.S. v. Jones, 469 F.3d 563, 567 (6th Cir. 2006) (withdrawal of plea violated terms of agreement, nullified agreement, and permitted government to use statement). *Compare* U.S. v. Newbert, 504 F.3d 180, 184 (1st Cir. 2007) (agreement not breached by motion to withdraw plea on basis of new evidence establishing

truthful and that defendant is not to personally or "through counsel" made representations materially different from statements made or information provided. Violation of these provisions, even by counsel rather than the defendant personally, permits use of admissions.[35]

Proffer agreements sometimes give the prosecution the right to use "derivative evidence"—evidence other than the defendants' statements themselves but obtained by the prosecution's use of those statements. Admissibility of such evidence has been upheld, at least where the proffer agreement "clearly" gives the prosecution the right to use information contained in statements that themselves cannot be used.[36]

Waivers might be subject to a perhaps-implied requirement of good faith on the part of the prosecution.[37] Thus a defendant might be relieved of a waiver in a proffer agreement upon proof that the prosecution never intended to try and reach a plea agreement but instead participated for the purpose of obtaining usable admissions by the defendant.

*Permissible Use of Plea Bargain Admissions.* The federal provisions permit use in perjury prosecutions of otherwise inadmissible pleas and statements related to pleas and plea negotiations. State provisions often[38] but not always provide similarly.[39] As a result of 1980 amendment, the federal provisions also embody a provision permitting the use of such statements against a defen-

---

innocence).

[35]*See generally* U.S. v. Dales, 425 Fed. Appx. 178, 180 (3d Cir. 2011) (agreement breached when defense counsel in opening statement and cross-examination "made implicit representations" contrary to statement by the defendant that he did not personally participate in the robbery). *Accord* U.S. v. Shaw, 354 Fed. Appx. 439, 443 (2d Cir. 2009) (because defense counsel implied facts that contradicted defendant's proffer statements, trial court did not err in admitting the proffer statements); U.S. v. Petrosian, 446 Fed. Appx. 826, 828 (9th Cir. 2011) (trial testimony justified trial judge in finding defendant was not completely truthful in his statement given in proffer session and thus in admitting proffer statement).

[36]*See* U.S. v. Merz, 396 Fed. Appx. 838, 841 (3d Cir. 2010) (joining other circuits in holding this result is justified by applying "contract law prin-

ciples").

[37]*Cf.* U.S. v. Annette, 2012 WL 1890237 (D. Vt. 2012) ("the Court does not see any evidence that the government entered the proffer session in bad faith"); State v. Miller, 1997 WL 674673 (Ohio Ct. App. 2d Dist. Montgomery County 1997) (unreported) (discussing and rejecting defendant's contention that proffer agreement was invalided by State's "bad faith").

[38]*E.g.,* State v. Bennett, 179 W. Va. 464, 370 S.E.2d 120, 125 (1988) (statutory exception permitting use of defendant's plea bargaining statements in later perjury prosecution did not renders protection inadequate and trial judge properly demanded that defendant testify as to guilt in proceeding to accept plea of guilty).

[39]*See* State v. Simpson, 450 N.W.2d 819, 821–22 (Iowa 1990) (refusing to read perjury exception into state provision).

dant when some other statement made in the course of the same plea proceedings or negotiations has been introduced and the statement at issue "ought in fairness be considered contemporaneously with it."[40]

*Use of Admissions to Impeach Testifying Defendant.* Whether an admission otherwise subject to exclusion may be used to impeach a defendant who testifies is not explicitly addressed under the federal provisions. The original version of Federal Rule 410 contained an explicit but limited exception permitting the use of "voluntary and reliable statements" made in court and on the record, even if they were otherwise inadmissible under Rule 410, but only "where offered for impeachment purposes." Congress eliminated this language in the 1975 amendment of the rule. The Second Circuit has held that this "unusually clear legislative history" demonstrates a Congressional intention "to preclude use of statements made in plea negotiations for impeachment purposes"[41] and other federal courts have agreed.[42] State provisions generally do not address the matter,[43] and the silent provisions are usually read to bar impeachment use of the statements.[44]

## § 161    "Tacit" and "adoptive" confessions and admissions[1]

Under the general rules regarding admissions,[2] the prosecution is generally permitted in a criminal case to prove that an accusatory statement was made in the hearing of the defendant and that the defendant's response was such as to justify the inference that he agreed with or "adopted" the statement. The adopting response may, of course, be an express affirmative agreement with

---

[40]*See* U.S. v. Mezzanatto, 998 F.2d 1452, 1454 (9th Cir. 1993), rev'd on other grounds 513 U.S. 196 (1995) (this provision is "an exception to prevent selective admission of plea negotiation statements. If a defendant introduces a statement made during plea negotiations, the prosecution may introduce other relevant plea negotiation statements so that the jury receives a full account of the issue presented"). See generally § 56 supra, considering the effect of introducing part of a writing or conversation.

[41]U.S. v. Lawson, 683 F.2d 688, 690–93 (2d Cir. 1982).

[42]*See* U.S. v. Acosta-Ballardo, 8 F.3d 1532, 1536 (10th Cir. 1993).

[43]*Compare* Neb. Rev. Stat. Ann. § 27-410 ("voluntary and reliable state-

ments made in court on the record" are admissible when offered for impeachment purposes). Under the Alaska rules, such statements are admissible, apparently as substantive evidence, when offered as prior inconsistent statements. Alaska R. Evid. 410(b).

[44]*E.g.,* Gillum v. State, 1984 OK CR 61, 681 P.2d 87, 89 (Okla. Crim. App. 1984).

**[Section 161]**

[1]*See generally* West's Key Number Digest, Constitutional Law ☞4664, 4666; West's Key Number Digest, Criminal Law ☞405.5, 410.30 to 410.39; West's Key Number Digest, Witnesses ☞347.

[2]See § 262 infra as to the nature of admissions.

the statement.[3] It may also be conduct from which the defendant's belief in the accuracy of the statement can be inferred;[4] where this is the case, the evidence amounts to what in this text is regarded as an "adoptive" confession.[5] Adoption can be also inferred from the defendant's failure to deny the accusation, so a type of adoptive admission can arise from either silence or an "equivocal response" not a clear denial.[6] Where the accusation is so adopted by the defendant's silence, the evidence thereby rendered admissible, the accusation and the defendant's adopting silence, is a "tacit" confession.[7]

The foundation necessary has been articulated in various ways. Best put, admission requires preliminary proof (1) of an accusatory statement that a person who considered himself innocent would, under the circumstances, deny; (2) that the defendant heard and understood the accusatory statement; (3) that the defendant had the opportunity and ability to deny the statement; and (4) that the defendant manifested his adoption of it or, in the case of a tacit admission, adopted it by his silence.[8]

Here, as in civil litigation, admission is based on the assumption that human nature is such that innocent persons will usually deny false accusations. Critical reconsideration of this assumption, especially as it applies in the criminal context, had led to increasing limitations upon adoptive confessions in criminal litigation. Use of this evidence in criminal trials is also affected by federal and state constitutional considerations. These matters, especially as they concern tacit confessions adopted by defendants' silence, implicate the requirements imposed by the privilege against compelled self-incrimination in general, the Fifth Amendment's requirements as specifically developed in *Miranda v. Arizona*,[9] and general considerations of minimal procedural fairness.

---

[3]*E.g.,* U.S. v. Young, 814 F.2d 392, 395–96 (7th Cir. 1987) (when told police had obtained a fingerprint at the crime scene, defendant responded, "Yeah, I guess it must be mine."). See generally § 261 infra.

[4]Nodding of the head, for example, will sometimes suffice. Gregory v. State, 518 N.E.2d 799, 800 (Ind. 1988). *See also* State v. Hunt, 325 N.C. 187, 381 S.E.2d 453, 457–58 (1989) (testimony that after another speaker described details of the killings, defendant looked at the speaker "like he had better hush" was sufficient).

[5]See generally § 261 infra.

[6]*See* House v. State, 535 N.E.2d 103, 110 (Ind. 1989). See generally § 262 infra (admissions by silence).

[7]Wills v. State, 82 Md. App. 669, 573 A.2d 80, 84 (1990).

[8]*See* U.S. v. Joshi, 896 F.2d 1303, 1311 (11th Cir. 1990); State v. Lambert, 705 A.2d 957, 962–63 (R.I. 1997); Strohecker v. Com., 23 Va. App. 242, 475 S.E.2d 844, 849 (1996).

[9]Miranda v. Arizona, 384 U.S. 436, 86 S. Ct. 1602, 16 L. Ed. 2d 694 (1966).

*Doyle v. Ohio*[10] held that federal Due Process barred cross-examination of a testifying defendant by use of pretrial silence after the defendant was taken into custody and warned pursuant to *Miranda* of the right to remain silent. The Supreme Court characterized silence after such warnings as "insolubly ambiguous," and appeared to be influenced by that conclusion. Subsequent decisions by the Court made clear, however, that *Doyle's* holding was based instead on the perceived unfairness of explicitly representing to a suspect that the suspect has the right to silence and then penalizing the suspect for exercising that right.[11] Finding the rationale for the prohibition applicable, the Supreme Court subsequently barred the substantive use of post-warning custodial silence to prove guilt.[12]

*Doyle's* rationale, so construed, would seem to not apply if the silence relied upon occurred before the defendant was advised of the right to remain silent. Consequently, the Supreme Court's Due Process case law poses no barrier to cross-examination use of silence prior to receipt of the *Miranda* assurance of the right to remain silent.[13] Although the cases explicitly found no barrier to impeachment use, it follows that federal Due Process also permits pre-warning silence to be used substantively—as the basis of a tacit confession—to prove a suspect's guilt.

Even in the absence of warnings, it is quite possible the criminal justice system effectively conveys to people at least some of the essence of the *Miranda* rights, and particularly that one has a right to remain silent in dealings with law enforcement. Much the same unfairness might be found in following this general dissemination of a right of silence with use at trial of pre-warning silence to prove guilt, despite the Supreme Court's failure to find sufficient unfairness to trigger federal Due Process.

A number of lower courts have concluded—despite the apparent limits of the Supreme Court's case law—that the Fifth Amendment bars the use of silence if the defendant was in custody although no explicit warning of the right to silence was given.[14] Some have extended this bar to silence before the defen-

---

[10]Doyle v. Ohio, 426 U.S. 610, 96 S. Ct. 2240, 49 L. Ed. 2d 91 (1976).

[11]Fletcher v. Weir, 455 U.S. 603, 607, 102 S. Ct. 1309, 71 L. Ed. 2d 490 (1982); Jenkins v. Anderson, 447 U.S. 231, 240, 100 S. Ct. 2124, 65 L. Ed. 2d 86 (1980).

[12]Wainwright v. Greenfield, 474 U.S. 284, 295, 106 S. Ct. 634, 88 L. Ed. 2d 623 (1986) (*Doyle* barred the use of

defendant's silence to rebut defendant's claim of insanity).

[13]Fletcher, 455 U.S. at 607 (pre-warning silence); Jenkins, 447 U.S. at 240 (pre-custody silence).

[14]*E.g.*, State v. VanWinkle, 229 Ariz. 233, 273 P.3d 1148, 1151 (2012) (following holdings of a majority of federal appellate courts that "post-custody, pre-*Miranda* silence cannot

dant was taken into custody.[15] Others, however, have limited the bar to situations covered by *Doyle* and subsequent Supreme Court decisions—those in which the *Miranda* warning of the right to remain silent was given.[16]

Apart from Due Process concerns, silence—whether pre or post-warning—might constitute invocation of the right to remain silent and its use to prove guilt as the basis of a tacit confession might then be an impermissible burden on the exercise of the self-incrimination privilege that creates the right to remain silent. As is developed in section 127, there is considerable authority for the proposition that the Fifth Amendment and perhaps some state law versions of privilege bar the use of pre-warning silence on this constitutional ground.

The factors considered in developing and formulating constitutional limits on the use of silence as the basis for tacit confessions have also been considered by courts addressing possible evidence law limits on this sort of evidence. This is particularly the case with what *Doyle* suggested was the "insolubly ambiguous" nature of silence.

Generally, modern courts have been increasingly critical of the traditional assumption that silence in the face of an accusation is

---

be used as evidence of a defendant's guilt"); State v. Ellington, 151 Idaho 53, 253 P.3d 727, 734 (2011) ("this Court has held that a defendant's right to remain silent attaches upon custody, not arrest or interrogation, and thus a prosecutor may not use any post-custody silence to infer guilt in its case-in-chief"). *Accord* People v. Tom, 139 Cal. Rptr. 3d 71, 88 (Cal. App. 1st Dist. 2012) ("we now join the federal circuits holding that the right of pretrial silence under *Miranda* is triggered by the inherently coercive circumstances attendant to a de facto arrest and therefore the government may not introduce evidence in its case-in-chief of a defendant's silence after arrest, but before *Miranda* warnings are administered, as substantive evidence of defendant's guilt"). *See generally,* State v. Kulzer, 186 Vt. 264, 2009 VT 79, 979 A.2d 1031, 1035–37 (2009) (collecting split federal and state decisions on whether the prosecution may use a defendant's pre-arrest, pre-*Miranda* silence may be used in the prosecution's case in chief where the defendant does not testify but not reaching issue).

[15]*E.g.,* Com. v. Molina, 2011 PA Super 237, 33 A.3d 51, 63 (2011) (en banc) ("We find it of no moment whether the silence occurred before or after the arrest or before or after *Miranda* warnings were administered. The Fifth Amendment was enacted to protect against self-incrimination, whether they are in custody or not, charged with a crime, or merely being questioned during the investigation of a crime."). *Accord* State v. Powell, 132 Ohio St. 3d 233, 2012-Ohio-2577, 971 N.E.2d 865, 895–96 (2012) (applying State v. Leach, 102 Ohio St. 3d 135, 2004-Ohio-2147, 807 N.E.2d 335 (2004)); State v. Gallup, 2011 UT App 422, 267 P.3d 289, 294–97 (Utah Ct. App. 2011).

[16]*E.g.,* U.S. v. O'Keefe, 461 F.3d 1338, 1346–47 (11th Cir. 2006) (pre-arrest and pre-warning silence is not protected); State v. Johnson, 811 N.W.2d 136, 147–48 (Minn. Ct. App. 2012) (same); Salinas v. State, 369 S.W.3d 176, 178–79 (Tex. Crim. App. 2012), cert. granted, 2013 WL 135534 (U.S. 2013) (same).

reliable proof that the silent person agrees with the accusation. Less than unequivocal expressed agreement with the accusation—and especially silence—may—given widespread knowledge of *Miranda*—reflect not agreement but instead a decision to invoke what even an innocent suspect believes to be an available and useful right of silence that may reduce the risk of wrongful prosecution or conviction.

The Supreme Court has held that the minimal probative value of a defendant's silence renders evidence of such silence inadmissible to impeach as a matter of federal evidence law.[17] The Connecticut Supreme Court held on state law grounds that an adoptive admission based on silence is admissible only if no explanation other than assent to the accusatory statement is "equally consistent."[18] Some courts have more severely curtailed prosecution use of tacit admissions.[19] The Alabama Supreme Court, for example, barred all use of either pre-or post-arrest silence, explaining that "neither logic nor common experience any longer support the tacit admission rule, if indeed, either ever supported it."[20]

Others courts have held that admissibility turns on case-specific probative value/risk of undue prejudice balances, and some have encouraged trial judges to engage in more critical appraisals of the competing considerations.[21]

---

[17]U.S. v. Hale, 422 U.S. 171, 179, 95 S. Ct. 2133, 45 L. Ed. 2d 99 (1975); Stewart v. U. S., 366 U.S. 1, 5, 81 S. Ct. 941, 6 L. Ed. 2d 84 (1961); Grunewald v. U.S., 353 U.S. 391, 421, 77 S. Ct. 963, 1 L. Ed. 2d 931 (1957).

[18]State v. Vitale, 197 Conn. 396, 497 A.2d 956, 961 (1985).

[19]Adams v. State, 261 P.3d 758, 765 (Alaska 2011) (evidence of a defendant's pre-arrest silence will usually be inadmissible under Evidence Rule 403 due to its inherently low probative value and its high risk of unfair prejudice); Wills v. State, 82 Md. App. 669, 573 A.2d 80, 83–84 (1990) (reviewing case law and holding that "evidence of an accused's post-arrest, pre-*Miranda* warning, silence for impeachment is inadmissible because the probative value, if any, of such evidence, is clearly outweighed by its potential for unfair prejudice").

[20]Ex parte Marek, 556 So. 2d 375, 381 (Ala. 1989). *Accord* Jarrett v. State, 265 Ga. 28, 453 S.E.2d 461, 463 (1995) ("we now conclude that a witness in a criminal trial may not testify as to a declarant's statements based on the acquiescence or silence of the accused," overruling prior decisions); People v. DeGeorge, 73 N.Y.2d 614, 543 N.Y.S.2d 11, 541 N.E.2d 11, 13–14 (1989) (silence, either before or after arrest, cannot be used "in the absence of unusual circumstances").

[21]*E.g.*, People v. Collier, 426 Mich. 23, 393 N.W.2d 346, 350–51 (1986) (admissibility of admission adopted by silence before contact with law enforcement is within discretion of trial judge, but judge should approach issue with "caution" and require preliminary demonstration that it was "natural" to expect defendant to speak).

### § 162    Use of otherwise inadmissible confessions for impeachment

The exclusionary sanctions applicable to confessions are subject to the limitations applicable to exclusionary sanctions generally, including the limitation which often permits the prosecution to use inadmissible evidence to impeach a defendant who testifies in his own defense at trial.[1] Confession law's complexity, and especially the distinction between the voluntariness requirement and other exclusionary rules, results in particular difficulties applying the impeachment exception to confession law.

In a line of cases beginning with *Harris v. New York*,[2] the Supreme Court held that the impeachment exception to federal constitutional exclusionary requirements permits the use of confessions obtained in violation of *Miranda v. Arizona*[3] and at least some Sixth Amendment right to counsel requirements for such impeachment purposes.[4] Those obtained in violation of "core" Sixth Amendment demands, however, seemed possibly to be inadmissible even for this purpose.[5]

Rejecting any distinction among Sixth Amendment violations, the Court in *Kansas v. Ventris*[6] held that apparently all confessions obtained in violation of the Sixth Amendment right to counsel could be used for impeachment. The Sixth Amendment violation occurs when the confession is elicited, not when it is used. The Court found no reason to distinguish these cases from all others in which use at trial of tainted evidence does not itself constitute a violation and thus use for impeachment is constitutionally acceptable.[7]

*Harris'* impeachment exception to the federal constitutional

---

**[Section 162]**

[1]See generally § 183 infra.

[2]Harris v. New York, 401 U.S. 222, 91 S. Ct. 643, 28 L. Ed. 2d 1 (1971).

[3]Miranda v. Arizona, 384 U.S. 436, 86 S. Ct. 1602, 16 L. Ed. 2d 694 (1966).

[4]Michigan v. Harvey, 494 U.S. 344, 353, 110 S. Ct. 1176, 108 L. Ed. 2d 293 (1990) (confession obtained after Sixth Amendment right to counsel applied and police violated it by reapproaching the defendant after he invoked his right to counsel could be used for impeachment); Harris, 401 U.S. at 225 (confession obtained after insufficient warning admissible to impeach); Oregon v. Hass, 420 U.S. 714, 723, 95 S. Ct. 1215, 43 L. Ed. 2d 570 (1975) (confession obtained by interrogation conducted after suspect invoked right to counsel admissible to impeach).

[5]Harvey, 494 U.S. at 353–54 (record fails to show whether defendant's waiver was knowing and voluntary and thus whether statement was obtained by a violation of "the 'core value' of the Sixth Amendment constitutional guarantee" rendering it inadmissible even for impeachment purposes).

[6]Kansas v. Ventris, 556 U.S. 586, 129 S. Ct. 1841, 173 L. Ed. 2d 801 (2009).

[7]Ventris, 556 U.S. at 1847.

exclusionary sanctions attaching to confessions does not extend to certain situations in which voluntariness concerns are implicated. In *Mincey v. Arizona*[8] the Court found constitutional error in the use of an involuntary confession to impeach a testifying defendant. "[A]ny criminal trial use against a defendant of his involuntary statement," the Court announced, "is a denial of due process . . . ."[9] This is apparently because involuntariness—unlike *Miranda* violations—render confessions at least somewhat untrustworthy, and consequently less valuable as indicators of defendant perjury. The prosecution's interest in using them for impeachment is therefore reduced. Further, law enforcement activity that has sufficient impact to render confessions involuntary is more offensive to constitutional values than activity that merely violates *Miranda's* prophylactic rules. This increases the need for maximum deterrence, which is provided by excluding the confessions for all purposes. In these cases, then, the need for full deterrence outweighs the prosecution's reduced interest in using the confessions even for the limited purpose at issue.

As in other exclusionary sanction situations, state courts and legislatures remain free to reject the federal constitutional model and to apply state law exclusionary requirements unqualified by impeachment exceptions. Some have done so.[10]

### § 163   Determining admissibility and credibility[1]

The close relationship between some requirements of admissibility and the weight that confession evidence is properly given in determining guilt have generated considerable disagreement on the role of judge and jury in resolving the various issues presented when the prosecution offers evidence of a defendant's confession. Some of the issues, of course, are constitutional ones.

*Roles of Judge and Jury.* In *Jackson v. Denno,*[2] the Supreme Court held that the due process clause of the Fourteenth Amendment requires that upon proper demand the trial judge determine the voluntariness of a challenged confession. *Jackson* held constitutionally impermissible what had previously been known as the "New York procedure," under which the trial judge

---

[8]Mincey v. Arizona, 437 U.S. 385, 98 S. Ct. 2408, 57 L. Ed. 2d 290 (1978).

[9]Mincey, 437 U.S. at 398 (emphasis in original). *See also* New Jersey v. Portash, 440 U.S. 450, 458, 99 S. Ct. 1292, 59 L. Ed. 2d 501 (1979) (grand jury testimony given under grant of immunity "is the essence of coerced testimony" and cannot be used to impeach the witness at his later criminal trial).

[10]See generally § 183 infra.

**[Section 163]**

[1]*See generally* West's Key Number Digest, Criminal Law ☞413.20 to 413.69.

[2]Jackson v. Denno, 378 U.S. 368, 84 S. Ct. 1774, 12 L. Ed. 2d 908 (1964).

conducted a preliminary inquiry and excluded a challenged confession only if its involuntariness was so clear as to present no issue. If the evidence presented a fair question as to voluntariness or any factual matters relevant to voluntariness, the confession was submitted to the jury with directions to determine voluntariness and to consider the confession on the issue of guilt or innocence only if it was found to be voluntary.

Under the New York procedure, the Court reasoned, jurors might first conclude that a defendant committed the crime charged and then be unable or disinclined to determine the voluntariness of a challenged confession without regard to its accuracy. This would, of course, violate the right to have voluntariness determined without regard to reliability.[3] Alternatively, the jurors might first address the confession and conclude that it was involuntary but reliable; they might then be unable or disinclined to ignore that confession in assessing the sufficiency of the prosecution's evidence on guilt. This would endanger the right to have guilt or innocence determined without consideration of an involuntary confession.[4]

Defendants have no federal constitutional right to jury consideration of claims of involuntariness rejected by trial judges. The Court in *Lego v. Twomey*[5] found neither a basis for concluding that juries are somehow "better suited" than trial judges to determine voluntariness,[6] nor convincing grounds for regarding trial judges' resolutions of voluntariness challenges as sufficiently unreliable to entitle defendants to "a second forum for litigating [their] claim[s]."[7]

Defendants do have a federal Due Process right to contest the credibility—as distinguished from the voluntariness—of a confession admitted into evidence. Once the prosecution is permitted to introduce evidence that the defendant made incriminating admissions, the Court held in *Crane v. Kentucky*,[8] the defendant is entitled to introduce evidence concerning the circumstances under which he made them if those circumstances bear upon the credibility of the admissions.[9]

Federal constitutional considerations, then, permit the trial

---

[3]*See* Rogers v. Richmond, 365 U.S. 534, 81 S. Ct. 735, 5 L. Ed. 2d 760 (1961), discussed in § 149 supra.

[4]The same fatal defects were found in an almost identical procedure whereby the prosecution was required to make only a "prima facie case that the alleged confession was freely and voluntarily made" and the ultimate determination of voluntariness was left to the jury. Sims v. State of Ga., 385

U.S. 538, 541, 87 S. Ct. 639, 17 L. Ed. 2d 593 (1967).

[5]Lego v. Twomey, 404 U.S. 477, 92 S. Ct. 619, 30 L. Ed. 2d 618 (1972).

[6]Lego, 404 U.S. at 489.

[7]404 U.S. at 490.

[8]Crane v. Kentucky, 476 U.S. 683, 106 S. Ct. 2142, 90 L. Ed. 2d 636 (1986).

[9]When, if ever, this right in-

judge to be given sole responsibility for resolving voluntariness issues. Under this "orthodox" approach, the trial judge resolves all factual disputes and determines voluntariness. No issues related to voluntariness are submitted to the jury. Many jurisdictions follow this procedure.[10]

Federal constitutional requirements also permit what is known as the Massachusetts or "humane" procedure[11] under which the trial judge makes a full inquiry into and determines voluntariness. If the trial judge finds the challenged confession voluntary, however, the issue of voluntariness is then submitted to the jury for reconsideration, and the jury is instructed to consider the confession on the defendant's guilt only if it first finds it voluntary. A number of jurisdictions take this approach.[12]

The wisdom of this approach is questionable.[13] Most if not all considerations relating to voluntariness will also be relevant to credibility, so the defendant will have an opportunity to present them to the jury. Whether jurors are ever or often able or inclined to distinguish credibility and voluntariness and to disregard a credible but involuntary confession is at best doubtful, and the task of adequately submitting both matters to the jury without

---

cludes the right to introduce expert testimony on such matters as the effect of various interrogation techniques on particular types of suspects has split the courts. If such expert testimony is inadmissible under a reasonable application of state evidence law, however, exclusion almost certainly does not violate *Crane's* Sixth Amendment mandate. *See* People v. Kowalski, 492 Mich. 106, 141 n.89, 821 N.W.2d 14, 36 n.89 (2012) (although trial court erred in excluding some offered expert testimony regarding defendant's psychological characteristics arguable related to why he might have given false confession, this did not violate Sixth Amendment as applied in *Crane* because *Crane* permits states to exclude evidence on evidence law reliability grounds).

[10]*E.g.,* Liu v. State, 628 A.2d 1376, 1387 (Del. 1993) ("The trial judge is the sole arbiter of the admissibility of the defendant's statements. There is no threshold determination of voluntariness for the jurors; their role is simply to determine the reliability or credibility of the statement. 'Accordingly, no specific instruction on voluntariness is required.'").

[11]*See* Com. v. Selby, 426 Mass. 168, 686 N.E.2d 1316, 1319 (1997).

[12]*E.g.,* State v. Schackart, 175 Ariz. 494, 858 P.2d 639, 648 (1993) ("Once the trial judge preliminarily determines that a confession is admissible, he or she must, if requested by the defense, instruct the jury to disregard the confession unless it is found to be voluntary."); Hannon v. State, 2004 WY 8, 84 P.3d 320, 343 n.5 (Wyo. 2004) (Wyoming follows the Massachusetts rule, which requires submission of the confession and the surrounding circumstances to the jury for its determination of the confession's voluntariness.").

[13]*See generally* Deeds v. People, 747 P.2d 1266, 1271–72 (Colo. 1987) (expressing doubt that jurors can isolate and determine voluntariness or disregard confessions they find involuntary, and concluding that best approach is to tell juries only that "it is the sole prerogative of the jury to determine what weight, if any, is to be given to the confession and any testimony directly related to the confession").

confusing the jurors is a difficult and perhaps impossible one. Careful submission of credibility, then, is preferable to the humane procedure.

What is submitted to a jury depends, of course, on the jurisdiction's approach. Under *Crane*, a defendant challenging before the jury the credibility of the prosecution's evidence that he confessed is certainly entitled to adequate jury instructions on the jury's obligation to evaluate credibility. Under nonconstitutional law, juries are often told that they are to consider, in light of all the circumstances, the weight to give to such evidence,[14] and this is probably sufficient under *Crane*.[15]

Some jurisdictions go further at least in certain types of cases, as for example by instructing juries to view with caution evidence that the defendant made an oral admission of guilt[16] or even to so view evidence that the accused made an out-of-court incriminating statement.[17] Recent developments regarding recording of out-of-court statements by suspect have sometimes included requirements of jury instructions concerning the special risks of evidence of unrecorded statements; this is considered in Section 158 supra.

Jurisdictions following the humane procedure require juries to address the voluntariness of any self-incriminating statements they find the accuseds made. This is a different task than determining the weight to be given such statements in light of their apparent credibility, and a jury is to be told to first

---

[14]*See* State v. Cunningham, 344 N.C. 341, 474 S.E.2d 772, 782 (1996), reaffirming its earlier approval of the following instruction:

There is evidence which tends to show that the Defendant confessed that he committed the crime charged in this case. If you find that the Defendant made that confession, then you should consider all the circumstances under which it was made in determining whether it was a truthful confession and the weight you will give to it.

[15]*See* State v. Robinson, 82 Haw. 304, 922 P.2d 358, 366–67 (1996) (defendant whose "defense" was primarily an attack on the reliability and credibility of her written confession was "entitled to have the jury instructed that it may accord such weight and effect to her inculpatory statement as the jury feels it deserves

under all the circumstances").

[16]State v. Baldwin, 296 N.J. Super. 391, 686 A.2d 1260, 1263 (App. Div. 1997) (explaining that the instruction is based on "the generally recognized risk of inaccuracy and error in communication and recollection of verbal utterances and misconstruction by the hearer").

[17]State v. Harris, 156 N.J. 122, 716 A.2d 458, 489 (1998) ("Criminal defendants are entitled to an instruction that jurors [are to] use caution in evaluating testimony concerning out-of-court statements."); Smithwick v. State, 199 Ga. 292, 34 S.E.2d 28, 34 (1945) (trial court was correct in instructing jury that admissions by the defendant should be "scanned with care").

determine voluntariness and then, if it finds the confession voluntary, to consider what if any weight to give to it.[18]

*Hearing and Burden of Proof. Jackson* means that generally a trial judge is required to hold a hearing[19] on the admissibility of a challenged confession[20]—a "Jackson v. Denno hearing"—if the party against whom it is offered objects and requests such a hearing.[21] A few courts, regarding some confession requirements as too important to fall to defense counsel's default, require that even in the absence of a demand for a hearing, trial judges conduct a hearing, entertain evidence, and determine voluntariness of a proffered confession.[22]

A defendant's federal constitutional right to a fair determination of voluntariness means that a trial judge's conclusion that a challenged confession is voluntary "must appear from the record

---

[18]Witt v. State, 892 P.2d 132, 140–41 (Wyo. 1995) (since Wyoming follows humane procedure, trial judge erred in telling jury only that it must determine whether to consider statements made by the defendant and, if so, how much weight to give them in light of all the circumstances including the voluntariness of the statements). The error in *Witt* was not a federal constitutional one, because federal constitutional law does not require a jury determination of voluntariness and the instruction given implemented the defendant's right under *Crane* to have the jury assess credibility.

[19]*Jackson* is widely regarded as establishing a right to have the hearing on voluntariness conducted out of the presence of the jury. But apparently no constitutional violation is committed by having the hearing in the presence of the jury if the confession is properly found voluntary by the judge, since the jury hears no evidence it is not otherwise entitled to hear, and the hearing is not somehow deficient because of the jury's presence. Watkins v. Sowders, 449 U.S. 341, 101 S. Ct. 654, 66 L. Ed. 2d 549 (1981).

[20]*Jackson* dealt with the procedure required to resolve a defendant's due process voluntariness challenge to the admissibility of an offered confes-

sion. But there has been a general tendency to regard *Jackson's* requirements as also applicable to other federal constitutional challenges to confessions' admissibility. *E.g.,* U.S. v. Danley, 564 F.2d 813, 815 (8th Cir. 1977) (trial judge must hold hearing and resolve *Miranda* challenges, citing *Jackson*).

[21]*See, e.g.,* U.S. v. Espinoza-Seanez, 862 F.2d 526, 535–36 (5th Cir. 1988) (trial court did not err in failing to hold hearing on admissibility of confession where defense did not both object to admissibility of confession and make clear that hearing was desired). In Wainwright v. Sykes, 433 U.S. 72, 86, 97 S. Ct. 2497, 53 L. Ed. 2d 594 (1977), the Supreme Court made clear that *Jackson* did not require a hearing in the absence of a defense objection to the admissibility of a confession.

[22]Page v. State, 614 S.W.2d 819, 821 (Tex. Crim. App. 1981) (even in absence of request for hearing, trial judge had duty to respond to objection to voluntariness of confession by holding hearing and resolving issue); State v. Smith, 181 W. Va. 700, 384 S.E.2d 145, 149 (1989) (trial court has mandatory duty under state law to hear evidence and determine voluntariness of confession regardless of whether request for hearing was made).

with unmistakable clarity."[23] It is not constitutionally necessary, however, that the trial judge make formal findings of fact on contested subissues or write a formal opinion.[24] Nevertheless, sound policy and particularly the practicalities of effective appellate review strongly suggest specific findings concerning disputed subquestions of fact as well as a clear ultimate determination of the major issues.

*Lego* held that when a defendant challenges the prosecution's proffer of a confession, the federal constitution requires that the prosecution prove the voluntariness of the confession but that the prosecution need only establish this by a preponderance of the evidence. Voluntariness does not have to be established beyond a reasonable doubt or even by clear and convincing evidence.[25]

No basis had been presented for believing that traditional determinations of admissibility based on a preponderance of the evidence were unreliable or otherwise "wanting in quality." Whatever might be accomplished by imposing a higher standard, the Court concluded, would be outweighed by the cost of denying juries evidence probative on defendants' guilt or innocence.[26] Fourteen years later, the Court summarily held that the prosecution's burden of proving compliance with Fifth Amendment *Miranda* requirements is no greater.[27]

States remain free to impose higher standards. Many do require the prosecution to establish voluntariness and sometimes compliance with other requirements, such as those imposed by self-incrimination demands, by clear and convincing evidence[28] or even beyond a reasonable doubt.[29]

---

[23]Sims v. State of Ga., 385 U.S. 538, 544, 87 S. Ct. 639, 17 L. Ed. 2d 593 (1967).

[24]Sims, 385 U.S. at 544.

[25]Lego, 404 U.S. at 482–89.

[26]404 U.S. at 489.

[27]Colorado v. Connelly, 479 U.S. 157, 168, 107 S. Ct. 515, 93 L. Ed. 2d 473 (1986).

[28]State v. Aponte, 800 A.2d 420, 427 (R.I. 2002) (burden of proof governing a jury's consideration of criminal confession issues is "clear and convincing evidence").

[29]State v. Belonga, 163 N.H. 343, 42 A.3d 764, 772 (2012) ("Our State Constitution requires the State to prove beyond a reasonable doubt that the defendant's statements were made

voluntarily.") (quoting State v. Aubuchont, 147 N.H. 142, 784 A.2d 1170, 1175 (2001)). *Accord* State v. Hunt, 25 So. 3d 746, 754 (La. 2009) ("before a confession or inculpatory statement made during a custodial interrogation may be introduced into evidence, the State must prove beyond a reasonable doubt that the defendant was first advised of his *Miranda* rights, that he voluntarily and intelligently waived those rights, and that the statement was made freely and voluntarily and not under the influence of fear, intimidation, menaces, threats, inducement, or promises"); State v. Dodge, 2011 ME 47, 17 A.3d 128, 132 n.4 (Me. 2011); Richardson v. State, 74 So. 3d 317, 322 (Miss. 2011). *Compare* State v. Lawrence, 282 Conn. 141, 920 A.2d 236, 248–49 (2007) (re-

fusing to overrule precedent construing state constitution as requiring
voluntariness to be proved by only a
preponderance of the evidence).

The burden may differ depending on which decision is involved.
South Carolina law, for example, provides that the trial judge is to determine whether voluntariness is proved
by a preponderance of the evidence but
the jury must find voluntariness
proved beyond a reasonable doubt. *See*
State v. Parker, 381 S.C. 68, 671 S.E.2d
619, 622 (Ct. App. 2008).

# Chapter 15

# The Privilege Concerning Improperly Obtained Evidence

## § 164  Introduction

Traditionally, out-of-court impropriety in the manner by which evidence was obtained did not affect its admissibility.[1] This was

---

**[Section 164]**

[1]Adams v. People of State of New York, 192 U.S. 585, 594, 24 S. Ct. 372, 48 L. Ed. 575 (1904) ("the weight of authority as well as reason" dictate that courts not pause to inquire as to the means by which competent evidence was obtained).

primarily, of course, because the courts regarded the need for all probative evidence to assure the most accurate resolution of lawsuits as more important than other objectives that might be furthered by excluding relevant but improperly obtained evidence.[2] In addition, however, courts regarded inquiries into possible impropriety in the development of evidence as too costly and time-consuming to justify whatever other objectives might be furthered by excluding evidence because of impropriety in obtaining it.[3]

Probably the most important recent development in the law of evidence as applied in criminal litigation has been the rejection of this approach and the resulting increase in requirements that evidence be excluded because of the manner in which it was obtained—so-called "exclusionary rules."[4]

Discussions sometimes assume the existence of "the exclusionary rule," suggesting that there is only one remedial requirement involved. This is unfortunate and misleading. Litigation and discussion is often dominated by considerations of the Supreme Court's construction of the Fourth Amendment to the United States Constitution as requiring the exclusion in both state and federal criminal prosecutions of evidence tainted by a violation of

---

Exclusion of evidence as a response to a party's violation of procedural requirements applicable to litigation has been and continues to be available in a number of contexts. Trial judges generally have discretion to respond to violations of discovery orders or witness sequestration rules by excluding the evidence as to which discovery was withheld or the testimony of the witness who violated the sequestration rule. E.g., Fed. R. Civ. P. 37(b)(2)(B) (if party fails to obey an order permitting discovery, court may enter order prohibiting the disobedient party from introducing designated matters in evidence). Such uses of exclusion are distinguishable in several ways from the rules that are the subject of this chapter. First, those uses of exclusion are to enforce rules that implement courts' own ability to process litigation. Second, when trial courts exercise their discretion in favor of exclusion, that should generally reflect a judgment that the underlying violation affected the ability of the court to assure that the evidence would be given only proper weight.

Thus, exclusion simply reflects the courts' exercise of their power to enforce litigation procedural requirements that may affect the reliability of evidence. The "exclusionary rules" that are the subject of this chapter, on the other hand, reflect the use of evidence admissibility to enforce legal requirements not directly related to litigation and based upon policies unrelated to the reliability of evidence.

[2]See 8 Wigmore, Evidence § 2183 (McNaughton rev. 1961).

[3]8 Wigmore, Evidence § 2183.

[4]These requirements are appropriately characterized as rules of privilege rather than rules of competency; see the discussion in §§ 72 and 72.1 supra concerning the distinction between rules of privilege and those of competency. Generally speaking, their purpose is not to facilitate the accurate ascertainment of facts by safeguarding against unreliable or misleading evidence but rather to further other interests embodied in the requirements violated by the manner in which the evidence was obtained.

that provision. But this ignores that exclusion may be required because evidence was obtained by violating other legal requirements, many of them not embodied in the federal constitution. Moreover, the contents of these exclusionary requirements need not necessarily be the same as that of the Fourth Amendment exclusionary demand.

Generally, then, discussion best avoids simplistic reference to "the exclusionary rule" as a single rule covering a range of situations. Instead, this area should be conceptualized as containing numerous possible exclusionary rules or sanctions. An exclusionary sanction may attach to any legal requirement that could be violated in the gathering of evidence. There are potentially as many exclusionary sanctions as there are legal requirements of this sort. The Fourth Amendment exclusionary sanction may provide a benchmark for analysis of issues presented by other exclusionary sanctions. But it is important to recognize that other such sanctions may differ in content from the Fourth Amendment's rule. Whether and how they should differ are hard issues that tend to be obscured by discussion of "the exclusionary rule."

It is, of course, difficult to separate discussion of exclusionary sanctions from consideration of the underlying rules enforced by these sanctions. Nevertheless, the contents of those rules are not matters of evidence law. Consequently, this chapter focuses upon the exclusionary consequences rather than the underlying legal requirements violated.

Many legal requirements relating to the admissibility of confessions, such as the *Miranda* requirements and directives that an arrested person be promptly presented before a magistrate, are probably exclusionary sanctions within the meaning of this chapter. For convenience, however, these are treated in Chapter 14, devoted generally to confessions.

## § 165 Policy bases for exclusionary sanctions[1]

Exclusionary sanctions result in exclusion of what would

---

**[Section 165]**

[1]The purposes which exclusionary rules might serve have been discussed primarily in the context of the federal constitutional requirements, but this discussion can quite easily be generalized. How the Supreme Court has developed the conceptual bases for these federal constitutional requirements is considered later. See § 167 infra. While this case law is a model that might be applied in other contexts, the Court's selection of those objectives legitimately served and the comparative significance given them is certainly not beyond reasonable dispute. Some state courts' development of state exclusionary requirements, for example, have rejected at least parts of this model in developing the conceptual bases for these state law rules. See § 168 infra.

otherwise be relevant and competent evidence, and therefore involve a considerable cost. Consequently, they bear a significant burden of justification. Such justification might be provided by several quite different functions which these sanctions might serve.

*Promotion of Accurate Results.* Can exclusionary rules be defended on the ground that they result in rejection of evidence that might otherwise increase the risk that trials would lead to inaccurate results? Some exclusionary sanctions may be supported, at least to some extent, on this basis. If counsel's presence at lineups reduces the risk of suggestiveness, for example, exclusion of eyewitness testimony tainted by the witness's identification of the defendant at a lineup conducted in violation of this right might to some extent result in rejection of unreliable evidence that might otherwise be credited beyond what can be defended on objective grounds.

Most exclusionary sanctions, however, cannot be supported on these grounds. To the contrary, the fact that the evidence excluded by these requirements is not only relevant and competent but also highly reliable increases the difficulty of justifying the requirements.

*Prevention of Future Violations.* A major function served by exclusionary sanctions, of course, is the prevention of future violations of the underlying legal requirements. Prevention might be effectuated in at least two quite different ways: deterrence and "education" or "assimilation."

Deterrence consists of motivating persons to consciously choose not to violate legal requirements because of a desire to avoid rendering evidence inadmissible. Usually in exclusionary sanction debates this means encouraging law enforcement officers to comply with legal requirements in a conscious effort to assure the admissibility of the products of their investigative efforts. But detractors of the exclusionary sanction approach argue that any expectation that deterrence will work effectively is naive, in part because law enforcement officers will often perceive the threat of exclusion as far less meaningful than other considerations influencing their conduct.

Exclusion will be a possibility only if the case is actively contested. Most criminal cases are not ultimately litigated, so the technical admissibility of evidence will not be a consideration. In the infrequent cases in which exclusion becomes a real possibility, the threat materializes only long after the officers' role in the case is finished. A threat to exclude, made in the context of plea bargaining and protracted processing of criminal cases, may be a threat of such minimal and distant significance that it cannot be expected to overcome, in the officers' minds, other considerations that suggest different courses of action.

In actuality, other considerations may be more immediately pressing and make stronger cases for officers' attention. If an officer believes that compliance with legal requirements endangers his personal safety, he is unlikely to ignore that risk because of the possibility of legal challenges to the admissibility of the products of his actions at some distant time. Similarly, the expectations of the officer's peers and immediate supervisors may well conflict with what the law requires and may compete quite effectively with evidentiary rules for the officer's response.

Moreover, the legal requirements with which the officer is expected to comply may be so unclear as to frustrate efforts to ascertain and follow them. Or they may appear to the officer as unrealistic, meaningless or both, and thus invite circumvention.

There is even a risk that to the extent an exclusionary sanction may convey a meaningful deterrent message to law enforcement officers, the result may be that officers will find it most advantageous to completely forego formal prosecution and instead rely upon "street justice" to encourage what they perceive as desirable behavior. If the result of an evidentiary rule is to encourage law enforcement agencies to engage in informal and largely extra-legal activities rather than to encourage them to comply with legal requirements so that prosecution remains possible, the rules have arguably effectuated the worst of all possibilities.

Perhaps the lesson is that generalization about the likely deterrent effect of exclusionary sanctions is difficult or impossible. Some law enforcement activities may be far more subject to being influenced by evidentiary rules than others.[2] Some legal requirements might far more than others lend themselves to effective implementation by means of exclusionary requirements.

Prevention of undesired law enforcement activity, however, may be accomplished in ways other than deterrence. The Supreme Court has noted the possibility that the long-term effect of excluding evidence may be to demonstrate the seriousness with which society regards the underlying legal requirements. This, in turn, may cause law enforcement officers and policymakers to incorporate the requirements into their value system and, presumably, to accept them unconsciously as demanding compliance regardless of the consciously-perceived effect of noncompliance.[3]

How effective exclusionary sanctions are in enforcing various

---

[2]See Terry v. Ohio, 392 U.S. 1, 13, 88 S. Ct. 1868, 20 L. Ed. 2d 889 (1968) (exclusionary rule has limitations as a tool of judicial control and "in some contexts the rule is ineffec-tive as a deterrent").

[3]See Stone v. Powell, 428 U.S. 465, 492, 96 S. Ct. 3037, 49 L. Ed. 2d 1067 (1976).

legal requirements in different contexts remains addressed largely on the basis of intuition. Some empirical research has been undertaken, but in part because of severe methodological problems it is inconclusive.[4]

*Judicial Integrity Considerations.*[5] Exclusionary sanctions might be justified in whole or in part on the basis of what the Supreme Court in *Elkins v. United States*[6] called "the imperative of judicial integrity."[7] But two very different approaches are sometimes confused in discussions of judicial integrity.

One argument is that because evidence was improperly obtained, courts' use of that evidence is simply and inherently "wrong" and thus to be avoided.[8] Of course, the nature of the argument means that it is incapable of utilitarian analysis or empirical verification. At its base, it rests upon an intuitive notion of "right" or "integrity."[9] Whether any such notion of "right" can provide strong support for a costly evidentiary rule, of course, is at best problematic.[10]

Another argument often regarded as a judicial integrity

---

[4]The classic study is Oakes, Studying the Exclusionary Rule in Search and Seizure, 37 U. Chi. L. Rev. 665 (1970). *See also* Spiotto, Search and Seizure: An Empirical Study of the Exclusionary Rule and its Alternatives, 2 J. Legal Studies 243 (1973). *See generally* Kamisar, Does the Exclusionary Rule Affect Police Behavior?, 62 Judicature 70 (1978). Joseph, The Case for The Exclusionary Rule, 14 Human Rights 38, 43 (1987), suggests that probably only anecdotal evidence will ever be available on the effectiveness of exclusion as a deterrent.

[5]*See generally* Bloom & Fentin, "A More Majestic Conception:" The Importance of Judicial Integrity in Preserving the Exclusionary Rule, 13 U. Pa. J. Const. L. 47 (2010). *See also* Stewart, The Road to Mapp v. Ohio and Beyond: The Origin, Development and Future of the Exclusionary Rule in Search-and-Seizure Cases, 83 Colum. L. Rev. 1365, 1382–83 (1983).

[6]Elkins v. U.S., 364 U.S. 206, 80 S. Ct. 1437, 4 L. Ed. 2d 1669 (1960).

[7]Elkins, 364 U.S. at 222.

[8]*Cf.* 364 U.S. at 223 ("[C]ourts [should not] be accomplices in the will-

ful disobedience of a Constitution they are sworn to uphold."). *See also* U. S. v. Payner, 447 U.S. 727, 746, 100 S. Ct. 2439, 65 L. Ed. 2d 468 (1980) (Marshall, J., dissenting) (if a court permits evidence resulting from deliberately illegal activity to be used, "it places its imprimatur upon such lawlessness and thereby taints its own integrity").

[9]This, of course can be met by a similar intuitive argument: "Is not the court which excludes illegally obtained evidence in order to avoid condoning the acts of the officer by the same token condoning the illegal acts of the defendant?" Barrett, Exclusion of Evidence Obtained by Illegal Searches, A Comment on People v. Cahan, 43 Cal. L. Rev. 565, 582 (1955).

[10]Justice Stewart argued that even Justice Holmes acknowledged that only his personal value decision supported his assertion that using tainted evidence was "less evil" than permitting guilty criminals to escape. Stewart himself took the position that no such value judgment can justify a federally-imposed exclusionary requirement. Stewart, The Road to Mapp v. Ohio and Beyond, 83 Colum. L. Rev. at 1383.

consideration has, in contrast, a clearly utilitarian end and thus is—in theory at least—susceptible to efforts to verify it. This approach was articulated by Justice Brandeis in *Olmstead v. United States*:[11]

> In a government of laws, existence of the government will be imperiled if it fails to observe the law scrupulously . . . . Crime is contagious. If the Government becomes a lawbreaker, it breeds contempt for law; it invites every man to become a law unto himself; it invites anarchy.[12]

This means, he continued, that the government, like a private litigant, should be denied access to the courts if it comes with unclean hands. If the government bases its request for aid from the courts on illegally obtained evidence, "aid is denied despite the defendant's wrong. It is denied in order to maintain respect for law; in order to promote confidence in the administration of justice; in order to preserve the judicial process from contamination."[13]

Essentially, this argument is that if illegally seized evidence is used by the government acting through its courts, government in general and its courts in particular will lose the respect of the governed and consequently will be rendered less able to perform their governing functions. In the case of courts, this means that they will be less able to resolve disputes among citizens.

Despite the rhetorical flourish with which Justice Brandeis demonstrated this argument can be made, it may simply be inconsistent with reality. Whether the courts' ability to command respect and compliance is affected by evidentiary rules is, of course, open to doubt. But to the extent that it is, this argument may distort the effect of those rules. General respect for the judiciary may well suffer when the courts are perceived as ignoring reliable evidence because of impropriety in the manner it was obtained, particularly if doing so requires the acquittal of persons clearly guilty of serious antisocial acts.

*Remedy for Wrongs Done in the Illegality.*[14] Superficially, at least, exclusionary sanctions would seem to perform a unique and perhaps appropriate remedial function, and thus might be justified on that basis. The law's objective, the argument might run, should be to place a wronged person as close to his previous condition as is feasible. Only an exclusionary sanction can replace

---

[11]Olmstead v. U.S., 277 U.S. 438, 48 S. Ct. 564, 72 L. Ed. 944 (1928).

[12]Olmstead, 277 U.S. at 485 (Brandeis, J., dissenting).

[13]277 U.S. at 484.

[14]*Cf.* Schroeder, Restoring the Status Quo Ante: The Fourth Amendment Exclusionary Rule as a Compensatory Device, 51 Geo. Wash. L. Rev. 633 (1983).

such a person in a position in which he need not fear the use against him of the fruits of wrong done to him.[15]

On the other hand, the substance of the underlying legal requirements violated may make clear that persons whose rights are violated have no legitimate interest in being free of criminal liability that looms only because of the violations of their rights. If they have no such legitimate interest, the fact that an exclusionary sanction frees them of such liability is of little or no significance.

The right to be free of unreasonable searches, for example, may protect only persons' interest in being free of the privacy invasion occasioned by such searches. That this privacy interest enables them to withhold from the government evidence of their criminal activity would then be at most an undesirable side effect of the privacy right. If the right to be free from unreasonable searches is so conceptualized, no person who is unreasonably searched has a legitimate interest in having the government deprived of the power to use against them evidence found as a result of that search. Their interest in an effective remedy for the violation of their privacy, then, does not include an interest in being returned to a condition in which they need not fear the government's use of the discovered evidence against them in a criminal prosecution.

If the underlying legal requirements are so conceptualized, the tendency of exclusionary sanctions to provide unique protection against criminal liability is of no legitimate remedial significance. Since the victims of the underlying wrongs have no legitimate interest in being free of the use of the evidence against them, the unique ability of exclusionary sanctions to bring about this result does not significantly support the exclusionary sanctions.

Even if exclusion does tend to some extent at least respond in a logical manner to the harm done, it may not be "appropriate" because it provides an excessive remedy.[16] This is especially the case if exclusion of evidence frustrates the prosecution. Acquittal of a demonstrably guilty person may simply be too heavy a cost even to make a victimized person whole.

### § 166 Federal constitutional exclusionary sanctions: (a) Development

Federal constitutional exclusionary sanctions have served as a

---

[15] *Cf.* White, Forgotten Points in the "Exclusionary Rule" Debate, 81 Mich. L. Rev. 1273, 1278 n. 21 (1983) ("The most natural and complete remedy [for violation of the right to be free from unreasonable searches] is to place the parties so far as possible in the situation that would have existed had the wrong never occurred.").

[16] Schroeder, Restoring the Status Quo Ante, 51 Geo. Wash. L. Rev. at 656.

model for modern exclusionary requirements. The Supreme Court's case law developing the federal sanctions—and the decisions molding the Fourth Amendment exclusionary requirement in particular—have similarly framed much of the discussion of exclusionary requirements in general.

Exclusion as a response to Federal constitutional illegality in obtaining evidence appears to have originated in confusion concerning the substance of Fourth and Fifth Amendment protection. In *Boyd v. United States*,[1] an unsuccessful claimant in a forfeiture action sought relief from a judgment of forfeiture on the ground that the trial court erred in receiving into evidence an invoice which the claimant had been compelled to produce by order of the trial court. Both the Fourth and Fifth Amendments were invoked. The Supreme Court held that the compulsory production of the document was subject to scrutiny under the Fourth Amendment.[2] To determine whether it was reasonable, the Court turned to the Fifth Amendment's prohibition against compelled self-incrimination. Finding an "intimate relationship" between the two provisions, the Court concluded that compelled production or other seizure of a person's private books or papers to be used in evidence against him was violative of the Fifth Amendment. Ultimately, the Court held that the admission into evidence of the invoice, given the manner in which it was obtained, violated both the Fourth Amendment prohibition against unreasonable searches and seizures and the Fifth Amendment prohibition against compelled self-incrimination.[3]

Twenty years later, in *Adams v. New York*,[4] the Court nevertheless refused to require exclusion where only the defendant's Fourth Amendment rights were violated. Such cases were governed by what the Court described as "the weight of authority

---

[Section 166]

[1]Boyd v. U.S., 116 U.S. 616, 6 S. Ct. 524, 29 L. Ed. 746 (1886). *Boyd* has been described by the Court as containing the "roots" of the Fourth Amendment exclusionary rule adopted in Weeks v. U.S., 232 U.S. 383, 34 S. Ct. 341, 58 L. Ed. 652 (1914). Stone v. Powell, 428 U.S. 465, 483 n.19, 96 S. Ct. 3037, 49 L. Ed. 2d 1067 (1976).

[2]Boyd, 116 U.S. at 622.

[3]116 U.S. at 634–35. While it is certainly arguable that no specific exclusionary sanction can be found in the language of the Fifth Amendment, that provision's prohibition against a person being "compelled . . . to be a witness against himself" does address some evidence admissibility matters. At least some members of the Court may have regarded any exclusionary sanctions created by the federal constitution as having their basis in this wording of the Fifth Amendment. *See* Mapp v. Ohio, 367 U.S. 643, 666, 81 S. Ct. 1684, 6 L. Ed. 2d 1081 (1961) (Black, J. concurring) (Fourth and Fifth Amendments together require exclusion of evidence obtained in violation of Fourth Amendment's prohibition against unreasonable searches and seizures).

[4]Adams v. People of State of New York, 192 U.S. 585, 24 S. Ct. 372, 48 L. Ed. 575 (1904).

as well as reason," embodied in the rule that courts will not pause to inquire as to the means by which competent evidence is obtained.[5]

A decade later, however, in *Weeks v. United States*,[6] the Court embraced exclusion as a Fourth Amendment remedy. The Fourth Amendment as it applied in federal criminal litigation, *Weeks* held, imposed an exclusionary sanction. "If letters and private documents can thus be [improperly] seized and held and used in evidence against a citizen accused of an offense," the Court reasoned, "the protection of the Fourth Amendment declaring his right to be secure against such searches and seizures is of no value, and, so far as those thus placed are concerned, might as well be stricken from the Constitution."[7]

*Weeks*, of course, was inapplicable to state litigation, and doubt remained even whether the Fourth Amendment itself was binding on the states. In *Wolf v. Colorado*,[8] the Court for the first time directly addressed these issues. Concluding that the core of the Fourth Amendment, the security of one's privacy against arbitrary intrusion by the police, was basic to a free society and therefore implicit in the concept of ordered liberty, the Court held that under *Palko v. Connecticut*[9] the Fourth Amendment prohibition against unreasonable searches and seizures was enforceable against the States through the Due Process clause of the Fourteenth Amendment.

But *Wolf* then distinguished the prohibition against unreasonable searches and seizures from the exclusionary remedy applied in federal criminal litigation and found the latter not binding on the States. By 1961, however, the Court was prepared to reconsider *Wolf's* second conclusion.

In *Mapp v. Ohio*,[10] this second holding of *Wolf* was reversed. Since *Wolf*, the majority explained, more than half of those states considering whether to adopt an exclusionary sanction as a matter of state law had decided to do so. The weight of the relevant authority, then, could no longer be said to oppose the *Weeks* rule. More important, however, the Court read experience as contradicting *Wolf's* assumption that remedies other than an exclusionary rule could be relied upon to enforce Fourth Amendment rights. The experience and decisions of the state courts as well as the Supreme Court's own decisions recognized the "obvious futil-

---

[5]Adams, 192 U.S. at 594.

[6]Weeks v. U.S., 232 U.S. 383, 34 S. Ct. 341, 58 L. Ed. 652 (1914).

[7]Weeks, 232 U.S. at 393.

[8]Wolf v. People of the State of Colo., 338 U.S. 25, 69 S. Ct. 1359, 93 L. Ed. 1782 (1949).

[9]Palko v. State of Connecticut, 302 U.S. 319, 58 S. Ct. 149, 82 L. Ed. 288 (1937).

[10]Mapp v. Ohio, 367 U.S. 643, 81 S. Ct. 1684, 6 L. Ed. 2d 1081 (1961).

ity of relegating the Fourth Amendment to the protection of other remedies . . . ."[11] Consequently, the *Weeks* exclusionary rule was held an essential part of both the Fourth and Fourteenth Amendments and therefore binding on the states as well as the federal government.[12]

*Mapp* was undoubtedly a bold holding made on minimal grounds. Functionally, the Supreme Court read the general terms of the Fourth Amendment as delegating to the federal courts the power to develop remedies appropriate to enforcement of the clear substantive commands of the provision. The framers must have anticipated that the guarantees of the provision be enforceable in federal courts. Since they failed to provide for remedies that enabled this, they must have intended that the courts have authority to develop such remedies as are appropriate given such considerations as the magnitude of the threats posed to the underlying guarantees and the effectiveness of less costly alternatives than exclusion of resulting evidence.

Having determined that an exclusionary sanction was an essential part of the Fourth Amendment right to be free from unreasonable searches and seizures, the Court proceeded to apply it uncritically to other federal constitutional rights.[13] It has made clear, however, that these various federal constitutional exclusionary sanctions are not identical in content.[14]

---

[11]Mapp, 367 U.S. at 652.

[12]The Fourth Amendment exclusionary remedy is triggered only by a violation of Fourth Amendment law, which does not somehow incorporate state law concerning the same subject. Virginia v. Moore, 553 U.S. 164, 169, 128 S. Ct. 1598, 170 L. Ed. 2d 559 (2008) (arrest by state officer in violation of state law requirement of arrest warrant is not unreasonable for Fourth Amendment purposes and does not trigger Fourth Amendment exclusionary requirement).

[13]In Miranda v. Arizona, 384 U.S. 436, 86 S. Ct. 1602, 16 L. Ed. 2d 694 (1966) (see generally § 150 supra), for example, once the Court held that the Fifth Amendment, as applied to custodial interrogation of suspects, imposed certain requirements such as the right to counsel and certain admonishments, it did not pause before attaching an exclusionary sanction to these rights.

Beginning in 1967, the Court similarly held that a defendant's right to counsel at trial implicates an exclusionary remedy that demands that the resulting conviction not be used in evidence or for other purposes. Burgett v. Texas, 389 U.S. 109, 114, 88 S. Ct. 258, 19 L. Ed. 2d 319 (1967) (citing *Mapp*). *See also* Loper v. Beto, 405 U.S. 473, 92 S. Ct. 1014, 31 L. Ed. 2d 374 (1972) (prior conviction obtained in violation of right to counsel cannot be used to impeach testifying defendant); Baldasar v. Illinois, 446 U.S. 222, 100 S. Ct. 1585, 64 L. Ed. 2d 169 (1980) (Sixth Amendment bars use of misdemeanor conviction for which no jail time was imposed to later enhance another misdemeanor into a felony).

[14]See § 176 infra ("fruit of the poisonous tree" does not apply to Fifth Amendment exclusionary aspect of *Miranda* holdings).

Until *Hudson v. Michigan*,[15] it was generally assumed that any violation of at least the Fourth Amendment triggered exclusionary rule analysis under *Mapp*. *Hudson*, however, held that at least one category of Fourth Amendment violations will not do so.[16] Fourth Amendment violations consisting of entry of premises to execute a search warrant in a "no knock" manner violating Fourth Amendment requirements simply cannot support an exclusionary rule challenge to evidence found in the premises.

*Hudson's* conceptual basis is somewhat unclear. Some of the Court's discussion suggests the holding rests on the lack of proof in these cases of sufficient factual causation between the Fourth Amendment violation and the discovery of the challenged evidence.[17] Other parts suggest that whatever factual causation may exist is usually if not inevitably of a sort that demands a finding that the taint was attenuated and thus the evidence is admissible despite the factual causation.

Overall the *Hudson* discussion indicates that the holding rested on neither causation nor attenuation of taint grounds. Rather, the Court is now willing to identify categories of Fourth Amendment violations that are, as a matter of Fourth Amendment exclusionary sanction law, insufficient to trigger the exclusionary remedy. A defendant's challenge to admissibility of evidence relying on such a violation must fail without inquiry into whether the defendant has proved causation or the prosecution has established attenuation of the taint.

Why were no knock entry violations held insufficient to trigger the exclusionary requirement, and what does this suggest regarding what other violations might be similarly characterized? *Hudson* was not entirely clear. Certainly the result was influenced by the Court's perceptions that the Fourth Amendment announcement requirement is one particularly difficult for officers to understand and meet. It also took into account that these cases often involve at most a minimal causal link between the violation and the discovery of the evidence and present factors militating in favor of a finding of attenuation of taint. It was also undoubt-

---

[15]Hudson v. Michigan, 547 U.S. 586, 126 S. Ct. 2159, 165 L. Ed. 2d 56 (2006). The implications of *Hudson* are considered in Tomkovicz, Hudson v. Michigan and the Future of Fourth Amendment Exclusion, 93 Iowa L. Rev. 1819, 1835–85 (2008).

[16]*Accord* Sanchez-Llamas v. Oregon, 548 U.S. 331, 348, 126 S. Ct. 2669, 165 L. Ed. 2d 557 (2006) ("we have ruled that the Constitution requires the exclusion of evidence ob-

tained *by certain violations of the Fourth Amendment*") (emphasis provided).

[17]Hudson, 547 U.S. at 592 ("In this case, of course, the constitutional violation of an illegal *manner* of entry was *not* a but-for cause of obtaining the evidence.") (emphasis in original). The general need for a defendant to show a causal link between illegal conduct and acquisition of challenged evidence is addressed in § 176.

edly influenced by the majority's increasing disenchantment with exclusion of evidence as a constitutional remedy.

In addition, however, *Hudson* indicated that exclusion is appropriate as a response only to Fourth Amendment requirements that protect Fourth Amendment interests in shielding evidence from government observation or physical seizure. The requirement of announcement before entering premises to execute a warrant protects other Fourth Amendment interests—the security of "life and limb" and property and certain aspects of privacy and dignity. Since the challenge to the evidence did not rest on interests related to the protection of evidence from government acquisition, *Hudson* explained, "the exclusionary rule is inapplicable."[18]

Post-*Mapp* applications of the federal constitutional exclusionary requirements generally assumed these requirements are mandatory. If the facts before a trial judge trigger one of the rules but no recognized exception to the exclusionary demand, the judge is required to exclude the evidence. The judge has no general discretion to admit or exclude evidence based on the judge's case specific evaluation of the propriety or wisdom of exclusion.[19]

The continuing validity of this assumption was cast into doubt by *Herring v. United States*.[20] *Herring* held that in at least one context exclusion is not required—or apparently permitted—if a defendant shows only a "negligent" violation of the Fourth

---

[18]547 U.S. at 593–95. Admissibility of evidence on a case-specific showing that the taint of illegality was attenuated is addressed in § 179.

Tomkovicz observed that Justice Kennedy's concurrence suggests he may not be prepared to recognize a new exception that would "afford judges a sharp new tool for cutting holes in the suppression remedy." Tomkovicz, Hudson v. Michigan, 93 Iowa L. Rev. at 1880.

This does not, of course, affect suppression as a state law remedy. *See* Berumen v. State, 182 P.3d 635, 637 (Alaska App.2008) (despite *Hudson*, suppression of evidence is state law remedy for serious violations of state statutory announcement requirement).

[19]At least one federal court found more discretion in the federal doctrine. If the structured analysis indicates evidence must be excluded, the Seventh Circuit held, the trial judge nevertheless has the power to further inquire whether—given the further facts of the case—exclusion would be consistent with those policies on which the Fourth Amendment exclusionary requirement is based. In the event that this analysis suggests those policies would not be best served by exclusion, the court has authority to admit the evidence. Thus "where the violation of the Fourth Amendment in a particular case causes no discernible harm to the interests of an individual protected by the particular constitutional prohibition at issue . . . , the exclusion of evidence for the trial is a disproportionately severe and inappropriate sanction." U.S. v. Espinoza, 256 F.3d 718 (7th Cir. 2001), describing the holding of U.S. v. Stefonek, 179 F.3d 1030 (7th Cir. 1999).

[20]Herring v. U.S., 555 U.S. 135, 129 S. Ct. 695, 172 L. Ed. 2d 496 (2009).

Amendment. Specifically *Herring* held exclusion was not required by a showing that the challenged evidence was tainted by an arrest made in reliance on police records erroneously indicating—as a result of negligent recordkeeping by officers of another county—a warrant was outstanding for the defendant. Whatever deterrence might be provided by excluding evidence tainted by merely negligent police recordkeeping, *Herring* held, is not worth the cost.[21]

Where *Herring* applies, it appears to require a defendant seeking exclusion of evidence under *Mapp* to at least show more as a basis for triggering exclusionary rule analysis than a mere Fourth Amendment violation. This analysis can be triggered by a showing of "deliberate, reckless, or grossly negligent conduct." Alternatively, at least "in some circumstances" a showing of "recurring or systemic negligence" will suffice.[22] Justice Breyer suggested in dissent that trial courts will have to engage a "case-by-case, multifactored inquiry into the degree of police culpability."[23]

If *Herring* applies, it may permit or require more than an inquiry into whether the defendant has shown at least gross negligence or reoccurring or systemic negligence. It may in at least some situations allow trial courts to balance on a case-by-case basis the proven law enforcement culpability against the need for deterrence in the type of situation presented.

Obviously, identifying those situations to which *Herring* applies presents a major issue of Fourth Amendment exclusionary rule law. The Court noted that that the constitutionally-deficient law enforcement conduct before it related to maintaining law enforcement records, and specifically an arrest warrant database.[24] *Herring* may apply only to such situations.

In *Herring*, the merely negligent held insufficient to trigger exclusionary rule analysis was by law enforcements officers of a county other than that employing the arresting officers. This apparently caused the *Herring* majority to characterize the negligence as "attenuated from" the law enforcement action directly causing the acquisition of the evidence.[25] Perhaps, then, *Herring* applies only where the constitutionally-deficient law enforcement conduct is attenuated in this manner from the law enforcement that in a direct sense infringed the objecting defendant's Fourth Amendment protected interests.

---

[21]Herring, 555 U.S. at 144 n. 4.

[22]555 U.S. at 144.

[23]555 U.S. at 158 (Breyer, J., dissenting).

[24]555 U.S. at 146 (referring to

"recordkeeping errors by the police" and "maintaining a warrant system").

[25]555 U.S. at 137 ("the error was the result of isolated negligence attenuated from the arrest").

*Herring* might be read as an expansion of the so-called "good faith" exception[26] to the Fourth Amendment exclusionary requirement. But the Court's discussion did not focus on the government's defensive response to *Herring's* challenge to the admissibility of the evidence. Rather, it suggested the defect was one in the attack itself: a defendant—at least in the context involved—must show more than a merely "negligent" law enforcement violation of Fourth Amendment requirements.

Recent developments reflect the Supreme Court's increasing disenchantment with exclusionary remedies for federal constitutional rights; this is developed in the next section. Quite predictably, therefore, in 2009 the Court summarily rejected a suggestion that it should craft a new and broad "exclusionary rule" barring state courts from admitting testimony from "jailhouse snitches."[27]

## § 167 Federal constitutional exclusionary sanctions: (b) Policy bases and analytical approach

As the Supreme Court developed the federal constitutional exclusionary requirements, primarily the Fourth Amendment sanction, it narrowed the policy considerations on which those requirements are based. It also formulated a consistently-applied approach to framing the subissues raised in developing the contents of those requirements. In the course of this process, the Court made several basic choices regarding the potentially-relevant policy considerations.

First, the Court has made clear that the federal constitutional rules do not serve a significant legitimate remedial function.[1] This is because as the Court envisions the constitutionally-cognizable injuries done, exclusion of evidence simply does not tend to make victims whole. "[T]he ruptured privacy of the victims' homes and effects," it explained in the context of search and seizure law, "cannot be restored. Reparation comes too late."[2]

If exclusion of evidence cannot restore the violated privacy, why cannot it at least reduce one effect of the privacy violation by replacing the victim to a position wherein he does not face criminal prosecution based on evidence obtained as a result of the violation of his privacy interests? The Court has not directly ad-

---

[26]See § 182.

[27]Kansas v. Ventris, 556 U.S. 586, 593 n.*, 129 S. Ct. 1841, 173 L. Ed. 2d 801 (2009).

**[Section 167]**

[1]*E.g.*, Stone v. Powell, 428 U.S. 465, 485, 96 S. Ct. 3037, 49 L. Ed. 2d

1067 (1976) (*Mapp's* exclusionary requirement "is not calculated to redress the injury to the privacy of the victim of the search or seizure").

[2]Linkletter v. Walker, 381 U.S. 618, 637, 85 S. Ct. 1731, 14 L. Ed. 2d 601 (1965).

dressed this question. But most likely it views the prosecution's possession of and ability to use incriminating evidence as entirely unrelated to the legitimate interests of the defendant. The prosecution has a right to possession of this evidence; the defendant has no ultimate right to withhold it from the prosecution. To the extent that an improper search results in the prosecution being able to implement its interest in obtaining such evidence, the search violates no protected interests, that is, no constitutionally-cognizable "rights," of the defendant. The wrong to the defendant consisted entirely of violating his privacy. To the extent that this violation of privacy factually resulted in the prosecution obtaining access to incriminating evidence, this in no way contributes to the constitutionally-offensive aspects of the search, that is, those aspects as to which the defendant has a legitimate claim to remedy.

Consequently, to deprive the prosecution of the ability to use this evidence would in no way restore the defendant in a manner to which he has any legitimate claim. His only legitimate claim is for restoration of his violated privacy, which is in no way accomplished by depriving the prosecution of evidence.

The second basic decision made by the Court was adoption of the view that considerations of judicial integrity have only a "limited role" in Fourth Amendment theory and, consequently, in determining the content of the provision's exclusionary mandate.[3] This was accomplished by holding that the "primary meaning" of judicial integrity in this context is such that it is violated when, but only when, courts' use of illegally obtained evidence encourages future violations of the sort that provided the prosecution access to the evidence at issue.[4] Consequently, whether particular use of illegally obtained evidence offends judicial integrity considerations involves essentially the same question as whether it serves a preventive purpose: will the admission of the evidence encourage future illegality of the sort committed to obtain the evidence at issue?[5]

A third basic policy decision concerns what almost by default

---

[3]Powell, 428 U.S. at 484.

[4]U.S. v. Janis, 428 U.S. 433, 458 n.35, 96 S. Ct. 3021, 49 L. Ed. 2d 1046 (1976). The Court's discussion also suggested that judicial integrity would be implicated if the use of the evidence itself constituted a violation of the defendant's rights. In such situations, it suggested, the taint arising from commission of the violation would itself be offensive and require rejection of the evidence. But in the Fourth Amendment context, the use of resulting evidence in no manner intrudes upon the defendant's protected interests. Janis, 428 U.S. at 458 n. 35.

[5]428 U.S. at 458 n. 35.

A substantial minority of the Court continues to hold a broader view of the considerations supporting the Fourth Amendment exclusionary requirement. These justices thus have a "more majestic" perception of the exclusionary requirement itself. Justice

has become the basic justification for the federal constitutional requirements—the need to prevent future violations of the underlying constitutional demands. Traditionally, the Court appeared to assume that this would be accomplished by conscious deterrence—law enforcement officers would be motivated by the exclusionary sanction to consciously comply with the constitutional rules. In *Stone v. Powell*,[6] with regard to the preventive function of the Fourth Amendment exclusionary rule, the Court indicated that the long-term "educative" effect is "[m]ore important[ ]" than the tendency of the threat of exclusion to consciously deter officers from future violations.[7] Nevertheless, it has not followed this pronouncement and in post-*Powell* analyses has assumed that prevention is accomplished primarily if not exclusively by deterrence.

A final policy decision was evidenced more recently in the Court's case law. Beginning with *Herring v. United States*,[8] the Court has stressed the importance of the "culpability" of the law enforcement conduct in determining the exclusionary consequences of that conduct.[9] To some extent, this is closely related to its emphasis on deterrence. "The extent to which the exclusionary rule is justified by . . . deterrence principles," it announced in *Herring*, "varies with the culpability of the law enforcement conduct."[10] But the case law also suggests the Court has come to view exclusion as a punishment imposed on law enforcement that must be justified by a demonstration that the triggering conduct was blameworthy. Later in *Herring* the Court observed:

> To trigger the exclusionary rule, police conduct must be sufficiently deliberate that exclusion can meaningfully deter it, and sufficiently

---

Ginsburg—writing for four members of the Court in Herring v. U.S., 555 U.S. 135, 129 S. Ct. 695, 172 L. Ed. 2d 496 (2009)—acknowledged that deterring future violations of the provision is "a main objective" of the exclusionary requirement. She added, however, that the exclusionary requirement "also serves other important purposes." It avoids undermining the public distrust of government caused by government benefiting from its own unlawful conduct. Further, she continued, exclusion of evidence "is often the only remedy effective to redress a Fourth Amendment violation." Herring, 555 U.S. at 151–53 (Ginsburg, J., dissenting).

The *Herring* majority acknowl-edged the dissenters' view, noting that it "would exclude evidence even where deterrence does not justify doing so." But it added the Court's cases reject the dissenters' conception of the Fourth Amendment exclusionary requirement. 555 U.S. at 141 n. 2.

[6]Stone v. Powell, 428 U.S. 465, 96 S. Ct. 3037, 49 L. Ed. 2d 1067 (1976).

[7]Powell, 428 U.S. at 492.

[8]Herring v. U.S., 555 U.S. 135, 129 S. Ct. 695, 172 L. Ed. 2d 496 (2009).

[9]Herring, 555 U.S. at 143–146.

[10]555 U.S. at 143.

culpable that such deterrence is worth the price paid by the justice system.[11]

This suggests a need for culpability independent of the need for the deliberateness necessary to invoke the deterrence rationale.

Building on these basic decisions regarding the relevant considerations, the Court has developed a consistent formula for framing specific subissues regarding the content of the federal constitutional exclusionary rules. First articulated in *United States v. Calandra*,[12] this approach puts the issue as one of proposed expansion of the exclusionary requirement beyond the core demand that evidence obtained as a direct result of activity violating the constitutional requirements be excluded when offered by the prosecution to prove the defendant's guilt in the prosecution's case-in-chief at a criminal trial. The analysis requires identification of, first, the increased effectiveness of the exclusionary sanction in accomplishing its purpose that would result from the proposed expansion, and, second, the costs of doing so. The critical question is whether the incremental increase in effectiveness is worth the cost that must be paid.[13]

Generally, in inquiring into the potential for increased effectiveness the Court focuses upon deterrence and inquires as to the incremental deterrent effect which would be achieved by the proposed expansion.[14] With regard to the costs, of course, the loss of reliable evidence of offenders' guilt is the major concern. But in addition the Court has taken into account other considerations, such as administrative costs and disruption of the criminal justice system in general and criminal trials in particular. In *Calandra*, for example, the specific issue before the Court was whether the Fourth Amendment exclusionary rule should be applied to grand jury proceedings by permitting witnesses to decline to respond to questions based upon information obtained in violation of the witnesses' Fourth Amendment rights. Permitting this, the majority stressed, would require that grand jury investigations be frequently halted for extended inquiries into the manner in which particular information was acquired. The result would be serious

---

[11]555 U.S. at 144. This was applied in Davis v. U.S., 131 S. Ct. 2419, 180 L. Ed. 2d 285 (2011), in support of extending the good faith exception to officers who conduct warrantless searches in strict compliance with then-binding appellate precedent. Davis, 131 S.Ct. at 2428 (such officers' conduct is neither "deliberate enough to yield 'meaningfu[l]' deterrence, [nor] culpable enough to be 'worth the price paid by the justice system' ").

[12]U.S. v. Calandra, 414 U.S. 338, 94 S. Ct. 613, 38 L. Ed. 2d 561 (1974). The analysis had clearly been used earlier. *E.g.*, Alderman v. U.S., 394 U.S. 165, 174–175, 89 S. Ct. 961, 22 L. Ed. 2d 176 (1969).

[13]*E.g.*, Calandra, 414 U.S. at 349–351; Alderman, 394 U.S. at 174–175.

[14]Calandra, 414 U.S. at 351.

interference with the effective and expeditious discharge by grand juries of their historic role and functions.[15]

In recent case law, a majority of the Court has shown increasing willingness to give minimal weight in its analyses to those considerations traditionally favoring reliance on exclusion of evidence. In *Hudson v. Michigan*,[16] for example, the majority suggested legal and social changes since *Mapp* have made reliance on the costly remedy of exclusion less necessary and less appropriate. Law enforcement agencies have become more professional, it added, and have emphasized internal discipline.[17]

Nearly as dramatic has been the willingness of a majority of the Court to characterize exclusion of evidence as a disfavored and last resort remedy under federal constitutional and nonconstitutional law. If the Vienna Convention on Consular Relations authorizes the federal courts to develop a judicial remedy for violations of the Convention, the Court explained in *Sanchez—Llamas v. Oregon*,[18] that remedy must conform with United States domestic law. Domestic United States law, it then made clear, accepts exclusion of evidence only where that approach provides more a more effective and less-costly remedy than alternatives. That is not the case, *Sanchez-Llamas* held, with violations of the Convention.[19]

What *Hudson* and *Herring* portend for the future of federal constitutional exclusionary requirements is far from clear. In *Hudson*, Justice Kennedy concurred in part to express confidence that "the continued operation of the exclusionary rule, as settled and defined by our precedents, is not in doubt."[20] No such confidence was expressed three years later by any of the Justices in *Herring*.

Given the relevant policy considerations, the Court expressly stated in *Hudson*, "[s]uppression of evidence . . . has always been our last resort . . . ."[21] Whether this is accurate as a statement of historical fact is at best questionable. Clearly, however, it accurately states the position of a majority of the current Court.

---

[15]414 U.S. at 350.

[16]Hudson v. Michigan, 547 U.S. 586, 126 S. Ct. 2159, 165 L. Ed. 2d 56 (2006).

[17]Hudson, 547 U.S. at 598–99.

[18]Sanchez-Llamas v. Oregon, 548 U.S. 331, 126 S. Ct. 2669, 165 L. Ed. 2d 557 (2006).

[19]Sanchez—Llamas, 548 U.S. at 347–40.

[20]548 U.S. at 603 (Kennedy, joining parts I through III of Court's opinion and concurring in the judgment).

[21]Hudson, 547 U.S. at 591. *Accord* Herring, 547 U.S. at 140 (quoting from *Hudson*).

## § 168   State constitutional exclusionary sanctions

Despite the prominence of *Mapp v. Ohio.*[1] and Fourth Amendment case law in exclusionary sanction discussion, the exclusionary remedy was first developed in state constitutional litigation.[2] State decisions provide bases of increasing importance for modern exclusionary sanctions, independent of *Mapp* and its progeny. Proponents of exclusion as a means of enforcing legal requirements, dissatisfied with the Supreme Court's development of federal rights and exclusionary remedies, have increasingly sought to persuade state courts to develop state constitutional rights—and state constitutional exclusionary requirements—as more rigorously protective of those suspected or accused of crime.

States' power to accept or reject an exclusionary approach was confirmed by the Supreme Court in *California v. Greenwood.*[3] Under California law, the warrantless search of Greenwood's trash constituted an unreasonable search under a state constitutional provision similar to the Fourth Amendment, yet state constitutional law did not require exclusion of the resulting evidence. All agreed that *Mapp* and its rationale did not require, as a matter of Fourth Amendment law, exclusion of evidence obtained in violation of the state constitution but not in violation of any federal provision. Further, the Court held, the Due Process Clause of the Fourteenth Amendment did not bar the state from depriving Greenwood of a remedy for police conduct violating state but not federal constitutional law. California could have defined unreasonable searches as encompassing no more official activity than was covered by the Fourth Amendment. Since the state has the power to permit police activity not barred by the Fourth Amendment, it necessarily also has the lesser included power to prohibit such activity but to enforce that prohibition by means other than excluding evidence from criminal trials.[4]

State constitutional provisions, like their federal counterparts, seldom expressly address the admissibility of evidence obtained in violation of them. When a state court is asked to construe such provisions to require the exclusion of evidence, then, it must

---

[Section 168]

[1]Mapp v. Ohio, 367 U.S. 643, 81 S. Ct. 1684, 6 L. Ed. 2d 1081 (1961).

[2]State v. Sheridan, 121 Iowa 164, 96 N.W. 730 (1903); State v. Slamon, 73 Vt. 212, 50 A. 1097 (1901). Ironically, after Weeks v. U.S., 232 U.S. 383, 34 S. Ct. 341, 58 L. Ed. 652 (1914), both states rejected their early pro-exclusionary rule positions. In State v. Tonn, 195 Iowa 94, 191 N.W.

530 (1923), *Weeks* and the "federal rule" were rejected and *Sheridan* was overruled. In State v. Stacy, 104 Vt. 379, 160 A. 257 (1932), the Vermont court announced that intervening cases had overruled *Slamon*.

[3]California v. Greenwood, 486 U.S. 35, 108 S. Ct. 1625, 100 L. Ed. 2d 30 (1988).

[4]Greenwood, 486 U.S. at 44–45.

choose whether or not to interpret its constitution with the same vigor and flexibility exercised by the Supreme Court in *Mapp*.[5] Thus, state courts are faced with the same basic question as the Supreme Court faced in *Mapp*—does general language prohibiting certain official conduct require or permit exclusion of evidence resulting from prohibited conduct? Seldom have state courts addressed directly and creatively the difficult question of whether such general constitutional provisions provide the courts with authority to mandate as pervasive and controversial requirements as exclusionary sanctions. Language accepting an exclusionary sanction for violations of state constitutions has sometimes simply offhandedly crept into discussion[6] and become accepted law without any focused and careful consideration as to the propriety of this position.[7] In some situations, state judicial attention has been focused upon whether a state exclusionary sanction should be developed as identical in content to federal constitutional exclusionary sanctions, rather than on whether a state exclusionary sanction is even justified. State constitutional exclusionary rules, then, have sometimes developed with little or no careful scrutiny of their propriety or wisdom.

Several courts have addressed in more depth the propriety of construing their state provisions as the Supreme Court construed the Fourth Amendment in *Mapp*. Each has chosen to follow the

---

[5]Occasionally the task is made easier by considerations not present in *Mapp*. Especially where a state constitution is of relatively recent origin, reliable evidence of an actual understanding on the part of the framers or adopters may be available. If so, of course, that understanding controls. *See* State v. Pokini, 45 Haw. 295, 367 P.2d 499 (1961) (1950 Constitutional Convention's Committee of the Whole Report makes clear that failure of provision to expressly provide for exclusion reflected only disagreement on how to best implement intention that illegally seized evidence be excluded).

[6]*See* State v. Thomas, 349 So. 2d 270, 273 (La. 1977) ("Any evidence produced as a result of an illegal search and seizure is tainted and thus inadmissible under the state and federal constitutions.").

[7]*See* Com. v. Russo, 594 Pa. 119, 934 A.2d 1199, 1207–10 (2007) (after

*Mapp*, "exclusionary decisions arose that were rendered exclusively under [Pa. Const.] Article I, Section 8," but "no decision of this Court has squarely purported to examine and disapprove of the long and unbroken line of pre-*Mapp* decisions holding that . . . Article I, Section 8 contained no exclusionary remedy whatsoever"). *See also* State v. Walker, 2011 UT 53, 267 P.3d 210, 216 (Utah 2011) (Lee, J., concurring) (Utah Supreme Court's recent case law discussions suggesting Utah Constitution contemplates an exclusionary rule "enshrine this sweeping remedy without any consideration of the original meaning of the constitutional provision in question. They also casually cast aside settled, longstanding precedents of this court that held the contrary."). *Accord* People v. Johnson, 66 N.Y.2d 398, 497 N.Y.S.2d 618, 488 N.E.2d 439, 446 n.3 (1985); State v. Carter, 322 N.C. 709, 370 S.E.2d 553, 555 (1988).

*Mapp* approach.[8] The most significant consideration in these analyses has been the courts' perceptions that exclusionary sanctions have become generally accepted and thus are appropriately read into a state provision in the absence of a demonstrated reason to read the state provision otherwise. As the intermediate Connecticut appellate court explained in accurately predicting that the state's highest court would recognize a state constitutional exclusionary rule:

> [T]he [exclusionary] rule has gained overwhelming judicial acceptance as the most effective method of guaranteeing the protection against unreasonable invasion of privacy secured by constitutional search and seizure provisions.[9]

Perhaps most amazing is the lack of diversity in the holdings. No highest state court seems recently to have squarely held that a state provision analogous to the Fourth, Fifth or Sixth Amendment does not require exclusion.[10]

A state court's adoption of a state constitutional exclusionary rule, and even its explicit approval of *Mapp's* interpretive ap-

---

[8]*See* State v. Dukes, 209 Conn. 98, 547 A.2d 10 (1988); Com. v. Ford, 394 Mass. 421, 476 N.E.2d 560 (1985); State v. Novembrino, 105 N.J. 95, 519 A.2d 820 (1987). In State v. Garner, 331 N.C. 491, 417 S.E.2d 502, 509–10 (1992), the North Carolina Supreme Court traced its less critical adoption of a state constitutional exclusionary rule.

[9]State v. Brown, 14 Conn. App. 605, 543 A.2d 750, 763 (1988).

[10]The intermediate Maryland court observed that the state has opted against an exclusionary rule. Fitzgerald v. State, 153 Md. App. 601, 837 A.2d 989, 1035 n.4 (2003). The state's highest court, on further consideration, noted the trend among the states towards recognizing exclusionary rules but did not reach whether Maryland's search and seizure provision contains one. 864 A.2d 1006, 1020 (Md. 2004). The intermediate court reaffirmed its position in Padilla v. State, 180 Md. App. 210, 949 A.2d 68, 77–85 (2008). *Accord* Ford v. State, 184 Md. App. 535, 967 A.2d 210, 232 (2009). In Brown v. State, 397 Md. 89, 916 A.2d 245, 251 (2007), the high court—citing *Fitzgerald*—commented, "there is no general exclusionary provision in Maryland for . . . violations [of the Maryland Declaration of Rights]."

The Michigan search and seizure provision ends with the sentence: "The provisions of this section shall not be construed to bar from evidence in any criminal proceeding any narcotic drug, firearm, bomb, explosive or any other dangerous weapon, seized by a peace officer outside the curtilage of any dwelling house in this state." Mich. Const Art. 1, § 11. Does this mean that in other situations the state provision does require exclusion of evidence obtained in violation of its requirement? In People v. Goldston, 470 Mich. 523, 682 N.W.2d 479 (2004), the Michigan court held it did not. Rather, the provision reflected the 1961 framers' desire for an exclusionary rule more limited than the Fourth Amendment one but a further perception that federal constitutional law precluded the state from limiting exclusion of evidence seized within the curtilage of a residence. Goldston, 682 N.W.2d at 488–89. The provision "does not restrict [the Michigan Supreme Court's] authority regarding evidence not enumerated in the antiexclusionary clause," and therefore the court "remains free to repudiate or modify the exclusionary rule by virtue of the fact

proach, does not mean that it is technically or logically bound to follow the Supreme Court's lead in developing the state remedy or even in framing the issues. Most importantly, the state court remains free to redefine for state law purposes the considerations bearing upon how the state remedy will be developed and the comparative importance of those considerations.

The Supreme Court has emphasized the federal constitutional exclusionary sanctions' function in deterring future violations of the substantive requirements of the amendments and has framed exclusionary rule issues so as to tailor the remedies to serve that function.[11] Some state courts have taken the same approach to state provisions.[12]

A few state courts have rejected this framework in developing their own state constitutional exclusionary sanctions. The Oregon Supreme Court, for example, explained:

> [T]his court . . . explicitly has rejected the view that the Oregon exclusionary rule is predicated upon a deterrence rationale. Instead, this court has held that the Oregon exclusionary rule is a constitutionally mandated rule that serves to vindicate a defendant's personal rights. In other words, the right to be free from unreasonable searches and seizures under Article I, section 9 [of the Oregon Constitution], also encompasses the right to be free from the use of evidence obtained in violation of that state constitutional provision. . . . [T]he aim of the Oregon exclusionary rule is to restore a defendant to the same position as if "the government's officers had stayed within the law."[13]

This emphasis on providing an effective remedy has also been embraced by some other courts.[14] While these courts have not extensively developed the bases or significance of this position, it

---

that it is a judicially created rule, not a constitutional rule." 682 N.W.2d. at 487.

[11]See § 167 supra.

[12]*E.g.*, Anderson v. State, 961 N.E.2d 19, 32 (Ind. Ct. App. 2012) ("Indiana search and seizure jurisprudence, like Fourth Amendment doctrine, identifies deterrence as the primary objective of the exclusionary rule.").

[13]State v. Hall, 339 Or. 7, 115 P.3d 908, 920 (2005) (citations omitted).

[14]The Washington Supreme Court, for example, explained that "the state exclusionary rule exists primarily to vindicate personal privacy rights, and strictly requires the exclu-

sion of evidence obtained by unlawful governmental intrusions." State v. Chenoweth, 160 Wash. 2d 454, 158 P.3d 595, 605 n.4 (2007). *Accord* State v. Panarello, 157 N.H. 204, 949 A.2d 732, 735 (2008) (state constitutional exclusionary requirement "serves to: (1) deter police misconduct; (2) redress the injury to the privacy of the victim of the unlawful police conduct; and (3) safeguard compliance with State constitutional protections"); State v. Guzman, 122 Idaho 981, 842 P.2d 660, 672 (1992) (Idaho exclusionary rule "should be applied in order to . . . provide an effective remedy to persons who have been subjected to an unreasonable government search and/or seizure[;] avoid having the judiciary commit an additional constitutional violation by considering evidence

appears to reject the Supreme Court's assumption that exclusion of evidence resulting from official lawlessness does not provide an appropriate remedy to those who suffer privacy intrusions or other harms from that official lawlessness.

Some state courts view state constitutional exclusionary requirements as serving a broader view of judicial integrity than the Supreme Court has found implicated in the federal constitutional requirements. The Hawaii Supreme Court, for example, has held that the Hawaii constitutional exclusionary requirement is to be construed in part as best furthers the policy that "the courts should not place their imprimatur on evidence that was illegally obtained by allowing it to be admitted into evidence in a criminal prosecution."[15]

State judicial independence in this area has resulted in some restrictive modifications of state constitutions. Florida's state constitutional search and seizure provision has long provided that evidence obtained in violation of it was inadmissible. In 1982, this was supplemented with a specific directive that it be construed "in conformity with" the Supreme Court's construction of the Fourth Amendment, thus limiting exclusion of evidence to those situations in which the evidence "would be inadmissible under decisions of the United States Supreme Court construing the 4th Amendment to the United States Constitution."[16] In the same year, California voters created a state constitutional "Right to Truth-in-Evidence" section providing that except as enacted by a two-thirds vote of both houses of the state legislature, "relevant evidence shall not be excluded in any criminal proceeding."[17] This has effectively deprived the California courts of power to develop state constitutional exclusionary sanctions requiring exclusion of relevant evidence where such exclusion is not mandated by the federal constitution.

### § 169    Exclusion for nonconstitutional illegality: (a) In general

Both federal and state constitutional requirements apply only where a defendant establishes that challenged evidence was obtained as a result of a violation of a constitutional rights. But

---

which has been obtained through illegal means; and . . . preserve judicial integrity").

[15]State v. Torres, 125 Haw. 382, 262 P.3d 1006, 1018 (2011) (quoting State v. Bridges, 83 Haw. 187, 925 P.2d 357, 366 (1996) (overruled on other grounds by, State v. Torres, 125 Haw. 382, 262 P.3d 1006 (2011)). See

also Com. v. Brown, 456 Mass. 708, 925 N.E.2d 845, 851 (2010) (one of the purposes justifying state constitutional exclusionary rule "is the protection of judicial integrity through the dissociation of the courts from unlawful conduct").

[16]Fla. Const. Art. 1, § 12.

[17]Cal. Const. Art. I, § 28(f)(2).

criminal defendants frequently seek exclusion as a remedy for violation of nonconstitutional legal requirements. When, if ever, exclusion is available on such bases presents a more difficult question than is often recognized.[1] Modern law's acceptance of exclusion as an appropriate remedy for the violation of constitutional requirements has tended too often to lead to uncritical acceptance of exclusion as similarly available upon a showing of any illegality. This is simply not the case.

Challenges to relevant evidence on grounds that it was obtained in violation of nonconstitutional legal requirements raises several distinguishable concerns addressed in the next three sections. First is whether courts have legislatively-provided authority to exclude evidence on these bases.[2] Second is whether courts have autonomous authority to exclude evidence on these grounds.[3] Third is the content of any such exclusionary requirements as exist.[4]

Generally, the number and nature of nonconstitutional legal requirements potentially affecting the development of evidence suggests that an exclusionary sanction be more sparingly applied than it is with regard to constitutional requirements. The Michigan Supreme Court explained:

> The exclusionary rule is particularly harsh in that it is neither narrowly tailored nor discerning of the magnitude of the error it is intended to deter. By taking no cognizance of the effect of a police error upon a particular defendant, or of the actual guilt or innocence of a defendant, the exclusionary rule [applied to nonconstitutional illegality] lacks proportionality.[5]

Earlier, the same court had suggested that applying an exclusionary sanction to violations of nonconstitutional law would be to discard highly relevant evidence in response to "a technical deficiency" in official conduct.[6] But this suggestion that all nonconstitutional requirements are mere technical ones oversimplifies the matter as much as uncritical application of exclusion to all illegality in obtaining evidence.

## § 170    Exclusion for nonconstitutional illegality: (b) Legislative requirements

Legislatures unquestionably have authority to direct that legal

---

**[Section 169]**

[1]*E.g.*, State v. Coffee, 54 S.W.3d 231, 233–34 (Tenn. 2001) (uncritically excluding evidence because magistrate issuing warrant failed to comply with requirement of Rules of Criminal Procedure that such a magistrate prepare and retain a copy of an issued warrant).

[2]See § 170 infra.

[3]See § 171 infra.

[4]See § 172 infra.

[5]People v. Hawkins, 468 Mich. 488, 668 N.W.2d 602, 609 n.9 (2003).

[6]People v. Sobczak-Obetts, 463 Mich. 687, 625 N.W.2d 764, 772 (2001).

requirements be implemented by excluding evidence obtained in violation of those requirements, or to give courts of the jurisdiction discretionary power to develop exclusionary remedies. Exercises of this authority may be explicit or implicit, and the two possibilities are best considered separately.

*Explicit Legislative Exclusionary Requirements.* A few jurisdictions have relatively broad statutory requirements of exclusion. Since 1925, Texas has statutorily excluded from criminal trials evidence obtained in violation of the laws or constitutions of either the United States or Texas.[1] North Carolina has a somewhat narrower provision, requiring the suppression of certain evidence obtained in violation of its Criminal Procedure Act.[2] These provisions, however, are exceptional. Most states have neither any general explicit legislative directive for exclusion of illegally obtained evidence nor explicit delegation to the courts of authority to develop any such exclusionary requirement.[3]

Somewhat more frequently, legislatures have provided exclusionary remedies for particular statutes. The primary example is the federal electronic surveillance statute,[4] which contains its own statutory exclusionary remedy.[5] Under this statute, states are authorized to provide by state law for state law enforcement officers to engage in certain electronic surveillance, and state statutes enacted pursuant to this contain exclusionary requirements similar or identical to that in the federal statute.[6]

Other statutory provisions also sometimes explicitly require exclusion.[7] Exclusion may be authorized indirectly, as in the Tennessee "implied consent" statute which provides that it is not to affect the admissibility of evidence in prosecutions for aggravated assault or homicide by the use of a motor vehicle.[8] Apparently it may affect admissibility in other prosecutions.

---

**[Section 170]**

[1]Tex. Code Crim. Proc. art. 38. 23.

[2]N.C. Gen. Stat. § 15A-974.

[3]The Georgia Supreme Court has read a general statutory authorization for a person aggrieved by an unlawful search and seizure to move to suppress evidence "so obtained" as embodying a state statutory exclusionary requirement. *See* Gary v. State, 262 Ga. 573, 422 S.E.2d 426, 428–29 (1992) (construing Ga. Code § 17-5-30).

[4]Omnibus Crime Control and Safe Streets Act of 1968, tit.II, codified as 18 U.S.C.A. §§ 2510 et seq.

[5]18 U.S.C.A. § 2515.

[6]*E.g.*, Tex. Code Crim. Proc. Ann. art. 18.20, §§ 2, 14(b).

[7]*E.g.*, Cal. Veh. Code § 40803(a) (evidence is inadmissible in speeding prosecution if it was obtained by use of "speed trap"). *Cf.* Ohio Evid. R. 601(C) (officer who made traffic arrest is not competent witness if officer "was not using a properly marked vehicle as defined by statute or was not wearing a legally distinct uniform as defined by statute").

[8]Tenn. Code Ann. § 55-10-406(d). *See also* Nardone v. U.S., 302 U.S. 379, 58 S. Ct. 275, 82 L. Ed. 314 (1937) (statutory prohibition against divulging or publishing the contents of communications obtained in violation of

Legislatures occasionally make clear that exclusion is not available. Oregon provides generally that courts may not exclude relevant and otherwise admissible evidence on the ground that it was obtained in violation "of any statutory provision," unless exclusion is required by the United States or Oregon Constitution, the rules of evidence, or the rights of the press.[9] More frequently, legislatures provide that specific statutory provisions are not to serve as the basis of exclusion.[10]

*Implied Legislative Exclusionary Requirements.* Legislative authority to exclude evidence may sometimes be implied from statutory provisions that lack the sort of explicit requirement discussed above, and courts have recognized this. When a statute is appropriately construed as authorizing or requiring exclusion, however, has proved to be a difficult question for many courts.

In several early cases, the Supreme Court uncritically held that evidence obtained in violation of certain federal statutory requirements must be excluded.[11] It left unclear, however, whether these holdings rested on readings of legislative intent or were rather exercises of the Court's own power to develop exclusionary requirements.

Some lower courts have been willing on quite scant bases to find implied legislative exclusionary requirements. In *United States v. Chemaly*,[12] for example, the court held that federal legislation limiting currency searches at the border required exclusion of evidence obtained in violation of its terms. Emphasizing the long acceptance among courts of exclusion as a remedy for even nonconstitutional illegality, the court reasoned that Congress assumed that in the absence of an explicit directive to the contrary courts would enforce the statute by excluding evi-

---

the statute also mandated exclusion of that information when it was offered by the Government in a criminal prosecution).

[9]Or. Rev. Stat. Ann. § 136.432.

[10]*E.g.*, Ariz. Rev. Stat. Ann. § 13-3925(A) (evidence seized pursuant to a search warrant is not to be excluded for a violation of Chapter 39 of Arizona Statutes, except as constitutionally required); N.J. Stat. Ann. § 2A:161A-10 (violation of specified statutory provisions "shall not affect the admissibility of evidence seized pursuant to a strip search or body cavity search").

[11]Miller v. U.S., 357 U.S. 301, 78 S. Ct. 1190, 2 L. Ed. 2d 1332 (1958) (violation of statutory requirement of prior announcement before entering to execute search warrant required exclusion); Grau v. U.S., 287 U.S. 124, 53 S. Ct. 38, 77 L. Ed. 212 (1932) (search warrant issued on showing insufficient to support statutorily-required determination that premises were used for storage or manufacture of liquor). *See also* Sabbath v. U.S., 391 U.S. 585, 88 S. Ct. 1755, 20 L. Ed. 2d 828 (1968). *Miller* was confusingly characterized in Sanchez-Llamas v. Oregon, 548 U.S. 331, 348–49, 126 S. Ct. 2669, 165 L. Ed. 2d 557 (2006), as based on the conclusion that the statutory requirement violated implicated important Fourth Amendment interests.

[12]U.S. v. Chemaly, 741 F.2d 1346 (11th Cir. 1984).

dence obtained in violation of it;[13] therefore, congressional silence regarding exclusionary sanctions was an implied directive that such a remedy be applied. There is a discernible tendency on the part of some courts to pursue this analysis under statutes imposing requirements similar to, but more stringent than, constitutional mandates. This is apparently on the assumption that when a legislature imposes requirements similar to constitutional ones enforced by exclusionary sanctions, it ordinarily assumes that its statutory directives will also be enforced by such sanctions.[14]

The Iowa Supreme Court reaffirmed—and expanded—its earlier decision to exclude evidence because officers violated a statutory provision giving a person arrested a right to contact an attorney or family member. It acknowledged "the general presumption against implied statutory exclusionary rules," but explained that "an exclusionary rule is warranted for violations of those statutes . . . which involve fundamental rights or have constitutional overtones."[15]

Most courts, however, are more reluctant to find unexpressed legislative directives that exclusionary sanctions be available.[16] The case discussions emphasize several considerations. If other

---

[13]Chemaly, 741 F.2d at 1354 n. 2.

[14]*E.g.*, State v. Jordan, 742 N.W.2d 149, 154 (Minn. 2007) (evidence tainted by execution of search warrant in nighttime in violation of statutory requirements must be suppressed because admitting the evidence "would subvert the basic purpose of [the statute]"); State v. Flynn, 123 N.H. 457, 464 A.2d 268 (1983) (state privacy act created "constitutional-type safeguards and thus exclusion was an appropriate remedy).

[15]State v. Moorehead, 699 N.W.2d 667, 675 (Iowa 2005) (exclusion is required not only of breath test taken after violation of statute but also of defendant's oral statement, "I'm drunk as hell.").

The Pennsylvania court required exclusion of evidence linked to Pennsylvania officers' pursuit of a suspect into Delaware and their failure to take the apprehended suspect before a Delaware magistrate. It described the situation as one in which "constitutional rights are not in the forefront," but apparently lurking in the background. Com. v. Sadvari, 561 Pa. 588, 752 A.2d 393, 398–99 (2000)

(also noting "[s]uppression is also appropriate to encourage future compliance with Delaware's procedures and, in a more general sense, to safeguard the individual right to be free from unlawful seizures").

[16]*See* U.S. v. Clenney, 631 F.3d 658, 667 (4th Cir. 2011) (violation of Electronic Communications Privacy Act of 1986 would not permit exclusion of evidence); Velasquez-Tabir v. I.N.S., 127 F.3d 456, 460–61 (5th Cir. 1997) (per curiam) (no provision of the National Labor Relations Act indicates a Congressional intent that evidence obtained in violation of the Act be excluded); U.S. v. Edgar, 82 F.3d 499, 510–11 (1st Cir. 1996) (violation of Fair Credit Reporting Act was not ground for suppression in criminal proceeding where Congress did not provide for such a remedy); People v. Clayton, 207 P.3d 831 (Colo. 2009) (state statute giving arrested person right to communicate with family members does not authorize exclusion of evidence tainted by a violation of the statute); State v. Smith, 154 N.H. 113, 908 A.2d 786, 788–90 (2006) (statute defining territorial jurisdiction of police officers but silent on remedy did

statutes passed by the legislative body have expressly directed exclusion, legislative failure to similarly provide in the statute at issue suggests to many courts a legislative intention that no such remedy be available for statutes silent on the matter.[17] If the overall purpose of legislation is to increase law enforcement power, courts have also reasoned, the legislature is unlikely to have intended to impede this general objective by imposing an exclusionary sanction, and thus courts should be reluctant to read one into such statutes.

At least one court requires that an intent to affect the admissibility of evidence be expressly stated in the statute relied upon by the defendant. The Michigan Supreme Court took this position, overruling earlier decisions uncritically excluding evidence for violation of statutes and court rules.[18]

Another announced that exclusion was available only if, first, the statute was designed to protect against improper government conduct, Second, the specific violation must have infringed "the legislative intent or 'spirit' behind the law, such that to effectuate the purpose behind the statue the evidence should be suppressed."[19]

---

not reflect legislative intent to create exclusionary remedy). *See generally* U.S. v. Thompson, 936 F.2d 1249, 1251–1252 (11th Cir. 1991) (concluding after careful analysis that federal "Pen Register" statute, 18 U.S.C.A. §§ 3132 et seq., contains no implied exclusionary sanction). *Accord* U.S. v. Forrester, 512 F.3d 500, 511–13 (9th Cir. 2008), (exclusion of evidence is not authorized by federal "pen register" statute).

A violation of the New York statutory physician-patient privilege does not give rise to a right to exclusion of tainted evidence. People v. Greene, 9 N.Y.3d 277, 849 N.Y.S.2d 461, 879 N.E.2d 1280, 1281–82 (2007).

A number of courts have held that exclusion is not an available remedy for a violation of federal or state legislation protecting the privacy of medical records. *E.g.*, State v. Mubita, 145 Idaho 925, 188 P.3d 867 (2008); Dorsey v. State, 185 Md. App. 82, 968 A.2d 654, 677 (2009).

[17]U.S. v. Benevento, 836 F.2d 60,

69–70 (2d Cir. 1987) (emphasizing federal electronic surveillance statute); Sun Kin Chan v. State, 78 Md. App. 287, 552 A.2d 1351, 1362–63 (1989) (where wiretap statute contained explicit exclusionary requirement and pen register statute did not, none would be read into the pen register statute).

[18]People v. Hawkins, 468 Mich. 488, 668 N.W.2d 602, 612–13 (2003) ("application of the exclusionary rule is inappropriate unless the plain language of the statute indicates a legislative intent that the rule be applied"). *Cf.* U.S. v. Clenney, 631 F.3d 658, 667 (4th Cir. 2011) ("In the statutory context, suppression is a creature of the statute, and its availability depend on the statutory text . . . ."); U.S. v. Cray, 673 F. Supp. 2d 1368, 1376 (S.D. Ga. 2009) ("Violation of a statute will not result in suppression unless the statute itself specifies exclusion as a remedy.").

[19]State v. Britton, 2009 SD 75, 772 N.W.2d 899, 905 (S.D. 2009).

The Wisconsin Supreme Court in *State v. Popenhagen*[20] abandoned its earlier insistence that a statute expressly provide for an exclusionary remedy. It then found sufficient legislative authorization for an exclusionary remedy in a statute authorizing the issuances of subpoenas in language recognizing that motions could be addressed to a court which issued a subpoena. Motions, it reasoned, include motions to suppress evidence obtained as a result of a subpoena issued in violation of the statutory requirements.[21]

On balance, courts should be reluctant to find implied authority in statutes for exclusion of evidence. Exclusion is an exceptionally costly remedy, and its propriety is highly questionable. Legislative silence almost certainly reflects, in most cases, the absence of a consensus that the provisions being enacted are appropriately enforced by such a remedy. Unless there is reasonably clear evidence of such a consensus, generally reflected in the terms of the statute itself, a statute should not be regarded as empowering the courts to exclude evidence obtained in violation of its requirements.

*Popenhagen's* approach, practically speaking, is not one based on even implied legislative provision for exclusionary remedies. As the dissent noted, under the majority's approach almost any statute could be read as authorizing suppression.[22] The Wisconsin court was in effect asserting judicial authority to develop an exclusionary remedy where the legislature has not barred that approach.

### § 171  Exclusion for nonconstitutional illegality: (c) Judicially developed requirements[1]

In the absence of legislative or constitutional authorization, courts may nevertheless have independent power to develop and apply exclusionary requirements. Some courts claim such power

---

[20]State v. Popenhagen, 2008 WI 55, 309 Wis. 2d 601, 749 N.W.2d 611 (2008).

[21]Popenhagen, 749 N.W.2d at 625–29. Properly read, it explained, its case law establishes that a trial court "has discretion to suppress or allow evidence obtained in violation of a statute that does not specifically require suppression of evidence obtained contrary to the statute, depending on the facts and circumstances of the case and the objectives of the statute." 749 N.W.2d at 627.

[22]749 N.W.2d. at 638 ("If the language of the statute provides for suppression, then almost any statute from this point forward does so as well.") (Ziegler, J., concurring in part and dissenting in part).

**[Section 171]**

[1]*See generally* Dix, Nonconstitutional Exclusionary Rules in Criminal Procedure, 27 Am. Crim. L. Rev. 53, 74–90 (1989).

without identifying its source.[2] If the matter is carefully examined, such judicial power might be based either upon the authority given many courts to promulgate rules relating to procedure and evidence or upon the power claimed by some courts to exercise what is often called "supervisory authority" over litigation and the behavior of some persons whose actions in some way affect that litigation.

*Rulemaking Power.*[3] Many American courts have power to promulgate rules of evidence and procedure, granted by statute or constitutional provision. This power has been implemented through widespread adoption of evidence rules. Might this power permit a court to promulgate an exclusionary rule applicable to violation of nonconstitutional, as well as perhaps constitutional, legal requirements?

Such action has been taken by the Alaska Supreme Court, which adopted a general exclusionary rule as part of its Criminal Rules and then incorporated this into its Evidence Rules. Under Alaska Rule of Evidence 412, evidence "illegally obtained" may not be used over proper objection by the defendant in a criminal prosecution "for any purpose," with limited exceptions applicable to perjury prosecutions.

Whether this is an appropriate exercise of the rulemaking power is at best problematic. Rulemaking authority is given to courts in large part because of their exceptional ability to address such matters as how to most efficiently and effectively arrive at accurate resolutions in litigated cases. The extent to which exclusionary requirements will interfere with these interests is, of course, an important consideration in deciding whether an exclusionary sanction is appropriate. But far more important are such considerations as the extent to which violations occur and whether other measures hold reasonable promise of discouraging them. The final decision must balance the costs of an exclusionary sanction and the potential benefits of it. This decision is no more than peripherally within courts' area of particular expertise and is clearly the sort of judgment that is ordinarily for legislative decision. Given the nature of exclusionary sanctions, despite their "evidentiary" form, they are best regarded as beyond general judicial evidentiary and procedural rulemaking authority.

*Courts' "Supervisory" Power—The Federal Model.* Some American courts have held, or indicated in dicta, that they have supervisory authority over judicial proceedings broader than ordinary rule-making power. This authority may give those courts

---

[2]*E.g.*, Copley v. Com., 361 S.W.3d 902, 906–07 (Ky. 2012) (explaining when under Kentucky law a violation of a rule of criminal procedure warrants exclusion of evidence).

[3]*See generally* Comley, 361 S.W.3d at 75–78.

the power to judicially-develop exclusionary requirements invoked by violation of nonconstitutional legal requirements. Whether such authority exists in particular jurisdictions and, if so, whether it authorizes such rigorous judicial lawmaking often poses difficult issues.

The most widely-noted model for such authority is the Supreme Court's reliance upon what it has described as its "supervisory power" authority to develop such exclusionary rules for litigation in the lower federal courts. Whether the Court's perception of its power is soundly based is, at best, questionable.

The seminal Supreme Court decision is *McNabb v. United States*,[4] holding that suppression was required of evidence obtained in violation of what was then the statutory requirement that an arrested person be presented before a magistrate without unnecessary delay. In *Rea v. United States*,[5] the Court held that a federal officer who had obtained evidence in violation of Rule 41 of the Federal Rules of Criminal Procedure should be enjoined from using that evidence in a state prosecution. Implicitly, *Rea* approved the suppression of this evidence in the federal litigation and explicitly held that Rea was entitled to the additional injunctive relief he sought. Both decisions rested upon what the Court described as its "supervisory power."[6] In *McNabb*, the Court equated an exclusionary rule with other rules of evidence, particularly those, apparently rules of privilege, that are based on considerations other than simply "evidentiary relevance."[7] Development of legal requirements of both sorts, the Court concluded, was permissible pursuant to its "duty" to establish and maintain "civilized standards of procedure and evidence" in the federal courts.[8] *Rea's* discussion went further and suggested that the underlying power was not only to provide for the proper processing of litigation but also to "prescribe standards for law enforcement . . . to protect the privacy of the citizen . . . ."[9]

Since *Rea*, the Court has continued to insist that it has such power. It has obviously, however, become more reluctant to exercise it and in fact has not found occasion to do so. In *Lopez v. United States*,[10] for example, the Court reaffirmed its "inherent power" to exclude "material" evidence because of illegality in the manner it was obtained, but commented that this power should

---

[4]McNabb v. U.S., 318 U.S. 332, 63 S. Ct. 608, 87 L. Ed. 819 (1943).

[5]Rea v. U. S., 350 U.S. 214, 76 S. Ct. 292, 100 L. Ed. 233 (1956).

[6]McNabb, 318 U.S. at 341; *Rea*, 350 U.S. at 217.

[7]McNabb, 318 U.S. at 341.

[8]318 U.S. at 340.

[9]Rea, 350 U.S. at 217–218.

[10]Lopez v. U.S., 373 U.S. 427, 83 S. Ct. 1381, 10 L. Ed. 2d 462 (1963).

be "sparingly exercised."[11] Since Lopez could show no "manifestly improper" conduct by the law enforcement officers, invoking the power in his case would not be justified. In *United States v. Caceres*,[12] the Court suggested that it had the power to exclude evidence on a "limited individualized approach" for the violation of federal administrative regulations.[13] But exclusion under this power would not be appropriate in the case before it, the Court concluded, since the investigators had made a reasonable, good faith attempt to comply with what they understood to be the applicable legal requirements, and the actions they took would clearly have been permitted had they followed the regulations.[14]

Most recently, the Court in *United States v. Payner*[15] considered an argument that it should exercise its supervisory power to exclude evidence obtained by "gross illegality" from a person other than the defendant who moved to suppress it. Again reaffirming its supervisory exclusionary power, the Court offered that "Federal courts may use their supervisory power in some circumstances to exclude evidence taken from the defendant by 'willful disobedience of law.' "[16] But it then made clear that the exercise of this power is to be informed by the same considerations and conclusions reached in developing the federal constitutional exclusionary requirements.[17] The Fourth Amendment case law makes clear that as a general rule, the purposes of exclusion are adequately achieved if the remedy is made available to those whose interests were violated by the underlying illegality.[18] This should also apply where exclusion might be justified under the supervisory power, and thus under that power federal courts should not suppress otherwise admissible evidence on the ground that it was unlawfully obtained from a third party not before the court.[19]

Both the scope and legitimacy of the supervisory power as applied and discussed in this line of cases have been severely criticized.[20] The Supreme Court's refusal, since *McNabb* and *Rea*, actually to exercise what it continues to insist is the federal courts' supervisory power to develop exclusionary rules for

---

[11]Lopez, 373 U.S. at 440.

[12]U. S. v. Caceres, 440 U.S. 741, 99 S. Ct. 1465, 59 L. Ed. 2d 733 (1979).

[13]Caceres, 440 U.S. at 756.

[14]440 U.S. at 757. *Accord* U.S. v. Ani, 138 F.3d 390 (9th Cir. 1998) (under *Caceres*, violation of Customs Service regulation requiring "reasonable cause" for inspection of mail from foreign country did not require suppression of resulting evidence).

[15]U. S. v. Payner, 447 U.S. 727, 100 S. Ct. 2439, 65 L. Ed. 2d 468 (1980).

[16]Payner, 447 U.S. at 735 n. 7.

[17]447 U.S. at 734–35.

[18]See § 175 infra.

[19]Payner, 447 U.S. at 735.

[20]Professor Beale has argued that the supervisory power, as such, simply does not exist, and that the phrase is

nonconstitutional violations suggests that the tribunal is becoming at least ambivalent concerning the legitimacy of this authority.

The lower federal courts continue to assume that some power to develop exclusionary rules exists, perhaps most significantly, implicitly relying on *Rea*, that violations of some of the nonconstitutional requirements for search warrants imposed by Rule 41 of the Federal Rules of Criminal Procedure under some circumstances require or permit exclusion.[21] The courts are, however, increasingly reluctant to exercise this power.[22]

In *Sanchez—Llamas v. Oregon*[23] the Court first explained *McNabb* and other cases as ones in which "the excluded evidence arose directly out of statutory violations that implicated important Fourth and Fifth Amendment interests."[24] In the next paragraph, however, the Court suggested that they rested at

---

a misleading label attached to several different forms of judicial power. Beale, Reconsidering the Supervisory Power in Criminal Cases: Constitutional and Statutory Limits on the Authority of the Federal Courts, 84 Colum. L. Rev. 1433, 1520 (1984). These include the power to establish procedural rules. But this power, she argued, does not extend to development of exclusionary requirements that are designed to control law enforcement practices for reasons unrelated to the fairness, reliability, or efficiency of the federal litigation process. Beale, Reconsidering the Supervisory Power, 84 Colum. L. Rev. at 1474–77.

The Court itself is apparently drawing back somewhat. *Lopez* strongly suggested, the *Rea* dictum notwithstanding, that the supervisory power did not authorize the federal courts to develop standards for law enforcement conduct with little or no implications for federal court litigation. *See* Hill, The Bill of Rights and the Supervisory Power, 69 Colum. L. Rev. 181, 214 (1969) (majority of Court has never accepted the view that supervisory power permits exclusion of evidence resulting from police practices violative of no statutory or constitutional standards but regarded as reprehensible from an independent judicial perspective).

[21]The seminal Court of Appeals decision is U.S. v. Burke, 517 F.2d 377 (2d Cir. 1975), discussed in § 172 infra. *Burke* is widely accepted although often distinguished. *E.g.*, U.S. v. Luk, 859 F.2d 667, 670–72 (9th Cir. 1988) (collecting cases from various circuits).

[22]*E.g.*, U.S. v. Carona, 630 F.3d 917, 922–23 (9th Cir. 2011) (district court did not abuse its discretion in refusing to exercise its supervisory power to exclude evidence obtained by prosecutor's violation of rule relating to conduct of attorneys); U.S. v. Cain, 524 F.3d 477, 483 (4th Cir. 2008) (district court erred in exercising supervisory power to exclude statement because Government interviewed defendant without complying with Criminal Justice Act Plan); U.S. v. Irvine, 699 F.2d 43, 46 (1st Cir. 1983) (case before court is not one of exceptional situations in which under *Caceres* evidence might be suppressed because of administrative regulation violation). *See also* U.S. v. Comstock, 805 F.2d 1194 (5th Cir. 1986); U.S. v. Frazin, 780 F.2d 1461, 1464 (9th Cir. 1986).

[23]Sanchez-Llamas v. Oregon, 548 U.S. 331, 126 S. Ct. 2669, 165 L. Ed. 2d 557 (2006).

[24]Sanchez—Llamas, 448 U.S. at 348.

least in part on the basis that the statutory right violated was a right "connected to the gathering of evidence."[25]

In *Corley v. United States*,[26] the Court held the *McNabb* exclusionary requirement still effective regarding confessions made after delay in presentment that both exceeded six hours and was unreasonable or unnecessary. *Corley* did not revisit or discuss the conceptual basis for the basic exclusionary mandate.

*Courts' "Supervisory" Power—State Court Decisions.* State courts may also have supervisory powers similar to that invoked in *McNabb-Rea*, and these might be relied upon as a basis for state court developed exclusionary requirements. Generally, however, state courts have engaged in little discussion of this possibility. When state tribunals mention supervisory power, they tend to avoid explicit comment upon whether they possess such power and whether it would support development of exclusionary sanctions. Rather, they simply find that the situations before them are not sufficient to invoke any such sanctions as they might have power to develop.[27] Even state courts embracing such power to exclude evidence generally provide little substantive discussion of the basis for this power and the decision to exercise it in particular situations.[28]

In what is probably the leading state court decision, *State v. Pattioay*,[29] the Hawaii Supreme Court held that its inherent supervisory authority to prevent and correct "errors and abuses"

---

[25]448 U.S. at 349 (right to consular notification under Vienna Convention, "in contrast to" the right violated in *McNabb*, "is at best remotely connected to the gathering of evidence").

In Virginia v. Moore, 553 U.S. 164, 172, 128 S. Ct. 1598, 170 L. Ed. 2d 559 (2008), the Court described its decision in U.S. v. Di Re, 332 U.S. 581, 68 S. Ct. 222, 92 L. Ed. 210 (1948), as resting on the Court's supervisory power over the federal courts. *Di Re*, *Moore* explained, reasoned that Congress intended to require that arrests for federal crimes comply with the requirements of the state in which the arrest took place. But this did not explain why *Di Re* held that the statutory invalidity of the arrest required suppression of the evidence obtained by that arrest.

[26]Corley v. U.S., 556 U.S. 303, 129 S. Ct. 1558, 173 L. Ed. 2d 443 (2009); see § 156 supra.

[27]*E.g.*, People v. Dyla, 142 A.D.2d 423, 536 N.Y.S.2d 799, 811 (2d Dep't 1988), holding that an arrest by a parole officer without a statutorily-required warrant did not require exclusion of the resulting evidence. "[W]e decline," the court summarily explained, "to exercise whatever inherent 'supervisory power' we may have to . . . order suppression."

[28]Com. v. Mason, 507 Pa. 396, 490 A.2d 421 (1985) (in selected situations evidence obtained in violation of the Pennsylvania Rules of Criminal Procedure would be suppressed in criminal litigation). The basis for this action was not made clear, although the opinion suggests reliance upon a state law version of supervisory power. Mason, 490 A.2d at 424 (quoting a reference to supervisory power in Com. v. Walls, 255 Pa. Super. 1, 386 A.2d 105, 107 (1978)).

[29]State v. Pattioay, 78 Haw. 455, 896 P.2d 911 (1995).

in the lower courts permitted it to develop exclusionary remedies mandating exclusion of evidence obtained in violation of nonconstitutional legal requirements. The power, it cautioned, is to be exercised with restraint and discretion and only in exceptional circumstances.[30]

*Pattioay* appeared to conceptualize the use of illegally obtained evidence by parties to litigation in an effort to obtain favorable action by the courts as sufficient abuse of the courts to justify exercise of the supervisory power. This in turn led it to adopt a rationale for exclusion broader than the deterrent-based federal constitutional rules. Use in a criminal trial of evidence tainted by official illegality, it emphasized, "would be to justify the illegality."[31] Even if exclusion does not sufficiently serve to deter illegality of the sort involved, then, such exclusion is justified as a means of precluding judicial "justification" of the underlying illegality in a manner that would offend notions of what some courts and commentators regard as judicial integrity.

In general, American courts have been insufficiently critical regarding their power, or the lack thereof, to develop exclusionary sanctions for nonconstitutional violations in obtaining evidence. This is no doubt due in large part to the prominence of federal constitutional exclusionary rule case law in any consideration of exclusionary sanction matters. On one hand, this case law encourages an uncritical assumption that courts have power to develop similar exclusionary requirements for nonconstitutional illegality.[32] On the other, resentment at being constitutionally compelled to accept what is regarded by some as an unwise remedy for constitutional violations encourages equally uncritical

---

[30]*Pattioay* itself required exclusion of evidence obtained in violation of the federal Posse Comitatus Act, 18 U.S.C.A. § 1385.

A split court applied exclusion to another statutory situation. State v. Wilson, 92 Haw. 45, 987 P.2d 268 (1999) (exclusion is required of evidence resulting from officer's failure to adequately warn drunk driving suspect of risks of criminal prosecution), reaffirmed—again over dissent on the exclusionary rule issue—in State v. Garcia, 96 Haw. 200, 29 P.3d 919 (2001). It also indicated that exclusion would be available as a result of a violation of a statutory requirement that officers make reasonable effort to convey to an attorney a message from an arrested person. It found exclusion not required on the facts of the case

because the defendant failed to demonstrate a connection between the statutory violation and the statement sought to be suppressed. State v. Edwards, 96 Haw. 224, 30 P.3d 238, 251–54 (2001).

[31]Pattioay, 896 P.2d at 925.

[32]*E.g.*, People v. Shreck, 107 P.3d 1048, 1054–55 (Colo. App. 2004) (statutory violation would not require exclusion, although proof of willful and recurrent violations might demand exclusion); People v. Garcia, 10 A.D.3d 535, 782 N.Y.S.2d 32 (1st Dep't 2004) (any violation of record confidentiality provisions did not require exclusion of evidence because "there are no . . . factors requiring suppression in this case").

rejection of exclusion as an authorized remedy where such a remedy is not constitutionally mandated.

Whether the courts of a particular jurisdiction have the power to develop exclusionary sanctions, and whether they should exercise any such power as they may have, must depend in large part upon the nature and breadth of judicial authority in that jurisdiction and the tradition with which it has been developed and applied. Proper resolution of these issues, in any case, requires careful consideration of the argument that the major factors in deciding whether exclusionary sanctions are appropriate are factors that require legislative rather than judicial action.

## § 172  Exclusion for nonconstitutional illegality: (d) Substance of exclusionary requirements[1]

The exclusionary requirements developed as part of federal constitutional law are, as an initial matter, unqualified. This means that a showing that evidence was obtained as a factual result of a violation of the underlying constitutional requirement demands exclusion of that evidence. Most exclusionary requirements applicable to nonconstitutional violations, on the other hand, are qualified. A right to exclusion, in other words, often demands that a defendant show more than a violation of a nonconstitutional legal requirement and that the challenged evidence was obtained as a factual result of that violation.

The limits or qualifications of these nonconstitutional exclusionary sanctions is developed in this section. Three types of limitations can usefully be distinguished.

First, those nonconstitutional legal requirements whose violation will trigger a possible right to exclusion have sometimes been limited. The case law suggests several approaches towards so limiting exclusionary requirements. Exclusionary requirements could be applied only if the legal requirement applies generally or frequently to official activity designed to collect evidence for use in criminal prosecutions. Given the evidentiary motivation of those affected by the legal requirements, exclusion might be expected to most effectively encourage compliance with the law in these cases.[2]

Exclusion might also be limited to those legal requirements

---

[Section 172]

[1]See generally Dix, Nonconstitutional Exclusionary Rules in Criminal Procedure, 27 Am. Crim. L. Rev. 53, 91–109 (1989).

[2]See Sanchez-Llamas v. Oregon, 548 U.S. 331, 349, 126 S. Ct. 2669, 165 L. Ed. 2d 557 (2006) (exclusion would be inappropriate remedy for violation of the right to consular notification contained in the Vienna Convention because that right "is at best remotely connected to the gathering of evidence" and "has nothing whatsoever to do with searches or interrogations"); State

that are related in some sufficient way to constitutional commands.[3] Perhaps the cost of exclusion is justified only if the violated legal requirement protects the same or similar interests as are protected by constitutional rules, although the legal requirement that is violated by infringements is not significant or basic enough to give rise to a constitutional intrusion.

Case law under the federal electronic surveillance regulatory scheme suggests that at least in the context of a set of legislative requirements, exclusion may reasonably be mandated only upon proof of a violation of a statutory requirement directly or importantly related to the underlying legislative objective. Although the federal statutory exclusionary sanction is unqualified, the Supreme Court has held that it is triggered only by those statutory provisions that "directly and substantially implement" the congressional purpose of reasonably limiting use of electronic surveillance techniques.[4] Consequently, failure to secure approval of an application for a surveillance order from the Attorney General or Assistant Attorney General did require exclusion of the resulting evidence,[5] but a failure simply to specify on the documents the official who had in fact authorized the application did not.[6] State exclusionary requirements embodied in similar state electronic surveillance statutes have been similarly construed.[7]

If a legal requirement does not directly and substantially imple-

---

v. Sundberg, 611 P.2d 44, 52 (Alaska 1980) (exclusion not required by excessive use of force to make arrests because such activity generally does not involve a quest for evidence).

[3]*E.g.*, Sanchez—Llamas, 548 U.S. at 348 (in "[t]he few cases in which we have suppressed evidence for statutory violations . . . the excluded evidence arose directly out of statutory violations that implicated important Fourth and Fifth Amendment interests"); State v. Flynn, 123 N.H. 457, 464 A.2d 268, 273 (1983) (exclusion of evidence obtained in violation of state "privacy" act is appropriate in part because act creates "constitutional-type safeguards"); Com. v. Price, 543 Pa. 403, 672 A.2d 280, 285 (1996) (exclusion is appropriate where "a violation of the law implicates constitutional concerns and/or fundamental rights").

The Iowa Supreme Court has indicated exclusion is possible only if the statute violated "involves a fundamental right of the defendant," which

is the case if confer a "right . . . grounded in fundamental fairness to the accused." State v. Dentler, 742 N.W.2d 84, 89 (Iowa 2007).

[4]U. S. v. Chavez, 416 U.S. 562, 574, 94 S. Ct. 1849, 40 L. Ed. 2d 380 (1974).

[5]U. S. v. Giordano, 416 U.S. 505, 527, 94 S. Ct. 1820, 40 L. Ed. 2d 341 (1974). *See also* U. S. v. Donovan, 429 U.S. 413, 432–39, 97 S. Ct. 658, 50 L. Ed. 2d 652 (1977) (suppression was not required by violation of requirement that application identify all those likely to be overheard if order issues or that post-interception notice be given to all identifiable persons whose conversations were intercepted).

[6]Chavez, 416 U.S. at 574.

[7]*E.g.*, State v. Quinn, 436 N.W.2d 758, 767 (Minn. 1989) (following *Giordano* in determining when evidence must be suppressed under state wiretap statute).

ment a constitutionally-related purpose or the ultimate objective of a legislative scheme, the courts tend to label it "technical" and to treat it as insufficient to trigger an exclusionary sanction.[8]

A second type of limitation upon nonconstitutional exclusionary sanctions makes exclusion available only to those defendants who show more than simply that the evidence at issue was obtained by means of a violation of a sufficient legal requirement. Often the case law requires a showing of either an "intentional" violation of the underlying legal requirement or prejudice in some sense as a result of that violation.[9] As this approach is applied, prejudice means that the defendant suffered the harm that the legal requirement was designed to prevent. When this approach is invoked in response to proof that officers failed to follow nonconstitutional requirements for search warrants, for example, prejudice apparently requires proof that the search would not have occurred had the requirements been met or at least that the search would have been significantly less intrusive if this had been the case.

Exclusion may be required if but only if the acquisition of the evidence did not involve a "good faith" effort to determine and comply with the law. The Florida courts have taken this position with regard to the statutory procedure for obtaining medical records.[10]

A similar but more flexible analysis would provide for exclusion

---

[8]State v. Smith, 367 N.W.2d 497, 504–05 (Minn. 1985) (obtaining information from welfare officials in violation of statutory limits "was a technical violation which did not subvert the basic purpose of the statute" and hence did not render evidence inadmissible); Com. v. Wholaver, 605 Pa. 325, 989 A.2d 883, 898 (2010) (lack of date on warrant was "technical defect").

[9]See Murray v. State, 855 P.2d 350, 355 (Wyo. 1993). The seminal case is U.S. v. Burke, 517 F.2d 377, 386–87 (2d Cir. 1975), holding that exclusion of evidence obtained by a search warrant issued or executed in violation of nonconstitutional requirements is required only if "(1) there was prejudice in the sense that the search might not have occurred or would not have been so abrasive if the Rule had been followed, or (2) there is evidence of intentional and deliberate disregard of a provision in the Rule." Accord U.S. v. Chaar, 137 F.3d 359, 362 (6th Cir.

1998) (violation of rule requirement that record of telephonic search warrant application be made and filed requires suppression of evidence only if the violation is prejudicial or intentional); Copley v. Com., 361 S.W.3d 902, 906–07 (Ky. 2012) (exclusionary may be warranted if there is prejudice to the defendant or proof of deliberate disregard of legal requirement); State v. Sheldon, 344 S.C. 340, 543 S.E.2d 585, 586 (Ct. App. 2001) (evidence obtained in violation of statutory provision relating to authority to investigate collisions involving law enforcement officers "is not necessarily inadmissible in the absence of a demonstration of prejudice resulting from the violation").

[10]Sneed v. State, 876 So. 2d 1235, 1238 (Fla. 3d DCA 2004) (evidence excluded where officer did not know of any legal requirements for obtaining records and failed to contact an attorney for the state to determine the proper procedure for obtaining such

only upon proof of a legal violation that was in some sense "substantial."[11] Under a North Carolina statute embodying a demand for a substantial violation of law,[12] determining whether an underlying violation was substantial requires consideration of: (a) the importance of the particular interest protected by the legal requirement; (b) the extent of the deviation from lawful conduct; (c) the extent to which the violation was willful; and (d) the extent to which exclusion will tend to deter future violations of the same sort.

A third type of limitation upon the right to exclusion gives a trial court discretionary authority to exclude evidence where on the facts of the case before the court exclusion is determined to sufficiently further the objectives of exclusionary sanctions to warrant the cost involved. This was the thrust of *Commonwealth v. Mason*,[13] in which the Pennsylvania Supreme Court explicitly announced that a showing that evidence had been obtained in violation of the Pennsylvania Rules of Criminal Procedure established only that "exclusion may be an appropriate remedy."[14] Exclusion is to be in fact ordered only if the trial judge, after considering the nature of the case and the particular facts, determines that exclusion and its costs would be proportional to the benefits to be gained. Trial judges were cautioned to give particular emphasis to the likelihood that exclusion would prevent future misconduct similar to that which gave rise to the violation before the court.[15]

A similar approach to the Alaska Evidence Rule barring use of "illegally obtained" evidence[16] was adopted by the Alaska Court of Appeals:

[F]actors to consider in determining whether to apply the exclusion-

---

records). *Sneed* noted that "suppression . . . in this case would serve the exclusionary rule's historic purpose by encouraging police officers to become familiar with the proper legal procedures before impulsively seizing private patient records." Sneed, 876 So.2d at 1238.

[11]*See* Model Code of Pre-Arraignment Procedure § 290.2(2) to (4) (Official Draft 1975).

[12]N.C. Gen. Stat. Ann. § 15A-974(2).

[13]Com. v. Mason, 507 Pa. 396, 490 A.2d 421 (1985).

[14]Mason, 490 A.2d at 426 (emphasis in original), reaffirmed in Com. v. Perez, 577 Pa. 360, 845 A.2d 779, 787

n.7 (2004).

[15]Mason, 490 A.2d at 424. The *Mason* court subsequently stressed the importance in the analysis of evidence of widespread and otherwise uncontrollable governmental conduct and whether the illegality suggests the challenged evidence is unreliable. Com. v. Wholaver, 605 Pa. 325, 989 A.2d 883, 898 (2010). *Cf.* State v. Moody, 208 Ariz. 424, 94 P.3d 1119, 1142 (2004) (if defendant showed violation of court rule requirement that defendant be permitted to contact counsel before execution of warrant for physical characteristics, defendant "failed to demonstrate why suppression would be appropriate in this case").

[16]See § 171 supra.

ary rule in cases where a government officer violated a statute . . . are: (1) "whether the statutory requirement . . . restriction [was] 'clear and widely known;' " (2) whether the statute was primarily enacted to protect the rights of individual citizens rather than to generally benefit society; (3) whether admission of the evidence would make courts accomplices to the willful disobedience of the law; and (4) whether the police have engaged in "widespread or repeated violations" of the statute.[17]

## § 173    Use of illegally obtained evidence in noncriminal litigation[1]

Most exclusionary sanction issues arise in criminal litigation.[2] Perhaps because of American courts' increasing acceptance of exclusion as a response to illegality in obtaining evidence, however, litigants sometimes attempt to invoke exclusionary remedies in various types of civil litigation. When, if ever, exclusionary sanctions are appropriate outside of criminal litigation presents a number of difficult questions.

Distinctions here as elsewhere must be drawn among the various exclusionary sanctions that do or might exist. The Supreme Court's case law addressing the application of the federal constitutional exclusionary requirements outside of criminal litigation provides an attractive model that has been widely but not universally followed in other contexts.

Soon after *Mapp v. Ohio*,[3] the Supreme Court held the Fourth Amendment exclusionary rule applicable in a state proceeding for forfeiture of an automobile on the basis that the vehicle had been used in a crime.[4] Forfeiture was clearly a penalty for a criminal act, the Court reasoned, and it would therefore be incongruous to

---

[17]State v. Avery, 211 P.3d 1154, 1159 (Alaska Ct. App. 2009) (quoting Berumen v. State, 182 P.3d 635, 641 (Alaska Ct. App. 2008)). In *Berumen*, evidence tainted by a violation of a "knock and announce" statute was held inadmissible. "The 'knock and announce' requirement is both clear and widely known," it is "clearly designed to protect the individual rights of homeowners, hotel room occupants, and others who expect privacy in a building or vessel," the violation was "flagrant," and the case law and record in the case suggest "there may be widespread or repeated violations of the statute." In *Avery*, however, evidence was admissible despite the recording of a telephone call in violation

of Department of Corrections policy; this was primarily because the policy was not widely known and apparently did not reflect actual practice.

**[Section 173]**

[1]*See generally* West's Key Number Digest, Evidence ⬦154.

[2]Application of exclusionary requirements in criminal litigation but in contexts other than trial is considered in § 174 infra.

[3]Mapp v. Ohio, 367 U.S. 643, 81 S. Ct. 1684, 6 L. Ed. 2d 1081 (1961).

[4]One 1958 Plymouth Sedan v. Com. of Pa., 380 U.S. 693, 85 S. Ct. 1246, 14 L. Ed. 2d 170 (1965).

exclude the evidence in a criminal prosecution but admit it in a forfeiture proceeding based on the same criminal activity.[5]

The matter was addressed again in *United States v. Janis,*[6] a civil proceeding for a tax refund in which the Government counterclaimed for the unpaid balance of the assessment. The assessment was based upon information concerning Janis' illegal bookmaking activities; that information had been obtained by state law enforcement officers acting pursuant to a defective search warrant but nevertheless in the "good faith" belief that the search was lawful. Use of the evidence was permissible, the Court reasoned, because "exclusion from federal civil proceedings of evidence unlawfully seized by a state criminal law enforcement officer has not been shown to have a sufficient likelihood of deterring the conduct of the state police so that it outweighs the societal costs imposed by the exclusion."[7]

*Janis* involved an intersovereign situation—the government that committed the illegality in obtaining the evidence was not the same government that sought to use it. Thus the Court's result may have rested in part upon a conclusion that excluding evidence in a federal civil proceeding is unlikely to influence state officers. In *I.N.S. v. Lopez-Mendoza,*[8] however, the Court arrived at a similar result in an intrasovereign case. At issue was whether evidence obtained in violation of the Fourth Amendment by federal immigration officers was admissible in a federal civil deportation proceeding. *Janis,* the Court nevertheless observed, provided the framework for analysis: the likely social benefits of excluding the evidence must be balanced against the likely costs.[9] The intrasovereign nature of the situation suggested that the deterrent benefits were likely to be greater than in *Janis.* But other

---

[5]*One 1958 Plymouth Sedan* is apparently still authoritative. U.S. v. $186,416.00 in U.S. Currency, 590 F.3d 942, 949 (9th Cir. 2010) (The Fourth Amendment exclusionary rule applies to civil forfeiture proceedings," citing *One 1958 Plymouth Sedan*); People v. $11,200.00 U.S. Currency, 2011 WL 3612233 (Colo. App. 2011), cert. granted, 2012 WL 4472952 (Colo. 2012).

But "while *One 1958 Plymouth Sedan* has not been overruled and, thus, is still applicable, several subsequently decided cases indicate that the underpinnings of [the decision] have been weakened." In re Forfeiture of $180,975, 478 Mich. 444, 734 N.W.2d 489, 493–94 (2007). *See also* U.S. v. Marrocco, 578 F.3d 627, 642 (7th Cir.

2009) (Easterbrook, C.J., concurring).

If the Fourth Amendment rule does apply, there is some question whether some version of the rule that identity is not excludable, see § 178 infra, means that the property itself cannot be excluded. *See* U.S. v. $482,627.00 in U.S. Currency, More or Less, 2005 WL 1140603 (W.D. Tex. 2005).

[6]U.S. v. Janis, 428 U.S. 433, 96 S. Ct. 3021, 49 L. Ed. 2d 1046 (1976).

[7]Janis, 428 U.S. at 454.

[8]I.N.S. v. Lopez-Mendoza, 468 U.S. 1032, 104 S. Ct. 3479, 82 L. Ed. 2d 778 (1984).

[9]Lopez-Mendoza, 468 U.S. at 1041.

considerations suggested they would still be quite small: the Government itself disciplines officers who violate the Fourth Amendment and excludes evidence arising from intentional violations, and INS officers know that there is only a small likelihood that any arrestee will actually challenge the officers' actions in a formal proceeding.[10] On the cost side, application of the rule would impede the busy deportation system. Since immigration enforcement often involves continuing violations of the law, application of an exclusionary rule in this context "would require the courts to close their eyes to ongoing violations of the law," a cost of a particularly offensive character.[11] The *Janis* balance, the Court concluded, came out against application of the Fourth Amendment exclusionary rule.[12]

Under *Janis* and *Lopez-Mendoza*, whether the federal constitutional exclusionary rules are applicable in civil litigation turns upon whether the increased prevention of unconstitutional conduct accomplished by application of the exclusionary requirement to civil cases of the sort at issue is worth the costs of so expanding those sanctions. The two decisions suggest that the Court is generally satisfied that sufficient prevention is provided by exclusion of unconstitutionally obtained evidence in criminal litigation. A civil litigant seeking to show that exclusion is justified under *Janis-Lopez-Mendoza* has an extremely difficult task.

Lower courts are understandably hesitant to exclude evidence in civil contexts. Nevertheless, at least some remain reluctant to characterize the federal constitutional sanctions as never applicable to noncriminal litigation.[13]

There is general agreement that whether the federal constitutional exclusionary rule applies in a technically noncriminal proceeding depends at least in part upon the type of proceeding. Many analyses also require consideration of the facts of the specific case, assuming that parties' objections to evidence require case-specific analyses. Several courts have distinguished at least five factors that are relevant to these analyses:

(1) the nature of the noncriminal proceeding;

(2) whether the proposed use of unconstitutionally seized material is intersovereign or intrasovereign;

(3) whether (in intrasovereign situations) the search and the noncriminal proceeding were initiated by the same agency;

(4) whether there is an explicit and demonstrable understanding between the two governmental agencies; and

---

[10]468 U.S. at 1044–45.

[11]468 U.S. at 1046.

[12]468 U.S. at 1050.

[13]Some, however, seem to adopt a rigid approach of blanket nonapplica- bility. Naguit v. Selcke, 184 Ill. App. 3d 80, 132 Ill. Dec. 547, 539 N.E.2d 1353, 1355 (5th Dist. 1989) (no authority exists for extension of exclusionary rule to administrative proceeding to discipline physician).

(5) whether the noncriminal proceeding fell within the "zone of primary interest" of the officers that conducted the search.[14]

The *Janis-Lopez-Mendoza* analysis is most likely to lead to exclusion when unconstitutionally obtained evidence is offered in proceedings which, although civil, are brought by governmental authorities for what is essentially a public purpose. Governmental activity may be conducted with the prospect of such litigation in mind, and thus exclusion in such litigation may discourage impropriety in the investigatory activity. There is widespread agreement, for example, that the exclusionary rule applies in proceedings to have a child declared delinquent.[15] Such rules have also been applied in proceedings to collect a tax on illegal drugs[16] and a school disciplinary hearing.[17]

Under the *Janis-Lopez-Mendoza* approach, it is quite unlikely that the federal constitutional rules will ever be applicable in civil actions between private parties.[18] If the evidence was wrongfully obtained by public officers, exclusion would not penalize them and officers would not likely be influenced in their future conduct by such exclusion.[19] If the evidence was wrongfully obtained by private persons,[20] the Supreme Court would almost certainly reason that exclusion would at most deter similar

---

[14]Vara v. Sharp, 880 S.W.2d 844, 850 (Tex. App. Austin 1994) (quoting from Wolf v. C.I.R., 13 F.3d 189, 194–95 (6th Cir. 1993)). *See* Hamilton's Henry the VIII Lounge, Inc. v. Department of Consumer & Industry Services, 2006 WL 1360288 (Mich. Ct. App. 2006) (unpublished) (applying *Wolf* analysis); State, Indiana Dept. of Revenue v. Adams, 762 N.E.2d 728 (Ind. 2002) (same).

[15]*E.g.*, In re Nicholas R., 92 Conn. App. 316, 884 A.2d 1059, 1062 (2005) ("juvenile delinquency proceedings are quasi-criminal . . . and as such the exclusionary rule does apply"). The Supreme Court noted but did not reach the matter in New Jersey v. T.L.O., 469 U.S. 325, 332–33, 105 S. Ct. 733, 83 L. Ed. 2d 720 (1985).

[16]Vara, 880 S.W.2d at 850. *Contra* State, Indiana Dept. of Revenue v. Adams, 762 N.E.2d 728 (Ind. 2002) (split court).

[17]Juan C. v. Cortines, 223 A.D.2d 126, 647 N.Y.S.2d 491, 495 (1st Dep't 1996), rev'd on other grounds 679 N.E.2d 1061 (N.Y. 1997).

[18]*See, e.g.*, Boyles v. Preston, 68 Conn. App. 596, 792 A.2d 878, 887–89 (2002) (evidence suppressed in criminal prosecution was properly admitted in civil suit for sexual harassment).

[19]Hughes v. Tupelo Oil Co., Inc., 510 So. 2d 502 (Miss. 1987) (evidence wrongfully obtained by police officer admissible in wrongful death action, because to exclude it would penalize the defendant rather than the officer who engaged in the misconduct). *See also* Divine v. Groshong, 235 Kan. 127, 679 P.2d 700, 707 (1984) ("We see no reason to extend the exclusionary rule to civil cases in which neither the State nor its officers are parties.").

[20]In such cases, of course, the party objecting to the evidence would face the initial hurdle of establishing a constitutional violation. Private actions generally are not covered by federal constitutional provisions, which protect citizens only against official activity. *See* Burdeau v. McDowell, 256 U.S. 465, 41 S. Ct. 574, 65 L. Ed. 1048 (1921) (private person's wrongful invasion of another's privacy does not constitute a "search" within

private action in the future, a concern beyond the scope of the underlying federal constitutional rules being enforced.[21]

Most courts, moreover, do not apply the federal constitutional exclusionary rules to administrative proceedings concerning employment or professional disciplinary matters,[22] school disciplinary proceedings,[23] drivers' license suspension or revocation proceedings,[24] civil tax assessment or collection proceedings,[25] or even child protection proceedings[26] or actions to compel

---

the meaning of the Fourth Amendment).

[21]Bogart v. Jack, 727 S.W.2d 447 (Mo. Ct. App. W.D. 1987) (letters obtained wrongfully by plaintiff admissible in action for alienation of wife's affections and criminal conversation with wife). *Contra* Williams v. Williams, 8 Ohio Misc. 156, 37 Ohio Op. 2d 224, 221 N.E.2d 622 (C.P. 1966) (evidence wrongfully obtained by husband inadmissible in divorce proceeding).

[22]*See* City of Omaha v. Savard-Henson, 9 Neb. App. 561, 615 N.W.2d 497, 503–10 (2000) (following majority approach that exclusionary rule is not applicable in administrative proceedings); Kerr v. Pennsylvania State Bd. of Dentistry, 599 Pa. 107, 960 A.2d 427, 434–35 (2008) (Fourth Amendment exclusionary rule did not apply in civil disciplinary proceedings of State Board of Dentristry).

[23]Thompson v. Carthage School Dist., 87 F.3d 979, 980–82 (8th Cir. 1996) (following the majority of decisions).

[24]The majority of a split court in Miller v. Toler, 229 W. Va. 302, 729 S.E.2d 137 (2012), explained:

[I]f the exclusionary rule is extended to civil license revocation or suspension proceedings there would be minimal likelihood of deterring police misconduct because the real punishment to law enforcement for misconduct is derived by excluding unlawfully seized evidence in the criminal proceeding. When this minimal deterrent benefit is compared to the societal cost of applying the exclusionary rule in a civil, administrative driver's license revocation or suspension proceeding that was

designed to protect innocent persons, the cost to society outweighs any benefit of extending the exclusionary rule to the civil proceeding.

729 S.E.2d at 143. *Accord* Nevers v. State, Dept. of Admin., 123 P.3d 958, 961–66 (Alaska 2005) (neither Fourth Amendment nor state constitutional exclusionary requirements applied to driver's license revocation proceedings); Martin v. Kansas Dept. of Revenue, 285 Kan. 625, 176 P.3d 938, 949 (2008) (sufficient deterrence accomplished by applying exclusionary rule in criminal litigation); Beller v. Rolfe, 2008 UT 68, 194 P.3d 949, 954 (Utah 2008) (need to protect public from impaired drivers outweighs whatever increased deterrence might result from applying exclusionary rule). *Contra* Loyal Order of Moose Lodge 1044 of Troy v. Ohio Liquor Control Comm., 105 Ohio App. 3d 306, 663 N.E.2d 1306, 1309 (2d Dist. Miami County 1995) (applying exclusionary rule in proceeding to revoke liquor license).

[25]Grimes v. C.I.R., 82 F.3d 286, 288–89 (9th Cir. 1996); Kivela v. Department of Treasury, 449 Mich. 220, 536 N.W.2d 498, 500–501 (1995).

[26]State ex rel. A.R. v. C.R., 1999 UT 43, 982 P.2d 73, 79 (Utah 1999) (Fourth Amendment exclusionary rule does not apply to child welfare proceedings, because what little deterrence achieved is "far outweighed" by the need to provide for the safety and health of children in peril by permitting courts to consider even unconstitutionally obtained evidence). *Accord* People ex rel. A.E.L., 181 P.3d 1186 (Colo. App. 2008); State of N.M. ex rel. CYFD v. Michael T., 143 N.M. 75, 2007-NMCA-163, 172 P.3d 1287, 1290

treatment for impaired persons.[27] Some attempt to draw finer lines; several courts have held that the Fourth Amendment exclusionary rule does not apply under federal Occupational Safety and Health Act proceedings to correct a violation but it does apply to proceedings to punish past violations by assessing penalties for them.[28]

In a plurality portion of the lead opinion, *Lopez-Mendoza* left open the possibility that the Fourth Amendment exclusionary rule might apply in noncriminal actions such as deportation proceedings upon proof that the evidence was obtained by "egregious violations of Fourth Amendment or other liberties that might transgress notions of fundamental fairness and undermine the probative value of the evidence obtained."[29] One court has held that proof of "bad faith"—that the officers should have known their conduct was unreasonable and hence unconstitutional—requires exclusion, even if the violation did not affect the probative value of the evidence at issue.[30] Perhaps if the underlying official activity is particularly offensive, the increased need to discourage such activity justifies the costs of adding to the exclusionary disincentive by rejecting its fruits even in civil litigation.

State courts, of course, are technically free to reject the approach taken in *Janis* and *Lopez-Mendoza* and to construe state

---

(Ct. App. 2007).

[27]Conservatorship of Susan T., 8 Cal. 4th 1005, 36 Cal. Rptr. 2d 40, 884 P.2d 988, 995–96 (1994) (Fourth Amendment exclusionary rule inapplicable in proceedings for appointment of a conservator for mentally-impaired person, although the improper entry of the home was made by an employee of the agency seeking the conservatorship and apparently was made for purposes of obtaining evidence regarding the need for treatment that would be assured by the conservatorship). *Accord* Matter of Guardianship and Conservatorship of Larson, 530 N.W.2d 348, 350 (N.D. 1995).

[28]Smith Steel Casting Co. v. Brock, 800 F.2d 1329, 1334 (5th Cir. 1986). *Accord* Trinity Industries, Inc. v. Occupational Safety and Health Review Com'n, 16 F.3d 1455, 1461–62 (6th Cir. 1994). *See* Lakeland

Enterprises of Rhinelander, Inc. v. Chao, 402 F.3d 739, 744 (7th Cir. 2005) ("We need not decide here whether to join the Fifth and Sixth Circuits in distinguishing between corrective and punitive OSHA proceedings for purposes of the applicability of the exclusionary rule.").

[29]I.N.S. v. Lopez-Mendoza, 468 U.S. 1032, 1050–51, 104 S. Ct. 3479, 82 L. Ed. 2d 778 (1984). *See* Lopez-Rodriguez v. Mukasey, 536 F.3d 1012, 1015–16 (9th Cir. 2008), rehearing en banc denied sub nom Lopez-Rodriguez v. Holder, 560 F.3d 1098 (9th Cir. 2009) (evidence tainted by egregious Fourth Amendment violation was subject to exclusion in proceeding before Board of Immigration Appeals).

[30]Gonzalez-Rivera v. I.N.S., 22 F.3d 1441, 1448 (9th Cir. 1994) (detention of person on the basis of race shows bad faith and requires exclusion).

constitutional provisions as fully applicable to civil litigation.[31] The Oklahoma Supreme Court exercised this power in *Turner v. City of Lawton*,[32] holding evidence unconstitutionally obtained inadmissible in an administrative proceeding to dismiss a firefighter. The court accepted the state search and seizure provision as creating a right to exclusion as a necessary remedy for the preceding violation of privacy, regardless of the necessity for exclusion to discourage future violations of the underlying legal requirements. In order to achieve the remedial objective of the state exclusionary requirement, then, the Oklahoma court extended its rule to civil litigation in order to replace the wronged person as close as possible to his condition before the wrongful search occurred.[33]

One court has more ambiguously indicated that trial judge's discretion in admitting evidence gives them some authority in civil proceedings to exclude evidence illegally obtained.[34]

## § 174 Use of illegally obtained evidence in criminal proceedings on matters other than guilt

Evidence may be offered against a criminal defendant in the course of criminal litigation but other than at the trial on guilt or innocence. It may, for example, be used in an effort to have pre-trial release denied or revoked, at a preliminary hearing to determine whether a defendant is to be "bound over" for grand jury consideration or trial, before a grand jury in support of a proposed indictment charging the defendant with an offense, at sentencing in support of a more severe disposition, in support of an effort to revoke probation once granted, or to substantiate a claim that parole after imprisonment should be denied or revoked. An exclusionary rule's determination that illegally obtained evidence must be inadmissible to prove defendants' guilt does not require the further conclusion that such evidence should be unavailable for any or all of these or similar purposes.

The Fourth Amendment issue was addressed most extensively

---

[31]*See* Sims v. Collection Div. of Utah State Tax Com'n, 841 P.2d 6, 15–16 (Utah 1992) (state constitutional exclusionary rule applies "where the proceeding in which exclusion is sought is quasi-criminal in nature or where there is a particularized need for deterrence to restrain improper law enforcement activities" and both considerations dictated its application to proceeding to enforce tax imposed on illegal drugs).

[32]Turner v. City of Lawton, 1986 OK 51, 733 P.2d 375 (Okla. 1986).

[33]Turner, 733 P.2d at 381–82.

[34]O'Brien v. O'Brien, 899 So. 2d 1133, 1137 (Fla. 5th DCA 2005) (state Security of Communications Act did not require exclusion of electronic communication intercepted in violation of the statute, but "[b]ecause the evidence was illegally obtained" trial court in divorce proceeding did not abuse its discretion in excluding it).

in *Pennsylvania Board of Probation v. Scott*,[1] in which the Supreme Court made clear that the critical question is whether the deterrence benefits of so expanding the Fourth Amendment exclusionary rule would outweigh the costs incurred. At issue in *Scott* was specifically whether evidence obtained in violation of the Fourth Amendment could be used to establish that a convicted defendant had violated the conditions of his parole. The costs of requiring exclusion in parole revocation proceedings would be exceptionally high, the Court reasoned, indicating that exclusionary rule issues would delay and impede the necessarily flexible and administrative procedures of parole revocation.

Probably more important, the deterrent benefits would most likely be low. Where law enforcement officers do not know that suspects are parolees, the remote possibility that this may be the case—and thus that fruits of misconduct will be unusable for parole violation purposes—is unlikely to influence the officers. Regular law enforcement officers who know a suspect is a parolee are unlikely to be influenced by the admissibility of the fruits of their actions in parole revocation proceedings. Parole officers specifically charged with parole concerns, on the other hand, are less likely than regular officers to perceive themselves engaged in the "adversarial" process of ferreting out crime, and thus are likely to respond adequately to less costly alternatives to exclusion, such as departmental training and discipline and civil damage liability.[2]

*Scott's* assessment of law enforcement officers' motivations is arguably quite naive. The state court below, like some others, sought a more sophisticated balance by directing that the Fourth Amendment exclusionary rule be applied where—but only where—the defendant challenging the evidence established that the officer who obtained it knew the suspect was a parolee. Thus the state court sought to limit application of the rule to those situations in which deterrent benefits were most certain. Rejecting this approach, the Supreme Court clearly concluded that even in these cases the potential deterrent benefit was minimal. In addition, however, it reasoned that a need to address the officers' awareness in exclusionary rule litigation would unacceptably increase the complexity of applying the rule and consequently the costs of doing so.[3]

---

**[Section 174]**

[1]Pennsylvania Bd. of Probation and Parole v. Scott, 524 U.S. 357, 118

S. Ct. 2014, 141 L. Ed. 2d 344 (1998).

[2]Scott, 524 U.S. at 368–69.

[3]524 U.S. at 368.

*Scott* thus supplemented the earlier holding in *United States v. Calandra*[4] that the Fourth Amendment does not require that evidence obtained in violation of its terms be kept from influencing grand jury decisions to indict. Together, *Scott* and *Calandra* leave no doubt that the Supreme Court is firmly convinced that exclusion at trial from the guilt-innocence process will generally satisfy federal constitutional requirements. Defendants are unlikely to be able to convince the Court that law enforcement officers unaffected by the admissibility of evidence at trial are likely to be sufficiently influenced by its admissibility for other purposes to justify what the Court regards as the considerable cost of expanding the federal constitutional exclusionary demands to proceedings other than the determination of guilt at trial.

The Supreme Court has not addressed the applicability of the federal constitutional exclusionary rules at pretrial stages except for grand jury proceedings. Most likely, considerations of practicality tip the scales in favor of not apply exclusionary sanctions for granting, limiting, or revoking pretrial release.[5] The Vermont Supreme Court, however, has held the prosecution may sometimes be required to make a prima facie case for admissibility.[6] It stressed that a finding the prosecution has failed to make this showing would not control whether the evidence must be suppressed for purposes of trial.[7]

Applicability of the federal constitutional requirement at preliminary hearings has likewise not been definitely decided.[8] In federal litigation, however, Rule 5.1(e) of the Federal Rules of Criminal Procedure specifically provides that "[a]t the preliminary hearing, the defendant . . . may not object to evidence on the ground that it was unlawfully acquired."[9] A number of state statutes and rules follow this approach.[10] At least a few permit challenges at the preliminary hearing.[11] The Hawai'i Supreme Court, over dissent, held that both state and federal constitutional

---

[4]U.S. v. Calandra, 414 U.S. 338, 94 S. Ct. 613, 38 L. Ed. 2d 561 (1974).

[5]State v. Delaurier, 488 A.2d 688, 691–92 (R.I. 1985) (federal constitutional exclusionary requirement does not apply in a proceeding to revoke bail).

[6]State v. Passino, 154 Vt. 377, 577 A.2d 281, 285 (1990), reapproved in State v. Avgoustov, 180 Vt. 595, 2006 VT 90, 907 A.2d 1185, 1187 (2006).

[7]Passino, 577 A.2d at 285 n. 2.

[8]In Giordenello v. U.S., 357 U.S. 480, 484, 78 S. Ct. 1245, 2 L. Ed. 2d

1503 (1958), the Court commented that the judicial officer conducing a preliminary hearing under the then-current Rules of Criminal Procedure "ha[d] no authority to adjudicate the admissibility at [the defendant's] later trial of the heroin taken from his person. That issue was for the trial court."

[9]Fed. R. Crim. P. 5.1(e).

[10]*E.g.*, Ky. R. Crim. P. 3.14(3).

[11]Cal. Penal Code § 1538.5(f) (providing for a motion to suppress at a felony preliminary hearing); Idaho Crim. R. § 5.1(b) ("if at the preliminary hearing the evidence shows facts

considerations require exclusion of illegally obtained evidence from the preliminary hearing.[12]

Whether the federal constitutional requirements apply post-trial in sentencing has also not been resolved by the Court. Almost certainly, however, the Court would reason, under *Scott* and *Calandra*, that whatever minimal incremental deterrence would be achieved by so applying the requirements would be outweighed by the costs. Particular weight would undoubtedly be given to the cost involved in requiring sentencing courts to exercise their considerable discretion without the benefit of all relevant and reliable evidence. Many lower courts hold—or at least state unqualifiedly—that these exclusionary requirements do not apply at sentencing.[13] Some, however, leave open that they may apply in exceptional circumstances, such as where the defendant shows the officers sought the evidence at issue for the purpose of increasing the severity of the defendant's sentence.[14]

State courts again are free to reject the *Scott-Calandra* ap-

---

which would ultimately require the suppression of evidence sought to be used against the defendant, such evidence shall be excluded and shall not be considered by the magistrate in his determining probable cause."); Iowa R. Crim. P. 2.2(4)(c) ("Rules excluding evidence on the ground that it was acquired by unlawful means are not applicable [at the preliminary hearing.").

[12]State v. Wilson, 55 Haw. 314, 519 P.2d 228 (1974).

[13]People v. Rose, 384 Ill. App. 3d 937, 323 Ill. Dec. 597, 894 N.E.2d 156, 163 (2d Dist. 2008) ("the exclusionary rule does not apply to the sentencing phase of criminal proceedings"); Brown v. City of Danville, 44 Va. App. 586, 606 S.E.2d 523, 533 (2004) ("We now hold that the exclusionary rule does not apply during sentencing proceedings . . . .").

[14]U.S. v. Hinson, 585 F.3d 1328, 1335 (10th Cir. 2009) ("The exclusionary rule does not bar the admission of the fruits of an illegal search at sentencing unless the illegal search was conducted with the intent to obtain evidence that would increase the defendant's sentence."); U.S. v. Perez, 581 F.3d 539, 544 (7th Cir. 2009) ("There is a possibility that the exclusionary rule might apply at sentencing where

the police deliberately violated the defendant's constitutional rights for the purpose of acquiring evidence to increase a defendant's prospective sentence."); U.S. v. Skilling, 554 F.3d 529, 592–93 (5th Cir. 2009) ("Ordinarily, a district court can consider illegally obtained evidence at sentencing even if that evidence is not admissible at trial, although . . . we may look, case-by-case, to whether the admission of the evidence will encourage the government to obtain evidence illegally."); U.S. v. Stark, 499 F.3d 72, 80–81 (1st Cir. 2007) (not deciding whether suppressed evidence may be used at sentencing if police misconduct was egregious because police acted with intent to increase the defendant's sentence).

The Alaska courts have indicated that illegally obtained evidence would be inadmissible at sentencing "if the evidence was obtained as a result of 'gross or shocking police misconduct' or if the police engaged in an unlawful search or seizure knowing at the time that the suspect was facing trial or sentencing on other charges." State v. Batts, 195 P.3d 144, 155 (Alaska Ct. App. 2008) (quoting Elson v. State, 659 P.2d 1195, 1204 n.28, 1205 (Alaska 1983)).

proach or the Supreme Court's application of it to some or all nontrial stages of criminal proceedings. An Oregon court has done so by holding that the Oregon constitutional exclusionary requirement, intended not simply to deter but also to adequately vindicate the right to privacy, requires that evidence obtained in an unreasonable search or seizure be excluded from sentencing. Adequate vindication requires assurance that those whose rights are violated be free from increased punishment based on the fruits of the violations.[15]

## § 175   "Standing" and personal nature of rights[1]

The Fourth Amendment exclusionary rule and most other exclusionary sanctions permit a criminal defendant to seek suppression of evidence only on the basis of a claim that the evidence was obtained in an improper manner that violated the defendant's own rights.[2] Put negatively, this requirement of "standing" precludes a defendant from objecting to evidence on the basis that it was obtained illegally but in a manner that violated only the rights of another person. Courts sometimes suggest that this reflects the "personal" nature of the rights enforced by exclusionary requirements,[3] but in actuality the standing requirement is best conceptualized as an aspect of the exclusionary remedy rather than of the underlying rights.

*Fourth Amendment Standing.* The Fourth Amendment standing requirement was first developed under pre-*Mapp v. Ohio*[4] law.[5] It was explained in *Jones v. United States*[6] as based upon language in the Federal Rules of Criminal Procedure authorizing a motion to suppress only by "[a] person aggrieved by an unlawful search and seizure." This was read by the Court as applying

---

[15]*See* State v. Swartzendruber, 120 Or. App. 552, 853 P.2d 842, 844–45 (1993).

**[Section 175]**

[1]*See generally* West's Key Number Digest, Criminal Law ☞392.41; West's Key Number Digest, Searches and Seizures ☞161 to 165.

[2]A defendant challenging the admissibility of evidence on exclusionary sanction grounds has the burden of establishing standing. *E.g.*, People v. Hunter, 17 N.Y.3d 725, 926 N.Y.S.2d 401, 950 N.E.2d 137, 138 (2011) ("well settled that a defendant seeking suppression of evidence obtained as the result of an alleged illegal search must prove standing to challenge the search"); Miller v. State, 2009 WY 125, 217 P.3d 793, 801 (Wyo. 2009).

[3]*E.g.*, Hill v. State, 1972 OK CR 211, 500 P.2d 1080, 1090 (Okla. Crim. App. 1972) (standing is "at least in part an outgrowth of the personal nature of certain constitutional rights").

[4]Mapp v. Ohio, 367 U.S. 643, 81 S. Ct. 1684, 6 L. Ed. 2d 1081 (1961).

[5]*See* Goldstein v. United States, 316 U.S. 114, 62 S. Ct. 1000, 86 L. Ed. 1312 (1942), discussed in Wong Sun v. U.S., 371 U.S. 471, 492, 83 S. Ct. 407, 9 L. Ed. 2d 441 (1963).

[6]Jones v. U.S., 362 U.S. 257, 80 S. Ct. 725, 4 L. Ed. 2d 697 (1960).

the "general principle" that constitutional protections can be claimed only by those parties to litigation that belong to the class of persons for whose sake the constitutional protection is given.[7] The Fourth Amendment exclusionary requirement is not designed to exclude evidence on grounds of unreliability or prejudicial effect. Rather, it is a means of making effective the underlying Fourth Amendment protection against official invasion of privacy and the security of property. "[I]t is," the Court concluded, "entirely proper to require of one who seeks to challenge the legality of a search as the basis for suppressing relevant evidence that he allege, and if the allegation be disputed that he establish, that he himself was the victim of an invasion of privacy."[8] After *Mapp*, this approach was incorporated into the Fourth Amendment exclusionary rule as applied to the states.[9]

As first announced and applied, the standing requirement was sometimes read as invoking a distinct body of law distinguishable from that defining the content of the Fourth Amendment's coverage. In *Rakas v. Illinois*,[10] however, the Supreme Court rejected such an approach and made clear that the inquiry necessitated by the Fourth Amendment standing requirement involves application of the case law defining the scope of Fourth Amendment coverage and, in particular, the extent of a particular defendant's rights under that provision.[11] When a defendant objects to the admissibility of the results of a search or seizure, the standing question is whether, under substantive Fourth Amendment law, the search or seizure violated the rights of the objecting defendant.

*Rakas* also adopted a quite restrictive view of substantive Fourth Amendment law, at least as applied to searches of automobiles. A mere passenger in an automobile, the Court held, has no privacy interest in the automobile. Officers' search of the vehicle, then, does not violate the Fourth Amendment rights of the passenger, and the passenger consequently cannot challenge the reasonableness of such a search.[12]

Careful application of *Rakas* requires consideration of all possible poisonous trees. A passenger in a stopped automobile is seized.[13] The passenger clearly has standing to raise the reasonableness of that seizure and may be able to establish that a search of the vehicle is the fruit of that seizure.

---

[7]Jones, 362 U.S. at 261.

[8]362 U.S. at 261.

[9]*E.g.*, Mancusi v. DeForte, 392 U.S. 364, 366–67, 88 S. Ct. 2120, 20 L. Ed. 2d 1154 (1968).

[10]Rakas v. Illinois, 439 U.S. 128, 99 S. Ct. 421, 58 L. Ed. 2d 387 (1978).

[11]Rakas, 439 U.S. at 139.

[12]439 U.S. at 148–49.

[13]Brendlin v. California, 551 U.S. 249, 127 S. Ct. 2400, 168 L. Ed. 2d 132 (2007) (passenger in vehicle is seized when vehicle is stopped because driver is believed to have committed a traffic

The Supreme Court has justified the Fourth Amendment's standing limitation in terms of the underlying policy concerns:

> The deterrent values of preventing the incrimination of those whose rights the police have violated have been considered sufficient to justify the suppression of probative evidence even though the case against the defendant is weakened or destroyed. But we are not convinced that the additional benefits of extending the exclusionary rule to other defendants would justify further encroachment upon the public interest in prosecuting those accused of crime and having them acquitted or convicted on the basis of all the evidence which exposes the truth.[14]

*Nonconstitutional Federal Exclusionary Requirements.* The Supreme Court has developed and applied standing as a limit on another, nonconstitutional exclusionary requirement. In *United States v. Payner*,[15] the Court rejected the argument that federal exclusionary requirements based on the courts' supervisory power should not require standing as did the constitutional requirements. The "same social interests" are implicated by both supervisory power exclusionary requirements and the Fourth Amendment exclusionary rule, it reasoned, and the values assigned to those interests do not change when the basis for the exclusionary sanction is the supervisory power rather than the Fourth Amendment. Consequently, even construction of the supervisory power exclusionary sanction is governed by the Court's conclusion that any increased deterrence that would be provided by abandoning standing is outweighed by the inevitable increased loss of reliable evidence.[16]

The Supreme Court has similarly read statutory exclusionary sanction language as incorporating a requirement of standing. Under the federal electronic surveillance statute, suppression of the results of an improper interception of a covered communication is required upon the motion of any "person against whom the interception was directed.[17] Without discussing the specific terminology chosen by Congress, the Court has held that the legislative history of the statute indicated a Congressional purpose to permit objections to evidence only by persons with standing under existent standing rules.[18]

*"Automatic" Standing.* Fourth Amendment law beginning in 1960 relaxed ordinary standing requirements in limited situations covered by what was characterized as the "automatic" stand-

---

offense and thus passenger has standing to challenge the seizure).

[14]Alderman v. U.S., 394 U.S. 165, 174–75, 89 S. Ct. 961, 22 L. Ed. 2d 176 (1969).

[15]U. S. v. Payner, 447 U.S. 727,

100 S. Ct. 2439, 65 L. Ed. 2d 468 (1980).

[16]Payner, 447 U.S. at 735–36.

[17]18 U.S.C.A. § 2510(11).

[18]Alderman, 394 U.S. at 175 n. 9.

ing rule. Under this rule, a defendant charged with possession of an item at the time of a search or seizure was permitted to challenge that search or seizure regardless of general standing requirements.[19] In part, the automatic standing rule was based on concern that in the cases covered defendants would often have to make an admissible judicial confession of guilt, i.e., possession, to establish standing. Such defendants' testimony establishing standing, given at the hearing on the admissibility of the item, might well be admissible against the defendants at trial. The resulting "dilemma," the Court concluded, was unacceptable.[20] As the Court has recognized in *United States v. Salvucci*,[21] this part of the rationale was destroyed by *Simmons v. United States*,[22] holding that testimony given at a motion to suppress evidence is not admissible against the defendant at a subsequent trial. A defendant who, to establish standing, judicially admits possession need not fear that the prosecution will use that admission at trial to establish his guilt.

But the automatic standing rule was also based in part upon perceived offensiveness of contradictory prosecutorial arguments that defendants had close enough relationships to items to be guilty of possession of them but not sufficient relationships to give them standing to challenge the searches by which the prosecution obtained the items.[23] In *Salvucci*, however, the Court concluded that there was no inherent inconsistency between such claims.[24] Since the automatic standing rule had therefore "outlived its usefulness in [the] Court's Fourth Amendment jurisprudence," it was overruled.[25]

The standing requirement is firmly entrenched in the Fourth Amendment and probably in those other exclusionary requirements over which the Supreme Court has substantive development power. But in *Alderman* the Court acknowledged that

---

[19]The rule was announced in Jones v. U.S., 362 U.S. 257, 263, 80 S. Ct. 725, 4 L. Ed. 2d 697 (1960). Brown v. U.S., 411 U.S. 223, 93 S. Ct. 1565, 36 L. Ed. 2d 208 (1973), made clear that the rule was limited to those situations in which the possession on which the charge was based was possession at the time of the search which the defendant sought to challenge.

[20]Jones, 362 U.S. at 263–64. In part, the Court reasoned that this situation provided offensive encouragement for defendants to perjure themselves by seeking to establish standing while maintaining defenses to the charges on their merits. 362 U.S. at 262.

[21]U. S. v. Salvucci, 448 U.S. 83, 100 S. Ct. 2547, 65 L. Ed. 2d 619 (1980).

[22]Simmons v. U.S., 390 U.S. 377, 88 S. Ct. 967, 19 L. Ed. 2d 1247 (1968).

[23]Jones, 362 U.S. at 263–64.

[24]Salvucci, 448 U.S. at 90–93.

[25]448 U.S. at 85.

Congress or states could extend the right of exclusion to persons without standing in the Fourth Amendment sense.[26]

*Standing Under State Law Exclusionary Requirements.* State courts developing state law exclusionary requirements have generally, but not universally, followed the Supreme Court's Fourth Amendment model. The most dramatic deviation was that of the California Supreme Court, which in 1955 announced that all of the reasons persuading it to adopt exclusionary requirements suggested further that defendants should be able to invoke those requirements regardless of whether they had been the victims of the illegality relied upon.[27]

The California court's rejection of standing rested on several bases. First, the California court sought greater assurance of a deterrent effect than satisfied the Supreme Court, and this was provided by requiring exclusion regardless of the challenging defendant's standing. In addition, however, the California tribunal gave greater weight to judicial integrity considerations than has the Supreme Court. It conceptualized judicial integrity as broader than the Supreme Court's later analysis finding judicial integrity implicated only if judicial use of evidence encourages future violations of the underlying legal requirement. Judicial integrity, as broadly conceptualized, was compromised by use of illegally obtained evidence regardless of whether the victims of the illegality were before the court.[28]

Whatever the controlling rationale, the California approach was nullified by the 1982 amendment to the state constitution barring judicial development of exclusionary sanctions.[29]

The Louisiana courts, in contrast, continue to construe that state's Constitution as dispensing with any standing requirement regarding unreasonable searches and seizures.[30]

Several state courts have retained a standing requirement as a matter of state constitutional law but have held that it is more

---

[26]Alderman v. U.S., 394 U.S. 165, 175, 89 S. Ct. 961, 22 L. Ed. 2d 176 (1969).

[27]People v. Martin, 45 Cal. 2d 755, 290 P.2d 855 (1955).

[28]*See also* In re Lance W., 37 Cal. 3d 873, 210 Cal. Rptr. 631, 694 P.2d 744, 762 (1985) (Mosk, J., dissenting) (explaining rationale for *Martin* rule in terms of "[t]he need to deter police misconduct, the ineffectiveness of all other remedies but the exclusionary rule, and the importance of avoiding judicial participation in unlawful acts").

[29]In re Lance W., 694 P.2d at 751–52. The constitutional amendment is discussed in § 168 supra.

[30]The Louisiana Constitution's search provision specifies: "Any person adversely affected by a search or seizure conducted in violation of this Section shall have standing to raise its illegality in the appropriate court." La. Const. Art. 1, § 5. This has been construed as permitting even defendants whose privacy was not invaded by a search to challenge discovered evidence; the underlying purpose was read as maximizing the deterrent effect of the exclusionary remedy. State

readily met than the Fourth Amendment requirement as construed by the Supreme Court. The New Jersey Supreme Court concluded that Fourth Amendment law, as construed and applied in *Rakas*, has "the potential for inconsistent and capricious application," and "will in many instances produce results contrary to commonly held and accepted expectations of privacy." It consequently held that a defendant need only assert a possessory, proprietary or participatory interest in either the area searched or the item seized in order to have standing.[31] The Vermont Supreme Court also took this approach.[32]

A few state courts retain automatic standing as a matter of state constitutional law. This has been the position of the highest courts in, among other states, Massachusetts[33] and Pennsylvania.[34] Most state courts, however, have followed the Supreme Court's lead and rejected automatic standing.[35]

Disagreement with the Supreme Court's Fourth Amendment case law, such as *Rakas*, may be best addressed as a matter of the substantive law triggering the exclusionary sanction rather than exclusionary rule law. If the result in *Rakas* is inappropriate, the blame may be attributable to the Court's definition of protected privacy rather than the exclusionary rule law that links the ability to challenge evidence to whether the defendant's privacy was violated.

---

v. Culotta, 343 So. 2d 977 (La. 1976). *Accord* State v. Cunningham, 88 So. 3d 1196, 1200–01 (La. Ct. App. 4th Cir. 2012).

[31]State v. Alston, 88 N.J. 211, 440 A.2d 1311, 1319 (1981), reaffirmed in State v. Carvajal, 202 N.J. 214, 996 A.2d 1029, 1034 (2010).

The major significance of this approach is that a defendant may challenge evidence based on a "participatory" interest in the place or property. Under State v. Bruns, 172 N.J. 40, 796 A.2d 226, 235–36 (2002), this requires in the context of a physical item a culpable role in the criminal activity generating and using the item and some contemporary connection between the defendant and the person from whom it was obtained. Bruns, 796 A.2d. at 237.

[32]State v. Wood, 148 Vt. 479, 536 A.2d 902, 908 (1987).

[33]Com. v. Sell, 504 Pa. 46, 470 A.2d 457 (1983). *Accord* Com. v. Bostick, 2008 PA Super 233, 958 A.2d 543, 552 (2008).

[34]Com. v. Amendola, 406 Mass. 592, 550 N.E.2d 121, 126 (1990). *Accord* Com. v. Mubdi, 456 Mass. 385, 923 N.E.2d 1004, 1011–14 (2010). Automatic standing was also adopted in and State v. Settle, 122 N.H. 214, 447 A.2d 1284, 1286 (1982) and State v. Jones, 146 Wash. 2d 328, 45 P.3d 1062, 1064–65 (2002).

[35]State v. Davis, 283 Conn. 280, 929 A.2d 278, 302–03 (2007) (joining majority of states considering the matter and rejecting automatic standing). *See, e.g.*, State v. Juarez, 203 Ariz. 441, 55 P.3d 784, 786–90 (Ct. App. Div. 1 2002) (refusing to adopt automatic standing as a matter of state constitutional law); State v. Taua, 98 Haw. 426, 49 P.3d 1227, 1239–41 (2002) (same).

## § 176    Scope of exclusion: (a) Evidence acquired as a result of illegality ("fruit of the poisonous tree")[1]

Some—but not all—prohibitions against the use of improperly obtained evidence extend beyond evidence obtained as an immediate and direct result of the impropriety. Many, following the "fruit of the poisonous tree" aspect of the Fourth Amendment exclusionary rule, demand the exclusion of all derivative evidence—evidence obtained as a factual result of the impropriety—unless an exception to the exclusionary demand applies. The relationship between this approach and what is often regarded as the separate "independent source" rule presents a continuing problem discussed in the next section.

*Fourth Amendment "Fruit of the Poisonous Tree" Rule.* In *Silverthorne Lumber Co. v. United States,*[2] the Supreme Court construed the Fourth Amendment exclusionary rule as requiring exclusion of evidence obtained even as an indirect result of violation of defendants' Fourth Amendment rights.[3] If a defendant establishes a Fourth Amendment violation—a "poisonous tree"—and that evidence was obtained as a factual result of that violation—that the evidence is "fruit" of the poisonous tree—the defendant is entitled to have the evidence excluded unless the prosecution establishes the applicability of an exception to the general requirement of exclusion. American courts have generally—and arguably uncritically—accepted that other exclusionary sanctions must or at least should be similarly defined.

If a defendant establishes that law enforcement officers, who possessed adequate basis for a search, were motivated to make a second search by information obtained in a first and unreasonable search, the Supreme Court held in *Murray v. United States,*[4] the results of the second search are fruit of the initial illegality. This is so even if the second search was made pursuant to a warrant which was obtained without use of the results of the first

---

**[Section 176]**

[1]*See generally* West's Key Number Digest, Criminal Law ⚷392.39.

[2]Silverthorne Lumber Co. v. U.S., 251 U.S. 385, 40 S. Ct. 182, 64 L. Ed. 319 (1920).

[3]Silverthorn Lumber Co., 251 U.S. at 392 (where documents were suppressed as obtained in an unreasonable search and returned to petitioners, Government could not use information obtained from those documents to subpoena them from petitioners because the essence of the Fourth Amendment "is that not merely evidence [unreasonably] acquired shall not be used before the Court but that it shall not be used at all"). *See also* Wong Sun v. U.S., 371 U.S. 471, 484–91, 83 S. Ct. 407, 9 L. Ed. 2d 441 (1963) (Fourth Amendment requires exclusion not only of physical, tangible materials obtained during or as a "direct" result of an unreasonable search but also evidence that as a consequence of the search the defendant made incriminating oral admissions).

[4]Murray v. U.S., 487 U.S. 533, 108 S. Ct. 2529, 101 L. Ed. 2d 472 (1988).

and unreasonable search. The challenged evidence nevertheless is a result or fruit of the first and unreasonable search.[5]

Generally, the taint flows only forward and renders inadmissible only that evidence obtained after, and as a factual consequence of, the unreasonable search. Moreover, part of a search may be reasonable and other parts may be unreasonable. Officers searching pursuant to a valid search warrant, for example, may search within the terms of the warrant and discover and seize some evidence. But at various times, they may exceed the scope of search authorized by the warrant and during some of these transgressions they may find and seize other evidence. Usually, only that evidence located and seized while the officers were engaged in the unreasonable aspects of the search, that is, while they were acting beyond the authority of the warrant, is tainted by the officers' improper action and thus rendered inadmissible.[6]

If evidence was acquired by exploiting illegality only in the sense that the illegality prevented illegal removal or destruction of the evidence, exclusion is not required. The Fourth Amendment position, the Supreme Court's discussion in *Segura v. United States*[7] suggests, is based on the policy position that defendants not be permitted to benefit from the loss of opportunities to engage in conduct barred by law.[8]

Amazingly, the Fourth Amendment fruit of the poisonous tree rule developed with little discussion of its rationale or justification. In 1984, however, the Supreme Court retrospectively explained the "core rationale" for the rule in terms of standard Fourth Amendment exclusionary sanction analysis: Although the fruit of the poisonous tree rule increases the cost of the exclusionary sanction, that cost is justified by the need to provide sufficient deterrence assuring adequate disincentive for the prohib-

---

[5]Murray, 487 U.S. at 543.

[6]Waller v. Georgia, 467 U.S. 39, 104 S. Ct. 2210, 81 L. Ed. 2d 31 (1984) (where officers executing valid search warrant seized more items than was permissible, Fourth Amendment required only suppression of those items improperly seized).

[7]Segura v. U.S., 468 U.S. 796, 104 S. Ct. 3380, 82 L. Ed. 2d 599 (1984).

[8]Segura, 468 U.S. at 816. *Segura* suggested that this result might be required by attenuation of taint analysis: If the defendants had in fact been able to engage in illegal efforts to remove or destroy the property, those efforts would have attenuated the taint of the initial illegality and rendered the evidence admissible. Since those efforts if taken could not have legitimately created a right to exclusion, a loss of the opportunity to engage in those efforts should not suffice to render otherwise admissible evidence unavailable to the prosecution. *Accord* U.S. v. Blackwell, 416 F.3d 631, 633 (7th Cir. 2005) (speculation that guns might have been hidden during delay to obtain a warrant did not render inevitable discovery rule inapplicable); Hughes v. Com., 87 S.W.3d 850, 853 (Ky. 2002) (rejecting argument that but for illegal search leading to body, defendant might have been able to remove and conceal body).

ited conduct. Only by threatening officers with the inadmissibility of the indirect as well as the direct results of their Fourth Amendment transgressions can adequate incentive for avoiding those transgressions be provided.[9]

*Initial Requirement of "But For" Causation.* As a consequence of the fruit of the poisonous tree rule, under exclusionary rules generally a defendant must show both an illegality sufficient to trigger the exclusionary sanction and a causal relationship between that illegality and the prosecution's possession of the evidence challenged. If but only if that relationship is shown does attention turn to whether the prosecution can show that the evidence is nevertheless admissible because of the nature of that relationship (attenuation of taint)[10] or despite that relationship (inevitable discovery).[11]

Fourth Amendment case law indicates that the defendant must show that "but for" the illegality, prosecution authorities would not have acquired the challenge evidence.[12] The major question is whether this should be applied literally, so that causation is shown if the defendant demonstrates that prosecution authorities would not have gained possession of the evidence precisely when and as they did but for the illegality.[13]

The matter is put quite effectively by the search warrant "no-knock" cases, in which the only Fourth Amendment violation is the officers' failure to announce their authority to enter and to permit the occupants to admit them. Often the evidence suggests

---

[9]Nix v. Williams, 467 U.S. 431, 442–43, 104 S. Ct. 2501, 81 L. Ed. 2d 377 (1984).

[10]See § 179 infra.

[11]See § 181 infra.

[12]*E.g.*, Wong Sun v. U.S., 371 U.S. 471, 487, 83 S. Ct. 407, 9 L. Ed. 2d 441 (1963) (defendant's showing that evidence "would not have come to light but for the illegal actions of the police" turns attention to whether the evidence "has been come at by exploitation of that illegality or instead by means sufficiently distinguishable to be purged of the primary taint"). *Accord* Segura v. U.S., 468 U.S. 796, 816, 104 S. Ct. 3380, 82 L. Ed. 2d 599 (1984) (referring to whether officers' actions "could be considered the 'but for' cause for discovery of the evidence"); Williams, 467 U.S. at 443 (evidence showed that statement obtained in violation of Sixth Amendment in fact led police to victim's body, which pre-

sented question of whether inevitable discovery nevertheless rendered evidence of body admissible).

[13]In U.S. v. Ramirez, 91 F.3d 1297 (9th Cir. 1996), the court determined that during an entry to execute a warrant officers had violated the Fourth Amendment by unnecessarily breaking the glass in a window. It summarily concluded that the evidence showed necessary but for causation between the Fourth Amendment violation and later acquisition of evidence during the execution of the warrant. 91 F.3d at 1302. The Supreme Court found no Fourth Amendment violation, and commented that it need not decide "whether . . . there was sufficient causal relationship between the breaking of the window and the discovery of the [evidence] to warrant suppression of the evidence." U.S. v. Ramirez, 523 U.S. 65, 71 n.3, 118 S. Ct. 992, 140 L. Ed. 2d 191 (1998).

that the unreasonable unannounced entry caused the officers to discover and seize the challenged evidence only slightly sooner than would have been the case had they paused to make a proper entry.

In *Hudson v. Michigan*,[14] discussed substantively in Section 166, all nine members of the Court agreed that a violation of the Fourth Amendment requires exclusion of evidence only if the violation was a but-for cause of obtaining the evidence. The Justices split 5 to 4—or perhaps 4 to 5—on whether the necessary but-for causality exists in a "no knock" search warrant entry situation.[15] A clear majority, however, took the view that in these cases either there is no but-for causality or the but-for causality that exists necessarily means the taint of the violation is attenuated.[16]

*Hudson*, then, confirmed that under the Fourth Amendment exclusionary rule "but for" causation is required. It also made

---

[14]Hudson v. Michigan, 547 U.S. 586, 126 S. Ct. 2159, 165 L. Ed. 2d 56 (2006).

[15]Justice Scalia's opinion for the Court clearly stated that but-for causation was lacking. Hudson, 547 U.S. at 591 (but-for causality lacking because even if they had not made unconstitutional no knock entry "the police would have executed the warrant they had obtained, and would have discovered the gun and drugs inside the house"). Justice Breyer, writing for the four dissenters, clearly concluded but-for causation existed. He explained that the unconstitutional entry "was a necessary condition of their presence in [the] home; and their presence in [the] home was a necessary condition of their finding and seizing the evidence." Further, "their discovery of evidence in [the] home was a readily foreseeable consequence of their entry and their unlawful presence within the home." Consequently, and "taking causation as it is commonly understood in the law," the unreasonable manner of entry was a but-for cause of obtaining the evidence. 547 U.S. at 615 (Breyer, J., dissenting).

Justice Kennedy purported to join the majority opinion's analysis of but-for causation. He inconsistently, however, explicitly wrote that in his view "the causal link between a viola-

tion of the knock-and-announce requirement and a later search is too attenuated to allow suppression," For this reason, he concluded, the violation "cannot properly be described as having caused the discovery of evidence." 548 U.S. at 603–04 (Kennedy, J., joining parts I through III of Court's opinion and concurring in the judgment). Despite his having joined Justice Scalia's reasoning that but-for causation was lacking, then, he appeared to view the situation as one involving a but-for causal relationship that necessarily established that the taint of the violation was attenuated.

[16]Professor Alschuler has argued that despite conventional wisdom and the justices' assertions, the Court generally has not required a but-for causal link between a constitutional violation and acquisition of the challenged evidence. Alschuler, The Exclusionary Rule and Causation: Hudson v. Michigan and its Ancestors, 93 Iowa L. Rev. 1741, 1745 (2008). Sound Fourth Amendment policy, he suggested, means that the proper inquiry would be "whether the government's illegal conduct facilitated the discovery of evidence either by reducing the labor required to make this discovery or by improving the odds of its occurrence." Alschuler, The Exclusionary Rule and Causation, 93 Iowa L. Rev. at 1776.

clear the justices disagree on precisely what this requires and thus when it does not exist.

*Limits on Excludable "Fruit" Under Fourth Amendment Law.* Insofar as Fourth Amendment law requires exclusion of fruit of the poisonous tree, there is one indication that at least as applied to some situations the fruits doctrine is qualified by some objective limits on those fruit subject to the exclusionary requirement.

When law enforcement officers violate a defendant's Fourth Amendment rights by unreasonably entering his home to there make an otherwise proper arrest of him, the Supreme Court held in *New York v. Harris*,[17] a defendant simply cannot challenge the admissibility of statements made by him subsequent to that arrest and after he was removed from his home. This is apparently the case regardless of the strength of his claim that such a statement was caused by the illegal entry and without the prosecution needing to establish the applicability of any exception to the exclusionary requirement.

*Harris* reflects the Court's conclusion that in the specific context there presented, an adequate balance of deterrence expectations and costs requires that defendants be permitted to challenge the admissibility of some fruits of an unreasonable entry—statements made as a result of that entry and while the defendant is still being detained in the unreasonably entered home. Permitting such defendants' to challenge the admissibility of statements obtained later, however, would trigger loss-of-evidence and increased-litigation costs exceeding whatever marginal deterrence against unreasonable entries of homes might be expected.

Under *Harris*, the fruit of the poisonous tree doctrine is clearly not sacrosanct, even in the Fourth Amendment context. The definition of challengeable fruit may be limited, where that can be done with reasonable clarity and when the characteristics of the type of situation at issue suggest such action as a means of achieving optimum balance between the deterrent benefits and costs of exclusion.

*Harris* may have been superseded by *Hudson v. Michigan*,[18] discussed in Section 166. *Hudson* held that a Fourth Amendment violation consisting of making an otherwise permissible entry of premises to execute a valid search warrant but in noncompliance with Fourth Amendment "knock and announce" requirements would simply not invoke the constitutional exclusionary remedy. Perhaps *Harris*-type entry without a warrant will now similarly not constitute a poisonous tree triggering the exclusionary rule.

---

[17]New York v. Harris, 495 U.S. 14, 110 S. Ct. 1640, 109 L. Ed. 2d 13 (1990).

[18]Hudson v. Michigan, 547 U.S. 586, 126 S. Ct. 2159, 165 L. Ed. 2d 56 (2006).

Most likely, however, the possibility that seeking a warrant would prevent the entry entirely means that *Harris* remains effective.

*Applicability of "Fruits" Rule to Other Exclusionary Requirements.* In a series of cases leading up to *United State v. Patane*,[19] the Supreme Court made clear that the fruit of the poisonous tree rule as developed in Fourth Amendment case law is not a necessary concomitant of a federal constitutional exclusionary requirement.

In *Patane*, a split majority of the Court held that the exclusionary remedy for a violation of *Miranda v. Arizona*,[20] although a Fifth Amendment matter, required only the exclusion of the out-of-court statement obtained by interrogation conducted in violation of the requirements of *Miranda*. Physical evidence,[21] testimony of witnesses,[22] and subsequent statements by the suspect[23] are not rendered inadmissible simply because they were obtained as a result of the excluded statement.[24]

The Justices split in *Patane* over whether the nature of the *Miranda* requirements were such that the *Miranda* exclusionary rule conceptually permitted a fruit of the poisonous tree aspect. Justice Thomas's plurality opinion announcing the judgment rested heavily upon his conclusion that the *Miranda* requirements were not direct constitutional constraints on the police and for this reason simply did not conceptually permit an exclusionary penalty extending to derivative evidence. Thus, these justices reasoned, the Court need not—and in fact could not—reach whether excluding derivative evidence would be sound constitutional policy.[25] Justice Kennedy's ground for concurring in the result reached by the plurality relied less on this rationale than on a judgment that the evidence at issue—physical items obtained by using information in an inadmissible statement— was reliable and particularly useful to the accurate resolution of contested criminal cases.[26]

A majority of the *Patane* Court, then, appeared to agree that that the nature of the *Miranda* exclusionary sanction did not preclude developing that sanction as extending to fruit of *Miranda* violations. They agreed that whether the *Miranda* federal constitutional exclusionary requirement should and would extend

---

[19]U.S. v. Patane, 542 U.S. 630, 124 S. Ct. 2620, 159 L. Ed. 2d 667 (2004).

[20]Miranda v. Arizona, 384 U.S. 436, 86 S. Ct. 1602, 16 L. Ed. 2d 694 (1966).

[21]Patane, 542 U.S. at 642.

[22]Michigan v. Tucker, 417 U.S. 433, 94 S. Ct. 2357, 41 L. Ed. 2d 182 (1974).

[23]Oregon v. Elstad, 470 U.S. 298, 105 S. Ct. 1285, 84 L. Ed. 2d 222 (1985).

[24]See generally § 159 supra.

[25]Patane, 542 U.S. at 641.

[26]542 U.S. at 644–45 (Kennedy, J., concurring in the judgment).

to fruit of the poisonous tree depended on balancing the value of excluding fruit as a means of deterring conduct violating the constitutional provision against the costs of doing so.[27] That majority disagreed on how the balancing should come out. Justice Kennedy, writing for himself and Justice O'Connor, concluded that "[i]n light of the important probative value of reliable physical evidence, it is doubtful that exclusion can be justified by a deterrence rationale sensitive to both law enforcement interests and a suspect's rights during an in-custody interrogation."[28] Justice Souter, writing for himself and Justices Stevens and Ginsburg, concluded that the need to avoid creating an incentive for police to ignore the *Miranda* requirements by permitting use of derivative evidence is worth the price it involves.[29]

Shortly before deciding *Patane*, the Supreme Court remanded *Fellers v. United States*[30] for a determination whether a showing that officers elicited a statement from Fellers in violation of his Sixth Amendment right to counsel requires suppression of later statements "on the ground that they were fruits of previous questioning conducted in violation of the Sixth Amendment . . . ."[31] The court of appeals held that the rationale for not applying a fruits rule to a violation of the *Miranda* Fifth Amendment requirements also controlled where the offered tree was poisoned by a violation of the Sixth Amendment.[32]

As the Court's case law culminating in *Patane* recognizes, whether an exclusionary requirement properly extends to derivative evidence or fruits should turn on whether so extending it will serve the purposes of the exclusionary requirement well enough to justify the cost paid by the increased loss of reliable evidence. A major consideration, of course, is the importance of legal requirement being enforced. Where an exclusionary sanction applies to violation of a nonconstitutional legal requirement, the nonconstitutional nature of that legal requirement suggests its respect is somewhat less important and thus argues against defining the sanction as extending to derivative evidence.[33]

---

[27]542 U.S. at 645 (Kennedy, J., joined by O'Connor, J., concurring in the judgment), 645 (Souter, J., joined by Stevens and Ginsburg, J.J., dissenting).

[28]542 U.S. at 645 (Kennedy, J., concurring in the judgment).

[29]542 U.S. at 645–46 (Stevens J., dissenting).

[30]Fellers v. U.S., 540 U.S. 519, 124 S. Ct. 1019, 157 L. Ed. 2d 1016 (2004).

[31]Fellers, 540 U.S. at 525.

[32]U.S. v. Fellers, 397 F.3d 1090 (8th Cir. 2005).

[33]*See* U.S. v. Tedford, 875 F.2d 446, 451 (5th Cir. 1989) (fruit of the poisonous tree rule is not invoked

## § 177    Scope of exclusion: (b) Evidence with an "independent source"

In *Silverthorne Lumber Co. v. United States*,[1] Justice Holmes announced for the Supreme Court that facts acquired in violation of the Fourth Amendment do not, for that reason, "become sacred and inaccessible." "If," he continued, "knowledge of them is gained from an independent source they may be proved like any others . . . ."[2] The "independent source" rule or "concept," based on this comment in *Silverthorne Lumber Co.*, has been a source of some uncertainty in exclusionary rule analysis. Among the problems has been distinguishing independent source from "inevitable discovery" as discussed in Section 181[3]

In *Murray v. United States*,[4] the Supreme Court emphasized that the independent source "concept" has been used in two distinguishable ways. Justice Holmes' *Silverthorne Lumber Co.* dictum used it to describe situations in which the prosecution has both tainted and untainted evidence of a particular fact and offers only the untainted evidence to prove that fact.[5] For example, police might improperly arrest X, question him, and obtain from him an admission to being in the vicinity of V's home the night it was burglarized. But an alert citizen might report to police seeing X in V's neighborhood on the night of the break-in. The fact that the prosecution obtained inadmissible evidence indicating X's presence near the scene of the offense would not bar it from proving his presence, because it could do so by evidence with an "independence source," that is, evidence obtained in a manner not factually related to the improper arrest. This, *Murray* indicated, was the more specific and most important use of the term independent source.

The other and more general use of the term, *Murray* continued, describes situations in which all of the prosecution's evidence of a particular fact is untainted by its improper activity.[6] For example, police might improperly arrest X and question him, but X may not reveal anything about the location of his victim's body. A citizen, however, may report to police that she observed X hide a body in a particular location; police following up on this information might then discover the body. The prosecution's evidence

---

when the exclusionary sanction is one triggered by a nonconstitutional requirement of the Federal Rules of Criminal Procedure).

**[Section 177]**

[1]Silverthorne Lumber Co. v. U.S., 251 U.S. 385, 40 S. Ct. 182, 64 L. Ed. 319 (1920).

[2]Silverthorne Lumber Co., 251 U.S. at 392.

[3]See § 181 infra.

[4]Murray v. U.S., 487 U.S. 533, 108 S. Ct. 2529, 101 L. Ed. 2d 472 (1988).

[5]Murray, 487 U.S. at 538.

[6]487 U.S. at 537–38.

regarding the body is admissible despite the improper arrest of X because that evidence has an independent source.

Conceptually, the *Murray* discussion makes clear, "independent source" is simply a label reflecting a conclusion that particular challenged evidence was not obtained in a manner causally related to the Fourth Amendment violation. The rule or— "concept"—merely describes several ways in which the prosecution can argue that a defendant seeking to invoke the exclusionary rule has not established the necessary causal link between the triggering illegality and the obtaining of the challenged evidence.[7]

In *United States v. Wade*,[8] however, the Supreme Court addressed the situation in which the prosecution offers a witness to make an in-court identification, the defendant shows the witness identified the defendant at a lineup conducted in violation of the defendant's Sixth Amendment right to counsel, and the prosecution argues the witness's observation of the crime is an independent source for the offered testimony. To prevail, the Court made clear, the prosecution must shoulder the burden of proof and that burden is clear and convincing evidence.[9] *Wade* may reflect the Court's view that independent source analysis in the lineup/eyewitness context presents unique risks of inaccurate application and this justifies—in this context—placement of the burden on the prosecution and increasing that burden to clear and convincing evidence.

Some courts uncritically place the burden of proof regarding independent source generally on the prosecution[10] without considering the tension between that position and a defendant's apparent burden of establishing that challenged evidence is the fruit of the conduct relied upon as the poisonous tree. Others require the defendant to make some sort of preliminary showing of causation, after which the prosecution has the burden of establishing that

---

[7]State v. Poaipuni, 98 Haw. 387, 49 P.3d 353, 359 (2002) ("[a]lthough we have characterized the independent source doctrine as an 'exception' to the exclusionary rule, it is, in essence, simply a corollary of the fruit of the poisonous tree doctrine").

[8]U.S. v. Wade, 388 U.S. 218, 87 S. Ct. 1926, 18 L. Ed. 2d 1149 (1967).

[9]Wade, 388 U.S. at 242.

[10]*E.g.*, U.S. v. Forbes, 528 F.3d 1273, 1279 (10th Cir. 2008) ("The government bears the burden of showing, by a preponderance of the evidence, that there is truly an independent source for the challenged evidence."); U.S. v. Alvarez-Manzo, 570 F.3d 1070, 1077 (8th Cir. 2009) ("to purge the taint, *i.e.* prevent the application of the 'fruit of the poisonous tree' doctrine, the government bears the burden of demonstrating that the voluntary consent was an independent, lawful cause of the search").

an independent source in some sense negates this preliminary showing.[11]

Courts have been particularly troubled by the problems presented where officers have acted improperly but the prosecution relies upon evidence obtained in the execution of a later search warrant. When can a subsequently-issued warrant as an independent source of the challenged evidence? If the warrant is obtained without disclosing to the magistrate any information not derived from the illegality but the officers were motivated to seek the warrant because of that illegality, *Murray* made clear, the warrant could not constitute an independent source.[12] Suppose the information derived from the illegality is submitted to the magistrate but it is accompanied by other untainted information itself sufficient to support the issuance of the warrant? *Murray* suggests the warrant can be an independent source only if the tainted information did not nevertheless influence the magistrate's decision to issue the warrant.[13] The lower courts, however, have eschewed any inquiry into the issuing magistrate's decision making. Under this approach, a warrant can constitute an independent source of evidence sized under it if there was sufficient untainted information submitted to the magistrate to support issuance of the warrant.[14]

_____

[11]State v. Johnson, 335 Or. 511, 73 P.3d 282, 286–87 (2003), for example, adopted the approach of what it described as that of some federal courts, under which the defendant must first establish a "factual nexus" between the unlawful police conduct and the challenged evidence. This nexus must include, at a minimum, a "but-for" relationship. Then the burden of proof shifts to the prosecution to show that the unlawful conduct has not tainted the evidence because the evidence was discovered through independent means. *Accord* State v. Cardenas, 143 Idaho 903, 155 P.3d 704, 709–10 (Ct. App. 2006).

[12]See § 176 supra.

[13]Murray v. U.S., 487 U.S. 533, 542, 108 S. Ct. 2529, 101 L. Ed. 2d 472 (1988) ("the search pursuant to warrant [would not be] in fact a genuinely independent source of the information and tangible evidence at issue . . . if information obtained during [the earlier illegal] entry was presented to the

Magistrate *and affected his decision to issue the warrant*") (emphasis supplied).

[14]*E.g.*, U.S. v. Jenkins, 396 F.3d 751, 758 (6th Cir. 2005) (if the untrained information is sufficient to support the warrant, the tainted information will not have affected the magistrate's decision "in a substantive, meaningful way" as is required to bar reliance on the warrant as an independent source); Com. v. Tyree, 455 Mass. 676, 919 N.E.2d 660, 676–77 (2010) ("Evidence obtained during a search pursuant to a warrant that was issued after an earlier illegal entry and search is admissible as long as the affidavit in support of the application for a search warrant contains information sufficient to establish probable cause to search the premises 'apart from' observations made during the initial illegal entry and search."). *Accord, e.g.*, U.S. v. Swope, 542 F.3d 609, 614 (8th Cir. 2008); State v. Spring, 128 Wash. App. 398, 115 P.3d 1052, 1055 (Div. 1 2005) (Despite some language in the

## § 178   Effect of illegality upon "jurisdiction" over criminal defendants and exclusion of "identity"

The very presence of many criminal defendants before trial courts could be regarded as the "fruit" of earlier official illegalities and hence in some way tainted by that activity. This is particularly so when the illegality consist of improper arrests, in the absence of which the defendants would almost certainly have never been apprehended. Nevertheless, there is agreement that ordinary illegality in an investigation does not deprive the trial court of "jurisdiction" in any sense or otherwise interfere with the court's power to proceed with the trial. Thus it does not provide a basis for a motion to dismiss the charges or for other relief which automatically ends the proceedings.[1]

As a matter of federal constitutional law, the Supreme Court has held since *Ker v. Illinois*,[2] decided in 1886, that there is no federal constitutional bar to a court exercising jurisdiction over the person of a criminal defendant regardless of manner in which the presence of the person was obtained. After this was reaffirmed in *Frisbie v. Collins*,[3] it became widely-called the *Ker-Frisbie* rule.

---

opinion, *Murray* did not change prior law involving no inquiry into magistrate's actual motivation).

A New Mexico court adopted a somewhat different approach. State v. Trudelle, 142 N.M. 18, 2007-NMCA-066, 162 P.3d 173 (Ct. App. 2007) ("under Article II, Section 10 of the New Mexico Constitution, a judge may not validate illegal police conduct by issuing a warrant that contains tainted information, even if the judge makes a notation that the warrant would have issued without the tainted information").

**[Section 178]**

[1]The Supreme Court has observed that "[it] may some day be presented with a situation in which the conduct of law enforcement agents is so outrageous that due process principles would absolutely bar the government from invoking judicial processes to obtain a conviction . . . ." U.S. v. Russell, 411 U.S. 423, 431, 93 S. Ct. 1637, 36 L. Ed. 2d 366 (1973). The Second Circuit has indicated that outrageous illegality in bringing a defendant into the jurisdiction may be such

a situation. U.S. v. Toscanino, 500 F.2d 267 (2d Cir. 1974). Whether in some situations due process as construed in *Toscanino* may require dismissal remains unclear. *See generally* U.S. v. Best, 304 F.3d 308, 312 (3d Cir. 2002) (Supreme Court's decisions give reason to doubt soundness of *Toscanino*, even on its "flagrant facts"). *Compare* Sneed v. State, 872 S.W.2d 930, 937 (Tenn. Crim. App. 1993) ("outrageous conduct by Tennessee officials in willful disregard of our extradition law violates due process and, in our view, suspends the jurisdictional authority of our courts in the criminal prosecution," and remanding for hearing on whether defendant can support claim).

[2]Ker v. People of State of Illinois, 119 U.S. 436, 7 S. Ct. 225, 30 L. Ed. 421 (1886).

[3]Frisbie v. Collins, 342 U.S. 519, 72 S. Ct. 509, 96 L. Ed. 541 (1952). *See also* U. S. v. Crews, 445 U.S. 463, 474, 100 S. Ct. 1244, 63 L. Ed. 2d 537 (1980) (illegally arrested defendant cannot claim that his presence at trial was the "suppressible 'fruit' " of his arrest).

The *Ker* approach was reaf-

In *United States v. Blue*,[4] the Court explained why this was not changed by the Court's commitment in *Mapp v. Ohio*[5] and its progeny to exclusionary sanctions as the primary means of implementing many federal constitutional rights:

> Our numerous precedents ordering the exclusion of . . . illegally obtained evidence assume implicitly that the remedy does not extend to barring the prosecution altogether. So drastic a step might marginally advance some of the ends served by exclusionary rules, but it would also increase to an intolerable degree interference with the public interest in having the guilty brought to book.[6]

That interference, of course, would be caused by depriving the prosecution of all possibility of convicting the defendant. Exclusionary sanctions, where applied, always leave open at least the theoretical possibility that the defendant can be convicted by evidence with an independent source.

Reluctance to read exclusionary sanctions as depriving courts of the power to proceed against defendants may affect analysis of other exclusionary sanction issues. In *United States v. Crews*,[7] for example, the victim made an in-court identification of the defendant, who had been illegally arrested. The Court of Appeals held that the defendant's presence at trial had been used by the prosecution in presenting that testimony; the witness testified that she was comparing her memory of the perpetrator with the defendant's appearance, with which she was familiar because she observed him in the courtroom, and on that basis she concluded that he was the perpetrator. This constituted an impermissible evidentiary use of the fruits of the illegal arrest, the Court of Appeals concluded.

Five members of the Supreme Court, however, rejected this approach and characterized Crews' argument as precluded by *Ker*

---

firmed in U.S. v. Alvarez-Machain, 504 U.S. 655, 660–662, 112 S. Ct. 2188, 119 L. Ed. 2d 441 (1992), leaving open the possibility that the federal courts may be without jurisdiction of a defendant brought into the county in violation of treaty provisions. Alvarez-Machain failed to persuade the Court that his abduction in Mexico and transportation into the United States was a violation of treaty. *Alvarez-Machain*, 504 U.S. at 669–70. *See generally* U.S. v. Noriega, 117 F.3d 1206, 1213 (11th Cir. 1997) ("Under *Alvarez-Machain*, to prevail on an extradition treaty claim, a defendant must demonstrate, by reference to the express language of a treaty and/or the established practice thereunder, that the United States affirmatively agreed not to seize foreign nationals from the territory of its treaty partner. Noriega has not carried this burden, and therefore, his claim fails.").

[4]U.S. v. Blue, 384 U.S. 251, 86 S. Ct. 1416, 16 L. Ed. 2d 510 (1966).

[5]Mapp v. Ohio, 367 U.S. 643, 81 S. Ct. 1684, 6 L. Ed. 2d 1081 (1961).

[6]Blue, 384 U.S. at 255.

[7]U. S. v. Crews, 445 U.S. 463, 100 S. Ct. 1244, 63 L. Ed. 2d 537 (1980).

and its progeny.[8] A holding that a defendant's face can be considered suppressible evidence, Justice White explained, "would be tantamount to holding that an illegal arrest effectively insulates one from conviction for any crime where an in-court identification is essential." This, he concluded, was inconsistent with the rationale of *Ker's* successors.[9]

A majority of the Court is strongly committed to the proposition that federal constitutional exclusionary sanctions should not, directly or indirectly, be applied or expanded to completely bar criminal proceedings.

Four years after *Crews*, the Court in *I.N.S. v. Lopez-Mendoza*,[10] and without discussing *Crews*, added:

> The "body" or identity of a defendant or respondent in a criminal or civil proceeding is never itself suppressible as a fruit of an unlawful arrest, even if it is conceded that an unlawful arrest, search, or interrogation occurred.[11]

State courts have adopted the *Ker-Frisbie* approach that illegality in the investigation and development of evidence does not affect the jurisdiction of the courts over the defendant or the prosecution. It does not require or even permit dismissal of the prosecution.[12] Exclusionary sanctions, in other words, are no more than evidence rules that affect the admissibility of certain evidence.

One isolated judicial defense of the position that an unlawful arrest should fatally taint the jurisdiction of the trial court was

---

[8]Crews, 445 U.S. at 477 (White, J., concurring in the result) (joined by The Chief Justice and Rehnquist, J.); 445 U.S. at 477. (Powell, J., concurring in part, joined by Blackmun, J.). Justice Marshall did not participate in the case.

[9]445 U.S. at 478, relying on *Frisbie v. Collins*.

[10]I.N.S. v. Lopez-Mendoza, 468 U.S. 1032, 104 S. Ct. 3479, 82 L. Ed. 2d 778 (1984).

[11]Lopez-Mendoza, 468 U.S. at 1039–40.

[12]E.g., State v. Murphy, 358 S.W.3d 126, 131 (Mo. Ct. App. S.D. 2011) ("Appellate courts have uniformly rejected arguments that because an arrest or detention was in some manner allegedly illegal, the convicting court either (1) lacked jurisdiction to try and convict the defendant, or (2) should have dismissed the charging document altogether."). *Accord* Bush v. State, 92 So. 3d 121 (Ala. Crim. App. 2009), cert. denied, (Mar. 23, 2012); Com. v. Dobbins, 594 Pa. 71, 934 A.2d 1170, 1180 (2007).

Courts have sometimes suggested that extraordinary circumstances—not present in the cases—might support or require dismissal. State v. Miller, 257 Kan. 844, 896 P.2d 1069, 1075–77 (1995) ("compelling circumstances" that might warrant dismissal of charges because of an illegal arrest not present, and thus trial court erred in dismissing prosecution because of illegality of arrest); Com. v. Jacobsen, 419 Mass. 269, 644 N.E.2d 213, 217 (1995) (circumstances showed neither "egregious misconduct" nor serious threat that defendant could not get a fair trial, and thus trial court erred in dismissing prosecution because of illegal arrest).

predicated largely upon considerations of broadly-defined judicial integrity:

> By basing the court's jurisdiction on an illegal warrantless arrest of the defendant in his home, the court legitimizes the illegal conduct which produced the arrest. Courts should not be parties to invasions of the constitutional rights of citizens.[13]

Lower courts have disagreed on the implications of *Crews* and *Lopez-Mendoza's* comment that the identify of a defendant is never suppressible fruit of an improper arrest. The New York Court of Appeals concluded that "a defendant may not invoke the fruit-of-the-poisonous-tree doctrine when the only link between improper police activity and the disputed evidence is that the police learned the defendant's name," and the Supreme Court dismissed review as improvidently granted.[14] One court, in contrast, dismissed the *Lopez-Mendoza* comment as simply restating the *Ker-Frisbie* rule that jurisdiction over a defendant is not affected.[15] Another suggested this limited a defendant's ability to challenge the admissibility of evidence the prosecution already and legally acquired on the basis that the relevance of that evidence was learned by identity-type information obtained as a result of an unconstitutional arrest.[16]

## § 179   Exceptions to exclusion: (a) Attenuation of taint

The Fourth Amendment exclusionary sanction, and most others modeled upon it, are subject to exception for evidence obtained after the "taint" of the illegality triggering the exclusionary requirement has become "attenuated." Given the nature of this exception, it applies only to "derivative" evidence that is subject to challenge initially only because it is "fruit of the poisonous tree."

This exception, unlike the "independent source" doctrine, does not rest on the lack of an actual causal link between the original illegality and the obtaining of the challenged evidence. Rather,

---

[13]State v. Smith, 131 Wis. 2d 220, 388 N.W.2d 601, 612 (1986) (Abrahamson, J., concurring).

[14]People v. Tolentino, 14 N.Y.3d 382, 900 N.Y.S.2d 708, 926 N.E.2d 1212, 1216 (2010), cert. dismissed as improvidently granted, 131 S. Ct. 1387 (2011).

[15]*Accord* State v. Maldonado-Arreaga, 772 N.W.2d 74, 79 (Minn. Ct. App. 2009) ("there is no general principle that biographical information is exempt from the exclusionary rule

[and therefore] when biographical evidence is obtained through unconstitutional governmental action and a party challenges the admissibility of the evidence, the exclusionary rule applies"); State v. Moscone, 161 N.H. 355, 13 A.3d 137, 144 (2011) ("the Court's statement that the identity of a defendant is never suppressible as the fruit of an illegal arrest is limited solely to jurisdiction").

[16]U.S. v. Fofana, 666 F.3d 985, 987–88 (6th Cir. 2012).

the exception is triggered by a demonstration that the characteristics of that causal link are such that the impact of the original illegality upon the obtaining of the evidence is sufficiently minimal that exclusion is not required despite the causal link.[1]

In *United States v. Leon*,[2] the Supreme Court explained that in the federal constitutional context, the attenuation of taint doctrine is the product of the principles underlying the federal constitutional exclusionary requirements. To some extent, it identifies those cases in which the taint upon evidence is so minimal that admitting the evidence does not compromise the integrity of the court.[3] More importantly, however:

> [T]he "dissipation of taint" concept . . . "attempts to mark the point at which the detrimental consequences of illegal police action become so attenuated that that the deterrent effect of the exclusionary rule no longer justifies its cost."[4]

The attenuation of taint qualification to the federal exclusionary requirements, of course, does not mean that other exclusionary demands must be similarly limited. Nevertheless, court have—perhaps uncritically—assumed that other exclusionary requirements extending to fruit of the poisonous tree are also qualified by similar limitations.[5]

Generalization as to what is sufficient to establish attenuation of taint is difficult.[6] Most of the Supreme Court case law applies

---

**[Section 179]**

[1]*See* Nardone v. U.S., 308 U.S. 338, 341, 60 S. Ct. 266, 84 L. Ed. 307 (1939) (although "[s]ophisticated argument" may establish a causal connection between the illegality and the challenged evidence, "such connection may have become so attenuated as to dissipate the taint"). *See also* Wong Sun v. U.S., 371 U.S. 471, 487, 83 S. Ct. 407, 9 L. Ed. 2d 441 (1963) (drawing the distinction). Maguire, Evidence of Guilt, 221 (1959), cited in *Wong Sun* as a basis for attenuation of taint, arguably failed to distinguish the attenuation notion from independent source.

[2]U.S. v. Leon, 468 U.S. 897, 104 S. Ct. 3405, 82 L. Ed. 2d 677 (1984).

[3]Leon, 468 U.S. at 911 n. 7.

[4]468 U.S. at 911, quoting Brown v. Illinois, 422 U.S. 590, 609, 95 S. Ct. 2254, 45 L. Ed. 2d 416 (1975) (Powell, J., concurring in part).

[5]For an unusual recognition that a state exclusionary requirement need not necessarily follow the federal model, see Bell v. State, 724 S.W.2d 780, 787 (Tex. Crim. App. 1986) (adopting approach of Supreme Court case law for purposes of state statutory exclusionary rule, because that case law "appears to be the best available framework" for determining whether the effect of illegality is sufficient to justify exclusion).

[6]Justice White has suggested that exclusion ought to be required if, but only if, the challenged evidence was foreseen by the officers at the time of their conduct or, in the exercise of reasonable care, should have been foreseen. Harrison v. U.S., 392 U.S. 219, 230–34, 88 S. Ct. 2008, 20 L. Ed. 2d 1047 (1968) (White, J., dissenting). If discovery of evidence was or could have been foreseen, the threat of its exclusion can be expected to discourage officers in similar situations from

the doctrine to situations in which a confession made by a defendant in custody begun in violation of the Fourth Amendment is challenged as an inadmissible fruit of the arrest. Drawing general standards from those discussions presents some difficulties. Nevertheless, there is frequent agreement[7] that whether the taint of illegality is sufficiently attenuated to render admissible evidence found as a factual result of that illegality is determined by considering three factors: (1) the temporal relationship between the illegality and the discovery of the challenged evidence;[8] (2) the number and nature of "intervening circumstances"; and (3) the purpose and flagrancy of the official misconduct.[9] Often,

---

engaging in similar conduct, no attenuation should be found, and such evidence should be excluded. But if discovery of the evidence was not and could not have been anticipated, exclusion cannot be expected to affect law enforcement conduct, attenuation should be found, and the evidence should be admitted.

Justice White's approach is, of course, conceptually true to what the Court has identified as the major principle underlying the federal constitutional exclusionary sanctions and the attenuation doctrine in particular. But accurately determining foreseeability in the varying situations presented by criminal cases may be impossible.

[7]E.g., U.S. v. Gross, 662 F.3d 393, 401–02 (6th Cir. 2011); State v. Page, 140 Idaho 841, 103 P.3d 454, 459 (2004). State v. Martin, 285 Kan. 994, 179 P.3d 457, 463 (2008); Cox v. State, 421 Md. 630, 28 A.3d 687 (2011); People v. Bradford, 15 N.Y.3d 329, 910 N.Y.S.2d 771, 937 N.E.2d 528, 531 (2010).

[8]The longer period of time between the primary illegality and obtaining the challenged evidence, the more likely it is that the taint of that illegality has become attenuated. See Rawlings v. Kentucky, 448 U.S. 98, 108–09, 100 S. Ct. 2556, 65 L. Ed. 2d 633 (1980) (45 minutes between illegal detention and making of statement was a "relatively short period of time" that might under some circumstances preclude attenuation of the taint, but

on the facts before the Court attenuation had occurred).

[9]Thus attenuation of taint is less likely to have occurred if the illegality was an extensive deviation from the underlying legal requirement. Rawlings, 448 U.S. at 110 (giving considerable weight to conclusion that the detention of the suspects to seek a search warrant was at most of uncertain Fourth Amendment acceptability). Accord Weems v. State, 167 S.W.3d 350, 363 (Tex. App. Houston 14th Dist. 2005)(improper arrest was not "flagrantly abusive" where it was made on information "not so lacking in indicia of probable cause as to render belief in [the existence of probable cause] entirely unreasonable").

Even more significant is whether the illegality was committed for the subjective purpose of seeking evidence of the sort at issue. U. S. v. Ceccolini, 435 U.S. 268, 279–80, 98 S. Ct. 1054, 55 L. Ed. 2d 268 (1978) (giving considerable weight to showing that the illegal search there was not conducted with the intent of locating evidence and, particularly, without the expectation of locating evidence of the sort at issue). Accord People v. Clay, 349 Ill. App. 3d 517, 285 Ill. Dec. 653, 812 N.E.2d 473, 480 (1st Dist. 2004) (in finding taint of arrest not attenuated, court stressed "police arrested defendant on a fishing expedition for evidence"). Compare U.S. v. Akridge, 346 F.3d 618, 628 (6th Cir. 2003) (evidence that improper search was made for evidence of drug activity argues against attenuation, but attenuation

however, this agreement provides little helpful guidance in making the final judgment. In *United States v. Ceccolini*,[10] the Court observed that "[o]bviously no mathematical weight can be assigned to any of the [relevant] factors . . . ."[11] This is an understatement.

What number and type of intervening circumstances are sufficient to attenuate a particular taint is an especially difficult question. The more intervening events, clearly, the more likely the taint is to have been attenuated. Some case law suggests that if one of the intervening circumstances involves judicial action, this is entitled to particular significance in finding attenuation.[12] A major thread running through the attenuation cases is the significance of proof that the chain of events involved a voluntary decision by someone to cooperate with investigating authorities.[13] If the decision was that of the defendant, the factor is entitled to particular weight.[14]

Some courts have characterized the third factor as the most important "because it is directly tied to the exclusionary rule's purpose—deterring police misconduct."[15] Where after an unreasonable stop an officer learns an arrest warrant exists, for example, arrests on that warrant, and as a result of that arrest obtained evidence, the taint of the stop is less likely to be attenuated if the evidence shows the stop was made for the purpose of determining whether any such warrants existed.[16]

The difficulty of applying attenuation analysis is illustrated by the Supreme Court's application of it to the situation in which

---

is suggested by evidence that police "were not specifically in search of the particular evidence sought to be suppressed in this case").

[10]U. S. v. Ceccolini, 435 U.S. 268, 98 S. Ct. 1054, 55 L. Ed. 2d 268 (1978).

[11]Ceccolini, 435 U.S. at 280.

[12]If officers during an improper detention learn that there is an outstanding judicially-issued arrest warrant for the suspect and later during the detention obtain evidence, the discovery of the warrant is likely to attenuate the taint of the initially improper detention. *E.g.*, U.S. v. Johnson, 383 F.3d 538, 545–46 (7th Cir. 2004). *Accord* State v. Page, 140 Idaho 841, 103 P.3d 454, 460 (2004) (stressing that attenuation would not occur if officer learned of warrant only after evidence was obtained).

[13]*E.g.*, People v. Medina, 110 Cal. App. 4th 171, 1 Cal. Rptr. 3d 546, 551 (2d Dist. 2003) (attenuation sufficient to dissipate taint requires "at least an intervening independent act by the defendant or a third party").

[14]In *Wong Sun*, for example, the Court's conclusion that Wong Sun's confession was admissible appeared to turn in large part upon the Court's conclusion that his decision to confess was voluntary. Wong Sun v. U.S., 371 U.S. 471, 491, 83 S. Ct. 407, 9 L. Ed. 2d 441 (1963).

[15]State v. Gorup, 279 Neb. 841, 782 N.W.2d 16, 33 (2010) (agreeing with some federal courts).

[16]State v. Grayson, 336 S.W.3d 138, 148 (Mo. 2011) ("Such a fishing expedition is precisely the sort of overreaching police behavior that the exclusionary rule is intended to deter.")

the challenged evidence consists of the in-court testimony of a witness located by exploitation of information obtained as a result of an improper search or seizure. In *Ceccolini*, the Court refused to adopt a per se rule under which such evidence could never be the excludable fruit of a Fourth Amendment violation.[17] But it did hold that the attenuation analysis should be applied in such cases in a manner appropriately accommodated to the situation. When a criminal defendant seeks suppression of live-witness testimony, "a closer, more direct link between the illegality and that kind of testimony is required," as compared to cases in which exclusion of other kinds of evidence is sought.[18] This apparently means that attenuation is to be more readily found, given that the evidence at issue—eyewitness testimony—is of exceptional importance and therefore exclusion is appropriate only if the facts show a particularly close relationship between the illegality and discovery of the evidence.

In *Ceccolini*-type cases as in other potential attenuation situations, the case for attenuation is dramatically strengthened by a showing of an intervening autonomous decision. The willingness—or eagerness—of the witness to testify is an important consideration.[19]

The Supreme Court in *Hudson v. Michigan*,[20] discussed substantively in section 166, introduced a new aspect of attenuation of taint analysis under Fourth Amendment law. *Hudson* acknowledged that attenuation of taint can occur "when the causal connection is remote." It then added:

> Attenuation also occurs when, even given a direct causal connection, the interest protected by the constitutional guarantee that has been violated would not be served by suppression of the evidence obtained.[21]

This, of course, suggests that attenuation may occur in some situations without reference to the characteristics of the causal link between the Fourth Amendment violation and acquisition of the challenged evidence.

---

[17]U. S. v. Ceccolini, 435 U.S. 268, 274–75, 98 S. Ct. 1054, 55 L. Ed. 2d 268 (1978).

[18]Ceccolini, 435 U.S. at 278. *Accord* U.S. v. Akridge, 346 F.3d 618, 628 (6th Cir. 2003).

[19]*See* Akridge, 346 F.3d at 626 (stressing "the degree of free will exercised by the witness," determined by among other factors whether the more direct fruits of the illegality were used in questioning the witness). *Accord* U.S. v. Wipf, 397 F.3d 677, 684 (8th Cir. 2005) (witness "testified willingly"). Consent will attenuate the taint of an improper detention only if that consent is an act of free will, unaffected by the taint of the illegality." Com. v. Arias, 81 Mass. App. Ct. 342, 963 N.E.2d 100, 107 (2012) (quoting Com. v. Loughlin, 385 Mass. 60, 430 N.E.2d 823, 825 (1982)).

[20]Hudson v. Michigan, 547 U.S. 586, 126 S. Ct. 2159, 165 L. Ed. 2d 56 (2006).

[21]Hudson, 547 U.S. at 593.

*Hudson* itself did not make entirely clear the extent to which its holding—that a no knock entry to execute a search warrant does not trigger the Fourth Amendment exclusionary requirement[22]—rested on attenuation of taint grounds. Best read, *Hudson* simply considered, in identifying a category of Fourth Amendment violations not triggering the exclusionary sanction, the frequently with which case-by-case attenuation of taint analysis in those cases would result in the challenged evidence being found ultimately admissible.

The Washington Supreme Court in *State v. Eserjose*[23] left open whether the exclusionary rule of article I, section 7 of the Washington Constitution is subject to an attenuation of taint exception. Four members of the court argued that it should not be:

> An attenuation exception . . . is fundamentally at odds with our article I, section 7 protection. . . . [T]his attenuation exception allows illegally obtained evidence to be admitted. Nor does such a doctrine respect our paramount concern of protecting individual privacy, as it would deny a remedy to those whose privacy has been unconstitutionally invaded. Additionally, application of the exception would necessarily be speculative, a departure from our otherwise nearly categorical exclusionary rule.

> More importantly, nothing in the attenuation doctrine . . . suggests how time, intervening circumstances, or less egregious misconduct can infuse the fruits of an illegal seizure with the authority of law required by article I, section 7. . . . Evidence obtained in violation of a person's constitutional rights, even if attenuated, still lacks the authority of law and should be suppressed.[24]

## § 180   Exceptions to exclusion: (b) Intervening illegal conduct

If, in response to officers' illegality sufficient to trigger an exclusionary sanction, suspects engage in further criminal conduct, the courts have regarded that further criminal conduct as bases for law enforcement action somehow independent of the initial illegalities. Thus evidence of those further illegalities, or

---

[22]See § 166 supra.

[23]State v. Eserjose, 171 Wash. 2d 907, 259 P.3d 172 (2011).

[24]Eserjose, 259 P.3d at 189 (Johnson, J., dissenting).

evidence derived from them, is admissible despite the original improper conduct of the officers.[1]

Often the further illegality consists of forcible resistance to the officers' conduct. In the leading decision, *United States v. Bailey*,[2] the defendant responded to his arguably improper arrest by struggling with the arresting officer. "But for" the unlawful arrest the officer would not have observed the defendant's resistance—because it would not have occurred. Nevertheless, the constitutional deficiency of the arrest did not require exclusion of evidence regarding the resistance. In a more rigorous application of the analysis, a Texas court applied it to a situation in which a suspect responded to an unlawful search of his car by grabbing the contraband and placing it in his mouth. Although the unlawfulness of the search precluded the prosecution from proving the defendant's possession before his criminal effort to destroy the contraband, the *Bailey* analysis permitted the prosecution to prove his criminal possession of it during and after his grabbing the drug.[3]

The precise nature of the doctrine being applied in these cases is not clear.[4] Some courts[5] appear to regard the doctrine as simply a specialized application of the attenuation of taint doctrine,[6] under which intervening voluntary criminal conduct usually and perhaps inevitably attenuates the taint of illegality preceding that conduct. This approach, of course, is consistent with the gen-

---

**[Section 180]**

[1]*E.g.*, U.S. v. Hunt, 372 F.3d 1010, 1012–13 (8th Cir. 2004) ("When a defendant commits a new and distinct crime during an unlawful detention, the Fourth Amendment's exclusionary rule does not bar evidence of the new crime."). *Accord* U.S. v. Sprinkle, 106 F.3d 613, 619–20 (4th Cir. 1997); People v. Smith, 870 P.2d 617, 619–20 (Colo. App. 1994); Brown v. City of Danville, 44 Va. App. 586, 606 S.E.2d 523, 530–32 (2004).

[2]U.S. v. Bailey, 691 F.2d 1009 (11th Cir. 1982).

[3]Holmes v. State, 962 S.W.2d 663, 669 (Tex. App. Waco 1998).

[4]The doctrine's relationship to exclusionary sanction law is sometimes obscured because—in the context of challenged to evidence obtained from arrests—courts pose the issue as whether the responsive criminal acts

provides "independent grounds" for the arrests. *E.g.*, State v. Dawdy, 533 N.W.2d 551, 556 (Iowa 1995) ("Because Dawdy's resistance provided an independent ground for Dawdy's arrest, the search of his person was valid as a search incident to an arrest.").

[5]*E.g.*, Holmes, 962 S.W.2d at 669 (voluntary commission of an unlawful act "generally operates as an intervening circumstance which purges any taint flowing from the unlawful arrest").

[6]People v. Doke, 171 P.3d 237, 240 (Colo. 2007) (defendant's criminal acts directed against deputies "are sufficiently attenuated from any illegal conduct of the deputies"); State v. Courville, 2002 MT 330, 313 Mont. 218, 61 P.3d 749, 753–54 (2002) (evidence of defendant's criminal conduct is so attenuated from the initial policy illegality that it lost its constitutional taint).

eral significance given in attenuation analysis to intervening voluntary conduct.[7]

Other courts appear to regard the doctrine as a separate exception to exclusionary requirements, based on considerations distinguishable from those supporting the attenuation of taint doctrine.[8] The New Hampshire Supreme Court in 2008 announced that it would then "join the overwhelming weight of authority in adopting the new crime exception to the exclusionary rule."[9] Under this "rule," if a person responses to an officer's unlawful entry, search or seizure by an officer with a physical attack or threat of such an attack upon the officer, evidence of this new criminal act is admissible despite the officer's illegal conduct,[10]

The rule is generally based on the proposition that whatever incremental deterrence of official illegality accomplished by excluding this evidence would be outweighed by the costs involved. Among those costs is the loss of the opportunity to discourage unlawful and perhaps violent responses to questionable law enforcement activity or perhaps actually encouraging such responses.[11] The Colorado court also commented that excluding such evidence would result in only minimal deterrence,[12] apparently on the assumption that officers' responses to attacks on them is unlikely to be affected by later admissibility or inadmissibility of evidence.

The exception is generally assumed to apply only if the defendant engaged in further criminal acts. An unwise response to official illegality that simply reveals a past digression by the defendant will not invoke it.[13] One court reasoned that the rationale for the exception—discouraging violent responses to even improper law enforcement conduct—did not justify the exception's application to evidence that a suspect responded to an unconstitutional detention by giving a false name to the office.[14]

Several courts have held that the exception only permits use of

---

[7]See § 179 supra.

[8]State v. Brocuglio, 264 Conn. 778, 826 A.2d 145, 155 (2003) (adopting "the new crime exception"); Com. v. Davis, 53 Va. Cir. 140, 2000 WL 1211539 (2000) (many courts have recognized a "distinct crime" exception to the poisonous tree doctrine).

[9]State v. Panarello, 157 N.H. 204, 949 A.2d 732, 737 (2008).

[10]Panarello, 949 A.2d at 736 (quoting from 3 W. LaFave et al., Criminal Procedure § 9.4(f), at 464–65 (3d ed. 2007)).

[11]U.S. v. Bailey, 691 F.2d 1009, 1017 (11th Cir. 1982).

[12]People v. Doke, 171 P.3d 237, 240–41 (Colo. 2007).

[13]See U.S. v. Ramirez, 91 F.3d 1297, 1303 (9th Cir. 1996), rev'd on other grounds 523 U.S. 65 (1998) (where defendant responded to officers' illegally entry by legally firing his gun into the ceiling, Government was barred from using evidence of this actions to prove his prior offense of illegal possession of the gun).

[14]People v. Brown, 345 Ill. App.

evidence of the new criminal conduct. Thus where an officer suspected drug activity and attempted an improper stop, and the suspect struggled, and the officer eventually recovered drugs, the exception permitted use of evidence of the suspect's resisting detention. It did not, however, permit the use of evidence of the drugs. This discourages criminal responds to police conduct, removes a potential incentive for improper law enforcement action, "preserves the integrity of the rationale underlying much of our constitutional seizure analysis."[15]

## § 181  Exceptions to exclusion: (c) Inevitable discovery[1]

Many exclusionary requirements are subject to an exception often called the "inevitable discovery" rule. Evidence otherwise inadmissible becomes usable under this exception upon a showing that if the evidence had not been improperly secured as it was, the prosecution would nevertheless "inevitably" have obtained it in a "legitimate" manner.[2]

Unlike the so-called independent source rule,[3] which is invoked by proof that the challenged evidence was in actual fact not obtained as a factual result of the illegality, this exception rests on proof regarding hypothetical scenarios. This characteristic also distinguishes inevitable discovery from attenuation of taint,[4] which is invoked by a showing regarding the actual causal link between the illegal conduct and obtaining the evidence.

---

3d 363, 280 Ill. Dec. 431, 802 N.E.2d 356 (4th Dist. 2003) ("[r]efusing to provide identification does not raise the same policy concerns as assaulting a law enforcement officer"). Another court limited the exception to criminal acts that endanger others. State v. Badessa, 185 N.J. 303, 885 A.2d 430, 437 (2005) (illegal stop precluded use of evidence of defendant's criminal refusal to submit to breathalyzer test).

[15]State v. Beauchesne, 151 N.H. 803, 868 A.2d 972, 984 (2005). *Accord* Jones v. State, 745 A.2d 856, 864–65 (Del. 1999). *Cf.* State v. Bergerson, 659 N.W.2d 791, 798 (Minn. Ct. App. 2003) (where defendant fled without resisting from improper traffic stop, flight did not purge the taint of the stop and render admissible drugs found in search of car after defendant was apprehended).

**[Section 181]**

[1]*See generally* West's Key Number Digest, Criminal Law ⟿392.39(12)

[2]The few cases are split on whether the alternative means of obtaining the evidence must actually have been legitimate or whether, instead, it is sufficient that those means although illegal were ones the defendant lacks standing to challenge. *Compare* U.S. v. Scott, 270 F.3d 30, 44–45 (1st Cir. 2001) (unconstitutional means which defendant lacks standing to challenge can support inevitable discovery) with U.S. v. Johnson, 380 F.3d 1013, 1017–18 (7th Cir. 2004) (permitting prosecution to rely on improper alternative means defendant lacked standing to challenge would create incentive for law enforcement to violate the law). *See also* State v. Ackward, 281 Kan. 2, 128 P.3d 382, 396 (2006) (following *Johnson*).

[3]See § 177 supra.

[4]See § 179 supra.

Inevitable discovery was incorporated into federal constitutional exclusionary analysis in *Nix v. Williams*,[5] a Sixth Amendment right to counsel case. The rationale for the exclusionary remedy, the Court reasoned, ordinarily requires only that the prosecution be denied any advantages that might flow from its misconduct. This preventive purpose does not require that the prosecution be put in any worse a position than it would be in had it not committed the primary illegality.[6] Since no reason exists to deny the prosecution any advantage it can establish that it would have enjoyed had its officers eschewed improper action, only an inevitable discovery exception can properly limit the exclusionary requirement as dictated by its rationale.

State courts have tended to construe state exclusionary requirements as qualified by an exception somewhat similar to *Williams's* federal constitutional doctrine.[7] A significant number, however, have been persuaded by the risk that the exception may be misapplied in operation to limit the exception more rigorously than the Supreme Court found appropriate in fashioning the exception to the federal constitutional exclusionary sanctions.

*Williams* rejected the contention that the nature of the issues posed by the exception requires an unusually high burden of proof on the prosecution.[8] Some state courts, however, have reasoned that the conjecture inherent in application of the exception justifies imposing upon the prosecution the task of proving the exception applies by clear and convincing evidence.[9]

*Williams* also rejected the holdings below that the exception requires a showing that the evidence was obtained by officers acting in actual "good faith," reiterating that even where officers act in bad faith the purposes of the exclusionary requirement do not

---

[5]Nix v. Williams, 467 U.S. 431, 104 S. Ct. 2501, 81 L. Ed. 2d 377 (1984).

[6]Williams, 467 U.S. at 442–43.

[7]*E.g.*, State v. Garner, 331 N.C. 491, 417 S.E.2d 502, 510 (1992) (rejecting argument that state constitutional exclusionary rule does not and should not include inevitable discovery exception); State v. Flippo, 212 W. Va. 560, 575 S.E.2d 170, 188 (2002). *Compare* Chest v. State, 922 N.E.2d 621, 625 n.6 (Ind. Ct. App. 2009) ("inevitability has not been adopted as an exception to the exclusionary rule under the Article 1, Section 11 of the Indiana Constitution"). The Texas statutory exclusionary sanction has been construed as subject to no inevitable discovery exception. State v. Johnson, 939 S.W.2d 586 (Tex. Crim. App. 1996) (statutory exclusionary requirement not subject to inevitable discovery exception).

[8]Williams, 467 U.S. at 444 n. 5 ("inevitable discovery involves no speculative elements but focuses on demonstrated historical facts capable of ready verification or impeachment" and consequently presents no justification for requiring more of the prosecution than proof by a preponderance of the evidence).

[9]*See* State v. Flippo, 212 W. Va. 560, 575 S.E.2d 170, 191 (2002) (collecting cases and opting for preponderance of the evidence standard under state constitutional law).

justify putting the prosecution in a worse position than it would have occupied had its officers acted properly.[10] Several state courts, however, have required that the officers have acted in good faith. The Alaska Supreme Court, for example, concluded that an unqualified exception poses a sufficient risk of encouraging law enforcement "shortcuts" to demand that as a matter of state constitutional law it be limited to situations in which the officers did not act in bad faith to accelerate the discovery of the challenged evidence.[11]

The exception is generally agreed to require proof that the prosecution would—not might or could—have obtained the challenged evidence in a proper manner.[12] Courts differ somewhat in their statements of the applicable standard. The Montana court colorfully stated that "[i]t must appear that, as certainly as night follows day, the evidence would have been discovered without reference to the violation of the defendant's rights."[13] Others have announced that legitimate discovery must be "truly inevitable"[14] or "certain as a practical matter."[15] Federal circuits differ. Some require only a reasonable probability that the evidence would have been obtained properly. Others direct the exception be limited to situations in which the trial courts find, with a high level of confidence, that each of the contingencies necessary to the legal discovery of the contested evidence would be resolved in the prosecution's favor.[16]

Some courts have sought to minimize the risk that inevitability will be uncritically found by requiring that the prosecution establish that the legitimate discovery of the evidence would have occurred as a result of an alternative line of investigation that was actually being actively pursued at the time of the illegal conduct.[17]

---

[10]Williams, 467 U.S. at 445–46.

[11]Smith v. State, 948 P.2d 473, 481 (Alaska 1997). *Compare* State v. White, 76 Wash. App. 801, 888 P.2d 169, 173–74 (Div. 1 1995) (prosecution must prove that the police did not act unreasonably or in an attempt to accelerate discovery).

[12]State v. Lee, 976 So. 2d 109, 127 (La. 2008) ("Integral to the proper application of the inevitable discovery doctrine is a finding that law enforcement *would* have inevitably secured the evidence by lawful means, not simply that they *could* have.") (emphasis in original).

[13]State v. Allies, 186 Mont. 99, 606 P.2d 1043, 1053 (1979). *Accord* State v. Pearson, 2011 MT 55, 359 Mont. 427, 251 P.3d 152, 157 (2011).

[14]People v. Hyde, 285 Mich. App. 428, 775 N.W.2d 833, 840 (2009).

[15]Com. v. Linton, 456 Mass. 534, 924 N.E.2d 722, 743 (2010).

[16]*See* U.S. v. Marrocco, 578 F.3d 627, 640 (7th Cir. 2009) (collecting cases and discussing different approaches).

[17]*E.g.*, U.S. v. Ochoa, 667 F.3d 643, 650 (5th Cir. 2012) (prosecution must demonstrate "the Government was actively pursuing a substantial

Perhaps the leading case, *United States v. Cherry*,[18] reasoned in part that without proof that police had begun active pursuit of the legal line of investigation at the time of their illegal conduct, application of the inevitable discovery exception based on that legal line of investigation would involve the sort of "speculative elements" that *Williams* assumed were not involved in the exception.[19] Others reject this requirement,[20] although proof that such an alternative investigation was actually underway strongly supports the contention that it had the independence necessary to trigger the exception.[21]

Clearly some courts are uncomfortable with the inevitable discovery exception, especially as applied to some types of situations, and this discomfort has given rise to a variety of possible limitations on the doctrine. Some discussions suggest that the exception is not to be applied where the illegality is particularly serious or infringes a central aspect of the governing law.[22] Oth-

---

alternate line of investigation at the time of the constitutional violation"); U.S. v. Delancy, 502 F.3d 1297, 1314–15 (11th Cir. 2007) (in Eleventh Circuit, "the prosecution must demonstrate that the lawful means which made discovery inevitable were being actively pursued prior to the occurrence of the illegal conduct"); Clay v. State, 290 Ga. 822, 725 S.E.2d 260, 267–68 (2012); Rowell v. State, 83 So. 3d 990, 996 (Fla. 4th DCA 2012); State v. Avery, 2011 WI App 124, 337 Wis. 2d 351, 804 N.W.2d 216, 226 (Ct. App. 2011).

[18]U.S. v. Cherry, 759 F.2d 1196 (5th Cir. 1985), reaffirming the approach taken in U.S. v. Brookins, 614 F.2d 1037 (5th Cir. 1980).

[19]Cherry, 759 F.2d at 1205 n. 10.

[20]U.S. v. D'Andrea, 648 F.3d 1, 12 (1st Cir. 2011) (analysis must be "flexible enough to handle the many different fact patterns that will be presented"). Proof that officers at least intended to pursue the lawful means before deviating onto the impermissible path may be necessary. State v. Perez, 147 Wash. App. 141, 193 P.3d 1131, 1132 (Div. 2 2008) (prosecution's reliance on inevitable discovery by search warrant failed because proof

showed officers never had intent to seek warrant).

The Alaska Supreme Court has required that the prosecution prove that the offered method of discovery would have involved "proper and predictable investigatory procedures." A procedure is "predictable" under this requirement only if considering the quality and value of sources in the possession of the officers and their "experience, ability, and knowledge," those procedures "would have been apparent to the investigator in the absence of any benefits provided by hindsight." Smith v. State, 948 P.2d 473, 480–81 (Alaska 1997).

[21]*See* U.S. v. Larsen, 127 F.3d 984, 986 (10th Cir. 1997).

[22]*See* U.S. v. Madrid, 152 F.3d 1034, 1041 (8th Cir. 1998) ("severity of the police misconduct" is relevant to whether inevitable discovery renders evidence admissible, and exception would not be applied where officers not only entered a home without a warrant but detained the occupants and engaged in a "continued, prolonged illegal search"); State v. Payano-Roman, 2005 WI App 118, 284 Wis. 2d 350, 701 N.W.2d 72, 77 n.3 (Ct. App. 2005), decision rev'd on other grounds without reaching issue, 2006 WI 47, 290 Wis.

ers suggest that it is not to be applied to in which excessive speculation would necessarily be involved.[23]

The exception might, as some courts have held, be limited to "derivative" as contrasted with "primary" or "direct" evidence. Under this distinction, direct or primary evidence is that which is actually discovered and seized during the illegal conduct. Derivative evidence, on the other hand, is evidence obtained later by means of information derived from illegal conduct.[24] Some courts have limited the exception to evidence of the latter sort.[25] If the exception is limited to derivative evidence, it becomes an exception not to the basic exclusionary requirement but only to the corollary that renders inadmissible all fruit of the poisonous tree. Most courts have refused to limit the exception to derivative evidence.[26] Perhaps, however, they have failed to fully explore the possibility that such a limitation might be the most appropriate way of preventing the exception from effectively nullifying some or most of the legal requirements enforced by exclusionary requirements.

State courts and legislatures are not, of course, bound to include this exception in state exclusionary requirement, and some have rejected it. A split Washington Supreme Court held in *State v. Winterstein*[27] that the state constitutional exclusionary rule had no inevitable discovery exception. The majority relied in part on its conclusion that the doctrine "is necessarily

---

2d 380, 714 N.W.2d 548 (2006) (inevitable discovery did not apply to evidence obtained by forced administration of laxative because search involved "invasion of the body"); State v. Holland, 176 N.J. 344, 823 A.2d 38, 47–48 (2003) (state constitutional exception applies only if the initial impropriety did not involve "flagrant police misconduct").

[23]The courts are split, for example, on whether the exception applies to render admissible evidence concerning oral statements. *Compare* State v. Lopez, 78 Haw. 433, 896 P.2d 889, 910 (1995) ("because we believe that applying the 'inevitable discovery' doctrine to oral statements, including confessions and consents to search, would amount to 'surmise and speculative inference' beyond that in which we are willing to engage at the expense of our constitution, we hold that it only applies to the admissibility of tangible physical evidence"), *with* U.S. v. Vasquez De Reyes, 149 F.3d 192, 195

(3d Cir. 1998) (declining to limit exception to tangible objects but finding that government failed to establish applicability of exception on facts before the court).

[24]*See* Murray v. U.S., 487 U.S. 533, 536–37, 108 S. Ct. 2529, 101 L. Ed. 2d 472 (1988).

[25]*E.g.*, State v. Jorgensen, 526 N.E.2d 1004, 1008 (Ind. Ct. App. 1988); People v. Stith, 69 N.Y.2d 313, 514 N.Y.S.2d 201, 506 N.E.2d 911, 913–914 (1987). *Accord* People v. Thurman, 79 A.D.3d 1662, 917 N.Y.S.2d 784, 786–87 (4th Dep't 2010) (applying distinction between primary and derivative evidence).

[26]Williams v. State, 372 Md. 386, 813 A.2d 231, 252–53 (2002); State v. Flippo, 212 W. Va. 560, 575 S.E.2d 170, 188 n.22 (2002); People v. Burola, 848 P.2d 958, 961–62 (Colo. 1993).

[27]State v. Winterstein, 167 Wash. 2d 620, 220 P.3d 1226 (2009).

speculative."[28] More importantly, it emphasized that the Washington exclusionary requirement—unlike the Fourth Amendment exclusionary rule—is designed to protect privacy by providing a remedy whenever privacy is impermissibly invaded. This rationale for the state law requirement is inconsistent with the inevitable discovery exception's denial of a remedy where deterrent considerations are viewed as insufficient to support exclusion.[29]

## § 182   Exceptions to exclusion: (d) "Good faith"

Whether illegally obtained evidence should be excluded if the officers who gathered it mistakenly believed (or could have believed) that their actions complied with legal requirements is among the most controversial issues posed by existing exclusionary requirements. A limited "good faith" exception to the federal constitutional exclusionary rules for at least some situations of this sort has been recognized by the Supreme Court. State courts and legislatures have sometimes, but not always, followed suit.

*Federal Constitutional Exception.* In *United States v. Leon*[1] and *Massachusetts v. Sheppard*[2] the Supreme Court held that evidence obtained in searches conducted pursuant to defective search warrants was nevertheless admissible if the prosecution established that reasonable officers would have believed the warrants and therefore the searches constitutionally permissible. Three years later, in *Illinois v. Krull*,[3] the Court similarly held admissible evidence obtained in a warrantless search upon proof that given an invalid statute purporting to authorizing the search, a reasonable officer would have believed the search constitutionally permissible.

The "good faith" label attached to the doctrine developed in *Leon*, *Sheppard* and *Krull* is arguably misleading.[4] The exception does not require proof that the officers actually and subjectively—in "good faith," as that term is generally used—believed

---

[28]Winterstein, 220 P.3d at 1232.

[29]220 P.3d at 1231–33. The majority also suggested that since the exception permitted courts' reliance on evidence actually tainted by unconstitutional conduct, it was inconsistent with the state exclusionary rule's objective of "protect[ing] the integrity of the judicial system by not tainting the proceedings with illegally obtained evidence." 220 P.3d at 1231–33.

**[Section 182]**

[1]U.S. v. Leon, 468 U.S. 897, 104 S. Ct. 3405, 82 L. Ed. 2d 677 (1984).

[2]Massachusetts v. Sheppard, 468 U.S. 981, 104 S. Ct. 3424, 82 L. Ed. 2d 737 (1984).

[3]Illinois v. Krull, 480 U.S. 340, 107 S. Ct. 1160, 94 L. Ed. 2d 364 (1987).

[4]Herring v. U.S., 555 U.S. 135, 142, 129 S. Ct. 695, 172 L. Ed. 2d 496 (2009) (*Leon* perhaps confusingly called the required objectively reasonable reliance "good faith"); People v. Machupa, 7 Cal. 4th 614, 29 Cal. Rptr. 2d 775, 872 P.2d 114, 115 n.1 (1994) (using term "good faith" only with reluctance, because *Leon* holding itself

their actions within constitutional limits. The inquiry is whether under all the circumstances "a reasonably well trained officer" would have known that the actions at issue were constitutionally impermissible.[5] If not, the exception applies whether the officer actually making the search knew the actions were improper. In fact, and despite the general statement of the rule, the exception does not require proof that the officers actually—subjectively—relied on the warrant or legislation.

Emphasizing the preventive purpose of the Fourth Amendment exclusionary rule,[6] *Leon*, *Sheppard* and *Krull* reasoned that in at least some situations the rule cannot be expected to deter objectively reasonable law enforcement activity and should not be applied in an effort to do so.[7] This is particularly so, *Leon* continued, where officers have obtained a search warrant. The magistrate has responsibility for determining such matters as whether probable cause exists; officers cannot be expected to question magistrates' resolution of those issues.[8] "Penalizing the officer for the magistrate's errors, rather than his own," the Court concluded, "cannot logically contribute to the deterrence of the Fourth Amendment violations."[9] Similarly, *Krull* reasoned, officers cannot ordinarily be expected to question the judgment of a legislature that passed a statute authorizing a search, so no contribution to deterrence can logically be expected from penalizing the officer for errors of the legislature.[10] Consequently, any benefits derived from excluding evidence in such situations cannot justify the substantial costs of exclusion.[11]

Given that officers' ability to rely on a warrant[12] or legislation[13] must be objectively reasonable, exclusion is required despite a warrant or authorizing statute if the defect in the warrant[14] or statute[15] is so clear that a reasonably well trained officer would recognize that defect. In the case of reliance upon a warrant, *Leon* added, exclusion is required if the officer in applying for the warrant misled the issuing magistrate by including information he knew was false or would have known was false except for his

---

"focuses expressly and exclusively on the objective reasonableness of an officer's conduct, not on his or her subjective 'good faith,' " and thus the term " 'good faith' exception" is "misleading").

[5]Leon, 468 U.S. at 922 n. 23.

[6]468 U.S. at 906–07.

[7]468 U.S. at 919.

[8]468 U.S. at 920.

[9]468 U.S. at 920.

[10]Illinois v. Krull, 480 U.S. 340, 349, 107 S. Ct. 1160, 94 L. Ed. 2d 364 (1987).

[11]Leon, 468 U.S. at 922.

[12]468 U.S. at 923.

[13]Krull, 480 U.S. at 354.

[14]Leon, 468 U.S. at 923.

[15]Krull, 480 U.S. at 355.

reckless disregard for the truth[16] or if the warrant was issued by a magistrate lacking the impartiality required by the Fourth Amendment.[17]

Eight years after *Krull*, the Court decided *Arizona v. Evans*,[18] which it later characterized as" appl[ying] the good-faith exception in a case where the police reasonably relied on erroneous information concerning an arrest warrant in a database maintained by judicial employees."[19] *Herring v. United States*[20] applied *Evans* to "a case where police employees erred in maintaining records in a [similar] warrant database" and the defendant showed only simple negligence and no systemic error or reckless disregard of constitutional requirements.[21] *Davis v. United States*[22] held the Fourth Amendment exception applied to a situation involving no basis for reliance on a warrant or statute. Rather, in *Davis* the Government showed state officers acting within the Eleventh Circuit made the search in a manner permissible under the Eleventh Circuit's interpretation of Supreme Court Fourth Amendment case law rejected—after the search—by the Court. The Fourth Amendment good faith exception, *Davis* held, means "[e]vidence obtained during a search conducted in reasonable reliance on binding precedent is not subject to the exclusionary rule."[23]

*Davis* explained:

The basic insight of the *Leon* line of cases is that the deterrence benefits of exclusion "var[y] with the culpability of the law enforcement conduct" at issue. When the police exhibit "deliberate," "reckless," or "grossly negligent" disregard for Fourth Amendment rights, the deterrent value of exclusion is strong and tends to outweigh the

---

[16]*Leon*, 468 U.S. at 923. The Supreme Court has held as a matter of Fourth Amendment law that a search warrant is constitutionally invalid if a defendant shows that the officer intentionally or with reckless disregard for the truth submitted to the issuing magistrate false facts necessary to the finding of probable cause. *See* Franks v. Delaware, 438 U.S. 154, 98 S. Ct. 2674, 57 L. Ed. 2d 667 (1978).

[17]*Leon*, 468 U.S. at 923, citing Lo-Ji Sales, Inc. v. New York, 442 U.S. 319, 99 S. Ct. 2319, 60 L. Ed. 2d 920 (1979) (magistrate accompanied officers to location of search and participated in it). Despite some implications of *Leon's* language, evidence is probably admissible under the exception regardless of whether the magistrate

was in fact sufficiently neutral if a reasonable officer would have believed the issuing magistrate sufficiently neutral. *See* O'Connor v. Madera County Superior Court, 76 Cal. Rptr. 2d 138, 144 (App. 5th Dist. 1998).

[18]Arizona v. Evans, 514 U.S. 1, 115 S. Ct. 1185, 131 L. Ed. 2d 34 (1995).

[19]Davis v. U.S., 131 S. Ct. 2419, 2428, 180 L. Ed. 2d 285 (2011).

[20]Herring v. U.S., 555 U.S. 135, 129 S. Ct. 695, 172 L. Ed. 2d 496 (2009).

[21]Davis, 131 S.Ct. at 2428 (so characterizing *Herring*).

[22]Davis v. U.S., 131 S. Ct. 2419, 180 L. Ed. 2d 285 (2011).

[23]Davis, 131 S.Ct. at 2429.

resulting costs. But when the police act with an objectively "reasonable good-faith belief" that their conduct is lawful, or when their
conduct involves only simple, "isolated" negligence, the " 'deterrence
rationale loses much of its force,' " and exclusion cannot "pay its
way."[24]

Applying this, *Davis* continued:

Although the search turned out to be unconstitutional . . . , all
agree that the officers' conduct was in strict compliance with then-
binding Circuit law and was not culpable in any way.

Under our exclusionary-rule precedents, this acknowledged
absence of police culpability dooms Davis's claim. Police practices
trigger the harsh sanction of exclusion only when they are deliberate enough to yield "meaningfu[l]" deterrence, and culpable enough
to be "worth the price paid by the justice system." The conduct of
the officers here was neither of these things. The officers who
conducted the search did not violate Davis's Fourth Amendment
rights deliberately, recklessly, or with gross negligence. Nor does
this case involve any "recurring or systemic negligence" on the part
of law enforcement. The police acted in strict compliance with binding precedent, and their behavior was not wrongful. Unless the
exclusionary rule is to become a strict-liability regime, it can have
no application in this case.[25]

The major issue posed by this line of cases is whether the
Fourth Amendment exception will be extended to other and
perhaps all situations in which reasonable officers would regard
their conduct as complying with federal constitutional standards.
Until *Herring* and *Davis*, the Court's discussions suggested the
exception was limited to situations in which the facts proved a
fairly-objective basis for an officer's objectively reasonable good
faith belief that the conduct was constitutional—an erroneous decision by some authority a police officer could not ordinarily be
expected to question. This could be a decision by a legislature—
reflected in a constitutionally-ineffective statute—or a judicial decision—reflected in an invalid warrant or a judicial misrepresentation that a valid warrant was outstanding.[26] On its facts, *Davis*
did not deviate from this—the appellate then-binding though erroneous case law was similar to the invalid warrants of *Leon* and
*Sheppard* and the ineffective statute of *Krull*.

The stated rationales for *Davis* and *Herring* as discussed in

---

[24]131 S.Ct. at 2427–28 (citations
omitted).

[25]131 S.Ct. at 2428–29.

[26]King v. Com., 302 S.W.3d 649,
657 (Ky. 2010). *See* State v. Mendoza,
748 P.2d 181, 185 (Utah 1987) ("good
faith" exception applies only if the officers relied upon some "outside au-

thority," such as an invalid warrant or
statute, which expressly authorized
their search).

One federal circuit has, how-
ever, since before *Leon* applied a broad
exception applicable to all law enforcement action. U.S. v. Williams, 622
F.2d 830, 846–47 (5th Cir. 1980) (en
banc).

*Davis*, however, placed little or no emphasis on the existence of an erroneous decision by an entity officers could not reasonably be expected to disregard. Rather, *Davis* stressed instead the lack of officer culpability rising above mere negligence. Such culpability, of course, will also be lacking in many situations involving no erroneous decision by an authoritative entity.

*Davis* strongly suggests some version of the good faith exception will eventually apply where the facts show no more than that a reasonable police officer would have realized the conduct was unconstitutional. A defendant seeking suppression, in other words, will have to refute the prosecution's prima facie case—or perhaps even a simple claim—of "good faith." This refutation will—consistent with *Davis*—require a showing the officer acted "deliberately, recklessly, or with gross negligence" or of "recurring or systemic [mere] negligence" on the part of law enforcement.

Pre-*Davis*, however, most lower courts assumed the Fourth Amendment exception applied only where the facts showed some authoritative basis for a belief the action was constitutional. It did not, for example, permit admission of evidence obtained in a search made by an officer who mistakenly but perhaps reasonably believed grounds existed for a warrantless exigent circumstances search.

When a reasonable officer could not regard a search warrant as constitutionally valid under *Leon* and *Sheppard* was addressed by the Supreme Court in *Groh v. Ramirez*.[27] The good faith exception would be inapplicable where a warrant contained no description whatsoever of the property or persons to be seized. The Supreme Court stressed that the officer himself had prepared the document, and that even a "simple glance" might have revealed the "glaring deficiency."[28]

*Leon's* good faith exception—at least as defined prior to *Davis*—raised a number of subquestions. Some courts declined to apply the exception where officers executing a valid search warrant erroneously exceed their authority under a valid warrant. The only error in such situations is that of the officers executing the warrant. Arguably, there thus remains sufficient likelihood that exclusion might encourage greater care in ascertaining the existence or effect of warrants.[29] If *Davis* has the implications suggested earlier in this section, of course, the exception would cover these situations.

---

[27]Groh v. Ramirez, 540 U.S. 551, 124 S. Ct. 1284, 157 L. Ed. 2d 1068 (2004).

[28]Groh, 540 U.S. at 563–64.

[29]Sadie v. State, 488 So. 2d 1368, 1378 (Ala. Crim. App. 1986) ("the 'good-faith exception' is not applicable because the officers clearly acted out-

Another question is whether the right of officers to rely on a facially valid warrant precludes a defendant from establishing that the warrant itself was tainted by earlier misconduct and thus evidence obtained as a result of the warrant's execution is excludable fruit of that original poisonous tree. Under the better view, a warrant can trigger the exception only if the warrant itself was untainted. If the warrant was issued on the basis of excludable evidence, the warrant and evidence obtained pursuant to it are all fruit of the original poisonous tree. Such laundering of tainted information through a magistrate should not render the fruits doctrine inapplicable.[30] The matter might be viewed not as a good faith exception problem but rather as whether the warrant is or could be an independent source of the challenged evidence; this is addressed in Section 176.

*State Constitutional Requirements.* State courts have differed in their construction of state constitutional exclusionary requirements. Some, of course, have followed the Supreme Court's approach and read state constitutional requirements as qualified by *Leon*-like exceptions.[31] Others, including the Supreme Courts of New Mexico[32] and Washington,[33] have refused to read such an exception into their constitutions.[34] Wisconsin in 2001 adopted a

---

side the confines of the description in the affidavit" and "it was the officers who made the determination of the place to be searched. Where the error does not fall on the issuing magistrate, but rather on the officers, the exception does not apply"). *Accord* State v. Johnson, 605 So. 2d 545, 548 (Fla. 2d DCA 1992) (exception only applies where officers act in an objectively reasonable fashion in executing a search warrant that is subsequently found invalid, and not where items were seized beyond authority of valid warrant).

Much the same result is reached under substantive Fourth Amendment law holding that a search is reasonable if it is of an area the officer reasonably believes to be covered by the terms of the warrant. *See* Maryland v. Garrison, 480 U.S. 79, 107 S. Ct. 1013, 94 L. Ed. 2d 72 (1987).

[30]Fitzgerald v. State, 153 Md. App. 601, 837 A.2d 989, 1019–20 (2003) ("in the case of an antecedent Fourth Amendment violation which contributes to a warrant application, the 'fruit of the poisonous tree' doctrine

'trumps' the officer's 'good faith' reliance under *Leon* and *Sheppard*). *Accord* U.S. v. Williams, 574 F. Supp. 2d 530, 557–58 (W.D. Pa. 2008), aff'd on other grounds, 416 Fed. Appx. 130 (3d Cir. 2011), cert. denied, 132 S. Ct. 573, 181 L. Ed. 2d 421 (2011).

[31]*E.g.*, Wendt v. State, 876 N.E.2d 788, 790 (Ind. Ct. App. 2007)) (Hopkins v. State, 582 N.E.2d 345, 351 (Ind. 1991), holding "the federal good-faith exception . . . [is] applicable to the prohibition of unreasonable search and seizure found in art. 1, § 11 of the Indiana Constitution," has not been implicitly overruled). *Accord* People v. Goldston, 470 Mich. 523, 682 N.W.2d 479, 489 (2004) (following "numerous" jurisdictions adopting good faith requirement as a matter of state constitutional law and overruling prior Michigan case law).

[32]State v. Guzman, 122 Idaho 981, 842 P.2d 660 (1992).

[33]State v. Afana, 169 Wash. 2d 169, 233 P.3d 879 (2010).

[34]*Accord* State v. Marsala, 216

somewhat narrower exception than was provided for under *Leon-Sheppard-Krull*.[35]

These state tribunals have, to some extent, rejected the Supreme Court's assumption that the effect of the exception on the deterrent value of the exclusionary requirement can be measured and that it is acceptable given the cost incurred by the loss of reliance evidence.[36] More importantly, however, some state courts have rejected the Supreme Court's assumption that the deterrent analysis is appropriate, and have found the exception unacceptable given the broader policy bases of state exclusionary requirements. The New Mexico Supreme Court, for example, reasoned that the exception was incompatible with the purpose of the state constitutional requirement "to effectuate in the pending case the constitutional right of the accused to be free from unreasonable search and seizure." "Denying the government the fruits of unconstitutional conduct at trial," the court concluded, "best effectuates the constitutional proscription of unreasonable searches and seizures by preserving the rights of the accused to the same extent as if the government's officers had stayed within the law."[37]

In addition, the New Mexico court reasoned, the state provision serves important considerations of judicial integrity, defined more broadly than that consideration in Fourth Amendment analysis, and the exception is inconsistent with this state law objective.[38] The Iowa court also stressed the remedial function of the state's

---

Conn. 150, 579 A.2d 58 (1990); State v. Cline, 617 N.W.2d 277, 288–93 (Iowa 2000); State v. Gutierrez, 116 N.M. 431, 863 P.2d 1052, 1066 (1993); State v. Novembrino, 105 N.J. 95, 519 A.2d 820 (1987); People v. Bigelow, 66 N.Y.2d 417, 497 N.Y.S.2d 630, 488 N.E.2d 451 (1985); State v. Carter, 322 N.C. 709, 370 S.E.2d 553 (1988); State v. Oakes, 157 Vt. 171, 598 A.2d 119 (1991). In State v. Koivu, 152 Idaho 511, 272 P.3d 483, 491 (2012), the Idaho court refused to overrule State v. Guzman, 122 Idaho 981, 842 P.2d 660 (1992), rejecting a good faith exception. *Cf.* State v. Bearden, 326 S.W.3d 184, 188 (Tenn. Crim. App. 2010) ("Tennessee . . . has not adopted [a] 'good faith exception.' ").

[35]State v. Eason, 2001 WI 98, 245 Wis. 2d 206, 629 N.W.2d 625, 648 (2001) ("we require that in order for the good faith exception to apply, the State must show that the process used

attendant to obtaining the search warrant included a significant investigation and a review by a police officer trained in, or very knowledgeable of, the legal vagaries of probable cause and reasonable suspicion, or a knowledgeable government attorney").

[36]Cline, 617 N.W.2d at 292 (disagreeing with Supreme Court's cost-benefit analysis, because Court's view of substantial costs attributable to lack of exception "is simply not supported"). *Accord* Guzman, 842 P.2d at 672 (agreeing with *Oakes*, 598 A.2d at 126).

[37]Gutierrez, 863 P.2d at 1067. *Accord* Afana, 233 P.3d at 380 (good faith exception is inconsistent with state provision designed primarily to protect privacy rather than to deter police misconduct).

[38]Gutierrez, 863 P.2d at 1068. *Accord* Cline, 617 N.W.2d at 289–90 ("Judges would become accomplices to

constitutional exclusionary rule and the impediment a good faith exception would place to performing that function.[39] Moreover, it rejected the Supreme Court's conclusion that exclusion of evidence is either ineffective in or unnecessary for assuring that judges and legislators perform adequately.[40]

*Nonconstitutional Exclusionary Requirements.* State statutory exclusionary requirements may be phrased to or construed as containing no good faith exception. The Georgia Supreme Court has so construed its provision,[41] and the Texas statutory exclusionary rule[42] has an exception limited to evidence obtained in reasonable reliance on warrants actually issued on probable cause.[43]

## § 183 Exceptions to exclusion: (e) Use of illegally obtained evidence to impeach testifying defendant[1]

Most exclusionary sanctions bar only the use of improperly obtained evidence at trial to prove the guilt of the defendant. Thus they are subject to an exception or qualification that permits the use of such evidence to cross-examine and impeach a defendant who testifies at trial.

In *Harris v. New York*[2] the United States Supreme Court reaffirmed its pre-*Mapp v. Ohio*[3] holding in *Walder v. United States*[4] that federal constitutional exclusionary requirements sometimes permit the use of otherwise inadmissible evidence to impeach a testifying defendant.[5] *United States v. Havens*[6] made clear that evidence tainted by violations of the Fourth Amendment could be

---

the unconstitutional conduct of the executive branch if they allowed law enforcement to enjoy the benefits on the illegality.").

[39]617 N.W.2d at 289.

[40]617 N.W.2d at 290 (good faith exception inappropriately encourages "lax practices by government officials in all three branches of government").

[41]Gary v. State, 262 Ga. 573, 422 S.E.2d 426 (1992). *Accord* Miley v. State, 279 Ga. 420, 614 S.E.2d 744, 745 (2005).

[42]Tex. Code Crim. Proc. art. 38. 23(b).

[43]*See* Gordon v. State, 801 S.W.2d 899, 912–13 (Tex. Crim. App. 1990) (under statutory exception, warrant must in fact have been issued on a sufficient showing and officers' reasonable belief that the information submitted

was sufficient to establish probable cause will not render the evidence admissible).

[Section 183]

[1]*See generally* Kainen, The Impeachment Exception to the Exclusionary Rules: Policies, Principles, and Politics, 44 Stan. L. Rev. 1301 (1992).

[2]Harris v. New York, 401 U.S. 222, 91 S. Ct. 643, 28 L. Ed. 2d 1 (1971).

[3]Mapp v. Ohio, 367 U.S. 643, 81 S. Ct. 1684, 6 L. Ed. 2d 1081 (1961).

[4]Walder v. U.S., 347 U.S. 62, 74 S. Ct. 354, 98 L. Ed. 503 (1954).

[5]Walder, 347 U.S. at 65–66.

[6]U.S. v. Havens, 446 U.S. 620, 100 S. Ct. 1912, 64 L. Ed. 2d 559 (1980).

used for impeachment. Statements elicited in violation of *Miranda v. Arizona*,[7] *Harris* held, could be used to impeach. But a statement that is involuntary, *Mincy v. Arizona*[8] confirmed, cannot be. Statements elicited in violation of the Sixth Amendment right to counsel as it applies to pretrial elicitation of self-incriminating statement were held usable for impeachment in *Michigan v. Harvey*[9] and this was reaffirmed in *Kansas v. Ventris*.[10]

Justice Scalia's opinion for the Court in *Ventris* clarified the rationale for the cases' distinction:

> Whether otherwise excluded evidence can be admitted for purposes of impeachment depends upon the nature of the constitutional guarantee that is violated. Sometimes that explicitly mandates exclusion from trial, and sometimes it does not. The Fifth Amendment guarantees that no person shall be compelled to give evidence against himself, and so is violated whenever a truly coerced confession is introduced at trial, whether by way of impeachment or otherwise. The Fourth Amendment, on the other hand, guarantees that no person shall be subjected to unreasonable searches or seizures, and says nothing about excluding their fruits from evidence; exclusion comes by way of deterrent sanction rather than to avoid violation of the substantive guarantee. Inadmissibility has not been automatic, therefore, but we have instead applied an exclusionary-rule balancing test. The same is true for violations of the Fifth and Sixth Amendment prophylactic rules forbidding certain pretrial police conduct.[11]

Impeachment use of evidence, under *Ventris*, is necessarily impermissible only if the trial use of the evidence is itself at least a part of the violation of the defendant's right on which exclusion for guilt-innocence purposes is based. This explains *Mincy's* holding that involuntary statements cannot be used for impeachment. In the other situations, the violations of the defendants' rights are complete before trial begins. Whether the exclusionary remedy is appropriately applied to bar impeachment use in those situations depends on a balancing of the incremental deterrence that would be accomplished by so expanding exclusion against the costs of doing this.

In all situations in which it has engaged in this balancing analysis, the Court has concluded that given the deterrence accomplished by excluding evidence offered on guilt, little—and

---

[7]Miranda v. Arizona, 384 U.S. 436, 86 S. Ct. 1602, 16 L. Ed. 2d 694 (1966).

[8]Mincey v. Arizona, 437 U.S. 385, 98 S. Ct. 2408, 57 L. Ed. 2d 290 (1978).

[9]Michigan v. Harvey, 494 U.S. 344, 110 S. Ct. 1176, 108 L. Ed. 2d 293 (1990).

[10]Kansas v. Ventris, 556 U.S. 586, 129 S. Ct. 1841, 173 L. Ed. 2d 801 (2009).

[11]Ventris, 556 U.S. at 590.

thus insufficient—additional deterrence would be provided by excluding unconstitutionally obtained evidence offered only to impeach the testifying defendant. The value of what little deterrence might be achieved, further, would be outweighed by the exceptionally high and offensive cost of permitting potential perjury to go unchallenged. Consequently, impeachment use is permissible.[12]

*Walder* had suggested that impeachment use of unconstitutionally obtained evidence was permissible only if the testifying defendant went beyond simply denying guilt and testified to collateral matters. Such a position would leave a defendant free to present at least a basic contention of innocence without giving up the right to be free from unconstitutionally obtained evidence.[13] *Harris*, however, rejected this approach. Thus, impeachment is permitted on the basis of testimony by a defendant simply denying guilt of the charged crime.[14]

Further, *Harris* and its progeny sometimes allow impeachment on the basis of testimony given on cross-examination as well as on direct. This is permitted, under *United States v. Havens*,[15] only if the testimony on cross-examination was in response to questions "plainly within the scope of the defendant's direct examination."[16] Whether a defendant's testimony on direct reasonably suggests inquiry by the prosecution on cross-examination into events involving tainted information is "necessarily case specific," and trial judges have considerable discretion in resolving particular cases.[17]

Impeachment is permitted as long as there is some "inconsistency" between the otherwise inadmissible evidence and the defendant's trial testimony.[18] The Supreme Court has suggested

---

[12]556 U.S. at 593 ("Our precedents make clear that the game of excluding tainted evidence for impeachment purposes is not worth the candle. The interests safeguarded by such exclusion are "outweighed by the need to prevent perjury and to assure the integrity of the trial process.") (quoting Stone v. Powell, 428 U.S. 465, 488, 96 S. Ct. 3037, 49 L. Ed. 2d 1067 (1976)).

[13]Walder v. U.S., 347 U.S. 62, 65, 74 S. Ct. 354, 98 L. Ed. 503 (1954). (a defendant "must be free to deny all the elements of the case against him without thereby giving leave to the Government to introduce by way of rebuttal evidence illegally secured by it . . .").

[14]Harris v. New York, 401 U.S. 222, 225, 91 S. Ct. 643, 28 L. Ed. 2d 1 (1971).

[15]U.S. v. Havens, 446 U.S. 620, 100 S. Ct. 1912, 64 L. Ed. 2d 559 (1980).

[16]Havens, 446 U.S. at 627.

[17]See U.S. v. Morla-Trinidad, 100 F.3d 1, 5–6 (1st Cir. 1996) (collecting cases).

[18]See State v. Browning, 199 W. Va. 417, 485 S.E.2d 1, 11 (1997) (following weight of authority that only "inconsistency" is required and otherwise inadmissible statement offered to impeach need not "actually contradict[ ]" or be "diametrically opposed"

that impeachment use must be "otherwise proper,"[19] indicating that local rules limiting impeachment might somehow be incorporated into the federal constitutional exception. There is no basis or rationale for constitutionally requiring a state to follow its ordinary cross-examination and impeachment rules when *Harris-Walder* evidence is offered. As a matter of nonconstitutional evidence law, there seems neither basis nor rationale for disregarding limits on impeachment simply because the witness is a criminal defendant and the evidence is inadmissible to prove guilt because of constitutional exclusionary requirements.[20] On the other hand, there is no justification for applying a stricter standard than applies to other evidence offered to impeach.[21]

Only a defendant's personal testimony at trial will trigger the opportunity to use otherwise excluded evidence. In *James v. Illinois*[22]—although only by a close 5 to 4 vote—the Court declined to expand the exception to permit the use of unconstitutionally obtained evidence to "impeach"—or rebut—defense testimony from witnesses other than the defendant. Such an expanded exception would weaken the deterrent value of the basic exclusionary requirement.[23] Further, permitting such rebuttal use of testimony would discourage defendants from presenting potentially meritorious defensive contentions, since defense counsel lack control over non-defendant witnesses.[24]

It follows from *James* that unconstitutionally obtained evidence is not somehow rendered admissible by defense counsel's opening statement.[25] Of course, unconstitutionally obtained evidence does not become admissible to prove guilt because it is of-

---

to trial testimony).

[19]Havens, 446 U.S. at 628.

[20]In State v. Electroplating, Inc., 990 S.W.2d 211, 226 n.17 (Tenn. Crim. App. 1998), however, the court surprisingly stated: "We see no reason nor basis for imposing [a requirement that the prosecution's use of constitutionally-infirm evidence under *Walder* and *Harris* satisfy the impeachment provisions of the evidence rules]." In *Electroplating, Inc.*, the evidence at issue was relevant to a substantive issue, inadmissible under federal constitutional law to prove guilt, but offered to contradict a factual assertion by the defendant in his testimony. For purposes of the state's prohibition against contradicting a witness with extrinsic evidence on a collateral matter, the court held, the

factual assertion contradicted by this evidence was not collateral. Thus it was not required to hold an evidence rule unsatisfied.

[21]State v. Whittle, 685 N.W.2d 461, 464–65 (Minn. Ct. App. 2004) (defendant offered no authority in support of argument that impeachment value should have to be greater when offered evidence was inadmissible under *Miranda*).

[22]James v. Illinois, 493 U.S. 307, 110 S. Ct. 648, 107 L. Ed. 2d 676 (1990).

[23]James, 493 U.S. at 317–318.

[24]493 U.S. at 318.

[25]State v. Rutter, 93 S.W.3d 714, 726–27 (Mo. 2002) (defendant did not waive right to have evidence excluded by opening statement comment that

fered in the prosecution's rebuttal case rather than its case-in-chief.[26]

Although the Supreme Court has never expressly so held, defendants are undoubtedly entitled to a limiting jury instruction directing the jurors to consider the evidence only on the defendant's credibility and not on guilt.[27]

State courts addressing the contents of state—generally constitutional—exclusionary requirements have seldom been willing to reject any impeachment exception.[28] Nevertheless, they have expressed concern regarding the scope and effect of exceptions based on the Supreme Court's federal constitutional model.[29] To the extent that state exclusionary requirements rest on broader rationales than the federal constitutional ones, of course, impeachment exceptions may be less appropriate in the state context.[30]

Some state tribunals, responding to such concerns, have adopted impeachment exceptions more limited than *Walder-Harris*. The Vermont Supreme Court, for example, emphasized what it viewed as the need to preserve a defendant's right to an unfettered opportunity to testify in his own defense. On this basis it rejected the *Havens* approach and held that evidence obtained in violation of the state provision could only be used to

---

he intended to present evidence on the subject).

[26]People v. Trujillo, 49 P.3d 316, 322 (Colo. 2002).

[27]Com. v. Wright, 415 Pa. 55, 60-61, 202 A.2d 79 (1964) ("where such evidence is properly admitted, the trial court must carefully instruct the jury that it is not to be used to determine if the defendant committed the crime, but solely for the purpose of evaluating the defendant's credibility"). *Accord* Brown v. State, 226 Ga. App. 140, 486 S.E.2d 370, 372 (1997); Brewer v. State, 501 S.W.2d 280, 283 (Tenn. 1973).

[28]The leading rejection of the exception was People v. Disbrow, 16 Cal. 3d 101, 127 Cal. Rptr. 360, 545 P.2d 272 (1976). *Disbrow* was nullified by amendment to the state constitution. See § 168 supra. Com. v. Triplett, 462 Pa. 244, 341 A.2d 62 (1975) also rejected *Harris*. But in 1984, Pa. Const. art. I, § 9 was amended to provide, "The use of a suppressed voluntary

admission or voluntary confession to impeach the credibility of a person may be permitted and shall not be construed as compelling a person to give evidence against himself." Thus impeachment use is permissible. *See* Com. v. Baxter, 367 Pa. Super. 342, 532 A.2d 1177, 1178 (1987).

[29]*See* State v. Burris, 145 N.J. 509, 679 A.2d 121, 131–33 (1996) ("continu[ing]" the impeachment exception to the state constitutional exclusionary rule, but acknowledging "genuine concerns" regarding its use that "counsel a use of the rule that is carefully circumscribed to assure that it will not be abused").

[30]State v. Iseli, 80 Or. App. 208, 720 P.2d 1343, 1344 (1986) (state rule's remedial function of restoring search victims to the position they would be in had no improper search been conducted suggests that improperly obtained evidence be unavailable to the prosecution for any purpose).

impeach a defendant's testimony on direct examination.[31] Hawaii, rejecting *Harris* but not *Walder*, held that evidence obtained in an unconstitutional search may not be used to impeach a testifying defendant's testimony "as to his actions," but may be used to contradict testimony regarding "the corroborative circumstances."[32]

---

[31]State v. Brunelle, 148 Vt. 347, 534 A.2d 198, 203 (1987).

[32]State v. Santiago, 53 Haw. 254, 492 P.2d 657, 664 (1971) (rejecting *Harris*), reaffirmed in State v. Kane, 87 Haw. 71, 951 P.2d 934, 941 (1998). *Compare* State v. Gomes, 59 Haw. 572, 584 P.2d 127, 129 (1978) ("the inadmissible evidence obtained by the prohibited search could be referred to in order to impeach, not appellant's testimony as to his actions, but his testimony as to the corroborative circumstances").

# Title 7.  Relevancy and Its Counterweights

## Chapter 16

# Relevance

§ 184    Relevance as the presupposition of admissibility
§ 185    The meaning of relevancy and the counterweights

## § 184    Relevance as the presupposition of admissibility

In the law of evidence, truth matters. To facilitate judgments based on an accurate understanding of the facts, the system of proof presupposes that the parties may present to the court or jury all the evidence that bears on the issues to be decided. Of course, many rules, such as those involving privilege, hearsay, and judicial economy, limit this system of free proof and keep probative evidence from the finder of fact. Nevertheless, unless there is some such distinct ground for refusing to hear the evidence, it should be received.[1] Conversely, if the evidence lacks probative value, it should be excluded.[2] Federal Rule of Evidence 402 and the corresponding Revised Uniform Rule adopt these two

---

**[Section 184]**

[1]State v. Collins, 335 N.C. 729, 440 S.E.2d 559, 562 (1994) (inasmuch as "every circumstance calculated to throw any light upon the supposed crime is admissible and permissible," evidence that the defendant did not support his children and did not send them gifts following his wife's death was properly admitted in a homicide prosecution); 1A Wigmore, Evidence § 28, at 969 n.2 & 975 (Tillers rev. 1983) (presenting pages of citations); cf. Holmes v. South Carolina, 547 U.S. 319, 330, 126 S. Ct. 1727, 164 L. Ed. 2d 503 (2006) (holding that exclusion of defense evidence of third-party guilt denied defendant a fair trial when the exclusion could not be said "to focus the trial on the central issues by excluding evidence that has only a very

weak logical connection to the central issues").

[2]E.g., People v. Hamilton, 45 Cal. 4th 863, 89 Cal. Rptr. 3d 286, 200 P.3d 898, 940 (2009) ("The trial court . . . lacks discretion to admit irrelevant evidence."); State v. Nesbit, 978 S.W.2d 872 (Tenn. 1998) (evidence that the defendant who admitted to shooting the deceased had a beeper and $602.00 in cash on him when arrested was improperly admitted because it "was not relevant to the existence of any issue that the jury was required to decide"). See generally Thayer, Preliminary Treatise on Evidence 264–66 (1898); 1 Wigmore, Evidence §§ 2, 27-29a (Tillers rev. 1983). Where one party offers irrelevant evidence and the other party, having failed to object, seeks to counter this evidence, the additional irrelevant evidence may be admissible

"axioms" of the common law. These rules succinctly provide that "relevant evidence is admissible" unless excluded by other laws or rules and that irrelevant evidence "is not admissible."

## § 185  The meaning of relevancy and the counterweights

To say that relevant evidence is generally admissible, while irrelevant evidence is not, would be of little value without a suitable definition of relevance. This section clarifies the meaning of relevance. It then outlines the factors that can make even relevant evidence inadmissible.

There are two components to relevant evidence: materiality and probative value.[1] Materiality concerns the fit between the evidence and the case. It looks to the relation between the propositions that the evidence is offered to prove and the issues in the case. If the evidence is offered to help prove a proposition that is not a matter in issue, the evidence is immaterial. What is "in issue," that is, within the range of the litigated controversy, is determined mainly by the pleadings, read in the light of the rules of pleading and controlled by the substantive law.[2] Thus, in a suit for worker's compensation, evidence of contributory negligence would be immaterial, whether pleaded or not, since a worker's negligence does not affect the right to compensation.[3] In an action to enjoin the enforcement of a statute prohibiting "partial-birth abortions" as void for vagueness, expert testimony as to a fetus's capacity to sense pain is immaterial, since it re-

---

as a form of "fighting fire with fire." See supra § 57.

**[Section 185]**

[1]*See, e.g.,* 1 Wigmore, Evidence § 2, at 18 (Tillers rev. 1983); James, Relevancy, Probability and the Law, 29 Calif. L. Rev. 689, 690–91 (1941).

[2]The matters in the range of dispute may extend somewhat beyond the issues defined in the pleadings. Under flexible systems of procedure, issues not raised by the pleadings may be tried by express or implied consent of the parties. *E.g.,* Fed. R. Civ. P. 15(b)(2).

[3]*Cf.* Mydlarz v. Palmer/Duncan Const. Co., 209 Mont. 325, 682 P.2d 695 (1984) (evidence of carelessness erroneously admitted, since contributory negligence is not a defense under Scaffolding Act). For other applications

of the materiality requirement, see U.S. v. Cassidy, 616 F.2d 101 (4th Cir. 1979) (whether United States' possession and use of nuclear weapons violates international law is immaterial in prosecution for desecrating the walls of the Pentagon); People v. Grant, 45 Cal. 3d 829, 248 Cal. Rptr. 444, 755 P.2d 894 (1988) (the grisly nature of the executions of convicted offenders sentenced to death is immaterial in a capital case); Reliance Steel & Aluminum Co. v. Sevcik, 267 S.W.3d 867, 868 (Tex. 2008) (in a highway accident case, it was reversible error to show that "the defendant's annual revenues were $1.9 billion" because "[n]either a plaintiff's poverty nor a defendant's wealth can help a jury decide whose negligence caused an accident").

lates only to the state's interest in enacting the law and not to the claim of vagueness.[4]

In addition to evidence that bears directly on the issues, leeway is allowed even on direct examination for proof of facts that merely fill in the background of the narrative and give it interest, color, and lifelikeness.[5] Maps, diagrams, charts, photographs, videotapes, and computer animations can be material as aids to the understanding of other material evidence.[6] Moreover, the parties may question the credibility of the witnesses and, within limits, produce evidence assailing and supporting their credibility.[7]

The second aspect of relevance is probative value, the tendency of evidence to establish the proposition that it is offered to prove. Federal Rule and the Uniform Rule of Evidence 401 incorporate these twin concepts of materiality and probative value. They state that " '[r]elevant evidence' means evidence having any tendency to make the existence of any fact that is of consequence to the determination of the action more probable or less probable than it would be without the evidence." A fact that is "of consequence" is material,[8] and evidence that affects the probability that a fact is as a party claims it to be has probative force.

---

[4]Planned Parenthood of Cent. New Jersey v. Verniero, 22 F. Supp. 2d 331 (D.N.J. 1998).

[5]*E.g.*, Old Chief v. U.S., 519 U.S. 172, 187–88, 117 S. Ct. 644, 136 L. Ed. 2d 574 (1997) (noting that "making a case with testimony and tangible things not only satisfies the formal definition of an offense, but tells a colorful story with descriptive richness" and remarking that the government in a criminal case may be allowed to introduce evidence to show "that a guilty verdict would be morally reasonable as much as to point to the discrete elements of a defendant's legal fault"); U.S. v. Freeman, 816 F.2d 558 (10th Cir. 1987) (hearsay accusations admissible to explain why police had defendants under surveillance when counterfeit money was passed). *But see* U.S. v. Harwood, 998 F.2d 91 (2d Cir. 1993) (error to admit hearsay testimony that defendant had a large supply of LSD as background to explain why officers approached defendant for an undercover buy).

[6]*E.g.*, Brookhaven Landscape & Grading Co., Inc. v. J. F. Barton

Contracting Co., 676 F.2d 516 (11th Cir. 1982) (chart contrasting anticipated and actual locations of boulders encountered in excavation admissible); Patton v. Archer, 590 F.2d 1319, 1323 (5th Cir. 1979) (chart of commodity price fluctuations admissible); *cf.* In re Air Crash Disaster at John F. Kennedy Intern. Airport on June 24, 1975, 635 F.2d 67, 73 (2d Cir. 1980) (proper to exclude chart of glide slope path that did not conform to stipulated facts). See generally infra §§ 213 to 214.

[7]U.S. v. Abel, 469 U.S. 45, 52, 105 S. Ct. 465, 83 L. Ed. 2d 450 (1984) (membership of defendant and his witness in prison gang that required its members to commit perjury for one another shows bias, which is relevant "because the jury, as finder of fact and weigher of credibility, has historically been entitled to assess all evidence which might bear on the accuracy and truth of a witness' testimony"); U.S. v. Robinson, 530 F.2d 1076 (D.C. Cir. 1976). See generally supra Ch. 5.

[8]U.S. v. Carriger, 592 F.2d 312, 315 (6th Cir. 1979). The Advisory Committee Note to Rule 401 criticizes

There are at least two ways to think about whether an item of evidence has probative value. First, one can simply ask, "Does learning of this evidence make it either more or less likely that the disputed fact is true?" Take, for example, evidence that a defendant charged with assaulting a neighbor has a reputation for being nonviolent. Knowing that someone has this reputation seems to make it less likely that he would commit an assault, presumably because we accept the underlying generalization that a smaller proportion of people with a reputation for nonviolence assault their neighbors than is the case for people generally. If we denote the reputation evidence as $E$ and the hypothesis that the defendant committed the assault as $H$, then we can say that the probability of the hypothesis $H$ given the evidence $E$ is less than the probability of $H$ without considering $E$. In symbols, $P(H \mid E) < P(H)$. (The vertical bar is read as "given" or "conditioned on," and "<" means "is less than.") Because $E$ changes the probability of the assault, it is relevant.[9]

Sometimes, however, this direct mode of reasoning about the probability of an hypothesis will be more difficult to apply because the effect of $E$ on the probability of $H$ will not be so apparent.[10] A second approach considers the probability of the evidence given the hypothesis, $P(E \mid H)$. Evidence that is more likely to arise when $H$ is true than when $H$ is not true supports $H$; evidence

---

the term "material" as "loosely used and ambiguous." At times, the term has been used somewhat differently than the way in which we have defined it. *E.g.*, Morgan, Basic Problems of Evidence 183 (1962).

[9]*Cf.* Hess v. State, 20 P.3d 1121, 1125 (Alaska 2001) (where a defendant charged with sexual assault contended that there was consent and the state elicited testimony that defendant previously forced another woman to engage in sex with him, it was error to exclude defendant's proof that he was acquitted of the prior charge of sexual assault because "[e]ven though the defendant's acquittal does not prove that he was innocent of the prior act, a jury may reasonably infer a greater probability of innocence from the fact of acquittal. . . . [A]lthough the acquittal does not prove that Hess was innocent of the prior charge, the . . . jury might plausibly have reasoned that the fact of the acquittal made it

less likely that [defendant] recklessly disregarded [the first alleged victim's] wishes. It might also plausibly have reasoned that the fact of the acquittal made it less likely that [defendant] had a propensity to recklessly disregard a companion's lack of consent. The jury therefore might also plausibly have reasoned that the fact of the acquittal made it less likely that [defendant] recklessly disregarded [the second alleged victim's] wishes. [The] acquittal was therefore relevant.").

[10]*See* Kaye, The Double Helix and the Law of Evidence 192–208 (2010); Lempert, Modeling Relevance, 75 Mich. L. Rev. 1021 (1977); Kaye, The Relevance of "Matching" DNA: Is the Window Half Open or Half Shut?, 85 J. Crim. L. & Criminology 676 (1995); Lyon & Koehler, The Relevance Ratio: Evaluating the Probative Value of Expert Testimony in Child Sexual Abuse Cases, 82 Cornell L. Rev. 43 (1996).

that is less likely to arise under $H$ than not-$H$ supports not-$H$.[11] Evidence of either type is probative of $H$. But evidence that is just as likely to arise when $H$ is true as when $H$ is false is of no use in deciding between $H$ and not-$H$—it is irrelevant.[12] In the example of the assault and the reputation for nonviolence, it seems less probable that a person who committed the assault would have such a reputation than that a person who did not commit the assault would have that reputation. Therefore, P($E$ | $H$) > P($E$ | not-$H$), and the evidence has probative value—it points toward not-$H$.

Indeed, the "likelihood ratio" of P($E$ | $H$) to P($E$ | not-$H$) can be used to quantify the probative value of the evidence $E$[13]—the larger the ratio, the more strongly the evidence supports the hypothesis $H$.[14] Consider a behavioral pattern said to be characteristic of abused children.[15] If research established that the behavior is equally common among abused and non-abused chil-

---

[11]Edwards, Likelihood: An Account of the Statistical Concept of Likelihood and its Application to Scientific Inference (1972); Royall, Statistical Evidence: A Likelihood Paradigm (1997).

[12]Keynes, A Treatise on Probability 120 (1st ed. 1921).

[13]*See, e.g.,* Edwards, Comment, 66 B.U. L. Rev. 623 (1986); Kaye, Comment: Quantifying Probative Value, 66 B.U. L. Rev. 761 (1986). Other measures of probative value have been advanced. *E.g.,* Friedman, A Close Look at Probative Value, 66 B.U. L. Rev. 733 (1986); Tillers & Schum, Charting New Territory in Judicial Proof: Beyond Wigmore, 9 Cardozo L. Rev. 907, 939–40 (1988). Some of these alternatives are criticized in Kaye & Koehler, The Misquantification of Probative Value, 27 Law & Hum. Behav. 645 (2003).

[14]The likelihood ratio can be interpreted as the ratio of (1) the odds in favor of $H$ given the evidence $E$ to (2) the odds without $E$. *See* Friedman, Assessing Evidence, 94 Mich. L. Rev. 1810 (1996); Lempert, Modeling Relevance, 75 Mich. L. Rev. 1021 (1977). When used in this sense, it is called the "Bayes factor." The Bayes factor thus measures just how much the evidence multiplicatively changes

the odds that $H$ is true. For example, if the odds (without regard to $E$) are 1:3 (corresponding to a probability of 1/4) and the Bayes factor for $E$ is 18, then the odds are increased to 18:3 (or 6:1, corresponding to a probability of 6/7).

Despite the numerical equivalence between the likelihood ratio and the Bayes' factor, accepting the likelihood ratio as a measure of probative value does not commit one to a fully Bayesian theory of evidence. Kaye, Likelihoodism, Bayesianism, and a Pair of Shoes, 53 Jurimetrics J. 1 (2012). And of course the conditional probabilities that appear in the likelihood ratio may involve contestable judgments. *See* Berger et al., Evidence Evaluation: A Response to the Court of Appeal Judgment in $R$ $v$ $T$, 51 Sci. & Justice 43, 45 (2011); Allen & Pardo, The Problematic Value of Mathematical Models of Evidence, 36 J. Legal Stud. 107 (2007).

[15]*See* Lyon & Koehler, The Relevance Ratio: Evaluating the Probative Value of Expert Testimony in Child Sexual Abuse Cases, 82 Cornell L. Rev. 43 (1996). This example involves but a single item of evidence, with no question as to the credibility of the source of the information. Expressing the probative value of a body of interrelated evidence in terms of the

dren, then its likelihood ratio would be one, and evidence of that pattern would not be probative of abuse. If the behavior were two times more common among abused children, then it would have rather modest probative value. And if it were a thousand times more common among abused children, its probative value would be far greater.

Probative evidence often is said to have "logical relevance," while evidence lacking in substantial probative value[16] may be condemned as "speculative"[17] or "remote."[18] Speculativeness usually arises with regard to dubious projections into the future or questionable surmises about what might have happened had the facts been different. For example, a calculation of lost wages in a wrongful death case that arbitrarily assumes that the deceased's salary would have grown at a constant rate year after year can be excluded as speculative.[19] Remoteness relates not to the passage of time alone, but to the undermining of reasonable infer-

---

underlying likelihood ratios can be very complex. *See, e.g.,* Kadane & Schum, A Probabilistic Analysis of the Sacco and Vanzetti Evidence (1996); Schum, Evidential Foundations of Probabilistic Reasoning (1994); Friedman, A Diagrammatic Approach to Evidence, 66 B.U. L. Rev. 571 (1986).

[16]That substantial probative value is required for evidence to be relevant is not apparent from the wording of Federal and Uniform Rule 401, but it is a pragmatic response that can be understood as a blend of rules 401 and 403. *See* Crump, On the Uses of Irrelevant Evidence, 34 Hous. L. Rev. 1 (1997); *cf.* Friedman, Irrelevance, Minimal Relevance, and Meta-Relevance, 34 Hous. L. Rev. 55, 65 (1997) (suggesting that rule 401 be revised to define "relevant evidence" as evidence that has "substantial probative value").

[17]Carlton v. H. C. Price Co., 640 F.2d 573, 579 (5th Cir. 1981) ("speculative for the jury to guess at a figure [for future medical expenses] in excess of those provided by the expert testimony"); Hull v. Merck & Co., Inc., 758 F.2d 1474, 1477 (11th Cir. 1985) (testimony of medical expert that exposure to chemicals was cause of plaintiff's illness made speculative by assumptions of facts not in evidence); State v. Conlogue, 474 A.2d 167 (Me. 1984)

(psychiatrist's opinion that, two years prior to incident at bar, mother accused of child abuse "might possibly be developing a psychosis").

[18]Holmes v. South Carolina, 547 U.S. 319, 326–27, 126 S. Ct. 1727, 164 L. Ed. 2d 503 (2006) ("evidence tending to prove that another person may have committed the crime with which the defendant is charged . . . may be excluded where it is speculative or remote"). *Compare* Sampson v. Missouri Pac. R. Co., 560 S.W.2d 573 (Mo. 1978) (seven-year-old hospital records concerning alcoholism of plaintiff in negligence action too remote) *with* State v. Green, 232 Kan. 116, 652 P.2d 697 (1982) (evidence that a husband charged with murdering his wife with an ax had thrown a hatchet at her nearly a year before not too remote). *See also* Gilstrap v. State, 261 Ga. 798, 410 S.E.2d 423 (1991) ("Where 'similar transaction' evidence has been admissible otherwise, lapses of time of 11 years and of 19 years have not demanded that the evidence was inadmissible. It should be clear, however, that an event 31 years in the past is too remote." To which a concurring opinion cautioned that "remoteness in time is not, alone, a sufficient standard.") (citations and note omitted).

[19]Hoffman v. Sterling Drug, Inc., 485 F.2d 132 (3d Cir. 1973) (error to

ences due to the likelihood of supervening factors. For example, testimony that the defendant in an automobile accident case was speeding just a few minutes before the collision is relevant to whether defendant was speeding at the moment of the collision,[20] but testimony that defendant exceeded the speed limit two years before the accident is likely to be excluded as too remote.[21] The two-year-old incident offers some indication that the driver was speeding, but many factors affect how fast a driver goes at a particular time, and these factors would change over a two-year period.[22]

Under our system, molded by the tradition of jury trial and predominantly oral proof, a party offers his evidence not en masse, but item by item. An item of evidence, being but a single link in the chain of proof,[23] need not prove conclusively the proposition for which it is offered.[24] It need not even make that proposition appear more probable than not.[25] Whether the entire body of one party's evidence is sufficient to go to the jury is one question. Whether a particular item of evidence is relevant to the case is quite another.[26] It is enough if the item could reasonably show that a fact is slightly more probable than it would appear without that evidence.[27] Even after the probative force of the evidence is spent, the proposition for which it is offered still can

---

admit expert calculations of future earnings that simply assumed a six percent annual salary increment).

[20]*See* Hill v. Rolleri, 615 F.2d 886, 891 (9th Cir. 1980) (speed of bus ten minutes before accident not too remote).

[21]The testimony also runs afoul of the rule against character evidence. See infra § 189 (character for care in civil cases).

[22]As this example also suggests, evidence excluded as "remote" often has some probative value, but not enough in light of the countervailing concerns discussed below. *See, e.g.,* U.S. v. Ravich, 421 F.2d 1196, 1204 n.10 (2d Cir. 1970); State v. Morowitz, 200 Conn. 440, 512 A.2d 175 (1986) ("remoteness . . . is one factor to be considered").

[23]*See* McCandless v. U.S., 298 U.S. 342, 56 S. Ct. 764, 80 L. Ed. 1205 (1936); Oseman v. State, 32 Wis. 2d 523, 145 N.W.2d 766 (1966).

[24]Doe v. New York City Dept. of Social Services, 649 F.2d 134, 147 (2d Cir. 1981); People v. Scott, 29 Ill. 2d 97, 193 N.E.2d 814, 822–23 (1963); Com. v. Yesilciman, 406 Mass. 736, 550 N.E.2d 378 (1990) (need "only provide a link in the chain of evidence").

[25]Bush v. Jackson, 191 Colo. 249, 552 P.2d 509 (1976); State v. Davis, 351 Or. 35, 261 P.3d 1197, 1205 (2011) ("the inference that the proponent of the evidence wishes to be drawn from the evidence need not be the necessary, or even the most probable, one.").

[26]State v. Irebaria, 55 Haw. 353, 519 P.2d 1246 (1974); State v. Giles, 253 La. 533, 218 So. 2d 585 (1969). The distinction is between relevance—a binary quantity in that an item of evidence either is or is not relevant—and probative value—a continuous quantity that varies from very weak (or even nonexistent) to exceeding strong (practically conclusive).

[27]Mutual Life Ins. Co. of New York v. Hillmon, 145 U.S. 285, 12 S. Ct. 909, 36 L. Ed. 706 (1892) (discussing the admissibility of certain letters written by Walters and expressing an

seem quite improbable.[28] Thus, the common objection that the inference for which the fact is offered "does not necessarily follow" is untenable.[29] It poses a standard of conclusiveness that very few single items of circumstantial evidence ever could meet.[30] A brick is not a wall.

But if even very weak material items of evidence are relevant, what sort of evidence is irrelevant for want of probative value? The long-standing distinction between "direct" and "circumstantial" evidence offers a starting point in answering this question.[31] Direct evidence is evidence which, if believed, resolves a matter

---

intention of going with Hillmon on a trip to Colorado, and reasoning that these "letters were competent, not as narratives of facts communicated to the writer by others nor yet as proof that he actually went away from Wichita, but as evidence that, shortly before the time when other evidence tended to show that he went away, he had the intention of going, and of going with Hillmon, which made it more probable both that he did go and that he went with Hillmon than if there had been no proof of such intention"); Home Ins. Co. v. Weide, 78 U.S. 438, 440, 20 L. Ed. 197, 1870 WL 12732 (1870) ("It is well settled that if the evidence conduces to any reasonable degree to establish the probability or improbability of a fact in controversy, it should go to the jury"); U.S. v. Jordan, 485 F.3d 1214, 1218 (10th Cir. 2007) ("The bar for admission under Rule 401 is 'very low.' . . . This is because the degree of materiality and probativity necessary for evidence to be relevant is 'minimal' and must only provide a 'fact-finder with a basis for making some inference, or chain of inferences.'") (quoting U.S. v. McVeigh, 153 F.3d 1166, 1190 (10th Cir. 1998)); U.S. v. Pugliese, 153 F.2d 497, 500 (C.C.A. 2d Cir. 1945) (Learned Hand, J.) ("All that is necessary . . . is that each bit may have enough rational connection with the issue to be considered a factor contributing to an answer").

[28]U.S. v. Curtis, 568 F.2d 643 (9th Cir. 1978); Byrd v. Lord Bros. Contractors, Inc., 256 Or. 421, 473 P.2d 1018 (1970).

[29]See, e.g., Douglass v. Eaton Corp., 956 F.2d 1339, 1344 (6th Cir. 1992) ("Even if a district court believes the evidence is insufficient to prove the ultimate point for which it is offered, it may not exclude the evidence if it has even the slightest probative value."); Supreme Pork, Inc. v. Master Blaster, Inc., 2009 SD 20, 764 N.W.2d 474, 488 (S.D. 2009) ("a tendency" suffices).

[30]Most circumstantial evidence commonly received could not pass so stringent a test. For instance, when a violent death is shown, evidence that the defendant accused of homicide was the beneficiary of a policy on the life of the deceased will be admitted. See generally 2 Wigmore, Evidence §§ 385, 390–91 (Chadbourn rev. 1979) (relevance of facts showing motive as evidence of doing an act). So too with evidence that the accused had an opportunity to commit the killing, 1A Wigmore, Evidence § 131 (Tillers rev. 1983), or that he expressed an intention to do so shortly before the death. 1A Wigmore, Evidence §§ 102–03. Motive, opportunity and design, taken together, may make guilt more probable than not, but singly each falls far short of establishing so high a probability.

[31]Perry's Adm'x v. Inter-Southern Life Ins. Co., 248 Ky. 491, 58 S.W.2d 906 (1933); People v. Bretagna, 298 N.Y. 323, 83 N.E.2d 537 (1949); Patterson, The Types of Evidence: An Analysis, 19 Vand. L. Rev. 1 (1965). The distinction is conceptually useful, but it has no direct importance in passing on the relevance of particular

in issue. Circumstantial evidence also may be testimonial,[32] but even if the circumstances depicted are accepted as true, additional reasoning is required to reach the desired conclusion. For example, a witness' testimony that he saw A stab B with a knife is direct evidence of whether A did indeed stab B. In contrast, testimony that A fled the scene of the stabbing would be circumstantial evidence of the stabbing (but direct evidence of the flight itself). Similarly, testimony of a witness that he saw A at the scene would be direct evidence that A was there, but testimony that he saw someone who was disguised and masked, but had a voice and limp like A's, would be circumstantial evidence that the person seen was A.[33]

In terms of this dichotomy, direct evidence from a qualified witness[34] offered to help establish a provable fact can never be irrelevant.[35] Circumstantial evidence, however, can be offered to help prove a material fact, yet be so unrevealing as to be irrele-

---

evidence. Both sorts of evidence are quite convincing on some occasions, but not nearly so telling in other instances. *See, e.g.,* U.S. v. Andrino, 501 F.2d 1373, 1378 (9th Cir. 1974) ("circumstantial evidence is not less probative than direct evidence, and, in some instances, is even more reliable"). Yet, it has been said that jurors tend to undervalue some forms of circumstantial evidence relative to direct evidence and are not easily satisfied without the latter form of evidence. Heller, The Cognitive Psychology of Circumstantial Evidence, 105 Mich. L. Rev. 241 (2006).

[32]For discussions of the difficulties implicit in this simplified definition and in Wigmore's more refined but unusual characterization of "real," "testimonial" and "circumstantial" evidence, see 1A Wigmore, Evidence §§ 24–25 (Tillers rev. 1983); Patterson, The Types of Evidence: An Analysis, 19 Vand. L. Rev. 1 (1965).

[33]Privette v. Faulkner, 92 Nev. 353, 550 P.2d 404 (1976); *cf.* U.S. v. Eatherton, 519 F.2d 603 (1st Cir. 1975). Likewise, a crucial issue in Williams v. Illinois, 132 S. Ct. 2221, 183 L. Ed. 2d 89 (2012), was whether a laboratory had correctly analyzed the DNA in samples sent to it. Because no one from the laboratory testified, there was no direct evidence on this

point. At a lineup, however, the victim of the rape identified a man who turned out to have the same DNA type as that reported to be present in semen in the vaginal swab sent to the laboratory. This coincidence, a plurality of the Supreme Court reasoned, was powerful circumstantial evidence that the laboratory had analyzed the correct samples and had done so accurately. What else could explain the fact that the reported DNA type matched "the very man whom the victim identified in a lineup and at trial as her attacker"? 132 S.Ct. at 2238 (plurality opinion). Although the coincidence was less dramatic than the plurality suggested—the man she identified was placed in the lineup only because he possessed the reported DNA type—the victim's identifications of him are at once direct evidence that he was the rapist and circumstantial evidence that the laboratory analyzed his DNA rather than anyone else's.

[34]As discussed supra Ch. 7, the court might find a witness incompetent to testify.

[35]A judge or jury is free to disbelieve any witness, but that possibility does not make the testimony irrelevant. For a formal analysis of the effect of credibility on probative value, see Schum & Martin, Formal and Empirical Research in Cascaded Infer-

vant to that fact. For instance, evidence that the government awarded a firm a lucrative contract is irrelevant on the issue of whether the firm damaged property leased to it because there is no reason to suppose that firms that handle large government contracts are more likely to damage such property than other lessees.[36]

In short, to say that circumstantial evidence is irrelevant in the sense that it lacks probative value is to say that knowing the evidence does not justify any reasonable inference about the fact in question.[37] Cases involving such evidence are few and far between.[38] That more than one inference could be drawn is not enough to render the evidence irrelevant. Fleeing the scene of a crime, for instance, could mean that the defendant, being con-

---

ence in Jurisprudence, 17 Law & Soc'y Rev. 105 (1982).

[36] City of Cleveland v. Peter Kiewit Sons' Co., 624 F.2d 749 (6th Cir. 1980). Evidence of wealth may, however, be admissible on the issue of punitive damages. Grant v. Arizona Public Service Co., 133 Ariz. 434, 652 P.2d 507, 522 (1982). In combination with a failure to file tax returns, evidence of excessive wealth may be admissible to show drug dealing. See U.S. v. Humphrey, 287 F.3d 422 (6th Cir. 2002), overruled in part on other grounds by United States v. Leachman, 309 F.3d 377 (6th Cir. 2002). But cf. U.S. v. Carter, 969 F.2d 197, 200 (6th Cir. 1992) (evidence of a failure to file federal income tax returns "is not probative on the issue of whether [defendant] engaged in a [single] cocaine transaction").

[37] U.S. v. Schipani, 289 F. Supp. 43, 56 (E.D. N.Y. 1968) (denying motion to suppress) (the test for relevancy is "whether a reasonable man might have his assessment of the probabilities of a material proposition changed by the piece of evidence"); Stewart v. People, 23 Mich. 63, 1871 WL 3011 (1871). The process of drawing inferences from circumstantial evidence involves inductive, not deductive reasoning. See Skyrms, Choice and Chance: An Introduction to Inductive Logic (4th ed. 2000); Salmon, The Foundations of Scientific Inference (1967).

[38] For cases finding facts completely lacking in probative value, see, for example, Mohammed v. Otoadese, 738 N.W.2d 628, 632 (Iowa 2007) (that a patient whose vocal cords were paralyzed brought an unrelated tort action for a slip-and-fall against a convenience store was not relevant to the malpractice claim against the surgeon); State v. Davis, 351 Or. 35, 261 P.3d 1197, 1207 (2011) (given that a mother took her child to the hospital June 25 "and that, over the course of several hours, the [child] was fully examined and subjected to testing to determine what was wrong with her," proof of the mother's "'deliberate withholding' of her fear (or belief) . . . does not make it more likely that the [child] actually was then suffering from a brain injury" that day, and "[e]ven under the low threshold for relevance, [her] belief in the possibility of a brain injury on June 25 does not, even slightly, . . . . decrease the probability that the fatal injuries occurred on June 29 or 30"); Com. v. Briggs, 608 Pa. 430, 12 A.3d 291, 339–40 (2011), cert. denied, 132 S. Ct. 267, 181 L. Ed. 2d 157 (2011) (that a man accused of shooting two police deputies voluntarily appeared at a court hearing was not relevant to show that, because he "did not fear being arrested or incarcerated," he did not have the state's "suggested motive that he killed the deputies because he did not want to be taken into custody").

scious of guilt for the crime charged, actually is guilty;[39] or it could mean that defendant is innocent but fled to avoid being apprehended for some other reason entirely.[40] However, the premise that, in general, people who flee are more likely to be guilty than those who do not is at least plausible, and as long as there is some plausible chain of reasoning that leads to the desired conclusion, the evidence is probative of that conclusion.[41] As a result, most evidence seriously offered at trial has *some* probative value.[42] Even when the courts denominate evidence as devoid of probative value, one may often wonder whether the evidence is not more properly excludable on grounds of materiality or insufficient probative value given the countervailing considerations that can bar the use of relevant evidence.[43]

Yet, how can a judge know whether the evidence could reasonably affect an assessment of the probability of the fact to be

---

[39]*See* Allen v. U.S., 164 U.S. 492, 499, 17 S. Ct. 154, 41 L. Ed. 528 (1896) ("the law is entirely well settled that the flight of the accused is competent evidence against him as having a tendency to establish his guilt"); U.S. v. Levine, 5 F.3d 1100, 1107 (7th Cir. 1993) (explicating the logic of flight as tending to establish guilt).

[40]*See* Alberty v. U.S., 162 U.S. 499, 511, 16 S. Ct. 864, 40 L. Ed. 1051 (1896) ("men who are entirely innocent do sometimes fly from the scene of a crime through fear of being apprehended as the guilty parties, or from an unwillingness to appear as witnesses").

[41]*See* State v. Hampton, 317 Or. 251, 855 P.2d 621, 623 (1993) ("The possibility that an inconsistent or contradictory inference may reasonably be drawn from the offered item of evidence does not destroy that item's relevancy so long as the inference desired by the proponent is also a reasonable one."); Byrd v. Lord Bros. Contractors, Inc., 256 Or. 421, 473 P.2d 1018, 1020 (1970) (where plaintiff was struck by concrete falling from a freeway overpass being repaired by defendant, evidence that four or five boys were running some six blocks away was admissible to suggest that they might have dropped the concrete even though "the boys could have come from numerous other places than the overpass and

could have been running for any one of the various reasons that boys run").

[42]*Compare* Crump, On the Uses of Irrelevant Evidence, 34 Hous. L. Rev. 1 (1997) (arguing that all facts are logically relevant), *with* Friedman, Irrelevance, Minimal Relevance, and Meta-Relevance, 34 Hous. L. Rev. 55 (1997) (maintaining that some facts are logically irrelevant).

[43]*See, e.g.,* Jenkins v. Anderson, 447 U.S. 231, 247, 100 S. Ct. 2124, 65 L. Ed. 2d 86 (1980) (dissenting opinion arguing that the fact that defendant, who stabbed another allegedly in self-defense yet waited two weeks before going to the police is "so unlikely to be probative" of the falsity of his trial testimony that it is "simply irrelevant" as impeachment evidence); U.S. v. Carter, 522 F.2d 666, 684 (D.C. Cir. 1975) (error to admit photo of drawing found on desk pad and "doodles" found at scene of robbery where FBI agent testified that more experienced agents had told him that no valid comparisons could be made); Energy Transp. Systems, Inc. v. Mackey, 650 P.2d 1152, 1156 (Wyo. 1982) (owner's testimony on what land is worth to him "has no probative value in a condemnation case"). For a discussion of the admissibility of evidence that is generally agreed to have no inferential value (on the issue of negligence), see infra § 201 (proof of liability insur-

inferred? In some instances, scientific research may show that the fact in issue is more likely to be true (or false) when such evidence is present than when it is not.[44] Ordinarily, however, the answer must lie in the judge's personal experience, general knowledge, and understanding of human conduct and motivation.[45] If one asks whether an attempted escape by a prisoner charged with two serious but factually unconnected crimes is relevant to show consciousness of guilt of the first crime charged,[46] the answer will not be found in a statistical table of the attempts at escape by those conscious of guilt as opposed to those not conscious of their guilt. The judge can only ask, could a reasonable juror believe that the fact that the accused tried to escape makes it more probable than it would otherwise be that the accused was conscious of guilt of the crime being tried? If the answer is affirmative, then the evidence is relevant. In other situations, the judge may need to consider not only whether the evidence reasonably could support the proposition for which it is offered, but also whether its absence might warrant the opposite inference.[47] That is, where a jury would expect to receive a certain kind of evidence, testimony explaining why that evidence is not available could be helpful and should be considered relevant.[48]

In sum, relevant evidence is evidence that in some degree advances the inquiry. It is material and probative. As such, it is admissible, at least prima facie. But this relevance does not ensure admissibility. There remains the question of whether its value is worth what it costs. A great deal of evidence is excluded on the ground that the costs outweigh the benefits. Rule 403 of the Federal and Uniform Evidence Rules categorize most of these

---

ance).

[44]*See* Strong, Questions Affecting the Admissibility of Scientific Evidence, 1970 U. Ill. L.F. 1, 2–4; Michael & Adler, The Trial of an Issue of Fact (pt. 1), 34 Colum. L. Rev. 1224, 1297 (1934).

[45]People v. Engelman, 434 Mich. 204, 453 N.W.2d 656 (1990) (whether pedophilia is gender-specific).

[46]*E.g.*, U.S. v. Myers, 550 F.2d 1036 (5th Cir. 1977) (articulating the logical steps required to infer guilt from flight and concluding that the evidence was irrelevant because of weakness in certain of these steps); People v. Yazum, 13 N.Y.2d 302, 246 N.Y.S.2d 626, 196 N.E.2d 263 (1963) (relevant);

State v. Crawford, 59 Utah 39, 201 P. 1030 (1921) (irrelevant); State v. Piche, 71 Wash. 2d 583, 430 P.2d 522 (1967) (relevant). See infra § 263.

[47]*See* Simon v. C.I.R., 830 F.2d 499 (3d Cir. 1987) (failure of taxpayers to provide testimony from persons involved in structuring financial transactions); Kaye, Do We Need a Calculus of Weight to Understand Proof Beyond a Reasonable Doubt?, 65 B.U. L. Rev. 657 (1986); Lindley & Eggleston, The Problem of Missing Evidence, 99 Law Q. Rev. 86 (1983).

[48]Saltzburg, A Special Aspect of Relevance: Countering Negative Inferences Associated with the Absence of Evidence, 66 Cal. L. Rev. 1011 (1978).

costs.[49] This rule codifies the common law power of the judge to exclude relevant evidence "if its probative value is substantially outweighed by the danger of unfair prejudice, confusion of the issues, or misleading the jury, or by considerations of undue delay, waste of time, or needless presentation of cumulative evidence."[50]

---

[49]Other social policies sometimes influence relevance rulings. *E.g.*, People v. Hackett, 421 Mich. 338, 365 N.W.2d 120 (1984) (need to protect victims of sex crimes from humiliation of questioning on unrelated sexual conduct); Com. v. Morgan, 358 Pa. 607, 58 A.2d 330 (1948) (need to protect rape victims from humiliation of physically demonstrating details of rape); Garvik v. Burlington, C.R. & N.R. Co., 124 Iowa 691, 100 N.W. 498 (1904) (indecency cited as a factor warranting exclusion). The propriety of relying on such factors to exclude relevant evidence under Rule 403 is disputed in Imwinkelried, The Meaning of Probative Value and Prejudice in Federal Rule of Evidence 403: Can Rule 403 Be Used to Resurrect the Common Law of Evidence?, 41 Vand. L. Rev. 879 (1988). Where evidence of a defendant's political or social views is involved, the First Amendment may compel a more searching inquiry into the probative value of the evidence or a different balance of prejudice and probative value. *See* Dawson v. Delaware, 503 U.S. 159, 112 S. Ct. 1093, 117 L. Ed. 2d 309 (1992); Faulkner, Evidence of First Amendment Activity at Trial: The Articulation of a Higher Evidentiary Standard, 42 UCLA L. Rev. 1 (1994); *cf.* White, The Statutory and Constitutional Limits of Using Protected Speech as Evidence of Unlawful Motive Under the National Labor Relations Act, 53 Ohio St. L.J. 1 (1992).

[50]For discussions and criticisms of this codification and the many cases applying it, see, for example, Gold, Federal Rule of Evidence 403: Observations on the Nature of Unfairly Prejudicial Evidence, 58 Wash. L. Rev. 497 (1983); Lewis, Proof and Prejudice: A Constitutional Challenge to the Treat-

ment of Prejudicial Evidence in Federal Criminal Cases, 64 Wash. L. Rev. 289 (1989); Tanford, A Political-Choice Approach to Limiting Prejudicial Evidence, 64 Ind. L.J. 831 (1989). The original Uniform Rules were slightly different. Uniform Rule 45 (1953) included the possibility that evidence would unfairly and harmfully surprise a party who has not had reasonable opportunity to anticipate that such evidence would be offered as a factor be weighed against probative value. Model Code of Evidence Rule 303(1) (1942) likewise includes surprise as a factor.

Whether surprise could justify exclusion of evidence at common law is doubtful. See 6 Wigmore, Evidence §§ 1845, 1849 (Chadbourn rev. 1976). *But see* 1A Wigmore, Evidence §§ 29a, 194, 979 (Tillers rev. 1983); Tanford, A Political-Choice Approach to Limiting Prejudicial Evidence, 64 Ind. L.J. 831 (1989). Still, some cases mention the unfair surprise arising when an opponent, having had no reasonable ground to anticipate the evidence, is unprepared to meet it, as grounds for exclusion. People v. Collins, 68 Cal. 2d 319, 66 Cal. Rptr. 497, 438 P.2d 33 (1968); State v. Martin, 472 So. 2d 91, 96 (La. Ct. App. 5th Cir. 1985); Stoelting v. Hauck, 32 N.J. 87, 159 A.2d 385 (1960); Thompson v. American Steel & Wire Co., 317 Pa. 7, 175 A. 541 (1934). Unfair surprise is not included in the Federal Rules and the Revised Uniform Rules on the theory that the appropriate remedy is a continuance. Fed. R. Evid. 403 advisory committee's notes. Of course, a distinct issue occurs when the surprise results from a breach of a rule of pleading or discovery. Exclusion then may be used to enforce such rules. *E.g.*, 6 Wigmore, Evidence § 1848 (Chadbourn rev. 1976); Bursey v. Bursey, 145 N.H. 283, 761 A.2d 491, 493 (2000); *cf.* Michigan

Such factors often blend together in practice, but we shall elaborate on them briefly in the rough order of their importance. First, there is the danger of prejudice. In this context, prejudice (or, as the rule puts it, "unfair prejudice") does not simply mean damage to the opponent's cause—for that can be a sign of probative value, not prejudice.[51] Neither does it necessarily mean an appeal to emotion.[52] Prejudice can arise, however, from facts that arouse the jury's hostility or sympathy for one side without regard to the probative value of the evidence.[53] Thus, evidence of convictions for prior, unrelated crimes might lead a juror to think that since the defendant already has a criminal record, an erroneous conviction would not be quite as serious as it would otherwise be.[54] A juror influenced in this fashion may be satisfied with a somewhat less compelling demonstration of guilt than should be required.[55] This rationale has been used in innumerable contexts—for example, to preclude inquiry into a medical expert's work in abor-

---

v. Lucas, 500 U.S. 145, 111 S. Ct. 1743, 114 L. Ed. 2d 205 (1991) (defendant accused of raping his ex-girlfriend, who failed to give timely, required notice of his intent to use evidence of his own past sexual conduct with the ex-girlfriend, could be precluded from introducing that evidence).

[51]E.g., Foley v. City of Lowell, Mass., 948 F.2d 10, 15 (1st Cir. 1991) (in a civil rights action against a city for condoning police brutality, the outrageousness of the police conduct on separate occasions "is a hallmark of probative value: the more outrageous the occurrences, the more probable that a policy of tolerance was in place"). Evidence that the facts are contrary to one party's contentions always is damaging, but this cannot be ground for excluding the evidence. Borden, Inc. v. Florida East Coast Ry. Co., 772 F.2d 750 (11th Cir. 1985); State v. Rollo, 221 Or. 428, 351 P.2d 422, 427 (1960) (an advocate "is entitled to hit as hard as he can above, but not below, the belt").

[52]E.g., State v. Dist. Ct. (Armstrong), 267 P.3d 777, 781, 127 Nev. Adv. Op. No. 84 (Nev. 2011).

[53]State v. Flett, 234 Or. 124, 380 P.2d 634, 636 (1963) ("to produce passion and prejudice out of proportion to its probative value"); Lease America

Corp. v. Insurance Co. of North America, 88 Wis. 2d 395, 276 N.W.2d 767 (1979) (causes jury to base decision on something other than established propositions in the case).

[54]See Old Chief v. U.S., 519 U.S. 172, 182, 117 S. Ct. 644, 136 L. Ed. 2d 574 (1997).

[55]Lempert, Modeling Relevance, 75 Mich. L. Rev. 1021 (1977) (change in an ideal, hypothetical juror's "regret matrix" distorts his appreciation of the burden of persuasion). This form of prejudice arises in many situations. See Harless v. Boyle-Midway Division, American Home Products, 594 F.2d 1051, 1058 (5th Cir. 1979) (proof that a 14-year-old boy had smoked marijuana on one occasion introduced for use in valuing the loss of his life held to be error, since the evidence was "highly prejudicial" yet "tenuous" and of "slight value" on the issue of damages); Meller v. Heil Co., 745 F.2d 1297, 1303 (10th Cir. 1984) (two hashish pipes containing marijuana residue found in decedent's rucksack inadmissible in absence of medical foundation showing that such drug use diminishes life expectancy); People v. Corey, 148 N.Y. 476, 42 N.E. 1066, 1071 (1896) (syphilis); Dunkle v. State, 2006 OK CR 29, 139 P.3d 228 (Okla. Crim. App. 2006) (witchcraft).

tion clinics after the expert had testified about the cause of infertility in a woman who used an intrauterine device,[56] to cut salacious scenes from a videotape of a two-million-dollar birthday party given by a corporate CEO accused of looting the company to pay for half of the party and for many other extravagances,[57] to preclude disclosure of the value of stock given to a White House official charged with illegal lobbying,[58] to preclude expert testimony on the extrapolation of a single blood alcohol test to a much earlier time,[59] to limit the number and nature of gruesome photographs of murder victims,[60] and to exclude videotapes of an injured plaintiff's rehabilitative therapy or daily activities.[61] Second, whether or not "emotional" reactions are at work, relevant evidence can confuse,[62] or worse, mislead a trier of fact who is not properly equipped to judge the probative worth of the evidence.[63] Third, certain proof and the answering evidence that

---

[56]Nickerson v. G.D. Searle & Co., 900 F.2d 412, 419 (1st Cir. 1990) ("fierce emotional reaction that is engendered in many people when the subject of abortion surfaces in any manner").

[57]Sorkin, Birthday Party Video Takes Center Stage at Kozlowski Trial, N.Y. Times, Oct. 29, 2003, at C4.

[58]Judge Won't Let Prosecutors Say Nofziger Received Wedtech Stock, Hous. Chron., Jan. 23, 1988, at 6.

[59]E.g., State v. Dist. Ct. (Armstrong), 267 P.3d 777, 127 Nev. Adv. Op. No. 84 (Nev. 2011).

[60]Berry v. State, 290 Ark. 223, 718 S.W.2d 447, 449–450 (1986); State v. Hennis, 323 N.C. 279, 372 S.E.2d 523, 526–27 (1988); Com. v. Powell, 428 Pa. 275, 241 A.2d 119, 121 (1968).

[61]Bannister v. Town of Noble, Okl., 812 F.2d 1265 (10th Cir. 1987) (giving guidelines for evaluating "day-in-the-life" films); Haley v. Byers Transp. Co., 414 S.W.2d 777, 780 (Mo. 1967) ("impact of these films would have been to create . . . sympathy . . . out of proportion to the real relevance of the evidence").

[62]Hamling v. U.S., 418 U.S. 87, 94 S. Ct. 2887, 41 L. Ed. 2d 590 (1974); Shepard v. U.S., 290 U.S. 96, 104, 54 S. Ct. 22, 78 L. Ed. 196 (1933) ("When the risk of confusion is so great as to

upset the balance of advantage, the evidence goes out"); Adams v. Providence and Worcester Co., 721 F.2d 870 (1st Cir. 1983); Renfro Hosiery Mills Co. v. National Cash Register Co., 552 F.2d 1061, 1069 (4th Cir. 1977) ("voluminous and complex" exhibits could have been excluded on the ground that they "had little if any probative value" and, among other defects, "might well have been confusing to a layman").

[63]Lempert, Modeling Relevance, 75 Mich. L. Rev. 1021 (1977), calls this an "estimation problem" with regard to the likelihood ratio. Fear that jurors will overestimate the worth of scientific and statistical evidence has limited the use of this type of evidence. See infra Ch. 20. Many psychological studies disclose some conditions under which people systematically err in drawing inferences from data. See, e.g., Judgment Under Uncertainty: Heuristics and Biases (Kahneman et al. eds., 1982); Gold, Jury Wobble: Judicial Tolerance of Jury Inferential Error, 59 S. Cal. L. Rev. 391 (1986); Heller, The Cognitive Psychology of Circumstantial Evidence, 105 Mich. L. Rev. 241 (2006). Kahan, The Economics—Conventional, Behavioral, and Political—of "Subsequent Remedial Measures" Evidence, 110 Colum. L. Rev. 1616 (2010), argues that the danger of overweighting should not lead to exclusion in civil cases when

it provokes might unduly distract the jury from the main issues.[64] Finally, the evidence offered and the counterproof could consume an inordinate amount of time.[65]

---

the other evidence of liability is relatively close.

[64]This condition could result from evidence that is so sensational and shocking that the jury would think of nothing else. Evidence of this nature is likely to be excluded. *E.g.*, Garvik v. Burlington, C.R. & N.R. Co., 124 Iowa 691, 100 N.W. 498, 500 (1904) ("shocking and indecent" jury view of penis to decide whether man was capable of sexual intercourse); Com. v. Morgan, 358 Pa. 607, 58 A.2d 330 (1948) (sobbing rape victim ordered to demonstrate body position maintained when she was raped on physician's examining table). Of course, these are extreme cases. More commonly, evidence that is disturbing or even gruesome is admitted as long as it has significant probative value. *E.g.*, Government of Virgin Islands v. Albert, 241 F.3d 344, 349 (3d Cir. 2001) (holding that the videotape of a murder scene, while explicit and gruesome, had probative value that was not substantially outweighed by prejudice and was admissible); State v. Kell, 2002 UT 106, 61 P.3d 1019, 1030 (Utah 2002) (holding that the videotape of a murder in progress has a high probative value that is not substantially outweighed by the prejudice of the fact that the video is "disturbing and difficult to watch").

A more common and subtle form of "distraction" can occur when the jury is tempted to rely on one type of evidence to the detriment of other important, but seemingly less revealing, evidence. *See, e.g.*, People v. Golochowicz, 413 Mich. 298, 319 N.W.2d 518, 528 (1982) (speculating that "if evidence of the identity of the criminal actor is weak or tenuous, revelation that he has committed an unrelated similar crime may, by reason of its tendency to distract the jury from the identification issue, tempt it to compromise or ignore that central element of the case while focusing on

the clearer proof of the defendant's other misconduct").

[65]U.S. v. Socony-Vacuum Oil Co., 310 U.S. 150, 230, 60 S. Ct. 811, 84 L. Ed. 1129 (1940) ("Terminal points are necessary even in a conspiracy trial involving intricate business facts and legal issues."); Renfro Hosiery Mills Co. v. National Cash Register Co., 552 F.2d 1061, 1069 (4th Cir. 1977) ("exhibits had little if any probative value but rather considerable potential for prolongation of the trial"); State v. Cavallo, 88 N.J. 508, 443 A.2d 1020, 1025 (1982) (preliminary showing of reliability required for expert testimony on psychological profile of rapists to prevent a "battle of experts" that "would consume substantial court time and cost both parties much time and expense"); *cf.* Reeve v. Dennett, 145 Mass. 23, 11 N.E. 938, 943–944 (1887) (Holmes, J.) ("so far as the introduction of collateral issues goes, that objection is a purely practical one—a concession to the shortness of life").

In a sense, time-consumption is the fundamental reason to exclude relevant evidence. It might be thought, for example, that "estimation" problems could be solved by supplying the jury with supplementary information or expert instruction in how to handle certain types of evidence that are prone to be misunderstood. *E.g.*, Finkelstein & Fairley, A Bayesian Approach to Identification Evidence, 83 Harv. L. Rev. 489 (1970). Similarly, one could try to counter evidence condemned as prejudicial for inducing jurors to weaken the applicable standard of proof by educating jurors more extensively in the meaning of the burden of persuasion. Nagel, Bringing the Values of Jurors in Line with the Law, 63 Judicature 189 (1979). But even if such strategies always had the desired effects, the probative value of the evidence rarely would justify the

Analyzing and weighing the pertinent costs and benefits is no trivial task. Wise judges may come to differing conclusions in similar situations. Even the same item of evidence may fare differently from one case to the next, depending on its relationship to the other evidence in the case,[66] the importance of the issues on which it bears, and the likely efficacy of cautionary instructions to the jury.[67] Accordingly, much leeway is given trial judges[68]

---

time and effort that would be consumed.

[66]*See* Sprint/United Management Co. v. Mendelsohn, 552 U.S. 379, 387, 128 S. Ct. 1140, 170 L. Ed. 2d 1 (2008) ("Relevance and prejudice under Rules 401 and 403 are determined in the context of the facts and arguments in a particular case, and thus are generally not amenable to broad per se rules."); U.S. v. 87.98 Acres of Land More or Less in the County of Merced, 530 F.3d 899, 907 (9th Cir. 2008) (exclusion of testimony about communications to developers of the strengths of electromagnetic fields was proper when "[t]he probative value of the testimony would have added relatively little, however, to the evidence that was presented at trial."); Friedman, A Close Look at Probative Value, 66 B.U. L. Rev. 733 (1986); Gold, Federal Rule of Evidence 403: Observations on the Nature of Unfairly Prejudicial Evidence, 58 Wash. L. Rev. 497 (1983). If other evidence, which does not carry the same dangers with it, could be used to establish the same fact, then the marginal probative value of the evidence in question is slight or non-existent. Old Chief v. U.S., 519 U.S. 172, 117 S. Ct. 644, 136 L. Ed. 2d 574 (1997) (in a prosecution for possession of a handgun by a felon, it is error to admit evidence of the name or nature of the defendant's prior conviction for assault causing serious bodily injury when the defendant offers to stipulate to the previous felony conviction); U.S. v. 88 Cases, More or Less, Containing Bireley's Orange Beverage, 187 F.2d 967, 975 (3d Cir. 1951) (error to introduce pictures of guinea pigs dying in agony from vitamin C deficiency after being

put on diet of orange drink); U.S. v. Layton, 767 F.2d 549 (9th Cir. 1985) (tape recording of Jim Jones' remarks that included sounds of children dying in mass suicides in Jonestown, Guyana, was properly excluded, partly because the same substantive point could be established by less inflammatory testimony).

For cases on the power of the court to prevent excessive cumulation of witnesses, see U.S. v. Fernandez, 497 F.2d 730, 735–36 (9th Cir. 1974) (proper to exclude testimony of 17 witnesses to prove facts as to which five had already testified); People v. Cardenas, 31 Cal. 3d 897, 184 Cal. Rptr. 165, 647 P.2d 569, 572 (1982) ("The fact that appellant and the witnesses were also members of [a Chicano youth gang] was cumulative and added little to further the prosecutor's objective of showing that the witnesses were biased because of their close association with appellant.").

[67]*See* U.S. v. Guerrero, 803 F.2d 783, 786 (3d Cir. 1986); U.S. v. Stevens, 595 F.2d 569, 571–72 (10th Cir. 1979). Usually, this last factor is offered, perhaps optimistically, as a reason to admit the troublesome evidence. *Cf.* Carter v. Kentucky, 450 U.S. 288, 302–03 n.20, 101 S. Ct. 1112, 67 L. Ed. 2d 241 (1981) (citing "modern empirical support" for the "long-standing" and "obvious" view that the judge's "lightest word or intimation . . . may prove controlling"). Yet, there are situations in which it is clear that a curative instruction would be futile (*e.g.*, Sprankle v. Bower Ammonia & Chemical Co., 824 F.2d 409, 416–17 n.10 (5th Cir. 1987)), and most studies of instructions to disregard evidence or to use it for only one purpose do not

who must fairly weigh probative value against probable dangers.[69] The standard of review on appeal—"abuse of discretion"[70]—is highly deferential.[71] Nevertheless, discretion can be abused,[72] and

---

reveal that these instructions work. *See* Devine et al., Jury Decision Making: 45 Years of Empirical Research on Deliberating Groups, 7 Psychol. Pub. Pol'y & L. 622, 666 (2001) ("In general, limiting instructions have proven to be ineffective and have even been associated with a paradoxical increase in the targeted behavior."); Kassin & Studebaker, Instructions to Disregard and the Jury: Curative and Paradoxical Effects, in Intentional Forgetting: Interdisciplinary Approaches 414, 422 (Golding et al. eds., 1998) (research yields mixed, often discouraging results on the effects of instructions to disregard); Steblay et al., The Impact on Juror Verdicts of Judicial Instruction to Disregard Inadmissible Evidence: A Meta-Analysis, 30 Law & Hum. Behav. 469 (2006) (judicial instructions to ignore evidence are not fully effective, but providing a rationale for compliance increases compliance); *cf.* Wistrich et al, Can Judges Ignore Inadmissible Information?, The Difficulty of Deliberately Disregarding, 153 U. Pa. L. Rev. 1251 (2005).

[68]*See* Sprint/United Mgmt., 552 U.S. 379 (holding that the court of appeals erred in assuming that the district court applied a per se rule to exclude testimony of nonparties alleging discrimination by supervisors of the defendant company who played no role in the adverse employment decision challenged by the plaintiff); U.S. v. Hanson, 618 F.2d 1261, 1266 (8th Cir. 1980) ("much leeway"); U.S. v. Beasley, 809 F.2d 1273, 1278–79 (7th Cir. 1987) ("Trial judges have a comparative advantage because they alone see all the evidence in context . . . . Discretion, when exercised, will rarely be disturbed."). For discussions of the scope of discretion and the need for leeway, see, for example, Leonard, Appellate Review of Evidentiary Rulings, 70 N.C. L. Rev. (1992);

Leonard, Power and Responsibility in Evidence Law, 63 S. Cal. L. Rev. 937 (1990); Richard M. Markus, A Better Standard for Reviewing Discretion, 2004 Utah L. Rev. 1279; Peter Nicolas, De Novo Review in Deferential Robes?: A Deconstruction of the Standard of Review of Evidentiary Errors in the Federal System, 54 Syracuse L. Rev. 531 (2004) (explicating the components of the abuse-of-discretion standard in various contexts).

[69]*See, e.g.,* Sprint/United Mgmt., 552 U.S. at 388 ("whether evidence of discrimination by other supervisors is relevant in an individual ADEA case is fact based and depends on many factors, including how closely related the evidence is to the plaintiff's circumstances and theory of the case," and "[a]pplying Rule 403 to determine if evidence is prejudicial also requires a fact-intensive, context-specific inquiry [that] is within the province of the District Court in the first instance.").

[70]The standard for appellate review of the trial court's balancing has been stated in various ways, but the usual standard is simply abuse of discretion. *E.g.*, General Elec. Co. v. Joiner, 522 U.S. 136, 118 S. Ct. 512, 139 L. Ed. 2d 508 (1997) (rejecting a stricter standard for scientific evidence); Old Chief v. U.S., 519 U.S. 172, 183, 117 S. Ct. 644, 136 L. Ed. 2d 574 (1997); Mohammed v. Otoadese, 738 N.W.2d 628, 631 (Iowa 2007).

[71]*E.g.*, Sprint/United Mgmt., 552 U.S. at 384 ("Under this deferential standard, courts of appeals uphold Rule 403 rulings unless the district court has abused its discretion."); U.S. v. Jordan, 485 F.3d 1214, 1218 (10th Cir. 2007) (" 'An abuse of discretion occurs when the district court's decision is arbitrary, capricious, or whimsical, or results in a manifestly unreasonable judgment.' Our deference to the trial court is based upon its first-hand ability to view the witnesses and evi-

some appellate courts have urged trial courts to articulate the reasoning behind their relevance rulings.[73] In certain areas, such as proof of character, comparable situations recur so often that relatively particularized rules channel the exercise of discretion.[74] In others, less structured discretion remains prominent.[75] One way or another, however, admissible evidence must satisfy the cost-benefit calculus we have outlined.[76]

---

dence and assess credibility and probative value. . . . Accordingly, the district court's decision . . . 'will not be disturbed unless the appellate court has a definite and firm conviction that the lower court made a clear error of judgment or exceeded the bounds of permissible choice in the circumstances.' ") (quoting U.S. v. Weidner, 437 F.3d 1023, 1042 (10th Cir. 2006)).

[72]*E.g.*, Old Chief, 519 U.S. at 191 (when an element of a crime is a prior conviction and "the prior conviction is for an offense likely to support conviction on some improper ground, the only reasonable conclusion was that the risk of unfair prejudice did substantially outweigh the discounted probative value of the record of conviction, and it was an abuse of discretion to admit the record when" the defendant offered to stipulate to the prior conviction); State v. Richmond, 289 Kan. 419, 212 P.3d 165 (2009).

[73]*E.g.*, Miller v. Poretsky, 595 F.2d 780, 786, 794 n.41 (D.C. Cir. 1978) (concurring opinion also embraced by majority, observing that "[t]he weighing process should be conducted explicitly on the record."); John McShain, Inc. v. Cessna Aircraft Co., 563 F.2d 632, 635 (3d Cir. 1977) ("the balance required is not a pro forma one. . . . The substantiality of the consideration given to competing interests can be best guaranteed by an explicit articulation of the trial court's reasoning"); U.S. v. Anderson, 933 F.2d 1261, 1269–70 (5th Cir. 1991) ("When requested by a party, a trial court must articulate on the record its findings as to the . . . probative value/prejudice evaluation" of other-crimes evidence, and "[w]hen the admissibility of external offense evidence is a close ques-

tion, . . . even without a request; it should pinpoint the element or elements . . . that the evidence will prove and explain why the evidence's probative value is not 'substantially outweighed' by its 'undue prejudice.' "); State v. Barringer, 32 Wash. App. 882, 650 P.2d 1129, 1132 (Div. 1 1982) ("The mere conclusion of a trial court that the probative value of the evidence outweighs the prejudice to the defendant is not enough . . . . [I]t is helpful for appellate review if the trial court articulates on the record the factors considered").

[74]See infra Ch. 17 (character and habit evidence); infra § 203 (scientific evidence). The "relevance rules" that have been extracted from repeated decisions about various types of evidence operate to exclude certain categories of evidence offered for particular purposes. When the evidence is introduced for some other purpose, however, admission is not required. The trial judge has discretion to exclude the evidence if the usual counterweights warrant it. *See* infra § 186.

[75]See infra Ch. 18 (similar happenings and transactions); infra § 202 (pretrial experiments). Even in the absence of a codified rule, appellate courts may look askance at rulings that inexplicably deviate from establish patterns. *See, e.g.*, Miller v. Poretsky, 595 F.2d at 796 ("The frequency with which other acts evidence has been admitted in discrimination cases without question or apparent ill consequences suggests that a judicial rule favoring its normal admission has arisen already de facto.").

[76]For more detailed applications of these principles, see supra § 12 (opinions on merits of the case); § 36

(self-contradiction on collateral matters); § 42 (extrinsic evidence of misconduct affecting credibility); § 43 (impeachment by evidence of conviction of crime); § 47 (impeachment by contradiction on collateral matters); infra ch. 17 to 20 (other "relevance rules"); § 266 (offers to compromise disputed claim); § 267 (safety measures after an accident).

Some courts and textwriters have described the weighing of marginal costs and benefits as a matter of "legal relevancy" in that "legally relevant" evidence must have a "plus value" beyond a bare minimum of probative value. Post v. U.S., 407 F.2d 319, 323 (D.C. Cir. 1968), quoting Frank R. Jelleff, Inc. v. Braden, 233 F.2d 671, 679 (D.C. Cir. 1956), quoting 1A Wigmore, Evidence § 28 (Tillers Rev. 1983). Wigmore was the major exponent of this view, and Thayer the proponent of the "logical relevance" school of thought that the Federal and Uniform Rules follow. The notion of "plus value" is at best an imprecise way to say that the probative value and the need for the evidence must outweigh the harm likely to result from admission, and most modern courts and writers do not rely on such potentially misleading terminology. *See* 1A Wigmore, Evidence § 28, at 975 (Tillers rev. 1983).

# Chapter 17

# Character and Habit

## § 186  Character, in general

Evidence of the general character of a party or witness almost always has some probative value, but in many situations, the probative value is slight and the potential for prejudice large.[1] In other circumstances, the balance shifts the other way. Instead of engaging exclusively in the case-by-case balancing outlined in Chapter 16, however, the courts pass on the admissibility of evidence of character and habit according to a number of rules with some exceptions that reflect the recurring patterns of such proof and its usefulness.[2] These rules categorically exclude most

---

**[Section 186]**

[1]See supra § 185. On the meaning of the term "character," see infra § 194.

[2]See generally Leonard, The New Wigmore, A Treatise on Evidence: Evidence of Other Misconduct and Similar Events (2009); Spencer, Evidence of Bad Character (2d ed. 2009). For a comparative perspective, see Damaska, Propensity Evidence in Continental Legal Systems, 70 Chi.-Kent L. Rev. 55 (1994). On the history of the development of the Anglo-American approach, see McKinney v. Rees, 993 F.2d 1378, 1381 n.2

(9th Cir. 1993) (explaining that rule against using other acts evidence for character purposes "has persisted since at least 1684 to the present, and is now established not only in the California and federal evidence rules, but in the evidence rules of thirty-seven other states and in the common-law precedents of the remaining twelve states and the District of Columbia," and listing statutes and cases from all American jurisdictions); Leonard, In Defense of the Character Evidence Prohibition: Foundations of the Rule Against Trial by Character, 73 Ind. L.J. 1161 (1998). Another perspective on the rule can be found in Sanchirico,

"character evidence"—defined as evidence offered solely to prove a person acted in conformity with a trait of character on a given occasion. This exclusionary rule applies to businesses and other organizations as well as natural persons.[3]

Character evidence that is not categorically excluded is admissible, subject to the other rules of evidence.[4] In particular, many courts emphasize the need for careful case-by-case balancing of probative value against the prejudice associated with this type of evidence.[5]

Before turning to the details of the rules, it may be helpful to sketch two general considerations that are central to shaping and applying them. The first is the purpose for which the evidence of character is offered. If a person's character is itself an issue in the case, then character evidence is crucial and skepticism of inferences from very general character traits to highly situation-specific conduct is less apposite. But if the evidence of character merely is introduced as circumstantial evidence of what a person did or thought, it is less critical. Other, and probably better, evi-

---

Character Evidence and the Object of Trial, 101 Colum. L. Rev. 1227 (2001) (presenting an incentive-based theory of the character rules that is said to diverge from the truth-seeking rationale) (criticized, Imwinkelried, The Dubiety of Social Engineering Through Evidence: A Reply to Professor Sanchirico's Recent Article on Character Evidence, 51 Drake L. Rev. 283 (2003)).

[3]*See, e.g.*, Kentucky Farm Bureau Mut. Ins. Co. v. Rodgers, 179 S.W.3d 815 (Ky. 2005); 1 Edward J. Imwinkelried, Uncharged Misconduct Evidence § 2:4, at 2 to 7 (2005); Kim, Character Evidence of Soulless Persons: The Applicability of the Character Evidence Rule to Corporations, 2000 U. Ill. L. Rev. 763, 810 (arguing, however, that the purposes of the character evidence rule, protection of "human autonomy considerations" do not apply to corporations, and therefore, the character evidence rule should not apply to corporations).

[4]If a rule forbids the use of evidence for a particular purpose, then there is no need for ad hoc balancing of probative value as against preju-

dice, distraction, and the like (described supra § 185). The exclusionary rule already reflects the judgment that the outcome of the balancing test should preclude admission. It does not follow, however that character evidence introduced for another purpose must be admitted. To the contrary, it is subject to the strictures governing all relevant evidence.

[5]*E.g.*, U.S. v. Noah, 130 F.3d 490, 495–96 (1st Cir. 1997); State v. Rose, 206 N.J. 141, 19 A.3d 985, 997 (2011) (calling for "careful and pragmatic evaluation of the evidence to determine whether [is] probative worth . . . is outweighed by its potential for undue prejudice"—a "more exacting [standard] than Rule 403 . . . ."); State v. Goebel, 36 Wash. 2d 367, 218 P.2d 300, 306 (1950) ("this class of evidence . . . should not be admitted even though falling within the generally recognized exceptions to the rule of exclusion, when the trial court is convinced that its effect would be to generate heat instead of diffusing light, or . . . where the minute peg of relevancy will be completely obscured by the dirty linen hung upon it").

dence of the acts or state of mind may be available,[6] and the exclusionary rule creates an incentive to produce it.[7] Furthermore, jurors may regard personality traits as more predictive of individual behavior than they actually are.[8] Exclusion is therefore much more likely when the character evidence is offered solely to help prove that a person acted in one way or another. Thus, Federal Rule of Evidence 404(a), which basically codifies common law doctrine, provides that subject to enumerated exceptions,[9] "[e]vidence of a person's character or character trait is not admissible to prove that on a particular occasion the person acted in accordance with the character or trait."[10] In the manner of the common law, the rule does not exclude evidence just because it reveals a person's character. It excludes such evidence only when

---

[6]*See* Lempert & Saltzburg, A Modern Approach to Evidence 237 (2d ed. 1983) (arguing that "however relevant character evidence is in the abstract, its incremental relevance in the context of a specific case is likely to be low.").

[7]Lempert et al., A Modern Approach to Evidence 340 (4th ed. 2011).

[8]Lempert et al., A Modern Approach to Evidence 336–37 (4th ed. 2011) (discussing psychological research and theories). "In addition, there is a good deal of psychological evidence that character traits are, generally speaking, dynamic rather than static aspects of personality. Character traits and conduct reflecting them vary over time and across situations, and they change as people and mature, as contexts change, and when competing aspects of personality are called into play." Lempert et al., A Modern Approach to Evidence 337 (4th ed. 2011) (footnote omitted). *See also* Méndez, The Law of Evidence and the Search for a Stable Personality, 45 Emory L.J. 221 (1996); Anderson, Note, Recognizing Character: A New Perspective on Character Evidence, 121 Yale L.J. 1912, 1931–35 (2012). *Contra* State v. Martinez, 2008-NMSC-060, 145 N.M. 220, 195 P.3d 1232, 1236 (2008) ("Modern scientific research now confirms what human beings have always observed in their own family and community relationships, that the average person is able

to explain, and even predict, a subject's behavior with a significant degree of accuracy."); Reed, The Character Evidence Defense: Acquittal Based on Good Character, 45 Cleveland St. L. Rev. 345, 356 (1997) (reviewing the psychological literature and emphasizing that "[n]early every scientist who studied individual human behavior found human behavior is characterized by consistency of cross-situational behavior patterns."); Sanchirico, Character Evidence and the Object of Trial, 101 Colum. L. Rev. 1227, 1241 (2001) (stating that recent research suggests that a "defendant's cross situational attributes, as evidenced by past acts, may be quite probative" and proposing that the rules governing character evidence are best conceptualized as a system of incentives to regulate behavior outside of the courtroom). The emerging view in the psychology of personality is "interactionism," a kind of compromise between the once dominant trait theory and its successor, situationism. *See* Imwinkelried, Reshaping the "Grotesque" Doctrine of Character Evidence: The Reform Implications of the Most Recent Psychological Research, 36 Sw. U. L. Rev. 741 (2008).

[9]There are three exceptions in Rule 404(a). They are taken up later in this chapter.

[10]Federal Rules 413 to 415 set forth additional exceptions to the rule of exclusion codified in Rule 404(a).

it is part of a particular mode of reasoning—a chain of inferences that employs the evidence to establish that the person (1) is more inclined to act or think in a given way than is typical, and (2) is therefore more likely to have acted or thought that way on a particular occasion. Because the character-evidence rule is directed at reasoning based on inferred behavioral dispositions or propensities, it can be described as a "propensity rule"[11] that only curtails the admission of "propensity evidence."[12]

The second consideration is the type of evidence offered to establish an individual's character. Character is susceptible of proof by evidence of conduct that reflects some character trait, by a witness's testimony as to the witness's opinion based on personal observations, or by testimony as to reputation generally. As one moves from the specific to the general in this fashion, the pungency and persuasiveness of the evidence declines, but so does its tendency to arouse undue prejudice, to confuse and distract, and to raise time-consuming side issues. Traditionally, where character evidence could come in at all, the relatively neutral and unexciting reputation evidence was the preferred type.[13] Thus, prior to the adoption of the Federal Rules, the other methods of proving character could be employed only in narrowly defined situations. Roughly stated, when character was being

---

[11]*E.g.*, People v. Chapman, 2012 IL 111896, 358 Ill. Dec. 640, 965 N.E.2d 1119, 1128 (Ill. 2012); Damaska, Propensity Evidence in Continental Legal Systems, 70 Chi.-Kent L. Rev. 55 (1994); Kuhns, The Propensity to Misunderstand the Character of Specific Acts Evidence, 66 Iowa L. Rev. 777 (1981); Redmayne, Recognising Propensity, 2011 Crim. L.R. 117.

[12]*E.g.*, People v. Chapman, 2012 IL 111896, 358 Ill. Dec. 640, 965 N.E.2d 1119, 1122 (Ill. 2012); State v. Lovett, 2012-NMSC-036, 286 P.3d 265 (N.M. 2012); Com. v. Mouzon, 53 A.3d 738 (Pa. 2012). Of course, not all evidence of propensity is evidence of character. Anderson, Note, Recognizing Character: A New Perspective on Character Evidence, 121 Yale L.J. 1912 (2012). An amputee may have a tendency to limp, a person with a cold may have a tendency to sniffle, and an individual with Parkinson's disease may have a tendency to shake under stress, but these propensities are not traits of character because the behaviors are not particularly blameworthy

or praiseworthy, and jurors are not likely to misestimate the ability of these conditions to predict the behavior on a given occasion. At the other pole, portraying a wife accused of murdering her husband-to-be for no apparent reason as "a bad mother, an unloyal fiancée, a self-absorbed manipulator, and even, quite literally, a witch" to show that "despite the lack of any readily apparent motive, she was the kind of person who would shoot her husband-to-be" is, quite clearly, propensity evidence of character. Dunkle v. State, 2006 OK CR 29, 139 P.3d 228, 238 (Okla. Crim. App. 2006).

[13]U.S. v. Polsinelli, 649 F.2d 793, 795 (10th Cir. 1981) ("The witness was not allowed to express a personal opinion of defendant's character, no matter how close or long his association with the defendant."); Com. v. United Food Corp., 374 Mass. 765, 374 N.E.2d 1331, 1336–37 (1978) (reputation of lounge as a place for prostitution not provable by evidence of specific incidents).

used as circumstantial evidence of conduct, it could be proved only by reputation evidence. When character was in issue, it could be proved by specific instances or by reputation.[14]

Federal Rule of Evidence 405(a), however, allows opinion testimony as well as reputation testimony to prove character whenever any form of character evidence is appropriate.[15] Some states go farther, allowing proof of those specific acts that have been the subject of a criminal conviction.[16] And, as at common law, when character is "in issue," as discussed in the next section, it also may be proved by testimony about specific acts.

## § 187   Character in issue

A person's characteristic behaviors may be a material fact that under the substantive law determines rights and liabilities of the parties. For example, because truth is a defense in an action for defamation, in an action of slander for the statement that the plaintiff "is in the habit of picking up things," the defendant can introduce evidence of plaintiff's thefts to prove that the statement was true.[1] A complaint for negligence may allege that the defen-

---

[14]There were, however, deviations from this pattern in various jurisdictions. *See, e.g.*, 5 Wigmore, Evidence §§ 1608–21 (Chadbourn rev. 1974); 7 Wigmore, Evidence §§ 1981–85 (Chadbourn rev. 1978).

[15]This liberalization was controversial. The federal Advisory Committee noted that "[i]n recognizing opinion as a means of proving character, the rule departs from usual contemporary practice in favor of that of an earlier day." Quoting Wigmore, it argued for "evidence based on personal knowledge and belief as contrasted with 'the second-hand, irresponsible product of multiplied guesses and gossip which we term' reputation." The House Committee on the Judiciary, fearing that "wholesale allowance of opinion testimony might tend to turn a trial into a swearing contest between conflicting character witnesses," deleted this departure from the then-prevailing common law in its proposed draft. H. Comm. on the Judiciary, Fed. Rules of Evidence, H.R. Rep. No. 650, 93rd Cong., 1st Sess., at 7 (1973). During House debate, the language was rein-

stated. 120 Cong. Rec., pt. 2, H2370 (1974).

[16]*E.g.*, N.J.R.E. 405(a) ("When evidence of character or a trait of character of a person is admissible, it may be proved by evidence of reputation, evidence in the form of opinion, or evidence of conviction of a crime which tends to prove the trait. Specific instances of conduct not the subject of a conviction of a crime shall be inadmissible.").

**[Section 187]**

[1]Talmadge v. Baker, 22 Wis. 625, 1868 WL 1628 (1868). *See also* Bylers Alaska Wilderness Adventures Inc. v. City of Kodiak, 197 P.3d 199, 208 (Alaska 2008) (Coast Guard's "letter of concern" admissible in response to a defamation action for statements about a charter boat operator's misdeeds); Pierson v. Robert Griffin Investigations, Inc., 92 Nev. 605, 555 P.2d 843, 844 (1976) (libel plaintiff's crimes committed more than ten years earlier); Walkon Carpet Corp. v. Klapprodt, 89 S.D. 172, 231 N.W.2d 370, 374 (1975) (reputation for past misdeeds admissible in regard to de-

dant allowed an unfit person to use a motor vehicle[2] or other dangerous object,[3] or that an employer was negligent in hiring or failing to supervise an employee with certain dangerous character traits.[4] In deciding who should have custody of children, fitness to

---

fendant's counterclaim of slander for statements concerning excessive drinking and sexual promiscuity).

Reputation (not character) comes into issue when defendant seeks to mitigate damages by showing that plaintiff's reputation was bad. Meiners v. Moriarity, 563 F.2d 343, 351 (7th Cir. 1977); Wrabek v. Suchomel, 145 Minn. 468, 177 N.W. 764 (1920); Proper v. Mowry, 90 N.M. 710, 568 P.2d 236, 243–44 (Ct. App. 1977); Corabi v. Curtis Pub. Co., 441 Pa. 432, 273 A.2d 899, 920 (1971). Specific acts may not be used to make this showing "unless they were generally known in the [relevant] community." Shirley v. Freunscht, 303 Or. 234, 735 P.2d 600, 603 (1987). *But see* Schafer v. Time, Inc., 142 F.3d 1361, 1371–73 (11th Cir. 1998) (in a libel action for falsely identifying plaintiff as a double agent implicated in the bombing of Pan Am flight 103 in 1992, the defendant, Time Magazine, was "permitted to question [plaintiff] about a felony conviction, a possible violation of his subsequent parole, convictions for driving under the influence, an arrest for writing a bad check, failure to file tax returns, failure to pay alimony and child support, and . . . efforts to change his name and social security number" on the theory that the claim for damages to reputation placed plaintiff's reputation in issue; however, the court neglected to inquire into whether these acts were generally known and therefore had an effect on reputation). Naturally, character traits may affect damages in other contexts. *See, e.g.,* cases cited, Admissibility of evidence of character or reputation of party in civil action for assault on issues other than impeachment, 91 A.L.R.3d 718.

[2]Allen v. Toledo, 109 Cal. App. 3d 415, 167 Cal. Rptr. 270 (4th Dist. 1980) (evidence of son's previous ac-

cidents admissible to prove father's knowledge that son was unfit to drive car); Curley v. General Valet Service, Inc., 270 Md. 248, 311 A.2d 231, 240–41 (1973) (testimony concerning driver's record of traffic offenses known to employer sufficient to permit finding of negligent entrustment); Bock v. Sellers, 66 S.D. 450, 285 N.W. 437, 440 (1939) (father liable for allowing son who "had a reputation in that community for fast and reckless driving" to drive his car knowing that the boy "had had four accidents while driving his father's cars.").

[3]In re Aircrash In Bali, Indonesia on April 22, 1974, 684 F.2d 1301 (9th Cir. 1982) (pilot's training record admissible to prove incompetence and airline's knowledge).

[4]Hirst v. Gertzen, 676 F.2d 1252, 1263 (9th Cir. 1982) (previous brutal acts of sheriff toward prisoners admissible in civil rights action arising from death of prisoner to show government negligence in supervising sheriff's activities as a jailer); American Airlines, Inc. v. U.S., 418 F.2d 180, 197 (5th Cir. 1969) (prior inadequate performance in landing airplane under adverse conditions admissible to show employer's negligence in allowing this pilot to land aircraft); Ayuluk v. Red Oaks Assisted Living, Inc., 201 P.3d 1183, 1195 (Alaska 2009) (in a suit against an assisted living facility arising from an employee's alleged sexual assault of a resident, it was improper to exclude evidence that a worker viewed pornography on another job and that another resident had bruises at the end of the worker's shift because this was "conduct that could reasonably alert supervisors of the need for further inquiry and supervision."); Morrow v. St. Paul City Ry. Co., 74 Minn. 480, 77 N.W. 303 (1898) (liability to servant for negligent failure

provide care is of paramount importance.[5] Nuisance claims naturally require proof of the conduct constituting the nuisance.[6] Civil rights and employment discrimination cases challenging alleged business practices require proof of the discriminatory practices.[7] When character has been put in issue by the pleadings in such cases, evidence of character must be brought forth.[8]

In view of the crucial role of character in this situation, the courts usually hold that it can be proved by evidence of specific acts. The hazards of prejudice, surprise and time-consumption implicit in this manner of proof are more tolerable when character is itself in issue than when this evidence is offered as an indirect indication of how the defendant behaved on a specific occasion. Federal Rule 405 reflects this approach.[9]

In deciding whether character is truly in issue, courts must ascertain whether a character trait is an "operative fact"—one that under the substantive law determines rights and liabilities

---

to select a competent fellow-servant); Supreme Pork, Inc. v. Master Blaster, Inc., 2009 SD 20, 764 N.W.2d 474 (S.D. 2009) (contractor's liability for lack of due care in selecting a subcontractor).

[5]Care and Protection of Martha, 407 Mass. 319, 553 N.E.2d 902 (1990) (adoption of abused child); Dauer v. Dauer, 169 Minn. 148, 210 N.W. 878, 879 (1926) (divorce action involving "children whose custody and care is to be determined").

[6]Com. v. United Food Corp., 374 Mass. 765, 374 N.E.2d 1331, 1337–38 (1978) (evidence of specific instances of prostitution on premises as well as general reputation evidence properly relied on to show that lounge constituted a public nuisance).

[7]E.g., Vinson v. Taylor, 753 F.2d 141, 146 (D.C. Cir. 1985) ("evidence tending to show Taylor's harassment of other women working alongside Vinson is directly relevant to the question whether he created an environment violative of Title VII"). Such evidence also may be admitted as circumstantial evidence of intent or acts under the business habit or custom exception to the rule against character evidence. See infra § 195.

[8]See, e.g., U.S. v. Masters, 622 F.2d 83, 88 (4th Cir. 1980) (evidence of other dealings in firearms admissible to prove defendant's status as a dealer subject to licensing requirement); U.S. v. Pauldino, 443 F.2d 1108, 1113 (10th Cir. 1971) (prosecution under statute that requires that defendant be shown to be in business of gambling, but court confused this point with exception for evidence of other crimes that shows common plan); Christy v. U.S., 68 F.R.D. 375, 378 (N.D. Tex. 1975) (rejecting government's contention that criminal record of inmate who allegedly raped a visitor at a prison was privileged from discovery in victim's suit claiming that government was negligent in assigning prisoner to minimum custody institution).

[9]Whenever a party may introduce evidence of character, Fed. R. Evid. 405(a) allows proof "by testimony about the person's reputation or by testimony in the form of an opinion." In addition, "[o]n cross-examination of the character witness, the court may allow an inquiry into relevant specific instances of the person's conduct." Beyond these two generally applicable modes of proof, "[w]hen a person's character or character trait is an essential element of a charge, claim, or defense," Rule 405(b) permits evidence of "relevant specific instances of the person's conduct."

of the parties.[10] "The relevant question should be: would proof, or failure of proof, of the character trait by itself actually satisfy an element of the charge, claim, or defense? If not, then character is not essential and evidence should be limited to opinion or reputation."[11]

Yet, some older cases do not simply permit evidence of specific acts to prove character when it is in issue. They insist on it.[12] But there is no reason to exclude reputation evidence, which ordinarily is the preferred mode of proof of character. Proof by means of opinion testimony is slightly more debatable, but most of the arguments against opinion evidence do not apply when character is in issue. For example, the possibility that specific acts may be inquired into on cross-examination (which may prompt barring specific act evidence when character is not in issue) is hardly of concern, since the door to such evidence already is open.[13]

---

[10]State v. Lehman, 126 Ariz. 388, 616 P.2d 63, 66 (Ct. App. Div. 2 1980); West v. State, 265 Ark. 52, 576 S.W.2d 718, 719 (1979). *See also* Gibson v. Mayor and Council of City of Wilmington, 355 F.3d 215, 232 (3d Cir. 2004) (charges that a police officer lied to his superiors did not put his general character as "a dishonest or untruthful cop" in issue within the meaning of Rule 405); State v. Whitford, 260 Conn. 610, 799 A.2d 1034, 1049–52 (2002) (a claim of self-defense does not put a homicide victim's character for violence in issue so as to allow proof of victim's acts of violence when intoxicated); State v. Jenewicz, 193 N.J. 440, 940 A.2d 269, 281 (2008) ("The better view is that a victim's violent character is not an essential element of self-defense" and hence cannot be proved by specific acts that did not lead to a criminal conviction"). The Model Code permits all forms of character evidence "[a]s tending to prove a trait of a person's character when it is one of the facts necessary to establish a liability or defense or is a factor in the measure of damages. . . ." Model Code Evid. R. 305 (1942).

[11]U.S. v. Keiser, 57 F.3d 847, 856 (9th Cir. 1995).

[12]McGowin v. Howard, 251 Ala. 204, 36 So. 2d 323, 325 (1948) (entrusting automobile); Young v. Fresno

Flume & Irr. Co., 24 Cal. App. 286, 141 P. 29, 32 (1st Dist. 1914) (liability to employee based on unfitness of fellow employee); Guedon v. Rooney, 160 Or. 621, 87 P.2d 209, 217 (1939) (entrusting automobile). Even in recent times, at least one state requires specific-act evidence when character is in issue. Conn. R. Evid. 4–5(c).

[13]Because an opinion held by someone familiar with an individual may rest on facts too detailed to be worth reciting yet still may be useful in evaluating character, many courts allow such opinion evidence when the character involved is for the so-called nonmoral traits of care, competence, skill or sanity. Marine Towing Co. v. Fairbanks, Morse & Co., 225 F. Supp. 467 (E.D. Pa. 1963) (expert opinion as to skill of engine repair crew); Lewis v. Emery, 108 Mich. 641, 66 N.W. 569 (1896) (competency of fellow employee at sawmill); 7 Wigmore, Evidence § 1984 (Chadbourn rev. 1978). On the other hand, as to the traits of moral character like peaceableness and honesty, courts that follow the tradition barring opinion evidence of the character of an accused as circumstantial evidence of conduct on a particular occasion presumably would frown on opinion evidence even when character is in issue. In re Monaghan, 126 Vt. 53, 222 A.2d 665, 672–73 (1966) (opinions as to character of applicant for

The phrase "character in issue" sometimes invites confusion. A defendant in a criminal case generally can bring in evidence of good character to show that he is not the type of person who would have committed to offense charged.[14] Although courts sometimes speak loosely of this strategy as putting the defendant's character in issue,[15] the defendant is using character solely as circumstantial evidence. When the defendant makes his character an issue in this manner, it merely means that the prosecution is allowed to bring forth certain kinds of rebuttal evidence of bad character.[16] It does not justify evidence of specific acts, opinions, and reputation by either party. That free-wheeling approach to character evidence is limited to the unusual situation in which an offense, claim, or defense for which character is an essential element is pled.

## § 188 Character as circumstantial evidence: General rule of exclusion

Even when a person's character is not itself in issue as defined in the preceding section, litigants may seek to introduce character-type evidence. In ascertaining whether such evidence is admissible, the purpose for which the evidence is offered remains of the utmost importance. In some cases, even though a person's character is not itself in issue, evidence of a character trait may be relevant to proving a material fact that is distinct from whether the person acted in conformity with that trait on an occasion that is the subject of the litigation.[1] In other words, the evidence has "special" or "independent" relevance as part of a

---

admission to bar inadmissible). *But see* Wilson v. Wilson, 128 Mont. 511, 278 P.2d 219, 222 (1954) (opinion as to fitness of parent admissible in custody proceeding), overruled on other grounds in Trudgen v. Trudgen, 134 Mont. 174, 329 P.2d 225 (1958).

[14]See infra § 191.

[15]*E.g.*, State v. Gomez, 367 S.W.3d 237, 246 (Tenn. 2012).

[16]See infra § 191.

[Section 188]

[1]As noted in the previous section, the courts usually state that various character traits of a decedent are in issue with regard to damages in an action for wrongful death. *See, e.g.*, St. Clair v. Eastern Air Lines, Inc., 279 F.2d 119, 121 (2d Cir. 1960) (observing that "[u]ndoubtedly, personal hab-

its and qualities are to some degree relevant considerations in determining an individual's earning ability and the support that his family would have received from him but for his death," but cautioning that "[e]xcept as they may show a propensity of the decedent to spend his money in ways which do not inure to the benefit of his family, the details of his personal life are not in issue"); Schmitt v. Jenkins Truck Lines, Inc., 170 N.W.2d 632, 655 (Iowa 1969) ("the trier of fact is entitled to consider on this issue of damages decedent's characteristics and habits including her . . . industriousness, disposition to earn, [and] frugality or lavishness"). The character traits here are used as circumstantial evidence, to predict how a party would have acted accordingly in the future, but there is no better evidence that can be

chain of reasoning that does not include the propensity inference described in § 186.[2]

Thus, where extortion is charged, the defendant's reputation for violence may be relevant to the victim's state of mind.[3] In these cases the reputation itself, not the character that it tends to prove, is the significant fact; reputation is not used as evidence of how the person with the character traits behaved on a given occassion.[4] Thus, a plaintiff alleging assault and subsequent emotional distress may introduce evidence of the defendant's past conduct to show the extent of her fear and its emotional impact.[5] Likewise, a defendant charged with assault or homicide who argues self-defense may offer evidence of his knowledge of the victim's violent nature on the theory that it shows his reasonable belief that he needed to resort to force.[6]

In contrast, evidence that an individual is the kind of person who behaves in certain ways almost always has some value as

---

used in making such predictions, and the predictions are not situation-specific. Therefore, it makes sense to deem this proof of propensity as outside the exclusionary rule. This future-looking evidence is not, in the words of Rule 404(a), offered to show how the person acted "on a particular occasion."

[2]U.S. v. Hicks, 575 F.3d 130, 142 (1st Cir. 2009) ("First, a court must ask whether the proffered evidence has a 'special' relevance, i.e., a non-propensity relevance."); State v. Torres, 283 Neb. 142, 812 N.W.2d 213, 230 (2012), cert. denied, 133 S. Ct. 244, 184 L. Ed. 2d 129 (2012) ("Evidence that is offered for a proper purpose is often referred to as having a 'special' or 'independent' relevance, which means that its relevance does not depend upon its tendency to show propensity.").

[3]U.S. v. DeVincent, 546 F.2d 452, 456–57 (1st Cir. 1976) (within trial court's discretion to admit testimony concerning defendant's twenty-year-old conviction for armed robbery and ten-year-old murder indictment as relevant to borrower's state of mind); Carbo v. U.S., 314 F.2d 718 (9th Cir. 1963) (proper to admit evidence of reputation of member of extortion conspiracy as strong-arm man to show impact on victims); cf. U.S. v. McClure,

546 F.2d 670, 672–73 (5th Cir. 1977) (error to exclude testimony offered by defendant accused of selling heroin that the government's "contingent fee informant" had coerced other persons into making heroin sales to him after the defendant's sale).

[4]See supra § 185.

[5]Brandner v. Hudson, 171 P.3d 83 (Alaska 2007) (in a suit for assault and negligence brought against a surgeon by a co-worker at the hospital who was grasped, dragged to her office, and pushed into a chair, causing a knee injury and post-traumatic stress disorder, it was proper to admit four-year-old domestic violence petitions filed against the physician by his wife but read by the plaintiff soon after the incident).

[6]See U.S. v. Keiser, 57 F.3d 847, 852–53 (9th Cir. 1995) (surveying case law on the admissibility of specific-act as opposed to reputation or opinion evidence to show the defendant's state of mind); State v. Jenewicz, 193 N.J. 440, 940 A.2d 269, 278–79 (2008) ("where the accused has knowledge of the victim's prior violent acts, it tends to show the reasonableness of the accused's belief that the use of self-defense against the victim was necessary").

circumstantial evidence of how this individual acted (and perhaps with what state of mind) in the matter in question. For instance, on average, persons reputed to be violent probably commit more assaults than persons known to be peaceable.[7] Yet, evidence of character in any form—reputation, opinion from observation, or specific acts—generally will not be received to prove that a person engaged in certain conduct or did so with a particular intent on a specific occasion,[8] so-called circumstantial use of character. The reason is the familiar one of prejudice outweighing probative value. Character evidence used for this purpose, while typically being of relatively slight value, usually is laden with the dangerous baggage of prejudice, distraction, and time-consumption.[9] As indicated in Section 185, prejudice can arise in two ways— misestimation of probative value and departure from legal norms. Misestimation would occur if jurors were to think that a character trait is more predictive than it actually is, or if they were to create incorrect, broad character portraits from isolated traits.[10] And, jurors would depart from the norms that they are expected to apply if they were to view a conviction of an accused who actually is innocent of the specific charges as less serious because of the bad acts or traits of character that he has displayed.[11]

At the same time, there are important exceptions to this general rule of exclusion, and this rule, it bears repeating, applies only when the theory of relevance is that the person or organization has a trait that it usually follows and therefore probably followed on the occasion in question.[12] In light of the various true exceptions to the rule as well as the limits within which the rule operates, some writers prefer to state the general rule as one of

---

[7]*See* Dinakar & Sobel, Violence in the Community as a Predictor of Violence in the Hospital, 52 Psychiatric Services 240, 240–41 (2001) (reporting that "[c]linicians generally believe that a history of violence may be a key predictor of future violence" but finding that in the small sample of patients studied, "a history of violence may not predict violence in the hospital"); Klassen & O'Connor, Demographic and Case History Variables in Risk Assessment, in Violence and Mental Disorder: Developments in Risk Assessment 229 (Monahan & Steadman eds. 1994) (reporting that past acts of violence are the best predictor of future violent behavior).

[8]See supra § 186.

[9]See supra § 186.

[10]Note, Recognizing Character: A New Perspective on Character Evidence, 121 Yale L.J. 1912, 1929 (2012).

[11]Old Chief v. U.S., 519 U.S. 172, 182, 117 S. Ct. 644, 136 L. Ed. 2d 574 (1997); Lempert, Modeling Relevance, 75 Mich. L. Rev. 1021 (1977); Anderson, Note, Recognizing Character: A New Perspective on Character Evidence, 121 Yale L.J. 1912, 1930 (2012).

[12]U.S. v. Bowie, 232 F.3d 923, 930 (D.C. Cir. 2000) ("The rule does not prohibit character evidence generally, only that which lacks any purpose but proving character.").

admissibility subject to exceptions for exclusion.[13] The next six sections consider various applications of the rule of exclusion and the most important exceptions to it.

## § 189   Character for care in civil cases

The rule against using character evidence solely to prove conduct on a particular occasion has long been applied in civil cases,[1] notwithstanding suggestions that exclusion is not justified

---

[13]*E.g.*, Model Code Evid. R. 306 (1942) ("evidence of a trait of a person's character is admissible for the purpose of proving his conduct on a specified occasion, except . . . ."). As we have noted, the Federal and Uniform Rules state the general rule as one of exclusion. See supra § 186. Historically, the terms "inclusionary" and "exclusionary" have been contentious and confusing. *See* 1 Edward J. Imwinkelried, Uncharged Misconduct Evidence §§ 2:25 to 2:30 (2005). At one time, English and American courts suggested that all uncharged misconduct of a defendant was inadmissible—subject to certain exceptions such as proof of motive or intent. This phrasing of the rule was denominated the "exclusionary" view. The original view (and the one that prevails today) is that the rule is "inclusionary" in that there is no exhaustive list of exclusions. In other words, the general rule of exclusion works by including within the general ban on character evidence only a subset of all character evidence— that which rests solely on a theory of disposition or propensity. Thus, the uses of evidence of character traits enumerated in Federal Rule 404(b) do not constitute a complete list of permissible, nonpropensity uses but merely illustrate uses of character evidence falling outside the use included in the general ban. State v. Gunby, 282 Kan. 39, 144 P.3d 647, 659 (2006) ("We hereby state unequivocally that the list of material facts in K.S.A. 60-455 is exemplary rather than exclusive. It may be that other crimes and civil wrongs evidence is relevant and admissible to prove a material fact other than the eight listed."); Thomas J. Reed, Admitting the Accused's Criminal History: The Trouble with Rule 404(b), 78 Temp. L. Rev. 201 (2005). See infra § 190. In Britain, the Criminal Justice Act 2003 reformulated British character law to be inclusionary: "it now allows prosecutors to adduce evidence of a defendant's bad character provided it passes through one of seven gateways." Culberg, Note, The Accused's Bad Character: Theory and Practice, 84 Notre Dame L. Rev. 1343, 1343 (2009). For discussion of how the English Court of Appeals has applied the new rule, see Redmayne, Recognising Propensity, 2011 Crim. L.R. 117.

[Section 189]

[1]*E.g.*, Coursen v. A.H. Robins Co., Inc., 764 F.2d 1329, 1335 (9th Cir. 1985) (proper to exclude evidence that manufacturer made false claims of efficacy, where evidence "did nothing except generally show defendant in a bad light") (internal quotation marks omitted); Crain v. Crain, 104 Idaho 666, 662 P.2d 538, 545 (1983) (error to introduce evidence in paternity action of mother's reputation as "sexual libertine"); Rittenhoffer v. Cutter, 83 N.J.L. 613, 83 A. 873 (N.J. Ct. Err. & App. 1912) (assault and battery); Slough, Other Vices, Other Crimes: An Evidentiary Dilemma, 20 U. Kan. L. Rev. 411 (1972); Slough, Relevancy Unraveled, 5 U. Kan. L. Rev. 404, 440–44 (1957); infra § 192 & Ch. 18. In civil, as in criminal cases, however, evidence of other wrongs often is used for another purpose than to prove conduct on a particular occasion. *E.g.*, Williams v. Mensey, 785 F.2d 631 (8th

in this context.[2] The rule is invoked most uniformly when specific act evidence is proffered.[3] Of course, we are speaking of specific acts other than those at bar. No doubt, evidence that someone acted negligently says something about that person's character. But we are concerned here with character as circumstantial evidence, that is, as evidence of a propensity to behave in a certain way which, in turn, makes it more likely that such behavior occurred on the occasion in question. When this is the theory of admissibility, the character evidence is inadmissible, but a previous accident or negligent act that does something more than show character or predisposition may be admissible.[4]

Negligence cases illustrate the point.[5] Evidence of negligent conduct of the defendant or his agent on other occasions may

---

Cir. 1986) (evidence of previous prison fights); Sweet v. Roy, 173 Vt. 418, 801 A.2d 694, 706–07 (2002) (plaintiff who alleged that the manager of a trailer park vandalized her mobile home to force her to leave and thereby make space for a new tenant who would not only lease the space but also would rent a home provided by the park was permitted to introduce testimony of other residents about damage to their homes to show the manager's larger plan to maximize revenue). Section 190 catalogs most of these purposes. See also infra Ch. 18.

[2]See Falknor, Extrinsic Policies Affecting Admissibility, 10 Rutgers L. Rev. 574, 581–84 (1956); cf. Uviller, Evidence of Character to Prove Conduct: Illusion, Illogic, and Injustice in the Courtroom, 130 U. Pa. L. Rev. 845 (1982) (broader criticism). The Model Code and the Uniform Rules, prior to the 1974 revision, permitted the use of character evidence to prove conduct in civil cases, except on the issue of negligence. See Model Code Evidence Rule 306 (1942); original Unif. R. Evid. 47 & 48. Whether the rule should bar a civil defendant from proving his good character when the allegations against him state a criminal offense also has engendered debate, see infra § 192, as has its application to civil assault and battery cases in which the identity of the first attacker is in dispute. See infra § 193.

In 1994, Congress added Fed. R. Evid. 415, which makes admissible other acts of sexual assault or child molestation in "a civil case involving a claim for relief based on a party's alleged sexual assault or child molestation."

[3]Lataille v. Ponte, 754 F.2d 33 (1st Cir. 1985) (error to admit prisoner's disciplinary record of assaults, hostage taking, weapons possession, arson and attempted escape, to show that prisoner, who claimed guards had beaten him, was a violent person); Hirst v. Gertzen, 676 F.2d 1252, 1262 (9th Cir. 1982) (sheriff's purportedly similar acts of taunting and brutalizing Indian prisoners, in a private civil rights action arising from the death of an Indian prisoner who hanged himself in his jail cell).

[4]Dallas Ry. & Terminal Co. v. Farnsworth, 148 Tex. 584, 227 S.W.2d 1017, 1020 (1950) (in an action for an injury allegedly due to the abrupt starting of a street car, testimony that the driver had started abruptly once before on the same trip admissible to show motorman was nervous and in a hurry). For an analysis of the problem of differentiating between acts offered to prove propensity and acts offered for another purpose, see Kuhns, The Propensity to Misunderstand the Character of Specific Acts Evidence, 66 Iowa L. Rev. 777 (1981).

[5]For applications of the rule and its exceptions in other civil cases, see,

reflect a propensity for negligent acts, thus enhancing the probability of negligence on the occasion in question, but this probative force has been thought too slight to overcome the usual counterweights.[6] In an action for malpractice against a surgeon, for example, a similarly botched surgery on another patient is not admissible to show that a surgeon was negligent in performing the surgery on the plaintiff,[7] but previous post-operative infections in patients may be admissible to show knowledge of a problem requiring precautions.[8] The same categorical approach

e.g., Miller v. Poretsky, 595 F.2d 780, 783–85 (D.C. Cir. 1978) (landlord's discrimination against other black tenants); Com. of Pa. v. Porter, 659 F.2d 306, 320 (3d Cir. 1981) (en banc) (pattern or practice of violating constitutional rights); Moorhead v. Mitsubishi Aircraft Intern., Inc., 828 F.2d 278 (5th Cir. 1987); Brown v. Miller, 631 F.2d 408 (5th Cir. 1980) (punitive damage award upset because independent bad act used in civil rights action); Cohn v. Papke, 655 F.2d 191, 193–94 (9th Cir. 1981) (improper to inquire into sexual preferences of plaintiff in civil rights action alleging brutality by police officers who arrested him for soliciting a homosexual act); Brundridge v. Fluor Federal Services, Inc., 164 Wash. 2d 432, 191 P.3d 879, 888 (2008) (observing that "[f]ederal courts have long recognized that in the civil employment context, evidence of employer treatment of other employees is not [always] impermissible character evidence; rather it may be admissible to show motive or intent for harassment or discharge."). See infra Ch. 18.

[6]Moorhead v. Mitsubishi Aircraft Intern., Inc., 828 F.2d 278 (5th Cir. 1987) (error to admit pilot's low marks at flight school refresher course); Nelson v. Hartman, 199 Mont. 295, 648 P.2d 1176, 1178 (1982) (evidence that a truck driver was an unlicensed and habitual traffic offender "could not be used to prove any specific of negligence" in an automobile accident case); Brownhill v. Kivlin, 317 Mass. 168, 57 N.E.2d 539, 540 (1944) (evidence that deceased had previously caused two

fires by going to sleep while smoking properly excluded in action against estate for deceased's allegedly burning down a garage in which she perished); Zucker v. Whitridge, 205 N.Y. 50, 98 N.E. 209, 210–13 (1912) (collecting cases); Supreme Pork, Inc. v. Master Blaster, Inc., 2009 SD 20, 764 N.W.2d 474, 486, 489 (S.D. 2009) (agreeing with the dissent that a subcontractor's past violations of the building code and a previous fire resulting from its failure to provide adequate ventilation would be inadmissible character evidence if offered "only [to] prove [the] character" of the subcontractor or contractor as typically doing "sloppy work," but reasoning that the incidents were admissible to prove "the foreseeability of harm, the risk of the danger with respect to the lack of safety measures, [the subcontractor's] lack of knowledge about installing exhaust chimneys in a manner that maintains the required clearances between combustibles and heat, and [the contractor's] lack of due care in selecting a subcontractor"); Thornburg v. Perleberg, 158 N.W.2d 188, 191 (N.D. 1968) (improper for plaintiff in automobile accident case to ask defendant driver on cross-examination, "you have a constant record of accidents and traffic violations, do you not?"); 1A Wigmore, Evidence § 65.1 (Tillers rev. 1983).

[7]Kunnanz v. Edge, 515 N.W.2d 167 (N.D. 1994).

[8]Farr v. Wright, 833 S.W.2d 597 (Tex. App. Corpus Christi 1992). For additional discussion of the character-evidence rules in medical litigation, see Ginsberg, Good Medicine/Bad

applies to evidence of other negligent acts of the plaintiff,[9] as well as other instances of careful conduct.[10]

Most courts also reject proof of an actor's character for care by means of reputation evidence[11] or opinion testimony.[12] In the past, a minority of courts had admitted these types of evidence, often under the guise of evidence of "habit," when there were no eyewitnesses to the event.[13] A few even did so if there were

---

Medicine and the Law of Evidence: Is There A Role for Proof of Character, Propensity, or Prior Bad Conduct in Medical Negligence Litigation?, 63 S.C. L. Rev. 367, 377 (2011); Gardner, Comment, Help Me Doc! Theories of Admissibility of Other Act Evidence in Medical Malpractice Cases, 87 Marq. L. Rev. 981 (2004).

[9]George v. Morgan Const. Co., 389 F. Supp. 253, 264–65 (E.D. Pa. 1975) (plaintiff's safety record not admissible to show contributory negligence); Nesbit v. Cumberland Contracting Co., 196 Md. 36, 75 A.2d 339, 342 (1950) (improper to cross-examine plaintiff, who drove car into pile of dirt and rocks that defendant left on highway, about convictions for reckless driving and driving without a license); cf. Reyes v. Missouri Pac. R. Co., 589 F.2d 791 (5th Cir. 1979) (four prior misdemeanor convictions for public intoxication improperly admitted to show that plaintiff was intoxicated when run over by defendant's train).

[10]Gates v. Rivera, 993 F.2d 697, 700 (9th Cir. 1993) (holding that, in a § 1983 excessive force case, the district court erred in allowing the defendant to testify that, in his sixteen-and-one-half years as a police officer, he never shot anyone); Puckett v. Soo Line R. Co., 897 F.2d 1423, 1428 n.6 (7th Cir. 1990); Ryan v. International Harvester Co. of America, 204 Minn. 177, 283 N.W. 129, 131 (1938) (proper to prevent defendant's driver from testifying that he had never previously had a collision); McCaffrey v. Puckett, 784 So. 2d 197 (Miss. 2001) (testimony that no complaints against defendant chiropractor had been filed with State Board of Chiropractic Examiners was

improperly admitted to show defendant's character for care); Zucker v. Whitridge, 205 N.Y. 50, 98 N.E. 209 (1912) (testimony that plaintiff customarily exercised caution before crossing train tracks improperly admitted).

[11]Denbeigh v. Oregon-Washington R. & Navigation Co., 23 Idaho 663, 132 P. 112, 115 (1913) (testimony that engineer "was known as a prudent and careful engineer" properly excluded); Phinney v. Detroit United Ry. Co., 232 Mich. 399, 205 N.W. 124 (1925) (testimony of conductor that motorman had a reputation for recklessness inadmissible); 1A Wigmore, Evidence § 65 (Tillers rev. 1983).

[12]Harriman v. Pullman Palace-Car Co., 85 F. 353, 354 (C.C.A. 8th Cir. 1898) (error to admit evidence that porter alleged to have injured plaintiff "was usually careful, competent, courteous and attentive"); Louisville & N.R. Co. v. Adams' Adm'r, 205 Ky. 203, 265 S.W. 623 (1924) (error to receive testimony that decedent killed at crossing was a careful driver); Greenwood v. Boston & M.R.R., 77 N.H. 101, 88 A. 217 (1913) (testimony of decedent's coworkers that decedent was careful in his work). But a history of being careful about a particular danger may come in as habit rather than character. Hussey v. Boston & M.R.R., 82 N.H. 236, 133 A. 9, 12 (1926) (evidence of lineman's "habitual care in the presence of charged wires" properly received in a case with no witnesses to accident). See infra § 195.

[13]Hawbaker v. Danner, 226 F.2d 843, 847 (7th Cir. 1955) ("habits of due care"); Pritchett v. Steinker Trucking Co., 108 Ill. App. 2d 371, 247 N.E.2d

eyewitnesses with conflicting stories.[14] The Federal and Uniform Rules do not make such fine distinctions.[15] The prevailing pattern is to exclude all forms of character evidence in civil cases when the evidence is employed merely to support an inference that conduct on a particular occasion was consistent with a person's character.[16]

This pattern persists despite psychological studies of "accident proneness." It had been argued that research establishing that drivers with inadequate training, defective vision, and certain attitudes and emotional traits are at risk for automobile accidents[17] should prompt a relaxation of the rule against evidence of character for negligence.[18] The argument seems to be that because a small number of drivers with identifiable characteristics account for the bulk of the accidents, they must drive improperly as a routine matter, and this provides a better-than-usual basis for inferring that the accident in issue resulted from such negligent driving. Presumably, the reform would be to admit evidence of previous accidents combined with proof that the particular driver fits the "accident proneness" profile.

A somewhat different proposal asks that aggregate and individual data concerning the actions of physicians should be admissible in malpractice cases.[19] For example, in deciding whether the removal of a patient's appendix was unnecessary surgery, the

---

923, 926–27 (4th Dist. 1969); Missouri-Kansas-Texas R. Co. v. McFerrin, 156 Tex. 69, 291 S.W.2d 931, 941–42 (1956).

[14]Glatt v. Feist, 156 N.W.2d 819, 825 (N.D. 1968) (habit evidence allowed in state that had applied the "no eyewitness" rule in a case in which the eyewitness testimony conflicted).

[15]See Rules 404 to 405, described supra § 186.

[16]Reyes v. Missouri Pac. R. Co., 589 F.2d 791 (5th Cir. 1979); Barbieri v. Cadillac Const. Corp., 174 Conn. 445, 389 A.2d 1263 (1978); Feliciano v. City and County of Honolulu, 62 Haw. 88, 611 P.2d 989, 991 (1980); infra § 200.

[17]See Maloney & Rish, The Accident-Prone Driver: The Automotive Age's Biggest Unsolved Problem, 14 U. Fla. L. Rev. 364 (1962); James & Dickinson, Accident Proneness and Accident Law, 63 Harv. L. Rev. 769, 772–75 (1950); Trautman, Logical or

Legal Relevancy—A Conflict in Theory, 5 Vand. L. Rev. 385, 399–400 (1952).

[18]James & Dickinson, Accident Proneness and Accident Law, 63 Harv. L. Rev. 769, 703 (1950); Trautman, Logical or Legal Relevancy—A Conflict in Theory, 5 Vand. L. Rev. 385, 401 (1952); cf. Maloney & Rish, The Accident-Prone Driver: The Automotive Age's Biggest Unsolved Problem, 14 U. Fla. L. Rev. 364, 378 (1962). But see Boodman, Safety and Systems Analysis, with Applications to Traffic Safety, 33 Law & Contemp. Prob. 488, 510 (1968) ("There are no reliable indicators of accident proneness"); Woody, Accident Proneness, 1981 Med. Trial Techniques Q. 74, 81 ("there is no clear-cut personality composite for the presumed accident prone personality").

[19]Note, The Medical Practice Computer Profile: Profile of the Doctor's Actions in a Serious of Similar Cases, 7 U.C.D. L. Rev. 523 (1974); Malpractice: Admissibility of evidence that

jury might be invited to consider whether the defendant physician performs appendectomies far more frequently than his colleagues. Although evidence of previous accidents or similar happenings should not be freely admitted,[20] a suitable expert testifying about a departure from the customary standard of care should be permitted to rely on such information and to explain this analysis to the jury. Moreover, where the statistically measured departure from the customary pattern is itself so great as to make it plain that the defendant is behaving differently from the norm, this statistic should be provable. Conversely, a defendant might wish to establish statistically that a pattern is within the normal range. The statistical pattern can be proved without going into the prejudicial, distracting, or time-consuming details of other incidents. The value of the evidence is greatest in cases where each surgery or other event, viewed in isolation, could be a matter of reasonable professional judgment. In these situations, the need for such evidence justifies taking the risks associated with defendant's seeking to prove reasonable care in each of the other incidents.[21]

## § 190    Bad character as evidence of criminal conduct: Other crimes

If anything, the rule against using character evidence to prove conduct on a particular occasion applies even more strongly in criminal cases. Indeed, some courts have intimated[1] or held[2] that the rule has constitutional underpinnings in this context. In crim-

---

defendant physician has previously performed unnecessary operations, 33 A.L.R.3d 1056; *cf.* U.S. v. Johnson, 634 F.2d 735, 736–37 (4th Cir. 1980) (admitting testimony of government auditor that physician charged with tax evasion who had character witnesses attest to her honesty actually reported four times as many services per Medicaid patient as other Virginia physicians).

[20]As Lempert & Saltzburg, A Modern Approach to Evidence 211 n.41 (2d ed. 1983), caution, "[t]here are at least two good reasons for [being reluctant to allow evidence of accident proneness]. First, accident proneness does not mean that one's negligence was responsible for a particular accident or series of accidents. Ordinary clumsiness or inattentiveness or a predilection for risk may mean that one is likely to be in more than his

share of accidents without engaging in behavior which ever rises to the level of negligence or contributory negligence. Second, involvement in a series of accidents may simply involve an unusual run of bad luck." The "bad luck" hypothesis is examined more fully infra § 196. *See also* Lempert et al., A Modern Approach to Evidence 336–37 (4th ed. 2011) (describing biases that could lead jurors in an automobile accident case to overvalue accident-proneness evidence).

[21]Whether or not one accepts the desirability of this limited inroad on the ban on character evidence, a consistent, narrow pattern of behavior may be admissible as a habit rather than a character trait. See infra § 195.

**[Section 190]**

[1]Government of Virgin Islands v. Toto, 529 F.2d 278, 283 (3d Cir. 1976) (prosecution's evidence of other crimes

inal cases, the rule means that unless and until the accused gives evidence of his good character,[3] the prosecution may not introduce evidence of his bad character.[4] Nor may the prosecution do so by insinuations,[5] implications,[6] or direct comments.[7] The evidence of

---

undermines presumption of innocence); U.S. v. Daniels, 770 F.2d 1111, 1118 (D.C. Cir. 1985) ("gives meaning to the central precept of our system of criminal justice, the presumption of innocence"); U.S. v. Foskey, 636 F.2d 517, 523 (D.C. Cir. 1980) (" 'a concomitant of the presumption of innocence,' " is that "It is fundamental to American jurisprudence that 'a defendant must be tried for what he did, not for who he is' "); State v. Manrique, 271 Or. 201, 531 P.2d 239, 241 (1975) ("constitutional right to be informed of the nature of the charge against him and to be held to answer only the crime named in the indictment"); DiBiagio, Intrinsic and Extrinsic Evidence in Federal Criminal Trials: Is the Admission of Collateral Other-Crimes Evidence Disconnected to the Fundamental Right to a Fair Trial?, 47 Syracuse L. Rev. 1229 (1997).

[2]Inasmuch as the common law has long excluded proof of most other crimes and wrongs merely to show a criminal disposition, the courts had no occasion to decide whether a broad exclusionary rule for this evidence is constitutionally compelled. Cf. Dowling v. U.S., 493 U.S. 342, 110 S. Ct. 668, 107 L. Ed. 2d 708 (1990) (deciding that double jeopardy and collateral estoppel doctrines do not bar proof of other crime for which defendant was acquitted). Modern legislation and rulemaking that has overturned the rule in cases of domestic violence and sexual assault and abuse has prompted conflicting holdings. These cases are discussed later in this section.

[3]See infra § 191.

[4]Michelson v. U.S., 335 U.S. 469, 475–76, 69 S. Ct. 213, 93 L. Ed. 168 (1948); U.S. v. Harris, 331 F.2d 185 (4th Cir. 1964) (reputation); Ex parte Thompson, 376 So. 2d 766 (Ala. 1979) (reputation); People v. Madson, 638

P.2d 18 (Colo. 1981) (prior conviction); 1A Wigmore, Evidence §§ 55, 57 (Tillers rev. 1983). See Fed. R. Evid. 404(a).

[5]The rule of exclusion encompasses questions which, though answered negatively, insinuate that the accused committed other crimes. U.S. v. Shelton, 628 F.2d 54, 56–57 (D.C. Cir. 1980) (assault conviction reversed because government cross-examined defendant and defense witness so as to suggest that they "were members of the drug underworld involved in all sorts of skullduggery").

[6]U.S. v. Fosher, 568 F.2d 207, 213 (1st Cir. 1978) ("mug shots from a police department['s] 'rogues' gallery"); U.S. v. Williams, 739 F.2d 297, 299–300 (7th Cir. 1984) (detective's testimony that he knew defendant as "Fast Eddie"); Miller v. State, 436 N.E.2d 1113, 1120 (Ind. 1982) ("mug shot"); cf. State v. Hicks, 133 Ariz. 64, 649 P.2d 267, 273 (1982) (testimony as to defendant's "known prints" did not come within rule); State v. Jackson, 770 N.W.2d 470, 484 (Minn. 2009) (in a prosecution for murder by shooting for the benefit of a gang, drinking beer with gang members was not admissible as general character evidence but was admissible to show "affiliation with the Bloods"); People v. Jackson, 232 Ill. 2d 246, 328 Ill. Dec. 1, 903 N.E.2d 388 (2009) (presence of defendant's DNA profile in a state database of DNA profiles of convicted offenders and some other individuals was admissible to explain how he became a suspect when the jury was not informed of the nature of the database).

[7]U.S. v. Schuler, 813 F.2d 978, 980 (9th Cir. 1987) (Rule 404(a) violation to suggest that laughing during testimony recounting threats against the President showed defendant to be "of bad character because he considered the charges . . . to be a joke").

or statements about bad character would not be irrelevant, but particularly in the setting of the jury trial, the dangers of prejudice, confusion and time-consumption outweigh the probative value.[8]

This broad prohibition includes the specific and frequently invoked rule that the prosecution may not introduce evidence of other criminal acts of the accused unless the evidence is introduced for some purpose other than to suggest that because the defendant is a person of criminal character, it is more probable that he committed the crime for which he is on trial.[9] As Federal Rule 404(b) puts it:

> Evidence of a crime, wrong, or other act is not admissible to prove a person's character in order to show that on a particular occasion the person acted in accordance with the character . . . . This evidence may be admissible for another purpose, such as proving motive, opportunity, intent, preparation, plan, knowledge, identity, absence of mistake, or lack of accident . . . .[10]

As the rule indicates, there are numerous uses to which evidence of criminal acts may be put, and those enumerated are neither mutually exclusive nor collectively exhaustive.[11] Nor are the enumerated purposes all of the same type. Some are phrased in

---

[8]Michelson v. U.S., 335 U.S. 469, 475–76, 69 S. Ct. 213, 93 L. Ed. 168 (1948) ("The inquiry is not rejected because character is irrelevant; on the contrary, it is said to weigh too much with the jury and to so overpersuade them as to prejudge one with a bad general record and deny him a fair opportunity to defend against a particular charge. The overriding policy of excluding such evidence, despite its admitted probative value, is the practical experience that its disallowance tends to prevent confusion of issues, unfair surprise and undue prejudice."); Boyd v. U.S., 142 U.S. 450, 458, 12 S. Ct. 292, 35 L. Ed. 1077 (1892) (proof of earlier robberies "only tended to prejudice the defendants with the jurors, to draw their minds away from the real issue, and to produce the impression that they were wretches whose lives were of no value"); People v. Cardenas, 31 Cal. 3d 897, 184 Cal. Rptr. 165, 647 P.2d 569 (1982) (reversing due to cumulative prejudice from evidence that defendant charged with attempted murder and related offenses was addicted to narcotics and that de-

fendant and defense witnesses all belonged to the same Chicano youth gang); Whitty v. State, 34 Wis. 2d 278, 149 N.W.2d 557 (1967) (describing "four bases" for the rules excluding proof of prior crimes); Kalven & Zeisel, The American Jury 160 (1966) (when a defendant's criminal record is known and the prosecution's case has contradictions, the defendant's chances of acquittal are 38% compared to 68% otherwise). A contrarian position and analysis of empirical research can be found in Larry Laudan & Ronald J. Allen, The Devastating Impact of Prior Crimes Evidence and Other Myths of the Criminal Justice Process, 101 J. Crim. L. & Criminology 493 (2011).

[9]People v. Molineux, 168 N.Y. 264, 61 N.E. 286, 294 (1901); 1A Wigmore, Evidence §§ 57, 58.1, 58.2, 192 (Tillers rev. 1983).

[10]Fed. R. Evid. 404(b)(1), (2).

[11]U.S. v. Miller, 895 F.2d 1431 (D.C. Cir. 1990) (to show that witness feared defendant); U.S. v. Tafoya, 757 F.2d 1522, 1525–28 (5th Cir. 1985) (attempted assassinations to show unreported income on theory that "[i]t is

terms of the immediate inferences sought to be drawn (such as plan or motive) while others are phrased in terms of ultimate facts (such as knowledge, intent or identity) which the prosecution seeks to establish.[12] With these points in mind, examination is in order of the principal purposes for which the prosecution may introduce evidence of a defendant's bad character. There are at least ten such "quasi-exceptions." (They are not true exceptions because there is no rule against admitting evidence of other crimes per se—the rule excluding proof of other crimes is confined to evidence of extrinsic crimes that are probative only through propensity reasoning.)[13] Following this listing, some general observations will be offered about the use of other-crimes evidence for these purposes.

The permissible purposes include the following.

(1) *To prove the existence of a larger plan,*[14] *scheme,*[15] *or conspiracy,*[16] *of which the crime on trial is a part.*

---

unlikely that one would attempt three killings in exchange largely for expenses or continue killings for over a year if not paid for the first one"); State v. Jeffers, 135 Ariz. 404, 661 P.2d 1105 (1983) (murder defendant's prior assaults on witness and accomplice to explain why defendant did not report the murder promptly and to counter defendant's insinuation that the accomplice lied to gain immunity); Rucker v. State, 291 Ga. 134, 728 S.E.2d 205 (2012) (photographs of tattoos depicting violence were admissible at a trial for murder and kidnapping on the issues of the timing and effect of defendant's alleged mental illness); State v. Gunby, 282 Kan. 39, 144 P.3d 647, 657 (2006) (rejecting a line of cases that "incorrectly limited the material facts supporting admission of other crimes and civil wrongs evidence to those eight explicitly set forth in the statute . . . .").

[12]*See* Stone, Exclusion of Similar Fact Evidence: America, 51 Harv. L. Rev. 988, 1026 n.190 (1938) ("Motive, intent, absence of mistake, plan and identity are not really all on the same plane. Intent, absence of mistake, and identity are facts in issue—facta probanda. Motive, plan, or scheme are facta probantia, and may tend to show any facta probanda").

[13]U.S. v. Bowie, 232 F.3d 923, 930 (D.C. Cir. 2000) ("The rule does not prohibit character evidence generally, only that which lacks any purpose but proving character."). The last item in this list—evidence of an accused's character for veracity—involves propensity reasoning as to whether the accused is testifying truthfully, but not to the allegedly criminal conduct that the prosecution must prove.

[14]Lewis v. U.S., 771 F.2d 454, 456 (10th Cir. 1985) (testimony that defendant accused of burglary of a post office, first burglarized a garage to obtain a cutting torch that he then used in the post office burglary); U.S. v. Parnell, 581 F.2d 1374 (10th Cir. 1978) (previous fraudulent scheme admissible as "direct precursor" of conspiracy to purchase grain with forged cashiers checks); U.S. v. Lewis, 693 F.2d 189, 192 (D.C. Cir. 1982) (testimony concerning stolen money orders not charged in indictment admissible to show that defendant was "the mastermind of a common scheme"); State v. Toshishige Yoshino, 45 Haw. 206, 364 P.2d 638 (1961) (evidence of first robbery admissible in prosecution for second where defendant and others robbed first victim and obtained from him the name and address of their next victim); State v. Long, 195 Or. 81,

For example, when a criminal steals a car to use it in a robbery, the automobile theft can be proved in a prosecution for the robbery.[17] Although some courts construe "common plan" more broadly[18] (especially in sexual abuse and domestic violence

---

244 P.2d 1033 (1952) (in prosecution for killing owner of truck, proper to prove as part of planned course of action that defendant used the truck the next day for a robbery in which he shot an FBI agent while fleeing); State v. Ciresi, 45 A.3d 1201, 1214 (R.I. 2012) (police officer's involvement in crimes committed with or on behalf of his informants admissible to demonstrate a "pattern of cultivating and protecting criminal informants . . . for his own financial and professional gain"); Admissibility, under Rule 404(b) of the Federal Rules of Evidence, of Admissibility, under Rule 404(b) of the Federal Rules of Evidence, of evidence of other crimes, wrongs, or acts similar to offense charged to show preparation or plan, 47 A.L.R. Fed. 781.

[15]The common-plan quasi-exception includes crimes committed in preparation for the offense charged. U.S. v. Cepulonis, 530 F.2d 238 (1st Cir. 1976) (testimony that bank robbers shot at a police officer and a passing motorist and evidence of a shotgun not used in the robbery properly admitted to show that defendants' plan was to distract police by firing and that they had assembled weapons for this purpose); U.S. v. Carroll, 510 F.2d 507, 509 (2d Cir. 1975) (other crimes done to determine if conspirators capable of handling mail truck robbery admissible in prosecution for attempted robbery of the mail truck).

[16]U.S. v. Bermudez, 526 F.2d 89 (2d Cir. 1975) (upholding admission of "traces of narcotics" and narcotics related equipment seized in home of conspirator six weeks after conspiracy to distribute cocaine ended); Admissibility in federal conspiracy prosecution of evidence of defendant's similar prior criminal act, 20 A.L.R. Fed. 125.

If the "other crimes" evidence is part of the conspiracy charged, then it is direct rather than circumstantial evidence of the offense charged. Consequently, there is no reason to analyze the evidence in terms of the permissible purposes for other-crimes evidence. U.S. v. Angelilli, 660 F.2d 23, 39 (2d Cir. 1981). Some courts invoke the quasi-exception anyway. U.S. v. De La Torre, 639 F.2d 245, 250 (5th Cir. 1981) ("the guns were partial payment for the drugs and thus were an integral part of the conspiracy" and hence admissible "to show common plan or scheme"); U.S. v. Marino, 658 F.2d 1120, 1123 (6th Cir. 1981). Similar confusion arises with respect to the "complete story" rationale discussed at the end of this list.

[17]U.S. v. Leftwich, 461 F.2d 586 (3d Cir. 1972).

[18]*See* People v. Catlin, 26 Cal. 4th 81, 26 Cal. 4th 1060c, 109 Cal. Rptr. 2d 31, 26 P.3d 357 (2001) (evidence that defendant poisoned his elderly mother with the herbicide paraquat was admissible, as part of a common plan, in prosecution for killing his fourth wife in the same manner); People v. Balcom, 7 Cal. 4th 414, 27 Cal. Rptr. 2d 666, 867 P.2d 777, 784 (1994) ("Consider the example of a defendant who is alleged to have taken money hidden in a freezer during the commission of the charged offense. Evidence that, during the commission of a subsequent crime, the defendant searched a freezer for valuables would be relevant to establish a common design or plan. The relevance of this evidence would be the same whether the defendant had formulated the plan to search freezers for valuables prior to the charged offense, or instead learned during the commission of the charged offense that some individuals hide valuables in their freezers, incorporating this knowledge into a plan that the defendant employed in com-

cases),[19] each crime should be an integral part of an over-arching plan explicitly conceived and executed by the defendant or his confederates.[20] This will be relevant as showing motive, and hence the doing of the criminal act, the identity of the actor, or his intention.

---

mitting the later, uncharged offense.").

[19]People v. Ewoldt, 7 Cal. 4th 380, 27 Cal. Rptr. 2d 646, 867 P.2d 757 (1994) (overruling People v. Tassell, 36 Cal. 3d 77, 201 Cal. Rptr. 567, 679 P.2d 1 (1984), which held that evidence of uncharged misconduct is admissible to establish a common design or plan only if such evidence demonstrates a "single, continuing conception or plot" in favor of the view that such evidence is admissible if the uncharged misconduct "shares sufficient common features with the charged offenses to support the inference that both the uncharged misconduct and the charged offenses are manifestations of a common design or plan"); State v. DeJesus, 288 Conn. 418, 953 A.2d 45, 75–76 (2008) (conceding that "the liberal standard [applied in many previous cases] to establish the existence of a common scheme or plan in *sex crime* cases . . . does not focus on the existence of an overall scheme or plan in the defendant's mind that encompasses the commission of the charged and uncharged crimes [and therefore does not comport with] "the 'true' common scheme or plan exception").

[20]U.S. v. Varoudakis, 233 F.3d 113, 119 (1st Cir. 2000) (error to admit evidence of defendant's burning his car on the theory that this act, along with defendant's hiring someone to burn his failing restaurant two years later, were part of a common plan to collect insurance proceeds); U. S. v. O'Connor, 580 F.2d 38, 42 (2d Cir. 1978) (bribes six months earlier "not sufficiently probative of a definite project directed toward completion of the crime in question"); U.S. v. Anderson, 933 F.2d 1261, 1272 n.7 (5th Cir. 1991) ("it is not enough to show that each crime was planned in the same way; rather,

there must be some overall scheme of which each of the crimes is but a part"); U.S. v. Dothard, 666 F.2d 498, 502 (11th Cir. 1982) ("Courts have admitted extrinsic act evidence to show a defendant's design or plan to commit the specific crime charged, but never to show a design or plan to commit 'crimes of the sort with which he is charged' "); People v. Engelman, 434 Mich. 204, 453 N.W.2d 656 (1990) (photographing and touching partially clad minors not shown to be a common scheme); State v. Cox, 781 N.W.2d 757, 771 (Iowa 2010) (defendant "essentially committed crimes of availability against his [younger] cousins, which demonstrates nothing more than propensity"); State v. Gallegos, 2007-NMSC-007, 141 N.M. 185, 152 P.3d 828, 838 (2007) (rejecting the theory that a guard at a juvenile detention facility charged with sexual contact and indecent exposure with minors was pursuing a common plan with different victims because "the fact that . . . two crimes were 'planned' in the same way is not enough. . . . There must be some overall scheme of which each of the crimes is but a part."); Com. v. Perkins, 519 Pa. 149, 546 A.2d 42 (1988) (court equally divided over admissibility of trespass to nearby home four hours after rape and burglary); *cf.* Brett v. Berkowitz, 706 A.2d 509, 516 (Del. 1998) (in a civil action by a client against her former lawyer for sexual harassment, evidence that the lawyer "had prior relations with other clients is not admissible to prove the presence of a plan or scheme" because "[m]ere repetition of sexual behavior is not evidence of a plan or scheme"). For commentary, see authorities cited, 1 Imwinkelried, Uncharged Misconduct Evidence § 3:24 (2005).

(2) *To prove other crimes by the accused so nearly identical in method as to earmark them as the handiwork of the accused.*[21]

The phrase of which authors of detective fiction are fond, modus operandi, may be employed in this context.[22] Much more is demanded than the mere repeated commission of crimes of the same class, such as repeated murders,[23] robberies[24] or rapes.[25]

---

[21]People v. Peete, 28 Cal. 2d 306, 169 P.2d 924 (1946) (prior homicide by defendant accused of shooting the deceased from behind at close range in an attempt to sever the spinal cord, then burying the body, was admissible to identify defendant as the murderer where the previous homicide involved a bullet from behind, severing the spinal cord at the neck, and burial of the body); Whiteman v. State, 119 Ohio St. 285, 164 N.E. 51 (1928) (evidence of other robberies by defendants wearing uniforms, impersonating officers and stopping cars, thus "earmarking" them as the perpetrators of the offense charged); Com. v. Wable, 382 Pa. 80, 114 A.2d 334 (1955) (three truck drivers on Pennsylvania turnpike shot in same week at about same time of day with same gun at about same angle).

[22]People v. Barbour, 106 Ill. App. 3d 993, 62 Ill. Dec. 641, 436 N.E.2d 667, 672 (1st Dist. 1982) (distinguishing modus operandi from the common plan, scheme or conspiracy quasi-exception); Haw. R. Evid. 404(b) ("Evidence of other crimes, wrongs, or acts . . . may, however, be admissible where such evidence is probative of . . . modus operandi . . . .").

[23]U.S. v. Woods, 484 F.2d 127, 134 (4th Cir. 1973) (evidence that defendant accused of suffocating her eight-month-old pre-adoptive foster son had custody of or access to nine children who suffered at least 20 cyanotic episodes resulting in the death of seven of them "admissible generally under the accident and signature exceptions"); State v. Williams, 234 Kan. 233, 670 P.2d 1348, 1352 (1983) ("a close question," but previous murder admissible where defendant had been drinking at a party before each mur-

der, the victims were women who were several years older than defendant, lived near him, were attacked in their homes then moved to another location, sexual molestation was apparent motive, and killer or killers inflicted long slicing wounds as well as massive stabbing abdominal wounds); People v. Golochowicz, 413 Mich. 298, 319 N.W.2d 518, 526 (1982) (although the question was too close to warrant reversal in itself, "there was not the requisite 'distinguishing, peculiar or special characteristics' " where "two unmarried male victims were both strangled, one bloodlessly and one after a beating, and their personal property of various kinds . . . stolen from their residences and later sold to friends of the defendant").

[24]U.S. v. Myers, 550 F.2d 1036, 1046 (5th Cir. 1977), ("An early afternoon robbery of an outlying bank situated on a highway, by revolver-armed robbers wearing gloves and stocking masks, and carrying a bag for the loot, is not such an unusual crime that it tends to prove that one of the two individuals involved must have been the single bandit in a similar prior robbery."); State v. Randolph, 284 Conn. 328, 933 A.2d 1158, 1179–81 (2007) (finding that the dissimilarities between two robberies of two restaurants on the same street and the lack of uniqueness of the similar characteristics made the signature quasi-exception inapposite); U.S. v. Phillips, 599 F.2d 134, 136–37 (6th Cir. 1979) ("Here there was only general testimony that defendant had committed other bank robberies—no common plan or distinctive pattern, no 'signature,' not even a similarity."); Sutphin v. Com., 1 Va. App. 241, 337 S.E.2d 897, 900 (1985) (reversible error to connect defendant to robbery, involv-

The pattern and characteristics of the crimes must be so unusual and distinctive as to be like a signature.[26] For example, in *Rex v.*

---

ing a cinder block thrown through a glass door, by evidence of previous conviction for breaking and entering by throwing a brick through a glass door, since "[b]reaking a glass door with a piece of cinder block or similar object is not a sufficiently distinctive method of attempting unlawful entry to prove identity."). Some courts are less careful. *E.g.*, State v. Smith, 146 Ariz. 491, 707 P.2d 289, 297 (1985) ("evidence of . . . three Circle K robberies was . . . admissible to . . . prove that defendant was the one who had committed the charged robbery and murder at the Low Cost Market, a convenience store similar to Circle K markets").

[25]*Compare* State v. Sauter, 125 Mont. 109, 232 P.2d 731, 732 (1951) (in charge of forcible rape in automobile after picking up victim in barroom, other rapes following similar pickups were "too common . . . to have much evidentiary value in showing a systematic scheme or plan"), *with* McGahee v. Massey, 667 F.2d 1357, 1360 (11th Cir. 1982) (where man wearing a white, see-through bikini bathing suit approached a woman sunbathing at beach and raped her, it was within trial court's discretion to permit testimony that twice during the previous month the defendant, wearing a red see-through bathing suit, had exposed himself to other women at the same beach to demonstrate "the manner of operation, identity and type of clothing worn by the defendant"); Williams v. State, 110 So. 2d 654, 663 (Fla. 1959) (that defendant hid in back seat of woman's car at shopping center and fled when woman screamed admissible to prove that six weeks later the defendant raped another woman outside the same shopping center after hiding in the back seat of her car); *cf.* U.S. v. Gano, 560 F.2d 990 (10th Cir. 1977) (permissible to show that defendant social worker charged with carnal knowledge of female under age of 16

had sexual relations with the girl's mother and had sold marijuana to mother and given marijuana to daughter); State v. Roscoe, 145 Ariz. 212, 700 P.2d 1312, 1317 (1984) (defendant singled out as rapist and killer of eight-year-old girl by prior California conviction involving a 17-year old victim, where both bodies were found in remote areas with clothes removed, shoes placed side by side, blouses torn open in front, gagged with socks, hands tied behind back with articles of clothing, and indications of vaginal and oral sex); State v. Morowitz, 200 Conn. 440, 512 A.2d 175 (1986) (podiatrist sedated female patients, sent assistant out of office, had patients disrobe and wear surgical gowns over their underwear, administered valium by injection, and had intercourse with sleeping patients; expert testimony showed that sedating and disrobing were not standard practices for ambulatory surgical procedures).

As the facts in some of these cases may suggest, the courts tend to find distinctive similarities in sex cases more readily than in other situations. In addition, if the rapist's method of operation is calculated to create the appearance of consent on the part of the victim, the similar acts evidence may be admitted to negate the defense of consent. Oliphant v. Koehler, 594 F.2d 547, 550–54 (6th Cir. 1979). *But see* People v. Barbour, 106 Ill. App. 3d 993, 62 Ill. Dec. 641, 436 N.E.2d 667, 673 (1st Dist. 1982) (error to introduce evidence of two prior incidents in which defendant had allegedly raped women whom he had known briefly socially since "identity was never in issue" and the fact that "two of defendant's former victims testified that they did not consent to defendant's sexual advances is wholly irrelevant to . . . this complainant's consent").

[26]*Compare* U.S. v. Pisari, 636 F.2d 855, 859 (1st Cir. 1981) (use of

*Smith*,[27] the "brides of the bath" case, George Joseph Smith was accused of murdering Bessie Mundy by drowning her in the small bathtub of their quarters in a boarding house. Mundy had left all her property to Smith in a will executed after a bigamous marriage ceremony. The trial court allowed the prosecution to show that Smith "married" several other women whom he drowned in their baths after they too left him their property. In all the drownings, Smith took elaborate steps to make it appear that he was not present during the drownings. The Court of Criminal Appeal affirmed the resulting conviction on the ground that the evidence in connection with Mundy's death alone made out a prima facie case, and the other incidents were properly admitted "for the purpose of shewing the design of the appellant."

(3) *To show, by similar acts or incidents, that the act in question was not performed inadvertently, accidentally,*[28] *involuntarily,*[29] *in self-defense,*[30] *or without guilty knowledge.*[31]

---

knife in prior robbery was not sufficient signature or trademark to warrant admission on charge of robbery of postal installation by knife), *with* U.S. v. Sliker, 751 F.2d 477, 487 (2d Cir. 1984) (bank fraud "schemes were identical . . . in the idiosyncratic details [for both] depended on the use of phony bank checks issued by the same non-existent offshore bank as well as on prearrangement with an 'officer' of the bank to confirm the validity of the checks"), *and* U.S. v. Woods, 613 F.2d 629, 635 (6th Cir. 1980) ("We find the circumstances of this case reveal a 'signature' on the crimes insofar as each was an armed robbery by robbers wearing ski masks, goggles and jumpsuits and using a stolen vehicle for a getaway car."). *See generally* People v. Haston, 69 Cal. 2d 233, 70 Cal. Rptr. 419, 444 P.2d 91 (1968). A civil case considering this theory, but rejecting it as obviously inadequate for want of sufficient similarities, is Hirst v. Gertzen, 676 F.2d 1252, 1262 (9th Cir. 1982) (described supra § 189).

[27]Rex v. Smith, (1915) 11 Cr. App. R. 229, described in Marjoribanks, For the Defence: The Life of Edward Marshall Hall 321 (1929).

[28]U.S. v. Witschner, 624 F.2d 840, 843 (8th Cir. 1980) (in prosecution for mail fraud based on submitting fraud-

ulent medical insurance claims, evidence relating to patients not mentioned in the indictment admissible to show "that submission of the false medical reports was not an accident"); U.S. v. Harris, 661 F.2d 138, 142 (10th Cir. 1981) (where father accused of murdering eight year old son claimed the fatal injuries occurred because he tripped while carrying the child on his shoulders, evidence of many bone fractures sustained by the infant months before were admissible, since "particularly in child abuse cases" the "admissibility of other crimes, wrongs or acts to establish intent and an absence of mistake or accident is well established"); U.S. v. Woods, 484 F.2d 127 (4th Cir. 1973); State v. Craig, 219 Neb. 70, 361 N.W.2d 206, 213 (1985) (15 prior incidents of mock wrestling with adopted daughter as prelude to fondling genitalia admissible to refute accused's claim that any disrobing in the course of wrestling with daughter on specific occasion charged was accidental); State v. Lapage, 57 N.H. 245, 294, 1876 WL 5314 (1876) (where there were repeated deaths of children in defendant's care, the court referred to a "class of cases . . . in which it becomes necessary to show that the act for which the prisoner was indicted was not accidental, *e.g.*, where the prisoner had shot the same person twice within a short time, or where the same person had fired a rick of grain twice, or where several deaths by poison had taken place in the same family, or where the children of the same mother had mysteriously died"); State v. Tanner, 675 P.2d 539, 548 (Utah 1983) (previous brutal treatment of small child by mother charged with manslaughter admissible to prove "absence of accident or mistake" and, more problematically, "pattern of behavior toward the victim"); State v. Norlin, 134 Wash. 2d 570, 951 P.2d 1131 (1998) (evidence of prior injuries to child admissible in child abuse prosecutions to show absence of accident only if state connects defendant to those injuries by preponderance of evidence); 2 Wigmore, Evidence § 312 (Chadbourn rev. 1979); Imwinkelried, The Use of Evidence of an Accused's Uncharged Misconduct to Prove Mens Rea: The Doctrines Which Threaten to Engulf the Character Evidence Prohibition, 51 Ohio St. L.J. 575, 586–93 (1990); Orfinger, Battered Child Syndrome: Evidence of Prior Acts in Disguise, 41 Fla. L. Rev. 345 (1989).

[29]U.S. v. Basile, 771 F.2d 307 (7th Cir. 1985) (in view of defense contention that defendant accused of fraud in connection with insurance claim for car theft was unwitting victim of domineering friend, it was proper to admit defendant's tape recorded statements that two previous claims for stolen cars were fraudulent); U.S. v. Holman, 680 F.2d 1340, 1349 (11th Cir. 1982) (other smuggling incidents to rebut defense of coercion); U.S. v. Smith, 552 F.2d 257 (8th Cir. 1977) (intoxication); U.S. v. Hearst, 563 F.2d 1331 (9th Cir. 1977) (evidence of other crimes to negate anticipated defense of duress by publisher's daughter held for ransom by terrorist group and charged in bank robbery committed by group).

[30]Stone v. State, 94 So. 3d 1078, 2012 WL 2433519 (Miss. 2012); State v. Payano, 2009 WI 86, 320 Wis. 2d 348, 768 N.W.2d 832 (2009).

[31]Huddleston v. U.S., 485 U.S. 681, 108 S. Ct. 1496, 99 L. Ed. 2d 771 (1988) (defendant's other sales of stolen property obtained from same suspicious source admissible to prove his knowledge that goods in question were stolen); U.S. v. Lee, 558 F.3d 638 (7th Cir. 2009) (when the owner and operator of the Tokyo Oriental Health Spa denied knowing that the spa was a front for a prostitution business, testimony that a "masseuse" at another "spa" she owned two years earlier was forced to provide sexual services for customers was admissible to show knowledge); U.S. v. DeLoach, 654 F.2d 763, 768–69 (D.C. Cir. 1980) (false promises to secure labor certificates for other aliens admissible to rebut defendant's disavowal of knowledge of false information); U.S. v. Ross, 321 F.2d 61 (2d Cir. 1963) (proper to cross-examine about defendant's employment in other firms that sold worthless securities by similar methods to refute claim of securities fraud defendant that he was an unwitting tool of his employer); U.S. v. Johnson, 634 F.2d 735 (4th Cir. 1980) (evidence that physician accused of tax evasion submitted fraudulent Medicaid billing properly admitted to rebut claim that she was too devoted to patients to worry about finances); People v. Marino, 271 N.Y. 317, 3 N.E.2d 439 (1936) (evidence of previous sale of stolen car); De La Paz v. State, 279 S.W.3d 336, 347 (Tex. Crim. App. 2009) ("the 'I saw what no one else saw' defense [on the part of a police officer charged with orchestrating fake drug busts] becomes considerably less probable when one hears that appellant saw two other fake drug deals that no one else saw and others denied that they occurred"); People v. Williams, 6 Cal. 2d 500, 58 P.2d 917 (1936) (where larceny defendant claimed he had picked a purse from a bag on the floor of a store, thinking it had been lost, detectives' testimony that the defendant took another woman's purse from another bag in the same manner was

*Rex v. Smith* falls in this category.[32] The death of one bride in the bath might be an accident, but three drownings cannot be explained so innocently. Another classic example of the "improbability" logic is the "baby farming" case of *Makin v. Attorney General of New South Wales*.[33] The remains of thirteen infants were discovered in places where the couple, John and Sarah Makin were living or had lived, and the Crown charged the Makins with the murder of two of these children. One was identified by his clothing and hair. His mother testified that the Makins had agreed to adopt her son in exchange for only three pounds.[34] The jury convicted the Makins of murdering the boy whose remains had been identified. On appeal, the couple argued that all the evidence concerning other missing children should not have been admitted. The Privy Council rejected this argument. Although its opinion did little to explain the basis for this conclusion, counsel for the Crown had stressed that "the recurrence of the unusual phenomenon of bodies of babies having been buried in an unexplained manner in a similar part of premises previously occupied" implied that the deaths were "wilful and not accidental." In these cases, the similarities between the act charged and the extrinsic acts need not be as extensive and striking as is required

---

admissible); 2 Wigmore, Evidence, §§ 301, 310, 324 (Chadbourn rev. 1979); McKusick, Techniques in Proof of Other Crimes to Show Guilty Knowledge and Intent, 24 Iowa L. Rev. 471 (1939).

This reasoning frequently is invoked in drug cases. *E.g.*, U.S. v. Wixom, 529 F.2d 217 (8th Cir. 1976) (evidence that defendant accused of distributing heroin had distributed an ounce of heroin on another occasion properly admitted to show that he knew he was distributing heroin); U.S. v. Lopez-Martinez, 725 F.2d 471, 475 (9th Cir. 1984) ($1000 payment to defendant in 1974 for hauling 340 pounds of marijuana across border to rebut claim that defendant thought that he was smuggling marijuana rather than heroin when he received $1000 for carrying 1.5 pounds in 1982). *But cf.* U.S. v. Hernandez-Miranda, 601 F.2d 1104 (9th Cir. 1979) (error to admit evidence of smuggling marijuana in a backpack to show knowl-

edge of heroin concealed in a car).

[32]Later incarnations of *Smith* include People v. Lisenba, 14 Cal. 2d 403, 94 P.2d 569 (1939) (drowning wives to collect insurance benefits), and, less clearly, State v. Langley, 354 N.W.2d 389 (Minn. 1984) (husband claimed he found wife dead in bathtub, with bruises on her body and with electric hair dryer in the water; history of husband's battering of wife admissible). For more recent English cases invoking the no-coincidence rationale, see Redmayne, Recognising Propensity, 2011 Crim. L.R. 117.

[33]Makin v. Attorney General of New South Wales, (1894) A.C. 57, 1893 WL 9238 (P.C.).

[34]The evidence also included some damaging admissions and suspicious behavior plus testimony of other mothers whose children had disappeared after these women had left them with John and Sarah with payments too small to support them for very long.

under purpose (3), and the various acts need not be manifestations of an explicit, unifying plan, as required for purpose (1).[35]

In some instances, it is possible to express numerically the
probability of the concatenation of events occurring by accident,
as when an abnormal number of cardiac arrests in a hospital occurs in the presence of a particular doctor or nurse. In these situations, testimony as to the entire sequence and its improbability
has been admitted.[36] There is some debate as to whether the no-
accident logic is just propensity reasoning in disguise,[37] but it
clearly differs from the usual propensity chain of inferences—
that (1) a defendant who committed a similar offense is predisposed to commit the offense charged, and therefore (2) it is more
probable that he did so. The no-accident reasoning is that (1)
looking at each event in isolation, it would be difficult to say
whether the defendant was responsible; but (2) looking at the
events as a whole, either the defendant is remarkably unlucky or
he is the cause of both events.[38] The different logical structure
makes a requirement of strong proof that defendant was
responsible for the other incidents inapposite.[39]

(4) *To establish motive.*[40]

The evidence of motive may be probative of the identity of the

---

[35]U.S. v. DeLoach, 654 F.2d 763,
769 (D.C. Cir. 1980) (prior frauds that
were admitted to negate defendant's
claim of mistake or lack of knowledge
"would not be admissible to show . . .
identity from a pattern of operations
so distinctive that only he could have
submitted the fraudulent forms in this
fashion").

[36]Fienberg & Kaye, Legal and
Statistical Aspects of Some Mysteri-
ous Clusters, 154 J. Royal Statistical
Soc'y (A) 61 (1991).

[37]*Compare* Imwinkelried, The Use
of Evidence of an Accused's Uncharged
Misconduct to Prove Mens Rea: The
Doctrines Which Threaten to Engulf
the Character Evidence Prohibition,
51 Ohio St. L.J. 575 (1990), *with*
Rothstein, Intellectual Coherence in
Evidence Codes, 28 Loy. L. Rev. 159,
1262–63 (1995), *and* Redmayne, Recognising Propensity, 2011 Crim. L.R.
117.

[38]*See* Fienberg & Kaye, Legal and
Statistical Aspects of Some Mysterious Clusters, 154 J. Royal Statistical

Soc'y (A) 61 (1991) (explicating the difference in terms of probability theory).

[39]Tucker v. State, 82 Nev. 127,
412 P.2d 970, 972 (1966), exemplifies
this pitfall. In 1957, Tucker informed
the police that he awoke to find a
bullet-ridden, dead body in his living
room. A grand jury investigation
proved inconclusive. In 1963, he notified the police that he woke up to find,
in his living room, the body of a second
man who had been shot. At Tucker's
trial for the murder of second man, the
state introduced evidence of the first
incident, and the jury convicted. The
Nevada Supreme Court reversed. It
reasoned that it did not need to decide
if the no-accident quasi-exception applied because the state lacked "plain,
clear and convincing evidence that the
defendant committed [the prior] offense." 412 P.2d at 972. This was
wrong. The whole point of the no-
accident theory is to aggregate events
that are individually inconclusive but
collectively compelling.

[40]U.S. v. Haldeman, 559 F.2d 31,
88 (D.C. Cir. 1976) (evidence of con-

criminal[41] or of malice or specific intent.[42] Thus, evidence that a store had fired an employee for stealing money from the cash register was admissible "to explain why he would return to that same store to rob it."[43]

---

spiracy of government officials to break into psychiatrist's office to obtain records of an opponent of government's war policy admissible to show motive for Watergate cover-up conspiracy); U.S. v. Wasler, 670 F.2d 539, 542 (5th Cir. 1982) (evidence of fraudulent loans admissible to show motive for allegedly fraudulent extension of loan by manager of federal credit union, since "[h]ad Wasler not managed to reduce his monthly payments, a default on the unauthorized loans might well have raised questions whose answers would have proved unpleasant"); U.S. v. Cyphers, 553 F.2d 1064 (7th Cir. 1977) (testimony that shortly after a bank robbery a defendant asked a government informer to purchase $1000 worth of heroin for him admissible to show motive for robbery); U.S. v. Ulland, 643 F.2d 537, 541 (8th Cir. 1981) (described supra § 187); People v. Cardenas, 31 Cal. 3d 897, 184 Cal. Rptr. 165, 647 P.2d 569, 573 (1982) (evidence of narcotics addiction erroneously admitted to show financial motive for attempted robbery of food store, noting that "[p]rior cases have upheld the admission of [such evidence] where obtaining narcotics was the direct result of the crime committed" but not "where the object of the charged offense was to obtain money or an item other than narcotics"); People v. Ciucci, 8 Ill. 2d 619, 137 N.E.2d 40 (1956) (illicit relationship and child by younger woman admissible to show motive for murder of legitimate children and wife who would not grant divorce); State v. Long, 195 Or. 81, 244 P.2d 1033 (1952) (testimony that defendant accused of murder used victim's truck to commit a robbery shortly afterward admissible); Com. v. Heller, 369 Pa. 457, 87 A.2d 287 (1952) (evidence of illicit relations with sister-in-law and of attempt to have her get divorce admissible against defendant accused of murdering his wife); State v. Gaines, 144 Wash. 446, 258 P. 508 (1927) (evidence that daughter was threatening to end incestuous relationship with defendant charged with murdering daughter); 2 Wigmore, Evidence § 390 (Chadbourn rev. 1979).

[41]State v. Green, 232 Kan. 116, 652 P.2d 697, 701 (1982) (where the "defendant claimed in essence that someone had broken into his wife's house to rob her and inflicted the fatal wounds prior to his arrival . . . evidence of the defendant's prior assaults on his wife was of great probative value on the issue of identity"); State v. Lopez, 45 A.3d 1 (R.I. 2012); cf. State v. Bainbridge, 108 Idaho 273, 698 P.2d 335 (1985) (unrelated extramarital affairs of defendant improperly emphasized in establishing defendant's sexual motive and hence his identity as killer of cashier found dying and partly disrobed).

[42]U.S. v. Benton, 637 F.2d 1052, 1056–57 (5th Cir. 1981), ("While motive is not an element of any offense charged . . . appellant's knowledge that Zambito might implicate him in the Florida homicides constituted a motive for appellant wanting to kill Zambito . . . . This evidence of motivation was relevant as tending to show the participation of appellant in the crime and to show malice or intent which are elements of the crimes charged."). In an assault or homicide case, evidence of the victim's violent history may be admissible to support a self-defense claim. See infra § 193.

[43]State v. Reid, 286 Kan. 494, 186 P.3d 713 (2008) (as described in State v. Wells, 289 Kan. 1219, 221 P.3d 561, 569 (2009)).

This reasoning commonly is applied in cases in which a husband charged with murdering his wife had previously assaulted or threatened her, evincing not merely a general disposition toward violence, but a virulent hostility toward a specific individual.[44] A few states have adopted a specific rule to allow evidence of past acts of domestic violence, by the same defendant against the same victim, to be admitted in prosecutions involving domestic violence without worrying about the purpose for the evidence.[45] In other words, a true exception to the propensity rule applies, and a defendant is not entitled to a limiting instruction.

The unusual probative value of a specific motive also can justify admission when the defendant is charged with conduct that interferes with the enforcement of the law. The prosecution then may prove that the defendant committed a crime that motivated the interference.[46] Finally, a variation of the reasoning permits proof of a consciousness of guilt as evidenced by criminal acts of

---

[44]*E.g.*, Spencer v. State, 703 N.E.2d 1053 (Ind. 1999); State v. Green, 232 Kan. 116, 652 P.2d 697, 701 (1982); Ortega v. State, 669 P.2d 935, 944 (Wyo. 1983) (neighbor's testimony that husband accused of murdering wife previously had argued with wife, pushed her down, and urinated on or near her, admissible for "insight into a person's feelings for another which may help establish motive"); Lempert et al., A Modern Approach to Evidence 351 (4th ed. 2011) (suggesting that "the propensity rule" should be defined so that it does not prohibit proof of "the defendant's record of committing crimes against a particular victim"); Park, Character Evidence Issues in the O.J. Simpson Case—Or Rationales of the Character Evidence Ban, With Illustrations from the Simpson Case, 67 U. Colo. L. Rev. 747, 753 (1996) (defending the use of evidence of prior assaults against the same victim as demonstrating an "intervening emotion" that motivates the alleged crime).

[45]People v. Johnson, 185 Cal. App. 4th 520, 110 Cal. Rptr. 3d 515 (1st Dist. 2010) (rejecting a due process challenge to Cal. Evid. Code § 1109 on the ground that the trial still must exclude when the risk of prejudice is excessive and upholding admission of

a history of violence as sufficiently probative); People v. Chapman, 2012 IL 111896, 358 Ill. Dec. 640, 965 N.E.2d 1119 (Ill. 2012) (interpreting Illinois' same-victim-in-the-household statute to apply in a murder prosecution); Alaska R. Evid. 404(b)(4).

[46]U.S. v. Siegel, 536 F.3d 306 (4th Cir. 2008) (murdering the victim of extensive fraud to prevent him from reporting it); State v. Simborski, 120 Conn. 624, 182 A. 221 (1936) (evidence that defendant, who was accused of murdering police officer who was seeking to arrest him, had committed two burglaries a short while before was admissible to show motive and as res gestae); People v. Odum, 27 Ill. 2d 237, 188 N.E.2d 720 (1963) (evidence in a murder prosecution that an earlier indictment for a different crime had named the deceased as a witness against defendant); Grandison v. State, 305 Md. 685, 506 A.2d 580, 605 (1986) (indictment in federal narcotics case admissible in state prosecution for hiring an assassin to kill witness in federal case); State v. Helling, 391 N.W.2d 648 (S.D. 1986) (prior DWI convictions admissible to show motive for flight from accident and fabrication of "phantom driver" story). See infra § 263.

the accused that are designed to obstruct justice[47] or to avoid punishment for a crime.[48]

The motive theory should not apply, however, when the "motive" is so common that the reasoning that establishes relevance verges on ordinary propensity reasoning[49] or when "motive" or "intent" is just another word for propensity.[50] Prior incidents involving guns, for example, are not admissible just to show that defendant was motivated by a desire to derive "a thrill from creating violence."[51]

(5) *To establish opportunity.*[52]

---

[47]People v. Spaulding, 309 Ill. 292, 141 N.E. 196 (1923) (killing sole eyewitness to crime); State v. Shaw, 199 Mont. 248, 648 P.2d 287 (1982) (testimony that defendant threatened prosecution's key witness admissible to prove consciousness of guilt); State v. Trujillo, 95 N.M. 535, 624 P.2d 44 (1981) (flight and escape); State v. Edwards, 383 S.C. 66, 678 S.E.2d 405, 408 (2009) ("witness intimidation evidence, if linked to the defendant, may be admitted to show a consciousness of guilt"); Gibbs v. State, 201 Tenn. 491, 300 S.W.2d 890 (1957) (in prosecution for murder, evidence that defendant also killed daughter when she discovered body admissible (along with evidence that defendant had killed husband first, then the wife when she discovered this) to show motive and as "inseparable components of a completed crime"). See infra § 265.

[48]People v. Gambino, 12 Ill. 2d 29, 145 N.E.2d 42 (1957) (escape and attempted escape while awaiting trial); State v. Brown, 231 Or. 297, 372 P.2d 779 (1962) (stealing cars to escape).

[49]U.S. v. Varoudakis, 233 F.3d 113, 120 (1st Cir. 2000) (explaining that:

> As proof of motive, the car fire testimony is offered as circumstantial evidence that [the defendant] committed the [restaurant] fire. It involves an inference of propensity as "a necessary link in the inferential chain." Put most simply, the government argues that [the defendant's] commission of the car fire arson in response to financial stress

makes it more likely that he committed the restaurant arson in response to financial stress. Contrast this forbidden inference with the permissible inference to be drawn in which the prior bad act—say, a botched robbery by the defendant that was frustrated by the ineptitude of his cohort—provided the motive for the defendant's subsequent assault on his cohort. There, the prior bad act would provide circumstantial evidence of the commission of the assault without the involvement of any propensity inference.)

(internal citation omitted). *See also* Lempert et al., A Modern Approach to Evidence 350 (4th ed. 2011) (pointing out that the value of inferring a motive is significant when the defendant's motive is not obvious but that "[t]he case for other-crimes evidence [to show motive] is less compelling when the jury is more likely to assume that a sufficient motive exists."). Nonetheless, some courts problematically admit evidence of previous illegal drug use on the theory that it shows a need for money, thereby motivating robberies. *E.g.*, State v. Hughes, 286 Kan. 1010, 191 P.3d 268 (2008).

[50]State v. Wells, 289 Kan. 1219, 221 P.3d 561, 568–570 (2009) (earlier acts of child molesting); State v. Kirsch, 139 N.H. 647, 662 A.2d 937 (1995) (same).

[51]U.S. v. Brown, 880 F.2d 1012, 1014 (9th Cir. 1989).

[52]1A Wigmore, Evidence § 131 (Tillers rev. 1983).

Other crimes sometimes are admissible to show that defendant had access to or was present at the scene of the crime[53] or possessed certain distinctive or unusual skills or abilities employed in the commission of the crime charged.[54] For example, a defendant might be shown to have neutralized sophisticated burglar alarm systems in other burglaries,[55] to be a skilled shoplifter,[56] or to know how to build pipe bombs with "a time delay and . . . an explosive filler, igniter, power source, and wiring."[57] Of course, the skill or knowledge must be rare if it is to possess enough probative value to offer a meaningful alternative to propensity reasoning.[58]

(6) *To show, without considering motive, that defendant acted with malice, deliberation, or the requisite specific intent.*[59]

Thus, weapons seized in an arrest have been held admissible to

---

[53]U.S. v. DeJohn, 638 F.2d 1048, 1052 (7th Cir. 1981) (testimony of YMCA security guard and city police officer revealing that on other occasions defendant had obtained checks from a mailbox at YMCA was "highly probative of the defendant's opportunity to gain access to the mailboxes and obtain the checks that he cashed" with forged endorsements); State v. Lemon, 497 A.2d 713 (R.I. 1985) (testimony that defendant robbed a restaurant in Providence admissible to refute alibi that he was in Boston at the time).

[54]As with the other purposes canvassed here, this rationale is applied loosely at times, without sufficient attention to the requirement that the skill be unusual. *E.g.,* U.S. v. Studley, 892 F.2d 518 (7th Cir. 1989); U.S. v. Garcia, 880 F.2d 1277 (11th Cir. 1989).

[55]*See* U.S. v. Barrett, 539 F.2d 244 (1st Cir. 1976).

[56]State v. Priebe, 221 Minn. 318, 22 N.W.2d 1 (1946) (proof of other acts of shoplifting was "a permissible method of showing defendant's capacity, skill, or means to do the act charged in the complaint," but the court did not explain how this skill was unusual).

[57]U.S. v. Zajac, 748 F. Supp. 2d 1327, 1335 (D. Utah 2010).

[58]*Compare* People v. Griffin, 33 Cal. 4th 536, 15 Cal. Rptr. 3d 743, 93 P.3d 344 (2004) (that defendant had learned slaughtering techniques while working at a meat company was admissible to suggest that he was the one who used the techniques on the victim) *with* People v. Gonzales, 54 Cal. 4th 1234, 144 Cal. Rptr. 3d 757, 281 P.3d 834, 857 (2012), cert. denied, 2013 WL 57426 (U.S. 2013) ("no specialized techniques were employed in the abuse . . . . The more bizarre forms of abuse . . . (being hung from a hook in a closet and branded with the grill of a hair dryer) required no expertise. . . .").

[59]*Compare* U.S. v. Beechum, 582 F.2d 898, 911 (5th Cir. 1978) (en banc) (evidence that defendant had possessed two stolen credit cards for ten months admissible to prove that he intended to keep a planted silver dollar taken from the mails rather than to return it to postal authorities, as he claimed, on the theory that "because the defendant had unlawful intent in the extrinsic offense, it is less likely that he had lawful intent in the present offense"); U.S. v. Draiman, 784 F.2d 248, 254 (7th Cir. 1986) (two previously inflated insurance claims following burglaries admissible to show specific intent in mail fraud prosecution arising from third fraudulent claim following burglary), *and* U.S. v. Jackson, 761 F.2d 1541, 1543–44 (11th Cir. 1985) (proof of physician's participation in subsequent similar fraud is "textbook example" of admissibility

show an "intent to promote and protect" a conspiracy to import illicit drugs.[60] Other incidents of a high school coach's physical contact with students were admissible to shed light on whether his physical contact with two students' breasts was "for the purpose of sexual gratification."[61]

(7) *To prove identity.*

Although this is indisputably one of the ultimate purposes for which evidence of other criminal conduct will be received and frequently is included in the list of permissible purposes for other-crimes evidence, it is rarely a distinct ground for admission. Almost always, identity is the inference that flows from one or

---

under Rule 404(b)), *with* U.S. v. Foskey, 636 F.2d 517, 524 (D.C. Cir. 1980) ("The mere fact that a person was [arrested] in the company of another who possesses drugs simply is not sufficient to justify a conclusion that he himself knowingly possessed drugs [when arrested together with the same person] two-and-one-half years later," since "the linchpin element of intent in the prior incident" is missing); U.S. v. Guerrero, 650 F.2d 728, 734 (5th Cir. 1981) (error to admit testimony of a patient who had obtained a prescription from defendant physician accused of illegally dispensing controlled substances to an undercover agent to the effect that defendant had a reputation for being free with pills and that she obtained and used the pills for nonmedical purposes after giving a false medical history, since "absent some evidence that defendant acted with unlawful intent in prescribing to [the witness patient], it cannot be said that [her] testimony is in any way relevant to the question of his intent in prescribing to [the undercover agent]"), *and* State v. Meehan, 260 Conn. 372, 796 A.2d 1191, 1206 (2002) (evidence that police officer charged with larceny for stealing money during the search of drug dealer had taken money from another suspect during a pat-down search of a different suspect was improperly admitted to prove specific intent because it "does not render it more or less likely that the defendant, during a subsequent, unrelated search . . . , had the specific intent to appropriate the money"). *Also compare*

State v. Featherman, 133 Ariz. 340, 651 P.2d 868, 873 (Ct. App. Div. 1 1982) (to prove that defendant murdered his estranged wife, where decomposed body was found in garbage dump, testimony that defendant had hit her over the head with a baseball bat two months prior to her death was admissible as "directly relevant to his intent the night she was killed"), *with* State v. Robtoy, 98 Wash. 2d 30, 653 P.2d 284, 292 (1982) (evidence of unrelated murder ten months earlier erroneously admitted to prove premeditation since it only shows a propensity for premeditated murder). *See* 2 Wigmore, Evidence §§ 363–65 (Chadbourn rev. 1979). *But see* Imwinkelried, The Use of Evidence of an Accused's Uncharged Misconduct to Prove Mens Rea: The Doctrines Which Threaten to Engulf the Character Evidence Prohibition, 51 Ohio St. L.J. 575, 586–93 (1990); Ordover, Balancing the Presumptions of Guilt and Innocence: Rules 404(b), 608(b), and 609(a), 38 Emory L.J. 135, 157 (1989) ("evidence of an unconnected prior crime is always evidence of propensity and never evidence of a specific intent to commit the crime charged").

[60]U.S. v. Marino, 658 F.2d 1120, 1123 (6th Cir. 1981) (seizure of shotgun, pistol, and ammunition admissible in connection with conspiracy to import a $3.7 million shipment of cocaine).

[61]People v. Wilson, 214 Ill. 2d 127, 291 Ill. Dec. 615, 824 N.E.2d 191, 193 (2005).

more of the theories just listed. The second (larger plan), third (distinctive device), and sixth (motive) seem to be most often relied upon to show identity.[62] Certainly, the need to prove identity should not be, in itself, a ticket to admission. In addition, the courts tend to apply stricter standards when the desired inference pertains to identity as opposed to state of mind.[63]

(8) *To show a passion or propensity for unusual and abnormal sexual relations.*[64]

Initially, proof of other sex crimes was confined to offenses involving the same parties,[65] but many jurisdictions now admit proof of other sex offenses with other persons,[66] at least as to of-

---

[62]*E.g.*, U.S. v. Bruner, 657 F.2d 1278 (D.C. Cir. 1981) (assaults of coconspirators and victims of "Fat Lady Conspiracy" admissible to show defendant's role as ringleader); State v. King, 111 Kan. 140, 206 P. 883 (1922) (evidence that bodies of missing persons were on defendant's premises and that their effects were in his possession admissible to prove that he had killed an employee who had disappeared, whose effects were in defendant's possession, and whose burned body was found ten years later on defendant's premises).

[63]U.S. v. Myers, 550 F.2d 1036, 1045 (5th Cir. 1977) ("a much greater degree of similarity between the charged crime and the uncharged crime is required when the evidence of the other crime is introduced to prove identity than when it is introduced to prove a state of mind").

[64]Burke v. State, 624 P.2d 1240 (Alaska 1980) ("lewd disposition" with same person); Brackens v. State, 480 N.E.2d 536 (Ind. 1985) (uncharged prior molestation of seven-year-old niece admissible to show "depraved sexual instinct"); Vogel v. State, 315 Md. 458, 554 A.2d 1231 (1989) (prior illicit sexual acts similar to those charged with same victim); State v. Schut, 71 Wash. 2d 400, 429 P.2d 126 (1967) (prior acts of incest with victim admissible to show lustful inclination towards victim); 1A Wigmore, Evidence § 62.2 (Tillers rev. 1983); *cf.* State v. Crossman, 229 Kan. 384, 624 P.2d

461, 464 (1981) (where illicit sexual acts between an adult and child are charged, similar prior acts are admissible to establish the relationship between the parties, a continuing course of conduct between them, or to corroborate the testimony of the complaining witness). For criticism of this exception to the propensity rule, see, for example, Lempert et al., A Modern Approach to Evidence 480–85 (4th ed. 2011).

[65]State v. Searle, 125 Mont. 467, 239 P.2d 995 (1952) (sodomy); State v. Start, 65 Or. 178, 132 P. 512 (1913); State v. Williams, 36 Utah 273, 103 P. 250 (1909) (statutory rape). Naturally, if evidence of other sex crimes is admitted for another purpose, this limitation has no effect. *See* State v. Jensen, 153 Mont. 233, 455 P.2d 631, 634 (1969).

[66]State v. Ferrero, 229 Ariz. 239, 274 P.3d 509, 511 (2012) (Ariz. R. Evid. 404(c) codifies certain cases from the 1970s to "expressly [permit] evidence of other similar crimes, wrongs, or acts to prove the defendant's character trait giving rise to an aberrant sexual propensity to commit the charged offense"); McLean v. State, 934 So. 2d 1248, 1262 (Fla. 2006) (grafting earlier case law on Florida's rule governing evidence of other sex offenses to require: (1) clear and convincing evidence, (2) analysis of factors including "the similarity of the prior acts to the act charged regarding the location of where the acts occurred,

fenses involving sexual aberrations.[67] Furthermore, courts in many jurisdictions do not overtly admit evidence of sex crimes with other victims as revealing an incriminating propensity but achieve a similar result by stretching to find a nonpropensity purpose.[68] Federal Rules of Evidence 413 and 414, added by Congress in 1994, allow the broadest conceivable use of "similar

---

the age and gender of the victims, and the manner in which the acts were committed," and (3) avoiding having the other offenses become a "feature of the trial"); McKim v. State, 476 N.E.2d 503 (Ind. 1985) (girlfriend's testimony of defendant's physical abuse and forced sexual intercourse with her was admissible to show "depraved sexual instinct" in prosecution for incest, rape and molestation of teenage daughter); State v. Schlak, 253 Iowa 113, 111 N.W.2d 289, 291 (1961) (evidence that defendant accused of sexually molesting a 15-year-old girl had attacked others upheld as showing his motive— "to gratify his lustful desire by grabbing or fondling young girls"); State v. Bolden, 257 La. 60, 241 So. 2d 490 (1970); State v. Edwards, 224 N.C. 527, 31 S.E.2d 516 (1944) (incest); Ordover, Admissibility of Patterns of Similar Sexual Conduct: The Unlamented Death of Character for Chastity, 63 Cornell L. Rev. 90 (1977); Chandler, Comment, Balancing Interests Under Washington's Statute Governing the Admissibility of Extraneous Sex-offense Evidence, 84 Wash. L. Rev. 259 (2009).

[67]State v. McFarlin, 110 Ariz. 225, 517 P.2d 87 (1973) (overruling cases establishing an unqualified propensity rule); State v. Snelgrove, 288 Conn. 742, 954 A.2d 165, 176 (2008) ("because of the unusually aberrant and pathological nature of the crime of child molestation, prior acts of similar misconduct, as opposed to other types of misconduct, are deemed to be highly probative because they tend to establish a necessary motive or explanation for an otherwise inexplicably horrible crime") (quoting State v. DeJesus, 288 Conn. 418, 953 A.2d 45, 76 (2008)); Com. v. Shively, 492 Pa. 411, 424 A.2d 1257, 1259–60 (1981)

(plurality opinion seeking to overrule more lenient treatment of evidence of other sex crimes recognized in Com. v. Kline, 361 Pa. 434, 65 A.2d 348 (1949)).

[68]*See, e.g.,* U.S. v. Hadley, 918 F.2d 848, 851 (9th Cir. 1990) (other instances of isolating student victims and performing "acts of sexual gratification upon them" is "sufficient to allow admission . . . as evidence of intent"); State v. DeJesus, 288 Conn. 418, 953 A.2d 45, 49 (2008) ("because strong public policy reasons continue to exist to admit evidence of uncharged misconduct in sexual assault cases more liberally than in other cases, we will maintain the liberal standard, but do so as a limited exception to the prohibition on the admission of uncharged misconduct evidence in sexual assault cases to prove that the defendant had a propensity to engage in aberrant and compulsive criminal sexual behavior"); State v. Randolph, 284 Conn. 328, 933 A.2d 1158, 1170 (2007) ("In cases that do not involve sex crimes, . . . we apply a more stringent standard to determine whether evidence of uncharged misconduct is admissible to establish a common scheme or plan"); State v. Sawyer, 279 Conn. 331, 904 A.2d 101, 104 n.1 (2006) (overruled by, State v. DeJesus, 288 Conn. 418, 953 A.2d 45 (2008)) ("our holdings in sexual assault cases that prior sexual misconduct is viewed more liberally than other types of prior misconduct should not be disturbed"); State v. DeLong, 505 A.2d 803, 805–06 (Me. 1986) (citing tradition of admissibility of evidence of extrinsic sexual relations and holding proof of uncharged incidents of incest admissible "to show the relationship between the parties that in turn sheds light on defendant's motive (i.e., attraction toward the victim),

crimes" in sexual assault and child molestation cases,[69] making "evidence of defendant's commission" of other such offenses "admissible . . . for its bearing on any matter to which it is relevant." Both the manner in which Congress adopted these rules[70] and their content have been the subject of widespread criticism.[71] Federal courts have rebuffed due process and other

---

intent (i.e., absence of mistake), and opportunity (i.e., domination of the victim)"); Montgomery v. Com., 320 S.W.3d 28, 33–35 (Ky. 2010) (incidents of inappropriately touching friends of stepdaughter in their sleep during sleepovers admissible to show modus operandi in prosecution for sexually abusing stepdaughter in the same way; however, the defense was that the stepdaughter fabricated the claim, not that another man had snuck into the trailer); State v. T.W., 220 Mont. 280, 715 P.2d 428, 431–32 (1986) (characterizing both assaults as part of a common scheme, the Supreme Court held that the trial court erred in excluding evidence that a brother accused of incest with his 15-year-old sister of below average intelligence had molested her four years earlier, just before he had left home to join the army); State v. Craig, 219 Neb. 70, 361 N.W.2d 206, 213 (1985) (mock wrestling with adopted daughter as prelude to fondling establishes modus operandi); Findley v. State, 94 Nev. 212, 577 P.2d 867 (1978) (evidence that the defendant, charged with placing his hand on the "private parts" of a young girl, had behaved similarly with two women nine years earlier allowed to show intent or lack of mistake where defendant testified and denied the act); State v. Davidson, 2000 WI 91, 236 Wis. 2d 537, 613 N.W.2d 606 (2000) (applying a "greater latitude" rule for the admissibility of sexual crimes to conclude, over a powerful dissent, that a previous touching of an adolescent girl is admissible to show "motive" and "plan" in an unrelated and more serious sexual assault of another adolescent girl); Carey v. State, 715 P.2d 244 (Wyo. 1986) (cross-examination of defendant about prior accusation of rape

permissible on theory that previous rape impeaches credibility); Bryden & Park, "Other Crimes" Evidence in Sex Offense Cases, 78 Minn. L. Rev. 529 (1994); Gregg, Other Acts of Sexual Misbehavior and Perversion as Evidence in Prosecutions for Sexual Offenses, 6 Ariz. L. Rev. 212 (1965); Trautman, Logical or Legal Relevancy-A Conflict in Theory, 5 Vand. L. Rev. 385, 406 (1951).

[69]Rule 415 extends these exceptions to the rule against other-crimes evidence to civil cases for damages "predicated on" such criminal acts. See Aiken, Sexual Character Evidence in Civil Actions: Refining the Propensity Rule, 1997 Wis. L. Rev. 1221.

[70]The Judicial Conference opposed the amendments and also drafted a more circumscribed alternative version. Nonetheless, Congress passed the original version. When the Uniform Rules were redrafted, the drafting committee unanimously rejected the new propensity rules, in part because they "would permit the admission of unfairly prejudicial evidence by focusing on convicting a criminal defendant for what the defendant *is* rather than what the defendant *has done*." Prefatory Note, Uniform Rules of Evidence Act 2 (2009), available at http://www.uniformlaws.org/shared/do cs/rules%20of%20evidence/uroea__fina l__99%20with%2005amends.pdf).

[71]Duane, The New Federal Rules of Evidence on Prior Acts of Accused Sex Offenders: A Poorly Drafted Version of a Very Bad Idea, 157 F.R.D. 95 (1994); Livnah, Branding the Sexual Predator: Constitutional Ramifications of Federal Rules of Evidence 413 Through 415, 44 Clev. St. L. Rev. 169 (1996); Nance, Foreword: Do We Really

constitutional challenges.[72] These opinions reason that the safeguard of case-by-case balancing of probative value (including the value of propensity inferences, of course) and prejudicial effect are adequate to assure fair trials.[73] Similar legislation has had a mixed reception in the states, with some courts striking down laws departing from the modern common law ban on propensity evidence.[74]

Unlike the quasi-exceptions for which other-crimes evidence is admissible to support reasoning that differs in some meaningful way from the ordinary propensity chain of inferences, the sex-crime exception flouts the general prohibition of evidence whose only purpose is to invite the inference that a defendant who committed a previous crime is disposed toward committing crimes, and therefore is more likely to have committed the one at bar. Although one can argue for such an exception in sex offense cases in which there is some question as to whether the alleged victim consented (or whether the accused might have thought there was consent),[75] a more sweeping exception is difficult to justify. It rests either on an unsubstantiated empirical claim that one

---

Want to Know the Defendant?, 70 Chi.-Kent L. Rev. 3 (1994) (summarizing arguments against the rules); Natali & Stigall, "Are You Going to Arraign His Whole Life?": How Sexual Propensity Evidence Violates the Due Process Clause, 28 Loy. U. Chi. L.J. 1 (1996); Orenstein, No Bad Men!: A Feminist Analysis of Character Evidence in Rape Trials, 49 Hastings L.J. 663 (1999); Raeder, American Bar Association Criminal Justice Section Report to the House of Delegates, reprinted in 22 Fordham Urb. L.J. 343 (1995); Sheft, Federal Rule of Evidence 413: A Dangerous New Frontier, 33 Am. Crim. L. Rev. 57 (1995).

[72]U.S. v. Coutentos, 651 F.3d 809, 819 (8th Cir. 2011) (Rule 414); U.S. v. Mound, 149 F.3d 799, 801 (8th Cir. 1998) (Rule 413); U.S. v. Castillo, 140 F.3d 874 (10th Cir. 1998) (Rule 413).

[73]U.S. v. LeMay, 260 F.3d 1018, 1031 (9th Cir. 2001) (Rule 414); U.S. v. Charley, 189 F.3d 1251, 1259 (10th Cir. 1999) (Rule 414); U.S. v. Enjady, 134 F.3d 1427 (10th Cir. 1998) (Rule 413). For a summary of the developing law on applying Rule 403 in this context, see Raeder, Litigating Sex Crimes in the United States: Has the Last

Decade Made Any Difference?, 6 Int'l Commentary Evid. 2:6, 29–30 (2009).

[74]*Compare* State v. Cox, 781 N.W.2d 757 (Iowa 2010) (Rule 413-type statute violates due process as applied to a different victim); State v. Ellison, 239 S.W.3d 603, 607–08 (Mo. 2007) (Rule 413-type statute violates due process-type provisions of Missouri Constitution), *with* People v. Falsetta, 21 Cal. 4th 903, 89 Cal. Rptr. 2d 847, 986 P.2d 182, 189–93 (1999) (statute admitting propensity evidence of sex crimes does not violate due process); People v. Donoho, 204 Ill. 2d 159, 273 Ill. Dec. 116, 788 N.E.2d 707, 720–21 (2003) (statute admitting propensity evidence of sex crimes constitutional under the Federal and Illinois Constitutions); State v. Reyes, 744 N.W.2d 95 (Iowa 2008) (People v. Watkins, 491 Mich. 450, 818 N.W.2d 296 (2012) (the statute copying Rule 414 does not violate the separation of powers doctrine).

[75]*See* Bryden & Park, "Other Crimes" Evidence in Sex Offense Cases, 78 Minn. L. Rev. 529 (1994) (arguing that other-rape evidence should be admissible in acquaintance rape cases and child sexual abuse cases); Park,

rather broad category of criminals[76] are more likely to be repeat offenders than all others[77] or on a policy of giving the prosecution some extra ammunition in its battle against alleged sex criminals.[78]

(9) *To complete the story of the crime on trial by placing it in the context of nearby and nearly contemporaneous happenings.*[79]

---

The Crime Bill of 1994 and the Law of Character Evidence: Congress Was Right About Consent Defense Cases, 22 Fordham Urb. L.J. 271 (1995); *cf.* Colb, "Whodunit" Versus "What Was Done": When to Admit Character Evidence in Criminal Cases, 79 N.C. L. Rev. 939 (2001) (advocating abolition of the ban against character evidence in cases in which "there is no dispute about identity").

[76]Recidivism rates seem to vary according to the type of sex offense. *See* Furby et al., Sex Offender Recidivism: A Review, 105 Psychol. Bull. 3 (1989); Prentky et al., Recidivism Rates Among Child Molesters and Rapists: A Methodological Analysis, 21 Law & Hum. Behav. 635, 655 (1997). *See generally* Tim Bynum, Center for Sex Offense Management, Recidivism of Sex Offenders, May 2001, available at http://www.csom.org/pubs/recidsexo f.html; Hanson & Bussière, Predicting Relapse: A Meta-Analysis of Sexual Offender Recidivism Studies, 66 J. Consulting & Clinical Psych. 348 (1998).

[77]*See* Baker, Once a Rapist? Motivational Evidence and Relevancy in Rape Law, 110 Harv. L. Rev. 563, 578–80 (1997); Bryden & Park, "Other Crimes" Evidence in Sex Offense Cases, 78 Minn. L. Rev. 529, 572 (1994); Greenfield, U.S. Dep't of Justice Bureau of Justice Statistics, Pub. No. NCJ-163392, Sex Offenses and Offenders: An Analysis of Data on Rape and Sexual Assault 26 (1997); Reed, Reading Gaol Revisited: Admission of Uncharged Misconduct Evidence in Sex Offender Cases, 21 Am. J. Crim. L. 127, 149, 154–55 (1993); The Evidence Project, 171 F.R.D. 330, 479 (1997); Rose, Caging the Beast: Formulating Effective Evidentiary

Rules to Deal with Sexual Offenders, 34 Am. J. Crim. L. 1 (2006); Rose, Should the Tail Wag the Dog? The Potential Effects of Recidivism Data on Character Evidence Rules, 36 N.M. L. Rev. 341, 342, 350, 364–65 (2006); Cossey, Comment, A Dangerous Leap: The Admission of Prior Offenses in Sexual–Assault and Child–Molestation Cases in Arkansas, 61 Ark. L. Rev. 107, 123 (2008) (reviewing recidivism statistics).

[78]*See* The Evidence Project, 171 F.R.D. 330, 476 (1997). Of course, many crimes are difficult to prove, and it is not clear why prosecutors should have special dispensations when it comes to proving sex crimes. Gregg, Other Acts of Sexual Misbehavior and Perversion as Evidence in Prosecutions for Sexual Offenses, 6 Ariz. L. Rev. 212, 235 (1965).

[79]U.S. v. Masters, 622 F.2d 83 (4th Cir. 1980) (upholding admission of taped conversations of the defendant with undercover agents despite reference to other sales and acts on grounds that the evidence was necessary to complete the story of the crime on trial as well as to prove that the defendant was "dealing"; on the latter point, see supra § 187); U.S. v. Ulland, 643 F.2d 537, 540–41 (8th Cir. 1981) (testimony as to financially troubled ventures admissible to show "immediate context" in prosecution for fraud in procuring checks); State v. Villavicencio, 95 Ariz. 199, 388 P.2d 245 (1964) (upholding introduction of evidence of sale of narcotics to one person in prosecution for sale to another, where evidence showed that both sales took place at same time and place); State v. Brown, 199 Conn. 47, 505 A.2d 1225, 1229–30 (1986) (evidence that robbery defendant was living with and receiv-

For example, in a prosecution for the murder of one child, the state was allowed to show that the defendant shot the child along with his other children and his wife while they were asleep.[80] Similarly, when police found drugs in a washing machine in an apartment complex, they were allowed to testify that the defendant, on trial only for possession, resisted arrest with nearly superhuman power when they found him hiding in a nearby dryer.[81]

It may seem axiomatic that uncharged crimes that are part of the "same transaction,"[82] that are "intrinsic"[83] to, or "inextricably intertwined"[84] with the crime actually charged do not offend the propensity rule. However, these phases, like the unhappy Latin incantation, "res gestae,"[85] often obscure what they purport to

---

ing earnings of young prostitute admissible to complete the story, where prostitute suggested that defendant rob her customer); State v. Klotter, 274 Minn. 58, 142 N.W.2d 568, 571 (1966) (where guns taken in burglary of sporting goods store and burglary that same night of home of friend of defendant's family located five miles away were found in defendant's possession, the events were "connected closely enough in time, place and manner"). A related use of other-crime evidence is to complete the story of how defendant came to be a suspect in the case at bar. *E.g.*, People v. Jackson, 232 Ill. 2d 246, 328 Ill. Dec. 1, 903 N.E.2d 388, 399 (2009) (citing cases of "case law relating to the admission of evidence explaining the course of an investigation").

[80]People v. Ciucci, 8 Ill. 2d 619, 137 N.E.2d 40 (1956).

[81]U.S. v. Marrero, 651 F.3d 453 (6th Cir. 2011), cert. denied, 132 S. Ct. 1042, 181 L. Ed. 2d 766 (2012).

[82]U.S. v. Brooks, 670 F.2d 625, 628–29 (5th Cir. 1982) (evidence that marijuana as well as cocaine was found in defendant's car at a border patrol checkpoint was properly admitted as proving "an uncharged offense arising out of the same transaction or series of transactions as the charged offense" of possession of cocaine with intent to distribute).

[83]U.S. v. Green, 617 F.3d 233 (3d Cir. 2010) (describing the loose use of this term in Rule 404(b) cases and proving a narrow definition).

[84]U.S. v. Bowie, 232 F.3d 923, 928 (D.C. Cir. 2000) ("Every circuit now applies some formulation of the inextricably intertwined 'test.' ").

[85]U.S. v. Krezdorn, 639 F.2d 1327, 1332 (5th Cir. 1981) ("an appellation that tends merely to obscure the analysis underlying the admissibility of the evidence."); State v. Price, 123 Ariz. 166, 598 P.2d 985, 987 (1979) ("This principle that the complete story of the crime may be shown even though it reveals other crimes has often been termed 'res gestae.' [W]e choose to refer to [it] as the 'complete story' principle."); State v. Gunby, 282 Kan. 39, 144 P.3d 647, 661 (2006) (endorsing Morgan's and Wigmore's view that the phrase "res gestae" is an impediment to clear thought); State v. Rose, 206 N.J. 141, 19 A.3d 985, 1011 (2011) ("invocations of res gestae as the basis for the admission of evidence do lack the analytic rigor, precision, and uniformity that evidential rulings were intended to have under the codified Evidence Rules."). For cogent summaries of such criticism, see U.S. v. Green, 617 F.3d 233 (3d Cir. 2010); Imwinkelried, The Second Coming of Res Gestae: A Procedural Approach to Untangling the "Inextricably Intertwined" Theory for Admitting Evidence

sible purpose should be clear,[105] and the issue on which the other crimes evidence is said to bear should be the subject of a genuine controversy.[106] For example, if the prosecution maintains that the

---

not bar admission). At least where the evidence of essentially identical crimes dispels the reasonable doubt that might be present when each crime is viewed in isolation, an acquittal should not preclude the proof of the earlier offense. *See, e.g., Oliphant*, 594 F.2d 547 (conviction following two previous acquittals and other complaints of rapes under similar circumstances that were arranged to suggest consent of the victims, the same defense being raised in the case at bar).

[105] U.S. v. Beasley, 809 F.2d 1273, 1279 (7th Cir. 1987) ("The district judge must . . . identify the exception that applies to the evidence in question"); U.S. v. Youts, 229 F.3d 1312, 1317 (10th Cir. 2000) ("The government must 'articulate precisely the evidentiary hypothesis by which a fact of consequence may be inferred' from the other acts evidence" and "the trial court [must] identify specifically the permissible purpose for which such evidence is offered and the inferences to be drawn therefrom.") (citations omitted); Masters v. People, 58 P.3d 979, 996 (Colo. 2002) ("It is not sufficient for the party seeking admission of other acts evidence to merely list the litany of permissible uses for such evidence. On the contrary, the prosecution 'must articulate a precise evidential hypothesis by which a material fact can be permissibly inferred from the prior act independent of the use forbidden by CRE 404(b).' ") (quoting People v. Spoto, 795 P.2d 1314 (Colo. 1990)); People v. Golochowicz, 413 Mich. 298, 319 N.W.2d 518, 523–24 (1982) ("the prosecutor's first duty is to identify, with specificity, the purpose for which the evidence is admissible," and trial judges should require "a showing by the prosecutor as to how such evidence is relevant" to this specified justification); State v. McGlew, 139 N.H. 505, 658 A.2d 1191, 1195 (1995) ("the State, in offering ev-

idence of other wrongs under Rule 404(b), must state the specific purpose for which the evidence is offered and must articulate the precise chain of reasoning by which the offered evidence will tend to prove or disprove an issue actually in dispute, without relying upon forbidden inferences of predisposition, character, or propensity."); State v. Gallegos, 2007-NMSC-007, 141 N.M. 185, 152 P.3d 828, 836 (2007) ("Part of the proponent's responsibility is also to cogently inform the court [of] . . . the rationale for admitting the evidence to prove something other than propensity. In other words, 'more is required to sustain a ruling admitting [other-acts] evidence than the incantation of the illustrative exceptions contained in the Rule.' "); Brundridge v. Fluor Federal Services, Inc., 164 Wash. 2d 432, 191 P.3d 879, 887–88 (2008); State ex rel. Caton v. Sanders, 215 W. Va. 755, 601 S.E.2d 75, 81 (2004) ("The specific and precise purpose for which the evidence is offered must clearly be shown from the record and that purpose alone must be told to the jury in the trial court's instruction").

[106] Kaufman v. People, 202 P.3d 542, 554 (Colo. 2009) (Although "the trial court found that evidence of knife possession was admissible for the independent purpose of proving identity because such evidence suggested that Kaufman was included in the pool of potential assailants, Kaufman . . . presented a theory of self-defense, thus negating any challenge to identity."); Campbell v. State, 974 A.2d 156, 161 (Del. 2009) ("If the State elects to present . . . evidence [of other crimes] in its case-in-chief it must demonstrate the existence, or reasonable anticipation, of . . . a material issue" or an "ultimate fact in dispute in this case."); State v. Gallegos, 152 P.3d at 838–39 (proof of a guard's sexual contact or indecent exposure with more than one prisoner

other crime reveals defendant's guilty state of mind, then his intent should be disputed.[107] Thus, if the defendant does not deny that the acts were deliberate, the prosecution may not introduce the evidence merely to show that the acts were not accidental.[108] Likewise, if the accused does not deny performing the acts charged, the exceptions pertaining to identification are unavailing.[109]

---

was totally unnecessary to show opportunity, which was "wholly undisputed"); People v. Golochowicz, 413 Mich. 298, 319 N.W.2d 518, 524 (1982) ("evidence of other misconduct is not admissible in this state to negate mistake or accident, to prove motive, to show intent, to demonstrate the defendant's plan, scheme or system, or to prove his identity, unless one or more of these factors are genuinely in issue—not 'in issue' in the sense that criminal intent, identity, [etc.] are nearly always in issue to some greater or lesser degree in every case, but in issue or 'material' in the sense that they are genuinely controverted matters."); Thompson v. The King, [1918] App.C. 221, 232 ("The mere theory that a plea of not guilty puts everything material in issue is not enough . . . . The prosecution cannot credit the accused with fancy defences in order to rebut them at the outset with some damning piece of prejudice.").

[107]U.S. v. Figueroa, 618 F.2d 934, 941 (2d Cir. 1980) (where codefendants suggested that they were selling coffee "grinds" rather than heroin as a "rip-off," the government could not use defendant's prior involvement on issue of intent because "no one . . . claimed that the trio was unwittingly selling . . . heroin, thinking it was some other substance"); Thompson v. U.S., 546 A.2d 414, 421 (D.C. 1988) ("If the 'intent exception' warranted admission of evidence of a similar crime simply to prove the intent element of the offense on trial, the exception would swallow the rule."). Thus, some cases hold that the quasi-exceptions pertaining to intent are not available to the prosecution where the act charged unequivocally reveals the requisite

intent. State v. Barker, 249 S.W. 75, 77 (Mo. 1923) (auto theft); People v. Lonsdale, 122 Mich. 388, 81 N.W. 277 (1899) (abortion).

Old Chief v. U.S., 519 U.S. 172, 117 S. Ct. 644, 136 L. Ed. 2d 574 (1997), has undermined the general consensus of the federal courts that a defendant's stipulation as to intent bars the use of other-crimes evidence to prove intent. *See* 1 Saltzburg et al., Federal Rules of Evidence Manual § 404.02[16] (10th ed. 2011) (describing this trend). The reasoning in *Old Chief*, however, merely indicates that the government cannot always be forced to accept a stipulation as to an element of the crime. It does not resolve the distinct question of whether a particular prejudicial form of proof is admissible when the only legitimate use of the evidence to establish an undisputed point. *Old Chief* may suggest that a mechanical rule that an offer to stipulate precludes evidence of intent (including other-crimes evidence) is unjustified. But it certainly does not imply that when the government has no real need to prove intent with other-crimes evidence, it should be allowed to resort to that evidence under the guise of proving intent.

[108]State v. Morgan, 315 N.C. 626, 340 S.E.2d 84, 92 (1986) (prior assaults and threats not admissible to show that fatal discharge of shotgun was not inadvertent or accidental, where accused contended that he acted in self-defense).

[109]U.S. v. DeVaughn, 601 F.2d 42, 46 (2d Cir. 1979) ("Since the concession that was offered would have established beyond question [defendant's] presence . . . and his identity as the recipient of the quinine, thus

Finally, even if one or more of the valid purposes for admitting other-crimes evidence is appropriately invoked, there is still the need to balance its probative value against the usual counterweights described in § 185.[110] When the sole purpose of the other-crimes evidence is to show some propensity to commit the crime at trial, there is no room for ad hoc balancing. The evidence is then unequivocally inadmissible—this is the meaning of the rule against other crimes evidence. But the fact that there is an accepted logical basis for the evidence other than the forbidden one of showing a proclivity for criminality does not ensure that the jury will not also rely on a defendant's apparent propensity toward criminal behavior.[111] Accordingly, modern authority recognizes that the problem is not merely one of pigeonholing, but of classifying and then balancing.[112] In deciding whether the danger of unfair prejudice and the like substantially outweighs the

---

removing identity as an issue, the other-crime evidence was not admissible to prove identity."); Miller v. State, 436 N.E.2d 1113, 1120 (Ind. 1982) (error in rape case to admit mug shot from prior charge where "there was simply no issue of identification"). *Contra* U.S. v. DeJohn, 638 F.2d 1048, 1052 n.4 (7th Cir. 1981) (genuine controversy requirement applies only to intent or motive).

[110]U.S. v. Cook, 538 F.2d 1000, 1003–04 (3d Cir. 1976); U.S. v. Beasley, 809 F.2d 1273, 1279 (7th Cir. 1987); Hicks v. State, 690 N.E.2d 215, 221 (Ind. 1997); People v. Golochowicz, 413 Mich. 298, 319 N.W.2d 518, 527–29 (1982); State v. Morgan, 315 N.C. 626, 340 S.E.2d 84, 93 (1986).

[111]A jury instruction is required to limit the jury's consideration of the evidence to the proper purpose. *E.g.*, Kaufman v. People, 202 P.3d 542, 553 (Colo. 2009); Campbell v. State, 974 A.2d 156, 161 (Del. 2009); State v. Gunby, 282 Kan. 39, 144 P.3d 647 (2006); State v. Nelson, 221 W. Va. 327, 655 S.E.2d 73, 78 (2007); Leach, "Propensity" Evidence and FRE 404: A Proposed Amended Rule With Accompanying "Plain English" Jury Instructions, 68 Tenn. L. Rev. 825, 866–869 (2001) (arguing for a "looser" form of Rule 404 that provides more discretion for the trial court and a plain English jury instruction to en-

sure proper consideration of propensity evidence). However, the efficacy of such instructions is doubtful. U.S. v. Daniels, 770 F.2d 1111, 1118 (D.C. Cir. 1985) ("To tell a jury to ignore the defendant's prior convictions in determining whether he or she committed the offense being tried is to ask human beings to act . . . well beyond mortal capacities."); Government of Virgin Islands v. Toto, 529 F.2d 278, 283 (3d Cir. 1976) ("A drop of ink cannot be removed from a glass of milk."); Dunn v. U.S., 307 F.2d 883, 886 (5th Cir. 1962) ("one cannot unring a bell; after the thrust of the saber it is difficult to say forget the wound"); U.S. v. DeCastris, 798 F.2d 261, 264 (7th Cir. 1986) ("this is like telling someone not to think about a hippopotamus").

[112]Huddleston v. U.S., 485 U.S. 681, 108 S. Ct. 1496, 99 L. Ed. 2d 771 (1988); U.S. v. Lavelle, 751 F.2d 1266, 1275 (D.C. Cir. 1985) ("Introducing evidence of prior bad acts for a legitimate purpose, however, does not automatically cleanse the evidence."); U.S. v. Hodges, 770 F.2d 1475, 1479 (9th Cir. 1985) (in performing Rule 403 balancing, "extrinsic acts evidence 'is not looked upon with favor'"); U.S. v. Fosher, 568 F.2d 207, 212–13 (1st Cir. 1978); People v. Cardenas, 31 Cal. 3d 897, 184 Cal. Rptr. 165, 647 P.2d 569, 572 (1982); Kaufman v. People, 202 P.3d 542, 552 (Colo. 2009); Campbell v. State, 974 A.2d 156, 161 (Del. 2009);

incremental probative value, a variety of matters must be considered, including the strength of the evidence as to the commission of the other crime,[113] the similarities between the crimes,[114] the interval of time that has elapsed between the crimes,[115] the need for the evidence,[116] the efficacy of alternative proof, and the degree to which the evidence probably will rouse the jury to overmastering hostility.[117]

## § 191　Good character as evidence of lawful conduct: Proof by the accused and rebuttal by the government

The prosecution, as we saw in the preceding section, generally is forbidden to initiate evidence of the bad character of the defendant merely to imply that, being a bad person, he is more likely to commit a crime. This rule, in turn, is a corollary of the more general proscription on the use of character as circumstantial evidence of conduct. Yet, when the table is turned and the defendant in a criminal case seeks to offer evidence of his good character to imply that he is unlikely to have committed a crime, the general rule against propensity evidence is not applied.[1] In both situations, the character evidence is relevant circumstantial

---

People v. Golochowicz, 413 Mich. 298, 319 N.W.2d 518, 521, 524, (1982); Brundridge v. Fluor Federal Services, Inc., 164 Wash. 2d 432, 191 P.3d 879, 888 (2008); State v. Nelson, 221 W. Va. 327, 655 S.E.2d 73, 78 (2007).

[113]Com. v. Donahue, 519 Pa. 532, 549 A.2d 121 (1988).

[114]U.S. v. Lee, 558 F.3d 638, 647 (7th Cir. 2009) (operating a "practically identical" spa as a brothel); U.S. v. Cvijanovich, 556 F.3d 857, 864 (8th Cir. 2009) ("similar in kind and close in time"); State v. Carpenter, 361 N.C. 382, 646 S.E.2d 105, 110 (2007) (applying "the requirements of similarity and temporal proximity" to find that evidence of an earlier drug sale was improperly admitted).

[115]U.S. v. Lee, 558 F.3d 638, 647 (7th Cir. 2009) (operating a "practically identical" other spa as a brothel two years before the one in question was a "time frame . . . close enough to be relevant"); U.S. v. Kendall, 766 F.2d 1426, 1436 (10th Cir. 1985) ("The uncharged crime or act must be close in time to the crime charged."); U.S. v.

Hodges, 770 F.2d 1475, 1480 n.4 (9th Cir. 1985) ("proximity in time").

[116]U.S. v. Morton, 50 A.3d 476, 482 (D.C. 2012).

[117]Cases discussing these considerations are collected in Graham, Handbook of Federal Evidence § 404.5 (7th ed. 2011); 2 Imwinkelried, Uncharged Misconduct Evidence, § 8 (2011). Another factor sometimes mentioned as entitled to consideration is surprise. People v. Kelley, 66 Cal. 2d 232, 57 Cal. Rptr. 363, 424 P.2d 947 (1967). The remedy here would seem to be notice, State v. Spreigl, 272 Minn. 488, 139 N.W.2d 167 (1965), or a continuance. Fed. R. Evid. 404(b)(2) and various state rules require notice.

**[Section 191]**

[1]*See generally* 1A Wigmore, Evidence §§ 55–60 (Tillers rev. 1983); 3A id. § 925 (Chadbourn rev. 1970); Reed, The Character Evidence Defense: Acquittal Based on Good Character, 45 Cleveland St. L. Rev. 345, 382–86 (1997). It is said that the practice of permitting evidence of good character began in the reign of Charles II with

evidence, but when the accused chooses to rely on it to exonerate himself, the problem of prejudice is altogether different. Now, knowledge of the accused's character may prejudice the jury in his favor, but the magnitude of the prejudice or its social cost is thought to be less.[2] Thus, the common law and the federal rules permit the defendant, but not the government, to open the door to character evidence.[3]

Not all aspects of the accused's character are open to scrutiny under this exception. The prevailing view is that only pertinent traits—those involved in the offense charged[4]—are provable.[5]

---

regard to capital cases. Reddick v. State, 25 Fla. 112, 25 Fla. 433, 5 So. 704 (1889). Later, the practice spread to cases in which the other testimony left guilt in doubt. *See* Daniels v. State, 18 Del. 586, 2 Penne. 586, 48 A. 196 (1901). Such limitations have long since been abandoned. Edgington v. U. S., 164 U.S. 361, 17 S. Ct. 72, 41 L. Ed. 467 (1896).

[2]The difference in the rule as regards the prosecution and the defense has been characterized as an amelioration of the "brutal rigors" of the early criminal law. Maguire, Evidence—Common Sense and Common Law 204 (1947). But to say that the defendant deserves the benefit of all reasonable doubts and that good character may produce a reasonable doubt assumes what should be demonstrated—that the doubt is not the product of unfair prejudice as defined supra § 185. Thus, one must consider whether a parade of character witnesses convinces most jurors that the defendant has led an exemplary life even when his past is not so unblemished and whether many defendants with checkered backgrounds will be in a position to produce such witnesses. Furthermore, to the extent that the ability to collect impressive character witnesses is concentrated among those accused of white collar rather than street crimes, one may question the fairness of an asymmetrical rule.

[3]*See, e.g.*, State v. Martin, 256 N.W.2d 85 (Minn. 1977); State v. Hood,

346 N.W.2d 481, 485 (Iowa 1984); Fed. R. Evid. 404(a)(1).

[4]It might be thought that character traits tend to occur in clusters, so that evidence of a trait not involved in the crime charged has some probative value as to the trait in question. This argument overlooks the fact that if the general correlation between the traits actually holds for the defendant at bar, then he should be able to provide more direct evidence of the pertinent trait.

[5]State v. Squire, 321 N.C. 541, 548, 364 S.E.2d 354, 358 (1988); Admissibility of evidence of pertinent trait under Rule 404(a) of the Uniform Rules of Evidence, 56 A.L.R.4th 402. A distinct situation, involving different rules, can arise if the accused takes the stand as a witness. If he does not testify that he has character traits that are inconsistent with the charges against him, the prosecution cannot introduce, by way of rebuttal, evidence that he lacks these traits. The rules under discussion here are simply inapplicable. But the prosecution may impeach credibility by evidence of bad character for veracity. The veracity of any witness at the time he testifies is open to this attack. At common law, however, the accused could not support his veracity-character before the prosecution attacked it. *E.g.*, State v. Howland, 157 Kan. 11, 138 P.2d 424 (1943) (defendant's evidence of veracity in statutory rape case properly excluded (1) as propensity evidence because not the trait involved in the crime, and (2) as supporting credibility

One charged with theft might offer evidence of honesty,[6] while someone accused of murder might show that he is peaceable, but not vice versa.[7] A few general traits, like being law-abiding, seem relevant to almost any accusation.[8]

The common law has vacillated as regards the methods of establishing the good character of the accused. A rule of relatively recent origin limits proof to evidence of reputation for the pertinent traits.[9] This constraint prevents a witness from giving a personal opinion[10] and also prohibits testimony concerning specific acts or their absence.[11]

---

because state had not attacked character for veracity). These matters, and the changes wrought by the Federal Rules, are addressed supra §§ 41 to 44.

[6]Manna v. State, 945 A.2d 1149, 1155 (Del. 2008) (error to exclude defendant's evidence of his reputation for honesty and truthfulness in a trial for armed robbery of a 7–11 convenience store by three men with t-shirts wrapped around their faces); State v. Martinez, 2008-NMSC-060, 145 N.M. 220, 195 P.3d 1232 (2008) (honesty and truthfulness are pertinent traits in a prosecution for solicitation of burglary); State v. Kramp, 200 Mont. 383, 651 P.2d 614, 618 (1982) (truth, integrity, honesty and veracity are pertinent traits in a prosecution for stealing a compressor from a construction site).

[7]For other examples, see U.S. v. Jackson, 588 F.2d 1046 (5th Cir. 1979) (truthfulness not pertinent to narcotics charges); Aaron v. U.S., 397 F.2d 584, 585 (5th Cir. 1968) (illicit affair with a woman not pertinent to charges of willfully making false entries in bank records, embezzlement, and misapplication of bank funds); State v. Altamirano, 116 Ariz. 291, 569 P.2d 233 (1977) (brother's testimony as to defendant's part-time employment and fact that defendant was not a heroin addict not pertinent to traits involved in sale of heroin); State v. Howland, 157 Kan. 11, 138 P.2d 424 (1943) (veracity not pertinent to rape charge); State v. Hortman, 207 Neb. 393, 299 N.W.2d 187 (1980) (veracity not pertinent to charges of assault and abuse

of an incompetent); Admissibility of evidence of pertinent trait under Rule 404(a) of the Uniform Rules of Evidence, 56 A.L.R.4th 402; When is evidence of trait of accused's character "pertinent" for purposes of admissibility under Rule 404(a)(1) of the Federal Rules of Evidence, 49 A.L.R. Fed. 478.

[8]U.S. v. Hewitt, 634 F.2d 277, 278–80 (5th Cir. 1981) (a trait of character is "no less pertinent for being general"); State v. Squire, 321 N.C. 541, 548, 364 S.E.2d 354, 358 (1988) ("a character trait of a general nature which is nearly always relevant in a criminal case is the trait of being law-abiding").

[9]See 7 Wigmore, Evidence §§ 1981, 1986 (Chadbourn rev. 1978) (history and policy behind rule); Ross, "He Looks Guilty": Reforming Good Character Evidence to Undercut the Presumption of Guilt, 65 U. Pitt. L. Rev. 227, 238 n.34 (2004) (reporting that 11 states continue to exclude opinion testimony of defendant's good character).

[10]E.g., Com. v. Walker, 442 Mass. 185, 812 N.E.2d 262, 274 (2004) (adhering to this "settled rule" because "[i]t is difficult to see how testimony from a multitude of witnesses, each expressing his or her personal opinion of the defendant's character, would assist a jury. Personal opinions, without more, simply cannot substantiate a defendant's good character.").

[11]Commonwealth v. Walker, 812 N.E.2d at 274. A witness who testifies that he lives in the defendant's community and has never heard of the

The Federal Rules reinstate the earlier common law approach.[12] Rule 405(a) provides, in part, that:

> When evidence of a person's character or character trait is admissible, it may be proved by testimony about the person's reputation or by testimony in the form of an opinion.[13]

This liberalization was not achieved without debate.[14] It allows expert opinion testimony about an accused's character traits,[15] subject to the court's residual power to screen for prejudice, distraction, and time-consumption.[16] Nevertheless, like the common law rules, it does not allow evidence of particular incidents.

---

defendant's character for the pertinent undesirable trait is qualified to testify that defendant's character for this trait is reputed to be good. People v. Van Gaasbeck, 189 N.Y. 408, 82 N.E. 718, 722 (1907); Negative proof of good character or reputation of defendant in criminal case, 67 A.L.R. 1210.

[12]Model Code of Evidence Rule 306(2)(a) and the original version of the Uniform Rules, Rules 46 & 47, also permitted opinion testimony based on personal observation of conduct, and a few states had clung to the earlier tradition. Freeman v. State, 486 P.2d 967 (Alaska 1971); State v. Blake, 157 Conn. 99, 249 A.2d 232 (1968) (dictum); State v. Hartung, 239 Iowa 414, 30 N.W.2d 491 (1948).

[13]For cases on opinion testimony under this rule, see Opinion evidence as to character of accused under Rule 405(a) of Federal Rules of Evidence, 64 A.L.R. Fed. 244.

[14]See supra § 186.

[15]U.S. v. Hill, 655 F.2d 512 (3d Cir. 1981) (reversible error to exclude testimony of psychologist that defendant was unusually susceptible to government inducements offered to support entrapment defense); U.S. v. Roberts, 887 F.2d 534 (5th Cir. 1989) (error to exclude psychologist's testimony that defendant's personality was consistent with that of a person who might undertake a private undercover operation to expose drug dealers); U.S. v. Staggs, 553 F.2d 1073 (7th Cir. 1977) (reversible error to exclude testimony of psychologist that defendant accused

of assaulting a federal officer was more likely to hurt himself than to direct his aggressions toward others); People v. Stoll, 49 Cal. 3d 1136, 265 Cal. Rptr. 111, 783 P.2d 698 (1989) (error to exclude psychologist's testimony that defendant had "a normal personality function," making it "unlikely" that she sexually abused children); State v. Hood, 346 N.W.2d 481, 484–85 (Iowa 1984) (psychological evaluation of wife as "passive-dependent" personality admissible to show that it was unlikely that she would murder husband); cf. Admissibility of expert testimony as to criminal defendant's propensity toward sexual deviation, 42 A.L.R.4th 937. Not all jurisdictions are open to this brand of expert testimony. See N.C. R. Evid. 405(a) (prohibiting "[e]xpert testimony on character or a trait of character . . . as circumstantial evidence of behavior"); Reed, The Character Evidence Defense: Acquittal Based on Good Character, 45 Cleveland St. L. Rev. 345 (1997) (arguing for greater receptivity to expert testimony about stable character traits).

Psychological testimony about character is to be distinguished from evidence of a mental condition or state, especially when the latter does not carry with it the opprobrium of bad character. E.g., U.S. v. West, 670 F.2d 675, 682 (7th Cir. 1982) (Rule 404(a) does not govern defendant's right to call expert to testify that he was not intelligent enough to know that he was being bribed).

[16]See supra § 185.

For example, a federal inspector charged with accepting a bribe from a meat packer can call a character witness to show his reputation for being honest, but he may not call other meat packers to testify that he did not solicit bribes from them.[17]

Where reputation evidence is employed, it may be confined to reputation at approximately the time of the alleged offense.[18] Traditionally, only testimony as to the defendant's reputation in the community where the accused resided was allowed,[19] but urbanization has prompted the acceptance of evidence as to reputation within other substantial groups of which the accused is a constantly interacting member, such as the locale where defendant works.[20]

When defendant does produce evidence of his good character as regards traits pertinent to the offense charged, whether by way of reputation or opinion testimony, he frequently is said to have placed his character "in issue."[21] The phrase is potentially misleading. That a defendant relies on character witnesses to indicate that he is not predisposed to commit the type of crime in question does not transform his character into an operative fact

---

[17]U.S. v. Benedetto, 571 F.2d 1246 (2d Cir. 1978). *See also* Government of Virgin Islands v. Petersen, 553 F.2d 324 (3d Cir. 1977) (evidence of membership in Rastafarians, who believe in non-violence, properly excluded); U.S. v. Hill, 40 F.3d 164, 169 (7th Cir. 1994) (improper to prove honesty by evidence that postal employee charged with stealing a check did not steal later "test letters"); State v. Mahoney, 188 N.J. 359, 908 A.2d 162, 170–71 (2006) (in the prosecution of a lawyer for stealing clients' funds entrusted to him, "defendant's character witnesses could properly 'testify as to their opinion or the defendant's reputation in the community as to honesty, trustworthiness, [and] integrity' [but not as to] defendant's military service, defendant's interactions with other attorneys and clients, or defendant's perceived skills as a lawyer").

[18]Lomax v. U.S., 37 App. D.C. 414, 1911 WL 20176 (App. D.C. 1911); People v. Willy, 301 Ill. 307, 133 N.E. 859, 864 (1921); Com. v. White, 271 Pa. 584, 115 A. 870 (1922) (remoteness within trial judge's discretion); Strader v. State, 208 Tenn. 192, 344 S.W.2d

546 (1961).

[19]Baugh v. State, 218 Ala. 87, 117 So. 426 (1928).

[20]U.S. v. Oliver, 492 F.2d 943 (8th Cir. 1974) (college roommates of seven weeks acquaintance); U. S. v. White, 225 F. Supp. 514, 522 (D. D.C. 1963), (dictum that community "is not necessarily a geographical unit, but is rather composed of the relationships with others which arise where a man works, worships, shops, relaxes and lives"); Hamilton v. State, 129 Fla. 219, 176 So. 89 (1937) (admitting reputation in locality where accused worked as hotel employee); State v. Jackson, 373 S.W.2d 4 (Mo. 1963); Admissibility of testimony as to general reputation at place of employment, 82 A.L.R.3d 525; *cf.* supra § 44 (similar considerations with respect to a witness' character for veracity). *See* 5 Wigmore, Evidence §§ 1615–16 (Chadbourn rev. 1974); infra § 322.

[21]*E.g.*, Greer v. U.S., 245 U.S. 559, 38 S. Ct. 209, 62 L. Ed. 469 (1918); West v. State, 265 Ark. 52, 576 S.W.2d 718 (1979).

upon which guilt or innocence may turn.[22] Defendant simply opens the door to proof of certain character traits as circumstantial evidence of whether he committed the act charged with the requisite state of mind.

Ordinarily, if the defendant chooses to inject his character into the trial in this sense, he does so by producing witnesses who testify to his good character. By relating a personal history supportive of good character, however, the defendant may achieve the same result.[23] Whatever the method, once the defendant gives evidence of pertinent character traits to show that he is not guilty, his claim of possession of these traits—but only these traits[24]—is open to rebuttal by cross-examination or direct testimony of prosecution witnesses.[25] The prosecution may cross-examine a witness who has testified to the accused's reputation to probe the witness' knowledge of the community opinion, not only generally, but specifically as to whether the witness "has heard" that the defendant has committed particular prior[26] criminal acts that conflict with the reputation vouched for on direct examination.[27] Likewise, if a witness gives his opinion of defendant's character, then the prosecution can allude to

---

[22]On the proper meaning of character in issue, see supra § 187.

[23]*See* Admissibility of evidence of pertinent trait under Rule 404(a) of the Uniform Rules of Evidence, 56 A.L.R.4th 402. See supra § 57. Courts generally allow a defendant leeway "to let the jury know who he is." State v. Stokes, 215 Kan. 5, 523 P.2d 364, 366 (1974) ("background information" and "biographical data" such as "place of birth, education, length of residence in the community, length of marriage, size of family, occupation, place of employment, service in armed forces" are not character evidence entitling prosecution to respond with evidence of bad character).

[24]U.S. v. Wooden, 420 F.2d 251 (D.C. Cir. 1969) (ruling that the prosecution could cross-examine a burglary-and-larceny defendant's proposed character witness about defendant's convictions for drunkenness was improper); State v. Kramp, 200 Mont. 383, 651 P.2d 614, 618 (1982) (cross-examination of a theft defendant's

character witness about defendant's traffic offenses was improper).

[25]1A Wigmore, Evidence § 58 (Tillers rev. 1983).

[26]Inquiry into reputation as affected by the charges at bar is improper. U.S. v. Curtis, 644 F.2d 263, 268–69 (3d Cir. 1981); U.S. v. Morgan, 554 F.2d 31 (2d Cir. 1977).

[27]*See* U.S. v. Manos, 848 F.2d 1427, 1430–31 (7th Cir. 1988); 3A Wigmore, Evidence § 988 (Chadbourn rev. 1970); Cross-examination of character witness for accused with reference to particular acts or crimes—modern state rules, 13 A.L.R.4th 796. The logic of this form of impeachment is that since the crimes occurred, they caused community talk, but either (a) the witness has not heard it, which shows his ignorance of defendant's true reputation, or (b) the witness has heard of it but is dissembling or else applying a low standard of "goodness." *See* Michelson v. U.S., 335 U.S. 469, 477–87, 69 S. Ct. 213, 93 L. Ed. 168 (1948).

pertinent bad acts by asking whether the witness knew of these matters in forming his opinion.[28]

This power of the cross-examiner to reopen old wounds is replete with possibilities for prejudice. Accordingly, certain limitations should be observed. The general responsibility of trial courts to weigh probative value against prejudice does not vanish because reference to other crimes or wrongs takes the form of insinuation or innuendo rather than concrete evidence.[29] The extent and nature of the cross-examination demands restraint and supervision. Some questions are improper under any circumstances. For instance, questions about the effect of the current charges on reputation or opinion usually are barred on the ground that it is unfairly prejudicial to ask the witness to indulge in a hypothetical assumption of the defendant's guilt.[30] As a precondition to cross-examination about other wrongs, the prosecutor should reveal, outside the hearing of the jury, what his basis is for believing in the rumors or incidents he proposes to

---

[28]Government of Virgin Islands v. Roldan, 612 F.2d 775, 778 (3d Cir. 1979) (proper for government to ask on redirect whether witness who testified on cross that defendant "is a man that never bother anybody" knew of defendant's previous murder conviction); U.S. v. Manos, 848 F.2d 1427, 1430–31 (7th Cir. 1988); State v. Lehman, 126 Ariz. 388, 616 P.2d 63 (Ct. App. Div. 2 1980); Com. v. Piedra, 20 Mass. App. Ct. 155, 478 N.E.2d 1284 (1985) (although it was "not clear error" to permit cross-examination of defendant's character witness about witness's knowledge of specific instance of defendant's bad conduct that occurred 18 years prior to trial, a judge "should consider the propriety of the use of such stale information").

There is a body of seemingly casuistic case law on the circumstances, if any, under which reputation-only witnesses can be asked what they know as distinguished from what they have heard. *See* Michelson v. U.S., 335 U.S. 469, 488, 69 S. Ct. 213, 93 L. Ed. 168 (1948) ("grotesque structure," but worth preserving); Cross-examination of character witness for accused with reference to particular acts or crimes—

modern state rules, 13 A.L.R.4th 796. Eschewing the dubious distinction between questions of the form "Have you heard" as opposed to "Do you know," Federal and Revised Uniform Rule 405(a) simply provide that "[o]n cross-examination, inquiry is allowed into relevant specific instances of conduct."

[29]U.S. v. Bright, 588 F.2d 504 (5th Cir. 1979); U.S. v. Lewis, 482 F.2d 632, 639 (D.C. Cir. 1973).

[30]U.S. v. Mason, 993 F.2d 406, 410 (4th Cir. 1993); U.S. v. Polsinelli, 649 F.2d 793 (10th Cir. 1981) (opinion witness); U.S. v. Hewitt, 663 F.2d 1381, 1391 (11th Cir. 1981) (although the government could ask defendant's reputation witnesses whether they had heard of a pending indictment elsewhere, to ask whether hearing this fact would cause a witness to retract her testimony that defendant's reputation was good was "highly improper" because "the government had already shown that [she] knew little of [defendant's] reputation in the community by exposing her ignorance of his pending trial," and the witness was not an expert qualified to say how the community would react under hypothetical conditions).

ask about.[31] The court then should determine whether there is a substantial basis for the cross-examination.[32] When cross-examination is allowed, a jury instruction explaining the limited purpose of the inquiry may be advisable.[33]

The other prosecutorial counterthrust to the defendant's proof of good character is not so easily abused. The government may produce witnesses to swear to defendant's bad reputation[34] or, in most jurisdictions, their opinion of defendant's character.[35] As with defense character witnesses, the strictures concerning pertinent traits and remoteness apply.[36] The courts had divided over the admissibility as rebuttal evidence of judgments of convictions for recent crimes displaying the same traits,[37] but with the

---

[31]It has been clear for some time that propounding a question in bad faith about a prior crime or wrong is ground for reversal. State v. Keul, 233 Iowa 852, 5 N.W.2d 849 (1942). But such reversals are rare.

[32]A number of cases recommend or require this type of procedure. U.S. v. Duke, 492 F.2d 693 (5th Cir. 1974); U.S. v. Reese, 568 F.2d 1246 (6th Cir. 1977); People v. Yoshio Futamata, 140 Colo. 233, 343 P.2d 1058 (1959); State v. Hinton, 206 Kan. 500, 479 P.2d 910 (1971); State v. Carey, 210 W. Va. 651, 558 S.E.2d 650, 659 (2001); State v. Nelson, 221 W. Va. 327, 655 S.E.2d 73, 79–80 (2007); see also Cross-examination of character witness for accused with reference to particular acts or crimes—modern state rules, 13 A.L.R.4th 796.

The use of arrest records for cross-examination has troubled many courts. The federal practice, upheld over a vigorous dissent in Michelson v. U.S., 335 U.S. 469, 69 S. Ct. 213, 93 L. Ed. 168 (1948), allows it. Some jurisdictions have declined to follow Michelson. Com. v. Scott, 496 Pa. 188, 436 A.2d 607 (1981); State v. Kramp, 200 Mont. 383, 651 P.2d 614, 618 (1982). Even in federal courts, the fact of a previous arrest, by itself, no matter how well documented, should not constitute a sufficient basis for cross-examination. Cf. U.S. v. McCollom, 664 F.2d 56, 58 (5th Cir. 1981) (cross-examination by reference to previous arrest for theft proper where lack of conviction resulted from a dismissal because defendant made restitution, so that "a good faith factual basis for the alleged prior misconduct exists").

[33]Michelson v. U.S., 335 U.S. 469, 484–85, 69 S. Ct. 213, 93 L. Ed. 168 (1948).

[34]3A Wigmore, Evidence § 988 (Chadbourn rev. 1970).

[35]The rules concerning the mode of proof—reputation versus opinion—do not depend on which party introduces the evidence. See supra § 186. Under a 2000 amendment to Federal Rule 404(a)(2)(A), the prosecution also can adduce one category of reputation and opinion evidence about the defendant's character in response to "evidence of the . . . pertinent trait." In this situation, "the prosecutor may offer evidence to rebut" evidence of the same trait. Fed. R. Evid. 404(a)(2)(A).

[36]State v. Jackson, 181 W. Va. 447, 383 S.E.2d 79 (1989) (20-year-old incident of child sexual abuse too remote); Admissibility of evidence of accused's good reputation as affected by remoteness of time to which it relates, 87 A.L.R.2d 968.

[37]The majority of the cases rejected the evidence. See, e.g., Eley v. U. S., 117 F.2d 526 (C.C.A. 6th Cir. 1941); State v. Myrick, 181 Kan. 1056, 317 P.2d 485 (1957); Zirkle v. Com., 189 Va. 862, 55 S.E.2d 24 (1949). The argument against the use of convic-

adoption of the federal rules, few jurisdictions allow any proof of specific instances of misconduct as rebuttal evidence.[38]

## § 192 Character in civil cases where crime is in issue

As explained in the preceding section, in criminal cases the law relaxes its ban on evidence of character to show conduct to the extent of permitting a defendant to produce evidence of good character. In civil litigation it is not unusual for one party to accuse another of conduct that amounts to a criminal offense. For instance, much of the conduct that is the subject of civil antitrust, securities, and civil rights cases as well as a substantial proportion of more traditional civil actions, could also provide grist for the public prosecutor's mill.

Where the homologous crimes are largely regulatory or administrative, it may seem inappropriate to accord the civil party the same dispensation given criminal defendants whose lives or liberties are in jeopardy. But what of the party whose adversary's pleading or proof accuses him of what would be an offense involving moral turpitude, as in an action for conversion, a complaint arising from an alleged incident of police brutality, or a suit for a breach of a fire insurance policy in which the insurer refuses to pay because it believes that the insured set the fire? Some courts have thought that the damage that may be done to the party's standing, reputation and relationships warrants according the civil defendant the same special dispensation.[1] These

---

tions for this purpose is much weaker than the one against the use of convictions to impeach the accused when he takes the stand as a witness. *See* supra § 43. If the defendant stays off the stand, the jury may well infer that he is guilty despite instructions to the contrary, but no such inference is likely from the failure to open the door to reputation. In any event, the issue seems largely academic, since the prosecution can advert to the conviction on cross-examination.

[38]U.S. v. Benedetto, 571 F.2d 1246, 1250 (2d Cir. 1978) (dictum); U.S. v. Pantone, 609 F.2d 675, 680 (3d Cir. 1979); State v. Lehman, 126 Ariz. 388, 616 P.2d 63, 66 (Ct. App. Div. 2 1980); supra § 186.

[Section 192]

[1]*See, e.g.*, Hein v. Holdridge, 78 Minn. 468, 81 N.W. 522, 523 (1900) (emphasizing difficulty of meeting charges of "indecent assault, seduction and kindred cases" that affect "his fortune, his honor, his family"). More recent incarnations in Colorado, Texas, and two aberrant U.S. Court of Appeals opinions—Perrin v. Anderson, 784 F.2d 1040 (10th Cir. 1986), and Crumpton v. Confederation Life Ins. Co., 672 F.2d 1248 (5th Cir. 1982)— are described in Alprin, Comment, Character Evidence in the Quasi-Criminal Trial: An Argument for Admissibility, 73 Tul. L. Rev. 2073 (1999).

courts therefore permitted the party to introduce evidence of good reputation for the traits involved.[2]

But this has never been the majority view. Since the consequences of civil judgments are less severe than those flowing from a criminal conviction, most courts have declined to pay the price that the concession would demand in terms of possible prejudice, consumption of time, and distraction from the issue.[3] Although the balance may be arguable,[4] the Federal and Uniform Rules of Evidence adhere to the majority position. Rule 404 bars evidence of character in civil as well as criminal cases to show how a person probably acted on a particular occasion,[5] and the grace given by Rule 404(a)(1) to an "accused" who wishes to

---

[2]Mourikas v. Vardianos, 169 F.2d 53, 59 (C.C.A. 4th Cir. 1948) (conversion); Peoples Loan & Inv. Co. v. Travelers Ins. Co., 151 F.2d 437, 440–41 (C.C.A. 8th Cir. 1945) (whether deceased was aggressor); Mays v. Mays, 153 Ga. 835, 113 S.E. 154 (1922); State v. Oslund, 199 Minn. 604, 273 N.W. 76 (1937) (bastardy proceeding); Hein v. Holdridge, 78 Minn. 468, 81 N.W. 522 (1900) (error to exclude evidence of chastity of man sued for seducing plaintiff's daughter); Waggoman v. Fort Worth Well Machinery & Supply Co., 124 Tex. 325, 76 S.W.2d 1005 (1934) (embezzlement counterclaim).

[3]Bosworth v. Bosworth, 131 Conn. 389, 40 A.2d 186 (1944) (cruelty in divorce case); Northern Assur. Co. v. Griffin, 236 Ky. 296, 33 S.W.2d 7 (1930) (setting fire); Baker v. First Nat. Bank, 1936 OK 10, 176 Okla. 70, 54 P.2d 355 (1936) (replevin); Greenberg v. Aetna Ins. Co., 427 Pa. 494, 235 A.2d 582 (1967) (setting fire); Eisenberg v. Continental Cas. Co., 48 Wis. 2d 637, 180 N.W.2d 726 (1970) (fraud). *See generally* 1A Wigmore, Evidence § 64 (Tillers rev. 1983); Adv. Comm. Note, Fed. R. Evid. 404(a).

[4]*See* Alprin, Comment, Character Evidence in the Quasi-Criminal Trial: An Argument for Admissibility, 73 Tul. L. Rev. 2073 (1999).

[5]*See supra* § 189. Some complications arise in assault and battery cases. *See generally* Admissibility of evidence of character or reputation of party in civil action for assault on

issues other than impeachment, 91 A.L.R.3d 718. When the issue is simply whether the defendant committed the act, the majority approach described above excludes defendant's evidence of his character for peacefulness. Feliciano v. City and County of Honolulu, 62 Haw. 88, 611 P.2d 989 (1980); Kornec v. Mike Horse Mining & Milling Co., 120 Mont. 1, 180 P.2d 252 (1947). But when the defendant pleads self-defense, he usually may show plaintiff's reputation for turbulence if he proves it was known to him. Feliciano v. City & Cnty. of Honolulu, 611 P.2d at 728–29; Phillips v. State, 550 N.E.2d 1290 (Ind. 1990) (victim's bad reputation for peace and quietude properly admitted, but "reputation" for carrying a gun properly excluded as specific act evidence); Admissibility of evidence of character or reputation of party in civil action for assault on issues other than impeachment, 91 A.L.R.3d 718; *cf.* Com. v. Stewart, 483 Pa. 176, 394 A.2d 968 (1978) (evidence of a single previous violent act of deceased's admissible to show homicide defendant's fear). The rationale is that the evidence then shows defendant's reasonable apprehension, and therefore is not used to prove that plaintiff acted in conformity with the character trait. Of course, this is also not an instance of the defendant's introducing evidence of his own good character. Likewise, since the exceptions described supra § 190 apply in civil as well as criminal cases, evidence of defendant's bad character

introduce evidence of his or her good character does not extend to civil defendants.

## §193 Character of victim in cases of assault, murder, and rape

A well established exception to the rule forbidding character evidence to prove conduct applies to homicide and assault cases in which there is a dispute as to who was the first aggressor.[1] Under this exception, the accused can introduce evidence of the victim's character for turbulence and violence.[2] The evidence must be directed to the victim's reputation or opinion rather than

---

may be used to show malice to justify punitive damages. Finally, when there is a dispute as to who committed the first act of aggression, many courts, regardless of their alignment on the general question of defendant's use of good character evidence, seem to admit evidence of the good or bad character of both parties for peacefulness as shedding light on their probable acts. Perrin v. Anderson, 784 F.2d 1040, 1045 (10th Cir. 1986) (dictum allowing police in private civil right suit to show by reputation or opinion testimony that deceased, whom they allegedly killed without justification, often reacted violently to uniformed officers); Feliciano v. City & Cnty. of Honolulu, 611 P.2d at 992; Klaes v. Scholl, 375 N.W.2d 671 (Iowa 1985) (proof of aggressive character of arrestee who sued, and was sued by the arresting officer, for civil assault, was admissible to show who was the aggressor, but cross-examination on specific acts of past violence was improper); Carrick v. McFadden, 216 Kan. 683, 533 P.2d 1249 (1975); Linkhart v. Savely, 190 Or. 484, 227 P.2d 187 (1951). *But see* Sims v. Sowle, 238 Or. 329, 395 P.2d 133 (1964). This result cannot be justified by saying that character here is "in issue." *E.g.*, Bugg v. Brown, 251 Md. 99, 246 A.2d 235 (1968); *cf.* Crumpton v. Confederation Life Ins. Co., 672 F.2d 1248 (5th Cir. 1982) (misapplying Rule 404(a)(1) to allow opinion evidence of good character to rebut insurer's argument that neighbor killed policyholder because he had raped her five days earlier). The issue is clearly

conduct on a particular occasion, and nothing more. The candid recognition that there is a special need beyond that in most cases of charges of crime in civil actions to know the dispositions of the parties seems called for.

**[Section 193]**

[1] *See generally* 1A Wigmore, Evidence §§ 62, 63 (Tillers rev. 1983); Behan, When Turnabout Is Fair Play: Character Evidence and Self-defense in Homicide and Assault Cases, 86 Or. L. Rev. 733 (2007); Slough, Relevancy Unraveled–Part II, 5 U. Kan. L. Rev. 404, 440 (1957); 40A Am. Jur. 2d, Homicide § 292; Admissibility of evidence of pertinent trait under Rule 404(a) of the Uniform Rules of Evidence, 56 A.L.R.4th 402; Admissibility of evidence as to other's character or reputation for turbulence on question of self-defense by one charged with assault or homicide, 1 A.L.R.3d 571. It has been said that the common law (and Rule 404(a)(2)) permits one accused of any crime to prove that the victim's character was such that acting in accordance with it would have diminished or cancelled the culpability of the defendant. Uviller, Evidence of Character to Prove Conduct: Illusion, Illogic, and Injustice in the Courtroom, 130 U. Pa. L. Rev. 845, 856 (1982).

[2] Lawrence v. State, 29 Ariz. 247, 240 P. 863 (1925); State v. Wilson, 235 Iowa 538, 17 N.W.2d 138 (1945); Freeman v. State, 204 So. 2d 842 (Miss. 1967); State v. Mitchell, 214 W. Va. 516, 590 S.E.2d 709, 715 (2003);

to specific acts—evidence of past acts of violence generally is not a permissible mode of proof.[3] In response, the prosecution may adduce evidence that the victim was a characteristically peaceful person.[4]

This line of proof and counterproof openly relies on the victim's tendency to act in accordance with a general trait of character—a violent or a peaceful disposition. Consequently, it does not require proof that the defendant was aware of the victim's violent reputation or acts.[5] But such awareness could have additional relevance. It could help to justify defendant's conduct by showing that the

---

1A Wigmore, Evidence § 63 (Tillers rev. 1983); Admissibility of evidence as to other's character or reputation for turbulence on question of self-defense by one charged with assault or homicide, 1 A.L.R.3d 571.

[3]Government of Virgin Islands v. Carino, 631 F.2d 226, 229 (3d Cir. 1980) (assault with intent to commit mayhem); U.S. v. Piche, 981 F.2d 706, 712–13 (4th Cir. 1992) (excluding evidence of participation in other racially motivated fights); Perrin v. Anderson, 784 F.2d 1040 (10th Cir. 1986) (previous violent encounters with police); State v. Whitford, 260 Conn. 610, 799 A.2d 1034, 1050 (2002) ("Our reluctance to permit proof of the victim's violent character through specific acts evidence is in keeping with the practice endorsed by both the federal rules of evidence and the majority of other jurisdictions to have considered the issue."); Klaes v. Scholl, 375 N.W.2d 671 (Iowa 1985) (although proof of the aggressive character of arrestee who sued, and was sued by the arresting officer, for civil assault, was admissible under Iowa Rule of Evidence 404(a)(2)(B) to show who was the aggressor, cross-examination on specific acts of past violence was improper); State v. Hale, 119 Ohio St. 3d 118, 2008-Ohio-3426, 892 N.E.2d 864, 881–882 (2008) (in response to the claim that the defendant killed the deceased to protect himself from a rape, the state called witnesses to testify about the victim's peaceful character, and the defense then presented a witness to testify that in 1998, the victim had performed oral sex on him, forcibly and against

his will; the last testimony was properly limited because it was specific-act evidence); Admissibility on issue of self-defense (or defense of another), on prosecution for homicide or assault, of evidence of specific acts of violence by deceased, or person assaulted, against others than defendant, 121 A.L.R. 380. See supra § 186. Some opinions lose sight of this limitation. E.g., Owens v. State, 270 Ga. 199, 509 S.E.2d 905 (1998). Others recognize an exception to the ban on specific-act evidence of the victim's violent character for convictions. State v. Smith, 222 Conn. 1, 608 A.2d 63, 72–73 (1992) ("In this state, convictions of violent crimes constitute a narrow exception to the general prohibition on evidence of specific acts to prove the violent character of a homicide victim, because the dangers of injecting collateral issues confusing to a jury and prolonging the trial are minimal when only convictions may be admitted."). Finally, a minority position is that even specific acts are admissible as long as they shed light sufficient light on the issue of who the first aggressor was. Randolph v. Com., 190 Va. 256, 56 S.E.2d 226, 264–65 (1949).

[4]State v. Brock, 56 N.M. 338, 244 P.2d 131 (1952). It is generally agreed that this evidence does not belong in the prosecution's main case. See, e.g., State v. Hicks, 133 Ariz. 64, 649 P.2d 267 (1982).

[5]Ex parte Miller, 330 S.W.3d 610 (Tex. Crim. App. 2009) (quoting Yantis v. State, 49 Tex. Crim. 400, 94 S.W. 1019, 1021 (1906): "If there were threats of an uncommunicated charac-

defendant reasonably believed that he was in immediate danger and needed to respond with the deadly (or other) force that he actually employed. Used only for this purpose, the evidence does not transgress the policy against employing character evidence to show conduct.[6] This "quasi-exception" for character evidence that shows reasonable fear is universally available,[7] but a minority of jurisdictions still do not embrace the true exception for victim-character evidence. They will not admit evidence of the victim's violent or belligerent propensity to show who was the first aggressor.[8]

In the minority jurisdictions, obviously the defendant must know of the victim's reputation or specific acts[9] if the evidence is to be admissible,[10] and the defendant cannot argue that the victim's aggressive character proves that the victim was the first attacker. In the majority jurisdictions, the defendant can use the victim-character evidence to determine who attacked whom, but he cannot refer to specific acts that he knew nothing about.

Federal Rule 404(a)(2) adopted the majority position by enumerating a true exception. It speaks to "pertinent"[11] character traits of the victims of crimes generally and specifically to the trait of nonviolence in homicide cases. It exempts from the usual rule of exclusion a defendant's "evidence of an alleged victim's pertinent trait"[12] and the prosecution's "evidence to rebut it";[13] and, "in a homicide case, the prosecutor may offer evidence of the

---

ter, [defendant] could then prove the dangerous character of deceased as a man likely to execute such threats, in order that the jury might determine who was most likely the aggressor").

[6]Government of Virgin Islands v. Carino, 631 F.2d 226, 229 (3d Cir. 1980) (prior conviction for manslaughter admissible pursuant to Fed. R. Evid. 404(b) to "demonstrate the fear" of defendant).

[7]Smith v. U.S., 161 U.S. 85, 88–89, 16 S. Ct. 483, 40 L. Ed. 626 (1896); 2 Wigmore, Evidence § 246 (Chadbourn rev. 1979). See supra § 190.

[8]*E.g.*, State v. Holland, 2012 ME 2, 34 A.3d 1130, 1135 (Me. 2012).

[9]State v. Hardin, 91 W. Va. 149, 112 S.E. 401, 402 (1922).

[10]State v. Osimanti, 299 Conn. 1, 6 A.3d 790, 800 (2010) (observing that in 1978, "we joined a majority of courts when we expanded this rule to allow the accused to introduce evidence of the victim's violent character to prove that the victim was the aggressor, regardless of whether such character evidence had been communicated to the accused prior to the homicide."); State v. Holland, 34 A.3d at 1135; 1A Wigmore, Evidence § 63 (Tillers rev. 1983); Uviller, Evidence of Character to Prove Conduct: Illusion, Illogic, and Injustice in the Courtroom, 130 U. Pa. L. Rev. 845, 856 (1982).

[11]See supra § 191.

[12]Fed. R. Evid. 404(a)(2)(B).

[13]Fed. R. Evid. 404(a)(2)(B)(i). In addition, Rule 404(a)(2)(B)(ii) allows the prosecution to "offer evidence of the defendant's same trait."

alleged victim's trait of peacefulness to rebut evidence that the victim was the first aggressor."[14]

That the character of the victim is being proved renders inapposite the usual concern over the untoward impact of evidence of the defendant's poor character on the jury's assessment of the case against the defendant. There is, however, a risk of a different form of prejudice. Learning of the victim's bad character could lead the jury to think that the victim merely "got what he deserved" and to acquit for that reason.[15] Nevertheless, at least in murder and perhaps in battery cases as well, when the identity of the first aggressor is really in doubt, the probative value of the evidence ordinarily justifies taking this risk.

In some jurisdictions, a claim of self-defense may not trigger, in itself, the prosecution's power to introduce rebuttal evidence of the victim's nonviolent nature. By one view, such counterproof is allowed only when the accused opens the door specifically by evidence of the victim's character for belligerence.[16] The rule quoted above clearly follows the contrary view in homicide cases. Since a dead victim cannot attest to his peaceable behavior during the fatal encounter, Rule 404(a)(2)(C) provides that whenever the accused claims self-defense and offers any type of evidence that the deceased was the first aggressor, the government may reply with evidence of the peaceable character of the deceased.[17] A similar exception to the general rule against the use of character to prove conduct pertained to the defense of consent in sexual assault cases. In the past, the courts generally admitted evidence of the victim's character for chastity,[18] although there were diverging lines of authority on whether the proof could be by specific in-

---

[14]Fed. R. Evid. 404(a)(2)(C).

[15]Crawley v. State, 137 Ga. 777, 74 S.E. 537 (1912) ("a crime is no less punishable if committed against a bad person than if it were perpetrated against a good person.").

[16]People v. Hoffman, 195 Cal. 295, 232 P. 974, 980 (1925). This has the advantage to the accused of permitting him to give evidence of self-defense and still keep out altogether this "collateral" evidence of character, in keeping with the general tradition against using evidence of character to show conduct. It restricts the opportunity for the appeal to pity and vengeance implicit in the praise of the character of the deceased. See supra § 191.

[17]1 Wigmore, Evidence, § 63 n. 21 (3d ed. 1940), argued for this approach, discussed more fully in 1A Wigmore, Evidence § 63, at 1372–73 (Tillers rev. 1983). It had substantial judicial support. *E.g.*, Sweazy v. State, 210 Ind. 674, 5 N.E.2d 511 (1937); State v. Holbrook, 98 Or. 43, 192 P. 640 (1920). A few decisions achieved the same effect by more dubious reasoning. *E.g.*, State v. Rutledge, 243 Iowa 179, 47 N.W.2d 251 (1951); State v. Brock, 56 N.M. 338, 244 P.2d 131 (1952).

[18]Gish v. Wisner, 288 F. 562, 562 (C.C.A. 5th Cir. 1923) (observing in civil case that "in a prosecution or suit for an assault with intent to commit rape, the rule is established by the great weight of authority that the general reputation for chastity of the

stances[19] and on whether the prosecution could put evidence of chastity in its case in chief.[20]

In the 1970s, however, nearly all jurisdictions enacted criminal "rape shield" laws "to protect rape victims from degrading and embarrassing disclosure of intimate details about their private lives, to encourage reporting of sexual assaults, and to prevent wasting time on distracting collateral and irrelevant matters."[21] The reforms ranged from barring all evidence of the victim's character for chastity to merely requiring a preliminary hearing to screen out inadmissible evidence on the issue.[22]

Federal Rule of Evidence 412 lies between these extremes. As originally promulgated, Rule 412 applied only to prosecutions for sexual assault.[23] Reversing the traditional preference for proof of character by reputation,[24] in criminal cases the rule bars all reputation and opinion evidence of the victim's past sexual conduct, but permits evidence of specific incidents if certain conditions are

---

complaining witness, who claims to be the victim, is material as bearing upon the vital question of her consent or nonconsent"). *But cf.* Kearse v. State, 88 S.W. 363, 364 (Tex. Crim. App. 1905) (defense witness's testimony that he had kissed prosecutrix properly excluded because there was no showing that defendant "was cognizant of such improper conduct" and "[f]urthermore, the fact that prosecutrix may have kissed [the] witness . . . would be no argument that she would kiss appellant").

[19]*Compare* State v. Wood, 59 Ariz. 48, 122 P.2d 416 (1942) (specific instance as well as reputation), *with* State v. Yowell, 513 S.W.2d 397 (Mo. 1974) (reputation only).

[20]*Compare* People v. Stephens, 18 Ill. App. 3d 971, 310 N.E.2d 824 (1st Dist. 1974) (allowed in state's case on theory that nonconsent is an element of that case), *with* Roper v. State, 375 S.W.2d 454 (Tex. Crim. App. 1964) (issue of consent is not raised by not-guilty plea alone). *See* Admissibility of prosecution evidence on issue of consent, that rape victim was a virgin, absent defense attack on her chastity, 35 A.L.R.3d 1452.

[21]U.S. v. Torres, 937 F.2d 1469, 1472 (9th Cir. 1991). *See generally* 1A Wigmore, Evidence § 62 (Tillers rev. 1983); Berger, Man's Trial, Woman's

Tribulation: Rape Cases in the Courtroom, 77 Colum. L. Rev. 1 (1977); Galvin, Shielding Rape Victims in the State and Federal Courts: A Proposal for the Second Decade, 70 Minn. L. Rev. 763 (1986); Letwin, "Unchaste Character," Ideology, and the California Rape Evidence Laws, 54 S. Cal. L. Rev. 35, 35–89 (1980); Ordover, Admissibility of Patterns of Similar Sexual Conduct: The Unlamented Death of Character for Chastity, 63 Cornell L. Rev. 90 (1977); Tanford & Bocchino, Rape Victim Shield Laws and the Sixth Amendment, 128 U. Pa. L. Rev. 544 (1980); Modern status of admissibility, in forcible rape prosecution, of complainant's general reputation for unchastity, 95 A.L.R.3d 1181.

[22]*E.g.*, Pierson v. People, 2012 CO 47, 279 P.3d 1217, 1220 (Colo. 2012) (the standard for admitting evidence of an alleged victim's past sexual conduct in a hearing required by the Colorado rape shield law is the balancing of probative value and its counterweights).

[23]Congress added Rule 412 three years after the Federal Rules of Evidence went into effect by enacting the Privacy Protection for Rape Victims Act of 1978, Pub. L. No. 95-540, 92 Stat. 2046 (1978).

[24]See supra § 186.

met. Procedurally, the proponent of the evidence ordinarily must give written notice before trial, and the court must conduct an in camera hearing before admitting the disfavored evidence.[25] Substantively, in criminal cases Rule 412 distinguishes between evidence of past sexual behavior of the victim with the accused and sexual conduct involving other individuals. If the evidence pertains to past conduct with an accused who claims consent, it may be admitted to prove or disprove consent.[26] But if the evidence pertains to acts of the victim with other individuals, the defendant may use it only to prove that someone else was the "the source of semen, injury, or other physical evidence."[27] Finally, the rule specifies that if the constitution mandates it, the defendant may introduce evidence of the victim's prior sexual conduct.[28]

Resort to an undefined, residual provision to avoid an otherwise unconstitutionally sweeping ban on proof of the victim's character is inferior to an articulation of the full range of allowable uses of sexual history evidence. It places trial courts in the awkward position of having to make constitutional rulings rather than being able to apply a self-contained and structured rule of evidence. Uniform Rule of Evidence 412 and many state laws and provide a more structured approach that seems preferable to the obscurity of the federal rule.[29]

Be that as it may, a number of cases have identified circumstances in which a defendant is constitutionally entitled to introduce evidence of an alleged victim's sexual conduct under the due process or confrontation clauses.[30] For example, in *Olden*

---

[25]Fed. R. Evid. 412(c).

[26]Fed. R. Evid. 412(b)(1)(B).

[27]Fed. R. Evid. 412(b)(1)(A). *See* U.S. v. Richards, 118 F.3d 622 (8th Cir. 1997) (this provision does not entitle a defendant who introduces evidence that semen was found inside the victim to prove that the victim had intercourse with several other men the same evening that the alleged assault occurred); U.S. v. Begay, 937 F.2d 515 (10th Cir. 1991) (error to prevent defendant from cross-examining child about prior sexual contacts that might have caused the child's physical conditions); Caldwell v. State, 6 So. 3d 1076, 1080 (Miss. 2009) ("victim's premature knowledge of sexual matters is [not] an "injury" for purposes of Rule 412").

[28]Fed. R. Evid. 412(b)(1)(C).

[29]*See* ABA Criminal Justice Section Comm. on Rules of Criminal Procedure and Evidence, Federal Rules of Evidence: A Fresh Review and Evaluation, 120 F.R.D. 299, 340 to 351 (1987) (proposing alternative to Rule 412). The situations under which these rules allow admission of the victim's past sexual conduct is described infra this section and discussed further in Galvin, Shielding Rape Victims in the State and Federal Courts: A Proposal for the Second Decade, 70 Minn. L. Rev. 763 (1986).

[30]*E.g.*, Barbe v. McBride, 521 F.3d 443 (4th Cir. 2008) (when the prosecution presented expert testimony that the child who defendant allegedly abused suffered post-traumatic stress disorder and argued that the PTSD was evidence of his abuse, the right to

*v. Kentucky*,[31] the Supreme Court held that a rape defendant's right to confront his accusers entitled him to inquire into the alleged victim's cohabitation with another man to show that she had a reason to falsely accuse the defendant.[32]

---

confrontation was violated by barring defendant from cross-examining the expert about the girl's accusations of abuse by other men); U.S. v. Bear Stops, 997 F.2d 451 (8th Cir. 1993) (evidence that a sexually assault by three boys might have produced the behaviors that the government attributed to defendant's alleged abuse); Ex parte Dennis, 730 So. 2d 138 (Ala. 1999) (due process requires admission of evidence that a third person's sexual activity with the victim caused the physical condition presented by the prosecution as evidence of rape); State v. Rolon, 257 Conn. 156, 777 A.2d 604 (2001) (precocious knowledge); State v. Colbath, 130 N.H. 316, 540 A.2d 1212, 1216–17 (1988) ("open, sexually suggestive conduct in the presence of patrons of a public bar"); State v. Stephen F., 2008-NMSC-037, 144 N.M. 360, 188 P.3d 84 (2008) (refusal to allow juvenile to question victim about punishment that she received from her parents for a prior sexual encounter, to establish a motive to fabricate her rape allegation); State v. Williams, 21 Ohio St. 3d 33, 487 N.E.2d 560 (1986) (exclusion of evidence of consensual sex with other men in a rape prosecution in which consent was the only contested issue and the victim testified that she had never consented to sexual intercourse with any man because she was a lesbian); State v. Pulizzano, 155 Wis. 2d 633, 456 N.W.2d 325 (1990) (precocious knowledge); Epstein, True Lies: The Constitutional and Evidentiary Bases for Admitting Prior False Accusation Evidence in Sexual Assault Prosecutions, 24 Quinnipiac L. Rev. 609, 656 (2006); Fishman, Consent, Credibility, and the Constitution: Evidence Relating to a Sex Offense Complainant's Past Sexual Behavior, 44 Cath. U. L. Rev.

709 (1995); Johnston, How the Confrontation Clause Defeated the Rape Shield Statute: Acquaintance Rape, the Consent Defense and the New Jersey Supreme Court's Ruling in State v. Garron, 14 S. Cal. Rev. L. & Women's Stud. 197 (2005); LaTesta, Rape Shield Statutes and the Admissibility of Evidence Tending to Show a Motive to Fabricate, 46 Cleve. St. L. Rev. 489, 498 (1998).

[31]Olden v. Kentucky, 488 U.S. 227, 109 S. Ct. 480, 102 L. Ed. 2d 513 (1988).

[32]A state court had prevented this inquiry, not on the basis of a rape shield law, but on the ground that it was unfairly prejudicial because the jury would have learned that the victim, a white woman, was living with a black man. Drawing on *Olden*, one court summarized situations in which the right to confront one's accusers or to present a full and fair defense requires the admission of past sexual behavior as including the following: "to expose a possible motive to lie," "to rebut the presumption of a victim's sexual naiveté," and "to respond when the prosecution has 'opened the door' by offering evidence of the victim's chastity." State v. Robinson, 2002 ME 136, 803 A.2d 452, 457 (Me. 2002). For an exchange of views on the Supreme Court's cases on these rights as applied to the limited review permitted in federal habeas corpus review of state convictions, see Gagne v. Booker, 680 F.3d 493 (6th Cir. 2012), cert. denied, 133 S. Ct. 481, 184 L. Ed. 2d 302 (2012) (en banc) (habeas corpus relief not available for the exclusion of a past incident of group sex with different individuals and an offer to engage in group sex with a defendant and his father).

A 1994 amendment extends the federal rape shield law to all civil cases "involving alleged sexual misconduct."[33] This augmented rule surely reaches civil suits for sexual assaults that could be (or were) the subject of criminal actions, and it probably extends to civil rights claims for sexual harassment.[34] However, the shield is weaker in the civil context than in criminal cases, where the rule excludes all evidence of the victim's sexual character—no matter how probative—that is not within the categorical exceptions. In contrast, Rule 412(b)(2) adopts a balancing test with the scales tilted against admission. It forbids admission of any type of evidence for sexual disposition unless the "probative value substantially outweighs the danger of harm to any victim and of unfair prejudice to any party."[35]

Under state laws, evidence of the victim's sexual experience generally is admissible, upon notice, for specified purposes:[36] to demonstrate that the victim, having had previous voluntary sexual relations with defendant, consented to the alleged at-

---

[33]Fed. R. Evid. 412(a). The amendment is part of the Violent Crime Control and Enforcement Act of 1994, Pub. L. No. 103-322, 108 Stat. 1796 (1994). It implements the changes to the rule proposed by the Advisory Committee on the Federal Rules of Evidence. These changes had been rejected by the Supreme Court in favor of a slightly different version. At the state level, "only a few jurisdictions have adopted protections for civil plaintiffs." Hines, Note, Bracing the Armor: Extending Rape Shield Protections to Civil Proceedings, 86 Notre Dame L. Rev. 879, 880 (2011).

[34]See Rodriguez-Hernandez v. Miranda-Velez, 132 F.3d 848 (1st Cir. 1998); A.W. v. I.B. Corp., 224 F.R.D. 20 (D. Me. 2004); Socks-Brunot v. Hirschvogel Inc., 184 F.R.D. 113 (S.D. Ohio 1999); Advisory Comm. Note to 1994 Amendment. Some of the difficulties in applying Rule 412 to sexual harassment claims are discussed in, e.g., Bell, Note, Shielding Parties to Title VII Actions For Sexual Harassment from the Discovery of Their Sexual History—Should Rule 412 of the Federal Rules of Evidence be Applicable to Discovery?, 12 Notre Dame J.L. Ethics & Pub. Pol'y 285

(1998); Klein, Note, Evidentiary Hurdles in Defending Sexual Harassment Suits: Amended Rule 412 and Rule 415 of the Federal Rules of Evidence, 9 Cornell J.L. & Pub. Pol'y 715 (2000); Springer et al., Survey of Selected Evidentiary Issues in Employment Law Litigation, 50 Baylor L. Rev. 415 (1998); Hilsheimer, Note, But She Spoke in an Un-ladylike Fashion! Parsing Through the Standards of Evidentiary Admissibility in Civil Lawsuits after the 1994 Amendments to the Rape Shield Law, 70 Ohio St. L.J. 661 (2009); Monnin, Note, Proving Welcomeness: The Admissibility of Evidence of Sexual History in Sexual Harassment Claims Under the 1994 Amendments to Federal Rule of Evidence 412, 48 Vand. L. Rev. 1155 (1995).

[35]This is, of course, a much stricter standard than the permissive balancing test of Rule 403. See supra Ch. 16.

[36]See, e.g., Fishman, Consent, Credibility, and the Constitution: Evidence Relating to a Sex Offense Complainant's Past Sexual Behavior, 44 Cath. U. L. Rev. 709 (1995).

tack;[37] that the victim has a motive falsely to accuse defendant;[38] that the witness characteristically fantasizes sexual assaults;[39] that the witness knowingly brings false accusations of sexual misconduct;[40] that a young child who gave a detailed account of a sexual assault already possessed the knowledge to do so;[41] or that someone else may have been the source of semen or trauma to the witness.[42]

A recurring difficulty under all the statutes arises in determining the conduct that is shielded from inquiry. The shield laws certainly apply to direct evidence of other acts of sexual intercourse or contact, for these laws are intended to protect victims from the embarrassment of having to disclose intimate sexual details. Concern for personal privacy and for not discouraging victims from complaining extends as well to private behavior that implies sexual intercourse or contact, such as the use of

---

[37]State v. Sanchez-Lahora, 261 Neb. 192, 622 N.W.2d 612 (2001); State v. Garron, 177 N.J. 147, 827 A.2d 243 (2003); State v. Gonyaw, 146 Vt. 559, 507 A.2d 944 (1985) (reversible error to exclude evidence of victim's recent consensual sexual intercourse with defendant and history of their consensual activity); *cf.* State v. Hopkins, 221 Neb. 367, 377 N.W.2d 110, 117 (1985) (inquiry into prior sexual relations with rapist inadmissible without proof that victim consented in these instances).

[38]People v. Hackett, 421 Mich. 338, 365 N.W.2d 120, 124 (1984); State v. Madsen, 772 S.W.2d 656 (Mo. 1989) (but rationale inapposite to facts); State v. Morgan, 66 Or. App. 675, 675 P.2d 513 (1984) (testimony that alleged rape victim and defendant had sexual intercourse about six times in the month and a half that they had been dating admissible under provision of state's Rule 412 that covers evidence showing "motive or bias of the alleged victim," since defendant's theory was that woman falsely accused him when she learned that he had slept with her best friend).

[39]State v. Anderson, 211 Mont. 272, 686 P.2d 193, 201 (1984). Uninspired incantation of a "fantasy defense" will not suffice. State v. Clarke, 343 N.W.2d 158, 162 (Iowa 1984) (evidence of prior oral sex inadmissible,

since a person who has engaged in such activity is no more likely than one who has not to fantasize its occurrence).

[40]*See* People v. Mandel, 48 N.Y.2d 952, 425 N.Y.S.2d 63, 401 N.E.2d 185, 187 (1979); State v. DeSantis, 155 Wis. 2d 774, 456 N.W.2d 600, 608 (1990) (discussing the defendant's burden to prove the falsity of a prior accusation and affirming exclusion of "sketchy, vague, remote, disputed and cumulative" testimony about allegedly false prior accusation).

[41]Summitt v. State, 101 Nev. 159, 697 P.2d 1374 (1985) (assault of six-year-old two years earlier and involving, as in case at bar, intercourse, fellatio and fondling); *cf.* State v. Pulizzano, 155 Wis. 2d 633, 456 N.W.2d 325 (1990) (state rape shield law, which did not provide for this exception, is unconstitutional as applied to exclude proof for this purpose).

[42]*See* State v. McQuillen, 236 Kan. 161, 689 P.2d 822 (1984) (discussing implications of allowing evidence of "rape trauma syndrome"). Naturally, when the government does not claim that the rapist deposited semen, defendant may not rely on this exception to introduce evidence that the victim's recent sexual activity might account for traces of semen. State v. Dabkowski, 199 Conn. 193, 506 A.2d 118 (1986).

contraceptives[43] or the presence of venereal disease.[44] As one moves to conduct that is less directly linked to sex acts, however, the applicability of a rape shield law becomes more arguable. Should modes of dress, prior accusations of rape, and statements about sexual desires or knowledge be considered "sexual conduct" or "sexual behavior" that is exempt from inquiry or proof?[45] The statutes and cases are divided.[46]

---

[43]U.S. v. Galloway, 937 F.2d 542 (10th Cir. 1991); Gilbert v. Com., 838 S.W.2d 376, 380 (Ky. 1991) (stepdaughter's request for birth control devices).

[44]State v. Carmichael, 240 Kan. 149, 727 P.2d 918, 925 (1986).

[45]Most statutes use such terms. The amended federal rule speaks of "sexual predisposition" as well as "sexual behavior." Fed. R. Evid. 412(a) (1) & (2). The advisory committee explains that this language "is intended to exclude evidence that does not directly refer to sexual activities or thoughts but that the proponent believes may have a sexual connotation for the factfinder." It justifies this expansive interpretation on the ground that even if the behavior being proved is public rather than private, admission would cause the victim potential embarrassment. In addition, it discerns a previously unstated objective of Rule 412—"safeguarding the victim against stereotypical thinking."

[46]See Socks-Brunot v. Hirschvogel Inc., 184 F.R.D. 113, 123 (S.D. Ohio 1999) (holding that plaintiff's use of profanity in the workplace is shielded); State v. Kelekolio, 74 Haw. 479, 849 P.2d 58, 77 (1993) (evidence of a sexual assault complainant's fantasies were not barred by Hawaii Rule of Evidence Rule 412, because the rule was "specifically designed to protect alleged sexual assault victims from being impeached by evidence of past sexual conduct, as distinguished from past sexual cognition"); State v. Garron, 177 N.J. 147, 827 A.2d 243, 255 n.3 (2003) (referring to amendment to

shield law to "limit admissibility of victim's manner of dress at time of offense"); Ga. Code Ann. § 24-2-3(a) (deeming inadmissible evidence relating to the victim's "past sexual behavior" such as evidence of her "marital history, mode of dress, general reputation for promiscuity, nonchastity, or sexual mores contrary to the community standards"); Fishman, Consent, Credibility, and the Constitution: Evidence Relating to a Sex Offense Complainant's Past Sexual Behavior, 44 Cath. U. L. Rev. 709 (1995); Hilsheimer, Note, But She Spoke in an Un-ladylike Fashion! Parsing Through the Standards of Evidentiary Admissibility in Civil Lawsuits after the 1994 Amendments to the Rape Shield Law, 70 Ohio St. L.J. 661, 683 (2009).

It is generally agreed that false allegations of sexual abuse are not "sexual conduct." E.g., People v. Jackson, 477 Mich. 1019, 726 N.W.2d 727 (2007), The argument that rape shield laws do not apply to acts of prostitution generally has been rejected, but evidence of prior acts of prostitution may be admissible when sufficiently supportive of a defense argument that the alleged rape was a consensual act of prostitution. See State v. Gregory, 158 Wash. 2d 759, 147 P.3d 1201 (2006) (upholding exclusion of prior acts of prostitution that were remote and dissimilar to the circumstances at bar). But see Portlock, Note, Status on Trial: The Racial Ramifications of Admitting Prostitution Evidence under State Rape Shield Legislation, 107 Colum. L. Rev. 1404 (2007).

The rape shield laws have withstood constitutional attacks.[47] They reflect the judgment that most evidence about chastity has far too little probative value on the issue of consent to justify extensive inquiry into the victim's sexual history.[48] Given the recognition of this notion in the case law emerging during the period preceding their enactment,[49] however, whether special rape shield laws were necessary to alter the law is questionable. Furthermore, there is scant evidence that the reforms have achieved the goals of increasing reports or convictions of rapes.[50] Thus, the true value of the rape shield laws may be symbolic rather than instrumental.

## § 194  Evidence of character to impeach a witness

The familiar practice of impeaching a witness by producing evidence of bad character for veracity amounts to using a character trait to prove that a witness is testifying falsely. As such, it involves a species of propensity reasoning and is subject to the argument that the jury will overvalue it.[1] Unlike propensity evidence to show the conduct alleged in a complaint, indictment, or information, however, the propensity inference from impeachment evidence of a witness's general truthfulness normally goes only to the conduct of the witness while testifying. Its purpose is to suggest that the witness should be believed now—not that the

---

[47]See Michigan v. Lucas, 500 U.S. 145, 111 S. Ct. 1743, 114 L. Ed. 2d 205 (1991) (upholding preclusion of evidence as sanction for defendant's failure to comply with notice-and-hearing requirements); Doe v. U.S., 666 F.2d 43, 47–48 (4th Cir. 1981) (collecting state cases in note 9); State v. Clarke, 343 N.W.2d 158 (Iowa 1984); Com. v. Joyce, 382 Mass. 222, 415 N.E.2d 181 (1981); People v. Hackett, 421 Mich. 338, 365 N.W.2d 120 (1984); State v. Pulizzano, 155 Wis. 2d 633, 456 N.W.2d 325 (1990); Haxton, Comment, Rape Shield Statutes: Constitutional Despite Unconstitutional Exclusions of Evidence, 1985 Wis. L. Rev. 1219; Constitutionality of "rape shield" statute restricting use of evidence of victim's sexual experiences, 1 A.L.R. 4th 283.

[48]People v. LaLone, 432 Mich. 103, 437 N.W.2d 611 (1989); State v. Oliveira, 576 A.2d 111 (R.I. 1990); Cong. Rec. S18580 (daily ed. Oct. 12, 1978) (remarks of Rep. Holtzman).

[49]U.S. v. Driver, 581 F.2d 80 (4th Cir. 1978); U.S. v. Kasto, 584 F.2d 268, 271–72 (8th Cir. 1978), overruling Packineau v. U.S., 202 F.2d 681 (8th Cir. 1953) (involvement with persons other than the defendant); McLean v. U. S., 377 A.2d 74 (D.C. 1977); State v. Hill, 309 Minn. 206, 244 N.W.2d 728, 731 (1976).

[50]Raeder, Litigating Sex Crimes in the United States: Has the Last Decade Made Any Difference?, 6 Int'l Commentary Evid. 2:6 (2009) (advocating stronger shield laws and stricter applications of them); Rice, The Evidence Project: Proposed Revisions to the Federal Rules of Evidence, 171 F.R.D. 330, 490 n. 179 (1997) (collecting studies); Spohn, The Rape Reform Movement: The Traditional Common Law and Rape Law Reforms, 39 Jurimetrics J. 119, 129 (1999) (collecting studies).

[Section 194]

[1]See supra § 186.

witness probably did or did not act as alleged in the civil complaint or criminal charge. When the witness is not a party, the threat that evidence will induce the jury to penalize or reward parties because of *their* bad or good character is usually absent. Moreover, the need for the evidence of a witness's character is greater. As a result, a distinct set of rules govern witness-character evidence. The chapter on impeachment discusses these rules.[2]

## § 195   Habit and custom as evidence of conduct on a particular occasion

Although the courts frown on evidence of traits of character when introduced to prove how a person or organization acted on a given occasion, they are more receptive to evidence of personal habits or of the customary behavior of organizations.[1] To understand this difference, one must appreciate the distinction between habit and character. The two are easily confused. People sometimes speak of a habit for care, a habit for promptness, or a habit of forgetfulness. They may say that an individual has a bad habit of stealing or lying. Evidence of these "habits" would be identical to the kind of evidence that is the target of the general rule against character evidence.[2] Character is a generalized description of a person's disposition, or of the disposition in respect to a general trait, such as honesty, temperance or peacefulness, that usually is regarded as meriting approval or diapproval.[3] Habit, in the present context, is more specific. It denotes one's

---

[2]See supra Ch. 5.

**[Section 195]**

[1]*See generally* 1A Wigmore, Evidence § 92 (Tillers rev. 1983); Green, Relevancy and Its Limits, 1969 Ariz. St. L.J. (Law & Soc. Order) 533, 549–51; Falknor, Competency of Proof of "Customary" Negligence in Support of Charge of Specific Act of Negligence, 12 Wash. L. Rev. & St. B.J. 35 (1937); Lewan, The Rationale of Habit Evidence, 16 Syracuse L. Rev. 39 (1964). Habit or routine practice evidence under Uniform Evidence Rule 406, 64 A.L.R.4th 567; Proof of mailing by evidence of business or office custom, 45 A.L.R.4th 476.

[2]U.S. v. Mascio, 774 F.2d 219, 222 n.5 (7th Cir. 1985) ("habit" of performing "insurance jobs," i.e., disposing of cars for owners who then file fraudulent insurance claims, is not an

acceptable form of habit evidence); Lapierre v. Sawyer, 131 N.H. 609, 557 A.2d 640 (1989) ("habit" of losing temper when falling behind in racquetball games); DeLeon v. Kmart Corp., 735 So. 2d 1214, 1218 (Ala. Civ. App. 1998) ("habit" of frequently telephoning police to complain of mistreatment by store employees). Sometimes the cases lose sight of this. *E.g.*, U.S. v. Luttrell, 612 F.2d 396 (8th Cir. 1980) ("habit" of not filing tax returns). The length of time separating each instance of a supposedly habitual practice is a factor in identifying a habit.

[3]U.S. v. McDowell, 762 F.2d 1072 (D.C. Cir. 1985) (bulletproof vest found in apartment of alleged drug dealer not character evidence under Rule 404(a)); U.S. v. Sampol, 636 F.2d 621, 656 n.21 (D.C. Cir. 1980) (defense theory that cross-examination of government witness as to his role in other

regular response to a repeated situation.[4] If we speak of a character for care, we think of the person's tendency to act prudently in all the varying situations of life—in business, at home, in handling automobiles and in walking across the street. A habit, on the other hand, is the person's regular practice of responding to a particular kind of situation with a specific type of conduct.[5] Thus, a person may be in the habit of bounding down a certain stairway two or three steps at a time, of patronizing a particular pub after each day's work, or of driving his automobile without using a seatbelt. The doing of the habitual act may become semi-automatic, as with a driver who invariably signals before changing lanes.[6]

---

assassinations was permissible to prove a habit was "patently without merit"); Levin v. U.S., 338 F.2d 265 (D.C. Cir. 1964) (acting in conformity with religious beliefs). The prohibition against character evidence arises in part because of the prejudicial nature of the traits that the parties commonly seek to expose. In deciding which personal characteristics qualify as traits of character, this consideration may be important.

[4]U.S. v. Holman, 680 F.2d 1340 (11th Cir. 1982) (one previous attempt to convince skipper of fishing vessel to smuggle marijuana could not show a habit of coercing owners of boats into smuggling drugs); Meyer v. U.S., 464 F. Supp. 317, 321 (D. Colo. 1979) ("regular response to a repeated situation"). Although it overstates the point, at least one text has said that "the distinction is between Pavlov and Freud." Wright and Miller's Federal Practice and Procedure, Evidence § 5233, at 354 (citing 2 Weinstein & Berger, Weinstein's Evidence 404–11 (1975)). It has also been noted that "one could reasonably testify to having observed habitual behavior, but character is almost always a matter of opinion.

[5]Model Code of Evidence Rule 307(1) (1942) defined habit in this way: "Habit means a course of behavior of a person regularly repeated in like circumstances. Custom means a course of behavior of a group of persons regularly repeated in like circumstances."

[6]For more examples, compare Weil v. Seltzer, 873 F.2d 1453, 1461 (D.C. Cir. 1989) (prescribing and misrepresenting steroids to allergy patients not of the "non-volitional, habitual type that assures its probative value"); U.S. v. Troutman, 814 F.2d 1428, 1455 (10th Cir. 1987) ("[e]xtortion or refraining from extortion is not a semi-automatic act and does not constitute habit"); State v. Whitford, 260 Conn. 610, 799 A.2d 1034, 1052 (2002) ("strangling people while . . . intoxicated" is not a habit because habit evidence does not "encompass specific instances of intentional violent conduct"); Brett v. Berkowitz, 706 A.2d 509, 517 (Del. 1998) (a lawyer's "alleged sexual behavior toward his clients, in that it entails some amount of judgment and decisionmaking, is too complex and is susceptible to too much variation to qualify as habit evidence"), with Howard v. Capital Transit Co., 97 F. Supp. 578 (D. D.C. 1951) (decedent's habit of using defendant's buses to return from work); Whittemore v. Lockheed Aircraft Corp., 65 Cal. App. 2d 737, 151 P.2d 670 (2d Dist. 1944) (practice of pilot to occupy left-hand seat when he would fly the plane); State v. Hedger, 115 Idaho 598, 768 P.2d 1331 (1989) (always arranging for child care when away at night); Fissette v. Boston & Maine R.R., 98 N.H. 136, 96 A.2d 303 (1953) (looking and listening at railroad crossing); Halloran v. Virginia Chemicals Inc., 41 N.Y.2d 386, 393 N.Y.S.2d 341, 361 N.E.2d 991 (1977) (mechanic's practice

Evidence of habits that come within this definition has greater probative value than does evidence of general traits of character.[7] Furthermore, the potential for prejudice is substantially less. By and large, the detailed patterns of situation-specific behavior that constitute habits are unlikely to provoke such sympathy or antipathy as would distort the process of evaluating the evidence.[8]

As a result, many jurisdictions accept the proposition that evidence of habit is admissible to show an act. These courts only reject the evidence categorically if the putative habit is not suf-

---

of using an immersion coil to heat cans of Freon for refilling air conditioning units); Glatt v. Feist, 156 N.W.2d 819 (N.D. 1968) (crossing street outside crosswalk at particular place); Charmley v. Lewis, 302 Or. 324, 729 P.2d 567 (1986) (crossing the same street in the same crosswalk nearly every day on way to grocery store); Bown v. City of Tacoma, 175 Wash. 414, 27 P.2d 711 (1933) (riding on cars in alley where accident occurred); French v. Sorano, 74 Wis. 2d 460, 247 N.W.2d 182 (1976) (hiding money in car); Admissibility of evidence of habit or routine practice under Rule 406, Federal Rules of Evidence, 53 A.L.R. Fed. 703.

[7] Character may be thought of as the sum of one's habits, although doubtless it is more than this. Unquestionably, the uniformity of an habitual response is far greater than the consistency with which one's conduct conforms to character or disposition. Even though character comes in only exceptionally as evidence of an act, surely any sensible person in investigating whether a given individual did a particular act would be greatly helped in his inquiry by evidence as to whether that individual was in the habit of doing it.

[8] Of course, there are important exceptions to this generalization. E.g., Perrin v. Anderson, 784 F.2d 1040, 1045 (10th Cir. 1986) (deceased's habit of responding to uniformed police with extreme violence); Brett v. Berkowitz, 706 A.2d 509 (Del. 1998) (a lawyer's offensive touchings and other sexual behavior toward his clients); State v. Franklin, 52 N.J. 386, 245 A.2d 356

(1968) (history of chronic alcoholism). But even if habit evidence, strictly defined, ordinarily is unlikely to be prejudicial in the sense of distorting the evaluative process, it may pose "estimation" problems. See supra § 185. For example, "[a] murderer, in the habit of taking the six o'clock bus home from work, may kill someone at six-fifteen, counting on evidence of habit to establish an alibi." Lempert & Saltzburg, A Modern Approach to Evidence 249 (2d ed. 1983) (concluding that these problems are not unduly severe). Surely, this is a concern that underlies the refusal of the court in Levin v. U.S., 338 F.2d 265 (D.C. Cir. 1964), to accept testimony as to the religious "habits" of the accused, offered to prove that he was at home observing the Sabbath rather than obtaining money through larceny by trick. In suggesting that religious practices cannot be habits, however, Levin (id. at 272) goes too far. Religiously motivated practices, though volitional, can be undertaken with sufficient regularity to rise to the level of habits, and a jury ordinarily can be trusted to appreciate the degree to which a criminal motive will lead one to deviate from habit. If regularly observed religious practices are not admissible as habit, it must be because the religious overtones of the habit would tempt the jury to misapply the law—a proposition whose truth is hardly obvious. But mere evidence of religious belief would not show an habitual religious practice. Rather, it would indicate a disposition toward religious behavior—a character trait.

ficiently regular or uniform,[9] or if the circumstances are not sufficiently similar[10] to outweigh the dangers of prejudice, distraction and time-consumption.[11] The Federal,[12] Uniform,[13] and

---

[9]This is tantamount to saying that there is not a sufficient indication of the existence of a habit. *See, e.g.,* U.S. Football League v. National Football League, 842 F.2d 1335, 1373 (2d Cir. 1988) (three or four instances of disregard of antitrust advice over a 20 year period do not show "a pattern of behavior"); Reyes v. Missouri Pac. R. Co., 589 F.2d 791, 795 (5th Cir. 1979) (four prior convictions for public intoxication over a 3.5 year period not sufficiently regular to rise to the level of habit evidence); Simplex, Inc. v. Diversified Energy Systems, Inc., 847 F.2d 1290, 1293–94 (7th Cir. 1988) (insufficient evidence of habitually late and defective performance of contracts); G.M. Brod & Co., Inc. v. U.S. Home Corp., 759 F.2d 1526, 1532–33 (11th Cir. 1985) (testimony of subcontractor that defendant company breached five contracts with him in a year and a half, and breached contracts with others, erroneously admitted to show company's habitual breaching of contracts with small businesses, since company dealt with thousands of different small subcontractors under many different circumstances); State v. Whitford, 260 Conn. 610, 799 A.2d 1034, 1051 (2002) (two or three incidents in which a man attempted to strangle others while he was intoxicated were insufficient to demonstrate a habit); Hardesty v. Coastal Mart, Inc., 259 Kan. 645, 915 P.2d 41, 47–48 (1996) (six prior falls or injuries over a three-year time span, even if they were caused by plaintiff's not looking where she was going, do not establish a habit of "not looking where she is going" while walking).

[10]Mueller v. Buscemi, 230 P.3d 1153, 1157 (Alaska 2010) (plaintiff attributed her fall in a parking lot to the owner's failure to keep it clear of ice and to have adequate lighting and "offered eight photographs which appear to show a water heater, ceiling tiles, a fire extinguisher, a sink, and a wall" on defendant's commercial properties, but these putative examples of improper maintenance were not "numerous enough to base an inference of systematic conduct and to establish [a] regular response to a repeated specific situation").

[11]Levin v. U.S., 338 F.2d 265 (D.C. Cir. 1964). Because intemperance is a potentially prejudicial habit, evidence of "habitual intemperance" seems to produce the conflicting results. Partly, the problem stems from the fact that the term may denote a general disposition for excessive drinking (a trait) or a practice of drinking a certain number of glasses of whiskey every night at home (a habit). Thus, the probative force of what is loosely called the habit of intemperance to prove drunkenness on a particular occasion depends on the regularity and details of the characteristic behavior. *Compare* Loughan v. Firestone Tire & Rubber Co., 749 F.2d 1519, 1523 (11th Cir. 1985) ("evidence of [tire mechanic's] drinking over an extended period of time, coupled with evidence of [his] regular practice of carrying a cooler of beer" sufficient "to establish a drinking habit" to support defendant's theory that defendant mounted tire assembly improperly), *and* State v. Kately, 270 N.J. Super. 356, 637 A.2d 214 (App. Div. 1994) (drinking one to two six-packs of beer at a field with a group of three or four friends almost every night for about one year), *with* Mydlarz v. Palmer/Duncan Const. Co., 209 Mont. 325, 682 P.2d 695, 704 (1984) ("evidence of general drinking problem" erroneously admitted to show why painter fell off ladder). For additional cases, see Admissibility of evidence showing plaintiff's antecedent intemperate habits, in personal injury motor vehicle accident action, 46 A.L.R.2d 103.

Model[14] Rules all follow this pattern. In the past, however, some jurisdictions excluded evidence of habit altogether,[15] and others admitted it only if there were no eyewitnesses to testify about the events that were said to have triggered the habitual behavior.[16]

Even the jurisdictions that were reluctant to accept evidence of personal habits were willing to allow evidence of the "custom" of a business organization,[17] if reasonably regular and uniform.[18] This may be because there is no confusion between character

---

[12]Federal and Uniform Rule 406 provides: "Evidence of the habit of a person or of the routine practice of an organization, whether corroborated or not and regardless of the presence of eyewitnesses, is relevant to prove that the conduct was in conformity with the habit or routine practice."

[13]Uniform Rule 406 also includes a provision that Congress deleted from the proposed federal rules: "Habit or routine practice may be proved by testimony in the form of an opinion or by specific instances of conduct sufficient in number to warrant a finding that the habit existed or that the practice was routine." Unif. R. Evid. 406 (rev. 2005). The House Committee on the Judiciary deleted the subdivision, as stated in the Committee Report, "believing that the method of proof of habit and routine practice should be left to the courts to deal with on a case-by-case basis." H. Comm. on the Judiciary, Fed. Rules of Evidence, H.R. Rep. No. 650, 93d Cong., 1st Sess., at 5 (1973).

[14]Model Code of Evidence Rule 307(2) (1942): "Evidence of a habit of a person is admissible as tending to prove that his behavior on a specified occasion conformed to the habit. Evidence of a custom of a group of persons is admissible as tending to prove that their behavior on a specified occasion conformed to the custom."

[15]See, e.g., Com. v. Nagle, 157 Mass. 554, 32 N.E. 861 (1893); Zucker v. Whitridge, 205 N.Y. 50, 98 N.E. 209 (1912); Fenton v. Aleshire, 238 Or. 24, 393 P.2d 217 (1964); Note, Evidence of Habit and Custom in Massachusetts Civil Cases, 33 B.U. L. Rev. 205 (1953).

[16]See, e.g., Missouri-Kansas-Texas R. Co. v. McFerrin, 156 Tex. 69, 291 S.W.2d 931, 941–42 (1956); Proof of mailing by evidence of business or office custom, 45 A.L.R.4th 476; see supra § 189 (minority exception to rule excluding character evidence on issue of particular negligent conduct when there are no eyewitnesses). The no-eyewitness rule seems unwise. The need for evidence of a true habit is no less because the eyewitnesses disagree or for some other reason (such as the very absence of eyewitnesses), the issue of fact is in doubt. Likewise, the prejudice of the evidence, if any, is no less when eyewitnesses are unavailable. Cereste v. New York, New Haven & Hartford R. Co., 231 F.2d 50, 53 (2d Cir. 1956).

[17]Massachusetts continues in this tradition. Com. v. Wilson, 443 Mass. 122, 138, 819 N.E.2d 919, 933 (2004) (owner's personal, not business, habit of locking door would be inadmissible); Palinkas v. Bennett, 416 Mass. 273, 276, 620 N.E.2d 775, 777 (1993).

[18]U.S. v. Oddo, 314 F.2d 115 (2d Cir. 1963) (customary practices of Immigration and Naturalization Service); Spartan Grain & Mill Co. v. Ayers, 517 F.2d 214, 219 (5th Cir. 1975) (evidence of how a firm handled eggs generally erroneously excluded where the firm was seeking damages for failure of eggs to hatch because of improper feed sold to it); Eaton v. Bass, 214 F.2d 896 (6th Cir. 1954) (custom of inspecting trucks); Russell v. Pitts, 105 Ga. App. 147, 123 S.E.2d 708 (1961) (customary sterilization procedures in medical center); Com. v. Torrealba, 316 Mass. 24, 54 N.E.2d 939 (1944) (custom of store to give sales slip with each pur-

traits and business practices, as there is between character and habit, or it may reflect the belief that the need for regularity in business and the organizational sanctions that may exist when employees deviate from the established procedures give extra guarantees that the questioned activity followed the usual custom.[19] Thus, evidence that a letter was written and signed in the course of business and put in the regular place for mailing usually will be admitted to prove that it was mailed.[20] Similarly, regular adherence to a standard protocol of informing research subjects of the known risks and benefits of a drug can counter allegations that some subjects were not properly informed.[21] But admissible business practices can include ones that depart from official or acknowledged company policy.[22]

---

chase received as evidence that goods found in defendant's possession, with no record of sale, were stolen); Santarpio v. New York Life Ins. Co., 301 Mass. 207, 210, 16 N.E.2d 668, 669 (1938) (custom of submitting insurance applications); Prudential Trust Co. v. Hayes, 247 Mass. 311, 314–315, 142 N.E. 73, 73–74 (1924) (custom of sending letters); Buxton v. Langan, 90 N.H. 13, 3 A.2d 647 (1939) (rule or practice of defendant's shop for employees to test brakes before renting out car); cases cited 1A Wigmore, Evidence § 93 (Tillers rev. 1983).

In a large number of cases, however, evidence of business routine standing alone has been held insufficient to prove the completion of an act. Corroboration that the routine was followed was required. Leasing Associates, Inc. v. Slaughter & Son, Inc., 450 F.2d 174 (8th Cir. 1971) (stating that the majority rule required corroboration); U.S. v. Oddo, 314 F.2d 115 (2d Cir. 1963). Following what appears to be the more reasonable view (see Mohr v. Universal C.I.T. Credit Corp., 216 Md. 197, 140 A.2d 49 (1958); Slough, Relevancy Unraveled (pt. 2), 5 U. Kan. L. Rev. 404, 409, 450–451 (1957)), Federal Rule 406 expressly rejects the corroboration requirement.

[19]*See, e.g.*, U.S. v. Seelig, 622 F.2d 207 (6th Cir. 1980) (error to exclude expert testimony as to the custom of pharmacists regarding the sales of over-the-counter exempt drugs).

[20]U.S. v. Scott, 668 F.2d 384, 388 (8th Cir. 1981); U.S. v. Gomez, 636 F.2d 295, 297 (10th Cir. 1981); U.S. v. Ziperstein, 601 F.2d 281, 295 (7th Cir. 1979); General Mills, Inc. v. Zerbe Bros., Inc., 207 Mont. 19, 672 P.2d 1109 (1983).

[21]Wetherill v. University of Chicago, 570 F. Supp. 1124 (N.D. Ill. 1983).

[22]Hazelwood School Dist. v. U.S., 433 U.S. 299, 309 n.15, 97 S. Ct. 2736, 53 L. Ed. 2d 768 (1977) (pre-Title VII discrimination in hiring teachers might "support the inference that such discrimination continued" after law became effective); Rosenburg v. Lincoln American Life Ins. Co., 883 F.2d 1328, 1336 (7th Cir. 1989) (insurer's routine fraudulent practice of "selling conditional insurance, waiving such conditions, and later asserting them as defenses"); Holley v. Seminole County School Dist., 755 F.2d 1492, 1505 (11th Cir. 1985) (where teacher alleged that school board dismissed her in response to her political activity, it was error to grant summary judgment for board after excluding teacher's evidence that board had not punished others who had engaged in similar political activities); Com. of Pa. v. Porter, 659 F.2d 306, 320 (3d Cir. 1981) (incidents of a policeman's unlawful arrests, searches, assaults and harassments "admissible under Rule 406 to show a pattern or routine practice of a defendant or organization"); U.S. v.

The existence of the personal habit or the business custom may be established by a knowledgeable witness's testimony that there was such a habit or practice.[23] Evidence of specific instances may also be used.[24] Naturally, there must be enough instances to permit the finding of a habit,[25] the circumstances under which the habit or custom is followed must be present,[26] and, as always, there are the limitations for cumulativeness, remoteness, unnec-

---

Callahan, 551 F.2d 733 (6th Cir. 1977) (error to exclude testimony that the routine of a construction company was to pay off local unions for the sake of expediency rather than out of fear of injury).

[23]Typically, this is the method employed. *See, e.g.*, Meyer v. U.S., 638 F.2d 155 (10th Cir. 1980) (dentist's testimony that it was his custom and habit to warn patients of risks of surgery to remove molars was adequate to support trial court's finding that dentist warned patient even though she denied being warned and the dentist had no specific recollection of warning her); 1A Wigmore, Evidence § 93 (Tillers rev. 1983); 2 Wigmore, Evidence § 375 (Chadbourn rev. 1979); Unif. R. Evid. 406 (rev. 2005).

[24]Perrin v. Anderson, 784 F.2d 1040, 1046 (10th Cir. 1986) ("adequate testimony [of police officers] to establish that [person killed in police investigation of traffic accident] invariably reacted with extreme violence to any contact with a uniformed police officer"); Wetherill v. University of Chicago, 570 F. Supp. 1124 (N.D. Ill. 1983) (physicians' and patients' testimony in sufficient instances to establish a practice of obtaining subjects' consent for drug study); State v. Sigler, 210 Mont. 248, 688 P.2d 749, 753 (1984) (neighbors' testimony about previous acts of needless, brutal discipline of infant admissible to show habitual pattern of violence to infant in prosecution for his murder); Reagan v. Manchester St. Ry., 72 N.H. 298, 56 A. 314 (1903); 2 Wigmore, Evidence §§ 375–76 (Chadbourn rev. 1979). But there is a thin line between particular instances to prove habit or custom and particular instances to show character

for care. *See, e.g.*, Frase v. Henry, 444 F.2d 1228, 1232 (10th Cir. 1971) (applying Kansas law). See supra § 189.

[25]*See, e.g.*, Strauss v. Douglas Aircraft Co., 404 F.2d 1152, 1158 (2d Cir. 1968); Wilson v. Volkswagen of America, Inc., 561 F.2d 494, 511–12 (4th Cir. 1977); Coats & Clark, Inc. v. Gay, 755 F.2d 1506, 1511 (11th Cir. 1985) ("the methods employed by a single warehouser at a single location are not sufficiently probative of the custom of the warehouse industry generally"); State v. Mary, 368 N.W.2d 166, 168–69 (Iowa 1985) (10–12 observations of nurse drawing blood samples adequate to show habitual features of her procedure); Weisenberger v. Senger, 381 N.W.2d 187, 191 (N.D. 1986) (insufficient number of observations to establish habit of driving on extreme right of narrow country roads); Steinberg v. Arcilla, 194 Wis. 2d 759, 535 N.W.2d 444 (Ct. App. 1995) (anesthesiologist's regular response of positioning arms of patients in certain way during each of 65 to 70 cases per month); Lewan, Rationale of Habit Evidence, 16 Syracuse L. Rev. 39 (1964); Model Code Evid. R. 307(3) ("many instances"); *cf.* Gasiorowski v. Hose, 182 Ariz. 376, 897 P.2d 678, 682 (Ct. App. Div. 1 1994) (improper placement of catheters in three operations, leading to suspension of anesthesiologist's hospital privileges, combined with defendant's testimony of "his routine practice as threading past the six black dots" were admissible as evidence of "routine practice of threading epidural catheters to excessive depth").

[26]Petricevich v. Salmon River Canal Co., 92 Idaho 865, 452 P.2d 362 (1969).

essary inflammatory quality, and so on.[27]

---

[27]*See* supra § 185. Thus, citing illustrations to the Model Code of Evidence Rule 307, the Federal Advisory Committee mentions the possibility of admitting testimony by W that on numerous occasions he had been with X when X crossed a railroad track and that on each occasion X had first stopped and looked in both directions, but that offers of ten witnesses, each testifying to a different occasion, might be excluded in the discretion of the court. Adv. Comm. Note to Fed. R. Evid. 406(b).

# Chapter 18

# Similar Happenings and Transactions

## § 196    Other claims, suits, or defenses of a party

Should a party be permitted to cast doubt on the merits of the claim at bar by demonstrating that an opponent has advanced similar claims or defenses against others in previous litigation?[1] Inescapably, two conflicting goals shape the rules of evidence in this area. Exposing fraudulent claims is important, but so is protecting innocent litigants from unfair prejudice. The easy cases are those in which one of these considerations clearly predominates. If the evidence reveals that a party has made previous, very similar claims and that these claims were fraudulent, then almost universally the evidence will be admissible[2] despite the dangers of distraction and time-consumption with regard to the quality of these other claims,[3] and despite the gen-

---

**[Section 196]**

[1]*See generally* 3A Wigmore, Evidence §§ 963, 981 (Chadbourn rev. 1970); Cross-examination of plaintiff in personal injury action as to his previous injuries, physical condition, claims, or actions, 69 A.L.R.2d 593. Evidence of other claims offered for other purposes raises different concerns than those addressed in this section. *See, e.g.,* Callihan v. Burlington Northern Inc., 201 Mont. 350, 654 P.2d 972 (1982) (involving prior settlements that would show a preexisting condition); Ginsberg, Good Medicine/ Bad Medicine and the Law of Evidence: Is There a Role For Proof of Character, Propensity, Or Prior Bad Conduct in Medical Negligence Litigation?, 63 S.C. L. Rev. 367, 378–79 (2011) (previous medical malpractice claims inad-

missible to prove a physician's malpractice). See infra § 200.

[2]Smith v. State Farm Fire and Cas. Co., 633 F.2d 401, 402–04 (5th Cir. 1980) (holding, however, that in an action on a fire insurance policy the trial court did not abuse its discretion in excluding evidence of four other fires destroying dwellings belonging to the decedent even though there was evidence that the decedent had burned three of these buildings to collect insurance); Sessmer v. Commonwealth, 268 Ky. 127, 103 S.W.2d 647 (1936) (evidence of other unfounded claims admissible to show system and plan in disbarment proceeding for conspiring to blackmail by asserting fictitious claims).

[3]Lowenthal v. Mortimer, 125 Cal. App. 2d 636, 270 P.2d 942, 945–46

eral prohibition on using evidence of bad character solely to show conduct on a given occasion.[4] At the other pole, if the evidence is merely that the plaintiff is a chronic litigant with respect to all sorts of claims, the courts consider the slight probative value overborne by the countervailing factors. This evidence they usually exclude.[5]

In between lie the harder cases. Suppose the evidence is that the party suing for an alleged loss, such as fire damage to his property or personal injury in a collision, has made many previous claims of similar losses. The evidence surely is relevant. The probability of so many similar accidents happening to the same person by chance alone can be vanishingly small.[6] Yet, rare events do happen. There will always be some people who suffer the slings

---

(2d Dist. 1954) ("To negative any inference of unreasonable contentiousness, plaintiffs would be entitled to attempt an adequate explanation.").

[4]See supra Ch. 17. Although this result may seem little different from the use of evidence of other frauds in an action for deceit (see infra § 197), in those cases admission is justified to show knowledge, intent, or a common scheme, rather than to imply that the allegations at bar are more likely to be true because the defendant has a deceitful nature. For a case of prior claims said to be part of common scheme, see Mathis v. Phillips Chevrolet, Inc., 269 F.3d 771, 776 (7th Cir. 2001) (actions for employment discrimination by car salesman against car dealers).

[5]Outley v. City of New York, 837 F.2d 587, 591–94 (2d Cir. 1988) (holding that it was improper to cross-examine about previous suits, not shown to be fraudulent, against police officers and government agencies); Raysor v. Port Authority of New York and New Jersey, 768 F.2d 34, 40 (2d Cir. 1985) (error to cross examine pro se litigant suing for false arrest and malicious prosecution about "his apparently extensive pro se litigation on other matters"); Lowenthal v. Mortimer, 125 Cal. App. 2d 636, 270 P.2d 942 (2d Dist. 1954) (error to allow defendant in an automobile accident case to cross-examine plaintiffs about 15 other suits not involving

personal injuries); Palmeri v. Manhattan Ry. Co., 133 N.Y. 261, 30 N.E. 1001, 1002 (1892) (evidence that plaintiff was an "habitual litigant" properly excluded in suit for slander and false imprisonment). Many courts disapprove of references to unconnected litigation even when it involves prior claims of the same genre. See, e.g., Middleton v. Palmer, 601 S.W.2d 759, 762 (Tex. Civ. App. Dallas 1980) (stating general rule); Knight v. Hasler, 24 Wis. 2d 128, 128 N.W.2d 407, 410 (1964) (error to permit cross-examination of plaintiff about two prior personal injury claims); cf. Hemphill v. Washington Metropolitan Area Transit Authority, 982 F.2d 572 (D.C. Cir. 1993) (per curiam) (improper to give an instruction regarding a "claims minded-plaintiff" where defendant did not contend that prior claims regarding a series of injuries to plaintiff were fabricated, but cross-examination was allowed).

[6]Mintz v. Premier Cab Ass'n, 127 F.2d 744, 745 (App. D.C. 1942) ("Negligent injury is not unusual, but it is unusual for one person, not engaged in hazardous activities, to suffer it repeatedly within a short period and at the hands of different persons."); cf. San Antonio Traction Co. v. Cox, 184 S.W. 722, 724 (Tex. Civ. App. San Antonio 1916) (holding that proof that plaintiff's relatives had made at least 17 different claims for injuries allegedly incurred alighting from defendant's streetcars was properly ex-

and arrows of outrageous fortune.[7] In itself, this fact gives no

cluded because there was no evidence of plaintiff's involvement in the other claims or his participation in a conspiracy, but opining that "[w]e think it so highly improbable that all these claims could be honest ones, that a jury would be justified in inferring that fraud had been practiced with regard to some of them").

This logic is not without its problems. The simplest probability model of the situation posits that each negligently caused accident has the same fixed probability ($p$) of happening. It follows that the probability ($P$) of an unbroken series of $n$ accidents is given by $pn$. In other words, the probability of all the accidents depends on how many accidents there are ($n$) and how likely each such accident is to occur ($p$). Unless $p$ is one, the value of probability $P$ for the series approaches zero as $n$ becomes very large. This model commonly is illustrated by the process of tossing a coin. For example, with an evenly balanced coin, the probability $P$ of obtaining two heads in a row is $(1/2)^2 = 1/4$, but the probability of ten heads in a row is only $(1/2)^{10} = 1/1024$.

This argument is easy to misunderstand or misapply. Even if the probability model holds, the low probability that a long series of similar, negligently caused accidents will happen to the same person does not lower the probability that a particular one (including the one in question) occurred. After all, the fact that the probability of the series of ten heads is only 1/1024 does not change the probability (1/2) for a head on a particular toss, and the fact that nine heads in a row have appeared does not make it less probable that the coin will come up a head on the tenth toss.

Nevertheless, a small $P$-value may well suggest that some aspect of the probability model does not fit the reality. There are several ways in which it might be wrong. Possibly, the only defect in the model is that the

value of the probability $p$ for each accident is too low. This could support the claimant's position that the last accident was bona fide. However, especially with large numbers of accidents, this reasoning will not be persuasive.

A less circular conclusion that could be drawn from the small $P$-value is that the form of the model is wrong—that something other than a series of independent accidents caused by someone else's negligence has befallen the claimant. There are two possibilities. The plaintiff could be honest but accident-prone. *See* Barnes v. Norfolk Southern Ry. Co., 333 F.2d 192, 197 (4th Cir. 1964) (proper to exclude company correspondence about employee's previous accidents when purpose was to show that "because Barnes had a history of prior accidents with the railroad, the probabilities were high that he was contributorily negligent on the day of the accident"); Nourse v. Welsh, 23 A.D.2d 618, 257 N.Y.S.2d 96, 97 (4th Dep't 1965) (cross-examination about prior accidents improperly "pursued for the obvious purpose of planting in the minds of the jurors that appellant was 'accident prone' "). The difficulty with this reasoning is that it runs squarely up against the bar to character evidence as proof of conduct on a particular occasion. *See* supra Ch. 17.

The remaining possibility is that plaintiff is fraudulently disposed or at least "claim-minded." But using this inference to conclude anything about the claim in issue also violates the character rule. Consequently, if an abnormal incidence of claims is an acceptable indication that the present one lacks merit, a forthright acknowledgment that this constitutes a true exception to the rule against using character to prove conduct seems called for.

[7]Applying the probability model of the previous note to a large enough collection of identical individuals, it

indication of prejudice. Presumably, a jury can come to a reasonable judgment as to the relative likelihood of the alternatives.[8] Nevertheless, there is a form of prejudice inherent in this situation. The jury may disapprove of a person precisely because that person is litigious.[9] The judge, balancing probative value against prejudice, should admit the evidence only if there is a basis for concluding that the other claims were fabricated.[10]

This foundation could be supplied by distinct evidence of fraud,[11] or it might be inferred when the probability of coincidence seems

---

can be shown that the probability that at least one person will suffer any finite number of negligently caused accidents approaches one. If we keep tossing enough coins ten times each, sooner or later we will discover one that comes up heads all ten times.

[8]Mintz v. Premier Cab Ass'n, 127 F.2d at 745 ("It was for the jury to decide from all the evidence, and from its observation of appellant on the stand, whether she was merely unlucky or was 'claim-minded' ").

[9]Mathis v. Phillips Chevrolet, Inc., 269 F.3d at 776 ("substantial danger of jury bias against the chronic litigant"); Raysor v. Port Authority of New York and New Jersey, 768 F.2d 34, 40 (2d Cir. 1985) ("litigiousness may have some slight probative value, but that value is outweighed by the substantial danger of jury bias against the chronic litigant"); Lowenthal v. Mortimer, 125 Cal. App. 2d 636, 270 P.2d 942, 945–46 (2d Dist. 1954) ("litigiousness, in the eyes of most people, reflects . . . upon character" and can generate "the hostility ordinarily felt against one who constantly requires services of a court of law for the adjustment of life's problems"). Any other plausible inference seems also to raise a problem of prejudice.

[10]A dictum in Hinkle v. Hampton, 388 F.2d 141, 144 (10th Cir. 1968), seems to go further. It would exclude all "evidence of other or collateral transactions." The courts in the District of Columbia go to the other extreme. They have said that whenever there have been other claims, it is up to the jury to decide whether the

claimant is "unlucky or claim-minded." Mintz v. Premier Cab Ass'n, 127 F.2d 744, 745 (App. D.C. 1942) (cross-examination of plaintiff about two prior personal injury claims); Manes v. Dowling, 375 A.2d 221, 223 (D.C. 1977) (evidence of four subsequent personal injury claims admissible even though only one was of another parking lot accident); Evans v. Greyhound Corp., 200 A.2d 194, 196 (D.C. 1964) (proper to cross-examine plaintiff suing for a fall while a passenger aboard a bus about two previous settled claims). But see Hemphill v. Washington Metropolitan Area Transit Authority, 982 F.2d 572 (D.C. Cir. 1993) (concurring opinion questioning the viability of this line of authority).

[11]If the probability of coincidence is not negligible, so that extrinsic evidence of falsity seems called for, that evidence should pertain to the prior claims. See McDonough v. City of Quincy, 452 F.3d 8, 20 (1st Cir. 2006) (upholding the exclusion of proof that a police officer lost one previous suit against the city "after he was denied a promotion [because] while that lawsuit was unsuccessful, there is nothing suggesting that it was fraudulently filed"); Gastineau v. Fleet Mortg. Corp., 137 F.3d 490 (7th Cir. 1998) (holding that evidence of three lawsuits against former employers was admissible in an action against a fourth employer, where one earlier action involved the creation of a fraudulent document and there were non-character uses for the evidence); Warner v. Transamerica Ins. Co., 739 F.2d 1347, 1350–51 (8th Cir. 1984) (claim for house fire occurring 15 days before insured's business

so negligible as to leave fraud as the only plausible explanation.[12] The likelihood of repeated, substantially identical claims depends on the number of claims and the probability of each incident.[13] In addition, the degree of similarity among the claims is important, inasmuch as a series of disparate but bona fide claims seems more likely than a string of very similar ones.[14]

So far, we have discussed evidence of a party's other claims introduced to raise a question about the instant claim or suit. Ev-

---

fire inadmissible without proof that house fire was arson); Garcia v. Aetna Cas. and Sur. Co., 657 F.2d 652, 654–55 (5th Cir. 1981) (error to allow cross-examination about previous fire that destroyed an insured building without any proof that the insured claimants caused the earlier fire); Union Carbide Corp. v. Montell N.V., 28 F. Supp. 2d 833 (S.D. N.Y. 1998) (excluding evidence of a single prior claim not shown to be fraudulent); Lewis v. Voss, 770 A.2d 996, 1008 (D.C. 2001) (error to admit evidence "without a factual predicate showing fraud or frivolous complaints, that, because of two prior claims, [plaintiff] had a 'motive' or 'interest' to file suit against [defendant]"); Mohammed v. Otoadese, 738 N.W.2d 628, 632 (Iowa 2007) (error to cross-examine witness in a medical malpractice suit about what she knew of a lawsuit against a convenience store for a slip-and-fall brought by a patient whose vocal cords were paralyzed allegedly as a result of malpractice); Daigle v. Coastal Marine, Inc., 482 So. 2d 749, 750 (La. Ct. App. 1st Cir. 1985) (error to introduce chart of amounts claimed for seven other back injuries without some evidence of fraud in any of these claims).

[12]Westfield Ins. Co. v. Harris, 134 F.3d 608 (4th Cir. 1998) (error to exclude evidence of plaintiff's six prior house-fire claims and one prior truck-fire claim); Dial v. Travelers Indem. Co., 780 F.2d 520 (5th Cir. 1986) (evidence of two subsequent fires shortly after fire for which insured filed a claim admissible to show intent or plan where these fires were set by arsonist; insured had motive to set them and was present at them); Hammann v. Hartford Acc. and Indem.

Co., 620 F.2d 588, 589 (6th Cir. 1980) (upholding admission of evidence of four prior fires in insurance recovery action as bearing on motive and intent); Wagschal v. Sea Ins. Co., Ltd., 861 F. Supp. 263 (S.D. N.Y. 1994); Bunion v. Allstate Ins. Co., 502 F. Supp. 340, 342 (E.D. Pa. 1980); Williamson v. Haynes Best Western of Alexandria, 688 So. 2d 1201, 1222–23 (La. Ct. App. 4th Cir. 1997) (independent proof that "nineteen insurance claims in the last ten years were totally or in part fraudulent" was not necessary to make the pattern admissible to show fraud, and the prior claims also were admissible to show the claimants' "ability and experience to execute a complex fraudulent scheme").

[13]See Mintz v. Premier Cab Ass'n, 127 F.2d 744 (App. D.C. 1942).

[14]Compare Bunion v. Allstate Ins. Co., 502 F. Supp. 340, 342 (E.D. Pa. 1980) (no showing of "any similarity among the accidents"), and Testa v. Moore-McCormack Lines, Inc., 229 F. Supp. 154, 159 (S.D. N.Y. 1964) (longshoreman's previous, very similar claim for slipping on grease inadmissible, since there was only one such prior claim), with Westfield Ins. Co. v. Harris, 134 F.3d 608 (4th Cir. 1998) (error to exclude evidence of prior, strikingly similar claims under fire insurance policies), and Wagschal v. Sea Ins. Co., Ltd., 861 F. Supp. 263 (S.D. N.Y. 1994) (evidence of plaintiffs' insurance claims for two previous fires admitted where there was proof that both those fires and the one giving rise to the claim at bar were of incendiary origin).

idence of a witness' past accusations or defenses introduced to attack the veracity of that witness presents comparable problems.
In these situations, a litigant might seek to prove that the other
accusations have been false as circumstantial evidence that the
testimony just delivered is also false. Although this is a species of
character evidence to show conduct, it usually will be admissible
to impeach the witness.[15] Even without proof that the other accusations were false, the very fact that the witness repeatedly accuses many others of the same kind of behavior may seem too
extraordinary to be explained as a mere coincidence. The logic

---

[15]Gastineau v. Fleet Mortg. Corp.,
137 F.3d 490 (7th Cir. 1998) (holding
admissible evidence of plaintiff's fabrication of a document to support his
case on the eve of trial); People v.
Mascarenas, 21 Cal. App. 3d 660, 98
Cal. Rptr. 728, 734 (2d Dist. 1971) (error to exclude testimony about earlier
fabricated charge of selling drugs offered to impeach 16-year-old police
informant who aspired to becoming a
federal narcotics agent); State v. Cappo,
345 So. 2d 443, 445 (La. 1977) (error
to bar defendant from cross-examining
state's witness falsely accusing others
of crimes); Fairfield Packing Co. v.
Southern Mut. Fire Ins. Co., 193 Pa.
184, 44 A. 317 (1899) (evidence that
employee of and witness for plaintiff
made intentional false statement in
another proof of loss for same fire);
State v. Izzi, 115 R.I. 487, 348 A.2d
371 (1975) (error to exclude criminal
assault defendant's proffered testimony of three other hospital attendants that 15 year old with a history
of mental illness repeatedly accused
attendants of causing injuries that
were actually self-inflicted).

Allegations of prior, similar
false claims arise with some frequency
when the complaining witness is a
minor or a woman alleging rape. See
People v. Hurlburt, 166 Cal. App. 2d
334, 333 P.2d 82, 84–88 (1st Dist. 1958)
(rape prosecutrix); People v. Hackett,
421 Mich. 338, 365 N.W.2d 120, 125
(1984) (rape); People v. Evans, 72
Mich. 367, 40 N.W. 473, 478 (1888);
Impeachment or cross-examination of
prosecuting witness in sexual offense
trial by showing that similar charges
were made against other persons, 71

A.L.R.4th 469. Most courts hold that
when it is clear that the prior claims
were untrue, the evidence is not barred
by rape shield laws. See supra § 193.
Indeed, a defendant in a criminal case
may have a constitutional right to
inquire into prior, false claims on
cross-examination. U.S. v. Bartlett,
856 F.2d 1071, 1088 (8th Cir. 1988);
U.S. v. Stamper, 766 F. Supp. 1396,
1400–01 (W.D. N.C. 1991); State v.
Anderson, 211 Mont. 272, 686 P.2d
193, 200 (1984). But the question of
the minimum acceptable quantum of
proof that the prior allegations of
sexual assault were untruthful has
generated a spectrum of answers. See
State v. DeSantis, 155 Wis. 2d 774,
456 N.W.2d 600 (1990) (judge need
only find evidence "sufficient to support a reasonable person's finding that
the complainant made prior untruthful accusations"); Smith v. State, 259
Ga. 135, 377 S.E.2d 158, 160 (1989)
(reasonable probability of falsity); State
v. Anderson, 211 Mont. 272, 686 P.2d
193 (1984) (admittedly or demonstrably false); Roundtree v. U.S., 581 A.2d
315, 323 n.22 (D.C. 1990) (within
discretion of trial court to preclude
cross-examination of 17-year-old prostitute about prior reports of rape or
sexual abuse by family members, boy-
friends of family members, and pimps
on at least eight occasions when "there
was 'no substantial basis' for concluding that the woman had fabricated her
prior claims of sexual assault," but
judge would have had to allow the
cross-examination if the defendant
had "shown convincingly" that the
prior allegations were false).

and issues here are perfectly analogous to those already addressed with regard to the filing of repeated, similar suits or claims.[16] However, in keeping with the customary relaxation of the standard of admissibility on cross-examination,[17] it is generally easier to elicit admissions about the other claims on cross-examination than it is to introduce the evidence by the testimony of the proponent's witnesses.[18]

## §197 Other misrepresentations and frauds

In cases alleging fraud or misrepresentation, proof that the defendant perpetrated similar deceptions frequently is received in evidence.[1] Such admission is not justified on the theory of "once a cheat, always a cheat," for that would contravene the ban on using character traits solely as propensity evidence of conduct on the occasion.[2] Rather, at least one of three well entrenched

---

[16]When the witness is a party, the relevance of the other claims is twofold. There is not only an indication that the party-witness is the sort of person who institutes false actions or raises false defenses, but also the suggestion that the party-witness is generally untruthful. Since both "claim-mindedness" and veracity come into play, courts that reject the "claim-mindedness" proof may allow the cross-examination of the party-witness. See Bunion v. Allstate Ins. Co., 502 F. Supp. 340, 342 (E.D. Pa. 1980). The party-witness may also make specific statements on direct examination that open the door to cross-examination about other claims. Atkinson v. Atchison, Topeka & Santa Fe Ry. Co., 197 F.2d 244, 246 (10th Cir. 1952) (cross-examination tending to impeach plaintiff's testimony of particular careful driving habits); Hinkle v. Hampton, 388 F.2d 141, 144 (10th Cir. 1968) (impeaching plaintiff's testimony about extent of previous injuries).

[17]See supra § 29.

[18]Myrtle v. Checker Taxi Co., 279 F.2d 930, 934 (7th Cir. 1960) (cryptic observation about scope of cross-examination of plaintiff about prior injuries); Bunion v. Allstate Ins. Co., 502 F. Supp. 340, 342 (E.D. Pa. 1980); cf. U.S. v. King, 505 F.2d 602, 610 (5th Cir. 1974) (evidence of repeated fraud "is viewed more favorably when it is introduced . . . on cross-examination").

**[Section 197]**

[1]See Whittaker Corp. v. Execuair Corp., 736 F.2d 1341, 1347 (9th Cir. 1984) (error to exclude proof of instances of "palming off" plaintiff's product as defendant's prior to filing of complaint and barred by statute of limitations, because such evidence may "show the nature and character of transactions under scrutiny or [may] establish a course of conduct"); 2 Wigmore, Evidence §§ 301–304, 321 (Chadbourn rev. 1979); Comment, Admissibility of Similar Transactions to Prove the Principal Transaction, 2 UCLA L. Rev. 394, 405 (1955); cf. supra § 190 (criminal cases). Early English and American cases are discussed in Leonard, The New Wigmore, A Treatise on Evidence: Evidence of Other Misconduct and Similar Events §§ 2.4.1(b) & 3.3.3 (2009).

[2]See U.S. v. Mills, 138 F.3d 928 (11th Cir. 1998) (in a trial of a couple for Medicare fraud, it was error to admit evidence that the wife concealed a jewelry purchase from customs inspectors because that incident merely revealed a general tendency to lie). See supra Ch. 17.

alternate theories typically is available.[3] To begin with, evidence of other frauds may help establish the element of knowledge—by suggesting that defendant knew that the alleged misrepresentation was false[4] or by indicating that defendant's participation in an alleged fraudulent scheme was not innocent or accidental.[5]

Second, the evidence may be admissible with respect to the closely related element of intent to deceive.[6] When other misrepresentations are used to show intent or knowledge, they

---

[3]Castle v. Bullard, 64 U.S. 172, 186, 23 How. 172, 16 L. Ed. 424, 1859 WL 10635 (1859) ("well recognized exceptions to the general rule"). The purposes for which the evidence may be admissible in civil cases have already been illustrated in the criminal context in § 190. The three outlined purposes listed in the text are not exhaustive. See, e.g., Lee v. Hodge, 180 Ariz. 97, 882 P.2d 408 (1994) (holding that trial evidence improperly excluded evidence that automobile repair shop intentionally damaged other customers' cars in various ways, since this evidence tended to show that the damage to plaintiffs' car engine was the intentional result of fraudulent practices rather than an accidental feature of sloppy workmanship).

[4]Penn Mut. Life Ins. Co. v. Mechanics' Sav. Bank & Trust Co., 72 F. 413, 422 (C.C.A. 6th Cir. 1896) ("It certainly diminishes the possibility that an innocent mistake was made in an untrue and misleading statement, to show similar but misleading statements of the same person about the same matter, because it is less probable that one would make innocent mistakes . . . in repeated instances than in one instance"), quoted in Morrison v. U.S., 270 F.2d 1, 5 (4th Cir. 1959); cf. U.S. v. Walls, 577 F.2d 690, 696–97 (9th Cir. 1978) (defaults on prior loans admissible to show lack of intent to repay); De La Paz v. State, 279 S.W.3d 336 (Tex. Crim. App. 2009) (when a police officer charged with perjury and falsifying police reports admits making the alleged perjured statements but denies their falsity and knowledge of their falsity, earlier, nearly identical acts of perjury are

admissible to prove the officer knew the statements were false).

[5]Weiss v. U. S., 122 F.2d 675, 692–93 (C.C.A. 5th Cir. 1941) ("As to the other building frauds which Hart admittedly perpetrated on the state, and in which Weiss claims to have been an innocent actor, the evidence was admissible. . . . [A] man may be many times the dupe of another, but it is less likely that he should be so oftener than once"); Matter of Brandon's Estate, 55 N.Y.2d 206, 448 N.Y.S.2d 436, 433 N.E.2d 501 (1982) (prior judgments of undue influence admissible in an action alleging another instance of undue influence on an elderly woman by the owner of a nursing home, on the theory that "[w]here guilty knowledge or an unlawful intent is in issue, evidence of other similar acts is admissible to negate the existence of an innocent state of mind").

[6]U.S. v. Oppon, 863 F.2d 141 (1st Cir. 1988) (previous acts of misrepresenting citizenship); Edgar v. Fred Jones Lincoln-Mercury of Oklahoma City, Inc., 524 F.2d 162, 167 (10th Cir. 1975) (other instances of turning back automobile odometers admissible under Oklahoma law); Fulwider v. Woods, 249 Ark. 776, 461 S.W.2d 581 (1971) (action for rescission for misrepresenting water supply on property); 2 Wigmore, Evidence §§ 302, 321 n.1 (Chadbourn rev. 1979); cf. U.S. v. Marine, 413 F.2d 214, 216 (7th Cir. 1969) (criminal fraud); Admissibility to establish fraudulent purpose or intent, in prosecution for obtaining or attempting to obtain money or property by false pretenses, of evidence of similar attempts on other occasions,

need not be identical nor made under precisely the same circumstances as the one in issue.[7]

Finally, if the uttering of the misrepresentations or the performance of the fraudulent conduct is contested, then other misrepresentations or fraudulent acts that are evidently part of the same overall plan or scheme may be admissible to prove the conduct of the defendant.[8] The requirement of a common plan or scheme is well recognized, but it appears to be of questionable value in civil cases. When there is conflicting testimony as to the making of the misrepresentation at issue, the value of evidence of other, very similar misrepresentations[9]—whether or not part of

---

78 A.L.R.2d 1359; Admissibility, in forgery prosecution, of other acts of forgery, 34 A.L.R.2d 777).

[7]U.S. v. Faust, 850 F.2d 575 (9th Cir. 1988) (forging a letter indicative of intent in forging checks); U.S. v. Fitterer, 710 F.2d 1328 (8th Cir. 1983) (earlier insurance fraud indicative of intent in a mail fraud case); U.S. v. Hardrich, 707 F.2d 992 (8th Cir. 1983) (earlier utterance of a forged instrument indicative of intent in uttering forged treasury checks).

　　Some courts allow subsequent deceptive conduct to be considered on the issue of intent but not knowledge. *See, e.g.,* Early v. Eley, 243 N.C. 695, 91 S.E.2d 919, 923 (1956) (evidence that defendants subsequently purchased stocks like those sold to plaintiffs and suffered loss admissible to show absence of fraudulent intent in sale to plaintiffs); 2 Wigmore, Evidence § 316 (Chadbourn rev. 1979); *cf.* Johnson v. State, 75 Ark. 427, 88 S.W. 905, 908 (1905) (subsequent conduct admissible to show criminal intent to defraud).

　　Whether before or after the events at bar, other deceptions cannot come in with respect to intent or knowledge if these matters are not prerequisites to liability and punitive damages are not sought. Johnson v. Gulick, 46 Neb. 817, 65 N.W. 883, 884 (1896) (deceit); Karsun v. Kelley, 258 Or. 155, 482 P.2d 533 (1971) (action under state Blue Sky Law for false statements inducing stock purchases); Standard Mfg. Co. v. Slot, 121 Wis. 14,

98 N.W. 923, 924–25 (1904) (action on a contract).

[8]Mudsill Min. Co. v. Watrous, 61 F. 163, 179 (C.C.A. 6th Cir. 1894) (evidence that defendants had "salted" ore samples that other intended buyers took from mine is "competent and cogent evidence tending to establish their complicity in the like fraud now under consideration" since all the fraudulent acts were "in furtherance of same general design" to make a sale); Carofino v. Forester, 450 F. Supp. 2d 257, 271 (S.D. N.Y. 2006) (admitting, in a civil suit based on a psychiatrist's fraudulent billing, a psychiatrist's conviction for a pattern of fraudulent billings); Kindred v. State, 254 Ind. 127, 258 N.E.2d 411, 415 (1970) (repeated use of credit card in prosecution for forgery); Altman v. Ozdoba, 237 N.Y. 218, 142 N.E. 591, 592–93 (1923) (other forgeries with respect to defense that promissory note forged); Karsun v. Kelley, 258 Or. 155, 482 P.2d 533 (1971) (substantially the same statements made to two other customers admissible as part of general plan to sell securities in violation of state Blue Sky Law); Shingleton Bros. v. Lasure, 122 W. Va. 1, 6 S.E.2d 252, 253–54 (1939) (misrepresentations inducing credit account); 2 Wigmore, Evidence § 304 (Chadbourn rev. 1979).

[9]Of course, if the identity of the perpetrator of the fraud were in doubt, then other fraudulent acts of the party so like the conduct in suit and so distinctive as to earmark them as the

the same plan or scheme—in resolving the controversy should be sufficient to outweigh the danger of prejudice. As it is, the courts often manage to discern a larger plan when the various acts could well be described as separate transactions.[10]

## § 198    Other contracts and business transactions

Evidence concerning other contracts or business dealings may be relevant to prove the terms of a contract, the meaning of these terms, a business habit or custom, and occasionally, the authority of an agent.[1] As to many of these uses, there is little controversy. Certainly, evidence of other transactions between the same parties readily is received when relevant to show the

---

work of the same person should be admissible to show that the party was the perpetrator. See supra § 190.

[10]For example, in Matter of Brandon's Estate, 55 N.Y.2d 206, 448 N.Y.S.2d 436, 433 N.E.2d 501 (1982), the Appellate Division had upheld the admission of two prior judgments of undue influence "as tending to establish a common scheme or plan under which appellants inveigle into Murphy's place of residence aged and ailing residents of her nursing home for the purpose of stripping them of their life savings." Noting that the courts often are too ready to find a common plan, the Court of Appeals rejected this reasoning. It explained that "[u]nlike the intent exception, mere similarity between the acts is an insufficient predicate for admissibility under the common scheme or plan exception. . . . Indeed, there must be such a clear concurrence of common features—i.e., time, place and character—that 'the various acts are naturally to be explained as caused by a general plan of which they are the individual manifestations.'" 433 N.E.2d at 504. Here, it concluded, "there was no showing that the [prior] incidents had any direct connection, either in fact or in Mrs. Murphy's mind, with the fraud or undue influence visited upon Alice Brandon." Despite the striking similarities in the treatment of three elderly women, the Court of Appeals

determined that the incidents could well be characterized as "separate and independent transactions entered into as the occasion arose." 433 N.E.2d at 505. With *Brandon*, compare Baldwin v. Warwick, 213 F.2d 485, 486 (9th Cir. 1954) (testimony that defendants had drugged the drinks of other real estate agents and then won heavily from them at cards admissible to show an "overall scheme" that included drugging plaintiff's drinks at various bars at which plaintiff shook dice with defendants after having shown them certain real estate), and Kabel v. Brady, 519 So. 2d 912 (Ala. 1987) (representations to patients that Medicare covers chiropractic services).

**[Section 198]**

[1]*See generally* 2 Wigmore, Evidence § 377 (Chadbourn rev. 1979); Comment, Admissibility of Similar Transactions to Prove the Terms of the Contract, 2 UCLA L. Rev. 394 (1955); supra § 195 (policies and practices of a business as circumstantial evidence of intent or acts on a particular occasion). Such evidence also may be admissible to impeach a witness's credibility, Potomac Leasing Co. v. Bulger, 531 So. 2d 307, 310 (Ala. 1988), or to demonstrate bad faith. Farmers & Merchants Bank of Centre v. Hancock, 506 So. 2d 305, 312–14 (Ala. 1987) (no other instances of repossession of collateral for loans prior to their maturity dates).

meaning they probably attached to the terms of a contract.[2] Likewise, when the existence of the terms is in doubt, evidence of similar contracts between the same parties is accepted as a vehicle for showing of a custom or continuing course of dealing between them, and as such, as evidence of the terms of the present bargain.[3] Also, when the authority of an agent is in question, other similar transactions that the agent has carried out on behalf of the principal are freely admitted.[4] Finally, evidence of misconduct in other business dealings may be relevant to claims of bad faith or knowledge in the transaction at bar, as when an insurer repeatedly refuses to make proper payments of underinsured motorist claims.[5]

In the past, many courts had balked when contracts with others were offered to show the terms or the making of the contract in suit.[6] It is hard to understand why any hard and fast line should be drawn. As an historical matter, these decisions perhaps

---

[2]Hartford Steam Boiler Inspection & Ins. Co. v. Schwartzman Packing Co., 423 F.2d 1170, 1173–74 (10th Cir. 1970) (prior contracts for insurance between same parties defining coverage broadly with specific exclusions of named items admissible to show meaning of later policy); Aetna Ins. Co. v. Northwestern Iron Co., 21 Wis. 458, 1867 WL 1710 (1867) (testimony as to usual course of business of marine insurance companies admissible to "prove the understanding of the parties"); Bourne v. Gatliff, (1844) 11 C. & F. 45, 49, 70, 8 Eng. Rep. 1019 (H.L.) (to ascertain meaning of bill of lading provision on delivery of goods, previous transactions may be looked to); cf. U.C.C. §§ 1-205, 2-202 (course of dealing between parties).

[3]Hyde v. Land-of-Sky Regional Council, 572 F.2d 988, 990 n.4 (4th Cir. 1978) (prior written contract of employment admissible to prove terms of oral contract for continued employment); Burns v. Gould, 172 Conn. 210, 374 A.2d 193 (1977) (prior written contract between the parties to develop a nursing home that plaintiff said was "in line with" an alleged oral contract to develop a second nursing home properly admitted to prove the terms of the oral contract); Terminal Grain Corp. v. Rozell, 272 N.W.2d 800 (S.D. 1978) (evidence of past dealings admis-

sible to show that corn seller's silence did not constitute acceptance of grain terminal's offer to purchase corn); Karp v. Coolview of Wis., Inc., 25 Wis. 2d 299, 130 N.W.2d 790, 792 (1964) (travel agent's prior extensions of credit to corporation admissible on issue of whether extension was to corporation or to individual). But an isolated previous instance, without an offer to prove more instances in a continued course of dealing, may not be admitted. Roney v. Clearfield County Grange Mut. Fire Ins. Co., 332 Pa. 447, 3 A.2d 365 (1939) (previous instance of insurance agent's filling in form without adequate information inadmissible).

[4]Parker v. Jones, 221 Ark. 378, 253 S.W.2d 342, 344 (1952) (prior instances of treating as agent).

[5]Ennen v. Integon Indem. Corp., 268 P.3d 277, 288 (Alaska 2012) (insurer's treatment of other claims "supported the superior court's conclusion that [the insurer] knew of the statutes governing UIM provisions and that [it] therefore should have known that it was not properly paying [the insured's] claim.").

[6]Herlihy Mid-Continent Co. v. Northern Indiana Public Service Co., 245 F.2d 440, 444 (7th Cir. 1957) (plaintiff might have made different agreements with different persons); Johnson v. Gulick, 46 Neb. 817, 65

may be explained as manifestations of the perennial confusion between the sufficiency of an item of evidence to prove the proposition for which it is offered and its relevance to that proposition.[7] In addition, these decisions reflect the beguiling power of the mystical phrase *res inter alios acta*.[8] Yet, it seems clear that contracts of a party with third persons may show the party's customary practice and course of dealing and thus supply useful insights into the terms of the present agreement.[9] Indeed, even if there are but one or two such contracts, they may be useful

---

N.W. 883, 884 (1896) ("no reasonable presumption can be formed as to the making or executing of a contract by a party with one person, in consequence of the mode in which he has made or executed similar contracts with other persons. [W]here the question between a landlord and his tenant is whether the rent was payable quarterly or half-yearly, it has been held irrelevant to consider what agreements subsisted between the landlord and other tenants, or of what time their rents would become due"); Turpin v. Branaman, 190 Va. 818, 58 S.E.2d 63, 65–66 (1950) (defendant's offer to show that his practice was to execute written contracts when buying apples for himself and oral ones when buying as broker rejected as irrelevant to issue of whether he bought apples from plaintiffs for himself or as broker).

[7]See supra § 185.

[8]The maxim *"Res inter alios acta, aliis neque nocere neque prodesse potest"* means "A thing done between some can neither harm nor profit others." The maxim *"Res inter alios acta alteri nocere non debet"* states a key tenet of the principle of res judicata—that a person is not bound by litigation in which that individual does not participate. Although the shortened version of these maxims still appeals to some judges, invocation of the phrase serves more often than not to obscure any real analysis. 2 Wigmore, Evidence § 458 (Chadbourn rev. 1979).

[9]Cibro Petroleum Products, Inc. v. Sohio Alaska Petroleum Co., 602 F. Supp. 1520, 1551–52 (N.D. N.Y. 1985) (the presence of a clause permitting cancellation upon notice in contracts negotiated with other parties admissible to show that the absence of a notice of cancellation clause in the contract at bar implies that the parties did not intend to allow cancellation); Joseph v. Krull Wholesale Drug Co., 147 F. Supp. 250, 258 (E.D. Pa. 1956) (evidence of practice of making corporate officers' contracts terminable at will admissible to show whether the one in issue was for definite term); Moody v. Peirano, 4 Cal. App. 411, 88 P. 380, 382 (1st Dist. 1906) (other sales of wheat from same shipment as "White Australian" properly admitted to show that defendant also warranted wheat sold to plaintiff to be White Australian); In re Isom's Estate, 193 Kan. 357, 394 P.2d 21, 29 (1964) (similar oral contracts to make will admissible to show existence of contract in suit); Krause v. Eugene Dodge, Inc., 265 Or. 486, 509 P.2d 1199, 1204 (1973) (fraud defendant's evidence about sales to others admitted to show the meaning of "new" car); Micke v. Jack Walters & Sons Corp., 70 Wis. 2d 388, 234 N.W.2d 347, 349 (1975) (in ascertaining whether a term in an employment contract existed, the testimony of a former employee about what he had been told when hired was admissible with respect to the "corporate habit or routine practice" of the manager who claimed that he told "all the men" he hired about the term in question); Super Tire Market, Inc. v. Rollins, 18 Utah 2d 122, 417 P.2d 132, 135–36 (1966) (seller's evidence of policy not to give warranties admissible to show absence of warranty on tires). See supra § 195 (habit evidence).

evidence.[10] When, in a certain kind of transaction, a business has adopted a particular mode of handling a bargaining topic or standardized feature, such as a warranty, discount or the like, it is often easier for it to cast a new contract in the same mold than it is to work out a new one. Moreover, some practices become so accepted in an industry that they may shape the meaning of most contracts in that field. As to these, evidence in the form of contracts or transactions involving neither of the parties may nevertheless be probative of the commercial relationship that exists between the parties.[11]

Inasmuch as there is no general danger of unfair prejudice inherent in evidence of other business transactions, strict rules or limits on admissibility are inappropriate. The courts should admit such evidence in all cases where the testimony as to the terms of the present bargain is conflicting and where the judge finds that the risk of wasted time and confusion of issues does not substantially outweigh the probative value of the evidence of the other transactions. Many jurisdictions therefore leave evidence of other contracts or business dealings to the trial judge to evaluate on a case by case basis.[12]

## § 199    Other sales of similar property as evidence of value

When the market value of property needs to be determined,

---

[10]*E.g.*, Moody v. Peirano, 88 P. at 382 ("The number and frequency of the sales in which the warranty had been made, and their proximity in time to the sale made to the plaintiff, would be circumstances addressed to the discretion of the court").

[11]The substantive law recognizes the pertinence of "usage of trade" in interpreting and supplementing the terms of a contract. *E.g.*, In re Acceptance Ins. Companies Inc., 567 F.3d 369, 378 (8th Cir. 2009) (when contract terms are ambiguous, resort to extrinsic evidence is permitted, including an expert's testimony "based upon his experience in the industry, his understanding of the language used in reinsurance contracts, and the intent of the parties to the contract"); Posttape Associates v. Eastman Kodak Co., 537 F.2d 751, 757–58 (3d Cir. 1976) (knowledge that film manufacturers typically limit their liability to replacing defective film could establish

"agreement" to limit liability to producer of documentary films suing supplier for lost profits); U.C.C. §§ 1-205(2) to 1-205(6). In fields in which contracts are individualized and little in the way of standard practices have developed, evidence of unrelated contracts may not have enough bearing on the transaction in issue to be worth the distraction and time-consumption. *See, e.g.*, Mass Appraisal Services, Inc. v. Carmichael, 404 So. 2d 666, 674 (Ala. 1981); Rangen, Inc. v. Valley Trout Farms, Inc., 104 Idaho 284, 658 P.2d 955, 961 (1983) (credit practices utilized with other customers were "not relevant" to the credit practice at bar).

[12]Minnesota Farm Bureau Marketing Corp. v. North Dakota Agr. Marketing Ass'n, Inc., 563 F.2d 906, 911 (8th Cir. 1977) (no abuse of discretion to exclude prior grain contracts with two other farmers that were dissimilar to the contract at issue).

the price actually paid in a competitive market for comparable items is an obvious place to look.[1] Indeed, when presented with the sometimes wildly disparate estimates of professional appraisers, courts have remarked that the sales prices of comparable properties are the best evidence of value.[2] The testimony of witnesses with first-hand knowledge of other sales,[3] or reliable price lists, market reports, or the like[4] may be received to show the market price.

The less homogeneous the product, the more difficulty there is in measuring market value in this way. Thus, cases involving land valuation, especially condemnation cases, frequently discuss the admissibility of evidence of other sales. A dying rule excludes the evidence entirely save in exceptional circumstances.[5] The dominant view gives the judge discretion to admit evidence of other sales.[6] The inquiry focuses on whether these sales have been sufficiently recent, and whether the other land is sufficiently

---

**[Section 199]**

[1]Cases abound. *See* Valuation of mineral interests in federal condemnation proceedings, 40 A.L.R. Fed. 656; Admissibility on issue of value of real property of evidence of sale price of other real property, 85 A.L.R.2d 110; Measure and elements of damages, in action other than one against a carrier, for conversion, injury, loss, or destruction of livestock, 79 A.L.R.2d 677. Of course, comparable sales are not the only possible source of evidence. *See, e.g.,* Admissibility, in eminent domain proceeding, of evidence as to price paid for condemned real property on sale prior to the proceeding, 55 A.L.R.2d 791; Valuation for taxation purposes as admissible to show value for other purposes, 39 A.L.R.2d 209.

[2]U.S. v. 421.89 Acres of Land, More or Less, in Marion, Polk and Warren Counties, State of Iowa, 465 F.2d 336, 339 (8th Cir. 1972) (approving of jury instruction to this effect); United States v. Bloom, 237 F.2d 158, 163 (2d Cir. 1956); Warwick Musical Theatre, Inc. v. State, 525 A.2d 905, 910 (R.I. 1987).

[3]Harlan & Hollingsworth Corp. v. McBride, 45 Del. 85, 69 A.2d 9, 14 (1949) (machinery).

[4]Although such reports would be hearsay if offered to show the actual

sales recited, Doherty v. Harris, 230 Mass. 341, 119 N.E. 863 (1918), they should be admissible as evidence of what traders would have paid for such property. Friedman Iron & Supply Co. v. J. B. Beaird Co., 222 La. 627, 63 So. 2d 144, 153 (1952) (trade journal); Curtis v. Schwartzman Packing Co., 61 N.M. 305, 299 P.2d 776, 778 (1956) (automobile dealers' "Blue Book"); 6 Wigmore, Evidence § 1702 (Chadbourn rev. 1976); Fed. R. Evid. 803(17); U.C.C. § 2-723 (proof of market price of goods); infra § 321. In addition, an expert witness may be permitted to refer to the extent that experts in the field reasonably rely on such materials. *See* Kaye et al., The New Wigmore, A Treatise on Evidence: Expert Evidence §§ 4.6-4.7 (2d ed. 2011). See also supra § 15.

[5]This minority approach often is called the "Pennsylvania rule" (despite that state's abrogation of the rule by statute). *See* Admissibility on issue of value of real property of evidence of sale price of other real property, 85 A.L.R.2d 110.

[6]U.S. v. 320.0 Acres of Land, More or Less in Monroe County, State of Fla., 605 F.2d 762, 801 (5th Cir. 1979) ("sound trial practice is to admit a liberal number of the 'most comparable' sales available, leaving it to the factfinder to assess the ultimate probative worth of any and all sales admitted,"

nearby and alike as to character, situation, usability, and improvements, as to make it clear that the two tracts are comparable in value.[7] A weaker standard for similarity applies when the other sales are used as the basis for an expert judgment as to value instead of being introduced as independent evidence of value.[8]

---

and even some sales that reflect a noncompensable enhancement in value resulting from the government's operations may be admitted); U.S. v. 0.161 Acres of Land, more or less, situated in City of Birmingham, Jefferson County, Ala., 837 F.2d 1036, 1044 (11th Cir. 1988); Ex parte Graham, 380 So. 2d 850, 852–53 (Ala. 1979); Duke Power Co. v. Winebarger, 300 N.C. 57, 265 S.E.2d 227 (1980); City of Paducah v. Allen, 111 Ky. 361, 23 Ky. L. Rptr. 701, 63 S.W. 981 (1901) ("here is where 'money talks' "); Ramsey County v. Miller, 316 N.W.2d 917 (Minn. 1982) (overruling the prior line of cases); Admissibility on issue of value of real property of evidence of sale price of other real property, 85 A.L.R.2d 110.

[7]U.S. v. 84.4 Acres of Land, More or Less, in Warren County, State of Pa., 348 F.2d 117, 119 (3d Cir. 1965) (similarly sized and developed golf courses within 50 mile radius); Washington Metropolitan Area Transit Authority v. One Parcel of Land in Fairfax County, Va., 780 F.2d 467, 471–72 (4th Cir. 1986) (error to allow testimony about value of improved properties to show value of similar but unimproved land); U.S. v. 3,727.91 Acres of Land, More or Less, In Pike County, State of Mo., 563 F.2d 357, 361 (8th Cir. 1977) (average price for acreage that included agricultural land and timber not a reliable indicator of market value of levees and ditches on the land); Fairfield Gardens, Inc. v. U.S., 306 F.2d 167 (9th Cir. 1962) (properties too dissimilar); Department of Conservation v. Aspegren Financial Corp., 72 Ill. 2d 302, 21 Ill. Dec. 153, 381 N.E.2d 231, 235 (1978) (differences in water supply, sewage facilities and population densities too great for properties to be comparable); Tolman v. Carrick, 136 Vt. 188, 385 A.2d 1119 (1978) (error to exclude evidence of sale merely because property was in another town); Admissibility on issue of value of real property of evidence of sale price of other real property, 85 A.L.R.2d 110; cf. Howell v. Texaco Inc., 2004 OK 92, 112 P.3d 1154, 1159 (Okla. 2004) ("If the market value at the wellhead is not established by an actual arm's-length sale at the best price available, then the market value may be constructed by evidence of the prevailing market price . . . . Arm's-length wellhead sales or offers of purchase from the same well and close in time to the sale at issue are proof of the prevailing market price. Proof of arms'-length sales from other wells in the vicinity can also be used to establish the prevailing market price . . . . The more similar in quality, quantity, delivery pressure, and geographical location of gas produced from other wells, the more probative and compelling are their sales in determining the prevailing market price."). The proponent has the burden of showing similarity. U. S. ex rel. and for Use of Tennessee Valley Authority v. Powelson, 319 U.S. 266, 273, 63 S. Ct. 1047, 87 L. Ed. 1390 (1943); Ashland Oil, Inc. v. Phillips Petroleum Co., 554 F.2d 381, 387 (10th Cir. 1975) (en banc) ("Evidence of 'other sales' [of helium] falls far short of establishing a market without comparability being clearly established."); Arkansas State Highway Commission v. Witkowski, 236 Ark. 66, 364 S.W.2d 309, 311 (1963); Dawson v. Papio Natural Resources Dist., 206 Neb. 225, 292 N.W.2d 42 (1980).

[8]Piney Woods Country Life School v. Shell Oil Co., 726 F.2d 225,

Since the value sought is what, on average, a willing buyer would have paid a willing seller, prices on other sales of a forced character, such as execution sales or condemnation awards for other tracts,[9] generally are inadmissible.[10] Many courts also exclude the condemnor's evidence of prices it paid to other owners on the theory that sales made in contemplation of condemnation do not approximate the relevant market price.[11] Other courts, following what seems the better reasoned view, allow such evidence in the judge's discretion.[12]

---

239 (5th Cir. 1984) ("objections against uncomparable sales [of natural gas go] to the weight which the [factfinder] should attach to the expert's opinion"), quoting Weymouth v. Colorado Interstate Gas Co., 367 F.2d 84, 91 (5th Cir. 1966); U.S. v. 429.59 Acres of Land, 612 F.2d 459, 462 (9th Cir. 1980); City of Lincoln v. Realty Trust Group, Inc., 270 Neb. 587, 705 N.W.2d 432 (2005) (expert opinion based on similar sales prices admissible without a showing that the methodology is "reliable" within the meaning of Daubert v. Merrell Dow Pharmaceuticals, Inc., 509 U.S. 579, 113 S. Ct. 2786, 125 L. Ed. 2d 469 (1993)); Kamrowski v. State, 37 Wis. 2d 195, 155 N.W.2d 125 (1967). Indeed, a qualified expert should be allowed to use sales of dissimilar properties in constructing a statistical model that predicts the price at which any particular property will sell. Alevizos v. Metropolitan Airports Commission, 317 N.W.2d 352 (Minn. 1982) (regression analysis admissible); cf. State v. Dillingham Corp., 60 Haw. 393, 591 P.2d 1049, 1060 (1979) (permissible for expert to testify about admittedly noncomparable "data properties").

[9]Whewell v. Ives, 155 Conn. 602, 236 A.2d 92 (1967); Nantahala Power & Light Co. v. Sloan, 227 N.C. 151, 41 S.E.2d 361 (1947).

[10]Knabe v. State, 285 Ala. 321, 231 So. 2d 887 (1970); Waldenmaier v. State, 33 A.D.2d 75, 305 N.Y.S.2d 381 (3d Dep't 1969); Admissibility on issue of value of real property of evidence of sale price of other real property, 85 A.L.R.2d 110.

[11]Evans v. U.S., 326 F.2d 827, 831 (8th Cir. 1964); Alaska State Housing Authority v. Du Pont, 439 P.2d 427 (Alaska 1968); Socony Vacuum Oil Co. v. State, 170 N.W.2d 378, 382 (Iowa 1969); Kirkpatrick v. State, 53 Wis. 2d 522, 192 N.W.2d 856, 857–58 (1972); Admissibility on issue of value of real property of evidence of sale price of other real property, 85 A.L.R.2d 110; cf. Washington Metropolitan Area Transit Authority v. One Parcel of Land in Montgomery County, Md., 548 F.2d 1130 (4th Cir. 1977) (condemnor's offer to owner of tract in question not admissible). Most decisions exclude the evidence of prices paid by the condemnor even when the owner offers it as an admission by the condemnor. Alaska State Housing Authority v. Du Pont, 439 P.2d 427 (Alaska 1968); Stewart v. Com. for Use and Benefit of Department of Highways, 337 S.W.2d 880 (Ky. 1960). The reasoning is that the condemnor may be willing to pay a premium to acquire the land promptly and without litigation.

[12]The rationale is that the price paid would not be too far out of line, since neither party to the sale was compelled to agree on a price (as the seller is in an execution sale). While the owner knows that he may have his land taken by eminent domain, he also knows that then he will be entitled to a judicial appraisal of fair market value. The owner may be willing to accept a lower price to avoid the costs of litigation, but the condemnor may also tolerate paying a higher price to obtain the property promptly without having to make his case in court. Depending

Of course, any other sale must be genuine, and the price must be paid or substantially secured.[13] Although actual sale prices rather than asking prices typically are required,[14] unaccepted offers made by a party may be admissible as statements of a party-opponent.[15] When the evidence of unaccepted offers comes from the mouth of the seller, however, the traditional rule is that the

---

on the skills of the negotiators, the agreed upon prices may come close to the market value (or, more precisely, to the seller's and buyer's estimates of what a court would find this value to be). Thus, evidence of the prices that the condemnor has paid to other owners has been accepted as shedding sufficient light on the value of the property. Transwestern Pipeline Co. v. O'Brien, 418 F.2d 15 (5th Cir. 1969); Com., Dept. of Highways v. McGeorge, 369 S.W.2d 126 (Ky. 1963); Admissibility on issue of value of real property of evidence of sale price of other real property, 85 A.L.R.2d 110; *cf.* In re City of Bethlehem, Northampton County v. Weidner, 474 Pa. 75, 376 A.2d 641 (1977) (evenly divided on this point). In any event, it seems clear that when there is no threat to exercise the power of eminent domain, the simple fact that the purchaser has such power will not render the evidence of the sale inadmissible. Cain v. City of Topeka, 4 Kan. App. 2d 192, 603 P.2d 1031, 1033–34 (1979).

[13]Macnaughtan v. Com., 220 Mass. 550, 108 N.E. 357 (1915) (option and sale admittedly made to influence legislation); McAulton v. Goldstrin, 66 Haw. 14, 656 P.2d 96, 97 (1982) (in the "absence of any details indicating the bona fides of the alleged offer," plaintiff's testimony that he had received certain offers for his car "lacked any probative value"); Redfield v. Iowa State Highway Commission, 252 Iowa 1256, 110 N.W.2d 397, 401–02 (1961) (speculative term contract); Comment, 39 Yale L.J. 748 (1929). On the "cash or equivalent" rule, see Surfside of Brevard, Inc. v. U.S., 414 F.2d 915 (5th Cir. 1969); Redfield, 110 N.W.2d at 402.

[14]*E.g.*, State ex rel. Price v. Parcel No. 1-1.6401 Acres of Land, More or Less, in City of Dover, East Dover Hundred, Kent County, 243 A.2d 709, 711 (Del. 1968); McAulton v. Goldstrin, 66 Haw. 14, 656 P.2d 96, 97 (1982) (offers to buy car prior to accident); Perlmutter v. State Roads Commission, 259 Md. 253, 269 A.2d 586, 587 (1970). This rule normally applies to options to buy or sell. U.S. v. Smith, 355 F.2d 807, 811–12 (5th Cir. 1966). It also covers offers concerning the land in question. *See* Department of Conservation, for and on Behalf of People v. Kyes, 57 Ill. App. 3d 563, 15 Ill. Dec. 34, 373 N.E.2d 304, 307 (2d Dist. 1978); State v. Lincoln Memory Gardens, Inc., 242 Ind. 206, 177 N.E.2d 655, 659 (1961). Asking prices are excluded, not because they have no probative value, but because efforts to determine their genuineness would be too costly. Missouri Baptist Hosp. v. U. S., 213 Ct. Cl. 505, 555 F.2d 290 (1977); State By and Through State Highway Commission v. Morehouse Holding Co., 225 Or. 62, 357 P.2d 266, 267–68 (1960). Some courts admit evidence of asking prices more freely. Bingham v. Bridges, 613 F.2d 794 (10th Cir. 1980) (applying Oklahoma law). The matter is treated in a series of annotations: Unaccepted offer for purchase of real property as evidence of its value, 25 A.L.R.4th 571; Unaccepted offer to sell or buy comparable real property as evidence of value of property in issue, 25 A.L.R. 4th 615; Unaccepted offer to sell or listing of real property as evidence of its value, 25 A.L.R.4th 983.

[15]Springer v. City of Chicago, 135 Ill. 552, 26 N.E. 514 (1891); Durika v. School Dist. of Derry Tp., 415 Pa. 480, 203 A.2d 474 (1964). See infra Ch. 26.

testimony is too unreliable to warrant admission,[16] because "[o]ral and not binding offers are so easily made and refused in a mere passing conversation, and under circumstances involving no responsibility on either side, as to cast no light upon the question of value"[17] and because "the person making such offer . . . may have so slight a knowledge on the subject as to render his opinion of no value."[18] Unaccepted offers are admitted more easily when the offeror is available for examination[19] or when there have been no consummated sales.[20] In addition, some courts allow expert appraisers to refer to such offers as part of the basis for their valuation,[21] although this theory does not make the offers admissible for their truth.[22]

## § 200  Other accidents and injuries

The admissibility of evidence of other accidents and injuries is raised frequently in negligence and product liability cases.[1] At one time, a few courts, influenced by *Collins v. Inhabitants of Dorchester*,[2] applied a rigid rule of exclusion.[3] The modern cases commit the matter to the trial judge for a weighing of the advantages and disadvantages of admitting or excluding the evidence;[4]

---

[16]Richard O. Duvall & David S. Black, Once Upon an Offer: Use of Unaccepted Offers to Purchase Real Estate As Evidence of Valuation in Condemnation Proceedings, Appraisal J., Jan. 2002, at 1.

[17]Sharp v. U.S., 191 U.S. 341, 349, 24 S. Ct. 114, 48 L. Ed. 211 (1903).

[18]Sharp, 191 U.S. at 348. The Court observed that "[h]e may have wanted the land for some particular purpose disconnected from its value. Pure speculation may have induced it, a willingness to take chances that some new use of the land might, in the end, prove profitable." 191 U.S. at 348.

[19]Schymanski v. Conventz, 674 P.2d 281, 286 (Alaska 1983).

[20]City of Chicago v. Lehmann, 262 Ill. 468, 104 N.E. 829 (1914).

[21]City of Atlanta v. Hadjisimos, 168 Ga. App. 840, 310 S.E.2d 570, 573 (1983); County of St. Clair v. Wilson, 284 Ill. App. 3d 79, 219 Ill. Dec. 712, 672 N.E.2d 27, 29–30 (5th Dist. 1996).

[22]*See generally* Kaye et al., The New Wigmore, A Treatise on Evidence:

Expert Evidence § 4.7 (2d ed. 2011). See supra § 15.

**[Section 200]**

[1]*See generally* 2 Wigmore, Evidence §§ 252, 457–58 (Chadbourn rev. 1979); Leonard, The New Wigmore, A Treatise on Evidence: Evidence of Other Misconduct and Similar Events § 14 (2009); Hare, Admissibility of Evidence Concerning Other Similar Incidents in a Defective Design Product Case: Courts Should Determine "Similarity" by Reference to the Defect Involved, 21 Am. J. Trial Advoc. 491 (1998); Morris, Proof of Safety History in Negligence Cases, 61 Harv. L. Rev. 205 (1948); Admissibility of Evidence of Prior Accidents or Injuries at Same Place, 15 A.L.R.6th 1; Products Liability: Firearms, Ammunition, and Chemical Weapons, 96 A.L.R.5th 239; Products liability: admissibility of evidence of other accidents to prove hazardous nature of product, 42 A.L.R.3d 780.

[2]Collins v. Inhabitants of Dorchester, 60 Mass. 396, 6 Cush. 396, 1850 WL 4592 (1850).

many cases stress the discretion so reposed in the trial judge.[5] In light of the prejudice that such evidence can carry with it, and because of the rule that evidence of other accidents or their absence is not admissible solely to show a character or propensity for careful or careless behavior,[6] most judges will scrutinize it carefully. Usually, a non-propensity purpose and a showing of sufficient similarity in the conditions giving rise to the various accidents are required.[7] Of course, exactly identical circumstances cannot be realized,[8] but the burden of showing substantial

---

[3]Hudson v. Chicago & N.R. Co., 59 Iowa 581, 13 N.W. 735 (1882); Bremner v. Inhabitants of Newcastle, 83 Me. 415, 22 A. 382 (1891).

[4]Brooks v. Chrysler Corp., 786 F.2d 1191, 1198 (D.C. Cir. 1986) (emphasizing the delay that would result from admitting a report on other accidents, "as Chrysler would have attempted to rebut the substance of each of the 330 complaints"); Lindquist v. Des Moines Union Ry. Co., 239 Iowa 356, 30 N.W.2d 120 (1947); Robitaille v. Netoco Community Theatres of North Attleboro, Inc., 305 Mass. 265, 25 N.E.2d 749 (1940).

[5]Jones & Laughlin Steel Corp. v. Matherne, 348 F.2d 394, 400 (5th Cir. 1965) (upholding admission); Nelson v. Brunswick Corp., 503 F.2d 376, 380 (9th Cir. 1974) (upholding exclusion of evidence of explosions and fires during resurfacing of other bowling alleys with the observation that "whether to admit such evidence is a matter generally for the trial court to decide, keeping in mind the collateral nature of the proof, the danger that it may afford a basis for improper inferences, the likelihood that it may cause confusion or operate to unfairly prejudice the party against whom it is directed and that it may be cumulative, etc."); Kopfinger v. Grand Central Public Market, 60 Cal. 2d 852, 37 Cal. Rptr. 65, 389 P.2d 529 (1964) (upholding admission of evidence of other falls in other locations in same store); Claveloux v. Downtown Racquet Club Associates, 246 Conn. 626, 717 A.2d 1205 (1998) (upholding exclusion of another player's falling on a racquet-

ball court); Estate of Klink ex rel. Klink v. State, 113 Haw. 332, 152 P.3d 504, 526–27 (2007) (upholding exclusion of eight other automobile accidents due to wet conditions on a highway).

[6]See supra § 189.

[7]For statements of the need for substantial similarity, see Brooks v. Chrysler Corp., 786 F.2d 1191, 1195 (D.C. Cir. 1986) (accidents involving out-of-groove dust boot not admissible to show defective design or notice in case of crash due to brake piston seizure with a properly sealed dust boot); McKinnon v. Skil Corp., 638 F.2d 270, 277 (1st Cir. 1981) (also emphasizing the trial judge's discretion to exclude evidence that meets this requirement if necessary to avoid "unfairness, confusion and undue expenditure of time"); Amatucci v. Delaware and Hudson Ry. Co., 745 F.2d 180 (2d Cir. 1984) (in FELA action by engineer who claimed working conditions caused heart condition, it was reversible error to admit testimony that seven or eight other engineers had heart attacks, since the circumstances and medical histories in these incidents were unknown); Julander v. Ford Motor Co., 488 F.2d 839, 845–47 (10th Cir. 1973) (evidence of seven pending suits for alleged design defect in automobile steering mechanism improperly admitted in absence of showing that the other accidents occurred under similar circumstances).

[8]See Jones & Laughlin Steel Corp. v. Matherne, 348 F.2d 394, 400–01 (5th Cir. 1965) ("The differences between the circumstances of the ac-

similarity falls on the proponent of the evidence.[9] As regards the permissible purposes, in practice these tend to blend together in that more than one typically is available.[10] For clarity of analysis,

---

cidents could have been developed to go to the weight to be given to such evidence"; defendant "had ample opportunity to explore these differences upon cross-examination or by its own witnesses"); Lopez v. Three Rivers Elec. Co-op., Inc., 26 S.W.3d 151, 160 (Mo. 2000) ("A prior accident that meets the requirements of similarity, even though remote, may be highly material. Remoteness of time goes to the weight of the evidence in most circumstances, not to its admissibility. . . . In the present case, where the evidence of the earlier accident was of sufficient like character, occurred under substantially the same circumstances, and resulted from the same cause, the trial court did not abuse its discretion in admitting evidence of the 1975 accident."); Kissock v. Butte Convalescent Center, 1999 MT 322, 297 Mont. 307, 992 P.2d 1271, 1275 (1999) (slip and fall on icy sidewalk days before slip and fall in icy parking lot was sufficiently similar to show notice of dangerous conditions despite "subtle, climatological differences" in that the first occurred "one day after a two-week series of snowstorms and freezing temperatures," while the second accident "occurred after a week of warm temperatures with conditions melting in the day and freezing at night").

[9]Mueller v. Buscemi, 230 P.3d 1153, 1156 (Alaska 2010) (because "It was [plaintiff's] burden to prove that her fall and these other falls occurred under substantially similar circumstances," other falls on defendant's property were properly excluded where "[t]he only similarity . . . identified . . . was that two of them allegedly occurred on the same day as her accident. Neither occurred in the same parking lot as her fall, and falls at other locations around [the] building are not necessarily probative of the conditions that existed in the build-

ing's rear parking lot."); Union Pacific R.R. Co. v. Barber, 356 Ark. 268, 149 S.W.3d 325, 337 (2004) (rejecting defendant's proposed rule excluding evidence of past "near-misses" at a railroad crossing in favor of the established doctrine that "admission . . . is considered on a case-by-case basis and the burden rests on the party offering the evidence to prove that the necessary similarity of conditions exists."); Burton v. CSX Transp., Inc., 269 S.W.3d 1, 11–12 (Ky. 2008) (although an expert was permitted to refer to a workplace study "linking solvent exposure and brain damage or cognitive impairment," the trial court properly prohibited the witness from stating that the subjects of the study worked at the same company as plaintiff, because the plaintiff "has not shown where he laid a foundation showing that the CSX workers involved in the . . . study were subject to similar conditions at work as he was."); Watson v. Ford Motor Co., 389 S.C. 434, 699 S.E.2d 169, 179–80 (2010) ("Courts require a plaintiff to establish a factual foundation to show substantial similarity because evidence of similar incidents may be extremely prejudicial.").

[10]Ramos v. Liberty Mut. Ins. Co., 615 F.2d 334, 339 (5th Cir. 1980) (collapse of similar mast on offshore oil rig two years earlier erroneously excluded, since the first accident was relevant to the manufacturer's "notice of the defect, its ability to correct the defect, the mast's safety under foreseeable conditions, the strength of the mast, and, most especially, causation"); McClure v. Walgreen Co., 613 N.W.2d 225, 234 (Iowa 2000) (noting that evidence of previous incorrectly filled prescriptions is relevant to determine punitive damages); Supreme Pork, Inc. v. Master Blaster, Inc., 2009 SD 20, 764 N.W.2d 474, 486, 489, (S.D. 2009) (a previous fire resulting from a

however, we shall try to isolate each valid purpose for admitting evidence of other accidents.

To begin with, the evidence may be admissible to prove the existence of a particular physical condition, situation, or defect. For instance, the fact that several persons slipped and fell in the same location in a supermarket can help show that a slippery substance was on the floor.[11] At the same time, this proof is a bit sensational. Unless the defendant strenuously disputes the presence of the condition, the court may reject the evidence of the similar accidents as unduly prejudicial and cumulative.

Second, the evidence of other accidents or injuries may be admissible to help show that the defect or dangerous situation

---

subcontractor's failure to provide adequate ventilation admissible to prove "the foreseeability of harm, the risk of the danger with respect to the lack of safety measures, [the subcontractor's] lack of knowledge about installing exhaust chimneys in a manner that maintains the required clearances between combustibles and heat, and [the contractor's] lack of due care in selecting a subcontractor.").

[11]Bitsos v. Red Owl Stores, Inc., 459 F.2d 656, 659–60 (8th Cir. 1972) (that another person had fallen down steps in the same year and had complained of the need to clean the stairs was "circumstantial evidence that [a] foreign substance had been . . . on the steps" when plaintiff slipped and fell); Simon v. Town of Kennebunkport, 417 A.2d 982 (Me. 1980) (error to exclude testimony that in the two years before an elderly woman fell on a sidewalk, 100 people stumbled or fell at the same spot); Cameron v. Small, 182 S.W.2d 565, 570 (Mo. 1944) (evidence that others had slipped on a ramp admissible as "tending to prove . . . that the surface of the ramp was unsafe, if the slipping of others occurred under the same conditions at that same place, and from the same cause, as the slipping of the plaintiff"); Ringelheim v. Fidelity Trust Co. of Pittsburgh, 330 Pa. 69, 198 A. 628, 629 (1938) ("proof that other persons had fallen at the same place on the same day" on a floor allegedly made slippery by an excess of polish "would show almost conclusively that the cause of such accidents was one common to all, namely, the condition of the floor, and not a mere coincidence of fault or ill luck of the individual victims").

Other cases of this kind include Gulf States Utilities Co. v. Ecodyne Corp., 635 F.2d 517, 519 (5th Cir. 1981) (error in a bench trial to exclude evidence of structural failure of similar towers that defendant built for others); DeMarines v. KLM Royal Dutch Airlines, 580 F.2d 1193 (3d Cir. 1978) (proof that six out of 191 passengers felt discomfort admissible to show abrupt change in cabin pressure); Bailey v. Kawasaki-Kisen, K.K., 455 F.2d 392, 397 (5th Cir. 1972) (reversible error to exclude evidence that boom fell a second time to show that the winch "was in some way defective"); Denison v. Wiese, 251 Iowa 770, 102 N.W.2d 671 (1960) (loose seats on bar stools); Albers Mill. Co. v. Carney, 341 S.W.2d 117 (Mo. 1960) (testimony by other farmers as to moldy food from same lot admissible to show moldiness of food that plaintiff's turkeys ate); Parker v. Bamberger, 100 Utah 361, 116 P.2d 425 (1941) (defect in signal device); cf. Glover v. BIC Corp., 987 F.2d 1410, 1421 (9th Cir. 1993) (error to exclude evidence of other fires in home of to show that house fire was caused by careless use of stove by intoxicated decedent rather than by a defective lighter).

caused the injury.[12] Thus, instances in which other patients placed on the same drug therapy contracted the same previously rare disease is circumstantial evidence that the drug caused the disease in plaintiff's case.[13] As typically developed at trial, such evidence of other accidents is a crude version of a retrospective epidemiologic study.[14] Since many unsuspected factors could contribute or cause the observed effects,[15] the conditions of the other injuries and the present one must be similar.[16] Some courts look to four "factors . . . when admitting evidence of other incidents

---

[12]Bailey v. Kawasaki-Kisen, K.K., 455 F.2d 392, 397 (5th Cir. 1972) (reversible error to exclude evidence that boom fell a second time to show that excess grease on the cables and drum of the winch was the cause of the injury a longshoreman sustained while dashing out of the way when boom fell a few minutes earlier). Evidence of similar injuries under similar circumstances—but without the alleged actions or omissions of the defendant— also may be admissible. Dick v. Lewis, 636 F.2d 1168, 1169 (8th Cir. 1981) (lay testimony about birth defects of other members of family admissible to refute claim that medical malpractice in handling the delivery caused cerebral palsy, spastic paraplegia, and mental retardation in 20-year-old plaintiff).

[13]Herbst et al., Association of Maternal Stilbesterol Therapy with Tumor Appearance in Young Women, 284 New Eng. J. Medicine 878 (1971) (first study linking a previously rare disease in young women with a drug prescribed to their mothers); Liability of manufacturer or seller for injury caused by drug or medicine sold, 79 A.L.R.2d 301; cf. Gober v. Revlon, Inc., 317 F.2d 47, 49–50 (4th Cir. 1963) (allergic reactions to "Wonder Base" for nail polish); Carter v. Yardley & Co., 319 Mass. 92, 64 N.E.2d 693, 694–95 (1946) (reactions of other perfume users admissible to show that same perfume burned plaintiff's skin); Products liability: mascara and other eye cosmetics, 63 A.L.R.4th 105.

[14]For discussions of epidemiologic and statistical proof of causation, see infra § 210. The evidence of other

incidents that is implicit in more careful statistical studies of the association between a suspected causative agent and a disease or injury should be admissible as forming the basis for the expert's opinion. See Kaye et al., The New Wigmore, A Treatise on Evidence: Expert Evidence § 4.6 (2d ed. 2011). See supra § 15.

[15]"Spurious correlations" are easily found in much observational data. Hans Zeisel, Say It with Figures (6th rev. ed. 1985). Even experimental data can be all but useless when possible causes are "confounded." Moore, Statistics: Concepts and Controversies (6th ed. 2001). For elementary expositions of the scientific logic of proving causation, see Kaye et al., The New Wigmore, A Treatise on Evidence: Expert Evidence § 12.5 (2d ed. 2011); Zeisel & Kaye, Prove It with Figures: Empirical Methods in Law and Litigation (1997).

[16]Compare Calhoun v. Honda Motor Co., Ltd., 738 F.2d 126, 133 (6th Cir. 1984) (manufacturer's recall letter stating that heavy rain reduced performance of motorcycle's rear brake pad was not admissible to show that this defect caused accident after plaintiff washed motorcycle at car wash), and Rexall Drug Co. v. Nihill, 276 F.2d 637, 642–645 (9th Cir. 1960) (evidence of "strawy, dry and frizzy" hair from home permanent solution inadmissible to show that the treatment caused plaintiff's baldness), with Smith v. Ingersoll-Rand Co., 214 F.3d 1235, 1248–49 (10th Cir. 2000) (differences in size and wheels of milling machines were not such as to overcome the "substantial similarity among the

to support a claim that the present accident was caused by the same defect: (1) the products are similar; (2) the alleged defect is similar; (3) causation related to the defect in the other incidents; and (4) exclusion of all reasonable secondary explanations for the cause of the other incidents."[17]

Although the use of evidence of other accidents to prove the existence of a condition (the first purpose listed above) can overlap the use of the evidence to prove that the condition caused plaintiff's injuries,[18] ordinarily, the need to use the evidence for this second purpose is plainer. Causation is frequently in genuine dispute, and circumstantial evidence may be of great value in pursuing this elusive issue. Thus, receptivity to evidence of similar happenings to show causation is heightened when the defendant contends that the alleged conduct could not possibly have caused the plaintiff's injury.[19]

Third, and perhaps most commonly, evidence of other accidents or injuries may be used to show the risk that defendant's conduct created.[20] If the extent of the danger is material to the case, as it almost always is in personal injury litigation, the fact that the

---

variables relevant to the plaintiff's theory of defect," namely, "the lack of visibility from the operator's platform and the feasibility of equipping the machines with mirrors.").

[17]Watson v. Ford Motor Co., 389 S.C. 434, 699 S.E.2d 169, 179 (2010).

[18]In the slip-and-fall cases as well as some of the other cases cited earlier, the finder of fact is invited to deduce from the presence of other accidents (1) that there were certain physical conditions (2) that caused all the injuries, including plaintiff's. But in other situations, only (2) justifies the evidence, since (1) is not in doubt. Johnston v. Yolo County, 274 Cal. App. 2d 46, 79 Cal. Rptr. 33 (3d Dist. 1969) (curve design of road as a cause of accidents); Poston v. Clarkson Const. Co., 401 S.W.2d 522 (Mo. Ct. App. 1966) (blast damage to nearby houses, not to prove blast, but to show cause of damage to plaintiff's house). Then there are cases in which (1) is the focal point of the controversy, and it is understood that if (1) holds, then so does (2). Gulf, C. & S.F. Ry. Co. v. Brooks, 73 S.W. 571 (Tex. Civ. App. 1903) (evidence of a later collapse of a gate and the ensuing replacement of a bolt in the hinge admissible to show that bolt was previously missing when the coal retained by the gate fell from tender and injured fireman).

[19]Wojciechowski v. Long-Airdox Division of Marmon Group, Inc., 488 F.2d 1111, 1116 n.7 (3d Cir. 1973); Ringelheim v. Fidelity Trust Co. of Pittsburgh, 330 Pa. 69, 198 A. 628 (1938) (evidence of other falls to refute testimony that polish hardens in five minutes); Texas & N. O. R. Co. v. Glass, 107 S.W.2d 924, 926 (Tex. Civ. App. Waco 1937) (testimony as to fires set by other oil burning locomotives admissible to refute testimony of railroad's experts that its oil burning locomotive would not emit sparks large enough to cause a fire). In food and drug cases the consumer often is rebutting a contention that he became ill from some other cause or that he is hypersensitive.

[20]Mitchell v. Fruehauf Corp., 568 F.2d 1139, 1147 (5th Cir. 1978) (applying Texas law to hold that other instances of meat swinging in refrigerated truck trailers and tipping them over admissible to show unreasonably dangerous design); Rimer v. Rockwell Intern. Corp., 641 F.2d 450, 456, 22

same conditions produced harm on other occasions is a natural and convincing way of showing the hazard.[21] The requirement of substantial similarity is applied strictly here.[22] However, statistical analyses in which the differences are likely to be randomly distributed should be more readily admissible than testimony about particular accidents.[23]

Finally, the evidence of other accidents commonly is received to prove that the defendant knew, or should have known, of the

---

Ohio Op. 3d 216 (6th Cir. 1981) (error to exclude evidence of 24 other aircraft accidents caused by alleged design defect in fuel intake system); Gulf Hills Dude Ranch, Inc. v. Brinson, 191 So. 2d 856, 861 (Miss. 1966) (other accidents on same slippery floor); Turner v. City of Tacoma, 72 Wash. 2d 1029, 435 P.2d 927, 931 (1967) (bumping into fire escape on sidewalk). In product liability cases, a reduced incidence of accidents with an alternative design may be admissible to show a design defect. Jackson v. Firestone Tire & Rubber Co., 788 F.2d 1070, 1078–80 (5th Cir. 1986) (applying Texas law).

[21]Of course, where the danger is obvious enough, evidence of other accidents would seem unnecessary and hence unduly prejudicial and time-consuming. City of Birmingham v. McKinnon, 200 Ala. 111, 75 So. 487 (1917) (stake and wire two feet above sidewalk).

[22]E.g., Vigil v. Burlington Northern and Santa Fe Ry. Co., 521 F. Supp. 2d 1185, 1221 (D.N.M. 2007) ("a high degree of similarity is essential" to demonstrate "[t]he dangerous nature of the [railroad] crossing," but it was present despite the installation of a stop sign after an earlier accident). For cases in which the requirement was held not satisfied, see Kelsay v. Consolidated Rail Corp., 749 F.2d 437, 441–45 (7th Cir. 1984) (two accidents at railroad crossing in previous decades too dissimilar); Lolie v. Ohio Brass Co., 502 F.2d 741, 745 (7th Cir. 1974) (evidence that other metal cable clips used to hold power lines in coal mines released when line was pulled sharply inadmissible in absence of any

showing that the clips were of the same quality and had the same characteristics as those defendant manufactured); Mobbs v. Central Vermont Ry., Inc., 155 Vt. 210, 583 A.2d 566, 569 (1990) (other accidents at other railroad crossings); Royal Mink Ranch v. Ralston Purina Co., 18 Mich. App. 695, 172 N.W.2d 43 (1969) (other experiences with mix of feed from different supplier inadmissible to show effect of defendant's feed on mink); Perry v. City of Oklahoma City, 1970 OK 66, 470 P.2d 974, 980 (Okla. 1970) (inadequate detail about circumstances of accidents).

[23]Seese v. Volkswagenwerk A.G., 648 F.2d 833, 846 (3d Cir. 1981) (government statistics showing that on average VW vans were more likely to eject occupants in collisions were admissible despite the fact that there were many variables, such as speed and type of accident, that differ from case to case); Branham v. Ford Motor Co., 390 S.C. 203, 701 S.E.2d 5, 21 (2010) (if "the rate or number of rollover accidents of the Bronco II was greater as compared to other vehicles in its class, such evidence may well be relevant on whether the Bronco II was unreasonably dangerous. [W]e are [not] persuaded by . . . Ford's general argument that many accidents may be attributable to inexperienced or impaired drivers . . . . [T]here is no suggestion in this record that inexperienced or impaired drivers disproportionately favored the Bronco II, thus skewing the comparative rollover accident data."); see infra Ch. 20 (scientific evidence).

danger.[24] Of course, if defendant's duty is absolute, this theory is inapposite. In negligence cases, however, the duty is merely to use reasonable care to maintain safe conditions. Even in many strict product liability cases, demonstrating that the product is defective or unreasonably dangerous for its intended use requires an analysis of foreseeable risks.[25]

---

[24]Hecht Co. v. Jacobsen, 180 F.2d 13, 17 (D.C. Cir. 1950) (similar accident with escalator on different floor years earlier indicated need to replace with a safer model); Gober v. Revlon, Inc., 317 F.2d 47, 51 (4th Cir. 1963) (previous complaints of allergic reactions to "Wonder Base" for nail polish); Young v. Illinois Cent. Gulf R. Co., 618 F.2d 332, 339 (5th Cir. 1980) (two recent prior accidents at grade crossing admissible to show that "a reasonably prudent railroad . . . would have taken precautions"); Soden v. Freightliner Corp., 714 F.2d 498 (5th Cir. 1983) (five other lawsuits arising from post-collision fires admissible to show notice of unreasonably dangerous fuel system in diesel trucks); Bailey v. Southern Pac. Transp. Co., 613 F.2d 1385, 1389 (5th Cir. 1980) (evidence of other accidents at different times of day and with cars approaching from opposite direction at crossing at which warning bell and signal light did not function admitted to show hazard and notice); Gardner v. Southern Ry. Systems, 675 F.2d 949, 952 (7th Cir. 1982) (evidence of another fatal collision of truck and train at same crossing under similar conditions 15 months earlier should have been admitted "to show that the railroad had prior knowledge that a dangerous and hazardous condition existed"); Borden, Inc. v. Florida East Coast Ry. Co., 772 F.2d 750, 756 (11th Cir. 1985) (in action against railroad and vandals arising from crash of derailed freight train into ice cream warehouse, it was error to exclude proof of vandalism of unknown origin to same type of switching device six months earlier and less than a mile away, to show foreseeability of vandalism to switch); Worsham v. A.H. Robins Co., 734 F.2d

676, 686–87 (11th Cir. 1984) (reports of pelvic disease from "Dalkon Shield" intrauterine device admissible); Palmer v. A.H. Robins Co., Inc., 684 P.2d 187, 199 (Colo. 1984) (reports of septic abortions due to "Dalkon Shield" admissible); General Motors Corp. v. Lupica, 237 Va. 516, 379 S.E.2d 311 (1989) (complaints of power steering failures due to foreign particles in system); 2 Wigmore, Evidence § 252 (Chadbourn rev. 1979).

Customer complaints arising from similar experiences but not culminating in accidents may help establish that defendant had actual notice of the danger. Gardner v. Q. H. S., Inc., 448 F.2d 238, 244 (4th Cir. 1971) (complaints concerning flammability problems with hair curlers); New York Life Ins. Co. v. Seighman, 140 F.2d 930, 932 (C.C.A. 6th Cir. 1944) (custodian received complaint about defective railing on third floor landing); Farley v. M M Cattle Co., 529 S.W.2d 751, 755 (Tex. 1975) (previous incident in which horse named "Crowbar" had run toward another horse used to show cattle ranch's awareness that Crowbar was dangerous).

[25]Jackson v. Firestone Tire & Rubber Co., 788 F.2d 1070, 1083 (5th Cir. 1986) (applying Texas law); Rexrode v. American Laundry Press Co., 674 F.2d 826, 829 n.9 (10th Cir. 1982) ("Under both federal and Kansas law, it is clear that evidence of the occurrence of other accidents involving substantially the same circumstances as the case at issue is admissible, pursuant to a strict liability theory, to establish notice, the existence of a defect, or to refute testimony by a defense witness that a given product was designed without safety hazards"); Branham v. Ford Motor Co., 390 S.C.

When the evidence of other accidents is introduced to show notice of the danger, subsequent accidents are not admissible under this rationale.[26] The proponent probably will want to show directly that the defendant had knowledge of the prior accidents, but the nature, frequency[27] or notoriety[28] of the incidents may well reveal that defendant knew of them or should have discovered the danger by due inspection. Since all that is required is that the previous injury or injuries be such as to call defendant's attention to the dangerous situation that resulted in the litigated accident, the similarity in the circumstances of the accidents can be considerably less than that which is demanded when the same evidence is used for one of the other valid purposes.[29]

Having surveyed the utility of a history of accidents in establishing liability, we now consider the admissibility of a history of safety for exculpatory purposes.[30] One might think that if proof of similar accidents is admissible in the judge's discretion

---

203, 701 S.E.2d 5, 220 (2010) (adopting a pure risk-utility test for alleged design defects).

[26]Magayanes v. Terrance, 739 F.2d 1131, 1136 (7th Cir. 1983) (notice to city of defective design of police transport vehicle cannot be shown by subsequent accident); Julander v. Ford Motor Co., 488 F.2d 839, 846 (10th Cir. 1973); Ozark Air Lines, Inc. v. Larimer, 352 F.2d 9 (8th Cir. 1965); Hyde v. Wages, 454 So. 2d 926, 931 (Ala. 1984) (subsequent accidents not admissible to show notice); Branham v. Ford Motor Co., 390 S.C. 203, 701 S.E.2d 5, 17–20 (2010) (post-manufacture studies of truck roll-overs inadmissible to show a defect know at the time of manufacture). In contrast, evidence admissible for one of the other valid purposes may relate to subsequent accidents. Jackson v. Firestone Tire & Rubber Co., 788 F.2d 1070, 1084 (5th Cir. 1986) (subsequent accidents admissible to show danger); Bailey v. Kawasaki-Kisen, K.K., 455 F.2d 392 (5th Cir. 1972); Taylor v. Northern States Power Co., 192 Minn. 415, 256 N.W. 674 (1934).

[27]Moore v. Bloomington, D. & C.R. Co., 295 Ill. 63, 128 N.E. 721, 722 (1920).

[28]Lombar v. Village of East Tawas, 86 Mich. 14, 48 N.W. 947 948 (1891).

[29]Jackson v. Firestone Tire & Rubber Co., 788 F.2d 1070, 1083 (5th Cir. 1986); Gardner v. Southern Ry. Systems, 675 F.2d 949, 952 (7th Cir. 1982); Ormsby v. Frankel, 255 Conn. 670, 768 A.2d 441, 451–52 (2001); Pierce v. Platte-Clay Elec. Co-op., Inc., 769 S.W.2d 769 (Mo. 1989). *But see* Fell v. Kewanee Farm Equipment Co., A Div. of Allied Products, 457 N.W.2d 911 (Iowa 1990) (insufficient similarity even under relaxed requirement); Powers v. Kansas Power & Light Co., 234 Kan. 89, 671 P.2d 491, 499 (1983) (plaintiff allowed to prove that serious accidents involving cranes hitting high voltage lines are common, but plaintiff not allowed to introduce evidence of specific claims and suits against defendant arising from such accidents, where plaintiff made no showing that these other claims were factually similar).

[30]*See generally* Leonard, The New Wigmore, A Treatise on Evidence: Evidence of Other Misconduct and Similar Events § 14.5 (2009); Morris, Studies in the Law of Torts 87–89 (1952) (history of no accidents often more probative than history of accidents); Admissibility of evidence of absence of other accidents or injuries at place where injury or damage occurred, 10 A.L.R.5th 371; Products liability: admissibility of evidence of

to show that a particular condition or defect exists, or that the injury sued for was caused in a certain way, or that a situation is dangerous, or that defendant knew or should have known of the danger, then evidence of the absence of accidents during a period of similar exposure and experience likewise would be receivable to show that these facts do not exist. Indeed, it would seem perverse to tell a jury that one or two persons besides the plaintiff tripped on defendant's stairwell while withholding from them the further information that another thousand persons descended the same stairs without incident.[31]

Yet, for many years decisions laid down just such a general rule against proof of absence of other accidents.[32] Admittedly, there are special problems with proving the nonexistence of something. In particular, an absence of complaints does not necessarily mean that accidents have not been occurring. "Stair climbers other than the plaintiff may have tripped but not fallen, or fallen without being hurt, or been hurt without complaining, or complained to someone other than the witness who testifies to the lack of complaints. Moreover the plaintiff may have been the first to pass after a deteriorating condition became sufficiently dangerous to cause a serious accident."[33] While these factors should be considered in balancing probative value against the

---

absence of other accidents, 51 A.L.R. 4th 1186.

[31]Croskey v. BMW of North America, Inc., 532 F.3d 511, 517 (6th Cir. 2008) ("On retrial plaintiff will also be allowed to put on similar incidents evidence to prove his design defect claim. To rebut that evidence, defendants should be allowed to put on evidence of the total number of cars sold during that same time with the same radiator neck piece to demonstrate the likelihood of failure of the radiator neck. Evidence of a small number of incidents versus the total number of similar model cars on the road has been permitted to refute evidence of prior accidents."); Birmingham Union Ry. Co. v. Alexander, 93 Ala. 133, 9 So. 525, 527 (1891) ("The negative proof in the one case, equally with the affirmative proof in the other, serves to furnish the means of applying to the matter the practical test of common experience.").

[32]Hlavaty v. Song, 107 Ariz. 606, 491 P.2d 460, 463 (1971) (slipping off chair); Dill v. Dallas County Farmers'

Exchange No. 177, 267 S.W.2d 677, 681 (Mo. 1954) ("testimony that no other invitee had ever fallen in defendant's store would tend to confuse issues"); Sanitary Grocery Co. v. Steinbrecher, 183 Va. 495, 32 S.E.2d 685, 686–87 (1945) (since "evidence must be confined to the point in issue," it was proper to exclude testimony that 1000 customers had entered store each day for 11 months without cutting themselves on sharp corner of shelf); Goins v. Wendy's Intern., Inc., 242 Va. 333, 410 S.E.2d 635, 636 (1991) ("an established rule of evidence"; Schiro v. Oriental Realty Co., 7 Wis. 2d 556, 97 N.W.2d 385 (1959) (injury on part of lawn that plaintiff had used without mishap for 24 years); Admissibility of evidence of absence of other accidents or injuries at place where injury or damage occurred, 10 A.L.R.5th 371.

[33]Lempert et al., A Modern Approach to Evidence 311 (4th ed. 2011); see Vermont Food Industries, Inc. v. Ralston Purina Co., 514 F.2d 456, 464–65 (2d Cir. 1975) (complaints may not be passed from regional to national headquarters).

usual counterweights, they do not justify a flat rule of exclusion.[34] In some cases, excluding such proof of safety may be justified on the ground that the persons passing in safety were not exposed to the same conditions as those that prevailed when the plaintiff's injury occurred.[35] The evidence of a thousand safe descents down the stairs would be far less convincing if it were revealed that all of these were made in daylight, while the two or three accidents occurred at night in poor lighting. However, the possibility that a very general safety record may obscure the influence of an important factor merely counsels for applying the traditional requirement of substantial similarity.[36] When the experience sought to be proved is so extensive as to be sure to include an adequate number of similar situations, the similarity requirement should be considered satisfied.[37]

Neither can the broad proscription be justified by the other

---

[34]*See* Jones v. Pak-Mor Mfg. Co., 145 Ariz. 121, 700 P.2d 819, 824–26 (1985) (extensive dicta on the foundation required and the factors to be considered in admitting evidence of lack of complaints or accidents). Courts often insist that "the proponent of the evidence must establish that if there had been prior accidents, the witness probably would have known about them." Jones, 700 P.2d at 825 (remarking that "[t]his portion of the evidentiary predicate will, in most cases, be formidable.").

[35]Pittman v. Littlefield, 438 F.2d 659, 662 (1st Cir. 1971) (error to admit testimony that bags of plaster had never previously fallen from storage bin when plaintiff alleged that bin was secured improperly in this instance); Wray v. Fairfield Amusement Co., 126 Conn. 221, 10 A.2d 600 (1940) (absence of accidents on roller coaster should have been limited to passenger riding in seat where plaintiff alleged the strap was defective); Taylor v. Town of Monroe, 43 Conn. 36, 1875 WL 1824 (1875) (safety history of bridge did not include previous experience with runaway horses).

[36]This is the approach followed in Walker v. Trico Mfg. Co., Inc., 487 F.2d 595, 599 (7th Cir. 1973) (failure to show that 45 other blow-mold machines and the circumstances of their use were sufficiently similar). *See also*

Buford v. Riverboat Corp. of Mississippi-Vicksburg, 756 So. 2d 765, 770 (Miss. 2000) (cautioning that "parties who propose to introduce such ["no falls"] evidence . . . should be mindful that the proponent of the evidence has the burden of laying the proper foundation for the evidence" and "[e]vidence along the lines of 'I worked there for four years and never saw anyone fall' without more is the sort of reckless testimony that can mislead the jury."). A drastic application of the similarity requirement can be found in Vermont Food Industries, Inc. v. Ralston Purina Co., 514 F.2d 456, 464–65 (2d Cir. 1975) (absence of complaints at national headquarters about nutritional value of chicken feed "not probative" in part because nutritional value fluctuates with storage life and other variables).

[37]Pandit v. American Honda Motor Co., Inc., 82 F.3d 376 (10th Cir. 1996) (safety record properly admitted where "Honda used a charge warning light system of the same design in all of its 1981 Accords and in a total of nearly 1.9 million automobiles between 1973 and 1981"); Webb v. Thomas, 133 Colo. 458, 296 P.2d 1036, 1040 (1956) (over 12,000 persons using swimming pool up to time of trial with only plaintiff injured from diving in shallow end); Stein v. Trans World Airlines, Inc., 25 A.D.2d 732, 268 N.Y.S.2d 752 (1st Dep't 1966) (error to exclude evidence

considerations that affect the admissibility of evidence. The problems of prejudice and distraction over "collateral issues" seem much more acute when it comes to proof of other accidents than when evidence of an accident-free history is proffered. Indeed, the defendant will seldom open this door if there is any practical likelihood that the plaintiff will dispute the safety record.

Consequently, few recent decisions can be found applying a general rule of exclusion.[38] A large number of cases recognize that lack of other accidents may be admissible to show (1) absence of the defect or condition alleged,[39] (2) the lack of a causal relationship between the injury and the defect or condition charged,[40] (3) the nonexistence of an unduly dangerous situation,[41] or (4)

---

that many thousands had walked through same area in air terminal without slipping); Erickson v. Walgreen Drug Co., 120 Utah 31, 232 P.2d 210, 214 (1951) (error to exclude evidence that no one had slipped on terrazzo entranceway, regardless of weather conditions, for the 15 years during which at least 4000 persons entered the store every day); Mobbs v. Central Vermont Ry., Inc., 155 Vt. 210, 583 A.2d 566, 576 (1990); Stark v. Allis-Chalmers & Northwest Roads, Inc., 2 Wash. App. 399, 467 P.2d 854, 858 (Div. 1 1970) (no similar accident with 10,000 allegedly faultily designed tractors).

[38]*See* Jones v. Pak-Mor Mfg. Co., 145 Ariz. 121, 700 P.2d 819, 824–26 (1985) (explicitly rejecting the previous rule of per se inadmissibility in defective product design cases). Most modern cases assume or quickly conclude that the safety record is admissible and focus on the similarity requirement. *Cf.* Magayanes v. Terrance, 739 F.2d 1131, 1134 (7th Cir. 1983) (plaintiff, who was injured when his body struck the metal interior of an unpadded police "squadrol" car, evidently did not object to police testimony that of several hundred persons transported by one officer in various squadrols, only plaintiff had been injured).

[39]Becker v. American Airlines, Inc., 200 F. Supp. 243 (S.D. N.Y. 1961)

(safety history of altimeter); Birmingham Union Ry. Co. v. Alexander, 93 Ala. 133, 9 So. 525, 527 (1891) ("the defendant should be allowed the benefit of proof that the track, as it was at the time, was constantly crossed by other persons, under similar condition, without inconvenience, hindrance, or peril, as evidence tending to show the absence of the alleged defect or that it was not the cause"); Jones v. Pak-Mor Mfg. Co., 145 Ariz. 121, 700 P.2d 819, 824–26 (1985) (exclusion of evidence of lack of similar accidents with garbage truck designed in 1947 upheld because proponent's offer of proof not sufficiently detailed to establish proper foundation); Menard v. Cashman, 93 N.H. 273, 41 A.2d 222 (1945) (absence of falls on stairway).

[40]Harrison v. Sears, Roebuck and Co., 981 F.2d 25, 30 (1st Cir. 1992); DeMarines v. KLM Royal Dutch Airlines, 580 F.2d 1193, 1200 (3d Cir. 1978) (no other passengers claimed injuries from change in cabin pressure); Birmingham Union Ry. Co. v. Alexander, 93 Ala. 133, 9 So. 525, 527 (1891); Rayner v. Stauffer Chemical Co., 120 Ariz. 328, 585 P.2d 1240, 1243 (Ct. App. Div. 1 1978) (200 tests in which herbicide did not damage potatoes); Lawler v. Skelton, 241 Miss. 274, 130 So. 2d 565 (1961) (effects of insecticide sprayed on various persons).

[41]Zheutlin v. Sperry & Hutchin-

want of knowledge (or of grounds to realize) the danger.[42]

---

son Co., 149 Conn. 364, 179 A.2d 829 (1962) (50,000 others had used curb without falling); McCarty v. Village of Nashwauk, 282 Minn. 262, 164 N.W.2d 380, 382 (1969) (error to exclude evidence of absence of prior accidents on sidewalk); Wollaston v. Burlington Northern, Inc., 188 Mont. 192, 612 P.2d 1277, 1282 (1980) (no prior railroad crossing accidents); Wozniak v. 110 South Main St. Land and Development Improvement Corp., 61 A.D.2d 848, 402 N.Y.S.2d 69, 70 (3d Dep't 1978) (no other falls in hotel parking lot); Rathbun v. Humphrey Co., 94 Ohio App. 429, 52 Ohio Op. 145, 113 N.E.2d 877 (8th Dist. Cuyahoga County 1953) (amusement ride placed near trees used by thousands without complaint); Baker v. Lane County, 37 Or. App. 87, 586 P.2d 114, 117–18 (1978) (no other instances of children being injured at

fairgrounds by reaching through outside fence to hold rope tethering horses).

[42]McCarty v. Village of Nashwauk, 282 Minn. 262, 164 N.W.2d 380, 382 (1969) (absence of falls on sidewalk); Pierce v. Platte-Clay Elec. Co-op., Inc., 769 S.W.2d 769 (Mo. 1989) (collecting cases to document "recent trend . . . to allow such evidence to rebut proof of notice of a danger"); Wilk v. Georges, 267 Or. 19, 514 P.2d 877, 881 (1973) (absence of falls on planks in garden nursery). Of course, the purposes are overlapping, and not all opinions spell them out distinctly. *See, e.g.,* Borrelli v. Top Value Enterprises, Inc., 356 Mass. 110, 248 N.E.2d 510 (1969) (absence of complaints of electric shock from carpet sweeper).

# Chapter 19

# Insurance Against Liability

## § 201 Insurance against liability as proof of negligence

A formidable body of cases holds that evidence that a party is or is not insured against liability is not admissible on the issue of negligence.[1] Federal Rule of Evidence 411 codifies this line of cases. It states that "evidence that a person was or was not insured against liability is not admissible to prove whether the person acted negligently or otherwise wrongfully."[2] The rule is

---

**[Section 201]**

[1]*See generally* Leonard, The New Wigmore: Selected Rules of Limited Admissibility §§ 6.1 to 6.13 (2002); 2 Wigmore, Evidence § 282a (Chadbourn rev. 1979); Calnan, The Insurance Exclusionary Rule Revisited: Are Reports of its Demise Exaggerated?, 52 Ohio St. L.J. 1177 (1991); Propriety and prejudicial effect of trial counsel's reference or suggestion in medical malpractice case that defendant is insured, 71 A.L.R.4th 1025; Prejudicial effect of bringing to jury's attention fact that plaintiff in personal injury or death action is entitled to workers' compensation benefits, 69 A.L.R.4th 131; Counsel's argument or comment stating or implying that defendant is not insured and will have to pay verdict himself as prejudicial error, 68 A.L.R.4th 954; Admissibility of evidence, and propriety and effect of questions, statements, comments, etc., tending to show that defendant in personal injury or death action carries liability insurance, 4 A.L.R.2d 761.

[2]Fed. R. Evid. 411; *cf.* Kan. Stat. Ann. § 60-454 ("Evidence that a person was, at the time a harm was suffered by another, insured wholly or partially against loss arising from liability for that harm is inadmissible as tending to prove negligence or other wrongdoing."). *See also* Admissibility, after enactment of Rule 411, Federal Rules of Evidence, of evidence of liability insurance in negligence actions, 40 A.L.R. Fed. 541.

limited to insurance for liability[3] and does not include other forms of insurance.[4]

This rule rests on two premises. The first is the belief that insurance coverage reveals little about the likelihood that one will act carelessly. Subject to a few pathological exceptions, financial protection will not diminish the normal incentive to be careful, especially when life and limb are at stake.[5] Similarly, the argument that insured individuals or firms are more prudent and careful, as a group, than those who are self-insurers[6] seems tenuous[7] and also serves to counteract any force that the first argument may have. Thus, the relevance of the evidence of coverage is doubtful. In addition, there is concern that the evidence would be prejudicial—that the mention of insurance invites higher awards than are justified,[8] and conversely, that the sympathy that a jury might feel for a defendant who must pay out of his

---

[3]"Insurance," in this sense, should include all agreements that protect against liability. *See* Matosantos Commercial Corp. v. SCA Tissue North America, LLC., 369 F. Supp. 2d 191, 194 (D.P.R. 2005) (citing federal cases); Kilpatrick v. Wiley, Rein & Fielding, 2001 UT 107, 37 P.3d 1130, 1149 (Utah 2001) (holding that evidence of an indemnity agreement is admissible, but only to show bias and the jury is given a limiting instruction). *But see* Galaxy Computer Services, Inc. v. Baker, 325 B.R. 544, 551 n.2 (E.D. Va. 2005) (particular indemnification agreement not treated as liability insurance). For a contrary view, see Kava v. American Honda Motor Co., Inc., 48 P.3d 1170 (Alaska 2002). For an analysis of the meaning of "liability insurance" for this purpose, see Leonard, The New Wigmore: Selected Rules of Limited Admissibility § 6.7.1 (2002).

[4]Dill v. Montana Thirteenth Judicial Dist. Court, 1999 MT 85, 294 Mont. 134, 979 P.2d 188, 192–93 (1999) (holding that evidence of underinsured motorist insurance is not excluded under Mont. R. Evid. 411); Atkins v. Stratmeyer, 1999 SD 131, 600 N.W.2d 891, 896 (S.D. 1999) (holding that evidence of health insurance is not excluded under South Dakota rule).

[5]Brown v. Walter, 62 F.2d 798, 800 (C.C.A. 2d Cir. 1933) (L. Hand, Cir. J., "There can be no rational excuse [for mentioning insurance] except the flimsy one that a man is more likely to be careless if insured. That is at most the merest guess, much more than outweighed by the probability that the real issues will be obscured."); Carrel v. National Cord & Braid Corp., 447 Mass. 431, 852 N.E.2d 100, 114 (2006) ("That National Cord carried liability insurance (voluntarily or because customers required it to) is not relevant to the question of what risks and dangers it foresaw or should have foreseen."). Where one's accident history directly affects premiums, the marginal effect on care should be especially slight.

[6]Slough, Relevancy Unraveled, 5 U. Kan. L. Rev. 675, 710 (1957).

[7]Moreover, it is but another way of saying that because an individual is usually prudent (as evidenced by the fact that he is thoughtful enough to buy insurance), he probably acted prudently in the circumstances of the accident. Such character evidence generally is disallowed. See supra § 189 (evidence of character for care).

[8]Eichel v. New York Cent. R. Co., 375 U.S. 253, 255, 84 S. Ct. 316, 11 L. Ed. 2d 307 (1963) ("It has long been recognized that evidence showing that defendant is insured creates a substantial likelihood of misuse."); Posttape Associates v. Eastman Kodak

own pocket could interfere with its evaluation of the evidence under the appropriate standard of proof.[9] Although empirical research into these possible forms of prejudice yields no clear answers, the "shallow pocket" hypothesis seems better supported.[10]

Despite these concerns and the general rule that evidence of the fact of insurance coverage is inadmissible to show negligence or reasonable care,[11] such evidence frequently is received. As with the exclusionary rules discussed in Chapters 17 (Character and Habit) and 18 (Similar Happenings and Transactions), the evidence may be admitted for some other purpose, providing of course that its probative value on this other issue is not substantially outweighed by its prejudicial impact.[12] The purposes

---

Co., 537 F.2d 751, 758 (3d Cir. 1976) ("Knowledge that a party is insured may also affect a verdict if the jury knows that some of the loss has been paid by insurance or that it would satisfy a judgment against a defendant."); Langley v. Turner's Exp., Inc., 375 F.2d 296, 297 (4th Cir. 1967) (danger that "the jury may award damages without fault if aware that there is insurance coverage to pay the verdict"); Wilson v. Farm Bureau Mut. Ins. Co., 714 N.W.2d 250, 267 (Iowa 2006) (evidence of insurance would cause the jury to return a larger verdict against the underinsured motorist than it would have if it were unaware that insurance existed."); Price v. Yellow Cab Co. of Philadelphia, 443 Pa. 56, 278 A.2d 161, 166 (1971) (identifying this as "the chief reason" for the exclusionary rule).

[9]*See* Dias v. Healthy Mothers, Healthy Babies, Inc., 2002 MT 323, 313 Mont. 172, 60 P.3d 986, 990 (2002). See supra § 185 (discussing this form of prejudice).

[10]*See* Vidmar, The Performance of the American Civil Jury: An Empirical Perspective, 40 Ariz. L. Rev. 849 (1998). For additional descriptions and criticisms of empirical studies of the effect of disclosing whether a defendant is insured, see Broeder, The University of Chicago Jury Project, 38 Neb. L. Rev. 744, 753–54 (1959); The

Insurance Exclusionary Rule Revisited: Are Reports of its Demise Exaggerated?, 52 Ohio St. L.J. 1177 (1991); Green, Blindfolding the Jury, 33 Tex. L. Rev. 157, 165 (1954); Kalven, The Jury, the Law, and the Personal Injury Damage Award, 19 Ohio St. L.J. 158, 171 (1958); Notes, 10 U. Fla. L. Rev. 68, 74 (1957), 29 Tex. L. Rev. 949, 955–56 (1951), 11 Ohio St. L.J. 370, 375 (1950).

[11]Cases stating or applying the rule excluding evidence or mention of the fact that a party has liability insurance can be found in almost all jurisdictions. Even when the fact of insurance is disclosed, the amount of coverage is inadmissible to show inability to pay. Reed v. General Motors Corp., 773 F.2d 660, 662–64 (5th Cir. 1985) (discussing federal and Louisiana law).

[12]For cases excluding evidence that fits into a permissible category, see Kingery v. Barrett, 249 P.3d 275, 285 (Alaska 2011); Garfield v. Russell, 251 Cal. App. 2d 275, 59 Cal. Rptr. 379, 382 (2d Dist. 1967); Gerry v. Neugebauer, 83 N.H. 23, 136 A. 751, 753 (1927) (impeachment); Cruz v. Groth, 2009 SD 19, 763 N.W.2d 810 (S.D. 2009) (impeachment). For a discussion of the balancing process that is needed for all relevant evidence, see supra § 185.

for which such evidence may be offered are several.[13] Federal and Uniform Rule 411 states that "the court may admit this evidence for another purpose, such as proving a witness's bias or prejudice or proving agency, ownership, or control."[14]

The fact that persons rarely purchase liability insurance to cover contingencies for which they are not responsible makes the evidence relevant to questions of agency,[15] ownership,[16] and control.[17] The fact of insurance can be relevant to the bias of a witness in a number of ways. For example, the witness may be an investigator or other employee of the insurance company.[18] In some jurisdictions, however, the courts strive to mask the fact

---

[13]*See generally* Comment, 26 Corn. L. Q. 137 (1940).

[14]As originally adopted, the "other purpose" part of the rule read: "[t]his rule does not require the exclusion of evidence of insurance against liability when offered for another purpose, such as proof of agency, ownership or control, or bias or prejudice of a witness."

[15]Hunziker v. Scheidemantle, 543 F.2d 489, 495 (3d Cir. 1976) (liability insurance may be admitted to show that pilot of light aircraft was acting as agent if adequate foundation is laid); McCoy v. Universal Carloading & Distributing Co., 82 F.2d 342, 344 (C.C.A. 6th Cir. 1936) (whether driver of truck was agent or independent contractor); Eldridge v. McGeorge, 99 F.2d 835, 841 (C.C.A. 8th Cir. 1938) (whether owner or driver of truck was an employee); Cook-O'Brien Const. Co. v. Crawford, 26 F.2d 574, 575 (C.C.A. 9th Cir. 1928) (whether worker injured by explosion was employee); Cherry v. Stockton, 75 N.M. 488, 406 P.2d 358, 360 (1965) (whether owner or driver of truck was employee); Biggins v. Wagner, 60 S.D. 581, 245 N.W. 385, 386–87 (1932) (same).

[16]Newell v. Harold Shaffer Leasing Co., Inc., 489 F.2d 103, 110 (5th Cir. 1974) (check for repair bill from insurance company naming defendant as the insured properly received under Mississippi law "on the issue of ownership and agency"); Dobbins v. Crain Bros., Inc., 432 F. Supp. 1060, 1069 (W.D. Pa. 1976) (ownership, possession, and custody of barge); Layton v.

Cregan & Mallory Co., 263 Mich. 30, 248 N.W. 539 (1933) (ownership of automobile); Anderson v. Ohm, 258 N.W.2d 114, 118 (Minn. 1977) (same); *cf.* Leavitt v. Glick Realty Corp., 362 Mass. 370, 285 N.E.2d 786, 787 (1972) (evidence of liability insurance to show ownership or control of building is not admissible when these matters are not disputed).

[17]Pinckard v. Dunnavant, 281 Ala. 533, 206 So. 2d 340, 342–43 (1968) (management and maintenance of premises); Appelhans v. Kirkwood, 148 Colo. 92, 365 P.2d 233, 239 (1961) (proof that father insured vehicle driven by son); Perkins v. Rice, 187 Mass. 28, 72 N.E. 323, 324 (1904) (defendant admitted ownership of premises but denied control of elevator).

[18]Ingalls Shipbuilding Corp. v. Trehern, 155 F.2d 202, 203–04 (C.C.A. 5th Cir. 1946) (cross-examination to show that defendant's witness was insurance adjuster); Vindicator Consol. Gold Mining Co. v. Firstbrook, 36 Colo. 498, 86 P. 313, 314 (1906) (cross-examination to show witness acting as agent for insurance company); Pickett v. Kolb, 250 Ind. 449, 237 N.E.2d 105, 106 (1968) (error to sustain objection to question "who paid you to do this inspection?"); Baker v. Kammerer, 187 S.W.3d 292, 296 (Ky. 2006) ("abuse of discretion to prevent disclosure of the fact that a witness presented as an "investigator" of an "incident [that] had been investigated by police" worked for an insurance company); Mac Tyres, Inc. v. Vigil, 92 N.M. 446, 589 P.2d 1037, 1039 (1979) (abuse of dis-

that the witness works for an insurance company (as opposed to some other kind of employer).[19] Evidence that an expert witness has the same insurance carrier as the defendant is normally not admissible; however if there is a substantial connection between the witness and the insurance carrier evidence of such a relationship may be admissible.[20] Most appellate courts defer broadly to

---

cretion to exclude deposition of witness admitting to having lied to insurance representative); Rigelman v. Gilligan, 265 Or. 109, 506 P.2d 710, 714 (1973).

When plaintiff's witness is impeached by a prior inconsistent written statement prepared by an insurance adjuster and plaintiff disputes the correctness of the statement, the majority of courts allow the plaintiff to show the insurance company's employee prepared the statement for plaintiff's signature. Complete Auto Transit, Inc. v. Wayne Broyles Engineering Corp., 351 F.2d 478, 481–82 (5th Cir. 1965); Roland v. Beckham, 408 S.W.2d 628, 633 (Ky. 1966); Brave v. Blakely, 250 S.C. 353, 157 S.E.2d 726, 730 (1967). *Contra* Texas Co. v. Betterton, 126 Tex. 359, 88 S.W.2d 1039 (Comm'n App. 1936).

[19]*See* O'Donnell v. Bachelor, 429 Pa. 498, 240 A.2d 484, 486, 489, (1968) (error to limit cross-examination to show that defendant's insurer employed investigator-witness, for "[o]nce a witness commits himself to the ocean of legal controversy, he must, under cross-examination, disclose the flag under which he sails." To which a dissent replied that disclosing the presence of the insurance company reveals "not only the flag, but the seamstress who sewed it"—a reference to the rule of some states that the impeachment be limited to showing that the witness was employed "on behalf of the defendant"); *see also* Jones v. Munn, 140 Ariz. 216, 681 P.2d 368 (1984) (witness may be cross-examined to establish that he is an investigator for defendant's "representative"); Matthews v. Jean's Pastry Shop, Inc., 113 N.H. 546, 311 A.2d 127 (1973).

[20]*See* Bonser v. Shainholtz, 3 P.3d 422, 425–27 (Colo. 2000) (evidence of

an expert's role as co-founder of insurance trust satisfies the substantial connection test and is admissible to establish bias); Oliveira v. Jacobson, 846 A.2d 822, 828 (R.I. 2004) (proper to ask, "for the purposes of impeaching his credibility or showing his potential for bias," a medical doctor testifying to the absence of malpractice about the fact that he had been paid $35,000–$40,000 a year for services as a board member of a medical malpractice insurance company and that he omitted this information on his curriculum vitae submitted to demonstrate his qualifications); Yoho v. Thompson, 345 S.C. 361, 548 S.E.2d 584, 585 (2001) (evidence of expert's involvement in consultant work for insurance company satisfies the substantial connection test and is therefore admissible to establish bias); Lombard v. Rohrbaugh, 262 Va. 484, 551 S.E.2d 349 (2001) (evidence of business dealings between expert witness and insurance carrier admitted to show bias). *But see* Kansas Medical Mut. Ins. Co. v. Svaty, 291 Kan. 597, 244 P.3d 642 (2010) (discovery requests for medical malpractice insurance company's records are not reasonably calculated to lead to discovery of admissible evidence of bias of expert witness simply because defendant and expert practice in same state and purchase insurance in same market); Reimer v. Surgical Services of Great Plains, P.C., 258 Neb. 671, 605 N.W.2d 777, 780–81 (2000) (probative value of evidence of physician and expert having the same insurance carrier does not overcome prejudice, and evidence is not admissible to show bias); Hoffart v. Hodge, 9 Neb. App. 161, 609 N.W.2d 397, 407–08 (2000) (evidence of an expert's connection to an insurance carrier is only admissible to show bias if the expert

the trial court on the balance of probative value to show bias and prejudice, but some seem disposed to demand admission when the financial interest of the witness in the insurer is clear.[21] Cross-examination affords the usual means of revealing the relationship between the company and the witness.[22]

Plainly, these purposes do not exhaust the possibilities. Evidence of insurance may be admitted when it is an inseparable part of an admission of a party bearing on negligence or damages.[23] And, there are some less common uses.[24]

---

witness has some interest in the outcome of the case sufficient to overcome the prejudice of admitting the evidence, and participating in the same insurance program does not satisfy this test).

[21]*See* Woolum v. Hillman, 329 S.W.3d 283, 288 (Ky. 2010) ("The only bright-line solution to this problem has been developed by the Supreme Court of Ohio, which . . . has conclusively held that 'in a medical malpractice action, evidence of a commonality of insurance interests between a defendant and an expert witness is sufficiently probative of the expert's bias as to clearly outweigh any potential prejudice evidence of insurance might cause.' Ede v. Atrium S. OB-GYN, Inc., 71 Ohio St. 3d 124, 1994-Ohio-424, 642 N.E.2d 365, 368 (1994); *see also* Davis v. Immediate Medical Services, Inc., 80 Ohio St. 3d 10, 1997-Ohio-363, 684 N.E.2d 292 (1997). The Ohio Supreme Court drew from the general truth-seeking nature of the rules of evidence, along with the specific exception for bias under Rule 411, in creating its bright-line rule favoring the inclusion of such evidence.

[22]Mideastern Contracting Corporation v. O'Toole, 55 F.2d 909, 912 (C.C.A. 2d Cir. 1932) (L. Hand, Cir. J., "The defendant need not have put in the statement [that the plaintiff allegedly made] at all; when it chooses to do so, it laid open to inquiry its authenticity, and that inevitably involved the relation of the person who took it"); Eppinger & Russell Co. v. Sheely, 24 F.2d 153, 155 (C.C.A. 5th Cir. 1928) (proper to ask physician

testifying for defendant whether he was retained by employer's insurer); Charter v. Chleborad, 551 F.2d 246 (8th Cir. 1977) (error to prohibit plaintiff in medical malpractice action from establishing on cross-examination that defendant's witness (an attorney who testified that plaintiff's expert witness had a bad reputation for truth and veracity) represents defendant's liability carrier from time to time); Dempsey v. Goldstein Bros. Amusement Co., 231 Mass. 461, 121 N.E. 429 (1919) (to show bias of physician who testified that plaintiff had no permanent injuries); Gibson v. Grey Motor Co., 147 Minn. 134, 179 N.W. 729 730 (1920) (insurance investigator); *cf.* Ikerd v. Lapworth, 435 F.2d 197, 208 (7th Cir. 1970) (Indiana law permits asking expert who is paying him even when the answer would disclose the existence of insurance, but this exception does not apply when the expert does not testify); Averett v. Shircliff, 218 Va. 202, 237 S.E.2d 92, 96 (1977) (proper to prohibit impeachment of appraisers in this manner since they were not regular employees but independent appraisers who worked for many insurance companies).

[23]If the reference to insurance can be severed without substantially lessening the probative value of the admission, this should be done. Cameron v. Columbia Builders, Inc., 212 Or. 388, 320 P.2d 251, 254 (1958); Connor v. McGill, 127 Vt. 19, 238 A.2d 777, 780 (1968). But where the reference to insurance is an "integral part" of the admission, the whole statement may be received. Herschensohn v. Weisman, 80 N.H. 557, 119 A. 705 (1923) (pas-

Furthermore, there are two other ways in which the fact of insurance can be brought home to the jury. Witnesses have been known to make unexpected and unresponsive references to insurance.[25] In these situations, the judge may declare a mistrial,[26] but it is a rare case in which he will do more than strike the reference and instruct the jury to ignore it.[27] Finally, in the

senger warned driver to be more careful lest he have an accident and kill somebody, and defendant driver said "Don't worry, I carry insurance for that"); Reid v. Owens, 98 Utah 50, 93 P.2d 680, 685 (1939) (The reference to insurance in the statement "My boy is careless, and he drives too fast. . . . We have taken out insurance to protect him [and] if you won't prosecute . . . we will do all we can to help you get that $5,000 insurance" was "itself freighted with admission").

[24]Posttape Associates v. Eastman Kodak Co., 537 F.2d 751, 758 (3d Cir. 1976) (to show awareness of trade usage limiting liability for defective film to replacement value); Hannah v. Haskins, 612 F.2d 373, 375 (8th Cir. 1980) (cross-examination allowed where plaintiff adverted to insurance payments on direct examination and they may have been relevant to the nature and extent of plaintiff's injuries); Morton v. Zidell Explorations, Inc., 695 F.2d 347 (9th Cir. 1982) (ship owner's purchase of insurance on vessel being refitted admitted to indicate awareness that shipyard did not bear risk of loss or damage to the vessel); Fleegel v. Estate of Boyles, 61 P.3d 1267, 1271–72 (Alaska 2002) (relevant to defendant's "financial condition as it related to punitive damages"); Williams v. Security Nat. Bank of Sioux City, Iowa, 358 F. Supp. 2d 782, 788 (N.D. Iowa 2005) (former trustee's letter to its liability insurer was admissible in remainder beneficiaries' action alleging that trustee mismanaged trust to show trustee's efforts to minimize its own liability by attempting to legitimize its erroneous distributions to life beneficiary); N.D.Iowa 2005); Busick v. St. John, 856 So. 2d 304 (Miss. 2003) (evidence that plaintiff's

health insurance paid for physical therapy was admitted to impeach plaintiff's testimony that she suffered permanent injuries and ceased physical therapy only because she could no longer afford it); Mickelson v. Montana Rail Link, Inc., 2000 MT 111, 299 Mont. 348, 999 P.2d 985, 992 (2000) (holding that evidence of plaintiff's failure to find work due to fear of loss of benefits is admissible to show a failure to mitigate damages); Kubista v. Romaine, 87 Wash. 2d 62, 549 P.2d 491, 496 (1976) (evidence that defendant's insurer had encouraged plaintiff to go to school to learn a new trade and had promised to take care of him admissible in rebuttal of defense that plaintiff could have mitigated damages by going back to work earlier).

[25]Isler v. Burman, 305 Minn. 288, 232 N.W.2d 818, 822 (1975) (pastor twice referred to church's insurance even though counsel had told him not to); Lowe v. Steele Const. Co., 368 N.W.2d 610 (S.D. 1985).

[26]Garber v. Martin, 261 Or. 410, 494 P.2d 858 (1972). Reversal is nearly automatic where the disclosure is deliberate and stressed by counsel in questioning or argument. Pickwick Stage Lines v. Edwards, 64 F.2d 758, 762–63 (C.C.A. 10th Cir. 1933); James Stewart & Co. v. Newby, 266 Fed. 287 (4th Cir. 1920); Lowe v. Steele Const. Co., 368 N.W.2d 610 (S.D. 1985).

[27]Dindo v. Grand Union Co., 331 F.2d 138, 141 (2d Cir. 1964) ("the specific question asked required only a yes or no answer, and the witness voluntarily brought in the insurance company"); Lenz v. Southern Pac. Co., 493 F.2d 471, 472 (5th Cir. 1974) (counsel's "single inadvertent reference" to railroad investigator as "insurance investigator"); Pullman v.

examination of prospective jurors, most jurisdictions allow questions about employment by or interest in insurance companies.[28]

---

Land O'Lakes, Inc., 262 F.3d 759, 763 (8th Cir. 2001) (upholding denial of mistrial motion where the "issue of insurance coverage was not highlighted for the jury and there was no further mention of insurance after the district court admonished appellees' counsel and [plaintiff] to refrain from mentioning insurance coverage for the remainder of the trial"); Hazeltine v. Johnson, 92 F.2d 866, 869–70 (C.C.A. 9th Cir. 1937); Muehlebach v. Mercer Mortuary & Chapel, Inc., 93 Ariz. 60, 378 P.2d 741, 745 (1963); Inama v. Brewer, 132 Idaho 377, 973 P.2d 148, 154 (1999) (holding that plaintiff's comments about insurance company paying for her damaged car do not warrant a mistrial when jury was instructed to disregard the statements); Evans v. Howard R. Green Co., 231 N.W.2d 907, 914–15 (Iowa 1975); Carver v. Lavigne, 160 Me. 414, 205 A.2d 159, 162 (1964) ("unpredictably elicited from an undoubtedly guileless witness"); Dias v. Healthy Mothers, Healthy Babies, Inc., 2002 MT 323, 313 Mont. 172, 60 P.3d 986, 989 (2002); Cramer v. Peavy, 116 Nev. 575, 3 P.3d 665 (2000) (holding that defendant's improper reference to worker's compensation benefits is not cause for a mistrial when the jury receives proper limiting instructions); DeSpain v. Bohlke, 259 Or. 320, 486 P.2d 545, 546–47 (1971) (physician's reference to patients' nervousness as a result of being " 'hounded' by the insurance company"); Gumenick v. U. S., 213 Va. 510, 193 S.E.2d 788, 796 (1973). *But see* Behrens v. Nelson, 86 S.D. 312, 195 N.W.2d 140, 141 (1972) (inadvertence rule not applicable where, contrary to his counsel's advice, plaintiff referred to insurance on direct examination).

[28]In some jurisdictions the trial judge may allow or disallow the questioning, and in general, many refinements and variations exist as to consultation with the court in advance and as to the questions that may be asked. It is usually said that the questions must be propounded in good faith. Such "good faith" involves establishing that the party is in fact insured, that prospective jurors may be associated with a liability carrier or otherwise unusually concerned with insurance policies or premiums. For cases and general discussions, see Drickersen v. Drickersen, 604 P.2d 1082, 1084–85 (Alaska 1979) (prospective juror's reference to rising insurance rates justified questioning entire panel on this point); King v. Westlake, 264 Ark. 555, 572 S.W.2d 841, 843–44 (1978) (questions about effect of verdict on insurance premiums); Harvey v. Castleberry, 258 Ark. 722, 529 S.W.2d 324 (1975) ("Are any of you policyholders in any mutual insurance company writing automobile liability insurance policies?"); Robinson v. Faulkner, 163 Conn. 365, 306 A.2d 857, 863–64 (1972) (question about "interest or participation or connection with casualty companies"); Rosenthal v. Kolars, 304 Minn. 378, 231 N.W.2d 285, 287 (1975) (whether jurors or any of their close relatives had been employed as claims adjusters for company that writes medical malpractice insurance); Ballinger v. Gascosage Elec. Co-op., 788 S.W.2d 506 (Mo. 1990) ("the 'insurance question' approved in numerous appellate decisions"); Lowe v. Steele Const. Co., 368 N.W.2d 610 (S.D. 1985) (improper to observe during voir dire that "insurance companies are always the defendants in these kinds of cases").

Some writers have proposed obtaining information about individual jurors with less prejudice by examining the venire before drawing panels for particular cases, Note, 52 Harv. L. Rev. 166 (1938), or by a questionnaire. Note, 43 Mich. L. Rev. 621 (1944); *see also* Calnan, The Insurance Exclusionary Rule Revisited: Are Reports of Its Demise Exaggerated?, 52 Ohio St. L.J. 1177 (1991); Eklund v. Wheatland County, 2009 MT 231, 351 Mont. 370,

Despite its nearly universal acceptance, the wisdom of the general prohibition on injecting insurance into the trial, as it currently operates, is questionable. When the rule originated, insurance coverage of individuals was exceptional. In the absence of references to insurance at trial, a juror most probably would not have thought that a defendant was insured. Today, compulsory insurance laws for motorists are ubiquitous, and liability insurance for homeowners and businesses has become the norm. Most jurors probably assume that defendants are insured.[29] Yet, few courts will allow a defendant to show that he is uninsured,[30] unless the plaintiff has opened the door to such evidence.[31] At a minimum, such a defendant, and indeed any party, should be entitled to an instruction that there has been no evidence as to whether any party is insured because the law is that the presence or absence of insurance should play no part in the case.[32]

More fundamentally, the underlying soundness of the general rule forbidding disclosure of the fact of insurance has been the object of scathing criticism.[33] Stripped to its essentials, the debate is not really over the application of the doctrines of relevancy and its counterweights. Hardly anyone questions the premise that the evidence is irrelevant to the exercise of reasonable care. Neither does anyone contend that a party has a right to put irrele-

---

212 P.3d 297, 303 (2009) (permissible to preclude plaintiff who was suing the county for "severe injuries" from mentioning insurance during voir dire, when counsel could still "question potential jurors . . . about their beliefs as taxpayers and their concerns on the financial outcome of the case"); State ex rel. Nationwide Mut. Ins. Co. v. Karl, 222 W. Va. 326, 664 S.E.2d 667 (2008) (permissible for counsel to inquire during voir dire about connections with "Nationwide Trial Division," a captive law firm).

[29]This realization has not escaped the courts. B-Amused Co. v. Millrose Sporting Club, Inc., 168 F. Supp. 709, 710 (E.D. N.Y. 1958) ("In this day and generation, nearly every juryman knows that the average negligence case is being defended by an insurance company. . . . The idea seems to die hard that what jurors know in their everyday business experience they close their minds to, when deliberating as jurors."); Young v. Carter, 121 Ga. App. 191, 173 S.E.2d 259, 261 (1970) (concurring opinion observing

that "Any juror who doesn't know there is insurance in the case by this time [after voir dire] should probably be excused [as] an idiot."); Connelly v. Nolte, 237 Iowa 114, 21 N.W.2d 311, 320 (1946) (The juror "doesn't require a brick house to fall on him to give him an idea"); see also Broeder, Voir Dire, 38 S. Cal. L. Rev. 503, 525 (1965).

[30]See Piechuck v. Magusiak, 82 N.H. 429, 135 A. 534 (1926) ("a form of the inadmissible plea of poverty").

[31]Stehouwer v. Lewis, 249 Mich. 76, 227 N.W. 759, 761 (1929); Whitman v. Carver, 337 Mo. 1247, 88 S.W.2d 885, 887 (1935).

[32]For suggestions as to the content of such instructions, see Diamond & Vidmar, Jury Room Ruminations on Forbidden Topics, 87 Va. L. Rev. 1857, 1909–11 (2001).

[33]See Calnan, The Insurance Exclusionary Rule Revisited: Are Reports of its Demise Exaggerated?, 52 Ohio St. L.J. 1177 (1991) (collecting criticisms).

vant evidence into the record.[34] Rather, the arguments for the abandonment of the policy of secrecy are either pragmatic or idealistic. The pragmatic argument is straightforward. The conspiracy of silence is hard to maintain. Its costs include extensive and unnecessary arguments, reversals, and retrials stemming from elusive questions of prejudice and good faith. This state of affairs might be tolerable if the revelations of insurance were truly fraught with prejudice. But, as we have suggested, most jurors probably presuppose the existence of liability insurance anyway, and the heart of the policy of nondisclosure is surrendered when jurors are examined about their connection with insurance companies. Consequently, the extent to which evidence of coverage or its absence is prejudicial is unclear.[35] Even the direction in which such prejudice might work is obscure.[36] In sum, the rule has become a hollow shell,[37] expensive to maintain and of doubtful utility.[38]

The other principal argument against the rule of secrecy is

---

[34]See supra § 184 (only relevant evidence is admissible). It might be said, however, that the identity of the insurer and the amount of coverage are relevant as "background facts." Green, Blindfolding the Jury, 33 Tex. L. Rev. 157, 165 (1954). See supra § 185.

[35]Muehlebach v. Mercer Mortuary & Chapel, Inc., 93 Ariz. 60, 378 P.2d 741, 744 (1963) ("the prejudicial content of a reference to liability insurance is largely a matter of the past. And, it has, in part, been made a thing of the past by the expenditures of vast sums of money by insurance companies to educate prospective jurors of the claimed relation between large verdicts and insurance rates").

[36]Shingleton v. Bussey, 223 So. 2d 713, 718 (Fla. 1969) ("revelation of the interest of an insurer . . . should be more beneficial to insurers than the questionable 'ostrich head in the sand' approach which may mislead jurors to think that insurance coverage is greater than it is"); Safeco Ins. Co. of America v. U.S. Fidelity & Guar. Co., 101 N.M. 148, 679 P.2d 816, 820 (1984) ("trial courts should recognize that the prejudicial tendencies [of revealing that a defendant is insured] can go in both directions").

[37]An indication of the prevalence of references to insurance in tort litigation comes from a study of 45 such cases in Tucson, Arizona. Trial testimony referred to insurance in 35% of the trials. Shari Seidman Diamond & Neil Vidmar, Jury Room Ruminations on Forbidden Topics, 87 Va. L. Rev. 1857, 1876 (2001). Insurance was mentioned by a witness in 10/25 of the motor vehicle cases and in 4/15 of the non-motor vehicle cases. "[J]urors spontaneously initiated jury room discussions about insurance in four-fifths of the remaining thirty-one cases." Shari Seidman Diamond & Neil Vidmar, Jury Room Ruminations on Forbidden Topics, 87 Va. L. Rev. 1857, 1884 (2001).

[38]Accord Leonard, The New Wigmore: Selected Rules of Limited Admissibility § 6.13 (2002); cf. Schwartz, Should Juries Be Informed that Municipality Will Indemnify Officer's 1983 Liability for Constitutional Wrongdoing?, 86 Iowa L. Rev. 1209 (2001) (arguing that due to the widespread criticism of Federal Rule of Evidence 411 and the need for the jury to know the truth, the rule should be amended to exclude evidence of governmental indemnification in § 1983 actions).

more difficult to evaluate, but standing alone, it is less persuasive. It arises from a certain conception of fairness—a conception that holds that the jury should know who the "real" parties in interest are. The insurance company, which under its policy has the exclusive right to employ counsel, defend the suit, and control the decision as to settling or contesting the action, is a party in all but name.[39]

Unfortunately, this argument begs the question. If the substantive law is that the depth of the defendant's pocket has nothing to do with liability or damages, then why should the jury be apprised of this fact? To be sure, in many cases the relative wealth of the parties is manifest. A multinational corporation cannot disguise itself as a struggling member of the proletariat. But where admittedly irrelevant characteristics can be removed from the courtroom without great strain, it is hard to see why they should be retained. In the end, therefore, it is the more pragmatic analysis that should be decisive. The benefits of a half-hearted policy of secrecy are not worth the costs. If disclosure of the fact of insurance really is prejudicial, the corrective is not a futile effort at concealment, but the usual fulfillment by the court of its function of explaining to the jury its duty to decide according to the facts and the substantive law, rather than upon sympathy, ability to pay, or concern about proliferating litigation and rising insurance premiums.

---

[39]In various jurisdictions, doctrines of joinder, subrogation or direct action may permit the insurance company to be named as a defendant. City Stores Co. v. Lerner Shops of District of Columbia, Inc., 410 F.2d 1010 (D.C. Cir. 1969) (subrogation); Note, 74 Harv. L. Rev. 357 (1960); Row, Comment, Admissibility of Insurance Policy Limits, 45 La. L. Rev. 1299 (1985) (Louisiana law).

# Chapter 20

# Experimental and Scientific Evidence

## I. SCIENTIFIC TESTS IN GENERAL

### § 202  Pretrial experiments

The dominant method of factual inquiry in the courts of law is observational. Witnesses relate what they have seen under naturally occurring conditions, and the judge or jury, observing the witnesses, accepts or rejects their testimony with varying degrees of confidence. In many fields of science, naturalistic observations of people or things are also a principal means of gathering information (though the observations are made in a more structured fashion and are presented and analyzed in a different way). In some scientific disciplines, the major method for collecting data involves manipulating the environment. In its simplest and ideal form, a controlled experiment holds constant all extraneous variables so that the experimenter can measure the impact of the one factor of interest.[1]

The opportunities for applying the experimental method to factual controversies that arise in litigation are immense, but they generally go unrecognized and unused.[2] Some of the more frequently encountered types of experiments are tests of the composition[3] or physical properties[4] of substances or products, tests of the flammability or explosive properties of products,[5] tests of

---

**[Section 202]**

[1]A grasp of the basic principles of experimentation in the sciences can be of great value to the attorney involved in the design and presentation of experiments conducted for litigation. The considerations that make a scientific experiment respected within the scientific community and those that should make an experiment convincing to a jury (and defensible as against expert attack) are largely the same. Acquaintance with this field is even more obviously relevant to the courtroom presentation of pre-existing scientific experiments. For elementary discussions of experimental design, see 1 Faigman, et al., Modern Scientific Evidence: The Law and Science of Expert Testimony §§ 5:40 to 5:44, 6:9 to 6:11 (2011–2012 ed.); Kaye et al., The New Wigmore, A Treatise on Evidence: Expert Evidence § 12.5 (2d ed. 2011); Zeisel & Kaye, Prove It with Figures: Empirical Methods in Law and Litigation (1997).

[2]Courtroom experiments and demonstrations are considered infra § 217. For additional discussion of legal aspects of pretrial experiments, see 2 Wigmore, Evidence §§ 445–60 (Chadbourn rev. 1979).

[3]5 Faigman, et al., Modern Scientific Evidence: The Law and Science of Expert Testimony §§ 42:1 et seq. (2011–2012 ed.) (drug testing); Committee on Scientific Assessment of Bullet Lead Elemental Composition Comparison, National Research Council, Forensic Analysis: Weighing Bullet Lead Evidence (2004); Admissibility of evidence of neutron activation analysis, 50 A.L.R.3d 117.

[4]Alonzo v. State ex rel. Booth, 283 Ala. 607, 219 So. 2d 858, 879 (1969) (error to deny production of incriminating tape recordings for electronic testing of possible alterations); Patricia R. v. Sullivan, 631 P.2d 91 (Alaska 1981) (tests of temperatures attained by heater); Dritt v. Morris, 235 Ark. 40, 357 S.W.2d 13 (1962) (slipperiness of concrete floor due to sweeping compound); Howard v. Omni Hotels Management Corp., 203 Cal. App. 4th 403, 136 Cal. Rptr. 3d 739 (4th Dist. 2012) (measurements of coefficient of friction of bathtub); Admissibility of experimental evidence to determine chemical or physical qualities or character of material or substance, 76 A.L.R.2d 354. See infra § 207.

[5]Stumbaugh v. State, 599 P.2d 166, 169–72 (Alaska 1979) (experiment to show how arson defendant could have set fire with materials found in premises); Guinan v. Famous Players-Lasky Corporation, 267 Mass. 501, 167 N.E. 235, 245 (1929) (tests of the flammability and explosive properties of scraps of motion picture film); Schmidt v. Plains Elec., Inc., 281 N.W.2d 794, 800–01 (N.D. 1979) (flammability of drapes positioned near heater); Faigman, et al., Modern Scientific Evidence: The Law and Science of Expert Testimony §§ 39:1 et seq. (2011–2012 ed.); Admissibility of experimental evidence to determine chemical or physical qualities or character of material or substance, 76 A.L.R.2d 354; Admissibility of experimental evidence as to explosion, 76 A.L.R.2d 402; cf. Admissibility of evidence as to experiments or tests in civil action for death, injury, or property damage against electric power company or the

the effects of drugs and other products on human beings or other organisms,[6] tests of firearms to show characteristic, identifying features, or capabilities,[7] tests of the visibility of objects or persons under certain conditions,[8] tests of the speed of moving vehicles and of the effectiveness of brakes, headlights or other components.[9] Some of these experiments can be simple affairs, such as driving an automobile along a stretch of road to determine where a particular object on the road first becomes visible. Others are more complicated, requiring sophisticated machinery, statistical analysis of the results, or other specialized knowledge

---

like, 54 A.L.R.2d 922.

[6]3 Faigman, et al., Modern Scientific Evidence: The Law and Science of Expert Testimony §§ 22:1 et seq. (2011–2012 ed.) (toxicology); Admissibility of experimental evidence to determine chemical or physical qualities or character of material or substance, 76 A.L.R.2d 354.

[7]Canada Life Assur. Co. v. Houston, 241 F.2d 523, 537 (9th Cir. 1957) (dropping rifle to see whether it would discharge on impact); Nicholson v. State, 570 P.2d 1058, 1064–65 (Alaska 1977) (trajectory experiment); State v. Baublits, 324 Mo. 1199, 27 S.W.2d 16 (1930) (trajectory tests rejected); 4 Faigman, et al., Modern Scientific Evidence: The Law and Science of Expert Testimony §§ 35:1 et seq. (2011–2012 ed.) (firearms and toolmarks identification); Admissibility, in homicide prosecution, of evidence as to tests made to ascertain distance from gun to victim when gun was fired, 11 A.L.R.5th 497; Admissibility of testimony that bullet could or might have come from particular gun, 31 A.L.R.4th 486; Expert evidence to identify gun from which bullet or cartridge was fired, 26 A.L.R.2d 892; cf. Admissibility, in criminal case, of results of residue detection test to determine whether accused or victim handled or fired gun, 1 A.L.R.4th 1072.

[8]McDaniel v. Frye, 536 F.2d 625, 626, (5th Cir. 1976) (visibility of truck); Stevens v. People, 97 Colo. 559, 51 P.2d 1022, 1024–25 (1935) (whether headlight would illuminate oncoming car at particular place); Butts v. U.S.,

822 A.2d 407, 414 (D.C. 2003) (study showing that "an unimpaired driver, under conditions similar to those on the night of the accident, could detect a pedestrian from a distance of 300 feet"); Carpenter v. Kurn, 348 Mo. 1132, 157 S.W.2d 213, 215 (1941) (distance at which an observer could tell that a person sitting on railroad tracks is a human being); Norfolk & W. Ry. Co. v. Henderson, 132 Va. 297, 111 S.E. 277, 281 (1922) (visibility of object the size of deceased two year old girl on railroad track); Admissibility of experimental evidence to show visibility or line of vision, 78 A.L.R.2d 152.

[9]Bauman v. Volkswagenwerk Aktiengesellschaft, 621 F.2d 230, 233–34 (6th Cir. 1980) (simulating sideswipe accident by banging on door handle with rubber mallet); Nanda v. Ford Motor Co., 509 F.2d 213, 223 (7th Cir. 1974) (striking car with a ram to see whether the force would dislodge fuel pipe); Ramseyer v. General Motors Corp., 417 F.2d 859, 864 (8th Cir. 1969) (simulation of 100,000 miles of driving wear on Corvair steering gear); Smith v. State Roads Commission, 240 Md. 525, 214 A.2d 792 (1965) (automobile swerve test); Admissibility of experimental evidence, skidding tests, or the like, relating to speed or control of motor vehicle, 78 A.L.R.2d 218; cf. Opinion testimony as to speed of motor vehicle based on skid marks and other facts, 29 A.L.R.3d 248; Admissibility in evidence, in automobile negligence action, of charts showing braking distance, reaction times, etc, 9 A.L.R.3d 976.

or procedures.[10] Testimony describing the experiments may be received as substantive evidence,[11] or it may form the basis for an expert opinion.[12] Although scientific or engineering experts conduct most pretrial experiments, the simplest experiments are often the most convincing, and scientific sophistication is not always necessary or cost-effective.[13]

Pretrial experiments will be admitted as evidence if their probative value is not substantially outweighed by the usual counterweights of prejudice, confusion of the issues, and time consumption.[14] The only form of prejudice that might operate in this context is that of giving experimental results more weight than they deserve. As discussed in the next section, this can be a barrier to admissibility when the interpretation of the experiment would require expert scientific testimony. The extent to

---

[10]See infra §§ 203 to 211. Some courts borrow from the cases involving pretrial experiments in evaluating the admissibility of results of computer simulations. Alcorn v. Union Pacific R.R. Co., 50 S.W.3d 226, 245 (Mo. 2001) ("A computer simulation is similar to evidence of experiment [which] is admissible when the experiment was made under conditions substantially similar in essential particulars to the condition which prevailed at the time of the occurrence in the suit. . . .").

[11]*E.g.*, Pullman v. Land O'Lakes, Inc., 262 F.3d 759, 765 (8th Cir. 2001) (because the results of a experiment in feeding cows allegedly toxic "steam flaked soybeans" were not presented by experts, it was not necessary to apply the special standards for scientific evidence (see infra § 203)).

[12]Of course, in this situation, the expert will be held to the normal standards for expert testimony. *E.g.*, Fireman's Fund Ins. Co. v. Canon U.S.A., Inc., 394 F.3d 1054, 1058–59 (8th Cir. 2005) (applying the "reliability" standard of Daubert v. Merrell Dow Pharmaceuticals, Inc., 509 U.S. 579, 113 S. Ct. 2786, 125 L. Ed. 2d 469 (1993), and Kumho Tire Co., Ltd. v. Carmichael, 526 U.S. 137, 119 S. Ct. 1167, 143 L. Ed. 2d 238 (1999), to exclude an incomplete pretrial test of a heating element said to have ignited a fire).

[13]May Department Stores Co. v. Runge, 241 F. 575 (C.C.A. 8th Cir. 1917) (holding that the trial court erred in excluding testimony of an experiment showing that a gate to an elevator shaft could not be raised high enough to allow a 200-pound "truck" that fell on plaintiff to be pushed into the shaft, and noting that "such evidence is even more persuasive than the testimony of witnesses who casually looked at the articles in some time past."); Marbra v. State, 904 So. 2d 1169, 1173–74 (Miss. Ct. App. 2004) (firearms expert's inability to get defendant's pistol to discharge by holding it by the barrel and striking it against a hard surface admissible as lay testimony); Johnson for Johnson v. Young Men's Christian Ass'n of Great Falls, 201 Mont. 36, 651 P.2d 1245, 1248–49 (1982) (tossing diving ring into pool at location where drowning victim was found and timing how long it took two boys to retrieve it "supported the conclusion that it took one to one and one-half minutes to retrieve the victim from the pool," an elapsed time too short to have caused permanent brain damage); Larson v. Meyer, 161 N.W.2d 165 (N.D. 1968) (whether tractor could pull milk truck out of rut without overturning).

[14]*See* Hasson v. Ford Motor Co., 19 Cal. 3d 530, 138 Cal. Rptr. 705, 564 P.2d 857 (1977) (discussing these considerations as they pertain to experiments). See supra § 185.

which the presentation will be distracting or time-consuming will vary from case to case. As for probative value, the courts often speak of the need for similarity between the conditions of the experiment and those that pertained to the litigated happening.[15] The burden of showing substantial similarity is on the proponent.[16]

---

[15]Cases emphasizing the importance of similar conditions abound. Hall v. General Motors Corp., 647 F.2d 175, 180 (D.C. Cir. 1980) (experiments with automobile drive shaft taped rather than bolted at rear inadmissible); Gladhill v. General Motors Corp., 743 F.2d 1049, 1051–52 (4th Cir. 1984) (crucial difference in angle of front wheels when brakes locked); Renfro Hosiery Mills Co. v. National Cash Register Co., 552 F.2d 1061, 1066 n.7 (4th Cir. 1977) (tests on mere prototype of computer under extreme conditions inadmissible to show that production model was unreliable under normal operating conditions); Shipp v. General Motors Corp., 750 F.2d 418, 427 (5th Cir. 1985) (different vehicle, roof and passenger compartment, and multiple rather than single rollover); Barnes v. General Motors Corp., 547 F.2d 275, 277 (5th Cir. 1977) (error to admit experiment in which test automobile with engine largely disconnected from frame was driven with accelerator "mashed to the floor" when actual vehicle had engine mount with roll-stop feature); Jackson v. Fletcher, 647 F.2d 1020, 1023–24, (10th Cir. 1981) (acceleration experiment with a truck that weighed about half what the truck involved in the accident weighed "could have produced a result desired by defendants but not a true depiction"); Love v. State, 457 P.2d 622, 628 (Alaska 1969) (experiment to determine whether vessel would drift into restricted waters inadmissible for lack of similarity); People v. Bonin, 47 Cal. 3d 808, 254 Cal. Rptr. 298, 765 P.2d 460 (1989) (wrapping T-shirt around arm not sufficiently similar to strangulation with T-shirt to ascertain whether ligature marks on neck could have come from T-shirt); Smith v.

State Roads Commission, 240 Md. 525, 214 A.2d 792 (1965) (automobile swerve test performed with sober driver, different vehicle, drier road conditions, and daylight illumination inadmissible as having nothing in common with accident except that both took place at the same curve); W.G.O. ex rel. Guardian of A.W.O. v. Crandall, 640 N.W.2d 344, 348 (Minn. 2002) (admission of the accident reconstruction expert's experiment with his wife's vehicle—of a different year, make and model—of repeatedly driving his wife's car at 30 mph, locking up the brakes, and jumping out to view the surface of the road where he observed that the skid marks were "visible to the naked eye" was improperly admitted to show that a driver did not apply her brakes as she claimed because the experiment was not "conducted under conditions and circumstances substantially similar to those existing when the accident occurred"); Buford v. Riverboat Corp. of Mississippi-Vicksburg, 756 So. 2d 765, 768 (Miss. 2000) (proponent of expert testimony about the coefficient of friction "failed to lay a proper foundation that the conditions of the crosswalk [when measured by the expert] were substantially similar to what they were on the day that [plaintiff] fell"); Spurlin v. Nardo, 145 W. Va. 408, 114 S.E.2d 913 (1960) (demonstrating that automobile mechanic with 35 years driving experience can stop a car descending a hill without using foot brakes not sufficiently similar); Products liability: admissibility of experimental or test evidence to disprove defect in motor vehicle, 64 A.L.R.4th 125.

[16]E.g., Renfro Hosiery Mills Co. v. National Cash Register Co., 552 F.2d

In practice, however, the similarity requirement is not applied to all pretrial experiments, or if it is nominally applied, the notion of "similarity" becomes almost infinitely flexible. In the words of one state supreme court, "[s]ubstantial similarity does not require identity of conditions, but only that degree of similarity which will insure that the results of the experiment are probative."[17] The requirement is at its strictest when the experiment expressly seeks to replicate the event in question to show that things could (or could not) have happened as alleged.[18] But even in these case-specific experiments, differences between the experimental and actual conditions that only could make it harder for the experiment to be favorable to the proponent should be no obstacle to admission.[19] Furthermore, an event can never be perfectly reenacted or simulated. There are too many details to keep track of, and some defy precise recreation. For example, the human agent in the happening to which the experiment pertains may be deceased, the vehicle may be destroyed, the surrounding circumstances may be known only vaguely, or the process of duplicating what actually happened may be too

---

1061, 1065–66 (4th Cir. 1977); Barnes v. Gen. Motors Corp., 547 F.2d at 277; Tunnell v. Ford Motor Co., 330 F. Supp. 2d 731, 746 (W.D. Va. 2004) (testing inadmissible "because Ford has not provided sufficient data from the restraints control module in the crashed vehicles to ascertain whether the change in velocity (Delta-V) in the crash test is the same as that in the Athey vehicle"); Robinson v. Morrison, 272 Ala. 552, 133 So. 2d 230, 235 (1961) (visibility); Hightower v. Alley, 132 Mont. 349, 318 P.2d 243, 247 (1957) (experiment to measure time required to walk a given distance rejected where plaintiff's counsel, who was 11 years younger than plaintiff, did the walking); Enghlin v. Pittsburg County Ry. Co., 1934 OK 466, 169 Okla. 106, 36 P.2d 32, 37 (1934) (experiment to find maximum speed of streetcar approaching intersection).

[17]Hermreck v. State, 956 P.2d 335, 339 (Wyo. 1998) (holding admissible an experiment using a ten-year-old girl on a 20-inch bicycle to determine how long it would take a seven-year-old boy on a 16-inch; bicycle to go from a standing start at the side of the road to the place where defendant's truck struck the bicycle), quoted in State v. Martin, 182 Vt. 377, 2007 VT 96, 944 A.2d 867, 879 (2007) (upholding, for lack of sufficient similarity and excessive impact, the exclusion of a "dramatic and vivid" videotape of a re-enactment offered to show how a hybrid sailboat might have capsized).

[18]State v. Martin, 182 Vt. 377, 2007 VT 96, 944 A.2d 867, 879 (2007) (exclusion of expert's re-enactment of the capsizing of a hybrid sailboat-motorboat was within the trial court's discretion to balance prejudice against probative value).

[19]People v. Spencer, 58 Cal. App. 197, 208 P. 380, 393 (3d Dist. 1922) (audibility test); Downing v. Metropolitan Life Ins. Co., 314 Ill. App. 222, 41 N.E.2d 297 (3d Dist. 1941) (using larger men than deceased to see whether deceased could have reached gun and shot himself); cf. State v. Boyer, 406 So. 2d 143 (La. 1981) (failure to simulate sound of falling rain not fatal in test showing that gunshot would have been more audible than telephone).

dangerous.[20] Consequently, although the similarity formula is sometimes overrigidly applied,[21] most courts recognize that the requirement is a relative one.[22] If enough of the obviously important factors are duplicated in the experiment, and if the failure to control other possibly relevant variables is justified, the court may conclude that the experiment is sufficiently enlightening that it should come into evidence.[23] This determination typically is subject to review only for an abuse of discretion.[24]

---

[20]*But see* Louisville Gas & Elec. Co. v. Duncan, 235 Ky. 613, 31 S.W.2d 915 (1929) (superintendent persuaded a miner to place himself in the same position as another miner who had been electrocuted).

[21]Some courts evince a distinct distaste for experimental evidence. Navajo Freight Lines v. Mahaffy, 174 F.2d 305, 310 (10th Cir. 1949) ("Evidence of this kind should be received with caution, and only when it is obvious to the court, from the nature of the experiments, that the jury will be enlightened rather than confused. In many instances, a slight change in the conditions under which the experiment is made will so distort the result as to wholly destroy its value as evidence, and make it harmful rather than helpful."). This aversion would be appropriate if experiments were generally of little or no probative value and strongly prejudicial. Compare supra §§ 186 to 194 (character evidence). More plausibly, the distrust of experimental evidence can be explained by the fact that many attorneys feel more comfortable with historical evidence based on personal recollections. However, there is no inherent reason that the average trial lawyer could not be equally skilled at discerning and elucidating for the jury any "slight changes" that would "wholly destroy" a defective proof by experiment. Rayner v. Stauffer Chemical Co., 120 Ariz. 328, 585 P.2d 1240, 1245 (Ct. App. Div. 1 1978) ("appellants were given ample opportunity to cross-examine the appellee's experts on these tests in order to illustrate any dissimilarities in conditions").

[22]Ramseyer v. General Motors Corp., 417 F.2d 859, 864 (8th Cir. 1969) ("Perfect identity between experimental and actual conditions is neither attainable nor required. . . . Dissimilarities affect the weight of the evidence, not admissibility"); U.S. v. Metzger, 778 F.2d 1195, 1204 (6th Cir. 1985) ("the substantially similar standard is a flexible one which . . . does not require that all variables be controlled"); Lever Bros. Co. v. Atlas Assur. Co., 131 F.2d 770, 777 (C.C.A. 7th Cir. 1942) (" 'Substantial similarity' . . . is a relative term . . . . There are no hard and fast rules."); Jackson v. Fletcher, 647 F.2d 1020, 1027 (10th Cir. 1981) (conditions "need not be identical but they ought to be sufficiently similar so as to provide a fair comparison"); Love v. State, 457 P.2d 622, 628 (Alaska 1969) (substantial similarity "does not require an identity of conditions but only that degree of similarity which will insure that the results of the experiment are probative."); Hansen v. Howard O. Miller, Inc., 93 Idaho 314, 460 P.2d 739 (1969) (braking experiment admissible despite differences in automobile make, weight and tire size).

[23]Patricia R. v. Sullivan, 631 P.2d 91, 101 (Alaska 1981) ("Of course, it can be argued that a 10-inch scrap of fiberglass wall insulation is not a fair substitute for a child in a blanket [who burned her face on a heater], but that goes more to the weight than the admissibility of the test."); Bowden v. State, 297 Ark. 160, 761 S.W.2d 148 (1988) (visibility test); Butts v. U.S., 822 A.2d 407, 414–15 (D.C. 2003) (that "the mannequin used in the study was

On the other hand, the similarity requirement either is not applied or is highly diluted when the pretrial experiment does not purport to replicate the essential features of a particular happening.[25] There are many perfectly acceptable experiments of this nature. For example, if one party contends that certain acts or omissions could not produce—under any circumstances—the result in question, then the other party may conduct an experiment to falsify this hypothesis. Of course, the closer the experiment is to the conditions that actually pertained, the more useful the experiment will be, but merely refuting the opposing party's sweeping claim may be sufficiently valuable to make the evidence admissible.[26]

---

of a lighter complexion than Mr. Tucker, that there was no same-lane traffic factored into the experiment, and that the street light above the point of impact was lit during the experiment were 'fertile field for cross-examination' rather than grounds for exclusion" in that "[t]he study was conducted at night, while it was raining, on a wet roadway, in the same model car as the one appellant was driving, traveling at the same speed as appellant, with a mannequin dressed in dark clothing" and "the dissimilarities are of the type that could easily be, and in fact were, explained to the jury"); State v. Ritt, 599 N.W.2d 802, 812 (Minn. 1999) ("No event can be perfectly reenacted however, and dissimilarities that are neither material nor misleading do not bar admission of experimental evidence"); Erickson's Dairy Products Co. v. Northwest Baker Ice Machine Co., 165 Or. 553, 109 P.2d 53, 55 (1941) (experiment to determine whether wallboard might have caught fire from welding operation using section of wallboard not involved in the fire); Maskrey v. Volkswagenwerk Aktiengesellschaft, 125 Wis. 2d 145, 370 N.W.2d 815, 825 (Ct. App. 1985) (differences in demonstration of automobile collision to show design defect not severe, given demonstration's purpose of illustrating problem with design).

[24]Hall v. General Motors Corp., 647 F.2d 175, 180 (D.C. Cir. 1980) ("The trial judge has broad leeway . . .

her finding will not be upset unless it is clearly erroneous"); Barnes v. General Motors Corp., 547 F.2d 275 (5th Cir. 1977) (admission held to be an abuse of discretion); Wagner v. International Harvester Co., 611 F.2d 224, 232–33 (8th Cir. 1979); Derr v. Safeway Stores, Inc., 404 F.2d 634, 639 (10th Cir. 1968) ("The trial court is, of course, the first and best judge whether conditions of the experiment are sufficiently similar and enlightening to render the testimony based thereon admissible. And we must not disturb the court's ruling on these critical issues unless we are convinced it is clearly wrong."); State v. Lindsey, 284 N.W.2d 368, 374 (Minn. 1979) (requiring a "clear showing of abuse"); Schmidt v. Plains Elec., Inc., 281 N.W.2d 794, 800–01 (N.D. 1979).

[25]Pandit v. American Honda Motor Co., Inc., 82 F.3d 376 (10th Cir. 1996) (relying on limiting instructions to this effect).

[26]Chambers v. Silver, 103 Cal. App. 2d 633, 230 P.2d 146 (2d Dist. 1951) (where defendant claimed that he lost control because main leaf in spring at front wheel broke when wheel crossed a two inch deposit of soil on road, it was error to exclude experiment in which another vehicle with same suspension system was driven over 2 × 4 boards at 45–50 m.p.h.); State v. Don, 318 N.W.2d 801, 805 (Iowa 1982) (police experiment showing how long it took to drive from one place to another admissible to demonstrate

Similarly, the proponent may offer to prove that something was not the cause of the actionable result by means of an experiment showing that some other agent can bring about the same result.[27] For example, when homeowners claimed in *Coon v. Utah Construction Co.*[28] that vibrations from defendant's heavy trucks on an adjacent highway enlarged cracks in the foundation and masonry walls, the construction company commissioned tests of the level of vibrations. The vibrations in the house were no greater when the company's trucks went by than when other traffic did—and a person walking on the floor caused much greater vibration.

Finally, the experiment may be introduced solely to illustrate or demonstrate[29] a scientific principle[30] or empirical finding[31] that

---

that even if evidence in support of alibi defense were believed, defendant still would have had opportunity to commit the crime).

[27]*See also* Szeliga v. General Motors Corp., 728 F.2d 566 (1st Cir. 1984) (demonstration that nondefective car wheel can be torn off axle from high speed impact with concrete block); Lincoln v. Taunton Copper Mfg. Co., 91 Mass. 181, 191, 9 Allen 181, 1864 WL 3442 (1864) (detecting copper in grasses not exposed to contamination from defendant's mill); 2 Wigmore, Evidence § 448 (Chadbourn rev. 1979).

[28]Coon v. Utah Const. Co., 119 Utah 446, 228 P.2d 997 (1951).

[29]In part, the distinction between a simulation of the events in question and a demonstration of a general principle or finding turns on whether the jury is likely to perceive the "demonstration" as a reenactment. *See* Muth v. Ford Motor Co., 461 F.3d 557, 566 (5th Cir. 2006) (upholding "[t]he district court['s rejection of] Ford's demonstration as not quite similar enough, yet that same demonstration too closely resembles the disputed accident to effectively present abstract principles without misleading the jury."); Gladhill v. General Motors Corp., 743 F.2d 1049, 1051 (4th Cir. 1984) (defendant's experiment went beyond "a demonstration to illustrate

a principle" and was held to stricter standard of similarity).

[30]Muth v. Ford Motor Co., 461 F.3d 557 at 556 ("When the demonstrative evidence is offered only as an illustration of general scientific principles, not as a reenactment of disputed events, it need not pass the substantial similarity test."); Gilbert v. Cosco Inc., 989 F.2d 399, 402 (10th Cir. 1993) ("experiments which purport to recreate an accident must be conducted under conditions similar to that accident, while experiments which demonstrate general principles used in forming an expert's opinion are not required to adhere strictly to the conditions of the accident"); Brandt v. French, 638 F.2d 209, 212–13 (10th Cir. 1981) ("mechanical principles relative to . . . how a motorcycle leans when it turns"); Harkins v. Ford Motor Co., 437 F.2d 276, 278 (3d Cir. 1970) (no need to show similarity where demonstrations with other automobiles showed "general principles of physics universal in their application").

[31]Slakan v. Porter, 737 F.2d 368, 378 (4th Cir. 1984) (in civil rights action for injuries to prisoner caused by guards using high pressure hoses, videotape to show force exerted by hose accurately depicted force); Abernathy v. Superior Hardwoods, Inc., 704 F.2d 963 (7th Cir. 1983) (holding admissible defendant's film

a jury, perhaps with the aid of an expert witness,[32] can apply to the specifics of the case.[33] Thus, experiments showing general properties of materials are admitted without confining the experiments to the conditions surrounding the litigated situation. Most of these analyses are referred to as tests rather than experiments. When this label is attached, the question becomes one, not of similarity, but of authentication—making sure that the right material was tested and that it underwent no essential alterations before testing. With all these limited-purpose experiments, the issue, as always, is whether, on balance, the evidence will assist the jury.

At a conceptual level, the "substantial similarity" standard is

---

depicting how logs were unloaded, but sound track properly excluded because microphone not positioned where plaintiff had been); Ramseyer v. General Motors Corp., 417 F.2d 859 (8th Cir. 1969) (experiment to show normal wear and tear on automobile component); Patricia R. v. Sullivan, 631 P.2d 91, 98–101 (Alaska 1981) (tests to determine how hot the surfaces of a heater would get and whether safety device would operate); Rankin v. Com., 327 S.W.3d 492, 498–99 (Ky. 2010) (film of two-year-old brother of a deceased and physically abused baby admissible not as a re-enactment, but only to show that the brother was unable to lift a teddy bear (filled with sand to weigh as much as the baby) out of a car seat admissible to refute defendant's claim that he had found the baby out of the car seat in which he had left her, with the two-year-old kneeling on baby's neck); C. F. Church Division of American Radiator & Standard Sanitary Corp. v. Golden, 1967 OK 130, 429 P.2d 771, 775 (Okla. 1967) (flammability of cellulose nitrate, a compound used in product); Horn v. Elgin Warehouse Co., 96 Or. 403, 190 P. 151 (1920) (in action for breach of warranty that wheat was Red Chaff, evidence that the wheat germinated to produce Red Chaff was admissible without any showing of similarity in planting and growing conditions); Nordstrom v. White Metal Rolling & Stamping Corp., 75 Wash. 2d 629, 453 P.2d 619, 627 (1969) (testing ladder in various positions with various weights

to see when it would tip over was admissible not "to show how the accident happened, but to show how it could have happened"). Cases in which an expert testifies to laboratory experiments designed to reveal the conditions under which eyewitness testimony is unreliable also fall in this category. See infra § 206.

[32]Millers' Nat. Ins. Co., Chicago, Ill. v. Wichita Flour Mills Co., 257 F.2d 93, 99 (10th Cir. 1958) (physics principles applicable to dust explosions).

[33]Gilbert v. Cosco Inc., 989 F.2d 399, 402 (10th Cir. 1993) ("experiments which purport to recreate an accident must be conducted under conditions similar to that accident, while experiments which demonstrate general principles used in forming an expert's opinion are not required to adhere strictly to the conditions of the accident."); Midwestern Wholesale Drug, Inc. v. Gas Service Co., 442 F.2d 663, 665 (10th Cir. 1971) (experiments with another heater properly admitted "to render intelligible the expert testimony regarding the normal operation of such heaters"); Rankin v. Commonwealth, 327 S.W.3d at 498–99 ("If, on the other hand, the experiment is not meant to simulate what happened, but rather to demonstrate some general principle bearing on what could or what was likely to have happened, then the similarity between the experimental and the actual conditions need not be as strong.").

somewhat frustrating. Its value lies in calling attention to the possible effect of differences on the implications of an experiment for the situation at bar. However, the requisite degree of similarity is not always obvious. One could say that when experiments reveal properties or traits that clearly apply under a wide range of conditions, substantial similarity is present even if the conditions are quite different. After all, there is little point in controlling for irrelevant conditions, and if physical theory indicates that the gross differences are superficial and inconsequential, the circumstances are similar in the relevant respects. More generally, whenever the marginal benefits of a more refined experiment do not exceed the marginal costs and the experiment is probative, the substantial-similarity requirement should be deemed satisfied.

Although some opinions adopt such an approach to finding substantial similarity, others treat the requirement as stating a preference for duplicating conditions to the greatest extent feasible. Yet, many useful experiments fall short of this Procrustean demand, and the courts that speak in these terms usually do not exclude an experiment just because a slightly more fastidious one could have been conducted. One device that they use to achieve a sensible result is to accept experiments elucidating "properties" as falling outside the rule demanding maximum similarity.[34] Nevertheless, these cases rarely provide an analysis of what makes the experimental findings pertain to general properties or traits and why a more detailed simulation is unnecessary. For instance, in *Council v. Duprel*,[35] the Supreme Court of Mississippi held an experiment with herbicides admissible, because it "was not an effort to duplicate the conditions existing on appellant's farm" but merely an attempt "to establish the fact that 2,4-D is far more destructive to cotton than 2,4,5-T." Of course, the question for the jury was whether 2,4-D was more destructive on appellant's farm, and an experiment could have been designed to control for possible differences in soil conditions, humidity, and other variables. But if the herbicidal quality of the

---

[34]Walden v. Department of Transp., 27 P.3d 297, 306 (Alaska 2001) (because "a purpose of [the] experiment was to demonstrate the "traits and capacities" of Willow sand—namely, the effect of Willow sand on the coefficient of friction of the road—the test conditions need not be identical to the conditions of [the] accident"); Palleson v. Jewell Co-op. Elevator, 219 N.W.2d 8, 15–16 (Iowa 1974) (laboratory experiment to simulate events leading to explosion of gas burner admissible despite objections as to dissimilarities because it showed "general traits and capacities of materials" and "principles developed from certain demonstrated phenomena," namely, how a leaf fragment allegedly left in device during installation would cause gas to leak and how clearing the line in the manner purportedly done would have removed the leaf).

[35]Council v. Duprel, 250 Miss. 269, 165 So. 2d 134 (1964).

chemical is largely independent of these variables, it can be considered a general property, and controlling for those variables would have been of little value. Thus, deciding when an experiment is acceptable as an investigation of a "property" as opposed to a recreation of the conditions of the accident involves the same inquiry as deciding when the experimental conditions are substantially similar to the ones of interest.

In short, whether the experiment is an overt effort at recreation or a simple study of general properties, the core question is whether matching the variables that are different would make the experiment so much more revealing as to be worth the additional effort and expense. Focusing directly on marginal costs and benefits gives some definition to the substantial-similarity test; indeed, it makes that language superfluous.

Some courts are less receptive to experiments commissioned for a specific lawsuit than to those undertaken solely to obtain scientific knowledge of greater generality.[36] The latter have the advantage of being untainted by any interest in the litigation.[37] Of course, scientists rarely are devoid of self-interest or biases, but the process of exposing one's work to the scrutiny of the scientific community through publication acts as an important check. This has led many courts to emphasize the importance of "peer review,"[38] a trend that gained considerable momentum following the Supreme Court's reference in *Daubert v. Merrell Dow Pharmaceuticals*,[39] to "peer review" as a consideration in ascertaining the admissibility of scientific evidence.[40]

But many of the case-specific experiments that are the subject of this section do not lend themselves to publication in scholarly

---

[36]*E.g.*, Brock v. Merrell Dow Pharmaceuticals, Inc., 874 F.2d 307, 313 (5th Cir. 1989) ("courts must . . . be extremely skeptical of medical and other scientific evidence that has not been subjected to thorough peer-review"); Foster v. Agri-Chem, Inc., 235 Or. 570, 385 P.2d 184 (1963) (agricultural experiment station's tests of the effect of fertilizer on wheat yields). *See generally* Kaye et al., The New Wigmore, A Treatise on Evidence: Expert Evidence § 7.5.2 (2d ed. 2011).

[37]Foster v. Agri-Chem, Inc., 235 Or. 570, 385 P.2d 184 (1963) ("greater latitude should be shown in admitting" experiments conducted for the sole purpose of obtaining scientific knowledge . . . because this type of evidence

is free from the taint of interest or bias that might accompany the usual 'experiment' ").

[38]*E.g.*, Richardson by Richardson v. Richardson-Merrell, Inc., 857 F.2d 823 (D.C. Cir. 1988) (unpublished analysis inadequate to support expert's opinion that the drug Bendectin is a human teratogen).

[39]Daubert v. Merrell Dow Pharmaceuticals, Inc., 509 U.S. 579, 113 S. Ct. 2786, 125 L. Ed. 2d 469 (1993) (discussed infra § 203).

[40]For a description of the nature of "peer review," see Kaye et al., The New Wigmore, A Treatise on Evidence: Expert Evidence § 7.3.2(b) (2d ed. 2011).

journals. Instead, courts must look to other indicia of reliability.[41] Because such post hoc inquiries can be difficult to undertake, it might be more fruitful to consider procedures to improve the design and implementation of case-specific experiments before they are conducted. Consideration might be given to excluding experiments unless the adversary has had reasonable notice, an opportunity to make suggestions, and to be present during the experiment.[42] Also worthy of consideration is appointment by the court of an impartial person to conduct or supervise an experiment.[43] Such prophylactic procedures could lead to findings that would invite much less in the way of time-consuming or distracting attack and defense at trial.

## § 203 Admissibility and weight

To deal effectively with scientific evidence, attorneys must know more than the rules of evidence. They must know something of the scientific principles as well. While they can rely on suitably chosen experts for advice about the more arcane points, they must have a sufficient grasp of the field to see what is essential

---

[41]The opinions in Kumho Tire Co., Ltd. v. Carmichael, 526 U.S. 137, 119 S. Ct. 1167, 143 L. Ed. 2d 238 (1999), underscore the need to establish reliability when the testimony about the experiment comes from an expert. *See* Hoffman, If the Glove Don't Fit, Update the Glove: The Unplanned Obsolescence of the Substantial Similarity Standard for Experimental Evidence, 86 Neb. L. Rev. 633 (2008).

[42]*See* Fortunato v. Ford Motor Co., 464 F.2d 962, 966 (2d Cir. 1972) (dictum that [t]est results should not even be admissible as evidence, unless made by a qualified, independent expert or unless the opposing party has the opportunity to participate in the test."). Under present practice, lack of notice and opportunity to be present are not grounds for rejection, but they may be argued on weight. U.S. v. Love, 482 F.2d 213, 218–19 (5th Cir. 1973) (no Sixth Amendment right to have defense expert present for chemical tests); Burg v. Chicago, R.I. & Pac. Ry. Co., 90 Iowa 106, 57 N.W. 680, 683 (1894) (visibility test). The recommendation offered here would allow rejection of experimental evidence on these

grounds in appropriate circumstances to encourage better designed experiments and to obviate objections that could have been raised in advance. The proposal would not apply to routine laboratory tests, but would cover experiments initiated *post litem motam* for the purpose of litigation.

[43]A notable example appeared in the course of the grand jury investigation of the White House's involvement in the Watergate break-in in 1974. A panel of six court-appointed experts agreeable to the Watergate Special Prosecutor and the White House conducted extensive tests to determine the cause of a notorious 18.5 minute gap on a subpoenaed tape recording of a conversation between President Nixon and an aide that took place shortly after the break-in. The experts' report made it plain that the gap consisted of intentional erasures made after the tape had been subpoenaed. The grand jury concluded that only a handful of people could have been responsible for these erasures, but it never secured sufficient evidence to prosecute any of these individuals. Watergate Special Prosecution Force, U.S. Dep't of Justice, Report 53 (1975).

and what is unnecessary detail and verbiage if they are to develop or counteract the evidence most effectively. In this chapter, we cannot explore in any depth the vast body of knowledge that comes into play in the forensic applications of science and medicine. Only a superficial sampling of a few areas will be attempted. We shall focus on some of the problems that can arise in making measurements and in interpreting data. Sections 204 through 207 deal with laboratory, clinical, or field tests (organized somewhat arbitrarily by scientific discipline) in which statistical analysis of the data does not play a major role. Sections 208 through 211 concern studies in which statistical analyses are prominent. In the remainder of this section, we discuss some general points concerning the admissibility of all such evidence and the weight that it should receive.[1]

Most of the case law centers on the threshold question of admissibility. The principles of relevancy outlined in Chapter 16 are as applicable to scientific evidence as to any other kind, and the doctrines governing all expert testimony discussed in Chapter 3 operate here as well. The screening of scientific evidence under these general principles can be described as a relevancy-helpfulness review.[2] However, many courts apply a more specialized rule for admissibility when expert witnesses are called to testify about scientific tests or findings. Two approaches are dominant—general acceptance and scientific soundness. Under the former, the proponent must show that the scientific community agrees that the principles or techniques on which the expert relies are capable of producing accurate information and conclusions. Under the latter standard, general acceptance remains an important consideration, but the court must consider other factors to decide for itself whether the expert's methodology is scientifically valid. Both the general-acceptance and the scientific-soundness tests require a binary determination. Evidence either possesses the necessary quality and is admissible (subject to the other rules of evidence), or it lacks the essential quality and is inadmissible. In contrast, a third approach—the relevancy-plus standard—considers the degree of general accep-

---

[Section 203]

[1]For more detailed treatments of scientific evidence, see Faigman et al., Modern Scientific Evidence: The Law and Science of Expert Testimony (2011–2012 ed.) (five volumes, with chapters by scientists); Giannelli & Imwinkelried, Scientific Evidence (4th ed.2007) (two volumes); Kaye et al., The New Wigmore, A Treatise on Evidence: Expert Evidence (2d ed. 2011).

[2]Kaye et al., The New Wigmore, A Treatise on Evidence: Expert Evidence § 6.2 (2d ed. 2011).

tance, the extent of scientific soundness, and still other factors in evaluating probative value.[3]

The notion of a special rule for scientific evidence originated in 1923 in *Frye v. United States*.[4] Frye was a murder prosecution in which the trial court rebuffed defendant's effort to introduce results of a "systolic blood pressure test," a forerunner of the polygraph. On appeal, the defendant relied on the traditional rule governing expert testimony, but the Court of Appeals for the District of Columbia, without explanation or precedent, superimposed a new standard:

> Just when a scientific principle or discovery crosses the line between the experimental and demonstrable stages is difficult to define. Somewhere in this twilight zone the evidential force of the principle must be recognized, and while courts will go a long way in admitting expert testimony deduced from a well-recognized scientific principle or discovery, the thing from which the deduction is made must be sufficiently established to have gained general acceptance in the particular field in which it belongs.[5]

The opinion did not state clearly whether "the thing" that needed "to have gained general acceptance" was the link between conscious insincerity and changes in blood pressure or the ability of an expert to measure and interpret the changes, or both. The court concluded, however, that the deception test lacked the requisite "standing and scientific recognition among physiological and psychological authorities."[6]

Many courts adopted the *Frye* standard in the ensuing years with scant discussion.[7] The theories or tests that have fallen prey

---

[3]On the distinction between relevance and probative value, see supra § 185. The line between the scientific-soundness standard and the relevancy analysis is perhaps less clear than we have suggested. If soundness only means that there is some minimal scientific basis for scientific testimony, then it merely screens out speculative testimony that lacks sufficient probative value to be admissible in light of the potential for prejudice, confusion, and consumption of time.

[4]Frye v. U.S., 293 F. 1013, 34 A.L.R. 145 (App. D.C. 1923).

[5]Frye, 293 Fed. at 1014.

[6]293 Fed. at 1014. Years after the conviction, another person confessed to the murder. Wicker, The Polygraphic Truth Test and the Law of Evidence, 22 Tenn. L. Rev. 711, 715 (1953). *But see* Starrs, "A Still Life Watercolor": Frye v. United States, 27 J. Forensic Sci. 684, 690 (1982) (stating that claims of Frye's innocence are baseless).

[7]Kaminski v. State, 63 So. 2d 339, 340 (Fla. 1952); Boeche v. State, 151 Neb. 368, 37 N.W.2d 593, 597 (1949). Once adopted, the standard was applied selectively. *See* Reed v. State, 283 Md. 374, 391 A.2d 364, 403 (1978) (dissenting opinion complaining that *Frye* was not applied in leading cases admitting expert testimony based on fingerprints, ballistics, intoxication tests, and X-rays); Giannelli, The Admissibility of Novel Scientific Evidence, 80 Colum. L. Rev. 1197, 1219–21 (1980). It was applied consistently only in polygraph cases. *See*

to its influence include polygraphy,[8] graphology,[9] hypnotic and drug induced testimony,[10] voice stress analysis,[11] voice spectrograms,[12] various forms of spectroscopy or inferences from the spectra,[13] infrared sensing of aircraft,[14] retesting of breath samples for alcohol content,[15] computer simulations of the movements of bodies in accidents,[16] psychological profiles of battered women and child abusers,[17] post traumatic stress disorder as indicating rape,[18] effect of "weapon focus" on eyewitness identification,[19] penile plethysmography as indicating sexual deviancy,[20] therapy to recover repressed memories,[21] astronomical calculations,[22] ear prints,[23] blood-group typing,[24] and DNA testing.[25] In the jurisdictions that follow *Frye*, the proponent of the evidence must prove general acceptance by surveying scientific publica-

---

McCormick, Scientific Evidence: Defining a New Approach to Admissibility, 67 Iowa L. Rev. 879, 884 (1982).

[8]See infra § 206, (B).

[9]State v. Anderson, 379 N.W.2d 70, 79 (Minn. 1985).

[10]See infra § 206, (C).

[11]See infra § 206, (B).

[12]See infra § 207.

[13]U.S. v. Brown, 557 F.2d 541, 556–57 (6th Cir. 1977) (ion microprobe mass spectroscopy as applied to hair samples); Clemons v. State, 392 Md. 339, 896 A.2d 1059 (2006) (analysis of the elemental composition of bullets to infer their origin); People v. Roraback, 242 A.D.2d 400, 662 N.Y.S.2d 327, 331 (3d Dep't 1997) (Fourier Transform Infrared Spectrophotometer to determine origin of cement samples).

[14]U.S. v. Kilgus, 571 F.2d 508, 510 (9th Cir. 1978) (customs officer tried to use military forward looking infrared tracking system to distinguish the aircraft he had previously followed from others of the same type).

[15]Com. v. Neal, 392 Mass. 1, 464 N.E.2d 1356, 1364–65 (1984).

[16]State v. Sipin, 130 Wash. App. 403, 123 P.3d 862 (Div. 1 2005).

[17]See infra § 206, (D).

[18]See infra § 206, (D).

[19]People v. LeGrand, 8 N.Y.3d 449, 835 N.Y.S.2d 523, 867 N.E.2d 374, 376 (2007).

[20]People v. John W., 185 Cal. App. 3d 801, 229 Cal. Rptr. 783 (1st Dist. 1986); Billips v. Com., 274 Va. 805, 652 S.E.2d 99 (2007) (holding that even in at sentencing, it was error to introduce plethysmograph test when the state did not show it was generally accepted).

[21]Franklin v. Stevenson, 1999 UT 61, 987 P.2d 22 (Utah 1999).

[22]U.S. v. Tranowski, 659 F.2d 750, 755–57 (7th Cir. 1981) (analysis of shadow length to determine time at which photograph taken).

[23]State v. Kunze, 97 Wash. App. 832, 988 P.2d 977 (Div. 2 1999).

[24]Huntingdon v. Crowley, 64 Cal. 2d 647, 51 Cal. Rptr. 254, 414 P.2d 382 (1966) (Kell-Cellano test not generally accepted as giving accurate results); State v. Damm, 62 S.D. 123, 252 N.W. 7, 104 A.L.R. 430 (1933) (medical sciences not shown to be sufficiently agreed on "the transmissibility of blood characteristics"), aff'd, 64 S.D. 309, 266 N.W. 667 (1936) (science found unanimously agreed); *cf.* People v. Brown, 40 Cal. 3d 512, 230 Cal. Rptr. 834, 726 P.2d 516 (1985) (multi-gel electrophoresis of dried bloodstains to identify serum proteins), rev'd on other grounds, California v. Brown, 479 U.S. 538, 107 S. Ct. 837, 93 L. Ed. 2d 934 (1987); People v. Young, 425 Mich. 470, 391 N.W.2d 270 (1986) (same).

[25]State v. Bible, 175 Ariz. 549,

tions,[26] judicial decisions,[27] or practical applications,[28] or by presenting testimony from scientists as to the attitudes of their fellow scientists.[29]

---

858 P.2d 1152 (1993) (computation of random match probability); Hayes v. State, 660 So. 2d 257 (Fla. 1995), rev'd on other grounds, 403 U.S. 443 (1971) (band-shifting correction via a monomorphic probe). See infra §§ 205 & 210.

[26]State v. Superior Court In and For Cochise County, 149 Ariz. 269, 718 P.2d 171 (1986); *cf.* Dowd v. Calabrese, 585 F. Supp. 430, 432 (D.D.C. 1984) (opinion poll of psychophysiologists on usefulness of polygraph "cannot substitute for time-honored procedures" such as "articles in learned journals, seminars, [and] acceptance at institutions of higher learning").

[27]Com. v. Mendes, 406 Mass. 201, 547 N.E.2d 35 (1989); State v. Heath, 264 Kan. 557, 957 P.2d 449, 464–65 (1998) (widespread judicial acceptance of battered child syndrome obviates need for *Frye* hearing); Lahey v. Kelly, 71 N.Y.2d 135, 524 N.Y.S.2d 30, 518 N.E.2d 924, 928–29 (1987). Unless the question of general acceptance has been thoroughly and thoughtfully litigated in the previous cases, however, reliance on judicial practice is a hollow ritual. *See* Kaye et al., The New Wigmore: A Treatise on Evidence: Expert Evidence § 6.3.3(d)(1) (2d ed. 2011); Kaye, The Double Helix and the Law of Evidence (2010).

[28]*E.g.*, Medley v. U.S., 155 F.2d 857, 859 (App. D.C. 1946) (rejecting a *Frye* challenge to an application of spectroscopy in order to identify a metal on the ground that "it is now in general use in scientific research and industrial analysis"); Hammond v. State, 569 A.2d 81 (Del. 1989) (physician's reliance on particular blood alcohol test for treatment decisions satisfies reasonable reliance standard).

[29]Jones v. U.S., 548 A.2d 35 (D.C. 1988) (discussing interplay of all these factors). Where the published indications of general acceptance are un-

equivocal and undisputed, courts have taken a kind of judicial notice of this acceptance. *E.g.*, State v. Tomanelli, 153 Conn. 365, 216 A.2d 625 (1966) (Doppler shift radar); Hayes v. State, 660 So. 2d 257 (Fla. 1995) (DNA profiling); Blackwell v. Wyeth, 408 Md. 575, 971 A.2d 235, 241 (2009) ("On occasion, the validity and reliability of a scientific technique may be so broadly and generally accepted in the scientific community that a trial court may take judicial notice of its reliability. Such is commonly the case today with regard to ballistics tests, fingerprint identification, blood tests, and the like."); State v. Armstrong, 179 W. Va. 435, 369 S.E.2d 870 (1988) (bitemarks). See infra §§ 204 & 205. Conversely, when there is legitimate debate about the acceptance or validity of a scientific test or principle, courts should not take "judicial notice." *E.g.*, People v. McKown, 226 Ill. 2d 245, 314 Ill. Dec. 742, 875 N.E.2d 1029 (2007) (holding that the trial and appellate courts erred in taking judicial notice that the horizontal gaze nystagmus test for alcohol intoxication was generally accepted). The "judicial notice" here is not the one that applies to adjudicative (case-specific) facts. State v. Branch, 243 Or. App. 309, 259 P.3d 103, 111 (2011); Strong, Language and Logic in Expert Testimony: Limiting Expert Testimony by Restrictions of Function, Reliability, and Form, 71 Or. L. Rev. 349, 367 n. 80 (1992). The underlying point is that there is no need for pretrial hearings as to the acceptance or validity of unquestionably established methods. Kaye et al., The New Wigmore: A Treatise on Evidence: Expert Evidence § 7.5.5 (2d ed. 2011).

Opinion polls also have been introduced to show the attitude of a group of scientists. *E.g.*, Benn v. U.S., 978 A.2d 1257, 1267 (D.C. 2009); Lee v. Martinez, 2004-NMSC-027, 136 N.M. 166, 96 P.3d 291 (2004). These are no substitute for the traditional

Especially since the early 1970s, however, the *Frye* standard was subjected to critical analysis, limitation, modification, and finally, outright rejection.[30] Some courts found the *Frye* standard satisfied in the teeth of expert testimony that the technique in question was too new and untried and the test results too inconclusive for court use.[31] While asserting the continuing vitality of the *Frye* standard, other courts held that general acceptance goes to the weight rather than the admissibility of the evidence.[32] Still others reasoned that the standard applies only to

---

types of evidence, which go well beyond top-of-the head remarks from individuals who may or may not be fully informed about the technique in question. Kaye et al., The New Wigmore: A Treatise on Evidence: Expert Evidence § 6.3.3(d)(4) (2d ed. 2011).

[30]McCormick, Scientific Evidence: Defining a New Approach to Admissibility, 67 Iowa L. Rev. 879, 884 (1982), details these developments. Although he concludes that the test reached its peak in a series of cases excluding voice spectrographic identifications, it has shown new vigor in subsequent cases excluding testimony of witnesses whose memories were stimulated by hypnosis (*see* infra § 206(C)) and was a major barrier to the admission of DNA profiling evidence in the first decade of that technology's forensic application. *See* Kaye, The Double Helix and the Law of Evidence (2010); infra §§ 205 & 210. The dearth of critical analysis in the first 50 years since *Frye* was decided has been attributed to the fact that most courts confronted with polygraph evidence thought it clear that the testimony should be suppressed and applied the standard with little comment. Other forms of scientific evidence tended to be accepted readily. In the past three decades or so, however, the courts have witnessed a dramatic increase in the volume and complexity of scientific evidence. *See* National Research Council Committee on Identifying the Needs of the Forensic Science Community, Strengthening Forensic Science in the United States:

A Path Forward (2009).

[31]U.S. v. Stifel, 433 F.2d 431, 438 (6th Cir. 1970) (neutron activation analysis of bomb fragments); U.S. v. Yee, 134 F.R.D. 161 (N.D. Ohio 1991) (DNA profiling admissible under general acceptance standard despite conflicting testimony about quality control, database, and effects of population structure), aff'd sub nom. U.S. v. Bonds, 12 F.3d 540 (6th Cir. 1993); Coppolino v. State, 223 So. 2d 68 (Fla. 2d DCA 1968) (test for presence of succinylcholine chloride specially developed to determine whether defendant had injected a lethal dose of this anesthetic into his wife); State v. Washington, 229 Kan. 47, 622 P.2d 986, 992 (1981) (holding that despite a biochemist's testimony on the unreliability of enzyme analysis in identifying a blood sample, the "method is sufficiently accepted as reliable by the scientific community").

[32]State v. Olivas, 77 Ariz. 118, 267 P.2d 893 (1954) (breathalyzer); People v. Marx, 54 Cal. App. 3d 100, 126 Cal. Rptr. 350 (2d Dist. 1975) (bitemark evidence); Jenkins v. State, 156 Ga. App. 387, 274 S.E.2d 618, 619 (1980) (electrophoresis with blood samples), overruled on other grounds by Herndon v. State, 232 Ga. App. 129, 499 S.E.2d 918 (1998); Com. v. Cifizzari, 397 Mass. 560, 492 N.E.2d 357, 364 (1986) (bitemark evidence); *cf.* Kramer v. U.S., 579 F. Supp. 314, 318 (D. Md. 1984) ("*Frye* is relevant in that it guides the Court in assessing the weight to accord to [the expert's] testimony").

tests for truthfulness,[33] to relatively esoteric applications of science,[34] to the "hard sciences"[35] or to very general principles or methodology rather than to the body of studies or results being applied to reach a conclusion in the case at bar.[36] Many opinions

---

[33]People v. Allweiss, 48 N.Y.2d 40, 421 N.Y.S.2d 341, 396 N.E.2d 735 (1979) (microscopic comparison of hair).

[34]Adkins v. Dirickson, 523 F. Supp. 1281, 1287 (E.D. Pa. 1981) ("tachograph [see infra § 204] operates on simple, understandable principles removed from the frontiers of science"); Ex parte Dolvin, 391 So. 2d 677, 679–80 (Ala. 1980) (odontologist's comparison of teeth in a skull with those in a photograph is a "physical comparison" rather than a scientific experiment or test); State v. Hasan, 205 Conn. 485, 534 A.2d 877 (1987) (podiatrist's determination that sneakers matched defendant's feet); Com. v. Gordon, 422 Mass. 816, 666 N.E.2d 122, 138–39 (1996) (forensic chemist's "personal observations" about the specificity of the ortho-tolidine testing for traces of blood not subject to *Frye* because her experience with the test was not "dependent on scientific theories or principles"); State v. Chiellini, 557 A.2d 1195 (R.I. 1989), overruled on other grounds by State v. Werner, 615 A.2d 1010 (R.I. 1992) (microscopic analysis and interpretation of "blood spatter pattern" not a "scientific test").

[35]*See* People v. Stoll, 49 Cal. 3d 1136, 265 Cal. Rptr. 111, 783 P.2d 698 (1989) (psychologist's opinion that defendants were not sexually deviant not subject to *Frye* standard); People v. Beckley, 434 Mich. 691, 456 N.W.2d 391 (1990) ("child sexual abuse accommodation syndrome" as explaining a child's behavior following the alleged abuse not subject to *Frye*); *see generally* Slobogin, Psychiatric Evidence in Criminal Trials: To Junk or Not to Junk?, 40 Wm. & Mary L. Rev. 1 (1998) (proposing a more sensitive framework to applying *Frye* or other tests to psychiatric testimony). For criticism of the "hard sciences" limitation, see Kaye

et al., The New Wigmore: A Treatise on Evidence: Expert Evidence ch. 8 (2d ed. 2011).

[36]U.S. v. Williams, 583 F.2d 1194, 1198 (2d Cir. 1978) (spectrographic analysis of voice admissible under traditional balancing test because "[w]e deal here with the admissibility or non-admissibility of a particular type of scientific evidence, not with the truth or falsity of an alleged scientific 'fact' or 'truth' "); Ibn-Tamas v. U. S., 407 A.2d 626, 638 (D.C. 1979) (psychologist's study of characteristics of battered women need not be generally accepted if the methodology used to study the phenomenon has general scientific acceptance); *cf.* State v. Hodges, 239 Kan. 63, 716 P.2d 563, 569 (1986) (methodology and theory underlying expert opinion about presence of battered woman syndrome, and not the application of that methodology, must be generally accepted); Douglas v. Lombardino, 236 Kan. 471, 693 P.2d 1138, 1148 (1985) (fact that a minority of experts believe that a drug is cardiotoxic not a bar to admissibility, since general acceptance is required of "new scientific tests or techniques, rather than an opinion arrived at through accepted tests and techniques"); Com. v. Cifizzari, 397 Mass. 560, 492 N.E.2d 357, 364 (1986) ("to admit bite mark evidence, including an expert opinion that no two people have the same bitemark, a foundation need not be laid that such evidence has gained acceptance in the scientific community. What must be established is the reliability of the procedures involved, such as X-rays, models, and photographs."); State v. Armstrong, 110 Wis. 2d 555, 329 N.W.2d 386, 393 n.14 (1983) (*Frye* pertains to phenomenon of hypnosis rather than to testimony of previously hypnotized witness).

simply ignored the standard,[37] and many others blithely equated it with a requirement of showing the accuracy and reliability of the scientific technique.[38] Finally, in the 1970s and 1980s, a strong minority of jurisdictions expressly repudiated *Frye*.[39]

The adoption of the Federal Rules of Evidence intensified the retreat from *Frye*. These rules do not explicitly distinguish between scientific and other forms of expert testimony, and they do not mention general acceptance. As originally adopted, Rule 702 majestically provided that "[i]f scientific, technical, or other specialized knowledge will assist the trier of fact to understand the evidence or to determine a fact in issue, a witness qualified as an expert by knowledge, skill, experience, training, or education,

---

[37]U.S. v. Baller, 519 F.2d 463 (4th Cir. 1975) (voice spectrograph); Brown v. Darcy, 783 F.2d 1389 (9th Cir. 1986) (polygraph tests too inaccurate and prejudicial to be admissible under Rule 702 unless opposing party stipulates to admission); People v. LaSumba, 92 Ill. App. 3d 621, 47 Ill. Dec. 202, 414 N.E.2d 1318, 1321–22 (4th Dist. 1980) (testing bloodstain for esterase-D enzyme); State v. Satterfield, 3 Kan. App. 2d 212, 592 P.2d 135, 140 (1979) (blood spattering); State v. Beachman, 189 Mont. 400, 616 P.2d 337 (1980) (rejecting polygraph evidence).

[38]U.S. v. Franks, 511 F.2d 25, 33 n.12 (6th Cir. 1975) ("We deem general acceptance as being nearly synonymous with reliability. If a scientific process is reliable, or sufficiently accurate, courts may also deem it 'generally accepted.'"), quoted in U.S. v. Distler, 671 F.2d 954, 961 (6th Cir. 1981); U.S. v. Gwaltney, 790 F.2d 1378, 1381–82 (9th Cir. 1986) ("general acceptance" proved by expert testimony as to "validity of the antibody theory" and "scientific basis underlying the immunobead assay procedure" identifying anti-sperm antibodies in defendant's semen); State v. Hurd, 86 N.J. 525, 432 A.2d 86, 91 (1981), quoting State v. Cary, 49 N.J. 343, 230 A.2d 384, 389 (1967) ("According to our most recent formulation . . ., the results of scientific tests are admissible only when they have 'sufficient scientific basis to produce uniform and reasonably reliable results

and will contribute materially to the ascertainment of truth.'"); cases cited, McCormick, Scientific Evidence: Defining a New Approach to Admissibility, 67 Iowa L. Rev. 879, at 892 n. 83 (1982).

[39]U.S. v. Downing, 753 F.2d 1224 (3d Cir. 1985) (expert testimony on eyewitness identifications); Whalen v. State, 434 A.2d 1346, 1354 (Del. 1980) (field test for semen); State v. Hall, 297 N.W.2d 80, 84–85 (Iowa 1980) (blood spatter analysis); State v. Catanese, 368 So. 2d 975, 980 (La. 1979) (general acceptance standard "is an unjustifiable obstacle to the admission of polygraph test results," but results inadmissible in criminal cases under balancing analysis); State v. Williams, 388 A.2d 500, 503–04 (Me. 1978) (voice spectrograph); State v. Williams, 4 Ohio St. 3d 53, 446 N.E.2d 444, 447–48 (1983) ("scientific nose-counting" not required for spectrogram to be admissible); State v. Brown, 297 Or. 404, 687 P.2d 751 (1984); Phillips By and Through Utah State Dept. of Social Services v. Jackson, 615 P.2d 1228, 1234–35 (Utah 1980) ("sufficient proof of reliability and an adequate explanation of the pertinent variables and potential inaccuracies" of HLA test for paternity not established in the record); Watson v. State, 64 Wis. 2d 264, 219 N.W.2d 398, 403 (1974) (conflict in scientific opinion of hair identification method a matter of credibility for the jury); Cullin v. State, 565 P.2d 445, 453–54 (Wyo. 1977).

may testify thereto. . . ." Some courts construed the omission of any direct reference to "general acceptance" as evincing a legislative intent to overturn the well-established common law requirement.[40]

Although the more convincing view is that the rules left the viability of the general acceptance standard open to further common law development,[41] in *Daubert v. Merrell Dow Pharmaceuticals*,[42] the Supreme Court determined that the federal rules "superseded" *Frye*[43] and "displaced" general acceptance as "the exclusive test for admitting expert scientific testimony."[44] Plaintiffs in *Daubert* were two young children born with missing or malformed limbs. Together with their parents, they sought damages from the maker of Bendectin, a drug approved by the Food and Drug Administration as safe and effective for the relief of nausea and vomiting during pregnancy. Plaintiffs' case foundered when they were unable to point to any published epidemiological studies concluding that Bendectin causes limb reduction defects. The district court granted summary judgment for Merrell Dow, and the Ninth Circuit Court of Appeals affirmed on the theory that under *Frye*, there could be no admissible expert testimony of causation without some peer-reviewed, published studies showing a statistically significant association between exposure to Bendectin and limb reduction defects. Having determined that *Frye* no longer governed, the Supreme Court remanded the case to the court of appeals, which adhered to its original decision on other grounds.[45]

However, the Supreme Court did not simply hold, as had the courts in a significant minority of federal and state jurisdictions, that with *Frye*'s demise, the relevancy-plus standard governs scientific expert testimony. Instead, it read into the phrase "scientific . . . knowledge" in Rule 702 a requirement of a "body of known facts or . . . ideas inferred from such facts or accepted as

---

[40]Contrasting cases are arrayed in McCormick, Scientific Evidence: Defining a New Approach to Admissibility, 67 Iowa L. Rev. 879, at 885 n. 56 (1982).

[41]Downing, 753 F.2d at 1235 ("the Federal Rules of Evidence neither incorporate it nor repudiate it"); Christophersen v. Allied-Signal Corp., 939 F.2d 1106, 1111, 1115–16 (5th Cir. 1991) (en banc); Giannelli, *Daubert*: Interpreting the Federal Rules of Evidence, 15 Cardozo L. Rev. 1999 (1994).

[42]Daubert v. Merrell Dow

Pharmaceuticals, Inc., 509 U.S. 579, 113 S. Ct. 2786, 125 L. Ed. 2d 469 (1993).

[43]Daubert, 509 U.S. at 589 n.6.

[44]Daubert, 509 U.S. at 589.

[45]Daubert v. Merrell Dow Pharmaceuticals, Inc., 43 F.3d 1311 (9th Cir. 1995) (even if unpublished epidemiological reanalyses of data used in previous studies were admissible, they would not show a substantial enough association between Bendectin and limb reduction defects to overcome a motion for summary judgment).

truths on good grounds" in accordance with "the methods and procedures of science."[46] In addition, the Court emphasized that scientific analysis must "fit" the facts of the case.[47] The Court then offered an abstract discussion of how the requirement of scientifically "good grounds" might be satisfied. It suggested inquiring into such matters as the degree to which a theory has been tested empirically, the extent to which it has been "subjected to peer review and publication," the rate of errors associated with a particular technique, and the extent of acceptance in the scientific community.[48]

*Frye*'s general-acceptance standard and *Daubert*'s scientific-soundness inquiry do not exhaust the range of "tests" for scientific evidence, and neither opinion offers any reasons for choosing among the many possibilities. Proponents of the general acceptance test argue that it assures uniformity in evidentiary rulings, that it shields juries from any tendency to treat novel scientific evidence as infallible, that it avoids complex, expensive, and time-consuming courtroom dramas, and that it insulates the adversary system from novel evidence until a pool of experts is available to evaluate it in court.[49] Most commentators agree, however, that these objectives can be met with less drastic

---

[46]Daubert, 509 U.S. at 590.

[47]509 U.S. at 591. Whether the necessary "fit" is something more than what is required under the general doctrine of the inadmissibility of irrelevant evidence (see supra § 184) is not apparent from the Court's opinion. In a later toxic tort case, the Court used language that might be employed to give additional content to "fit." In General Elec. Co. v. Joiner, 522 U.S. 136, 118 S. Ct. 512, 139 L. Ed. 2d 508 (1997), the majority opinion observed that "[a] court may conclude that there is simply too great an analytical gap between the data and the opinion proffered." Thus, proof that a chemical causes tumors in mice at very high doses might be relevant to whether the chemical is a human carcinogen at low dosages (see supra § 185), but the extrapolation from across species and dosages might constitute "too great an analytical gap" to provide the requisite "fit." However, such fit is implicit in the concept of validity. *See* Kaye et al., The New Wigmore, A Treatise on Evidence: Expert Evidence (2d ed. 2011).

[48]509 U.S. at 594. For a detailed analysis of these factors, see Kaye et al., The New Wigmore, A Treatise on Evidence: Expert Evidence § 6.3.2 (2d ed. 2011). In Kumho Tire Co., Ltd. v. Carmichael, 526 U.S. 137, 119 S. Ct. 1167, 143 L. Ed. 2d 238 (1999), the Supreme Court wrote that "*Daubert*'s general holding—setting forth the trial judge's general 'gatekeeping' obligation—applies not only to testimony based on 'scientific' knowledge, but also to testimony based on 'technical' and 'other specialized' knowledge." 526 U.S. at 141. The Court further concluded "that a trial court may consider one or more of the more specific factors that *Daubert* mentioned when doing so will help determine that testimony's reliability." 526 U.S. at 141. However, the *Kumho* Court cautioned that "the test of reliability is 'flexible,' and *Daubert*'s list of specific factors neither necessarily nor exclusively applies to all experts or in every case." 526 U.S. at 141.

[49]U.S. v. Addison, 498 F.2d 741 (D.C. Cir. 1974) (voice spectrogram), questioned in U.S. v. McDaniel, 538

constraints on the admissibility of scientific evidence. In addition to the *Daubert* approach of looking directly to reliability or validity rather than to the presence or absence of general acceptance, it has been suggested that a panel of scientists rather than judges screen new developments for validity or acceptance,[50] that a substantial acceptance test be substituted for the general acceptance standard,[51] that scientific evidence be admitted freely, coupled with testimony of an expert appointed by the court if it finds that the testimony would be subject to "substantial doubt in peer review by the scientific community,"[52] and that the traditional standards of relevancy and the need for expertise—or a somewhat more detailed relevancy-plus analysis[53]—should govern.[54]

The last method for evaluating the admissibility of scientific evidence is the most appealing. General scientific acceptance is a proper condition for taking judicial notice of scientific facts, but it is not suitable as a determinant of the admissibility of scientific evidence. Any relevant conclusions supported by a qualified

---

F.2d 408, 413 (D.C. Cir. 1976); U.S. v. Amaral, 488 F.2d 1148 (9th Cir. 1973) (psychology of eyewitness testimony); State ex rel. Collins v. Superior Court, In and For Maricopa County, 132 Ariz. 180, 644 P.2d 1266 (1982); People v. Leahy, 8 Cal. 4th 587, 34 Cal. Rptr. 2d 663, 882 P.2d 321 (1994) (horizontal gaze nystagmus test for alcohol intoxication); Reed v. State, 283 Md. 374, 391 A.2d 364, 370–72 (1978) (voice spectrogram); State v. Cavallo, 88 N.J. 508, 443 A.2d 1020 (1982).

[50]*See, e.g.,* Kantrowitz, Controlling Technology Democratically, 63 Am. Sci. 505 (1975); Martin, The Proposed "Science Court," 75 Mich. L. Rev. 1058 (1977). For criticism of the idea, see Bazelon, Coping with Technology Through the Legal Process, 62 Cornell L. Rev. 817, 827–28 (1977); Sofaer, The Science Court: Unscientific and Unsound, 9 Envtl. L. Rev. 1 (1978).

[51]*See* U.S. v. Gould, 741 F.2d 45, 49 (4th Cir. 1984) (compulsive gambling disorder as establishing insanity defense not substantially accepted); U.S. v. Baller, 519 F.2d 463, 465 (4th Cir. 1975); *cf.* Latin et al., Remote Sensing Evidence and Environmental Law, 64 Cal. L. Rev. 1300, 1380 (1976)

(reasonable acceptance standard); Minton, Note, Expert Testimony Based on Novel Scientific Techniques: Admissibility Under the Federal Rules of Evidence, 48 Geo. Wash. L. Rev. 774, 787 (1980) (preponderance of experts standard).

[52]Elliot, Toward Incentive-Based Procedure: Three Approaches for Regulating Scientific Evidence, 69 B.U. L. Rev. 487, 507 (1989).

[53]McCormick, Scientific Evidence: Defining a New Approach to Admissibility, 67 Iowa L. Rev. 879 (1982); Strong, Questions Affecting the Admissibility of Scientific Evidence, 1970 U. Ill. L.F. 1 (advocating some special rules for applying the general principles).

[54]Berger, A Relevancy Approach to Novel Scientific Evidence, 115 F.R.D. 89, 89 to 91 (1987) (admissible when probative value outweighs prejudice, time-consumption, etc.); Imwinkelried, The Standard for Admitting Scientific Evidence: A Critique from the Perspective of Juror Psychology, 28 Vill. L. Rev. 554 (1983) (questioning need for special rule for scientific evidence); Trautman, Logical or Legal Relevancy, 5 Vand. L. Rev. 385, 395–96 (1952).

expert witness[55] should be received unless there are distinct reasons for exclusion. These reasons are the familiar ones of prejudicing or misleading the jury or consuming undue amounts of time.[56]

This traditional approach to the evidence does not make scientific testimony admissible on the say-so of a single expert.[57] Nei-

---

[55]With increasing specialization and overlapping of fields of expertise, the question of whether an expert is properly qualified can be difficult. A recurring problem is the tendency of laboratory technicians or test equipment operators to testify to inferences or probability calculations based on their test results. *See, e.g.,* People v. Kelly, 17 Cal. 3d 24, 130 Cal. Rptr. 144, 549 P.2d 1240, 1250 (1976) ("Nash has an impressive list of credentials in the field of voice print analysis. However, these qualifications are those of a technician and law enforcement officer, not a scientist."); State v. Priester, 301 S.C. 165, 391 S.E.2d 227 (1990) (error for technician to testify to intoxicating effect of blood alcohol level). Even a scientist eminently qualified in one area may not be knowledgeable in another. *See* Kaye et al., The New Wigmore, A Treatise on Evidence: Expert Evidence § 3.2 (2d ed. 2011). Generally, cross-examination should expose such deficiencies.

[56]See generally supra § 185. In this context (and in other areas involving expert testimony) a dominant danger is that the jury will give the opinions or theories of some experts more credence than they deserve. History is full of theories, propounded and accepted by many honest, reputable and persuasive experts, that cannot withstand empirical testing. *E.g.,* Goodwin & Goodwin, The Tomato Effect: Rejection of Highly Efficacious Therapies, 251 J.A.M.A. 2387 (1984); Lasagna, Consensus Among Experts: The Unholy Grail, 19 Persp. Biol. & Med. 537 (1976); Risinger et al., Exorcism of Ignorance as a Proxy for Rational Knowledge: The Lessons of Handwriting Identification "Expertise," 137 U. Pa. L. Rev. 731

(1989). Sometimes, juries are appropriately skeptical of these theories, but especially when the expertise involves matters outside common experience, their injection can retard rather than advance the inquiry. Where expert tests and procedures are amenable to rigorous validity testing (like the double-blind testing of drugs for efficacy), and where external proficiency testing of the experts utilizing these techniques is feasible, such testing should be a prerequisite to admissibility; and, if the testimony is allowed, the jury should be informed of the results of the validity and proficiency tests. *But see* Imwinkelried, Coming to Grips with Scientific Research in *Daubert's* "Brave New World": The Courts' Need to Appreciate the Difference Between Validity and Proficiency Studies, 61 Brook. L. Rev. 1247 (1995) (arguing that proficiency studies are inadmissible character evidence).

[57]See State v. Catanese, 368 So. 2d 975, 981 (La. 1979) (polygraph); State v. Philbrick, 436 A.2d 844, 861 (Me. 1981) (error to allow detective to testify to reconstructing sequences of shootings from blood spatters in car when pathologist could not determine sequence, there was no literature on using spatterings to deduce a sequence, and detective's knowledge was limited to what he learned in a 3-week training course at "blood-spatter school"); State v. Boutilier, 426 A.2d 876, 879 (Me. 1981) (state trooper's use of an inapposite formula (which he claimed to have checked by empirical testing) to calculate speed from skid marks should have been excluded, since there was no testimony that "the methodology had sufficient scientific basis, or recognition to vouch for its reliability," but "[w]e do not intimate that 'general scientific acceptance' is a

ther does it go to the other extreme of insisting on a fully formed scientific consensus. It permits general scientific opinion of both underlying principles and particular applications to be considered in evaluating the worth of the testimony.[58] In so treating the yeas and nays of the members of a scientific discipline as but one indication of the validity, accuracy, and reliability of the technique, the traditional balancing method focuses the court's attention where it belongs—on the actual usefulness of the evidence in light of the full record developed on the power of the scientific test.

Furthermore, unlike the general acceptance and scientific soundness standards, the relevancy approach is sensitive to the perceived degree of prejudice and unnecessary expense associated with the scientific technique in issue. Not every scrap of scientific evidence carries with it an aura of infallibility. Some methods, like bitemark identification and blood-splatter analysis, are demonstrable in the courtroom. Where the methods involve principles and procedures that are comprehensible to a jury, the concerns over the evidence exerting undue influence and inducing a battle of the experts have less force.[59] On the other hand, when the nature of the technique is more esoteric, as with some types of statistical analyses and biochemical tests, when subjective judgments are misleadingly presented as hard science, or when the inferences from the scientific evidence sweep broadly or cut deeply into sensitive areas, a stronger showing of probative value should be required.[60] This could result in the categorical exclusion of certain types of evidence, such as polygraphic lie detection and statements made while under the influence of a "truth" serum. By attending to such considerations, the rigor of the requisite foundation can be adjusted to suit the nature of the evidence and the context in which it is offered.[61]

Using a legal standard that recognizes that scientific validity

---

sine qua non of a proposed method of determining facts; what we do regard as requisite . . . is a showing of sufficient reliability."); Merrell Dow Pharmaceuticals, Inc. v. Havner, 953 S.W.2d 706, 712 (Tex. 1997) ("it is not so simply because 'an expert says it is so'"); Phillips By and Through Utah State Dept. of Social Services v. Jackson, 615 P.2d 1228, 1234–37 (Utah 1980) (HLA tests for paternity).

[58]See McCormick, Scientific Evidence: Defining a New Approach to Admissibility, 67 Iowa L. Rev. 879 (1982).

[59]Ex parte Dolvin, 391 So. 2d 677 (Ala. 1980) ("physical comparisons" admitted); People v. Marx, 54 Cal. App. 3d 100, 126 Cal. Rptr. 350 (2d Dist. 1975) (bitemark analysis admitted); State v. Hall, 297 N.W.2d 80 (Iowa 1980) (blood spatter analysis admitted).

[60]See, e.g., People v. Collins, 68 Cal. 2d 319, 66 Cal. Rptr. 497, 438 P.2d 33 (1968) (probability calculations); State v. Catanese, 368 So. 2d 975, 981 (La. 1979) (polygraph).

[61]See Developments in the Law: Confronting the New Challenges of

and acceptance are matters of degree rather than yes-or-no judgments diminishes the severity of many of the problems that have plagued the general acceptance and scientific soundness standards. Courts in *Frye* and *Daubert* jurisdictions[62] have been forced to draw (and tempted to manipulate) an often obscure line between "scientific" evidence and other expert or lay testimony.[63] Focusing at the outset on the costs and benefits of the particular evidence makes it less crucial to decide exactly when evidence is so "scientific"[64] or "novel"[65] that the special test for novel scientific

---

Scientific Evidence, 108 Harv. L. Rev. 1481, 1498–1509 (1995) (calling attention to "functional criteria" such as those listed here).

[62]The problem is mitigated in jurisdictions that follow Kumho Tire Co., Ltd. v. Carmichael, 526 U.S. 137, 119 S. Ct. 1167, 143 L. Ed. 2d 238 (1999), in addition to *Daubert*.

[63]*See, e.g.,* Logerquist v. McVey, 196 Ariz. 470, 1 P.3d 113 (2000) (testimony as to accuracy of alleged recovered repressed memories not subject to *Frye*); Kuhn v. Sandoz Pharmaceuticals Corp., 270 Kan. 443, 14 P.3d 1170 (2000) (differential diagnosis not subject to *Frye*); State v. O'Key, 321 Or. 285, 899 P.2d 663, 674 (1995) (discussing the conflict in opinions deciding whether a policeman's observations of oscillations in the movement of an individual's eyes (nystagmus) that can occur as a result of intoxication is "scientific evidence"). *See generally* Kaye et al., The New Wigmore, A Treatise on Evidence: Expert Evidence ch. 8 (2d ed. 2011).

[64]*Compare* State v. Bresson, 51 Ohio St. 3d 123, 554 N.E.2d 1330, 1336 (1990) (the "HGN test [the Horizontal Gaze Nystagmus test performed by a police officer observing the angle on onset of oscillations of the eyeball when tracking an object moving to the side of head] cannot be compared to other scientific tests such as a polygraph examination, since no special equipment is required in its administration"), *with* People v. McKown, 226 Ill. 2d 245, 314 Ill. Dec. 742, 875 N.E.2d 1029, 1036 (2007) ("We agree with those jurisdictions that hold HGN

testing to be scientific."). As interpreted in Kumho Tire Co., Ltd. v. Carmichael, 526 U.S. 137, 119 S. Ct. 1167, 143 L. Ed. 2d 238 (1999), *Daubert* requires a special showing of reliability for all expert testimony, although the nature of the showing may vary with the subject matter.

[65]State v. Hodgson, 512 N.W.2d 95, 97 (Minn. 1994) (bitemark identification admissible despite defendant's assertion of lack of general acceptance because it "is not a novel or emerging type of scientific evidence," but is "routinely used"); Hulse v. State, Dept. of Justice, Motor Vehicle Div., 1998 MT 108, 289 Mont. 1, 961 P.2d 75, 92–93 (1998) (*Daubert* limited to novel scientific evidence, a category that does not include the horizontal gaze nystagmus test for alcohol intoxication); Com. v. Puksar, 597 Pa. 240, 951 A.2d 267, 275 (2008) ("*Frye* . . . applies only to proffered expert testimony involving novel science," not to the testimony of a forensic pathologist about the manner of death that other pathologists derided as "fantastic" and "ridiculous"). The better view is that any special test for scientific evidence applies whether the evidence is familiar or novel. The proponent of familiar scientific evidence, like the proponent of novel evidence, should be able to demonstrate soundness or general acceptance if there is a significant challenge to the evidence. *See* Kaye et al., The New Wigmore, A Treatise on Evidence: Expert Evidence § 9.3 (2d ed. 2011); Strong, Language and Logic in Expert Testimony: Limiting Expert Testimony by Restrictions of Function, Reliability, and Form, 71 Or. L. Rev.

evidence applies. Similarly, predictability is not easily attained in the face of ambiguity and disagreement as to how general the acceptance in the scientific community must be,[66] who can speak for that community,[67] and the "particular field" to which the scientific evidence belongs[68] and in which it must be accepted.[69] Although such issues arise under any effort to assess the probative value of scientific evidence, they are far less critical when a court can consider the number of fields in which a technique is used, the rigor required in those fields,[70] and the degree of its acceptance in those fields, without having to label the technique as generally accepted.[71] Finally, attending to the probative value of

---

349 (1992).

[66]U.S. v. Metzger, 778 F.2d 1195, 1204 (6th Cir. 1985) (testimony of expert with master's degree in chemistry that "numerous crime laboratories" use thin-layer chromatography to detect monomethylamine nitrate plus one paper on the subject in a professional journal establishes general acceptance).

[67]See People v. Young, 425 Mich. 470, 391 N.W.2d 270 (1986) (requiring "disinterested and impartial" witnesses, as opposed to those scientists or technicians whose "livelihood was . . . intimately connected with the new technique," to vouch for general acceptance); D.H. Kaye, Science in Evidence 85 (1997).

[68]See People v. Brown, 40 Cal. 3d 512, 230 Cal. Rptr. 834, 726 P.2d 516 (1985) (questionable whether testimony of police chemist that method for identifying proteins in dried blood was "an accepted practice in the field of forensic chemistry and are utilized by large numbers of law enforcement agencies" would have been established "acceptance by impartial scientists in field of forensic chemistry"), rev'd on other grounds, California v. Brown, 479 U.S. 538, 107 S. Ct. 837, 93 L. Ed. 2d 934 (1987); Com. v. Lykus, 367 Mass. 191, 327 N.E.2d 671, 677 (1975) (general acceptance of voice spectrogram need only be shown among those who would be expected to be familiar with its use); People v. Young, 425 Mich. 470, 391 N.W.2d 270 (1986) (because "[t]he community of scientists

having direct empirical experience with electrophoresis of evidentiary bloodstains does not seem 'sufficiently large,' " the relevant group is geneticists and other "scientists having experience with electrophoresis"). State v. Dirk, 364 N.W.2d 117 (S.D. 1985) (Frye test met by expert's testimony that technique used in forensic laboratories).

[69]1 Faigman, et al., Modern Scientific Evidence § 1:5 (2011–2012 ed.) ("The general acceptance test thus degenerates into a process of deciding whose noses to count. . . . because the pertinent field can be so easily manipulated, the test by itself provides courts with little protection against shoddy science.").

[70]1 Modern Scientific Evidence § 1:5 (2011–2012 ed.) ("Different fields have widely differing standards.").

[71]In theory, Daubert can be applied to reach the same results as the broader relevancy analysis proposed here. Indeed, some courts have seen the opinion as confirming the relevancy approach applied in opinions predating Daubert. E.g., State v. O'Key, 321 Or. 285, 899 P.2d 663 (1995). Certainly, in rejecting general acceptance as the touchstone of admissibility, the Daubert opinion encourages more flexible treatment of scientific evidence. As introduced by the Court, the scientific soundness threshold is arguably quite low—it could be read to exclude only "subjective belief or unsupported speculation" and "inference[s] or assertion[s] [not] derived by

conclusions as well as methodologies softens the brittle distinction between the two that can be awkward to apply in *Frye* jurisdictions (and in *Daubert* jurisdictions that have not softened the distinction by later decisions[72] or amendments[73] to their rules of evidence).[74]

Of course, it might be argued that the relevancy-plus approach is no less amorphous and manipulable than the general acceptance and scientific soundness standards.[75] There is truth in this charge, but courts and commentators have identified the varied considerations that determine the balance of probative value and

---

the scientific method." 509 U.S. at 590. Evidence that clears this low hurdle then would be assessed under the usual helpfulness and relevancy standards. *See* 509 U.S. at 591 & 595. This framework would be equivalent to starting with the relevancy standard. *See* State v. Porter, 241 Conn. 57, 698 A.2d 739 (1997) (adhering to exclusionary rule for polygraph evidence even assuming that polygraphic lie detection satisfies *Daubert*). In practice, however, courts applying *Daubert* can set the soundness bar considerably higher, and it is not hard to present the "scientific method" as demanding rigorous validation and extensive publication. *See* Foster & Huber, Judging Science: Scientific Knowledge and the Federal Courts (1997).

[72]*See* General Elec. Co. v. Joiner, 522 U.S. 136, 118 S. Ct. 512, 139 L. Ed. 2d 508 (1997) ("conclusions and methodology are not entirely distinct from one another").

[73]After the Supreme Court elaborated on *Daubert* in *General Electric v. Joiner* and *Kumho Tire Co. v. Carmichael*, Federal Rule of Evidence 703 was amended to provide not only that "the testimony is the product of reliable principles and methods" (*Daubert's* scientific soundness standard), but also that "the testimony is based on sufficient facts or data" and "the expert has reliably applied the principles and methods to the facts of the case."

[74]For efforts to separate methodology from conclusion for the purpose of applying a screening test for scien-

tific evidence, see 1 Faigman, et al., Modern Scientific Evidence § 1:18 (2011–2012 ed.); Kaye et al., The New Wigmore, A Treatise on Evidence: Expert Evidence § 9.2 (2d ed. 2011); Kaye, The Dynamics of *Daubert*: Methodology, Conclusions, and Fit in Statistical and Econometric Studies, 87 Va. L. Rev. 1933 (2001).

[75]*See* Kreiling, Scientific Evidence: Toward Providing the Lay Trier with the Comprehensible and Reliable Evidence Necessary to Meet the Goals of the Rules of Evidence, 32 Ariz. L. Rev. 915, 925–27 (1990). It has been said that the choice of any of these specific legal formulae matters less than the manner in which they are applied. Kaye et al., The New Wigmore, A Treatise on Evidence: Expert Evidence §§ 7.3.2 & 7.4.2 (2d ed. 2011). There is some empirical evidence to confirm this. *See* Edward K. Cheng & Albert H. Yoon, Does *Frye* or *Daubert* Matter? A Study of Scientific Admissibility Standards, 91 Va. L. Rev. 471 (2005) (study of tort cases finding that the change to *Daubert* had no significant impact on the rate at which defense counsel removed cases to federal courts); Jennifer L. Groscup et al., The Effects of *Daubert* on the Admissibility of Expert Testimony in State and Federal Criminal Cases, 8 Psychol. Pub. Pol'y & L. 339, 342, 344 (2002) (analyzing 372 federal and 321 state criminal appellate decisions from 1988 to 1999 and concluding that the adoption of a *Daubert* standard had no statistically significant effect on the rate at which scientific evidence was admitted in state or federal courts).

prejudice of scientific evidence.[76] Applying these to various types of scientific evidence offers a more honest and sensitive basis for making admissibility decisions than the more cramped tests that have characterized this area of the law of evidence.

Whatever the standard for admissibility may be in a particular jurisdiction, arguments as to the weight that the jury should give to the evidence will be important. Indeed, skills in building cases with admissible scientific evidence and demolishing these same structures have become valuable as the forensic applications of science have grown more commonplace.[77] Attention to possible infirmities in the collection and analysis of data can cut superficially impressive scientific evidence down to its proper size. To begin with, one might consider the process by which the forensic scientist makes raw measurements.[78] Does subjective judgment play any role? If so, do different experts tend to find very different measured values, so that the measurement process is unreliable?[79] Are the variations randomly distributed about some true mean, or are they biased in one direction or another, so that even if they are reliable, their accuracy is suspect? Then there are problems of interpretation. Is the quantity being measured the real item of interest, or at least a suitable proxy for that vari-

---

[76]See State v. O'Key, 321 Or. 285, 899 P.2d 663 (1995); U.S. v. Downing, 753 F.2d 1224 (3d Cir. 1985). Building on various state and federal opinions, one former state supreme court justice outlined the following factors for consideration in weighing probative value against possible prejudice:

(1) the potential error rate in using the technique, (2) the existence and maintenance of standards governing its use, (3) presence of safeguards in the characteristics of the technique, (4) analogy to other scientific techniques whose results are admissible, (5) the extent to which the technique has been accepted by scientists in the field involved, (6) the nature and breadth of the inference adduced, (7) the clarity and simplicity with which the technique can be described and its results explained, (8) the extent to which the basic data are verifiable by the court and jury, (9) the availability of other experts to test and evaluate the technique, (10) the probative significance of the evidence in the circumstances of the case, and (11) the care with which the technique was employed in the case.

McCormick, Scientific Evidence: Defining a New Approach to Admissibility, 67 Iowa L. Rev. 879, 911–12 (1982) (footnotes omitted). See also Trautman, Logical or Legal Relevancy, 5 Vand. L. Rev. 385 (1952).

[77]See Imwinkelried, The Methods of Attacking Scientific Evidence (4th ed. 2004).

[78]"Measurement," in this context, includes qualitative observations of the presence or absence of some characteristic or property.

[79]Here, the term "unreliable" is used in its technical sense, to refer to the reproducibility of results. Instruments (including human observers) that generate substantially different values each time a measurement of the same variable is made under the same conditions are said to be unreliable. See Kaye et al., The New Wigmore, A Treatise on Evidence: Expert Evidence § 12.7 (2d ed. 2011). In many situations, individually unreliable measurements can be combined to yield more reliable summary statistics, as when the scores of several judges are averaged in athletic competitions.

able? In brief, considering the probable errors introduced at each stage of the scientific analysis, is the final result likely to be reliable, accurate, and meaningful?[80] The remainder of this chapter describes particular scientific (and pseudo-scientific) tests and studies both with regard to these weight-related factors and to the validity of the reasoning of the scientific experts who bring their specialized knowledge and training to the courtroom.

Before turning to particular areas and types of scientific evidence, however, one additional feature of scientific evidence deserves mention. The fundamental problem of scientific expert testimony is that judges and juries are compelled to evaluate scientific claims with little or no prior knowledge of the field. We call on scientists because they have knowledge that legal decision makers lack, then we ask those decision makers to evaluate intelligently that mysterious knowledge. How can they perform this task without becoming "amateur scientists"?[81] Procedures permitting and encouraging professional scientists to contribute their expertise to screening and assessing scientific evidence can help resolve this conundrum. In particular, requiring adequate pretrial disclosure of the witness's scientific reasoning in written form for review by other scientists could be valuable.[82] And, a

---

[80]The term "validity" often is used to denote these last two qualities. That is, a valid technique or measuring device returns reasonably accurate values of the variables that the scientist purports to be measuring. A valid method or measure is reliable, but not all reliable (consistent) measures are valid. *See* Kaye et al., The New Wigmore, A Treatise on Evidence: Expert Evidence § 12.7 (2d ed. 2011). Although courts commonly use the term "reliability" to mean "that which can be relied upon" for some purpose such as establishing probable cause or crediting a hearsay statement, when experts testify as to "reliability," it may be well to keep this distinction in mind.

[81]Daubert, 509 U.S. at 601 (Rehnquist, C.J., concurring in part and dissenting in part).

[82]For a proposal to provide pretrial, scientific peer review of the methodology that a scientific expert proposes to use in court, see Nesson & Demers, Gatekeeping: An Enhanced

Foundational Approach to Determining the Admissibility of Scientific Evidence, 49 Hastings L.J. 335 (1998). Other writing calling for more meaningful disclosure and pretrial review includes NIST Expert Working Group on Human Factors in Latent Print Analysis, Latent Print Examination and Human Factors: Improving the Practice through a Systems Approach (Kaye ed. 2012); National Research Council Committee on Identifying the Needs of the Forensic Science Community, Strengthening Forensic Science in the United States: A Path Forward 186 (2009); Giannelli, Wrongful Convictions and Forensic Science: The Need to Regulate Crime Labs, 86 N. Car. L. Rev. 163 (2007); Kaye & Freedman, Reference Guide on Statistics, in Reference Manual on Scientific Evidence 83 (Federal Judicial Center ed., 2d ed. 2000); Havard, Expert Scientific Evidence Under the Adversarial System: A Travesty of Justice?, 32 J. Forensic Sci. Soc'y 225 (1992); Lord Woolf, Access to Justice: Final Report (1996), summarized in 5

century of calls for court-appointed, testifying experts or expert advisers or managers may have had some effect.[83]

## II. PARTICULAR TESTS

### § 204 Physics and electronics: Speed detection and recording

Forensic applications of physics and electronics include motor vehicle accident reconstruction, analysis of tape recordings, and detecting and recording speed and other aspects of the movements of vehicles.[1] This section surveys the evidentiary features of speed detection and recording devices.

*(A) Mechanical Timing Devices.*

The branch of classical mechanics that deals with the motion of objects is called kinematics. The physicist defines average velocity as the distance travelled along a given direction in a specified time period divided by the length of this time period. Speed is the absolute value of velocity. (The difference between speed and velocity is that the latter includes information as to the direction of travel, while the former merely states how fast the object moved.) Acceleration is the change in velocity for a unit of time divided by the time elapsed. It states how quickly an object is speeding up, slowing down, or changing direction. Measuring such quantities without some mechanical aid is difficult to do accurately, although

---

Expert Evidence 71 (1997).

[83]General Elec. Co. v. Joiner, 522 U.S. 136, 118 S. Ct. 512, 139 L. Ed. 2d 508 (1997) (Breyer, J., concurring); Gross, Expert Evidence, 1991 Wis. L. Rev. 1113; Hand, Historical and Practical Considerations Regarding Expert Testimony, 15 Harv. L. Rev. 40 (1901). For discussions of the procedures and the powers of courts to seek scientific assistance directly, see Kaye et al., The New Wigmore, A Treatise on Evidence: Expert Evidence §§ 11.2 & 11.3 (2d ed. 2011); Ellen E. Deason, Court-appointed Expert Witnesses: Scientific Positivism Meets Bias and Deference, 77 Or. L. Rev. 59 (1998); Note, Improving Judicial Gatekeeping: Technical Advisors and Scientific Evidence, 110 Harv. L. Rev. 941 (1997). *But see* Cheng, Independent Judicial Research in the *Daubert* Age, 56 Duke L.J. 1263, 1270–71 (2007). Commentators also have called for reforms in the system that produces

scientific evidence in criminal cases— mandatory accreditation of forensic laboratories, periodic proficiency testing of analysts, enforceable codes of ethics, funding for basic research, and the formal separation of crime laboratories from police and prosecutorial offices. A leading example is National Research Council Committee on Identifying the Needs of the Forensic Science Community, Strengthening Forensic Science in the United States: A Path Forward (2009).

**[Section 204]**

[1]Here, as elsewhere in this chapter, the assignment of particular techniques to a scientific discipline such as physics, chemistry, biology, medicine, or psychology is inevitably somewhat arbitrary, since these disciplines overlap. The "criminalistics" techniques mentioned infra § 207 are drawn from most of these fields.

it can be easy enough to ascertain whether one vehicle is moving faster or slower than another.[2] A more elaborate application of these principles of kinematics to the detection and conviction of traffic offenders is recorded in an English case at the turn of the century in which a constable took readings from a watch with a second hand.[3] A progression of more sophisticated timing mechanisms followed, from the stopwatch,[4] as employed by a stationary observer[5] or by observers in aircraft,[6] to the Visual Average Speed Computer and Record (VASCAR).[7] When a suspected violator's vehicle reaches a clearly marked point, such as an intersection, the operator activates the timer. When the police car reaches the same point, the operator activates a mechanism for recording the distance the police car travels as measured by its odometer. When the target vehicle reaches a second clearly marked point down the road, the police officer shuts off the timer, and when the police car arrives at this second point, he turns off the distance switch. The computer divides the measured distance by the measured time elapsed and displays this average speed.[8]

---

[2]Speedometer readings from the chase car or motorcycle have long been admitted. City of Spokane v. Knight, 96 Wash. 403, 165 P. 105 (1917). Some courts allow trained police officers to testify as experts in estimating speed visually. *E.g.*, State v. Chambers, 241 Neb. 66, 486 N.W.2d 481 (1992); Barberton v. Jenney, 126 Ohio St. 3d 5, 2010-Ohio-2420, 929 N.E.2d 1047 (2010). *But see* State v. Ostdiek, 351 S.W.3d 758, 768–69 (Mo. Ct. App. W.D. 2011) (ambiguous testimony of excess speed was not sufficient to support a verdict for speeding).

[3]Gorham v. Brice, (1802) 18 T.L.R. 424 (K.B. Div.).

[4]If the accuracy of the stopwatch has not "been verified through an independent test for accuracy," however, the speed calculation may be inadmissible. State v. Chambers, 233 Neb. 235, 444 N.W.2d 667 (1989). The stopwatch method can be refined by laying sensitive tubes across the roadway at an appropriate distance apart and using the signals generated by passing cars to start and stop a timer. City of

Webster Groves v. Quick, 323 S.W.2d 386 (Mo. Ct. App. 1959); Proof, by radar or other mechanical or electronic devices, of violation of speed regulations, 47 A.L.R.3d 822. Photographic methods, including stroboscopic analysis, also have been used to secure convictions. Com. v. Buxton, 205 Mass. 49, 91 N.E. 128 (1910).

[5]State v. Cook, 194 Kan. 495, 399 P.2d 835 (1965).

[6]Myren, Measurement of Motor Vehicle Ground Speed from Aircraft, 52 J. Crim. L., Criminology & Police Sci. 213 (1961); Automobiles: speeding prosecution based on observation from aircraft, 27 A.L.R.3d 1446.

[7]Moenssens et al., Scientific Evidence in Civil and Criminal Cases § 4.05 (4th ed. 1995); Proof, by radar or other mechanical or electronic devices, of violation of speed regulations, 47 A.L.R.3d 822.

[8]Elementary calculus establishes that an average velocity cannot exceed the largest instantaneous velocity during the averaging period.

Initially, the courts required expert testimony concerning the principles and operation of the VASCAR.[9] However, the kinematic principles, which date back to the time of Galileo and Newton, are so well established that they, like the ability of an electronic computer to divide two numbers, easily can be the subject of a kind of judicial notice.[10] The more serious issue, which goes to the weight and (in an extreme case, the admissibility) of the evidence, is the accuracy of the device under operational conditions. Errors can arise from a poorly calibrated odometer, from turning on and off the switches at the wrong times, and so on. A foundation indicating that the device is properly calibrated and the operator well trained in its use is usually required.[11]

### (B) Tachographs and Data Recorders.

A speed detector and recorder not so closely tied to police work is the tachograph. It consists of a tachometer and a recording mechanism that furnishes, over time, the speed and mileage of the vehicle to which it is attached.[12] It is used on trains, trucks and busses. Its readings have been admitted in civil and criminal

---

[9]People v. Leatherbarrow, 69 Misc. 2d 563, 330 N.Y.S.2d 676 (County Ct. 1972); People v. Persons, 60 Misc. 2d 803, 303 N.Y.S.2d 728 (Spec. Sess. 1969).

[10]State v. Finkle, 128 N.J. Super. 199, 319 A.2d 733 (App. Div. 1974); State v. Frankenthal, 113 Wis. 2d 269, 335 N.W.2d 890, 891 n.1 (Ct. App. 1983) ("the VASCAR is simply a modern, scientific invention used to speed up and simplify a task which a person of average intelligence could perform"). The requirements for judicial notice of "adjudicative facts" do not apply to "legislative facts" that cut across cases. State v. Branch, 243 Or. App. 309, 259 P.3d 103, 111 (2011); Strong, Language and Logic in Expert Testimony: Limiting Expert Testimony by Restrictions of Function, Reliability, and Form, 71 Or. L. Rev. 349, 367 n. 80 (1992).

[11]See Com. v. Vishneski, 380 Pa. Super. 495, 552 A.2d 297 (1989) (applying statutory standards for calibration); State v. Chambers, 241 Neb. 66, 486 N.W.2d 481 (1992) (police officer's explanation of calibration not sufficiently coherent to show accuracy). Compare Tiffin v. Whitmer, 32 Ohio Misc. 169, 60 Ohio Op. 2d 367, 61 Ohio Op. 2d 291, 290 N.E.2d 198 (Mun. Ct. 1970) (evidence established accuracy of system and proper training and expertise of operator), and State v. Frankenthal, 113 Wis. 2d 269, 335 N.W.2d 890, 890–91 (Ct. App. 1983) (VASCAR adequately verified with "a certified stopwatch at a distance premeasured by a certified steel tape" and with "a certified speedometer"), with City of St. Louis v. Martin, 548 S.W.2d 622 (Mo. Ct. App. 1977) (evidence insufficient to support conviction where police verified accuracy of VASCAR with a stopwatch but never verified accuracy of the stopwatch); see also Presumption and burden of proof of accuracy of scientific and mechanical instruments for measuring speed, temperature, time, and the like, 21 A.L.R.2d 1200.

[12]See generally Conrad, The Tachograph as Evidence of Speed, 8 Wayne L. Rev. 287 (1962); Cooney, Comment, The Evidentiary Use of Tachograph Charts in Civil Litigation, 92 Dick. L. Rev. 483 (1988); Admissibility in Evidence, in Civil Action, of Tachograph or Similar Paper or Tape Recording of Speed of Motor Vehicle, Railroad Locomotive, or the Like, 18 A.L.R.6th 613.

cases, on a showing the particular device works accurately and an identification of which portion of the record generated pertains to the events in issue.[13]

A more advanced kinematic recording instrument is the aircraft flight recorder.[14] It records time, airspeed, altitude, attitude (orientation of axes relative to some reference line or plane, such as the horizon), magnetic heading, vertical acceleration, and other instrument readings. These records can be extremely valuable in analyzing aircraft crashes. Admissibility turns on evidence of authenticity and expert testimony to explain how the machine operates and to interpret the marks on the chart.[15] Similar devices, known as Event Data Recorders, are installed in trains and some commercial and private trucks, buses, and automobiles.[16] To date, no doubts have been raised about their general acceptance or validity for recording kinematic information immediately before crashes.[17]

### (C) Radar.

Radar equipment provides another means of measuring

---

[13]*Compare* Bell v. Kroger Co., 230 Ark. 384, 323 S.W.2d 424 (1959) (erroneously admitted where device had not been checked since its installation in truck three years before accident and the graph conflicted sharply with the truck driver's testimony as to the number of stops he had made); Malinowski v. United Parcel Service, Inc., 792 A.2d 50, 54 (R.I. 2002) (holding that speed recording from tachograph taken from truck involved in an accident was properly excluded where there were indications that the device was not functioning correctly); *and* Texas & N. O. R. Co. v. Lemke, 365 S.W.2d 148 (Tex. 1963) (tape inadmissible without linking the indication of acceleration to any specific location), *with* Adkins v. Dirickson, 523 F. Supp. 1281 (E.D. Pa. 1981) (device is sturdy and reliable and argument over accuracy only goes to weight of the evidence); Hall v. Dexter Gas Co., 277 Ala. 360, 170 So. 2d 796 (1964) (admissible); Whitton v. Central of Ga. Ry. Co., 89 Ga. App. 304, 79 S.E.2d 331 (1953) (admissible in train-automobile collision case); Thompson v. Chicago & E. I. R. Co., 32 Ill. App. 2d 397, 178 N.E.2d 151 (1st Dist. 1961) (train speed tape admissible).

[14]*See generally* DeLory, Flight Recording as Evidence in Civil Litigation, 9 Val. U. L. Rev. 321 (1974).

[15]*See* American Airlines, Inc. v. U.S., 418 F.2d 180 (5th Cir. 1969).

[16]Glancy, Retrieving Black Box Evidence From Vehicles: Uses and Abuses of Vehicle Data Recorder Evidence in Criminal Trials, Champion, May, 2009, at 12.

[17]Matos v. State, 899 So. 2d 403 (Fla. 4th DCA 2005) (*Frye* satisfied); Com. v. Zimmermann, 70 Mass. App. Ct. 357, 873 N.E.2d 1215, 1221 (2007) (holding that reliability under *Daubert* had been adequately established and observing that "Although as yet there are not many decisions on the admissibility of EDR data, most seem to support admission."); State v. Shabazz, 400 N.J. Super. 203, 946 A.2d 626 (2005) (general acceptance and reliability established); Askland, The Double Edged Sword That Is the Event Data Recorder, 25 Temp. J. Sci. Tech. & Envtl. L. 1, 3 (2006) ("EDRs have consistently satisfied the 'general acceptance' standard in *Frye* hearings."); Comment, Every Time You Brake, Every Turn You Make–I'll Be Watching You: Protecting Driver Privacy in

velocity.[18] Military or aircraft pulse-type radar uses the velocity-distance-time relationships previously discussed. The radar antenna transmits microwave radiation in pulses. The equipment measures the time it takes for a pulse to reach the target and for its echo to return. Since the radiation travels at a known speed (the speed of light), this fixes the distance to the target. The changes in the distances as determined from the travel times of later pulses permit the target's velocity to be computed. Police radar relies on different principles.[19] In its simplest form, the radar speedmeter used by police agencies transmits a continuous beam of microwaves of uniform frequency, detects the reflected signals, and measures the difference in frequency between the transmitted and reflected beams. It converts this frequency difference into the speed of the object that has reflected the radiation. This conversion is based on the Doppler effect. Electromagnetic radiation coming from an object moving relative to the observer is shifted to a higher frequency if the object is approaching, and to a lower frequency if the object is receding.[20] For the range of velocities of interest in traffic court, the extent of

---

Event Data Recorder Information, 2006 Wis. L. Rev. 135, 145 ("Unsurprisingly, because EDR data is similar in nature to other computerized data that is routinely collected, courts have held that EDR data meets evidentiary standards."); Admissibility of Evidence Taken from Vehicular Event Data Recorders (EDR), Sensing Diagnostic Modules (SDM), or "Black Boxes", 40 A.L.R.6th 595. *But see* People v. Muscarnera, 16 Misc. 3d 622, 842 N.Y.S.2d 241, 252 (Dist. Ct. 2007) (granting a *Frye* hearing on the admissibility of results of automobile black box data).

[18]*See generally* 2 Wigmore, Evidence §§ 417b, 665a (Chadbourn rev. 1979); National Highway Traffic Safety Administration, U.S. Department of Transportation, Traffic Radar: Is it Reliable? (1980); Kopper, The Scientific Reliability of Radar Speedmeters, 33 N.C. L. Rev. 343 (1955); McCarter, Legal Aspects of Police Radar, 16 Clev.-Mar. L. Rev. 455 (1967); Trichter & Patterson, Police Radar 1980: Has the Black Box Lost its Magic?, 11 St. Mary's L.J. 829 (1980); Comment, 48 Fordham L. Rev. 1138 (1980).

[19]Some courts rely on the impressive precision of military and air traffic control radar to conclude that police radar meets the general acceptance test discussed supra § 203. *E.g.*, Com. v. Whynaught, 377 Mass. 14, 384 N.E.2d 1212 (1979). Although the conclusion is correct, this reasoning overlooks the substantial differences in design, construction and theory of operation of Doppler-effect radar and pulsed radar.

[20]The Austrian physicist Christian Johann Doppler demonstrated and described the frequency shift of sound waves due to relative motion. A common illustration of the phenomenon is the heightened pitch of the whistle on an approaching train, followed by the lowered pitch as the train recedes. Perhaps this explains why the court in People v. Walker, 199 Colo. 475, 610 P.2d 496, 498 (1980), made the scientific blunder of suggesting that Doppler effect radar involves sound waves. Physicists now appreciate that all electromagnetic radiation and other forms of energy transmission exhibit the Doppler effect. Landsberg & Evans, Mathematical Cosmol-

this Doppler shift is directly proportional to the relative speed.[21] When the radar set is at rest relative to the ground, it therefore gives the speed of the vehicle being tracked.

A more complicated version of the Doppler shift detector processes signals received at two distinct frequencies. This refinement allows the unit to be used conveniently in a moving vehicle. The shift in frequency of the beam as reflected off the road surface gives the speed of the police vehicle. The shift in frequency as reflected off the target vehicle gives its speed relative to the police car. In effect, circuitry in the radar unit adds the relative speed to the police car's speed to yield the ground speed of the target.

Most of the early cases admitting radar evidence of speeding involved testimony showing not only that the target car had been identified[22] and that a qualified operator had obtained the reading from a properly functioning device, but also explaining the Doppler effect, its application in the radar speedmeter, and the scientific acceptance of this method of measuring speed.[23] Within a few years, the courts began to take a type of judicial notice of the underlying scientific principles and the capability of the device to measure speed with tolerable accuracy.[24] Expert testimony on these subjects is no longer essential.[25]

The question of what must be proved to establish that the

---

ogy 154–58 (1st ed. 2d printing 1979).

[21]Hoyle, Astronomy and Cosmology: A Modern Course 237 (1975) (proportionality is a non-relativistic approximation); Kopper, The Scientific Reliability of Radar Speedmeters, 33 N.C. L. Rev. 343 (1955); McCarter, Legal Aspects of Police Radar, 16 Clev.-Mar. L. Rev. 455, 346–50 (1967).

[22]Honeycutt v. Com., 408 S.W.2d 421 (Ky. 1966) (one vehicle adequately singled out of a group); Com. v. Bartley, 411 Pa. 286, 191 A.2d 673 (1963) (one vehicle in a line of five adequately identified).

[23]State v. Moffitt, 48 Del. 210, 100 A.2d 778 (Super. Ct. 1953); Hardaway v. State, 202 Tenn. 94, 302 S.W.2d 351 (1957) (dictum); cf. People v. Persons, 60 Misc. 2d 803, 303 N.Y.S.2d 728 (Spec. Sess. 1969) (VASCAR).

[24]State v. Tailo, 70 Haw. 580, 779 P.2d 11 (1989); State v. Dantonio, 18 N.J. 570, 115 A.2d 35 (1955); State v. Hanson, 85 Wis. 2d 233, 270 N.W.2d 212 (1978) (moving radar); Proof, by

radar or other mechanical or electronic devices, of violation of speed regulations, 47 A.L.R.3d 822.

[25]State v. Spence, 418 So. 2d 583, 587 (La. 1982); Com. v. Whynaught, 377 Mass. 14, 384 N.E.2d 1212 (1979); State v. Calvert, 682 S.W.2d 474, 477 (Mo. 1984); People v. Knight, 72 N.Y.2d 481, 534 N.Y.S.2d 353, 530 N.E.2d 1273 (1988) (moving radar); Mills v. State, 99 S.W.3d 200, 202 (Tex. App. Fort Worth 2002); City of Bellevue v. Lightfoot, 75 Wash. App. 214, 877 P.2d 247 (Div. 1 1994) State v. Hanson, 85 Wis. 2d 233, 270 N.W.2d 212 (1978) (moving radar); Proof, by radar or other mechanical or electronic devices, of violation of speed regulations, 47 A.L.R.3d 822. Many states enacted statutes to this effect. Hardaway v. State, 207 Ga. App. 150, 427 S.E.2d 527 (1993); Fitzwater v. State, 57 Md. App. 274, 469 A.2d 909 (1984); State v. Chambers, 241 Neb. 66, 486 N.W.2d 481 (1992); Sweeny v. Com., 211 Va. 668, 179 S.E.2d 509 (1971).

specific instrument was operating accurately has provoked more controversy. Decisions range from holdings that the evidence is inadmissible without independent verification of the accuracy of the system at the time and place of the measurement[26] to holdings that lack of evidence of testing goes to the weight but not the admissibility of the results.[27] In many jurisdictions, statutes provide for admissibility and specify the requisite type of showing of accuracy.[28] Revelations that police radar units operating under field conditions may not be as reliable as had once been assumed underscore the importance of demonstrating the accuracy of the equipment.[29]

Regardless of whether the jurisdiction has a particularized rule for the extent and type of testing needed for admissibility, evi-

---

[26]People v. Walker, 199 Colo. 475, 610 P.2d 496 (1980) (inadmissible when only one tuning fork used to check receiver and that fork was not itself tested for accuracy within the last year); Com. v. Whynaught, 377 Mass. 14, 384 N.E.2d 1212 (1979) (acceptability of testing left to discretion of trial court); City of Jackson v. Langford, 648 S.W.2d 927 (Mo. Ct. App. E.D. 1983) (proof that unit was tested near time of arrest was lacking); State v. Carman, 10 Neb. App. 373, 631 N.W.2d 531, 536–37 (2001) ("no evidence [was] produced that the tuning forks used . . . to test [the] radar were in any way properly tested, calibrated, or certified as a reliable gauge of a radar unit's accuracy"); State v. Doria, 135 Vt. 341, 376 A.2d 751 (1977); Myatt v. Com., 11 Va. App. 163, 397 S.E.2d 275 (1990) (inadmissible when tested with two tuning forks, but without admissible evidence that tuning forks were accurate); State v. Hanson, 85 Wis. 2d 233, 270 N.W.2d 212 (1978); Latin et al., Remote Sensing Evidence and Environmental Law, 64 Cal. L. Rev. 1300, 1413–14 (1976); Proof, by radar or other mechanical or electronic devices, of violation of speed regulations, 47 A.L.R.3d 822; cf. State v. Gerdes, 291 Minn. 353, 191 N.W.2d 428 (1971) (conviction cannot rest entirely on radar measurement with device not externally tested).

[27]State v. Dantonio, 18 N.J. 570, 115 A.2d 35 (1955) (dictum); People v. Dusing, 5 N.Y.2d 126, 181 N.Y.S.2d 493, 155 N.E.2d 393 (1959); Proof, by radar or other mechanical or electronic devices, of violation of speed regulations, 47 A.L.R.3d 822. This seems to be the minority view. See Com. v. Whynaught, 377 Mass. 14, 384 N.E.2d 1212 (1979).

[28]The statutory requirements for verifying the accuracy of the instrument range from the general to the specific. Compare State v. Chambers, 241 Neb. 66, 486 N.W.2d 481 (1992), with Wiggins v. State, 249 Ga. 302, 290 S.E.2d 427 (1982). They may not apply, however, in cases other than speeding prosecutions. Department of Highway Safety and Motor Vehicles v. Nelson, 823 So. 2d 828, 829 (Fla. 1st DCA 2002) (testimony admissible in a prosecution under an implied consent law as opposed to a "proceeding with respect to an alleged violation of provisions of law regulating the lawful speed of vehicles") (internal quotation marks for Florida statute omitted).

[29]See N.Y. Times, Nov. 27, 1979, § C, at 1 ("Florida police clocked a . . . tree and a house moving at 28 miles an hour"); Trichter & Patterson, Police Radar 1980: Has the Black Box Lost its Magic?, 11 St. Mary's L.J. 829 (1980); Comment, 48 Fordham L. Rev. 1138 (1980).

dence pertaining to the accuracy of the reading is admissible.[30] There are many ways in which errors can creep into the system.[31] Stationary radar readings will be wrong if the transmission frequency changes, if the receiver misevaluates the frequency difference, if the radar is not held motionless, or if radiation from another source is attributed to the suspect's vehicle.[32] Moving radar, being a more complex device, has more room for error.[33] Acceleration of the patrol car, "cosine error," and "shadowing" can lead the instrument to underestimate the patrol car's speed, and hence to overstate the target vehicle's speed.[34]

Some of these sources of error can be minimized or excluded by careful operating procedures and on-site tests. These include the use of tuning forks vibrating at frequencies such that their linear motions will cause the speedmeter to register particular speeds if it is receiving properly, use of an internal, electronically activated tong for the same purpose, and simply checking that, when aimed at another police car, the radar reading corresponds with that car's speedometer reading. Of course, after a few years of use, tongs may not vibrate at the presumed frequency, an internal oscillator may need adjustment, and a car's speedometer may not be accurate. At least on the question of admissibility, however, most courts recognize that independent errors are unlikely to be identical.[35] They tend to hold that some combination of these

---

[30]Dooley v. Com., 198 Va. 32, 92 S.E.2d 348, 350 (1956) (to rebut presumption mandated by statute).

[31]For more detailed analysis than is provided here, see Moenssens et al., Scientific Evidence in Civil and Criminal Cases § 4.03 (4th ed. 1995); Goodson, Technical Shortcomings of Doppler Traffic Radar, 30 J. Forensic Sci. 1186 (1985); Trichter & Patterson, Police Radar 1980: Has the Black Box Lost its Magic?, 11 St. Mary's L.J. 829 (1980); Comment, 48 Fordham L. Rev. 1138 (1980).

[32]Myatt v. Com., 11 Va. App. 163, 397 S.E.2d 275 (1990) (error to exclude expert testimony on the last possibility).

[33]People v. Knight, 72 N.Y.2d 481, 534 N.Y.S.2d 353, 530 N.E.2d 1273 (1988).

[34]"Cosine error" can arise when the radar echo comes from a target that is not directly in front of the radar unit. It results from the fact that the Doppler shift is a function of the component of the relative velocity along the line of sight. See Comment, 48 Fordham L. Rev. 1138, 1142–43 (1980). "Shadowing" occurs when the reflection indicating the speed of the police car comes from slow moving objects rather than stationary ones. Comment, 48 Fordham L. Rev. 1138, 1143–44 (1980). Tests of police radar units for these and other errors are described in the NHTSA report, National Highway Traffic Safety Administration, U.S. Dep't of Transportation, Traffic Radar: Is it Reliable? (1980).

[35]State v. Shimon, 243 N.W.2d 571, 573 (Iowa 1976); State v. Hebert, 437 A.2d 185, 186 (Me. 1981); State v. Graham, 322 S.W.2d 188, 197 (Mo. Ct. App. 1959); State v. Kramer, 99 Wis. 2d 700, 299 N.W.2d 882, 885–86 (1981).

methods is sufficient to warrant admissibility.[36] Furthermore, a number of decisions, sometimes aided by statute, hold that tested radar readings can amount to proof beyond a reasonable doubt.[37]

### (D) Laser Pulses.

Yet another device uses a laser to generate pulses of infrared radiation about every billionth of a second.[38] Like pulse radar, this laser-based speed detection device measures the reflection times of the pulses to determine the speed of the reflecting object via the distance-time-velocity formulas. The physical principles that the device relies on are eminently sound, and the only possible ground for questioning the scientific basis of such speed measurements is whether the instrument properly implements

---

[36]State v. Shimon, 243 N.W.2d at 573 (admissible with testing by a single tuning fork and tracking of another police car whose speedometer was independently calibrated); Fitzwater v. State, 57 Md. App. 274, 469 A.2d 909 (1984) (admissible with speedometer check and testing with two tuning forks); State v. Hebert, 437 A.2d 185 (Me. 1981) (admissible with tests of receiver with two tuning forks to measure a range of speeds, internal oscillator, and tracking of another police car); State v. Calvert, 682 S.W.2d 474, 477 (Mo. 1984) (admissible when tested by two external tuning forks, an internal fork, and a certified speedometer); State v. Kramer, 99 Wis. 2d 700, 299 N.W.2d 882, 885 (1981) (two tuning forks); Comment, 48 Fordham L. Rev. 1138 (1980); Proof, by radar or other mechanical or electronic devices, of violation of speed regulations, 47 A.L.R.3d 822. State statutes and regulations also are prominent here. State v. Kincaid, 235 Neb. 89, 453 N.W.2d 738 (1990) (two external tuning fork tests and internal calibration test sufficient to satisfy statute); State v. Chambers, 233 Neb. 235, 444 N.W.2d 667 (1989) (stopwatch is not "electronic speed measurement device" subject to statutory requirements for admissibility). Most courts to consider the point hold that the external tuning forks need not be tested for accuracy. State v. Tailo, 70 Haw. 580, 779 P.2d 11 (1989).

Many of these rulings may seem odd since even when the detailed formulas for ensuring accuracy are not satisfied, the evidence almost always still meets the normal test for relevance. See supra § 185. The more exacting formulas may be justified, however, on the theory that the jury would overestimate the force of the evidence because of the aura of reliability and accuracy associated with radar and electronics. Although a jury could be educated about the different types of radar and the weaknesses of police radar, the particularized rules of testing would be the more efficient way to proceed if the incidence of erroneously high readings is large. If this error rate is in fact high, then the stringent rules serve to lay to rest many residual doubts about the evidence in a cost-effective way.

[37]See, e.g., Yolman v. State, 388 So. 2d 1038 (Fla. 1980) (upholding as constitutional a statute creating a presumption on the basis of radar evidence if the operator is certified and the equipment tested every six months by a tuning fork test); People v. Stankovich, 119 Ill. App. 2d 187, 255 N.E.2d 461 (2d Dist. 1970) (single tuning fork); Kansas City v. Hill, 442 S.W.2d 89 (Mo. Ct. App. 1969) (two tuning forks); Peterson v. State, 163 Neb. 669, 80 N.W.2d 688 (1957) (tracking another police car).

[38]See Richardson, Laser Technology in Traffic Enforcement: Better Late than Lased, 21 Colo. Law. 713 (1992).

them. After some hesitation,[39] the courts have agreed that laser devices can measure vehicular speed accurately.[40] Indeed, not only do some courts accept the general principles of laser-based speed detection, but they even dispense with hearings on the general acceptance or validity of specific instruments[41] and admit the evidence when the proponent demonstrates compliance with the manufacturer's recommendations for proper operation and calibration.[42] The better view, however, is that "[a]lthough the

---

[39]Izer v. State, 236 Ga. App. 282, 511 S.E.2d 625 (1999) (reviewing cases and declining to admit the evidence where the state made no effort to prove scientific soundness or general acceptance), superseded by statute as stated in Van Nort v. State, 250 Ga. App. 7, 550 S.E.2d 111 (2001); People v. Canulli, 341 Ill. App. 3d 361, 275 Ill. Dec. 207, 792 N.E.2d 438, 445 (4th Dist. 2003) (reversing a speeding conviction because the "trial court erred in admitting the results of the Lidar laser unit without conducting a *Frye* hearing" when "the issue of scientific acceptance of laser technology to measure the speed of vehicles has not been adequately litigated"); Hall v. State, 264 S.W.3d 346, 350 (Tex. App. Waco 2008) ("LIDAR technology is novel scientific evidence which may be admissible only after its reliability has been judicially determined in a 'full-blown 'gatekeeping' hearing' ").

[40]Goldstein v. State, 339 Md. 563, 664 A.2d 375 (1995) (admissible where neither the general principles of laser-based speed detection nor the feasibility of the technology was contested; alleged flaws in the design of the particular device not part of the *Frye* inquiry into general acceptance); Matter of Admissibility of Motor Vehicle Speed Readings Produced by LTI Marksman 20-20 Laser Speed Detection System, 314 N.J. Super. 233, 714 A.2d 381 (Law Div. 1998) (validity testing showed the laser-based device to be accurate and generally more conservative than radar), aff'd sub nom. State v. Abeskaron, 326 N.J. Super. 110, 740 A.2d 690, 694 (App. Div. 1999); People v. DePass, 165 Misc. 2d 217, 629 N.Y.S.2d 367 (J. Ct.

1995) (testimony of astrophysicist concerning principles of operation and other uses of laser-based distance and velocity measurements established general acceptance).

[41]State v. Williamson, 144 Idaho 597, 166 P.3d 387, 390 (Ct. App. 2007) ("On the basis of decided cases and law in other jurisdictions . . ., we hold that laser speed detection devices are generally reliable"); People v. Mann, 397 Ill. App. 3d 767, 337 Ill. Dec. 410, 922 N.E.2d 533, 538 (2d Dist. 2010) (previous "decisions [in other jurisdictions] are ample authority that the use of LIDAR to measure the speed of moving vehicles is based on generally accepted scientific principles"); Goldstein v. State, 339 Md. 563, 664 A.2d 375, 380 (1995); *cf.* State v. Hall, 269 Neb. 228, 691 N.W.2d 518, 523 (2005) ("assum[ing], without deciding, that the ProLaser III was a "radio microwave, mechanical, or electronic speed measurement device" governed by a special statute providing for admissibility, it was not necessary for the trial court to rule that the device was sufficiently reliable and valid for speed readings to be admissible under Rule 702); State v. Branch, 243 Or. App. 309, 259 P.3d 103 (2011) (taking "judicial notice" of the scientific principles underlying a laser-based measurement of distance).

[42]State v. Assaye, 121 Haw. 204, 216 P.3d 1227 (2009); State v. Ali, 679 N.W.2d 359, 364 (Minn. Ct. App. 2004); Columbus v. Barton, 106 Ohio Misc. 2d 17, 733 N.E.2d 326 (Mun. Ct. 1994); State v. de Macedo Soares, 190 Vt. 549, 2011 VT 56, 26 A.3d 37, 40 (2011).

underlying principles of laser technology may be the same from one device to another, generally judicial notice as to the reliability of a speed-measuring device is device-specific."[43] That is, the proponent of the evidence should bear the burden of showing that the instrumentation validly implements the recognized scientific principles to produce reliable measurements of speed, either indirectly—by evidence of general acceptance (in *Frye* jurisdictions)—or directly—by evidence of scientific soundness (in *Daubert* jurisdictions).[44] Only after a suitable period of judicial acceptance without significant controversy should a court rely on previous opinions as the sole basis for establishing general scientific acceptance or validity for instrumentation.[45]

## § 205 Biology and medicine: drunkenness and blood, tissue, and DNA typing

The forensic applications of the biological sciences and medicine are far too extensive and varied to be discussed fully here, but we shall consider two groups of laboratory tests of biological samples that commonly provide crucial evidence. These are chemical tests for drunkenness and immunogenetic and other tests for blood, tissue and DNA types.

*(A) Drunkenness.*

Physiologically, the amount of alcohol in the brain determines the degree of intoxication.[1] Except in an autopsy, however, a

---

[43]State v. Starks, 196 Ohio App. 3d 589, 2011-Ohio-2344, 964 N.E.2d 1058, 1067 (12th Dist. Warren County 2011); *accord* State v. Green, 417 N.J. Super. 190, 9 A.3d 172 (App. Div. 2010).

[44]On the nature of these showings, see Kaye et al., The New Wigmore, A Treatise on Evidence: Expert Evidence § 6.3.3 & 7.3.2 (2d ed. 2011); supra § 203.

[45]In response to the concern voiced in Goldstein v. State, 339 Md. 563, 664 A.2d 375, 381 (1995), that "[i]f every brand of every instrument were subject to a discrete [*Frye*] evaluation, trial courts would be mired in hearings concerning devices incorporating scientific principles, possibly including calculators and magnifying glasses," it is clear that modifications or upgrades to a device should not defeat the previous acceptance of that

device if expert testimony establishes that the change is minor and does not detract from the accuracy of the instrument. State v. Starks, 964 N.E.2d at 1061. Furthermore, when companies sell comparable instruments such as calculators or personal computers under different brand names, a court can take judicial notice of the fact that the devices work in the same manner and as advertised—as shown by the acceptance of the components and the various brands in the marketplace.

[Section 205]

[1]*See* Garriott's Medical-Legal Aspects of Alcohol (Garriott ed., 5th ed. 2008); Garriott, Alcohol Testing: Scientific Status, in 5 Faigman, et al., Modern Scientific Evidence: The Law and Science of Expert Testimony § 41:22 (2011–2012 ed.); 2 Giannelli & Imwinkelried, § 22.02, at 368 (4th ed. 2007); Taylor & Oberman, Drunk

direct measurement of this quantity is not feasible.[2] Nevertheless, samples of blood, urine, saliva, or breath can be taken, and the alcohol level in these samples can be measured. Using these measurements to determine whether a person is intoxicated raises two technical problems—the accuracy of the measurement itself and the relationship between the concentration of alcohol in the sample and the degree of intoxication. There is room for concern on both these points.

Analysis of blood samples gives the most accurate results.[3] Various chemical and other techniques are available to measure the concentration of ethyl alcohol in the sample.[4] When proper procedures are followed and the sample is correctly obtained and preserved, these give reliable estimates. Of course, there is always room for error in measurements.[5] Estimates are not necessarily true values. The probable range of errors that arise even when chemical or other tests are performed properly should be quantified and described along with the more familiar "point estimates" of alcohol concentration long encountered in court.[6]

Even where the measured values are very precise, moving from an estimated value for the blood alcohol concentration (BAC) to the degree of intoxication during the crucial period creates uncertainty. Substantial variability in tolerances for alcohol, absorption rates, and clearance rates, both among individuals

---

Driving Defense § 6.02 (7th ed. 2010). For a catalog of scientific publications, see National Institute on Alcohol Abuse and Alcoholism, Alcohol and Alcohol Problems Science Database, http://etoh.niaaa.nih.gov/Introduction.htm.

[2]And even autopsies do not actually entail measurements using brain tissue to ascertain alcohol intoxication. On post-mortem determinations of alcohol levels, see Garriott, Alcohol Testing: Scientific Status, in 5 Faigman, et al., Modern Scientific Evidence: The Law and Science of Expert Testimony §§ 41:64 to 41:69 (2011–2012 ed.).

[3]See Taylor & Oberman, Drunk Driving Defense §§ 6.01 & 8.02 (7th ed. 2010); Fitzgerald & Hume, The Single Chemical Test for Intoxication: A Challenge to Admissibility, 66 Mass. L. Rev. 23 (1981).

[4]See Garriott, Alcohol Testing: Scientific Status, in 5 Faigman, et al.,

Modern Scientific Evidence: The Law and Science of Expert Testimony §§ 41:32 to 41:57 (2011–2012 ed.).

[5]See Bureau International des Poids et Mesures, Evaluation of Measurement Data—Guide to the Expression of Uncertainty in Measurement (2008); Moenssens et al., Scientific Evidence in Civil and Criminal Cases § 3.09 (4th ed. 1995).

[6]State v. Fausto, No. C076949 (Wash. Dist. Ct. Sept. 21, 2010) (Order Suppressing Defendant's Breath-Alcohol Measurements in the Absence of a Measurement for Uncertainty), available at http://www.motorists.org/dui/uncertainty-breath-test.pdf; Ted Vosk, DWI, Champion, Nov. 2010, at 48; cf. Gullberg, Estimating the Measurement Uncertainty in Forensic Blood Alcohol Analysis, 36 J. Analytical Toxicology 153 (2012) (describing methodology for estimating uncertainty).

and within the same individual from one situation to another,[7] complicates efforts to deduce the true extent of intoxication at the time of an arrest or accident.[8] In particular, one cannot assume that BAC inevitably is higher at the time of an accident than it is afterwards, for the concentration rises after drinking, then drops.[9] Extrapolations based on direct measurements of BAC therefore seem more perilous than is generally recognized,[10] and there have been suggestions that BAC should be measured at several different times to ascertain whether the first reading is from the early period of rising BAC or the later period of declining BAC.[11]

---

[7]*See* Jones, Disappearance Rate of Ethanol from the Blood of Human Subjects: Implications in Forensic Toxicology, 38 J. Forensic Sci. 104, 112 (1993) ("Human beings show an enormous variation in their response to alcohol."); Jones & Jonsson, Food-Induced Lowering of Blood-Ethanol Profiles and Increased Rate of Elimination Immediately After a Meal, 39 J. Forensic Sci. 1084 (1994).

[8]State v. Downey, 2008-NMSC-061, 145 N.M. 232, 195 P.3d 1244, 1249 (2008) (summarizing expert testimony on the importance of individual variables); Com. v. Gonzalez, 519 Pa. 116, 546 A.2d 26 (1988) (expert unable to extrapolate BAC to earlier time without knowing when last drink was consumed); Stewart v. State, 129 S.W.3d 93, 93 (Tex. Crim. App. 2004) ("trial judge admitted . . . breath alcohol test results but refused to permit the State's expert to give retrograde extrapolation testimony, because the . . . expert . . . conceded that he did not have enough information to determine what [defendant's] alcohol concentration would have been at the time she drove.").

[9]State v. Downey, 195 P.3d at 1252; Stewart v. State, 129 S.W.3d at 93 ("the blood alcohol concentration shown by the results of the tests taken at the police station could have been higher, lower, or the same as results that would have been obtained immediately after Stewart drove, because Stewart's body could have been absorbing or eliminating alcohol at the time of the test."). For graphs, see Jones,

Disappearance Rate of Ethanol from the Blood of Human Subjects: Implications in Forensic Toxicology, 38 J. Forensic Sci. 104, 109–11 (1993).

[10]*See* Com. v. Jarman, 529 Pa. 92, 601 A.2d 1229 (1992) (reversing a conviction "given the lapse of one hour between appellant's driving and the taking of a blood sample, the small amount by which the test result exceeded the 0.10% level, the 10% margin of error in the test, and the testimony provided by the Commonwealth's expert witness that appellant's blood alcohol level may indeed have been below 0.10% before the test was administered"); Kimberly S. Keller, Sobering Up *Daubert*: Recent Issues Arising in Alcohol-Related Expert Testimony, 46 S. Tex. L. Rev. 111 (2004).

[11]*See* State v. Olivas, 77 Ariz. 118, 267 P.2d 893 (1954); Com. v. Neal, 392 Mass. 1, 464 N.E.2d 1356, 1369 (1984) (value of two tests); State v. Dist. Ct. (Armstrong), 267 P.3d 777, 127 Nev. Adv. Op. No. 84 (Nev. 2011) (affirming exclusion of extrapolation based on a single test result); Fitzgerald & Hume, The Single Chemical Test for Intoxication: A Challenge to Admissibility, 66 Mass. L. Rev. 23 (1981) (arguing that unless a second sample is analyzed to determine whether the level is rising or falling, the single test result should not be admissible); Nichols, Toward a Coordinated Judicial View of the Accuracy of Breath Testing Devices, 59 N.D. L. Rev. 329 (1983) (advocating measurements at two times); Patiser, Note, In Vino Veritas: The Truth About

However, even with two measurements, the situation may not be clearcut.[12]

Determinations resting exclusively on concentration of alcohol contained in a sample of breath (BrAC) pose additional problems. To be sure, various instruments have been shown to be accurate in measuring BrAC in laboratory studies, and arguments that particular instruments are not generally accepted or sufficiently accurate for the purpose of determining BrAC usually fail.[13] As with tests of blood, however, errors can arise from operating conditions, individual biological variability, and extrapolation to the time in question. Moreover, there is an inherent problem with breath testing. A formula must be used to convert BrAC to BAC. Traditionally, a single number is used as a multiplier in making this conversion, but the true value of this parameter is debatable.[14] Certainly, the conversion ratio varies among individuals and even within the same individual over time.[15] Although most studies suggest that the conventional figure of 2100 tends to understate the blood alcohol level,[16] a small fraction of individuals will have blood alcohol concentrations that are lower than those deduced from this value.[17]

These cautions concerning the scientific proof do not necessar-

---

Blood Alcohol Presumptions in Drunk Driving Law, 64 NYU L. Rev. 141 (1989) (advocating multiple testing).

[12]*See* 2 Giannelli & Imwinkelried, Scientific Evidence § 22.04 (4th ed. 2007).

[13]*E.g.,* State v. Crea, 119 Idaho 352, 806 P.2d 445, 447 (1991) ("scientific acceptance of the Intoximeter 3000 is well established in Idaho and many other jurisdictions"); 5 Faigman, et al., Modern Scientific Evidence: The Law and Science of Expert Testimony § 41:8 (2011–2012 ed.).

[14]Fraiser, Mississippi Informed Consent Law: A Survey of Decisions Responding to Recent Scientific Research on Tests for Intoxication, 72 Miss. L.J. 1037, 1046–50 (2003).

[15]*E.g.,* Garriott, Alcohol Testing: Scientific Status, in 5 Faigman, et al., Modern Scientific Evidence: The Law and Science of Expert Testimony § 41:43 (2011–2012 ed.) ("The actual blood:breath ratio can vary considerably."); Jones & Andersson, Variability of the Blood/Breath Alcohol Ratio in Drinking Drivers, 41 J. Forensic Sci.

916, 919 (1996) ("The blood-breath ratio is a moving target, and the notion of a constant value for all subjects under all conditions is imaginary.").

[16]Garriott, Alcohol Testing: Scientific Status, in 5 Faigman, et al., Modern Scientific Evidence: The Law and Science of Expert Testimony § 41:43 (2011–2012 ed.) ("A ratio of 2300:1 has been shown to be more accurate in post-absorption subjects . . . giving them a slightly lower reading than if a direct blood alcohol were measured."); 2 Giannelli & Imwinkelried, Scientific Evidence § 22.03[b] (4th ed. 2007).

[17]State v. Downie, 117 N.J. 450, 569 A.2d 242 (1990) (using the standard ratio usually understates BAC, but it may overstate BAC about one time in 45); Garriott, Alcohol Testing: Scientific Status, in 5 Faigman, et al., Modern Scientific Evidence: The Law and Science of Expert Testimony §§ 41:35 to 41:53 (2011–2012 ed.); Jones & Andersson, Variability of the Blood/ Breath Alcohol Ratio in Drinking Drivers, 41 J. Forensic Sci. 916 (1996) (studying nearly 800 drivers with both

ily make the blood and breath test evidence inadmissible. On the contrary, when the tests are properly conducted and analyzed, the evidence can be of great value in deciding questions connected with intoxication. Since the links from breath alcohol concentration to blood alcohol level to intoxication, as well as the accuracy of measurements made under ideal conditions are well established,[18] under the usual principles governing scientific evidence, the test results should be admissible if founded on a showing of authenticity and satisfactory care in the collection of the sample and its analysis.[19] Expert testimony ordinarily would be needed to establish that the party with the measured or inferred BAC was intoxicated during the period in question.[20] Some courts

---

breath and blood tests and finding that the blood-breath ratio was less than 2100 in only 34 (4%) after adjusting for the metabolism of alcohol during the interval between the two tests and in 156 individuals (20%) without this adjustment). *But see* State v. Johnson, 717 S.W.2d 298, 301 (Tenn. Crim. App. 1986) (reporting that in "a double blind scientific study . . . of 134 persons arrested in Tennessee for driving under the influence, . . . [i]n 21% of the cases the breath test was higher than the blood test," and for these 27 individuals, "the mean difference between the breath and blood tests was .012%."). *See also* 2 Giannelli & Imwinkelried, Scientific Evidence § 22.03[b] (4th ed. 2007) (discussing studies).

[18]U.S. v. Smith, 776 F.2d 892, 899 (10th Cir. 1985) ("testing breath samples for blood alcohol content has general acceptance in the scientific community"); State v. Downie, 117 N.J. 450, 569 A.2d 242 (1990) ("as long as proper procedures are followed, the breathalyzer's accuracy] should remain a subject of judicial notice"); People v. Mertz, 68 N.Y.2d 136, 506 N.Y.S.2d 290, 497 N.E.2d 657 (1986) ("the scientific reliability of breathalyzers in general is no longer open to question").

[19]Ballou v. Henri Studios, Inc., 656 F.2d 1147 (5th Cir. 1981) (error to exclude expert testimony about intoxication based on finding that blood sample from deceased who drove into a truck parked on the shoulder of a

highway contained .24% alcohol); McGough v. Slaughter, 395 So. 2d 972, 977 (Ala. 1981) (foundation insufficient for "admission under general evidence principles"); State ex rel. Collins v. Seidel, 142 Ariz. 587, 691 P.2d 678 (1984); State v. Dille, 258 N.W.2d 565, 567–69 (Minn. 1977) (foundation sufficient for admission under statute providing that "the court may admit evidence of the amount of alcohol in the person's blood, breath, or urine as shown by a medical or chemical analysis"); 5 Faigman, et al., Modern Scientific Evidence: The Law and Science of Expert Testimony § 41:8 (2011–2012 ed.); Challenges to use of breath tests for drunk drivers based on claim that partition or conversion ratio between measured breath alcohol and actual blood alcohol is inaccurate, 90 A.L.R. 4th 155; Evidence of automobile passenger's blood-alcohol level as admissible in support of defense that passenger was contributorily negligent or assumed risk of automobile accident, 5 A.L.R.4th 1194.

[20]Mattingly v. Eisenberg, 79 Ariz. 135, 285 P.2d 174 (1955); State v. Dacey, 138 Vt. 491, 418 A.2d 856, 859 (1980); Watts, Tests for Intoxication, 45 N.C. L. Rev. 34 (1966). *But see* Stewart v. State, 129 S.W.3d 93 (Tex. Crim. App. 2004) (a later BrAC measurement is relevant to show impairment even without expert extrapolation and may be considered along with other evidence of impairment); Fraiser, Mississippi Informed Consent Law: A Survey of Decisions Responding to

have emphasized the need for care in admitting retrograde extrapolations,[21] but arguments that the extrapolation process itself is so uncertain as to be inadmissible under *Frye* or *Daubert* have not prevailed.[22]

In the context of traffic offenses, specialized statutes and regulations provide shortcuts to the application of the common

---

Recent Scientific Research on Tests for Intoxication, 72 Miss. L.J. 1037, 1052–56 (2003) (describing conflicting case law on the effect of a failure to provide retrograde extrapolation in a "per se" DUI prosecution).

The sources of error outlined above could diminish the weight or even preclude the admission of this testimony. U.S. v. DuBois, 645 F.2d 642 (8th Cir. 1981) (expert's attempt to extrapolate to BAC at time of accident when defendant had consumed more alcohol after the accident); State v. Dist. Ct. (Armstrong), 267 P.3d 777, 127 Nev. Adv. Op. No. 84 (Nev. 2011); Stewart v. State, 129 S.W.3d 93 (Tex. Crim. App. 2004). When the time of testing is too remote or the manner of testing grossly erroneous, exclusion is proper. Because the inference of intoxication requires knowledge of physiology and toxicology, an expert qualified to report measurements of blood or breath alcohol is not necessarily qualified to testify to the level of intoxication associated with these measurements. See supra § 203.

[21]State v. Dist. Ct. (Armstrong), 267 P.3d 777, 779, 127 Nev. Adv. Op. No. 84 (Nev. 2011) (state's retrograde extrapolation properly excluded under Rule 403 "[b]ecause the prosecution in this case had to rely on the results from a single blood sample and a number of the factors that affect the mathematical calculation necessary to a retrograde extrapolation were unknown"); Mata v. State, 46 S.W.3d 902, 916 (Tex. Crim. App. 2001) (despite disagreements in the scientific literature, "the science of retrograde extrapolation can be reliable in a given case," but "the expert must demonstrate some understanding of the difficulties associated with a retrograde

extrapolation," "must demonstrate an awareness of the subtleties of the science and the risks inherent in any extrapolation," and "must be able to clearly and consistently apply the science"; moreover, "[t]he court . . . should also consider (a) the length of time between the offense and the test(s) administered; (b) the number of tests given and the length of time between each test; and (c) whether, and if so, to what extent, any individual characteristics of the defendant were known to the expert in providing his extrapolation.").

[22]*E.g.*, State v. Vliet, 95 Haw. 94, 19 P.3d 42, 60 (2001) (taking "judicial notice that Widmark's formula is widely viewed as reliable"); Com. v. Senior, 433 Mass. 453, 744 N.E.2d 614, 619 (2001) ("the Commonwealth provided, through its toxicology expert, . . . ample evidence that retrograde extrapolation is a reliable method of determining blood alcohol levels"); Smith v. State, 942 So. 2d 308 (Miss. Ct. App. 2006); State v. Teate, 180 N.C. App. 601, 638 S.E.2d 29 (2006); State v. Burgess, 188 Vt. 235, 2010 VT 64, 5 A.3d 911, 915 (2010) ("retrograde extrapolation is generally considered to meet the admissibility requirements of *Daubert*"); 5 Faigman, et al., Modern Scientific Evidence: The Law and Science of Expert Testimony § 41:7 (2011–2012 ed.) (reviewing cases); Admissibility and Sufficiency of Extrapolation Evidence in DUI Prosecutions, 119 A.L.R.5th 379; *cf.* Olson v. Ford Motor Co., 481 F.3d 619, 628 (8th Cir. 2007) ("The fact that two witnesses did not regard the formulas used by Dr. Donelson as reliable does not mean that testimony based on the formulas was inadmissible under Rule 702.").

law principles and evidence codes in determining the admissibility of blood and breath test evidence.[23] In proceedings involving driving or control of a vehicle while under the influence of intoxicating liquor, these laws typically make chemical test evidence of BAC admissible as long as it is obtained by certified persons following procedures that the state department of health has prescribed.[24] If the procedures are sufficiently rigorous,[25] then

---

[23]*See* State v. Bender, 382 So. 2d 697, 699 (Fla. 1980) (citing statutes); Construction and application of statutes creating presumption or other inference of intoxication from specified percentages of alcohol present in system, 16 A.L.R.3d 748. Most of these statutes are restricted to prosecutions for driving while intoxicated. Moenssens et al., Scientific Evidence in Civil and Criminal Cases § 3.12 (4th ed. 1995). As a rule, attempts to invoke the statutorily prescribed presumptions and procedures in other prosecutions or civil actions have not been crowned with success. State v. Bender, 382 So.2d 697, at 700; Mattingly v. Eisenberg, 79 Ariz. 135, 285 P.2d 174, 177 (1955); Construction and application of statutes creating presumption or other inference of intoxication from specified percentages of alcohol present in system, 16 A.L.R.3d 748. *But see* Divine v. Groshong, 235 Kan. 127, 679 P.2d 700, 708–09 (1984) (rebuttable presumption of intoxication applies in civil proceedings). Even in the type of case to which the statute clearly applies, the more general evidentiary principles still can be critical. The state may rely on a test not yet approved pursuant to the statutory scheme. *See* State v. Mills, 133 Vt. 15, 328 A.2d 410 (1974) (gas chromatography admissible). Or it may seek to introduce proof without having followed the statutory prescription. *See* State v. Trahan, 576 So. 2d 1 (La. 1990) (adherence to promulgated procedures required for presumptions, but not necessarily for admission of the evidence); State v. Deloit, 964 S.W.2d 909, 914 (Tenn. Crim. App. 1997) ("the state has the alternative of proceeding under . . . the more onerous condi-

tions described in the Tennessee Rules of Evidence"); State v. Brooks, 162 Vt. 26, 643 A.2d 226 (1993) ("Compliance with the statutory rule-making requirement is mandatory only to the extent that the State wishes to benefit from the presumption of validity."). *Contra* State v. Watson, 51 Wash. App. 947, 756 P.2d 177 (Div. 3 1988) (breathalyzer result inadmissible). Likewise, a party may call on "general evidence principles" in a civil action in which statutory procedures are available but not followed. *See* McGough v. Slaughter, 395 So. 2d 972, 977 (Ala. 1981); State ex rel. Collins v. Seidel, 142 Ariz. 587, 691 P.2d 678 (1984); Divine v. Groshong, 679 P.2d at 706 ("If the blood sample is taken under appropriate conditions to guard against contamination, if the chemical testing is properly conducted by competent personnel . . ., then those results are admissible in a civil action whether or not they are taken in conformity with the statute.").

[24]Before the statutes were adopted, cases on the analysis of breath samples had divided, with a majority admitting the evidence. *Compare* People v. Bobczyk, 343 Ill. App. 504, 99 N.E.2d 567, 570 (1st Dist. 1951), *with* People v. Morse, 325 Mich. 270, 38 N.W.2d 322 (1949) ("general scientific recognition that the breath test applied by the Hager Drunkometer will afford an accurate index of the alcoholic content of the blood" not established); *cf.* People v. Boscic, 15 N.Y.3d 494, 912 N.Y.S.2d 556, 938 N.E.2d 989 (2010) (prosecution must show that a breath analyzer was in proper working order, and Department of Health regulations listing approved devices and requiring calibration

the results of this testing can trigger two rebuttable presumptions:[26] if BAC at the relevant time[27] was at or above a specified level (such as 0.08%), that the individual was under the influence; and if BAC was at or below a smaller level (such as 0.05%), that he was not. An intermediate reading is usually deemed "competent evidence" for consideration along with the other evidence in the case. In most jurisdictions, a party offering test results pursuant to such a statute must lay a foundation by producing witnesses to explain how the test is conducted, to identify it as duly approved under the statutory scheme, and to vouch for its correct administration in the particular case.[28]

within 12 months will assist in this task).

[25]State v. Rowell, 517 So. 2d 799 (La. 1988) (gas chromatography test conforming to regulations inadmissible because regulations did not provide for maintenance of the chromatograph, preservation of the sample, validation of calibration samples and proficiency testing of operator).

[26]On the nature of the presumptions, see Lattarulo v. State, 261 Ga. 124, 401 S.E.2d 516, 518 (1991) (inasmuch as "[t]he challenged provisions do not relieve the state of its burden of proving that the accused was 'under the influence' and was driving, [and] the jury may not be instructed that the blood-alcohol level creates a presumption of guilt, . . . the challenged provisions do not create an unconstitutional presumption"); People v. Calvin, 216 Mich. App. 403, 548 N.W.2d 720, 723 (1996) ("The presumptions against the accused . . . must be construed as permissive or rebuttable to ensure that the burden of proving all elements of the offense beyond a reasonable doubt remains on the prosecution."); State v. Dacey, 138 Vt. 491, 418 A.2d 856 (1980) (permissive inference rather than mandatory presumption). Some conclusive presumptions have been struck down as unconstitutional. McLean v. Moran, 963 F.2d 1306 (9th Cir. 1992) (invalidating Nevada statute).

[27]There are local variations as to whether BAC at the time of testing or at the extrapolated figure for an earlier time triggers the presumptions. *Compare* People v. Mertz, 68 N.Y.2d 136, 506 N.Y.S.2d 290, 497 N.E.2d 657 (1986) (reviewing anticlinal cases and, to avoid a possibly unconstitutional presumption, reading a statute permitting chemical tests within two hours of arrest to mean that a high BAC reading in this period is only "prima facie evidence" of a "per se" violation), *with* State v. Tischio, 107 N.J. 504, 527 A.2d 388, 389 (1987) (because high BAC measured "within a reasonable time after the defendant was driving his vehicle" satisfies "per se" statute, "extrapolation evidence . . . is not admissible"); *cf.* State v. Korhn, 41 Conn. App. 874, 678 A.2d 492 (1996) (presumption equating measured BAC with BAC at the time of operation of motor vehicle did not impermissibly shift burden of proof).

[28]Schirado v. North Dakota State Highway Com'r, 382 N.W.2d 391 (N.D. 1986) (conviction reversed for failure to establish compliance with regulations defining fair administration of breath alcohol test); State v. Bobo, 909 S.W.2d 788 (Tenn. 1995) (failure to lay foundation of compliance with statute for breath alcohol test requires exclusion even if the deviation worked to the benefit of the defendant); City of West Allis v. Rainey, 36 Wis. 2d 489, 153 N.W.2d 514 (1967) (expert testimony not required for admissibility and presumptions); 2 Giannelli & Imwinkelried, Scientific Evidence § 22.06 (4th ed. 2007); Necessity and sufficiency of proof that tests of blood alcohol concentration were conducted

By the early 1980s, as concern with the carnage due to drunken driving escalated,[29] nearly all states placed still more emphasis on chemical testing by providing for the admissibility of BrAC measurements obtained with approved equipment and procedures,[30] and all states have enacted "per se" laws making it a crime to drive while having a BAC or BrAC (or in several states, a urine alcohol concentration) in excess of a specified amount.[31] Some of these statutes seek to circumvent defense challenges to converting BrAC to BAC by redefining the offense in terms of breath rather than blood alcohol.[32] Indeed, to avoid the need to

---

in conformance with prescribed methods, 96 A.L.R.3d 745. This evidence must show that the instrument was in proper working order and the chemicals were of a kind and mixed in the proper proportions. People v. Freeland, 68 N.Y.2d 699, 506 N.Y.S.2d 306, 497 N.E.2d 673 (1986); People v. Campbell, 73 N.Y.2d 481, 541 N.Y.S.2d 756, 539 N.E.2d 584 (1989) (blood alcohol tests conducted by hospital technician); People v. Mertz, 68 N.Y.2d 136, 506 N.Y.S.2d 290, 497 N.E.2d 657 (1986) (breathalyzer).

[29]*See* 2 Giannelli & Imwinkelried, Scientific Evidence § 22.01 (4th ed. 2007).

[30]*See, e.g.,* Dougherty v. State, 259 Ga. App. 618, 578 S.E.2d 256 (2003) (upholding Division of Forensic Sciences (DFS) rules and regulations mandating quarterly inspections and calibration, and that machine operators attend breath analysis certification course, met the statutory requirement that DFS promulgate satisfactory techniques and methods for chemical testing of alcohol in blood).

[31]*See* Valentine v. State, 215 P.3d 319, 324 (Alaska 2009) (rebuttable presumption for 0.08 BrAC); Roberts v. State, 329 So. 2d 296 (Fla. 1976) (BAC statute constitutional); State v. Tanksley, 809 N.W.2d 706 (Minn. 2012) (statutory limit on urine alcohol concentration obviated the need from a hearing on the correlation between urine concentration and BAC); State v. Kuhl, 276 Neb. 497, 755 N.W.2d 389 (2008) (adherence to statutory scheme

supports a conviction notwithstanding unrebutted, but not necessarily convincing, expert testimony that the "inherent margin of error" in the breath-alcohol analyzer is too large to demonstrate that the true BrAC exceeded the statutory limit); Murray City v. Hall, 663 P.2d 1314 (Utah 1983) (statute construed as creating rebuttable presumption for BAC of .08 to .10 and conclusive presumption for BAC of .10 or more held constitutional); Patiser, Note, In Vino Veritas: The Truth About Blood Alcohol Presumptions in Drunk Driving Law, 64 NYU L. Rev. 141 (1989). For a database on legislation, see National Institute on Alcohol Abuse and Alcoholism, Alcohol Policy Information System, Blood Alcohol Concentration (BAC) Limits: Adult Operators of Noncommercial Motor Vehicles, http://www.alcoholpolicy.nia aa.nih.gov/Blood_Alcohol_Concentra tion_Limits_Adult_Operators_of_ Noncommercial_Motor_Vehicles.h tml.

[32]*See* People v. Bransford, 8 Cal. 4th 885, 35 Cal. Rptr. 2d 613, 884 P.2d 70 (1994) (evidence that the conversion factor applicable to defendant was less than 2100 inadmissible under per se law); State v. Brayman, 110 Wash. 2d 183, 751 P.2d 294 (1988) (redefinition of offense constitutional); *cf.* State v. Downie, 117 N.J. 450, 569 A.2d 242 (1990) (construing a "blood alcohol" per se law as intended to mean "breath alcohol"). For additional cases on the constitutionality of this stratagem, see 2 Giannelli & Imwinkelried, § 22.01, at 362, & § 22.08[c] (4th ed. 2007); Validity, construction, and application

present or consider testimony extrapolating from later to earlier measurements, some statutes created a presumption as to what the alcohol level was at the time of driving,[33] and some statutes even redefined the offense to consist of having a given BAC or BrAC within several hours after operating a motor vehicle.[34] The typical result is a potentially confusing mosaic of laws and rules in which a set of overlapping offenses with various statutory provisions for admitting evidence of BAC or BrAC in traffic cases is superimposed on the more general evidence code or common law rules.[35]

### (B) Blood, Tissue, and DNA Types.

Another group of chemical tests—those that identify blood, tissue and DNA types—are often the subject of courtroom testimony. DNA testing has come to dominate the field, but inasmuch as the particularized case law and legislation began in response to blood and tissue typing, we begin with an exposition of the earlier technologies.

Elucidating the biochemical mechanisms by which a multicel-

---

of statutes directly proscribing driving with blood-alcohol level in excess of established percentage, 54 A.L.R.4th 149.

[33]*E.g.*, State v. Stutliff, 97 Idaho 523, 547 P.2d 1128, 1130 (1976) ("this statute does not require extrapolation back but establishes that the percentage of blood alcohol as shown by chemical analysis relates back to the time of the alleged offense for purposes of applying the statutory presumption"). The law was repealed and replaced in 1984 and further stiffened in 1987. *See* Elias-Cruz v. Idaho Dept. of Transp., 153 Idaho 200, 280 P.3d 703 (2012).

[34]*Compare* State v. Baker, 720 A.2d 1139 (Del. 1998) (striking down as vague and overbroad a statute making it a crime to have an "alcohol concentration" of .10 or more "within four hours after the time of driving"), *and* Com. v. Barud, 545 Pa. 297, 681 A.2d 162 (1996) (same result as to statute making it a crime to have a BAC above .10 within three hours after operating a motor vehicle), *with* Bohannon v. State, 269 Ga. 130, 497 S.E.2d 552 (1998) (statute making it "a crime to have a blood-alcohol con-

centration of .10 or greater, as measured within three hours of driving" is not vague or overbroad); Sereika v. State, 114 Nev. 142, 955 P.2d 175 (1998) (statute making it a crime to be "found by measurement within 2 hours after driving . . . to have 0.10" BAC is not vague or overbroad); Com. v. Finchio, 592 Pa. 577, 926 A.2d 968 (2007) (within-two-hours per se law does not create an irrebuttable presumption and complies with due process); *and* Com. v. Duda, 592 Pa. 164, 923 A.2d 1138 (2007) (same); *cf.* Valentine v. State, 215 P.3d 319 (Alaska 2009) (within-four-hours per se statute satisfies due process, but the addition to a traditional DUI statute of a provision barring scientifically valid "delayed absorption" evidence violates due process).

[35]Consequently, there may be more than one way to lay a foundation for the scientific evidence. State ex rel. Collins v. Seidel, 142 Ariz. 587, 691 P.2d 678 (1984). Likewise, evidence may be admissible or sufficient to prove one offense but not another. Valentine v. State, 215 P.3d 319 (Alaska 2009); Com. v. Gonzalez, 519 Pa. 116, 546 A.2d 26 (1988).

lular organism distinguishes between self and non-self—between its own cells and foreign substances—is a major research problem in biology.[36] The topic is fundamental to understanding the way in which the body responds to infections from microorganisms, to grafts of foreign tissues or materials, and to blood transfusions, and it is central to the study of allergies, tumors, and autoimmune diseases. Research in this field reveals that sticking out of the surface of cells are various molecules, called in this context, antigens. For instance, individuals with type A blood have the molecule known as an A antigen on their red blood cells.[37] The red blood cells are not the only ones to possess antigens. Human Leucocyte Antigens (HLA) are found on the surface of most human cells, and there is an elaborate nomenclature for these. The full set of antigens that a cell possesses thus distinguishes it from the cells of other organisms. It is conceivable that each person is uniquely identifiable in this way. In addition to the immunologically crucial antigens, cells and bodily fluids contain chemicals such as enzymes and other proteins that can differ from one person to another.[38]

Most enzymes and serum proteins are identified by a technique called electrophoresis, in which an electric field is applied to separate the molecules according to their electric charge. Although electrophoresis is a standard technique in biochemistry,[39] its application to aged or dried blood stains was marked by controversy.[40] Difficulties arose because thin gel multisystem testing is used only in crime laboratories, because few outside investigations of the effects of aging and environmental contami-

---

[36]See generally Dean, Blood Groups and Red Cell Antigens (2005); Delves et al., Roitt's Essential Immunology (11th ed. 2006).

[37]We are simplifying for ease of exposition. In fact, there are several distinct antigens that are included within type A blood. Consequently, the type A blood group can be divided into various subgroups corresponding to the presence or absence of the particular antigens. Ignoring subdivisions, type B blood corresponds to the B antigen, type AB to the combination of the A and B antigens, and type O blood lacks both the A and B antigens.

[38]Ballantyne, Serology Overview, in Encyclopedia of Forensic and Legal Medicine 53 (Payne et al. eds., 2005); Gaensslen, Sourcebook on Forensic Serology, Immunology, and Biochemistry (1983).

[39]Maddox, Understanding Gel Electrophoresis, 345 Nature 381 (1990).

[40]See People v. Brown, 40 Cal. 3d 512, 230 Cal. Rptr. 834, 726 P.2d 516 (1985), rev'd on other grounds, 479 U.S. 538 (1987) (inadequate showing that Frye test satisfied); People v. Harbold, 124 Ill. App. 3d 363, 79 Ill. Dec. 830, 464 N.E.2d 734, 746 (1st Dist. 1984) ("There is some dispute among scientists as to the accuracy of results derived from electrophoretic testing of dried blood stains"); People v. Young, 418 Mich. 1, 340 N.W.2d 805, 814 (1983); Kaye, The Double Helix and the Law of Evidence 13–18 (2010); Admissibility, in criminal cases, of evidence of electrophoresis of dried evidentiary bloodstains, 66 A.L.R.4th 588.

nation were undertaken, and because crime laboratories did not submit to routine proficiency testing. Nevertheless, almost all appellate courts that encountered challenges to electrophoretic identifications concluded that both the multisystem and the more generally used electrophoretic procedures are scientifically accepted and that the findings can be admitted into evidence.[41]

A different type of test is used to detect antigens. The antigens react with other biologically produced molecules, called antibodies. Serologic tests consist of exposing a suspected antigen to its corresponding antibody and observing whether the expected reaction occurs. Errors involving misinterpretation, mislabeling, poor reagents, and the like are always possible, but workers in this field report that with stringent procedures and quality control standards, the risk of error can be made very small.[42]

The forensic use of these tests arose principally in two areas—identifying the perpetrators of violent crimes or sexual offenses from traces of blood[43] or semen[44] and ascertaining parentage in

---

[41]Many opinions seem rather uncritical. State v. Beaty, 158 Ariz. 232, 762 P.2d 519 (1988) (analysis ends with the undiscriminating observation that "PGM or blood grouping tests are a well-recognized and admissible means for identification of blood and semen samples"); People v. Thomas, 204 Ill. App. 3d 890, 149 Ill. Dec. 932, 562 N.E.2d 396 (4th Dist. 1990) (taking judicial notice of unspecified forms of electrophoresis among forensic scientists); State v. Fenney, 448 N.W.2d 54 (Minn. 1989) ("taking forensics as the relevant field," electrophoresis of dried blood is generally accepted and isoelectric focusing results are admissible); State v. Dirk, 364 N.W.2d 117 (S.D. 1985) (*Frye* test met by expert's testimony that forensic laboratories use the technique). The leading case rejecting multisystem testing is People v. Young, 425 Mich. 470, 391 N.W.2d 270 (1986). *Young* does not rely on the frequently superficial opinions of other courts. Instead, it demands that thin-gel multisystem electrophoresis of aged bloodstains be independently and rigorously validated. *See* Kaye, The Double Helix and the Law of Evidence 16–18 (2020).

[42]Hunt, Investigation of Serological Evidence—A Manual for Field Investigators (1984); Henningsen, Error Risks in Paternity Diagnosis by Bloodgrouping, in Inclusion Probabilities in Parentage Testing (R.H. Walker ed. 1983). Dried bloodstains require special preparation and analysis. Lee, Identification and Grouping of Bloodstains, in Forensic Sciences Handbook 267 (Saferstein ed. 1982). For some enumerations of possible sources of error in serologic tests, see Anonymous v. Anonymous, 10 Ariz. App. 496, 460 P.2d 32, 35 (Div. 2 1969); Jackson v. Jackson, 67 Cal. 2d 245, 60 Cal. Rptr. 649, 430 P.2d 289, 292 n.1 (1967) (dissenting opinion).

[43]*See* Admissibility, weight, and sufficiency of blood-grouping tests in criminal cases, 2 A.L.R.4th 500.

[44]*See* Admissibility, in prosecution for sex-related offense, of results of tests on semen or seminal fluids, 75 A.L.R.4th 897. In these cases, other chemical tests also may be used to determine whether a stain is actually blood, whether it is human blood, and how long it has been exposed.

child support cases,[45] criminal cases,[46] and other litigation.[47] In general, the courts moved from an initial position of mistrust of such evidence[48] to the present stage of taking judicial notice of the scientific acceptance or acceptability of serologic and related tests.[49] From the outset, it was recognized that if the suspect's antigens do not match those in the sample found at the scene of a crime, then the incriminating trace does not consist of his blood. For a considerable time, however, there was a difference of judicial opinion concerning evidence of a match. Since some combinations of antigens are relatively common, a few courts dismissed the positive test results for these antigens as irrelevant.[50] The better view—and the overwhelming majority po-

---

[45]Admissibility and weight of blood-grouping tests in disputed paternity cases, 43 A.L.R.4th 579; Admissibility, weight and sufficiency of Human Leukocyte Antigen (HLA) tissue typing tests in paternity cases, 37 A.L.R.4th 167.

[46]E.g., State v. Spann, 130 N.J. 484, 617 A.2d 247 (1993); State v. Jackson, 320 N.C. 452, 358 S.E.2d 679 (1987); State v. Hartman, 145 Wis. 2d 1, 426 N.W.2d 320 (1988).

[47]Davis, Note, Are You My Mother? The Scientific and Legal Validity of Conventional Blood Testing and DNA Fingerprinting to Establish Proof of Parentage in Immigration Cases, 1994 B.Y.U. L. Rev. 129 (1994); Admissibility and weight of blood test results in immigration preference or derivative citizenship proceedings under Immigration and Nationality Act (8 U.S.C.A. secs. 1101 et seq.), 46 A.L.R. Fed. 176.

[48]See Huntingdon v. Crowley, 64 Cal. 2d 647, 51 Cal. Rptr. 254, 414 P.2d 382 (1966) (Kell-Cellano test not generally accepted as giving accurate results); State v. Damm, 62 S.D. 123, 252 N.W. 7, 104 A.L.R. 430 (1933), aff'd, 64 S.D. 309, 266 N.W. 667 (1936) (medical sciences not shown to be sufficiently agreed on "the transmissibility of blood characteristics") (science found unanimously agreed); Phillips By and Through Utah State Dept. of Social Services v. Jackson, 615 P.2d 1228 (Utah 1980) (HLA testing); Kaye,

The Double Helix and the Law of Evidence 7–12 (2010).

[49]E.g., Moore v. McNamara, 201 Conn. 16, 513 A.2d 660 (1986) (dictum); Com. v. Beausoleil, 397 Mass. 206, 490 N.E.2d 788 (1986); Houghton v. Houghton, 179 Neb. 275, 137 N.W.2d 861, 869 (1965); Matter of Abe A., 56 N.Y.2d 288, 452 N.Y.S.2d 6, 437 N.E.2d 265 (1982); Kofford v. Flora, 744 P.2d 1343 (Utah 1987); State v. Meacham, 93 Wash. 2d 735, 612 P.2d 795, 797 (1980).

[50]State v. Peterson, 219 N.W.2d 665, 671 (Iowa 1974); People v. Macedonio, 42 N.Y.2d 944, 397 N.Y.S.2d 1002, 366 N.E.2d 1355 (1977); People v. Robinson, 27 N.Y.2d 864, 317 N.Y.S.2d 19, 265 N.E.2d 543 (1970); State v. Woodall, 182 W. Va. 15, 385 S.E.2d 253 (1989) (dictum that Type O match common to 45% of population "borders on irrelevancy"). The Iowa Supreme Court retreated from its dictum in Peterson. See State v. Mark, 286 N.W.2d 396, 412–13 (Iowa 1979). After acknowledging that "the relative rarity of the assailant's type of blood [goes] to weight rather than admissibility" (Matter of Abe A., 56 N.Y.2d 288, 452 N.Y.S.2d 6, 437 N.E.2d 265 (1982)), the New York Court of Appeals finally and flatly overruled Robinson and Macedonio in People v. Mountain, 66 N.Y.2d 197, 495 N.Y.S.2d 944, 486 N.E.2d 802 (1985). See Kaye, The Double Helix and the Law of Evidence 20–24 (2010).

sition[51]—is that positive findings are neither irrelevant nor so inherently prejudicial as to justify a rule against their admission.[52]

Serologic tests have been used in paternity litigation at least since the 1930s.[53] The underlying logic is based on elementary principles of human genetics. Roughly speaking, portions of the DNA contained in the chromosomes of the nucleus of a cell—the genes—direct the synthesis of proteins. Different versions (or alleles) of these genes oversee the synthesis of the different antigens. Consequently, by ascertaining which antigens are present in an individual (the phenotype), one learns something about that individual's alleles (the genotype).[54] As such, the antigens

---

[51]*See* People v. Lindsey, 84 Cal. App. 3d 851, 149 Cal. Rptr. 47, 54–55 (2d Dist. 1978) (collecting cases); Perry v. State, 524 N.E.2d 316 (Ind. 1988); Com. v. Yarris, 519 Pa. 571, 549 A.2d 513 (1988) (population frequency of 13%); People v. Mountain, 66 N.Y.2d 197, 495 N.Y.S.2d 944, 486 N.E.2d 802 (1985); Kaye, The Admissibility of "Probability Evidence" in Criminal Trials (pt. 2), 27 Jurimetrics J. 160 (1987); Admissibility, weight, and sufficiency of blood-grouping tests in criminal cases, 2 A.L.R.4th 500.

[52]In one leading case, Shanks v. State, 185 Md. 437, 45 A.2d 85 (1945), the accused was charged with rape. The state proved that blood found on the coat of the accused, like that of his alleged victim, was type O. The defendant argued that since 45% of the population had type O blood, the evidence should have been excluded as too remote. The court reasoned that "[t]he objection of remoteness goes to the weight of the evidence rather than its admissibility. To exclude evidence merely because it tends [only] to establish a possibility . . . would produce curious results not heretofore thought of. [T]hat the accused was somewhere near the scene of the crime would not, in itself, establish a probability [exceeding .5] that he was guilty, but only a possibility, yet such evidence is clearly admissible as a link in the chain." 45 A.2d at 87. Likewise, in Com. v. Statti, 166 Pa. Super. 577, 73 A.2d 688, 692 (1950), the court held

that "the admissibility of this evidence is not affected by the fact that Type O blood is common to perhaps 45% of the people of the world. It was still competent as some evidence, just as evidence of how an assailant was dressed, however conventionally, would be competent though by no means conclusive of identity." Some courts treated the positive findings as admissible solely to corroborate the other evidence pointing to the defendant. Com. v. Mussoline, 429 Pa. 464, 240 A.2d 549 (1968).

[53]*See* Flippen v. Meinhold, 156 Misc. 451, 282 N.Y.S. 444, 446 (City Ct. 1935) (construing "Chapter 196 of the Laws of 1935, . . . which . . . provides that the court shall direct 'any party to the action and the child of any such party to submit to one or more blood grouping tests . . . wherever it shall be relevant to the prosecution or defense of an action' " as not authorizing orders to prove rather than disprove an alleged father's paternity).

[54]How much one learns depends on some details of the particular genetic system. Human chromosomes come in pairs. One is inherited from the mother, the other from the father. The cell nucleus thus contains two of each gene—one on each chromosome. If the two genes both act to express antigens, then the genotype giving rise to these antigens is known in its entirety. Such a system is said to be codominant, because neither allele dominates the other. The genetic sys-

are genetic markers. Knowing the phenotypes of the child, mother, and putative father and applying the laws of inheritance, a geneticist can say whether it would be possible for a child with the observed phenotype to have been born to the mother and the alleged father. That is, the medical expert can state that the biological father—whoever he may be—must have certain genetic characteristics, which can be compared to those that the alleged father has. In this way, a man falsely accused—one who does not have the necessary characteristics—can be excluded.[55]

With an appropriate foundation, such negative test results are nearly always admissible,[56] although the weight accorded to an

---

tem underlying the HLA antigens is of this simple type. However, with HLA it is common to speak of "haplotype" rather than genotype. The haplotype is half of the genotype. It is the set of HLA alleles along one of the chromosomes. The other chromosome usually has a different haplotype. Because the same allele can appear in both haplotypes or a haplotype may have an allele that does not react with any of the known antisera, it is not always possible to specify uniquely a person's haplotypes on the basis of his HLA phenotypes.

Instead of the genes being codominant, one "dominant" allele can function to the exclusion of its "recessive" partner. With these genetic systems, the phenotype does not always provide an unequivocal indication of the genotype. For example, the classic red blood cell types are thought to be the result of three alleles, designated A, B, and O. A person with type A blood could have the genotype AA or AO (since the O allele gives rise to neither A nor B antigens). Without testing other members of the family, there is no way to tell from serologic tests. For details on the genetic markers once used in parentage testing, see Morris & Gjertson, Parentage Testing: Scientific Status, in 4 Faigman, et al., Modern Scientific Evidence: The Law and Science of Expert Testimony §§ 32:9 to 32:11 (2011–2012 ed.).

[55]As with any empirical statement, absolute certainty is unattainable. In particular, an exclusion presupposes that simple Mendelian genetics is at work and that there has been no laboratory error. Furthermore, due to "silent" genes and weakly reacting reagents, not all exclusions are unambiguous. *Cf. Oi Lan Lee v. District Director of Immigration and Naturalization Service at Los Angeles, Cal.,* 573 F.2d 592, 595 n.2 (9th Cir. 1978) (recognizing that certainty in blood test exclusions, as in all scientific determinations, is "a matter of degree").

[56]*See* Little v. Streater, 452 U.S. 1, 101 S. Ct. 2202, 68 L. Ed. 2d 627 (1981) (holding that due process requires the state to finance blood tests for indigent paternity defendants and observing that "unlike other evidence . . . blood test results, if obtained under proper conditions by qualified experts, are difficult to refute"); Beach v. Beach, 114 F.2d 479, 480–81 (App. D.C. 1940); Houghton v. Houghton, 179 Neb. 275, 137 N.W.2d 861, 868 (1965); Admissibility and weight of blood-grouping tests in disputed paternity cases, 43 A.L.R.4th 579.

Two doctrines may interfere with the admissibility or weight of exculpatory immunologic evidence. Most jurisdictions allow the defense of *exceptio plurium concubentium*, which permits the defendant in a paternity proceeding to escape liability by showing that the mother had sexual relations with some other man during the possible period of conception. *See* Ellman & Kaye, Probabilities and Proof: Can HLA and Blood Group

exclusion varies. A few cases can be found upholding liability despite serologic proof of nonpaternity.[57] Perhaps the most notorious involved the comedian Charlie Chaplin.[58] In most states, however, a properly conducted blood test that excludes the defendant is conclusive.[59]

Positive immunogenetic findings are another matter. The traditional rule in this country was that serologic tests are inadmissible for this purpose.[60] At one time, when only a few, widely shared antigens were known, this approach made some sense. For example, under the early ABO system, a positive test result merely meant that the accused was, on average, one of the 87% of the male population possessing the requisite genotypes.[61] Such evidence is not very probative, and the fear that the jury

---

Testing Prove Paternity?, 54 NYU L. Rev. 1131, 1134 n.2 (1979). Second, in a few jurisdictions the presumption of legitimacy accorded a child born of a married mother during wedlock is well-nigh conclusive. Michael H. v. Gerald D., 491 U.S. 110, 109 S. Ct. 2333, 105 L. Ed. 2d 91 (1989); Jackson v. Jackson, 67 Cal. 2d 245, 60 Cal. Rptr. 649, 430 P.2d 289 (1967) (biological parentage irrelevant if conception occurs during cohabitation, but in conjunction with other evidence blood tests may show that conception did not occur in this period); John M. v. Paula T., 524 Pa. 306, 571 A.2d 1380 (1990) (putative father could not compel husband to take blood test despite HLA test said to show 97.47% probability for putative father).

[57]One child support decision of this ilk, State v. Camp, 286 N.C. 148, 209 S.E.2d 754, 756–57 (1974), provoked a statute, N.C. Gen. Stat. Ann. § 8-50.1(a)(1), making a definitive exclusion conclusive. Section 631(4) of the Uniform Parentage Act of 2000 does the same.

[58]Berry v. Chaplin, 74 Cal. App. 2d 652, 169 P.2d 442, 450–51 (2d Dist. 1946).

[59]Jackson v. Jackson, 253 Ga. 576, 322 S.E.2d 725, 727 (1984) (statute mandating jury instruction to find nonpaternity if jurors believe exclusionary test results were truthfully reported and correctly conducted does not require such a finding where ex-

pert did not know chain of custody); Jordan v. Mace, 144 Me. 351, 69 A.2d 670 (1949); Hanson v. Hanson, 311 Minn. 388, 249 N.W.2d 452, 453 (1977) (reviewing the weight generally accorded exclusionary results); Houghton v. Houghton, 179 Neb. 275, 137 N.W.2d 861, 870 (1965); cf. Oi Lan Lee v. District Director of Immigration and Naturalization Service at Los Angeles, Cal., 573 F.2d 592, 594–95 (9th Cir. 1978) (exclusions conclusive in Immigration and Naturalization Service proceedings). The view that a negative test result is conclusive if the accuracy of the testing is not attacked directly is an application of the doctrine that where uncontroverted physical facts contradict the testimony of a witness, that testimony cannot be accepted and a verdict based on it cannot be sustained. Anonymous v. Anonymous, 10 Ariz. App. 496, 460 P.2d 32, 35 (Div. 2 1969) ("To hold [that results which excluded the husband as the father of his wife's child were not conclusive] would be tantamount to this court, by judicial decree, declaring the laws of motion and gravity to be repealed").

[60]Isaacson v. Obendorf, 99 Idaho 304, 581 P.2d 350, 354–55 (1978); J. B. v. A. F., 92 Wis. 2d 696, 285 N.W.2d 880, 881–84 (Ct. App. 1979); Krause, Illegitimacy: Law and Social Policy 127–31 (1971).

[61]See Joint AMA-ABA Guidelines: Present Status of Serologic Testing in Problems of Disputed Parentage, 10 Fam. L.Q. 247, 257–58 (1976).

would give it more weight than it deserved, cloaked as it was in the garb of medical expertise, prompted many courts to exclude it as unduly prejudicial.[62] With the plethora of genetic markers that became known, however, it was commonplace to determine that the biological father had immunogenetic traits shared by one in several thousand men of the same race. As laboratories came to test reliably for more and more antigens, positive test results became too probative to be ignored.[63]

As a result, evidence that the accused has immunogenetic traits consistent with the claim that he is the biological father was received regularly. In most states, this was a consequence of statutory innovation.[64] In other instances, it was an example of the common law lugubriously digesting a technological advance.[65] The battle over the admissibility of serologic and related tests to

---

[62]*See, e.g.,* State ex rel. Freeman v. Morris, 156 Ohio St. 333, 46 Ohio Op. 188, 102 N.E.2d 450, 452 (1951).

[63]Ellman & Kaye, Probabilities and Proof: Can HLA and Blood Group Testing Prove Paternity?, 54 NYU L. Rev. 1131 (1979); Polesky & Krause, Blood Typing for Paternity, Current Capacities and Potential of American Laboratories—A Survey, 10 Fam. L.Q. 287 (1976) (collecting data on the capacity of blood banks and other laboratories to do serologic and related tests). An unexplained failure to test all the men whom a complainant indicates might have been the father or to perform a reasonably comprehensive battery of tests on each man may warrant exclusion of the evidence or a negative inference concerning it. *See* Ellman & Kaye, Probabilities and Proof: Can HLA and Blood Group Testing Prove Paternity?, 54 NYU L. Rev. 1131, 1158–61 (1979).

[64]Kaye & Kanwischer, Admissibility of Genetic Testing in Paternity Litigation: A Survey of State Statutes, 22 Fam.L.Q. 109 (1988); Litovsky & Schultz, Scientific Evidence of Paternity: A Survey of State Statutes, 39 Jurimetrics J. 79 (1998); Uniform Parentage Act § 12 (1973) ("Evidence relating to paternity may include . . . blood test results" and "medical or anthropological evidence . . . based on tests performed by experts"). Many of these statutes are awkwardly drafted

or poorly conceived. For instance, the phrase "blood tests" can invite arguments. Crain v. Crain, 104 Idaho 666, 662 P.2d 538 (1983) (HLA typing is not a blood group test, and as such, was not subject to strictures of former statute on blood testing); Com. v. Beausoleil, 397 Mass. 206, 490 N.E.2d 788 (1986) (HLA typing is not a "blood grouping test" within the meaning of a statute excluding test results that do not exculpate the alleged father); Phillips By and Through Utah State Dept. of Social Services v. Jackson, 615 P.2d 1228, 1233 (Utah 1980) (Uniform Parentage Act as enacted in Utah "was not intended to apply to HLA tests" as opposed to "blood test based on red blood cell groupings"); Ellman & Kaye, Probabilities and Proof: Can HLA and Blood Group Testing Prove Paternity?, 54 NYU L. Rev. 1131, 1139 n. 4 (1979). More troublesome aspects of the statutes relate to the admission of calculations of the "probability of paternity" and presumptions based on these probabilities. *See* Kaye, Presumptions, Probability and Paternity, 30 Jurimetrics J. 324 (1990). See infra § 211.

[65]McQueen v. Stratton, 389 So. 2d 1190 (Fla. 2d DCA 1980); Hennepin County Welfare Bd. v. Ayers, 304 N.W.2d 879, 882 (Minn. 1981) ("where a proper foundation is laid, blood test results that confirm paternity are admissible"); Ellman & Kaye, Probabilities and Proof: Can HLA and

prove paternity is over, but disputes over efforts to give an exact statement of the "probability of paternity" linger.[66]

Red blood cell grouping, blood serum protein and enzyme analysis, and HLA typing went a long way toward identifying individuals in suitable cases, but they were overshadowed by forensic adaptations of DNA technology.[67] There is no single method of DNA typing. As with conventional immunogenetic testing, the probative value of the laboratory findings depends on the procedure employed, the quality of the laboratory work, and the genetic characteristics that are discerned. We shall describe some of these procedures and the theory that lies behind them, and then consider the case law.

DNA is found in all nucleated cells, including those in bodily fluids such as blood and saliva. The DNA molecule has two long strands that spiral around one another, forming a double helix. Within the double helix are units, called nucleotide bases, that link one strand to the other, like the steps of a spiral staircase. There are four of these bases, which can be referred to by their initials, A, T, G and C. The A on one strand pairs with T on the other, and the G bonds to C. The lengthy sequence of AT and GC "stairs" within the DNA includes all the genes and regulatory sequences (for turning certain genes on and off and modulating the output of genes). The genes are stretches of base pairs whose order determines the composition of proteins and related products synthesized by various cells. These DNA sequences are called "coding" because the order of the base pairs specifies the order of the subunits that make up the protein for which the gene codes. However, most of the DNA in human beings (and many other organisms) is noncoding. Indeed, much of it has no known function, and even within functional regions, the variants in many sequences from one person to another are of little or no consequence to health or bodily function. But whether functional or not, essentially all the DNA in all of an individual's bodily cells are faithful copies of the DNA in the fertilized cell that grew into that individual.

Examining cell surface antigens (such as the ABO and HLA

---

Blood Group Testing Prove Paternity?, 54 NYU L. Rev. 1131, 1132 n. 7 (1979) (HLA tests); Kolko, Admissibility of HLA Test Results to Determine Paternity, 9 Fam. L. Rep. 4009 (1983).

[66]See infra § 211.

[67]*See generally* Kaye, The Double Helix and the Law of Evidence (2010); National Research Council Committee on DNA Forensic Science: An Update, The Evaluation of Forensic DNA

Evidence (1996); Kaye & Sensabaugh, Reference Guide on DNA Evidence, in Reference Manual on Scientific Evidence 129 (3d ed. 2011). Other techniques of genetic analysis occasionally surface in court. *E.g.*, Cobey v. State, 73 Md. App. 233, 533 A.2d 944 (1987) (error under *Frye* to admit Olson's quinacrine staining of chromosomes to incriminate defendant in rape resulting in aborted pregnancy).

systems) or blood serum enzymes or proteins gives some information about the DNA sequences that code for these particular substances—if the markers differ, then the underlying DNA must differ. In contrast, DNA typing works with the DNA molecule itself and is not limited to identifying variations in coding sequences. With appropriate technology, one can detect differences in the base pair sequences anywhere in the DNA molecules of human cells. Because 99.9 percent of the DNA sequence in any two people is identical, the technical challenge is to detect the relatively rare stretches of DNA, also called alleles, that vary among individuals. Two categories of procedures have been used, and more are under development. In PCR-based testing, small portions of DNA molecules are "amplified" by heating and cooling with an enzyme called DNA polymerase. Even if the sample contains only a small number of DNA molecules to start with, the polymerase induces a chain reaction that generates millions of identical fragments. Various procedures then can be used to characterize these small DNA fragments. At present, the most popular PCR-based technology is STR testing. STRs (short tandem repeats) consist of repeated occurrences of a core pattern of a few bases, such as (AATG)(AATG) . . . (AATG).[68] Depending on the number of repeats, these portions of DNA differ in their lengths—the more repeats, the longer the allele. The number of repeats can be detected with a form of electrophoresis that leads to peaks at distinct locations (for different alleles) on a graph known as an electropherogram.[69]

As with serologic tests, a single allele may be common in the population and hence not especially revealing. However, a series of STRs can narrow the percentage of the population that could have been the source of the sample, and testing for ten, twenty, or even more STRs usually is feasible—and very discriminating.[70]

Another form of PCR-based testing uses mitochondrial DNA

---

[68]Butler, Fundamentals of Forensic DNA Typing (2010); Goodwin et al., An Introduction to Forensic Genetics (2d ed. 2011); Kaye, The Double Helix and the Law of Evidence (2010); National Research Council Committee on DNA Forensic Science: An Update, The Evaluation of Forensic DNA Evidence (1996); Kaye & Sensabaugh, Reference Guide on DNA Evidence, in Reference Manual on Scientific Evidence 129 (3d ed. 2011).

[69]For a more complete explanation of how the graph is produced and examples of electropherograms, see, for example, Kaye, The Double Helix and the Law of Evidence (2010); Kaye & Sensabaugh, Reference Guide on DNA Evidence, in Reference Manual on Scientific Evidence 129 (3d ed. 2011).

[70]E.g., Butler, Fundamentals of Forensic DNA Typing (2010); Goodwin et al., An Introduction to Forensic Genetics (2d ed. 2011); Kaye, The Double Helix and the Law of Evidence (2010); National Research Council Committee on DNA Forensic Science: An Update, The Evaluation of Forensic DNA Evidence (1996); Kaye & Sensabaugh, Reference Guide on DNA Evidence, in Reference Manual on Scientific Evidence 129 (3d ed. 2011).

(mtDNA). Mitochondria are small structures outside of the cell nucleus, in which certain molecules are broken down to supply energy. The mitochondrial genome is minuscule compared to the chromosomal genome in the cell nucleus.[71] Like nuclear DNA, however, it has discrete alleles that can be detected with sequencing procedures that determine the sequence of the base pairs one after the other.[72] The mitochondrial DNA has three features that make it useful for forensic DNA testing. First, the typical cell, which has but one nucleus, contains between 75 to 1,000 identical mitochondria. Hence, for every copy of chromosomal DNA, there are hundreds of copies of mitochondrial DNA. This means that it is possible to detect mtDNA in samples containing too little nuclear DNA for conventional typing. Second, the mtDNA contains a region of about a thousand base pairs that varies greatly among most individuals. Finally, mitochondria are inherited mother to child, so that siblings, maternal half-siblings, and others related through maternal lineage possess the same mtDNA sequence.[73] This last feature makes mtDNA particularly useful for associating persons related through their maternal lineage—associating skeletal remains to a family, for example. However, the mt-DNA alleles are not as distinctive as a series of STR alleles; hence, an mtDNA match is much less definitive.

The typing procedure that dominated the first decade or so of forensic DNA cases is known as RFLP (restriction fragment length polymorphism) testing. It involves "digesting" DNA into fragments with enzymes ("restriction enzymes") from bacteria,[74] separating the restriction fragments according to length by gel

---

[71]In contrast to the haploid nuclear genome of over three billion base pairs, the mitochondrial genome is a circular molecule 16,569 base pairs long. Butler, Advanced Topics in Forensic DNA Typing: Methodology 406 (2011); Pakendorf & Stoneking, Mitochondrial DNA and Human Evolution, 6 Ann. Rev. Genomics & Hum. Genetics 165 (2005).

[72]Butler, Advanced Topics in Forensic DNA Typing: Methodology 413 (2011); Pakendorf & Stoneking, Mitochondrial DNA and Human Evolution, 6 Ann. Rev. Genomics & Hum. Genetics 165 (2005).

[73]Evolutionary studies suggest an average mutation rate for the mtDNA control region of one nucleotide difference every 300 generations, or one difference every 6,000 years. Conse-

quently, one would not expect to see many examples of nucleotide differences between maternal relatives. On the other hand, differences in the bases at a specific sequence position among the copies of the mtDNA within an individual have been seen. This heteroplasmy, which is more common in hair than other tissues, counsels against declaring an exclusion on the basis of a single base pair difference between two samples. Kaye & Sensabaugh, Reference Guide on DNA Evidence, in Reference Manual on Scientific Evidence 129 (3d ed. 2011).

[74]A restriction enzyme binds to DNA when it encounters a certain short sequence (usually four to eight base pairs) and cleaves the DNA at a specific site within that sequence. Digesting a sample of DNA with such an enzyme usually gives rise to frag-

electrophoresis,[75] blotting the array of fragments onto a nylon membrane, tagging the fragments with a radioactive probe,[76] then placing X-ray film to the membrane to give an image with dark bands at the locations of the tagged fragments.[77] The process can be repeated with other probes, and each probe yields a picture (known as an autoradiogram) with one or two bands. There will be one band if DNA in the sample came from a person who inherited the same allele from each parent; but more commonly, there will be two bands per probe because the individual inherited one allele from one parent and a different allele from the other parent. The locations of the bands from all the probes is the DNA "profile" seen on an autoradiograph.

With RFLP testing, the region within the long DNA molecules that are profiled depends on the particular combination of probe and restriction enzyme. Within some regions are stretches of DNA known as VNTRs (variable number of tandem repeats). Like STRs, VNTRs result from repetitions of core sequences. However, the repeated units are much longer (about 30 to 60 base pairs), and so are the alleles (which can consist of many thousands of base pairs). A probe that detects the core repetitive sequence will detect these variable length fragments. Because the number of repeating units at a VNTR locus varies greatly within a population, the probes that detect this type of repetitive

---

ments ranging from several hundred to several thousand base pairs in length. National Research Council Committee on DNA Forensic Science: An Update, The Evaluation of Forensic DNA Evidence (1996).

[75] The broken pieces of DNA are loaded into small holes cut into one end of a slab of gel. Because DNA fragments have a negative charge, applying an electric field to the gel pulls all the fragments toward the positive pole. Larger fragments have more difficulty moving through the gel, so after a while, the smaller fragments migrate farther. When the electric current is turned off, equally long pieces of DNA will lie in a band near their starting point, and equally short pieces will be in a band toward the other end of the gel. The length of any particular fragment can be measured by comparing the distance it has travelled to the distances that standard fragments of known size placed in a parallel slot in the gel have migrated. National Research Council Committee on DNA

Forensic Science: An Update, The Evaluation of Forensic DNA Evidence (1996).

[76] A "probe" is a short strand of DNA with a radioactive or chemiluminescent "tag" at one end. A sequence such as ATTGCTAT, for instance, will bind to a longer DNA fragment that contains the "complementary" sequence . . . TAACGATA . . . . (The rule is that A binds to T and C binds to G.)

[77] Here, however, the purpose of the probe is not to test for the presence of a given sequence, but merely to mark a fragment so that its length can be measured. Although the underlying variation consists of differences in the sequence of nucleotide bases, only the length of the fragments is ascertained via a particular restriction enzyme and probe. In this sense, the measured "alleles" are just the different lengths of the restriction fragments.

DNA are exquisitely informative. However, gel electrophoresis is not capable of measuring the lengths of VNTRs down to the level of a single repeat unit. This limitation made for some complications in deciding whether two VNTR bands "match" and how many people in the general population might be found to have similarly matching bands.[78]

A major advantage of the polymerase chain reaction over immunogenetic and RFLP testing is that it requires very little biological material, and it permits smaller (more degraded) DNA fragments to be analyzed. PCR-based procedures also can be automated and take less time to complete. For such reasons, they dominate forensic testing.

The judicial reception of DNA evidence can be divided into at least five phases.[79] The first phase was one of rapid acceptance. Initial praise for RFLP testing in homicide, rape, paternity, and other cases was effusive. Indeed, one judge proclaimed "DNA fingerprinting" to be "the single greatest advance in the 'search for truth' . . . since the advent of cross-examination."[80] In this first wave of cases, expert testimony for the prosecution rarely was countered, and courts readily admitted RFLP findings.[81]

In a second wave of cases, however, defendants pointed to problems at two levels—controlling the experimental conditions of the analysis, and interpreting the results.[82] Some scientists questioned certain features of the procedures for extracting and analyzing DNA employed in forensic laboratories, and it became apparent that declaring matches or non-matches among the RFLPs due to VNTR loci in two samples was not always trivial.[83] Despite these concerns, most cases continued to find forensic

---

[78]*See* People v. Venegas, 18 Cal. 4th 47, 74 Cal. Rptr. 2d 262, 954 P.2d 525 (1998); Kaye, The Relevance of "Matching" DNA: Is the Window Half Open or Half Shut?, 85 J. Crim. L. & Criminology 676 (1995).

[79]For a more elaborate review of this legal history, see Kaye, The Double Helix and the Law of Evidence (2010).

[80]People v. Wesley, 140 Misc. 2d 306, 533 N.Y.S.2d 643 (County Ct. 1988).

[81]E.g., Andrews v. State, 533 So. 2d 841 (Fla. 5th DCA 1988); People v. Wesley, 140 Misc. 2d 306, 533 N.Y.S.2d 643 (County Ct. 1988); Spencer v. Com., 238 Va. 275, 384 S.E.2d 775 (1989) (early version of DQα test properly admitted where "[t]he record is replete with uncontradicted expert

testimony that no 'dissent whatsoever (exists) in the scientific community'"); State v. Woodall, 182 W. Va. 15, 385 S.E.2d 253 (1989) (taking judicial notice of general scientific acceptance where there was no expert testimony, but holding that inconclusive results were properly excluded as irrelevant); Admissibility of DNA identification evidence, 84 A.L.R.4th 313.

[82]For a comprehensive survey of possible sources of error and ambiguity in VNTR profiling, see Thompson & Ford, The Meaning of a Match: Sources of Ambiguity in the Interpretation of DNA Prints, in Forensic DNA Technology 93 (Farley & Harrington eds., 1990).

[83]*See* U.S. v. Yee, 134 F.R.D. 161 (N.D. Ohio 1991); Anderson, DNA Fingerprinting on Trial, 342 Nature

RFLP analyses to be generally accepted,[84] and a number of states provided for admissibility of DNA tests by legislation.[85] Concerted attacks by defense experts of impeccable credentials, however, produced a few cases rejecting specific proffers on the ground that the testing was not sufficiently rigorous.[86] Moreover, a minority of courts, perhaps concerned that DNA evidence might well be conclusive in the minds of jurors, added a "third prong" to the general acceptance standard.[87] This augmented *Frye* test requires not only proof of the general acceptance of the ability of science to

---

844 (1989); Thompson & Ford, Is DNA Fingerprinting Ready for the Courts?, New Scientist, Mar. 31, 1990, at 38; Kolata, N.Y. Times, Jan. 29, 1990, at A1 col. 1 (reporting that "[l]eading molecular biologists say a technique promoted by the nation's top law-enforcement agency for identifying suspects in criminal trials through the analysis of genetic material is too unreliable to be used in court"; but the accuracy of this report is seriously questioned in Moenssens, DNA Evidence and Its Critics—How Valid Are the Challenges?, 31 Jurimetrics J. 87 (1990)).

[84]*E.g.*, U.S. v. Yee, 134 F.R.D. 161 (N.D. Ohio 1991); State v. Pennington, 327 N.C. 89, 393 S.E.2d 847 (1990) (uncontradicted expert testimony that false positives are impossible); Glover v. State, 787 S.W.2d 544 (Tex. App. Dallas 1990) (admissible in light of other decisions where "[a]ppellant did not produce any expert testimony").

[85]Md. Code Ann., Cts. & Jud. Proc. § 10-915 ("In any criminal proceeding, the evidence of a DNA profile [defined as "an analysis of genetic loci that has been validated according to standards established by [TWGDAM and the DNA Advisory Board of the FBI]" is admissible to prove or disprove the identity of any person"); Minn. Stat. Ann. § 634.25 ("In a criminal trial or hearing, the results of DNA analysis . . . are admissible in evidence without antecedent expert testimony that DNA analysis provides a trustworthy and reliable method of identifying characteristics in an individual's genetic material upon a showing that the offered testimony meets

the standards for admissibility set forth in the Rules of Evidence."); Melson, Legal and Ethical Considerations, in Kirby, DNA Fingerprinting: An Introduction 189, 199–200 (1990).

[86]People v. Castro, 144 Misc. 2d 956, 545 N.Y.S.2d 985 (Sup 1989) (principles of DNA testing generally accepted, but "[i]n a piercing attack upon each molecule of evidence presented, the defense was successful in demonstrating to this court that the testing laboratory failed in its responsibility to perform the accepted scientific techniques and experiments"); State v. Schwartz, 447 N.W.2d 422, 428 (Minn. 1989) ("DNA typing has gained general acceptance in the scientific community," but "the laboratory in this case did not comport" with "appropriate standards"); Norman, Maine Case Deals a Blow to DNA Fingerprinting, 246 Science 1556 (1989); Sherman, DNA Tests Unravel?, Nat'l L.J., Dec. 18, 1989, at 1, 24–25.

[87]This innovation was introduced in People v. Castro, 144 Misc. 2d 956, 545 N.Y.S.2d 985 (Sup 1989). It soon spread. *See* U.S. v. Two Bulls, 918 F.2d 56 (8th Cir. 1990), vacated for rehearing en banc, app. dismissed due to death of defendant, 925 F.2d 1127 (8th Cir. 1991) ("it was error for the trial court to determine the admissibility of the DNA evidence without determining whether the testing procedures . . . were conducted properly"); Ex parte Perry, 586 So. 2d 242 (Ala. 1991). For cases declining to graft a "third prong" to *Frye*, see, for example State v. Bible, 175 Ariz. 549, 858 P.2d 1152 (1993); Hopkins v. State, 579 N.E.2d

produce the type of results offered in court, but also of the proper application of an approved method on the particular occasion.[88] Such matters are better handled not as part of the special screening test for scientific evidence, but as aspects of the balancing of probative value and prejudice.[89]

A different attack on DNA profiling begun in cases during this period proved far more successful and led to a third wave of cases in which many courts held that estimates of the probability of a coincidentally matching VNTR profile were inadmissible.[90] These estimates relied on a simplified population-genetics model for the frequencies of VNTR profiles, and some prominent scientists claimed that the applicability of the mathematical model had not been adequately verified.[91] A heated debate on this point spilled over from courthouses to scientific journals and convinced the supreme courts of several states that general acceptance was lacking.[92] A 1992 report of the National Academy of Sciences proposed a more "conservative" computational method as a compromise,[93] and this seemed to undermine the claim of scientific acceptance of the less conservative procedure that was in general use.[94]

In response to the population-genetics criticism and the 1992

---

1297 (Ind. 1991); State v. Vandebogart, 136 N.H. 365, 616 A.2d 483 (1992); State v. Cauthron, 120 Wash. 2d 879, 846 P.2d 502 (1993).

[88]Later, some courts insisted on such a showing as part of the demonstration of scientific soundness required under *Daubert*. U.S. v. Martinez, 3 F.3d 1191 (8th Cir. 1993). It even was argued that proficiency testing of specific analysts or laboratories was necessary to satisfy *Frye* or *Daubert*. This argument is unconvincing. *See* Imwinkelried, Coming to Grips with Scientific Research in *Daubert*'s "Brave New World": The Courts' Need to Appreciate the Difference Between Validity and Proficiency Studies, 61 Brook. L. Rev. 1247 (1995).

[89]*See supra* § 203. *See* Berger, Laboratory Error Seen Through the Lens of Science and Policy, 30 U.C. Davis L. Rev. 1081 (1997).

[90]*See* National Research Council Committee on DNA Forensic Science: An Update, The Evaluation of Forensic DNA Evidence 205–11 (1996) (exhaustively tabulating cases); Kaye,

DNA Evidence: Probability, Population Genetics, and the Courts, 7 Harv. J. L. & Tech. 101 (1993).

[91]Kaye, The Double Helix and the Law of Evidence (2010); William C. Thompson, Evaluating the Admissibility of New Genetic Identification Tests: Lessons from the "DNA War," 84 J. Crim. L. & Criminology 22 (1993). In the light of the totality of information on the distribution of various genes in populations, the criticism of the simple random-mating model was overblown. Kaye, The Double Helix and the Law of Evidence (2010); Devlin & Roeder, DNA Profiling: Statistics and Population Genetics, in 1 Modern Scientific Evidence 710 (Faigman et al. eds., 1997).

[92]*See* Kaye, The Double Helix and the Law of Evidence (2010).

[93]National Research Council Committee on DNA Technology in Forensic Science, DNA Technology in Forensic Science (1992).

[94]*See* Kaye, The Forensic Debut of the NRC's DNA Report: Population Structure, Ceiling Frequencies and the

report came an outpouring of critiques of the report and new studies of the distribution of VNTR alleles in many population groups. Relying on the burgeoning literature, a second National Academy panel concluded in 1996 that the usual method of estimating frequencies of VNTR profiles in broad racial groups was sound.[95] In the corresponding fourth phase of judicial scrutiny of DNA evidence, the courts almost invariably returned to the earlier view that the statistics associated with VNTR profiling are generally accepted and scientifically valid.[96]

In a fifth phase of the judicial evaluation of DNA evidence, the courts concluded that the newer PCR-based methods rested on a solid scientific foundation and were generally accepted in the scientific community.[97] Thus, in little more than a decade, DNA typing made the transition from a novel set of methods for identification to a "gold standard" for forensic technology.[98] However, one should not lump all forms of DNA identification together. New techniques and applications continue to emerge. These range

---

Need for Numbers, 96 Genetica 99 (1995), published in slightly different form in 34 Jurimetrics J. 369 (1994).

[95]National Research Council Committee on DNA Forensic Science: An Update, The Evaluation of Forensic DNA Evidence (1996). The 1996 report provides more refined methods for estimating allele frequencies in ethnic subpopulations.

[96]People v. Reeves, 91 Cal. App. 4th 14, 109 Cal. Rptr. 2d 728 (1st Dist. 2001) (with the exception of the defendant's expert, controversy over random match probability calculations has been resolved); People v. Miller, 173 Ill. 2d 167, 219 Ill. Dec. 43, 670 N.E.2d 721 (1996) ("while there has been some controversy over the use of the product rule in calculating the frequency of a DNA match, that controversy appears to be dissipating"); Armstead v. State, 342 Md. 38, 673 A.2d 221 (1996) ("the debate over the product rule essentially ended in 1993"); Com. v. Fowler, 425 Mass. 819, 685 N.E.2d 746 (1997) (product rule with and without ceilings for VNTRs now meets test of scientific reliability in light of 1996 NRC Report), departing from Com. v. Lanigan, 413 Mass. 154, 596 N.E.2d 311 (1992) (dispute over population structure evinces lack of general acceptance); Kaye The Double Helix and

the Law of Evidence (2010).

[97]*E.g.*, U.S. v. Coleman, 202 F. Supp. 2d 962 (E.D. Mo. 2002) (mtDNA testing satisfies *Daubert*, and a finding of a match can be presented fairly to reveal that the type is not unique); State v. Pappas, 256 Conn. 854, 776 A.2d 1091 (2001) (mtDNA results and statistics admissible under *Daubert*); Com. v. Rosier, 425 Mass. 807, 685 N.E.2d 739 (1997) (STR testing and product-rule calculations admissible); Kaye & Sensabaugh, Reference Guide on DNA Evidence, in Reference Manual on Scientific Evidence 129 (3d ed. 2011).

[98]For instances of the presentation of DNA analysis as the gold standard for forensic science, see, for example, National Research Council Committee on Identifying the Needs of the Forensic Science Community, Strengthening Forensic Science in the United States: A Path Forward (2009); Garrett, Judging Innocence, 108 Colum. L. Rev. 55, 64 & 64 n.32; Giannelli, Wrongful Convictions and Forensic Science: The Need to Regulate Crime Labs, 86 N.C. L. Rev. 163, 171 (2007); Saks & Koehler, The Coming Paradigm Shift in Forensic Identification Science, 309 Science 892, 893 (2005).

from the use of new genetic systems and new analytical procedures[99] to the typing of DNA from plants and animals.[100] Even
with existing systems, efforts to push PCR to its limits in copying
only DNA fragments from a few cells ("low template" or "touch"
DNA samples) have generated controversy.[101] So have the
procedures analysts follow in interpreting mixed stains and
software designed to automate or assist in the interpretive
process.[102] Before admitting such evidence, it will be necessary to
inquire into the biological principles and knowledge that would
justify inferences from these new technologies or applications.[103]

## § 206　Psychology: Lie detection; drugs and hypnosis; eyewitness testimony; profiles and syndromes

The law and its procedures have long attracted the interest of
psychologists. Although the preeminent contributions of psychologists and psychiatrists as expert witnesses have come in presenting clinical diagnoses or evaluations in criminal and other cases,[1]
at this point, we shall describe less conventional forensic
applications. Specifically, this section surveys issues arising from

---

[99]Kaye & Sensabaugh, Reference
Guide on DNA Evidence, in Reference
Manual on Scientific Evidence 129 (3d
ed. 2011).

[100]State v. Leuluaialii, 118 Wash.
App. 780, 77 P.3d 1192 (Div. 1 2003)
(expert testimony of canine STR match
and associated probabilities was improper without proof of general acceptance); Imwinkelried, Canine DNA, 46
Crim. L. Bull. No. 4, Art. 6, Summer
2010; Kaye & Sensabaugh, Non-human
DNA Evidence, 39 Jurimetrics J. 1
(1998).

[101]People v. Megnath, 27 Misc. 3d
405, 898 N.Y.S.2d 408 (Sup 2010) (*Frye*
does not apply to "touch DNA" because
the procedures are not novel, and
anyway the modifications are generally accepted); R. v. Reed, [2009] (CA
Crim Div.) EWCA Crim. 2698, ¶ 74
("Low Template DNA can be used to
obtain profiles capable of reliable interpretation if the quantity of DNA
that can be analysed is above the
stochastic threshold [of] between 100
and 200 picograms."); Kaye &
Sensabaugh, Reference Guide on DNA
Evidence, in Reference Manual on
Scientific Evidence 129 (3d ed. 2011).

[102]*E.g.*, Com. v. Foley, 2012 PA
Super 31, 38 A.3d 882 (2012) (software
satisfies *Frye* standard); Kaye, The
Double Helix and the Law of Evidence
(2010).

[103]*E.g.*, Harrison v. State, 644
N.E.2d 1243 (Ind. 1995) (error not to
hold *Frye* hearing on PCR-based
method). For suggestions to assist in
evaluating new developments in DNA
testing, see Kaye & Sensabaugh,
Non-human DNA Evidence, 39 Jurimetrics J. 1 (1998).

**[Section 206]**

[1]Barefoot v. Estelle, 463 U.S.
880, 103 S. Ct. 3383, 77 L. Ed. 2d 1090
(1983) (psychiatrist's predictions of
future violence admissible in capital
sentencing hearing despite professional skepticism over the ability of
mental health experts to make such
predictions); 2 Faigman, et al., Modern
Scientific Evidence: The Law and
Science of Expert Testimony, chs. 9,
10, 12 (2011–2012 ed.) (insanity and
diminished capacity; predictions of
violence; projective techniques); Appelbaum, Reference Guide on Mental
Health Evidence, in Reference Manual
on Scientific Evidence 813 (3d ed.
2011).

expert testimony about physiological indicators of deception, "truth" drugs and hypnosis, eyewitness identifications, and "profiles" of certain types of offenders or victims.

*(A) Detection of Deception.*

Popular belief has it that lying and consciousness of guilt are accompanied by emotion or excitement that expresses itself in bodily changes—the blush, the gasp, the quickened heartbeat, the sweaty palm, the dry mouth. The skilled cross-examiner may face the witness with his lies and involve him in a knot of new ones, so that these characteristic signs of lying become visible to the jury. This is part of the demeanor of the witness that the jury is told it may observe and consider upon credibility.[2]

Internal stress also has been thought to accompany the process of lying. It is said that more than 4,000 years ago the Chinese would try the accused in the presence of a physician who, listening or feeling for a change in the heartbeat, would announce whether the accused was testifying truthfully.[3] The modern "lie detectors" operate on the same general principle. While an interrogator puts questions to the suspect, the polygraph monitors and records several autonomic physiological functions, such as blood pressure, pulse rate, respiration rate and depth, and perspiration (by measuring skin conductance). In the most commonly used procedure, the "diagnosis" is made by comparing the responses to "control" questions with the reactions to "relevant" questions.[4] Control questions attempt to force the subject to lie about some common transgression. In an embezzlement case, for

---

[2]*See* 3A Wigmore, Evidence § 946 (Chadbourn rev.1970); Fisher, The Jury's Rise as Lie Detector, 107 Yale L.J. 575 (1997). For efforts of psychologists to identify behavioral indicators of lying, see Boyd et al., Detection of Deception (2006); Vrij, Detecting Lies and Deceit: Pitfalls and Opportunities (2d ed. 2008); Wellborn, Demeanor, 76 Cornell L. Rev. 1075, 1082–88 (1991).

[3]Morland, An Outline of Scientific Criminology 59–60 (2d ed. 1971). "Saliva tests" have also been used, the method of implementation varying according to the culture. The Chinese required the suspect to chew a mouthful of rice flour, then looked to see if it had remained dry. Bedouins required suspected liars to lick a hot iron. A burned tongue was a sign of lying. In Britain the test was to swallow a "trial slice" of bread and cheese. Inability to

swallow was thought to reveal deception. Saks & Hastie, Social Psychology in Court 192 (1978). *See also* Langley, The Polygraph Lie Detector, 16 Ala. Law. 209–10 (1955).

[4]Moenssens et al., Scientific Evidence in Civil and Criminal Cases § 20.07 (4th ed. 1995); Office of Technology Assessment, U.S. Congress, Scientific Validity of Polygraph Testing: A Research Review and Evaluation—A Technical Memorandum 13–23 (1983); Vrij, Detecting Lies and Deceit: Pitfalls and Opportunities 298–304 (2d ed. 2008); Honts et al., The Case for Polygraph Tests, in 5 Faigman, et al., Modern Scientific Evidence: The Law and Science of Expert Testimony § 40:22 (2011–2012 ed.); Iacono & Lykken, The Case Against Polygraph Tests, in 5 Faigman, et. al., Modern Scientific Evidence: The Law and Science of Expert Testimony §§ 40:47

instance, a control question might be, "Have you ever stolen anything?"[5] A relevant question is one that relates to the particular matter under investigation.[6] If the autonomic disturbances associated with the relevant items seem greater or more persistent, then the subject is judged to be dissembling.[7] In making this judgment, most federal and local law enforcement agencies employ some type of numerical scoring system.[8] Other analysts apply a less structured procedure[9] and insist that polygraphic lie

---

to 40:62 (2011–2012 ed.). Interrogation without "control questions" is known as "relevant-irrelevant" testing, since the investigator merely looks for a difference in responses to questions that are relevant to the incident under investigation and those that are irrelevant. The consensus in the scientific community is that "relevant-irrelevant" testing is not revealing, and the technique is not normally used in specific incident examinations. Office of Technology Assessment, U.S. Congress, Scientific Validity of Polygraph Testing: A Research Review and Evaluation—A Technical Memorandum 17 (1983); Vrij, Detecting Lies and Deceit: Pitfalls and Opportunities 296–98 (2d ed. 2008); Honts et al., The Case for Polygraph Tests, in 5 Faigman, et. al., Modern Scientific Evidence: The Law and Science of Expert Testimony § 40:21 (2011–2012 ed.).

[5]In a variation of this procedure, the examiner instructs the subject to lie about certain questions. These "directed lies" serve as the "controls." Honts et al., The Case for Polygraph Tests, in 5 Faigman, et. al., Modern Scientific Evidence: The Law and Science of Expert Testimony § 40:23 (2011–2012 ed.); Iacono & Lykken, The Case Against Polygraph Tests, in 5 Modern Scientific Evidence: The Law and Science of Expert Testimony § 40:51 (Faigman et al. eds. 2011–2012).

[6]"Irrelevant" questions (for example, "Did you ever go to school?") also are asked. Contrivances such as the "card test" may be used to heighten the suspect's faith in the machine, and

hence his anxiety over answering incriminating questions falsely. Reid & Inbau, Truth and Deception: The Polygraph ("Lie Detection") Technique 42–43 (2d ed. 1977); Kleinmuntz & Szucko, On the Fallibility of Lie Detection, 17 Law & Soc'y Rev. 85, 88–89 (1981).

[7]See Moenssens et al., Scientific Evidence in Civil and Criminal Cases § 20.07 (4th ed. 1995); Vrij, Detecting Lies and Deceit: Pitfalls and Opportunities 302–04 (2d ed. 2008).

[8]Iacono & Lykken, The Case Against Polygraph Tests, in 5 Faigman, et. al., Modern Scientific Evidence: The Law and Science of Expert Testimony § 40:49 (2011–2012 ed.); Raskin, The Polygraph in 1986: Scientific, Professional and Legal Issues Surrounding Application and Acceptance of Polygraph Evidence, 1986 Utah L. Rev. 29, 37.

[9]Kleinmuntz & Szucko, On the Fallibility of Lie Detection, 17 Law & Soc'y Rev. 85, 89 (1981). These analysts may rely on numerous factors, including the apparent intelligence and educational background of the suspect. Behavioral cues that are said to be symptomatic of deceptiveness or truthfulness include squirming, yawning, coughing, sniffling, gurgling, pausing, refusing to look the examiner in the eye, being late for the appointment, wanting to leave as soon as possible, becoming abusive and argumentative after the card test, being cooperative (but not overly polite), and displaying confidence in the machine and its operator. Reid & Inbau, Truth and Deception: The Polygraph ("Lie Detection") Technique 17, 19, 23,

detection is a "clinical judgment" that depends on "intrinsic emotional states," "medical conditions," and "unique" interviews.[10]

The validity and reliability[11] of the control-question test are hotly contested.[12] Polygraph examiners claim that, properly administered, it is a highly effective means of detecting deception, and they cite figures such as 80%, 90%, 92%, 99%, and even 100% for its accuracy.[13] Although some controlled experiments

---

293–95 (2d ed. 1977). *But see* Reid & Inbau, at 296 ("sole or even major reliance should not be placed upon behavior symptoms: they should be considered only in the context of the entire Polygraph examination").

[10]Moenssens et al., Scientific Evidence in Civil and Criminal Cases § 20.12 (4th ed. 1995).

[11]As indicated supra § 203, these terms have a specialized meaning in science. Reliability refers to reproducibility of results (consistency), while validity relates to ability to measure whatever it is that one purports to measure (here, truthfulness). *See, e.g.,* Blinkhorn, Lie Detection as a Psychometric Procedure, in The Polygraph Test: Lies, Truth and Science 30, 31–35 (Gale ed.1988).

[12]Iacono & Lykken, The Case Against Polygraph Tests, in 5 Faigman, et. al., Modern Scientific Evidence: The Law and Science of Expert Testimony § 40:45 (2011–2012 ed.); Saxe et al., The Validity of Polygraph Testing, in On the Witness Stand: Controversies in the Courtroom 14 (Wrightsman et al. eds., 1987); Vrij, Detecting Lies and Deceit: Pitfalls and Opportunities 304–15 (2d ed. 2008).

[13]U.S. v. Oliver, 525 F.2d 731, 737 (8th Cir. 1975) (the expert polygrapher "personally testified that he had conducted more than 50,000 examinations which were subjected to verification through supporting admissions, confessions, or additional evidence. The accuracy of his diagnosis was estimated in excess of 90 percent"); Am. Polygraph Ass'n, Frequently Asked Questions about Validated Techniques and the Meta-Analysis, at 8, Jan. 9, 2012, available at http://www.polygrap

h.org/files/validated__techniques__fa q__1-9-2012.pdf ("The 95% confidence interval for unweighted accuracy was .798 to .940, with a mean of .869. . . . Event-specific diagnostic techniques, conducted around a single known or alleged problem, have [higher] accuracy levels . . . ."); Am. Polygraph Ass'n, The Validity and Reliability of Polygraph Testing, http://www.polygra ph.org/betasite/apa5rev.htm, visited Aug. 10, 2005 (reporting that "field examinations confirmed by independent evidence [showed] an average accuracy of 92% [and that] laboratory simulations of polygraph examinations [produced] an average accuracy of 80%"); Department of Defense, The Accuracy and Utility of Polygraph Testing (1984); Moenssens et al., Scientific Evidence in Criminal Cases § 14.09, at 712 (3d ed. 1986) ("it is reported that when the technique is properly applied by a trained, competent examiner, it is very accurate in its indications, with a known error percentage of less than one percent. That conclusion is based on the examinations of over 100,000 persons suspected or accused of criminal offenses or involved in personnel investigations initiated by their employers, almost all of which examinations were conducted at the extensive facilities of John E. Reid and Associates. It is also supported by validation studies reported in Journal articles"); Wallach, Letter, Sci. News, Dec. 17, 1983, at 397 ("In my 30-odd years of experience . . . I've found that skilled operators can approach 100 percent accuracy in verifying true statements"); Wittenberg & Simmons, Truth or Consequences, Ore. St. Bar J., Nov. 1997, 23, 25 ("In a summary of all real crimes cases from 1980 through 1990,

and other studies have been interpreted as showing that such accuracy is possible,[14] most psychologists and other scientists reviewing the literature are not impressed with these bold assertions. They see methodological flaws undermining the conclusions,[15] they suggest figures in a much lower range,[16] and they point out that the percentage figures of "accuracy" are inappropriate measures of validity.[17] Attempts to determine the rate of false

---

accuracy rates . . . [averaged] above 90%."); *cf.* Lykken, The Lie Detector and the Law, 8 Crim. Defense, May–June 1981, at 20, 23 (citing inflated claims concerning now discredited lie detection techniques).

[14]Honts et al., The Case for Polygraph Tests, in 5 Faigman, et al., Modern Scientific Evidence: The Law and Science of Expert Testimony § 40:26 (2011–2012 ed.) ("[H]igh quality laboratory studies indicate that the CQT is a very accurate discriminator of truthful and deceptive subjects. Overall, these studies correctly 91% of the subjects and produced approximately equal numbers of false positive and false negative errors."); Raskin, The Polygraph in 1986: Scientific, Professional and Legal Issues Surrounding Application and Acceptance of Polygraph Evidence, 1986 Utah L. Rev. 29, 43 (tbl. 1) (accuracy in five laboratory studies ranged from 91 to 96% when "inconclusive" results were counted as "correct," 85 to 88% otherwise).

[15]Carroll, How Accurate is Polygraph Lie Detection?, in The Polygraph Test: Lies, Truth and Science 19 (Gale ed., 1988); Committee to Review the Scientific Evidence on the Polygraph, National Research Council, The Polygraph and Lie Detection 2 (2003) ("The general quality of the evidence for judging polygraph validity is relatively low: the substantial majority of the studies most relevant for this purpose were below the quality level typically needed for funding by the National Science Foundation or the National Institutes of Health."); Office of Technology Assessment, U.S. Congress, Scientific Validity of Polygraph Testing: A Research Review

and Evaluation—A Technical Memorandum 41–43 & 48–50 (1983) (discussing problems of interpreting and relying on various studies and reviews of studies); Vrij, Detecting Lies and Deceit: Pitfalls and Opportunities 317–21 (2d ed. 2008).

[16]Committee to Review the Scientific Evidence on the Polygraph, National Research Council, The Polygraph and Lie Detection 3 (2003) ("Estimates of accuracy from these 57 studies are almost certainly higher than actual polygraph accuracy of specific-incident testing in the field"); Vrij, Detecting Lies and Deceit: Pitfalls and Opportunities 322–29 (2d ed. 2008).

[17]*See* Vrij, Detecting Lies and Deceit: Pitfalls and Opportunities 314–15 (2d ed. 2008); *cf.* Kleinmuntz & Szucko, On the Fallibility of Lie Detection, 17 Law & Soc'y Rev. 85, 86–87 (1981) (overall rate of agreement between two analysts is not a useful measure of inter-rater reliability). The overall accuracy, or hit rate, could be 100% even if the polygraph technique had no value at all. If a polygraph operator declares all suspects to be liars, and the rate of conviction in that jurisdiction is 100%, then the examiner will be "proved" right in every case. If the analyst picks 90% of the suspects—entirely at random—and declares that these are lying, and if the conviction rate is 90%, then the expected hit rate is (90%) (90%) = 81%. The hit rate statistic is even more misleading if the examination itself influences the disposition of the case. For a more general analysis of the relation between the various "accuracy" statistics and the probative value of a declaration of deception or truthful-

positives—of saying that someone is lying when he is actually telling the truth—also have been controversial. Some writers claim that these errors rarely occur[18] but there are also studies and analyses that put the expected rate of false positives in excess of 35%.[19] The skeptics also dispute the underlying theory.[20] At best, the control question technique registers physiological cor-

---

ness, see Kaye et al., The New Wigmore, A Treatise on Evidence: Expert Evidence § 7.3.2(c) (2d ed. 2011); Kaye, The Validity of Tests: Caveant Omnes, 27 Jurimetrics J. 349 (1987).

[18]Raskin, The Polygraph in 1986: Scientific, Professional and Legal Issues Surrounding Application and Acceptance of Polygraph Evidence, 1986 Utah L. Rev. 29, 43 (Table 1) (false positive rates in five laboratory studies ranged from 0 to 17 percent, false negatives from 0 to 10 percent); Raskin & Podlesny, Truth and Deception: A Reply to Lykken, 86 Psychol. Bull. 54 (1979).

[19]Office of Technology Assessment, U.S. Congress, Scientific Validity of Polygraph Testing: A Research Review and Evaluation—A Technical Memorandum 97 (1983) (false positives in criminal incident field studies ranged from 0 to 75%, false negatives from 0 to 29.4%; false positives in laboratory studies analogous to criminal investigations ranged from 2 to 50.7%, false negatives from 0 to 28.7%). But see Raskin, The Polygraph in 1986: Scientific, Professional and Legal Issues Surrounding Application and Acceptance of Polygraph Evidence, 1986 Utah L. Rev. 29, 45 (criticizing certain field studies included in the OTA review). See also Carroll, How Accurate is Polygraph Lie Detection?, in The Polygraph Test: Lies, Truth and Science 22 (Gale ed., 1988) (9–33% false positives in laboratory studies), 26 (37–55% false positives in field studies); Kleinmuntz & Szucko, A Field Study of the Fallibility of Polygraphic Lie Detection, 308 Nature 449 (1984) (28% false positives, 26% false negatives); Kleinmuntz & Szucko, On the Fallibility of Lie Detection, 17

Law & Soc'y Rev. 85, 96 (1981) (reporting their own study showing that correlation coefficients between diagnoses (of six examiners given polygraph records of 50 truthful and 50 untruthful subjects) and whether or not the examinees were actually telling the truth ranged from .45 to .55, with false positives ranging from 18 to 50%, and citing other studies finding false positive rates of 49 and 55%); Lykken, The Lie Detector and the Law, 8 Crim. Defense, May–June 1981, at 20 (estimating an average of 36–39% false positives). But see also Raskin, The Polygraph in 1986: Scientific, Professional and Legal Issues Surrounding Application and Acceptance of Polygraph Evidence, 1986 Utah L. Rev. 29; Raskin & Podlesny, Truth and Deception: A Reply to Lykken, 86 Psychol. Bull. 54 (1979).

[20]Committee to Review the Scientific Evidence on the Polygraph, National Research Council, The Polygraph and Lie Detection 2 (2003):

Almost a century of research in scientific psychology and physiology provides little basis for the expectation that a polygraph test could have extremely high accuracy. Although psychological states often associated with deception (e.g., fear of being judged deceptive) do tend to affect the physiological responses that the polygraph measures, these same states can arise in the absence of deception. Moreover, many other psychological and physiological factors (e.g., anxiety about being tested) also affect those responses. Such phenomena make polygraph testing intrinsically susceptible to producing erroneous results. This inherent ambiguity of the physiological measures used in the polygraph suggests that further investments in improving polygraph technique and interpretation will bring only modest improvements in accuracy.

relates of anxiety, which is not the same thing as consciousness of guilt or lying. Questions can provoke inner turmoil even when they are answered truthfully.[21] As one critic has put it, "the polygraph pens do no special dance when we are lying."[22] In addition, there are numerous countermeasures that a suspect can use to mislead the analyst, some of which are said to be effective and difficult to detect.[23] It is feared that if the polygraph came into widespread use in court cases, these could cause the rate of false negatives—saying that the suspect is telling the truth when he is lying—to become intolerably high.

---

[21]Kleinmuntz & Szucko, On the Fallibility of Lie Detection, 17 Law & Soc'y Rev. 85, 87 (1981) ("there is no reason to believe that lying produces distinctive physiological changes that characterize it and only it. . . . No doubt when we tell a lie many of us experience an inner turmoil, but we experience a similar turmoil when we are falsely accused of a crime, when we are anxious about having to defend ourselves against accusations, when we are questioned about sensitive topics—and, for that matter, when we are elated or otherwise emotionally stirred"). Those who support the technique, however, might counter that a skilled examiner takes time to put the subject at ease before taking any readings and that some of these sources of anxiety should affect responses to all questions and therefore not interfere with the differential analysis.

[22]Lykken, as quoted in Kleinmuntz & Szucko, On the Fallibility of Lie Detection, 17 Law & Soc'y Rev. 85, 88 (1981); cf. People v. Zackowitz, 254 N.Y. 192, 172 N.E. 466 (1930) (Cardozo, J.) ("The sphygmograph records with graphic certainty the fluctuations of the pulse. There is no instrument yet invented that records with equal certainty the fluctuations of the mind.").

[23]Committee to Review the Scientific Evidence on the Polygraph, National Research Council, The Polygraph and Lie Detection 4 (2003) ("Countermeasures pose a potentially serious threat to the performance of polygraph testing . . . ."); Office of Technology Assessment, U.S. Congress, Scientific Validity of Polygraph Testing: A Research Review and Evaluation—A Technical Memorandum 87–92 & 100–01 (1983); Saks & Hastie, Social Psychology in Court 199 (1978); Yarmey, The Psychology of Eyewitness Testimony 173 (1979); Gudjonsson, Lie Detection: Techniques and Countermeasures, in Evaluating Witness' Evidence 143–51 (Lloyd-Bostock & Clifford eds. 1983); Honts et al., Mental and Physical Countermeasures Reduce the Accuracy of Polygraph Tests, 79 J. Applied Psychol. 252 (1994); Honts et al., The Case for Polygraph Tests, in 5 Modern Scientific Evidence: The Law and Science of Expert Testimony § 40:33 (Faigman et al. eds. 2011–2012) (countermeasures produce false negatives or inconclusive but not false positives); Raskin, The Polygraph in 1986: Scientific, Professional and Legal Issues Surrounding Application and Acceptance of Polygraph Evidence, 1986 Utah L. Rev. 29, 49–52 (discussing drugs and physical countermeasures). But see Committee to Review the Scientific Evidence on the Polygraph, National Research Council, The Polygraph and Lie Detection 4 (2003) ("It is unknown whether a deceptive individual can produce responses that mimic the physiological responses of a nondeceptive individual well enough to fool an examiner trained to look for behavioral and physiological signatures of countermeasures.").

Another group of devices that measure a physiological response to detect when a person is consciously concealing knowledge are the voice stress analyzers. They analyze the frequency spectrum of a speaker's voice to detect subaudible, involuntary tremors said to result from emotional stress. The scientific literature on these lie detection devices indicates that they have no validity.[24]

Finally, neuroscientists have experimented with instruments that measure blood flow (fMRI)[25] or electrical activity within the brain (EEG).[26] Despite enthusiastic reports from the small number of scientists seeking to use such instruments for detect-

---

[24]Committee to Review the Scientific Evidence on the Polygraph, National Research Council, The Polygraph and Lie Detection 167–68 (2003); Hollien, The Acoustics of Crime: The New Science of Forensic Phonetics 288 (1990) ("very difficult, if not impossible, to defend the validity of this approach"); Lykken, A Tremor in the Blood: Uses and Abuses of the Lie Detector 173 (2d ed. 1998) ("the voice stress 'lie test' has roughly zero validity"); Saks & Hastie, Social Psychology in Court 202 (1978) ("no scientific evidence to support the claim that they are accurate beyond chance levels"); Vrij, Detecting Lies and Deceit: Pitfalls and Opportunities 338–39 (2d ed. 2008); Hollien et al., Voice Stress Evaluators and Lie Detection, 32 J. Forensic Sci. 405, 415 (1987) ("a device that will permit the detection of lying from the voice analysis alone presently does not exist"); Horvath, Detecting Deception: The Promise and the Reality of Voice Stress Analysis, 27 J. Forensic Sci. 340 (1982) ("the scientific evidence reported to date shows that voice stress analyzers are not effective in detecting deception: none of these devices has yet been shown to yield detection rates above chance levels in controlled situations"). Kelly R. Damphousseat et al., Assessing the Validity of Voice Stress Analysis Tools in a Jail Setting, Mar. 31, 2007, at 53 (NCJRS doc. no. 219031, available at https://www.ncjrs.gov/pdffiles1/nij/grants/219031.pdf) (of 87 subjects who tested positive for cocaine use within the past 72 hours, 40 deceptively stated that they had not used cocaine in this period, but voice-stress analysis only correctly indicated deception for eight of the 40 (a sensitivity of 20%); however, of the 47 respondents who were not deceptive, the voice-stress analysis programs correctly classified 42 as truthful, for a specificity of 89%). Thus, the courts almost invariably exclude voice stress evidence. Barrel of Fun, Inc. v. State Farm Fire & Cas. Co., 739 F.2d 1028, 1030, 1032 (5th Cir. 1984); People v. Lippert, 125 Ill. App. 3d 489, 80 Ill. Dec. 824, 466 N.E.2d 276, 47 A.L.R. 4th 1183 (5th Dist. 1984); Neises v. Solomon State Bank, 236 Kan. 767, 696 P.2d 372, 377–78 (1985).

[25]Kozel et al., Functional MRI Detection of Deception After Committing a Mock Sabotage Crime, 54 J. Forensic Sci. 220 (2009); Langleben, Detection of Deception with fMRI: Are We There Yet?, 13 Leg. & Criminol. Psychol. 1 (2008); Seaman, Black Boxes, 58 Emory L.J. 427 (2008); Simpson, Functional MRI Lie Detection: Too Good to be True?, 36 J. Am. Acad. Psychiatry & L. 491 (2008); Spence, The Deceptive Brain, 97 J. Royal Soc'y Med. 6 (2004).

[26]The theory is that specific patterns (designated P300 and MERMER) in the EEG (electroencephalograph) reveal the processing of the details of a crime stored in the brain. Farwell & Smith, Using Brain MERMER Testing to Detect Concealed Knowledge Despite Efforts to Conceal, 46 J. Forensic Sci. 135 (2001); Keckler, Cross-examining the Brain: A Legal Analysis of Neural Imaging for Credibility Impeachment, 57 Hastings L.J. 509, 519–21 (2006).

ing deception or memories,[27] robust demonstrations of reliability and validity remain to be seen.[28]

The courts have not greeted the modern methods of lie detection with enthusiasm.[29] Indeed, *Frye v. United States*,[30] the case that announced the general-acceptance standard for the admissibility of scientific evidence, involved a primitive version of the polygraph.[31] In the succeeding decades, many courts treated the early decision as if it established that polygraph results were inadmissible regardless of any improvements in the technology.[32]

---

[27]Farwell et al., Brain Fingerprinting in Field Conditions, 43 Psychophysiology S37 (2006); Farwell & Richardson, Brain Fingerprinting in Laboratory Conditions, 43 Psychophysiology S38 (2006); Farwell & Smith, Using Brain MERMER Testing to Detect Concealed Knowledge Despite Efforts to Conceal, 46 J. Forensic Sci. 135 (2001) (reporting over 99% accuracy in laboratory research and real-life field applications); *see also* Allen & Iacono, A Comparison of Methods for the Analysis of Event-related Potentials in Deception Detection, 34 Psychophysiology 234 (1997).

[28]*See* Wagner, Can Neuroscience Identify Lies?, in A Judge's Guide To Neuroscience: A Concise Introduction 13 (2010); Adelsheim, Functional Magnetic Resonance Detection of Deception: Great as Fundamental Research, Inadequate as Substantive Evidence, 62 Mercer L. Rev. 885 (2011); Keckler, Cross-examining the Brain: A Legal Analysis of Neural Imaging for Credibility Impeachment, 57 Hastings L.J. 509, 521, 527–37 (2006); Law, Cherry-picking Memories: Why Neuroimaging-based Lie Detection Requires a New Framework for the Admissibility of Scientific Evidence under FRE 702 and *Daubert*, 14 Yale J. L. & Tech. 1 (2011); Langleben, Detection of Deception with fMRI: Are We There Yet?, 13 Leg. & Criminol. Psychol. 1 (2008); Monteleoneet et al., Detection of Deception Using fMRI: Better than Chance, But Well Below Perfection, 2 Social Neurosci. 1747 (2008); New, If You Could Read My Mind: Implications of Neurological

Evidence for Twenty—First Century Criminal Jurisprudence, 29 J. Legal Med. 179 (2008); Pardo, Neuroscience Evidence, Legal Culture, and Criminal Procedure, 33 Am. J. Crim. L. 301 (2006); Rosenfeld, "Brain Fingerprinting:" A Critical Analysis, 4 Scientific Rev. Mental Health Practice 20 (2005); Simpson, Functional MRI Lie Detection: Too Good to be True?, 36 J. Am. Acad. Psychiatry & L. 491 (2008); Seaman, Black Boxes, 58 Emory L.J. 427 (2008); Shen & Jones, Brain Scans as Evidence: Truths, Proofs, Lies, and Lessons, 62 Mercer L. Rev. 861 (2011).

[29]For an historical review, see 1 Giannelli & Imwinkelried, Scientific Evidence § 8.04 (4th ed. 2007).

[30]Frye v. U.S., 293 F. 1013, 34 A.L.R. 145 (App. D.C. 1923) (rejected by, State v. Walstad, 119 Wis. 2d 483, 351 N.W.2d 469 (1984)) and (rejected by, State v. Brown, 297 Or. 404, 687 P.2d 751 (1984)) and (rejected by, Nelson v. State, 628 A.2d 69 (Del. 1993)) and (rejected by, State v. Alberico, 116 N.M. 156, 861 P.2d 192 (1993)) and (rejected by, State v. Moore, 268 Mont. 20, 885 P.2d 457 (1994)) and (rejected by, State v. Faught, 127 Idaho 873, 908 P.2d 566 (1995)) and (rejected by, People v. Shreck, 22 P.3d 68, 90 A.L.R.5th 765 (Colo. 2001)).

[31]*See* Marston, Psychological Possibilities in the Deception Tests, 11 J. Crim. L. & Criminology 551 (1921). See supra § 203.

[32]For two strenuous but futile efforts to lay the necessary foundation, see People v. Davis, 343 Mich. 348, 72 N.W.2d 269 (1955); People v. Leone,

With the erosion of the general-acceptance requirement[33] and the explosive growth of polygraphy in American government and business,[34] however, a substantial number of courts were willing to take a fresh look at the evidentiary value of the most commonly used polygraph tests.[35] Three principal positions on admissibility have emerged, with considerable back and forth movement into and out of each category.[36] First, there is the traditional rule that the test results are inadmissible when offered by either party, either as substantive evidence or as relating to the credibility of a witness.[37] As a corollary, the willingness[38] or unwilling-

---

25 N.Y.2d 511, 307 N.Y.S.2d 430, 255 N.E.2d 696 (1969).

[33]See supra § 203.

[34]See H.R. Rep. No. 208, 100th Cong., 1st Sess. 3 (1987) (employer polygraph testing tripled in 10 years). With some exceptions, the Employee Polygraph Protection Act of 1988, 29 U.S.C.A. §§ 2001 to 2009, forbids polygraph testing by employers. For discussions of statutory and other limitations on the practice, see, for example, Lundell, Polygraphs and Employment: A BNA Special Report (1985); Goldzband, The Polygraph and Psychiatrists, 35 J. Forensic Sci. 391 (1990); Note, Lie Detectors in the Workplace: The Need for Civil Actions Against Employers, 101 Harv. L. Rev. 806 (1988); Driscoll, Note, The Employee Polygraph Protection Act of 1988: A Balance of Interests, 75 Iowa L. Rev. (1990); Validity and construction of statute prohibiting employers from suggesting or requiring polygraph or similar tests as condition of employment or continued employment, 23 A.L.R.4th 187.

[35]See U.S. v. Prince-Oyibo, 320 F.3d 494 (4th Cir. 2003) (surveying cases); Giannelli, Polygraph Evidence: Post-*Daubert*, 49 Hastings L.J. 895 (1998); Admissibility in State Criminal Case of Results of Polygraph (Lie Detector) Test—Post-Daubert Cases, 10 A.L.R.6th 463; Admissibility in Federal Criminal Case of Results of Polygraph (Lie Detector) Test—Post-Daubert Cases, 140 A.L.R. Fed. 525.

[36]For example, in Brown v. Darcy, 783 F.2d 1389 (9th Cir. 1986), the Ninth Circuit overruled its line of cases that gave the trial court discretion to admit unstipulated polygraph evidence. Then it overruled *Brown* in U.S. v. Cordoba, 104 F.3d 225 (9th Cir. 1997).

[37]*E.g.*, U.S. v. Prince-Oyibo, 320 F.3d 494 (4th Cir. 2003) (concluding that even if polygraph evidence could be shown to be admissible under *Daubert*, it would take an en banc ruling to overturn the Fourth Circuit's firmly established per se rule); People v. Harris, 47 Cal. 3d 1047, 255 Cal. Rptr. 352, 767 P.2d 619, 649–50 (1989); State v. Miller, 202 Conn. 463, 522 A.2d 249, 260–61 (1987); State v. Shively, 268 Kan. 573, 999 P.2d 952 (2000) (computer-scored polygraph examinations are not admissible under *Frye*); Underwood v. State, 37 So. 3d 10, 13 (Miss. 2010); Com. v. Mendes, 406 Mass. 201, 547 N.E.2d 35, 40 n.4 (1989); State v. A.O., 198 N.J. 69, 965 A.2d 152, 161 (2009) (collecting cases to establish that "Twenty eight states bar the admission of polygraph evidence outright."); State v. Lyon, 304 Or. 221, 744 P.2d 231 (1987); Sturzenegger v. Father Flanagan's Boy's Home, 276 Neb. 327, 754 N.W.2d 406, 421 (2008); State v. Werner, 851 A.2d 1093, 1104 (R.I. 2004) (applying *Daubert*); State v. Dery, 545 A.2d 1014 (R.I. 1988) (applying *Frye*); In re Fuller, 2011 SD 22, 798 N.W.2d 408, 414 n.4 (S.D. 2011) ("This Court has repeatedly held that polygraph tests are not

ness[39] of a party or witness to submit to examination is also inadmissible.[40] Second, a substantial minority of jurisdictions have carved out an exception to the rule of unconditional exclusion. In these jurisdictions the trial court has the discretion to receive polygraph testimony if the parties stipulated to the admission of the results prior to the testing and if certain other conditions are met.[41] Third, in a small number of jurisdictions, admission even in the absence of a stipulation is said to be

---

admissible in the courts of this state."); Rathe Salvage, Inc. v. R. Brown & Sons, Inc., 191 Vt. 284, 2012 VT 18, 46 A.3d 891 (2012) (applying Rule 403).

[38]People v. Muniz, 190 P.3d 774, 785 (Colo. App. 2008) (collecting many cases holding that willingness to undergo testing is inadmissible); Admissibility of evidence of polygraph test results, or offer or refusal to take test, in action for malicious prosecution, 10 A.L.R.5th 663; Admissibility of polygraph or similar lie detector test results, or willingness to submit to test, on issues of coverage under insurance policy, or insurer's good-faith belief that claim was not covered, 7 A.L.R.5th 143; Propriety and prejudicial effect of comment or evidence as to accused's willingness to take lie detector test, 95 A.L.R.2d 819.

[39]Kosmas v. State, 316 Md. 587, 560 A.2d 1137, 1140 (1989) ("In a long line of cases anchored by the often quoted opinion of the Minnesota Supreme Court in State v. Kolander, 236 Minn. 209, 52 N.W.2d 458, 465 (1952), it is universally held that evidence of the defendant's willingness or unwillingness to submit to a lie detector examination is inadmissible."); State v. Sexton, 368 S.W.3d 371, 409–10 (Tenn. 2012) ("any reference to a possible polygraph examination or the refusal to submit to such an examination had no place in this trial"); Propriety and prejudicial effect of comment or evidence as to accused's willingness to take lie detector test, 95 A.L.R.2d 819.

[40]But see People v. Jefferson, 184 Ill. 2d 486, 235 Ill. Dec. 443, 705 N.E.2d 56 (1998) (fact that defendant had appeared to undergo a polygraph

test was admissible for the limited purpose of helping to rebut claim that inculpatory statements given in lieu of the test were coerced); State v. Lavoie, 2010 ME 76, 1 A.3d 408, 413 (Me. 2010); Admissibility of polygraph evidence at trial on issue of voluntariness of confession made by accused, 92 A.L.R.3d 1317. In earlier days, courts admitted evidence of the refusal of an accused to submit to a superstitious test of guilt on the theory that a jury could find that if the defendant believed (however erroneously) in its efficacy, the refusal was an implied admission. State v. Wisdom, 119 Mo. 539, 24 S.W. 1047 (1894); 2 Wigmore, Evidence § 275(3) (Chadbourn rev. 1979). Even today, a few courts allow a defendant's willingness to undergo an examination to be admitted if sufficiently probative of consciousness of innocence. E.g., State v. Gonzalez, 2011 WI 63, 335 Wis. 2d 270, 802 N.W.2d 454, 456 n.3 (2011) ("Although polygraph test results are always inadmissible, an offer to take a polygraph test may be admissible.").

[41]The seminal case is State v. Valdez, 91 Ariz. 274, 371 P.2d 894, 900 (1962). Its progeny are listed in U.S. v. Piccinonna, 885 F.2d 1529, 1533–34 n.18 (11th Cir. 1989) (en banc), State v. Perry, 139 Idaho 520, 81 P.3d 1230, 1235 (2003), and State v. A.O., 198 N.J. 69, 965 A.2d 152, 161 (2009) (eighteen states); Admissibility of lie detector test taken upon stipulation that the result will be admissible in evidence, 53 A.L.R.3d 1005. In many of these "stipulation" jurisdictions, the evidence is admissible for a limited purpose. See, e.g., State v. Valdez, 91 Ariz. 274, 371 P.2d 894 (1962). At least one state implements the stipulation-

discretionary with the trial judge.[42] Even in these jurisdictions, however, admission of unstipulated results is so rare as to be aberrational.[43]

The widespread and strongly rooted reluctance to permit the introduction of polygraph evidence is grounded in a variety of concerns. The most frequently mentioned is that the technique is not generally accepted in the scientific community or is "unreliable" due to inherent failings, a shortage of qualified operators,[44] and the prospect that "coaching" and practicing would become

---

only rule by statute. People v. Wilkinson, 33 Cal. 4th 821, 16 Cal. Rptr. 3d 420, 94 P.3d 551, 569 (2004) (holding that, in light of "the deep division in the scientific and legal communities regarding the reliability of polygraph evidence," this statute does not deprive criminal defendants of any constitutional right to present exculpatory evidence).

A few opinions also state that polygraph results can be admitted to impeach or corroborate a witness's testimony. *E.g.*, Piccinonna, 885 F.2d at 1536 (dictum approving of admissibility, subject to Fed. R. Evid. 608, "when . . . the party planning to use the evidence at trial [provides] adequate notice to the opposing party [and gives the] opposing party was given reasonable opportunity to have its own polygraph expert administer a test covering substantially the same questions"). In U.S. v. Henderson, 409 F.3d 1293, 1303 (11th Cir. 2005), however, the same court of appeals pointedly observed that "we have yet to hold that exclusion of polygraph evidence at trial was an abuse of discretion under *Piccinonna*."

[42]U.S. v. Rumell, 642 F.2d 213, 215 (7th Cir. 1981); State v. Dorsey, 88 N.M. 184, 539 P.2d 204 (1975).

[43]One court, reviewing the cases on discretionary admission, concluded that such discretion is exercised soundly "only when special circumstances exist." U.S. v. Piccinonna, 885 F.2d 1529, 1534 (11th Cir. 1989) (en banc). Another observed that "unilaterally obtained polygraph evidence is almost never admissible under Evidence Rule 403." Conti v. C.I.R., 39

F.3d 658, 663 (6th Cir. 1994); *see also* U.S. v. Ross, 412 F.3d 771, 773 (7th Cir. 2005) ("[C]ourts have routinely rejected unilateral and clandestine polygraph examinations like the one taken here, citing concern that a test taken without the government's knowledge is unreliable because it carries no negative consequences, and probably won't see the light of day if a defendant flunks."); *cf.* U.S. v. Semrau, 693 F.3d 510 (6th Cir. 2012) (exclusion of fMRI testimony was warranted because "the test was unilaterally obtained without the Government's knowledge," and "the use of lie detection test results solely to bolster a witness' credibility is highly prejudicial, especially where credibility issues are central to the verdict.") (internal citations and quotation marks omitted). The courts of New Mexico, however, admit polygraph evidence freely. Tafoya v. Baca, 103 N.M. 56, 702 P.2d 1001 (1985) (admissible under state rule 707).

[44]Honts & Perry, Polygraph Admissibility: Changes and Challenges, 16 Law & Hum. Behav. 357, 375 (1992) ("Polygraph examiners in the United States, as a whole, are poorly trained. Their techniques lack standardization, and polygraph tests are subject to manipulation by unethical examiners. Given this state of affairs, the work-product of most of the polygraph professionals should rightly be questioned."). *But see* Honts et al., The Case for Polygraph Tests, in 5 Modern Scientific Evidence: The Law and Science of Expert Testimony § 40:39 (Faigman et al. eds. 2011–2012) (referring to improvements in qualifications and training). Even with

commonplace if the evidence were generally admissible.[45] Because there is intense disagreement in the literature as to the premise that even a truly expert polygrapher is capable of distinguishing truthful statements from intentional falsehoods in realistic situations at rates significantly above chance levels,[46] admissibility under the *Frye* standard is, at best, doubtful.[47] Likewise, whether polygraphy possesses the modicum of demonstrated validity demanded under the federal rules as interpreted in *Daubert v. Merrell Dow Pharmaceuticals* is open to grave question.[48] Estimating a realistic error rate seems to be especially difficult.[49]

---

qualified operators, many factors can affect the validity of the examiners' conclusions. *See* Office of Technology Assessment, U.S. Congress, Scientific Validity of Polygraph Testing: A Research Review and Evaluation—A Technical Memorandum 83–92 (1983). Examinations of victims and attempts to assess states of mind are particularly questionable. Raskin, The Polygraph in 1986: Scientific, Professional and Legal Issues Surrounding Application and Acceptance of Polygraph Evidence, 1986 Utah L. Rev. 29, 46–49 & 54.

[45]These concerns are well outlined in State v. Porter, 241 Conn. 57, 698 A.2d 739 (1997); People v. Baynes, 88 Ill. 2d 225, 58 Ill. Dec. 819, 430 N.E.2d 1070 (1981); Com. v. Vitello, 376 Mass. 426, 381 N.E.2d 582, 596–99 (1978); People v. Barbara, 400 Mich. 352, 255 N.W.2d 171 (1977); Abbell, Polygraph Evidence: The Case Against Admissibility in Federal Criminal Trials, 15 Am. Crim. L. Rev. 29 (1977).

[46]Iacono & Lykken, The Case Against Polygraph Tests, in 5 Faigman, et al., Modern Scientific Evidence: The Law and Science of Expert Testimony § 40 (2011–2012 ed.).

[47]U.S. v. Scheffer, 523 U.S. 303, 118 S. Ct. 1261, 140 L. Ed. 2d 413 (1998) ("there is simply no consensus that polygraph evidence is reliable"); Com. v. Mendes, 406 Mass. 201, 547 N.E.2d 35, 39 (1989) ("there remains no consensus among experts"); State v. Dery, 545 A.2d 1014, 1017 (R.I. 1988); Honts & Perry, Polygraph Admissibility: Changes and. Challenges, 16 Law &

Hum. Behav. 357, 360, 360 (1992) ("The accuracy of the control question test is a matter of contentious and polemic debate in the scientific literature."); 1 Giannelli & Imwinkelried, Scientific Evidence § 8.03, at 429 (4th ed. 2007) ("validity . . . remains controversial"). There have been efforts to counter the profound disagreements among knowledgeable scientists by taking surveys of members of professional organizations. *See* Honts et al., The Case for Polygraph Tests, in 5 Faigman, et al., Modern Scientific Evidence: The Law and Science of Expert Testimony § 40:38 (2011–2012 ed.); Lykken, A Tremor in the Blood: Uses and Abuses of the Lie Detector 177–88 (2d ed. 1998). A few courts have paid considerable attention to these surveys. U.S. v. Orians, 9 F. Supp. 2d 1168, 1174 (D. Ariz. 1998); U.S. v. Varoudakis, 1998 WL 151238 (D. Mass. 1998); U.S. v. Cordoba, 991 F. Supp. 1199 (C.D. Cal. 1998) (identifying methodological flaws in these surveys). This simple nose-counting is a retrograde development. *See* Dowd v. Calabrese, 585 F. Supp. 430, 432 (D.D.C. 1984) (opinion poll of psychophysiologists on usefulness of polygraph "cannot substitute for time-honored procedures" such as "articles in learned journals, seminars, [and] acceptance at institutions of higher learning").

[48]*See* U.S. v. Scheffer, 523 U.S. 303, 118 S. Ct. 1261, 140 L. Ed. 2d 413 (1998); Committee to Review the Scientific Evidence on the Polygraph, National Research Council, The Polygraph and Lie Detection (2003);

Yet, the decisive arguments against admission go beyond the search for the artificial level of "acceptance" or "reliability" compelled by *Frye* and *Daubert*. After all, a great deal of lay testimony routinely admitted is at least as unreliable and inaccurate, and other forms of scientific evidence involve risks of instrumental or judgmental error.[50] Rather, the more compelling argument against admissibility adjusts the requisite quantum of acceptance

---

Kleinmuntz & Szucko, On the Fallibility of Lie Detection, 17 Law & Soc'y Rev. 85, 87 (1981) ("the reliability of the polygraph is difficult to gauge," and, as to validity, "polygraphic interrogation does poorly indeed"); Office of Technology Assessment, U.S. Congress, Scientific Validity of Polygraph Testing: A Research Review and Evaluation—A Technical Memorandum 96 (1983) ("there is at present only limited scientific evidence for establishing the validity of polygraph testing."); Saxe & Ben-Shakhar, Admissibility of Polygraph Tests: The Application of Scientific Standards Post-*Daubert*, 5 Psychol., Pub. Pol'y & L. 203 (1999). For cases concluding that modern polygraphy does not satisfy *Daubert*, see U.S. v. Gilliard, 133 F.3d 809, 812 (11th Cir. 1998) (upholding the exclusion of "a hybrid control question technique"); U.S. v. Varoudakis, 1998 WL 151238 (D. Mass. 1998); U.S. v. Orians, 9 F. Supp. 2d 1168 (D. Ariz. 1998); U.S. v. Cordoba, 991 F. Supp. 1199, 1207–08 (C.D. Cal. 1998) (finding, inter alia, that "there are no controlling standards to ensure proper protocol or provide a court with a yardstick by which a particular defendant's examination can be measured"); U.S. v. Pitner, 969 F. Supp. 1246, 1250 (W.D. Wash. 1997) (citing cases); State v. Lavoie, 2010 ME 76, 1 A.3d 408, 412 (Me. 2010) ("The scientific evidence simply does not support the reliability or validity of polygraph examinations."). *Contra* Lee v. Martinez, 2004-NMSC-027, 136 N.M. 166, 96 P.3d 291 (2004) (applying a remarkably elastic version of *Daubert* to reach this result).

[49] *E.g.*, U.S. v. Semrau, 693 F.3d 510 (6th Cir. 2012) (fMRI test). The 2003 NRC Report emphasizes that "[t]he lack of understanding of the processes that underlie polygraph responses makes it very difficult to generalize from the results obtained in specific research settings or with particular subject populations to other settings or populations, or from laboratory research studies to real-world applications." Committee to Review the Scientific Evidence on the Polygraph, National Research Council, The Polygraph and Lie Detection 3 (2003). Although this difficulty prevents any confident estimation of the error rate of the procedure in practice, the report suggests that "errors are not infrequent." Committee to Review the Scientific Evidence on the Polygraph, National Research Council, The Polygraph and Lie Detection 123 (2003). As to validity, the report cautiously states that "features of polygraph charts and the judgments made from them are correlated with deception in a variety of controlled situations involving naive examinees untrained in countermeasures: for such examinees and test contexts, the polygraph has an accuracy greater than chance." Committee to Review the Scientific Evidence on the Polygraph, National Research Council, The Polygraph and Lie Detection 122–23 (2003).

[50] *Cf.* Frederick Schauer, Essay, Can Bad Science Be Good Evidence? Neuroscience, Lie Detection, and Beyond, 95 Cornell L. Rev. 1191 (2010) (observing that the loss in excluding bad, but not worthless, science may be greater than that of admitting it).

or validity to the type of evidence in question.[51] If the probative value of polygraph readings is slight (or would be if the barriers to admissibility were dropped), then their value easily is outweighed by the countervailing considerations.[52] These counterweights are the danger that jurors would be unduly impressed with the "scientific" testimony[53] on a crucial and typically determinative matter,[54] that judicial and related resources would be squandered in producing and coping with the expert testimony,[55] and that routine admissibility would put undesirable pressure on defendants to forfeit the right against self-incrimination.[56]

Some of these concerns may be overstated,[57] and the miscellaneous other reasons that courts sometimes give for excluding polygraph tests may not withstand analysis. It sometimes is said that polygraph results would not aid the jury because the credibility of a witness is susceptible to resolution without expert

---

[51]See supra § 203 (arguing for the relevancy-plus test).

[52]State v. Brown, 297 Or. 404, 687 P.2d 751, 775 (1984) ("probative value of polygraph evidence is far outweighed by reasons for its exclusion").

[53]U.S. v. Alexander, 526 F.2d 161, 168 (8th Cir. 1975) ("polygraph evidence . . . is likely to be shrouded with an aura of near infallibility, akin to the ancient oracle of Delphi"); Com. v. Walker, 392 Mass. 152, 466 N.E.2d 71, 74 (1984); State v. A.O., 198 N.J. 69, 965 A.2d 152, 160 (2009) ("to many citizens who serve on juries, polygraph evidence—presented by experts and arrayed in scientific language—has an aura of infallibility. That impression 'can lead jurors to abandon their duty to assess credibility and guilt' and rely instead on the examiner's expert opinion.") (footnote omitted).

[54]United States v. Alexander, 526 F.2d at 169; Brown v. Darcy, 783 F.2d 1389, 1396–97 (9th Cir. 1986).

[55]Com. v. Walker, 392 Mass. 152, 466 N.E.2d 71 (1984); State v. Grier, 307 N.C. 628, 300 S.E.2d 351 (1983); State v. Lyon, 304 Or. 221, 744 P.2d 231, 236 (1987).

[56]U.S. v. Bursten, 560 F.2d 779, 785 (7th Cir. 1977) ("trial by machine"). This may be part of a more generalized dignitary concern. State v. Lyon, 304 Or. 221, 744 P.2d 231 (1987) (Linde, J., concurring) ("the polygraph seeks to turn the human body against the personality that inhabits it"); Silving, Testing of the Unconscious in Criminal Cases, 69 Harv. L. Rev. 683 (1956).

[57]Theorizing about the devastating impact of polygraph evidence is inevitably somewhat inconclusive. For expressions of opinion contrary to the received wisdom, see McMorris v. Israel, 643 F.2d 458, 462–63 (7th Cir. 1981) ("Scientific evidence . . . has become more a part of the ordinary trial so that jurors may be more likely to use polygraph evidence with discretion"). For a list of experimental studies not finding any dramatic effects, see Honts et al., The Case for Polygraph Tests, in 5 Modern Scientific Evidence: The Law and Science of Expert Testimony § 40:43 (Faigman et al. eds. 2011–2012). Of course, the real question is not whether this evidence has some impact. It is whether it has more of an effect than its actual probative value would warrant and, if so, how much more. See supra § 186.

testimony.[58] But talk of "prejudice to the jury process,"[59] of "usurp-[ing] the jury's function,"[60] and affirmations that "the jury system is [not] yet outmoded,"[61] or that "the jury is the lie detector,"[62] may reflect this cramped view of the scope of expert testimony in addition to the previously catalogued concerns. The real issue, of course, is not whether juries can decide which witnesses to believe without polygraph or other such testing, but rather how much this testing would enhance those decisions—and at what cost.

Even from this more balanced perspective, however, opening up the matter to the discretion of the trial courts—without providing more detailed standards than the usual balancing prescription—could lead to untoward results.[63] Nor is the "stipulation-only" approach satisfactory.[64] Whether polygraph testimony should be admitted is doubtful, but if it is to be received, clear standards should be developed as to whether such testimony is admissible solely for impeachment purposes,[65] how important the

---

[58]U.S. v. Alexander, 526 F.2d 161, 169 n.16 (8th Cir. 1975) ("polygraph evidence is not necessary since the jury is capable of performing the function served by the polygraph").

[59]People v. Anderson, 637 P.2d 354, 362 (Colo. 1981).

[60]State v. Perry, 139 Idaho 520, 81 P.3d 1230, 1235 (2003); Rathe Salvage, Inc. v. R. Brown & Sons, Inc., 191 Vt. 284, 2012 VT 18, 46 A.3d 891, 899 (2012).

[61]U.S. v. Stromberg, 179 F. Supp. 278, 280 (S.D. N.Y. 1959).

[62]U.S. v. Barnard, 490 F.2d 907, 912 (9th Cir. 1973) (quoted in U.S. v. Scheffer, 523 U.S. 303, 118 S. Ct. 1261, 140 L. Ed. 2d 413 (1998) (plurality opinion)); Rathe Salvage, Inc., 46 A.3d at 899.

[63]State v. Dean, 103 Wis. 2d 228, 307 N.W.2d 628, 653 (1981) ("The lack of such standards heightens our concern that the burden on the trial court to assess the reliability of stipulated polygraph evidence may outweigh any probative value the evidence may have."). Furthermore, this court doubted that satisfactory standards could evolve judicially. Dean, 307 N.W.2d at 653 ("adequate standards have not developed in the seven years since Stanislawski to guide the trial

courts in exercising their discretion in the admission of polygraph evidence").

[64]Recognizing that the presence of a stipulation does not enhance the validity or reliability of the examiner's conclusions, many courts have declined to relax their traditional exclusionary rule to recognize stipulations. Pulakis v. State, 476 P.2d 474, 479 (Alaska 1970); People v. Anderson, 637 P.2d 354, 361–62 (Colo. 1981); People v. Baynes, 88 Ill. 2d 225, 58 Ill. Dec. 819, 430 N.E.2d 1070, 1077 (1981); State v. Lyon, 304 Or. 221, 744 P.2d 231 (1987); State v. Frazier, 162 W. Va. 602, 252 S.E.2d 39, 49 (1979). North Carolina, Oklahoma and Wisconsin have defected from the ranks of "stipulation-only" jurisdictions. State v. Grier, 307 N.C. 628, 300 S.E.2d 351, 361 (1983); Fulton v. State, 1975 OK CR 200, 541 P.2d 871 (Okla. Crim. App. 1975); State v. Dean, 103 Wis. 2d 228, 307 N.W.2d 628 (1981).

[65]U.S. v. Piccinonna, 885 F.2d 1529, 1536 (11th Cir. 1989) (en banc). For a time, Massachusetts allowed polygraph evidence only to corroborate or impeach the testimony of a defendant who had agreed to be tested. Com. v. Walker, 392 Mass. 152, 466 N.E.2d 71 (1984); Com. v. Vitello, 376 Mass. 426, 381 N.E.2d 582, 597 (1978). In Com. v. Mendes, 406 Mass. 201, 547

testimony must be in the context of the other evidence in the case for admissibility to be warranted,[66] what level of training and competence examiners should have, what precautions should be taken against deceptive practices on the part of examinees,[67] and what procedures would be best to give an independent or opposing expert a meaningful opportunity to view or review the examination and analysis.[68] When all is said and done, the game simply does not seem worth the candle. A categorical rule of exclusion for polygraph results is a logical and defensible corollary to the general principles of relevancy.[69] The case against admitting diagnoses of deception from the newer neuroimaging technologies

N.E.2d 35, 41 (1989), the Supreme Judicial Court abandoned this experiment, observing that "our hope that polygraphy would mature to the point of general scientific acceptance has not materialized."

[66]Commonwealth v. Vitello, 381 N.E.2d at 596 n. 23; State v. Dean, 307 N.W.2d at 634 n. 7 (the argument for admissibility is most "compelling" when the finder of fact must choose between the conflicting stories of the complaining witness and the defendant with little or no corroborating evidence).

[67]As with calibration checks of radar equipment (see supra § 204), this may be an instance in which jurisdictions that are willing to admit such evidence should insist on "cost-effective" precautions to prevent errors even though the evidence would be at least minimally relevant without them.

[68]United States v. Piccinonna, 885 F.2d at 1536 (requiring adequate notice and reasonable opportunity for opposing side to administer its own test); U.S. v. Alexander, 526 F.2d 161, 170 n.17 (8th Cir. 1975); Abbell, Polygraph Evidence: The Case Against Admissibility in Federal Criminal Trials, 15 Am. Crim. L. Rev. 29 (1977); cf. supra § 201 (suggesting cooperation in design and execution of pretrial experiments).

[69]State v. Porter, 241 Conn. 57, 698 A.2d 739, 768–69 (1997) ("admis-

sion of the polygraph test would be highly detrimental to the operation of Connecticut courts, both procedurally and substantively. . . . [A]ny limited evidentiary value that polygraph evidence does have is substantially outweighed by its prejudicial effects. We therefore reaffirm our per se rule against the use of polygraph evidence in Connecticut courts."); Rathe Salvage, Inc. v. R. Brown & Sons, Inc., 191 Vt. 284, 2012 VT 18, 46 A.3d 891, 901 (2012) (because the "limited, if not absence of, probative value is substantially outweighed by risks of confusion, delay, and time wasted on collateral issues related to variables in administration of the polygraph[, t]here was no error in the trial court's per se exclusion of polygraph evidence under Rule 403[, and] the trial court was not required to conduct a *Daubert* hearing to assess its reliability under Rule 702."). Being founded in part on the reasonable judgment that the evidence uniformly is low in probative value, the "per se" rule constitutionally can be applied to exclude evidence that a defendant in a criminal case passed a polygraph test. U.S. v. Scheffer, 523 U.S. 303, 118 S. Ct. 1261, 140 L. Ed. 2d 413 (1998); Porter, 698 A.2d at 777–79; People v. Richardson, 43 Cal. 4th 959, 77 Cal. Rptr. 3d 163, 183 P.3d 1146, 1194–95 (2008). On this and other constitutional claims of admissibility, see 1 Giannelli & Imwinkelried, Scientific Evidence § 8.05 (4th ed. 2007).

is even stronger, since such cutting-edge technologies are less well studied yet potentially more impressive to jurors.[70]

*(B) Drugs and Hypnosis.*

Psychologists and psychiatrists have used hypnosis and hypnotic drugs for diagnosis and therapy. Resort to these techniques became prevalent in the treatment of traumatic war neuroses during World War II, and the methods have been applied to the treatment of hysterical amnesias, catatonic conditions, and psychosomatic disorders.[71] They have also been employed to test the truthfulness of a witness' testimony as well as to enhance recall.[72]

Although the scientific study of hypnosis began over 200 years ago, a single, satisfactory explanation of the phenomenon has yet to emerge.[73] The scientific studies do make it clear, however, that people who are hypnotized or given "truth serum" do not always

---

[70]In first appellate opinion on fMRI-truth testing, the U.S. Court of Appeals for the Sixth Circuit held, on the basis of expert testimony at a pretrial hearing and a review of some of the scientific literature, that the technique had not been established as valid under *Daubert* (and that it lacked general scientific acceptance). U.S. v. Semrau, 693 F.3d 510 (6th Cir. 2012). A trial court in New York excluded fMRI evidence, writing that "even a cursory review of the scientific literature demonstrates that the plaintiff is unable to establish that the use of the fMRI test to determine truthfulness or deceit is accepted as reliable in the relevant scientific community." Wilson v. Corestaff Services L.P., 28 Misc. 3d 425, 900 N.Y.S.2d 639, 642 (Sup 2010). For developments in other countries, see Church, Note, Neuroscience in the Courtroom: An International Concern, 53 Wm. & Mary L. Rev. 1825 (2012); Gaudet, Note, Brain Fingerprinting, Scientific Evidence, and *Daubert*: A Cautionary Lesson from India, 51 Jurimetrics J. 293 (2011).

[71]Hilgard, Hypnotic Susceptibility (1965); Erickson, Naturalistic Techniques of Hypnosis, 1 Am. J. Clinical Hypnosis 3 (1938); Packer, The Use of Hypnotic Techniques in the Evaluation of Criminal Defendants, 9 J. Psychiatry & L. 313 (1981). Highly

controversial at first, hypnosis gradually gained acceptance within the scientific and medical communities for use in experimental and clinical work. *See* Hilgard, Hypnotic Susceptibility 3–5 (1965).

[72]*See generally* Bryan, Legal Aspects of Hypnosis (1962); Cook, Hypnotism and the Courts (1987); McConkey & Sheehan, Hypnosis, Memory, and Behavior in Criminal Investigation (1995); Depres, Legal Aspects of Drug-Induced Statements, 14 U. Chi. L. Rev. 601 (1947); Dession et al., Drug Induced Revelation and Criminal Investigation, 62 Yale L.J. 315 (1953).

[73]Council on Scientific Affairs, American Medical Association, Scientific Status of Refreshing Recollection by the Use of Hypnosis, 253 J.A.M.A. 1918, 1919 (1985). Many reviews of the scientific literature have appeared in past decades, and they are in general agreement on the key points regarding the hypnotic state and the recall of memories. The summary of the literature in this paragraph is based on the following review articles and books: Bryan, Legal Aspects of Hypnosis (1962); Loftus, Eyewitness Testimony (1979); McConkey & Sheehan, Hypnosis, Memory, and Behavior in Criminal Investigation (1995); Lynn & Nash, Truth in Memory:

tell the truth. Indeed, subjects have been known to feign, quite convincingly, a hypnotized state. Even though some studies suggest that in certain circumstances hypnosis can enhance memory, the effect is not apparent in experimental studies, and it is clear that hypnosis can alter memory. Hypnotized persons are highly suggestible, and some authorities believe that when a hypnotist encourages a subject to relate everything he can possibly remember, the subject produces fragments and approximations of memory in an effort to be cooperative. In addition, the subject may accept as his own recollections distortions inadvertently suggested by the hypnotist. Finally, the hypnotic session may reinforce the witness's confidence in erroneous memories.

Forensic applications of hypnosis can generate a variety of constitutional and evidentiary issues.[74] A party might seek admission of statements a witness made while under hypnosis or

---

Ramifications for Psychotherapy and Hypnotherapy, 36 Am. J. Clinical Hypnosis 194, 199–200 (1994); Nash & Nardon, Scientific Status, in 2 Faigman, et al., Modern Scientific Evidence: The Law and Science of Expert Testimony §§ 19:8 to 19:30 (2011–2012 ed.); Orne et al., Hypnotically Refreshed Testimony: Enhanced Memory or Tampering with Evidence?, Issues & Practices in Crim. Just. 41 (1985); Orne, The Use and Misuse of Hypnosis in Court, 27 Int'l J. Clinical & Experimental Hypnosis 311 (1979); Patrye et al., Supreme Court of Canada Addresses Admissibility of Posthypnosis Witness Evidence, 50 Canadian Psych. 98 (2009); Saks & Hastie, Social Psychology in Court (1978); Smith, Hypnotic Memory Enhancement of Witnesses: Does It Work?, 94 Psychol. Bull. 387 (1983), reprinted in On the Witness Stand: Controversies in the Courtroom 78 (Wrightsman et al. eds., 1987); Spiegel, Hypnosis and Evidence: Help or Hindrance?, 3 Annals N.Y. Acad. Sci. 73, 78 (1979); Yarmey, The Psychology of Eyewitness Testimony 177 (1979); Note, Are the Courts in a Trance? Approaches to the Admissibility of Hypnotically Enhanced Witness Testimony in Light of Empirical Evidence, 40 Am. Crim. L. Rev. 1301 (2003); Note, The Admissibility of Testimony Influenced by Hypnosis, 67 Va. L. Rev. 1203 (1981).

[74]For example, a confession resulting from an interrogation with drugs is a paradigm of an involuntary confession. See Townsend v. Sain, 372 U.S. 293, 307–08, 83 S. Ct. 745, 9 L. Ed. 2d 770 (1963) (evidentiary hearing required on habeas corpus petition with respect to confession obtained 15 hours after narcotic addict undergoing withdrawal symptoms had been injected with phenobarbital and hyoscine); cf. Leyra v. Denno, 347 U.S. 556, 74 S. Ct. 716, 98 L. Ed. 948 (1954) (confession obtained by a "psychiatrist with considerable knowledge of hypnosis" was involuntary). Perhaps a suspect could waive his constitutional protections, but his inability to exercise his normal judgment to request that the interrogation cease or that he consult with counsel complicates matters. See, e.g., Sparer, Some Problems Relating to the Admissibility of Drug Influenced Confessions, 24 Brook. L. Rev. 96 (1957); Stewart, Hypnosis, Truth Drugs, and the Polygraph, 21 U. Fla. L. Rev. 541 (1969). Commenting on a defendant's failure to undergo narcoanalysis is improper and can lead to reversal of a conviction. State v. Levitt, 36 N.J. 266, 176 A.2d 465, 469–70 (1961). But see People v. Draper, 304 N.Y. 799, 109 N.E.2d 342, 343 (1952). For additional discussion of constitutional questions raised by hypnosis, see 1 Giannelli & Imwinkel-

narcoanalysis to show directly the existence of certain facts, to impeach or buttress credibility, or to show the basis for a psychiatric or psychological opinion. Similarly, a party might offer the in-court testimony of a previously hypnotized or drugged witness.

The courts have been most reluctant to admit such statements or testimony. In the first case to raise the issue, a California court stated in 1897 that "the law of the United States does not recognize hypnotism."[75] Since then the courts nearly always excluded statements made under hypnosis[76] or narcoanalysis,[77] regardless of whether these statements are offered as substantive evidence or as bearing on credibility.

Posthypnotic testimony as to recollections enhanced or evoked under hypnosis has produced more divergent holdings.[78] A few courts have said that such testimony is generally admissible with objections as to its accuracy bearing on the weight that the finder of fact should give it.[79] But even in these jurisdictions there is a tendency to insist on rigorous safeguards for the hypnotically

---

ried, Scientific Evidence § 12.06 (4th ed. 2007).

[75]People v. Ebanks, 117 Cal. 652, 49 P. 1049, 1053 (1897), overruled on other grounds, People v. Flannelly, 60 P. 670 (Cal.1900) (excluding testimony about statements given under hypnosis).

[76]People v. Shirley, 31 Cal. 3d 18, 181 Cal. Rptr. 243, 723 P.2d 1354 (1982) (reviewing cases); Strong v. State, 435 N.E.2d 969, 970 (Ind. 1982) (composite drawing produced from witnesses' description given under hypnosis inadmissible because "evidence derived from a witness while he is in a hypnotic trance is inherently unreliable"); Com. v. Juvenile, 381 Mass. 727, 412 N.E.2d 339, 341 (1980) ("[i]t is generally accepted that testimony while under hypnosis and evidence of what a subject said while under hypnosis are inadmissible"); 1 Giannelli & Imwinkelried, Scientific Evidence § 12.04 (4th ed. 2007).

[77]Lindsey v. U.S., 16 Alaska 268, 237 F.2d 893, 896 (9th Cir. 1956) (tape recording of sodium pentothal interrogation inadmissible to restore credibility after impeachment); State v. Hudson, 289 S.W. 920, 921 (Mo. 1926) ("truth telling serum" is a "claptrap"

on a par with "the magic powers of philters, potions and cures by faith").

[78]For reviews or collections of the opinions, see 2 Faigman, et al., Modern Scientific Evidence: The Law and Science of Expert Testimony §§ 19:3 to 19:7 (2011–2012 ed.); 1 Giannelli & Imwinkelried, Scientific Evidence § 12.05 (4th ed. 2007); Note, Are the Courts in a Trance? Approaches to the Admissibility of Hypnotically Enhanced Witness Testimony in Light of Empirical Evidence, 40 Am. Crim. L. Rev. 1301 (2003); Admissibility of hypnotically refreshed or enhanced testimony, 77 A.L.R.4th 927.

[79]Kline v. Ford Motor Co., Inc., 523 F.2d 1067, 1069–70 (9th Cir. 1975); cases cited, McQueen v. Garrison, 619 F. Supp. 116, 128–29 (E.D. N.C. 1985); Pearson v. State, 441 N.E.2d 468, 472–73 (Ind. 1982); Hopkins v. Com., 230 Va. 280, 337 S.E.2d 264, 271 (1985); Chapman v. State, 638 P.2d 1280, 1282–85 (Wyo. 1982). The first case to admit hypnotically refreshed testimony, Harding v. State, 5 Md. App. 230, 246 A.2d 302 (1968), was overruled in Collins v. State, 52 Md. App. 186, 447 A.2d 1272, 1283 (1982); cf. Polk v. State, 48 Md. App. 382, 427 A.2d 1041 (1981) (remanding for determination of admis-

refreshed memories to be admissible.[80] The far more prevalent view is that testimony about the posthypnotic memories is inadmissible.[81]

There are two exceptions to this per se rule of exclusion. First, the usual rule permits a witness to testify to memories recorded and preserved before the hypnotic session.[82] To that extent at least, the witness remains competent to testify. Under this excep-

---

sibility under general scientific acceptance test). Some courts describe their approach as a totality-of-the-circumstances standard, which may reflect a lesser degree of receptiveness to the evidence. *See* Borawick v. Shay, 68 F.3d 597, 608 (2d Cir. 1995); Mersch v. City of Dallas, Tex., 207 F.3d 732, 735 (5th Cir. 2000); State v. Iwakiri, 106 Idaho 618, 682 P.2d 571, 578 (1984); Roark v. Com., 90 S.W.3d 24 (Ky. 2002); State v. Cheeseboro, 346 S.C. 526, 552 S.E.2d 300, 308–09 (2001).

[80]U.S. v. Harrelson, 754 F.2d 1153 (5th Cir. 1985); U.S. v. Valdez, 722 F.2d 1196 (5th Cir. 1984) (excluding testimony but declining to adopt per se rule); Sprynczynatyk v. General Motors Corp., 771 F.2d 1112, 1122–23 (8th Cir. 1985) (burden on proponent, with safeguards); U.S. v. Adams, 581 F.2d 193, 199 n.12 (9th Cir. 1978); Pearson v. State, 441 N.E.2d 468 (Ind. 1982); State v. Hurd, 86 N.J. 525, 432 A.2d 86, 95–97 (1981) (elaborating strict procedural safeguards); State v. Armstrong, 110 Wis. 2d 555, 329 N.W.2d 386, 394–95 (1983) (burden on proponent to prove that hypnotic session was not impermissibly suggestive); cases cited, McQueen v. Garrison, 619 F. Supp. 116, 129 (E.D. N.C. 1985); *cf.* U.S. v. Solomon, 753 F.2d 1522, 1525–26 (9th Cir. 1985) (statements made, with safeguards, under influence of sodium amytal admitted, when not identified to jury as having been made under narcoanalysis). Adherence to such safeguards is an important factor in jurisdictions that look to "the totality of the circumstances." *See, e.g.,* Borawick v. Shay, 68 F.3d 597 (2d Cir. 1995); State v. Iwakiri, 106 Idaho 618, 682 P.2d 571 (1984). In State v. Moore,

188 N.J. 182, 902 A.2d 1212 (2006), the New Jersey Supreme Court reconsidered—and rejected—the safeguards promulgated in State v. Hurd, 86 N.J. 525, 432 A.2d 86 (1981), in favor of the per se rule of inadmissibility.

[81]*E.g.,* People v. Sutton, 233 Ill. 2d 89, 330 Ill. Dec. 198, 908 N.E.2d 50, 62 (2009) (identification of defendant at a lineup seven years after hypnosis was "per se inadmissible"); People v. Lee, 434 Mich. 59, 450 N.W.2d 883 (1990); State v. Moore, 188 N.J. 182, 902 A.2d 1212, 1220–23 (2006) (reviewing the development of the case law and concluding that "Today, as the debate continues, four states consider hypnotically refreshed testimony per se admissible, with the trier of fact determining its weight, . . . six allow such testimony when certain procedural safeguards are met, . . . twenty-six have adopted variations on the per se inadmissible rule, . . . and nine have adopted some type of 'totality of the circumstances' test"); People v. Hults, 76 N.Y.2d 190, 557 N.Y.S.2d 270, 556 N.E.2d 1077 (1990) (inadmissible to impeach complaining witness). Commentary tends to favor the per se rule of exclusion. *See* Diamond, Inherent Problems in the Use of Pretrial Hypnosis on a Prospective Witness, 68 Cal. L. Rev. 313 (1980); Orne et al., Hypnotically Refreshed Testimony: Enhanced Memory or Tampering with Evidence?, Issues & Practices in Crim. Just. 41 (1985).

[82]*E.g.,* State ex rel. Collins v. Superior Court, In and For Maricopa County, 132 Ariz. 180, 644 P.2d 1266, 1279 (1982) (supplemental opinion); People v. Wilson, 116 Ill. 2d 29, 106 Ill. Dec. 771, 506 N.E.2d 571 (1987).

tion, proof that these memories existed prior to hypnosis must go well beyond a subject's posthypnotic recollections of the timing of his or her memories. Once hypnotized, it may be impossible for the subject to separate untainted, prehypnotic recollections from later, possibly tainted or confabulated memories.[83]

The desirability of this exception is debatable. For a time, California excluded *all* testimony of a hypnotized witness—even testimony consistent with statements made before the hypnotic session.[84] This strict rule responds to the concern that the hypnotic session enhances the witness's confidence in all his recollections, thereby insulating the witness from meaningful cross-examination. The strict rule also obviates the need to determine whether the hypnotic session has tainted the witness's current testimony about the earlier statements or the events. In that regard, courts applying the exception for preserved memories sometimes look for compliance with various safeguards that help establish that the hypnosis does not taint the testimony about prehypnotic statements.[85]

Second, in *Rock v. Arkansas*,[86] the Supreme Court held that the constitution precludes categorical exclusion of the hypnotically refreshed testimony of a criminal defendant who cannot present a meaningful defense without that testimony.[87] Even so, a

---

[83]Orne et al., Hypnotically Refreshed Testimony: Enhanced Memory or Tampering with Evidence?, Issues & Practices in Crim. Just. 41, 42 (1985) (urging compliance with stringent guidelines, including videotaping of hypnotic session); Orne, The Use and Misuse of Hypnosis in Court, 27 Int'l J. Clinical & Experimental Hypnosis 311 (1979) (proposing standards).

[84]People v. Brown, 40 Cal. 3d 512, 230 Cal. Rptr. 834, 726 P.2d 516 (1985), rev'd on other grounds, 479 U.S. 538; People v. Guerra, 37 Cal. 3d 385, 208 Cal. Rptr. 162, 690 P.2d 635, 663–65 (1984). Propelled by Cal. Evid. Code § 795, in People v. Hayes, 49 Cal. 3d 1260, 265 Cal. Rptr. 132, 783 P.2d 719 (1989), California joined the many other jurisdictions refusing to apply the exclusionary rule to testimony about events recalled and recorded prior to the hypnotic session, at least

in criminal cases.

[85]Contreras v. State, 718 P.2d 129, 139–40 (Alaska 1986); State v. Lopez, 181 Ariz. 8, 887 P.2d 538, 540 (1994) ("Because the officers were later hypnotized, . . . safeguards [along the lines of those proposed by Orne were necessary] to prevent tainting the post-hypnosis testimony."); Com. v. Kater, 388 Mass. 519, 447 N.E.2d 1190, 1198 n.8 (1983); (Orne guidelines "acceptable," but "they should not be applied inflexibly.").

[86]Rock v. Arkansas, 483 U.S. 44, 107 S. Ct. 2704, 97 L. Ed. 2d 37 (1987).

[87]*Rock* does not affect the admissibility of testimony from hypnotized witnesses other than the defendant. Burral v. State, 352 Md. 707, 724 A.2d 65 (1999). Neither does it require admission of testimony from a defendant while under hypnosis. Rault v. Butler, 826 F.2d 299 (5th Cir. 1987).

defendant's testimony may be excluded unless rigorous safeguards are employed during hypnosis.[88]

Most of the courts adopting a per se exclusionary rule for hypnotic and posthypnotic statements relied on the *Frye* test[89] of general scientific acceptance,[90] although the same result can reached by examining scientific validity under *Daubert*[91] or inquiring directly into the relative costs and benefits of the testimony. Indeed, the more modern cases support their invocation and application of the general acceptance standard by examining scientific testimony or literature on the value of hypnosis for recovering memories[92] and by referring to the usual concerns with scientific evidence—its suspected tendency to overawe the jury[93] and to consume time and resources—in a matter of particular sensitivity.[94]

---

[88]State v. Butterworth, 246 Kan. 541, 792 P.2d 1049 (1990); State v. Moore, 188 N.J. 182, 902 A.2d 1212 (2006).

[89]See supra § 203.

[90]Contreras v. State, 718 P.2d 129, 134–36 (Alaska 1986) (alternative holding); State ex rel. Collins v. Superior Court, In and For Maricopa County, 132 Ariz. 180, 644 P.2d 1266 (1982); People v. Shirley, 31 Cal. 3d 18, 181 Cal. Rptr. 243, 723 P.2d 1354 (1982); State v. Haislip, 237 Kan. 461, 701 P.2d 909, 926 (1985); Burral v. State, 352 Md. 707, 724 A.2d 65 (1999); Com. v. Kater, 388 Mass. 519, 447 N.E.2d 1190, 1197 (1983) (collecting cases); People v. Gonzales, 415 Mich. 615, 329 N.W.2d 743 (1982); Alsbach v. Bader, 700 S.W.2d 823, 828–30 (Mo. 1985); State v. Moore, 188 N.J. 182, 902 A.2d 1212, 1226–27 (2006) (applying *Frye* and observing that "[m]any courts considering hypnotically refreshed testimony have asked whether such testimony meets the standard for the admissibility of scientific evidence set forth in *Frye*"); People v. Hughes, 59 N.Y.2d 523, 466 N.Y.S.2d 255, 453 N.E.2d 484 (1983); State v. Martin, 101 Wash. 2d 713, 684 P.2d 651, 654–56 (1984). *But see* State v. Brown, 337 N.W.2d 138 (N.D. 1983) (*Frye* does not apply to hypnotically induced testimony of a lay witness); State v. Armstrong, 110 Wis. 2d 555, 329

N.W.2d 386, 393 (1983) (*Frye* applies to phenomenon of hypnosis rather than to hypnotically refreshed testimony).

[91]*See* State v. Medrano, 127 S.W.3d 781 (Tex. Crim. App. 2004) (adhering to the totality-of-the-circumstances standard and safeguards adopted under *Frye* for hypnotically-enhanced memories). However, some courts reason that *Daubert* is inapplicable. Borawick v. Shay, 68 F.3d 597 (2d Cir. 1995) ("*Daubert* concerns [only] the admissibility of data derived from scientific techniques or expert testimony").

[92]People v. Shirley, 31 Cal. 3d 18, 181 Cal. Rptr. 243, 723 P.2d 1354 (1982) ("for this limited purpose [of ascertaining general scientific acceptance] scientists have long been permitted to speak to the courts through their published writings in scholarly treatises and journals"); Stokes v. State, 548 So. 2d 188 (Fla. 1989).

[93]Shirley, 723 P.2d at 1354 (hypnosis is invested with a "misleading aura of certainty which often envelops a new scientific process, obscuring its currently experimental nature"); Coleman et al., What Makes Recovered-Memory Testimony Compelling to Jurors?, 25 Law & Hum. Behav. 317, 324–25 (2001); Johnson & Hauck, Beliefs and Opinions About Hypnosis Held by the General Public: A System-

When an expert uses narcoanalysis or hypnosis to determine whether a subject is insane, incompetent, or mentally incapacitated, the case for admissibility is much stronger.[95] A few courts have excluded expert opinions based on these techniques,[96] but this position seems difficult to defend even under the restrictive general-acceptance standard. Most courts recognize that the opinions of the experts may be admitted and that the revelation of the details of what the subject said while under hypnosis or drugs is within the trial judge's discretion.[97] Thus, the trial court may permit the expert to give an explanation of the underlying

---

atic Evaluation, 42 Am. J. Clinical Hypnosis 10, 17 (1999); Yapko, Suggestibility and Repressed Memories of Abuse: A Survey of Psychotherapists' Beliefs, in Child Sexual Abuse and False Memory Syndrome 215, 220–23 (Robert A. Baker ed., 1998); Note, Are the Courts in a Trance? Approaches to the Admissibility of Hypnotically Enhanced Witness Testimony in Light of Empirical Evidence, 40 Am. Crim. L. Rev. 1301, 1323–24 (2003) (reviewing studies). *But see* Scheflin et al., Special Methodologies in Memory Retrieval: Chemical, Hypnotic, and Imagery Procedures, in Retrospective Assessment of Mental States in Litigation: Predicting the Past 369, 402 (Simon & Shuman eds., 2002) (asserting that there is "no empirical basis" for the view); Greene et al., Impact of Hypnotized Testimony on the Jury, 13 Law & Hum. Behav. 61 (1989) ("jurors view hypnotic testimony with a certain amount of skepticism").

[94]State ex rel. Collins v. Superior Court, In and For Maricopa County, 132 Ariz. 180, 644 P.2d 1266, 1296–97 (1982) (citing George Orwell's classic novel *1984* to underscore the proposition that "there are few dangers so great in the search for truth as man's propensity to tamper with the memory of others"); State v. Mack, 292 N.W.2d 764, 770 (Minn. 1980) (adverting to "the difficulty and expense of calling experts qualified to testify to the uses of hypnosis"). As noted in connection with the former minority rule against post-hypnotic testimony about pre-hypnotic memories and statements, an additional concern is that a witness

whose apparent memories have been evoked under hypnosis will have an artificially and unjustifiably high level of confidence in all his recollections, thereby insulating the witness from meaningful cross-examination.

[95]*See* Sadoff, Psychiatric Involvement in the Search for Truth, 52 ABAJ 251 (1966).

[96]People v. Ford, 304 N.Y. 679, 107 N.E.2d 595 (1952) (opinion on sanity based on sodium amytal interview inadmissible); cf. People v. Fournier, 86 Mich. App. 768, 273 N.W.2d 555, 561 (1978) (expert opinion as to intent based on sodium brevital interview); State v. Sinnott, 24 N.J. 408, 132 A.2d 298 (1957) (opinion of sexual propensities derived from sodium pentothal examination). Expert opinion testimony as to truthfulness derived from hypnotic techniques is almost invariably inadmissible. Mental health professionals do not seem to have any special ability to separate truth from falsehood in narcoanalytic and hypnotic sessions. Diamond, Inherent Problems in the Use of Pretrial Hypnosis on a Prospective Witness, 68 Cal. L. Rev. 313, 337 (1980).

[97]People v. Modesto, 59 Cal. 2d 722, 31 Cal. Rptr. 225, 382 P.2d 33 (1963) (error to exclude tape recording of hypnotic session pertinent to expert opinion on intent without balancing probative value against prejudicial effect); Lemmon v. Denver & R.G.W.R. Co., 9 Utah 2d 195, 341 P.2d 215, 219 (1959) (sodium amytol interview admissible with regard to diagnosis of amnesia).

information along with an opinion, but still curb the introduction of the statements made under hypnosis or narcoanalysis.[98]

*(C) Eyewitness Testimony.*

For many years, expert testimony has been received to show that mental disorders may have affected the testimony of eyewitnesses. In the 1970s, criminal defendants also began to call on psychologists to offer expert opinions on the factors that ordinarily influence the reliability of eyewitness identifications. Typically, the expert testifies to generalizations from experiments in which students or other subjects have witnessed a film or other enactment or description of the kind of events that are the subjects of courtroom testimony. In such studies, the accuracy of the recall of faces or facts is then tested under a variety of conditions. The overall findings indicate that such witnesses often make mistakes, that they tend to make more mistakes in cross-racial identifications as well as when the events involve violence, that errors are easily introduced by misleading questions asked shortly after the witness has viewed the simulated happening, and that the professed confidence of the subjects in their identifications bears no consistent relation to the accuracy of these recognitions.[99]

Testimony about such research findings has been received in some cases and rejected in others.[100] By and large, rejection was the norm, especially in the 1970s and 1980s, when the evidence

---

[98]People v. Hiser, 267 Cal. App. 2d 47, 72 Cal. Rptr. 906, 915–16 (5th Dist. 1968) (tape recording of sodium pentothal and hypnotic interviews properly excluded); People v. Myers, 35 Ill. 2d 311, 220 N.E.2d 297, 310 (1966) (testimony detailing defendant's response during sodium pentothal interview properly excluded); State v. Chase, 206 Kan. 352, 480 P.2d 62 (1971) (proper to exclude videotape of sodium amytal interview); State v. Harris, 241 Or. 224, 405 P.2d 492, 498–500 (1965) (tape recording of hypnotic interview); State v. White, 60 Wash. 2d 551, 374 P.2d 942 (1962) (tape recordings of sodium amytol and desoxyn interviews, properly excluded).

[99]*See generally* State v. Henderson, 208 N.J. 208, 27 A.3d 872 (2011) (making recommendations and describing the state of psychological knowledge as described in a hearing ordered by the New Jersey Supreme

Court); Cutler & Penrod, Mistaken Identity: The Eyewitness, Psychology, and the Law (1995); 2 Handbook of Eyewitness Psychology: Memory for People (Lindsay et al. eds. 2006); Elizabeth Loftus, Eyewitness Testimony (1979); Loftus & Doyle, Eyewitness Testimony: Civil and Criminal (1997); Wells, Scientific Status, in 2 Faigman, et al., Modern Scientific Evidence § 16:16 to 16-48 (2011–2012 ed.); Fulero, System and Estimator Variables in Eyewitness Identification: A Review, *in* 2 Psychological Expertise in Court 57 (Lieberman & Krauss 2009); TerBeek, A Call for Precedential Heads: Why the Supreme Court's Eyewitness Identification Jurisprudence Is Anachronistic and Out-of-step with the Empirical Reality, 31 Law & Psychol. Rev. 21 (2007); Wells & Olson, Eyewitness Testimony, 54 Ann. Rev. Psychol. 277–95 (2003).

[100]People v. Enis, 139 Ill. 2d 264, 151 Ill. Dec. 493, 564 N.E.2d 1155

seemed novel. Given the extreme deference usually accorded trial court decisions on the need for expert testimony, these decisions were almost invariably upheld.[101] By 1990, a handful of appellate courts had held that exclusion of expert testimony on highly pertinent aspects of eyewitness identifications constituted an abuse of discretion[102] or that this testimony is not categorically excluded.[103] But one opinion after another displayed a distinct distaste for such testimony.[104] A few jurisdictions seemed to prohibit it entirely.[105] In 1995, the Court of Appeals for the First Circuit would only say that "[q]uite recently, several circuits have suggested that such evidence warrants a more hospitable reception. . . . It may be that a door once shut is now somewhat ajar."[106] In 1997, the Eleventh Circuit spoke of a continuing "attitude of disfavor"[107] and was unimpressed with "nascent case law more receptive to expert testimony on eyewitness reliability."[108]

The unsympathetic opinions argued that since an appreciation

---

(1990) (collecting cases); Bloodsworth v. State, 307 Md. 164, 512 A.2d 1056 (1986) (collecting cases); 2 Faigman, et al., Modern Scientific Evidence § 16:2 to 16-6 (2011–2012 ed.); 1 Giannelli & Imwinkelried, Scientific Evidence § 9.02(d) (4th ed. 2007); Admissibility, at criminal prosecution, of expert testimony on reliability of eyewitness testimony, 46 A.L.R.4th 1047.

[101]U.S. v. Watson, 587 F.2d 365, 369 (7th Cir. 1978) ("It is a matter in which the trial court has broad discretion"); Hager v. U.S., 856 A.2d 1143 (D.C. 2004); State v. Lawhorn, 762 S.W.2d 820, 823 (Mo. 1988) ("Almost uniformly, state and federal courts have upheld the trial court's exercise of discretion"); People v. Lee, 96 N.Y.2d 157, 726 N.Y.S.2d 361, 750 N.E.2d 63, 67 (2001). The cases also reject claims that exclusion of defense experts on the topic violates constitutional rights to compulsory process or due process. Johnson v. Wainwright, 806 F.2d 1479 (11th Cir. 1986); State v. Kemp, 199 Conn. 473, 507 A.2d 1387 (1986) (overruled by, State v. Guilbert, 306 Conn. 218, 49 A.3d 705 (2012)); Heath v. U.S., 26 A.3d 266, 275–85 (D.C. 2011).

[102]State v. Chapple, 135 Ariz. 281, 660 P.2d 1208, 1224 (1983); People v. McDonald, 37 Cal. 3d 351, 208 Cal. Rptr. 236, 690 P.2d 709 (1984) (sole

evidence linking black defendant to street robbery of an Hispanic was conflicting testimony of eyewitnesses, and six defense witnesses supported the accused's alibi defense); State v. Taylor, 50 Wash. App. 481, 749 P.2d 181, 185 (Div. 1 1988).

[103]U.S. v. Downing, 753 F.2d 1224 (3d Cir. 1985); U.S. v. Smith, 736 F.2d 1103 (6th Cir. 1984).

[104]*E.g.*, State v. Chapple, 135 Ariz. 281, 660 P.2d 1208, 1227 (1983) (dissenting opinion); State v. Malmrose, 649 P.2d 56, 61 (Utah 1982) ("such testimony would amount to a lecture to the jury about how they should perform their duties").

[105]*See* McMullen v. State, 714 So. 2d 368, 371 (Fla. 1998) (categorizing caselaw); Bomas v. State, 412 Md. 392, 987 A.2d 98 (2010) (reviewing caselaw on three approaches—prohibitory, discretionary, and favored); Vallas, A Survey of Federal and State Standards for the Admission of Expert Testimony on the Reliability of Eyewitnesses, 39 Am. J. Crim. L. 97 (2011) (categorizing caselaw).

[106]U.S. v. Brien, 59 F.3d 274, 277 (1st Cir. 1995).

[107]U.S. v. Fred Smith, 122 F.3d 1355, 1357 (11th Cir. 1997).

[108]Smith, 122 F.3d at 1358.

of the limitations on eyewitnesses' perceptions and memory is within the ken of a lay jury, broad brush psychological testimony about these mechanisms would not appreciably assist the jury[109] and that cross-examination is sufficient to expose unreliable identifications.[110] They pointed also to the standard concerns with scientific evidence—that lay jurors will overstate its importance and that its introduction will entail undue expense and confusion.[111] Some courts were dubious of the scientific validity of the psychological research.[112] The more poorly reasoned opinions spoke of invading the province of the jury.[113]

---

[109]U.S. v. Fosher, 590 F.2d 381, 383 (1st Cir. 1979); Dyas v. U. S., 376 A.2d 827, 832 (D.C. 1977) (not "beyond the ken of the average layman," nor would expert testimony "aid the trier in his search for the truth."); Johnson v. State, 438 So. 2d 774, 777 (Fla. 1983) ("a jury is fully capable of assessing a witness's ability to perceive and remember . . . without the aid of expert testimony"); State v. Ammons, 208 Neb. 797, 305 N.W.2d 812, 814 (1981) ("The accuracy or inaccuracy of eyewitness observation is a common experience of daily life").

[110]U.S. v. Christophe, 833 F.2d 1296, 1299 (9th Cir. 1987) ("We adhere to the position that skillful cross examination of eyewitnesses, coupled with appeals to the experience and common sense of jurors, will sufficiently alert jurors to specific conditions that render a particular eyewitness identification unreliable."); U.S. v. Thevis, 665 F.2d 616, 641 (5th Cir. 1982) ("the problems of perception and memory can be adequately addressed in cross-examination and . . . the jury can adequately weigh these problems through common sense evaluation").

[111]Fosher, 590 F.2d at 383; Thevis, 665 F.2d at 641 ("open the door to a barrage of marginally relevant psychological evidence"); People v. Enis, 139 Ill. 2d 264, 151 Ill. Dec. 493, 564 N.E.2d 1155 (1990) (the expert generalizations are of doubtful applicability and could create the misleading impression "that all expert testimony is unreliable"); Com. v. Francis, 390 Mass. 89, 453 N.E.2d 1204 (1983).

[112]U.S. v. Christophe, 833 F.2d 1296, 1299 (9th Cir. 1987) ("Psychologists do not generally accept the claimed dangers of eyewitness identification in a trial setting."); U.S. v. Watson, 587 F.2d 365, 369 (7th Cir. 1978) (affirming exclusion because scientific field inadequately developed); Caldwell v. State, 267 Ark. 1053, 594 S.W.2d 24 (Ct. App. 1980) ("The field of perception and memory is alleged to be a science," but "the science of human perception testimony is new"); Porter v. State, 94 Nev. 142, 576 P.2d 275, 278 (1978) ("not a recognized field of expertise"). Several circuits emphasized the need to prove scientific soundness. E.g., U.S. v. Brien, 59 F.3d 274, 277 (1st Cir. 1995) (inadequate showing under *Daubert*, but "[t]here is more expert literature on the subject, more experts pressing to testify, and possibly more skepticism about the reliability of eyewitnesses"); U.S. v. Amador-Galvan, 9 F.3d 1414, 1417–18 (9th Cir. 1993).

[113]U.S. v. Brown, 540 F.2d 1048, 1054 (10th Cir. 1976) ("opinion evidence cannot usurp the functions of the jury or be received if it touches the very issue before the jury"); State v. Stucke, 419 So. 2d 939, 945 (La. 1982) ("invades the province of the jury and usurps its function"); State v. Hill, 463 N.W.2d 674 (S.D. 1990). Such pronouncements are unnecessary rhetoric, stating a conclusion but not giving a reason. People v. McDonald, 37 Cal. 3d 351, 208 Cal. Rptr. 236, 690 P.2d 709 (1984); Benn v. U.S., 978 A.2d 1257, 1274 (D.C. 2009) ("If expert testimony can assist the jury, it per-

Nevertheless, the matter could not be disposed of this easily. Concern over the reliability of eyewitness testimony lies at the heart of the Supreme Court's right to counsel[114] and due process[115] decisions in cases involving lineups and other pretrial identification procedures. It may well be that without some counteracting influence, juries give too much weight to the witness's assertions of recognition. Studies consistently expose eyewitness misidentification as the leading cause of false convictions in rape and, to a lesser extent, homicide cases.[116] To contend that juries know how to evaluate the reliability of the identifications without expert assistance,[117] while simultaneously maintaining that the assistance would have too great an impact on the jury's deliberations, smacks of makeshift reasoning.[118] Admittedly, there are dangers—some obvious and some subtle—in

---

force does not usurp the jury's function."). If they were taken at face value and applied in other areas, the results would be intolerable. See, for example, supra §§ 204 (radar evidence of speeding) & 205 (blood alcohol evidence of drunkenness and biological evidence of paternity).

[114]U.S. v. Wade, 388 U.S. 218, 87 S. Ct. 1926, 18 L. Ed. 2d 1149 (1967). But see Kirby v. Illinois, 406 U.S. 682, 92 S. Ct. 1877, 32 L. Ed. 2d 411 (1972).

[115]Manson v. Brathwaite, 432 U.S. 98, 111–12, 97 S. Ct. 2243, 53 L. Ed. 2d 140 (1977); Neil v. Biggers, 409 U.S. 188, 198, 93 S. Ct. 375, 34 L. Ed. 2d 401 (1972); Stovall v. Denno, 388 U.S. 293, 87 S. Ct. 1967, 18 L. Ed. 2d 1199 (1967).

[116]Garrett, Convicting the Innocent: Where Criminal Prosecutions Go Wrong 8–9, 279 (2011); Gross et al., Exonerations in the United States 1989 Through 2003, 95 J. Crim. L. & Criminology 523, 543 (2005).

[117]The eyewitness researchers have responded to the judicial pronouncements that jurors know all they need to know without expert testimony. Applying the tools of their trade, these researchers have undertaken further studies to reveal what jurors know about the factors that seem to affect eyewitness performance, how closely this lay knowledge tracks the research findings, and what effect expert testimony has on jury delibera-

tions. See Cutler & Penrod, Mistaken Identity: The Eyewitness, Psychology, and the Law 171–251 (1995); Wells, Scientific Status, 2 Faigman, et al., Modern Scientific Evidence § 16:45 (2011–2012 ed.); Benton et al., Eyewitness Memory is Still Not Common Sense: Comparing Jurors, Judges and Law Enforcement to Eyewitness Experts, 20 Applied Cognitive Psychol. 115 (2006); Magnussen et al., Beliefs About Factors Affecting the Reliability of Eyewitness Testimony: A Comparison of Judges, Jurors and the General Public, 24 Applied Cognitive Psychol. 122 (2010); Vidmar & Shuller, Juries and Expert Evidence: Social Framework Testimony, 52 Law & Contemp. Probs. 133, 160–66 (1989); Wise & Safer, A Comparison of What U.S. Judges and Students Know and Believe About Eyewitness Testimony, 40 J. Applied Social Psychol. 1400 (2010).

[118]However, some research suggests that expert description of the weaknesses of eyewitness reports induces jurors to give those reports less credit than they deserve. See Mosteller, Legal Doctrines Concerning the Admissibility of Expert Testimony Concerning Social Framework Evidence, 52 Law & Contemp. Probs. 85, 89–92 (1989); Sanders, Expert Testimony in Eyewitness Facial Identification Cases, 17 Tex. Tech. L. Rev. 1409, 1459–64 (1986).

translating laboratory and classroom demonstrations of witness fallibility into conclusions about the accuracy of a particular witness's identification in a real life setting.[119] Nevertheless, it seems clear that the researchers have something to offer, and that when a case turns on uncorroborated eyewitness recognition, the courts should be receptive to expert testimony about the knowledge, gleaned from methodologically sound experimentation, of the factors that may have produced a faulty identification and that are present in the case at bar. Although the researcher must be circumspect in stating inferences about a particular witness's testimony,[120] the pertinent research findings can assist

---

[119]Loh, Psycholegal Research: Past and Present, 79 Mich. L. Rev. 659, 686–91 (1981) (psychological studies give information about average performance of all kinds of persons under conditions that may be structured to promote inaccuracies in the identifications). For skeptical analysis of the benefits of importing the research studies into the courtroom, see Ebbesen & Konecni, Eyewitness Memory Research: Probative v. Prejudicial Value, 5 Expert Evidence 2, 3 (1997) ("the courts have been misled about the validity, consistency, and generalizability of the research. . . . Research on eyewitness memory continues to lack external validity or generality. . . ."); Egeth & McCloskey, Expert Testimony About Eyewitness Behavior: Is it Safe and Effective?, in Eyewitness Testimony: Psychological Perspectives 238 (Wells & Loftus eds., 1984); Elliott, Expert Testimony About Eyewitness Identification (A Critique), 17 Law & Hum. Behav. 423 (1993); Konecni & Ebbesen, Courtroom Testimony by Psychologists on Eyewitness Identification Issues: Critical Notes and Reflections, 10 Law & Hum. Behav. 117 (1986); McCloskey et al., The Experimental Psychologist in Court: The Ethics of Expert Testimony, 10 Law & Hum. Behav. 1 (1986); cf. Lindsay & Wells, What Do We Really Know About Cross-Racial Eyewitness Identification?, in Eyewitness Testimony: Psychological Perspectives 219 (Wells & Loftus eds., 1984) (cross-racial identification research lacks adequate explanatory theories and has produced inconsistent results).

[120]Loftus, Eyewitness Testimony 200 (1979) ("Any psychologist who attempted to offer an exact probability for the likelihood that a witness was accurate would be going far beyond what is possible"). Although there is no longer any specific prohibition on allowing an expert to express an opinion on an "ultimate" fact (see supra § 12), the need to avoid undue prejudice can justify curtailing testimony. Thus, it has been held that it is proper to allow a clinical psychologist to "testify regarding those factors which he believed could influence eyewitness identifications," but to prevent him "from stating to the jury his own opinion as to the reliability of [the particular] identification." Hampton v. State, 92 Wis. 2d 450, 285 N.W.2d 868, 872 (1979). See also State v. Chapple, 135 Ariz. 281, 660 P.2d 1208, 1219 (1983) ("the 'generality' of the testimony is a factor which favors admission. Witnesses are permitted to express opinions on ultimate issues but are not required to testify to an opinion on the precise questions before the trier of fact"); State v. Guilbert, 306 Conn. 218, 49 A.3d 705, 729 (2012) ("An expert should not be permitted to give an opinion about the credibility or accuracy of the eyewitness testimony itself"); State v. Fontaine, 382 N.W.2d 374, 378 (N.D. 1986); State v. Buell, 22 Ohio St. 3d 124, 489 N.E.2d 795, 804 (1986).

the jury in evaluating a crucial piece of evidence.[121] While expert testimony on the psychology of eyewitness identifications may not be necessary or appropriate in many cases,[122] in those instances in which the case turns on the eyewitness testimony and the expert's assistance could make a difference, the scientific knowledge generally should be admitted, either through expert testimony or judicial instructions[123] concerning factors affecting eyewitness accuracy that are important to assessing the identification in question and that are not well understood by most jurors.[124]

Indeed, in rejecting the argument that admission of an eyewitness identification made in highly suggestive circumstances—but for which the state was not responsible—violates the right to due

---

[121]See, e.g., U.S. v. Sullivan, 246 F. Supp. 2d 696 (E.D. Ky. 2003) (admitting defendant's expert testimony because it is scientifically valid and would be helpful to the jury); Stein, The Admissibility of Expert Testimony about Cognitive Science Research on Eyewitness Identification, Law, Probability & Risk 295 (2003).

[122]E.g., U.S. v. Langan, 263 F.3d 613 (6th Cir. 2001) (psychologist's testimony on eyewitnesses properly excluded under Daubert for lack of fit); U.S. v. Hall, 165 F.3d 1095 (7th Cir. 1999) (same); People v. Young, 7 N.Y.3d 40, 817 N.Y.S.2d 576, 850 N.E.2d 623 (2006) (exclusion not an abuse of discretion given the particular facts); People v. Lee, 96 N.Y.2d 157, 726 N.Y.S.2d 361, 750 N.E.2d 63 (2001) (although expert psychological testimony on eyewitness identification satisfies Frye, it was not an abuse of discretion to exclude such testimony in the circumstances of the case).

[123]A few commentators have concluded that pattern jury instructions for eyewitness identifications and other "social framework" evidence should supplant rather than supplement expert testimony. Walker & Monahan, Social Frameworks: A New Use of Social Science in Law, 73 Va. L. Rev. 559, 592–98 (1987). Contra Mosteller, Legal Doctrines Concerning the Admissibility of Expert Testimony Concerning Social Framework Evidence, 52 Law & Contemp. Probs. 85, 112 (1989). For cases on the need

for and adequacy of judicial instructions on the infirmities of eyewitness testimony, see U.S. v. Tipton, 11 F.3d 602, 606 (6th Cir. 1993); State v. Dyle, 899 S.W.2d 607 (Tenn. 1995) (identifying different approaches in the caselaw). Although the Supreme Court assumes that "[e]yewitness-specific jury instructions, which many federal and state courts have adopted" are valuable in ensuring that jurors evaluate eyewitness testimony properly, it has been reported that experiments on the efficacy of such instructions indicate that "judges' instructions do not serve as an effective safeguard." Cutler & Penrod, Mistaken Identity: The Eyewitness, Psychology, and the Law 255–64 (1995). For still another device to present jurors with research results, see State v. Alger, 115 Idaho 42, 764 P.2d 119 (Ct. App. 1988) (Scientific American article admissible under learned treatise exception to hearsay rule).

[124]See, e.g., U.S. v. Smithers, 212 F.3d 306 (6th Cir. 2000); People v. McDonald, 37 Cal. 3d 351, 208 Cal. Rptr. 236, 690 P.2d 709, 727 (1984); Bomas v. State, 412 Md. 392, 987 A.2d 98 (2010); People v. Santiago, 17 N.Y.3d 661, 934 N.Y.S.2d 746, 958 N.E.2d 874 (2011); Comment, 73 Cal. L. Rev. 1402, 1416–29 (1985); Mosteller, Legal Doctrines Concerning the Admissibility of Expert Testimony Concerning Social Framework Evidence, 52 Law & Contemp. Probs. 85, 89–92 (1989).

process of law, the Supreme Court in *Perry v. New Hampshire*,[125] took solace in the fact that in some states "in cases involving eyewitness identification of strangers or near-strangers, trial courts will routinely admit expert testimony [on the dangers of such evidence]."[126] Although it seems doubtful that this practice is truly routine,[127] appellate courts have generally moved from a position of skepticism and hostility to an increasingly open stance toward presenting jurors with the research findings on the psychology of eyewitness testimony.[128]

### (D) Profiles and Syndromes.

Psychological studies sometimes show a correlation between certain traits or characteristics and certain forms of behavior. When this is the case, one can construct a diagnostic or predictive "profile" for such behavior.[129] For instance, studies of "accident prone" persons indicate that such factors as having poor eyesight, being relatively young or old, and acting impulsively, aggressively or rebelliously are prevalent in this group.[130] Physicians regard certain patterns of physical injuries in children, which they designate the "battered child syndrome,"[131] as indicating repeated physical abuse.[132]

---

[125]Perry v. New Hampshire, 132 S. Ct. 716, 181 L. Ed. 2d 694 (2012).

[126]Perry, 132 S.Ct. at 729 (quoting and adding bracketed material to State v. Clopten, 2009 UT 84, 223 P.3d 1103, 1113 (Utah 2009)).

[127]See U.S. v. Smith, 621 F. Supp. 2d 1207 (M.D. Ala. 2009) (urging more extensive use of such testimony in the Eleventh Circuit).

[128]E.g., State v. Guilbert, 306 Conn. 218, 49 A.3d 705, 713 (2012) (concluding that "the time has come to overrule" previous cases that treated "expert testimony on the issue [as] disfavored" and stating that "testimony by a qualified expert on the fallibility of eyewitness identification is admissible under [Connecticut's version of *Daubert*] when that testimony would aid the jury in evaluating the state's identification evidence."); Benn v. U.S., 978 A.2d 1257, 1277 (D.C. 2009) (describing changes since "our 1977 *Dyas* decision"); State v. Henderson, 208 N.J. 208, 27 A.3d 872 (2011); Com. v. Christie, 98 S.W.3d 485 (Ky. 2002) (overruling cases seeming to establish

a per se rule of inadmissibility); People v. Santiago, 17 N.Y.3d 661, 934 N.Y.S.2d 746, 958 N.E.2d 874 (2011) (reviewing New York cases and standards on exclusion of psychological testimony on eyewitness identification). For catalogs of all the caselaw, see U.S. v. Owens, 682 F.3d 1358, 1359 (11th Cir. 2012) (dissenting from denial of petition for rehearing en banc); Vallas, A Survey of Federal and State Standards for the Admission of Expert Testimony on the Reliability of Eyewitnesses, 39 Am. J. Crim. L. 97, 136–38 (2011).

[129]See generally Monahan, The Clinical Prediction of Violent Behavior (1981); Turvey, Criminal Profiling: An Introduction to Behavioral Evidence Analysis (2001); Monahan, A Jurisprudence of Risk Assessment: Forecasting Harm Among Prisoners, Predators, and Patients, 92 Va. L. Rev. 391 (2006).

[130]See supra § 189.

[131]Kempe et al., The Battered-Child Syndrome, 181 J.A.M.A. 17 (1962); Nelson, The Misuse of Abuse:

Likewise, analysis of individuals apprehended while smuggling drugs through airports shows that these persons tend to arrive from major points of distribution, to have little or no luggage with them, to look nervously about, to arrive in the early morning, and to have large amounts of cash in small bills.[133] Police often describe a flexible version of this profile in describing how a defendant came to their attention, explaining the nature of illegal drug smuggling, or suggesting that the defendant is in fact a courier.[134] Used for the last purpose, this profile evidence usually is inadmissible as evidence of bad character[135] or as an opinion on the defendant's intent.[136]

In civil commitment and criminal proceedings at which a

---

Restricting Evidence of Battered Child Syndrome, 75 Law & Contemp. Probs. 187 (2012).

[132]U.S. v. Boise, 916 F.2d 497, 503–04 (9th Cir. 1990) ("battered-child syndrome has gained general judicial recognition . . . as an accepted medical diagnosis"). Many courts admit evidence of injuries sustained while in the parent's care to rebut the parent's claim that the death or damage was accidental. See supra § 190. There also is a psychological version of the battered child syndrome. See 2 Faigman, et al., Modern Scientific Evidence: The Law and Science of Expert Testimony §§ 14:1 et seq. (2011–2012 ed.).

[133]See U.S. v. Sokolow, 490 U.S. 1, 109 S. Ct. 1581, 104 L. Ed. 2d 1 (1989) (dissenting opinion contending that the features in a drug courier are insufficient to establish reasonable suspicion for an investigative stop); Reid v. Georgia, 448 U.S. 438, 441, 100 S. Ct. 2752, 65 L. Ed. 2d 890 (1980) (per curiam) (the profile characteristics common to the suspect and the Drug Enforcement Administration's "informal" profile of drug couriers did not establish reasonable suspicion, since these characteristics merely "describe a very large category of presumably innocent travelers").

[134]U.S. v. Cordero, 815 F. Supp. 2d 821, 843 (E.D. Pa. 2011) ("The majority of courts have concluded that the testimony is inadmissible as substantive proof of guilt or innocence, but may be admitted for rebuttal or other,

non-substantive purposes such as explaining modus operandi or describing the background operational principles of a particular type of narcotics operation.") (citing Admissibility of drug courier profile testimony in criminal prosecution, 69 A.L.R.5th 425).

[135]U.S. v. Williams, 957 F.2d 1238, 1241 (5th Cir. 1992) ("drug courier profiles are not admissible as substantive evidence of guilt"); Salcedo v. People, 999 P.2d 833, 837 (Colo. 2000) ("Almost uniformly, courts and commentators have rejected the use of drug courier profiles as substantive evidence."); Giannelli & Imwinkelried, Scientific Evidence § 9.07(c) (4th ed. 2007); Becton, The Drug Courier Profile: "All Seems Infected that th' Infected Spy, As All Looks Yellow to the Jaundic'd Eye," 65 N.C. L. Rev. 417 (1987); Kadish, The Drug Courier Profile: In Planes, Trains, and Automobiles; and Now in the Jury Box, 46 Am. U. L. Rev. 747, 774–75 (1997) ("The majority of courts have concluded that expert testimony on the 'drug courier profile' [is inadmissible] when offered as substantive evidence of guilt . . . ."). But see U.S. v. Montes-Salas, 669 F.3d 240, 248 (5th Cir. 2012) ("Testimony about the usual practices of drug smugglers may be admitted when it is not "pure profile testimony" but rather is used to rebut the defendant's innocent explanation for his behavior.") (note omitted).

[136]U.S. v. Mendoza-Medina, 346 F.3d 121, 128 (5th Cir. 2003) ("[D]rug courier profiles can violate Federal

---

person's dangerousness to others is an issue, unvalidated clinical predictions of violence have long been admitted.[137] In the aftermath of *Daubert*, however, the use of statistical (actuarial) risk assessment instruments[138] has commanded more attention, even in *Frye* jurisdictions.[139]

More generally, we all evaluate information in the light of some set of factors that could be called a "profile." Jurors, for example, can be said to bring to the courtroom their preconceived "profiles" which they then apply to decide who is lying and who is telling the truth, and who is likely to have committed an offense and who is innocent. Although there is no fundamental difference between the psychological and medical profiles and the more common, impressionistic ones, some of the former may have been derived in a more systematic and structured way, and some may have been tested by verifying that they give correct diagnoses or predictions when applied to new cases. The correlations obtained in such prospective or cross-validated studies measure the validity of the better-defined profiles.[140]

Particularly in criminal cases, litigants have sought to

---

Rule of Evidence 704(b) when they are used to prove that the defendant was a courier and therefore knew that he was transporting drugs.") (footnotes omitted). *But see* Kaye et al., The New Wigmore, A Treatise on Evidence: Expert Evidence § 2.2.3(b) (2d ed. 2011) (describing competing theories of Rule 704(b), one of which would classify inferences based on external factors as opposed to psychological expertise as falling outside Rule 704(b)).

[137]*See* Barefoot v. Estelle, 463 U.S. 880, 103 S. Ct. 3383, 77 L. Ed. 2d 1090 (1983) (sentencing phase of capital case); U.S. v. Salerno, 481 U.S. 739, 107 S. Ct. 2095, 95 L. Ed. 2d 697 (1987) (pretrial detention).

[138]*See* Appelbaum, Reference Guide on Mental Health Evidence, in Reference Manual on Scientific Evidence 813, 827–50 (Committee on the Development of the Third Edition of the Reference Manual on Scientific Evidence and Federal Judicial Center eds., 3d ed. 2011); Monahan, A Jurisprudence of Risk Assessment: Forecasting Harm Among Prisoners, Predators, and Patients, 92 Va. L. Rev. 391 (2006); Monahan et al., Developing a

Clinically Useful Actuarial Tool for Assessing Violence Risk, 176 Brit. J. Psychiatry 312 (2000).

[139]*See, e.g.,* Jackson v. State, 833 So. 2d 243, 246 (Fla. 4th DCA 2002) (upholding the trial court's determination that the actuarial instruments "are generally accepted in the relevant scientific community as part of the overall risk assessment for sexual predators"); In re Commitment of Simons, 213 Ill. 2d 523, 290 Ill. Dec. 610, 821 N.E.2d 1184 (2004) (actuarial violence predictions in civil commitment proceeding satisfy *Frye*); 2 Faigman, et al., Modern Scientific Evidence chs. 10 & 11 (2011–2012 ed.); 1 Giannelli & Imwinkelried, Scientific Evidence § 9.10 (4th ed. 2007); Janus & Prentky, Forensic Use of Actuarial Risk Assessment with Sex Offenders: Accuracy, Admissibility and Accountability, 40 Am. Crim. L. Rev. 1443 (2003); Monahan, Violence Risk Assessment: Scientific Validity and Evidentiary Admissibility, 57 Wash. & Lee L. Rev. 901 (2000).

[140]*E.g.*, Rice et al., Cross Validation and Extension of the Violence Risk Appraisal Guide for Child Molesters and Rapists, 21 Law & Hum. Behav.

introduce expert testimony as to a long list of profiles[141] said to be scientifically constructed or validated.[142] These include the following:

- The "battered woman syndrome" (BWS)[143] has been invoked

---

231 (1997).

[141]*See* In re Marriage of Bates, 212 Ill. 2d 489, 289 Ill. Dec. 218, 819 N.E.2d 714, 733–34 (2004) (noting that "PAS [Parental Alienation Syndrome] is now the subject of legal and professional criticism," but not reviewing the lower court's finding of general acceptance); Kennedy, Psychological Syndrome Evidence, *in* 2 Psychological Expertise in Court 103 (Lieberman & Krauss 2009); Slobogin, Psychiatric Evidence in Criminal Trials: To Junk or Not to Junk?, 40 Wm. & Mary L. Rev. 1 (1998).

[142]As is apparent from previous notes, not all of the "profiles" and "syndromes" mentioned in this section can be considered scientifically constructed and validated. *See also* Salcedo v. People, 999 P.2d 833 (Colo. 2000) (detective's personal profile of drug courier was inadmissible); State v. Stevens, 78 S.W.3d 817 (Tenn. 2002) (inferences as to motivation from the nature of a crime scene were not shown to be reliable under *Kumho Tire v. Carmichael* by unexplained statement that "a study to determine the accuracy rate of its crime scene analysis . . . yielded a seventy-five to eighty percent accuracy rate" or by FBI agent's attestation that "the demand is just outstripping our resources to provide it"); State v. Fortin, 162 N.J. 517, 745 A.2d 509 (2000) (although "linkage analysis lacks sufficient scientific reliability to establish that the same perpetrator committed [two different] crimes," an expert who insisted that "a sexual predator's behavior is as unique as his fingerprints, his DNA, or as a snowflake" may testify as to the frequency with which a specific pattern of injuries to two victims was seen in the cases he had studied); Faigman, To Have and Have Not: Assessing the Value of

Social Science to the Law, 38 Emory L.J. 1005 (1989); Faust & Ziskin, The Expert Witness in Psychology and Psychiatry, 241 Science 31 (1988).

[143]The outpouring of writing on the problem of battered women is "truly prolific." Faigman, Review Essay: Discerning Justice When Battered Women Kill, 39 Hastings L.J. 207, 207 n.1 (1987). Many courts and commentators quickly embraced the theories of "cycles" and "learned helplessness" propounded in Walker, The Battered Woman (1979), and Walker, The Battered Woman Syndrome (1984). Faigman, Review Essay: Discerning Justice When Battered Women Kill, 39 Hastings L.J. 207, 209 n. 4 (1987). *But see* Faigman, Note, The Battered Woman Syndrome and Self-Defense: A Legal and Empirical Dissent, 72 Va. L. Rev. 619, 647 (1986) (since "the leading research suffers from significant methodological and interpretive flaws," "[t]he prevailing theories of battered woman syndrome have little evidentiary value in self-defense cases"). In the main, the criticism of the theory has not been refuted. Faigman & Wright, The Battered Woman Syndrome in the Age of Science, 39 Ariz. L. Rev. 67, 109–10 (1997) ("The battered woman syndrome remains little more than an unsubstantiated hypothesis that, despite being extant for over fifteen years, has yet to be tested adequately or, when adequately tested, has failed to be corroborated."); Mosteller, Syndromes and Politics in Criminal Trials and Evidence Law, 46 Duke L.J. 461, 482 (1996); Schuller & Rzeba, Scientific Status, *in* 2 Faigman, et al., Modern Scientific Evidence: The Law and Science of Expert Testimony §§ 13.25 to 13:29 (2011–2012 ed.). For a more favorable review of the theories and research into the impact of the expert testimony and the common

to support pleas of self-defense in murder cases,[144] to establish the killing was not premeditated,[145] to buttress defenses of duress in cases in which women aided their abusive partners in criminal activity,[146] to explain inconsistencies in a woman's statements or behavior,[147] and in various other situations.[148] Indeed, prosecutors have found uses for the syndrome,[149] as have civil litigants.[150]

- Prosecutors in sexual abuse cases have relied on the "rape trauma syndrome" (RTS, a form of post-traumatic stress disorder)[151] or related behaviors that are said to be common

---

lay perceptions of battered women, see Vidmar & Schuller, Juries and Expert Evidence: Social Framework Testimony, 52 Law & Contemp. Probs. 133, 148–55 (1989).

[144]Smith v. State, 268 Ga. 196, 486 S.E.2d 819, 822 (1997) (admissible); Com. v. Rodriquez, 418 Mass. 1, 633 N.E.2d 1039, 1042 (1994) ("may be admissible"); State v. Hennum, 441 N.W.2d 793, 798 n.2 (Minn. 1989) (listing self-defense cases); State v. Koss, 49 Ohio St. 3d 213, 551 N.E.2d 970 (1990) (admissible); State v. Urena, 899 A.2d 1281 (R.I. 2006) (admissible); 1 Giannelli & Imwinkelried, Scientific Evidence § 9.03(a) (4th ed. 2007); Faigman & Wright, The Battered Woman Syndrome in the Age of Science, 39 Ariz. L. Rev. 67 (1997).

[145]State v. Stewart, 228 W. Va. 406, 719 S.E.2d 876, 885 (2011).

[146]U.S. v. Willis, 38 F.3d 170 (5th Cir. 1994) (irrelevant to objective standard for duress defense); 1 Giannelli & Imwinkelried, Scientific Evidence § 9.03(b) (4th ed. 2007); Faigman & Wright, The Battered Woman Syndrome in the Age of Science, 39 Ariz. L. Rev. 67 (1997); Appel, Note, Beyond Self-Defense: The Use of Battered Woman Syndrome in Duress Defenses, 1994 U. Ill. L. Rev. 955.

[147]People v. Brown, 33 Cal. 4th 892, 16 Cal. Rptr. 3d 447, 94 P.3d 574, 582 (2004) (holding that even a single prior act of violence is admissible "to explain the behavior of domestic violence victims"); People v. Riggs, 44 Cal. 4th 248, 79 Cal. Rptr. 3d 648, 187

P.3d 363 (2008); State v. Borrelli, 227 Conn. 153, 629 A.2d 1105 (1993) (admissible); State v. Grecinger, 569 N.W.2d 189 (Minn. 1997) (admissible after defense attack on credibility); State v. Stringer, 271 Mont. 367, 897 P.2d 1063 (1995) (admissible); Dean v. State, 2008 WY 124, 194 P.3d 299 (Wyo. 2008).

[148]The uses catalogued here are described in 2 Faigman, et al., Modern Scientific Evidence: The Law and Science of Expert Testimony §§ 13:1 et seq. (2011–2012 ed.); Admissibility of expert testimony concerning domestic-violence syndromes to assist jury in evaluating victim's testimony or behavior, 57 A.L.R.5th 315.

[149]State v. Haines, 112 Ohio St. 3d 393, 2006-Ohio-6711, 860 N.E.2d 91 (2006) (a veritable diagnosis of battered-woman syndrome "went beyond the providing of a context for a witness's testimony into . . . whether [defendant] committed domestic violence"); 2 Faigman, et al., Modern Scientific Evidence: The Law and Science of Expert Testimony § 13:17 (2011–2012 ed.).

[150]Faigman & Wright, The Battered Woman Syndrome in the Age of Science, 39 Ariz. L. Rev. 67 (1997).

[151]PTSD is listed in American Psychiatric Association, Diagnostic and Statistical Manual of Mental Disorders—Text Revision 309.81 (4th ed. 2000). It has been suggested that since there is no rape-specific syndrome, the phrase "rape trauma syndrome" should be avoided. State v.

among victims of rape to negate a claim of consent,[152] to explain conflicting statements or actions of the complainant,[153] to prove criminal sexual penetration.[154] Conversely, defendants have introduced evidence that a complainant did not experience the syndrome's symptoms.[155]

---

Allewalt, 308 Md. 89, 517 A.2d 741, 751 (1986); State v. Taylor, 663 S.W.2d 235 (Mo. 1984); State v. Black, 109 Wash. 2d 336, 745 P.2d 12, 19 (1987); *cf.* Kennedy, Psychological Syndrome Evidence, in 2 Psychological Syndrome Evidence 103, 108 (Lieberman & Krauss 2009) ("In contrast to PTSD, this disorder does not enjoy widespread consensus as to its definition nor is it specifically included in the DSM-IV TR.").

[152]*Compare* State v. Huey, 145 Ariz. 59, 699 P.2d 1290, 1293–94 (1985); State v. Allewalt, 517 A.2d at 741; State v. Obeta, 796 N.W.2d 282 (Minn. 2011) (admissible); *with* People v. Bledsoe, 36 Cal. 3d 236, 203 Cal. Rptr. 450, 681 P.2d 291, 300–01 (1984); State v. McGee, 324 N.W.2d 232, 233 (Minn. 1982); State v. Taylor, 663 S.W.2d 235 (Mo. 1984); People v. Taylor, 75 N.Y.2d 277, 552 N.Y.S.2d 883, 552 N.E.2d 131 (1990); State v. Black, 109 Wash. 2d 336, 745 P.2d 12, 16–18 (1987) (inadmissible). For more cases and commentary, see 1 Giannelli & Imwinkelried, Scientific Evidence § 9.04 (4th ed. 2007); 2 Faigman, et al., Modern Scientific Evidence: The Law and Science of Expert Testimony §§ 15:1 et seq. (2011–2012 ed.); McCord, The Admissibility of Expert Testimony Regarding Rape Trauma Syndrome in Rape Prosecutions, 26 B.C. L. Rev. 1143, 1146–56, 1165–77 (1985).

[153]U.S. v. Winters, 729 F.2d 602 (9th Cir. 1984) (admissible to explain kidnapped victim's failure to escape or call for help); State v. Freeney, 228 Conn. 582, 637 A.2d 1088, 1093 (1994) (admissible to explain victim's failure to make escape attempts); People v. Hampton, 746 P.2d 947, 951 (Colo. 1987) (admissible to put delay in reporting rape "in context"); People v.

Taylor, 75 N.Y.2d 277, 552 N.Y.S.2d 883, 552 N.E.2d 131 (1990) (testimony that it is common for victim to remain calm and quiet after attack admissible); State v. Baby, 404 Md. 220, 946 A.2d 463 (2008) (holding that " 'rape trauma syndrome' evidence should first be subjected to *Frye-Reed* analysis"); Com. v. Gallagher, 519 Pa. 291, 547 A.2d 355 (1988) (inadmissible to explain why victim was unable to identify defendant as rapist two weeks after the rape).

[154]State v. Ross, 104 N.M. 23, 715 P.2d 471 (Ct. App. 1986); Taylor v. Com., 21 Va. App. 557, 466 S.E.2d 118, 122 (1996) (relevant to show "occurrence of a traumatizing event").

[155]Henson v. State, 535 N.E.2d 1189, 1193 (Ind. 1989) ("fundamentally unfair" to exclude proof of absence of syndrome when state can prove its presence in rape cases); State v. McQuillen, 236 Kan. 161, 689 P.2d 822, 836–37 (1984) (dictum); State v. Scheffelman, 250 Mont. 334, 820 P.2d 1293, 1299 (1991) ("The absence of evidence of psychological trauma does not prove that the offense did not occur."); State v. Jones, 83 Ohio App. 3d 723, 615 N.E.2d 713, 718–19 (2d Dist. Miami County 1992) (questioning value of this negative evidence). The absence of PTSD is not necessarily as probative as its presence. *See generally* Lyon & Koehler, The Relevance Ratio: Evaluating the Probative Value of Expert Testimony in Child Sexual Abuse Cases, 82 Cornell L. Rev. 43, 70–74 (1996). The probative value depends, in part, on the frequency of the syndrome among rape victims. If the syndrome is rare—if but a small percentage of women who are raped suffer from PTSD—then its absence in a particular case does little to enhance the probability that the complainant

- In sexual abuse cases involving children, prosecutors have relied on a similar "child sexual abuse accommodation syndrome" (CSAAS)[156] to prove the fact of abuse[157] or to explain the child's delay in reporting the abuse,[158] a retrac-

---

consented. On the other hand, if the base rate is high, there is some force to the argument for admitting defendant's proof of the absence of trauma. McCord, The Admissibility of Expert Testimony Regarding Rape Trauma Syndrome in Rape Prosecutions, 26 B.C. L. Rev. 1143, 1146–56, 1211 n. 425 (1985). A related question is whether, when the prosecution chooses not to rely on PTSD testimony to negate consent, a defendant may present expert testimony that PTSD is common after a sexual assault and then argue that the government's failure to show PTSD enhances the probability of consent. *Cf.* State v. Davidson, 351 N.W.2d 8, 12 (Minn. 1984) (discussing negative inferences from lack of fingerprints); Livermore, Absent Evidence, 26 Ariz. L. Rev. 27 (1984).

[156]Summit, The Child Sexual Abuse Accommodation Syndrome, 7 Child Abuse & Neglect 177 (1983) (arguing for the existence of this syndrome "in part from statistically validated assumptions regarding prevalence, age relationships and role characteristics of child sexual abuse and in part from correlations and observations that have emerged as self-evident"). Commentary on the evidentiary use or scientific foundations of this "syndrome" includes Giannelli & Imwinkelried, Scientific Evidence § 9.05 (4th ed. 2007); Myers, Evidence in Child, Domestic and Elder Abuse Cases §§ 6.20[B]; 6.22 (2005); Askowitz & Graham, The Reliability of Expert Psychological Testimony in Child Sexual Abuse Prosecutions, 15 Cardozo L. Rev. 2027 (1994); Hall, The Role of Psychologists as Experts in Cases Involving Allegations of Child Sexual Abuse, 23 Fam. L.Q. 451, 463–64 (1989) ("With the increasing quantity and sophistication of our research, it is becoming more clear that 'syndromes' and 'profiles' . . . do

not exist"); McCord, Expert Psychological Testimony about Child Complainants in Sexual Abuse Prosecutions, 77 J. Crim. L. & Criminology 1 (1986); Myers, Expert Testimony in Child Sexual Abuse Litigation: Consensus and Confusion, 4 U.C. Davis J. Juv. L. & Pol'y 1 (2010); Roe, Expert Testimony in Child Sexual Abuse Cases, 40 U. Miami L. Rev. 97 (1985); Younts, Evaluating and Admitting Expert Opinion Testimony in Child Sexual Abuse Prosecutions, 11 Duke L.J. 691 (1991); Note, Expert Testimony on Child Sexual Abuse Accommodation Syndrome: How Proper Screening Should Severely Limit its Admission, 26 Quinnipiac L. Rev. 497 (2008).

[157]U.S. v. Hadley, 918 F.2d 848, 852–53 (9th Cir. 1990) (admissible); Steward v. State, 652 N.E.2d 490, 494 (Ind. 1995) (listing many cases that have held CSAAS testimony inadmissible to prove that abuse occurred and following that pattern); People v. Peterson, 450 Mich. 349, 537 N.W.2d 857, 866 (1995) ("Most courts will not allow expert testimony in this area if offered to prove that the abuse occurred."); State v. Myers, 359 N.W.2d 604 (Minn. 1984) (upholding admission with 7-year-old victim); Bishop v. State, 982 So. 2d 371, 381 (Miss. 2008) (upholding the admission of an affirmative answer to the question, "Based on experience dealing with all these hundreds of children that have you [sic] interviewed through the years, based on your experience in this particular case with [C.C.], would you say that [C.C.'s] statements and her actions during these sessions are consistent with those of other children [who] have suffered this type of sexual abuse?").

[158]State v. J.Q., 130 N.J. 554, 617 A.2d 1196, 1211 (1993) (admissible to explain delay and willingness to visit the abuser); People v. Spicola, 16

tion of the accusation,[159] or other behavior apparently inconsistent with abuse.[160] They also have relied on expert testimony that children who report sexual abuse generally are truthful.[161]

- In child abuse and homicide cases, prosecutors have called witnesses to establish that defendants exhibited the "battering parent syndrome" or "child battering profile" to describe "the type of person who would abuse a child."[162] In the same vein, defendants have pointed to the presence of factors in

---

N.Y.3d 441, 922 N.Y.S.2d 846, 947 N.E.2d 620 (2011), cert. denied, 132 S. Ct. 400, 181 L. Ed. 2d 257 (2011) (six-year delay in reporting); State v. Petrich, 101 Wash. 2d 566, 683 P.2d 173, 179–80 (1984) (admissible to explain delay in reporting incest).

[159]Steward v. State, 652 N.E.2d 490, 496–99 (Ind. 1995) (listing cases and holding CSAAS testimony admissible for this purpose); Newkirk v. Com., 937 S.W.2d 690 (Ky. 1996) (inadmissible).

[160]Goodrich v. Morgan, 40 Tenn. App. 342, 291 S.W.2d 610 (1956) (error to admit expert testimony that abused children seem happy and add details to their accusations over time); People v. Beckley, 434 Mich. 691, 456 N.W.2d 391, 399 (1990).

[161]State v. Snapp, 110 Idaho 269, 715 P.2d 939, 941 (1986) (not error to strike a clinical psychologist's testimony that "a lot of times children become very honest when they come into a courtroom"); State v. Myers, 382 N.W.2d 91 (Iowa 1986) (testimony that studies show that 74/75 and 2499/2500 children are truthful erroneously admitted); State v. W.B., 205 N.J. 588, 17 A.3d 187, 202 (2011) (testimony that "the great majority of children, throughout the age groups, do not lie about child sexual abuse"); People v. Spicola, 16 N.Y.3d 441, 922 N.Y.S.2d 846, 947 N.E.2d 620 (2011), cert. denied, 132 S. Ct. 400, 181 L. Ed. 2d 257 (2011) (testimony about the rarity of cases of false accusations was permissible); State v. Logue, 372 N.W.2d 151, 154 (S.D. 1985) (error to admit

social worker's testimony that one-third of the 47 children whom she interviewed in cases of sexual abuse made unsubstantiated accusations and that victim in case at bar gained his sexual knowledge with defendant); State v. Kinney, 171 Vt. 239, 762 A.2d 833 (2000) (error to admit expert testimony that for child victims of sexual abuse, "False reporting, the percentages are very low. About two percent.").

[162]Nelson, The Misuse of Abuse: Restricting Evidence of Battered Child Syndrome, 75 Law & Contemp. Probs. 187, 198 (2012). The courts usually reject such testimony. People v. Walkey, 177 Cal. App. 3d 268, 223 Cal. Rptr. 132 (4th Dist. 1986) (inadmissible); Sanders v. State, 251 Ga. 70, 303 S.E.2d 13, 18 (1983) (inadmissible); State v. Loebach, 310 N.W.2d 58 (Minn. 1981) (inadmissible); State v. Pulizzano, 155 Wis. 2d 633, 456 N.W.2d 325, 335 (1990) (inadmissible); cf. U.S. v. Gillespie, 852 F.2d 475 (9th Cir. 1988) (characteristics of child molesters inadmissible); State v. Hickman, 337 N.W.2d 512 (Iowa 1983) ("psychiatrist who had made a study of the psychology of rapists and had examined defendant and his medical history" allowed to describe "various kinds of rapists and [characterize] defendant as of the class of aggressive, antisocial or sociopathic, hatred rapists" to rebut defendant's claim that sexual intercourse was consensual). See also 1 Giannelli & Inwinkelried § 9.07(a) (4th ed. 2007).

the profile in other individuals who might have abused the child.[163]

- So too, defendants accused of sexual offenses have offered testimony to the effect that they did not fit the profiles for sexual offenders.[164]

When the plaintiff or the government offers evidence that the defendant fits an incriminating profile, it may be excluded under the rule that prohibits evidence of character to show conduct on a particular occasion.[165] The same reasoning applies when a defendant, seeking to create doubt about his own conduct, produces evidence that another person fits the profile.[166] Yet, arguably the rule should not bar admission in all such cases.[167] After all, the rule rests on the premise that the marginal probative value of character evidence generally is low while the potential for distraction, time-consumption and prejudice is high. Where the profile is not itself likely to arouse sympathy or hostility, the argument for applying the rule against character evidence to prove conduct on a particular occasion is weakened.[168] Conversely, if it were shown that the profile was both valid and revealing—that it distin-

---

[163]People v. Gonzales, 54 Cal. 4th 1234, 144 Cal. Rptr. 3d 757, 281 P.3d 834, 856–57 (2012), cert. denied, 2013 WL 57426 (U.S. 2013); State v. Conlogue, 474 A.2d 167, 172 (Me. 1984).

[164]U.S. v. St. Pierre, 812 F.2d 417, 420 (8th Cir. 1987) (sex offender profile not generally accepted in scientific community); State v. Hulbert, 481 N.W.2d 329, 332 (Iowa 1992); State v. Cavaliere, 140 N.H. 108, 663 A.2d 96 (1995) (properly excluded because there is "no test or group of tests which can determine if a person is a sexual offender"); State v. Cavallo, 88 N.J. 508, 443 A.2d 1020 (1982) (testimony that defendant lacks the characteristics exhibited by rapists as encountered by psychiatrist in his practice properly excluded); cf. People v. Stoll, 49 Cal. 3d 1136, 265 Cal. Rptr. 111, 783 P.2d 698 (1989) (holding admissible a psychologist's opinion based on interviews and tests that defendants charged with child sexual abuse were not deviant or abnormal).

[165]On the general rule, see supra § 190.

[166]People v. Gonzales, 281 P.3d at 856–57 (Cal. 2012) (a family history of

child abuse is inadmissible character evidence to show that someone else is an abuser). *Contra* State v. Conlogue, 474 A.2d at 172 (Me. 1984) (trial court erred in excluding, as inadmissible character evidence, testimony offered to show that it was not the defendant, but rather the mother, who had a "history of child abuse [that] would predispose her to abuse her own child," who was responsible).

[167]*See* U.S. v. Sanet, 666 F.2d 1370 (11th Cir. 1982). See supra § 189 (profiles of physicians' billings and services).

[168]Many cases exclude incriminating profile evidence without analyzing it as character evidence. *E.g.*, Hall v. State, 15 Ark. App. 309, 692 S.W.2d 769, 773 (1985) (testimony "that in 75% to 80% of such cases the perpetrator is known to the children involved," that "children are almost always told not to tell what happened," that "50% of child sexual abuse cases occur in either the home of the child or the perpetrator," and that "the first offense is virtually always committed before the age of 40" was "not of proper benefit to the jury"); Duley v. State, 56 Md. App. 275, 467 A.2d 776, 779 (1983) (error to allow testimony that "[t]he persons

guishes between offenders and nonoffenders with great accuracy—then the balance might favor admissibility. It is far from clear, however, that any existing profile is this powerful.[169]

When the profile evidence is used defensively (to show good character, to restore credibility, or to prove apprehension in connection with a claim of self-defense), it falls outside of or under an exception to the rule against character evidence.[170] Admissibility then should turn on the extent to which the expert testimony would assist the jury viewed in the light of the usual counterweights.[171] The qualifications of the expert,[172] the degree of acceptance in the appropriate scientific community,[173] the reli-

---

who are involved in the Battered Child Syndrome often are young, somewhat immature, . . . in a stressful situation, and . . . [t]hey sometimes have been victims of quite harsh punishment themselves as they were growing up"); State v. Petrich, 101 Wash. 2d 566, 683 P.2d 173 (1984) (should exclude on retrial of defendant, accused of statutory rape of 13-year-old granddaughter, testimony by sexual assault center representative that in "85 to 90 percent of our cases, the child is molested by somebody they already know").

[169]For some skeptical assessments of various profiles, see People v. Bledsoe, 36 Cal. 3d 236, 203 Cal. Rptr. 450, 681 P.2d 291 (1984) (rape trauma syndrome); Flanagan v. State, 625 So. 2d 827 (Fla. 1993) ("sexual offender profile evidence is not generally accepted in the scientific community"); Steward v. State, 652 N.E.2d 490, 493 (Ind. 1995) (CSAAS "poses serious accuracy problems" and "does not detect sexual abuse"); People v. Beckley, 434 Mich. 691, 456 N.W.2d 391, 405 (1990) ("child sexual abuse syndrome evidence is essentially a therapeutic tool," and "experts who have tried to establish some universal symptomology of sexual abuse victims sometimes seem to belie their own theory"); Goodson v. State, 566 So. 2d 1142, 1146 (Miss. 1990) ("it is doubtful that there is any such thing as a scientifically established child sexual abuse profile"); Expert Witnesses in Child Abuse Cases: What Can And Should Be Said

in Court? (Ceci & Hembrooke eds., 1998); Schuller & Rzepa, Scientific Status, in 2 Faigman, et al., Modern Scientific Evidence: The Law and Science of Expert Testimony §§ 13:1 et seq. (2011–2012 ed.).

[170]See supra §§ 191 & 194.

[171]See supra § 203.

[172]Duley v. State, 56 Md. App. 275, 467 A.2d 776, 780 (1983) ("there is not one word of testimony showing how, when, or where the doctor, a pathologist, acquired his expertise on the profile of the battered child's parent"); People v. Beckley, 456 N.W.2d at 398–99 (although "[n]ot all psychiatrists, psychologists, and social workers will qualify to give expert testimony on the subject" of child sexual abuse, the psychologist, social worker, and counselor in this case were qualified).

[173]In jurisdictions that adhere to the *Frye* standard (see supra § 203), proof of general acceptance among scientists should be required. *E.g.*, State v. Cavallo, 88 N.J. 508, 443 A.2d 1020 (1982); *cf.* Doe v. Archdiocese of St. Paul, 817 N.W.2d 150 (Minn. 2012) (recovery of repressed memories). *But see* People v. Beckley, 434 Mich. 691, 456 N.W.2d 391 (1990) (refusing to apply *Frye* unless to expert testimony about sexually abuse children unless offered to diagnose the abuse). For more detail discussion of the applicability of *Frye* and *Daubert* to psychological and psychiatric testimony, see Kaye et al., The New Wigmore, A

ability and validity of using the profile for a particular purpose,[174] and the need for the evidence[175] in light of what most jurors know about the behaviors in question[176] thus affect the admissibility and of course the weight of the profile evidence.[177] For example, it is not clear how the "battered woman syndrome" helps show the reasonableness of the use of deadly force within the traditional doctrine of self-defense.[178] The effect of the syndrome evidence in

---

Treatise on Evidence: Expert Evidence § 8.8.3 (2d ed. 2011).

[174]*E.g.*, State v. Black, 537 A.2d 1154, 1157 (Me. 1988) (no validation of indicators of sexual abuse relied on by expert); People v. Taylor, 75 N.Y.2d 277, 552 N.Y.S.2d 883, 552 N.E.2d 131, 139 (1990) (Given "the therapeutic nature of the [rape trauma] syndrome, . . . its usefulness as a fact-finding device is limited and . . . where it is introduced to prove the crime took place, its helpfulness is outweighed by the possibility of undue prejudice."); State v. Rimmasch, 775 P.2d 388, 401–03 (Utah 1989) ("scientific literature raises serious doubts" about profile of sexually abused child); *cf.* Dorsey v. State, 276 Md. 638, 350 A.2d 665 (1976) (improper to admit police detective's testimony that 80% of people arrested for armed robbery deny involvement). Under *Daubert*, a particularly high threshold of validity might be required. *See* Faigman & Wright, The Battered Woman Syndrome in the Age of Science, 39 Ariz. L. Rev. 67 (1997).

[175]Articulating the inference for which the profile is offered can be crucial. Some courts that exclude rape trauma syndrome evidence to establish lack of consent, or child abuse accommodation syndrome to demonstrate the abuse, for example, may be receptive to the same evidence used to counter a defendant's suggestion that the victim's post-incident conduct is inconsistent with the claim of rape or abuse. *E.g.*, People v. Beckley, 434 Mich. 691, 456 N.W.2d 391 (1990) (child abuse); People v. Bledsoe, 36 Cal. 3d 236, 203 Cal. Rptr. 450, 681 P.2d 291, 298 (1984) (rape trauma syndrome).

[176]*Compare* State v. Thomas, 66 Ohio St. 2d 518, 20 Ohio Op. 3d 424, 423 N.E.2d 137, 140 n.51 (1981) (expert explanation of why battered women stay with men who injure them is superfluous), *with* State v. Kelly, 97 N.J. 178, 478 A.2d 364, 372 (1984) ("a battering relationship embodies psychological and societal features that are not well understood by lay observers"). A few courts rely on this factor to allow profile evidence in cases with children victims but not in similar cases with adult victims. *Compare* State v. Hall, 406 N.W.2d 503 (Minn. 1987) (14-year-old), *and* State v. Myers, 359 N.W.2d 604 (Minn. 1984) (7-year-old), *with* State v. McGee, 324 N.W.2d 232 (Minn. 1982), *and* State v. Saldana, 324 N.W.2d 227 (Minn. 1982).

[177]It has been said that such evidence is prejudicial because it "would tend to stereotype defendant." State v. Thomas, 66 Ohio St. 2d 518, 20 Ohio Op. 3d 424, 423 N.E.2d 137, 140 (1981). The claim that it is inherently prejudicial or wrong to use statistically validated characteristics of a class to infer something about a member of that class cannot withstand analysis. See infra § 208. Likewise, the objection that profile evidence invades the province of the jury, *e.g.*, Smith v. State, 247 Ga. 612, 277 S.E.2d 678, 680 (1981) (rejecting this argument), is too conclusory to be useful.

[178]*See generally* Faigman, Review Essay: Discerning Justice When Battered Women Kill, 39 Hastings L.J. 207, 215 (1987); Schopp et al., Battered Woman Syndrome: Expert Testimony and the Distinction Between Justification and Excuse, 1994 Ill. L. Rev. 45; Schulhofer, The Feminist Challenge in Criminal Law, 143 U. Pa. L. Rev. 2151

such situations is to redefine the substantive law.[179] This result suggests the need for a stronger scientific base than now exists for the expert testimony.[180]

The form or specificity of the testimony—whether the expert crosses the line between the general and the specific[181] or tries to evaluate the truthfulness of the witness[182] or a class of witnesses[183]—also is important. Even courts that allow generalized or "social framework" testimony to explain what otherwise ap-

---

(1995). The same concern arises with evidence that a defendant was an abused child. Nelson, The Misuse of Abuse: Restricting Evidence of Battered Child Syndrome, 75 Law & Contemp. Probs. 187, 201 (2012).

[179]Some commentators favor this anomaly on frankly "political" grounds. E.g., Mosteller, Syndromes and Politics in Criminal Trials and Evidence Law, 46 Duke L.J. 461 (1996).

[180]Faigman & Wright, The Battered Woman Syndrome in the Age of Science, 39 Ariz. L. Rev. 67 (1997); Morse, The Misbegotten Marriage of Soft Psychology and Bad Law, 14 Law & Hum. Behav. 595, 595–96 (1990) ("The psychological justification for the defense employs unacceptably soft science, and its legal support is confused and regressive.").

[181]U.S. v. Binder, 769 F.2d 595, 602 (9th Cir. 1985) ("testimony . . . was not limited to references to psychological literature or experience or to discussion of a class of victims generally"); People v. Beckley, 434 Mich. 691, 456 N.W.2d 391, 406–07 (1990) (eschewing "a direct opinion on the ultimate question of whether [child] abuse occurred"); State v. Hennum, 441 N.W.2d 793, 799 (Minn. 1989) ("testimony on battered woman syndrome will be limited to a description of the general syndrome and the characteristics which are present in an individual suffering from the syndrome"); State v. Haines, 112 Ohio St. 3d 393, 2006-Ohio-6711, 860 N.E.2d 91, 102 (2006) ("experts who are called to testify in domestic violence prosecutions must limit their testimony to the general characteristics of a victim suffering from the battered woman syn-

drome. The expert may also answer hypothetical questions regarding specific abnormal behaviors exhibited by women suffering from the syndrome, but should never offer an opinion relative to the alleged victim in the case."); Goodson v. State, 566 So. 2d 1142, 1146 (Miss. 1990). Other jurisdictions permit less circumspect testimony. E.g., State v. Edward Charles L., 183 W. Va. 641, 398 S.E.2d 123, 140–41 (1990) (sexual assault of a child).

[182]People v. Beckley, 434 Mich. 691, 456 N.W.2d 391, 407 (1990) ("any testimony about the truthfulness of this victim's allegations against the defendant would be improper"); Com. v. Gallagher, 519 Pa. 291, 547 A.2d 355, 357–58 (1988) (rape trauma); State v. Rimmasch, 775 P.2d 388 (Utah 1989) (applying Rule 608(a)(1) to child sexual abuse testimony).

[183]State v. Lindsey, 149 Ariz. 472, 720 P.2d 73, 76 (1986) (error to allow testimony that "[t]he one statistic that I have found [was] that it was possibly one percent that lied"); Powell v. State, 527 A.2d 276 (Del. 1987) (error to admit expert testimony that more than 90 percent of children reporting sexual abuse tell the truth); State v. Brodniak, 221 Mont. 212, 718 P.2d 322, 327–28 (1986) (error to allow testimony that "roughly two percent of the number of accusations [of sexual assault] are found to be unfounded" and that "[r]oughly two to three percent" of sexual assault complainants distort information); State v. W.B., 205 N.J. 588, 17 A.3d 187, 202 (2011) ("an assertion that only 5–10% of children exhibiting CSAAS symptoms lie about sexual abuse . . . cannot be tolerated.").

pear to be abnormal or unusual behavior, often vehemently reject expert opinions on the applicability of the profile or the credibility of a witness in a given case.[184]

In some ways, profile evidence resembles expert testimony, considered earlier in this section, describing the results of psychological research into eyewitness identifications. Defendants who have retracted their confessions also have offered expert testimony on the variables associated with false confessions.[185] In these instances, the expert provides background information that

---

[184]State v. Chapple, 135 Ariz. 281, 660 P.2d 1208, 1224 (1983) ("Nor do we invite opinion testimony in even the most extraordinary case on the likelihood that a particular witness is correct or mistaken in identification or that eyewitness identification in general has a certain percentage of accuracy or inaccuracy"); State v. Favoccia, 306 Conn. 770, 51 A.3d 1002 (2012) (even in "a delicate middle ground between the generalized behavioral testimony held admissible . . . and the more pointed diagnoses held inadmissible," "our concerns about indirect vouching . . . require us to limit expert testimony about the behavioral characteristics of child sexual assault victims . . . to that which is stated in general or hypothetical terms, and to preclude opinion testimony about whether the specific complainant has exhibited such behaviors."); State v. W.B., 205 N.J. 588, 17 A.3d 187, 200 (2011) ("Simply stated, CSAAS cannot be used as probative testimony of the existence of sexual abuse in a particular case."; "Any CSAAS expert testimony beyond its permissible, limited scope cannot be tolerated."); State v. Milbradt, 305 Or. 621, 756 P.2d 620, 624 (1988) ("we really mean it—no psychotherapist may render an opinion on whether a witness is credible in any trial conducted in this state").

[185]U.S. v. Benally, 541 F.3d 990, 996 (10th Cir. 2008) (upholding exclusion of expert testimony); Miller v. State, 770 N.E.2d 763, 770–74 (Ind. 2002) (testimony erroneously excluded); State v. Lamonica, 44 So. 3d 895 (La. Ct. App. 1st Cir. 2010) (excluding psychologist's testimony as un-

necessary given juror's ordinary knowledge and under *Daubert*); People v. Kowalski, 492 Mich. 106, 821 N.W.2d 14 (2012) ("because the claim of a false confession is beyond the common knowledge of the ordinary person, expert testimony about this phenomenon is [potentially] admissible" but "[a]n expert explaining the situational or psychological factors that might lead to a false confession may not comment on the truthfulness of a defendant's confession, vouch for the veracity of a defendant recanting a confession, or give an opinion as to whether defendant was telling the truth when he made the statements to the police.") (footnotes and internal quotation marks omitted); Com. v. Robinson, 449 Mass. 1, 864 N.E.2d 1186, 1190 (2007) (excluded as lacking general acceptance and scientific validity); State v. Free, 351 N.J. Super. 203, 798 A.2d 83 (App. Div. 2002) (inadmissible without proof of general acceptance); State v. Gilman, 226 W. Va. 453, 702 S.E.2d 276, 281 (2010) (psychiatrist testified "that there are twenty-five variables and factors associated with persons prone to making false confessions" and that "the Appellant had fourteen at the time of his confession."); *cf.* People v. Kogut, 10 Misc. 3d 305, 806 N.Y.S.2d 366 (Sup 2005) (testimony about psychological studies on the voluntariness of confessions admitted). *See also* Giannelli & Imwinkelried, 1 Scientific Evidence § 9.09 (4th ed. 2007); Leo et al., Psychological and Cultural Aspects of Interrogations and False Confessions: Using Research to Inform Legal Decision-Making, *in* 2 Psychological Expertise in Court 25 (Lieberman &

might contradict lay impressions and that the jury can apply to the case at hand, if persuaded to do so. This type of testimony has been denominated "social framework" evidence,[186] and neither the research into the variables affecting eyewitnesses and false confessions normally is normally presented as amounting to a profile or a syndrome.[187] Perhaps the greater initial receptivity of the appellate courts to psychological profile evidence stems from the fact that this type of testimony seems more like the clinical assessments routinely received from psychologists and physicians.[188] In addition, considering the subject matter of most of the psychological profiles that have come to the attention of the courts, it is likely that a growing sensitivity to women's and children's issues has played a major role.[189]

## § 207 Criminalistics: Identifying persons and things

Many of the techniques of scientific criminal investigation, or

---

Krauss 2009).

[186]See generally Monahan & Walker, Twenty-Five Years of Social Science in Law, 35 Law & Hum. Behav. 72 (2011).

[187]E.g., Kolb v. State, 930 P.2d 1238, 1241–42 (Wyo. 1996) ("The psychologist further testified [that] 'False Confession Syndrome' is not a diagnostic term in psychology").

[188]State v. Middleton, 58 Or. App. 447, 648 P.2d 1296, 1300 (1982) (since "admitted experts" were "explaining superficially bizarre behavior by identifying its emotional antecedents," their testimony "was as admissible as would be a doctor's testimony in a personal injury case that a party's physical behavior was consistent with a claimed soft tissue injury, although such an injury was not objectively verifiable"); cf. State v. Southard, 347 Or. 127, 218 P.3d 104 (2009) (child sexual abuse "diagnosis" is valid because it is based on valid techniques such as medical interviews, but the particular diagnosis was inadmissible under Rule 403). Yet, one could make expert testimony on eyewitness identification sound like profile evidence. One could simply say that the "profile" or "syndrome" of an accurate (or inaccurate) eyewitness identification consists of the various factors studied in

the experiments and that the identification in question "matches" this profile or is a "classic case" of this syndrome.

[189]Hoeffel, The Gender Gap: Revealing Inequities in Admission of Social Science Evidence In Criminal Cases, 24 U. Ark. Little Rock L. Rev. 41 (2001); Mosteller, Syndromes and Politics in Criminal Trials and Evidence Law, 46 Duke L.J. 461 (1996); 1 Giannelli & Imwinkelried, Scientific Evidence § 9.03, at 511 ("The widespread legal acceptance of BWS is a product of the work of feminist scholars, who have attacked the traditional law of self-defense as based upon a male-oriented perspective."). The clearest example of politics in syndrome evidence is the enactment of California rule 1107(a) ensuring the admissibility of "expert testimony [on] battered women's syndrome" for limited purposes. See People v. Brown, 33 Cal. 4th 892, 16 Cal. Rptr. 3d 447, 94 P.3d 574, 580 (2004) ("trial courts often continued to exclude such expert evidence . . . . Consequently, the Legislature in 1991 enacted [Cal. Evid. Code] section 1107 to ensure the admissibility of expert evidence on domestic violence for both the prosecution and the defense.").

criminalistics,[1] are aimed at identifying people or things.[2] Fingerprinting, studying the trajectories and characteristics of bullets and firearms, examining questioned documents,[3] detecting and identifying poisons and other drugs, microscopically comparing hairs and fibers, and matching blood stains[4] are among the better known examples. In addition, there is a vast array of less familiar techniques for detecting and analyzing "trace evidence" of criminal or other activity. These include other applications of microanalysis, forensic odontology,[5] anthropology, entomology, and somewhat esoteric chemical and physical tests used in connection with fingerprints, firearms, glass fragments, hair, paints, explosions and fires, questioned documents, and recordings.

While these methods are unquestionably of great value in many investigations, their use in the courtroom can pose problems. To emphasize the scientific quality of the analysis, or in an effort to be as precise as possible, or in response to demands from the court or counsel, expert witnesses may state the results or implications of their tests in quantitative, probabilistic terms—a practice that causes difficulty for the courts.[6] Furthermore, some analytic procedures or tests are themselves specially adapted or developed for forensic purposes and well known primarily in law enforcement circles. Consequently, the test of general scientific acceptance does not always work well in this context,[7] and this incongruity can result in important opinions on the standards

---

**[Section 207]**

[1]"Criminalistics" refers to "the examination, evaluation, and interpretation of physical evidence." Dillon, Foreword, O'Hara & Osterburg, An Introduction to Criminalistics: The Application of the Physical Sciences to the Detection of Crime (1972). Despite the "criminal" root in the term, the topics surveyed in this section have obvious applications to many civil cases as well. Treatises that survey the scientific and legal developments in this field include 4 Faigman, et al., Modern Scientific Evidence: The Law and Science of Expert Testimony (2011–2012 ed.) (with chapters by forensic scientists); Giannelli & Imwinkelried, Scientific Evidence (4th ed. 2007).

[2]*See generally* Kaye et al., The New Wigmore, A Treatise on Evidence: Expert Evidence (2d ed. 2011); Robertson & Vignaux, Interpreting

Evidence: Evaluating Forensic Science in the Courtroom (1995).

[3]Section 205 of the second edition of this treatise was devoted to this topic. Authentication of documents by proof of handwriting is treated infra § 223.

[4]See supra § 205(B).

[5]Admissibility and Sufficiency of Bite Mark Evidence as Basis for Identification of Accused, 1 A.L.R.6th 657.

[6]This complication is taken up infra § 211.

[7]*See* Kaye et al., The New Wigmore, A Treatise on Evidence: Expert Evidence (2d ed. 2011); Saks, Merlin & Solomon: Lessons from the Law's Formative Encounters with Forensic Identification Science, 49 Hastings L.J. 1069 (1998) (reviewing the history of judicial acceptance of various forms of forensic identification

governing the admissibility of scientific evidence.[8] Although the newest, technologically sophisticated tests or procedures tend to be validated for forensic use and to receive outside scrutiny, historically much of forensic science has been a practical craft, lacking an academic tradition that prized rigorous validation of methods and assumptions.[9] Two examples—identification of latent fingerprints and spectrographic analysis of human voices—will serve to illustrate these observations.

### (A) Fingerprinting

Fingerprints may have been used as a means of identification in ancient China, but their use in criminal investigations in the Western world began in the late 19th Century.[10] In the United States, fingerprints were introduced in evidence for the first time in *People v. Jennings*,[11] a 1910 murder trial in Illinois.[12] Four witnesses testified for the prosecution that they had examined thousands of fingerprints in their careers and that the fingerprints in question came from the defendant. The Illinois Supreme Court upheld the resulting conviction, concluding "that there is a scientific basis for the system of finger print identification . . . [and] that this method of identification is in such general and common use that the courts cannot refuse to take judicial cognizance of it."[13] Yet, the ability of examiners to match latent prints—those naturally deposited on paper, metal, glass, or other surface—to rolled, inked prints had never been carefully studied.

For nearly a century, neither these studies nor much other fundamental research into the premises and claims of fingerprint examiners was undertaken.[14] This state of affairs created a quandary: if *Frye* requires general acceptance among scientists

---

evidence and urging a fresh look, especially at techniques that are generally accepted among criminalists but lack careful, empirical validation).

[8]*See generally* Kaye et al., The New Wigmore, A Treatise on Evidence: Expert Evidence (2d ed. 2011); Faigman, et al., Modern Scientific Evidence: The Law and Science of Expert Testimony (2011–2012 ed.); Giannelli & Imwinkelried, Scientific Evidence (4th ed. 2007). See supra § 203.

[9]Comm. on Identifying the Needs of the Forensic Sci. Cmty., Nat'l Research Council, Strengthening Forensic Science in the United States: A Path Forward (2009); Mnookin et al., The Need for a Research Culture

in the Forensic Sciences, 58 UCLA L. Rev. 725 (2011).

[10]*See* Beavan, Fingerprints: The Origins of Crime Detection and the Murder Case that Launched Forensic Science (2001); Cole, Suspect Identities: A History of Fingerprinting and Criminal Identification (2001).

[11]People v. Jennings, 252 Ill. 534, 96 N.E. 1077 (1911).

[12]For a description of this case and the legal history of fingerprinting, see Mnookin, Fingerprint Evidence in an Age of DNA Profiling, 67 Brook. L. Rev. 13 (2001).

[13]People v. Jennings, 96 N.E.2d at 1082.

[14]*See* Comm. on Identifying the

(as opposed to fingerprint analysts) that the origin of a latent print can be attributed to a single individual with 100% confidence (as fingerprint examiners traditionally reported),[15] or if *Daubert* demands scientific demonstrations of the validity of the assumptions of those working in the field or scientifically plausible estimates of error rates in actual identifications, how can such testimony of infallible individualization continue to be admissible?

No opinion provided a satisfactory answer.[16] Instead, courts have been content with long usage in law enforcement and in the courtroom in lieu of acceptance and extensive research in the scientific community.[17] They have accepted litigation-driven, unpublished studies that probably could not withstand scientific peer review as scientific fact.[18] They have confused a second examiner's approval of a co-worker's conclusion with scientific peer review.[19] They have maintained that the lack of many publicized cases of false identifications means that the false-positive error rate is es-

---

Needs of the Forensic Sci. Cmty., Nat'l Research Council, Strengthening Forensic Science in the United States: A Path Forward (2009); Mnookin, Fingerprint Evidence in an Age of DNA Profiling, 67 Brook. L. Rev. 13, 19 (2001).

[15]NIST Expert Working Group on Human Factors in Latent Print Analysis, Latent Print Examination and Human Factors: Improving the Practice Through a Systems Approach (Kaye ed. 2012).

[16]For a detailed review of the case law, see 4 Faigman, et al., Modern Scientific Evidence: The Law and Science of Expert Testimony §§ 33:1 et seq. (2011–2012 ed.).

[17]U.S. v. Baines, 573 F.3d 979, 990–91 (10th Cir. 2009) (relying on testimony of an FBI agent of "an error rate of one per every 11 million," but recognizing that it surely is higher); U.S. v. Crisp, 324 F.3d 261, 268–69 (4th Cir. 2003); U.S. v. Sullivan, 246 F. Supp. 2d 700, 703 (E.D. Ky. 2003) (relying on testimony that "the standard methodology used by fingerprint examiners . . . has been in use for some time" to find "that [it] is gener-

ally accepted in the fingerprint analysis and forensic science fields").

[18]Kaye, Questioning a Courtroom Proof of the Uniqueness of Fingerprints, 71 Int'l Stat. Rev. 521 (2003) (criticizing the FBI-commissioned "50K study" introduced in U.S. v. Mitchell, 365 F.3d 215 (3d Cir. 2004)); Champod & Evett, A Probabilistic Approach to Fingerprint Evidence, 51 J. Forensic Identification 101, 101–22 (2001) (expressing incredulity with regard to the study). Yet, the government continued to rely on the largely meaningless study. Baines, 573 F.2d at 987.

[19]U.S. v. Havvard, 117 F. Supp. 2d 848 (S.D. Ind. 2000); *cf.* Baines, 573 F.2d at 990 (accepting the premise that an operational quality check is one form of the peer review spoken of in *Daubert* but noting that because the second examiner had the notes of the first analyst, the review in the case was not "the independent peer review of true science"); Mitchell, 365 F.3d at 238–39 (3d Cir. 2004) (accepting this faulty premise). *Contra* Sullivan, 246 F.Supp.2d at 703; U.S. v. Llera Plaza, 188 F. Supp. 2d 549 (E.D. Pa. 2002).

sentially zero.[20] And, when all else fails, they have observed that "the *Daubert* standard offers a list of flexible factors to be used as appropriate for various types of expert testimony"[21] as if flexibility itself is a ground for admitting the evidence.

The courts go to these extremes because, even without extensive scientific study, it seems obvious that fingerprint comparisons are probative and valuable. The difficulty lies in saying how probative they are and in pretending that a probability is a certainty.[22] Experiments testing the validity and reliability of fingerprint analysts show that trained analysts using their personal judgments and thresholds can achieve low false positive rates (a fraction of a percent) and moderate false negative rates (around 10% or less) in matching latent prints to exemplars.[23] Experiments also reveal that expectation bias can affect the outcomes in some cases.[24] But with blind verification and procedures to reduce the chance of cognitive bias, fingerprint matches can be very strong evidence of identity.[25]

At the same time, the traditional description of a match as *necessarily* excluding everyone else in the world as a possible source of the latent print plainly exceeds the bounds of what is scientifically demonstrable, even though only two or three opinions have disapproved of the practice.[26] Fortunately, there is no shortage of alternative ways to explain the meaning of a match. These

---

[20]U.S. v. Havvard, 117 F. Supp. 2d 848 (S.D. Ind. 2000).

[21]U.S. v. Havvard, 260 F.3d 597, 600 (7th Cir. 2001). *See also* Baines, 573 at 992 (also emphasizing that "our review here is deferential, limited to the question of whether the district judge abused her considerable discretion").

[22]*See* Kaye, Beyond Uniqueness: The Birthday Paradox, Source Attribution and Individualization in Forensic Science Testimony, to be published in 11 Law, Probability & Risk (2012), available at http://lpr.oxfordjournals.o rg/content/early/2012/11/05/lpr.mgs 031.full.pdf+html.

[23]Tangen et al., Identifying Fingerprint Expertise, 22 Psych. Sci. 995 (2011) (false positive rate of 3/444 = 0.68% and false negative rate of 35/444 = 7.88%); Ulery et al., Accuracy and Reliability of Forensic Latent Fingerprint Decisions, 108 Proc. Nat'l Acad. Sci. USA 7733 (2011) (false positive rate of 6/3628 = 0.02% and false

negative rate of 450/4113 = 10.9%). Using a second, independent examiner in a verification step, as some laboratories do, would reduce these error rates considerably.

[24]NIST. Expert Working Group on Human Factors in Latent Print Analysis, Latent Print Examination and Human Factors: Improving the Practice Through a Systems Approach (Kaye ed. 2012).

[25]For suggested procedures, see NIST Expert Working Group on Human Factors in Latent Print Analysis, Latent Print Examination and Human Factors: Improving the Practice Through a Systems Approach (Kaye ed. 2012); Reese, Note, Techniques for Mitigating Cognitive Biases in Fingerprint Identification, 59 UCLA L. Rev. 1252 (2012).

[26]U.S. v. Llera Plaza, 179 F. Supp. 2d 492 (E.D. Pa. 2002), withdrawn from bound volume and opinion vacated and superseded on reconsideration, 188 F. Supp. 2d 549

include statements (when justified) that the matching features are very unusual in the general population, that it would be improbable to find another source that matches so well in a geographic area, and that the match is much more probable when the latent print and the exemplar come from the same individual than when they originate from different people.[27] In addition, automated systems for estimating the probabilities of matches for prints of varying quality and completeness under competing hypotheses about the true source are coming close to fruition.[28]

### (B) Voice Spectrograms

Identification of speakers by means of spectrographic analysis of their voices illustrates the premature adoption for courtroom use of a seemingly impressive identification technique. Complex sound waves, such as those involved in speech, can be understood mathematically as sums of simple waveforms of various frequencies. The frequency spectrum of such a sound wave is, in effect, a list of each such constituent frequency and its relative importance in describing the composite sound. Since the 1940s or 1950s, electronic devices that analyze sound waves into these frequency components have been available. A spectrogram is a graphic representation of this information, that is, a picture of the frequency spectrum of a sound wave.[29] In the 1960s, it was proposed that the spectral characteristics of a speaker's voice could identify that speaker. The theory was that individuals have different but largely stable patterns in the way they manipulate their lips, teeth, and so on in speaking. From the outset, this

---

(E.D. Pa. 2002); U.S. v. Zajac, 2010 WL 3546782 (D. Utah 2010); State v. Rose, No. K06-0545 (Md. Cir. Ct. Oct. 19, 2007).

[27] Kaye et al., The New Wigmore, A Treatise on Evidence: Expert Evidence ch. 15 (2d ed. 2011); NIST Expert Working Group on Human Factors in Latent Print Analysis, Latent Print Examination and Human Factors: Improving the Practice Through a Systems Approach (Kaye ed. 2012).

[28] See NIST Expert Working Group on Human Factors in Latent Print Analysis, Latent Print Examination and Human Factors: Improving the Practice Through a Systems Approach (Kaye ed. 2012); Neumann et al., Quantifying the Weight of Evidence from a Forensic Fingerprint Comparison: A New Paradigm, 175 J.

Royal Stat. Soc'y: Series A 371 (2012). These should not be confused with the algorithms that search databases of digitalized exemplar prints to produce a list of more or less similar prints for human inspection. The current AFIS (Automated Fingerprint Identification System) algorithms produce lists without estimates of the likelihoods for each candidate in the list. NIST Expert Working Group on Human Factors in Latent Print Analysis, Latent Print Examination and Human Factors: Improving the Practice Through a Systems Approach (Kaye ed. 2012).

[29] For examples, see Comm. on the Evaluation of Sound Spectrograms, National Research Council, On the Theory and Practice of Voice Identification 4–5 (1979); Kersta, Speaker Recognition and Identification by Voiceprints, 40 Conn. B.J. 586 (1966).

hypothesis has been controversial.[30] If it is false, then comparisons of spectrograms should not produce consistently correct identifications. Despite a few early (and seemingly extravagant) claims of accurate identifications,[31] subsequent studies providing better approximations of realistic forensic conditions reported misidentifications at rates ranging from 18% (12% false negatives and 6% false positives) to 70 and 80% (including 42% false positives).[32] Many scientists therefore doubt the reliability and validity of the current technique.[33]

Most courts applying the general scientific acceptance test to

---

[30]*See* Comm. on the Evaluation of Sound Spectrograms, National Research Council, On the Theory and Practice of Voice Identification 2 (1979) ("the assumption that intraspeaker variability is less than . . . interspeaker variability . . . is not adequately supported by scientific theory and data"); Faigman, et al., Modern Scientific Evidence: The Law and Science of Expert Testimony §§ 38:1 et seq. (2011–2012 ed.); Bolt et al., Speaker Identification by Speech Spectrograms: A Scientist's View of Its Reliability for Legal Purposes, 47 J. Acoustic Soc'y Am. 597 (1970); Thomas, Voiceprint—Myth or Miracle, in Scientific and Expert Testimony 1015, 1026 (Imwinkelried ed., 2d ed. 1981) ("controlled scientific experiments indicate that frequently the vocal equipment and its use by two different speakers produce results more similar than the results produced by the same speaker on two different occasions").

[31]Initial studies were conducted under artificial conditions that bore little resemblance to forensic applications. Thomas, Voiceprint—Myth or Miracle, in Scientific and Expert Testimony 1015, 1035–37 (Imwinkelried ed., 2d ed. 1981). Later studies failed to examine some important variables. Comm. on the Evaluation of Sound Spectrograms, National Research Council, On the Theory and Practice of Voice Identification 58 (1979) ("What is in doubt is the degree of accuracy with which identifications can be made under all sorts of conditions, especially in forensic conditions . . . The presently available experi-

mental evidence about error rates consists of results from a relatively small number of separate, uncoordinated experiments. These results alone cannot provide estimates of error rates that are valid over the range of conditions usually met in practice.").

[32]*See* Thomas, Voiceprint—Myth or Miracle, in Scientific and Expert Testimony 1015, 1020, 1042–43 (Imwinkelried ed., 2d ed. 1981) (reviewing studies). *See also* Bolt et al., Speaker Identification by Speech Spectrograms: Some Further Observations, 54 J. Acoustic Soc'y Am. 531, 534 (1973) ("laboratory evaluations of these methods show increasing errors as the conditions for evaluation move toward real-life situations"). These statistics should be supplemented to take into account the error rates that would be expected if the scientific method did not work at all. Unfortunately, this is not easily accomplished, since "the scientific results reported to date do not provide quantitative information about the improvement in accuracy, if any, associated with the use of voicegrams." Comm. on the Evaluation of Sound Spectrograms, National Research Council, On the Theory and Practice of Voice Identification 25 (1979).

[33]*See* National Research Council Comm. on the Evaluation of Sound Spectrograms, On the Theory and Practice of Voice Identification 58–70 (1979); Hollien, The Acoustics of Crime: The New Science of Forensic Phonetics 230 (1990) ("its validity is in question (due to insufficient and/or negative research)"); Bonastre et al., Person

voice spectrographic evidence have held the evidence inadmissible.[34] In fact, this evidence inspired some of the most spirited and thoughtful defenses of the general acceptance standard for scientific evidence.[35] On the other hand, faith in the method and a belief that jurors will not find it overly impressive prompted some courts to bend the *Frye* test to the breaking point to conclude that the evidence should be admissible.[36] Use of the technique has declined, however,[37] and in *Daubert* jurisdictions,

---

Authentication by Voice: A Need for Caution, in Eurospeech 2003—Interspeech 2003, Proceedings of the 8th European Conference on Speech Communication and Technology, Geneva, Switzerland, Sept. 1–4, 2003 ("Given the current state of knowledge, there are no methods, either automatic or based on human expertise, that enable one to state with certainty that a person is (or is not) the speaker in a particular recording. This is particularly true when one is trying to authenticate a short utterance with strong background noise, recorded with poor quality equipment over unknown channels by a speaker who may have disguised or artificially modified his or her voice.").

[34]U.S. v. Addison, 498 F.2d 741 (D.C. Cir. 1974), questioned in U.S. v. McDaniel, 538 F.2d 408, 413 (D.C. Cir. 1976); State v. Gortarez, 141 Ariz. 254, 686 P.2d 1224, 1236 (1984); People v. Kelly, 17 Cal. 3d 24, 130 Cal. Rptr. 144, 549 P.2d 1240 (1976); People v. Drake, 748 P.2d 1237 (Colo. 1988); Cornett v. State, 450 N.E.2d 498, 503 (Ind. 1983); Reed v. State, 283 Md. 374, 391 A.2d 364 (1978); Windmere, Inc. v. International Ins. Co., 105 N.J. 373, 522 A.2d 405 (1987); Admissibility and Weight of Voice Spectrographic Analysis Evidence, 95 A.L.R.5th 471. For reviews of the legal history of speaker identification by spectrographic analysis and other methods, see 1 Giannelli & Imwinkelried, Scientific Evidence ch. 10 (4th ed. 2007); Solan & Tiersma, Hearing Voices: Speaker Identification in Court, 54 Hastings L.J. 373 (2003). Additional discussion of cases can be found in Faigman, et al., Modern Scientific

Evidence: The Law and Science of Expert Testimony §§ 38:1 et seq. (2011–2012 ed.).

[35]Defining the relevant scientific community has been something of a problem in these cases. *Compare* Reed v. State, 283 Md. 374, 391 A.2d 364 (1978), *with* Com. v. Lykus, 367 Mass. 191, 327 N.E.2d 671 (1975).

[36]U.S. v. Williams, 583 F.2d 1194 (2d Cir. 1978); U.S. v. Baller, 519 F.2d 463 (4th Cir. 1975); U.S. v. Smith, 869 F.2d 348 (7th Cir. 1989); Admissibility and Weight of Voice Spectrographic Analysis Evidence, 95 A.L.R.5th 471. Many of these courts took the research of Dr. Oscar Tosi as establishing the accuracy of the technique. Tosi, Voice Identification: Theory and Legal Applications (1979). Some distinguished scientists drew the opposite conclusion. *See* Speaker Identification by Speech Spectrograms: Some Further Observations, 54 J. Acoustic Soc'y Am. 531, 533 (1973) (stating that "we regard the 5% to 10% false identification rates seen [by Tosi] as artificial minima which are likely to increase when conditions depart from the laboratory situation" and adding that "[t]he Tosi experiments, in fact, show considerable disagreement among different panels of observers as to what constitutes a match").

[37]*See* U.S. v. Drones, 218 F.3d 496, 503–04 (5th Cir. 2000); Koenig, Selected Topics in Forensic Voice Identification, Crime Lab. Digest, Oct. 1993, at 78, 80 (reporting that as of 1993, the only crime laboratories that were continuing to use the technique on a regular basis were the FBI and the New York City Police Department).

courts are increasingly likely to exclude the evidence.[38] Whatever standard may be applied, it seems that unless further research makes the validity of the technique plainer, the courts will remain divided over or opposed to the admissibility of voice spectrographic identification.[39]

## III. STATISTICAL STUDIES

### § 208 Surveys and opinion polls

Samuel Johnson once remarked that "You don't have to eat the whole ox to know the hide is tough."[1] In the past, courts required litigants to dismember and devour an ox or two to prove a point—either because of skepticism about the value of sampling and opinion polling[2] or because of the hearsay rule.[3] In *Irvin v. State*,[4] for example, the Florida Supreme Court upheld the trial judge's

---

[38]U.S. v. Simmons, 431 F. Supp. 2d 38 (D.D.C. 2006) (following cases excluding voice spectrograms); U.S. v. Angleton, 269 F. Supp. 2d 892, 897 (S.D. Tex. 2003) (holding that *Daubert* is not satisfied and observing that "few reported cases have subjected voice spectrograph identification methods to a *Daubert* analysis. Even the cases that found the admission of such expert testimony not to be clear error express doubts about the reliability, scientific validity, and acceptance of voice spectrographic analysis.").

[39]*See* State v. Morrison, 871 So. 2d 1086, 1086–87 (La. 2004) (reversing trial court's order excluding "the defense expert's testimony regarding aural/spectrographic voice identification" because no hearing was held and "the present record does not provide this Court with an adequate basis for determining whether the trial judge properly exercised his gate-keeping function under *Daubert* . . .", despite evidence presented by defendant that voice identification analysis has been subjected to peer review and publication, has a known error rate, and has a degree of acceptance in the relevant scientific community."); Solan & Tiersma, Hearing Voices: Speaker Identification in Court, 54 Hastings L.J. 373, 422 (2003) (observing that "throughout the 1980s and early 1990s . . . courts continued to be . . . seri-

ously divided" and "[t]his disagreement has not abated"). The NRC Report studiously avoids taking a position on the legal issues, except to say that "the technical uncertainties . . . are so great as to require that forensic applications be approached with great caution" and to recommend that "if it is used in testimony, then the limitations of the method should be clearly and thoroughly explained to the fact finder, whether judge or jury." Comm. on the Evaluation of Sound Spectrograms, National Research Council, On the Theory and Practice of Voice Identification 2 (1979).

**[Section 208]**

[1]As quoted in Moore, Statistics: Concepts and Controversies 3 (2d ed. 1985).

[2]*See, e.g.*, Spowls, The Admissibility of Sample Data into a Court of Law, 4 UCLA L. Rev. 222 (1957).

[3]In most large surveys, many individuals are employed to do the interviewing or other forms of data collection. Furthermore, when opinion polls are in issue, the individuals whose opinions were sampled are not testifying in court. Testimony as to the findings therefore is usually thought to involve hearsay, and historically this has been the major objection to survey evidence. Various arguments to circumvent or overcome the hearsay

refusal to admit a public opinion survey in a pretrial hearing on the theory that the poll was "hearsay based upon hearsay" and that it was "useless" in revealing public attitudes toward the defendant, a black who had been convicted of rape but alleged that the verdict was the result of racial prejudice.[5] The court regarded as much more informative the opinions given by selected witnesses who testified in court that the defendant could get a fair trial in the county, and it cited as an "illustration of the friendliness of the white people for the colored in the community . . . the recent construction of an elaborate memorial to a colored soldier who had been killed in World War II."[6]

With the development and implementation of scientific survey methods, the courts are much more receptive to proof based on sample data.[7] The Federal and Uniform Rules circumvent hearsay objections by allowing an expert to form an opinion on the basis of a survey produced in a reasonably reliable manner.[8] Specially commissioned surveys or samples have been used to support motions for a change of venue in response to pretrial publicity,[9] to show consumer perceptions in trademark and misleading

---

rule have been used by courts electing to receive the evidence. *See, e.g.,* Schering Corp. v. Pfizer Inc., 189 F.3d 218 (2d Cir. 1999) (applying state-of-mind and residual exceptions); Texas Aeronautics Commission v. Braniff Airways, Inc., 454 S.W.2d 199, 203 (Tex. 1970) ("admissible whether it is considered to be nonhearsay or within the state of mind exception to the hearsay rule"); Zeisel, The Uniqueness of Survey Evidence, 45 Cornell L.Q. 322 (1960).

[4]Irvin v. State, 66 So. 2d 288 (Fla. 1953).

[5]Irvin v. State, 66 So.2d at 291–92

[6]Irvin, 66 So.2d at 292.

[7]*See generally* Kaye et al., The New Wigmore, A Treatise on Evidence: Expert Evidence § 12.6 (2d ed. 2011); Zeisel & Kaye, Prove It with Figures: Empirical Methods in Law and Litigation (1997); Becker, Public Opinion Polls and Surveys as Evidence: Suggestions for Resolving Confusing and Conflicting Standards Governing Weight and Admissibility, 70 Or. L. Rev. 463 (1991); Diamond, Survey Research, in Reference Guide on Survey Research, in Reference Manual on Scientific Evidence 359 (Federal Judicial Center & Comm. on the Third Edition of the Reference Manual on Scientific Evidence, Nat'l Research Council eds., 3d ed. 2011).

[8]Rule 703 departs from the common law in permitting an expert to testify to an opinion based on facts or data that are not admissible in evidence and to testify about this underlying information as long as it is "of the type reasonably relied on by experts in the particular field." In theory, the evidence is not introduced for its truth, but only to show the basis for the expert's belief. The federal Advisory Committee's Note to this rule refers to survey evidence, observing that "[t]he rule also offers a more satisfactory basis for ruling upon the admissibility of public opinion poll evidence. Attention is directed to the validity of the techniques employed rather than to relatively fruitless inquiries into whether hearsay is involved."

[9]*See* U.S. v. Campa, 419 F.3d 1219 (11th Cir. 2005) (reversing convictions of individuals, accused of acting as unregistered Cuban intelligence agents working within the United States and supporting and implement-

advertising cases,[10] to unmask community standards in obscenity prosecutions,[11] and for numerous other purposes.[12] Advocates

---

ing a plan to shoot down a civilian aircraft outside of Cuban and United States airspace, for the failure to grant a change-of-venue motion that was supported by specially commissioned opinion polls and other evidence of anti-Castro sentiment in Miami-Dade Country); State v. Hickman, 337 N.W.2d 512, 515 (Iowa 1983) (survey introduced by prosecution); Zeisel & Kaye, Prove It with Figures: Empirical Methods in Law and Litigation 135–46 (1997); Zeisel & Diamond, The Jury Selection in the Mitchell-Stans Conspiracy Trial, 1976 Am. B. Found. Research J. 151. Of course, the admissibility of a poll does not mean that it will succeed in demonstrating such widespread prejudice as would warrant a continuance or change in venue. U.S. v. Haldeman, 559 F.2d 31 (D.C. Cir. 1976) (voir dire examination may be given more weight than defendants' poll); U.S. v. Collins, 972 F.2d 1385 (5th Cir. 1992).

[10]Admissibility and weight of consumer survey in litigation under trademark opposition, trademark infringement, and false designation of origin provisions of Lanham Act (15 U.S.C.A. secs. 1063, 1114, and 1125), 98 A.L.R. Fed. 20. Classic cases include U.S. v. 88 Cases, More or Less, Containing Bireley's Orange Beverage, 187 F.2d 967 (3d Cir. 1951), and Zippo Mfg. Co. v. Rogers Imports, Inc., 216 F. Supp. 670 (S.D. N.Y. 1963).

[11]U.S. v. Pryba, 900 F.2d 748, 757 (4th Cir. 1990) (telephone survey properly excluded); People v. Nelson, 88 Ill. App. 3d 196, 43 Ill. Dec. 476, 410 N.E.2d 476 (2d Dist. 1980) (survey showing that "a majority . . . of Illinois residents consider it acceptable for adults to view sexually explicit materials" was excluded erroneously, but testimony of the expert that these results showed no "consensus" was properly excluded as confusing, distracting, and unnecessary); Saliba v. State, 475 N.E.2d 1181, 1185 (Ind. Ct.

App. 1985) ("opinion poll is uniquely suited to a determination of community standards"); Com. v. Trainor, 374 Mass. 796, 374 N.E.2d 1216 (1978) ("[a] properly conducted public opinion survey, offered through an expert in conducting such surveys, is admissible in an obscenity case if it tends to show relevant standards," but the survey in question was properly excluded); Carlock v. State, 609 S.W.2d 787 (Tex. Crim. App. 1980) (survey erroneously excluded); County of Kenosha v. C & S Management, Inc., 223 Wis. 2d 373, 588 N.W.2d 236, 253 (1999) (although "a survey may be admitted for the purpose of shedding light on community standards," "telephone surveys which ask respondents to opine about the availability and acceptance of 'actual depictions of sexual activity' in magazines and videos in their communities are not relevant to the determination of obscenity in a particular instance, particularly where the respondent is to opine about sexually explicit material in the abstract."); Admissibility of evidence of public-opinion polls or surveys in obscenity prosecutions on the issue whether materials in question are obscene, 59 A.L.R.5th 749 (concluding that "[t]he courts are divided on the admissibility of evidence of public-opinion polls or surveys on the issue whether materials are obscene.").

[12]E.g., C. A. May Marine Supply Co. v. Brunswick Corp., 649 F.2d 1049 (5th Cir. 1981) (survey of customers of dealer whose franchise was cancelled); Baumholser v. Amax Coal Co., 630 F.2d 550 (7th Cir. 1980) (survey of residents as to property damage from blasting operations); Pittsburgh Press Club v. U.S., 579 F.2d 751 (3d Cir. 1978) (tax-exempt club's mail survey of its members as to their sponsorship of income-producing uses of club facilities); Rosado v. Wyman, 322 F. Supp. 1173, 1180 (E.D. N.Y. 1970) (determining welfare benefits); Boucher v. Bomhoff, 495 P.2d 77, 80–81, (Alaska

have also relied on pre-existing research involving sample data in product liability, food and drug, environmental, constitutional, and other cases.[13] The modern opinions have said that case-specific surveys are generally admissible if they are conducted according to the principles accepted by social scientists and statisticians for gathering and analyzing survey data.[14] This section therefore gives an overview of these principles—adherence to which affects the weight as well as the admissibility of survey evidence.[15] In a great many cases, courts have examined whether the conclusions of the survey researchers rest on data collected in

---

1972) (survey as to effect of misleading language prefacing ballot measure); Sufficiency of random sampling of drug or contraband to establish jurisdictional amount required for conviction, 45 A.L.R.5th 1. Courts have occasionally undertaken their own sampling studies. *E.g.*, Meeropol v. Meese, 790 F.2d 942, 956–57 (D.C. Cir. 1986) (in camera inspection of every hundredth document that FBI claimed was exempt from disclosure under Freedom of Information Act); In re Chevron U.S.A., Inc., 109 F.3d 1016 (5th Cir. 1997) (flawed procedure to select sample of 30 cases for trial to ascertain damages applicable to 3,000 cases); *cf.* Cimino v. Raymark Industries, Inc., 151 F.3d 297 (5th Cir. 1998) (use of sample cases in asbestos cases to estimate total damages violated Seventh Amendment); Hilao v. Estate of Marcos, 103 F.3d 767 (9th Cir. 1996) (approving of trying only a sample of all the claims filed); Blue Cross and Blue Shield of New Jersey, Inc. v. Philip Morris, Inc., 113 F. Supp. 2d 345, 375–76 (E.D. N.Y. 2000) (sampling to ascertain the aggregate cost of a single plaintiff's health insurance claims allowed); Scottsdale Memorial Health Systems, Inc. v. Maricopa County, 224 Ariz. 125, 228 P.3d 117 (Ct. App. Div. 1 2010) (sampling of hospitals' claims against county for emergency room bills of patients was permissible in principle, but a special master's report failed to establish the accuracy of the sampling); Walker & Monahan, Sampling Evidence at the

Crossroads, 80 S. Cal. L. Rev. 969 (2007).

[13]See infra § 209. *See* Atkins v. Virginia, 536 U.S. 304, 122 S. Ct. 2242, 153 L. Ed. 2d 335 (2002) (using polling results to ascertain public attitudes toward the death penalty).

[14]C. A. May Marine Supply Co. v. Brunswick Corp., 649 F.2d 1049 (5th Cir. 1981) ("Surveys and customer questionnaires are admissible, if they are pertinent to the inquiry, upon a showing that the poll is reliable and was conducted in accordance with accepted survey methods"); Baumholser v. Amax Coal Co., 630 F.2d 550 (7th Cir. 1980) ("To qualify a study or opinion poll for admission into evidence, there must be a substantial showing of reliability. There must be some showing that the poll is conducted in accordance with generally accepted survey principles and that the results are used in a statistically correct manner").

[15]*See, e.g.,* C. A. May Marine Supply Co. v. Brunswick Corp., 649 F.2d 1049 n.10 (5th Cir. 1981). Once a survey has been shown to conform to "conventional methodology," its arguable deficiencies usually are said to affect its weight rather than its admissibility. *See, e.g.,* SquirtCo. v. Seven-Up Co., 628 F.2d 1086, 1091 (8th Cir. 1980); Harolds Stores, Inc. v. Dillard Dept. Stores, Inc., 82 F.3d 1533, 1544 (10th Cir. 1996); Jellibeans, Inc. v. Skating Clubs of Georgia, Inc., 716 F.2d 833, 844 (11th Cir. 1983).

such a way as to permit fair inferences about the relevant factual questions.[16]

Although many refinements are possible, the basic ideas behind scientific survey techniques are simple enough.[17] The researcher tries to collect information from a manageable portion (a sample) of a larger group (a population) in order to learn something about the population. Usually some numbers are used to characterize the population, and these are called parameters. For example, the proportion of all consumers who would mistake one product for another because of a similarity in the brand names is a population parameter. Sample data lead to statistics, such as the proportion of the persons in the sample who are confused by the similarity. These sample statistics are then used to estimate the population parameters. If 50% of the sample studied exhibited confusion between the products with the similar brand names, then one might conclude that 50% of the population would be confused. Under some circumstances, statistical methods enable the researcher not only to make an estimate, but to indicate how much such an estimate could differ from the unknown parameter just because of the luck of the draw—that is, to quantify the sampling error that may be lurking in the estimate.

Sampling underlies almost every pertinent research effort. Descriptive surveys, like those introduced in connection with change of venue motions, are almost always confined to a sample of the entire population. Surveys looking for causal explanations (such as a survey of homicide rates in states that do and states that do not have capital punishment) usually involve samples. Even experiments designed to investigate causation, such as a trial of a new drug, typically produce only sample data. Many such surveys are nonverbal. Since an employer's records can be inspected, no one needs to poll the current employees to obtain

---

[16]*E.g.*, Firefly Digital Inc. v. Google Inc., 817 F. Supp. 2d 846 (W.D. La. 2011) (admitting Lanham Act survey over a *Daubert* objection); THOIP v. Walt Disney Co., 788 F. Supp. 2d 168 (S.D. N.Y. 2011) (excluding a Lanham Act survey for methodological flaws); Malletier v. Dooney & Bourke, Inc., 525 F. Supp. 2d 558 (S.D. N.Y. 2007) (excluding a Lanham Act survey under Rule 403 for lack of fit and cumulative flaws in the survey).

[17]For introductions to the theory of sampling and survey research, see Kaye et al., The New Wigmore, A Treatise on Evidence: Expert Evidence § 12.6 (2d ed. 2011); Zeisel & Kaye, Prove It with Figures: Empirical Methods in Law and Litigation ch. 7 (1997); Diamond, Survey Research, in Reference Guide on Survey Research, in Reference Manual on Scientific Evidence 359 (Federal Judicial Center & Comm. on the Third Edition of the Reference Manual on Scientific Evidence, Nat'l Research Council eds., 3d ed. 2011); Kaye & Freedman, Reference Guide to Statistics, in Reference Manual on Scientific Evidence 211, 223–27, 239, 242–47, 278–79 (Federal Judicial Center & Comm. on the Third Edition of the Reference Manual on Scientific Evidence, Nat'l Research Council eds., 3d ed. 2011).

data on the distribution of wages paid to men as opposed to women. Other surveys are personal or verbal, as we know from experience with survey interviewers and written questionnaires.

What factors are likely to make such surveys produce accurate as opposed to misleading estimates? We can identify two major categories of errors: random errors and nonrandom errors.[18] There are many potential sources of nonrandom, or systematic errors. In personal surveys, these include the specification of the population to be sampled,[19] the technique for eliciting responses,[20] the wording of the questions,[21] the method for choosing and finding respondents,[22] and the failure to pose questions that address the

---

[18]*See generally* Barnett, Sample Survey Principles and Methods (3d ed. 2003); Groves et al., Survey Methodology (2d ed. 2009); Gonzalez et al., Standards for Discussion and Presentation of Errors in Survey and Census Data, 70 J. Am. Stat. Ass'n 5 (1975).

[19]Reddy Communications, Inc. v. Environmental Action Foundation, 477 F. Supp. 936, 947 (D.D.C. 1979) ("survey failed to account for the specific public exposed to . . . publications" that were available only by mail upon specific request and not "distributed or sold in the public marketplace where uninformed or easily gullible readers might be exposed to them").

[20]For example, postcards mailed in response to a newspaper advertisement containing a questionnaire about a product may introduce "nonresponse" bias, since disgruntled customers tend to respond in disproportionately large numbers. *Cf.* U.S. v. Shine, 571 F. Supp. 2d 589, 598–99 (D. Vt. 2008) (noting that "[o]f the returned jury questionnaires a substantial number of responders elected not to answer the race and ethnicity questions. This may have introduced bias in the sample if non-responders tend to be disproportionately of one race or ethnicity."); Com. v. Trainor, 374 Mass. 796, 374 N.E.2d 1216 (1978) ("There was no indication that the method of selection of the subjects to be interviewed assured a representative sample of the citizens of Boston. One might suspect that certain persons

would decline to participate because of the method by which they were approached").

[21]Pittsburgh Press Club v. U.S., 579 F.2d 751 (3d Cir. 1978); Quality Inns Intern., Inc. v. McDonald's Corp., 695 F. Supp. 198, 219 (D. Md. 1988) (misleading visual presentation); Carlock v. State, 609 S.W.2d 787, 790 n.3 (Tex. Crim. App. 1980).

[22]For example, the locations and time of day or night at which interviews are conducted can affect the characteristics of the sample. To avoid bias in selecting the units on which data is to be obtained, the sampling frame must be representative of the population, and the units in the sampling frame must have nonzero probabilities of being selected. In quota sampling, the sample is hand-picked by the interviewers to resemble the population in some key ways. The method seems logical, but it often gives bad results because of unintentional bias on the part of the interviewers. "Convenience samples" which, like the newspaper advertisement poll, make no effort to secure a representative sample, are especially likely to produce biased results. Nevertheless, courts rely on convenience samples under certain conditions. *See* Quality Inns Intern., Inc. v. McDonald's Corp., 695 F. Supp. 198, 207–08 (D. Md. 1988) (mall intercept survey); Diamond, Survey Research, in Reference Guide on Survey Research, in Reference Manual on Scientific Evidence 359

proper issues.[23] Unless those sources of nonrandom error cancel each other out, any estimates made on the basis of the sample data will be biased.[24] Making the sample size larger offers no protection against bias. It only produces a larger number of biased observations.

Random errors arise at two levels. The first is with respect to the observations on each unit sampled. In a nonverbal study, a measuring instrument (such as an instrument to determine breath alcohol content) might well give slightly different readings even on identical samples. A person seeking to get rid of an interviewer may say whatever pops into mind.[25] The process for making individual measurements or observations is rarely perfectly reliable. The second kind of random error results from variability from one sample to the next. One sample of air expelled from the lungs may be slightly different from the next in its concentration of alcohol. Even though great care may be taken to assure that the people selected for interviews are representative of the population, there can be no guarantee that another sample selected by the same procedure would give identical responses. As such, even if all the answers or measurements are individually free from error, sampling variability remains a source of statistical, or chance error.

If methods known as probability sampling are employed, however, the magnitude of the sampling error (but not of the

---

(Federal Judicial Center & Comm. on the Third Edition of the Reference Manual on Scientific Evidence, Nat'l Research Council eds., 3d ed. 2011).

[23]This type of error seems to be uncomfortably prevalent in surveys intended for use in court. *See, e.g.,* C. A. May Marine Supply Co. v. Brunswick Corp., 649 F.2d 1049 (5th Cir. 1981) (survey offered to prove lost profits from a franchise termination was correctly excluded, since "[e]vidence tending to show business goodwill is not germane unless it demonstrates a 'going concern' value," and "general predisposition to purchase products at May Marine is not reflective of how many of a certain item would have been purchased"); Muha v. Encore Receivable Management, Inc., 558 F.3d 623, 625–26 (7th Cir. 2009) (question drafted by plaintiffs' lawyer was not appropriate); U.S. v. Pryba, 678 F. Supp. 1225, 1228–31 (E.D. Va. 1988) (questions must focus on materials alleged to be obscene); Reddy

Communications, Inc. v. Environmental Action Foundation, 477 F. Supp. 936, 947 (D.D.C. 1979) ("The interviewees . . . were shown two illustrations . . . in a context devoid of any background information and totally foreign from the usual manner in which the public would come in contact with either of the figures"); People v. Norwood, 37 Colo. App. 157, 547 P.2d 273 (App. 1975) (survey showing that most city residents had heard of pending murder trial did not prove that they were prejudiced).

[24]If the direction or magnitude of the bias can be determined, the results nonetheless may be useful.

[25]The individual also may lie. If the persons being questioned have a motive to fabricate, the sample data may be biased. *See, e.g.,* Pittsburgh Press Club v. U. S., 579 F.2d 751 (3d Cir. 1978).

nonrandom errors) can be estimated. Probability sampling also has been shown to be very effective in producing representative samples. The reason is that unlike human beings, blind chance is impartial. Probability sampling uses an objective chance process to pick the sample. It leaves no discretion to the interviewers. As a result, the researcher can compute the chance that any particular unit in the population will be selected for the sample. Stated another way, a probability sample is one in which each unit of the sampling frame has a known, nonzero probability of being selected. Other samples, either "convenience" samples or "quota" samples, do not have this property, and they are acceptable only in special circumstances.[26] A common type of probability sampling is simple random sampling, in which every unit has the same probability of being sampled. It amounts to drawing names at random without replacement.

The statistics derived from observations or measurements of random samples permit one to estimate the parameters of the population. In a consumer confusion survey for instance, some proportion of the sample of consumers who are interviewed will indicate confusion between the products. If the sample is a simple random sample, and if there are no nonrandom errors, then this sample proportion is an unbiased estimator of the proportion for all consumers. But it is only an estimate. Another random sample probably would not include precisely the same persons, and it probably would produce a slightly different proportion of responses indicating confusion. There is no single figure that expresses the extent of this statistical error. There are only probabilities. If one were to draw a second random sample, find the proportion of confused consumers in this group, then do the same for a third random sample, a fourth, and so on, one would obtain a distribution of sample proportions fluctuating about some central value.[27] Some would be far away from the mean, but most would be closer. Pursuing this logic in a rigorous way, the statistician computes a "confidence interval" and gives an "interval estimate" for the population proportion. The analyst may report that at a 90%

---

[26]Debra P. by Irene P. v. Turlington, 730 F.2d 1405, 1411 n.11 (11th Cir. 1984) (results of a survey of students about the skills that they had been taught found persuasive despite the possibility of discretionary selection of classes to be surveyed within each randomly selected school).

[27]The center of this distribution is characterized by the mean of all the sample proportions. The statistic known as the variance (or the square root of this quantity, the standard deviation) describes the width of the distribution of the sample proportions. For large samples, the sample proportions follow a bell shaped curve known as the normal distribution such that about two-thirds of the sample proportions lie within one standard deviation on either side of the mean. For more details, see Kaye et al., The New Wigmore, A Treatise on Evidence: Expert Evidence § 12.8.1 (2d ed. 2011).

confidence level, the population proportion is 50% plus or minus 10%. This means that if the same method for drawing samples and interviewing the customers were repeated a very large number of times, and if a 90% confidence interval were computed about each sample, 90% of the resulting interval estimates would be correct. This many would include the population proportion, whatever that number happens to be.

Although testimony as to confidence intervals often is received in cases involving survey evidence, its meaning apparently remains obscure in many cases.[28] Note that a confidence of, say 90% does not necessarily mean that the interval estimate has a 90% probability of being correct.[29] Strictly speaking, all that the classical statistical methodology reveals is that the particular interval was obtained by a method that gives intervals that would capture the true proportion in 90% of all possible samples. But each such interval estimate could be different. Thus, the "confidence" pertains to the process rather than to any particular result. Therefore, the common view that "[a] 95% confidence interval means that there is a 95% probability that the 'true' [value] falls within the interval"[30] is mistaken.[31] Despite this difficulty in interpreting a confidence interval, the technique does give the finder of fact an idea of the risk of error in equating the sample proportion to the population figure. If the interval is small, even for a high level of "confidence," then the sample

---

[28]*See, e.g.,* Turpin v. Merrell Dow Pharmaceuticals, Inc., 959 F.2d 1349, 1353 (6th Cir. 1992) ("If a confidence interval of '95 percent between 0.8 and 3.10' is cited, this means that random repetition of the study should produce, 95 percent of the time, a relative risk somewhere between 0.8 and 3.10."); Hilao v. Estate of Marcos, 103 F.3d 767 (9th Cir. 1996); Cimino v. Raymark Industries, Inc., 751 F. Supp. 649 (E.D. Tex. 1990) (that a quantity fell within a 99% confidence interval said to be more revealing than its lying within the narrower 95% interval). These statements are either wrong or garbled.

[29]*See* Kaye, Apples and Oranges: Confidence Coefficients and the Burden of Persuasion, 73 Cornell L. Rev. 54, 61–62 (1987). A statistical procedure that does produce this probability is presented in Bright et al., Statistical Sampling in Tax Audits, 1988 Law & Soc. Inquiry 305.

[30]DeLuca by DeLuca v. Merrell Dow Pharmaceuticals, Inc., 791 F. Supp. 1042 (D.N.J. 1992).

[31]Nevertheless, the point eludes many courts. *E.g.,* Gomez v. Astrue, 695 F. Supp. 2d 1049, 1055 n.3 (C.D. Cal. 2010) ("A 90% confidence interval means that the investigator is 90% confident that the true estimate lies within the confidence interval."); Cook v. Rockwell Intern. Corp., 580 F. Supp. 2d 1071, 1089 n.15 (D. Colo. 2006) ("if a value is estimated as falling in a certain range at a 90 percent confidence level, then there is a probability of 90 percent that the true value falls within the given range."); Coleman v. State, 341 S.W.3d 221, 245 n.77 (Tenn. 2011) (after giving a correct definition, the court added that "a confidence interval [is] 'a range of values so defined that there is a specified probability that the value of a parameter of a population lies within it,'" quoting the Oxford English Dictionary).

proportion is reasonably accurate, at least in the sense that taking more, or larger samples probably would give similar results.

The width of the confidence interval depends on three things. For a given sample, there is a trade-off between the level of confidence and the narrowness of the interval. One can be sure that the population proportion lies somewhere between zero and one. The confidence is 100% but the interval is so broad as to be useless. Lowering the confidence level narrows the range of the estimate, but there is more risk in concluding that the population value lies within the narrower interval. Second, for a given confidence and a fixed sample size, the width of the interval depends on how homogeneous the population is. If nearly every consumer would be confused (or nearly no one would be), then there will be minimal sampling variability, since almost all the possible samples can be expected to look alike. Hence, the confidence interval for any sample will be very narrow. On the other hand, if the population is highly variable, then there are more chances to draw aberrant samples, and the computed confidence interval for any sample will be larger. Third, whatever the makeup of the population, larger samples give more reliable results than smaller ones. However, the point of diminishing returns rapidly is reached in that adding the same amount to the sample size does little to narrow the confidence interval.[32] It is wrong to believe that one always needs to sample a substantial proportion of a large population to obtain an accurate estimate of a population parameter.[33]

In assessing the statistical error of a survey, therefore, the courts should look to the interval estimates rather than to untutored intuitions as to how large a sample is needed. Deciding what level of confidence is appropriate in a particular case, however, is a policy question and not a statistical issue. Finally, in making use of surveys, it is important to remember that the statistical analysis does not address the nonrandom sources of

---

[32]The width of the confidence interval is inversely proportional to the square root of the sample size. Thus, if the sample size is increased from, say, 50 to 200, the confidence interval is cut in half. To achieve another reduction of one-half, however, it is necessary to increase the sample size not by another 350, but by 600, to reach a size of 800. A third reduction of one-half would require a sample of 3200, and things only get worse as we continue. In sampling from very large populations, then, it is not the percentage of the population that is sampled that is important, but the absolute size of the sample. A sample of 100 is about as good for a population of 30,000 as it is for one of 3,000.

[33]See Zeisel & Kaye, Prove It with Figures: Empirical Methods in Law and Litigation 108–10 (1997); Kaye, Likelihoodism, Bayesianism, and a Pair of Shoes, 53 Jurimetrics J. 1 (2012) (noting the unreasonable demand regarding sample size in R. v. T., (2010) EWCA Crim 2439; (2011) 1 Cr. App. R. 9, 2010 WL 5652779).

error. A small confidence interval with a high confidence coefficient is not worth much if the data collection is badly flawed.

## § 209    Correlations and causes: Statistical evidence of discrimination

Survey evidence, as we described it in the previous section, involves sampling from some population, deriving statistics from the sample data, and offering some conclusion about the population in light of these sample statistics. In this section, we describe applications and extensions of this approach used to supply and interpret evidence on the issue of causation.[1] When causation is at issue, advocates have relied on three major types of information—anecdotal evidence, observational studies, and controlled experiments.[2] Anecdotal reports can provide some information, but they are more useful as a stimulus for further inquiry than as a basis for establishing association or causation. Observational studies can establish that one factor is associated with another, but considerable analysis may be necessary to bridge the gap from association to causation. Controlled experiments are ideal for ascertaining causation, but they can be difficult to undertake.

"Anecdotal evidence" means reports of one kind of event following another. Typically, the reports are obtained haphazardly or selectively, and the logic of "post hoc, ergo propter hoc" does not suffice to demonstrate that the first event causes the second. Consequently, while anecdotal evidence can be suggestive,[3] it can also be quite misleading. For instance, some children who live

---

**[Section 209]**

[1]In and of itself, statistical analysis can never prove that some factor A causes some outcome B. It can show that in a sample of observations, occurrences of B tend to be associated with those of A, and it can suggest that this statistical association probably would be observed for repeated samples. But the association, even though "statistically significant," need not be causal. For instance, a third factor C could be causing both A and B. Thus, over some time period, there could be a correlation between the number of people smoking cigarettes and the number of certain crimes committed, but if told that the population (and hence the number of smokers) was growing rapidly during this time, no one would think that this proves

that smoking causes crime. Experimental design and some forms of statistical analysis can help control for the effects of other variables, but even these methods simply help formulate, confirm, or refute theories about causal relationships. *See generally* Panel on Methods for Assessing Discrimination, National Research Council, Measuring Racial Discrimination 77–89 (Blank et al. eds., 2004).

[2]The description of these types of data that follows is abridged from Kaye & Freedman, Statistical Proof, in 1 Faigman, et al., Modern Scientific Evidence: The Law and Science of Expert Testimony § 6.9 (2012–2013 ed.).

[3]In medicine, evidence from clinical practice is often the starting point for the demonstration of a causal ef-

near power lines develop leukemia; but does exposure to electrical and magnetic fields cause this disease? The anecdotal evidence is not compelling because leukemia also occurs among children who have minimal exposure to such fields.[4] It is necessary to compare disease rates among those who are exposed and those who are not. If exposure causes the disease, the rate should be higher among the exposed, lower among the unexposed. Of course, the two groups may differ in crucial ways other than the exposure. For example, children who live near power lines could come from poorer families and be exposed to other environmental hazards. These differences could create the appearance of a cause-and-effect relationship, or they could mask a real relationship. Cause-and-effect relationships often are subtle, and carefully-designed studies are needed to draw valid conclusions. Thus, some courts have deemed attempts to infer causation from anecdotal reports unsound methodology.[5]

Typically, a well-designed study will compare outcomes for subjects who are exposed to some factor—the treatment group—and other subjects who are not so exposed—the control group. A distinction must then be made between controlled experiments and observational studies. In a controlled experiment, the investigators decide which subjects are exposed to the factor of interest and which subjects go into the control group. In most observational studies, the subjects themselves choose their exposures. Because of this self-selection, the treatment and control groups of observational studies are likely differ with respect to important factors other than the variable whose effects are of primary interest. These other factors are called confounding variables or lurking variables. With observational studies on

---

fect. One famous example involves exposure of mothers to German measles during pregnancy, followed by blindness in their babies.

[4]*See* Committee on the Possible Effects of Electromagnetic Fields on Biologic Systems, National Research Council, Possible Health Effects of Exposure to Residential Electric and Magnetic Fields (1997); Zeisel & Kaye, Prove It with Figures: Empirical Methods in Law and Litigation 66–67 (1997). There are serious problems in measuring exposure to electromagnetic fields, and results are somewhat inconsistent from one study to another. For such reasons, the epidemiologic evidence for an effect on health is inconclusive. Edward W. Campion, Power Lines, Cancer, and Fear, 337

New Eng. J. Med. 44 (1997) (editorial).

[5]In re Denture Cream Products Liability Litigation, 795 F. Supp. 2d 1345, 1354 (S.D. Fla. 2011) ("The Eleventh Circuit, although it has not has not completely excluded the possibility that causation may be established by case studies, has been very hostile when experts have relied on them to infer causation."); Dixon v. Ford Motor Co., 206 Md. App. 180, 47 A.3d 1038, 1048 (2012), cert. granted, 429 Md. 303, 55 A.3d 906 (2012) ("we agree . . . that 'case reports' and other anecdotal evidence are not probative of either general or actual causation") (note omitted); Kaye et al., The New Wigmore, A Treatise on Evidence: Expert Evidence § 12.5.1 (2d ed. 2011).

the health effects of power lines, family background is a possible confounder; so is exposure to other hazards.[6]

Whether the data come from observational or experimental studies, the conclusions that can be drawn will involve further statistical assessments. Parties in environmental and product liability cases typically rely on statistical reasoning to establish that a chemical or other agent is carcinogenic or toxic. In civil rights cases, parties seeking to prove (or disprove) that a class or an individual has been subjected to unlawful discrimination may find statistical evidence useful. In antitrust litigation, a party may use statistical analysis to show illegal conduct and its effects. In business litigation generally, a party may apply statistical techniques to estimate lost profits or other damages resulting from illegal conduct. In these and many other sorts of cases, the statistics, and inferences drawn from them, if in accordance with normal statistical practice, will be admissible via the testimony of a suitably qualified expert.

The weight that may be given such testimony will depend, of course, on the skill of counsel and the ability and preparation of the witness. In addition, the methods that the expert uses to analyze and interpret that data, so as to assist the court or jury in understanding it, will be crucial in determining the admissibility and impact of the evidence. This section outlines one of the statistical concepts most frequently encountered in connection with sophisticated statistical proofs. Because most cases addressing the usefulness of this concept arose in discrimination litigation, it draws on a few of the developments in this area to illustrate some general points about the presentation of statistical evidence.

The courts have relied heavily on statistical evidence in cases in which a criminal defendant alleges that he was indicted by an unconstitutionally selected grand jury or an unconstitutionally empaneled petit jury.[7] There is no constitutionally permissible basis for systematically excluding, say, members of defendant's race from the population of citizens who are eligible for jury duty.

---

[6]Likewise, an "experiment" that compares the interpretations of DNA analysts in an actual case to those asked to review the same data under unspecified conditions is essentially an observational study. It does not control for even the most obvious confounding variables. Kaye, The Design of "The First Experimental Study Exploring DNA Interpretation," 52 Sci. & Justice 126 (2012) (discussing Dror & Hampikian, Subjectivity and Bias in Forensic DNA Mixture Interpretation, 51 Sci. & Justice 204 (2011)).

[7]Castaneda v. Partida, 430 U.S. 482, 97 S. Ct. 1272, 51 L. Ed. 2d 498 (1977) (grand jury); Kaye, Statistical Evidence of Discrimination in Jury Selection, *in* Statistical Methods in Discrimination Litigation (Kaye & Aickin, eds. 1986); Zeisel, Dr. Spock and the Case of the Vanishing Women Jurors, 37 U. Chi. L. Rev. 1 (1969) (petit jury).

Where direct evidence of discrimination is unavailable, or where additional proof is desired, statistical methods have been pressed into service. The usual procedure is to compare the proportion of the persons eligible for jury service who are in the class allegedly discriminated against[8] with the corresponding proportion appearing on jury venires or pools. Substantial underrepresentation over a significant period of time is taken as evidence of discrimination.[9]

In early cases, the courts made purely intuitive assessments of the disparity in the proportions.[10] In time, formal statistical reasoning to evaluate the quantitative evidence became *de rigueur*.[11] The logic begins from the assumption that selection of potential jurors is a random process, like blindly drawing differently colored marbles from an urn, in which the chance that a person will be selected is the same in each instance. Under the "null" hypothesis that everyone has an equal chance of being selected, the probability of picking a member of the protected class each time is simply the overall proportion of these individuals in the

---

[8]This population proportion typically is obtained from census data. Inasmuch as the population changes over time and not every adult is eligible for jury service, some complications can arise. U.S. ex rel. Barksdale v. Blackburn, 610 F.2d 253, 262, 266 (5th Cir. 1980); Kaye, Statistical Evidence of Discrimination in Jury Selection, *in* Statistical Methods in Discrimination Litigation 13 (D.H. Kaye & Mikel Aickin, eds. 1986); Kaye, Statistical Evidence of Discrimination, 77 J. Am. Stat. Ass'n 773, 780 (1982).

[9]The courts usually measure the disparity by the difference between the population proportion (as deduced from census data) and the sample proportion (the actual rate of representation of jury venires). U.S. ex rel. Barksdale v. Blackburn, 610 F.2d 253, 256–57, (5th Cir. 1980) (reviewing Supreme Court decisions). Other measures, however, are more appropriate. *See* Washington v. People, 186 P.3d 594 (Colo. 2008); Kaye, Statistical Evidence of Discrimination, 77 J. Am. Stat. Ass'n 773, 780 (1982). There can be other statistical evidence of discrimination in a selection process. A particular pattern in the assignment of jurors can be suspicious. United States ex rel. Barksdale v. Blackburn,

610 F.2d at 268–69; Kaye, Statistical Evidence of Discrimination in Jury Selection, *in* Statistical Methods in Discrimination Litigation 13 (D.H. Kaye & Mikel Aickin, eds. 1986).

[10]Swain v. Alabama, 380 U.S. 202, 85 S. Ct. 824, 13 L. Ed. 2d 759 (1965); Finkelstein, The Application of Statistical Decision Theory to Jury Discrimination Cases, 80 Harv. L. Rev. 338 (1966).

[11]*E.g.*, Moultrie v. Martin, 690 F.2d 1078, 1082–83 (4th Cir. 1982) (stating that hypothesis testing is mandatory for any statistical demonstration of racial discrimination). This rule is criticized in Kaye, Is Proof of Statistical Significance Relevant?, 61 Wash. L. Rev. 1333 (1986), and Kaye, Hypothesis Testing in the Courtroom, *in* Contributions to the Theory and Practice of Statistics (Gelfand ed. 1986). In addition, the statistical analysis undertaken by the *Moultrie* court is questioned on technical grounds in Finkelstein & Levin, Statistics for Lawyers (2d ed. 2001), and Kaye, Statistical Evidence of Discrimination in Jury Selection, *in* Statistical Methods in Discrimination Litigation 13 (D.H. Kaye & Mikel Aickin, eds. 1986).

eligible population. The alternative to this hypothesis is not always specified clearly, but it usually amounts to the claim that the chance of picking a protected class member is not equal to the population proportion.[12] The statistical analyst calculates the probability that so few members of the protected class would be chosen for jury service if each selection were made by the random process described above. This probability is called a "*p*-value." It states the chance that a disparity at least as large as the one observed would come about as a matter of bad luck or coincidence. The *p*-value thus expresses how improbable or surprising the extreme outcome is when null hypothesis is true. If the *p*-value is very small, it is taken to indicate that the null hypothesis is implausible.[13] If the *p*-value is large, it is taken to indicate that this hypothesis is consistent with the data. The *p*-value thus serves as an index of the statistical force of the quantitative evidence—the smaller the *p*-value, the more unlikely it is that the statistical disparity was the result of the chance process. It should be noted, however, that even though small *p*-values are needed to reject the null hypothesis (coincidence) as implausible, the *p*-value does not directly measure the probability of coincidence. Confusing the probability that the disparity would arise simply by coincidence with the probability that coincidence is in fact the explanation for the disparity is so common[14] that it goes by its own name—the transposition fallacy.[15]

---

[12]Whether they are stated or not, only two such alternative hypotheses are ever considered in the mathematical analysis described here. A "one-sided" hypothesis states that the chance for selecting any member of the protected class for jury duty is less than the population proportion. In contrast, a "two-sided" hypothesis does not state on which side of the population proportion the true probability of selection falls. It only asserts that the individual selection probability differs from the population proportion. A "one-tailed" test considers the one-sided alternative; a "two-tailed" test uses the two-sided alternative. Both these alternative hypotheses are stated within the context of the probability model that posits independent random selections of jurors with the same chance of selection for members of the protected class every time. In employment discrimination cases a few courts have disapproved of one-tailed testing. *E.g.*, Palmer v. Shultz, 815 F.2d 84 (D.C. Cir. 1987). This position seems overdrawn. In re Phenylpropanolamine (PPA) Products Liability Litigation, 289 F. Supp. 2d 1230, 1241 (W.D. Wash. 2003); Kaye, Is Proof of Statistical Significance Relevant?, 61 Wash. L. Rev. 1333, 1358 n. 113 (1986).

[13]Procedurally, this will result in the statistics on underrepresentation being said to establish a prima facie case of discrimination, at least if there is some other evidence suggesting discrimination or the opportunity to discriminate. Most commentators agree that a gross disparity that cannot plausibly be explained by the null hypothesis should be enough, in itself, to establish the prima facie case. *See* Kaye, Statistical Evidence of Discrimination, 77 J. Am. Stat. Ass'n 773, 776 (1982).

[14]*E.g.*, H.B. Rowe Co., Inc. v. Tippett, 615 F.3d 233, 245 (4th Cir.

The *p*-value is by no means the only quantity that indicates the strength of statistical evidence. For various reasons, some statisticians and scientists do not think that it is the best.[16] One problem with its use in court is the tendency of some expert witnesses or judges to assume that because there is an arbitrary convention of insisting on *p*-values of .05 or less before labeling scientific findings "statistically significant," this same number should be required before the factfinder may rely on the quantitative results.[17] If the *p*-value is not to be misleading, its meaning must be clearly understood.[18] The factfinder must realize that the *p*-value is not itself evidence. Neither is it a statement of how

---

2010) ("[T]he t-value of 3.99 . . . was statistically significant at a 95 percent confidence [sic] level. In other words, there was at least a 95 percent probability that prime contractors' under-utilization of African American subcontractors was not the result of mere chance"); Yorkey v. Diab, 601 F.3d 1279, 1284 (Fed. Cir. 2010) ("[T]he standard confidence [sic] level of p < 0.05 indicates at least a 95% probability that a significant statistical relationship does not exist between two sets of values."); Brown v. Nucor Corp., 576 F.3d 149, 156 (4th Cir. 2009) ("a .05 level of significance, i.e., there is only a 5% probability that the result is due to chance"); In re Ephedra Products Liability Litigation, 393 F. Supp. 2d 181, 191 (S.D. N.Y. 2005) ("P = .05 means that there is one chance in twenty that a result showing increased risk was caused by a sampling error."); In re Phenylpropanolamine (PPA) Products Liability Litigation, 289 F. Supp. 2d 1230, 1236 n.1 (W.D. Wash. 2003) ("P-values measure the probability that the reported association was due to chance"); Washington v. People, 186 P.3d 594, 597 (Colo. 2008) ("the likelihood that the underrepresentation of African–Americans on jury panels . . . occurred by chance was 0.008%"); King v. Burlington Northern Santa Fe Ry. Co., 277 Neb. 203, 762 N.W.2d 24, 38 (2009) ("A significance level of .05 presents a 5-percent probability that researchers observed an association because of chance variations.") (footnote and later clarification omitted).

[15]*See* Kaye et al., The New Wigmore, A Treatise on Evidence: Expert Evidence § 12.12.8.2(b) (2d ed. 2011). See infra § 210.

[16]Barnette, Comparative Statistical Inference (3d ed. 1999); Edwards; Likelihood: An Account of the Statistical Concept of Likelihood and its Application to Scientific Inference (1972); Royall, Statistical Evidence: A Likelihood Paradigm (1997); Fienberg, Comment: The Increasing Sophistication of Statistical Assessments of Evidence in Discrimination Litigation, 77 J. Am. Stat. Ass'n 784 (1982); Peter R. Killeen, An Alternative to Null-Hypothesis Significance Tests, 16 Psych. Sci. 345 (2005); Natrella, The Relationship Between Confidence Intervals and Tests of Significance, 14 Am. Statistician 20 (1960).

[17]*See, e.g.,* Castaneda v. Partida, 430 U.S. 482, 496 n.17, 97 S. Ct. 1272, 51 L. Ed. 2d 498 (1977); Moultrie v. Martin, 690 F.2d 1078, 1082–83 (4th Cir. 1982).

[18]The writing and testimony of experts does not always provide a satisfactory explanation. Some presentations use technical terms like "significance" and "confidence" in ways that suggest that a statistician can tell a court or jury how certain it can be of one or another conclusion. Braun, Statistics and the Law: Hypothesis Testing and Its Application to Title VII Cases, 32 Hastings L.J. 59, 87 (1980) ("the techniques developed in this article, when properly applied, are irrefutable in what they demonstrate.

large the observed underrepresentation is.[19] It is merely one measure of the probative force of statistical evidence, and an incomplete measure at that.[20] This is not to deny that it is a useful concept. Properly understood, it may assist the court or jury in assessing the statistical evidence.

This approach also is used in employment discrimination cases.[21] There is more difficulty in defining the relevant population from which employees are drawn,[22] there are more variables

When led to a rejection of the null hypothesis at a level of significance of .05, a court can be 95% confident that a disparity of treatment of the relevant groups exists."). But concepts of significance and confidence do not translate so easily into statements about beliefs. Shafer, A Theory of Evidence (1976). See supra § 208 (explaining the meaning of a confidence interval). It could be argued that to avoid misleading a jury, experts should not be permitted to speak of a "confidence" level. Kaye, Is Proof of Statistical Significance Relevant?, 61 Wash. L. Rev. 1333 (1986).

[19]U.S. v. LaChance, 788 F.2d 856, 865–66 (2d Cir. 1986) (mean number of allegedly excluded jurors small when measured per grand jury panel); McCleskey v. Kemp, 753 F.2d 877, 897–98 (11th Cir. 1985) (statistically significant logistic regression coefficient demonstrating increased probability of capital sentence for killers of whites did not show sufficient disparity to demonstrate unconstitutionality); Washington v. People, 186 P.3d 594 (Colo. 2008) (highly statistically significant disparities were too small to constitute a violation of the constitution; however, the court ordered a change in the selection procedure); Kaye et al., The New Wigmore, A Treatise on Evidence: Expert Evidence § 12.8.2(c) (2d ed. 2011).

[20]It is incomplete because it speaks only to the risk of an erroneous finding for the plaintiff conditional on the null hypothesis. Barnette, Comparative Statistical Inference (3d ed. 1999); Henkel & McKeown, Unlawful Discrimination and Statistical

Proof: An Analysis, 22 Jurimetrics J. 34 (1981); Kaye, The Numbers Game: Statistical Inference in Discrimination Cases, 80 Mich. L. Rev. 833, 844 n. 41 (1982) (book review); Kaye, Statistical Significance and the Burden of Persuasion, 46 Law & Contemp. Prob. 13 (1983).

[21]E.g., Hazelwood School Dist. v. U.S., 433 U.S. 299, 97 S. Ct. 2736, 53 L. Ed. 2d 768 (1977) (using $z$-statistics but not giving the corresponding $p$-values); N.A.A.C.P. v. North Hudson Regional Fire & Rescue, 665 F.3d 464, 472 (3d Cir. 2011), cert. denied, 132 S. Ct. 2749, 183 L. Ed. 2d 616 (2012) (prima facie case of disparate impact of a municipal residency requirement for firefighters was established by large disparity between proportions of African-Americans in the regional labor force and the proportion in the local fire department when the $p$-value was so small as to leave " 'virtually no probability' that the discrepancies are the result of chance"); Latino Officers Ass'n City of New York, Inc. v. City of New York, 558 F.3d 159 (2d Cir. 2009) (disparities unconvincing in the absence of a significance test); Segar v. Smith, 738 F.2d 1249 (D.C. Cir. 1984).

[22]E.g., Wards Cove Packing Co., Inc. v. Atonio, 490 U.S. 642, 109 S. Ct. 2115, 104 L. Ed. 2d 733 (1989); N.A.A.C.P. v. North Hudson Regional Fire & Rescue, 665 F.3d 464, 473–74 (3d Cir. 2011), cert. denied, 132 S. Ct. 2749, 183 L. Ed. 2d 616 (2012); Hemmings v. Tidyman's Inc., 285 F.3d 1174, 1185–87 (9th Cir. 2002); Gastwirth, Statistical Reasoning in Law and Public Policy (1988); Shoben, Defining the Relevant Population in Employ-

to consider,[23] the sample sizes tend to be smaller,[24] and the mechanics of computing $p$-values may differ,[25] but the meaning of the $p$-value and of "statistical significance" is the same.[26] When complicated statistical models are used to account for the effects

---

ment Discrimination Cases, in Kaye & Aickin, Statistical Methods in Discrimination Litigation 55 (1986).

[23]*E.g.*, Ste. Marie v. Eastern R. Ass'n, 650 F.2d 395, 400–01 (2d Cir. 1981) (failure to account for differences in qualifications of male and female employees made statistics with vanishingly small $p$-values "totally wanting in probative value"); Pouncy v. Prudential Ins. Co. of America, 668 F.2d 795, 803 (5th Cir. 1982) ("appellant's statistical evidence is deficient because it 'fails to take into account the fact that a number of factors operate simultaneously to influence the amount of salary [an employee] receives.' . . . The discrepancies between the mean salary of black employees and the mean salary of white employees hired in specific years may be explained by . . . different job levels, different skill levels, previous training, and experience: all may account for unequal salaries in an environment free of discrimination"); Adams v. Ameritech Services, Inc., 231 F.3d 414, 424 (7th Cir. 2000) (study admissible despite omission of certain variables); Coble v. Hot Springs School Dist. No. 6, 682 F.2d 721, 730–33 (8th Cir. 1982) (because "the probative value of appellant's statistical data is undermined by the small sample size for promotions and the failure to [use regression analysis to] consider the effect of education and experience together on salary," no prima facie case was established). *But see* Bazemore v. Friday, 478 U.S. 385, 106 S. Ct. 3000, 92 L. Ed. 2d 315 (1986) ("plainly incorrect" to refuse to credit a regression study that did not include "all measurable variables thought to have an effect on salary level," since the study had substantial probative value); Kaye, Statistical Evidence: How to Avoid the "Diderot Effect," 2 Inside Litigation 21 (1988).

[24]Some courts have implied that a small sample size makes a $p$-value or confidence interval less meaningful. Rivera v. City of Wichita Falls, 665 F.2d 531, 536 n.7 (5th Cir. 1982) ('the application of probability theories to samples as limited as 35 is, of itself, problematic'); Equal Employment Opportunity Commission v. American Nat. Bank, 652 F.2d 1176, 1193 n.12 (4th Cir. 1981); Coble v. Hot Springs School Dist. No. 6, 682 F.2d 721, 730 (8th Cir. 1982). This view seems misguided. *Cf.* E.E.O.C. v. Steamship Clerks Union, Local 1066, 48 F.3d 594, 604 (1st Cir. 1995) (" '[e]ven small samples are not per se unacceptable' "). A small sample size merely affects the method of computing these quantities and reduces the ability of the statistical test to discriminate between the hypotheses. In technical terms, the smaller sample size diminishes the power of the test—it has less of an a priori chance of detecting a true difference. At the same time, choosing to reject the null hypothesis if the $p$-value is less than some fixed number (the significance level) creates the same risk of a false positive (an incorrect decision that would favor the plaintiff) whatever the sample size may be. Therefore, the smaller sample size only increases the risk of a false negative (an incorrect decision for the defendant), and a very small $p$-value is indicative of a real result for a small sample, just as it is for a large one.

[25]Kaye, Hypergeometric Confusion in the Fourth Circuit, 26 Jurimetrics J. 215 (1986); Sugrue & Fairley, A Case of Unexamined Assumptions: The Use and Misuse of the Statistical Analysis of Castaneda/Hazelwood in Discrimination Litigation, 24 B.C. L. Rev. 925 (1983).

[26]When discriminatory intent is an element in the cause of action, and when this intent cannot be established

of many variables, however, many subtle errors are possible,[27] and an uncritical acceptance of the estimates derived from these models and their calculated $p$-values can be dangerous.[28] In short, for this form of scientific testimony, the battle is not usually over the admissibility of statistical evidence in general or over the use of concepts like the $p$-value to assess the evidence.[29] Rather, the battlelines are drawn when it comes to the admissibility of obviously flawed applications,[30] to the weight that should be given the

---

solely by proof of disparate impact, the legal significance of the statistical data and, hence, of any $p$-value is attenuated.

[27]Aickin, Issues and Methods in Discrimination Litigation, in Statistical Methods in Discrimination Litigation 211 (Kaye & Aickin eds., 1986); Peterson, Pitfalls in the Use of Regression Analysis for the Measurement of Equal Employment Opportunity, 5 Int'l J. Policy Analysis & Information Systems 43 (1981). Regression models are not the only techniques for multivariate analysis, and any $p$-value or confidence interval for an estimate derived from a regression model rests on a set of restrictive assumptions that may not hold in practice. Kaye & Freedman, Reference Guide to Statistics, in Reference Manual on Scientific Evidence 211 (Federal Judicial Center & Comm. on the Third Edition of the Reference Manual on Scientific Evidence, Nat'l Research Council eds., 3d ed. 2011). Consequently, in some cases another approach may be superior. Greiner, Causal Inference in Civil Rights Litigation, 122 Harv. L. Rev. 533 (2008).

[28]Given enough latitude in the number of variables and the form of a statistical model, a statistician eventually can construct a particular model that will fit the data remarkably well and have low $p$-values for the quantities of interest. This same model easily can be worthless in the sense that it probably would not work well with any other data. Yet, models with as many as 128 variables have been relied on in court. The Evolving Role of Statistical Assessments as Evidence

in the Courts (Fienberg ed., 1988). Another problem is the tendency of some courts to misuse the descriptive statistic R-squared when, as is almost always the case, there are statistics or $p$-values that are much more to the point. *See, e.g.,* Valentino v. U.S. Postal Service, 511 F. Supp. 917, 944 (D.D.C. 1981) (defendant's model said to give a better estimate of a regression coefficient merely because it "measured many more variables" and yielded a larger R-squared).

[29]*But see* Kadane, A Statistical Analysis of Adverse Impact of Employer Decisions, 85 J. Am. Stat. Ass'n 925 (1990); Comment, Legal Standards and Statistical Proof in Title VII Litigation: In Search of a Coherent Disparate Impact Model, 139 U. Pa. L. Rev. 455 (1990).

[30]Munoz v. Orr, 200 F.3d 291 (5th Cir. 2000) (plaintiffs' expert's statistical analysis properly excluded as unreliable under *Daubert* for problems ranging "from particular miscalculations to his general approach to the analysis" including tables that did not add to anywhere near 100%, failure to do regression and thereby account for pertinent variables); People Who Care v. Rockford Bd. of Educ., School Dist. No. 205, 111 F.3d 528, 537–38 (7th Cir. 1997) (under *Daubert*, "a statistical study that fails to correct for salient explanatory variables, or even to make the most elementary comparisons, has no value as causal explanation and is therefore inadmissible in a federal court"); Sheehan v. Daily Racing Form, Inc., 104 F.3d 940, 942 (7th Cir. 1997) ("failure to exercise the degree of care that a statistician would

evidence,[31] and to transforming methods and conventions of statistical inference into rules of law.[32]

## IV.  PROBABILITIES AS EVIDENCE

### § 210   Identification evidence, generally

The previous two sections discussed the use of probability calculations in connection with statistical studies. When the statistical analyst takes properly collected sample data, computes statistics such as a proportion, a difference between two means, or a regression coefficient, and calculates a $p$-value or a confidence interval for each such statistic, the courts are willing to rely on the probabilities in assessing the force of the statistical evidence. Especially in criminal cases, however, the courts are more reluctant to admit probability calculations intended to show the identity of a wrongdoer.[1] This section examines the admissibility of probability calculations relating to the myriad forms of identification evidence—eyewitness testimony, DNA tests, fingerprints, bitemarks, questioned document examinations,

---

use in his scientific work, outside of the context of litigation" rendered a statistical analysis that failed to account for an obvious confounding variable inadmissible under *Daubert*).

[31]Valuable suggestions from a distinguished panel of judges, lawyers, professors and statisticians for improving the process by which statistical testimony is generated and evaluated are developed in The Evolving Role of Statistical Assessments as Evidence in the Courts (Fienberg ed., 1988). *See also* Kaye, Improving Legal Statistics, 34 Law & Soc'y 301 (1991) (elaborating on a few of these recommendations, especially those designed to narrow statistical disputes prior to trial).

[32]*Compare* Palmer v. Shultz, 815 F.2d 84, 96 n.3 (D.C. Cir. 1987) ("we do not believe that we can allow the threshold at which statistical evidence alone raises an inference of discrimination to be lower than 1.96 standard deviations"), *with* Gay v. Waiters' and Dairy Lunchmen's Union, Local No. 30, 694 F.2d 531, 551–53 (9th Cir. 1982) ("It would be improper to posit a quantitative threshold above which statistical evidence of racial impact is sufficient as a matter of law to infer

discriminatory intent, and below which it is insufficient as a matter of law"), *and* DeLuca by DeLuca v. Merrell Dow Pharmaceuticals, Inc., 911 F.2d 941 (3d Cir. 1990) (expert may present opinion that drug causes birth defects despite epidemiologic studies with $p>.05$). *See generally* Kaye & Freedman, Reference Guide to Statistics, in Reference Manual on Scientific Evidence 211 (Federal Judicial Center & Comm. on the Third Edition of the Reference Manual on Scientific Evidence, Nat'l Research Council eds., 3d ed. 2011); Lempert, Statistics in the Courtroom: Building on Rubinfeld, 85 Colum. L. Rev. 1098, 1098–99 (1985) ("For a decade I have questioned the unthinking use of the .05 level of statistical significance to evaluate the importance of empirical research results to legal proceedings"); Monahan & Walker, Social Facts: Scientific Methodology as Legal Precedent, 76 Cal. L. Rev. 877 (1988) (criticizing *Palmer*).

**[Section 210]**

[1]*See* Admissibility, in criminal case, of statistical or mathematical evidence offered for purpose of showing probabilities, 36 A.L.R.3d 1194.

microanalysis, and so on.[2] The next section focuses on the role of probability calculations in paternity litigation.

At the outset, two preliminary points of clarification may be helpful. First, although the phrase "probability evidence" is a convenient shorthand for testimony or argument involving probability calculations, the term is something of a misnomer. The probabilities are not themselves evidence. They are numbers ranging from zero to one that may be used in drawing conclusions from the statistical or other evidence.[3] The topic of this section is whether or when overtly attaching a probability number to identification evidence is permissible. A somewhat different question is whether statistical evidence alone is sufficient to support a verdict. Psychologists have detected an aversion to decisions based on "naked statistical evidence" under certain conditions,[4] and philosophers and legal commentators have presented theories to justify or to counter the apparent opposition of some courts to verdicts that seem to rest exclusively on naked statistical evidence.[5] Positions have ranged from denying that there is any generally accepted rule of law precluding such verdicts, to offering economic (incentive-based) justifications for such a rule, to opposing verdicts based on an explicit probability for fear that they will undermine the expressive function of verdicts, to reconceptualizing the burden of persuasion, to positing unconventional theories of probability.[6]

Second, it should be clear that any global objection to using

---

[2] For descriptions of or references to the techniques of scientific criminology, see supra § 207. Probability calculations also are offered to show identity in civil cases. Brook, The Use of Statistical Evidence of Identification in Civil Litigation, 29 St. Louis U. L.J. 293 (1985); Meier & Zabell, Benjamin Pierce and the Howland Will, 75 J. Am. Stat. Ass'n 497 (1980). Compare supra § 209 (probabilities used in inferring causation).

[3] When counsel use such numbers as rhetorical flourishes to emphasize the strength of the evidence, no question of the admissibility of evidence is raised. Hicks, Famous Jury Speeches 216–29 (1925) (in arguing that a document was not authentic, counsel told the jury to "[t]ake up your table of logarithms and figure away until you are blind, and such an accident could not happen in as many thousand, billion, trillion, quintillion years as you

can express by figures"). Of course, the arguments may be objectionably misleading or unfair, and we shall encounter some examples of dubious closing arguments in a later note.

[4] Niedermeier et al., Jurors' Use of Naked Statistical Evidence: Exploring Bases and Implications of the Wells Effect, 76 J. Personality & Social Psychol. 533 (1999); Wells, Naked Statistical Evidence of Liability: Is Subjective Probability Enough?, 62 J. Personality & Social Psychol. 739 (1992). The phrase "naked statistical evidence" may have originated in Kaye, Naked Statistical Evidence, 89 Yale L. J. 601 (1980) (book review).

[5] For a review and critique of the epistemological theorizing, see Pundik, The Epistemology of Statistical Evidence, 15 Int'l J. Evid. & Proof 117 (2011).

[6] See, e.g., U.S. v. Hannigan, 27 F.3d 890, 895 (3d Cir. 1994) (Becker,

group statistics to draw inferences on individual instances is untenable. Courts sometimes suggest that evidence about a class of objects cannot be used to support a conclusion about a particular member of the class—especially when the inference concerns personal behavior.[7] When it comes to inanimate objects, however, the courts are much quicker to recognize the usefulness of generalizations derived from the experience of others. For example, government statistical reports showing that Volkswagen vans are more likely to eject occupants in an accident than are other vans are readily admissible.[8] A statistician might try to reconcile these intuitions by reasoning that the group-based judgments about people are weaker because there is more variability among human beings or the circumstances they confront than there is among mere objects like Volkswagen vans.[9] But surely this depends on the characteristics in question. People are very similar in some dimensions and highly variable in others. So are Volkswagen vans. And even as to the highly variable features, it seems hard to deny that the statistical evidence as to people is relevant under Rule 402.[10]

A more convincing explanation for resistance to the introduction of probabilities derived from experience with groups of

---

J., concurring); Cohen, The Probable and the Provable 74 (1977) (proposing an ordinal theory of probability); Allen, Rationality, Mythology and the "Acceptability of Verdicts" Thesis, 66 B.U. L. Rev. 541 (1986); Brook, The Use of Statistical Evidence of Identification in Civil Litigation: Well-Worn Hypotheticals, Real Cases, and Controversy, 29 St. Louis U. L.J. 293 (1985); Kaye, The Limits of the Preponderance of the Evidence Standard: Justifiable Naked Statistical Evidence and Multiple Causation, 1982 Am. Bar Foundation Research J. 487; Nance, Allocating the Risk of Error: Its Role in the Theory of Evidence Law, 13 Leg. Theory 129 (2007); Nesson, The Evidence or the Event? On Judicial Proof and the Acceptability of Verdicts, 98 Harv. L. Rev. 1357 (1985).

[7] U.S. v. Shonubi, 103 F.3d 1085 (2d Cir. 1997) (evidence of the quantities of heroin swallowed in balloons by other drug smugglers was not adequate in proving that defendant smuggled more than 1 kilogram of heroin over eight smuggling trips from Nigeria); U.S. v. Rangel-Gonzales, 617

F.2d 529, 532 (9th Cir. 1980) (that very few aliens, when advised of right to consult with Consulate, do so, "would not appear to have any bearing on what this particular individual would have done"); Koehler, When Do Courts Think Base Rate Statistics Are Relevant?, 42 Jurimetrics J. 373 (2002).

[8] Seese v. Volkswagenwerk A.G., 648 F.2d 833, 846 (3d Cir. 1981).

[9] *Cf.* United States v. Rangel-Gonzales, 617 F.2d at 532 n. 3 ("the party offering the evidence must at least show that the conduct of others . . . occurred in comparable circumstances"); Dorsey v. State, 276 Md. 638, 350 A.2d 665, 669 (1976) (manifest error to permit a detective to testify that 75–80% of his robbery arrests led to convictions, in part because of "the absence of any showing of similarity between the appellant's arrest and those other investigations").

[10] *See* Kaye, Paradoxes, Gedanken Experiments and the Burden of Proof, 1981 Ariz. L.J. 635, 639–40; supra § 185

individuals might be that where the statistical indicators pertain to volitional conduct, the courts are cautious because they place great weight on a conception of human autonomy and dignity that the coldly statistical analysis would undermine. To put it another way, shying away from the statistical predictions reflects a belief that everyone should have the opportunity to depart from the statistical norm.[11]

This more refined and overtly normative theory does not deny the truism that all evidence is statistical or probabilistic.[12] Plainly, we rely on generalizations derived from experience with other members of the same group all the time. Law schools admit students with high grades and test scores in part because other students with these credentials have achieved success. Banks issue credit cards based on ratings that reflect the behavior of other individuals. Surgeons perform drastic operations on patients because other patients have experienced beneficial effects in the past. Legislatures enact statutes making it an offense to drive with a blood alcohol concentration exceeding an amount seen to impair the functioning of a sample of persons. Juries tend to convict or acquit defendants because of hunches or beliefs about how certain classes of people behave, and they award dam-

---

[11]*Cf.* Underwood, Law and the Crystal Ball: Predicting Behavior with Statistical Inference and Individualized Judgment, 88 Yale L.J. 1408 (1979). *But see* Hamer, Civil Standard of Proof Uncertainty: Probability, Belief and Justice, 16 U. Sydney L. Rev. 506, 534 (1994) (autonomy is no basis for a rule against statistical evidence).

[12]U.S. v. Veysey, 334 F.3d 600, 606 (7th Cir. 2003) ("Statistical evidence is merely probabilistic evidence coded in numbers rather than words."); Riordan v. Kempiners, 831 F.2d 690, 698 (7th Cir. 1987) ("All evidence is probabilistic—statistical evidence merely explicitly so"); DePass v. U.S., 721 F.2d 203, 207 (7th Cir. 1983) (dissenting opinion) ("most knowledge, and almost all legal evidence is probabilistic . . . and probabilities that are derived from statistical studies are no less reliable in general than the probabilities that are derived from direct observation, from intuition, or from case studies of a single person or event"); David Rosenberg, The Causal Connection in Mass Exposure Cases: A "Public Law" Vision of the Tort System, 97 Harv. L. Rev. 849, 870 (1984) ("The entire notion that "particularistic" evidence differs in some significant qualitative way from statistical evidence must be questioned. . . . 'Particularistic' evidence, however, is in fact no less probabilistic than is the statistical evidence that courts purport to shun. "Particularistic" evidence offers nothing more than a basis for conclusions about a perceived balance of probabilities.") (footnotes omitted); Saks & Kidd, Human Information Processing and Adjudication: Trial by Heuristics, 15 Law & Soc'y 123, 151–54 (1980–81) (decrying "the myth of particularized proof"). For further analysis, see Probability and Inference in the Law of Evidence: The Limits and Uses of Bayesianism (Tillers & Green eds., 1988); Koehler & Shaviro, Veridical Verdicts: Increasing Verdict Accuracy Through the Use of Overtly Probabilistic Evidence and Methods, 75 Cornell L. Rev. 247 (1990); Shaviro, Statistical-Probability Evidence and the Appearance of Justice, 103 Harv. L. Rev. 530–54 (1989).

ages in wrongful death cases with the assistance of mortality tables that reflect the experiences of many other men or women.[13] We are all guilty of such "profiling." We could not survive without it.[14]

So, too, any expert giving any opinion on whether the scientific test identifies the defendant as being the person who left the incriminating trace, such as a fingerprint, bullet, or bloodstain, necessarily bases this conclusion on an understanding or impression of how similar the items being compared are and how common it is to find items with these similarities.[15] If these beliefs have any basis in fact, it is to be found in the general experience of the criminalists or more exacting statistical studies of these matters.[16] In brief, the reluctance to allow testimony or argument about probabilities must be justified, if at all, on the basis of something other than an undifferentiated claim about the logical or epistemological weakness of relying on probabilities derived from statistics about other persons or things. In fact, more conventional concerns about probability evidence surface in the decisions in this area. These relate to the probative value of the explicit quantification and the tendency of the seemingly impressive numbers to mislead or confuse the jury.[17]

To begin with, for more than a hundred years there have been

---

[13]*See also* Lewis v. N.J. Riebe Enterprises, Inc., 170 Ariz. 384, 825 P.2d 5 (1992) (permissible to consider the fact that many carpenters are unemployed three months out the year in arriving at damages for an injured carpenter).

[14]*See* Schauer, Profiles, Probabilities, and Stereotypes (2003).

[15]*See* Com. v. Drayton, 386 Mass. 39, 434 N.E.2d 997, 1005 (1982).

[16]*See* Aitken & Taroni, Statistics and the Evaluation of Evidence for Forensic Scientists (2d ed. 2004); Robertson & Vignaux, Interpreting Evidence: Evaluating Forensic Science in the Courtroom (1995); NIST Expert Working Group on Human Factors in Latent Print Analysis, Latent Print Examination and Human Factors: Improving the Practice Through a Systems Approach (Kaye ed. 2012).

[17]The leading exposition of these concerns is Tribe, Trial by Mathematics: Precision and Ritual in the Legal Process, 84 Harv. L. Rev. 1329 (1971). *See also* Broun & Kelly, Playing the

Percentages and the Law of Evidence, 1970 U. Ill. L.F. 23 (1970). For commentary arguing that these dangers are overstated, see Kaye & Koehler, Can Jurors Understand Probabilistic Evidence?, 154 J. Royal Stat. Soc'y Series A 75 (1991); Koehler & Shaviro, Veridical Verdicts: Increasing Verdict Accuracy Through the Use of Overtly Probabilistic Evidence and Methods, 75 Cornell L. Rev. 247 (1990); Saks & Kidd, Human Information Processing and Adjudication: Trial by Heuristics, 15 Law & Soc'y 123, 151–54 (1980–81); Thompson, Are Juries Competent to Evaluate Statistical Evidence?, 52 Law & Contemp. Prob. 9 (1989); Wagner, Book Review, 1979 Duke L.J. 1071. A related argument, mentioned earlier, is that if the probability evidence is all there is to go on, it may force a quantification, and thence a degradation, of the burden of persuasion or the presumption of innocence. *See* Nesson, The Evidence or the Event?, On Judicial Proof and the Acceptability of Verdicts, 98 Harv. L. Rev. 1357 (1985); Nesson, Reasonable Doubt and Permissive Inferences, 92

attempts to compute the probability of observing a conjunction of certain incriminating characteristics by assuming that each characteristic is statistically independent and that the probabilities of these presumably independent characteristics could be obtained by introspection.[18] In the most notorious of these cases,[19] *People v. Collins*,[20] police apprehended a man and a woman fitting descriptions supplied by eyewitnesses near the scene of a robbery. The prosecutor proposed figures for the frequencies of such things as an interracial couple in a car, a girl with a pony tail, a partly yellow automobile, a man with a mustache, and so on. A mathematics professor testified to the rule that the joint probability of a series of independent events is the product of the probabilities of each event. Applying this rule to the "conservative estimates" that he had propounded, the prosecutor concluded that there was but one chance in 12 million that any couple possessed the distinctive characteristics of the defendants, and he argued that "the chances of anyone else

---

Harv. L. Rev. 1187 (1978). Tribe, Trial by Mathematics: Precision and Ritual in the Legal Process, 84 Harv. L. Rev. 1329 (1971).

[18]Miller v. State, 240 Ark. 340, 399 S.W.2d 268, 270 (1966) (taking the probability that two randomly selected soil samples would have the same color to be 1/10, that they would have the same texture to be 1/100, and the same density, 1/1000, the expert testified that "[o]n random basis when you get two samples to match all these, it would be one in one million"); People v. Collins, 68 Cal. 2d 319, 66 Cal. Rptr. 497, 438 P.2d 33 (1968); People v. Risley, 214 N.Y. 75, 108 N.E. 200, 203 (1915) (expert calculated that the probability of defendant's typewriter producing letters with peculiarities that matched those on an allegedly forged document was "one in four thousand million"); *cf.* Hicks v. Scurr, 671 F.2d 255, 258 (8th Cir. 1982) (probability of another individual having similar fingerprints said to be "one in approximately seven million"); Com. v. Drayton, 386 Mass. 39, 434 N.E.2d 997, 1005 (1982) (fingerprint examiner stated on re-direct examination that the probability that prints with 12 points of similarity could be made by

two different people was "one out of 387 trillion"); State v. Sneed, 76 N.M. 349, 414 P.2d 858 (1966) (expert's calculation of 240 billion to one odds for a combination of characteristics, including the use of the alias "Robert Crosset," was improperly admitted even though there was some empirical basis (including an examination of the frequencies of names in a telephone directory) for the probabilities that were multiplied together, because "the validity of the estimates [had] not been demonstrated"); Meier & Zabell, Benjamin Pierce and the Howland Will, 75 J. Am. Stat. Ass'n 497 (1980) (testimony in 1867 that 30 matches in the strokes of a contested signature on a will revealed that it had been traced, since the probability of so many matches arising by chance was "once in 2,666 millions of millions of millions").

[19]For colorful information on the case, see Fisher, Evidence 70–74 (2d ed. 2008); Kaye, The Double Helix and the Law of Evidence 24–25 (2011).

[20]People v. Collins, 68 Cal. 2d 319, 66 Cal. Rptr. 497, 438 P.2d 33 (1968).

besides these defendants being there, . . . having every similarity, . . . is something like one in a billion."[21]

In *People v. Collins* and other such cases, the appellate courts hold that it is error to admit such testimony on the ground that the hypothesized values that are multiplied together are sheer speculation.[22] In addition, *Collins* and opinions in similar cases decry the use of the multiplication rule on the ground that the events are obviously far from independent.[23] Because the fallacious computations and are presented in the guise of expert analysis, they are excluded under the principle that their prejudicial impact clearly outweighs their probative value.[24]

In another group of cases, there are some data for calculating

---

[21]Collins, 438 P.2d at 37.

[22]Miller v. State, 240 Ark. 340, 399 S.W.2d 268, 270 (1966) ("Dr. Mathews had made no tests on which he could reasonably base his probabilities . . . nor did he base his testimony on studies of such tests made by others;" hence "[a]dmission of the unsubstantiated, speculative testimony on probabilities was clearly erroneous"); People v. Risley, 214 N.Y. 75, 108 N.E. 200 (1915) ("The statement of the witness was not based upon actual observed data, but was simply speculative"); *cf.* Branion v. Gramly, 855 F.2d 1256 (7th Cir. 1988) (speculative probability calculation in defendant's brief).

[23]As applied in *Collins*, this criticism of the probability calculation is not as powerful as it first might appear to be. A more general formula for computing the probability of a joint event is available when the conjoined events are dependent; it too involves multiplying a series of probabilities. Since one could apply this more appropriate formula to suitably manufactured probabilities to reach the same result, the use of the multiplication rule is the lesser of the two evils. *See* Fairley & Mosteller, A Conversation About *Collins*, 41 U. Chi. L. Rev. 242 (1974); Finkelstein & Fairley, A Bayesian Approach to Identification Evidence, 83 Harv. L. Rev. 489 (1970).

[24]Occasionally, prosecutors will manufacture probabilities and multiply them à la *Collins* to argue that the chance of a coincidental misidentification is negligible. At least one court has held that such expositions are not improper—coming from the prosecutor rather than an expert witness. Roach v. State, 451 N.E.2d 388, 391–93 (Ind. Ct. App. 1983) (prosecutor, using blackboard, concluded that "the possibility that all these things happened" was "[o]ne in ten million"); *cf.* Rowan v. Owens, 752 F.2d 1186, 1188 (7th Cir. 1984) (*Collins*-like computation on the part of appellate court reviewing the sufficiency of the evidence); People v. Redman, 135 Ill. App. 3d 534, 90 Ill. Dec. 361, 481 N.E.2d 1272 (4th Dist. 1985) (prosecutor's mistaken computation not reversible error in absence of contemporaneous objection); State v. Chavez, 100 N.M. 730, 676 P.2d 257 (Ct. App. 1983) (prosecutor's irrelevant computation not so fundamental an error as to require reversal in absence of contemporaneous objection). However, without a careful explanation of the relationship between the probability of a coincidental misidentification and the distinct probability that the defendant left the incriminating traces, a closing argument involving the multiplication of hypothetical probabilities is likely to mislead the jury. Even with a proper and complete exposition of the mathematical reasoning, the exposition may not have much value to many jurors. Accordingly, without a reasonable foundation for the frequencies in question, such quantitative argument should not be allowed.

the joint probability. While many forensic experts are content to describe the points of similarity between the incriminating traces and material taken from the defendant or his belongings and to leave it to the jury to decide how unlikely it would be to find all these similarities by mere coincidence,[25] from time to time, the experts testify to vanishingly small probabilities.[26] The appellate responses to estimates that have some empirical basis are more

---

[25]U.S. v. Hickey, 596 F.2d 1082, 1084, 1089 (1st Cir. 1979) (inspection of hairs revealed that the samples were "microscopically identical," and hence that the incriminating hairs "could have" been the defendant's); U.S. v. Cyphers, 553 F.2d 1064, 1071–72 (7th Cir. 1977) ("the expert's opinion that the hairs found on the items used in the robbery 'could have come' from the defendants was entitled to be admitted for whatever value the jury might give it"); U.S. v. Hicks, 103 F.3d 837, 846 (9th Cir. 1996) (overruled by, U.S. v. W.R. Grace, 526 F.3d 499 (9th Cir. 2008)) (testimony that DNA testing "only [showed] that Hicks could not be excluded as a contributor to the sample" was properly admitted); State v. West, 274 Conn. 605, 877 A.2d 787 (2005) (upholding microscopic hair comparisons when the criminalist explained that it is impossible to determine whether a particular hair fragment comes from a particular individual and that it is possible for two different individuals to have hair that is microscopically indistinguishable); State v. Washington, 229 Kan. 47, 622 P.2d 986, 988 (1981) (although foreign pubic hairs left on murder victim showed 21 microscopic similarities and no differences when compared to defendant's, expert was unable to say that the foreign hairs "came from [defendant] beyond any scientific doubt"); State v. Noel, 157 N.J. 141, 723 A.2d 602 (1999) (testimony as to a match in the elemental composition of bullets found in defendant's belongings, at the crime scene, and in the victim's body along with the examiner's opinion that randomly selected bullets would not match was admissible even though no statistics on the general percentage of

such matching bullets were presented).

[26]U.S. v. Massey, 594 F.2d 676, 679 (8th Cir. 1979) (expert testified that "the Canadians have done a study where they have come up with a chance of one in 4,500 these hairs could have come from another individual"); State v. Garrison, 120 Ariz. 255, 585 P.2d 563, 566–67 (1978) (expert testified that "the probability factor of two sets of teeth being identical in a case similar to this is, approximately, eight in one million"); Com. v. Drayton, 386 Mass. 39, 434 N.E.2d 997, 1005 (1982) (chance of two people leaving fingerprints that have 12 points of similarities is "one out of 387 trillion"); Wilson v. State, 370 Md. 191, 803 A.2d 1034, 1047 (2002) (physician obtained the figure of 1/100,000,000 by multiplication in a case involving two deaths in of infants in same family); State v. Coolidge, 109 N.H. 403, 260 A.2d 547, 559 (1969) (matches among particles of clothing would occur coincidentally with a probability of 1/1027); State v. Sneed, 76 N.M. 349, 414 P.2d 858 (1966) (240 billion to one odds for a combination of characteristics, including the use of the alias "Robert Crosset"); cf. People v. Trujillo, 32 Cal. 2d 105, 194 P.2d 681, 684 (1948) ("the chances were one in a hundred billion that this number of matches [among fibers from clothing] would be a coincidence"); Fienberg & Kaye, Legal and Statistical Aspects of Some Mysterious Clusters, 154 J. Royal Stat. Soc'y Series A 61 (1991) (reporting cases of expert testimony on clusters of deaths in hospitals or elsewhere said to have probabilities such as "9.1 in a trillion" in the absence of foul play). There have been cases in which the reported

---

divided.[27] When the probabilities of the individual characteristics or events are well founded, there are three possibilities regarding the joint events to consider—the events could be statistically independent, positively correlated (tending to occur together), or negatively correlated. When statistical independence is established, multiplication of the individual probabilities is allowed.[28] When the events seem positively correlated, however, the simple multiplication rule yields an excessively small probability, and admission of the testimony constitutes error.[29] When the underlying events or characteristics are negatively correlated, multiplication of the unconditional probabilities understates how improb-

---

population frequencies of DNA profiles are in the billionths, trillionths, quadrillionths, and beyond. *E.g.*, Snowden v. State, 574 So. 2d 960 (Ala. Crim. App. 1990) (" 'approximately one in eleven billion,' with a 'minimum value' of one in 2.5 billion and a 'maximum' value of one in 27 trillion"); Engram v. State, 341 Ark. 196, 15 S.W.3d 678 (2000) ("one in 600 trillion"); Com. v. Jones, 2002 PA Super 368, 811 A.2d 1057, 1061 (2002) (one in two quadrillion).

[27]*Compare* Massey, 594 F.2d at 679–81 (where an expert referred to a study indicating that the probability of matching hair samples by coincidence was 1/4500 but could not explain this study, it was plain error for the prosecutor to argue that the evidence was "better than 99.44 percent . . . better than Ivory soap, if you remember the commercial" because "[b]y using such misleading mathematical odds the prosecutor 'confuse[d] the probability of concurrence of the identifying marks with the probability of mistaken identification' "), *Wilson*, 803 A.2d at 1047 (infant deaths), *and* State v. Carlson, 267 N.W.2d 170 (Minn. 1978) (hair), *with* U. S. ex rel. DiGiacomo v. Franzen, 680 F.2d 515 (7th Cir. 1982) (hair); State v. Garrison, 120 Ariz. 255, 585 P.2d 563, 566–67 (1978); People v. Trujillo, 32 Cal. 2d 105, 194 P.2d 681, 685–86 (1948); Prewitt v. State, 819 N.E.2d 393 (Ind. Ct. App. 2004) (pathologist's testimony that only 4 in 10,000 suicides are forehead wounds of intermediate range); Coolidge, 260 A.2d at 558–61

(particles of clothing), rev'd on other grounds, 403 U.S. 443; State v. Clayton, 646 P.2d 723, 727 (Utah 1982) (probability testimony about hair admissible). For a synthesis of the cases, see Kaye, The Double Helix and the Law of Evidence 24–35 (2011).

When the probabilities are derived from studies that the expert is not prepared to defend, a hearsay objection may be effective. *See* State v. Scarlett, 121 N.H. 37, 426 A.2d 25, 28 (1981). See supra § 15; infra § 324.2. *But see* State v. Garrison, 120 Ariz. 255, 585 P.2d 563 (1978); State v. Clayton, 646 P.2d at 725–27.

[28]*E.g.*, U.S. v. Gwaltney, 790 F.2d 1378, 1381–82 (9th Cir. 1986); People v. Miller, 173 Ill. 2d 167, 219 Ill. Dec. 43, 670 N.E.2d 721 (1996).

[29]Wilson, 803 A.2d (error to multiply probabilities in a case involving two deaths in of infants in same family, since genetic factors might result in a higher incidence of multiple cases of Sudden Infant Death Syndrome (SIDS) within a family). A similarly naive calculation in the testimony of a former president of the Royal College of Paediatrics and Child Health in the United Kingdom provoked a public rebuke from the Royal Statistical Society, fueled arguments for a reversal of the mother's conviction, and led the General Medical Council to strike him from the medical register for gross professional misconduct. Gosline, Top Paediatrician Guilty of Professional Misconduct, New Scientist, July 15, 2005.

able the joint event is. As such, the conservative computation should be admissible to show that the event is improbable. In the exceptional case that finds error even in the admission of computations that the court considers well founded,[30] the rationale seems to be that the jury would misconstrue the meaning of the probability or overemphasize the number, or that it would be too difficult to explain its true meaning.[31]

---

[30]State v. Carlson, 267 N.W.2d 170, 175 (Minn. 1978), squarely held that it was error to admit a probability "based on empirical scientific data of unquestioned validity." Ironically, the study on which the probability estimates in that case were founded has since been impugned. See The Evolving Role of Statistical Assessments as Evidence in the Courts 64–67 (Fienberg ed., 1989); Aitken & Robertson, A Contribution to the Discussion of Probabilities and Human Hair Comparisons, 32 J. Forensic Sci. 684 (1987); Barnette & Ogle, Probabilities and Human Hair Comparison, 27 J. Forensic Sci. 272 (1982); Miller, Procedural Bias in Forensic Science Examinations of Human Hair, 11 Law & Hum. Behav. 157 (1987); Note, Splitting Hairs in Criminal Trials: Admissibility of Hair Comparison Probability Estimates, 1984 Ariz. St. L.J. 521 (1984). The Minnesota Supreme Court extended its exclusionary rule to encompass well established estimates of the frequencies with which combinations of genetic markers appear in the population to avoid a "potentially exaggerated impact on the trier of fact." State v. Boyd, 331 N.W.2d 480, 482 (Minn. 1983). Then it limited the rule to the end product of the calculation; the jury may be informed of the frequency of each independent genetic marker, but not of the number that is the product of these relative frequencies. State v. Joon Kyu Kim, 398 N.W.2d 544 (Minn. 1987). After that, it arbitrarily exempted DNA evidence from this exclusionary rule. State v. Bloom, 516 N.W.2d 159 (Minn. 1994). The entire line of cases and the argument that "there is a real danger that the jury will use the evidence as a measure of the defendant's guilt or innocence, and that the evidence will thereby undermine the presumption of innocence, erode the values served by the reasonable doubt standard, and dehumanize our system of justice," Boyd, 331 N.W.2d at 483, has been rejected by every other jurisdiction to face the question as well as by the Minnesota legislature, at least as to the probabilities associated with genetic markers. See State v. Schwartz, 447 N.W.2d 422, 428–29 n.5–6 (Minn. 1989). Although not conclusive, the empirical literature does not support the claim that jurors will overweight testimony on probabilities. Kaye et al., Statistics in the Jury Box: How Jurors Respond to Mitochondrial DNA Probabilities, 4 J. Empirical Leg. Stud. 797 (2007); Kaye & Koehler, Can Jurors Understand Probabilistic Evidence?, 154 J. Royal Stat. Soc'y Series A 75 (1991); Thompson, Are Juries Competent to Evaluate Statistical Evidence?, 52 Law & Contemp. Prob. 9 (1989).

[31]See People v. Collins, 68 Cal. 2d 319, 66 Cal. Rptr. 497, 438 P.2d 33 (1968) ("Mathematics, a veritable sorcerer in our computerized society, while assisting the trier of fact in the search for truth, must not cast a spell over him"); State v. Carlson, 267 N.W.2d 170, 176 (Minn. 1978) ("psychological impact of the suggestion of mathematical precision" cannot be dispelled, and "[t]estimony expressing opinions or conclusions in terms of . . . probability can make the uncertain seem all but proven, and suggest, by quantification, satisfaction of the requirement that guilt be established 'beyond a reasonable doubt' "). For a different view, see State v. Clayton,

In evaluating these decisions, it is important to distinguish between explicit calculations of the probability of guilt or coincidence and the presentation of relevant background statistics.[32] If the offender, whoever he or she might have been, left a bloodstain at the scene of the crime that matches the defendant's blood types, the scientific evidence cannot be interpreted intelligently without some knowledge of how frequently these blood types occur in the relevant population.[33] We have already remarked that if the expert offers any conclusion as to whether the defendant left the incriminating trace, he or she is relying, either explicitly or sub rosa, on estimates of these quantities. Without being informed of such background statistics or the relative likelihoods

---

646 P.2d 723, 727 n.1 (Utah 1982) ("We do not share that philosophy having a higher opinion of the jury's ability to weigh the credibility of such figures when properly presented and challenged").

[32]People v. Harbold, 124 Ill. App. 3d 363, 79 Ill. Dec. 830, 464 N.E.2d 734, 749 (1st Dist. 1984) ("the State went much farther [than population frequencies] and expressed the similarity between the perpetrator and the defendant in terms of the likelihood of a random match"); State v. Washington, 229 Kan. 47, 622 P.2d 986, 994–95 (1981) (citing cases to support the proposition that in contrast to probabilities not based on adequate data, "population percentages on the percentage of certain combinations of blood characteristics, based on established facts, are admissible as relevant to identification"). Even in State v. Carlson, 267 N.W.2d 170, 175 (Minn. 1978), the court held that it was error to allow an explicit estimate of the probability of misidentification based on hair samples, but it did not suggest that there was any error in expert testimony that "only .85 percent of the population would have blood with the same combination of . . . characteristics as the victim's blood and the matching stains found on [defendant's] jacket."

[33]Sensabaugh, Biochemical Markers of Individuality, in Forensic Science Handbook 338, 403 (Saferstein

ed. 1982) ("the interpretation of individualization typing results is intimately tied to population frequency statistics; without being provided the appropriate statistical information the triers of fact have no rational basis for deciding the significance of a type-for-type match"). This observation applies to more than blood typing. Even fingerprint evidence, which the courts often assert uniquely identifies individuals, merely establishes a probability. Obtaining reliable estimates of the population frequencies, however, can be difficult if not impossible. See Comm. on Scientific Assessment of Bullet Lead Elemental Composition Comparison, National Research Council, Forensic Analysis: Weighing Bullet Lead Evidence (2004); Barnette & Ogle, Probabilities and Human Hair Comparison, 27 J. Forensic Sci. 272 (1982); Osterburg, An Inquiry into the Nature of Proof, 9 J. Forensic Sci. 413, 420–26 (1964) (survey indicating that fingerprint experts vary in their estimates of the frequency of particular print characteristics). Defining the relevant population is not always easy, Kingston, A Perspective on Probability and Physical Evidence, 34 J. Forensic Sci. 1336 (1989), and all too often, the sample statistics are treated as if they permit an exact statement of the population parameters. See Berry, Inferences Using DNA Profiling in Forensic Identification and Paternity Cases, 6 Statistical Sci. 175 (1991).

for different sources,[34] the jury is left to its own speculations (or exposed to inadequately validated claims of uniqueness).[35] When the available data do not permit a reasonable calculation, but it is obvious that the match is probative, this may be tolerable.[36] But where reasonable estimates of the population frequencies are available, they should not be kept from the jury.[37] Thus, courts

---

[34]The term "likelihood" here has a specialized meaning. Kaye et al., The New Wigmore, A Treatise on Evidence Expert Evidence § 14.2 (2d ed. 2011); Kaye, Likelihoodism, Bayesianism, and a Pair of Shoes, 53 Jurimetrics J. 1 (2012). See supra § 185.

[35]For conflicting views on the possibility of demonstrating the uniqueness of traces such as fingerprints and toolmarks, compare Saks & Koehler, The Individualization Fallacy in Forensic Science Evidence, 61 Vand. L. Rev. 199 (2008) (inherently impossible because all evidence is probabilistic), with Kaye, Probability, Individualization, and Uniqueness in Forensic Science Evidence: Listening to the Academies, 75 Brook. L. Rev. 1163 (2010) (possible but extremely difficult to establish the requisite probability that a feature set is unique), and Kaye, Identification, Individuality, and Uniqueness: What's the Difference?, 8 Law, Probability & Risk 85 (2009) (distinguishing between claims of individualization and claims of uniqueness). Of course, there is no compelling reason for testimony of global uniqueness. E.g., Cole, Forensics Without Uniqueness, Conclusions Without Individualization: The New Epistemology of Forensic Identification, 8 Law, Probability & Risk 233 (2009); Koehler & Saks, Individualization Claims in Forensic Science: Still Unwarranted, 76 Brook. L. Rev. 1187 (2011). For some alternatives, see Kaye et al., The New Wigmore, A Treatise on Evidence: Expert Evidence ch. 15 (2d ed. 2011); Expert Working Group on Human Factors in Latent Print Analysis, Latent Print Examination and Human Factors: Improving the Practice Through a Systems Approach (Kaye ed. 2012). See supra § 207(A).

[36]State v. Noel, 157 N.J. 141, 723 A.2d 602 (1999). In dealing with DNA evidence, a number of courts held the fact of a match inadmissible in the absence of an uncontroversial estimate of the frequency of the matching DNA types. E.g., State v. Bible, 175 Ariz. 549, 858 P.2d 1152 (1993); State v. Cauthron, 120 Wash. 2d 879, 846 P.2d 502 (1993). This departure from established practice apparently resulted from a statement in a report of a committee of a National Academy of Sciences that a match without a probability attached to it was "meaningless." Comm. on DNA Technology in Forensic Science, Nat'l Research Council, DNA Technology in Forensic Science 74 (1992). The reasoning of the courts that have relied on this statement is faulty. See Kaye, The Double Helix and the Law of Evidence (2010); cf. National Research Council Committee on DNA Forensic Science: An Update, The Evaluation of Forensic DNA Evidence (1996) (suggesting that testimony of match without a statement of a numerical probability is scientifically acceptable).

[37]U.S. v. Green, 680 F.2d 520, 523 (7th Cir. 1982) (testimony on frequency of genetic markers in population properly admitted); State v. Pearson, 234 Kan. 906, 678 P.2d 605, 618 (1984) ("evidence of population percentages concerning the possibility of certain combinations of blood characteristics, based on established facts, is admissible as relevant to identification"); Com. v. Gomes, 403 Mass. 258, 526 N.E.2d 1270, 1279–80 (1988); State v. Nicholas, 34 Wash. App. 775, 663 P.2d 1356 (Div. 1 1983) (testimony that 60% of male population would have semen matching that found in vaginal smear from rape victim admis-

routinely admit testimony estimating such frequencies, often without objection.[38]

To be sure, there are risks in this policy. A juror who hears that only one out of every five, or for that matter, one out of every 10,000 persons, possesses the traits that characterize the true offender, may be tempted to subtract this statistic from one to arrive at the incorrect conclusion that the remainder is the probability that the defendant is guilty. In the statistical literature, this reasoning is known as the transposition fallacy.[39] Nevertheless, it should not be so difficult for defense counsel to

---

sible).

[38]*E.g.*, U.S. v. Gwaltney, 790 F.2d 1378, 1382–83 (9th Cir. 1986) (Defendant "has no quarrel with the statistical evidence that he was part of the 29% of the population who are Type A secretors or that his PGM 1 plus 1 (sic) group constitutes 40% of the population."); State v. Hjerstrom, 287 N.W.2d 625, 628 (Minn. 1979) ("chips of glass found in [burglary defendant's clothing] had the same dispersion and refraction index as glass in the window which was broken by the burglars in gaining entrance, and . . . only 5% of all glass in the United States" had these characteristics); State v. Dirk, 364 N.W.2d 117, 120 (S.D. 1985) (testimony that 18–19% of population had incriminating immunogenetic markers); Hopkins v. Com., 230 Va. 280, 337 S.E.2d 264, 267 (1985) ("Laboratory analysis showed that the cigarette filter found near the victim's remains was a kind of filter found in Price Breaker cigarettes, in 13% of all cigarettes sold, and in 4% of all cigarette brands").

Estimated base rates for false identifications or accusations typically are held to be inadmissible, as indirect opinions on the credibility of witnesses. See cases cited, supra § 206(D). This result seems justified where there is no satisfactory independent criterion for determining the frequency of false identifications or accusations. In the absence of such a criterion, the estimated base rates cannot be scientifically validated, and their prejudicial effect clearly outweighs their probative value.

[39]See supra § 209. Transposition manifests itself in dozens of judicial opinions. *E.g.*, Adams v. Ameritech Services, Inc., 231 F.3d 414, 424, 427 (7th Cir. 2000); Ottaviani v. State University of New York at New Paltz, 875 F.2d 365, 372 n.7 (2d Cir. 1989); Rivera v. City of Wichita Falls, 665 F.2d 531, 545 n.22 (5th Cir. 1982); Morris v. State, 811 So. 2d 661 (Fla. 2002); State v. Ferguson, 20 S.W.3d 485 (Mo. 2000); State v. Rogers, 355 N.C. 420, 562 S.E.2d 859 (2002). The prosecutor in *Collins* made this mistake, as did the prosecutor in Wilson v. State, 370 Md. 191, 803 A.2d 1034 (2002), who argued to the jury that "[i]f you multiply his numbers, instead of 1 in 4 million, you get 1 in 10 million that the man sitting here is innocent. That was what a doctor, their expert, told you." The prosecutor and the criminalist in the trial for which a writ of habeas corpus was upheld in Brown v. Farwell, 525 F.3d 787 (9th Cir. 2008), also misconstrued the probability that DNA would match by coincidence as the probability of that the match was nothing more than coincidence. Although transposition is not generally correct, when there are only two possibilities—that the trace evidence comes from defendant or that the match is coincidental—and when the probability of the latter event is exceedingly small, the transposition may be approximately correct. See Kaye, "False, But Highly Persuasive": How Wrong Were the Probability Estimates in *McDaniel v. Brown*?, 108 Mich. L. Rev. First Impressions 1 (2009); Meier & Zabell, Benjamin Pierce and the Howland Will, 75 J.

correct any such misapprehension by pointing out that the frequency estimate merely establishes that the defendant is one member of a class of persons who have the incriminating characteristics.[40] The distribution of these characteristics in the population at large simply determines whether this class of persons whom the scientific evidence would identify as a possible offender is large or small.[41]

In principle, a statistician could do more than state the frequency at which the scientific tests would implicate persons. First, in those cases in which the identifying characteristics were not the very basis on which the defendant was picked from the general population,[42] the expert could be explicit about the $p$-value for the findings.[43] Second, valiant efforts have been made to calculate conditional probabilities pertaining to the number of

---

Am. Stat. Ass'n 497, 502 (1980).

[40]Kaye, The Double Helix and the Law of Evidence (2010); Ellman & Kaye, Probabilities and Proof: Can HLA and Blood Group Testing Prove Paternity?, 54 NYU L. Rev. 1131, 1146 (1979); Thompson, Are Juries Competent to Evaluate Statistical Evidence?, 52 Law & Contemp. Prob. 9, 31–35 (1989) (describing jury simulation studies). *Contra* Jonakait, When Blood Is Their Argument, 1983 U. Ill. L.F. 369.

[41]People v. Lindsey, 84 Cal. App. 3d 851, 149 Cal. Rptr. 47 (2d Dist. 1978) ("The chemist stated that approximately 36 percent of the population would secrete type 'O' blood antigenes [sic] into bodily fluids such as semen"); Shanks v. State, 185 Md. 437, 45 A.2d 85, 90 (1945) ("if the jury or judge is told that 45% of the population have 'O' blood, we cannot assume that this statement would be disregarded and not given its proper weight"); State v. Carlson, 267 N.W.2d 170, 175 (Minn. 1978) (incriminating genetic markers would be found in .85% of population).

[42]Obviously, the assumption that the suspect has been selected for testing on the basis of traits that are statistically independent of those that the test detects does not hold in a case like *People v. Collins*. There, the selection of the suspects is highly correlated with the characteristics in question. *See* Branion v. Gramly, 855

F.2d 1256, 1264 (7th Cir. 1988). Neither does it apply when the suspect is located by an automated search of a DNA database. The proper probability analysis in these situations has produced a good deal of confusion. *See* Kaye et al., The New Wigmore, A Treatise on Evidence: Expert Evidence § 14.4 (2d ed. 2011) (analyzing the issue and the leading opinions). The view that the method of selection does not significantly change the relevant probability is presented forcefully in Balding, Errors and Misunderstandings in the Second NRC Report, 37 Jurimetrics J. 469 (1997); Donnelly & Friedman, DNA Database Searches and the Legal Consumption of Scientific Evidence, 97 Mich. L. Rev. 931 (1999); and Kaye, Rounding Up the Usual Suspects: A Legal and Logical Analysis of DNA Database Trawls, 87 N. Car. L. Rev. 425 (2009).

[43]*But see* People v. Harbold, 124 Ill. App. 3d 363, 79 Ill. Dec. 830, 464 N.E.2d 734, 749 (1st Dist. 1984) (error to characterize population frequency as the probability of a random match). Roughly speaking, the $p$-value is the probability of the evidence given the null hypothesis. See supra § 209 (discussing $p$-values in discrimination cases). If the null hypothesis in this context is that the trace evidence did not come from the defendant, then the $p$-value is the probability that the scientific test or identification procedure would give a positive result for a

people in some populations who have the incriminating characteristics. Indeed, the opinion in *People v. Collins* sported a mathematical appendix purporting to show that the conditional probability of there being more couples with the characteristics of the Collins's given that there was at least one such couple was 0.41.[44] One could imagine admitting testimony about these probabilities.[45] Third, when it is feasible to compute the likelihood ratio that indicates the probative value of the evidence,[46] an expert might present this quantity. This approach has been followed in a growing number DNA cases[47] and is generally accepted among European forensic scientists.[48] Finally, the expert could apply Bayes' rule to show jurors how the frequency data would increase a previously established probability that the

---

person selected at random from the relevant population. Thus, if the test is perfectly accurate, it is simply the proportion of people in the relevant population with the incriminating traits.

    Although there are dangers in having criminalists whose expertise does not extend to the theory of statistical inference testify about probabilities (or for attorneys to try to describe them), see, for example, State v. Garrison, 120 Ariz. 255, 585 P.2d 563 (1978) (dissenting opinion); The Evolving Role of Statistical Assessments as Evidence in the Courts (Fienberg ed., 1988); Kirk & Kingston, Evidence Evaluation and Problems of General Criminalistics, 9 J.Forensic Sci. 434 (1964), it also should be kept in mind that jurors acting on their own initiative may interpret a population frequency estimate as a probability.

[44]Collins, 438 P.2d at 42–43. This calculation involves an approximation to the binomial distribution with the population size taken to be the reciprocal of the hypothesized frequency of the identifying characteristics. This assumption about the population size is contrived. *See* Fairley & Mosteller, A Conversation About *Collins*, 41 U. Chi. L. Rev. 242 (1974). For proposed refinements, improvements, and other analyses of the "duplication probability," see Charrow & Smith, A Conversation About "A Conversation About *Collins*," 64 Geo. L.J. 669

(1976); Finney, Probabilities Based on Circumstantial Evidence, 72 J. Am. Stat. Ass'n 316 (1977); Lenth, On Identification by Probability, 26 J. Forensic Sci. Soc'y 197 (1986); Smith & Charrow, Upper and Lower Bounds for Probability of Guilt Based on Circumstantial Evidence, 70 J. Am. Stat. Ass'n 555 (1975); Stripinis, Probability Theory and Circumstantial Evidence, 22 Jurimetrics J. 59 (1981).

[45]Presumably, the defense might offer them to defuse the impact of numbers like the one-out-of-twelve-million figure in *Collins*.

[46]See supra § 185.

[47]*E.g.*, Coy v. Renico, 414 F. Supp. 2d 744, 760 (E.D. Mich. 2006) (likelihood ratios for DNA evidence satisfy *Daubert* and are admissible); State v. Ayers, 2003 MT 114, 315 Mont. 395, 68 P.3d 768 (2003) (a suitably explained likelihood ratio is admissible, but refusing to apply *Daubert* on the unconvincing ground that *Daubert* is inapplicable to scientific evidence that is not novel); Kaye et al., The New Wigmore, A Treatise on Evidence: Expert Evidence § 14.2.2 (2d ed. 2011).

[48]*See* NIST Expert Working Group on Human Factors in Latent Print Analysis, Latent Print Examination and Human Factors: Improving the Practice through a Systems Approach (Kaye ed. 2012); Kaye, Likelihoodism, Bayesianism, and a Pair of Shoes, 53 Jurimetrics J. 1 (2012).

person tested is the one who left the incriminating traces.[49] This last proposal has been attacked on both philosophical[50] and practical[51] grounds. It has been said in reply that the pragmatic objections are the more persuasive.[52] Certainly, having an expert testify to the "probability of guilt" given the evidence would be inadvisable.[53] But whether the benefits of using this method of statistical inference solely to educate the jury by displaying the probative force of the evidentiary findings would be worth the

---

[49]*See* Good, Probability and the Weighing of Evidence 66–67 (1950); Kaye et al., The New Wigmore, A Treatise on Evidence: Expert Evidence § 14.3 (2d ed. 2011); Cullison, Identification by Probabilities and Trial by Arithmetic, 6 Hous. L. Rev. 1 (1969); Ellman & Kaye, Probabilities and Proof: Can HLA and Blood Group Testing Prove Paternity?, 54 NYU L. Rev. 1131 (1979); Fairley, Probabilistic Analysis of Identification Evidence, 2 J. Legal Stud. 493 (1973); Finkelstein & Fairley, A Bayesian Approach to Identification Evidence, 83 Harv. L. Rev. 489 (1970); Kaye, Likelihoodism, Bayesianism, and a Pair of Shoes, 53 Jurimetrics J. 1 (2012). The mechanics of this approach are briefly stated in the next section. The usual suggestion is that the expert present an illustrative chart showing how, in view of the frequency with which the incriminating traits are to be found in the relevant population, the identification evidence would affect a broad spectrum of prior probabilities. The expert need not ask the jurors to choose any particular prior probability to express their estimate of the strength of the non-test evidence. Berry, Inferences Using DNA Profiling in Forensic Identification and Paternity Cases, 6 Statistical Sci. 175 (1991), proposes that statisticians go beyond this, and counsel jurors to form prior and posterior probabilities. Balding, Comment On: Why the Effect of Prior Odds Should Accompany the Likelihood Ratio When Reporting DNA Evidence, 3 Law, Probability & Risk 63 (2004), suggests that "Bayes' theorem in . . . forensic settings can readily be conveyed to judges and jurors using informal language, and . . . that

this approach has the best prospect of assisting the legal decision-making process."

[50]*See* Probability and Inference in the Law of Evidence: The Limits and Uses of Bayesianism (Tillers & Green eds., 1988); Brilmayer & Kornhauser, Review: Quantitative Methods and Legal Decisions, 46 U. Chi. L. Rev. 116 (1978).

[51]See Tribe, Trial by Mathematics: Precision and Ritual in the Legal Process, 84 Harv. L. Rev. 1329 (1971) (Bayesian calculations "dwarf soft variables," threaten the presumption of innocence and encourage jurors to err by misestimating and misusing the prior probability of guilt).

[52]Ellman & Kaye, Probabilities and Proof: Can HLA and Blood Group Testing Prove Paternity?, 54 NYU L. Rev. 1131 (1979); Kaye, The Laws of Probability and the Law of the Land, 47 U. Chi. L. Rev. 34 (1979).

[53]*See* Kaye, Comment: Uncertainty in DNA Profile Evidence, 6 Statistical Sci. 196 (1991). Nor does this seem to be what most proponents of Bayesian presentations have recommended. *See* Ellman & Kaye, Probabilities and Proof: Can HLA and Blood Group Testing Prove Paternity?, 54 NYU L. Rev. 1131, 1146 (1979); Finkelstein & Fairley, A Comment on "Trial by Mathematics," 84 Harv. L. Rev. 1801 (1971); Kaye, Rounding Up the Usual Suspects: A Legal and Logical Analysis of DNA Database Trawls, 87 N. Car. L. Rev. 425 (2009) (criticizing the English Court of Appeals for prohibiting defendants from describing the impact of DNA evidence on a prior probability).

costs in terms of time-consumption and possible confusion is a closer question.[54] Outside of the parentage testing area, Bayesian calculations rarely are seen in court.[55]

In general, it appears that the explicit use of the theories of probability and statistical inference, either as a basis for the opinions of the experts themselves or as a course of education for jurors in how to think about scientific identification evidence, remains controversial.[56] As long as counsel and the experts do not try to place a scientific seal of approval on results not shown to be scientifically based, however, there is room for judicious use of these theories to put the identification evidence in reasonable perspective.

## § 211  Paternity testing

Problems of questioned or disputed parentage have plagued mankind, perhaps ever since the origin of the species. The Talmud tells of a case in which a widow married her brother-in-law before the required three-month waiting period after the death of her husband. She gave birth to a child scarcely six months later. The rabbis reasoned that either the child was a full term baby fathered by the deceased husband or a premature child of the second husband. Since the mother had shown no visible signs of pregnancy three months after her first husband's death, the matter was not easy to settle. As one rabbi said, "it is a doubt."[1]

Many legislators, courts, and commentators have concluded that genetic and statistical methods permit such doubts to be dispelled. Section 205(B) described the methods of detecting genetic markers and the principles of human genetics that allow this information to be applied to resolve cases of disputed parentage. We saw that states now admit the results of DNA, blood, and tissue typing tests not merely to exclude the alleged father as the biological father, but, when he is not excluded, to help prove that he is the father. To assist the trier of fact in

---

[54]*Compare* Finkelstein & Fairley, A Comment on "Trial by Mathematics," 84 Harv. L. Rev. 1801 (1971), *and* Kaye, DNA Evidence: Probability, Population Genetics and the Courts, 7 Harv. J. L. & Tech. 101 (1993), *with* Tribe, A Further Critique of Mathematical Proof, 84 Harv. L. Rev. 1810 (1971).

[55]Criminal and civil cases are collected in Kaye et al., The New Wigmore, A Treatise on Evidence: Expert Evidence § 14.3.2 (2d ed. 2011).

[56]For further analysis, see Kaye et al., The New Wigmore, A Treatise on Evidence: Expert Evidence ch. 14 (4th ed. 2011).

[Section 211]

[1]For a Bayesian interpretation of the rabbinical arguments, see Rabinovitch, Probability and Statistical Inference in Ancient and Medieval Jewish Literature 58–60 (1973). As to the presumption of the husband's paternity, see supra § 205(B); infra § 343.

interpreting positive results, the expert, under generally applicable evidentiary principles,[2] may give reliable estimates of the frequencies that characterize the distribution of the pertinent genotypes or genetic markers in the male population. That is, if the population data warrant it, the expert may testify to the proportion of men that the test would exclude—a parameter that is sometimes converted into the "probability of exclusion."[3] To this extent, the procedures are essentially the same as those that apply to scientific identification evidence generally.[4]

Yet, many experts believe that testimony limited to the test results and the probability of exclusion is incomplete and sometimes misleading.[5] They prefer to testify to "the probability of paternity,"[6] and almost all jurisdictions allow such testimony

---

[2]See supra § 210.

[3]In practice, "probability of exclusion" may be used to denote two distinct concepts. Some experts use it to refer to the proportion of the male population that a single test or the battery of tests would exclude as the biological father without regard to the phenotypes of the mother and child tested in any given case. *See, e.g.,* State ex rel. Hausner v. Blackman, 7 Kan. App. 2d 693, 648 P.2d 249, 253 (1982) ("The HLA test alone has a probability of exclusion of 78 percent to 80 percent and when it is used in addition to the six other tests, the probability of exclusion rises to at least 91 percent to 95 percent"); Joint AMA-ABA Guidelines: Present Status of Serologic Testing in Problems of Disputed Parentage, 10 Fam. L.Q. 247, 253–58 (1976). This figure is a measure of the ability of the tests to exclude falsely accused males across a spectrum of cases. It is sometimes called a "mean" or a "cumulative" probability of exclusion. *See* Joint AMA-ABA Guidelines: Present Status of Serologic Testing in Problems of Disputed Parentage, 10 Fam. L.Q. 247 (1976). It is useful to the laboratory in deciding which tests to include in its standard battery, but it is not well suited to measuring the power of the tests employed in a particular case where the genotypes or phenotypes of the mother and child are known. In this situation, the "probability of exclu-

sion" that should be testified to is, in effect, the proportion of males in the relevant population who do not have the incriminating genotypes (those that the biological father, whoever he was, could have had, given the types of the mother and child).

[4]See supra § 210. *But see* State ex rel. Hausner v. Blackman, 7 Kan. App. 2d 693, 648 P.2d 249, 253 (1982); Com. v. Beausoleil, 397 Mass. 206, 490 N.E.2d 788 (1986); Kofford v. Flora, 744 P.2d 1343 (Utah 1987) (prohibiting presentation of the probability of exclusion unless accompanied by "probability of paternity").

[5]*See, e.g.,* Peterson, A Few Things You Should Know About Paternity Tests (But Were Afraid to Ask), 22 Santa Clara L. Rev. 667, 677–81 (1982). The scientists and physicians do not all agree on which approach is scientifically the soundest. *See* Inclusion Probabilities in Parentage Testing (Walker ed., 1983).

[6]Michael H. v. Gerald D., 491 U.S. 110, 113, 109 S. Ct. 2333, 105 L. Ed. 2d 91 (1989) ("98.07% probability that [appellant] was Victoria's father"); Clark v. Jeter, 486 U.S. 456, 108 S. Ct. 1910, 100 L. Ed. 2d 465 (1988) ("blood tests . . . showed a 99.3% probability that Jeter is Tiffany's father"); Ellman & Kaye, Probabilities and Proof: Can HLA and Blood Group Testing Prove Paternity, 54 N.Y.U. L. Rev. 1154 (1979); Walker, Probability

in civil cases.[7] Yet, even though most states have statutes that permit positive test results to be received into evidence,[8] not all of these statutes say whether the probabilities derived from the test results also are admissible.[9] At the other extreme, statutes adopted across the country not only allow such testimony, but rely on the "probability of paternity" to trigger a presumption of paternity.[10] In the absence of a statute explicitly authorizing the

---

in the Analysis of Paternity Test Results, *in* Paternity Testing 69 (Silver ed. 1978). Other terms have been used in lieu of "probability." *See, e.g.,* People ex rel. Shockley v. Hoyle, 338 Ill. App. 3d 1046, 273 Ill. Dec. 850, 789 N.E.2d 1282, 1289 (2d Dist. 2003) ("The result of the test showed the 'estimated plausibility of paternity' to be 94.35% or 'likely.' "); State ex rel. Williams v. Williams, 609 S.W.2d 456, 457 (Mo. Ct. App. W.D. 1980) ("there was an 81.15% possibility that Ronald was the father"); State v. Jackson, 320 N.C. 452, 358 S.E.2d 679, 680 (1987) (geneticist testified for prosecution in rape case involving the birth of a child to an eleven-year-old girl that the "likelihood of paternity" ranged from 93.4% to 99.1%). These "plausibilities" and "possibilities" are computed in the same way as the probability of paternity. Sometimes the symbol W or the phrase "likelihood of paternity" (which should not be confused with the likelihood ratio discussed infra this section) are employed.

[7]*See* Ellman & Kaye, Probabilities and Proof: Can HLA and Blood Group Testing Prove Paternity?, 54 NYU L. Rev. 1131 (1979); Kaye, The Probability of an Ultimate Issue: The Strange Cases of Paternity Testing, 75 Iowa L. Rev. 75 (1989); Kolko, Admissibility of HLA Test Results to Determine Paternity, 9 Fam. L. Rep. 4009 (1983). There has been some judicial resistance to the "probability of paternity" in criminal cases. *See* Kaye, Science in Evidence ch. 10 (1997). However, no special rule for the use of these numbers in criminal as opposed to civil cases seems justified. Griffith v. State, 976 S.W.2d 241 (Tex. App. Amarillo 1998); 4 Faigman,

et al., Modern Scientific Evidence: The Law and Science of Expert Testimony § 32:7 (2011–2012 ed.).

[8]Kaye & Kanwischer, The Admissibility of Genetic Testing in Parentage Litigation: A Survey of State Statutes, 22 Fam. L.Q. 109 (1988); Litovsky & Schultz, Scientific Evidence of Paternity: A Survey of State Statutes, 39 Jurimetrics J. 79 (1998). See supra § 205(B).

[9]Commissioner of Social Services of Lewis County on Behalf of Farr v. O'Brien, 130 Misc. 2d 586, 496 N.Y.S.2d 947, 948 (Fam. Ct. 1985) (dictum that "the Family Court Act does not specifically mandate the acceptance of the . . . probability of paternity").

[10]In re Jesusa V., 32 Cal. 4th 588, 10 Cal. Rptr. 3d 205, 85 P.3d 2 (2004) (resolving conflicting statutory presumptions); Mulligan v. Corbett, 426 Md. 670, 45 A.3d 243, 247 (2012) ("[A] statistical probability of the alleged father's paternity of at least 99.0% . . . may be received into evidence and constitutes a rebuttable presumption of his paternity."); Kaye, Presumptions, Probability and Paternity, 30 Jurimetrics J. 323 (1990) (demonstrating that the probabilities listed in these statutes do not necessarily indicate the fraction of cases in which the resulting presumption will be correct, and arguing that these statutes are undesirable). Much of the impetus for these statutes came from the Welfare Reform Act of 1996, 42 U.S.C. § 666(a)(5)(G), which requires these laws as a condition for federal financial assistance to states, and the Uniform Parentage Act of 2000 carried this trend to its ultimate conclusion, making the results of paternity tests effectively conclusive. 4 Faigman, et al.,

expert to give the "probability of paternity," admissibility should turn on whether probability testimony is sufficiently likely to aid the jury in properly assessing the probative value of the positive findings. To answer this question, one must first understand what the "probability of paternity" is. This section indicates how this probability is computed.[11] It then argues that one version of this approach is not suited for courtroom use and suggests some alternative methods of assisting the jury or court to weigh the positive test results along with the other evidence in the case to reach a decision as to paternity.[12] Finally, it discusses special concerns that have been raised about probability computations involving DNA typing. It concludes with the suggestion that in most cases, testimony as to the numerical probability of paternity is no longer necessary.

The probability of paternity, as conventionally computed, is a deceptively simple application of an elementary result in probability theory discovered by the Reverend Thomas Bayes in the nineteenth century. Bayes' formula can be interpreted as showing the effect of a new item of evidence on a previously established probability.[13] Suppose we let $B$ stand for the event that the alleged father is the biological father, we let Odds($B$) designate the odds in favor of this event (before we learn the outcome of the laboratory tests),[14] and we use the letter $T$ to denote the test evidence (the types of the mother, child and father). Many testifying experts take the prior odds to be 1 (that is, 50-50) on the theory that doing so shows that they are neutral as between plaintiff and defendant.[15] Although this conception of "neutrality" cannot

---

Modern Scientific Evidence: The Law and Science of Expert Testimony § 32:6 (2011–2012 ed.).

[11]Other references on this point include Paternity Testing (Silver ed. 1978); Inclusion Probabilities in Parentage Testing (Walker ed., 1983); Biomathematical Evidence of Paternity (Hummel & Gerchow ed. 1982); Paternity Testing by Blood Grouping (2d ed. Sussman 1976); Morris & Gjertson, Scientific Status, *in* 4 Faigman, et al., Modern Scientific Evidence: The Law and Science of Expert Testimony §§ 32:8 to 32:19 (2011–2012 ed.).

[12]The argument sketched here relies heavily on Aickin & Kaye, Some Mathematical and Legal Considerations in Using Serological Tests to Prove Paternity, *in* Inclusion Probabilities in Parentage Testing 155 (R.H. Walker ed. 1983); Ellman & Kaye, Probabilities and Proof: Can HLA and Blood Group Testing Prove Paternity?, 54 NYU L. Rev. 1131 (1979); and Kaye, The Probability of an Ultimate Issue: The Strange Cases of Paternity Testing, 75 Iowa L. Rev. 75 (1989).

[13]References in law journals to the elementary version of Bayes' formula are given supra §§ 184, 210.

[14]A probability $P$ for some outcome corresponds to odds of $P / (1 - P)$ to 1 in favor of that outcome. For example, if the probability of paternity is $P = 1/2$, the odds are 1/2 divided by $1 - 1/2$, or 1 to 1.

[15]State v. Hartman, 145 Wis. 2d 1, 426 N.W.2d 320, 322 (1988) (noting

withstand examination,[16] adopting these odds does amount to assuming that the accusation of paternity is as likely to be true as to be false. Bayes' rule tells us how to update these odds to account for the test results $T$. In particular, it says to multiply the prior odds by a quantity called the likelihood ratio to produce the new odds that the alleged father is the biological father, which we write as Odds($B \mid T$), for the odds of $B$ given the test results $T$. In symbols, Odds($B \mid T$) = LR Odds(B), where LR is an abbreviation for likelihood ratio. For the standard assumption that the prior odds are 1, the posterior odds of paternity are just Odds($B \mid T$) = LR.

This likelihood ratio can be computed as the ratio of two probabilities.[17] The numerator is the probability that the types $T$ would be found if the alleged father really were the biological father. The denominator is the probability that the types $T$ would be found if the alleged father were not the biological father. In other words, the likelihood ratio states how many times more

---

expert testimony that "[f]ifty percent . . . shows that the laboratory is completely neutral"); Butcher v. Com., 96 S.W.3d 3, 8–9 (Ky. 2002) ("The use of a prior probability of .5 is a neutral assumption. The statistic merely reflects the application of a scientifically accepted mathematical theorem. . . ."); Jessop v. State, 368 S.W.3d 653, 669 (Tex. App. Austin 2012) (describing and accepting, as scientifically mandated in molecular biology, testimony that "being at the mid-point of possible values, [a prior probability of 1/2] translates into a neutral assumption—paternity and non-paternity have equal weight"); Griffith v. State, 976 S.W.2d 241 (Tex. App. Amarillo 1998) (testimony that a prior probability of one-half was "standard" and "neutral").

[16]*See* Kaye et al., The New Wigmore, A Treatise on Evidence: Expert Evidence § 14.3.2, at 651 (2d ed. 2011) (concluding that the opinions are "muddled" and "the arbitrary selection of one-half as the prior probability that the defendant is the source is difficult to defend"); Kaye, The Probability of an Ultimate Issue: The Strange Cases of Paternity Testing, 75 Iowa L. Rev. 75, 94 (1989). The misunderstanding of the "standard" and "neutral" assumption of one-half for a prior

probability is acute in Jessop v. State, 368 S.W.3d 653 (Tex. App. Austin 2012). There, the court doggedly insisted that "a 0.5 prior-probability assumption assigns no more culpability to appellant than it does to any other random male individual." 368 S.W.2d at 675. If this were true, then every other male individual living at the 1,700-acre YFZ Ranch in Texas would have to be assigned this same 0.5 probability. The probability that at least one of them was the father of the child born to the underage mother then would exceed, by many times over, the maximum possible value of 1 permitted by the laws of probability. In other words, to say that the one defendant has a prior probability of one-half is actually to say that he has far more probability than any other randomly selected man on the ranch. This is hardly a "neutral" assumption that treats, a priori, all random male individuals as equally likely to be innocent.

[17]Being a ratio of two conditional probabilities, the likelihood ratio is not itself a probability. Unlike probabilities, which are bounded by 0 and 1, the likelihood ratio can exceed one. The larger the ratio, the more probative the evidence. See supra § 185.

probable it is that the tests would show the types $T$ if the alleged father were the biological father than if he were not.[18] It often is referred to as the "paternity index." The computation of the numerator is relatively simple. It is just the probability that a man with the phenotypes of the alleged father and a woman with the mother's types would produce an offspring with the child's types.[19] The computation of the denominator is trickier. The denominator is the probability that a man other than the alleged father would produce an offspring with the child's types. But which man? Some "alternative men" could not produce this type of child. They are the ones whom the tests would exclude. Others would have the same probability of producing this type of child as does the alleged father. These are the ones who have the same types that he does. Still others would produce this type of child with other probabilities. Their types differ from the alleged father's but are still consistent with the genotypes of the biological father. The conventional solution is to invent a "random man"—a hypothetical entity whose genotypes are a kind of average across all these men. Assuming that the estimates of the population allele frequencies are completely free from error,[20] the computation can proceed.

---

[18]Regrettably, the transposition fallacy (see supra §§ 210 & 211) produces misinterpretations such as the following: "The paternity index is a value reflecting the likelihood that a tested man is the father of the child as opposed to an untested man of the same race. It . . . means that he is that many more times likely to be the father than any other randomly selected male of his race." Butcher v. Com., 96 S.W.3d 3 (Ky. 2002) (quoting Griffith v. State, 976 S.W.2d 241, 243 (Tex. App. Amarillo 1998)). *See also* State v. Beasley, 960 So. 2d 1182, 1184 (La. Ct. App. 2d Cir. 2007) ("DNA tests yielded a paternity index . . . making Beasley 133 million times more likely to be the father than a randomly-selected black male."). As stated in the text, the paternity index involves probabilities computed on the assumption that the tested man is the father on the assumption that a randomly selected man is. It does not give the probability that the assumptions are true. To invert the conditional probabilities requires Bayes' rule, and that necessitates a value for the prior odds.

[19]Without testing relatives of the defendant, only the types of the alleged father can be known. The usual practice is to assume that the probability that the alleged father has the obligatory genotypes or haplotypes is given by the relative frequency of these types in the population at large. Aickin, Some Fallacies in the Computation of Paternity Probabilities, 36 Am. J. Hum. Genetics 904 (1984), challenges this procedure.

[20]Particularly with rare alleles or haplotypes in serological and HLA types, the estimates of population frequencies are questionable. *See* Selvin, Some Statistical Properties of the Paternity Ratio, *in* Inclusion Probabilities in Paternity Testing (Walker ed., 1982); Juricek, Electrophoresis: A Continuation of the Discussion, 29 J. Forensic Sci. 704 (1984) (letter); Reisner et al., Studies of Random Black and White Populations in North Carolina: HLA Antigen Profile, 21 Tissue Antigens 14 (1983). In some situations, erroneous estimates of gene or haplotype frequencies "can have severe effects on the

Suppose, for example, that given the estimated allele frequencies, it is 5,000 times more likely to obtain a child with the observed types from a man with the alleged father's types than from the imaginary "random man." Bayes' formula then states that Odds($B \mid T$) = 5000 Odds ($B$). For prior odds of 1, this means that the odds that the alleged father is the biological father are 5000 to 1. The corresponding probability of paternity is 5000/5001 = .9998, or 99.98%. These are the kind of numbers that the experts testifying to the "probability of paternity" produce.

Should the results of these calculations ever be admissible? Resorting to the "random man" to form the likelihood ratio and postulating prior odds of 1 create problems for a courtroom presentation. It is tempting to dismiss the choice of the prior odds as contrived, speculative, and lacking any scientific basis.[21] It sounds like some of the classic cases in which an expert multiplied together probabilities that had no basis in fact.[22] Here, however, there are some hard data suggesting that these prior odds understate the incidence of truthful accusations of paternity and therefore favor the alleged father, who would be the objecting party.[23]

Nonetheless, to serve up any single number computed in this fashion as "the" probability of paternity connotes more than the mathematical logic can deliver. Most persons hearing that the probability of paternity is 99.98% would think that the alleged father's role in the affair is conclusively confirmed. Indeed, the experts have developed standardized phrases, which they call

---

calculation of a probability of paternity when using the HLA system." Reading & Reisner, The Effect of Differences in Gene Frequency on Probability of Paternity, 30 J. Forensic Sci. 1130, 1138 (1985).

[21]Everett v. Everett, 150 Cal. App. 3d 1053, 201 Cal. Rptr. 351, 360 (2d Dist. 1984); Alinda V. v. Alfredo V., 125 Cal. App. 3d 98, 177 Cal. Rptr. 839, 840 (1st Dist. 1981); Sensabaugh, Biochemical Markers of Individuality, in Forensic Science Handbook 339, 403 (Saferstein ed. 1982) ("There is, of course, no objective basis for the estimation of this prior probability by the serologic expert").

[22]See supra § 210.

[23]Chakravarti & Li, Estimating the Prior Probability of Paternity from the Results of Exclusion Tests, 24 Forensic Sci. Int'l 143 (1984); Ellman & Kaye, Probabilities and Proof: Can HLA and Blood Group Testing Prove Paternity?, 54 NYU L. Rev. 1131, 1150–51 (1979); Heise et al., A Critical Analysis of Paternity Determination Using HLA and Five Erythrocyte Antigen Systems, 4 Am. J. Forensic Medicine & Pathology 15 (1983); Hummel et al., The Realistic Prior Probability from Blood Group Findings for Cases Involving One or More Men, in Biomathematical Evidence of Paternity 73–87 (Hummel & Gerchow ed. 1982); Silver, An Introduction to Paternity Testing, in Paternity Testing xi–xii (Silver ed., 1978). This empirical justification raises the issue of using an average figure for the veracity of claimants to judge the merits of an individual claim. Ellman & Kaye, Probabilities and Proof: Can HLA and Blood Group Testing Prove Paternity?, 54 NYU L. Rev. 1131 (1979). See supra § 210.

"verbal predicates," to characterize the numbers.[24] Yet, in view of the way in which the "probability of paternity" is calculated, many men—all those who share the alleged father's types—would have had "probabilities of paternity" of 99.98% had they been tested. Some nonexcluded men (for serological amd HLA types) might have even higher "probabilities of paternity." In more than one case, a man later shown to be sterile had a "probability of paternity" exceeding 95% as determined from HLA typing.[25] Unless an expert can somehow explain that the calculated "probability of paternity" is not the chance that the alleged father, as distinguished from all other possible fathers, is the biological father, the expert should not be allowed to put this "probability" before the jury. Furthermore, it would appear that any accurate explanation of why the "probability of paternity" does not mean the probability that the alleged father, rather than any other man, is the biological father, and then of what it does mean, would be hopelessly confusing. Consequently, testimony as to the "probability of paternity," computed with a fixed and undisclosed prior probability of one-half, should not be allowed.[26] Such testimony seems unable to fulfill its only legitimate function—assisting the jury in weighing the positive test results along with

---

[24]Carlyon v. Weeks, 387 So. 2d 465, 466 (Fla. 1st DCA 1980) ("the plausibility of paternity for Miles is 99.9%, making paternity 'practically proved' in the terminology of Hummel"). In their canonical version, the "predicates" range from "not useful" (less than 80%) to "practically proved" (99.80–99.90%). What should be said if the probability of paternity were still higher is not specified. Joint AMA-ABA Guidelines: Present Status of Serologic Testing in Problems of Disputed Parentage, 10 Fam. L.Q. 247, 262 (1976).

[25]O'Bannon v. Azar, 435 So. 2d 1144 (La. Ct. App. 4th Cir. 1983) (affirming verdict for defendant who had 99.91% paternity probability but who previously had a successful vasectomy); Cole v. Cole, 74 N.C. App. 247, 328 S.E.2d 446 (1985) (reversing finding of paternity based on a 95.98% paternity probability where it was undisputed that the alleged father previously had a successful vasectomy).

[26]Plemel v. Walter, 303 Or. 262, 735 P.2d 1209 (1987). Virtually all commentators outside of the paternity testing community concur. 1A Wigmore, Evidence § 165a, at 1797–98 (Tillers rev. 1983) (however, aspects of Wigmore's explanation of the "probability of paternity" are incorrect; authorities cited, Kaye, The Probability of an Ultimate Issue: The Strange Cases of Paternity Testing, 75 Iowa L. Rev. 75, 95 n. 96 (1989); Berry, DNA Fingerprinting: What Does It Prove?, Chance: New Directions in Statistics and Computing, Summer 1990, at 15, 24 ("For a laboratory to assume that the prior probability of paternity or of guilt is 1/2, or any other particular value, is misleading at best. . . . The resulting posterior probability is assuredly not the probability of paternity."). Neither do paternity testing experts who understand the foundations of the "probability of paternity" wish to hide the value of the prior probability. Committee on Parentage Testing, American Association of Blood Banks, Standards for Parentage Testing Laboratories (1988) (Standard P8.243: "prior probabilities . . . shall be stated").

the other evidence in the case.[27] The same rule of exclusion should apply to the "verbal predicates" that some experts attach to probabilities of paternity.[28]

This rule would not prohibit the introduction of the genetic evidence and an explanation of its significance. The fact that competently performed genetic tests prove the alleged father's phenotypes or genotypes to be consistent with the claim of paternity is always relevant and useful evidence. The strength of this evidence, like other forms of identification evidence, can be shown to some extent by testimony about the probability of exclusion or, better, the likelihood ratio.[29]

There is also a strong argument for using a Bayesian approach to help the jury evaluate the evidence. Instead of viewing the evidence from the position of a laboratory, which, having nothing else to go on, is driven to such artifacts as using prior odds of one, one can adjust the focus to the trial, where other evidence is available to the decisionmaker. As noted in section 210, the expert could show the jury how the test results would affect not merely a prior probability of one-half, but a whole spectrum of prior

---

[27]The probability would be of more value if the entire trial were conducted as an exercise in Bayesian inference with the laboratory evidence being the first datum. The probability that laboratories now calculate could become the next prior probability, to be modified according to the likelihood ratio for the next piece of evidence, and so on. When all the evidence was in and counted, the final probability of paternity would determine the outcome. But it seems pointless to stop the chain of computations at the first step, and it is potentially misleading and confusing to process only one type of evidence in this way.

[28]Plemel v. Walter, 303 Or. 262, 735 P.2d 1209, 1214 n.5 (1987); Angela B. v. Glenn D., 126 Misc. 2d 646, 482 N.Y.S.2d 971, 975 (Fam. Ct. 1984) ("the so-called 'Hummel's predicate' . . . roughly corresponded to a form chart for parimutuel horse racing"); Kaye, The Probability of an Ultimate Issue: The Strange Cases of Paternity Testing, 75 Iowa L. Rev. 75 (1989); Kaye, Plemel as a Primer on Proving Paternity, 24 Willamette L. Rev. 867, 882–83 (1988). The "verbal predicates" convey less information than the numbers to which they are attached. In

some cases they are even more misleading than a statement of the "probability of paternity." County of Ventura v. Marcus, 139 Cal. App. 3d 612, 189 Cal. Rptr. 8, 12 (2d Dist. 1983) (because the "verbal predicate" of "undecided" is attached to probabilities in the .80–.90 range, the court reached the patently false conclusion that "It is therefore equally valid to infer therefrom that he is not the father as to infer that he is the father"); State ex rel. Williams v. Williams, 609 S.W.2d 456, 457 (Mo. Ct. App. W.D. 1980) ("the expert testified that a possibility or probability of paternity of less than 80% is no help at all in determining paternity. He stated that he preferred a probability of more than 90%"). The expert's testimony should be complete enough to permit the jury to decide for itself how much is enough. There are means of explaining the significance of the positive test findings that allow this, but the translation of dubious probability calculations into conclusions that do not draw on the qualifications and specialized knowledge of the expert is hardly the way to proceed.

[29]See supra § 210.

probabilities. It could be made clear to the jurors that the purpose of this exposition is not to compel them to assign a prior probability to the other evidence in the case, but to permit them to gauge the strength of the positive test findings and to weigh these findings, along with the other evidence,[30] in the manner that they think best. By using variable instead of fixed prior odds, the expert can display the statistical force of the evidence without attempting to quantify—on the basis of incomplete information—the one thing that the jury must decide with the benefit of all the evidence in the case: the probability of paternity.[31]

Even if an illustrative rather than a fixed prior probability is used to generate the probability of paternity, however, it is important to recognize that the likelihood ratio does not include all the information pertinent to assessing the laboratory findings. As we have described it (and as typically computed), this ratio assumes that there is no ambiguity or doubt about the determination of phenotypes or genotypes and the frequencies of the related alleles in the relevant population.

Given the cornucopia of DNA loci that can tested and the fresh and uncontaminated samples that can be obtained from the mother, child, and putative father, however, the statistical issues rarely should be significant. Indeed, the need to put any numbers before the jury is questionable. The exquisite power of DNA loci

---

[30]Opinions holding that verdicts of nonpaternity may be returned in the face of very large paternity probabilities recognize this need to blend the genetic findings with the nonscientific evidence. *See* Chisolm v. Eakes, 573 So. 2d 764 (Miss. 1990).

[31]This quantity, however computed, should not be confused with a confidence coefficient, a significance level, or a *p*-value, as a few courts and commentators are wont to do. Kaye, The Probability of an Ultimate Issue: The Strange Cases of Paternity Testing, 75 Iowa L. Rev. 75, 103–04 (1989). These very different probabilities are defined supra § 209.

Only a few opinions explicitly consider the necessity for variable, as opposed to fixed, prior odds. In Plemel v. Walter, 303 Or. 262, 735 P.2d 1209, 1219–20 (1987), the Supreme Court of Oregon decreed that a particular table of priors and posteriors must be used if the defendant questions whether the prior probability is one-half. In Com.

v. Beausoleil, 397 Mass. 206, 490 N.E.2d 788 (1986), the Supreme Judicial Court of Massachusetts rejected in dicta the proposal that an expert who wishes to discuss the posterior probability of paternity do so with respect to a wide range of priors. Recognizing "the basic flaw" in computing the "probability of paternity" with a fixed prior probability, the court announced that henceforth the immunogenetic evidence of paternity would be inadmissible unless the posterior probability exceeds 0.95 and certain other conditions are satisfied. Where the conditions are met, the Court would "leave to defense counsel the task of highlighting on cross-examination the exact nature of the probability of paternity calculation and its weaknesses." 490 N.E.2d at 797 n. 19. A detailed analysis and criticism of the Massachusetts guidelines is developed in Kaye, The Probability of an Ultimate Issue: The Strange Cases of Paternity Testing, 75 Iowa L. Rev. 75 (1989).

to discriminate among individuals makes detailed calculations of the troublesome "probability of paternity" largely beside the point in many cases. Considering that genetic tests can produce posterior probabilities well in excess of 0.99 for virtually any plausible prior probability in the ordinary case,[32] it has been suggested that:

> [W]e are approaching the point where explicit statistical analysis can be relegated to the background. Today, exclusions rarely are interpreted in terms of a paternity index or a probability of paternity, presumably because these numbers are so close to zero as to give no more guidance to a judge or jury than a simple statement that if the test results are correct, then it is practically impossible for the tested man to be the father. Likewise, an inclusion for which the paternity index is clearly astronomical perhaps may be more profitably described as demonstrating that it is practically impossible for the putative father to be anything but the biological father.[33]

Even so, this optimism should be tempered by the recognition that it is always conceivable—and sometimes fairly plausible—that the possible father is a brother, a son, or a father of the tested man. A likelihood ratio for the hypothesis that the biological father is such a close relative will be much smaller than the usual paternity index for the alternative of a random man. A simple solution would to give the likelihood ratio for such relatives along with the observation that the test, if performed correctly, essentially eliminates the possibility of an unrelated man being the father.

---

[32] *E.g.*, State v. Beasley, 960 So. 2d 1182, 1184 (La. Ct. App. 2d Cir. 2007) (likelihood ratio of 133,000,000); Jessop v. State, 368 S.W.3d 653, 670 (Tex. App. Austin 2012) (15-locus STR testing yielded a likelihood ratio of 57,040,000. Likelihood ratios in cases investigating siblingship and other familial relations are less definitive.

[33] Kaye, DNA Paternity Probabilities, 24 J. Fam. L. 279, 303–04 (1990); see also State v. Spann, 130 N.J. 484, 617 A.2d 247, 262 (1993) ("As a practical matter, the complex issues raised by admitting evidence of HLA test results in paternity and criminal cases are likely to become less and less important, indeed totally irrelevant, once acceptable scientific standards permit a broader forensic use of DNA 'fingerprinting.' It is generally accepted that DNA identifying techniques will exclude from consideration the DNA sequences of all but identical twins, making DNA testing the functional equivalent of a fingerprint.").